MW00807651

Fairbairn's book of crests of the families of Great Britain and Ireland

James Fairbairn

Nabu Public Domain Reprints:

You are holding a reproduction of an original work published before 1923 that is in the public domain in the United States of America, and possibly other countries. You may freely copy and distribute this work as no entity (individual or corporate) has a copyright on the body of the work. This book may contain prior copyright references, and library stamps (as most of these works were scanned from library copies). These have been scanned and retained as part of the historical artifact.

This book may have occasional imperfections such as missing or blurred pages, poor pictures, errant marks, etc. that were either part of the original artifact, or were introduced by the scanning process. We believe this work is culturally important, and despite the imperfections, have elected to bring it back into print as part of our continuing commitment to the preservation of printed works worldwide. We appreciate your understanding of the imperfections in the preservation process, and hope you enjoy this valuable book.

FAIRBAIRN'S BOOK OF CRESTS OF THE FAMILIES OF GREAT BRITAIN AND IRELAND

BEING A FOURTH EDITION

REVISED AND ENLARGED

IN TWO VOLUMES

VOL. I

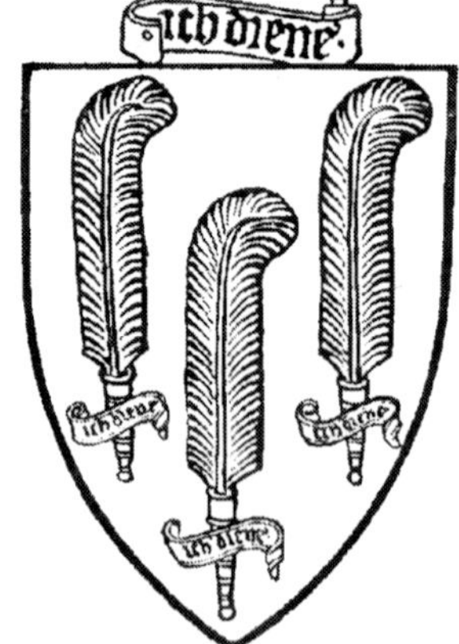

T. C. & E. C. JACK

LONDON W.C. 34 HENRIETTA STREET & ED[illegible]

Allen County Public Library
900 Webster Street
PO Box 2270
Fort Wayne, IN 46801-2270

PREFACE TO THE PRESENT EDITION

"FAIRBAIRN'S BOOK OF CRESTS" was first published 1859, and since that date had passed through some number of Editions prior to the year 1892, when the work was very thoroughly overhauled and revised under our direction.

The book had long ago established itself as a recognised work of reference, and as an indispensable adjunct to every library; and being suitable to the needs and purposes of jewellers and engravers, it had also from its first publication been adopted and accepted as the standard work of reference for business and trade purposes. By far the larger proportion of armorial orders placed in the hands of tradesmen for execution are carried out with the assistance of "Fairbairn."

The ever-increasing number of new families and new grants of arms, and the constant immigration of families of foreign origin using crests hitherto found in no English book of reference, create from time to time the necessity of extensive additions to the entries which the text contains. The large edition which we published in 1892 having been entirely exhausted, we availed ourselves of the opportunity afforded by the necessity of reprinting the volume to again submit the work to such revision as was required to bring it up to the present date.

This, we believe, will enable the book to maintain fully its old position and reputation as the only authoritative and the most complete collection of Crests and Mottoes in use in this country, a position in which it has hitherto had no rival. The question of the right of any particular person to the crest to which a claim is made depends upon proof of descent from the original grantee. Such proof often amounts to a highly controversial discussion, and it has seemed to us that we were not called upon for the purposes of the present work to adopt any such standard; rather otherwise, because the omission of a crest in consequence of a lack of proof of pedigree would create a hindrance to the use of the book by those handicraftsmen who need to refer to its pages.

34077

We therefore can give no guarantee of the official accuracy on the point of rightful inheritance. The existence of the original corpus of the book, which, when compiled, was never based upon the requirement of an official imprimatur for each crest, precludes therein any adoption of the official standard.

The additions to the text in the present edition have been considerable, but the overwhelming bulk of these additions has been obtained from sources not in themselves official, certainly, but purporting to be based upon information having a more or less official character. Such being the case, we can unhesitatingly assert that in the present edition the proportion of officially authorized crests is infinitely higher than in any previous edition of the work, not even excepting the edition of 1892. As to the remainder, the position is now as it was then; we have no exact knowledge, and the crests may or may not be authoritative.

THE PUBLISHERS.

EXTRACT FROM THE EDITOR'S PREFACE TO THE REVISED EDITION OF 1892.

HE origin of Heraldry has puzzled wiser and abler heads than mine; indeed, it would be folly to attempt, in the Preface to a Work of this character, to discuss the matter at all; but the whole subject may be said to resolve itself into the query, "Where does mere ornamentation end, and where does Heraldry '*as we know it*' begin?" The generally received opinion seems to be that the Crusades were coeval with, if, indeed, they were not the cause of, the birth of Heraldry, its laws, and its emblems.

Undoubtedly Arms—*i.e.*, the charges and field depicted upon the escutcheon—were of prior origin to crests. Consequently there are many Coats-of-Arms to which no Crest has ever been assigned, and which have no such ornament attached or belonging to them, but I have only come across one solitary Crest which possessed a legitimate existence without a corresponding and complementary Coat-of-Arms pertaining to it. This one (borne by a family of Buckworth) arose through a peculiar combination of circumstances, and has been rectified nearly a century.

The Crest is that part of the complete achievement which is placed upon and surmounts the coronet, wreath, or chapeau, which in its turn is above the mantling or lambrequin which it is supposed to attach to the helmet. Anciently, whilst the coronets and chapeaux were reserved for the rank to which they appertained, none below the rank of the knightly families were permitted to place their Crest upon a wreath. But both these laws—and more is the pity—have long been relegated to oblivion; and at the present day, unless the Crest be specially blazoned, as upon a chapeau, or issuing from a coronet (as to the different forms of which refer to the GLOSSARY), both of which are required to be mentioned in its Blazon, it must always be placed upon a wreath or torse. This is supposed to be a skein of coloured silk and a gold or silver cord twisted together, and at the present day is always of the principal—*i.e.*, the first-mentioned in the Blazon—colour and metal of the Arms, of which *six* alternate "twists" must be visible, the metal occurring first at the dexter end (see Plate 1, No. 2). When a "fur" occurs upon the Arms instead of either metal or colour, the ground tincture of the fur should be taken.

In the next place, I wish to explain the laws governing the usage and adoption of Crests. It is ***not***, as I have often been solemnly assured, "simply a matter of choice" and personal fad or fancy upon the part of the bearer, and the sooner it is fully understood the better it will be that His Majesty's College of Arms in Queen Victoria Street, London; Lyon Office, in the New General Register House in Edinburgh; and Ulster's Office, in the Record Tower of Dublin Castle, are absolutely the only legitimate or authoritative Offices of Arms within His Majesty's Dominions. So recently as 1804 the Law Offices of the Crown reported to H.M. King George III. that "the Heralds have the original cognizance of Pedigrees and Coat-Armour." Who, then, has the right to display Armorial Bearings? That it is a matter of the Law of the Land, in addition to conformity to Heraldic regulations, may not be generally known, but in the Warrants directing the Visitations of the various counties and districts during the sixteenth and seventeenth centuries, to be made in obedience to the Royal Commissions, the right is clearly laid down, and at the present day exists under as well defined limits as those which govern and regulate the Peerage. In England—for in the three countries the laws are not the same—direct legitimate male descent is required to be proved from some person to whom Armorial Bearings were recorded and allowed at the Visitations, or to whom Arms have since been granted or exemplified, and, failing such descent, it is necessary to petition for the favour of the Earl Marshal's Warrant to the Kings of Arms that a Patent of Armorial Bearings shall be issued to you, if it be so desired. In Ireland, the same qualifications are necessary to inherit Armorial Bearings; but in addition, and in Ireland only, it is within the power and authority of Ulster King of Arms, in cases where a Coat-of-Arms has been borne continuously by a family for four or more generations, but without lawful authority, according to his discretion, to *confirm* those Arms and their usage within specified limitations, with the addition of some mark which shall be readily recognisable as a sign of confirmation. In Scotland, the right to bear the Arms or Crest of a family is absolutely confined to the *heir male* only. All younger sons are required to matriculate their Arms and Crests in Lyon Court, when some mark of cadency is added, and their younger sons again in their turn must do likewise, and have a *further* and additional sign of cadency added to the Bearings. Though not a regulation, it appears to have been a very frequent practice upon each occasion of such matriculation to entirely alter the Crest, which accounts for the very large number of utterly different Crests in existence for the same family amongst the Scottish Ordinaries of Arms.

There is no such thing as the "prescriptive right to Arms," as to which some people talk glibly. Others of their persuasion have other little plausibilities, equally corrupt, which they bring into prominence. And it is a fairly safe plan to pursue to reject as bogus all Arms and Crests which boast no other origin than the heraldic stationer who, for a trifling fee, professes, on receipt of "name and county," to find armorial bearings for any applicant.

Mottoes in England and Ireland are not necessarily hereditary, and unless attached to, or in any way forming a part of, the Arms or Crest, may be altered, assumed, or discarded at the will of the bearer, and borne in any position in relation to his Arms or Crest that he may fancy; but in Scotland the Motto forms a part of the grant, and is unchangeable, and is also usually required to be borne upon an escroll *above* the Crest. A practice has lately very extensively arisen of using with a single surname two or more Crests. With a very few exceptions, it is only allowable so to do in cases where one of these be of honourable augmentation, or where one or both be governed by some special grant; and in cases where, by the assumption of one or more additional surnames, or by a change of surname, such additional Crests—usually one for each surname—have been exemplified in accordance with the terms of the Royal License.

No Lady whatsoever is allowed by the Laws of Heraldry to in any way bear or use, in her own right, either Crest or Motto ; and Arms only in a special and distinctive manner.

The collection of Mottoes, with their Translations, which must of necessity form one of the features of the Book, it has been thought well to submit to the revision of the Rev. James Wood (Editor of "Nuttall's Dictionary," New Edition), though, in justice to the erudition of this gentleman and his scholarly attainments, it should be known that I have throughout *insisted* upon the various Mottoes being spelt in the manner and retained in the actual form in which I have understood them *to be used*, even at the expense of accurate and scholastic spelling. Our ancestors had their own ideas—frequently peculiar—as to the method of spelling, and he would need be a Vandal who would cause unnecessary alterations in their quaint conceptions. And in addition, in some half-dozen cases, in order to preserve some pun—no doubt atrocious—I have asked for some translation to be allowed to stand which has not always been as literal a rendering as was possible of the foreign tongue, for we of the ancient and honourable Science and Brotherhood of Armory dearly love a pun. The Key to the Plates has been done in the offices of my Publishers, and in many other matters connected with the revision and publication of this Edition of 'FAIRBAIRN' I have experienced much kindness consideration, and assistance at their hands.

The whole of the Illustrations of the last Edition have been carefully examined. Some have been altered and some rejected, and over One Thousand New Crests have been added to those previously appearing. It has been one great anxiety that the Illustrations, however slightly they might differ, should not be quoted as correct unless they actually were so, and this will account for the large proportion of the references being mentioned as only for purposes of comparison. The Book was originally Compiled and Engraved in Scotland, by a Scotsman, and it is a well-known fact that both Scotch blazonry and emblazonment are far freer and "looser" than when controlled by the "garrulous minuteness" of the English school of Arms. This matter has been ably argued out (but, methinks, to a wrong conclusion), and explained in the latest book upon the subject which has left the press (Woodward & Burnett's "Treatise of Heraldry"). One sentence will explain my views. When a Blazon can be otherwise *correctly* depicted in two or more separate ways (and here I am not referring to mediæval or antique styles of draughtmanship), and further, when *one* of those ways only is painted upon the Grant or Exemplification, why should it be open to discussion as to the possible accuracy of any other form ? If one form be *right*, why is not any other shape or position *wrong ?*

For example, the term which, more than any other, has given me trouble on this score is one applied to birds—to wit, "rising." My own idea is that this should be as upon Plate 88, No. 2. Plate 77, No. 5, is the other extreme, and is an accepted interpretation of the term in Scotland ; but I have seen in the Offices and College of Arms authoritative paintings of every other possible position of the wings, short of their being "close," occurring in Coats-of-Arms or Crests, and blazoned simply as "rising." A little uniformity upon this and other points in the Heraldry of the Three Kingdoms might be desirable.

"FAIRBAIRN'S BOOK OF CRESTS," first published in the year 1859, was originally compiled by a certain JAMES FAIRBAIRN, and was revised by LAWRENCE BUTTERS, Seal Engraver in Ordinary to Her Majesty for Scotland. Its sale hitherto has been chiefly amongst Jewellers and Seal Engravers. Perhaps this accounts for the lamentable fact that many Crests have crept within its pages which can but be described as *bogus*. To have deliberately and in cold blood verified the thirty or forty thousand Crests which the Book in its previous Editions made mention of would have been a work of so many years' duration, and of so vast an expense, that it could by no possibility have ever repaid such expenditure. I have not attempted to do this, and consequently I do not pretend that this Edition is absolutely "sans peur et sans reproche," but I have detected and discarded a vast quantity that were without authority, as a moment's comparison between the two Editions will readily show.

LONDON, *1st October*, 1892.

CONTENTS OF VOL. I.

PART I.—INDEX OF SURNAMES.

PART II.—(1.) MOTTOES.

(2.) KEY TO PLATES.

(3.) DICTIONARY OF TERMS.

PART I.

INDEX OF SURNAMES.

ABBREVIATIONS.

arg.	argent
az.	azure
erm.	ermine
gu.	gules
ppr.	proper
purp.	purpure
sa.	sable

Definitions of Heraldic terms will be found in the DICTIONARY OF TERMS.

ALPHABETICAL INDEX OF THE CRESTS

OF THE

FAMILIES OF GREAT BRITAIN AND IRELAND AND THE COLONIES

NOTE.—The reference numbers mean, as in Aaron, plate 222, crest 3. As some assistance to engravers, and rather than leave a larger proportion than was otherwise inevitable of the crests without any reference to an illustration, the term *cf.* (*compare*) has been used, and means that the reference is given only for comparative purposes, the plate not corresponding precisely with the blazon; this term, however, being only used where the difference is but slight. It will be noticed that in the illustrations of many of the new crests the colour-lines appear in the form in which they are usually used in heraldic engraving, in order to render such illustrations perfectly correct renderings of particular crests. In cases where the same engraving would be correct if of another colour, it has been thought better to use the term "compare" (*cf.*) to prevent such illustrations being considered absolutely accurate.

A.

Aaron, Aarons, and **Aaroons,** a lady's arm from the elbow in pale ppr. 222. 3

Abadain or **Abaudain,** a savage wreathed about the head and loins with laurel leaves, and holding over the shoulder a club, all ppr. 186. 1

Abadam, a dexter hand holding a broken spear, all ppr. 214. 10

Abadam of Middleton Hall, Carmarthen, out of a ducal coronet or, a demi-lion gardant gu. *Aspire.—Indulge not.* *cf.* 10. 8

Abarle, a flute in pale ppr. 168. 3

Abarough or **Abarow,** Somers., a ferret arg., collared or, lined az. 134. 9

Abarrow, Hants, a demi-female habited, holding in her hands a quiver of arrows, all ppr.

Abaudain, *see* Abadain.

Abbat, a unicorn's head ppr. 49. 7

Abbeford, Leics., on a chapeau ppr., a water-bouget sa. 168. 2

Abberbury, a hawk, wings expanded and inverted, resting its dexter claw on a mount ppr. 87. 9

Abberbury, a camel's head sa. 132. 7

Abbetot, Warw., a dexter hand holding a cutlass in pale ppr., hilted or. 213. 8

Abbett, a unicorn's head ppr., collared az. *cf.* 49. 7

Abbey of London, an eagle's head erased ppr. 83. 2

Abbey, same crest. *Spei mea cœlo.*

Abbey, a leopard rampant ppr. *cf.* 26. 2

Abbey, Henry, Esquire, J.P., of Fairlee, Brighton, an eagle displayed arg., between two cross crosslets or, each wing charged with a cross crosslet gu.

Abbis, Abbiss, Abis, or **Abys,** Norf., a spur az., leather sa., the buckle of the first. 178. 8

Abborne, a dexter arm vested az., cuffed or, holding in the hand ppr. a baton in bend sinister gu., tipped with gold.

Abbot, Henry Napier, M.A., solicitor, 5, Downside Road, Clifton, Bristol, a demi-unicorn erm., armed and maned arg., gorged with a collar az., studded or. *Perseverando.* 292. 4

Abbot (Rt. Hon. Reginald Charles Edward), **Baron Colchester,** of Colchester, Essex, out of a ducal coronet or, a unicorn's head erm., armed, maned and tufted of the first, between six ostrich-feathers arg., quilled also or. *Deo patriæ amicus.—Perseverando.*

Abbot, out of a ducal coronet a unicorn's head or, between two ostrich-feathers arg. 48. 14

Abbot of Lincoln, a unicorn's head erased arg., attired and crined or, charged with a bar gemel sa.

Abbot, a demi-unicorn erm., armed and maned arg., collared az., studded or. 48. 10

Abbot or **Abbott,** a hand holding a dagger, point downwards, dropping blood. 213. 6

Abbot, a fox passant ppr., charged on the shoulder with a water-bouget arg. *Labore.* *cf.* 32. 1

Abbot, a snail ppr. 141. 8

Abbot, a cubit arm erect, vested and cuffed erm., holding in the hand a crescent arg. *cf.* 206. 8

Abbot of Castleacre, Norf., a griffin sejant or. 62. 10

Abbot, a griffin sejant az., bezantée. *cf.* 62. 10

Abbot, Devonsh., a griffin sejant az., platée, winged and beaked or. *cf.* 62. 10

Abbott, *see* Tenterden, Baron.

Abbott, John, Esquire, of Braemar House, Lancaster Gate, Paddington, London, W., in front of two crosiers saltirewise sa., a unicorn's head erased or. *Labore.*

Abbott, John Theodore, surgeon, 5, Church Road, Tunbridge Wells, out of a ducal coronet a unicorn's head or, between two ostrich-feathers arg. *Deo patriæ amicis.*

Abbs, Durh., the sun in splendour. *Noli irritare leonem.* 162. 2

Abbs, out of a ducal coronet or, an eagle's head with wings displayed arg., collared of the first. *In te Domine speravi.*

Abby, a cross crosslet az. 165. 2

Abcot or **Abcott,** a rose per pale or and az., barbed counterchanged. *cf.* 149. 1

Abday, an eagle's head erased ppr. 83. 2

Abden, a swan's head ppr., between wings az. 101. 6

Abdey, an eagle's head erased ppr., beaked or. 83. 2

Abdy and **Abdey,** Essex, an eagle's head erased ppr. 83. 2

Abdy of Stapleford-Abbot, Essex, same crest.

Abdy, Sir William Neville, Bart., of Albyns, near Romford, Essex, an eagle's head erased ppr., beaked or. *Tenax et fidelis.* 83. 2

Abech, out of a mural coronet, an arm from the elbow vested az., cuffed or, holding a mullet gu. *cf.* 206. 12

Abeck or **Habeck,** out of a mural coronet a cubit arm, vested az., cuffed arg., holding in the hand a mullet gu. *cf.* 206. 12

a'Beckett, *see* Beckett.

À Beckett, the late Hon. William Arthur Callander, J.P., of Wilton, Middle Brighton, Melbourne, Victoria, Australia, a fleur-de-lis az. surmounted with a lion's head erased erm., the whole debruised by a bendlet sinister wavy or. *Foys sapience et chevalerie.* 260. 14

À'Beckett, William Gilbert, Esquire, M.A., LL.M., Cambs., Barrister-at-law of the Inner Temple, of Melbourne, same crest and motto.

A Beckett, Arthur Hayward, Esquire, of Ballintrae, Mornington, co. Victoria, same crest and motto.

Abel and **Abell,** Essex and Kent, an arm in armour embowed ppr., holding a sword arg., hilted or, the arm enfiled with a wreath arg. and gu. 195. 3

Abel, Essex, an arm in armour embowed, holding in the hand a couteau, all ppr.

Abel, Bart., in front of a dexter arm embowed in armour, the hand grasping a thunderbolt, a torch fessewise fired, all ppr. *Ohne Rast Zum Ziel.* 251. 8

Abeleyn, a peacock ppr. 103. 7

Abelhall or **Ablehall,** a lion's head erased sa., between two wings or. 19. 7

Abeline, Ablin or **Ablyn,** a sword in pale enfiled with a savage's head ppr.

Abell, *see* Abel. 191. 9

Abell, Kent, a boar's head couped and erect sa., armed or, transpierced by an arrow in bend sinister, the shaft arg., the pheon az.

Abelon or **Abilon,** a mitre ppr., labelled gu. *cf.* 180. 5

Abelyn or **Abelyne,** on a globe ppr., an eagle, wings expanded and inverted gu. *cf.* 159. 7

Abenhall or **Ablehall,** two branches of laurel issuing cheveron-ways vert. 151. 15

Abeny, a hand vested, holding a mill-rind ppr. 207. 4

Aber, a demi-talbot rampant arg., ducally gorged gu. 55. 12

Aberbury, Oxon., a hawk, wings expanded and inverted, resting the dexter claw on a mount ppr. 87. 9

Aberbuthnet, a dove within an adder in orle ppr. *Innocue ac provide.* 92. 11

Aberbuthnet of Fiddes, a peacock ppr., *Tam interna, quam externa.* 103. 7

Aberbuthnet of Findowrie, a peacock issuing. *Interna præstant.* 103. 10

Aberbuthnot, Scotland, a peacock ppr. 103. 7

Aberbuthnot, Scotland, a peacock's head erased ppr., beaked or. *Laus Deo.* 103. 1

Abercorn, Duke, Marquess, and **Earl of,** and **Duke of Chatelherault** (Hamilton), out of a ducal coronet or, an oak fructed and penetrated transversely in the main stem by a frame-saw ppr., the frame or, the blade inscribed with the word "*Through.*" *Sola nobilitas virtus.* 143. 13

Abercorne, Scotland, a boar's head couped ppr. 43. 1

Abercorne, Scotland, two daggers in saltier ppr. 169. 8

Abercrombie of that ilk, Scotland, on a mount an oak-tree fructed, all ppr. *Tace.* 143. 14

Abercrombie, a cross Calvary gu. *In cruce salus.* 166. 1

Abercrombie of Fetternier, a cross crosslet fitched gu. *In cruce salus.* 166. 2

Abercrombie of Tullibody, a bee volant ppr. *Vive ut vivas.* 137. 2

Abercromby, a bee volant ppr. *Vive et vivas.* 137. 2

Abercromby, Baron, of Aboukir, Fern Tower, Crieff, Perthsh., Abercromby, a bee volant ppr. *Vive ut vivas.* 137. 2

Abercromby, Alexander, Esquire (M.D., F.R.C.S. Edinburgh), residing at Cape Town, Cape Colony, a bee volant or. *Vive ut vivas.* 270. 4

Abercromby, Sir George William, Bart., of Birkenbog, a falcon rising ppr., belled or. *Mercy is my desire.—Petit alta,* and *Vive ut vivas.* 88. 2

Abercromby, a cross Calvary gu. *In cruce salus.* 166. 1

Abercromby, Banff, on a mount an oak-tree acorned, all ppr. *Tace.* 143. 14

Aberdare Baron (Bruce), a cubit arm in armour in bend, grasping in the gauntlet a sceptre ppr. *Fuimus.—Ofner na ofne angau.*

Aberdeen, Earl of (*now* Gordon *only*), two arms holding a bow and arrow straight upwards in a shooting posture and at full draught, all ppr. *Fortuna sequatur.*

Aberdeen, Earl of (*formerly* Hamilton-Gordon), of Haddon House, Aberdeen: (1) Two arms from the shoulder naked holding a bow ppr., to let an arrow fly (*for Gordon*). 202. 2. (2) Out of a ducal coronet or, an oak-tree fructed and penetrated transversely in the main stem by a frame-saw inscribed with the word "*Through,*" all ppr., the tree charged with an escutcheon arg., thereon a heart gu. (*for Hamilton*). *Fortuna sequatur.* *cf.* 143. 13

Aberdein, of Cairnbulg, Aberdeensh., Scotland, a dexter hand holding an annulet ppr. *Intemerata fides.* 216. 1

Aberdour, Lord, *see* Morton, Earl of.

Aberdour, an anchor with cable, and a sword in saltire, all ppr. *Hinc spes effulget.* 169. 9

Aberdwell or **Abredrobell,** a greyhound arg., current towards a tree vert. 58. 11

Abergavenny, Marquess of (Nevill), Nevill Eridge Castle, Tunbridge Wells, a bull arg., pied sa., armed or, charged on the neck with a rose, barbed and seeded ppr. *cf.* 45. 2. *Another,* out of a ducal coronet or, a bull's head sa. *cf.* 44. 11. *Ne vile velis.* Badges: (1) A rose gu., seeded or, barbed vert. (2) A portcullis or.

Aberigh, on a mount a ferret ppr. 134. 10

Aberherdour, Aberkerdour, and **Aberkirdor,** Scotland, a sword in pale ppr. *Pro rege et patria.* 170. 2

Aberkirdor and **Aberkirdour,** Scotland, on the point of a sword in pale a garland, all ppr. *Pro rege.* 170. 1

Aberkirdor, Scotland, within the horns of a crescent arg., a buckle az. 163. 15

Aberneathy, Scotland, a ship under sail ppr. *Salus per Christum.* 160. 13

Aberneathy, a parrot holding in the dexter claw a pear. 101. 13

Abernethy of Rothmay, a parrot feeding on a bunch of cherries, all ppr. *Salus per Christum.* 101. 8

Abernethy of Auchinloich, a parrot ppr. *In Christo salus.* 101. 4

Abernethy, Scotland, a cross crosslet fitched gu. *In Christo salus.* 166. 2

Abernethy of Corskie, in the sea a ship in distress. *Salus per Christum.* 160. 14

Abernethy, Scotland, a ship under sail ppr. *Salus per Christum.* 160. 13

Abernethy, a three-masted ship in a storm. 160. 14

Aberton or **Aburton,** on a human heart gu., an eagle's claw erased ppr. 113. 14

Abett, a unicorn's head gu., collared or. *cf.* 49. 7

Abilem, a man's head in profile issuing ppr. *cf.* 190. 14

Abingdon, Earl of, and **Baron Norreys,** Wytham Abbey, Oxford (Bertie), a Saracen's head couped at the breast ppr., ducally crowned or, charged on the chest with a fret az. *Virtus ariete fortior.* 245. 5

Abingdon of Dowdeswell, Glouc., an arm in armour embowed ppr., garnished or, holding in the hand an ancient mace sa., headed and studded also or, girt round the arm near the shoulder with a sash tied in a bow arg., fringed gold. 199. 3

Abingdon, a dexter arm in armour embowed ppr., holding in the hand a sword by the blade point downwards. 195. 6

Abingdon, a bull rampant. 45. 11

Abingdon, Worcs., an eagle close or. 76. 2

Abingdon, Worcs., an eagle displayed or, crowned az. *cf.* 74. 14

Abinger, Baron, Inverlochy Castle, Kingussie, Inverness-sh. (Scarlett), a Tuscan column chequy or and gu., supported on either side by a lion's gamb ermines, erased gu. *Suis stat viribus.* 239. 10

Able, an arm in armour embowed, the hand grasping a sword, all ppr. 195. 2

Ablehall, a lion's head erased sa., between two wings or. 19. 7

Ablyn, a sword in pale enfiled with a savage's head ppr. 191. 9

Abney-Hastings, Bart., *see* Hastings.

Abney-Hastings, *see* Donington, Baron.

Abney, Sir William de Wiveleslie, K.C.B., of Measham Hall, Derbysh., a demi-lion rampant or, holding between the paws a pellet. *Fortiter et honeste.* *cf.* 11. 7

Aboat, a griffin sejant. 62. 10

Aboril and **Abrol,** Worcs., a lion's head ppr., vomiting flames gu. 17. 1

Abot, a unicorn's head erased ppr. 49. 5

Aboyne, Earl of, *see* Marquess of Huntly.

Abrahall, Heref., a hedgehog ppr. 135. 8

Abraham, the sun in splendour or. 162. 2

Abraham, Thomas Fell, Esquire, of Riverham, Grassendale Park, Lancs, upon a mount vert in front of two fronds of fern a rook ppr. *Veritas libertas.* 244. 4

Abraham, Alfred Clay, Esquire, F.I.C., of 87, Bold Street, Liverpool, same crest and motto.

Abrahams and **Abram,** the sun rising from a cloud ppr. 162. 5

Abram of Lorraine, a bee or. 137. 4

Abrey, a chevalier on horseback at full speed, holding a broken spear, all ppr. 189. 5

Abriscourt, Oxon., a hare close among grass ppr. 136. 12

Abrol or **Aboril,** Worcs., a lion's head vomiting flames ppr. 17. 1

Abrook and **Abrooke,** a wolf's head erased sa. 30. 8

Absalem, Absolom, and **Absolon,** a fleur-de-lis or. 148. 2

Abtot, a bear couchant arg., collared and muzzled or. 34. 6
Aburton, on a human heart gu., an eagle's foot erased ppr. 113. 14
Abuscourt and **Abustourt,** a hare close among grass ppr. 136. 12
Accorne, Scotland, an oak-tree vert. *Stabo.* 143. 5
Aceck, Acbiche, or **Hackbeck,** a cross pattée erm. *cf.* 165. 7
Acford, a horse's head sa., bridled or. 51. 5
Acguillum, a dexter hand holding a holly branch, all ppr. *cf.* 209. 14
Acham, Plenyth, Cornw., a lion sejant or, collared and lined sa. 7. 4
Acham or **Aclam,** a demi-lion arg., holding a maunch gu.
Achany, Scotland, out of a crescent, a cross crosslet fitched sa. *Per ardua ad alta.* 166. 9
Achard, a crescent inflamed ppr. 163. 12
Acheley, London and Shropsh., an eagle's head erased gu., winged or, in beak a branch of lilies arg., leaved vert.
Acheley, a griffin's head erased ppr. 66. 2
Acheley, a demi-swan gu., winged or, holding in the beak a flower arg.
Acher, Kent, a bull's head erased gu. 44. 3
Acheson, Scotland and Ireland, a cock ppr. 91. 2
Acheson, Earl of Gosford and **Viscount Acheson,** a cock gu., standing on a trumpet or. *Vigilantibus.* 91. 6
Acheson of Glencairney, Bart., same crest and motto.
Acheson, Scotland, an eagle displayed. 75. 2
Acheson, a sandglass ppr. 177. 15
Achieson, Scotland, an astrolabe ppr. *Observe.* 167. 7
Achilles or **Achillis,** a savage's head affrontée, ducally crowned ppr. *cf.* 192. 9
Achmuty, an arm embowed in armour ppr., holding a broken spear az. *Dum spiro spero.* 197. 2
Achym, a crescent or. 163. 2
Achym or **Acklame,** a lion sejant gardant or, collared and chained sa. *cf.* 7. 4
Achym, Cornw., a lion sejant or, collared and lined sa. 7. 4. *Another,* a demi-lion arg., holding a maunch gu.
Ackelom, a sagittarius shooting a bow ppr. 53. 2
Ackerman, Ackermann, or **Acraman,** out of a palisado coronet or, an arm embowed ppr., vested gu., cuffed arg., holding in the band an oak branch vert, fructed or. 205. 1
Ackers, Benjamin St. John, of Huntley Manor, Glouc., upon a mount, in front thereof three sprigs of oak slipped and fructed, a dove rising, holding in the beak a like sprig of oak, all ppr. *La liberté.* 295. 9
Ackers, a Doric column or. *cf.* 176. 3
Ackers of Moreton Hall, Chester, a dove rising, holding in the beak an olive-branch, all ppr. *La liberté.* 94. 5
Ackford, a horse's head sa., bridled or. 51. 5
Ackhurst, a demi-lion arg., holding in the dexter paw an acorn slip vert, fructed or. *cf.* 12. 3
Acklam or **Aclome,** Yorks, a demi-lion arg., holding a maunch gu.
Acklame, a lion sejant or, collared and lined sa. 7. 4
Ackroyd or **Ackeroyd,** a dog sleeping ppr. 57. 13
Ackroyd, William, of The Wheatley's, Yorks, out of a mural coronet, a stag's head. *Veritate victoria.*
Ackworth, a griffin's head erased ppr. 66. 2
Ackworth, Kent, a griffin segreant. *Vincit qui patitur.* 62. 2
Acland, a falcon trussing a bird. *cf.* 79. 7
Acland, a dexter hand couped fesseways holding a rose-branch.
Acland, Sir Charles Thomas Dyke, Bart., of Columb-John, Devons., on a sinister arm in fess vested az., the hand in a glove arg., a peregrine falcon ppr., beaked and belled or. *Inébranlable.* 86. 14
Acland, Rear-Admiral Sir William A. Dyke, Bart., Rocklands, Chudleigh, South Devonsh., same crest and motto.
Acland, Bart., Killerton, Devonsh., and Holnicote, Somers., on a sinister arm in fesse vested az., gloved arg., a hawk perched of the last, beaked and belled or. *Inébranlable.* 86. 14
Acland, Alfred Dyke, Esquire, of 38, Pont Street, London, a couped arm lying fesseways to the sinister az., gloved arg., thereon a falcon perched ppr., beaked, membered, and belled or. *Inébranlable.*
Acland, Charles Thomas Dyke, Esquire, of Killerton, Exeter, same crest and motto.
Acland, Theodore Dyke, Esquire, of 74, Brook Street, London, same crest and motto.
Acland, Fuller-Palmer-, Bart., Somers.: (1) For *Acland,* on a sinister arm, in fess vested az., gloved arg., a hawk perched arg., beaked and belled or. 86. 14. (2) For *Palmer,* a demi-panther gardant, flames issuing out of mouth and ears, holding a palm-branch ppr. 23. 12. (3) For *Fuller,* on a ducal coronet gu., a lion's head arg., *Palma virtuti* for Palmer over the crest and *Inébranlable* for Acland underneath the arms. 17. 5
Acland, Hon. John Barton Arundel, M.A., of Holnicote, Mount Peel, Rangitata, Canterbury, New Zealand, Member of the Legislative Council of New Zealand, a man's hand, couped at the wrist, in a glove, lying fesseways, thereon a falcon, perched, all ppr. *Inébranlable* 86. 14
Acland, Sir Henry Wentworth Dyke, Bart., K.C.B., M.D., D.C.L., LL.D., F.R.S., a sinister arm lying fesseways vested az., the hand in a glove arg., thereon a falcon perched ppr., beaked and belled or. 86. 14
Acland-Troyte, Hugh Leonard, Esquire, of Hunsham, Court Bampton, Devon, (1) an eagle's wing sa., charged with five estoiles or, environed with a snake ppr, the wing charged for distinction with a cross crosslet or (for Troyte). (2) On a man's hand couped at the wrist, in a glove fesseways, a falcon perched all ppr (for Acland). *A Deo in Deo.*
Acland-Troyte, John, Edward Esquire, M.A., same crest and motto.
Acland-Troyte, Rev. Reginald Henry Dyke, M.A., of Presbytère St. André, Pau, France, same crest and motto.
Acle, Devonsh., an annulet or, stoned sa. 167. 14
Acleham or **Aclehum,** a demi-lion vert holding an escutcheon gu. *cf.* 14. 2
Aclome, a demi-lion arg., holding a maunch gu.
Acock, out of a mural coronet a swan issuing ppr.
Acock, out of a ducal coronet a demi-swan issuing ppr. *cf.* 99. 5
Acombe, a dexter arm in armour embowed sa., garnished or, tied round with a ribbon arg. and gu., holding in the hand a broken tilting-spear. *cf.* 197. 2
Acotts or **Acottis,** a lion rampant gu., supporting a standard ppr., flag az., charged with a saltier arg. 3. 7
A'Court, Bart., an eagle displayed sa., charged with two chevronels arg., holding in the beak a lily, slipped ppr. *Grandescunt aucta labore.*
A'Court, a lion's head erased, regardant gu. 17. 6
A'Court-Holmes, *see* Heytesbury, Baron.
A'Court-Repington, Charles Henry Wyndham, Esquire, M.A., of Amington Hall, Warw. (1) A demi-heraldic antelope gu., armed, ungu., and tufted or, billettée arg. (for Repington). (2) An eagle displayed sa., on the breast two chevronels or, holding in the beak a lily ppr. *Virtus propter se.*
Acraman, out of a palisado coronet or, an arm embowed ppr., vested gu., cuffed arg., holding in the band an oak-branch vert, fructed or. 205. 1
Acraman, same crest. *Esse quam videri.* 205. 1
Acre, Westml., a triangular harrow ppr. 178. 4
Acres and **Acris,** an eagle displayed ppr., charged on the breast with a pellet. 75. 1
Acton, Baron (Dalberg-Acton), of Aldenham Hall, Shropsh., on a wreath of the colours a circular wreath arg. and gu., therein a leg in armour ppr., garnished or, bent at the knee and couped at the middle of the thigh, blood dropping therefrom gu. 193. 5. *Another,* the same crest without the circular torse.
Acton, Edward William Frederick, Esquire, J.P., of the Leasowes, Bridgnorth, within a torse, a human leg and thigh in armour couped and dropping blood, all ppr.
Acton, Augustus Wood-, of Acton Scott, Shropsh., same crest.
Acton of West Aston, Ireland, same crest. *Adjuvante Deo.*
Acton, Chesh., a demi-lion rampant, regardant arg., grasping a spear or, enfiled with a boar's head sa., couped gu. 9. 10
Acton, a demi-lion regardant, holding a spear enfiled with a savage's head.
Acton, Worc., an arm in armour, embowed ppr., garnished or, the hand grasping a sword arg., hilt of the second enfiled with a boar's head, couped sa., dropping blood.
Acton, William Robert, Esquire, J.P., of Wolverton Hall, Pershore, an arm in

armour, embowed ppr., holding in the hand a sword arg., hilt or, enfiled with a boar's head couped at the neck sa., distilling blood. *Vaillance avance l'homme.*

Acton, a pine-tree vert, fructed or. 144. 13

Acton, Ireland, a pellet between two wings gu. *cf.* 110. 4

Acworth, a griffin's head erased ppr. 66. 2

Acworth, an armed arm or, issuant out of a coronet of strawberry-leaves gu., the hand grasping a serpent ppr., holding in the mouth an annulet sa.

Adagh, a demi-lion rampant arg., guttée-de-sang, holding in the paws three blue pinks. *Mea gloria fides.*

Adair, *see* Waveney, Baron.

Adair, Bart., of Kinghilt, a man's head couped and bloody ppr. *Loyal au mort.*

Adair of Heatherton Park, Somers., same crest. *Loyal à mort.*

Adair, Cumb. and Scotland, a Saracen's head couped and impaled with a spear. *I dare.* 191. 8

Adair, Sir Frederick Edward Shafto, Bart., of Flixton Hall, Suff., a man's head affrontée couped at the neck and bloody ppr. *Loyal au mort.*

Adair, Allan Shafto, Esquire, J.P., of Bank of England, Plymouth, same crest and motto.

Adair, Scotland, on a sword in pale a Saracen's head affrontée, dropping blood all ppr., the sword hilted and pommelled or. *Arte et marte.—Fortitudine.* 101. 11

Adam, Hants, a crescent gu. 163. 2

Adam, on a mount vert a sword ppr., and a cross crosslet fitchée gu., in saltier, banded of the last. *cf.* 166. 12

Adam, James, M.D., Malling Place, West Malling, Kent, a cross crosslet fitchée gu., and a sword in saltire ppr.

Adam of Culross, a cross crosslet fitchée gu., surmounted of a sword in saltier ppr. *Crux mihi grata quies.* 166. 12

Adam of Runcorn, two swords in saltier, and a cross crosslet, fitched in pale, *Dominus ipse faciet.* 166. 14

Adam, Sir Charles Elphinstone, Bart., of Blair Adam, Kinross, a cross crosslet fitchée gu., surmounted of a sword in saltire ppr. *Crux mihi grata quies.* 166. 12

Adam, Scotland, a hand holding a cross crosslet, fitched gu. *Crux mihi grata quies.* 221. 14

Adam, Scotland, a passion-cross or, charged with a man's heart ppr. *In cruce salus.* *cf.* 165. 4

Adam of Walden, Essex, a talbot passant az., bezantée, collared arg. *cf.* 54. 5

Adam, an eagle volant ppr.

Adam or **Adams**, a griffin's head, gu., between two wings or, beaked az. *cf.* 67. 7

Adam or **Adams**, a griffin's head gu., between two wings or, pellettée. *cf.* 67. 7

Adams of Ahavagurrah, Ireland, a griffin's head erased az. *Malo mori quam fœdari.* 66. 2

Adams, Cambs, a griffin's head gu., between two wings or. *cf.* 67. 7

Adams, Lincs, a griffin's head couped gu., beaked az., between two wings or, pellettée. *cf.* 67. 7

Adams of Cheaton, Shropsh., a griffin's head erased erm., beaked gu., charged with a chevron vairée or and az. *cf.* 66. 2

Adams, a griffin's head erased erm., beaked gu., charged with a chevron chequy or and sa. *cf.* 66. 2

Adams, a griffin's head between two wings, addorsed vert, charged on the breast with a cross or.

Adams, William, Esquire, of Drumelton House, Cootehill, and Erne View, co. Cavan, Ireland, a griffin's head couped gu., between two wings sa., each charged with three bezants. *Ingenium superat vires.* *cf.* 67. 7

Adams, Yorks, a demi-griffin erm., winged and beaked az., holding an escallop or. *cf.* 65. 1

Adams, Francis, of Clifton, Glouc., a demi-griffin segreant or. *Tout ou rien.* 64. 2

Adams of Ansty Hall, Warwick, a talbot passant az., semée of bezants, collared arg. *Sub cruce veritas.* *cf.* 54. 5

Adams, *see* **Woollcombe-Adams.**

Adams, Notts, a talbot sa., semée of cinquefoils or, resting the dexter paw upon a mullet of the last.

Adams, Samuel Thomas, Esquire, a talbot sa., semée of cinquefoils or, and resting the dexter paw upon a mullet also or.

Adams, Bath, out of a crown vallery or, a demi-lion affrontée arg., semée of mullets gu.

Adams, Devonsh., out of a ducal coronet or, a demi-lion gardant arg. *cf.* 10

Adams, out of a ducal coronet or, a demi-lion affrontée ppr.

Adams, Carmarthensh., out of a ducal coronet or, a demi-lion affrontée gu. *Aspire, persevere, and indulge not.*

Adams, London, a lion rampant or. 1. 13

Adams of Holyland, Pembroke, a martlet arg. *Certior in cœlo domus.* *cf.* 95. 2

Adams, a martlet sa., holding in the beak a mullet or. *Cruce duce.* *cf.* 95. 5

Adams, a raven sa. *cf.* 107. 2

Adams, Middx., an eagle volant regardant. 79. 5

Adams, an eagle regardant, wings elevated sa., pendant from the neck an escutcheon or, charged with a cat's face vert, resting the dexter claw on a crescent also or. 77. 3

Adams, Rev. James Williams, V.C., B.A., the Rectory, Postwich, Norwich, same crest.

Adams, on a mount vert an eagle reversed and regardant, wings expanded ppr., beak and legs or, holding in the beak a mullet sa., the sinister claw resting on a crescent reversed gold.

Adams, London, on a bezant a demi-eagle sa.

Adams, Bart., a greyhound's head couped. *cf.* 61. 2

Adams, Shropsh., a greyhound's head erased erm. 61. 4

Adams, Ireland, a boar's head or, couped gu. *cf.* 43. 1

Adams, London and Ireland, a boar's head arg., couped gu. *cf.* 43. 1

Adams, London, a wolf's head erased erm. 30. 8

Adams, a wolf's head erased ppr. 30. 8

Adams, Rev. William Fulford, of the Rectory, Weston-sub-Edge, Glouc., a dexter arm embowed in armour ppr., garnished or, the elbow charged with a torteau, the gauntlet also ppr., grasping a cross crosslet fitchée sa. *Libertas et natale solum.*

Adams of Bowdon, Devonsh., a dexter arm, in armour ppr., embowed, grasping a cross crosslet fitched sa., charged on elbow with a torteau. *Libertas et natale solum.*

Adams, Percy, Fulford, Lancaster Road, Wimbledon, a dexter arm embowed in armour, the hand in a gauntlet ppr., grasping a cross crosslet sa., the arm charged on the elbow with a torteau. *Libertas et natale solum.*

Adams, a dexter arm in armour embowed, holding in the hand a cross crosslet. 198. 5

Adams, Ireland, an arm couped at the shoulder, embowed ppr., vested gu., holding in the hand a flag sa., charged with a bee. 204. 12

Adams, Very Rev. Samuel, M.A., of Northlands, co. Cavan, Ireland, Dean of Cashel and Prebendary of Terebrine, in the Diocese of Elphin, J.P., on a mount vert a cross crosslet fitchée or, charged with a bleeding heart gu. *In cruce salus.* *cf.* 166. 6

Adams, Ambrose Douglas, Esquire, on a mount vert, a cross crosslet fitchée or, charged with a bleeding heart gu. *In cruce salus.*

Adams, James Craig Bate de Lisle, Esquire, same crest and motto.

Adams, John Hervey Stuart, Esquire, of Northlands, Carrickmacross, same crest and motto.

Adams, Leslie Piers, Esquire, same crest and motto.

Adams, Maxwell Richard William Peers-, Esquire, same crest and motto.

Adams, Peers - Newsham, Esquire, same crest and motto.

Adams, Samuel Allen, Esquire, of Northlands, Carrickmacross, same crest and motto.

Adams, a cat-a-mountain gardant arg., collared az., resting the dexter forepaw on a terrestrial globe ppr. *Suaviter sed fortiter.* *cf.* 26. 5

Adamson, Newcastle-upon-Tyne, a cross crosslet gu. 165. 2

Adamson of Aberdeenshire and late of Ewell, Surrey, a cross crosslet fitchée az. *Crux mihi grata quies.* 166. 2

Adamson, Scotland, a cross crosslet fitched, and sword in saltier ppr. 166. 12

Adamson, a tilting-spear, broken in three pieces, two in saltier, surmounted by the head-piece in pale, pointed or, banded gu. 175. 2

Adamson, John George, Esquire, a talbot passant az., collared, charged on the shoulder with a cross invected, and holding in the dexter paw a key in pale, all or. *Watch and ward.*

Adamson of Brampton Place, Bexley Heath, Kent, a cross crosslet fitchée az. *Crux mihi grata quies.*

Adamson, Lawrence William, Esquire, LL.D., of Eglingham Hall, Northumb., a talbot passant az., collared, charged on the shoulder with a cross invected, and holding in the dexter paw a key in pale, all or. *Watch and ward.*

Adamson, William Shaw, Esquire, J.P., of Careston Castle, Brechin, co. Forfar, a sword ppr., hilted and pommelled or, and a cross crosslet fitchee gu. in saltier, all between two branches of laurel, also ppr. *Crux mihi grata quies.* 266. 4

Adamson, William Rushton, Esquire, of Rushton Park, Robertsbridge, Sussex, a talbot passant az., bezantee and collared or. *Avant.* cf. 54. 5

Adamson, a lion passant, holding in the dexter paw a cross crosslet fitched gu. cf. 6. 2

Adare, Baron, *see* Dunraven, Earl of.

Adcock or **Addcock,** a fox's head ppr. 33. 4

Addagh, a lion rampant. *Mea gloria fides.* 1. 13

Addams, a griffin's head between two wings gu. cf. 67. 7

Addcock or **Adcock,** a fox's head ppr. 33. 4

Addenbrooke, on the banks of a river an otter party per pale arg. and sa., and charged with two crescents counter-changed.

Addenbrooke, Edward Homfrav, the Platts, Kidderminster, crest as fore-going. *Nec temere nec timide.*

Addenbrooke, Herbert Henry Hodgetts, Esquire, same crest.

Addenbrooke, Rev. James Jennings, of Whixhall, Salop, same crest.

Adderbury, Sussex, an embattled tower, ppr. 156. 2

Adderley, Warw. and Staffs, on a chapeau gu., turned up erm., a stork arg. 105. 3

Adderley, Hubert John Broughton, Esquire, of Barlaston Hall, Stoke on Trent: (1) Same crest as above. (2) A sea-dog's head couped gu., eared and finned.

Adderley of Ham's Hall, Warw., same crest.

Adderley, Baron Norton, same crest. *Addere legi justitiam decus.*

Adderley, Hon. Henry Arden, of Fillongley Hall, Coventry, same crest and motto.

Adderly, Staffs and Scotland, a rose gu. 149. 2

Adderton, a hand holding a scimitar. 213. 5

Adderton and **Atherton,** Shropsh., a cubit arm grasping a truncheon. 214. 6

Addey, Kent, on a mount a stag lodged, all ppr. 115. 12

Addington, Devonsh., a leopard sejant gardant arg., pelettee.

Addington, Baron (Hubbard), in front of a fasces fessewise ppr., an eagle's head erased arg., collared fleurettee gu. *Alta petens.* 245. 4

Addington, a cat passant ppr. 26. 4

Addington, *see* Sidmouth, Viscount.

Addis, Adis, or **Ades,** out of a tower ppr. a demi-lion az. 157. 11

Addison, a tower arg. 156. 2

Addison, a pair of wings erect ppr. 109. 6

Addison, a unicorn's head erased, transpierced by an arrow, in bend sinister guttee. *Let the deed shaw.*

Addison, Sudbury, a unicorn's head erased arg., pierced through the neck with an arrow and charged on the breast with three annulets.

Addison, Staffs, a demi-unicorn couped arg., armed, ungu., and crined or, the sinister foot resting on an escutcheon gu., charged with a leopard's face of the second.

Addison, William Henry, Esquire, of Newark, Kent, and of Robertson, Cape Colony, South Africa, a snake nowed or, in front of a demi eagle, wings displayed sa., holding in the beak a snake entwined round the neck ppr. *Addecet honeste vivere.* 81. 5

Addlington or **Adlington,** Devonsh. and Lincs, a goat's head erased ppr. 128. 5

Addreston or **Aderston,** a martlet gu. cf. 95. 5

Addurston, a swan's neck and wings arg., beaked gu., gorged with a ducal coronet or.

Addy or **Addey,** on a mount a stag lodged, all ppr. 115. 12

Adean, a stag's head cabossed ppr. 122. 5

Adeane, Charles Robert Whorwood, of Babraham, Cambs, a griffin's head collared between two wings. 67. 7

Adeane, Rear-Admiral Edward Stanley, C.M.G., of 28, Eaton Place, S.W., same crest.

Adelin, a chevalier on horseback, at full speed, brandishing a sword, all ppr. 189. 10

Adelmare, the sea vert, thereon a dolphin naiant ppr.

Adelsorf, two wings elevated sa. 109. 6

Adelston or **Adeston,** an escutcheon arg., charged with a cinquefoil gu.

Adenstoun, Adingstoun, or **Adinston,** a dexter hand holding a cross pattee fitched. 221. 12

Aderley, Blackhall, Staffs, a leopard's head couped or, pierced through the mouth with a sword-blade broken arg.

Aderson, a cup or, with three branches of laurel issuing therefrom vert. 177. 2

Aderton, a hand holding a scimitar ppr. 213. 5

Aderstone, a martlet gu. 95. 5

Adey, a leopard's face or, jessant de lis gu. 22. 5

Adey, Adrey, or **Ady,** on a mount vert, a stag lodged arg., attired and ducally crowned or. cf. 115. 12

Adey, *see* Adye.

Adger, a swan with wings addorsed regardant arg., murally crowned gu., resting its dexter foot on an escallop or. 99. 7

Adie, Aedie, and **Addie,** Crieff and Scotland, a cross crosslet and sword in saltier ppr. *Crux mihi grata quies.* 166. 12

Adingstoun or **Adinston,** Scotland, a dexter hand holding a cross patee fitchee. 221. 12

Adis, out of a tower ppr., a demi lion az. 157. 11

Adkins, a lion rampant gu., supporting a flagstaff with ropes ppr., flag arg., charged with a cross of the first. cf. 3. 7

Adlam, a hand gu., holding a hawk's lure or. 217. 8

Adlam, William, of Chew Magna, Somers., on a mount vert, and in front of rays of the sun, an eagle ppr., collared sa. *Tyme proveth truth.*

Adlard, a hand holding a dagger erect, all ppr. 212. 9

Adler of Haverstoke, Essex, a demi eagle, wings displayed sa., charged on the breast with an etoile or. cf. 80. 2

Adlercron, Rodolph Ladeveze, Esquire, F.R.G.S., of Broom Hall, Horsham, Sussex, a demi-eagle displayed sa., langued gu., ducally crowned or, the dexter wing per fesse arg., and az., the sinister per fesse of the last and or. *Quo fata vocant.*

Adlington, a goat's head erased arg. 128. 5

Adlington, Henry Smith, of the Hall Holme, Hale, Shipdham, Thetford, Norf., same crest. *Per antiquam cartam.*

Adlington, an heraldic antelope's head erased arg. cf. 127. 11

Adlyn, on a mount vert, a martlet or. 95. 7

Adney, an eagle's head, holding in the beak an acorn, slipped and leaved ppr. cf. 84. 10

Adolphus, a demi lion rampant murally crowned, holding a knight's helmet between the paws.

Adshead and **Adshade,** an antelope trippant ppr. 126. 6

Adson, Scotland, an oak tree. *Stand sure.* 143. 5

Ady, Kent, on a mount vert, a stag lodged arg., attired and ducally crowned or. cf. 115. 12

Ady or **Adry,** a leopard's face or, jessant de-lis gu. 22. 5

Adye, a leopard passant gardant. cf. 24. 3

Adye and **Adyer,** Kent and Durh., a cherub's head ppr. 189. 9

Adyn, Dorchester, a lion's head ppr. cf. 17. 8

Adys, a cock crowing erm. 91. 2

Aermine, on a mount vert, an erm. arg., the tip of the tail sa. 134. 10

Aeth, a demi-griffin or, holding in the dexter claw a battle-axe gu. 64. 11

Affleck, Scotland, an eagle rising ppr. 77. 5

Affleck of Balmanno, Scotland, two wings issuing. *Rerum sapientia custos.* 109. 6

Affleck, Bart., of Dalham Hall, Newmarket, an ear of wheat or, between two fern branches ppr. *Pretiosum quod utile.* 239. 11

Affleck of that ilk, same crest and motto.

Affordbie of Affordby, Lincs, a horse's head erased sa., bridled or. cf. 51. 5

Agad, a heraldic antelope's head. 127. 10

Agall, on a chapeau ppr., a bull statant sa. cf. 45. 9

Agan, on a ducal coronet or, a stag's head cabossed ppr. cf. 122. 5

Agar, Ireland, a demi-lion rampant or. *Via trita via tuta.* 10. 2

Agar, Earl of Normanton, a demi-lion rampant or. *Via trita via tuta.* 10. 2

Agar-Ellis, Viscount Clifden, *see* Clifden.

Agar-Robartes, *see* Robartes, Baron.

Agard, Lancs, a bugle-horn arg., garnished or, stringed sa. 228. 11

Agard, Lancs, an ibex's head or, semée of hurts, maned, horned, tufted, and collared az.

Agas of Wymondham, Norf., a Moor's head sa., wreathed arg. and gu. 192. 13

Agbury, Kent and Glouc., a bird supporting a flag, charged with a cross. 78. 14

Ager or **Auger** of Bishopbourn, Kent and Glouc., a bull's head erased gu., attired or. 44. 3

Agg or **Auge,** a Moor's head couped sa., wreathed arg. and az. 192. 13

Aggs, on a chapeau ppr. a bull statant sa. *cf.* 45. 9

Aglionby, Rev. Francis Keyes, Christ Church Vicarage, Westminster, a demi-eagle displayed or. 81. 6

Agmondesham of Horsley, Surrey, a stag trippant or. 117. 8

Agmondisham or **Agmundesham,** Surrey, a stag lodged ppr. 115. 7

Agnew, the sun shining on the stump of a tree ppr. 145. 5

Agnew, a crow statant, wings expanded, transfixed with an arrow, all ppr. 107. 11

Agnew or **Agneu** of Sheuchan and Lothian, Scotland, an eagle issuant and regardant ppr. *Consilio non impetu.* 80. 10

Agnew of Lochryan, an eagle rising regardant, holding in dexter claw a sword ppr. *Consilio et impetu.* 77. 10

Agnew of Castle Wiger, an eagle rising regardant ppr. *Consilio non impetu.* 77. 4

Agnew, Hon. Sir James Wilson, K.C.M.G., M.D., M.R.C.S., of Macquarie St. Hobart, Tasmania, Member of the Executive Council, and formerly Member of Legislative Council, Chief Secretary and Premier of the said Colony, an eagle issuant rising, with wings expanded and regardant ppr., charged on the breast with a trefoil slipped vert. *Consilio non impetu.*

Agnew, Charles Stewart, Esquire, J.P., of Hobart, Tasmania, an eagle issuant rising and regardant ppr., charged on its breast with a trefoil slipped vert. *Consilio non impetu.*

Agnew, Sir Andrew, of Lochnaw, Bart., an eagle issuing regardant ppr. *Consilio non impetu.* 80. 10

Agnew, Sir William, Bart., 11, Great Stanhope St., W., an eagle regardant, wings expanded ppr., each wing charged with a pale or, holding in its mouth a sword pointing upwards ppr., the dexter claw resting on a saltier couped gu. *Consilio et impetu.* 236. 5

Agnew, Scotland, an eagle rising regardant ppr. *Si non consilio, impetu.* 80. 10

Agnew, John Vans, of Barnbarroch, Scotland: (1) An eagle issuant regardant ppr. (*for Agnew*). 80. 10. (2) A lion rampant, in dexter paw a pair of scales ppr. (*for Vans*). *Consilio non impetu.—Be faithful.*

Agrevell, a bezant. *cf.* 159. 14

Agruall, a lion's face gardant between two wings ppr. 21. 4

Aguilar and **Aguillar,** an eagle's head erased, holding in the beak a fleur-de-lis, all ppr. 84. 12

Aguillon, Yorks, a pelican vulning herself ppr. 98. 1

Agworth, a torteau. 159. 14

Ahanny or **Ahany,** Scotland, out of a crescent a cross crosslet fitched sa. *Per ardua ad alta.* 166. 9

Ahem, Ireland, a vine ppr. 152. 9

Aher, a sand-glass sa., winged gu. 113. 11

Ahlfeldt, Frederic Carl, Esquire, a brack arg., collared and sejant on a cushion gu., tasselled or. *Fortitudine suavitate.* 59. 8

Ahrends, an eagle ppr. *Post nubila phœbus.* 76. 2

Aicken, Aiken, or **Aikin,** a fountain throwing up water ppr. 159. 13

Aickinson, a demi-lady, holding in the dexter hand a tower, and in the sinister a palm-branch. 183. 8

Aickman and **Aikman,** Scotland, an oak-tree fructed ppr. *Sub robore virtus.* 143. 2

Aidgmam, a demi-eagle or, charged on the breast with a thistle ppr. *cf.* 81. 6

Aifler, two wings in lure. 113. 1

Aighton, Lancs, a snake coiled up ppr. 142. 2

Aigler or **Ayler,** two wings in lure. 113. 1

Aigles, Northumb., a hunting-horn ppr. 228. 11

Aiken, a fountain throwing up water ppr. 159. 13

Aiken, *see* **Chetwood-Aiken.**

Aiken, Scotland, a cross crosslet fitched gu. *In cruce salus.* 166. 2

Aiken, Ireland, an ox-yoke az., stapled or. 178. 6

Aiken, James, of Dalmoak, co. Dumbarton, a dexter hand couped at the wrist, holding a garland of oak-leaves ppr. *In robore decus.*

Aikenhead or **Aitkenhead,** a demi-savage holding in the dexter hand three laurel-sprigs fructed ppr. *Rupto robore nati.* *cf.* 186. 4

Aikenhead, Frank, Esquire, Naval and Military Club, 94, Piccadilly, W., a demi-man affrontée holding in his dexter hand a branch of laurel slipped and fructed, all ppr., and resting his sinister on a chaplet of oak, also ppr., fructed. *Rupto robore nati.* 258. 10

Aikenhead, Scotland, an oak-tree fructed ppr. *Annoso robore quercus.* 143. 2

Aikin or **Aicken,** an oak-tree vert. *Sub robore virtus.* 143. 5

Aikman, a man ppr., holding a standard gu., vested arg., the coat az. 187. 9

Aikman of Cairnie, an oak-tree fructed ppr. *Sub robore virtus.* 143. 2

Aikman, Thomas Stokes George Hugh Robertson, of Ross, Hamilton, N.B., an oak-tree ppr. *Sub robore virtus.*

Aikman of Bromlinton, an oak-tree fructed ppr. *Sub robore virtus.* 143. 2

Aile and **Ailes,** a dexter arm embowed, the fist clenched ppr. 202. 2

Ailesbury, Marquess and **Earl of, Earl of Cardigan, Earl Bruce, Viscount Savernake,** etc. (Brudenell-Bruce), Savernake Forest, Marlborough, Wilts: (1) A lion statant az., tail extended (*for Bruce*). *c.f.* 4. 8. (2) A sea-horse naiant ppr. (*for Brudenell*). *Think and thank.—Fuimus.* 46. 5

Aillen, Edinburgh, a pelican in her piety ppr. *Non sibi.* 98. 8

Ailmer or **Aylmer,** London, a goat passant or.

Ailsa, Marquess of (Kennedy), Culzean Castle, Maybole, a dolphin naiant ppr. *Avis la fin.* 140. 5

Aime and **Aine,** a pillar barry of four gu. and or, winged ppr. 113. 10

Aimgevyne of Theshelthorpe, Lincs, a vine or, bearing three bunches of grapes ppr. *cf.* 152. 9

Aines, Ainge, Ainger, Aitken, a common boat ppr. 179. 6

Ainge, London, a cross formée fitchée or, between two wings az. *cf.* 110. 7

Ainlie, an arm holding a laurel chaplet ensigned with a bird. *cf.* 205. 6

Ainsley or **Ainslie** of Blackhill, a pelican's head erased ppr. *Pietas tutissima virtus.* 98. 2

Ainsley, Bart., Scotland, an arm embowed brandishing a scimitar ppr. *Pro rege et patria.* 201. 1

Ainsley and **Ainslie,** Scotland, an arm embowed grasping a scimitar, all ppr. *Pro rege et patria.* 201. 1

Ainslie, Bart., Lincs, a dexter arm embowed holding a scimitar ppr. *Pro rege et patria.* 201. 1

Ainslie of Pilton, Bart., on a chapeau a dexter arm embowed grasping a scimitar ppr. *Pro patria sæpe, pro rege semper.*

Ainslie, a hand holding a scimitar ppr. 213. 5

Ainslie, Quebec, an eagle's head erased ppr. *Pietas tutissima virtus.* 83. 2

Ainslie: (1) An eagle's head erased ppr. *Pietas tutissima virtus.* 83. 2. (2) A dexter arm embowed grasping a scimitar, all ppr. *Pro rege et patria.* 201. 1

Ainslie, an arm holding in the hand two branches of laurel, ensigned with a bird. *cf.* 205. 6

Ainsworth, Richard Henry, of Smithills Hall, Lancs, a man in armour, holding in his dexter hand a battle-axe ppr. *Mea gloria fides.*

Ainsworth, David, of the Flosh, Cleator, Whitehaven, Cumb., a falcon rising with wings displayed and inverted. *Surgo et resurgam.*

Ainsworth, John Stirling, Esquire, of Harecroft, Gosforth, Cumb., and Ardanaiseig, Kilchrenan, Argyll, same crest and motto.

Ainsworth, Lieutenant-Colonel David, Backbarrow, North Lancs, a falcon, wings expanded and inverted, belled ppr. *Surgo et resurgam.* 87. 1

Air, Scotland, the stump of an oak-tree, new branches sprouting ppr. 145. 2

Aird, Scotland, a cock ppr. *Vigilantia.* 91. 2

Aird, Sir John, Bart., 14, Hyde Park Terrace, W., on a bull rail fessewise a lion rampant erect, holding between the paws a rivet, all ppr. *Vigilantia.* 251. 7

Aird, a cubit arm holding a hawk's lure, all ppr.

Airey, a cinquefoil gu. 148. 12

Airey, Lieutenant-Colonel Henry Parke, Esquire, D.S.O., of Victoria Barracks, Oxford Street, Paddington, Sydney, out of the battlements of a tower or, a dexter and a sinister arm embowed in armour ppr., the hands also ppr., holding a cinquefoil az. *Je le tiendrai.*

Airey, a leg in armour, couped at the thigh ppr., garnished and spurred or. 193. 1

Airlie, Earl of (Ogilvy), Airlie Castle, a lady from the waist, affrontée ppr., holding a portcullis gu. *A fin.* 183. 7

Airmine of Osgodsby, Bart., on a mount vert, an erm. passant arg. 134. 10

Airth, Scotland, a cock crowing ppr. 91. 2

Airth, Scotland, a stag's head erased, at gaze ppr.

Aiscough, a cross crosslet fitched az. *In hoc signo vinces.* 166. 2

Aiselbie or **Aislabie,** Yorks, a lion's head erased gu., gorged with three lozenges, conjoined in fess arg. *cf.* 17. 8

Aisincourt, a demi-eagle displayed with two heads. *cf.* 82. 1

Aiskell, Aiskill, and **Askill,** in the sea an anchor, in pale ppr. 161. 6

Aislabie, *see* Aiselbie.

Aitcheson, Scotland, a cock ppr., wattled and combed. *Vigilantibus.* 91. 2

Aitchison of Rochsolloch, the same.

Aitchison, Henry H., M.D., Wallsend-on-Tyne, a cock ppr., combed and wattled gu. *Vigilantibus.*

Aitchison, *see* **Acheson.**

Aitchison of Pittenweem, an astrolabe ppr. *Observe.* 167. 7

Aitchison, Robert Swan, Esquire, M.D., of 74, Great King Street, Edinburgh, an eagle's head erased sa. *Vigilantibus.*

Aitken, James, Esquire, of Saltcoats and Darroch, Stirling, Scotland, an oak-tree ppr. *Robore et vigilantia.* 143. 5

Aitken of Aitkenside, a cross crosslet fitched gu. *In cruce salus.* 166. 2

Aitken, Colonel R. Easton, V.D., Glasgow, a mailed arm embowed, holding a cross crosslet fitched. *In cruce salus.* 295. 13

Aitken, James H., Esquire, Garteows, Falkirk, N.B., a cross crosslet fitchée. *In cruce salus.* 166. 2

Aitken of Edenhurst, Timperley, Chesh., a cross crosslet fitchée az. *In cruce salus.*

Aitken of Thornton, Fifeshire, a cross crosslet fetchée gules. *In cruce salus.* 166. 2

Aitken, Aitkin, and **Atkin,** a boat ppr. 179. 6

Aitken, James, Esquire, Shipowner, Glasgow, a cock sa., collared and chained or. *Robore et vigilantia.*

Aitkenhead, Scotland, a demi-savage holding in his dexter hand three laurel sprigs fructed ppr. *cf.* 186. 4

Aitkenhead, Scotland, an oak-tree ppr. *Rupto robore nati.* 143. 5

Aitkens, a dexter arm in armour embowed, holding in the hand ppr. a cross crosslet fitched erect arg. 198. 5

Aitkenson, a demi-lady holding in her dexter hand a tower, and in her sinister a palm-branch. 183. 8

Aitkenson, a cock ppr. 91. 2

Aitkine, Scotland, a cross crosslet fitched gu. *In cruce salus.* 166. 2

Aitkinson, Scotland, a cock ppr. 91. 2

Aito or **Auito,** Devonsh., issuing out of a cloud a dexter arm ppr., grasping a sword erect arg., hilted or, enfiled with a Moor's head in profile sa., wreathed about the temples arg., and with pearls in the ears.

Aiton of that ilk, Scotland, Bart., a dexter hand pulling a rose ppr. *Et decerptæ dabunt odorem.* 218. 13

Aiton of Dunmure, same crest and motto.

Aiton and **Aitoune,** a rose gu. *Virtute orta occidunt rarius.* 149. 2

Aiton of Kippo, a rose-tree vert, flowered gu. *Et decerptæ dabunt odorem.* 149. 14

Aiton of Kinaldie, same crest.

Aitoune of Inchdairnie, same crest and motto.

Akarys, Akers, Akeris, and **Akyris,** a griffin's head gu. 66. 1

Akarys, a demi-griffin or. 64. 2

Akaster, a demi-griffin or. 64. 2

Akeland and **Akland,** on a sinister arm in fesse vested az., gloved arg., a hawk perched of the last, beaked and belled or. 86. 14

Akeland, a hawk belled ppr. 85. 2

Akelitz, Akelits, or **Hakelut,** a halbert issuing ppr. 172. 1

Akenhead, Scotland, an oak-tree ppr. 143. 5

Akenhead, a cock ppr. 91. 2

Akenhead, a demi-savage holding in the dexter hand a bunch of acorns. *Rupto robore nati.*

Akenside, an arrow ppr. 173. 5

Aker, a triangular harrow. 178. 4

Akeris, a griffin's head gu. 66. 1

Akerman or **Ackerman,** out of a pallisado coronet or, an arm embowed, vested gu., cuffed arg., holding in the hand ppr. an oak-branch vert, fructed of the first. 205. 1

Akeroyd and **Akroyd,** a dog sleeping ppr. 57. 13

Akers, a Doric column or.

Akers-Douglas, Rt. Hon. Aretas, M.P., of Chilston Park and Malling Abbey, Kent: (1) A dexter arm in armour embowed ppr., garnished or, grasping in the hand a dagger in bend sinister, also ppr., hilt and pommel gold (*for Douglas*). 195. 3. (2) A dexter cubit arm vested bendy or and az., the hand ppr. holding a banner, also bendy or and az., charged with a Saracen's (or Irish Kerne's) head between eight cross crosslets, fringed and tasselled or (*for Akers*). *Sapientia et veritas.—Je vive en esperance.*

Akiris, Akeris, or **Akyris,** a griffin's head gu. 66. 1

Akland, on a sinister arm in fesse, vested az., gloved arg., a hawk perched of the last, beaked and belled or. 86. 14

Akland, the same, but the hawk hooded.

Akroyd, in front of a stag's head ppr., three spear-heads sa., encircled by a wreath of oak also ppr. *In veritate victoria.*

Alabaster and **Allebaster,** a feather arg., enfiled with a ducal coronet or. 114. 13

Aland, Ireland, a leopard passant gardant or.

Aland, Lord Fortescue, same crest. *Forte scrutum salus ducem.*

Alanson, Allanson, and **Allenson,** a lion rampant gardant gu., supporting a cross or.

Alanson, on a mount vert, a lion rampant gardant gu., supporting a long cross or. 3. 15

Alate, a unicorn's head arg., collared sa. *cf.* 49. 11

Albalanda, a boar passant gu. 40. 9

Albam, an urchin ppr. 135. 8

Alban, a lion's head erased, pierced in breast with an arrow. *cf.* 17. 13

Albani, d', Arthur James Louis Francis, Esquire, of Newmarket, on a wreath of the colours two ostrich-feathers in saltire az., thereon perched a martlet or. *Vestigia nulla retrorsum.*

Albany, Shropsh., London, Beds, and Middx., a dolphin hauriant or. 140. 11

Albany, London, Shropsh., and Beds, out of a ducal coronet gu. a demi-dolphin hauriant or.

Albany, Shropsh., out of a ducal coronet a dolphin hauriant embowed or.

Albany, Duke of (H.R.H. Prince Leopold), on a coronet composed of crosses patée and fleur-de-lis a lion statant gardant and crowned with a like coronet or, and differenced with a label of three points arg., the centre point charged with St. George's cross, and each of the other points with a heart gu.

Albaster, Staffs, a feather in pale arg., enfiled with a ducal coronet or. 114. 12

Albemarle, Earl of (Keppel), Quidenham Park, Attleborough, Norf., out of a ducal coronet or, a swan's head and neck arg. *Ne cede malis.* *cf.* 100. 10

Albeney, a yoke in bend ppr. 178. 6

Albeney, Berks, a stock-dove az., holding in the beak a branch vert, fructed gu. 92. 5

Alberough or **Albrough,** a castle, at the sinister base a thistle-bush ppr. 155. 6

Alberry of Wickingham, Berks, a dove az., holding in its beak a branch fructed. 92. 5

Albert, a demi-savage, wreathed about the middle with leaves, over his shoulder a sledge-hammer, all ppr. *cf.* 186. 11

Alberton, a pennon in bend gu., the staff headed sa. and tasselled or. 176. 12

Albertus, Poland, the hull of a ship, with only main-mast, and the top without tacking or. *Deus dabit vela.*

Albery, a stock-dove az., holding in its beak a branch, leaves and stalk vert, fructed gu. 92. 5

Albon, Albone, Allebone, and **Allibone,** a bull's head affrontée. 44. 8

Alborough, Somers., a fox arg., collared and lined or.

Albrecht, a dexter cubit arm erect ppr., holding a fleur-de-lis or. *cf.* 215. 5

Albrecht or **Albreght,** a dexter hand in fesse ppr., holding a fleur-de-lis or. 221. 9

Albyn, a lion's gamb issuing sa., holding a spear or, on the top a flag gu. 35. 9

Alcester, Baron (Admiral Sir Frederick Beauchamp Paget Seymour, G.C.B.), out of a ducal coronet or, a phœnix in flames ppr. *Foy pour devoir.*

Alchorn, a human heart gu., ducally crowned or, between two wings arg. 110. 14

Alcock, Staffs, a cock gu. 91. 2

Alcock, Ireland, a cock arg., combed and wattled gu., spurred az. *Vigilanter.* 91. 2

Alcock of Silvertost, Northamp., a cock erm., beaked, membered, crested, and wattled or. 91. 2

Alcock of Wilton Castle, Ireland, a cock arg., standing on a globe, armed, combed, and gilled or. *Vigilate.*

Alcock, Ireland, on a pomeis charged with a cross patée or, a cock statant sa. *Vigilate.*

Alcock, Philip Clayton, Esquire, of Wilton Castle, Enniscorthy, same crest and motto.

Alcock, Kent, out of a ducal coronet az., a demi-swan erm., wings expanded, and ducally crowned or. *cf.* 99. 5

Alcock-Beck, *see* Beck-Alcock.

Alcock-Stawell-Riversdale. William Thomas Jonas, Esquire: (1) Out of a mural crown or, a dexter arm in armour couped at the elbow ppr., charged with an ogress, the hand grasping a sword in bend sinister, also ppr. (*for Riversdale*). (2) On a cap of maintenance gu., turned up erm., a falcon rising arg., in his beak a scroll, thereon "*En parole je vis*" (*for Stawell*). (3) A cock arg., combed and wattled gu., spurred az., and above it, on an escroll, the motto "*Vigilanter*" (*for Alcock*). *Hæc inimica tyrannis.* 91. 2

Alcock-Stawell, Jonas William, Esquire, of Kilbrittain Castle, Cork: (1) On a cap of maintenance gu., turned up erm., a falcon rising arg., in his beak a scroll, thereon *En parole je vis* (*for Stawell*). (2) A cock arg., combed and wattled gu., spurred az., and above it, on an escroll, the motto. *Vigilanter.*

Aldam, out of a ducal coronet a plume of five ostrich-feathers. 114. 13

Aldborough or **Aldeburghe**, Yorks, an ibex passant or.

Aldborough, Earl of (Stratford), Ireland, a dexter arm in armour embowed, holding in the hand ppr. a scimitar az., hilted and pommelled or. *Virtuti nihil obstat et armis.* 196. 10

Aldborough and **Aldeborough**, an escallop or, between two wings az. 141. 10

Alde, a torteau. 159. 14

Alden or **Aldon**, Herts and Middx., out of a ducal coronet or, a demi-lion gu. 16. 3

Alden, Herts and Middx., out of a ducal coronet per pale gu. and sa., a demi-lion rampant or. 16. 3

Alden, out of a coronet arg., a bat's wing gu., surmounted of another arg.

Aldenham, Baron (Gibbs), Aldenham House, Elstree, Herts, in front of a rock ppr., a dexter arm in armour embowed, the hand gauntletted ppr., holding a battle-axe in bend sinister sa. *Tenax propositi.* 231. 1

Alder, a griffin's head gu. 66. 1

Alderford, Norf., a rat ppr. 136. 11

Alderington, a dexter hand holding a hawk's lure ppr. 217. 8

Alderley, a mailed dexter arm embowed ppr., grasping a cross-hilted sword also ppr., hilted or, transfixing a boar's head sa.

Aldersey, Hugh, Esquire, J.P., of Aldersey Hall and Spurstow, Chester, a demi-griffin segreant gu., beaked and legged or, issuing from a plume of five feathers of the last. *Alnus semper floreat.* 240. 5

Aldham, issuant from a mount vert four ostrich-feathers arg., conjoined at the points by a mill-rind or.

Alderson, Norf., from a plume of feathers arg., a griffin rising of the same. 64. 9

Alderson, from behind a mount vert, thereon a branch of alder, the sun rising ppr.

Alderson, a pillar ppr. 176. 3

Alderson, Middx.: (1) A dove, in its beak an olive-branch ppr. (*for Alderson*). 92. 5. (2) A boar's head couped or (*for Lloyd*). 43. 1

Alderton, Suff., a crescent arg. 163. 2

Aldewinckle, Aldewincle, Aldewinkell, Aldwinckle, and **Aldwinkle**, a wyvern, wings addorsed, ducally crowned, vomiting fire. 70. 10

Aldham, Shrimpling, Norf., a talbot's head erased or, collared sa., lined gu. *cf.* 56. 2

Aldhouse, Aldhowse, Aldehowse, Aldous, or **Aldus**, a bird rising gu. 87. 3. (*The above crest was exhibited at the Visitation of Suffolk, anno 1664, by John Aldhowse of Moulton, in that county, when he recorded his pedigree. It was, however, "respited for further proof," which does not appear to have been made.*)

Aldirford, a monkey's head ppr. 136. 14

Aldjo, a stump of an oak sprouting new branches ppr. 145. 2

Aldon, out of a ducal coronet or, a demi-lion gu.

Aldred, an arm in armour embowed, holding a cross crosslet fitched in pale. 198. 5

Aldrich, a bull passant arg., armed or. *Fortitudo vincet.* *cf.* 45. 2

Aldrich-Blake, *uses* the same.

Aldrich, a griffin segreant. 62. 2

Aldridge, Charles Powlett, of St. Leonard's Forest, Sussex, an arm couped below the shoulder vested az., charged with a bezant, the hand holding a quill arg. *Dirige.*

Aldridge, Herbert Henry, Esquire, same crest and motto.

Aldridge, John Barttelot, Esquire, same crest and motto.

Aldridge or **Aldrige**, a phœnix in flames ppr. 82. 2

Aldridge, a phœnix in flames ppr., charged on the breast and on each wing with a bezant.

Aldrington, a dexter hand holding a hawk's lure ppr. 217. 8

Aldwell, Lieutenant-Colonel Theobald Butler, M.A., co. Moyne, Tipperary, Ireland, an osprey with wings elevated ppr., resting the dexter claw upon an escutcheon of the *Butler* arms, viz., "or, a chief indented az."

Aldwell, Rev. Basil S., of St. Luke's, Portsea, Hants, same crest.

Aldwinckle, *see* Aldewinckle.

Aldwinkle, *see* Aldewinckle.

Aldworth, R., Esquire, of Newmarket, Ireland, a dexter arm in armour embowed, the hand grasping a sword, all ppr. *Nec temere, nec timide.*

Aldworth, Robert, Esquire, of Westlake, West Coker, Yeovil, Somerset, and Newmarket Court, Newmarket, co. Cork, same crest and motto.

Aldworth, Scotland, a torteau. 159. 14

Aldworth, a demi-dragon rampant arg., holding a cross crosslet fitchée gu.

Aldworth, a sand-glass winged. 113. 11

Alen, Ireland, a heraldic tiger holding a rose.

Alen, Ireland, a demi-heraldic tiger quarterly or and gu., gorged with a collar counterchanged, chained of the first, and holding between the paws a juilie flower of three branches ppr. *Fortis et fidelis.*

Alençon, France, a greyhound arg. *cf.* 60. 2

Alephe, London, a cock's head erased. 90. 1

Aleston or **Alston**, a lion passant regardant gu., ducally gorged and chained. *cf.* 6. 1

Alexander, Earl of Stirling, a bear sejant erect ppr. *Per mare, per terras.* 34. 8

Alexander, Major George Agar, Colamore Lodge, Dalkey, co. Dublin, crest as above.

Alexander, Porydstone, Ayr, a bear sejant. *Per mare, per terras.* 34. 8

Alexander, Very Rev. John, of Mulrankin Rectory, Wexford, same crest and motto.

Alexander, a bear rampant ppr.

Alexander, Scotland, an elephant passant ppr. *Per mare, per terras.* *cf.* 133. 9

Alexander, Sir Claud, Bart., J.P., of Ballochmyle, co. Ayr, Scotland, an elephant ppr. *Perseverantia vincit.* 133. 9

Alexander-Sinclair, Edwyn Sinclair, Esquire, of Freswick, Caithness-sh., an elephant passant ppr. *Perseverantia vincit.*

Alexander, *see* Caledon, Earl of. 195. 2

Alexander, a dexter arm in armour embowed, holding a sword ppr., pommel and hilt or. 195. 2

Alexander, Summerhill, Kent, a hand holding a sword ppr. 212. 13

Alexander, Kent, a cubit arm erect, holding a sword ppr., pommel and hilt or. 212. 3

Alexander, Sir Lionel Cecil, Bart., Kentstown, co. Meath, a dexter arm embowed, holding a dagger ppr., charged on the wrist with a mullet or. *Per mare, per terras.*

Alexander, James Dalison, D.L., Hampsell Manor, Eridge, Sussex, an arm in armour embowed ppr., holding a dagger of the last, hilt and pommel or. *Per mare, per terras.*

Alexander, Granville Henry Jackson, Esquire, J.P. and D.L., of Forkhill, co. Armagh, an arm in armour embowed, the hand grasping a sword, all ppr., and charged on the elbow with an annulet sa. *Per mare, per terras.*

Alexander, Lesley William, Esquire, J.P., of 29, Campden Grove, Kensington, an arm embowed in armour ppr., in the hand a sword, all ppr., pommel and hilt or. *Per mare, per terras.*

Alexander, London, an arm in armour embowed, the hand grasping a sword, all ppr. 195. 2

Alexander, Henry, Esquire, D.L., of Forkhill, co. Armagh, Ireland, an arm in armour embowed, the hand grasping a sword in bend sinister ppr., on the elbow an annulet sa. *Per mare, per terras.* *cf.* 195. 2

Alexander of Pitkellie, two dexter hands conjoined in fesse. *Ora et labora.* 224. 2

Alexander of Auchmull, a hand holding a pair of scales ppr. *Quod tibi ne alteri.* 217. 13

Alexander of Boghall, a hand holding a quill-pen. *Fidem servo.* 217. 10

Alexander, Scotland, a talbot arg., collared gu. 54. 2

Alexander, Hants, a talbot's head erased arg., collared gu. *Nil desperandum.* 56. 1

Alexander of Kinglassie, a horse's head couped gu., bridled arg. *Ducitur non trahitur.* 51. 5

Alexander, a horse's head arg., bridled sa. *Ducitur non trahitur.* 51. 5

Alexander, a cock arg., beaked and membered gu. 91. 2

Alexander, Stirling, a beaver ppr. *Per mare, per terras.* 134. 8

Alexander of Powis, same crest and motto.

Alexander, Scotland, on a mount vert, an otter passant ppr. *Per mare, per terras.* *cf.* 134. 5

Alexander, Scotland, a serpent waved in fesse ppr. *Ingenium vires superat.* 142. 6

Alexander, Scotland, a serpent coiled in fesse. *Ingenium vires superat.*

Alexander, Halifax, Yorks, a demi-lion gardant, wickling with its dexter paw a battle-axe ppr., the sinister paw resting on a cross fleury, and gorged with a collar az., charged with two bezants.

Alford, Berks and Sussex, a boar's head arg., with a broken spear in the mouth, handle thrust down the throat or. 42. 10

Alford, Surrey, Yorks, and Shropsh., a boar's head erect arg., in the mouth three feathers of a pheasant's tail ppr. 41. 12

Alford, Charles John, Esquire, F.R.G.S., of 30, Wilbury Road, Brighton, an escallop inverted arg., surmounting a crosier in bend sinister or. *Vive ut vivas.* 261. 16

Alford, Edward Fleet, Esquire, F.R.G.S., F.L.S., of 26, the Boltons, South Kensington, same crest and motto.

Alford, Rev. Josiah George, of Stoke Bishop Vicarage, Bristol, same crest and motto.

Alford, Robert Gervase, Esquire, F.R.G.S., of 30, Wilbury Road, Brighton, same crest and motto.

Alford, Suff., a hind's head ppr. 124. 1

Alford, Viscount, *see* Brownlow, Earl.

Alfounder, Essex, an arm couped at the elbow and erect, vested gu., cuffed arg., holding in the hand ppr. three nails or, all between two wings of the second. 207. 9

Alfrey and **Allfrey,** an ostrich-head and neck between two ostrich-feathers arg. 97. 14

Alfrey and **Allfrey,** an ostrich-head and neck between two ostrich-feathers arg., gorged with a ducal coronet or. 97. 9

Algar and **Alger,** a greyhound's head sa., charged with four bezants or. 61. 12

Algar, Claudius George, Esquire, solicitor, 17, Abchurch Lane, London, E.C., a greyhound's head. *Honore et amore.* 61. 12

Algeo, the stump of a tree ppr. *Non deficit alter.*

Algeo, Captain Henry James, of Ballybrack, co. Dublin, the stump of a tree ppr. *Non deficit alter.*

Algeo, Lewis, Esquire, of Glenboz Manor, Hamilton, co. Leitrim, the stump of a tree ppr. *Non deficit alter.*

Algie, Algeo, and **Algoe,** a bear rampant supporting a staff raguly. 34. 9

Algist, a dexter and a sinister arm, couped in saltier, each from the shoulder, vested gu., cuffed or, and holding in the hand ppr. a scimitar arg., hilted of the second. 203. 10

Algloval, a goat statant arg.

Algoe, Scotland, a bear sejant erect, supporting a staff. 34. 7

Algoe, *see* Algie.

Algood and **Allgood,** two arms in armour embowed, holding up a flaming heart, all ppr. 194. 7

Algood, Northumb. and Devonsh., two arms in armour embowed ppr., holding in the hands a human heart gu., inflamed or, charged with a tower triple-towered arg. 194. 10

Alicock, Northamp., a cock erm., combed and wattled or. 91. 2

Alie, a dexter hand holding up the sun ppr.

Alington, Baron (Alington), a talbot passant ppr., billettée or. *Dieu est tout.* *cf.* 54. 1

Alington, of Swinhope, Lincs, a talbot passant erm. 54. 1

Alington, Baron (Sturt), Crichel, Wimborne, a demi-lion rampant gu., holding a banner of the last charged with a rose arg., the staff and fringe or. *En Dieu est tout.* 251. 2

Alington, Vice-Admiral Arthur Hildebrand, J.P., of Swinhope, North Thoresby, S.O., Lincs, a talbot passant erm. *Non pour haine.—En Dieu est tout.*

Alington, Julius, Esquire, J.P., of Little Barford, St. Neot's, co. Hunts, same crest and motto.

Alison, Scotland, a tree ppr., with a bell hung on the branches on each side. *Crescit sub pondere virtus.* 143. 10

Alison, Scotland, an oak-tree ppr., with a weight hanging on each side. *Crescit sub pondere virtus.* 143. 10

Alison, Scotland, an eagle's head erased ppr. *Vincit veritas.* 83. 2

Alison, Rev. A., Scotland, an eagle's head erased ppr. *Vincit veritas.* 83. 2

Alison, Major-General Sir Archibald, K.C.B., 2nd Bart., 93, Eaton Place, same crest and motto.

Alison and **Allison,** Scotland, a falcon's head erased ppr. *Vincit veritas.* 88. 12

Aljoy, Scotland, the stump of an oak-tree, new branches sprouting. *Non deficit alter.* 145. 2

Alkene, Askue, or **Ayskew,** a man's head affrontée, couped at shoulders. *cf.* 190. 5

Allaire, on a lily a butterfly volant ppr.

Allam of Normanhurst, Romford, on a mount vert, a bull passant gu. *Nil sine labore.* 45. 7

Allan, Scotland, a talbot's head erased sa. *Spero.* 56. 2

Allan, James, Esquire, shipowner, Glasgow, a talbot's head erased sa. *Spero.* 56. 2

Allan, Bryce, Esquire, shipowner, Liverpool, a talbot's head erased sa. *Spero.* 56. 2

Allan, Alexander, Esquire, shipowner, Glasgow, a talbot's head erased sa. *Spero.* 56. 2

Allan, Alexander, of Aros House, near Tobermory, Isle of Mull, N.B., same crest and motto.

Allan, R. S., of 15, Woodside Terrace, Glasgow, same crest and motto.

Allan, Robert Gilkison, Esquire, of Rosemont, Aigburth, Liverpool, a talbot's head erased sa. *Spero.*

Allan, Scotland, a comet ppr. *Lucco et terreo.* 164. 10

Allan, Durh., a demi-lion rampant ppr., holding up a rudder gu. *Fortiter gerit crucem.* 11. 11

Allan, Scotland, a dexter arm bendways grasping a sabre ppr. *Dirigat Deus.*

Allan, Scotland, a cross crosslet fitched gu. *Fide et labore.* 166. 2

Allan of Middlesex and of Errol, Scotland, an eagle rising ppr. *Fortiter.* 77. 5

Allan of Eastwood, Mid-Lothian, the same.

Allan, *see* Havelock-Allan.

Allan of Blackwell Grange, Durh., a demi-lion rampant arg., ducally crowned gu., holding in the dexter paw a cross-potent or, and supporting with the sinister a rudder of the second. *Fortiter gerit crucem.* 11. 9

Allan, Barton, Yorks, same crest and motto.

Allanby, Henry Charles Rynman, of Monk's Tower, Lincoln, a crescent gu., issuant therefrom a demi-lion rampant ppr., holding between the paws a horseshoe, also gu. *Fide et labore.* 266. 3

Allanby, *see* **Montgomerie.**

Alland, a bear's paw erect ppr. 36. 6

Allanson, a demi-eagle, wings expanded. *Virtute et labore.* 80. 2

Allanson, Yorks and Lancs, a demi-griffin, wings displayed erm., collared gemelle.

Allanson, *see* Alanson.

Allanson-Winn, *see* Headley, Baron.

Allanson and **Allenson,** on a mount vert, a lion rampant gardant or, supporting a long cross gu. 3. 15

Allanson, John Bath, Carnarvon, Wales, issuant from a mount vert, a demi-lion guardant or, holding in the paws a cross gu. *Labor et honor.*

Allardas, Allardice, Allerdyce, Scotland, a torteau between two wings az. *cf.* 110. 4

Allardice, a dove and olive-branch. *Amicitia sine fraude.* 92. 5

Allardice and **Allerdice** of that ilk, a naked man from the middle grasping in his dexter hand a scimitar, all ppr. *In defence of the distressed.—My defence.* 186. 3

Allardice, Barclay-, David Stuart, of Belmont Avenue, Providence, Rhode Island, U.S.A.: (1) A naked man from the middle, holding in his dexter hand a scimitar ppr. (*for Allardice*). 186. 3. (2) A Bishop's mitre or (*for Barclay*). *In defence of the distressed.—In cruce spero.* *cf.* 180. 5

Allardice, Barclay-, Robert, Esquire, of Rose Hill, Lostwithiel, Cornw.: (1) A naked man from the middle, in his dexter hand a scimitar, all ppr. (2) A bishop's mitre or (*for Barclay*). *In defence of the distressed.—In cruce spero.*

Allardice, formerly of Dunninald an ear of wheat and a palm-branch in saltier ppr. *Bene qui pacifici.* 154. 10

Allatt, a unicorn's head arg., collared sa. cf. 49. 11

Allatt, on a demi-bezant issuing a bee-hive, bees swarming ppr.

Allaunson, Durh., a pheon arg., the shaft broken or. 174. 10

Allaunson, on a mount vert, a lion rampant gardant gu., supporting a long cross or. 3. 15

Allaway and **Alloway,** an anchor in pale ppr. 161. 1

Allaway and **Alloway,** on an anchor a dove, holding in its beak an olive-branch, all ppr. cf. 94. 4

Allaway, Heref., two anchors in saltier sa., thereon a dove holding in the beak a branch of olive ppr. *Dei dono sum quod sum.*

Allcard, Lancs, a demi-swan, wings elevated arg., semée of mullets az., holding in the beak a bulrush ppr. *Semel et semper.*

Allchin, William Henry, M.D., 5, Chandos Street, Cavendish Square, W., a human heart gu., ducally crowned or, between two wings displayed arg. *Non est mortale quod opto.*

Allcock, *see* Alcock.

Allcroft, Herbert John, of Stokesay Court, Salop, out of the battlements of a tower a demi-lion ppr., holding in the dexter paw a flagstaff, therefrom flowing to the sinister a banner sa., charged with a tower arg., and resting the sinister paw on an escutcheon, also arg., charged with a fleur-de-lis sa. *Dat Deus incrementum.*

Allden, Alldin, and **Alldon,** a scimitar and a caduceus in saltier, ensigned with a round hat. cf. 171. 1

Allebaster, *see* Alabaster and Arblaster.

Allebone, *see* Albon.

Alger, *see* Algar.

Alleet, Ireland, a demi-unicorn salient regardant arg., horned and maned or. 48. 9

Allen, Middx., *see* Allan.

Allen, James Franklin Swithen, Esquire, M.D., M.Ch., R.U.I., of Pietermaritzburg, Natal, South Africa, an ogress charged with a talbot's head erased or. *Fidelis morte tam vitæ.* 263. 6

Allen, Viscount, Ireland, a bezant charged with a talbot's head erased sa. *Triumpho morte tam vitâ.* cf. 57. 1

Allen, the late William, of Wink House, Thurnscoe, Yorks, a talbot's head erased ppr., collared gu. *Semper vigilans.*

Allen, Samuel, Esquire, M.A., LL.D., J.P., Barrister-at-law, of Lisconnan, Dervock, co. Antrim, Ireland, a bezant charged with a talbot's head erased sa., gorged with a chaplet of fern ppr. *Malo mori quam fœdari.* 57. 1

Allen, Chelsea, a talbot's head erased per pale, indented arg. and gu., collared and chained sa.

Allen, Colonel Ralph Edward, of Bathampton, Somers., same crest.

Allen, London, a talbot passant sa., collared gu., ears and chain or. cf. 54. 5

Allen, Benjamin Haigh, of Clifford Priory, Heref., same crest.

Allen, Jefferys Philip Thomas, of Lyngford, Taunton, same crest.

Allen, George Edmund, of Wickeridge, Ashburton, Devonsh., same crest.

Allen of Grove, Kent, on a ducal coronet or, lined erm., a bloodhound passant sa., collared of the first, armed gu. cf. 54. 9

Allen, Kent, on a ducal coronet or, lined erm., a bloodhound statant sa., collared or. cf. 54. 9

Allen, on a mount vert, a hound statant sa. 57. 4

Allen, Kent, a talbot passant or, collared gu. cf. 54. 1

Allen, Kent, on a mount vert, paled round or, a hound sa., collared or.

Allen, a demi-greyhound rampant paly of six arg. and sa., collared gu., holding between the paws a crescent or.

Allen, Yorks, a demi-greyhound rampant sa., holding in his dexter paw a crescent arg. *Diligenter et fideliter.*

Allen, Marcus, Esquire, a bezant charged with a talbot's head erased sa., gorged with a chaplet of fern ppr. *Malo mori quam fœdari.*

Allen, Samuel, Esquire, J.P., same crest and motto.

Allen, Berks, a bird, wings elevated. *Triumpho morte tam vitâ.*

Allen, Chesh., a martlet or, wings elevated sa., collared gu. cf. 95. 11

Allen, Chester, a martlet rising or, winged sa. cf. 95. 11

Allen or **Alleyn,** Chesh., Suff., and Wilts, a martlet arg., winged and holding in the beak an acorn or, leaved vert.

Allen, Pembroke, the same crest. *Amicitia sine fraude.*

Allen of Inchmartin, Perthsh., and Eveley, Hants, an eagle rising ppr. *Fortiter.* 77. 5

Allen of London, a dove holding in its beak an olive-branch. *At spes solamen.—Amicitia sine fraude.* 92. 5

Allen, George Baugh, Esquire, of 5, Albert Terrace, Regent's Park, same crest. *Amicitia sine fraude.*

Allen, Henry Seymour, of Cresselly, Pembroke, a dove holding in its beak an olive-branch. *Amicitia sine fraude.* 92. 5

Allen of Hazel Hill, Neyland, Pembrokesh., a dove holding in the beak an olive-branch, all ppr.

Allen, Somers., a partridge, wings elevated.

Allen, a cock or, combed, wattled, and legged gu. 91. 2

Allen, Middx., an eagle rising ppr. *Fortiter.* 77. 5

Allen of Errol, an eagle perched, wings expanded. *Fortiter.* 77. 5

Allen, Ralph Edward, Esquire, of 10, Hanover Square, W., a Cornish chough with wings endorsed ppr. *Jamais arrière.*

Allen, Scotland, a demi-lion gu. *Remember.* 10. 3

Allen of Thaxted, Essex, Bart., and Fenchurch, Middx., a demi-lion az., holding a rudder. 11. 11

Allen, Berks, a naked demi-female, holding in her dexter hand a spear erect, all ppr.

Allen, Ireland, a demi-tiger rampant gu. *Virtus auro præferenda.* cf. 25. 10

Allen, Richmond Robert, M.D., of 2, West Hill, Dartford, Kent, a demi-heraldic tiger gu. *Virtus auro præferenda.*

Allen, Devonsh., a mullet gu., pierced or.

Allen, van, William Harman, Esquire, Ph.D., 435, Fifth Avenue, New York, U.S.A., two wings displayed gu., each charged with a chevron arg. 110. 2

Allen, out of a ducal coronet or, a horse's head arg. *Sine labe decus.* 51. 7

Allen, Hogge-: (1) The battlements of a tower ppr., therefrom issuing a horse's head per chevron engrailed arg. and gu. (*for Allen*). (2) Two spears in saltire in front of an oak-tree eradicated and fructed, all ppr. (*for Hogge*). *Quercus glandifera amica porcis.* cf. 50. 4

Allen, Edward, Esquire, of Stowford Lodge, Ivybridge, South Devonsh., a lion's head erased. *Diligenter et fideliter.*

Allen, a griffin's head erased, per fesse arg. and gu. 66. 2

Allen, London, a demi-griffin, holding a branch vert, fructed or. cf. 64. 2

Allen, an arm vested az., the hand holding a hunting-horn gu., garnished or. *Vivite fortes.*

Allen, Captain Robert Calder, R.N., C.B., 72, Shirland Gardens, Maida Vale, London, an arm vested az., the hand holding a hunting-horn gu., garnished or. *Vivite fortes.*

Allen, Surrey, issuing out of flames of fire an arm couped at the elbow erect, holding in the hand a human heart, all ppr. 216. 11

Allen, out of a ducal coronet or, two falchion-swords, saltireways, all ppr.

Allen, a snake coiled supporting two pennons in saltier. 175. 12

Allen, Lancs, out of a coronet a wolf's head erm., maned or.

Allen, the late George, Esquire, of Queen's Terrace, Windsor, on a mount vert, a wheat-ear ppr., rising and regardant, holding in the beak an ear of wheat or, between four similar ears of wheat, two on either side. *God giveth the increase.* 271. 7

Allen, Rev. George Cantrell, M.A., of Cranleigh School, Surrey, same crest and motto.

Allenson and **Alleson,** a talbot's head or, collared and ringed az., between two wings expanded of the last.

Allenson, a demi-lion rampant gardant, holding a cross gu.

Allerdyce, *see* Allardyce.

Allerton, Baron (Jackson), Allerton Hall, Leeds, a horse or, holding in the mouth an ear of wheat slipped vert, and resting the foreleg on three annulets, one and two interlaced gu. *Essayes.*

Allerton, a lion's head gu., collared sa. 18. 6

Alles and **Allez,** a thistle ppr. 150. 5

Allestowe or **Hallestowe,** a hand holding the butt-end of a broken spear.

3 1833 02617 9272

Allestry, a demi-lion rampant az, brandishing a scimitar arg, hilted or 14 10
Allett of Iwood, Somers, a unicorn's head arg, collared sa *cf* 49 11
Allett, a unicorn's head erased arg, collared with a bar gemel sa, horned or *cf* 49 5
Alley, a lion's face or, between two wings sa 21 4
Alley, Ireland, out of a ducal coronet or, a mullet gu, between two laurel-branches vert.
Alleyn and **Allyn,** Devonsh, a demi lion rampant az, supporting a rudder or 11. 11
Alleyn, a demi lion gu, supporting a rudder sa 11 11
Alleyn and **Allyn,** a demi lion rampant az, fretty arg, holding a rudder gu *cf* 11 11
Alleyn, issuing out of flames of fire, an arm couped at the elbow and erect, holding a human heart, all ppr 216 11
Alleyne, Sir John Gay Newton, Bart, of Alleyn Dale Hall, Barbados, and Chevin, Belper, Derbysh, out of a ducal coronet or, a horse's head arg *Non tua te moveant sed publica vota.* 51 7
Allez, *see* Alles
Allfrey, an ostrich head between two ostrich-feathers arg 97 14
Allfrey, Herbert Cyril (late of Wokefield Park, Berks), an ostrich head and neck gorged with a coronet or, between two ostrich-feathers arg 97 9
Allgood Rev James, M A, of Nunwick, Northumb, two arms in armour embowed ppr, holding in the hands a human heart, inflamed, charged with a tower, triple towered arg *Age omne bonum* 194 10
Allgood, Rev James, M A, same crest and motto
Allhusen, Augustus Henry Eden, Esquire, Stoke Court, Stoke Pogis, Bucks, a demi-lion rampant gardant az, holding in the dexter paw a passion cross or, all between two open buffalo-horns of the last *Devant si je puis* 11 13
Allhusen, William Hutt, Esquire, of 15, Kensington Palace Gardens W a demi lion guardant az, holding in the dexter paw a passion-cross or, between two open buffalo horns of the last *Devant si je puis*
Allhusen, Wilton, Esquire, of 61, Eaton Place, S W, a demi-lion guardant az, holding in the dexter paw a passion cross or, between two open buffalo horns of the last *Honour first.*
Allibane, a spaniel sejant ppr 57 9
Allibone, *see* Albon
Allicock and **Allicocke,** a cock ppr 91 2
Allieson or **Allison,** a demi savage brandishing a scimitar ppr 186 3
Allin, Suff, a snake coiled up and environed with flags or rushes ppr
Allin, a partridge, wings expanded
Allin, Bart (1) A sword erect arg, hilt and pommel or 170 2 (2) On an open Bible a hand couped closed holding a sword erect
Allingbridge, a castle triple-towered ppr, flag displayed arg, charged with a cross sa 155 8
Allingham, a church and spire environed with trees ppr 158 11
Allington, out of a ducal coronet or, a buck's head ppr, attired of the first, pierced through the neck with an arrow of the same, barbed and flighted arg
Allington, a talbot or, langued gu *cf* 54 2
Allington, of Horse Heath, Cambs, a talbot passant erm 54 1
Allington, a talbot passant erm *Non pour haine* 54 1
Allison, *see* Alison
Allison, a pheasant holding in the dexter claw a key, and in the beak an ear of barley ppr 90 12
Allison, Scotland, an eagle's head erased ppr *Vincit veritas* 83 2
Allison, the late Colonel James John, D L, J P, of Beaufront Roker, Sunderland a peacock in pride ppr *Vincit veritas* 103 12
Allison, Robert Andrew, of Scaleby Hall, Carlisle same crest and motto
Allison, Col William Henry, J P, D L, of Undercliffe, Durh, same crest and motto
Alliston, Frederick Prat, Esquire, of Kamesburgh, Beckenham, Kent, in front of an eagle's head erased holding in the beak a sprig of the cotton-tree slipped and fructed, all ppr, a shuttle fesseways or, thread pendent gu *Renovate animos*
Allix, Noel Charles Noel, Willoughby Hall, Lincs, a wolf's head erased ppr 30 8
Allmack, a tower ppr *Cavendo tutus* 156 2
Allman, Sussex, a leg in armour couped above the knee ppr, spurred or 193 1
Allnett and **Allnutt,** a thunderbolt ppr 174 13
Allot and **Allott,** an arm couped at the shoulder and embowed ppr, the elbow resting on the wreath, vested gu, grasping a sword enfiled with a leopard's head 204 4
Allot and **Allott,** the same, but the arm not vested
Allot of Hague Hall, Yorks, a dexter cubit arm erect vested or, charged with a fesse double cotised wavy az, the cuff arg, holding in the hand ppr a mullet or *Fortiter et recte* 266 2
Allot, John George, Esquire, of Eastfield, Louth, Lincs, same crest and motto
Allott, Yorks a cubit arm erect, vested gu, cuffed or, holding in the hand ppr a mullet of the second *cf* 206 13
Allott, Rev Henry Hepworth, of the Rectory, Stifford, Grays, Essex, a dexter arm couped at the elbow, habited or charged with a fesse double cotised wavy az, cuff arg, the hand ppr holding a mullet or *Fortiter et recte* 266 2
Allott, Rev Robert James, of Westgate, Louth, Lincs, same crest and motto
Alloway, an anchor in pale ppr 161 1
Alloway, an anchor in pale ppr, thereon a dove holding an olive branch ppr *cf* 94 4
Allport, Cannock, Staffs, and Shropsh, a demi lion erminois, gorged with a mural coronet gu
Allpress of St James's Street, Westminster, on a mount vert, an eagle with two hands displayed per pale nebuly az and gu, resting each claw upon a pomegranate leaved and slipped or *Mors levior quam dedecus*
Allsop, Allsup, and **Alsope,** a dove holding in its beak an olive-branch ppr. 92 5
Allsopp, Baron Hindlip, *see* Hindlip
Alltham and **Altham,** a demi-lion gu, supporting the rudder of a ship sa 11 11
Allvey and **Alvey,** a plough ppr 178 7
Allwright or **Alwright,** on a chapeau a greyhound statant, all ppr 58 4
Allye, Tewkesbury, Glouc, a leopard's head or, between two wings sa.
Allye, Dorset, a stag's head erased per pale arg and or, attired of the first, gorged with a collar embattled and counter-embattled gu, charged with three escallops of the second
Allyn, a tree eradicated vert, fructed with branches of berries gu
Almack, Suff, a tower arg, thereon a flag having inscribed on it "*Pax.*" *Mael. al sicker* 157 13
Alman, of Pearnsey, Sussex, a leg in armour, spurred or, couped in the middle of the thigh 193 1
Almanerlaval, a tower ppr 156 2
Almard, a stag trippant ppr 117 8
Almayne, on a ducal coronet or, a cinquefoil gu
Almears or **Almeers,** a long cross crossed on three grieces arg 166 6
Almer and **Almor,** a palmer's staff erect or
Almericus, a nag's head erased arg, ducally gorged or *cf* 51 4
Almewake and **Alnwick,** on a chapeau a cock, all ppr 91 12
Almiger, on a ducal coronet ppr, a tiger sejant gu 24 11
Almond, three cinquefoils az, stalked and leaved vert
Almond, a globe vert garnished and ensigned with a cross patee or. 159 12
Almot, Alnot, and **Alneot,** a thunderbolt ppr 174 13
Alms, a stag's head erased or 121 2
Alnwick, on a chapeau a cock, all ppr 91 12
Alpe, a bull's head erased sa 44 3
Alphe, Hants, out of a ducal coronet or, a hawk's head arg 89 4
Alphe, Hants, out of a ducal coronet an eagle's head ppr *cf* 83 14
Alpin, Scotland, a man's head couped affrontee ppr *Virtutis regia merces* 190 10
Alport, Staffs, Warw, and Shropsh, a demi-lion erminois, gorged with a mural coronet gu
Alred, Holderness, Yorks, a griffin's head ppr 66 1
Alsop and **Alsope,** *see* Allsop
Alsop, Derbysh and Leics, a dove, wings expanded or, beaked and legged gu, holding in its beak an ear of wheat of the first
Alsop, a dove, in its beak an ear of wheat, all ppr, and in its dexter claw a key erect sa 92 1
Alsoppe, London a dove arg legged gu between two ostrich feathers sa
Alspath and **Alspach,** two spears in saltire az

Alstantan or **Alstanton,** out of a mural coronet or, an arm in armour embowed holding a dagger, all ppr

Alston, Crewe, Odell, Beds, an estoile or, between the horns of a crescent arg *Immotus* 163 4

Alston or **Alstone,** of Chelsea, Bart, and of Mile End, Bart, same crest

Alston, a star ppr. *E tenebris lux* 164 3

Alston, Charles Henry, Esquire, of Letterawe, Loch Awe Argyll, N B, a demi eagle rising ppr, on each wing a crescent reversed gu *In altum* c/ 80 2

Alston, George, Esquire, of Hill House, Newbury, Berks, same crest and motto

Alston, William, Esquire, of Stockbriggs, Lanarksh, same crest and motto

Alston, William Charles, Esquire, of Elmdon Hall, near Birmingham, same crest and motto

Alston, William Hamilton, Esquire, of Oakburn, Helensburgh, N B, a demi eagle rising ppr *In Altum* 80 2

Alston, a lion passant regardant gu 6 1

Alston, Scotland, a demi eagle rising ppr *In altum* 80 2

Alston, Charles Henry, Esquire, merchant, Glasgow, a demi eagle rising ppr, on each wing a crescent reversed gu *In altum* c/ 80 2

Alston, Westerton, an eagle issuing, wings expanded ppr *Sursum* 80. 2

Alstone, Colonel, Scotland, a demi eagle, wings expanded and inverted ppr, on each wing a crescent reversed gu *In altum* c/ 80 2

Alstone of Newton, Suff, Assington, and Marleford, out of a crescent arg, an etoile or *Immotus* c/ 163 4

Altamont, Earl of, *see* Sligo, Marquess of

Altham and **Alltham,** a demi-lion gu, supporting a rudder sa 11 11

Altham, Cook- (1) A demi-lion or, holding a ship's rudder sa (*for Altham*) 11 11 (2) A talbot sejant sa., collared or, reposing the dexter fore paw on an escutcheon arg, charged with an estoile az (*for Cook*) *Pro Deo et Catholica fide* c/ 55 3

Altham, Edward, Esquire (1) A demi lion or, charged with three mullets and erased gu, holding a ship's rudder sa (2) A talbot sejant sa, collared or, reposing the dexter forepaw on an escutcheon arg, charged with an estoile az *Pro Deo et Catholica fide*

Altham, John Altham Surtees, Esquire, same crest and motto

Althan or **Althaun,** a demi-archer vested, shooting ppr 187 6

Althorp, Viscount, *see* Spencer, Earl of

Althoun, a dexter hand apaumée ppr 222 14

Alvanley, Baron (Arden), out of a ducal coronet or, five ostrich feathers arg, charged with a crescent. *Patientia vinces* 114 3

Alvarde, Ipswich, *see* Alverd

Alvares, a demi-lion rampant ppr, holding in the dexter paw a mascle az

Alvas, Alves, and **Alvis,** Scotland, a garb or *Deo favente* 153 2

Alvensleben, Baron de, out of a marquess's coronet ppr, a staff raguly per pale gu and or, couped, surmounted by a rose

Alverd, Alured, or **Alvarde,** a mill-rind or 165 11

Alverstone, Baron (Webster), Winterfold, Cranleigh, Surrey, a swan's head and neck erased ppr, encircled by an annulet az, and holding in the beak a like annulet. *Veritas puritas* 245 2

Alves and **Alvis,** *see* Alvas

Alwaye, Streetely, Beds, a hind's head arg, between two holly branches vert, fructed with berries gu

Alwood and **Allwood,** a demi-stag salient ppr, attired or 119 2

Alwyn, Essex, a lion's gamb erect and erased sa., enfiled with a mural coronet or c/ 36 1

Alye, a lion's face or, between two wings sa. 21 4

Alye, a leopard's face or, between a pair of wings displayed sa

Alye, Dorset, a stag's head erased per pale arg and or, on the neck a fesse crenelle gu, charged with three escallops of the second

Alyson, Kent, a pheon arg, with part of broken shaft or 174 10

Amand, Amane, or **Amarme,** a pomegranate ppr 152. 4

Amarle or **Armarle,** a lion passant or, resting its dexter paw on a mullet gu

Amary Essex, a cat's head and neck affrontée arg, holding in the mouth a rat sa. 25 1

Amberley, Viscount, *see* Russell, Earl of

Ambesace and **Amboraes,** out of a ducal coronet or, a man's head in profile ppr

Ambler, a mascle or 167 9

Ambler and **Anbler,** two dexter hands conjoined supporting a royal crown

Ambler, Kirkton, Lincs, a demi leopard arg, holding a laurel crown ppr

Amborow, Anbury, or **Anborow,** a bear's head erased sa, muzzled or 35 2

Ambridge, a cross crosslet fitched in pale gu, surmounted by two swords in saltier ppr 166 14

Ambros, Ambrose, and **Ambross,** a hand holding a billet arg 215 11

Ambrose, William Henry, Esquire, 45, St James's Square, Notting Hill, W, and Lanarksh, issuant from the battlements of a tower or, a cubit arm ppr, holding in the hand a billet in bend sinister, also or *J'espere en Dieu* 215 13

Ambrose, a cherub's head between two wings 189. 9

Ambrose, a pelican in her piety or, charged on the breast with a shamrock ppr *In Heaven is all my trust* c/ 98 14

Ambry or **Ambrey,** a wolf's head erm, holding in the mouth a rose branch 29 7

Amcot and **Amcots,** a squirrel sejant gu, cracking a nut or 135 7

Amcotes and **Amcotts,** Weston Cracroft, of Kittlethorpe Park, Newark and Amcotts, Lincs (1) A squirrel sejant gu, collared, and eating an acorn or (2) A stock ppr, supporting with his dexter foot a battle-axe staff or, headed arg 135. 7

Amcots, a squirrel sejant gu, collared or 135 4

Amcotts, Bart, a boar's head couped and erect arg, issuing out of the mouth an estoile or

Amcotts, *see* Cracroft-Amcotts

Ameers, a long cross crossed on three grieces arg 166 6

Amenton, an antelope's head ppr c/ 126 2

Amerace, a mascle arg 167 9

Amerdley, a heart inflamed gu, winged or 110 6

Ameredith of Marston, Devonsh, a demi-lion rampant sa, ducally gorged and lined or c/ 10 7

Ameredith of Tamerton, the same crest

Amerex and **Americe,** a torteau charged with a talbot's head arg, erased or 57 5

Amerie, a dexter hand ppr, holding a fleur-de-lis in pale or c/ 215 5

Amery of Park House, Stourbridge, out of a mural coronet, a talbot's head *Tu ne cede malis* 56 6

Amery, London, same crest and motto

Ames, Frederick, Esquire, of Hawford Lodge, near Worcs, a rose arg, slipped and leaved ppr, and in front thereof an annulet or 244 11

Ames, Henry St Vincent, Esquire of Cote House, Westbury on Trym, Bristol same crest *Fama candida rosa dulcior*

Ames, Louis Eric, Esquire, of Linden, Morpeth, same crest and motto

Ames, Lionel Gerard, of The Hyde, Bedford, a rose arg, slipped and leaved vert, in front thereof an annulet or *Non sibi* c/ 149 5

Ames and **Amos,** a square collegiate cap sa 180 9

Amherst Earl (Amherst), Montreal, Sevenoaks, Kent, on a mount vert, three tilting-spears points upwards or, headed arg, one in pale and two in saltier, environed with a chaplet of laurel vert *Constantia et virtute* 175 11

Amherst, of Hackney, **Baron** (Tyssen Amherst), Didlington Hall, Brandon, Norf (1) In the centre, on a mount vert, three tilting-spears, one in pale and two in saltire or, headed arg, encircled by a wreath of laurel ppr (*for Amhurst or Amherst*) 175 11 (2) Upon the dexter side, in front of a trefoil slipped vert, a dexter arm fessewise couped, vested gu, cuff az, the hand ppr holding a cross crosslet fitchee erect, also gu (*for Daniel*) 207 8 (3) Upon the sinister side, a demi lion rampant per fesse wavy or and az, ducally crowned gu, and holding between the paws an escutcheon of the second charged with an estoile of the first (*for Tyssen*) *Victoria concordia crescit* (*Amherst*), *Toujours prêt* (*Daniel*), *Post mortem virtus virescit* (*Tyssen*) 14 2

Amherst, Hon Joceline George Herbert, of Holmesdale, Darlington, Western Australia, on a mount vert, three like spears, one erect and two in saltire, girt with a wreath of laurel ppr *Constantia et virtute*

Amhurst, *see* Amherst

Amias, Norf, a buck's head erased arg, attired or, the neck gorged with a wreath arg and sa c/ 121 2

Amidas, London, a branch of oak ppr, acorned or c/ 151 3

Amiel, a hunting-horn sans strings sa 228 11

Amiens, Viscount, Ireland, *see* Aldborough, Earl of.

Amitesly, Glouc., a bezant charged with a pale indented gu. *cf.* 159. 6

Amler, Shropsh., an eagle's head erased. 83. 2

Amo, a negress's head from the breasts affrontée, the face smiling ppr., with ear-rings or. 182. 4

Amoek, a man's head from the shoulders in profile ppr., vested gu., wreathed arg. and sa.

Amock, a savage's head from the shoulders, vested gu., wreathed arg., and sa.

Amond or **St. Amond,** Scotland, three cinquefoils az., stalked and leaved vert.

Amond, out of a mural coronet a griffin's head. 67. 10

Amond, Scotland, out of a mural coronet a griffin's head ducally gorged. 67. 6

Amond, Scotland, an arm in armour embowed brandishing a scimitar, all ppr. 196. 10

Amorie or **D'Amorie,** Glouc., out of a mural coronet or, a talbot's head az., eared of the first. 56. 6

Amory, out of a ducal coronet or, a plume of seven ostrich-feathers arg., four and three.

Amory, *see* Heathcote-Amory.

Amos and **Ames,** a square collegiate cap sa. 180. 0

Amos of St. Ibbs, Herts, a stag's head. *Sapere aude.* 121. 5

Amosley, a horse at full speed sa. 52. 8

Amouth, a battle-axe and the top of a javelin in saltier ppr.

Amphlet, Staffs, a dromedary ppr. 132. 2

Amphlett, Richard Holmden, K.C., of Wychbold Hall, Worcs., a dromedary ppr., bridled sa.

Amphlett, Rev. Charles, of Earlscombe, Worcs., on a mount vert, a dromedary statant ppr., charged with three cinquefoils sa. *Vincit qui patitur.*

Amphlett, Edward Greenhill, J.P., of Worthing, Sussex, on a wreath arg. and az., a dromedary statant ppr., with halter and line reflexed over the back or, charged on the body with two lozenges arg. *Chi legge regge.* 292. 15

Amphlett, Charles Edward, Captain 6th (Inniskilling) Dragoons, same crest and motto.

Amphlett, a dromedary ppr., bridled sa. *Honour before honours.*

Amphlett, John, Esquire, Clent, Stourbridge, a dromedary statant, bridled ppr.

Ampthill, Baron (Russell), Government House, Madras, a goat statant arg., armed and unguled or, charged with a mullet sa. for difference. *Che sara sara.* 307. 1

Amsden and **Amsdon,** a cross-fleury fitched or, fleury gu., between two wings ppr.

Amson of Lees, Chesh., a cock blackbird ppr. between two ostrich-feathers arg.

Amson, a crane ppr. 105. 9

Amy of Jersey, out of a ducal coronet or, a peacock's head ppr., holding a sprig vert. *Hostis honori invidia.*

Amy or **Amye,** Cambs., out of a ducal coronet or, an eagle's head ppr., in beak a sprig vert.

Amyand, a naked arm embowed ppr., holding three ears of corn bladed, all or. *La vie durante.* *cf.* 202. 6

Amyand of Moreas Court, Heref., Bart., a crow ppr. 107. 14

Amyas, Norf., a stag's head erased or, gorged with a wreath arg. and sa., tied at the end.

Amyas, Tilbury, Essex, a hind trippant ppr., collared gu. *cf.* 124. 14

Amyat and **Amyatt,** a ram passant ppr. *cf.* 129. 5

Amyatt, Southampton, a ram passant arg. *cf.* 129. 5

Amys, Essex, a hind trippant arg., collared gu *cf.* 124. 12

Anables, a stag at gaze ppr. 117. 3

Anby and **Anbley,** a dexter hand ppr., holding a cross patée fitched in pale gu. 221. 12

Ancaster, Earl of (Heathcote-Drummond-Willoughby), Normanton Park, Stamford: (1) A saracen's head affrontée, couped at the shoulders ppr., ducally crowned or. (2) On a ducal coronet or, a sleuth-hound arg., collared and leashed gu. (3) On a mural crown az., a pomey as in the arms, between two wings displayed erm. *Loyaute me oblige.*

Ancher and **Anchor,** Kent, a bull's head erased gu. 44. 3

Ancketill, Ireland, an oak-tree ppr., acorned or. *Vade ad formicam.* 143. 2

Ancketill of Anketill's Grove, co. Monaghan, same crest and motto.

Ancketill, Dorset, on a mount vert, an oak-tree ppr. 143. 14

Ancketill, Dorset, the root of an oak-tree erased, out of it a live branch sprouting ppr., acorned or.

Ancram, Earl of, *see* Lothian, Marquess of.

Ancram, Hill House, Frome, an anchor erect sa. *Hold fast.* 161. 1

Andby, Andy, or **Andey,** Devonsh., on the stump of a tree a crane statant, all ppr. 105. 12

Andby, a dexter hand ppr., holding a cross patée fitchée in pale gu. *cf.* 221. 12

Andegarvia, an escarbuncle sa. 164. 12

Andelby, an escutcheon gu., charged with a cross moline or.

Anderdon, Hants, a dexter arm in armour, embowed ppr, garnished or, the hand apaumée, also ppr. 200. 1

Anderley, a dolphin haurient devouring a fish ppr. 140. 6

Anderson-, Pelham, Earl of Yarborough, *see* Yarborough.

Anderson, *see* Macaulay-Anderson.

Anderson, Bart., Yorks, a water-spaniel passant or. *Gnaviter.* 57. 9

Anderson, Warw., a talbot passant or. 54. 1

Anderson, Scotland, a crescent or. *Gradatim.* 163. 2

Anderson, an oak-tree ppr. *Stand sure.* 143. 5

Anderson of Airdbreck, an oak-tree ppr. *Stand sure.* 14. 35

Anderson, Sir Alexander, of Aberdeen, an oak-tree ppr. *Stand sure.* 143. 5

Anderson of Liverpool, an oak-tree, and equally pendant therefrom two weights ppr. *Pro Deo certo.* 143. 10

Anderson, Bart., of Fermoy, Ireland, a tree ppr., surmounted of a saltier humettée sa. *Stand sure.*

Anderson, James Henry, Esquire, of Portarlington Road, West Bournemouth, upon a mount vert, an oak-tree ppr., in front thereof three cross crosslets fitchée, one in pale and two in saltier sa. *Stand sure.*

Anderson of New South Wales, a yew-tree ppr. *Sic viret virtus.—Ubi solum ibi certum.*

Anderson, Scotland, a stag lodged ppr. *Recte quod honeste.* 115. 7

Anderson, on a mount a stag lodged, all ppr. 115. 12

Anderson, Alnwick, a stag lodged amidst rushes, the neck pierced with an arrow or, headed arg.

Anderson of Jesmond House, Northumb., on a mount vert, a stag lodged, wounded in breast by an arrow, in mouth an ear of wheat, all ppr., charged on side with a bugle-horn or. *Nil desperandum, auspice Deo.*

Anderson, London and Scotland, a phœnix in flames ppr. *Providentia.* 82. 2

Anderson, Penley, Herts, a spaniel-dog passant ppr. 57. 9

Anderson, merchant, London, a phœnix in flames ppr. *Dominus providebit.* 82. 2

Anderson, an eagle issuing, wings expanded and inverted ppr., gazing at the sun gu.

Anderson, an eagle issuing. *Qui honeste fortiter.*

Anderson, an eagle issuing, holding in the dexter claw an olive-branch, all ppr. *Qui honeste fortiter.* 80. 3

Anderson, Walter N., of Toronto, Ontario, an eagle issuing, holding in the dexter claw an olive-branch ppr. *Qui honeste fortiter.* 80. 3

Anderson of Whiteburgh, a crescent arg. *Ut se crescit clarescit.* 163. 2

Anderson, Archibald, Esquire, of 30, Oxford Square, London, a crescent arg. *Gradatim.* 163. 2

Anderson of Newbigging, a mullet az. *Nil conscire sibi.* 164. 2

Anderson, Glasgow, a cloud ppr. *Recte quod honeste.* 162. 13

Anderson of Glasgow, an elephant's head couped ppr. 133. 2

Anderson, out of a ducal coronet or, a stag's head affrontée, in the mouth a dart ppr. *cf.* 119. 13

Anderson, London, out of a ducal coronet arg., a hind's head or, pierced through the neck with an arrow sa., feathered of the first. 124. 6

Anderson, Newcastle, an eagle's head erased arg., holding in the beak an arrow in pale gu., headed and feathered or.

Anderson, George, Esquire, M.A., J.P., of Little Harle Tower, Newcastle-upon-Tyne (*as recorded in the College of Arms*), in front of a falcon's head erased sa, guttée d'or, holding in the beak an arrow palewise, head downwards ppr., three hearts or. 88. 8. A falcon's head erased sa., guttée, beaked and eyed or, holding in the beak an arrow in bend dexter head downwards ppr. *Vigilans et certus.* 88. 13

Anderson, Bradley, Durh., on a chapeau gu., turned up erm., a griffin's head erased arg., charged on the neck with a fetterlock sa.

Anderson, Kenneth Lockwood Morrison, Esquire, of Cluny, Swanage, Dorset, issuing from waves of the sea a sea-horse's head ppr., holding in the mouth a trident or, and on an escroll below the shield. *Stand sure.*

Anderson, Ireland, on a mount a leopard couchant gardant, crowned with an antique crown. cf. 24. 9

Anderson-Pelham, Hon. Evelyn Cornwallis, of 29, Belgrave Square: (1) A peacock in his pride arg. (*for Pelham*). (2) A water-spaniel or (*for Anderson*). *Vincit amor patriæ.*

Anderson of Linkwood, a hand holding a pen all ppr. *Honesty is the best policy.* 217. 10

Anderson, Sussex, a hand holding a pen. *Honesty is the best policy.* 217. 10

Anderson of Tushielaw, Stirling, a sword in pale, between two branches of laurel in orle ppr. *Pro bello vel pace.* 170. 3

Anderson, Mill Hill, Middx., three ostrich-feathers encircled with a chain or, on the centre one a crescent.

Anderson, Aberdeen, a cross-staff erect, marked with the degrees of latitude. *Per mare.*

Anderson, a ship in full sail ppr. 160. 13

Anderton, a dexter arm in armour embowed ppr., garnished or, the hand apaumée ppr. 200. 1

Anderton, Lancs, a curlew arg.

Anderton, William Arthur Alphonsus Joseph Ince (Major), of Euxton, Lancs, a curlew ppr. *We stoop not.*

Anderton, E., Esquire, Trunstone, Westdown, Ilfracombe, a curlew arg. *Supero non cedo.*

Anderton, a stork ppr. 105. 11

Anderton of Brondyffryn, Denbighsh., a stork arg., holding in the beak three cinquefoils slipped or, and resting the dexter leg on a shackbolt sa.

Anderton, Wilfrid Francis, Esquire, of Haighton, Preston, Lancs, issuant out of a crescent vert, a buck's head, holding in the mouth an ear of wheat ppr. *Aude incipe.* 228. 2

Andesley, a sword ppr., and a cross crosslet sa., in saltier. 166. 12

Andlaw, an eagle's head sa. 83. 1

Andover, Viscount, *see* Suffolk, Earl of.

Andrade, a wolf's head or. 30. 5

Andre or **Andree,** a mill-rind az. 165. 11

Andrea or **St. Andrew,** a cinquefoil arg. 148. 12

Andrea, a hurt, charged with a lion's head erased, collared gu. cf. 19. 1

Andrew, Devonsh., a stag's head erased sa., attired or. 121. 2

Andrew of Tredinick, Cornw., a stag at gaze, holding in his mouth a wheat ear, all or, charged on the side with two mascles interlaced az. *Prospice.*

Andrew of Nethertarvit, a star or. *Give and forgive.* 164. 3

Andrew of Clockmill, a dexter hand holding a laurel-branch ppr. *Virtute et fortuna.* 219. 9

Andrewes, Rutl., a demi-lion or, ducally crowned arg., holding up in the dexter paw a human heart gu.

Andrewes, Suff., a stag's head erased arg., charged with a crescent for difference. 119. 8

Andrewes, a Moor's head in profile, couped at the shoulders ppr. 192. 13

Andrewes, a Moor's head in profile sa., banded arg. 192. 13

Andrews, Bart., of Denton, Northamp., a blackamoor's head in profile, couped at shoulders, wreathed about the temples, all ppr. 192. 13

Andrews, Bart., of Shaw Place, Berks, out of an Eastern coronet or, a blackamoor's head couped ppr., in the ear a pendant or. *Victrix fortunæ sapientia.* 192. 6

Andrews, a Moor's head in profile, couped at the shoulders ppr. 192. 13

Andrews, Oxon., a dexter arm vested vert, cuffed arg., holding in the hand a branch ppr. *Nec careo, nec curo.*

Andrews, Surrey, a stag's head erased arg. *Quod honestum utile.* 121. 2

Andrews, Richard, Southampton, a stag's head erased arg. 121. 2

Andrews, Scotland, a hand holding a branch of laurel ppr. *Virtute et fortuna.* 219. 9

Andrews, Suff., an acorn vert. cf. 152. 1

Andrews, a Moor's head couped ppr. 192. 13

Andrews, Suff., a stag's head erased or. 121. 2

Andrews, Hants, a greyhound's head couped per pale or and sa., charged on the neck with a saltier humettée between two roundles in fess, all counterchanged.

Andrews, of Lathbury, Bucks, of Norf. and Suff., a stag's head erased arg. 121. 1. (*For the Suffolk branch,* charged with a crescent for difference.) 119. 8

Andrews, Middx., on a naval coronet or, a dove volant with an olive-branch in the beak, all ppr.

Andrews, Suff., a bird, wings expanded az., holding in its beak a laurel-branch vert. 94. 5

Andrews, upon a mount vert, a dove holding in the beak an olive-leaf slipped ppr., and charged on the breast with an escallop gu.

Andrews, Warw., a demi-lion az., gorged with a collar or, charged with three mullets of the first. cf. 10. 9

Andrews, London and Hants, an arm erect habited vert., cuffed arg., charged on the sleeve with a quatrefoil or, and holding in the hand a branch of the first fructed of the third.

Andrews of Rivington, Lancs, a Moor's head in profile, couped at the shoulders ppr., in ear a pendant arg. *Fortiter defendit.* 192. 13

Andros, on a tower a lion rampant sa. 157. 12

Andros, Guernsey, a blackamoor's head, couped at the shoulders and wreathed about the temples, all ppr.

Andson, Angus, a fir-tree seeded ppr. *Stand sure.* 144. 13

Aneleche, an eagle, wings expanded ppr. 77. 5

Anelshey, Glouc., a bezant charged with a pale indented gu. cf. 159. 6

Anesworth, *see* Ainsworth.

Aneys, a sword in bend ppr. 170. 5

Angas or **Anges,** an ostrich-head erased arg., holding in the beak a horse-shoe ppr.

Ange, a cross formée or, between two wings az. 110. 7

Ange, a cross formée fitchée or, between two wings az. cf. 110. 7

Angel, Angle, Anegall, or **Anegal,** on a chapeau a tower, all ppr. cf. 156. 2

Angeldon, London, a knot sa., between two wings or.

Angell, London, out of a ducal coronet or, a demi-pegasus arg., crined gu. cf. 47. 5

Angell, Surrey, same crest. *Stare super vias antiquas.*

Angell, on a mount vert, a swan arg., ducally gorged or, beaked and legged gu. cf. 100. 7

Angellis or **Angles,** a lion's gamb erect, holding a cross pattée fitched or. cf. 36. 9

Anger and **Angier,** Kent, a martlet flying over a castle, ruined in the sinister tower ppr. cf. 155. 2

Anger, an escarbuncle or. 164. 12

Angersteen and **Angerstein,** a lion's head erased gu., holding in the mouth a quatrefoil vert.

Angerstein of Weeting Hall, Norf., between two elephants' trunks a stork, holding in its dexter claw a stone, all ppr.

Angesteen, a crane ppr., holding in the dexter claw a mullet arg. cf. 105. 6

Angeville of Thethelthorpe, Lincs, a branch of three roses arg., stalked and leaved vert. 149. 8

Angevine and **Angevyne,** Lincs, same crest.

Anglesey, Marquess of (Paget), Beaudesert, Lichfield, Staffs, a demi-heraldic tiger sa., maned, armed, ducally gorged and tufted arg. *Per il suo contrario.* 25. 7

Angolesme, the sail of a ship ppr. 160. 9

Angolisme, a lion's gamb sa. cf. 36. 4

Anguilla, a bezant charged with a talbot's head erased sa. cf. 57. 1

Anguish, Norwich, a snake nowed ppr., between two branches of fern vert. *Latet anguis in herba.*

Angus, a quadrangular castle. 155. 4

Angus, Scotland, a lion crowned with an antique crown or. *Fortis est veritas.*

Angus, John, Esquire, Aberdeen, a lion passant gardant gu., armed and langued az. *Fortis est veritas.* 4. 3

Anhelet, a gem ring or, the stone gu. 167. 14

Anke or **Ankor,** a bull's head erased gu. 44. 3

Anketel, a rose gu. 149. 2

Anketell of Shaftesbury, on a mount vert, an oak-tree ppr. 143. 14

Anketell, the stump of an oak-tree, the branches sprouting, acorned ppr.

Anketell of Anketell, Ireland, an oak-tree ppr. *Vade ad formicam.* 143. 5

Anketell-Jones, Henry Moutray Ernest, Esquire, M.A., J.P., Burrishoole House, Newport, co. Mayo, on a chapeau, a stag at gaze. *Cœlitus mihi vires.*

Ankor, a bull's head erased gu. 44. 3

Ankyrsley, a hunting horn sans strings vert, veruled arg cf 228 11
Anlaby, on a mount an oak-tree ppr 143 14
Anleby, Yorks, an arrow in pale, enfiled with a ducal coronet or 174 3
Anlet and **Anlett,** Yorks, on a rock a fire-beacon ppr 177 14
Anley, a dexter arm, the hand gloved and holding a hawk's lure ppr cf 217 8
Anmers or **Anners,** Chesh, a lion's head erased ppr 17 8
Anmetesley, a bezant charged with a pale indented gu cf 159 6
Anna and **De Anna,** a bezant cf 159 14
Annabell, Annable, and **Annables,** a stag at gaze ppr 117 3
Annaly, Baron (White), a cubit arm ppr, charged with a chevron engrailed gu, thereon a cross crosslet or, holding in the hand three roses of the second, slipped ppr *I e et virtute* 245 10
Annand, Surrey, a griffin segreant ppr *Sperabo* 62 2
Annand of Annandale, a rose stalked and leaved ppr *Quod honestum utile* 149 5
Annandale, Scotland, same crest and motto.
Annandale, a spur erect or, winged arg 111 12
Annat, Scotland, a boar sa, transfixed with an arrow 40 14
Anncell, a stag's head affrontee, ducally gorged 119 14
Anncey and **Anncy,** on a mural coronet a stag sejant ppr 116 4
Anne, a woman's head couped at the breasts ppr, vested arg, the hair dishevelled or
Anne, Major Ernest Lambert Swinburne, of Burgwallis, Yorks (1) A maiden's head couped at the shoulders ppr, crined or (*for Anne*) 182 5 (2) A leopard's face gu between two dragons' wings ppr, each charged with a fret sa (*for Charlton*) 10 3
Anne of Trickley, Yorks, a buck's head cabossed arg 122 5
Anneles, a mermaid ppr, the tail vert. 184 8
Annelshie, a bezant charged with a pale indented gu cf 159 6
Annesley, Ireland, a demi-lady supporting a portcullis 183 7
Annesley, Oxon, a Moor's head in profile, couped sa, wreathed about the temples arg and az *Virtutis amore* 192 13
Annesley, Viscount Valentia, *see* Valentia.
Annesley, Earl (Annesley), Castlewellan, co Down a Moor's head in profile couped at the shoulders ppr, wreathed above the temples arg and az *Virtutis amore*
Annesley of Arley Castle, Staffs (1) A Moor's head in profile couped ppr, wreathed about the temples arg, and az (*for Annesley*) 192 13 (2) A bull's caboshed ppr, between two flags gu (*for Macleod*) *Hic murus ahaneus —Virtutis amore —Hold fast* 43 5
Annesley, a Saracen's head in profile, wreathed arg and az 190 14
Annesley, William Gore, Esquire, of Delgany, Polstead Road, N, Oxford, a Moor's head couped at the shoulders in profile ppr, wreathed about the temples arg and az *Virtutis amore* 241 13
Annesley, a buck's head or 121. 5
Annes, Anness, and **Annis,** a mascle or 167 9
Anngell, Kent, out of a ducal coronet or, a demi pegasus arg crined gu cf 47 5
Anningson, Bushell, M A, Walthamead, Cambridge, a scaling ladder in bend arg 301 15
Annot, Annott, or **Annat,** a boar passant sa, transfixed with an arrow ppr 40 14
Annyslay, a Moor's head couped sa 192 13
Anscell or **Anstrell** of Barford, Beds, a demi lion az., ducally gorged and lined or cf 10 7
Ansdell, a dexter hand ppr, holding a buckle or 223 11
Anselbie and **Anselby,** an arrow in pale, enfiled with a ducal coronet or 174 3
Ansell, a demi-lion ppr, ducally gorged and lined or cf 10 7
Ansert, a demi lion rampant, imperially crowned, holding in the dexter paw a sword wavy ppr 14 14
Ansley, a blackamoor's head in profile couped at the shoulders ppr, gorged with a collar or, charged with three escallops cf 192 13
Anslow-Alabone, M, M D, 20, Lower Seymour Street, Portman Square, W, a lion's head erased, transfixed through the neck with an arrow in bend point downwards 297 1
Anson, Sir William Reynell, Bart, of Birch Hall, Lancs, out of a ducal coronet or, a spear erect ppr *Nil desperandum*
Anson, Earl of Lichfield (1) Out of a ducal coronet or, a spear-head ppr (2) A greyhound's head, couped erm, charged on neck with two bars-gemelle or *Nil desperandum*
Anson, Sir Archibald Edward Harbord Anson, Esquire, of Southfield, Silver hill, St Leonard's-on-Sea, out of a ducal coronet or, a spear head erect ppr *Nil desperandum*
Anson-Horton, Henry, Esquire, of Catton Hall, Burton-on-Trent (1) Out of the waves of the sea ppr, a tilting spear erect or, headed and enfiled with a dolphin arg, finned gold (*for Horton*) (2) Issuant from a coronet or, a spear-head erect ppr
Anstavill, a castle triple-towered, a demi-lion rampant issuing out of the middle tower 155 10
Anstay, Anstee, Anstey, and **Anstie,** a martlet or 95 2
Anstead, Ansted, or **Antished,** a cross formee or, charged with five torteaux cf 165 7
Anstell, Cornw, a cross formee arg, guttee de-poix cf 165 7
Anstey, Rev Henry, M A, Slapton Rectory, Leighton Buzzard, a martlet or *Esse quam videri* 95 2
Anstie, a leopard's face ppr, jessant de-lis gu 22. 5
Anstis, Cornw, out of a ducal coronet, five ostrich feathers, all ppr 114 13
Anstis or **Anstice,** a dexter cubit arm vested per pale embattled, holding in the hand a griffin's head erased ppr 211 6
Anston, a martlet issuing ppr
Anstrell, *see* Anscell
Anstrother, out of a ducal coronet or, a demi man in armour ppr, in hand a spear sa, headed arg
Anstruther of that ilk, Bart, two arms in armour embowed, grasping in the gauntlets a battle-axe, all ppr *Periissem ni periissem* 194 12
Anstruther, Henry Torrens, Esquire of Gillingshill, Pittenween, same crest and motto
Anstruther of Hintlesham, Suff., same crest and motto
Anstruther, Inverkeithing, same crest and motto
Anstruther, Airdrie, same crest.
Anstruther, Carmichael-, Sir Windham, Bart, Scotland (1) The same as above (*for Anstruther*) 237 18 (2) An arm in armour erect grasping a broken spear ppr (*for Carmichael*) *Toujours prêt* 210 9
Anstruther, Sir Ralph William, Bart of Balcaskie Pittenweem, Fifesh, two arms in armour, counter embowed, holding in the hands a battle-axe, all ppr *Periissem ni periissem* 237 18
Anstruther-Duncan, Alexander William, Esquire, of Naughton, Fife, N B, two arms in armour, holding in the gauntlets a battle axe ppr *Periissem ni periissem* 237 18
Anstruther, Lieutenant-Colonel Robert Hamilton, of Hintlesham Hall, Ipswich (1) Two arms in armour, holding in the gauntlets a battle-axe, all ppr (2) Out of a wreath of laurel or, a horse's head paly of six sa and arg *Periissem ni periissem.*
Ansty, a martlet or 95 2
Anteshey and **Antesley,** a bezant charged with a pale indented gu cf 159 6
Anthonisz, Richard Gerald, of Colombo, Ceylon, a lozenge gu, between wings arg *Waarheid eer vrijheid.*
Anthonisz, Hon Peter Daniel, M D, C M G, M L C, of Galle, Ceylon, a lozenge gu between two wings erect arg 110 3
Anthony of London, a demi goat ppr, charged with a bezant, armed and attired or cf 128 2
Anthony of Chalfont St Giles, Bucks, a demi-ram per fesse erm and sa, horns and hoofs or, charged on the body with a bezant thereon a leopard's face gu *None pour haine*
Anthony and **Antoale,** London, a goat's head arg 128 12
Anthony, a goat's head or 128 12
Anton of Stoatfield, Lincs, Middx, London, and Ireland, out of a mural coronet, a lion's head arg 19 12
Antony or **Antonie,** Suff, a goat's head gu 128 12
Antram, Dorset, a demi griffin az *Prudentia et animo* 64 2
Antrim, Earl of (M'Donnell), Glenarm Castle, Antrim (1) A dexter arm embowed fesseways, couped at the shoulder, vested or, cuffed arg, holding in the hand ppr a cross crosslet fitched in pale az (*for M'Donnell*) 203 9 (2) A sun in splendour or (*for Kerr*) *Sero sed serio —Toujours prêt* 162 2
Antrobus, Sir Edmund, Bart, Amesbury Abbey, Salisbury, a unicorn's head couped arg., horned and maned or

gorged with a wreath of laurel vert, issuing out of rays of the sun ppr. *Dei memor, gratus amicis.*

Antrobus, John Coutts, of Eaton Hall, Chester, same crest and motto.

Antrobus of London, same crest.

Antwisel or **Antisell,** an eagle, wings expanded and inverted ppr. 76. 13

Anvers, Chesh., a branch with three roses ppr. 149. 8

Anvers, De, a wyvern sa. 70. 2

Anvory, a dexter hand holding a holly-branch ppr.

Anwell and **Anwyl,** England, and Parkin, Merionethsh., an astrolabe ppr. 167. 7

Anwick, London, a dexter arm gu., the hand holding a broken tilting-spear or. 214. 10

Anwill and **Anwyl,** Wales, two hands issuing out of clouds pulling an anchor out of the sea ppr. 224. 13

Anwyl, Robert Charles, of Llugwy, Machynlleth, an eagle displayed or. *Eryr eryrod eryri.*

Anwyt, an eagle displayed ppr. 75. 2

Aoluite, on a chapeau, a lion statant, tail extended, all ppr. 4. 8

Apeele, a fleur-de-lis or, between two wings arg. *cf.* 110. 5

Apesley, Surrey and Sussex, the same crest.

Ap-Enyions, a sheaf of arrows ppr., banded gu. *Virtuti fido.* 173. 3

Ap-Griffith, out of a cloud a dexter and a sinister arm shooting an arrow, all ppr. *cf.* 200. 2

Aphe, Hants, out of a ducal coronet arg. a parrot's head or.

Aphery, a trefoil slipped vert. 148. 9

Ap-Howell, a gauntlet erect holding a sword, all ppr. 210. 4

Apifer, a hand holding a spiked club ppr. *cf.* 214. 6

Apiliard or **Appleyard** of East Carlton, Norf., a demi-heraldic tiger quarterly gu. and az., the tail of the last tufted or, holding in the mouth a rose gu., stalked and leaved vert. *cf.* 25. 13

Apilston, a pelican in her piety, wings displayed or, vulned ppr. 98. 14

Aplegath or **Aplegarth** of Rapley, Hants, a demi-heraldic tiger gu., bezantée armed and tufted or, charged with a bend of the last. *cf.* 25. 13

Apleton, *see* Appleton.

Apletree, Hants, a goat passant arg. *cf.* 129. 5

Apleyard, an owl arg. 96. 5

Appelton and **Appolton,** a camel couchant ppr. *cf.* 132. 4

Apperley of Morben, Montgomeryshire, a pine-apple sa. 152. 8

Applebee, a martlet or. 95. 2

Appleby, Leics., an apple or, stalked and leaved vert.

Appleby, F. H., Brigade-Surgeon Lieutenant-Colonel, Barnbygate House, Newark, same crest. *Fructu arbor cognoscitur.*

Appleford, a demi-savage holding in the dexter hand a sword, and in the sinister a baton, ensigned with a royal crown, all ppr. *cf.* 186. 14

Appleford, Essex and Berks: (1) An apple or, having a leaf on either side vert (*for Appleford*). (2) A demi-savage holding in the dexter hand a sword, and in the sinister a baton ensigned with a royal crown (*for Woodville*). *Dum spiro spero.* *cf.* 186. 14

Appleton or **Apleton,** Suff., an elephant's head couped sa., eared or, in the mouth a snake vert, coiled about the trunk. *cf.* 133. 2

Appleton, James Enderby, M.R.C.S., Linda, Poole Road, Bournemouth, same crest. *Omne bonum Dei donum.*

Appleton, Suff., out of a ducal coronet or, three pine-apples vert, the tops purfled of the first.

Applewhaite of Stoke Ask, Suff., a cubit arm erect, holding in the hand an open book. 215. 10

Appleyard of Shotsham, Norf., an owl arg. 96. 5

Appleyard, a demi-dragon ppr., holding in the dexter claw a scimitar arg. *cf.* 73. 10

Appleyard, *see* Apiliard.

Aprece, Bucks and Hants, an otter ppr., collared and lined or. *cf.* 134. 5

Aprece, Bucks and Hants, a spear erect arg. *Labora ut æternum vivas.* 175. 9

Apreece, Bart., of Washingley Hall, Hunts, a spear-head erect arg., imbrued ppr. *Vix labora ut in æternum vivas.* 174. 12

Apreece, a civet-cat ppr., pierced through the middle with a spear-head erect.

Aprice, Heref., a cock, wings expanded gu., holding in the beak a rose ppr., leaved and stalked vert.

Ap-Rice, a boar's head erect arg., pellettée, between two oak-branches vert, fructed or.

Apsey, a dove with an olive-branch in its beak volant over water, all ppr. 93. 11

Apsley, Lord, *see* Bathurst, Earl of.

Apsley, Sussex, a fleur-de-lis or, between two wings arg. *cf.* 110. 5

Apted, Surrey, a stag's head erased or. *Semper eadem.* 121. 2

Apthorp, Rev. G. F., 13, De Parys Avenue, Bedford, a mullet pierced az. *Nemo nisi Christus.*

Apuldrefield, on a chapeau gu., turned up erm., a man's head in profile, couped at the neck, wearing a cap arg., fringed at the front and back gu.

Aquitar, London, a demi-lion rampant or, murally crowned az., holding in the dexter paw a laurel-branch slipped ppr.

Arabin, the sun rising behind a mountain ppr. 162. 10

Arabin of Beech Hill, Essex, and Drayton, Middx., an eagle's head erased between two wings sa., ducally crowned or. *Nec temere, nec timide.*

Arabyn, a griffin's head erased ppr., ducally crowned or, between two wings arg.

Arblaster or **Allebaster,** Staffs, a feather in pale, enfiled with a ducal coronet, all ppr. 114. 12

Arblester, Areblaster, and **Arablester,** out of a ducal coronet a greyhound's head arg., collared or. *cf.* 61. 7

Arbuckle, Scotland, a ram ppr. 131. 13

Arburthnet of Findoury, Scotland, a peacock ppr. *Interna præstant.* 103. 7

Arburthnet of Catherlan, a peacock's head couped ppr., charged with a mullet or. *Sit laus Deo.* *cf.* 103. 2

Arburthnet, same crest. *Tam interna, quam externa.*

Arbuthnot, Viscount (Arbuthnot), Arbuthnott House, Fourdoun, Kincardineshire, Scotland, a peacock's head couped ppr., beaked or. *Laus Deo.* 103. 2

Arbuthnot of Arbuthnothaugh, a peacock's head couped ppr. *Deus me sustinet.* 103. 2

Arbuthnot, Sir Robert Keith, Bart., 105, Cadogan Gardens, S.W., a peacock's head ppr. *Innocent and true.* 103. 2

Arbuthnot, Scotland, a peacock's head couped ppr., beaked or. *Laus Deo.* 103. 2

Arbuthnot, Hugh Gough, Esquire, of 40, Princes Gate, London, a peacock's head ppr. *Innocent and true.*

Arbuthnot of Fiddes, a peacock ppr. *Tam interna, quam externa.* 103. 7

Arbuthnot of Montrose, a dove with an adder in orle ppr. *Innocue ac provide.* 92. 11

Arbuthnot of Weymouth, a ship under sail ppr. *Fluctuo sed affluo.* 160. 13

Arbuthnot, a cross pattée or. 165. 7

Arcedeckne or **Archdeckne,** a dexter arm in armour embowed, holding in the hand a scimitar. 196. 10

Arcedeckne-Butler, James Fitzwalter, Esquire: (1) Out of a ducal coronet or, a plume of five ostrich-feathers, therefrom a demi-falcon rising arg., a label of the last upon a crescent az., for difference (*for Butler*). (2) A cubit arm erect, vested arg., charged with three chevronels sa., the hand ppr., grasping a sword in bend sinister arg., pommel and hilt or (*for Arcedeckne*). *Timor Domini fons vitæ.*

Arcedeckne-Butler, St. John Henry, Esquire, of Coreen, Talawakelle, Ceylon, same crests, and motto.

Arcester, Glouc., on a bezant, an escarbuncle sa.

Archard, Kent, out of a ducal coronet a demi-fish ppr. 139. 14

Archbald and **Archibald,** Scotland, a decrescent arg. *Ut reficiar.* 163. 1

Archbald and **Archibald,** Scotland, a palm-branch erect ppr. *Dilat servata fides.* 147. 1

Archbold, Ireland, a lion's head couped erm., guttée-de-sang. *cf.* 21. 1

Archbold, Worcs. and London, a dove rising arg. 94. 2

Archdale and **Archedale,** London, out of a ducal coronet or, a heraldic tiger's head arg., maned and tufted sa. 25. 3

Archdale, Edward Mervyn, Esquire, of Riversdale, Ballinamallard, co. Fermanagh, out of a ducal coronet an heraldic tiger's head arg., maned, tufted, and armed sa. *Data fata secuta.*

Archdale, Mervyn A., M.B., East Riding Asylum, Beverley, Yorks, out of a ducal coronet a talbot. *Ferendo et sperendo.*

Archdall, Rev. William Frederick, M.A., the Rectory, Glanmire, R.S.O., co. Cork, same crest. *Data fata secuta.*

Archdall, out of a ducal coronet gu., a heraldic tiger's head arg., langued gu., tufted sa. *Data fata secutus.* 25. 3

Archdall of Castle Archdall and Trillic, Ireland (1) Out of a ducal coronet or, a heraldic tiger's head arg, named, tufted, and armed sa (*for Archdall*) 25 3 (2) On a chapeau ppr, a hand vested az, grasping a sword ppr, hilt and pommel or (*for Montgomery*) (3) A squirrel sejant ppr (*for Mervyn*) *Data fata secuta—Honneur sans repos—De Dieu tout* cf 135 2

Archdall, Ireland, a cross pattee erm cf 165 7

Archdall or **Archdell**, out of a ducal coronet or, a griffin's head 67 9

Archdeacon, Cornw, a martlet flying over a tower ppr cf 156 9

Archdecon, co Cork, a dexter cubit arm vested arg, and charged with three chevronels sa, the hand grasping a sword ppr

Archebold or **Archbold**, Staffs, a lion's head erased arg, collared gu 18 6

Archedale, *see* Archdale

Archer-Burton, *see* Burton

Archer, Arthur Montfort, M D, Dee Hills Lodge, Chester, a sagittarius passant drawing a bow, all ppr *Sola bona quæ honesta*

Archer, Robert Samuels, M D, 15, St Domingo Grove, Liverpool, crest and motto as above

Archer, Hubert Graves, Esquire, a centaur *Sola bona quæ honesta*

Archer, Baron Archer (*extinct*), of Umberslade, Warw, out of a mural coronet gu, a dragon's head arg *Sola bona quæ honesta* 72 11

Archer, Thomas Lancelot, M R C S, 82, Vincent Square, Westminster, out of a mural coronet or, a wyvern's head and neck gu *Sola bona quæ honesta*

Archer, Lincs, a dragon's head per pale gu and az, between two wings expanded, the sinister wing or, the dexter arg, issuing out of a mural coronet per pale of the last and third

Archer, out of a mural coronet or, a wyvern's head gu *Deus salutem disponit* 72 11

Archer, a demi dragon holding in the dexter claw a dart

Archer, Essex, a griffin's head erased arg, pierced through the neck by a spear in bend sinister, point downwards

Archer of Chelmsford, Essex, a griffin's head erased arg, pierced by a spear in bend sinister, collared gu, charged with two crosses patee, in the beak a slip of oak fructed ppr

Archer de Boys, Essex (1) A wyvern arg 69 5 (2) A leg couped at the thigh, embowed at the knee quarterly sa and arg, spur and leather or cf 193 8

Archer-Houblon, George Bramston, Esquire, of 73, Upper Berkeley Street (1) A lion's head erased or (*for Houblon*). (2) A wyvern arg (*for Archer*) (3) A leg in armour, couped at the thigh ppr, garnished and spurred or (*for Eyre*)

Archer, Essex, a wyvern arg 69 5

Archer, Charles Gordon, of Trelaske, Cornw, a quiver full of arrows fesseways 174 4

Archer, Cornw, on a quiver full of arrows lying fesseways, a serpent, all ppr

Archer, Essex and Kent, a bull's head erased gu 44 3

Archer of Bourne, Kent, a bull's head erased gu, armed or 44 3

Archer, Ireland, a mound az, banded and crossed or 159 12

Archer, Ireland, a ducal coronet ppr *Pro rege et patria* 228 10

Archer, William Henry Davies, Esquire, B A, LL M, J P, of Brickendon, Longford Tasmania, *uses* a bear's gamb holding an arrow in bend, all ppr *Malo mori quam fœdari—Le fin couronne l'œuvre* cf 38 4

Archer, Joseph, Esquire, J P, of Panshanger, Longford, Tasmania, *uses* a bear's gamb holding an arrow in bend, all ppr *Malo mori quam fœdari—Le fin couronne l'œuvre* cf 38 4

Archer, Scotland, a dexter hand and sinister arm issuing from the wreath, drawing an arrow in a bow to the head ppr 200 2

Archer, an archer habited vert, in the dexter hand a bugle-horn arg, raised to the mouth, holding in the sinister a bow erect, across the shoulders a quiver full of arrows

Archer, Essex, a leg in armour embowed, couped at the thigh quarterly sa and arg, spurred or 193 1

Archever, Scotland, two arms drawing an arrow in a bow to the head *Ready* 200 2

Archibald, *see* Archbald

Archibald, Blackhall, Scotland, a decrescent arg *Ut reficiar* 163 1

Archibald, a branch of palm trees slipped ppr. *Dilat servata fides* 147 1

Archibald, Ireland, a palm-branch slipped in bend ppr, in front thereof a mount vert, thereon an estoile or *Palma non sine pulvere*

Archibald, Hon Sir Adams George, K C M G, C M G, Q C, D C L, of Halifax, and of The Cottage, Truro, Nova Scotia, in the Dominion of Canada, a palm-branch slipped in bend ppr, in front thereof a mount vert, thereon an estoile or *Palma non sine pulvere*

Archibald, Charles Falcon, Esquire, of Rusland Hall, Ulverston, a palm-branch slipped in bend ppr, in front thereof a mount vert, thereon an estoile or *Palma non sine pulvere*

Archideckne, a dexter arm in armour embowed, holding in the hand a dagger 196 5

Arcy, D', Ireland, a tilting-spear broken in three pieces ppr, head in pale, other two in saltier, banded gu 175 2

Ard, a cock ppr *Vigilantia* 91 2

Ardaff, a demi-lion arg, guttée-de-sang, holding in the paws a lily of three flowers az, slipped and leaved vert

Ardagh, a demi lion rampant or, pellettee, holding three lilies arg, slipped and leaved vert

Ardee, Lord, *see* Meath, Earl of

Ardem, a cross Calvary az 166 1

Arden, *see* Haddington, Earl of

Arden, Baron (Perceval), *see* Egmont, Earl of

Arden, Baron Alvanley, Chester, out of a ducal coronet or, a plume of five feathers arg, charged with a crescent gu *Patientia vinces* 114 3

Arden or **Arderne**, Beds and Warw, a plume of feathers az, charged with a martlet or

Arden, a thistle stalked and flowered ppr cf 150 2

Arden, Oxon, a boar passant quarterly or and az 40 9

Arden, Warw, on a chapeau gu, turned up or, a boar passant of the last cf 40 8

Arden, Percy, of Pontfaen, co Pembroke, a mount vert, thereon a boar passant arg, semee-de-lis az, langued gu, armed and ungu. or *Doluere dente lacessiti* 249 14

Arden, on a chapeau gu, turned up erm, a boar passant or cf 40 8

Arden, East Burnham, Bucks, a boar passant or, semee-de lis gu *Doluere dente lacessiti* cf 40 9

Arden, on a chapeau gu, turned up erm, a wild boar passant or, charged with three annulets 40 8

Arden, Warw and Staffs, on a chapeau az, turned up erm, a wild boar passant or *Quo me cunque vocat patria* cf 40 8

Arden, Douglas, Esquire, a mount vert, thereon a boar passant arg, semee-de-lis az, langued gu, armed and unguled or *Doluere dente lacessiti*

Arden, Percy, Esquire, of A7, Albany, Piccadilly, same crest and motto

Arden, Richard Edward, Esquire, of East Burnham House, near Slough, Bucks same crest and motto

Arden, George Edward, Esquire, on a chapeau az, turned up erm, a wild boar statant or *Quo me cunque vocit patria*

Arden of Gresham, Norf, same crest and motto

Arden, Middx, on a mount vert, a boar passant arg, semee-de-lis az, langued gu, armed and ungu or *Doluere dente lacessiti*

Arden, Oxon, a lion's gamb erased gu, holding a cross pattee fitchee 36 9

Arderes, Meriden, Warw, a demi-lion ar, gorged with a collar or, charged with three mullets of the first cf 10 9

Ardern, in a coronet or, a pyramid of leaves vert cf 151 14

Arderne, a plume of feathers arg, banded or

Arderne, Chesh and Lancs, out of a ducal coronet or, a plume of five feathers, three or, two az 114 13

Arderne, issuing from a ducal coronet or, a double plume of feathers gu, the ends turned downwards of the first 114 4

Arderne, Chesh, out of a ducal coronet or, seven feathers arg, tipped gu

Arderne, Warw, a boar passant or 40 9

Arderne, on a chapeau az, turned up erm, a boar passant or cf 40 8

Arderne, on a chapeau gu, turned up erm, a wild boar passant or, charged with three annulets 40 8

Ardes of Sharington, Bucks, within a catherine-wheel sa, ducally crowned or, the sun in splendour

Ardes, a catherine-wheel or, pierced sa, ducally crowned of the first

Ardilaun, Baron (Guinness), Ashford, near Cong, co Galway (1) A boar passant quarterly or and gu, a crescent

for difference (*for Guinness*). 40. 9. (2) On a pillar arg., encircled by a ducal coronet or, an eagle preying on a bird's leg erased ppr. *Spes mea in Deo.* 248. 1
Arding, Alfred Charles, Esquire, J.P., B.A., of Brazier's Park, Checkenden, Oxon.: (1) A demi-griffin vert, the wing charged with three escallops, two and one or, and holding in the mouth a tilting-spear in bend ppr. (*for Arding*). (2) Issuant from a rock a flame of fire ppr., environed by a chain or (*for Wells*). *Semper fidelis.*
Ardington or **Arthington,** Yorks, a dove holding in its beak an olive-branch ppr. 92. 5
Ardis, a demi-lion rampant gu., holding in its dexter paw a rose or, leaved vert. 12. 1
Ardrossan, Baron, Scotland, *see* Eglinton, Earl of.
Ardyn, a cross Calvary az. 166. 1
Ardyn, on a chapeau gu., turned up erm., a boar passant or. *cf.* 40. 8
Arel of France and England, a boar's head erect, between two ostrich-feathers. 41. 14
Areskin, a dexter hand holding an escutcheon. *cf.* 219. 7
Areskine, Scotland, a demi-griffin, holding in its dexter claw a sword ppr. *Ausim et confido.* 64. 6
Areskine of Dun, a griffin's head erased, holding in the beak a sword in bend, all ppr. *In Domino confido.* 66. 10
Areskine, Scotland, an arm in armour embowed, gauntleted, holding a sword, all ppr. 195. 1
Arlece, Arlois, or **Arforce,** a scaling-ladder az. 158. 14
Argahast, a Doric column ppr.
Argal, a lion's head erased gu. 17. 2
Argall, Argell, or **Argill,** a lion's head erased ppr. 17. 8
Argall of Low Hall, Essex, a sphinx, wings expanded ppr. 182. 12
Argall, a sphinx or, winged arg. 182. 12
Argall, an arm in armour embowed supporting a battle-axe, all ppr.
Argente and **Argentine,** Camb., a demi-lion gu., holding a covered cup arg.
Argenton, a martlet sa. 95. 2
Argentre, an eagle's head erased gu. 83. 2
Argles, Thomas Atkinson, of Eversley, Milnthorpe, Westml., a lion's head erased gu. *Patriæ non sibi.* 17. 2
Arguilla, on a bezant a talbot's head erased sa. *cf.* 57. 2
Argum, Argun, or **Argune,** a hand erect issuing from a cloud and holding an open book, all ppr. 215. 1
Argyll, Duke of (Campbell, K.G., K.T., P.C.), Inverary Castle, Argyll, a boar's head erased or, armed arg., langued gu. *Vix ea nostra voco.—Ne obliviscaris.* 42. 2
Ariel and **Ariell,** an anchor cabled and a sword in saltier, all ppr. 169. 9
Aries, Ireland, a satyr holding in his dexter hand a sword and in his sinister a partizan, all ppr. *Fides mihi panoplia.* *cf.* 189. 3
Arkell or **Arkle,** a griffin sejant arg., holding in his dexter claw a garland of laurel vert. 62. 9
Arkinstall, Camb., on a mount vert, a greyhound sejant erm. 59. 3
Arkley, Scotland, within two thistles disposed in orle flowered ppr., a rose gu., barbed and seeded of the first. *Bene qui sedulo.*
Arkroyd, a dog sleeping. 57. 13
Arkwright, Arthur Chandos, Esquire, of Thoby Priory, Brentwood, Essex, an eagle rising or, in its beak an escutcheon pendent by a ribbon gu., thereon a hank of cotton arg. *Multa tuli fecique.*
Arkwright, Arthur William, Esquire, same crest and motto.
Arkwright, Rev. Edwin, of 36, Seymour Street, London, same crest and motto.
Arkwright, Esmé Francis Wigsell, Esquire, of Sanderstead Court, Croydon, Surrey, same crest and motto.
Arkwright, Francis, Esquire, of Overton, near Marton, Wellington, New Zealand, same crest and motto.
Arkwright, Frederic Charles, Esquire, of Willersley, Matlock, same crest and motto.
Arkwright, Herbert Robert, Esquire, of Knuston Hall, Irchester, same crest and motto.
Arkwright, John Hungerford, Esquire, of Hampton Court, Leominster, same crest and motto.
Arkwright, John Thomas, Esquire, of Hatton House, near Warw., same crest and motto.
Arkwright, Loftus Joseph, Esquire, of Parndon Hall, Little Parndon, Harlow, Essex, same crest and motto.
Arkwright, Richard, Esquire, of Farnham, Surrey, same crest and motto.
Arkwright, William, Esquire, of Sutton Scarsdale, Chesterfield, same crest and motto.
Arkwright, Rev William Harry, Esquire, of the Vicarage, Wicksworth, Derbysh., same crest and motto.
Arkybus, a lion's head erased arg. 17. 8
Arle, a boar's head erect between two ostrich-feathers. 41. 14
Arlote or **Arlott,** on a chapeau a leopard passant gardant, three blades of rushes on each side, all ppr.
Armesbury and **Armesburg,** Essex, two hands conjoined, each issuing from a cloud, all ppr. 224. 1
Armeston of Burbage, Leics., a dragon's head erased vert, scaled or, charged with a crescent of the same for difference. *cf.* 71. 2
Armestone, Leics., a dragon's head erased ppr. *cf.* 71. 2
Armestrang or **Armstrong,** Scotland, an arm embowed ppr. *Invictus maneo.* 202. 2
Armestrang, Armstrang, or **Armstrong,** Scotland, a hand issuing out of a cloud, holding a club, all ppr. *Invicta labore.* 214. 9
Armet, *see* Armit.
Armfield-Marrow, Peter, Esquire, between two roses arg., seeded or, barbed vert, a maiden's head couped at the shoulders ppr., crined, also gold, the neck encircled with a garland of roses arg., barbed or, seeded vert. *Fidite virtute.*
Armiger or **Armeier** of North Creake, Norf., on a ducal coronet or, an heraldic tiger sejant gu., crined and tufted of the first. 25. 12
Armine of Osgodby, Lincs, on a mount vert, an erm. ppr. 134. 10
Armistead, a dexter arm in armour embowed ppr., holding the butt-end of a broken spear or. *Suivez la raison.* 197. 7
Armit and **Armitt,** on a mount vert, a bull passant ppr. 45. 7
Armit, Armet, or **Armuet,** a demi-lion rampant gu., holding between the paws a helmet, the visor closed, arg.
Armitage of Egremont, Chesh., an arm bendwise or, vested gu., crusuly and cuffed of the first, holding a holly-branch erect, slipped and fructed ppr. *Fortiter et fideliter.*
Armitage, Yorks, a dexter arm embowed, vested or, cuffed arg., grasping in the hand ppr. a sword by the blade, also ppr., hilt of the first point down ward.
Armitage, Charles Ingram, of High Royd, Honley, same crest.
Armitage, George Pollard, of Milnsbridge, Yorks, a dexter arm embowed, couped at the shoulder, vested or, cuffed arg., holding in the hand ppr. a staff gu., pointed and headed or. *Semper paratus.*
Armitage, Sir Elkanah, of the Priory, Pendleton, Manchester, in front of a dexter arm embowed, vested gu., cuffed arg., the hand grasping the blade of a sword in bend sinister, the point downwards, pommel and hilt or, an escutcheon of the last charged with a cross potent gu.
Armitage, Benjamin, Esquire, of Holme Hall, Bakewell, Derbysh., same crest.
Armitage, Charles Smith, Esquire, of the Lee Wood Hotel, Buxton, Derbysh., same crest.
Armitage, Vernon Kirk, Esquire, of Swinton Park, Manchester, same crest. *Deo duce ferro comitante.*
Armitage, Walter Stanley, Esquire, of 34, Cambridge Square, Hyde Park, London, in front of an arm embowed vested az., cuffed arg., the hand grasping by the blade a sword ppr., pommel and hilt or, a dexter gauntlet fesseways also or. *Deo duce ferro comitante.* 233. 5
Armitstead, a dexter and a sinister arm embowed in armour, each hand grasping a spear erect ppr. *Pro Rege Patria.*
Armitstead, Rev. John Richard, M.A., of Cranage Hall, Chesh., same crest and motto.
Armitstead, George, Esquire, of Kinloch Laggan, Kingussie, N.B., crest as above.
Armo, three passion-nails ppr., one in pale and two in saltier.
Armony, a stag gu. 117. 5
Armorer, a gauntlet bendwise, holding the shaft of a broken tilting-spear, all ppr.
Armory, Ireland, an eagle's head or. 83. 1
Armour, Scotland, a dexter hand holding an esquire's helmet, all ppr. *Cassis tutissima virtus.* 217. 12
Armour, Donald, M.B., 89, Harley Street, W., crest and motto as above.
Armstrang of Mangerton, an arm in armour embowed ppr. 200. 1
Armstrong of Whittock, an arm embowed gu. *Invictus maneo.* 202. 2

Armstrong, Heref. and Worcs., an arm embowed ppr. *Invictus maneo.* 202. 2

Armstrong, an arm in armour, couped at the shoulder, embowed fessewise. *cf.* 200. 4

Armstrong of Willow Bank, Ireland, an arm in armour. *In Deo robur meus.*

Armstrong, Thomas St. George, Esquire, of Garry Castle House, Banagher, King's Co., same crest. *Vi et armis.*

Armstrong of Ballycumber, Ireland, a dexter arm in armour arg., the hand ppr. *Vi et armis.* 200. 1

Armstrong, Harkness, Rig Canobie, same crest and motto.

Armstrong of Hemsworth, Yorks, same crest and motto.

Armstrong, a dexter arm in armour embowed, hand apaumée ppr. 200. 1

Armstrong, Norf., a dexter arm in armour embowed arg., the hand clenched ppr. *Vi et armis.* *cf.* 200. 1

Armstrong, Scotland, an arm embowed, couped, cuffed arg., vested gu., holding a sword, all ppr. *Strength.*

Armstrong, an arm in armour grasping a sword az., hilted and pommelled or. *Invictus maneo.* 195. 2

Armstrong, Scotland, an arm issuing out of a cloud holding a club ppr. *Invicta labore.* 214. 9

Armstrong, King's Co., Ireland, an armed arm holding a broken tilting-spear ppr. 210. 9

Armstrong, Sir Andrew Harvey, Bart., Gallen Priory, Ferbane, King's Co., Ireland, an arm in armour embowed, the hand grasping the trunk of an oak-tree eradicated, all ppr. *Invictus maneo.*

Armstrong, Sir George Carlyon Hughes, Bart., 39, Cadogan Square, S.W., in front of an arm couped at the shoulder, embowed and barwise in pale, garnished or, fists clenched, a trefoil slipped vert. *Vi et armis.*

Armstrong, George Elliot, Esquire, of 24, Hans Road, S.W., same crest and motto.

Armstrong of Termonfechan, Louth, out of a mural coronet or, an armed arm embowed, the hand grasping an oak-tree eradicated ppr. *Invictus maneo.*

Armstrong, a dexter arm vambraced, the hand ppr. grasping a leg in armour, couped at the thigh of the same.

Armstrong, Marcus Beresford, Esquire, J.P., of Chaffpool, near Ballymote, same crest and motto.

Armstrong, Lieutenant-Colonel Richard, 6, Ashburn Place, London, S.W., same crest and motto.

Armstrong-MacDonnell, Charles Randal, of New Hall and Kilkee, co. Clare: (1) A dexter arm embowed fesseways, vested or, cuffed arg., the hand ppr. holding a cross crosslet fitchée erect az., the arm charged with a crescent gu. (*for MacDonnell*). *cf.* 203. 9. (2) A dexter arm embowed and lying vambraced fesseways ppr., the elbow resting upon the wreath and charged with a mullet gu., the hand grasping an armed leg couped at the thigh and bleeding, also ppr. *Toujours prêt.—Vi et armis.*

Armstrong, Baron, of Cragside, Rothbury, Northumb., and Jesmondene, Newcastle-upon-Tyne, within a garland of oak vert, an arm vambraced and embowed, resting upon the elbow, holding in the hand a sledge-hammer, all ppr. *Fortis in armis.* 234. 2

Armstrong, Baron, *see* Watson-Armstrong.

Armuet, *see* Armit.

Armytage, London and Yorks, a demi-lion arg., holding in the dexter paw a cross botonnée gu.

Armytage, Sir George John, Bart., of Kirklees, Yorks, a dexter arm embowed, couped at the shoulder, vested or, the cuff arg., holding in the hand ppr. a staff gu., pointed and headed or. *Semper paratus.*

Armytage, Arthur Henry, Esquire, of Marton Hall, Bridlington, Yorks, a dexter arm embowed, couped at the shoulder, habited or, the cuff arg., holding in the hand ppr. a staff gu., headed and pointed or. *Semper paratus.*

Armytage, Francis Reginald, Esquire, of Windsor House, Shrewsbury, same crest and motto.

Armytage, Godfrey, Esquire, of Carr Lodge, Horbury, Wakefield, same crest.

Armytage, Percy, Esquire, same crest and motto.

Armytage, George, Esquire, J.P., of Ingleby, Winchelsea, Victoria, Australia, and of 59, Queen's Gate, London, S.W., a dexter arm embowed, couped at the shoulder, habited or, the cuff arg., holding in the hand ppr. a dagger of the second, pommel and hilt of the first. *Semper paratus.* 204. 1

Arnald or **Arnauld,** a demi-cat gardant ppr. 26. 12

Arnall-Thompson, Harry Thompson, Esquire, of Haworth, Keighley, Yorks, and Ansty Frith, Leicester: (1) In front of two flagstaves ppr., flowing from each a pennon gu., a lion couchant sa., charged on the shoulder with a bezant (*for Thompson*). (2) In front of a demi-leopard regardant ppr., semée of annulets gu., holding between the paws a torteau charged with a pheon, a staff raguly fesseways, also gu. (*for Arnall*).

Arneel, Arnied, or **Arneil,** Scotland, an eel naiant vert. *Sans peur.* 142. 10

Arnet, on a mount vert, a bull passant ppr. 45. 7

Arnet, Scotland, a crescent or. *Speratum et completum.* 163. 2

Arnett, Arnot, and **Arnott,** on a tower ppr., a flag displayed az. *Another,* the flag arg. 157. 13

Arneway, Arnaway, and **Arnold,** Bucks and Lincs, a crosier or. 170. 14

Arnewood, Hants, out of a ducal coronet a demi-leopard.

Arney, Chamberry, Dorset, on a mural coronet or, three arrows arg. through a heart gu., two in saltier and one in pale.

Arnison, Major W. B., of Beaumont, Penrith, Cumb., in front of a fern-brake a stag lodged ppr., resting the dexter forefoot upon an estoile or. *Ditat servata fides.* 115. 13

Arnold, a hand ppr., holding a bunch of grapes purp., leaved vert. 219. 6

Arnold, a demi-tiger arg., pellettée, holding between the paws a fireball sa.

Arnold, Henry Fraser James Coape-, of Wolvey Hall, co. Warw., a demi-tiger regardant sa., bezantée maned and tusked, and holding between his paws a pheon or. *Ut vivas vigila.*

Arnold, London, a demi-heraldic tiger sa., bezantée, maned and tufted or, holding a broad arrow, the shaft gu., feathers and pheon arg.

Arnold of Missenden, Bucks, same crest. *Nil desperandum.*

Arnold, a demi-leopard regardant ppr., bezantée, holding a pheon or. *Ut vivas vigila.*

Arnold, Devonsh., out of a ducal coronet an antelope's head. *cf.* 126. 2

Arnold, Cromer, Norf., Bellesford, Suff., and Kent, a dolphin naiant arg. 140. 5

Arnold, Chilwick, Herts, an eagle's head erased gu., gorged with a mural coronet arg., holding in its beak an acorn slipped vert. *cf.* 84. 10

Arnold, Ireland, a feather and a sword in saltier. 170. 6

Arnold-Forster, Edward Penrose, of Cathedine, Burley-in-Wharfedale, a dolphin naiant.

Arnot of Balcormo, a crescent or. *Speratum et completum.* 163. 2

Arnot, Arrat, and **Arrot,** Scotland, a hand holding a dagger erect ppr. *Pax armis acquiritur.* 212. 9

Arnott, Sir John Alexander, Bart., 68, Merrion Square, Dublin, on a rock a tower ppr., therefrom a flag flying to the sinister az. *Speratum et completum.* 239. 12

Arnott of Arlary, same crest and motto.

Arnott, Fermanagh, a cubit arm erect in armour, the hand grasping a dagger, all ppr. *Speratum et completum.* 210. 2

Arnway, Lincs, a crosier or. 170. 14

Aron, a lady's arm from the elbow in pale. 222. 3

Arpin, an arm in armour holding a holly-branch, all ppr. 200. 14

Arran, Earl of (Gore), Castle Gore, Ballina, co. Mayo, a wolf rampant arg., collared gu. *In hoc signo vinces.* *cf.* 28. 2

Arras, out of a tower gu. embattled or, a lion's head of the last.

Arrat, Scotland, *see* Arnot.

Arrat of that ilk, Scotland, a dexter hand holding a sword erect ppr., hilted and pommelled or. *Antiquam assero decus.* *cf.* 212. 9

Arris, Scotland, a satyr, holding in his dexter hand a partizan. *cf.* 189. 3

Arrol, Scotland, a demi-lion rampant holding in the dexter paw a scimitar. *Courage.* 14. 10

Arrol, Archibald, Esquire, 18, Blythswood Square, Glasgow, a demi-lion gu., armed and langued az., holding in the dexter paw a scimitar ppr. *Courage.* 14. 10

Arrol, William Auchincloss, Esquire, of Torwood Hill Row, Dumbartonsh., same crest and motto.

Arrot of that ilk, Scotland, a dexter hand holding a sword in pale ppr. *Antiquum assero decus.* *cf.* 212. 9

Arrot, *see* Arnot.

Arrowood or **Arwood,** Lancs, a savage holding in his dexter hand a club resting on the wreath, all ppr.

Arrowsmith, seven arrows ppr., points upwards, and tied with a ribbon.

Arrowsmyth of Huntingfield Hall, Suff., seven arrows ppr., enfiled with a ducal coronet or. *cf.* 173. 9

Arscot, Devonsh., a demi-man affrontée in Turkish habit, holding in his dexter hand a scimitar held over his head, his sinister resting on a tiger's head issuing out of the wreath. 185. 7

Arscott, same crest.

Arssick, Arsike, Arsycke, and **Arsyke,** a talbot sejant ppr., resting his dexter paw on a shield gu. 55. 3

Arther and **Arthur,** a mullet of six points gu. 164. 3

Arthington, *see* Ardington.

Arthur, Dublin, a falcon volant ppr., jessed and belled or. *cf.* 88. 3

Arthur, Sir Matthew, Bart., of Carlung, West Kilbride, Ayrsh., on a rock a pelican in her piety ppr. *Fac et spera.* 295. 5

Arthur, William Francis John Rae, Esquire, a pelican in her piety, full-faced and wings elevated, all ppr. *Fac et spera.*

Arthur of Springfield, Essex, a pelican in her piety sa., the nest or, vulning herself gu. 98. 14

Arthur, Rev. Thomas Freke, M.A., of Hawley House, Barnstaple, a pelican in her piety sa., the nest or, her young also sa., vulning herself gu.

Arthur, Rev. William Wells, B.A., the Rectory, Atherington, Barnstaple, same crest.

Arthur, Scotland, a pelican in her piety in a nest vert. *Fac et spera.* 98. 14

Arthur, a pelican in her piety sa., the nest or, her young of the first, and on her breast a crescent. *cf.* 98. 14

Arthur, Sir George Compton Archibald, Bart., 4, Sackville Street, W., in front of two swords in saltire ppr., pommels and hilts or, a pelican in her piety sa., the nest of the second. *Stet fortuna domus.* 239. 5

Arthur, Tasmania, upon the capital of an Ionic column ppr., in a nest of the same, a pelican in her piety sa., charged on the wing with a quartrefoil or. *Teneo tenuere majores.* 98. 9

Arthur, Ireland, a falcon, wings addorsed az., belled or. *Impelle obstantia.* 88. 2

Artindale of Brown Hill, Burnley, Lancs, a demi-pegasus or, winged fretty gu., holding between the hoofs a mullet of six points. *In lumine luce.* 47. 12

Artked, a dexter arm embowed, resting on the elbow, holding in the hand a cross crosslet fitched in pale sa.

Arton, a candlestick or.

Artus, an eagle's head, holding in the beak a quill ppr.

Arundel and Surrey, Earl of, *see* Norfolk, Duke of.

Arundel, Baron (Arundel), of Trerice, Cornw., on a chapeau gu., turned up erm., a martlet arg. 95. 1

Arundel, Ireland, on a chapeau gu., turned up erm., a swallow arg. *Cruce dum spiro fido.* *cf* 96. 3

Arundel, Harris-, Devonsh.: (1) A stag's head ppr., attired or (*for Arundel*). 121. 5. (2) On a chapeau sa., turned up erm., a martlet of the last. 95. 1. (3) An eagle rising erm., beaked and spurred or (*for Harris*). *De Hirundine.* —*Nulli prœda.*—*Kar Deu.*—*Res. pub. tra.* 77. 5

Arundell, Cornw., on a mount a horse passant arg., against a tree ppr.

Arundell Hunter-, *see* Hunter.

Arundell, Viscount Galway, *see* Galway.

Arundell of Wardour, Baron (Arundel), Wardour Castle, Tisbury, Wilts, a wolf passant ar. *Deo data.* 28. 10

Arwell or **Arwell,** a hand holding a helmet ppr. 217. 12

Asadam, a rook feeding sa. 107. 4

Asborne, a lion's gamb erect, holding a flag arg., charged with an eagle displayed sa. *cf.* 35. 12

Asburner, an ash-tree ppr. 144. 11

Asche, Aschey, or **Ascher,** in the sea, a ship in full sail ppr. 160. 13

Ascon, a mascle arg. 167. 9

Ascough, *see* Askew.

Ascough of Blibers, Lincs, an ass arg. *cf.* 125. 11

Ascough, Lincs, an ass passant sa. 125. 7

Ascough and **Ascue,** an ass's head erased arg. *cf.* 125. 10

Ascum, a fleur-de-lis sa. 148. 2

Aselock or **Aslake,** Suff., a talbot's head sa., guttée d'eau. *cf.* 56. 12

Asen, a martlet gu. *cf.* 95. 5

Aserburne, an ash-tree ppr. *Quicquid crescit, in cinere perit.* 144. 11

Asgile, Bart., London, a sphinx gardant, wings addorsed arg., crined or. *Sui oblitus commodi.* 182. 12

Asgil, London, same crest and motto.

Asgill, London and Hants, on a mural coronet or, a sphinx couchant, gardant, the body brown, face and breasts ppr., winged or. *Sui oblitus commodi.*

Ash, an old man's head in profile ppr., wreathed and stringed or and az.

Ash, Stalsted, Kent, on a rock a goose, wings addorsed ppr. 102. 1

Ash, Warw., a cockatrice gu. 68. 5

Ash, a cockatrice's head erased. 68. 12

Ash of Ashbrook, Ireland, a squirrel. *Non nobis sed omnibus.* *cf.* 135. 2

Ashawe, Lancs, out of a ducal coronet or, an arm embowed, vested with leaves vert, holding in the hand a cross pattée fitchée arg. 198. 1

Ashawe, the same, only holding a cross crosslet fitchée arg.

Ashbee, an eagle displayed with two heads arg. *Be just and fear not.* 74. 2

Ashberton, on a chapeau ppr., a communion cup or.

Ashbey, *see* Ashby.

Ashborne or **Ashburne,** Ireland, a tower triple-towered ppr. 157. 6

Ashborne, a lion's gamb erect, holding a flag arg., charged with eagle displayed sa. *cf.* 35. 12

Ashbourne, Baron (Gibson), 12, Merrion Square, Dublin, on a bank of reeds a pelican in her piety, all ppr. *Pandite cœlestes portœ.* 242. 9

Ashbrook, Viscount (Flower), Castle Durrow, Durrow, Queen's Co., Ireland, a raven ppr., holding in the beak an ermine-spot sa. *Mens conscia recti.* *cf.* 107. 14

Ashburne and **Ashburner,** Camb., an ash-tree ppr. *Quicquid crescit in cinere perit.*—*Actio virtutis laus.* 144. 11

Ashburnham, Earl of (Ashburnham, Knight of Malta, and Knight Grand Cross of the Pontifical Order of Pius), Ashburnham Place, Battle, Sussex, out of a ducal coronet or, an ash-tree ppr. *Le roi et l'estat.* 145. 9

Ashburnham, Bart., Bromham, Sussex, same crest. *Will God, and I shall.*

Ashburnham of Ashburnham, Sussex, out of a ducal coronet or, an ash-tree ppr. *Will God, and I shall.* 145. 9

Ashburnham, Major-General Sir Cromer, of Brooklands, Wellington, Salop, same crest and motto.

Ashburnham or **Ashbrenham,** a griffin's head ppr., collared arg. *cf.* 67. 7

Ashburton, Baron (Baring), the Grange, Alresford, Hants, a mullet erminois between two wings arg. *Virtus in arduis.* 239. 2

Ashbury, *see* Ashborne.

Ashbury, a lion's gamb erased or, holding a spear, pendant therefrom a flag arg., charged with a martlet gu. *Æquitate ac diligentia.* *cf.* 35. 12

Ashby of Greenfields, Shropsh.: (1) On a mural coronet arg., a leopard's face or (*for Ashby*). *cf.* 22. 2. (2) A demi-lion rampant, holding in the dexter paw a sword (*for Maddock*). 14. 12 *Be just and fear not.*

Ashby, Major George Ashby: (1) On a mural crown arg., a leopard's face affrontée or (*for Ashby*). (2) A demi-lion couped or, fretty gu., holding in the dexter paw a dagger erect arg., pommel and hilt gold. *Be just and fear not.*

Ashby, John Shuckburgh, same crests and motto.

Ashby, Nicholas Hermann, Esquire, of Quenby Hall, Leics., upon a mural coronet arg., a leopard's face or. *Be just and fear not.* *cf.* 22. 2

Ashby, Leics., a ram's head arg., attired or. 130. 1

Ashby, Leics., an eagle close arg., ducally crowned or. *cf.* 76. 2

Ashby, Middx., an eagle, wings expanded arg., ducally crowned or. *cf.* 77. 5

Ashby, George Ashby Hermann, Esquire, upon a mural crown arg., a leopard's face or. *Be just and fear not.*

Ashcombe, Baron (Cubitt), Denbies, Dorking, a column ppr., in front two scimitars in saltire or. *Felix qui prudens.* 245. 1

Ashcomb or **Vishcomb,** Berks, on a chapeau ppr., a demi-eagle displayed sa., ducally crowned or. *cf.* 80. 12

Ashcroft of Grange House, Oakhill Park, Old Swan, Liverpool, out of park-pales or, an ash-tree ppr., therefrom pendant by a riband gu. an escutcheon of the first, charged with an ash-branch, slipped, leaved, and fructed vert. *Floruit fraxinus.*

Ashdoun or **Ashdown,** a lion's head gu., collared or, and bezantée.

Ashdown, Kent, a bull's head couped. *Numen et omnia.* 44. 10

Ashe, Bart., Twickenham, a cockatrice or, combed and wattled gu. 68. 5

Ashe, Devonsh., a cockatrice close or, legged and beaked gu.

Ashe of Ashfield, Ireland, and of Wilts, a cockatrice or, combed, wattled, and armed gu *Fight —Non nobis sed omnibus* 68 4
Ashe or **Eshe,** Devonsh, a cockatrice arg, charged on the breast with a tre foil, slipped gu 68 4
Ashenden, a lion's gamb erased gu, holding up the hilt of a broken sword ppr 38 2
Ashenden, a lion rampant supporting an arrow in pale, point downwards 2 4
Ashenhurst of Beardhall, Derbysh, a cockatrice, tail nowed, with a serpent's head sa, comb, wattles, and head gu, in the beak a trefoil vert
Asher, a ship in full sail ppr 160 13
Asherburne and **Ashburner,** Cumb, an ash tree ppr *Quicquid crescit in cinere perit —Actio virtutis laus* 144. 11
Asherst, Lancs a fox passant ppr 32 1
Asheton, Great Lever, Lancs, a boar's head couped arg, armed and bristled gu *In Domino confido* 43 1
Asheton or **Assheton,** a mower, his face and hands ppr, his habit vested per pale arg and sa counterchanged, holding a scythe, the blade arg, the handle or *cf* 188 12
Asheton-Tonge, *see* Tonge
Asheton or **Ashton,** a demi-angel, wings expanded, hands closed as in prayer, vested arg, face and hands ppr, hair, wings, and girdle or
Ashfield, a wolf passant or 28 10
Ashfield, a wolf current erm 28 4
Ashfield, Norf and Suff, a griffin passant arg 63 2
Ashfield, Suff, a wyvern statant arg *cf* 70. 2
Ashford of Ashford, Devonsh and Cornw, issuing out of a chaplet of oak-leaves vert, a Moor's head in profile sa, wreathed arg
Ashford, Baron, *see* Albemarle, Earl of
Ashfordby, Wilts, an ass's head erased or, gorged with a collar sa, charged with three mullets or *cf* 125 12
Ashhurst, Lancs, a fox statant ppr *Vincit qui patitur* *cf* 32 2
Ashhurst, William Henry, of Waterstock, Oxon., same crest and motto
Ashinghurst, a cockatrice close sa, wattled and legged gu, the tail nowed, ending with a serpent's head, holding in the mouth of cockatrice a trefoil vert
Ashley, Chesh, a bear's head muzzled ppr 34 14
Ashley, Lord, *see* Ashley Cooper
Ashley of Wimborne, Dorset, on a chapeau gu, turned up erm, a bull passant sa, gorged with a ducal coronet and armed or *cf* 45 9
Ashley-Cooper, Rt. Hon Sir Anthony, **Earl of Shaftesbury** and **Baron Ashley,** on a chapeau gu, turned up erm, a bull passant sa, gorged with a ducal coronet or, armed and ungu of the same *Love, serve* *cf* 45 9
Ashlin, a fir tree ppr 144 13
Ashman, Wilts, a hautboy in pale 168. 1
Ashmead-Bartlett, Sir Ellis, of 6, Grosvenor Street, in front of a tower ppr, a demi-swan with wings elevated arg, collared sa *Mature*
Ashmole, Staffs, a greyhound courant sa *cf* 58 5
Ashmole, Staffs, on a mount, a greyhound courant sa 58 2
Ashmore, Ireland, a demi-eagle displayed, with two heads or, each royally crowned ppr *cf* 82 1
Ashmore, Lieutenant-Colonel Charles, Belfast, a star of six points wavy arg, between two laurel branches vert *Cave adsum.*
Ashoe, a hawk ppr, belled or 85 2
Ashondon, a lion rampant supporting an arrow erect, point downward 2 4
Ashpitel, a demi dragon erased sa, winged, collared, and armed or *Omnia certa fac* *cf* 73 10
Ashton, Baron (Williamson), Ryelands, Lancaster, a demi eagle displayed or, guttee-de-poix, each wing charged with a fesse, and holding in beak two trefoils in saltire sa. *Murus æneus conscientia sana*
Ashton, Leics, a boar's head couped arg 43 1
Ashton, Percy, Morton House, near Worcs, a boar's head erased sa *In Domino confido*
Ashton, a stag statant regardant arg, attired and ungu or, gorged with chaplet of laurel ppr
Ashton, *see* Burchardt-Ashton
Ashton, Lancs, a boar's head couped arg *In Domino confido.* 43 1
Ashton of Middx, Staffs, of Spalding, Lincs, and Sheering, Essex, out of a mural coronet arg, a griffin's head gu, ducally gorged and beaked or 67 6
Ashton, Thomas Gair, of Hyde, Chesh, on a mount vert, a mower ppr, vested paly arg and sa, in the act of whetting his scythe, also ppr *Vide et virtute* *cf* 188 12
Ashton, Ireland, a man armed cap à pie striking with a scythe ppr *Quid non resolutio*
Ashton of Little Orm Hall, Staffs, on a mount vert, a mower with his scythe, all ppr *Fide et virtute*
Ashton, Arundel Mackenzie, Esquire, of Stockport, Chesh, on a mount vert, a mower ppr, vested paly arg and sa, in the act of whetting his scythe, also ppr
Ashton, *see* Asheton
Ashton, a lion's head erased ppr 17 8
Ashton of Manchester, upon a mount vert, an heraldic tiger rampant or, gorged with a collar dancettee, and holding between the paws a mullet sa *Agere pro aliis*
Ashton-Gwatkin, Rev Walter Henry Trelawny of the Rectory Wrotham, Kent, on a mount vert, a garb or, in front thereof a Cornish chough with wings expanded sa *Duw a bortha y brain*
Ashtown, Baron (Trench), Woodlawn, co Galway, an arm in armour embowed, holding a sword, all ppr *Virtutis fortuna comes* 105 2
Ashurin of Bretforton Manor, Evesham, Worcs., a Moor's head couped at the shoulders in profile ppr wreathed about the temples arg and az *Audax vincendo* 192 13
Ashurst, a wolf passant ppr 28 10
Ashurst of Waterstock, Oxon, a fox statant ppr. *Vincit qui patitur* *cf* 32 2
Ashwell, on a chapeau a garb ppr 153 10
Ashwood, on a chapeau the sun, all ppr *cf* 162 2
Ashworth, Heyford, Oxon, on a mount vert, a fox ppr *cf* 32 2
Ashworth of Egerton Hall, Turton, Bolton-le-Moors, Lancs, on a mount vert, a fox ppr *Fac recte nil time* *cf* 32 2
Ashworth, Lancs, same crest. *Appetitus rationi pareat*
Ashworth, George Binns, of Birtenshaw House, Bolton, Lancs, upon a rock a fox ppr, supporting with the dexter foreleg a passion cross invected or
Ashworth, Henry, Esquire of Birtenshaw House, Bolton, Lancs same crest.
Ashworth, Edward, of Staghills, Waterfoot, Manchester, in front of two crosslets bottonée fitchee in saltire or, a fox passant ppr, charged on the body with two fleurs-de lis in fesse, also gold *Vincit amor patriæ* 244 1
Ashworth, a savage's head affrontée ppr 190 12
Ashworth, on a mount vert, an ash-tree ppr *cf* 144 11
Ashworth, Ireland, on a chapeau a garb ppr 153 10
Ashworth, Hants, on a mount vert, a fox ppr *Cœlum non animum* *cf* 32 2
Aske of Aske, Lancs, an old man's head in profile ppr, wreathed or and az, and tied with a bow of the colours
Aske, a dragon's head couped arg 71. 1
Askeam or **Askeham,** a dolphin az 140 5
Askeby, Askely, Asklaby, Asklakby, or **Asklakeby,** a sundial on a pedestal ppr 176 7
Asken or **Askene,** an ass's head sa 125 12
Asketine or **Askentine,** of West Peckham, Kent, two lions' gambs erect sa, supporting a crescent or 39 6
Askew, an ass ppr *cf* 125 11
Askew or **Askue,** London, an ass's head ppr, gorged with three bars or, between two wings or and arg
Askew, Lincs, an ass arg *cf* 125 11
Askew and **Ascough,** Northumb and Scotland, an arm ppr, holding a sword arg, hilt or, enfiled with a Saracen's head couped ppr, wreathed or and sa, blood issuing gu *Fac et spera.* *cf* 212 14
Askew of Pallinsburn, Northumb, same crest *Patientia casus exsuperat omnes*
Askew, Henry Hugh, Esquire, a naked arm ppr, grasping a sword arg, pommel and hilt or, enfiled with a Saracen's head couped, distilling drops of blood, all also ppr, wreathed about the temples
Askew-Robertson, Watson, Esquire, of Ladykirk, Berwick, and Pallinsburn, Cornhill, co Northumb (1) A dexter cubit arm ppr, charged (for distinction) with a cross crosslet gu, the hand holding an imperial crown, also ppr 270. 5 *Virtutis gloria merces (for Robertson of Ladykirk)* (2) A dexter hand holding on a poignard erect ppr, hilt and pommel or, a Saracen's head couped and imbrued ppr, wreathed about the temples with a torse arg and gu, tied with ribands

of the same colours, and above, on a scroll. *Fac et spera (for Askew). Patientia casus exsuperat omnes (for Robertson of Ladykirk).* 270. 6
Askham, a dolphin az.
Askill, *see* Aiskell.
Askwith, Yorks, a mascle gu. 167. 9
Askwith, of Ripon, Yorks, a cross crosslet fitchée between two wings. *Honestas quam splendida.* 111. 3
Aslack, Aslake, and **Asloke,** of Holme, Norf., a talbot's head sa., guttée-d'eau. *cf.* 56. 12
Aslacton, a moorcock's head erased sa.
Aslakby or **Aslakeby,** a sundial on a pedestal ppr. 176. 7
Aslake, *see* Aselock.
Aslin, London, a demi-horse ppr. 53. 3
Aslin, Aslyn, or **Asslan,** an escutcheon charged with a rose gu. *cf.* 149. 7
Aspall, a dragon's head couped or. 71. 1
Aspall, a man's head bearded ppr., on his head a cap gu.
Aspath, two spears in saltier.
Aspin, Bucks, a dragon's head or, between two aspen-branches ppr.
Aspinall, Preston, Lancs, a demi-griffin erased sa., collared, winged, and beaked or. *Ægis fortissima virtus.*
Aspinall, Ralph John, J.P., of Standen Hall, Lancs, same crest and motto.
Aspinwall, Samuel J., Chestergate, Macclesfield, a demi-griffin sa., collared beaked and clawed or. *Ægis fortissima virtus.*
Aspland, Arthur Palmer, Esquire, of Wernest Lodge, Gee Cross, Chesh., in front of a ram's head couped sa., armed or, three mascles interlaced fessewise arg. *Ex libertate veritas.* *cf.* 130. 1
Aspland, Lindsay Middleton, Esquire, LL.D., same crest and motto.
Asprey, London, a demi-griffin erased sa. *Redoutable et fougueux.*
Asscoti or **Ascotti,** an eagle displayed with two heads ppr., imperially crowned or. *Dum spiro spero.* *cf.* 74. 2
Assent, out of a ducal coronet a horse's head arg., bridled gu. *cf.* 51. 7
Assey, Suff., a demi-lion rampant ppr., crowned with an Eastern crown gu., and holding in his paws a sword erect, also ppr.
Assheton and **Asshetton,** a boar's head couped gu. (*another*, or). 43. 1
Assheton, Ralph, of Downham and Cuerdale, Lancs, on a cap of maintenance a mower vested, and capped quarterly arg. and sa., the sleeves and stockings counterchanged, holding a scythe az., handled or, the point of the blade towards the dexter. *Nec arrogo nec dubito.*
Assheton, Ralph Cokayne, Esquire, of Hall Foot, Clitheroe, same crest and motto.
Assheton, Rev. Richard Orme, the Gable House, Bilton, Rugby, Warw., same crest and motto.
Astbury, Frederick James, Esquire, of Hilton Park, Prestwich, on a mural coronet, a dove with wings expanded ppr., holding in the dexter claw an estoile or. *Devotione et labore.*
Astel or **Astle,** Staffs, a seahorse couchant, ducally gorged. *cf.* 46. 5

Astell, a cross crosslet or, entwined by a serpent vert. *Sub cruce glorior.* 165. 6
Astell, Richard John Vereker, of 16, Sloane Gardens, S.W.: (1) A cross crosslet or, environed with a serpent vert. 165. 6. (2) A lion's head erased purp., gorged with a coronet or, and guttée-de-larmes. *Sub cruce glorior.*
Astell, Somerset Charles Godfrey Fairfax, Esquire, of West Lodge, Puddlehinton, Dorchester: (1) A cross crosslet or, entwined with a serpent vert. (2) A lion's head erased purp., gorged with a ducal coronet or, and guttée-de-l'armes. *Sub cruce gloria glorior.*
Asterby, Lincs, an oak-tree ppr. 143. 5
Astery, Asterlley, or **Esterley,** an estoile between two wings ppr. *cf.* 112. 1
Astle, *see* Astel.
Astley, Baron Hastings, out of a ducal coronet or, a plume of five ostrich-feathers arg. 114. 13. And also, on a chapeau gu., turned up erm., a ducal coronet or, issuing therefrom a pillar gu., surmounted by five ostrich-feathers arg. *Justitiæ tenax.*
Astley, Rev. Hubert Delavel, of Benham Hall, Newbury: (1) Out of a ducal coronet or, a plume of five feathers arg. (2) On a chapeau gu., a ducal coronet or, thereout a plume of feathers arg., incased gu. *Justitiæ tenax.*
Astley, Ludford-, of Ansley Park, near Atherstone, Warw., on a cap of maintenance a plume of seven ostrich-feathers gu.
Astley, Warw., out of a ducal coronet or, a plume of seven ostrich-feathers gu., surmounted by another plume of the first.
Astley, Sir John Dugdale, Bart., of Everley, Wilts, on a chapeau ppr., a plume of ostrich feathers gu.
Astley, Essex, on a chapeau a plume of feathers arg., banded gu., environed with a ducal coronet or. 114. 11
Astley-Corbett, Sir Francis Edmund George, Bart., of Elsham Hall, in the county of Lincs, on a wreath of the colours an elephant statant arg., tusked or, the trappings sa., fimbriated or, on his back a castle triple-towered of the last. 133. 11
Astley, Sir John, K.G., *temp.* Hen. VI., out of a ducal coronet or, a harpy arg., ducally gorged and crined of the first.
Aston, a bull's head or, armed per fesse sa. and arg. *cf.* 44. 3
Aston, Baron Aston, of Forfar, a bull's head couped sa. *Numini et patriæ asto.* 44. 10
Aston, Harold Edgar, solicitor, 71, Edgware Road, W., same crest and motto.
Aston, Lord Aston, Staffs and Ireland, a bull's head or, the horns arg., tipped sa. *cf.* 44. 3
Aston, a chapeau gu., turned up erm., on each side thereof within the erm. a bull's horn ppr.
Aston, a fox's head ppr. 33. 4
Aston, an etoile ppr. *E tenebris lux.* 164. 1
Aston of Aston, Chester, an ass's head ppr. *Prêt d'accomplir.* 125. 12
Aston, Chesh., an ass's head per chevron arg. and sa. 125. 12

Aston of Fairnham, Bart., Hants, an ass's head ppr. 125. 12
Aston, Staffs, Chesh., and Lancs, an ass's head ppr. *Prêt d'accomplir.* 125. 12
Aston, Chesh., an ass's head per pale arg. and sa. 125. 12
Aston, Staffs and Lancs, an ass's head per pale arg. and sa. *Prêt d'accomplir.* 125. 12
Astonne, an ass's head gu. 125. 12
Astor, William Waldorf, Esquire, of 18, Carlton House Terrace, S.W., an eagle with wings displayed. *Ad astra.*
Astrie, Henbury, and Astry, Wood End, Beds, a stag's head erased gu., attired or. 121. 2
Astrovel, a buckle or. 178. 5
Astrye, Beds, an ostrich or, wings endorsed, holding in the beak a horse-shoe. *cf.* 165. 7
Aswell, Cornw., a cross formée arg., guttée-de-poix. *cf.* 165. 7
Aswell, *see* Ashwell.
Atbarough or **Atborough,** Somers., a martin arg., collared and lined or. *cf.* 134. 9
Atcherley, of Marton, Shropsh., a demi-bustard couped gu., wings elevated or, holding in the beak a lily arg., slipped vert. *Spe posteri temporis.*
Atcherley, Llewellyn William, Esquire, same crest and motto.
Atcherley, Richard Topping Beverley, Esquire, same crest and motto.
Atcheson of Pittenweem, an astrolabe ppr. *Observe.* 167. 7
Atcheson, Scotland, a cock standing on a trumpet ppr. *Vigilantibus.* 91. 6
Atchison, a cock ppr. *Vigilantibus.* 91. 2
Atcliff, Atcliffe, Atclyff, or **Atclyffe,** a cross crosslet arg. 165. 2
Atetse, a Cornish chough ppr. 107. 14
Atfield, an arm embowed throwing an arrow fesseways, all ppr. 201. 14
Atfoe, on a chapeau a lion's head erased, all ppr. 17. 9
Athanray, Ireland, out of a ducal coronet a goat's head. 128. 14
Athawes, Edward James, Esquire, of Neville House, Streatham, a lion rampant.
Athelstan or **Athelston,** a hand holding a sword in pale, enfiled with a savage's head couped and wreathed. 212. 14
Athelstane, a mound gu., banded and crossed or. 159. 12
Atherley and **Atherly,** a lion's head erased sa. 17. 8
Atherley, on a chapeau a stork ppr. 105. 3
Atherley, Arthur Harry Howard, Esquire, J.P., of Landguard Manor, near Shanklin, Isle of Wight, on a chapeau gu., turned up erm., a stork ppr. *Pro patria.*
Atherton, Durh., upon a fountain a sparrow-hawk close ppr.
Atherton, Lancs, on a perch a hawk belled ppr. 85. 13
Atherton or **Atterton,** Lancs, a hawk ppr., legged and beaked or. 85. 2
Atherton, Rev. Robert, Bolnhurst Rectory, St. Neot's, Hunts, a hawk ppr., legged and beaked or. *Onward.* 85. 2
Atherton, Lancs, a swan arg. 99. 2
Atherton, Lancs, a swan az., ducally gorged and lined or. *cf.* 99. 2

Atherton, Taynton House, Glouc, a swan az, ducally gorged and lined or *Nec elatus, nec dejectus* cf 99 2

Atherton of Atherton, Yorks, a demi-swan arg, beaked gu, gorged with a ducal coronet or

Atherton, a swan, wings expanded, gorged with a collar and lined, and issuing from ducal coronet cf 99 5

Athill, Charles Harold, Esquire, F S A, *Richmond Herald*, a plume of three ostrich-feathers erect arg, interlaced with as many annulets fessewise or *Crescam ut prosim* 115 5

Athlone, Earl of (De Ginkell), Ireland, a pair of wings erect arg, charged with two bars dancettee *Malo mori quam fœdari* cf 109 6

Athlumney, Baron (Somerville), Navan, Meath, Ireland, a demi lion rampant sa, charged on the shoulder with a cross crosslet fitchee and two mullets arg *Crains Dieu tant que tu viveras* 10 5

Athol, Scotland, an arm in armour brandishing a scimitar ppr 196 10

Athole, Duke of (Stewart Murray), a demi-savage ppr, wreathed about the head and waist vert, holding in the dexter hand a dagger, also ppr, pommel and hilt or, and in his sinister a key of the last *Furth fortune and fill the fetters* 186 2

Athorpe, a hawk ppr 85 2

Athorpe, Rev. George Middleton, of Morthen Hall, near Rotherham, a falcon ppr, belled or, the dexter claw resting on an escutcheon of the arms viz per pale nebulee arg and az, two mullets in fesse counterchanged 85 11

Athorpe, Robert (1) Same crest as above (2) Middleton (3) A mount vert, thereon a cross cluchée or, charged in the centre with a fleur-de lis sa

Athurton, a swan arg, ducally gorged and lined or cf 99 2

Athwat, a horse's head erm, out of a plume of five ostrich-feathers gu cf 51 11

Athy, Ireland, a lion passant or *Duci et non trahi* 6 2

Atkey, Frederick Walter, Esquire, of Clevelands, Wimbledon, a griffin segreant or gorged with a collar gemel holding between the claws a cross moline, and the dexter foot resting on a garb fessewise gu *Labore fides*

Atkin, *see* Ames

Atkin, Ireland, an ox-yoke az, stapled or 178. 6

Atkin-Roberts, John Roberts Esquire of Glassenbury Park, Cranbrook, Kent (1) On a mount vert, an eagle displayed erm, wings arg, gorged with a chaplet of ivy ppr (*for Roberts*) 74 10 (2) Two greyhounds' heads, addorsed and erased arg, guttee-de-sang gorged with a collar vair and each holding in the mouth a trefoil slipped sa (*for Atkin*) *Post funera virtus* cf 60 12

Atkins, Yelverton, Norf, a demi tiger erm, collared and lined or cf 23 8

Atkins, London, an etoile 164 1

Atkins or Atkyns, Totteridge, Herts, and Glouc, two greyhounds' heads erased, addorsed arg and sa, collared and ringed counterchanged *Vincit cum legibus arma* 60. 12

Atkins, Frederick Thomas, Esquire, banker, Madras, India, in front of two greyhounds' heads addorsed and erased arg, gorged with a collar flory and counter flory az, as many fleurs-de lis of the last 60 14

Atkins of Yelverton, Norf, a demi lion rampant erm, langued gu, armed and ducally gorged or, with a chain affixed to the coronet, pendant between the paws and reflexed thence over the back, also or cf 10 7

Atkins of Waterpark, Cork, a pelican vulning herself ppr *Be just and fear not* 98 1

Atkins, a pelican ppr, preying on a wyvern vert

Atkins, Ireland, a nag's head erased sa, bridled arg *Honor et virtus* cf 50 8

Atkinson, a pheon or *Deo adjuvante* 174 11

Atkinson, Newcastle, a pheon az 174 11

Atkinson of Tarbottle, Northumb, a pheon or 174 1

Atkinson, Sheffield, a pheon or *Aut homo aut nullus* 174 11

Atkinson of Newark, Notts, a pheon or *Nil sine labore* 174 11

Atkinson, late Rt Hon Richard of Highfield House, Rathgar co Dublin, and of 31, College Green, Dublin, Lord Mayor of the said city 1857 and 1861 the battlements of a castle arg the towers at either end flommant ppr, thereon a pheon erect, point downwards or *Esperance en Dieu*

Atkinson of Rehins, and of Ballylahan, co Mayo, Ireland, an eagle displayed with two heads arg, charged on the breast with a fleur-de lis sa *Est pii Deum et patriam diligere* cf 74 2

Atkinson of Cangort, Ireland, an eagle with two heads displayed az, beaked and legged gu *Deo et regi fidelis* 74 2

Atkinson of Woolley Grange, Bradford on-Avon, Wilts, Walls End, and Benwell, Northumb, an eagle displayed with two heads sa, suspended from the neck a bugle-horn stringed arg, and holding in each claw a rose gu, slipped and leaved ppr *Deo et regi fidelis*

Atkinson, Buddle, Esquire, an eagle displayed with two heads sa, gorged with a bugle-horn stringed arg, in each claw a rose slipped ppr, seeded or *Deo regi fidelis*

Atkinson, Charles, Esquire, of Rehins, Ballylahan, co Mayo, an eagle displayed with two heads arg, charged on the breast with a fleur-de-lis sa *Est pii Deum et patriam diligere*

Atkinson, Guy Montague, Esquire, Cangort Shinrone, King's Co, an eagle displayed with two heads az beaked and legged gu *Deo et regi fidelis*

Atkinson, Edwin Crossley Esquire, of Micklegate House, Pontefract, Yorks, an eagle, wings expanded arg, holding a fleur de-lis in the beak, beaked and legged gu *Tempus omnia revelat* cf 77. 5

Atkinson, Thomas Henry Hollis Bradford, Esquire, of Angerton, near Morpeth, Northumb, on a mount between two roses stalked and leaved ppr, a pheon az *Crede Deo*

Atkinson, London, Northumb, and Somers, an eagle, wings expanded arg, beaked and legged gu 77 5

Atkinson, Notts, a demi-eagle, wings displayed or, collared sa. cf 80 2

Atkinson, Nicholas, Esquire, Senior Puisne Judge of the Supreme Court of Justice in British Guiana, of Roraima Broadhurst Gardens Hampstead, a falcon, wings elevated and endorsed gu, bezantee, gorged with a collar gemel arg supporting with the dexter leg an escutcheon az charged with a rose arg *Deo et patriæ fidelis* cf 87 10

Atkinson, Rev Francis Home, of Morland Hall, Westml, a roundel per fesse az and gu, charged with an eagle, with two heads displayed or

Atkinson of Rampsbeck Lodge, Cumb, a falcon, wings expanded cf 87 1

Atkinson, a swan, wings addorsed, swallowing a fish ppr 99 10

Atkinson, a lion's head erased ppr 17 8

Atkinson, a wolf's head erased sa 30 8

Atkinson of Angerton Northumb, on a mount, and between two roses stalked and leaved ppr, a pheon az *Crede Deo*

Atkinson, Cambs, a sea-lion sejant arg, holding in the dexter paw an escallop or

Atkyn and Atkyns, an arm in armour embowed ppr, holding in the gauntlet a cross formee fitched az, fleury or

Atkyns, *see* Atkins

Atkyns of Saperton Hall, Glouc, on a mount vert, two greyhounds' heads addorsed arg and sa, collared and ringed counterchanged *Vincit cum legibus arma* cf 60 12

Atkyns of Great Berkhampstead, Herts, a stork arg, wings and tail sa, beaked and legged gu, preying on a dragon vert

Atlee, two lions' heads addorsed ppr, and collared cf 18 2

Atlee and Atley, Sussex, two lions' heads addorsed ppr 17 3

Atley, on an escutcheon arg, a pheon az

Atmore and Attemore, a mermaid ppr, crined or, comb and mirror of the last 184 8

Atsley, a leopard's head erased or, spotted sa, and ducally gorged of the first cf 23 2

Atsoe or Atfoe, on a chapeau ppr, a lion's head erased gu 17 9

Attelound or **Attelounde,** a hound couchant gardant ppr (*Another*, arg) cf 57 11

Atterton, *see* Atherton

Atterton, Lancs, a swan arg, ducally gorged and lined or cf 99 2

Attfield, an arm embowed throwing an arrow in fess, all ppr 201 14

Atton or Attone, out of a ducal coronet two lions' gambs in saltier sa 39 10

Attree, Alfred Augustus Town, Esquire, on a mount an oak-tree, and in front thereof a serpent nowed, all ppr *Sperate futurum*

Attree, Frederick William Town, Esquire, of Royal Engineers, Chatham, same crest and motto.

Attwood, a demi-lady, holding in her dexter hand a pair of scales, all ppr. 183. 2

Attwood, Worcs., issuing from a coronet a swan's head.

Attwood, Thomas A. C., Esquire, M.A. Oxon., of Malvern Wells, Worcs., of the family of Attwood, formerly of Hawne House, Corngreave's Hall, and the Leasowes, near Halesowen, in the same county, and of the city of Birmingham, beneath an oak-tree a demi-swan, wings expanded ppr. *Possunt quia posse videntur.* 100. 5

Attwood, formerly of Park Attwood, Wolverley Court, and Perdiswell, Worcs., issuing from a ducal coronet a swan's head and neck between two wings displayed ppr.

Atty of Penley Hall, Warw., on a ducal coronet an erm. passant. *Eamus quo ducit fortuna.*

Atwater, between the attires of a stag, affixed to the scalp or, a rose gu. *cf.* 149. 9

Atwell, Devonsh., a lion rampant erminois, holding between the paws an annulet or.

Atwood, Rev. George Dewhurst, Hinton, Brackley, Northamp., a dove ppr. *Humani nil alienum.* 92. 2

Atwood, an antelope's head ppr *cf.* 126. 2

Atwood, Ireland, an arm in fess, holding in the hand a cross crosslet fitched erect. 221. 10

Atwood, Suff., a cubit arm in armour erect arg., holding in the hand ppr. a battle-axe.

Atwood of Bromfield, Essex, on a branch of a tree trunked lying fesseways or, a fleur-de-lis arg., between two sprigs vert.

Aty, Atye, or **Attye,** an erm. passant ppr. 134. 6

Atye of Newington, Middx., same crest.

Aubemarle, an ear of wheat bladed and a palm-branch in saltier ppr. 154. 10

Aubert, London, a talbot passant ppr., with a broken collar between his fore-legs, a line affixed to the collar reflexed over the back, and passing between the hind-legs, with a double bow at the end, all or. *Fide et fortitudine.* 54. 3

Aubertin of Yeulands, Banstead, Surrey, two banners of the arms (viz., az. on a fesse or, between three plates in chief and a cross moline in base arg., an eagle displayed sa.) in saltire. *Esto fidelis.*

Aubert, John Daniel, Esquire, a tilting-spear erect ppr., passing through a hauberk or coat of mail or. *Aides Dieu.*

Aubin and **St. Aubin,** on a rock a Cornish chough, all ppr. 107. 2

Aubin, Cornw., on a rock ppr., an eagle rising arg.

Aubley or **Aubly,** a dexter hand ppr., holding a cross pattée fitched gu. in pale. *cf.* 221. 12

Aubrey, Bart. (*extinct*), an eagle's head erased or. *Solem fero.* 83. 2

Aubrey, Charles Aubrey, Esquire, of Dorton House, Bucks: (1) An eagle's head erased or (*for Aubrey*). 83. 2. (2) Issuant from a wreath of quatrefoils gu., an arm embowed, vested arg., charged with two escallops, also gu., the hand holding a scimitar ppr. (*for Ricketts*). *Solem fero.*

Aubyn, St., Somers., a squirrel sejant erm., collared and lined or. *cf.* 135. 4

Aubyn, an eagle, wings displayed ppr. 77. 5

Aucher of Bourne, Kent, Bart., a bull's head erased gu., armed or. 44. 3

Auchinleck of that ilk, Scotland, an ear of rye ppr. *Pretiosum quod utile.* 154. 1

Auchinleck, Ireland, a wheat-stalk bladed and eared, all ppr. *Pretiosum quod utile est.* 154. 3

Auchinleck of Balmano, Scotland, two wings issuing ppr. *Rerum sapientia custos.* 109. 6

Auchmuty, Scotland, an arm in armour embowed holding a spear, all ppr. 197. 1

Auchmuty, an arm in armour embowed ppr., holding in the hand the lower part of a broken spear az. *Dum spiro spero.* 197. 7

Auchmuty, General Sir Samuel Benjamin, G.C.B., on a wreath of the colours an arm embowed in armour ppr., holding the lower part of a broken spear bendways az. *Dum spiro spero.* 197. 7

Auchterlonie, Scotland, an eagle displayed ppr. *Deus mihi adjutor.* 75. 2

Auchterlony of Guynd, same crest.

Auchterlony, Scotland, a lion's head erased sa., collared or. 18. 6

Auckland, Baron (Eden), Kitley, Plymouth, an arm in armour embowed ppr., holding a garb or, the upper part of the arm encircled by an annulet gu. *Si sit prudentia.* 251. 10

Audborough, an escallop or, between two wings az. 141. 10

Audeley, a mullet of six points or, between two wings az. 112. 1

Auden, Rev. T., of Condover, Shrewsbury, a scimitar and caduceus in saltire, ensigned with a pilgrim's hat. *Cresco et spero.* 295. 12

Audin, a lion passant or, holding in the dexter paw a banner gu., thereon a cross arg. 5. 13

Audin, a lion rampant arg., holding in the dexter paw an ancient battle-axe of the same.

Audley of Waldon, Essex, on a chapeau gu., turned up erm., a wyvern, wings addorsed quarterly or and az. *cf.* 70. 4

Audely, a Saracen's head couped ppr., wreathed arg. and purp. 190. 14

Audley or **Audly,** a martlet sa.

Audley, Baron (Thicknesse-Touchet): (1) A cubit arm erect, vested, paly of six or and gu., holding a scythe ppr., the blade downwards (*for Thicknesse*). (2) Out of a ducal coronet or, a swan rising arg., ducally gorged (*for Touchet*). *Je le tiens.*

Audley, Boston, Lincs, a man's head couped at the shoulders sa., with a cap or, turned up erm.

Audouin, Ireland, a stag's head erased ppr. *Chassé pour foi.* 121. 2

Audry, Wilts, a stag trippant ppr. 117. 8

Audym, a lion rampant crowned per pale or and arg., supporting a paschal banner disvelloped arg., staff and cross gu. *cf.* 3. 7

Audym and **Audyn** of Dorchester, a lion passant crowned or, bearing on his shoulders a paschal banner disvelloped arg., staff and cross gu. *cf.* 5. 13

Auffrick, two arms in armour embowed, holding in the hands a gem ring, all ppr. *cf.* 194. 11

Auforus, a mullet or. 164. 2

Aufrere, a lion rampant gu. *Esto quod esse videris.* 1. 13

Auge, a savage's head couped ppr., wreathed arg. and sa. 190. 14

Auger of Bordeaux, France, and of Ireland, on a mount an oak-tree, thereon perched a jay, all ppr.

Aughterlony, an eagle displayed ppr. *Deus mihi adjutor.* 75. 2

Auld, Scotland, the sun rising out of a cloud ppr. *Major virtus quam splendor.* 162. 5

Auld, a lion's head erased ppr. 17. 8

Auld or **Aulde,** Scotland, a cherub's head ppr., the wings in saltier. *Virtute et constantia.* 189. 13

Auldis, Scotland, the trunk of an oak-tree with a branch sprouting forth on either side vert. *Non deficit alter.* 145. 2

Auldjo, the stump of a tree, leaves sprouting, all ppr. 145. 2

Aumarle, Aumerle, and **Amerle,** an arrow in pale ppr. 173. 5

Auncell, a lion passant ppr. 6. 2

Auncell, a stag's head affrontée ppr., ducally gorged or. 119. 14

Aundeligh, a sceptre in pale or. 170. 10

Aungate, on a torteau an étoile or.

Aunger, an escarbuncle or. 164. 12

Aunger, London, a demi-griffin or. 64. 2

Aungier, Earl of Longford (*extinct*), a griffin segreant az., langued gu., the beak, forelegs, and claws or, and holding between the claws an escarbuncle of the same. *Scio cui confido.*

Aunsham, an escallop or, between two palm-branches vert. 141. 4

Aurd, a buck's head erased ppr. 121. 2

Aurelis, a demi-youth ppr., vested arg., the coat az., buttoned or.

Auriol of London and Brussels, an eagle rising, the dexter wing erect, the sinister close.

Aust and **Auste,** a garb ppr. 153. 2

Austen or **Austin** of Bexley, and of Grovehurst and Broadford, Kent, on a mural coronet or, a stag sejant arg., attired of the first.

Austen-Cartmell, James, Esquire, of 100, Lexham Gardens, Kensington, and New Square, Lincoln's Inn, London. (1) A lion rampant per fesse nebuly vert and gu., guttée-d'or, and resting the forepaws upon a tent (?) or (*for Cartmell*). (2) In front of the battlements of a tower ppr., thereon a stag sejant arg., attired and resting the dexter forefoot upon a quatrefoil or, a lion's gamb erased fessewise gu. (*for Austen*). *Immer frey.*

Austen, Lieutenant-Colonel Henry Haversham Godwin, of Shalford House, Surrey, on a leopard's face az., a falcon rising or. *Ne quid nimis.*

Austen Leigh, *see* Leigh.

Austin-Gourlay, *see* Gourlay

Austin, Sir John, Bart., Red Hill, Castleford, Normanton, a dexter arm embowed in fesse, couped at the shoulder, vested or, cuff indented erm, the hand ppr grasping a cross botony fitchee gu, resting on the arm a mullet of the last 234 3

Austin, a lion's gamb erased ppr 36 4

Austin, Surrey, a passion-cross or, between two wings erect sa cf 111 6

Austin, Rt Rev William Piercy, D D, first Bishop of Guiana, a demi-lion or, holding between the paws a passion-cross gu, and charged on the body with three fusils, two and one az

Austin, a paschal lamb arg 131 2

Austin of Doddington Grove, Surrey, on a ducal coronet or, a paschal lamb ppr *Crux nostra corona* cf 131 2

Austin, Rev William Edward Cranford, Rector of Stoke Abbott, Dorset, an eagle displayed with two heads per pale or and gu on each wing a crescent counterchanged *Virtute non vi* cf 74 4

Austin, Scotland, an arm couped at the shoulder embowed ppr, vested vert, cuffed or, the arm resting upon the elbow and holding in the hand a cross crosslet fitchee gu 203 9

Austrey, Hartington, Beds, a demi-ostrich arg, the wings gu

Austrey of Sommerton, Hunts, an ostrich-head erased arg, between two ostrich-wings gu, holding in the beak a horse shoe sa

Austyn, a buck's head cabossed 122 5

Austyn, out of a ducal coronet or, a stag's head at gaze ppr cf 119 13

Auverquerque, on a chapeau az, turned up erm, a lion rampant gardant or cf 2 5

Auverquerque, a griffin's head sa 66 1

Auvray, France, a demi savage with a club over the dexter shoulder, all ppr 186 5

Avagour and Avougour, England and France, a parrot's head between two wings ppr 101 10

Avebury, Baron (Lubbock), High Elms, Farnborough R S O, a stork, wings elevated erm, supporting an antique shield az, bordered or, charged with a lion rampant guardant arg 236 12

Aveland, Baron, *see* Heathcote

Avelin or **Evelin** of Long Ditton, Surrey, a demi hind erm, vulned in the shoulder gu

Aveline, Windsor and Frogmore, Berks, a lion's head erased arg, holding in the mouth in pale a sword, also arg, hilt and pommel or

Aveline, France, a griffin's head erased or 66 2

Aveling of Wisbeach, a griffin passant or, winged and ducally gorged az, and resting the dexter claw on a cross crosslet fitchee of the same 63 6

Aveling, Stephen T, Esquire, Restoration House, Rochester, the same crest *Omnibus optimus*

Aveling, James Thomas, of Estover, Cambs, crest as above

Avenant of Shelsley Walsh, Worcs, a parrot's head erased vert, between two wings expanded per pale az and gu, collared gemelle or, holding in the beak of the third an olive-branch of the first 101 14

Avenayne or **Avenar,** a buck's head cabossed ppr 122 5

Avenel, Avanet, or **Avenett,** out of a baron's coronet a hand grasping a scimitar, all ppr cf 213 5

Avenel, Avenele, Aveneyle, or **Avenyle,** a buck's head cabossed ppr 122 5

Avenet, Avenett, or **Avnett,** a torteau charged with a lion's head erased or cf 19 3

Avenon, London, a parrot's head erased vert, between two wings expanded per pale az and gu, collared gemelle or, holding in the beak of the third an olive branch of the first 101 14

Averill of Broadway, Worcs, a buck's head cabossed gu 122 5

Averinges, a raven sa 107 14

Avern, Warw, a horse's head erm 50 12

Avery or **Averey,** of Tillingly, Warw, a leopard couchant arg, bezantee ducally gorged or cf 24 10

Avery of Huwish, Somers, and Enfield, Middx, two lions' gambs or, supporting a bezant 39 4

Avison, a dexter hand, vested and cuffed, holding an anchor 208 3

Avison, a hand issuing from a cloud holding an anchor 223 4

Avonmore, Viscount (Yelverton), Belle Isle, Roscrea, co Tipperary, Ireland, a lion passant regardant gu *Renascentur* 6 1

Awborn, a unicorn passant or, gorged with a ducal coronet, and chained sa 48 6

Awbrey, an eagle's head erased or 83 2

Awdrey, Oxon, on a lion's gamb ppr, a cheveron or, charged with a mullet sa 39 2

Awdry, Delmé Henry Seymour, of Seend, Wilts, out of a ducal coronet or, a lion's head az *Nil sine Deo* 17 5

Awdry, Thomas, of Notton House, Wilts, same crest

Awdry, Charles, Esquire, of Shaw Hill, Melksham, in front of a lion's head erased az, gorged with a collar gemel arg, a cinquefoil between two crescents fesseways or *Nil sine Deo*

Awdry, Herbert, Esquire, of Notton House, Chippenham, same crest and motto

Awdry, Thomas, Esquire, of Ardath, Salisbury, same crest and motto

Awdry, Rev Vere, Esquire, of Ampfield, Romsey, same crest and motto

Awdry, Rev William, of the Vicarage, Amport, Andover, Hants, same crest and motto

Awger or **Ager,** Kent and Glouc, a bull's head erased gu, attired arg

Awing, on a quartrefoil quarterly gu and vert, a lion's head on a wreath arg

Awmack, a tower ppr *Cavendo tutus* 156 2

Awndye, Devonsh, on a lion's gamb ppr, a cheveron or, charged with a mullet sa 39 2

Awnsam, an escallop-shell or, between two palm branches vert 141 4

Awston of London, a greyhound's head couped arg, gorged with a plain collar sa., charged with three bezants cf 61 2

Ayde, Norf., a demi lion rampant gardant or, supporting a battle axe arg 16. 12

Aygle, a bugle horn arg 228 11

Aylemer and **Aylener,** Ireland, on a ducal coronet or, a sea-aylet, wings displayed sa 108 6

Ayler, *see* Aigler.

Ayles, a dexter arm embowed, the fist clenched ppr 202 2

Aylesbury, *see* Ailesbury.

Aylesbury (1) A staff in pale raguly or cf 147 10 (2) A dragon's head or, gorged with three bars gu.

Aylesbury, Henry Aylesbury Walker, of Packwood, Warw (1) Upon the trunk of a tree eradicated ppr, a dragon's head erased or, gorged with a collar gemel az (2) On a mount vert a crescent az, within a chain in orle or *Virtutis amore*

Aylesford, Earl of (Finch), Packington Hall, Coventry, a griffin passant sa *Aperto vivere voto* 63 2

Aylet of Howells, Essex, an arm gu, holding a sword arg, hilted or *Not in vain* 212 3

Aylett of Braintree, Essex, a demi-unicorn regardant arg, crined and armed or 48 9

Ayleward, Aylward, and **Aylwarde,** Norf, between the horns of a crescent or, a cross pattee gu 163 6

Aylford and **Aylnford,** flames of fire between two branches of palm in orle, all ppr 146 12

Ayliffe of London and Brinksworth, Wilts, out of a ducal coronet or, an oak-tree ppr, fructed of the first cf 143 5

Aylmer, Baron (Aylmer), out of a ducal coronet or, a demi-Cornish chough rising ppr *Steady*

Aylmer of Derry House, Ireland, out of a ducal coronet a Cornish chough rising, all ppr *Hallelujah*

Aylmer, Gerald Percy Vivian, of Walworth, Durh, same crest and motto

Aylmer, Sir Arthur Percy Fitz Gerald Bart, of Donadea Castle, Kildare, same crest and motto

Aylmer, John Algernon, Esquire, of Courtown, Kilcock, co. Kildare, same crest and motto

Aylmer, Ireland, a sea-aylet with wings displayed sa, on a ducal coronet or 108 6

Aylmer of Howden Hall, Essex, on a marquess's coronet or, an aylet's head erased sa, beaked gu, between two eagles' wings expanded of the first

Aylmer, *see* Hendrick-Aylmer

Ayloffe, a bear sejant regardant against the stump of a tree

Ayloffe, a demi lion rampant or 10 2

Ayloffe of Braxted Magna, Essex, and Framfield, Sussex, a demi-lion or, collared gu 10 9

Aylward, *see* Toler-Aylward.

Aylward-Kearney, James, Esquire, of Shankhill Castle, co Kilkenny, Ireland (1) A gauntleted hand fessways or, holding a dagger erect arg, pommel and hilt of the first (*for Kearney*) (2) Out of a ducal coronet or, an arm embowed, vested az, cuffed arg, the hand ppr grasping an anchor in bend sinister gold, and in an escroll above the motto, *Verus et fidelis semper* (*for Aylward*) *Sustine et abstine*

Aylwin, *see* Alwyn.

Aylworth of Devonsh., Glouc., and Kent, an arm vested sa., issuing out of rays or, holding in the hand ppr. a human skull arg. 208. 10

Ayncotes, a covered cup or, between two wings sa.

Ayncotts, a squirrel sejant gu., collared or. 135. 4

Aynesworth, Lancs, two battle-axes in saltier ppr. *Courage sans peur.* 172. 4

Aynesworth or **Aynsworth,** a falcon, wings expanded and inverted ppr., belled or. *Courage sans peur.* 87. 1

Aynscomb of Mayfield, Sussex, a cubit arm erect, holding in the hand ppr. a fleur-de-lis sa. *cf.* 215. 5

Aynscomb and **Ayniscamp,** Sussex, same crest.

Aynsley of Little Harle Tower, Northumb., a man in armour holding in the dexter hand a sword erect ppr., hilted and pommelled or, in his sinister a shield of the Aynsley arms, viz., gu. on a bend erm., between two quatrefoils or, three mullets of six points sa. *Furth fortune and fill the fetters.*

Aynsley, Capt. John Francis Murray, R.N., Hall Court, Hants, a man in armour holding in the dexter hand a sword erect ppr., pommel and hilt or, and in the sinister in front of his breast a shield gu., charged with a bend arg., thereon three mullets of six points or (*Aynsley*). *Furth fortune and fill the fetters.*

Aynworth, two battle-axes in saltier ppr. 172. 4

Aype, an antelope trippant arg., collared sa. *cf.* 126. 6

Ayre, Notts, on a ducal coronet or, a wyvern vert. 70. 9

Ayre, Yorks, a leg in armour couped at the thigh, all ppr., garnished and spurred or. *Veritas vincit.* 193. 1

Ayre, Lincs, a leg erect in armour per pale arg. and sa., couped at the thigh gu., knee-cap and spur or. *Læto ære florent.* 193. 2

Ayrton (late Rt. Hon. Acton Smee, Chief Commissioner of Works), a demi-lion rampant erm., holding a pennon per pale gu. and az., thereon a leopard's face or. *Pro aris et focis.*

Ayscough, Durh., an ass's head erased arg. *cf.* 125. 12

Ayscough, an ass erm. *cf.* 125. 11

Ayscough, Newcastle, an arm ppr. holding a sword arg., hilted or, enfiled with a Saracen's head couped ppr., wreathed or and sa., dropping blood gu. *Fac et spera.* *cf.* 212. 14

Aysingcourt or **Aysyngcourt,** an eagle's head between two wings ppr. 84. 2

Ayskey and **Ayskew,** *see* Alkene.

Ayson of London and Essex, out of a mural coronet arg., a griffin's head gu., ducally gorged or. 67. 6

Aysscough, an ass passant ppr. 125. 7

Ayton, a hand holding a hawk's lure ppr. 217. 8

Ayton, *see* Aiton and Aitoun.

Aytoun, Scotland, a hand pulling a rose ppr. *Decerptæ dabunt odorem.* 218. 13

Aytoun, Fife, Scotland, a rose gu. *Virtute orta occidunt rarius.* 149. 2

Aytoun, Kinaldie, Fife, a rose-tree vert, flowered gu. *Et decerptæ dabunt odorem.* 149. 14

Aytoun-Sinclair, Roger, of Inchdairnie, co. Fife: (1) A hand holding a rose ppr. (*Aytoun*). (2) A phœnix in flames (*Sinclair*). (1) *Decerptæ dabunt odorem* (*Aytoun*). (2) *Fides* (*Sinclair*).

B.

Baad or **Bad,** Scotland, a dexter hand ppr. holding a trident az. 214. 12

Babb or **Babe,** Dorset, a dexter hand erect, pointing with two fingers to the sun ppr. 222. 10

Babbwell or **Babwell,** a gate or. 158. 9

Babe of Castle Derver, Louth, on a mound a babe in swaddling-clothes, all ppr.

Babeham or **Babehaw** of London, a demi-man ppr., wreathed on the head with a knot gu., holding in his dexter hand a wing sa., guttée-d'or. *cf.* 186. 7

Baber, Middx., and Somers., on a mount vert, a cock, wings expanded arg., combed, wattled, and legged gu. 91. 7

Babington of Dethickin, Oxon., and Derbysh., a demi-bat displayed gu. 137. 12

Babington, Rev. John Albert, of Cossington, co. Leics., a dragon's head between two dragons' wings gu. *Foy est tout.*

Babington, Francis Evans, Esquire, of South Lodge, Halesworth, Suff., same crest and motto.

Babington, Thomas Zachary Dodson, Esquire, of Redlands, Parksome, Dorset, same crest and motto.

Babington, Oxon. and Derbysh., a dragon's head erased between two wings gu. *cf.* 72. 7

Babington of Rotheley Temple, Leics., a dragon's head between two wings gu. *Foy est tout.* 72. 7

Babington, Lodley, Leics., a fox's head ppr. 33. 4

Babington, out of a ducal coronet a demi-eagle displayed ppr. *In solitos docuere nisus.* 80. 14

Babrampore, the Maharaja Dirg Bijye Sing of, on the trunk of a tree eradicated fesseways, and sprouting to the dexter, a falcon surmounted by a rainbow, all ppr.

Babthorp, Yorks, a cockatrice's head erased arg., beaked, combed, and wattled or. 68. 12

Babwell, Middx., a gate or. 158. 9

Bacche or **Bache,** Somers., a savage's head affrontée between two branches of laurel in orle ppr. 192. 14

Bacchus, Henry, Esquire, the Manor House, Lillington, Warw., an eagle displayed or. *Aquila non capit muscam Bacchus.* 75. 5

Bacchus, Charles Henry, Esquire, in front of a rock ppr., thereon an eagle displayed or, an eagle's leg fesseways, erased at the thigh, also or. *Aquila non capit muscam.*

Bacchus, Rev. Francis Joseph, of the Oratory, Edgbaston, Birmingham, same crest and motto.

Bacchus, George Reginald, Esquire, same crest and motto.

Bacchus, Rev. John Northcote, the Presbytery, Henley-on-Thames, same crest and motto.

Bacchus, Robert Sidney, Esquire, of Burghfield Manor, Reading, same crest and motto.

Bacchus, William Ernest, Esquire, of Hornton Grounds, Banbury, same crest and motto.

Bache, Stanton, a demi-lion rampant, regardant pean, holding between his paws a bezant. *cf.* 11. 7

Bache, Thomas, Esquire, of Coventry, on a mount vert, a demi-lion gardant sa., bezantée, gorged with a wreath of oak or, holding between the paws a woolpack ppr.

Bacheler, Berks, a dragon's head erased or, vulned in the neck gu. *cf.* 72. 5

Bacheler, Bachelor, and **Bachelour,** a leg erased above the knee ppr. 193. 10

Back of Eaton, Norwich, a griffin passant per pale wavy gu. and arg., collared or, wings elevated erminois, the dexter claw supporting a woolpack arg.

Back, Philip Edward, Esquire, of Mancroft Towers, Oulton, Suffolk, same crest.

Back, William, Esquire, M.D., same crest and motto.

Backhouse, Sir Jonathan Edmund, Bart., the Uplands, Darlington, in front of a rock ppr., thereon an eagle displayed vert, holding in each claw a passion cross or, a serpent on its back, the tail nowed, also ppr. 259. 4

Backhouse, Charles F., M.R.C.S., L.R.C.P., The Terrace, St. Ives, Cornw., same crest. *Confido in Deo.*

Backhouse, out of a ducal coronet an arm in armour brandishing a scimitar, all ppr. *cf.* 196. 10

Backhouse, on a snake embowed, its tail nowed, an eagle displayed. *Confido in Deo.*

Backhouse, an eagle vert, wings close, preying on a snake ppr. *Confido in Deo.*

Backhouse, Charles James, of St. John's, Wolsingham, Durh., in front of a rock ppr., thereon an eagle displayed vert, holding in each claw a passion cross or, a serpent on its back, the tail nowed, also ppr. *Confido in Deo.*

Backhouse, Edward, Esquire, of Hurworth Grange, Croft, Darlington, same crest and motto.

Backie, a sword and a cross crosslet fitched in saltier ppr. 166. 12

Backie or **Baikie,** Orkney, a flame of fire ppr. *Commodum non damnum.* 177. 10

Backwell, London, out of a mural coronet or, a demi bull sa

Bacon, Sir Hickman Beckett, 11th Bart of Redgrave and 12th Bart of Milden hall, Suff, Premier Bart, a boar passant erm *Mediocria firma* 40 9

Bacon, Rev Thomas, M A, late Rector of Wiggonholt and Greatham, Sussex, a boar arg, resting the dexter fore foot on a fret sa

Bacon of Daisy Hill, Londonderry, a boar passant erm, charged on the body with a mullet or *Mediocria firma* cf 40 9

Bacon of Sutton Bonnington, Notts, on a mount vert, a boar statant arg, bristled and tusked or, semee of mullets sa, and holding in the mouth a ragged staff vert. *Mediocria firma* 40 10

Bacon of Harlston, Norf, a demi-boar or, armed and bristled az 40 13

Bacon of Newton Cup, Durh, and Stewart Pilc, Northumb, a demi wild boar rampant gardant az, bristled, armed, and ungu or, langued gu, holding in the mouth a tilting spear arg, stricken in shoulder and vulned ppr 41 2

Bacon, a boar's head couped or, holding in the mouth a griffin's head erased az

Bacon, Hants, a tiger sejant gu, pierced through the breast with a broken spear or, headed arg *Another*, the spear arg

Bacon, Nicholas Henry, of Raveningham Hall, Norf, a boar passant erm *Mediocria firma*

Bacon, Rev M J, of Swallowfield Vicarage, Reading, a talbot's head sa, erased gu, holding in the mouth a deer's leg or *Proba conscientia*

Bacon of Twyhouse, Somers, a grey hound's head erased sa, holding in the mouth a stag's foot or 61 5

Bacon, Kenrick Verulam, Esquire, the Lodge, Hale, Farnham, Surrey, a boar statant erm, bristled, armed, and ungu or, debruised by a bendlet sinister wavy gu *Mediocria firma*

Bacon, Hesset, Norf, a talbot's head sa, erased gu, holding in the mouth a deer's leg or

Bacot, William George, M D, Carfax, Marlborough Road, Bournemouth, out of a ducal coronet or, a goat's head arg, attired of the first *Antiquum obtinens*

Badby, London, a sphinx passant gardant ppr, wings addorsed 182 12

Badcock of Kensington, Middx, and Essex, a stag lodged gardant between two branches of laurel in orle, all ppr 115 11

Badcock, Devonsh, a demi-cock gu

Badd of Fareham, Hants, a lion's head erased, gardant arg, ducally crowned az cf 18 11

Baddeley, a phœnix in flames, all ppr *Deum time, et dedecus* 82 2

Badder, on the stump of a tree in fess, couped and eradicated, a lion sejant 7 9

Baddiford, of Dartmouth, Devonsh, an eagle's head or, crowned with a coronet flory sa, between two branches of lily arg, stalked and leaved vert cf 84 6

Baddiford, an eagle's head or surmounted by a cross crosslet sa, between two branches of thistle ppr 84 7

Badeley, John, Leigh's Hall, Essex, and **Baddeley**, Essex and Suff, a boar's head and neck couped arg *Principiis obsta* 41 1

Badelismere or **Badelsmere**, Yorks, a lion's gamb erased sa, holding a laurel-branch vert cf 37 4

Baden-Powell, Baden Fletcher Smyth, Major Scots Guards (1) A lion passant or in the paw a broken tilting spear in bend ppr, pendent therefrom by a riband gu, an escocheon resting on the wreath sa, charged with a pheon or (*for Powell*) (2) Out of a crown vallery or, a demi lion gu, on the head a like crown, charged on the shoulder with a cross patee arg and supporting with the paws a sword erect ppr pommel and hilt or (*for Baden*) *Ar nid yw Pwyil nyd yw*

Baden-Powell, Donald Esquire (son of Sir George Baden Powell), of 114, Eaton Square same crests and motto

Baden-Powell, Henry Warington Smyth, Esquire K C of 8, St George's Place, London same crests and motto

Baden-Powell, Major General Robert Stephenson Smyth, C B, same crests and motto

Baden-Powell, Sir George, K C M G, same crests and motto

Badenach-Nicolson, Arthur, Esquire of Glenbervie House Drumlithie, Fordoun N B, a lion's head erased or *Nil sistere contra*

Badger, a badger ppr 33 10

Badger, a buck's head cabossed sa, between the attires a greyhound current arg, collared gu 122 11

Badham, an eagle displayed with two heads arg, charged on the breast with a saltier gu *Virtus astra petit* 74 1

Badham-Thornhill, Laurence John, Esquire, of Carrigmahon, Monkston, co Cork (1) A double-headed eagle displayed (*for Badham*) (2) A thorn bush, thereon a robin redbreast ppr (*for Thornhill*) *Conquer or die.*

Badley, Suff, a demi lion rampant arg, charged with two bendlets az cf 10 2

Baett or **Batt**, a demi lion or, guttee-de sang cf 10 2

Bageley or **Bagley**, on the top of a spear, issuing, a wyvern sans legs, tail nowed 69 6

Bagenal, Beauchamp Frederick, Esquire, of Benekerry, Carlow, heraldic ante lope sejant vert, attired, ungu, ducally gorged and chained or

Bagenhall, Staffs, a dragon's head erased gu, gorged with a bar gemelle or cf 71 2

Bagenholt, a horse courant bridled ppr cf 52 1

Bagg, two wings endorsed gu and arg, the latter charged with a cinquefoil az cf 109 12

Baggalay, the late Sir Richard, Attorney-General, Surrey, a goat's head erased arg, charged on the neck with three fleurs de lis, one and two az *Stemmata quid faciunt* 243 8

Baggallay, Claude, Esquire, of The Grange, East Grinstead, Sussex, a goat's head erased arg, charged on the neck with three fleurs de lis one and two az *Stemmata quid faciunt*

Baggallay, Ernest, Esquire, of the Moat, Cowden, Kent, same crest and motto.

Baggallay, Henry Charles, Esquire, of Onslow Gardens, S W, same crest and motto.

Baggally, a dexter arm in armour em bowed ppr, garnished or, holding a sword, also ppr *Dulce periculum* 195 2

Bagge, Sir Alfred Thomas, Bart, of Stradsett Hall, Norf, two wings ad dorsed or, semee of annulets gu *Spes est in Deo* 239 4

Bagge, Thomas Edward, Esquire, of Gaywood Hall, King's Lynn, same crest and motto

Bagge, a sword in pale, supporting a garland of laurel, all ppr 170 1

Bagge or **Bagg**, Plymouth, Devonsh, a cinquefoil az, between two wings, the dexter gu, the sinister arg

Baggeley, Chesh, a ram's head az, armed and charged with three lozenges or 130 11

Baggeley, Chesh, a ram's head az, armed or 130 1

Baggs, a rose charged with a thistle ppr 149 3

Bagholt and **Bagholt**, on a ducal coronet or, a leopard sejant gardant ppr

Baghot, a stag's head cabossed sa, between the attires a greyhound courant arg, collared gu 122 11

Baghot-De la Bere, Rev John, of Buxted St Mary Vicarage, Uckfield, Sussex (1) Out of a ducal coronet or, a plume of eight ostrich-feathers, five and three per pale arg and az 263 7 (*for De la Bere*) (2) A stag's head cabossed sa, and between the attires a greyhound courant arg, collared gu *In cruce salus* 263 8

Bagley, an arm in armour embowed, holding a sword, all ppr 195 2

Bagnall, Kent, a dragon's head erased gu, gorged with two bars or cf 71 2

Bagnall, John, Esquire, Water Orton, near Birmingham, and **Benjamin Bagnall**, Esquire, Ellerslie, Eaton Gardens, Hove, Sussex, a lion rampant holding between the paws an hour glass *Fugit hora* 1 5

Bagnall, Staffs and Wales, an antelope sejant arg, billettée sa, ducally gorged, lined, armed, and tufted or 126 4

Bagnall of Wicklow and Worcs a heraldic antelope sejant arg, billettee sa, horns and tail or, collared and chained of the same, the chain reflexed over the back cf 126 4

Bagnall, Ireland, a heraldic antelope sejant vert, crined, ducally gorged, and chained or

Bagnall-Wild, Ralph Bagnall Esquire, M A, J P, of Costock, Notts (1) A demi stag sa, guttee-d'or, attired and resting the sinister foot on an escallop or (*for Wild*) 119 4 (2) Upon the trunk of a tree fesseways, eradicated and sprouting ppr, a heraldic antelope sejant az, bezantee, gorged with a collar gemel and attired or (*for Bagnall*) 127 9 *Sur et loyal*

Bagne and **Bague**, on a chapeau a pelican vulning herself, all ppr 98 7

Bagnel, Bagnell, Bagnill, or **Bagnoll,** a galley, sails furled ppr. 160. 6

Bagnell, an ancient galley, oars in action. 160. 7

Bagnell, a goat rampant, ducally gorged and staked to the ground.

Bagot, Christopher Neville, Esquire, of Aughrane Castle, co. Galway, Ireland, out of a ducal coronet or, a goat's head erm., horned of the first. *Antiquum obtinens.* 128. 14

Bagot, Arthur Henry Louis, Esquire, out of a ducal coronet or, a goat's head arg., armed of the first, and charged with a crescent gu. *Antiquum obtinens.*

Bagot, Charles Fitzroy Alexander Hallifax, Esquire, same crest and motto.

Bagot, John Christopher, Esq., of Ballyturin, Gort, co. Galway, same crest and motto.

Bagot, Richard, Esquire, of 42, Lowndes Street, S.W., same crest and motto.

Bagot, Baron, Blithfield, Rugeley, Staffs, out of a ducal coronet or, a goat's head arg., attired of the first. *Antiquum obtinens.* 128. 14

Bagot of Kilcoursey, King's Co., same crest and motto.

Bagot of Pype Hall, Staffs, same crest and motto.

Bagot, Josceline Fitzroy, of Levens Hall, Westml., out of a ducal coronet or, a goat's head arg., armed of the first, and charged with a crescent gu. *Antiquum obtinens.*

Bagot of Castle Bagot, co. Dublin, same crest. *Pour Dieu et mon roi.*

Bagshaw, of South Okendon, Essex, a bugle-horn or. 228. 11

Bagshaw, of Delaridge, Derbysh., an arm couped at the elbow, erect ppr., grasping a bugle-horn sa., stringed vert. *cf.* 217. 4

Bagshawe, issuing from clouds an arm erect ppr., holding in the hand a bugle-horn sa. *cf.* 217. 4

Bagshawe, of Oakes, Norton, and Wormhill Hall, Derbysh., issuing from clouds a dexter cubit arm, holding in the hand ppr. a bugle-horn or, the handle sa., within the strings a rose gu. *Forma, flos; fama, flatus.*

Bagshawe, Frederic, M.D., 35, Warrior Square, St. Leonard's, issuing from clouds a dexter cubit arm couped, holding in the hand ppr. a bugle-horn. *Forma, flos; fama, flatus.*

Bagshawe, Clement Walsh, Esquire, of 24, East Cliff, Dover, issuing out of clouds a dexter arm ppr., holding in the hand a bugle-horn or, the handle sa., within the strings a rose gu. *Forma, flos; fama, flatus.*

Bagshawe, Francis Westby, Esquire, of the Oaks, Sheffield, same crest and motto.

Bagshawe, Greaves-, William Henry, of Ford Hall, Derbysh., and Banner Cross, Yorks: (1) A dexter cubit arm couped holding in the hand ppr. a bugle-horn sa., stringed vert (*for Bagshawe*). *cf.* 217. 4. (2) On a mount vert, a stag trippant or, holding in the mouth a slip of oak ppr. (*for Greaves*). *Forma, flos; fama, flatus.—Deo non fortuna.* *cf.* 118. 2

Bagshawe, a dexter cubit arm erect ppr., the hand holding a bugle-horn sa., stringed vert. *Forma, flos; fama, flatus.*

Bagshole and **Bagshote,** an acorn slipped and leaved ppr. 152. 1

Baguley, J. M., Esquire, Whitecliffe, Alfriston, Sussex, a ram's head az., attired or, charged with three lozenges of the second.

Bagwell, Richard, Esquire, J.P., of Marlfield, Ireland, out of a mural coronet a demi-bull, all ppr. *In fide et in bello fortes.*

Bagwell-Purefoy, Wilfrid, Esquire, of Greenfield, Tipperary, a hand in armour grasping a broken lance, all ppr. *En bonne-foy.*

Baighton, a heron's head erased, holding in its beak an eel, all ppr. 104. 2

Baigrie, Robert, C.B., Lieutenant-Colonel Bombay Staff Corps, in front of the battlements of a tower, thereon an armed leg couped above the knee ppr., garnished and spurred or, a mount vert.

Baikie, Alfred, of Tankerness, Orkney, a flame of fire. *Commodum non damnum.* 177. 10

Bailey, Lt.-Col. Edmund Wyndham Grevis, J.P., of Nepicar House, Wrotham, Kent, in front of a demi-lion erminois, holding in his dexter paw a cross pattée fitchée gu., a trunk of a tree eradicated fesseways and sprouting ppr. *Nec temere, nec timide.*

Bailey, James, Esquire, of Shortgrove, Newport, Essex, in front of a cubit arm vested per pale az. and gu., cuff arg., the hand ppr., holding a crosier surmounted by a mullet, both or, three mullets of the last. *Deo duce.*

Bailey, Baron Glanusk, *see* Glanusk.

Bailey, John Lockhart, Esquire, of Llangorse House, Prince's Park, Liverpool, same crest and motto.

Bailey, Llewellyn Crawshay, Esquire, of Llangorse House, Prince's Park, Liverpool, same crest and motto.

Bailey of Norwich, a cubit arm erect, vested bendy of six az. and sa., the cuff arg., holding in the hand ppr. a crosier, and surmounted by an estoile, both or. *Deo duce.* 207. 2

Bailey, J. G., Esquire, M.S., M.D., Santa Ana, Orange County, California, U.S.A. (eldest son of the late Sir James Bailey), a cubit arm erect, vested bendy of six az. and sa., the cuff arg., holding in the hand ppr. a crosier surmounted by an estoile, both or. *Deo duce.* 207. 2

Bailey, Shropsh., a griffin segreant gu., guttée d'or. *Another,* guttée d'eau. *cf.* 62. 2

Bailey, a cat salient gardant. 26. 3

Bailey, a demi-lady, holding in her dexter hand a tower, and in her sinister a laurel-branch vert. 183. 8

Bailey, the late John Eglington, Esquire, F.S.A., of Stretford, Lancs, in front of an anchor in bend sinister ppr., a female figure vested vert, supporting with her dexter hand an escutcheon gu., charged with a martlet arg., and resting with the sinister on the stock of the anchor. *Vallum œnium esto.* 184. 1

Bailey, Ronald, Esquire, in front of an anchor in bend sinister ppr., a female figure vested vert, supporting with the right hand an escocheon gu., charged with a martlet arg., and resting the left on the stock of the anchor. *Vallum œnium esto.*

Bailey, Rev. James Sandford, of Ightham Place and Nepicar House, Kent, in front of a demi-lion erminois, holding in the dexter paw a cross pattée fitchée gu., the trunk of a tree eradicated fessewise and sprouting ppr. *Nec temere, nec timide.* 231. 14

Bailey, Sir William Henry, of Sale Hall, Chesh., a griffin segreant arg., wings chequy of the first and az., holding in the dexter claw a flagstaff, therefrom flowing to the sinister a banner gu., semée of annulets, and resting the sinister claw on a pheon sa. *Non terra sed aquis.*

Bailhache, Jersey, a ship ppr. *Vive memor lethi, fugit hora.* 160. 13

Bailie, a hand holding a dagger. *Quid clarius astris?* 212. 9

Baillie-Hamilton-Arden, Earl of Haddington, *see* Haddington.

Baillie, Cochrane-, Lord Lamington, *see* Lamington.

Baillie, Kennedy-, of Ardtrea, Armagh, Ireland: (1) A boar's head couped arg. (*for Baillie*). 43. 1. (2) A dolphin naiant az. (*for Kennedy*). *Quid clarius astris?* 140. 5

Baillie, of Hoperig, East Lothian, a boar's head couped. *Quid clarius astris?* 43. 1

Baillie, James Evan Bruce, of Douchfour, Inverness, a boar's head couped. *Quid clarius astris.* 43. 1

Baillie, Bart., a boar's head erased ppr. *Ubi bene ibi patria.* 42. 2

Baillie, James William, Esquire, of Ilston Grange, Leicester, a boar's head couped. *Quid clarius astris?*

Baillie-Gage, Thomas Robert, Esquire, of 38, Northumberland Road, Dublin: (1) A ram passant arg., armed and hoofed or, holding in the mouth a trefoil slipped vert (*for Gage*). *cf.* 131. 13. (2) A boar's head couped, holding in the mouth a sprig of oak, all ppr. (*for Baillie*). *Courage sans peur.* 42. 7

Baillie of Rosehall, Scotland, a cat sejant ppr. *Spero meliora.* 26. 8

Baillie of Corstorphine, a crow ppr. *Be not wanting.* 107. 14

Baillie, Scotland, a cockatrice, wings expanded. 68. 6

Baillie of Monktown, co. Ayr, an eagle regardant, his wings raised ppr. *Libertas optima rerum.* *cf.* 77. 10

Baillie of Walston, a dove volant, in its beak an olive-branch ppr. *Patior et spero.* 93. 10

Baillie of Carnbrae, on the point of a sword in pale ppr., hilt and pommel or, a laurel wreath fructed, also ppr. *Perseverantia.* 170. 1

Baillie of Hardington, Scotland, a hand holding a pen ppr. *Fides servata ditat.* 217. 10

Baillie, Scotland, the sun in splendour ppr. *Clarior astris.* 162. 2

Baillie of Jerviswood, a crescent or. *Major virtus quam splendor.* 163. 2

Baillie of Balmudyside, the morning star ppr. *Vertitur in lucem.* 164. 1

Baillie, Inshaughy, Ireland, a star of eight points arg., out of a cloud ppr. *Nil clarius astris.* 164. 11

Baillie, Sir Robert Alexander, Bart, of Polkemet, Linlithgow, an etoile of eight points or, out of a cloud ppr *In caligine lucit* 164 11

Baillie, Hon William Douglas Hall, of Kennington, Picton, Marlborough, New Zealand, Member of the Legislative Council of New Zealand, a star of eight points arg, issuant from a cloud ppr *Quid clarius astris?* 164 11

Baillie, Sir Robert Alexander, Bart, of Ognez, Toorak, near Melbourne, Victoria, and Benerembah, Hay, New South Wales, Australia, out of a cloud ppr, an estoile of eight rays or *In caligine lucel* 164 11

Ballward of Horsington, Somers, a bull's head couped arg cf 44 3

Baily, out of a ducal coronet a wyvern's head ppr 72 4

Baily, Thomas Farmer, Esquire, of Hall Place, Kent, a goat's head erased az, bezantee, attired or *Vestigia nulla retrorsum* cf 128 5

Bain, late Sir James, D L, J P, F R S, F R G S, Jarrington, Cumb, and 3, Park Terrace, Glasgow, a dexter arm embowed gu, the hand grasping a dirk ppr *Et arte et marte*

Bain of Craggs, Little Broughton, Cockermouth, a dexter arm embowed gu, the hand grasping a dirk ppr *Et arte et marte*

Bain, a dexter arm in armour embowed ppr, garnished or, grasping a dagger, also ppr *Et marte et arte* 195 4

Bain of Berwick, Northumb, a hand holding a scroll of paper ppr *Virtute* 215 6

Bain of Morriston, Lanark, a dexter hand ppr, holding a rose gu, slipped and leaved vert *Benedic nobis Domine* 218 10

Bain of Lynton, Devonsh, a dexter hand ppr, holding a rose gu, slipped and leaved vert *Benedic nobis Domine* 218 10

Bain or **Baine**, a lion rampant gu, between two wings or 9 2

Bainbridge, Bainbrigg, Bainbrigge, or **Bambridge**, Leics and Derbysh, on a mount vert, a goat sa, armed and ungu or, and collared and belled arg 129 3

Bainbridge, George B, Esquire, Espley Hall, Morpeth, Northumb, a stag's head erased *Avance*

Bainbridge, an arm from the shoulder issuing from the sea, holding an anchor, corded, all ppr 202 7

Bainbrigge, William Parker Yates, J P, 71, Lissenden Mansions, Highgate Road, N W, on a mount vert, a goat statant sa, horned, ungu and collared arg *Virtute non armis fido*

Baines, a wild duck among flags ppr 102 5

Baines, a cubit arm holding a dagger ppr 212 3

Baines, Peteonly, Scotland, a dexter hand holding a dagger ppr *Vel arte vel marte* 212 9

Baines, Rev Albert Charles of Little Wymondley, Stevenage, Herts, a dexter arm embowed, vested az, cuff arg, the hand grasping a jaw bone ppr, on the arm a cross pattée or 264 15

Baines, Athelstan Arthur, Esquire, of 29, First Avenue, Hove, Brighton, same crest

Baines, Egerton Charles Augustus, Esquire, same crest

Baines, Rev Frederick Samuel, of 41, Medina Villas, Hove, Brighton, same crest.

Baines, Jervoise Athelstane, Esquire, of Kensington Park Gardens, same crest

Baines, John, Esquire, same crest

Baines, Louis Adolphus, Esquire, same crest

Baines, Rev Montague Charles Alexander, of Carlby Rectory, Stamford, same crest *Furor arma ministrat*

Baines, Bell Hall, Yorks, a cubit arm erect, holding in the hand a leg bone, in bend sinister arg

Baines, William Mortimer Esquire, of Bell Hall, Naburn, Yorks, a dexter hand couped ppr, holding a shin-bone arg

Baines, a bone and a palm branch in saltier ppr 147 4

Baird, Sir Alexander, Bart, of Urie, Stonehaven, Kincardine, a griffin's head erased or *Dominus fecit*

Baird, William, Esquire, of Elie House, Fife, same crest and motto

Baird, John George Alexander, Esquire, of 89, Eaton Square, S W, same crest and motto

Baird, Sir David, Bart, of Newbyth, East Lothian (1) A Mameluke on horseback, holding in his dexter hand a scimitar, all ppr 189 8 (2) A boar's head erased or *Vi et virtute* 42 2

Baird, Maturin-, *see* Maturin-Baird

Baird, Sir William James Gardiner, Bart, of Saughton Hall, co Edinburgh, Scotland, a boar's head erased or *Vi et virtute* 42 2

Baird, Sir John Kennedy, of 31, Cadogan Place, London, a boar's head erased or *Vi et virtute*

Baird, Scotland, a boar's head erased ppr, and another charged with a crescent 42 2

Baird of Cambusdoon, Ayr, an eagle's head erased *Dominus fecit* 83 2

Baird of Frankfield, Scotland, an eagle's head ppr *Vi et virtute* 83 2

Baird, an eagle's head erased ppr *Dominus fecit* 83 2

Baird of Knoydart, Inverness, and of Lochwood, Lanark, a griffin's head erased or *Dominus fecit* 66 2

Baird, Auchmedden, Scotland, a griffin's head erased ppr *Dominus fecit* 66 2

Baird, a cockatrice, wings addorsed gu. 68 5

Baird-Hay, James George, Esquire, of Belton, Haddington, Scotland, a goat's head erased arg, armed or. *Spare nought* 128 5

Baird, Scotland, a dove, wings expanded ppr *Virtute et honore* 94 3

Baird, of Craigton, Scotland, a ship in full sail ppr *Adsit Deus non demovebor* 160 13

Bairnsfather or **Barnesfather**, Scotland, a boar's head couped or 43 1

Bairstow, out of a crescent a demi-eagle displayed 81 4

Baisley of Ricketstown, co Carlow, an arm in armour embowed ppr, the hand holding a shepherd's crook pointed with the head of a bearded arrow, all ppr

Bake, a demi man in armour wielding a sword, all ppr 187 1

Baker, Bart (now Rhodes), Devonsh, a dexter arm embowed, vested az, charged with three annulets interlaced or, cuffed arg, holding in the hand an arrow in bend sinister ppr. *True unto death*

Baker, a naked dexter arm embowed, holding an arrow ppr 201 13

Baker, a dexter arm in armour embowed, holding an arrow ppr 198 4

Baker, Derbysh, a dexter arm embowed in armour, grasping a caduceus in bend surmounting the truncheon of a tilting-spear in bend sinister splintered, all ppr *Dum spiro spero*

Baker, Chester and Shrewsbury, out of a ducal coronet a dexter arm embowed, vested or, the hand gauntleted and holding a broken tilting spear without hurr or vamplate, in bend of the same, on shaft a ring enfiled with a garland vert

Baker, out of a cloud a dexter arm in fess, raising a garb, all ppr 223 12

Baker, a dexter hand gu, holding a club sa 214 6

Baker, a naked dexter arm, holding a purse 202 1

Baker of London, and of Northfield, Worcs, a hand issuing out of clouds ppr, holding a cross Calvary sa *Nemo sine cruce beatus*

Baker of Skerton House, Old Trafford, Manchester, two arms embowed in armour grasping a tilting-spear fesse-wise, the head to the sinister ppr, pendant from the staff a spur leathered or *Ex monte alto* 194 3

Baker, Philip of Shelbourne, Wake Green Moseley same crest and motto

Baker, Mayfield, Sussex, on a tower sa, an arm in mail embowed ppr, holding a piece of plate-iron az (described also as a flint-stone ppr)

Baker, Hon Sir Richard Chaffey, K C M G, J P, of Adelaide South Australia Member of the Legislative Council of South Australia, a dexter arm embowed ppr, charged with two cinquefoils az, holding a lozenge, also az thereon a swan's head and neck erased or *Carpe diem*

Baker, John Richard, Esquire, same crest and motto

Baker, Sissinghurst, Kent, a dexter cubit arm holding a swan's head erased arg, beaked gu 220 9

Baker, Rev Robert Lowbridge, of Ramsden, Charlbury, Oxford, a dexter arm in mail ppr, the under vest seen at the elbow vert, the hand also ppr, grasping a swan's neck erased or, beaked gu, and gorged with a ducal coronet of the last

Baker, Kent, an arm embowed, vested with green leaves, holding in the hand ppr a swan's head erased or

Baker of Lismacue, co Tipperary, a dexter naked hand and arm holding a swan's head erased arg *Honos virtutis satelles* 220 9

Baker of Wareslcy, Worcs, a naked dexter arm embowed ppr, grasping a swan's head erased or, ducally gorged and beaked gu.

Baker of West Hay, Somers., a dexter arm in mail, the under-vest seen at the elbow vert, holding in the hand ppr. a swan's neck erased or, beaked and gorged with a ducal coronet gu.

Baker, Granville Edwin Lloyd, of Hardwicke, Glouc., a hairy, wild man's arm vert, hand and elbow ppr., holding a swan's head erased or and arg., ducally gorged gu. 220. 9

Baker, George Edward, Esquire, M.A., of Freshford, co. Somers., Fellow and Bursar of Magdalen College, Oxford, a tower sable and issuing from the battlements thereof a dexter arm in armour embowed holding in the hand a baton ppr. *Sola meus turris Deus.* 314. 8

Baker, Thorngrove, Worcs., and Lypeat Park, Glouc., a swan's head erased or, ducally gorged gu. *Persevero.* 101. 5

Baker, Lawrence James, Esquire, of Ottershaw Park, Ottershaw, Surrey, in front of a swan's head erased arg., an estoile or, between two bezants. *Sedulo et honeste.*

Baker, Lawrence Ingham, Esquire, of Eastcote Lodge, Pinner, same crest and motto.

Baker of Bowden, Chesh., London, and Windsor, a swan's head erased arg., collared gu., holding in the beak a trefoil az.

Baker, Sir Samuel White, F.R.S., F.R.G.S., F.R.S.A., K.M., M.A., D.L., J.P., Sandford Orleigh, Newton Abbot, Devonsh., a swan's head erased arg., gorged with a naval coronet and between two cinquefoils az. *Persevere.*

Baker of Wattisfield and Wrentham, Suff., a demi-ostrich, wings expanded, holding in its beak a horseshoe. *cf.* 96. 8

Baker, an ostrich-head erased or, holding in the beak a horseshoe arg.

Baker, Radnorsh., a hawk's head arg., between two wings gu., holding in the beak three ears of wheat of the last. *cf.* 89. 1

Baker, Ireland, an eagle displayed sa. 75. 2

Baker, a phœnix in flames, all ppr. 82. 2

Baker, Sir Randolph Littlehales, Bart., of Ranston, Blandford, Dorset, and Ashcombe, Sussex: (1) A nag's head erased arg., charged on the neck with a cross pattée fitchée gu., holding in the mouth a trefoil slipped vert (*for Baker*). 51. 2. (2) Between two wings elevated or, an armed arm embowed ppr., garnished or, the hand in a gauntlet grasping an arrow in bend sinister entwined by a branch of olive, also ppr. (*for Littlehales*). *Finis coronat opus.* 198. 10

Baker, Sir George Sherston, Bart., of Upper Dunstable House, Richmond, Surrey, a demi-lion rampant, per fesse indented erminois and pæan, holding between the paws an escallop arg., charged with an erm. spot. *Fidei coticula crux.* 13. 10

Baker, Durh., a lion rampant arg. 1. 13

Baker, Ferdinand, of Elemore Hall, Durh.: (1) A lion rampant arg., charged on the shoulder with a saltier az., and holding between the paws an escutcheon of the last, thereon a maunch or (*for Baker*). 3. 4. (2) A griffin passant per pale or and erm., resting the dexter claw on an escutcheon sa., charged with a tower or (*for Tower*). *Love and dread.* 63. 9

Baker of London and Worcs., a cockatrice erm., combed and wattled gu. 68. 4

Baker, William Clinton, Esquire, of Bayfordbury, Herts, a cockatrice per fesse indented erminois and pæan, combed and wattled gu., gorged with a collar az., and in the beak a quatrefoil slipped vert. *So run that ye may obtain.*

Baker, Wingfield-, of Orsett Hall, Essex: (1) For *Baker*, a cockatrice erm., combed and wattled gu. 68. 4. (2) For *Wingfield*, a griffin passant vert. 63. 2

Baker, Westbrook, of Cottesmore, Rutland, a greyhound's head erased ppr., charged with a fess between six ears of wheat or. *Non sibi sed patriæ.*

Baker, a greyhound's head erased arg., gorged with a fess engrailed sa., fimbriated or, charged with three fleur-de-lis of the last.

Baker, William Meath, of Hasfield Court, Glouc., out of a ducal coronet or, a goat's head arg., attired or. *Ars bona violentia.*

Baker, Lincs. and Smallborough, Norf., a demi-unicorn erased arg., armed and maned or. *cf.* 48. 7

Baker, a bear's head couped or. 43. 1

Baker, a rose-tree vert, flowered or. 149. 14

Baker, Rev. Robert Lowbridge, of Ramsden House, Oxford, a dexter arm in mail, the under-vest seen at the elbow vert, the hand ppr. grasping a swan's neck erased or, gorged with a ducal coronet gu., beaked also of the last.

Baker, Kent, and of Battel, Sussex, a musk-rose branch vert, flowered arg., seeded or. 149. 8

Baker of London, on a mount vert, a tower arg., between two laurel-branches ppr.

Baker of Walton, Norf., on a chapeau az., turned up erm., a stag's head cabossed or. 122. 10

Baker-Wilbraham, George Barrington, Esquire, a wolf's head erased arg., charged on the neck with a cross crosslet az. for distinction (*for Wilbraham*). (2) A dexter arm embowed vested az., charged with three annulets interlaced or, cuffed arg., holding in the hand ppr. an arrow of the last. *In portu quies.*

Baker-Cresswell, Addison Francis, Cresswell, Morpeth, Northumb.: (1) On a mount vert a torteau charged with a squirrel sejant arg. (*for Cresswell*). 135. 11. (2) A goat's head erased arg., armed and crined or, gorged with a collar gemel and charged on the neck with a saltire gu. (*for Baker*). *Cressa ne careat.*

Balam, Norf. and Suff., a lion's head erased gu., collared and lined or, charged on the neck with a cinquefoil arg.

Balam of Walstoken, Norf., and Barton, Suff., out of a ducal coronet or, a demi-cock gu., wings displayed, combed and wattled or. 91. 14

Balberney, Scotland, a stag lodged ppr. 115. 7

Balbirnie-Vance, Robert Anstruther, Esquire, J.P., formerly of Balmerino, Victoria, a lion rampant or, gorged with a collar gu., and holding in the dexter paw a pair of balances ppr., and charged on the shoulder with a cinquefoil of the second. *Be faithful.*

Balcarres, Earl of, Scotland (Lindsay), *see* Crawford, Earl of.

Balchen, an anchor erect, and from its cross-beam a square banner pendant charged with three fleur-de-lis in fesse.

Balcombe, Kent, a bear passant ppr., collared and chained or. *Tenebo.* *cf.* 34. 1

Baldberney or **Balbirney,** Scotland, a morion ppr. 180. 1

Balderney, on a mount a stag lodged, all ppr. 115. 12

Balderston or **Balderstones,** Scotland, a hand holding a lancet ppr. *Vulnere sano.* 216. 14

Balderstone, Scotland, out of a cloud a dexter arm in fess ppr., holding in the hand a cross pattée fitched az. 223. 6

Baldock of Petham, Kent, on a mount vert, a greyhound sejant, the dexter paw resting on an escallop arg. 59. 1

Baldock of Cauleston, Norf., an eagle close, gazing at the sun. 76. 1

Baldrie or **Baldry,** a trefoil slipped vert. 148. 9

Baldry, out of a gillyflower gu., a demi-man habited.

Baldwin, a squirrel sejant or. *cf.* 135. 4

Baldwin, a squirrel sejant or, holding a sprig of hazel vert. *Vim vi repello.* 135. 2

Baldwin, Colonel William John Atkinson, of Dalton-in-Furness, Lancs, a squirrel sejant or, charged on the body with a fesse az., and supporting with the fore-legs an ostrich feather erect arg. *Vim vi repello.* 233. 3

Baldwin of Shrewsbury, on a wreath above a cap of maintenance a cockatrice, wings endorsed arg.

Baldwin and **Baldwyn** of Diddlebery, on a mount vert, a cockatrice arg., beaked, combed, and wattled or, ducally gorged and lined of the last. *Per deum meum transilio murum.* *cf.* 68. 7

Baldwin, Frederick Benjamin Judge, surgeon, Draycott House, Bodicote, Banbury, a cockatrice arg., ducally gorged or. *Est voluntas Dei*

Baldwin of Clohina, Ireland, a dove, in its beak an olive-branch ppr. *Est voluntas Dei.* 92. 5

Baldwin, Captain William, of Chingford, Dunedin, New Zealand, Honorary Resident Magistrate for that Colony, *uses* standing on a cross a dove, holding in its beak an olive-branch. *Sequere me est voluntas Dei.*

Baldwin of Stede Hill, Kent, a lion rampant az., holding in its paws a cross crosslet fitched or.

Bale of Carleton-Curlew, Leics., a demi-lion gu., supporting a broken spear or.

Bales of Norton, Northamp, a lion sejant gu, resting the dexter paw on a cross pattee fitched or

Bales of Wilby, Suff, a tiger's head erased sa, armed or, gorged with a fess wavy az (*Another*, on a mount vert, a lion sejant erm) 7 7

Balfour, Bart, Denmilne, Fife, a crescent or *God gives increase* 163 2

Balfour of Randerston, a crescent 163 2

Balfour-Melville, John Mackintosh, Esquire, of Piling, Edinburgh, and Strathkinness, Fife (1) On the dexter side a dexter hand holding an olive-branch ppr *Adsit Deus* (*for Balfour*) 219 9. (2) On the sinister side a crescent arg *Denique cœlum* (*for Melville*) 163 2

Balfour of Teling, Scotland, a dexter hand holding an olive-branch, all ppr *Adsit Deus* 219 9

Balfour, Arthur Mackintosh, Esquire, Sussex Artillery, Brighton, a dexter hand holding an olive branch ppr *Adsit Deus*

Balfour, Hon James, of Tyalla, Toorak, Melbourne, same crest and motto

Balfour of Trenaby, Orkney, a dexter arm in armour erect, the hand holding a baton in bend gu, tipped arg *Forward.* cf 209 9

Balfour, Scotland, a hand in armour holding a truncheon ppr *Forward* 209 9

Balfour of Balmouth, an otter's head couped *Forward, non temere* 134 1

Balfour of Dunbog, a tower arg, masoned sa, ensigned with an otter's head erased of the last *Nil temere*

Balfour, a mermaid holding in her dexter hand an otter's head erased, all ppr cf 184 10

Balfour of Mountquhanny, Fife, a mermaid ppr, holding in her dexter hand an otter's head erased sa, and in her sinister a swan's head, also erased ppr *Omne solum forti patria*

Balfour of Dunbog, a mermaid ppr, holding in her dexter hand a boar's head erased sa *Omne solum forti patria* 184 10

Balfour of Burleigh, Baron (Bruce), Kennet, Alloa, Clackmannan (1) On the dexter side, on a rock a mermaid ppr, holding in her dexter hand an otter's head erased sa, and in her sinister a swan's head erased, also ppr (*for Balfour*) *Omne solum forti patria* (2) On the sinister side, a dexter arm in armour from the shoulder, resting on the elbow, the hand holding a sceptre, all ppr (*for Bruce*) *Fuimus*

Balfour, James William, Esquire, of Balfour Castle, Kirkwall, a dexter arm in armour erect ppr, the hand holding a baton in bend gu, tipped arg *Forward*

Balfour, William Edward Ligonier, Esquire, of Boodle's Club, St James, same crest and motto

Balfour, Lt-Col John Edmond Heugh, D S O, of The Manor, Sidmouth, a dexter hand and arm erect, holding in bend a branch of laurel slipped, all ppr *Adsit Deus*

Balfour, Major Kenneth Robert, M P, of Stagsden House, Bournemouth same crest and motto

Balfour of Grange, on the battlements of a castle arg, a woman standing attired gu, holding in her dexter hand an otter's head *Nil temere* 155 7

Balfour, Gerald William, M A of 67, Addison Road, W a palm tree ppr *Virtus ad æthera tendit*

Balfour, Edward, of Balbirnie, Fife, a palm tree ppr *Virtus ad æthera tendit.* 144 1

Balfour, Charles Barrington, Esquire, of Newton Don, Kelso, same crest and motto

Balfour, Edward, Esquire, of Balbirnie, Markinch, N B, same crest and motto

Balfour, Rt Hon Arthur James, of Whittinghame, Scotland, same crest and motto

Balfour of Townley Hall, Ireland, on a perch or, a hawk close ppr, beaked and belled, also or, round the neck a ribbon gu *Omne solum forti patria* cf 85 13

Balfour of Forret, an eagle rising, ppr *Dieu aidant* 77 5

Balfour-Kinnear, George Thomas, of Cross and Bristane, Orkney, Esquire, Writer to the Signet, 6, Doune Terrace, Edinburgh, an anchor ppr *Spem fortuna alit* 161 11

Balfour, Major Francis Walter of Fernie Castle, co Fife, a mermaid ppr, holding in her dexter hand an otter's head erased sa, and in the sinister a swan's head erased ppr *Omni solum forti patria.*

Balfour, Scotland, an heraldic tiger passant sa 25 5

Balfour-Hay, see Paterson Balfour-Hay

Balgonie, Lord, *see* Leven, Earl of

Balguy of Duffield, Derbysh, a bear passant ppr, collared and chained or cf 34 1

Baliol, Scotland, a decrescent and an increscent arg 163 7

Ball of Scotto, Norf, a demi lion rampant gardant sa 10 8

Ball, a demi-lion rampant, holding between the paws a ball

Ball, Northamp, out of clouds ppr, a demi lion rampant sa, semee of estoiles arg, holding a globe or

Ball, an arm erect or, holding in the hand a fire ball, all ppr 216 6

Ball, a cubit arm vested gu, the cuff arg, grasping in the hand a fire ball ppr

Ball, Sir Robert Stawell, of The Observatory, Cambridge, an arm vambraced embowed arg, charged with two ogresses the hand grasping a fire ball fired, all ppr *On* 241 12

Ball, Sir Charles Bent same crest and motto

Ball, John Stewart Valentine, Esquire, same crest and motto

Ball, Thomas Hand, Esquire, of 236, Chestnut Street, Philadelphia, U S A, an escallop or, charged with a fire ball all proper

Ball of Boughton, Greenhall, and Irby, Chesh, out of a ducal coronet an arm in armour embowed, holding in the hand a fire ball, all ppr

Ball, Bart (*extinct*), of Blofield, Norf, out of a naval coronet a cubit arm erect in naval uniform, holding in the hand a grenade bursting ppr

Ball or Ballagrove, near Drogheda, a griffin's head erased arg, langued gu, beaked or *Fulcrum dignitatis virtus* 66 2

Ball of London, a caltrap az, embrued gu 174 14

Ball, Lancs, a turtle-dove ppr 92 2

Ballantine Dykes, *see* Dykes

Ballantyne of Holylee, Scotland, a demi-griffin, holding in the dexter claw a sword erect ppr *Nec cito, nec tarde* 64 6

Ballard of Ballards, in Horton, near Canterbury, Kent, a demi-griffin, wings addorsed erm, beaked and armed or 64 2

Ballard of Evesham, co Worcs, a griffin's head erased erm 66 2

Ballard of Cradley, Heref, a demi griffin erm, supporting a broken tilting spear ppr 65 3

Balle, an arm holding a fire ball ppr 216 6

Ballenden of Broughton, a hart's head couped ppr, attired or, between the attires a cross crosslet fitched of the last *Sic itur ad astra* cf 120 12

Ballenden, St Clair Grahame, L R C P, Holborn Lodge, Sedgley, Dudley, crest and motto as above

Bellenger, a dragon's head with wings addorsed ppr cf 72 1

Ballentine, a demi-griffin sa, wings addorsed erm, holding in the dexter claw a sword erect arg, hilt and pommel or 64 6

Ballett of Hatfield, Essex, out of a mural coronet or, a demi-eagle displayed sa 80 8

Ballidon, Derbysh, a demi lion vert, crowned or, holding a cross crosslet of the last cf 11 10

Ballingall, Hugh, Esquire, J P, D L, of Ardarroch, Dundee, a demi eagle displayed vert, between two lilies issuing out of the wreath ppr *Decore* 250. 15

Ballinghall, late Sir George, F R S, Regius Professor of Military Surgery in the University of Edinburgh, an eagle displayed with two heads, per pale embattled or and gu *Fortitudine et decore* 74 2

Ballow of Westminster, two arms embowed, vested sa, cuffed arg, the hands ppr, conjoined, holding an etoile of eight points or

Balls-Headley, Walter, Esquire, M A, M D, F R C P, of Collins Street, Melbourne, and Redholme, Kensington, Road, South Yarra, Victoria, uses a martlet *Celer et vigilans.* 95 4

Bally of Bath, on a mount vert, in front of an oak tree fructed ppr, two swords in saltire, also ppr, pommels and hilts or

Balm and **Balme,** a hat turned up or, with three ostrich feathers arg 115 4

Balm, a trefoil slipped or *Fideliter* 148 9

Balmanno of Affleck, Scotland, a dexter hand grasping a scimitar, all ppr *Fortiter* 213 5

Balmanno or Balmano, Scotland, an eagle displayed gu, holding in each claw a sword ppr 75 6

Balnaves of Carnbody, a dexter hand holding a ball ppr *Hinc origo* 216 3

Balnaves or **Balneaves,** a dexter hand holding a ball sa *Fortitudine et velocitate* 216 3

Balscott, on a ducal coronet or, a lion passant gardant arg. *cf.* 6. 4

Balsillie, Scotland, a dexter hand ppr., holding a cross crosslet fitched gu. 221. 14

Balston, Kent, a dove holding an olive-branch in its beak, all ppr. *J'espère.* 92. 5

Balston, Reginald Mansfield, Esquire, in front of a dove holding in the beak a sprig of olive ppr., three fleur-de-lis fesseways sa. *J'espère.*

Balston, Richard James, Esquire, of Springfield, Maidstone, same crest and motto.

Baltrey, on a mural coronet or, a goat's head erased quarterly arg. and erm.

Balvaird, Scotland, a hand holding a hunting-horn ppr. *Non omnibus dormio.* 217. 4

Bambell, out of a ducal coronet or, a pelican vulning herself sa. *cf.* 98. 1

Bamber, Lancs, a bull's head erased gu., armed or. *Fortis et egregius.* 44. 3

Bamber, Ireland, a bull's head couped gu. *cf.* 44. 3

Bambrough, Rendlesham, Suff., a skull-cap arg.

Bamburg, Yorks, a wolf's head erased vert, bezantée. *cf.* 30. 8

Bamfield or **Bamfylde,** a lion's head erased sa., ducally crowned or. 18. 8

Bamfield or **Baumfield,** a lion's head erased sa., ducally crowned gu., charged on the neck with an annulet or. *cf.* 18. 8

Bamfield, Cornw. and Devonsh., a lion statant gardant, holding in the dexter paw an anchor, the flukes resting on the wreath. 5. 10

Bamford of Bamford, Derbysh., on a chapeau a serpent nowed. 142. 9

Bamford, Arthur J. J., Esquire, of Misterton Hall, Lutterworth, Leics., in front of a dexter arm embowed, holding a flagstaff ppr., therefrom flowing a banner arg., charged with a mascle gu., three annulets interlaced fesseways of the last. *Perseverantia vincit.* *cf.* 199. 10

Bamme, Baum, or **Baume,** out of a ducal coronet a griffin's head, holding in the beak a key, all ppr. 65. 14

Bampfylde (Rt. Hon. Sir Augustus Frederick George Warwick), **Baron Poltimore,** Devonsh., a lion's head erased sa., ducally crowned or. *Delectare in domino.* 18. 8

Banard or **Banyard** of Stakey, Norf., a lion's gamb erased sa., charged with a martlet, or for difference. *cf.* 36. 4

Banastre, Shropsh., a peacock ppr. 103. 7

Banbury, Sir Frederick George, Bart., Warneford Place, Highworth, Wilts, a demi-antelope ppr., holding between the forepaws a cross pattée and charged on the shoulder with a garb gu. *Moneo et munio.* 232. 7

Banbury or **Bandbury,** Oxon., a falcon regardant, holding in its dexter claw a garland of laurel, all ppr. 85. 4

Bance of London and Callow, Berks, out of a ducal coronet or, a lion's gamb holding a cross crosslet fitched sa. 36. 11

Banckes, *see* Bankes, and Banks, and Bank.

Bancks, a griffin segreant arg., holding a cross formée fitchée gu.

Bancroft of London, a garb between two wings expanded, all or. 153. 14

Bancroft, Sir Squire, 18, Berkeley Square, W., in front of a garb banded between two wings or, each wing charged with a cross crosslet, four annulets fesseways and interlaced az. *Vi et virtute.* 244. 17

Band of Wookey House, Somers., an eagle rising or. *Dieu est mon aide.* 77. 5

Band, Essex, on a chapeau an owl ppr., wings expanded or. 96. 6

Bandenell of Netherbury, a griffin statant ppr. 63. 8

Banderstone, *see* Balderstone.

Bandinel, a helmet close, crested with a plume of feathers ppr. 180. 4

Bandon, Earl of, *see* Bernard.

Banester or Banaster, Lancs, a peacock in pride, the body and wings or, the tail ppr. 103. 2

Banester, Leics. and Staffs, a peacock sitting ppr., gorged with a collar gu., charged with three bezants.

Banester, Surrey, a peacock ppr. 103. 7

Banester, a crab erect. 141. 5

Banester, a lobster or. 141. 2

Banger, a greyhound's head erased, per fess gu. and or. 61. 4

Bangor, Viscount (Ward), Castle Ward, Downpatrick, co. Down, a Saracen's head affrontée, couped below the shoulders ppr., wreathed about the temples or and az., and adorned with three ostrich-feathers. *Sub cruce salus.* 190. 5

Banister, a torteau. 159. 14

Banke or **Banck** of London and Yorks, on the stump of a tree couped a stork close, all ppr. 105. 12

Banke or **Banckes,** Glouc. and Lancs, a griffin segreant arg., holding a cross formée fitched gu.

Bankes of London and Middx., a man's head couped at the shoulders sa., on his head a chapeau gu., turned up erm.

Bankes of Kingston Lucy, Dorset, a blackamoor's head affrontée, couped at the shoulders ppr., in the ears earrings or, on the head a chapeau gu., turned up erm., adorned with a crescent, issuant therefrom a fleur-de-lis or. *Velle vult quod Deus.*

Bankes, Walter Ralph, of Corfe Castle, Dorsetshire, same crest and motto.

Bankes of Revesby Abbey, Lincs, on the stump of an oak-tree couped, sprouting out new branches, a stork statant arg., beaked or, ducally gorged gu. *Nullius in verba.* 105. 4

Bankes of Winstanley, Wigan, on the stump of a tree a stork statant ppr., ducally gorged gu. 105. 4

Banks, Yorks, an eagle's head couped arg. 83. 1

Banks of Leeds, Yorks, an eagle's head erased sa., between two fleur-de-lis arg. 84. 9

Banks, Herbert Delamark, Esquire, of Oxney Court, near Dover, Kent, on a mount vert, a stone column of the Tuscan order, fesseways, thereon a stork ppr., the dexter claw resting on a fleur-de-lis or. *Perseverando.* 104. 1

Banks, a dragon's head erased arg. *Ripa caret taciturna ventis.* *cf.* 71. 2

Banks of Aylesford, Kent, a dragon's head erased arg. *cf.* 71. 2

Banks, Sir John, of Golagh, Monaghan, a dragon's head erased per pale sa. and gu. *Fide et fortitudine.*

Banks, Yorks, on a mount vert, a dragon rampant arg., supporting a cross pattée or.

Banks, Edwin Hodge, of Highmoor, Wigton, Cumb., upon the trunk of a tree eradicated and sprouting to the dexter ppr., an eagle regardant, wings elevated sa., charged upon the breast and upon each wing with a fleur-de-lis or. *Dum spiro spero.*

Banks, Middx., a blackamoor's head affrontée, couped at the shoulders ppr., in the ears earrings or, and on his head a chapeau gu., turned up erm.

Banks, Dorset, a blackamoor's head affrontée, couped at the shoulders ppr., in the ears earrings or, and on his head a chapeau gu., turned up erm., charged with a crescent, issuing therefrom a fleur-de-lis or.

Banks of Aylesford, Kent, on a mount vert, a stag statant, attired and ungu or, behind a tree ppr. *cf.* 116. 13

Banks, John Daniel, solicitor, Notary Public, West End House, Prescot, an eagle's head couped arg. *Nullius in verba.*

Banks of London, an arm in armour embowed arg., garnished or, issuing out of clouds ppr., holding in the hand, also ppr., a falchion arg., hilt and pommel or, and on the falchion a chaplet vert.

Bannatine and **Bannatyne,** Scotland, a demi-griffin. 64. 2

Bannatyne of Corhouse, a demi-griffin holding in the dexter claw a sword erect, all ppr. *Nec cito, nec tarde.* 64. 6

Bannatyne of Kames, same crest and motto.

Bannatyne of Newhall, a demi-griffin holding in the dexter claw a sword in fesse ppr. *Dum spiro spero.*

Bannatyne, Scotland, a griffin's head erased. 66. 2

Banner of London, an arm in armour embowed, holding in the hand ppr. a banner gu., fringe and staff arg., charged with a fleur-de-lis or. *Nil sine numine.* *cf.* 199. 9

Banner of London, a demi-wolf ppr., ducally gorged and chained or, holding between its paws a mullet of six points of the same. 31. 6

Bannerman, Bart., of Elsick, Scotland, a demi-man in armour affrontée, his dexter hand grasping a sword, all ppr. *Pro patria.* 187. 1

Bannerman, W. Bruce, Esquire, F.S.A., of Croydon, a demi-man in armour affrontée, his dexter hand grasping a sword, all ppr., and his sinister hand holding a banner displayed arg., thereon a canton az., charged with a saltire of the field. *Pro patria.* 292. 12

Bannerman of Edinburgh, same crest and motto.

Bannerman, James Murray, of Wyastone Leys, Heref. A demi-man in armour holding in the dexter hand a sword, all ppr. *Pro patria.*

Bannerman, Scotland, a demi-priest habited ppr., in the act of prayer. *Hæc præstat militia.*

Bannerman, Campbell-, Rt. Hon. Sir Henry, M.P., of Hunton Court, Kent: (1) A demi-man in armour ppr (*for Bannerman*). (2) A boar's head erased ppr. (*for Campbell*). *Patriæ fidelis.—Ne obliviscaris.* 42. 2

Bannester and **Bannister,** an arm in armour couped in fess, holding a scimitar in pale arg., enfiled with a boar's head couped ppr. *cf.* 211. 9

Banning, *see* Greaves-Banning.

Banning of London, an ostrich arg., holding in the beak a key or. 97. 5

Bannister, an arm in armour couped fessways ppr., holding a scimitar arg. in pale, enfiled with a boar's head couped, also ppr. *cf.* 211. 9

Bannister of Guonchall, Leics., a peacock sitting ppr., gorged with a collar gu., charged with three bezants.

Bantry, Earl of (Hedges-White): (1) A stork arg., beaked and membered or, charged with a crescent gu. (*for White*). (2) A swan's head and neck erased ppr. (*for Hedges*). *cf.* 101. 5. (3) A leg booted, armed, and spurred, couped at the thigh, per pale gu. and arg., spurred or (*for Eyre*). *The noblest motive is the public good.*

Banworth, on a ducal coronet a griffin sejant, resting the dexter claw on an escutcheon. 62. 11

Baptista of Castile, out of a ducal coronet or, a dragon's head vert, in flames of fire ppr. 72. 14

Baptist-Browne of Italy, a dragon's head between two wings sa., gorged with a bar gemelle or, the dexter ear gu., the sinister arg., the wings purfled or.

Baratty, an eagle regardant, wings expanded, holding in its dexter claw a sword, all ppr. 77. 10

Barban or **Barbon,** a leopard's head and neck ppr. 22. 10

Barbe, St., of Lymington, Hants, a wyvern sa. 70. 2

Barbenson, Thomas Nicholas, Esquire, of Alderney, three mullets or, in front of a mount vert, thereon an olive-tree ppr., and on the dexter side thereof, rampant to the sinister, a lion gu. *Semper fidelis.* 3. 11

Barber, Scotland, a dexter hand holding a cross crosslet fitched gu. 221. 14

Barber, Scotland, a dexter hand holding a cross pattée fitched gu. 221. 12

Barber, Thomas Philip, Esquire, B.A., J.P., Lamb Close House, Greasley, Notts, out of a ducal coronet, a bull's head. *In Deo spes.* 44. 11

Barber, Suff., out of a ducal coronet gu., a bull's head arg. *cf.* 44. 11

Barber of London, on a mural coronet gu., a bull's head erased arg.

Barber, Herts, out of a ducal coronet or, a bull's head per pale arg. and gu. *cf.* 44. 11

Barber-Starkey, William Joseph, Esquire, of Aldenham Park, Bridgnorth, Shropsh., a stork arg., semée of estoiles az. *Homo proponit. Deus disponit.*

Barberie or **Barberrie,** a dexter hand holding an arrow, point downwards, all ppr. *Suivez raison.* 214. 4

Barbon of London, a leopard's head and neck arg., spotted sa. 22. 10

Barbon, *see* Barban.

Barbor of Stamford, Lincs, London, and Suff., out of a ducal coronet or, a bull's head arg., charged on the neck with a cinquefoil gu. *cf.* 44. 11

Barbor, on a staff raguly in fess an eagle displayed with two heads az., each ducally crowned or, the inside of the wings and the legs also or.

Barbour, a Calvary-cross gu. *Nihilo nisi cruce.* 166. 1

Barbour, George, of Bolesworth Castle, Chesh., in front of a mount vert, thereon a cross Calvary arg., a garb fessewise or. *Nihilo nisi cruce.*

Barby, Devonsh. and Northamp., a heraldic tiger statant arg., attired with four horns, turned round like those of a ram or.

Barchaud, a dove arg., winged or, beaked, legged, and collared gu., charged on the breast with a crescent of the last, holding in its beak an olive-branch vert, and resting its dexter claw on a mill-rind, erect az.

Barclay, Sir David Edward Durell, Bart., of Pierston, a sword in pale arg., hilt and pommel or. *Crux Christi nostra corona.* 170. 2

Barclay-Allardice, *see* Allardice.

Barclay of London, same crest and motto.

Barclay, Scotland, a hand holding a dagger in pale ppr. *Crux Christi nostra corona.* 212. 9

Barclay, Charles Alexander, Esquire, of Aberdour House, Fraserburgh, co. Aberdeen, a hand holding a dagger ppr. *Aut agere, aut mori.*

Barclay, Charles Herbert, Esquire, of Inchedura, North Berwick, N.B., same crest and motto.

Barclay, Robert, Esquire, of Bury Hill, Dorking, Surrey, a mitre or, and in an escroll. *In cruce spero.*

Barclay, a dexter hand holding a sword ppr., hilted and pommelled or. *Aut agere, aut mori.* 212. 13

Barclay, an arm couped and embowed, resting the elbow on the wreath, holding in the hand three ears of wheat, all ppr. 202. 6

Barclay, Scotland, a mitre ppr. *In cruce spero.* *cf.* 180. 5

Barclay, Robert, of Higham, Bury St. Edmunds, same crest and motto.

Barclay, a mitre or, charged with an escallop gu. *Dieu avec nous.* *cf.* 180. 5

Barclay, Rev. Joseph, LL.D., Rector of Stapleford, Herts, and Bishop of Jerusalem, a mitre or, charged with an escallop gu. *Dieu avec nous.* *cf.* 180. 5

Barclay of Touch, Scotland, a cross pattée gu. *Crux salutim confert.* *cf.* 165. 7

Barclay of Balmakewan, Scotland, a cross pattée gu. *Sola cruce salus.* *cf.* 165. 7

Barclay of Wavertree, a cross pattée gu., surmounted by an Eastern crown or. *Mieux être que paroître.*

Barclay of Burford Lodge, Surrey, same crest.

Barclay, Sweden, a passion-cross gu., surmounted by a celestial crown or. *Crux Christi solamen offert.*

Barclay, Scotland, a dove holding in its beak an olive-branch ppr. *Cedant arma.* 92. 5

Barclay, a demi-griffin regardant az., supporting a flag erect charged with a crescent. 64. 14

Barclay of Johnston, Scotland, the sun issuing out of a cloud ppr. *Servabit me semper Jehovah.* 162. 5

Barcroft, Henry, Esquire, of the Glen, co. Armagh, a demi-bear rampant gu., muzzled and charged on the shoulder with a trefoil slipped or. 263. 10

Barcroft of Meer Green, Worcs., a wolf rampant gu. 28. 2

Bard of Caversfield, Bucks, a lion's gamb couped and erect or, grasping a horse's leg erased sa. 38. 12

Bardin, a demi-youth ppr., holding over his shoulder a broken axe.

Bardolf, Bardolfe, or **Bardolph,** out of a ducal coronet or, a dragon's head of the same, wings expanded gu.

Bardolph of London, out of a mural coronet gu., a dragon's head between two wings of the last, each charged with a mascle or.

Bardswell, Charles William, M.A., Recorder of Kingston-on-Thames, the Beacon, Surbiton, a peacock in his pride ppr. *Non nobis nascimur.*

Bardwell, an arm in armour holding in the hand a broken spear, the pieces in saltier. 209. 10

Bardwell, Thomas Newman Frederick, Esquire, D.L., Bolton Hall, Wilberfoss, Yorks, a demi-goat erm., armed and attired or. *Bear thee well.* 129. 10

Bare, Ireland, a wolf's head sa. 30. 5

Barentine or **Barrentine,** an eagle displayed arg., between the attires and over the scalp of a stag or.

Bareth, Ireland, a lozenge gu. *cf.* 110. 3

Barett, a demi-leopard gardant ppr. *cf.* 23. 4

Bareu or **Barew,** a holly-branch vert. 147. 7

Barfoot of Midlington Place, Hants, a stag statant, gorged with a ducal coronet. *cf.* 117. 5

Barfoot or **Barford,** out of a ducal coronet, a cubit arm in armour, the hand grasping a sword in bend sinister ppr.

Barford or **Berford,** Rutl., a bear passant sa. *cf.* 34. 1

Bargrave or **Bargrove,** Kent, on a mount vert a pheon gu., point downwards, between two laurel-branches of the first.

Barham, Baron (Noel), a buck at gaze arg., attired or. *Tout bien ou rien.* 117. 3

Barham or **Braham,** Suff. and Surrey, a wolf's head arg. 30. 5

Barham of Staines, Middx., a stork among bulrushes, all ppr. 104. 3

Bariff, Northamp., on a mount vert a beaver passant ppr., gorged with a plain collar and ring or. *cf.* 134. 4

Baring of Larkbeer, Devonsh., a mullet erminois, between two wings arg. *Probitate et labore.* *cf.* 111. 5

Baring, Baron Ashburton, *see* Ashburton.

Baring, Viscount Baring and **Earl of Northbrook,** *see* Northbrook.

Baring, Baron Revelstoke, *see* Revelstoke.

Baring, a dexter cubit arm in armour, holding in the hand a caltrap, all ppr. 210. 7

Baring-Gould, Rev. Baring, of 65, Lee Park, Lee, Kent, a demi-lion rampant az. bezantée. *Toujours sans tache.—Probitate et labore.*

Baring-Gould, Francis, Esquire, of Merrow Grange, Surrey, same crest and motto.
Baring-Gould, Rev. Sabine, of Lew Trenchard, North Devon, same crest and motto.
Baring, Harold Herman John, High Beach, Essex, a mullet erminois between two wings arg. *Probitate et labore.* 239. 2
Baring, William Henry, of Norman Court, Hants, crest and motto as above.
Barkas or **Barcas,** an arm from the shoulder holding a roll of bark ppr. *Fari quæ sentiat.*
Barke, an arm from the shoulder holding in the hand a spade ppr. 202. 12
Barkeley, Somers., a unicorn statant gu., armed or. *cf.* 48. 5
Barkeley, a mitre gu., charged with a chevron, between ten crosses formée arg. *cf.* 180. 5
Barkeley, Okenbury, Cornw., on a mount vert, a stag lodged ppr. 115. 12
Barkeman of London, two arms in armour embowed or, holding between the hands ppr. a bundle of arrows arg., banded gu. 194. 6
Barker, Bart., Bocking Hall, Essex, a bear sejant or, collared sa. *cf.* 34. 8
Barker, Thomas, Esquire, of Roslyn Hall, Sydney, New South Wales, a bear sejant sa., muzzled and gorged with a collar gemelle or, holding in the paws an escutcheon gu., charged with an escallop arg.
Barker, Christopher Dove, Esquire, of Radnor House, Great Malvern, issuant from an annulet or, a bear's head erased sa., muzzled of the first, charged with a bend nebuly arg., thereon three torteaux. *Virtus tutissima cassis.*
Barker, Ponsonby-, of Kilcooly, Ireland: (1) A bear sejant or, collared sa. (*for Barker*). *cf.* 34. 8. (2) In a ducal coronet az., three arrows, one in pale and two in saltier, points downward, enveloped with a snake ppr. (*for Ponsonby*). 173. 2
Barker, a bear's head sa., muzzled or. 34. 14
Barker, Rev. Alfred Gresley, Stanlake Park, Reading, on a rock arg., a hawk close or. *In solo Deo salus.*
Barker, Norf., a bear's head erased gu., muzzled or. 35. 2
Barker of Newbury, Berks, Great Horwood, Bucks, etc., a bear's head erased gu., muzzled or, between two wings erect, the dexter az., the sinister of the second. 35. 5
Barker, George Rickard, Esquire, Hemsby Hall, Norf., a bear's head couped gu., muzzled or, between two torteaux.
Barker of Over and Vale Royal, Chesh., a falcon arg., standing on a hawk's lure gu., stringed or. *cf.* 85. 14
Barker, Shropsh., on a rock a hawk ppr. 86. 7
Barker of Wollerton, Shropsh., on a rock arg., a hawk close or. 86. 7
Barker, Raymond-, Reginald Henry, of Fairford Park, Glouc.: (1) On a rock arg., a hawk close or (*for Barker*). 86. 7. (2) Out of a mural coronet a demi-eagle displayed or, charged on the body with three torteaux in pale. *Virtus tutissima cassis.* 80. 8
Barker of Haughmond, Shropsh., an eagle rising regardant arg., beaked and winged or. 77. 4
Barker of Chelsum, Bucks, a turtle-dove ppr., holding in its beak a rose gu., stalked and leaved vert. *cf.* 92. 5
Barker of Bockenhall, Essex, an ostrich-head erased or, holding in the beak a horse-shoe arg.
Barker, Middx., Kent, and Surrey, out of a ducal coronet or, an eagle displayed sa., beaked and legged gu. *cf.* 75. 2
Barker of Albrighton Hall, Salop, same crest. *Juvante Deo floret industria.*
Barker of Holbeach, Norf., out of a ducal coronet or, a griffin's head ppr. *Fide sed cui vide.* 67. 9
Barker, Hurst., Berks and Warw., a naked boy ppr., holding an arrow.
Barker, Berks, a naked man holding a spear in pale ppr.
Barker, Berks, a demi-Moor ppr., in his dexter hand an arrow or, feathered and headed arg., on his sinister arm a shield, also or, and over his shoulder a sash gu.
Barker of Ipswich, Suff., same crest.
Barker, William Oliver, Esquire, M.D., of Dunboyne, co. Meath, and of Gardiner's Row, Dublin, a demi-Moor ppr., over his sinister shoulder a sash gu., holding in his dexter hand an arrow or, feathered and headed arg., and on his sinister arm a shield or, charged with a crescent sa. *Mors potius macula.*
Barker of Ipswich, a greyhound sejant arg., collared and ringed or, having attached to the latter a line of the same, entwined round the body and held to the ground by the dexter hind-foot.
Barker, Rutland, a bear sejant ppr. *cf.* 34. 8
Barkesworth or **Barksworth,** Yorks, out of a ducal coronet two arms, dexter and sinister, vested and embowed, and in each hand an ostrich-feather. 203. 2
Barkey of Bremen, Germany, and of Dublin, a lion's gamb couped sa., between two ostrich-feathers, the dexter arg., the sinister gu.
Barkham, an arm couped at the shoulder in a maunch, embowed in fess, the elbow resting on the wreath. 203. 1
Barkham of London, two arms in armour embowed ppr., holding a sheath of five arrows or, feathered arg., and banded with a ribbon gu. *Diligentia fortuna mater.* 194. 6
Barksteade of London, out of a ducal coronet or, an arm in armour embowed ppr., grasping a sword arg., hilt and pommel of the first. 195. 10
Barkworth, Yorks, a demi-lion rampant arg. *Esto quod esse videris.* 10. 2
Barlande, a lion rampant gu., supporting a garb ppr. 1. 7
Barlay or **Barley,** a boar's head or, tusked az., charged on the breast with a mullet of the same. 41. 3
Barley, Derbysh., a boar's head erased or, in the mouth a quatrefoil az.
Barley of London, a dexter cubit arm vested, charged with a fess vair cottised, cuff arg., holding in the hand a staff.
Barley, a demi-stag party per pale, charged with three bars wavy counter-changed. *cf.* 119. 2
Barling, Kent, a lion rampant gu., supporting a garb ppr. *Perspicax audax.* 1. 7
Barloss, a cock or, combed, legged, and wattled gu. 91. 2
Barlow, Very Rev. William Hagger, Dean of Peterborough, on a Mercury's cap or, the wings arg., an eagle's head erased ppr.
Barlow, Sir Thomas, Bart., in front of a staff erect, entwined by a serpent ppr. an eagle's neck erased with two heads arg., thereon a rose gu. *Sicut aquila juvenescam.* 232. 9
Barlow, Lancs, two eagles' heads erased and conjoined arg., beaked or. 84. 11
Barlow of Sheffield, on a Mercury's cap or, the wings arg., an eagle's head erased ppr., collared erm. 84. 1
Barlow of Slebege, Pembroke, a demi-lion arg., holding in the dexter paw a cross crosslet fitched sa. 11. 10
Barlow, an eagle's head erased ppr., holding in the beak an escallop-shell.
Barlow of Upton House, near Manchester, a gauntleted hand bendways ppr., grasping two eagles' heads conjoined and erased at the neck sa. *En foi prest.*
Barlow, Alexander Kay, Esquire, of Wivenhoe Hall, Essex, same crest and motto. 84. 11
Barlow, William Wycliffe, Esquire, of Pitt Manor, near Winchester, same crest and motto.
Barlow-Massicks, Thomas, Esquire, of the Oaks, Millom, Cumb., a cross pattée az., surmounted by a leopard's face jessant-de-lis or. *Vestigia nulla retrorsum.*
Barlow of Dublin, issuant from a billet raguly vert, a demi-eagle without wings, per pale arg. and or, and charged on the breast with two chevronels sa. 80. 11
Barlow, Sir Richard Wellesley, Bart., out of an Eastern crown or, a demi-lion arg., supporting in the paws a cross crosslet fitchée az., between on the dexter side a branch of olive, and on the sinister a branch of palm ppr. *Si pius in primis.—Dilige pacem.* 251. 5
Barlow, a demi-lion rampant gardant arg., gorged with a collar gu., thereon three bezants, holding between the paws a cross moline of the second charged with a bezant.
Barnaby, a demi-Moor ppr., holding in his dexter hand a rose gu.
Barnaby, a boar's head erased, per fess nebuly sa. and or. 41. 5
Barnaby of Colchester, Essex, a demi-greyhound gu., collared and ringed arg., holding between the paws a branch of laurel vert.
Barnaby, Worcs., an escallop sa. 141. 14
Barnaby, Shropsh., a leopard couchant sa. 24. 10
Barnack or **Barnake,** a bear's head sa., muzzled or, between two wings of the last. *cf.* 35. 5
Barnard, Rev. Dennis Jacob Johnson, of the School House, Stamford, a demi-lion arg., charged on the shoulder with

an escallop, holding between the paws a serpent nowed, the whole between two escallops, all az *Maintenant ou jamais* 295 6

Barnard, Baron (Vane), an armed hand couped at the wrist grasping a sword in bend sinister, all ppr, pommel and hilt or *Nec temere nec timide*

Barnard of Bartlow, Cambs, a demi-bear rampant sa, muzzled or 34 13

Barnard, Yorks, same crest

Barnard, Fulke Lancelot Wade, Esquire, of Portishead, Somers, same crest *Fer et perfer* 34 13

Barnard of London, out of a ducal coronet or, a demi-bear rampant sa, muzzled or 34 10

Barnard, Benjamin, Esquire, of Ham, Surrey, out of a mount vert, a demi-bear sa, muzzled, charged on the shoulder with a cross pattee fitchee, and the sinister paw resting on a cross crosslet or

Barnard of Notcliffe House, Tewkesbury, Glouc, a demi-bear rampant sa, semée of annulets or, and holding between the paws a buckle of the last *Ex concordia victoriæ spes* 34 11

Barnard of Cave Castle, Yorks (1) A bear rampant sa, muzzled or (*for Barnard* (2) A greyhound courant (*for Boldero*) *Festina lente* cf 58 2

Barnard, Norf. and Yorks, and Pirton, Oxon, a demi lion rampant arg, charged on the shoulder with a mullet within an annulet, holding in the paws a snake entwined az 9 14

Barnard, G W G, 4, Surrey Street, Norwich, a demi lion arg, charged on the shoulder with an escallop, holding between the paws a serpent nowed, the whole between two escallops, all az *Nunc aut nunquam* 260 13

Barnard, John, Esquire, of Lambeth, Surrey, a lion passant arg, billettée sa, supporting with the dexter paw an escutcheon gu, charged with a garb or *Mea gloria fides* 5 1

Barnard, London, an escallop-shell arg 141 14

Barnard, Herbert, Esquire of 69, Portland Square W on a mount vert, a demi bear sa muzzled charged on the shoulder with a cross patee fitchee and the sinister paw resting on a cross crosslet or

Barnard, John, Esquire, of 32, Montpellier Crescent, Brighton, a lion arg, billettee sa, supporting with the dexter paw a shield gu, charged with a garb or *Mea gloria fides*

Barnard, Joseph, Esquire, a demi-bear rampant sa, semee of annulets or, and holding between the paws a buckle of the last *Ex concordia victoriæ spes*

Barnardiston, Nathaniel, Esquire, of The Ryes, near Sudbury, Suff, a bittern or, standing among bulrushes ppr

Barnardiston, Nathaniel Walter, of the Ryes Sudbury, Suff, same crest

Barnardiston of Kiddington, Suff, an ass's head arg *Je trouve bien* 125 12

Barnardiston of Great Cotes, Lincs, among rushes ppr, a stork or 104 3

Barnato, of 23, Upper Hamilton Place, upon a rock ppr, two roses saltireways arg, stalked, leaved, and slipped vert, interlaced by a mascle or *Industria atque fortuna*

Barnawell, *see* Barnewell

Barnby, Yorks, a bear's head couped sa, muzzled or 34 14

Barne, Michael, Esquire, a falcon volant arg, ducally gorged and membered or, standing on a mount vert *Nec timide nec temere*

Barne, Miles, Esquire, of Sotterley, co Suff, same crest and motto

Barne, Seymour, Esquire, of Sotterley, co Suff, same crest and motto

Barne of Tiverton, Devonsh, in front of an oak tree ppr, growing out of a mount vert, an eagle with wings displayed sa, charged on the body and on each wing with a bezant, and resting the dexter claw on a leopard's face or *Avorum honori* 78 10

Barne of London, out of a ducal coronet or, and on a mount vert, a stag statant ppr 118 4

Barneby of Brockhampton, Heref, a lion couchant gardant sa *Virtute non vi* 7 10

Barneby, William Henry, of Longworth, Heref, same crest and motto

Barneby-Lutley, John Habington, Esquire, of Brockhampton, co Heref, same crest and motto

Barned, Lewis- Israel, Esquire, of Gloucester Terrace, Regent's Park, London, N W (1) A female in a sitting attitude vested az, and holding in the right hand a sickle ppr (*for Barned*) (2) Upon the trunk of a tree fess wise and eradicated ppr, a gryphon segreant or, holding in the dexter claw a trefoil vert (*for Lewis*) *Benigno numine*

Barnefield, a lion's head erased sa., ducally crowned gu 18 8

Barnes, Berks, a demi unicorn erm, armed, collared, and lined or cf 48 10

Barnes, Edmund, J P, 220, Camden Road, N W, same crest *Nec timide nec temere*

Barnes, Walter James, solicitor, Bideford, same crest and motto

Barnes, a demi greyhound ppr, holding in its paws a garb or

Barnes, a demi-lion or 10 2

Barnes, Cambs, a leopard passant arg, spotted sa, collared and lined or

Barnes, Pemberton-, of Haveringham-atte Bower, Romford, Essex (1) Upon a rock a leopard passant ppr, semée of estoiles, and a cross crosslet sa, for difference (*for Barnes*) (2) Upon the trunk of an oak tree eradicated and sprouting, towards the dexter ppr, a griffin passant or, guttee de poix (*for Pemberton*) *Mutare vel timere sperno*

Barnes, the descendants of the late Robert Barnes, Esquire, of Durham, upon a rock a bear ppr, muzzled or, and resting the dexter fore paw on a trefoil slipped vert *Forbear*, and the same crest with the motto *Fer fortiter* 34 2

Barnes of London, in rushes ppr, a duck arg 102 3

Barnes, a falcon, wings expanded arg, ducally gorged, beaked, and legged or

Barnes, Kent, on a mount vert, a falcon, wings expanded arg, ducally gorged, beaked and legged or

Barnes, Herts and Lancs, an etoile pierced or 164 5

Barnes of London, out of a cloud ppr, issuing rays paleways or, an arm erect vested of the second, holding in the hand, also ppr, a broken sword arg, hilt and pommel also or cf 210 12

Barnes, the late Alfred, of Ashgate Lodge, Chesterfield, Derbysh, in front of a cubit arm in armour the hand grasping a broken sword, all ppr, the wrist encircled by a wreath of oak or, five annulets interlaced and fessewise arg *Frangas non flectes*

Barnes, Arthur Gorell, Esquire, of Tupton Hall, Chesterfield, same crest and motto

Barnes, Frederic Gorell, Esquire, J P, D L, of Springfield Hawkhurst, Kent, same crest and motto

Barnes, Hon Sir John Gorell, K C, of 14, Kensington Park Gardens, same crest and motto

Barnes of Brookside, Manchester, a cubit arm issuant from rocks ppr, habited chequy arg and az, cuffed of the second, the hand grasping a broken sword ppr, and issuant from the rock behind the arm rays of the sun or *Deus noster refugium*

Barnes, Captain Richard Knowles, R N, on the embattlements of a tower gu, a wyvern az, gorged with a collar gemel or, the wings elevated of the last guttee-de-sang

Barnes, a demi savage, wreathed about the head and loins, holding a club in pale, all ppr

Barnes, same crest *Nec timide, nec timere*

Barnes, Robert, Esquire, upon a rock ppr, muzzled or, and resting the dexter fore-paw on a trefoil slipped vert *Fer fortiter*

Barnes, Rev George, M A, of the Rectory, St Albans, Wood Street, London, same crest and motto

Barnesfather, *see* Bairnsfather

Barnesley, Staffs and Surrey, an old man's head affrontee, couped at the breast ppr, charged with a mullet for difference

Barnet, a holly branch ppr 150 10

Barnett, Bertram, Knighton Grange, near Chichester, out of a ducal crown or, a demi bear sa, muzzled of the first

Barnett, Thomas, Esquire, of Knighton Grange Aldingbourne, Chichester out of a ducal coronet a bear's head muzzled *Nisi paret imperat*

Barnett of Stratton Park, Biggleswade, Beds, a fleur de lis arg 148 2

Barnevelt, a demi-buck gu 119 2

Barnewall, Sir Reginald Aylmer John de Barneval Bart Ireland, 23, Cliveden Place Eaton Square S W, from a plume of five ostrich-feathers or, gu, az vert, and arg, a falcon rising of the last *Malo mori quam fœdari*

Barnewell, Baron Trimlestown, Ireland, same crest and motto

Barnewall or Barnawelle of Stamford, Lincs, a boar's head erased arg,

34077

gorged with a collar embattled gu., charged with three bezants, in front a double ring or.

Barnewell of Cransley, Northamp., a wolf's head erased arg., gorged with collar raguly gu., charged with three bezants, in front a double ring or.

Barnewell, Ireland, an arm from the elbow erect, vested, holding in the hand two branches of laurel in orle, with martlet perched between and on the hand. 205. 6

Barney or **Berney**, Norf., a garb or. 153. 2

Barney, a hand in armour holding a pheon in pale ppr. 211. 7

Barney, Park Hall, Norf., a plume of seven feathers alternately az. and gu., four at the bottom and three at the top.

Barnfield, Shropsh. and Devonsh., a lion's head erased sa., ducally crowned gu. *cf.* 18. 8

Barnham, a crescent gu., between two branches of laurel in orle ppr. *cf.* 163. 10

Barnham, Bart. (*extinct*), Kent, a dragon's head arg., pellettée, between four dragon's wings sa., bezantée.

Barns-Graham, *see* Graham.

Barns, a garb or. *Peace and plenty.* 153. 2

Barns of Glasgow, a garb ppr., banded gu. *Peace and plenty.* 153. 2

Barns, Stephenson-, Colonel James, C.B., of Kirkhill: (1) A garb ppr., banded gu. (*for Barns*). 153. 2. (2) A dexter hand issuing out of a cloud, holding a laurel garland, all ppr. (*for Stephenson*), 218. 9; and for a crest of augmentation, a dexter arm in armour, issuing from a broken battlement, the hand holding a banner inscribed "*St. Sebastian.*" *Peace and plenty.—Cœlum non solum.*

Barns, a pellet. *cf.* 159. 14

Barnsdale, issuant from rays of the sun or, an eagle's head and neck arg., beaked gu.

Barnsley, a dragon passant arg., charged on the breast with a rose gu. *cf.* 73. 2

Barnsley, Shropsh., a man's head couped at the shoulders and affrontée ppr. *cf.* 190. 5

Barnwell of Mileham Hall, and Beeston, Norf., a wolf's head erased arg., gorged with a collar raguly gu., charged with three bezants. *Loyal au mort.* *cf.* 30. 11

Barnwell, Turnor-, of Bury St. Edmunds: (1) A wolf's head erased arg., gorged with a collar embattled and counter-embattled gu., charged with three bezants and chained or (*for Barnwell*). *cf.* 30. 11. (2) On a mount vert, a lion passant gardant arg., holding in his dexter paw a fer-de-moulin sa., and charged on the side with a fret gu. (*for Turnor*). *Malo mori quam fœdari.* *cf.* 6. 7

Barnwell, a wolf statant regardant ppr. *cf.* 28. 12

Barnwell, on a mount vert, a wolf statant regardant ppr. *cf.* 28. 12

Baron of Bradwell, Essex, a garb vert, eared or. 153. 2

Baron (alias Barnes of London), out of clouds ppr., issuing rays paleways or, an arm erect, habited of the last, holding in the hand ppr. a broken sword arg., hilted of the second.

Baron of Heywood, Lancs, a cubit arm in armour, the hand in a gauntlet grasping a tilting-spear erect ppr., suspended therefrom by a chain or, an escutcheon gu., charged with a mullet pierced, also or. 209. 12

Baron of Preston, Scotland, a demi-eagle displayed sa. *Alter ipse amicus.* 81. 6

Baron, Cornw., a talbot's head couped or. 56. 12

Baron or **Barron**, Scotland, on a mount vert, a pyramid ppr., environed with ivy. 179. 12

Baronsdale of London, out of an antique crown or, a stork's head arg., beaked gu.

Barough or **Barrow**, a lion passant az., resting his dexter paw on a ball or. *cf.* 6. 2

Barr, a branch of laurel fructed ppr. 151. 11

Barr, a lion's head erased gu., collared or. *Fortitudine.* 18. 6

Barr, an arm couped at the shoulder vested gu., embowed and lying fess-ways, the elbow resting upon the wreath, the hand towards the sinister holding a bow ppr. 204. 11

Barr, a demi-savage, the head and loins wreathed with leaves, all ppr. *cf.* 185. 2

Barran, Sir John, Bart., Chapel Allerton Hall, near Leeds, in front of a tower gu., charged with three mascles intertwined palewise, a lion's gamb fesse-wise erased or. *Amor patriæ.* 234. 12

Barrat or **Barratt**, a galley, her oars in saltier sa., the flags gu. 160. 10

Barratt and **Barrett**, a wyvern ppr., collared gu., chained or. *cf.* 70. 1

Barre or **Barrey**, an arm in armour, couped at the elbow in fesse, holding in the hand a sword in pale, ensigned with a Saracen's head affrontée. *cf.* 211. 11

Barreau, Jersey, a dexter hand in armour ppr., holding a passion-cross arg. *In hoc signo vinces.*

Barrel or **Barrell**, Heref., a talbot's head couped arg., eared gu. 56. 12

Barrentine, *see* Barentine.

Barret, a demi-unicorn arg., collared sa. 48. 10

Barrett-Lennard, *see* Lennard.

Barrett, a human heart or, between two wings az. *cf.* 110. 14

Barrett-Hamilton, Samuel, Esquire, J.P., of Kilmannock, co. Wexford, Ireland: (1) In front of two battle-axes in saltire an oak-tree fructed, all ppr., the trunk transfixed with a frame-saw or (*for Hamilton*). (2) A human heart gu., between two wings conjoined and expanded az., bezantée (*for Barrett*). Over the second crest, *Vivit post funera virtus.* Under the arms "*Through.*"

Barrett of Castle Barrett, Cork, a human heart or, between two wings conjoined sa., semée of étoiles or. *In uprightness God will support us.*

Barrett of Barrett's Country, co. Cork, a demi-lion rampant sa., ducally crowned per pale arg. and gu. 10. 11

Barrett, Heref., a lion rampant or, holding between his paws an escallop sa. *cf.* 1. 13

Barrett of Lea Priory, Kent, a lion couchant arg., the dexter paw resting on a mullet sa. *cf.* 7. 5

Barrett, Charles William Sessions, M.B., Argent Mead, Hinchley, Leics., a demi-unicorn arg., collared sa. *Frangas non flectes.*

Barrett of Aveley, Essex, a hydra with seven heads, the wings addorsed vert, scaled or. 73. 3

Barrett, Cambs, a griffin segreant regardant or, beaked, armed, and winged gu. *cf.* 62. 2

Barrett, Warw., a griffin segreant regardant gu., the wings elevated or. *cf.* 62. 2

Barrett, Louis Arthur, of Milton House, Berks, a wyvern, the wings erect or, collared and chained az. *Honor, virtus, probitas.*

Barrett of Attleborough, Norf., a wyvern erm., collared and chained sa., charged on the neck with an escallop of the last, the wings displayed.

Barrett of Shortney, Notts, a nag's head erased per pale gu. and az., gorged with two bars arg. *cf.* 51. 4

Barrett, Suff., a demi-greyhound arg., collared and lined sa. *cf.* 60. 8

Barrett, Suff., a helmet arg., garnished and plumed with feathers or. 180. 4

Barrett, on a globe a hawk, the wings expanded, all ppr. 159. 7

Barretto of London and Calcutta, out of a count's coronet a demi-tiger ppr., collared with three barrulets, and holding a star pagoda or.

Barrey, *see* Barre.

Barrie, Scotland, a demi-otter sa. 134. 11

Barriff, Northamp., on a mount vert, a beaver passant ppr., gorged with a plain collar and ring or. *cf.* 134. 4

Barriffe, *see* Beriffe.

Barrington of Barrington Hall, Essex, a Capuchin friar affrontée ppr., couped below the shoulders, vested paly arg. and gu., on the head a cap or. *Tout ung durant ma vie.* 192. 3

Barrington, Sir Vincent Hunter Barrington Kennett, 57, Albert Hall Mansions, S.W.: (1) A hermit's head in profile couped below the shoulders ppr., vested paly of six gu. and or, the cowl thrown back (*Barrington*). (2) Between two branches of palm a dexter arm embowed in armour ppr., garnished or, charged with an estoile gu., holding in the hand a helmet ppr. (1) *Ung durant ma vie.* (2) *Audi alteram partem.*

Barrington, Rt. Hon. John, Lord Mayor of Dublin, 1864, of Glenvar, co. Dublin, Ireland, on a wreath of the colours a mural crown ppr., out of which a hermit's bust in profile, vested paly arg. and gu., and having on the head a cowl, also paly arg. and gu. *Honesta quam splendida.*

Barrington, Viscount (Barrington), a Capuchin friar couped at the breast in profile, the hair sa., vested paly of six arg. and gu., on the head a cap or, the cowl hanging behind paly as the last. *Honesta quam splendida.*

Barrington, Nicholas William, M D, 97, St George's Road, Warwick Square, S W, same crest and motto

Barrington, Charles George, Esquire, of 13, Morpeth Mansions, Victoria Street, London, a Capuchin's bust in profile vested, with a cowl paly of six arg and gu *Honesta quam splendida* 251 1

Barrington, Edward, Esquire, of Cam panella, Killiney, co Dublin, crest as above, but issuing from a mural crown *Honesta quam splendida*

Barrington, Jonathan Pim, Esquire, of 70, Adelaide Road, Dublin same crest and motto

Barrington-White, James, Esquire, of Roxley Court, Hitchen, Herts, a crown vallary or, charged on the band with three pommes, issuing therefrom a demi-hermit, with the dexter arm elevated, vested paly gu and arg, the hand ppr grasping three roses gu on one stem slipped, barbed, and seeded ppr, on the head a cowl, also paly gu and arg *Ung durant ma vie* 233 4

Barrington, Sir Charles Burton, Bart, Ireland, out of a crown vallary or, a hermit's bust, vested paly of six arg and gu, a cowl of the last. *Ung durant ma vie* 190 9

Barritt of Jamaica, a talbot's head per fesse arg and erm, collared or, eared sa *cf* 56 1

Barron, Norf, a garb ppr 153 2

Barron, an eagle regardant, wings expanded, holding in the dexter claw a sword, all ppr 77 10

Barron, Edward Jackson, F S A, 10, Endsleigh Street, Tavistock Square, W C, same crest. *Vigilans*

Barron of Belmont House, Kilkenny, Ireland, a boar passant az *Fortuna juvat audaces* 40 2

Barron, Clarke Charles Netterville, of Hobons Street, Wellington, New Zealand, same crest and motto

Barron, Sir Henry Page Turner, Bart, C M G, of Glenanna and Barron Court, co Waterford (1) A boar passant az, armed and crined or, langued gu, charged with a cross pattee of the second *cf* 40 2 (2) A demi-lion rampant arg, langued gu *Audaces fortuna juvat*

Barrow, Sir Francis Laurence John, Bart, on a mount vert, a squirrel sejant cracking a nut, all ppr, charged on the shoulder with an anchor *Parum sufficit*

Barrow, Northamp, a demi-boar rampant or, charged with three billets between two bendlets sa *cf* 40 13

Barrow of Winthorpe, Norf, a stag's head couped arg 121 5

Barrow, Suff, a hind's head arg 124 1

Barrow, a horse's head ppr, charged with three bezants *cf* 51 4

Barrow, the late John, Esquire, Meathrop Hall, Westml (present representative, Mrs Williams, Holme Island, Grange-over-Sands), a squirrel cracking a nut, all ppr *Confido in Deo* 135 7

Barrow, Sir John Croker, Bart, Lancs, on a mount vert, a squirrel sejant cracking a nut, all ppr, charged on the shoulder with an anchor *Parum sufficit* 245 6

Barrow, John James, of Holmewood, Kent, on a perch ppr, a squirrel sejant or, collared and chained az, cracking a nut ppr *Non frustra*

Barrow, Bridgman Langdale, Esquire, of Sydnope Hall, near Matlock, same crest and motto

Barrow, John Burton, Esquire, of Ringwood Hall, Chesterfield, co Derbysh, same crest and motto

Barrow, George Martin, Esquire, of St John's Green, Essex, upon a mount vert, a squirrel sejant ppr, gorged with a collar gemel or, holding a rose arg, barbed, leaved, and slipped of the first

Barrow, Shropsh, a squirrel sejant gu, charged with a chevron or, cracking a nut ppr *cf* 135 7

Barrow of Southwell, Lincs, and Ringwood Hall, Derbysh, on a perch ppr, a squirrel sejant or, collared and chained, cracking a nut, all ppr *Non frustra*

Barrow, Cambs, an ostrich-head erased arg, holding in the beak a key or

Barrow, Glouc, an Amazonian woman ppr

Barrow, Lansdowne Grove, Bath, a demi bear sa, semee de-lis arg, muzzled or, holding in the dexter paw an arrow, point downwards ppr

Barrow, Alfred, Esquire, of London, issuant out of clouds a dexter arm embowed in armour ppr, garnished or, the hand also ppr, holding a bugle-horn sa, stringed vert, above the hand a fleur-de-lis of the second

Barrow, Ireland, on a mural coronet or, a dove holding in its beak an olive-branch ppr *cf* 92 5

Barrowcourt, Somers, out of a wreath of laurel vert, a demi-bull rampant or *cf* 45 12

Barrowe, a demi-lion rampant arg, holding in the dexter paw a cross crosslet fitched sa 11 10

Barrowman, Scotland, a demi-huntsman firing a gun, all ppr 187 2

Barrs, Staffs, upon a mount vert, in front of a gate or, the trunk of an oak tree eradicated and sprouting towards the dexter ppr

Barrs-Haden, of High Court, Staffs (1) In front of a cubit arm in armour, the hand grasping an arrow in bend sinister, a morion, all ppr (*for Haden*) (2) Upon a mount vert, in front of a gate or, the trunk of an oak-tree eradicated and sprouting towards the dexter ppr (*for Barrs*) *Disce pati*

Barry, Rt Hon Charles Robert, of 3, Fitzwilliam Square, East Dublin, a castle arg, and issuing from the battlements a wolf's head gu *Boutez en avant* *cf* 254 6

Barry of Ballyclough, Ireland same crest *Boutez en avant*

Barry, Bart, Ireland, same crest and motto

Barry, Standish-, Henry Arthur Bruno Robert of Lemlara, Carrigtwohill, Cork same crest and motto

Barry, Sir Francis Tress, Bart, 1, South Audley Street, W, issuant from a castle with two towers arg, a wolf's head sa, holding in the mouth a trefoil slipped vert, between four roses, two on either side gu, stalked and leaved ppr *Boutez en avant* 234 8

Barry, James Grene, Esquire J P D L, of Sandville House, Ballyneety, co Limerick, out of a castle arg, charged with a crescent az, a wolf's head sa *Boutez en avant*

Barry, Devonsh, a wolf's head sa, charged with a crescent or *cf* 30 5

Barry of Winscot, Devonsh, a wolf's head erased sa 30 8

Barry of Dublin, a wolf's head couped sa 30 5

Barry, Ireland, on a ducal coronet or, a wolf's head erased gu, collared of the first *Regi legi fidelis* *cf* 30 11

Barry, a lion's head erased gu, collared or *Fortitudine* 18 6

Barry of Stanley House, London Road, Forest Hill, S E, a gryphon gu, wings elevated and addorsed barry of six or and az, in its beak a rose arg leaved and slipped ppr, resting the dexter claw on a portcullis with chains sa *Boutez en avant*

Barry, a griffin's head erased per bend sinister vair and arg, gorged with a plain collar gu, charged with two mullets or

Barry of Roclaveston, Notts, the embattlement of a tower on a bar fessewise gu, charged with three roses in fess arg *A rege et victoria*

Barry, Otter-, of Emperor's Gate, London (1) The embattlements of a tower gu, charged with three roses in fesse arg (*for Barry*) (2) Two crosses pattee, and resting thereon a crescent, all or (*for Otter*) 163 8

Barry, *see* Bury-Barry

Barrymore, Earl, extinct, out of a castle with two towers arg, a wolf's head sa *cf* 254 6

Barrymore, Baron (Smith Barry, P C), a castle arg, issuant from the battlements thereof a wolf's head sa, charged with a cross pattée fitchee or *Boutez en avant* 254 6

Barsane or **Bartane,** a raven rising ppr *His securitas* 107 3

Barsham, Norf, a garb lying in fess 153 6

Barstow, John Jeremiah Jackson, of The Lodge, Weston super Mare, and Rossmoor, Yorks (1) In front of a horse's head arg, collared gemel sa, an increscent and a decrescent of the last 270 9 (2) In front of two trees ppr, a jackdaw standing on a demi-Catherine-wheel, both sa *Nil desperandum auspice Deo* 270 10

Bartan, Bartane, or **Bartam,** Scotland, a tent az, the flag gu 158 7

Bartane, *see* Barsane

Bartelot, Rev Richard Grosvenor, Church House, Salisbury, a demi eagle or, wings elevated az, pendent from the beak an escutcheon arg, charged with a cross patee fitchee gu *Sapiens incipit a fine*

Bartelott, a peacock arg 103 7

Bartelott, Smyth-, Sussex, a swan couchant arg, the wings expanded

Barthelet of London, out of a ducal coronet arg, two serpents endorsed az, scaled or, their tails coming up in saltire under their throats, the ends entering into their ears, langued and armed gu.

Bartholomew, *see* Bartolomew.

Bartholomew, E. Urquhart, Lieutenant, of Cransbrook, Lansdowne Road, Aldershot, a demi-goat rampant arg., gorged with a wreath of laurel vert. *I conquer by the wound.* 302. 10

Bartholomew of Glasgow, a demi-goat saliant sa., gorged with a wreath of laurel ppr. *Ad alta.* 302. 10

Bartlet, Rev. John Moysey de Ludbroke, of Ludbroke Manor, Devonsh., in front of a demi-swan, wings elevated arg., semée of crescents, and gorged with a collar indented gu., five roses fessewise of the last, barbed and seeded ppr. *Mature.*

Bartlett of Weston in Branscombe, Devonsh., a demi-griffin sa., collared gemel arg., holding a cinquefoil of the second.

Bartlett, Sir Ellis Ashmead, M.P., in front of a tower ppr., a demi-swan, wings elevated arg., collared sa. *Mature.* 100. 1

Bartlett-Burdett-Coutts, William Lehman Ashmead, Esquire, Holly Lodge, Highgate: (1) A man from the middle shooting an arrow from a bow, all ppr., charged for distinction with a cross crosslet or (*for Coutts*). 247. 11. (2) A lion's head erased sa., charged for distinction with a cross crosslet or (*for Burdett*). 247. 10. (3) In front of a tower ppr., a demi-swan, wings elevated arg., collared sa. (*for Bartlett*). 247. 12

Bartlett, a demi-eagle or, wings elevated az., pendent from the beak an escutcheon arg., charged with a cross pattée fitchée gu. *Sapiens incipit a fine.*

Bartlett, Rev. Robert Leach, of Thurloxton Rectory, Taunton, and Swanage, Dorset, same crest and motto.

Bartlett, Charles Leftwich Oldfield, Esquire, of Burton House, Sherborne, Dorset, same crest and motto.

Bartlett, late John Adams, Esquire, of Lytnon, Mossley Hill Road, Liverpool, on a mount vert, a moorcock sa., combed and wattled gu., holding in the beak an ear of wheat leaved and slipped ppr., resting the dexter claw on a crescent gu. *Deo favente cresco.* 89. 2

Bartlett, Thomas, Esquire, of 12, Pembroke Place, Liverpool, same crest and motto.

Bartlett, William, Esquire, of Highfield House, Knotty Ash, Liverpool, same crest and motto.

Bartlett, William, Esquire, of 12, Pembroke Place, Liverpool, same crest and motto.

Bartley of London, a lion passant, tail extended ppr. *Candide et secure.* 5. 11

Bartolomew or Bartholomew of Rochester, a demi-goat arg., gorged with a chaplet of laurel vert. *cf.* 129. 10

Bartolozzi, on a mount a poplar-tree, all ppr. *Labore et prudentia.* 144. 12

Barton, Scotland, *see* Bartan.

Barton, a wolf's head erased erm. 30. 8

Barton, a wolf's head erased or. 30. 8

Barton of Barton, Lancs, a boar's head couped gu. 43. 1

Barton, John, Esquire, J.P., Trentham, Wellington, New Zealand, same crest. *Nisi Dominus frustra.*

Barton, Baptist Johnstone, Esquire, J.P., of Greenfort, Letterkenny, co. Donegal, a boar's head gu. *Vis fortibus arma.*

Barton, Nathaniel, Esquire, J.P., of Straffan House, co. Kildare, Ireland, a boar's head erased ppr. *Fide et fortitudine.* 42. 2

Barton, Dunbar Plunkett, Esquire, of 13, Clare Street, Dublin, same crest and motto.

Barton, William Henry Hugh, Esquire, of Hereford Villa, Bronsford Road, Worcs., same crest and motto.

Barton of Grove, co. Tipperary, Ireland, a boar's head gu. *Quod ero spero.* 43. 1

Barton of Clonelly, co. Fermanagh, Ireland, same crest and motto.

Barton of Rochestown, Cahir, same crest and motto.

Barton of Glendalough, co. Wicklow, Ireland, same crest. *Fide et fortitudine.*

Barton, Ireland, a boar's head erased ppr. *Fide et fortitudine.* 42. 2

Barton, a dragon's head couped and crowned or.

Barton, Norf., a dragon's head couped or. 71. 1

Barton of Threxton House, Norf., a griffin's head erased ppr. *Fortis est veritas.* 66. 2

Barton of Edinburgh, a raven rising sa. *His securitas.* 107. 3

Barton, Charles Steventon, 1, Calverley Park, Tunbridge Wells, Kent, an owl ppr. *Fortis et veritas.* 96. 5

Barton, an owl arg., ducally gorged or. *cf.* 96. 5

Barton, Everard William, of Warstone House, Bewdley, on a mount vert, an owl arg., between two acorns slipped and leaved ppr. *I byde my time.* 253. 1

Barton, Charles Tom, Esquire, of the Hill, Wolverley, Worcs., same crest and motto.

Barton, Lancs, an acorn or, leaved vert. 152. 1

Barton, James Herbert Cooper, M.A., Solicitor, Cleveland House, Belle Vue, Shrewsbury, an acorn leaved and slipped ppr.

Barton of Stapleton Park, an acorn ppr., fructed or, with a leaf on either side. *Crescitur cultu.*

Barton, Yorks, issuant from a mount vert an acorn ppr., fructed or, with a leaf on either side vert, each charged with a martlet, also or. *Crescitur cultu.* 152. 1

Barton of Smithills, Manchester, an acorn or, leaved vert. 152. 1

Bartram, Cumb., an arm embowed, holding in the hand a scimitar, all ppr. 201. 1

Barttelot, Sir Walter, Bart., of Stopham House, Sussex: (1) A swan couchant arg., wings expanded and addorsed. 247. 1. (2) A castle with three turrets sa. *Mature.* *cf.* 155. 8

Barttelot, Brian Barttelot, Esquire, of Ditton, Torquay, Devonsh., a swan couchant with wings endorsed arg. *Mature.* 247. 1

Barwell, a talbot passant. 54. ?

Barwell, a demi-wolf salient erm. 32. 2

Barwell, a demi-lady holding in her dexter hand a garland of laurel ppr. 183. 5

Barwell of Norwich, an antelope's head erased arg., attired or. 126. 2

Barwell of Witham, a greyhound's head erased arg., collared or. *cf.* 61. 2

Barwick, Northumb., on a mount vert a stag or, attired sa. 117. 1

Barwicke, Essex, an escarbuncle, the centre az. and the rays arg. 164. 12

Barwis of Langrigg, Cumb., and Yorks, a bear muzzled. *Bear and forbear.* *cf.* 34. 1

Barwis of Iselekirk, Cumb., a hand cutting an ostrich-feather with a scimitar in saltire. *cf.* 213. 7

Barwise, William, M.D., Scarisbrick Road, Southport, a bear statant ppr., muzzled and chained. *Sustine et abstine.*

Bary, *see* De Bary.

Barzey of Shrewsbury, a squirrel sejant ppr., cracking a nut or. 135. 7

Basceilly, a torteau charged with a pale indented or. 159. 6

Basevi of Hove, Sussex, a buck's head erased ppr. 121. 2

Bashe, Herts and Heref., a griffin segreant per pale arg. and sa., gorged with a plain collar counterchanged, holding in the beak a broken spear. *cf.* 62. 2

Basier or **Basire**, a hand ppr., holding a buckle or. 223. 11

Basing, Baron (Sclater-Booth), out of a ducal coronet or, a demi-eagle displayed sa., holding in the beak a crescent of the first. Εἰ μὴ ἐν τῷ σταυρῷ.

Baskcomb of Chiselhurst, Kent, a talbot's head couped gu., charged on the neck with a cinquefoil erm. *Forti et fideli nihil difficile.* *cf.* 56. 12

Baskenford, a sword and an ear of wheat bladed in saltier, all ppr. *Armis et diligentia.* 154. 11

Baskerville, John, Esquire, of Crowsley Park, Henley-on-Thames, Oxford, a wolf's head erased or, pierced through the mouth by a broken spear in bend sinister point upwards arg., imbrued gu., and staff broken gold. *Spero ut fidelis.*

Baskerville, Mynors-, Ralph Hopton, Esquire, of Clyro Court, near Hay, same crest and motto.

Baskervile and **Baskerville**, Heref. and Warw., a lion's head pierced through the mouth with a spear.

Baskerville, Heref. and Warw., a wolf's head erased arg., holding in the mouth an arrow, the point downwards.

Baskerville, Wilts, a wolf's head erased or, in the mouth a broken spear of the same, headed arg., embrued gu.

Baskerville, a wolf's head erased arg., holding in the mouth a standard, thereon a flag.

Baskerville, Chesh., a forester vested vert, edgings or, holding over his dexter shoulder a crossbow of the last, in the other hand in a leash a hound passant arg.

Baskerville, a sheaf of rosemary ppr.

Baskervill-Glegg, *see* Glegg.

Basket or **Baskett,** of Isle of Wight and Dorset, a demi-lion or 10 2

Baskin of Ord, Scotland, a sword and a stalk of wheat in saltier, all ppr *Armis et diligentia* 154 11

Basnet, on a mount covered with long grass, an oak-tree, all ppr 143 14

Basnett, formerly of the Cloughs, Newcastle-under-Lyne an arm in armour embowed, holding in the hand a cutlass, all ppr cf 196 10

Baspoole of Beston, Norf, out of a ducal coronet or, a stag's head erm, attired of the first, wreathed about the neck arg and sa, and tied behind with two bows cf 120 7

Basquer of Isle of Wight, Hants, out of a mural coronet gu, a griffin's head or 67 10

Bass, out of a ducal coronet, two wings, all ppr 109 8

Bass, of Curzon Street, Mayfair, London, W, out of a mural crown gu, masoned arg, a demi-greyhound issuant, holding in the mouth a rose with two leaves, all ppr

Bass, Baron Burton, *see* Burton

Bass, Staffs, a demi lion gu, resting the sinister paw on a plate charged with a fleur-de lis az, on the shoulder three annulets, two and one, arg *Basis virtutum constantia* 13 11

Bassano, a silkworm moth ppr

Bassano, Alfred Hill, Esquire, of Heydon holme Old Hill, same crest. *Gratia nos dirige*

Bassano, Walter, Esquire of Heydon Cross, Old Hill, same crest and motto

Basse, a demi-lion gu, resting his sinister paw on an oval shield in cartouch or, charged with a fleur de-lis az

Basset, Arthur Francis of Tehidy, Cornw, a unicorn's head couped arg, horned, maned, and tufted or *Pro Rege et populo*

Basset, a unicorn's head couped arg, armed and maned or charged with two bars dancettee gu *Pro rege et populo* cf 49 9

Basset, Charles Henry, Esquire, of Pilton House, Barnstaple, and of Umberleigh, Devonsh, a unicorn's head couped arg, armed and crined or, charged on the neck with two bars indented gu, and for distinction with a cross crosslet of the same *Pro rege et populo* 49 9

Basset, of Watermouth, Ilfracombe, and Umberleigh, Essex (1) A unicorn's head couped arg, armed and crined or, charged on the neck with two bars, indented gu (*for Basset*) cf 49 9 (2) On a mount vert, a lamb passant arg, in the mouth a sprig of cinquefoil gu, slipped also vert (*for Davie*) cf 131 9

Basset and Bassett, a griffin segreant sa, semee-de-lis or, collared and chained of the last cf 62 2

Basset and Bassett, Glouc, a falcon with wings displayed arg cf 87 12

Basset, William Richard Basset, of Beaupre, Cowbridge, Glamorgansh, a stag's head cabossed and between the attires a cross fitchee arg *Gwell angau na chywilydd* cf 122 5

Bassett, Lord Bassett of Drayton, out of a ducal coronet or, a boar's head az, tusked of the first 41 4

Bassett, George Forbes, M A, Basset Mount, Basset, Southampton, a stag's head caboshed, and between the attires a cross pattee fitchee arg *Gwell angau na chywilydd*

Bassett, Ralph Thurston Esquire, of Crossways Cowbridge, Glamorgansh same crest and motto

Bassett, Alfred Barnard, of Fledborough Hall, Holyport, Berks, a boar's head erased or, gorged with a riband gu, suspending an escutcheon of the last charged with a bugle horn of the first *In arduis fortitudo* 250 14

Bassett or **Basset** of Langley, Derbysh, out of a ducal coronet or, a boar's head gu 41 4

Bassett of Womberly, Devonsh, a unicorn's head arg, charged with two bars dancettee gu *Pro rege et populo.* cf 49 9

Bassingborne, out of a ducal coronet or, a bull's head gu, ducally crowned of the first cf 44 11

Bassinges, three roses gu, stalked and leaved vert, issuing from the wreath 149 12

Bastable, a griffin's head couped gu, between two wings erect or *Regardez mort* 65 11

Bastard of Ashngton, Norf, an elephant's head, per chevron or and sa, eared of the last 133 2

Bastard, an arm in armour embowed, grasping a dagger ppr 195 4

Bastard, Baldwin John Pollexfen, of Kitley and Buckland Court, Devonsh, a dexter arm in armour embowed ppr, garnished or, the hand gauntleted grasping a sword in bend sinister, point downward, also ppr, hilt and pommel of the second *Pax potior bello* cf 195 6

Bastard, William Edmund Pollexfen, Esquire, of Lynham, Yealmpton, Devonsh, same crest and motto

Bastard, Rev William Pollexfen, of Cofflete, Torquay, same crest and motto

Basto, a horse's head couped arg cf 50 13

Batchelor or **Batchellor,** a leg erased above the knee ppr 193 10

Bate, Thomas, Esquire, of Kelsterton, Flint, North Wales, in front of a stag's head couped arg, attired or, pierced in the neck by an arrow in bend, point downwards ppr, a hand couped at the wrist fessewise, also or *Live to live* 237 2

Bate, Yorks, a stag's head arg, attired or, vulned through the neck with an arrow of the second, feathered and headed of the first

Bate, a bull's head couped erm, armed or cf 44 3

Bate, Derbysh, a cross pattee 165 7

Bate of Ashby-de-la-Zouch, Leics, a dexter hand apaumee *Dieu et ma main droite* 222 14

Bateman, Baron (Bateman-Hanbury), *see* Hanbury

Bateman, *see* Jones Bateman

Bateman, Sir Frederick of Upper St. Giles, Norwich, a crescent *Principiis obsta*

Bateman of Hartington Hall and Breadsall Mount, Derbysh, out of a crescent or, an etoile gu, between two eagles' wings of the first. *Sidus adsit amicum* 112 8

Bateman, Sir Alfred Edmund, K C M G, of Woodhouse, Wimbledon Park, same crest and motto

Bateman, Frederick Osborne Fitzherbert, Esquire, of Hartington Hall and Bread sall Mount, Derbysh, same crest and motto

Bateman, Hugh Alleyne Sacheverell, Esquire, of Etwall, Derbysh, same crest *Virtus ad sidera*

Bateman, Hugh Osborne, Esquire, same crest *Sidus adsit amicum*

Bateman, Rev John Fitzherbert, of 119, Fordwych Road, West Hampstead, N W, same crest and motto

Bateman of Middleton, Derbysh, same crest

Bateman, an increscent arg, between two wings, the dexter arg, the sinister gu

Bateman, Derbysh, out of a crescent or, an etoile gu 163 4

Bateman, a Muscovy duck's head couped, between two wings erect, expanded, all ppr *Nec prece, nec pretio*

Bateman of Whitechapel, Middx, out of a mural coronet arg, an eagle rising with a garland in its beak ppr

Bateman of Knypersley, Staffs, and Tolson Hall, Westml, a tower arg, issuant therefrom a demi eagle, wings elevated sa, charged on the breast with the chemical character of Mars or, and holding in the beak a wreath of oak ppr

Bateman, John, Esquire, of Moveron's Manor and Brightlingsea, Essex, same crest

Bateman, Robert, Esquire, of Benthall Hall Broseley, Shropsh, same crest

Bateman, Rev Rowland, M A, of Narowal, Punjab, India, same crest

Bateman, La Trobe-, Rev William Fairbairn, Ascot Rectory (1) In front of an eagle's head or, a crescent surmounted by a mullet gu, between two wings, also or, each charged with an escallop az (*for Bateman*) 252 14 (2) Out of clouds a dexter cubit arm ppr, the hand grasping an anchor fesseways or (*for La Trobe*) *Tutto si fa —Sidus adsit amicum*

Bateman of Oak Park, Kerry, a pheasant ppr *Nec prece, nec pretio* cf 90 8

Bateman of Bartholey, Monm, same crest and motto

Bates, Sir Edward Bertram, Bart., J P, a stag's head erased az, attired or, charged on the neck with two quatrefoils in pale, and pierced by as many arrows in saltire or *Labore et virtute* 120 6

Bates, a lion's head erased gu 17 2

Bates, Yorks, a demi lion rampant, holding in the dexter paw a thistle and in the sinister a fleur de lis, all ppr 13 12

Bates, late Cadwallader John of Langley Castle, Northumb, in front of a swan's head couped arg, the neck charged with six barrulets az, five fleurs-de lis, alternately or and gu *Virtutis comes invidia* 241 4

Bates, a dexter hand apaumee couped ppr *Cor et manus concordant* 222 14

Bates of Walsingham, Durham, an arm in armour embowed, the hand grasping a sword, the point to the dexter, all ppr. *Ernst und treu.* 195. 4

Bates of Milbourne Hall, Northumb., a naked man holding in his dexter hand a willow-wand ppr. *Et mano et corde.*

Bates, William R., Esquire, of Liverpool, on a mount vert, a savage wreathed about the waist with oak, and holding in the dexter hand three arrows conjoined, two in saltire and one in pale, points upwards, all ppr.

Bates of Denton, Sussex, an arm in armour embowed, holding a truncheon. *Manu et corde.*

Bates, Henry Stratton, Esquire, J.P., same crest and motto.

Bateson, Bart., **Baron Deramore,** *see* Deramore.

Bateson, Antrim, Ireland, a bat's wing sa. *Probitas verus honos.* 137. 10

Bath, Marquess of (Thynne), a reindeer statant or, collared sa. *J'ai bonne cause.* cf. 125. 9

Bath, a wolf's head sa., holding in the mouth a rose slipped ppr. 29. 7

Bath, Edward Henry, of Alltyferin, Carmarthensh., D.L. and J.P. for that co., High Sheriff 1892, a wolf's head erased sa., gorged with a collar vair, holding in the mouth a rose gu., slipped and leaved ppr. *He conquers who endures.* 295. 11

Bath, Ireland, a lion rampant arg., supporting in the paws a sword of the first pommel and hilt or.

Bather, a falcon close ppr., belled or. *Ut vivas vigila.* 85. 2

Batherne, of Penhow, Monm., out of rushes a demi-swan rising ppr.

Bathgate, Scotland, a bee volant ppr. *Vive ut vivas.* 137. 2

Bathurst, Bart., of Leachlade, Glouc. (*extinct*), on a mount vert, a bay horse statant. cf. 52. 5

Bathurst, Charles, Lydney Park, Glouc., a dexter arm in armour embowed, holding in the hand, all ppr., club with spikes or. *Tien ta foy.* 231. 2

Bathurst, Ven. Frederick, Archdeacon of Bedford, of Holwell Rectory, Hitchin, same crest and motto.

Bathurst, *see* Harvey-Bathurst.

Bathurst, Earl (Bathurst), a dexter arm in mail embowed, holding in the hand, all ppr., a spiked club or. *Tien ta foy.* 231. 2

Bathurst, Hervey-, Sir Frederick Edward William, Bart.: (1) A dexter arm in mail embowed, holding in the hand ppr. a club spiked or (*for Bathurst*). 231. 2. (2) A leopard sa., bezantée, collared and lined or, holding in the dexter paw a trefoil slipped vert (*for Hervey*). *Tien ta foy.—Je n'oublieray jamais.* 254. 12

Bathurst, Isle of Wight, a dexter arm in mail-armour, embowed ppr., charged with an annulet or, and holding in the hand, also ppr., a club with spikes or. cf. 199. 2

Bathurst, a tiger holding in the dexter paw a fleur-de-lis ppr.

Batley, Yorks, a demi-lion rampant gu., holding between the paws a bezant. 11. 7

Batley, Battley, Battaley, or **Batteley,** a castle double-towered, weeds growing round the sinister tower ppr. cf. 155. 6

Batnymersh, a dexter arm in armour, holding in the hand ppr. a baton sa., tipped arg.

Batt, Esquire, J.P., D.L., of Purdysburn, co. Down, and Ozier Hill, co. Wexford, Ireland, a crescent arg., charged with an escallop gu. *Virtute et valore.* cf. 163. 2

Batt, Thomas Edmond, Esquire, of Rathmullan House, co. Donegal, a crescent arg., charged with an escallop gu. *Virtute et valore.*

Batt, Hackney, a wolf passant ppr. 28. 10

Batt, *see* Baett.

Batt, Middx., a demi-lion or, guttée-de-sang, holding between the paws a marshal's staff in pale or, tipped sa. cf. 15. 9

Batt, Berks and Yorks, a demi-lion guttee-de-sang, holding between the paws a mill-rind sa., banded or. *Dominus a dextris.*

Battayll or **Battaille,** out of an antique crown or, a dexter cubit arm ppr., holding a cross crosslet fitched in pale gu.

Batten, Chisholm-, James Forbes Chisholm, Esquire, of Thornfalcon, near Taunton, and Kirkhill, R.S.O., Invernesshire, in front of the stump of an oak-tree, sprouting on either side ppr., three roses arg., barbed and seeded, also ppr. (*for Batten*). 233. 10. (2) A dexter hand holding a dagger erect ppr., on the point a boar's head erased or. *Feros ferio* (*for Chisholm*).

Batten, a hand couped in fess, charged with an eye. 221. 4

Batten of Yeovil, Somers.: (1) The trunk of an oak-tree couped at the top, issuing from towards the top two branches, all ppr. (2) A sea-lion erect, holding in the paws an anchor, all ppr. cf. 20. 3

Batten, George B., M.D., 2, Underhill Road, Lordship Lane, Dulwich, S.E., a dexter cubit arm issuing in bend grasping a battle-axe in bend sinister.

Batten, Henry Butler, Esquire, of Aldon, Yeovil, Somers., in front of the stump of an oak-tree, sprouting on either side ppr., three roses arg., barbed and seeded ppr. *Tenax propositi perstо.* 233. 10

Batten, Herbert Cary George, Esquire, of Fairlee, Isle of Wight, Keyford, Yeovil, same crest and motto.

Batten, Herbert Phelips, Esquire, of Lufton Manor, near Yeovil, Somers., same crest and motto.

Batten, John Mount, Esquire, Upcerne House, Dorchester, same crest. *Hold fast.*

Batten, John, F.S.A., of Aldon, Somers., out of a ducal coronet a camel's head az., gorged with a wreath of roses or.

Batten, Clifford, Esquire, of Mussoorie, United Provinces, India, a dexter arm in armour embowed holding in the hand a battle-axe fessewise, all ppr. *Fortiter.* 292. 8

Battersbee and **Battersby,** a ram passant erm., armed and ungu. or. cf. 129. 5

Battersby, Ireland, a ram passant erm., armed and ungu. or. *Ante honorem humilitas.* cf. 129. 5

Battersby, Worsley, Esquire, of Stannanaughts, Lancs, Cleveland, Somers., and of 72, Onslow Gardens, London, on a wreath of the colours a ram arg., armed or, charged on the body with two trefoils slipped vert, resting the dexter foreleg on a lozenge sa. *Labore vinces.* cf. 131. 10

Battersea, Baron (Flower), issuant out of clouds, a cubit arm erect ppr., the hand holding a rose and a lily arg., each slipped vert. *Flores curat Deus.* 257. 5

Battie, Wadsworth, Yorks, a stork with a fish in its beak, all ppr.

Battie, a kingfisher ppr. cf. 96. 9

Battie, a kingfisher ppr., ducally gorged and chained or, holding in its beak a fish arg. cf. 96. 9

Battie-Wrightson of Cusworth Park, Doncaster, upon a rock ppr., a unicorn rampant arg., resting the sinister foreleg on an escutcheon or, charged with a griffin's head erased az. 237. 4

Battine, a demi-Bengal artilleryman habited, holding in the dexter hand a flagstaff ppr., therefrom flowing to the sinister a banner gu., inscribed "*Bhurtpore*" in letters of gold.

Battye-Trevor, Charles Edmund Augustine Trevor, Esquire: (1) Upon a club fesseways ppr., a stork arg., collared and lined sa., holding in the beak a roach ppr. (*for Battye*). (2) On a mount vert, the trunk of an oak-tree, a branch sprouting from its dexter side, acorned ppr., upon the trunk a wyvern, tail nowed sa., wings elevated erminois (*for Trevor*). *Ducat amor Dei.*

Baud and **Baude,** a lion's head gardant, erased gu., ducally crowned or. cf. 18. 11

Baugh, Oxon., Glouc., and Shropsh., on a ducal coronet or, a talbot sejant sa. cf. 55. 2

Baumfield, *see* Bamfield.

Baumfield, Cornw., and Devonsh. a lion statant gardant, holding in the dexter paw an anchor, the flukes resting on the wreath. 5. 10

Baumford, *see* Bamford.

Baumford, Donington, Lincs, on a chapeau a serpent nowed. 142. 9

Baunceford, a lion rampant. 1. 13

Bausefield and **Bausfield,** out of a ducal coronet or, a griffin's head ppr. 67. 9

Bavand, Chesh., a boar's head or, pierced in the mouth with an arrow arg.

Bavant, Chester, on a chapeau gu., turned up erm., a boar's head couped sa., armed and langued gu. 42. 5

Bavent, Norf., a sheaf of six arrows in saltier sa., feathered arg., barbed or, banded gu. 173. 13

Bawde of Curringham, Essex and Beds, a satyr's head in profile sa., with wings to the side of the head or, the tongue hanging out gu. 190. 6

Bawdewyn or **Bawdwen,** a sceptre in pale or. 170. 10

Bawle, an arm embowed, vested gu., cuffed or, holding in the hand ppr. a branch of laurel vert.

Bawtre or Bawtree, Cambs, a lion's head erased gu 17 2

Bawtre, a goat's head erased arg 128 5

Bax, Alfred Ridley, Esquire, of Ivy Bank, Haverstock Hill, Hampstead, N W, two arms embowed, vested sa, cuffs arg, the hands ppr, holding a lyre or *Verus et fidelis*

Baxendale, Joseph William, of Hursley Park, Hants, issuant from a mount a fir tree ppr, between four trefoils, slipped two on either side vert

Bax-Ironside, Henry George Outram, Esquire, of Heronden House, Eastry, Kent (1) A cubit arm vested per pale az and gu, cuff arg, the hand ppr, holding a cross flory or (*for Ironside*) (2) A demi lion gu, charged on the shoulder with three cinquefoils arg, holding between the paws an Eastern crown or (*for Bax*) *In hoc signo vinces*, *Cavendo tutus*

Baxter, the late Rt Hon W E, of Kincaldrum, Forfarsh, Scotland, a lion rampant guardant sa *Vincit veritas* 2 5

Baxter, John Henry, Esquire, Gilston, Colinsburgh, Fifesh., Scotland, a lion rampant guardant sa *Vincit veritas* 2 5

Baxter, Edward A, Esquire, of Kincaldrum, near Forfar, a lion passant guardant sa *Vincit veritas*

Baxter of Atherstone, Warw, a falcon belled and jessed or *Virtute non verbis* cf 85 2

Baxter, Scotland, an escarbuncle sa 164 12

Baxter, Stannow, Norf, a lion's gamb erased or, holding a spear sa, headed arg, stringed and tasselled of the first 38 11

Baxter, an eagle's head couped 83 1

Baxter, Henry, Esquire, J P, of the Tower, Rainhill, Lancs, a demi eagle displayed sa., gorged with a collar gemel, charged on the breast and on each wing with an annulet, and holding in the beak three ears of wheat leaved and slipped, all or

Baxter, Richard, Esquire, of Leinster Gardens and Lincoln's Inn, London, a bat, wings expanded sa, each wing charged with an annulet or, and in the mouth an arrow fessewise ppr *Deeds, not words* cf 137 11

Bay of London and Hants, a dexter wing sa, charged with an escallop or cf 109 7

Bayard, a demi-horse 53 3

Bayen, a poplar tree vert 144 12

Bayford, an owl arg 96 5

Baylee or Bailie, *see* Bailey

Bayley or Bailey, Scotland, *see* Bailey

Bayley, a lion rampant ppr 1 13

Bayley, Shropsh, a lion statant gardant ppr, armed and langued gu *Si Deus pro nobis quis contra nos* 4 1

Bayley, London, a demi lion rampant gardant or, holding in the dexter paw a branch vert cf 12 10

Bayley, Bart, London and Kent, on a mount vert, behind a wall arg, a lion rampant of the same

Bayley, London, a dexter arm embowed, habited az, and charged with a fess vair, the hand ppr holding a staff or

Bayley of Hoddesdon, Herts, out of a ducal coronet or, a nag's head arg 51 7

Bayley, a boar's head erased ppr 42 2

Bayley, a griffin sejant erm, winged and armed or

Bayley and **Bailey,** Shropsh, a griffin segreant gu, guttee d'eau 62 2

Bayley-Worthington of Sharston Hall, near Northenden, a goat passant arg, semee of estoiles sa., in the mouth a sprig of laurel ppr *In optimum sed gratum*

Baylie, within seven mullets in orle or, a cross pattee gu 164 9

Baylis, Glouc, out of an eastern coronet or, charged on the band with an auricula flower, a bay-tree fructed, all ppr

Baylis, London, a demi antelope ppr, gorged with a collar or, buckled of the same 126 3

Baylol, Scotland, an increscent and decrescent arg 163 7

Bayloll, on a mount vert, a lion rampant collared, holding in the dexter paw an arrow, all ppr cf 2 6

Bayly of London, an arm couped at the elbow and erect, habited gu, charged with a fesse vair, the cuff arg, holding in the hand ppr a mullet of six points or cf 206 13

Bayly, Wicklow, a boar's head erased ppr *Quid clarius astris?* 42 2

Bayly, Somers, a goat's head az, bezantee, attired or cf 128 12

Bayly, Hugh Wansey M A, New Oxford and Cambridge Club, same crest *Verum ob consilium*

Bayn, Scotland, a dexter hand grasping a dagger in pale or *Et marte, et arte* 212 9

Bayn, a Saracen's head in profile ppr, wreathed and stringed behind arg and az 190 4

Baynard, of Blagdon, Somers, a demi unicorn rampant or, armed ppr, crined sa 48 7

Baynard of Stukey, Norf, a bear's paw erased sa, charged with a martlet or

Baynbridge or Baynbrigge, a stag's head erased arg attired or 121 2

Baynbridge Buckeridge-, Cambs, a dexter cubit arm erect, couped at the elbow vested, charged with three bars ermi nois, holding in the gauntlet ppr a cross crosslet fitched sa

Baynbrige, Derbysh, a cubit arm armed with a gauntlet or, holding a battle-axe

Baynbrigge, Leics, upon a mount vert, a goat passant sa., armed, ungu, belled, and collared arg 129 3

Baynbrigge, Derbysh, a bloodhound passant or, collared vert, garnished of the first cf 54 5

Bayne, of Tulloch, Scotland, a dexter hand grasping a dirk in pale ppr *Et marte, et arte* 212 9

Bayne, a pellet between two wings arg cf 111 9

Bayne, *see* Baine

Bayne, Scotland, a hand holding a scroll of paper ppr *Virtute* 215 6

Bayne, Lancs, an etoile or 164 1

Baynes, Sir Christopher William Walter, Bart, of Harefield Place, Middx, a cubit arm erect, vested az, cuffed erminois, holding in the hand a jawbone arg *Furor arma ministrat*

Baynes, Cumb, Essex, and London, the same crest

Baynes of Blackburn, a cubit arm erect ppr, vested arg, the hand grasping a shuttle or, all within a wreath of the cotton plant, flowered and fructed ppr *Arte et industria* 208 15

Baynes or Baines, Surrey, a dove volant regardant or, holding in its beak a myrtle branch ppr

Baynham, a beaver ppr 134 8

Baynham, Kent and Glouc, a bull's head couped at the neck or cf 44 3

Baynham, Glouc, out of a mural coronet gu, a bull's head arg cf 44 11

Bayning, Baron (Powlett), a buck statant sa, attired or, charged on the body with a mullet arg *Stare super vias antiquas* cf 117 5

Baynton and Bayntun, Wilts, a griffin's head erased sa, beaked or cf 66 5

Baynton, a goat passant ppr cf 129 5

Bayntun, Rolt-, Bart (*extinct*), of Seacombe Park, Herts, a griffin's head erased sa, beaked or cf 66 5

Bayons and Bayos, a horse at full speed, holding in his mouth a spear head ppr cf 52 8

Bazalgette, Joseph Esquire, a lion rampant arg, gorged with a collar az charged with two crosses flory or, holding in the dexter forepaw a sword erect ppr, pommel and hilt of the third, and the dexter hind paw resting on a crescent or

Bazalgette, Edward, Esquire, c o. London County Council, Spring Gardens

Bazeley or Bazley, a hand holding a chapeau between two branches of laurel in orle, all ppr 217 5

Bazilie or Bazely, a crow sa. *Be not wanting* 107 14

Bazley, Sir Thomas Sebastian, Bart, a cubit arm ppr, charged with a bee volant or, the hand holding a chapeau gu, turned up or, the whole between two branches of oak vert *Finem respice* 254 9

Beach, Hicks-, Rt Hon Sir Michael Edward, Bart (1) A demi-lion rampant arg, ducally gorged or, holding in the paws an escutcheon az, charged with a pile or (*for Beach*) 236 4 (2) A buck's head couped at the neck or, gorged with a wreath of laurel ppr (*for Hicks*) *Tout en bon heure* 120 3

Beach of Oakley Hall, Hants (1) A demi lion rampant arg, ducally gorged or, holding in the paws an escutcheon az, charged with a pile, also or (*Beach*) 236. 4 (2) Crest as above

Beach, Beds and Kent, out of a ducal coronet or, a demi lion arg 16 3

Beachcroft, a beach tree ppr, behind six park pales arg

Beaconsfield, Earl of, *see* Disraeli

Beadle of South Ella, Yorks, a stag's head erased or, attired and ducally gorged gu cf 121 2

Beadnell, Henry Christopher Thomas, of Gogarth, Montgomerysh, a grey hound's head ppr, erased gu, gorged with a rosary and a bell pendent therefrom arg *Nec timide, nec temere.*

Beadon of Gotten House, Somers., a lion with a human face passant or. *Esse quam videre.*

Beaghan of Dunluce, co. Antrim, Ireland, a bezant between two wings paly sa. and gu., per fesse counterchanged. *cf.* 111. 9

Beaghan, Ireland, two swords in saltier, points downward. *cf.* 171. 12

Beak and **Beake,** out of a ducal coronet the horns, scalp, and ears of an ox.

Beake or **Beeke,** Dorset, an ostrich-head arg., holding in the beak a horse-shoe or.

Beal, Sussex, a lion's head erased. *Tout hardi.* 17. 8

Beal or **Beall,** a demi-wolf sa., holding a spear in pale, tasselled ppr. 29. 4

Beale, Surrey, a unicorn's head sa., erased gu., armed and crined or. 49. 5

Beale, Cork, Ireland, and London, a unicorn's head erased or, charged with an etoile gu. *Malo mori quam fœdari.* *cf.* 49. 5

Beale of London, a unicorn's head erased or, semée-d'etoiles gu. *cf.* 49. 5

Beale of Heath House, Shropsh., a unicorn's head erased or, semée-d'etoiles gu. *cf.* 49. 5

Beames, between six sun-rays a garb ppr., charged with three mullets, two and one arg. *Bene vivere bis vivere.*

Beamish, Bernard-, of Raheroon, Cork, a demi-lion rampant gu., charged on the shoulder with a trefoil slipped or. *Virtus insignit audentes.* *cf.* 10. 5

Beamish, Richard Henrik, Esquire, of Ashbourne, Glounthaun, co. Cork, Ireland, a demi-lion rampant gu., charged on the shoulder with a trefoil slipped or. *Virtus insignit audentes.* *cf.* 10. 5

Beamish, Alten Augustus William, Esquire, of 27, Philbeach Gardens, S.W., same crest and motto.

Beamish, Francis Bernard Servington, Esquire, same crest and motto.

Beamish, James Caulfield, Esquire, of Camphull, Dromore West, co. Sligo, same crest and motto.

Beamish, North Ludlow Axel, Esquire, of Ashgrove, co. Cork, same crest and motto.

Beamish or **Bemish,** a pair of scales ppr. 179. 8

Bean or **Beane,** a lion rampant, holding between the paws a plumb-rule sa. 3. 2

Beanlands, Rev. Arthur John, M.A., the Rectory, Victoria, British Columbia, a leopard's head erased or.

Bearcroft, a demi-bear rampant muzzled. 34. 13

Beard of North Kells, Lincs, a lion's gamb couped or, grasping a horse's leg, erased above the knee sa. 38. 12

Beard, Aberton, Sussex, on a chapeau gu., turned up erm., a tiger couchant or, maned, armed, and tufted sa.

Beard, *see* Bard.

Beardmore or **Berdmore,** on a mitre sa., semée of crosses pattée arg., a cheveron of the last. *cf.* 180. 5

Beardmore of Uplands, Hants, a griffin's head erased. *Providentiæ me committo.* 66. 2

Beardmore, a wolf rampant. 28. 2

Beardoe, of Manchester, Lancs, a demi-bear, holding in the dexter paw a bundle of six arrows in saltier ppr., headed or, flighted arg.

Beardsley, Richard Henry, Bay Villa, Grange-over-Sands, a demi-leopard, holding in the dexter paw a sprig of laurel, all ppr. *A cruce salus.* 294. 1

Beare or **Beere,** Kent, on a garb in fess or, a raven sa.

Beare, of Beare, Huntsham and Morebath, Devonsh., a bear's head sa., muzzled or. *Bear and forbear.* 34. 14

Bearhaven, Viscount, *see* Bantry.

Beasley, a demi-leopard, holding in the dexter paw a sprig of laurel ppr. 23. 9

Beasley, Dublin, a demi-leopard ppr., holding between its paws a plate charged with a trefoil slipped vert. *Labor omnia vincit.*

Beath or **Beith,** Scotland, a dragon's head vomiting fire ppr. *Fortuna virtute.* 72. 3

Beath or **Bieth,** Scotland, a dragon's head couped ppr. *Fortuna virtute.* 71. 1

Beath, Scotland, a wolf's head erased. *Fortuna virtute.* 30. 8

Beathell: (1) Out of a ducal coronet a boar's head and neck. 41. 4. (2) An eagle's head between two wings displayed az., charged on the neck with an etoile or. *cf.* 84. 2

Beatie or **Beattie,** Scotland, a star issuing from a crescent or. *Lumen cœleste sequamur.* 163. 4

Beatie or **Beatty,** a castle sa. *cf.* 155. 8

Beaton, a lion passant sa. *Fortis in arduis.* 6. 2

Beatson of Rossend, Fife, a bee erect, wings expanded ppr. *Cum prudentia sedulus.* 137. 1

Beatson, Stuart Brownlow, Esquire, Union Bank of London, Charing Cross Branch, a bee volant *en arrière* ppr. *Cum prudentia sedulus.*

Beatson of Contell, Fife, Scotland, a bridge of three arches arg. *Pro patria.* 158. 4

Beattie of Aberdeen, Scotland, *see* Beatie.

Beatty, Ireland, on a ducal coronet a lion passant gardant ducally crowned. 6. 4

Beatty, W. J., M.D., Van Mildert House, Stockton-on-Tees, a demi-lion rampant, holding in the dexter paw a crescent. *Fortiter et fideliter.*

Beaty, two keys in saltier ppr. *cf.* 168. 11

Beauchamp, Earl of (Lygon), a savage's head affrontée, couped at the shoulders and wreathed round the head ppr. *Ex fide fortis.* *cf.* 192. 14

Beauchamp, Proctor-, Sir Reginald William, Bart., of Langley Park, Norf.: (1) On a mount vert, a greyhound sejant arg., spotted of a brown colour, collared or. (2) An heraldic tiger. *Toujours fidèle.* 59. 2

Beauchamp, Edmund Beauchamp, D.L., Trevince, Gwennap, Cornw., a demi-sea-horse reguardant arg., holding in his paws a heart gu. *Auspice Teuro.*

Beauchamp of Hoult, Essex, a swan's head and neck arg., beaked gu., between two wings sa. 101. 6

Beauchamp, Earl of Warwick, out of a ducal coronet or, a demi-swan arg.

Beauchamp, out of a ducal coronet or, a swan's head gu.

Beauchamp of Powycke, Glouc., a tiger passant or, vulned in the shoulder gu. 27. 11

Beauchampe, Glouc. and Warw., out of a coronet gu., a swan's head and neck arg., beaked of the first.

Beauchatt, a cat's head erased gardant gu. 26. 14

Beauclerk, *see* St. Alban's, Duke of.

Beauclerk, Aubrey de Vere, Esquire, of Ardglass Castle, co. Down. *See* St. Albans, Duke of.

Beaufey or **Beaufoy,** a demi-griffin, holding between the claws a close helmet az. *cf.* 64. 1

Beaufice, a Paschal lamb passant arg., bearing a banner pink, the staff ppr., surmounted by cross. 131. 2

Beaufort, Duke of (Somerset), a portcullis or, nailed az., with chains pendent thereto, also or. *Mutare vel timere sperno.* *cf.* 178. 3

Beaufort, Leicester Paul, Esquire, of the Cottage, Strathfield, Turgis, Winchfield, Hants, a female figure habited of the second, encircled round the waist with a belt or, holding in her dexter hand a mirror ppr., in her left hand a book, between two wings erect arg. *Deus meus turris fortis.*

Beaufoy, Beaufo, or **Beawfo,** a tree vert, on a ribbon round the stem the motto "*Sub tegmine fagi.*"

Beauman of Hyde Park, co. Wexford, a cubit dexter arm in armour holding a sword, all ppr. *Fortiter.* 210. 2

Beaumont, Baron (Stapleton), a man's head couped at the shoulders in profile ppr., wreathed about the temples arg. and sa. *Mieulx je serra.* 191. 12

Beaumont, Sir George Howland William, Bart., of Stoughton Grange, Leics., on a chapeau az., semée-de-lis or, turned up erm., a lion passant of the second. *Erectus non elatus.* 254. 10

Beaumont of Barrow-upon-Trent, on a chapeau gu., turned up erm., a lion passant or. *Erectus non elatus.* 4. 9

Beaumont, Francis Henry, of Buckland, Surrey, on a chapeau az., semée-de-lis or, turned up erm., a lion passant or. *Erectus non elatus.* 254. 10

Beaumont, De, a demi-lion gardant sa. 10. 8

Beaumont, Leics. and Suff., a lion passant or. 6. 2

Beaumont, Devonsh., a stork or heron, wings expanded arg. 105. 2

Beaumont, Suff., a bear's head erased ppr. 35. 2

Beaumont, Captain Lewis Anthony, R.N., upon a rock a cubit arm erect ppr., holding in the hand a cross crosslet fitchée sa., and surmounted by a mullet of six points or.

Beaumont, Henry Frederick, Esquire, of Whitley Beaumont, Huddersfield, a bull's head erased quarterly arg. and gu. *Fide sed qui vide.*

Beaumont, Wentworth Blackett, Esquire, of Bretton Park, Wakefield, same crest and motto.

Beaumont, Wentworth Canning Blackett, Esquire, of Bywell Hall, Stockfield-on-Tyne, same crest and motto.

Beaumont, Wentworth-Blackett, of Bretton Hall, Yorks, same crest and motto.

Beaumont, a bull's head quarterly arg and gu cf 44 3
Beaumont, Leics, and Beaumont Hall, Suff, an elephant, on its back a tower triple-towered arg, garnished or (*Another*, the tower or) 133 11
Beauram, a lion's head erased arg, pelletee cf 17 8
Beauvoir, a griffin's head between two wings ppr 65 11
Beauvoir, London, a demi dragon, wings addorsed ppr 73 10
Beauvons and Beavons, a bull's head sa cf 44 3
Beavan or Bevan, over a mount vert, a dove hovering ppr, in its beak a gem-ring or *Semper virtute constans* 21 5
Beavan, a lion's head erased az, holding in the mouth a rose gu
Beaver, a beaver ppr 134 8
Beaver, Hugh, Esquire, of the Temple, near Manchester, a mount vert, thereon in front of three arrows, one in pale and two in saltire, points downwards, a beaver passant ppr
Beaver, Robert Atwood, M D, Sturminster Newton, Dorset, same crest *Industria et virtute*
Beaver, A Atwood, of Beauvoir, Bournemouth same crest and motto
Beaver, a leopard statant ppr 24 2
Beavis, Devonsh, a pheon arg (*Another* or) 174 11
Beawfice, a Paschal lamb passant arg, supporting a flag, the banner pink, the staff or, surmounted by a cross 131 2
Beawpell, out of a mural coronet a hand ppr, vested gu, holding a sword wavy az
Beazley, Edwin Arthur, Esquire, of Merefield, Oxton, Birkenhead, a demi-leopard ppr, holding in dexter paw a lily arg, stalked, leaved, and slipped vert, and resting the sinister paw on a fleur de-lis or *Steadfast*
Beazley, Frank Charles, Esquire, of Fern Hill, Claughton, Birkenhead, same crest and motto
Beazley, James Henry, Esquire, of Oak Dene, Noctorum, Birkenhead, same crest and motto.
Beazley, Robert Clover, Esquire, of Waterford Road, Birkenhead, same crest and motto
Bebb of Donnington Grove, Berks (1) An esquire's helmet ppr, resting in a crescent gu, the helmet charged with a cross crosslet of the second for distinction (*for Bebb*) (2) Out of an Eastern crown or, a cubit arm erect, vested sa, cuffed erm, the hand holding a wreath of laurel ppr (*for Lawrell*) *Per vim et virtutem —Præmium virtutis honor*
Bebington of Bebington, Chesh, out of a ducal coronet or, a demi-eagle displayed sa, bezantee cf 80 14
Bec or Beck, on a chapeau gu, turned up erm, a lion's head erased of the first. 17 9
Beccles, a dexter arm in armour embowed ppr, holding in the hand, also ppr, a cross pattee
Beche, Berks, a cubit arm, vested or, cuffed gu, holding in the hand ppr an escarbuncle of the last 207 7

Becher of Chancellor House, Tunbridge and Beds, a demi-lion erased arg, its body enfiled with a ducal coronet or cf 10 2
Becher, Wrixon-, Sir Henry, Bart, of Ballygiblin, co Cork, Ireland, out of a ducal coronet or, a demi lion erm, gorged with a plain collar vair *Bis vivit qui bene* cf 16 3
Beck of London, a raven ppr, between two wings or
Beck, Norf, out of the sea ppr, a sea-wolf arg, finned or, holding between the paws a cross pattee gu
Beck, *see* Bec
Beck, Lt Col Charles Harrop, C B, of Upton Priory, Macclesfield, Chesh, a raven ppr, between two wings or *Assiduitas*
Beck of Woodside, Surrey, a staff raguly fessewise or, thereon a blackbird, holding in the beak a sprig of holly ppr *Cruce insignis*
Beck, Alcock-, William, of Esthwaite Lodge a cross potent or, perched thereon a blackbird ppr holding in its beak an annulet of the first *Animum rege*
Beck, Wales, on a mount vert, a pelican arg, vulning herself gu cf 98 1
Beck, Suff, a peacock ppr 103 7
Beck, Peter Arthur, Esquire, of Trelydan Hall Gillfield, near Welshpool a peacock's head couped az, holding in the beak an annulet or between two wings expanded of the last, semee of annulets of the first *Spem pretio non emam*
Beck of Creeting St Mary and Needham Market, Suff, a peacock's head erased or, holding in the beak a serpent entwined about the neck ppr, between two wings az, each charged with three bezants *Unitate fortior* cf 103 3
Beck, Rev Edward Josselyn, of the Rectory, Rotherhithe, a peacock's head erased or, holding in the beak a serpent entwined about the neck ppr, between two wings az, each charged with three bezants *Unitate fortior*
Becke of Berks and Lincs, a peacock's head erased or, gorged with two bars dancettee sa, between two wings az, each charged with three bezants pale ways. 102 2
Beckering and Bekering, Yorks, a crow perched on an oak-tree
Becket, Ireland, a Cornish chough ppr 107 14
Beckett of Courthither, Cornw (Visitation 1623), a Cornish chough, wings expanded sa, beaked and legged gu, ducally gorged or cf 107 3
Beckett or à Beckett, of Penleigh, Wilts, a fleur-de-lis az, charged with a lion's head erased erm *Foys, sapience, et chevalerie* (*The arms of Beckett are of very ancient date, as per the Visitations of Wiltshire in 1565 and 1623, but the crest belonging thereto was granted in the year* 1808 *to the Rev. Thomas à Beckett Turner of Penleigh and Littleton, Wiltshire, and to his younger brother William and their descendants*) 19 8
Beckett-Turner, William, of Littleton, Wilts (1) A lion passant gardant erminois, charged upon the body with three trefoils in fesse slipped vert, and holding in the dexter paw a fer-de-moline sa (*for Turner* 6 8 (2) A fleur de lis az, charged with a lion's head erased erm (*for Beckett*) 19 8
Beckett, Rt Hon Sir Edmund, LL D, Q C, Baron Grimthorpe, of Grimthorpe, Yorks, a boar's head couped or, pierced by a cross pattee fitched erect gu *Prodesse civibus*
Beckett, Ernest William, Esquire, of Kirkstall Grange, Leeds, a boar's head couped or, pierced by a cross pattee fitchee erect sa *Prodesse civibus*
Beckett, a dexter arm embowed in armour ppr, about the elbow a wreath or and az, holding in the hand, also ppr, a baton of the second cf 200 3
Beckford, London, Wilts, and Leics, a stork's head erased, holding in the beak a fish, all ppr
Beckford, Clarence, Esquire, of Victoria Street, Westminster, S W, a stork's head erased, collared, and chained reflexed az, between two roses arg, barbed, seeded, leaved, and slipped ppr. *De Dieu tout*
Beckford of Ruxley Lodge, Surrey, a heron's head erased or, collared, holding in the beak a fish arg *De Dieu tout*
Beckford of Fonthill, Wilts (1) A heron's head erased or, gorged with a collar flory and counterflory gu, holding in the beak a fish arg (2) Out of a ducal coronet or, an oak-tree fructed ppr., the stem penetrated transversely by a frame-saw, also ppr, differenced with a shield pendent from a branch of the tree, charged with the arms of Latimer, viz, gu, a cross patonce or *De Dieu tout*
Beckford, Love-, of Basing Park, Hants, a heron's head erased or, holding in the beak a fish ppr
Beckham, a horse's head arg, pierced through the neck with a broken tilting-spear or, and holding in the mouth the top of the spear embrued gu
Beckingham of Hoe, Norf, a demi griffin arg, armed sa, wings addorsed gu, holding in the dexter claw a cutlass arg, hilted or cf 64 6
Beckingham, Essex, a demi griffin sa, holding in its dexter claw a cutlass arg, hilt and pommel or cf 64 6
Beckley, Beckly, or Bickley, Devonsh, a cross pattee gu., between two wings or 110 7
Beckman, London, an ostrich head couped arg, gorged with a fess dancettee sa, between two palm-branches ppr 96 10
Beckwell or Bekewell, a horse shoe ppr 158 6
Beckwith or Bickwith, a stag's head erased ppr 121 2
Beckwith, Durh, a stag's head couped ppr 121 5
Beckwith, an antelope ppr 126 12
Beckwith of Thurcroft, Yorks, an antelope ppr, holding in the mouth a branch vert *Jouir en bien* cf 126 12
Beckwith, Henry John, J P, of Millichope Park, Shropshire, and Silksworth near Sunderland, an antelope trippant holding in the mouth a branch *Jouir en bien*

Beckwith, Bart., of Aldborough, Yorks, same crest and motto

Beckwith, Yorks, a stag's head quarterly per fess indented or and gu *Another,* or and az 121 5

Beckwith, Yorks, a stag's head couped sa. 121 5

Beckwith, Durh, a roebuck's head couped sa 121 5

Beckwith, a dove holding in the beak three ears of wheat, all ppr cf 92 5

Beckwith and **Beckworth,** Yorks, an eagle's head or, beaked gu, charged with two bends vert, all between two wings, one arg, the other sa cf 84 2

Beckquet, a falcon rising sa, ducally gorged or *Celeritas* 87 2

Bective, Earl, *see* Headfort, Marquess

Becton, a demi heraldic tiger ppr, ducally gorged and chained or cf 25 12

Becton, a demi heraldic tiger ducally gorged and chained, holding between the paws a mullet of six points cf 25 12

Bedall, Essex, a buck's head gu, attired or, between the attires a bough of a tree leaved ppr cf 121 5

Beddington, Hyam Leopold, Esquire, of Cornwall Terrace, St Marylebone, London, a lion rampant arg, gorged with a collar gemelle az, holding in the fore-paws a flagstaff erect ppr, therefrom flowing to the dexter a banner az, charged with a chaplet of roses arg, and resting the dexter hind paw on a mullet of six points or *Ex fide fortis* 2 10

Beddington, Claude, Esquire, of 51, South Street, Park Lane, W same crest *Be strong and of good courage*

Beddington, Herbert Melville, Esquire, of 8, Cornwall Terrace, Regent's Park, N W, same crest and motto

Beddington, Maurice, Esquire, of 91, Lancaster Gate, London, W, same crest

Beddington, Alfred Henry, Esquire, 8, Cornwall Terrace, Regent's Park, London, N W, on a wreath of the colours a lion rampant arg, gorged with a collar gemelle az, holding in the fore paws a flagstaff erect ppr, therefrom flowing to the dexter a banner az, charged with a chaplet of roses arg, and resting the dexter hind-paw on a mullet of six points or *Be strong and of good courage* 2 10

Beddington, Samuel Henry, Esquire, of Hyde Park Square, London, W, a lion rampant arg, gorged with a collar gemelle az, holding in the fore paws a flagstaff erect ppr, therefrom flowing to the dexter a banner az, charged with a chaplet of roses arg, and resting the dexter hind paw on a mullet of six points or *Deus nobis quis contra* 2 10

Beddoe, John, M D, the Chantry, Bradford on Avon, Wilts, a stag's head and neck erased ppr, pierced through the neck by an arrow or *Qui invidet minor est*

Bedell of Rumford, Essex, an arm in armour couped at the elbow and erect, the hand grasping a cutlass by the blade arg, hilted or

Bedell and **Bedolfe,** Staffs and Bedolph's Hall, Essex, an arm embowed, vested az, holding in the hand ppr a sword arg, hilt and pommel or, pierced into the side of a squirrel sejant regardant or, the side of the squirrel guttee de-sang

Bedell of Hamerton, Hunts, out of a palisado coronet a buck's head or, attired az cf 120 7

Bedell-Sivright, William Henry Revell, Esquire, of North Cliff, North Queensferry, Fifeshire, Scotland, a dexter hand holding a thunderbolt ppr *Recte ferio* 216 4

Bedell, a stag's head couped gu, attired or, the branches az, between the attires a thistle of the second stalked and leaved vert cf 121 5

Bedewell or **Bedwell,** on a rock a fort in flames ppr 155 1

Bedford, Duke (Russell), a goat passant arg, armed or *Che sara sara* cf 129 5

Bedford, Cornw, an eagle rising from an anchor arg *Vertie sans peur*

Bedford, a hand ppr, holding a sphere erect or 216 3

Bedford, John, Esquire, of Oughtibridge and Birley House, Yorks, in front of a bear's paw erased sa, holding a terrestrial globe ppr, an annulet arg *Gare le pied fort* 231 5

Bedford, Henry Hall, Esquire, same crest and motto

Bedford of More Hall, Bolsterstone, Sheffield, same crest and motto

Bedford of Henloc, Beds and London, a demi lion sa., ducally crowned or, holding between the paws a sphere, also or cf 11 7

Bedford, Edward, solicitor and Notary Public, 12, Priory Crescent, Southover, Lewes, Sussex, a demi lion rampant holding between the paws an imperial crown *Animum fortuna sequatur* 300 9

Bedford, a demi-lion rampant ppr, holding in the dexter paw a trefoil slipped vert cf 13 13

Bedford, a demi lion rampant az, holding in the dexter paw a fleur-de-lis or cf 13 2

Bedford, Ryland-, a demi lion rampant sa, murally crowned or, holding between the paws a bezant *Animum fortuna sequatur*

Bedingfield of Beckhall, Norf, an eagle displayed or *Despicio terrena* 75 2

Bedingfield, Paston-, Sir Henry George, Bart, Oxburgh, Norf, a demi-eagle wings expanded gu *Despicio terrena solem contemplor.* Badge, a fetterlock az 80 2

Bedingfield of Ditchingham, Norf, a demi eagle wings expanded gu *Aquila non capit muscas,* or *Despicio terrena* 80 2

Bedingfield, James, of Bedingfield House, Eye, Suffolk, same crest and motto

Bedingfield, a demi-eagle wings expanded or *Despicio terrena* 80 2

Bedingfield, a unicorn's head erased sa, the horn wreathed or and arg 49 5

Bedle or **Bedell,** London, a stag's head erased or, attired and ducally gorged gu cf 121 2

Bedo and **Bedon,** of Putney, Surrey, a boar's head couped and erect gu cf 43 3

Bedolfe, *see* Bedell

Bedwell of the Manor East Kennett, near Marlborough, out of a ducal coronet a griffin's head 67 9

Bee of Basingstoke, Hants, a dragon's head or, pierced through with an arrow gu, flighted and feathered arg

Bee, Norf, a dragon's head erased or, collared vair 71 2

Beebee, a beehive ppr *Se defendendo* cf 137 7

Beeby, a mullet or 164 2

Beech, Rowland John, of Brandon Lodge, Warw, and the Shawe, Staffs, in front of a bugle horn stringed az, a stag's head cabossed or *Sub tegmine fagi* 122 8

Beecham, Joseph, Esquire, Ewanville, Huyton, near Liverpool, a swan's head and neck erased arg, between two escallop-shells or, holding in the beak a like escallop shell *Nil sine labore.* 101 2

Beecher of London, a demi lion erased arg, enfiled round the body with a ducal coronet or cf 10 2

Beechey and **Beechy,** a hurt. cf 159. 14

Beeching, Sussex, a winged spur *Ag noscor eventu* 111 12

Beeching, James Plumer George, Esquire, of Spring Grove, Isleworth, a beech-tree, the sun rising from behind the stem, in front a fountain, all ppr

Beecroft, Berks, on a chapeau vert, turned up or, a wyvern, wings expanded az *Pro virtute* cf 70 11

Beecroft of Bishop-Wearmouth, two arms embowed, dexter and sinister, in armour ppr, holding in the fingers an annulet gu cf 194 11

Beedham of Ashfield, Kimbolton, Hunts, on a mural crown ppr, a bird, wings expanded arg, beaked and legged gu, resting its dexter claw on an escutcheon of the second charged with a human heart of the third *God be in my bede*

Beeke, *see* Beake

Beekensball, Lancs, an arm erect couped below the elbow holding a garland gu 218 6

Beer and **Beere,** *see* Beare

Beerhaven, Viscount, *see* Bantry, Earl of

Beers of Leslie Hill, Ireland, on a garb in fesse or, a raven sa *In Deo spes mea*

Beesley or **Beesly,** out of a mural coronet two branches of palm in saltier ppr, surmounting a spear in pale 175 1

Beeston, Beestone, or **Beiston,** a heart gu, within a fetterlock sa cf 181 7

Beeston of Beeston Castle, Chesh, on a mount vert, a castle or, issuant therefrom an arm in armour embowed ppr, garnished of the second, brandishing a sword ppr, hilted, also or

Beetham, Richmond, Esquire, J P, of Christchurch, Canterbury, New Zealand, Resident Magistrate for Christchurch and Sheriff of Timaru, South Canterbury, a stag lodged gu *Per ardua surgam* 115 7

Beetham, late Albert, out of a ducal coronet or, an elephant's head trunked and tusked or *Per ardua surgam*

Beevor, Sir Hugh Reeve, Bart., of Hethel, Norf, a beaver passant ppr *Suaviter in modo, fortiter in re.* 236 7

Beevor of Heckmondwike, Yorks, the same crest. *Nil desperandum*

Beg or **Begg,** Scotland, a cross crosslet fitched between two branches of palm in orle ppr cf 166 5

Begbie, Francis Warburton, Esquire, M R C S, a lion's gamb erased, holding a spear-head ppr, and in an escroll over the same this motto *Sans peur*

Begbie, Rev A J, M A, of the Rectory, Horton, Chipping Sodbury, Glouc, a cock ppr, charged on the breast with a hurt, the dexter claw resting on a mullet of six points or *In Deo con fidentia*

Begbie, Colonel Elphinstone Waters, C B, of Clifton Lodge, Winchester, same crest and motto

Begg, Dublin, a naked arm embowed ppr, holding in the hand a long cross gu

Begg, Ireland, a hand fesswise couped at the wrist ppr, holding a cross formee fitchee purpure

Begg, out of a mural coronet a demi-savage ppr, wreathed round the middle vert, holding in the dexter hand a cock's head and in the sinister a club resting on the shoulder

Beggar or **Begger,** a pelican's head and neck erased vulning herself 98 2

Beggs of Shropsh, a Cornish chough ppr 107 14

Behethland, from a cloud in the sinister a dexter hand fesseways holding a club in pale, all ppr 223 5

Behrens, Sir Jacob, of Springfield House, Bradford, Yorks, a demi bear arg, muzzled sa, holding in the dexter paw a mullet of six points gu, and resting the sinister paw on an escutcheon gu, charged with a bee volant ppr *Esse quam videri*

Behrens, Charles, Esquire, of Holm-Acre, Altrincham, Chesh, same crest and motto

Behrens, Gustav Nathan, Esquire, same crest and motto

Beighton of Werksworth, on a mural coronet or, a greyhound erm, collared of the first

Beilby, Warw, a leopard's face 22 2

Beilby, a hawk close ppr 85 2

Beirne or **O'Beirne,** Connaught, a dexter arm in armour embowed, the hand grasping a sword, all ppr 195 2

Beist or **Biest** of Atcham, Shropsh, a sinister arm couped above the elbow, vested sa, cuffed arg, the hand ppr holding a bow stringed, also ppr

Beiston, *see* **Beeston**

Beith or **Bieth,** Scotland, a dragon's head couped vert *Fortuna virtute* 71 1

Beke, Beeke, or **Beack,** Durh, out of a ducal coronet gu, two bulls' horns erm

Beke, out of a ducal coronet a boar's head and neck 41 4

Beke or **Beck,** Berks and Lincs, a hare's head

Beke, Norf, a dragon's head erased or, collared vair 71 2

Bekett, within a wreath or and vert, garnished with laurel leaves of the second, a falcon rising arg, legged and beaked gu, and ducally gorged or

Belasis, a stag's head erased arg *Bonne et belle assez* 121 2

Belasyse of Newborough, Yorks, **Viscount Fauconburgh,** and a Bart, a stag's head erased ppr, attired or, holding in the mouth an acorn leaved vert. *Bonne et belle assez* cf 119 11

Belcher, Northamp, a demi-hawk or, wings expanded sa 88 11

Belcher of Gilsborough, Northamp., Staffs, and Warw, a greyhound's head erased erm., eared az, gorged with a collar gu, rimmed and ringed or cf 61 2

Belches, Scotland, a horse's head arg, bridled gu *Keep tryst* 51 5

Belches of Tofts, Scotland, the stump of an oak-tree eradicated shooting branches ppr *Revirescit* 145 2

Belches and **Belsches,** Scotland, a greyhound's head couped arg, collared az *Fulget virtus intaminata* 61 2

Beldam, a lion rampant arg 1 13

Beldam-Johns, Frederick Meadows, Esquire, of Fowlmere Manor, Royston, a garb banded or, pendent from the band by a ring, also or, an escutcheon vert, charged with a dexter hand couped at the wrist or *Dat Deus incrementum*

Beldero, Suff, a greyhound current gu, collared and ringed or cf 58 2

Belew or **Bellew,** Devonsh, an arm embowed, vested vert, holding in the hand ppr a bell or

Beley, late of St John's Hill, Surrey, a griffin sejant or, winged vair, resting the dexter claw on a plate *Auspice Deo vinces* cf 62 10

Belfarge or **Belfrage,** Scotland, on a ducal coronet or, a hawk belled ppr 85 9

Belfast, Earl of, *see* Donegal Marquess of

Belfield of London and Herts, a demi-heraldic tiger arg, armed and tufted or, pierced through the body with the broken staff of a flag, the flag hanging between the fore legs party per fess wavy arg and az

Belfield of Malmains, Glouc, same crest *Ubi amor ibi fides*

Belfour, Belfore, Belloure, and **Balfour,** a hautboy in pale ppr 168 1

Belfrage, *see* Belfarge

Belgrave, William, of Kilworth and Belgrave, Leics, and Preston Hall, Rutland, a ram's head arg 130 1

Belgrave of Cockfield, Suff, out of a ducal coronet a fleur de lis

Belhaven and Stenton, Baron (Hamilton), Wishaw House Lanarksh, Scotland a nag's head couped arg, bridled gu *Ride through* 51 5

Belhouse, a squirrel sejant per pale arg and az, the tail or, the fore feet against an oak branch vert, fructed or

Belhouse, a wolf s head party per pale or and az 30 5

Belhald of Thorpe, Northamp, a lion's head couped gu, billettee arg cf 21 1

Bell of Stoneycross, Leics, a demi-man affrontee habited in russet leather and gloved grasping in the dexter hand a hawk rising ppr, suspended therefrom a lure, the sinister hand resting on a trefoil slipped both or *Magna est veritas*

Bell, a hawk close ppr, beaked and belled or *Perseverantia* 85 2

Bell, Richard Moore, Claremont, Brighton Road, Sutton, Surrey, a hawk close ppr, belled or *Perseverantia*

Bell, Berks and Bucks, a hawk, wings expanded arg, beaked and belled or, jessed gu cf 87 12

Bell, Charles Wentworth, Esquire, of Bronsil, Eastnor, near Ledbury, Heref, on a rock ppr, between two antlers az, a hawk close, also ppr, around the neck a riband az, pendent therefrom a bell or *Dextra fideque*

Bell, Spencer-, James, Esquire, of Fawe Park, Cumb (1) A beaver statant erm (*for Bell*) 134 8 (2) Out of a ducal coronet or, a griffin's head arg, collared gu, between two wings expanded of the second (*for Spencer*) *Dieu defend le droit* cf 67 1

Bell, Charles Loraine, of Woolsington, Northumb, between two escallops sa, a falcon close ppr, belled and jessed or, holding in the beak a wing erect, also or *Bell assez bel* 85 2

Bell, Sir Isaac Lowthian, Bart, of Rounton Grange, Yorks, a hawk or, holding in its beak a lure az, and resting its dexter claw on a sun in splendour of the first *Perseverantia* 86 2

Bell, John Charles, Esquire, of 61, Portland Place, London, W, in front of the stock of a tree a branch of olive and a sword in saltire, all ppr, thereon a hawk, wings close arg, belled or, charged on the body with two bars az *Fortis qui prudens*

Bell, Thomas, Esquire, 23, Windsor Terrace, Newcastle on Tyne, in front of a mount vert, thereon a falcon rising ppr, belled and jessed or, three roses fessewise of the last *Industria et probitate* 87 5

Bell, a falcon close ppr, belled or *Prend moi tel que je suis* 85 2

Bell of Bellview, co. Fermanagh, Ireland, on a ducal coronet or, a falcon rising ppr, collared gu, belled of the first

Bell, Thomas Fotherley, M B, the Red House, Heckington, Lincs, a falcon belled ppr *Prend moi tel que je suis*

Bell, on a mount an eagle rising ppr *Vian affectat Olympo* cf 78 1

Bell, on a rock ppr, a martlet erminois cf 95 2

Bell, a hawk's bell stringed ppr

Bell, Scotland, a bell or 168 7

Bell, in front of a tree ppr, a bear resting his dexter fore-paw on a bell

Bell, Essex, a talbot passant erm 54 1

Bell, Scotland, a demi lion rampant ppr *Dextra fideque* 10 2

Bell, Matthew, of Bourne Park, Canterbury, a lion's head erased ppr *Lege et labore*

Bell of Ewell, Surrey, and of Scatwell Muir of Ord, Scotland, formerly of Provosthaugh, Scotland, on a mount vert, a roebuck feeding ppr *Signum pacis amor* 116 9

Bell, Matthew Montgomerie Esquire, of 72, Great King Street, Edinburgh, a stag grazing ppr *Signum pacis amor* 256 18

Bell of Jamaica, a stag's head erased gu., attired arg *Fulget virtus* 121 2

Bell of Fortoun, Scotland, a stag's head erased ppr *Ardenter amo* 121 2

Bell, Thomas, Esquire, Rossie, Perth, a stag's head erased gu *Fulget virtus* 121 2

Bell of Ealing, a stag's head ppr, attired or *Signum pacis amor* 121 5

Bell, Sir James, 1st Bart., of Marlborough Terrace, Glasgow, a stag's head couped ppr., attired or. *Signum pacis amor.*

Bell, Scotland, a dexter hand with the two last fingers folded down ppr. *Confido.* 222. 11

Bell, Joseph, Esquire, surgeon, 2, Melville Crescent, Edinburgh, *uses* a garb. *Quid utilius.* 153. 2

Bell, Middx., a portcullis ppr. 178. 3

Bell, George Robert, Esquire, a stone masoned arch ppr., suspended from the keystone thereof a bell or.

Bell, London, a human heart winged ppr. *Forward, kind heart.* 112. 10

Bell, Glouc., an arm embowed, vested gu., holding in the hand ppr. a battle-axe, the staff gu., the head arg.

Bell, Scotland, a cubit arm in armour grasping a scimitar, all ppr. *Pro rege et patria.*

Bell, Walter Leonard, M.D., 123, London Road, Lowestoft, Suff., a garb or. *Quid utilius.*

Bell, William Abraham, Esquire, of Pendell Court, Bletchingley, Surrey, a figure of Justice vested chevronny of six arg. and gu. *Hujus stat fœdere Mundus.*

Bellairs of Kirby Bellars, a lion's gamb erased gu. *In cruce mea fides.* 36. 4

Bellairs, Lincs, out of a mural coronet or, a demi-lion rampant gu., holding between the paws a cross crosslet fitchée or.

Bellairs, Lincs, out of a mural coronet or, a demi-lion rampant gu., holding in the paws a staff ppr., thereon a banner displayed of the arms of Walford, viz., arg. a fesse, and in chief a lion passant gu. *cf.* 16. 7

Bellairs of Barton End, Staffs: (1) Out of a mural crown or, a demi-lion rampant gu., holding between the paws a cross crosslet fitchée, also gold. (2) A horse's head couped arg., in the mouth a leaf of oak ppr. *Virtus tutissima cassis.*

Bellairs, Lieutenant-General Sir William, of Clevedon, Somers., same crests. *Virtus tutissima cassis.*

Bellairs, George Clarke, Esquire, of Southbourne-on-sea, Hants: (1) Out of a mural crown or, a demi-lion rampant gu., langued az., holding between his paws a cross crosslet fitchée or. (2) A horse's head couped arg., in the mouth a leaf of oak ppr. *Virtus tutissima cassis*, and *Nihil sine cruce.*

Bellairs, Lincs, a horse's head couped arg., holding in the mouth a wreath of oak vert.

Bellam, Ballam, and **Bellome**, out of a ducal coronet or, a cock's head between two wings gu., combed and wattled of the first.

Bellamy, an arm couped and erect, vested sa., cuffed arg., holding in the hand ppr. a sceptre or, surmounted by a crescent arg.

Bellars of New Lodge, Herts, a lion's gamb erased ppr. 36. 4

Bellas, a stag's head erased per fesse, indented arg. and gu., attired or, holding in the mouth a fleur-de-lis az. *cf.* 121. 2

Bellasis or **Bellasses**, on a mount a palm-tree ppr. 144. 3

Bellasis, Durh., a stag's head erased ppr., attired or. 121. 2

Bellasis or **Bellassis**, Yorks, a lion couchant gardant az. *Bonne et belle assez.* 7. 10

Bellasis of Marton, Westml., a mount vert, thereon a lion couchant gardant az., in front of a tent ppr., lined gu. 9. 4

Bellasis, Edward, Esquire, *Lancaster Herald*, of 22, Prince of Wales' Terrace, W., a mount vert, thereon a lion couchant gardant az., in front of a tent ppr., lined gu. 9. 4

Bellasis, Yorks, a stag's head erased, in mouth an oak-branch fructed ppr. *cf.* 121. 2

Bellenden of Auchinoule, co. Edinburgh, a hart's head couped, between the attires a cross crosslet fitchée or. *Sic itur ad astra.* 120. 12

Bellerby, Yorks, a dexter hand couped at wrist, pierced through the palm with an arrow in bend sinister, all ppr.

Bellere, a spur rowel az. 164. 8

Bellet, Chesh., a fox's head erased sa. 33. 8

Bellet of Norf. and Wilts, an arm in armour couped at the elbow, holding in the gauntlet a baton or, tipped at both ends sa. 209. 9

Bellew of Stockleigh, Devonsh., an arm embowed, vested, the hand ppr. grasping a chalice, pouring water into a basin, also ppr. *Tout d'en haut.*

Bellew of Okehampton, a dexter arm embowed vested vert, cuffed arg., the hand or, grasping a chalice pouring water into a basin, also ppr.

Bellew, William Legassicke, Esquire, same crest and motto.

Bellew, a boar passant sa. 40. 9

Bellew, a hyena passant. *cf.* 127. 13

Bellew, Baron (Bellew), of Barmeath, co. Louth, Ireland, an arm in armour embowed, holding a sword ppr. *Tout d'en haut.* 195. 2

Bellew, an arm in armour embowed, holding in the hand a dagger, point downwards.

Bellew, Grattan-, Sir Henry Christopher, Bart., of Mount Bellew, co. Galway, Ireland: (1) An arm in armour embowed ppr., charged with a crescent for difference, grasping in the hand a sword ppr., pommel and hilt or (*for Bellew*). 234. 4. (2) A dove ppr., holding in its dexter claw a sceptre and standing on a tun or (*for Grattan*). *Tout d'en haut.* 248. 7

Bellewe of Newstead, Lincs, a buck's head erased or, guttée-de-larmes, the dexter attire arg., the sinister az., guttée counterchanged. *cf.* 121. 2

Belli of Courtlands, Surrey, on the battlements of a tower gu., a lion rampant erm., holding in the dexter fore-paw a sword erect ppr., pommel and hilt or, the dexter hind-paw resting on a caltrap of the last. *Per acuta belli.*

Bellingham, Lincs and Yorks, a buck's head couped arg., on a branch twisted or and az., leaved vert.

Bellingham, Ireland, a stag's head erased sa., attired or, charged with a fleur-de-lis of the last. *cf.* 120. 5

Bellingham, Sir Alan Henry, Bart., of Castle Bellingham, co. Louth, Ireland, a buck's head couped or. *Amicus amico.—Ainsi il est.* 121. 5

Bellingham of Brumby, Lincs and Sussex, a stag's head arg., attired or, gorged with a chaplet vert. 120. 3

Bellingham, Bart. (*extinct*), of Hilsington, Westml., a stag's head erased az., attired or. 121. 2

Bellingham of Orston, Wilts, a demi-buck supporting a banner charged with the family arms, viz., arg. on a pile or, between two bugle-horns sa., stringed or, two boar's heads couped in chief sa., and in base a rose gu., stalked and leaved vert.

Bellingham of Hissington, a bugle-horn arg. 228. 11

Bellis, a hand in armour, holding a holly-branch, all ppr. 209. 14

Bellismo, out of water the top of a spear in pale, sustaining on its point a dolphin naiant. 140. 10

Bellomont, a cross moline lozenge-pierced gu. *cf.* 165. 11

Bellot, a fox's head erased sa. 33. 8

Belmore, Earl (Lowry-Corry): (1) A cock ppr. (*for Corry*). 91. 2. (2) A garland of laurel vert between two branches of the same (*for Lowry*). 257. 12. *Virtus semper viridis.*

Belmour, a griffin's head. 66. 1

Beloe, an ancient Greek lyre or, the chords arg., the band gu., garnished of the first. *Vita et pectore puro.*

Belper, Baron (Strutt), in front of rays of the sun ppr., a cubit arm erect, vested, bendy of six or and sa., cuffed arg., holding in the hand a roll of paper ppr. *Propositi tenax.* 248. 2

Belsches, *see* Belches.

Belsches-Wisheart, on a chapeau a trunk of an oak-tree eradicated, sprouting out branches with leaves ppr. *Revirescit.—Fulget.*

Belsches of that ilk, a greyhound's head couped arg., collared az. *Fulget virtus intaminata.*

Belshes, Invermay, a horse's head couped arg., bridled gu. *Keep tryst.—Revirescit.* 51. 5

Belson, a hand holding a key in bend sinister. 217. 7

Belstede, Belsted, Belstide, or **Beltead**, Norf., a seax az., hilted or. 171. 2

Belt of Bossall Hall, Yorks, on a mount vert, a cross pattée fitchée in pale gu. *cf.* 166. 3

Beltoft or **Beltofts**, a cock sa., beaked, combed, and wattled gu. 91. 2

Beltoft or **Beltofts**, Lincs, out of a ducal coronet a hand holding a sword, all ppr. 212. 11

Belvale, two arms in armour embowed, holding in the hands a heart inflamed ppr. 194. 7

Belward, a pheon sa. 174. 11

Belyn, Chesh., a unicorn's head erased arg., armed or, charged on the neck with four bars gu. *cf.* 49. 7

Bempde, a winged spur. 111. 12

Ben and **Benne** of Newport-Cranley, Surrey, an heraldic tiger passant erm., ducally gorged and tufted or. *cf.* 25. 5

Benbow of Newport, Shropsh., a harpy close or, the face ppr., the head wreathed with a chaplet of flowers gu. *cf.* 189. 1

Bence of Aldborough, Benhall, and Kingsfield, Suff., a tower arg., charged with a fret gu. *cf.* 156. 2

Bence, Edward Starkie, Kentwell Hall, Suff., a tower or, charged with a fret gu. *Virtus castellum meum.*

Bence of Thorington, Suff, a castle triple-towered *Virtus castellum meum* cf 155 8

Bence-Lambert, Colonel Guy Lenox, C.M.G., of Thorington Hall Darsham, Suff, a centaur ppr, charged on the shoulder with a cross crosslet or *Ut quocunque paratus*

Bencler, a stag's head cabossed, between the attires a bugle horn strung, all arg cf 122 5

Bendall, Middx, a demi-lion double-queued az, holding an anchor ppr cf 12 12

Bendlowes, Essex, a centaur with bow and arrow, all or 53 2

Bendyshe, Rev Richard, of Barrington, Cambs, and Bendish of Steeple-Bamstead, Essex, out of a ducal coronet or, a talbot's head, all or *Utraque Pallade* 57 12

Bene, a buck's head erased, per pale embattled, holding in the mouth a rose slip ppr, thereon three roses arg cf 121 2

Benegall, a battering-ram fesseways

Benett of Norton Bavant and Westbury, Wilts, out of a mural coronet or, a lion's head arg, charged with a mullet, also or cf 19 12

Benett, Wilts, a demi-lion rampant gu, holding between the paws a bezant. 11 7

Benett, Staffs, a horse's head arg cf 50 13

Benge, an eagle displayed ppr 75 2

Benger, Kent, a cockatrice per pale or and vert, wings expanded counterchanged 68 6

Bengough, Rev. Edward Stuart, M A, of the Rectory, Hemingby, Horncastle, two crosses pattee arg, thereon resting a lion's head erased sa., charged with an ermine spot or *Per acuta belli*

Bengough, Major General Harcourt Mortimer, C B, of The Beech House, Whitwell, Herts, same crest and motto

Benhan, Bengham, or **Benham,** a chart ppr 159 11

Benjamin, on a chapeau a flame of fire, all ppr 180 10

Benley, a sand glass gu 177 15

Benn, Joseph, Esquire, of Horton Grange, Bradford, Yorks, on a wreath of the colours an alpaca's head couped at the neck between two sprigs of oak fructed ppr *Cura atque industria* 125 2

Benn, William Henry, Esquire, of Willaston, Harrogate, same crest and motto

Benne, London, an heraldic tiger passant erm, ducally gorged and tufted or

Bennet, a ship in full sail ppr 160 13

Bennet, Earl of Tankerville, *see* Tankerville

Bennet of London, a double scaling-ladder or 158 12

Bennet, Norf, two dolphins, the one or, the other arg, entwined in saltier, erect on their tails 140 3

Bennet, a Cornish chough ppr 107 14

Bennet of London, on a mount vert, a martin ppr

Bennet of Laleston, Glamorgansh, a goat's head erased sa. *Aut nunquam tentes, aut perfice* 128 5

Bennet of Grubet, Bart, a hand issuing out of a cloud ppr, holding a cross pattee fitched gu *Benedictus qui tollit crucem.* 223 6

Bennet, a dexter hand holding a cross pattée fitched gu *Benedictus qui tollit crucem* 221 12

Bennet, Ireland, an arm couped at the elbow, holding a thistle slipped, all ppr 218 2

Bennet, Scotland, a demi-lion holding in its dexter paw a cross crosslet fitched *Benedictus qui tollit crucem.* 11 10

Bennet, Scotland, a demi lion holding in the dexter paw a cross pattee gu

Bennet of Abington, out of a mural coronet or, a lion's head gu, charged with a bezant cf 19 12

Bennet of Steeple-Ashton, Wilts, a demi-lion rampant arg, crowned or, supporting a tower ppr

Bennet, Leigh-, Henry Currie, of Thorpe Place, Surrey, out of a mural coronet or, a lion's head gu *Dux vitæ ratio* cf 19 12

Bennet of Rougham Hall Suff, and of Tollesbury, Essex out of a mural coronet or, a lion's head gu charged on the neck with a bezant *Bene tenax* cf 19 12

Bennett of Thorpe Place, Surrey, out of a mural coronet or, a lion's head gu, charged with a bezant *Dux vitæ ratio* cf 19 12

Bennett, William, Esquire, of Bank House Grimsby, in front of a demi-lion or, gorged with a collar invected gu, holding between the paws a bezant, an escallop surmounting two branches of oak fructed in saltire ppr *Deo juvante*

Bennett of Bennett's Court, Ireland, out of a mural coronet or, a demi lion rampant arg, holding in the dexter paw a bezant *Serve the King*

Bennett, Surrey and Berks, out of a mural coronet or, a lion's head gu, charged on the neck with a bezant cf 19 12

Bennett of Faringdon, Berks, a lion's head charged with a bezant *De bon valoir servir le roi* cf 21 1

Bennett, a demi lion rampant gu, holding in the dexter paw a bezant

Bennett of Finsbury, a demi lion rampant or, holding in its dexter paw a bezant

Bennett, Jackson-, John Charles, Esquire (1) Out of a mural coronet or, a dem. lion rampant arg, holding between the paws a bezant (*for Bennett*) cf 11 7 (2) An arm embowed in armour, the hand grasping a battle axe, all ppr, the arm charged with a mullet gu (*for Jackson*) *Serve the king* cf 200 6

Bennett of Stourton, Stourbridge, on a mount vert, a horse's head couped arg, pierced through the neck by an arrow, in bend sinister, point downwards, ppr *Irrevocabile*

Bennett, Glamorgansh, a goat's head erased sa, bearded and double armed or, langued gu *Aut nunquam tentes, aut perfice*

Bennett of Willaston Hall, Chesh, and Bedstone, Shropsh, on a mount vert, a greyhound passant or, collared gu, studded arg *De bon vouloir servir le roy*

Bennett of Pyt House, Wilts, on a whelk-shell or, a Cornish chough sa, beaked and legged gu *Nihi consulit Deus*

Bennett, Newcastle, a castle or, with fire flaming therefrom ppr, charged with three pellets cf 155 9

Bennett of Dublin, an arm couped at the elbow, holding in the hand a thistle, all ppr 218 2

Bennie, Benny, Benzie, or **Binnie,** Scotland, a horse's head bridled ppr *Virtute et opera* 51 5

Benning, a demi horse saddled and bridled cf 53 6

Benningham, Ireland, a horse at full speed with the point of a broken spear in its mouth cf 52 8

Bennion, *see* Benyon

Bennis, Dublin, a dexter hand couped at the wrist, lying fesseways and grasping a reaping-hook, all ppr

Bennitt, William Ward, Esquire, of Stokegreen House, Slough, Bucks, upon a mount vert, a horse's head couped arg, pierced through the neck by an arrow in bend sinister, point downwards ppr *Irrevocabile*

Benolt, a stag current ppr cf 118 13

Benon of Aldington, Sussex, on a mount vert, a griffin segreant, wings elevated arg cf 62. 2

Bensay, Berks, a horse saddled and bridled *Virtute et opera* 52 4

Bense or **Benst,** a sea-lion holding a cross patonce 20 4

Bensley, Bart, of Marylebone, a dexter hand holding a plume of ostrich-feathers

Bensley or **Bensly,** a sand-glass gu 177 15

Benson, a bear's head erased ppr, muzzled and collared or cf 35 2

Benson of Utterby, Lincs, a bear's head erased arg, muzzled gu *Inconcussa virtus* 35 2

Benson, General Robson, 15, Lansdown Crescent, Bath, in front of a bear's head couped sa, gorged with a collar and muzzled or, two crosses pattee, also or cf 34 14

Benson, a bear's head erased arg, collared and muzzled gu, and holding in the mouth a trefoil slipped of the last *Fay bien, crain rien* cf. 35 2

Benson, Robert Hugh, Esquire, a bear's head arg, erased gu, gorged with a collar gemel, and muzzled of the second, and holding in the mouth a trefoil slipped in bend sa *Fay bien crain rien*

Benson, Arthur Christopher, Esquire, of Eton College, Windsor, same crest and motto

Benson, Edward Frederick, Esquire, same crest and motto

Benson of Baysbrown and Hawkshead, Lancs, a bear's head erased arg, muzzled, gorged with a collar, and pendent therefrom an escutcheon az, charged with a trefoil or *Si Deus quis contra* cf 35 2

Benson of Dublin, a bear's head couped ppr, muzzled and collared with a chaplet of cinquefoils or cf 34 14

Benson, Thomas Starling, Esquire, of North Cray Place, Kent, the sun rising from clouds ppr, in front a demi lion gu, charged on the shoulder with a trefoil arg., the sinister paw resting on an escutcheon az., thereon a bear's head erased of the third, collared and muzzled, also gu. *Opes parit industria.* 14. 6

Benson, George Vere, M.A., barrister-at-law, a demi-lion rampant, holding in the dexter paw a mullet of five points. *Miseris succurrere.*

Benson, a talbot's head erased arg., ducally crowned or. 56. 9

Benson, the sun surmounted by a rainbow, each end of the latter issuing out of clouds, all ppr.

Benson, Ralph Beaumont, of Lutwyche, Shropsh., a military long-tailed chestnut horse, maned and tailed sa., richly caparisoned, bitted and bridled ppr., the saddle-cloth az., the girth arg., and suspended round the neck a shield, also az., charged with a pine-apple ppr. *Leges arma tenent sanctas commercia leges.*

Bensted, Benstead, Benst, or **Bense,** a sea-lion holding a cross patonce. 20. 4

Bent of Batsford, Staffs, a demi-lion az., holding between its paws a bezant. *Nec temere, nec timide.* 11. 7

Bent, a demi-lion az., holding between its paws a bezant. *Nec temere, nec timide.* 11. 7

Bent, a demi-lion az., holding between its paws a lozenge arg. *cf.* 13. 1

Bent of Wrexham Lodge, Bucks, a demi-lion rampant, per fesse az. and gu., gorged with a collar indented, and holding between its paws a bull's head cabossed or. *Tutamen Deus.*

Benthall or **De Benthall** of Benthall, Shropsh., on a ducal coronet or, a leopard statant arg., spotted sa.

Bentham, a lion rampant arg. 1. 13

Bentham, on a cross fleury fitched quarterly gu. and arg., between two wings of the first, each charged with a rose of the second, seeded or, barbed vert, the sun also or. 112. 7

Bentick, a chevalier standing beside his horse holding the bridle, all ppr. 53. 11

Bentick, a ship at sea in full sail, all ppr. 160. 13

Bentinck, *see* Portland, Duke of.

Bentinck, Henry Aldenburg, of Terrington St. Clement, Norf., and of Indio, Bovey Tracey, Devonsh., out of a ducal coronet or, two arms counter-embowed, vested gu., on the hands gloves or, each holding an ostrich-feather arg. 203. 2

Bentinck, Count (William Charles Philip Otho Bentinck), out of a ducal coronet or, two arms counter-embowed, vested gu., on the hands gloves, also or, each holding an ostrich-feather arg. 203. 2

Bentley of Birch House, Lancs, a wolf rampant erm., ducally gorged or. *Benigno numine.* *cf.* 28. 2

Bentley, a spaniel dog passant arg. *Vive ut vivas.* *cf.* 57. 7

Bentley, James, Esquire, of Highbury Place, Middx., a talbot passant arg., supporting with the dexter fore-paw an escutcheon of the arms, viz., or, on a bend cotised sa., a lion's face between two chaplets of oak of the field.

Bentley, Edward, Esquire, of Ely Place, London, a talbot passant arg., the dexter paw resting on an antique shield vair, charged with an annulet or.

Bentley, Richard, Esquire, of Upton, near Slough, Bucks, same crest. *Fide et fiducia.*

Bentley, a demi-lion rampant. 10. 2

Bentley, a demi-lion rampant grasping a thunderbolt or.

Benton, Wilts, on a mount vert, a lamb carrying a flag az. 131. 14

Benton, a griffin's head erased arg. 66. 2

Benvil or **Benvill,** a demi-swan rising ppr. 100. 9

Benweil or **Benwell,** a greyhound sejant, collared, with wings addorsed. 59. 9

Benwell of Oxford and London, a garb or, entwined by a serpent ppr., the head issuing through the ears of corn to the sinister. *cf.* 153. 1

Benwin, out of a ducal coronet gu., a boar's head erect arg., langued of the first.

Benyngton, Essex, a lion's head erased arg., semée of torteaux gu., ducally crowned or. 18. 9

Benyon-De Beauvoir, *see* De Beauvoir.

Benyon of Sussex and Suff., on a mount vert, a griffin sejant arg. *cf.* 62. 10

Benyon, Shropsh., on a mount vert, a griffin sejant arg. *cf.* 62. 10

Benyon, James Herbert, of Englefield, Berks, a griffin sejant or, gorged with an Eastern crown gu., holding in the beak a Guernsey lily ppr. (*for Benyon*). *cf.* 62. 10. (2) A lion's head erased and murally crowned arg., charged with a fesse indented erm. (*for Fellowes*). *Vincam vel moriar.* 18. 3

Benzie, Scotland, a horse's head bridled ppr. *Virtute et opera.* 51. 5

Berblock of London, in a guantlet in fess ppr., garnished or, lined gu., the lower part of a spear in pale of the second.

Berdmore or **Beardmore,** a mitre sa., semée of crosses pattée arg., charged with a chevron of the last. *cf.* 180. 5

Bere, Kent, and Oakenham, Berks, on a garb in fess or, a bird sa.

Bere, Richard, Timewell House, Devonsh., a bear's head erased sa., muzzled or. 35. 2

Bere, a heraldic tiger sejant az., bezantée, maned and tufted or.

Berearly, London, a cross potent fitched between two wings expanded.

Bereford, Staffs, an ostrich-head between two palm-branches. *cf.* 96. 10

Berenger and **Beranger,** England and France, on a mount a tree vert. 143. 14

Berens, Kent, a demi-bear salient sa. 34. 13

Berens, Richard Benyon, Esquire, of Kevington, St. Mary Cray, Kent, a demi-bear. *Nil nisi cruce.*

Berens, of Spratton Grange, Northamp., a demi-bear erect, holding between the paws a sword, all ppr. *Deus protector meus.* *cf.* 34. 13

Bereseth, a griffin's head erased ppr., collared or. *cf.* 66. 2

Beresford, Marquess of Waterford, *see* Waterford.

Beresford, Baron Decies, Ireland, *see* Decies.

Beresford-Ash, William Randall Hamilton, Esquire, of Ashbrook, Derry: (1) A squirrel sejant ppr., holding in its paws a trefoil slipped vert (*for Ash*). (2) A dragon's head erased vert, pierced through the neck with a broken tilting-spear, the point thrust through the upper jaw, all ppr., a crescent or for difference (*for Beresford*). *Nil nisi cruce.*

Beresford-Massy, John George, Macbie Hall, Peebles: (1) Out of a ducal coronet or, a bull's head gu., armed sa., charged with a martlet of the first (*for Massy*). *cf.* 44. 11. (2) A dragon's head erased az., charged with a crescent or, and pierced through the neck with a broken spear, the broken point thrust through the upper jaw, also or, and on an escroll above the crest the motto *Nil nisi cruce.* *Pro libertate patria.*

Beresford, Viscount and **Baron** (Beresford—*extinct*), out of a mural coronet or, a dragon's head per fesse wavy az. and gu., pierced through the neck with a broken tilting-spear in bend of the first, and holding the upper part of the spear in the mouth. *Nil nisi cruce.*

Beresford, Charles Edward de la Poer, Esquire, a dragon's head erased arg., pierced through the neck with a broken spear or, point arg., thrust through the upper jaw. *Nil nisi cruce.*

Beresford, William James Montgomery, Esquire, same crest and motto.

Beresford, Ralph Barre de la Poer, Esquire, of Learmont, co. Londonderry, same crest and motto.

Beresford, Mostynde de la Poer, of 76, Jermyn Street: (1) Same crest as above. (2) A stag's head cabossed ppr., attired or, between the horns a crucifix of the last. *Nil nisi cruce.*

Beresford, Pack-: (1) Issuant from a mural crown or, a dragon's head per fess wavy arg. and gu., the lower part of the neck transfixed by a broken spear, in the mouth the remaining part of the spear, the point upwards or (*for Beresford*). (2) A mural crown arg., and issuing therefrom a lion's head gu., gorged with a wreath or (*for Pack*). *Nil nisi cruce.*

Beresford-Peirse, Sir Henry Monson de la Poer, Bart., of Bedale Hall, Yorks: (1) A cross crosslet fitchée or, surmounted with a mural crown gu. (*for Peirse*). 279. 5. (2) Out of a naval crown or, a dragon's head per fess wavy arg. and gu., the lower part of the neck transfixed with a broken tilting-spear, and in the mouth the remaining part of the spear, point upwards of the first (*for Beresford*). *Non sine pulvere palma.—Nil nisi cruce.* 279. 6

Beresford, Kent, and Bentley, Derbysh., a dragon's head erased az., pierced through the neck with a broken spear or, part of same in the mouth, headed arg.

Beresford, Charles William, surgeon, Markgate House, Narborough, Leics., same crest. *Nil nisi cruce.*

Beresford, Major-General John Beresford, of Craig Dhu Varren, Portrush, co.

Antrim, an arm vambraced ppr, the hand bare, holding a pheon thereof gu *Tribus virtus*

Beresford-Drummond, Francis Colebrooke, Esquire, a falcon, wings expanded, hooded, jessed, and belled ppr, charged on the breast with a mullet or *Lord have mercy*

Beresford, a dolphin hauriant 140 11

Berey of Croston, Lancs, between two wings erm, an eagle's head couped or 84 2

Bergaigne or **Bergaine,** a demi-lion holding in its dexter paw a sword arg 14 12

Berger, a lion's gamb erased sa, holding a dagger ppr 38 8

Bergne-Coupland, Alexander Hugh, Esquire, of Skellingthorpe Hall, Lincoln (1) A swan, wings addorsed arg, semee of escallops gu and resting the dexter foot on a like escallop (*for Coupland*) cf 99 7 (2) A demi-lion gu, gorged with a collar gemelle or, holding in the dexter paw two arrows saltirewise, points downwards ppr, and resting the sinister paw on a fleur-de-lis az (*for Bergne*) *Æquo adeste animo*

Beridge, Rev Basil James Harold, Gosfield Place, Essex, in front of a bear's head erased sa, three escallops inverted or *In solo Deo salus* 249 13

Beriffe, of Colchester, Essex, out of a mural coronet gu, a demi lion rampant or, ducally crowned of the first, and holding in its dexter paw a trefoil slipped vert

Beriffe, Essex, in grass vert, a beaver passant ppr, collared or cf 134 4

Beringer, Bucks and Hants, a stem of holly-tree raguled and trunked lying fesseways sprouting out a branch in pale, leaved and fructed, all ppr

Beringham or **Berringham,** Worcs, a cross moline az 165 11

Beringham, an arm in armour embowed holding in the hand a spiked club, all ppr cf 199 2

Berington of Winsley, Heref, and of Little Malvern Court, Worcs, a greyhound's head couped arg, gorged with a collar gu 61 2

Berington, Chesh, out of a ducal coronet or, a greyhound's head arg, collared gu cf 61 7

Berington, Bradwell, Chesh, out of a ducal coronet or, a greyhound's head arg, collared gu, charged with three plates cf 61 7

Berkeley, Roland Comyns of Cotheridge, Worcs, a bear's head couped arg, muzzled gu *Dieu avec nous* 34 14

Berkeley, Maurice Henry, Esquire, of St Cloud, Worcs., same crest and motto

Berkeley, Thomas Mowbray Martin, Esquire, same crest and motto

Berkeley, Robert Valentine, of Spetchley, Worcs, same crest and motto

Berkeley, Comyns, M R C P, 53, Wimpole Street, W, same crest and motto

Berkeley, a unicorn passant gu, armed and crined or cf 48 5

Berkeley, Earl of, Viscount Dursley (Rt Hon Randal Thomas Moreton Berkeley), a mitre gu, labelled and garnished or, charged with a chevron between ten crosses pattee, six and four, arg *Dieu avec nous* cf 180 5

Berkenhead, out of a ducal coronet a hand holding a sheath of arrows, points downward, all ppr 214 2

Berkhead, Crostwhite, Cumb, a goat's head erased, party per fess or and gu, attired sa 128 5

Berkhead or **Berkenhead,** a goat salient arg, attired or, resting the dexter fore-foot on a garb of the last

Berkley, a unicorn passant gu, armed and crined or cf 48 5

Berkley, a bear's head couped arg, muzzled gu 34 14

Bermingham, an heraldic antelope's head erased arg, maned and attired or cf 127 10

Bermingham, an owl erm, crowned or cf 96 5

Bermingham and **Birmingham,** Warw, two lions' gambs in saltier sa 39 14

Bernall, a demi-lion rampant gu 10 2

Bernard, a bear passant ppr, muzzled or cf 34 1

Bernard of Nettleham, Lincs, and Nether Winchendon, Bucks, a demi-bear sa, muzzled and collared or *Bear and forbear* 307 14

Bernard, Hunts, a demi bear sa, muzzled and collared or *Nisi paret imperat* 307 14

Bernard, John Mackay, Esquire, of Dunsinnan and Buttergask, Perth, a demi-bear arg., muzzled and lined gu *Bear and forbear*

Bernard, Dr Charles John Skegness Lincolnshire, a demi-bear rampant muzzled and collared *Bear and forbear* 307 14

Bernard, Earl of Bandon, and **Viscount Bernard,** Castle Bernard, Bandon, Ireland a demi lion arg, holding a snake ppr *Virtus probata florebit* cf 9 14

Bernard, of Palace Anne, Ireland, a demi lion arg, holding between its paws a snake ppr *Virtus probata florebit* cf 9 14

Bernard, Percy Broderic, Castle Harket, Tuam, same crest and motto

Berners of Tharfield, Herts, a monkey ppr, collared about the loins and lined or cf 136 8

Berners, Charles Hugh, of Woolverstone Park, Suff, a monkey ppr, environed about the loins and lined or, holding a scroll with the motto *Del fuego Io avola* cf 136 8

Bernes, Cambs, a leopard passant arg, spotted sa, collared and lined or cf 24 2

Berney, Sir Henry Hanson, Bart, of Parkhall, Norf, a plume of ostrich-feathers arg, and gu alternately *Nil temere, neque timore* 251 6

Berney, Thomas, Clifton House, Bramley Hill, Croydon, same crest

Berney, Augustus, Esquire, of Bracon Hall, Norf, out of a ducal coronet a plume of five ostrich feathers arg *Nil temere, neque timore*

Berney of Kirkbridge, Norf, same crest and motto

Berney, an eagle's head ppr, gorged with an Eastern coronet or, and in the mouth a palm-branch vert, between two wings erm

Berney, Norf, a sheaf of reeds or cf 153 2

Bernheim, a fleur-de-lis, on the top three grass spires, each containing seven piles gu

Bernil and **Birnall,** a greyhound's head between two roses stalked and leaved 61 11

Berns of Soham, Cambs, an ounce arg, spotted sa, collared and chained or cf 24 12

Berondon and **Berondowne,** Northumb, a unicorn rampant ppr 48 2

Berowe and **Berew,** Glouc, a sea-horse's head erased sa, bezantee, maned and finned or

Berreton, out of a ducal coronet a bear's head and neck muzzled 34 3

Berrey, a hand holding a dagger 212 3

Berriedale, Lord, *see* Caithness, Earl of

Berring, out of a ducal coronet or, a greyhound's head ppr 61 7

Berringham, *see* Beringham

Berrington, Arthur Vendigaid Davies, Esquire, J P, D L, of Pant y Goitre, Abergavenny (1) An estoile gu (*for Berrington*) 164 1 (2) A wolf salient arg (*for Davies*) *Solem fero* cf 28 1

Berry or **Berrie,** Westerbogie, Scotland, a demi lion gu, holding in the dexter paw a cross crosslet fitched az *In hoc signo vinces* 232 3

Berry, William, Esquire, of Tayfield, Fife, Scotland, a demi-lion rampant gu, armed and langued az, holding in his dexter paw a cross crosslet fitchée, also az *In hoc signo vinces —L'esperance me comforte* 11 5

Berry, Robert, of 5, University Gardens, Glasgow, same crest and motto

Berry of Ballynegall, Westmeath (1) A griffin's head and neck per pale indented gu and arg, charged with a trefoil counterchanged (*for Berry*) cf 66 1 (2) A demi lion rampant az, holding between his paws an escallop or (*for Gibbons*) *Nihil sine labore* 13 10

Berry, Henry F, Assistant Keeper of the Records in Ireland and Colonel Edward Ring Berry, a griffin's head erased arg, and charged on the neck with three torteaux in pale *Ne cede malis* cf 66 2

Berry, Edward Ring, Esquire, of 2, Hyde Park Gate, South Kensington, S W, same crest and motto

Berry, Henry Fitzpatrick, Esquire, of 60, Morehampton Road Dublin same crest

Berry of Berry-Narbor, Devonsh, a griffin's head erased per pale, indented arg and gu 66. 2

Berry, William Bertram Esquire, of Kersewell, Carnwath Lanarksh, a ram's head ppr, issuing from an antique crown or *J'avance*

Berry, an eagle's head ppr, gorged with an Eastern coronet or, in the beak a laurel slip vert

Berry, Bart. (*extinct*), of Catton, Norf, between two wings elevated erm, an eagle's head couped ppr, gorged with an Eastern crown or, in the beak a palm branch ppr *Per ardua*

Berry, out of an Eastern coronet or, a demi-talbot rampant ppr

Berry, between the horns of a crescent or, a cross pattee gu 163 6

Berry, Henry, Esquire, of Eshald House, Rothwell, Yorks, in front of a demi-gryphon arg., holding between the claws a fret gu., a like fret. *Vincit omnia veritas.*

Berryman, Devonsh., a horse's head erased sa. 50. 8

Bertie, a savage's head couped at shoulders ppr., ducally crowned or. *Loyauté m'oblige.* 192. 9

Bertie, Earl of Lindsey, *see* Lindsey.

Bertie, Earl of Abingdon, *see* Abingdon.

Bertie-Greatheed, *see* Greatheed.

Bertie, Bart., of Nether Hall, Essex, a man's head affrontée couped at the shoulders ppr., ducally crowned or, charged on the breast with a sinister bendlet wavy gobony arg. and az. *Loyauté m'oblige.*

Bertie, a pear-tree fructed ppr. 144. 10

Bertles or **Bertleys,** Chesh., a lion rampant az., holding a tree erased at the roots ppr.

Bertram, a bull's head erased ppr., ducally gorged or. 44. 2

Bertram of Grafford, Jersey, a demi-lion arg. 10. 2

Bertram of Grouville, Jersey, a demi-lion arg., holding between its paws an escutcheon of the arms, viz., or, an orle az.

Bertram of Nisbet, co. Roxburgh, Scotland, issuing out of an antique crown or, a ram's head ppr. *J'avance.* cf. 130. 8

Bertram, William, Esquire, of Kersewell, Carnwath, co. Lanark, a ram's head ppr., issuing from an antique crown or. *J'avance.*

Bertram, Julius, of Sishes, Stevenage, Herts, an eagle displayed sa., holding in the mouth a fleur-de-lis or, and in each claw a chaplet of roses gu., leaved, also or. *Aquila non capit muscas.*

Bertrand, a hand holding a pistol ppr. 221. 8

Bertwhistle, a dolphin naiant ppr. 140. 5

Berwick, Duke of, *see* Fitzjames.

Berwick, Baron (Noel-Hill): (1) On the battlements of a tower ppr., a hind statant arg., collared and chained or (*for Hill*). 124. 10. (2) A buck at gaze arg., attired or (*for Noel*). 117. 3. (3) A stag's head caboshed sa., holding in the mouth a sprig of oak ppr. (*for Harwood*). *Qui uti scit ei bona.* cf. 122. 5

Berwick, Lancs, two ears of wheat in saltier ppr. 154. 4

Bery of Bury, Devonsh., a griffin's head erased party per pale indented arg. and gu. 66. 2

Bery or **Barry** of Winscot, Devonsh., a wolf's head erased sa. 30. 8

Besant, Philip Eustace, Esquire, of Frognal End, Hampstead, N.W., issuant from clouds ppr., a palm-tree or, thereto attached by a chain, gold, and resting on the wreath an escocheon sa., charged with two bezants in pale.

Beseley, Lancs and Yorks, an arm in armour embowed, resting on the elbow, couped at the shoulder, holding a club, all ppr. 199. 4

Beseley, Yorks, a castle triple-towered arg., on the centre tower a standard floating to the sinister sa., charged with a saltier of the first. cf. 155. 8

Beseley, Besley, or **Besly,** a lion rampant holding between his paws a ducal coronet. 3. 6

Beseley, Besley, or **Besly,** out of a mural coronet two branches of palm in saltier, surmounted by a spear in pale ppr. 175. 1

Besiles or **Besills,** a hand holding a bunch of grapes, all ppr. 219. 6

Besley and Besly, *see* Beseley.

Besly, *see* Wood-Besly.

Besney, Heref., out of a ducal coronet a demi-griffin arg. 64. 4

Besook, on a mural coronet a beaver passant ppr. (*Another,* statant.) cf. 134. 8

Bessborough, Earl (Ponsonby), in a ducal coronet az., three arrows, one in pale and two in saltire, points downwards, entwined by a snake ppr. *Pro rege lege grege.* 173. 2

Bessell, a demi-lion affrontée, in each paw a slip of columbine ppr., flowered purp.

Bessemer, the late Sir Henry, Knt., Knight Commander of the Austrian Order of St. Francis Joseph, and Knight Grand Cross of the Legion of Honour of France, of Denmark Hill, Surrey, a demi-griffin az., charged with three fleur-de-lis chevronwise or, supporting a torch erect fired ppr. *Onward ever.* 228. 7

Best, Baron Wynford, *see* Wynford.

Best-Fairfax, Kent, out of a mural coronet or, an ostrich issuant arg., holding in its beak a cross crosslet of the first.

Best, out of a mural coronet or, an ostrich-head arg., holding in the beak a cross crosslet of the first.

Best, Kent, out of a ducal coronet or, an ostrich-head between two wings arg., holding in the beak a cross crosslet of the first. cf. 97. 11

Best, Glouc. and Kent, out of a ducal coronet or, an ostrich-head between two wings arg. cf. 97. 11

Best of Chilston, Kent, out of a mural coronet or, a demi-ostrich issuant arg., holding in the beak a cross crosslet fitched or.

Best, Major Mawdistly Gaussen, of Park House, Boxley, Kent, same crest. *Sola cruce.*

Best, London, a peacock with wings elevated or, holding in the beak a serpent reflexed over the back az.

Best, London and Kent, out of a ducal coronet gu., a demi-peacock, the wings displayed or, holding in the beak a snake ppr., entwined round the body.

Best of Eastbury, Surrey, a griffin's head erased sa. *Haud nomine tantum.* 66. 5

Best, a griffin's head erased sa. 66. 5

Best of Elmswell, Little Driffield, and South Dalton, Yorks, a cubit arm vested gu. and cuffed arg., holding a falchion ppr.

Best, Marmaduke Head, of Donnington, Berks, a cubit arm vested gu., cuffed arg., holding a falchion ppr. *Optimus est qui optime facit.*

Best, Haden-, George Alfred Haden, Esquire, of Haden Hill, Rowley Regis, Staffs: (1) In front of a rock ppr., thereon a pheon az., a boar's head couped or (*for Best*). 270. 11. (2) In front of a cubit arm in armour, the hand grasping an arrow in bend sinister, a morion, all ppr. (*for Haden*). 270. 12

Bestall, a bee erect and volant ppr. *Utile dulci.*

Beste of Middleton-Quernhow, Yorks, the sinister arm of an archer couped and embowed in fess, habited gu., holding a bow in pale ppr., strung arg. cf. 204. 11

Beste, Digby-, of Botleigh Grange, Hants, and Abbotsham Court, Devonsh.: (1) An archer's arm habited gu., holding a bow in pale, strung or (*for Beste*). 204. 11. (2) An ostrich arg., holding in the beak a horse-shoe or (*for Digby*). *Solo Deo gloria.* 97. 8

Bestick, a demi-lion rampant az., holding between the paws a bezant. *In Deo salus.* 11. 7

Bestney, Herts, out of a ducal coronet a demi-griffin arg. 64. 4

Beston, a demi-talbot holding in the mouth an arrow. 55. 10

Bestoricke or **Bestorike,** a demi-talbot holding in the mouth an arrow. 55. 10

Bestow, a crescent arg. 163. 2

Bestroe and **Bestrow,** an elephant's head erased per chevron or and sa., armed of the last. 133. 3

Besville, a dragon's head erased gu. cf. 71. 2

Beswick, London and Kent, a demi-lion ppr., holding between its paws a bezant. 11. 7

Beswick of Beswick, Kent, a demi-lion ppr., double-queued, holding between its paws a bezant. cf. 11. 7

Beswick of Gristhorpe, Yorks, a demi-lion rampant or, holding between its paws a bezant. *Denique cœlum.* 11. 7

Beswick, of Winnington, Chesh., a demi-lion or, holding between its paws a bezant. 11. 7

Beswicke-Royds, Clement Robert Nuttall, Pyke House, Littleborough, Manchester: (1) A leopard sejant sa., bezantée, gorged with a collar arg., the dexter fore-paw resting on a pheon or (*for Royds*). (2) A demi-lion rampant or, holding between its paws a bezant (*for Beswicke*). *Semper paratus.*

Beswycke, a demi-lion rampant gu., holding in the dexter paw a bezant. cf. 11. 7

Betagh, Ireland, two anchors in saltier. 161. 7

Betagh, a camel's head erased arg., bridled gu. cf. 132. 9

Betenham or **Betnam,** Kent, a bear's head erased sa., muzzled and billetée or. cf. 35. 2

Betenson, Bettenson, or **Betterson,** Kent, a lion's head erased sa., collared arg. *Qui sera sera.* 18. 6

Betenson, Devonsh., a griffin's head couped ppr. 66. 1

Betham, Bucks, out of a ducal coronet or, an elephant's head arg. 133. 1

Bethell, Dorset, a demi-eagle, wings displayed az., charged on the body with an etoile of six points or. cf. 80. 2

Bethell, Heref. and Yorks, between two wings displayed az., an eagle's head, couped of the same, charged on the neck with an etoile or. cf. 84. 2

Bethell, Guy Vivian, Esquire, out of a crown vallery or, an eagle's head sa between two wings az, and charged on the breast with an estoile or *Ap Ithel* 250. 3

Bethell, Slingsby Westbury, Esquire, same crest and motto

Bethell, Baron Westbury, out of a crown vallery or, an eagle's head sa, between two wings az, and charged on the breast with an estoile or *Ap Ithel* 250 3

Bethell, William, of Walton Abbey, York, out of a ducal coronet or, a boar's head couped sa 41 4

Bethell, Alfred James, Esquire, of Middlethorpe Lodge, York, same crest

Bethell, Commander George Richard, of Sigglesthorne, Hull, same crest and motto

Bethell, William, Esquire, of Rise Park, Hull, same crest and motto

Bethell or **Bythell,** out of a ducal coronet or, a boar's head and neck arg 41 4

Bethome, out of a ducal coronet an elephant's head arg 133 1

Bethune, Bart, Scotland, an otter's head, erased ppr *Debonnair* 134 3

Bethune, Patton-, of Clayton Priory, Burgess Hill, Sussex (1) A demi-otter issuant arg (*for Bethune*) 134 11 (2) Upon two swords saltirewise ppr, pommels and hilts or, a falcon rising arg, guttee de larmes (*for Patton*) *Virtute adepta —Debonnaire*

Bethune, an otter's head couped ppr *Urbane* 134 1

Bethune, Charles Congleton, of Balfour, co Fife, an otter's head erased arg *Debonnair* 134 3

Bethune, Scotland, an otter's head couped arg *Debonnair* 134. 1

Bethune of Blebo Scotland, an otter issuing arg *Debonnair* 135 11

Bethune, Alexander Esquire of Blebo, Cupar, Fifesh a demi-otter rampant arg *Debonnair*

Bethune of Nethertarvit, a physician's quadrangular cap sa. *Resolutio cauta* 180 7

Bethune of Great Berwick, Shropsh, a demi-lion rampant *Nunquam non paratus* 10 2

Bethwater, a fawn's head cabossed or

Betnam, *see* Betenham

Beton, Beaton, Betton, and **Betune,** a lion passant sa *Fortis in arduis* 6 2

Betray, an arm embowed vested gu, cuffed arg, holding in the hand ppr a torteau

Betson of Glassermount, Scotland, a bee volant in pale ppr *Cum prudentia sedulus* 137 2

Betson of Contle, Scotland, a bridge of three arches ppr *Pro patria* 158 4

Betsworth, out of a tower arg, a demi lion or, ducally crowned az, holding in his dexter paw a battle axe arg *cf* 157 11

Bettenson or **Bettinson** of Seven Oaks, Kent, a lion's head erased sa, collared arg *Qui sera sera* 18 6

Bettes, out of a ducal coronet or, a buck's head gu, attired of the first, gorged with a collar arg, charged with three cinquefoils of the second *cf* 120 7

Bettes, Hants, out of a ducal coronet or, a bull's head arg 44 11

Bettescombe of Vere's Watton, Dorset, an olive-branch ppr *Non omnis moriam.* 151 11

Bettesworth of Tyning, co Sussex, on the stump of a tree vert, a lion sejant per fesse or and arg, holding in the dexter paw a battle axe gu, headed of the third 9 5

Bettesworth, out of a tower arg, a demi lion rampant per fess or and arg, crowned az, holding in the paws a battle axe, the handle or, headed arg *cf* 157 11

Bettie or **Betty,** a goat's head erased and collared ppr *cf* 128 7

Bettison, Warw, a lion's head erased sa, collared arg *Qui sera sera* 18 6

Betton of Great Berwick and Overton, Shropsh, a demi-lion rampant *Nunquam non paratus* 10 2

Betton, *see* Beton

Betts, a leopard passant gardant ppr 24 4

Betts, Augustine Matthew, of Euthella, Goulburn, New South Wales, out of a naval coronet arg, a demi-lion gu, holding a sail arg, charged with an anchor sa

Betts of Preston Hall, Kent, out of the battlements of a tower ppr, a stag's head arg, charged with a cinquefoil sa *Ostendo non ostento* *cf* 120 10

Betts of Wortham Hall, Suff, out of a ducal coronet or, a buck's head gu, attired of the first 120 7

Bettsworth, out of a tower arg, a demi-lion rampant crowned az, holding in the paws a battle-axe, handle or, headed arg *cf* 157 11

Betty, a demi-lion holding in the dexter paw a crescent arg

Betty, a goat's head erased and collared ppr *cf* 128 7

Betune, a demi-bear rampant 34 13

Betune, *see* Beton

Beufo, a beech-tree with a saw through it ppr

Beugo, an arm in armour embowed, wielding a scimitar turned to the dexter, all ppr *Qui nos vincet?—Pro Deo, patria, et rege*

Beuzevill, a lion's head ppr, platee *cf* 21 1

Bevan or **Bevin,** Cornw, a griffin passant or 63 2

Bevan of Fosbury, Wilts, and Trent Park, Middx, a griffin passant or, semee of annulets gu, holding in the dexter claw two annulets interlaced, also gu *Deus præsidium* 63 5

Bevan, Roland Yorke, Esquire, same crest and motto

Bevan, Sydney, Esquire, of Fosbury Manor, Hungerford, Wilts, same crest and motto

Bevan, Wilfred Arthur, Esquire, same crest and motto

Bevan, Paul, Esquire, M A (Cantab), A C A, 46, Queen's Gate Terrace, London, S W, a griffin passant or, semée of annulets gu, and holding in its dexter claw two annulets interlaced of the last *Non sine industria* 63 5

Bevan of Ashted, Surrey, on a mural coronet arg, a griffin passant or, gorged with an Eastern coronet gu

Bevan, Thomas, Esquire, D L J P High Sheriff of the City of London and of Middx, 1878-79, and High Sheriff of Kent, 1895, of Stone Park Kent, upon the battlements of a tower ppr, a gryphon or, gorged with a collar gemel az, resting the dexter claw on an escutcheon arg, charged with a hurt *Semper virtuti constans* 63 11

Bevan of Pen y Coed, Carmarthensh, a mount vert, thereon an eagle rising ppr, holding in the beak an annulet or, enriched with a ruby ppr *Semper virtute constans*

Bevan, *see* Beavan

Bevans or **Beavins,** a weaver's shuttle in pale, threaded ppr 176 14

Beveley, a bull's head sa, ducally crowned or

Bevens of Dublin, a cubit arm erect, vested az, the hand ppr, grasping a garb or *cf* 218 1

Bevereham and **Beverham,** Ireland, out of a coronet or, an arm in armour, holding a sword, all ppr

Beveridge-Duncan, *see* Duncan

Beveridge, Kent, Chichester, and Scotland, out of a ducal coronet or, a demi-beaver ppr

Beverley, between two wings expanded a nail erect

Beverley of Beverley, Yorks, a bull's head erased arg *Ubi libertas, ibi patria* 44 3

Beverley, Earl of, *see* Northumberland, Duke of

Beverley of Dublin, on a mount vert, a wolf passant arg, pierced through the neck with an arrow sa

Bevers of Hogsdon, a demi-wyvern vert, armed gu 69 12

Bevers, a beaver sejant ppr *Et finem spiro* 134 8

Beversham of Holbrook Hall, Suff, out of a tower arg, a demi lion gu 157 11

Bevil, a bull's head gu, armed or

Bevil and **Bevile,** Suff, a dove volant, with an olive-branch in its beak ppr 93 10

Bevill, Beville, or **Bevin,** Cornw, a griffin passant gu 63 2

Bevill, a griffin passant or, collared sa *cf* 63 2

Beville of Killegarth, a griffin passant or *Futurum invisible* 63 2

Bevin, *see* Bevill

Bevis, a pheon az 174 11

Bew, a peacock's head couped and erect ppr 103 2

Bewcham or **Bewsham,** a hand issuing from the wreath and pruning a vine ppr *cf* 221 11

Bewes of St Neots, Cornw, on a chapeau gu, turned up erm, a pegasus rearing of a bay colour, mane and tail sa, wings or, holding in the mouth a sprig of laurel ppr 263 4

Bewes, Cecil Edward, Esquire, of 3, the Esplanade, Plymouth, same crest *Major ab advertis*

Bewes of Beaumont, near Plymouth, the same crest *Major ab odvertis*

Bewicke, Calverley, Esquire, of Bewicke, Newcastle, and Close House, Northumb, a goat's head erased arg, armed, maned and gorged with a mural coronet gu *In cœlo quies* *cf* 128 5

Bewicke, Calverley Theodore Esquire, of 1 Warwick Road, S W, same crest and motto

Bewicke-Copley, Robert Calverley Alington, Sprotborough, Doncaster: (1) Out of a ducal coronet or, charged with a cross crosslet gu. (for distinction) five ostrich-feathers arg. (*Copley.*) (2) A goat's head erased at the neck arg., armed, maned, and gorged with a mural coronet gu. (*Bewicke.*) *In cruce vinco.*

Bewley, Sir Edmund Thomas, of 40, Fitzwilliam Place, Dublin, an ibex's head or, issuant from the centre of a rose gu., stalked and leaved ppr. *Virtutis gloria merces.* 271. 11

Bewley, Suff., an ibex's head or, issuing out of the centre of a rose gu., barbed vert.

Bewley, Lincs, a Moor's head affrontée vested in a cowl, all ppr.

Bewris or **Bewrys,** a lion's head arg., charged with two chevronels sa., ducally crowned or.

Bewshin, out of a ducal coronet or, a lion's gamb holding a palm-branch ppr. 36. 10

Bexley, Baron (Vansittart), upon two crosses pattée arg., a demi-eagle couped sa., the wings elevated. *Grata quies.*

Beyard, on a tower arg., the loopholes and gateway sa., a lion rampant gu. 157. 12

Beykle, a cross pattée gu., between two wings or. 110. 7

Beynham of Grove, Herts, a beaver ppr. 134. 8

Beynham, Hunts, a raven ppr. 107. 14

Beynon of Trewern, Pembrokesh., a lion rampant sa. *Heb Dduw heb ddim a Duw a digon.* 1. 10

Beynon of Bath, a lion rampant ppr., holding between its paws a rose or, barbed vert. *cf.* 1. 6

Beynon, *see* Crowther-Beynon.

Beynon, a lion rampant arg., semée of cross crosslets vert, holding between the fore-paws an escutcheon, also arg., thereon a greyhound's head erased pean, and charged on the shoulder for distinction with a rose gu. *Integer vitæ.*

Beynon of Carshalton, Surrey: (1) A lion rampant arg., semée of cross crosslets vert, holding between the paws an escutcheon of the first, charged with a greyhound's head erased pean (*for Beynon*). (2) A griffin's head erased pean, holding in the beak a mill-rind or (*for Batley*).

Beynton, a griffin's head erased sa. 66. 5

Bibby Hesketh, Charles Hesketh, Esquire, D.L., of the Rookery, North Meols, Southport, co. Lancaster: (1) A mount vert, thereon in front of an eagle with two heads displayed ppr., a garb or, banded gu. (*for Hesketh*). (2) In front of a cubit arm erect, holding a sword in bend sinister ppr., pommel and hilt or, a mullet of six points between two escallops fesseways arg. (*for Bibby*). *Quod tibi hoc alteri.*

Bice of Dublin, a falcon preying on a partridge, all ppr. 77. 12

Bickerstaffe, in front of the sun in splendour a unicorn rampant, all ppr. 48. 1

Bickersteth, Rev. Samuel, the Vicarage, Lewisham, S.E., a dexter arm in armour embowed holding in the hand a battle-axe. *Frappe fort.*

Bickersteth, *see* Langdale, Baron.

Bickersteth, a dexter arm embowed in armour ppr., garnished or, about the elbow a wreath of oak vert, in the hand a roll of paper ppr. *Frappe fort.* 266. 1

Bickersteth, Lieutenant-Colonel Robert, of 70, Cromwell Road, S.W., same crest and motto.

Bickerton, Hussey-, Bart., of Upwood, Hunts: (1) A dexter arm in armour embowed, holding a dagger, all ppr., and for augmentation suspended from the arm by a crimson ribbon an escutcheon gu., charged with a mullet and increscent fesseways or (*for Bickerton*). *cf.* 196. 5. (2) A hind trippant ppr., ducally gorged and chained or (*for Hussey*). *Pro Deo et rege.* *cf.* 124. 12

Bickerton, a martlet or. 95. 2

Bickley, Bart., of Attleborough, Norf., a hind's head ppr., collared arg. *cf.* 124. 5

Bickley of Bickleigh, Devonsh. and Sussex, Cambs and Middx, the same crest.

Bicknall or **Bicknell,** an angel praying between two branches of laurel in orle. 184. 2

Bicknell, Algernon Sidney, Esquire, a dragon couchant regardant, wings expanded sa., gorged with a collar or, holding in the dexter claw a cross flory. *Surge biconyll.*

Bicknoll, a dragon's head erased vert. *cf.* 71. 2

Bicknor, Bickenor, or **Bykenore,** a pheon erm. 174. 11

Bicknor, *see* Bykenor.

Bickwith, Yorks, *see* Beckwith.

Biddell, Biddle, or **Biddelle,** Glouc., a demi-heraldic tiger rampant gu., ducally gorged or. *Deus clypeus meus.* 25. 12

Biddulph, Myddelton, of Chirk Castle, Denbigh: (1) A wolf salient arg., charged on the shoulder with a trefoil slipped vert (*for Biddulph*). 268. 9 (2) Out of a ducal coronet or, a bloody hand ppr. (*for Myddelton*). *In veritate triumpho.*

Biddulph, Michael, of Ledbury, Heref.: (1) A wolf salient arg., charged on the shoulder with a trefoil slipped vert. 268. 9. (2) A wolf sejant regardant arg., vulned on the shoulder gu. *Sublimiora petimus.* 278. 10

Biddulph, a wolf sejant regardant arg., vulned in the shoulder gu. 278. 10

Biddulph, Sir Theophilus George, Bart., of Birdingbury Hall, Warw., a wolf rampant arg., vulned in the shoulder ppr. *cf.* 28. 2

Biddulph, Wright-, of Burton Park, Sussex: (1) A wolf salient arg. *cf.* 28. 1. (2) Out of a ducal coronet or, a dragon's head ppr. 72. 4

Biddulph, George Tournay, Esquire, of Douglas House, Petersham, a wolf salient arg., charged on the breast with a trefoil slipped pert. *Sublimiora petamus.* 268. 9

Biddulph, General Sir Michael Anthony Shrapnel, K.C.B., of 2, Whitehall Court, S.W., a wolf sejant regardant arg., vulned on the shoulder gu. *Sublimiora petamus.* 278. 10

Biddulph, Michael, Esquire, of 19, Ennismore Gardens, London, S.W., a wolf sejant regardant arg., vulned in the shoulder gu. 278. 10

Biddulph, General Sir Robert, United Service Club, Pall Mall, same crest. *Sublimiora petamus.*

Biddulph, Cleve Court, Somers., a wolf salient arg. *cf.* 28. 1

Biddulph Colclough, Francis Digby, Esquire, of Tintern Abbey, co. Wexford, Ireland: (1) A demi-eagle displayed sa., gorged with a ducal coronet or, and charged on the breast with a cross crosslet arg. (*for Colclough*). *cf.* 81. 2. (2) A wolf rampant arg., guttée-de-sang, gorged with a bar gemelle az., and charged with a trefoil slipped ppr. (*for Biddulph*). *His calcabo gentes.* 28. 5

Biddulph, Lieutenant-Colonel M. W., Rathrobin, Tullamore: (1) A wolf salient arg. 278. 9 (2) A wolf sejant regardant arg., vulned in the shoulder gu. 278. 10

Bidgood of Exeter, Devonsh., a dexter hand erect in armour or, holding an adder ppr.

Bidgood of Rockbeare Park, Devonsh., the same crest, charged for distinction with a cross crosslet gu.

Bidlake, Somers., a cock holding in the beak a trefoil, all ppr. 91. 5

Bidlake, same crest. *Virtute non astutia.*

Bidon, between two wings a lion rampant. 9. 2

Bidulph, Kent, a wolf salient arg., vulned in the shoulder gu. *cf.* 28. 1

Bidwell or **Bydewell,** Devonsh., a hand couped in fess holding a curling-stone. 221. 2

Bidwell, a martlet sa. 95. 5

Bidwill, John Orbell, Esquire, J.P., of Pihautea, Featherstone, Wellington, New Zealand, *uses* an escallop. 141. 14

Bie, two oak-branches in saltier ppr. 151. 1

Bielby, a hawk close ppr. 85. 2

Biest, Shropsh., *see* Beist.

Biest, a fetterlock ppr. 168. 12

Bieth, *see* Beith.

Bifield or **Byfield,** London, a cross crosslet fitched gu., between two palm-branches vert. *cf.* 166. 5

Big, Bigg, or **Bigge,** three savages' heads conjoined in one neck, one looking to the sinister, one to the dexter, and one upwards, wreathed vert. 191. 5

Big, Bigg, or **Bigge,** Essex, a cockatrice's head couped ppr., beaked and crowned or, between two wings displayed vert. *cf.* 68. 8

Bigberry and **Bigbury** of Bigbury, Devonsh., a hand holding a leg in armour, couped above the knee and spurred, all ppr. 220. 11

Bigelow, Melville Madison, Esquire, Ph.D., Cambridge, Massachusetts, U.S.A., a ram's head az., attired arg., the neck charged with three lozenges or. *Finis coronat opus.* 130. 11

Bigg of Benendon, Kent, Haines Hill, Berks, Chilton Folyatt, Wilts, and Hants, a rhinoceros ppr. 226. 2

Bigg, Bart. (*extinct*), of Lenchwich, Worcs., an arm embowed vested, couped at the shoulder, holding in the hand a serpent ppr., the tail environing the arm.

Bigg of Iping, Sussex, and Arnwood, Hants, an eagle's head couped ppr, ducally crowned or, between two wings elevated of the first *cf* 84 2
Bigg, out of a mural coronet seven Loch aber axes ppr 172 9
Biggar of Woolmet, co Edinburgh, Scotland, a pelican's head couped and vulning itself ppr *Giving and for giving* *cf* 98 2
Biggar or **Bigger**, a pelican's head vulning ppr *cf* 98 2
Biggar, Ireland, a demi pelican sa, vulning herself ppr
Bigge, *see* Bigg
Bigge of Long Horsley, Northumberland, a cockatrice's head couped sa, beaked and crowned or, wings erect vert.
Bigge, Francis Edward, Esquire, Hennapyn, Cockington, Torquay, a cockatrice's head couped and murally crowned or between two wings erect az
Bigge or **Biggs**, an eagle's head erm, ducally crowned or, between two wings arg *cf* 84 2
Biggs, Yeatman-, of Stockton House, Wilts (1) In front of a javelin erect ppr, a leopard's head affrontee erased az, charged with two fleurs de lis fessewise or (*for Biggs*) 243 10 (2) A goat's head erased sa, armed, bearded, and charged with a gate or (*for Yeatman*) 243. 11
Biggs, London, a leopard's face gu *cf* 22 2
Biggs, London, a lamb couchant arg *cf* 131 12
Biggs, a dexter hand charged with a bendlet arg, holding a serpent vert 220 2
Bigham, Hon Sir John Charles, of 10, Palace Gate, Kensington, a horse per pale or and sa, charged on the body with three horse-shoes fesseways counterchanged, and resting the dexter fore-leg on a cross pattee gu *J'avance*
Bigland, George, of Bigland Hall, Lancs, a lion passant regardant gu, holding in the dexter paw an ear of big wheat stalked and bladed or *Gratitude — Spes labor levis* *cf* 6 1
Bignell, a Wyvern gu, the wings elevated and addorsed or, resting the dexter claw on an anchor of the last *cf* 69 5
Bignold, Charles Arthur Bathurst, Esquire, of Eaton Hall, Norwich a lion passant regardant gu, holding in his fore-paw an ear of big wheat or
Bigot or **Bigott**, a martlet sa *cf* 95 5
Bigsby of Stowmarket, Suff, and Arnovale, Notts, an eagle displayed or, armed gu *Ad astra — Nitamur semper ad optima* 75 2
Bigwood, a hand erect issuing from a cloud holding a club in bend sinister 214 9
Bilesby of Bilesby, Lincs, a lion's head erased arg 17 8
Bill, a stork's head erased ppr 106 1
Bill, Charles, of Farley Hall, Staffs, a pelican's head erased arg, vulning itself. *Omne solum patria* 98 2
Billam of Billam and Wales, and of Newall Hall, Yorks, a dexter arm grasping an arrow ppr *Azincourt* 214 4
Billcliffe of Turganby, Kent, a naked arm couped at the elbow and erect holding a battle axe, all ppr *cf* 213 11
Billers of London, a snail in its shell ppr 141 8
Billesworth, a squirrel sejant cracking a nut, all ppr *Another*, collared or 135 7
Billet or **Billot**, Norf, and Ashe, Devonsh, a hand and arm couped at the elbow in armour ppr, holding in the gauntlet a baton or *cf* 209 9
Billiat, Joseph, Esquire, of Aisthorpe Hall, Lincs, a duck close or, holding in the beak a billet arg, between two bulrushes ppr *Ung Dieu ung Roy* 271. 17
Billich, a rat salient sa
Billing, Norf., a dexter arm in armour ppr, holding in the hand an anchor
Billing and **Billinge** of Deding, Oxon, and Billinge, Lancs, an arm couped at the shoulder and embowed in fess, the elbow resting upon the wreath and holding a spear in pale 201 11
Billing, a mount semee of quatrefoils 179 10
Billing or **Billinge**, a buck trippant ppr 117 8
Billingham, a lion rampant ppr 1 13
Billingham, a lion rampant double-queued arg *Another*, or 1 14
Billinghurst, Surrey, issuant from a human heart a branch of roses, all ppr
Billinghurst of Newport, Isle of Wight, an eagle displayed or, holding in the beak a cross crosslet fitched arg *cf* 75. 2
Billings, Beds, an arm embowed, vested, holding a covered cup 203 4
Billingsley, on a mount vert, a leopard couchant or, spotted sa *cf* 24 9
Billington of Dublin, out of a mural crown sa., a sun in splendour or *cf* 162 2
Bilney, Norf, a demi griffin arg, holding between the claws a buckle sa
Bilsdon, a ram's head couped or 130 1
Bilson or **Billson**, Hants, a bugle horn or, stringed arg, and tasselled of the first 228 11
Binckes, Bincks, or **Binks**, a winged column gu 113 10
Bindley, out of flames ppr, a phœnix rising of the same *Nunc et idem* 82 2
Bindley or **Bindly**, out of a mural coronet a dexter arm embowed wielding a sword ppr *cf* 201 4
Bindlosse, Borwick, Lancs, and Westml, a demi-horse arg, ducally gorged az *cf* 53 3
Bindon, Ireland, on a mount vert, a bull passant arg *Stet non timeat* 45 7
Binet, Jersey, a woman couped at the knees, habited medievally, between the attires of a stag, all ppr *Il le vueil*
Bing, Middx, *see* Byng.
Bing, Kent, a demi-pegasus regardant or, holding in pale a flag gu *cf* 47 9
Binge, Kent, an antelope erm, attired or 126 12
Bingham, Rt Hon John George Barry, **Baron Clanmorris**, a rock, thereon an eagle rising, all ppr *Spes mea Christus* *cf* 77 5
Bingham, Richard Charles William, Esquire, of Melcombe Bingham, Dorchester, on a rock ppr, an eagle rising or *Spes mea Christus*
Bingham, Baron (Bingham), *see* Lucan, Earl of
Bingham of Binghams-Melcombe, Dorset, on a rock ppr, an eagle rising or *Spes mea Christus* *cf* 77 5
Bingham, Sir John Edward, Bart, of West Lea, Ranmoor, Sheffield, an eagle, wings expanded ppr, resting the dexter claw on a garb fessewise vert and charged on each wing with a cross patee azure *Spes mea Christus* 254 3
Bingham, Ireland, on a mount vert, an eagle rising ppr *cf* 78 1
Bingham, Denis, Esquire, of Bingham Castle, Belmullet, co Mayo, on a mount vert, a falcon rising ppr, beaked, belled, and membered or *Spes mea Christus*
Bingham, Dorset, an arm couped at the elbow erect ppr, habited az, charged on the sleeve with a cross formee arg, cuffed of the same, and holding in the hand ppr a laurel branch vert
Bingham-Cox of Woodlands, Northaw, Herts, and of Botherop, Glouc (1) Between a stag's attires attached to the scalp ppr, a cockatrice gu, holding in the beak an ear of wheat or (*for Cox*) (2) A wing erect arg, between two catherine-wheels az (*for Bingham*)
Bingley, a cross crosslet, charged with an escallop between two wings 111 8
Bingley, T H, Esquire, of Whitley Hall, Ecclesfield, Yorks, West Riding, three arrows, one in pale and two in saltire or, the points downwards, barbed and flighted arg, in front thereof, suspended by a ribbon gu, an escutcheon sa, charged with a pheon, also arg *Beatus qui implevit* *cf* 173 1
Bingley of Blyth, Notts, on a pellet a cross formee arg, charged with an annulet gu, and between two wings or
Bingley, Middx and Flintsh, a pheon arg, between two wings or, and behind all a pellet.
Bingley, Notts, on a pellet a cross formee arg
Bingley and **Bingly**, a phœnix in flames ppr 82 2
Binks, Durh, a lion's head erased between two wings, all or 19 7
Binks, an eagle's head erased, ducally gorged, holding in the beak a pheon 83 10
Binks, *see* Binckes
Binney, a dexter hand ppr, holding a sword in pale az, hilt and pommel or 212 9
Binney, James, Esquire J P, D L M A, Barrister at-law, of Pampisford Hall Cambridge on a wreath of the colours a barbel in front of two bulrushes in saltire, all ppr *Bene* 271 10
Binning, Lord, *see* Haddington, Earl of
Binning of Walliford, Scotland, a demi-horse furnished for a waggon ppr *Christo duce feliciter*
Binning of Carloury Hall Scotland, a horse's head furnished for a waggon ppr *Virtute doloque* 50 12

Binns, Worcs., a martlet. *Labore et diligentia.* 95. 4

Binns of Sheffield. a lion rampant az., gorged with a collar flory and counterflory or, holding in the fore-paws a sword erect ppr., pommel and hilt of the second, the dexter hind-paw resting on a saltier, also or. *Deus providebit.*

Binns, a mortar mounted ppr. 169. 10

Binns, Ireland, a hand holding a close helmet az. 217. 12

Binny or **Binney,** a dexter hand holding a sword in pale az., hilt and pommel or. 212. 9

Binny of Fearn, Scotland, a horse's head arg., bridled gu. *Virtute et opera.* 51. 5

Binny or **Binnie,** Scotland, a horse's head bridled ppr. *Virtute et opera.* 51. 5

Birch, a hare courant sa. *Libertas.* cf. 136. 3

Birch, a hare courant sa., collared or. cf. 136. 3

Birch, Bart., Lancs, on a mount vert, a hare sa., collared arg. *Libertas.*

Birch of Birch Hall, Lancs, Lincs, and London, a fleur-de-lis arg., entwined by a serpent ppr. 148. 8

Birch, Lancs and Shropsh., a demi-bird (eagle ?) wings displayed sa. 80. 2

Birch of Croydon, Surrey, an eagle rising az., holding in the dexter claw a banner flowing to the dexter gu., thereon three crosses clechée, two and one, the staff point and tassels or. cf. 78. 14

Birch of Wrotham Hall, Norf., a fleur-de-lis arg., with a serpent entwined ppr. *Prudentia et simplicitate.* 148. 8

Birch, Henry, Thame, Oxon., a fleur-de-lis or, surmounted by a hurt, entwined by a serpent and between two palm-branches ppr. *Sincera fide agere.*

Birch, Newell-, of Henley Park, Oxford, same crest and motto.

Birch of Kilkenny, Ireland, a griffin's head erased, holding in the beak a birch-branch ppr., and charged on the shoulder with a lozenge sa.

Birchall of Bowden Hall, Glouc., a lion rampant arg., and resting his fore-paws against the sinister side of a tree, all ppr. *Quare verum.*

Birchall, John Dearman, Esquire, of Bowden Hall, Gloucester, a lion rampant arg., resting its fore-paws against the sinister side of a tree, all ppr. *Quare verum.*

Birch-Reynardson, Charles, Esquire, of Holywell Hall, Stamford: (1) A lion's head erm., murally crowned chequy arg. and gu. (*for Reynardson*). (2) A fleur-de-lis arg., and a trefoil slipped vert, entwined by a serpent ppr. (*for Birch*). *Virtus est vitium fugere,* and *Prudentia simplicitate.*

Birch-Reynardson, Vere Henry, Esquire, of Rushington Manor, Totton, Hants, same crests and mottoes.

Birch-Reynardson, William John, Esquire, of Adwell House, Tetsworth, same crests and mottoes.

Birchett of Rye, Sussex, an heraldic tiger sejant vert, ducally gorged and maned or.

Birchill of Birchill, Chesh., a lion rampant az., supporting a tree vert.

Bird of Drybridge, Heref., a martlet gu. *Cruce spes mea.* cf. 95. 5

Bird, a martlet, the wings expanded gu., charged on the breast with a mullet or. cf. 95. 11

Bird of Broxton, Chesh., a martlet gu. cf. 95. 5

Bird of Hackney, Middx., a martlet rising gu. cf. 95. 11

Bird, on a dolphin ppr., an eagle with wings expanded or.

Bird, Charles Henry, Esquire, M.A., J.P., of Crookbey, Cockerham, Lancs, three mullets of six points fessewise arg., thereon a martlet gu. *Cruce spes mea.*

Bird, Westminster, a ring-dove ppr., resting its dexter claw on a rose or.

Bird of Denston, Suff., out of a ducal coronet arg., a greyhound's head couped or. 61. 7

Bird, London and Warw., a greyhound's head vert, erased gu., gorged with a collar dove-tailed or. 235. 5

Bird, William Macdonald, Esquire, of 26, Harrington Gardens, South Kensington, London, a greyhound's head vert, erased gu., collar dove-tailed or. *Recte certe.* 235. 5

Bird, Derbysh., on a mount vert, the stump of a tree couped and eradicated, thereon a falcon, wings addorsed, all ppr. cf. 87. 11

Bird, out of an Eastern coronet a demi-lion holding in the dexter paw a cross crosslet.

Birde, a griffin's head erased bendy of six sa. and arg. 66. 2

Birdwood, Sir George Christopher Molesworth, M.D., K.C.I.E., C.S.I., LL.D., of 7, Apsley Terrace, Acton, London, W., a martlet. 297. 7

Birkbeck, London: (1) A bow erect entwined by an oak-branch ppr., acorned or. (2) An oak-branch ppr., acorned or, and a rose-branch flowered gu., intertwined and erected. *Fide sed cui vide.*

Birkbeck, Sir Edward, Bart., of Horstead Hall, Norf., upon a rock in front of a hazel-branch slipped and fructed a bow palewise, all ppr. 248. 3

Birkbeck, Henry, Esquire, of Westacre High House, Swaffham, Norf., upon a rock a bow in pale, stringed and intertwined with a hazel-branch, all ppr.

Birkbeck, William John, Esquire, same crest.

Birkbeke or **Birkberke,** a nut-branch vert, fructed or.

Birkby, on a chapeau gu., turned up erm., a garb or, banded arg. 153. 10

Birkenhead of Backford, Chesh., a goat salient arg., attired or, resting the fore-feet on a garb of the last.

Birkenhead, Chesh., out of a ducal coronet or, an arm embowed ppr., holding in the hand three arrows of the first.

Birkes, an ear of wheat and a palm-branch in saltier ppr. 154. 10

Birket of Birket House, Chesh., a ram's head erased arg. 130. 6

Birket and **Birkett,** on a hand couped at the wrist an eagle rising ppr. cf. 78. 12

Birle, Essex, an arm couped at the shoulder in fess, vested arg., cuffed sa., holding in the hand ppr. a cross formée fitched or, charged on the arm with three torteaux.

Birley, Henry Langton, of Carr Hill, near Kirkham and Staind, Lancs, a demi-boar sa., armed ungu., and bristled or, gorged with a chain of the last, and supporting a branch of teazle ppr., and charged on the shoulder with a millrind. *Omni liber metu.*

Birley, Hugh Arthur, Esquire, of Woodside, Knutsford, same crest and motto.

Birley of Woodend, Cumb., a demi-boar sa., collared arg., the chain reflexed over the back or., supporting a branch of wild teazel ppr., and charged on shoulder with a mill-rind, also arg. *Omni liber metu.*

Birley of Halliwell Hall, and Moss Lee, Lancs, and of Manchester, same crest and motto.

Birmingham, Norf., two lions gambs in saltier sa. 39. 14

Birmingham, a goat's head erased. 128. 5

Birn, Ireland, a dexter hand apaumée couped gu. 222. 14

Birnal or **Birnall,** a greyhound's head between two roses stalked and leaved. 61. 11

Birnie of Broomhill, Scotland, a lion's head erased ppr. *Sapere aude, incipe.* 17. 8

Birnie of Saline, Scotland, a dexter hand ppr., holding an anchor erect or, environed with clouds, also ppr. *Arcus, artes, astra.* 223. 4

Birom, Lancs, an urchin sa. 135. 8

Biron, a mermaid with a glass and a comb, all ppr. *Crede Byron.* 184. 8

Birrell, an arm in armour embowed brandishing a scimitar, all ppr. 196. 10

Birt, a flounder.

Birt, Kent, a demi-leopard guardant gu., guttée-d'eau, charged with two bars wavy or, supporting with the paws an anchor arg., cable sa., all between two branches of oak fructed ppr. *Facta non verba.*

Birte, Devonsh., a dexter arm embowed in fess issuing from a cloud in the sinister holding in the hand a garland of laurel, all ppr. 200. 12

Birtwesill, a dolphin naiant ppr. 140. 5

Bischoff, of Leeds and London (originally of Basle, Switzerland), a crosier erect or, between two wings of an imperial eagle, the dexter arg., the sinister sa.

Biscoe, Henry Stafford Tyndale, Esquire, of Holton Park, Oxon., on a mount vert, in front of an oak-tree a greyhound courant ppr., collared or, seizing a hare, also ppr. *Confido non confunda.* 58. 14

Biscoe of Kingillie, co. Inverness, Scotland, a greyhound courant sa., seizing a hare or. cf. 58. 14

Biscoe, Thomas Ramsay, Esquire, of Newton, Kirkhill, Inverness-sh., a greyhound sa., seizing a hare ppr. *Post virtutem curro.*

Bisdée, Alfred J., surgeon, Norris Lodge, Hoddesdon, Herts, on a mural coronet a fleur-de-lis. *Dieu est ma foi.*

Biset, Scotland, the stump of an oak-tree shooting branches ppr. *Exitus acta probat.* 145. 2

Bish, on a chapeau, a demi-lion rampant. 15. 14

Bishe of Burston, Surrey, on a mural crown or, a sword erect arg., pommel and hilt of the first, the blade impaling a leopard's face gu. cf. 22. 1

Bishop, a griffin's head erased sa., between two laurel branches vert.

Bishop, Dorset and Somers., an eagle's head erased, party per fesse or and gu., beaked of the last. 83. 2

Bishop of Evesham, Worcs., out of a mural coronet arg., a griffin's head sa., beaked or. 67. 10

Bishop, Charles, Cwm-Rythan, Llandovery, a double-headed eagle displayed ppr. *Ung je serviray.*

Bishop, Charles Joseph, Esquire, of Hillside, St. Helen's, an eagle's head erased per fesse erm. and or, charged with two lozenges paleways, and holding in the beak a pheon sa. *Pro Deo.*

Bishoppe of Bristol, Somers., a griffin sejant arg., resting its dexter claw on an escutcheon, also arg. *cf.* 62. 11

Bishopston, Warw., an arm issuing from a cloud in fess, holding a terrestrial globe. 223. 1

Bishton, out of a castle triple towered, an arm in armour embowed, all ppr., grasping a dagger, also ppr., hilted or. *cf.* 155. 3

Bispham, Lancs. on a chapeau gu., turned up erm., a lion passant arg., resting the dexter claw on an escutcheon of the first.

Bispleam, a stag's head cabossed erm., attired or. 122. 5

Biss, an eagle preying on a partridge, all ppr. 77. 12

Biss, Durh. and Somers., on a mount vert, two serpents entwined erect and respecting each other ppr. *Ayez prudence.—Nil conscire sibi.*

Bisse, Ireland, on a mount vert, two snakes interlaced or, respecting each other ppr.

Bissell, a demi-eagle with wings displayed sa., charged on the neck with an escallop-shell or. *cf.* 80. 2

Bissell, Frederick Edward, M.D., Kingstone, near Heref., a demi-eagle sa. with wings displayed, charged on the breast with an escallop shell or. *Deus nobiscum quis contra.*

Bisset, the trunk of an oak-tree sprouting ppr. *Reviresco.* 145. 2

Bisset, the stump of a tree eradicated and erased, therefrom a branch sprouting ppr. *Repullulat.*

Bisset, Fenwick- : (1) The trunk of an oak-tree sprouting afresh (*for Bisset*). 145. 2. (2) A phœnix in flames gorged with a mural crown ppr. (*for Fenwick*). *Abscissa virescit.—Perit ut vivat.* *cf.* 82. 2

Bisset, a hand couped in fess holding a sword in pale, on the point a garland of laurel, all ppr. *cf.* 221. 7

Bisset, Scotland, the trunk of a tree ppr., a shield arg. pendent from one of its branches. *Revirescit.* 145. 8

Bissett, Captain Maurice Elrington, of Lessendrum, Huntly, N.B., and Rev. Mordaunt Elrington Bissett, the trunk of an oak-tree sprouting afresh ppr. *Abscissa virescit.* 145. 2

Bisshe, Essex, a hind trippant arg. 124. 12

Bisshop of Brandean House, Hants: (1) An eagle's head erased per fesse or and gu., beaked of the last. 83. 2. (2) On a ducal coronet or, a griffin sejant arg., resting the dexter claw on an escutcheon of the last. *Pro Deo et ecclesia.* 62. 11

Bisshopp, Bart. (*extinct*), of Parham Park, Sussex, on a ducal coronet or, a griffin sejant arg., resting its dexter claw on an escutcheon of the last. *Pro Deo et ecclesia.* 62. 11

Bisshopp, Baron, of Harringworth: (1) On a ducal coronet or, a griffin sejant arg., resting its dexter claw on an escutcheon of the last. (2) On a flag folded round a halberd in fess, a falcon arg. *Pro Deo et ecclesia.*

Bissland, Bilsland, or **Bullsland,** co. Renfrew, a bull's head. *Certum pete finem.* *cf.* 44. 3

Bisson, a blackbird ppr. *Bis dat qui cito dat.* *cf.* 106. 2

Bisson, F. S. de Carteret, City Asylum, Nottingham, same crest and motto.

Bistley, a Doric column or.

Bistley, a cross pattée gu., between two wings or. 110. 7

Bitfield, a demi-wolf rampant, pierced through the shoulder and transfixed by a flagstaff.

Bitterley of Cowdrey, Sussex, out of a ducal coronet a hand vested, holding the sun ppr. 209. 2

Blaauw, Henry Thomas Gillman, of Beechland, Sussex, a demi-lion rampant ppr. *Festina lente.* 10. 2

Blabley, Devonsh., a tiger's head erased arg., issuing out of rays or.

Blachford, Baron (*extinct*), *see* Rogers, Bart.

Blachford of London, a demi-swan rising, the wings expanded arg., guttée-de-larmes. 100. 9

Blachford of London and Dorset, a demi-swan rising arg., guttée-de-poix. 100. 9

Blachford, William Henry, Esquire, of Ham, Surrey, a demi-swan erased arg., guttée-de-larmes, gorged with an Eastern crown or, wings elevated bendy wavy of the second and gu.

Black of Aberdeen, Scotland, a demi-lion ppr. *Non crux, sed lux.* 10. 2

Black, Charles Bertram, Esquire, 38, Drummond Place, Edinburgh, a demi-lion rampant sa., armed and langued gu. *Non crux, sed lux.* 10. 1

Black of Wigtown, Scotland, a star or, rising out of a cloud ppr. *Spes lucis æternæ.* 164. 11

Black of Glasgow, a kangaroo sejant ppr. *Via crucis, via lucis.* 136. 7

Black of Craigmaddie, co. Stirling, Scotland, a demi-lion rampant ppr., gorged with a collar or. *Non crux, sed lux.* 10. 9

Black, Norman Spens, Esquire, of 1, Grove Avenue, Blackrock, co. Dublin, a demi-lion rampant ppr., gorged with a collar or. *Non crux sed lux.*

Black, Charles Bertram, Esquire, c/o. Messrs. A. and C. Black, Publishers, Soho, London, W.C., a demi-lion rampant sa., armed and langued gu. *Non crux, sed lux.*

Black, William George, Esquire, of Ramoyle, Dowanhill Gardens, Glasgow, same crest and motto.

Black, Charles Christopher, of the Inner Temple, a mount vert, thereon a cat gardant ppr., holding between the paws an escutcheon az., charged with a boar's head erased or.

Black, a reindeer's head ppr., collared. *cf.* 122. 1

Black, an arm embowed, vested, purfled at the shoulder, the part above the elbow in fesse lying upon the wreath, the hand in pale holding a branch of palm ppr. 203. 7

Black of London, an arm in armour embowed ppr., wielding in the hand, also ppr., a scimitar arg. *Spe vires augentur.* 196. 10

Blackader of Blackader, Scotland, an adder in pale sa., holding in the mouth a rose gu., leaved and stalked. *Vise à la fin.*

Blackborn, Blackborne, or **Blackburn,** Yorks, out of a cloud shedding forth rays an arm from the elbow erect vested gu., holding a broken sword of the last. *cf.* 208. 13

Blackburn, an antelope's head erased arg. 126. 2

Blackburn, out of a ducal coronet or, a demi-lion rampant ppr., holding in the dexter paw a mullet sa., gorged with a plain collar arg., charged with three mullets of the third. *Bonne et belle assez.*

Blackburn, Scotland, an arm couped at the shoulder and embowed, the elbow resting on the wreath, holding in the hand a bombshell fired ppr. 202. 5

Blackburn of Wavertree Hall, Lancs, and Hawford Lodge, near Worcs., on a trumpet or, a cock statant ppr. 91. 6

Blackburne, Robert Ireland, of Hale Hall, Liverpool, and Orford, Lancs, upon a mount vert, a trumpet or, thereon a cock gu., beaked, combed, wattled, spurred, and charged on the breast with a cinquefoil or. *Come ut ico sue.* 237. 16

Blackburne of Richmond, Yorks, a horse's head couped arg. *cf.* 50. 13

Blackburne-Maze, William Peter, Esquire, of Shaw House, Newbury, Berks: (1) An eagle displayed erminois, charged on the breast and on each of the wings with a cinquefoil gu. 237. 15. (*for Maze*). (2) On a mount vert, a trumpet fesseways or, thereon a cock gu., beaked, wattled, armed, and charged on the breast with a cinquefoil or (*for Blackburne*). 237. 16. *Garde ta bien aimee.*

Blacke, Suff. and Essex, a hand couped in fess ppr. 221. 6

Blakeney, John Henry, L.R.C.P., Woodford, Bristol Road, Edgbaston, Birmingham, a dexter arm in armour embowed, holding in the hand a sword, all ppr.

Blackensteiner, out of a coronet or, a plume of three feathers, the centre one arg., the others gu.

Blackeny, a harpy gardant ppr. 189. 1

Blacker of Carrick Blacker, Ireland, an arm in armour holding a battle-axe ppr. *Pro Deo et rege.*

Blacker of Madras, a dexter arm in armour embowed, the hand gauntleted and grasping a battle-axe, all ppr. *Pro Deo et rege.*

Blacker, Murray MacGregor, Esquire, a dexter armed arm embowed ppr., the hand gauntleted and grasping a battle-axe ppr. *Pro Deo et rege.*

Blacker, William, Esquire of Castle Martin, Newbridge, co Kildare, same crest and motto

Blacker, a nag's head couped az, bridled or 51 5

Blacker, Bucks, and of Old Sarum, Wilts, two lions' heads erased, collared and addorsed 18 2

Blacker, Bucks, a horse's head couped az, bridled or 51 5

Blacker-Douglas, St John Thomas, Esquire, of Elm Park, Armagh (1) A cubit arm erect ppr, grasping a human heart gu, and charged with a trefoil slipped vert (*for Douglas*) (2) A dexter armed arm embowed ppr, the hand gauntleted, grasping a battle-axe ppr *Forward*, and *Pro Deo et rege*

Blacket, Major General Sir Edward William, Bart., A D C, of Matfen Hall, Northumb, a hawk's head erased ppr *Nous travaillerons en l'espérance* 88 12

Blacket and **Blackett**, a hawk's head couped ppr cf 89 1

Blackett, Edward Umfreville, of Wylam, Northumb, a hawk's head erased ppr *Nous travaillerons dans l'espérance* 88 12

Blackett-Ord, John Reginald, Esquire, Whitfield Hall, Whitfield, R S O, Northumb, upon a mount vert, an elk's head erased ppr, pellettee (*for Ord*) *Nous travaillerons dans l'espérance*

Blackford, *see* Blachford

Blackhall, Scotland, an annulet or, stoned vert 167 14

Blacknall of Totnes, Devonsh, a tiger's head erased arg, issuing out of rays or

Blackie and **Blackley**, Lancs, a dragon's head vert, ducally gorged or cf 72 9

Blackie of Edinburgh, a tiger salient ppr *Spero in Deo.*

Blackie, Robert, Esquire, 7, Great Western Terrace, Glasgow, Publisher, a wolf's head erased ppr *Virtute et fidelitate* 30 8

Blackie, James Robertson, Esquire, of Ferndean, Cove, Dumbartonsh, and Northbank, Glasgow, a wolf's head erased ppr *Virtute et fidelitate*

Blackiston, London, a cock or 91 2

Blackley or **Blakey** of Blackley Hall, Lancs, a dragon's head vert, ducally gorged or cf 72 9

Blackman, a demi Moor in fetters, crowned with an Eastern coronet

Blackman, London, a griffin erm

Blackman, a demi griffin vert, semee of crescents arg, collared gu *Fide et fiducia* cf 64 2

Blackmore, Devonsh, a Moor's head in profile sa, erased at the neck ppr, and round the neck a chaplet of roses or, leaved vert.

Blackmore, an arm in armour embowed ppr, garnished or, supporting a standard, the banner of the last, the staff of first, pointed arg cf 199 9

Blackmore, out of a mural coronet or, an arm in armour embowed ppr, garnished or cf 200. 1

Blackmore, a demi griffin segreant erm 64 2

Blacknell, Warw and Berks, an arm embowed, vested gu, cuffed arg, holding in the hand ppr four feathers, each per pale of the second and first

Blackney or **Blackeney** of Norf., a harpy gardant ppr 189 1

Blacknoll and **Blakenhall**, issuing out of a cloud az, a hand fessewise ppr, holding a plume of six feathers alternately arg and gu

Blackshame, an acorn or, stalked and leaved vert. 152 1

Blackstone of Castle Priory, Wallingford, Berks, a cock gu 91 2

Blackwall, London, a dexter hand gauntleted, holding a pheon, all ppr 211 7

Blackwall of Blackwall, Derbysh, two arms embowed, habited in mail ppr, the hands arg, holding between them by the nose and ear a greyhound's head couped sa, collared chequy or and gu

Blackwall, John of Hendre Llanrast, North Wales same crest *Fidelitas*

Blackwall-Evans, John Blackwall, of Blackwall, Derbysh (1) On a ducal coronet or, a boar's head erased fessewavs gu (*for Evans*) (2) Two arms embowed, habited in mail ppr, holding by the nose and ear a greyhound's head couped at the neck sa, collared chequy or and gu (*for Blackwell*)

Blackwell of Ampney Park, Glouc, two arms in scale armour embowed, holding between the hands ppr a greyhound's head couped at the neck gu, collared sa

Blackwell, a martlet 95 4

Blackwell of Sprouston Hall, Norf a swan's head and neck erased arg, ducally gorged or 101 5

Blackwell, a dove issuing

Blackwell, Middx, a demi lion holding between its paws an anchor ppr *Petit ardua virtus* 12 12

Blackwill, a demi-lion holding between its paws an anchor ppr 12 12

Blackwood, Captain Sir Francis, Bart, on a chapeau gu, turned up erm, a crescent arg *Per vias rectas* 245 3

Blackwood of Ballyleidy, Ireland, on a cap of maintenance gu, turned up erm, a crescent arg

Blackwood, Baron, Ireland, the sun in splendour *Per vias rectas*

Blackwood, Hamilton-Temple-, Marquess of Dufferin and Ava, *see* Dufferin and Ava

Blackwood, Scotland, a hand holding a couteau sword ppr *Virtute parta tuemini* 213 5

Blackwood, on a mount vert, an escutcheon arg, between two laurel branches ppr cf 146. 14

Blackwood, Edinburgh, rays or beams of the sun ppr *Per vias rectas*

Bladen of Glastonbury, Somers, a greyhound's head erased ppr *Toujours fidele* 61 4

Bladen, Ireland, on a ducal coronet a griffin passant, wings elevated or, holding in its beak an arrow ppr *Spe et labore* cf 63 2

Bladerike, a lion's head erased, pierced through the mouth with a sword in fess, all ppr cf 17 8

Blades of Broxwell Hall, Surrey, a demi-tiger rampant gardant couped, supporting with the paws a staff erect ppr, therefrom a banner flowing to the sinister az, fringed or, charged with two swords in saltire arg, pommels and hilts of the third, surmounted of the Roman fasces paleways of the same, the axe headed also arg, interlaced with a double chain collar or, and from the neck pendent by a blue ribbon a star pagoda, also ppr

Blades, Yorks, a talbot's head erased sa 56 2

Bladewell and **Bladwell**, Suff, Staffs, and Norf, a demi-lion per pale indented arg and gu 10. 2

Blagdon of Boddington Manor House, Cheltenham, a lion rampant bearing a cross

Blage, on a broken tilting spear or, a lion passant arg, crowned of the first

Blagrave, Henry Barry, of Calcot Park, Berks (1) A falcon ppr, belled or 85 2 (2) An oak-tree eradicated ppr (3) Three palm branches ppr *Pro marte et arte*

Blagrave of Bulmarsh Court, Berks (1) An oak-tree eradicated vert (2) A falcon ppr 85 2

Blagrove, a palm-tree fructed ppr 144 1

Blagrove, Henry, Esquire, of Abshott, Hants, a cocoa-tree fructed ppr, therefrom pendent by a chain or, an escutcheon gu, charged with a greave of the second

Blaikie or **Blackie**, Scotland, a wolf's head erased ppr *Virtute et fidelitate* 30 8

Blaikie of Craigiebuckler Scotland, a Moor's head ppr *Fidelis* 192 13

Blaine, Sir Robert Stickey, of Summerhill, Bath, *uses* a sword erect ppr, pommel and hilt or *Pax aut bellum* 170 2

Blair, Hunter-, Rev Sir David Oswald, Bart, O S B, the Abbey, Fort Augustus, N B, a stag's head caboshed ppr *Vigilantia, robur, voluptas* 122 5

Blair, Frederick Gordon, of Blair, Ayr, a stag lodged ppr *Amo probos* 115 7

Blair, Patrick Esquire of 11 Ainslie Place Edinburgh a dove with wings expanded *Virtute tutus*

Blair of Balthayock, Perth, a dove, wings expanded ppr *Virtute tutus* 94 2

Blair, Ireland, a stag lodged ppr 115 7

Blair of Watton Grove, Surrey, a dove with wings expanded, holding in his beak an olive-branch ppr *Virtute tutus* 94 5

Blair (1) A dove, wings expanded ppr, charged on the breast with a torteau for distinction (*for Blair*) cf 94 2 (2) A wyvern with wings displayed vert (*for Stopford*) cf 70 8

Blair, Alexander, Esquire, 35, Moray Place, Edinburgh, *uses* a dove, wings expanded and inverted ppr *Virtute tutus* 94. 2

Blair, a boar's head couped.

Blair of Dunsky, a boar's head couped ppr *Virtute et honore* 43 1

Blair, Scotland, a crescent arg *God be my guide* 163 2

Blair of Balmill, Scotland, a Roman head armed ppr *Facies qualis mens talis* 191 6

Blair of France, a garb or *Virtute tutus* 153 2

Blair of Lethenty, Scotland, a garb ppr *Nec temere, nec timide* 153 2

Blake, Baron Wallscourt, *see* Wallscourt

Blake, *see* Aldrich Blake

Blake, Wilts, on a chapeau gu, turned up erm, a martlet sa 95 1

Blake, Bart, Durh, a martlet arg, charged on the breast with a fret gu cf 95 4

Blake of Horstead, Norf, on a morion ppr, a martlet arg *Bene præparatum pectus*

Blake, Jex-, Rev Francis William, of Swanton Abbot, Norf (1) On a morion ppr, a martlet arg (2) A horse's head erased arg, maned or, holding in the mouth a broken spear or *Bene præparatum pectus*

Blake, Suff, a mountain-cat passant gardant ppr cf 26 4

Blake, Charles Joseph, Esquire, of Heath House, Maryborough, Queen's Co, a cat-a-mountain passant guardant ppr *Virtus sola nobilitat*

Blake, George Francis, Esquire, of Merlin Park, co. Galway, same crest and motto

Blake, Sir Henry Arthur, K C.M G, of Myrtal Grove, Youghal, same crest and motto

Blake, Henry Claude, Esquire, Athlone, Pursuivant of Arms, Office of Arms, The Castle, Dublin, same crest charged with a crescent for difference and motto.

Blake, Martin Joseph, Esquire, of Old Square, Lincoln's Inn, W C, same crest and motto

Blake, Colonel Maurice Charles, C B, of Towerhill, Cloongullane and Muckanagh, co Mayo, same crest and motto

Blake, Robert Joseph, Esquire, same crest and motto

Blake, Thomas Joseph, Esquire, a cat a mountain passant guardant ppr *Virtus sola nobilitat*

Blake, Valentine Joseph, Esquire, of Brookhill, Claremorris, co Mayo, same crest and motto

Blake, a mountain cat passant ppr *Virtus sola nobilitat* 26 4

Blake of Renvyle, co Galway, a mountain cat passant ppr *Virtus sola nobilitat* 26 4

Blake, Sir Valentine, Bart, of Menlough Castle, co. Galway, Ireland, a cat passant gardant ppr *Virtus sola nobilitas* cf 26 4

Blake, a boar's head sa., gorged with a collar arg, holding in the mouth a lion's gamb erased or

Blake, Bart, Sir Patrick James Graham, of Langham, Suff, a leopard passant gardant ppr *Confido et probitate* cf 24 2

Blake, Ireland, a leopard passant gardant ppr *Virtus sola nobilitat* cf 24 2

Blake, Essex, a dragon's head erased arg, pellettee cf 71 2

Blake-Daly, John Archer, Esquire, of Raford, Kiltulla, near Athenry, a greyhound courant sa., collared, in front of an oak tree ppr, fructed gold

Blake, De Burgh, Charles Ormsby, Esquire, of Merlin Park, Merlinstown (1) A cat a mountain sejant guardant ppr, collared and chained or, and above *Ung Roy, ung foy, ung loy* (2) A mountain cat passant guardant ppr *Virtus sola nobilitat*

Blake - Humfrey, Lieutenant Colonel Thomas, of Heggatt Hall, Horstead, Norwich (1) On a ducal coronet an eagle or, and charged on the breast for distinction with a cross crosslet gu (*for Humphrey*) 277 11 (2) On a morion ppr, a martlet arg *Cœlestem spero coronam* 277 12

Blakeborne, Yorks, out of a cloud shedding forth rays, an arm from the elbow erect, vested gu, holding a broken sword ppr cf 208 13

Blakely of Thorp Hamlet, Norf, a unicorn passant az, guttee d'or, and ducally gorged arg, resting the dexter foot on an escutcheon or, charged with a pale vair *Allons Dieu ayde* 48 4

Blakemore of the Leys, Monmouthsh, a Moor's head in profile sa, gorged round the neck with a chaplet of roses or, leaved vert *Pro Deo, pro rege, pro patria, et lege*

Blakeney, Baron (Blakeney), out of clouds ppr, an arm erect vested az, the hand grasping a sword, both also ppr *Auxilium meum ab alto* cf 210 12

Blakeney-Lyon-Stewart, Thomas, Esquire, of Ballymenagh, co Tyrone, Ireland (1) Out of an embattlement ppr, a demi-lion rampant gu (*for Stewart*) cf 10 3 (2) Within two branches of laurel a lady to the girdle habited in white, holding in her dexter hand a thistle and in her sinister a trefoil, all ppr (*for Lyon*) (3) Out of clouds ppr, an arm erect couped at the elbow, vested per pale or and az, and charged with an escallop counter changed, holding in the hand a dagger, both also ppr, pommel and hilt or (*for Blakeney*) *Forward*

Blakeney, John, Esquire of Abbert Castle Galway out of a ducal coronet or, an arm erect couped at the elbow, vested gu, cuffed arg, holding in the hand a sword ppr, hilt and pommel of the first *Auxilium meum ab alto*

Blakeney, John Henry L R C P, of Woodford, Bristol Road Edgbaston, a dexter arm in armour embowed, holding in the hand a sword all ppr

Blakeney, out of a ducal coronet or, an arm erect, couped at the elbow, vested gu, cuffed arg, holding in the hand a sword ppr, hilt and pommel of the first *Auxilium meum ab alto*

Blakeney, an arm erect, couped at the elbow, vested gu, cuffed arg, holding in the hand a sword ppr, hilt and pommel or *Auxilium meum ab alto*

Blakeney, Ireland, out of a plume of three ostrich feathers an eagle rising ppr 80 6

Blakenhall or **Blacknoll,** issuing out of a cloud az, a hand ppr, in fess, holding a plume of six feathers, two, two, and two arg and gu, alternately

Blakeny or **Blackney,** Norf, a harpy gardant ppr 189 1

Blaker of Salisbury, Wilts, a demi horse sa, ducally gorged or cf 53 3

Blaker of Portslade, Sussex, a horse's head sa, maned and bridled or 51 5

Blaker, Nathaniel Payne, M R.C S, 29, Old Steine, Brighton, same crest

Blakeston or **Blakiston,** Durh, a cock or, collared, combed, and wattled gu cf 91 2

Blakeway, a tiger's head spotted

Blakey, Suff, a dragon's head couped at the neck vert, gorged with a coronet arg cf 72 9

Blakie or **Blackie,** Scotland, a wolf's head erased ppr *Virtute et fidelitate* 30 8

Blakiston, Sir Horace Nevile, Bart., of Lynton, Westby Road, Boscombe, Bournemouth, a cock gu *Doe well and doubt not*

Blakiston, Hon Charles Robert, of Christchurch, New Zealand, late Member of the Legislative Council, and Augustus Frederick Noel Blakiston, also of New Zealand, *use* a cock gu *Doe well and doubt not* 91 2

Blakiston of Blakiston, Durh, a cock or 91 2

Blakiston-Houston, John, Esquire, of Orangefield and Roddens, Belfast (1) A sand-glass ppr (2) A cock statant gu, charged with an annulet or *Doe well and doubt not*

Blakit, a falcon's head erased ppr 88. 12

Blamore, Glouc, a tiger sejant vert, collared and chained or cf 27 6

Blanch, a leopard's head gardant erased gu cf 23 3

Blanchard, Lancs, on a chapeau an arm in armour embowed, holding a battle-axe

Blanchard, Wilts and Somers, on the point of a sword in pale a mullet 169. 3

Blancharden of Blancharden, Kent, a cock's leg armed with a spur sa, erased at the thigh, and issuing therefrom a plume of five ostrich feathers, alternately or and az

Blanchfield of Blanchfieldstown, Ireland, an arm erect vested per pale, alternately indented gu and erm, the hand ppr, holding a sword arg, pommel and hilt or

Blanck of Guildford, Surrey, a dragon s head couped vert, collared and chained arg, holding in the mouth a firebrand of the last, flaming ppr

Blanckagam, a dove holding in its beak an olive branch, all ppr 92 5

Blanckley, a falchion erect ppr, hilt and pommel or, pierced through a leopard's face, also ppr *Pro rege et lege* cf 22 1

Blanckmaynes or **Blanchmaynes,** a leopard's head gardant erased or cf 23 3

Blanceminster, on the trunk of a tree lying in fess, and sprouting one branch, a falcon close

Bland, a griffin's head couped, collared, the wings addorsed cf 67. 11

Bland, Notts, out of a ducal coronet or, a leopard's head ppr 23 11

Bland, Davison-, John, of Kippax Park, Yorks, out of a ducal coronet or, a lion's head ppr *Sperate et virile fortes* 17 5

Bland, Loftus Henry Bland, Esquire, K.C., of Blandsfort, Queen's Co., Ireland, out of a ducal coronet or, a lion's head ppr., charged with a crescent gu. *Quo fata vocant.* cf. 17. 5

Bland, Major-General Edward Loftus, of Woodbank, Whiteabbey, co. Antrim, out of a ducal coronet or, a lion's head ppr., charged with a crescent gu. *Quo fata vocant.*

Bland, John Humphry, Esquire, of Fernagh, Whiteabbey, co. Antrim, same crest and motto.

Bland of London and Norwich, out of a vallary coronet or, a lion's head ppr., charged with a bend sa., thereon three pheons, also or. *Potior origine virtus.*

Bland, a holly-branch vert. 150. 10

Bland, a cock gu. 91. 2

Bland of London and Yorks, same crest. *Vigilante.*

Bland of Randall's Park, Leatherhead, Surrey, a cock gu., beaked, legged, and wattled or, charged on the breast with a pheon of the last. cf. 91. 2

Bland, James Franklin, Esquire, J.P., of Derryquin Castle, co. Kerry, Ireland, a cock ppr., charged on the breast with a pheon or. *Eloquentia sagitta.* cf. 91. 2

Bland, John Franklin, Esquire, of Hollywood, Kenmare, a cock ppr., charged on the breast with a pheon or. *Eloquentia sagitta.*

Blandford, Marquess of, *see* Marlborough, Duke of.

Blandford, Dorset, a dexter hand holding a pistol ppr. 221. 8

Blandy, Frederick, Esquire, of Birchamp House, Colford, Glouc., a demi-lion regardant gu., holding between the paws an urn sa., with flames issuing ppr. *Ex urna resurgam.*

Blane, Sir Seymour John, Bart., of Blanefield, Ayrsh., a sword erect ppr., hilt and pommel or. *Paritur pax bello.* 170. 2

Blaney or **Blayney,** London, a horse's head couped arg., in complete armour ppr., bridled az. 51. 13

Blaney, a horse's head erased sa. 50. 8

Blaney of Berks, a horse's head erased sa. *Hope well and have well.* 50. 8

Blaney, Heref., a nag's head couped arg., maned and tufted sa., bridled gu. 51. 5

Blaney, Heref., a fox passant arg. 32. 1

Blantyre, Baron (Rt. Hon. Charles Stewart), Scotland, a dove holding an olive-leaf in its beak, all ppr. *Sola juvat virtus.* 92. 5

Blaquier, De Baron (Blaquier), a garb ppr., banded or. *Tiens à la vérité.* 153. 2

Blatchford of Osborne, Isle of Wight, a swan's head and neck erased sa., between two wings arg. cf. 101. 6

Blathwaite, on a rock ppr., an eagle rising arg. cf. 77. 5

Blathwayt, Rev. Wynter Thomas, of Dyrham Park, Gloucs., and of Langridge and Porlock, Somers., on a rock ppr., an eagle rising arg. *Virtute et veritate.* cf. 77. 5

Blaumester, a demi-savage holding a club over his shoulder, all ppr. 186. 5

Blaverhasset, a dexter hand holding a hunting-horn sans strings ppr., verruled or. 217. 4

Blaw of Castle Hill, Scotland, an armed hand holding a sword in pale, all ppr. 210. 4

Blaxland, Edward Tremayne, Esquire, of Fordwich, Broke, *vid* Whittingham, New South Wales, Australia, (1) An eagle displayed with two heads ppr., guttée-de-sang (*for Blaxland*). 74. 2. (2) A lion's gamb erect and erased gu., enfiled with a ducal coronet erm. (*for Sandwell*). *Juste et fortiter.* cf. 36. 3

Blaxton, a goat passant or. cf. 129. 5

Blaydes, of Ranby Hall, Notts, a talbot's head erased sa. *Pro Deo, rege, et patria.* 56. 2

Blaydes, a thistle vert, flowered gu. cf. 150. 2

Blaydes, a demi-leopard salient ppr., holding in the dexter paw a sword arg., hilt and pommel or.

Blaydes of Oulton House, Yorks, a demi-leopard, collared and chained or, holding in the dexter paw a sword erect ppr.

Blaydes-Marvel, Yorks, a talbot's head erased sa. *Pro Deo, rege, et patria.* 56. 2

Blayne, Berks, a greyhound's head arg., collared az. 61. 2

Blayney of London, a horse's head couped arg., in complete armour ppr., the bridle az. 51. 13

Blayney of the Lodge, Evesham, Worcs., a fox passant arg. *I rest to rise.* 32. 1

Blayney, an erm. passant arg. 134. 6

Blayney, Baron (*supposed to be extinct*), a nag's head couped arg., bridled gu., on the forehead a plate of armour, in the centre of which a spike, all ppr. *Integra mens augustissima possessio.* 51. 13

Blayney, a fox passant arg. 32. 1

Bleamire and **Bleaymire** of Westml. and Cumb., a heraldic tiger sejant gu., collared and chained or.

Bleddyn or **Bleeddyn,** a boar passant sa., bristled arg. 40. 9

Bledlow of London, in the sea an anchor ppr. 161. 6

Blencowe of Marston Hall, Oxon., a sword in pale, hilt upwards, pierced through a human heart, all ppr., between two wings arg. cf. 110. 8

Blencowe, John Alexander, of Marston St. Lawrence, Northamp., same crest. *Quorsum vivere mori, mori vita.*

Blencowe, Robert Campion, Esquire, of Bincham Chailey, Lewes, same crest and motto.

Blencowe, Henry Prescott George, Thoby Priory, Essex, a sword in pale arg., hilt in chief or, enfiladed with a human heart gu., all between two wings expanded arg. *Quorsum vivere mori, mori vitæ.*

Blenerhasset, Suff., a wolf sejant gu., his tail flected over his back, langued az. 29. 3

Blenkinsopp, Leaton-, George Ilderton, of Hoppyland Castle, Durh., and Humbleton Hall, Northumb.: (1) A lion rampant or (*for Blenkinsopp*). 1. 13. (2) Out of a mural coronet two wings expanded arg., each charged with a cross crosslet fitched sa. (*for Leaton*). *Dieu defende le droit.* 227. 11

Blenman of Croscombe, Somers., a dexter arm couped and erect ppr., vested sa., the ruffle arg., at the wrist a diamond button, holding in the hand a roll of parchment ppr. 208. 8

Blennerhasset, Ireland, in the sea a pillar ppr. 176. 2

Blennerhassett, Sir Rowland, Bart., of Blennerville, co. Kerry, Ireland, a wolf sejant ppr. *Fortes fortuna juvat.* 29. 3

Blennerhassett of Ballyseedy, a wolf sejant ppr. *Fortes fortuna juvat.* 29. 3

Blennerhassett, Rowland Ponsonby, Esquire, of 52, Hans Place, S.W., a wolf sejant ppr. *Fortes fortuna juvat.*

Blenshell or **Blinshall,** Aberdeen, a holly-leaf vert. *Deo fervente florebo.*

Blesby or **Blesbie** of Blesbie, Lincs, a griffin's head erased or. 66. 2

Bleset or **Blesset,** an eagle displayed ppr. 75. 2

Blesson or **Blessone,** a martlet arg. 95. 2

Bletsho of Winington, Beds, a wolf's head or, semée of hurts murally gorged az. cf. 30. 5

Blewet, Blewett, and **Bluet,** Cornw., and Holcombe Regis, Devonsh., a squirrel sejant or, collared and lined gu., holding in the paws an acorn of the first leaved vert.

Blewet, Blewitt, and **Bleuett** of Grenham, Somers., a mort head ppr. 193. 11

Blewitt, London, Somers., and Monm., a squirrel sejant ppr., eating an acorn or. *Spes mea in Deo.* 135. 7

Blick, Bucks, a leopard passant arg., semée of mullets sa. cf. 24. 2

Blick of the Lodge, Islip, Oxon., a leopard passant arg., semée of mullets sa. *Ne timere caute eo.*

Blick and **Blicke,** a hawk's lure az., ringed or. 178. 11

Bligh or **Blighe,** Cornw., a dexter arm couped at the elbow holding in the hand a battle-axe. cf. 213. 11

Bligh, a griffin's head erased or. 66. 2

Bligh, Kent, a griffin's head erased or. *Finem respice.* 66. 2

Bligh, Earl of Darnley, Ireland, a griffin's head erased or. *Finem respice.* 66. 2

Blinckarne or **Blincarne,** Kent, a demi-lion, holding in the dexter paw a cross engrailed gu.

Bliss, an arm from the elbow, holding in the hand a bundle of four arrows, points downwards. cf. 214. 3

Bliss of the Temple, London, a dexter cubit arm erect, holding by the lower limb a cross couped gu., fleury or. *Virtus sola felicitas.*

Bliss of Chipping-Norton, Oxon., a garb ppr. 153. 2

Bliss, Sir Henry William, K.C.I.E., 10, Cornwall Gardens, S.W., a garb or.

Blissett, a sword in pale, enfiled with a thistle ppr. cf. 170. 2

Blithe, London and Lincs, a tower, on the battlements a lion passant, all arg. cf. 157. 12

Blithe of London, a lion sejant gu. 8. 8

Blithe, Derbysh., a peacock or, in its beak a serpent reflexed over the neck ppr. cf. 103. 7

Blithman of London, a demi-bear arg., muzzled gu., holding between its paws a battle-axe of the last.

Blizard, a fleur-de-lis az. 148. 2

Blizard or **Blizzard,** a lady's arm erect, on the wrist a bracelet. 222. 6

Blobold, two lions' gambs erect and erased in saltire, the dexter uppermost, between two demi-spears or.

Block, Samuel Richard, Esquire, of London, and of Kentish Town, Middx., a mount vert, thereon an eagle with wings elevated ppr., seizing with the dexter claw an owl arg.

Block, Major Arthur Hugh, R.A., of Zimulgherry, Deccan, India, same crest and motto.

Block, John Saumarez Talbot, Esquire, of 15, Talbot Square, London, same crest and motto.

Block, Samuel Cecil Macartney, Esquire, same crest and motto.

Blockley, the sun shining on a demi-eagle with two heads in flames ppr. *cf.* 82. 12

Blockney, Ireland, out of a ducal coronet az., a boar's head and neck or. 41. 4

Blockney, the same, collared gu. *cf.* 41. 4

Blodlow, a lion rampant sa. 1. 10

Blodwell, Suff., a demi-lion per pale, indented arg. and gu. 10. 2

Bloer of London, a cubit arm vested vert, holding in the hand ppr. a pomme. *cf.* 205. 13

Blofeld, Thomas Calthorpe, of Hoverton House, Norf., a plume of three ostrich-feathers arg. *Domino quid reddam.* 115. 1

Blois, Sir Ralph Barrett Macnaghten, Bart., of Cockfield Hall, Yoxford, Suff., a gauntlet erect ppr., holding a fleur-de-lis arg. *Je me fie en Dieu.* 254. 5

Blois, De, and **Bloys,** a lion rampant gardant gu. 2. 5

Blomberg, two eagles' wings addorsed ppr. *cf.* 109. 12

Blomberg, out of a ducal coronet a demi-lion rampant double-queued. *cf.* 10. 6

Blome of Seven Oaks, Kent, a peacock's tail erect or. *Post virtutam curro.* *cf.* 115. 6

Blomefield, Leonard, Esquire, of Belmount, near Bath, Somers., a demi-heraldic tiger az., tufted and crined or, holding in the mouth a branch of broom of the same, and holding in the paws a sword erect, broken at the point ppr., pommel and hilt or.

Blomefield, Sir Thomas Wilmot Peregrine, Bart., of Attleborough, Norf., out of a mural coronet arg., a demi-heraldic tiger az., armed and tufted or, collared of the first, holding a broken sword ppr. 245. 8

Blomer or **Bloomer** of Hagthorpe, Glouc., an heraldic tiger sejant vert, ducally gorged, and the chain reflexed over the back or.

Blomfeild, Blomefield, or **Bloomfield,** two wings displayed ppr. 109. 6

Blomfield, Suff., a demi-heraldic tiger rampant arg., holding between its paws a broken sword.

Blommart, an arm couped and embowed, resting the elbow on the wreath, holding a sword in pale enfiled with a savage's head couped.

Blond, Le, Ireland, on a chapeau gu., turned up erm., a gamecock ppr. *cf.* 90. 2

Blondel, a Saracen's head ppr. 190. 5

Blondell, a dexter hand holding a battle-axe, all ppr. 213. 12

Blondevill or **Blonville,** a Cornish chough ppr. 107. 14

Blood, a buck's head erased ppr., attired or, holding in the mouth an arrow of the second.

Blood, Ireland, a talbot's head sa., collared or. *cf.* 56. 1

Blood, Major-General Sir Bindon, K.C.B., of Cranagher, Ennis, co. Clare, issuant from waves of the sea a demi-figure of Neptune, all ppr. *Honor virtutis præmium.*

Blood, Charles Holcraft, Esquire, same crest and motto.

Blood, Frederick William, Esquire, same crest and motto.

Blood, John, Esquire, of Ballykilty, Ardsollus, co. Clare, same crest and motto.

Blood, Joseph Fitzgerald, Esquire, of 8, Lorne Road, Birkenhead, same crest and motto.

Blood, Neptune Fitzgerald, Esquire, of Vrede, Orange River Colony, South Africa.

Bloodworth, a dexter hand couped in fess gu., holding a cross crosslet fitched in pale sa. 221. 10

Bloom, a cubit arm erect, vested az., cuffed arg., holding in the hand ppr. some slips of broom, stalked vert, blossomed or.

Bloomfield, Baron, Ireland, out of a mural coronet or, charged with two cinquefoils in fess az., a bull's head ppr. *Fortes fortuna juvat.*

Bloomfield, a fox's head ppr. 33. 4

Bloomfield, a bull's head ppr. *cf.* 44. 3

Bloomfield of Kilthroe, co. Tipperary, Ireland, a bull's head erased sa., armed and langued or. *Fortes fortuna juvat.* 44. 3

Bloomfield, two wings issuing ppr. 109. 6

Bloor or **Bloore,** an arm in armour embowed, holding a cutlass, all ppr. *cf.* 196. 10

Bloss of Ipswich, Suff., a demi-angel, holding in the dexter hand a griffin's head erased. 183. 3

Blosse, Lynch-, Sir Henry, Bart., of Castle Carra, co. Mayo, Ireland, a lynx passant coward arg. *Nec temere, nec timide.*

Blossom or **Blossome,** out of a ducal coronet a hand holding a swan's head and neck erased. 220. 7

Blossome or **Blossun,** a ram passant ppr. *cf.* 131. 13

Bloundell or **Blundell,** a squirrel sejant or, cracking a nut ppr. 135. 7

Bloundell of Carlington, Beds, a squirrel sejant gu., collared and holding a nut or. *cf.* 135. 7

Blount of Maple-Durham, Oxon., on a ducal coronet or, a wolf passant sa.

Blount, Baron Mountjoy of Thurveston and **Earl of Newport** (*extinct*), on a ducal coronet or, a crescent of the same.

Blount, London and Glouc., a sea-lion rampant erm., ducally crowned or. *cf.* 20. 5

Blount, Darell-, John, Esquire, of Maple-Durham, Oxon.: (1) The sun in splendour, charged in the centre with an eye, all ppr. (*for Blount*). (2) Out of a ducal coronet or, a man's head in profile, couped at the shoulders and bearded ppr., wreathed round the temples or and az., on the head a cap, also az., fretty arg., tasselled of the first, and turned up erm., for difference a cross crosslet az. (*for Darell*). *Lux tua vita mea.*

Blount, the sun or, charged with a gauntlet sa., garnished or.

Blount of Kinlet: (1) An armed foot in the sun ppr. 162. 12. (2) On a chapeau gu., turned up erm., a lion passant of the first, ducally crowned or. *cf.* 4. 9

Blount of Wadeley, Shropsh., and London, a lion passant gu., crowned or. *cf.* 6. 2

Blount, Sir Walter de Sodington, Bart., of Sodington, Worcs., an armed foot in the sun ppr. *Lux tua via mea.* 162. 12

Blount, late Walter Aston Edward, Esquire, an armed foot in the sun, all ppr. *Lux tua via mea.* 162. 12

Blount, Sir Edward Charles, K.C.B., of Imberhorne, Sussex, a sun in splendour charged with a gauntlet ppr. *Lux tua via mea.*

Blount, behind the rays of the sun or, a bull's head sa.

Blount, in the sun a griffin's head erased, all ppr. 162. 14

Blount, Archibald Henry, of Orleton, Heref., a cross sa., in the sun in splendour or. *Mors crucis mea salus.*

Blount (alias Croke), in a crescent az., two swans' heads reversed and interlaced arg., in the beak of each an annulet gu. 100. 11

Blouyle, Suff., a demi-lion rampant per pale indented arg. and gu. 10. 2

Blow, two wings conjoined arg. 109. 6

Blower, out of a mural coronet or, a demi-eagle displayed vert, vulned in the breast by an arrow of the first, feathered arg. 80. 7

Bloxam of Bloxam, Oxon., and Rugby, Warw., an anchor in bend sinister or, cabled az.

Bloxam and **Bloxham,** a shuttle az. 176. 14

Bloxholmedax, in front of a tree vert, a boar passant arg.

Bloxsome of the Rangers, Glouc., a wyvern's head erased or, transfixed by a spear-head in pale sa. *Non timere sed fortiter.*

Bloye, a mullet gu., between two branches of palm in orle vert. 146. 8

Bloys of Ipswich, Suff., a gauntlet ppr., purfled or, holding a fleur-de-lis of the last.

Bluck, a bull's head erased gu., armed or. 44. 3

Bludder or **Bluder,** Lincs. and Middx., a lion's head erased arg., pierced through the neck with a broken spear of the same.

Bludder, Bluder, or **Bluther,** London, a lion's head erased arg., pierced through neck with the blade of a sword of the last, the wound gu. *cf.* 17. 13

Bludworth, a naked arm embowed ppr., guttée-de-sang, holding a wreath of laurel vert. 202. 4

Bluet and **Bluett** of Holcombe Court, Holcolm-Regis, Devonsh., a squirrel sejant or, collared and lined gu., and holding in its paws an acorn of the first, leaved vert. *In Deo omnia.*

Bluett, Colonel Charles Edward Lane, of Tormohun House, Torquay, a squirrel sejant or, in his paw an acorn vert, fructed or. *In Deo omnia.*

Blufield, a demi-greyhound, wounded in the breast with an arrow ppr.

Blumberg, Ludwig Alexander, Esquire, of Palace Gardens, Kensington, and Victor George Blumberg, Esquire, on a mount vert, a lion's head erased or, semée of estoiles sa. *Concordia vim dat.* cf. 17. 8

Blund, a cock's head erased gu. 90. 1

Blundell, Ireland, on a tower an eagle rising ppr. 156. 8

Blundell, an arm in armour embowed, the hand holding a scimitar, all ppr. *Unus et idem ferar.* 196. 10

Blundell, a unicorn's horn ppr.

Blundell, a demi-lion rampant sa., holding in the paws a cross-tau fitchée erect arg.

Blundell, William Joseph, Esquire, the Hall, Crossby, Liverpool, same crest.

Blundell, Charles Joseph Weld, of Ince Blundell, Lancs, and Cardington, Beds: (1) A squirrel sejant gu., collared, and holding a nut or, charged on the body with a bezant for distinction. (2) A wyvern sa. guttée-d'eau, collared, chained, and winged or. *Nil sine numine.*

Blundell, a hawk holding in the dexter claw an ear of wheat ppr. 85. 7

Blunden, Ireland, on the point of a spear a dolphin naiant ppr. 140. 9

Blunden, Sir William, M.D., Bart., of Castle Blunden, co. Kilkenny, Ireland, a demi-lion rampant per fesse sa. and arg., armed and langued gu. *Cedamus amori.* 10. 2

Blunden of Bishop's Castle, Shropsh., a demi-griffin or, gorged with a fess erm. cf. 64. 2

Blundeston, a wolf passant arg. 28. 10

Blundestone and **Blunstone,** Suff., the sun rising ppr. *Post nubes lux.*

Blunt, the sun in splendour or. 162. 2

Blunt, on a mount vert, a sun in splendour ppr. 162. 3

Blunt of Wallop House, Hants, the sun in glory, charged on the centre with an eye issuing tears, all ppr. *Inter lachrymas micat.*

Blunt, Sir William, Bart., of Heathfield Park and Ringmer, Sussex, same crest. *Lux tua vita mea.—Inter lachrymas micat.*

Blunt, Wilfrid Scawen, Esquire, 104, Mount Street, Grosvenor Square, a lion statant, crowned or, on a cap of maintenance. *Respiciendo prospiciende.*

Blunt, the sun in splendour or, charged in the centre with a slipper.

Blunt, out of a coronet or, a bull's head couped near the shoulders sa. cf. 44. 11

Blunt, Notts, a wolf passant sa. 28. 10

Blyth, Sir James, Bart., 33, Portland Place, W., in front of a mound vert, thereon a bull statant arg., ringed and chained or, three roses gu. *Spero meliora.* 250. 18

Blyth, Scotland, an arm in armour embowed, holding by the middle of the blade a drawn sword point downwards, all ppr. 195. 6

Blyth, a buck's head ppr. *Spero meliora.* 121. 5

Blyth, a stag's head erased gu., attired or, gorged with a chaplet vert. 120. 3

Blythe, Bodmin, Cornw., a griffin's head erased or. 66. 2

Blythe, Yorks, a buck's head erased or, attired of the same, collared az. cf. 121. 2

Blythe of Cornw., an arm embowed, habited per pale or and az., cuffed arg., holding in the hand ppr. a battle-axe, staff of the second, headed of the third.

Blythe, Norf., a stag's head couped gu., gorged with a chaplet of laurel ppr. 120. 3

Blythe, in a wreath erm. and gu., a roebuck's head erased of the second, attired or, gorged with a chaplet vert. cf. 120. 3

Blythe of Norton, Derbysh., a roebuck's head erased, attired or, gorged with a chaplet vert. 120. 3

Blythswood, Baron (Campbell), Blythswood House, Renfrew, N.B.: (1) A lymphad sa. (2) An oak-tree with a lock hanging from one of the branches, all ppr. *Vincit labor.—Quæ serata secura.*

Boade, a ram's head gorged with a fess indented sa., charged with three escallops arg. cf. 130. 1

Boag or **Bogg,** a sand-glass ppr. 177. 15

Boag, Sir Robert, of Belfast, and of Violet Lodge, Groomport, co. Down, Ireland, an hour-glass between two oak-branches in orle ppr. *Regit omnia tempus*

Boak, a beacon fired ppr. 177. 14

Board of Bordhill, Sussex, and Lindfield, a stag erm.

Board, an antelope statant or. *Perforatus.* 126. 12

Boardman, a lion sejant, collared and lined or. 7. 4

Boardman, William, Esquire, of Farrington House, Penwortham, Lancs, a stag's head sa., erased gu., crusily and attired or. cf. 121. 2

Boase, Cornw., a demi-lion charged with three bezants on the shoulder, and with a star on the hip, holding in its paws five arrows, four in saltier and one in fess at the top.

Boatfield, five arrows sa., enfiled with a ducal coronet or. 173. 9

Bock, a hawk's leg and wing conjoined, the first belled and jessed, all ppr. 113. 5

Bocket, a horse's head between two wings addorsed.

Bocking, Suff., on a chapeau gu., turned up erm., a leopard passant ppr. 24. 1

Bockingham, Suff., on a chapeau a lion statant gardant, collared and ducally crowned. cf. 4. 2

Bockland or **Bocklande,** a bull's head erased arg., ducally gorged sa. 44. 2

Bockland or **Bocklande,** a hawk close regardant arg., beaked and belled or.

Bockley, the sun shining on a demi-eagle with two heads in flames ppr. cf. 82. 12

Boddam of Enfield, Middx., of Kirklington Park, Notts, and Essex, a stag trippant ppr. 117. 8

Boddicott, Bodicote, or **Bodycoat,** a weaver's shuttle in pale az., threaded arg. 176. 14

Boddington or **Bodington,** a lion's gamb grasping a scimitar, all ppr. 38. 13

Boddington or **Boddinton,** a demi-lion rampant gu., holding in the dexter paw a cross crosslet fitched arg. 11. 5

Boddington (anciently of Brinklow, Warw.), Reginald Stewart Boddington, Esquire, 15, Markham Square, Chelsea, S.W., a demi-lion rampant gu., holding in the dexter paw a cross crosslet fitched arg. *Vincit veritas.* 11. 5

Boddington, Henry, Esquire, J.P., of Pownall Hall, Wilmslow, Chesh., a demi-lion az., gorged with a collar gemel, and holding in the dexter paw a cross crosslet fitchée or, resting the sinister on a lozenge az., charged with a cross crosslet, also fitchée or. *Vincit veritas.* 11. 8

Boddy, Evan Marlett, Esquire, F.R.C.S. (Edinburgh), 109, Ashted Row, Birmingham, a staff erect raguly gu., enfiled with a ducal coronet or. *Vi corporis et animi.* 147. 12

Bode, of Feversham, Kent, a greyhound's head couped arg., collared and ringed sa., the collar charged with three escallops of the first. cf. 61. 2

Bodell, a dexter arm embowed vested stabbing with a sword a squirrel sejant regardant ppr.

Bodelsgate, Cornw., a horse's head erased arg. 51. 4

Boden, Lancs, a stork's head erased arg., between two lilies ppr. *Diligentia et vigilantia.*

Boden, Henry, of the Friary, Derbysh., a swan, the wings extended ppr. *Contra audentior ito.* 99. 12

Boden, Marshall, Esquire, of Burton Crescent, St. Pancras, Middx., an eagle rising or, charged on the breast with a rose gu., and perched upon four mascles conjoined in fesse of the same.

Bodenfield, an eagle's head erased between two wings arg., ducally crowned or. cf. 84. 2

Bodenham of Rotherwas, Heref., a dragon's head erased sa. *Veritas liberabit.* cf. 71. 2

Bodenham, Heref., out of a ducal coronet or, a wing sa. 109. 4

Bodenham, Heref., a dragon's head erased sa. cf. 71. 2

Bodicote, a weaver's shuttle in pale az., threaded arg. 176. 14

Bodington, a demi-lion rampant gu., holding in his dexter paw a cross crosslet fitched arg. 11. 5

Bodington, a lion's gamb grasping a scimitar ppr. 38. 13

Bodkin of Annagh, Ireland, a wild boar ppr. *Crom-a-boo.* 40. 9

Bodkin, Rev. Dr., the Cloisters, Cheltenham, same crest and motto. 297. 4

Bodkin, a leopard's face or. 22. 2

Bodkin, a pillar sa. 176. 3

Bodley or **Bodlegh** of Dunscombe, in Crediton, Devonsh., on clouds az., encircled with rays or, a ducal coronet of the last.

Bodley of Streatham, Surrey, a bull's head or *cf* 44 3

Bodley, a demi wolf holding btewecn its paws a ducal coronet, all ppr *cf* 31 12

Bodrigan or **Bodrugan**, a dexter hand erect, round the wrist a ribbon

Bodwida, a dexter arm in armour embowed ppr, holding a fleur-de-lis or 199 14

Body, a staff raguly and erect gu, enfiled with a ducal coronet or 147 12

Body, Charles Ash, Esquire, of the Cedars, Sydenham Hill, a demi-lion or, charged with two bars sa, holding in the dexter paw a distaff in bend sinister ppr, and supporting with the sinister an eagle's head erased gu *Omne bonum desuper* 249. 12

Bodychan, Sparrow, Henry Glendeor, of Gwynn du, Bodychan, Anglesey, a sparrowhawk *Honestas optima politia*

Bodyham, a pegasus at full speed wings addorsed and ducally gorged, *cf* 47 1

Boehm, Sir Edgar Collins, Bart, Bramlands, Woodmancote, Sussex, a hat sa, charged on the turn-up with three bezants fesseswise *Sola mea testis* 234 9

Boehm, Bohem, and **Boeham**, between two elephants' trunks per fesse arg and sa, a horse-shoe of the first

Boevey, Crawley-, Sir Thomas Hyde, Bart, Flaxley Abbey, Glouc, on a mount vert, a heron ppr, collared or, holding in the dexter claw a saltire of the last *Esse quam videri* 239 6

Bog and **Bogg**, *see* Boag

Boger, an eagle, wings expanded, supporting a flag *cf* 78 14

Boger, Captain Edmund, R N, on a tower or charged with two lozenges in fess vairce arg and gu, a dove with an olive-branch in its beak, all ppr

Boger, Walter Deeble, of Wolsdon, Cornw in front of a cubit arm ppr, holding a dibble in bend or, and a rose gu, leaved and slipped in bend sinister ppr, a cinquefoil, also or

Boger, Francis Herbert, Esquire, of Melbourne, Australia, same crest

Boger, John Richard, Esquire, of 29, St Edmund's Terrace, Regent's Park, same crest as Boger of Cornw

Boger, Percival Sylvester, Esquire, of Saltash, Cornwall, same crest as Boger of Cornw

Boger, William Henry, Esquire, of Fowey, Cornw, same crest as Boger of Cornw

Bogg, Suttern, Lincs, a bat displayed arg, armed or 137 11

Boggis or **Boggs**, the sail of a ship ppr 160 9

Boggis-Rolfe (1) A raven on a branch sprouting at the dexter end (*for Rolfe*) (2) The sail of a ship ppr (*for Boggis*) *Avancez*

Bogie and **Boggie**, a lamb supporting a flag *Deus pastor meus* 131 2

Bogle, Scotland, a rose slipped and leaved ppr *Dulcedine* 149 5

Bogle, Captain John du Terreau, R E, in front of a primrose gu, stalked and leaved vert, a fret or *Dulcius ex aspersus*

Bogle of Daldowie, Scotland, a primrose stalked and leaved ppr, thereon a bee feeding sa *E labore duleedo*

Bogle of Hamilton's Farm, Ayr, and Shettlestone, Lanark, a ship in full sail ppr *Spe meliore vehor* 160 13

Bogle, Gilbert, 42, Heaton Grove, Newcastle-on Tyne, on waves of the sea a ship of three masts in full sail ppr

Bogle, a tower ppr 156 2

Bogley, a cross Calvary sa, on three grieces gu 166 1

Bohem, a horse-shoe arg, between two elephants' trunks per fesse of the same and sa

Bohun, De, a wolf current ppr 28 4

Bohun of Tressingfield, Suff, on a chapeau a quatrefoil pierced erm, in the centre thereof a bezant *cf* 148 10

Bohun or **Boone**, Lincs, out of a ducal coronet gu, a cup arg, between two elephants' tusks or

Bohun, Earls of Hereford, Essex, and Northampton (*extinct*), on a chapeau gu, turned up erm, a lion statant gardant and ducally crowned or *cf* 4 2

Boidell, a greyhound's head erased az 61 4

Boileau, Chester, a heart inflamed ppr 181 13

Boileau, Sir Maurice Colborne, Bart, of Tacolnestone Hall, Norf, in a nest or, a pelican in her piety ppr, charged on the breast with a saltier couped gu, the nest resting in a foreign coronet *De tout mon cœur*

Bois, a stag's head arg, attired gu, between the attires a mound or *cf* 121 5

Bois, a lion rampant gu 1 13

Bokeland, a lion rampant, holding between his fore paws a pair of scales, all ppr

Bokeland, an eagle's head couped gu, between two wings chequy or and vert 84 2

Bokenham, Norf, three mullets in chevron 164 7

Bokenham, Norf, a lion rampant gu 1 13

Bokinge or **Boking** of Boking, Suff, a man's head couped at the shoulders arg, the hair vert *cf* 190 13

Bolaine or **Boloine** of London, a bull's head couped arg *cf* 44 3

Boland, Devonsh, out of a ducal coronet or, a cubit arm erect, holding in the hand three arrows in bend sinister, all ppr 214 3

Bolbeck or **Bolebeck**, a lion sejant, supporting with his dexter paw a broken lance, all ppr *cf* 8 11

Bolckow, Charles Ferdinand Henry, of Marton Hall, Yorks, a boar passant az, in front of seven acorns or, leaved and stalked ppr *Suscipere et finire* *cf* 40 2

Bolcole, a demi-reindeer ppr, collared, traced, and charged on the shoulder with an étoile or

Bold or **Bolde**, out of a ducal coronet gu, a griffin's head sa, between two wings displayed or *cf* 67 1

Bold of Bold, Lancs, a griffin segreant sa, armed and legged or 62 2

Bolden, John Leonard, of Hyning, Lancaster (1) Out of a ducal coronet or, a tiger's head arg 27 3 (2) A swan or *Pour bien désirer* 99 2

Boldero and **Bolderowe**, a pomeis *cf* 159 14

Boldero, Rev John Simon, Amblecote Vicarage, Stourbridge, a greyhound courant

Boldero, Rev John Herbert, Rattlesden, Suff, a greyhound sejant gu, collared or *Audax ero* 59 4

Bolders, Boldorne, and **Boldron**, a greyhound current gu, collared or *cf* 58 2

Bolding, late George Frederick, Esquire, of 224, Hagley Road, Edgbaston, in front of a demi-seahorse ppr, a garb fesseways or *Sto pro veritate* 253 12

Boldrowe, Suff, a lion's gamb arg, grasping a saltier az

Bolebec or **Bolebeck**, a lion sejant supporting with his dexter paw a broken lance, all ppr *cf* 8 11

Boleine, a bull's head couped arg, langued gu, charged on the neck with a crescent or

Boles, out of a mural coronet az, a lion's head arg 19 12

Boleyn, Bollens, or **Bollin**, two branches of thorn in orle ppr *cf* 146 6

Bolger, a dexter arm couped and embowed fesseways ppr, holding in the hand three ears of rye leaved or 202 6

Bolger of St Austins, Ireland, an escallop reversed or *Deus nobis hæc otia fecit* 141 9

Bolhalth, from the top of a tower issuing from the wreath an arm embowed holding a spear in fess, all ppr 201 10

Bolingbroke and St John, Viscount (St John), Lydiard Park, Swindon, Wilts, on a mount ppr, a falcon rising and belled or, ducally gorged gu *Nec quærere, nec spernere honorem*

Bolitho, Thomas Bedford, of Trewidden, Penzance, Cornw, in front of a fern-brake a cubit arm and hand erect ppr, vested az, charged with three bezants cuffed arg, the hand holding a fleur-de-lis sa *Re Deu*

Bolitho, John Borlase, Esquire, in front of a fern-brake ppr, a cubit arm erect vested az, charged with three bezants, cuffed arg, in the hand ppr a fleur de-lis sa *Re Deu*

Bolitho, Otho Glynn, Esquire, of Poltair, Cornw, same crest and motto

Bolitho, Thomas Bedford, Esquire, of Trewidden, near Penzance, same crest and motto

Bolitho, Thomas Robins, Esquire, of Trengwainton, Hea Moor, Cornw, R S O, same crest and motto

Bolitho, William Edward Thomas, Esquire, of York House, Penzance, same crest and motto

Bolland of Clapham, Surrey, an eagle's head erased ppr, gorged with a collar erm, holding in the beak a peg sa

Bolland, a hart trippant ppr, attired or 117 8

Bollardt of Antwerp and Dublin, a griffin's head erased arg. 66 2

Bolle and **Bolles**, Bart. (*extinct*), of Bolles Hall, Lincs, a demi boar wounded in the breast with a broken spear *cf* 40. 13

Bollen, a talbot gu., collared and leashed or. cf. 54. 5

Bollens and **Bolleyn**, two branches of thorn disposed in orle ppr. cf. 146. 6

Bollers, an arm vested, couped and embowed in fesse, the elbow resting on the wreath, holding a cross crosslet fitchée. 203. 9

Bolles, Middx., and of Scampton, Lincs, a buck's head arg., attired or. 121. 5

Bolles and **Bolls**, Suff., a cock crowing or, combed, wattled, legged, and armed gu. 91. 2

Bolleyn and **Bollin**, *see* Boleyn and Bollens.

Bollingbroke, Bollingbrook, and **Bollinsbrook**, a Spanish hat az., turned up arg., in front three feathers of the last. 115. 4

Bolney, Berks, and of Bolney, Sussex, a skeleton's head couped at the shoulders ppr., holding in the mouth a firebrand or, flammant at both ends ppr.

Bolourd, out of a ducal coronet or, a demi-eagle gu. 80. 4

Bolron, a dove volant sa. cf. 93. 13

Bolron, an arm in fess couped at the shoulder and embowed, the elbow resting on the wreath, the hand holding a sword in pale, enfiled with a savage's head. 201. 7

Bolster, George, Esquire, of Springville, Kanturk, co. Cork, a cubit arm erect in armour ppr., charged with three plates in pale, the hand bare grasping a scimitar, also ppr., hilt and pommel or. *Vi et virtute.* 263. 5

Bolster, Thomas, Esquire, of Springville, Kanturk, co. Cork, same crest and motto.

Bolstred and **Bolstrode**, a bull's head and neck between two wings expanded gu., armed arg. 43. 10

Bolt or **Boult**, a stork ppr. 105. 11

Bolter, a lion's head erased sa., imperially crowned or. cf. 17. 14

Bolthorpe, a demi-tiger salient or, ducally gorged arg., cf. 25. 10

Bolton, Baron (Orde-Powlet), Bolton Hall, Leyburn, Yorks, and Hackwood Park, Basingstoke, a falcon rising and belled or, charged on the breast and wings with three étoiles in fess gu., gorged with a ducal coronet az., and holding in the beak a salmon ppr. *Aymez loyaulte.* 239. 9

Bolton, Henry Hargreaves, Esquire, of Heighside, Newchurch-in-Rossendale, Lancs, three bird-bolts, two in saltire and one in fesse ppr., thereon a falcon close, belled and jessed or. *Sursum corda.* 255. 15

Bolton, Henry Hargreaves, jnr., Esquire, of High Brake, Huncoat, Accrington, Lancs, same crest and motto.

Bolton of Bolton, Lancs, a hawk arg., belled or. 85. 2

Bolton, Edwin, Esquire, of Carbrook, Larbert, Stirlingsh., a falcon close sa., armed, jessed, and belled or. *Industria et virtute.* cf. 85. 2

Bolton of Bective Abbey, co. Meath, a hawk arg., belled or. 85. 2

Bolton of Woodbridge, Suff., a falcon close arg., charged on the breast with a trefoil slipped vert, beaked and belled or. cf. 85. 2

Bolton, on a mount vert, a hawk rising sa., belled and charged on the breast with two bird-bolts in saltire or.

Bolton of Cranwich, Norf., on a mount vert, a falcon erm., beak and bells or, holding in the beak a trefoil slipped of the first.

Bolton, a falcon arg. 85. 2

Bolton, a falcon arg., with the wings expanded or. 87. 1

Bolton-Massy of Brazil, co. Dublin, and of Ballywire, co. Tipperary: (1) Out of a ducal coronet or, a bull's head gu., armed sa. (*for Massy*). cf. 44. 11. (2) A falcon belled ppr., jessed az. (*for Bolton*). *Pro libertate patria.* cf. 85. 2

Bolton, a tun erect ppr., transpierced by an arrow fesswise or.

Bolton, Boltone, or **Boltoun**, a horse saddled and bridled at full speed. 52. 1

Bolton, a hind's head per pale indented arg. and az., holding in the mouth a broad arrow or, feathered and headed arg. cf. 124. 1

Bolton or **Boulton**, Lancs and Yorks, a buck's head erased arg., attired or, gorged with a chaplet vert, and pierced through the neck with an arrow of the second.

Bomford, North-, Captain John: (1) A griffin segreant arg., charged on the shoulder with a cross crosslet fitchée gu. (*for Bomford*). cf. 62. 2. (2) A wyvern's head erased vert, langued gu., collared and chained or (*for North*). *Justus et fidelis.* cf. 71. 2

Bomford, Ireland, an eagle displayed holding in the dexter claw a dagger. 75. 7

Bomont, an ostrich, the wings expanded arg.

Bon, Le, of Farneaux, Normandy, out of a ducal coronet or, a plume of ostrich-feathers arg. *Confido.*

Bonamy, Guernsey, a plume of three feathers or. 115. 1

Bonar of Kimmerghame, Berwick, a sword in pale ppr. *Denique cœlum.* 170. 2

Bonar, John Andrew Macdonell, Glenburn, Granville Road, Sevenoaks, a sword in pale, the blade ppr., the hilt and pommel or. *Denique cœlum.* 302. 14

Bonar, a dexter hand charged on the palm with an eye and holding a heart bleeding ppr. *Præstat tuto quam cito.*

Bond, Isle of Purbeck, Dorset: (1) An eagle rising sa., charged with a fess or. (2) A demi-pegasus az., winged and semée of estoiles or. *Non sufficit orbis.* cf. 47. 5

Bond, Nathaniel, of Creech Grange, Dorset: (1) An eagle's wing sa., charged with a fesse or. 247. 4. (2) A demi-pegasus az., winged and semée of estoiles or. *Non sufficit orbis.*

Bond of Peckham, Surrey, and Saltash, Cornw., a demi-pegasus az., winged and semée of estoiles or. cf. 47. 5

Bond or **Bonde**, an old man's head in profile ppr., the hair sa.

Bond, Ireland, an ostrich-head between two branches of palm in orle. cf. 96. 10

Bond, John Gregory, Greatwood, Penryn, Cornw., a lion sejant ppr.

Bond of Coolamber, co. Longford, Ireland, a lion sejant arg. 8. 8

Bond, Bart. (*extinct*), on a mount vert, a lion sejant arg. cf. 8. 8

Bond, Gerald Denis, Esquire, of Holme Priory, Wareham, a wing sa., charged with a fesse or. 247. 4

Bond, William Henry, Esquire, of Fryern Court, Hants, same crest.

Bond, M'Geough-, Joshua Walter, of Drumsill, co. Armagh, Ireland: (1) A lion sejant arg., charged on the shoulder with an annulet sa. (*for Bond*). cf. 8. 8. (2) A dexter arm embowed, the hand grasping a scimitar in the act of striking, all ppr. (*for M'Geough*). *Nemo me impune lacessit.* 201. 1

Bond of Cawbery and Walford, Heref., and of Newland and Redbrook, Glouc., a demi-lion. 10. 2

Bonde, an old man's head in profile ppr., the hair sa.

Bonde of Coventry, Warw., a demi-griffin gu., bezantée, holding in the beak a twig vert, seeded or. cf. 64. 2

Bondiville, Yorks, a stag's head ppr. 121. 5

Bone, a bone and a palm-branch in saltier ppr. 147. 4

Bone or **Boun**, a sword and a key in saltier ppr. 171. 10

Boneham and **Bonham**, a pheon in pale, point downwards, with part of the broken shaft remaining therein. 174. 10

Bonekill, Scotland, a demi-man in armour brandishing in his dexter hand a sword, all ppr. 187. 1

Bonekill, Scotland, a dexter hand holding a buckle or. 223. 11

Bonell of Duffield, Derbysh., a demi-lion rampant sa. 10. 1

Bonest and **Bonus**, London, a talbot's head couped arg. 56. 12

Bonfoy or **Bunfoy** of Hease, Middx., an arm couped and erect in armour ppr., holding in the gauntlet a cross Calvary gu. *En bonne foy.*

Bonham, Wilts, the stump of a tree in fess sprouting ensigned with a fleur-de-lis. 145. 13

Bonham, Essex, a mermaid ppr. *Esse quam videri.* 184. 5

Bonham, Edward William, Esquire, H.M. Consul, Calais, France, a mermaid ppr., holding in her dexter hand a looking-glass and in her sinister a comb. *Esse quam videri.* 184. 5

Bonham, Sir George Francis, Bart., Knowle Park, Cranleigh, Surrey, upon a rock a mermaid holding in her dexter hand a wreath of coral and in her sinister a mirror, all ppr. *Esse quam videri.*

Bonham of Petersfield, Hants, a dragon's head arg., guttée-de-sang. cf. 71. 1

Bonham, *see* Boneham.

Boniface, Sussex, a talbot passant sa. 54. 1

Bonnell, Norf., a lion rampant or, holding between his paws a cross crosslet az.

Bonnell of Isleworth, Middx., a lion rampant or, holding between the paws a cross crosslet, and charged on the shoulder with an annulet, both az.

Bonnell of London, a demi-lion erased or, pellettée, queue-fourchée interlaced, supporting a spear of the first.

Bonnell, Ireland, a demi-lion az, holding between the paws a cross crosslet fitchee or. *Terris peregrinus et hospes* cf 11 10

Bonner, a unicorn's head couped between two wings and holding in the mouth a trefoil

Bonner, Oxon, a talbot's head arg, collared az, studded, rimmed, and ringed or cf 56. 1

Bonnet of France and London, a unicorn's head couped vert, purfled and crined or *Rara bonitas* 49 7

Bonnett, a cubit arm in armour lying in fesse and holding a cross crosslet fitched az. 211. 14

Bonney, a square padlock ppr 168 13

Bonney, a martlet ppr *Ne quid nimis* 95 4

Bonney, Rev Thomas George 23 Denning Road, N W, same crest and motto

Bonniman, Scotland, a spur between two wings ppr 111 13

Bonnor, G, Esquire, 42, Queen's Gate Terrace, Kensington, a demi-talbot or, gorged with a collar gemelle az, holding between the paws an hourglass ppr *A la bonne heure*

Bonsall, John Joseph of Fronfraith co Cardigansh, Aberystwith and Llanwnn Montgomerysh, Wales, a dexter hand grasping a cross flory gu *Pro patria* 221 14

Bonsall, Thomas William, Morben, Montgomery, same crest and motto

Bonshaw, a dexter hand issuing from a cloud in fess holding a sword in pale, on the point a garland of laurel, all ppr *Mente manuque* cf 223 10

Bonsor, Henry Cosmo Orme, Kingswood Warren, Epsom, Surrey, on a staff raguly in fess or, a wolf passant sa, collared, and the chain reflexed over the back of the first, the dexter paw resting on a rose gu, barbed and seeded ppr cf 29 1

Bontein, Scotland, a cubit arm erect holding a sword ppr *Fortiter et fide* 132 12

Bontein, a cross crosslet fitchee in pale surmounted by two palm branches in saltier

Bontein and **Bonteine**, Scotland, an armillary sphere ppr *Soli Deo gloria* 159 10

Bontein, John, Esquire, a demi eagle issuing out of a ducal coronet ppr *Copiose et opportune*

Bontein, James Shelley, Esquire, Glen cruitten, Oban, Argyllsh same crest and motto

Bonten, a griffin segreant holding in the dexter claw a sword in pale cf 62 2

Bontien, out of a ducal coronet a demi eagle issuing ppr *Copiose et opportune*

Bontine and **Bontien** of Ardoch, Dumbarton, Scotland, a bunting bird standing on a garb, all ppr *Copiose et opportune*

Bonton, a cubit arm erect holding a mill rind, all ppr

Bonus and **Bonest** of London, a talbot's head couped arg 56. 12

Bonvile, Devonsh, a stag's head ppr 121 5

Bonvill, a demi-lion rampant supporting an anchor ppr 12 12

Bonwick, Surrey, a lion's head erased gu, charged with an etoile or cf 17 8

Bonynge, Charles William, Esquire, of 42, Prince's Gate, London, an ostrich ppr, charged with an escallop sa, and holding in the beak a key of the same *Virtute decoratus*

Bonython, Sir John Langdon Esquire of Carclew, Adelaide, South Australia, a fawn feeding ppr *In Deo spes mea* 124 13

Boodam, an etoile of eight rays or cf 164 4

Boodle, a horse's head, the neck transpierced with a spear in bend ppr 50 11

Booer, a wolf's head erased erm 30 8

Booker, London and Notts, a swan ppr, collared and lined az 99 1

Booker, Lieutenant-Colonel Josias, of Demerara, in the West Indies, on a mount vert, a swan ppr, collared and lined, and charged on the breast with a fleur-de lis az *Deo non fortuna*

Booker, Ireland, a crow feeding ppr 107 4

Booker of Cobrey Park, Heref, a demi-eagle displayed *Ad cœlum tendit* 81 6

Bookey, a dove volant arg, holding in the beak a sprig vert cf 93 10

Bookey of Ardenode, co Kildare, Ireland, from a morion az, a buck's head couped ppr *Tenax et fidus*

Boon or **Boone**, a bell ppr 168 7

Boon or **Boone**, a hand holding a sheaf of arrows, points downwards, all ppr 214 3

Boord, Sir (Thomas) William Bart, Oldbury Place Ightham Kent a goat arg, guttee de-poix resting the dexter leg on an escutcheon gu charged with a martlet of the first *Virtute et industriâ* 239 1

Boord, Borde, or **Board**, of Cuckfield and Lingfield, Sussex, a goat statant erm, armed or 129 5

Boorman of East Peckham, Kent, a bee volant between two oak-branches fructed, all ppr

Boorne of London and Essex, an heraldic tiger sejant gu, maned, tufted, and tailed or cf 25 7

Boorne, out of a ducal coronet a stag's head arg 120 7

Boorne of Battle, Sussex, a stag's head erased gu, attired arg, and guttee d'eau cf 121 2

Boors, an eel naiant az 142 10

Boot or **Boote**, a greyhound couchant between two branches of laurel in orle 60 5

Booth, Sclater-, Baron Basing, *see* Basing

Booth, Chesh, a figure of St Catherine ppr, vested vert, crowned with a ducal coronet within a nimbus and crined or, holding in her dexter hand a catherine-wheel or, and in her sinister a sword, the point downwards

Booth, Derbysh, a St Catherine ppr, kneeling in prayer, vested arg, crowned or, holding in the dexter hand a catherine wheel and in the sinister a sword point downwards

Booth, Haworth, Benjamin Blaydes Hullbank House, near Hull, Yorks (1) A St Catherine robed and crowned as a queen kneeling in prayer holding in her dexter hand a catherine-wheel and in her sinister a sword, point downwards (2) A stag's head gu, attired or gorged with a laurel-wreath arg *Quod ero spero* 120 3

Booth of Hoe Place, Woking, a lion passant arg *Quod ero spero* 6 2

Booth, Robert Home Brooke, of Glendon Hall, Northamp., a lion passant arg *Quod ero spero* 6 2

Booth, John Firth, Manor House, Lees, near Oldham, a lion passant *Quod ero spero*

Booth, James Erskine Wise, Esquire of Lara, Annomoe co Wicklow, upon a wreath of laurel a lion passant *Nec temere nec timide*

Booth or **Boothe** of Barton, Lancs, and Dunham Massey, Chesh, a lion passant arg 6 2

Booth of Twemlow, Chesh, a lion passant per pale wavy arg and erm, charged on the shoulder with a hank of cotton ppr cf 6 2

Booth, Gore-, Sir Josslyn Augustus Richard, Bart, Ireland (1) A lion passant arg *Quod ero spero* 6 2 (2) A wolf rampant arg *In hoc signo vinces —Genti æquus utrique* 28 2

Booth, Sir Charles, Bart, of Portland Place, Middx, and Great Catworth, Hunts, a lion passant arg, gorged with a bar gemelle and holding in the dexter paw a chaplet of laurel vert *Deus adjuvat nos*

Booth of Salford, Lancs, two laurel-branches vert in orle, thereon a lion passant arg *Non mihi, sed Deo et regi*

Booth, George H, 3, St George's Place, Victoria Gardens, Brighton on a garland of laurel a lion passant

Booth of Kellingham, Lincs, a boar's head erased and erect sa, armed or, holding in the mouth a spear-head arg

Booth, Philip Henry, J P, Gildersome, near Leeds, a lion passant *Quod ero spero*

Booth, Berks, a porcupine's head erased cf 136 2

Booth, a fasces ppr 171 4

Boothby, Sir Brooke, Bart, of Broadlow, Ash, Derbysh, a lion's gamb erased and erect or *Mors Christi, mors mortis mihi* 36 4

Boothby, Charles Edward, Esquire, of 1, Palmeira Square, Brighton, Sussex, same crest and motto

Bootle - Wilbraham, *see* Skelmersdale, Baron

Bootle, a leopard couchant or, spotted gu 24 10

Bootle, a demi lion rampant regardant ppr, holding between the paws an antique oval shield gu, rimmed or, charged with a cross patonce crossed arg

Booty, Suff, on a mount vert, a hand ppr, couped at the wrist, holding a sword arg, hilted or cf 212 13

Bor of Dublin two wings endorsed gu and or, on the former a fleur de lis of the last *Sicut iris florebit* cf 109 12

Boraster and **Boraston**, Heref, Worcs, and Berks, out of a mural coronet sa, a griffin's head or, gorged with a fess between two vars gemelle gu cf 67 10

Bordelays, Bordeleys, Bordeley, or **Bordeloys,** Camb, an Indian goat salient, holding in the mouth a branch of trefoil.

Boreel, Sir Jacob William Gustavus, Bart., of Meervliet, Velsen, Holland, a demi-man sa., wreathed about the head and loins, holding in his dexter hand an arrow in bend sinister, point upwards ppr.

Boreham or **Borham,** on a mural coronet ppr., a serpent nowed vert. 142. 12

Boreham, H. W., M.B., Elm Bank, Teignmouth, same crest. *Destruendo conservatis.*

Borelands, a broken lance ppr. *Press through.* 175. 6

Boreley and **Borseley,** Wilts, in front of a rock, a Cornish chough ppr. *cf.* 102. 6

Borell or **Burrell,** Heref., and Brommer Park, Northumb., a naked arm embowed ppr., charged with three pellets, holding in the hand a branch vert, fructed or.

Boreman, on the stump of a tree, an eagle rising ppr. 79. 12

Boreston or **Borreston,** a parrot vert, breasted gu. 101. 4

Borgoine, a marigold, on the top thereof a bee, all ppr. *cf.* 151. 12

Borham, *see* Boreham.

Borington, Viscount, *see* Morley, Earl of.

Borlacy of London, a stag's head erased ppr., holding in the mouth a riband with the motto "*Spes mea Deus.*"

Borland and **Borelands,** Scotland, a broken lance ppr. *Press through.* 175. 6

Borlase of Bookmer, Bucks, and of Cornw., a wolf passant regardant arg., struck in the shoulder with an arrow or, held in the mouth. *Te digna sequere.* *cf.* 28. 6

Borman, Devonsh. and Somers., a bull's head erased or, armed sa. 44. 3

Borminghall, a wolf's head erased gu. 30. 8

Borne, Kent, a lion sejant or, collared az., resting the dexter forepaw on a pellet *cf.* 6. 11

Borodaile, a dragon's head erased ppr. *cf.* 71. 2

Boron, a dragon's head and wings sa., collared or. *cf.* 72. 7

Borough, Bart. (*extinct*), of Baseldon Park, Berks, three plates surmounted by a plume of five ostrich-feathers arg. *Suivez moi.*

Borough, Shropsh., a fleur-de-lis arg. 148. 2

Borough of Sandwick, Kent, a dove standing on a snake, all ppr. 92. 10

Borough, Lincs, and of Richmond, Yorks, a swan's head and neck arg., beaked gu. *cf.* 101. 6

Borough or Burgh, a falcon rising erm., belled and ducally gorged or. 87. 2

Borough, John Sidney Burton, of Chetwynd Park, Newport, co. Salop, and of Edgmond, Shropsh., on a mount an eagle regardant, wings expanded, all ppr., the dexter claw supporting the shield of Pallas or. *Virtute et robore.*

Borough, George Thomas, Esquire, an eagle ppr., holding the shield of Pallas in its claws. *Virtute et robore.*

Borough, two wings addorsed erm. 109. 12

Borradaile, Borrodaile, or **Boradaile,** out of a tower, a demi-greyhound, holding between his paws a branch of laurel, all ppr. *cf.* 157. 8

Borrer, of Henfield, Sussex, a buck's head ppr., erased and fretty arg., holding in his mouth an auger of the first. *Fide laboro.*

Borrer, Arthur Hardress, Esquire, of 6, Durham Place, Chelsea, S.W., a buck's head erased ppr, fretty arg., holding in the mouth an auger of the first.

Borrer, Major Cary Hampton, J.P., D.L., Somerhill Lodge, Hove, Sussex, same crest.

Borrer, Rev. Charles Alexander, of Horseheath, Linton, Cambs, same crest.

Borrer, Walter Charles Freshfield Clifford, Esquire, of Pickwell, Cuckfield, Sussex, same crest. *Deo cari nihilo carent.*

Borrer, William, Esquire, of Brook Hill, Cowfield, Horsham, same crest. *Fide laboro.*

Borreston, *see* Boreston.

Borrett of London, a boar's head and neck erased, of a sandy colour and bristled or, the neck transpierced with a broken spear of the second, the end held in the mouth.

Borron, a paschal lamb ppr. *Per tela per hostes impavidi.* 131. 2

Borrow, Derbysh., on a mount an eagle regardant, wings expanded, all ppr., supporting with the dexter claw the shield of Pallas or.

Borrowes, Sir Kildare Dixon, Bart., Gilltown, co. Kildare, Ireland, a lion gardant murally crowned, all or. *Non vi virtute.*

Borrowes of Gilltown, Newbridge, co. Kildare, a lion sejant arg., ducally crowned or. *Non vi virtute.*

Borrowes or **Borrows,** Ireland, a boar's head erased in fess, with a sword thrust through the under jaw in pale, and issuing out of the mouth.

Borrowes or **Borrows,** a crane supporting with the dexter claw an anchor. 105. 10

Borrowman, Scotland, a demi-man in armour brandishing in his dexter hand a sword, all ppr. *Pro patria.* 187. 1

Borselle, over the stump of an oak-tree an eagle volant ppr.

Borsley, in front of a rock, a Cornish chough ppr. *cf.* 102. 6

Borston, a dagger in pale az., hilt and pommel or.

Borthwick of Gordonshall, Scotland, a withered rose-bush sprouting anew from the root. *Virtus post facta.*

Borthwick, Baron (Borthwick), a Moor's head in profile couped ppr., wreathed arg. and sa. *Qui conducit.* 192. 13

Borthwick (Baron Glenesk), on a staff raguly fessewise sa., a blackamoor's head in profile couped ppr. *Qui conducit.* 209. 15

Borthwick, John, Esquire, of Heriot, Midlothian, a blackamoor's head in profile couped. *Qui conducit.*

Borthwick, Scotland, a savage's head couped ppr. *Qui conducit.* 191. 1

Borthwick of Stow, Scotland, a dexter hand couped and apaumée, charged with an eye ppr. *Mente manuque.* 222. 4

Borthwick, Browne-, of Hope Park, Midlothian, a cubit arm erect ppr., grasping a fleur-de-lis or. *Delectat et ornat.* *cf.* 215. 5

Borthwick of Hartside, Scotland, a hart's head erased gu., attired or, devouring a serpent ppr. *Cœlitus datum.* 121. 7

Borthwick of Muirhouse, Scotland, a pelican with wings expanded or, vulning herself ppr. *Ex vulnere salus.* 98. 1

Borthwick of Crookston, Scotland, a Moor's head couped ppr. *Fide et spe.*

Borthwick of Mayshiels, Scotland, an eagle rising ppr. *Nec deerit operi dextra.* 77. 5

Borton, Suff., a boar's head ppr. 41. 1

Borton of Stapleford, a boar's head couped or, holding in the mouth a branch of laurel ppr.

Borton, General Sir Arthur, G.C.B., K.C.B., G.C.M.G., 105, Eaton Place, London, S.W., in front of a sword paleways point downwards ppr., pommel and hilt gold, a boar's head couped sa., holding in the mouth a sprig of laurel fructed, also ppr. *In Deo confido.*

Bosanquet, Percival, Esquire, J.P., of Ponfield, near Hertford, a demi-lion rampant ppr. *Per damna per cædes.*

Bosanquet, Samuel Courthope, Dingestow Court, Monm., a demi-lion rampant, couped gu.

Bosanquet, Charles Bertie Pulleine, Esquire, of Rock Hall, Alnwick, Northumb., same crest.

Bosanquet, Theodore, Esquire, West Down House, Bradworthy, North Devonsh., a demi-lion rampant ppr.

Bosanquet, Smith-, Horace James, Esquire, of Broxbournebury, Broxbourne, Herts: (1) A demi-lion gu., gorged with a collar nebuly or, and holding between the paws a mullet of six points of the first within an annulet of the second (*for Bosanquet*). (2) An elephant's head erased or, eared gu., charged on the neck with three fleur-de-lis, two and one az. (*for Smith*). *Per damna, per cædes.—Tenax in fide.* *cf.* 133. 3

Boscawen, Boscawen Trevor Griffith, Trevalyn, Denbigh, a lion passant sa.

Boscawen, Cornw., a falcon ppr. 85. 2

Boscawen (Rt. Hon. Evelyn Edward Thomas, **Viscount Falmouth**), a falcon close ppr., belled or. *Patience passe science.* 85. 2

Bosgrave, a boar's head erased arg., between two oak-branches vert, fructed or. 42. 1

Bosne and **Bosney,** a cockatrice displayed. 68. 14

Bosom, Bosome, and **Bossum,** Cornw., a tree growing out of a mount ppr. 143. 14

Boss, Durh., out of a naval coronet, an arm holding a billet, all ppr. *Cada uno es hijo de sub obras.*

Bostock of Abingdon, Berks, an antelope or, gorged with a collar gu. 126. 12

Bostock, Shropsh., a martlet arg. 95. 4

Bostock of Bostock, Chesh., and Whixall, Shropsh., on the stump of a tree eradicated arg., a bear's head erased sa., muzzled or.

Bostock of Oxford, Kent, a crescent arg., therefrom issuant a bear's head pean erased gu., muzzled or.

Bostock, Francis, Horsham, Sussex, same crest

Boston, Baron (Irby), a Saracen's head in profile ppr, wreathed arg and sa *Honor fidelitatis præmium* 190. 14

Boston, Scotland, a dove between two branches of laurel in orle, all ppr 92 12

Boston, a horse's head in armour ppr 51. 13

Bosum of Windley, Norf, a talbot's head erased arg, eared and ducally crowned or 56 9

Bosvile, Thomas Bolle, Ravenfield Park, near Rotherham, or **Bosville,** Yorks, a bull statant arg, the hinder part behind a clump of oak trees ppr *Intento in Deum animo*

Bosville, Alexander Wentworth Macdonald, Thorpe Hall, Bridlington (1) A bull passant arg, armed sa., issuant from a burst of oaks ppr, and charged on the shoulder with a rose gu (2) A cubit arm in fesse couped in armour ppr, charged with a bendlet sinister az, the hand ppr holding a cross crosslet erect fitchee gu *Virtus propter se Per mare per terram*

Boswall, Sir George Lauderdale Houston, Bart, Blackadder, Edrom, Berwicksh (1) A cubit arm grasping a sword ppr 239 7 (2) A sandglass winged ppr (*Houston*) *Fortiter* —" *In time* " 239 8

Boswell, Bart, of Auchinleck, Ayr, a falcon ppr, hooded gu, belled or *Vraye foi* 292 3

Boswell, John Irvine, Crawley Grange, Newport Pagnell, a falcon close ppr, hooded *Vraye foy* 292 3

Boswell, Claud Patrick, Esquire, of Balmuto, Fifeshire, a falcon ppr, hooded gu, jessed and belled or *Vraye foi* 292 3

Boswell, Yorks, out of a wood ppr, a bull passant arg

Boswell, Yorks and Kent, a lion's head 21 1

Boswell of Glassmount, Scotland, a lark volant ppr *Nothing venture, nothing have* cf 93 10

Boswell of Dowen, Scotland, same crest *I hope for better*

Boswell, John Douglas, Garrallan, Ayr (1) A falcon ppr, hooded gu, belled or (*Boswell*) (2) A heart ppr (*Douglas*) (1) *Vraye foy* (2) *Fortis et fidelis*

Bosworth, a lily slipped and leaved ppr 151 2

Bosworth, a demi-lion rampant ppr *Animus valet* 10 2

Botatort or **Botetourt,** Norf, out of a mural coronet, six spears in saltier ppr 175 8

Boteler of Teston, Kent, two eagles supporting a vine ppr *Aquilæ vitem pocula*

Boteler of Hatfield Woodhall, Herts, an arm in armour embowed, holding in the hand a sword ppr 195 2

Boteler, a covered cup or, between two wings, the dexter arg, the sinister az

Boteler or **Botler** of Bewsey, a unicorn salient arg, armed or, tied round the neck with a sash of the last

Botell and **Bothell,** Essex, a marigold ppr 151 12

Boteller, a covered cup or

Boterwike, a hawk, holding in its dexter claw an ear of wheat ppr 85 7

Boteshed, a stag's head arg 121 5

Botetourt, *see* **Botatort**

Botevile, Boteville, or **Bonteville,** Shropsh, a reindeer or *J'ay bonne cause* cf 125 9

Both or **Bothe,** on a tower embattled, a flag displayed 157 13

Bothell, *see* Botell

Botheras, Cornw, a demi lion rampant ppr *Pro Deo et patria* 10. 2

Bothwell, Lord Holyroodhouse, Scotland, a naked boy pulling down the top of a green pine-tree, all ppr *Obduram adversus urgentia* 189 6

Botiler, a cinquefoil gu 148 12

Botley, Berks, a boar's head and neck sa, ducally gorged or *Probitate* cf 41 6

Botockshed, a stag's head arg 121 5

Botreaulx or **Botreaux,** a dove standing on a hill, all ppr 92 3

Botreulx or **Botreux,** Cornw, two laurel branches in saltier ppr

Botsford, Hon Amos Edwin, of the city of Ottawa and parish of Sackville, in the Dominion of Canada, Lieutenant-Colonel Reserve Militia, co Westml, *uses* a bird close *Digna sequens*

Bott, Staffs, on a glove a falcon ppr 86 12

Botteler and **Bottiller,** Ireland, a cock's head and neck vert, combed, wattled, beaked, and ducally gorged or, between two dragons' wings expanded arg cf 68 8

Botteley, Botilly, or **Botley,** a boar's head and neck sa, ducally gorged or cf 41. 6

Bottell, an escallop az 141 14

Bottiller, a cinquefoil gu 148 12

Bottlesham, an escallop-shell between two wings 141 10

Bottomley, Yorks, out of a tower, a demi-lion ppr *Fortiter fideliter et feliciter* 157 11

Bottomley of Wade House, Halifax, Yorks, upon a mount vert, an Angola goat in front of a palm-tree ppr, resting the dexter foot upon an escutcheon gu, charged with a shuttle palewise or *Fideli certa merces*

Bottonley, a hawk standing on a fish, all ppr 86 6

Bottrell, Shropsh, a quiver erect sa, garnished or, strapped gu, the buckle also or, replenished with arrows arg

Bouche, a Saracen's head, couped at the shoulders and affrontee ppr, wreathed arg and sa 190 5

Boucher, *see* Bouchier and Bourchier

Boucher, Alfred Richard, Esquire, of Trenean, St Germans, Cornw, a demi-sea horse ppr, collared and lined gu, between the fins a water-bouget sa *Deo favente*

Boucher, Edward Graham, of Fairfield, Lymington, Hampshire, same crest and motto

Boucher and **Bouchier,** an owl ppr *Non vi sed voluntate* 96 5

Boucher of Salisbury, Wilts, a greyhound sejant arg, collared and lined or cf 59 4

Boucher, an old man's head in profile couped at the shoulders ppr, on his head a cap turned down in front

Boucherett of Willingham and Stallingborough, Lincoln, a cockatrice or *Prima voce salutat* 68 5

Bouchier of Little Stambridge, Essex, a greyhound sejant arg, ducally gorged or cf 59 4

Boudier of Jersey, a crescent az *Dieu et la réligion* 163 2

Bouge of Thurcaston, Leics, a bat displayed arg, armed or 137 11

Bough, Scotland, the stump of an oak-tree sprouting branches ppr *Quod ero spero* 145 2

Boughey of Colton, Staffs, an angel praying between two branches of laurel in orle ppr 184 2

Boughey, Fletcher-, Sir Thomas, Bart, of Aqualate, Newport, Shropshire (1) A plate charged with a pheon per pale erm and sa, the point downward (*for Fletcher*) 242 5 (2) Out of an Eastern crown or, points alternately of the last and arg, a buck's head erm, attired aad collared of the first (*for Boughey*) *Nec quærere, nec spernere, honorem* 242 4

Boughs, the stump of a tree sprouting ppr, from one of the branches a shield pendent gu 145 8

Boughton, a stork's head erased, holding in the beak an eel, all ppr cf 104 2

Boughton, a stork's head arg, beaked gu, holding therein a snake ppr 106 3

Boughton, Warw, a lion's head couped or 21 1

Boughton, a goat's head couped per pale arg pellettee, and gu bezantee, attired, or cf 128 12

Boughton, Bouse-, Sir Charles Henry, Bart., of Lawford Hall, Warw A man's head ppr, the hair, beard, and whiskers sa, the head surrounded and crossed by a ribbon knotted at the top and flowing from either temple arg (*for Rouse*) A stork's head erased chevrony of four sa and arg, holding in the beak or, a snake ppr (*for Boughton*) *Omne bonum Dei donum* cf 106 3

Boulby or **Bowlby,** two branches of thorn in orle 146 4

Bould and **Boulde,** of Bould, Lancs, out of a ducal coronet or, a griffin's head sa., beaked gu, between two wings of the first cf 67 1

Bouling, a garb or 153 2

Boulsted and **Boulstred,** Devonsh, a bull's head between two wings gu, armed arg 43 10

Boult, a morion ppr 180 1

Boult, a heron ppr 105 9

Boultbee, a stag's head erased ppr 121 2

Boultbee or **Boultbie,** out of a ducal coronet, a demi boar ppr cf 40 13

Boulter of Bristol, two bird-bolts in saltire, and thereon a dove rising ppr

Boulton, Norf, and Yorks on a holly-bush vert, fructed gu, a hawk rising ppr

Boulton of Gibbon Grove, Surrey, a hawk with wings expanded arg, collared legged, and belled gu, the dexter foot supporting an escutcheon az, charged with a fleur de lis or cf 87 7

Boulton James, Esquire, of 13A, Great Marlborough Street, London, W, upon a mount vert, an eagle with wings displayed, holding in the beak a branch of holly, and between two branches of holly, all ppr.

Boulton, Percy, M.D., 15, Seymour Street, Portman Square, W., a hawk belled ppr. *Dum spiro spero.*

Boulton of Forebridge Villa, Staffs, on a fer-de-moulin, a hawk pierced with an arrow. *Mens conscia recti.*

Boulton, Matthew Ernest, Tew Park, Oxford, a hind's head per pale az. and or, erased gu., in the mouth an arrow in bend, point downwards ppr. *Faire son devoir.*

Boulton, a horse at full speed saddled and bridled. 52. 1

Boulton, *see* Bolton.

Boulton, Lincs, a tun erect ppr., transfixed by a bird-bolt fesseways or. *Dux vitæ ratio.*

Boulton, James Forster, Toronto, Ontario, Canada, same crest and motto.

Boulton of Soho, Staffs, a hind's head erased per pale az. and or, holding in the mouth an arrow in bend point downwards. *Faire sum devoir.* cf. 124. 3

Boulton, Samuel Bagster, Copped Hall, Totteridge, on a holly-bush a falcon rising, holding in its dexter paw a bird bolt in pale, point downwards, and in its beak a sprig of holly, all ppr. *I will never quit.* 244. 10

Bound, on the top of a tower, a lion rampant. 157. 12

Bounn or **Boun,** a sword and a key in saltier ppr. 171. 10

Bourch, Ireland, a demi-lion rampant gu., holding in his dexter paw a fleur-de-lis or. 13. 2

Bourcher, Bourchir, or **Bourchier,** a man's head in profile ppr., couped at the shoulders, crowned with a ducal coronet or, and issuing therefrom a cap tasselled and turned forward gu. cf. 190. 8

Bourcher, Worcs., on a mount vert, a greyhound sejant arg., ducally gorged and lined or. cf. 59. 2

Bourchier, a greyhound salient or.

Bourchier, Essex and London, a greyhound sejant arg., ducally gorged or. cf. 59. 4

Bourchier, *see* Bouchier and Bourcher.

Bourchier, a mullet of six points. 164. 3

Bourchier-Chilcott, Thomas, 4, Stone Buildings, Lincoln's Inn, W.C.: (1) Out of a ducal coronet a mount ppr., thereon a stag statant gu. (2) A man's head in profile couped at the shoulders ppr., on the head a ducal coronet or, issuing therefrom a cap tasselled and turned forward gu. *Le bon temps viendra.*

Bourchier, Henry James, Baggotstown, near Bruff, co. Limerick, on a cap of maintenance gu., turned up erm., a griffin arg. *Le bon temps viendra.—Vincere vel mori.*

Bourdelain and **Bourdillon,** on a chapeau a martlet. (*Another,* with the wings endorsed.) 95. 1

Bourden, a bunch of grapes ppr. 152. 7

Bourdon, a gillyflower ppr. 151. 8

Bourdon, Scotland, a lion rampant arg., holding a battle-axe ppr.

Bourges of Westport, Dorset, a camel's head erased ppr., bezantée. cf. 132. 7

Bourke, Earl of Mayo, *see* Mayo.

Bourke, Baron Connemara, *see* Connemara.

Bourke, Viscount Bourke, of Mayo (*dormant*), on a chapeau gu., turned up erm., a lion sejant arg., ducally gorged or. *Audaces fortuna juvat.* cf. 7. 6

Bourke of Ballintober, co. Mayo, Ireland, on a chapeau gu., turned up erm., a lion sejant arg.

Bourke of St. Andrews, Holborne, Middx., a lion couchant gardant, the tail issuing from between the hind-legs or charged on the shoulder with a fleur-de-lis az. *Chacun le sien.* 7. 11

Bourke of Thornfield, Ireland, a mountain-cat sejant gardant ppr., collared and chained or. *In cruce salus.* 26. 13

Bourke, Lord Castle Connell, the same crest.

Bourke, Lord Brittas, the same crest. *Vinctus sed non victus.*

Bourn, Surrey, between two wings a peacock's head, holding in the beak a serpent, the tail coiled round the neck, all ppr. 103. 3

Bourne, Ireland, between two wings a peacock's head, holding in the beak a serpent, the tail coiled round the neck, all ppr. 103. 3

Bourne, London, out of clouds ppr., an arm erect, vested or, cuffed arg., holding in the hand, also ppr., a pheon by the point sa.

Bourne of Chesterton, Oxon., a pegasus current, wings addorsed gu., semée d'etoiles or, and holding in the mouth a rose of the first, stalked and leaved ppr., seeded of the second. cf. 47. 2

Bourne, John, of Hilderstone Hall, Staffs, on a mount vert, a pegasus salient per fesse or and gu., charged on the body with two fountains ppr., holding in the mouth a trefoil slipped vert. *Hæc omnia transeunt.* 47. 4

Bourne of Wells, Somers., a demi-heraldic tiger arg., armed, maned, and tufted sa., gorged with a collar erminois. cf. 25. 13

Bourne of Stalmine Hall, Lancaster, an heraldic tiger sejant or, guttée-de-sang, resting the dexter paw on a cross pattée gu. *Esse quam videri.* 255. 19

Bourne, Bart., of Hackinsall, Lancs, same crest. *Semper vigilans.*

Bourne, Rev. George Drinkwater, of Weston Subedge, Gloucs., same crest and motto.

Bournes, George Smith, Esquire, of Rossport House, Belmullet, Ireland, a garb between two doves respecting each other, all ppr. *Vincit qui patitur.*

Bousfield, William, 33, Stanhope Gardens, Queen's Gate, S.W., out of a ducal coronet an eagle's head ppr.

Bousfield, out of a ducal coronet an eagle's head ppr. cf. 83. 14

Boustead, a lion's head erased, and on it a chapeau, all ppr. 21. 10

Boutcher, Emmanuel, Esquire, a greyhound sejant arg., collared, and with the line reflexed over the back or, semée of estoiles sa., and resting the dexter paw on a water-bouget of the last. *Be fast.* 59. 6

Bouteville, *see* Boteville.

Boutfleur, a fleur-de-lis az. 148. 2

Boutflower, Andrew, M.R.C.S., Stenecourt, Kersal, Manchester, a fleur-de-lis. 294. 15

Bouverie, Campbell-, *see* Campbell.

Bouverie, *see* Radnor, Earl of.

Bouverie, John Augustus Sheil, of Delapré Abbey, Northamp., a demi-eagle with two heads displayed sa., ducally gorged or, charged on the breast with a cross crosslet arg. *Patria cara, carior libertas.* 302. 2

Bouverie, De, a demi-eagle displayed with two heads sa., gorged with a ducal coronet or, and charged on the breast with a cross crosslet arg. 302. 2

Bouvier, an eagle with wings expanded and inverted ppr. cf. 77. 4

Bouwen, a tent gu., garnished or. 158. 7

Bouwens, in front of a demi-lion guardant or, between two wings vair arg. and sa., three roses fesseways arg., barbed and seeded ppr. *Nec temere, nec timide.*

Bover of Appleton, Chesh., a goat's head couped sa., armed and charged on the neck with a fleur-de-lis or. cf. 128. 12

Bovey of Wordon Abbey, Beds and Stow, Cambs., a lion's gamb erect and erased per fesse or and gu., holding a bow of the second, stringed of the first.

Bovil and **Bolvile,** Suff., a demi-friar holding in his dexter hand a crucifix. cf. 187. 7

Bovile, Bovyle, and **Bovyll,** a bull passant quarterly sa. and or. cf. 45. 2

Bow, Scotland, a lion's head erased ppr., *Fideliter.* 17. 8

Bowater of London, out of clouds a rainbow ppr.

Bowcher, out of a ducal coronet or, a demi-pelican vulning herself arg.

Bowdan and **Bowden** of Bowden, Chesh., a bezant charged with a lion's head erased gu., collared arg. cf. 19. 1

Bowden, Derbysh., a heron's head erased or. 104. 11

Bowden of Stroud Green, Croydon, Surrey, in front of a battle-axe and a tilting-spear in saltier or, a heron's head erased sa. cf. 104. 11

Bowden-Smith, Nathaniel, Vice-Admiral, K.C.B., a talbot passant. *Suaviter in modo, fortiter in re.*

Bowditch of Bowditch, Dorset, seven arrows or, barbed and feathered arg., six in saltier, one in pale. 173. 7

Bowdler, Shropsh., on a mount vert, a Cornish chough ppr. 107. 9

Bowdler, a dexter arm embowed grasping an arrow, all ppr. 201. 13

Bowdler, Richard Hope, Esquire, of Kirkham, Lancs, a dexter arm embowed, holding in the hand an arrow, all ppr. *Innocue ac provide.* 201. 13

Bowdon, of Beightonfields, Derbysh: (1) A heron's head erased ppr., beaked and charged on the neck with three erm. spots sa. cf. 104. 11. (2) Out of a ducal coronet or, a demi-eagle displayed ppr. *Vanus est honor.* 80. 14

Bowdon, Butler-, John Erdeswicke, of Pleasington Hall, Lancs: (1) A heron's head erased ppr., beaked and charged on the neck with three erm. spots (*for Bowdon*). cf. 104. 11. (2) A covered cup or, charged with an erm. spot (*for Butler*). *Comme je trouve.—Vanus est honor.*

Bowell of Berry Court, Hants, a lion's head erased barry of six arg and gu cf 17 4

Bowen-Colthurst, *see* Colthurst.

Bowen, a stag trippant ppr *Cautus a futuro* 117. 8

Bowen of Kittle Hill and Swansea, a stag statant, vulned in the back with an arrow, all ppr 117 10

Bowen of Courtwood, Queen's Co , Ireland, on a mount vert, a stag lodged gu , attired or, holding in the mouth a trefoil slipped ppr , and charged with a crescent or, for difference *Virtus vincit invidiam* cf 115 12

Bowen of Ballyadams, Queen's Co , on a mount vert, in front of an oak tree ppr , fructed or, a stag lodged gu , attired and ungu of the third, holding in the mouth a trefoil slipped of the first cf 115 10

Bowen, Henry Charles Cole Esquire of 15, Herbert Place, Dublin, a stag's head *Caustus in futuro*

Bowen, Webb-, of Camrose, Pembrokesh , a lion rampant sa 1 10

Bowen, James Bevan, of Llyngwair, co Pembrokesh , a lion rampant or, holding between his paws a Bowen knot of the same *Audaces fortuna juvat*

Bowen, Ireland, a demi lion rampant, holding in his paws a flag of St George, all ppr *In hoc signo vinces* cf 15 2

Bowen, George Edward, Esquire, of Portaferry, co Down, a demi-lion rampant, holding in his paws a flag bearing the standard of St. George, all ppr *In hoc signo vinces*

Bowen, Rev Arthur James, of Troedyrawr Cardigansh , a lion rampant or, holding in the paws a knot or *Audaces fortuna juvat* 51 5

Bowen, George Bevan, Esquire, Stradmore Llandyssil, Cardigansh , same crest and motto

Bowen, a falcon close ppr , belled or *Esse quam videri* 85 2

Bowen, Oxon , an arm couped at the elbow and erect vested sa , cuffed erm , holding in the hand ppr a chaplet of laurel vert cf 205 4

Bowen, Ireland, a hand issuing from a cloud in fess, holding a sphere 223 1

Bowen, Rt. Hon Sir George Ferguson, G C M G , D C L , LL D , M A , of 16, Lowndes Street, S W , on a mount vert, within a crown vallarial arg , a falcon rising regardant ppr , holding in the dexter claw a lile fleur de-lis

Bowen, George William Howard, Esquire, of Ickleton, Great Chesterford, Essex, same crest and motto

Bowen-Colthurst, Robert Walter Travers, Esquire, of Oakgrove, and Dripsey Castle, Cork (1) A colt courant sa , charged on the shoulder with a crescent sa (*for Colthurst*) (2) On a mount vert, a falcon close ppr , belled or *Justum et tenacem*

Bowen-Miller, Ormsby, Esquire, J P and D L , of Blindwell, Tuam, co. Galway (1) A wolf's head erased az (*for Miller*) (2) A falcon close ppr , belled or (*for Bowen*) *Nil conscire sibi*

Bower, Herbert Morris, Esquire, of Elmcrofts, and Trinity Hill, Ripon, a boar passant arg , semee of escallops sa *Fortis propositi tenax*

Bower or Booer of London, a wolf's head erased erm 30 8

Bower, Sir Graham John, K C M G , of Reduit, Mauritius, a griffin's head *Ad metam*

Bower of Oxenfield, Durh , a human leg couped at the thigh dropping blood ppr , charged above the knee with a plate cf 193 10

Bower of Wellham and Scorton, Yorks, a human leg couped at the thigh transpierced above the knee by a broken spear in bend ppr *Esse quam videri* cf 193 10

Bower of Kellerby, Yorks, same crest

Bower of Iwerne House, Dorset, a talbot's head arg *Hope well and have well* 56 12

Bower, James Bower of Claremont, Teignmouth, Devonsh , in front of a talbot's head couped sa , gorged with a collar gemel or, a tilting-spear fesse wise, the head to the dexter, also or *Hope well, love well*

Bower, Henry Syndercombe, Fontmell Parva, Blandford, a talbot's head couped arg *Hope well and have well*

Bower of Kinnettles, Scotland, a dexter and a sinister arm shooting an arrow from a bow, all ppr *Ad metam* 200 2

Bower, Yorks, an escallop arg 141 14

Bower, a bow and a sheaf of arrows in saltire all ppr *Ad metam* 173 12

Bower, Major Robert Lister of Northallerton a human leg transpierced by a broken spear in bend ppr *Esse quam videri*

Bower, Captain Edmund Thomas Chivers, of Broxholme, Yorks, on a mount vert, a quiver az , garnished or, and filled with arrows ppr , in saltire with a bow unstrung, also ppr *Veritas prævalevit* 267 16

Bowerbank, a demi savage ppr , wreathed about the head and middle with leaves vert cf 186 1

Bowerman or Bowreman, Devonsh and Wilts, a goat's head erased or, the horns twisted or and sa. 128 5

Bowerman, a goat's head erased or

Bowers of Chichester, Sussex, a lion passant arg , collared and chained or, holding in the dexter paw a bow bent of the second stringed of the first

Bowes, Earl of Strathmore and Kinghorn, and **Baron Bowes,** *see* Strathmore

Bowes of Streatlam, Durh , a sheaf of arrows or, feathered and headed arg , banded az 173 3

Bowes of Bradley Hall, Durh , a sheaf of arrows or, flighted and headed arg , bound in a girdle az *Sans variance et mon droit —In multis in magnis, in bonis expertus* 173 3

Bowes, Richard, of Darlington, and of Monkend Hall, Croft on Tees, Yorks of the family of Bowes of Yorks and London A demi-leopard gardant gu , holding between the paws a bundle of arrows or, barbed arg , and banded with a ribbon az. *Jaculis nec arcu —Bonne et belle assez* 23 5

Bowes of London, a demi leopard rampant gardant gu , holding between the paws a bundle of arrows or, pointed arg , banded az 23 5

Bowes, Lord Bowes of Clonlyon, co Meath, Ireland, a demi lion rampant gu , armed and langued az , holding in the dexter paw five arrows points downwards ppr *Quærere verum*

Bowet or **Bewet,** Yorks, on a chapeau gu , turned up erm , a leopard arg , ducally gorged or cf 24 1

Bowida, a dexter arm in armour embowed, holding in the hand ppr a fleur-de lis or 199 14

Bowie, Scotland, a demi-lion az , holding in the dexter paw a dagger ppr *Quod non pro patria* cf 14 12

Bowker, Hon Robert Mitford, of Craigie burn, Somerset East, Cape Colony, *uses* a Bourchier knot (*incorrect*) 165 14

Bowland, Essex and London, out of a ducal coronet an arm in armour couped at the elbow or, holding in the hand a sword arg , pommel of the first cf 209 11

Bowland, two demi ducks wings displayed and inverted respecting each other, the dexter arg , the sinister sa , beaked or

Bowlby, two branches of thorn in orle 146 4

Bowlby, Edward Salvin, Gilston Park, Herts, three annulets interlaced or, between two thorn-branches ppr *Je la change qu'en mourant*

Bowle, a demi-bittern regardant

Bowler, a boar's head couped per pale az and gu , bezantee cf 41 1

Bowles of London, and of Myddleton House, Waltham Cross, Herts, a demi boar rampant erminois, the sinister shoulder pierced with an arrow or, headed arg *Ut tibi sic alteri* cf 40 13

Bowles, Henry Carington Bowles, Esquire, of Myddelton House, Enfield, a demi-boar erect erminois, the sinister shoulder pierced with an arrow arg *Ut tibi sic alteri*

Bowles, Henry Ferryman, Esquire, of Forty Hall, Enfield, same crest and motto

Bowles, Lt -Col Thomas John, J P of Milton Hill, Slaventon, Berks, a demi boar az , ungu and bristled or, pierced through the chest with an arrow of the second, headed arg cf 40 13

Bowles of North Aston, Oxon , and of Gosberkirk, Lincs, same crest

Bowles, Charles Eyre Bradshaw, Bradshaw Hall, Derbysh , a demi boar pierced in the left breast by an arrow

Bowles, Heref and Herts, out of a ducal coronet or, a boar's head couped sa , between two wings gu , billettee of the first

Bowles of London, out of a ducal coronet or, a griffin's head sa , beaked, and between two wings of the first 67 1

Bowles of London, a buck's head arg , attired or 121 5

Bowley, a mullet of five points pierced, and through the perforation a sword

Bowley, a sword in pale between two branches of laurel in orle 170 3

Bowman, Scotland, a demi-blackamoor shooting an arrow from a bow, all ppr cf 185 6

Bowman, a stag trippant vulned in the shoulder with an arrow, all ppr cf 117 8

Bowman of Ashenyards, Scotland, a quiver of arrows in pale ppr. *Sublimia cures.* cf. 174. 4

Bowman, on the stump of a tree ppr., a quiver vert, of arrows gu., flighted az., suspended by a belt sa.

Bowman, Scotland, a quiverful of arrows suspended from an oak-tree couped at the top, all ppr. *Numine et arcu.*

Bowman of Hethleton, Dorset, on a staff raguled, couped and erect arg., a quiver of arrows gu., flighted of the first, buckled on the staff with a belt sa.

Bowman, Sir William Paget, Bart., on a mount vert, the stump of a tree ppr., around the upper part a belt sa., therefrom pendent on the dexter side a quiver gu., filled with arrows arg. *Quondam his vicinus armis.* 251. 9

Bowman, Alfred John, Esquire, of Rusthall Lodge, Tunbridge Wells, on a wreath of the colours, a stag gorged with a chaplet of olive ppr., attired or, pierced on either side by an arrow in bend sinister gu., and resting the dexter leg on an antique shield or, transfixed by an arrow in bend, also gu. *Vulneratus sed non victus.* 257. 16

Bowman of Wissingset, Norf., a sword in pale arg., hilt and pommel or, on each side of the blade a demi-annulet indented of the second.

Bown, a hand holding an escutcheon charged with a rose. cf. 219. 7

Bownas, out of a ducal coronet a sceptre environed by two serpents between two wings, all ppr. 170. 13

Bownas, on a mount vert, a swan with the wings displayed erm., and each charged with a lozenge gu., holding in the beak an arrow ppr.

Bownder of Limerick, a demi-lion rampant or, guttée-de-sang, holding in the dexter paw a sword ppr., pommel and hilt of the first, enfiled with a mural crown of the first. cf. 14. 12

Bowne and **Bowyn,** on the top of a tower issuing from the wreath an eagle with wings addorsed ppr., holding in the beak an acorn slipped and leaved vert. 76. 10

Bownell, a savage's head from the shoulders helmeted, all ppr. cf. 192. 7

Bownes, an oak-tree ppr., therefrom an escutcheon pendent gu.

Bownes, out of a ducal coronet a cock's head, all ppr. 90. 6

Bowre of Donhead, St. Andrews, Dorset, a talbot's head sa. 56. 12

Bowrie, Scotland, a demi-lion az., holding in the dexter paw a dagger, all ppr. *Quod non pro patria.* cf. 14. 12

Bowring, a parrot vert, feeding on a bunch of cherries ppr. 101. 8

Bowring, John Frederick Edward, Esquire, of Forest Farm, Windsor Forest, Berks, a demi-lion rampant or, grasping in the dexter paw an arrow in bend sinister, and in the sinister paw an Oriental bow paleways ppr. *Nunquam mutans.*

Bowring, Edgar Alfred, Esquire, of 30, Eaton Place, London, same crest and motto.

Bowring, John Frederick Edward, of Forest Farm, Windsor Forest, same crest and motto.

Bowring, Lewin Bentham, Esquire, East India United Service Club, same crest.

Bowser and **Bowssar** of Stone, Glouc., a demi-talbot gu., gorged with a collar chequy or and az., charged on the body with three guttées-d'or. cf. 55. 11

Bowyer, Sir George Henry, Bart., of Denham Court, Bucks, and Radley, Berks, a falcon rising and belled or. 87. 1. *Contentement passe richesse.* (*The foregoing is the crest as registered in the College of Arms, but, as appears from the Visitations, the family have at other times made use of the following crests: (1) A demi-man ppr., shooting with a bow and arrow arg., the arrow tipped or.* 186. 6. *(2) On a ducal coronet or, an heraldic tiger sejant arg.* 25. 7. *(3) An arm couped at the elbow and erect habited gu., charged with three bends and cuffed or, holding in the hand ppr., a dragon's head erased.* cf. 208. 7. *(4) Out of a tower gu., a demi-dragon rampant or.* cf. 157. 5.)

Bowyer, an eagle's head erased arg., holding in the mouth an anchor gu. by the middle of the shank, the flukes downward.

Bowyer of Knipersley, Staffs, Lincs, and Sussex, out of a tower gu., a demi-dragon rampant or. cf. 157. 5

Bowyer, Hants, a cubit arm erect holding in the hand a serpent coiled round the arm, all ppr. 220. 2

Bowyer, on a mount vert, a tower triple-towered gu., thereon a demi-dragon or.

Bowyer, an arm couped at the elbow and erect, vested gu., cuffed arg., holding in the hand a fish.

Bowyn, *see* Bowne.

Box, Oxon., an arm couped at the elbow in fess, vested gu., cuffed arg., holding erect in the hand ppr. a branch of box vert, at the elbow another branch erect.

Box, a demi-griffin or, winged az., the first feather, also or, holding between the claws a fireball of the same inflamed gu.

Boxall, Sir Charles Gervaise, K.C.B., Battlemead, Maidenhead, two anchors in saltire and cabled surmounted by an escutcheon pendent by a ribbon, all az., charged with a fret arg.

Boxall, W. P. G., M.A., K.C., of Ivory's, Cowfold, Sussex, same crest. *Spes mea in Deo.*

Boxall and **Boxell,** an eagle's leg erased in fess holding a feather in pale. 113. 12

Boxall, a gadfly ppr.

Boxell, Sussex, out of a ducal coronet a boar's head and neck, all or. *Per tela per hostes.* 41. 4

Boxhall, Boxhull, and **Boxmell,** Sussex, two anchors in saltier az. 161. 7

Boxsted and **Boxstead,** a hand issuing pulling a thistle. 218. 5

Boyare, out of a castle gu., a demi-dragon or. cf. 157. 5

Boyce or **Boyse,** a lion rampant. 1. 13

Boyce and **Boyse,** England and Scotland, a star of six points or, within a crescent arg. 163. 4

Boyce or **Boyse,** Ireland, a castle triple-towered, out of middle tower a demi-lion rampant. 157. 11

Boyce, Robert Henry, Esquire, C.B., of Ee Yuan, Hampton Wick, out of a tower ppr., a demi-lion rampant gu., holding between the paws an escarbuncle or. *Semper fidelis.* 263. 3

Boycott, *see* Wight-Boycott.

Boycott, *see* Morse-Boycott.

Boycott of Boycott, Hinton, and Rudge, Shropsh., out of a mural coronet an arm in armour embowed casting a grenado, all ppr. *Pro rege et religione.* 197. 10

Boycott, Henry, Esquire, the Firs, Ironbridge, Shropsh., out of a mural coronet an arm in armour embowed casting a grenado, all ppr. *Pro rege et religione.* 197. 10

Boyd, John, Maxpoffle, Roxburgsh., Scotland, a dexter hand erect pointing with the thumb and two forefingers ppr. *Confido.* 222. 11

Boyd of Pitcon, a dexter hand pointing with the thumb and two forefingers to the sun ppr. *Spes mea in cœlis.* 222. 10

Boyd, William Henry, Esquire, J.P., D.L., of Ballymacool House, co. Donegal, Ireland, a dexter hand couped at the wrist erect pointing upwards with the thumb and first two fingers ppr., the hand charged with a trefoil or. *Confido.* cf. 222. 11

Boyd, George Fenwick, J.P., Moor House, Durh., in front of a dexter hand couped at the wrist pointing upwards with the thumb and two fingers ppr., four lozenges conformed in fesse az. *Confido.* 222. 1

Boyd, Ven. Charles Twining, of Columba, Ceylon, same crest and motto.

Boyd, William, Esquire, of North House, Long Benton, Newcastle, same crest and motto.

Boyd, Captain John Theodore Thomas, of Glenfern, St. Kilda, Melbourne, Victoria, Australia, formerly of the 11th Regiment of Infantry, a dexter hand couped at the wrist erect pointing with the thumb and first two fingers, the others turning down. 222. 11

Boyd, Stanley, M.B., 134, Harley Street, W., out of a ducal coronet or, a dexter hand erect, the third and fourth fingers folded down. *Confido.*

Boyd of Pinkell, Scotland, a cross moline sa. *Prudentia me sustinet.* 165. 11

Boyd, Sir John, of Maxpoffle, Roxburgh, Scotland, (late Lord Provost of Edinburgh), a dexter hand pointing upwards with the thumb and two fingers ppr. *Confido.* 222. 11

Boyd of Trochrig, Scotland, a sundial or. *Eternitatem cogita.* 176. 7

Boyd, Bart., of Danson, Kent, three ostrich-feathers sa. *Confido.* 115. 1

Boyd, Scotland a star of five points or. *Virtus nobilitat.* 164. 2

Boyd-Rochfort: (1) Out of a ducal coronet or, a hand erect with the third and fourth fingers folded (*for Boyd*). cf. 222. 11. (2) On a mural crown or, a robin redbreast ppr., charged with a cross pattée, also or (*for Rochford*). *Confido.—Candor dat viribus alas.* cf. 108. 10

Boyd-Rochfort, George Arthur, Esquire, of Middleton Park, Castletown, co. Westmeath, same crests and mottoes.

Boydell, Chesh, a stag statant pierced in the side with an arrow in bend sinister 117 10
Boydell, a Saracen's head couped ppr, thereon a cap gu, turned up erm, the end hanging down with a bell attached to it or
Boyer and **Boyes**, a lady's arm from the elbow erect ppr, enfiled with a brace let sa 222 6
Boyer, a demi griffin segreant 64 2
Boyer, an arm from the elbow erect, vested, cuffed, holding in the hand ppr three trefoils slipped vert
Boyes, Charles Crofton, Esquire, of Kawaran Falls Station, Otago, New Zealand, a sword erect ppr, hilted and pommelled or *Ex animo* 170 2
Boyes, a hand holding a cross pattee fitched ppr 221 12
Boyes and **Boys**, Scotland, a dog sejant ppr *Attendez vous* 57 9
Boyle, a griffin's head erased or, gorged with a ducal coronet az, holding in the beak a branch of laurel fructed ppr 66 11
Boyle, Ireland, a human heart gu, between a cross and a sword in saltire ppr
Boyle, Rt. Hon Sir Richard Edmund St Lawrence, K P, **Earl of Cork and Orrery, and Viscount and Baron Boyle**, on a ducal coronet or, a lion's head erased per pale crenellee arg and gu *Honor virtutis præmium —God's Providence is my inheritance* cf 19 10
Boyle, Sir Charles Cavendish K C M G, same crest and second motto
Boyle, Earl of Shannon and **Viscount Boyle**, *see* Shannon
Boyle, Rt Hon Sir David G C M G, **Earl of Glasgow**, an eagle displayed with two heads per pale embattled arg and gu *Dominus providebit* 74 2
Boyle of Shewalton, Ayr, same crest and motto
Boymen, Boynam, Bonham, and **Boynan**, the trunk of a tree in fess, ensigned between the branches with a fleur de lis. 145 13
Boyne, Viscount (Hamilton - Russell), Brancepeth Castle, Durh (1) A goat passant arg, collared gemelle, and charged on the body with an escallop sa. (*for Russell*) cf 129 5 (2) Out of a ducal coronet or, an oak ppr, fructed of the first, and penetrated transversely in the main stem by a frame-saw, also ppr (*for Hamilton*) *Nec timeo, nec sperno* 143 8
Boynell and **Boyville**, a boy pulling a branch from a tree cf 189 6
Boynton, Sir Griffith Henry, Bart, of Barmston, Yorks, a goat passant sa, guttee d'argent, armed, crined, and ungu or *Il tempo passa.*
Boynton, a goat passant sa, armed or, ducally gorged arg cf 129 5
Boynton, on a cinquefoil gu, a talbot's head erased sa, guttee d'or
Boynton, an arm from the elbow holding in the hand a millrind
Boys, De, Essex, a wyvern arg 70 1
Boys, Kent, a demi-dog gobonated sa and or, holding an oak-branch leaved and fructed of the last
Boys, a dog sejant ppr 57 9
Boys, Lincs, a stag's head couped arg, attired gu, between the attires a mound and a cross or
Boys of Hoston, Norf, an owl arg, ducally crowned or, in a holly-bush ppr
Boys, Kent, on a chapeau az, turned up erm, a demi lion arg, ducally crowned or 15 14
Boys of Betshanger, Kent, a demi lion arg, ducally crowned or 10 11
Boyse, a buck's head erased attired gu 121 2
Boyson, an eagle vert, with wings displayed erminois, armed or 77 5
Boyton, a crow transfixed with an arrow, the wings expanded ppr 107 11
Boyton, co Tipperary, Ireland, a falcon close ppr, holding in the beak a spur or, leathered sa *Per damna, per cædes.*
Boyton, Rev. Canon of the Deanery, Londonderry, and Convoy House, co Donegal, same crest and motto
Boyville, De, a demi-eagle displayed with two heads or cf 82 1
Boyzell, a talbot's head sa, holding in the mouth a stag's horn or
Brabant, Devonsh, a rose gu, slipped and leaved vert, and the point of a lance or, in saltier cf. 150 1
Brabant, His Honour Herbert William, of St John's, Wanganui, New Zealand, Resident Magistrate at Wanganui, and Judge of the Native Land Court of New Zealand, a falcon close *Dum spiro spero* 85 2
Brabantine, a dog passant arg, collared or, the collar charged with three leopards' faces sa
Brabazon, Leics, over a mount vert, a falcon volant or cf 88 3
Brabazon, Colthurst-, of Danesfort, co Kerry, Ireland, on a mount vert, a falcon rising or, charged on the breast with a cross crosslet gu *Vota vita mea* cf 87 1
Brabazon, Major General John Palmer, of Brabazon Park, Swinford, co Mayo, and 10, Wilton Crescent, London, S W, on a mount vert, a falcon rising, belled or, charged with a fleur de lis az *Vota vita mea*
Brabazon, William Philip, Esquire, of Brook House, Lymm, near Warrington, same crest and motto
Brabazon, Earl of Meath and **Baron Brabazon**, *see* Meath
Brabourne and **Brabon** of London and Devonsh, a mewed hawk ppr, armed az, jessed and belled or cf 86 8
Brabourne, Baron (Knatchbull Hugessen), Smeeth Paddocks, near Ashford (1) An oak tree ppr between two wings elevated, the pinions az, feathered or (*for Hugessen*) 236 3 (2) On a chapeau az, turned up erm, an ounce statant arg, spotted sa (*for Knatchbull*) *In crucifixa gloria mea.* 24 1
Braby, James, J P, Rudgwick, Sussex, a martlet ppr *Ex industria decus*
Bracays and **Brakes**, a demi leopard rampant gardant ppr cf 23 4
Bracciano, Rome, on a ducal coronet an eagle displayed sa, gazing at a comet to the sinister ppr
Braccinaro, a dexter arm vested az., cuffed arg, holding in the hand a sprig of roses ppr
Brace, a lion's face ppr, ducally crowned or, within two laurel-branches in orle vert cf 21 11
Brace, Worcs, an arm in armour embowed holding in the hand, all ppr, a sword arg, hilted or 195 2
Brace, Frank Addison Esquire, of Doveridge Hall Derbysh, an arm embowed vested in chain mail arg, the hand grasping a scimitar ppr *Festina lente*
Brace, a dexter arm embowed in chain armour, the hand grasping a sword ppr, pommel and hilt or, attached to the blade a flag az, charged with an anchor of the second
Brace, out of a naval crown or, a dexter arm embowed in chain armour, the hand holding the flag of the kingdom of Holland in the year 1808, all ppr
Bracebridge, Suff, on a mount vert, a wolf passant arg cf 28 10
Bracebridge and **Brasbridge**, Lincs, the stump of a tree ppr, raguled or
Bracebridge, Warw, a staff raguly arg *Be as God will* cf 147 10
Bracegirdle of Bracegirdle Green, Chesh, two augers erect and addorsed conjoined with a girdle gu
Bracester, on a cloud a mullet of six points cf 164 11
Bracey, a unicorn sejant, resting the dexter foot against an oak-tree ppr 48 3
Bracher, Berks a demi leopard rampant gardant ppr *Primi et ultimi in belleo.* cf 23 4
Bracken of Hillam Hall, South Milford, Yorks, a catherine-wheel *Viguer de dessus* 167 2
Brackenbury, a savage's head couped ppr 190 12
Brackenbury of Skendleby, Lincs, a lion couchant gardant sa, at the foot of an oak tree ppr *Sans recueiller jamais*
Brackenridge of Ashfield Park, co Tyrone, a pile gu, charged with a rose arg, barbed vert, seeded or, between two wings az *Virtute et industria* 111 4
Brackesby, a boar's head and neck couped gu bristled or 41 1
Brackley, Viscount, *see* Ellesmere, Earl of
Brackshaw, a buck's head couped ppr 121 5
Bracy, De, Shropsh, a falcon standing on the trunk of a tree in fess, and sprouting a branch on the dexter side
Bracy of Maddresfield, a human heart pierced sa
Bracy or **Bracey**, a garb environed by two snakes ppr 153 3
Brad, a griffin sejant erect holding between the fore claws a battle axe
Bradberry, a demi-dove arg, fretty gu, holding in the beak a slip of barberry vert, fructed ppr
Bradbridge, Bredbridge, or **Brodbridge**, a leopard's head erased arg, pellettee ducally gorged or, between two spears ppr headed of the first.
Bradbrook, William, M R C S, Bletchley, Bucks, a dexter arm embowed in chain mail holding in the hand a cross crosslet fitchee interlaced with a mascle az *Firma nobis fides*

Bradburne and **Bradbourne** of Bradburne and London, a pine-tree vert, fructed or. 144. 13

Bradbury of Derby and London, a dove issuing volant arg., fretty gu., in its beak a slip of barberry vert, fructed gu.

Bradbury, W. Lawrence, Esquire, of Whitefriars, London, E.C., a demi-dove volant arg., fretty gu., holding in the beak a slip of barberry vert, fructed of the second. *Carpe diem.*

Bradbury, Lancs, a demi-wood-pigeon arg., the body fretty gu., and each wing charged with a buckle. *Æquitas actionem regula.*

Bradbury, Thomas Haigh, Esquire, of Bradley, Huddersfield, Yorks, a demi-woodpigeon, wings displayed arg., each wing charged with a round buckle, the tongue pendent sa., and in the beak a sprig of barberry, leaved and fructed over the branch of a tree fessewise ppr. *Æquitas actionem regula.*

Bradbury, Essex and Suff., a boar's head erect between two ostrich-feathers ppr. 41. 14

Bradbury, Augustus Beaty, Esquire, of Edinburgh, between two ears of wheat or, a sword erect point downwards ppr., pendent from the hilt by a chain or, an escutcheon arg., charged with a heart gu. *Amicitia cum virtute.* 154. 8

Bradby, a serpent half erect and nowed, in its mouth a garland of laurel ppr. 142. 7

Braddick of Boughton Mount, near Maidstone, a dapple-gray horse statant, the dexter fore-foot resting upon an escutcheon vert, charged with a stag's head caboshed or.

Braddon, the late Sir Edward Nicholas Coventry, K.C.M.G., of 5, Victoria Street, S.W., a man's face affrontée between two arms in armour counter-embowed, the hands gauntleted. *Aut mors aut libertas.*

Braddyll, an anchor in pale surmounted by a fleur-de-lis. 161. 9

Braddyll, Lancs, a badger passant or. *Cognoies toy mesme.* 33. 10

Braddyll, Thomas Richmond Gale, Esquire, of Conishead Priory, Lancs: (1) A badger passant or (*for Braddyll*). (2) A unicorn's head ppr., charged with two palets az., over all an anchor or (*for Gale*). *Cognoies toy mesme.* 33. 10

Brade, a beehive with bees volant ppr. 137. 7

Bradestone, Bradstone, and **Bradston,** out of a ducal coronet, two lion's gambs in saltier ppr. 39. 12

Bradfield, Norf., a hand holding two branches of palm in orle. 218. 7

Bradfoot, Braidfoot, and **Bradfute,** Scotland, a demi-griffin segreant or, armed gu. 64. 2

Bradford, Earl of, *see* Bridgeman.

Bradford, Robert Dickie, Aldbrough, Hull, a lion rampant holding between its paws a wreath of roses. *Generous though powerful.*

Bradford, Yorks, a peacock's head ppr., holding in the beak a snake entwined round the neck vert. *cf.* 103. 3

Bradford of Swindon, Wilts, a stag's head erased or. 121. 2

Bradford, General Sir Edward, Bart., G.C.B., G.C.V.O., 50, South Audley Street, W., a stag's head erased or, charged on the neck with a mural crown, and suspended from the mouth a bugle-horn stringed sa. *Humani nihil alienum.* 259. 1

Bradford, Ireland, a camel's head sa. 132. 7

Bradgate, Leics., an arm in armour ppr., banded with a ribbon vert, couped below the elbow in bend, holding in the hand ppr. the upper part of a broken spear gu., the point downwards arg.

Bradhull, Lancs, a badger passant or. 33. 10

Bradley and **Bradeley,** a boar sa., bristled and ungu. or, gorged with a garland vert. 40. 6

Bradley, Lancs and London, a boar's head couped gu. 43. 1

Bradley, Ireland, a bull's head cabossed ppr. 43. 8

Bradley of Stourbridge, Worcs., a grey-hound statant. *Vigilans et audax.* *cf.* 60. 2

Bradley of Gore Court, Kent: (1) A dexter arm embowed in armour, holding a battle-axe, all ppr. (*for Bradley*). 200. 6. (2) A heraldic antelope's head erased, armed, and crined or, langued gu. (*for Dyne*). *cf.* 127. 11

Bradley, on a thorn-bush a nightingale ppr. *cf.* 145. 7

Bradley, Ireland, a martlet or, holding in the beak a cross formée fitchée sa. *cf.* 95. 8

Bradling, an arm in armour couped at the shoulder embowed and lying in fess, the elbow on the wreath, holding in the hand a sword, all ppr.

Bradney, a hawk ppr., belled and jessed or. *cf.* 85. 2

Bradney, Joseph Alfred, Esquire, J.P. and D.L., of Bradney, in the county of Somerset, and of Tal-y-Coed, in the county of Monmouth, a hawk close ppr., legged, jessed, and belled or, holding in the beak a trefoil vert, and in the dexter claw a cross pattée fitchée sa. *Mors gloria forti.* 86. 5

Bradney of Bayford Lodge, Wincanton, Somers., Spring Grove, Bishopstoke, Hants, a hawk close ppr., belled, jessed, and legged or, holding in its dexter foot a cross pattée fitchée sa., and in its beak a trefoil vert. *Mors gloria forti.*

Bradney, Joseph Alfred, Esquire, of Tal-y-Coed, near Monmouth, same crest and motto.

Bradsay and **Bradsey,** a demi-greyhound collared. 60. 8

Bradshagh, Bradshaigh, and **Bradshaw,** Chesh., Lancs, and Leics., on a mount vert, a stag at gaze ppr., under a vine-tree, also ppr., fructed purp. *Qui vit content tient assez.* 116. 14

Bradshaw of Barton Blount, Derbysh., a hart gu., standing under a vine-branch vert. *Qui vit content tient assez.* *cf.* 116. 14

Bradshaw, Frank, Lifton Park, Devonsh., a mount vert, thereon a stag statant ppr., gorged with a collar gemel or, between two oak-trees, also ppr. *Tu ne cede malis.*

Bradshaw, Lancs, on a mount a stag ducally gorged standing under a vine fructed, all ppr. *Non nobis solum nati sumus.* *cf.* 116. 14

Bradshaw of Milecross, co. Down, Ireland, on a mount vert, a buck statant beneath an oak-tree ppr. *Deus mihi spes et tutamen.* 116. 13

Bradshaw, Northumb., a stag trippant under an oak-tree, all ppr. *Dieu et mon devoir.* *cf.* 116. 12

Bradshaw, Shropsh., a wolf's head erased arg., collared and lined. *cf.* 30. 11

Bradston, a dove with an olive-branch in the beak ppr. 92. 5

Bradston and **Bradeston,** Glouc., out of a ducal coronet or, a boar's head sa. 41. 4

Bradstreet, Ireland, a unicorn's head between two laurel-branches in orle. 49. 14

Bradstreet, Sir Edmund Simon, Bart., Castilla, Clontarf, co. Dublin, Ireland, an arm in armour embowed, the hand grasping a scimitar, all ppr. *Virtute et non vi.* 196. 10

Bradwarden, a demi-otter rampant. 134. 11

Bradwell, Chesh., a rock ppr. 179. 7

Brady of Ely, Cambs, a cherub ppr., crined and winged or. *In Deo fides.* 189. 9

Brady, Ireland, a cherub ppr., the wings or. 189. 9

Brady, A. Newton, Esquire, Maryville, Ennis, co. Clare, a cherub's head and neck ppr., between two wings or.

Brady, Geale-: (1) A cherub's head and neck ppr., between two wings or (*for Brady*). *cf.* 189. 9. (2) A unicorn's head and neck or, charged with an anchor sa. (*for Geale*). *Claritate dextra.* *cf.* 49. 7

Brady, on a mount vert, a griffin sejant or, beaked sa., supporting with the dexter claw an escutcheon arg. *cf.* 62. 11

Brady, Cambs, on a mount vert, a griffin sejant or, beaked gu. *cf.* 62. 10

Brady, Sir Francis William, Bart., K.C., Sorrento Cottage, Dalkey, co. Dublin, a martlet or, charged on the breast with a trefoil slipped vert. *Vincit pericula virtus.* *cf.* 95. 2

Brady of London, Devonsh., and Hants, an arm in armour embowed holding in the hand an olive-branch fructed, all ppr. *cf.* 199. 12

Brady, Ireland, a hand cutting at a feather with a scimitar ppr. 213. 7

Brady, Browne-, Thomas, Esquire, of Newgrove, Tulla, co. Clare; Kilbegs, Blessington, co. Wicklow; and Cartron, Burren, co. Clare, an eagle displayed with two heads per pale arg. and sa., the dexter wing charged with a pellet and the sinister with a plate. *Nec timeo, nec sperno.*

Brae, Thomas, Esquire, of Bengal, upon a mount vert, an eagle rising ppr., crowned with an Eastern crown or, charged on the breast with a hurt, and on each wing with a fleur-de-lis az.

Bragden and **Bragdon** of London, a boar issuant out of a rock, all ppr.

Brage or **Bragge** of London and Essex, out of a ducal coronet per pale arg and or, a bull's head sa, armed of the second 44 11
Brages and **Bruges** of London, on an anchor or, a scroll bearing the motto *Mihi cœlum portus* cf 161 1
Bragg or **Bragge,** Scotland, and of West Clandon, Surrey, out of a ducal coronet or, a bull's head sa 44 11
Bragg, Somers, a lion's head erased arg, collared vaire or and az 18 13
Bragg, Berks, an ostrich feather enfiled with a ducal coronet *Per virtutem scientiam* 114 12
Bragge, Scotland, a hand holding a sword *Honorat mors* 212 13
Bragge, *see* Brage
Braham of London and Finchley, Middx, on a bar dancettee arg, a phœnix erm, winged az, the flames of fire ppr, and holding in the beak a lyre or
Braham of London and Berks, out of a ducal coronet or, a plume of five ostrich-feathers sa 114 13
Braham, four ostrich-feathers sa, enfiled with a ducal coronet or
Braham of London and Bucks, a cubit arm erect, vested bendy wavy of four az. and gu, holding in the hand ppr a fish arg
Braham, a wolf's head couped arg 30 5
Braid, a demi-lion gu *Floreat majestas* 10 3
Braidfoot, Scotland, a demi-griffin or 64 2
Braidwood, Scotland, an oak-tree fructed ppr *Vigueur de dessus* 143 5
Braikenridge, George Weare, Esquire, of Broomwell House, Somers, on a wreath of the colours (or and vert) a beehive or between two rose-branches ppr *Bello ac pace paratus* 294 2
Braikenridge, George John, the Grove, Bush Hill, Middx, same crest and motto
Braikenridge, William Jerdone, Esquire, Claremont, Clevedon, and 16, Royal Crescent, Bath, same crest and motto
Brailsford, out of a ducal coronet a dragon's head 72 4
Brailsford, Lincs, a unicorn's head arg, erased gu, armed and maned or, entwined by a serpent ppr, and charged on the neck with a pomme, thereon a cross arg *In Jehovah fides mea.* 49 2
Braimor, Scotland, an arm in armour embowed throwing a pheon hafted 108 7
Brain or **Braine,** a hurt charged with a talbot's head erased or cf 57 5
Brain, Samuel Arthur, Esquire, of Roxburgh, Penarth, South Wales, a leopard's head couped arg, charged with a pale gu, and encircled by a branch of oak vert. *Ardua tendo*
Braine or **Brayne,** Glouc, a leopard's head arg 22 10
Braithwait, Yorks, a greyhound couchant arg, collared and lined gu cf 60 1
Braithwait, on a mount vert, a greyhound couchant. cf 60 1
Braithwaite, Robert, 26, Endymion Road, Brixton Hill, S W, a greyhound couchant arg, collared and chained or *Sub cruce salus*
Braksdall, a sheaf of arrows ppr, feathered and banded gu 173 3
Brakyn of Chesterton, Cambs, a hawk's head erased arg, ducally gorged or cf 88 12
Brakyn, a whale's head erect arg, charged with a bend between two bendlets az, thereon three lozenges or, all between two cinquefoils of the last, stalked and leaved vert
Bramble, Dorset, a demi-lion rampant gu, ducally crowned or, and holding in the dexter paw a cross pattee fitchee of the last *Temere ne sperne* cf 10 11
Bramble, James Roger, Lieutenant-Colonel, J P, F S A, Seafield Weston-super-Mare, same crest and motto
Bramfell, out of a ducal coronet an arm embowed wielding a scimitar cf. 201 2
Bramhall, Yorks and Chesh, a lion passant or *Sanguine Christe tuo* 6 2
Bramhall, a lion passant or, charged on the shoulder with a crescent for difference cf 6 2
Bramley, a pheasant ppr cf 90. 8
Brampston, a fetterlock az 168 12
Brampton, Baron (Hawkins), 5, Tilney Street, Park Lane, W, on a fasces fesswise ppr, a fox passant or *Toujours prest* 234 7
Brampton of Attleborough, Norf, out of a mural coronet a talbot's head gu, eared arg 56 6
Brampton of Brampton, Norf, on a tiger arg bridled a naked man astride ppr, wreathed about the temples arg and gu
Bramston, Lieutenant Colonel Thomas Harvey, of Skreens, Essex, a lion sejant or, gorged with a collar sa, charged with three plates cf 7 4
Bramston, a tun fesseways or, thereon a raven sa, holding in the beak a carnation-branch ppr
Bramwell, out of a ducal coronet or, two lion's gambs in saltier ppr 39 10
Bramwell, Baron (Rt Hon Sir George William Wilshere Bramwell), two lion's gambs erased in saltier or, supporting a sword in fesse, the point to the dexter ppr *Diligenter* 39 3
Bramwell, Sir Frederick Joseph, Bart, Holmwood, Edenbridge, Kent, the same crest and motto
Branch, out of a ducal coronet or, a cock's head az, combed gu, holding in the beak a branch vert cf 90 6
Branche of London, out of a ducal coronet or, a cock's head az, beaked of the first, combed and wattled gu 90 6
Brancker, a cubit arm vested sa, cuffed arg, holding in the hand ppr a lozenge of the first
Brand of Laurieston, Scotland, a vol ppr 113 1
Brand, Suff and London, out of a ducal coronet or, a leopard's head gardant arg, semee of roundles of various colours cf 23 11
Brand of London, a leopard's head and neck erased gardant quarterly arg and or, semée of pellets, pomeis, and torteaux cf 23 3
Brand, Hon Arthur George, of Pelham House, Lewes, Osborne House, Wisbech, 50, Park Street, W, out of a crown vallery or, a leopard's head arg, semee of escallops and gorged with a collar gemel gu *Pour bien desirer*
Brand, Scotland, two elephants' probosces couped, flexed, and reflexed arg, the dexter charged with three mascles, the sinister with three spur rowels sa *Aye forward*
Brand, in front of a tree a stag statant ppr cf 116 13
Brand, on the stump of a tree in fess erased, shooting forth a new branch, an eagle statant regardant
Brand, Surrey, out of a ducal coronet or, a cockatrice's head gu, between two wings ppr 68 11
Brand, a vol with a baton or in pale, ensigned on the top with the unicorn of Scotland *Advance*
Brander, *see* Dunbar Brander
Brander, an elephant passant arg cf 133 9
Brander, Hants, a phœnix in flames ppr 82 2
Brander, Surrey and Scotland, a dove regardant holding in the beak an olive branch ppr *Silentio et spe* 92 4
Brander, an arm from the elbow ppr, vested chequy or and az, holding a branch of palm of the first
Brandeston, a dexter hand couped in fess gu 221 6
Brandford of London, an eagle rising or, holding in the beak a sprig of oak fructed vert cf 77 2
Brandling, Northumb, the stump of a tree couped and erased, from the top issuing flames, from the sinister side a sprig acorned and leaved, all, ppr *Fide et virtute* cf 145 14
Brandon, Duke of, *see* Hamilton, Duke of
Brandon, Suff, a lion's head erased or, guttee de poix, crowned with a ducal coronet party per fess arg and gu cf 18 8
Brandon of London, a lion's head erased arg, charged with two bars gu, on each of which three bezants cf 17 8
Brandram, a lamb passant arg, charged with a pile wavy between two fer-de-moulines sa, on the pile a bee volant or 131 6
Brandreth, Beds (1) An escallop arg, in front thereof a sword erect point downwards ppr (*for Brandreth*) (2) A gauntlet fesswise ppr, thereon a mullet pierced or (*for Gibbs*) *Nunquam non paratus*
Brandreth, a Paschal lamb couchant arg cf 131 12
Brandreth, Staffs and Lincs, same crest
Brandreth of Leese, Cheshire and the Manor, Buckland Newton, Dorchester, Dorset, same crest *Fortunam honestant virtute*
Brandt, a stag rising out of a bush ppr 116 1
Brandwood, Durh, a yew-tree ppr 143 1
Branfill of Upminster Hall, Essex, out of a cloud a naked arm holding a sword, all ppr *Not in vain* 223 10
Brangan of Dublin, a cubit arm erect vested vert cuffed arg, the hand ppr, holding a cross moline or 207 4
Branscomb, Branscombe, and **Bronscomb,** a lion passant regardant ducally gorged and chained, all ppr 6 3

Brant, a lion passant or. 6. 2
Branthwaite, Brantwayte, and **Braithwaite** of London, on a rock ppr., an eagle rising arg.
Brantingham, Devonsh., an oak-tree ppr. 143. 5
Branton-Day, Ralph, Esquire, of Great Sarratt Hall, Rickmansworth, Herts, on a mount vert, thereon two hands conjoined ppr., cuffed arg., fixed to a pair of wings, the dexter erminois, charged with a mullet pierced sa., and the sinister ermines charged with a mullet pierced arg. *Surge dies est.*
Brasbridge, Warw., a staff raguly arg. *cf.* 147. 10
Bras-de-Fer, Jersey, an eagle displayed sa. 75. 2
Brash, Scotland, a hand erect issuing from a cloud holding an anchor in pale ppr. 219. 2
Brash, Edward Alexander, surgeon, 35, Southernhay West, Exeter, same crest.
Brashier or **Brasier**, Ireland, a demi-lion rampant per pale or and sa. *Amor patriæ.* 10. 2
Brasier or **Brazier**, a dove holding in its beak an olive-branch ppr. 92. 5
Brassey, a hand throwing a dart ppr. *cf.* 214. 4
Brassey, Baron (Sir Thomas Brassey, K.C.B.), Normanhurst, Battle, a mallard arg., beaked and legged gu. *Arduis sæpe metu nunquam.* 102. 4
Brassey, Albert, Esquire, J.P., of Heythrop, Chipping Norton, Oxon., and 29, Berkeley Square, S.W., a mallard ppr. *Arduis sæpe metu nunquam.*
Brassey, Henry Leonard Campbell, of Preston Hall, Aylesford, Kent, Sefton Lodge, Newmarket, same crest and motto.
Brassy, a unicorn sejant resting the dexter foot against an oak-tree ppr. 48. 3
Brathwayte of Westminster, a greyhound couchant arg., collared and lined gu., studded and ringed or. *cf.* 60. 1
Bratshaw, a bugle-horn stringed. 228. 11
Bratt, Staffs, two greyhounds' heads erased, collared, and addorsed ppr. 60. 12
Brattle, between a laurel and a myrtle branch in saltier a battle-axe, all ppr. 172. 12
Braunch, out of a ducal coronet or, a demi-lion rampant pierced in the breast with an arrow. *cf.* 16. 3
Braunch and **Braunche**, on a garb or, a bird sa.
Braund, Samuel, Esquire, of Devon House, Prospect, South Australia, issuant from clouds a dexter cubit arm in armour holding in the hand a brand raguly inflamed, all ppr., the arm charged with a cross bottony gu. *Fidelis ad extremum.*
Braving, Wilts, a demi-talbot gu., guttée-d'or, ducally crowned arg.
Brawne of London and Surrey, out of a mural coronet or, a dragon's head sa. 72. 11
Bray of Shere, Surrey, a flax-breaker or
Bray, Edward, Esquire, same crest.
Bray, Reginald More, Esquire, of 17, the Boltons, S.W., same crest.
Bray of Langford Hill, Cornw., out of a ducal coronet az., a griffin's head erm., beaked or. 67. 9
Bray, an ounce ppr. 24. 2
Bray, an arm erect vested az., holding in the hand ppr. a chaplet vert. *cf.* 205. 4
Bray, Beds and Sussex, a lion passant gardant or, between two wings addorsed vairé or and az.
Braybroke, Suff., a maiden's head ppr., crined or, wreathed with a garland of violets and leaves of the first. *cf.* 182. 10
Braybrooke, Baron (Neville), of Audley End, Saffron Walden, Essex, a bull statant arg., pied sa., collared and chained or. *Ne vile velis.* *cf.* 45. 2
Braybrooke, a Minerva's head affrontée, all ppr. *cf.* 182. 1
Braye, Baron (Verney-Cave), Stanford Hall, Market Harborough: (1) A greyhound courant sa., collared arg., and holding in the mouth an escroll, thereon the motto *Gardez* (*for Cave*). (2) A demi-phœnix beholding a ray of the sun, all ppr. (*for Verney*). *Un tout seul.—Gardez.* *cf.* 82. 2
Braye, Cornw., *see* Bray.
Braye, out of a ducal coronet or, a plume of five ostrich-feathers, three arg., two az., on the top of the plume a griffin's head gu. *cf.* 114. 13
Braye, H. H., surgeon, Hurstmonceux, 31, King Edward Road, Hackney, N.E., a hemp braye (or flax-breaker) or. 302. 13
Braylesford and **Brayliord**, Derbysh., out of a ducal coronet or, a stag's head affrontée ppr. 119. 13
Brayne, Glouc., from behind a mount vert, the sun rising ppr. 162. 7
Braynton, a griffin's head erased ppr. 66. 2
Braytoft, Lincs, a demi-lion rampant gu., crusily arg. *cf.* 10. 3
Brazier, *see* Brasier and Brashier.
Breach, an escarbuncle gu. 164. 12
Breach of Cirencester, Glouc., an antelope sejant ppr. *cf.* 126. 4
Breadalbane, Marquess and Earl of, and Baron, Earl of Ormelie, etc. (Rt. Hon. Sir Gavin Campbell), Taymouth Castle, Aberfeldy, Scotland, a boar's head erased ppr. *Follow me.* 42. 2
Bream of London, a cubit arm erect vested bendy of six or and az., cuffed of the first, the hand grasping a fish ppr. *God is my defender.*
Breanon, Scotland, an arm in armour embowed, holding a sword. 195. 2
Breant, a demi-griffin regardant, holding a flag charged with a saltier. *cf.* 64. 14
Brearey or **Breary**, the bust of a nun couped at the shoulders affrontée, veiled ppr. *Jesu seul bon e bel.*
Brearly, a cross potent fitchée gu., between two wings arg.
Breary, *see* Brearey.
Breawse, a human heart transfixed with a sword in bend sinister, all ppr. 181. 6
Brebner of Lairney, Scotland, a cock's head erased gu. 90. 1
Breche, out of a cup arg., three roses stalked and leaved ppr. 173. 3
Breck or **Breek**, a demi-lion ppr. *Firmus maneo.* 10. 2
Brecknock and **Brecknoy**, an arm erect issuing from clouds holding an anchor in pale. 219. 2
Brecknock, Earl of, *see* Camden, Marquess.
Bredel of London, an owl ppr. *Nitor in adversum.* 96. 5
Bredon, Alexander Macaulay, Esquire, Scarborough, Yorks, a demi-lion rampant arg., holding in the dexter paw a cross pattée fitchée gu., the sinister paw resting on a passion-nail or. *Vincit veritas.*
Bredon, Matthew Boyd, Esquire, of Ballinataggart House, Portadown, Dowth Lodge, Drogheda, and 39, Ovington Square, S.W., same crest and motto.
Bredon, Robert Edward, Esquire, of Shanghai, same crest and motto.
Bree, a hand couped in fess. 221. 6
Breedon, Berks and Northamp., a demi-lion arg., holding in its dexter paw a cross pattée fitched gu. *cf.* 11. 10
Breek, a demi-lion ppr. *Firmus maneo.* 10. 2
Breen, Henry Hegart, Esquire, F.S.A., Administrator of the Government of the Island of St. Lucia and its dependencies, two arms in armour embowed and interlaced ppr., in the dexter hand a sword, also ppr., and in the sinister hand a passion-cross gu.
Brees and **Breeze**, a stag at gaze or. 117. 3
Breeton, a naked arm embowed holding in the hand ppr. a wreath of laurel vert. 202. 4
Brember of London, two arms in armour embowed holding a battle-axe, all ppr. 194. 12
Bremer, Devonsh., out of a naval coronet or, the sails arg., a dexter cubit arm in armour holding in the hand, gauntleted or, a sword ppr., hilt and pommel of the first, between two branches of oak or, the arm charged with an anchor erect sa. *A la vérité.* 210. 10
Bremner, England and Scotland, a dexter arm vambraced holding in the gauntlet a pheon erect. *Per tela, per hostes.* *cf.* 211. 7
Bremner, a cock's head erased. 90. 1
Brenan, Ireland, out of a mural coronet a demi-eagle displayed. *cf.* 80. 7
Brenan and **Brennan**, Ireland, a wheel gu. 167. 1
Brenan, an arm in armour embowed, the hand grasping a dagger, all ppr. *Sub hoc signo vinces.* 195. 4
Brenchesley and **Brenchley**, an annulet or, within it an escutcheon az., charged with a cross patonce of the first. 167. 6
Brenchley, Kent, a dexter arm couped near the elbow holding a branch of laurel ppr. 219. 9
Brende, Norf., a lion rampant gardant arg. 2. 5
Brende, Suff., the fore-part of a lion gu., united to the hind-part of a dragon vert, sejant.
Brendon, an eagle displayed. 75. 2
Brenlee, a demi-griffin. 64. 2
Brennan, *see* Brenan.
Brent, Glouc., Kent, and Somers., a dragon's head between two wings expanded arg. 72. 7

Brent, a lion rampant 1 13
Brent, a wyvern's head between two wings arg, charged on the breast with three ermine spots, one and two cf 72 7
Brentingham, an oak tree ppr 143 5
Brenton, Bart, out of a naval coronet or, the circle thereof inscribed "Spartan," a swan arg, guttee-de-sang *Go through*
Brenton, a swan arg 99 2
Brenton, a demi savage affrontée, bandcuffed ppr 186 12
Breos, De, an eagle rising regardant ppr cf 77. 4
Breres, Lancs, a nag's head erminois cf 50 12
Brereton of Brinton, Norf., a bear ppr, muzzled or *Opitulante Deo* cf 34 1
Brereton or **Brewerton,** a bear's head and neck or, muzzled sa 34 14
Brereton, Ireland, a demi unicorn collared 48 10
Brereton, Ireland, out of a ducal coronet or, a bear's head couped sa, muzzled of the first 34 3
Brereton, John Alfred, Major-General, Riversdale, Ramsey, Isle of Man, same crest *Opitulante Deo*
Brereton, Chesh and Norf, a bear's head and neck erased sa, muzzled gu, studded or 35 2
Brereton, on a chapeau az, turned up erm, a dragon with wings elevated gu cf 73 4
Brereton, Bart. (*extinct*), of Honford, Chesh, out of a ducal coronet or, a bear's head charged with a crescent in chief and a cross crosslet ppr 34 3
Brerwood or **Brierwood,** Chester, two swords in saltier gu, pommels and hilts or, enfiled with an earl's coronet ppr cf 171 12
Bres er, out of a crown vallary a lion's head cf 17 5
Bresingham, on a chapeau ppr, a demi lion rampant gardant or cf 15 14
Brest, an arm ppr, vested sa, holding in the band a bow arg
Bretargh, Lancs, a lion's gamb holding an ostrich feather *Fari qui sentient* 37 3
Bretherton, Rev Humphrey William, of Eccleston Rectory, Chorley, Lancs, a cross raguly flory sa, therefrom pendent by a riband gu, a stag's head caboshed arg *Per aspera ad dulcia crucis*
Bretherton, Norris, Esquire, of Runshaw Hall, Euxton, Lancs, and Nateby Lodge, Garstang, same crest and motto
Bretherton, Frederick Annesley Stapelton, the Hall, Rainhill, Lancs, in front of a demi-unicorn arg, a portcullis sa
Breton or **Bretton,** London, Essex, Staffs, and Leics, on a lion's gamb az, a chevron or, charged with a mullet sa 39 2
Breton, on a lion's gamb az, and between three billets arg, a chevron or, charged with a mullet sa cf 39 2
Breton, Norf, a demi talbot gu, eared, collared, and lined or, holding in his feet the line coiled up
Breton, Northamp., on a mural coronet gu, a boar's head couped sa cf 42 11
Breton, a wolf paly of eight or and az 28 10
Bretrook, a horse saddled and bridled, at full speed 52 1
Brett, a sphinx passant cf 182 12
Brett, Charles Henry, Esquire, of Gretton Malone Road, a falcon ppr, jessed gu, belled and vervelled or *Vilia contemnit aucupia*
Brett, William Bailey, Esquire, of 58, Merrion Avenue, Blackrock, co Dublin, same crest and motto
Brett, Ireland, a crane regardant wings addorsed, resting the dexter foot on a stone 105 5
Brett, Glouc and Leics, on a tower arg, a man's head ppr
Brett, a garb *Velis id quod possis* 153 2
Brett, Staffs, a lion's gamb erect erased arg, grasping a dragon's head erased vert
Brett, Kent and Devonsh, a lion passant gu 6 2
Brett of Moore Place, Esher, Surrey, a lion passant gu, charged on the shoulder with a cross bottony fitchee or, and holding in the dexter fore paw a fasces ppr *Vicimus* 262 7
Brett of Ocle Court, Heref, on a chapeau gu, turned up erm, a lion passant of the first 4 9
Brett, Kent, a griffin's head between two wings az, beaked or cf 67 7
Brett, a demi-lion queue fourchee arg, langued and armed gu cf 10 2
Brettell, a demi-eagle displayed az, upon a mill-rind or, holding in the beak an ear of corn of the last
Brettell, Henry Cartwright, Esquire, solicitor, of Dudley, *uses* a demi eagle displayed or, winged vair 229 2
Brettridge, Bucks, an arm holding a sword ppr, pommelled and hilted or 212 13
Brew, a park gate gu 158 9
Brew-Mulhallen, Vivian, Esquire of Sidmanton Lodge, Bray, co Wicklow, and Donerea Lodge, Kilcool (1) An escallop or (*for Mulhallen*) (2) A lion rampant per fesse or and gu, charged on the breast with a cross crosslet fitchee sa (*for Brew*) *Always ready*
Brewdnell, from an old castle in ruins a martlet rising sa
Brewer or **Breuer,** Kent, out of a mural coronet an arm from the elbow erect, vested gu, billettee or, holding in the hand ppr a battle-axe arg
Brewer or **Breuer,** a mermaid holding a mirror and a comb ppr 184 8
Brewer, a syren charged with a mullet, for difference her human part ppr, her tail scaled or and gu, divided by parallel lines wavy
Brewerton, *see* Brereton
Brewes, De, out of a ducal coronet gu, a lion's gamb 36 12
Brewin, Leics, a unicorn passant arg, armed, maned, and tufted or, collared and charged on the body with three mullets pierced in fesse az cf 48 5
Brewin, Arthur, Esquire, 64 Austin Friars, E C., on a chapeau ppr, a unicorn statant arg *Be fast*
Brewley, a lion rampant ppr, platee, holding in the paws a shield erm, thereon a bend gu, charged with three chevrons or
Brews or **Brewis,** out of a ducal coronet or, a cock's head ppr 90 6
Brews, Brewse, and **Brewes,** a lion passant az 4 3
Brews or **Brewse,** a demi-Hercules clothed with a skin holding over the shoulder a club ppr
Brews or **Brewes,** out of a ducal coronet gu, a lion's gamb ppr 36 12
Brewster and **Brewsted,** Scotland, a leopard's head erased az, bezantee cf 23 2
Brewster, Northamp, a leopard's head erased sa, bezantee cf 23 2
Brewster, French- (1) A leopard's head erased az, bezantee, holding in the mouth a trefoil slipped vert (*for Brewster*) (2) A dolphin naiant ppr (*for French*) *Verité soyez ma garde* 140 5
Brewster of Whitfield, Essex, a demi-lion holding in the dexter paw a club over his shoulder, all ppr
Brewster of Dublin, a wolf's head couped gu, the neck charged with a trefoil slipped or, and pierced through with an arrow sa, barbed and feathered arg. *Probitas cum fortitudine.* cf 29 6
Brewster of Essex, a beaver's head erased sa *Verité soyez ma garde* 134 3
Brey, a hill ppr *By degrees.*
Breyton, on a mount vert, a wild duck ppr 102 1
Brian, a demi savage ppr cf 186. 5
Brian, a beacon flammant or 177 14
Briand and **Briant,** out of a mural coronet a bundle of arrows banded
Brice, a demi-fleur de-lis arg
Brice, a stag trippant. 117 8
Brice, Hants and Somers, a lion's head erased erm, pierced through with an arrow or, headed and feathered arg
Brice, Ireland, an arm holding a cutlass, all ppr *Do well, and doubt not* 213. 5
Brice, Ireland, a cubit arm erect ppr, grasping a scimitar arg, hilt and pommel or cf 213 8
Brichen, Scotland, an arm in fess issuing out of clouds grasping a club in the hand, all ppr 223 5
Brickdale, on a ducal coronet or, a dolphin naiant az 140 4
Brickdale, Somers, out of a ducal coronet or, a demi lion rampant supporting a spear ppr, thereon a standard az, fringed and tasselled of the first, charged with a sheaf of five arrows pheoned of the same, flighted arg, pointed and banded gu
Brickdale, Somers, a sheaf of seven arrows or, flighted arg, headed and banded gu
Brickenden, a lion's gamb erased holding a rose branch slipped ppr 37 10
Brickenden, a demi wyvern vert 69 10
Brickhurst, Lincs, out of a mural coronet or, a tiger's head and neck arg cf 27 1
Brickwood, a demi savage affrontee ppr, wreathed about the head and loins with leaves vert, and holding in his dexter hand a slip of oak of the last cf 186 4

Brid, London, an eagle's head bendy of eight arg. and sa., ducally gorged or.

Bridall, Middx., a lion's gamb erased az., armed gu., holding a demi-lance broken arg., headed gu. 38. 9

Bride, two eagle's heads erased and addorsed ppr. 84. 11

Brideoake, Robert Farrar, Croft, near Warrington, a tree ppr., the trunk clasped by a pair of hands fesseways couped at the wrists.

Bridge, Heref. and Essex, two wings arg., on each a chevron engrailed sa., charged with a chaplet or.

Bridge, Henry Hamilton, Esquire, J.P., of Fairfield and Ashcott, Waipawa, Napier, New Zealand, two wings arg., on each a chevron engrailed sa., charged with a chaplet or. *Post hominem animus durat.*

Bridge, Surrey, a stag's head arg. *Nec minus fortiter.* 121. 5

Bridge, an eagle with wings displayed holding in the beak a branch. *Me juvat ire pet altum.*

Bridge, Vice-Admiral Cyprian A. G., R.N., 30, Green Street, Grosvenor Square, London, W., an eagle rising, in its beak an olive-branch, all ppr. *Me juvat ire per altum.* 77. 2

Bridge, a chaplet of oak or, between two wings elevated sa., each charged with a bridge of one arch, embattled, and at each end a tower ppr.

Bridgeman of Coney-Weston Hall, Norf., a trefoil slipped vert. 148. 9

Bridgeman, Lancs, Warw., and Shropsh., a fox sejant ppr. 32. 11

Bridgeman, Earl of Bradford, Weston Park, Shifnal, a demi-lion arg., holding between the paws a garland of laurel or. *Nec temere, nec timide.* 260. 2

Bridgen, a demi-mariner vested in russet ppr., round the waist a sash, and on the head a cap gu., in his dexter hand a sphere or, the sinister arm resting on an anchor of the last. 186. 10

Bridger or **Briger,** Glouc., a dragon's head vert, transfixed with the end of a spear ppr. in bend sinister. 72. 10

Bridger, Kent, out of a ducal coronet or, a crab gu. cf. 141. 5

Bridger, Harry, of Buckingham House, Sussex, a crab gu. 141. 5

Bridges, Bart., of Goodneston, Kent (*extinct*), out of a ducal coronet or, a Moor's head in profile ppr., wreathed about the temples arg., and of the first, gorged with a collar of the same, and pendent therefrom a cross patée of the third. *Je garderay.*

Bridges, Edinburgh, a demi-lion gu. *Maintien le droit.* 10. 3

Bridges, on a tower a hawk with wings displayed, all ppr. cf. 156. 8

Bridges, an anchor in pale ppr. 161. 1

Bridges or Brydges, Essex, a boar passant arg., pierced through the neck with a broken spear, headed of the first, embrued gu. cf. 40. 14

Bridges, Glouc., a man's head from the shoulders in profile ppr., vested paly of six arg. and gu., semée of roundels counterchanged and wreathed of the last and az.

Bridges, on a tower arg., masoned sa., a dove rising ppr. 156. 11

Bridgewater, a demi-stag or, attired sa. 119. 2

Bridgman, Warw., a demi-lion rampant arg., holding between the paws a garland of laurel ppr. 260. 2

Bridgstock, a raven sa., holding in the dexter claw an escallop.

Bridon, Suff., a hawk's head erased sa., charged with three bezants, one and two. cf. 88. 12

Bridport, Viscount (Hood), Royal Lodge, Windsor Park, a Cornish chough ppr., supporting with the dexter claw an anchor or. *Steady.* 245. 9

Bridson of Bryerswood, Windermere, Westml., a demi-mariner in profile ppr., vested and capped az., collared arg., girdles or, grasping in the dexter hand an anchor erect of the last, and resting the sinister hand on a wreath of coral gu. *Tutus in undis.*

Bridson, Major Thomas Ridgway, of Rock End, Torquay, Devonsh., and Bridge House, Bolton, Lancs, same crest and motto.

Brien, Ireland, two lion's gambs couped and erect gu., armed az., supporting a sword ppr., pommel and hilt or.

Brien, Ireland, a cross pattée gu., between the horns of a crescent or. 163. 6

Brien, Edward Henry, M.D., Stanley Villa, New Chester Road, Rock Ferry, issuing from clouds a dexter arm embowed ppr., holding in the hand a sword of the last.

Brierly, London, a cross potent fitchée gu., between two wings arg.

Briers, Beds, a demi-leopard rampant gardant erased az., gorged with a collar arg., charged with three mullets pierced gu.

Brierly, John Swallow, Esquire, of Delrow, Aldenham, Herts, in front of an oak-tree ppr., an escutcheon arg., guttée-de-sang, charged with a cross nebuly gu., between two roses of the last, both stalked and leaved of the first. *Ad utrumque paratus.*

Brierwood, two swords in saltier gu., pommels and hilts or, enfiled with an earl's coronet ppr. cf. 171. 12

Brig, an arm in armour embowed holding a dagger ppr. 196. 5

Brigden, Sussex, an arm in armour embowed ppr., garnished or, wielding a sword arg., hilt and pommel gold. *Mea gloria fides.* 195. 2

Briger, *see* Bridger.

Brigges, Westml., a fox ppr. 32. 1

Briggs, Bart. (*extinct*), Shropsh., on the stump of a tree eradicated or, sprouting two new branches vert, a pelican or, vulning herself ppr. *Virtus est Dei.* cf. 98. 6

Briggs, Bart. (*extinct*), Barbadoes, upon the stump of a tree erased and couped and charged with a trefoil ppr., a pelican vulning herself, wings elevated arg. *Virtus est Dei.—Ne traverse pas le pont.* 98. 6

Briggs, Major-General David, of Strathairly, Largo, Fife, a pelican in her piety. *Sola virtus invicta.*

Briggs, Joseph Lyder, Esquire, J.P., of Maynards, and of Welch Town in the island of Barbadoes, in the West Indies, on a wreath of the colours upon the stump of a tree erased and couped and charged with a trefoil ppr., a pelican vulning herself, wings elevated arg. *Ne traverse pas le pont.* 98. 6

Briggs, a tiger's head couped affrontée.

Briggs, Shropsh., an arm embowed covered with leaves vert, holding in the hand ppr. a bow gu., strung sa., and an arrow arg.

Briggs, Yorks, on a mount vert, a laurel-branch erect ppr., in front a lion passant erm., the dexter paw resting on a pheon sa. *Fortiter et fideliter.*

Briggs, Berks, a demi-dragon vert, wings az. *Felicior quo certior.* 73. 10

Brigham, Yorks, on a cloud a crescent between two branches of palm in orle. cf. 146. 10

Brigham or **Briggam,** Yorks, a boar's head in bend couped sa.

Brigham of Foxley House, Chester, out of a ducal coronet a plume of feathers. *In cruce salus.* 114. 3

Brighouse, Lincs, out of a mural coronet or, a tiger's head arg. cf. 27. 1

Bright, Ireland, a hand erect ppr., vested sa., issuing out of a cloud shedding forth rays, holding a mort-head of the first. 208. 10

Bright, Allan Heywood, Esquire, of Liverpool, a crescent arg., and between the horns an estoile or.

Bright, late Benjamin, of Barton Court, Colwell, Heref., same crest. *Post tenebras lucem.*

Bright, Charles Edward, Esquire, of 98, Cromwell Road, London, S.W., same crest and motto.

Bright, George, Esquire, of 25, Victoria Square, Clifton, Bristol, same crest and motto.

Bright, Heywood, Esquire, of Sandheys, West Derby, Liverpool, same crest and motto.

Bright, Rev. James Franck, D.D. (Oxon.), of University College, Oxford, same crest and motto.

Bright, Tyndall, Esquire, of Liverpool same crest and motto.

Bright, William Robert, Esquire, same crest and motto.

Bright, a dragon's head. 71. 1

Bright, Hon. Henry Edward, of Gawler and Willaston, South Australia, Member of the Legislative Council, *uses* a sun in splendour issuing out of clouds. *In arduis fortitudo.* 162. 5

Bright, Bart., Harrow-weald, a mass of clouds and issuant therefrom a sun in splendour, all ppr. 162. 5

Bright, Sussex, the sun in splendour or, issuing from clouds ppr. *Lumen umbra Dei.* 162. 5

Bright, a demi-lion rampant holding a battle-axe headed gu. *Post tenebras lucem.* 15. 4

Bright, Chesh., a demi-griffin holding in the dexter claw a mullet sa. cf. 64. 2

Bright, Suff., a dragon's head gu., vomiting flames of fire ppr., collared and lined or. cf. 72. 3

Bright, Shropsh., a dragon's head erm., vomiting flames of fire ppr., gorged with a collar sa., charged with three cross crosslets fitchée or. *Nunquam non paratus.* cf. 72. 3

Brightman or **Britzman,** Surrey, out of rays or, an arm in armour embowed ppr, garnished of the first, holding in the gauntlet a sword arg, hilted also or, the arm tied round with a sash or and purp

Brigid, Ireland, out of a cloud ppr, an etoile of eight rays 164 11

Brignac, a reindeer's head cabossed 122 4

Brignall, an eagle with two heads displayed charged on the breast with a saltier 74 1

Brigstocke, William Player, Brent-Eleigh Hall, Lavenham, Suff, a raven ppr, holding in the dexter claw an escallop or 291 9

Brigwood, a demi-savage affrontée wreathed about the head and middle with leaves and holding in the dexter hand a slip of oak, all ppr cf 186 4

Brimacombe, R, Colebrooke Lodge, Putney Heath, S W, on a mount vert, an owl with wings displayed and inverted, charged on each wing with a pale, thereon a roundel *Sapienter*

Brin, Ireland, a dexter hand couped gu 222 14

Brinckman, Sir Theodore Henry, Bart, St Leonard's, Windsor, a pair of wings, each quarterly arg and az *Perseverando* 109 6

Brind, Frederick William, Esquire, the Court Lodge, Chelsfield, Kent, a dexter cubit arm erect, holding the head of a broken spear, all ppr *Nil sine labore* 214 13

Brindesley, an escallop-shell per pale or and sa 141 14

Brindley of Union Hall, Staffs, on a mount vert, a demi lion regardant erm, holding in the mouth a sprig of oak, the dexter paw holding an olive-branch ppr, the sinister paw resting on an escutcheon az, charged with two chevronels or 14 4

Brindley and **Brinley,** a wyvern holding in the mouth a hand ppr 70 3

Brine, two swords in saltier ppr, surmounted by a cross crosslet fitched gu 166 14

Brine, Dorset, a lion rampant arg, billettee, and holding between the paws a cross moline gu

Brine, Ernest Augustus, Esquire, of Poole, Dorset, a lion rampant arg, semee of billets, and holding in the fore paws a cross moline gu *Confido*

Brine, Rev Algernon Lindsay, of Margate Kent, same crest and motto

Brine, Capt Arthur (late R M L I), of Frith Cottage, Torquay, same crest and motto

Brine, Rev George Augustus, M A, of Beechgrove, Honiton, Devonsh, same crest and motto

Brine, Rev James Edward Bouverie, of Nuward Eliya, Ceylon, same crest and motto

Brine, Colonel John Jones, H E I C S, same crest and motto

Brine, Admiral Lindesay, R.N, Athenæum Club, Pall Mall, S W, same crest and motto

Brine, Percival Forbes, Esquire, same crest and motto

Brine, Philip Arthur Sherard, Esquire, of Richmond, Virginia, U S A, same crest and motto

Bringhorne, Kent, on a wolf's head erased sa, a pile or

Bringham, a cat salient gardant ppr 26 3

Bringhurst, Leics, an arm in armour embowed arg, holding a club sa, spiked or cf 199 2

Bringhurst, Ireland, a dragon's head erased arg, gorged with a collar compony or and gu 71 2

Brinkhurst, a demi-lion arg, ducally crowned or, holding in each paw a bezant cf 10 11

Brinkley, Richard Grapes, Esquire, of Ardagh and Fortland, co Sligo, Ireland, on a wreath of the colours a cross potence engrailed surmounted by an estoile, all or *Mutabimur*

Brinkley, John Lloyd, Esquire, of Fortland, Faskey, co Sligo, a cross patonce engrailed gu, surmounted of an estoile arg *Mutabimur*

Brinkley, John Turner, Esquire, of Northgate, Warw, same crest and motto

Brinklow or **Bringlow,** a demi lion or, supporting a flaming sword gu, hilt of the first

Brinkworth of Bath, on a mount vert, a willow-tree ppr

Brins, a talbot's head collared swallowing a bird, with wings expanded. cf 57 3

Brinton, on a wreath arg and gu, in front of a saltire gu, a beacon sa, fired ppr cf 177 8

Brinton, John, Esquire, of Moor Hall, Stourport, same crest *Lux et salus*

Brinton, Reginald Seymour, Esquire, J P, of Croft, Kidderminster, same crest ΒΙΟΣ ΠΑΙΓΝΙΑ ΣΠΟΥΔΑΙΑ

Brisac, an arm embowed ppr, vested gu, holding a covered cup or 203 4

Brisban or **Brisbane,** Scotland, an anchor in pale with a serpent wreathed about it, all ppr *Animum prudentia firmat* 161 3

Brisbane, Scotland, an ant hillock, semee of ants ppr *Virtuti damnosa quies*

Brisbane, a demi-savage holding over his shoulder a club ppr 186. 5

Brisbane, Charles Thomas, Esquire, of Brisbane, Ayr (1) Dexter, the crest of honourable augmentation, viz, out of a naval crown or, a dexter arm embowed in the uniform of a captain of the Royal Navy, the hand grasping a cutlass ppr, hilted and pommelled or, and from the hand pendent by a ribbon arg, fimbriated az, a gold medal, representing that given by His Majesty George III to Sir Charles Brisbane *Curacoa* 204 2 (2) Sinister, the family crest, viz, a stork's head erased holding in the beak a serpent writhing ppr *Certamine summo.* cf 106 3

Brisbane and **Brishon,** Scotland, a heron's head erased holding in the beak an eel, all ppr *Certamine summo* 104 2

Brisbane (1) A stork's head erased holding in the beak a serpent wavy ppr (*for Brisbane*) cf 106 3 (2) A lion issuant gardant ppr, holding in his dexter paw a cross crosslet fitchee gu (*for Makdougal*) *Certamine summo —Fear God.* 11 12

Brishon or **Brisbone,** on a chapeau a lion rampant holding an arrow, point downward cf 2 4

Brisco, Sir Musgrave Horton, Bart, Crofton Hall, Wigton, Cumb, a greyhound current sa, seizing a hare ppr. 254 8

Briscoa, a pennon gu, charged with a crescent arg, the staff in bend sa, headed or cf 176 12

Briscoe and **Briscowe,** a pheon between two arms in armour embowed supporting a Saracen's head affrontee 194 9

Briscoe and **Briscowe,** Ireland, a Saracen's head affrontee ppr 190. 5

Brise-Ruggles, Archibald Weyland, Spains Hall, Braintree, Essex (1) A tower or, transpierced with four darts in saltier and inflamed ppr (*for Ruggles*) (2) An alligator rampant (*for Brise*) *Struggle*

Brislay, a cock pheasant ppr, standing among flowers az, leaved vert cf 90 8

Bristed, a dexter hand holding a spur ppr 217 14

Bristol, Marquess of (Hervey), Ickworth Park, Bury St Edmunds, a leopard passant sa, bezantee, ducally gorged and chained or, holding in the dexter paw a trefoil slipped vert *Je n'oublierai jamais*

Bristow, Herts, out of a crescent or, a demi eagle displayed az 81 4

Bristow of Broxmore Park, Wilts, out of a crescent or, a demi-eagle displayed az *Vigilantibus non dormientibus* 81 4

Bristow, Collyer- (1) Issuant out of a crescent or, a phœnix ppr, charged on each wing with a cross crosslet az (*for Bristow*) (2) A boar's head erased or, guttee de-sang, holding in the mouth a staff raguly bendwise gu (*for Collyer*) *Avance*

Bristowe, Rev Charles John, of Bees thorpe Hall, Notts, same crest and motto

Bristowe, Hubert Carpenter, M D, the Cottage, Wrington, Somers., same crest and motto

Britain, a dexter hand ppr, holding a key or 217 7

Britain, Briton, Britten, and **Britton,** out of a naval coronet a mermaid holding in her dexter hand a purse and in her sinister a comb ppr cf 184. 14

Britley, on a chapeau a demi-lion holding in the dexter paw a mullet. cf 15 14

Brittain or **Brittaine,** an eagle's claw erased in fess holding a quill 113 12

Britten, an ear of wheat and palm-branch in saltier ppr 154 10

Britten, a wolf passant ppr *Cassis tutissima virtus* 28 10

Britton, Arthur Henry Daniel, Esquire, of Vercroft, Clyde Road, Redland, Bristol, on a wreath of the colours, a lion's gamb erect and erased az, guttee d'eau between two mullets of six points, also az *Salut a tous* 264 2

Britton, Philip William Poole Carlyon-, Hanham Court, Glouc (1) A lion's gamb erect and erased az, guttee-d'eau between two mullets of six points, also az (*Britton*) 264 2 (2) A demi lion rampant gu, ducally crowned or, collared arg., holding between the paws a bezant and charged on the shoulder with a cross crosslet of the second (*Carlyon*). 260. 10. *Salut à tous.—Turris tutissima virtus.*

Britweesil, a salmon naiant ppr. 139. 12

Briwer or **Briwere,** out of a cloud a dexter arm holding an open book ppr. 215. 1

Brixton or **Brixtone,** a demi-horse rampant arg. 53. 3

Broad, His Honour Judge Lowther, of Ronaki, Nelson, New Zealand, *uses* a demi-savage holding in the dexter hand three arrows and pointing with the sinister to an imperial crown. *Fortior leone justus.* 186. 13

Broad, on a chapeau gu., turned up erm., a leopard's face arg. *Another,* ppr.

Broad, on a chapeau a tiger's head ducally crowned.

Broadbelt, an eagle displayed ppr. 75. 2

Broadbent, Sir William Henry, Bart., K.C.V.O., of Longwood, Huddersfield, in front of a pheon, the staff rompu, a serpent nowed, all ppr. 251. 11

Broadbent or **Brodbent,** a pheon arg., the point embrued ppr., the staff broken near the point or. 174. 10

Broadbent, a dexter arm ppr., holding in the hand a covered cup or. 217. 11

Broade, Stanier-Philip-: (1) On a mount vert, a bear's head erect or, transfixed by an arrow fesswise ppr. (*for Broade*). 243. 5. (2) In front of a griffin's head erased ppr., three escallops or (*for Stanier*). *Pro Deo et rege.—Pietate fortior.* 243. 6

Broadhead, Bart., Yorks, a demi-lion rampant ppr., collared and chained or, supporting an escutcheon erm., charged with an eagle displayed gu. *Perseverando.*

Broadhead, on a chapeau a garb ppr. 153. 10

Broadhurst, a mermaid holding in her dexter hand a dagger ppr. 184. 7

Broadhurst, a lion's head couped ppr., collared vairé arg. and gu. *cf.* 18. 13

Broadhurst, a swan erm., swimming in water ppr., charged on the breast with an étoile sa., the wings expanded or, fretty raguly az.

Broadley, a stag's head erased ppr. *Mitis sed fortis.* 121. 2

Broadley, London, a talbot passant ppr. *Non immemor beneficii.* 54. 1

Broadley, London, a stag's head erased ppr. *Non immemor beneficii.* 121. 2

Broadley, Henry Broadley Harrison, Welton House, Beverley, Yorks: (1) Within a chaplet of roses ppr., a cross pattée fitched sa. 243. 13. (2) A demi-lion rampant or, charged with a bend vair arg. and gu., supporting with the sinister paw a shield arg., thereon two branches of laurel saltirewise vert. *Nihil viget simile.* 243. 14

Broadmead, William Bucknell, Enmore Castle, Somers., on a fret az., a stag's head erased, holding in the mouth an acorn slipped ppr. *Semper fidelis.*

Broadmead, Henry, Esquire, a fret az., thereon a stag's head erased, holding in the mouth an acorn slipped ppr. *Semper fidelis.*

Broadmead, Rev. Philip Palfrey, of Olands, Milverton, Somers., same crest and motto.

Broadmead, Thomas Palfrey, Esquire, of Enmore Park, Bridgwater, same crest and motto.

Broadmead, William Bucknell, Esquire, of Enmore Castle, Bridgwater, same crest and motto.

Broadockshaw and **Brodockshaw,** a stag's head arg. 121. 5

Broadrick, Lieutenant-Colonel Edward, a spear-head arg., consanguined and within a chaplet of oak fructed, all ppr. *Decens et honestum.*

Broadrick, George, Esquire, of Broughton House, Broughton Road, Ipswich, same crest and motto.

Broadrick, Yorks, a spear's head arg., embrued and within a chaplet of oak fructed, all ppr. *Decens et honestum.*

Broadstone, in a cloud a crescent between two palm-branches. 146. 10

Broadwood, London and Sussex, a yew-tree leaved and eradicated ppr., on the trunk an annulet or, transfixed by three arrows, one in fess, two in saltier of the last. *Semper virens.*

Broadwood, a pine-tree ppr., charged with nine cones gu., the trunk eradicated, also ppr. *Semper virens.* 144. 13

Broadwood, James Henry Tschudi, Esquire, of Lyne, Capel, Surrey, and Pleystowe, Capel, Dorking, a pine-tree eradicated and fructed ppr., surmounted by three arrows, two in saltire, points downwards, and one in fess, point to the dexter, also ppr., encircled around the stock by an annulet or. *Semper virens.*

Broadwood, John Alexander Redman, Esquire, of Laugharne, co. Carmarthensh., same crest and motto.

Broadwood, Thomas Capel, Esq., same crest and motto.

Brocas, London, a Moor's head couped at the shoulders, radiated ppr.

Brock, John, Esquire, of Glastonbury, Somers. *Justice to all.*

Brock, Scotland, on a chapeau gu., a dove rising ppr. 94. 10

Brock, Essex, a pegasus az. 47. 1

Brock, Clutton-, Worcs.: (1) A demi-lion gardant gu., on the body a chevron or, charged with three trefoils slipped vert, holding between his paws an arrow of the second barbed and feathered arg. (*for Brock*). (2) An owl on a myrtle-branch (*for Clutton*). *Virescit vulnere virtus.* *cf.* 96. 5

Brock or **Brocke,** Chesh., a demi-lion rampant gu., holding in the dexter paw a dart or, feathered of the first. *cf.* 13. 6

Brock, out of a mural crown arg., a demi-Canadian Indian, the dexter hand supporting a tomahawk erect ppr. *Canada.*

Brock, an escallop or. 141. 12

Brockas or **Brokas,** Hants, a lion sejant erect, holding in his dexter paw a cross pattée fitched, and resting the sinister on a pyramid. *cf.* 8. 12

Brockbank of the Croft, Kirsanton, Lancs, a stag at gaze ppr. 117. 3

Brockdon, Devonsh., a stag's head erased per chevron arg. and gu., attired or. 121. 2

Brocket of the Ryes, Essex, a stag lodged sa., ducally gorged and lined or. *cf.* 115. 7

Brocket, a stag's head erased, pierced through the neck with an arrow.

Brocket, a brocket or young deer lodged ppr. *cf.* 124. 8

Brocket or **Brockhill,** Kent, a badger sa. 33. 10

Brockhill, Kent, on a mount vert, a badger sa. 33. 12

Brockholes, a fret arg. 165. 10

Brockholes, Lancs, a brock or badger passant sa. *cf.* 33. 10

Brockholes, Fitzherbert-, William Joseph, of Claughton Hall, Lancs: (1) A brock (or badger) passant sa. (*for Brockholes*). *cf.* 33. 10. (2) A cubit arm in armour erect ppr., the hand clenched within a gauntlet (*for Fitzherbert*). *Ung je serviray.*

Brocklebank, Ralph, Esquire, of 9, Faulkner Square, Liverpool, in front of a mount vert, thereon a cock ppr., three escallops in fesse or. *God send grace.*

Brocklebank, Thomas, Esquire, of the Roscote, Heswall, Chester, same crest and motto.

Brocklebank, Sir Thomas, Bart., of Greenlands, Cumb., an anchor fessewise sa., thereon a cock arg., combed and wattled gu., charged on the breast with an escallop, also sa. *God send grace.* 257. 2

Brocklehurst, a brock ppr. *Veritas me dirigit.* 33. 10

Brocklehurst, William B., of Butley Hall, Chester, and of Hurdsfield House, near Macclesfield, a brock sa., holding in the mouth a slip of oak fructed ppr., in front of a mount vert, thereon two oak-trees, also ppr. *Veritas me dirigit.* 254. 1

Brocklehurst, Philip Lancaster, Esquire, of Swythamley Park, near Macclesfield, Staffs, same crest and motto.

Brocklehurst, Robert, of St. Clare, West Derby, Lancs, on a rock in front of two oak-branches fructed in saltire, a brock, all ppr. 292. 7

Brockman of Beachborough, Kent, on a sword erect arg., hilt and pommel or, a stag's head cabossed ppr., attired of the second, the blade through the head and bloody at the point.

Brocton, Shropsh., a hand holding up a ducal coronet capped and tasselled, between two branches of laurel in orle. 217. 3

Brodbent, a pheon arg., the point guttée-de-sang, the staff broken near the head or. 174. 10

Broderwicke of Langford, Berks, out of a coronet or, a spear-head arg., imbrued. *cf.* 174. 12

Brodhurst, a demi-swan, the wings vairée, charged on the breast with an escutcheon. *Virescit vulnere virtus.* *cf.* 100. 9

Brodhurst, a demi-swan or. 100. 9

Brodie or **Brody,** Sussex and Scotland, a hand holding a sheaf of arrows ppr. *Unite.* 214. 3

Brodie of Brodie, Moraysh., a dexter hand holding a bunch of arrows, all ppr. 214. 3

Brodie, Ian Ashley Moreton, Esquire, of Brodie, Brodie Castle, Forres, N.B., a dexter hand holding three arrows, all ppr.

Brodie, Alexander, of Lethen, Nairn a dexter hand holding five arrows, all ppr *Be mindful to unite*

Brodie, William Haig, M D, Lethen, Battle, Sussex, a dexter hand holding five arrows in bend sinister, all ppr *Be mindful to unite*

Brodie, Sir Benjamin Vincent Sellon, Bart, of Boxford, Suff, a dexter cubit arm erect, holding in the hand a civic wreath vert, with three arrows arg, one in fesse, two in saltire. *Unite* 254 11

Brodie, a lion's gamb erased sa, holding a palm-branch ppr cf 36 7

Brodie, Sir Thomas Dawson, Bart, of Idvies, Forfarsh, a dexter hand holding a bunch of five arrows ppr *Be mindful to unite* 214 3

Brodie-Innes, John William, Esquire of 15, Royal Circus Edinburgh, N B (1) A mullet az *Be trust (for Innes)* (2) A hand holding a sheaf of arrows ppr *Unite (for Brodie)*

Brodley, London and Lancs, a boar's head couped gu 43 1

Brodnax, Kent and Chesh, out of a mural coronet a demi eagle or, winged gu, gorged with a collar of the second, charged with three cinquefoils arg

Brodockshaw, a stag's head arg 121 5

Brodribb, Ernest George, Esquire, of Melbourne Club, Melbourne, Australia, a mount vert, therefrom springing three roses gu stalked and leaved ppr, interlaced with as many mascles, also interlaced fesseways or *Prudentia tutus*

Brodribb, Frank Claudius, Esquire, of Wyallah, Toowoomba, and Kurrowah, Darling Downs, Queensland, same crest and motto.

Brodribb, Owen Adams Kennedy, Esquire, same crest and motto

Brodribb, Rev William Kennedy, B A, of Putley Rectory, Ledbury, Heref, and Frank Claudius Brodribb, Esquire, J P, of Wyallah, Toowoomba, Queensland, upon a mount vert, three mascles fessewise interlaced or, and interlacing three roses erect gu, stalked and leaved of the first *Prudentia tutus* 149 13

Brodrick, Surrey, a spear-head arg, embrued gu 174 12

Brodrick, *see* Brodrick-Cloete

Brodrick, Charles Cumberland, Lynbridge House, Tavistock, Devon, out of a ducal coronet or, a spear-head arg, embrued gu *A cuspide corona*

Broese, a crane, holding in its claw a stone ppr 105 6

Brogden, out of a ducal coronet or, a hand ppr, holding a rose gu, slipped and leaved vert. 218 11

Brogden, London, a demi lion ducally crowned, holding between its paws a cross formee cf 11. 2

Broge, Brogg, and **Broige,** Scotland, a dexter hand holding a sword, all ppr *Honorat mors* 212 13

Brograve, London, Herts, Norf, Warw, and Lancs, an eagle displayed, with two heads erm, each ducally crowned or *Finis dat esse* cf 74 2

Brohier or **Broheir,** in a crescent an arrow in pale 163 13

Broke, a fox's head ppr 33 4

Broke, the late Sir Philip, Bart, of Nacton (1) Of honourable augmentation, issuant from a naval crown or, a dexter arm embowed, encircled by a wreath of laurel ppr, the hand grasping a trident erect of the first. (2) A brock passant ppr *Sævumque tridentem servamus* cf 33 10

Broke, Shropsh, a badger ppr 33 10

Broke, Horace, Esquire, of Gladwyns, Harlow, Essex, a brock or badger passant ppr

Brokelsbey and **Brokelsby,** Lincs, a brock or badger ppr 33 10

Brokesby, Leics, a boar's head couped at the neck gu, bristled or 43 1

Bromage, out of a ducal coronet a dexter arm in armour embowed, the hand holding a scimitar, all ppr *Deus dux certus* cf 196 10

Bromell, a Bacchus' head, couped at the shoulders ppr, vested gu

Bromborough, out of a ducal coronet or, a cubit arm habited az, cuffed arg, holding in the hand an oak-branch ppr, fructed of the first

Brome, Broom, and **Broome,** Oxon, an arm couped at the elbow and erect, vested bendy wavy of six or and gu, holding in the hand ppr a bunch of broom vert, seeded of the first

Brome of West Malling, Kent, an arm vested gu, turned up arg, holding in the hand ppr a slip of broom vert, flowered or *Domine, dirige nos*

Brome, a cock arg, wings elevated az, beaked, combed, legged, and wattled gu cf 91 7

Bromeall, a demi-lion rampant, double-queued ppr 10 6

Bromeley, Cambs, on a wreath and issuing out of a mural coronet or, a demi lion rampant sa, holding a standard vert, charged with a griffin passant of the first cf 16. 7

Bromell, a demi eagle displayed, with two heads, each ducally crowned cf 82 7

Bromewich and **Bromwich,** Glouc, Heref, and Herts, out of a ducal coronet or, a unicorn's head sa. *Another*, guttee-d'or *Another*, out of a mural coronet 48 12

Bromfield, Kent and Chesh, a demi-tiger az, armed, maned, and tufted or, holding erect a broken sword arg, hilt and pommel of the second

Bromfield, Staffs, a lion passant gardant or, gorged with a wreath of the first and az cf 4 3

Bromflet or **Bronslet,** Lancs, on a chapeau sa, turned up arg, a wyvern vert, ducally crowned or 70 4

Bromflete, out of a ducal coronet or, a wolf's head gu cf 30 5

Bromhall, Beds, a demi-lion or, holding between the paws a cross crosslet fitched sa cf 11 10

Bromhall, London and Chesh, a lion passant or 6 2

Bromhead, Sir Benjamin Parnell, Bart, Thurlby Hall, Lincs, out of a mural coronet gu, a unicorn's head arg, armed and crined or, holding in the mouth a rose gu, slipped and leaved ppr *Concordia res crescunt*

Bromhead, Ireland, a pelican vulning herself ppr 98 1

Bromige, out of a mural coronet or, a talbot's head az, eared gold *Fides servata dilat* 56 6

Bromilow, a demi lion rampant, holding in the dexter paw a cross crosslet fitchee 11 10

Bromley, Baron Montford, *see* Montford

Bromley, Chesh, Staffs, and Yorks, out of a ducal coronet or, a demi lion rampant arg, supporting a standard sa, flag gu, charged with a lion passant gardant of the first. cf 16. 7

Bromley, Shropsh, a lion's gamb erect arg cf 36 4

Bromley, Shropsh, a cock pheasant ppr cf 90. 8

Bromley, Sir Henry, Bart, Eaststoke, Notts, a pheasant sitting ppr *Pensez forte*

Bromley, Shropsh, same crest

Bromley-Davenport, *see* Davenport.

Bromley-Wilson, Maurice, Esquire, of Dallam Tower, Milnthorp, Westml (1) A crescent or, therefrom flames issuant ppr (*for Wilson*) (2) A pheasant ppr (*for Bromley*)

Brompton, a lion rampant or 1 13

Bromwich, out of a ducal coronet or, a unicorn's head sa, guttee d'or cf 48 12

Bronan, *see* Brougham

Brond or **Brounde,** London and Suff, a demi-griffin or, holding a battle-axe embowed, the handle gu, the head arg 64 11

Bronker, Kent and Middx, a talbot passant gu, resting the dexter paw on a garland of flowers ppr cf 54 1

Bronker, Wilts, a cubit arm erect, vested sa, cuffed arg, holding in the hand ppr a lozenge of the first

Bronscomb or **Branscomb,** a lion regardant, ducally gorged and chained ppr 6 3

Brook, Chesh, a badger passant ppr cf 33 10

Brook, London, on a mount vert, in front of an oak-tree, a badger passant ppr, the dexter fore-paw resting on a chaplet or

Brook or **Brooke,** Bucks, a hawk's lure with the line formed into a bow knot between two wings, all ppr cf 110 10

Brook, a fleur-de lis arg, around it a serpent entwined ppr 148 8

Brooke, Bransby, Sonning, near Reading, Berks, a demi lion rampant guardant, holding between the paws an arrow in pale, point downwards ppr.

Brooke, Sir Richard Marcus, Bart, of Norton Priory, Chesh, a brock ppr *Faste without fraude* 33 10

Brooke, Earl of, and **Baron,** *see* Warwick, Earl of

Brooke of Mere Hall, Chester, a badger passant ppr *Vis unita fortior* cf 33 10

Brooke, John Townshend, Esquire, of Houghton Hall, Shifnel, Shropsh, on a mount vert a brock per pale sa and arg *Virtus est Dei*

Brooke, Lieutenant Colonel Arthur, of Brock Wood, Burwash, Sussex, and Junior United Service Club, St James's, a brock or badger ppr *Vis unita fortior* 33 10

Brooke, Harry Vesey, Esquire, J P, D L, of 1, Lauderdale Road, Maida Vale, N W, and Fairley Aberdeenshire, same crest *Gloria finis*

Brooke, Rev. James Mark Saurin, of 20, Gledhow Gardens: (1) A brock or badger ppr. 277. 10. (2) A dexter arm from the elbow, vested bendy sinister azure and sa., grasping an oak-root sa. *Ex fonte perenni. Reason contents me.* 277. 9

Brooke of Handford, Chester, same crest. *Pro avitâ fide.*

Brooke, William John, of Haughton Hall, Shropsh., a brock or badger ppr. *Virtus est Dei.*

Brooke, Sir Arthur Douglas, Bart., of Colebrook, co. Fermanagh, a brock passant arg. *cf.* 33. 10

Brooke, Edward, Esquire, of Pabo Hall, near Conway, a brock ppr. 33. 10

Brooke, Shropsh., on a mount vert, a badger passant ppr. 33. 12

Brooke, on an Eastern coronet a brock ppr., ducally gorged or. *Dum spiro spero.*

Brooke, a goat's head erased sa., armed and bearded or. 128. 5

Brooke, an Indian goat's head, bendy of six gu. and az., erased per fess or, eared and armed of the last.

Brooke, Yorks, a sword erect arg., hilted or, thereon two serpents entwined and respecting each other ppr. round the hilt. *Non est mortale quod opto.*

Brooke, Sir Thomas, Bart., of Armitage Bridge, Huddersfield, in front of a sword erect, point upwards, the blade entwined by two serpents respecting each other ppr., a boar's head erased sa. *Est nec astu.* 42. 13

Brooke, Edward, Esquire, of Thorpe Almondbury, Yorks, in front of a sword erect, the blade entwined by two serpents respecting each other ppr., a boar's head erased sa. *Est nec astu.*

Brooke, John Arthur, Esquire, of Fenay Hall, Huddersfield; Fearn Lodge, Ardgay, Ross-sh., Esquire, same crest and motto.

Brooke, John Kendall, Esquire, of Sibton Park, near Yoxford, Suff., same crest and motto.

Brooke, Ven. Joshua Ingham, Esquire, of the Vicarage, Halifax, same crest and motto.

Brooke, Rev. Richard England, M.A., Cambs, Grantchester, Dene, Bournemouth, same crest and motto.

Brooke, William, Esquire, of Northgate Mount, Honley, Yorks, same crest and motto.

Brooke, William, Esquire, same crest and motto.

Brooke, Edgar William, same crest and motto.

Brooke, Edward, of Ufford Place, Suff., on a chapeau gu., turned up erm., a wing erect and displayed of the first, charged with a chevron arg., and thereon a lion rampant sa., crowned or. 109. 2

Brooke, E. Arden, Esquire, 71, Ivy Road, Cricklewood, London, N.W., on a wreath of the colours, a brock passant ppr. *Vis unita fortior.*

Brooke, Hants, a lion rampant or. 1. 13

Brooke, Hants, a demi-lion rampant erased or. *cf.* 10. 2

Brooke, a demi-lion gu., holding between the paws a broad arrow or, feathered and headed arg.

Brooke, on a ducal coronet a cock ppr., combed and wattled gu. 90. 6

Brooke, a griffin's head erased, charged with a fess dancettée, and in base with a cross crosslet fitched gu. *cf.* 66. 2

Brooke, Staffs, a stork or crane or. 105. 11

Brooke, Shropsh., a heron or. 105. 9

Brooke, De Capel-, Sir Arthur Richard, Bart., of Oakley, Northamp., a demi-seahorse arg., maned and finned or. *Spes mea in Deo.* 46. 7

Brooke, Bart., Chester, a man in armour, holding in his dexter hand a spear, and on his sinister arm a shield, all ppr. 188. 4

Brooke, Bucks, out of a coronet or, a plume of six ostrich-feathers or and sa. alternately. *cf.* 114. 13

Brookes, on a mount a bear muzzled and chained. 34. 5

Brookes or **Brooks,** three organ-pipes, two in saltier, one in pale or, enfiled with a garland of laurel vert. *cf.* 168. 10

Brookesby, a boar's head couped gu., bristled or. 43. 1

Brookesby, a boar's head erect and erased gu., langued az., tusked arg. 43. 3

Brookfield, Arthur Montagu, Esquire, of Leasam, Rye, and of Kensington, London, a cubit arm erect in armour ppr., holding in the hand a sickle palewise, also ppr., and two ears of wheat in saltire, stalked and bladed or. *Beware the reaping.*

Brookfield, John Storrs, B.A., M.D., J.P., Middx., of Brondesbury, London, N.W., and Hill Place, Upminster, Essex, on a chapeau a brock, all ppr. 305. 9

Brooking, an escallop or, surmounted by a crescent az. *Crux fidei calcar.* *cf.* 141. 12

Brooking, a sword in pale, enfiled with a savage's head couped ppr. 191. 9

Brookman or **Brockman,** Kent, on a sword erect arg., hilt and pommel or, a stag's head cabossed ppr., attired of the second, the blade through the head and embrued at the point.

Brookman, a crane, holding in the dexter claw a stone. 105. 6

Brooks, *see* Burd-Brooks.

Brooks, *see* Close-Brooks.

Brooks, a badger ppr. 33. 10

Brooks, Maurice, Esquire, J.P., of Oaklawn, Bird Avenue, Milltown, Dublin, on a mount vert, a badger passant ppr., resting the dexter paw on a civic crown vert. *Respice, aspice, prospice.*

Brooks, Bedford, on a mural coronet an otter ppr. *Ut omnis vita labitur.*

Brooks, John Hatfield, J.P., D.L., Flitwick Manor, Ampthill, on a mural coronet an otter ppr. *Ut omnis vita labitur.* 292. 13

Brooks or **Brookes,** Scotland, a beaver passant. *Perseverando.* 134. 8

Brooks, a bear ppr., muzzled and chained. 34. 1

Brooks, Lancs, a demi-lion holding between the paws an arrow ppr. *Finem respice.*

Brooks, the late Sir William Cunliffe, Bart., of Barlow Hall, Manchester, a demi-lion arg., charged on the shoulder with a fountain, holding in the paws a harpoon in bend sinister ppr. *Finem respice.* 12. 14

Brooks, Lancs, a demi-lion rampant vert, charged on the shoulder with a fountain, and holding between the paws an anchor. *Finem respice.*

Brooks, Francis Augustus, M.D., St. Felix, Felixstowe, a dexter arm in armour embowed, holding in the hand the lower part of a broken tilting spear.

Brooks, a lion passant. 6. 2

Brooksbank, Yorks, a hart's head couped ppr., attired or, gorged with two bars wavy az.

Brooksbank, Edward Clithrow, Esquire, of Healhaugh Old Hall, Tadcaster, same crest.

Brooksbank, Walter Lamplugh, Esquire, of Lamplugh Hall and Manor of Lamplugh, same crest.

Brooksbank, William Lyon, Esquire, late of Bromley, Kent, a stag's head couped erm., attired or, charged with two bars nebuly az., and holding in the mouth a palm-branch slipped in bend vert.

Brooksbank, a stag statant ppr., attired or, gorged with a collar dancettée vert, therefrom pendent an escutcheon or, charged with a rose gu.

Broom and **Broome,** *see* Brome.

Broome, Heref., a demi-eagle or, winged sa., holding in the beak a slip of broom vert. *cf.* 80. 2

Broome, Notts, a cockatrice arg., winged az., beaked, legged, combed, and wattled gu. 68. 5

Broomfield, a hand issuing from a cloud in fess, pointing to a serpent, head erect ppr. 223. 7

Broomhead-Colton-Fox, Barnard Platts, Esquire, of Wales and of Sheffield, both in the West Riding of the county of York, Solicitor of the Supreme Court of Judicature: (1) In the centre, on a wreath of the colours, a fox passant gu., guttée-d'or, resting the dexter fore-paw upon an annulet encircling an escallop, both or (*for Fox*). (2) On the dexter side, on a wreath of the colours, upon a rock ppr., in front of a cross crosslet erect and fitchée sa., a boar passant arg., charged on the body with two roses gu., barbed and seeded ppr. (*for Colton*). (3) Upon the sinister side, on a wreath of the colours in front of a unicorn's head erased erm., maned, horned, and holding in the mouth a fleur-de-lis or, a staff raguly fessewise, also or (*for Broomhead*). *Per fidem et patientiam.*

Bronté, Duke of, *see* Bridport, Viscount.

Broon, a branch of holly and a cross crosslet fitched in saltier. 166. 10

Broster, Chester, a dexter hand ppr., vested barry of five arg. and gu., holding a palm-branch vert.

Brothers, a demi-greyhound sa., holding in the feet a dart gu., feathered arg. *cf.* 60. 11

Brotherton, a hand holding a club in pale ppr. *cf.* 214. 6

Brotherton of Stubbings House, Maidenhead: (1) An eagle displayed ppr. 75. 2. (2) A bear's head erased at the neck arg., holding in the mouth an arrow or, pheoned and feathered of the first.

Brouchan, *see* Brougham.

Brough, a swan ppr. 99. 2

Brough, William Spooner, Esquire, Leek, a swan's head and neck erased *Sincerite*

Brough, Lincs, a lion sejant, collared and lined or 7 4

Brough, Scotland, a buffalo's head sa 44 1

Brougham and Vaux, Baron (Brougham), Brougham Hall, Penrith, Westml, an arm in armour embowed, holding in the gauntlet a lucy arg, and charged on the elbow with a rose gu *Pro rege, lege, grege* 236 2

Brougham, Broughan, Bronhan, and **Brouchan,** Wales, out of a ducal coronet gu, a dexter hand brandishing a sword ppr 212 11

Broughton, Essex and Beds, an eagle's head erased sa, holding in its beak a snake arg, and charged on the breast with two chevrons of the last

Broughton-Rouse, Edward Broughton, M A, LL M, Corpus Christi College, Cambridge (1) A man's head affrontee, couped at the shoulders, the hair and beard sa, bound with a fillet arg (*for Rouse*) 190 13 (2) Three ostrich feathers arg, issuing from the wreath (*for Broughton*) *La fortune passe partout —Dii facientes adjuvant* 115 2

Broughton, Berks, out of a ducal coronet or, a boar's head sa, bristled of the first, gorged with a collar arg, charged with three escallops gu cf 41 4

Broughton, Sir Delves Louis, Bart, of Broughton, Staffs and Chesh, a sea-dog's head gu, eared and finned arg

Broughton, Shropsh, a talbot passant gu *Another*, a talbot statant gu 54 1

Broughton, Somers, on a mount vert, a spaniel couchant erm cf 57 11

Broughton, Staffs, a squirrel sejant gu cf 135 4

Broughton, Shropsh, an owl arg, charged on the breast with three snakes in fret vert cf 96 5

Broughton, Baron, *see* Hobhouse

Broughton-Adderley, Hubert John, Esquire, of Barlaston Hall, Stoke-on Trent, Coton Hall, Sudbury Derbysh, on a chapeau gu, turned up erm, a stork arg

Broun, Sir William, Bart., of Colstoun, Scotland, a lion rampant, holding in its dexter paw a fleur de lis or *Floreat majestas* 2 7

Broun, Lieutenant-Colonel, Montague Cecil, Cavalry Club, Piccadilly, W, on a ducal coronet or, a lion rampant ppr, holding in his dexter paw a fleur-de-lis or *Floreat majestas* 291 8

Broun-Morison, John Broun, Esquire, D L, J P, R C A (King's Body guard of Scotland), of Finderlie Kinross, and Murie, Perthsh (1) On the dexter side three Moors' heads conjoined in one neck ppr, banded or, one looking upwards, the others to the dexter and sinister (*for Morison*) 191 5 (2) On the sinister side a lion rampant ppr, holding in the dexter fore-paw a fleur de lis arg (*for Brown*) *Prudentia præstat —Floreat majestas* 2 7

Broun of Johnstounburn, co Haddington, a rose slipped and barbed ppr *Armat et ornat*

Broun, same crest and motto

Broun, a dexter arm from the elbow erect, holding in the hand ppr a book 215 4

Broun, a vine ppr *Præmium virtutis honor* 152 9

Brouncker, an arm in armour embowed, holding in the gauntlet a sword ppr 195 1

Brouncker, Francis Henry Ernest, of Boveridge, Dorset, out of battlements sa, a dexter cubit arm vested arg, charged with two bendlets wavy of the first, holding in the hand ppr a lozenge in pale, also arg, charged with a cross pattee sa *Duty* 207 1

Bround or **Brounde,** Suff, a demi griffin or, holding a battle axe embowed arg, the handle gu cf 64 11

Brounker, Ireland, the Roman fasces ppr 171 4

Brounker, a lion's gamb erased ppr, holding a bezant 39 13

Brounlee, a demi-peacock issuing ppr 103 10

Browell, a dexter hand holding a scimitar ppr 213 5

Browell, the late Rev William Robert, of the Rectory, Beaumont, Essex, a rock ppr, thereon in front of an anchor cabled in bend sinister sa, an eagle rising, also ppr *Virtute quam astutia*

Brown of Clonboy, co Clare, an eagle displayed *Virtus dabit, cura servabit* 75 2

Brown, *see* M'Kerrell-Brown

Brown, Worcs, a demi eagle displayed, with two heads az, charged on the breast with the Roman fasces erect, surmounting two swords in saltire and encircled by a chaplet or

Brown, Rev Dixon Dixon, of Unthank Hall, Northumb, two escallops or, thereon resting an eagle displayed vert holding in the beak a cross crosslet fitchee of the first *Suivez raison* cf 74 11

Brown, Thomas Edwin Burton Esquire of Ryslaw, 185, Willesden Lane Brondesbury, an eagle displayed *Spectemur agendo*

Brown and **Browne,** an eagle displayed vert. *Suivez la raison* 75 8

Brown, Warw, an eagle regardant, holding in his dexter talon a fleur-de-lis or *Labor omnia vincit* cf 76 6

Brown, Forsyth- (1) An eagle rising regardant ppr, holding in its dexter talon a fleur de lis or (*for Broun*) (2) A demi-griffin az, issuant out of an antique crown or (*for Forsyth*) *Labor omnia vincit —Instaurator ruinæ*

Brown, Robert, junior, F S A, Priestgate House, Barton-on-Humber, a demi eagle displayed ppr *Fortitudine et prudentia*

Brown, an eagle displayed vert, crowned with a mural coronet or, and charged on the breast with a garland of laurel of the last *Suivez moi* cf 74 14

Brown, an eagle's head erased ppr *Vi et virtute* 83 2

Brown, Herts, a griffin's head erased sa, beaked and eared or, charged on the neck with a bar-gemelle arg and a trefoil slipped erm *Si sit prudentia* cf 66 4

Brown, of Compton Ashbourne, Derbysh, and Southport, Lancs in front of a gryphon's head erased per pale sa and arg, gorged with a collar flory counter-flory counterchanged, five bezants fessewise *Si sit prudentia* 302 6

Brown and **Browne,** a griffin's head erased or 66 2

Brown, Scotland, a cock ppr *Docendo disco* 91 2

Brown and **Browne,** Durh, a stork's head couped at the neck, nowed ppr, between two wings arg

Brown of London, a hawk ppr, belled or, standing on a bird's leg erased à la quise and conjoined to a wing all gu *Nil sine causa*

Brown, on a lure a falcon rising ppr cf 87 1

Brown, Norf, on a mount vert, an ostrich arg, winged, beaked, legged, and collared or cf 97 2

Brown, a lion passant 6 2

Brown, Berks, a lion rampant *Spero* 1 13

Brown, Scotland, a lion rampant ppr *Famæ studiosus honestæ* 1 13

Brown, Scotland, a lion rampant *Spero* 1 13

Brown, Scotland, a lion rampant charged with a cinquefoil between two fleurs-de lis *Si sit prudentia*

Brown, a lion rampant, holding in the dexter paw a fleur-de-lis or *Floreat majestas* 2 7

Brown, Adam, Esquire, of Hamilton, Ontario, a lion rampant charged with a fleur de lis or *Floreat majestas* cf 1 13

Brown, Scotland, a lion rampant sa, holding in his dexter fore-paw a fleur-de lis or *Floreat majestas* 2 7

Brown, Scotland, a lion rampant ppr, holding in his dexter fore paw a cross crosslet fitchee gu, and in his sinister a fleur de-lis or *Vitam impendere vero*

Brown, Scotland, a demi-lion gu, holding in the dexter paw a fleur-de lis or *Floreat majestas* 13 2

Brown, James Millar, Esquire, of the Buluwayo Club, Buluwayo, South Africa, a demi lion rampant vert, holding in his dexter paw a fleur-de lis or *Floreat majestas*

Brown, a demi lion rampant ppr, holding in the dexter paw a fleur-de-lis or 13 2

Brown, Andrew Cassels, M D, Dacre Hill, Rock Ferry, Cheshire, same crest *Floreat majestas*

Brown, same crest *Gaudeo*

Brown, same crest. *Tandem licet sero*

Brown, a demi lion rampant, holding in the dexter paw a trefoil vert cf 13 13

Brown, Yorks, a demi-lion rampant erased or, between two elephants' trunks ppr *Persevera Deoque confido*

Brown, William James, Esquire, of Burghwallis Hall, Doncaster, Mibigill Lodge, co. Sutherland, same crest and motto

Brown, Candler-, Ireland, a demi lion rampant gu, holding between the paws a fleur-de-lis erminois, and charged on the shoulder with a cross crosslet arg *Gaudeo* cf 13 5

Brown, Bart, Westminster and Scotland, a demi-lion gu, holding in the dexter paw a fleur de lis or. 13 2

Brown, Sir John, of Endcliffe Hall, Sheffield, a lion sejant ppr., charged with two barrulets sa., and supporting with the dexter paw an escutcheon arg., thereon a bee volant, also ppr. *Nec sorte, nec fato.* 8. 1

Brown, John, Esquire, of Caxton Road, Broomhill, Sheffield, same crest and motto.

Brown, Sir William Richmond, Bart., of Astrop, Northamp., a bear's paw erect and erased arg., issuant out of a wreath of oak vert, and holding a sinister hand ppr. *Est concordia fratrum.* 37. 9

Brown, Sir Alexander Hargreaves, of Broome Hall, Holmwood, Surrey, and 12, Grosvenor Gardens, London, S.W., same crest and motto. 254. 7

Brown, a lion's gamb erect and erased gu., holding a wing arg.

Brown-Gilpin of Sedbury Park, Yorks: (1) A lion's gamb erased arg., armed and charged with a bar gemelle gu., the paw holding two eagle's wings conjoined sa. (*for Brown*). 37. 11. (2) An arm embowed in armour, the hand grasping a branch of laurel, all ppr. (*for Gilpin*). *cf.* 199. 12

Brown of Woodplumpton, Lancs, a lion's gamb erased or, fretty, and holding a mullet of six points sa.

Brown or **Broun,** Scotland, a vine-tree ppr. *Præmium virtutis honor.* 152. 9

Brown, Scotland, a rose gu., stalked and leaved ppr. *Armat et ornat.* 149. 5

Brown, Germany and Scotland, a dolphin naiant ppr. *Virtus dedit, cura servabit.* 140. 5

Brown, Walter, Esquire, of Currie, Gorebridge, Midlothian, and 21, Ann Street, Edinburgh, N.B., a ship under sail ppr. *Caute et sedulo.* 270. 3

Brown, a ship under sail ppr. *Caute et sedulus.*

Brown, Scotland, a ship in full sail in the sea, all ppr. *Deus adesto.* 160. 13

Brown, Horatio Robert Forbes, Esquire, a ship in the sea firing the signal for sailing, all ppr. *Deus adesto.*

Brown, on a mount a hare current ppr. 136. 3

Brown, Sir William Roger, of Highfield, Hilperton, Wilts, in front of a cubit arm erect, vested az., cuffed arg., the hand ppr. holding a balance suspended gold, a mount vert, thereon a garb fessewise or. *Fortuna et labore.*

Brown, a hare courant ppr. *cf.* 136. 3

Brown-Borthwick, London, a hand ppr., holding a fleur-de-lis or. *Delectat et ornat.* *cf.* 215. 5

Brown, Scotland, a hand holding an open book ppr. *Deus evehit pios.* 215. 10

Brown, a dexter hand holding a sword, all ppr. *La vertu est la seule noblesse.* 212. 13

Brown, Alfred, Esquire, of Durhan, Natal, a hillock vert, in front of a dexter arm embowed in armour, the hand grasping a dagger, the point to the dexter ppr., pommel and hilt or, pendent from the arm by a riband gu., an escutcheon or, charged with an oak-tree eradicated ppr. *Honor meus vita mea.*

Brown, Sir Charles Gage Brown, K.C.M.G., M.D., F.R.C.P., LL.D., of 88, Sloane Street, S.W., a cubit arm erect holding in the hand a steering-wheel, all ppr. *Spes ultra.*

Brown, Charles Herbert Gage, Esquire, of 85, Cadogan Place, S.W., same crest and motto.

Brown, Scotland, a hand holding a closed book ppr. *Delectat et ornat.* 215. 4

Brown or **Browne,** Scotland and Ireland, an arm in armour embowed, couped at the shoulder and resting the elbow on the wreath, holding in the hand a sword ppr.

Brown, Cornish-: (1) A demi-man ppr., wreathed round the temples or and gu., charged on the body with five escallops saltireways or, and holding in the dexter hand a battle-axe ppr. (*for Brown*). (2) Upon a ragged staff or, a Cornish chough, wings expanded ppr. (*for Cornish*). *Deus pascit corvos.* *cf.* 107. 3

Brown Westhead-, George Marion York, Shelton, Stoke-on-Trent: (1) Within a fetterlock or, a Saracen's head couped ppr., wreathed round the temples arg. and sa. (2) A demi-eagle displayed with two heads az., charged on the breast with the fasces erect surmounting two swords in saltire, and encircled by a chaplet or. *Ora et labora.*

Brown, out of a vallary coronet or, a buck's head sa., attired or. *f.* 120. 7

Browne, Marquess of Sligo, *see* Sligo.

Browne, Baron Kilmaine, *see* Kilmaine.

Browne, Earl of Kenmare, *see* Kenmare.

Browne-Cave, *see* Cave.

Browne, Baptist-, *see* Baptist.

Browne, Bart., of Johnstown, Dublin, an eagle displayed vert. *Suivez la raison.* 75. 8

Browne, du Moulin-, Charles Anthony, Esquire, of Rusina, Leamington: (1) An eagle displayed vert (*for Browne*). 75. 8. (2) A leopard's face or, transfixed through the mouth with two tilting-spears saltirewise ppr., and surmounted by a fleur-de-lis gu. *Suivez raison.—In te Domine speravi.* 22. 8

Browne of Liverpool, Lancs, an eagle displayed with two heads per pale az. and gu., the wings or, and each wing charged with a fleur-de-lis sa. *cf.* 74. 2

Browne, Hon. Thomas Hillman, of Guildford Lodge, Queenstown, Cape Colony, an eagle displayed vert. *Suivez raison.* 75. 8

Browne, Lancs, an eagle displayed arg., charged on the wings with two bars sa. *cf.* 75. 2

Browne, Knox-: (1) An eagle displayed with two heads vert, charged on each wing with a fleur-de-lis or (*for Browne*). *cf.* 74. 2. (2) On a perch a falcon close ppr., charged on the breast with a pheon sa. (*for Knox*). *Suivez raison.—Moveo et proficio.* *cf.* 85. 13

Browne, Thomas Browne, Esquire, of Newgrove, co. Clare, Ireland, an eagle displayed with two heads per pale arg. and sa., the dexter wing charged with a pellet and the sinister with a plate. *Nec timeo, nec sperno.* 74. 4

Browne, Windham, Esquire, an eagle displayed with two heads per pale arg. and sa., the dexter wing charged with a pellet, and the sinister with a plate. *Nec timeo, nec sperno.* 74. 4

Browne of Janeville, Down, an eagle displayed vert. *Suivez la raison.* 75. 8

Browne, Dodwell Francis, Esquire, of Rathian, Castlebar, co. Mayo, and Colombo, Ceylon, same crest and motto.

Browne, Captain Dominick Sidney, J.P., D.L., and High Sheriff, 1896, of Breaghwy, Castlebar, and 3, Berkeley House, Berkeley Square, W., an eagle displayed vert. *Suivez raison.*

Browne, Henry George, Esquire, of Montcagle, Shanklin, Isle of Wight, same crest and motto.

Browne, Rev. Henry George Cavendish, B.A., of the Rectory, Bredon, Tewkesbury, same crest and motto.

Browne, Sir James Frankfort Manners, K.C.B., of 19, Roland Gardens, S.W., same crest and motto.

Browne, Robert John, Esquire, of Ceolarne, Silchester Road, Kingstown, co. Dublin, same crest and motto.

Browne of Mount Kelly, Galway, same crest and motto.

Browne of Bronwylfa, co. Flint, an eagle displayed vert. *Spectemur agendo.* 75. 8

Browne, Sussex and Berks, same crest and motto.

Browne of Browne's Hill, co. Carlow, an eagle displayed with two heads sa. *Fortiter et fideliter.* 74. 2

Browne, on an Eastern crown or, an eagle displayed with two heads sa., *Hoc age.* *cf.* 74. 2

Browne, Arthur Blennerhassett, Esquire, of Riverstown, co. Cork, same crest and motto.

Browne, Essex, an eagle displayed with two heads sa. 74. 2

Browne, an eagle displayed with two heads per pale az. and gu., winged or. 74. 2

Browne, Bart., Sussex, an eagle displayed vert. 75. 8

Browne, Rev. Robert Melvill Gore, of East Woodhay Rectory, Newbury, same crest. *Suivez raison.*

Browne, William-, of Rathbane, Limerick, on a marquess's coronet ppr., an eagle displayed gu., winged and membered or *Suivez la raison.* *cf.* 75. 2

Browne, Kent, a vulture, wings addorsed, displuming a mallard's wing, all ppr. 79. 13

Browne, Galway, two eagles' heads couped and conjoined sa. *cf.* 84. 11

Browne, an eagle's head erased arg., holding in the beak an arrow ppr. *cf.* 83. 2

Browne, Wilts, a demi-eagle displayed or, surmounted by two palm-branches in saltire. *Suivez raison.* *cf.* 81. 6

Browne, a griffin's head erased gu. *Probitas veritas honos.* 66. 2

Browne of Moyne, Galway, a griffin's head erased arg. *Fortiter et fideliter.* 66. 2

Browne of Greenville, Galway, same crest and motto.

Browne, a griffin's head erased or, collared arg. *cf.* 66. 2

Browne of Caughley, Shropsh., a griffin's head erased per pale gu. and sa., gorged with a collar or, charged with two trefoils slipped vert.

Browne of Weymouth, Dorset, a griffin's head erased sa, beaked or 66 5

Browne of Tallantire Hall, Cumb, a griffin's head vert between two wings *Traducere ævum leniter* cf 67 7

Browne of Browne Hall, Mayo, a griffin's head erased arg, langued gu *Fortiter et fideliter* 66 2

Browne, Heref, a demi-griffin vert winged and legged or

Browne, a demi griffin vert, wings elevated or 64 5

Browne, Notts, a cock pheasant az, combed and beaked gu, collared or 90 10

Browne, Beale-, Desmond John Edward, Salperton, Gloucester (1) (Browne) A demi-eagle double headed displayed sa, charged on the breast with a leopard's face or (*for Browne*) (2) A unicorn's head erased arg semee of estoiles gu (*for Beale*) *Sperat in Deo*

Browne, a peewit arg, in a nest or

Browne of Norwich, out of a ducal coronet a crane's claw, all ppr cf 113 13

Browne, a stork's head couped at the neck and nowed ppr, between two wings arg

Browne of Islington, a crane az, beaked and legged or, the crown of the head gu, holding in the beak an ear of wheat of the second cf 105 14

Browne, on a mural coronet gu, a crane's head erased erm, charged on the neck with an escallop az *Verum atque decens* cf 104 10

Browne, a stork's head holding in the beak an acorn slipped vert, fructed or, between two wings expanded az each charged with an escallop of the second

Browne, Shropsh, out of a mural coronet gu, a stork's head erm cf 104 10

Browne, Suff, a demi stork, wings expanded ppr, the neck nowed

Browne, Norf., on a chapeau a crane *Pietate* 105 3

Browne, a crane's head and neck erased az, ducally gorged or, holding in the beak a bezant

Browne, Ireland, out of a mural crown gu, a stork's head and neck erm, beaked az cf 104 10

Browne, Dorset, on a mount vert, a hare current arg 136 3

Browne, Derbysh, a lion rampant arg, ducally crowned or, supporting a tilting spear ppr, headed of the first

Browne, a demi-lion ducally gorged and chained or cf 10 7

Browne, a lion rampant ppr 1 13

Browne, Chester, a demi-lion rampant arg *In te Deus speravi* 10 2

Browne, Sir Benjamin Chapman, J P, of Westacres, Newcastle on-Tyne, a demi-lion rampant ppr. *Ne cede malis*

Browne, a demi-lion rampant ppr *Ne cede malis*

Browne, a lion sejant sa, resting the dexter paw on an escutcheon arg, charged with a mullet of the first cf 8 1

Browne, Bucks, a heraldic tiger az, maned, tufted, and armed or cf 25 5

Browne, Charles Michael Edward, Esquire, of L'Hermitage, St Cyre, Indre et Loire, France, same crest *Qui non ciconia tigris*

Browne, Middx, a tiger passant ppr 24 7

Browne, a bear's paw couped and erect or, grasping a falchion arg 38 13

Browne, out of a mural coronet or, a tiger's head sa cf 27 1

Browne, Suff, a lion's gamb erased and erect gu, holding a ring arg

Browne, a lion's gamb erased and erect gu, holding a wing arg

Browne, Middx, a buck's head erased ppr, attired or 121. 2

Browne, Sussex, a stag ppr, attired, ducally gorged, and lined or cf 117. 5

Browne, Leics, a boar's head erased sa, pierced through the neck with a broken spear or, headed arg

Browne-Lecky, Conolly William Lecky, Esquire, of Aughentaine Castle, co Tyrone Ireland (1) A boar's head erased ppr, charged with a rose gu (*for Lecky*) (2) A lion rampant or, resting his sinister fore-paw on an escutcheon gu, charged with a fleur-de-lis or (*for Brown*) *Utere dum potes*

Browne-Lecky, Raymond Saville, Esquire, of Aughentain, co Tyrone, Ireland (1) A boar's head erased ppr, charged with a rose gu (*for Lecky*) (2) A lion rampant or, resting his sinister fore paw on an escutcheon gu, charged with a fleur-de lis or (*for Brown*) *Utere dum potes*

Browne, a bull salient ppr, collared and lined or

Browne, John Michael, Hall Court, Heref, a bull salient ppr, collared and chained or 64. 5

Browne, a sword erect arg, embrued at the point gu cf 170 2

Browne, on a mount vert, three anchor-stocks sa, two in saltire and one in pale, enfiled by a crown arg

Browne, Herts, a dragon's head arg, guttee de-poix, between two wings expanded sa, guttee-d'eau 72 7

Browne, Devonsh and Heref, a demi-man sa, wreathed about the middle and temples, holding in his dexter hand a hammer or cf 186 11

Browne of Wymondham Norf (1) An escallop arg, charged with a cross moline gu, between four torteaux cf 141 14 (2) A demi talbot rampant arg, pellettee, holding a spear erect or

Browne, Norf, an arm erect vested bendy or and az, holding in the hand ppr a fetterlock gu

Browne of London, a bee-hive with bees volant ppr *Virtus et industria* 137 7

Browne of London, a cubit arm vested gu, cuffed arg, holding in the hand ppr a sword erect, also ppr, hilted or, enfiled with a leopard's head of the second *Virtus curâ servabit*

Browne an arm couped and erect vested az, cuffed erm, holding in the hand ppr a caltrap or cf 206 14

Browne, Limerick, an armed arm holding a sword ppr *Fidem servabo genusque* 210. 2

Browne, Shropsh, a man's leg couped at the knee booted and spurred ppr

Browne of Writtle, Essex, a breastplate or, leathered sa, buckled of the first, issuant above a plume of feathers arg and gu

Browne, Wexford, Ireland, a stag's head erased arg, attired or, guttee de-sang 121. 2

Browne-Clayton, William Clayton, of Brown's Hill, co Carlow, an eagle displayed with two heads sa. *Fortiter et fideliter*

Brownell, Yorks, an escallop arg 141 14

Brownell, Derbysh, out of a ducal coronet a triple plume of twelve ostrich feathers arg, five, four, and three. 114 6

Brownfield, a lion passant arg, semee of pheons gu, supporting with the dexter paw a cross pattee fitchee or *Laborant numen adest*

Brownhill, Scotland, the sun rising from behind a mountain ppr *Radii omnia lustrant* cf 162 7

Browning of Comley, Glouc, on a chapeau gu, turned up erm, a pair of wings endorsed

Browning, out of a ducal coronet a cockatrice's head cf 68 13

Browning, Ireland, a dexter arm embowed holding in the hand a battle-axe ppr 201 5

Browning, a sinister arm from the elbow issuing from a cloud in the dexter, the hand above a serpent's head, erect from the middle, and looking toward the sinister ppr 223 7

Browning, George Elliot, Eden Bank, Wetheral Cumb, a sinister arm from the elbow issuing from a cloud in the sinister, the hand above a serpent's head erect from the middle and looking toward the dexter ppr *In Deo salus* 302 8

Browning, Thomas Wise, Carass Court, Croom, co Limerick, a lion's head erased ppr

Browning, Oscar, King's College, Cambs, on a cap of maintenance party per fess az and arg, a pair of wings addorsed *Be just and fear not —Pour le Roy et la Loy*

Brownlee and Brownlie, Scotland, an arm in armour brandishing a sword 210 2

Brownlee and Bronlie, a demi peacock issuing ppr 103 10

Brownlee and Brownlie, Scotland, an eagle displayed, charged on the breast with an annulet cf 75 2

Brownlow, Ireland, a goat's head erased arg 128 5

Brownlow, Ireland, a goat's head erased arg, collared gu cf 128 7

Brownlow, Earl (Cust), Belton House, Grantham, Lincs, a lion's head erased sa, gorged with a collar paly, wavy of six arg and az *Esse quam videri* 18. 6

Brownlow, London and Lincs, on a chapeau gu, turned up erm, a greyhound passant or, collared of the first cf 58 4

Brownlow, Baron, Lurgan, on a chapeau az, turned up erm, a greyhound statant gu *Esse quam videri* 58 4

Brownlow, General Sir Charles Henry, G C B, of Warfield Hall, Bracknell, Berks, upon a chapeau az, turned up erm, a greyhound gu, collared or *Esse quam videri*

Brownrig or **Brownrigg,** a lion rampant holding in his dexter paw a fleur de-lis ppr 2 7

Brownrigg, Sir Douglas Egremont, Bart., White Waltham, Maidenhead. (1) As an augmentation, a demi-Kandian holding in the dexter hand a sword, and in his sinister the crown of Kandy. (2) Out of a mural coronet or, a sword erect ppr., pommel and hilt of the first, entwined by a serpent vert. *Virescit vulnere virtus.*

Brownrigg, a sword erect environed by a snake, all ppr.

Brownsmith, in a frame lozenge-shaped, five arrows points downward, one in pale, four in saltier. 173. 4

Brownsword, a pegasus current ppr. 47. 1

Broxholme, Lincs, a bear statant against an elm-tree, all ppr.

Broyn, two lion's gambs sa., holding up an escutcheon arg. 39. 1

Bruce, *see* Baron Balfour of Burleigh.

Bruce, Baron Thurlow, *see* Thurlow.

Bruce, Brudenell-, Marquess of Ailesbury and **Earl Bruce**, *see* Ailesbury.

Bruce, Earl of Elgin, *see* Elgin.

Bruce, Baron Aberdare, *see* Aberdare.

Bruce, *see* Cumming-Bruce.

Bruce, *see* Hamilton-Tyndall-Bruce.

Bruce of Kennet, Clackmannan, a hand holding a sceptre ppr. *Fuimus.*

Bruce, Knight-, Lewis Bruce, Rivermead, Sunbury: (1) A cubit arm in armour in bend grasping a sceptre, all ppr. (*for Bruce*). (2) On a spur lying fesseways or, a hawk with wings elevated ppr. (*for Knight*). *Fuimus.*

Bruce, Sir William Cuningham, Bart., of Vyëra, Ascot, Berks, on a chapeau ppr. an arm from the shoulder couped and embowed fessewise in armour holding in the hand a sceptre ensigned on the point with an open crown, all ppr. *Fuimus*; also, *Do well and doubt not.* *cf.* 197. 4

Bruce, Kilroot, co. Antrim, a cubit arm holding a scimitar ppr. *Do well and doubt nought.* 213. 5

Bruce of Scoutbush, Ireland, a hand holding a scimitar ppr. *Do well, doubt nought.* 213. 5

Bruce, Scotland, a horse's head erased arg., bridled gu. *Be true.* *cf.* 51. 4

Bruce, James, Esquire, of the Manor House, Benburb, co. Tyrone, a horse's head arg., bridled gu., and charged on the neck with a cinquefoil of the last. *Do well and doubt not.*

Bruce, William Robert, Esquire, of Rockford, Blackrock, Dublin, same crest and motto.

Bruce, John, J.P., 21, Drumsheugh Gardens, Edinburgh, a cubit arm erect holding a heart ppr.

Bruce, John, of Sumburgh, Shetland Islands, same crest and motto.

Bruce, Samuel, Esquire, of Norton Hall, Campden, Glouc., a horse's head couped arg. *Do well and doubt not.*

Bruce, Henry Le Geyt, K.C.B., a lion statant az. *Fuimus.*

Bruce, a horse's head erased sa., bridled gu. *Fuimus.* *cf.* 51. 4

Bruce of Pittarthie, Scotland, a horse's head couped and furnished ppr. *True.* 5. 5

Bruce, Newton, Scotland, an eagle's head couped ppr. *Spes mea superne.* 83. 1

Bruce, Mowance, Scotland, a dexter hand holding a heart ppr. *Omnia vincit amor.* 216. 9

Bruce, Scotland, a naked arm embowed issuing out of a cloud and holding a human heart ppr. *Semper fidelis.*

Bruce, Scotland and England, a lion passant az. (*Another*, or.) 6. 2

Bruce, Robert, Esquire, of 6, Warwick Square, London, S.W., a lion passant az., holding in his dexter paw a trefoil slipped ppr. *Fuimus.*

Bruce, Sir Henry Hervey, Bart., Downhill, co. Londonderry, Ireland, a lion passant az., holding in his dexter paw a trefoil slipped vert. *Fuimus.* *cf.* 6. 5

Bruce of Balcaskie, Scotland, the setting sun ppr. *Irrevocabile.*

Bruce, Scotland, a star or. *Ad summa virtus.* 164. 3

Bruce, Scotland, a lion rampant. *Fuimus.* 1. 13

Bruce of Wester Kinloch, Scotland, a star or. *Ad summa virtus.* 164. 3

Bruce of Garvet, Scotland, a hand holding a sword ppr. *Venture forward.* 212. 13

Bruce, Scotland, an arm embowed, holding in the hand a cutlass, all ppr. *Do well, doubt nought.* 201. 2

Bruce of Arnot, Scotland, the sun rising from a cloud ppr. *Nec me qui, cætera vincit.* 162. 5

Bruce, Robert Cathcart, M.D., 10, Courtfield Road, S.W., on a cap of dignity a dexter arm in armour couped at the shoulder and embowed fessewise holding in the hand a sceptre ensigned with an open crown, all ppr. *Fuimus.*

Bruce, Hon. Sir Gainsford, of Yewhurst, Bromley, Kent, in front of a torch erect fired ppr., a lion statant with tail extended or, charged on the body with two fleurs-de-lis fesseways gu. *Do well and doubt not.*

Bruce, Sir George Barclay, K.B., of 64, Boundary Road, London, N.W., same crest, and *Be trew.*

Bruch, a demi-eagle displayed sa. 81. 6

Bruckshaw or **Bruckshow**, a sea-chart ppr. 159. 11

Brudenal and **Brudenell**, a battle-axe in pale surmounted by a branch of laurel and a branch of rue in saltier ppr. *cf.* 172. 12

Brudenell-Bruce, *see* Ailesbury, Marquess of.

Brudenell, Leics. and Northamp.: (1) An arm embowed covered with leaves vert, holding in the hand ppr. a spiked club or, slung to the arm with a line of the last. 199. 1. (2) A talbot arg., ducally gorged gu. *cf.* 54. 2. (3) A sea-horse arg. *En grace affie.* 46. 5

Brudnell, a sea-horse arg. *En grace affie.* 46. 5

Bruen, *see* Bruning.

Bruen or Bruin, a pedlar ambulant arg., with a crutch in his dexter hand and a pack on his back or.

Bruen, Chesh., a fisherman vested per pale arg. and sa., counterchanged, holding in his dexter hand a fisherman's staff, and in his sinister a landing-net thrown over the shoulder or.

Bruer, a mermaid ppr. 184. 5

Bruere, out of a mural crown per pale arg. and or, a cubit arm erect, vested gu., cuffed of the first, holding in the hand a halbert in bend sinister ppr.

Bruges, De, a cross Calvary gu. 166. 1

Bruges, an anchor erect sa., charged with a saltire or, entwined by the cable ppr. *Omne solum forti patria.* *cf.* 102. 2

Bruges, Ludlow-, William Penruddocke, of Seend, near Melksham: (1) Same crest as above. (2) A demi-marten couped sa. *Mihi cœlum portus.—Omni solum forti patria.*

Bruges, London, on an anchor sa., stock or, a scroll with the motto *Mihi cœlum portus.* *cf.* 161. 1

Bruges, Glouc., Wilts, and Essex, a Saracen's head in profile, couped at the shoulders ppr., vested arg., semée of torteaux, and wreathed of the second and sa.

Bruget, out of a ducal coronet or, a swan's head and neck between two wings arg. *cf.* 101. 6

Bruin, *see* Bruen.

Bruining, *see* Bruning.

Brumfield, a pheon az. 174. 11

Brumherd, a mermaid with a comb and a glass, all ppr. 184. 5

Brummel or **Brummell**, a dove with an olive-branch ppr. 92. 5

Brumstead, a demi-griffin arg., wings elevated or, holding in the dexter claw a cross formée fitched gu. *cf.* 64. 2

Brun, a stag lodged sa. 115. 7

Brune, a goat passant arg., armed or. *cf.* 129. 5

Brune-Prideaux, Cornw. and Dorset, a man's head in profile couped at the shoulders, on the head a chapeau gules, turned up arg.

Brune, Prideaux-, Charles Glynn, of Prideaux Place, Padstow, Cornw.: (1) A goat passant per pale indented arg. and sa., armed and ungu. or, pendent from a collar gu. a shield, thereon the arms of Brune, viz., azure, a cross moline or (*for Brune*). (2) As above (*for Prideaux*). *Toujours prêt.*

Bruneck, an eagle's head erased sa. 83. 2

Brunet, a cockatrice displayed gu. 68. 14

Bruning, Bruen, Bruining, a demi-lion double queued gu., guttée-d'eau, ducally crowned arg.

Brunner, Sir John Tomlinson, Bart., Druids Cross, Wavertree, Liverpool, in front of a wing erect gu., a fountain playing ppr., charged on the basin with a rose gu. *Bibe si sapis.* 234. 1

Brunsell, Notts, a lion's gamb erased or, holding a rose arg., stalked and leaved vert. 37. 10

Brunsfield and **Brunsfields**, Scotland, a demi-chevalier brandishing a sword ppr. 187. 1

Brunton, a beacon in flames ppr. *Fax mentis incendium gloriæ.* 177. 14

Brunton, an anchor sa. 161. 1

Brunwin, a lion's head erased or, fretty sa. 17. 8

Bruse, out of a ducal coronet or, a lion's head gu. 17. 5

Bruse, Norf., a Saracen's head in profile ppr., wreathed arg. and gu. 190. 14

Bruse, an eagle rising regardant ppr. 77. 4

Bruse, out of a ducal coronet or, a demi-lion az. 16. 3

Brusell and **Brussell**, a lion's head erased gu 17 2

Bruskett, out of a ducal coronet or, a demi-lion az 16 3

Bruton or **Brutyn**, Exeter, a demi wolf ducally crowned holding between the paws a mullet ppr cf 31 6

Brutton, a cat sejant gardant ppr 26 8

Brutton, a sphere ppr 159 1

Bruyer and **Bruyeres**, a bear's paw erased cf 36 6

Bruyn or **Bruyn**, Surrey and Essex, a goat arg, armed or 129 5

Bruyn and **Bruyne**, on a chapeau gu, an ibex of the same

Bruzead, a cat sejant sa cf 26 8

Bryan, Loftus Anthony, Esquire, of Upton and Borrmount, co Wexford, Ireland, on a mural crown ppr, a lion rampant gu, collared gemelle or, and charged on the shoulder with a cinquefoil arg *Ferro mea recupero.*

Bryan, a greyhound current regardant erm, collared or cf 58 2

Bryan, Kilkenny, a sword in pale ppr, pommel and hilt or, between two lions' gambs couped and erect gu *Fortis et fidelis*

Bryan, Kent, on a garb in fess a bird

Bryan, Wexford, a Saracen's head erased at the neck sa

Bryan, Ireland, a demi-savage ppr cf 186 5

Bryan, on a dexter hand couped in fess a hawk close ppr cf 86 8

Bryan, issuing out of clouds a naked arm embowed, the hand grasping a dagger, all ppr

Bryan, on a chapeau gu, turned up erm, a hunting horn sa, garnished or cf 228 11

Bryan, De, Ireland, a dexter hand holding an escallop-shell or 216 2

Bryant, Middx, out of a ducal coronet or, a demi lion az *Fortiter et fideliter* 16 3

Bryant, a flag az, charged with a saltier arg cf 176 13

Bryant, John Henry, M D, 8, Mansfield Street, Portland Place, W, same crest

Bryant, Thomas, Surgeon, 27, Grosvenor Street, W, same crest *Sub hoc signo vinces*

Bryce, a cock ppr holding in its beak an ear of corn cf 91 2

Bryce, a griffin's head erased or 66. 2

Bryce, Scotland, a dexter arm holding in the hand a cutlass ppr. *Do well, doubt nought* 213 5

Bryce, Scotland, out of a cloud in the sinister a dexter hand holding a pair of scales ppr *Fiat justitia*

Brydall, Middx, a lion's gamb erect and erased az, holding a broken lance arg, headed or 38 9

Bryden, Berwicksh, a hawk's head erased ppr, charged with three bezants, one and two *Keep watch* cf 88 12

Bryden, Scotland, a lion passant az 6 2

Brydges, Bart, Kent, the bust of a man, head ppr, hair and beard sa, vest arg, collar gu, cap or, band and tassel of the third, the cap and vest charged each with a pheon, the point downwards of the second

Brydges, Jones-, Sir Harford James, Bart, of Boultibrook, Heref (1) Two wings addorsed arg, each charged with a bend, engrailed sa (*for Brydges*) cf 109 12 (2) On a cushion gu, garnished and tasselled or, a representation of the royal crown of Persia (3) A crow sa, resting the dexter claw on the star of the Order of the Crescent (*for Jones*) *Deus pascit corvos*

Bryen or **Brian** (1) A beacon in flames or 177 14 (2) An heraldic tiger current az, bezantee cf 25 5

Bryers, Lancs, a nag's head erm 50 13

Brykes, a wolf's head erased pierced with an arrow ppr cf 30 8

Brykes or **Byrkes**, a wolf's head erased per pale or and az, holding in the mouth an arrow of the first feathered gu cf 30 8

Brymer, Scotland, a hand gauntleted holding a pheon ppr. *Per tela, per hostes* 211 7

Brymer, William Ernest, Esquire, of Ilsington House, Dorchester, and 8, St James's Street, London, a plume of six ostrich-feathers alternately gu and arg, charged with an escutcheon of the last, thereon a catherine-wheel of the first *Virtute*

Brymton, Brympton, and **Brumpton**, out of a ducal coronet ppr, a lion's gamb 36 12

Brympton and **Brumpton**, the same charged with a bezant cf 36 12

Bryne, a lion's gamb holding a hawk's lure, all ppr

Brysilly, a cock-pheasant purpure cf 90 8

Bryson, Brysoun, Bryssan, or **Bryssone**, Scotland, a spur rowel ppr 164 8

Bryson of Craigton, a hand holding a horn ppr *Ever ready.—Vivit post funera virtus* 217 4

Bryson, a ship under sail *God, with my right* 160. 13

Bubb of Carlisle, Cumb, on a mount vert, a unicorn sejant arg, crined and armed or, resting the dexter foot on a shield per pale of the last and erm

Bubb, Henry, Esquire, of Ullenwood near Cheltenham, same crest *Liberté tout entière*

Buccleuch and Queensbery, Duke of, (Montagu Douglas Scott, K G), Dalkeith House, Edinburgh, a stag trippant ppr, attired and ungu or *Amo* 117 8

Buch, a man's head in profile with ass's ears cf 190 6

Buchan, Earl of (**Erskine**), Gogmagog Hills, Cambridge, a dexter arm couped below the elbow holding a club, all ppr *Judge nought* cf 214 6

Buchan, Scotland, a demi-lion rampant holding between his paws a laurel branch ppr *Fortior qui melior*

Buchan, Scotland, a lion holding in his dexter paw a twig of olive ppr *Fortior quo milior*

Buchan, Scotland, a lion's head erased gu 17 2

Buchan, Ireland, a wolf sejant sa 29 3

Buchan, Scotland, a sunflower ppr *Non inferiora secutus* 157 12

Buchan, William, Esquire, Peebles, same crest and motto

Buchan, Scotland, the sun shining on a sunflower ppr *Fortior qui melior*

Buchan, Fordyce- (1) The sun shining on a sunflower in full bloom, all ppr (*for Buchan*) (2) A camel's head couped ppr (*for Fordyce*) *Non inferiora secutus* 132 7

Buchan, Major John Inverarity, of Finhaven, Stevenson Street, Studley Park, Kew, near Melbourne, an oak tree eradicated fesseways ppr, thereon a lion rampant per fesse indented or and az, holding in the dexter fore-paw a branch of laurels slipped, also ppr *Facta non verba*

Buchan-Hepburn, *see* Hepburn

Buchan-Sydserff, Thomas J P, of Ruchlaw Prestonkirk, Scotland, an eagle's head couped gu *Virtute promoveo*

Buchanan, *see* Leith Buchanan

Buchanan, *see* Fergusson Buchanan

Buchanan, Scotland, a dexter hand holding up a ducal cap ppr, tufted on the top with a rose gu, all within two laurel-branches in orle vert. *Clarior hinc honos* 217 2

Buchanan, Scotland, the same crest. *Audaces juvo*

Buchanan, Sir Eric Alexander, Bart, of Dunburgh, Stirlingsh, an armed dexter hand holding a cap of dignity purpure, the facing erm *Nunquam victus* cf 210 8

Buchanan, an armed dexter hand ppr, holding a ducal cap purpure, turned up erm *Nunquam victus* cf 210 8

Buchanan, Carrick- of Drumpellier House, Coatbridge, Lanarksh, a hand holding up a ducal cap purpure, tufted on the top with a rose gu, within two branches of laurel disposed orleways ppr *Audaces juvo*

Buchanan, Cross-, a cubit arm erect ppr, holding a sword, also ppr, hilted and pommelled or 212 9

Buchanan, Herbert Blackwood Esquire, of Throsk, Stirlingsh, a dexter hand grasping a scimitar ppr *Audaciter*

Buchanan, a dexter hand holding a dagger in pale ppr *Sanguine inscribam* 219 9

Buchanan, Scotland, a hand holding a sword ppr *God, with my right* 212 13

Buchanan, Scotland, a hand holding a sabre in bend ppr *Audacia et industria* 212 13

Buchanan, a dexter hand grasping a scimitar ppr *Audaciter* 213 5

Buchanan, of Ardoch, Dumbarton, two hands grasping a two-handed sword ppr *Clariora sequor* 213 3

Buchanan, Gray-, James Ross, Esquire, of Scotstown, Eastfield, Cambuslang, N B (1) Two hands grasping a two-handed sword ppr (*for Buchanan*). 213 3 (2) An anchor in the sea ppr (*for Gray*) *Clariora sequor.—Fast* 161 8

Buchanan, Scotland, a hand holding a lance in bend ppr *Secundo curo.* 214 11

Buchanan, Scotland, a dagger erect ppr *Nobilis est ira leonis* 169 2

Buchanan, Thomas Alexander, Esquire, of Powis, near Stirling, N B, a sword erect in pale ppr, hilted and pommelled or *Virtute gladii parvi.—Nobilis est ira leonis*

Buchanan, William Cross, Esquire, a cubit arm erect ppr., holding a sword, also ppr., pommel and hilt or.

Buchanan, William Frederick, Esquire, of Clar Innis, Sydney, N.S.W., and Killarney, Narrabii, N.S.W., in front of a dexter hand couped at the wrist ppr., holding an escutcheon sa., charged with a rose arg., barbed and seeded of the first, two branches of laurel slipped and fructed in saltire of the last. *Clarior hinc honos.* 269. 19

Buchanan, Scotland, a sinister arm embowed in fess, vested, holding in the hand a bent bow or. *Par sit fortuna labori.* 204. 11

Buchanan, Scotland and England, two hands conjoined and couped in fess. 224. 2

Buchanan, Scotland, a lion's gamb erased and erect ppr. *Nobilis est ira leonis.* 36. 4

Buchanan, Scotland, a dove holding in its beak an olive-branch, all ppr. *Nuncia pacis.* 92. 5

Buchanan, Ireland, a demi-unicorn or. 48. 7

Buchanan, Scotland, a rose slipped gu. *Ducitur hinc honos.* 149. 5

Buchanan, Francis C., Esquire, Clarinish Row, Dumbartonsh., an eagle rising ppr. *Audax omnia perpeti.* 77. 5

Buchanan, John Young, Esquire, of Christ's College, Cambridge, same crest and motto.

Buchannan, Scotland, a dexter hand holding a bow in bend ppr. 214. 5

Buchannan, George, Esquire, of Flowergate Cross, Whitby, Yorks, a dexter hand ppr., holding a ducal cap purpure, turned up erm., tufted on the top with a rose gu., all within two branches disposed orleways, also ppr. *Audaces juvo.* 217. 3

Buche, out of a ducal coronet or, a demi-boar sa., pierced in the neck with an arrow ppr.

Buck, a demi-lion rampant ppr., ducally crowned or, holding in its paws a bow or.

Buck, Lincs, a portcullis az., garnished and chained or. *cf.* 178. 3

Buck of Denholme Yorks, a portcullis az., garnished and chained or. *Nosce teipsum.* *cf.* 178. 3

Buck, Hants, an arm in armour embowed ppr., garnished or, holding a scimitar arg., hilted of the second. 196. 10

Buck, Norf., a buck lodged ppr 115. 7

Buck, a buck's head couped ppr. 121. 5

Buck, Glouc., a buck's attire arg., fixed to the scalp or.

Buck, a buck's attire fixed to the scalp sa.

Buck, between a buck's attires fixed to the scalp, a lion rampant holding over the sinister shoulder a battle-axe, all ppr.

Buck, Lincs, a Saracen's head in profile ppr., wreathed or and az., on his head a cap of the second, the neck charged with two bars gemelle of the same, the shoulders habited of the third.

Buckby, on a chapeau gu., turned up erm., a garb or, banded arg. 153. 10

Bucke, Cambs, a buck at gaze erm., in front of an olive-tree ppr. 116. 12

Bucke, Kent, an arm in armour embowed ppr., garnished or, holding in the hand a cutlass arg., hilt of the second. 196. 10

Buckeridge, Middx., a stag current ppr. *cf.* 118. 13

Buckeridge, a dexter arm erect couped at the elbow, habited per pale indented az. and vert, charged with three bars erminois, holding in the gauntlet ppr. a cross crosslet fitchée sa.

Bucket, a lily and a holly-branch in saltier ppr. 151. 10

Buckfield, Buckfold, and **Buckfould,** a buck ppr., attired or, in a field vert, paled around of the first.

Buckingham, a lion rampant gu. 1. 13

Buckingham, London, on a chapeau az., turned up erm., a demi-swan, wings expanded ppr., membered or, ducally gorged gu.

Buckingham and Chandos, Duke of, Earl Temple (Temple - Nugent - Brydges - Chandos-Grenville): (1) A garb vert (*for Grenville*). 153. 2. (2) On a ducal coronet a martlet or (*for Temple*). 95. 12. (3) The bust of an old man in profile couped below the shoulders ppr., habited paly of six arg. and gu., semée of roundels, counterchanged, wreathed round the temples of the second and az. (*for Brydges*). (4) A Saracen's head couped at the shoulders and affrontée ppr., wreathed about the temples arg. and sa. (*for Chandos*). *Templa quam dilecta.* 190. 5

Buckinghamshire, Earl of (Hobart-Hampden), Hampden House, Great Missenden, Bucks: (1) A talbot statant erm., collared, ringed, and lined gu., the end of the line tied in a knot over the back (*for Hampden*). *cf.* 54. 5. (2) A bull passant per pale sa. and gu., bezantée, in the nose a ring or (*for Hobart*). *Auctor pretiosa facit.—Vestigia nulla retrorsum.* *cf.* 45. 2

Buckland, Bucks, on a mount vert, a stag lodged ppr. 115. 12

Buckland and **Buckle,** Somers., on a chapeau gu., turned up erm., a talbot sejant or. 54. 14

Buckle, Sussex, out of a ducal coronet, a demi-ounce arg. *Nil temere tenta nil timide.*

Buckle, Vice-Admiral Charles Matthew, of 3, Lowndes Street, S.W., same crest. *Nec temere, nec timide.*

Buckle, Christopher Reginald, Esquire, of Norton House, Aldingbourne, Chichester, same crest and motto.

Buckle, Cuthbert Robert, Esquire, same crest and motto.

Buckle, Rev. Edward Valentine, of Banstead, Surrey, same crest and motto.

Buckle, a lion's head erased. 17. 8

Buckle, out of a ducal coronet or, a demi-leopard arg.

Buckle or **Buckel,** London, out of a ducal coronet or, a bull's head arg. 44. 11

Buckler, Dorset, Hants, and Wilts, and Charles Alban Buckler, Esquire, *Surrey Herald Extraordinary,* a dragon's head couped sa., collared with two gemelles and guttée-d'or. *Fidelis usque ad mortem.* 71. 3

Buckley, Lancs, a bull's head erased arg. 44. 3

Buckley, Wilts, out of a ducal coronet or, a bull's head arg., armed of the first. *Nec temere, nec timide* 44. 11

Buckley, Yorks, out of a fern-brake ppr., a bull's head sa.

Buckley, Sir Edmund, Bart., of Dinas Mawddwy, Merionethsh., on a mount in front of a bull's head sa., two fern-branches ppr., over all a bendlet sinister wavy or. *Nec temere, nec timide.* 234. 5

Buckley, Glouc., a bull's head erased sa., ducally gorged or, holding in the mouth a flagstaff bendwise ppr., therefrom pendent a white banner charged with a cross pattée gu. *Sed soli Deo.*

Buckley, Hon. Sir Henry Burton, of 7, Melbury Road, Kensington, W., upon a mount vert, a demi-stag at gaze gu., attired and gorged with a collar, a chain attached reflexed over the back or, supporting a garb of the last. *To my utmost.*

Buckley, Kent, a demi-eagle rising ppr. 80. 2

Buckley, Chesh., a griffin's head gu., between two wings of the same bezantée 65. 11

Buckley, a stag's head. 121. 5

Buckmaster, Lincs, Devonsh., and Northamp., a demi-lion sa., holding in the dexter paw a fleur-de-lis or, and charged on the shoulder with three annulets conjoined of the same. *cf.* 13. 2

Buckminster, Northamp., a demi-lion rampant sa., supporting a battle-axe erect or, headed arg. *cf.* 15. 5

Bucknall, a buck's head cabossed sa. 122. 5

Bucknall of Turin Castle, Mayo, a buck's head cabossed sa., attired or. 122. 5

Bucknel or **Bucknell,** a dexter hand issuing from a cloud in fess, holding a ball ppr. *cf.* 223. 1

Buckner, William Henry Pierce, of Coastguard, Fraserburgh, Aberdeen, a buck courant erminois, in front of a beech-tree, issuant from a mount ppr. *Fide surgimus ad spem.*

Buckner, a fleur-de-lis gu., with an adder entwined, the head issuing from the centre leaf ppr. *cf.* 148. 8

Buckston of Bradborne, Derbysh., a pelican or, vulning herself gu. *Fructum habet caritas.* 98. 1

Buckton, Northumb., a goat's head erased per fess indented arg. and sa., armed or. 128. 5

Buckton, James Douglas, Bruche Hall, Warrington, a stag trippant holding in the mouth a branch of laurel. *Veritas.*

Buckton or **Buketon,** Yorks, a demi-shark issuing regardant, gorging a negro ppr. 139. 2

Buckton, De, a goat's head couped per fess arg. and sa., armed or and vert. *cf.* 128. 12

Buckworth, Surrey, a demi-lion arg., holding in the dexter paw a cross crosslet fitched gu. 11. 10

Buckworth, Richard, Esquire, of Cockley Cley Hall, Norf., *uses* a demi-lion holding a cross crosslet fitchée (*of no authority*). 11. 10

Buckworth-Herne-Soame, Sir Charles, Bart., Dawley, Shropsh.: (1) On a lure arg., garnished and lined or, a hawk of the last, charged on the breast with a cross crosslet fitchee sa (*for Soame*) 85 14 (2) In an esquire's helmet, the beaver raised, a man's face, all ppr (*for Buckworth*) 191 10

Buckworth, Bart, Surrey, in an esquire's helmet, the beaver raised, a man's face, all ppr 191 10

Bucton, a hand issuing from a cloud in fess, reaching to a garland of laurel ppr 223 3

Budd, Ireland, an heraldic tiger passant gu 25 5

Budd, a dragon's head couped, the neck transpierced with a spear 72 10

Budd, a hurt charged with a star of seven points or

Buddicom, Harry William, Esquire, of Penbedw, Mold, co Flint, and Villa Capella, Borighera, Italy, in front of a beacon fired ppr, issuant from the flames thereof a demi-lion gu, gorged with a collar gemel or, holding in the dexter paw a sword in bend sinister of the first, pommel and hilt or, a cross pattee between two escallops of the last *Virtute et vigilantia.* 260 19

Buddicom, William Squire, Esquire, of Ticklerton Court, Church Stretton, Salop, same crest and motto

Budds, a ram passant arg *Another*, or 131 13

Budge, Scotland, a dexter hand holding a dagger ppr *Stricta parata neci* 212 3

Budgen, a lion's gamb sa, holding a spear tasselled in bend sinister cf 38 11

Budgett, James Smith, Esquire, of Stoke Park, Guildford, Surrey in front of two palmer's staves in saltire or, a water bouget az. *Hoc etiam præterebit* 168 6

Budorshide and **Budoxhead**, Cornw, a stag's head erased arg 121 2

Budworth, a sinister arm couped ppr, vested az, holding towards the sinister a bent bow of the first 204 11

Budworth, Essex, a wolf's head erased ppr *Beowulf* 30 8

Bugge, a bat affrontee, the wings expanded or 137 11

Bugge, Essex, out of a ducal coronet or, a Moor's head in profile sa, wreathed of the first and az cf 192 6

Buggen, Buggin, and **Buggens**, a Doric column arg, entwined with laurel vert 176 4

Buggen, Buggin, and **Buggine**, Kent and London, a cockatrice, displayed arg, crested and membered or 68 14

Buggine, an heraldic antelope sejant arg, armed, tufted, and ungu sa. cf 126 4

Buist of Perth, a swan naiant, the wings addorsed, and devouring a perch, all ppr *Assiduitate.* cf 99 13

Bukaleel, out of a ducal coronet or, a bull's head arg, armed of the first 44 11

Buketon, Yorks, a demi shark issuing, swallowing a negro ppr 139 2

Bukill, a talbot's head arg 56 12

Bulbec and **Bulbeck**, Essex, a lion's head regardant ppr cf 17 6

Bulbec and **Bulbeck**, a hand holding a sealed letter ppr

Bulbeck, Kingston, a bull passant vert, ungu, maned, and armed or 45 2

Bulcock, London and Devonsh, a lion's head gu, within a chain in orle issuing or 19 5

Bulfin, Patrick, Esquire, J P, of Wordtown House, Rathfarnham, co Dublin, a demi-lion rampant or, holding in the dexter paw a civic crown vert, and charged on the shoulder with a trefoil slipped, also vert *Vincit veritas*

Bulimore, a demi-lion rampant sa 10 1

Bulkeley, Ireland, Bucks, and Chesh, out of a ducal coronet or, a bull's head arg, armed of the first. *Nec temere, nec timide* 44 11

Bulkeley, a bull's head and neck erased per pale arg and sa 44 3

Bulkeley, a bull's head and neck couped per pale arg and sa, armed or and of the first cf 44 3

Bulkeley or **Bulkely**, Ireland, a bull's head couped at the neck sa cf 44 3

Bulkeley-Owen, Rev Thomas Mainwaring Bulkeley, Justice of the Peace for the county of Shropsh (1) Two eagles' heads conjoined and erased party per fesse or and gu, membered of the last (*for Owen*) 84 14 (2) Out of a ducal coronet or, a bull's head arg, armed of the first (*for Bulkeley*) *Eryr eryrod eryri —Nec temere, nec timide* 44 11

Bulkeley, Williams-, Sir Richard Henry, Bart, Baron Hill, Beaumaris, Wales (1(Out of a ducal coronet or, a bull's head arg, armed of the first, and charged with a cheveron sa (*for Bulkeley*) cf 44 11 (2) A stag's head caboshed arg (*for Williams*) *Nec temere, nec timide.* 122 5

Bull of London, on a wreath a cloud ppr, thereon a celestial sphere az, replenished with the circles or, and beautified with the zodiac, inscribed with the signs Aries Taurus, Gemini, Cancer *Sol, mi re fa*

Bull of London, a lion's head erased sa, ducally crowned or 18 8

Bull, Ireland, a rose gu 149 2

Bull, a bull's head and neck erased sa 44 3

Bull, Ireland, a bull's head affrontee couped gu, murally crowned or cf 44 8

Bull, London, Yorks, and Norf, a bull's head erased sa, charged with six annulets or, one, two, and three cf 44 3

Bull, Oxon, a bull's head cabossed gu, armed or, between two wings of the last cf 43 8

Bull, a bull's head cabossed between two wings or cf 43 8

Bull, William James, M P, Vencourt, Hammersmith, a bull's head caboshed and winged sa, armed or *Excelsior Dei gratia*

Bull, Warw, a bull passant sa, armed or, holding in the mouth a scroll cf 45 2

Bullen, Lincs, a bull's head couped sa, armed or cf 44 3

Bullen, *see* Symes Bullen

Bullen, Tatchell-, John Bullen Tatchell, of Marchwood, near Bridport (1) Out of a naval coronet or the sails arg, a bull's head of the first, charged on the neck with an anchor sa, between two wings az (*for Bullen*) (2) On a mount vert in front of an oak tree fructed ppr a bow and arrow in saltire or surmounted by a lion's face gu (*for Tatchell*) *A rege et victoria* cf 43 10

Bullen, John Bullen Symes, Esquire, of Catherston, Charmouth, Dorset, out of a naval crown gold, the sails arg, a bull's head or, charged on the neck with an anchor sa, between two wings az *A rege et victoria*

Buller, Cornw (1) An eagle on a rock supporting a banner (2) A Saracen's head ppr *Aquila non capiat muscas* 190 5

Buller, *see* Churston, Baron

Buller, Cornw and Somers, a Moor's head affrontee couped ppr, wreathed about the temples arg and az *Aquila non capiat muscas*

Buller, John Follett, of 20 Carlton Crescent, Southampton, same crest and motto

Buller, Manningham-, Sir Morton Edward, Bart Dilhorn Hall, Cheadle, Staffordsh (1) A Saracen's head affrontee couped ppr (*for Buller*) cf 190 5 (2) Out of a ducal coronet gu, a talbot's head or, collared, also gu, therefrom a line terminating in a knot sa (*for Manningham*)

Buller, Admiral the late Sir Alexander of Erle Hall, Plympton, South Devon, and Belmore House, West Cowes, Isle of Wight, a Saracen's head affrontee couped at the shoulders ppr *Aquila non capit muscas*

Buller, Charles Francis, Esquire, same crest and motto

Buller, John Dashwood, Esquire, of Down Hall, Epsom, same crest and motto

Buller, General Rt Hon Sir Redvers Henry, of Downes, Crediton, same crest and motto

Buller, Sir Walter Lawry K C M G, F R S, of Papaitonga Estate Wellington, New Zealand, same crest

Bulley, a heart inflamed ppr 181 13

Bullingham, Lincs, an escallop arg, between two palm-branches vert 141 4

Bullivant, a demi lion or, charged on the breast with a fleur de lis vert, and holding between the paws a tower sa

Bullivant, Cecil H, 15, Ravenstone Road, Stratford, E, a demi-lion rampant or, charged on the breast with a fleur de lis, holding in the paws a tower ppr *Gratia Dei sufficit*

Bullman, out of a ducal coronet a bull's head ppr *Pro patria* 44 11

Bullman, Rev Job George, of Oakwood, West Enfield, Middx, on a mount vert, a bull passant arg, the dexter forefoot resting on a ball az *Patienter* 299 7

Bulman, out of a ducal coronet a bull's head ppr *Pro patria* 44 11

Bulman, Northumb, on a mount vert, a bull passant arg, resting the dexter foot on a hurt cf 45 7

Bulmar, a demi-lion rampant holding an escallop shell 13 10

Bulmer, a demi-bull rampant gu, armed or, charged with an escallop between two billets in pale or cf 45 12

Bulmer or **Bullmer,** Essex and Yorks, a bull passant gu., armed and ungu. or. *cf.* 45. 2

Bulmer, a demi-bull rampant gu., armed or. 45. 12

Bullo and **Bulow,** an arm embowed, the hand clenched ppr. 202. 2

Bullock, London, on a mount vert, a bee-hive or, thereon a bee displayed ppr. *cf.* 137. 7

Bullock, seven arrows, six in saltier and one in pale gu., feathered and headed arg., enfiled with a mural coronet of the last. *cf.* 173. 7

Bullock, Edward, Esquire, Barrister-at-law, Recorder of Buckingham, 5, Pump Court, Inner Temple, and 4, Porchester Square, London, five Lochaber axes, the handles or, blades ppr., bound with a scarf gu., tassels or. *Nil conscire sibi.* 172. 13

Bullock, Walter Henry, Esquire, of Faulkbourn Hall, Witham, Essex, same crest and motto.

Bullock, Essex, five battle-axes, the staves or, heads sa., tied together with a line and bow-knot gu. *cf.* 172. 13

Bullock, five pole-axes ppr., encircled by a ribbon az. *cf.* 172. 13

Bullock, Watson-, Essex: (1) Five antique halberds, the blades ppr., the handles or, encircled with a ribbon of the last, the cord tied in a knot gu. (*for Bullock*). *Nil conscire sibi. cf.* 172. 13. (2) A dexter arm in armour embowed, holding in the gauntlet a palm-branch ppr. (*for Watson*). *Esperance en Dieu.* *cf.* 199. 12

Bullock, Somers., on a mount vert, five black-bills erect, banded with a wreath of olive ppr., therefrom pendent an escutcheon az., charged with a cross crosslet or.

Bulstree and **Boulstree,** out of a mural coronet a stag's head. *cf.* 121. 6

Bulstrode, Beds and Bucks, a bull's head and neck gu., armed arg., between two wings of the first. 43. 10

Bulstrode, Christopher Victor, M.A., M.B., 105, Broadhurst Gardens, Hampstead, a bull's head and neck between two wings expanded gu., attired or. *Thinke and thanke.*

Bult, an arm in armour couped and embowed, resting the elbow on the wreath, a sash tied at the shoulder gu., holding a club. 199. 3

Bulteel of Flete, Devonsh., out of a ducal coronet gu., a pair of wings arg., billettée of the first. *cf.* 109. 8

Bulteel, John George, of Pamflete, Ivebridge, Devonsh., same crest.

Bulteel and **Bultell,** Somers., a bull's head gu., between two wings or. 43. 10

Bulwer, Norf., a horned wolf's head erased erm., crined and armed or. *Adversis major par secundis.*

Bulwer, General Sir Edward Earle Gascoigne, of the Grange, Heydon, Norwich, same crest and motto.

Bulwer, Sir Henry Ernest Gascoyne, K.C.M.G., same crest and motto.

Bulwer, Colonel William Earle Gascoyne Lytton, C.B., J.P., of Heydon Hall, Norwich, and Quebec House, East Dereham, Norf., same crest and motto.

Bulwer-Lytton, the Rt. Hon. Sir Victor Alexander George Robert, **Earl of Lytton** and **Viscount Knebworth,** of Knebworth, Herts: (1) A bittern in flags ppr., charged with a rose gu., barbed and seeded ppr. (*for Lytton*). *cf.* 104. 3. (2) An heraldic tiger's head erased erm., armed and crined or (*for Bulwer*). *cf.* 25. 4. (3) A dove regardant arg., holding in the beak an olive-branch ppr., fructed or (*for Wiggett*). *Hoc virtutis opus.* 92. 4

Bulwer, Lieutenant-Colonel James Redfoord, of Temple Gardens, London, E.C., M.A., Q.C., Recorder of Cambridge, sometime Treasurer of the Honourable Society of the Inner Temple, in front of a goat's head erased erm., armed or, a portcullis with chains sa. *Spes sibi quisque.* *cf.* 128. 5

Bulworth, out of a ducal coronet or, a stag's head between two branches of palm ppr. *cf.* 120. 7

Bulworth, a stag's head erased ppr. 121. 2

Bumstead and **Bumsted,** out of a cloud a hand erect pointing to a star, all ppr. 222. 7

Bunbury, Sir Henry Charles John, Bart., of Stanney Hall, Chesh., two swords in saltier through the mouth of a leopard's face or, the blades ppr., hilts and pommels of the first. *Firmum in vita nihil.—Esse quam videri.* 22. 7

Bunbury, M'Clintock-: (1) Two swords in saltire arg., hilted or, pierced through the mouth of a leopard's face of the last (*for Bunbury*). 22. 7. (2) A lion passant ppr. (*for M'Clintock*). *Vis unita fortior.* 6. 2

Bunbury-Tighe, Edward Kenwick, Esquire, of Woodstock, Inistioge, co. Kilkenny: (1) A wolf's head erased ppr., gorged with a collar az., thereon a cross crosslet or, between two bezants (*for Tighe*). (2) Two swords in saltire arg., hilted or, pierced through the mouth of a leopard's face of the last (*for Bunbury*). 22. 7. *Firmum in vita nihil.—Summum nec metuam diem nec optem.* 30. 4

Bunbury, Ireland, a hand in fess issuing from a cloud and reaching to a garland of laurel, all ppr. 223. 3

Bunbury, Richardson-, the Rev. Sir John, Bart., of Castle Hill, co. Tyrone, Ireland: (1) In front of a tree ppr., on a mount vert, a leopard's head, paly of six arg. and sa., transfixed by two arrows in saltier, also ppr. (*for Bunbury*). 236. 11. (2) A lion rampant erm., holding in the mouth a trefoil slipped vert, and between the fore-paws a torteaux, charged with a cross crosslet or (*for Richardson*). *Virtus paret robor.* 236. 10

Bunce, Kent, a demi-boar az., pierced through the neck with a broken spear gu., headed arg. *Sic vivere, vivetis.* *cf.* 41. 2

Bunch, Scotland, a stork ppr. 105. 11

Buncombe, Somers., a demi-lion gu., charged on the shoulder with a water-bouget arg., supporting a spear, thereon a banner of the first, fringed of the second, and charged with a cross flory or.

Bund, Worcs., an eagle's head erased or. 66. 2

Bund, Willis-, John William, of Wick Episcope, Worcester: (1) An eagle's head erased ppr. (*for Bund*). 66. 2. (2) Two lion's gambs erased, the dexter argent, the sinister gules, supporting an escutcheon or (*for Willis*). *Non nobis Domine.* 39. 1

Bund, Willis-, two lion's gambs erased or, supporting a griffin's head erased. *Optivo floreo nomine.* 250. 5

Bundy, Worcs., a hand holding an eagle's leg erased, all ppr. *Certum pete finem.* 220. 12

Bunford, out of a ducal coronet a demi-lion gu. 16. 3

Bungey, an eagle with wings endorsed arg., standing on a laurel-branch vert, fructed or.

Bunn, an ostrich-head arg., collared gu., between two palm-branches vert. *cf.* 96. 10

Bunnell, on a ducal coronet a Cornish chough rising ppr. 108. 6

Bunney and **Bunny,** Yorks and Durh., a goat's head erased sa., attired or, charged on the sinister horn with two annulets conjoined of the last. *Monte dessus* *cf.* 128. 5

Bunny of Ryton, Durh., a goat's head erased sa., charged with a mullet. *Monte dessus.* *cf.* 128. 5

Bunten, Scotland, a hand grasping a sword ppr. *Fortiter et fide.* 212. 13

Bunten and **Bunting,** Scotland, a bunting-bird on a garb, all ppr. *Copiose et opportune.* *cf.* 153. 2

Bunten, James Clark, Esquire, of Dun-Alastair, Perthsh., a demi-eagle displayed ppr. *Copiose et opportune.*

Bunting, a hand issuing from a cloud holding two branches of laurel in orle. 218. 9

Bunting, an armillary sphere ppr. 159. 10

Bunton, on a ducal coronet a talbot passant collared and lined. 54. 9

Bunyard, Kent, a buck springing. *Renovato nomine.* 117. 2

Burard, on a ducal coronet or, an étoile of eight points ppr. 164. 4

Burbage, a boar's head erased arg., between two branches vert. 42. 1

Burbidge, between the attires of a stag attached to the scalp or, a boar's erect and erased sa. 43. 2

Burbridge, out of a ducal coronet az., two arms embowed, vested gu., gloved or, holding in each hand an ostrich-feather arg. 203. 2

Burbyche, Middx. and Heref., a boar's head and neck erased arg., bristled or, between two oak-branches vert, fructed of the second. *cf.* 41. 5

Burcetre, a comet ppr. 164. 10

Burch, an eagle with wings expanded gu. 77. 5

Burch, Nathaniel Geach, Esquire, of Edenwood, Sydenham Hill, London, S.E., upon a canoe ppr., an eagle displayed sa., charged on the breast and upon each wing with a birch-leaf slipped or, holding in the beak a like leaf. *Strune fortis.*

Burchall, Heref, a lion rampant az, supporting a tree vert

Burchall and **Burchill**, out of a ducal coronet two hands dexter and sinister, in saltier, each grasping a scimitar, the edges outward, all ppr

Burchar, London and Essex, a greyhound sejant arg, ducally gorged or cf 59 4

Burchardt-Ashton, Frederic, Esquire, and Arthur Burchardt-Ashton, Esquire, both of Pole Bank, Gee Cross, Werneth, Chesh (1) In front of a boar's head erased gu, between two mullets of six points sa, pierced arg, a javelin erect ppr (*for Ashton*) (2) Upon a mount vert, a castle with two towers sa, issuant therefrom a demi-woman affrontee ppr, habited az, holding in the dexter hand a heart gu, and supporting with the sinister hand a javelin ppr (*for Burchardt*)

Burche, an eagle with wings expanded gu 77 5

Burchett, a winged spur ppr 111 12

Burckhead and **Burkett**, a goat rampant arg armed or, and between the feet a garb of the first

Burd and **Byrde**, London, an eagle's head erased, bendy of eight arg and sa, ducally gorged or 83 11

Burd-Brooks, of Heathfield House, Beckenham, Kent, a demi lion arg, charged on the shoulder with a fountain ppr, and holding in the paws a harpoon in bend sinister, also ppr *Finem respice* 12 14

Burdekin, Sidney, Esquire, of Sydney, New South Wales a seahorse erect ppr resting the sinister paw on an anchor erect sa the whole between two coral branches gu *Virtus summa nobilitas*

Burden, a heart transfixed by a sword in bend sinister 181 6

Burdenbroke, an otter's head erased close sa 134 3

Burder, a mount vert, thereon in front of an oak tree a stag lodged regardant ppr, attired and ungu or, suspended from the neck by a line a bugle of the last *Labor omnia vincit*

Burdett, Sir Charles Grant, Bart, of Burthwaite, Yorks, on a tower arg, a martlet with wings displayed or 156 9

Burdett, Arthur Hugo de Burdet, Esquire, of Coolfin, Banagher, King's Co, same crest

Burdett, Sir Francis, Bart., of Foremark, Derbysh, a lion's head erased sa, langued gu 17 8

Burdett, a lion's head couped sa 21 1

Burdett-Coutts, *see* Coutts

Burdett, Bart, Ireland, a lion's head erased sa 17 8

Burdett, Warw and Yorks, a thistle ppr 150 7

Burdon, Durh, a lion rampant standing on the sinister hind-foot, supporting himself by a pilgrim's staff or

Burdon, Roland Esquire of Castle Eden, Durham, same crest

Burdon, a gilliflower or 151 8

Burdon of Newcastle on-Tyne (1) An eagle rising regardant or, each wing charged with a cross crosslet az, holding in the dexter claw a trumpet of the first (*for Burdon*) (2) Upon three annulets interlaced gu, a stork arg, beaked, legged and collared gu, holding in the beak a salmon ppr (*for De Butts*) *Honor virtutis* 104 4

Burdon, Augustus Edward, Esquire, of Hartford House, Cramlington, Northumb, same crests and motto

Burdon-Sanderson, Richard, Esquire, of Waren House, Belford, Northumb, and Otterburn Dene, Otterburn R S O Northumb, a wolf's head arg, erased gu, collared and chain reflexed behind the neck or between a branch of palm and another of laurel and for distinction on the neck a saltire humettee gu *Clarior ex obscuro* 287 15

Burdus or **Burduss**, Middx, an elephant erm on a mount vert and under a tree ppr cf 133 12

Bure, an eagle ppr 76 2

Burfoot, London, on a wreath an Eastern crown, thereon a pine apple leaved and crowned with leaves growing from the top, all or cf 152 8

Burford, Earl, *see* St Albans, Duke of

Burg, a falcon standing on a serpent nowed ppr 86 3

Burgace, **Burgass**, **Burgas**, and **Burgase**, two pigeons billing ppr 93 2

Burge, a branch of olive ppr 151 11

Burges, Lincs, on a mural coronet chequy or and sa, a round buckle of the first, the tongue erect in pale cf 178 5

Burges, Essex and Ireland (1) A dove rising arg, beaked and membered gu, holding in its beak a palm-branch ppr (*for Burges*) cf 94 5 (2) A demi lion rampant gu langued az holding in the dexter paw an annulet enclosing a fleur-de lis arg (*for Lloyd*) *Tace aut face* cf 1 13

Burges, Colonel Ynyr Henry, of Parkanaur, Dungannon, co Tyrone, same crests and motto

Burges, Ireland, a camel's head couped gu, bezantee cf 132 7

Burges, W E P, Major, the Ridge, Chipping-Sodbury, a camel's head gu, bezantee *Levius fit patientia*

Burgess, Sussex and Berks, a camel's head ppr, erased gu, bezantee *Levius fit patientia* cf 132 7

Burgess, a lion rampant 1 13

Burgess, a griffin's head erased 66 2

Burgess, a greyhound's head ppr, bezantee 61 12

Burgess, a fleur-de-lis or *Le bon temps viendra* 148 2

Burgh, Baron Downes, *see* Downes

Burgh, De, *see* Clanricarde, Marquess of

Burgh, an arm in armour couped and embowed fesswise, the elbow on the wreath, the hand apaumee ppr, ribboned and bowed cf 200 1

Burgh, Shropsh, an eagle statant, the wings expanded 77 5

Burgh, a falcon rising erm, belled and ducally gorged or 87 2

Burgh, a mountain-cat sejant gardant ppr, collared and chained or 26 13

Burgh, De Hussey- (1) A catamountain sejant gardant ppr, collared and chained or (*for De Burgh*) 26 13 (2) A hind trippant arg on a mount vert and under a tree ppr (*for Hussey*) *A cruce salus*

Burgh, a fleur-de-lis arg, environed with a serpent vert 148 8

Burghall, Ireland, a wolf's head erased sa 30 8

Burghclere, Rt Hon Herbert Colston Gardner, Baron, of Debden Hall, Saffron Walden, and 48, Charles Street, Berkeley Square, W, a demi-griffin az, collared and chained, and charged on the shoulder with a saltire wavy or, and holding between the claws an anchor erect with a piece of cable attached *Valet anchora virtus* 239 3

Burghep or **Burghepe**, a friar's head in profile ppr, couped at the shoulders, vested gray

Burghersh, Baron, *see* Westmoreland, Earl of

Burghersh, Devonsh and Norf, out of a mural coronet gu, a demi lion double-queued arg cf 10 6

Burghersh, two stumps of trees, couped and argnly, in saltier ppr, banded vert 147 9

Burghill, Suff. and Wales, a lion's head erased arg 17 8

Burghill, a lion's head arg, crowned with a Saxon crown or cf 17 12

Burghley, Baron, *see* Exeter, Marquess of

Burghley and **Burgly**, a winged greyhound sejant cf 59 9

Burgin, a sword and a key in saltier ppr 171 10

Burgis, a camel's head ppr 132 7

Burgoigne or **Burgoyne**, Cambs and Devonsh, an heraldic antelope sejant arg, attired, tufted and maned sa cf 126 4

Burgon, a cock crowing or 91 2

Burgon, Longstanton, Herts, an heraldic tiger sejant arg, maned and tufted sa

Burgone and **Burgoyne**, Oxon, on a ducal coronet or, a lion passant gu 6 6

Burgoyne, Sir John Montagu, Bart, of Sutton Park, Beds, a talbot sejant or, eared sa, gorged with a plain collar gu 55 1

Burk, under the shade of two trees a stag lodged ppr

Burke, a demi bull rampant armed and ungu or, gorged with a chaplet vert cf 45 14

Burke, Viscount, *see* Clanricarde, Marquess of

Burke, Sir John Bernard, C B, LL D, late *Ulster King of Arms*, Knight Attendant and Registrar of the Most Illustrious Order of St Patrick, of Tullemaine House, Dublin, and the Record Tower, Dublin Castle, a catamountain sejant gardant ppr, collared and chained or, and charged on the breast with a cross couped of the last *Ung roy, ung foy, ung loy* cf 26 13

Burke, Henry Farnham Esquire, C V O, F S A, *Somerset Herald*, a catamountain sejant gardant ppr, collared and chained or, charged on the breast with a cross couped gold *Ung roy, ung foy, ung loy* cf 26 13

Burke, Ashworth Peter, Esquire, of Elm Hall, co Tipperary, same crest and motto

Burke, Arthur Augustine Meredyth, Esquire, a catamountain sejant gardant ppr., collared and chained or, and charged on the breast with a cross or. *One king, one faith, one law.*

Burke, Charles Carrington, Esquire, of Michenhall, Godalming, same crest and motto.

Burke, Edward Plunkett, Esquire, same crest and motto.

Burke, Francis Eustace, Esquire, of Terriers, High Wycombe, Bucks, same crest and motto.

Burke, Harold Arthur, Esquire, of 7, Victoria Road, Kensington, same crest and motto.

Burke, John Edward, Esquire, same crest and motto.

Burke, Ulick John, Esquire, of Woodcote Manor, co. Southampton, same crest and motto.

Burke, Walter St. George, Esquire, of Auberies, Sudbury, Suff., same crest and motto.

Burke, Sir Henry George, Bart., of Marble Hill, Ireland, a catamountain sejant gardant ppr., collared and chained or. *Ung roy, ung foy, ung loy.* 26. 13

Burke, Ireland, a catamountain sejant gardant ppr., collared and chained or. 26. 13

Burke, Ireland, a cat sejant ppr. *A cruce salus.* *cf.* 26. 8

Burke, Sir Theobald Hubert, Bart., of Glinsk, co. Galway, Ireland, out of a ducal coronet or, a plume of five ostrich-feathers arg. *In hoc signo vinces.* 114. 13

Burke, a demi-lion rampant az., holding a cross or. 11. 14

Burket and **Burkett,** a garb or. *Impendam, expendar.* 153. 2

Burket, Burkett, and **Burkitt,** a dexter arm embowed brandishing a club ppr. 202. 10

Burkett, *see* Burckhead.

Burkett, a goat rampant arg. 129. 2

Burkin, Suff., a crab ppr. 149. 5

Burland, a demi-savage brandishing a scimitar ppr. 186. 3

Burland, a griffin's head erased and collared. *cf.* 66. 2

Burleigh, a stag's head erased gu. 121. 2

Burleigh, a demi-boar ppr., armed, ungu., and bristled or, and gorged with a chain of the last supporting a thistle ppr. *cf.* 40. 13

Burles, a squirrel sejant cracking a nut, all ppr. 135. 7

Burleton and **Burlton,** a garb. 153. 2

Burley, Leics. and Wilts, a demi-boar ppr., armed, ungu., and bristled or, and gorged with a chain of the last supporting a thistle ppr. *cf.* 40. 13

Burlington, Earl of (Cavendish), a snake nowed ppr. *Cavendo tutus.* 142. 4

Burlinson, Durh., a demi-lion holding between the paws a rose arg., barbed vert. *cf.* 16. 6

Burlton, a dexter and a sinister arm vested holding up a cross crosslet fitched.

Burlton, Thomas Davies, Esquire, J.P. for co. Heref., of Eaton Hill, Leominster, a demi-gryphon couped, wings elevated and addorsed arg., holding in the dexter claw a horse-shoe, and resting the sinister on a fleur-de-lis, both az. *Mens sana in corpore sano.* 241. 14

Burly or **Burley,** Suff., a squirrel sejant supporting a ragged staff or.

Burman, a demi-peacock az. 103. 10

Burmester, a cross patée az., within six mullets in a circle or. *cf.* 164. 9

Burmey, a dexter hand ppr., holding an anchor erect or, environed with clouds arg. *Arcus, artes, astra.* 219. 2

Burn or **Burne,** a hurt. *cf.* 159. 14

Burn, Scotland, a hand ppr., holding a cross crosslet fitched az. *Vincit veritas.* 221. 14

Burn, London, a cubit arm vested or, charged with a bend az., thereon a buckle between two estoiles of the first, and holding in the hand ppr. a bugle-horn sa., thereon a wreath of oak ppr.

Burn, an arm erect, vested sa., cuffed arg., holding in the hand ppr. a fleur-de-lis or.

Burn, Scotland and London, a dexter hand holding a horn ppr. *Ever ready.* 217. 4

Burn, Ireland, a wolf's head erased ppr. 30. 8

Burn, Perthsh., two dragons in saltire ppr. *Tendit ad astra fides.* 169. 8

Burn, a demi-tiger erm., holding between the paws a fountain.

Burn-Callander, Henry, Esquire, J.P., of Preston Hall, Dalkeith, N.B.: (1) Out of an Eastern crown or, a cubit arm ppr. (*for Callander*). (2) Two daggers in saltire ppr. (*for Burn*). *Tendit ad astra fides.*

Burnaby, Sir Henry, Bart., of Broughton Hall, Oxon., out of a naval coronet a demi-lion rampant gardant or, holding in the dexter paw a staff ppr., thereon a flag gu. *Pro rege.* 16. 9

Burnaby and **Burneby,** Middx., a demi-man sa., holding in the dexter hand a bunch of columbine flowers ppr., and round his neck a rope or, with the end hanging down on the sinister side. *Pro rege.*

Burnaby, Algernon Edwyn, of Baggrave Hall, Leics., a demi-moryon boye tawney, through his ear a double ring of silver, about his neck a flat chain of the same, holding in his hand a bourage plant flowered azure, stalked and leaved vert. *Pro Rege.*

Burnard, Robert, Esquire, 3, Hillsborough, Plymouth, on a rock ppr., an escallop arg., between the attires of a stag, also ppr. *Bear and forbear.* 141. 13

Burnard, Charles Frederick, Esquire, of Chatsworth Lodge, Compton Gifford, Plymouth, and Huccaby House, Lydford, Devon, same crest and motto.

Burnby and **Burneby,** Middx., on a mount a stag rising from under a tree, all ppr. *cf.* 116. 5

Burne, *see* Burn.

Burnell, London, a greyhound sejant arg. 59. 4

Burnell, Norf., a tower in flames ppr.

Burnell, a lion's gamb erased sa., grasping a rose gu., slipped and leaved vert. 37. 10

Burnell, Pegge-: (1) A lion's gamb erect and erased sa., holding in the paw a bunch of violets ppr. (*for Burnell*). (2) The sun rising in splendour, the rays alternately sa., or, and arg. (*for Pegge*). *Caritas fructum habet.*

Burnes of Montrose: (1) Out of a mural crown per pale vert and gu., the rim inscribed "*Cabool*" in letters arg., a demi-eagle displayed or, transfixed by a javelin in bend sinister ppr. *cf.* 80. 8. (2) Out of an Eastern crown or, an oak-tree withered renewing its foliage ppr. *Ob patriam vulnera passi.*

Burness of Grove House, Leytonstone, and of Tilbury, both in Essex, a demi-pegasus sa., winged or. *Perseverantia vincit.* 47. 5

Burnet, Wilts, a vine couped ppr. *Virescit, vulnere virtus.* 152. 9

Burnet, Peebles, Scotland, a vine-branch slipped ppr. *Tandem fit surculus arbor.* 152. 9

Burnet, Scotland, a hand with a cutlass cutting a vine-branch ppr. *Tandem fit surculus arbor.*

Burnet, Scotland, a branch of holly slipped ppr. *Nec fluctu, nec flatu.* 150. 10

Burnet, Scotland, a holly-branch ppr. *Virtute cresco.* 150. 10

Burnet or **Burnett,** Northumb., a holly-branch vert, fructed gu. *Virtute cresco.* 150. 10

Burnet, Scotland, a boar's head erased az. *Quidni pro sodali.* 42. 2

Burnet of Craigmyle, Scotland, a dexter hand holding a palm-branch ppr. *Quæ vernant crescent.* 219. 11

Burnet, Rev. Alexander George, of Kemnay House, Kemnay, Aberdeen, same crest and motto.

Burnet, on a mount out of a ducal coronet a hand with a knife pruning a vine ppr.

Burnett, Sir Thomas, Bart., of Leys, Aberdeen, a hand with a knife pruning a vine-tree ppr. *Virescit vulnere virtus.* 251. 3

Burnett, Kent, in a mural crown or, a mount vert, thereon a vine-tree ppr., fructed or, on the sinister an arm issuing from a cloud, holding in the hand a knife pruning the vine, also ppr. *Virescit vulnere virtus.*

Burnett, Scotland, issuing out of a cloud in sinister a hand in fess grasping a pruning-knife ppr.

Burnett, John George, Esquire, of Powis House, Aberdeen, and 21, Walker Street, Edinburgh, a dexter hand holding a palm-branch ppr., and in an escroll above the same. *Quæ vernant crescent.*

Burnett, Ireland, a holy lamb regardant arg., holding the standard of St. Patrick ppr.

Burnett, a bull's head ducally gorged and crowned. *cf.* 44. 2

Burney, Kent, an arm in a maunch in fess, holding in the hand a cross patée fitched. *Omne bonum desuper.* *cf.* 203. 3

Burney, Arthur George, United University Club, Pall Mall East, S.W., out of a maunch gu., charged with an ancient lyre or, stringed arg., a hand ppr. holding a cross patée fitchée, erect sa. *Omne bonum desuper.* 237. 3

Burney, Henry Edward, Esq, of Wavendon Tower, Bletchley, Bucks, same crest *Gang warily*

Burney or Burnie, Scotland, a lion's head erased gu *Sapere aude incipe* 17 2

Burney or **Burnie,** a bull's head ducally gorged and crowned cf 44 2

Burnham, Baron (Levy-Lawson), Hall Barn, Beaconsfield Bucks (1) In front of a terrestrial globe ppr, a winged morion or 257 7 (2) A ram arg, holding in the mouth a trefoil slipped vert, and resting the dexter fore-leg on a quatrefoil or *Of old I hold* 257 8

Burnham, Berks, out of a ducal coronet a hand holding a dagger in pale, the blade wavy *Basis virtutem constantia* 212 1

Burnham, Lincs, out of a ducal coronet a hand holding a dagger in pale, the blade wavy 212 1

Burnham, a leopard's head erased ppr 23 10

Burnham, James, Esquire, Ladysmith, Western Elms Avenue, Reading Berks, a leopard's head erased ppr *Time Deum et ne timeas* 23 10

Burnie, *see* Burney

Burnley-Campbell, Hardin, Esquire, of Ormidale, Colintraive, Argyllsh, a dexter hand in pale holding a dirk erected, both ppr *Pro patria semper*

Burnman, Devonsh, a bull's head erased or armed gobony or and sa 44 3

Burns, Scotland, two hands issuing from clouds conjoined in fess ppr, holding up a laurel branch vert cf 224 3

Burns, a woodlark perching on a sprig of bay tree ppr *Woodnotes wild Better a wee bush than nae bield* 295 7

Burns, Bart, of Wemyss House, Wemyss Bay, Renfrewsh, a dexter hand ppr, holding a hunting horn sa, garnished vert. *Ever ready* 297 8

Burns, John William, Esquire, of Kilmahew, Cardross, Dumbartonsh, and Cumbernauld House, Cumbernauld, Dumbartonsh, same crest and motto

Burns, Scotland and England, a dove with wings expanded az 94 2

Burns-Gibson, John, M D, Harlesden, N W, a pelican in her piety *Morior ut vivamus*

Burns-Hartopp, James, Esquire, of Dalby Hall, Melton Mowbray, Scraptoft Hall, Leics, Waterville, and Kilgarvan, co Kerry (1) Out of a ducal coronet or, a pelican issuing arg, charged on the neck with a cross crosslet for distinction, vulning herself ppr (*for Hartopp*) (2) A hand ppr holding a hunting-horn sa, garnished or *Ever ready*

Burns-Lindow, Isaac William, Esquire, of Irton Hall, Holmrock, via Carnforth, Cumberland, a lion rampant gu, semee of buckles or, and holding between the paws a fountain *Vi et virtute*

Burnside, Scotland, a crescent arg *Gradatim plena* 163 2

Burnside, a branch of oak ppr. 151 3

Burnyeat, issuant from flames ppr, a bear's head per pale or and az, gorged with a collar flory-counter flory counter-changed

Burnyeat, William, Esquire, of Mill Grove, Moresby, Whitehaven same crest

Burr, Rev George Frederick M S A L Mus, Highfields Park, Hales-Owen Worcs, 'Halesowen," Blacklands Hastings, Sussex, a wyvern with wings displayed and tail nowed *Virtus honoris janua*

Burr, a lion's head ppr, collared or cf 18 6

Burr, Berks, out of a mural crown inscribed with the word '*Ternate*' a Malay holding in his dexter hand the colours of Ternate, all ppr *Virtus verus honos*

Burra, in front of a griffin's head erased sa, semee of annulets or, a fret of the last cf 66 2

Burra, James Salkeld, Esquire, of Bockhanger, Ashford, Kent, same crest *Pactum serva*

Burra, Robert, Esquire, of the Gate, Sedbergh, Yorks R S O, same crest *Per siste*

Burrall, *see* Porter Burrall

Burrard, Bart, of Lymington (*extinct*), Hants, out of a mural crown per pale or and arg, an arm in bend, the hand grasping a sword, and about the arm a wreath of laurel, all ppr

Burrard, Sir Harry Paul, Bart, of Walhampton, Isle of Wight, out of a naval coronet or, a cubit arm erect ppr. charged with a cross patee gu, holding in the hand a trident in bend sinister, point downward, of the first 236 8

Burrard, Hants, a dexter arm embowed, the hand grasping a sword ppr 201 4

Burrell, *see* Gwydvr, Baron

Burrell, Northumb, an armed arm ppr, holding a branch of burdock vert *Adhæreo*

Burrell, Boreel, Burell, or **Bereel,** Kent and Sussex, an arm embowed ppr holding in the hand a branch of laurel vert 228 6

Burrell, John Lawrence, Esquire, Newcastle-on Tyne, *uses* a dexter naked arm embowed, holding in the hand a branch of laurel 228 6

Burrell, Sir Merrik Raymond, Bart Knepp Castle, Horsham, Sussex, a naked arm embowed, holding in the hand a branch of laurel, all ppr *Sub libertate quietem* 228 6

Burridge, Devonsh, a demi-mariner ppr, the waistcoat gu, cap az, and neckerchief arg, supporting a rudder sa

Burrish, out of a tower per pale arg and gu, a demi-lion rampant double-queued or cf 157 11

Burrough or **Borough,** Lincs, an eagle with wings expanded erm 77 5

Burrough, Rev Charles, M A, of Eaton Bishop Rectory, Heref, a griffin's head arg, beaked or, charged on the neck with two chevronels vert *Vive ut vivas* 226 13

Burroughes, Henry Randall Esquire of Burlingham Hall Norwich a griffin's head erased arg, between two chevrons vert. *Animo et vide*

Burroughs, Norf, a griffin's head arg, charged with two chevronels vert 226 13

Burroughs, Bart, Ireland, on an Eastern crown or, a lion passant gu *Audaces fortuna juvat* cf 6 6

Burroughs, Lieutenant General Frederick William Traill, C B of Trumland House, Rousay, Orkney a lion passant gules *Audaces fortuna juvat*

Burroughs, Scotland, a lion passant gu *Audaces fortuna juvat* 6 2

Burrow, Scotland and England, a lion passant gardant arg *Deus nobis hæc otia fecit* 4 3

Burrow, a falcon erm with wings expanded 87 1

Burrowes, a lion sejant arg 8 8

Burrowes and **Burrows,** a lion sejant arg, ducally crowned or cf 8 8

Burrowes of Stradone, co Cavan, a lion sejant gardant sa, ducally crowned or, langued gu *Non vi sed virtute*

Burrowes, Thomas Cosby, Esquire, of Lismore House, Crossdoney, co Cavan, same crest and motto

Burrowes, Thomas James, Esquire, of Stradone House, Cavan, and 44, Thurlow Square, S W, same crest and motto

Burrowes and **Burrows,** an eagle, wings displayed erm, ducally gorged or cf 78 1

Burrowes and **Burrows,** two wings addorsed erm 109 12

Burrowes and **Burrows,** Ireland, a stag trippant 117 8

Burrows of Sydenham, Oxon, between two fleur-de-lis erminois, an eagle, the wings elevated and addorsed ppr, ducally gorged and charged on the breast with a cinquefoil or *Together*

Burrows, Sir Frederick Abernethy, Bart, 33 Ennismore Gardens, S W, an eagle with wings expanded or, collared az, holding in the beak a spear-head, and resting the dexter claw on a fleur de-lis, both of the last *Et vi et virtute* 236 1

Burrows, an ostrich-feather erect, enfiled by a ducal coronet

Burrs, a demi-antelope collared 126 3

Bury, a fox's head couped ppr 33 4

Burslam or **Burslem,** a pestle and mortar 177 13

Bursted, a wyvern gu 70 1

Burt, George, Esquire, D L, of Purbeck House, Swanage, Dorset, in front of two cross crosslets fitchee in saltire or, a bugle-horn sa, tipped, garnished, and veruled or, the strings gu, interlacing the cross crosslets, and all in front of a rock ppr *Know thyself* 228 4

Burt, John Mowlem, Esquire, of Purbeck House, Swanage, and 19, Grosvenor Road, S W, same crest and motto

Burt, Hon Septimus, of Strawberry Hill, Perth, a bugle horn sa, stringed gu *All for the better*

Burt-Marshall, James, Esquire, of Luncarty, Perthsh, and of Liverpool, a dove holding in its beak an olive-branch ppr *Virtute tutus* 92 5

Burtchaell of Brandondale, co Kilkenny, Ireland, on a mount vert, a lion rampant sa, supporting on the sinister side an oak tree ppr *Quo fata vocant* 263 1

Burtchaell, Charles Henry, Esquire, same crest and motto

Burtchaell, David, Esquire, of Port Fairy, Victoria, same crest and motto

Burtchaell, David Edward, Esquire, same crest and motto.

Burtchaell, George Dames, Esquire, of 44, Morebampton Road, Dublin, same crest and motto.

Burtchaell, Richard Rothe, Esquire, of Brandondale, Graignamanagh, co. Kilkenny, Ireland, same crest and motto.

Burthogge, Devonsh., a demi-wolf or, gorged with a bar gemelle az. *cf.* 31. 5

Burton, Baron (Bass), of Rangemore and Burton-on-Trent, Staffs, a demi-lion rampant gu., resting the sinister paw upon a plate charged with a fleur-de-lis az., and charged upon the shoulder with three annulets, two and one arg. *Basis virtutum constantia.* 13. 11

Burton, *see* Lingen-Burton.

Burton, Yorks and Shropsh., on a wreath of the colours a dexter gauntlet az., couped at the wrist. 209. 5

Burton of Longner Hall, Shropsh.: (1) On a wreath of the colours a dexter gauntlet az., couped at the wrist (*for Burton*). 209. 5. (2) Out of a ducal coronet or, seven leeks, roots upwards ppr. (*for Lingen*). *Dominus providebit.* 147. 5

Burton, Sir Charles William Cuffe, Bart., of Pollacton, co. Carlow, Ireland, on a ducal coronet or, a dexter gauntlet, the palm inwards, all ppr. *Deus providebit.*

Burton of Falde Hall, Staffs, Lindley and Bedworth, Leics., and Dronfield, Derbysh.: (1) Upon a mount vert, a beacon arg., inflamed ppr. 177. 8. (2) Out of a ducal coronet or, a cypress-tree ppr. 145. 9. (3) On a ducal coronet or, a wyvern with wings endorsed az., collared gold. *Lux vitæ.* *cf.* 70. 9

Burton, Derbysh., out of a ducal coronet or, a wyvern with wings endorsed az., collared, also or. *cf.* 70. 9

Burton, the late Sir Richard, of Sacket's Hill House, St. Peters, Isle of Thanet, a beacon or, fired ppr., surmounted by two branches of laurel in saltire vert. *Vigilans.* *cf.* 177. 14

Burton, Alfred, Esquire, M.R.C.S.E., of 13, Dover Street, W., at one time Physician to His Excellency the Lord Lieutenant of Ireland, an embattled wall ppr., charged with a crescent gu., thereon a beacon arg., fired ppr. *Lux vitæ.*

Burton of Foggathorpe, Bubwith, Yorks, E.R., of Childrey, Berks, and of Walton Hall, Bucks, in front of two arms embowed in armour, the hands ppr., holding a fleur-de-lis arg., six annulets, interlaced fesseways, also arg. *Sans changer.* 194. 1

Burton, Archer- of Woodlands, near Emsworth, Hants: (1) On a mount vert, an owl arg., ducally crowned or, holding in the dexter claw a rose gu., slipped of the first (*for Burton*). (2) A dragon's head erased gu., gorged with a crown vair, and holding in the mouth an arrow, point downwards or (*for Archer*). *Amicus vitæ solatium.*

Burton of Polethorpe, Rutl., and Stockerston, Leics., Bart. (*extinct*), an owl arg., ducally crowned or. *cf.* 96. 5

Burton of Somersby, Lincs, an owl ducally crowned holding in the dexter claw a star, all or. *Cari Deo nihil carent.*

Burton, Bindon Francis Burton, M.D., 1, Park Villas, Polsloe Road, Exeter, out of a ducal coronet a dexter gauntlet, the palm inwards, all ppr. *Dominus providabit.*

Burton, David Fowler, Esquire, of Cherry Burton, Yorks: (1) Upon a mount vert, a perch or, thereon a parrot, also vert, the dexter claw resting upon an escallop arg., and holding in the beak a cherry stalked ppr. (*for Burton*). (2) A mount vert, thereon a stag regardant or, the dexter fore-foot resting on a cinquefoil of the same (*for Robinson*).

Burton, General Fowler, Esquire, of Stoke Damerel, Devonport, same crests.

Burton of Inglethorp, Derbysh., on a mount vert, a tower arg., triple-towered or. *cf.* 157. 6

Burton of Stapleforth, Notts, a boar's head couped or, holding in the mouth a branch vert.

Burton, Langhorne Burton, Esquire, of the Uplands, South Cliffe, Scarborough, an owl erm., membered and ducally crowned or, the dexter claw resting on an estoile sa. *Cari Deo nihil carent.*

Burton, Essex, on the top of a ruined castle arg., a falcon volant or. *cf.* 156. 8

Burton, Yorks, a cubit arm erect, habited per pale arg. and gu., cuffed of the first, holding in the hand ppr. a walking staff of the second, headed, rimmed, and ferruled or.

Burton-Mackenzie, Evan North, of Kilcoy, Ross-sh., Scotland: (1) On the dexter side, an arm embowed in chain-mail, couped at the shoulder, holding a broadsword in bend ppr. (*for Mackenzie*). (2) On the sinister side a stag's head caboshed or, pierced between the attires with an arrow ppr. (*for Fraser*). Over the crests, *Fide parta fide aucta.* Under the arms, *Dia's mo dhuthaich.*

Burtz, a squirrel sejant resting his fore-paws on a staff raguly.

Burwasch, Burwasche, or **Burwash**, the helm of a ship ppr. 179. 1

Burwell, a Saracen's head couped at the shoulders ppr. 190. 5

Burwell, Suff., a lion's gamb erect and erased or, holding three burr-leaves vert

Burwood, a boar's head ppr. 41. 1

Bury, Viscount, *see* Albemarle, Earl of.

Bury, Lincs and Somers., a demi-dragon arg., wings, ears, and claws sa. 73. 10

Bury, cos. Cork and Limerick, Ireland, a boar's head couped at the neck or, tusked arg., langued gu., transfixed through the neck by a spear ppr.

Bury, William Pennefather Arthur Forbes Phineas, Esquire, of Curraghbridge, co. Limerick, and Carrigrenane, Little Island, co. Cork, same crest. *Virtus sub cruce crescit.*

Bury, Earl of, and **Viscount Charleville** and **Baron Tullamore** (*extinct*), Ireland: (1) A boar's head couped or, transpierced through the neck from behind with an arrow ppr. (*for Bury*). (2) Out of a ducal coronet or, a Moor's head couped at the shoulders ppr., wreathed round the temples or and az. (*for Moore*). *Virtus sub cruce crescit.*

Bury, Howard-, Captain Kenneth, of Charleville Forest, King's Co.: (1) A boar's head couped at the neck or, tusked arg., langued gu., transfixed through the neck by a spear ppr., and charged for difference with a cross crosslet vert (*for Bury*). (2) On a chapeau gu., turned up erm., a lion statant gardant, the tail extended or, ducally gorged arg., and charged on the body with a crescent, also gu., for difference (*for Howard*). *Virtus sub cruce crescit.—Nous maintiendrons.* *cf.* 4. 8

Bury, *see* Berry.

Bury, Devonsh., a griffin's head erased party per pale or and gu. 66. 2

Bury, Devonsh., a tiger's head erased erm., crined sa., gorged with a collar az., charged with a bezant between two fleurs-de-lis or. 22. 12

Bury, Rev. William Edward, the Rectory, Screveton, Notts, a demi-wyvern arg., wings and feet sa., purfled or. *Virtus sub cruce crescit.*

Bury, a fox's head couped ppr. 33. 4

Bury-Barry, James Robert Barry, Esquire: (1) Out of a castle arg., a wolf's head couped sa., langued gu. (*for Barry*). (2) A boar's head couped at the neck or, tusked arg., langued gu., transfixed through the neck by a spear ppr., point downwards, and charged with a crescent for difference gu. (*for Bury*), and over it the motto "*Virtus sub cruce crescit.*" *Boutez en avant.*

Burye, a dove regardant holding in the beak an olive-branch ppr. 92. 4

Busbie, a bee erect, head downwards, the wings expanded ppr. *cf.* 137. 1

Busbridge, Essex, an arm in mail erect holding in the band a cutlass ppr.

Busbridge, Perry Barr, Warw., a stag's head cabossed. 122. 5

Busby and **Bushby**, a stag's head arg., erased gu., pierced through the back of the neck with an arrow sa., headed and barbed of the first. *cf.* 121. 2

Busfeild, John, Esquire, of Laurel Bank, Ripon, a cubit arm in armour ppr., a fleur-de-lis within an annulet or.

Busfeild, William, of Pant-y-Ochin, Wrexham, same crest. *Medio tutissimus ibis.*

Busfield of Upwood, Yorks: (1) A cubit arm in armour erect ppr., holding in the hand a fleur-de-lis or (*for Busfield*). 210. 6. (2) An eagle's head erased (*for Atkinson*). *Medio tutissimus ibis.* 83. 2

Bush, Bushe, or **Bussche**, the trunk of a tree with branches ppr., pendent therefrom an escutcheon arg. 145. 8

Bush of Dylton, Wilts, a goat's head erased arg., armed or. 128. 5

Bush, Thomas, Esquire, a goat's head couped arg., the sinister horn az., and the dexter purpure. *Hope me encourageth.*

Bush, a stag statant. 117. 5

Bushby, Henry North Grant, Esquire, J.P., of Wormley-Bury, Broxbourne, Herts, upon a mount vert, a stag's head erased ppr., guttée-de-sang, the neck transfixed by an arrow in bend sinister, point to the dexter, also ppr. *Fructu non foliis.* 250. 13

Bushby, Sussex and Cumb., a crow picking ppr. 107. 4

Bushby, *see* Busby.

Bushe, a goat's head arg, armed sa, charged on the neck with a crescent for difference *Hope me encourageth* cf 128 12
Bushe, Erasmus, Esquire, of 32, Bullingham Mansions, Kensington, London, W, same crest and motto
Bushe of Glencairn Abbey, Waterford, a goat's head couped arg, attired or *Moderata durant* 128 12
Bushe of Kingstown, co Dublin, Ireland, a goat's head erased per fesse arg and az, armed or *Nil metuens superavi* 128 5
Bushe, Arthur, Esquire, a goat's head arg *Moderata durant*
Bushe, Cecil Josiah Lambton, Esquire, same crest and motto
Bushe, Charles, Esquire, same crest and motto
Bushe, George, Esquire, same crest and motto
Bushe, Horace Kendal, Esquire, same crest and motto
Bushe, Percy, Esquire, same crest and motto
Bushe, Seymour C H, Esquire, same crest and motto
Bushe, William Daxon, Esquire, same crest and motto
Bushe, Ireland, a cross pattee fitched arg, between two ears of wheat in orle
Bushell, Warw, an arm from the elbow in armour holding a caltrap 210 7
Bushell or **Busshell**, Chesh, a cherub's head between two wings ppr 189 9
Bushell, Lancs, a water bouget between two wings arg, each charged with a hurt *Dum spiro spero*
Bushnan, London, a sinister arm embowed, vested sa, cuffed arg, holding in the hand a roll of parchment ppr
Bushnell, on a ducal coronet or, a wyvern sans feet 70 9
Bushrudd, Dorset, an heraldic tiger's head arg, crined and tufted sa, collared gu cf 25 4
Bushy or **Bushey**, a boar's head erased sa 41 5
Busk, France, a stag trippant ppr *Suaviter sed fortiter* 117 8
Busk of Ford's Grove, Middx a stag at gaze ppr *Suaviter sed fortiter* 117 3
Busk and **Buske**, out of a ducal coronet or, a fish's head az 139 14
Busse, *see* Bushe
Bussell, Warw, a cherub's head between two wings ppr 189 9
Bussell, issuing from clouds two dexter hands conjoined, holding up an olive-branch, all ppr cf 224 3
Bussell, a crane's head erased arg 104 11
Bussie, an eagle displayed az 75 2
Bustard, Devonsh, a bustard's head arg, between two wings gu, between the neck and the wings two ears of wheat erect or
Busteed, an eagle rising ppr 77 5
Busterd, Ireland, a cannon mounted ppr 169 12
Bustin, an escallop between two branches of palm ppr 141 4
Busvargus or **Bosvargus** of Bushvargus, Cornw, a Cornish chough ppr 107 14
Butcher, a lion passant gu, holding in the dexter paw a crescent arg 5 6
Butcher, a branch of a cotton-tree fructed ppr *Be steady*
Butcher, Arthur Herbert, Esquire, of Elmslea, Birkenhead, co Chester, a branch of a cotton tree fructed ppr *Be steady*
Butcher, Major Henry Townsend, same crest and motto
Butcher, John George, Esquire, of 32, Elvaston Place, London, S W, same crest and motto
Butcher, Samuel Esquire (son of Major-General Arthur Butcher) c o Messrs Thomas Cook and Son, Banking Department, Ludgate Circus, E C, same crest and motto
Butcher, Samuel Henry, Esquire, of Danesfort, Killarney, co Kerry, and 6, Tavistock Square, London, W C, same crest and motto
Butcher, Rev Samuel John, M A, Clerk in Holy Orders, Vicar of Weston Beggard, Heref, same crest and motto
Bute, Marquess and Earl of (Crichton Stuart), Mount Stuart, Rothesay, Isle of Bute (1) A demi-lion rampant gu (*for Stuart*) 10 3 (2) A dragon vert, flames issuing from the mouth ppr (3) A wyvern ppr, holding in the mouth a sinister hand couped gu *Nobilis est ira leonis —Avito viret honore* cf 70 10
Buthall, a wyvern ppr, charged on the breast with a hand couped at the wrist gu cf 70 1
Butler, Marquess of Ormonde, *see* Ormonde
Butler, Earl of Lanesborough, *see* Lanesborough
Butler, Earl of Carrick, *see* Carrick
Butler, Earl of Kilkenny, *see* Kilkenny
Butler, Earl of Glengall, *see* Glengall
Butler, Baron Dunboyne, *see* Dunboyne
Butler, *see* Fyfe Butler
Butler, *see* Arcedeckne Butler
Butler-Clough, *see* Clough
Butler, *see* Boteller and Botteller and Buttler
Butler-Bowdon, *see* Bowdon
Butler, Sir Thomas Pierce, Bart, of Cloughgrenan, co Carlow, Ireland, out of a ducal coronet or, a plume of five ostrich-feathers, and therefrom a falcon rising arg *Comme je trouve* 248 9
Butler, Ireland, out of a ducal coronet or, a plume of five ostrich-feathers, therefrom a falcon rising arg *Comme je trouve* 248 9
Butler, John Piers, Esquire, a falcon displayed ppr, rising out of a plume of five ostrich-feathers arg *Comme je trouve*
Butler, Rev Charles Ewart, M A, Corpus Christi College, Cambridge, a horse statant arg, charged on the body with a pale az, thereon a cross crosslet or, and holding in the mouth a quatrefoil slipped gu *Deo duce Christo luce* 295 8
Butler-Creagh, Captain Walker Blake (1) A horse's head erased arg, caparisoned gu, in the headstall of the bridle a laurel-branch vert, and charged on the neck for distinction with a fleur de lis sa (*for Creagh*) (2) A plume of five ostrich feathers arg, charged with a covered cup gu, and issuant from the plume a falcon rising ppr (*for Butler*) *Virtute et numine —Comme je trouve*
Butler-Kearney, Charles James, Esquire, of Drom, co Tipperary, Ireland (1) A gauntleted hand fesseways or, holding a dagger erect arg, pommel and hilt of the first (*for Kearney*) (2) Out of a ducal coronet or, a plume of five ostrich-feathers arg, and issuant therefrom a demi falcon also arg, and on an escroll above, "*Timor Domini fons vitæ*" *Sustine et abstine.* 248 9
Butler, Francis Theobald, M D, 3, Pelham Crescent, Hastings, out of a ducal coronet a plume of five ostrich-feathers, and rising therefrom a demi-falcon with wings expanded and inverted, all ppr *Timor Domini fons vitæ* 248 9
Butler, Captain Antoine Sloet, of 12, St James's Terrace, Clonkeath, co Dublin, same crest *Comme je trouve*
Butler, William, Esquire, of Wilton, co Kilkenny, same crest and motto
Butler, Dublin, out of a mural coronet or, a plume of five ostrich-feathers arg, therefrom a phœnix issuant, wings expanded az holding in his beak a trefoil slipped of the first *Esse quam videri*
Butler, a covered cup or, banded sa, and a ball on the top of the second
Butler, Scotland, an uncovered cup or *Sapienter uti bonis* 177 4
Butler and **Boteler**, Kent, a covered cup or, between two wings, the dexter of the same the sinister az
Butler, a covered cup or
Butler, Devonsh, a lion's gamb erased gu, holding a covered cup or cf 38 14
Butler, Fowler-, Major-General Robert Henry, of Pendeford Hall, Wolverhampton (1) A covered cup or surmounting two palm branches in saltire vert, between two wings quarterly or and sa. *Depressus extoller* (*for Butler*) (2) A cubit arm vested az, holding in the hand ppr a lure vert, feathered arg lined or, twisted round the arm *Garde le Roy* (*for Fowler*)
Butler, an arm embowed, vested az, ruffle of indented lace arg, the hand ppr, holding a covered cup erect az 203 4
Butler, Derbysh, an arm embowed, vested az, cuffed arg, holding in the hand a bunch of grapes ppr
Butler, two arms in armour embowed ppr, purfled or, holding in the hands, also ppr, a round buckle of the second cf 194 11
Butler, London, an eagle with wings addorsed, holding in the dexter claw a vine branch, all ppr
Butler, F K L, London Institution, Finsbury Circus, E C, a grape-vine issuing from a mount between two eagles with their wings elevated and addorsed, respecting each other *Aquila vitem pocula vitam*
Butler, Herts, a dexter arm in armour gauntleted az, garnished or, holding a sword sa, hilted of the second 210 4
Butler, a male griffin segreant arg, armed, beaked, collared, and chained or *Je ferai bien*
Butler, Middx, a greyhound sejant or, collared gu, ringed, also or cf 59 2
Butler, Cyril Kendall, of Bourton House, Shrivenham, Berks, a falcon, wings endorsed and inverted, resting the dexter claw on a covered cup or *Tu contra audentior ito*

Butler, Hedley Ormonde, 26, Grove Park Gardens, Chiswick, W., same crest. *Labor omnia vincit improbus.*

Butler of Elmore, Chipstead, Surrey, a greyhound sejant arg., charged with two bars az., and resting the dexter paw on a covered cup or. *Labor omnia vincit.* 59. 12

Butler, Ireland, a demi-cockatrice displayed vert, wings elevated arg., combed, beaked, and ducally gorged or.

Butler, Humphrey, Esquire, Commander R.N., same crest.

Butler or **Botteler,** Cambs, a cockatrice's head and wings, the head vert, the wings arg., ducally gorged, combed, and wattled or. 68. 10

Butler-Danvers, Leics.: (1) A wyvern or (*for Danvers*). 70. 1. (2) A demi-cockatrice couped vert, combed, beaked, wattled, and ducally gorged or (*for Butler*). *Liberté toute entière.*

Butler of Kirkland, Lancs, a horse passant arg., pellettée and furnished or. *Beneficii memor.* cf. 52. 6

Butler, Philip, Esquire, of Gattalunga, Adelaide, Australia, a horse statant arg., charged on the body with a pale az., thereon a cross crosslet or, and holding in the mouth a quatrefoil slipped gu. *Doe duce Christo luce.*

Butler, Cotes, Lincs, a horse's head erased, quarterly arg. and sa. 51. 4

Butler, Lancs, a unicorn salient arg., armed or, gorged with a sash of the last. cf. 48. 2

Butler, Samuel, Esquire, of Henbury Hill, Westbury-on-Trym, near Bristol, a unicorn salient or, holding in the mouth a rose gu., barbed, seeded, slipped, and leaved ppr., and resting the sinister fore-foot upon a covered cup az. *Fac recte et nil time.* 263. 2

Butler, William Henry, Esquire, of Summerhill House, St. George, Bristol, same crest and motto.

Butler, a demi-stag az., collared or, supporting between the legs a covered cup per pale az. and or. *Tandem implebitur.*

Butler-Bowdon, John Erdeswick, Esquire, of Pleasington Hall, Blackburn, Lancs, and Southgate House, Chesterfield: (1) A heron's head erased ppr., beaked and charged on the neck with three erm. spots (*for Bowdon*). (2) A covered cup or, charged with an erm. spot sa. (*for Butler*). *Vanus est honor.*

Butler-Bowdon, Lancelot George, Esquire, of Barlborough House, Chesterfield, same crests and motto.

Butler, Ireland, a lamb statant erm.

Butt, Kent, a lion sejant, holding in the dexter paw a broken spear. cf. 8. 11

Butt of Tavistock Square, London, a horse's head couped sa., semée of estoiles or, the mane plaited ppr., on the head a skull-plate of the second with two feathers az. cf. 50. 14

Butt, Isaac, Esquire, LL.D., of Dublin, a horse's head erased arg., charged on the neck with a trefoil vert, the mane plaited or, on the head a plume of three ostrich-feathers of the first. *Possunt quia, posse videntur.*

Butt, George Berkeley, Esquire, same crest and motto.

Butt-Gow, Philip, Esquire, of Dorville Road, Lee, Kent, a dexter arm in armour embowed holding a broad-sword enfiled with a boar's head, all ppr. *Caraid ann am fheum.*

Butter, Archibald Edward, Esquire, J.P., of Faskally, Pitlochry, Perthsh., two arms issuing from clouds, and drawing a bow with an arrow paleways, all ppr. *Diriget Deus.*

Butter, a camel's head couped ppr. 132. 7

Butter of Gormack, Scotland, issuing from clouds two arms drawing a bow with an arrow, all ppr. *Diriget Deus.* cf. 200. 2

Butter, Dr. John K., M.D., of Highfield House, Cannock, Staffs, issuing from clouds, two arms drawing a bow with an arrow, all ppr. *Furth fortune.* 294. 13

Butterfield, Hants, out of a ducal coronet or, a dragon's head with the wings elevated vert. 72. 1

Butterfield of Clapham, Surrey, out of a ducal coronet or, a demi-dragon with wings elevated arg., charged on each wing with a butterfly volant az.

Butters, Scotland, two naked arms issuing shooting an arrow from a bow, all ppr. 200. 2

Butterworth, Scotland, a hand issuing from a cloud in fess pointing to a serpent nowed, the head erect, all ppr. 223. 7

Butterworth, a sphere resting on a cloud ppr. 159. 5

Butterworth, Joseph Henry, Esquire, an eagle with wings elevated erminois, resting its dexter claw on an escutcheon az., charged with a cross crosslet or. *Per ardua Deo favente.*

Buttery, Northamp., an heraldic tiger passant arg., tufted and maned or, supporting with the dexter paw an escutcheon.

Button, a ram statant arg., armed and unguled or, collared gu., pendent thereto a bell of the second. cf. 129. 3

Button, Wilts, a wyvern erect on the tail sa.

Button or Budden, a bull's head ppr., charged with a cross botonée or. cf. 44. 3

Button of Alton, Wilts, on each side of a chapeau gu., turned up erm., a horn or, waved as those of an ox.

Buttress, London, an eagle displayed. *In periculis audax.* 75. 2

Butts, Suff. and Norf., a horse's head arg., armed and bridled or, on the head a plume of three feathers of the first and second. 50. 14

Butts, Norf., a horse's head sorrel, the mane plaited arg. and or, on the head a skull-plate az., and two feathers of the third and fourth. cf. 50. 14

Butts, Suff., a horse's head caparisoned, all ppr., from the top of the head issuant two feathers, the dexter or, the sinister sa. cf. 50. 14

Butts, De, a ferret passant ppr. 134. 6

Butts of Dorking, Surrey, an arm couped at the elbow and erect ppr., grasping in the hand a fish arg. 220. 4

Buxhull, a Saracen's head ppr., crowned or. 192. 9

Buxton, Sir Thomas Fowell Victor, Bart., of Bellfield, Dorset, and of Runton, Norf., a buck's head couped gu., attired or, gorged with a collar of the last, therefrom pendent an escutcheon arg., charged with an African's head sa. *Do it with thy might.* 248. 6

Buxton, Henry Edmund, Esquire, of Fritton, Great Yarmouth, same crest and motto.

Buxton, Sidney Charles, Esquire, of 7, Grosvenor Crescent, S.W., same crest and motto.

Buxton, Alfred St. Clair, Surgeon, 44, Devonshire Street, Portland Place, W., a stag's head couped gu., attired or. *Quicquid assequitur manus tua ut facias pro facultate tua fac.*

Buxton, Norf. and Derbysh., a pelican or, with wings expanded, vulning herself gu. 98. 1

Buxton, a demi-doe ppr.

By, Sussex, a demi-lion or, holding in the dexter paw a fleur-de-lis az. 13. 2

By and **Bye,** two oak-branches in saltier. 151. 1

Byam, Somers., a wolf passant or, collared and lined vert. cf. 28. 10

Byam, Sussex and Somers.: (1) A wolf passant or, collared and lined vert. cf. 28. 10. (2) A dragon's head erased ppr., holding in the mouth a sinister hand couped gu., dropping blood. *Claris dextera factis.* 72. 6

Byam, a dragon's head erased ppr., holding in the mouth a sinister hand couped gu., dropping blood. 72. 6

Byass, Worcs., between two wings az., a wing arg., charged with an escutcheon of the first, thereon a fleur-de-lis of the second. *By assiduity.* 249. 11

Byass, Robert Nicholl, Esquire, of Wyck Hill, Stow-on-Wold, same crest and motto.

Byass, Sidney Hutchinson, Esquire, of Glanoqur, Bridgend, Glamorgan, same crest and motto.

Byatt, Suff., out of an Eastern crown or, a dove rising ppr.

Byeknor, *see* Bykenor.

Byde, Herts, an arm erect ppr., vested az., cuffed arg., holding in the hand an anchor sa., the fluke or. 208. 3

Byde, a demi-griffin az., armed and winged or, holding a garb of the last. cf. 65. 5

Bydewell or **Bidwell,** a hand couped at the wrist in fess holding a curling-stone. 221. 2

Bye, *see* By.

Byeing, an angel pointing upward ppr.

Byer and **Byers,** Northamp., a griffin's head party per pale gu. and az., charged with a pheon arg. cf. 66. 1

Byerly, Byerley, and **Byorley,** London and Yorks, two lion's gambs ppr., holding a cross crosslet or. 39. 12

Byers, Scotland, a cock regardant ppr. *Marte suo tutus.* 91. 9

Byest, Shropsh., *see* Beist.

Byfeld or **Byfield,** London, a cross crosslet fitched sa., between two palm-branches vert. cf. 166. 5

Byfield, *see* Bifield.

Byfield, on a man's head bearded and affrontée a chapeau ppr.

Byfield, London, an antelope trippant ppr. 126. 6

Byfield, an antelope trippant ppr., collared or. cf. 126. 6

Byfleet, Cambs, a Saracen's head affrontee ppr, wreathed with a ribbon arg, tied in a bow-knot on the sinister side *cf* 190 5
Byford and **Bytford**, Heref a lion's gamb erect or, holding an eagle's leg erased at the thigh sa 38 10
Byford or **Bayford**, an owl arg 96 5
Bygan, Yorks, an erm ppr *cf* 134 2
Bygbery, Devonsh, a hand holding a leg in armour couped above the knee and spurred ppr 220 11
Bygod or **Bygode**, Yorks, on a chapeau arg, turned up gu, charged with two bars az, a dolphin embowed and devouring the cap or
Bygot, seven arrows or, one in pale and six in saltier 173 7
Byirley, a lion's gamb holding up a human heart, all ppr 39 11
Bykenor and **Bicknor**, Kent an antelope's head gu, armed arg, collared or *cf* 126 2
Bykenor, a pheon erm 174 11
Byles, out of a ducal coronet or, a lion's head per bend embattled arg and gu 17 5
Bylney, Norf, out of a tower a demi griffin sa 157 5
Byne, a hind regardant or, resting the dexter foot on a ball sa *cf* 124 11
Byng, Earl of Strafford, *see* Strafford
Byng, Viscount Torrington, *see* Torrington
Byng, Middx, a heraldic antelope statant erm, armed, crined, and ungu or *Tuebor* *cf* 127 5
Byng, Cranmer- (1) A heraldic antelope trippant erm, attired, tusked, crined, and ungu or (*for Byng*) 127 5 (2) A crane's head erm, erased gu, pierced through the neck by an arrow in bend sinister or, barbed and flighted arg (*for Cranmer*) *Tuebor*
Byng, Cranmer-, Lieutenant-Colonel Alfred Molyneux, Quendon Hall Newport same crests and motto
Byngham, a hand ppr holding three branches of cinquefoil gu, leaved vert, and charged on the sleeve sa. with a cross arg 205 12
Byngley of Broughton, Flintsh, a pellet charged with a pheon arg, between two wings erect or
Byngley or **Bynley**, a harp or 168 9
Byorley, *see* Byerley
Byrch, Essex, on a mount a birch-tree ppr
Byrch, Beds, a hare courant sa *cf* 136 3
Byrch, a hare courant sa, collared or *cf* 136 3
Byrch, Kent and Sussex, an eagle rising ppr, holding in the dexter claw a banner az, charged with a cross clechee or, the staff, point, and tassels of the same 78 14
Byrch, Essex, a squirrel sejant eating an apple, and holding a branch of birch in the sinister foot
Byrch, Essex, a squirrel sejant, bendy wavy of six or and az, holding a branch of birch vert
Byrchett or **Birket**, of Kent and Rye, Sussex, a tiger vert, gorged with a ducal coronet or *cf* 27 14
Byrdall, a stag's head erased ppr 121 2
Byrde, Kent, a stag's head cabossed arg, between the attires or, a bird of the last 122 9
Byrde, Lincs, a demi-lion sa, guttee-de sarg *cf* 10 1
Byrde, Captain Henry of Pentre House, Goytrey, near Pontypool, same crest *Quid leone fortius*
Byrde, on a dolphin embowed ppr, an eagle with wings addorsed or
Byres, a cock regardant ppr *Marte suo tutus* 91 9
Byres Moir-, George, of Tonley Whitehouse, Aberdeensh, same crest and motto
Byres of Coates, a bee volant or *Rule be ours* 137 1
Byres, Scotland, a catherine wheel 167 2
Byres, *see* Byers
Byrmyncham, a cap per pale indented arg and sa, between two wings expanded or
Byrn, Ireland and England, a mermaid ppr 184 5
Byrne, Ireland, a mermaid ppr, charged with three escallops or, holding in her dexter hand a mirror and in her sinister a dart
Byrne, Thomas Joseph Esquire, J P, of Rossmakea Dundalk a mermaid holding in her dexter hand a mirror, and in her sinister a comb, all ppr, and charged below the waist with an escallop gu *Certavi et vici* 292 5
Byrne, Hon Sir Edmund Widdrington, K B, of 33, Lancaster Gate, W, a mermaid ppr holding in her dexter hand a mirror and in her sinister a comb between two dexter hands apaumee couped at the wrists arg *Certavi et vici*
Byrne, of Cabinteely, Dublin, a mermaid holding in her dexter hand a mirror and in her sinister hand a comb, all ppr *Certavi et vici* 184 5
Byrne and **Byrn**, a hand issuing from a cloud in pale holding a garb 218 3
Byrom, Lancs, a hedgehog sa 135 8
Byrom, Lancs, a hedgehog sa, charged for distinction with a cross crosslet arg *Arme a tous points* *cf* 135 8
Byrom, Edward Esquire, of Culver, near Exeter, and Kersall Cell, Lancs, Grimston Garth, Hull, same crest and motto
Byrom, out of a ducal coronet or, a tree vert 145 9
Byron, Rt. Hon George Frederick William, **Baron Byron**, of Rochdale, Lancs, a mermaid with a comb and a mirror, all ppr *Crede Byron* 184 5
Byron of Bayford, Herts, and Couldon, Surrey, a mermaid ppr holding in her dexter hand an escutcheon suspended by a ribbon az, and in her sinister a mirror
Byrtwhysell, Lancs, a dolphin ppr 140 5
Byshe, on a chapeau gu, turned up erm, a demi lion or 15 13
Byshe, a mule passant arg
Byshoppe Dublin, an eagle displayed gu 75 2
Bysse, on a mount vert, two snakes interwoven and erect, respecting each other or
Bystley, a cross pattee gu, between two wings or 110 7
Bythell of Winchester, out of a ducal coronet or, a boar's head and neck arg 41 4
Bythesea of Week House, Wilts, and Freshford, Somers, an eagle displayed arg, charged on the breast with the Roman fasces erect, surmounting two swords in saltier, and encircled by a chaplet ppr, and on each wing with a cross crosslet fitchee gu *Mutare vel timere sperno* *cf* 75 2
Bythesea, Rear-Admiral John, C B, of 22, Ashburne Place, S W, same crest and motto
Bythesea, Samuel Francis Glossop, Esquire, of 36, Adelaide Crescent, Brighton same crest and motto
Bythesea, Kent, out of a mural coronet arg, masoned sa, a griffin's head ducally gorged ppr 67 6
Bywater, out of a ducal coronet, a hand in armour holding a scimitar, all ppr 209 11

C

Cabbell, Benj Bond, Esquire, of Cromer Hall, Norf, an arm in armour embowed grasping a sword, all ppr 195 2
Cable, Ernest, Esquire, of Calcutta, in front of a fret sa, an escutcheon or, charged with a padlock of the first
Cabot, an escallop or 141 12
Cabourne, Cabron, and **Cabrone**, of Thrasthrop, Lincs, out of a ducal coronet or, a lozenge arg, charged with a martlet sa 180 11
Cabytott, Norf, a greyhound current az, collared and ringed or. *cf* 58 2
Cacher, London, out of a ducal coronet or, a demi leopard arg, spotted and collared of the first *cf* 23 13
Caddel, Scotland, a tower gu, loopholes and portway or 156 2
Caddell and **Cadell**, Scotland, a stag's head ppr *Vigilantia non cadet* 121 5
Caddey, a pile charged with a cross pattee fitched or
Caddon, an arm in armour embowed holding in the hand an arrow in pale, surmounted by a bow stringed in fess, the cord crossing in saltire over the arrow 198 9
Caddy, a cross crosslet vert 166 2
Cade, Kent, a demi-cockatrice winged gu, combed or
Cade, Derbysh, a demi-lion rampant gu 10 3
Cade, Derbysh and Essex, a demi-lion rampant gu, charged on the shoulder

with a bezant, and holding in the dexter paw a fleur-de-lis or. *cf.* 13. 2

Cade, Francis Joseph, M.A., Teighmore, Cheltenham, a demi-lion rampant gu. *Generositate.*

Cadell, London, a stag's head couped sa., collared arg., pendent from the collar an escutcheon of the arms—viz., arg., a cross engrailed vert, in the first quarter a stag's head caboshed. *Deo duce.* *cf.* 120. 8

Cadell, M. G. I., M.D., 15, Talbot Road, Bayswater, W., a stag's head erased. *Vigilantia non cadet.* 121. 2

Cadell, Colonel Thomas, of Cockenzie House, Prestonpans, a stag's head ppr. *Vigilantia non cadet.* 121. 2

Cadell, *see* Caddell.

Cadicott, a dexter hand per fess gu. and arg., holding a battle-axe. 213. 12

Cadicott, a demi-ape ppr. *cf.* 136. 13

Cadiman, London and Norf., a rock ppr. surmounted by a fleur-de-lis or. *cf.* 179. 7

Cadman, a stork's head royally crowned ppr. 104. 7

Cadman of Westbourne House, Yorks, same crest. *Deus et patria.*

Cadman, Rev. John Montagu, M.A. (Cantab), of The Vicarage, Sedbergh, Yorks., in front of a rock a stork's head, both ppr., ducally crowned or. *Deus et patria.* 237. 19

Cadman, Rev. William Snape, M.A., Vicar of Boxley, Kent, same crest and motto.

Cadman, Charles William, Copmanhurst, Broomhill, Sheffield, same crest and motto.

Cadman, John Heaton, Ackworth, same crest and motto.

Cadogan, Earl (Cadogan), Culford Hall, Bury St. Edmunds, out of a ducal coronet or, a dragon's head vert. *Qui invidet minor est.* 72. 4

Cadurcis, a griffin's head erased gu., holding in the beak a trefoil vert, gorged with a ducal coronet or. *cf.* 71. 8

Cadwoodley, an antelope trippant per pale gu. and or, attired of the last. 126. 6

Cady, a merlin ppr., chained, tasselled and belled or.

Cadye, Glouc., on a mount vert, a cockatrice arg., combed and wattled gu., ducally gorged and chained or. 68. 7

Cæsar, Hunts, a cross pattée. 165. 7

Cæsar, a dolphin embowed ppr., in the sea vert. *cf.* 140. 5

Cafe, Claremont, Sidmouth, Devonsh., in front of a sword erect, point downwards arg., hilted or, an escutcheon az., charged with a Saracen's head couped, also arg. *Coup sur coup.* 171. 8

Cafe, Charles Haydon Wilkinson, Esquire, same crest and motto.

Cafe, General William Martin, V.C., of Wetherby Place, South Kensington, same crest. *From Caf to Caf.*

Cage, Kent, a stag trippant erm., attired or, charged on the shoulder with an annulet gu. 117. 9

Cahan and **Cahane,** Ireland, an arm embowed holding a sword ppr. 201. 4

Cahill, Ireland and England, a lion's gamb holding a scimitar ppr. 38. 13

Cahill and Cahil, Ireland, a demi-bull rampant sa., gorged with a chaplet vert. 45. 14

Cahill, John Nugent, Esquire, J.P., of Ballyconra, co. Kilkenny, Ireland, an anchor erect entwined with a cable ppr., out of the dexter fluke an oak-branch, also ppr. *In Domino confido.* 299. 10

Cahill, John, M.D., 12, Seville Street, Lowndes Square, S.W., same crest and motto.

Cahn, Cahan, and **Cahun,** Scotland, a stag's head erased. *Si je puis.* 121. 2

Cahurta, a stag erm., attired or. 121. 5

Caillard of Wingfield House, Wilts, a quail ppr. *Aid-toi, Dieu t'aidera.* *cf.* 89. 12

Caillard, same crest and motto.

Cain and **Caine,** a demi-antelope per fesse arg. and az., collared and attired or. 126. 3

Cain, William Joseph, Esquire, of Woodbourne Square, Douglas, Isle of Man, in front of a demi-heraldic antelope gu., armed and gorged with a collar gemel or, semée of plates, supporting between its legs a mullet of six points, pierced arg., a rock ppr. *Esto quod esse videris.*

Caird, a demi-friar issuing, holding in his hand a staff erect ppr.

Caird, Henryson-, James Alexander, of Cassencary, Creetown, N.B., a dexter hand fesseways couped at the wrist ppr., holding a star of six points ensigned with a crescent arg. *Virtus sola nobilitat.* 286. 11

Cairleon, a cross moline lozenge-pierced erm. *cf.* 165. 11

Cairncross of Balmashaner, Scotland, a dagger in pale ppr. *Certamine parta.* 169. 2

Cairne, Scotland, a hand holding a fish ppr. 220. 4

Cairnes, Scotland, a fleur-de-lis. *Effloresco.* 148. 2

Cairnes, Scotland, a cinquefoil ppr. *Effloresco.* 148. 12

Cairnes, on a tower a martlet statant ppr. 156. 9

Cairnie, Scotland, a ship under sail. ppr. 160. 13

Cairnie, on a cinquefoil vert, a martlet sa. *Ad alta.*

Cairns, Earl (Cairns), Lindisfarne, near Bournemouth, a martlet arg., charged with a trefoil slipped vert. *Effloresco.* *cf.* 95. 4

Cairns, Scotland, a bell az. *Sub spe.* 168. 7

Cairns, Scotland, a palm-tree ppr. *Virtus ad æthera tendit.* 144. 15

Cairns of Pilmor, a cinquefoil ppr. *Effloresco.* 148. 12

Cairns, Scotland, a stag's head erased ppr., between the attires a cross crosslet fitched. *Semper fidelis.* 120. 12

Caithness, Earl of (Sinclair), 59, Inverness Terrace, W., a cock ppr. *Commit thy work to God.* 91. 2

Calamount, an antelope's head erased erm., attired arg. 126. 2

Calamy, a hedgehog ppr. 135. 8

Calandrine, a demi-eagle displayed arg., holding in the beak a scroll, thereon the motto *Sursum.* 81. 14

Calcot, *see* Caldecot.

Calcott, Hants, a lion sejant collared and lined. *Dieu avec nous.* 7. 4

Calcraft of Ingress, Kent, and Rempston, Dorset, a greyhound current sa., collared and ringed arg., charged on the body with a pallet wavy or. *cf.* 58. 2

Calcraft, William Montague, Esquire, of Rempston, Wareham, Dorset, same crest.

Calcraft of Ancaster Hall, Lincs, a greyhound current sa., charged with a cross crosslet or. *cf.* 58. 1

Caldecot, Oxon., a demi-heraldic tiger or, tufted, maned, and attired with two straight horns sa., the horns wreathed of the first and last.

Caldecot, Chesh., an ostrich ppr. 97. 2

Caldecott, a demi-lion rampant or, charged on the shoulder with a cinquefoil gu. *cf.* 10. 2

Caldecott, Colonel Charles Thomas, of Holbrook Grange, Rugby, a demi-lion rampant gu., charged on the shoulder with a cinquefoil arg. *In utrumque paratus.*

Calder, a stag's head cabossed ppr. 122. 5

Calder, within a serpent in orle a boar's head erased and erect. 41. 11

Calder of Lynegar, a stag's head cabossed sa. *Vigilans non cadit.* 122. 5

Calder, a swan ppr., crowned or. *Be mindful.* 99. 4

Calder, Bart., Scotland, a swan swimming in a loch, bordered with flags ppr. *Vigilans non cadet.* 99. 8

Calder, in water a duck swimming ppr. 102. 7

Calderwood of Pittedy, a dexter hand holding a palm-branch ppr. *Veritas premitur non opprimitur.* 219. 9

Calderwood of Polton, a phœnix in flames ppr. *Virtus sibi præmium.* 82. 2

Calderwood, Scotland, a beehive ppr., with bees volant. 137. 7

Calderwood, Scotland, a dove holding in its beak a palm-branch ppr. *Spero.* *cf.* 92. 5

Caldicote, a lion statant gardant ppr., supporting an esquire's helmet embellished or. *Si Deus pro nobis quis contra nos.* *cf.* 4. 1

Caldmore, a demi-Turk vested holding in his dexter hand a staff headed with a crescent.

Caldron, a dexter hand holding a palm-branch slipped ppr. 219. 11

Caldwall of Alston, Staffs, a cock's head arg., beaked, combed, and wattled gu., between two wings expanded sa., holding in the beak a cross pattée fitchée or. 90. 7

Caldwell, Bart., Ireland, out of a ducal coronet a sceptre or, entwined with two serpents vert, between two wings ppr. 170. 13

Caldwell, Scotland, a fountain throwing up water ppr. 159. 13

Caldwell, issuing out of a mural crown or, a dexter arm in armour, the hand holding a sword in bend, all ppr. *Fac et spera.* *cf.* 210. 2

Caldwell, a demi-lion grasping a broken scimitar, all ppr. *cf.* 10. 2

Caldwell, Charles Henry Bulwer, Esquire, of New Grange, co Meath, the Cedars, Windlesham, Surrey, issuant from a naval crown or, a demi-lion the dexter paw grasping a scimitar ppr, pommel and hilt gold, the sinister resting on an anchor erect, also ppr *Ense libertatem petit*

Caldwell, Colonel Robert Townley, of Brook House, Cambridge, and Inneshewen, Aboyne, N B, out of an Eastern crown arg, the rim inscribed "Gooty" in letters sa a demi-lion rampant holding in his dexter paw a falchion ppr, and supporting in his sinister paw an escutcheon az charged with a representation of a medal conferred upon Sir Alexander Caldwell in commemoration of his services at the siege of Seringapatam, pendent from a ribbon tenné *Virtus et spes*

Caldwell, out of an Eastern crown or, a demi lion gu, holding in the dexter paw a sword ppr, pommel and hilt of the first, supporting between the paws two flag-staves in bend sinister, the one being that of the Union flag of Great Britain surmounting the other with the staff broken, being a flag swallow-tailed vert, semee of mullets arg *Virtus et spes*

Caldwell, Hugh, Esquire, of Blackwood, near Newport, Monm, a demi lion rampant, holding in its dexter paw a broken scymitar, all ppr *Aspiro* 275 2

Caldwell, Norf, a demi-cock rising 90 9

Caldwell, Bart, Quebec, out of a ducal coronet or, a dexter cubit arm in pale ppr, grasping a cross Calvary gu *Sapere aude*

Caldwell, Staffs, a lion couchant arg, gorged with two bars, the upper sa, the lower vert, holding between the paws a cold well ppr *Niti facere experiri*

Caldwoodley, Devonsh, an antelope trippant 126 6

Calebot, Norf, a greyhound current az, collared and ringed or *cf* 58 2

Caledon, Earl of (Alexander), Caledon, co Tyrone, Ireland, an arm in armour embowed ppr, holding in the hand a sword of the last *Per mare, per terras* 195 2

Calender and **Callandar**, Scotland and Ireland, out of an Eastern coronet or, a dexter hand holding up a billet ppr 215 14

Calibut, a stag's head at gaze az *cf* 119 12

Call, Sir William George Montagu, Bart, of Whiteford, Cornw, a demi lion rampant holding in his paws a trumpet fessewise arg *Grata manu* *cf* 9 15

Callagan and **O Callagan**, Ireland, a naked arm embowed holding in the hand a sword with a snake entwined round the blade, the head towards the hand, all ppr *cf* 201 3

Callagan, a morion ppr 180 1

Callandar and **Callender**, a dexter hand holding a billet ppr *I mean well* 215 11

Callander, George Frederick William, of Craigforth, Stirling, and Ardkinglass, Argyll, a dexter hand ppr, holding a billet or *I mean well* 215 11

Callander, Bart, Stirlingsh, out of an Eastern crown or, a dexter cubit arm ppr, holding in the hand a billet *Et domi et foris* 215 14

Callander and **Callendar**, two elephants' probosces addorsed per fess gu and or 123 10

Callarde and **Calliarde**, Norf, a demi lion sa, supporting a double scaling ladder or

Callender-Brodie, John Sharp, Esquire, of Idvies, Forfar, and 26, Moray Place, Edinburgh, a dexter hand holding a sheaf of arrows ppr *Be mindful to unite* (*for Brodie*) A dexter hand ppr, holding a billet or *I mean well* (*for Callender*)

Calley, Colonel Thomas Charles Pleydell, Burderop Park, Wilts, a demi lion holding in the dexter paw a battle-axe arg, handle gu, and charged on the shoulder with a bend of the last, thereon three mullets of the first *Callide et honeste* 15 6

Callis, out of a ducal coronet a cockatrice's head between two wings, all ppr 68 11

Callore, on a ducal coronet a sheaf of arrows environed by a serpent 173 11

Calloum, a sinister arm in armour embowed to the sinister ppr holding a battle-axe handle downwards or

Callow, on a ducal coronet a peacock ppr 103 8

Callwell, Scotland, a hand erect ppr, holding a cross pattee fitchee gu 221 12

Calmady of Langdon Hall Devonsh, a Pegasus sa, ungu and collared or *Similis frondescit virga metallo* *cf* 47 1

Calrow of Adlington, Chesh, and Walton Lodge, near Preston, Lancs, a beehive, thereon perched a dove with wings elevated, holding in the beak a sprig of olive, all ppr *Industria*

Calshill, a dexter wing erect or 109 7

Calston, the moon in her complement *cf* 162 4

Calthorp and **Calthrop**, Suff and Norf, a boar's head and neck az, armed and bristled or 41 1

Calthorpe, Bart, a boar's head and neck couped vert

Calthorpe, Baron (Gough Calthorpe), Elvetham, Winchfield, Hants (1) A boar's head couped at the neck az (2) A boar's head couped arg pierced through the cheek with a broken spear *Gradu diverso via una*

Calthorpe, Lieutenant General the Hon Somerset John Gough, Perry Hall, Birmingham, same crests and motto

Calthrop, Hollway-, Henry Calthrop, Esquire, of Stanhoe Hall, Norf (1) In front of a boar's head couped at the neck az, collared gemelle or, three annulets interlaced of the last (*for Calthrop*) 41 7 (2) A goat's head couped arg, semee of crescents, and holding in the mouth two trefoils slipped, all gu (*for Hollway*) *Quærere verum* 128 6

Caltoft, Lincs, a rose gu, between two laurel branches vert 149 11

Calton of Catsworth, Hunts, a talbot passant arg, collared and lined or 54 5

Calton of Babram, Cambs, a boar passant arg 40 9

Calverley and **Calveley**, Chesh and Yorks, out of a ducal coronet or, a calf's head affrontee sa 43 6

Calverley, Sussex and Surrey, a horned owl arg *En caligine veritas* 96 5

Calverley of Cockerham, Lancs, a horned owl arg, guttée de-poix *cf* 96 5

Calverley, John Selwyn, Oulton Hall, Yorks, a horned owl arg

Calverley, Edmond Leveson, Esquire, of 18, Cheyne Gardens, S W, same crest.

Calverley, Horace Walter, Esquire, of 38, South Eaton Place, S W, same crest

Calverley-Rudston, Trevor Wheeler, of Allerthorpe Hall Pocklington, Yorks, a bear's paw erect pean, grasping a cross moline erminois

Calvert, out of a mural coronet arg, two spears erect, therefrom two forked pennons flowing to the dexter one erminois, the other pean, the staves gu

Calvert, out of a ducal coronet or, two staves with pennons flying to the dexter side, the dexter of the first, the sinister sa

Calvert, Archibald Motteux, Ockley Court, Surrey, same crest *Fatti masghii parole femine*

Calvert, John Jackson, Esquire, of Woodlands, Marrickville, near Sydney, N S W, Clerk of the Parliaments, N S W (1) A mount vert, thereon an owl erm, gorged with a collar az, pendent therefrom an escocheon sa, charged with three gouttes, two and one, arg (*for Calvert*) (2) A goat's head az, erased, armed, and crined or, charged on the neck with a pheon of the last (*for Jackson*) *cf* 128 5

Calwodley, an antelope trippant per pale gu and or, attired of the last 126 6

Calwood, a dexter hand holding a palm-branch vert 219 11

Cam and **Camm**, a dove between two laurel-branches in orle 92 12

Camac and **Camic**, a martlet sa 95 5

Cambell, Essex, a bear's head couped per fess or and az, muzzled gu 34 14

Cambell, a lion's head affrontee ppr *cf* 18 11

Cambell, a swan ppr, ducally crowned or, between two laurel branches vert *cf* 99 4

Cambell, a swan ppr, crowned or 99 4

Cambell, a boar's head couped in fess. 43 1

Camber, Essex, a Saxon crown per pale sa and arg, between two wings expanded, counterchanged 110 9

Camborne, Cornw, three broken spears or, tied together with a band gu, two in saltier, one in pale

Cambridge, Duke of, upon a coronet composed of crosses pattee and strawberry leaves a lion statant guardant and crowned with a like coronet, all or, differenced by a label of three points arg, the centre point charged with the cross of St George, and each of the other points with two hearts in pale gu

Cambridge and **Cambrige**, a lion passant gardant ppr 4 3

Cambridge, a griffin's head erased or, holding in the beak a cross crosslet fitched of the same. *cf.* 66. 2

Cambridge, Pickard- of Bloxworth House, Dorset: (1) A griffin's head erased sa., semée of trefoils, holding in the beak a cross botony fitchée or (*for Cambridge*). (2) A lion sejant arg., charged on the shoulder with an ermine spot, and gorged with a collar gemelle sa., supporting with the dexter fore-paw an escutcheon gu., charged with a fleur-de-lis within a bordure or (*for Pickard*). *Esse quam videri.*

Camden, Marquess (Pratt), Bayham Abbey, Lamberhurst, Kent: (1) An elephant's head erased arg. (*for Pratt*). 133. 3. (2) A dragon's head erased vert, holding in the mouth a sinister hand couped at the wrist gu., and about the neck a chain, and pendent therefrom a portcullis or (*for Jeffreys*). *Judicium parium, aut lex terræ.* *cf.* 72. 6

Camden, on a pile or, six estoiles gu.

Camden, a cross pattée per pale sa. and arg., between two wings counterchanged. 110. 7

Camel, a camel's head. 132. 7

Cameron, Sir Charles, Bart., Balclutha, Greenock, N.B., on a rock ppr. five arrows points downwards barbed and feathered az., enfiled with an annulet gu. *Pro patria.* 254. 2

Cameron, a sheaf of five arrows tied with a band gu. 173. 3

Cameron, Donald, Esquire, Chief of Clan Cameron, of Achnacarry, Spean Bridge, Inverness-sh., and of Lochiel: (1) A dexter arm in armour embowed brandishing a sword, all ppr. (2) A sheaf of five arrows tied with a band gu. *Pro rege et patria.—Unite.* 195. 2

Cameron, Scotland, an arm in armour embowed brandishing a broadsword ppr. *Pro rege et patria.* 195. 2

Cameron of Glendessary, an arm in armour holding in the hand a sword ppr. *Hinc orior.* 210. 2

Cameron, Allan Gordon, Letterwalton, Ledaig, Argyllsh., same crest. *Pro Rege et patria.*

Cameron, Bart. (*extinct*), Scotland: (1) Out of a mural coronet or, a dexter arm in armour embowed, the hand grasping a sword, all ppr. 195. 9. (2) As an honourable augmentation, a Highlander of the 92nd Foot up to the middle in water, grasping in his dexter hand a broadsword, and in his sinister a banner inscribed "*92nd*," all within a wreath of laurel. Over the crests "*Arriverette*"; under the arms "*Maya.*"

Cameron, Sir Roderic William, of Glennevis, Canada, and Clifton Berney, Staten Island, New York, a cubit arm erect ppr., the hand grasping a flagstaff in bend sinister, also ppr., therefrom flowing a banner arg., charged with a lymphad sa. *Hinc orior.* 267. 15

Cameron, Hants, a dexter arm in armour embowed ppr., holding in the hand a sword, also ppr., hilt and pommel or. 195. 2

Cameron, John, Esquire, of Meiklehill House, Kirkintilloch, N.B., same crest. *Pro rege et patria.*

Cameron, Henry Lovett, Millbrook House, Shepperton, same crest. *Pro rege et patria.*

Cameron, a lion's gamb sa., holding a flag arg., charged with an eagle with two heads displayed, also sa. 35. 12

Camfield and **Camfyld,** Norf., out of a tower a demi-lady ppr.

Camfield, an arm erect couped at the elbow, vested, holding in the hand three wheat-ears ppr. *cf.* 205. 7

Camic, *see* Camac.

Camm, *see* Cam.

Camm, a cross gu., charged with a crescent or.

Camm, John Brooke Maker, M.A., Burnham Grange, Bournemouth, on a Greek cross of the second, a crescent of the first. *Per crucem ad lucem.*

Cammell, Charles, Esquire, of the Hall, Hutton's Ambo, Yorks., a camel's head erased arg., gorged with a collar gemelle sa., holding in the mouth a trefoil slipped sa. *Perseverando.* 296. 10

Cammell, Charles David Wilson, Ashwicke Hall, Marshfield, Chippenham, same crest and motto. 132. 10

Cammell, Bernard Edward, Esquire, of Folly Court, Wokingham, Berks, same crest and motto.

Cammell, Archibald Allen, Esquire, of Brookfield Manor, Hathersage, Sheffield, same crest and motto.

Camoys, Baron (Stonor), Stonor Park, Henley-on-Thames, on a wreath or and az., a rock arg., charged with spots gu. and az., and a dove pecking thereat with a stone gu. in its beak. 259. 12

Camoys or **Camays,** a lion's head erased az., holding in the mouth a trefoil slipped vert. *cf.* 17. 8

Camp, a griffin's head erased, ducally gorged, holding in the beak a branch of laurel, all ppr. 66. 11

Campbell, Duke of Argyll, *see* Argyll.

Campbell, Marquess of Breadalbane, *see* Breadalbane.

Campbell, Earl of Loudoun, *see* Loudoun.

Campbell, Earl Cawdor, *see* Cawdor.

Campbell, Lord Stratheden and Campbell, *see* Stratheden.

Campbell, Baron Clyde, *see* Clyde.

Campbell, *see* M'Iver-Campbell.

Campbell-Davys, *see* Davys.

Campbell-Douglas, *see* Douglas-Campbell-Douglas.

Campbell-Orde, Bart., *see* Orde.

Campbell, Earl of Islay, a boar's head couped. *Memini.* 43. 1

Campbell, Baron, a boar's head erased gyrony of eight or and sa. *Audacter et aperte.* 42. 2

Campbell of Ormidale, Argyllsh., a boar's head couped or. *Ne obliviscaris.* 43. 1

Campbell, Major-General Frederick Lorn, 12, Cranley Gardens, S.W., a boar's head erased or. *Nil tibi.—Ciod a sin dulse.*

Campbell of Asknish, a boar's head couped or. *Nunquam obliviscar.* 43. 1

Campbell, MacIver Forbes Morison MacIver, of Ballochyle, Argyllsh., a boar's head couped ppr. *I will not forget.* 43. 1

Campbell, William Rose, Esquire, of Ballochyle, Argyllsh., same crest and motto. 43. 1

Campbell, Colin George Pelham, Stonefield, Argyllsh., a boar's head couped transpierced by a sword and a javelin in saltire. *Non obliviscar.*

Campbell, a boar's head couped sa. *Usque ad aras.* 43. 1

Campbell of Lix, Argyllsh., a boar's head couped ppr. *Deo volente.* 43. 1

Campbell, Major-General Patrick John, the Albany, Piccadilly, same crest. *Nil tibi.*

Campbell, Colonel Aylmer M'Iver, of Askuish, Argyllsh., a boar's head couped or. *Nunquam obliviscar.* 43. 1

Campbell of Monzie, Perth, a boar's head erased ppr. *Follow me.* 42. 2

Campbell, Rt. Hon. James Alexander, of Stracathro, Forfarsh., a boar's head erased ppr. *Ne obliviscaris.* 42. 2

Campbell, Sir Guy Theophilus, Bart., of the Lodge, Thames Ditton, Surrey, and Scotland, a boar's head in fess erased or, langued gu. *Follow me.* 42. 2

Campbell, John, Esquire, of Rathfern, White Abbey, co. Antrim, same crest. *Ne obliviscaris.*

Campbell of Mochaster, Scotland, a boar's head erased chequy or and sa. *Sequor.* 42. 2

Campbell of Lochdochart, a boar's head erased ppr. *Recte sequor.* 42. 2

Campbell of Port Glasgow, a boar's head erased ppr. *Deo volente.* 42. 2

Campbell, a boar's head erased ppr. *Follow me.* 42. 2

Campbell, James, Esquire, of Craignish and Ardnagreggan, Callander, N.B., a boar's head erased ppr. *Fit via vi.* 42. 2

Campbell, James, Esquire, of Tullichewan Castle, Alexandria, Dumbartonsh., same crest and motto.

Campbell of London and Middlesex, a boar's head erased or. 42. 2

Campbell-Bannerman, Sir Henry, M.P., of 6, Grosvenor Place, and Hunton Court, Kent: (1) On the dexter side a demi-man in armour ppr. (*for Bannerman*). 187. 1. (2) On the sinister side a boar's head erased ppr. (*for Campbell*). *Patriæ fidelis.—Ne obliviscaris.* 42. 2

Campbell, Alexander, Esquire, of Cammo, Midlothian, a boar's head erased sa., armed and langued gu. *Follow me.* 42. 2

Campbell, Duncan, Esquire, of Inverneill and Ross, Argyllsh., a boar's head erased or, langued gu. *Fit via vi.* 42. 2

Campbell, Sir Gilbert Edward, Bart., of Carrick-Buoy, Ireland, an Eastern crown surmounted by a boar's head erased ppr. *Ne obliviscaris.* *cf.* 42. 2

Campbell of Lawers, a boar's head erect and erased az. *Fac et spera.* 43. 3

Campbell of Colgrain, Dumbarton, a boar's head erect and erased or, armed and langued az. *Fac et spera.* 43. 3

Campbell of Park, a boar's head erased and erect or, langued az. *Fac et spera.* 43. 3

Campbell, Henry A., Esquire, of Eastwell Park, Ashford, Kent, a boar's head erased and erect or, langued az. *Fac et spera.* 43. 3

Campbell, Henry Alexander, Esquire, of Lynford Hall, Mundford, Norf, a boar's head erect and erased or *Fac et spera* 43 3

Campbell, William Middleton, Esquire, of Camis-Eskan, Helensburgh, N B, and Fen Place, Turner's Hill, Sussex, same crest and motto

Campbell, a dove holding in its beak an olive-branch ppr *Gaudium adfero* 92 5

Campbell of Gargunnock, a stork ppr *Refero* 105 11

Campbell, Scotland, a swan gorged with ducal coronet ppr *Be mindful* cf 99 2

Campbell of Ardchattan Priory Argyllsh a swan with wings elevated arg, crowned with an Eastern crown or *Be mindful* cf 99 4

Campbell of Calder, a swan ppr, crowned or *Be mindful* cf 99 2

Campbell, Sir John William, Bart, of Ardnamurchan and Airds, same crest and motto cf 99 2

Campbell of Moy, Elgin, Scotland, a swan rising ppr, crowned or *Be ever mindful* 99 4

Campbell of Auchmannoch, Ayrsh, a two headed eagle displayed gu, in a flame of fire or *I byde my tyme* (2) Three ears of barley bladed ppr 74 6

Campbell, Arthur, Esquire, of Catrine House, Ayrsh, W S, crest as first above, same motto

Campbell, issuing out of water a demi-eagle displayed with two heads, above it the sun shining ppr 82 10

Campbell, Ireland, the wings of an eagle conjoined ppr *Ulterius et melius* 113 1

Campbell of Fairfield, Ayrsh, an eagle's head erased ppr *Constanter et prudentia* 66 2

Campbell of Skerrington, an eagle's head *Constans et prudens* 66 1

Campbell, Scotland, an eagle's head couped ppr *Constanter et prudentia* 66 1

Campbell of Treesbank, Ayrsh, a phœnix head erased or *Constanter et prudentia*

Campbell of Sornbeg, Ayrsh, same crest and motto

Campbell, George James, of Cessnock, a phœnix's head erased or *Constanter et prudenter*

Campbell of Glassnock, Ayrsh, a phœnix head couped ppr *Constans et prudens*

Campbell of Shawfield and Islay, a griffin segreant holding the sun between its claws ppr *Fidus amicus* 62 6

Campbell, Somerset-, Captain Walter Douglas, of Holly Grove, Windsor Park, same crest and motto

Campbell, James Carter, Esquire, J P, of Ardpatrick, Tarbert, Argyllsh (1) A griffin segreant holding the sun between the fore-paw (2) Two oars of a galley in saltire *Terra mare fide*

Campbell of Woodhall, Lanarksh, a griffin segreant holding in his claws the sun ppr *Fidus amicus* 62 6

Campbell, Sir Archibald Spencer Lindsey, Bart, of Succoth Scotland and 23, Moray Place, Edinburgh a camel's head couped ppr *Labor omnia superat* 132 7

Campbell of Inveraw, a hart's head ppr *Pro aris et focis* 121 5

Campbell of Glenfeochin, a stag's head ppr *Mar bu mhianu dom —Fortitudine et prudentia* 121 5

Campbell of Glenfeachar, a goat statant az, armed and ungu or, holding in the month a sprig of ivy ppr *Marbu mhianu leon* 129 9

Campbell, a lion sejant affrontee and erect gardant, holding in the dexter paw a sword, and in the sinister a crown of laurel *Victoriam coronat Christus* cf 7 3

Campbell, Sir James, Bart, of Aberuchill, Perthsh, Kilbryde Castle, Dunblane, Perthsh, and Whitemead Park, Coleford, Glouc, a lion affrontee gu, crowned with laurel, and holding in the dexter paw a sword ppr, hilted and pommelled or, and in the sinister a dag or Highland pistol, also ppr *Sequitur victoria forteis*

Campbell, John Logan, Esquire, M D, F R C G, of Kilbryde, Auckland, New Zealand, a lion affrontee gu, crowned with laurel, and holding in the dexter paw a sword ppr, hilted and pommelled or, and in the sinister a dag or Highland pistol, also ppr *Sequitur victoria forteis*

Campbell of Glenlyon, a demi lion rampant ppr, gorged with a collar gyronny of eight or and sa, and holding in his dexter paw a heart gu, crowned or *Quæ recta sequor*

Campbell, Sir Archibald Ava, Bart, Scotland (1) On a mount vert, a Burmese warrior on horseback armed and accoutred ppr (2) Out of an Eastern crown or, a demi-lion ppr, supporting with the dexter paw a man's heart gu, crowned or *Perseverantia victor*

Campbell, Suff, a lion's head affrontée ppr *I beare in minde* cf 18 1

Campbell, London, a demi hound az, gorged with a ducal coronet or *Festina lente —Dieu pour nous* 55 12

Campbell, Lieutenant-Colonel Duncan of South Hall Colintraive, N B a hart's head erased ppr *Pro aris et focis*

Campbell, Graham-, Robert Charles, of Shervin, Lochgilphead (1) A hart's head erased ppr (2) An escallop or *Pignus amoir —Pro aris et focis*

Campbell, Scotland, a ship at anchor ppr *Vincit labor* 160 4

Campbell of Ardkinlis, a galley, her oars in action sa *Set on* 160 7

Campbell, Sir Archibald Campbell, Bart, of Blythswood, Renfrewsh, J P, D L 160 6 (1) A lymphad sa 160 6 (2) On a cap of maintenance ppr, a salamander vert, encircled with flames of fire, also ppr 138 2 (3) A human heart ensigned with an imperial crown ppr *Vincit labor —Jamais arriere* cf 181 2

Campbell - Horsfall, Charles Esquire M B, Ch B (Vict Univ) of Clevedon Somerset (1) A dexter cubit arm holding a tilting spear in bend sinister 214 11 (2) A boar's head erased *Audaces juvo* 42 2

Campbell of Skipness Castle, Argyllsh, two oars of a galley in saltier *Terra marique fides* 179 3

Campbell of Auchawilling, two oars of a galley in saltier *Armis et fide* 179 3

Campbell, same crest *Vi et fide*

Campbell, Rev Archibald Ean of All Souls' Vicarage, Leeds, same crest *Terra mare que fides*

Campbell, Alexander James Henry, of Dunstaffnage, Argyllsh, an anchor in pale reversed az *Vigilando* cf 161 1

Campbell, Pleydell-Bouverie- (1) Two oars of a galley in saltire ppr (*for Campbell*) 179 3 (2) A demi eagle displayed with two heads sa, ducally gorged or, and charged on the breast with a cross crosslet arg (*for Bouverie*) *Vis et fides —Patria cara, carior libertas*

Campbell of Glenfalloch, Perth, a human heart gu, pierced through with an arrow bendwise ppr *Thus far* 181 10

Campbell, Cockburn-, Sir Thomas, Bart, of Gartsford, Scotland (1) A cubit arm erect, holding in the hand a scimitar ppr (*for Campbell*) 213 5 (2) A cock ppr (*for Cockburn*) *Without fear —Vigilans et audax* 91 2

Campbell of Barbieston, Ayrsh, a hand and arm holding a dagger, with the sun above in his splendour, all ppr *Honore et armis* cf 212 3

Campbell, Captain John, Madras Native Infantry, a dexter hand couped in fess, grasping a dagger erect gu *I forget not*

Campbell, Sir Hugh Hume, Bart, of Marchmont, Berwick, a dexter hand issuing from a heart and grasping a scimitar, all ppr *True to the end —Fides probata coronat* 213 4

Campbell, Scotland, an arm in armour embowed holding in the hand a dagger *Paratus sum* 196 5

Campbell of Ottar, Scotland, a hand in pale holding a dirk erect ppr *Pro patria semper* 212 9

Campbell, Burnley-, Lieutenant-Colonel Hardin, of Ormidale, Colintraive, Argyllsh, same crest and motto

Campbell, Archibald Argyle, of Lochnell, Argyllsh, a dexter hand holding a spear in bend *Audaces juvo —Arma parata fero* 214 11

Campbell, Colin, Esquire of Ardfin House Jura, Argyllsh, a hand holding a lance ppr *Audaces juvo* 214 11

Campbell, James Archibald, Esquire, of Craigie, Ayrsh, a dexter hand and arm couped at the elbow and erect ppr, holding a spur or *Forget me not* cf 217 14

Campbell of Craigie House, Ayrsh, same crest and motto

Campbell, James Archibald, Esquire of Barbreck near Lochgilphead, a hand holding a spear *Arma parata fero*

Campbell, Scotland, a dexter hand holding a spur or *Memor esto* 263 9

Campbell, Albert Johnstone, Esquire, of 17, Cleveland Gardens, Hyde Park, London, W, same crest and motto

Campbell, Sir Norman Montgomery Abercrombie, Bart, of Auchinbreck, a dexter hand ppr, holding a spur or *Forget not* 217 14

Campbell, William, of Skerrington, Ayrsh, and 12, Randolph Crescent Edinburgh a dexter arm in armour, holding in the hand a garland of laurel, all ppr *Campi fero præmia belli*

Campbell-Colquhoun, Rev. John Erskine, of Killermont, and Garscadden, Dumbartonsh., N.B., Ledeameroch, Dumblane, and Chartwell, Westerham, Kent: (1) A hand ppr., holding a buckle or. (2) a boar's head erect and erased or, langued az. *Omnia firmat (for Colquhoun). Fac et spera (for Campbell).*

Campbell of Duntroon, issuing out of the top of a tower two arms drawing an arrow in a bow, all ppr. *Agite pro viribus.* 99. 4

Campbell of Netherplace, a hand issuing from a cloud, holding a signet letter ppr. *Optime quod opportune.* 215. 7

Campbell-Müller-Morrison of Hetland, Dumfriessh., three Moors' heads conjoined in one neck sa., banded az., the faces looking to the chief, dexter, and sinister respectively. 191. 5

Campbell, Sir Duncan Alexander Dundas, Bart., of Barcaldine, Scotland, a man in full Highland garb holding in his dexter hand a broadsword, on his sinister arm a shield, all ppr. *Paratus sum.* 183. 5

Campbell, Scotland, a dexter hand holding a lance in bend sinister. *Arma parata fero* 214. 11

Campbell, Scotland, a demi-man in a coat of mail holding in his dexter hand a sword, and on his sinister arm a shield az., charged with a unicorn's head and neck, couped arg., horned and maned or. *Quid non pro patria.*

Campbell-Swinton, John Liulf, Esquire, of Kimmerghame, Dunse, N.B., a boar chained to an oak-tree fructed, all ppr. *J'espère.* 232. 1

Campden, Viscount, *see* Gainsborough, Earl of.

Campe, a griffin's head erased, ducally gorged, and holding in the beak a branch of laurel, all ppr. 66. 11

Camper, an anchor between two wings. 161. 12

Camperdown, Earl of (Haldane-Duncan), on waves of the sea a dismasted ship ppr. *Secundis dubiisque rectus.*

Campion, London, Devonsh., and Essex, out of a ducal coronet or, a talbot's head sa. 293. 4

Campion, Harold Gilmore, Boscawen, Rydal Road, Streatham, same crest.

Campion, William Henry, Esquire, of Danny, Hurstpierpoint, Sussex, a turkey-cock arg., combed and wattled gu.

Campion and **Campyon,** a turkey in pride ppr., combed and wattled gu. 108. 5

Campion and **Campyon,** a bear's head and neck per pale erm. and sa., muzzled or. 34. 14

Camville, on a mount a leopard sejant ppr. 24. 12

Canby, a mound sa., ensigned with a cross patée.

Canceller and **Cancellor,** an arm couped at the shoulder embowed in fess, resting upon the elbow and supporting a flag displayed az., charged with a crescent arg. 202. 13

Cancelor and **Candisherler,** a dexter hand ppr., holding a covered cup or. 217. 11

Candeler, London, a goat's head couped sa., attired arg. 128 12

Candish, Suff., an ostrich-head az., gorged with a collar sa., rimmed or, and charged with three bezants.

Candishe, a wolf's head couped az., collared or. 30. 9

Candler-Brown, *see* Brown.

Candler, Norf., a shark's head erased ppr. 139. 6

Candler, Worcs., an angel ppr., vested arg., holding in the dexter hand a sword, the blade wavy of the first, hilt and pommel or. *Ad mortem fidelis.*

Candler of Kilkenny, Ireland, an angel affrontée habited az., girded and winged or, holding in the dexter hand a flaming sword ppr., and in the sinister a palm-branch ppr. *Ad mortem fidelis.*

Candler, a goat's head couped sa., armed and maned arg. 128. 12

Candler, Suff., an eagle rising regardant ppr. 77. 4

Cane, a human heart gu., charged with a cinquefoil or. 181. 1

Cane, a leopard rampant, gorged with a mural coronet. *cf.* 27. 2

Cane, *see* Du Cane.

Canham, two palm-branches in orle ppr. 146. 2

Caning, a quatrefoil ppr. 148. 10

Cankrien, Yorks, a demi-lion rampant erminois, holding between the paws a palmer's scrip sa., the strap and tassels or.

Cann, Devonsh., a leopard statant ppr. 24. 2

Cann, George Dunning, M.A., LL.M., 6, Lyndhurst Road, Exeter, and Dishcombe, Okehampton, Devonsh., same crest. *Maculis immaculabilis.*

Cann, Cornw., a cross crosslet fitched, between two wings conjoined.

Cann, Bart. (*extinct*), of Crompton Greenfield, Glouc., out of a mural coronet or, a plume of five ostrich-feathers arg. *cf.* 114. 13

Cann, Skoulding-, of Gilston, Herts: (1) Out of the battlements of a tower ppr., a rose gu., slipped and leaved, also ppr., between four feathers gu. and arg., and arg. and gu. (*for Cann*). (2) An owl arg., collared sa., holding in the dexter claw a thistle slipped ppr. *Perimus licitis.*

Canning, Viscount Stratford de Redcliffe, *see* Stratford.

Canning, Baron Garvagh, *see* Garvagh.

Canning, De Burgh-, *see* Clanricarde, Marquess of.

Canning, Viscount (Canning), a demi-griffin az., guttée-d'or. *Ne cede malis, sed contra.* 64. 2

Canning, Gordon-, William James, Hartpury, Glouc.: (1) A demi-lion rampant arg., holding in the dexter paw a battle-axe ppr. (*for Canning*). *cf.* 15. 6. (2) A stag's head erased ppr. (*for Gordon*). *Dum vigilo tutus.—Bydand.* 121. 2

Canning, a demi-lion rampant arg., holding in the dexter paw a battle-axe ppr. *cf.* 15. 6

Canning, a demi-lion rampant erm., supporting a battle-axe ppr. 15. 4

Canning, Arthur Richard, of Bryn-y-mor, Woolston, Southampton, a demi-lion rampant arg., holding in the dexter paw a battleaxe ppr. *Ne cede malis sed contra.*

Canning, a demi-lion rampant arg., charged with three trefoils vert, holding in the dexter paw an arrow, point downwards. *Ne cede malis, sed contra.*

Cannock, Lincs, a demi-buck couped arg., attired and ducally gorged or, one foot resting on the wreath. *cf.* 119. 2

Cannon, Scotland, between the horns of a crescent arg., a buckle az. 163. 15

Cannon, Pembrokesh., Wales, a cannon sa., mounted on a carriage or. 169. 12

Cannynge, issuing from clouds two dexter hands conjoined and gauntleted, holding up a heart inflamed, all ppr. 211. 2

Cant of Dryburnford, a dove ppr. *Altius reposita* 92. 2

Cantelow, Heref., and **Cantelupe,** a leopard's face gu., jessant-de-lis or. 22. 5

Cantelow, Ireland, a demi-bull per pale or and az. 45. 12

Canterbury, Viscount (Manners-Sutton), on a chapeau gu., turned up erm., a peacock in pride ppr. *Poury parvenir.* 103. 5

Cantillion, Ireland, an arm embowed holding a dagger ppr. *cf.* 201. 4

Cantillon, Ireland, a dexter arm embowed ppr., holding a dart or, feathered arg. 201. 14

Cantilon, Ireland, a hand holding an arrow point downward. 214. 4

Cantis of Canterbury, Kent, a hart's head erased ppr., attired or, gorged with a collar arg., charged with three roses gu., barbed and seeded ppr. *cf.* 121. 2

Cantlow, a boar passant. 40. 9

Canton, Ireland, on a chapeau ppr., a boar passant per pale arg. and vert. *cf.* 40. 8

Canton, Kent, on a chapeau a lion's head erased ppr. 17. 9

Canton, Loftus Henry, Pentlow, Eastbourne, same crest. *Penser avant parler.*

Cantrell, an arm in armour embowed, holding in the hand a sword by the middle in fess, all ppr. *cf.* 195. 6

Cantrell-Hubbersty, Albert Cantrell, Esquire, of Tollerton Hall, Notts: (1) In front of a griffin's head erased arg., charged with a fesse engrailed vert, a mole fesseways or (*for Hubbersty*). (2) In front of a tower arg., a rock ppr., thereon a boar passant sa. armed or, charged on the body with two roses arg. (*for Cantrell*). *Propositi tenax* over the Hubbersty crest, and *Pectus fidele et apertum* over the Cantrell crest.

Cantrell and **Cantrill,** a tower arg., the port way sa. *Another,* gu. 156. 2

Cantwell, a hand ppr., holding an annulet or. 216. 1

Cantwell, Ireland, a leopard's head couped ppr. 22. 10

Canzler of Burghausen, Bavaria, a hart rampant ppr., holding in the mouth a branch of a tree vert between two elephant's tusks gu. and arg.

Cape, a lion passant gu., holding in the dexter paw a sword in pale ppr., hilt and pommel or. *cf.* 6. 2

Capel of the Grove, Painswick, Glouc., a plume of three ostrich-feathers, two arg. and one gu. *Sic vita humana.* 115. 1

Capel of Swanwick, Somers, a demi lion rampant or, holding in the dexter paw a cross crosslet fitchee gu 11 10

Capel-Carnegy-Arbuthnott, James Carnegy Capel, Esquire (1) A peacock's head and neck couped ppr (2) A hand grasping a thunderbolt ppr *Interna prœstat —Dread God*

Capel Coningsby, Earl of Essex, *see* Essex

Capel, Arthur, J P, Bulland Lodge, Wiveliscombe, Somers, a demi-lion rampant supporting a cross crosslet fitchee or *Fide et fortitudine*

Capell, an anchor cabled gu, bezantee 161 2

Capell, Heref and Glouc, a plume of three ostrich feathers, the centre one arg, the others gu 115 1

Capes, a cross fleury fitched gu, flory or 166 7

Capling of London, out of the centre tower of a castle triple-towered a demi-lion rampant, all ppr 155 10

Capon, a demi lion gu 10 3

Capp, a winged spur or 111 12

Cappell, Rev Louis, D D, in front of a palmer's staff erect a catherine wheel or, between two wings az, guttee d'or 111 10

Capper, Warw and Staffs, a dexter arm couped and embowed, vested az, cuffed erminois, holding in the hand a banner az, the staff or, fringed and charged with a bee volant of the same

Capper of London, Middx, and Herts, a ram's head and neck couped, charged on the neck with a rose *cf* 130 1

Capper, a ram's head erased 130 6

Capps, Norf, a demi antelope or *cf* 126 5

Capron, a demi man in armour with a lance and a shield, all ppr

Capron, Rev George Hallilev, of Southwick Hall, Northamp, a cross fleury or, in front of a demi-man affrontée in armour ppr, garnished of the first, holding in the dexter hand an arrow, the barb downwards, also ppr, the sinister hand resting on the cross *Vigilate et orate —Sub cruce salus* 187 3

Capron, Rev Charles Henry Ward, B A, of Westown Lodge, Worthing, same crest *Sub cruce salus*

Caradoc or **Cradock, Baron Howden,** *see* Howden

Carbery, Baron (Evans-Freke), Ireland (1) A bull's head couped sa, collared and chained or (*for Freke*) *cf* 44 3 (2) A demi lion rampant regardant or, between the paws a boar's head couped sa (*for Evans*) *Libertas*

Carbery, a wyvern's head erased gu *cf* 71 2

Carbinell, out of a ducal coronet an arm in armour brandishing a scimitar ppr 209 11

Carbronel, Carbonnell, or **Carbonelle,** a demi-lion az, crowned gu, charged on the shoulder with three plates *cf* 10. 11

Carbonel or **Carbonell,** a sword in bend ppr 170 5

Carbutt, Sir Edward Hamer, Bart, in front of a mount vert, two ears of wheat saltirewise or, perched thereon a raven ppr *In accord and concord* 257 11

Carey, a lion's gamb erased sa, holding a letter ppr

Card of London, out of a cloud a hand holding a letter ppr 215 7

Card, a demi-lion rampant 10 2

Cardale of London, a linnet ppr *Studendo et contemplando inde fessus* 94 11

Carden, Sir John Craven, Bart, of Templemore co Tipperary Ireland, a pheon sa *Fide et amore* 174 11

Carden, Sir Frederick Walter, Bart, London, a fasces fessewise or, thereon a wolf's head erased sa, pierced in the neck by an arrow in bend sinister, point downwards, embrued ppr, also or *Fide et amore* 29 12

Carden, Bucks, a wolf's head erased sa, pierced with an arrow arg *cf* 29 6

Carden, a wolf statant sa, holding in his mouth an arrow palewise ppr *cf* 29 2

Cardew, out of a ducal coronet a plume of four feathers 114 1

Cardiffe, on a chapeau gu, turned up or, a martlet sa 95 1

Cardiff, Ireland, a gillyflower slipped and leaved ppr 151 8

Cardigan, Earl of, *see* Ailesbury, Marquess of

Cardigan, a lion's gamb erect and erased or holding an antique mace az 38 1

Cardin, a wolf statant sa, holding in the mouth an arrow palewise ppr *cf* 29 2

Cardinal, Essex, a dromedary ppr *cf* 132 2

Cardinal, Durrant Edward, J P, F R G S 18, Cromwell Road, Brighton and Tendring Manor, Colchester, an African camel ppr

Cardington, a bull passant per fess arg and sa *cf* 45 2

Cardonnel, De, a dove ppr *L'esperance me console* 92 2

Cardonnell, Northumb, a goldfinch ppr, on the breast a trefoil vert *cf* 106 4

Cardozo, Samuel Nunez, Esquire, of Hackney, London, a demi savage affrontee ppr, holding in his dexter hand a stalk of tobacco of three leaves ppr, and his sinister resting on a triangle or

Cardross, Baron, *see* Buchan, Earl of

Cardwell, a knight in complete armour ppr, visor up, on the top of the helmet a plume of feathers gu, holding in his dexter hand a battle axe of the first *cf* 188 2

Cardwell, Viscount (Cardwell), a man in armour, holding in the dexter hand a war-mace, all ppr, charged on the breast with a cross patee gu *Agissez honnêtement —Vaillant et veillant* *cf* 188 2

Cardwell, a tower ppr, domed or, with a flag thereon sa 157 15

Careless, *see* Carlos

Carell, a sword in pale surmounted by two crosses crosslet fitchee in saltire

Carew, a lion passant sa *En esperance je vis —Felice chi puo* 6 2

Carew Baron (Carew), an heraldic antelope trippant sa, armed and crined or *Nil admirari* 126 6

Carew, Sir Henry Palk, Bart, of Haccombe, Devonsh, the round top of a mainmast set off with palisadoes or, and a demi-lion issuing thereout sa *Nil conscire sibi* 257 4

Carew, Charles Robert Sydenham, Esquire, of Colliprest House, Tiverton, Devonsh, same crest and motto

Carew, an heraldic antelope trippant az, attired, maned, tufted, and ungu or 126 6

Carew, the late Russell, Carpenders, Watford, same crest. *Nil conscire sibi*

Carew, Pole-, Sir Reginald, K C V O, a mast of a ship sa, on the round-top a demi lion of the last surrounded with spears ppr 257 4 A second crest (*for Pole*), a lion's gamb gu, armed or, is sometimes used

Carew, Robert Thomas, Esquire, of Ballinamona Park, Waterford, an antelope passant gu, crined and combed or

Carey, a swan rising ppr *Sine macula* 99 12

Carey, Ireland, on a mount a fire beacon ppr 177 8

Carey or **Cary,** a maiden's head ppr 182 3

Carfrae, Scotland, a tower embattled arg *Fortis in fide* 156 2

Carfrae, James A Alston Esquire, of Holme Lodge, Wimbledon Common, London, S W, same crest and motto

Cargill, Scotland, a demi angel ppr, on the head a cross pattee *cf* 183 12

Cargill, Scotland, a martlet ppr 95 4

Cargill, a martlet arg *In Domino confido* 95 4

Carington, Rt Hon Sir Charles Robert, **Baron Carrington,** an elephant's head erased or eared gu, charged on the neck with three fleur-de lis, two and one az *Tenax in fide* *cf* 133 3

Carington, a peacock's head erased az, ducally gorged or *cf* 103 11

Carington, Herbert Hanbury Smith Ashby, Folville Manor Melton Mowbray, and Grangethorpe, Rusholme, Manchester (1) Out of a ducal coronet or, a unicorn's head arg armed and crined or (2) A peacock's head erased ppr, ducally gorged or *Fides semper firma*

Carkettle, Scotland, a griffin's head erased ppr 66 2

Carleill of Sewerby, Yorks, a Moor's head in profile, couped at the shoulders ppr 192 13

Carleton, a dexter arm embowed and naked to the elbow, the shirt folded above the elbow arg, and vested over gu, the hand grasping an arrow in bend sinister point downwards ppr *cf* 201 13

Carleton, a unicorn's head sa, the horn twisted of the first and second 48 12

Carleton, L S, Surgeon Lieutenant-Colonel, Newnham on Severn, same crest *Quærere verum*

Carleton, Viscount Carleton, Ireland, out of a ducal coronet a unicorn's head arg, armed and crined of the first *Quærere verum* 48 12

Carleton, Baron, *see* Shannon, Earl of

Carleton, Baron Dorchester, *see* Dorchester

Carleton, the Hon Dudley Massey, of Greywell Hill, Winchfield, Hants, a dexter arm embowed ppr, vested above the elbow gu., edged arg., the hand grasping an arrow in bend sinister point downwards ppr. *Quondam his vicimus armis.*

Carleton, General Henry Alexander, C.B., of 12, Marlborough Buildings, Bath, out of a ducal coronet or, a unicorn's head arg., the horn twisted of the first and second, maned and tufted of the first. *Nunquam non paratus.*

Carlile, a martlet or, holding in the beak a sprig of two roses gu., leaved and stalked vert. cf. 95. 2

Carlile, James William, Esquire, D.L., J.P., of Ponsbourne Park, Herts, two dragons' heads addorsée vert. *Humilitate.* 72. 8

Carlile, Walter William, Esquire, of Gayhurst, Newport Bagnell, Bucks, same crest and motto.

Carlile, Edward Hildred, Esquire, of Helme Hall, Meltham, Yorks, same crest and motto.

Carlill, Cumb. and Westml., an arm in armour embowed holding in the hand ppr. a spear arg. cf. 197. 1

Carlill, an arm in armour embowed or, garnished gu., holding in the hand ppr. a baton of the first. cf. 200. 3

Carline, William Arthur, M.D., Lincoln, a demi-griffin. *Vivimus dum vivamus.*

Carling, Bristol, a buck's head erased ppr. *Tout droit.* 121. 2

Carlingford, Baron, and **Baron Clermont** (Rt. Hon. Sir Chichester Samuel Parkinson-Fortescue), K.P.: (1) An heraldic tiger ppr., supporting with his fore-paw a plain shield arg. (*for Fortescue*). cf. 25. 5. (2) A falcon with wings addorsed ppr., belled or, and charged on the breast with a pellet and holding in the beak an ostrich-feather arg. (*for Parkinson*). *Forte scutum salus ducum.—Si celeres quatit pennas.*

Carlisle, Earl of (Howard), on a chapeau gu., turned up erm., a lion statant gardant, the tail extended or, ducally gorged arg., and charged with a mullet sa., for difference. *Volo non valeo.* cf. 4. 7

Carlisle, William Thomas, Esquire, of Lincoln's Inn, in front of a blackamoor's head in profile, couped at the shoulders ppr., wreathed about the temples arg. and gu., two mullets of eight points or. cf. 192. 13

Carlos, a sword arg., hilt and pommel or, and a sceptre of the last in saltier, enfiled with a civic crown vert. *Subditus fidelis regis est regni salus.* 170. 7

Carlow, Viscount, see Portarlington, Earl.

Carlton, an arm embowed ppr., holding in the hand an arrow. 201. 13

Carlyle, Scotland, two dragons' heads and necks addorsed vert. *Humilitate.* 72. 8

Carlyle of Limekilns, Scotland, a dexter arm holding a writing-pen ppr. *Humilitate.* 217. 10

Carlyll, Stephen, 7, Hanover Terrace, Regent's Park, W., a Moor's head in profile couped at the shoulders ppr. Motto as above.

Carlyon of Tregrehan, Cornw., a demi-lion rampant gu., ducally crowned or, collared arg., holding between its paws a bezant *Turris tutissima virtus.* 260. 10

Carlyon, Arthur Spry Gwavas, Esquire, J.P., of Gwavas, Tikokino, Hawkes Bay, New Zealand, same crest and motto

Carlyon, Alexander Keith, Esquire, of Mount Park, Harrow, Middx., same crest and motto.

Carlyon, George Richard, Esquire, of Tregrehan, Cornw., same crest and motto.

Carlyon, Rev. Henry Chichele, M.A., of Delhi, Punjab, India, same crest and motto.

Carlyon, Gerald Winstanley, Esquire, same crest and motto.

Carlyon, T. A., Esquire, Connemara, Darracott Road, Boscombe Park, Bournemouth, a demi-lion rampant gu., ducally crowned or, collared arg., holding between the paws a bezant. *Turris tutissima virtus.* 260. 10

Carlyon, Thomas Alfred, Esquire, c.o. Captain Carlyon-Britton, 14, Melbury Mansions, S.W., same crest and motto.

Carlyon, Thomas Baxter, Esquire, of Royal Arsenal, Woolwich, same crest and motto.

Carlyon-Britton, see Britton.

Carlyon, in the sea a pillar ppr. 176. 2

Carmalt of Langrigg, Cumb., a dragon's head erased per pale or and vert, gorged with collar, charged with three escallops counterchanged. cf. 71. 2

Carmarden and **Carmarthen,** a lion's gamb erect and erased or. 36. 4

Carmarthen, Marquess of, see Leeds, Duke of.

Carmichael of Balmblae, a woman's head and neck issuing. *Fortune helps the forward.* 182. 3

Carmichael of Carspherne, Scotland, a dexter hand and arm in armour brandishing a tilting-spear ppr. *Toujours prest.* cf. 210. 9

Carmichael, James, Esquire, of Arthurstone, Meigle, Perthsh., same crest and motto.

Carmichael, John, Esquire, of Cork: (1) Issuing from a mural crown a dexter arm in armour embowed, the hand holding a broken spear in bend sinister point downwards, all ppr., the arm charged with a cross patée gu. (*for Carmichael*). (2) Out of a mural crown ppr., an ostrich's head az., holding in the beak a horse-shoe or, and charged on the neck with a cross crosslet fitchée of the last (*for M'Ostrich*). *Toujours prest.*

Carmichael, Gibson-, Sir Thomas David, Bart., of Skirling; (1) An arm in armour embowed holding a broken lance, the top pendent ppr. (*for Carmichael*). 197. 3. (2) A pelican in her piety ppr. (*for Gibson*). *Toujours prest.—Pandite cœlestes portæ.* 98. 14

Carmichael, Evelyn George Massey, M.A., Library Chambers, Temple, a cubit arm erect in armour holding in the hand a broken spear, all ppr.

Carmichael, Ireland, an arm from the elbow in armour, holding a pheon ppr.

Carmichael of Maulslei, an arm in armour holding in the hand a broken spear ppr., and charged with a mullet or. *Toujours prest.* cf. 197. 3

Carmichael, Sir James Morse, Bart., a cubit arm in armour holding in the hand a tilting-spear ppr. *Toujours prest.* cf. 210. 11

Carmichael-Ferrall, Captain John Jervis O'Ferrall, R.N., of Angher Castle, co. Tyrone: (1) Out of a ducal coronet or, a dexter hand gu. (*for Ferrall*). (2) An arm embowed in armour grasping a broken lance, all ppr., charged with a trefoil or (*for Carmichael*).

Carminow, Carmynow, or **Carmenow,** a dolphin naiant or. 140. 5

Carminow of Tregarrick, Cornw., a dolphin naiant or. *Cala raggi wethlow.* 140. 5

Carnaby, a bull's head per chevron or and gu. cf. 44. 3

Carnaby, a lion's head issuing sa., charged with a chevron arg. cf. 21. 1

Carnac, on a crescent per pale gu. and erm., a sword ppr., hilt and pommel or, point upwards. 169. 4

Carnac, Rivett-, Sir James Henry Sproule, Bart., Derby: (1) Out of a crescent erm., the interior part gu., a sword erect ppr., pommel and hilt or (*for Carnac*). 169. 4. (2) An arm erect couped at the elbow, vested per pale arg. and sa., holding in the hand ppr. a broken sword of the first, hilt and pommel or (*for Rivett*). *Sic itur ad astra.*

Carnarvon, Earl of (Herbert), a wyvern, the wings elevated vert, holding in the mouth a sinister hand couped at the wrist gu. *Ung je serviray.* 70. 3

Carncross, a dagger erect arg., hilted and pommelled or, between two branches of laurel ppr. *Certamine parta.* 170. 3

Carnduff, David, Esquire, 22, Queen Street, Edinburgh (formerly Bengal Educ. Dept.), a dexter hand grasping a banner arg., charged with a saltire couped az. *Tenax propositi.*

Carne, Nash, Colgiamorgan, a pelican displayed with two heads sa., issuing from a ducal coronet ppr. *En tout loyal.—Fy ngobaith sydd yn nuw.*

Carne, John Devereux Vann Loder Nicholl, St. Donat's Castle, Glamorgan, a pelican displayed with two heads sa., issuing from a ducal coronet ppr. *En toute loyale,* and also *Fy ngobaith sydd yn nuw.*

Carnegie of Kennaird Angus, a dexter hand holding a thunderbolt ppr. *Deum timete.* 216. 4

Carnegie, James, of 13, Prince's Garden, a dexter hand couped at the wrist, holding in fess a thunderbolt shafted paleways winged arg. *Deum timete.*

Carnegie, Lord, of Crimonnogate, Lonmay, Aberdeensh., and Elsick, Kincardinesh., same crest. *Dred God.*

Carnegie, Earl of Northesk, see Northesk.

Carnegie of Pitarow, Bart., a demi-eagle displayed az., beaked and membered gu. *Video alta sequorque.* 81. 6

Carnegie of Ballindarg, a dexter arm vambraced ppr., holding an escutcheon az., charged with a St. Andrew's cross arg. *Loyal in adversity.*

Carnegie of Craigo, a star ppr. *Alis aspicet astra.* 164. 3

Carnegie, Rt. Hon. Sir James, K.T., **Earl of Southesk, Baron Carnegie** of Kinnaird and Leuchars, in Scotland, **Baron Balinhard** of Farnell, Forfarsh., in the United Kingdom, and a Baronet of Nova Scotia, Kinnaird Castle, Brechin, N.B., a thunderbolt ppr., winged or. *Dread God.* 247. 6

Carnegie, Claud Cathcart Strachan, of Tarrie, Forfarsh, same crest and motto

Carnegie, John, B A, Cranborne, Widmore Road, Bromley, Kent, on a thunderbolt ppr, an eagle to the sinister regardant and with wings expanded and inverted *Time deum*

Carnegie of Lour, a leopard's head erased ppr *Armis et animis* 23 10

Carnegie of Finhaven, Forfarsh, a leopard's head affrontee ppr *Tache sans tache* cf 23 3

Carnegie of Newgate, two dexter hands gauntleted issuing out of a cloud conjoined and supporting a flaming heart ppr *Armis et animis* 211 2

Carnegie, a demi-eagle displayed az, beaked gu, looking to a star or *Video alta sequorque* cf 81 6

Carnegy (1) A lion passant ppr, holding in his dexter fore paw a banner az, charged with a saltire arg cf 5 13 (2) A demi-leopard ppr *Tache sans tache* cf 23 13

Carnegy, Patrick Alexander Watson, Lour, Forfarsh, a demi-leopard ppr. *Tache sans tache*

Carnell, Yorks, an arm in armour embowed holding a sword, all ppr 195 2

Carney, a swan's head and neck erased holding in the beak an annulet

Carney, Ireland, a gauntleted hand lying fessways holding a sword erect, all ppr cf 211 8

Carnie, out of a cloud a hand in fess pointing to a crosier in pale, all ppr 223 2

Carniquet, Scotland, a swan with wings addorsed arg, ducally gorged and chained or cf 99 3

Carnoek, Scotland, a hand ppr, holding a fleur de lis az cf 215 5

Carnsew, a hound passant regardant ppr cf 54 1

Carnwath, Earl of, and **Baron Dalzell,** Scotland (Dalzell), a dagger erect ppr., pommel and hilt or *I dare* 169 2

Caron, Hon Sir Joseph Philippe Rene Adolphe, K C M G, K C, P C, of Daly Street, Ottawa, Canada, Minister of Militia and Defence for the Dominion of Canada, *uses* a fleur de lis *Suaviter in modo, fortiter in re* 148 2

Carpendale, Rev Maxwell, Rector of Tamlaght, in the diocese of Armagh, a hawk's head erased ppr, charged with a cross crosslet or *Data fata secutus* cf 88 12

Carpendale, Major Maxwell John, same crest

Carpenter, on a stand a globe ppr *Per acuta belli* 150 4

Carpenter, Hon Walter Cecil of Kiplin Northallerton a globe in a frame or charged for distinction with a cross crosslet az *Per acuta belli*

Carpenter, a stag's head arg, between two wings addorsed az

Carpenter, a demi lion rampant gu, ducally crowned or collared sa cf 10 11

Carpenter, Barbadoes, a demi-lion rampant gu, holding between the paws a cross pattee vert *Audaces fortuna juvat* 11 2

Carpenter, Worcs, a coney sejant arg cf 136 1

Carpenter, Somers, a snail passant ppr, the shell arg 141 8

Carpenter of Cobham, Surrey, a grey hound's head erased per fess sa and arg 61 4

Carpenter, Earl of Tyrconnel, *see* Tyrconnel

Carpenter, a falcon with wings expanded arg, beaked, legged, and belled or 87 1

Carpenter, an arm in armour embowed holding in the hand ppr a hammer or

Carpenter, an arm in armour grasping in the hand a passion nail, all ppr

Carpenter, Ireland, an alligator ppr cf 138 11

Carpenter-Garnier, John, Esquire, of Rookesbury Park, Fareham, Hants (1) In front of a lion's head erased az, gorged with a wreath of oak, three fleurs-de lis or (*for Garnier*) (2) An arm embowed in armour ppr, the hand grasping a staff or, between two wings of the last, semee of estoiles az (*for Carpenter*)

Carr, Thomas, M D, 15, Albert Terrace, Blackpool, a unicorn s head erased ppr *Pro Christo et pro patria* 298 10

Carr, Knt of Hart (badge on standard), a stag's head barry of eight arg and gu, trochings or, one annulet of the first upon the said trochings *Por Dysserver*

Carr of Hetton, Northumb, the same *Pour Deservir* (over crest)

Carr of St Helen, Auckland, Durh (from Hetton), a stag's head couped arg, attired or

Carr of Sleaford, Lincs, Bart, a stag's head couped arg, on the neck two bars gemelles gu (sometimes charged with a fleur de-lis)

Carr of Hedgeley Northumb and Dunstan on Hill, Durh, on a wreath of the colours a stag's head couped arg, gorged with two bars gemelles between as many annulets gu *Por Dysserver*

Carr, Rev Charles Ridley, of Exmouth, Devonsh, same crest and motto

Carr, Cuthbert Ellison, Esquire, same crest and motto

Carr, Henry, Esquire, same crest and motto

Carr, Vice Admiral Henry John, of United Service Club, S W same crest and motto

Carr, Martin Raymond, Esquire, same crest and motto

Carr, Ralph Clement, Esquire, same crest and motto

Carr-Ellison, *see* Ellison

Carr of Eshott Heugh, Northumb, a stag's head erased ppr, gorged with a collar gemelle, and the neck encircled with an annulet gu, on the attires a riband, also gu, passing through an annulet or *Pour deservir*

Carr, Thomas William, Esquire, same crest and motto

Carr, Rev Thomas William, of Long Rede, Barming, Maidstone, Kent, same crest *Pour deservir*

Carr of Hillingdon, Middx, a stag's head couped arg, horned or, on the neck an estoile sa between two bars gemelle gu

Carr of Bristol, a hart's head arg, horned or, about his neck two gemelles gu (sometimes charged with a martlet)

Carr of Horbury, Yorks, a stag's head couped per bend embattled arg and gu, charged on the neck with two estoiles counterchanged

Carr of Eshott, a stag's head erased ppr. *Nil desperandum* 121 2

Carr, Rev Edmund Holbrooke Hall, Derby, a stag's head erased ppr, charged on the neck with a mullet of six points or between two thistles slipped and leaved ppr *Tout droit*

Carr, William, of Starkhouse and Giggleswick, Yorks, a stag's head couped arg, attired or, on the neck two bars gemelles or *Ad sidere tollite vultus*

Carr, William, Esquire, J P, of Ditchingham Hall Ditchingham Norf, a stag's head couped ppr charged on the neck with three bars or *Ad sidere tollite vultus*

Carr-Gomm, Francis Culling, Esquire, of the Chase, Farnham Royal, Bucks (1) Two lions' gambs in saltire sa, erased gu, charged for distinction with a cross crosslet arg, and each holding a seax erect ppr, hilt and pommel or (*for Gomm*) (2) A stag's head erased ppr, gorged with a collar gemelle, and the neck encircled with an annulet gu, on the attires a riband, also gu, passing through an annulet or (*for Carr*) (1) (*Gomm*) *Per costanza e speranza* and (2) (*Carr*) *Pour deservyr*

Carrack, *see* Carrick

Carrant, Somers, a bull's head caboshed per pale gu and arg, armed, counterchanged 43 8

Carre, Scotland, a stag's head erased or *Tout droit* 121 2

Carre, Riddel-, Thomas Alexander, of Cavers, Carre Lilliesleaf Roxburghsh, Scotland (1) A stag's head erased ppr, attired with ten tynes or (2) A demi greyhound ppr *Tout droit*— *Hope to share*

Carrell, Sussex on a mount vert, a stag lodged regardant arg, attired or 115 9

Carrell, Sussex, on a mount vert, an ibex arg, maned and horned or

Carrell, Sussex and Kent, a lion's head erased vert, between two wings arg and sa, charged on the neck with two bends or cf 19 7

Carrick, Earl of, Ireland (Butler), out of a ducal coronet a plume of five ostrich feathers arg, thereupon a falcon rising of the last *Soyez ferme*

Carrick, Scotland, a demi-lion or, in the dexter paw a thistle ppr, in the sinister a fleur-de lis gu 13 12

Carrick and **Carrack,** an ostrich arg, beaked and legged or, holding in the beak a broken spear of the last, headed of the first

Carrick, Glouc, an ostrich arg, beaked and legged or, holding in the beak a staff of the same, thereon a flag gu *Garde bien*

Carrick, an ostrich ppr *Garde bien* 97 2

Carridge of London, on a mount vert, a spear-hook sa

Carrie, Ireland, an arm in armour embowed, holding in the hand a dart point downwards all ppr 198 4

Carrier, Hants, out of a ducal coronet or, a dragon's head vert 72 4

Carrill, *see* Carrel.

Carrington, John Bodman, Esquire, of Laggis, Netherhall Gardens, Hampstead, London, N.W., a lion sejant per bend sinister or and arg., semée of annulets, and holding in the mouth a mallet in bend gu., resting the dexter paw upon a torteau. *Absque labore nihil.*

Carrington, Earl (Wynn-Carrington), an elephant's head erased or, eared gu., charged on the neck with three fleur-de-lis two and one az. *Tenax et fidelis.* *cf.* 133. 3

Carrington, London and Yorks, out of a ducal coronet or, unicorn's head sa. 48. 12

Carrington, Sir Frederick, K.C.B., K.C.M.G., of College Lawn, Cheltenham, same crest.

Carrington, out of a ducal coronet arg., a unicorn's head sa., maned and armed of the first. 48. 12

Carrington, Oxon., out of a ducal coronet or, a unicorn's head sa., crined arg., the horn twisted of the last and second. 48. 12

Carrington, Chesh., a unicorn's head arg., armed and crined or. 49. 7

Carrington, Thomas, Esquire, of Sharrow Hurst, Sheffield, three horse-shoes or, thereon a unicorn's head erased sa. *Ferro non gladio.* 49. 1

Carrington, Arthur, Esquire, of Langdale, Bedford, same crest. *Semper paratus.*

Carrington, an eagle close. 76. 2

Carrington, Warw., a peacock's head erased ppr., ducally gorged or. *cf.* 103. 1

Carritt, John Price, of Chateau de la Croisière, Gistel, Belgium: (1) An eagle displayed with two heads sa., crowned with a four-balled coronet or (*for Carritt*). 74. 8. (2) A lion rampant regardant sa. (*for Lloyd-Price*). 2. 11. (3) A bull's head sable, behind it the rays of the sun or (*for Blount*). *Fide et bello fortis.*

Carrol or **Carroll,** Ireland, a tent gu. 158. 7

Carrol, Knt., of London, on a mount vert, a stag lodged regardant arg., attired or. *Semper eadem.* 115. 9

Carrol or **Carroll,** Ireland, on the stump of an oak sprouting a hawk ppr., belled or. *cf.* 86. 11

Carroll, a bear's head sa., muzzled or, between two wings of the last. *cf.* 35. 5

Carroll of Ballynure, co. Wicklow, same crest. *In fide et in bello fortes.* *cf.* 86. 11

Carroll, Rev. Frederick, of Ashford and Munduff, co. Wicklow, and Woodhouse, near Halifax, Yorks, Vicar of Pollington, near Peterborough, Northamp., on the stump of a tree sprouting to the dexter side ppr., a falcon rising per pale arg. and gu., belled and jessed or. *Flecti non frangi.* 87. 8

Carroll, Coote Alexander, Esquire, of Ashford, co. Wicklow, Ireland, on the stump of a tree sprouting to the dexter a falcon rising belled ppr., charged on the breast with a cross fleury sa. *Flecti non frangi.* *cf.* 87. 12

Carron, Scotland, a camel's head per fess arg. and az. 132. 7

Carrowe of London, a mainmast broken, the round-top set off with palisadoes or, headed arg., a lion issuant thereout sa., collared per pale of the first and second.

Carruthers of Howmains, a seraph volant ppr. *Promptus et fidelis.* 184. 11

Carruthers of Annandale, a seraph standing vested ppr. *Paratus et fidelis.* 184. 1

Carruthers, a cherub's head ppr.

Carruthers, Francis John, of Dormont, Lockerbie, a seraph volant ppr. *Promptus et fidelis.* 264. 16

Carruthers, Mitchell-: (1) A cherub's head ppr. (*for Carruthers*). 189. 9. (2) St. Michael in armour holding a spear in his dexter hand, the face, neck, arms and legs bare, all ppr., the wings arg. and hair auburn. *Promptus et fidelis.* —*Virtute cresco.* 189. 11

Carry, a cross Calvary ppr. 165. 4

Carryngton, *see* Carrington.

Carsain, Scotland, a dexter hand holding a scimitar ppr. *Ne m'oubliez.* 213. 5

Carse, Scotland, a falcon's head. *Velocitate.* *cf.* 88. 12

Carse or **Carss,** Scotland, between the horns of a crescent a cross crosslet fitched or. *In cruce salus.* 166. 9

Carsey of Dykelborough, Norf., an arm couped at the elbow and erect, vested az., purfled and cuffed arg., holding in the hand a bunch of gilliflowers ppr. *cf.* 205. 14

Carsewell and **Carswell,** Scotland, a lion's head within a fetterlock. *cf.* 19. 4

Carsewell, a lion passant, the tail extended ppr. 5. 11

Carson, an elephant statant. *Fortitudine et prudentia.* 133. 9

Carson, Bucks, an elephant's head erased, the trunk elevated ppr. *Virtute et valore.* *cf.* 133. 3

Carson of Accarsane, Cape Town, Cape of Good Hope, a dexter hand ppr., holding a crescent arg. *Teneo et credo.* 216. 8

Carstairs, Scotland, the sun shining on a primrose ppr. *Te splendente.* 150. 8

Cart, England and Scotland, a stag's head holding in the mouth a serpent, all ppr. 121. 7

Cart, Scotland and England, a hand holding a club in pale, all ppr. *cf.* 214. 6

Cartell, a tower triple-towered arg., masoned sa. 157. 6

Carter, Northamp., a talbot's head arg. 56. 12

Carter, Northamp., a talbot's head arg., charged with a mullet gu. *cf.* 56. 12

Carter, Cornw., on a mural coronet sa., a talbot passant arg. *cf.* 54. 1

Carter of Watlington Park, on a mural crown or, a talbot passant arg., charged with three buckles az. *Sub libertate quietum.*

Carter, a talbot sejant resting the dexter paw on a catherine-wheel per pale arg and gu. *cf.* 55. 3

Carter of Robertstown and Rathnally, co. Meath, Ireland, on a mural crown or, charged with three hurts, a talbot passant arg. *Victrix patientia duris.*

Carter, Frederick Walter, 24, Ainslie Place, Edinburgh, a talbot's head couped ppr., charged with a mullet arg. *Espérance.* 299. 6

Carter of London, on a mount vert, a greyhound sejant arg., sustaining an escutcheon of the last charged with a cart-wheel vert.

Carter, Hants, a lion's head erased. *Fear not.* 17. 8

Carter, Cornw., a lion's head erased arg. 17. 8

Carter, Yorks, a lion's head erased or, fretty sa. *cf.* 17. 8

Carter, a lion's head, holding in the mouth a comet-star ppr.

Carter, Ireland, a demi-lion rampant sa., holding between the paws a cross lozengy gu., each lozenge charged with a plate.

Carter, Yorks, out of a mural coronet or, a demi-monkey ppr. 163. 13

Carter, Major William Graydon, 1st Batt. Essex Regt., out of a mural crown or, masoned az., a demi-monkey ppr. 163. 13

Carter, Kent, a dexter arm in armour embowed ppr., holding in the hand a roll of paper.

Carter, Edward, Esquire, of Birmingham, a cubit arm erect, vested gu., charged with two roses paleways arg., barbed and seeded, the hand grasping a carbine in bend sinister between two branches of oak fructed, all ppr. *Few words, fair faith.*

Carter, George William, Esquire, of Cliff End House, Scarborough, issuant from the battlements of a tower a demi-monkey ppr., holding between the hands an escutcheon or, charged with a round buckle sa. *Fortitudine.*

Carter, Sir Gilbert Thomas, of 34, Charing Cross, London, S.W., and Government House, Nassau, Bahamas, upon the trunk of a tree fessewise eradicated and sprouting to the dexter a crowned crane ppr., resting the dexter leg on an escutcheon az., charged with a lion's head erased arg. *Nemo me major nisi me justior.* 253. 13

Carter, John, Esquire, of Harrogate and Langrick Grange, near Boston, Lincs, out of the battlements of a tower arg., a demi-monkey gu., charged on the shoulder with a bezant, and holding between the hands a shuttle of the first. *Spes in salute.*

Carter, John Burroughes, Esquire, of the Manor House, Northwold, Norfolk, a talbot sejant erm., the dexter fore-paw supporting an escocheon per pale arg. and az., a catherine-wheel counter-changed. *Sacro grotus cineri.*

Carter, John Robert, Esquire, in front of a tau purpure a demi-cart-wheel or. *In hoc signo vinces.* 269. 7

Carter-Campbell, Thomas Tupper, Esquire, of Fascadel, Ardishaig, Argyllsh., a boar's head erect erased or, armed and langued az. *Fac et spera.*

Carteret, Baron (Thynne), a reindeer statant or. *Loyal devoir.* *cf.* 125. 9

Carteret, on a mount vert, a squirrel sejant ppr. *cf.* 135. 5

Carteret, on a branch of a tree a squirrel sejant cracking a chestnut, all ppr. *Loyal devoir.*

Carteret, Guernsey, a squirrel sejant gu, cracking a nut ppr, on a branch of laurel springing up before him vert

Carthew, Scotland, a wild duck ppr 102 10

Carthew, a falcon rising ducally gorged and belled ppr 87 2

Carthew of Dublin, a dragon's head erased az, langued gu, charged on the neck with a trefoil slipped or cf 71 2

Carthew, Ranulphus John, J P, Woodbridge Abbey, Suff and 154, Kensington Palace Gardens London W, upon a rock an auk ppr holding in the beak a besant *Bedhoh fyr ha heb drok* 275 5

Carthew-Yorstoun, Morden, Esquire, of East Tinwald, Dumfries, N B, and Irvine House, Caobie, N B (1) A tower ppr (*for Yorstoun*) (2) A murr ppr, ducally gorged or *Mens conscia recti —Let us be wise without evil*

Cartier, George Ettienne, Esquire, of Montreal, an anchor in bend sinister sa, cabled ppr, pendent therefrom by a gold chain an escutcheon gu, charged with a fleur-de lis or *France et sans dol* 161 5

Cartiles, Northumb, a talbot passant per pale, indented or and vert 54 1

Cartland, Ireland, a demi eagle rising ppr 80 2

Cartland, John Howard, Esquire, of the Priory, King's Heath Worcs, in front of a demi eagle rising couped ppr, holding in the beak an ear of wheat leaved and slipped, a garb fesseways or *Loyal a devoir* 249 10

Carthtch, two hands wielding a two handed sword ppr 213 3

Cartmell, *see* Austen Cartmell

Cartwright, a lion's head arg, charged on the neck with a catherine-wheel sa cf 21 1

Cartwright, a griffin's head erased or, pierced through the neck with a broken lance ppr, vulned gu cf 66 2

Cartwright-Enery, Captain Stewart Durance Davies (1) On a rock a falcon close ppr, holding in its beak an annulet gu (*for Enery*) cf 86 7 (2) A griffin's head erased or, charged with a rose gu, and pierced through the neck with a lance broken in the middle, vulned, above it on an escroll the motto, *Defend the fold* (*for Cartwright*) *Sans changer*

Cartwright, William Cornwallis, Aynhoe, Northampton, a wolf's head erased or, pierced through the neck with a spear arg *Defend the fold* 275 4

Cartwright, George, 1, Campden House Terrace, W, same crest and motto

Cartwright of Thwaite St Mary and Ellingham, Norf (1) A wolf's head or, erased gu, transpierced by a broken tilting-spear saltirewise ppr (*for Cartwright*) (2) Out of a ducal coronet a demi-tiger arg (*for Cobb*) *Fuimus*

Cartwright, Ernest Henry, Myskyns, Ticehurst Sussex, a wolf's head erased or, gutté-de poix gorged with a collar nebuly gu, between on either side three cinquefoils slipped vert *Defend the fold* 299 4

Cartwright, Rev Anson William Henry, of Brimley House, Teignmouth, out of a chaplet of roses gu, a dexter arm embowed in armour, the hand ppr, holding a catherine-wheel, also gu *Nil desperandum*

Cartwright, Hon Sir Richard John, K C M G, P C, M P, of the Maples, Frontenac, and of King Street, Kingston, Ontario, Canada, a wolf's head erased or, pierced through the neck with the broken blade of a sword arg *Defend the fold* cf 30 8

Cartwright, a wolf's head erased per fesse embattled or, and gules between two branches of laurel in orle 253 21

Cartwright, William, Esquire, of Brimley House, West Teignmouth, Devonsh, out of a chaplet of roses gu, a dexter arm embowed in armour, the hand ppr, holding a catherine-wheel, also gu

Carus of Keudall, Westml, an eagle wings expanded sa, beaked and legged or, charged with a cinquefoil arg cf 77 5

Carus-Wilson, Rev William, Vicar of Preston-next Faversham (1) A crescent or, issuing flames of fire ppr (*for Wilson*) (2) A hawk rising sa, beaked, belled, and collared or, from the collar an escutcheon pendent arg, charged with a wolf's head sa, vulned ppr (*for Carus*) *Non nobis solum*

Carus-Wilson, Edward Shippard, Esquire, of Penmount, near Truro, same crests and motto

Carus-Wilson, Cecil Esquire, same crests and motto

Carver, between two wings a peacock's head holding in its beak a snake, the tail coiled round the neck, all ppr 103 3

Carver, out of a ducal coronet or, a Saracen's head couped at the shoulders ppr cf 190 5

Carvick, of Wyke Yorks, and Moat Mount, Highwood Hill, Middx, an ostrich arg, beaked and legged or, holding in the mouth a broken spear of the last, headed of the first *Be steadfast* cf 97 2

Carvile of Berwick on-Tweed, an arm in armour embowed ppr, garnished or, holding in the hand a sword arg, hilt and pommel of the second *Sola virtus triumphat* 195 2

Carvill, a goat passant sa, armed or cf 129 5

Carwardine, Herts, a wolf passant arg, holding in the mouth an arrow sa, embrued gu cf 28 2

Carwell, a leopard's head erased gardant ppr

Cary, Colonel Lucius Falkland Brancaleone, of Torr Abbey, Devonsh, a swan ppr *Virtute excerptæ* 99 2

Cary of White Castle, Donegal, a swan ppr *Sine macula* 99 2

Cary, Stanley Edward George, of Follaton Park, Devonsh (1) A swan ppr (*for Cary*) 99 2 (2) A dexter hand in armour holding a sword, all ppr (*for Fleming*) *Virtute excerptæ* 210 2

Cary, Robert Sgedden Sulvarde, Esquire, of Torr Abbey, Torquay, same crest as first one above and same motto

Cary, a swan, the wings elevated arg, beaked and legged gu, a crescent surmounted with a mullet, also gu, for difference *Comme je trouve* cf 99 12

Cary of London, a swan ppr, with wings erect, charged on the breast with a rose sa cf 99 12

Cary, a horse's head armed with a shield plate bridled or 51 13

Cary, a demi-lady vested 182 8

Cary, a maiden's head ppr 182 3

Cary, Ireland, two hands couped and conjoined ppr, holding a cross crosslet fitched az (*Another*, gu) 224 11

Cary of London, a lion couchant gardant ppr 7 10

Cary-Elwes, Valentine Dudley Henry of Billing Hall, Northampton (1) Five arrows one in pale and four in saltire, all points downwards, interlaced with a serpent, all ppr 270 7 (2) A swan with wings elevated and endorsed ppr *Deo non fortuna —In utroque fidelis* 270 8

Caryer of Canterbury, Kent, a dove with wings elevated arg, membered gu, bearing an olive-branch, all ppr, within a circle of glory rayonne or cf 93 14

Carysfort, Earl (Proby), an ostrich head erased arg, ducally gorged or, holding in the beak a key of the last *Manus hæc inimica tyrannis*

Casaer, Scotland, a dolphin haurient 140 11

Casamajor, a lion rampant sa 1 10

Casborne of Newhouse, Pakenham, Suff, a lion passant or, gorged with a ducal coronet gu *Puro de fonte* cf 6 2

Case and **Casse**, on a winged globe a dove rising, all ppr 159 9

Case, Scotland, a cubit arm in armour or, holding in the hand gauntleted a sword arg, hilt and pommel of the first, round the arm a scarf tied in a bow arg and gu

Case of West Chester, a cubit arm vested erm, cuffed az, holding in the hand ppr a round buckle or *Distantia jungit*

Casement, Roger, Esquire, J P, of Magherin-temple, Ballycastle, co Antrim on a wreath of the colours a mural crown gu, issuing therefrom a demi tiger rampant gardant ppr charged with a mullet of the first, and crowned with an Eastern crown or, holding in the paws a sword erect ppr, pommel and hilt gold, the point encircled with a wreath vert *Dum spiro spero* 249 9

Casement, out of a mural crown per pale gu and az, a demi-leopard gardant ppr, crowned with an Eastern crown or, holding a sword passing through a wreath of laurel vert

Casey, a demi-talbot gu cf 55 11

Casey, a demi-talbot per fess or and gu cf 55 8

Casey, out of a ducal coronet two branches of laurel in orle 146 9

Casey, Ireland, issuing out of a cloud a hand in fess holding a garb 223 12

Casey of Dublin, out of a ducal coronet or, a demi eagle displayed ppr *Per varios casus* 80 14

Casey, Arthur Edrom Comerford, Esquire, of H M Bengal Civil Service, out of a ducal coronet or, a demi-eagle displayed ppr, charged on the breast with a bugle-horn stringed gold *O'Cathasaigh cloidhimh Leirge* cf 80 14

Casey, Hon James Joseph, C M G, of Ibrickane, Acland Street, St. Kilda, and of Weeroona, Port Philip Bay, both in Victoria, Australia, Chairman of the General Sessions, a rock, thereon an eagle rising regardant holding in the beak a dagger. *Vigore et virtute.*

Cash, out of a mural coronet or, a garb ppr., and thereon a bird perched. 153. 9

Cashall, a lion rampant supporting a plumb-rule arg. 3. 2

Cashen, Berks, a rose-sprig with leaves and buds. *Rosam ne rode.* 149. 8

Cashine, an arm holding a sword in an oak-bush, all ppr.

Casley (formerly **De Chastelai**). Willbraham John Braddick Casley, Esquire, of Coatham, Redcar, Yorks, a lion rampant ppr., armed and langued gu. *Malo mori quam fœdari.* 1. 13

Caslon, a spear-head ppr. 174. 12

Casmajor, a lion rampant sa. 1. 10

Cason of Steeple Morden, Cambs and Herts, a cubit arm vested purp., cuffed arg., holding in the hand a firelock ppr.

Cass of Hackney, Middx., and Scotland, a pair of scales ppr. 179. 8

Cass, an eagle's head erased gu., charged with a fountain, and holding in the beak three ears of wheat or. *Ubique patriam reminisci.*

Cass, Arthur Herbert, Esquire, of United Service Club, Pall Mall, W., same crest and motto.

Cass, Captain Charles Herbert Davis, same crest and motto.

Cass, Rev. Frederick Charles, same crest and motto.

Cass, Bernard Croft, Esquire, of Maylands, Heaton, Bradford, Yorks, same crest and motto.

Cass, Charles Parkinson, Solicitor, Keighley, Yorks, same crest and motto.

Cassan, Ireland, on a chapeau a fleur-de-lis between wings ppr. *cf.* 110. 5

Cassan of Sheffield House, Ireland, issuant from an earl's coronet ppr., a boar's head and neck erased or, langued gu. *Juvant arva parentum.*

Cassan, Matthew Sheffield, Esquire, of Sheffield House, Maryborough, Queen's Co., same crest and motto.

Casse, out of a ducal coronet or, a demi-eagle displayed ppr. 80. 14

Cassel or **Cassell,** a hawk regardant supporting with the dexter claw a garland of laurel, all ppr. 85. 4

Cassels, Charles James Hodgson, formerly of 11, Brunswick Street, Hillside, Edinburgh, a dolphin naiant embowed or. *Avise la fin.* 140. 5

Cassels, Larrett, Esquire, of the Dominion Bank, Ottawa, Canada, same crest and motto.

Cassels, a castle ppr. *Galea spes salutis.* *cf.* 155. 8

Cassidi, Francis Richard, of Glenbrook, Magherafelt, co. Down, a spear broken into three pieces, two in saltire, and the head in pale ppr., banded gu. *Frangas non flectes.*

Cassidi of Glenbrook, Magherafelt, co. Londonderry, Ireland, a spear broken in three pieces, two in saltier, the head in pale, banded gu. *Frangas non flectes.* 175. 2

Cassidy, an arm holding a sword with a snake entwined around it ppr. *Firm and faithful.*

Cassie, a hind's head. 124. 1

Cassilis, Earl, *see* Ailsa, Marquess of.

Cassils, Scotland, an arm in armour embowed holding in the hand a fleur-de-lis. 199. 14

Casson, from a tower a dove rising az. 156. 8

Casstle, out of a castle triple-towered a griffin issuant. *cf.* 155. 10

Cassy, a crow feeding ppr. 107. 4

Cassy, an eagle displayed with two heads vert. 74. 2

Casteja, Marie Emmanuel Alvar de Biaudos Scarisbrick, Marquis de, of Scarisbrick Hall, near Ormkirk: (1) A dove sa., beaked and legged gu., holding in the beak an olive-branch ppr., charged for distinction with a cross crosslet or (*for Scarisbrick*). (2) De Biaudos.

Castell, Norf., a dragon's head couped gu. 71. 1

Castell, a tower arg., in flames at the top ppr.

Castell, Cambs, a tower triple-towered sa., purfled or. 157. 6

Castell, Ireland, on a tower triple-towered arg., an arm in armour erect holding in the hand an ogress ppr.

Castell, Ireland, a cross fleury fitched vert, fleury or. 166. 7

Castellain, a unicorn's head couped or. *Fidel je garderay.* 49. 7

Castello, James, Esquire, 35, Porchester Terrace, Hyde Park, a demi-lion rampant.

Castelton, *see* Castleton.

Castelyon, Lincs, on a tower a lion passant or. *cf.* 156. 2

Caster, Norf., a savage standing on a serpent ppr. 188. 3

Castilion and **Castillon,** Berks, a lion's head erased gardant ducally crowned. *cf.* 18. 11

Castle of London, a tower in flames ppr.

Castle, Egerton, M.A., F.S.A., 49, Sloane Gardens, S.W., same crest. *Pactum serva.*

Castle of London, a dexter arm couped and embowed in fess ppr., vested gu., cuffed or, holding in the hand a pennon charged with a bee volant of the third, the staff of the first. 204. 12

Castle-Stuart, Sir Henry James Stuart-Richardson, fifth Earl and Viscount of Stuart Hall, Stewartstown, and Drum Manor, Cookstown, both in co. Tyrone: (1) A lion rampant arg., holding a wreath of oak-leaves fructed ppr., and charged on the shoulder with a cross formée gu. (*for Richardson*). (2) A unicorn's head arg., armed or (*for Stuart*). *Forward.*

Castlecomb, an arm in armour embowed ppr., garnished or, holding in the hand a pistol ppr. *cf.* 197. 12

Castle-Cuffe, Viscount, *see* Desert, Earl.

Castlehow, a castle ppr., therefrom issuant a lion az., supporting a passion cross or. *cf.* 155. 10

Castlelock of Faversham, Kent, out of a mural coronet or, a demi-griffin segreant sans ailes or, holding in the talon a cross crosslet fitched of the last.

Castlemaine, Baron (Handcock), Ireland, a demi-lion rampant az., holding between the paws a fusil arg., charged with a cock gu. *Vigilate et orate.* 236. 6

Castleman, a lion rampant between two wings. 9. 2

Castleman of Coberley, Glouc., a demi-man in armour holding in his dexter hand a flag of defiance displayed over his head, his sinister on the pommel of his sword, all ppr.

Castleman, of Chettle, Blandford, formerly of Wimborne and Hinton St. Mary, Dorset, a demi-man in armour holding in his dexter hand a dagger, all ppr., and in his sinister a key or. *Without God castles are nothing.* 299. 3

Castlereagh, Viscount, *see* Londonderry, Marquess of.

Castlerosse, Viscount, *see* Kenmare, Earl.

Castleton, Suff., a dragon passant, wings addorsed vert. 73. 2

Castleton, Surrey, Suff., and Lincs, a dragon's head between two wings expanded gu. 72. 7

Castleton, Surrey, a demi-dragon with wings addorsed gu. 73. 10

Castletown, Baron (Fitzpatrick), a dragon on its back ppr., surmounted by a lion passant sa., the whole debruised by a bendlet sinister wavy arg. *Fortis sub forte fatiscet.* *cf.* 73. 8

Castlewellan, Baron, *see* Annesley, Earl of.

Castlyn, a tower ppr., with a flag gu. 157. 13

Caston, a lion's gamb erased sa., holding a cross pattée, fitched in pale erm. 36. 9

Caswall, Wilts, and **Caswell,** Middx., a dexter arm couped at the shoulder in mail holding in the hand ppr. a cross crosslet fitched or. *cf.* 198. 2

Caswell, Middx, an arm in armour embowed grasping a broken spear, all ppr. 197. 2

Catcher, out of a ducal coronet ppr., a demi-leopard arg., collared and lined or. *cf.* 23. 14

Catcher, a garb or, banded vert. 153. 2

Catchmay, a demi-lion issuant az., gorged with a coronet or. 10. 7

Cater, London, Berks, Hunts, and Leics., a demi-griffin arg., beaked and legged gu. 64. 2

Cater, A. Parker, Esquire, of Avondale, Rugeley, Staffs, and St. Mary's Grove, Stafford, same crest. *Nihil sine labor.* 64. 2

Cater of London and Berks, a lion's head erased barry of six or and az. 17. 4

Caterall of Catherall, Lancs, a cat passant or. 26. 4

Caterall of Horton, Chesh., on a chapeau az., turned up erm., a cat passant ppr.

Catesby, a leopard passant ppr. *cf.* 24. 2

Catesby, Northamp., an antelope's head couped arg., between the attires or, two battle-axes erect ppr.

Catesby or **Cattesbye,** Bucks, a lion passant sa., crowned or. *cf.* 6. 2

Catesby, Northamp. and Bucks, a leopard passant gardant arg., pellettée. 24. 4

Catesnelboge, an anchor ppr. 161. 1

Cathcart, Earl (Cathcart), a dexter hand couped above the wrist and erect ppr., grasping a crescent arg. *I hope to speed.* 216. 8

Cathcart, of Carbiston, Ayrsh., a dexter hand couped at the wrist holding a crescent arg. *I hope to speed.* 216. 8

Cathcart of Knockdolian Castle, Ayrsh., same crest and motto.

Cathcart, Sir Reginald Archibald Edward, Bart., Scotland, a dexter hand holding up a heart royally crowned, all ppr. *By faith we are saved.* *cf.* 216. 9

Cathcart, a pyramid arg., environed by a vine vert. *cf.* 179. 12

Catherens, Catherns, and **Catharines**, a griffin or, pellettée. 63. 8

Catheryns, a griffin statant or, guttée-de-poix. *cf.* 63. 8

Cathery, a boar's head couped sa., holding in the mouth three arrows. 42. 9

Cathie, Scotland, a stag's head couped ppr. 121. 5

Cathrope, on a mount a stag current. 118. 13

Cathrow-Disney, *see* Disney.

Catley, a hand erect holding a sealed letter ppr. *cf.* 215. 7

Catlin and **Catlyn**, a leopard's head couped at the neck and regardant arg., ducally gorged and lined or.

Catlin, a demi-leopard rampant gardant arg., pellettée, ducally gorged vert, between two wings of the last.

Catlin or **Catlyn**, Beds and Northamp., a lion's head erased arg., collared and lined or. *cf.* 18. 6

Catlin, Kent, a lion sejant gardant or, between two wings adorsed barry of six of the first and az.

Caton, Rev. Redmond Bewley, Great Fakenham Rectory, Suff., issuant from a castle with two towers arg., charged with three crosses crosslet fitchée in fesse sa., a Saracen's head affrontée ppr., wreathed round the temples or and gu. *Cautus metuit foveam lupus.*

Cator, Albemarle, of Beckenham Place, Kent, a lion's head erased erminois, charged on the neck with two bars engrailed gu. *Nihil sine labore.* *cf.* 17. 8

Cator, Albemarle, Esquire, of Woodbastwick Hall, Norwich, and Trewsbury, Coates, Cirencester, same crest and motto.

Catt, a horned owl ppr. 96. 5

Catt, George Henry, Esquire, of Villa Amalthea, Hythe, Southampton, in front of an esquire's helmet ppr., a gauntlet fesseways, also ppr. *Fortis qui prudens.* 267. 14

Cattelin, a demi-leopard rampant gardant arg., pellettée, ducally gorged vert, between two wings of the last.

Catterall of Crook, Lancs, a cat passant gardant arg. *cf.* 26. 4

Catteshye, *see* Catesby.

Cattle, Lancs, a wolf's head az. 30. 5

Cattley, a demi-cat rampant gardant supporting an anchor. *cf.* 26. 12

Cattley, *see* Catley.

Catton, a horned owl arg. 96. 5

Catton, Oxford, on a tun a dog sejant.

Catty, a goat's head erased arg. 128. 5

Catzius, an estoile or, within a garland of laurel vert.

Catznellage, the attires of a stag or. *Ne supra.* 123. 5

Caudwell, Eber, Surgeon, 8, Battersea Rise, S.W., a cock's head couped holding a cross patée fitchée, all between two wings. *In deo spes.*

Cauley, from a plume of three ostrich-feathers an eagle rising ppr. 80. 6

Caulfeild of Drumcairne, Tyrone, a dragon's head erased gu., gorged with a bar gemelle arg. *Deo duce, ferro comitante.* *cf.* 71. 2

Caulfeild of Raheenduff, Queen's Co.; of Bloomfield, Westmeath; of Donamon Castle, co. Roscommon, same crest and motto.

Caulfeild, out of a mural coronet a hand holding a sword wavy. *cf.* 212. 4

Caulfeild, *see* Charlemont, Earl of.

Caulfeild, of Matlock House, Twickenham, Middx., a dragon's head erased gu., gorged with a collar gemelle arg. *Deo duce, ferro comitante.* 276. 2

Caulfeild, Algernon Thomas St. George, Esquire, of Donamon Castle, Roscommon, same crest and motto. 276. 2

Caulkin, Warw., out of a ducal coronet a demi-lion rampant ppr. *Vincit qui se vincit.* 16. 3

Caundis, out of an antique crown or, a lion's head gu. *cf.* 17. 5

Caunter, a naked arm erect couped at the elbow holding a palm-branch ppr. *Quam non torret hyems.* 219. 11

Caus, a cinquefoil per pale arg. and az. 148. 12

Causton, Surrey, a demi-leopard with a lion's tail arg., collared per pale az. and gu.

Causton, Richard Knight, Esquire, a demi-leopard rampant arg. *In Deo spes.*

Causton, Essex, a cubit arm erect vested gu., cuffed arg., charged with two bends wavy sa., holding in the hand ppr. a round buckle or.

Causton, a wolf's head erased or. 30. 8

Cautley, Nathaniel, Esquire, of Shelf Hall, Halifax, Yorks: (1) Two swords in saltire ppr., pommels and hilts or, surmounted by a cross flory or (*for Cautley*). (2) On a mount vert, an Angora goat in front of a palm-tree ppr., resting the dexter foot upon an escutcheon gu., charged with a shuttle paleways or (*for Bottomley*). *Fideli certa merces.*

Cauty, a catherine-wheel az. 167. 2

Cauvin, Scotland, a dexter hand holding a dagger point downwards. *cf.* 213. 6

Cavaler of London, a horse's head sa., maned, bridled, and armed or, on his head a plume of three feathers, the first arg., the second or, the third gu. 50. 14

Cavall, a naked man holding a palm-tree ppr.

Cavan, Earl of, and **Baron** (Lambart), Ireland, on a mount vert, a centaur per pale gu. and arg., drawing a bow, also gu., the arrow or. *Ut quocunque paratus.* *cf.* 53. 2

Cavanagh, out of a crescent arg., a garb or.

Cavanagh, Ireland, a stag lodged between two branches of laurel. 115. 11

Cave, Sir Charles Daniel, Bart., a daisy-flower slipped ppr., a greyhound's head issuant therefrom, per pale arg. and sa., guttée counterchanged.

Cave, Verney-, Baron Braye, *see* Braye.

Cave, a greyhound current sa., collared or. *Cave, Deus videt.* (*Another*, collared arg.) *cf.* 58. 2

Cave, Glouc., a greyhound courant sa., holding in the mouth a scroll bearing the motto, *Cave.*

Cave-Browne-Cave, Sir Mylles, Bart., of Stanford, Northants: (1) A greyhound courant sa., holding in his mouth an escroll with the motto, *Gardez* (*for Cave*). (2) A stork ppr., beaked and membered or (*for Browne*). 105. 11

Cave, Leics., out of a flower arg., stalked and leaved vert, a greyhound's head per pale erm. and ermines. 61. 14

Cave of Belmont, Millhill, and Queensberry House, Richmond, Surrey, a greyhound sejant or, pellettée, resting the dexter paw on a cross moline gu. *Cave, Deus videt.* *cf.* 59. 4

Cave, Basil Shillito, Esquire, C.B., H.B.M.'s Agency and Consulate-General, Zanzibar, and 14, Redcliffe Square, London, S.W., same crest and motto.

Cave, George, Esquire, of the Old Palace, Richmond, Surrey, same crest and motto.

Cave, Thomas, Esquire, same crest and motto.

Cave, Sir Charles Daniel, of Cleve Hill, Glouc., a daisy-flower slipped ppr., issuant therefrom a greyhound's head per pale arg. and sa., guttée counterchanged. *Cave.* 257. 3

Cave-Orme, George Alington, Esquire, of Vicarage House, Teddington, a dolphin naiant arg., charged on the body with two escallops gu., and between as many branches of coral of the last.

Cavel, an unicorn sejant arg.

Cavell of Trehaverrock, Cornw., a calf's head couped gu. *Karanza whilas karanza.*

Cavenagh, issuing out of clouds two dexter hands grasping an oak-stump ppr., sprouting anew ppr. 224. 10

Cavenagh, a stag lodged between two branches of laurel vert. 115. 11

Cavenagh-Mainwaring, James Gordon, Esquire, of Whitmore Hall, Staffs: (1) Out of a ducal coronet or, an ass's head ppr. (*for Mainwaring*). (2) Upon a mount between two trefoils slipped vert a crescent az., therefrom issuant a garb or. *Devant si je puis.*

Cavendish, Duke of Devonshire, *see* Devonshire.

Cavendish, Baron Chesham, *see* Chesham.

Cavendish, Baron Waterpark, *see* Waterpark.

Cavendish, Sussex, a wolf's head or, collared gu. 30. 9

Cavendish, a serpent nowed vert. 142. 4

Cavendish, Alfred Edward John, Esquire, a snake nowed ppr. *Cavendo tutus.*

Cavendish, Captain Cecil Charles, same crest and motto.

Cavendish, Charles George, Esquire, same crest and motto.

Cavendish, Ernest Lionel Francis, Esquire, same crest and motto.

Cavendish, Francis William Henry, Esquire, same crest and motto.

Cavendish, Reginald Richard Frederick, Esquire, same crest and motto.

Cavendish, Victor Christian William, Esquire, of Holker Hall, Carnforth, same crest and motto.

Cavendish, William Henry Alexander George Delmar, Esquire, same crest and motto.

Caw, Scotland, a stag's head holding in the mouth a serpent, all ppr. 121. 7

Cawarden, a wolf's head erased sa., pierced with an arrow arg. *cf.* 30. 8

Cawdor, Earl (Campbell), a swan ppr. *Be mindful.* *cf.* 99. 2

Cawdor, a sheaf of arrows sa., barbed and feathered or, banded gu. 173. 3

Cawley, out of a plume of three ostrich-feathers an eagle rising ppr. 80. 6

Cawley, Frederick, Esquire, of Brooklands, Prestwich, Manchester, upon a mount vert a swan's head erased arg., between six bulrushes stalked and leaved, three on either side or.

Cawley, Hugh, Esquire, of Alderley Edge, same crest and motto.

Cawodley and **Cawoodley** of Cawodley and Stridley, Devonsh., a hawk's leg az., joined at the knee to a wing arg., belled or. 113. 5

Cawson of London, out of a ducal coronet or, a unicorn's head arg., ducally gorged, lined and ringed sa. *cf.* 48. 12

Cawston, George, Esquire, of the Manor House, Cawston, Norf., and 56, Upper Brook Street, W., in front of an oak-tree ppr., a falcon arg., charged on the wing with a cross crosslet sa., preying on a hare az. *Sohou, Sohou.* 249. 8

Cawthorne, George J., Esquire, of Beauchêne, Fox Hill, Upper Norwood, London, S.E., and of Stretton House, Leamington Spa., a thorn-tree, and on the top thereof a rook perched and cawing ppr., all between two wings sa., each charged with a chess rook or. *At spes non fracta.* 106. 8

Cawthorne, a raven ppr. 107. 14

Cawthorne, Yorks, an arm embowed ppr., holding in the hand a cross patonce or.

Cawthra of Toronto, Canada, upon a quiver fessewise filled with arrows or, a boar's head couped az., holding in the mouth two arrows saltirewise, the points resting on the quiver, also or. *Maintien le Droit.* 228. 1

Cawthra, Henry, Esquire, of Yeadon Hall, Toronto, Canada, same crest and motto.

Cawton, a dromedary sa., bezantée. 132. 2

Cay, *see* Kay.

Cay of Bishop-Wearmouth, Durh., a griffin's head erased sa., holding in the beak a key az. *Patria cara carior libertas.* 66. 6

Cay, a hawk ppr., and flotant behind him a pennon vert, tied round the neck and charged with the arms, viz., az., a bend or, debruised by a label of three points arg.

Cay of Charlton Hall, Northumb., a royal eagle gorged with a collar and banner vert, bearing a rose arg. *Sit sine spinâ.*

Cayle, Ireland, a demi-stag holding in the mouth a rose slipped and leaved. 119. 1

Cayley, Sir George Everard Arthur, Bart., Yorks, a demi-lion rampant or, charged with a bend gu., thereon three mullets arg., and holding in the dexter paw a battle-axe arg., the handle gu., garnished or. *Nul q'um per lucem ac tenebras mea sidera sanguine surgent.* 15. 6

Cayley, Digby Leonard Arthur, Esquire, of Lovely Hall, Salesbury, near Blackburn, same crest and motto.

Cayley of Low Hall, Yorks, a demi-lion rampant or, charged with a bend gu., thereon three mullets arg., and holding in the dexter paw a battle-axe arg., the handle gu., garnished or. 15. 6

Cayley, Hugh, Esquire, of Wydale, Yorks, a demi-lion rampant or, charged with a bend gu., thereon three mullets arg., in the paws a battle-axe az., handle also gu., tufted or.

Cayley, Sir Richard, of 62, Clarendon Road, W., same crest.

Cayley-Webster, Herbert, Capt., late 7th Brigade South Irish Division, Royal Artillery, of Junior Naval and Military Club: (1) A dragon's head couped (*for Webster*). 275. 6. (2) A lion rampant holding in the paws a battle-axe (*for Cayley*). *Fides et justitia.* 275. 1

Cayly and **Cayley,** a mascle vert. 167. 9

Cayzer, Sir Charles, M.P., of Gartmore, Perthsh., a sea-lion erect ppr., holding in the dexter paw a fleur-de-lis, and supporting with the sinister an estoile, both or. *Caute sed impavide.* 271. 19

Cazalet, a casque, and in front thereof a tilting-spear fessewise, all ppr.

Cazalet, Clement H. Langston, Tanhurst, near Dorking, Surrey, and 2, Bedford Court Mansions, Bedford Square, London, W.C., same crest. *Spero meliora.*

Cazalet, William Marshall, Esquire, of Fairlawn, Tunbridge, Kent, a casque ppr.

Cazenove, a sword in pale az., hilted or. 170. 2

Cazenove, Arthur Philip, Esquire, of 51, Cadogan Place, S.W., two demi-lions guardant, addorsed, tails interlaced, that on the dexter or, that on the sinister az., each gorged with a collar counterchanged, and holding between the paws a rose as in the arms.

Cecil, Marquess of Exeter, *see* Exeter.

Cecil, Marquess of Salisbury, *see* Salisbury.

Cecil, six arrows in saltier or, barbed and flighted arg., girt together by a belt gu., buckled and garnished of the first, and over the arrows a morion-cap. 173. 10

Cecil, Lord William, of Burghley House, Stamford, on a chapeau gu., turned up erm., a garb or, supported by two lions rampant, the dexter arg., the sinister az., the garb charged with a mullet, also az., for difference. 3. 5

Cecil, a garb or, supported by two lions rampant, the dexter arg., the sinister az. *cf.* 3. 5

Ceily or **Ceely,** an arm in armour, holding in the hand a pheon, point upward, all ppr. 211. 7

Celey, Cornw., a tiger sejant arg. 27. 6

Cely or **Ceely,** Essex, a bundle of quills ppr. 113. 6

Cely, a dexter hand with the two first fingers erect. 122. 11

Cenino, an escallop between two palm-branches ppr. 141. 4

Cervington, Devonsh., a tun or, and issuing out of the bung-hole five roses of the same stalked and leaved ppr. 154. 4

Cevilioc, an arm in armour embowed, round the shoulder a ribbon tied in a bow, and holding in the hand a knotted club. 199. 3

Ceyley, *see* Cayley.

Chabnor, Herts, a pheon or. 174. 11

Chace, a lion rampant or, holding between its paws a cross patonce gu. *cf.* 1. 13

Chad, Bart. (*extinct*), Norf., a falcon, wings expanded ppr., beaked, legged, and membered or, supporting in the dexter claw a cross potent per pale gu. and arg.

Chad, Scott-, Joseph Stonehewer, Thursford Hall, East Dereham, Norf.: (1) Same crest as above. (2) Crest of Scott.

Chadborn, Glouc., a demi-griffin az. 64. 2

Chadborn, C. N., M.R.C.S., Glouc., a demi-griffin sa. *Quo fata vocant.* 293. 2

Chaderton, a griffin's head couped gu. 66. 1

Chadock, a martlet arg. 95. 4

Chadock and **Chaddock,** on a ducal coronet or, a martlet gu. 95. 12

Chads, a unicorn's head couped between two laurel-branches ppr. 49. 14

Chadwell, out of a ducal coronet a dexter hand holding by the neck a swan's head erased ppr. 220. 7

Chadwick, on a ducal coronet or, a martlet gu. 95. 12

Chadwick, Notts, Staffs, and Lancs, a lily arg., stalked and leaved vert. *In candore decus.* 151. 2

Chadwick, Hugo Mavesyn, Esquire, of Shenstone, Lichfield, same crest. *Stans cum rege.*

Chadwick, Alfred, Esquire, of Frankham, Mark Cross, Sussex, a lily stalked and leaved ppr., between two quatrefoils or. *Nil desperandum.*

Chadwick of Healey, Lancs: (1) A lily arg., stalked and leaved vert. 151. 2 (2) A talbot's head gu., pierced through the neck with an arrow or, and gorged with a collar charged with the arms of Hansacre, viz., erm., three chess rooks gu. *Juxta salopiam.—Stans cum rege.*

Chadwick of Puddleston Court, Leominster, a white lily stalked and leaved surmounted by two crosses crosslet fitched in saltier. *In candore decus.* 151. 2

Chadwick, Harry, Esquire, of Chad Wyche, Bovey Tracey, Devonsh., in front of two cross crosslets fitchée in saltire the flower and stem of a lily slipped ppr. *In candore decus.*

Chadwick of High Bank, Lancs, in front of a lily stalked and leaved ppr., a martlet arg. *Deo fidens proficio.*

Chadwick, Edward Marion, Esquire, of the city of Toronto, Canada, a martlet arg., holding in its beak a white lily slipped and leaved ppr., borne fesseways, the flower to the sinister. *In candore decus.—Toujours prêt.*

Chadwick, His Honour Austin Cooper of Guelph, Canada, same crest and mottoes.

Chadwick, Alfred, M.D., Clyde House, Heaton Chapel, Stockport, a white lily stalked and leaved ppr. *In candore decus.*

Chadwick, Cooper-: (1) A martlet sa., charged on the breast with a crescent arg., holding in the beak a lily slipped and leaved ppr. (*for Chadwick*). (2) On a mount vert, a bull passant per pale arg. and sa., gorged with a collar dancettée az. (*for Cooper*). cf. 45. 7

Chafe, Dorset and Devonsh., a demi-lion rampant az., bezantée, langued gu., holding between the paws a lozenge arg. (*Not recorded.*) cf. 13. 1

Chaffers, on a mural crown gu., charged with three mullets of eight points or, a chaffinch ppr.

Chaffin, on a mural crown a mullet of eight plain rays or. cf. 164. 4

Chafin or **Chaffin**, Dorset, a talbot passant or. 54. 1

Chafy-Chafy, Rev. Wm. Kyle Westwood, M.A., Rous Lench, Court Evesham, on a mount vert, between two branches of palm, a peacock in his pride, all ppr. *Fide et fiducia.* 103. 14

Chaigneau, Ireland, a lion's head erased gu. 17. 2

Chalbots, two anchors in saltier ppr. 161. 7

Chalie, in water a swan naiant with wings addorsed. 99. 9

Chalke of Long Ashton, Westbury, and Yatton, Somers., Avington, Berks, and Shelborne, Wilts, out of a ducal coronet or, a demi-swan rising arg., crested gu. cf. 100. 12

Chalke, Alfred Raymond, Esquire, of Coryton Terrace, Mutley, Plymouth, in front of a demi-swan, wings expanded or, a fountain, each wing charged with a cinquefoil gu. *Semper virtute vivo.*

Chalkhill, Middx., out of a ducal coronet or, a horse's head erm., maned of the first. 51. 7

Chalklen, on a mural coronet a sheaf of seven arrows, points upward.

Challen, Sussex, a castle arg., thereon a flag. *Spes, salus, decus.* 155. 8

Challen-Gratwick, Sussex, a demi-horse salient. *Gloria Deo.* 53. 3

Challenge, Glouc., an eagle's head sa. 83. 1

Challenor, Sussex, a wolf statant regardant arg., pierced through the shoulder with a broken spear or, the upper part in his mouth, the lower resting on the wreath.

Challon, a mermaid holding in her dexter hand a mirror ppr. cf. 184. 5

Challoner and Chaloner, a demi-sea-wolf rampant or. *Sicut quercus.*

Chalmers of Aldbar, Forfarsh., an eagle rising ppr. *Spero.* 77. 5

Chalmers, Patrick, Aldbar Castle, near Brechin, same crest and motto.

Chalmers of Balnecraig, Scotland, same crest and motto.

Chalmers, an eagle rising regardant ppr., *Spero.* 77. 4

Chalmers, Sir David Patrick, H.M. Advocate for Gold Coast Colony, an eagle rising regardant ppr. *Spero.* 77. 4

Chalmers of Leith Mount, Scotland, on a mount vert, an eagle rising ppr., holding in his dexter talon a sword ppr. *Spero.*

Chalmers, John Henry, Gentleman, of Holcombe, Moretonhampstead, South Devonsh., a falcon, wings addorsed ppr., semée-de-lis, between two quatrefoils, all gu. *Quid non Deo juvante.*

Chalmers, His Honour Judge Mackenzie, of Leamington, upon an Eastern crown an eagle rising, wings displayed ppr., collared and murally crowned, and supporting with the dexter claw a flagstaff erect, therefrom flowing to the sinister a banner arg., charged with a lion passant gu. *Spero.* 78. 13

Chalmers, Dalzell, Barrister, 1, the Mansions, Earl's Court, S.W., same crest and motto.

Chalmers, Scotland, a hawk rising ppr., jessed and belled or. *Promptus et fidelis.* 87. 1

Chalmers, a falcon belled ppr. *Non præda, sed victoria.* 85. 2

Chalmers of Westburn, Aberdeen, a dove holding an olive-branch in her beak ppr. *Spero.* 92. 5

Chalmers, David Montague Alexander, Esquire, of Beaconhill, Murtle, Aberdeen, and 18, Golden Square, Aberdeen, same crest and motto.

Chalmers, John Gray, Esquire, of Aberdeen, same crest and motto.

Chalmers, W. Bryce, 21, Cromwell Crescent, S.W., same crest and motto.

Chalmers, Scotland, a demi-lion holding in the dexter paw a fleur-de-lis gu. *Quid non Deo juvante.* 13. 2

Chalmers of Kildonnan, a demi-lion holding in his dexter paw a sabre ppr. *Non temere.* 14. 12

Chalmers, Scotland, a lion's head erased sa. *Avancez.* 17. 8

Chalmers of Ashentrees, Scotland, a sinister hand holding up a pair of scales ppr. *Lux mihi laurus.* cf. 217. 13

Chamber, a demi-eagle with two heads displayed per pale sa. and arg., the heads imperially crowned or. cf. 82. 7

Chamber, Middx., Cornw., and Essex, a bear passant sa., muzzled, collared, and lined or. cf. 34. 1

Chamber, Notts, out of a chaplet of roses gu., leaved vert, a greyhound's head arg., gorged with a belt az., buckled and studded or, from the belt in front a chain and ring of the last.

Chamber, Leics., out of a coronet or, an otter's head arg.

Chamberlain, Sir Henry Hamilton Errol, Bart., 16, Chester Street, Belgrave Square, S.W., of London, an eagle displayed ppr., the dexter claw resting on an armillary sphere or. *Spes et fides.* 254. 4

Chamberlain and **Chamberlayne**, a swan with wings addorsed, crowned ppr. 99. 4

Chamberlain, out of a mural coronet gu., a demi-lion rampant or, holding in the dexter paw a key arg.

Chamberlain, Rt. Hon. Joseph, M.P., 40, Prince's Gardens, London, S.W., out of a mural coronet a demi-lion rampant holding between the paws a key erect, wards upwards. *Je tiens ferme.*

Chamberlain, a bear's head erased arg. 35. 2

Chamberlain and **Chamberlan**, a pheon with part of the shaft broken ppr. 174. 10

Chamberlain or **Chamberlayn**, an ass's head couped arg. 125. 12

Chamberlain and **Chamberlaine**, Glouc., Oxon., and Yorks, out of a ducal coronet or, an ass's head arg. 125. 10

Chamberlain, an ass's head erased arg., ducally crowned or.

Chamberlayn, Cambs, an ass's head erased ppr., ducally gorged or.

Chamberlayne, Ingles-, Henry, of The Hyde, Glouc.: (1) Out of a ducal coronet an ass's head. 125. 10. (2) A lion's head erased charged with three trefoils. *Virtuti nihil invium.* cf. 17. 8

Chamberlayne, out of a ducal coronet gu., the head of an ass arg. 125. 10

Chamberlayne, William Tankerville, of Stoney Thorpe, Warw., out of a ducal coronet or, an ass's head ppr. *Prodesse quam conspici.* 125. 10

Chamberlayne, Tankerville, Esquire, of Cranbury Park, Hants, out of a ducal coronet or, an ass's head arg. *Mors potior maculâ.* 125. 10

Chamberlayne, Stanes Brocket Henry, Barrister-at-Law, Wetherley Hall, Atherstone, same crest and motto.

Chamberlayne, Ireland, a pegasus. 47. 1

Chamberlayne, Tankerville James, of Cyprus, 27, Upper Mount Street, Dublin, and 41, Lancaster Gate, W., a pegasus arg. *Nemo me impune lacessit.*

Chamberlen of London, a dexter arm couped and embowed fesseways holding in the hand a grenade fired, all ppr. 202. 5

Chamberlin of London, out of a Saxon coronet an ostrich holding in the beak a key.

Chambers of Fox Hall, Ireland, a falcon close belled ppr. *Spero dum spiro.* 85. 2

Chambers, a falcon belled ppr. *Non præda, sed victoria.* 85. 2

Chambers, Scotland, a falcon rising and belled ppr. *Facta non verba.* 87. 1

Chambers, Charles Edward Stuart, Esquire, of Cardney, Dunkeld, N.B., same crest and motto.

Chambers of Wimbledon, London, S.W., out of a ducal coronet or, a demi-eagle displayed gu., winged or. *Non præda, sed victoria.* 80. 13

Chambers, out of a ducal coronet or, a demi-eagle displayed gu., winged of the first. 80. 13

Chambers, Richard Edward Elliot, Esquire, out of a ducal coronet or, charged with a cross humettée gu., a demi-eagle displayed of the last, winged and collared of the first. *Non præda, sed victoria.*

Chambers, Edmund Frederic, Esquire, of the Hurst, near Alfreton, Derbysh., in front of a fret or, a stork, the wings expanded ppr., each wing charged with a cinquefoil, also or. *In fide fortis.* 104. 12

Chambers, Ireland, on a mount a tree ppr. 143. 14

Chambers, G. F., Lethen Grange, Sydenham, S.E., an arm in armour embowed ppr., charged with a cross couped gu., holding in the hand, also ppr., a scimitar arg., hilt and pommel or. *Vi et virtute.* cf. 196. 10

Chambers, an ass's head erased arg. cf. 125. 12

Chambers, Sir George Henry, Langley Lodge, Beckenham, Kent, in front of an ass's head erased sa., collared gemelle, an anchor fessewise or.

Chambers, a leg in armour, garnished and spurred, couped at the thigh, the thigh resting upon the wreath, the toe pointing to the sinister. *Deo ac bello.* *cf.* 193. 8

Chambers, Leics., out of a ducal coronet or, three holly-leaves vert.

Chambers, a bear passant sa., muzzled, collared, and chained or. *cf.* 34. 1

Chambers, George Wilton, of London and Clough House, Yorks, on a mount vert, a bear passant ppr., muzzled and gorged with an Eastern crown, from the muzzle a chain pendent and reflexed over the back, all or. *cf.* 34. 5

Chambers, Oxon., a greyhound's head erased arg., round his neck a belt az., buckled or. *cf.* 61. 4

Chambers, Ireland, a greyhound's head erased arg., collared sa., garnished or. *Vivam te laudare.* *cf.* 61. 2

Chambers of London, within a mountain vert, a man working in a copper-mine, holding in his hand a pick-axe elevated ppr., his cap, shirt, drawers, and nose arg., his shoes sa., the planet Venus rising behind the mountain or.

Chambley and **Chambly,** above a globe a ship ppr. 160. 1

Chambre, Shropsh.: (1) A greyhound's head erased arg., collared az., buckled and studded or, from the belt in front a chain and ring of the last. *cf.* 61. 2. (2) A camel's head quarterly arg. and or, collared gu., between three annulets of the last.

Chambré, Hunt Walsh, Esquire, of Dungannon House, co. Tyrone, a greyhound's head erased arg., collared az., therefrom a cord knotted and terminated by a ring or. *Tutamen pulchris.*

Chambre of London, a cock gu., holding in its dexter claw three wheat-ears or. *cf.* 91. 2

Chambre of Halhead Hall and Kendal, Westmoreland, a cock gu., holding in his dexter claw three wheat-ears or. *En Dieu est tout.* *cf.* 91. 2

Chambre, Ireland, a greyhound's head erased arg., collared az., therefrom a cord knotted and terminated by a ring or. *Tutamen pulchris.*

Chambre, a rose-branch ppr. 149. 8

Chambres, Reginald Gordon, a greyhound's head erased arg., collared az., leashed with knotted leash or. *A fyn duw a fydd.*

Chamier, a cubit arm in bend vested az., charged with five fleurs-de-lis in saltire or, cuffed erm., holding in the hand a scroll, and thereon an open book ppr., garnished of the second.

Chamier of Dublin, out of a French noble coronet ppr., a cubit arm in bend vested az., charged with five fleurs-de-lis in saltire or, cuffed erm., holding in the hand a scroll, and thereon an open book ppr., garnished gold. *Aperto vivere voto.*

Chamier, Adrian Charles, Captain, 46, Nevern Square, S.W., same crest. *Aperto vivere voto.*

Chamier, Lieutenant-General Stephen, C.B., 64, Inverness Terrace, W., same crest and motto.

Chamley of Dublin, a demi-griffin segreant erm., beaked and winged or, holding between the claws a helmet arg., garnished or. *Cassis tutissima virtus.* *cf.* 64. 1

Chamond, Cornw., a lion sejant. 8. 8

Chamond and **Chaumond,** a griffin sejant or. 62. 10

Chamond, on a chapeau ppr., a fleur-de-lis gu., between two wings of the first. *cf.* 110. 5

Champ, a stag ppr. 117. 5

Champagne, a bunch of grapes slipped and leaved vert. 152. 7

Champain, a demi-lion rampant gardant gu. 10. 8

Champayn, Scotland, a bear's head couped sa. 34. 14

Champernon, a lion's head erased arg., semée of pellets ducally crowned or. 18. 9

Champernonne and **Champernowne,** out of a ducal coronet an ostrich rising holding in the beak a horse-shoe, all ppr. 96. 8

Champeroun, a dexter hand holding a rose-branch ppr. 218. 10

Champernowne, a swan sitting ppr., holding in the beak a horse-shoe or.

Champernowne, Arthur Melville, Dartington Hall, Totnes, same crest.

Champernowne, a demi-lion arg., holding a cross formée fitchée or. *cf.* 11. 10

Champion, an arm in armour embowed and erect ppr., garnished or, holding in the gauntlet a chaplet of laurel vert. 199. 12

Champion, Albert Edward Gurney, 3, Fourth Avenue Mansions, Hove, Brighton, same crest. *Semper fidelis.*

Champion of London, an arm erect couped at the elbow, vested gu., charged with three bars or, holding in the hand ppr. a rose-branch of the last.

Champion, an arm erect vested arg., cuffed gu., holding a chaplet of laurel vert.

Champion, a turkey-cock ppr. 108. 5

Champion of London, a leopard's head erased gardant or, ducally gorged sa. *Præclarius quo difficilius.* *cf.* 23. 8

Champion of London, a winged spur ppr. *Speed.* 111. 12

Champion De Crespigny, *see* De Crespigny.

Champney of London, a leopard's head erased gardant or, ducally gorged sa. *cf.* 23. 8

Champney, a lion's gamb erased supporting a torteau. 39. 13

Champneys, a demi-Moor side-faced, habited or, cuffs, cape, and ornaments on the shoulders gu., wreathed about the temples also or and gu., and holding in the dexter hand a gem-ring or, stoned az.

Champreys, same crest. *Pro patria non timidus perire.*

Chance (the descendants of the late Wm. Chance, Esquire, of Birmingham, who died 1828), on a wreath of the colours a demi-lion rampant gu., semée of annulets or, holding between the paws a sword erect entwined by a wreath of oak, all ppr. *Deo non fortuna.* 246. 5

Chance, Alexander Macomb, Esquire, of Lawnside, Edgbaston, Birmingham, same crest and motto.

Chance, Arent De Peyster, Esquire, of Wheatfields, Powick, Worcs., same crest and motto.

Chance, Arthur Lucas, Esquire, of Great Alne Hall, Alcester, same crest and motto.

Chance, Edward Ferguson, Esquire, of Sandford Park, Steeple Alston, Oxon., same crest and motto.

Chance, Frederick William, Esquire, of Morton, Carlisle, same crest and motto.

Chance, George, Esquire, of 28, Leinster Gardens, London, W., same crest and motto.

Chance, George Ferguson, Esquire, of Clent Grove, near Stourbridge, same crest and motto.

Chance, Henry, Esquire, of Leamington, same crest and motto.

Chance, Sir James Timmins, of 51, Prince's Gate, London, S.W., and 1, Grand Avenue, Hove, Sussex, a demi-lion rampant gules, semée of annulets or, holding between the paws a sword erect, entwined by a wreath of oak, all ppr. *Deo non fortuna.*

Chance, John Homer, Esquire, of Edgbaston, Birmingham, same crest and motto.

Chance, Joseph Selby, Esquire, of Carlisle, same crest and motto.

Chance, William Edward, Esquire, of Aldby Park, York, same crest and motto.

Chancelor or **Chancellor,** Scotland, an eagle displayed sa. *Que je surmonte.*

Chancellor of Shieldhill, by Biggar, Lanarksh., same crest and motto.

Chancey, Northamp., an arm erect vested arg., enfiled with a ducal coronet or, holding in the hand ppr. a battle-axe, the staff gu., headed of the first. *cf.* 207. 10

Chancey, out of a ducal coronet or, a griffin's head gu., charged with a pale az., between two wings displayed of the last, the inner part of the wings of the second. 67. 1

Chancey, Essex and Norf., out of a ducal coronet or, a griffin's head with wings endorsed bendy gu. and az., beaked of the first. 67. 1

Chandew, a pelican's nest with three young birds in it ppr.

Chandlee, Thomas, Esquire, of Balltore, Athy; Samuel Chandlee, Esquire, of Gaul's Mills, Waterford; and Richard Shackleton Chandlee, Esquire, of Greenoge, Terenure, Dublin, Ireland, a dexter hand couped at the wrist ppr., holding a sword in bend sinister arg., pommel and hilt or, the wrist charged with a garb vert. *Pax et copia.* 212. 5

Chandlee, William, Esquire, of Brighton Square, Rathmines, Dublin, same crest and motto.

Chandler of London, a bull's head sa., attired arg. *cf.* 44. 3

Chandler, a pelican in her piety sa., the nest vert. 98. 8

Chandois and **Chandos,** a stag's head gu., between the attires a cross pattée az. 120. 9

Chandos, *see* Buckingham, Duke of.

Chandos, out of a ducal coronet or, a dragon's head sa. 72. 4
Chandos, Herts, an old man's head in profile ppr., the hair gray, wreathed arg.
Chandos-Pole, Reginald Walkelyne, Esquire, of Radbourne Hall, Derbysh., and Sidling Court, Dorchester: (1) A falcon rising ppr., belled and jessed or. (2) A man's head ppr., wreathed about the temple arg.
Chandos-Pole-Gell, Harry Anthony, Esquire, of Hopton Hall, Derbysh.: (1) A greyhound statant sa., collared or, on the shoulder a cross crosslet or, for difference (*for Gell*). (2) A falcon rising ppr., belled and jessed or (*for Pole*). (3) A man's head ppr., wreathed about the temples arg. (*for Chandos*).
Channer, a demi-sea-wolf rampant ppr.
Channing, a blackamoor's head in profile couped below the shoulders.
Channy, Herts, out of a ducal coronet a demi-eagle displayed or. 80. 14
Channsy or **Chansey,** a griffin's head erased holding in the beak a key. 66. 6
Chantrell, a tower arg., in the portal a boar's head sa.
Chantry, a lion rampant gu., supporting a pillar sa.
Chapan, a hawk rising ppr. 87. 1
Chape or **Chappe,** Norf., a dexter hand gauntleted holding a pheon point upward ppr. 211. 7
Chapell, Ireland, a demi-lion rampant vert, holding in the dexter paw a chaplet or. *cf.* 10. 2
Chaplin of Coliston, Scotland, a griffin's head erased gu. *Labor omnia vincit.* 66. 2
Chaplin, Rt. Hon. Henry, of Blankney and Tathwell, Lincs, a griffin's head erased or, murally gorged vert. *cf.* 66. 2
Chaplin, Cecil, 21, Grafton Street, Bond Street, W., same crest.
Chaplin of London and Hants, a griffin's head erased arg., ducally gorged or. *cf.* 66. 2
Chaplin, Nugent, Campden House Chambers, Campden Hill, W., same crest. *Sapiens qui assiduus.*
Chaplin of Anerley Park, Upper Norwood, London, S.E., in front of a cross potent or, a caduceus fesseways ppr. *Labore et fide.* 268. 7
Chapman, Sir Montagu Richard, Bart., Killua Castle, Clonmellon, Westmeath, Ireland, an arm in armour embowed holding a broken spear encircled with a wreath of laurel, all ppr. *Crescit sub pondere virtus.*
Chapman, two spears' heads in saltire in front of a dexter arm embowed in armour, the hand gauntleted and grasping a broken tilting-spear enfiled with an annulet or. *Crescit sub pondere virtus.*
Chapman, Joseph John, M.A., 17, St. Hilda Terrace, Whitby, same crest and motto.
Chapman, Hillvar David, Kilhendre, Ellesmere, Salop, same crest.
Chapman, Alfred Daniel, Milton Ernest Hall, Bedford, same crest.
Chapman, Arthur Wakefield, Crooksbury, Farnham, same crest.
Chapman, Horace Edward, Esquire, of Donhead House, Salisbury, Wilts, same crest and motto.
Chapman, Major-General Ingram Francis, of Lambourn, Glendinning Avenue, Weymouth, same crest and motto.
Chapman, Cambs, a dexter arm in armour couped and erect, holding in the hand a lance, all ppr. 210. 11
Chapman, Scotland, a hand holding a sword in pale, thrust through a boar's head erased ppr. 212. 6
Chapman, Ireland, issuing out of a cloud a hand erect, holding a sword wavy, all ppr. 212. 4
Chapman of London and Yorks, a buck's head per chevron arg. and gu. 121. 5
Chapman of London, a heraldic antelope's head erased sa., attired and crined or, pierced in the neck by an arrow of the last, headed arg., embrued gu. *cf.* 127. 10
Chapman, Somers., a buck's head cabossed sa., attired or, between the attires two arrows in saltier of the last, feathered arg. 122. 7
Chapman of Frewen Hall, Oxon., and Hill End, Chesh., a stag's head erased sa., attired and semée of crescents or. *Crescit sub pondere virtus.* *cf.* 121. 2
Chapman of London, out of a crescent per pale or and gu., a unicorn's head of the last, maned, armed, and guttée-d'or.
Chapman, a falcon arg., beaked and legged gu., supporting a garb or.
Chapman, Scotland, a hawk regardant ppr., holding in the dexter claw a garland of laurel. 85. 4
Chapman, Lincs, a fleur-de-lis or, between two olive-branches vert.
Chappeace, an eagle close ppr. 76. 2
Chappes, a hand gauntleted holding a pheon point upwards ppr. 211. 7
Chapple, on the stump of a tree couped, a falcon hooded ppr. *cf.* 86. 11
Chapple of London, on the stump of a tree a falcon hooded ppr. *Viresco.* *cf.* 86. 11
Chard of Pathe House, Somers., an eagle rising arg., the dexter claw resting on an escutcheon az., charged with a bugle-horn stringed or, gorged with a collar gemelle sa., and holding in the beak an oak-branch slipped ppr. *Nil desperandum.*
Chardin, Leics., a lion rampant or. 1. 13
Chardin, a dove ppr. 92. 2
Charingworth, a naked arm embowed holding a cutlass ppr. *cf.* 201. 1
Charlemont, Viscount (Caulfield), Roxborough Castle, Moy, Ireland, a dragon's head erased gu., gorged with a bar-gemelle arg. *Deo duce, ferro comitante.* *cf.* 71. 2
Charles, the late Rev. James, D.D., minister of Kirkcowan, Wigtown, Scotland, an eagle displayed sa. *Virtus auget honorem.* 75. 2
Charles, Devonsh., a demi-eagle displayed with two heads per pale or and erm. *cf.* 82. 1
Charles, a demi-griffin erm., holding a spear gu. *cf.* 65. 3
Charles of London, a demi-wolf erm., holding a halberd arg., tasselled or. *cf.* 29. 4
Charles, J. Roger, M.D., of Pelsall, near Walsall, and 27, West Street, Chichester, a demi-wolf gu., charged with two lozenges in pale erm., supporting with the paws a battle-axe arg., between two branches of oak fructed ppr. *Esse quam videri.*
Charlesworth, Yorks, a demi-eagle sa., the wings elevated fretty or, holding in the beak a mascle of the last. *Justitia et virtus.*
Charlesworth, Albany Hawke, Esquire, of Ferne, Donhead St. Andrew, Salisbury, and Grinton Lodge, Richmond, Yorks, same crest and motto.
Charlesworth, Charles Ernest, Esquire, of Owston Hall, near Doncaster, same crest and motto.
Charlesworth, out of a ducal coronet a cock's head, all ppr. 90. 6
Charleton, an arm embowed, habited gu., cuffed erm., holding in the hand ppr. a broad arrow.
Charlett, Newport-: (1) A stag's head or (*for Charlett*). 121. 5. (2) A fleur-de-lis or (*for Newport*). 148. 2
Charleville, Earl of, and **Viscount** and **Baron Tullamore,** Ireland, *see* Bury.
Charlewood or **Charlwood,** a Saracen's head ppr. 190. 5
Charlewood, an arrow in pale enfiled with a ducal coronet, all ppr. 174. 3
Charley, Sir William Thomas, D.C.L., K.C., D.L., V.D. Common Serjeant of the City of London, 1878-1892, Queen Anne's Mansions, London, S.W., on a chapeau gu., turned up erm., a falcon's head erased arg., charged with a cinquefoil of the first, and holding in the beak a corn bluebottle slipped ppr. *Justus esto et non metue.* *cf.* 89. 6
Charley, John Stouppe, Esquire, J.P., of Finaghy House, co. Antrim, and of the island of Aranmore, co. Donegal, Ireland, same crest and motto. *cf.* 89. 6
Charley and **Charnley,** a griffin passant, holding in the dexter claw a buckle. 63. 7
Charlton, Essex, out of a ducal coronet or, a demi-eagle displayed sa., holding in the beak a heart's-ease flower ppr. *cf.* 80. 14
Charlton, Shropsh., out of an Eastern coronet or, a leopard's head and neck affrontée gu. 246. 4
Charlton, St. John, Esquire, of Cholmondeley, Malpas, same crest. *Spero meliora.*
Charlton, a leopard's face gu. 22. 2
Charlton, Heref., a leopard's face gu. *Sans varier.* 22. 2
Charlton, Lechmere-, of Ludford, Heref.: (1) A leopard's face gu. (*for Charlton*). 22. 2. (2) Out of a ducal coronet or, a pelican vulning herself ppr. (*for Lechmere*). *cf.* 98. 1
Charlton, on a chapeau a leopard statant ppr. 24. 1
Charlton, William Henry, of Hesleyside, Bellingham, a lion's face gu., between two dragon's wings elevated ppr., on each a fret sa. *Sans varier.*
Charlton of Hesleyside, Northumb., a demi-lion rampant. *Sans varier.* 10. 2
Charlton, Northumb., two lion's gambs erect gu. *cf.* 36. 5
Charlton, Edward Francis Benedict, Esquire, a lion's face gu., between two dragon's wings elevated ppr., on each a fret sa. *Sans varier.*

Charlton, Ulric Edmund Emmanuel, Esquire, same crest and motto.

Charlton, William Lancelot Stanislas, Esquire, same crest and motto.

Charlton, Geoffrey Nicholas, of Chilwell, Notts, a swan's head and neck erased arg., beaked gu., gorged with a chaplet vert. *Stabil conscia æqui.* cf. 101. 5

Charlton, Oxon., out of a ducal coronet or, a unicorn's head sa., crined arg., the horn twisted of the last and second. 48. 12

Charlton, Sussex, an arm embowed, vested gu., cuffed erm., holding in the hand a broad arrow ppr.

Charnell, Warw. and Leics., out of a ducal coronet or, a demi-eagle displayed. 80. 14

Charnell, a peacock close or. 103. 7

Charnells, out of a ducal coronet a demi-plover or, the wings displayed arg.

Charney, on a rock a dove holding an olive-branch in its beak, all ppr. 93. 9

Charnock, Lancs, a lapwing ppr., charged with a mullet pierced for difference. 92. 2

Charnock, Beds, a lapwing ppr. *Soyez content.*

Charpentier, a dexter hand ppr., holding a fleur-de-lis gu. 215. 5

Charpentier, A., Rathmines House, Uxbridge, a dexter cubit arm ppr., holding a fleur-de-lis gu.

Charrington, issuing from a cloud a dexter hand pointing to a star, all ppr. 222. 7

Charrington, Hugh Spencer, Esquire, of Dove Cliff House, Burton-on-Trent, a demi-gryphon gu., gorged with a collar gemelle, charged on the shoulder with two annulets interlaced, and resting the sinister claw on a cross patée, all or, and holding in the dexter claw a branch of thorn-tree ppr. *Cassis tutissima virtus.* 258. 5

Charrington, Spencer, Esquire, of Hunsdon House, Hunsdon, near Ware, Herts, same crest and motto.

Charter of Bishop's Lydeard, Somers., in front of a cubit arm vested az., cuffed arg., the hand holding a scroll entwined by a branch of myrtle, all ppr., an escallop also arg. *Non sine jure.*

Charteris, *see* Wemyss, Earl of.

Charteris, Scotland, a dexter hand grasping a dagger ppr. *This is our chart.* 212. 3

Charteris, Scotland, a stork's head ppr. cf. 106. 1

Charteris, an arm issuing out of a cloud holding a sword aloft ppr. *Non gladio sed gratia.*

Charteris, Charters, and **Chartres,** a demi-cat rampant gardant ppr. 26. 12

Charteris, Richard Butler, Esquire, of Cahor Lodge, Tipperary, a swan ppr. *This our charter.*

Chartnay or **Chartney,** two arms in armour embowed wielding a battle-axe ppr. 194. 12

Chartres, *see* Charteris.

Chartsey, a dexter arm embowed holding up two olive-branches in orle ppr. 202. 4

Chartsey, a wolf passant sa., devouring a fish arg. cf. 28. 10

Chase, a griffin's head erased holding in the beak a key. 66. 6

Chase, Herts, a lion rampant sa., holding between the paws a cross flory or. cf. 1. 13

Chassereau, a demi-chevalier in armour brandishing a sword ppr. 187. 1

Chastelai, *see* Casley.

Chastelin, a fleur-de-lis or. 148. 2

Chastelon, on the point of a sword in pale a maunch. 169. 11

Chater, a stork ppr. *Jucundi acti labores.* 105. 11

Chatfield, a demi-Moor with a quiver on his back shooting an arrow from a bow, all ppr. 185. 6

Chatfield or **Chatfeild,** Sussex, a heraldic antelope's head erased arg., attired and ducally gorged gu. *Che sara sara.* cf. 127. 10

Chatteris, on a mount vert, a pheasant ppr., holding in its beak a fleur-de-lis or, and resting the dexter claw on a bezant. *Libertas.*

Chatterton, Bart., Ireland, an antelope's head erased arg., pierced through the back of the neck by an arrow ppr. *Loyal à mort.* cf. 127. 1

Chatterton, Smith-: (1) An antelope's head erased ppr., attired or, pierced through the back of the neck with an arrow, also ppr., gorged with a ducal coronet of the second, and charged on the neck with a cross crosslet gu. (*for Chatterton*). (2) Out of a crown vallery or, a unicorn's head az., armed, crined, and tufted of the first, and charged with a crescent of the same (*for Smith*). *Loyal à mort.* cf. 48. 12

Chatterton, Cambs, a demi-griffin gu., beaked, legged, and winged or. 64. 2

Chatting, a human heart gu., transpierced by a sword in bend sinister, point downward ppr. 181. 6

Chatto, Potts-: (1) A castle or, charged with a fleur-de-lis az., and surmounted with a cinquefoil, also az. (*for Chatto*). (2) A leopard sejant ppr., gorged with a collar fleury counter-fleury, therefrom a line reflexed over the back, and resting the dexter paw on a fleur-de-lis, all gu. *Omnibus amicus.*

Chattock, a dexter hand holding a lion's gamb ppr. cf. 220. 10

Chaucer, two lion's gambs arg. and gu., supporting an escutcheon party per pale counterchanged. 39. 1

Chaucer, Chauser, and **Chawcer,** a tortoise passant ppr. cf. 125. 5

Chaumond, on a chapeau ppr., a fleur-de-lis az., between wings. cf. 110. 5

Chaumond, *see* **Chamond.**

Chauncey, a savage's arm embowed holding a club, all ppr. 202. 10

Chauncey, a dexter hand striking with a dagger, all ppr.

Chauncy of Munden Parva, Herts, out of a ducal coronet or, a griffin's head gu., between two wings az., the inner parts of the wings gu. 67. 1

Chaundler, a pelican in her piety sa., the nest vert. 98. 8

Chauser, *see* Chaucer.

Chauster, two stag's attires ppr. 123. 5

Chausy, out of a ducal coronet or, a griffin's head paly of four az. and gu., between two wings expanded, the dexter az., quill feathers gu., the sinister gu., feathered az. 67. 1

Chavasse, Henry, Esquire, of Whitfield Court, Kilmeaden, Waterford, upon a rock ppr., an eagle's claw erased and erect or, grasping an arrow in bend of the last, barbed and flighted arg. *Loyaulté mon héritage.*

Chawcer, a tortoise passant ppr. cf. 125. 5

Chawner, an ermine passant ppr. 134. 6

Chawner of Newton Manor House, Hants, a sea-wolf's head erased sa. *Nil desperandum.*

Chaworth, Baron, *see* Neath, Earl of.

Chaworth, a tower ppr., on the top five ostrich-feathers arg.

Chaworth, an arm in armour embowed, the hand holding an arrow, all ppr. 198. 4

Chaworth, a dagger az., hilt and pommel or, and a cross crosslet fitched sa., in saltier. cf. 166. 12

Chaworth-Musters, John Patricius, Esquire, of Annesley Park, near Nottingham, and Wiverton Hall, near Bingham: (1) A lion sejant guardant or, supporting with the fore-paws a shield of the arms (*for Musters*)—i.e., Arg., on a bend gu., a lion passant guardant or, within a bordure engrailed of the second. 269. 15. (2) A tower arg., charged with a bendlet wavy gu., thereon a lion passant or, issuant from the battlements an ostrich feather sa., between four others of the first. 269. 16

Chawrey and **Chawsey,** an arm from the elbow erect ppr., vested per pale sa. and arg., holding in the hand a covered cup or. cf. 203. 4

Chawser and **Chawsers,** *see* Chaucer.

Chaytor, Yorks, a stag's head lozengy arg. and az. cf. 120. 4

Chaytor, Sir William Henry Edward, Bart., of Croft, Yorks, a buck's head couped lozengy arg. and sa., attired or, holding in the mouth a trefoil slipped vert. *Fortune le veut.* 120. 4

Chaytor, Clerveaux-, Clervaux Alexander, of Spennithorne Hall, Yorks: (1) A stag's head erased lozengy arg. and az., the dexter attired of the first, and the sinister of the second (*for Chaytor*). cf. 120. 4. (2) An eagle displayed (*for Clerveaux*). 75. 2. (3) A heron ppr. 105. 9

Cheales, an eagle's head erased or, ducally crowned arg. cf. 83. 2

Cheales, Rev. Alan, of Hagworthingham, Lincs, and Ellerslie, Tilehurst Road, Reading, an eagle's head erased or, ducally crowned az. *Bene vivere et lætari.*

Cheap of Rossie, Scotland, a garb or, banded vert. *Ditat virtus.* 153. 2

Cheape, George Clerk, Esquire, of Bentley Manor, Broomsgrove, Worcs., same crest and motto.

Cheape, James, Esquire, of Strathtyrum, St. Andrews, Fifesh., same crest and motto.

Cheape of Madeira, a garb or, banded gu. *Ditat virtus.* 153. 2

Checkland, two cubit arms erect ppr., holding two annulets interlaced sa., each arm charged with a cinquefoil gu. *Omne bonum, Dei donum.*

Checkland, George Edward, Thurnby Court, Ashby-de-la-Zouch, same crest and motto.

Checkland, William, Esquire, of Swannington House, Leics., same crest and motto.
Chedder and **Cheder**, on a chapeau gu., turned up arg., a lion passant gardant az., ducally crowned ppr. *cf.* 4. 5
Chedworth, Devonsh., a wolf's head sa., collared or. 30. 9
Chedworth, Devonsh., a demi-lion rampant gardant az., holding in the dexter paw a battle-axe ppr. 16. 14
Cheek, issuant from between the horns of a crescent a cross pattée fitchée gu. *cf.* 163. 6
Cheeke, on a chapeau a lion passant ppr. 4. 9
Cheeke, Somers. and Suff., a sword in pale ensigned with a cross pattée. 169. 5
Cheeke, Suff., out of a naval coronet or, a demi-mermaid holding a comb and mirror ppr. 184. 14
Cheere, a talbot passant az., collared or, resting his fore-paw on an escallop of the last. *cf.* 54. 2
Cheere, a talbot passant az., collared and ringed or. *Præmium virtutis honor.* *cf.* 54. 2
Cheese of Huntington Court, Heref., a lion's head erased or. *Omnia fert ætas.* 17. 8
Cheeseman and **Chesman**, a dexter hand holding a royal crown ppr. 217. 1
Cheetham of Rycroft House, Rochdale, and Brooklyn, Heywood, Lancs, a demi-griffin wings addorsed gu., bezantée, the mouth transfixed by a tilting-spear or, holding between the claws a bezant. *Ad mortem fidelis.*
Cheetham, of Singleton House, Broughton, Kent, in front of a demi-griffin segreant gu., resting the sinister claw on a cross potent sa., a plate. *Quod tuum tene.* 65. 4
Cheetham, Sydney William, M.R.C.S., 233, Romford Road, Forest Gate, E., a demi-griffin segreant gu., charged on the breast with a cross potent re-crossed or. *Quod tuum tene.*
Cheffield, Rutl., an arm in armour couped and embowed resting on the elbow, holding a sword, all ppr. *cf.* 195. 2
Chein and **Cheine**, on a chapeau two lions supporting a garb ppr. 3. 5
Chein and **Cheine**, Scotland, a cross pattée fitched arg. *Patienta vincit.* 166. 3
Cheisly or **Chesly**, Scotland, a rose ppr., slipped and leaved vert. *Fragrat post funera virtus.* 149. 5
Chelley, a leg in armour, couped below the knee and spurred, all ppr. 193. 4
Chelmick, Shropsh., a lion sejant gardant or, supporting with the dexter paw an escutcheon vert. *cf.* 8. 2
Chelmsford, Baron (Thesiger), 5, Knaresborough Place, S.W., a cornucopia in fess, the horn or, the fruit ppr., thereon a dove, holding in the beak a sprig of laurel ppr. *Spes et fortuna.* 93.
Chelsea, Viscount, *see* Cadogan, Earl.
Chelsum, a garb or. 153. 2
Chelsum, a greyhound current arg. *cf.* 58. 2
Cheltenham, a demi-eagle displayed ppr. 81. 6
Chemere, a peer's helmet or. *cf.* 180. 4
Chenell, an arm ppr., vested sa., cuffed or, holding in the hand a covered cup arg. *cf.* 203. 4
Cheney, a bull's scalp or, horned arg. 123. 8
Chenevix, a hand erect grasping a sword ppr., hilted and pommelled, and piercing a fleur-de-lis or. *cf.* 212. 3
Chenevix-Trench, Alfred, Esquire, of Villa Bona Ventura, Cadenabbia, Italy, a dexter arm in armour embowed, the hand grasping a cutlass, all ppr. *Virtutis fortuna comes.*
Chenevix-Trench, Colonel Charles, R.A., same crest and motto.
Chenevix-Trench, George Frederick, Esquire, same crest and motto.
Chenevix-Trench, Rev. Herbert Francis, of St. Peter's Vicarage, Isle of Thanet, same crest and motto.
Chenevix-Trench, Julius, Esquire, same crest and motto.
Chenevix-Trench, Philip Francis, Esquire, same crest and motto.
Chenevix-Trench, Samuel Richard, Esquire, same crest and motto.
Cheney of Badger Hall, Shifnal, Shropsh., a bull's horns and scalp arg. *Fato prudentia major.* (*See* Cure.) 123. 8
Cheoke, a bird's head sa.
Chepstow, an arm vambraced az., studded and garnished or, holding a sword ppr. 195. 2
Cherbron, a lion's gamb erect gu., holding a griffin's head erased or.
Chere, a talbot passant az., collared and ringed or. *Præmium virtutis honor.* *cf.* 54. 2
Cherley, a cross patonce between two stalks of wheat or, leaved ppr. 154. 13
Cherry, a demi-lion arg., holding an annulet gu. *cf.* 10. 2
Cherry, a demi-lion arg., holding a gem-ring or, enriched with a precious stone ppr. *cf.* 10. 2
Cherry, Rev. Benjamin Newman, Clipsham Rectory, Oakham, Rut., a stag couchant regardant.
Cherry-Garrard, Major-General Apsley, of Lamer Park, Wheathampstead, Herts: (1) A leopard sejant ppr. (*for Garrard*). (2) A demi-lion arg., the neck encircled with an annulet, and holding between the paws a fleur-de-lis within an annulet gu. (*for Cherry*). *Cheris l'espoir.*
Cherwood, a unicorn's head or, between two laurel-branches vert. 49. 14
Chesbrough, a demi-lion rampant gu., holding between the paws a cross pattée or. 11. 2
Cheselden, Cheseldon, Cheseldyne, and **Cheselton**, Rutl. and Leics., a talbot couchant arg., spotted sa., collared and lined or. *cf.* 54. 11
Chesham, Baron (Cavendish), Latimer, Chesham, Bucks, a snake nowed ppr. *Cavendo tutus.* 142. 4
Chesham, Lancs, out of a ducal coronet, a lion's gamb erect or. 36. 12
Chesham, Lancs, a falcon wings expanded ppr. 87. 1
Chesham, two arms embowed holding a chess castle or.
Cheshire, a talbot sejant supporting with his paws a shield charged with a garb. *cf.* 55. 3
Cheshire of Dublin, a leopard's face arg., jessant three roses gu., leaved vert.
Cheshire or **Chesshyre**, a hawk's lure purp. 178. 11
Cheslie, Chiesly, and **Chislie**, Scotland, an eagle displayed ppr. *Credo et videbo.* 75. 2
Cheslin of London, a tower arg. 156. 2
Cheslin, a fleur-de-lis per pale vert and az. 148. 2
Chesly, Scotland, a rose ppr., slipped and leaved vert. *Fragrat post funera virtus.* 149. 5
Chesman, *see* Cheeseman.
Chesney, a man's head bearded and wreathed ppr. 190. 4
Chesshyre, Essex, a hawk's lure purp., feathered or. 178. 11
Chester of Bush Hall, Herts, and Royston, Cambs, a demi-griffin segreant erm., beak, tongue, talons, and eyes ppr. *Vincit qui patitur.* 64. 2
Chester of Chichley Hall, Bucks, a ram's head couped arg., armed or. 130. 1
Chester of Amesbury, Glouc., a lion's gamb erased gu., holding a broken sword arg., hilted or. 38. 2
Chester of Blabie, Leics., a dragon passant arg. 73. 2
Chester, Henry Morris, Poyle Park, Surrey, a dragon passant erm. *Vincit qui patitur.*
Chester, Essex, a cutlass arg., hilt and pommel or, between two branches of laurel ppr. *cf.* 170. 3
Chesterfield, Earl of (Scudamore-Stanhope): (1) A tower az., and from the battlements thereof a demi-lion issuant or, ducally crowned gu., holding between the paws a grenade fired ppr. (2) Out of a ducal coronet or, a bear's paw sa. ppr. *A Deo et rege.* *cf.* 157. 10
Chesterfield, on a chapeau a greyhound statant ppr. 58. 4
Chesterman, a demi-griffin. *Semper fidelis.* 64. 2
Chesterton, a tiger's head erased.
Cheston, Suff., a dexter gauntlet in fess ppr., holding a sword arg., hilt and pommel or, on the blade a Saracen's head couped, distilling blood of the first. *Ex merito.* *cf.* 211. 11
Chetham, in the sea a rock ppr. 179. 5
Chetham, Suff., a griffin passant regardant arg., wings addorsed or, charged with a crescent gu. *cf.* 63. 14
Chettle, on a rock a wyvern, wings addorsed ppr. 69. 11
Chetum, Lancs, a demi-griffin gu., charged with a cross potent az. *Quod tuum tene.* *cf.* 64. 2
Chetwode, a sea-lion sejant. 20. 2
Chetwode, Sir George, Bart., of Chetwode, Bucks, and Oakley, Staffs, out of a ducal coronet or, a demi-lion rampant gu. *Corona mea Christus.* 16. 3
Chetwode, Wilmot-: (1) Out of a ducal coronet or, a demi-lion rampant gu. (*for Chetwode*). 16. 3. (2) Out of a crescent gu., a demi-man-tiger rampant arg., horned and ungu. or (*for Walwell*). (3) An eagle's head erased sa., holding in the beak an escallop gu., (*for Wilmot*). *Corona mea Christus.* *cf.* 83. 2
Chetwode, Ludford-, Warw.: (1) Out of a ducal coronet or, a demi-lion rampant gu. (*for Chetwode*). 16. 3. (2) A

boar's head couped erminois, holding in the mouth a cross pattée gu., the head charged with an escallop sa. (*for Ludford*).

Chetwood and **Chetwoode**, *see* Chetwode.

Chetwood-Aiken: (1) A cross crosslet fitchée gu. (*for Aiken*). Motto, *In cruce salus*. 166. 2. (2) Out of a ducal coronet or, a demi-lion issuant sa. (*for Chetwood*), and the motto, *Corona mea Christus*. 16. 3

Chetwood-Aiken, John, Esquire, of the Glen, Stoke Bishop, Glouc., same crests and mottoes.

Chetwyn, a human heart pierced with a passion-nail ppr. *cf.* 181. 4

Chetwynd, Viscount (Chetwynd), 25, Elvaston Place, S.W., a goat's head erased arg., armed or. *Probitas verus honos*. 128. 5

Chetwynd, Sir George, Bart., of Grendon, Warw., a goat's head erased arg., armed or. *Quod Deus vult fiet*. 128. 5

Chetwynd-Stapylton, Lieutenant-General Granville George, out of a ducal coronet or, a Saracen's head ppr. *Fide sed cui vide*.

Chetwynd-Stapylton, Henry Goulburn, Esquire, of Hilliers, Petworth, Sussex, same crest and motto.

Chetwynd-Stapylton, Miles, Esquire, same crest and motto.

Chetwynd-Stapylton, Rev. William, of Hallaton, Leics., same crest and motto.

Cheureuse, an eagle displayed or, winged arg. 75. 2

Chevalier, a demi-chevalier in armour brandishing a scimitar, all ppr. 187. 4

Chevallier, a lion's head erased arg., langued gu. *Fidei coticula crux*. 17. 8

Cheverell and **Cheverill**, two dexter hands conjoined holding a sword in pale, all ppr. 224. 7

Chevers, an arm in armour embowed, couped at the shoulder, the part above the elbow in fess, the hand in pale holding a close helmet ppr. 198. 11

Chevers, a demi-goat saliant arg., collared gu., crined and ungu. or. *En Dieu est ma foi*. *cf.* 128. 2

Chevers, John Joseph, Esquire, of Killyan House, Ballinasloe, co. Galway, same crest and motto.

Cheverton, Hants, out of a castle triple-towered a demi-lion, all ppr. *Invicta labore*. 155. 10

Chevil, an arm in armour embowed holding in the hand a sword, all ppr. 195. 2

Chew of London and Beds, a griffin sejant arg., guttée-de-sang, beaked, legged, and winged sa., the dexter claw resting on a catherine-wheel gu. *cf.* 62. 10

Chewton, Viscount, *see* Waldgrave, Earl.

Cheylesmore, Baron (Eaton), Cheylesmore, Coventry, a lion's head erased arg., devouring a tun or, gorged with a double chain of the same, suspended therefrom an escutcheon az., charged with a cross couped, also or. *Vincit omnia veritas*. 257. 1

Cheyn and **Cheyne**, a dexter hand holding an escallop ppr. 216. 2

Cheyne, of Esselmont, Scotland, a cross pattée fitched or. *Patientia vincit*. 166. 3

Cheyne of Straloch, a Capuchin's cap. *Fear God*.

Cheyne, Scotland, an ibex's head and neck gorged with a collar, with one link of a chain affixed thereto.

Cheyney, Kent, Beds, and Berks, a bull's scalp or, attired arg. 123. 8

Cheyney, Cambs, a cap or, turned up az., on each side a feather erect ppr.

Cheyney, a wolf passant vert, ducally gorged and lined or. *cf.* 28. 10

Cheyney, Bucks, a bear's head erased gu., environed round the neck twice with a chain passing through the mouth arg., ringed or. *cf.* 35. 2

Chibnall, a wolf's head ppr. 30. 5

Chibnall, Beds and Northamp., a dragon's head erased sa., ducally gorged and lined or. *cf.* 72. 9

Chichele and **Chichley**, a tiger passant arg., holding in his mouth a man's leg couped at the thigh ppr., the foot downwards.

Chicheley, Cambs, a tiger passant arg. *cf.* 27. 11

Chichester, Marquess of Donegal, *see* Donegal.

Chichester, Baron Ennishowen, *see* Ennishowen.

Chichester, Earl of (Pelham), Staunmer, Lewes, Sussex, a peacock in pride arg. Badge, a buckle or. *Vincet amor patriæ*. 103. 2

Chichester, William Henry, Esquire, of Grenofen, Tavistock, Devonsh., same crest and motto.

Chichester, Charles, of Hall, Devonsh., a heron rising with an eel in its mouth ppr. *Ferme en foy*. *cf.* 104. 13

Chichester: (1) A heron devouring a snake, all ppr. (*for Chichester*). 105. 8. (2) Out of a ducal coronet or, a demi-griffin segreant ppr. (*for Hopton*). *Invitum sequitur honor*. 64. 4

Chichester, Devonsh. and Dorset, a stork with wings addorsed ppr., holding in its beak a snake vert. 104. 13

Chichester, the late Rev. Arthur Chichester, of the Rectory, Badlesmere, Kent: (1) A heron, wings addorsed, in its beak an eel, all ppr. (*for Chichester*). (2) In front of a chaplet of holly fructed ppr., a torch erect or, fired ppr. (*for Burnard*). *Ardet in arduis*.

Chichester, Rev. Edward Arthur, of the Vicarage, Dorking, a stork rising with a snake in its beak, all ppr. *Invitum sequitur honor*.

Chichester-O'Neil, Rev. William, of Shane's Castle, co. Antrim, Prebendary of St. Michael's, in the city and diocese of Dublin: (1) An arm embowed in armour grasping a sword, all ppr. (*for O'Neil*). 195. 2. (2) A stork rising with a snake in its beak, all ppr. (*for Chichester*). *Lamh dearg Eirin*. 104. 13

Chichester, Sir Edward, Bart., of Youlston, Barnstaple, Devonsh., a bittern rising with an eel in its beak ppr.

Chichester, Nugent, Esquire, of Calverleigh Court, Tiverton, Devonsh.: (1) A goldfinch ppr. (*for Nagle*). (2) A heron rising with an eel in the beak ppr. (*for Chichester*). *Ferme en foy*.

Chichester-Constable, Walter George Raleigh, Esquire, of Burton Constable, Hull, Wycliffe Hall, Darlington, Scargill Lodge, Bernard Castle, Wood Hall, Hull, and Runnamoat, Roscommon: (1) A dragon's head couped barry of six arg. and gu., charged with nine lozenges or, three, three, and three (*for Constable*). (2) A stork rising holding in the beak a snake ppr. *Surgit post nubila Phœbus.—Ferme en foy*.

Chick, Sussex, a demi-pegasus rampant sa., enfiled round the body with a ducal coronet or. *Non temere*. 47. 7

Chiefly, a lion's head erased or. 17. 8

Chiene, on a chapeau two lions supporting a garb ppr. 3. 5

Chiesly, Scotland, a rose gu., stalked vert. *Fragrat post funera virtus*. 149. 5

Chiesly, Scotland, an eagle displayed ppr. *Credo et videbo*. 75. 2

Chilborne, Essex, a hawk's head erased az., holding in the beak a ring or, to which is attached an estoile of the last.

Chilcot, two garbs in saltire.

Chilcote and **Chilcott**, Surrey, out of a ducal coronet a mount ppr., thereon a stag at gaze gu. *Spero*. 118. 7

Child-Villiers, Earl of Jersey, *see* Jersey.

Child, Coles, Bromley Palace, Bromley, Kent, an eagle with wings expanded arg., holding in the beak a snake entwined round the neck and legs ppr.

Child, Bart. (*extinct*), of Surat, East Indies, and Dervill, Essex, a leopard's face or, between two laurel-branches ppr. *Spes alit*.

Child of Langley Bury, Herts, an eagle, wings expanded erm., holding in the beak a trefoil slipped vert. *cf.* 77. 2

Child, Hants and Shropsh., an eagle with wings expanded arg., round the neck a snake entwined ppr. *Imitare quam invidere*. 77. 8

Child, Cecil E. C., Vernham, Merton Hall Road, Wimbledon, same crest and motto.

Child, Sir Smith, Bart., of Newfield and Stallington Hall, Staffs., an eagle with wings elevated arg., entwined round the neck by a snake ppr., holding in the beak a cross crosslet fitchée, and each wing charged with a mullet of six points gu. *Imitari quam invidere*. *cf.* 77. 8

Child of London and Worcs., on a rock ppr., an eagle rising, the wings addorsed arg., gorged with a ducal coronet or, round the neck an adder entwined ppr. *cf.* 77. 8

Child, Herbert Henry, Rudhall, Ross, Heref., on a rock an eagle with wings endorsed and inverted, collared and chained, and resting the dexter claw on a serpent nowed. *Probitas verus honos*.

Child, Surrey, an eagle with wings expanded between two ears of big-wheat, holding in the beak a serpent entwined round the neck, all ppr. *Imitare quam invidere*. *cf.* 77. 8

Child, Hooke-, Albert Theodore, Esquire, of Finchley New Road, London: (1) Upon a fret gu., an eagle, the wings elevated arg., entwined round the neck by a serpent ppr., each wing charged with a trefoil slipped, also gu. (*for Child*). (2) Upon a mount, between two ears of wheat stalked and leaved or, an escallop az. (*for Hooke*). *Imitare quam invidere*.

Childe of Kinlet, Shropsh., and Northwicke, Worcs., an eagle with wings expanded arg., enveloped round the neck and body with a snake ppr. 77. 8

Childe-Freeman, Rev. Edward Leonard, of Edwyn Ralph Rectory, Bromyard, Worcs.: (1) An eagle with wings expanded arg., entwined round the neck by a serpent ppr. (*for Childe*). (2) On a mount vert, a cockatrice arg., wattled, combed, and beaked or, ducally gorged and lined, also or, and charged by a crescent sa. for difference. *Per Deum meum, transilio murum* (*for Baldwyn*). —*Pax et plenitudo.*

Childe-Pemberton, William Shakespear, 11, Granville Place, Portman Square, W.: (1) An eagle with wings expanded arg., standing upon and entwined round the neck by a snake ppr. (*Childe*). (2) On a mount vert, a cockatrice arg., wattled, combed, and beaked or, ducally gorged, lined, and ringed gold, a crescent sa. for cadency (*Baldwyn*). (3) In front of a griffin's head couped sa., a crescent or (*Pemberton*). *Per deum meum, transilio murum.*

Childers of Cantley, Yorks, a cubit arm erect habited in chain armour, and holding in the gauntlet ppr. an oval buckle, tongue erect az.

Chilmick, Shropsh., a lion sejant gardant or, supporting with the dexter paw an escutcheon vert. *cf.* 8. 2

Chilton, a boar's head couped at the neck or, holding in the mouth two roses, one arg., the other gu., leaved and stalked ppr.

Chilton, Kent, a griffin passant sa., bezantée. *cf.* 63. 2

Chilworth, Devonsh., a boar's head and neck erased sa., ducally gorged or. 41. 6

Chiney, an arm in armour embowed holding in the gauntlet a sabre, all ppr. 195. 2

Chinn, Glouc., on a ducal coronet or, a greyhound sejant arg. *cf.* 59. 4

Chinnery, Bart. (*extinct*), of Flintfield, Cork, Ireland, on a globe or, an eagle rising ppr., collared, also or. *Nec temere, nec timide.* *cf.* 159. 7

Chinnery-Haldane, Right Rev. James Robert Alexander, of Alltshellach Onich, Inverness-sh., Bishop of Argyll and the Isles: (1) On the dexter side an eagle's head erased or (*for Haldane*). 83. 2. (2) On the sinister side, perched on a globe or, an eagle rising ppr., collared of the first (*for Chinnery*). *Suffer.*—*Nec temere, nec timide.* *cf.* 159. 7

Chipchase, a demi-eagle displayed holding in the dexter claw a laurel-branch ppr. *cf.* 81. 6

Chipman, Somers., a leopard sejant arg., murally crowned gu. *cf.* 24. 13

Chipnam, Heref., a dexter and sinister arm shooting an arrow from a bow ppr. 200. 2

Chippendale and **Chippingdale,** of Craven, Yorks, Humberston, Leics., Blackenhall, Staffs, and of London, a lion's gamb erect arg., erased gu., holding a fleur-de-lis or. *Firmor ad fidem.*

Chipperfield of London, an eagle displayed gu. *Spernit pericula virtus.* 75. 2

Chirbrond, a winged heart ppr. 112. 10

Chirnside, Scotland, a hawk with wings expanded ppr. 87. 1

Chiseldine, a talbot couchant arg., spotted sa., eared and collared gu., chained or, the end of the chain in a bow-knot of the last. *cf.* 54. 11

Chisenal and **Chisenhall,** Lancs, a griffin segreant gu. 62. 2

Chisholm of that ilk, a dexter arm in armour embowed from the shoulder, the hand holding a scimitar in bend, all ppr. *Vi et virtute.* 196. 10

Chisholm, Sir Samuel, Bart., 20, Belhaven Terrace, Glasgow, a hand holding a boar's head erased ppr. *Colo communitatem.* 257. 9

Chisholm, Kent and Scotland, a hand couped below the wrist holding a dagger erect, all ppr., on the point a boar's head erased or, laugued gu. *cf.* 212. 2

Chisholm, Roderick Donald Matheson, of Erchless Castle, Inverness, a dexter hand holding a dagger erect ppr., on the point a boar's head couped gu. *Feros ferio.* 212. 2

Chisholm, England and Scotland, a dexter hand holding a sword erect ppr., on the point a boar's head couped gu. *Vi et arte.* 212. 2

Chisholm, The (J. Chisholm Gooden-Chisholm), of 33, Tavistock Square, London, a dexter hand holding a dagger erect ppr., on the point a boar's head couped gu. *Feros ferio.* 212. 2

Chisholme, out of a ducal coronet a dragon's head with wings addorsed. 72. 1

Chisholme of Comer, Scotland, a dexter hand holding a dagger in pale ppr. *Vi et virtute.* 212. 9

Chisholme, Scotland, a boar's head erased. 42. 2

Chislie, Scotland, an eagle displayed ppr. *Credo et videbo.* 75. 2

Chissell, three chisels arg., handles or, two in saltire, the handles downwards, and one in pale, the handle upwards.

Chiswell of London, a mermaid ppr. 184. 5

Chiswell of London, a dove with wings displayed arg., beaked and legged gu., standing on a bezant and holding in the beak a laurel-branch vert.

Chittinge, a talbot's head erased arg. 56. 2

Chittock, a demi-stag ppr., attired or. 119. 2

Chittock, an antelope trippant ppr. 126. 6

Chitty of London, a talbot's head couped or. 56. 12

Chitwood, on a mount vert, a crow sa. 107. 9

Chitwynde, a sword in pale ppr., on the point a boar's head erased. *cf.* 42. 4

Chivers, a comet star, the tail towards the sinister ppr. 164. 10

Choare, on top of a tower arg., the port sa., a row of five feathers or.

Choiseul, Ireland, a dexter and sinister hand supporting a two-edged sword in pale, all ppr. 213. 1

Choke, out of a ducal coronet or, a demi-stork displayed arg., beaked gu.

Choke, Berks, a stork's head ppr., beaked gu. *cf.* 106. 1

Cholmeley and **Cholmondley,** a demi-griffin segreant sa., winged and beaked or, holding in the claws a helmet ppr. *cf.* 64. 1

Cholmeley, Sir Hugh Arthur Henry, Bart., Easton Hall, Grantham: (1) A garb or. (2) A demi-griffin segreant sa., beaked, winged, and membered or, holding between the claws a helmet ppr., garnished of the second. *cf.* 64. 1

Cholmeley, Hugh Charles Fairfax, Esquire, Bransby Hall, Easingwold, Yorks: (1) On a helmet affronté arg. a garb or. (2) A demi-griffin segreant sa., beaked, winged, and membered or, bearing a helmet arg. *Cassis tutissima virtus.*

Cholmley, Bart., of Whitby and Hildenby, Yorks, a full-fronted helmet with grills arg., thereon a garb or. *A la volonté de Dieu.*

Cholmley of Whitby, Yorks, a demi-griffin segreant sa., beaked or, holding in the dexter claw a helmet arg. 64. 1

Cholmondeley, Marquess of (Cholmondeley), Cholmondeley Castle, Malpas, Chesh., a demi-griffin segreant sa., beaked, winged, and membered or, holding between the claws a helmet ppr., garnished of the second. *Cassis tutissima virtus.* *cf.* 64. 1

Cholmondeley, Rev. Richard Hugh, 62, Albert Gate Mansions, S.W., same crest and motto.

Cholmondeley, Baron Delamere, *see* Delamere.

Cholmonly of London, a helmet arg., garnished or, charged with three torteaux, one and two.

Cholwell, a leopard's face az. 22. 2

Cholwich and **Cholwick,** a lion's gamb erect and erased sa., supporting an ancient shield per pale or and arg. *cf.* 37. 2

Cholwich, Lear-, of Teignmouth, Devonsh.: (1) A lion's gamb erased sa., supporting an antique shield per pale erminois and erm. (*for Cholwich*). *cf.* 37. 2. (2) A demi-unicorn erminois supporting a staff raguly gu. (*for Lear*).

Cholwich and **Cholwick** of Cholwich, Devonsh., a fox's head couped sa. 33. 4

Cholwill or **Cholville,** Devonsh., a linnet ppr.

Chooke, an ibex's head erased arg., gorged with a crown gu., double-horned or.

Chope, Rev. R. R., St. Augustine's Vicarage, 117, Queen's Gate, S.W., a lion passant.

Chopinge of London, a tree vert, fructed or, the stem arg., charged with two bends wavy gu., on the sinister side of the stem a woodpecker ppr.

Chorley, Lancs and Staffs, on a chapeau gu., turned up erm., a hawk's head erased arg. 89. 6

Chough, a demi-lion rampant sa., collared arg., holding in the paws a halberd in pale or. *cf.* 15. 4

Chowne, a cubit arm erect in armour holding in the gauntlet ppr. a broad arrow sa., feathered arg.

Chrighton or **Crighton,** a dragon's head vomiting fire ppr. 72. 3

Chrisope, an antelope trippant ppr., collared and chained or. *cf.* 126. 6

Chrisope, a bear's head muzzled. 34. 14

Christall, Scotland, a fir-tree ppr. *Per augusta ad augusta.* 144. 13

Christian, Ireland, a lion couchant gardant ppr. 7. 10

Christian, a lion sejant gardant erect holding in the dexter paw a cross, and resting the sinister on a pyramid sa. *cf.* 8. 12

Christian, a unicorn's head erased arg., collared, maned, and armed or. 49. 11

Christian, out of a naval coronet a unicorn's head. *cf.* 48. 12

Christian of Ewanrigg, Cumb., a unicorn's head erased arg., armed and gorged with a collar invecked or. *Salus per Christum.* *cf.* 49. 11

Christian, the figure of Hope ppr., robed arg., leaning on an anchor or.

Christian, a greyhound current ppr. *cf.* 58. 2

Christie, Robert Maitland, of Durie, Fife, a dexter hand holding a letter ppr. *Pro rege.*

Christie, a cross Calvary gu. *Sit vita nomini congrua.* 166. 1

Christie, a brown bear passant muzzled, the chain reflexed over the shoulder or, on the back a bezant charged with a cross sa., the dexter paw resting on an escutcheon per pale of the last and gu. *Integer vitæ.* 269. 4

Christie, Augustus Langham, Esquire, of Tapeley Park, Instow, North Devonsh., and 42, Great Cumberland Place, London, W., same crest and motto.

Christie, William Langham, Esquire, of Glyndebourne, Lewes, Sussex, and 117, Eaton Square, S.W., same crest and motto.

Christie, Ireland, out of an earl's coronet a Moor's head from the shoulders, all ppr. 182. 2

Christie, a holly-slip leaved and fructed ppr. 150. 10

Christie, Thomas Craig, Esquire, of Bedlay Chryston, Glasgow, Lanarksh., a branch of holly leaved and fructed ppr. *Sic viresco.*

Christie, a holly-stump leaved and fructed ppr. *Sit vita nomini congrua.* 145. 10

Christie, John, Esquire, of Cowden and Glenfarg, Perth, and of Milnwood, Lanarksh., a withered holly-branch sprouting out leaves ppr. *Sic viresco.* 145. 10

Christie of Craigton, Scotland, a holly-branch withered with leaves sprouting anew ppr. *Sic viresco.* 145. 10

Christie, Hector, Esquire, of Langcliffe Place, near Settle, Yorks, same crest and motto.

Christie, Scotland, a holly-bush ppr. *Sic viresco.*

Christie-Miller, Sydney Richardson, Esquire, J.P., of Moira House, 21, St. James's Place, London; of Britwell Court, Burnham, Bucks; and of Craigentinny, Midlothian, Scotland: (1) A dexter hand erect holding an open book ppr. (*for Miller*). 279. 10 (2) A holly-stump withered sprouting out leaves ppr. (*for Christie*). *Manent optima cœlo.—Sic viresco.* 279. 9

Christie, a phœnix in flames ppr. 82. 2

Christie, a phœnix's head in flames ppr. 82. 9

Christison, Sir Alexander, Bart., of 40, Moray Place, Edinburgh, a Passion cross gu., on three grieces ppr. *Vitam dirigat.* 166. 1

Christison, John, Esquire, Writer to the Signet, of 40, Moray Place, Edinburgh, a Passion cross gu., on three grieces ppr. *Vitam dirigat.* 166. 1

Christmas, an arm embowed ppr., vested or, covered with leaves vert, supporting a staff couped and raguly arg.

Christmas, an arm ppr., charged with two bars or and gu., holding a double branch of roses flowered of the second, leaved vert.

Christopher, Norf., a unicorn's head erased arg. 49. 5

Christopher of Norton, Durham, two arms embowed, vested az., the hands ppr., supporting an anchor sa., cabled arg. *Arte conservatus. Deo conservatus.*

Christopher, Captain Alfred Charles Seton, of 9, Sloane Terrace Mansions, London, S.W., two arms embowed vested az., the hands ppr. supporting an anchor sa., cabled arg.

Christopher, Danby Stevens, Esquire, of 28, Argyll Street, London, W., same crest and motto.

Christopher, Henry Carmichael, Esquire, same crest and motto.

Christopher, Leonard William, Esquire, of Murre, Punjab, same crest and motto.

Christopher, Wilmot Conway, Esquire, same crest and motto.

Christopher, a stag's head cabossed ppr. 122. 5

Christopherson, Sussex, a demi-eagle regardant holding in the dexter claw a sword ppr. *Ardenter prosequor alis.*

Christy of Apuldrefield, Kent, a mount vert, thereon the stump of a holly-tree sprouting between four branches of fern, all ppr. *Sic viresco.*

Christy, Richard, Esquire, of Watergate, Emsworth, Sussex, same crest and motto.

Christy, Joseph Fell, Esquire, of Upton, Alresford, Hants, same crest and motto.

Christy, William Miller, Watergate, Emsworth, same crest and motto.

Chritchley, Ireland, a lion rampant per fesse, embattled gu. and az. *Honesta quam splendida.* 1. 13

Chrystie, a lion's gamb erased holding a dagger, all ppr. 38. 8

Chubb, Sir George Hayter, of Newlands, Chislehurst, Kent, in front of a demi-lion supporting between its paws a bezant charged with a rose gu., a key fesseways, wards upwards, or. 242. 2

Chubbe, Dorset, a demi-lion az., holding between the paws a bezant. 11. 7

Chudleigh, a savage ppr., wreathed about the loins and temples vert, and holding in the dexter hand a club spiked or.

Chudleigh, a savage ppr. in profile holding in the dexter hand a spiked club or, with a bugle-horn hung over the sinister shoulder, wreathed about the loins and temples vert.

Chun, a boar passant regardant pierced in the shoulder by an arrow, the end held in the mouth, all ppr.

Church, Essex, an arm in armour ppr., garnished or, holding in the hand a baton of the same.

Church, a hand holding a sword erect between two branches of laurel entwined round the blade. *Virtute.*

Church, Ireland, a talbot collared, all ppr. 54. 2

Church, a cloud ppr. 162. 13

Church, a demi-lion rampant or, brandishing in his dexter paw a battle-axe ppr., and resting his sinister paw on a cross gu.

Church, Samuel Church, Esquire: (1) In front of a Passion cross gu., a pelican in her piety arg., the wing charged with a rose, also gu., barbed and seeded ppr. (*for Church*). (2) A lion rampant regardant sa., semée of pheons, and holding between the paws a mascle or (*for Philips*). *Vulnera ecclesiæ liberorum vita.*

Church, Sir William Selby, Bart., K.C.B., Woodside, Hatfield, Herts, a greyhound's head sa., erased gu., collared az., and charged with two bezants. *Mea spes est in Deo.* 262. 4

Church, a greyhound's head erased sa., platée, collared or.

Churchar, Sussex, an heraldic tiger passant arg., maned and tufted or. 25. 5

Churche, Essex, a demi-greyhound sa., gorged with a collar or, charged with three lozenges gu., holding a trefoil of the second.

Churche, Shropsh., a greyhound's head erased erm., collared, lined, and ringed or. *cf.* 61. 2

Churchey, Wales, a greyhound's head erased sa., collared or, holding in the mouth a trefoil slipped gu.

Churchill, Duke of Marlborough, *see* Marlborough.

Churchill, Viscount (Spencer), G.C.V.O., Rolleston, Leics., out of a ducal coronet or, a griffin's head between two wings expanded arg., gorged with a bar-gemelle gu., armed of the first. *Dieu defend le droit.* *cf.* 67. 1

Churchill, Surrey and Dorset, out of a ducal coronet or, a demi-lion rampant arg. *Dieu defend le droit.* 16. 3

Churchill, Frederick, M.D., 4, Cranley Gardens, Queen's Gate, S.W., same crest.

Churchill, Charles Morant, Manor House, Buckland Ripers, Dorset, same crest.

Churchill, a lion couchant gardant arg., holding a flagstaff erect entwined with a branch of laurel ppr., flowing from the staff to the sinister a banner swallow-tailed gu., charged with an Eastern crown or.

Churchill, a lion couchant arg., holding a banner of the last charged with a cross.

Churchill, a savage's head affrontée, ducally crowned ppr. 192. 9

Churchouse, William John Franklin, Physician and Surgeon, Chard House, Long Buckby, Rugby, a demi-lion rampant holding between its paws a church bell. *Nunquam non fidelis.*

Churchman of London, on a garb in fess or, a cock arg., beaked, legged, and wattled gu. 91. 4

Churchward, Rev. Marcus Dimond Dimond-, Vicar of Northam, Bideford,

Devonsh., issuant from three lozenges conjoined in fesse gu., each charged with a fleur-de-lis or, a buck's head couped ppr. *Suaviter in modo.* *cf.* 121. 5

Churchyard, an arm in armour embowed holding in the hand a baton, and thereon suspended a laurel crown, all ppr.

Churchyard, Shropsh., a dexter arm embowed and vambraced, holding a broken spear environed with a chaplet. *En Dieu et mon roy.* *cf.* 197. 3

Churston, Baron (Yarde-Buller), of Churston Ferrers and Lupton, Devonsh., a Saracen's head affrontée couped ppr. *Aquila non capit muscas.* 190. 5

Churton, the late John, Esquire, of Moranned, Rhyl, Flintsh., out of the battlements of a tower ppr., a demi-lion gu., gorged with a collar gemel or, holding in the dexter paw a sword ppr., and resting the sinister paw on an escutcheon erm., charged with a ram's head erased sa., armed or. *Avancez.*

Churton, Shropsh., out of a mural coronet ppr., a demi-lion rampant gu., holding in the paw a sword ppr., pommel and hilt or. *Avancez.*

Chussell, three chisels arg., handles or, two in saltire, the handles downwards, and one in pale, the handle upwards.

Chute, Hants and Kent, a gauntlet ppr., holding a broken sword arg., hilt and pommel or.

Chute, Charles Lennard, of The Vyne, Hants, a dexter cubit arm in armour, the hand gauntleted grasping a broken sword in bend sinister ppr., hilt and pommel or.

Chute, Wiggett-: (1) A dexter cubit arm in armour, the hand gauntleted grasping a broken sword in bend sinister ppr., hilt and pommel or (*for Chute*). (2) A griffin's head couped sa., holding in the beak an ear of wheat ppr., between two wings arg., each charged with a mullet gu. (*for Wiggett*). *Fortune de guerre.*

Chute, Wiggett-, Rev. Devereux, of Sherborne St. John, Basingstoke, same crests and motto.

Chuter, a dexter hand holding a spur. 217. 14

Chyner, an antelope's head erased erm. 126. 2

Cidderowe, out of a tower arg., a demi-lion rampant sa. 157. 11

Ciely, Cornw., a tiger sejant arg. 27. 6

Cinsallagh, Ireland, a lion's head erased ppr. 17. 8

Cipriani, an eagle displayed sa., crowned gu. *cf.* 74. 14

Clabrock, Middx. and Kent, out of a ducal coronet or, a demi-ostrich arg., wings displayed erm., holding in the beak a horse-shoe sa. 96. 8

Clack, on a mount a holy lamb bearing a flag, all ppr. 131. 14

Clack, an old man's head couped at the shoulders, vested gu., wreathed arg.

Clack, Heref. and Berks, a demi-eagle or, winged erm. 80. 2

Clagett of London, Kent, and Surrey, an eagle's head erased erm., ducally crowned or, between two wings sa.

Clagstone, a falcon rising ppr. 87. 1

Clamond, Cornw., a griffin sejant or. 62. 10

Clanbrasil, Baron, *see* Roden, Earl of.

Clancarty, Earl of (Le Poer-Trench), Garbally, Ballinasloe, co. Galway: (1) An arm in armour embowed holding in the hand a sword, all ppr. 195. 2. (2) A lion rampant or, imperially crowned, holding in the dexter paw a sword arg., hilt and pommel or, and in the sinister a sheaf of arrows of the last. (3) A stag's head cabossed arg., attired and between the attires a crucifix or. *Consilio et prudentia.* 122. 13

Clancy, Ireland, and **Clanny,** Durh., a hand gauntleted holding a dagger in pale, on the point a wolf's head couped close, dropping blood gu.

Clancy, Ireland, a hand couped at the wrist erect, holding a sword impaling a boar's head also couped, all ppr. 212. 6

Clandinen, Ireland, a demi-lion holding a mullet of six points.

Clanmorris, Baron (Bingham), Newbrook, Ballyglass, co. Mayo, Ireland, on a rock an eagle rising, all ppr. *Spes mea Christus.*

Clanricarde, Marquess of (De Burgh-Canning), Portumna Castle, co. Galway: (1) A demi-lion rampant arg., charged with three trefoils vert, holding in the dexter paw an arrow pheoned and flighted ppr., the shaft or (*for Canning*). *cf.* 13. 6. (2) A cat-a-mountain sejant gardant ppr., collared and chained or (*for De Burgh*). *Nug roy, nug foy, nug loy.* 26. 13

Clanwilliam, Earl of (Meade), Gill Hall, Dromore, co. Down, Ireland, an eagle displayed with two heads sa., armed or. *Toujours prêt.* 74. 2

Clapcott, a buck's head couped sa., attired or. 121. 5

Clapham, Scotland, a dexter hand holding a helmet ppr. 217. 12

Clapham, a lion rampant sa., holding in the dexter paw a sword arg., pommel and hilt or.

Clapham, T. R., Austwick Hall, same crest.

Clapham of Burley Grange, Yorks, a lion rampant sa. *Post est occasio calva.* 1. 10

Clapp, a pike naiant ppr. 139. 12

Clapperton, Scotland, a talbot passant arg. *Fides præstantior auro.* 54. 1

Clapton, Hants, a dolphin hauriant, head downwards.

Clapton, Edward, M.D., 41, Eltham Road, Lee, S.E., a bay horse's head erased, bridled and charged with a quatrefoil or, gorged with a chain of the last, pendent therefrom a bell az. *Laudo et plaudo.*

Clare, Earl of (Fitzgibbon), a boar passant gu., bristled or, charged on the body with three annulets of the last. *Nil admirari.* *cf.* 40. 8

Clare, John Leigh, Esquire, of Hoylake, Birkenhead, upon a mill-rind fesseways or, a cock with wings expanded gu. *Vigilante.*

Clare, Leigh-, Octavius Leigh, Esquire, B.A., of Hindley Cottage, East Sheen, Surrey, same crest and motto.

Clare, Shropsh. and Worcs., a stag's head cabossed gu., attired ppr. 122. 5

Clarence and Avondale, H.R.H. the late Duke of, on a coronet composed of crosses pattée and fleur-de-lis, a lion statant gardant or, crowned with a like coronet and differenced with a label of three points arg., the centre point charged with St. George's cross.

Clarendon, Earl of (Villiers), the Grove, Watford, Herts, a lion rampant arg., ducally crowned or. *Fidei coticula crux.* 1. 12

Clarge, a ram's head couped arg., with two straight and two bent horns or.

Clarges, out of a ducal coronet a ram's head armed with four horns or.

Claridge, Essex, an eagle regardant. *Cum periculo lucrum.* 76. 6

Clarina, Baron (Massey), Elm Park, Limerick, Ireland, out of a ducal coronet or, a bull's head gu., armed sa. *Pro libertate patriæ.* 44. 11

Clark, a falcon rising. 87. 1

Clark, Sir John Forbes, Bart., Tillypronie, Tarland, Aberdeensh., a rock, therefrom rising a falcon ppr., belled or, and resting the dexter claw on a ducal coronet of the last. *Amat victoria curam.*

Clark, Sir James Richardson Andrew, Bart., Tidmarsh, near Reading, a demi-huntsman winding a horn holding in his sinister hand a whip, all ppr., between a stag's attires, the scalp in front arg. *Free for a blast.*

Clark, Andrew, Esquire, S.S.C., of 21, Bernard Street, Leith, and 19, Raeburn Place, Edinburgh, a falcon rising ppr. *Honore et virtute.* 87. 1

Clark of Bellefield, Trowbridge, and Cumberwell, near Bradford, Wilts, a swan arg., ducally gorged, and with a chain reflexed over the back or, charged on the wings with an estoile gu., and resting the dexter foot on a cross moline, also gu.

Clark of Bishop Wearmouth, Durh., a swan ppr., reposing his dexter foot on an ogress. *cf.* 99. 2

Clark, Frederick, Esquire, D.L., of Great Cumberland Place, London, upon the trunk of a tree eradicated fessewise, sprouting to the dexter, a lark rising ppr., charged on the breast with a rose gu., and holding in the beak three ears of wheat slipped or.

Clark, Charles Stanley Gordon, Esquire, two pellets, thereon a lark rising ppr., gorged with a collar gemel arg., and holding in the beak an ear of wheat leaved and slipped or. *Be advised.*

Clark, Henry Herbert Gordon, Esquire, of Mickleham Hall, near Dorking, same crest and motto.

Clark, Crawfurd A. Gordon, Esquire, same crest and motto.

Clark, Gilchrist-, of Speddoch, Dumfriessh., Scotland, within a serpent in a circle an estoile pierced or. *Animo et scientia.*

Clark, Norf., an eagle's leg gu., joined to a wing or. *cf.* 113. 5

Clark, a griffin's head erased. 66. 2

Clark, a demi-griffin ducally gorged. *cf.* 64. 2

Clark, a mullet of six points arg. *Animo et scientia.* 164. 3

Clark of London, a cross pattée or, between two eagles' wings erect az. *Absit ut glorier nisi in cruce.* 110. 7

Clark of Dowlais House, Merthyr Tydvil, a lion rampant supporting a shield gyronny of eight. *Tryandtryst.* cf. 1. 4

Clark of Buckland Tout Saints, Devonsh., a demi-lion gu., collared or, charged on the shoulder with an estoile arg., and holding in the dexter paw a baton sa. *Victor mortalis est.* cf. 15. 9

Clark, Archibald Henry, Beaumont Lodge, Paignton, same crest and motto.

Clark, Godfrey Lewis, 44, Berkeley Square, a lion rampant or, supporting a shield gu., charged with a cross erm. placed upon a saltire or. *Try and tryste.—Non major alio, non minor.*

Clark of Achareidh, Nairn, Scotland, a bear sejant arg., muzzled, collared, and chained ppr., holding a battle-axe erect, also ppr. *Sans changer.*

Clark, a talbot's head erased or. 56. 2

Clark, a talbot's head couped or, gorged with a collar az., charged with a plate. cf. 56. 1

Clark, a dragon's head erased az. *Fortitudo.* cf. 71. 2

Clark, The Goddards, Snaith, Yorksh., a stag's head cabossed.

Clark of Belford, Northumb., a dragon's head erased az., guttée-d'or, gorged with a collar embattled, counter-embattled, and charged on the neck with three annulets interlaced, also or. *Fortitudo.*

Clark, Bucks and Beds, a goat arg., against a tree ppr. 129. 8

Clark, Ireland, on a mural coronet az., a stag sejant or. 116. 4

Clark of Steeple, co. Antrim, Ireland, a boar's head erased sa., transfixed through the jaws with a broken spear ppr. *Non eget jaculis.*

Clark, a fox's head gu. 33. 4

Clark, Towers-, of Wester Moffat, Lanarksh.: (1) A dexter hand holding a scimitar bendways ppr., hilted and pommelled or (*for Clark*). 213. 5. (2) A tower or, masoned sa. (*for Towers*). *Fortiter.—Turris fortis mihi Deus.* 156. 2

Clark, a hand holding a dagger in bend sinister. 212. 3

Clark, James Jackson, Esquire, of Largantogher House, Maghera, co. Londonderry, Ireland, out of a mural crown an arm embowed in armour, the hand holding a dagger, all ppr., the arm charged with a trefoil vert. *Virtute et labore.* cf. 195. 9

Clark, Sir Andrew, Bart., of Cavendish Square, London, between the attires of a stag affixed to the scalp arg., a demi-huntsman winding a horn, and holding in his sinister hand a whip, all ppr. *Free for a blast.* cf. 187. 12

Clark, Andrew, F.R.C.S., 71, Harley Street, W., a demi-huntsman winding a horn, and holding in his sinister hand a whip, all ppr. *Free for a blast.*

Clark, Stewart, Esquire, of Dundas Castle, South Queensferry, an anchor cabled gu. *Sure and steadfast.* 161. 2

Clark, a pheon ppr. 174. 11

Clark or **Clarke,** Derbysh., in a gem ring or, set with a diamond sa., a pheon arg. cf. 167. 12

Clark, Sir John Maurice, Bart., of 14, Rothesay Place, Edinburgh, a battle-axe in pale ppr. *In Deo speravi.* 172. 3

Clarke, Grahame- Leonard John, Frocester Manor House, Stonehouse, Glouc., an escallop quarterly gu. and erminois.

Clark-Kennedy, John William James, Esquire, of Knockgray, Carsphairn, Kirkcudbright, N.B.: (1) A demi-man in the uniform of the Royal Dragoons holding in his dexter hand a sword, and sinister a French eagle, all ppr. (2) A dolphin naiant ppr. *Avise la fin.*

Clarke, Sir Charles, Bart., of Dunham Lodge, Norfolk, a mount vert, thereon a lark with wings elevated or, holding in the beak an ear of wheat ppr., the dexter claw resting on an annulet sa. 259. 7

Clarke, Hon. Sir Rupert Turner Havelock, Bart., in front of an arm embowed in armour holding in the hand an arrow in bend sinister ppr., three escallops. *Signum quærens in vellere.* 248. 4

Clarke of Cork, on the stump of a tree couped, eradicated, and sprouting on each side, a lark perched ppr., the wings expanded, holding in the beak two wheat-ears or.

Clarke, formerly of Wayste Court, Abingdon, Berks, in front of a mount overgrown with clover a lark rising ppr., charged on the breast with a cross patée arg., and holding in the beak an ear of wheat or. *Carpe diem.*

Clarke, a lark rising, holding in the beak an ear of wheat, all ppr. *Carpe diem.*

Clarke, a lark with wings expanded, holding in the beak an ear of wheat, all ppr. cf. 94. 5

Clarke, Alexander Felix, Esquire, of 38, English Quay, St. Petersburg, Russia, upon a mount vert, a swan arg., charged on the body with two pellets fesseways, holding in the beak an ostrich feather or. *Si bene facias nil metuas.* 256. 15

Clarke-Travers, Sir Guy Francis Travers, Bart., of Rossmore, co. Cork: (1) An heraldic tiger passant arg. (*for Travers*). 25. 5. (2) On the stump of a tree couped, eradicated, and sprouting on each side a lark perched ppr., wings expanded, holding in the beak two wheat-ears or (*for Clarke*). *Nec temere, nec timide.—Constantia et fidelitate.*

Clarke, a peacock's head erased ppr., holding in the beak a trefoil slipped vert. cf. 103. 1

Clarke, a swan ppr. 99. 2

Clarke, Durh. and Ireland, a swan ppr., resting the dexter foot on an ogress. cf. 99. 2

Clarke, a swan rising arg., ducally gorged and chained or. cf. 99. 3

Clarke, James Richard Plomer, Welton Place, near Daventry, Northamp., same crest.

Clarke, an eagle with wings expanded sa., beaked and membered or. 77. 5

Clarke, Lincs, a sinister wing or. 109. 7

Clarke of Arlington, Berks, a cross pattée or, between a pair of eagles' wings erect az. *Absit ut glorier nisi in cruce.* 110. 7

Clarke, Surrey, on a ducal coronet or, a cross pattée of the same between two eagles' wings expanded sa. cf. 110. 7

Clarke, Heref., a lion rampant vert, holding a pen arg.

Clarke, a demi-lion rampant or. 10. 2

Clarke of London and Glouc., out of a ducal coronet or, a demi-lion ppr. 16. 3

Clarke of London and Yorks, a demi-lion rampant or, holding a cross crosslet fitched az. 11. 10

Clarke, out of a mural coronet a demi-lion rampant holding a pennon gu. cf. 16. 7

Clarke, out of a mural coronet a demi-lion rampant, in the dexter paw a pennon, resting the sinister on an escutcheon.

Clarke, Suff., an elephant's head quarterly gu. and or. 133. 2

Clarke, Thomas, Esquire, of Masson House, Matlock, Bath, Derbysh., in front of an heraldic tiger's head erased sa., maned or, gorged with a collar gemel arg., two fleur-de-lis also arg. *Vincit qui patitur.*

Clarke, Beds, a goat salient arg., attired or, against a pine-tree ppr. 129. 8

Clarke, Bart., Ireland, out of an Eastern crown gu., a demi-dragon with wings elevated or. *Constanter et fidelitate.*

Clarke, Berks, out of a ducal coronet a dragon's head. *Pro legibus et regibus.* 72. 4

Clarke, Kent, a demi-griffin arg., issuing from flames ppr. *In medio tutissimus.* cf. 64. 2

Clarke, Westminster, a demi-griffin, the wings endorsed or, gorged with a collar engrailed az. cf. 64. 2

Clarke, Surrey, a bear sejant arg., supporting a battle-axe erect az.

Clarke of Ashgate and Norton Hall, Derbysh., a bear rampant az., collared and chained sa., holding a battle-axe gu.

Clarke, Montague de Salis McKenzie Gordon Augustus, Achareidh, Nairn, a bear sejant arg., muzzled, collared, and chained ppr., holding a battle-axe erect ppr. *Sans changer.—Dan ni h-andan.*

Clarke of Elm Bank, Leatherhead, Surrey, a bear rampant erm., gorged with a naval crown or, the line reflexed over the back gu., supporting a battle-axe erect ppr. *Mœnibus crede ligneis.*

Clarke, George Jackson, Esquire, of the Steeple, Antrim, Ireland, a boar's head erased sa., transfixed through the jaws with a broken spear ppr. *Non eget jaculis.*

Clarke, Colonel Thomas, D.L., ex-Sheriff of the City of London, of the Gables, 35, Upper Hamilton Terrace, London, N.W., on a wreath of the colours, in front of a horse's head couped erminois, a spur erect leathered gu. *Fortis in arduis.* 51. 8

Clarke of Dublin, a horse's head erased or, charged with a cross pattée gu. cf. 51. 4

Clarke, Suff., a nag's head erased sa. 50. 8

Clarke, Kent, a unicorn's head erased arg., crined and armed or, gorged with a collar gu., charged with three plates. cf. 49. 11

Clarke, Ireland, a sea-horse vert. 46. 5

Clarke, Ireland, a demi-ram erminois. *Vir gregis.* 130. 13

Clarke, Kent, a fleur-de-lis per pale arg. and sa. 148. 2

Clarke, Suff., a conger-eel's head erect and erased gu., collared with a bar gemelle or. 139. 3

Clarke, Essex, a greyhound sejant sa. 59. 4

Clarke, Kent and Essex, a greyhound's head couped or, charged with a cinquefoil az.

Clarke, Cambs, a talbot's head erased or. 56. 2

Clarke of Summerhill, Lancs, out of a ducal coronet or, a demi-bull rampant erm., armed of the first. *Esperance en Dieu.* cf. 45. 8

Clarke of London, a talbot's head or, gorged with a fesse engrailed az., charged with three lozenges of the first. cf. 56. 12

Clarke, Sir Philip Houghton, Bart., of Shirland, Notts, an arm couped near the wrist ppr., holding a sword in pale arg., hilted or. 212. 9

Clarke, out of a mural coronet arg., a cubit arm in armour holding a scimitar ppr., hilted or. cf. 209. 11

Clarke, an arm embowed in armour ppr., holding in the gauntlet an arrow or, headed and feathered arg. cf. 198. 4

Clarke, the Hon. Sir Rupert Turner Havelock, Bart., of Rupertswood, Bourke County, Victoria, Australia, and 30, Park Lane, London, W., Member of the Legislative Council of Victoria, in front of a dexter arm embowed in armour, the hand in a gauntlet ppr., grasping an arrow in bend sinister or, flighted arg., three escallops, also or. *Signum quærens in vellere.* 198. 6

Clarke, Joseph, Esquire, J.P., of Mandeville Hall, Toorak, near Melbourne, Victoria, Australia, same crest and motto.

Clarke, the late Thomas Sinclair, of Knedlington, Yorks, on a chapeau az., turned up erm., two wings expanded out of a ducal coronet, between them the word "Elmer" in Saxon characters. *The time will come.*

Clarke of London, on a plate arg., the letter Y gu.

Clarke, Derbysh., in a gem ring or, set with a diamond sa., a pheon arg. cf. 167. 12

Clarke of Hyde Hall, Chesh.: (1) A pheon ppr. 174. 11. (2) An eagle with wings expanded sa., beaked and membered or. 77. 5

Clarke, Richard Hall, Bridwell, Cullompton, Devonsh., a lark rising holding in its beak an ear of wheat ppr. *Carpe diem.*

Clarke, Heref., an escallop quarterly gu. and or. 141. 14

Clarkeson, Clarkesonn, and **Clarkson,** a hand and arm couped below the elbow lying fesseways in a coat of mail ppr., holding in the hand a sword erect arg., hilt and pommel sa., on the blade a pennon flotant gu.

Clarkson, an arm in armour embowed holding a couteau-sword, all ppr. *Per ardua.* cf. 196. 10

Clason and **Classon,** Scotland, a rose-branch ppr. 149. 8

Clater, a dexter hand holding a crescent. 216. 8

Claude, a demi-unicorn rampant collared ppr. 48. 10

Claus, on the point of a sword in pale a cross pattée. 169. 5

Clauson, Chas., Esquire, between two wings arg., a mullet of five points or. *Spes et fides.* 111. 5

Clauson, Albert Charles, Esquire, of 8, Old Square, Lincoln's Inn, W.C., a mullet of ten points encircled by an annulet or, between two wings sa., the dexter charged with three bendlets, and the sinister with as many bendlets in sinister arg. *Spes et fides.*

Clauson, Major John Eugene, C.M.G., R.E., 44, Stanhope Gardens, Queen's Gate, S.W., same crest and motto.

Clavedon, a pelican vulning herself ppr. 98. 1

Clavel and **Clavell,** a human heart in flames, all ppr. 181. 13

Clavel, Clavell, and **Claville,** a buck's head erased and pierced between the attires by an arrow. cf. 121. 2

Claver, Bucks, a lion's gamb couped and erect or, holding a key sa. cf. 35. 1

Clavering of Callaly Castle, Northumb., a man's head affrontée couped at the shoulders, between two wings ppr. *Ad cœlos volans.*

Clavering, Northumb., a cherub's head with wings erect. *Ad cœlos volans.* 189. 9

Clavering, Sir Henry Augustus, Bart., of Axwell, Durh., out of a ducal coronet or, a demi-lion az. *Nil actum si quid agendum.* 16. 3

Clavering, Napier-, the Rev. J. W., Axwell Park, Durh.: (1) A dexter arm from the elbow ppr., the hand grasping a crescent arg. (2) The top of an embattled tower arg., masoned sa., issuing therefrom six lances disposed saltirewise, three and three with pennons az. *Nil actum si quid agendum.—Sans tache.—Ready, aye ready.*

Claxson, Glouc., on a mount vert, a stag lodged arg., attired and ungu. or, supporting with the dexter foot an escutcheon gu., charged with a porcupine arg. *Sapere aude, incipe.* cf. 115. 12

Claxton, a hedgehog arg. 135. 8

Claxton, Durh., on a ducal coronet or, a hedgehog arg. 135. 14

Claxton, a hedgehog sa., bezantée. cf. 135. 8

Clay, *see* Pelham-Clay.

Clay or **Claye** of London and Shropsh., a lion's head per pale vert and sa., charged with an escallop arg. cf. 21. 1

Clay, Claye, and **Cley,** Derbysh., two wings expanded arg., semée of trefoils slipped sa. 109. 11

Clay, Henry, Esquire, M.A., J.P., D.L., of Piercefield Park, Chepstow, Monmouthsh., in front of two wings arg., semée of trefoils slipped sa., a mount vert, and thereon two estoiles gu. *Clarior virtus honoribus.* 292. 11

Clay of Ford Manor, Surrey, and Arthur J. Clay, Esquire, of Holly Bush, Staffs, same crest and motto.

Clay, Sir Arthur Temple Felix, Bart., Ardmeallie, Huntley, N.B., two wings arg., each charged with a chevron engrailed between three trefoils slipped sa. *Per orbem.* cf. 109. 6

Clay, Alfred, Esquire, an annulet sa., surmounted by a martlet arg., between two wings also arg., guttée-de-poix, each wing charged with three trefoils or and two sa.

Clay, Arthur Travis, Esquire, of Holly Bank, Rastrick, Yorks, same crest and motto.

Clay, John William, Esquire, same crest.

Clay, Charles John, Esquire, of West House, Cambridge, upon a rock ppr., a pheon az., in front thereof a key fesseways ward upwards, and to the sinister of the last. *Propositi tenax.*

Claydan, an arm in armour brandishing a sword, all ppr. *Probitatem quam divitias.* 210. 2

Claydon, a demi-lion rampant az., vulned on the shoulder gu., murally crowned arg., holding in the paws a cross flory fitched of the second.

Clayton, Fitzroy Augustus, Esquire, of Fyfield House, Maidenhead, Berks, a leopard's gamb erased arg., holding a pellet.

Claye, *see* Clay.

Claye, Frank Reginald, Esquire, Long Eaton, Derbysh., two wings expanded arg., semée of trefoils slipped sa. 109. 11

Clayfield, a Moor's head couped sa. 192. 13

Clayhills-Henderson, George David, Esquire, of Invergowrie, Dundee, Forfarsh., Hallyards Meigle, Perthsh., Thornton-le-Moor, Yorks, a hand holding an imperial crown ppr. *Corde et animo.*

Clayhills, Scotland, an arm holding an imperial crown ppr. *Corde et animo.* cf. 217. 1

Clayley, a greyhound's head arg., between two rose-slips flowered gu., stalked and leaved vert. 61. 11

Clayton-East, Bart., *see* East.

Clayton of Crooke, Lancs, an arm embowed vested sa., holding a sword point downwards.

Clayton, an arm in armour embowed, holding in the hand a sword point downward ppr. 195. 4

Clayton, Bart., (extinct) of Adlington, Lancs, a dexter arm embowed, grasping in the hand a dagger ppr., the point to the dexter. *Probitatem quam divitias.* cf. 201. 4

Clayton, the late J. Bertram, 42, Wilton Crescent, same crest.

Clayton of Lostock Hall, Leyland, Lancs, a dexter arm embowed in armour, the hand in a gauntlet grasping a sword in bend sinister, the point downwards ppr., pommel and hilt or, pendent from the wrist by a riband an escutcheon of the last, charged with a griffin's head erased az.

Clayton, Sir William Robert, Bart., D.L., of Marden Park, Surrey, a leopard's gamb erased and erect arg., holding a pellet. *Virtus in actione consistit.—Quid leone fortius?* 39. 13

Clayton of Hedgerley Park, Bucks, a leopard's gamb erased and erect grasping a pellet. *Virtus in actione consistit.—Quid leone fortius?* 39. 13

Clayton, Major, E. G., Kingswood, Woking, same crest and motto.

Clayton, out of a mural coronet or, a leopard's paw arg., holding a pellet. *cf.* 39. 13

Clayton, the late Nathaniel, Esquire, of East Cliff, Lincs, upon the battlements of a tower a lion's gamb erect and erased ppr., grasping a pellet, encircled by a wreath of oak vert.

Clayton of Enfield, a dove with an olive-branch in its beak, all ppr. *Quod sors, fert, ferimus.* 92. 5

Clayton, Norf. and Shropsh., a unicorn couchant arg., maned, armed, and ungu. or, and under the dexter foot a bezant.

Cleaber, an arm erect vested arg., holding in the hand ppr. a chaplet of thorns vert.

Clealand, on a sinister gauntlet in fess a falcon, all ppr. *cf.* 86. 13

Cleasby, Richard Digby, Esquire, of Penoyre, Brecon, a mount vert, thereon a demi-lion regardant arg., gorged with a collar az., charged with three lozenges or, holding between them an inescutcheon gu., thereon a whelk arg. *Fide sed cui vide.*

Cleather, Cornw., a cubit arm vambraced holding in the hand gauntleted a dagger arg., the blade wavy. *cf.* 210. 4

Cleather, G. G., 97, Oxford Gardens, W., same crest.

Cleather a sand-glass gu., winged arg. 113. 11

Cleaveland, a greyhound's head sa., charged with three bezants. *cf.* 61. 12

Cleaver, a lion's gamb couped or, holding a key sa. *cf.* 35. 1

Cleavland, a greyhound's head sa., charged with three bezants one and two. *cf.* 61. 12

Cleborne, a wolf's head erased sa. *Virtute invidiam vincas.* 30. 8

Cleborne, a wolf rampant, holding in the dexter paw an annulet. *Beware.—Ne oblivescaris.* *cf.* 28. 2

Clebury, Shropsh., a goat's head erased sa., armed or. 128. 5

Clederow of London, out of a tower arg., a demi-lion sa. 157. 11

Cleeve, a fox's head erased sa. 33. 8

Cleeve, a hand holding a buckle. 223. 11

Cleg or **Clegg,** out of a ducal coronet or, a demi-lion rampant, imperially crowned, all ppr. *cf.* 16. 3

Clegat, an eagle's head erm., ducally crowned and beaked or, between two wings sa. *cf.* 84. 2

Clegg, Harry, Esquire, of Plas Llanfair, P.G., Anglesey, in front of a demi-lion per fesse nebuly arg. and gu., holding in the dexter paw a cross crosslet crossed sa., three acorns erect and fesseways slipped and leaved ppr. *In veritate triumpho.* 244. 14

Clegg of Allerton, Lancs, an eagle rising arg. 76. 13

Clegg of Little Clegg, Lancs, a griffin's head couped. *Qui potest capere capiat.* 66. 1

Cleghorn, a cubit arm erect holding in the hand a pair of scales equally poised, all ppr. 217. 13

Cleghorn, a dexter hand issuing from a cloud in sinister holding a laurel-branch, all ppr. *Insperata floruit.* *cf.* 223. 3

Cleghorn, an arm in armour embowed, throwing a dart ppr. *Sublime petimus.* 198. 4

Cleiland or **Cleilland,** Scotland, on a sinister hand couped and gloved ppr., a falcon statant. *For sport.—Non sibi.* 186. 14

Cleiveland of the Lowe, Lindridge, Worcs., the head and neck of an osprey erased ppr. 83. 2

Cleland, Rose-, of Rath-Gael House, Ireland: (1) On a sinister glove a hawk ppr. (*for Cleland*). 86. 12. (2) A rose gu., seeded and slipped ppr., between two wings erm. (*for Rose*). *For sport.—Je pense à qui pense plus.* *cf.* 149. 5

Cleland-Henderson, Major-General John William, formerly of Roke Manor, Hants: (1) Upon the dexter side, a cubit arm erect vested az., the hand ppr., grasping a chain, therefrom suspended an escutcheon arg., charged with two estoiles in chief and a crescent in base gu. (*for Henderson*). 208. 9. (2) Upon the sinister side, a falcon or, on a sinister glove ppr. (*for Cleland*). *Virtus sola nobilitat.—Non sibi.* 86. 12

Cleland, Scotland, a falcon rising ppr. *Si je pourois.* 87. 1

Cleland, William Henry, of Rooks Nest, Banstead, Surrey, and 34, Brunswick Square, Hove, Brighton, on a mount vert, a falcon ppr., belled and jessed or, between two dexter hands couped at the wrist, also ppr. *Je pense à qui pense plus.* 249. 7

Cleland, on a sinister glove a falcon belled ppr. *Non sibi.* 86. 12

Cleland, a Moor's head sa., wreathed arg. 192. 13

Clelland, Scotland, a rose gu., leaved and stalked vert. *Fragrat, delectat, et sanat.* 149. 5

Clelland, Scotland, a buck at gaze ppr. *Ne cedem insidiis.* 117. 3

Clement, Ashburnham-, Sir Anchitel Piers, Bart., Broomham, Hastings, out of a ducal coronet or, an ash-tree ppr. *Will God, and I shall.*

Clement, Dorset and Devonsh., on a mount, vert, a griffin sejant or. *cf.* 62. 10

Clement, Norf., a lion passant arg., guttée-de-sang. 6. 2

Clement of Lower Clapton, Middx., a lion passant arg., guttée-de-sang, gorged with a collar and charged on the body with two crosses crosslet in fesse gu. *cf.* 6. 2

Clement, Ireland, a cross moline or. 165. 3

Clements, Francis Leonard, Esquire, same crest. *Nil sine Deo.*

Clements, Henry Topham, Esquire, of Belmont, East Hothly, Sussex, same crest and motto.

Clements of Rathkenny, Ireland, same crest. 165. 3

Clements, Colonel Henry Theophilus, of Ashfield Lodge, Cootehill, Ireland, a hawk statant ppr. *Patriis virtutibus.* 85. 2

Clements, Baron, *see* Leitrim, Earl of.

Clements, Lucas-, of Rathkenny, co. Cavan: (1) A hawk close ppr., belled and jessed or (*for Clements*). *cf.* 85. 2. (2) A demi-griffin arg., beaked and membered or (*for Lucas*). *Patriis virtutibus* 64. 2

Clements, William, Burton-on-Trent, crest same as the first above, motto as above.

Clements, co. Cavan, a fawn's head erased ppr. 124. 3

Clements, a falcon close. 85. 2

Clements, a leopard gardant per pale gu. and erm., ducally gorged or. 24. 3

Clements, Ireland, out of a ducal coronet or, a lion's gamb sa., holding a cross crosslet fitched of the first. 36. 11

Clementson, an arm from the elbow ppr., vested paly gu. and or, cuffed counter-changed, holding a palm-branch of the first.

Clemsby, a tower ppr. 156. 2

Clench or **Clenche,** a reindeer's head caboshed ppr. 122. 4

Clench, Suff., out of a Saxon crown or, an arm erect vested gu., cuffed arg., holding in the hand ppr. a club vert, spiked of the first. 206. 2

Clench, E. Payton, Esquire, of 16, Hanover Square, London, W., out of a Saxon crown or, an arm erect vested gu., cuffed arg., holding in the hand ppr. a club vert, spiked of the first. *Tien le droit.* 206. 2

Clendon, a stag's head ppr., between the attires a cross pattée arg. 120. 9

Clent, Worcs., two lion's gambs erect sa., holding a chaplet vert, flowered or.

Clepan, Clephan, and **Clephane,** Scotland, a dexter hand holding a helmet ppr. *Ut sim paratior.* 217. 12

Clepole, Notts, a fleur-de-lis arg., enfiled with a ducal coronet or. 148. 1

Clere, Norf., the sun or, between two wings az., on each a crescent of the first.

Clere, out of an antique Irish crown or, five ostrich-feathers arg. *Virtute non verbis.* *cf.* 114. 13

Clere, Norf., out of a ducal coronet or, a plume of ostrich-feathers arg. 114. 13

Clere, Norf., a camel's head ducally gorged ppr., bridled gu. *cf.* 132. 9

Clerk, Sir George Douglas, Bart., J.P., of Penicuik, Edinburgh, a demi-huntsman winding a horn ppr. Over the crest, *Free for a blast*; under the arms, *Amat victoria curam.* 187. 12

Clerk, Robert Mildmay, Esquire, J.P., of Westholme, and Charlton House, Shepton Mallet, Somers., same crest.

Clerk, Edmund Hugh, Esquire, of Burford, Shepton Mallet: (1) An Æsculapius' wand. (2) A huntsman in green ppr. (*for Clerk*). *Amat victoria curam,* and *Free for a blast.*

Clerk, Scotland, a dexter arm couped at the elbow brandishing a broadsword, all ppr. *Fortiter ubique.*

Clerk, Scotland, an Æsculapius' rod ppr. *Sat cito, si sat tuto.*

Clerk, Norf., a demi-forester ppr., on his breast a star arg. *Amat victoria curam.*

Clerk, an oak-tree fructed ppr. *In robore decus.* 143. 5

Clerk-Rattray, Lieutenant-General Sir James, of Craighall, Rattray, N.B.: (1) On the dexter side a star or, and thereon a flaming heart ppr. (*for Rattray*). *Super sidera votum.* And upon the sinister side a demi-huntsman winding a horn ppr., habited vert. *Free for a blast.*

Clerke, a greyhound's head or, charged on the neck with a cinquefoil az. *cf.* 61. 4

Clerke, out of a naval coronet or, a Moor's head ppr. *cf.* 192. 6
Clerke, out of clouds ppr., a hand arg., holding a branch vert. *cf.* 219. 9
Clerke, Shropsh. and Hants, a wolf's head erased per pale arg. and vert. *Ut prosim aliis.* 30. 8
Clerke, Sir William Francis, Bart., of Hitcham, Bucks, a ram's head couped ppr. 130. 1
Clerke, a swan ppr. 99. 2
Clerke, on a partridge ppr., an eagle's leg gu., winged at the thigh or.
Clerke, a pheon arg. 174. 11
Clerke, an eagle's head erased arg., holding in the beak a branch of laurel vert. *cf.* 83. 2
Clerke, an arm holding an arrow arg., feathered or. 214. 4
Clerke, a boar's head gu., holding in the mouth a sword in bend ppr. *cf.* 42. 6
Clerkson of Kirkiton and Mansfield Woodhouse, Notts, a hand and arm clad in complete armour lying fesseways ppr., couped below the elbow gu., grasping in the gauntlet a sword erect arg., hilt and pommel or, on the blade a split pennon of the second flotant towards the sinister.
Clermont, Baron, *see* Carlingford, Baron.
Clermont, a savage ppr., wreathed about the head and middle with leaves vert, standing on a serpent of the last. 188. 3
Clermont, a pole-cat ppr. 135. 13
Clervaux, Yorks, an eagle displayed ppr. 75. 2
Clerveaux-Chaytor, *see* Chaytor.
Clesby, Yorks, a reindeer trippant ppr. 125. 9
Clesby, an ensign ppr., his coat gu., holding a banner of the last. 188. 6
Cletherow and **Clyderowe,** a Roman soldier in armour ppr, holding a spear. 188. 2
Cleve, a griffin passant with wings addorsed, ducally gorged or. 63. 3
Cleve and **Clive** of London and Shropsh., a wolf's head per pale dancettée arg. and sa. 30. 5
Cleveland, Duke of (formerly Vane): (1) A dexter hand in a gauntlet ppr., bossed and ringed or, brandishing a dagger, also ppr. (*for Vane*). (2) On a chapeau gu., turned up erm., a lion passant gardant or, gorged with a collar componée of the second and az., and crowned with a five-leaved ducal coronet of the last (*for Fitzroy*). *Nec temere, nec timide.* *cf.* 4. 2
Cleveland, Duke and Marquess of, Earl of Darlington, Viscount and Baron Barnard of Barnard Castle, and **Baron Raby of Raby Castle,** Durh. (His Grace the late Sir Harry George Powlett, K.G., D.C.L.), a falcon rising or, belled of the last and ducally gorged gu. *Aymes loyaulté.* 87. 2
Cleveland, a demi-old man ppr., vested az., with a cap gu., turned up with a hair front, holding in his dexter hand a spear headed arg., on top thereof a line ppr., passing behind him and coiled up in his sinister hand.
Cleveland, a demi-man affrontée ppr., in a military habit gu., with a belt and sash, and holding the Union flag ppr. 187. 9
Cleveland, a bishop's mitre ppr. *cf.* 180. 5
Cleveland of Tapley, Devonsh., a cubit arm erect, vested az., cuffed arg., holding in the hand ppr. a dagger of the second, hilt and pommel or. *Audaces juvat.*
Cleves, two elephants' probosces addorsed sa. 123. 10
Clevland, a hand holding a sword arg., hilted and pommelled or. *Fortuna audaces juvat.* 212. 13
Cley, *see* Clay.
Cleybroke, out of a ducal coronet or, a demi-ostrich arg., with wings displayed erm., holding in the beak a horse-shoe sa. 96. 8
Cleypole, out of a ducal coronet or, a fleur-de-lis arg. *cf.* 148. 2
Clibborn, Thomas Strettel, Esquire, of Holmesby, Elizabeth Bay, Sydney, New South Wales, Australia, and of the Castle, Moate, co. Westmeath, Ireland, out of a ducal coronet or, a wolf's head sa. *Virtus vincit invidiam.* 30. 8
Clibborn, out of a ducal coronet a wolf's head sa. *Virtus vincit invidiam.*
Clifden, Viscount, *formerly* (Agar-Ellis), a female figure naked ppr., her hair flowing down to her waist. *Non haec sine numine.*
Clifden, Viscount (Agar-Robartes), Lanhydrock, near Bodmin a lion rampant, or, holding a flaming sword erect ppr., pommel and hilt or. *Quæ supra.*
Cliff, a lion rampant arg. 1. 13
Cliff, William, Esquire, of Claremont, West Derby, Lancs, in front of a willow-tree ppr., a gryphon's head erased or.
Cliff-M'Culloch, William Edward, Esquire, of St. Clare, West Derby, Liverpool, a hand throwing a dart ppr. *Vi et animo.*
Cliffe, a griffin passant with wings addorsed arg., ducally gorged or. 63. 3
Cliffe, Anthony, Esquire, J.P., D.L., of Bellevue, co. Wexford, a wolf's head erased quarterly per pale indented or and sa. *In cruce glorior.* 30. 8
Cliffe, Essex and Devonsh., an archer ppr., the coat vert, shooting an arrow of the first. 188. 9
Cliffe, Clyff, and **Clyffe,** two lion's paws in saltier erased, each holding a seax, all ppr. 39. 5
Clifford, Frederick, Esquire, K.C., of 24, Collingham Gardens, South Kensington, S.W., in front of a demi-infant affrontée (representing the infant Hercules) grasping in each hand elevated a serpent nowed, all ppr. *Nec sine labore fructus.*
Clifford of Chudleigh, Baron (Clifford), Ughbrooke Park, Chudleigh, Devonsh., out of a ducal coronet or, a demi-wyvern rising gu. *Semper paratus.* 70. 9
Clifford, Sir George Hugh Charles, Bart., of Flaxbourne, in the province of Marlborough, New Zealand, out of a ducal coronet a demi-wyvern rising gu. *Semper paratus.* 70. 9
Clifford, the late Sir Robert Cavendish Spencer, Bart., Yeoman Usher of the Black Rod, a leopard gardant supporting in his dexter fore-paw a spear erect, all ppr. *Virtus mille scuta.*
Clifford of Perristone, Heref., a griffin segreant sa. *Semper paratus.* 62. 2
Clifford of Annesley, Wexford, a hand ppr., holding a fleur-de-lis or. *Dulcis amor patriæ.* *cf.* 215. 5
Clifford, Glouc., a dexter hand couped in fesse holding a fleur-de-lis. *Dulcis amor patriæ.* 221. 9
Clifford, Henry Francis, of Frampton, Glouc., a hand ppr. holding a fleur-de-lis or. *Dulcis amor patriæ.* *cf.* 215. 5
Clifford, Ireland, a dexter hand apaumée gu. 222. 14
Clifford, a talbot's head erased gu., eared or. 56. 2
Clifton of Clifton Hall, Notts: (1) Out of a ducal coronet gu., a demi-peacock per pale arg. and sa., wings expanded and counterchanged (*for Clifton*). (2) A lion sejant gardant winged or, with a glory round the head arg., semée of crosses pattée gu., and supporting an ox-yoke of the first (*for Markham*). *Tenez le droit.*
Clifton, George, Claremont, Dryburgh Road, Putney, crest same as first of the above.
Clifton, Juckes-, Bart., Notts, out of a ducal coronet gu., a demi-peacock per pale arg. and sa., the wings expanded counterchanged. *Tenez le droit.* *cf.* 103. 13
Clifton, an arm in fess vested az., holding in the hand ppr. a hawk arg. 86. 14
Clifton, Lancs and Yorks, an arm in armour embowed ppr., garnished or, holding in the gauntlet a sword arg., hilted of the second. 195. 1
Clifton-Dicconson, Charles, Esquire, of Wrightington Hall, Lancs: (1) A bezant, thereon a hind's head vert, erased and holding in the mouth a cross crosslet fitchée gu. (*for Dicconson*). (2) A dexter arm in armour embowed ppr., garnished or, holding in the gauntlet a sword in bend sinister, also ppr., hilt and pommel or (*for Clifton*). *Adverso fortior.* 195. 1
Clifton of Clifton, a dexter arm in armour embowed, holding in the hand a sword ppr. *Mortem aut triumphum.* 195. 2
Clifton, Augustus Wykeham, Esquire, of Warton Hall, Lytham, same crest and motto.
Clifton, John Talbot, Esquire, of Clifton and Lytham Hall, Preston, Lancs, same crest and motto.
Clifton-Mogg, William, Brynwern Hall, Newbridge-on-Wye, South Wales: (1) A cock ppr., about the neck a chain or, pendent therefrom an escutcheon arg., charged with a crescent gu. (2) Out of a ducal crest coronet gu., a demi-peacock per pale arg. and sa., the wings expanded counterchanged.
Clifton-Hastings-Campbell, Hon. Gilbert Theophilus Clifton: (1) Issuant from flames or, an eagle with two heads displayed gu., and in an escroll above. *I byde my time.* (2) A bull's head erased sa., armed and gorged with a coronet or (*for Hastings*). (3) A dexter arm embowed in armour, the hand in a gauntlet or, grasping a sword arg., pommel and hilt or (*for Clifton*). *Truth winneth troth.*
Clifton, Baron, *see* Darnley, Earl.

Clinch or **Clynch**, on a hand couped in fess, gauntleted, an eagle rising ppr. 78. 12

Clinkscales, a dexter arm embowed in mail and holding a sword ppr. *Manu forti.*

Clinton, Baron (Hepburn-Stuart-Forbes-Trefusis): (1) In the centre, a gryphon sejant, wings elevated or, resting its dexter claw on an antique shield arg. (*for Trefusis*). *cf.* 62. 11. (2) Dexter, issuant out of a baron's coronet a dexter hand holding a scimitar ppr. (*for Forbes*). *cf.* 213. 5. (3) Sinister, a dexter hand grasping a sword ppr. (*for Stuart*). *Tout vient de Dieu.—Nec timide, nec temere.—Avaunt.* 212. 13

Clinton of London, Herts, and Scotland, out of a ducal coronet gu., five ostrich-feathers arg., banded by a ribbon az. *cf.* 114. 13

Clinton, De, on a mount a stag feeding, all ppr. 116. 9

Clinton, *see* Newcastle, Duke of.

Clippingdale, S. D., Esquire, of 36, Holland Park Avenue, London, W., a sea-horse ppr., holding in its mouth a branch of coral gu., and supporting an anchor erect and cabled or. *Sapientia domus erecta est.* 46. 8

Clipsham, a boar's head couped sa. *Fortiter.* 43. 1

Clitherow, issuing out of a tower arg., a demi-lion rampant sa. 157. 11

Clitherow, Colonel Edward John Stracey, Boston House, Brentford: (1) Out of a tower or, a demi-lion rampant sa. (2) A lion rampant erminois, ducally crowned and supporting a cross patée fitchée gu.

Clive, Viscount, *see* Powis, Earl of.

Clive, *see* Windsor, Baron.

Clive, a boar's head erased at the neck sa. *Credo, ama et regna.* 42. 2

Clive, Percy Archer, of Whitfield, Heref., a griffin passant arg., ducally gorged gu. *Audacter et sincere.*

Clive, General Edward Henry, of 25, Ennismore Gardens, S.W., same crest and motto.

Clive, Lord Clive, Ireland, same crest and motto.

Clive, a horse's head sa., between two wings arg. 51. 3

Clive, a griffin passant with wings addorsed arg., langued gu., ducally gorged or. *Credo, ama et regna.*

Clive, a griffin wings addorsed arg., ducally gorged or. 63. 3

Clive, a hand holding a buckle or. 223. 11

Cloake, out of a plume of five ostrich-feathers an eagle rising, all ppr. *cf.* 80. 6

Clobery, Devonsh., a goat's head erased sa., attired or. 128. 5

Clobery of Bradstone, Devonsh., an antelope's head erased arg., attired or. 126. 2

Clock or **Cloke**, a demi-bear rampant sa. 34. 13

Clode, a demi-lion holding a lozenge pierced arg. *cf.* 10. 2

Cloete, Hendrick, Esquire, of Alphen, Wynberg, Cape Colony, and Alphen Villa, Pretoria, Transvaal, two javelins in pale points upwards, interlaced with as many saltireways, banded gu., between two wings per fesse arg. and gu. *Ubi cras.* 231. 15

Clogston, an eagle with wings expanded. 77. 5

Clogstoun of London, on a mount ppr., a hawk rising, also ppr., belled and crowned with an antique crown or, and charged on the breast with a rose gu. *Turris mihi fortis Deus.*

Cloke, Kent, a demi-bear rampant sa. 34. 13

Clonbrock, Baron (Dillon), of Clonbrock, co. Galway, Ireland, on a chapeau gu., turned up erm., a falcon rising ppr., belled or. *Auxilium ab alto.* *cf.* 87. 1

Cloncurry, Baron (Lawless), of Cloncurry, co. Kildare, Ireland, out of a ducal coronet or, a demi-man in armour in profile, his visor closed, holding in his dexter hand a sword, all ppr., the helmet adorned with a plume of three feathers, the exterior two gu., the centre one arg. *Virtute et numine.*

Clonmell, Earl of (Scott), Bishop's Court, Straffan, co. Kildare, a buck trippant ppr. *Fear to transgress.* 117. 8

Clonmore, Lord, *see* Wicklow, Earl of.

Clopton, Suff., a wolf's head per pale or and az. 30. 5

Close, a garb or. 153. 2

Close, a garb or, pierced transversely by a spear ppr., headed arg. *Clausus mox excelsior.* 153. 8

Close-Brooks, John Brooks, Esquire, Banker, of Birtles Hall, Chelford, Chesh.: (1) A demi-lion arg., charged on the shoulder with a fountain ppr., and holding in the paws a harpoon in bend sinister, also ppr. (*for Brooks*). 12. 14. (2) A garb or, transfixed by a spear fesseways, point to the dexter ppr. (*for Close*). *Finem respice.* 153. 8

Close, Surgeon-Captain Napier, Ravensworth, Chard, a demi-lion arg., holding in the paws a battle-axe. *Fortis et fidelis.*

Close, Robert Campbell, Esquire, of Streyncham, Stanmore, New South Wales, a garb arg. *Fortis et fidelis.* 153. 2

Close, Major Maxwell Archibald, of Drumbanagher, Armagh, out of an Eastern crown a demi-lion vert, holding a battle-axe or, headed arg. *Fortis et fidelis.* *cf.* 15. 4

Close or **Closs**, a boar sa., among weeds vert. 40. 5

Clotworthy, Devonsh., a stag's head erased sa., attired and charged on the neck with two mullets in pale arg., pierced by an arrow or, feathered and headed of the second, vulned gu. *cf.* 121. 2

Clotworthy, Ireland, a boar passant or. 40. 9

Clough of Thorpe Stapleton, Yorks, a demi-lion rampant erm., holding between the paws a battle-axe, the handle sa., headed arg. 15. 4

Clough of Plas Clough, Denbighsh.: (1) A demi-lion rampant az., holding in the dexter paw a sword arg., pommel and hilt or (*for Clough*). 281. 7. (2) An arm embowed, vested az., with a ruffle of point lace arg., holding in the hand ppr. a covered cup or (*for Butler*). *Sine macula macla.* 281. 8

Clough, Lloyd-, Wales: (1) A demi-lion rampant az., holding in the dexter paw a sword erect arg., hilt and pommel or (*for Clough*). 14. 12. (2) A hart trippant arg., attired or, holding in the mouth a snake vert (*for Lloyd*). *Sine macula macla.* *cf.* 117. 8

Clough-Taylor, Edward Harrison, Esquire, of Firby Hall, Yorks, a leopard passant per pale ppr. and erm., the dexter paw resting on a shield of the arms, *i.e.*, a shield erm. on a pale engrailed sa., three lions passant or.

Clough-Taylor, Horatio George, same crest.

Clough, Walter Owen, Esquire, upon a mount vert, in front of a battle-axe erect sa., a leopard's face jessant-de-lis or.

Cloun and **Clun**, a chevalier in armour ppr., holding in his dexter hand a marshal's baton arg., tipped sa. 188. 7

Cloun and **Clune**, a wolf collared and lined holding in the dexter paw a trefoil, all ppr.

Clove, a camel's head couped or. 132. 7

Clovel or **Clovell**, a bull passant gu. *cf.* 45. 2

Clover, George Robert, Esquire, of Ramlé, Birkenhead, Chesh., a camel's head erased or, charged with three trefoils slipped in pale sa., and holding in the mouth a like trefoil. *Ut vinclo vir verbo ligitur.* 300. 6

Clovile, Clovell, Clovyle, and **Clonvyle**, Essex, an ostrich arg., holding in its beak a scroll with this motto, *All is in God. Another:* A demi-ostrich arg., with wings expanded, holding in its beak a nail or. *cf.* 97. 2

Clowberry, a goat's head erased arg., armed or. 128. 5

Clowes of London and Warw., a demi-lion vert, ducally crowned or, holding a battle-axe of the last, headed arg. 15. 4

Clowes, a demi-lion vert, crowned. *Quod tuum tene.*

Clowes, Henry Arthur, Norbury, Ashborne, a demi-lion vert, crowned. *Quod tuum tene.*

Clowes, William, Esquire, of 51, Gloucester Terrace, Hyde Park, London, W., a demi-lion rampant vert, ducally crowned, holding in the dexter paw a battle-axe in bend sinister or, and resting the sinister paw on an escutcheon arg., charged with a crescent az.

Clown, a chevalier in armour ppr., holding in his dexter hand a tilting-spear with a pennon unfolded. *cf.* 188. 2

Clud and **Cludde**, a bull's head per chevron gu. and erm. *cf.* 44. 3

Cludde, Shropsh., an eagle with wings expanded ppr., preying on a coney arg. 79. 6

Cludde of Cluddeley and Orleton, Shroph., a hawk ppr., belled or, preying on a grey coney, also ppr., vulned in the head gu.

Cluff, Richard, Esquire, J.P., of Kildress House, Cookstown, co. Tyrone, a dexter arm in armour embowed holding in the hand a sword, all ppr. *Fide et fortitudine.*

Clulow, Yorks, on a garb in fess a lion passant gardant. 5. 12

Clulow of Echingham, Sussex, a mount vert, thereon a demi-lion az., fretty arg., collared or, holding in the dexter paw an olive-branch vert, and supporting with the sinister a pillar of stone ppr.

Clun and **Clune,** *see* Cloune.
Clun, a wolf collared and lined holding in the dexter paw a trefoil ppr.
Clunie, Scotland, a sand-glass winged. 113. 11
Clunie, Scotland, a tree ppr. 143. 5
Clutterbuck, out of a ducal coronet a hand holding a rose slipped and leaved, all ppr. 218. 11
Clutterbuck of Eastington, Glouc., a buck statant arg., between two laurel-branches ppr.
Clutterbuck, Thomas, Warkworth, Northumb., same crest.
Clutterbuck of London, Middx., and Wilts, a buck sejant gu., between two laurel-branches ppr.
Clutton, Heref., on a mount vert the stump of a tree, thereon an owl, all ppr.
Clutton of Charlton Hall, Chester, a cock or. 91. 2
Clutton-Brock, *see* Brock.
Clyde, Baron (Campbell), on a mural crown a swan sa. *Be mindful.* *cf.* 99. 2
Clyderowe and **Cletherow,** a Roman soldier in complete armour with a spear, all ppr. 188. 4
Clyff and **Clyffe,** *see* Cliffe.
Clynch, a camel's head per fess or and az. 132. 7
Clynch, *see* Clinch.
Clyncke, a lion's head royally crowned, all ppr.
Clyplesby and **Clypsby,** a bull passant sa., plattée. *cf.* 45. 2
Clyve, *see* Clive and Cleve.
Coach of London, a gauntlet erect or, the hand clenched, from the fingers blood dropping gu.
Coach, a stag sejant gu., attired or, between two laurel-branches vert.
Coachman of London, a demi-lion rampant sa., crusily and holding between the paws a cinquefoil arg. *cf.* 10. 2
Coakley, a lion passant or, holding in the dexter paw an eagle's leg erased gu. *cf.* 6. 2
Coane, Scotland, a lily ppr. 151. 2
Coape, a dexter hand holding a sword erect ppr. 212. 9
Coape, a fleur-de-lis arg. 148. 2
Coape-Arnold, Henry Fraser James, Esquire, of Wolvey Hall, near Hinckley, and Goldhanger, Essex, a demi-tiger regardant sa., bezantée, maned and tusked, and holding between his paws a pheon or. *Ut vivas vigila.*
Coates of Eastwood, co. Down, Ireland, on a mount vert, a cock ppr., combed, wattled, and legged gu., and charged with a mullet of the last. *Vigilans et audax.* *cf.* 91. 2
Coates of Whitton, Radnorsh., upon a mount vert, a greyhound couchant arg., collared and lined or, resting the dexter paw on a rose gu. *Est voluntas Dei.*
Coates or **Coats,** a swan's head between two wings arg. 101. 6
Coates or **Cotes,** a cock gu., combed, wattled, and legged or. 91. 2
Coats or **Cotes,** Yorks and Shropsh., a cock ppr., combed, wattled, and legged gu. 91. 2
Coats or **Cotes,** an arm erect couped below the elbow, vested paly of six or and az., cuffed arg., holding in the hand a covered cup or.
Coats, a hand holding a helmet ppr. *Quo paratior.* 217. 12
Coats or **Cotes,** Ireland, two lions' gambs erased supporting a crescent. 39. 6
Coats or **Cotes,** Ireland, a cock ppr. *Watchful and bold* 91. 2
Coats or **Cotes,** Scotland, an anchor ppr. *Be firm.* 161. 1
Coats, Peter, Esquire, Thread Manufacturer, of 5, Garthland Place, Paisley, an anchor cabled and erect ppr. *Be firm.* 161. 2
Coats, James, Esquire, of Ferguslie House, Paisley, N.B., same crest and motto.
Coats, Glen-, Sir Thomas Glen, Bart., formerly **Thomas Coats** of Ferguslie, Paisley, same crest and motto.
Coats, James Monro, Esquire, 26, Upper Brook Street, London, W., an anchor gu. and in an escroll. *Be firm.* 275. 8
Cobb, an elephant passant or. *Virtutis stemmata.* *cf.* 133. 9
Cobb, Kent, out of a ducal coronet or, a demi-leopard rampant ppr.
Cobb, Norf., a swan's head or, holding in the beak a fish.
Cobb of Yarmouth, a duck's head erased or, holding in its beak a herring collared arg.
Cobb, a shoveller sa., beaked and legged or.
Cobb and **Cobbe,** Ireland, a dexter hand per fess gu. and or, brandishing a scimitar ppr. 213. 1
Cobbe of Swaraton, Hants, and of Newbridge, co. Dublin, out of a ducal coronet or, a pelican's head arg., vulning herself gu. *Moriens cano.—In sanguine vita.* *cf.* 98. 2
Cobbe, Lieutenant-General Alexander Hugh, C.B., of Army and Navy Club, out of a ducal coronet gu., a pelican's head and neck vulning itself ppr. *In sanguine vita,* and below the arms, *Moriens cano.*
Cobbe, Lieutenant-Colonel Charles Augustus, of Farnleigh, Baldwin's Hill, East Grinstead, same crest and mottoes.
Cobben, Cobbin, Cobbyn, Cobenn, and **Cobyn,** on a garb in fess a lion passant gardant. 5. 12
Cobbes, a shoveller sa.
Cobbett, Middx., a bird rising or, pellettée, holding in the beak a sprig of laurel ppr. 94. 1
Cobbold, a thunderbolt ppr. 174. 11
Cobbold of Ipswich, a lion passant gardant or. *Rebus angustis fortis.* 4. 3
Cobbold, C. Spencer, the Elms, Bath-easton, Bath, same crest. *Defendo et repugno.*
Cobbold, John Dupuis, the Holywells, Ipswich, same crest.
Cobham, Viscount, *see* Lyttleton.
Cobham, Lord Cobham, a Saracen's head ppr., wreathed about the temples or and gu. 190. 5
Cobham, Kent, an old man's head in profile couped at the shoulders ppr., with a long cap gu., turned up arg., fretty sa., a button at the top or. 192. 2
Cobham, Charles, Esquire, the Shrubbery, Gravesend, an old man's head in profile couped at the shoulders ppr., on the head a cap gu., turned up arg., fretty sa., buttoned upon the top or. *Scire, sapere, facere.* 192. 2
Cobham, Alexander William, Shinfield Manor, near Reading, same crest. *Concordia.*
Cobham, a dexter hand holding a dagger point downwards ppr.
Cobham, a hind's head arg., crowned with a palisado coronet or.
Cobham, Herts, a demi-lion rampant or. 10. 2
Coblegh, Cobleigh, and **Cobley,** an arm in armour embowed in fess, the elbow on the wreath, holding in the hand a sceptre, all ppr. 196. 9
Coblegh, Cobleigh, Coboleche, and **Cobligh,** a cock's head erased gu., combed, wattled, and guttée-d'or, holding in the beak a laurel-branch arg.
Cobley, a swan's neck with two heads ppr., guttée-de-poix, holding in each beak a cross crosslet fitchée arg.
Cobyn, Cobben, Cobbin, Cobbenn, and **Coblyn,** on a garb fesseways a lion passant gardant. 5. 12
Cochet, a talbot passant sa., spotted arg. 54. 1
Cochran, a spear's head and a garb in saltire ppr. *Armis et industria.*
Cochran, Alexander, Esquire, of Balfour, Aberdeen, a black horse passant ppr. *Virtute et labore.* 294. 11
Cochran-Patrick, Neil Kennedy, Esquire, of Woodside, Beith, N.B.: (1) A hand ppr., holding a saltire sa. (*for Patrick*). (2) A horse trotting sa., crined and ungu. or (*for Cochran*). *Ora et labora,* and *Virtute et labore.*
Cochrane, Earl of Dundonald, *see* Dundonald.
Cochrane-Baillie, Baron Lamington, *see* Lamington.
Cochrane or **Cochran,** Scotland, a horse passant arg. 52. 6
Cochrane, John Richard, Esquire, of Calder Glen, Lanarksh., a white horse passant ppr. *Domine in virtute tua.* 294. 11
Cochrane or **Cochran,** a hand issuing from a cloud raising a garb. 223. 12
Cochrane or **Cochran,** Scotland, a dexter hand holding a human heart ppr. *Concordia vincit.* 216. 9
Cochrane or **Cochran,** Scotland, a stag at gaze ppr., attired gu. *Vigilante salus.* 117. 3
Cochrane or **Cochran,** Scotland, a greyhound current arg. *Virtute et labore.* *cf.* 58. 2
Cochrane, Sir Henry, J.P., D.L., of Woodbrook, near Bray, co. Dublin, in front of two tilting-spears in saltire a bay-horse passant, all ppr. *Virtute et labore.* 236. 9
Cochrane, Thomas Belhaven Henry, Esquire, of Carisbrooke Castle: (1) (of augmentation) Issuing out of a naval crown or, a dexter arm embowed, vested az., cuffed arg., the hand holding a flagstaff ppr. thereon hoisted a flag of a rear-admiral of the White, being arg., a cross gu., and thereon the words "St. Domingo" in letters of gold. (2) A horse passant arg. 294. 11
Cock, Norf., an ostrich gu., ducally gorged and holding in the beak a horse-shoe or. 97. 1
Cock, on the stump of a tree ppr., a cock gu. *cf.* 91. 2

Cock or **Cocks,** a chevalier on horseback brandishing a sword, all ppr. 189. 10

Cock, Northumb. and Scotland, a cock ppr. 91. 2

Cock and **Cocke,** a cock arg., combed and wattled gu. 91. 2

Cock, Herts, an ostrich holding in the beak a horse-shoe, all ppr. 97. 8

Cock, Harold, Ridgebourne, Shrewsbury, in front of the stump of an oak-tree, one branch sprouting from the dexter side and fructed ppr., thereon a cock or, holding in the beak a sprig of oak, five mascles conjoined fessewise of the second. *Talent de bien faire.*

Cock, the late Alfred, Esquire, of 8, Kensington Park Gardens, London, W., same crest and motto.

Cockain, Cockayn, Cockayne, Cokaine, and **Cockayne,** a cock's head erased gu., crested and jelloped sa. *Virtus in arduis.* 90. 3

Cockburn, a cock ppr. 91. 2

Cockburn or **Cockburne,** Scotland, a cock gu. *In dubiis constans.* 91. 2

Cockburn, Hon. Sir John Alexander, K.C.M.G., M.D. (London), 10, Gatestone Road, Upper Norwood, a cock crowing ppr. 91. 2

Cockburn, Bart., of that Ilk, Scotland, a cock crowing. *Accendit cantu.—Vigilans et audax.* 91. 2

Cockburn, Admiral the late Sir George, G.C.B.: (1) Out of a naval crown or, two arms embowed, the dexter vested az., holding a pike erect ppr., the sinister habited gu., supporting the upper part of a musket with a bayonet fixed, also ppr. (2) A cock ppr. *Ita.—Vigilans et audax.* 91. 2

Cockburn, Scotland, a cock's head ppr. *I rise with the morning.* cf. 90. 1

Cockburn-Campbell, Bart.: (1) A dexter hand holding a scimitar ppr. Over is the motto, "*Without fear*" (*for Campbell*). (2) A cock ppr. (*for Cockburn*). Motto below the shield, "*Forward.*" 213. 5

Cockburn-Hood of Stainrigg House, Coldstream, N.B., a demi-archer clothed and accoutred ppr. *Swift and sure.—Olim sic erat.*

Cockburn, on a rock ppr., a leopard sejant per fess or and gu. 24. 12

Cockburn, Scotland, a dexter arm holding a broken spear in bend ppr. *Press through.* 214. 10

Cockburn, Surrey, a horse's head arg., bridled gu. *Quo duxeris adsum.* 51. 5

Cocke, a dexter hand couped, holding a dagger in pale, all ppr. 212. 9

Cocke, Scotland, a lion's gamb holding a sceptre in pale, all ppr. cf. 38. 7

Cocke, a bear's head arg., crowned or.

Cockeine, Kent, on a mural coronet arg., a cock of the same, beaked, barbed, and membered gu. cf. 91. 2

Cockell, on a mural coronet or, a cock gu., semée of roundles, resting the dexter claw on an escallop, and holding in the beak a sprig of laurel ppr.

Cocker, Lincs, a lion couchant gardant erm. 7. 10

Cockerham of Hillersdon and Collumpton, Devonsh., a cubit arm erect holding in the hand ppr. an anchor erect sa.

Cockerell, Glouc., within a crescent az., a tiger's face ppr., crowned with an Eastern crown or. 22. 6

Cockerell, between two wings a lion's face ppr. 21. 4

Cockerell, a Roman fasces ppr. 171. 4

Cockerith, a fire beacon ppr. 177. 14

Cockes, a hand holding a lion's gamb erased ppr. 220. 10

Cocket, Herts, a man's head in profile couped at the shoulders ppr., vested vert, the collar or, on the head a cap bendy wavy of the last and az., turned up, indented sa.

Cockett, a poplar-tree ppr. 144. 12

Cockett of Hadsor and Droitwich, Worcs., a man's head in profile couped below the shoulders ppr., on the head, upon a wreath arg. and sa., a cap bendy wavy or and az.

Cockfield, an eagle with wings addorsed, preying on a tortoise. 79. 8

Cockfield or **Cokefield,** on the stump of a tree an eagle with wings addorsed ppr. 79. 12

Cockle, a talbot passant gu., collared arg. cf. 54. 1

Cockman, a demi-eagle displayed sa. 81. 6

Cockram, George Edward, 15, Addison Road, W., a demi-lion rampant arg., holding in the dexter paw a cross crosslet fitchée gu. *Fuimus.*

Cockram, issuing out of clouds a cubit arm holding an anchor erect, the flukes upward ppr.

Cockram, a tree ppr. 143. 5

Cockrell, a leopard's face ppr. 22. 2

Cockridge, a cock ppr. 91. 2

Cockridge, a cock crowing ppr. 91. 2

Cocks, Earl Somers, *see* Somers.

Cocks, a cock ppr. 91. 2

Cocks, a hind's head erased, collared. cf. 124. 5

Cocks, Worcs., a buck lodged ppr. 115. 7

Cocks, Glouc. and Suff., on a mount vert, a stag lodged arg., attired sa. 115. 12

Cocks, John James Thomas Somers, Esquire, of 2, Fawcett Street, Earl's Court, S.W., on a mount vert, a stag lodged and regardant arg., attired and ungu. sa.

Cocks, a chevalier on horseback in armour, brandishing a sword, all ppr. 189. 10

Cocksedge, a cock gu., holding in the beak a violet ppr. cf. 91. 2

Cocksey, a tiger's head couped sa., charged on the neck with a cinquefoil between two bars or.

Cocksey, a bishop's mitre ppr. cf. 180. 5

Cocksey, on a garb in fess a cock ppr. 91. 4

Cockshutt, Lancs and Shropsh., a demi-griffin sa. 64. 2

Cockshutt, Herts, a demi-griffin arg., gorged with a collar gu., guttée-d'eau. cf. 64. 2

Cockworthy and **Cookworthy,** a cock gu. 91. 2

Codd, Norf., a heron's head erased ppr. 104. 11

Codd or **Codde,** England and Ireland, a hawk's leg erased, belled ppr. 113. 8

Codd, a physician's cap sa., tufted or. 180. 7

Codd or **Codde,** a square fort with four towers ppr. 155. 4

Codd, a sea-pie ppr.

Codd, a lion rampant gorged with a mural coronet and charged with two torteaux. cf. 1. 13

Codd of Kensington, Middx., on a mount vert, a lion rampant arg., pellettée, gorged with a mural crown gu., holding between the fore-paws an annulet or, the dexter hind-paw resting on a pellet.

Codd or **Codde,** Ireland, a lion's head erased holding in the mouth a sinister hand ppr. 21. 2

Coddington, Sir William, Bart., of Wycollar, Blackburn, in front of a boar's head erased or, fretty sa., a trefoil slipped vert. *Nil desperandum.*

Coddington and **Codinton,** on a chapeau an eagle, wings expanded and inverted, all ppr.

Coddington, Ireland, a hand holding a sword ppr. 212. 13

Coddington of Oldbridge, Ireland, a wolf's head erased or, charged with a trefoil slipped ppr. *Nil desperandum.* cf. 30. 8

Codenham, a lion's head erased or, langued az., charged on the neck with three trefoils slipped vert. cf. 17. 8

Codham, the same crest.

Codrington, Admiral the late Sir Edward, G.C.B., out of a naval coronet or, the sails arg., inscribed on the band in black letters, "*Navarin,*" the three naval flags of the allied Powers in that action, viz., Russia arg., a saltire az., England the union-jack, and France a white flag, the staves ppr. *Vultus in hostem.*

Codrington, Sir Gerald, Bart., of Dodington, Glouc., out of a ducal coronet or, a dragon's head couped gu. between two dragons' wings chequy or and az. *Immersabilis est vera virtus.*

Codrington, Col. Alfred Edward, of 110, Eaton Square, London, S.W., same crest and motto. *Vultus in hostem.*

Codrington, Sir Gerald William Henry, Bart., J.P., of Dodington Park, Glouc., same crest. *Immersabilis est vera virtus.*

Coe, two swords in saltier ppr., surmounted by a cross crosslet fitched sa. 166. 14

Coe, a martlet sa. *Præsto et persto.* 95. 5

Coe, Norf., an arm in armour embowed ppr., holding in the hand a chaplet vert. 199. 12

Coe, a crane supporting with the dexter claw an anchor, all ppr. 105. 10

Coe, a demi-eagle with two heads displayed. cf. 82. 1

Coesvelt, a demi-lion rampant gu., behind and above the latter a demi-hind salient issuant az.

Coey, Sir Edward, of Belfast, in front of a flagstaff ppr., the flag flowing to the sinister arg., and charged with a sinister hand gu., a greyhound courant, also arg. *Droit en avant.*

Coffield, on a cross fleury fitched gu., between two wings or, a crescent of the last. cf. 166. 8

Coffin, a camel's head erased or, bridled, lined, ringed, and gorged with a ducal coronet sa. *In tempestate floresco.* 132. 9

Coffin, Bart., on the stern of a ship or, a pigeon with wings addorsed arg., holding in the beak a laurel-sprig vert. *Extant recte factis præmia.*

Coffin, a long cross sa. 165. 4

Coffin, Pine-, John, of Portledge, Devonsh.: (1) A martlet az., charged on the breast with two bezants. *cf.* 95. 4. (2) A pine-tree ppr. *In tempestate floresco.* 144. 13

Coffin, Isaac Tristram, Esquire, of Magdalen Islands, British North America, the stern of a man-of-war or, thereon a hooded dove, wings elevated, and in the bill a branch of olive ppr. (a mullet for difference.) *Extant recte factis præmia.*

Coffy of Lynally, King's Co., Ireland, a man riding on a dolphin ppr. *Non providentia sed victoria.* *cf.* 189. 12

Coffyn, a martlet or, between two cinquefoils arg., stalked and leaved ppr. *cf.* 95. 2

Cogan, a lion's head erased gu., semée of mullets of six points or. *cf.* 17. 2

Cogan or **Coggan,** a talbot passant, collared and lined. *Constans fidei.* 54. 5

Cogan, William Henry Ford, M.A., J.P., of Tinode, co. Wicklow, Ireland, a talbot passant ppr., collared and chained or, charged on the shoulder with a cross bottony gu. *Constans fidei.* *cf.* 54. 5

Cogger, an arm in armour embowed holding in the hand a club, all ppr. 199. 6

Coggeshall, Suff., a stag lodged sa., attired or. 115. 7

Coggs of London, out of a mural coronet az., a griffin's head or, charged with a cog sa. *cf.* 67. 10

Coghill, a cock ppr. *Dum vivo canto.*

Coghill of Coghill, Yorks and Oxon., a cock with wings addorsed erm. *cf.* 91. 7

Coghill, Sir John Joscelyn, Bart., D.L., of Coghill, Yorks, on a mount vert, a cock with wings expanded or, beaked, combed, and wattled gu., charged on the breast with a bezant. *Non dormit qui custodit.* *cf.* 91 2.

Coghill, Percy de Geiger, 4, Sunnyside, Princes Park, Liverpool, a cock with wings expanded ppr. *Dum vivo canto.* 298. 4

Coghlan or **Coghlen,** a fret or. 165. 10

Coghlan, Ireland, a demi-lion rampant ducally crowned, holding in the dexter paw a sword, all ppr. *cf.* 14. 12

Coghlan, in a ducal coronet or, a mount vert, thereon a tower arg., issuant therefrom an arm embowed in armour, the hand grasping a scimitar, both also ppr. *Unione minima vigent.*

Coghlan, Major-General Sir William Marcus, Knight Commander of the Most Honourable Order of the Bath, out of an Irish crown or, an arm embowed in armour ppr., charged with a bomb fired sa., the hand grasping a scimitar, both also ppr. *Fortis in arduis.*

Coghlan, late William Maut Hay, Esquire, of 19, Redcliffe Square, S.W., out of an Irish crown or, an arm embowed in armour ppr., charged with a bomb fired sa. *Fortis in arduis.*

Coham of Coham and Dunsland, Devonsh., in front of a plume of five ostrich-feathers arg., two cross crosslets fitched in saltire az. *Fuimus et sub Deo erimus.*

Coham-Fleming, John Blyth, Esquire, of Coham, near Highampton, Devonsh.: (1) A goat's head erased ppr., collared or (*for Fleming*). *cf.* 128. 7. (2) In front of a plume of five ostrich-feathers arg., two cross crosslets fitchée in saltire az. (*for Coham*). *Let the deed show.—Fuimus et sub Deo erimus.*

Cohen, a bear's head couped sa., muzzled gu. 34. 14

Cohen, Samuel, Esquire, of Park Place, Brixton, London, S.W., a demi-lion issuant barry of eight arg. and gu., holding in the dexter paw an acorn slipped ppr. 12. 3

Cohn, Maurice, Esquire, of 21, Grosvenor Place, S.W., and the Range, Shepperton, Middx., upon a mount vert, a lion rampant or, holding between the fore-paws a torch fired ppr. between two maple-leaves of the first. *Lux dei ibi salus.*

Coin, two wings expanded. 109. 6

Cokaine and **Cokayne,** *see* Cockain.

Cokayne, George Edward, Esquire, M.A., F.S.A., of Exeter House, Rowhampton, *Clarenceux King of Arms,* a cock's head erased gu., beaked, crested, and jelloped sa. 90. 3

Cokayne-Cust, Henry John, Esquire, of Cockayne Hatley, Beds, Belton House, Grantham, 8, Carlton House Terrace, S.W.: (1) A lion's head erased sa., collared paly wavy of six arg. and sa. (*for Cust*). (2) A cock's head erased gu., beaked, crested, and jelloped sa. *Esse quam videri.*

Cokayne-Frith, Colin, Esquire, Highfield, Canterbury, above a grove of trees ppr., the sun in splendour or. *Virtus in arduis.*

Coke, Earl of Leicester, and **Viscount Coke,** *see* Leicester.

Coke, a dexter hand couped holding a dagger in pale ppr. 212. 9

Coke, the sun in splendour or. 162. 2

Coke, Colonel William Langton, 30, Nevern Square, S.W., same crest. *Non aliunde pendere.*

Coke of Brookhill Hall, Derbysh., same crest and motto. 162. 2

Coke, Edward Beresford, Esquire, same crest and motto.

Coke, Francis Sacheverell, of the Priory, Titley, same crest and motto.

Coke, Major-General John Talbot, of Trusley Manor, Derbysh., same crest and motto.

Coke of Lower Moor House, Heref., same crest and motto.

Coke, Norf., on a chapeau az., an ostrich ppr., holding in the beak a horse-shoe or. 97. 13

Coke, William H., M.R.C.S., 17, High Street, Ashford, Kent, same crest. *Prudens qui patiens.*

Cokeningham, Yorks, a goat's head erased arg. 128. 5

Coker, Dorset, a Moor's head affrontée ppr., couped at the shoulders, wreathed arg. and gu. 192. 4

Coker, Dorset, a Moor's head in profile sa., wreathed arg. and gu. 192. 13

Coker of Bicester, Oxon., same crest. *Fiat justitia.* 192. 13

Cokerith, a fire-beacon ppr. 177. 14

Cokes, a hand holding a lion's gamb erased ppr. 220. 10

Cokeseged and **Cocksedge,** a cock gu., holding in the beak a violet ppr. *cf.* 91. 5

Cokfeld, out of a ducal coronet a lion's gamb. 36. 12

Cokyll, a talbot passant gu., collared arg. *cf.* 54. 5

Colbarne, out of a ducal coronet or, a stag's head erased arg., attired of the first. *Seur et loyal.* *cf.* 120. 7

Colbatch, Middx., a dexter arm embowed, habited per pale dancettée vert and az., cuffed erm., holding in the hand a pine-apple downwards slipped and leaved ppr.

Colbeck, Beds, on a chapeau gu., turned up erm., a lion's head erased or, pellettée. 17. 9

Colbey, an arm in armour embowed ppr., garnished or, holding in the gauntlet a sword, also ppr. 195. 1

Colborne, Baron Seaton, *see* Seaton.

Colborne, Baron (Ridley-Colbourne): (1) A stag's head couped ppr., gorged with a ducal coronet, and pendent therefrom a bugle stringed gu. (*for Colborne*). (2) A bull passant gu. (*for Ridley*). *Constans fidei.* *cf.* 45. 2

Colborne, Somers. and Wilts, out of a ducal coronet or, a reindeer's head arg., attired of the first. 122. 3

Colborne, George F., Cefn Parc, Newport, Monm., same crest. *Unita vis fortior.*

Colbran, Kent, a stag's head erased or. *Quod sors fert ferimus.* 121. 2

Colbrand, Sussex, a tiger sejant arg., maned or. 27. 6

Colbroke, Colebrook, and **Colebrock,** a spear in pale ppr. 175. 9

Colburn, out of a ducal coronet an antelope's head erased. *cf.* 126. 2

Colby, an arm in armour embowed ppr., garnished or, holding in the gauntlet a dagger ppr., hilt and pommel or. *cf* 196. 5

Colby, an arm in armour embowed ppr., garnished or, holding in the gauntlet a scimitar, all ppr. *cf.* 196. 10

Colby or **Coleby,** an arm in armour embowed ppr., garnished or, holding in the gauntlet a broken sword arg., hilt and pommel gu., embrued ppr.

Colby, Frederic Clarence Coplestone, Esquire, A.K.C., on a wreath of the colours or and az., and between two palm-branches, a dexter arm embowed in armour, the hand in a gauntlet grasping a broken sword, all ppr., and suspended from the hand a palmer's scrip or. *Non omnis frangar.* 196. 2

Colby, Rev. Samuel Reynolds, A.K.C., same crest and motto.

Colchester, Baron (Abbot), of Colchester, Essex, out of a ducal coronet or, a unicorn's head erm., armed, crined, and tufted of the first, between six ostrich-feathers arg., quilled gold. *Deo patriæ amicis.—Perseverando.*

Colchester of London and Warw., a demi-lion ppr., holding between the paws an étoile gu. *cf.* 10. 2

Colchester-Wemyss, Magnard Willoughby, Westbury Court, Westbury-on-Severn, a swan ppr.

Colcleugh, a lion passant gardant or, collared gu., holding an anchor sa. *cf.* 5. 10

Colclough, *see* Biddulph-Colclough.

Colclough or **Colcloughe,** a hind's head ppr., vulned gu. 124. 1

Colclough, Staffs, a demi-eagle displayed sa., ducally gorged or. *cf.* 81. 2

Colclough, Rosborough-, of Tintern Abbey, co. Wexford, Ireland: (1) A demi-eagle displayed sa., gorged with a ducal coronet or (*for Colclough*). *cf.* 81. 2. (2) On a dexter hand in fess a dove close with a branch of olive in his beak, all ppr. (*for Rosborough*). *God is my shield.—His calcabo gentes.*

Colde and **Colfe,** in flames of fire ppr., a ram arg., armed or. *cf.* 131. 13

Coldham of Midhurst, Sussex, a dragon's head gu., pierced with a spear or, headed arg. 72. 10

Coldham of Anmer Hall, Norf., a griffin's head erased gu., transfixed with an arrow arg. 66. 13

Coldham-Fussell, James Cecil, Esquire, of Hodnet, Falcon Street, St. Leonard's, New South Wales, between two laurel-branches ppr., a fusil or, charged with a cross flory sa. *Δια.* 147. 13

Coldicott, a dexter hand ppr., holding a billet gu. *Sum quod sum.* 215. 1

Coldstream, Scotland, a swan naiant with wings addorsed. *Live in hope.* 99. 9

Cole, Earl of Enniskillen, and **Viscount Cole,** *see* Enniskillen.

Cole, Northumb., an arm erect ppr., holding in the hand a scorpion sa. 220. 1

Cole of Holybourne, Hants, a naked arm holding in the hand a scorpion ppr., armed or. *Deum cole regem serva.—Esto quod esse videris.* 220. 1

Cole, Clayton-, Alfred, of 64, Portland Place, same crest. *Fide et fiducia.*

Cole, a bull current winged.

Cole of London, a bull's head couped sa. *cf.* 44. 3

Cole, out of a ducal coronet or, a bull's head gu., armed of the first. 44. 11

Cole, late William Cole, Esquire, Banker, of Exeter, a bull's head couped at the neck sa., armed or, between two branches of oak fructed ppr. *cf.* 43. 12

Cole, Brownlow, Esquire, a bull's head couped sa., attired or, between two branches of oak couped sa., fructed or. *Deum cole regem serva.*

Cole, Rev. William Alston, 21, Morton Crescent, Exmouth, same crest and motto.

Cole, Charles Francis, Esquire, same crest and motto.

Cole, Lancs, a lion's head erased gu., pierced in the neck by an arrow. *cf.* 17. 2

Cole, Essex, a leopard's head erased arg., collared and chained or, holding in the mouth an oak slip vert. *cf.* 23. 10

Cole, Herts, a demi-dragon az., winged or, holding a chaplet vert. *cf.* 73. 10

Cole, Rev. George Lamont, formerly of Wallisford Manor, Wellington, Somers., a demi-dragon ppr., holding between the claws two cross crosslets fitchée in saltire arg. *Deum cole regem serva.* *cf.* 73. 10

Cole, a demi-dragon vert, holding in its dexter claw a javelin armed or, feathered arg. *cf.* 73. 10

Cole, Cornw., a demi-dragon holding an arrow or, headed and feathered arg. *cf.* 73. 10

Cole, Edward Campbell Stuart, of Stoke Lyne, Exmouth, same crest. *Deum cole regem serva.*

Cole, Middx., Oxon., and Ireland, a demi-griffin segreant vert, grasping in its dexter claw an arrow with the point downwards or, barbed and feathered arg. *Deum cole regem serva.* *cf.* 64. 2

Cole, Francis Burton Owen, Esquire, of Brandrum, Monaghan, Lysmeirchion, Denbigh, same crest and motto.

Cole, Somers., an eagle displayed arg. 75. 2

Cole, Somers., an eagle displayed arg., ducally gorged or. *cf.* 75. 2

Cole, Oxon., a bundle of arrows arg., belted and buckled or. 173. 3

Cole-Baker, Lyster, M.D., Bayfield, Kent Road, Southsea, a dexter arm in armour embowed holding in the hand a swan's head erased and ducally gorged. *Honor virtutis satelles.*

Colebrock and **Colebrook,** *see* Colbroke.

Colebrooke, Sir Edward Arthur, Bart., of Crawford, Lanarksh., a wyvern with wings expanded or, resting the dexter claw upon an antique escutcheon gu., *Sola bona quæ honesta.*

Coleby, *see* Colby.

Colegrave, on a mural coronet gu., two arrows in saltier or, flighted arg.

Colegrave of Cann Hall, Essex, and Little Ellingham, Norf., an ostrich-feather erect az., and two arrows in saltire or, barbed and flighted arg., banded by a mural crown gu. *Fidei constans.*

Coleman, a horse's head erased ppr. 51. 4

Coleman of London and Leics., a nag's head erased sa., maned and bridled arg., tasselled or. *cf.* 51. 5

Coleman of Bexley Lodge, Norwich, a cross patonce gu., surmounted by a unicorn's head erased arg., charged with three roses in chevron of the first. *Be just and fear not.*

Coleman, out of a ducal coronet a greyhound's head, all ppr. 61. 7

Coleman, a demi-greyhound sa., collared arg., holding between the feet a mullet of the first. *cf.* 60. 8

Coleman of Merriot, Somers., a bull's head erased gu., charged with a crescent arg. *cf.* 44. 3

Coleman of Brandon Parva, Norf., and of Napier, New Zealand, upon a mount vert, in front of a shepherd's crook erect gu., a lamb grazing arg. *Esto sol testis.*

Coleman, Wilts., a caltrap or, between two wings arg. 299. 11

Coleman, Henry William, J.P., Wyther Lodge, Kirkstall, Leeds, same crest. *Resolve well.—Persevere.*

Colemere and **Colmore,** a harpy with wings expanded ppr. 189. 4

Colemere, Collmore, and **Collymore,** a Moor's head in profile, couped below the shoulders ppr., wreathed or and gu. 192. 13

Colen, a sword and a pastoral staff in saltier.

Colepeper, a falcon with wings expanded arg., beaked, legged, and belled or. 87. 1

Coleridge, Baron (Coleridge), of Ottery St. Mary, Devonsh., on a mount vert, therefrom issuing ears of wheat ppr., in front of a cross gu., an otter, also ppr. *Qualis vita, finis ita.* 134. 7

Coleridge, Devonsh., same crest. *Time Deum cole regem.* 134. 7

Coleridge, Stephen William Buchanan, Esquire, of 7, Egerton Mansions, South Kensington, London, S.W., same crest and motto.

Coleridge, a griffin's head ppr., between two wings or. 65. 11

Coles, on a tower a lion rampant ppr. 157. 12

Coles, Ireland, a horse trotting arg., saddled and bridled sa. *cf.* 52. 2

Coles, out of a ducal coronet or, a demi-dragon vert, holding in the dexter claw an arrow of the first, headed and feathered arg. *cf.* 73. 10

Coles, Somers., on a mount vert, an eagle displayed arg., ducally gorged and membered or. *cf.* 74. 10

Coles, Charles Edward, C.M.G., Cairo, same crest.

Coles, around a marble pillar ppr., garnished or, a snake entwined vert.

Coles of Old Park, Clapham Common, Surrey, upon a mount vert, a column erect entwined by a serpent holding in the mouth a branch of olive, all ppr.

Coles, Colonel Charles Horsman, of 10, Palmeira Avenue, Hove, Sussex, same crest. *Persevere.*

Coles, Edward George, Esquire, same crest and motto.

Coles, an arm in armour embowed ppr., holding in the hand a serpent entwined round the arm vert.

Coles, a hand holding a sword in pale, enfiled with a boar's head couped ppr. 212. 6

Coleshill, Viscount, *see* Digby, Baron.

Colet, a hand holding a battle-axe ppr. 213. 12

Coley, a dexter arm in armour ppr., holding a scimitar arg., hilt and pommel or.

Colfox, out of a ducal coronet or, a demi-wolf gu., devouring a hand arg.

Colfox, out of a tower ppr., a demi-greyhound az., holding a branch vert. 157. 8

Colfox, William, Esquire, of Westmead, near Bridport, a fox ppr., charged on the body with two fleur-de-lis in fesse sa., and resting the sinister paw on a fleur-de-lis gu. *Lux lex, libertas.* 238. 7

Colhoun of Carrickbaldvey, co. Donegal, a buck's head erased per pale vert and arg., charged with two mullets in pale counterchanged. *Viget sub cruce.*

Coling, a demi-griffin segreant ppr., holding between the claws a fusil gu., charged with a crescent arg. *cf.* 64. 2

Colladon, issuing out of the sea a dexter arm ppr., holding an anchor cabled sa. 202. 7

Collamore and **Collmore,** a negro's head and shoulders couped sa., wreathed or and gu. 192. 13

Colland, a fish-wheel or.

Collar, a tiger's head erased or. *cf.* 27. 3

Collard of Barmston, Essex, a demi-lion rampant sa., supporting a cross-bow or.

Collard of Collard and Southcott, Devons., a demi-lion rampant sa., holding a scaling-ladder or.

Collard of Broomfield, Herne, Kent, same crest. *Nomini noceas.*

Collard of Hamilton Terrace, St. John's Wood, London, N.W., in front of a battle-axe erect or, a bull's head erm., erased gu., gorged with a collar vair. *Ubi libertas ibi patria.*

Collas, Jersey, a plain cross or. *Crux spes unica.*

Collay, Chesh., Herts, Warw., an elephant's head gu., between two wings sa.

Colle of Newcastle, Northumb., a dexter hand holding a scorpion ppr. 220. 1

Colledge, Thomas Richard, Esquire, a mount vert, thereon in front of a pomegranate leaved and stalked ppr. a snake nowed, also ppr.

Collee, a griffin segreant arg., armed and beaked or. 62. 2

Collen or **Collin,** Essex, a griffin's head erased or, collared vert. *cf.* 66. 2

Collen and **Collin,** a griffin's head erased or, collared erm. *cf.* 66. 2

Collen, a griffin's head erased vert, collared erm. *cf.* 66. 2

Collen or **Collin,** a demi-griffin or, collared az. *cf.* 65. 8

Collens or **Collins,** Dorset, a dove arg. *Volabo ut requiescam.* 92. 2

Collens and **Collensweil,** a cubit arm holding a firebrand, all ppr.

Colles, Somers., on a mount vert, an eagle displayed arg., ducally gorged and membered or. *cf.* 74. 10

Colles, a griffin's head couped or, between two oak-branches vert, fructed of the first. *cf.* 66. 1

Colles, Ireland, issuing out of a cloud a dexter hand holding a sword wavy, all ppr. 212. 4

Colles of Luckley, Grimley and Leigh Court, Worcs., a sea-pie with wings expanded or, guttée-de-poix, standing on a dolphin lying on its back of the first.

Colles, Richard, Millmount, Kilkenny, a sea-pye sa., guttée-d'eau, seizing on a fish ppr., wounded and bleeding. *Temperato splendeat usu.*

Collet of London and Suff., a hind trippant arg. 124. 12

Collet, Sir Mark Wilks, Bart., D.L., of St. Clere, Ightham, Kent, a hind arg., holding in the mouth a sprig of oak fructed and slipped ppr., and supporting with the dexter fore-leg a rose, also arg., within an annulet sa. *Dum spiro spero.* 262. 5

Collet, Suff., a hind's head erased at the neck arg., gorged with a mural crown sa. *cf.* 124. 3

Colleton, Sir Robert Augustus William, Bart., 158, King Henry's Road, N.W., a stag's head erased ppr. 121. 2

Collett, Suff., a hind's head couped arg., gorged with a collar engrailed sa.

Collett of London and of Locker's House, Hemel Hempstead, Herts, a stag ppr., supporting with the dexter foot an escutcheon sa. 295. 2

Collett, Rev. Edward, of Hayton Vicarage, Retford, same crest.

Colley, a griffin segreant arg., beaked and legged or. 62. 2

Colley, Ireland, a sinister hand holding a bow, all ppr. 214. 5

Colley, co. Kildare, Ireland, a dexter cubit arm habited gu., encircled below the cuff arg. with a ducal coronet or, the hand grasping a scimitar ppr., hilted and pommelled of the third. *Virtutis fortuna comes.*

Colley, George Pomeroy Arthur, Esquire, formerly of Mount Temple, Clontarf, co. Dublin, same crest and motto.

Colley, an arm erect holding a spear in bend ppr., with the banner of St. George appended thereto. *Unica virtus necessaria.*

Colliar or **Collyar,** Staffs, a demi-negro ppr., with pearls in the ears arg., holding in the dexter hand an acorn-branch fructed or.

Collick, a lion passant holding in the dexter paw a cross crosslet fitched. *cf.* 6. 2

Collier, out of a naval coronet or, on the circle the words "*St. Sebastian,*" a cross pattée fitched or, between two wings displayed pean.

Collier, Arthur Bevan, Esquire, of Cartha-Martha, Callington, Cornw., a demi-man affrontée ppr., holding in the dexter hand an oak-branch ppr., fructed or, and resting the sinister hand on an escutcheon az., charged with two keys saltireways or. *Persevere.*

Collier, John Francis, Esquire, of County Court, Liverpool, same crest and motto.

Collier, Mortimer Calmady, Esquire, of Foxhams, Horrabridge, same crest and motto.

Collier, Lieutenant-Colonel Mortimer John, V.D., of Foxhams, Horrabridge, S. Devonsh., same crest and motto.

Collier, William Frederick, Esquire, of Woodtown, Horrabridge, S. Devonsh., same crest.

Collier, a cross pattée fitched between two wings or. *cf.* 110. 7

Collier, a unicorn rampant arg., armed or. 48. 2

Collier, Dorset, a wyvern with wings addorsed arg. 70. 1

Collier, a unicorn's head arg., erased and armed or. 49. 5

Collimore of London, a demi-man in profile, vested gu., the collar turned over and billettée or, on his head a cap gu., wreathed and ensigned with a crescent of the second, and holding in the dexter hand a sceptre or, on the top thereof a crescent arg.

Collin, *see* Collen.

Collin, Notts, a talbot's head erased per fess indented or and arg., eared and charged on the neck with a cross formée gu. 56. 14

Collin, a demi-lion sa., holding in the dexter paw a broken lance or.

Collin, a griffin passant gu. 63. 2

Collin, on a chapeau gu., turned up erm., a griffin passant per pale sa. and gu. *cf.* 63. 13

Collingborne, Northumb., on a roundle quarterly or and az., a cross pattée counterchanged.

Collingborne, Devonsh. and Wilts, a demi-woman ppr., the hair dishevelled or, vested erm., the sleeves gu., holding in the dexter hand a covered cup of the second. *cf.* 183. 4

Collings, a sphere ppr. 159. 1

Collings, Essex, a griffin's head erased or, collared vert. *cf.* 66. 2

Collings, a cubit arm erect, the hand holding a torch, all ppr.

Collings, Charles D'Auvergne, M.D., the Grange, Guernsey, a horse's head erased arg., bridled and charged on the neck with three fleur-de-lis, two and one az. *Fidelis in omnibus.* *cf.* 51. 5

Collington, a stag's head erased ppr. 121. 2

Collingwood, Baron Collingwood: (1) The stern of the *Royal Sovereign* man-of-war in waves between a branch of laurel and a branch of oak, all ppr. (2) A stag at gaze under an oak-tree ppr. *Ferar unus et idem.* *cf.* 116. 12

Collingwood, Norf., a buck's head arg., attired or. 121. 5

Collingwood, Northumb., a stag at gaze in a holly-bush ppr. *Nil conscire sibi.*

Collingwood, Edward John, Esquire, of Lillburn Tower, Alnwick, same crest. *Ferar unus et idem.*

Collingwood, Rev. Robert Gordon, Dissington Hall, ten miles north-west of Newcastle-on-Tyne, same crest, the stag charged for distinction with a cross crosslet sa. *Ferar unus et idem.*

Collingwood, a dove holding in its beak an olive-branch. 92. 5

Collins, Digby, of Truthan, Cornw., a dove with wings expanded ppr. *Volabo ut requiescam.* 94. 2

Collins, John Stephen, Esquire, J.P., of Ardnalee, Carrigro Lane, co. Cork, Ireland, a pelican arg., vulning herself gu., gorged with a plain collar az. *Dant vulnera vitam.*

Collins, Henn-, Hon. Sir Richard, of 3, Bramham Gardens, Earl's Court, London, S.W., same crest and motto.

Collins, a demi-griffin arg. 64. 2

Collins, Shropsh., a demi-griffin segreant or, collared erm. *cf.* 65. 8

Collins of London, Kent, Shropsh., and Sussex, a demi-griffin or, beaked and legged gu., collared erm. *cf.* 65. 8

Collins, Rev. Henry, Knaresborough, a demi-griffin or, armed gu. *Tendimus.*

Collins, J. Rupert, M.D., General Hospital, Cheltenham, same crest. *Grip fast.*

Collins, Somers., a demi-griffin or, collared arg. *Deum et regem.* *Another,* collared erm. *cf.* 65. 8

Collins of Wythall, Walford, Heref.: (1) A demi-griffin or, collared erm. *cf.* 65. 8. (2) A dexter arm embowed habited arg., the hand ppr., holding a scimitar or. *Fide et virtute.—Colens Deum.*

Collins, John Stratford, Whythall, Walford, Ross-sh., crest same as second above. Same mottoes.

Collins, a demi-griffin segreant or, collared with a bar gemelle gu. *Favente Deo et sedulitate.* *cf.* 64. 2

Collins, Kent, a demi-griffin segreant or, beaked, legged, and ducally gorged arg. *cf.* 64. 2

Collins, Major-General Edward Archibald Cowling Hall, Bedale, Yorks, same crest.

Collins, a demi-griffin arg., armed gu. 64. 2

Collins, Charles M., Esquire, of Kelvindale, Lanarksh., a demi-griffin or, holding in his dexter claw a rose gu., and a thistle ppr., both slipped and leaved vert. *Fide et virtute.* *cf.* 64. 2

Collins, Charles Millington, Esquire, of Kelvindale and Maryhill, Lanarksh., a demi-griffin or, holding in the dexter claw a thistle and a rose gu., both slipped and leaved vert. *Fide et virtute.*

Collins, Edward Tennison, Esquire, of St. Edmunds, Howth, co. Dublin, on a wreath of the colours, a demi-griffin segreant or, armed and langued gu., charged on the shoulder and wing with two trefoils slipped in fesse vert. *Favente Deo et sedulitate.*

Collins, Joseph Tenison, Esquire, of Society Street, Ballinasloe, co. Galway, Ireland, on a wreath of the colours a demi-griffin segreant or, armed and langued gu., charged on the shoulder and wing with two trefoils slipped in fesse vert. *Favente Deo et sedulitate.* cf. 64. 2

Collins of Betterton, Berks, a griffin's head erased vert, crowned or. *Per collem collem.* 66. 9

Collins, Rev. John Ferdinando, same crest and motto.

Collins, Oxon., a griffin's head couped. *Si je puis.* 66. 1

Collins, Sussex, a griffin's head erased gu. *Labor omnia vincit.* 66. 2

Collins, Essex, on a chapeau gu., turned up erm., a griffin statant per pale arg. and gu. cf. 63. 13

Collins, William, Esquire, of Rotterdam, Holland, a horse's head couped arg., bridled sa., charged on the neck with three fleur-de-lis, one and two az., and gorged with a wreath of laurel vert. cf. 51. 5

Collins, Devonsh., a camel's head erased ppr. *Sermoni consona facta.* cf. 132. 7

Collins, Ireland, a human heart transpierced by a Passion nail in pale ppr.

Collins, Devonsh., a cubit arm erect holding a lighted torch ppr.

Collins, Arthur Shuckburgh, Hillwood, near Nelson, New Zealand, same crest.

Collins, James Tertius, Esquire, of Churchfield, Edgbaston, Birmingham, in front of a demi-gryphon or, wings vert, gorged with a collar, gemel sa., five lozenges conjoined fesseways of the second.

Collinson, a squirrel ppr. cf. 135. 7

Collinson, Rev. Christopher Barber, Laxton Vicarage, near Newark, and of Beltoft, Belton, Lincs, a squirrel sejant. 297. 15

Collinson, Major-General Thomas Bernard, a squirrel sejant eating a nut ppr. 297. 15

Collinson, a rose gu., between two branches of laurel in orle ppr. 149. 11

Colliray, a martlet flying over a tower, all ppr. cf. 155. 2

Collis, Ireland, a dexter arm throwing a dart ppr. 214. 4

Collis, Edward, Esquire, of Ballinvarig: (1) On a rock a sea-pie ppr., charged on the breast with a cross crosslet or, and feeding on a fish, also ppr. (*for Collis*). 299. 13. (2) A cubit arm erect ppr., charged with two crescents in pale sa., holding in the hand an anchor of the last (*for Supple*). *Mens conscia recti.*

Collis, Lt.-Col. C. Herbert, Hagley, near Stourbridge, Worcs., a sea-pie with wings expanded or, guttée sa., standing on a dolphin lying on its back of the first. *Mens conscia recti.*

Collis, William Henry, 7, Barn Hill Road, Wavertree, Liverpool, same crest. *Finem respice.*

Collis-Sandes, Falkiner Sandes, Esquire, Barrister-at-Law, Oak Park, Tralee, co. Kerry: (1) On a mount vert, a griffin segreant or, collared fleurettée gu. (*for Sandes*). cf. 62. 2. (2) On a rock a sea-pie ppr., charged on the breast with a fountain and preying on a dolphin, all ppr. (*for Collis*). *Virtus fortunæ victrix.*

Collison of East Bilney, Norf., a demi-lion rampant ppr., holding between the paws a cinquefoil or, the centre leaf gu. cf. 10. 2

Collison, a bomb fired ppr. 177. 12

Collison and **Collisone,** Scotland, a falcon's head erased ppr. *Hoc virtutis opus.* 88. 12

Colliver, a hand holding a club ppr. 214. 6

Colliver, a dexter hand couped in fess gu. 221. 6

Collman, *see* Coleman.

Collow, Scotland, a hand holding a dagger in pale ppr. *Pro patriâ semper.* 212. 9

Colls, on a ducal coronet a griffin sejant with wings addorsed ppr., supporting an escutcheon arg. 62. 11

Collumbel, Lincs, on a chapeau gu., turned up erm., a dove close ppr., holding in the beak an ear of wheat or.

Collwell, Cambs, on a chapeau gu., turned up erm., a lion passant arg., gorged with a label of three points gu. cf. 4. 9

Colly, a griffin segreant sa., armed or. 62. 2

Collyear, a dexter hand ppr., holding a key az. 217. 7

Collyear, a unicorn rampant arg., armed and ungu. or. 48. 2

Collyer-Bristow, *see* Bristow.

Collyer, Dorset, a demi-unicorn arg., armed, crined, and ungu. or. 48. 7

Collyer, a unicorn's head couped ppr., maned and horned or.

Collyer, Daniel William, Cormiston, Lanarksh., same crest.

Collyer, a cross pattée fitched or, between two eagle's wings sa. cf. 110. 7

Collyer, a wyvern with wings addorsed sa. 70. 2

Collyer, two lions' heads erased, addorsed, and collared. 18. 2

Collyn, a griffin's head erased or, collared erm. cf. 66. 2

Collyngs, Suff., a nag's head sa., bridled or, the rein hanging down before with a ring at the end of it. cf. 51. 5

Colman, a caltrap or, between two wings arg.

Colman of Carshalton Park, Surrey, in front of two wings arg., each charged with an estoile az., a rock ppr., thereon a caltrap or. *Sat cito si sat bene.* 244. 15

Colman, Jeremiah, Esquire, J.P., D.L., of Gatton Park, Surrey, in front of two wings expanded arg., each charged with an estoile of six points wavy az., a rock ppr., thereon a caltrap or. *Sat cito si sat bene.* 244. 15

Colman, Russell James, Esquire, J.P., D.L., of Bracondale Woods, Norwich, the Clyffe, Corton, Lowestoft, same crest and motto.

Colman, Kent, a greyhound's head sa., gorged with a collar and ring arg., charged with three mullets sa. cf. 61. 2

Colmore, Cregoe-, William Berwick, Esquire, of Moor End, Charlton Kings, Glouc., out of a crescent or, a blackamoor's head in profile wreathed about the temples of the first and gu.

Colne or **Colney,** a talbot sejant per pale sa. and erm., collared arg. 55. 1

Colnet, Hants, a dragon's head ducally gorged and chained ppr. cf. 72. 9

Cologan or **MacColgan,** Ireland, a dexter arm in armour embowed holding a lance transfixing a stag's head couped, all ppr. *Virtus probata florescit.*

Colpepper, a martlet gu. between the horns of an ox.

Colpoys, out of a naval coronet a dexter hand apaumée. cf. 222. 14

Colquhoun, Sir James, Bart., of Colquhoun and of Luss, Dumbartonsh., a hart's head couped gu., attired arg. *Si je puis.* 121. 5

Colquhon, Scotland, a hart's head couped gu., attired arg. *Si je puis.* 121. 5

Colquhoun of Killermont, Dumbartonsh., a stag's head erased ppr. *If I can.* 121. 2

Colquhoun, Scotland: (1) A hart's head couped ppr. 121. 5. (2) A hand holding a buckle. 223. 11

Colquhoun, Bart., of Tilliquhoun, Scotland, a stag's head erased ppr. *Si je puis.* 121. 2

Colquhoun of Kennuoir, Scotland, a buck's head erased ppr. *Si je puis.* 121. 2

Colquhoun of Dunyelder, a laurel-branch slipped ppr. *Dum spiro spero.* 151. 13

Colquhoun of Kilmardony, a stag's head erased ppr. *Festina lente.* 121. 2

Colquhon of Drumpelder, a branch of laurel slipped ppr. *Dum spiro spero.* 151. 13

Colquhoun-Campbell, Rev. John Erskine, of Garscadden: (1) A dexter hand holding a buckle ppr. (2) A boar's head erected and erased or. *Omnia firmat.—Fac et spera.* 223. 11

Colquhoun, an arm from the elbow ppr., vested gu., the cuff indented or, holding a baton of the first, veruled of the last.

Colquhoun - Farquharson - Macdonald of the Crag, Montrose, Angus, St. Martin's Abbey, Perth, Banderan House, and Glenshee Lodge, Blairgowrie, Perthsh., a demi-lion gu., holding in his dexter paw a hand ppr. *Per mare, per terras.*

Colquitt, a hawk rising ducally gorged and belled ppr. 87. 2

Colquitt, Craven-, Fulwar Lewis George, on a chapeau gu., turned up erm., a gryphon statant of the second, beaked or. *Virtus in actione consistit.*

Colshill and **Colsill,** Essex and Cornw., an arm in armour couped at the shoulder, garnished or, holding a gauntlet ppr.

Colshull, an arrow in pale. 173. 5

Colson, two arms couped at the elbow and vested, holding in the hands an escutcheon or. 208. 2

Colston, a ship's boat ppr. 179. 6

Colston of London, a dolphin naiant sa. 140. 5

Colston of Filkins Hall, Oxon., a dolphin naiant ppr. *Go thou and do likewise.* 140. 5

Colston, Charles Edward Hungerford Atholl, Roundway Park, Devizes, a dolphin embowed, all ppr. Motto as above.

Colston, a spear's head in pale, enfiled with a savage's head couped ppr. 191. 7

Colt, the Rev. Sir Edward Harry Dutton, Bart., of 13, St. Leonard's Road, Exeter, a horse passant or. *Vincit qui patitur.* 52. 8

Colt, Suff., a nag's head erm. 50. 13

Colt, Essex, a colt at full speed sa., holding in the mouth part of a broken tilting-spear or, headed az., the remainder lying between his hind-legs. 52. 7

Colt, Suff., a colt passant arg. 52. 6

Colt, Kent, in a fire ppr. a ram arg., attired or. *cf.* 131. 13

Colt, Scotland, a hand throwing a dart ppr. *Transfigam.* 214. 4

Colt, Captain George Frederick Russell, J.P., D.L., of Gartsherrie House, Coatbridge, Lanarksh., N.B., a dexter naked arm embowed holding in the hand an arrow in bend sinister point downwards, all ppr. *Transfigam.* 201. 13

Colter and **Coulter,** Scotland, a harpy gardant ppr. 189. 1

Colthurst, Sir George St. John, Bart., of Ardrum, Inniscarra, co. Cork, a colt statant sa. *Justum ac tenacem.*

Colthurst, Joseph, Esquire, of Dripsey Castle, co. Cork, Ireland, a colt courant sa., charged on the shoulder with a crescent or. *Justum et tenacem.* *cf.* 52. 8

Colthurst, Bowen-, Robert Walter Travers, Esquire, of Oakgrove, co. Cork: (1) A colt courant sa., charged on the shoulder with a crescent or (*for Colthurst*). *cf.* 52. 8. (2) On a mount vert, a falcon close ppr., belled or (*for Bowen*). *Justum et tenacem.* *cf.* 85. 2

Colthurst-Vesey, George, Esquire, J.P., of Lucan House, near Dublin: (1) A hand in armour holding a laurel-branch all ppr. (*for Vesey*). (2) A colt statant sa. (*for Colthurst*). *Sub hoc signo vinces.*

Colthurst, Ireland, on the stump of a tree a crane perched ppr. 105. 12

Colthurst, a greyhound's head sa. between two roses gu., leaved and slipped ppr. 61. 11

Colthurst, Somers., a demi-lion rampant gardant arg. 10. 8

Coltman, Yorks, London, and Leics., a nag's head erased sa., maned and bridled arg., tasselled or. *cf.* 51. 5

Colton, *see* Broomhead-Colton-Fox.

Colton, Chesh., a boar passant arg., armed and bristled or, vulned in the shoulder gu. *cf.* 40. 9

Colton-Fox, John Staveley, Esquire, of Todwick Grange, Sheffield: (1) A fox passant gu., guttée-d'or, resting the dexter fore-paw on an annulet encircling an escallop, both or (*for Fox*). (2) Upon a rock ppr., in front of a cross crosslet erect and fitchée sa., a boar passant arg., charged on the body with two roses gu., barbed and seeded ppr. (*for Colton*). *Per fidem et patientiam.*

Columball, a camel's head ppr. *Pacem amo.* 132. 7

Columbine, on a cap of maintenance a dove. *Audaces fortuna juvat.* *cf.* 92. 2

Colvil and **Colville,** a demi-hind ppr.

Colvil and **Colville,** a demi-stag holding in the mouth a rose ppr. 119. 1

Colvil and **Colville,** Scotland, a hind's head couped ppr. *Obliviscar.* 124. 1

Colvil and **Colville,** Scotland, a hind's head couped arg. *Non obliviscar.* 124. 1

Colvil and **Colville,** Scotland, a hind's head arg., charged with a cross pattée sa *cf.* 124. 1

Colvil and **Colville,** Scotland, a talbot's head arg. *Ad finem fidelis.* 56. 12

Colvil and **Colville,** Scotland, a bull's head. *Ne obliviscaris.* *cf.* 44. 3

Colvil and **Colville,** Scotland, a demi-Hercules with a lion's skin and a club, all ppr. *Oublier ne puis.*

Colvil and **Colville,** a hand in pale issuing from a cloud holding a dagger wavy. 212. 4

Colvile of Gorne, Ireland, a hind's head arg., charged with a cross formée sa. *cf.* 124. 1

Colvile, a greyhound's head erased arg. 61. 4

Colvile, a demi-lion rampant or, holding in the dexter paw a cross moline gu. *cf.* 10. 2

Colvile, Augustus Henry Asgill, Esquire, of 16, Pevensey Road, St. Leonards-on-Sea, on a chapeau gu., a lion statant, tail extended arg., gorged with a label of five points of the first. *Persevere.*

Colvile, Edward Leigh Mansel, Esquire, same crest and motto.

Colvile, Fiennes Middleton, Esquire, C.B., of St. Mildred's, Guildford, same crest and motto.

Colvile, Rev. Gerald Henry, of Weston Rectory, Shifnal, same crest and motto.

Colvile, Henry Algernon, Esquire, same crest and motto.

Colvile, Major-General Sir Henry Edward, K.C.M.G., C.B., of Lullington, Burton-on-Trent, and Lightwater, Bagshot, Surrey, same crest and motto. *cf.* 4. 8

Colvile, Spencer Twisleton, Esquire, same crest and motto.

Colvile, Charles Frederick, 45, Emperor's Gate, South Kensington, on a chapeau gu., turned up erm., a lion statant arg., with extended tail, with a collar of three points of the first.

Colvile and **Colwall,** Kent, a bird rising ppr., holding in the beak a sprig vert. 94. 5

Colville, Lincs, a cock-pheasant with wings elevated ppr., holding in the beak a hawk's bell or.

Colville of Culross, Viscount (Colville), Culross Lodge, West Cowes, a hind's head couped arg. *Oublier ne puis.* 124. 1

Colvill, John Chaigneau, Esquire, a hind's head couped arg., and charged with a cross patée sa. *In hoc signo vinces.*

Colvill, Robert Frederick Steuart, Esquire, B.A., of Coolock House, co. Dublin, same crest and motto.

Colvin, Robert, Esquire, of Lough Eske, co. Donegal, a hind's head couped arg., charged with a trefoil slipped vert. *In hoc signo vinces.* *cf.* 124. 1

Colvin, Forrester Farnell, of Wymarks, Henfield, Sussex, a greyhound's head and neck erased erm., holding in the mouth a trefoil slipped ppr., and gorged with a chevron collar. *Audacter et sincere.* 264. 8

Colvin, Richard Beale, Monkhams Hall, Waltham Abbey, Essex, same crest and motto.

Colvin-Smith, Robert Curzon Molison, M.B., B.C., B.A., Cromer, Norf., an ostrich arg., holding in the beak a horse-shoe or. *Tu ne cede malis.*

Colwell, a talbot statant arg., spotted gu. and sa., collared az. 54. 2

Colwich, a bat displayed ppr. 137. 11

Colwick and **Colwyke,** issuing from a cloud a hand in pale holding a sealed letter, all ppr. 215. 7

Colwick and **Colwyke,** in the sea an anchor in pale ensigned with a dove, holding in its beak an olive-branch, all ppr. 94. 4

Colyar, De, Henry Anselm, 24, Palace Gardens Terrace, Barrister-at-law: (1) A cross crosslet fitchée between two wings. 281. 5. (2) A demi-Moor affrontée ppr. holding in his dexter hand an acorn slipped ppr. *Avance.* 281. 6

Colyear, Ireland, a unicorn rampant arg., armed and crined or. *Avand.* 48. 2

Colyer-Fergusson, Thomas Colyer, Ightham Mote, Ivy Hatch, near Sevenoaks, a dexter hand grasping a broken spear in bend, all ppr. *Vi et arte.*

Comb or **Combe,** Somers., a demi-lion sa., ducally gorged arg. 10. 7

Comb or **Combe,** Scotland, a crane holding in the beak a bunch of clover ppr. *cf.* 105. 14

Comb of Norton Ferrers and Tisburie, Somers., a demi-lion rampant sa., ducally gorged arg. 10. 7

Combe, Abram, of Strathearn, Dunmurry, co. Antrim, a crane holding in its beak a bunch of clover, all ppr. *Res non verba quæso.*

Combe, a dexter arm in armour embowed sa., garnished or, wreathed about the arm arg. and gu., and holding in the hand a broken tilting-spear of the second. 197. 5

Combe, Boyce Harvey, Esquire, J.P., of Oaklands, Westfield, near Battle, Sussex, a dexter arm in armour embowed, wreathed above the elbow with a ribbon, the hand grasping a broken tilting-spear, all ppr. *Nil timere, nec temere.* 197. 5

Combe, Charles, Esquire, of Cobham Park, Surrey, on a mount vert, between two short flagstaves, and flowing from each a pennon gu., a dexter arm in armour embowed ppr., garnished or, and wreathed about the upper part with a ribbon of the second, grasping in the hand a broken tilting-spear, all ppr. *Nil timere, nec temere.* 197. 9

Combe, Charles Harvey, of Cobham Park, Cobham, Surrey, same crest and motto.

Combe, Richard Thomas, Esquire, of Earnshill, Curry-Rivell, near Taunton, a morion in front of a dexter arm embowed in armour, holding a sword ppr., and charged with a pheon sa.

Comber, Suff., a greyhound's head sa., charged with three bezants, two and one. *cf.* 61. 12

Comber of Brotherton House, West Coker, Yeovil, a lynx's head or, pelletée.

Comber, same crest.

Comber, George, Esquire, of Rowley Brow, Knutsford, Chesh., a lynx's head couped or, pelletée.

Comber, John, same crest.

Comberford, Ireland, a peacock in pride ppr. 103. 12

Comberford of Kingsbury, Warw., out of a ducal coronet or, a peacock's head per pale of the last and gu., charged with six roses counterchanged.

Comberford, a dove volant holding in the beak an olive-branch ppr. 93. 10

Comberford, a pestle and mortar sa. 177. 13

Combermere, Viscount (Stapleton-Cotton), of Bhurtpore, in the East Indies, and of Combermere, Whitchurch, Chesh.: (1) A falcon ppr., wings expanded, belled or, holding in the dexter claw a belt ppr., buckled of the second. (2) Of honourable augmentation, upon a mount vert, a soldier of the 3rd Regiment of Light Dragoons mounted, all ppr., in the attitude of charging the enemy, and over the crest, in an escrol az., the word *Salamanca* in letters of gold. (3) Out of a ducal coronet or, a Saracen's head couped at the shoulders affrontée, wreathed round the temples arg. and sa. *In utraque fortuna paratus.*

Comberton, two lion's gambs sa., supporting a Doric pillar arg. 39. 8

Comberton, a demi-savage holding a hammer over his shoulder ppr. 186. 11

Combrey, Scotland, a sheaf of arrows, points upward ppr. *Ad metam.* *cf.* 173. 11

Comerford, a peacock in pride ppr. *So ho ho dea ne.* 103. 12

Comerford, Ireland, out of a ducal coronet or, a peacock's head ppr. *So ho ho dea ne.* *cf.* 103. 2

Comes of London, out of a ducal coronet or, a lion's gamb arg., holding a staff raguly sa., slipped at each end gu.

Commerell of Strood, Sussex, a dexter arm holding in the hand a laurel-branch, all ppr. 219. 9

Commolin, a fir-tree ppr. 144. 13

Compigne, a dexter hand per fesse arg. and az., holding up a covered cup or. 217. 11

Compion, a demi-talbot vert. *cf.* 55. 8

Comport, Kent, a demi-lion arg., charged with a quatrefoil gu., holding a torteau. *cf.* 11. 7

Compson, Shropsh., a garb or. 153. 2

Compton, Earl, *see* Northampton, Marquess.

Compton, a buck at gaze arg., attired or. *Tout bien ou rien.* 117. 3

Compton, Henry Francis, of the Manor House, Hants, a demi-dragon erased with wings elevated, the body enfiled with a ducal coronet. *cf.* 73. 6

Compton, Northamp., on a mount vert, a beacon or, inflamed ppr., on the beacon a label with this motto, *Nisi Dominus.—Je ne cherche qu'un.* 284. 7

Compton, Arthur Ernest, Esquire, in front of a beacon fired a lion couchant, supporting with the fore-paws an esquire's helmet, all ppr. *Nisi Dominus.* 267. 12

Compton, Beaumont Albert, Esquire, same crest and motto.

Compton, George William, Esquire, of Kimberley, South Africa, same crest and motto.

Compton, Henry James, Esquire, same crest and motto.

Compton, Walter George, same crest and motto.

Compton, Glouc., a beacon ppr. *Nisi Dominus.* 177. 14

Compton, Bart. (*extinct*), of Hartbury, a beacon inflamed ppr. *Dum spiro spero.* 177. 14

Compton, on a chapeau purp., turned up erm., a fleur-de-lis gu. *cf.* 148. 2

Compton of Court, co. Limerick: (1) A lion passant ppr., charged on the shoulder with a rose arg. (*for Compton*). *cf.* 6. 2. (2) A lion's head erased ppr. (*for Widenham*). *Clementia in potentia.—Be firm.* 17. 8

Comrie or **Comry**, Scotland, a demi-archer shooting an arrow from a bow, all ppr. *Ad metam.* 187. 6

Comyn, Francis, Ruabon House, Llandudno, an eagle displayed or. *Courage.*

Comyn, on a mount vert, two garbs in saltire or.

Comyn, Durh., two arms embowed, vested erm., holding between the hands ppr. a sheaf of cumin or.

Comyn, Durh., a sheaf of cumin or. 153. 2

Comyns, on a chapeau gu., turned up erm., a bloodhound sejant ppr. 54. 14

Comyns, a demi-unicorn couped holding a staff raguly sa. *Mallem mori quam mutare.*

Comyns, Rev. George Yonge, of Wood, Bishop's Teignton, Devonsh., same crest and motto.

Conacher, John, Esquire, a falcon rising az. *Audaciter et velociter.*

Conarton, Cornw., a talbot's head erased per pale or and gu., collared counterchanged. 56. 1

Conant, Ernest William Proby, of Lyndon House, Rutl., upon a wreath of the colours on a mount vert, a stag ppr. resting the dexter foot on an escutcheon gu., billety or. *Conanti dabitur.*

Concannon, Henry J., of Tuam, co. Galway, same crest and motto.

Concanon, Edmund John, Esquire, of Waterloo, co. Galway, Ireland, an elephant statant ppr., tusked or. *Con can an.—Sagesse sans tache.* 133. 9

Concanon, George Lewis Blake, Esquire, of King's College, Cambridge, same crest and motto.

Conder, Edward, Esquire, of Terry Bank, Kirkby Lonsdale, Westml., in front of a lymphad sa., sails furled and flags and pennons flying, and with oars in action, an anchor fessewise or, the flukes to the dexter. *Je conduis.* 160. 2

Condie, on a ducal coronet or, a lion passant az 6. 6

Conduitt of London, two caducei winged lying in fess or, thereon a peacock's head erased ppr.

Coneley or **Conelly**, a talbot couchant ppr. 54. 11

Conerley, a spaniel sejant ppr. 57. 9

Conesby, a cony sejant arg. 136. 4

Coney of Marton, Lincs, a demi-cony sa., holding a pansy flower purp., stalked and leaved vert.

Congalton and **Congilton**, Scotland, a bee ppr. *Multum in parvo.* 137. 4

Congleton, Baron (Parnell), of Congleton, Chesh., a boar's head erased or, between two wings gu., each charged with two chevronels arg. *Te digna sequere.* 257. 10

Congrave, Berks and Kent, a falcon with wings expanded ppr., belled or. 87. 1

Congreve, Bart., Staffs, a falcon with wings expanded ppr. *Persevere.—Non moritur cujus fama vivit.* 87. 1

Congreve, Berks, a falcon rising ppr. *Non moritur cujus fama vivit.* 87. 1

Congreve of Congreve, Staffs, a falcon rising with wings expanded. *Non moritur cujus fama vivit.* 87. 1

Coningesby, Coningsby, and **Conisbie**, a cony sejant arg. 136. 4

Coningsby, out of a ducal coronet or, a plume of ostrich-feathers, thereon a cony sejant, all ppr.

Coningham, on a ducal coronet or, a mount vert, thereon a stork of the first, in the beak a snake between two cinquefoils stalked and leaved ppr.

Coningham, Ireland, an anchor and sword in saltier ppr. 169. 9

Conlan, Captain George Nugent, a dexter cubit arm erect, vested az., cuffed arg., holding in the hand two laurel-branches ppr., and charged on the sleeve with a garb or, banded vert. *Virtus tutissima.*

Connack, out of a ducal coronet a demi-eagle issuing ppr. 80. 4

Connaught and Strathearn, H.R.H. the Duke of, upon a coronet composed of crosses patée and fleur-de-lis a lion statant gardant or, crowned with a like coronet and differenced with a label of three points arg., the centre point charged with the cross of St. George gu., and each of the other points with a fleur-de-lis az.

Connel or **Connell**, Scotland, a bee volant ppr. *Non sibi.* 137. 1

Connel or **Connell**, a goat current towards a tree, all ppr. 129. 6

Connell, Scotland, a bee erect ppr. 137. 1

Connell of Ashtown, co. Dublin, a stag's head erased arg., charged on the neck with a trefoil slipped vert. 121. 8

Connell, on a dexter hand apaumée in fess a bird perched. *cf.* 86. 8

Connell, a dexter hand ppr., vested sa., holding a rod arg. *Servus servorum Dei.*

Connell, Ireland, out of a tower a demi-griffin segreant ppr. 157. 5

Connellan, Ireland, an owl perched on the stump of an oak-tree ppr. *Iter utrumque.*

Connellan, James Hercules Fitzwalter Henry, Esquire, of Coolmore, Thomastown, co. Kilkenny, same crest and motto.

Connelley, Conelly, and **Conolly**, England and Ireland, a female holding in her dexter hand an anchor, and in her sinister a Saracen's head. 184. 9

Connelley, Connelly, Connely, Connolly, and **Conolly,** a talbot couchant ppr. 54. 11

Connemara, Baron (Bourke), P.C., G.C.I.E., of Connemara, co. Galway, a catamountain sejant gardant ppr., collared and chained or, charged with a mullet for difference. *A cruce salus.* 26. 13

Conner, an arm in armour embowed holding in the hand a dagger, all ppr. 196. 5

Conner, Henry Daniel, 16, Fitzwilliam Place, Dublin, same crest. *Meen sucker reague.*

Conner of Manch House, co. Cork, a dexter arm in armour embowed ppr., garnished or, holding in the hand a short sword ppr., hilt and pommel of the last. *Min, sicker, reag.* 195. 3

Conney of Bassingthorpe, Lincs, a talbot's head or, the tongue hanging out of his mouth distilling blood ppr. *cf.* 56. 12

Conney of Parley, Rutl., on a mount vert, a cony sejant or. *cf.* 136. 4

Connock, out of a ducal coronet an eagle's head and wings issuing ppr. 84. 3

Connocke, Cornw., out of a ducal coronet a demi-griffin segreant, all or. 64. 4

Connolly, *see* Connelley.

Connop, out of the horns of a crescent arg., an arm erect, vested az., cuffed of the first, holding in the hand a branch of oak ppr.

Connor, a hand holding a hawk's lure. 217. 8

Connor, Ireland, out of a ducal coronet a hand ppr., vested sa., holding the sun or. 209. 2

Connor of Corcamroe, a hand gauntleted holding a javelin in bend sinister, point downwards. 217. 8

Connor, James Henthorn Todd, M.R.C.S., L.S.A., Waynflete, Lyford Road, Wandsworth Common, S.W., a dexter arm in armour embowed holding in the hand a short sword ppr. *Activity and valour.*

Connour, Connor, and **Conor,** an arm in armour embowed holding a sword, all ppr. 195. 2

Conny and **Coney,** a cony sejant arg., holding in the mouth a pansy flower ppr., leaved vert.

Connybeare, on a rock a dove, wings endorsed, all ppr., holding a cross patée fitchée gu.

Conolly, a cubit arm erect, vested sa., cuffed arg., holding in the hand a chaplet of roses ppr.

Conolly, an arm in armour erect holding in the hand ppr. an annulet arg.

Conolly, late Charles John Thomas, Esquire, of Midford Castle, Somers., a cubit arm erect, vested az., cuffed arg., charged with a crescent of the last, the hand ppr. grasping a chaplet of roses or. *En Dieu est tout.*

Conolly, Captain Edward Michael, of Castletown, co. Kildare, a dexter cubit arm, vested az., cuffed arg., the hand ppr. grasping a chaplet or. *En Dieu est tout.*

Conolly, John Richard Arthur, Esquire, same crest and motto.

Conqueror, a spear-head ppr. *Victoria.* 174. 12

Conquest, Beds, a holly-tree ppr., fructed gu. 145. 6

Conradus, a unicorn's head erased or, collared sa., studded or. 49. 11

Conran, Scotland, a flame of fire between two palm-branches in orle, all ppr. 146. 12

Conran, a demi-stork with wings expanded holding in the beak a cross patée fitched.

Conran, two doves billing ppr. 93. 2

Conran, William Adam, Esquire, J.P., of Blacklands, Plympton, Devonsh., a hind's head erased arg., charged with a crescent for difference. *In Deo spes mea.* 124. 2

Conran, Gerald Marcell, Esquire, of Bradridge House, South Brent, Devonsh., same crest and motto.

Conran, Henry Arthur Lewis, Esquire, same crest and motto.

Conran, Ireland, a pillar entwined with woodbine ppr. 176. 4

Conroy, Ireland, a lion rampant vert, supporting a pennon gu. *cf.* 3. 7

Conroy, Knt., Ireland, a wreath of laurel ppr. *L'antiquité ne peut pas l'abolir.* 146. 5

Conroy, Sir John, Bart., M.A., of Llanbrynmair, Montgomery, a dexter cubit arm erect, vested or, cuffed erm., the hand grasping a wreath of laurel ppr. *cf.* 205. 6

Considen, *see* Constantine.

Considine, a hand issuing plucking a thistle ppr. 218. 5

Constable, Yorks, a ship in full sail or.

"As to the ship is anchor and cable,
So be thou to thy friend Constable."

160. 13

Constable: (1) A ship in full sail or (*for Constable*). 160. 13. (2) A lion passant arg. (*for Haggerston*). 6. 2

Constable, Surrey, a ship to the sinister sails furled, all or. *cf.* 160. 4

Constable, Strickland-, Henry, of Wassand, Yorks: (1) A ship with tackle, guns, and apparel all, or (*for Constable*). 160. 13. (2) A turkey-cock sa., membered and wattled gu. (*for Strickland*). 108. 5

Constable, Clifford-, Sir Frederick Augustus Talbot, Bart., Yorks: (1) A dragon's head barry of six arg. and gu., charged with nine lozenges or, and holding in the mouth a teazle ppr. (*for Constable*). *cf.* 71. 1. (2) Out of a ducal coronet or, a wyvern rising gu. (*for Clifford*). 70. 9. (3) From behind a body of dark clouds the sun rising from the rays, issuant in chief a lily of France, all ppr., surmounted by a scroll inscribed *Surgit post nubila Phœbus* (*also for Clifford*). *Semper paratus.*

Constable, Chichester-, Walter George R., Wycliff Hall, Darlington: (1) Crest same as first above. (2) A heron arg., devouring a snake vert. Same mottoes.

Constable, Scotland, a greyhound passant arg.

Constable, a greyhound passant ppr., collared gu. *Impiger et fidus.*

Constable, Scotland, out of a cloud in the sinister a hand pointing to a crosier on the dexter ppr. *Præclarior, quo propinquior.* 223. 2

Constable-Maxwell, Baron Herries, *see* Maxwell.

Constable, Ireland, an arm from the shoulder, the hand clenched ppr. 202. 2

Constable-Maxwell, the late Alfred Peter, Esquire, of Terregles, Kirkcudbright, a stag lodged in front of a holly-tree ppr. *Reviresco.*

Constable-Maxwell-Stuart, Henry, Esquire, of Traquair, Peeblessh., and Scarthingwell, Yorks, on a garb a crow ppr. *Judge nought.*

Constant, a human heart between a pair of wings, all ppr. *cf.* 110. 14

Constantine, a lion's gamb erased holding a broken sword ppr. 38. 2

Constantine and **Considen,** a Saracen's head ppr., and on the head a steel cap, the passett or, the ear-pieces tied under the chin with a riband gu.

Constantyne, a sword in bend sinister ppr., surmounted by a cross crosslet az. 166. 12

Contry of Brook, Kent, an ostrich's head and neck or, between two wings expanded az., each charged with a fleur-de-lis, also or. *cf.* 97. 10

Conway, Baron, *see* Hertford, Marquess of.

Conway, Edward, **Viscount de Conway,** in Belgium, the bust of a Moor in profile couped at the shoulders ppr., wreathed about the temples arg. and az., and charged upon the breast with a crescent arg. *Fide et amore.* *cf.* 192. 13

Conway, a Moor's head in profile couped ppr., wreathed arg. and az. *Fide et amore.* 192. 13

Conway of London, out of a ducal coronet a demi-cock with wings expanded gu., beaked and wattled az. 91. 14

Conway, England and Ireland, a Moor's head in profile ppr., banded arg. and az. 192. 13

Conway-Gordon, Francis Ingram, Esquire, of Lynwode Manor, Market Rasen, Lincs, issuing out of a mural crown or, a stag's head at gaze ppr., attired and charged on the neck with a crescent of the first. *Bydand* (below the shield).—*Animo non astutia.*

Conwell, Ireland, out of a ducal coronet or, a staff, also or, with two serpents entwined thereon ppr. *Age in æternum.* *cf.* 170. 13

Conwy, Rowley-, Maurice William, Esquire, of Bodrhyddan, Rhuddlan R.S.O., Flintsh., a wolf's head erased arg., collared and langued gu. (*for Rowley*). *Fide et amore.*

Cony, Cumb., a talbot's head or, the tongue hanging out and dropping blood ppr. *cf.* 56. 12

Cony or **Coney,** a cony sejant arg. 136. 4

Cony or **Coney,** Herts and Hunts, on a mount vert, a cony or. *cf.* 136. 1

Conybeare, Charles Augustus Vansittart, Esquire, of Oakfield Park, Wilmington, Kent, a rock, thereon a dove rising ppr., holding in the dexter foot a cross patée fitchée gu. *Usque conabor.*

Conybeare, Henry Grant Madan, Esquire, of Delmore, Ingatestone, Essex, same crest and motto.

Conyers, Lord (Lane-Fox), *see* Lane-Fox.
Conyers, a trefoil slipped vert. 148. 9
Conyers, Yorks and Durh., a sinister wing gu. *cf.* 109. 7
Conyers of Copped Hall, Essex, a bull's head erased or, armed sa., pierced through the neck with an arrow of the last, barbed and feathered arg., vulned gu. *cf.* 44. 3
Conyers, a Moor's head sa., wreathed and stringed arg. and az. 192. 13
Conyers of Willow Bank, Fulham, a demi-man in armour ppr., his scarf gu., holding in his dexter hand a falchion erect, transfixing a dragon, the head towards the sinister, also ppr.
Conyngham, Marquess (Conyngham), Bifrons, Canterbury, a unicorn's head erased arg., armed and maned or. *Over, fork over* 49. 5
Conyngham of Spring Hill, Ireland: A unicorn's head couped arg., armed and crined or. *Over, fork over.* 49. 7
Conyngham, a dexter arm in armour brandishing in the hand a sword, all ppr. 210. 2
Conyston, out of a ducal coronet or, a peacock's tail ppr. 115. 6
Coo, a crane supporting an anchor, all ppr. 105. 10
Coo, *see* Coe.
Cooch, Colonel Charles, an eagle displayed gu., charged on each wing with two crescents arg., and resting each claw upon a fleur-de-lis or. *Ad diem tendo.*
Cooche, Ireland, a dexter hand couped at the wrist holding a dagger, all ppr., between a pair of wings erect gu.
Coock or **Cook**, a talbot sejant resting the dexter paw on an escutcheon or. 55. 3
Coode, Richard Carlyon, Polapit Tamar, Launceston, a bald-headed coot ppr.
Cook-Altham, *see* Altham.
Cook, Sir Frederick Lucas, Bart., of 24, Hyde Park Gardens, issuing from a chaplet of roses gu., a dexter arm embowed ppr., holding in the hand a mullet of six points or, between two branches of oak vert. *Esse quam videri.*
Cook, Wyndham Francis, Esquire, of 69, Cadogan Square, S.W., same crest and motto.
Cook or **Cooke**, Hants, a dexter arm embowed ppr., holding in the hand a chaplet of laurel vert, surmounted by an étoile arg.
Cook or **Cooke**, Hants, a dexter arm embowed ppr., encircled with a wreath of laurel vert, holding in the hand an étoile or
Cook, Yorks and Northumb., a demi-lion gardant sa., ducally gorged or. *cf.* 10. 8
Cook of London, a demi-lion gu., holding in the dexter paw an étoile or. *cf.* 10. 2
Cook of Dublin, a demi-wolf arg., collared gu., studded or, holding in the dexter paw a fleur-de-lis of the last. *cf.* 31. 5
Cook, a caduceus fesseways ppr., in front of a demi-eagle couped az. *Omnia vincit labor.* *cf.* 80. 2
Cook, Northamp., an eagle displayed or, guttée-de-poix, armed sa., having about the neck a collar of the same. *cf.* 75. 2
Cook, a horse's head and neck couped. *cf.* 50. 13
Cook of London, an ostrich gorged with a ducal coronet holding in the beak a horse-shoe. *Haut et bon.* *cf.* 97. 8
Cook, Beds, an ostrich arg., holding in the beak a horse-shoe of the same. 97. 8
Cook, John, Esquire, W.S., of 11, Great King Street, Edinburgh, a sea-chart ppr. *Tutum monstrat iter.* 270. 1
Cook, Henry, of 22, Eglinton Crescent, Edinburgh, same crest and motto. 159. 11
Cook, John, Esquire, of Aberdeen, same crest and motto.
Cooke, a demi-lion rampant. 10. 2
Cooke of Cordangen, Ireland, a demi-lion rampant gu., holding between the paws a mullet or. *Tu ne cede malis, sed contra audentior ito.* 15. 8
Cooke, a demi-lion rampant erased holding between the paws a bezant. *cf.* 11. 7
Cooke, Sir William Henry Charles Wemyss, Bart., of Wheatley, Yorks, out of a mural crown arg., a demi-lion gardant sa., gorged with a ducal coronet or.
Cooke, Philip Bryan Davies, Esquire, of Owston, near Doncaster, and Gwysaney, near Mold, same crest. *Da Domine quod jubes, et jube quod vis.*
Cooke, Philip Tatton Davies, Esquire, of Maesalyn, Mold, same crest. *Spes tutissima cœlis.*
Cooke, Suff., a lion's head gardant erased arg.
Cooke of Peak, Yorks, a lion's head arg. 21. 1
Cooke of Walgrave, on a mount vert, a demi-unicorn erased, chequy arg. and az., winged gu.
Cooke, Charles Wallwyn Radcliffe, Esquire, M.P., of Hellens, Much Marcle, Heref., a unicorn's head or, between two wings endorsed az. 49. 13
Cooke, Essex and Glouc., a unicorn's head or, between two wings addorsed az. 49. 13
Cooke, a unicorn's head or, between two wings endorsed company gu. and az. *cf.* 49. 13
Cooke, Middx., on a mount vert, a unicorn sejant or, resting the dexter foot on a cross potent gu.
Cooke, Derbysh., the sun in splendour or. 162. 2
Cooke, Kent and Sussex, on a mount vert, a beaver passant or. 134. 4
Cooke, Devonsh. and Cornw., a demi-cat rampant gardant or, holding an oak-branch vert, fructed of the first. *cf.* 26. 12
Cooke, a falcon rising ppr. *Vis courageant fier.* 87. 1
Cooke, a demi-eagle with wings displayed per pale gu. and sa., ducally crowned or. *cf.* 80. 2
Cooke, out of a mural coronet or, an eagle's head arg. 83. 9
Cooke, out of a mural coronet chequy or and gu., an eagle's head arg., beaked or. *Vici.* 83. 9
Cooke, an ostrich holding in the beak a horse-shoe or. 97. 8
Cooke, Suff., on a chapeau sa., turned up erm., an ostrich arg., holding in the beak a horse-shoe of the last. *cf.* 97. 13
Cooke, Norf., on a chapeau az., turned up erm., an ostrich arg., holding in the beak a horse-shoe or. 97. 13
Cooke, George Richard, J.P., Fort William, Borrisoleigh, same crest. *Virtus ardua petit.*
Cooke, John Ormsby, Esquire, J.P., of Kilturra House, Ballymote, co. Sligo, and of Wells, co. Carlow, Ireland, on a chapeau az., turned up erm., an ostrich statant arg., holding in the beak a horse-shoe or, and in an escrol above the crest, "*Sans tache.*"—*Deo favente supero.* 97. 13
Cooke, a griffin's head erased sa., charged on the neck with a bar gemelle arg. 66. 4
Cooke, Scotland, a griffin's head arg. 66. 1
Cooke, Glouc., a griffin's head erased holding in the beak an annulet. *cf.* 66. 2
Cooke, Suff., a griffin segreant sa. 62. 2
Cooke of London, out of a ducal coronet or, a dragon's head arg. 72. 4
Cooke, a cockatrice with wings expanded. 68. 6
Cooke, Suff., a demi-cockatrice with wings addorsed ppr.
Cooke, a boar's head erased ppr. 42. 2
Cooke, Suff., an heraldic antelope's head erased or, semée of torteaux tusked, attired, and tufted gu. *cf.* 127. 4
Cooke, Ireland, a leopard's head erased pean. 23. 10
Cooke of Claines Red Morley, Oliver, and Staunton, Worcs., an heraldic tiger's head erased arg., ducally gorged gu., studded of the first. *Pro rege et patria.*
Cooke, Suff., a wolf's head arg., ducally gorged gu. *cf.* 30. 5
Cooke, Ireland, a demi-wolf arg., holding between the paws a fleur-de-lis az. *cf.* 31. 2
Cooke of Fulwell Heath, Essex, a wolf's head erased erm., holding in the mouth a trefoil slipped per pale or and az. *cf.* 30. 8
Cooke-Collis, Colonel William, D.L., C.M.G., Castle Cooke, Kilworth, co. Cork, a sea-pye sa., collared arg., bezante, preying on a fish ppr. *Mens conscia recti.* 295. 10
Cooke-Collis: (1) A sea-pye preying on a fish (*for Collis*). (2) A demi-lion rampant, (*for Cooke*). 275. 3
Cooke-Hurle, Joseph, Esquire, of Southfield House, Brislington, Bristol: (1) Issuant from the battlements of a tower or, a swan with wings extended arg., and each charged with a cross crosslet fitchée gu. (*for Hurle*). (2) On a mount vert, an eagle's head erased arg., semée of cinquefoils gu. (*for Cooke*). *Confide recte agens.*
Cooke-Trench, Thomas Frederick, Esquire, of Millecent, co. Kildare, Ireland: (1) An armed arm embowed holding a sword, all ppr. (*for Trench*). 195. 2. (2) A demi-wolf arg., holding between his paws a fleur-de-lis az. (*for Cooke*). *Virtuti fortuna comes.* *cf.* 31. 2
Cooke of Mylton, Warw., a wolf's head per pale gu. and or, gorged with two bars counterchanged. *cf.* 30. 5
Cooke, an arm erect vested paly of six or and gu., holding in the hand a bunch of columbines and roses arg., cuffed ppr. *cf.* 205. 14

Cooke, Worcs., out of a mural coronet or, an arm in armour embowed ppr., garnished of the first, holding a sword arg., hilt also or, on the arm two chevrons gu. *cf.* 195. 9

Cooke, J. Reginald, Solicitor, Ashborne, Derbysh., out of a ducal coronet a dexter arm in armour embowed to the sinister holding a scymitar.

Cooke, Norf., out of a mural coronet or, two wings expanded per pale of the first and sa. *cf.* 227. 11

Cooke, Cambs, a greyhound's head couped per pale or and gu., gorged with two bars counterchanged. *cf.* 61. 2

Cooke-Yarborough, Alfred, Esquire, of Hokianga, New Zealand: (1) A falcon close or, belled gold, preying on a mallard ppr. (2) A demi-lion guardant sa., gorged with a ducal coronet or. *Non sine pulvere palma.*

Cooke-Yarborough, Arthur, Esquire, of the Cottage, Wyberton, near Boston, same crest and motto.

Cooke-Yarborough, George Bryan, Esquire, of Campsmount, near Doncaster, same crest and motto.

Cooker, Devonsh., within the horns of a crescent gu., an etoile or. 163. 4

Cookes, out of a ducal coronet or, a negress's head affrontée sa., wreathed, and with ear-rings. *cf.* 182. 2

Cookes, Worcs., a hand holding a dagger ppr. 212. 9

Cookes of Bentley, Worcs., out of a mural coronet an arm in armour holding in the hand a short sword. *Deo, Regi, Vicino.* *cf.* 210. 2

Cookes, Rev. Thomas Horace, of Curraghmore, Banbury, out of a mural coronet or, an arm in armour ppr., charged with two chevronels gu., holding in the gauntlet a sword arg., pommel and hilt gold. *Deo, Regi, Vicino.*

Cookesey and **Cooksey,** on a garb in fess a cock standing ppr. 91. 4

Cookesey, Worcs., a bunch of cinquefoils stalked vert, flowered arg., bound gu.

Cookesey, Worcs., a talbot passant. *Prodesse quam conspici.* 54. 1

Cookesey, Worcs., a wolf's head sa., charged on the neck with a cinquefoil between two bars or. *cf.* 30. 5

Cookman, a griffin's head between two wings expanded or, ducally gorged az. *cf.* 65. 11

Cookson, *see* Hume-Cookson.

Cookson, *see* Fife-Cookson.

Cookson, *see* Saurey-Cookson.

Cookson, a demi-lion rampant bearing a staff raguly ppr. *Nil desperandum.* 15. 1

Cookson, Reynard-, of Whitehill Park, Durh.: (1) A demi-lion ppr., guttée-de-sang, grasping in both paws a club, also ppr. (*for Cookson*). (2) Upon a rock ppr., a wolf's head erased arg., semée of cross crosslets fitchée az. (*for Reynard*). *Ne quid nimis.*

Cookson, Charles George, Esquire, a demi-lion rampant ppr., gorged with a collar nebuly gu., holding in the dexter paw a club, also ppr., and resting the sinister on a spur-rowel, point upwards or.

Cookson, Henry, Theodore of Sturford Mead, Warminster, Wilts, same crest.

Cookson, John Blencowe, of Meldon Park, Morpeth, same crest.

Cookson, William Reginald, Esquire, Binfield Park, near Bracknell, Berks, same crest.

Cookson, a nag's head erased and bridled. *Nos non nobis.* *cf.* 51. 5

Cookson of Bedford, out of a mural crown or, a boar's head gu., gorged with a chain of gold, and transfixed by a spear from the sinister ppr. 244. 12

Cookworthy, *see* Cockworthy.

Cooley, a leopard's face jessant-de-lis or. 22. 5

Cooling, a griffin segreant arg., beaked and legged or. 62. 2

Coombes or **Coombs,** a dexter hand holding a cushion. 215. 9

Coombes or Combs, a dexter hand holding up an escutcheon. *cf.* 219. 7

Coombs, Carey Pearce, M.D., Castle Cary, Somerset, a dexter cubit arm habited holding up an escutcheon.

Coop or **Coope,** a demi-eagle with two heads displayed gu. *cf.* 82. 1

Coope of Rochetts, Brentwood, and of Berechurch Hall, Colchester, a fleur-de-lis or, in front of a dragon's head gu., gorged with a collar vair, all between two roses of the second stalked and leaved ppr.

Cooper, Ashley-, Earl of Shaftesbury, *see* Ashley.

Cooper-Chadwick, Richard, Esquire, of Killenure Castle, co. Tipperary, Ireland: (1) A martlet sa., charged on the breast with a crescent arg., holding in its beak a lily stemmed and slipped ppr. (*for Chadwick*). (2) On a mount vert, a bull passant per pale indented arg. and sa., and gorged with a collar dancettée az. (*for Cooper*). *cf.* 45. 7

Cooper, a demi-leopard gardant holding in the dexter paw a rose-branch slipped ppr.

Cooper, Wilts, a demi-leopard gardant ppr., ducally crowned arg., holding in the dexter paw a holly-branch fructed ppr.

Cooper of Dublin, a demi-lion rampant or. *Noli irritare leonem.* 10. 2

Cooper, James Cooper, Esquire, of Cooper's Hill, Clarina, co. Limerick, same crest and motto.

Cooper, a demi-lion rampant, holding in both paws a battle-axe, all ppr. *Fide et fortitudine.* 15. 4

Cooper, a lion's head arg., erased gu., gorged with a chaplet of laurel ppr. 17. 10

Cooper, Kent, Sussex, and Herts, a lion's gamb erect and erased or, holding a branch vert, fructed gu. *cf.* 37. 4

Cooper, Yorks, a lion sejant arg., supporting a battle-axe in pale sa., headed of the first. 8. 3

Cooper, William Charles, same crest and motto.

Cooper, William Smith Cowper, Toddington Manor, Dunstable, on a gazon vert, a lion sejant erminois holding in his dexter paw a battle-axe, and in the sinister a tilting-spear, all ppr. *Tuum est.*

Cooper, Samuel Joshua, Esquire, of Mount Vernon, Worsborough, near Barnsley, Yorks, on a mount vert, a lion sejant pæan, holding in his dexter paw a battle-axe erect or. *Tout vient de Dieu.* 271. 4

Cooper, Sir Daniel, Bart., G.C.M.G., of 6, De Vere Gardens, Kensington, W., a lion sejant or, collared az., supporting in the dexter paw a lance erect ppr. *Perseverantia omnia vincit.*

Cooper, the late Samuel Thomas, Esquire, of Bulwell, Notts, on a mount vert, in front of two battle-axes in saltire or, headed arg., a lion sejant ppr., collared of the second, supporting with the dexter paw a gad or square plate of steel ppr.

Cooper of Lewes, Sussex, on a mount vert, a lion passant gardant or, the dexter fore-paw resting on an escutcheon gu., charged with a leopard's face of the second.

Cooper, Beds and Middx., on a gazon vert, a lion sejant or, holding in his dexter paw a battle-axe, and in his sinister a tilting-spear, all ppr. *Tuum est.*

Cooper, Norf., out of a mural coronet arg., a spear erect ppr., fringed and tasselled or, pointed arg.

Cooper, Sir Astley Paston, Bart., D.L., of Gadebridge, Herts, out of a mural crown arg., a demi-spear erect ppr., fringed or, pointed arg., and in front thereof two palm-branches in saltire vert. *Nil magnum nisi bonum.* 175. 1

Cooper, Albert Beauchamp Astley, Esquire, of Temple Hill, East Budleigh, Devonsh., out of a mural crown arg., a spear erect ppr., fringed or, headed arg., surmounted of two palm-branches in saltire ppr. *Nil magnum nisi bonum.*

Cooper, Bart. (*extinct*), of Walcot, Somers., on a mount vert, a unicorn sejant arg., armed and crined or, in front of two tilting-spears in saltire, also or.

Cooper, Notts, on a mount vert, a unicorn sejant arg., armed and crined or, supporting a broken tilting-spear of the last.

Cooper of Thurgarton, Notts, a demi-man, his dress divided quarterly and counterchanged arg. and sa., sleeves slashed, and holding in his dexter hand a covered cup or, face and hands ppr., wreathed round the temples or and az., on his head a cap of the last.

Cooper, Harry, M.D., Fownhope, Surbiton Hill, Surrey, same crest. Motto as below.

Cooper of Markree Castle, Sligo, a demi-man affrontée, habited per pale arg. and sa., holding in the dexter hand ppr. a covered cup or, wreathed round the head arg. and az., on his head a cap gu. *Deo patria rege.*

Cooper, Rt. Hon. Edward Henry, P.C., of 42, Portman Square, W., same crest and motto.

Cooper, the late Joshua Harry, Esquire, of Dunboden, co. Westmeath, same crest and motto.

Cooper, William Synge, Esquire, same crest and motto.

Cooper, an arm erect ppr., holding in the hand a chaplet vert. 218. 4

Cooper, Scotland, a dexter arm embowed, holding in the hand a battle-axe ppr. *Pour ma patrie.* 201. 5

Cooper of Failford, Ayrsh.: (1) A dexter hand holding a garland of laurel, both ppr. 218. 4. (2) An oak-tree with a branch borne down by a weight, both ppr. *Virtute.—Resurge.* 143. 10

Cooper, a cubit arm erect holding two branches of laurel disposed in orle ppr. *Virtute.* 218. 4

Cooper, an arm embowed in armour ppr., holding a branch vert. *Frango dura patientia.*

Cooper, William Robert, Mayfield, Norwich, an ostrich holding in the beak a horse-shoe. *Virtute vincet.* 298. 8

Cooper, East Dereham, Norf., a falcon close ppr. 85. 2

Cooper, a phœnix in flames. 82. 2

Cooper, a sand-glass ppr. 177. 15

Cooper, Scotland, between the horns of a crescent an étoile of six points ppr. 163. 4

Cooper, a greyhound sejant sa. 59. 4

Cooper, Northumb., a cock's head erased or. 90. 1

Cooper, Glouc., on a mural coronet arg., a pelican vulning herself ppr. 98. 3

Cooper, Berks, on a garb or, a pelican vulning herself ppr. *cf.* 98. 1

Cooper, Durh., issuing from a tower a Moorish king's head in profile wreathed and chained.

Cooper-Key, on a cap of maintenance gu., turned up erm., a martlet sa. *Paulatim.*

Cooper, an oak-tree, a branch thereof borne down by a weight ppr. *Inclinata resurgo.* 143. 10

Cooper, William Craufurd, Esquire, of Failford, Mauchline, Ayrshire, on the dexter a hand holding a garland of laurel, both ppr. *Virtute.* On the sinister, upon a wreath arg. and az., an oak-tree with a branch borne down by a weight, both ppr. *Resurgo.*

Cooper, on a ducal coronet or, a war-horse passant arg., saddled and bridled gu. 52. 13

Cooper, Ireland, a cockatrice's head erased or, guttée-de-poix, beaked, crested, and jelloped gu. 68. 12

Cooper, a dove holding in its beak an olive-branch ppr. 92. 2

Cooper, George Alexander, Esquire, D.L., of Hursley Park, Winchester, and 26, Grosvenor Square, London, W., a dexter hand grasping a wolf's head erased, all ppr. *Virtute et fortitudine.* 231. 19

Cooper-Cooper, William, Esquire, F.S.A., of Toddington Manor, Dunstable, Beds, on a gazon vert, a lion sejant or and erminois, holding in his dexter paw a battle-axe, and in the sinister a tilting-spear, all ppr. *Tuum est.*

Cooper-Dean, James Edward, Esquire, of Littledown, Christchurch: (1) A demi-lion or, gorged with a collar nebuly, holding in the dexter paw a crescent, and resting the sinister paw upon an increscent, all gu. (*for Dean*). (2) In front of a cubit arm holding in the hand a scroll entwined by a branch of oak, all ppr., an annulet or (*for Cooper*). *Fortis in arduis.*

Coore, a tower triple-towered. 157. 6

Coote, Lincs, Norf., and Essex, a coot's head erased sa. 102. 12

Coote, Sir Algernon Charles Plumptre, Bart., of Ballyfin, Queen's Co., a coot close sa. *Vincit veritas.—Coute que coute.* 100. 10

Coote, Charles Robert Purdon, Esquire, of Ballyclough Castle and Bear Forest, Mallow, co. Cork, same crest and mottoes.

Coote, Eyre, Esquire, of West Park, Damerham, viâ Salisbury, same crest and mottoes.

Cootes, a cubit arm erect, vested paly of four or and az., holding in the hand ppr. a covered cup of the first.

Cope, Thomas, of Osbaston Hall, Leics., in front of a saltire couped az., a greyhound courant or. *Perseverando.* *cf.* 58. 2

Cope, Ireland, a harp gu. 168. 9

Cope, a fleur-de-lis per pale or and arg. 148. 2

Cope, Francis Robert, of The Manor House, Loughgall, Armagh: (1) Out of a fleur-de-lis or, charged with a mullet gu., a dragon's head of the second (*for Cope*). (2) On a chapeau az., turned up erm., a crescent or, therefrom issuant a trefoil slipped vert (*for Doolan*). *Æquo adeste animo.*

Cope, John Garland, Esquire, of Drummilly, Loughgall, co. Armagh, and 14, Pembridge Square, S.W., same crest and motto.

Cope, Sir Anthony, Bart., of Hanwell, Oxon., and Bramshill, Hants, a fleur-de-lis or, a dragon's head issuing from the top thereof gu. *Æquo adeste animo.*

Cope, Ricardo, M.R.C.S., St. Bartholomew's Hospital, London, same crest and motto.

Copeland, *see* Copland.

Copeland, a lion passant ppr. 6. 2

Copeland of Belnagan, co. Meath, Ireland, out of a ducal coronet a swan's head and neck, all ppr. *cf.* 100. 10

Copeland, a nag's head couped, bridled. 51. 5

Copeland, William Taylor, Esquire, a nag's head erased arg., charged on the neck with a trefoil vert, between two holly-branches fructed ppr. *Benigno numine.*

Copeland, Richard Pirie, Esquire, of, Kibblestone Hall, near Stone, Staffs, same crest and motto.

Copeland, William Fowler Mountford, Esquire, of Quarry House, St. Leonard's-on-Sea, same crest and motto.

Copeman, a tower arg., charged with an estoile gu., issuant from the battlements a talbot's head, also gu. *In arce salus.*

Copen, a dexter hand holding a pair of compasses. *Vivitur ingenio.*

Copenger, Norf., a falcon's leg belled and a wing conjoined ppr. 113. 5

Copenger of London, a buck's head arg. 121. 5

Copildike, Copledike, and **Copledyke,** Kent, a wyvern with wings addorsed statant on a wheel ppr. 69. 3

Copinger, Suff., a chamois-deer's head sa. 127. 3

Copinger, Kent, a ram's head sa. 130. 1

Copinger, Walter Arthur, Esquire, of the Priory, Manchester, and Tynycoed Tower, Dinas Mawddwy, Merionethsh., a leg in armour couped at the thigh, flexed at the knee, the foot in chief, the toe pointing to the dexter, all ppr., the spur or. *Virtute et fidelitate.* 193. 3

Copinger, a parrot's head between two wings vert, holding in the beak gu. a sprig of three marigolds ppr., leaved or. *cf.* 101. 10

Copland, Copeland, and **Cowpland,** a hand holding a military sash. 219. 3

Copland, Copeland, and **Cowpland,** a castle triple towered ppr., ensigned with a flag gu., charged with a cross arg. 155. 8

Copland, a horse's head and neck couped, bridled, and decked with oak-slips fructed, all ppr. *cf.* 51. 5

Copland, a nag's head couped arg., bridled between two laurel-branches in perspective vert. *cf.* 51. 5

Copland, a lion rampant winged. 20. 7

Copland of Collieston, Scotland, a knight in armour looking to the dexter, brandishing a sword in his right hand, and bearing in his left an imperial crown, all ppr. *Vici.*

Copland, a chevalier in armour on horseback, holding in his dexter hand a sword. 189. 10

Copland, out of a ducal coronet a swan's head and neck. *cf.* 100. 10

Copland of Aberdeen, a swan with wings addorsed and neck embowed ppr., gorged with a ducal coronet sa. *Æquo adeste animo.* *cf.* 99. 3

Copledike and **Copledyke,** *see* Copildyke.

Coplestone, Dorset and Devonsh., a wolf passant az. 28. 10

Coplestone, Dorset and Devonsh., a demi-heraldic tiger gu., maned and tufted or. 25. 13

Copley, Baron Lyndhurst, *see* Lyndhurst.

Copley, *see* Watson-Copley.

Copley, a dexter arm in armour embowed, wreathed with laurel, and charged with an escallop-shell, and holding a sword. *cf.* 195. 2

Copley, Yorks, a covered cup or.

Copley, Yorks, on a goat's head quarterly arg. and sa., attired or, four crescents counterchanged. *cf.* 128. 12

Copley, Suff., a griffin sejant regardant with wings expanded arg.

Copley, Surrey and Yorks, a griffin sejant arg., ducally gorged and lined or. *cf.* 62. 10

Copley, Bart. (*extinct*), Yorks, out of a ducal coronet or, a plume of four ostrich-feathers arg. 114. 1

Copley, Yorks, out of a ducal coronet or, a plume of eight ostrich-feathers arg., three and five. *In cruce vinco.*

Copley, Bewicke-, Major Robert Calverley Alington, Sprotborough Hall, Doncaster: (1) A ducal coronet or, issuant therefrom a plume of five ostrich-feathers arg., the rim charged with a cross crosslet gu. (2) A goat's head erased arg., armed, maned, and gorged with a mural crown gu. *In cruce vinco.*

Copoldyke, Lincs, a goat's head erased arg., armed and ducally gorged or. *cf.* 128. 5

Coppard, Sussex, a stag regardant arg., attired and ungu. or, collared gu., holding in the mouth two ears of barley couped vert. *In constantia decus.*

Coppard, Kent, a stag regardant arg. *Tutus si fortis.*

Coppen, out of an earl's coronet or, a demi-griffin of the same, armed sa., ducally gorged arg.

Coppen, Hon. George Selth, the Anchorage, Sorren-on-sea, Victoria, out of a ducal coronet a or, demi-griffin az., beaked and legged of the first. *Esse quam videri.*

Coppen, John Maurice, Esquire, of Ascot, Berks, out of the battlements of a tower ppr., a demi-gryphon or, holding between the paws a saltire az. *Copia sine penuria.* 242. 6

Coppendale, Middx., a stag at gaze ppr., attired or. 117. 3

Coppin, Norf., out of a ducal coronet or, a demi-griffin az., beaked and legged of the first. 64. 4

Coppin, on a ducal coronet a cock or. *cf.* 91. 2

Coppinger or **Coppenger,** a demi-lion rampant. 10. 2

Coppinger of London, same crest. *Virtute non vi.* 10. 2

Coppinger of Middleton and of Ballyvolane, Cork, same crest and motto. 10. 2

Coppinger or **Coppenger,** Ireland, a dexter cubit arm ppr., vested or, holding a holly-branch vert.

Coppinger, Suff., a goat's head erased or. 128. 5

Coppull, Lancs, a lion's head erased erm., charged with three guttes-d'or, two and one. *cf.* 17. 8

Copquitt-Craven, Fulwar Lewis George, Esquire, on a chapeau gu., turned up erm., a gryphon statant of the second beaked or. *Virtus in actione consistit.*

Copson, the stump of a tree couped at each end in fess ppr., shooting forth a branch spreading to dexter and sinister vert, ensigned with a fleur-de-lis or. 145. 13

Copwood, Herts, an eagle with wings addorsed or. 75. 8

Coquerel, Guernsey, a cock's neck with two heads erased gu., each collared or.

Cor, Scotland, an increscent and a decrescent or. 163. 7

Coram and **Corham,** Devonsh., a beaver passant or. *cf.* 134. 8

Corbally, Ireland, a trout naiant ppr. 139. 12

Corben, Corbin, and **Corbyn,** a dexter hand ppr., holding a cross pattée fitched az. 221. 12

Corben, Middx., a demi-lion rampant az., holding in his dexter paw a sword ppr. *Sapit qui reputat.* 14. 12

Corben, *see* Corbyn.

Corbet, William Joseph, of Spring Farm, Delgany, co. Wicklow, an elephant and castle. *Deus pascit corvos.*

Corbet, Captain Sir Walter Orlando, Bart., of Moreton Corbet, Acton Reynald Hall, near Shrewsbury: (1) An elephant statant arg., tusked or, the trappings sa., fimbriated gold, on his back a castle triple-towered of the last, and over the crest, upon an escroll the motto, "*Virtutis laus actio.*" 133. 11. (2) A squirrel sejant ppr., cracking a nut or, and over it upon an escroll the motto, "*Dum spiro spero.*" *Deus pascit corvos.* 135. 4

Corbet, Frederick Hugh Mackenzie, Esquire, of 27, Longridge Road, Earl's Court, S.W., same crests and mottoes.

Corbet, Henry Reginald, Esquire, of Adderley, Stoke, Child's Ereall, Market Drayton, same crests and mottoes.

Corbet, Reginald, Esquire, of Adderley Hall, Market Drayton, same crests and mottoes.

Corbet, Reginald George, Esquire, of 27, Longridge Road, Earl's Court, S.W., same crests and mottoes.

Corbet, Edward, of Longnor, Shropsh., a raven ppr., in its beak a holly-branch vert, fructed gu.

Corbet of London, on a mount vert, a squirrel sejant or, cracking a nut of the last leaved vert. 135. 5

Corbet, Rev. George William, B.A., of Sundorne Castle, Shropsh., Prebendary of Lichfield Cathedral, Rural Dean of Wrockwardine, Rector of Upton Magna, on a mount vert, an elephant statant arg., the trappings or and sa., on its back a castle triple-towered of the third, suspended therefrom by a riband gu. an escutcheon of the arms of Corbet, viz.: or, two ravens in pale ppr., a bordure engrailed gu., and for distinction in chief a cross crosslet, also gu. *Deus pascit corvos.* *cf.* 133. 11

Corbet of Towcross, Scotland, a raven's head erased sa. *Save me, Lord.*

Corbett, Lionel Edmund Henry, Esquire, same crest. *Deus pascit corvos.*

Corbett, Reginald William Uvedale, Esquire, of Ashfield Hall, Neston, Chesh., same crest and motto.

Corbett, Richard Cecil, Esquire, of Stableford Hall, near Bridgnorth, Salop, same crest and motto.

Corbett, Uvedale Bennett, Esquire, of Modyn, Chester, same crest and motto.

Corbett, Roger John, Esquire, of Impney, Droitwich, Ynys-y-Maengwyn, Towyn, Merionethsh., in front of a tower gu., an elephant arg., the trappings and saddle-cloth sa., charged with a raven or, and supporting with the trunk a tilting-spear erect ppr. *Deus pascit corvos.* 244. 18

Corbett, Walter John, Esquire, of Impney, Droitwich, same crest and motto.

Corbett, Holland-, Francis, Esquire, of Admington House, Glouc., a raven sa., charged with three ermine spots, two and one or, and holding in the beak a sprig of holly ppr.

Corbett of Warw., formerly of Dumbartonsh., a branch of a tree ppr., thereon a raven sa. *Deus pascit corvos.* 107. 10

Corbett, Archibald Cameron, Esquire, of 26, Hans Place, S.W., same crest and motto.

Corbett, Astley-, Sir Francis Edmund George, Bart., of Elsham Hall, Lincs, on a wreath of the colours an elephant statant arg., tusked or, the trappings sa., fimbriated gold, on his back a castle triple-towered of the last. 133. 11

Corbett, Vincent Charles Stuart Wortley, Chiltern Moor, Fence Houses, an elephant arg., armed or, with a castle triple-towered on the back. *Deus pascit corvos.*

Corbett-Winder, William, Esquire, of Vaynor Park, Berriew, Montgomerysh.: (1) Out of a crown vallery or, a buffalo's head sa., armed gold, in the mouth a branch of cherry-tree fructed ppr. (*for Winder*). (2) A raven, in the beak a holly-branch slipped ppr. (*for Corbett*). *Nulla pallescere culpa*, and *Deus pascit corvos.*

Corbin of Guernsey, a raven with wings elevated ppr., charged on the breast with an ermine spot, and on the wing with a cross pattée fitchée or. *Deus pascit corvos.*

Corbould-Warren, Rev. John Warren, of Tacolneston Old Hall, Norwich: (1) Upon a rock ppr., a wyvern arg., winged barry of six erm. and az. (*for Warren*). (2) Two arms embowed in armour with gauntlets ppr., each charged with a rose gu., and grasping a sword fesseways, point toward the dexter, also ppr., pendent from the blade by a chain an escutcheon or, thereon a raven sa. (*for Corbould*). *Sola virtus invicta.*

Corbreake and **Corbreyke,** a dexter hand holding a roll of paper ppr. 215. 6

Corbreake, a cross crosslet gu. 165. 2

Corby, on a chapeau a dove with wings addorsed, all ppr. 94. 10

Corby, in the sea ppr., a pillar arg. 176. 2

Corbyn, a lion rampant. 1. 13

Corbyn, two arms in armour embowed and in saltier, in the dexter hand a sword, and on the point a boar's head couped, and in the sinister a human heart, all ppr. *cf.* 194. 13

Corcor, *see* Corker.

Cordall, Sussex, a cockatrice vert, beaked, combed, jelloped, and crowned gu. 68. 4

Cordall, Norf. and Suff., a cockatrice vert, wings close, combed and wattled gu.

Cordall of London, a cockatrice vert, collared, combed, wattled, and legged sa. 68. 4

Cordel, Cordell, and **Cordelle,** a demi-savage holding in his dexter hand a scimitar and in his sinister a constable's baton ppr. 186. 14

Cordell, a cockatrice, wings close vert, wattled, beaked, and collared or.

Corderay and **Corderoy,** a human heart gu., ducally crowned or. *cf.* 181. 2

Cordin, a boar's head couped between two serpents in orle, nowed at the top and respecting each other.

Cordingley, out of a coronet vallery or, an arm embowed, vested az., holding in the hand an oak-branch fructed ppr. 205. 1

Cordner, General Edward James, Torbay Mount, Torquay: (1) A dexter arm embowed in armour holding a sword, all ppr. (*Cordner*). (2) An arm in armour erect, the hand grasping an oak-branch acorned, all ppr. (*Kennedy*). *Je suis prest.—Calea spes salutis.*

Cordon, *see* Cordin.

Core and **Corey,** of London and Norf., out of a ducal coronet a griffin's head between two wings or, each wing charged with three estoiles in pale gu. *cf.* 67. 1

Corfield, a hand holding two palm-branches in orle ppr. 218. 7

Corfield, F. J. A., Esq., 15, Gloucester Terrace, Lancaster Gate, London, W., a dexter hand ppr., holding two palm-branches in orle vert. *Palmam qui meruit ferat.*

Corfield, Frederick Channer, Esquire, of Ormonde Fields, Derbysh., and Chatwall Hall, Cardington, Shropsh., in front of a cubit arm erect, the hand grasping two palm-branches in orle, all ppr., a heart gu. *Serva fidem.*

Corham, *see* Coram.

Corie or **Cory**, a griffin's head gu., between wings or, each charged with a mullet of the first. *cf.* 65. 11

Coringham or **Coryngham**, a rook ppr. *cf.* 107. 5

Coriton or **Coryton**, a lion passant gardant gu. *Dum spiro spero.* 4. 3

Cork and Orrery, Earl of (Boyle), K.P., P.C., out of a ducal coronet or, a lion's head per pale, crenellée arg. and gu. *God's providence is my inheritance.* 17. 5

Cork, in front of a tree vert, a Paschal lamb passant with a staff and banner ppr. *cf.* 131. 2

Corke, issuing out of a cloud a hand erect pointing to a star, all ppr. 222. 7

Corker and **Corcor** of Dublin, a human heart ducally crowned between on either side three blades of grass, all ppr. *Sacrificium Deo cor contritum.*

Corker, Ireland, a demi-lion rampant erm., holding in the dexter paw an étoile or. 15. 7

Cormac or **Cormack**, on a rock a martlet, all ppr. *Sine timore.* *cf.* 95. 7

Cormick, Ireland, a hand couped in fess holding a sword in pale, on the point a garland of laurel, all ppr. 221. 7

Cornack, a sword in pale ppr., hilt and pommel or. 170. 2

Corneille, Ireland, a raven ppr. *cf.* 107. 5

Corneilles, a man's arm couped and embowed, the hand holding a branch of vine, fructed, leaved, and slipped, all ppr.

Cornelius, out of a cloud in the sinister a dexter hand in fess ppr., holding a cross patée fitched az. 223. 6

Cornell, Kent, out of a ducal coronet or, a demi-lion rampant arg. *Certum pete finem.* 16. 3

Corner, a lion's gamb erased holding an eagle's leg, also erased. 38. 10

Cornewall, Rev. Sir George Henry, Bart., M.A., of Moccas, Heref. : (1) A Cornish chough ppr. 107. 14. (2) A demi-lion rampant gu., ducally crowned or. *La vie durante.* 10. 11

Cornewall, Herbert Somerset Hamilton, Esquire, of 48, Haggard Road, Twickenham, on a chapeau gu., turned up erm., a lion statant ppr.

Corney, a lion's head erased per pale arg. and gu., charged on the neck with a rose counterchanged. *cf.* 17. 8

Corney of London, a bugle-horn arg., stringed gu. *Fac recte, nil time.* 228. 11

Corney, Hon. Bolton Glanvill, M.R.C.S., of Na Tua, in Yalo, Suva, Fiji, Member of the Legislative Council, a demi-wild-man affrontée, wreathed round the waist and temples with leaves, and supporting a club resting on the dexter shoulder. 185. 2

Cornfoot of Ryde, Isle of Wight, and Petersham, Surrey, a griffin segreant per fesse or and gu., the wings erm., the dexter claw grasping an arrow barbed and flighted ppr., the sinister claw resting on a mullet of the first. *cf.* 62. 2

Cornick of West Alington, Bridport, Dorset, upon a mount vert, a tower arg., in front thereof a garb fessewise.

Corningham, a rock ppr. 179. 7

Cornish-Brown, *see* Brown.

Cornish of Black Hall, Devonsh., a Cornish chough ppr. 107. 14

Cornish of Marazion, Cornw., a Cornish chough sa., wings addorsed, beaked and legged gu., standing on a branch of olive ppr.

Cornish, Kent and Essex, on a branch of a tree couped at each end in fesse ppr., with one sprig at the dexter end vert, a Cornish chough sa., with wings addorsed, beaked and legged gu.

Cornish, an eagle displayed. 75. 2

Cornish, Beds, out of a ducal coronet or, a demi-eagle displayed sa. *cf.* 80. 13

Cornock, *see* Hawkes-Cornock.

Corns, a stag trippant ppr. *Pacem amo.* 117. 8

Cornsley, a lion's gamb holding a sabre in pale ppr. *cf.* 38. 5

Cornwall, Shropsh., a Cornish chough ppr. *La vie durant.* 107. 4

Cornwall, Moses, Esquire, of Kimberley, South Africa, a Cornish chough ppr., holding in its beak a bezant. *La vie durant.* 256. 16

Cornwall, Shropsh. : (1) A Cornish chough ppr. 107. 14. (2) A wyvern gu. Same motto. 70. 1

Cornwall, Scotland, a Cornish chough hatching in the face of a rock, all ppr. *We big, you see, warily.* 102. 6

Cornwall, on a chapeau gu., turned up erm., a lion statant ppr. *cf.* 4. 8

Cornwall, a lion sejant gu., ducally crowned or. *cf.* 8. 8

Cornwall, Berks, a demi-lion rampant gu., ducally crowned or. 10. 11

Cornwall, Dorset, a boar's head couped or, in bend, the blade of a broken sword thrust down the throat ppr.

Cornwallis, Earl (Mann) : (1) A demi-dragon sa., guttée-d'eau (*for Mann*). 73. 10. (2) On a mount vert, a stag lodged regardant arg., attired and ungu. or, gorged with a chaplet of laurel vert, vulned in the shoulder ppr. (*for Cornwallis*). *Virtus vincit invidiam.* *cf.* 115. 9

Cornwallis, Fiennes Stanley Wykeham, Esquire, of Linton Place, Maidstone, Kent, same crest as first above, and same motto.

Cornwallis, Ireland, on a mount a hind statant, all ppr. *cf.* 124. 14

Cornwallis, a lion rampant gardant holding between the paws a ducal coronet, the whole between two standards.

Cornwallis-West, William Cornwallis, Esquire, of Ruthin Castle, Ruthin, Denbighsh., out of a ducal coronet or, a griffin's head az., beaked and eared or. *Jour de ma vie.*

Cornwell, Hubert V., 62, Albert Palace Mansions, Battersea Park, S.W., a demi-lion rampant.

Corp, a yew-tree ppr. 144. 11

Corrance of Parham Hall, Suff., a raven, the dexter claw resting on an escutcheon sa., charged with a leopard's face or. 107. 12

Corre, Ireland, a unicorn's head erased arg. 49. 5

Correy, out of a ducal coronet or, a demi-griffin ppr., the wings semée of trefoils sa. *cf.* 64. 4

Corrie or **Corry**, a demi-Cupid holding a hymeneal torch in pale or, inflamed gu. 185. 8

Corrie or **Corry**, Scotland and Ireland, a cock ppr. *Vigilans et audax.* 91. 2

Corrie, Alfred Wynne, Esquire, of Park Hall, Owestry, Salop, on a wreath of the colours, a cock ppr., holding in the beak a rose arg., leaved and slipped of the first, and resting the dexter claw on a saltire couped of the second. *Vigilans et audax.* 271. 14

Corrie, Edgar Valentine, same crest and motto.

Corrie, Edward Rowland, same crest and motto.

Corrie, Malcolm Stuart, Esquire, same crest and motto.

Corrie, William Malcolm, same crest and motto.

Corrie or **Corry**, Scotland, a demi-lion ppr. *Courage.* 10. 2

Corrigan, the late Sir Dominic John, Bart., M.D., of Merrion Square, Dublin, President of the King and Queen's College of Physicians in Ireland, a sword in pale, point downwards, in front thereof two battle-axes in saltire, all ppr. *Consilio et impetu.*

Corrington, *see* Carrington.

Corry, Lowry-, Earl Belmore and **Viscount Corry**, *see* Belmore.

Corry, Lowry-, Baron Rowton, *see* Rowton.

Corry, Sir William, Bart., of Dunraven, co. Antrim, a cock combed and wattled ppr., charged on the breast with a trefoil slipped vert. *Vigilans et audax.* *cf.* 91. 2

Corry, Thomas Charles Steuart, Esquire, M.D., etc., of Ormeau Terrace and Balmoral, Belfast, eldest son of the late Thomas Charles Steuart Corry, Esquire, J.P., D.L., and M.P. for co. Monaghan, of Rockcorry Castle, co. Monaghan, Ireland, out of a ducal coronet a griffin's head between two wings arg. *Forti tene manu.* 67. 1

Corry, Ireland, a griffin's head couped. 66. 1

Corry, Ireland, a cock holding in its beak an ear of wheat ppr. *Vigilans et audax.* *cf.* 91. 2

Corry, Ireland, an arm erect, vested az., cuffed or, holding in the hand a mill-rind sa. 207. 4

Corsane, Scotland, an eagle close crowned with an antique crown and gazing at the sun, all ppr. *Præmium virtutis gloria.* *cf.* 76. 1

Corsar or **Corser**, Scotland, a pegasus ppr. *Recto cursu.* 47. 1

Corsar, Scotland, a pegasus courant arg., winged and hoofed or. *Recto cursu.* 47. 1

Corse, Scotland, a cross crosslet fitched az. *Certum pete finem.* 166. 2

Corsellis, an antique lamp or, flamant ppr. 177. 5

Corser, Shropsh., a pegasus courant with wings elevated. *Recto cursu.* 47. 1

Corstorphine, a stork's head royally crowned arg. *Fortitur crucem sustine.*

Corstorphine, John Edward Ellice, of Kingsbarnes House, near St. Andrews, same crest and motto.

Corthine, Yorks, a demi-lion couped holding in the dexter paw an étoile, and the sinister resting on a torteau.

Cory, *see* Corie.

Cory of Yarmouth, Norf., out of a ducal coronet or, a griffin's head between two wings expanded ppr. *Virtus semper viridis.* 67. 1

Cory, Isaac R., Shere, Guildford, Surrey, out of a ducal coronet a griffin's head between two wings, each charged with three estoiles.

Cory: (1) A demi-griffin gu., wings expanded vairé or and gu., charged on the breast with an anchor or (*for Cory*). *cf.* 64. 2. (2) A demi-lion gardant ppr., collared sa., supporting a cross patée fitchée arg. (*for Eade*). *Scutum meum Jehova.*

Cory, Clifford John, Esquire, of Llantarnam Abbey, Monmouthsh., and St. Lythiau's, Glamorgansh., on a wreath of the colours (arg. and sa), in front of a griffin's head couped between two wings or, three roses fesseways gu., barbed and seeded ppr. *Virtus semper viridis.* 291. 3

Cory, John, Esquire, of 4, Park Crescent, Portland Place, W., same crest.

Cory, Saxton Campbell, Esquire, of Cranwells, Bath, same crest.

Cory, James Herbert, Esquire, of Tryn-y-pare, Whitchurch, Glamorgansh., in front of a griffin's head erased or, between two wings per pale of the last and gu., three quatrefoils sa. *Cor unum via una.*

Coryngham, *see* Coringham.

Coryton, a marigold ppr. 151. 12

Coryton of Pentillie Castle, Cornw., a lion passant gu. 6. 2

Cosard, Hants, a lion's head erased gu., ducally crowned or. 18. 8

Cosars, a buffalo's head erased ppr. 44. 1

Cosars, issuant from a castle triple-towered a demi-lion rampant ppr. 155. 10

Cosby, a cubit arm in armour holding in the hand two pieces of a broken spear, all ppr. 209. 10

Cosby, Ireland, a griffin segreant gu., supporting the two pieces of a broken spear or, the head arg.

Cosby, Robert Ashworth Godolphin, Esquire, of Stradbally Hall, Queen's Co., a griffin segreant, his wings erect gu., supporting a broken spear or, headed arg. *Audaces fortuna juvat.* 252. 7

Cosen, Norf., and **Cossen,** on a chapeau az., turned up erm., an heraldic tiger sejant or. *cf.* 27. 6

Cosens, a demi-griffin holding in both paws a battle-axe, all ppr. *cf.* 64. 2

Cosens, a cockatrice with wings erect or. 68. 4

Cosgrave, a tiger's head erased affrontée. 23. 3

Cosker, Ireland, a unicorn's head and neck couped or, winged az., charged with a crescent sa. *cf.* 49. 13

Cossar or **Cosser,** a chestnut horse passant ppr., saddled and bridled arg. 52. 4

Cossar or **Cosser,** on a thistle a bee ppr. 150. 9

Cossens, a Doric pillar gu. 176. 3

Cossens, *see* Cosens.

Cosson and **Cossen** of London and Cornw., a lion rampant or, guttée-de sang, ducally crowned of the first. 1. 2

Costello, a falcon close ppr., belled or. *Audaces fortuna juvat.* 85. 2

Costerton of Great Yarmouth, Norf., a lion passant supporting a fire-beacon, all ppr.

Costerton, Norf., on a mount vert, a lion statant erminois, in front of a beacon or, inflamed ppr. *Pro patriâ uro.*

Costley, a hand erect ppr., holding a cross crosslet fitched. 221. 14

Costomer of Yarmouth, on a chapeau gu., turned up erm., a lion or, between two wings of the first, each charged with as many bars of the second.

Cosway, a Moor's head couped at the shoulders ppr. 192. 13

Cosworth of Cosworth, Cornw., and London, a wyvern's head couped az., purfled or, langued gu. 71. 1

Cosyn, on a mount vert, a hare sejant sa., holding a bunch of flowers ppr.

Cosyn, Durh., an eagle. 76. 2

Cosyn, an anchor sa., environed by a serpent vert. 161. 3

Cosyns, *see* Cosins.

Cotell, on a ducal coronet or, a leopard sejant ppr. 24. 11

Coterell, *see* Cotrell and Cotterell.

Cotes of Woodcote, Shropsh., a cock ppr., combed, wattled, and legged or. 91. 2

Cotes, Morton Russell, Esq., F.R.G.S., M.J.S., of East Cliff Hall, Bournemouth, a cock, ppr. *Je defends le cote faible.* 91. 2

Cotes, Leics., a cock ppr., combed and wattled or. 91. 2

Cotes, Arthur, Esquire, of Seagry House, Chippenham, Wilts, a cock ppr., combed and wattled or. *Soli Dei honor et gloria.*

Cotes, Charles, Esquire, of Burcot, Leighton Buzzard, same crest and motto.

Cotes, Charles James, Esquire, of Pitchford Hall, Salop, and Woodcote Hall, Newport, Salop, same crest and motto.

Cotes, Bucks and Leics., a cock or, combed and wattled gu. 91. 2

Cotgrave, Cotgreve, and **Cotgrieve,** a comet-star towards the sinister ppr. *cf.* 164. 10

Cotgrave, out of a ducal coronet or, a demi-peacock ppr. 103. 13

Cotgreave, Knt., Chesh., a demi-peacock arg., charged on the breast with a fess indented gu., the wings elevated or, each charged with an erm. spot. *Antiquum obtinens.*

Cother, a pegasus' head between two wings arg. 51. 3

Cother, a dexter arm in armour embowed ppr., garnished or, holding in the hand, also ppr., a chaplet vert. 199. 12

Coton, Norf., an eagle rising or. 77. 5

Cotrel, Cotrell, and **Cottrell,** a talbot's head erased sa., collared and lined arg., the collar charged with three torteaux. *cf.* 56. 1

Cotrell and **Coterell,** a demi-savage holding in his dexter hand a club, and round the sinister arm a serpent entwined, all ppr. *cf.* 185. 3

Cotsford, out of a ducal coronet a griffin's head ppr. 67. 9

Cottell, Devonsh. and Somers., on a ducal coronet or, a leopard sejant ppr., charged with a crescent. *cf.* 24. 11

Cottenham, Earl of (Pepys), a camel's head erased or, bridled and gorged with a ducal coronet sa. *Mens cujusque is est quisque.* 132. 9

Cotter, Ireland, a lion passant regardant ppr. 6. 1

Cotter, two lion's gambs sa., supporting a pillar arg. 39. 8

Cotter, Sir James Laurence, Bart., of Rockforest, co. Cork, a dexter arm in armour embowed ppr., grasping in the hand a dart. *Dum spiro spero.* 198. 4

Cotterall, Cotterell, and **Cotterill,** a hand holding a glove ppr. 220. 5

Cotterell, Yorks, a talbot's head couped arg., eared and collared or. *cf.* 56. 12

Cotterell, Sir John Richard Geers, Bart., of Garnons, Heref., an arm in armour embowed, the hand in a gauntlet ppr., resting on an escutcheon arg., charged with a talbot's head sa., collared and lined or. *Non rapui sed recepi.*

Cottes, a hound's head or, collared gu., his mouth embrued with blood.

Cottesford, Oxon. and Devonsh., a bear couchant sa., muzzled and collared or. 34. 6

Cottesloe, Baron (Fremantle), of Swanbourne and of Hardwicke, Bucks, a demi-lion gu., issuing out of a mural crown or, holding a banner quarterly arg. and vert, the staff also or, and charged on the shoulder with a plate. *Nec prece, nec pretio.* *cf.* 16. 7

Cottesmore, an arm in armour holding in the hand two pieces of a broken spear ppr. 209. 10

Cottesmore, Oxon., a unicorn couchant arg.

Cottier, Charles Edward, Esquire, upon a fleur-de-lis fesseways, a cock combed and wattled ppr., holding in the beak an oak-leaf slipped vert. *Vigilantibus.*

Cottingham, on a chapeau ppr., a greyhound sejant arg. *cf.* 59. 4

Cottingham, Captain Edward Roden, Royal Marine Artillery, Eastney Barracks, Portsmouth, on a wreath of the colours between two scimitars a Saracen's head couped at the shoulders ppr., wreathed round the temples arg. and az. *Cadere non cedere possum. Utrinque paratus.—Pro rege mutavi.* 298. 11

Cottington, Glouc. and Wilts, a stag's head arg., attired or, gorged with a collar az., charged with three roses of the second. *cf.* 121. 9

Cottle, Somers., out of a crown vallery or, a mount vert, thereon an ounce sejant ppr.

Cotton, Lord Combermere, *see* Combermere.

Cotton, Bart., Cambs, a griffin's head erased arg. *Fidelitas vincit.* 66. 2

Cotton, Suff., a griffin's head erased arg. 66. 2

Cotton, a griffin's head erased holding in the beak a gauntlet ppr. *cf.* 66. 2

Cotton, a hawk's head erased. 88. 12

Cotton, Staffs and Worcs., a hawk ppr., beaked and legged or. 85. 2

Cotton, a hawk ppr., beaked and belled or, holding in the dexter claw a demi-garter sa., buckled of the second.

Cotton, Hants, London, and Shropsh., a falcon with wings expanded arg., beaked and legged or, holding in the dexter claw a belt az., the buckle of the second. 298. 6

Cotton, Charles, M.R.C.S., Hon. Assoc. Order of St. John of Jerusalem in England, 42, Spencer Square, Ramsgate, same crest. *Morum certus amor*

Cotton, Durh., a falcon ppr., beaked and belled or, holding in the dexter claw a belt, also ppr., the buckle of the second. *In utrâque fortuna paratus.*

Cotton, Henry Calverley, Esquire, of Abbeydale, Shrewsbury, same crest and motto.

Cotton-Jodrell, Lieutenant-Colonel and Hon. Col. Edward Thomas Davenant, C.B., of Reaseheath Hall, Nantwich, and Shallcross Manor, Whaley Bridge, Chesh.: (1) A cock's head and neck couped or, wings elevated arg., combed and jelloped gu. (*for Jodrell*). (2) A falcon rising with wings endorsed ppr., holding in the dexter claw a belt az., buckled and garnished or (*for Cotton*). *Vigilando.*

Cotton, Shropsh., a falcon arg., holding in his dexter claw a buckle or.

Cotton, a Cornish chough holding in its beak a cotton-hank, all ppr.

Cotton, Glouc., five snakes tied together ppr., the heads in chief.

Cotton, Surrey, on a mount vert, in front of a lion's head erased gu., gorged with a collar erm., a hank of cotton fesseways arg.

Cotton, Venerable Henry, LL.D., Archdeacon of Cashel, and Rector of Thurles, co. Tipperary, Ireland, out of a ducal coronet a demi-eagle displayed or, charged on the breast with a cross crosslet sa. *With God's blessing.* cf. 80. 14

Cotton, Honourable George Witherage, of Adelaide, South Australia, Member of the Legislative Council, uses an eagle displayed. *Aquila non capit muscam.* 75. 2

Cotton, Hunts, out of a ducal coronet or, a demi-eagle displayed arg. cf. 80. 13

Cotton, Leics. and Staffs, an eagle displayed arg. 75. 2

Cottrell, Yorks, a talbot's head couped arg., eared and collared or. cf. 56. 1

Cottrell, Middx., a talbot's head sa., collared and lined or, the collar charged with three escallops sa. *Nec temere, nec timide.* cf. 56. 12

Cottrell-Dormer, Charles, Esquire, of Rousham and Middle Aston, Oxon.: (1) A fox statant arg. (*for Dormer*). (2) On a wreath of the colours, a talbot's head couped sa., gorged with a collar with chain affixed thereto, between two crosses patée paleways or, the collar charged with three escallops, also sa. (*for Cottrell*). (3) On a ducal coronet or, a horse passant sa., bridled, saddled, and accoutred, also or (*for Upton*). *Semper paratus.*

Cottrell-Dormer, Clement Aldemar, Esquire, of Cokethorpe Park, Oxford, same crests and motto.

Couch and **Couche,** a demi-bear rampant. 34. 13

Coucher and **Cowcher,** a well ppr. 159. 15

Couchman, a demi-lion rampant sa., semée of cross crosslets arg., holding between the paws a cinquefoil of the last.

Couchtree, a hawk's head between two wings. 89. 1

Coudray, Coudrey, and **Coudry,** a lion's gamb erased az., holding a battle-axe or. 38. 3

Coulcher, Yorks, out of a vallery crown a buck's head, all ppr.

Couldwell, a sea-lion rampant vert. 20. 5

Coull, *see* Dixon-Coull.

Coull, a hand holding a book half open in pale, all ppr. *Cole Deum.*

Coulson, Northumb., in a nest ppr., a pelican in her piety arg., vulning herself gu. 98. 14

Coulson, Henry John Wastell, Esquire, of Langton Lodge, Blandford, Dorset, between two spears a pelican in her piety, all ppr. *Je mourrai pour ceux que j'aime.* 264. 14

Coulson of Blenkinsopp, Northumb., a pelican in her piety. Same motto. 98. 14

Coulson and **Coulston,** a dolphin naiant sa. 140. 5

Coulson and **Coulston,** Hants, an eagle with wings addorsed arg., preying on a dolphin ppr.

Coult, Scotland, an arm embowed, the hand grasping a dart, all ppr. *Transfigam.* 201. 13

Coulter, a harpy gardant. 181. 9

Coulthard, Cumb., a demi-lion rampant gu. 10. 3

Coulthart, John Ross, Esquire, of Coulthart, Wigtown, Collyn, Dumfries, and Croft House, Ashton-under-Lyne, Lancs, a war-horse's head and neck couped arg., armed and bridled ppr., garnished or. *Virtute non verbis.* 51. 13

Coulthurst, issuing from clouds two hands grasping the stump of a tree. 224. 10

Coultman, three ears of wheat ppr. cf. 154. 6

Coulton, a lion's gamb supporting an escutcheon. cf. 37. 2

Coults, Scotland, a demi-Moor shooting an arrow from a bow ppr. 186. 6

Couper, Sir George Ebenezer Wilson, Bart., K.C.S.I., C.B., C.I.E., out of a mural crown or, a hand holding a garland ppr. *Virtute.* cf. 218. 4

Couper, Scotland, a hand holding a garland ppr. *Virtute.* 218. 6

Couper, an arm holding a cutlass ppr. cf. 213. 5

Couper, a dexter arm erect, the band clenched gu.

Couper, on a mural coronet arg., a pelican with wings addorsed erm., beaked and legged or, vulned gu. 98. 3

Couper or **Coupir,** a cock's head gu. 90. 1

Couper, Scotland, a dove with a serpent nowed in its beak ppr. 139. 12

Coupland, a salmon naiant ppr. 129. 12

Coupland, Bergne-, *see* Bergne.

Courcy, De, Baron Kingsale, on a ducal coronet, or, an eagle displayed arg. *Vincit omnia veritas.* cf. 75. 2

Courcy, De, out of a mural coronet a hand holding a mullet ppr. cf. 206. 12

Court and **Covert,** out of a ducal coronet or, a unicorn's head arg., armed and crined of the first, charged with a mullet gu. cf. 48. 12

Court, a stag's head erased ppr. 122. 2

Court, A', a lion's head erased regardant. cf. 17. 6

Courtauld of Gosfield Hall, Essex, in front of a fleur-de-lis arg., three mullets fessewise gu. *Tiens à la verite.* cf. 148. 2

Courtauld, George, Esquire, of Cuthedge, Gosfield, Halstead, same crest and motto.

Courtayne, out of an Eastern crown or, a demi-talbot sa. *Salus per Christum.—Per mare, per terras.*

Courteene, Worcs., a demi-talbot sa. cf. 55. 8

Courteis, a demi-husbandman holding over his shoulder a ploughshare.

Courteis and **Courteys,** a wolf's head couped arg., collared and spiked sa., chained or. cf. 30. 11

Courtenay, Earl of Devon, *see* Devon.

Courtenay, a dolphin naiant ppr. 140. 5

Courtenay, a dolphin embowed arg., charged with four torteaux devouring the top of a ducal cap gu., in a coronet or.

Courtenay, out of a ducal coronet or, a plume of seven ostrich-feathers, four and three arg.

Courthope, Kent, a camel's head or, vulned in the neck gu. 132. 7

Courthope, Suff., a demi-stag salient gu., semée d'étoiles and attired or. 299. 14

Courthope, Frederic George, Esquire, of Southover, Lewes, Sussex, same crest.

Courthope, George John, of Whiligh, Ticehurst, Sussex, (Post-town, Hawkhurst,) Kent, a demi-stag salient gu., semée-d'étoiles and attired or.

Courthope, William John, of 29, Chester Terrace, Regent's Park, N.W., same crest.

Courthorp, Sussex, a cubit arm erect ppr., holding in the hand an anchor az., the flukes and ring or.

Courtis, a phœnix in flames ppr. 82. 2

Courtis, an oak-tree. 143. 5

Courtney, Ireland, a cherub with wings in saltier ppr. 189. 13

Courtney, Ireland, a cherub ppr. 189. 9

Courtney, Rt. Hon. Leonard Henry, P.C., 15, Cheyne Walk, a dolphin embowed. *Ut libertate serviamus.*

Courtney, a dolphin naiant arg. 140. 5

Courtney, Guy Budd, M.D., Ramsgate, same crest. *Ubi lapsus quid feci.*

Courtois and **Courtoys,** a mount vert.

Courtois and **Courtoys,** a castle triple-towered. cf. 155. 8

Courtown, Earl of (Stopford), a wyvern with wings displayed vert. *Patriæ infelici fidelis.* cf. 70. 8

Courtry, Kent, a falcon's head or, between two wings az., each charged with a fleur-de-lis of the first. cf. 89. 1

Cousen and **Cousin,** a ram's head erased gu. 130. 6

Cousins, Oxon., a falcon ppr. *Surgam.* 85. 2

Cousins, Scotland, a demi-eagle with wings expanded ppr. *Right and Reason.* 80. 2

Cousmaker and **Coussmaker,** an étoile or. 164. 1

Coussmaker, same crest. *Deo fretus sum.*

Couston, a sword and a garb in saltier, all ppr. 153. 7

Couts, Scotland, a stag's head erased. *Esse quam videri.* 121. 2

Coutts, *see* Bartlett-Burdett-Coutts and Money-Coutts.

Coutts, a demi-centaur ppr.

Cove, a lion's gamb holding a palm-branch ppr. 36. 7

Cove, Heref., out of a ducal coronet or, a dexter arm in armour embowed holding in the gauntlet a battle-axe ppr. *cf.* 200. 6

Covell of London, on a chapeau gu., turned up erm., a lion passant arg., charged with a file of three points gu., each charged with as many bezants. *cf.* 4. 9

Coventon, an heraldic tiger rampant gu., semée of estoiles armed and tufted or, supporting a tilting-spear ppr. *Invidere sperno.*

Coventry, Earl of (Coventry), a garb or, lying fesseways, thereon a cock gu., combed, wattled, and legged of the first. *Candide et constanter.* 91. 4

Coventry, John, Esquire, of Burgate House, Fordingbridge, Hants, a garb or, fesseways, thereon a cock gu., comb, wattles, and legs of the first. Same motto.

Coventry, on a chapeau gu., turned up arg., a cock pheasant ppr., beaked and membered of the first. *cf.* 90. 8

Coverdale and **Coverdall,** a lion rampant per fess or and gu. 1. 13

Covert, Sussex, Kent, and Surrey, a leopard's face or. 22. 2

Covert, Somers., out of a ducal coronet or, a unicorn's head arg., armed and crined of the first, charged with a mullet gu. *cf.* 48. 12

Covill and **Coville,** an arm in armour embowed ppr., bound with a shoulder ribbon tied in a knot gu., holding in the hand a club of the first. 199. 3

Cow, Cowe, Cowee, Cowey, and **Cowie,** a feather in pale ppr. *cf.* 114. 12

Cowan of Bo'ness, an escallop-shell or. *Sic itur in altum.* 141. 12

Cowan, the late Charles, Esquire, of Logan House and Westerlee, Edinburgh, and James Cowan, Esquire, of Edinburgh, an escallop arg. *Sic itur in altum.* 141. 14

Cowan, Charles William, Esquire, of Valleyfield, Penicuik, Midlothian, N.B., same crest and motto.

Cowan, John Marshall, M.D., 14, Woodside Crescent, Glasgow, an escallop or. *Sic itur in altum.*

Cowan, Robert William, Esquire, of Cochrane, N. W. T., Canada, same crest and motto.

Cowan, issuing out of clouds ppr., a cubit arm erect, also ppr., holding in the hand a heart gu. 216. 5

Cowan, James, Esquire, of Ross Hall, Renfrewsh., issuant out of a cloud a dexter hand ppr., holding a heart gu. *Vires et fides.* 216. 5

Cowan, a demi-lion double-queued ppr. 10. 6

Cowan, Bart. (*extinct*), of London, a demi-lion erm., gorged with a representation of the collar of the Lord Mayor of London ppr., and holding between the paws a saltire gu. *Aymez loyaulté.*

Cowan, Ireland, a lion rampant sa., ducally crowned or. 1. 12

Cowan, Middx. and Surrey, in front of a trunk of a tree erect, eradicated and fructed ppr., a stag arg., resting the dexter fore-foot on a caltrap or. *Sanctitas Deo.*

Cowan, Lewis P., 4, Albemarle Street, Piccadilly, in front of a trunk of a tree eradicated and fructed ppr., a stag arg., resting the dexter fore-foot on a caltrap or. Same motto.

Cowan, David, of 27, Linden Gardens, W., same crest and motto.

Cowan, Harry Douglas, of 4, Albemarle Street, W., same crest and motto.

Cowan, John Campbell, Esquire of U.S.A., same crest and motto.

Cowan, a fret gu. 165. 10

Coward of West Penard and Wells, Somers., a demi-greyhound sa., holding between his feet a stag's head cabossed arg., attired or.

Cowbrough and **Cowbrugh,** Scotland, a griffin's head between two wings ppr. 65. 11

Cowcey, Cowcie, and **Cowey,** out of a ducal coronet an arm in armour embowed, holding in the hand an anchor corded, all ppr.

Coweher, a bird holding a branch in its beak. 92. 5

Cowden, a demi-lion sa., charged with an annulet or. *cf.* 10. 1

Cowdrey, Hants, out of a ducal coronet or, an arm in armour embowed ppr., garnished of the first, holding in the gauntlet an anchor gu., the stock sa., and the cordage entwined round the arm of the last.

Cowe, Cowee, and **Cowey,** *see* Cow.

Cowey, De, a nag's head arg., bridled gu. 51. 5

Cowell-Stepney, Bart., *see* Stepney.

Cowell, Scotland, issuing out of a bush a lion's face ppr. 21. 9

Cowell, on a chapeau gu., turned up erm., a lion passant or, gorged with a label of the first. *cf.* 4. 9

Cowell of Harristown, co. Kildare, Ireland, a lion passant gardant gu., ducally crowned and plain-collared or. *Fortis et celer.* *cf.* 4. 3

Cowell, Major-General the Rt. Hon. Sir John Clayton, P.C., K.C.B., Master of the Queen's Household, Buckingham Palace, same crest and motto. *cf.* 4. 3

Cowell, Andrew Richard, Esquire, of Cullentra, co. Wexford, c.o. Messrs Grindley and Co., 55, Parliament Street, London, S.W., same crest and motto.

Cowell, Albert Victor John, Esquire, of Clifton Castle, Bedale, Yorks, same crest and motto.

Cowell, on a chapeau gu., turned up erm., a cow's head sans horns couped sa., bezantée. *Amour de la bonté.*

Cowen, on a winged globe an eagle rising, all ppr. 159. 9

Cowen, Richard John, F.R.C.S., 15, Half Moon Street, W., a dexter arm embowed in chain-mail, holding in the hand a sword. *Defying ye field.* 305. 8

Cowie, Scotland, a fleur-de-lis az. *Per cœli favorem.* 148. 2

Cowie, Surrey, on the stump of a tree sprouting new branches a falcon with wings expanded ppr. *cf.* 86. 11

Cowie, *see* Cow.

Cowley, Earl (Wellesley): (1) Out of a ducal coronet or, a demi-lion rampant gu., holding a forked pennon of the last flowing to the sinister, one-third per pale, from the staff arg., charged with the cross of St. George. 16. 1. (2) A cubit arm vested gu., cuff arg., encircled with a ducal coronet or, grasping a scimitar ppr., pommel and hilt or. *Porro unum est necessarium.*

Cowley of London, out of a ducal coronet or, a demi-lion erm. 16. 3

Cowley, on a mural coronet az., a leopard's face arg., jessant-de-lis or. *cf.* 22. 5

Cowling, on a lion's head erased az., a chapeau ppr. 21. 10

Cowmeadow, a demi-lion rampant arg., holding in the dexter paw a trefoil slipped vert. *cf.* 13. 13

Cowper, Earl (Cowper), a lion's gamb erect and erased or, holding a cherry-branch vert, fructed gu. *Tuum est.* *cf.* 37. 4

Cowper, a lion's gamb erased or, charged with two annulets az., transfixed by a sword ppr. fesswise, the point to the dexter, and holding a cherry-branch ppr., fructed gu. *Tuum est.*

Cowper, Frank, Esquire, M.A. (Oxford), of Grosvenor Club, Piccadilly, W., same crest and motto.

Cowper, Yorks, on a castle gu., the head of a Saracen king ppr., wreathed arg. and az., and crowned with a Saxon coronet or.

Cowper, Leics., a cockatrice's head erased arg., pellettée, beaked, combed, and wattled gu. *cf.* 68. 12

Cowper of London, a bull's head erased or, billettée sa., armed arg., between two wings expanded az.

Cowper, Cumb., a buffalo's head erased per fesse sa. and or, armed of the last, charged on the neck with a cross crosslet counterchanged, holding in the mouth a slip of oak ppr. *Industria et perseverantia.*

Cowper, Geoffrey Thomas Middleton Carleton, Esquire, of Carleton Hall, Penrith, Cumberland, same crest and motto.

Cowper, Shropsh., a lion's head arg., erased gu., gorged with a chaplet of laurel vert. 17. 10

Cowper, a lion sejant arg., holding a battle-axe of the same.

Cowper of London, a lion rampant sa., holding a tilting-spear paleways arg.

Cowper, Chesh., out of a mural coronet gu., a demi-wolf arg., supporting a garb or.

Cowper, Sussex, in a pheon arg., a laurel-sprig ppr., all between two wings gu.

Cowper, Scotland, a hand holding a wreath of laurel ppr. 218. 4

Cowper, Glouc., a hand holding a cutlass, all ppr. 213. 5

Cowper, a cubit arm erect, vested gu., cuff arg., holding in the hand a lantern suspended to a staff, all ppr. *Conduco*. 268. 2

Cowper, Henry Swainson, Esquire, F.S.A., of High House, Hawkshead, Lancs, same crest and motto.

Cowper-Essex, Thomas Christopher, Esquire, of Grove House, Seymour Place, S.W., Major 3rd Batt. Loyal North Lancs Regt.: (1) On the capital of an Ionic column ppr., a griffin's head couped sa., and charged on the neck with two quatrefoils or (*for Essex*). 268. 1. (2) A cubit arm erect, vested gu., cuffed arg., holding in the hand a lantern suspended to a staff, all ppr. (*for Cowper*). *Conduco*. 268. 2

Cowpland, *see* Copland.

Cowsfield, out of a ducal coronet a camel's head. *cf.* 132. 7

Cowtherne, on a mount vert a raven ppr. 107. 5

Cox, *see* Bingham-Cox.

Cox of Limerick, an antelope's head erased sa., attired or, transfixed through the neck by a broken spear ppr. *Fortiter et fideliter*. 127. 1

Cox of Broxwood, Heref., an antelope's head erased ppr., pierced through the neck by a spear. 127. 1

Cox, John George Snead, Broxwood Court, Pembridge, Heref., an ibex's head erased ppr., attired and eared or, pierced through the neck by a broken spear arg., headed gold. *Nil amplius oro*.

Cox, Herts, an antelope's head erased sa., pierced through the neck by a broken spear and vulned gu. 127. 1

Cox, Herts, an antelope's head erased sa., attired, bearded, and pierced through the neck with an arrow or. *cf.* 127. 1

Cox, Colonel William, Esquire, of Ballynoe, Ballingarry, Limerick, same crest *Fortiter et fideliter*.

Cox of Coolcliffe, Wexford, a goat's head erased sa. *Fide et fortitudine*. 128. 5

Cox of London, a goat's head erased arg. 128. 5

Cox, Bart., Ireland, a goat's head erased az., armed or. *Fide et fortitudine*. 128. 5

Cox, Ireland, a goat's head erased az., armed or, holding in his mouth a trefoil slipped vert. *Fide et fortitudine*. *cf.* 128. 5

Cox, Lieutenant-General Sir John William, Esquire, K.C.B., of 26, South Parade, Southsea, same crest and motto.

Cox of London and Glouc., a goat's head arg., attired or, holding in the mouth an oak-leaf az. *cf.* 128. 12

Cox, Herts, a goat's head erased sa., armed, bearded, and pierced through the neck by an arrow or, the wound guttée-de-sang. *cf.* 128. 5

Cox, Hon. George Henry, J.P., of Winbourn, Mulgoa, near Sydney, Beowang, Mount Wilson, Burrundulla, Mudgee, and Pine Ridge, Talbrugar, all in New South Wales, Member of the Legislative Council, a griffin's head erased sa., pierced through the neck with an arrow gu., headed and feathered arg. *Fortitudo in adversis*. *cf.* 66. 13

Cox, Edward Standish, Esquire, of Fernside, Rylstone, New South Wales, Australia, a griffin's head erased sa., pierced through the neck with an arrow gu., headed and feathered arg. *Fortitudo in adversis*. *cf.* 66. 13

Cox, Sussex, a griffin's head erased sa., pierced through the neck by an arrow gu., headed and feathered arg. *cf.* 66. 13

Cox, Norf., out of a ducal coronet a griffin's head between two wings. 67. 1

Cox, Ireland, a wyvern, the tail nowed ppr.

Cox of London, a cock gu., ducally crowned or. *cf.* 91. 2

Cox, Frederick, Hillingdon House, Uxbridge, same crest.

Cox of Kent, a demi-horse salient arg., charged on the neck with a thunderbolt ppr. *cf.* 53. 3

Cox of Charton, Farningham, Kent, and of Trevereux, Limpsfield, Surrey: (1) Of honourable augmentation, upon a bow fesseways or, a stag at gaze arg., attired, ungu., and gorged with a collar and chain reflexed over the back of the first. (2) A demi-horse arg., charged on the shoulder with a thunderbolt ppr. *Chescun son devoir*. *cf.* 53. 3

Cox, Lincs, on a mount a stag lodged regardant ppr. *Prodesse quam conspici*. 115. 9

Cox, Ireland, two hands conjoined in fess supporting a heart gu. 224. 4

Cox of London, an arm in armour ppr., garnished or, holding in the hand a battle-axe arg., the handle gu.

Cox, Scotland, issuing out of the sea an arm embowed, holding in the hand an anchor in bend sinister, cabled ppr. 202. 7

Cox, Alfred William, Esquire, of Glendoick, Glencarse, Perthsh., a dexter arm embowed issuing out of the sea, holding in the hand an anchor in bend sinister, cabled ppr. *Præmium virtutis honos*. 231. 4

Cox, William Henry, Esquire, of Snaigow, Dunkeld, Perthsh., same crest and motto.

Cox, Edward, Esquire, of Cardean, Meigle, N.B., same crest. *Præmium virtutis honor*.

Cox, an arm arg., charged with a bend az., holding in the hand a triple bunch of pinks, leaved ppr.

Coxan or **Coxen**, a lion rampant or, holding in the dexter paw a fleur-de-lis az. 2. 7

Coxe of London, a demi-lion rampant arg., collared sa., holding in the dexter paw a spear-head or. *cf.* 10. 0

Coxed, Oxon., out of an Eastern crown or, a griffin's head vert, langued ppr.

Coxhead, a lion passant paly of six or and gu. 6. 2

Coxon or **Coxson**, a cock arg., combed, wattled, and legged gu. 91. 2

Coxton, an antelope trippant ppr. 126. 6

Coxwell, Glouc., a dragon's head arg., between two dragon's wings expanded gu. 72. 7

Coxwell-Rogers, Rev. Augustus Mead, Esquire, of Mickleton Vicarage, Chipping-Campden: (1) A fleur-de-lis or (*for Rogers*). (2) A demi-dragon displayed arg. *Vigila et ora*.

Coxwell-Rogers, Rev. Richard, B.A., of Dowdeswell Rectory, Andoversford, Glouc., same crests and motto.

Coyle, Ireland, a hind's head erased or. 124. 3

Coyne, Staffs, a cubit arm erect, vested sa., slashed and cuffed or, holding in the hand ppr. a cutlass arg., embrued gu., the hilt and pommel or.

Coyne, Ireland, a sea-horse ppr. 46. 5

Coyne of Dublin, a sea-horse ppr. holding a fusil arg., charged with a fleur-de-lis sa.

Coyney, *see* Coyne.

Coyney or **Coyny**, an oak-branch ppr. 151. 3

Coys, Essex, out of clouds ppr., therefrom issuing rays or, an arm erect, the hand grasping a snake entwined round the arm, all ppr.

Coyte, Rev. Walter Beeston, M.A., Tower House, Aldeburgh-on-Sea, an eagle displayed.

Coytmore, a dagger in pale ppr. 169. 2

Cozens-Hardy, *see* Hardy.

Cozens, William Hardy, Esquire, of Letheringset Hall, Norf., a lion rampant or, guttée-de-sang and fretty gu. 3. 3

Cozens, a lion rampant sa., holding in the dexter paw a battle-axe az., hafted gu. *cf.* 1. 13

Cozens, James Brewster, Esquire, of Woodham-Mortimer Lodge, Essex, on a mount vert, a lion's gamb erect and erased sa., charged with a cross botonnée or. *Confido recte agens*.

Crab, Scotland, a salmon naiant ppr. 139. 12

Crab or **Crabbe**, an escutcheon az., charged with a fleur-de-lis or.

Crab or **Crabbe**, a lion's gamb erased holding a dagger ppr. 38. 8

Crabbie, the late John, Esquire, of 22, Royal Terrace, Edinburgh, a dexter arm embowed, the hand holding a crabstick in bend sinister ppr. *Nunquam non paratus*.

Crabtree, a hand erect holding a dagger in pale, all ppr. 212. 9

Cracherode, a demi-boar salient regardant or, wounded in the shoulder with an arrow ppr., held in the mouth. *cf.* 41. 2

Crackanthorp, a holly-tree ppr.

Crackanthorpe, Montague Hughes, Esquire, of Newbiggin Hall, Westmoreland, and of 65, Rutland Gate, St. Margaret's, Westminster, London, Q.C., Doctor of Civil Law of the University of Oxford, and a Bencher of Lincoln's Inn: (1) On a wreath of the colours a holly-bush fructed ppr. (*for Crackanthorpe*). (2) A demi-lion rampant ppr., gorged with a collar vair, holding in the dexter paw a staff raguly gu., and resting the sinister paw on a mullet, also gu., pierced arg. (*for Cookson*). *Mihi res subjungere conor*. *cf.* 15. 1

Cracklow, out of a crescent a flame of fire issuant ppr. 163. 12

Cracroft of Hackthorn, Lincs, a stork ppr., supporting with his dexter claw a battle-axe, the staff or, headed arg. *cf.* 105. 11

Cracroft (really Cracroft-Amcotts), Edward Weston, Esquire, of Hackthorn

Hall, Lincoln: (1) A squirrel sejant gu., collared or, eating an acorn of the last (*for Amcotts*). (2) A stork ppr., supporting with the dexter claw a battle-axe, the handle or, the head arg. (*for Cracroft*). The crest of Cracroft only is now used.

Cracroft-Amcotts, Weston, Esquire, of Kettlethorpe Hall, Newark, same crests and motto.

Crade, a demi-dragon sans wings or, the tail environed round the body.

Craddock or **Cradock,** Somers. and Wilts, a bear's head erased sa., billettée and muzzled or. cf. 35. 2

Craddock or **Cradock,** a bear's head couped arg., muzzled gu. 34. 13

Craddock or **Cradock,** out of a ducal coronet or, a lion's gamb holding a spear tasselled ppr. cf. 36. 14

Craddock or **Cradock,** Ireland, a lion rampant holding between his paws a ducal coronet. 3. 6

Craddock or **Cradock,** the stump of an oak-tree sprouting a branch on the sinister side ppr.

Craddock or **Cradock,** England and Wales, a horse passant sa. 52. 6

Cradock or **Caradoc, Baron Howden,** *see* Howden.

Cradock-Hartop, *see* Hartop.

Crafford or **Craford,** Kent and Essex, a hawk's head couped or. 88. 12

Craford, Northumb., an eagle's head between two wings arg. 84. 2

Craford, Berks, a deer's head ppr., and between the attires a cross. 120. 9

Crafton, a dolphin haurient swallowing a fish, all ppr. 140. 6

Crag or **Cragg,** on a chapeau gu., turned up erm., a fleur-de-lis between two wings az. cf. 110. 5

Cragg, William Alfred, Threekingham House, Falkingham, Lincs, an arm in armour embowed, holding in the hand a dagger.

Craggs, two arms embowed, each holding a scimitar ppr.

Craggs of Westminster, of Durh., and of Newland, co. Dublin, a dexter and a sinister arm couped above the elbows, armed az., garnished arg., grasping in the gauntlets a sword of the last, hilt and pommel or.

Craick, Scotland, an anchor ppr. *Providence.* 161. 1

Craig, Scotland, a chevalier on horseback holding in his dexter hand a broken spear, all ppr. *J'ai bonne esperance.* 189. 5

Craig or **Craige,** Scotland, a chevalier on horseback holding a broken lance in bend, all ppr. *Vive ut vivas.* 189. 5

Craig, Gibson-, Sir James Henry, Bart., of Riccarton, in Midlothian: (1) A knight on horseback in full armour, his dexter hand grasping a broken tilting-spear, all ppr. (*for Craig*). 189. 5 (2) A pelican in her piety ppr. (*for Gibson*). *Vive Deo et vives.—Pandite cœlestes portæ.* 98. 14

Craig, S. H., L.R.C.P., L.R.C.S., L.M., 124, Strond Green Road, N., crest and motto same as first of the above.

Craig, R. Hunter, Esquire, of West Dunmore, Stirlingsh., and West Park, Skelmorlie, Ayrsh., N.B., a chevalier armed cap-à-pie or, on a horse in full career sa., harnessed ppr., grasping a broken lance in bend, also ppr. *J'ai bonne esperance.*

Craig, William Young, Esquire, of Milton House, Alsager, Chester, a beaver sejant ppr. *Arte utile facio.* 263. 11

Craig, Ireland, a demi-lion gu., holding in the dexter paw a mullet or. cf. 10. 2

Craig, a lion's head vert, collared or. cf. 18. 6

Craig, Scotland, a pillar arg. 176. 3

Craigdallie, Scotland, a dexter hand pulling a thistle ppr. 218. 5

Craigdallie, Scotland, a lion rampant holding a battle-axe ppr.

Craigdallie, a pillar arg. 176. 3

Craige, *see* Craig and Craigg.

Craigg and **Craigie,** Scotland, a cornucopia ppr. *Honeste vivo.* 152. 13

Craigg, Craigge, or **Craige,** a boar passant arg. 40. 9

Craigie, Scotland, a pillar ppr. 176. 3

Craigie, Bart., of Garisay, Orkney, a boar passant arg., armed az. *Timor omnes abesto.* 40. 9

Craigie-Halkett of Hartill, Lanarksh., a falcon's head erased ppr. *Fides sufficit* (above).—*Honeste vivo* (beneath).

Craigie, David C., Esquire, Carshalton, Surrey, a knight on horseback in full armour, his dexter hand grasping a broken lance, all ppr. *Vive Deo ut vivas.* 299. 1

Craigy, Scotland, a boar passant arg., armed and langued gu. *Timor omnes abesto.* 40. 9

Craik, an eagle's leg erased at the thigh ppr. cf. 113. 8

Craik, Scotland, an anchor ppr. *Providence.* 161. 2

Craik, Ireland, a goat's head arg., armed gu. 128. 12

Craister, Northumb., a raven ppr. 107. 14

Crake, on a chapeau ppr., a talbot sejant or. 54. 14

Crakenthorp, three ears of wheat or. cf. 154. 6

Crakenthorpe, a pillar ensigned with a heart. 176. 5

Craker of London, on a chapeau ppr., a talbot sejant or. *Fides præstantior auro.* 54. 14

Cramer or **Crammer,** a gauntlet ppr. 209. 8

Cramer, Ireland, a fleur-de-lis or, between two wings conjoined and erect sa.

Cramer, John Thomas, Esquire, of Ballindinisk House, co. Cork, a fleur-de-lis between two wings expanded or, penned arg. *Inevitabile fatum.*

Cramer, on a mount a cock with wings expanded ppr. *Non dormit qui custodit.* 91. 7

Cramer, Ireland, out of a ducal coronet or, a talbot's head sa., eared arg. 57. 12

Crammond, Scotland, a tower arg., masoned sa. *My hope is constant in thee.* 156. 2

Cramond, a pelican vulning herself ppr. *Vulnera temno.* 98. 1

Cramp, a demi-lion rampant gu., holding a mullet or. *Fide et amore.* 15. 8

Cramphorne, Herts, a talbot's head erased erm., eared sa., gorged with a collar gu., charged with three cross crosslets fitched or. cf. 56. 1

Crampton, Ireland, a Roman fasces in pale ppr. 171. 4

Crampton, Bart., a demi-lion rampant or, holding between his paws a close helmet ppr. *Fortem posce animum.* cf. 10. 2

Crampton, George Cecil Croxton, Esquire, Ballyhook, Grange Con., co. Wicklow, same crest and motto.

Crampton, John Twisleton Ribton, of Termoncarra, Belmullet, same crest and motto.

Cramsie, James Sinclair, Esquire, of O'Harabrook, Ballymoney, co. Antrim, a stag's head couped, pierced through the neck with an arrow embrued ppr., and charged with a trefoil vert. *Labour omnia vincit.*

Cranage, Chesh., out of a mural coronet a demi-monkey ppr. 136. 13

Cranage, Chesh., out of a ducal coronet or, a demi-stork with wings expanded ppr.

Cranber, Suff., out of a ducal coronet a hand holding a sheaf of arrows ppr. 214. 2

Cranborne, Viscount, *see* Salisbury, Marquess of.

Cranbrook, Earl of (Gathorne Gathorne-Hardy), of Hemsted Park, Kent: (1) A dexter arm embowed in armour ppr., garnished or, entwined by a branch of oak vert, charged with two catherine-wheels, the one above and the other below the elbow gu., the hand grasping a dragon's head erased ppr. (*for Hardy*). 198. 12. (2) In front of a wolf's head erased arg., a staff raguly fessewise or (*for Gathorne*). *Armé de foi hardi.* cf. 30. 8

Crane, Suff., a crane ppr. 105. 9

Crane, Ireland, a wheel sa. 167. 1

Crane, a demi-hind or, ducally gorged az.

Crane, C. Albert, M.D., 31, Warwick Square, S.W., a demi-hind couped or. *Qui pascit corvos pascet grues.*

Craney, an arm embowed vested az., cuffed gu., holding a cutlass ppr. *Amor proximi.*

Cranfield, on a ducal coronet or, a fleur-de-lis between two ostrich-feathers arg.

Cranfield, out of a ducal coronet an antelope's head, all or. cf. 127. 6

Cranford, an eagle with wings expanded ppr., supporting a flag az. cf. 78. 14

Cranford, a cross moline sa. 165. 3

Cranley, Viscount, *see* Onslow, Earl.

Cranmer-Byng, Lieutenant-Colonel Alfred Molyneux, of Quendon Hall, Essex: (1) An heraldic antelope trippant erm., armed, crined, and hoofed or (*for Byng*). (2) A crane's head erm., erased gu., pierced through the neck by an arrow in bend sinister or, barbed and flighted arg. *Tuebor.—Nosce teipsum.*

Cranmer and **Cranmore,** Notts, a crane's head erased az., pierced through the neck by an arrow ppr., barbed and feathered arg., the neck vulned gu. cf. 104. 11

Cranmore, a crane's head erased arg., beaked gu., pierced through the neck with an arrow ppr., barbed and plumed arg., the neck vulned gu.

Cranston, a column arg., entwined with woodbine vert. 176. 4

Cranston, Scotland, a crane's head erased ppr. *I desire not to want.* 104. 11

Cranstoun, *see* Trotter-Cranstoun.

Cranstoun, Baron, Scotland, a crane roosting with its head under its wing, and holding up a stone with its dexter foot, all ppr. *Thou shalt want ere I want.*

Cranstoun, C. B., M.B., Broad Street, Ludlow, Shropsh., a crane holding in its dexter foot a stone, all ppr. Motto as above.

Cranstoun, Edmonstone-, Charles Joseph, Core House, Lanark, a crane statant vulning itself ppr.

Cranstoun, Scotland, a crane's head erased ppr. *I desire not to want.* 104. 11

Cranstoun, a crane arg. *Dum vigilo curo.* 105. 9

Cranton, a dromedary sa., collared or, bezantée, maned gu.

Cranwell, Lincs, a crane close arg. 105. 9

Cranwell, on a mount vert a hare current arg. 136. 3

Cranworth, Baron (Rolfe; *extinct*), a dove arg., holding in its beak a sprig of olive ppr., ducally gorged gu., the dexter claw resting on three annulets interlaced or. *Post nubila Phœbus.*

Cranworth, Baron (Gurdon), of Letton and Cranworth, a goat climbing up a rock, all ppr. *In arduis viget virtus.* 238. 1

Crass and **Crasse,** Durh., a crescent surmounted by a cross crosslet fitchée or. *Hodie non cras.* 166. 9

Crastein, a Cornish chough ppr. 107. 14

Crastein, a Cornish chough ppr., between two wings expanded gu.

Craster, on a ducal coronet or, a cock ppr. *cf.* 91. 2

Craster, Northumb., a raven ppr. 107. 14

Cra'ster, Thomas William, of Cra'ster, Alnwick, Northumb.: (1) A raven ppr., charged on the breast with an escallop or (*for Cra'ster*). *cf.* 107. 5. *Hodie felix cras ter.*

Cratford, Worcs., a demi-lion rampant gardant erminois, ducally gorged az. *cf.* 10. 8

Crathorne, Lincs, on a thorn-bush a bird ppr.

Crathorne, Yorks, on a mount vert, a bird sa. 92. 3

Crauford or **Craufurd,** a hand holding a lancet. 216. 14

Craufuird, formerly of Grange House, Ayrsh., a game-hawk hooded and belled ppr. *Durum patientiâ frango.* *cf.* 85. 1

Craufurd, Sir Charles William Frederick, Bart., of Kilbirney, Stirling, an ermine ppr. *Sine labe nota.* 134. 6

Craufurd, Houison-, Lieutenant-Colonel William Reginald, of Craufurdland, Ayrsh.: (1) A marble pillar surmounted by a man's heart ppr. (*for Craufurd*). *Stant innixa Deo.* 176. 5. (2) A dexter hand erect couped at the wrist (*for Howison*). *Sursum corda.* 222. 14

Craufurd, Henry John, Esquire, of Auchenames, Renfrewsh., and Crosbie, Ayrsh., a stag's head erased gu., between the attires a cross crosslet fitchée sa. *Tutum te robore reddam.* 120. 12

Craufurd, Hugh Ronald George, Esquire, of Portencross, Ayrsh., same crest and motto.

Craunton *see* Cranton.

Crause, out of a ducal coronet a hand holding a rose slipped and leaved ppr. 218. 11

Craven, Earl of (Craven), Yorks, on a chapeau gu., turned up erm., a griffin statant with wings elevated erm., beaked and armed or. *Virtus in actione consistit.* 63. 13

Craven, Fulwar-, Esquire, of Brock Hampton Park, Glouc., on a chapeau gu., turned up erm., a griffin statant of the second, beaked or. *Virtus in actione consistit.* 63. 13

Craven, Colquitt-, Fulwar Lewis George, of Brock Hampton Park, Cheltenham, same crest and motto.

Craven of Richardstown, Louth, on a chapeau gu., turned up erm., a griffin statant sa., wings addorsed, beaked, and semée-de-lis or. *Fortitudine crevi.* *cf.* 63. 13

Craven, Warw. and Berks, on a chapeau gu., turned up erm., a griffin passant of the last. *cf.* 63. 13

Craven, Berks, a griffin statant erm. *cf.* 63. 13

Craven, on a perch sa., a falcon az., with wings expanded, beaked and legged gu.

Craw of East Reston, an eagle gardant ppr., beaked and armed gu. *Cui debeo fidus.*

Craw of Netherhyer, a crow sa. *God is my safety.* *cf.* 107. 5

Craw of Heughead, on a garb a crow sa. *Nec careo, nec curo.*

Crawe, a hawk with wings expanded arg., charged on the breast with a cinquefoil az. *cf.* 87. 1

Crawfield, a lion rampant. 1. 13

Crawford and Balcarres, Earl of, *see* Lindsay.

Crawford, Berks, a deer's head ppr., and between the attires a cross or. 120. 9

Crawford of Drumsey, a stag's head erased gu., between the attires a cross crosslet fitched of the same. *Tutum te robore reddam.* 120. 12

Crawford of Haining, a hart's head couped ppr. *Hactenus invictus.* 121. 5

Crawford of Comlarg, issuing out of a cloud a dexter hand grasping a hart by the attires and bearing him to the ground, all ppr. *Tutum te robore reddam.* 116. 10

Crawford, a goat's head gu. 128. 12

Crawford, a crescent arg. 163. 2

Crawford, Scotland, a decrescent arg. *Sine labe lucebit.* 163. 1

Crawford, James Coutts, Esquire, of Overton, Lanarksh., and Miramart, Wellington, New Zealand, an increscent chequy arg. and az. *Fide et diligentia.* 163. 3

Crawford, James Dundas, Esquire, same crest and motto.

Crawford of Carsburn, and **Crawfurd** of Hamilton, a crescent arg., charged with a star. *Sine labe lucebit.* *cf.* 163. 2

Crawford, within the horns of a crescent a star. 163. 4

Crawford of Easter Seaton, an increscent chequy arg. and gu. *Fide et diligentia.* 163. 3

Crawford, a half-moon, the crescent chequy arg. and az., the face sa.

Crawford, a griffin's head erased between two wings. *cf.* 65. 11

Crawford of Jardinhill, a pair of balances on the point of a dagger in pale. *God save the right.* *cf.* 179. 11

Crawford of Crawfordburn, on the point of a dagger arg., hilted or, a pair of balances suspended of the last, stringed gu. *Quod tibi, hoc alteri.* *cf.* 179. 11

Crawford, on the point of a dagger erect a pair of balances, all ppr. *God show the right.* *cf.* 179. 11

Crawford, George Reginald, Esquire, of Arpley House, West Hill, Putney Heath, S.W., a dexter arm in armour embowed, holding a dagger ppr. *Sine labe nota.*

Crawford of Cloverhill, a garb ppr. *God feeds the crows.* 153. 2

Crawford, a castle triple-towered ppr. *cf.* 155. 8

Crawford, Scotland, a castle ppr. *cf.* 155. 8

Crawford, Scotland, a palm-branch ppr. *Calcar honeste.* 147. 1

Crawford of Crawfordsland, on the top of a marble pillar a man's heart, all ppr. *Stant innixa Deo.* 176. 5

Crawford of Crawfuird, Scotland, an ermine passant ppr. *Sine labe nota.* 134. 6

Crawford, Robert, Esquire, J.P., D.L., M.A., co. Donegal, of Stonewold, near Ballyshannon, co. Donegal, an erm. passant ppr., charged on the shoulders with a trefoil slipped or. *Sine labe nota.* 271. 16

Crawford of Ardmillan, Scotland, a falcon hooded and belled ppr. *Durum patientiâ frango.* *cf.* 85. 1

Crawford and **Crawfurd,** Scotland, a phœnix in flames ppr. *God show the right.* 82. 2

Crawford or **Crawforde,** a hand holding a lancet ppr. 216. 14

Crawfurd of Saint Hill, Sussex, a hawk hooded and belled ppr. *Durum patientiâ frango.* *cf.* 85. 1

Crawfurd, a garb ppr. *God feeds the crows.* 153. 2

Crawfurd, Scotland, a cinquefoil slipped vert. *Feliciter floret.* *cf.* 148. 12

Crawfurd, a goat's head gu. 128. 12

Crawfurd, a stag's head erased ppr. *Hactenus invictus.* 121. 2

Crawfurd, a stag's head erased ppr., and between his attires gu. a cross crosslet fitchée or. *Omnia Deo juvante.* 120. 12

Crawfurd, a dexter hand issuing out of a cloud grasping a hart by the attires and bringing him to the ground, all ppr. *Tutum te robore reddam.* 116. 10

Crawfurd-Stirling-Stuart, of Castlemilk and Milton, Lanarksh.: (1) A dexter naked arm issuant grasping a sword, all ppr., pommel and hilt or (*for Stuart*). (2) A Moor's head sa., banded about the temples arg. (*for Stirling*). (3) A crescent arg. (*for Crawfurd*).

Crawfurd, a castle triple-towered arg., masoned sa., loopholes and ports gu. *cf.* 155. 8

Crawfurd, James, Esquire, of Thornwood, Lanarksh., same crest. *Ex pugnavi.*

Crawfurd of Lanarksh., Scotland, a castle triple-towered arg., masoned sa., loopholes and ports gu. *cf.* 155. 8

Crawfurd, Macknight- of Lauriston Castle, Midlothian, and Kirkland House, West Kilbride, N.B.: (1) A sword erect in pale, having on the point a pair of balances, all pp. (*for Craufurd*). 179. 11. (2) A demi-lion rampant or (*for Macknight*). *Quod tibi hoc alteri.—Nil durum volenti.* 10. 2

Crawhall of Northumb. and Durh., on a garb or, a crow sa. *Nec careo, nec curo.*

Crawhall, a crow holding in the dexter claw a battle-axe. *Præsto et persto.*

Crawhall, George, of Burton Croft, Yorks, upon a mount vert a crow sa., holding in the dexter claw a battle-axe in bend ppr. *Præsto et persto.*

Crawley-Boevey, *see* Boevey.

Crawley, Sussex and Beds, a crane ppr., in the dexter claw a fleur-de-lis or. *cf.* 105. 9

Crawley, Francis, Esquire, of Stockwood, Luton, Beds, same crest. *Non omnia possumus omnes.*

Crawley, Ireland, a triangular harrow. 178. 4

Crawley, Dorset, a lion's head erased semée of hurts, gorged with a ducal coronet gu. 18. 5

Crawshaw, Baron (Brooks), a demi-lion ppr., maned arg., charged on the shoulder with a fountain, and holding in the paws a pheon in bend sinister ppr., stringed or.

Crawshaw, a greyhound current arg., collared gu. *cf.* 58. 2

Crawshaw, on a mount in front of a bull-dog, collared, a pile of balls. 57. 10

Crawshay, de Barri, Esquire, of Rosefield, Sevenoaks, Kent, on a mount vert, a mastiff dog standing over a pyramid of cannon-balls ppr. *Perseverance.*

Crawshay, Codrington Fraser, Esquire, of Lhanvair Grange, near Abergavenny, Monmouthsh., same crest and motto.

Crawshay, Francis Richard, Esquire, of Treforest, South Wales, same crest and motto.

Crawshay, Tudor, Esquire, of Dimlands, Llantwit-Major, Glamorgansh., same crest and motto.

Crawshay, William Thompson, Esquire, of Cyfarthfa Castle, Merthyr Tydvil, and Caversham Park, Reading, same crest. *Perseverance.*

Crawshay, a greyhound current sa. *cf.* 58. 2

Crawshay, Norf., a dog sa., standing over a heap of olives ppr.

Cray of Kent, a chevalier on horseback holding a sword in pale, all ppr. *cf.* 189. 10

Craycraft or **Crecroft,** a stork holding in the dexter claw a battle-axe ppr. *cf.* 125. 11

Craye, out of a ducal coronet or, a griffin's head arg., collared of the first. *cf.* 67. 9

Creagh, Ireland, a nag's head erased bridled ppr. *cf.* 51. 5

Creagh, *see* Butler-Creagh.

Creagh, *see* MacMahon-Creagh.

Creagh, Newcastle-on-Tyne, a horse's head couped arg., between two laurel-branches ppr. *cf.* 50. 2

Creagh, a horse's head erased arg., bridled gu., and decked with a slip of laurel ppr. *Virtute et numine.* *cf.* 51. 5

Creagh, Michael, Esquire, of the city of Dublin, a horse's head erased arg., caparisoned gu., in the headstall of the bridle a laurel-branch vert. *Virtute et numine.* *cf.* 51. 5

Creagh, John Bagwell, Esquire, of Hermitage, near Doneraile, same crest and motto.

Creagh, Ireland, an arm holding a dagger, point downward. *cf.* 213. 6

Creake, a stag trippant gu. 117. 8

Crealocke of Langerton, Littleham, Devonsh., a griffin's head erased sa., beaked or, langued gu., transfixed by a sword fesseways ppr., the hilt resting on the wreath, holding in the beak a sprig of laurel, also ppr. *Deo et gladio.*

Crean, Ireland, a hand plucking a thistle ppr. 218. 5

Crean, a water-bouget az. 168. 4

Creasy, a greyhound's head sa., collared arg. 61. 2

Creck, a swan arg. 99. 2

Crecroft, *see* Craycraft.

Cree, Scotland, an arm in armour embowed wielding a scimitar ppr. 196. 10

Cree, George Cecil, Ower Moigne Court, Dorset, a dexter hand holding a civic crown ppr. *The reward of integrity.*

Creeck, Scotland, a hand holding a crown of laurel ppr. *Volenti nil difficile.* *cf.* 218. 4

Creed, on an oak-branch vert a dove arg., holding in the beak a sprig ppr., charged on the breast with a cross patée gu.

Creed, a dove holding in its beak an olive-branch ppr. 92. 5

Creed, a demi-wolf regardant erminois, holding in the dexter paw an étoile gu.

Creed, a dragon's head gu. 71. 1

Creed, Thomas, M.D., Ballinstone, Parkwood Road, Boscombe, Hants, a thistle ppr.

Crees, Warw., on a mount a falcon with wings addorsed, ducally gorged, belled. *Gladio et virtute.* *cf.* 88. 2

Creese, a unicorn's head couped ppr. *Demique decus.* 49. 7

Creeton, a dragon passant vomiting fire ppr. *cf.* 73. 2

Creevey or **Crevy,** a griffin sejant per pale arg. and sa., winged or. 62. 10

Cregoe, an arm in armour embowed, cut off below the wrist and dropping blood, holding in the hand an arrow. *Fortuna audaces juvat.*

Cregoe-Colmore, William Barwick, Esquire, of Moor End, Charlton Kings, Cheltenham, out of a crescent or, a blackamoor's head in profile, wreathed about the temples or and gu.

Creighton, a bomb-shell fired ppr. 177. 12

Creirie, *see* M'Crire.

Creke, Cambs, in a crescent arg., a bundle of five arrows or, headed and barbed arg., tied with a ribbon gu.

Creke, *see* Crake.

Creketot, a stag's head erased or. 121. 2

Crelie, Ireland, a wolf's head erased arg. 30. 8

Cremer of London and Norf., a ram's head erased paly of six arg. and gu., attired of the first. 130. 6

Cremer, Wyndham Cremer, Esquire, of Beeston Hall, Cromer, Norf., a ram's head erased per pale wavy arg. and gu., armed or

Cremorne, Baron, *see* Dartrey, Earl of.

Crenway, on a chapeau gu., a boar passant or. *cf.* 40. 8

Crepping or **Creping,** Lincs, a lion passant ppr., holding in the dexter paw a crescent arg. 5. 6

Cresacre, a catamountain.

Crespigny, on a chapeau gu., turned up erm., a gauntlet ppr., holding a cutlass arg., the hilt and pommel or.

Crespine, Crespin, or **Crispin,** a hydra with seven heads vert. 73. 3

Cress or **Cresse,** Notts, a griffin's head couped sa. 66. 1

Cressall, two lion's gambs erased supporting a bezant. 39. 4

Cressenor or **Cressner,** a dexter arm couped and embowed fesseways, holding three wheat-stalks ppr. 202. 6

Cresset, Shropsh., a demi-lion rampant gardant arg., ducally crowned or, holding a beacon of the first fired ppr.

Cressey, out of a ducal coronet or, a demi-peacock ppr. 103. 13

Cressy, Charles Albert, Hill House, Walton, Ipswich, out of a ducal coronet a demi-eagle displayed ppr. *Cressa ne careat.*

Cresswell, *see* Baker-Cresswell.

Cresswell, Suff., a squirrel sejant cracking a nut, all ppr. 135. 7

Cresswell of London and Northumb., on a mount vert, a torteau charged with a squirrel sejant arg. 135. 11

Cresswell, Shropsh., a greyhound sejant arg. 59. 4

Cresswell, a dexter arm embowed, vested, slashed, holding in the hand ppr. a mace.

Cresswell, George, Esquire, of Oele Court, Hertford, between two eagle's wings gu., guttée-d'or, a bird bolt of the last, thereon a squirrel sejant ppr., holding in the paws a trefoil slipped vert. *Vincit amor patriæ.*

Cresswell, Ireland, a savage's head ppr., wreathed vert. *cf.* 190. 7

Cresswell, Baker-, Addison Francis, of Cresswell, Alnwick, Northumb.: (1) A mount vert, thereon a torteau charged with a squirrel sejant arg. (2) A goat's head erased arg., armed and crined or, gorged with a collar gemel, and charged on the neck with a saltire gu. *Cressa ne careat.*

Cressy, Lincs, out of a ducal coronet or, a demi-eagle displayed ppr. 80. 14

Cressy, a griffin's head couped sa. 66. 1

Creston, a lion passant resting his dexter paw on a torteau. *cf.* 6. 2

Creswell, Hants, a sinister arm in chain armour, holding in the hand ppr. a cross botonnée fitched or.

Creswell, Northamp., a Saracen's head ppr. 190. 5

Creswell of Pinkney Park, Wilts, a Saracen's head ppr., wreathed vert and arg., charged with a mullet gu. *Aut nunquam tentes, aut perfice.* 190. 5

Creswell, Northamp., on the branch of a tree fesseways vert a squirrel sejant gu., cracking a nut or, between two hazel-twigs of the first, fructed of the third.

Creswick, out of a ducal coronet or, an arm in armour embowed, holding in the hand a dagger ppr. *cf.* 196. 5

Creswick, Henry, Esquire, of Hawthorne House, Melbourne, Australia, a lion rampant double-queued sa., guttée-d'or, supporting a caduceus, also or. *Do right and fear not.* 3. 1

Creting, Kent, and **Cretinge,** Suff., a bear passant transpierced by an arrow in bend sinister. *cf.* 34. 4

Creveguer or **Creverguere,** a mountain in flames ppr. 179. 2

Crevy, *see* Creevey.

Crew, Chesh., out of a ducal coronet or, a lion's gamb arg. 36. 12

Crew, Durh., a ferret collared and lined. 134. 9

Crew, on a mount vert, a doe lodged ppr. 125. 4

Crewdson, William Dillworth, Esquire, J.P., of Helme Lodge, Kendal, Westml., a fox's head erased or, between two fleur-de-lis az., charged on the neck with an estoile of six points wavy of the last. *Sapientia tutus.*

Crewe, Earl of (Crewe-Milnes), Fryston Hall, Ferry Bridge, Yorks: (1) A garb or, charged with a fess dancettée az., thereon three mullets arg. (2) Out of a ducal coronet or, a lion's gamb arg., armed gu. *Scio cui credidi.*

Crewe, Baron (*extinct*), of Crewe, Chesh.: (1) Out of a ducal coronet or, a lion's gamb erect arg. (*for Crewe*). 36. 12. (2) A demi-lion rampant gardant or, holding in the paws a slip of olive ppr. (*for Offley*). *Sequor nec inferior.* *cf.* 10. 8

Crewe, Sir Vauncey Harpur, Bart., D.L., of Calke Abbey, Derbysh.: (1) Out of a ducal coronet or, a lion's gamb erect arg. (*for Crewe*). 36. 12. (2) A boar statant or, ducally gorged gu. (*for Harpur*). *Degeneranti genus opprobrium.*

Crewe, a boar passant sa. 40. 9

Crewe, Ireland, a dexter hand holding an open book ppr. 215. 10

Crewe-Read, Offley John, Esquire: (1) An eagle displayed sa. (*for Read*). (2) Out of a ducal coronet or, a lion's gamb arg., charged with a crescent gu. (*for Crewe*).

Crewker, an arm in armour embowed brandishing a scimitar. 196. 10

Crews, Crewse, or Cruse, Devonsh., on a mount vert a stork ppr., holding in its dexter claw an escallop arg. *Another,* holding a stone. 105. 1

Creyke of Rawcliffe, Yorks, on a garb or, a raven ppr. 258. 16

Creyke, Yorks, on a garb in fess or, an eagle with wings addorsed arg.

Creyke, Yorks, a crow with wings addorsed sa.

Creyke, Ralph, Esquire, of Rawcliffe Hall, Goole, and Marton, Bridlington, on a garb fesseways or, a rook, wings ppr. *À vie la verité.* 258. 16

Criall, out of a mural coronet a demi-lion rampant gardant gu., holding between the paws a key or.

Criche of London and Oxon., a demi-lion erm., crowned or, holding a cross formée fitched of the last. *cf.* 10. 11

Crichton, Viscount, *see* Erne, Earl of.

Crichton-Stuart, Marquess of Bute, *see* Bute.

Crichton, Scotland, a dragon's head couped vert, vomiting fire ppr. *God send grace.* 72. 3

Crichton, a dragon's head erased ppr. *Perseverantia.* *cf.* 71. 2

Crichton, a dragon vert, crowned and spouting out fire ppr.

Crichton, a galley, her oars in saltier sa. 160. 10

Crichton of London, a mastiff standing in a watching posture ppr. *Fidelis.*

Crichton of Woodhouselee, Scotland, a camel's head and neck couped ppr. *Perseverantia.* 132. 7

Crichton, Scotland, a pillar arg. *Stand sure.* 176. 3

Cricket or **Crickitt,** a lion passant gardant az. 4. 3

Cricket or **Crickitt,** Essex, a drake's head erased ppr.

Crickitt, Tom Shelton, Solicitor, Marine Lodge, Brighton, a drake's head erased ppr. *Accipe daque fidem.* 298. 12

Crickman, a stag lodged ppr. 115. 7

Cridland, Somers., issuing from clouds two dexter hands conjoined ppr. 224. 1

Crierie, *see* M'Cririe.

Crigan, Ireland, a harp ppr., ensigned with a human heart gu. *cf.* 168. 9

Criktoft, a demi-unicorn az. 48. 7

Crimes, Dorset, a martlet sa. 95. 5

Cringan, Crinan, and **Crinzian,** Scotland, a dexter arm in armour embowed, holding a dagger bendways, point downwards ppr. *Subito.* 195. 4

Crioll, environed with clouds ppr., a mullet or. *cf.* 164. 11

Cripps, an ostrich's head erased, gorged with a ducal coronet, and holding a horse-shoe in its beak, all ppr.

Cripps, Charles Alfred, M.P., M.A., K.C., Parmoor, Henley-on-Thames, same crest. *Fronti nulla fides.*

Cripps, Wilfred Joseph, Esquire, C.B., M.A., F.S.A., Cirencester, same crest and motto.

Cripps, Frederic William Beresford, of Ampney Park, Cirencester, same crest.

Cripps and Crips, an arm in armour embowed, holding a scimitar ppr. 300. 8

Cripps, William Charles, J.P., the Lawn, Camden Park, Tunbridge Wells, same crest.

Cririe, Scotland, a bee-hive sa., with bees volant or. *Industria.* 137. 7

Crisp, out of a ducal coronet or, the attires and scalp of a stag ppr. 123. 3

Crisp, a camelopard statant ppr. 132. 8

Crisp or **Crispe,** Kent, a camelopard arg., pellettée, attired, collared, and lined or.

Crisp or **Crispe,** Middx., a camelopard or, pellettée, attired and collared of the first, lined arg.

Crisp, Frederick Arthur, Esquire, of Grove Park, Denmark Hill, and of Broadhurst, Surrey, upon a rock ppr., a camelopard statant sa., semée of annulets, and gorged with a collar, thereto affixed a chain reflexed over the back, and holding in the mouth a horse-shoe, all or. *Dum tempus habemus operemur bonum.* 132. 11

Crisp, George Edwin, Esquire, of Playford Hall, Suff., same crest and motto.

Crisp, William Henry, Esquire, of the Cedars, Great Bealings, Suff., same crest and motto.

Crisp, Fred, Esquire, of White House, New Southgate, Middx., Moor Barns, Maddingley, and Girton, Cambridge, in front of a camelopard statant arg., semée of pellets, gorged with a collar with line reflexed over the back gu., three horse-shoes sa. *Mens conscia recti.* 233. 7

Crispie, a lion passant gu., his dexter paw resting on a bezant. *cf.* 6. 2

Crispin, a chevalier on horseback at full speed tilting with a lance, all ppr.

Crispin, a seven-headed hydra vert. 73. 3

Critchett, Sir George Anderson, M.A., 21, Harley Street, Cavendish Square, a starling ppr.

Critchley or **Critchlow,** a harp vert. 168. 9

Croachrod, a wolf regardant pierced through the body with a spear, the end in its mouth. *cf.* 28. 6

Croachrod, *see* Cracherode.

Croad or **Croade,** on a cloud a celestial sphere ppr. *cf.* 159. 5

Croall, David, Esquire, of Southfield, Liberton, Edinburgh, a horse's head couped gu. *I press forward.* *cf.* 50. 13

Croasdaile, a demi-man in armour holding in his dexter hand a sword ppr. 187. 1

Crobber, on a winged globe an eagle with wings expanded ppr. 159. 9

Crochrod, Essex and Suff., a demi-boar rampant regardant gu., armed or, transpierced by a broken spear arg., grasped in the mouth.

Crockat or **Crockett,** on a rock a solan goose ppr.

Crockat or **Crockett,** Scotland, a dog sleeping sa., spotted arg. *Tak' tent.* 57. 13

Crocker, Surrey, a horse passant arg. *Fama semper vivit.* 52. 6

Crocker, J. Hedley, M.D., Gort House, Petersham, Surrey, a raven ppr. *Deus alit eos.*

Crockett, a Cornish chough ppr. *Crow not, croak not.* 107. 14

Crockford, a dexter hand holding a roll of parchment ppr. 215. 6

Crode, a demi-dragon sans wings or, the tail environed round the body.

Croeker, a crow sa., crowned arg., holding in his beak an ear of wheat or.

Croft, Sir Herbert George Denman, Bart., D.L., J.P., of Croft Castle, Heref.: (1) A wyvern sa., vulned in the side gu. *cf.* 70. 2. *Esse quam videri.* (2) A lion passant gardant arg. *Tryumphe o Trespas.* 4. 3

Croft, Richard Benyon, Esquire, of Fanhams Hall, Ware, Herts, same crests and motto.

Croft, Sir John Frederick, Bart., Yorks, and Kent: (1) A lion passant gardant or, supporting an escutcheon arg., charged with the cross of St. George gu. (2) A lion passant gardant per pale indented gu. and erminois, the dexter fore-paw resting on an escutcheon arg., charged with a representation of the star of the Order of the Tower and Sword ppr. *Esse quam videri.—Valor e lealdade.*

Croft, Harry, Stillington Hall, Easingwold, Yorks, crest same as second above.

Croft, Yorks, a lion passant gardant sa., supporting with the dexter paw an escutcheon pæan, charged with a lion passant gardant or.
Croft, a wyvern vert. 70. 1
Croft, a dragon's head couped vert. 71. 1
Croft, a talbot sejant. *cf.* 55. 2
Crofton, Baron (Crofton), of Mote, co. Roscommon, Ireland, seven ears of wheat conjoined on one stalk or. *Dat Deus incrementum.—Pro patriâ et rege.*
Crofton, Sir Morgan George, Bart., D.L., of Mohill House, co. Leitrim, seven ears of wheat on one stalk ppr. *Dat Deus incrementum.*
Crofton, Rev. Addison, of Linton Court, Settle, same crest and motto.
Crofton, Rev. William d'Abzac, M.A., of Puckeridge, Standon, Ware, Herts, same crest and motto.
Crofton, Sir Malby, Bart., of Longford House, co. Sligo, seven ears of wheat on one stalk ppr. *Dat Deus incrementum.*
Crofton, out of a mount vert six ears of wheat or, bladed ppr. *cf.* 154. 7
Crofton, Ireland, an ear of wheat ppr. 154. 3
Crofton, an eagle's head erased, ducally gorged, holding in the beak a pheon, all ppr. 83. 10
Crofton, Ireland, a savage's head ppr. 190. 12
Crofts of Velvetstown, Cork, a bull's head caboshed sa., armed or, thereon a chevron of the last. *Virtute et fidelitate.* *cf.* 43. 8
Crofts, Christopher, of Velvetstown, Cork, a bull's head caboshed sa. *Virtute et fidelitate.*
Crofts of Cloheen, Cork, same crest and motto.
Crofts, a bull's head couped sa., armed or. *cf.* 44. 3
Crofts, Suff., a bull's head caboshed sa., armed or. 43. 8
Crofts, a bull's head caboshed arg., armed or. 43. 8
Crofts, a dragon's head vert, charged with three ermine spots. *cf.* 71. 1
Crofts, Heref. and Shropsh., a wyvern with wings addorsed az. 70. 1
Crofts, a lion passant gardant or. 4. 3
Crofts, on a chapeau az., turned up erm., an eagle's neck with two heads erased sa., gorged with an Eastern crown or.
Crofts, a talbot sejant erm. *cf.* 55. 2
Crog, or **Crogg** a crescent gu., charged with an étoile arg. *cf.* 163. 2
Crog or **Crogg**, a cross moline or, between two ears of wheat orleways of the same. 154. 14
Croke of Chilton and Chequers, Bucks, and Studley and Waterstock, Oxon., two swans' necks addorsed and interlaced issuing out of a crescent, all arg., and holding in each beak an annulet gu. 100. 11
Croke, John, Esquire, of the Abbey, Cirencester, Glouc., same crest. *Virtutis amore.*
Croke or **Crook**, a celestial and a terrestrial sphere ppr. 159. 3
Croker, Ireland, a demi-wyvern with wings expanded sa. 69. 12
Croker of Croker's Hele, Crokern Tor, and Lineham, Devonsh., a drinking-cup or, with three fleur-de-lis of the same issuing therefrom, and charged with a rose gu. *Je tiendray ma puissance par ma foi.* 177. 1
Croker of West Molesey, Surrey, a drinking-cup or, with three fleur-de-lis issuing therefrom ppr., and charged on the centre with a rose gu. *Deus alit eos.—J'ai ma foi tenu a ma puissance.* 177. 1
Croker, Devonsh. a raven ppr. 107. 14
Croker, Oxon., a raven ppr., ducally gorged or, holding in the beak an ear of wheat of the last. *cf.* 107. 6
Croker of London and Glouc., an arm in armour embowed ppr., garnished or, holding in the hand an anchor, also ppr.
Crokey, Yorks, a lion's head sa., erased gu. 17. 8
Crole, a unicorn's head erased arg., armed and crined or, between two elephants' trunks sa.
Crolly, a wolf passant sa. 28. 10
Cromartie, Earl of, Viscount Tarbat of Tarbat, **Baron Macleod** of Castle Leod, and **Baron Castlehaven**, all in the county of Cromartie (Rt. Hon. Francis Leveson-Gower): (1) A wolf passant arg., collared and chained or (*for Gower*). *cf.* 28. 10. (2) A goat's head erased erminois (*for Leveson*). 128. 5. (3) A cat-a-mountain salient ppr. (*for Sutherland*). *Frangas non flectes.* 26. 3
Crombie, a demi-lion rampant gardant or, holding in the dexter paw a fleur-de-lis gu. *cf.* 13. 2
Crombie, an eagle displayed gu. 75. 2
Crombie of Phesdo, Scotland, same crest. *Fear God.* 75. 2
Crome, Berks and Middx., out of a mural coronet or, a demi-lion sa., holding in the dexter paw a fleur-de-lis arg. *cf.* 13. 2
Cromer, Earl of (Baring), a mullet erminois between two wings arg. *Probitate et labore.*
Cromer, a ram's head couped gu., charged with two palets arg. *cf.* 130. 1
Cromer, Norf., a crow sa. *cf.* 107. 5
Cromer, a demi-lion arg., armed and langued gu. 10. 2
Cromer, a chevalier in armour standing beside a war-horse and holding the bridle, all ppr. 53. 11
Cromie, Bart., Ireland: (1) A dexter hand apaumée ppr. 222. 14. (2) A centaur with a bow and arrow ppr., the equestrian part grey. *Labor omnia vincit.* 53. 2
Cromie, Ireland, a dexter hand erect holding a cross crosslet fitched. 221. 14
Cromlyn, a fawn's head caboshed or.
Crommelin, De la Cherois-, of Carrowdore, co. Down, Ireland: (1) Out of a ducal coronet or, a swan rising ppr. (*for Crommelin*). *cf.* 99. 5. (2) An anchor az. (*for De la Cherois. Fac et spera.* 161. 1
Crompe of Stonelinch, Sussex, three quatrefoils erect or, stalked and leaved ppr. 148. 7
Crompe, a cat rampant sa. 26. 2
Crompton, Staffs and Lancs, a talbot sejant or, holding in the dexter paw a coil of rope of the same. *cf.* 55. 2
Crompton, Staffs., out of a mural coronet gu., a sea-horse's head or, the mane arg.
Crompton, Derbysh., a demi-horse sa., vulned in the chest by an arrow or, feathered arg. *Love and loyalty.* *cf.* 53. 3
Crompton, John Gilbert, Esquire, of Flower Lilies, Windley, Derbysh., same crest and motto.
Crompton-Roberts, Charles Montagu, Esquire, of Drybridge, Monmouth, and 52, Mount Street, London, W.: (1) A demi-lion guardant per bend dove-tailed or and gu., holding in the dexter paw a sword erect, ppr., and resting the sinister upon a pheon or (*for Roberts*). 306. 1. (2) A talbot sejant or, pellettee, resting the dexter paw upon an escutcheon az., charged with a lozenge arg. (*for Crompton*). *God and my conscience.* 306. 2
Crompton-Roberts, Major Henry Roger, of 16, Belgrave Square, London, S.W., same crests and motto.
Cromuel, Hants, an eagle displayed, holding in the dexter claw a sword. 75. 7
Cromwell, Earl of Essex, on a chapeau gu., turned up erm., a pelican or, guttée-de-larmes, vulned gu. *Semi mortuus qui timet.* 98. 7
Cromwell, Hants, a demi-lion rampant arg., guttée sa., holding a spear or, headed az.
Cromwell of Cheshunt Park, Herts, a demi-lion rampant arg., holding in the dexter paw a gem ring or. *Pax quæritur bello.—Mors meta laborum.* *cf.* 10. 2
Cron or **Crone**, seven arrows, six in saltier and one in pale or. 173. 7
Cron or **Crone**, a demi-fish az 139. 4
Crook, a sinister hand issuing from a cloud in the dexter pointing towards a serpent, the head erected ppr. 223. 7
Crook, an eagle displayed or. 75. 5
Crook, Scotland, an arm in armour embowed ppr., holding a fleur-de-lis or. 199. 14
Crook, a raven ppr. 107. 14
Crook, Lancs, a Cornish chough sa., beaked and legged gu. 107. 14
Crook, Herbert Evelyn, M.D., same crest. *Tiens à la verité.*
Crooke, Hants, a fleur-de-lis or, environed by a snake vert, its head issuing through the centre leaf. 300. 5
Crookes, Sir William, of 7, Kensington Park Gardens, W., an elephant quarterly or and vert, charged with two crosses pattées counterchanged, resting the dexter forefoot on a prism ppr. *Ubi crux ibi lux.* 230. 13
Crooks, Scotland, a demi-leopard ppr. *cf.* 25. 10
Crooks, Fleming, 72, South Audley Street, W., a demi-leopard rampant ppr. *Nihil sine Deo.* 299. 8
Crooks, an elephant quarterly or and gu. 133. 9
Crooks, Shropsh., an elephant quarterly or and gu. *Wisdom and strength.* 133. 9
Crookshank, Ireland, a wyvern with wings addorsed vomiting fire at both ends ppr. 69. 9
Crookshank, a dexter hand holding an ear of wheat, all ppr. 218. 14
Crookshank, Edgar March, Saint Hill, East Grinstead, a cubit arm erect in armour ppr., the naked hand also ppr., grasping a dagger pommelled and hilted or. *Conferre gladion.*

Crookshank, a demi-negro holding in the dexter hand a cocoa-nut ppr. *Per ardua.*

Croome of North Cerney House, Glouc., out of a mural crown or, a demi-lion sa., holding in the dexter paw a fleur-de-lis arg. *cf.* 13. 2

Croone, a lion's gamb erect and erased holding a snake, all ppr. 35. 3

Cropley of London and Middx., a lynx passant gardant ppr. *cf.* 127. 2

Cropley, Cambs and Hunts, a mountain-cat passant erm. 26. 4

Cropper, Thornburgh-, *see* Thornburgh.

Cropper, Lancs, a powter pigeon arg.

Cropper of Swaylands, Penshurst, Kent, upon a rock ppr., in front of two spears in saltire az., a cropper pigeon or. *Love every man, fear no man.* 94. 9

Cropper, James, of Ellergreen, Kendal, same crest and motto.

Cropper, Charles James, Esquire, of Ellergreen, Kendal, same crest and motto.

Cropper, Edward William, Esquire, of Fearnhead, Great Crosby, near Liverpool, same crest and motto.

Cropper, a triangular harrow ppr. 178. 4

Crosbey or **Crosbie**, Scotland, the stump of an oak-tree shooting new branches. *Resurgam.* 145. 2

Crosbie, Sir William Edward Douglas, Bart., of Maryborough, Queen's Co., three swords, two in saltire points downwards, the other in pale point upwards, environed by a snake, all ppr. *Indignante invidia florebit justus.*

Crosbie or **Crosbey**, Scotland, a quill and a sword in saltier ppr. 170. 4

Crosbie or **Crosby** Scotland, a holy lamb ppr., supporting the standard gu. *Nil desperandum.* 131. 2

Crosby, Ireland, a lion passant gardant arg. 4. 3

Crosby, between the horns of a crescent per pale arg. and gu., a cross flory or. *Te duce libertas!*

Crosby, two arms dexter and sinister couped in saltier ppr., vested, the dexter gu. and the sinister az., each brandishing a scimitar. 203. 10

Crosell, a stag's head at gaze gu., attired arg. *cf.* 119. 12

Crosfield, a lion rampant. *Virtus sub cruce crescit.*

Crosfield, William, of Annesley, Aigburth, Liverpool, same crest and motto.

Crosier, a cubit arm erect, vested gu., cuffed arg., holding a crosier or. *cf.* 207. 2

Crosland, Yorks, a cross flory quarterly gu. and arg. *Ultra pergere.*

Crosland, Walter, Esquire, of the Grange, Eaton Hastings, Faringdon, Berks, a cubit arm erect ppr., grasping a cross bottony gu., between two roses gu., stalked, leaved, and slipped, also ppr.

Crosley, Berks, a dragon's head sa., gorged with a collar or, charged with a cinquefoil gu. *cf.* 71. 2

Crosley, the late Sir Charles Decimus, of Kensington Gardens Terrace, Hyde Park, London, W., in front of a palm-tree ppr., an heraldic antelope arg., armed, ungu., and tufted or, resting the dexter foot upon a cross flory of the last. *Per crucem confido.* 127. 7

Crosroe, Ireland, an arm in armour embowed, holding in the hand a sword, all ppr. 195. 2

Cross-Buchanan, *see* Buchanan.

Cross, *see* Innes-Cross.

Cross, Viscount (Cross), of Broughton-in-Furness, Lancs, a griffin's head erased arg., gorged with a double chain or, therefrom pendent a mullet pierced sa., and holding in the beak a Passion nail, also sa. *Crede cruci.* 66. 14

Cross, William, Esquire, of Red Scar, Preston, Lancs, same crest and motto.

Cross, Scotland, a griffin segreant per fess gu. and sa., winged arg., the tips or. 62. 2

Cross, Carlton, of Crook Hall, Chorley, Lancs, in front of a griffin's head couped gu., langued gold, collared arg., three fleur-de-lis fesseways or. *Ex cruce flores.*

Cross, David, Esquire, of Ingliston, Renfrewsh., a griffin segreant sa., armed, beaked, and winged arg. *Sub cruce copia.* 62. 2

Cross, Alexander, Esquire, of Langbank, Renfrewsh., a griffin segreant sa., armed, beaked, and winged or. *Sub cruce copia.*

Cross, Robert, Esquire, of Leith and 13, Moray Place, Edinburgh, a griffin segreant sa., armed, beaked, and winged arg. *Sub cruce copia.*

Cross, Norf., a griffin passant arg. 63. 2

Cross, a dragon's head erased. *cf.* 71. 2

Cross, a dragon's head couped vert. 71. 1

Cross, Ireland, a stork ppr., holding in its beak a cross potent fitchée arg. *Certavi et vici.* *cf.* 105. 11

Cross, Geoffrey, 102, High Street, Ramsgate, a crane ppr., holding in its beak a cross botony arg. *Dum spiro spero in cruce fido.*

Cross, Ireland, two hands couped and conjoined in fess, holding a scimitar in pale ppr. *cf.* 224. 7

Cross, Chesh., on a mount vert, a stork erm., beaked and membered gu., resting his dexter claw on a cross crosslet of the last, and holding in the beak a plummet sa.

Cross, a lion passant gardant supporting an anchor ppr. 5. 10

Crossby, *see* Crosby

Crossdell, out of a mural coronet a cross patonce charged with a leopard's face, behind the cross two swords in saltier, points upwards.

Crosse, Yorks, a stork ppr., supporting with the dexter claw a crescent arg. *cf.* 105. 9

Crosse, Lancs, a stork ppr., holding in its beak a cross pomée arg. *cf.* 105. 9

Crosse of Crosse Hall, Liverpool, and Crosse Hall and Shaw Hill, Chorley, Lancs, a stork ppr., holding in its beak a cross botonnée arg. *cf.* 105. 11

Crosse, Thomas Richard, Esquire, of Chorley, Lancs, 38, Grosvenor Gardens, S.W., same crest. *Sub cruce salus.*

Crosse of London, on a chapeau gu., turned up erm., a stork az., resting the dexter claw on a cross moline arg. *cf.* 105. 3

Crosse, Rev. Marlborough, of the Vicarage, Terrington St. Clement, near King's Lynn, Norf., a gryphon's head erased gu., charged with a mullet of six points or, between two crosses potent, also gu. *Esse quam videri.* 241. 15

Crosse, Somers., a tower arg., flames issuing from the battlements ppr.

Crosse, a hand plucking a thistle ppr. 218. 5

Crosse, Scotland, a cross crosslet az. *Certum pete finem.* 165. 2

Crosse, Scotland, a cross crosslet fitched gu. Same motto. 166. 2

Crosse, Somers., a cross pattée fitchée gu., between two wings arg., each charged with a crosslet of the first. *Se inserit astris.*

Crossfield, a lion rampant. 1. 1

Crossfield, Talbot King, Esquire, of Stanningfield, Bury St. Edmunds; 8, Stone Buildings, Lincoln's Inn, London, a talbot passant or, holding in the mouth a cross crosslet fitchée az., and resting the dexter fore-leg on a cross couped of the second. *La croix ma foi.*

Crossing, Devonsh., a cross crosslet fitchée gu. 166. 2

Crossley, on a rock a swan ppr. *cf.* 99. 2

Crossley of Scaitcliffe, Lancs, a hind's head couped arg., holding in the mouth a cross moline fitchée, and charged upon the breast with a cross tau gu. *Credo et amo.*

Crossley, Sir Savile Brinton, Bart., J.P., M.P., of Somerleyton, Lowestoft, Suff., a demi-hind erased ppr., charged with two bars, and holding between the feet a cross crosslet or. *Omne bonum ab alto.* 262. 1

Crossman, Somers., a demi-lion erm., holding an escallop-shell sa. 13. 10

Crossman, Major-General Sir William, K.C.M.G., of Cheswick House and the Manor House, Holy Island, Northumb., on a wreath or and sa., in front of a goat's head erased arg., three cross crosslets fesseways gu. *In cruce spes mea.* 128. 8

Crosswell, an arm erect, vested, holding in the hand a club ppr.

Crost, out of a ducal coronet or, a swan's head between two wings ppr. 100. 10

Croste, Leics., a griffin's head arg. 66. 1

Crosthwaite, Ireland, a fox sejant or. 32. 11

Crosthwaite of Dublin, Ireland, a demi-lion rampant per fess ppr. and or. *Conquer or die.* 10. 2

Crosweller, a lion's head gardant and erased or, charged with a cross gu.

Crothers, Wallace George, Esquire, of Highfields, Chew Magna, Somers., on a club lying fessways ppr., an heraldic tiger passant or. *Sperandum est.* *cf.* 25. 5

Crotty, a hand holding up a scorpion ppr. 220. 1

Crotty, Ireland, a hind trippant gu. 124. 12

Crouch or **Crowch**, Herts and London, on a mount vert, a lamb couchant ppr. *cf.* 131. 12

Crouch, a sword in pale between two palm-branches in orle ppr. *cf.* 170. 3

Crouch, Sussex, same crest. *Sedulo et honeste tutela.*

Crouchard, a cross or, between two bucks' attires gu.

Crouchfield, on a mount a palm tree, all ppr 144 3
Crouchley, a leopard's face ppr 22 2
Croudace, Durh, an angel, the hands clasped on the breast, vested ppr *Promptus et fidelis* 184 12
Croughton, a leopard's head erased and affrontee, ducally gorged 23 8
Croughton, a dragon's head couped, holding in the mouth a glove cf 72 12
Crow, Ireland, a goat passant arg, armed and ungu sa. cf 129 5
Crow, Wales, a cock arg, combed, wattled, and membered or 91 2
Crow, Ireland, a camel's head couped arg, bridled and reined sa cf 132 7
Crow or **Crowe**, a camel's head or, vulned in the neck gu cf 132 7
Crow, Norf, five arrows sa, feathered arg, four in saltier and one in pale, banded gu 173 3
Crowch of London, on a mount vert, a lamb couchant arg cf 131 12
Crowch, a sword in pale between two branches of palm disposed orleways, all ppr cf 170 3
Crowcher, a lion couchant ppr, charged with a cross pattee or cf 7 5
Crowder, an escallop shell arg, charged with a mullet gu 141 6
Crowder of Clapham, Surrey, on the broken shaft of a tilting spear gu, an heraldic tiger passant arg cf 25 5
Crowder, Augustus George, J P, 6, Montagu Square, W, same crest *Carpe diem*
Crowder of London, on a mount vert, a tilting spear lying fessewise gu, there on an heraldic tiger passant or, wreathed round the middle with oak vert, holding a Roman fasces erect in the dexter paw ppr *En Dieu est ma fiance*
Crowe, *see* Crouch
Crowe, Thomas, Esquire, J P, D L., of Dromore House, co Clare, Ireland, on a mount vert, an Irish wolf-dog arg, collared gu *Skagh McEnchroe*
Crowe, Evan Barby, 10, Ladbroke Grove, W, a cock ppr *Sunt sua præmia laudi*
Crowe, out of a mural coronet an arm vested holding in the hand a mullet 206. 12
Crowfoot of Beccles, Suff, on a mount vert, a raven sa, supporting with the dexter claw a staff erect or, and en twined with a snake ppr *Cavendo*
Crowfoot, Edward Bowles, Esquire, same crest *Cavendo tutus*
Crowfoot, Rev John Henchman, of the Sub-Deanery, Lincoln, same crest and motto
Crowfoot, William Miller, Esquire, of Beccles, Suff, same crest and motto
Crowgay or **Crowgie**, an arm from the elbow holding in the hand a key ppr 217 7
Crowgey, a greyhound current arg cf 58 2
Crowhall, on a garb a crow, all ppr
Crowhall, on a rock a crow, all ppr *Nec cupias, nec metuas* 107 2
Crowhurst, Viscount, *see* Cottenham, Earl of
Crowley of Middx and Stourbridge, Worcs, on a mount vert, a sun in splendour ppr, charged with a rose gu cf 162 3
Crown or **Crowne**, a lion's head erased sa, ducally crowned arg 18 8
Crownall, a bull's horns and scalp ppr 123 8
Crownall, a dexter hand holding a dagger in pale point downward, all ppr cf 213 6
Crowther-Beynon, a lion rampant arg, semee of cross crosslets vert, and charged on the shoulder for distinction with a rose gu, holding between the fore paws an escutcheon, also arg, thereon a greyhound's head erased pean
Crowther-Beynon, Rev Samuel Bryan, of Beckenham, Kent, same crest
Crowton, a stag's head or 121 5
Croxton of Brookfield, Abergavenny, a dexter cubit arm vested az, cuffed arg encircled by a wreath of oak the hand supporting a cross botonnee fitchee in pale or on the dexter side of the wreath 249 6
Crozier, a stag's head cabossed ppr 122 5
Crozier, John George, Esquire, of Gortra House, co Fermanagh, a demi eagle displayed ppr, charged on the breast with a cross patee or *Vi et virtute*
Cruchley, *see* Crutchley
Cruck, a demi greyhound sa 60 11
Crucks, Scotland, a demi-leopard ppr. cf 23 13
Crucks, Scotland, a fetterlock az. 168 12
Cruden, a griffin's head ppr 66. 1
Crudgington and **Crudington**, a boar passant 40 9
Cruell or **Crull**, a centaur shooting an arrow from a bow ppr 52 2
Crugg, a falcon's head couped arg, collared gu, between two wings ad dorsed bendy of four or and sa
Cruice or **Cruise**, a demi-lion rampant or 10 2
Cruice or **Cruise**, Ireland, a greyhound's head erased or 61 4
Cruikshank of London, a hawk's head erased ppr *Audito et gradito* 88 12
Cruikshank, an arm in armour holding in the hand a sword ppr 210 2
Cruikshank of Stracathro, Scotland, a dexter hand in armour holding a dagger in pale ppr *Cavendo tutus* 210 4
Cruikshank, Augustus Walter, Esquire, of Langley Park, Montrose, Forfarsh, same crest and motto
Cruikshank, a boar's head couped, armed, and langued az 43 1
Cruikshanks, Scotland, an arm in armour holding a dagger in pale, and on its point a boar's head, all ppr cf 210. 4
Cruikshanks, a boar's head erased ppr *Vis fortibus arma* 42 2
Cruikshanks, Scotland, a boar's head couped, armed, and langued az 43 1
Crukes, on a garb in fess a pelican with wings addorsed vulning itself
Crule of Cambray, Spain, a demi-lion rampant holding a bezant 11 7
Crull, *see* Cruell
Crull or **Crulle**, an arm in armour in fess couped at the elbow, holding a broken lance in pale ppr, the head falling to the sinister
Crum, Alexander, Scotland, an oak-tree ppr *Fear God* 143 5
Crum, William Graham, Esq, of Thornlie bank, Glasgow, same crest and motto
Crumb, Scotland, an eagle displayed ppr *Fear God* 75 2
Crumbie, Scotland, an eagle with two heads displayed ppr 74 2
Crump or **Crumpe**, a cat salient gardant sa 26 3
Crump, Shropsh, a garb or 153 2
Crump, Crumpe, and **Crompe**, Sussex and Chesh, three quatrefoils or, stalked and leaved vert *Fixus adversa sperna* 148 7
Crump, Ernest Radclyffe, Huntingdon Court, Kington, Heref, same crest and motto 292 2
Crumpe, Sylverius, late of Hobart Town, Tasmania (1) On a mount vert, a cat salient gardant sa, charged with a cross crosslet fitchee or (*for Crumpe*) cf 26 3 (2) An arm in armour embowed, the hand grasping a sword entwined with a serpent, all ppr, and charged on the elbow with a trefoil clipped vert (*for Moriarty*) *Scandit sublimia virtus*
Crumpton, a fire beacon ppr 177 14
Cruse, *see* Crews
Cruso, a cross formee or *Virtus nobilitat* 165 7
Crutchfield, on a mount vert, a palm-tree ppr 144 3
Crutchley, on a chapeau a lion passant gardant ducally crowned cf 4 5
Crutchley or **Cruchley**, a talbot sejant arg cf 55 2
Crutchley, Percy Edward, of Sunninghill Park, Berks, on a mount vert, a talbot sejant arg, collared, and the line reflexed over the back or, the dexter fore paw resting on a torteau
Crutchley, Charles, Esquire, same crest.
Crutenden, a goat's head erased ppr 128 5
Cruttendon, an elk's head ppr
Crutwell, a hand holding a key ppr 217 7
Cruwys, George James, of Cruwys Morchard Court, Devonsh, on a mount vert, a stork ppr, holding in the dexter claw an escallop or 105 1
Cruwys, George James of Cruwys Morchard House, near Tiverton, on a mount vert a stork az, legged gu, resting the dexter leg on a stone ppr *Vigilate*
Crux of Kent, a demi eagle with wings expanded arg, holding in the beak a cross formee fitched sa cf 80. 2
Crymes, Surrey and Devonsh, a martlet vert 95 4
Crymes, an arm embowed in fess, vested or, holding in the hand a chaplet of laurel ppr
Crynes, a lion's head erased 17 8
Cubit or **Cubitt**, issuing out of clouds a dexter and a sinister hand combating with scimitars ppr 224 15
Cubit or **Cubitt**, Norf, an arm in armour embowed, the hand throwing an arrow ppr 198 4
Cubitt, of Denbies, Surrey, a Doric column ppr, in front thereof two falchions in saltire arg, pommels and hilts or *Felix qui prudens* 245 1
Cuckborne, on a chapeau gu, turned up erm, flames of fire ppr 180 10
Cudden, a wolf sejant az 29 3

Cuddon, Norf. and Suff., an arm embowed in armour, the hand grasping a bow strung and fully bent in fesse, the arrow in pale point upwards ppr. 235. 13
Cudmore and **Cudnor** of Kelvedon, Essex, a griffin passant or. 63. 2
Cudmore of Temple and Loxbeare, Devonsh., a griffin's head gu. 66. 1
Cudworth, Lancs, on a mount vert, an arm erect, couped at the elbow, vested erminois, holding in the hand a battle-axe headed sa., the handle or.
Cue, a demi-lion rampant or, holding between the paws a garb az. 12. 5
Cuerden and **Cureton,** a stag's head quarterly per fesse indented or and az., attired counterchanged. 121. 5
Cuellan, Van, of London, an angel ppr. with wings expanded, the outside or, the inside az., vested of the second, and holding in the dexter hand a spear sa.
Cuff, a demi-griffin ppr. 64. 2
Cuffe, Earl of Desart, *see* Desart.
Cuffe of Criche, Somers., an arm erect, habited bendy wavy arg. and az., cuffed erm., holding in the hand ppr. a battle-axe, also az., headed or. 207. 10
Cuffe, Wheeler-, Sir Charles Frederick Denny, Bart., D.L., of Leyrath, Kilkenny, an arm in armour embowed az., holding a baton gu. *Animus tamen idem.* 200. 3
Cuffe, an arm in armour embowed ppr., the hand holding the broken staff of a tilting-spear or. 197. 7
Cuiler, a broken spear in pale, the top falling to the sinister ppr. 175. 6
Cuillen, Ireland, a mermaid holding a comb and a mirror ppr. 184. 5
Culchech, an ox-yoke in bend sa. 178. 6
Culchech and **Culcheth,** issuing out of clouds two hands pulling an anchor from the sea, all ppr. 224. 13
Culcheth of Culcheth, Lancs, on a cap of maintenance gu., turned up erm., a blackamoor standing affrontée, holding in his dexter hand a dart, all ppr.
Cullamore of London, a demi-Turk in profile, vested gu., billettée or, the turban arg., the cap of the first, and on the top thereof a crescent of the third, holding in the dexter hand a Turkish sceptre of the second having on the top a crescent.
Cullen, Scotland, a pelican in her piety ppr. *Non sibi.* 98. 14
Cullen, an eagle displayed gu. 75. 2
Culleton of Culleton's Heraldic Office, 25, Cranbourn Street, London, W.C., a demi-lion rampant holding in the dexter paw a cross Calvary in bend sinister. *Nescit vox missa reverti.*
Culley of Coupland Castle and Fowberry Tower, Northumb., in front of an oak-tree ppr., a talbot statant per pale az. and or, gorged with a collar gemel arg., and holding in the mouth a lily slipped ppr. 278. 3
Culley, Rev. Matthew, of Coupland Castle Wooler, same crest. *Amicos semper amat.*
Culliford, two elephants' proboscis addorsed ppr. 123. 10
Culling, a griffin segreant arg. 62. 2
Cullowe of Tintagel, Cornw., a unicorn's head arg. 49. 7
Cullum, *see* Milner-Gibson-Cullum.
Cullum, Bart. (*extinct*), of Hawsted and Hardwick House, Suff., a lion sejant or, holding between its fore-paws a column arg., capital and base of the first. *Sustineatur.*
Culme-Seymour, Bart., *see* Seymour, Bart.
Culme of Dublin, a lion sejant ppr., supporting a column or, on the top a dove alighting arg. *Immobilis innocentia.*
Culmer, Devonsh., a leopard rampant ppr. *cf.* 27. 2
Culpeck, Surrey, a demi-unicorn or. *Honor et veritas.* 48. 7
Culpeper, a falcon arg., belled or. 85. 2
Culpepper of Astwood Court and Feckenham, Worcs., a falcon with wings expanded arg., beaked and belled or. 87. 1
Culverton, a pelican vulning herself ppr. 98. 1
Culy, a wolf's head erased erm. 30. 8
Cumber, Sussex, a lynx's head or, charged with three pellets, one and two.
Cumberland and Teviotdale, Duke of, Earl of Armagh, and **King of Hanover** (H.R.H. Prince Ernest Augustus William Adolphus George Frederick), upon a coronet composed of crosses pattée and strawberry-leaves a lion statant gardant or, crowned with a like coronet and charged with a label of three points arg., the centre point charged with a fleur-de-lis az., and each of the other points with the cross of St. George.
Cumberland, a hunting-horn gu., between two wings ppr. 112. 3
Cumberland, a demi-wolf salient sa. 31. 2
Cumberlege or **Cumberdedge,** Staffs, a unicorn's head erased az. 49. 5
Cumberlege-Ware, Charles Edward, Esquire, of Poslingford, Suff., in front of two spears in saltier ppr., a dragon's head gu., gorged with a collar gemelle arg. *Deo favente.*
Cumbrae-Stewart, Francis Edward, Esquire, J.P., of Montrose, Brighton, near Melbourne, and of Wildernesse, Beaconsfield, Mornington, Victoria, a demi-lion rampant gu. *Avito viret honore.* 10. 3
Cumby, a griffin's head erased gu. 66. 2
Cumine, Cuming, or **Cummin,** Scotland, a garb or. *Courage.* 153. 2
Cumine or **Cumming,** in a maunch gu., an arm ppr. 203. 3
Cumine or **Cumming,** Scotland, a dexter hand holding a sword ppr. 212. 13
Cumine or **Cumming,** Scotland, a dexter hand holding a sickle ppr. *Hinc garde nostra.* 219. 13
Cuming, Scotland, a lion rampant gu., holding in the dexter paw a dagger ppr. *Courage.* *cf.* 1. 13
Cumming, Scotland, an eagle rising ppr. *Nil arduum.* 77. 5
Cumming, a lion rampant ppr., armed and langued gu. *Courage.* 1. 13
Cumming-Bruce, Charles Lennox, Esquire, M.P., of Roseisle and Dunphail, Elgin, Scotland: (1) On the dexter side, on a cap of maintenance ppr., a dexter arm in armour from the shoulder embowed and resting on the elbow, also ppr., the hand holding a sceptre erect or (*for Bruce*). (2) On the sinister side, a lion rampant or, holding in his dexter fore-paw a dagger ppr. (*for Cumming*). *Fuimus.—Courage.* *cf.* 1. 13
Cumming, Gordon-, Sir William Gordon, Bart., D.L., of Altyre and Gordonstown, co. Elgin: (1) A lion rampant or, holding in the dexter paw a dagger ppr. *Courage.* (2) A cat sejant. *Sans crainte.* *cf.* 1. 13
Cumming of Auchray, a sword and a dagger saltireways ppr. *Courage.* *cf.* 171. 12
Cumming or **Cummyng,** two swords in saltire ppr. *Courage.* 171. 12
Cummings, a dexter hand ppr., vested az., holding a roll of paper arg. 208. 8
Cummins, Henry Alfred, Esquire, C.M.G., Major R.A.M.C., c/o Messrs. Holt and Co., 3, Whitehall Place, S.W., two arms embowed, vambraced, and hands ppr., holding a garb or, banded gu. *Hinc garbræ nostræ.*
Cummins, Brigadier-General James Turner, D.S.O., of Fort St. George, Madras, same crest and motto.
Cummins, William Edward Ashley, Esquire, of 17, St. Patrick's Place, Cork, and Woodville, Glanmire, co. Cork, same crest and motto.
Cunard, Sir Bache, Bart., J.P., on a rock ppr., a falcon with wings expanded arg., the dexter claw resting on a cinquefoil az. *By perseverance.* 259. 9
Cundall, Cundill, or **Cundy,** two ears of wheat in saltier ppr. 154. 4
Cundell, J. Ross, Esquire, of Leith, two ears of wheat in saltier ppr. *Spes aspera levat.* 154. 4
Cuningham, Scotland, a hand holding a lozenge or. 219. 10
Cuninghame, *see* Fairlie-Cuninghame.
Cuninghame, a dexter hand holding a plumb-rule ppr. *Ad amussim.*
Cuninghame, John William Herbert, Lainshaw, Ayr, N.B., same crest. *Over, fork over.*
Cuninghame, a dexter hand holding the upper part of an anchor by the ring ppr. *Enough in my hand.*
Cuninghame, a demi-lion gardant arg., holding in his dexter paw a scroll, and in his sinister a garb ppr. *Sedulo numen adest.*
Cuninghame of Caddell, Ayrsh., a unicorn's head couped arg., armed or. *Over, fork over.* 49. 7
Cuninghame, Sir Thomas Andrew Alexander Montgomery, Bart., of Corshill and Kirtonholm, Ayrsh., a unicorn's head erased ppr. *Over, fork over.* 49. 5
Cuninghame, John Alistair Erskine, Esquire, of Balgownie House, Culross, viâ Dunfermline, Fifesh., an oak-tree ppr. *Tandem.*
Cuninghame, William, Esquire, of Belmont, Ayrsh., N.B., a unicorn's head couped arg., gorged with a collar chequy az. and or. *So fork forward.*
Cuninghame, a unicorn's head erased ppr. *Over, fork over.* 49. 5
Cuninghame, a unicorn's head couped arg., gorged with a collar chequy az. and of the first. *So fork forward.* *cf.* 49. 11

Cuninghame, John Charles, Craigends, Renfrewsh., same crest and motto.
Cuninghame, Smith-, John Anstruther, Caprington Castle, Ayrsh.: (1) Crest same as above. (2) A ship in distress ppr., and over "*At spes infracta,*" also *Via tuta virtutis.*
Cuninghame, a unicorn sejant and grasping an oak-tree with his fore-feet, all ppr. *Mihi robori robur.* cf. 48. 3
Cunliffe, a hawk rising ppr. 87. 1
Cunliffe, Kent and Lancs, a greyhound sejant arg., collared or. cf. 59. 2
Cunliffe, Sir Robert Alfred, Bart., J.P., D.L., of Liverpool, Lancs, a greyhound sejant arg., collared sa. *Fideliter.* cf. 59. 2
Cunliffe, Captain Ellis Brooke, of Petton Park, Shrewsbury, and 18, Ennismore Gardens, S.W., same crest and motto.
Cunliffe, Pickersgill-, John Cunliffe, Esquire, of Hooley House, Surrey: (1) A greyhound sejant arg., collared sa. (*for Cunliffe*). cf. 59. 2. (2) On a rock ppr., an eagle with wings elevated sa., bezantée, holding in the beak a cross crosslet fitchée or (*for Pickersgill*). *Fideliter.*
Cunliffe, Pickersgill-, Harry, of Staughton Manor, Huntingdonshire, on a rock ppr., an eagle, wings elevated sa., bezantée, and holding in the beak a cross crosslet fitchée or. *Quæ recta sequor.*
Cunningham, *see* Gun-Cunningham.
Cunningham, *see* Miller-Cunningham.
Cunningham of Robertland, Scotland, a unicorn's head. *Fortitudine.* 49. 7
Cunningham, Scotland, a unicorn's head arg., maned and armed or. *Over, fork over.* 49. 7
Cunningham of Edinburgh, a unicorn's head sa., maned and armed or. *Over, fork over.* 49. 7
Cunningham of Bedland, a unicorn's head couped arg., armed and crined or. *Virtute et labore.* 49. 7
Cunningham, a unicorn's head erased ppr. *Sans varier.* 49. 5
Cunningham of Edinburgh, a unicorn's head erased arg. *Over, fork over.* 49. 5
Cunningham, a demi-unicorn or. 48. 7
Cunningham, on a mount vert, a unicorn couchant.
Cunningham, the trunk of an oak-tree with sprigs vert. *Tandem.* 145. 2
Cunningham of Lainshaw, Scotland, the stump of an oak-tree ppr., with one sprig vert. *Non obstante Deo.* 145. 2
Cunningham of Balgonie, an oak-tree ppr. *Tandem.* 143. 5
Cunningham, Bart., N.S., a dexter hand ppr. holding a lozenge or. *Curâ et candore.* 219. 10
Cunningham, a cubit arm erect, vested per pale or and az., cuffed arg., holding in the hand a pine-apple ppr.
Cunningham, a dexter hand holding the upper part of an anchor by the ring ppr.
Cunningham of Gattonside, Roxburghsh., a soldier fully equipped on horseback at full speed, and holding a sword in his dexter hand erect, all ppr. *Nec timeo, nec sperno.* 189. 10
Cunningham of Bomintoun, a demi-lady habited, holding in her dexter hand a pair of scales. *Præstat auro virtus.* 183. 2
Cunningham, Ireland, a lion's head erased or, semée of torteaux gu., ducally crowned az. 18. 9
Cunningham, out of a ducal coronet or, a dragon's head collared and chained, the wings addorsed. cf. 72. 1
Cunningham, out of a ducal coronet or, a mount vert, thereon a stork statant, holding in its beak a snake, the tail coiled, all ppr.
Cunningham of Baquhan, a boar's head couped az. *Curâ et constantiâ.* 43. 1
Cunninghame of Edinburgh, a maiden from the middle upwards in antique attire, holding in her dexter hand a balance ppr. *Virtus præstat auro.* 183. 2
Cunninghame, a martlet volant over water ppr. *Prospere qui sedulo.* cf. 96. 2
Cunninghame, Durh., the stump of an oak-tree sprouting ppr. 145. 2
Cunninghame, an arm in armour, holding in the hand a sword, all ppr. 210. 2
Cunninghame-Graham, Robert Bontine, Esquire, of Gartmore, Perthsh., and Finlaystone, Renfrewsh., an eagle displayed, in his dexter talon a sword in pale ppr. *For right and reason.*
Cunnington, a demi-lion rampant gu. 10. 3
Cunyngham, Dick-, Sir Robert Keith Alexander, Bart., of Prestonfield, Edinburgh, and of Lambrughton, Ayrsh., on the dexter side a dexter hand holding a plumb-rule ppr., on the sinister side a ship in distress ppr. *Ad amussin.*—*At spes infracta.*—*Via tuta virtutis.* 160. 14
Cunynghame, Sir Francis George Thurlow, Bart., of Milncraig, Ayrsh., a unicorn's head armed and crined or. *Over, fork over.* 49. 7
Cunynghame, Henry Hardinge Samuel, Esquire, C.B., M.A., of Barn Bridge, South Nutfield, Surrey, Home Office, Whitehall, and 134, Cromwell Road, S.W., a unicorn ungu., maned and armed or, lying on a mount vert. In an escroll above the crest. *Over, fork over.*
Cupholme, Lincs, a ram's head erased gu., armed or. 130. 6
Cuppage, a sundial arg. 176. 7
Cupper, Somers., on a mural crown arg., a pelican erm., vulning her breast gu., beaked and legged or. 98. 3
Cupplade, Lancs, a lion's head erased erm., charged with three guttes-d'or, two and one. cf. 17. 8
Cupples, a demi-man in military costume ppr., holding a banner az.
Cure, George Edward Capel, of Blake Hall, Ongar, Essex, out of a ducal coronet a griffin's head with wings expanded, all arg., charged on the neck with a rose gu. *Fais que droit arrive que pourra.* 67. 3
Cure, Colonel Alfred Capel, of Badger Hall, Shifnal, Shropsh.: (1) Out of a ducal coronet arg., a griffin's head between two wings expanded of the first, and charged on the neck with a rose gu. (*for Cure*). 67. 3. (2) A bull's scalp arg. (*for Cheney*). *Fato prudentia major.*—*Fais ce que doit arrive que pourra.* 123. 8
Cureton, *see* Cuerden.
Curle of Soberton, Hants, an eagle with wings expanded ppr., beaked and legged or. 77. 5
Curle, R. Barclay, Esquire, of Shieldhill, Biggar, Scotland, and New Club, Glasgow, a demi-eagle with wings expanded ppr. *Une foi.* 80. 2
Curle of London, on a mount vert, a hedgehog or. *Un Dieu, un Roy, un Foy.* cf. 135. 8
Curle of St. Margaret's Cottage, Bradwell-on-Sea, Essex, on a mount vert, a porcupine or. *Un Dieu, un Roy, un Foy.* 305. 5
Curley and **Curling,** on a mural coronet or, a dragon's head erased vert, ducally gorged and lined of the first, from the mouth issuing flames of fire ppr.
Curling, Kent, a savage's head in profile ppr., wreathed about the temples vert. 190. 7
Curran and **Curren,** Ireland, a parrot's head between two wings. 101. 10
Currel and **Curle,** Scotland, a bugle-horn stringed and knotted *Forward.* 228. 11
Currell, Devonsh., a peacock's head couped ppr. 103. 2
Curren, Scotland, a parrot's head between two wings ppr. 101. 10
Currer, Yorks, a lion's head erased arg., collared sa., rimmed and studded or, *Merite.* 18. 6
Currer of Clifton House, Yorks: (1) A lion's head erased arg., gorged with a collar sa., charged with three bezants (*for Currer*). cf. 18. 6. (2) A sword in pale arg., hilt and pommel or (*for Roundell*). *Merere.* 170. 2
Currey, a golden fleece ppr. 130. 2
Currey, Robert, Esquire, of Herne Hill, Surrey, between two oak-branches fructed ppr., an escutcheon gu., charged with a rose arg., barbed and seeded vert. *Espérance.* 149. 7
Currey of Erlwood, Windlesham, Surrey, and Fachlwyd, Hall, Ruthin, North Wales, a rose gu.
Currie or **Currey,** a rose arg., barbed and seeded vert. 149. 4
Currie, a golden fleece ppr. 130. 2
Currie, Ireland, an arm in armour embowed, holding in the hand a spear, all ppr. cf. 197. 1
Currie, Scotland, a demi-lion rampant ppr. *Courage.* 10. 2
Currie of Bush Hill, Middx., and Minley Manor, a cock gu. 91. 2
Currie, John Lang, Esquire, J.P., of Larra and Titanga, both co. Hampden, and Eildon, Grey Street, St. Kilda, Victoria, a cock gu. *Audax et vigilans.* 91. 2
Currie, Scotland, a cock crowing ppr. *Vigilans et audax.* 91. 2
Currie, Rev. Sir Frederick Larkins, Bart., M.A., Rector of Old Alresford, Hants, a cock ppr., resting its foot upon a rose arg., barbed and seeded ppr. cf. 91. 2
Currie, Henry William, Esquire, of Rushden House, Higham Ferrers, same crest and motto.
Currie, James Pattison, Esquire, of Sandown House, Esher, same crest.
Currie, Laurence, Esquire, of Minley Manor, Farnborough, Hants, same crest.
Curry, a cock gu. 91. 2

Curry of Manchester, a griffin's head erased arg., charged on the neck with an annulet gu., and holding in the beak another annulet az. *Aspiro.* cf. 66. 2

Curry and **Cory**, Ireland, out of a ducal coronet a griffin's head or, between two wings of the last, semée of estoiles sa. cf. 67. 1

Curry, a demi-lion arg. *Fortis et lenis.* 10. 2

Curryer of London, a cinquefoil vert. 148. 12

Curson of Keddleston, Derbysh., a popinjay with wings expanded or, beaked, legged, and collared gu. *Let Curson hold what Curson held.*

Curson, Derbysh., a cockatrice with wings addorsed and tail nowed gu. cf. 68. 5

Curson of Letheringsett, Norf., two arms in armour ppr., couped at the shoulders, garnished or, holding a sword fesseways, the hilt in the dexter gauntlet, the point to the sinister.

Curtayne, on a rock a leopard sejant ppr. 24. 12

Curteis of Appledore and Otterden Place, Kent, of Tenterden and Rye, and of Windmill Hill, Sussex, a unicorn passant or, between four trees ppr.

Curteis, a wolf's head couped arg., collared and spiked sa., chained or. cf. 30. 9

Curteis, Curtess, Curteys, Curtois, or **Curtoys,** a demi-husbandman vested az., holding over the shoulder an ox-yoke ppr. *Another,* holding over the shoulder a ploughshare. 187. 14

Curteis, Herbert, Esquire, of Windmill Hill Place, Hailsham, Sussex, a unicorn passant or, between four trees ppr. *Fortiter suaviter.*

Curteis, Rev. Thomas Samuel, of the Rectory, Sevenoaks, same crest. *Courtois sans bassesse.*

Curtis, an arm in mail, garnished arg.

Curtis, an arm in armour embowed, holding in the hand a sword ppr., garnished arg. 195. 2

Curtis, Sir Arthur Colin, Bart., of Gatcombe, Hants, out of a naval coronet or, an arm embowed, vested az., cuffed arg., supporting a flagstaff ppr., thereon a flag of the second, charged with a wolf's head or, and a canton gyronné of four gu. and az., thereon a cross of the third within a bordure of the first. *Per ardua.*

Curtis, Ireland, a hand holding four arrows, points downward. cf. 214. 3

Curtis of East Cliffe, Devonsh., an arm in armour embowed, holding in the hand ppr. a scimitar arg., hilt and pommel or. 196. 10. *Another crest,* an arm in armour erect, holding in the hand a sword, all ppr., hilt and pommel or. *Velle bene facere.* 210. 2

Curtis, an arm in mail ppr., holding in the hand a scimitar arg.

Curtis, Curtois, and Curtoys, *see* Curteis.

Curtis of Thornfield, Lancs, in front of a horse's head arg., holding in the mouth a fleur-de-lis az., a fasces fessewise ppr. *Perseverando vinco.* 51. 12

Curtis, Sir William Michael, Bart., of Cullands Grove, Middx., a ram's head couped arg., surmounted by two branches of oak in saltier ppr. *Gradatim vincimus.* cf. 130. 1

Curtis, Suff., a lion sejant ppr., supporting with his dexter paw an escutcheon of the arms, viz.: az., a chevron dancettée between three mural coronets or.

Curtis of Roscrea, co. Tipperary, Ireland, a dolphin naiant az., pierced in the side with a feather or. cf. 140.5

Curtis, Shropsh., a leopard's face or. 22. 2

Curtis, a greyhound's head between two roses. 61. 11

Curtler, Frederick Lewis, of Bevere House, Worcs., a lion's head erased bendy sinister or and az., ducally crowned of the first, from the mouth flames issuant ppr. *Labor omnia vincit.* cf. 17. 1

Curtoys of the Longhills, Lincs, an escallop. *Soyez courtois.* 141. 14

Curtoys, a triton holding in his sinister hand a trident. 185. 12

Curwen, a demi-savage regardant, wreathed about the head and middle with leaves, all ppr. 185. 1

Curwen, Alan De Lancy, of Workington Hall, Cumb., a unicorn's head erased arg., armed or. *Si je n'estoy.* 49. 5

Curwen, Rev. Edward Hasell, Plumbland Rectory, Carlisle, same crest and motto.

Curzon, Earl Howe and **Baron Scarsdale,** *see* those titles.

Curzon, Viscount, *see* Howe, Earl.

Curzon, Roper-, Baron Teynham, *see* Teynham.

Curzon, *see* Zouch, Baron de la.

Curzon, a popinjay rising or, collared gu. *Let Curzon holde what Curzon helde.*

Curzon, George Augustus, same crest and motto.

Cusac-Smith, Bart., out of a ducal coronet or, a unicorn's head az., armed or. *En Dieu est mon espoir.* 48. 12

Cusach, Cusack, and **Cusacke,** a spear enfiled with a savage's head couped ppr. 191. 7

Cusack of Killeen, Gerrardstown, Lismullen, and Clonard, co. Meath, Ireland, a mermaid sa., holding in the dexter hand a sword, and in the sinister a sceptre ppr. *Ave Maria, plena gratia.—En Dieu est mon espoir.* cf. 184. 7

Cusack, James William Henry Claud, of Abbeville House, Malahide, co. Dublin, same crest and mottoes.

Cusack, Sir Ralph Smith, of Furry Park, Raheny, Dublin, same crest.

Cusack-Smith, Sir (Thomas) Berry, K.C.M.G., of British Legation, Santiago, and British Consulate-General, Valparaiso, out of a ducal coronet or, a unicorn's head az. *En Dieu est mon espoir.*

Cusacke, a dexter hand holding a seax cutting at a quill, all ppr. 213. 9

Cush or **Cushe,** a cock sa., combed and wattled gu. 91. 2

Cushney of Aberdeen, Scotland, an anchor ppr., surmounted by a fleur-de-lis or. *Spes meum solatium.* 161. 9

Cussans or **De Cusance,** a dexter hand holding a boar's head in pale and erased, all ppr. 220. 6

Cussans of Jamaica, an eagle displayed gu., armed and langued az., charged on the breast with a bend arg., thereon with three fleurs-de-lis sa. *Dum spiro spero.* cf. 75. 2

Cust, Earl Brownlow, *see* Brownlow.

Cust, Sir Charles Leopold, Bart., of Leasowe Castle, Chesh., a lion's head erased sa., gorged with a collar paly wavy of six arg. and az. *Esse quam videri.* 18. 6

Cust, same crest. *Qui custodit caveat.*

Cust, Sir Reginald John, of 13, Eccleston Square, same crest.

Cust, Robert Needham, Esquire, LL.D., of 63, Elm Park Gardens, S.W., same crest. *Opera illius mea sunt.*

Cust of Stamford, Lincs, a lion's head erased sa., collared gobonée arg. and az. 18. 6

Cust, a dexter arm vested arg., the hand ppr. holding a scroll on which is the motto, "*In cruce salus.*"—*In morte quies.*

Custance, a covered cup.

Custance, Norf., out of a ducal coronet or, a phœnix gu., in flames ppr. 82. 5

Custance, Rev. Charles Edward Salwey, Lullington Vicarage, Burton-on-Trent, a demi-eagle displayed gu., on the breast a mullet of six points or. *Appetitus rationi pareat.*

Custance, Colonel Frederic Hambleton, C.B., J.P., Weston House, Norf., a demi-eagle displayed gu., charged on the breast with a star of six points or. *Appetitus rationi pareat.* cf. 81. 3

Cutberd, Cuthberd, Cuthbert, and **Cutbert,** a lion's head erased arg., gorged with a collar gu., charged with three cross crosslets fitched of the first. cf. 18. 6

Cuthbert of Canada, a cubit arm holding an arrow ppr. *Fortiter.* 214. 4

Cuthbert, Robert Thomas Powlett, of Rosedale, Westwood Park, Southampton, a dexter arm in armour, holding an arrow ppr. *Fortiter.*

Cuthbert of Castlehill, Inverness, and Rosshall Aberdeen, Scotland, a hand gauntleted holding a dart. *Nec minus fortiter.*

Cuthbert or **Cuthburt,** on a heart gu., an eagle's claw erased at the thigh ppr. 113. 14

Cuthbert, an arm in armour embowed, grasping a broken spear, all ppr. 197. 2

Cuthbert, Scotland, a cubit arm erect, the hand grasping a tilting-spear in bend sinister ppr. *Nec minus fortiter.* 214. 11

Cuthbert-Kearney: (1) A dexter arm in armour couped below the elbow in fesse, the hand bare grasping a dagger erect, all ppr. (*for Kearney*). (2) A demi-lion rampant or, debruised by an arrow point downwards gu. (*for Cuthbert*). *Semper fidelis.* cf. 10. 2

Cuthell or **Cuthill,** on a ducal coronet or, a leopard sejant, gorged ppr. cf. 24. 11

Cutlar-Fergusson, Robert, Esquire, of Craigdarroch, Monaive, Dumfries, N.B., a dexter hand grasping a broken spear in bend. *Vi et arte.*

Cutler, Suff., a dragon's head erased or, ducally gorged gu. 71. 8

Cutler of Bloherby, Leics., a dragon's head erased gu. cf. 71. 2

Cutler, Yorks, a dragon's head erased or, ducally gorged az. *cf.* 71. 8

Cutler, Colonel John Edward, J.P., of Valetta, Sheffield, a dragon's or wyvern's head erased or, ducally collared az. *Dum spiro spero.* 71. 8

Cutler of Westminster, a dragon's head erased az., gorged with a mural coronet or, holding in the mouth a laurel-branch vert.

Cutler of Ipswich, Suff., a demi-lion gu., holding between the paws a Danish battle-axe arg., staff or. 15. 4

Cuttes, an eagle displayed arg., beaked and membered gu. 75. 2

Cutting, a demi-griffin arg., collared az., holding between its claws an escallop or. *cf.* 65. 8

Cutts of Childerley, Cambs, a greyhound's head erased arg., collared gu., ringed or. *cf.* 61. 2

Cuyet, a goat's head erased sa. 128. 5

Cuyler, Sir Charles, Bart., of St. John's Lodge, Herts, on a mural crown ppr., a battle-axe erect surmounted by two arrows in saltier or, flighted arg., points upwards. *Deo non sagittis fido.*

Cyfer, a griffin's head ppr. 66. 1

D.

Dabbins, out of a mural coronet chequy arg. and sa., an acorn or, leaved vert. 152. 3

Dabernon, Devonsh., in a maunch gu., a hand apaumée ppr. 203. 1

Dabetot or **Dabitot**, Warw., a dove holding in its beak an olive-branch ppr. 92. 5

D'Abrichecourt, out of a ducal coronet or, a plume of feathers arg., debruised by two bars gu., each charged with three lozenges of the first.

Dabridgcourt, Hants and Warw., out of a ducal coronet or, four feathers arg., charged with two bars gu., on each three mascles of the first. *cf.* 114. 1

Daccomb of Stapleton, Dorset, a pair of wings conjoined ppr. 113. 1

Daccome of Croft Castle, Dorset, an oak-tree ppr., fructed or, round the tree a scroll with the motto, "*Virtutis robore robor.*"

Da Costa, a reindeer trippant ppr. 125. 9

D'Acre, an eagle rising ppr. 77. 5

Dacre, Baron, *see* Hampden, Viscount.

Dacre, an eagle rising sa. 77. 5

Dacre, a bull statant gu., the tail extended. *Forte en loyauté.* *cf.* 45. 2

Dacre, a demi-tiger ducally gorged and chained ppr.

Dacres, Heref., a buckle. 178. 5

Dacres, a dove az., charged on the neck with an escallop or, between two oak-branches vert, fructed of the second. *cf.* 92. 14

Dade of Woodton, Norf., and Tannington, Suff., a garb or, enfiled with a ducal coronet per pale az. and gu. 153. 5

Dadley, a naked arm embowed, holding in the hand two slips of columbine, all ppr. *In malos cornu.*

Daer, Lord, *see* Selkirk, Earl.

D'Aeth, Hughes-, of Knowlton Court, Kent, a griffin's head erased or, holding in the beak a trefoil slipped vert. *cf.* 66. 2

Dagget, an eagle displayed gu., charged with a bezant. 75. 1

Dagget, Scotland, a demi-talbot sa., collared or *cf* 55. 11

Dagley, a Minerva's head from the shoulders affrontée.

Dagworth, a lion's gamb erased holding the hilt of a broken sword ppr. 38. 2

Daille, Scotland, a swan's head and neck couped ppr. *Laudes cano heroum.* *cf.* 101. 5

Daintry, a bull's head and neck ducally gorged, all ppr. *cf.* 44. 2

Daisie, Scotland, a hawk's head erased ppr. 88. 12

Dakeham, Lincs and Shropsh., a dove or 92. 2

Dakyns, Derbysh., of Hackness, and of Linton, Yorks, out of a naval coronet or, a dexter arm embowed ppr., holding in the hand a battle-axe arg., round the wrist a ribbon az. *Strike, Dakyns, the devil's in the hempe.* *cf.* 201. 5

Dalavall, Northumb., a ram's head arg., armed or. 130. 1

D'Albani, Arthur James Louis Francis, Esquire, of Newmarket, on a wreath of the colours two ostrich-feathers in saltire az., thereon perched a martlet or. *Vestigia nulla retrorsum.*

Dalbiac, Yorks, a dove with wings expanded, holding in the beak an olive-branch. 94. 5

Dalbiac, same crest. *Pax et amor.*

Dalbie and **Dalby**, a crane regardant resting its dexter claw on a stone *cf.* 105. 5

Dalby, Sir William Bartlett, M.B., B.A. (Cantab.), F.R.G.S., of Red Lodge, Englefield Green, Surrey, in front of a dexter arm embowed to the sinister, holding in the hand an ancient lamp, a serpent nowed, all ppr. *Probitas verus honos.* 253. 15

Dalby of Castle Donnington, Leics., a demi-griffin segreant ppr. *In Deo spero.* 64. 2

Dalby, J. Lyttleton, M.R.C.S., 13, Buckingham Road, Brighton, same crest. *Fidelis et tenax.*

Dalby of Reading, Berks, a demi-griffin segreant ppr. 64. 2

Dalby, a demi-Hercules with lion's skin and club ppr.

Dale, a swan ppr. 99. 2

Dale, Northumb., a stork ppr. 105. 11

Dale, a stork arg., beaked, legged, and ducally gorged or. *cf.* 105. 11

Dale, on a chapeau gu., turned up erm., a heron arg., beaked, legged, and ducally gorged or. *cf.* 105. 3

Dale, Brodrick, Esquire, J.P., of Cleadon Meadows, Durh., and of Apperley Dene, Stocksfield, Northumb., upon a rock ppr., a heron arg., gorged with a collar gemelle gu., and resting the dexter foot on a fret or. *Spectemur agendo.* 258. 15

Dale, Sir David, Bart., West Lodge, Darlington, in front of two eagles' heads erased and addorsed ppr., an escutcheon az., charged with a bezant. *I byde my time.* *cf.* 84. 11

Dale of Newton-Montague, Dorset, a garb ppr. 153. 2

Dale, Edward Robert, Crane Villa, Salisbury, same crest.

Dale, Rutl., three battle-axes, one in pale and two in saltier, the handles or, the heads arg., enfiled with a chaplet of roses of the first. 172. 10

Dale, an arm embowed holding a sword in bend ppr. 201. 4

Dale, Scotland, an arm brandishing a scimitar ppr. 213. 5

Dales, a demi-lion rampant or, collared gu. 10. 9

Dalgety or **Dalgetty**, a lion rampant gardant az. 2. 5

Dalgety, Frederick John, Esquire, of Lockerley Hall, Romsey, Hants, a lion rampant guardant gu., gorged with a wreath of oak or, supporting a shield arg., thereon a thistle slipped ppr. *Vincit qui patitur.*

Dalgleish, Scotland, the trunk of an oak-tree sprouting forth new branches. *Revirescam.* 145. 2

Dalgleish, Sir William Ogilvy, Bart., of Errol Park, Errol, Perthsh., the stump of an oak-tree sprouting out branches and leaves, all ppr. *Revirescam.* 271. 2

Dalgleish, John James, Esquire, D.L., J.P., of Westgrange, Fifesh.; address—Brankston Grange, Bogside, Stirling, the stump of an oak-tree sprouting out branches and leaves ppr. *Revirescam.* 145. 2

Dalgleish, Laurence, Esquire, of Pitfirrane, Keavil and Roscobie, Fife, same crest and motto. 145. 2

Dalgleish of Scotscraig, Scotland, a book expanded ppr. *Deliciæ mei.* 158. 3

Dalgleish of Tinnygask, Fifeshire, the stump of an oak-tree sprouting out branches and leaves ppr. *Revirescam.* 145. 2

Dalglish-Bellasis, William, Esquire, a mount vert, thereon a lion couchant guardant az., in front of a tent ppr., lined gu. *Bon est bel assez.*

Dalhousie, Earl of, Lord Ramsay, of Kerrington (Rt. Hon. Sir Arthur George Maule Ramsay), of Midlothian: (1) A unicorn's head couped at the neck arg., armed or (*for Ramsay*). 49. 7. (2) A wyvern with two heads vomiting flames before and behind ppr. (*for Maule*). *Ora et labora.* 69. 9

Dalhurst, a crescent arg. 163. 2

Dalingrugge, a demi-lion ppr. 10. 2

Dallson, Kent and Lincs, a man in armour ppr., purfled or, holding in his dexter hand a battle-axe arg., the handle gu. *D'accomplir Agincourt.*
Dalkeith, Earl, *see* Buccleuch, Duke of.
Dall, a sword and a pen in saltier ppr. 170. 4
Dallas-Yorke, *see* Yorke.
Dallas, Sir George Edward, Bart., of Petsal, Staffs, a crescent per pale or and gu. *Lux venit ab alto.* 163. 2
Dallas, an increscent arg. *Lux venit ab alto.* 163. 3
Dallas, Scotland, a crescent. *Gradatim.* 163. 2
Dallas, a crescent per pale arg. and gu. 163. 2
Dallas, Scotland, an open lancet ppr. *Semper paratus.* 178. 9
Dallaway, a demi-lion rampant or. *Notandi sunt tibi mores.* 10. 2
Dallender of Poynings, Sussex, and Buckland, Surrey, an eagle's head vairée arg. and gu. 83. 1
Dalley, Ireland, a ferret collared and lined, all ppr. 134. 9
Dalley and **Dally,** a demi-angel issuing holding in her dexter hand a griffin's head erased ppr. 183. 3
Dalling, Bart. (*extinct*), of Burwood Park, Surrey, a cubit arm erect, holding in the hand a branch of oak fructed ppr. *cf.* 219. 9
Dalling, a cannon arched over with a chain, and within the arch a lion's head erased, all ppr. 19. 6
Dally, an arm erect, vested sa., cuffed arg., holding in the hand an arrow ppr.
Dallyson of Hornsey, Middx., the sun or, rising from clouds ppr. 162. 5
Dalmahoy of that Ilk, a dexter hand brandishing a sword, all ppr. *Absque metu.* 212. 3
Dalmeny, Lord, *see* Rosebery, Earl.
Dalmer of London, a demi-lion rampant erminois holding between the paws a mullet of six points arg., pierced vert. *cf.* 10. 2
Dalrymple, Earl of Stair, and **Viscount Dalrymple,** *see* Stair.
Dalrymple, *see* Hamilton-Dalrymple.
Dalrymple, Sir Walter Hamilton, Bart., of the Lodge, North Berwick, Haddington, a rock ppr., intended to represent the "Bass Rock." *Firm.*
Dalrymple, Sir Charles, Bart., of New Hailes, Midlothian, M.A., M.P. for the Borough of Ipswich, a rock ppr. *Firme.* 179. 7
Dalrymple, Elphinstone-, Sir Robert Græme, Bart., Old Rectory, Broad Chalk, Salisbury: (1) Two horns erect parted per fesse or and sa., counterchanged. (2) A rock ppr., over which the motto "*Firm.*" (3) An armed hand erect holding an ostrich-feather sa.
Dalrymple, Scotland, a rock ppr. *Quiescam.* 179. 7
Dalrymple, Bart., Scotland, out of a viscount's coronet a rock ppr. *Firm.* 179. 7
Dalrymple, Scotland, a rock ppr. *Atavis.* 179. 7
Dalrymple, Scotland, same crest. *Be firm.* 179. 7
Dalrymple, Scotland, same crest. *Steady.* 179. 7
Dalrymple-Hay: (1) A rock ppr. (*for Dalrymple*). 179. 7. (2) A falcon ppr., charged on the breast with an escutcheon gu. (*for Hay*). *Firm.—Serva jugum.* 85. 3
Dalrymple, a lion's head erased or. 17. 8
Dalrymple, Scotland, a hart's head ppr. 121. 5
Dalsiel of London, a demi-man in armour holding in his dexter hand a scimitar brandished aloft ppr. *I dare.* 187. 4
Dalston of Dalston Hall, Cumb., out of a ducal coronet or, a falcon's head ppr. 89. 4
Dalston, out of a ducal coronet or, an eagle's head ppr., holding in the beak a pellet. 83. 14
Dalton, *see* Wade-Dalton.
D'Alton, Count, of Greenastown, co. Tipperary, Ireland: (1) On a ducal coronet or, ornamented with pearls on the strawberry-leaves and between them, an eagle displayed sa., looking to the sinister langued gu., and crowned with a similar coronet. (2) Out of a coronet the same as the last a demi-lion rampant arg., armed and langued or, holding in the dexter paw an olive-branch vert. *Tristus et fidelis.*
Dalton, Fitzgerald Verity, Dean House, Dean, Kimbolton, out of a mural crown a demi-lion rampant guardant.
Dalton of Bispham, Lancs, a dragon's head vert, between two wings or. 72. 7
Dalton, a dragon's head vert, between two wings or, pellettée. 72. 7
Dalton of Kingston-on-Hull and Hawkeswell, Yorks, a dragon's head with wings displayed vert, gorged with a collar nebulée arg. *cf.* 72. 7
Dalton, a dragon's head vert, purfled and winged or. *God is my defender.* 72. 7
Dalton, a wyvern's head couped vert, gorged with a collar nebuly or, between two wings displayed, also vert, the inside of the wings of the second. *Patientia vincit.* *cf.* 72. 7
Dalton of Thurnham, a dragon's head vert, between two wings or. 72. 7
Dalton, Grant-, Alan, Esquire, of Shanks House, Somers., and Wyke Lodge, Winchester: (1) On a mount ppr., a dragon's head couped vert, between two wings or, each charged with a cross crosslet sa. (*for Dalton*). (2) A boar's head couped arg. (*for Grant*). *Stabit conscius æqui.* 43. 1
Dalton of Dunkirk Manor, Glouc., a demi-dragon vert. *Inter cruces triumphans in cruce.* 73. 10
Dalton, a ram's head couped arg., armed or. 130. 1
Dalton, Ireland, a seax ppr. 171. 2
Dalton, Portman-, Seymour Berkeley, 18, Eccleston Square, S.W.: (1) A dragon's head with wings displayed vert, the outside of the wings or, gorged with a collar nebulé of the last, a cross pattée arg. for difference. (2) A talbot sejant or.
Dalway, a demi-lion rampant gu., holding in his paws a staff erect ppr., on a banner appendant thereto and flotant to the sinister arg., a saltire of the first. *Esto quod audes.* *cf.* 15. 2
Dalway, Marriot Robert, same crest and motto.
Daly, Baron Dunsandle, *see* Dunsandle.
Daly, Ireland, in front of an oak-tree ppr., fructed or, a greyhound courant sa. *Deo fidelis et regi.* 58. 5
Daly, John Archer, Esquire, of Raford, Athenry, and Furbough, Glaway, in front of an oak-tree ppr., fructed or, a greyhound courant sa., collared gold. *Deo fidelis et regi.*
Daly, William Disney John Eyre, Esquire, of Onitchambo, Elsternwick, Melbourne, Australia, in front of an oak-tree fructed ppr., a greyhound courant sa. *Deo fidelia et regi.* 58. 5
Daly, Frederick Henry, M.D., 185, Amhurst Road, Hackney Downs, N.E., same crest and motto.
Daly, James Dominic, 57, Colmore Row, Birmingham, same crest.
Daly, James Dermot, of Castle Daly, Loughrea, same crest.
Daly, Ireland, a ferret collared and lined ppr. 134. 9
Daly, a demi-angel holding in the dexter hand a griffin's head erased ppr. 183. 3
Dalyell, Scotland, a demi-man in armour holding a scimitar, all ppr. 187. 4
Dalyell, a dexter hand holding a scimitar ppr., hilted and pommelled or. *I dare.—Right and reason.* 213. 5
Dalyell of Ticknevin, Carbery, co. Kildare, and Lingo, St. Andrews, a dexter hand grasping a scimitar, both ppr. *I dare.*
Dalzell, Earl of Carnwath, and **Baron Dalzell,** *see* Carnwath.
Dalzell, a dagger in pale ppr. 169. 2
Dalzell, Robert Stuart, Esquire, M.A., of Glenae House, Dumfries, a dagger erect az., pommel and hilt or. *I dare.*
Dalzell, a dexter hand issuing out of a cloud grasping a spear in bend ppr. *I dare.* *cf.* 214. 11
Dalziel, Scotland, a sword in pale ppr. *I dare.* 170. 2
Dalziel, same crest and motto. 213. 5
Dalziel of London, a demi-man in armour, brandishing in his dexter hand a scimitar ppr. *I dare.* 187. 4
Dalziel, a branch of laurel and a thistle issuing from two hands couped and conjoined, one gauntleted, the other ppr. 224. 8
Dalziell, a naked man ppr.
Dalziell, Bart., Scotland, a dexter hand holding a scimitar ppr. *I dare.* 213. 5
Dam of Hadham, Heref., out of a mural crown a hawk's head. *cf.* 89. 4
Damant, two lions' heads addorsed. 17. 3
Damer, Dawson-, Earl of Portarlington, *see* Portarlington.
Damer, Earl of Dorchester (*extinct*), out of a mural coronet or, a talbot's head az., eared of the first. *Tu ne cede malis.* 56. 6
Damer of Milton Abbey, Dorset, same crest. 56. 6
Damerley, a dexter hand brandishing a scimitar aloft, all ppr. 213. 5
Damerley, a lion's head erased within a chain or, disposed in orle. 19. 5
Dammant, a dexter hand brandishing a scimitar, all ppr. 213. 5
Damock, a gauntlet supporting a spear erect sa.

D'Amorie, Glouc., out of a mural coronet or, a talbot's head az., eared of the first. 56. 6

Damory, a wolf courant ppr. 28. 4

Damory, a long cross recrossed and standing on three grieces gu. 166. 6

Damory, Ireland, a demi-lion rampant gardant sa. 10. 8

Dampier of Collingshays, Somers., a demi-lion rampant sa., ducally crowned or. *Dominus petra mea.* 10. 11

Dampier, Henry Lucius, Esquire, C.I.E., of Fairholme, Parkstone, Dorset, a demi-lion rampant crowned with a ducal coronet. *Dominus petra mea.*

Dan or **Dann,** out of a mural coronet a demi-monkey rampant ppr. 136. 13

Danby of Danby, Yorks, a scorpion erect or.

Danby, Yorks, a crab erect or. 141. 5

Dancastle, Berks, a stag's head arg., attired or, vulned in the neck ppr. *cf.* 121. 5

Dance, Holland, Esquire, Berks and Hants, a horse's head az., caparisoned or, charged on the neck with an escutcheon arg., and thereon a lion's head erased gu.

Dance, out of a ducal coronet a nag's head affrontée.

Dance, a horse's head couped az., bridled gu. 51. 5

Dance, Colonel the late Sir Charles Webb, K.H., Herts, a horse's head couped sa., wreathed round the bottom of the neck with oak vert, the bit or, and the bridle of the first.

Dance of Dublin, out of a mural crown or, a goat's head az. *cf.* 128. 12

Dancer, Bart., of Modreeny House, co. Tipperary: (1) A talbot passant sa., collared or. (2) An arm embowed in armour and charged on the fore-arm with three estoiles in pale gu., holding a palm-branch ppr. *Vincit qui patitur.* *cf.* 54. 5

Dancer, a pheon with part of the broken shaft therein. 174. 10

Dancey of Donhead, St. Andrews, Wilts, a horse's head couped gu., bezantée, maned and bridled or. *cf.* 51. 6

Dand of Mansfield Woodhouse, Notts, on a mount vert, a swan arg., winged sa., beaked gu. 100. 7

Dandern, out of a ducal coronet or, a demi-ostrich with wings expanded arg. *cf.* 96. 8

Dandridge of Great Malvern, Worcs., a lion's head erased, charged with a mascle arg. *In adversis etiam fide.* *cf.* 17. 8

Dandy of Sapiston, Suff., a garb or, on the sinister side thereof a dove close arg.

Dane, a griffin's head erased or. 66. 2

Dane, a wolf statant arg. 29. 2

Dane of Wells, Somers., out of a ducal coronet or, a demi-lizard vert.

Danes or **Daneys,** a quadrangular castle. 155. 4

Danet, a greyhound's head couped arg., collared gu., studded and buckled or. 61. 2

Danford, a man in military costume ppr., holding in his dexter hand a flag displayed az. *cf.* 188. 6

Dangan, Viscount, *see* Cowley, Earl.

Dangar of Haverstock Hill, Middx., upon a mount vert, a demi-man affrontée in armour ppr., the helmet adorned with three feathers az., holding in the dexter hand a broken tilting-spear, also ppr., and supporting with the sinister an escutcheon sa., charged with a ram's head erased or. *Traditus non victus.* 187. 13

Dangar, Hon. Henry Carey, of Grantham, Sydney, and the Grove, Camden, New South Wales, Australia, same crest and motto. 187. 13

Dangerfield, a savage's head wreathed with laurel-leaves ppr. 190. 7

Dangerfield of Bromyard, Worcs., a griffin's head erased ppr. 66. 2

Danheck, a thistle ppr. *cf.* 150. 2

Danheck of London, a rose ppr. 149. 5

Daniel, *see* Amherst.

Daniel, Wilts and Yorks, a unicorn's head erased or. 49. 5

Daniel, a unicorn's head couped arg., armed or. *Nec timeo, nec sperno.* 49. 7

Daniel, a dexter naked arm erect, enfiled with a ducal coronet holding a sword. *Sub lege libertas.* 212. 7

Daniel, a galley with her oars in saltier. 160. 10

Daniel, Ireland, a bull passant ppr. *cf.* 45. 2

Daniel, William Henry, Esquire, J.P., of Lough Ree Lodge, Glasson, co. Westmeath, in front of a trefoil slipped vert, a dexter arm couped, vested gu., cuffed az., the hand ppr., holding a cross crosslet erect, also gu. *Toujours prêt.*

Daniel, Dorset, an arm couped in fess, vested az., cuffed or, holding in the hand ppr. a cross crosslet fitched in pale gu. *cf.* 207. 8

Daniell of Truro, Cornw., and **Daniels** of St. Austin's, Hants, on two oak-branches vert, fructed or, meeting saltierwise in base, a pelican erm. in her piety, the nest and young ppr. 98. 12

Daniell, Somers., Chesh., and Suff., a tiger passant regardant arg.

Daniell, Robert, Esquire, J.P., D.L., of New Forest, co. Westmeath, Ireland, a unicorn's head erased arg., armed and crined or, and charged with a crescent gu. *Pro fide et patria.* *cf.* 49. 5

Daniell, a wolf statant regardant gu. *Another,* sa. *cf.* 28. 12

Daniell, Scotland, a unicorn's head arg. 49. 7

Daniell, Arthur Stewart, M.A., Fairchildes, Wartingham, Surrey, same crest. *Nil sperno miror metuo.*

Daniell, Herts, Yorks, and Wilts, a unicorn's head erased or. 49. 5

Daniell, Somers. and Chesh., a unicorn's head couped arg. 49. 7

Daniell, Lieutenant-Colonel Edward Staines, Esquire, late 102nd Regt., on a roundel per fesse or and az., a lion rampant ppr., holding in the dexter paw a fleur-de-lis or.

Daniell, Robert George, Esquire, J.P., of New Forest, Kilbeggan, co. Westmeath, a unicorn's head erased arg., armed and crined or, charged with a crescent gu. *Pro fide et patria.*

Daniels, Hants, a dove holding in its beak an olive-branch ppr. 92. 5

Dankyrsley, Yorks, a demi-woman vested arg., playing on a harp or. 183. 6

Danmare, a lion's gamb sa., supporting an escutcheon gu. *cf.* 37. 2

Dannat, Dannant, or **Dannett** of Elmbridge, Worcs., and of Leics., Shropsh., and Warw., a greyhound's head erased arg., collared or, rimmed, and the ring gu., charged with three torteaux. *cf.* 61. 2

Danncey or **Dauncey,** Heref., a lion's head erased arg., collared gu. 18. 6

Dannsey, a nag's head gu., bezantée, maned and bridled or. *cf.* 51. 5

Dannsey and **Dauntesy,** a dragon's head erased vert. *cf.* 71. 2

Danrey of Laureth, Cornw., a horse passant saddled and bridled ppr. 52. 4

Dansey, a demi-savage wreathed round the middle, and holding in his dexter hand a slip of myrtle, all ppr. 186. 4

Dansey, Wilts, a horse's head couped arg., maned and bridled or. 51. 5

Dansey, Heref., a lion rampant per fess or and gu. 1. 13

Dansey of Easton Court, Heref., a lion's head erased arg., collared gu. 18. 6

Dansie, a sea-horse ppr. 46. 5

Danskine of Stirling, a beaver holding in his mouth a log of wood ppr. *Nec improvidus.* *cf.* 134. 8

Danson, a garb quarterly or and gu., banded az. 153. 2

Dant, a chough's head erased sa., beaked gu., blood dropping from the beak.

Danvers, Oxon. and Northumb., a parrot vert, holding in its beak an annulet or. 101. 11

Danvers, Leics. and Oxon., a parrot vert, winged gu., holding in its beak a round buckle or. *cf.* 101. 4

Danvers of Smithwick and Rothley, Leics., a parrot close vert, holding in its beak an oak-branch ppr., fructed with three acorns. *cf.* 101. 4

Danvers of London and Bucks, a fleur-de-lis erm., enfiled with a ducal coronet or. 148. 1

Danvers, a wyvern or. 70. 1

Danvers, a wyvern with wings addorsed or. 70. 1

Danvers, Sir Juland, K.C.S.I., of 103, Lexham Gardens, W., a wyvern with wings endorsed or. *Forte en loyalte.*

Danvers, Butler-: (1) A wyvern with wings elevated and tail nowed or, the dexter claw resting on an escutcheon arg., thereon a bend gu., charged with three martlets or (*for Danvers*). (2) A demi-cockatrice couped vert, the wings elevated arg., combed, beaked, wattled, and ducally gorged or (*for Butler*).

Danyell, a unicorn's head couped arg., armed or. *Nec timeo, nec sperno.* 49. 7

Dapifer, an eagle az. 76. 2

Darbishire of Penyffryn, Carnarvonsh., and Oakdene, Kent, out of clouds a dexter arm in armour embowed, all ppr., holding in the hand a cross voided and pointed sa. *Ubi amor ibi fides.—Durate et vincite.* 263. 12

Darbishire, Charles Henry, Esquire, J.P., C.C., of Plas Mawr, Penmaenmawr, issuant from clouds a dexter arm embowed holding in the hand ppr. a cross pointed and voided sa. *Ubi amor ibi fides.*

Darbishire, George Stanley, Esquire, J.P., of 18, Morella Road, Wandsworth Common, Surrey, same crest. *Durate et vincite.*

Darbishire, Henry Astley, Esquire, J.P., D.L., of Oakdene, Cowden, Kent, same crest and motto.

Darbishire, James Edward, Esquire, of Dunowen, Thurleigh Road, Wandsworth Common, Surrey, same crest and motto.

Darbishire, William Arthur, Esquire, J.P., D.L., B.A., of Penybryn, Carnarvon, North Wales, same crest.

Darby, Suff., a garb arg., banded or. 153. 2

Darby, a garb or, banded with a naval crown az., in front of an anchor placed in sinister bend sa. *Spero meliora.* 153. 4

Darby, Lincs, an heraldic antelope's head erased gu., maned, tufted, armed, and attired or. *cf.* 127. 10

Darby, an heraldic tiger attired with four horns turned round like ram's horns or.

Darby of London and Dorset, out of a tower arg., two wings, the dexter or, the sinister az. 156. 7

Darby, Alfred Edmund William, Esquire, J.P., of Little Ness, Shrewsbury, in front of two cross crosslets fitchée in saltier sa., a demi-eagle displayed couped erminois, the wings az., charged on the breast with an escallop of the last. *Utcunque placuerit Deo.* 81. 13

Darby, John Henry, of Penygarth, near Wrexham, same crest and motto.

Darby, Very Rev. John Lionel, Dean of Chester, of the Deanery, Chester, a garb or, banded with a naval crown az., in front of an anchor placed in sinister bend sa. *Spero meliora.*

Darby, Jonathan Charles, Esquire, J.P., D.L., of Leap Castle, Roscrea, King's Co., same crest and motto.

Darby, Griffith-, Christopher William, Esquire, J.P., of Padworth House, Reading: (1) A stag's head caboshed per pale gu. and az., attired or, between the attires an estoile of the last (*for Griffith*). (2) A garb arg. charged with an anchor erect sa. (*for Darby*).

Darcey and **Darcy,** a demi-lady attired, her hair dishevelled ppr., holding in her hand a branch of three cinquefoils vert. 183. 4

Darcie, Lincs and Durh., a woman's head couped at the breasts ppr., the hair flowing and dishevelled or, wreathed about the head with cinquefoils gu., pierced of the second. *cf.* 182. 5

Darcy, *see* Mervyn-D'Arcy-Irvine.

Darcy, Ireland, a cross sa.

Darcy, Ireland, a dexter arm embowed in chain armour, the hand grasping a spear in bend sinister, point downwards, all ppr.

Darcy or **D'Arcy,** England and Ireland, a spear broken in three pieces, the head in pale, the other pieces in saltier ppr., banded gu. 175. 2

D'Arcy, a bull ppr. *Un Dieu, un roi.* 45. 2

D'Arcy, a bull passant sa., armed, ungu., maned, and tufted or. *Je loue Dieu Grace attendant.* *cf.* 45. 2

D'Arcy, on a chapeau gu., turned up erm., a bull statant sa., armed or. *Un Dieu, un Roi.* *cf.* 45. 5

D'Arcy, a demi-woman, her hair flowing ppr., vested gu., holding in the dexter hand three red roses slipped and leaved vert. *Vertu cerche honneur.* 183. 4

D'Arcy, Hyacinth, Esquire, J.P., D.L., of New Forest, Ballinasloe, co. Galway, Fisher Hill, Castlebar, and Rockvale, Gort, a bull passant sa. *Un Dieu, un roy.*

D'Arcy, Martin Charlemange Macdonnell, of Doo Castle, co. Mayo, same crest.

D'Arcy, William Knox, Esquire, of Stanmore Hall, Stanmore, Middx., on a chapeau gu., turned up erm., a bull passant sa., armed or. *Un Dieu, un Roi.*

Dare, on a chapeau a demi-lion ppr., holding between its paws an increscent arg.

Dare, Essex, a demi-lion rampant az., bezantée, charged on the shoulder with a cross crosslet or, holding between the paws a lozenge of the same, charged with an increscent gu. *Loyauté sans tache.* 13. 1

Dare, Hall-, Robert Westley, Esquire, J.P., D.L., of Newtownbarry, Wexford, and Theydon Bois, Essex: (1) A demi-lion rampant az., bezantée, charged on the shoulder with a cross crosslet or, and holding between the paws a lozenge of the same charged with an increscent gu. (*for Dare*). 13. 1. (2) A horse's head couped sa., semée of mullets or, armed ppr., bridled arg., on the head two ostrich-feathers of the first and third, and holding in the mouth a battle-axe or (*for Hall*). *Loyauté sans tache.* 51. 10

Dare, an arm couped and embowed in fess, resting the elbow on the wreath and girt above the elbow with a ribbon, holding in the hand a slip of laurel, all ppr.

Darell-Blount, *see* Blount.

Darell, Cornw., a wolf passant ppr. 28. 10

Darell, Sir Lionel Edward, Bart., of Richmond, Surrey, out of a ducal coronet or, a man's head in profile, couped at the shoulders ppr., bearded sa., wreathed round the temples of the first and az., on the head a cap of the last, fretty arg., tasselled gold, turned up erm. *cf.* 190. 1

Darrell-Blount, John, Esquire, J.P., D.L., of Maple Durham, near Reading, Oxon. and Calehill, Ashford, Kent: (1) The sun in splendour charged in the centre with an eye, all ppr. (*for Blount*). (2) Out of a ducal coronet or, a man's head in profile couped at the shoulders and bearded ppr., wreathed round the temples or and az., on the head a cap, also az., fretty arg., tasselled gold and turned up erm., for difference a cross crosslet az. (*for Darell*). *Lux tua vita mea.*

Dark, an arm embowed purp., holding in the hand a streamer az., thereon an escutcheon arg., charged with a cross sa.

Darker of London, an arm embowed holding a bunch of hop-vine, all ppr. 202. 8

Darley of Aldby, Yorks, a horse's head couped gu., accoutred in armour arg., and bridled or. *Vivitur ingenio.* 51. 13

Darley, Warren-: (1) A horse's head couped arg., accoutred in armour ppr., bridled gu. (*for Darley*). 51. 13. (2) Out of a ducal coronet or, a plume of five ostrich-feathers gu., therefrom an eagle's claw ppr. *Dare.—Per mare, per terras.*

Darley, Ireland, out of a ducal coronet or, a demi-lion vert. 16. 3

Darley of Dublin, a horse's head arg., bridled gu. *Dare.* 51. 5

Darling, Quintin Richard, L.R.C.S., Bridge House, Eardisley, a demi-griffin segreant holding between its claws a flagon sa., banded arg. *Omnia vincit amor.*

Darling, Andrew, Esquire, of Toronto, Canada, a hand holding a heart. *Dei donum.* 216. 9

Darling, a hand gauntleted holding a pheon erect point upward. 211. 7

Darling of London, a lady ppr., vested in a loose robe arg., the body pink, flowing round her a robe az., holding in her dexter hand a cross crosslet fitched gu., and in her sinister a book ppr.

Darling, out of a mural coronet or, an arm in armour embowed ppr., holding up an escutcheon gu., charged with two swords in saltier arg., hilts and pommels or, encircled by the ribbon and medal of Corunna.

Darling, Scotland, a hand holding a heart ppr. *Dei donum.* 216. 9

Darling, Hon. Sir Charles John, of 18, Prince's Gardens, S.W., same crest and motto.

Darling, Rev. Frederick, M.A., of the Ridge, Hartfield, Sussex, out of a mural crown or, a dexter arm embowed in armour ppr., sustaining an inescutcheon gu., thereon two falchions in saltire, blades arg., hilts and pommels or, encircled by the ribbon and medal of Corunna. *Inspired I aspired.*

Darlington, Latimer John de Vere, Sefton House, Harrogate, same crest and motto.

Darlington: (1) A leopard's head erased or. 23. 2. (2) A winged pillar supporting a globe. *Cruce dum spiro spero.* *cf.* 113. 10

Darlington, a winged pillar. 113. 10

Darlston, Worcs., a hawk's head between two wings expanded barry of four arg. and sa., beaked or. 89. 1

Darnall, Darnel, or **Darnol,** a lion's head erased arg., between two wings or. 19. 7

Darnall, a lion's head erased az., between two wings gu. 19. 7

Darnell of Thornley, Durh., a lion's head erased az., the neck pierced by an arrow in bend gu., flighted sa., between two wings or. *Deus nobiscum.*

Darnell, Durh., on a cock-pheasant sitting ppr., a falcon's leg erased at the thigh ppr., and belled or. 90. 14

Darnley, Earl of (Bligh), Cobham Hall, Gravesend, a griffin's head erased or. *Finem respice.* 66. 2

Darnley, on a ducal coronet a martlet, all ppr. 95. 12

Daroch, a demi-negro holding in his dexter hand a dagger, all ppr. *Be watchful.*

Darrell, a goat's head erased arg., attired or. 128. 5

Darrell, an eagle preying on a child swaddled ppr. 77. 13

Darroch, a dove holding in the beak an olive-branch ppr. 92. 5

Darroch, Duncan, Esquire, of Gourock, Greenock, Renfrewsh., and Torridon, Auchnasheen, Ross-sh., a demi-negro holding in his dexter hand a dagger ppr. *Be watchful.*

Darsy, Ireland, a cross sa.

Dart or **Darte,** a flame of fire ppr. 177. 10

Dartey, a nag's head couped, armed, and bridled. 51. 13

Dartrey, Earl of, Baron Cremorne, of Castle Dawson, co. Monaghan (Vesey Dawson), an estoile of six points or. *Toujours propice.* 164. 3

Dartiquenave of London, a lion sejant or, semée-de-lis az., holding in the dexter paw an arrow gu.

Dartmouth, Earl of, Viscount Lewisham, Baron Dartmouth of Dartmouth, Devonsh. (Rt. Hon. William Heneage Legge), Patshull House, Wolverhampton, out of a ducal coronet of five leaves or, a plume of six ostrich-feathers alternately arg. and az. *Gaudet tentamine virtus.*

Dartrey, Earl of (Dawson), Dawtrey, co. Monaghan, an estoile or. *Toujours propice.*

Darvall or **Darwall,** a lion's head or, gorged with a collar gu., charged with three bezants. cf. 18. 6

Darwell, a lion's head erased or, ducally crowned gu. 18. 8

Darwen or **Darwin** of Cleatham, Lincs, a camel's head couped ppr. 132. 7

Darwin, the late Rear-Admiral Sacheverell Charles, of Fern, Hartington, Derbysh., in front of a demi-gryphon vert, holding between the claws an escallop or, three escallops fessewise arg. *Cave et aude.*

Darwin of Elston Hall, Notts: (1) A demi-griffin sa., semée of mascles or, charged on the shoulder with a cross patée of the second, resting the sinister claw on a shield arg., thereon a leopard's face jessant-de-lis gu. (*for Darwin*). 64. 12. (2) A cubit arm erect, vested bendy of six arg. and az., cuffed gu., the hand holding in saltire an oak-branch and a vine-branch, both fructed ppr. (*for Rhodes*). 206. 7

Darwin, Lieutenant-Colonel Charles Waring, J.P., of Dryburn, near Durham: (1) On a wreath of the colours a demi-griffin sa., semée of mascles or, resting the sinister claw upon a shield arg., charged with a leopard's face jessant-de-lis gu., and charged upon the shoulder (for distinction) with a cross patée or (*for Darwin*). (2) On a wreath of the colours a cubit arm erect, vested bendy of six arg. and az., cuffed gu., the hand holding in saltire an oak-branch and vine-branch, both fructed ppr. (*for Rhodes*). *Cave et aude.*

Darwin, Francis, Esquire, J.P., of Creskeld, Arthington, Leeds, same crest.

Darwin, Francis Alvey Rhodes, of Leathley Hall, Otley, Yorks, same crests.

Darwin, George Howard, F.R.S., of Newnham Grange, Cambridge, in front of a demi-griffin segreant vert, holding between the claws an escallop or, three escallops fesseways arg.

Darwin, Horace, Esquire, M.A., of the Orchard, Cambridge, same crest.

Darwin, Major Leonard, of 12, Egerton Place, S.W., same crest and motto.

Darwin, William Erasmus, of Ridgmount Basset, Southampton, same crest and motto.

Dasent, Arthur Irwin, Esquire, of Tower Hill, Ascot, Berks, formerly St. Vincent, W. I., a dexter arm in armour embowed grasping a falchion, all ppr. *Strike.* 196. 10

Dashwood of London, a griffin's head erased per fess erminois and gu. *Pro Magnâ Chartâ.* 66. 2

Dashwood of Stanford Park, Notts, a griffin's head erased per fess erminois and gu. 66. 2

Dashwood, Sir George John Egerton, Bart., D.L., of Kirtlington Park, Oxon., a gryphon's head erminois, erased gu. *Virtuti nihil invium.* 66. 2

Dashwood, Sir Edwin Abercromby, Bart., a griffin's head erased per fesse erminois and gu. 66. 2

Dassett, Warw., a dove arg., beaked gu. 92. 2

Dast, a flame of fire ppr. 177. 10

Dastin and **Daston** of Broadway, Worcs., a reindeer's head arg., couped gu., pierced through the neck by a broad arrow or, the arrow entering the back part of the neck.

Datmer, an eagle's head erased ppr. 83. 2

Daubeney, Lansdowne, Esquire, J.P., of Cote, Westbury-on-Trym, near Bristol, and Norton Court, Norton, Malreward, Bristol, a holly-bush ppr. *Badge,* two dragon's wings displayed arg. *Ad finem fidelis.*

Daubeney, George Walters, Cote, near Bristol, same crest. *Ad finem fidelis.*

Daubeney, William Arthur, Esquire, J.P., M.A., of the Island House, Midsomer Norton, near Bath, and Clevelands, near Dawlish, same crest and motto.

Dauglish, Henry William, of 54, Leinster Square, London, W., a camel's head and neck couped ppr. *Be hardy.*

Daubuz, a griffin's head with wings addorsed ppr. cf. 67. 11

Dauble, Cornw., a horse passant, saddled and bridled ppr. 52. 4

Dauglish of London, a camel's head and neck couped ppr. *Be hardy.* 132. 7

Daulbeny, an eagle with wings expanded or. 77. 5

Dauncey, Heref., a lion's head erased arg., collared gu. 18. 6

Daunecourt and **Daunscourt,** a negro's head couped at the shoulders, vested paly of six erm. and ermines, pendents at the ears or, wreathed on forehead, and with bats' wings to his head expanded sa. cf. 182. 6

Daunsey, a nag's head couped and bridled. 51. 5

Daunt, a cockatrice displayed ppr.

Daunt, a bugle-horn or, stringed sa. 228. 11

Daunt of Owlpen, Glouc., and Gortigrenane, co. Cork, a bugle-horn, stringed sa. *Vigilo et spero.* 228. 11

Daunt, Rev. Achilles, M.A., of Sherborne, Dorset, a bugle-horn or, stringed sa. *Vigilo et spero.*

Daunt, Esquire, Achilles Thomas, J.P., of Kilcascan Castle, Ballyneen, co. Cork, same crest and motto.

Daunt, Rev. Edward Stephen, of Greystones, co. Wicklow, same crest.

Daunt, Rev. William, of Queenstown, co. Cork, same crest and motto.

Dauntesy, a dragon's head erased vert. cf. 71. 2

Dauntesey, Robert Dauntesey, Esquire, of Agecroft, Lancs, a dragon's head erased vert, gorged with a collar dancettée or, and encircled by a chain of the same. *Virtus sola invicta.* cf. 71. 2

Dauntesey, Robert Dauntesey, of Agecroft Hall, Pendlebury, same crest and motto.

Dauntsey, out of a ducal coronet a dexter hand holding a fleur-de-lis. 215. 2

Dauvergeue, a horse's head sa., bridled or. 51. 5

Davall of London, an arm embowed holding a fleur-de-lis or.

Davall or **Davell,** Yorks, a terrestrial globe ppr. 159. 1

Davell, Yorks, a dexter hand apaumée, charged with an eye ppr. 222. 4

Davenant of Davenant, Essex, a sinister arm embowed, holding in the hand a chaplet of wheat or.

Davenport of Davenport, Chesh., a man's head in profile, couped at the shoulders ppr., with a rope round the neck or. 253. 20

Davenport, late Rear-Admiral Sir Salusbury Price, C.B., K.C.H., of Bramhall, Chesh., a man's head ppr., around the neck a rope or, charged for distinction on the neck with a cross crosslet fitchée sa.

Davenport, Cyril James Humphreys, V.D., F.S.A., the Library, British Museum, and 113, St. Mark's Road, W., same crest. *Audaces fortuna juvat.*

Davenport, Rev. George Horatio, of Foxley, Heref., in front of a man's head in profile, couped at the shoulders ppr., around the neck a rope or, two cross crosslets fitchée, in saltire, also or. *Mors Janua vitæ.*

Davenport, Sir Samuel, K.C.M.G., LL.D., J.P., of Beaumont, near Adelaide, South Australia, a felon's head couped ppr., haltered or. *Tu ne cede malis.*

Davenport-Handley, John William Handley, Esquire, of Clipsham Hall, Oakham, Rutlandsh.: (1) A goat passant sa., bearded, ungu., and armed or, charged on the body with two mascles interlaced arg. 253. 19. (*for Handley*). (2) A man's head in profile, couped at the shoulders ppr., around the neck a rope or, and charged on the breast with a cross crosslet fitchée sa. (*for Davenport*). *Audaces fortuna juvat.* 253. 20

Davenport, Bromley-, William, of Capesthorne, Chesh., and Baginton, Warw.: (1) A man's head in profile, couped at the shoulders ppr., around the neck a rope or (*for Davenport*). 253. 20. (2) Out of a ducal coronet or, a demi-lion issuant arg., charged for distinction on the shoulder with a cross crosslet fitchée sa., supporting a pennon flying towards the sinister gu., thereon a lion passant gardant of the first, the staff and spear erect ppr. (*for Bromley*). *Fear God, honour the King.*

Davernett, a woodpecker close ppr.

Daverport, a lion passant erm., ducally crowned or, resting the dexter paw on an escutcheon of the last.

Davers, a demi-savage holding in his dexter hand a club, and in his sinister a serpent nowed, all ppr. *cf.* 185. 3

Davers, Bart. (*extinct*), of Rougham, Suff., a jay ppr., holding in its beak an annulet or.

Davey, Baron (Davey), Verdley Place, Fernhurst, a demi-lion ppr., holding between the paws a mullet pierced gu., and supporting under the sinister paw a sword, point downwards, also ppr., hilt and pommel or.

Davey, an ostrich's head, holding in the beak a horse-shoe, between two feathers all ppr. 97. 12

Davey of Redruth, Cornw., a mount vert, thereon an eagle rising az., charged on the wing with a cinquefoil or, holding in the dexter claw a staff sa., therefrom flowing a pennon gu. *E perseverantia honor.* 264. 13

Davey, Sussex, a horse's head in armour, on top a plume of ostrich-feathers, all ppr. *Non inferiora.* 50. 14

Davey, Joshua Sydney, Esquire, J.P., of Bochym, Cury-Cross, Lancs R.S.O., Cornw., a mount vert, thereon an eagle rising with wings endorsed az., charged upon the wing with a cinquefoil or, and supporting in the beak and in the dexter talon a flagstaff erect, terminating with a cross botonnée sa., and therefrom flotant to the sinister a forked pennon gu. *E perseverantia honor.* 264. 13

David, a lamb passant arg., holding in the mouth a sprig vert, fructed gu. *cf.* 131. 9

David, a dove holding an olive-branch in its beak ppr. *Pax et copia.* 92. 5

David, Rev. William, M.A., of St. Fagan's Rectory, Cardiff, upon a mount vert, between two quatrefoils or, a dove holding in the beak a sprig of olive ppr., and gorged with a collar gemelle, also or. *Ffyddlon hyd angau.*

David, Arthur Evan, Esquire, on a mount vert, between two quatrefoils or, a dove holding in the beak a sprig of holly ppr., and gorged with a collar, also or. *Ffyddlon hyd angau.*

David, Evan Edgar, Esquire, J.P., M.A., of Fairwater House, Cardiff, same crest and motto.

David, Edmund Usher, Esquire, of Yscallog, Llandaff, Cardiff, same crest and motto.

David, Tannatt William Edgeworth, Esquire, same crest and motto.

David, William Ontario, Esquire, same crest and motto.

Davidge, Somers., a demi-lion arg., gorged with a collar gu., charged with three lions passant of the first. *cf.* 10. 9

Davidson, Scotland, a falcon's head couped ppr. *Viget in cinere virtus.* *cf.* 89. 1

Davidson, out of a mural coronet az., a lion's head gu. 19. 12

Davidson, Scotland, a pheon. 174. 11

Davidson of Cantray, Inverness, Scotland, a dexter hand holding a human heart, all ppr. *Sapienter si sincere.* 216. 9

Davidson of London, upon a mount vert, a dove with wings elevated az., holding in the beak two ears of corn, and the dexter foot resting on a pheon or. *Per augusta ad augusta.*

Davidson, a lamb bearing a cross and banner. 131. 2

Davidson of Muirhouse, Scotland, a phœnix in flames ppr. *Viget in cinere virtus.* 82. 2

Davidson of London, a stag courant or, pierced through the neck with an arrow arg.

Davidson, Madgwick George, 89, Westbourne Terrace, Hyde Park, W., upon a mount a demi-Highlander, affrontée, ppr., habited and capped vert, kilted chequy arg. and sa., his sporran also ppr., holding in the dexter hand a pheon or, and supporting with the sinister a human heart gu. *Sapienter si sincere.*

Davidson, Scotland, a youth from the middle holding in his dexter hand a man's heart, all ppr. *Sapienter si sincere.*

Davidson, Duncan, Esquire, J.P., D.L., of Inchmarlo, Banchory, N.B., a youth from the middle holding in his dexter hand a heart, all ppr. *Sapienter sincere.*

Davidson, Hugh, Esquire, of Cantray Croy, Gollanfield, N.B., a dexter hand holding a man's heart, all ppr. *Sapienter si sincere.*

Davidson, William, Esquire, of Muirhouse, Davidson's Mains, Midlothian, a phœnix in flames ppr. *Viget in cinere virtus.*

Davidson, William Edward, Esquire, K.C., of the Foreign Office, Downing Street, S.W., an eagle's head couped ppr. *Viget in cinere virtus.*

Davie, Bart., *see* Ferguson-Davie.

Davie, a talbot's head erased arg., collared, ducally crowned and eared or. *cf.* 56. 9

Davie, on a chapeau vert, turned up erm., a boar arg., armed and crined or, gorged with a bough ppr. *cf.* 40. 7

Davie, Scotland, an eagle's head couped ppr. *Sedulitate.* 83. 1

Davie, Ferguson-, Sir John Davie, Bart., Creedy Park, Crediton, Devonsh: (1) A paschal lamb regardant gu. (2) A kingfisher, wings elevated ppr., holding in the beak a branch of olive vert. *Auspice Christo.*

Davies-Evans, *see* Evans.

Davies, *see* Price-Davies.

Davies of Gwysaney, a lion's head couped quarterly arg. and sa. *Heb Dhuw heb ddym Dhuw a digon.* 21. 1

Davies of Marrington Hall, Shropsh., a lion's head erased arg., langued and ducally crowned gu. *Dum spiro spero.* 18. 8

Davies of Hanwell, Middx., a lion's head couped quarterly arg. and sa., ducally crowned or. *Honor virtutem coronat.*

Davies of London, a lion rampant. *Nisi dominus frustra.* 1. 13

Davies, John Birt, Esquire, of Birmingham, a lion rampant arg., charged with three cross crosslets gu., and holding between the paws a piece of cable nowed ppr. *Conatimur.*

Davies, on a chapeau sa., turned up or, a demi-lion rampant of the last. (*Granted to Sir Thomas Davies, Lord Mayor of London,* 1677.) 15. 12

Davies, Francis Pritchard, M.D., Kent County Asylum, Barming Heath, Maidstone, same crest. *Festina lente.*

Davies, on a chapeau sa., turned up or, a demi-lion rampant of the last, holding in its dexter paw a mullet. *cf.* 15. 14

Davies, Kent, a demi-lion rampant sa. 10. 1

Davies, a lion's gamb erased, holding a mullet of five points.

Davies of London and Shropsh., two lion's gambs erased, the dexter ermines, the sinister erm., holding a buckle or.

Davies, Sir William George, K.C.S.I., C.S.I., of 5, Barkston Gardens, London, S.W., a horse's head erased arg. *Esse quam videri.* 49. 5

Davies, Major-General Frederick John, Ashleigh, Teignmouth, a horse's head. *Esse quam videri.*

Davies, Ireland, a nag's head arg., charged with a caltrap sa. 51. 9

Davies, Clement, Esquire, of Birmingham, a lion rampant arg., charged with three cross crosslets gu., and holding between the paws a piece of cable nowed ppr. *Conatimur.*

Davies, Dayrell, Esquire, R.N., F.Z.S., F.R.G.S., of 26, Circus, Bath, a bull's head couped sa., charged with three estoiles chevronways, and in front thereof a spur leathered fesseways, rowel to the dexter or. *Per crucem ad astra.*

Davies, Alderman Sir Horatio, K.C.M.G., of Wateringbury Place, near Maidstone, on a fasces fesseways or, a boar's head couped arg., and transfixed by a sword imbrued in bend, point upwards, ppr., pommel and hilt or. *Dum spiro spero.*

Davies, Matthew Lewis Vaughan, J.P., D.L., of Tan-y-Bwlch, Aberystwith, North Wales, a leopard's head and neck erased and affrontée. *Duw yw digon.*

Davies, Theophilus Clive, Esquire, B.S., of Craigside, Honolulu, Hawaiian Islands, and Ravenside, Tunbridge Wells, a demi-lion sa., guttée-d'eau, supporting a harp or. *Ffyddlawn a gwir.*

Davies of St. Albans, Clarendon Road, Southsea, in front of three spears' heads, one erect and two in saltire sa., headed ppr., a lion rampant gu., charged on the shoulder with a fleur-de-lis arg. *Heb duw heb ddim duw a digon.*

Davies, Rev. Edward William Lewis, M.A., of Tyisha and Glyn-Rumney, Monmouthsh., and of the Circus, Bath, a bull's head couped sa., charged with three estoiles chevronwise, and in front thereof a spur leathered fessewise, rowel to the dexter, all or. *Per crucem ad castra.*

Davies of Ticknam, Somers., a griffin segreant or. 62. 2

Davies of Moor Court, Heref., same crest. 62. 2

Davies, a mullet of five points pierced between two wings expanded. *cf.* 111. 5

Davies of Court-y-Gollen, Crickhowell, Brecknocksh., a dragon's head, holding in the mouth a bloody hand. *Vive ut vivas.* 72. 6

Davies of Marsh, Shropsh., on a mount vert, a goat lodged arg., against a tree ppr.

Davies, Lieutenant-General Henry Fanshaw, of Elmley Castle, Pershore, on a mount vert, a goat couchant sa., guttée d'eau, under an oak-tree ppr. *Deus tutor.*

Davies, Francis Robert, of Hawthorn, Blackrock: (1) As above. (2) A dragon's head erased vert. (3) A dragon's head couped vert between two dragons' wings or.

Davies, William David, Esquire, of Cwmwysg, Senny Bridge, Brecconsh., and Holly Lodge, Hildrop Road, London, N., in front of two flag staves in saltire ppr., flowing from each a banner gu., charged with a shepherd's crook erect or, a lamb passant, also ppr. *Duw dy ras.* 238. 9

Davies, William Howell, Esquire, of Chatford House, Clifton Down, Clifton, Bristol, in front of a cross crosslet fitchée gu., a stag ppr., resting the dexter foreleg on a hawk's lure, also gu. *Amynedd a dewrder.*

Davies of Scoveston, Milford Haven, a wolf rampant crowned. *Y Bywyd dros y gwir.*

Davies-Evans, Herbert, Esquire, of High Mead, Llanybyther R.S.O., South Wales: (1) A wolf's head arg., guttée-de-sang, gorged with a collar gemelle and erased gu. (*for Evans*). (2) A lion rampant or, semée of crosses patée fitchée az., gorged with a collar dancettée, with a chain reflexed over the back sa. *Fide et virtute.*

Davies, Edward Jenner, Haywardsend, Stonehouse, Glouc., a talbot statant. *Vive ut vivas.*

Davies of Bristol, a demi-goat gardant arg., holding in the paws a leek ppr.

Davies-Lloyd, a demi-antelope sa., semée of mullets arg., holding between the legs a cross crosslet sa. *Sic itur ad astra.*

Davies, Somers., a fawn lodged ppr. *cf.* 125. 4

Davies, Saunders-, of Pentre, Pembroke: (1) A wolf salient arg. (*for Davies*). *cf.* 28. 2. (2) A demi-bull salient couped at the loins arg. (*for Saunders*). *Solem ferre possum.* *cf.* 45. 8

Davies of Prittlewell, on a chapeau gu., turned up erm., a boar passant arg., collared of the first. *cf.* 40. 8

Davies, Kent, a boar's head couped and erect or. *cf.* 43. 3

Davies, Sussex, on a ducal coronet or, a boar's head couped sa. *cf.* 43. 1

Davies of Everton, Hants, a dove with wings addorsed arg., holding in its beak a sprig vert bearing three roses or.

Davies, Francis Robert, Hawthorne, co. Dublin, on a mount vert, a goat lodged arg., against a tree ppr.

Davis, *see* Hart-Davis.

Davis-Goff, *see* Goff.

Davis, Kent, a wolf passant erm. 28. 1

Davis, Heref., out of a mural coronet ppr., a demi-wolf salient arg., holding a cinquefoil gu.

Davis of London and Westml., a demi-wolf rampant regardant, erased az., ducally gorged and chained or, holding in the paws a mullet of six points arg. 31. 4

Davis, a lion rampant. 1. 13

Davis of Leytonstone, Essex, a demi-lion issuant sa., charged on the shoulder with the fasces or, and holding between the paws a bomb fired pr. *Decide.* 12. 11

Davis of London, a lion's head erased ppr. *Ne tentes, aut perfice.* 17. 8

Davis, Arthur Holdsworth, M.B., 34, North Bridge Street, Sunderland, a lion's head erased, ducally crowned.

Davis, a lion's head erased or, ducally crowned gu. 18. 8

Davis, Colonel John, F.S.A., of Bifrons, Farnborough, Hants, Whitmead, Lilford, Surrey, and United Service Club, Pall Mall, London, W., a lion's head erased sa., charged with a caltrap or, upon two swords in saltire ppr., hilted and pommelled also or. *Ne tentes, aut perfice.* 19. 2

Davis, Charles Percy, Esquire, J.P., of Mount Camel, Redcastle, Victoria, *uses* a demi-lion rampant. *Inspice.* 10. 2

Davis, a leopard's head erased ppr. 23. 2

Davis, a lamb couchant. *cf.* 131. 12

Davis, a fawn lodged. 124. 8

Davis, Ireland, a dragon's head erased vert. *cf.* 71. 2

Davis, a boar's head erased ppr. 42. 2

Davis, Ireland, a nag's head couped arg., charged on the neck with a caltrap sa. *cf.* 51. 9

Davis, three arrows, one in pale and two in saltier ppr. *cf.* 173. 1

Davis, Sir Francis Boileau, Bart., of Hollywood, Glouc., two Indian pikes in saltier ppr., surmounted by a mullet pierced sa., between two wings vairée arg. and sa. *Utili secernere honestum.* 174. 7

Davis of Bristol, Somers., two arms embowed, vested erm., cuffed az., holding in the hands ppr. a mound or. 203. 12

Davis, James W., Esquire, F.S.A., F.G.S., F.L.S., Alderman and Mayor of Halifax, Chevenedge, Halifax, two arms embowed, habited erm., cuffed az., the hands ppr. supporting a mound or. *Ne tentes, aut perfice.* 203. 12

Davis, Hants, an arm in armour embowed holding in the hand a scimitar, all ppr. 196. 10

Davis, Ireland, an arm from the shoulder embowed holding a club, all ppr. 202. 10

Davis, Ireland, a dexter arm in armour embowed, the hand gauntleted and holding a battle-axe, all ppr. 200. 6

Davison, out of an earl's coronet or, a dove rising arg., holding in the beak a wheat-stalk, bladed and eared, all ppr.

Davison, Rashell, M.D., Featherwood, Northumb., out of an earl's coronet a dove arg., with an ear of corn in its mouth.

Davison, out of a mural coronet a stag's head affrontée, all ppr. *cf.* 119. 13

Davison, a stag's head couped between two wings or.

Davison, Shropsh., an eagle displayed arg., collared gu., holding in its beak an ear of wheat or. *cf.* 75. 2

Davison, late James Berwick, Esquire, of Probate Registry, Somerset House, a cross moline gu., entwined by a branch of olive or, thereon perched a dove erm.

Davison, Robert John William, Esquire, of Grammar School, Ilminster, same crest.

Daviss, out of a ducal coronet a hand holding a sword waved in pale, all ppr. 212. 1

Davoron, a hind ppr. *cf.* 124. 12

Davy, Devonsh., a dove holding in the beak an olive-branch ppr. 92. 5

Davy, Devonsh., a dove with wings addorsed ppr., holding in the beak a sprig vert, thereon three roses or. *cf.* 94. 5

Davy of Rose Ash and Beaford, Devonsh., a paschal lamb regardant arg., holding a pennon of the last, charged with a cross gu., the staff or. *cf.* 130. 2

Davy of Sussex Square, London, on a mount vert, a lamb passant regardant ppr., semée of estoiles sa., supporting a staff or, therefrom flowing a pennon arg., the ends gu., charged with a cross patée of the last. *El hombre propone, Dios dispone.* 131. 3

Davy of Ingoldisthorpe, Norf., out of a ducal coronet or, an elephant's head sa., armed arg., in front of the coronet a ring, thereto a line and ring or, reflexed over the trunk. *cf.* 133. 1

Davy, Bart. (*extinct*), out of a civic wreath or, an elephant's head sa., eared of the first, the tusks arg., the proboscis attached by a line to a ducal coronet around the neck, also or. *Igne constricto vita secura.*

Davy, Sussex, Suff., and Wilts, a lion sejant arg., supporting a column or.

Davy of Calton, Norf., a cannon or, mounted on a carriage gu. 169. 12

Davy, Scotland, a talbot's head erased or, ducally crowned. 56. 9

Davy, a talbot's head erased arg., ducally crowned, collared, and eared or. *cf.* 56. 9

Davye of Crediton and Cannotene, Devonsh., a halcyon bird breasted gu., the head and neck az., the tail ppr., the wings endorsed arg., holding in the beak a branch vert, with three roses or.

Davys, an ostrich holding in its beak a horse-shoe ppr. 97. 8

Daw, an eagle with wings expanded looking at the sun ppr.

Dawbeney, a mulberry-tree vert, fructed gu., debruised by a sinister bendlet.

Dawbeney, Devonsh., a leopard's face or, jessant-de-lis gu. 22. 5

Dawbeney, two lion's gambs erased, holding up a crescent or. 39. 6

Dawbeney, an elephant's head erased per fess or and vert. 133. 3

Dawbin, a Triton holding in his sinister hand a trident ppr. 185. 12

Dawbney, *see* Dawbeney.

Dawe, Somers., out of a ducal coronet a hand holding a swan's head erased, all ppr. 230. 7

Dawe, Dorset, a lion's gamb erased and erect arg., holding a fleur-de-lis or.

Dawes, Middx., a dexter arm embowed, vested gu., cuffed arg., holding in the hand ppr., an oak-slip vert, fructed with three acorns or.

Dawes of Burton Hill, Barlavington, Sussex: (1) Upon a mount vert, between two acorns slipped and leaved ppr., an arm embowed, vested sa., cuffed or, holding in the hand a sprig of myrtle ppr. (*for Dawes*). (2) An eagle's head erased gu., gorged with a collar gemel arg., suspended from the beak a padlock sa. (*for Willcock*). *Fear not.*

Dawes of Stapleton, Leics., on the point of a halberd erect or, a wyvern, the tail nowed and sans legs sa., bezantée, vulned gu. *cf.* 69. 6

Dawes, Staffs, and of Shawe Place, Lancs, a wyvern sa., bezantée, holding in its dexter claw a battle-axe erect az., handle or. *En Dieu est tout.* *cf.* 70. 2

Dawker, out of a palisado coronet an arm embowed, vested, holding in the hand a battle-axe in fess ppr.

Dawkins, William Gregory, of Over Morton, Oxon., a dexter arm embowed, couped at shoulder, holding in the hand a battle-axe of the last in bend ppr., charged on the blade with a rose gu. *cf.* 201. 5

Dawn and **Dawne,** a crane holding in its beak an oak-branch ppr. 105. 14

Dawnay, Baron, *see* Downe, Viscount.

Dawney and **Dawny,** a dexter wing or. 109. 7

Dawnsey, a nag's head couped az., bezantée, bridled or. *cf.* 51. 5

Daws, Sussex, a demi-man vested in green winding a hunting-horn ppr. *Hinc usque superna venabor.* 187. 12

Dawson-Damer, Earl of Portarlington, *see* Portarlington.

Dawson, Earl of Dartrey and Baron Cremorne, *see* Dartrey.

Dawson, a cat's head erased affrontée ppr., holding in the mouth a rat sa. *cf.* 25. 1

Dawson of Edwardston Hall, Suff., a tabby cat's head gardant erased, holding in the mouth a rat sa. *Vitæ via virtus.* *cf.* 25. 1

Dawson of Spaldingholme, Yorks, a cat's head affrontée, erased near the shoulders arg., spotted sa., holding in the mouth a rat of the last. *Vitæ via virtus.* *cf.* 25. 1

Dawson, Edward Alfred Finch, Esquire, of Launde Abbey, Leics., issuing from clouds a sinister cubit arm vested, the hand apaumée. *Manus hæc inimica tyrannis.*

Dawson of Weston-Askwith, Skipton-in-Craven, on a mount vert, in front of a quiver paleways or, with arrows therein ppr., a talbot statant sa., charged with two buckles or. *Perseverando.* 249. 20

Dawson, Lieutenant-Colonel Henry Philip, R.A. (*retired*), of Hartlington Hall, Burnsall, Skipton-in-Craven, a cat's head erased guardant arg., gorged with a mural crown or, in the mouth a rat fesseways ppr. *Amor meus crucifixus.*

Dawson, William Mosley, Esquire, of Lancliffe Hall, Giggleswick, Yorks, upon a staff raguly fessewise or, a cat's head erased affrontée ppr., gorged with a collar flory counterflory or, and holding in the mouth a rat fessewise, also ppr. *cf.* 25. 1

Dawson, Northumb., a talbot passant ppr. *Vitæ via virtus.* 54. 1

Dawson of Azerley, Yorks, on a mount vert a talbot statant sa. *cf.* 54. 2

Dawson, Christopher Holdsworth, Esquire, of Weston, Yorks, upon a mount vert in front of a quiver palewise or, with arrows therein ppr., a talbot statant sa., charged with two buckles of the second. *Perseverando.* 54. 6

Dawson, Cumb., a demi-talbot erm., eared az., holding an arrow or, flighted and pointed arg. *cf.* 55. 10

Dawson, a daw ppr.

Dawson, Benjamin Franklin, Esquire, a buckle fesseways or, thereon a daw sa. *Alte volat.*

Dawson of Castle Dawson, Ireland, an étoile of six points or. *Toujours propice.* 164. 3

Dawson, Sir John William, C.M.G., 293, University Street, Montreal, same crest.

Dawson, an estoile between two ears of wheat slipped, all or.

Dawson, Westropp-, of Charlesford, co. Wexford, Ireland: (1) On clouds ppr. an estoile or, on an escroll above the motto, *Toujours propice* (*for Dawson*). 164. 11. (2) An eagle's head couped erm., charged with an annulet gu. (*for Westropp*). *Tourne vers l'occident.* *cf.* 83. 1

Dawson, on a chapeau gu., turned up erm., a cockatrice or. *Deeds, not words.* *cf.* 68. 9

Dawson, Ireland, a tower arg. alighting thereon a falcon with wings addorsed sa. 156. 11

Dawson, Lincs, an arm in armour embowed ppr., garnished or, holding in the gauntlet a battle-axe of the last. 200. 6

Dawson, Yelverton, Esquire, M.D., of Southbourne, Hants, same crest.

Dawson, a hand erect and apaumée, charged with an eye, all ppr. 222. 4

Dawtrey of Moor House and Dodding, hurst, Sussex, a unicorn arg. *cf.* 48. 5

Dax, between the horns of a crescent a cross pattée. 163. 6

Dax, an antelope's head erased. *cf.* 127. 4

Day of Beaufort, Kerry, two hands clasping each other, couped at wrist, conjoined to a pair of wings ppr. *Sic itur ad astra.* 224. 12

Day, two hands conjoined ppr., affixed to two wings expanded, the dexter or, the sinister az., each charged with a mullet counterchanged. *cf.* 224. 12

Day, Robert, Esquire, J.P., F.S.A., M.R.I.A., of Myrtle Hill House, Cork, two hands clasping each other in fesse ppr., conjoined at the wrists to a pair of wings, the dexter or, the sinister az., the former charged with a mullet and the latter with a crescent counterchanged. *Sic itur ad astra.*

Day, Hon. Sir John, of 25, Collingham Gardens, S.W.: (1) A martlet az. (2) A demi-lion double-queued gu., supporting a staff raguly or. *A solis ortu.*

Day, Fitzgerald-, of Spring Hill, co. Kerry, two dexter hands clasped together ppr., each conjoined to a wing expanded quarterly or and az., counterchanged, over the hands a mullet gu. *Sic itur ad astra.* *cf.* 224. 12

Day, Richard, Esquire, M.D., of Auckland, New Zealand; Robert Day, Esquire, of Cork; and the Rev. William Tottenham Day, M.A., Rector of Rathclarin, in the Diocese of Ross, two hands clasping each other in fesse ppr., conjoined at the wrists to a pair of wings, the dexter or, the sinister az., the former charged with a mullet and the latter with a crescent counterchanged. *Sic itur ad astra.* *cf.* 224. 12

Day, Arthur James, Northlands House, Southampton, two hands clasping each other in fesse ppr. conjoined at the wrists to a pair of wings the dexter or, the sinister az., each charged with a mullet counterchanged. *Sic fidem teneo.*

Day, a demi-cockatrice with wings expanded.

Day of London, a greyhound's head erased arg., collared, ringed, and lined gu., the end nowed. *cf.* 61. 2

Day of Ampthill House, Ampthill Square, London; Stratton House, Swindon, Wilts; Holly Hill, Harvil, Gravesend, Kent, upon a mount vert a greyhound's head erased arg., collared and with a line affixed thereto gu., and in front a fountain.

Day, William Henry, Esquire, M.D., of Holly Hill, Kent, and Stratton St. Margaret, Wilts, same crest.

Dayman of Mambury, a demi-lion holding in the dexter paw a fusil gu., charged with a fleur-de-lis erm.

Dayman, a demi-lion rampant, ducally gorged and chained or. *Toujours prest.* *cf.* 10. 7

Dayrell of Lillingston Dayrell, Bucks, a goat's head erased ppr. *Securè vivere mors est.* 128. 5

Dayrell, Edmund Marmaduke, Esquire, J.P., same crest and motto.

Dayrell, Rev. Richard, out of a ducal coronet a goat's head erased ppr. *Virtus mille scuta.*

Dayrell of Shudy Camps Park, Cambs, on a ducal coronet a goat's head erased, all ppr. *Virtus mille scuta.* *cf.* 128. 14

Dayrolles of Henley Park, Surrey, a mullet of six points or. 164. 3

Dea, an arm couped below the wrist in fess, vested gu., the cuff dancettée arg., holding in the hand ppr. a broken sword of the last, hilt and pommel or.

Deacle, out of a mural coronet arg., an eagle rising or, holding in the beak a rose gu.

Deacons of Wasperton, Warw., an eagle's head erased arg., between two wings sa. *cf.* 84. 2

De Aguilar of London, a lion rampant or, charged with a plate. *cf.* 1. 13

Deaken or **Deakin,** out of a mural coronet gu., a leopard's head or, ducally gorged of the first. 23. 7

Deakin, J. Buckley, Esq., 14 Ullet Road, Liverpool, same crest. *Dum vigilo tutus.*

Deakin, Newton-, Charles Frederic, of Moseley Hall, Cheadle, Cheshire, Barrister-at-Law, a dexter arm embowed ppr., holding in the hand a battle-axe in bend sinister arg., pendent from the wrist by a riband az. an escutcheon arg., charged with a lion rampant sa., holding between the paws a cross pattée fitchée gu. *Stryke, Dakyns, the devil's in the hempe.* 201. 8

Deakin, Hon. Alfred, of Llanarth, Walsh Street, South Yarra, Melbourne, Victoria, Australia, representative for Essendon and Flemington in the Legislative Assembly of Victoria, out of a naval coronet or, a dexter arm embowed ppr., holding a battle-axe arg., on the wrist a ribbon az. *Stryke, Dakyns, the devil's in the hempe.*

Dealbeney, an ox-yoke in bend sa. 178. 6

Deale, Kent, within a snake in orle ppr., a dove arg., beaked and legged gu. 92. 11

Dealtry of Lofthouse Hall, Yorks, issuing out of a cloud a hand holding a stag by the attires. 116. 10

Dealtry, a fleur-de-lis arg. 148. 2

Dean, Ireland, a demi-lion az. 10. 2

Dean, a demi-lion rampant or, holding between the paws a crescent sa.

Dean of London, a griffin's head erased arg. 66. 2

Dean, a winged pillar ppr. 113. 10

Dean, Galway, Ireland, a wing or. 109. 7

Deane, Baron Muskerry, *see* Muskerry.

Deane-Morgan, *see* Morgan.

Deane, a demi-lion rampant or, holding in the dexter paw a crescent gu. *cf.* 10. 2

Deane, Ralph Hawtrey, Esquire, B.A., of 98, Sinclair Road, W., a demi-lion rampant holding in his dexter claw a crescent. *Virtuti mœnia cedant.*

Deane, Ireland, a lion's gamb erased gu. 36. 4

Deane of Mountjoy Square, Dublin, a demi-griffin segreant az., ducally crowned or, holding between the claws a harp ppr., and charged on the shoulder with a trefoil slipped or. *La foi me guide.*

Deane or Dane, Hants, a griffin's head erased or. 66. 2

Deane, Hants, a griffin's head erased or, between two wings erect vert.

Deane of Maplestead, Essex, and Blackburne, Lancs, a bear's head couped arg., muzzled or. 34. 14

Deane of Berkeley, Wexford, Ireland, a tortoise displayed ppr. *Ferendo non feriendo.*

Deane, Berkeley St. George, Esquire, of Glendaragh, Delgany, co. Wicklow, same crest and motto.

Deane, George Onslow, J.P., the Boyce Court, Dymock, Glouc., a griffin's head erased or, beaked gu., collared vert, bezantée, between two wings elevated of the third.

Deane, on a mount vert, a tortoise or. 125. 5

Deane, Deand, and **Dene,** a lion's head erased arg. 17. 8

Deane-Drake, Joseph Edward, Esquire, J.P., of Stokestown House, New Ross, Ireland: (1) A dexter arm embowed in armour grasping a pole-axe, all ppr. (*for Drake*). (2) A tortoise displayed ppr. (*for Deane*).

Deane-Freeman, John Joseph, Esquire, of Cloheen, co. Cork: (1) A demi-lion rampant gu. (*for Freeman*). (2) A tortoise displayed ppr. (*for Deane*). *Liberet auda* (*for Freeman*).—*Ferendo non feriendo* (*for Deane*).

Deane-Freeman, Richard, Esquire, of Sunnyside, Vernon Avenue, Clontarf, Dublin; Drumman Peake, Aghlorah, co. Galway; Garrankea, co. Limerick, same crests and mottoes.

De Angolesme, a boat's sail affixed to a mast, all ppr. 160. 9

Deans-Dundas, *see* Dundas.

Deans, Scotland, a sword in pale point upward ppr., hilt and pommel or. 170. 2

Deans of Longhermiston, Scotland, a sword in pale ppr., hilted and pommelled or, ensigned on the top with a cross pattée. *Arte vel marte.* 169. 5

Deans-Campbell, a crescent issuing out of a ducal coronet or. *Vel arte, vel marte.*

Dear and **Deare,** a horse at full speed, saddled and bridled. 52. 1

Dear, a deer's head erased ppr. 121. 2

Dearden, James Griffith, of Wytham Hall, Bourn, Lincs, a stag buffant ppr.

Dearden, Lancs, a stag trippant regardant. *Dum spiro spero.*

Dearman, out of a ducal coronet or, five cinquefoils gu., stalked and leaved ppr.

Deards, Herts and London, a Catherine-wheel ducally crowned or. *cf.* 167. 2

Deas, Scotland, on a daisy a bee feeding ppr. *Industria.*

Dease, Ireland, out of a ducal coronet a demi-ostrich with wings addorsed ppr 96. 11

Dease, Ireland, a lion rampant holding a dagger. *Toujours prêt.* *cf.* 1. 13

Dease of Turbotston, Coole, and Orangeton, co. Cavan, same crest and motto.

Dease, Sir Gerald Richard, of Celbridge Abbey, Celbridge, co. Kildare, same crest and motto.

Deasie, Scotland, a hawk's head erased ppr. 88. 12

Deasy, Capt. Henry Hugh Peter, in front of two trefoils slipped in saltire vert, a dexter arm erect, couped above the elbow ppr., holding in the hand a dagger in bend sinister arg., pommel and hilt or. *Toujours prêt.* 200. 10

Death, Kent, a griffin's head or, holding in the beak a trefoil vert. *cf.* 66. 1

Deaves, a lion's gamb erased gu., holding a dagger or. 38. 8

De Balinhard of Dublin, on a cap of maintenance gu., doubled erm., a lion statant gardant sa., crowned with a German prince's coronet or. *Tâche sans tache.*

De Barentine, Jersey, a demi-eagle displayed arg. 81. 6

De Bary, a star of six points between two wings elevated. *Fidus Deo et regi.* 112. 1

De Bathe, Sir Henry Percival, Bart., J.P., D.L., of Knightstown, co. Meath, a lion rampant arg., supporting in its paws a dagger of the first, pommel and hilt or. *Nec parvis sisto.* *cf.* 1. 13

De Beauvoir, Bart., Ireland: (1) A griffin's head and neck with wings addorsed arg., holding in the beak a branch of woodbine ppr. (*for De Beauvoir*). (2) An eagle displayed vert (*for Browne*). *Conduct is fate.* 75. 8

De Beauvoir, Benyon-: (1) A griffin's head and neck with wings addorsed and couped arg., holding in the beak a branch of woodbine ppr. (2) On a mount vert, a griffin sejant or, gorged with an Eastern coronet gu., holding in the beak a branch of woodbine ppr. (3) Out of a ducal coronet or, a dragon's head ppr., collared of the first. *cf.* 72. 4

De Beauvoir, a demi-dragon with wings addorsed ppr. 73. 10

De Bellomont, a cross moline lozenge pierced gu. 165. 1

Debenham, a dexter hand apaumée ppr., in a maunch or, cuffed gu. 205. 1

Debenham, Frank, Esquire, of FitzJohn's Avenue, Hampstead, N.W., a demi-lion per pale indented sa. and gu., holding in the dexter paw a key in bend ward upwards, and an arrow in bend sinister point downwards, and resting the sinister paw on a decrescent, all or. *Laborante honor debentair.* 241. 16

De Berry, Major-General George Frederick, Strood Hill, Rochester, Kent, out of a ducal coronet a dragon's head.

De Best of London, on a mural coronet or, a fleur-de-lis party per pale of the first and az., between two laurel-branches vert.

De Betum, an elephant ppr. 133. 9

De Blaquiere, Baron (Rt. Hon. Sir William de Blaquiere), of Ardkill, co. Londonderry, a garb ppr., banded or. *Tiens à la vérité.* 153. 2

De Blois, a lion rampant gardant gu. 2. 5

Debnam, a bear transfixed by a broken spear ppr. 34. 4

De Bohun, a wolf current ppr. 28. 4

De Bouche, a cloud ppr. 162. 13

Debram, a wheel between two wings.

De Breteville, a staff raguly in pale sa., surmounted by an eagle displayed gu. 75. 3

De Brevill, a hand holding a sheaf of arrows ppr. 214. 3

De Brewes, out of a ducal coronet gu., a lion's gamb or. 36. 12

De Bruges, a cross Calvary gu. 166. 1

De Bryan, Ireland, a dexter hand ppr. holding an escallop or. 216. 2

De Burg, a bull's head between two wings. 43. 10

De Burgh, *see* Burgh.

De Burgh, *see* Clanricarde, Marquess.

De Burgh, Middx., an arm in armour embowed fesseways, couped at the shoulder, the gauntlet apaumée ppr., stringed as a bugle-horn az., tassels gold. *Nec parvis sisto.*

De Burgh: (1) An armed arm embowed, the elbow resting on the wreath with the hand seen in the gauntlet ppr., stringed as a bugle az., tasselled or. (2) On a chapeau gu., turned up erm., a lion sejant arg., gorged with a ducal coronet or. *Nec parvis sisto.*—*A cruce salus.*—*Semper et ubique fidelis.*

De Burgh, Hugo Henry Patrick, of Ballinaperse, co. Wexford, a catamountain sejant guardant. *A cruce salus.*

De Burgh, Thomas John, of Oldtown, Naas, co. Kildare, same crest and motto.

De Burgh, Ulick, of Scarva Clones, co. Monaghan, same crest and motto.

De Burgh, a water-bouget az. 168. 4

De Burgo, Bart., Ireland, a mountain-cat sejant gardant ppr., collared and chained or. *Ung roy, ung foy, ung loy.* 26. 13

De Burton, Lt.-Col. Albert, J.P., D.L., of Buckminster Hall, Billingboro, Lincs, a dexter arm embowed in armour ppr., garnished or, the hand grasping a spear in fesse, the point towards the sinister and two arrows in saltire, the pheons towards the dexter, also ppr. *Ab illustri pago.*

De Butts, *see* Butts.

De-Capell-Brooke, Sir Arthur Richard, of Oakley, Northamp., a demi-sea-horse arg., finned and maned or. *Spes mea Deus.* 46. 7

De Cardonnel, a dove ppr. *L'esperance me console.* 92. 2

De Carteret, a reindeer's head cabossed. 122. 4

De Cetto, Baron Louis Charles Augustus Adrian, A.D.C. to His Excellency the Lord-Lieutenant of Ireland, and Maximilian Henry Æmilius de Cetto, Esquire, a plume of five ostrich-feathers alternately arg. and az., each charged with a mullet counterchanged. *Altiora peto.* 115. 3

De Chandew, a nest of young birds ppr. 113. 7

De Chastelai, *see* Casley.

Decies, Baron (Horsley-Beresford), of Beresford Lodge, Birchington, Kent, a dragon's head erased az., transfixed in the neck with a broken tilting-spear or, the broken-off point arg., thrust through the upper jaw and charged with a mullet for difference. *Nil nisi cruce.*

Decker of London, a mountain-cat current regardant ppr. 26. 7

De Clifford, Baron (Russell), Dalgan Park, Shrule, Tuam, a goat statant arg., armed or. *Che sara sara.* 129. 5

De Clinton, on a mount vert, a stag feeding ppr. 116. 1

De Colyar, *see* Colyar.

De Costa, a plume of ostrich-feathers or. 115. 1

De Courcy, Baron Kingsale, *see* Kingsale.

De Courcy-Wheeler, Henry Eliardo, Esquire, M.A., Barrister-at-law, Capt. 8th King's Royal Rifle Corps (Carlow Mil.), J.P., co. Kildare, of Robertstown House, Robertstown, co. Kildare, on a ducal crest coronet or, an eagle displayed gu., a crescent for difference. *Facie tenus.*

De Cowcy, a horse's head couped arg., bridled gu. 51. 5

de Crespigny, Champion-, Sir Claude, Bart., of Champion Lodge, Camberwell, Surrey, on a chapeau gu., turned up erm., a cubit arm mailed erect holding a broadsword ppr. *Mens sibi conscia recti.*

De Cryoll of London and Enfield, Middx., out of a mural crown a demi-lion rampant gardant gu., holding between the paws a key or.

De Cusance, a dexter hand holding up a boar's head erased and erect ppr. 220. 6

Dedan, a lion's head erased arg. 17. 8

De Den and **De Dena,** a dexter hand in fess couped, holding a sword in pale, on the point a garland, all ppr. 221. 7

De Dinan, on a cap of maintenance, a winged lion, sejant affrontée.

De Dreux, a ram's head erased arg., armed or. 130. 6

Dee of Mortlake, Surrey, a lion sejant gardant or, holding in the dexter paw a cross formée fitched az., on the cross a label with the motto, *Hic labor,* the sinister resting on a pyramid arg., on it a label with this motto, *Hoc opus.* 8. 12

Deeble, a dibble arg.

Deedes of Sandling Park, Kent, an eagle's head erased per fess nebulée gu. and arg., between two wings expanded sa. *Facta non verba.* 84. 5

Deerham, Norf., a bear sejant erect sa., muzzled, lined, and ringed or. *cf.* 34. 8

Deerhurst, Viscount, *see* Coventry, Earl.

Deering, out of a ducal coronet az., a dragon's head or. 72. 4

Deeves, out of a ducal coronet or, a unicorn's head gu., armed and crined of the first. 48. 12

De Eureux, five arrows gu., headed or, feathered arg., bound by a belt of the first, buckled of the second. 173. 3

D'Eureux, out of a ducal coronet or, a unicorn's head gu., armed and crined of the first. 48. 12

D'Eye, on a chapeau two wings displayed or. *cf.* 112. 9

D'Eyncourt, *see* Tennyson-D'Eyncourt.

D'Eyvil, an arm in armour embowed ppr., holding a club sa., spiked or. *cf.* 199. 2

De Ferrars, on a chapeau an eagle preying on a child swaddled, all ppr. 79. 3

De Ferrers, a pheon az. 174. 11

De Ferrieres, Charles Conrad Adolphus du Bois, of Hardwick Hall, Monmouth, upon a rock a raven ppr., holding in the dexter claw a sword, also ppr., pommel and hilt or. *Tout par et pour Dieu.* *cf.* 106. 9

De Flandre, Charles, Esquire, of 118, Princes Street, Edinburgh, a lion sejant affrontée sa., between two buffalo horns or. *Tousiours Prest.*

De Fortibus, an escarbuncle or. 164. 12

De Frece, Walter, of 26, Bedford Court Mansions, Bedford Square, W.C., a dexter cubit arm holding a star of eight points. *Astrum teneo.* 307. 3

De Freyne, Baron (French), French Park, Roscommon, a dolphin naiant ppr. *Malo mori quam fœdari.* 140. 5

De Garis, a lion passant gardant or. 4. 3

De Gaunt, a cross pattée fitched sa. 166. 3

De Gaury, Arthur J., Solicitor, of 1, Powis Gardens, Bayswater, W., a lion passant arg., armed and ducally crowned or. *Recta ubique.*

De Gaury, Francis Herbert Hillairet, Esquire, of 26, Castellain Road, London, W., same crest and motto.

Degge, Derbysh., and Callow Hill, Staffs, on a ducal coronet or, a falcon close arg., jessed and belled of the last. 89. 9

De Ginkell, *see* Athlone, Earl of.

Degon, on a ducal coronet a dolphin haurient ppr. *cf.* 140. 11

Dedon, a portcullis az. 178. 3

De Gray, a dart and a palm-branch in saltier ppr. 171. 7

De Grey, Baron Walsingham, *see* Walsingham.

De Grey, Hon. John Augustus, of Leiston Old Abbey, Suff., and Hill Street House Hill Street, Knightsbridge, a wyvern's head ppr. *Excitari non hebescere.*

De Grey, Earl, Baron Lucas and Grantham, *see* Ripon, Marquess of.

Dehaney, Ireland, a demi-bear rampant ppr. 34. 13

De Haney, a demi-bear salient arg., muzzled gu. 34. 13

De Harcla, a fret az. 165. 10

De Hatfield, on the stump of a tree sprouting branches an eagle with wings addorsed and inverted, all ppr.

De Havilland, John Thomas Ross, Guernsey, out of a coronet sa., a tower triple-towered arg., the portcullis gu. *Dominus fortissima turris.* *cf.* 157. 6

De Hochepied-Larpent, Major Sir George Albert, Bart., of Roehampton, Surrey: (1) A unicorn's head arg., crined or, the neck charged with a fleur-de-lis, and below with four annulets conjoined az. (*for Larpent*). (2) Out of a ducal coronet or, a crescent sa. (*for De Hochepied*). (3) Out of a ducal coronet or, a dexter hand issuant apaumée ppr. (*also for De Hochepied*). *Optivo cognomine crescit.*

De Hochepied-Larpent, Egmont, Esquire, of Gladstone Avenue, Malvern, Victoria, Australia, same crests and motto.

De Hochepied-Larpent, Frederick, Esquire, same crests.

De Hochepied-Larpent, Lionel Gerrard Harrison, Esquire, B.A., of Kelvedon, Essex, same crests.

De Hochepied-Larpent, Lionel Henry Planta, Esquire, I.S.C., of Holmwood, Lexden, Colchester, same crests and motto.

De Hochepied-Larpent, John Melville, 9th **Baron De Hochepied,** Baron and Magnate of the Kingdom of Hungary, of 27, Palmeira Square, Brighton: (1) Out of a royal diadem ppr., a crescent sa. (2) Out of a similar crown a dexter hand issuant apaumée ppr. (*both for De Hochepied*). *Optivo cognomine crescit.*

De Hoghton, Sir James, Bart., of Hoghton Tower, Preston, a bull passant arg., the ears, tips of the horns, mane, hoofs, and point of the tail sa. *Mal gre le tort.* *cf.* 45. 2

De Horne of Stanway Hall, Essex, a cup, round at the top erm., bordered with the eyes of peacock's feathers ppr.

De Horsey, Admiral Algernon Frederick Rous, of Melcombe House, Cowes, Isle of Wight, a horse's head couped arg., in armour or, bridled az., on the head a plume of three feathers, the dexter gold, the centre of the third and the sinister gu.

Deicrow, out of a mural crown a demi-lion rampant gardant gu., holding between the paws a key or.

Deighton, a fountain throwing up water ppr. 159. 13

Deinston, Scotland, a tree ppr., fructed gu. 143. 5

Dekewer and **Dekener,** Middx., out of a tower vert, a tiger's head ppr., collared or. 157. 9

De Keyser, Alderman Sir Polydore, of Chatham House, Grove Road, Clapham Park, a mallet sa., between two branches of palm slipped vert. *Respice, aspice, prospice.* 176. 8

De Kierzkowski-Steuart, *see* Kierzkowski.

De la Barr of London, a plume of three feathers, the centre one ppr., the others az. 115. 1

Delaber, a greyhound sejant sa., collared. *cf.* 59. 2

De la Bere, *see* Baghot-De la Bere.

Delabere, out of a ducal coronet ppr., a plume of ostrich-feathers per pale arg. and az. 263. 7

De la Bere, Henry Thomas, Esquire, of the Vicarage, Woodlands, Kingsclere, Hants, out of a ducal coronet or, five ostrich-feathers ppr.

De la Chambre, Sussex, an ass's head erased arg. cf. 125. 12

De la Cherois, Daniel, of the Manor House, Donaghadee, an anchor erect ppr. *Fac et spera.* 161. 1

De la Cherois, Samuel, Esquire, of Ballywilliam, near Donaghadee, same crest and motto.

De la Cherois-Crommelin, Frederick Armand, Esquire, J.P., of Carrowdore Castle, co. Down: (1) Out of a ducal coronet or, a swan rising ppr. (*for Crommelin*). (2) An anchor az. *Fac et spera.*

Delacour, John, Esquire, an Irish wolf-dog passant ppr., gorged with a collar gemelle gu., and charged on the shoulder with a trefoil slipped vert. *Fortis et fidelis.*

Deladowne, an arm vested az., cuffed or, holding in the hand ppr. a cup of the first, flames issuing therefrom ppr.

De la Faye of Wichbury, Wilts, a demi-lion rampant arg. 10. 2

Delafeld and **Delafield**, an ox's foot couped sa. 123. 7

De la Ferté, Charles Henry Joubert, Esquire, of the Ferns, Weybridge, Surrey, two pine-trees in saltire, eradicated and fructed ppr. *Omnia virtuti cedunt.* 238. 4

Delafield, a cross pattée gu., between two wings or. 110. 7

Delafield, Middx., a dove with wings expanded holding in the beak an olive-branch, all ppr. *Insignia fortunæ paria.*—*Fest.* 94. 5

De la Fons, a wolf sejant or. 29. 3

De la Fosse, a cock or. 91. 2

De la Fountaine, Essex, on a mount vert, a griffin sejant or, holding in the dexter claw an Eastern crown arg.

De la Garde, Jersey, a deer-hound or, collared and ringed gu.

De la Hadd, Kent, on a mount vert, a talbot sejant arg., eared sa., ducally gorged gu., on the dexter side of the mount a laurel-branch ppr.

Delahay, a pomeis charged with a lion's head erased arg., collared az. 19. 3

Delahay, Heref., a wolf's head. 30. 5

Delahill, a caltrap az. 174. 14

Delahyde of Moyglare, Meath, Ireland, a heron's head couped arg., ducally gorged or, beaked gu., holding in the beak a snake ppr.

Delaite, a cock or. 91. 2

Delaland, two hands conjoined supporting a human heart ppr. 224. 4

Delaland, a leopard's head issuing from a tower ppr. 157. 7

Delaleigh, out of a crescent or, a cross crosslet fitched sa. 166. 9

Delalynd, in the sea ppr., an anchor sa. 161. 6

Delalynd and **Delalynde**, an escallop gu., between two eagle's wings or. 141. 10

Delamaine, a chevalier in armour ppr., holding in the dexter hand a tilting-spear with the pennon unrolled. cf. 188. 2

Delamain, a demi-eagle displayed ppr. 81. 6

Delamaine, a man in military uniform az., holding a flag in bend gu. cf. 188. 6

Delamare, an eel naiant ppr. 142. 10

Delamare, a ship under sail in the sea ppr. 160. 13

Delamere, Baron (Cholmondeley), Vale Royal, Northwich, Chesh., a demi-griffin segreant sa., beaked, winged, ducally gorged and membered or, and holding between the claws a helmet ppr., garnished, also or. *Cassis tutissima virtus.* cf. 64. 1

Delamere, a pheasant ppr. cf. 90. 2

Delamote and **Delamotte**, an ostrich's head, holding in the beak a horse-shoe between two feathers, all ppr. 97. 12

Delamote, a lion passant gardant, collared vair. cf. 4. 3

De la Motte, a demi-lion gu., gorged with an Eastern crown or, the sinister paw resting on an escutcheon az., charged with two medals, that on the dexter being a representation of the medal commemorative of Seringapatam, and that on the sinister a representation of the medal commemorative of Egypt. *Providentia Dei conservet.*

De la Motte, Peter William, Esquire, M.R.C.P., of Staines, Middx., on a mount vert, a demi-lion rampant gu., against a tree, fructed ppr. *Providentia Dei conservet.* 291. 2

Delancey and **Delancy**, a demi-leopard gardant, supporting an anchor ppr. 23. 1

Delancey, a sinister arm in armour embowed holding in the hand a standard with flag. cf. 199. 9

Deland, a leopard's head issuing from a tower ppr. 157. 7

Deland, Suff., two dexter hands conjoined supporting a human heart ppr. 224. 4

Delane, an eagle displayed or, charged with a mullet sa. cf. 75. 2

Delane of Queen's Co., Ireland, now of Ascot House, Berks, a dexter arm embowed in armour grasping a flaming sword, all ppr. *In te Domine speravi.* 195. 8

Delaney and **Delany**, an antelope trippant ppr. 126. 6

Delaney and **Delany**, between two wings a swan statant ppr.

Delaney, Ireland, a buffalo's head erased gu. 44. 1

Delany, out of a ducal coronet a bull's head erased. 44. 11

Delap, James Bogle, Esquire, J.P., late Hon. Major, Royal Bucks Hussars, of Monellan, Killygordon, co. Donegal, and the Manor House, Lillingstone Lovel, Bucks, two arms embowed, the dexter ppr., holding a rose gu., slipped and leaved vert, the sinister in armour, the hand holding a sword, all ppr., pommel and hilt or. *Merito.*

Delap, Surrey, two arms embowed, the dexter ppr., holding in the hand a rose gu., the sinister in armour, and holding a sword ppr., hilt and pommel or. *Merito.*

Delap of London and Surrey, a cubit arm in armour per pale embattled or and az., holding in the hand a sword ppr., hilt and pommel of the first. 210. 2

Delap, a rose-branch with three roses, all ppr. 149. 14

De Lapasture, Count and **Marquis** in the Kingdom of France (Gerard Gustavus Ducarel), of Rowney Abbey, Ware, a lion's head regardant and erased or. cf. 17. 6

Delapinde, a lion's gamb erased arg., holding three pines or, leaved vert.

Delapipe, three organ-pipes or, entiled with a garland of laurel vert. 168. 10

Delaplaunch, a cross moline erm. 165. 3

Delaplaunch, a hunting horn sans strings sa., garnished or. 228. 9

De la Poer-Beresford, *see* Waterford, Marquess, and Decies, Baron.

De la Poer, Edmond James de Poher, J.P., D.L., a Count of the Papal States, a Knight of St. John of Jerusalem (Malta), claiming to be Baron le Power and Coroghmore, of Gurteen le Poer, Kilsheelan, Clonmel, a buck's head caboshed ppr., attired or, and between the attires a crucifix of the last. *Per crucem ad coronam.* 122. 13

Delapool, **Delapoole**, and **De la Poole**, a crosier gu. 170. 14

Delapoole, on a chapeau a leopard statant ppr. 24. 1

Delaport, a bird with wings expanded ppr. 94. 2

De la Pryme, Rev. Alexander, M.A., Wistow Lodge, Hunts, on a rock ppr. an eagle. *Per varios casus.*

De la Rever and **Delariver**, a shepherd's flute or. 168. 3

De la River and **Delariver**, Yorks, a lion's gamb holding a broken spear ppr. cf. 39. 9

Delarous, an armed arm erect holding in the hand a sword ppr. 210. 2

De la Rue, Sir Thomas Andros, Bart., 52, Cadogan Square, London, a brazier gu., fired, between two branches of laurel, issuant from the flames a serpent nowed and erect ppr. *Cherche la vérité.* 248. 5

De la Rue, Herbert, Esquire, J.P., of the Lodge, Six Mile Bottom, Newmarket, same crest and motto.

De la Rue, Warren William, Esquire, J.P., of the Cottage, Chippenham, near Newmarket, same crest and motto.

Delatune, Hants, an antelope trippant or. 126. 6

Delature, a lamb bearing a cross and banner. 131. 2

Delaune, Faunce-, Alured, Sharsted, Kent, a demi-lion rampant sa., langued gu., ducally gorged or, between two wings arg. *Ne tentes aut perfice.*

Delaune, the lion of St. Mark sejant, wings elevated, round the head a glory, all ppr., resting the dexter paw on the Gospel close or, covered gu., garnished of the second.

De la Vach and **Delavache**, a cow's tail ppr. 123. 12

Delavache, an ox-yoke in pale sa. cf. 178. 6

Delaval, Northumb., out of a ducal coronet or, a goat's head arg., armed of the first. *Dieu me conduise.* 128. 14

Delaval, a salamander in flames ppr. 138. 4

Delavall of Seaton Delaval, Northumb., a ram's head erased arg., armed or. 130. 6

Delavere, a stag salient ppr. 117. 2

Delavere, a catherine-wheel dropping blood, all gu. *cf.* 167. 2

Delawar, a bird's head couped arg., beaked gu. 83. 1

Delawarr, Earl (Sackville), Buckhurst, Sussex: (1) Out of a ducal coronet or, a griffin's head az., beaked and eared or (*for West*). 67. 9. (2) Out of a coronet composed of fleurs-de-lis an estoile arg. (*for Sackville*). *Jour de ma vie.* *cf.* 164. 4

Delechamber, Sussex, an ass's head erased arg. *cf.* 125. 12

Delegh, out of a crescent or, a cross crosslet fitched sa. 166. 9

Deleval, on a chapeau a lion's head erased, ducally crowned, all ppr. 21. 3

De Levis, out of the coronet of a Marquis of France or, a demi-eagle displayed sa. *Deo juvante.*

Delgarno, a sea-lion statant, holding in his dexter paw a cross moline. *cf.* 20. 4

De Ligne of Harlaxton, Lincs, on a mount vert, a lion sejant gardant or, the dexter paw resting on a caltrap az.

Deliers of London, a demi-lion rampant az., ducally crowned gu. 10. 11

Deline, a rock ppr. *Esse quam videri.* 179. 7

De L'Isle and **Dudley, Baron** (Sidney), of Penshurst, Kent: (1) A porcupine statant az., the quills, collar, and chain or. (2) A griffin's head erased arg., ducally gorged or. *Quo fata vocant.* *cf.* 136. 5

De Lisle, Major-General Alfred, a demi-eagle displayed or. *De insula.* 81. 6

De Lisle-Phillipps, March-, Everard, of Garendon Park and Grace Dieu Manor, Leics.: (1) A stag trippant ppr. (*for Lisle*). 117. 8. (2) A demi-griffin ppr. gorged or, holding an escutcheon az., charged with a lion rampant or (*for Phillipps*). 64. 10. (3) A demi-lion rampant quarterly az. and or, holding a Maltese cross or (*for March*). *En bon espoir.—Quod justum non quod utile.* 11. 3

De Lisle-Phillipps, March, Edwin Joseph Lisle, Charnwood Lodge, Coalville, Leics., crests as above.

De Lisle, a lion passant gardant. 4. 3

Delius, Johann Daniel, Esquire, Vice-Consul to His Majesty the King of Sweden and Norway at Bradford, Yorks, of Fulwith Grange, near Harrogate, Yorks, and 35, De Vere Gardens, Kensington, London, W., out of a coronet or, three ostrich-feathers arg. 114. 2

Delius of Cassel and Munster, Westphalia, out of a coronet or, having five pearls issuing from the rim, three ostrich-feathers arg. 114. 5

Dell, Alfred Percival, Esquire, of Thornpack Lodge, Teignmouth, issuing from a cloud a hand erect holding a garb. 218. 3

Dellaber, a tower ppr., thereon a flag arg., charged with a saltier sa. 157. 13

Dellaber, a greyhound sejant sa. 59. 4

Dellabere, Glouc., out of a ducal coronet or, a plume of five feathers party per pale arg. and az. 114. 13

Dellatre, Ireland, a mullet or, between two olive-branches vert. *cf.* 146. 8

Dellee, on a mount a dove, all ppr. 92. 3

Dellyne, on a ducal coronet a Cornish chough ppr.

Delmar, a lion sejant gu., collared dancettée, the dexter fore-paw resting on a fleur-de-lis or. *cf.* 6. 11

Delme and **Delmie,** a lion passant gu., in front of an anchor sa. *cf.* 6. 2

Delmé-Radcliffe, Lieutenant-Colonel Emilius Charles, Esquire: (1) A bull's head sa., armed or, gorged with a ducal coronet, and holding in the mouth a cross crosslet fitchée or (*for Radcliffe*). (2) In front of an anchor sa., a lion passant gu. (*for Delme*). *Caen, Crecy, Calais.*

Delmé-Radcliffe, Francis Augustus, Esquire, of Hitchin Priory, Hitchin, Herts, same crests and motto.

Delmé-Radcliffe, Rev. Henry Eliot, M.A., of South Tedworth, Hants, same crests and motto.

Delmé-Radcliffe, Ralph Hubert John, Esquire, same crests and motto.

Delmege, Captain James O'Grady, of Castle Park, Limerick, Ireland, a boar's head erect and erased per pale az. and gu., armed or. *Juveniam aut viam faciem.* 43. 3

De Lousada, Horace, **Duke de Losaday Losada,** and a grandee of the first class in the Kingdom of Spain, on a mount vert, a dove regardant arg., with wings expanded or, holding in its beak a sprig of olive ppr.

Del See, a demi-woman naked, her hair dishevelled, wreathed round the temples with cinquefoils gu.

Delsume, a pegasus' head arg., between two wings endorsed or.

Delves, Scotland and England, out of a ducal coronet or, a demi-eagle displayed arg. *Je ne puis.* 80. 14

Delves, out of a ducal coronet or, a demi-eagle displayed between two wings arg.

Delves, out of a ducal coronet or, a demi-heron with wings displayed arg.

Delves, a dolphin naiant az. 140. 5

Delvin, Lord, *see* Westmeath, Marquess.

De Mandeville, on a mount vert, a stag current regardant ppr. 118. 12

De Mardeston, a cross fleury fitched gu., fleury or. 166. 7

De Mardeston, Suff., out of a mural coronet a lion's head. 19. 12

De Massue, Melville Amadeus Henry Douglas Heddle Bruce de la Caillemotte, ninth **Marquis de Ruvigny et Raineval,** in the Kingdom of France: (1) A demi-savage, crowned and girt with laurel, holding with both hands a club all ppr. (2) Out of a ducal coronet or, a dexter arm in armour embowed ppr., garnished of the first, grasping in the hand a sword in bend sinister, also ppr., pommel and hilt also or. 195. 10. "*Duce Deo.*"—*Aimer sans crainte.*

De Mauley, Baron (Ponsonby), Langford House, Lechdale, of Canford, Dorset, out of a ducal coronet or, three arrows points downwards, one in pale and two in saltire, environed by a snake ppr. *Pro rege, lege, grege.* 173. 2

De Medewe, *see* Medewe.

Demeschines, a hand holding a cutlass ppr. *cf.* 213. 5

De Mewburgh, a cinquefoil. 148. 12

De Mohun, a lion's head regardant ppr.

De Moleyns, *see* Eveleigh-De Moleyns.

De Montacute, a griffin's head gu., between two wings or. 65. 11

De Montalt, Earl, *see* Montalt.

De Montgomery, a demi-savage holding in his dexter hand a sword, and in his sinister a marshal's baton ppr.

De Montmorency, Viscounts Frankfort and **Mountmorres,** *see* those titles.

De Montmorency, a peacock in pride ppr. 103. 12

De Montmorency, Rev. Waller, M.A., of Castle Morres, Knocktopher, co. Kilkenny, same crest. *Dieu ayde.* 103. 12

De Montmorency, on a ducal coronet or, a peacock in his pride ppr. *Dieu ayde.* *cf.* 103. 12

De Morton, a griffin segreant sa. 62. 2

De Mowbray, a fox current ppr. *cf.* 32. 8

Dempsey, a sphinx with wings addorsed ppr. *cf.* 182. 12

Dempsey, Ireland, out of a mural coronet seven battle-axes erect, all ppr. 172. 9

Dempster of Skibo, Sutherland, a leg-bone and a palm-branch in saltier, all ppr. *Mors aut vita decora.* 147. 4

Dempster, a demi-lion gu., holding in the dexter paw a sword in pale ppr. *Fortiter et strenue.* *cf.* 14. 12

Den, a blackamoor's head sa., banded arg. 192. 13

Den and **Denne,** Kent, on a staff raguly vert a stag lodged ppr., attired or. *cf.* 115. 7

Den and **Denne,** on a mount vert, a stag lodged regardant arg. 115. 9

Denbigh, Earl of, of Newnham-Paddox, a nut-hatch on a hazel-branch fructed, all ppr. *Virtutis præmium honor.*

Denby, an antelope trippant gu., collared arg. *cf.* 126. 6

Dench, a unicorn's head between two branches of laurel in orle ppr. 49. 14

Dendy of Griggs, Towerhill, Horsham, Sussex, on a mount between two slips of laurestinus vert, a bezant charged with a unicorn's head couped az. *Respicio sine luctu.*

Dendy, Richard Sidney, Esquire, F.R.G.S., of Bognor, Sussex, same crest.

Dendy, Robert Arthur, Esquire, B.A., same crest.

Dendy of Dorking, Surrey, on a mount vert, a swan arg., beaked gu., resting its dexter claw on a pheon ppr. *Per ardua stabilis esto.* *cf.* 100. 7

Dene, a lion's head erased arg. 17. 8

Dene, Devonsh., a dexter hand holding a cross crosslet fitched. 221. 14

Deneston, a cross fleury fitched gu., fleury or. 166. 7

De Newburg, a quatrefoil vert. 148. 10

D'Engaine and **Dengaine,** on a mount a stag feeding ppr. 116. 9

Dengayne, a tower sa., with a cupola gu., surmounted with a flag of the same. 157. 15

Denham, Scotland, a thistle and a rose-slip in saltier, all ppr. *Juvant aspera probum.* 150. 3

Denham, Scotland, a crane holding in its dexter claw a stone, all ppr. *Cura dat victoriam.* 105. 6

Denham, a lion's head erased erminois. 17. 8

Denhany, a demi-bear salient arg. 34. 13

Denholm, Scotland, a stag lodged ppr. 115. 7

Denis, a hand grasping a snake, all ppr. 220. 2

Denis, out of a ducal coronet a plume of five ostrich-feathers ppr. 114. 13

Denis-Tottenham, John, Esquire, J.P., of Ashfield, Rathfarnham, Dublin: (1) A lion rampant gu., charged with a crescent or (*for Tottenham*). (2) An heraldic tiger's head erased erm. (*for Denis*). *Ad astra sequor.*

Denison, Earl of Londesborough, *see* Londesborough.

Denison, a dexter arm vested gu., cuffed arg., pointing with the forefinger to an estoile or.

Denison, a dexter arm in bend vested vert, the hand ppr., pointing to a star or.

Denison, William Denison, of Ossington, a cubit arm bendwise, vested az., cuffed arg., the hand ppr., pointing with the fore-finger to a star or.

Denison of York, a dexter arm embowed, vested az., cuffed arg., the hand ppr., pointing to a mullet of six points of the second. 228. 12

Denison, late John, Esquire, of Brookfield House, Toronto, a dexter arm embowed, vested az., cuffed or, the hand pointing with the forefinger to a star of six points. *Perseverando.*

Denison, out of a naval coronet a demi-mermaid holding in her dexter hand a mirror, and in her sinister a comb ppr. 184. 14

Denison, Henry, Esquire, J.P., of Ossington Hall, near Newark, a sinister cubit arm in bend dexter, vested vert, cuffed erm., charged with a cross crosslet on the hand ppr., pointing with the fore-finger to an estoile.

Denison, William Evelyn, of Ossington Hall, near Newark, same crest.

Denison, Beckett-, a sinister cubit arm in bend dexter, vested vert, cuffed erm., charged with a cross crosslet or, the hand ppr., pointing with a forefinger to an estoile radiated of the third.

Denistoun, a dexter hand holding an antique shield sa., charged with a star or. 219. 7

Denman, Baron (Denman), of Dovedale, Derbysh., a raven rising ppr., holding in the beak an annulet or. *Prudentiâ et constantiâ.*

Denman, a demi-greyfriar vested ppr., holding in his dexter hand a lash. 187. 11

Denn, Sussex, out of a ducal coronet a camel's head or. *cf.* 132. 7

Denn, on a chapeau gu., turned up erm., a demi-peahen issuant with wings displayed ppr.

Denne, on a chapeau vert, turned up erm., a demi-peacock with wings expanded and elevated ppr.

Denne, Kent, on a chapeau vert, turned up erm., a peacock in pride ppr. 103. 5

Denne, Henry, Esquire, B.A., Barrister-at-Law, on a mount vert, a stag lodged erm , attired and resting the dexter fore-foot on a fleur-de-lis or.

Denne, Rev. Richard H., M.A., of Brimpsfield Rectory, near Gloucester, same crest.

Denne, *see* Den.

Denne, Herbert H., Esquire, of Fordwich, near Canterbury, same crest.

Dennestoun, Lord, Scotland, a dexter hand ppr., holding up an antique shield sa., charged with a star or. *Adversa virtute repello.* 219. 7

Dennet of London, a boar's head erased az. 42. 2

Dennett, a hand holding an escallop-shell erect, all ppr. 216. 2

Dennett, a demi-wolf sa., collared indented arg. *cf.* 31. 5

Denney and **Denny,** Essex and Norf., a cubit arm erect ppr., holding in the hand a bunch of barley or.

Dennie and **Denny,** Scotland, a hand erect pointing with two fingers to the sun. 222. 10

Dennis, Glouc., a demi-lion rampant az., bezantée. 10. 4

Dennis, a leopard's head and neck couped ppr. 22. 10

Dennis, a tiger's head erased arg.

Dennis, a tiger's head erased erm.

Dennis, Cornw., a dragon's head and neck couped. 71. 7

Dennis, a griffin's head erased erm. 66. 2

Dennis, a wolf sejant erect sa., collared and chained or. *Dieu à la mer.*

Dennis, Ireland, an heraldic antelope trippant. 127. 5

Dennis, Ireland, a castle with two towers arg., from each tower a banner floating to the sinister gu. *Suaviter sed fortiter.* *cf.* 155. 6

Dennis, a castle arg. with two towers, each surmounted with a cupola, from which a flagstaff, thereon a flag gu., charged with an Eastern crown or. *Suaviter sed fortiter.*

Dennis, Ireland, out of a ducal coronet a hand holding a sheaf of arrows ppr. 214. 2

Dennis, Kent, an arm couped at the elbow and erect in armour, grasping a snake, all ppr.

Dennis, W. Pen, Esquire, Pendine, Wrexham, in front of a tree an antelope trippant. *Suaviter sed fortiter.* 300. 15

Denniss, E. R. Bartley, Esquire, Barrister-at-Law, of 1, Essex Court, Temple, a leopard's head couped ppr. *Suaviter sed fortiter.*

Dennistoun, *see* Denistoun.

Dennistoun, Alexander, of Golfhill, Glasgow, N.B., a dexter arm in pale ppr., the hand holding an antique shield sa., charged with a mullet or. *Adversa virtute repello.*

Dennistoun, James Wallis, of that Ilk, J.P., of Auchenlea, Row, Dumbartonsh., same crest and motto.

Dennistoun, Richard Campbell, Esquire, same crest and motto.

Dennistoun, a squirrel sejant or. *cf.* 135. 7

Denny, out of a ducal coronet a plume of ostrich-feathers. 114. 13

Denny, Sir Robert Arthur, Bart., of Tralee, co. Kerry, a cubit arm vested az., turned up arg., holding five wheat-ears or. *Et mei messis erit.* 205. 5

Denny, H. E., M.D., Longtown, Cumberland, same crest.

Denny, Rev. Edward, M.A., of Kempley Vicarage, Glouc., a cubit arm vested az., turned up or, holding five wheat-ears or. *Et mea messis erit.*

Denny, Thomas Anthony, Esquire, F.R.G.S., of 7, Connaught Place, London, W., out of a mural coronet ppr., a cubit arm vested az., cuffed arg., the hand also ppr., holding five wheat-ears or. *Et mea messis erit.* *cf.* 205. 5

Denny, Richard Harrison, Esquire, of the Cottage, Framingham, Pigot, Norwich, a cubit arm erect ppr., the hand grasping three ears of wheat ppr., surmounting two cross crosslets in saltire gu. *Vincit omnia veritas.*

Denny, Ireland, a garb in fess ppr. 153. 6

Denny, a buck's head couped at the neck. 121. 5

Denny, a hand erect pointing with two fingers to the sun. 222. 10

Dennys, out of a ducal coronet a plume of five ostrich-feathers ppr. 114. 13

Dennys, General Julius Bentall, of Westbourne, Sidmouth, a griffin's head.

Dennys, *see* Denys.

Denouac, between two wings a globe, thereon an eagle with wings expanded ppr. *cf.* 159. 9

Denovan, Scotland, a stag trippant gu. 117. 8

Denshire, a lion regardant holding with both paws an anchor, all ppr.

Denston, out of a ducal coronet or, a dexter hand holding a sword-blade wavy in pale ppr. 212. 1

Densy, on a chapeau a stag trippant ppr. 118. 3

Dent, Surrey, a tiger's head couped arg.

Dent, Northumb., a tiger's head erased erm., maned sa., vomiting fire ppr.

Dent of Sudeley Castle, Glouc., an heraldic tiger's head erased erm., semée of lozenges az., flames issuing from the mouth ppr. *Concordia et industria.*

Dent, Edward John, of Shortflatt Tower, Belsay, Newcastle-on-Tyne: (1) A panther's head erased, incensed, and affrontée, transpierced by an arrow barbed and flighted, the pheon towards the dexter, all ppr. (*for Dent*). *cf.* 23. 6. (2) A swallow rising out of clouds ppr. (*for Hedley*).

Dent, Major John William, of Ribston Hall, Yorks, and Winterton, Lincs: (1) A demi-tiger sa., collared arg., resting the sinister paw on a lozenge erm. (2) On a mount a crane holding in the beak a rose slipped, and resting the dexter claw on a serpent nowed, all ppr. *Patientia et perseverantia.*

Dent, Francis, Esquire, of 1, Harcourt Buildings, Temple, E.C., same crests and motto.

Dent, Rev. Joseph Jonathan, M.A., of the Vicarage, Hunsingore, Wetherby, Lincs, same crests and motto.

Dent, William Dent, Esquire, of 23, Kelvin Grove, Prince's Park, Liverpool, same crests and motto.

Dent, Henry Francis Menethorpe, Malton, Yorks, same crests and motto.

Dent, a demi-wolf salient sa., gorged round the neck with a collar dancettée arg. *cf.* 31. 5

Denton, a stork ppr. 105. 11

Denton of Denton Hall, Cumb., an eagle sa. 26. 2

Denton, Sir George Chardin, K.C.M.G., of Bathurst, Gambia, West Africa, an eagle with wings displayed.

Denton, Cumb., a martlet sa. 95. 5

Denton, Camb., a lion couchant or. 7. 5

Denver, a demi-lion rampant az., holding with both paws a cross crosslet fitchée or. cf. 11. 10

Denys, in front of a tree vert, an antelope trippant ppr.

Denys, Sir Francis Charles Edward, Bart., of Easton-Neston, Northamp., a demi-lion erminois, collared gu., holding between the paws a French lily slipped ppr. *Hora e sempre.*

Depden, an anchor or, surmounted by a fleur-de-lis sa. 161. 9

Depden, a dexter and a sinister hand wielding a two-handed sword ppr. 213. 3

Depham, a cherub ppr. 189. 9

Depham, a lion passant ppr. 6. 2

De Placetes, a lion's head ppr., collared or. 18. 6

De Ponthieu, a tree vert. 143. 5

Deptun, an anchor or, enfiled by a fleur-de-lis sa. 161. 9

De Pudsey, an eagle's head gu., holding in the beak an acorn slipped and leaved vert. cf. 84. 10

Deram, a hand in fess couped holding a fleur-de-lis ppr. 221. 9

Deram, a pyramid entwined by a vine ppr. cf. 179. 12

Deramore, Baron (de Yarburgh-Bateson), of Heslington Hall, York, and Belvoir Park, co. Down, a bat's wing erect sa. 277. 8. (2) A falcon close or, preying upon a duck ppr. 277. 7. *Nocte volamus.—Non est sine pulvere palma.*

De Ramsey, Baron (Fellowes), of Ramsey Abbey, Hunts, a lion's head erased or, murally crowned arg., and charged with a fesse dancettée erm. *Patientia et perseverantia cum magnanimitate.* 18. 3

Deraw, a bundle of quills arg. 113. 6

Derby, Earl of, Baron Stanley of Bickerstaffe (Stanley, K.G.), Knowsley Hall, Prescot, on a chapeau gu., turned up erm., an eagle with wings extended or, preying on an infant in its cradle ppr., swaddled gu., the cradle laced gold. *Sans changer.* cf. 77. 13

Derby, a dromedary ppr. 132. 2

Dereham, Norf., a bear sejant erect sa., muzzled, lined, and ringed or, charged on the shoulder with an annulet arg. cf. 34. 8

Derham, Ireland, a demi-wolf per pale or and sa. 31. 2

Derham, two hands winged and clasped. 224. 12

Derhaugh, Suff., a heraldic tiger passant or, tufted and maned sa. 25. 5

De Renzy, Annesley Charles Castriot, a sword in pale, point upwards ppr. *Facta non verba.*

De Reuter, Baron, Paul Julius, of 18, Kensington Palace Gardens, a horse at full gallop, on his back a knight in complete armour arg., grasping in his dexter hand a lance in rest, and in his sinister a flash of lightning ppr. *Per mare per terras.*

Dering, Sir Henry Neville, Bart., of Surrenden-Dering, Kent, on a ducal coronet or, a mount vert, thereon a horse passant sa. *Stemni ne semni.* cf. 52. 13

Dering, George Edward, Lockleys, Herts, same crest as above. *Terrere nolo timere nescio.*

De Rinzy of Clobemon, co. Wexford, a lion rampant or. *Facta non verba.* 1. 13

De Rivers and **De Ryvers,** a tortoise passant ppr. cf. 125. 5

De Rivers, a bat displayed. 137. 11

Dermot or **Dermott,** a demi-lion holding a spear in pale thrust through a bear's head, all ppr.

Dermott, Ireland, a griffin's head erased or. 66. 2

Dernford, a cross crosslet fitched az., and a sword ppr., in saltier. 166. 12

Dernford, a sphinx passant gardant, wings addorsed ppr. 182. 12

De Romara, a stag's head at gaze ppr. cf. 119. 12

De Ros, Baron (Fitz-Gerald-De Ros), of Hamlake, Leics.: (1) On a chapeau gu., turned up erm., a peacock in pride ppr. (*for De Ros*). 103. 5. (2) A monkey statant ppr., environed round the loins and chained or (*for Fitz-Gerald*). *Crom a boo.* 136. 8

De Rouillon, Norf., a dolphin haurient sa. 140. 11

Derrick, on a spear-head a savage's head couped and dropping blood ppr. *Virtute non viribus.* cf. 191. 7

Derule, a demi-wolf gu. 31. 2

De Ruvigny et Raineval, Marquis, *see* De Massue.

Derwell, a harp or. 168. 9

Derwent, Baron (Vanden-Bempde-Johnstone), of Hackness, North Riding of Yorks: (1) A spur erect, rowel upwards, with wings elevated or, leathered gu., the buckle ppr. (*for Johnstone*). 111. 12. (2) Issuing from the battlements of a tower ppr., a demi-eagle with two heads displayed sa., the wings or, about the neck a pearl collar, therefrom a diamond pendant, and charged on the breast with a sword fesseways ppr., pommel and hilt gold. *Nunquam non paratus.* cf. 82. 6

Derwin, a demi-griffin holding in its claws an escallop. cf. 64. 2

De Ryvers, *see* De Rivers.

De Sales La Terrière, Colonel Fenwick Bulmer, Comte de Sales de St. Salvy, of Grove Place, Nursling, Hants, Exon of the King's Bodyguard of the Yeomen of the Guard, de geules un croissant d'or, en chef un aigle du même en fasce d'azure à trois étoilles d'or. *Ny plus ny moyns.*

De Salis, Rev. Henry Jerome Augustine Fane, Count of the Holy Roman Empire, Portnall Park, Virginia Water: (1) Out of a marquis's coronet or, a demi-woman ppr., crowned or, hair flowing down the back, winged in place of arms, and from the armpits az. (2) Out of a ducal coronet or, an eagle displayed sa., ducally crowned, also or. (3) Out of a ducal coronet a demi-lion rampant double-queued and crowned with a like coronet, all or, brandishing a sword ppr., hilt and pommel of the first, the lion cottised by two tilting-spears of the same, from each a banner paly of six arg. and gu., fringed also or. *Salix flectitur sed non frangitur.—Pro Deo rege et patria.*

Desanges, a cherub's head or. 189. 9

Desart, Earl of (Cuffe), Desart Court, Kilkenny, Ireland, a cubit arm erect couped below the elbow, vested or, charged with two bendlets undée az., the cuff erm., holding in the hand ppr. a pole-axe of the first, the staff of the second. *Virtus repulsæ nescia sordidæ.* cf. 207. 10

De Saumarez, Baron (Saumarez), of Saumarez, Guernsey, a falcon displayed ppr., with a crescent for difference. *In Deo spero.*

Desbarres, an arm couped at the shoulder and embowed, holding in the hand a spear in pale, all ppr. 201. 9

Desborough and **Desbrowe,** a bear's head couped sa., muzzled or. 34. 14

Desbrisay, a bell or. 168. 7

Desbrisay, a paroquet perched ppr. 101. 4

Desbrow, a bear's head and neck couped sa., muzzled or. 34. 14

Desbrowe, *see* Desborough.

Desbrowe, a talbot's head erased. 56. 2

Deschamps, a golden fleece girt round the middle with a collar or. 130. 10

De Senlize, a lion passant gardant, the tail extended gu. cf. 4. 3

De Silva, a lion rampant gu. 1. 13

Desland, Ireland, two hands couped and conjoined supporting a heart. 224. 4

Desmond, Earl of, Ireland, *see* Denbigh, Earl of.

Desmond, a lion passant gardant or, grasping a saltier gu. cf. 4. 3

Desnay, on a chapeau arg., turned up gu., charged with a fleur-de-lis or, a lion passant gu. cf. 4. 9

Desney, a wyvern sans legs vert. cf. 69. 14

Despard, Ireland, a hand holding a broken spear. 214. 10

Despard, on a ducal coronet or, a star of twelve rays arg. cf. 164. 4

Despard of Killaghy Castle, co. Tipperary, a dexter cubit arm in armour grasping a dagger with a broken blade, all ppr., hilted or. *Pugno, pugnas, pugnavi.*

Despencer, Baron Despencer, out of a ducal coronet per pale gu. and arg., between two wings a griffin's head of the last, beaked and eared of the first, ducally gorged per pale or, and of the second. cf. 67. 1

Despencer, Le, a griffin's head ppr. 66. 1

Despencer, two wings conjoined ppr.

Dess and **Desse,** on a chapeau gu., turned up erm., an owl with wings expanded or. *Vigilo.* 96. 6

Dessen, a porcupine sa., the spines tipped or. 136. 5

De St. Croix, a dexter arm embowed in armour ppr., holding in the hand a Passion cross. *In Deo confido.*

De St. Martin, an eagle's head or, between two wings sa. 84. 2

Des Vœux, Sir Charles Champagné Dalrymple, Bart., M.A., of Indiville, Queen's Co., a squirrel sejant ppr. *Altiora in votis.* cf. 135. 4

Des Vœux, Sir (George) William, G.C.M.G., of 35, Cadogan Square, London, S.W., same crest and motto.

De Tabley, Baron (Leicester-Warren), of Tabley House, County Palatine of Chester, on a chapeau gu., turned up erm., a wyvern arg., the wings elevated and expanded chequy or and az. *Tenebo.* cf. 70. 5

De Teissier, Philip Antoine, **Baron de Teissier** of the Kingdom of France, a cinier or crest-coronet. *Nemo me impune lacessit.*

De Teissier, a boar passant sa. (*used by some members of the family in England*). Same crest. 40. 9

Dethick, Derbysh. and Norf., a nag's head erased arg. 51. 4

Dethick, Durh., a horse's head couped arg., charged on the neck with a mullet on a crescent. *cf.* 50. 13

Dethicke, an eagle regardant with wings expanded and inverted ppr. 77. 4

Deton and **Detton,** a goat's head erased arg., collared gu. *cf.* 128. 5

Deton, on a tower arg., a crescent gu. 156. 4

De Tonge, Baron (Henri Asheton), of Château du Ragotin, Avranches, Manche, in front of a dexter arm in armour embowed, the hand grasping a grappling-iron in bend sinister sa., a lion sejant of the last, pierced in the shoulder by an arrow ppr. *Tenebo.* 197. 13

De Trafford, *see* Trafford.

De Ufford, a demi-eagle displayed sa. 81. 6

De Uphaugh, *see* Uphaugh.

D'Eureux, five arrows gu., headed or, feathered arg., bound by a belt of the first, buckled or. 173. 3

D'Eureux, out of a ducal coronet or, a talbot's head. 57. 12

De Vahl, *see* Samuel.

Devall, on a chapeau a greyhound sejant, all ppr. *cf.* 59. 4

De Vallado, Marquis De, *see* Walrond.

De Vallance, a greyhound's head gu. *cf.* 61. 2

Devan, a lion rampant arg., murally gorged or. *Non sibi solum.* *cf.* 1. 13

Devas, Horace George, Hartfield, Hayes, Kent, a lion rampant sa., collared or, langued gu., holding between the paws a shield arg., charged with a spear-head in pale sa. *Virtute et opero.*

Devas, Charles Frederic, Esquire, B.A., J.P., of Pickhurst Manor, Bickenham, same crest.

Devas, Horace, of Spondon Hall, Derby, same crest.

Devas, Thomas, of Mount Ararat, Wimbledon, Surrey, same crest.

Devaynes, a lion rampant holding between the paws a battle-axe ppr.

Devaynes, out of a baron's coronet a demi-dragon holding in the dexter claw a sword.

Devendale, a long cross az. 165. 4

Devenish, Sussex, a demi-tiger salient vert, holding in the dexter paw a cross crosslet fitched arg.

Devenish, Rev. William, B.A., of Mount Pleasant, Stokestown, co. Roscommon, a sheldrake arg., wings expanded sa., collared or. *Spero et captivus nitor.*

Devenish, Ireland, a sheldrake sa.

Devenport, on a mount vert, a hound sejant ppr., resting his dexter paw on a stag's head caboshed. *cf.* 55. 4

Devenshire, Cornw., an eagle ppr. 76. 2

Deveral and **Deverel,** the rays of the sun issuing from behind a cloud ppr. 162. 9

De Vere, *see* Vere.

Devere, the sun shining on a sunflower ppr. *cf.* 150. 6

Devereaux and **Devereux,** Ireland, a stag trippant ppr. 117. 8

Devereux, Viscount Hereford, *see* Hereford.

Devereux, out of a ducal coronet or, a talbot's head arg., eared gu. 57. 12

Devereux, a tower ppr. 156. 2

Deverson, a lion's head gardant and erased gu., collared or.

De Vesci, Viscount (Vesey), Abbey-Leix, Queen's Co., Ireland, a hand erect in armour, holding a laurel-branch, all ppr. *Sub hoc signo vinces.*

Deveston, a cross fleury fitched gu., fleury or. 166. 7

Devetts, issuing from clouds a cubit arm in fess, holding a sword erect enfiled with a boar's head erased. *cf.* 223. 10

De Veulle, a heart gu., between two wings or. *Veuille bien.* *cf.* 110. 14

Devey, a dexter arm embowed in fess, couped ppr., vested sa., holding a cross crosslet fitched gu. 203. 9

De Vic, a caltrap sa. 174. 14

De Visme, an eagle displayed ppr. 75. 2

De Visme, an allerion ppr.

De Vismes, Baron Henry Auriol Douglas, late Captain R.A., an eagle displayed with two heads sa. *J'aspire.* 74. 2

De Vitre, a demi-griffin or, holding between his paws a bunch of grapes purp., issuing out of an oak-wreath ppr., acorned or.

Devlin, Jeremiah, Esquire, of the City of New York, U.S.A., a griffin passant gu., charged on the shoulder with an Irish cross or. *Crux mea stella.* *cf.* 63. 2

Devoike, a dexter hand throwing an arrow ppr. 214. 4

Devon, Earl of (Courtenay), Powderham Castle, Exeter: (1) Out of a ducal coronet or, a plume of seven ostrich-feathers four and three arg. (2) A dolphin embowed ppr. *Quod verum tutum.—Ubi lapsus, quid feci.* 140. 5

Devon, a horse's head arg., thrust through by a spear sa., the head or. 50. 11

Devonshire, Duke of (Cavendish), Chatsworth, Derbysh., a serpent nowed ppr. *Cavendo tutus.* 142. 4

Devonshire, a cross moline or. 165. 3

De Waetor, the attires of a stag fixed to the scalp or. *cf.* 123. 5

Dewar, Scotland, a cock crowing ppr. *Gloria patri.* 91. 2

Dewar, James, Esquire, of Lassodie, Fife, a cock, the wings raised ppr. *Gloria patri.* *cf.* 91. 7

Dewar, Northumb., a holy lamb bearing the banner of St. Andrew ppr. *cf.* 130. 2

Dewar, Captain James Cumming, of Vogrie, Midlothian, a dexter arm vambraced brandishing a sword ppr., hilted and pommelled or. *Quid non pro patria.* 210. 2

Dewar, Albemarle O'Beirne Willoughby, of Doles, Hurstbourne, Tarrant, Andover, an anchor erect sa., cabled gu. *Dum spiro spero.*

Dewar, Sir Thomas Robert, M.P., J.P., of 36, St. James's Street, S.W., and the Grove, Pluckley, Kent, between two thistles leaved and slipped ppr., a cock gu., armed and spurred arg., charged on the breast with a cinquefoil or. *Gloria patri.* 267. 13

De Warren, a lion passant gardant az. 4. 3

Dewe, Bucks, a dragon's head between two dragon's wings expanded sa., on each a cinquefoil or. *cf.* 72. 7

Dewell and **Dewelle,** on a mount vert, a horse current arg., bridled sa. 52. 10

Dewelles, an ostrich's head and wings arg., ducally gorged gu., holding in the beak a horse-shoe az. *cf.* 97. 10

Dewers, an anchor cabled ppr. 161. 2

Dewes, Warw., a wolf's head erased or, collared vair, holding in the mouth a quatrefoil pierced gu., slipped ppr. *cf.* 30. 12

Dewey, Thomas Charles, Esquire, of South Hill Wood, Bromley, Kent, a dragon's head erased sa., holding in the mouth a sword in bend ppr., pommel and hilt or, between two dragon's wings of the last, on each a bend of the first, charged with a cinquefoil of the third. *Vir sapiens fortis est.*

Dewhurst, a wolf's head erased gu. 30. 8

Dewhurst, Lancs, a wolf's head erminois. *Spes mea in Deo.* 30. 5

Dewhurst, Lancs, a wolf's head erased erminois, collared az. *Spes mea in Deo.* 30. 11

Dewhurst, John Bonny, Esquire, of Aireville, Yorks, in front of a wolf's head erased or, guttée-de-poix, three saltires gu. *Spes mea in Deo.* *cf.* 30. 8

De Windt, Joseph Clayton, Esquire, of King Street, St. James's, London, W.C.: (1) A mill-rind fesseways or, thereon a pelican in her piety az., semée of estoiles or, the nest ppr. (*for De Windt*). (2) A demi-griffin or, billettée gu., holding between the claws a plummet of the first (*for Jennyns*). *Memor virtutis avitæ.*

Dewing, Norf., a greyhound's head erased arg., collared and ringed gu. *cf.* 61. 2

De Winton of Clifton, Glouc., a wyvern ppr. *Syn ar dy Hûn.* 70. 1

De Winton, Walter, of Maesllwch Castle, Radnor: (1) A wyvern's head erased vert, gorged with a collar embattled counter-embattled arg. *cf.* 71. 2. (2) A demi-lion rampant issuing from a mural crown, holding in his paws a rose-branch, and charged on the shoulder with a full-blown rose. *Syn ar dy Hûn.*

De Winton, Charles Henry, of Maesderwen, Brecon, same crests and motto.

De Winton, Sir Francis Walter, of Llanstephan, Llyswen, R.S.O., and York House, St. James's Palace, London, S.W., same crests and motto.

De Winton, Captain Thomas, of Wallsworth Hall, Sandhurst, Glouc., same crests and motto.

De Winton, Robert Henry, Esquire, of Graftonbury, Heref., a wyvern's head erased ppr., gorged with a collar embattled counter-embattled or, thereon two annulets sa., holding in the mouth an arrow in bend, the pheon downwards arg. *Syn ar dy Hûn.*

De Worms, Baron George, of the Austrian Empire, 17, Park Crescent, W. out of an Austrian baron's coronet five ostrich-feathers or, gu., or, az., and or. *Vinctus non victus.* 231. 7

Dewsbury, Glouc., on a mount vert, a martlet or. 95. 7

Dexter, a tree, pendent therefrom two weights. 143. 10

Dexter, Ireland, a naked arm embowed holding a scimitar, all ppr. 201. 1

Deycourt, a sword in pale enfiled with a leopard's face. 22. 1

Deymond, Deyman, or **Dyamond,** of Tiverton, a lady's arm from the elbow erect enfiled with a bracelet.

Deyncourt, the standard of St. George ppr. 176. 13

d'Eyncourt, Tennyson-, E. C., Bayons Manor, Lincs.: (1) A lion passant guardant arg., on the head a crown of fleur-de-lis or, the dexter forepaw supporting a shield charged with the arms of D'Eyncourt. (2) A dexter arm in armour, the hand in a gauntlet or, grasping a broken tilting-spear enfiled with a garland of laurel ppr. (*Tennyson*). *En avant* (*D'Eyncourt*.—*Nil temere* (*Tennyson*).

Deynes, Suff., out of a mural coronet or, a dragon's head sa., gorged with two bars of the first. *cf.* 72. 11

Deyvelle, Deyvill, and **Davell,** an arm in fess ppr., vested, holding a fleur-de-lis or. *Penses coment.*

Deyvil, a fleur-de-lis gu. 148. 2

D'Eyvill, an arm in armour embowed ppr., holding in the hand a club sa., spiked or. *cf.* 199. 2

Diable, *see* Dibble.

Diamont, a demi-lion or, holding in his dexter paw a fusil gu., charged with a fleur-de-lis of the first.

Dias, on a garland of laurel a lion passant, all ppr. 5. 15

Dibble, Diable, and **Dible,** on a chapeau a lion statant gardant, ducally gorged, the tail extended, all ppr. *cf.* 4. 7

Dibdin, a talbot passant collared ppr. *cf.* 54. 5

Dible, Dibley, Dibloy, and **Diblo,** a demi-Hercules holding over his shoulder a club ppr.

Dicconson, a hind's head or. 124. 1

Dicconson, Clifton-, Charles, Esquire, of Wrightington Hall, Lancs: (1) A bezant, thereon a hind's head vert, erased gu., holding in the mouth a cross crosslet fitchée of the last (*for Dicconson*). (2) A dexter arm in armour embowed or, holding in the hand ppr. a sword arg., pommelled and hilted, also or (*for Clifton*). *Adverso fortior.* 195. 2

Dicconson-Gerard, Hon. Robert Joseph, of 12, Stratton Street, W.: (1) Same crest as above. (2) A monkey statant ppr., environed about the middle with a plain collar and chained arg.

Dicey, a demi-lion or. *Fide et amore.* 10. 2

Dicey, a lion sejant erect gu., supporting between his paws an escutcheon arg. *cf.* 8. 4

Dicher, Shropsh., a bear passant arg. *cf.* 34. 5

Dichfield, Shropsh., a bear passant arg. *cf.* 34. 5

Dick, Bart., of Braid, Scotland, a stag's head erased ppr., attired or. *Virtute.—Publica salus mea merces.* 121. 2

Dick-Cunyngham, Bart.: (1) A dexter hand holding a plumb-rule ppr. (*for Cunynghom*). (2) A ship in distress ppr. (*for Dick*). *Ad amussim.—At spes infracta.—Via tuta virtutis.* 160. 14

Dick, Scotland, a ship in distress ppr. *At spes infracta.* 160. 14

Dick, Ireland, a horse's head armed ppr., bridled gu. 51. 5

Dick of Pitkerro, Forfar, Scotland, a dexter arm issuing out of a cloud, holding a pen, all ppr. *Diligentia et candore.* *cf.* 217. 10

Dick, a dagger and a sword in saltier, both ppr. *cf.* 171. 12

Dick, Quintin Dick, Esquire, of Carantrila, co. Galway, a leopard sejant ppr. *Semper fidelis.*

Dick, Quintin, Esquire, of Layer Tower, Essex, a cat sejant. *Semper fidelis.* 26. 8

Dick-Lander, Sir Thomas North, Bart., of the Grange, Agra Patnas, Ceylon, a tower with portcullis down, and the head and shoulders of a sentinel appearing above the battlements in a watching posture ppr.

Dicken, Charles Gauntlett, upon a rock ppr. a lion sejant sa., guttée-d'or, gorged with a collar or, supporting with the dexter forepaw an escutcheon arg., charged with a cross flory sa., surmounted by another. *Consilio ac virtute.*

Dicken, Charles Shortt, Esquire, C.M.G., of Harrington Mansions, 33, Harrington Road, S.W., same crest and motto.

Dicken, Frederick Rowland, same crest and motto.

Dicken, Colonel William Popham, C.B., same crest and motto.

Dickens, a hind's head. 124. 1

Dickens, an arm in armour couped in fess, the part from the elbow in pale, holding up an esquire's helmet, all ppr. 198. 11

Dickens, Suff., a lion rampant ppr., holding a cross flory sa.

Dickens, a lion couchant or, holding up in the dexter paw a cross patonce sa. *cf.* 7. 5

Dickens, a demi-leopard ppr. *Hostis honori invidia.* *cf.* 23. 13

Dickenson of Lyston Court, Glouc., a demi-lion rampant az. *Facta non verba.* 10. 2

Dickenson and **Dicconson,** Lincs, Yorks, and Staffs, a demi-lion rampant per pale erminois and az. 10. 2

Dickenson, a tiger sejant erm., ducally gorged or, holding in the dexter paw a broad arrow of the last, feathered arg.

Dickenson of London, a hand holding an ox-yoke ppr. 217. 6

Dickenson, issuing out of clouds a cubit arm erect, holding in the hand a branch of laurel, all ppr. *cf.* 218. 9

Dickenson, issuing out of clouds a cubit arm erect, holding in the hand three wheat-ears, all ppr.

Dickenson, an arm erect ppr., vested gu., holding an escarbuncle arg. 207. 7

Dickenson, Wilts, out of a ducal coronet or, a dexter arm ppr., holding in the hand a fleur-de-lis of the first. 215. 2

Dickenson, out of a ducal coronet a phœnix in flames, all ppr. 82. 5

Dickenson, a greyhound's head between two roses slipped and leaved, all ppr. 61. 11

Dickeson, a boar's head couped, holding in the mouth four arrows, all ppr. 42. 9

Dickey and **Dickie,** a ferret ppr. *cf.* 134. 9

Dickey, Archibald Alexander George, Esquire, M.D., L.R.C.S.I., L.R.C.P.I., of Higgin House, Colne, Lancs, on a mount a dove holding in its beak an olive-branch, all ppr. *La Paix.*

Dickie, Scotland, on a rock an alder-tree growing, both ppr.

Dickin, Shropsh., a lion sejant or, holding in the dexter paw a cross crosslet of the same. *Vincit veritas.* *cf.* 8. 8

Dickins, Kent, a lion sejant or, holding a cross flory sa. *In hoc signo vinces.*

Dickins, Thomas Bourne, LL.D., Emscote Vicarage, Warwick, same crest.

Dickins of Southbridge House, on a mount vert, a lion sejant sa., holding in the dexter paw a cross flory az. *Semper fidelis.* *cf.* 7. 7

Dickins, Scrase-, Charles Robert, of Coolhurst, Sussex, and Cherrington, Warw.: (1) A lion sejant sa., holding a cross flory or (*for Dickins*). (2) On the stump of a tree, entwined by a serpent ppr., a falcon, also ppr., beaked, membered, and belled or (*for Scrase*). *cf.* 86. 11

Dickins, William Park, Cherington Park, Shipstone-on-Stour, same crests.

Dickins, an arm in armour couped in fesse, from the elbow in pale, holding up an esquire's helmet, all ppr. 198. 11

Dickinson, out of clouds ppr., a cubit arm erect of the last, holding a branch of laurel vert. *cf.* 219. 9

Dickinson, William, of Kingweston, Somers., same crest. *Dei manus medicus.*

Dickinson, John Douglas, Esquire, of Glanhonddu, Breconsh., same crest.

Dickinson, a tiger sejant erm., ducally gorged or, holding in the dexter paw a broad arrow of the last, plumed arg.

Dickinson of Abbots' Hill, Herts, a demi-lion rampant or, holding in the dexter paw a fleur-de-lis az., and resting the sinister paw on a bezant. *cf.* 13. 2

Dickinson, Frederick, Esquire, of The Towers, Cockermouth, Cumb., a lion's head erased. *Virtutis premium honor.* 17. 8

Dickinson of Gildersome and Coalbrookdale, on a wreath or and az., a camel's head couped ppr., bridled gu., adorned with a plume of three ostrich-feathers alternately arg. and sa., and under the lower jaw a bell or. *Faint, yet pursuing.*

Dickinson, Major-General, E.I.C., upon a mount vert, an elephant ppr., supporting with his trunk a flagstaff, also ppr., therefrom flowing a flag az., charged with two spears in saltire or. *Fortuna sequitur.*

Dickman, a demi-horse rampant or. 53. 3

Dickman, an ostrich arg., holding in his beak a key az. *Diligentia.* 97. 5

Dickson, Bart., *see* Poynder.

Dickson, John W., of Dumfries, Scotland, and Ceylon, in front of an arm in armour embowed, brandishing a falchion ppr., a trident and a spear in saltier or. *Fortes fortuna juvat.* 196. 11

Dickson, Archibald, M.D., of Hartree and Kilbucho, in the counties of Peebles and Lanarksh., a dexter hand holding a scimitar ppr. *Fortes fortuna juvat.* 213. 5

Dickson of Arbroath, a dexter hand holding a sword in bend ppr., hilt and pommel or. *Fortes fortuna juvat.* 212. 13

Dickson, Scotland, a dexter hand holding a sword in bend ppr. *Fortes fortuna juvat.* 212. 13

Dickson, Arthur Benson, J.P., of Blackbeck, Abbots, Reading, and Underfield: (1) A dexter cubit arm in bend, holding in the hand a sword point upwards, also in bend, all ppr. (2) A goat's head erased ppr., charged on the neck with an escallop arg. *Fortes fortuna juvat.*

Dickson, James, of El Dayleeyeh, Cairo, Egypt, a dexter hand holding a sprig of everlasting ppr. *Dum vita spes.*

Dickson, Raynes Waite, Esquire, of Arnside, South Yarra, Melbourne, Victoria, on a boar's head erased arg., guttée-de-sang, muzzled gu., a bezant between two mullets fesseways or. *Fortes fortuna juvat.*

Dickson, Dickson-, William, out of battlements a naked arm embowed, holding a sword, all ppr. *Fortes fortuna juvat.*

Dickson, Samuel, Auchmuty, Esquire, J.P., D.L., of Clonlebarde, co. Limerick, Ireland, and of Beenham House, Berks, out of battlements a naked arm embowed, holding a sword in bend sinister, all ppr. *Fortes fortuna juvat.* cf. 201. 4

Dickson, Scotland, a human heart ppr., winged arg. *Cœlum versus.* 112. 10

Dickson, Ireland, issuing out of a tower a lion's head ppr. cf. 157. 7

Dickson, Raynes Waite, Esquire, of Arnside, Domaine Road, South Yarra, Melbourne, Victoria, Australia, in front of a bear's head erased arg., guttée-de-sang, muzzled gu., a bezant between two mullets fessewise or. *Fortes fortuna juvat.*

Dickson, Scotland, a hart lodged ppr., attired or, within two branches of laurel in orle vert. *Cubo sed curo.* cf. 115. 11

Dickson, Richard, Esquire, of Stockton-upon-Tees, on a mount vert, between two branches of palm, a buck lodged in front of a tree, all ppr. 115. 10

Dickson, on a mural crown or, a stag lodged ppr., attired or. cf. 115. 7

Dickson, a stag's head erased ppr., attired or. 121. 2

Dickson, James, Esquire, of Broad Street, London, an eagle displayed az., guttée-d'or, holding in the beak a thistle ppr., and resting each claw upon an escallop, also or. *Fides et libertas.* cf. 74. 11

Dicom and **Dicons,** Beds, a cock's head az., beaked or, combed and wattled gu 90. 1

Dicoine, Lincs, a unicorn's head erased quarterly erm. and gu., crined or, the horn gobony of the last and arg. 49. 5

Diconson, *see* Dickenson.

Diddier or **Didear,** a demi-griffin with wings expanded ppr. 64. 2

Dietz, issuing out of a ducal coronet the attires of a stag. cf. 123. 1

Difford and **Ditford,** a lion's head erased or, ducally crowned gu. 18. 8

Digby, Baron (Digby), of Geashill, King's Co., an ostrich holding in the beak a horse-shoe, all ppr. *Deo, non fortunâ.* 97. 8

Digby, an ostrich arg., holding in its beak a horse-shoe ppr. 97. 8

Digby of Osbertstown, Ireland, an ostrich arg., holding in its beak a horse-shoe or. *Deo, non fortunâ.* 97. 8

Digby, Wingfield-, of Sherborne Castle, Dorset: (1) An ostrich arg., holding in the beak a horse-shoe or (*for Digby*). 97. 8. (2) A griffin passant vert (*for Wingfield*). *Deo, non fortunâ.* 63. 2

Digby, Charles Wriothesly, Esquire, of Meriden Hall, Coventry, an ostrich arg., holding in the beak a horse-shoe or. *Deo, non fortunâ.* 97. 8

Digby, Henry Almarus, Esquire, of North Runeton Lodge, King's Lynn, same crest and motto.

Digby, Sir Kenelm Edward, K.C.B., of 57, Eaton Place, London, S.W., same crest and motto.

Digby, Lieutenant-Colonel William Benjamin, J.P., of Ballincurra, Mullingar, co. Westmeath, same crest and motto.

Digby, John, 1, Elm Court, Temple, E.C., same crest and motto.

Digges, Diggs, and **Dyges,** Kent, Surrey, and Wilts, an eagle's leg couped at the thigh sa., and plumed with three ostrich-feathers arg.

Diggs, Bart. (*extinct*), of Chilham and Wootton Court, Kent, an eagle's leg couped at the thigh sa., issuant therefrom three ostrich-feathers arg.

Dighton, Herts and Glouc., a lion's gamb erased or, holding a cross formée fitchée gu. 36. 9

Dighton, Conway, 2, Blenheim Terrace, Cheltenham, same crest. *Virtus incendit vires.*

Dighton, Lancs, and Sturton, Lincs, a squirrel sejant per pale arg. and gu., collared, and cracking a nut or. cf. 135. 7

Dighton, on a ducal coronet or, a hawk close arg., beaked and legged gu., belled of the first. 85. 9

Dighton, Lancs, on a ducal coronet arg., a martlet of the same. 95. 12

Dighton, a fountain throwing up water, all ppr. 159. 13

Dighton, an heraldic antelope arg. cf. 127. 5

Dikens, a bird's head, the neck az., the top of the head gu., beaked or.

Dikens, a lion's head erased gu., ducally crowned or. 18. 8

Dikes and **Dykes,** a lobster vert. 141. 2

Dikes or **Dykes,** a scorpion vert.

Dilke, Rt. Hon. Sir Charles Wentworth, Bart., of 76, Sloane Street, S.W., a dove arg., membered gu. *Leo inimicis, Amicis Columba.* 92. 2

Dilke, a dove close arg., beaked and legged gu. 92. 2

Dilke of Maxstoke Castle, Warw.: (1) A dove arg., beaked and membered gu. (*for Dilke*). 92. 2. (2) An antelope's head couped gu., armed, and charged on the neck with three annulets interlaced in fesse or (*for Fetherston*).

Dilkes, a mill-rind gu. 165. 11

Dillington, Norf., on a perch arg., a hawk close ppr., beaked, belled, and legged or. 85. 13

Dillington, a lion's head couped or, vulned with a broken spear ppr., guttée-de-sang.

Dillon, Earl of Roscommon and **Baron Clonbrock,** *see those titles.*

Dillon, Alfred, Esquire, of Aquitaine House, Elm Road, Beckenham, Kent, upon a rock ppr., a falcon rising arg., the whole between two crescents, and within the horns of each a mullet of six points. *Auxilium ab alto.* 249. 5

Dillon, Viscount (Dillon), of Costello Gallen, co. Sligo, Ireland, a demi-lion rampant gu., holding between the paws an estoile arg. *Dum spiro spero.* cf. 15. 8

Dillon, Dr. T. G., of Coolmeen, co. Roscommon, a demi-lion rampant gu., holding between the paws an estoile arg. *Dum spiro spero.*

Dillon, Sir John Fox, Bart., J.P., of Lismullen, co. Meath, on a chapeau gu., turned up erm., a falcon rising arg., beaked, legged, and belled or. *Auxilium ab alto.*

Dillon, Auguste Henri, **Comte Dillon,** of Assevent, Département du Nord, France, out of a ducal coronet or, a demi-lion gu., holding between the paws an estoile pierced of the first. *Dum spiro spero.* cf. 16. 3

Dillon of Chimwell and Hart, Devonsh., a demi-lion holding in the dexter paw an estoile issuing out of a crescent gu. cf. 15. 7

Dillon, Luke Gerald, Esquire, of Seaham, Durh., a demi-lion rampant holding between both paws an estoile of eight points or. *Dum spiro spero.* 15. 8

Dillon, a demi-lion holding in his dexter paw a mullet. *Dum spiro spero.* 15. 7

Dillon, Ireland, out of a marquess's coronet or, a falcon with wings expanded arg., beaked and legged or, between the wings an imperial eagle sa. *Auxilium ab alto.*

Dillon, John, Esquire, of 2, North Great St. George's Street, Dublin, a demi-lion rampant gu., holding between the paws a mullet or.

Dillon, General Sir Martin Andrew, K.C.B., of United Service Club, W., same crest.

Dillon-Trenchard, Henry Luke, Esquire, of Colinshays House, near Bruton, Somers.: (1) A dexter arm, vested az., cuffed or, holding in the hand a trenching-knife ppr. (*for Trenchard*). (2) On a chapeau gu., turned up erm., a hawk rising ppr. *Nosce teipsum.*

Dilwyn-Llewelyn, Sir John Talbot, Bart., J.P., D.L., of Penllegare, Llangyfelach, and of Ynis-y-gerwn, Cadoxton-juxta-Neath, Glamorgansh.: (1) On a wreath of the colours upon the trunk of a tree fessewise, eradicated and sprouting, a lamb passant ppr., supporting a staff in bend sinister or, therefrom flowing a banner gu., charged with three chevronels arg. (*for Llewelyn*). 131. 5. (2) On a wreath of the colours in front of a stag's head couped ppr., three trefoils slipped vert (*for Dillwyn*). *Craignez honte.* 120. 2

Dillwyn-Venables-Llewelyn, Charles Leyshon, Esquire, of Llysdinam Hall, Newbridge-on-Wye: (1) Upon the trunk of a tree fesseways, eradicated and sprouting, a lamb passant ppr., supporting a staff or, therefrom flowing a banner gu., charged with three chevronels arg. (2) A wyvern, wings expanded gu., each wing charged with a fesse arg., issuant from a weir-basket ppr., the dexter claw resting on a mullet az., for difference (*Venables.*) (3) In front of a stag's head couped ppr., three trefoils slipped vert (*for Dillwyn*). *Craignez honte.*

Dimmock, a boar's head couped ppr., between two laurel-branches vert.

Dimond, a cross crosslet in pale, surmounted by a sword in bend sinister, point downwards.

Dimsdale, Charles Robert Southwell, **Honourable Baron Dimsdale** of the Russian Empire, J.P., issuing out of a Russian baron's coronet a griffin's head erm.

Dimsdale, a griffin's head erased arg. *Magnus Hippocrates! tu nobis major.* 66. 2

Dimsdale, Sir Joseph Cockfield, Bart., of Upton, West Ham, Essex, a staff fesseways entwined by a serpent ppr., thereon a griffin's head erased arg. *Quod Deus vult fiet.* 262. 11

Dimsdale, a beaver ppr. 134. 8

Dine, Beds, a wyvern statant ppr. *J'ay espere mieux avoir.* 70. 1

Dineley, on a ducal coronet or, three darts, two in saltier and one in pale, with a serpent entwined ppr. 173. 2

Dines, a griffin passant. 63. 2

Dingdale, Lancs, a griffin's head between two wings endorsed or. *cf.* 67. 11

Dingham, a dexter hand erect, pointing with the two forefingers to the sun in splendour ppr. 222. 10

Dingham, in a round top or, six spears, in the centre a pennon arg., thereon a cross gu.

Dingle, William Alfred, Esquire, M.D., L.R.C.P., M.R.C.S., of 46, Finsbury Square, London, E.C., a demi-greyhound holding between the paws an escallop. *J'ai espoir mieux avoir.*

Dingley and **Ditley,** Yorks, a Roman head with a helmet couped at the neck, all ppr. 191. 6

Dingley, out of a ducal coronet a dragon's head or. 72. 4

Dingwall, Baron, *see* Cowper, Earl.

Dingwall-Fordyce, *see* Fordyce.

Dingwall, a human heart ppr. 181. 2

Dinham, an arm couped vested or, the hand arg., holding a lock of hair sa.

Dinnet, a bull's head gu. *cf.* 44. 3

Dinorben, Baron (Hughes), out of a crown vallery a demi-lion rampant arg., holding between the paws a pike-head ppr.

Dinwiddie, an eagle with wings addorsed and inverted, holding in the dexter claw a guinea-pig. *Ubi libertas ibi patria.*

Dinwordy, a cubit arm erect grasping in the hand a spear, all ppr. 214. 11

Dipford of London, a lion's head erased or, ducally crowned gu. 18. 8

Dirom, Scotland, a stag's head erased. 121. 2

Dirom of Mount Annan, Dumfries, a stag's head couped ppr. *Ducit dominus.* 121. 5

Dirom, Pasley-, Patrick Alexander, Esquire, Mount Annan, Annan, Dumfriessh.: (1) A stag's head ppr. (*for Dirom*). 121. 5. (2) A dexter arm in armour embowed grasping a dagger, all ppr. (*for Pasley*). *Ducit dominus.*—*Be sure.* 196. 5

Dirwyn, a peacock's head erased ppr. 103. 1

Discombe, Lincs, a unicorn's head erased. 49. 5

Dishington, Scotland, a man in armour kneeling. *Unica spes mea Christus.*

Dishington, Scotland, an escallop. *Unica spes mea Christus.* 141. 14

Diskens, on a chapeau a lion couchant. 7. 12

Disker and **Diskers,** on a mount vert a centaur passant regardant ppr. and arg., drawing a bow and arrow or, feathered of the third. *cf.* 53. 5

Disney, Lincs. and Bucks, a lion passant gardant gu. 4. 3

Disney, Edgar John, the Hyde, Essex, same crest.

Disney, Ireland, the same crest.

Disney, Very Rev. Brabazon William, B.D., Dean of the Diocese of Armagh, a lion passant gardant gu., charged on the breast with a fleur-de-lis or. *Vincit qui patitur.* *cf.* 4. 3

Disney, Frederick William, Esquire, of the Woodlands, Kingston Hill, Surrey, same crest and motto.

Disney, Lambert Brouncker, Esquire, same crest and motto.

Disney, Henry R. E., Esquire, same crest and motto.

Disney, Cathrow-, late James, Esquire, formerly *Somerset Herald*: (1) A lion passant gardant gu., charged with a cross patée fitchée or (*for Disney*). *cf.* 4. 3. (2) A dragon passant sa., winged or, resting the dexter claw on a leopard's face, jessant-de-lis of the last (*for Cathrow*). *cf.* 73. 2

Disney, the late Lieutenant-General Sir Moore, K.C.B., a lion's head couped gu., semée-de-lis or, and gorged with a mural crown arg. *Et decus et pretium recti.*

Disraeli, Coningsby Ralph, Esquire, of Hughenden Manor, issuant from a wreath of oak ppr., a castle triple-towered arg. *Forti nihil difficile.*

Ditchfield, Rev. Peter Hampson, M.A., F.S.A., F.R.H.S., of Barkham Rectory, near Wokingham, a porcupine. *In Deo fido.*

Ditford, on a mount or, a bull passant gu. 45. 7

Ditton, a demi-griffin segreant arg. 64. 2

Dive, Beds and Northamp., a wyvern with wings addorsed gu. *J'ai espere mieux avoir.* 70. 1

Divie and **Divvie,** Scotland, an eagle's head couped ppr. *Sedulitate.* 83. 1

Dix, a greyhound's head arg., ducally gorged gu., between two wings or.

Dix, a greyhound's head erased arg., ducally gorged gu., between two wings, the dexter sa., the sinister or, a crescent for difference.

Dixie, Sir Alexander Beaumont Churchill, Bart., of Bosworth House, Leics., an ounce sejant ppr., ducally gorged or. *Quod dixi, dixi.*—*Dei gratia grata.*

Dixie, a leopard sejant. *cf.* 24. 13

Dixie, an ounce sejant ppr., spotted sanguine, ducally gorged or. *Quod dixi, dixi.*

Dixon, Kent, a demi-hind sa., bezantée.

Dixon of Unthank Hall, Northumb.: (1) A mount vert, thereon a demi-hind arg., gorged with a collar, the line therefrom reflexed over the back gu., supporting a cross crosslet sa. (*for Dixon*). (2) Two escallops or, thereon resting an eagle displayed vert, holding in the beak a cross crosslet fitchée of the first (*for Brown*). *Suivez raison.* *cf.* 74. 11

Dixon-Coull, Robert, Esquire, of Middleton, Morpeth, Northumb.: (1) In front of a unicorn's head couped arg., gorged with a collar gemelle az., three annulets interlaced or (*for Coull*). (2) A demi-stag regardant ppr., charged on the shoulder with a pheon, and resting the dexter foot on a cross patée or (*for Dixon*). *Ad finem spero.*

Dixon, Norf., a stag's head erased per pale dancettée sa. and or, attired counterchanged. 121. 2

Dixon, Yorks, a stag's head erased. 121. 2

Dixon, Herts, on a mount vert, a tiger sejant erm., ducally gorged or. *cf.* 27. 6

Dixon, a tiger sejant collared and lined. *cf.* 27. 6

Dixon, Marmaduke, Esquire, J.P., of Eyrewell Park, West Eyreton, Canterbury, New Zealand, a lion rampant arg. *Respice finem.* 1. 13

Dixon of Seaton-Carew, Durh., a lion rampant holding in its dexter paw a fleur-de-lis, all ppr. *Auxilium meum ab alto.* 2. 7

Dixon, Berks and Chesh., a demi-lion rampant or. *Another,* arg. 10. 2

Dixon, Rt. Hon. Sir Daniel, Bart., of Ravensdale, co. Louth, a demi-lion rampant az., charged on the shoulder with a cross patonée surrounded by a civic crown or. *Fide et constantia.* 262. 8

Dixon, Thomas Henry, Esquire, of the Clappers, Gresford, Denbighsh., a lion's head erased per fesse arg. and gu., charged on the neck with three fleurs-de-lis of the last, and pierced through the mouth by an arrow, the point coming out at the back ppr., feathered arg. *Macte virtute esto.*

Dixon, Thomas, Esquire, J.P., C.C., High Sheriff 1903-1904, of Rheda, Frizington, Cumb., in front of a cubit arm grasping a scimitar ppr., pommel and hilt gold, a staff raguly fessewise or. *Quod dixi, dixi.* *cf.* 213. 5

Dixon, George Hodgson, Esquire, of Armathwaite Hall, Armathwaite R.S.O., Cumb., in front of an anchor in bend sinister sa., a dexter cubit arm erect ppr., holding in the hand an olive-branch, also ppr. *Peace.* 231. 9

Dixon, George Henry Hewitt, Esquire, of Carlisle, Alfred Street, North Sidney, same crest.

Dixon, Essex and Durh., a cubit arm vested erminois, cuffed arg., holding in the hand ppr. a roundle of the first. 215. 13

Dixon, William Smith, Esquire, of Govan Hill, Lanark, Scotland, a dexter hand ppr., holding a sword in bend sinister arg. *Fortes fortuna juvat.* 212. 13

Dixon, Sheffield, an arm embowed vested az., platée, cuffed arg., holding in the hand a garland of roses ppr. *Fide et constantia.* *cf.* 205. 3

Dixon, Thomas, Esquire, of Grensde House, Durh., in front of a cubit arm vested or, cuffed gu., the hand holding a fox's head erased ppr., a torteau. *Quod dixi, dixi.*

Dixon, Scotland, a dexter hand ppr., holding a sword in bend sinister arg. *Fortes fortuna juvat.* 212. 13

Dixon, Ireland, a pelican in her piety ppr. 98. 14

Dixon, Yorks, an eagle displayed sa. *Quod dixi, dixi.* 75. 2

Dixon, a demi-eagle displayed ppr., winged vair. *In recto fides.* 81. 6

Dixon, A. Juckes, Esquire, of 88, Station Road, King's Norton, Birmingham, and Bournville Lane, Stirchley, formerly of the Marsh, Wellington, Shropsh., an eagle's head couped between two wings. *In recto fides.* 84. 2

Dixon, Ireland, a demi-boar rampant vert, armed, tusked, maned, and tufted or, holding in the dexter paw a fleur-de-lis of the last. *cf.* 40. 13

Dixon, Scotland, a water-bouget. 168. 4

Dixon, Herts, a sphere arg., charged with a pale indented vert. 159. 6

Dixon-Hartland, Sir Frederick, Bart.: (1) A stag's head erased or, gorged with a collar-jewel, pendent therefrom by a chain, a key in bend all sable (*Hartland*). 281. 11. (2) A demi-lion couped per fesse indented or and sable, supporting with the sinister paw an antique shield of the second, charged with a talbot's head erased of the first. 281. 12

Dixon-Johnson, Charles William, Esquire: (1) An arm embowed in armour firing a pistol, all ppr. (*for Johnson*). (2) A cubit arm erected, vested erminois, cuffed arg., in the hand a roundel of the first (*for Dixon*).

Dixon-Johnson, Cuthbert Francis, Esquire, of Ayhleyheads, Durh., same crests and motto.

Dixwell, Kent and Warw., a lion's gamb couped az., holding an eagle's leg with a wing conjoined thereto sa. *cf.* 38. 10

Doane, Chesh., a sheaf of arrows or, headed and feathered arg., banded gu. 173. 3

Dobbie and **Dobie,** Scotland, a cross crosslet fitched gu. 166. 2

Dobbie and **Dobie,** Scotland, an eagle displayed ppr. *Non minima sed magna prosequor.* 75. 2

Dobbie, Scotland, a crescent az. 163. 2

Dobbin, Leonard, Esquire, of Armagh, and of Gardiner's Place, Dublin, out of a mural coronet an oak-branch acorned ppr., on the coronet a crescent or. *Re e merito.* *cf.* 152. 3

Dobbin, Ireland, a demi-lion or, supporting a long cross gu. 11. 14

Dobbin, a dexter hand holding a laurel-branch ppr., fructed gu. 219. 9

Dobbin, Sir Alfred Graham, of Frankfort, Montenotte, Cork, a cubit arm erect ppr., charged with two chevronels interlaced az., the hand grasping a spear passing through an annulet az., bent sinisterwise. *Deus dexter meus.*

Dobbin, Lieutenant-Colonel George Miller, J.P., of Drummulla House, Omeath, co. Louth, an oak-branch acorned ppr., the crown charged with a crescent or. *Re e merito.*

Dobbins and **Dobins,** a staff raguly surmounted by an eagle displayed ppr. 75. 3

Dobbs, a lion sejant affrontée. 7. 2

Dobbs, a lion sejant affrontée, holding in each fore-paw a dagger ppr. 7. 1

Dobbs, Ireland, a unicorn's head couped arg., maned, armed, and tufted or. 49. 7

Dobbs, Conway Edward, Esquire, J.P., of Glenariffe House, Parkmore, co. Antrim, and Dalguise, Monkstown, co. Dublin, a unicorn's head erased arg. *Amor Dei et proximi summa beatitudo.* 49. 5

Dobbs, Archibald Edward, Esquire, same crest and motto.

Dobbs, Montague William Edward, Esquire, J.P., D.L., of Clonkeevan, Donadea, co. Kildare, same crest and motto.

Dobbs, Robert Conway Esquire, of Campshire, Cappoquin, co. Waterford, same crest and motto.

Dobbyn of Waterford, Ireland, a hand couped holding a javelin, all ppr. *Deus dexter meus.* 214. 13

Dobede of Soham, Cambs, on a mount vert, a demi-lion erased arg., crowned or, holding an escutcheon erm., charged with two swords in saltire, surmounted by a fasces in pale within a wreath, all or. *Droit à chacun.*

Dobell, on a mount vert, a hart lodged between four bulrushes ppr. *cf.* 115. 12

Dobell of Falmere, Sussex, on a mount vert, a hind lodged arg. between four arrows stuck into the mount or. *Tutus in bello.* *cf.* 125. 4

Dobell, same crest. *Without help from above the arrow flies in vain.*

Dobell, Sussex, an eagle's head ppr. *Tout prest.* 83. 1

Dobie, a hand holding a scroll between two branches of laurel in orle, all ppr. 215. 3

Dobie, an eagle displayed. 75. 2

Dobie, *see* Dobbie.

Doble, Somers., on a mount vert, a doe lodged arg., pierced by four arrows in saltier or. *cf.* 125. 4

Dobree, Alfred, of 16, St. George's Terrace, Gloucester Road, on a mount vert, a thistle ppr. *Spe vivitur.* *cf.* 150. 5

Dobree, Bonamy, Esquire, of 4, Queen's Gate Place, London, S.W., same crest.

Dobree, Samuel, Esquire, J.P., of the Priory, Wellington, Somers., and Hughenden, Ealing, London, W., same crest and motto.

Dobree, on a ducal coronet a talbot passant, collared and lined or. 54. 9

Dobson, Hon. Sir William Lambert, of Hobart, Tasmania, *uses* two bear's paws in saltire gu. *Ut tibi sic alteri.* 39. 14

Dobson, Hon. Frank Stanley, B.A., LL.D., Q.C., F.L.S., of Melbourne, Victoria, Australia, Member of the Legislative Council, *uses* two lion's gambs erased in saltire gu. *Ut tibi sic alteri.* *cf.* 39. 14

Dobson, Northumb., two bear's paws in saltier ppr. 39. 14

Dobson, Norf., two lion's gambs erased and in saltire gu. *cf.* 39. 14

Dobson, Hugh Verner, Esquire, J.P., of Perridge House, Pilton, Shepton Mallet, two lion's gambs erased ppr., entwined by a chain or, and surmounted by a fleur-de-lis gu. *Robur cum virtute.*

Dobyns of London, out of a ducal coronet two lion's gambs in saltier. 39. 10

Dobyns, Heref., a falcon volant or. *Quod pudet hoc fugeat.* 88. 3

Dockenfield and **Dokenfield,** out of a ducal coronet or, an arm erect vested per pale gu. and arg., holding in the hand ppr. the sun in splendour of the first. 209. 2

Docker, a bridge of three arches ppr. 158. 4

Docker, His Honour Ernest Brougham, of Carhullen, Granville, New South Wales, Australia, *uses* a bridge with three arches ppr. *Stare super vias antiquas.* 158. 4

Dockingfield, a cubit arm erect, holding in the hand ppr. the sun or.

Dockrell, Maurice Edward, Esquire, J.P., of Camolin, Monkstown, co. Dublin, a demi-lion rampant gorged with a wreath of oak-leaves, all ppr., and charged on the shoulder with a crescent az. *Semper idem.* *cf.* 10. 2

Docksey, on a chapeau gu., turned up erm., a lion's head erased per pale az. and arg. *cf.* 17. 9

Dockware and **Dockwrae,** Yorks, within a fetterlock az., a heart gu. *cf.* 181. 7

Dockwra, a demi-lion rampant holding between the paws a plate charged with a pallet gu. *cf.* 11. 7

Docton and **Doketon,** a fleur-de-lis sa. 148. 2

Dod and **Dodd,** Ireland, a horse statant, saddled and bridled. *cf.* 52. 4

Dod and **Dode,** two hands couped and conjoined, the dexter in armour and the sinister ppr., supporting a branch of laurel and a thistle in orle, also ppr. 228. 10

Dod of Lower Hall, Broxton, Chesh., a hand erect couped ppr., holding a claw-hammer sa.

Dod, Shropsh., a serpent vert issuing from and piercing a garb ppr. *cf.* 153. 1

Dod and **Dodd,** Chesh. and Surrey, a garb or, environed by a snake ppr. *cf.* 153. 1

Dod, Wolley-, Rev. Charles, of Edge, Chesh., a garb arg., banded gu., environed with a snake, the head issuing from the middle of the garb ppr., and charged for distinction with a cross crosslet of the second (*for Dod*). (2) A man's head facing the dexter in chain-mail, couped at the shoulder ppr. (*for Wolley*). *In copia cautus.*

Dodd, G. Ashley, M.A., J.P., Godinton, Ashford, Kent, same crest as first above.

Dodd, John, Esquire, of the Hollies, Oldham, Lancs, in front of a garb or, environed by a serpent vert, a crow sa.

Dodd, Walter H., Esquire, L.R.C.P., of 5, Stanford Avenue, Brighton, a garb ppr., environed by a serpent vert issuing therefrom. *Cautus in copia.*

Dodding of Conishead, Lancs, a demi-lion or, holding a cross crosslet fitchée az. 11. 10

Dodds and **Dods,** Northumb. and Scotland, a ferret or. *cf.* 134. 13

Dodds, Honourable Alexander, of Merrenburn, North Shore, Sydney, New South Wales, Member of the Legislative Council of New South Wales, a wheat-sheaf. *Semper paratus.* 153. 2

Dodds, out of a ducal coronet a reindeer's head ppr. 122. 3

Doderidge, Devonsh., a lion's head erased gu., murally gorged or. *cf.* 17. 2

Dodge, Cooper-, *see* Cooper-Dodge.

Dodge, Walter Phelps, Esquire, of Chinnock Manor, Simsbury, Connecticut, U.S.A., a demi-sea-dog az., collared, finned, and purfled or. *Leni perfruar otio.*

Dodgin, an arm from the shoulder vested or, cuffed az., embowed in fess, the elbow on the wreath, holding a sword enfiled with a leopard's face ppr. 204. 4

Dodgson, Lancs, two lion's gambs erased in saltire gu. *Virtus semper eadem.* cf. 39. 14

Dodingsells, a wolf passant gu. 28. 10

Dodington, Shropsh., a lion's gamb erect or. cf. 36. 4

Dodington, Somers., a lion's gamb ppr., holding a flag gu., charged with a chevron or.

Dodington, Wilts, a stag lodged regardant arg., holding in the mouth an acorn or, stalked and leaved vert. cf. 115. 8

Dodington, Marriott-, Roger, of Horsington, Somers.: (1) On a mount vert, a stag lodged regardant arg., attired or, holding in the mouth an acorn of the last, leaved of the first (*for Dodington*). (2) On a rock ppr., a talbot paly of six arg. and sa., resting the dexter forepaw on an estoile of the last (*for Marriott*).

Dodmer and **Dodmore,** an arm vested quarterly gu. and sa., the hand holding two arrows vert.

Dodson, a demi-griffin segreant. 64. 2

Dodson, Richard Ball, Esquire, 1, Vicarage Gardens, Brighton, a demi-lion rampant arg., holding in the dexter paw a trefoil slipped gu., and resting the sinister upon a fleur-de-lis sa. *Credo.* 13. 13

Dodson, the head of Janus couped at the neck ppr. 191. 6

Dodson, three faces, two male and one female, conjoined in one neck, a male face on top and a male and female to the sinister and dexter respectively.

Dodswall and **Dodswell,** a lion's head erased ppr. 17. 8

Dodsworth, Smith-, Sir Matthew Blayney, Bart., J.P., D.L., of Newland Park, Yorks: (1) A dexter cubit arm in chain-mail or, the hand ppr. grasping a broken tilting-spear, the broken part imbrued gu. (*for Dodsworth*). (2) Out of a ducal coronet or, a boar's head az., bristled gold (*for Smith*). *Pro lege senatu que rege.* 41. 4

Dodsworth, a demi-lion supporting a long cross. 11. 14

Dodwell of Shankhill House, Dublin, a demi-lion arg., pellettée, armed and langued az. cf. 10. 2

Doe, a demi-lion supporting a ship's rudder ppr. 11. 11

Doe, Lancs, a garb or, with a coulter stuck within the band in bend sinister sa. cf. 153. 2

Doeg, a hand holding a thistle. 218. 2

Doget and **Dogett,** Kent, on a chapeau a bull collared, to the collar a bell pendent, all ppr. cf. 45. 5

Doggell, on a chapeau a wild bull gorged with a coronet ringed and lined. 45. 5

Dogget, Norf., a lion's head or, gorged with a mural coronet sa. cf. 21. 1

Dogherty and **Doherty,** England and Ireland, a wolf current erm. 28. 4

Dogherty and **Doherty,** Ireland, a boar regardant transfixed by an arrow. cf. 40. 14

Dogherty and **Doherty,** Ireland, a hand holding a sword. 212. 13

Doherty-Waterhouse, Captain Daniel Henry: (1) In front of an eagle's leg erased at the thigh or, issuant therefrom a wing in bend sa., a fountain, and charged for distinction on the thigh with a cross crosslet sa. (2) An arm in armour embowed ppr., charged with a cross crosslet fitchée or, the hand grasping a scimitar, also ppr. cf. 196. 10

Doidge, a demi-sea-dog az., collared, finned, and purfled or.

Doig, a falcon with wings expanded and inverted and belled, all ppr. 87. 1

D'Oiley and **D'Oyley,** a demi-wyvern vert, winged or. 69. 12

Dokerton, a fleur-de-lis ppr. 148. 2

Dolan, a decrescent gu. 163. 1

Dolben, Mackworth-: (1) A griffin sejant with wings endorsed ppr. (*for Dolben*). 62. 10. (2) A cock ppr. (*for Mackworth*). 91. 2

Dolben, Bart., Northamp., a griffin sejant with wings addorsed ppr. 62. 10

Dolben, a demi-bull arg., gorged with laurel-leaves vert. cf. 45. 14

Dolby, Essex and Leics., a demi-griffin arg., winged and beaked or. 64. 2

Doleman, an elephant's head erased sa. 133. 3

D'Olier, Edmund, Esquire, of Knocklin, Bray, co. Wicklow, a dove close arg., holding in his beak an ear of wheat or. *La bonté de Dieu.* cf. 92. 5

Doline, a fleur-de-lis az., between two wings arg.

Doling, a stag's head erased ppr. 121. 2

Dolins, a fleur-de-lis az., between two wings arg. cf. 110. 5

Dollabe, out of a ducal coronet ppr., a plume of five feathers per pale arg. and az. 114. 13

Dollar, an arm embowed, holding in the hand a falchion ppr., hilt and pommel or. 201. 4

Dolliffe, on a castle arg., three olive-sprigs vert.

Dolling, Robert Holleche, Esquire, J.P., Barrister-at-Law, of Magheralin, co. Down, and of Tamlaght O'Crilly, co. Derry, Ireland, a buck's head ppr., attired or, gorged with two bars dancettée arg. *Spero.* cf. 121. 5

Dolling of Worth, Isle of Purbeck, a stag's head couped per fesse dancettée ppr. and arg., gorged with a fesse dancettée sa., attired or. cf. 121. 5

Dolmage, Austin J., Esquire, of Rathkeale, co. Limerick, a boar's head erased and erect per pale az. and gu., armed or. *Inveniam aut faciam.*

Dolman, Berks, a garb arg., eared and banded or. 153. 2

Dolphin of Turoe, Galway, a dolphin haurient ppr. *Firmum in vitâ nihil.* 140. 11

Dolphin, a swan ppr. 99. 2

Dolphin, Northumb., a swan's head and neck between two swan's wings ppr. 101. 6

Dolphin, Rev. Canon Arthur R., M.A., the College, Durham, same crest.

Dolphin and **Dolphine,** a lion passant gardant or, holding in the dexter paw a mill-rind sa. 6. 7

Dolseby, a demi-griffin arg., winged or. 64. 2

Dolsey, a demi-woman naked, her hair dishevelled, wreathed round the temples with cinquefoils gu.

Dolton, a demi-lion. 10. 2

Domenichetti, William Lewis, Esquire, of Collingham, Notts, on a wreath of the colours a lion of St. Mark sejant gardant, winged and circled round the head, supporting an Irish harp, all or. *Nunquam non paratus.* 20. 9

Domenchetti, Rev. Richard Hippisley, of Belshford Rectory, Horncastle, same crest and motto.

Domere, a castle sa., masoned arg. 155. 4

Dominick, Bucks, a stag sejant or, attired gu., gorged with a naval coronet of the last, resting his dexter foot on an antique shield vert.

Domvile, Sir Compton Meade, Bart., of Templeogue and Santry, both in co. Dublin, a lion's head erased arg., ducally crowned or. *Qui stat caveat ne cadat.* 18. 8

Domvile, Herbert Winnington, Esquire, of Loughlinstown, co. Dublin, same crest and motto.

Domvile and **Domville,** Shropsh., issuing from a cloud a hand in fess stretching towards a garland of laurel in the dexter. 223. 3

Domville, Sir William Cecil Henry, Bart., of St. Alban's, Herts, out of a mural coronet gu., a demi-lion arg., supporting between its paws an escutcheon az., charged with three Oriental crowns, the points alternately radiated or.

Domville, Chesh., two lion's gambs erased in saltier arg. cf. 39. 14

Domville of Lymme Hall, Chester, a buck's head cabossed ppr. 122. 5

Domville, Ireland, a Saracen's head affrontée, couped at the neck and wreathed around the temples with laurel, all ppr. *Ung durant via vie.*

Don, Scotland, a dexter hand holding a pen ppr. *Suum cuique.* 217. 10

Don and **Donn,** out of a ducal coronet a mount, and thereon a stag at gaze, all ppr. 118. 7

Don-Wauchope, Bart.: (1) A garb or (*for Wauchope*). 153. 2. (2) A pomegranate ppr. (*for Don*). *Industria ditat.—Non deerit alter aureus.* 152. 4

Donald, issuing out of a cloud a dexter hand in fesse ppr., holding a cross patée fitched sa. 223. 6

Donald, Scotland, an arm in armour embowed, brandishing in the hand a sword, all ppr. *Toujours prêt.* 195. 2

Donald, Scotland, a garb ppr. *Fac et spera.* 153. 2

Donaldson-Hudson, *see* Hudson.

Donaldson of Douglas, Isle of Man, an eagle's head erased gu. *My hope is constant.* 83. 2

Donaldson, Charles George, Esquire, an eagle's head erased gu., collared dancettée or, holding in the beak a thistle and a trefoil entwined ppr. (*for Donaldson*). cf. 83. 2. (2) An arm embowed in armour ppr., charged upon the elbow with a catherine-wheel gu., the hand, also ppr., grasping an arrow, point downwards or, feathered arg. (*for Matthews*). *Toujours prêt.* cf. 198. 4

Donaldson, a cock crowing within two adders in orle, all ppr. *Prudenter vigilo.* 91. 1

Donaldson, Scotland, on a rock az., a raven sa. *My hope is constant in thee.* 107. 2

Donaldson, Scotland, the rudder of a ship ppr. *Steer steady.* 179. 1

Donaldson, a garb vert. *Nulli inimicus ero.* 153. 2

Donaldson, a Passion cross gu. *Sub cruce salus.* 165. 4

Donaldson of London, a hand holding a sword ppr. *My hope is constant in thee.* 212. 13

Donaldson, Scotland, a hand holding a sword ppr. *Aut pax, aut bellum.* 212. 13

Donaldson, Thomas Olinthus, of 49, Lee Terrace, Blackheath, S.E., same crest and motto.

Donaldson, a dexter hand holding a dagger in pale ppr., hilted or, pommelled arg. *Promptus.* 212. 9

Donaldson, a dexter arm vambraced, couped at the shoulder, brandishing a sword, all ppr. *In omnia promptus.* 195. 2

Donaldson-Hudson, Ralph Charles, Esquire, of Cheswardine Hall, Market Drayton: (1) Upon a mill-rind fesseways sa., a lion's head erased or, gorged with a bar gemelle indented gu. (*for Hudson*). (2) In front of a saltire az., a cubit arm erect grasping a dagger and charged with a thistle slipped, both ppr.

Donand, in front of a rock a Cornish chough, all ppr. 102. 6

Donand, a savage wreathed about the middle with leaves ppr. *cf.* 188. 3

Donavan, a hawk with wings displayed ppr. *cf.* 87. 12

Donavan, *see* Donovan.

Doncastell, Berks, a buck's head couped or, vulned in the neck gu. *cf.* 121. 5

Doncaster, Earl of, *see* Buccleuch, Duke of.

Done, a bugle-horn sa., garnished arg., stringed vert. 228. 11

Done, a bundle of arrows arg., barbed az., banded gu. 173. 3

Done, Chesh.: (1) A buck's head couped at the shoulders ppr. 121. 5. (2) Two sheaves of arrows in saltier or, banded gu. 173. 13

Donegall, Marquess of (Chichester), of Island Magee, co. Antrim, a stork ppr., with wings expanded, holding in its beak an eel ppr. *Invitum sequitur honor.—Honor sequitur fugientem.*

Donegan, Lieutenant-Colonel James Henry, J.P., of Carrigmore, Cork, a mural crown, thereon a robin-redbreast, all ppr. *Virtus non vertitur.* 108. 10

Donelan, a lion's gamb erased holding a sceptre in pale ppr. 38. 7

Donelan of Hillswood, Galway, a lion rampant. *Omni violentiâ major.* 1. 13

Donelan, James, Esquire, M.D., of Bruntsfield, Harrow-on-the-Hill, and 6, Manchester Square, W., a lion rampant grasping in his dexter paw a sprig of oak, all ppr. *Omni violentiâ major.*

Donelan and **Donnelan,** a greyhound sejant arg. 59. 4

Donelan, on a mount vert, a demi-lion rampant or. *cf.* 10. 2

Donelly of Bally Donelly, co. Tyrone, Ireland, a naked arm embowed grasping a straight sword ppr., hilt and pommel or, encircled with a pointed Irish crown of the last. *Lamh dearg eiren.* *cf.* 201. 4

Donelly and **Donnelly,** Ireland, a church with a spire ppr. 158. 10

Doneraile, Viscount (St. Leger), Doneraile, co. Cork, a griffin passant or. *Haut et bon.* 63. 2

Dongan, a lion passant or, resting the dexter paw on a helmet ppr. *cf.* 6. 2

Donhault, Northamp. and Oxon., a cherub or. 189. 9

Donington, Baron (Abney-Hastings): (1) A bull's head erased erm. armed and ducally gorged arg., and for distinction charged with a cross crosslet, also arg. (*for Hastings*). *cf.* 44. 2. (2) A demi-lion rampant or, the sinister paw resting upon an antique shield charged with the arms of Hastings, viz.: "arg., a maunch within a bordure engrailed sa.," and for distinction charged upon the shoulder with a cross crosslet (*for Abney*). *Tenebras meas.*

Donithein, a swan naiant among rushes. 99. 8

Donithorn, Cornw., a swan with wings addorsed naiant in a lake ppr. 99. 9

Donkin, in the sea a ship in distress ppr. 160. 14

Donkin, a leopard couchant ppr. 214. 10

Donnar, an arm in armour embowed ppr., garnished or, holding in the hand a truncheon arg.

Donne, Chesh., a bundle of arrows or, headed and feathered arg., banded gu. 173. 3

Donne, a wolf's head erased or. 30. 8

Donne, Rev. Charles Edward, 18, Ladbroke Road, Bayswater, W., a wolf's head erased arg. *Loyale au mort.*

Donnellan, *see* Donellan.

Donnellan, John Nicholas, Esquire, M.B., B.Ch., B.A.O., of Broomsgrove, Upperton Road, Eastbourne, a lion rampant holding in the dexter paw three oak-leaves, fructed ppr. *Omni violentiâ major.*

Donnellan, Patrick Sarsfield, 1,028 Spruce Street, Philadelphia, U.S.A., same crest and motto.

Donnelly, *see* Donelly.

Donnelly, Major-General Sir Charles Fretcheville Dykes, 59, Onslow Gardens, S.W., a naked arm embowed grasping a straight sword ppr., hilt and pommel or, encircled with a pointed Irish crown of the last. *Lamh dearg Eiren.*

Donnithorn, a Cornish chough close ppr. 107. 14

Donoughmore, Earl of (Hely-Hutchinson), of Knocklofty, Clonmel, Ireland, out of a ducal coronet a demi-cockatrice with wings elevated az. *Fortiter gerit crucem.* 301. 9

Donovan, Ireland, on a chapeau gu., turned up erm., a falcon alighting arg., the tips of the wings and the tail sa.

Donovan, Sir Henry, J.P., of Tralee, co. Kerry, Ireland, a falcon alighting ppr., holding in the beak a cross crosslet fitchée gu. *Adjuvante Deo in hostes.*

Donovan, St. John Henry, Esquire, of Seafield, Tralee, same crest and motto.

Donovan, Richard, Esquire, of Carolanty, Shinrone, Kings' Co., on a chapeau purpure, turned up erm., a falcon rising. *Adjuvante Deo in hostes.—Guillia ar animina abu.*

Donovan, William, Esquire, M.D., of Glandore, Erdington, Warw., on a chapeau ppr., an eagle rising with wings expanded and inverted. *Adjuvante Deo in hostes.*

Donovan, Sussex and Surrey, a hawk with wings displayed ppr. *Adjuvante Deo in hostes.* *cf.* 87. 12

Donovan, Ireland, a cross fleury fitched arg. 166. 7

Donwike, a dexter hand holding a tilting-spear, all ppr. 214. 11

Doolan, Ireland, a demi-lion rampant gardant holding in the dexter paw a battle-axe ppr. 16. 14

Doolan, Ireland, on a chapeau az., turned up erm., a crescent or, therefrom issuant a trefoil slipped vert.

Doolman, Ireland, a wolf passant az. 28. 10

Doore, a demi-heraldic tiger az., crined and tufted or, holding between the paws an escallop of the last. *cf.* 25. 13

Dopping, a dove volant az. *cf.* 93. 13

Dopping, Ireland, a demi-eagle displayed sa. 81. 6

Dopping, Ireland, a talbot's head gu., eared arg., collared and chained or. *cf.* 56. 12

Dopping, a talbot's head couped arg., collared gu., studded and chained or. *cf.* 56. 12

Dopping-Hepenstal, Lambert John, Esquire, J.P., Major R.E., of Derrycassan, co. Longford, Ireland: (1) A pelican in her piety ppr., charged on the breast with a cross crosslet gu. (*for Hepenstal*). *cf.* 98. 14. (2) A talbot's head arg., chained or, and gorged with a collar engrailed gu., thereon three bezants (*for Dopping*). *Virescet vulnere virtus.* *cf.* 56. 12

Dopping-Hepenstal, Captain Lambert John, of Derrycassan, Granard, co. Longford, and Altadore Castle, co. Wicklow, same crest.

Doran, Ireland, a bear's head couped in fesse between two branches of laurel in orle vert. 35. 11

Doran, out of a ducal coronet or, a talbot's head gu. 57. 12

Doran, Ireland, out of a ducal coronet or, a lion's head ppr. 17. 5

Doran, Ireland, out of a ducal coronet or, a lion's head erased arg., guttée-de-sang. *cf.* 17. 5

Doran, a lion's gamb sa., holding a battle-axe. *cf.* 38. 3

Dorannan, Ireland, an eagle rising ppr. 77. 5

Dorchester, Baron (Carleton), of Dorchester, Oxon., a dexter arm embowed and naked to the elbow, the shirt folded above the elbow arg., and vested over gu., the hand grasping an arrow in bend sinister, point downwards, ppr. *Quondam his vicimus armis.*

Dore, Hants, a tower embattled sa., on the top a lion rampant. *Fortis in arduis.* 157. 12

Dore, Samuel Lammas, Esquire, J.P. co. of London, of Pinner Hill, Pinner, between the horns of a crescent arg., a cross patée or. 163. 6

Dore, Wilts, on a mural coronet arg., an eagle rising purp., holding in its beak an antique shield per pale az. and gu., charged with three bees or.

Dorien, a demi-savage holding over his dexter shoulder a hammer. 186. 11

Dorington, *see* Dodington.

Dorington, Sir John Edward, Bart., M.P., J.P., D.L., M.A., of Lypiatt Park, Glouc., a stag's head erased ppr., charged with a bugle-horn sa., stringed gu., in front thereof an arrow fessewise ppr. *Strepitus non terret ovantem.* 262. 6

Dorington and **Dorrington,** a lion's gamb ppr., holding a flag gu., charged with a chevron or. *cf.* 35. 9

Dorman, Thomas, of Newgate House, Sandwich, Kent, a lion's gamb holding a tilting-spear. *In arduis viget virtus.* *cf.* 38. 11

Dormer, Baron (Dormer), of Wenge, Bucks, a falconer's right-hand glove fessewise arg., thereon perched a falcon with wings inverted, also arg., belled and beaked or. *Cio che Dio vuole io voglio.*

Dormer, on a dexter gauntlet a falcon close, all ppr. 86. 13

Dormer, a fox passant ppr., between two wings endorsed arg. *cf.* 32. 1

Dormere, a wyvern with wings displayed. 70. 8

Dormere, a castle sa., masoned arg. 155. 4

Dorn of London, a stag's head erased ppr. 121. 2

Dorn, two battle-axes addorsed in pale, environed by a serpent ppr. 172. 6

Dornford, two battle-axes in saltier addorsed ppr. 172. 4

Dorrell, a goat's head erased arg., armed or. 128. 5

Dorrell, an antelope's head couped arg., attired or. *cf.* 126. 2

Dorrely, a mullet of six points or. 164. 3

Dorrien, Herts, a cubit arm erect ppr., holding in the hand a trefoil slipped vert.

Dorrien, Smith-, of Haresfoot, Herts: (1) Issuant from the battlements of a tower arg., a dexter arm erect ppr., holding three trefoils vert (*for Dorrien*). (2) An elephant's head erased or, charged on the neck with three fleurs-de-lis sa. (*for Smith*). *Preines haleine tire fort.*

Dorrington, *see* Dodington.

Dorset, Duke of (Sackville), out of a coronet composed of eight fleurs-de-lis or, an étoile of the like number of points arg. *Aut nunquam tentes, aut perfice.* *cf.* 164. 4

Dorville, a rose slipped ppr. 149. 5

Dorville, a rose per fess gu. and arg. 149. 6

Dorward, Scotland, a cross patée fitched arg. *This I'll defend.* 166. 3

D'Osten-Möller, Charles Champion, Esquire: (1) On a Danish baron's coronet a fleur-de-lis or (*for Möller*). (2) In front of three peacock's feathers erect ppr., two keys in saltire or, between as many eagle's wings arg. (*for D'Osten*). *Die moller salich ihm.* 112. 12

Dotchen, Worcs., a stork's head erased arg., between two wings expanded sa. *cf.* 106. 1

Dotson, Cornw., a hand holding a sword ppr. 212. 13

Dotson of Heye, Cornw., a dexter arm in armour ppr., garnished or, holding a scourge with four lashes sa., the handle garnished and the lashes ended with spur-rowels of the second.

Dottin, Hants, a doe trippant ppr., charged on the body with three torteaux in fesse. *cf.* 124. 12

Doubleday, Middx., an arm in armour or, resting the gauntlet on an escutcheon az., thereon a mullet pierced of the first.

Douce of Debtling, Kent, an antelope's head. *Celer et vigilans.* *cf.* 126. 2

Dougal, Scotland, a bull's head cabossed ppr. 43. 8

Dougall, Scotland, a lion's head erased ppr., gorged with an antique crown or. *Auxilio Dei.—Stand fast.* *cf.* 17. 8

Dougall, Maitland-, William, Scotscraig, Fife: (1) A lion sejant affrontée gu., ducally crowned ppr., holding in the dexter paw a sword of the last, pommel and hilt or, in the sinister a fleur-de-lis az. (2) A lion's head erased ppr., gorged with an antique crown or. *Auxilio Deo.*

Dougan of London, a lion passant, the dexter paw couped at the joint.

Doughty-Tichborne, *see* Tichborne, Bart.

Doughty or **Douty,** a cubit arm erect, vested per pale crenellée or and arg., cuffed of the first, holding in the hand ppr. a mullet of six points sa., pierced or. *cf.* 206. 13

Doughty, a mullet gu. 164. 2

Doughty of Theberton Hall, Suff., a mullet sa. *Palma non sine pulvere.* 164. 2

Doughty, a dove rising holding in its beak an olive-branch ppr. 94. 5

Douglas, Marquess of, *see* Hamilton, Duke of.

Douglas, Duke of Buccleuch, Earl of Morton, Marquess of Queensberry, Earl of Wemyss, and **Earl of Selkirk,** *see those titles respectively.*

Douglas, *see* Akers-Douglas.

Douglas, *see* Home-Douglas.

Douglas, Baron (Douglas), Scotland, on a chapeau ppr., a salamander vert in flames, also ppr. *Jamais arrière.* 138. 2

Douglas, Monteath-: (1) On a chapeau gu., turned up erm., a salamander in flames ppr., charged on the shoulder for distinction with a cross crosslet or (*for Douglas*). 138. 2. (2) An oak-tree fructed, with a lock hanging from one of the branches, all ppr. (3) Out of an Eastern crown or, the rim charged with three bombs fired, an oak-tree, the stem transfixed by a sword fesse-ways, pommel and hilt to the dexter, all ppr. (*for Monteath*). *Jamais arrière.—Quæ serata secura.—Viresco.* 143. 11

Douglas, Henry Mitchell Sholto, of Lordington Manor, Sussex, on a chapeau gu., turned up erm., a salamander in flames ppr. *Jamais arrière.* 138. 2

Douglas, Lieutenant-Colonel William Charles, D.S.O., of Brigton, Douglastown, near Forfar, N.B., on a chapeau gu., turned up erm., a salamander vert in flames ppr. *Jamais arrière.*

Douglas, Ireland, a salamander in flames ppr. 138. 4

Douglas, Francis Archibald Brown, Esquire, 21, Moray Place, Edinburgh, a hand grasping a man's heart ppr. *Sicker.*

Douglas, Sir Kenneth, Bart., of Glenbervie, Kincardinesh., a salamander in flames ppr. *Jamais arrière.* 138. 4

Douglas, Scotland, a dragon in flames. *cf.* 73. 1

Douglas of Kinglassie, a sanglier between the clefts of an oak-tree, with a chain and lock binding them together, all ppr. *Lock sicker.* 40. 4

Douglas, Sir Arthur Percy, Bart., of Carr, a wild boar sticking between two clefts of an oak-tree, a chain and lock holding them together, all ppr. *Lock sicker.* 40. 4

Douglas-Campbell-Douglas, Rev. Sholto, of Douglas-Support, Lanarksh., Scotland, an oak-tree with a lock hanging from one of the branches ppr. *Quæ serata secura.*

Douglas, an oak-tree ppr., with a lock hanging from one of the branches. *Quæ serata secura.*

Douglas, Archibald Campbell, Mains, Dumbartonsh., same crest and motto.

Douglas, Scotland, an oak-tree ppr.

Douglas, a heart gu. *Fortis et fidelis.* 181. 2

Douglas of Killhead, Bart., a human heart gu., bezantée, imperially crowned and winged or. *Forward.* *cf.* 110. 14

Douglas, Scotland, a human heart gu., winged and crowned or, charged with a crescent chequy gu. and arg. *Forward* *cf.* 110. 14

Douglas, William Thomas Parker, Esquire, B.A., M.B., of Holmby, Speen, Newbury, a human heart crowned ppr., between two wings. *Jamais arrière.* 110. 14

Douglas of Castle-Douglas, Bart., a heart gu., imperially crowned or, winged arg., on each wing a mullet sa. *Audax et promptus.* *cf.* 110. 14

Douglas, a heart gu., bezantée, royally crowned, and between two wings, all ppr. *cf.* 110. 14

Douglas of Kelhead, a heart winged ppr. *Jamais arrière.* 112. 10

Douglas, a human heart gu., winged and ensigned with an imperial crown or. *Forward.*

Douglas of Salwarpe, Worcs., a human heart gu., ensigned with an imperial crown between two wings or. *Spero.*

Douglas, a man's heart imperially crowned ppr. and winged gu. *Forward.* *cf.* 110. 14

Douglas, James Tory, Esquire, of Hong Kong and Scotland, a hand grasping a man's heart ppr. *Sicker.* 216. 9

Douglas, Robert Hinde, same crest and motto.

Douglas, a hand holding a human heart ppr., ensigned with a crescent arg. *Meliora sperando.* *cf.* 216. 9

Douglas, Scott-, Sir George Brisbane, Bart.: (1) A cubit arm erect, holding in the hand a broken tilting-spear, all ppr. (*for Douglas*). (2) A lion's head erased, holding in the mouth a thistle, all ppr. (*for Scott*). *Do or die.—Pro patriâ.* 214. 10

Douglas, out of a cloud a dexter hand holding a broken tilting-spear. *cf.* 214. 10

Douglas of Cavers, a dexter hand holding a broken lance in bend ppr. *Do or die.* 214. 10

Douglas, Palmer-, Edward, Cavers, near Hawick, same crest and motto.

Douglas of Tilquhillie, Dumbartonsh., issuing out of a cloud a dexter hand holding a sword erect ppr. *God for us.* cf. 212. 9

Douglas, Kent, an arm in armour embowed ppr., garnished or, the hand grasping a dagger, also ppr., hilt and pommel of the second. 196. 5

Douglas, out of a bush a dexter hand issuant holding an oak-leaf, all ppr. *Tandem fit surculus arbor.*

Douglas of Bridgeford, a dexter hand grasping a sword erect, all ppr. *Petit ardua virtus.* 212. 9

Douglas, a wolf sejant ppr. 29. 3

Douglas of Tympindean, a plume of ostrich-feathers ppr. 115. 1

Douglas of Earnslaw, a boat in distress surrounded with clouds and stars shooting through the same, all ppr. *Durate.* cf. 174. 4

Douglas, Scotland, a martlet sa. *Sursum.* 95. 5

Douglas, Scotland, a peacock ppr. 103. 7

Douglas, a peacock's head issuing from a tower ppr.

Douglas, Scotland, a peacock's head ppr. 103. 2

Douglas, on the stump of a tree a falcon with wings expanded ppr., belled or, charged on the breast with a mullet az. *Sursum.* cf. 87. 12

Douglas, a demi-savage wreathed about the head and middle with leaves, and holding in his dexter hand a club, all ppr. 185. 2

Douglas, a griffin's head couped. 66. 1

Douglas, a greyhound's head sa. cf. 61. 2

Douglass of Grace Hall, Down, a dexter arm erect, holding in the hand a human heart, all ppr. *Forward.* 216. 10

Douglass, John Edward William James, Esquire, of Feugh Lodge, Banchory, N.B., a dexter hand issuing from clouds holding a sword erect ppr. *God for us.*

Douglass, Blacker-, St. John Thomas, Esquire, J.P., D.L., of Elm Park, co. Armagh, Ireland: (1) A cubit arm erect ppr., grasping a human heart gu., charged with a trefoil slipped vert (*for Douglass*). cf. 216. 9. (2) A dexter armed arm embowed, the hand gauntleted grasping a battle-axe, all ppr. (*for Blacker*). *Forward.—Pro Deo et rege.* 200. 6

Doulton, Henry Lewis, of Woolpits, Ewhurst, Surrey, and Bowling-Green House, Putney Heath, S.W., a demi-lion rampant sa., holding in the dexter paw a cross crosslet or, and resting the sinister on an escutcheon arg., charged with a vase ppr. *Le beau est la splendeur du vrai.*

Doune, Lord, *see* Moray, Earl of.

Dounie and **Downie,** Scotland, a cock ppr. *Courage.* 91. 2

Dounies, a wolf's head. 30. 5

Douro, Marquess of, *see* Wellington, Duke of.

Douthwaite, on a rock ppr., a fleur-de-lis per pale or and gu. cf. 148. 2

Dovaston, Shropsh., a dexter arm in armour embowed supporting a hatchet. *Percussus elevor.*

Dovaston, Milward Edmund, Esquire, M.R.C.S., L.S.A., F.O.S., of Hatchcroft House, Hendon, a dexter arm in armour embowed to the sinister supporting a battle-axe, all ppr. *Percussus elevor.*

Dove, a hunting-horn stringed. 228. 11

Dove, Scotland, a pegasus salient with wings addorsed and ducally gorged, all ppr. 47. 3

Dove of London, and Stradbroke, Suff., a dove arg., the wings sa., charged with a crescent for difference. cf. 92. 2

Dove, Surrey, in a chaplet vert, banded or, a dove ppr.

Dove, on a tower arg., a dove rising ppr. 156. 11

Dove, on a tower arg., a dove with wings expanded ppr. 156. 8

Dove, a dove with wings expanded ppr., holding in the beak a sprig vert. 94. 5

Dover, Hants, on a demi-tower triple-towered arg., a demi-cockatrice with wings expanded vert.

Dover, an owl arg. 96. 5

Dover, Baron, *see* **Clifden, Viscount.**

Doveton, the late Lieutenant-General Sir John, G.C.B., a dove with wings displayed supporting with the dexter claw a staff with a pennon, all ppr.

Dow, Scotland, a dove ppr. *Patience.* 92. 2

Dowbiggin, a reindeer's head cabossed ppr. 122. 4

Dowd, Ireland, a bird ppr. 92. 2

Dowdal and **Dowdall,** out of a ducal coronet a boar's head and neck collared or. cf. 41. 4

Dowdall and **Dowdal,** Ireland, a holy lamb ppr. 131. 2

Dowdall of Lecall, co. Louth, Ireland, a martlet gu., crowned arg. cf. 95. 4

Dowdall of Glaspistol, co. Louth, Ireland, a martlet arg., crowned or. cf. 95. 4

Dowdall and **Dowdal,** a dove ducally crowned ppr. cf. 92. 2

Dowdall, Ireland, a dove holding an olive-branch in its beak and ducally gorged, all ppr. *Fidelis usque ad mortem.* cf. 92. 5

Dowde, Ireland, a mailed arm holding in the hand a spear, all ppr., headed arg. 210. 11

Dowdeswell, Essex, issuing from clouds two hands wrenching asunder the trunk of a tree, all ppr. 224. 10

Dowding, a catherine-wheel az. 167. 2

Dowds, Ireland, a dove gu. 92. 2

Dowe, *see* Dow and Dove.

Dowell, a lion's head erased sa. 17. 8

Dowell, two lion's gambs erased in saltier, enfiled with a wreath of laurel.

Dowell, Admiral Sir W. Montagu, G.C.B., Ford, Bideford, North Devonsh., a lion, head erased.

Dowglas, Scotland, a dexter arm in armour embowed holding in the hand a sword, all ppr. 195. 2

Dowglas, Scotland, a hand holding a scimitar, all ppr. *Honor et amor.* 213. 5

Dowie, Scotland, a dove volant holding in its beak an olive-branch ppr. *Patience.* 93. 10

Dowie of Wimbledon, Surrey, the trunk of a tree eradicated fessewise and sprouting to the dexter ppr., surmounted by a dove volant holding in the beak a sprig of olive, also ppr., and gorged with a collar gemelle or.

Dowies, Norf., a wolf's head erm., charged with a mullet. cf. 30. 5

Dowine, Scotland, a dexter hand holding a dagger, all ppr. *Hold fast.* 212. 9

Dowker, out of a ducal coronet sa., a plume of five ostrich-feathers arg. 114. 13

Dowker, Ireland, two dexter hands couped and conjoined holding a human heart ppr. 224. 4

Dowland, a tiger passant gardant or. 27. 4

Dowler, a hand erect plucking a thistle ppr. 218. 5

Dowley, a demi-heraldic tiger gu., ducally gorged or. 25. 12

Dowling, Ireland, a lion's head erased az., gorged with two bars or. cf. 17. 8

Dowling, Vincent James, Esquire, J.P., of Line, Rylstone, New South Wales, Australia, *uses* a falcon belled and jessed, holding in the dexter claw a sword. *Fortis et egregius.*

Dowling, out of a mural coronet a dexter arm vested, holding in the hand a sword wavy.

Dowman, Yorks, out of a mural coronet a bundle of seven arrows banded gu.

Down and **Downs,** a cubit arm, holding in the hand a broken hammer. 221. 13

Downe, Viscount (Dawnay), Wykeham Abbey, Yorks, a demi-Saracen in armour, couped at the thighs, wreathed about the temples ppr., holding in the dexter hand a ring or, stoned az., and in the sinister a lion's gamb erased of the second, armed gu. *Timet pudorem.*

Downe, Surrey, a sea-lion erect gu., guttée-d'or. 20. 5

Downe, an arm vested arg., cuffed or, the hand ppr. holding a crescent of the second flammant ppr. cf. 206. 10

Downer, two hands conjoined in fesse, winged at the wrists. 224. 12

Downes, Baron (Burgh), Ireland: (1) A mountain-cat sejant gardant ppr., collared, and a chain reflexed over the back or (*for Burgh*). 26. 13. (2) A wolf's head erased ppr., charged on the neck with a mullet or (*for Downes*). *A cruce salus.* cf. 30. 8

Downes of Cowley, Glouc., and of Windsor, Berks, a stag's head gu., attired or 121. 5

Downes, Charles Villiers, Aspley Guise, Beds, upon two ears of wheat leaved and slipped or, a lapwing, wings addorsed ppr. *Soies content.* 270. 2

Downes, John Sheen, Esquire, of Newmarket, Ontario, Canada, same crest and motto.

Downes, Essex, a stag lodged arg. 115. 7

Downes, Arthur, Esquire, of 46, Gordon Square, W.C., Milford Lodge, Craven Arms, Shropsh., and the Priory, Berwick St. John's, Wilts, a hart lodged arg.

Downes, a buck's head erased ppr. 121. 2

Downes, Suff. and Norf., a wolf's head arg., charged with a mullet. cf. 30. 5

Downfield, a cock ppr. *Virtute et labore.* 91. 2

Downham, Ireland, a dexter arm embowed ppr., holding in the hand a club vert. 202. 10

Downie, Scotland, a ship under sail with a plough on deck, all ppr. *Ex undis aratra.*

Downie, a dagger and a cross crosslet fitched in saltier. 166. 12

Downie, a boar's head erased or. 42. 2

Downie, Scotland, a cock ppr. *Courage.* 91. 2

Downie, Scotland, out of a ducal coronet a cock's head. 90. 6

Downie, Mackenzie-, Alexander Francis, Esquire, of Holybourne, near Alton, a cock crowing ppr. *Courage.*

Downing, Cambs and Norf., an arm in armour embowed, a ribbon bowed at the wrist arg., holding in the hand ppr. a broad arrow, or, headed and feathered of the first. *cf.* 198. 4

Downing, Norf., a bear's head couped in fess. 43. 1

Downing, Ireland, a boar's head couped gu. 43. 1

Downing, Essex, out of a ducal coronet a swan or.

Downman, a hand holding a lancet ppr. 216. 14

Downs, *see* Downes.

Downs, out of a tower arg., a demi-lion rampant gu., holding a battle-axe ppr. *cf.* 157. 11

Downshire, Marquess of (Hill), Hillsborough Castle, co. Down, a reindeer's head couped gu., attired and plain collared or. *Per Deum et ferrum obtinui.*—*Ne tentes aut perfice.* *cf.* 122. 1

Downton, Shropsh., a dexter hand holding up a sword in pale, enfiled with a savage's head, all ppr. 212. 12

Dowse, issuing from clouds two dexter hands, each brandishing a scimitar ppr. 224. 15

Dowsing, Norf., a squirrel sejant cracking a nut, all ppr. 135. 7

Dowson, a lion rampant per fess or and gu. 1. 13

Dowson, Suff., a dove ppr. 92. 2

Dox and **Doxey,** a demi-savage holding in his dexter hand three arrows in pale, and the sinister pointing to an imperial crown, all ppr. 186. 13

Doxat, of Clare, Hants, out of a ducal coronet or, a demi-lion rampant double-queued arg. *cf.* 10. 6

Doyle and **Doyley,** Norf., out of a mural coronet arg., an arm embowed ppr., vested sa., cuffed of the first, holding in the hand a spear of the second. *cf.* 204. 7

Doyle, Sir Everard Hastings, Bart., 7, Grosvenor Gardens, W., out of a ducal coronet or, a buck's head ppr. *Fortitudine vincit.* 120. 7

Doyle, Ireland, a stag's head couped gu., ducally gorged or, attired arg. *cf.* 121. 5

Doyle, Bart. (*extinct*): (1) A Mameluke on horseback in the act of throwing a djirid, all ppr. (2) Out of an Eastern coronet or, a stag's head gu., attired or, charged on the neck with a mullet of eight points within an increscent arg. *Fortitudine vincit.*

D'Oyley, a buck's head cabossed arg. 122. 5

D'Oyley, Oxon., a demi-dragon with wings addorsed or. 73. 10

D'Oyley, Bart. (*extinct*), a demi-dragon with wings addorsed holding in the claws a fleur-de-lis. *cf.* 73. 10

Doyley, a demi-dragon vert, winged or. 73. 10

Doyley, a demi-dragon ppr. 73. 10

D'Oyly, Sir Warren Hastings, Bart., J.P., out of a ducal coronet or, an estoile arg., between two wings issuant and erect gu. *Do no ylle, quoth D'oylle.*

D'Oyly, William, Esquire, of 9, FitzGeorge Avenue, Kensington, London, W., a demi-dragon arg., wings elevated az., holding between the claws a fleur-de-lis sa. *Omne solum forti patria.*

Doyne, Ireland, a holly-tree vert. 145. 6

Doyne, Charles Mervyn, Esquire, of Wells, near Gorey, and Kellistown, co. Carlow: (1) A demi-eagle rising ppr. 80. 2. (2) A holly-bush ppr., in front thereof a lizard passant or.

Dracelow and **Drakelow,** a demi-husbandman holding in his dexter hand an ox-yoke ppr. 187. 14

Draffen, Joseph Wright, Esquire, of Connaught Terrace, Hyde Park, London, W., out of a ducal coronet or, a demi-lion rampant gu., gorged with a chaplet of trefoils ppr., supporting a spear, thereon a banner of the second, charged with a fleur-de-lis of the first, in an escroll over the crest *Lesmahagow.* *Per ardua surgo.*

Draghorn and **Dreghorn,** on rye grass a horse feeding, all ppr. *Utitur ante quæsitis.*

Drago, Cambs, a demi-eagle displayed per pale or and gu., the dexter wing charged with a fleur-de-lis of the last, the sinister with one of the first. *Invidiâ major.* *cf.* 81. 6

Dragoner, Middx., a pheon sa. 174. 11

Drake, *see* Fuller-Eliott-Drake, Bart.

Drake, a hand issuing out of clouds drawing a ship round a globe. *Perseverando.* 160. 3

Drake of Springfield, Devonsh.: (1) A dexter arm erect ppr., holding in the hand a battle-axe sa. 213. 12. (2) An eagle displayed gu. *Aquila non capit muscas.* 75. 3

Drake: (1) A dexter arm in armour embowed, grasping a pole-axe, all ppr. (*for Drake*). 200. 6. (2) A tortoise displayed ppr. (*for Deane*). *Sic parvis magna.*

Drake, England and Ireland, a dexter arm erect ppr., holding in the hand a battle-axe sa., headed arg. 213. 12

Drake, a cubit arm holding a battle-axe erect, all ppr. 300. 1

Drake, Tyrwhitt-, William Wykeham, of Shardeloes, Amersham, Bucks and Lincs: (1) A naked dexter arm erect holding in the hand a battle-axe arg., headed sa. (*for Drake*). 279. 12 (2) A savage ppr., wreathed vert, holding in both hands over his dexter shoulder a club or (*for Tyrwhitt*). 279. 11

Drake, an arm embowed arg., thereon two bendlets wavy gu., supporting a battle-axe, the staff sa., headed of the first. *cf.* 201. 5

Drake of Roriston, co. Meath, a wyvern with wings displayed and the tail nowed gu. *cf.* 70. 8

Drake, Ireland and England, a wyvern with wings addorsed arg. 70. 1

Drake, Norf., a reindeer's head couped arg.

Drake, a reindeer's head erased or, ducally gorged and attired sa. *cf.* 122. 1

Drakelow, *see* Dracelow.

Drakenford, an anchor and cable ppr. 161. 2

Drane, a demi-lion rampant ppr. 10. 2

Dransfield, Essex and Yorks, a sword in pale enfiled with a Turk's head, all ppr. 191. 9

Draper, Ireland, a galley with her oars in action ppr. 160. 7

Draper, Middx., Beds, and Oxon., a heraldic tiger's head vert, tufted or, pierced through the neck by an arrow of the last.

Draper, Bucks, a camel's head erm., bridled or, maned sa. *cf.* 132. 7

Draper, Leics. and Notts, a cubit arm erect, vested vert, cuffed and slashed arg., holding in the hand ppr. a covered cup or.

Draper, William, Esquire, M.R.C.S., De Grey House, York, same crest. *Vicit pepercit.*

Draper, Northumb., a cubit arm erect, vested erminois, holding in the hand ppr. a mullet of six points or. *cf.* 206. 13

Draper, a stag's head gu., attired or, charged on the neck with a fess between three annulets of the last. *Vicit pepercit.* *cf.* 121. 5

Draper of London, a stag's head erased gu., gorged with a fess between two bars gemelles arg., charged with a fleur-de-lis sa. *cf.* 121. 2

Draper, a buck's head couped gu., gorged with a fesse arg., thereon three fleurs-de-lis sa. *cf.* 121. 5

Drax, a demi-dragon with wings addorsed or. 73. 10

Drax, a demi-dragon with wings endorsed or, and issuing out of his mouth a scroll with this motto, *Mort en droit.* *cf.* 73. 10

Drax, Sawbridge-Erle-, Wanley Ellis, Holnest Park, Sherborne, Dorset, of Charborough Park, Dorset, and Ellerton Abbey, Yorks: (1) A demi-wyvern or (*for Drax*). 69. 12. (2) A demi-lion rampant az., holding in the dexter paw a hand-saw erect or (*for Sawbridge*). *Mort en droit.*

Drax, out of a ducal coronet or, an eagle's head ppr. *cf.* 83. 14

Draycote, Derbysh., a dragon's head erased gu., scaled or. *cf.* 71. 1

Draycot or **Draycott,** a dragon's head couped vert. 71. 2

Draycott or **Draycot,** a dragon's head erased gu. *cf.* 71. 2

Drayner, Kent, a lion sejant arg., holding in the paws a broken tilting-spear of the same. 8. 11

Drayner, Middx., a pheon or. 174. 11

Drayton of London, the sun in splendour or. *Non nobis solum.* 162. 2

Drayton, on a sun in splendour ppr. a Mercury's cap vert, winged arg. *cf.* 162. 2

Drayton, a dexter hand couped ppr., holding a cross crosslet fitched gu. 221. 14

Drayton, an eagle's leg couped or, the thigh az. *cf.* 113. 8

Dreghorn, *see* Draghorn.

Dreux, a ram's head arg., armed or. 130. 1

Drever, an eagle rising regardant holding in the beak a pomegranate, all ppr. *cf.* 77. 4

Drew, Ireland, a dexter hand erect holding a chapeau, all ppr., between two laurel-branches vert. 217. 5

Drew, Alexander, Esquire, of Holme Lodge, Burnley, Lancs, a lion's head erased.

Drew, Wilts, a lion's head erased gu., collared gobony or and az. 18. 6

Drew, a bull's head erased sa., armed or, holding in the mouth three wheat-ears of the last. *cf.* 44. 3

Drew, Julius Charles, Wadhurst Hall, Sussex, in front of a bull's head sa., gorged with a collar gemel, and holding in the mouth three ears of wheat, a garb fessewise, all or. *Deum adspice: Drogo nomen et virtus arma dedit.*

Drew, William Francis, Esquire, same crest and motto.

Drew, on a mount vert, a roebuck current or. 118. 13

Drew, Scotland, a cup or. 177. 4

Drewe, two arms from the shoulder couped in saltier ppr., vested arg., each holding a scimitar in pale of the first. 203. 10

Drewe-Mercer, Alfred, Esquire, of Elmhurst, Beadonwell Erith, Kent: (1) A heron's head couped holding in the beak an eel twined round the neck ppr., between two crosses patée az. (*for Mercer*). (2) Upon a mount vert, a stag courant ppr., in front of a gate or (*for Drewe*).

Drewell, Bucks, a dexter arm embowed ppr., vested or, cuffed gu., holding up a covered cup of the second. 203. 4

Drewett, Ormonde Drewett, of Jarrow Hall, Durh., in front of two palm-branches saltireways ppr., a fleur-de-lis gu. 148. 3

Drewry, a greyhound current sa., collared or. *cf.* 58. 2

Drewry, a greyhound courant arg. *cf.* 58. 2

Dreyer, John Louis Emil, Esquire, of the Observatory, Armagh, an arm vambraced, the hand gauntleted, grasping a trident bend sinisterways arg., the shaft ppr. *Uden arbeide ingen lykke.*

Dring, William Ernest, L.R.C.P., M.R.C.S., L.S.A., of Willsden, Buckhurst Hill, Essex, on a chapeau a phœnix in flames, all ppr. *Prudentia et animo.* 82. 11

Drinkwater, three ears of wheat, two in saltier and one in pale, enfiled with a ducal coronet, all or. *cf.* 154. 6

Drinkwater, the Deemster Sir William Leece, of Kirby, Douglas, Isle of Man, three ears of wheat, two in saltire and one in pale, enfiled with a ducal coronet, all or. *Sapiens qui assiduus.* *cf.* 154. 6

Drisdale, Ireland, within a chaplet or, a thistle slipped and leaved ppr.

Driver, a heart gu., winged or. 112. 10

Driver, a sinister arm in armour embowed, holding in the hand a laurel-wreath ppr. *cf.* 199. 13

Drogheda, Earl of, Viscount Moore of Drogheda, **Baron** (Moore), Moore Abbey, Monasterevan, co. Kildare, out of a ducal coronet or, a Moor's head ppr., wreathed about the temples arg. and az. *Fortis cadere, cedere, non potest.* 240. 12

Dromgoule, Ireland, an estoile rayed or.

Drought, under a tree a stag at gaze, all ppr. 116. 12

Drought, Ireland, a sceptre or. 170. 10

Drought, Thomas Armstrong, Esquire, of Lettybrook, Ireland, a rainbow issuant from clouds ppr. *Semper sitiens.*

Drought, Thomas Henry, Whigsborough, near Parsonstown, same crest and motto.

Drought, Richard Reynell, Esquire, of Glencarrig, Glenealy, co. Wicklow, same crest and motto.

Druce, an arm in armour embowed, the hand grasping a scimitar, all ppr. 196. 10

Druitt, out of a ducal coronet or, a plume of five ostrich-feathers arg., banded gu. *cf.* 114. 13

Druitt, a talbot passant, collared and lined. 54. 5

Drumlanrig, Viscount, *see* Queensberry, Marquess.

Drummond, Viscount Strathallan, *see* Strathallan.

Drummond, *see* Beresford-Drummond.

Drummond, Rt. Hon. George, **Earl of Perth and Melfort, Lord Drummond** of Cargill, **Lord Drummond** of Stobhall and Montifex, **Viscount Melfort and Forth, Hereditary Thane of Lennox, Hereditary Steward of Menteith and Strathearn, Duc de Melfort, Comte de Lussan and Baron de Valrose:** (1) On a ducal coronet a sleuth-hound ppr., collared and leashed gu. 54. 9. (2) On a ducal coronet a sun in splendour, all ppr. (3) Out of an Eastern crown a lion issuing affrontée gu., holding in the dexter paw a sword ppr., hilted and pommelled or, and in the sinister a thistle, also ppr. *Dei dono sum quod sum.—Ab uno ad omnes.—Gang warily.*

Drummond, on a ducal coronet a sleuth-hound standing ppr., collared and leashed gu. *Gang warily.* 54. 9

Drummond, Williams-, Sir James Hamlyn Williams, Bart., of Hawthornden, Mid Lothian, a demi-pegasus ppr., maned and winged or. *Hos gloria reddit honore.* 47. 5

Drummond, a pegasus ppr., maned and winged or. *Hos gloria reddit honore.* 47. 1

Drummond, a demi-pegasus ppr., armed and winged or. 47. 5

Drummond, England and Scotland, two arms drawing a bow and arrow ppr. *Arte et marte.* 200. 2

Drummond of the Boyce, Glouc., two arms drawing an arrow to the head ppr. *Marte et arte.* 200. 2

Drummond, Malcolm, Megginch Castle, Perth, two arms drawing an arrow to the head ppr. in a bow or. *Marte et arte.*

Drummond of Arncraig, two arms ppr. shooting an arrow from a bow or. *Marte et arte.* 200. 2

Drummond, issuing out of a mural coronet two arms drawing an arrow in a bow, all ppr. *Marte et arte.* *cf.* 200. 2

Drummond of Cultmalundy, a hand holding a heart ppr. *Cum corde.* 216. 9

Drummond of Invermay, a dexter hand holding a flaming heart ppr. *Loyal au mort.* *cf.* 216. 9

Drummond, John, of Strageath and Balquhandy, Perthsh., a dexter arm from the shoulder in armour embowed, the hand bare holding a falchion ppr. *Caute sed intrepide.* 196. 10

Drummond, Reginald Henry Tudor, Esquire, of Balquhandy, Dunning, Perthsh., same crest.

Drummond of Logie Almond, a dexter arm from the shoulder embowed brandishing in the hand a broadsword, all ppr. *Nil timeo.* 201. 4

Drummond, a dexter hand holding a spear ppr. *Per mare, per terras.* 214. 11

Drummond of Carlowrie, a dexter hand holding a curling-stone. *Have at all.* 221. 2

Drummond, on a dexter hand gloved, a hooded hawk ppr. *Prius mori quam fidem fallere.* 86. 8

Drummond, Andrew Cecil, of Cadland, Hants, a goshawk with wings expanded ppr. 87. 1

Drummond, a falcon rising ppr. 88. 2

Drummond of Cromlix, Scotland, a goshawk with wings displayed ppr., armed, jessed, and belled or. *Lord, have mercy.*

Drummond of Machany, a falcon hooded, jessed, and belled, all ppr. *Prius mori quam fidem fallere.* *cf.* 85. 1

Drummond of Madderty, a falcon ppr., armed, jessed, and belled or. *Lord, have mercy.* *cf.* 85. 2

Drummond, a goshawk with wings displayed ppr.

Drummond, a falcon close regardant holding in the dexter claw a garland of laurel, all ppr. 85. 4

Drummond of Cargill, an eagle volant.

Drummond, an eagle rising from a globe, all ppr. *Altiora peto.* 159. 7

Drummond, an eagle rising to the sinister, the head in the sun.

Drummond of Colnhalzie, on a rock a turtle-dove, all ppr. *Sto mobilis.* *cf.* 92. 3

Drummond of Monedie, a dove standing on an anchor in pale, all ppr. *Spes mea, res mea.*

Drummond, Stirling-Home-, Henry Edward, Blair Drummond, Stirling, a sleuth-hound's head ppr. *E cura quies.*

Drummond of Blair, a nest of young ravens ppr. *Deus providebit.* 113. 7

Drummond, a garb or, thereon a Cornish chough feeding ppr. *Ex hoc vivo.*

Drummond of Pitkellanie, a sword and a garb in saltier, both ppr. *Et marte, et arte.* 153. 7

Drummond of Riccarton, a lion rampant az., armed and langued gu. *Dum spiro, spero.* 1. 13

Drummond, a demi-lion az. *Dum spiro, spero.* 10. 2

Drummond of Midhope, three stars chevronways or. *Ad astra per ardua.* 164. 7

Drummond of Kildees, a garland of laurel ppr. *Si recte facias.* 146. 5

Drummond, a ship in distress ppr. 160. 14

Drummond, a pheon or. *Consequitur quodcunque petit.* 174. 11

Drummond, on a ducal coronet or, a greyhound statant arg. *cf.* 60. 2

Drumson, a dexter hand holding a battle-axe ppr. *Spectemur agendo.* 213. 12

Drury, a greyhound's head erased ppr. 61. 4

Drury, a greyhound courant arg. *cf.* 58. 2

Drury, Major Charles William, of Kingston, Ontario, Canada, a greyhound current ppr., *Non sine causa.* *cf.* 58. 2

Drury, Ireland, a battle-axe in pale ppr. 172. 3

Drury-Lowe, General Sir Drury Curzon, of Key Dell, Horndean, R.S.O., Hants: (1) A wolf passant arg. (*for Lowe*). (2) A greyhound courant sa., gorged with a plain collar, and charged with two mullets, all or.

Drury-Lowe, Richard Curzon Sherwin, Esquire, same crests.

Drury-Lowe, Robert Henry, Esquire, same crests.

Drury-Lowe, Vincent Francis Keppel, Esquire, same crests.

Drury-Lowe, William Drury Nathaniel, Esquire, of Locko Park, Derby, same crests.

Dry of London, on a ducal coronet a lion passant gardant, ducally crowned, all ppr. 6. 4

Dryden, Sir Alfred Erasmus, Bart., M.A., of Ambrosden, Oxon., and Canons Ashby, Byfield, Northamp., a demi-lion sustaining in the dexter paw a sphere or.

Dryland, Norf., a demi-man in military costume holding a banner displayed gu., charged with a cross arg.

Drysdale, Scotland, an anchor with a cable, all ppr. *Non sine anchorâ.* 161. 2

Drysdale, a crane's head crowned ppr. 104. 6

Drysdale, Scotland, a martlet sa. *Per varios casus.* 95. 5

Drysdale, Ireland, a thistle ppr. within a chaplet or.

Drywood, Essex, a greyhound's head per pale or and gu., collared az., between two wings counterchanged. *cf.* 61. 2

Drywood, Essex, an oak-branch fructed ppr. 151. 3

Duane, England and Ireland, a wolf's head erased ppr. 30. 8

Dubber, Surrey, out of a mural coronet gu., two wings expanded arg., each charged with a bend of the first, and thereon three crescents of the second.

Duberley and **Duberly**, Wales, a dexter arm embowed ppr. holding in the hand, also ppr., three wheat-ears or.

Duberley, Grey William, of Gaines Hall, St. Neots, Hunts, a dexter arm embowed ppr. holding in the hand three ears of wheat or. *Res, non verba.*

Duberley and **Duberly**, a cock holding in its beak a trefoil ppr. 91. 5

Duberly, Arthur Grey, Esquire, of the Barns, Fenlake, Beds, same crest and motto.

Duberly, James Grey, Esquire, of 41, Camperdown Place, Great Yarmouth, same crest and motto.

Dubisson, a gannet sa. *Nil impossibile.*

Du Bisson, on a chapeau ppr., a gannet sa. *Nil impossibile.*

Du Bois, a falcon close ppr., belled or. *cf.* 85. 2

Du Bois de Ferrieres of Hardwick Hall, Monmouth, upon a rock a raven ppr. holding in the dexter claw a sword, also ppr., pommel and hilt or. *Tout par et pour Dieu.*

Du Boulay of Donhead Hall, Wilts, out of a ducal coronet or, a dog's head collared.

Du Boys of London, a wheel or. 167. 1

Du Cane, Charles Henry Copley, of Braxted Park, Whitham, Essex, a demi-lion rampant sa., ducally crowned or, supporting an anchor erect of the last. *cf.* 13. 12

Du Cane, Richard, Esquire, of 25, Park Crescent, Portland Place, W., same crest.

Du Cane, Major-General Sir Edmund Frederick, K.C.B., Chevalier of the Order of the Rose, Brazil, of Kilnwich Hall, Beverley, Yorks, and 40, Queen's Gate Gardens, London, S.W., a demi-lion rampant sa., ducally crowned or, supporting with the paws an anchor erect of the last. *Par fermesse du quesne.* *cf.* 12. 12

Ducarel, Surrey, a cock gu. 91. 2

Ducat and **Duchet**, issuing from clouds two hands conjoined in fess holding a palm-branch, all ppr. 224. 3

Ducie, Earl of (Moreton), Tortworth, Falfield, Glouc., a moorcock's head or, combed and wattled gu., between two wings displayed az. *Perseverando.*

Ducie, a sea-lion, the fore-part or, the tail arg., supporting with the dexter paw an anchor az., the flukes of the first. *cf.* 20. 5

Ducie, two palm-branches in orle vert. 146. 2

Duck, Norf. and Devonsh., on a mount vert, a falcon az., with wings expanded or, beaked and legged of the same.

Duck, on an anchor erect or, a snake entwined ppr. 161. 3

Duckenfield, *see* Duckinfield.

Duckenfield, a demi-husbandman holding over his dexter shoulder a ploughshare, all ppr.

Duckensfield, on a tower embattled a flag displayed or. 157. 13

Ducker, James Ernest Townshend, Esquire, of 100, Friar Gate, Derbysh., a stag statant ppr., attired and ungu. or. *Hæc generi incrementa fides.*

Ducket, three wheat-ears ppr. 154. 6

Ducket of London and Wilts, a garb of lavender vert, flowered az., banded or. *cf.* 153. 2

Duckett, Sir George Floyd, Bart., D.L., of Hartham House, Wilts: (1) Out of a ducal coronet or, a plume of five ostrich-feathers, one, two, and three (*for Duckett*). (2) A garb of lavender vert, flowered az., banded or (*also for Duckett*). *cf.* 153. 2. (3) A sheldrake ppr., charged on the breast with a saltire gu. (*for Jackson*). *Je veux le droit.*

Duckett, Steuart James Charles, Esquire, J.P., of Russelstown Park, Carlow, same crests and motto.

Duckett, William, Esquire, of Duckett's Grove, Palatine, co. Carlow, and Newtown, co. Kildare, same crest.

Duckett, a cockatrice displayed ppr. 68. 14

Duckett-Steuart, Charles Edward Henry, Esquire, of Rutland Lodge, Carlow, a pelican in her piety arg., winged or, the nest and young ppr.

Duckinfield and **Duckingfield**, out of a ducal coronet or, a dexter arm vested gu., cuffed arg., holding in the hand the sun in splendour of the first. 209. 2

Duckworth, Bart. (*extinct*), Devonsh., a tower with the battlements thereof partly demolished, from the top flames issuant ppr., on the sinister side a sea-lion erect az., the paws pressing against the tower. *Disciplinâ, fide, perseverantiâ.* 281. 2

Duckworth, Rev. William Arthur, Orchardleigh Park, Somers., a griffin's head erased and surmounting four spear-heads conjoined in saltire ppr. *Non nobis solum.*

Duckworth, on a garb in fess or, a wild duck ppr.

Duckworth, Sir Dyce, of 11, Grafton Street, Piccadilly, upon a mount between two palm-branches vert, a garb fesseways or, charged with two crosses patée in fesse, and surmounted by a duck sa. *Perseverantia.*

Duckworth, Rev. Canon Robinson, C.V.O., D.D., of 5, Abbey Road, London, N.W., and Little Cloisters, Westminster Abbey, S.W., same crest and motto.

Duckworth, a lady holding in her dexter hand the sun and in her sinister the moon ppr. 184. 4

Duckworth, Herbert, Esquire, a griffin's head erased and surmounting four spear-heads conjoined in saltire ppr. *Non nobis solum.*

Duckworth, Russell, Esquire, of the Cloisters, Bath, same crest and motto.

Du Coin, three mullets in chevron. 164. 7

Ducye, *see* Ducie.

Duddingston and **Dudingstoun**, Scotland, a greyhound's head couped ppr. *cf.* 61. 12

Dudgeon, Henry, Esquire, of the Priory, Stillorgan, co. Dublin, a naked arm fesseways, couped at the shoulder and embowed at the elbow, the hand grasping a dudgeon or dagger, all ppr., pierced through a heart gu. *Deo fide ferro comitante.*

Dudgeon, a holly-branch vert and a cross crosslet fitched az. in saltier. 166. 10

Dudgeon, Scotland, issuing from a heart a hand grasping a scimitar, all ppr. 213. 4

Dudgeon, issuing from a human heart a hand grasping a sword. *cf.* 213. 4

Dudingstoun, *see* Duddingston.

Dudley, Earl of (Ward), out of a ducal coronet or, a lion's head az. *Comme je fûs.* 17. 5

Dudley, Lieutenant-Colonel Brigade-Surgeon William Edmondson, of 15, Sion Hill, Bath, Somers., a lion's head az., out of a ducal coronet or. *Droit et loyal.*

Dudley, out of a ducal coronet or, a lion's head az., collared and ringed of the first. *cf.* 17. 5

Dudley, out of a viscount's coronet or, pearled arg., a lion's head az., collared and ringed of the first.

Dudley-Janns, Rev. Sheldon Francis, of Glenarm Rectory, co. Antrim: (1) A lion rampant sa., collared gemelle arg., holding between the paws an escallop of the last (*for Janns*). *cf.* 1. 13. (2) A lion rampant double-queued az., holding between the paws a rose gu., entwined with a trefoil slipped and leaved vert, and in an escroll over the crest the motto, "*Mori quam fœdari*" (*for Dudley*).—*Honor virtutis præmium.* cf. 1. 14

Dudley, Francis, Esquire, of County Asylum, Bodmin, Cornw., a lion rampant, double-queued, holding between the paws a knot. *Mori quam fœdari.*

Dudley, a unicorn passant, collared and chained.

Dudley, Cambs, a buck's head erased arg., attired sa., the neck pierced by an arrow barbed and flighted ppr., and gorged with a collar gu., therefrom pendent an escutcheon of the second charged with a hand in bend, couped at the wrist or. 120. 14

Dudley of Clapton, Northamp., on a ducal coronet or, a woman's head with a helmet thereon, the hair dishevelled and the throat-latch loose ppr.

Dudley, an eagle with wings expanded sa. 77. 5

Dudly, an eagle with wings expanded sa. 77. 5

Dudman, a salmon naiant ppr. 139. 12

Duer, a branch of laurel vert. 151. 13

Duff, Duke of Fife, *see* Fife.

Duff, Robert William, of Fetteresso Castle, Stonehaven, Kincardinesh., a demi-lion rampant gu., holding in his dexter paw a dagger ppr. *Virtute et opera.* 14. 12

Duff, a demi-lion ppr., holding in his dexter paw a sword erect arg., hilt and pommel or, and in his sinister paw a human heart gu., with one wing to it. cf. 14. 12

Duff: (1) A demi-lion rampant holding in his dexter paw a sword in pale ppr., hilted and pommelled or. cf. 14. 12. (2) Out of a naval crown or, inscribed with the word "*Mars,*" a ship-of-war's mast, with the pendent half-mast lowered, all encircled with a wreath of laurel ppr. *Virtute et opera.—Cupressus honores peperit.*

Duff, a demi-lion gu., holding in his dexter paw a broadsword ppr., hilt and pommel or. *Deus juvat.* 14. 12

Duff, the same. *Deus juvabit.*

Duff, a demi-lion gu., holding in his dexter paw a scimitar ppr. *Virtute et opera.* 14. 8

Duff, a lion's head erased within a fetterlock ppr. 19. 5

Duff, Grant-, Rt. Hon. Sir Mountstuart Elphinstone, P.C., G.S.I., Lexden Park, Colchester, a buck's head ppr. *Virtute et opera.*

Duff, Scotland, a hand holding an escallop. *Omnia fortunæ committo.* 216. 2

Duff, Gordon Alexander, Hatton Castle, Aberdeen, Scotland, a stag's head ppr. *Virtute et opera.* 121. 5

Duff, Robert William, Fetteresso Castle, Kincardine, a demi-lion rampant gu., holding a sword in dexter paw ppr., pommel and hilt or. *Virtute et opera.*

Duff, a winged heart ppr. *Kind heart.* 112. 10

Duff, Gordon-, Thomas Duff, of Drummuir Castle, Keith, a man's heart ppr., winged or. *Kind heart.*

Duffe, Ireland, a greyhound courant arg., collared or. cf. 58. 2

Duff-Assheton-Smith, George William, Esquire, of Vaynol Park, near Bangor: (1) Issuant from a mural crown or, two arms embowed, vested az., cuffed arg., holding a pheon or (*for Smith*). (2) A mower in the act of mowing, vested per pale arg. and sa., sleeves and hose counterchanged, cap quarterly arg. and sa., scythe-handle or, blade ppr. (*for Assheton*).

Duff-Sutherland-Dunbar, Sir George, Bart., of Hempriggs, Caithness-sh., and Ackergill Tower, near Wick, Caithness-sh., a sword and key in saltire ppr.

Dufferin and Ava, Marquess of (Hamilton-Temple-Blackwood), Clandeboye, Belfast, Down: (1) On a cap of maintenance gu., turned up erm., a crescent arg. (*for Blackwood*). 245. 3. (2) On a ducal coronet or, a martlet or (*for Temple*). 95. 12. (3) A demi-antelope affrontée erm., attired and ungu. or, holding between his hoofs a heart gu. (*for Hamilton*).

Duffey, Arthur Cameron, Esquire, M.D., R.A.M.C., of 30, Fitzwilliam Place, Dublin, a tower ppr., thereon a banner of the arms displayed. *Deo, Patriæ, Amicis.*

Duffield, late Rev. Matthew Dawson, Canon of Middleham, Vicar of Stebbing, Essex, a dove holding in its beak an olive-branch, all ppr. *Esto semper fidelis.* 92. 5

Duffield, Dawson-, Yorks: (1) A dove holding in its beak an olive-branch ppr. (*for Duffield*). 92. 5. (2) A greyhound passant sa. (*for Dawson*).

Duffield, a bear's head couped sa., muzzled and collared. cf. 34. 14

Duffield of London, a talbot passant or, eared sa., gorged with a plain collar and ringed of the last. cf. 54. 5

Duffin, a griffin segreant ppr. 62. 2

Duffin, Middx., a griffin segreant quarterly arg. and gu., winged and armed or. 62. 2

Duffus, Baron (Dunbar), Scotland, a sword and a key in saltier, both ppr. *Sub spe.* 171. 10

Duffy, an angel ppr. 184. 12

Duffy, Ireland, two palm-branches in orle ppr. 146. 2

Du Fou, a pole-cat passant ppr. 135. 13

Dufrene, a tree ppr. 143. 5

Dugan and Duggan, a talbot statant ppr., collared arg. 54. 2

Dugdale, William Francis Stratford, Merevale Hall, Warwick: (1) A griffin's head and wings endorsed or, gorged with a Garter King of Arms coronet (*for Dugdale*). cf. 67. 11. (2) A dexter arm embowed, habited arg., holding in the hand ppr. a scimitar or (*for Stratford*). *Pestes patriæ pigrities.* cf. 204. 1

Dugdale, James Broughton, Wroxhall Abbey, Warwick, a gryphon's head erm., wings endorsed erminois, gorged with a collar az., therefrom pendent a cross moline gu. *Perseverando.*

Dugdale, Adam, Esquire, of Griffin Lodge, Blackburn, a griffin's head and wings endorsed erminois, gorged with a collar gemelle az., and charged on the neck with a cross moline gu. *Perseverando.*

Dugdale, Frank, Esquire, of Snitterfield, Stratford-on-Avon, same crest and motto.

Dugdale, James Boardman, Esquire, J.P., of Sandford, Wareham, Dorset, same crest and motto.

Dugdale, John Marshall, Esquire, J.P., D.L., of Llwyn, Llanfyllin, same crest and motto.

Dugdale, Arthur George, Esquire, J.P., of Stock House, Sturminster Newton, Dorset, a griffin's head and wings endorsed or, gorged with a Garter King of Arms coronet or. *Pestis patriæ pigrities.*

Dugdale, Lancs and Warw., a griffin's head between two wings addorsed or. *Pestis patriæ pigrities.* cf. 67. 11

Duggan, *see* Dugan.

Duggan, a demi-lion holding between the fore-paws a sword environed by a snake.

Dugmore, Norf., an eagle rising ppr. 77. 5

Dugnall, a cross patée per pale or and gu., between two wings counterchanged. 110. 7

Duguid, Scotland, a dove holding in its beak an olive-branch ppr. *Patientia et spe.* 92. 5

Duguid, Charles James Gordon, Esquire, of Aberdeen, a dove holding a laurel-branch in her beak ppr. *Patientia et spe.* 92. 5

Duguid, William M'Combie, at present residing in Aberdeen, same crest and motto. 92. 5

Duguid-M'Combie, Peter, of Cammachmore, Kincardinesh., and of Easterskene and Lynturk, Aberdeensh., Esquire: (1) On the dexter side, a wild cat sejant ppr. (*for M'Combie*). 25. 2. (2) On the sinister side, a dove holding a laurel-branch in her beak ppr. *Touch not the cat, but a glove.—Patientia et spe.* 92. 5

Du Halgoet, a Moor's head couped at the neck ppr. cf. 192. 13

Duheaume, Jersey, a dexter hand issuant from clouds holding a sprig of three roses, all ppr. 218. 12

Duhig, David John, Esquire, L.R.C.P.E., L.R.C.S.E., L.F.P.S.G., of Little Langtons, Hornchurch, Essex, in front of a holly-tree ppr., a lizard passant or. *Mullaach a bu.*

Duigan, William, Esquire, M.B., B.C., B.A., of 66, Woodstock Road, Oxford, a dexter arm in armour embowed holding in the hand a sword ppr. *Decreir.*

Duignan, William Henry, Esquire, of Gorway House, Walsall, Staffs, an owl at gaze ppr. *Historia magistra vitæ.*

Duine, Ireland, a dexter hand ppr. *Celer atque fidelis.* 222. 14

Duke, Suff., on a plume of five ostrich-feathers, three az., two arg., a sword of the second, hilted or.

Duke, Surrey, Kent, Wilts, and Devonsh., a demi-griffin or, holding a chaplet az. *Another,* the chaplet arg. cf. 64. 2

Duke, Rev. Edward Hungerford, Wickham Rectory, Fareham, Hants, same crest.

Duke, Sir James, Bart., Laughton Lodge, Laughton, Sussex, a demi-gryphon arg., winged az., holding in the beak a peacock's feather ppr., supporting a sword, also ppr., representing that of the city of London. *Gradatim vincimus.* 259. 2

Duke, Olliver Thomas, St. Kilda, The Ridgeway, Wimbledon, a demi-gryphon arg., charged with three annulets interlaced paleways az., holding in the dexter claw a chaplet of the last, and resting the sinister claw on a sword point downwards ppr., pommel and hilt or. *Gradatim vincimus.*

Dukenfield of Dukenfield, Bart., Chesh., out of a ducal coronet or, a dexter cubit arm erect, habited gu., cuffed arg., holding in the hand a sun in splendour. *Ubi amor, ibi fides.* 209. 2

Dukes, a tent ppr. 158. 7

Dukes, Shropsh., an arm in armour ppr., embowed to the sinister, garnished or, holding in the gauntlet a tilting-lance ppr., thereon a forked pennon flowing to the sinister per fess arg. and sa., fringed and tasselled of the second, and charged with an escutcheon of the arms of the Holy Trinity.

Dukley, a falcon's leg erased and belled, all ppr. 113. 8

Dulaney, a winged bull sejant resting his dexter fore-foot upon an open book.

Dumar, on a foreign helmet ppr., two elephants' trunks sa., each charged with a fess arg.

Dumaresq, Henry Rowland Gascoigne, Esquire, J.P., of Mount Ireh, Hadspen, Tasmania, Member of the House of Assembly for Longford, Member of Fisheries Board, a bull passant gardant ppr. *Dum vivo spero.* cf. 45. 2

Dumaresq and **Dumaresque,** out of a mural coronet a demi-lion holding a flag. cf. 16. 7

Dumas, a lion's gamb erased gu. 36. 4

Dumas, Henry John Philip, Esquire, J.P., of the Cedars, Clapham Common, London, S.W., Surrey, issuant from a chaplet of roses an arm embowed in armour ppr., charged with a fleur-de-lis az., and grasping a scythe in bend sinister, also ppr. *Adsum.* 238. 5

Dumbais, an arm in armour embowed fesseways, the shoulder on the wreath, holding a cross crosslet fitched.

Dumbleton, an eagle displayed per pale erm. and erminois. 75. 2

Dumbreck, Scotland, a dexter hand holding a sword in pale, on its point a boar's head couped ppr. *Nocentes prosequor.* 212. 2

Dumfries, Earl of, *see* Bute, Marquess of.

Dummer, Hants, a demi-lion az., holding in its dexter paw a fleur-de-lis or. 13. 2

Du Moulin-Browne, *see* Browne.

Du Mouline, an eagle with wings addorsed preying on an infant swaddled. 77. 13

Dun, five snakes erect on their tails, bound together in the middle by one snake in fess or.

Dun, Somers., three snakes erect gu., tied in the middle in a knot ppr.

Dun, Somers., out of a ducal coronet a bear's paw erect or, grasping a snake ppr. cf. 35. 3

Dun, Scotland, a dexter hand holding a key in bend sinister az. *Mecum habita.* 217. 7

Dun, a dexter hand couped at the wrist ppr. *Celer atque fidelis.* 222. 14

Dun and **Dunn,** within a serpent in orle a boar's head erased and erect, the snout upwards. 41. 11

Dun-Waters, James Cameron, of Craigton, Stirlingsh., a demi-talbot arg., holding in his mouth an arrow gu. *Toujours fidele.* 55. 10

Dunalley, Baron (Prittie), of Kilboy, co. Tipperary, Ireland, a wolf's head erased or. *In omnia paratus.* 30. 8

Dunbar, Baron Duffus, *see* Duffus.

Dunbar of Newton, Scotland, a dexter hand reaching to an astral crown ppr. *Spem vigilantia firmat.*

Dunbar, Sir Archibald, Bart., J.P., D.L., of Northfield, a dexter hand apaumée reaching at an astral crown ppr. *Spem vigilantia firmat.*

Dunbar, Sir Alexander James, Bart., of Boath, co. Nairn, a dexter hand apaumée ppr., reaching to two earls' coronets tied together. *Sub spe.*

Dunbar of Baldoon, Scotland, a horse's head arg., bridled gu. *Firmior quo paratior.* 51. 5

Dunbar, Sir Uthred James Hay, Bart., J.P., D.L., of Mochrum, co. Wigtown, a horse's head arg., bridled gu., a dexter hand couped fesseways ppr., holding the bridle. *In promptu.—Sub spe.—Candoris præmium honos.*

Dunbar, Scotland, a dexter hand couped ppr. 222. 14

Dunbar of Inchbreck, a dexter holding an ear of wheat ppr. *Sapiens non eget.* 218. 14

Dunbar of Leuchit, Scotland, a dexter hand holding a glove ppr. *Sapit qui laborat.* 220. 5

Dunbar of Machermore, Scotland, a lion's head erased arg., crowned with an antique crown or. *Fortis et fidelis.* cf. 17. 12

Dunbar, Sir George Duff Sutherland, Bart., a key and sword in saltire ppr. *Sub spe.*

Dunbar of Hempriggs, a demi-lion holding in the dexter paw a rose gu., slipped and leaved vert. *Ornat fortem prudentia.* 12. 1

Dunbar of Grange, a wreath of laurel ppr. *Sub spe.* 146. 5

Dunbar, two branches of laurel in orle. 146. 5

Dunbar, Sir Drummond Miles, Bart., of Durn, Banff, N.B., two sprigs of laurel in saltire ppr. *Spes dabit auxilium.*

Dunbar of Hillhead, a rose slipped gu. *Olet et sanat.* 149. 5

Dunbar, Ireland, a demi-eagle displayed with two heads imperially crowned.

Dunbar, a griffin's head erased, ducally gorged, and holding in the beak a pheon ppr.

Dunbar, Scotland, a sword and a key in saltier, both ppr. *Sub spe.* 171. 10

Dunbar, a book expanded ppr. *Consulat et ornat.* 158. 3

Dunbar-Brander, Captain James Brander, Esquire, J.P., D.L., of Pitgaveny House, near Elgin: (1) On the dexter side a dove holding a branch of laurel in its beak, both ppr., and in an escroll over, *Silentio et spe.* (2) On the sinister side a dexter hand apaumée pointing to an astral crown ppr. *Spem vigilantia firmat.*

Dunbar-Brunton, James, Esquire, M.B., C.M., of the Manor House, Leatherhead, and of Ladhope, Roxburghsh., N.B., a beacon inflamed, all ppr. *Fax mentis incendium gloriæ.* 177. 14

Dunbar-Buller, Charles William, Esquire, J.P., D.L., of Woburn, co. Down: (1) A Saracen's head affrontée couped at the shoulders ppr. (*for Buller*). (2) A demi-lion rampant or, armed, and charged on the shoulder for distinction with a cross crosslet gu., holding in the dexter paw a red rose ppr., leaved and barbed vert (*for Dunbar*). *Aquila non capit muscas.*

Dunbar-Dunbar, Rev. John Archibald, of Sea Park, Kinloss, and Glen of Rothes, co. Elgin, a dexter hand apaumée reaching to an astral crown ppr. *Sub spe.*

Dunblane, Viscount, *see* Leeds, Duke of.

Dunboyne, Baron of (Butler), Knoppogue Castle, Quin, co. Clare, out of a ducal coronet or, a plume of five ostrich-feathers, therefrom a demi-falcon rising, all arg. *Timor Domini fons vitæ.* cf. 114. 13

Duncan, Viscount, *see* Camperdown, Earl of.

Duncan, *see* Haldane-Duncan-Mercer-Henderson.

Duncan-Morison, *see* Morison.

Duncan, England and Scotland, a ship under sail. *Disce pati.* 160. 13

Duncan, Alexander Lauderdale, Knossington Grange, Oakham, a ship in distress ppr. *Disce pati.* 160. 14

Duncan, Alexander, Parkhill, Arbroath, N.B., same crest and motto.

Duncan, Alexander Robert, Esquire, of Sunnyside, Montrose, same crest and motto.

Duncan, William, Esquire, M.D., of Eythorne, near Dover, Kent, a ship in distress ppr. *Disce pati.*

Duncan, Beveridge-: (1) A ship under sail in the sea ppr., the maintop-sail and the foretop-sail each charged with a cinquefoil gu., and the foretack with a hunting-horn of the last stringed az. (*for Duncan*). cf. 160. 13. (2) Out of a mural crown or, a demi-beaver ppr. (*for Beveridge*). cf. 134. 11

Duncan, a hunting horn ppr. 228. 11

Duncan of Mairdrum, a boar's head erased ppr. 42. 2

Duncan, a dexter hand grasping a scimitar ppr., hilted and pommelled or. *Deo juvante vinco.* 213. 5

Duncan, Scotland, a greyhound ppr., collared or. cf. 60. 2

Duncan of Ardounie, a demi-greyhound ppr., collared or. *Vivat veritas.* 60. 8

Duncan, William McD., of Edgcote Rectory, a demi-greyhound collared gu. *Vivat veritas.*

Duncan, D. J. Russell, of 1, Harley Street, Cavendish Square, W., a demi-greyhound. *Vivat veritas.*

Duncan, John James, Esquire, J.P., of Hughes Park, Watervale, South Australia, a panther's head. *Prudentia ducit.*

Duncan, Ireland, a lion passant or, supporting with the dexter paw a close helmet arg., garnished of the first. cf. 6. 2

Duncannon, Viscount (Ponsonby), Ireland, *see* Bessborough, Earl of.

Duncanson, a dexter hand apaumée ppr. *Mens et manus.* 222. 14

Dunch, Berks, out of a ducal coronet or, an heraldic antelope's head az., maned and attired of the first.

Dunch, Berks, a demi-heraldic antelope az., bezantée, armed, maned, and attired or.

Duncombe, Earl of Feversham, *see* Feversham.

Duncombe, Alfred Charles, Esquire, of Calwich Abbey, Ashbourne, Derbysh., out of a ducal coronet or, a horse's hind-leg sa., the shoe arg. *Deo regi patriæ.* 123. 6

Duncombe, Pauncefort-, Sir Everard Philip Digby, Bart., J.P., of Great Brickhill Manor, Bucks: (1) Out of a ducal coronet or, a horse's hind-leg sa., the shoe arg., charged for distinction with a cross crosslet or (*for Duncombe*). *cf.* 123. 6. (2) A lion rampant arg., ducally crowned or (*for Pauncefort*). *Non fecimus ipsi.* 1. 12

Duncombe, Bucks, a talbot's head erased gu., eared sa., collared arg. *Non fecimus ipsi.* 56. 1

Duncombe, Scotland, a demi-lion ppr. 10. 2

Duncombe-Eden, Slingsby Arthur, Esquire, J.P., D.L., of Beamish Park, Chester-le-Street, Durh., a dexter arm embowed in armour arg., the upper encircled by an annulet gu., the hand grasping a garb bendways or.

Dundas, *see* Zetland, Earl of.

Dundas, Viscount Melville, *see* Melville.

Dundas of Blair Castle, Perth, a lion's head affrontée gu., looking through a bush of oak ppr. *Essayez.* 21. 9

Dundas, Sir Sydney James, Bart., of Beechwood, Midlothian, a lion's head affrontée in a bush of oak, all ppr. *Essayez.* 21. 7

Dundas of Dundas, Adam Alexander, Inchgarvie House, South Queensferry, N.B., a lion's head affrontée looking through a bush of oak ppr. *Essayez.* 21. 9

Dundas, Sir Robert, Bart., of Arniston, Gorebridge, Midlothian, and Polton House, Lasswade, N.B., same crest and motto.

Dundas, a lion's face affrontée within two branches of laurel in orle. 21. 11

Dundas, Whitley-Deans-, of Barton Court, Berks: (1) A lion's head affrontée ppr., ducally crowned or, looking through a bush of oak fructed, also ppr. (*for Dundas*). *cf.* 21. 7. (2) A buck's head couped arg., attired or, charged on the neck with a rose gu. for distinction (*for Whitley*). *cf.* 121. 5. (3) A sword erect ppr., on the top thereof a cross patée az. (*for Deans*). *Essayez.—Live to live.—Arte vel marte.* 169. 5

Dundas, a demi-lion gardant ppr., issuing out of a bush of oak vert. *Essayez.* *cf.* 10. 8

Dundas of Kinkevel, a lion's gamb erect ppr. *Essayez hardiment.* *cf.* 36. 4

Dundas, a lion's head couped or. *Essayez.* 21. 1

Dundas, on a chapeau a flame of fire, all ppr. 180. 10

Dundas, Scotland, a salamander in flames ppr. *Extinguo.* 138. 4

Dundas, Hamilton-, of Duddingston: (1) A dexter hand holding a mullet az. (*for Dundas*). 216. 7. (2) A hand grasping a spear in bend ppr. (*for Hamilton*). *Essayez.—Et arma, et virtus.* 214. 11

Dundas, Commander Colin Mackenzie, R.N., of Ochtertyre, Stirling, N.B., a dexter cubit arm erect, holding in the hand ppr. a mullet az. *Essayez.* 216. 7

Dundas of Duddingston, a dexter hand holding a star az. *Essayez.* 243. 9

Dundas, a hand holding a scroll. *Revise.* 215. 6

Dundonald, Earl of (Cochrane), Gwrych Castle, Abergele, North Wales, a horse passant arg. *Virtute et labore.* 52. 6

Dune, a mullet quarterly or and sa. 164. 2

Dunfermline, Baron (Abercromby), a bee erect ppr. 137. 1

Dunford, a wheat-ear slipped or. 154. 3

Dunford, a lion's head erased arg., holding in the mouth a dexter hand couped at the wrist ppr. 21. 2

Dunfee of London, a lion's head erased, pierced in the neck with a sword in bend dexter. *Esse quam videri.* 17. 13

Dungan, Ireland, a lion passant or, supporting with the dexter paw a close helmet arg., garnished of the first. *cf.* 6. 2

Dungan, Ireland, an orb arg., banded and surmounted by a cross patée or.

Dungannon, Viscount (Hill-Trevor), Ireland, a wyvern with wings elevated and tail nowed sa., ducally gorged or. *Quid verum atque decens.* 70. 2

Dungarvan, Viscount, *see* Cork, Earl of.

Dunglass, Lord, *see* Home, Earl of.

Dunham, Lincs. a martin passant or, between two spears erect ppr.

Dunies, Scotland and England, two palm branches in orle ppr. 146. 2

Dunk, a lion's head collared or. *cf.* 18. 6

Dunkellin, Lord, *see* Clanricarde, Marquess of.

Dunkin, an arm in armour couped at the elbow in fess, holding in the hand a cross crosslet fitched. 211. 14

Dunkin, Ireland, an eel naiant ppr. 142. 10

Dunkley, William Wilberforce, Esquire, F.R.C.P., Hon. Assoc. Grand Priory Order of Hospital of St. John of Jerusalem in England, a falcon's leg erased at the thigh, belled and jessed, all ppr. *Facta non verba.* *cf.* 113. 8

Dunleath, Baron (Mulholland), Ballywalter Park, Ballywalter, co. Down, an escallop gu. *Semper præcinctus.*

Dunlo, Viscount, *see* Clancarty, Earl of.

Dunlop, between the attires of a stag az., a cross patée arg. *cf.* 123. 5

Dunlop, Scotland, a rose ppr. *E spinis.* 149. 5

Dunlop, William Hamilton, of Doonside, Scotland, a dexter hand holding a dagger erect ppr. *Merito.* 212. 9

Dunlop, Scotland, a dexter hand holding a sword ppr. *Merito.* 212. 13

Dunlop, George James, Esquire, of the Hermitage, St. Mark's, Cheltenham, a dexter hand holding a dagger in bend sinister ppr. *Merito.—E spinis.* 212. 3

Dunlop, Scotland, a dexter hand holding a dagger in bend sinister ppr. *Merito.—E spinis.*

Dunlop, William Hamilton, Esquire, of Doonside, Ayrsh., N.B., a dexter cubit arm erect grasping a dagger, all ppr., the arm charged with a cinquefoil erm. *Merito.*

Dunluce, Viscount, *see* Antrim, Earl of.

Dunmill, Kent, a unicorn's head issuing ppr. *Nec tardo.* 49. 7

Dunmore, Earl of (Murray), of Blair, Moulin, and Tillymott, Scotland, a demi-savage wreathed about the head and loins with oak, holding in the dexter hand a sword erect ppr., pommel and hilt or, and in the sinister a key of the last. *Furth fortune and fill the fetters.* 186. 2

Dunn, Sir William, Bart., the Retreat, Lakenheath, Brandon, Suff., in front of a cornucopia fessewise or, an arm erect ppr., holding in bend sinister a key of the first. *Vigilans et audax.* 242. 3

Dunn, Alfred Calvert, Esquire, in front of a windmill ppr., an estoile between two mullets of six points or. *Perge sed caute.*

Dunn, Eustace Alexandria Andrew, same crest and motto.

Dunn, Frederick Williams, Esquire, of Park View House, Hackney, South Australia, same crest and motto.

Dunn, *see* Dun.

Dunn, Scotland, a dexter hand ppr., holding a key in bend sinister or. *Mecum habito.* 217. 7

Dunn and **Dunne,** two swords in saltier ppr., entwined by a ribbon az., thereto a key pendent sa. 171. 14

Dunn, Durh., five snakes erect on their tails, tied together round the middle by one snake in fess or.

Dunn, six snakes erect contrary posed, three and three, encircled with a ribbon.

Dunn, Scotland, on the point of a sword in pale a garland of laurel, all ppr. 170. 1

Dunn and **Dunne,** two lion's gambs supporting a pillar ppr. 39. 8

Dunn, William Allison, Esquire, M.R.C.S., of Millom, Cumb., in front of a bear's paw erect ppr., grasping a serpent entwined around it, three buckles, all or. *Facta non verba.* 231. 20

Dunn, Ireland, in front of a tree a lizard passant, all ppr. *Vigilans et audax.*

Dunn, Oxon., a Mamaluke on horseback, holding in his dexter hand a scimitar, all ppr. *Absque metu.* 189. 8

Dunn and **Dunne,** Ireland, three holly-leaves ppr., banded gu. 150. 12

Dunnage, a parrot holding in its beak a branch of cherry-tree, all ppr. *cf.* 101. 4

Dunnage, a sword in pale enfiled with a leopard's face. 22. 1

Dunnet, Scotland, on a rock a fox ppr. *Non terra, sed aquis.* *cf.* 32. 2

Dunning, Scotland and England, a demi-talbot rampant holding in its mouth an arrow. 55. 10

Dunning, an antelope's head couped at the neck ppr., attired or. *Studiis et rebus honestis.* *cf.* 126. 2

Dunning, Edwin Harris, Esquire, of Stoodleigh Court, Stoodleigh, North

Devonsh., Easterlands, Washfield, Tiverton, an antelope's head couped at the neck ppr., gorged with a chain gu., pendent therefrom an escutcheon arg., charged with two annulets interlaced fesseways sa., between as many acorns slipped and leaved ppr. *Fide et animo.*

Dunnington-Jefferson, Joseph John, Esquire, of Thicket Priory, Yorks: (1) A griffin sejant, wings endorsed or, gorged with a collar gemelle az., in the beak a lily slipped ppr. (*Jefferson*). (2) A horse courant arg., gorged with a collar gu., charged with a bezant between two annulets or (*for Dunnington*). *A cruce salus.*

Dunock, a wyvern. 70. 1

Dunphy, Henry Michael, Esquire, Barrister-at-Law, a pelican in her piety ppr., gorged with an antique Irish crown gu., the nest charged with a mullet, also gu. *Generosa virtus nihil timet.* cf. 98. 14

Dunraven and Mount Earl, Earl of (Wyndham-Quin): (1) A wolf's head erased erm. (*for Quin*). 30. 8. (2) A lion's head erased within a fetterlock and chain or (*for Wyndham*). *Quæ sursum volo videre.* 19. 4

Dunsandle and Clan Conal, Baron (Daly), of Dunsandle, co. Galway, in front of an oak-tree ppr., a greyhound courant sa. *Deo fidelis et regi.* 58. 5

Dunsany, Baron (Plunkett), of Dunsany Castle, co. Meath, Ireland, a horse passant arg. *Festina lente.* 52. 6

Dunscombe, Clement, Esquire, M.A., L.C.E., of the Laurels, Halliford-on-Thames, Middx., and Albert Mansions, 92, Victoria Street, Westminster, S.W., out of a ducal coronet or, a horse's fore-leg sa., hoof arg. *Fidelitas vincit.* 123. 6

Dunscombe, Parker, Esquire, same crest and motto.

Dunsford, Devonsh., out of a ducal coronet a demi-lion rampant. 16. 3

Dunsford, out of a mural coronet an eagle's head ppr. 83. 9

Dunsford, Follett, Esquire, of Cardigan, Southampton, and Royal Southampton Yacht Club: (1) On a mount a stag trippant regardant ppr. (2) A beehive ppr., bees volant. *Forward.—Industria temperantia et Gratia Dei.*

Dunsmure, Henry, Esquire, of Glenbruach, Callander, N.B., Scotland, an anchor or. *Spes anchora tuta.* 161. 1

Dunsmure, James, Esquire, M.D., F.R.C.S.E., of 53, Queen Street, Edinburgh, same crest and motto.

Dunsmure, Alexander, of Glenbruach, Perthsh., Scotland, an anchor erect or. 161. 1

Dunstable, a swan's head arg., between two wings sa. 101. 6

Dunstaville and **Dunstavile,** a demi-friar holding a lash. 187. 11

Dunster, out of the top of a tower arg., an arm embowed, vested gu., cuffed of the first, holding in the hand ppr. a tilting-spear sa. 204. 7

Dunston or **Duston,** a man's head in profile ppr. 191. 1

Dunston, Frederick Warburton, Esquire, of Burltons, Donhead, Salisbury, a cock gu., combed and wattled, and between the two antlers of a stag or. *Fortis et vigilans.*

Duntze, Sir George Alexander, Bart., a mullet between two eagle's wings. (*Not recorded.*) *Nunquam præponens.* 111. 5

Dunville, Robert Grimshaw, Esquire, of Redburn, Holywood, co. Down, and of Turf Club, Piccadilly, London, W., and John Dunville Dunville, Esquire, of 7, Norfolk Street, Park Lane, and of White's Club, St. James's Street, two lion's gambs erect and erased ppr. *Qui stat caveat ne cadat.* 36. 5

Dunwich, Viscount, *see* Stradbroke, Earl of.

Dupa or **Duppa,** an acorn slipped and leaved ppr. 152. 1

Duperier of Totnes, Devonsh., a lion's head erased and crowned or, langued gu. *Ni vanité, ni faiblesse.* 18. 8

Duperon, on a chapeau a martlet, all ppr. 95. 1

Dupont, a flag or, the staff ppr. 176. 15

Du Plat, Major-General Sir Charles Taylor, of Ashley, Winchfield, Hants, on a French noble coronet a plate and mullet of five points or. *Nil actum si quid agendum.*

Du Port, on a rock arg., guttée-de-sang, a falcon ppr., beaked and legged gu. 86. 7

Duppa, Kent, an arm in armour holding in the hand a lion's gamb erased or.

Dupplin, Viscount, *see* Kinnoul, Earl of.

Dupre, a rose per fess or and az. cf. 149. 6

Dupre, a rose slipped ppr. 149. 5

Dupre, William Baring, Wilton Park, Beaconsfield, Bucks, a lion rampant arg., resting the dexter hind-foot on a fleur-de-lis gu. cf. 1. 13

Dupree, a lion rampant arg. 1. 13

Dupuy, a demi-griffin. 64. 2

Durand, Sir Edward Law, Bart., Ruckley Grange, Shifnal, Salop, over a rock ppr. a crescent arg., between two laurel-branches or. *Esperance en Dieu.* 262. 9

Durand, Sir Henry Mortimer, G.C.M.G., of the British Embassy, Madrid, same crest.

Durand, a yew-tree ppr. 143. 1

Durand, a demi-lion gu. *In misericordia Dei confido.* 10. 3

Durant, Middx., a dragon passant gu., holding in the dexter claw a sword erect arg., the point embrued, the hilt and pommel or, and on the blade a ducal coronet of the last. cf. 73. 2

Durant, out of a ducal coronet or, a greyhound's head sa., charged with an étoile of the first. cf. 61. 9

Durant, a boar arg., bristled, armed, an ungu. or, pierced in the side with a broken spear ppr., vulned gu. cf. 40. 14

Durant, Charles Richard, of 13, Egerton Gardens, South Kensington, a boar bendy of six or and sa., pierced through the back by a sword in bend sinister ppr., and resting the dexter foot upon a cross crosslet gu. *Beati qui durant.* 40. 3

Durant, a fleur-de-lis arg. 148. 2

Durant, Thomas, Esquire, of 5, Guildhall Chambers, E.C., a boar passant, per fesse wavy arg. and gu., bristled and tusked az., and pierced through the body with a broken lance bendways sa., the head downwards or. *Beati qui durant.*

D'Urban, the sun shining on the stump of a tree ppr. 145. 5

Durban, Somers., a talbot passant regardant liver-coloured, charged on the shoulder with a bezant, the dexter paw supporting a lance or, headed ppr., thereon a banner displayed gu., charged with a gauntlet arg. 54. 4

Durban and **Durbin,** issuing from a cloud in the sinister a dexter arm holding a club, all ppr. 223. 5

D'Urban, William Stewart Mitchell, of Newport House, near Exeter, in front of a palm-tree a sphinx couchant. *Firme.*

Durborough, a demi-chevalier holding in his dexter hand a sword, all ppr. 187. 1

Durell of London, a Saracen's head affrontée ppr., on the head a cap az., fretty arg., tufted or, doubled erm., wreathed about the temples or and az. 190. 1

Durham, Earl of (Lambton), Lambton Castle, Durham, a ram's head cabossed arg., armed sa. *Le jour viendra.* 130. 7

Durham, a cannon mounted ppr. 169. 12

Durham, Scotland, a hand pulling a thistle ppr. *Vive Deo.* 218. 5

Durham, Scotland, an increscent gu. *Augeor dum progredior.* 163. 3

Durham, a dolphin ppr. 140. 5

Durham, a dolphin haurient. 140. 11

Durham of Ardownie, Scotland, a dolphin naiant ppr. *Ulterius.* 140. 5

Durham of Largo, Scotland, on a baron's coronet a dolphin, all ppr. *Victoria non præda.* cf. 140. 4

Durham of Grange, Scotland, two dolphins haurient addorsed ppr. *Ultra fert animus.* 140. 1

Durie and **Dury,** Scotland, a dove volant holding an olive-branch in its beak, all ppr. 92. 5

Durie and **Dury,** a dove regardant holding an olive-branch in its beak ppr. 92. 4

During, a hand in fess couped at the wrist and gauntleted holding a dagger, thereon a savage's head couped affrontée, all ppr. 211. 11

Durley, a horse's head couped az., gorged with an Eastern coronet or.

Durnard, Scotland, a cross patée fitched arg. *This I'll defend.* 166. 3

Durnford, a dagger in pale ppr. 169. 2

Durning, Lancs, a demi-antelope erased az. cf. 126. 5

Durning-Lawrence, Sir Edwin, B.A., LL.B., of King's Ride, Ascot, Berks, a wolf's head erased arg., crusily, and charged with a pair and compasses extended sa. *Per ardua stabilis.* 276. 3

Durno, Scotland, a hand holding a sword in pale. *Ex recto decus.*

Durno, a hand brandishing a sword ppr. 212. 9

Durrant, Ireland, on a ducal coronet a peacock, all ppr. 103. 8

Durrant, Derbysh., a lion rampant arg., holding in the dexter paw a fleur-de-lis or, and in the mouth a sword point downwards ppr., hilt and pommel of the second. cf. 2. 7

Durrant, Norf., a boar passant per fess wavy arg. and gu., bristled and tusked az., pierced through the body by a broken lance in bend sa., the head downwards or. *cf.* 40. 9

Durrant, Sir William Robert Estridge, Bart., of Scottow, Norf., a boar passant per fesse wavy arg. and gu., bristled and tusked az., and pierced through the body with a broken lance bendways sa., the head downwards gold. *Lobes pejor morte.*

Dursley, Viscount, *see* Berkeley, Earl.

Durward, Scotland, a demi-man ppr., vested gu., holding a gem-ring. 185. 9

Durward, a dexter hand holding a seax cutting at a pen, all ppr. 213. 9

Dury, *see* Durie.

Dusautoy, a hand holding a sickle ppr. 219. 13

Dusgate, Richard Dusgate, Esquire, of Fring Hall, King's Lynn, Norf., a lion's head erased sa. 17. 8

Dusseaux, a ram's head erased arg., armed or. 130. 6

Duston and **Dustone,** a man's head couped ppr. 190. 12

Duthie, a dexter arm erect ppr., holding a sword in pale of the last, hilt and pommel or. *Data, fata, secutus.* 212. 13

Dutton, Baron Sherborne, *see* Sherborne.

Dutton, a plume of five ostrich-feathers arg. *cf.* 114. 13

Dutton, Edward George, Esquire, M.R.C.S.E., L.S.A., M.B., of Sherborne, Lipson Road, Plymouth, a plume of five ostrich-feathers ppr. *Servabo fidem.*

Dutton, Chesh., out of a ducal coronet a plume of five ostrich-feathers gu., az., or, vert and tenné. 114. 13

Dutton of Burland Hall, Chester, out of a ducal coronet or, a plume of five ostrich-feathers arg., az., or, vert and gu. *Servabo fidem.* 114. 13

Dutton, Frank Macdermott, Esquire, of 74, Lancaster Gate, London, W., a fret fessewise gu., in front of a plume of five ostrich-feathers alternately or and arg. *Servabo fidem.* 231. 16

Dutton, Henry, Esquire, of Anlaby, Kapunda, South Australia, same crest and motto.

Duval and **Duvall,** a lion sejant per pale arg. and gu., supporting an escutcheon of the first, charged with a bend of the second. *cf.* 8. 8

Duval of London, on a globe a monkey sejant holding in its dexter fore-paw a slip of palm, all ppr.

Duval and **Duvall,** a dexter arm embowed holding in the hand a spear, all ppr.

Duvernet or **Duvernette,** a stag trippant ppr. 117. 8

Duxbury, on the stump of a tree growing out of a mount vert, a dove rising ppr. 93. 8

Dwaris, of London, a demi-lion rampant arg., pellettée, holding in the paws a battle-axe or. 15. 4

Dwire, Ireland, a hand holding a sword in bend sinister. 212. 13

Dwyre, out of a mural coronet a lion's head charged with a torteau. *cf.* 19. 12

Dwyre, Ireland, two lion's heads erased and addorsed ppr. 17. 3

Dy or **Dye,** on a ducal coronet or, a swan with wings addorsed and ducally gorged, all ppr.

Dyall, an armed arm holding a banner charged with a cross patée as in the arms.

Dyas, out of a ducal coronet a hand holding by the neck a swan's head erased. 220. 7

Dyas, Henry Mortimer, Esquire, of Bolton, Kells, co. Meath, a leopard's face. *Refulgens in tenebris.*

Dyce of Disblair, Aberdeen, Scotland, an escutcheon gu. *Dare.* (*From an old seal, 1745, not recorded in Lyon Office.*) 176. 10

Dyce, Aberdeen, Scotland, a demi-tiger gardant ppr., gorged with a mural crown gu., on the head an Eastern crown or, supporting in the paws a flagstaff, thereon hoisted a flag per bend embattled arg. and vert, surmounted by a sword in bend sinister ppr., pommel and hilt or. *Decide and dare.* (*Granted, 1797, to Lieutenant-General Alexander Dyce, H.E.I.C.S., Madras Establishment.*) 228. 5

Dyce, James Stirling, Esquire, of 8, Lawrence Mansions, Chelsea, London, S.W., a lion rampant gardant sa., murally gorged arg., sustaining a flagstaff ppr., thereon hoisted a banner party per bend embattled or and gu., charged with a leopard's face counterchanged, and in an escroll over the same this motto, *Decide and dare.* 1. 2

Dyce-Sombre: (1) Out of an Eastern crown or, a demi-tiger issuant vert, striped or, holding between the paws a flagstaff ppr., thereon hoisted a banner per bend embattled arg. and of the second, charged with a scimitar in bend sinister, also ppr., pommel and hilt of the first (*for Dyce*). 228. 8. (2) The "Chattie" or parasol of State of Sirdhana (*for Sombre*). *Favente numine.* (*Granted, 1838, to Colonel David Ochterlony Dyce-Sombre of Sirdhana, in the province of Agra, in the East Indies, sometime Commander of the Troops of the late Princess Begum Sumroo, Independent Sovereign of Sirdhana, elder son of Colonel George Alexander Dyce of Aberdeenshire*).

(*These four entries relate to the same family.*)

Dycer, a griffin's head erased arg., ducally gorged or. *cf.* 66. 11

Dycher, a bear passant arg. *cf.* 34. 5

Dychfield, Essex, Oxon., and Lancs, a porcupine. 136. 5

Dye, *see* Dy.

Dyer, Sir Thomas Swinnerton, Bart., of Tottenham, Middx., out of a ducal coronet or, a goat's head arg., armed of the first. *Terrere nolo, timere nescio.* 128. 14

Dyer, a goat's head erased arg., holding in the mouth a pansy ppr., stalked and leaved vert. *cf.* 128. 5

Dyer, Herts, a goat's head erased ppr., holding in the mouth a rose arg. *cf.* 128. 5

Dyer, out of a crown vallery or, a goat's head sa., armed and gorged with a collar gemelle of the first.

Dyer, out of a ducal coronet or, a goat's head arg., armed of the first. *Terrere nolo, timere nescio.* 128. 14

Dyer of Roundhill and Wincanton, Somers., and Stoughton, Hunts, out of a ducal coronet or, a goat's head sa., armed gold. 128. 14

Dyer, Sidney Reginald, M.D., the Rockery, Stafford, same crest. *Ché sarà sarà.*

Dyer, an old man's head in profile couped at the shoulders ppr., the hair arg., the beard sa., and his cap or, turned up chequy arg. and az.

Dyer, a demi-lion rampant gu., armed and langued az. *Ché sarà sarà.* 10. 3

Dyes, a demi-lion rampant vert. 10. 2

Dyke, Rt. Hon. Sir William Hart, Bart., P.C., of Horsham, Sussex, a cubit arm in armour, the hand in a gauntlet sa., garnished or, holding a cinquefoil slipped, also sa.

Dykes, Wilts, Kent, and Surrey, an eagle's head sa. 83. 1

Dykes, Ballantine-, Frecheville Hubert, Dovenby Hall, Cockermouth, a lobster vert. *Prius frangitur quam flectitur.* 141. 2

Dylke, a dove arg., beaked and membered gu. 92. 2

Dylkes, a dove holding in its beak an olive-branch, all ppr. 92. 5

Dymock, *alias* **Collier,** Staffs, a demi-negro ppr., with pearls in his ears arg., holding in the hand an oak-branch ppr., fructed or.

Dymock, Dymok, or **Dymoke,** Devonsh., out of a ducal coronet or, a rod raguly vert. 147. 10

Dymock, Shropsh., an arm in armour erect ppr., holding a tilting-spear sa., headed arg., embrued gu. *Pro rege et lege Dimico.* 210. 11

Dymock, Warw., a hand and arm in armour erect ppr., holding a tilting-spear sa., headed arg., embrued gu. *cf.* 210. 11

Dymock of Penley Hall, Flintsh., and Ellesmere, Shropsh., same crest. *Pro rege et lege Dimico.*

Dymock, T. Vaughton, of 7, Cavendish Place, Bath, a dexter arm in armour embowed to the sinister holding in the gauntlet a lance in bend sinister, all ppr. *Dimico pro rege.*

Dymoke of Scrivelsby, Lincs, **Honourable** the **King's Champion:** (1) A sword erect arg., hilt and pommel or. 170. 2. (2) A lion passant arg., ducally crowned or. *cf.* 6. 2. (3) The scalp of a hare, the ears erect ppr. *Pro rege Dimico.* 133. 11

Dymoke, Wells-, Edmund Lionel, Esquire, of Shrubs Hill, Sunningdale, Berks, the two ears of an ass sa. *Pro rege Dimico.* 123. 11

Dymoke, Frank Scaman, of Scrivelsby Court, Horncastle, Lincs, same crest and motto.

Dymon, a demi-lion holding in the dexter paw a fusil gu., charged with a fleur-de-lis or. *Semper constans.* *cf.* 13. 2

Dymond, Devonsh., a lady's arm from the elbow erect, enfiled with a bracelet. 222. 6

Dyndy, a dragon's head erased vert. *cf.* 71. 2

Dyne or **Dynne,** Norf., a plume of feathers or. 115. 1

Dyne and **Dynne**, Norf., out of a ducal coronet a merlin's sinister wing arg. 109. 4

Dyne, John Bradley, Esquire, M.A., of the Grove, Highgate, N., and 4, Stone Buildings, Lincoln's Inn, a heraldic antelope's head erased, collared arg. *Nec decipere nec decipi.*

Dyneley, out of a ducal coronet or, a dragon's head of the same. 72. 4

Dynevor, Baron (Rice), of Dynevor, Carmarthen, a raven sa. *Secret et hardi.* 107. 14

Dynham, a bell az. 168. 7

Dynham of Wortham, an arm couped or, the hand arg., holding a lock of hair sa. *Sis tenax.*

Dynham, in a round top or, six spears, in the centre a pennon arg., thereon a cross gu.

Dyon, on an escallop or, the point in base, a lion passant sa.

Dyott, Lieutenant-General Richard, of Freeford, Lichfield, a heraldic tiger passant arg., armed and langued gu., collared, chained (the chain reflexed over the back and passing between the hind-legs), and ringed, also gu.

Dyott, Lieutenant-General Richard, Freeford, Staffs, a tiger passant arg., armed or, collared, lined, and ringed gu.

Dyrward, Dyrwarne, and **Dyrrwarne**, a cup or. 177. 4

Dysart, Earl of (Tollemache), Perthsh., and of Buckminster Park, Grantham, a horse's head erased gu., between two wings expanded or, pelletée. *Confido, conquiesco.* cf. 51. 3

Dyson, Staffs, on a mount vert, a paschal lamb arg., the head surrounded by a nimbus or, with a banner ppr. cf. 131. 2

Dyve, between two bat's wings gu., a horse's head reversed vert.

Dyx, *see* Dix.

Dyx, a greyhound's head erased arg., ducally gorged gu., between two wings, the dexter or, the sinister sa.

Dyxon, a demi-hind sa., bezantée.

Dyxton, a palm-tree fructed and leaved all ppr. 144. 1

E.

Eade, Norwich, a leopard's face arg. 22. 2

Eadon, a mitre or, charged with a chevron gu. cf. 180. 5

Eady, a fleur-de-lis environed with a serpent. 148. 8

Eaens, on a mount vert, a Cornish chough ppr. 107. 5

Eagar, a quill in pale ppr.

Eagar, Rev. Alexander Ricchard, D.D., St.Gorran Vicarage,St. Austell,Cornw., on a wreath of the colours a demi-lion az., gorged with an antique Irish crown and charged on the shoulder with a mullet or. *Facta non verba.*

Eagle, Suff., a lion's gamb erect and erased or, grasping an eagle's leg erased at the thigh gu. 38. 2

Eagles, two lion's gambs in saltier ppr. 39. 14

Eaglesfield and **Eglesfield**, out of a tower a demi-greyhound holding in the dexter foot a branch of palm ppr. 157. 8

Eaines, a demi-lion rampant gu. 10. 3

Ealand, Yorks, an arrow in pale arg. 173. 5

Eales of London and Bucks, on an eel embowed vert an eagle displayed ppr.

Eales, a lion's gamb holding up a human heart ppr. 39. 11

Eales, Lionel George Nuttall, Esquire, a bear's paw erased fessewise az., holding a fleur-de-lis and encircled by an annulet, both or. *Nec parvis sisto.*

Eam of London and Berks, a demi-lion rampant sa. 10. 1

Eamer, a hind trippant az. 124. 12

Eamer of London, out of a ducal coronet a demi-lion rampant gardant ppr., collared or, holding in the dexter paw a dagger of the first. *Strenuè et prosperè.*

Eames, Somers., a demi-lion rampant sa. 10. 1

Eardley-Twistleton-Fiennes, Baron Saye and Sele, *see* Saye.

Eardley, a sword in pale ppr., enfiled with a leopard's face gu. 22. 1

Eardley, Bart. (*extinct*), of Hadley, Middx.: (1) A stag courant gu., attired or (*for Eardley*). cf. 118. 13. (2) A falcon with wings endorsed ppr., belled or, holding in the beak an acorn slipped and leaved, also ppr. (*for Smith*). *Spes decus et robur.* cf. 88. 2

Earl, a nag's head erased sa., maned or. 51. 4

Earl, on the point of a tilting-spear ppr., headed arg., a dolphin naiant of the first. 140. 9

Earl, Berks, a lion's head erased or, pierced by a broken dart ppr. cf. 17. 8

Earle, Lincs, a lion's head erased or, pierced through the head by a broken spear arg., point embrued gu. cf. 17. 8

Earle, Scotland, a nag's head erased sa., maned or. 51. 4

Earle, John, Esquire, B.A., of 4, the Crescent, Ripon, a horse's head couped. *Dum spiro spero.*

Earle, a lion's gamb erect and erased holding an arrow in bend sinister point downwards, all ppr. cf. 38. 4

Earle, Sir Henry, Bart., D.L., J.P., of Allerton Tower, Lancs, a lion's gamb erased holding an arrow in bend sinister point downwards ppr., and pendent by a chain or, an escutcheon gu., charged with an escallop, also or. *Servare modum.* 38. 4

Earle, Arthur, Esquire, F.R.G.S., J.P., of Chidwall Lodge, Wavertree, Liverpool, same crest.

Earle, Nicholas, Esquire, of Ashton-under-Lyne, Lancs, upon a mount vert, a lion's gamb erased az., grasping a battle-axe in bend sinister and encircled by a wreath of oak ppr. *Ne tentes aut perfice.* 38. 6

Earle, George Hudson, Esquire, of Rocklands, Torquay, a lion's head erased or, charged with two escallops gu. and in front of two spears in saltire ppr. *Magna est veritas.* 260. 8

Earles, a cross gu., between two wings erm.

Earlsfort, Lord, *see* Clonmell, Earl.

Earlsman of Westover, Isle of Wight, a greyhound's head couped arg., guttée-de-poix, collared az., rimmed and studded or. 61. 2

Earnley, Sussex, a savage's head affrontée couped at the shoulders, round the temples a wreath, issuing therefrom a plume of three ostrich-feathers, all ppr. cf. 192. 10

Earnshaw, a cross patée fitched or, fimbriated gu. 166. 3

East, Bart., a horse erm., supporting with the dexter fore-leg a cross Calvar in bend sinister sa. *Æquo pede propera.* cf. 52. 9

East, Herbert Hinton D'Este-, Esquire, of Bourton House, Moreton-in-the-Marsh, Glouc., a horse passant erm., the dexter fore-leg supporting a Passion cross in bend sinister sa. cf. 52. 9

East, D'Este-, Herbert, Esquire, of Bourton House, Moreton-in-le-Marsh, Glouc., same crest.

East, Bucks and Berks, a horse passant sa. *J'avance.* 52. 6

East, Clayton, Sir Gilbert Augustus, Bart., of Hall Place, Berks: (1) A horse passant sa. (*for East*). (2) Out of a mural crown gu., a leopard's paw erect arg., charged with a crescent and grasping a pellet (*for Clayton*). *J'avance.* cf. 39. 13

Eastchurch, the sun rising from behind a cloud ppr. 162. 5

Eastday, Kent, on a mount vert, a hind lodged ppr. 125. 4

Easten, Arthur Henry, Esquire, of the Durrant, Sevenoaks, Kent, an oak-tree.

Eastfield, a hawk with wings expanded ppr., beaked, legged, and belled or. 87. 1

Eastlake, Charles Lock, Long Sutton House, Langport, a griffin passant. *Utere sorte tua.*

Easthope, Surrey, out of a vallery coronet or, a horse's head arg., maned of the first, charged on the neck with two bendlets engrailed az. 50. 1

Eastland, an arm in armour embowed ppr., holding a fleur-de-lis or. 199. 14

Eastman, a swan collared and lined ppr. 99. 1

Eastnor, Viscount, *see* Somers, Earl.

Eastoft, a dagger and a pen in saltier ppr. *Artis vel martis.* cf. 170. 4

Eastoft, a stork with an eel in its beak ppr. cf. 105. 8

Easton, Devonsh., a yew-tree ppr. 143. 1

Easton, Scotland, a demi-chevalier in armour brandishing a sword, all ppr. 187. 1

Eastwood, *see* Murphy-Eastwood.

Eastwood, on a ducal coronet per pale or and gu., a lion passant gardant of the same, crowned ppr. 6. 4

Eastwood, Frederick, Esquire, of Buckden Mount, Huddersfield, upon the battlements of a tower ppr. a lion passant gu., guttée-d'or, supporting with the dexter fore-paw a battle-axe erect also ppr. *Oriens sylva.*

Eastwood, Harry Arnold, of Thorpe House, Almondbury, Huddersfield, same crest.

Eastwood, William Seymour, Esquire, of Esher Lodge, Esher, Surrey, upon the battlements of a tower per pale arg. and gu., and in front of a lance erect ppr., therefrom flowing to the sinister a pennant az., a lion passant gardant per pale of the second and first, resting upon the dexter forepaw a fountain ppr. *Nil desperandum.* 5. 7

Eastwood, Charles John Ebden, Baldslow Place, St. Leonard's-on-Sea, same crest. *Spes sibi quis que.*

Eastwood, C. Edmund, Esquire, of Malvern Wells, Worcs., on a wreath of the colours issuant from a wreath of oak a well ppr., thereon a swan arg., beaked and legged sa. *Per fidem vinco.* 100. 3

Eastwood, a boar passant ppr. 40. 9

Eastwood, Captain R. J. C., of Castletown, co. Louth, and The Fews, Ireland, a wild boar passant az., charged with a castle arg., and holding a branch of acorns in its mouth ppr. *Oriens sylva.* cf. 40. 9

Easum, on a mount five wheat-ears ppr. 154. 7

Eaten and **Eaton,** a crow's head erased ppr.

Eaton, Baron Cheylesmore, see Cheylesmore.

Eaton, Notts, an eagle's head erased sa., holding in the beak a sprig vert. *Vincit omnia veritas.* 84. 10

Eaton, Ireland, a beaver passant arg. cf. 134. 8

Eaton, out of a ducal coronet or, a bull's head sa., armed arg. 44. 11

Eaton, a boar's head erased holding in the mouth a sword. 42. 6

Eaton of Rainham Essex, a stork arg., beaked and legged gu., holding in the beak an ostrich-feather or. cf. 105. 11

Ebblewhite, Ernest Arthur, Esquire, of Tintern, Christchurch Road, Crouch End, N., a demi-wolf erm., holding between the paws a lyre or, and charged on the shoulder with a mullet of six points pierced arg. *En avant.* 246. 7

Ebden, Charles John, Baldslow Place, Sussex, a lion regardant sa., collared or, resting the dexter paw upon a fusil, also sa., and holding in the mouth a palm-branch ppr. *Spes sibi quis que.*

Eberstein, a peacock's head ppr. 103. 2

Ebhert, a salamander in flames ppr. 138. 4

Ebrington, Viscount, see Fortescue, Earl.

Ebsworth, a demi-wolf erm., supporting a spear tasselled. 29. 4

Ebury, Baron (Grosvenor), of Ebury Manor, Middx., a talbot statant or. *Virtus non stemma.* cf. 54. 2

Eccles, a gauntlet ppr. 209. 8

Eccles, Ecles, and **Exles,** Scotland and Ireland, a broken halberd az. *Se defendendo.* 172. 7

Eccles, William McAdam, Esquire, M.S. Lond., F.R.C.S. Eng., of 124, Harley Street, Cavendish Square, W., a broken halbert, the two parts in chevron. *Se defendendo.*

Eccles, William, Esquire, of Withy Grove, Bamber Bridge, Preston, upon a rock ppr., a cross pattée gu., and on either side three cinquefoils slipped vert. *Per ecclesiam ad cælum.*

Eccleston or **Eclestone,** a dexter hand holding a dagger in pale ppr. 212. 9

Eccleston or **Eclestone,** a magpie ppr.

Eccleston, Sheils-, same crest.

Echard, Suff., an ostrich with wings expanded holding in the beak a key. cf. 97. 5

Echingham of Dunbrody Abbey, co. Wexford, Ireland, an eagle ppr., holding in the dexter claw a staff or, thereon a pennon gu.

Echingham of Kent, a church-bell ppr. 168. 7

Echlin, John Godfrey, Esquire, of Dunloskin, Carrickfergus, a talbot passant arg., spotted sa., langued gu. *Non sine prædâ.* 54. 1

Echlin, Henry, Esquire, J.P., of Kirlish, co. Tyrone, a talbot passant arg., spotted sa., gorged with a collar az., and charged on the shoulder with a white rose ppr. *Non sine prædâ.* cf. 54. 5

Echlin, Sir Thomas, Bart., of Clonagh, co. Kildare, a talbot passant arg., spotted sa. *Rumor acerbe tace.* 54. 1

Eckersall, Middx., a dexter arm in armour embowed ppr. and inverted, charged with a lozenge arg., holding in the hand an esquire's helmet of the first, garnished or.

Eckersley, James Carlton, Ashfield, Wigan, an arm in armour embowed ppr., garnished and charged with two cinquefoils, the one above, the one below, the elbow or, holding in the hand an esquire's helmet between two branches of oak in saltire slipped, also ppr. *Allons mes enfants.*

Eckford, Scotland, a griffin statant or. 63. 8

Eckley of Credenhill Park Heref., a leopard's head erased gu. *Gesta prævenient verbis.* cf. 23. 2

Ecles, see Eccles.

Ecleston, Lincs, a cock-pheasant ppr. cf. 90. 8

Ecleston and **Eclestone,** see Eccleston.

Ecroyd, William Farrer, Esquire, J.P., D.L., of Lomeshaye, Lancashire, of Credenhill Park, Heref., and of Whitbarrow Lodge, Westml., in front of a demi-tower ppr., thereon a stag's head erased erminois, three spears, one in pale and two in saltire, also ppr. *In veritate victoria.*

Ecton, a hand holding a branch of palm ppr. 219. 11

Eddington, a phœnix in flames ppr. 82. 2

Eddington, Archibald Campbell, Esquire, of Ballangeich, co. Villiers, Victoria, Australia, uses a savage's head couped at the neck and distilling blood. *Data, fata, secutus.* 190. 11

Eddowes, a mitre bezantée, charged with a chevron. cf. 180. 5

Ede, a cross moline az., between two ears of wheat in orle ppr. 154. 14

Eden, Baron Auckland, see Auckland.

Eden, Sir William, Bart., D.L., of West Auckland, Durh., and Maryland, North America, a dexter arm in armour embowed ppr., the hand grasping a garb or, banded vert. *Si sit prudentia.*

Eden, Lieutenant-Colonel John Henry, of Bishopston Grange, Ripon, same crest and motto.

Eden, Durh., an arm embowed vested barry of four az. and gu., holding in the hand ppr. a bunch of wheat vert.

Eden, Kent and Suff., a plume of feathers arg. 115. 1

Eden, an ostrich holding in the beak a horseshoe ppr. 97. 8

Eden, Essex and Suff., a demi-dragon sans wings vert, holding a rose-branch flowered arg., stalked and leaved ppr.

Eden, an eagle volant ppr.

Edeworth, a lion's head erased. 17. 8

Edgar, Suff., a demi-ostrich rising, holding in the beak a horse-shoe. cf. 90. 8

Edgar of the Red House, near Ipswich, Suff., an ostrich's head between two wings expanded or, each charged with as many bends az., and holding in the beak a horse-shoe arg. 96. 12

Edgar, Scotland, a dagger and a quill in saltier ppr. *Potius ingenio quam vi.* cf. 170. 4

Edgar, Scotland, a withered oak-branch sprouting afresh ppr. *Apparet quod.* cf. 51. 3

Edgar, Wilfred Haythorne, Esquire, an arm in armour, the hand bare and grasping a dagger in bend sinister, point downwards, all ppr. *Maun do it.*

Edgar, Scotland, a hand holding a dagger point downward ppr. *Man do it.* cf. 213. 6

Edgcumbe, see Mount-Edgcumbe, Earl of.

Edgcumbe, Devonsh. and Cornw., a boar passant arg., armed, bristled, and membered or, gorged with a chaplet of oak vert, fructed of the second. *Au plaisir fort de Dieu.* 40. 6

Edgcumbe, Richard John Frederick, Esquire, of Edgbarrow, Crowthorne, Berks, a boar arg., accolled with a wreath of oak ppr., fructed or. *Au plaisir fort de Dieu.*

Edgcumbe, a boar's head in a dish, all arg.

Edgcumbe, Pearce-, Sir Edward Robert, Sandye Place, Sandy, Beds, a demi-boar supporting between the legs a javelin erect ppr., and gorged with a collar, therefrom suspended a bugle-horn stringed, both or. *Pro jure semper.* 255. 10

Edge of London and Staffs, a demi-sea-lion ppr.

Edge, Sir John, of Clonbrock, Queen's Co., Ireland, a reindeer's head couped ppr., collared and chained or, and holding in its mouth a trefoil vert. *Semper fidelis.* cf. 122. 1

Edge, John Dallas, Esquire, same crest and motto. cf. 122. 1

Edge, John Henry, Esquire, B.A., of Farnans, Ballickmoyler, Queen's Co., same crest and motto.

Edge, Thomas Lewis Kekewich, Esquire, of Strelley Hall, Nottingham, same crest and motto.

Edge, Notts, a reindeer's head couped ppr., collared and chained or. 122. 1

Edge, an ostrich's head erased between two wings.

Edgebury, alias Wilkinson, of Deptford, Kent, on a mount vert, a bird sa., supporting a pennon az. and gu., the ends flotant, the top arg., thereon a cross of the fourth, the staff or.

Edgell, Rev. Edward Bettenson, of Standerwick Court, Somers., a falcon rising arg., guttée-de-sang, belled or, resting the dexter claw on an antique shield of the first, charged with a cinquefoil gu. *Qui sera sera.* 87. 7

Edgell, Wyatt-, Arthur, of Milton Place, Surrey: (1) A demi-lion rampant holding in the dexter paw a cinquefoil gu., slipped and leaved vert (*for Edgell*). *cf.* 10. 2. (2) A demi-lion per pale crenellée or and sa., holding in the dexter paw an arrow gu., feathered and headed arg. (*for Wyatt*). *Honesta bona.* *cf.* 13. 6

Edgell, on a chapeau ppr., a dove with wings addorsed az. 94. 10

Edgelow, Arthur Wilberforce Hennen, M. and L.S.A., of Seymour House, 10, Merton Road, Wimbledon, a castle triple-towered charged with a fleur-de-lis. *Espère en Dieu.* 300. 2

Edgeworth, a lion's head erased arg. 17. 8

Edgeworth, Sneyd-, Ireland, on a ducal coronet a pelican in her piety, all or. *Constans contraria spernit.* *cf.* 98. 8

Edgeworth, Thomas Newcomen, Esquire, M.A., D.L., of Kilshrewly, Edgeworthstown, on a ducal coronet a pelican with wings endorsed and inverted vulning herself. *Constans contraria spernit.*

Edgill, a demi-lion rampant holding in the dexter paw a cinquefoil gu., slipped and leaved vert. *cf.* 10. 2

Edgworth, a cherub ppr. 189. 9

Edie, Scotland, a cross crosslet fitched gu., and a skean ppr. in saltier. *Crux mihi grata quies.* 166. 12

Edington, a savage's head couped and dropping blood, all ppr. 190. 11

Edington, a Saracen's head couped at the shoulders ppr., wreathed arg. and gu. 190. 5

Edington or **Edingtoun,** an arm in armour embowed, wreathed with laurel, holding in the hand a standard erect, all ppr., the flag charged with the sun or.

Edington, Scotland, a stag's head erased or. *Labor omnia vincit.* 121. 2

Edlin, a swan's head between two wings arg. 101. 6

Edmands, Surrey and Middx., a griffin's head erased arg., holding in the beak a cross crosslet fitched az., between two wings also arg., each charged with a thistle ppr. *Vincit veritas.*

Edmeades, Major-General Henry, R.A., of Nurstead Court, Gravesend, Kent, five arrows interlaced or, surmounted by a crescent sa. *cf.* 173. 3

Edmerston, a dexter hand throwing a dart ppr. 214. 4

Edmiston or **Edmistone,** Scotland, a camel's head and neck. 132. 7

Edmond, a demi-lion ppr., supporting a long cross gu. 11. 14

Edmond, on a chapeau a fleur-de-lis. *cf.* 148. 2

Edmond of Haverfordwest, Swansea, and Carmarthen, an arm in armour embowed holding in the hand a battle-axe, all ppr. *Persevere.* *cf.* 200. 6

Edmond, Captain Edmond Morgan Edmond, of Llanstephan, Carmarthen, same crest and motto.

Edmondes, Sussex, a dragon's head erased arg., charged on the breast with three pellets. *cf.* 71. 2

Edmondes, Hants and Sussex, a dragon's head erased quarterly vert and arg., semée of roundles counterchanged and charged with a crescent. 71. 2

Edmonds, Oxon., a griffin's head erased gu., holding in the beak a cross crosslet fitched or. *cf.* 66. 2

Edmonds of Dedington, Oxon.: (1) A griffin's head erased gu., holding in the beak a cross pattée fitchée or. *cf.* 66. 2. (2) On a globe arg., banded or, a griffin's head gu.

Edmonds, Cambs, a greyhound sejant sa., bezantée, collared or. *cf.* 59. 2

Edmonds, Bucks and Cornw., between two wings endorsed a lion couchant gardant, all or.

Edmonds, a sinister wing erect per pale or and arg. *cf.* 109. 7

Edmonds, Devonsh., on a chapeau gu., turned up erm., a fleur-de-lis or, between two wings az. *cf.* 110. 5

Edmonds, William, Esquire, of Wiscombe Park, Honiton, Devonsh., a rock ppr., thereon a fleur-de-lis vert, surmounted by a boar's head couped arg. *Absque labore nihil.*

Edmonds, Yorks, a three-masted ship in full sail ppr. 160. 13

Edmonds, an arm in armour embowed ppr., throwing a pheon az., the handle of the first. 198. 7

Edmonds, an arm in armour embowed holding in the hand a battle-axe, all ppr. *Agnus in pace, leo in bello.* *cf.* 200. 6

Edmondson of London, a lion rampant or, gorged with a bar gemelle gu., supporting a pennon az., the staff gu., headed arg. 3. 14

Edmondson, Yorks, a demi-lion sa., holding an escallop or. 13. 10

Edmondstone, Scotland, a camel's head and neck ppr. 132. 7

Edmondstone, Scotland, a demi-lion rampant gu., armed and langued az., holding in his paws a battle-axe ppr. *Be hardie.* 15. 4

Edmonstone, Scotland, a hand drawing a semicircle with a compass ppr. *Gadge and measure.*

Edmonstone, a squirrel sejant or. *cf.* 135. 4

Edmonstone-Montgomerie, William E., Esquire, of 200, Cromwell Road, Kensington, London: (1) On the dexter side—On a chapeau a dexter gauntlet erect ppr., the hand holding a dagger, also ppr., hilted and pommelled or (*for Montgomerie*). (2) On the sinister side—Out of a ducal coronet or, a swan's head and neck arg., beaked or (*for Edmonstone*). *Garde, garde.—Virtus auget honorem.*

Edmonstone, Sir Archibald, Bart., D.L., of Duntreath, Stirlingsh., out of a ducal coronet or, a swan's head and neck ppr. *Virtus auget honorem.* *cf.* 100. 10

Edmondstoune-Cranstoun, Charles Joseph, Esquire, of Corehouse, Lanarksh., a crane statant vulning itself ppr.

Edmund, on a chapeau gu., turned up arg., a lion passant gradant az., ducally gorged or. *cf.* 4. 5

Edmunds, Hants, a winged lion couchant gardant or.

Edmunds, Yorks, in the sea an ancient ship of three masts under sail, all ppr. *Votis tune velis.*

Edmunds, two hands in fess couped and conjoined, supporting a human heart, all ppr. 222. 4

Ednor, a griffin's head erased gu., beaked or. 66. 2

Ednowain, Wales, a boar's head couped sa., langued gu., tusked or, transfixed by a dagger ppr.

Edolphe, Kent, an ibex's head erased sa., maned, armed, and attired or.

Edon, Kent and Suff., a plume of feathers arg.

Edridge, a hawk standing on a fish ppr. 86. 6

Edridge of London and Norf., a lion's head erased gu. 17. 2

Edridge, Wilts, a lion rampant arg. 1. 13

Edrington, a goat's head ppr., collared erm. *cf.* 128. 12

Edward, a tortoise ppr. *cf.* 125. 5

Edward, a tortoise or. *Nec flatu, nec fluctu.* *cf.* 125. 5

Edward, a buck's head couped or. 121. 5

Edwardes, Baron Kensington, *see* Kensington.

Edwardes, Sir Henry Hope, Bart., J.P., of Shrewsbury, a man's head and shoulders affrontée in armour, the helmet open vizored ppr., garnished or. *A vyno Duw dervid.*

Edwardes, Hope-, Lieutenant-Colonel Herbert James, Netley, Shrewsbury: (1) Same as above. (2) A broken globe between two palm-branches ppr., and charged with three arrows, two in saltire and one in pale, point downwards or, the whole surmounted by a rainbow with clouds at each end ppr. *A vyno Duw dervid.*

Edwardes-Tucker of Sealy Ham, Pembroke, a bear's paw holding a battle-axe arg. *Vigilate.—Gardez la foy.* *cf.* 38. 3

Edwardes, Carmarthen, a demi-lion or, holding between the paws a Bowen-knot. *Aspera ad virtutum est via.* *cf.* 10. 2

Edwards-Moss, *see* Moss.

Edwards, Heref., out of a ducal coronet or, a demi-lion rampant gu., holding in his dexter paw a sword ppr. *cf.* 16. 3

Edwards, Glouc., a demi-lion rampant or, holding between his paws a castle arg. *cf.* 10. 2

Edwards, Frank, Esquire, J.P., D.L., of the Cottage, Knighton, Radnorsh., issuant from the battlements of a tower or, a wolf's head per pale erm. and gu., guttée-d'or, charged with a cross couped, also or. *A gar y gwir a gyfyr.* 246. 6

Edwards, a lion passant gardant or. 4. 3

Edwards, Bart., of Garth, Montgomery, a lion passant gardant per pale or and gu., resting the dexter paw on an escutcheon of the last, charged with a nag's head erased arg. *Y Gwir yn erbyn y byd.* cf. 4. 3

Edwards, late Colonel George Rowland, of Ness Strange, Shropsh., within a wreath arg. and sa., a lion rampant per fesse of the same. 9. 3

Edwards, Charles Edward Munroe, of Dolseran Road, Dolgelly, same crest. *Fidelis.*

Edwards, Wales, an oak-tree ppr., on the dexter side a gate, also ppr., on the sinister a lion rampant against the tree gu.

Edwards, a lion's head erased per bend sinister erm. and ermines. 17. 8

Edwards, a lion's head erased per bend sinister erm. and ermines, charged with four fleurs-de-lis. cf. 17. 8

Edwards of Old Court, co. Wicklow: (1) A lion's head erased ermines between two palm-branches issuing ppr. (*for Edwards*). cf. 17. 7. (2) An arm in armour embowed, the hand holding a sword within a sun in splendour ppr. (*for Kynaston*). *Heb Dduw, heb ddim, Dduw a digon.—Honor potestate honorantis.* 195. 7

Edwards, a lion's head erased ermines, between two palm-branches ppr. *Heb Dduw, heb ddim, Duw a digon.* cf. 17. 7

Edwards, Lieutenant-Colonel the Right Hon. Sir Fleetwood Isham, G.C.V.O., K.C.B., I.S.O., of St. James's Palace, S.W., issuant from a chaplet of roses gu., a lion's head erased per pale ermines and erm., gorged with a collar gemel or. *Integritate.* 225. 9

Edwards, a lion's gamb couped and erect erm., grasping a goat's leg erased sa., ungu. or.

Edwards, Cambs and Sussex, on a ducal coronet arg., a tiger passant or.

Edwards of London, on a ducal coronet or, a tiger passant sa., maned of the first.

Edwards, Devonsh., Hunts, and Shropsh., an ibex passant sa., bezantée, maned, armed, and attired with two straight horns or.

Edwards, an antelope trippant ppr. 126. 6

Edwards, Cornw., an antelope saliant sa., bezantée, attired or. 126. 7

Edwards, John, Esquire, of Trematon Hall, near Saltash, in front of two wheat-stalks ppr., a griffin's head erased per chevron or and az. *Perseverando.* cf. 66. 2

Edwards, on a mount vert, a wyvern arg. 69. 11

Edwards, a wyvern with wings displayed. 70. 8

Edwards, Howell Powell, Esquire, M.A., of Novington Manor, Sussex, a dragon's head erased vert, gorged with a collar vair, and charged with two quatrefoils in pale or, holding in the mouth a dexter hand couped at the wrist distilling drops of blood ppr., between two spear-heads erect arg. 244. 5

Edwards, Somers., an eagle displayed az. 75. 2

Edwards, an eagle's head erased sa., ducally gorged or. cf. 83. 2

Edwards, Norf., a martlet sa., charged on the wing with a cinquefoil or. cf. 95. 5

Edwards, Henry William Bartholomew, the Hall, Hardingham, Attleborough, Norf., same crest. *Quid leges sine moribus?*

Edwards, a turtle-dove holding in its beak an olive-branch, all ppr. 92. 5

Edwards, Sir John Henry Priestly Churchill, Bart., out of a vallery coronet or, a talbot's head arg., semée de-lis az. *Omne bonum, Dei donum.* 257. 6

Edwards, Arthur Hancock, Esquire, J.P., D.L., M.A., of Pyenest, Halifax, same crest and motto.

Edwards, out of a marquess's coronet a talbot's head. cf. 57. 12

Edwards, Warw., a talbot passant ppr. 54.

Edwards, F. Swinford, Esquire, of 55, Harley Street, W., out of the coronet of a marquess a talbot's head. *Gardez la foy.*

Edwards, Wales, a boar's head erased arg. 42. 2

Edwards, on a mount vert, a horse's head erased or, charged on the neck with a chevron gu., between two oak-branches ppr.

Edwards, John, Esquire, K.C., of Harcourt Buildings, Temple, London, E.C., a stag regardant arg., charged on the body with two fleurs-de-lis az., and resting the dexter fore-leg on an esquire's helmet ppr. 118. 1

Edwards, Beds, three ostrich-feathers arg. 115. 1

Edwards, Ireland, a crosier in pale or. 170. 14

Edwards of London, a hand gu., holding a cross pattée fitched or. 221. 12

Edwards, Sir James Bevan, K.C.M.G., C.B., of the Gables, Folkestone, a man's head in a helmet in profile. *A vynno Duw dervid.*

Edwards of Toxteth Park, Liverpool, and Broughton, Lancs, a man in complete armour, resting the dexter hand on a sword point downwards ppr., and supporting with his sinister an escutcheon of the arms, viz.: or, a pile az. and a chevron counterchanged between three horse's heads erased of the second. *A vynno Duw dervid.—Duw ydi ein cryfdwr.*

Edwards, George Frederick, Esquire, F.R.G.S., F.Z.S., of Alger House, 6, Highbury Crescent, London, N., in front of a man's head in profile, couped ppr., crined or, a fret of the last. *Gratia naturam vincit.*

Edwin, a Cornish chough ppr. 107. 14

Edwin, a lion sejant holding between the fore-paws an escutcheon, both party per chevron gu. and or. cf. 8. 4

Eel, a boar's head couped or. 43. 1

Eeles, a dexter arm in armour in fess couped holding in the hand a cutlass enfiled with a boar's head, all ppr. 211. 9

Effingham, Earl of (Howard), of Effingham, Surrey, on a chapeau gu., turned up erm., a lion statant gardant, his tail extended or, gorged with a ducal coronet arg., charged with a mullet sa., for difference. *Virtus mille scuta.* cf. 4. 4

Egan, a long cross gu. 65. 4

Egan, Ireland, a demi-eagle regardant. 80. 10

Egan, Ireland, on a tower or, a knight in complete armour couped at the knees holding in his dexter hand a battle-axe, all ppr. *Fortitudo et prudentia.*

Egerley, a Cornish chough ducally gorged, all ppr. 107. 6

Egerton, Earl of Wilton, *see* Wilton.

Egerton, Earl of Ellesmere, *see* Ellesmere.

Egerton, *see* Grey-Egerton, Bart.

Egerton of Tatton, Earl of (Egerton), Tatton, County Palatine of Chester, on a chapeau gu., turned up erm., a lion rampant, also gu., supporting an arrow palewise or, pheoned and flighted arg. *Sic donec.* cf. 2. 4

Egerton, Charles Augustus, the Banks, Robertsbridge, Sussex, same crest and motto.

Egerton, Duke of Bridgewater, on a chapeau gu., turned up erm., a lion rampant of the first, supporting a broad arrow erect or, headed and feathered arg. cf. 2. 4

Egerton, Hon. Alan de Tatton, of Rostherne Manor, Knutsford, same crest and motto.

Egerton, Charles Augustus, Esquire, J.P., of the Banks, Mountfield, Sussex, same crest. *Sic donec.*

Egerton, Sir Edwin Henry, K.C.B., of British Legation, Athens, same crest and motto.

Egerton, Hugh Edward, Esquire, same crest.

Egerton, Sir Robert Eyles, of Coed-y-Glyn, three arrows, two in saltire and one in pale or, headed and feathered sa., banded gu. *Virtuti non armis fido.*

Egerton, Reginald A., Esquire, Brookville, Raheny, co. Dublin, three arrows, two in saltire arg., and one in pale, points downwards or, barbed and feathered sa., banded with a ribbon gu. *Virtuti non armis fido.*

Egerton, Chesh. and Shropsh., a lion rampant gu., supporting an arrow ppr., headed and feathered arg. 2. 4

Egerton, Ireland, a lion sejant gu., supporting in the dexter paw a battle-axe arg., the staff of the first, and in the sinister a laurel-branch ppr. 8. 9

Egerton, a lion rampant ppr. 1. 13

Egerton, Chesh., a lion's gamb gu., holding a sword arg., hilt and pommel or. 38. 5

Egerton, three arrows arg., headed and feathered sa., banded or. 173. 1

Egerton, five arrows, one in pale and four in saltier. 173. 3

Egerton, a buck's head erased sa., attired or. 121. 2

Egerton, Chesh., a plume of feathers erm 115.

Egerton, an arm vested gu., holding in the hand ppr. a sword arg.

Egerton-Green, Claude Egerton, Esquire, of East Hill House, Colchester: (1) A stag's head arg., erased or, attired sa., gorged with a collar gemel gu., holding in the mouth a sprig of holly fructed ppr. (*for Green*). (2) On a chapeau gu., turned up erm., a lion rampant of the first, supporting an arrow in pale, the pheon downwards arg. (*for Egerton*).

Egerton-Warburton, Augustus, Esquire, of Bakerup, West Australia: (1) A

Saracen's head affrontée couped at the shoulders ppr., round the temples a wreath arg. and gu., issuing therefrom three ostrich-feathers or (*for Warburton*). (2) Three arrows, two in saltire and one in pale or, headed and feathered sa., bound with a ribbon gu. (*for Egerton*).

Egerton-Warburton, Rev. Geoffrey, of Warburton Rectory, Chesh., same crests.

Egerton-Warburton, George, Esquire, J.P., of Sandicroft, Northwich, Chesh., same crests.

Egerton-Warburton, George Grey, Esquire, J.P., of Yeriminup, Western Australia, same crests.

Egerton-Warburton, Horace, Esquire, of St. Werburghe's, West Australia, same crests.

Egerton-Warburton, Piers, Esquire, J.P., of Arley Hall, Northwich, Chesh., same crests.

Egerton-Warburton, Roland, Esquire of Stoneyhurst, West Australia, same crests.

Egg, out of a ducal coronet the attires of a stag. 123. 1

Eggerly, a Cornish chough ducally gorged, all ppr. 107. 6

Eggington, Gardiner, Esquire, of North Ferriby, Yorks, a talbot sejant arg., eared sa., gorged with a collar per fesse nebulée or and az., the dexter paw resting upon a sphere ppr. *Integer vitæ.* cf. 55. 1

Egginton, Arthur, Esquire, of South Ella, near Hull, same crest and motto.

Egginton, John Smyth, Esquire, J.P., of the Elms, Kirk Ella, Hull, same crest and motto.

Egginton-Ernle-Erle-Drax, John Lloyd, Esquire, of 7, Lypiatt Terrace, Cheltenham: (1) A demi-dragon or, charged for difference on the shoulder with an escallop gu. (*for Drax*). (2) In front of a lion's head erased or, gorged with two barrulets sa., three escallops fessewise arg. (*for Erle*). (3) A man's head in profile couped at the shoulders ppr., on the head a long cap barry of ten tasselled and tied or and sa., and charged on the neck for difference with a cross crosslet or (*for Ernle*). (4) On a mount vert, a talbot sejant erm., holding in the mouth an eagle displayed sa. (*for Egglinton*). *Mort en droit.*

Egloke, a griffin passant per pale or and az. 63. 2

Egleby and **Eglionby,** Warw., a demi-eagle with wings expanded or, charged with a mullet for difference. cf. 80. 2

Eglefelde and **Eglefield,** a dexter hand apaumée, charged with an eye ppr. 222. 4

Eglenton, Ireland, a lion rampant resting the fore-paw on an antique shield.

Egleston, a talbot's head erased sa., collared arg. 56. 1

Eglin, Joseph, Esquire, of Kingston-upon-Hull, on a mount vert, an eagle rising or, surmounted by an anchor and cable in bend sinister sa., holding in the dexter claw a rose gu., slipped vert.

Eglinton and Winton, Earl of (Montgomerie), Eglinton Castle, Irvine, a female figure ppr., representing Hope, anciently attired az., resting her dexter hand upon an anchor or, and holding in her sinister by the hair the head of a savage couped of the first. *Gardez bien.* 184. 9

Eglionby, *see* Egleby.

Egmanton, Lancs, a hand holding a cross pattée fitched gu. 221. 12

Egmont, Earl of (Perceval), Cowdray Park, Midhurst, Sussex, a thistle erect and leaved ppr. *Sub cruce candidâ.* cf. 150. 5

Egremond, a lion's head gu., imperially crowned or. 17. 14

Egremont, Earl of (Wyndham), a lion's head erased or, within a fetterlock of the same, the arch company-counter-company or and az. *Au bon droit.*

Eidingtoun, an arm in armour embowed, wreathed above the elbow with laurel, and supporting a standard charged with the rising sun.

Eills, John Lamport, Esquire, of Liverpool, an eagle's claw erased ppr., grasping a bezant, charged with a cross crosslet fitchée sa. *Teneo tuti memor futuri.*

Eiston, Scotland, out of a cloud the sun rising ppr. *Veritas.* 162. 5

Ekeney, on a chapeau ppr., a pheon az. cf. 174. 11

Ekington, *see* Ekinton.

Ekins, a lion's gamb sa., holding up a lozenge arg., charged with a cross crosslet fitched gu. 35. 10

Ekins, a lion's gamb sa., holding a cross crosslet fitched in bend gu. cf. 36. 11

Ekinton and **Ekington,** a sand-glass gu. 177. 15

Ekles, *see* Eccles.

Ekles, a broken halbert, the top hanging down az. *Se defendo.* 172. 7

Elam, Kent, between the attires of a stag, attached to the scalp, a boar's head erased and erect, all ppr. 43. 2

Eland and **Elland,** on a chapeau az., turned up or, a martlet gu. 95. 1

Eland and Elland, a demi-female holding in her dexter hand a garland of laurel. 183. 5

Elcham, a covered cup or, between two wings ppr.

Elcho, Lord, *see* Wemyss, Earl of.

Elcock, a stag salient ppr. 117. 2

Elcocke, Chesh., out of a mural coronet or, a demi-cock az., combed, beaked, and wattled of the first, and holding in the beak a wheat-ear ppr.

Elcocks, Chesh., out of a mural coronet or, a cock's head gu., holding in the beak a wheat-ear.

Eld of London and Staffs, a falcon rising or, beaked, membered, jessed, and belled gu., his beak embrued ppr. cf. 87. 1

Eld, Francis Frederick, J.P., Belvoir, Torquay, same crest.

Elder, a demi-unicorn rampant. 48. 7

Elder, Scotland, a dexter hand holding a roll of paper ppr. *Virtute duce.* 215. 6

Elder, Scotland, a dexter hand holding a palm-branch ppr. *Virtute duce.* 219. 11

Elderkar, *see* Ellerker.

Eldershaw, Scotland, a demi-lion rampant gu., ducally gorged or. 10. 7

Elderton, a fox's head ppr. 33. 4

Eldon, Earl of (Scott), Stowell Park, North Leach, Glouc., a lion's head erased gu., gorged with a chain, and therefrom a portcullis pendent or, and charged with a mullet arg. for difference. *Sit sine labe decus.* cf. 17. 2

Eldred, Essex, a Triton ppr., holding an escallop or.

Eldred, a dexter hand couped in fess, reaching to a laurel-crown, all ppr.

Eldres, a camel's head couped ppr. 132. 7

Eldres, a winged globe ppr. cf. 159. 9

Eldridge, out of a ducal coronet a peacock's tail ppr. 115. 6

Eldrington, Essex, a heron sa., membered gu. 105. 9

Elers, Carew Thomas, Esquire, of Oldbury, Kent, between two dove's wings ppr., an escutcheon of the arms, viz.: gyronny of twelve pieces arg. and gu., in the centre point an inescutcheon or. *Gloria virtutis umbra.*

Eley, Lincs, an arm erect vested arg., holding in the hand ppr. a fleur-de-lis sa.

Eley, Yorks, an arm in armour, holding in the hand a hawk's lure ppr.

Elfe or **Elphe,** an eagle's head couped. 83. 1

Elford, Bart., Devonsh., a demi-lion rampant erased per pale arg. and sa., ducally crowned or. *Difficilia quæ pulchra.* cf. 10. 11

Elfred, Sussex, on a mount vert, a lamb couchant arg., between two olive-branches ppr. 131. 12

Elgee, Percival Charles, Esquire, M.A., of 23, Bramham Gardens, S.W., a demi-man in profile habited in complete armour, the visor raised, and holding in his sinister hand a scimitar in pale, all ppr. *Corda semper fidelia.*

Elgie, on a ducal coronet a swan with wings addorsed and ducally crowned.

Elgin and Kincardine, Earl of (Bruce), a lion statant with the tail extended az. *Fuimus.* cf. 4. 8

Elgood, Edgar John, Esquire, of the Manor House, Sidcup, Kent, B.C.L., M.A. Oxon., J.P., co. Kent, in front of a mount vert, thereon a greyhound current sa., holding in the mouth a key in bend, wards upwards or, a pile of six pellets, one, two, and three. *Tenax propositi.* 292. 14

Elham, out of a mural coronet a fire-beacon between two wings ppr. 112. 5

Elibank, Baron (Murray), of Elibank, Selkirk, a lion rampant gu., holding between the paws a battle-axe ppr. *Virtute fideque.*

Elin, George H. A., of Old Southcote Lodge, Reading, on a mount a crocodiles tatant ppr. *Vincet qui perseverit.*

Elingham, an eagle's head couped ppr. 83. 1

Elliot, Baron, Earl St. Germans, *see* St. Germans.

Eliot, an elephant's head couped arg., collared gu. cf. 133. 2

Eliot, an elephant's head sa., armed and eared arg. 133. 2

Eliot, Surrey, a griffin's head couped between two wings addorsed sa., collared arg. cf. 67. 11

Eliot, issuing out of clouds a dexter arm embowed throwing a dart ppr. *cf.* 201. 14

Eliot, of Borthwickbrae, Scotland, a dexter hand erect holding a lance in bend ppr., headed arg. *Hoc majorum opus.* 214. 11

Eliott, Sir William Francis Augustus, Bart., D.L., F.R.S., of Stobs, Roxburghsh., a dexter hand in armour couped above the wrist, holding a scimitar in bend arg., pommel and hilt or, the wrist charged with a key sa.

Eliott, a dexter hand holding in bend sinister a flute round which a serpent is entwined, all ppr. *Non sine Deo.* *cf.* 217. 9

Eliott-Lockhart, William, Esquire, of Cleghorn, Lanarksh.: (1) On the dexter side a boar's head erased arg., armed and langued gu., and in an escroll over, *Sine labe fides.* (2) On the sinister side a dexter hand erect ppr., holding a lance in bend, also ppr. *Hoc majorum opus.* 214. 11

Eliston, an eagle's head arg., beaked and erased gu., murally gorged az. 83. 11

Elkin, a demi-heraldic antelope or, armed and tufted sa.

Elkings, a lion's gamb erect sa., holding a lozenge or, charged with a cross crosslet fitchée gu. 35. 10

Elkington of London and Leics., on a mural coronet chequy or and sa., embattled of the first, a demi-griffin arg., winged gu., holding in the dexter claw a gem-ring or, the gem of the second.

Elkington, George, Esquire, M.R.C.S., of Llwynguril, Merioneth., same crest. *Industria et Spe.*

Elkins, on a castle triple-towered ppr., a flag displayed gu. 155. 8

Ellacott, in a maunch or, cuffed gu., a hand clenched ppr. 203. 3

Ellames, Lancs, an elm-tree ppr. *Nec sperno, nec timeo.* 143. 1

Elland, on a chapeau az., turned up or, a martlet gu. 95. 1

Elland, a demi-woman holding in her dexter hand a garland of laurel. 183. 5

Ellard, a torteau charged with a stag or, standing on a mount vert. 116. 11

Ellard, on a mount vert, a stag or. 117. 1

Ellaway, five arrows, one in pale and four in saltier, points downwards, environed with a serpent, all ppr. *cf.* 173. 3

Ellenborough, Baron (Law), of Ellenborough, Cumb., a cock gu., chained round the neck and charged on the breast with a mitre or. *Compositum jus fasque animi.* *cf.* 91. 2

Ellerker and **Elderkar,** a dolphin az., tusked or, and a salamander's head erased of the same casting flames of fire addorsed within a crown counterchanged set upon a wreath or and az. 236. 2

Ellerton of Bodsyllan, Carnarvon, a buck trippant or, his neck encircled with a chaplet vert. *Spero infestis metuo secundis.* *cf.* 117. 8

Elles, Arthur Warre, Esquire, a gauntleted dexter hand grasping an asp ppr., the hand charged with a cross crosslet fitchée gu. *Sperno.*

Ellesmere, Earl of (Egerton), of Ellesmere, Shropsh., on a chapeau gu., turned up erm., a lion rampant, also gu., supporting an arrow or, feathered and headed arg. *Sic donec.*

Elleston, a demi-heraldic tiger holding between the paws a naval crown. *cf.* 25. 13

Ellesworth, a dexter arm in armour embowed holding in the hand a club, all ppr. 199. 6

Elletson, a griffin's head erased gu., ducally gorged or. *cf.* 66. 11

Elley, an anchor in pale az., entwined by a serpent vert. 161. 3

Elley of Hampstead, a cubit arm erect habited arg., holding in the hand ppr. a fleur-de-lis sa.

Ellice, Middx. and Herts, an arm erect couped below the elbow in armour, holding in the gauntlet a snake entwined round the arm, all ppr.

Ellice, a pelican in her piety ppr. 98. 14

Ellice, a mermaid holding a mirror and a comb ppr. 184. 5

Ellick, a wolf's head erased sa. 30. 8

Ellicomb, a buck's head erased, murally gorged and chained. *cf.* 121. 2

Ellicombe or **Ellacombe,** Glouc. and Devonsh., a stag's head erased, murally gorged and chained. *Nullis fraus tuta latebris.* *cf.* 121. 2

Ellicombe, Hugh Myddleton, Esquire, of Culverlands, Devonsh., a stag's head erased ppr., attired or, between the attires a cross patée fitchée, and gorged with a collar embattled counter-embattled gu., chained of the second.

Ellicombe, Devonsh., a dexter arm in armour embowed wielding a sword, all ppr. 195. 2

Ellicott, a hawk with wings expanded and belled, all ppr. 87. 1

Ellicott or **Ellacott,** in a maunch or, cuffed gu., a hand clenched ppr. 203. 3

Ellies, Scotland, a lily, the flower closed ppr. *Sub sole patebit.*

Ellington, a lion's gamb holding up a cross patée fitched sa. *cf.* 36. 9

Elliot - Murray - Kynynmound, Earl of Minto, *see* Minto.

Elliot or **Elliott,** a demi-sea-horse az., scaled or. 46. 7

Elliot or **Elliott,** of London, a demi-sea-horse az., finned or. 46. 7

Elliot, Sir George, Bart., D.C.L., M.P., D.L., of Penshaw, Durh., a demi-sea-horse az., charged with two fleurs-de-lis palewise, and resting the sinister foot on as many annulets interlaced or. *Labor et veritas.* 46. 12

Elliot or **Elliott,** an elephant's head or, eared and armed gu. 133. 2

Elliot or **Elliott,** out of a mural coronet an elephant's head collared.

Elliot, Christopher, Esquire, B.A., M.D., of 3, Beaufort Road, Clifton, Bristol, an elephant's head couped or. *Non eget arcu.*

Elliot of Laurieston, same crest. *Apto cum lare.*

Elliot of Binfield Park, Berks: (1) An elephant's head arg., erased gu., charged upon the neck with two barrulets invected vert (*for Elliot*). *cf.* 133. 3. (2) A mermaid holding a glass and a comb ppr. (*for Glasse*). 184. 5

Elliot or **Elliott,** a boar's head couped, pierced through the dexter eye by a broken spear.

Elliot or **Elliott,** Surrey, a griffin's head couped between two wings addorsed sa. *cf.* 67. 11

Elliot of London and Pembrokesh., a griffin's head or, issuant from an oak-wreath ppr., between two wings, also or, semée-de-lis gu. *cf.* 65. 11

Elliot, Scotland, a kingfisher ppr. *Quid pure tranquilis.* *cf.* 96. 9

Elliot, Ireland, over the sea a dove volant, holding in its beak an olive-branch ppr. 93. 11

Elliot, a demi-eagle gorged with a wreath, the wings elevated. *Nocet differre paratis.*

Elliot or **Elliott,** a demi-man in armour ppr. *Pro rege et limite.* *cf.* 187. 5

Elliot, John, Esquire, of Binks, Roxburghsh., a demi-man in armour arg., holding in his dexter hand a pike ppr. *Pro Deo, rege et limite.*

Elliot, William Claude, Esquire, of Harwood, Bonchester Bridge, Hawick, N.B., a gentleman in a watching posture holding a pike in his hand ppr.

Elliot, Scott-, William, of Arkleton, Langholm, Dumfriessh., a demi-chevalier in complete armour holding in his right hand a sword erect, all ppr. *Pro Rege et limite.*

Elliot, Fogge-, John Walton, of Elvet Hill, Durh.: (1) A dexter arm holding a cutlass ppr. (*for Elliot*). 213. 5. (2) A unicorn's head couped arg. (*for Fogge*). *Peradventure.* 49. 7

Elliot or **Elliott,** a dexter arm holding a cutlass ppr. *Peradventure.* 213. 5

Elliot or **Elliott,** a dexter hand holding a flute ppr. *Inest jucunditas.* 217. 9

Elliot, Bertram Charles, Esquire, of Brydone, Bitterne, Southampton, issuing from a cloud a dexter hand throwing a dart, all ppr. *Non eget arcu.* 214. 1

Elliot or **Elliott,** a dexter hand ppr., holding a crescent sa. 216. 8

Elliot, a dexter arm grasping a spear ppr. 214. 11

Elliot, George Stokoe, Esquire, M.D., F.R.C.S. Edin., of Southwell, Notts, a dexter arm embowed holding in the hand a scimitar, all ppr. *Per sacra, per ignes fortiter et recte.*

Elliot or **Elliott,** a nail erect ppr. 176. 11

Elliot, Edward Hay Mackenzie, Esquire, of Woleflee, Hawick, N.B., a ram ppr. *Vellera fertis oves.* 131. 13

Elliot or **Elliott,** an oak-tree ppr. *Fortiter.* 143. 5

Elliot or **Elliott,** an anchor cabled in pale ppr. *Candide et caute.* 161. 2

Elliot or **Elliott,** a dexter arm holding a dart, point downwards, all ppr. *Suaviter sed fortiter.* 214. 4

Elliot, Francis Edmund Hugh, Esquire, same crest and motto.

Elliot, Admiral Sir George, of 6, Castletown Road, West Kensington, S.W., same crest and motto.

Elliot, Rt. Hon. Sir Henry George, of Ardington House, Wantage, same crest and motto.

Elliott-Drake, Fuller-, *see* Drake.

Elliott, Ireland, an elephant's head couped sa., eared and tusked arg. 133. 2

Elliott, Ireland, an elephant's head couped arg., charged with three pellets in pale, tusked or. *cf.* 133. 2

Elliott, Henry Worton, Elmfield, Selley Oak, near Birmingham, same crest.

Elliott, Cornw., an elephant's head or, eared and armed gu. 133. 2

Elliott, Thomas Gosseline, Esquire, of Lansdown Terrace, Cheltenham, a griffin sejant gu., holding in his beak a snake ppr., and charged on the shoulder with a trefoil slipped or. *Occurrent nubes.*

Elliott, George Henry Blois, Esquire, of Farnborough Park, Hants, a mermaid holding a looking-glass and a comb in her hand ppr. (*for Glasse*).

Ellis, Agar-, Viscount Clifden, *see* Clifden.

Ellis, Baron Howard de Walden, *see* Howard.

Ellis, *see* Leslie-Ellis.

Ellis, Yorks, Leics., and Kent, a naked woman, her hair dishevelled ppr. *cf.* 184. 13

Ellis, John William, Esquire, M.B., Ch.B., of 18, Rodney Street, Liverpool, same crest and motto.

Ellis of Overleigh, Chesh., a female affrontée ppr., couped at the waist, habited gu., crined or. 182. 8

Ellis, a mermaid gu., crined or, holding in her dexter hand a mirror and in her sinister a comb of the second. 184. 5

Ellis, Williams-, Rev. John Clough, of Glasfryn, Carnarvon: (1) A mermaid gu., crined or, holding in her dexter hand a mirror and in her sinister a comb of the second. 184. 5. (2) An arm in armour embowed, holding in the hand a broken spear-head, all ppr. *Wrth ein ffrwythau ni'n hadnabyddir.—Gweithred a ddengis.*

Ellis, three escallops az., in front of a mermaid wreathed across the shoulder with red coral ppr. *Primus.*

Ellis, Sir John Whittaker, Bart., of Byfleet, Surrey, and Solent Lodge, Cowes, a female figure ppr., vested or, holding in the dexter hand a chaplet of roses gu. and in the sinister a palm-branch slipped vert. *Huic habeo non tibi.* 184. 6

Ellis, Herts, out of a ducal coronet or, a lion's head gu., crowned of the first. *Fort et fidèle.* *cf.* 17. 5

Ellis, Heaton-, Charles Henry Brabazon, Wyddial Hall, Buntingford, Herts, same crest and motto.

Ellis, Wales, on a chapeau az., turned up erm., a lion passant gu. 4. 9

Ellis, a demi-lion rampant arg., gorged with a collar gu., charged with three cross crosslets fitchée arg. *cf.* 10. 9

Ellis, between the horns of a crescent a stag's head cabossed. 122. 14

Ellis, Lincs, in a crescent gu., an escallop or. 141. 1

Ellis of London, out of grass ppr., a goat's head arg., armed of the first. *cf.* 128. 12

Ellis, Major-General Sir Arthur Edward Augustus, K.C.V.O., 29, Portland Place, on a mount vert, a goat's head erased arg.

Ellis of Chiselhurst, Kent, a goat's head couped or, charged with a pale sa., thereon three crescents arg.

Ellis, a fleur-de-lis arg. 148. 2

Ellis, Ireland, a swan with wings expanded, murally gorged, all ppr. *Mors mihi vita fide.* *cf.* 99. 12

Ellis, a garb per fess or and vert. 153. 2

Ellis, a garb vert, bezantée. 153. 2

Ellis of Saughton Mills, Scotland, a gauntlet surmounted by a dove holding an olive-branch in her beak, all ppr. *Pax finis belli.*

Ellis of Southside, Scotland, a gauntleted hand grasping an adder ppr. *Sperno.*

Ellis of Kempsey, Worcs., out of a mural crown or, a cubit arm in bend vested gu., cuffed az., the hand grasping a sword ppr., pommel and hilt of the first, the blade broken and encircled by a wreath of cypress, pendent from the wrist by a ribbon gu., fimbriated az., a representation of the Waterloo medal.

Ellis, Scotland, a lily close in the flower ppr. *Sub sole patebit.*

Ellis, Scotland, an eel ppr. *Sperans.* 142. 10

Ellis of Greenwoods, Stock, Essex, and the Warren, Wanstead, Essex, in front of a sun in splendour a dolphin naiant ppr., charged on the body with a cross couped sa. *Obsta.* 249. 4

Ellis-Viner, Rev. Alfred William: (1) A dexter arm embowed in armour, encircled at the elbow by a wreath of vine, and holding in the hand a gem-ring, all ppr. (2) A horse's head erased erm., gorged with a plain collar arg., thereon a cinquefoil between two crescents slipped sa., holding in the mouth a trefoil slipped ppr. *Labore et honore.*

Ellison, Durh., an eagle's head erased or. 83. 2

Ellison, an eagle's head erased per fess or and gu., murally gorged az. 83. 11

Ellison, Carr-, Ralph, Esquire, of Hedgeley, Northumb., and Dunstanhill, Durh.: (1) An eagle's head erased or, gorged with a collar vair, holding in the beak a branch of three roses gu., leaved and slipped ppr. (*for Ellison*). (2) A stag's head couped arg., attired or, charged on the neck with two bars gemel gu., the whole between two annulets of the last (*for Carr*). *Por dysserver.—Nec te quæsiveris extra.* *cf.* 17. 8

Ellison, a griffin's head erased ppr., collared or. *cf.* 66. 2

Ellison, Scotland, a cross crosslet fitched gu. 166. 2

Ellison, a lion passant gardant holding in its dexter paw an anchor. 5. 10

Ellison-Macartney, John William, Esquire, Barrister-at-Law, J.P., of the Palace, Clogher, co. Tyrone, Ireland: (1) A cubit arm erect, the hand grasping a rose-branch in flower, all ppr. (*for Macartney*). (2) A buck's head erased ppr., charged on the neck with a trefoil slipped vert (*for Ellison*). *Stimulat sed ornat.—Spe gaudeo.* 121. 8

Ellison-Macartney, Rt. Hon. William Grey, same crests and motto.

Ellison, a greyhound sa. *cf.* 60. 2

Elliston of London, an eagle's head erased ppr., ducally gorged arg. *cf.* 83. 10

Elliston, a griffin's head erased ppr., collared or. *cf.* 66. 2

Elliston, three mullets in chevron. 164. 7

Ellisworth, between the attires of a stag ppr., a rose gu. 149. 9

Ellnor, out of a ducal coronet or, an eagle's head sa., beaked gu., between two wings of the second, each charged with a bezant.

Elloway, a dragon's head gu. 71. 1

Ellwood, Yorks, on a mural coronet a stag sejant ppr. 116. 4

Elly, an arm erect vested arg., holding in the hand ppr. a fleur-de-lis sa.

Ellyot and **Ellyott,** an elephant's head couped arg. 133. 2

Ellyott of London, a demi-pegasus arg., maned, winged, and hoofed or. 47. 5

Ellyott, *see* Elliott.

Elmeet, Holland, a horse's head bridled ppr. 51. 5

Elmen, on a ducal coronet a wyvern. 70. 9

Elmes, Lancs and Northamp., out of a ducal coronet or, a woman's head and neck couped below the breasts ppr., crined of the first. 182. 9

Elmhirst, Rev. William Heaton, of Elmhirst, near Barnsley, Yorks, a mount vert, therefrom issuant rays of sun, in front of a hurst of elm-trees ppr. *In Domino confido.*

Elmhirst, James, Esquire, of Elm House, Thorne, near Doncaster, same crest and motto.

Elmhirst, Rev. Robert, of Farnham Lodge, near Knaresborough, same crest and motto.

Elmhurst, Lincs, a clump of elms ppr.

Elmley, Viscount, *see* Beauchamp, Earl.

Elmore, the top of a halberd ppr. 172. 1

Elmore, a Cornish chough ppr. 107. 14

Elmsall of Thornhill, near Wakefield, Yorks: (1) An elm-tree, the trunk entwined with a vine-branch fructed, all ppr. (*for Elmsall*). 144. 7. (2) On a mount vert, a stag trippant or, holding in the mouth a slip of oak ppr. (*for Greaves*). *Amicta vitibus ulmus.* *cf.* 118. 2

Elmsey, a falcon's head erased ppr. 88. 12

Elmslie, a demi-wolf holding a spear in pale, tasselled, all ppr. 29. 4

Elmsly, Scotland, a thistle leaved ppr. *Prenez garde.* *cf.* 150. 7

Elmy and **Elney,** on a chapeau a tower ppr.

Elnorth, on a mount an ermine passant. 134. 10

Elphingston, Scotland, a dove arg., holding a snake ppr. 92. 7

Elphingston, Scotland, a griffin sejant sa., holding in the dexter claw a laurel-wreath vert. 62. 9

Elphingston, Scotland, a griffin sejant sa., holding a sword in pale, and on the point thereof a Saracen's head, all ppr. *Do well, and let them say.* *cf.* 62. 7

Elphingston, Scotland, a demi-lady richly attired holding in her dexter hand a garland ppr. *Merito.* 183. 5

Elphingston, two arms in saltier, in the dexter hand a sword and in the sinister a branch of laurel, all ppr. *In utroque paratus.*

Elphingston, Scotland, a dexter hand holding a pen. *Sedulitate.* 217. 10

Elphingston, Scotland, a demi-greyhound arg. 60. 11

Elphingston, a demi-greyhound rampant, collared and ringed. 60. 8

Elphinstone, Baron (Buller-Fullerton-Elphinstone), of Elphinstone, Stirlingsh., Scotland, a lady from the middle richly habited gu., holding in her dexter hand a tower arg., and in her sinister a branch of laurel ppr. *Cause causit.* 183. 8

Elphinstone, Lord Balmerinoch, Scotland, a dove arg., with a snake ppr. linked about its legs. *Prudentia fraudis nescia.*

Elphinstone, Lord Coupar, Scotland, a stag lodged in front of a tree ppr. *Sub umbra.*

Elphinstone, Dalrymple-Horne-, Sir Græme Hepburn, Bart., of Horn and Logie, Elphinstone, Aberdeen: (1) Two horns erect parted per fesse or and sa., counterchanged (*for Horne*). *cf.* 123. 8. (2) A rock ppr., over which the motto, "*Firm*" (*for Dalrymple*). 179. 7. (3) A hand in armour erect holding an ostrich-feather sa. (*for Elphinstone*). *Moneo et munio.*

Elphinstone, Sir Howard Warburton, Bart., M.A., of Sowerby, Cumb., out of a mural crown gu., a demi-woman affrontée habited, holding in her dexter hand a sword erect ppr., pommel and hilt or, and in her sinister an olive-branch vert. *Semper paratus.* 262. 12

Elphinstone-Stone, Captain Webb Elphinstone: (1) In front of an anchor lying fesseways or, flukes to the dexter, a swan's head and neck couped arg., beaked sa. (*for Stone*). (2) Out of a mural crown gu., a lady from the middle well attired ppr., holding in her dexter hand a sword and in her sinister a laurel-branch, both also ppr. (*for Elphinstone*). *True to the end.* 262. 12

Elphinstone, a dexter hand holding a garb ppr. *Non vi sed virtute.* 218. 1

Elrick, Scotland, out of a ducal coronet a horse's head, all ppr. *Dum spiro, spero.* 51. 7

Elringtou, the Roman fasces in pale ppr. 171 4

Elrington, Ireland, a stork sa. 105. 11

Elsley of Patrick Brompton and Mount St. John, a sagittarius regardant ppr. and arg., holding a bow and arrow of the first, charged on the side with a rose gu., barbed and seeded ppr. *Sans Dieu rien.* *cf.* 53. 5

Elson, Sussex, a demi-eagle displayed arg., billettée sa., beaked or. 81. 6

Elston, Durh., a demi-lion holding in the dexter paw a mullet arg. 15. 7

Elston, on a chapeau an escallop between two wings, all ppr. 141. 11

Elswell, on a bezant a cross patée gu.

Elsworth, a heart winged and crowned, all ppr. 110. 14

Elton, Heref., a lion's head erased and affrontée, collared az. *cf.* 18. 11

Elton, Major William, of Heathfield, Taunton, a dexter arm embowed in armour ppr., garnished or, adorned with a scarf about the wrist tied vert, the hand in a gauntlet holding a falchion ppr., pommel and hilt or. *Artibus et armis.* 291. 4

Elton, Rev. Edward Daubeny, Hopton Rectory, Aston-on-Clun, a dexter arm embowed vambraced, holding fesseways a falchion, all ppr., and encircling the arm at the elbow a cordon nowed vert.

Elton of London and Berks, out of a mural coronet gu., an arm vested or, turned up arg., holding in the hand ppr. a mullet of the second. 206. 12

Elton, Sir Edmund Harry, Bart., of Clevedon Court, Somers., an arm in armour embowed ppr., garnished or, charged with two estoiles gu., holding in the gauntlet a scimitar, also ppr., pommel and hilt or, tied round the wrist with a scarf vert. *Artibus et armis.* *cf.* 196. 4

Elvet, a lion sejant or. 8. 8

Elvin, Charles Norton, Esquire, M.A., of Eckling Grange, East Dereham, Norf., issuing from rocks ppr., a demi-lion rampant or, holding between the paws a vine-branch fructed, also ppr. *Elvenaca floreat vitis.* 12. 2

Elwell, a dart erect, point downwards. 173. 5

Elwes of Hablesthorpe, Notts, and Worleby, Lincs, five arrows, four in saltire and one in pale or, flighted and barbed arg., entwined by a snake gu.

Elwes, Henry Hervey, Esquire, J.P., of East Hill, Colchester, same crest. *Deo non fortuna.*

Elwes, Cary-, Valentine Dudley Henry, Billing Hall, Northamp.: (1) Five arrows or, barbed and feathered arg., entwined by a snake ppr. (*for Elwes*). 270. 7. (2) A swan arg., wings endorsed (*for Cary*). *Deo non fortuna.—In utroque fidelis.* 270. 8

Elwill, Bart. (*extinct*), of Exeter, an arm erect vested sa., cuffed arg., holding in the hand ppr. a fleece or. 208. 12

Elwin, Elwyn, and **Elwynn,** a demi-savage holding over his dexter shoulder a hammer ppr. 186. 11

Elwon, T. L., Esquire, J.P., D.L., of Saltburn-by-the-Sea, Yorks, late Major 4th Battalion of Princess of Wales' Own Yorkshire Regiment, in front of a stag's head sa., attired and collared gemelle or, three mascles interlaced fesseways of the last. *Dum spiro, spero.* 120. 13

Elwood of Loghmaske, co. Mayo, Ireland, a lion rampant gu., resting the fore-paws on the trunk of an oak-tree ppr.

Elwood, an arm in armour embowed, holding in the hand a pickaxe, all ppr. *Fide et sedulitate.*

Elworth, on a mount an ermine passant ppr. 134. 10

Elworthy, a steel cap ppr. 180. 1

Elworthy, Henry Stuart, Esquire, F.R.C.S., of 16, Rosebery Gardens, Crouch End, N., same crest. *Fide et sedulitate.* 293. 14

Elwyn, a demi-savage holding over the dexter shoulder a hammer ppr. 186. 11

Ely, Marquess of (Loftus), Ely Castle, Enniskillen, co. Fermanagh, a boar's head erased and erect arg. *Prends moi tel que je suis.—Loyal à mort.* 43. 3

Ely, Ireland, a pheon point upwards gu. 174. 9

Elyard, an arm in armour embowed holding in the hand a scimitar. 196. 10

Elye, an arm in armour holding in the hand a hawk's lure ppr.

Elyott, Elyot, and **Eliot,** of Green Place, Wonersh, Surrey, a griffin's head couped with wings endorsed sa., collared arg. *cf.* 67. 11

Eman, a lion sejant erect regardant purp. *cf.* 8. 13

Embery, a dexter arm embowed fesseways holding in the hand a sword in pale, enfiled with a Saracen's head in profile, all ppr. 201. 7

Embery, a pillar az., environed by a serpent ppr., the masonry of the base arg. *cf.* 176. 3

Emenfield, a hand holding an escutcheon or, charged with a martlet ppr. *cf.* 219. 7

Emer, out of a ducal coronet or, a demi-lion rampant gardant ppr., holding in the dexter paw a sword, also ppr., hilt and pommel of the first.

Emeric de St. Dalmas of Hauteville, Guernsey (of the Piedmontese family of Emerico di San Dalmazzo), out of a count's coronet two palms in saltier or. *Ut palma florebit.* 147. 2

Emeris, Rev. John, of Southwood, in front of a bear's head and neck couped sa., gorged with a collar gemelle, three cinquefoils or. *Emeritus.* 41. 9

Emeris, Rev. William Charles, M.A., of Taynton Vicarage, Burford, Oxon., same crest.

Emerson, Northumb., a sinister wing ppr., charged with a bend or, and thereon three torteaux.

Emerson, Durh., a lion rampant vert, bezantée, holding a battle-axe gu., headed arg.

Emerson, Charles Arthur, Esquire, of Deighton Manor, Northallerton, a demi-lion guardant erased az., holding between the paws a hawk's lure, and gorged with a plain collar or, debruised by a bendlet sinister wavy of the last. *Fideliter et honeste.* 241. 2

Emerson, Eleazer Biggins, Esquire, of Tollesby Hall, Marton R.S.O., Yorks., same crest and motto.

Emerson, John James, Esquire, of Easby Hall, Great Ayton, R.S.O., Yorks, same crest and motto.

Emerson, Peter Henry, Esquire, M.B., B.A., M.R.C.S., of Foxwold, Southbourne-on-sea, near Christchurch, Hants, in front of a demi-lion vert, charged on the shoulder with two barrulets dancettée or, and holding in the paws a battleaxe erect, a club fessewise entwined by a serpent, also ppr. *Audacter et hilare.*

Emerson-Tennent, Sir James, LL.D., of Tempo Manor, co. Fermanagh, Ireland: (1) A boar's head erased gu., charged with two crescents in fesse or (*for Tennent*). (2) A demi-lion rampant vert, bezantée, gorged with an Eastern crown or, and holding in the paws a battle-axe, staff gu., axe arg. (*for Emerson*). *Deus protector noster.*

Emerson of Dublin, Ireland, a demi-lion rampant vert, semée of torteaux, armed and langued gu., holding between the paws a battle-axe, the staff of the last, headed arg. *cf.* 15. 4

Emerson, Lincs and Norf., issuing from a cloud rays of the sun, all ppr. 162. 9

Emerton, Wolseley Partridge, Esquire, D.C.L., Banwell Castle, Somers., issuant from the wreath arg. and sa., a swan with wings addorsed and elevated arg. (*for Emerton*). 100. 2. Mr. Emerton also uses a second crest, viz: A partridge rising with an ear of wheat in its beak, all ppr. (*for Partridge*). *Rara avis in terris.—Nihil nisi labore.* 89. 11

Emery, Kent, a demi-unicorn rampant erased gu., armed and ungu. or, crined sa. *cf.* 48. 7

Emery, out of a mural coronet ppr., a demi-horse arg., maned or, collared gu., studded, also or. *Fidelis et suavis.*

Emeryke, out of a ducal coronet or, a boar's head and neck sa., collared arg. *cf.* 41. 4

Emes and **Emme** of London and Berks, a demi-lion rampant sa. 10. 1

Emline or **Emlyn,** a demi-savage wreathed about the loins and temples, holding with both hands a club over the dexter shoulder, all ppr. *Honestum prætulit utili.* *cf.* 186. 1

Emly, Baron (Monsell), of Tervoe, co Limerick, a lion rampant ppr., holding between the paws a mullet sa. *Mone sale.*

Emly, Ireland, a lion's gamb holding a battle-axe, all ppr. *cf.* 38. 3

Emlyn, Viscount, *see* Cawdor, Earl.

Emme, a demi-lion rampant gardant sa. 10. 8

Emmerson, a cock ppr. 91. 2

Emmet or **Emmett,** on a chapeau a unicorn's head erased ppr. 49. 10

Emmot or **Emmott,** a hind sejant regardant resting the dexter foot on a beehive ppr. 125. 1

Emmott, Green-, Walter Egerton John, Esquire, J.P., of Emmott Hall, Colne, Lancs: (1) Out of a ducal coronet composed of five leaves erminois a demi-buffalo sa., armed and ungu. or. (2) A stag's head arg., erased or, attired sa., gorged with a collar gemel gu., holding in the mouth a sprig of holly fructed ppr. *Tenez le vraye.—Nec in arido de fit.*

Emmott, Alfred, Esquire, of 30, Ennismore Gardens, S.W., and Spring Bank, Oldham, in front of a demi-bull sa., armed or, semée of annulets and gorged with a collar gemel arg., and holding between the legs a plate, three escallops reversed or. 235. 6

Emmott, Charles, Esquire, of Snow Hall, Gainford, Darlington, same crest.

Empson, Arthur Reginald, Esquire, of Yokefleet Hall, near Howden, Yorks, a tent arg., adorned or, lined az., charged in the interior with a cross pattée of the first. *cf.* 158. 7

Empson, a lion sejant gardant or, holding in the dexter paw a long cross gu., the sinister resting on a triangle pierced sa.

Emslie or **Emsly,** Scotland, a thistle leaved ppr. *Prenez garde.* *cf.* 150. 5

Encombe, Viscount, *see* Eldon, Earl.

Endas or **Eneas,** a castle triple-towered ppr., domed gu. *cf.* 155. 8

Enderbie and **Enderby,** a swan sa. 99. 2

Enderby or **Enderbie,** a maunch, therein a hand clenched. 203. 3

Enderby or **Enderbie,** a whaling harpooner in the act of striking ppr.

Endsore, Staffs, a cubit arm vested gu., holding a sword arg., hilt and pommel or.

Enell, a mermaid holding a comb and a glass ppr. 184. 5

Enery, *see* Cartwright-Enery.

Enery, Ireland, a falcon close ppr. *Sans changer.* 85. 2

Enfield, Viscount, *see* Strafford, Earl.

Enfield, Essex, a hand holding an escutcheon or, charged with a martlet ppr. *cf.* 219. 7

Engaine, a tower sa., the cupola and flag gu. 157. 15

Engham, Kent, two lions' gambs erect or, holding up a fire-ball gu.

Engham, an arm embowed vested az., cuffed indented arg., the hand grasping a snake entwined about the arm vert.

England, a cherub ppr. 189. 9

Englebert, Dorset, two wings addorsed and charged with two bends. *cf.* 109. 12

Engledow, Charles John, Esquire, of Rostellan Castle, co. Cork, a greyhound's head couped sa., collared arg. *Sans changer.*

Engledue, a greyhound's head erased sa., collared arg. *cf.* 61. 2

Englefield, Wilts, an eagle displayed per pale az. and gu. 75. 2

Englefield, Wilts, a sinister arm vested per pale az. and gu., cuffed arg., holding in the hand ppr. a branch vert.

Engleheart, an arm in armour embowed holding in the gauntlet a sword, all ppr. 195. 1

Engleheart, Sir John Gardiner Dillman, of 28, Curzon Street, Mayfair, London, an angel ppr., winged, and crowned or, and issuant from a ducal coronet of the last, holding in his dexter hand a sword arg.

English, Percy James, Esquire, of 42, Egerton Gardens, Kensington, London, in front of a cinquefoil vert, an arrow palewise or, between two branches of oak slipped, leaved, and fructed ppr.

English, Robert, Esquire, of 21, Portman Square, London, W., and Scatwell, Ross-shire, in front of a rose-branch slipped ppr., five lozenges fesseways and conjoined or. *Virtus semper viridis.* 307. 4

English, a greyhound's head between two roses slipped and leaved. 61. 11

English, a rose-branch ppr., flowered gu. 149. 8

English, Thomas Harks, Esquire, L.R.C.P., Eng., M.R.C.S. Lond., of Netherby, Sleights, Yorks, an oak-tree ppr. *Per secula manens.*

English, on a mount vert, a lion sejant laying his dexter paw on an antique shield sa.

English, a demi-lion. 10. 2

English, of Farmley co. Dublin, a demi-lion rampant sa., holding between his paws an estoile of six points or. *Nisi dominus frustra.* *cf.* 15. 8

English, a hand ppr. holding a covered cup arg. 217. 11

English, Ireland, a pyramid entwined with Woodbine. *cf.* 179. 12

Engolisme, a torteau. 159. 14

Ennew, Essex, a lion's head erased gu. 17. 2

Ennis, an anchor az., surmounted by a fleur-de-lis. 161. 9

Ennis, Ireland, an ox-yoke in bend. 178. 6

Ennis, Bart., of Ballinahowen Court, Westmeath, a boar's head erased, pierced by an arrow, all ppr., charged with an estoile az. *Virtute et valore.*

Ennis, John, Esquire, J.P., D.L., of Ballinahown Court, co. Westmeath. Same crest and motto.

Ennishowen, Baron (Chichester), a stork holding in its beak a snake ppr. *Famæ vestigia retinens.* *cf.* 105. 8

Enniskillen, Earl of (Cole), Florence Court, Enniskillen, Fermanagh, a demi-dragon vert, langued gu., holding in the dexter claw a dart or, headed and feathered arg., and resting his sinister upon an escutcheon az., charged with a harp or, stringed arg. *Deum cole, regem serva.* *cf.* 73. 10

Ennismore, Viscount, *see* Listowel, Earl.

Ennys, Cornw., a hand holding a garb ppr. 218. 1

Enoke, Worcs., a demi-lion holding in its paws a serpent nowed ppr. *cf.* 10. 2

Enson of Burton-on-Trent, Staffs, an arm in armour ppr., garnished or, holding in the hand a sword arg., hilt and pommel of the second. 210. 2

Ensor, a lion rampant per fess or and sa., holding in the dexter paw a fleur-de-lis gu. 2. 7

Ensor, Norf., a unicorn's head arg., armed and crined or. 49. 7

Enswell and **Entwissell,** Lancs, on a mount vert, a hind ppr., collared arg. 124. 14

Enswell and **Entwissell,** a human heart gu. 181. 2

Entwisle, John Bertie Norreys, Esquire, of Foxholes, Rochdale, and Kilworth House, Rugby: (1) A hand fesseways, couped above the wrist ppr., holding a fleur-de-lis erect or. *cf.* 221. 9. (2) A dexter arm in armour embowed, holding with the hand and by the hair a Saracen's head erased and affrontée, all ppr. *Per ce signe a Agincourt.*

Enys, Francis Gilbert, Esquire, J.P., of Enys, Penryhn, Cornw., three ostrich-feathers erect arg. *Serpentes velut et columbæ.* 115. 2

Epitre, a cinquefoil pierced gu. *cf.* 148. 12

Epps, Kent, on a chaplet vert, flowered or, a falcon rising of the last.

Ercall, a dexter hand ppr., holding up a mullet of six points or, charged with a crescent sa.

Erdeswike, Staffs, out of a ducal coronet gu., a boar's head per pale arg. and sa., langued of the first. 41. 4

Erdington, a hand holding a ball sa. 216. 3

Eredy of London, out of a coronet two wings, all ppr. 109. 8

Erington or **Errington,** Northumb. and Wilts, a cock gu., combed and wattled sa. 91. 2

Erington, Northumb., a unicorn's head erased quarterly arg. and gu. 49. 5

Erisby, a broken halberd ppr. *Auxilio Dei.* 172. 7

Erisey of Erisey, Cornw., a cinquefoil erm. 148. 12

Erisey, Cornw., a stag trippant ppr. 117. 8

Erle-Drak, *see* Drax.

Erle, Dorset, a lion's head erased or, transpierced by a spear arg., embrued gu. *cf.* 17. 8

Erle, Twynihoe William, Esquire, of Millhall, Cuckfield, Hayward's Heath, and Bramshott Grange, Liphook, Hants, a lion's head erased pierced through the neck with a spear, all ppr. *Stet fortuna domus.*

Erley or **Erly,** a hand erect ppr., holding a gem ring or, the stone gu.

Ermine, an ermine ppr. 134. 6

Ermingland, Norf., out of an antique crown a demi-lion gu. 10. 3

Erne, Earl of (Crighton), Crom Castle, Newtown Butler, Fermanagh, a wyvern's head couped vert, vomiting flames of fire from the mouth and ears ppr. *God send grace.* cf. 72. 3

Ernelle, Kent, a chevalier on horseback wielding a scimitar, all ppr. 189. 10

Ernle and **Ernley** of Ernle, Sussex, an eagle displayed vert. 75. 2

Ernst, an eagle gazing at the sun ppr. 75. 1

Erpingham, a pyramid of leaves vert and sa., issuing out of a ducal crown or.

Errington, Northumb. and Essex, a unicorn's head erased per pale arg. and gu. 49. 5

Errington, a stag's head couped at the neck arg., attired or, the tongue hanging out gu. 121. 9

Errington, (formerly Stanley) Sir John Massy, Bart., of Hooton, Chesh., a stag's head and neck couped arg., attired or, the tongue hanging out gu.

Errington, Sir George, Bart., J.P., of Lackham Manor, Wilts, a unicorn's head erased quarterly arg. and gu., armed and crined or. 49. 5

Errington, Gladwin-, Gilbert Launcelot, Hinchley Wood House, Ashbourne, same crest and motto.

Errington, William Valentine, 17, Hans Place, S.W., a unicorn's head erased arg.

Errington, a cock gu., combed and wattled sa. 91. 2

Errol, Earl of (Hay), of Slains Castle, Cruden, Aberdeen, a falcon rising ppr. *Serva jugum.* 87. 1

Erskine, Earl of Buchan, Earl of Mar, Earl of Mar and Kellie, *see* Buchan and Mar, and Mar and Kellie.

Erskine, Baron (Erskine), of Restormel Castle, Cornw., a dexter arm embowed, the hand grasping a club, all ppr. *Trial by jury.* 202. 10

Erskine, Lord Erskine, a dexter hand grasping a club or. *Fortitudine.* 214. 6

Erskine, Scotland, a dexter hand holding a club raguly ppr. *Judge nought.* 214. 6

Erskine, Bart., of Torrie, Scotland, a cubit arm erect, the hand grasping a sword ppr., hilt and pommel or. *Fortitudine.* 212. 13

Erskine, a dexter hand and arm erect holding a dagger in pale. 212. 9

Erskine, Scotland, a dexter arm in armour grasping in the hand a sword ppr. *Je pense plus.* 210. 2

Erskine, Scotland, a dexter arm from the elbow ppr., holding a cross crosslet fitchée or. *Think well.* 221. 14

Erskine, a dexter arm in armour embowed holding a dagger erect. 196. 5

Erskine of Tinwald, Scotland, a dexter hand ppr. holding a skene in pale arg., hilted and pommelled or, within a garland of olive-leaves ppr. *Je pense plus.—Perspicax audax.*

Erskine, Scotland, a dexter hand holding a dagger in pale ppr., within an orle of laurel vert. *Je pense plus.—Perspicax audax.*

Erskine, Scotland, a cubit arm erect grasping a sword ppr., hilted or. 212. 3

Erskine, Scotland, a dexter arm embowed holding in the hand a scimitar. *Je pense plus.* 201. 1

Erskine of Alva, Scotland, a dexter arm in armour embowed and gauntleted grasping a sword ppr. *Je pense plus.* 195. 1

Erskine, Henry David, Esquire, C.V.O., J.P., D.L., of Cardross, Stirling, N.B., of Linlathen, Forfarsh., a sword erect bearing on the point a boar's head erased ppr. *Fortitudine non insidiis.* 42. 4

Erskine of Carnock, Fifesh., a sword erect bearing on the point a boar's head ppr. *Fortitudine.* cf. 42. 4

Erskine, a boar's head erased and erected ppr. *Fortitudine.* 43. 3

Erskine, Scotland, a griffin's head erased holding in the beak a sword in bend, all ppr. *In Domino confido.* 66. 10

Erskine, West-: (1) A griffin's head erased gu., charged with a mullet erm., holding in the beak a sword bendwise point upwards ppr. (*for Erskine*). cf. 66. 10. (2) Out of a mural crown ppr., a griffin's head az., charged with a trefoil slipped or (*for West*). *Jour de ma vie.—In Domino confido.* cf. 67. 10

Erskine, Scotland, a demi-griffin holding in its dexter claw a sword, all ppr. *Ausim et confido.* 64. 6

Erskine, Scotland, a demi-lion rampant gu. 10. 3

Erskine, Scotland, a demi-lion rampant gu., holding in the dexter paw a thistle ppr., and in the sinister a fleur-de-lis az. *Je pense plus.* 13. 12

Erskine, Knight-, Henry William, Pittodrie, Pitcaple, Aberdeen, same crest and motto.

Erskine, Kennedy-, Augustus John William Henry, Dun House, Montrose, N.B.: (1) A dolphin naiant ppr. (2) A griffin's head erased gu., charged with a mullet erm., holding in the beak a sword bendwise point upwards ppr.

Erskine, Sir Ffolliott Williams, Bart., D.L., of Cambo, Fifesh., a garb fessewise or, thereon a cock with wings expanded ppr., charged with a bend wavy sinister az. *Veillant et vaillant.*

Erthe, Scotland, a cock crowing. *Audax.* 91. 2

Erving, a hand holding a mill-rind.

Erving, on a plate a cross sa.

Erwin, Scotland, on a mount vert, a tree ppr., thereto chained a boar passant or, collar, chain, and padlock az. *Lock sick.*

Escales, out of a ducal coronet gu., seven ostrich-feathers arg.

Eschallers, Cambs, a mermaid having a double tail, displayed on either side.

Esclabor, a galley with her sails furled sa., flags gu. 160. 6

Escot or **Esscot,** Cornw., a lion passant per pale arg. and sa. 6. 2

Escott, an ostrich gu., holding in its beak a horse-shoe or. 97. 8

Esdaile of London, a demi-lion rampant holding in its paws a mullet of six points or. cf. 15. 8

Esdaile, Charles Edward Jeffries, Cothelestone House, Taunton, same crest.

Esdaile, a flag issuant sa. 176. 15

Esharton, a demi-lion per chevron or and vert. 10. 2

Eshelby, a rose arg., barbed and seeded ppr., between two wings vair, on each wing a fesse gu., charged with a bezant. *Excelle bene merendo.*

Esher, Viscount (Brett), of Esher, Surrey, a lion passant gu., charged on the shoulder with a cross botony fitchée or, and holding in the dexter fore-paw a fasces ppr. *Vicimus.* 262. 7

Esingold, a chevalier on horseback brandishing a sword ppr. 189. 10

Esler, Robert, Esquire, M.D., M.Ch., of 4, Queen's Road, Peckham, London, S.E., two proboscides couped, the dexter per fesse sa. and gu., the sinister per fesse sa. and or, each charged in base with a stripe counterchanged. *Ne vile velis.* 300. 10

Esmé and **Esmey,** a savage wreathed about the head and middle with leaves, holding in the dexter hand a club resting upon the wreath, all ppr.

Esmond, Ireland, a horned owl sa. 96. 5

Esmonde, Sir Thomas Henry Grattan, Bart., M.P., of Ballynastragh Gorey, co. Wexford, Ireland, out of a mural coronet gu., a knight's head in armour in profile with visor raised, all ppr., and in an escroll above the word "*Jerusalem.*" *Malo mori quam fœdari.*

Espeke, an ostrich's head between two wings arg., holding in the beak a horse-shoe az. cf. 97. 10

Espinasse, issuing from clouds two hands conjoined in fess, supporting a heart inflamed ppr. 224. 5

Essery, Richard Aubrey, Cefn Bryn, Penmaen, R.S.O., Glamorgansh., a stag trippant ppr.

Essex, Earl of (Capell), of Cassiobury, Watford, a demi-lion rampant or, holding in the dexter paw a cross crosslet fitchée gu. *Fide et fortitudine.* 11. 10

Essex of London, out of a mural coronet erm., a griffin's head or. 67. 10

Essex, out of a mural coronet erm., a demi-eagle displayed or, the wings vair. 80. 8

Essex, an eagle's head or, gorged with a ducal coronet per pale az. and sa. cf. 83. 1

Essex, Berks, an eagle's head or, holding in the beak a hawk's leg erased at the thigh gu.

Essex, Cowper-, late Thomas Christopher, Yewfield Castle, Outgate, Ambleside: (1) On the capital of an Ionic column a griffin's head couped sa., charged with two quatrefoils or. 268. 1. (2) A cubit arm erect vested gu. and cuffed arg., holding in the hand ppr. a lantern suspended from a staff, all ppr. 268. 2. *Conduco.*

Essington, Lincs, a horse's head erased arg. 51. 4

Essington, Glouc., a hand ppr., holding a fusil or. 219. 10

Essington of Ribbesford House, Bewdley, Worcs., on a mount vert, a fusil fesseways arg., in front of a cubit arm erect ppr., grasping a fusil. *Sea or land.*

Estanton, a wyvern or. 70. 1

Estatford, a dexter hand holding a sword by the blade in bend hilt upwards, all ppr.

Estcott, a seagull with wings expanded sa.

Estcourt, Sotheron-, Rt. Hon. George Thomas John, Estcourt, Tetbury: (1) Issuant from a mural crown per pale az. and gu., a demi-eagle displayed or, each wing charged with a mullet of six points, also az. (*for Estcourt*). 81. 1. (2) A double-headed eagle displayed per pale arg. and gu., charged on the breast and each head crowned with a mural coronet or, on each wing four cross crosslets counterchanged (*for Sotheron*).

Estcourt, out of a mural coronet az., a demi-eagle displayed ppr., beaked or. 80. 8

Estday, Kent, on a mount vert, a hind lodged arg. 125. 4

Este, a garb or, banded gu. 153. 2

Esteley and **Estley,** on a ducal coronet three daggers, one in pale and two in saltier or.

Estercombe, Somers., out of a ducal coronet or, a griffin's head az., beaked of the first. 67. 9

Esterley, Lincs, a mastiff passant arg.

Estewer, *see* Estower.

Estland and **Estlin,** an arm in armour embowed ppr., holding in the hand a fleur-de-lis or. 199. 14

Estling, a demi-talbot gu., holding in the dexter paw a battle-axe ppr.

Estmerton, two dexter hands in fess, couped and conjoined ppr., supporting a cross crosslet fitched sa. 224. 11

Estoft, Lincs, a lion's gamb quarterly gu. and arg., holding up a crescent or. 39. 15

Eston, Devonsh., on a mount vert, five ears of wheat erect or, stalked and leaved ppr. 154. 7

Estote, a fleur-de-lis gu. 148. 2

Estower and **Estewer,** a goat statant arg 129. 5

Estrange, Glouc., a chevalier on horseback at full speed holding a broken lance ppr. 189. 5

Estridge, Henry Whatley, Muiety House, Malmesbury, an ostrich ppr. *Deus tutamen.*

Estwood, a lion's head erased and crowned, all or. 18. 8

Estwood, *see* Eastwood.

Etelum, a talbot's head ducally crowned or. *cf.* 56. 9

Ethelstan, Lancs, an eagle displayed purp. 75. 2

Ethelstan and **Ethelston,** a broken spear. 175. 6

Ethelston, Robert Peel, Esquire, J.P., of Hinton, Whitchurch, Salop, a ram's head couped sa., charged with three cross crosslets or. *Dat et sumit Deus.* *cf.* 130. 1

Etheridge, a crescent charged with an étoile of six points. *cf.* 163. 2

Etherington, Yorks, a tower decayed on the sinister side, on a battlement thereof a leopard's face ppr.

Etienne of Guernsey, on a rock ppr., a salmon lying fesseways arg., holding in the mouth a rose gu., leaved and stalked vert.

Eton, a crow's head erased ppr.

Eton, a lion's head erased arg., devouring a tun or.

Etton, Chesh., a hand holding a dagger in pale thrust through a boar's head couped ppr. 212. 6

Ettrick, Baron, *see* Napier, Baron.

Ettrick of High Barnes, Durh., a demi-lion rampant gu., holding in the dexter paw a marshal's baton sa., tipped at each end or.

Etty, a lion rampant gardant. 2. 5

Ety, Yorks, a husbandman mowing with a scythe ppr. 188. 12

Euen, Scotland, a demi-lion holding in the dexter paw a mullet gu. *Audaciter.* 15. 7

Eure, a stag's head erased az., attired arg., charged with the sun or. 121. 14

Eure, a horse's head arg. *Artis vel Martis.* *cf.* 50. 13

Eure, Shropsh., two lions' gambs or, supporting an escallop-shell arg.

Eure, two lions' gambs erect gu., holding an escallop arg.

Eure, a talbot passant or. 54. 1

Eureux, five arrows, one in pale and four in saltier gu., headed or, feathered arg., bound by a belt of the first, buckled of the second. 173. 3

Eustace, a hand holding a close helmet ppr. 217. 12

Eustace, Ireland, a stag statant ppr. 117. 5

Eustace, a stag at gaze, and between the attires a crucifix, all ppr. *Cur me persequeris.* *cf.* 117. 6

Eustace, Rev. William, Vicar of Stradbally and Moyanna, Queen's Co., Ireland, a stag at gaze ppr., charged with a fleur-de-lis and a saltire wavy couped in fesse gu., and between the attires a crucifix arg. *Cur me persequeris.* 117. 6

Eustace, a stag's head caboshed, and between the attires a crucifix, all ppr. *Soli Deo gloria.* 122. 13

Euston, Earl of, *see* Grafton, Duke of.

Euston, a boar passant sa., armed, bristled and hoofed arg. 40. 9

Evans-Freke, *see* Carberry, Baron.

Evans-Fitz-Henry, *see* Fitz-Henry.

Evans, *see* Blackwall-Evans.

Evans, a lion passant sa. 6. 2

Evans, Major David Williams, of Glascoed, Llansantffraid, near Oswestry, a lion gardant arg., charged on the body with two crosses moline az., and resting the dexter fore-paw on an escutcheon erminois, thereon a cross moline between four lozenges, also az. *Festina lente.*

Evans, Edward, Esquire, of Bronwylfa, near Wrexham, a lion passant regardant arg., the body charged with three crosses moline gu., and resting the dexter paw upon a bundle of rods banded, also gu. *Libertas.*

Evans, Edward, Esquire, of Spital Old Hall, near Spital, Chesh., same crest and motto.

Evans, Edward Wallace, Esquire, of Whitbourne Hall, Worcs., same crest and motto.

Evans of Moreton Court, Heref., a lion rampant regardant bendy of six erm. and sa., supporting a tilting-spear erect ppr., enfiled with a boar's head erased, also sa. *Libertas.*

Evans, William, Esquire, of Lynnon, Carnarvon, the Roman faces fessewise, thereon a lion rampant holding in his dexter paw a scimitar, all ppr.

Evans, Davies-, Herbert, Esquire, Highmead, Llanybyther, Carmarthen: (1) A wolf's head arg., guttée-de-sang, gorged with a collar gemel and erased gu. (*for Evans*). 30. 11. (2) A lion rampant or, semée of crosses pattée fitchée az., gorged with a collar dancettée, with a chain reflexed over the back sa. (*for Davies*). *Fide et virtute.* *cf.* 1. 3

Evans, Franklen George, Esquire, J.P., of Llwynartha, Castleton, near Cardiff, between two crosses couped gu., a tower ppr., thereon a flagstaff of the last with a pennant flying to the sinister gu., charged with two mullets of six points arg. *Nisi Dominus frustra.* 263. 14

Evans, George, Esquire, of Gortmerron House, Dungannon, co. Tyrone, a demi-lion rampant regardant erminois, holding between the paws a boar's head couped sa. *Libertas.*

Evans, Josiah, Esquire, a nag's head erased arg., between two estoiles or. *A fynno Duw derfid.*

Evans, Lieutenant-General Sir De Lacy, G.C.B., out of a mural crown gu., a demi-lion regardant or, holding between the paws a boar's head couped sa. *Espana agradecida.* *cf.* 16. 5

Evans-Lombe, Edward Henry, Esquire, of Bylaugh Park, East Dereham, and Melton Hall, Wymondham, two tilting-spears in saltire or, each having a small pennon gu. *Propositi tenax.*

Evans, Sir Francis Henry, Bart., K.C.M.G., Tubbendens, Orpington, Kent, in front of a demi-lion gu., charged on the shoulder with a cross crosslet arg., an anchor fessewise, the flukes to the dexter ppr. *Omnia si patienter.* 262. 2

Evans, Thomas D'Arcy, Esquire, J.P., of Knockaderry, co. Limerick, Ireland: (1) A demi-lion rampant regardant or, holding between the paws a boar's head couped sa. (*for Evans*). (2) A tilting-spear broken in three pieces, the head in pale, the others in saltire ppr., banded gu. (*for D'Arcy*). *Libertas.* 175. 2

Evans, David, of Ffrwdgrech, near Brecon, a lion rampant. *Duw a Phol Daioni.*

Evans, Evan Laming, Esquire, M.A., M.D., F.R.C.S., of 36, Bryanston Street, Great Cumberland Place, London, W., a lion passant guardant. *Libertas.*

Evans, Ireland and Wales, a demi-lion rampant regardant or, holding between the paws a boar's head couped sa. *Libertas.*

Evans, Charles Payne, Esquire, J.P., D.L., of Llanstephan House, Llanstephan,

Radnorsh., upon two arrows in saltire a boar's head couped, all or. *Heb Dduw, heb ddim.* 41. 13

Evans, William Gwynne, Esquire, of Penlan Hall, Fordham, Essex. and Oaklands Park, Newnham, Glouc., upon a rock ppr., a boar's head couped sa., between two daggers erect or.

Evans, Sir David, K.C.M.G., of Ewell Grove, Surrey, upon the trunk of a tree couped and eradicated, and sprouting to the dexter, a boar's head erect and erased, all ppr. *Trwy rhinwedd ac olesterwydd*

Evans, David, Esquire, J.P., of Cleveland House, Grangetown, R.S.O., Yorks, in front of a javelin ppr., a dragon statant sa., holding in the mouth a rose gu., slipped and leaved ppr. *Ydewraf ennilla.* 267. 11

Evans-Gordon, Major-General Charles Spalding of Preston Cottage, Ightham, Sevenoaks, a demi-savage holding in his right hand an ear of wheat ppr. *Tam pace quam prælio.*

Evans, Derbysh., a boar's head erased in a charger, all arg.

Evans of Allestree Hall, Derbysh., out of a round dish or, a boar's head erased fessewise erminois.

Evans, England and Wales, on a ducal coronet or, a boar's head in fess erased sa. *cf.* 48. 2

Evans, Oliver Conrad Penrhys, Esquire, M.D., B.S., of 22, Church Street, Kidderminster, on a ducal coronet a boar's head erased close. *Probitas et libertas.*

Evans, James, Chepstow, Monmouthsh., a dexter hand gauntleted in fesse grasping a fleur-de-lis. *Deus nobis hæc fecimus.*

Evans, Heref., out of an earl's coronet an arm in armour embowed holding in the hand a sword, all ppr., the point embrued gu. *cf.* 195. 12

Evans of London and Shropsh., an arm embowed, vested gu., cuffed or, holding in the hand a gilliflower ppr., stalked and leaved vert.

Evans, Norf., a dexter cubit arm erect, vested barry wavy of six az. and or, cuffed arg., holding in the hand a parchment-roll ppr. *cf.* 208. 5

Evans, Heref., a cubit arm erect holding in the hand a torch inflamed, also erect, all ppr.

Evans, a paschal lamb passant bearing a banner, all ppr. 130. 2

Evans, Benjamin Hill, Esquire, F.Z.S., F.R.G.S., of the Mall, Ravenscourt Park, a paschal lamb bearing a banner, all ppr.

Evans, a stag trippant ppr., attired and unguled or. 117. 8

Evans, C. Wilfred Evans, Esquire, of Ely, an eagle displayed.

Evans, William Herbert, Forde Abbey, Chard: (1) A demi-lion rampant or, holding between his paws a boar's head couped sa. (2) A demi-griffin rampant or. *Libertas.*

Evans, John Carbery, Pymme's Park, Edmonton, N., on a ducal coronet or, a boar's head couped sa., langued gu. *Libertas.*

Evans, an eagle's head erased sa. 85. 2

Evans, Bucks, an eagle's head between two wings sa., holding in the beak a rose gu., stalked and leaved ppr. *cf.* 84. 2

Evans, Peter Fabyan Sparke, Esquire, J.P., of Trinmore, Clifton Downs, upon a rock a peacock ppr., charged on the breast with a quatrefoil or, resting the dexter foot on a sprig of oak leaved, fructed and slipped, also ppr. *Deo favente.*

Evans, Joseph, Esquire, J.P., Lord of the Manor of Parr, Lancs; of Hurst House and Haydock Grange, Lancs; Llanddoget Park, Denbighsh., and Maenan House, Carnarvonsh., a nag's head erased arg., between two estoiles or. *In cœlo quies.* *cf.* 51. 3

Evatt, a lion's gamb erased ppr., holding a torteau. 39. 13

Eveleigh-De Moleyns, Rt. Hon. Dayrolles Blakeney, **Baron Ventry**: (1) A savage's head affrontée couped below the shoulders ppr. (*for De Moleyns*). (2) A goat's head erased per chevron or and sa., armed of the last, holding in the mouth a branch of laurel ppr. (*for Eveleigh*). *Vivere sat vincere.* *cf.* 128. 5

Eveleigh of West Eveleigh, Clyst St. Lawrence, and Holcome, Devonsh., a goat's head erased per chevron or and sa., armed of the last, holding in the mouth a branch of laurel ppr. *cf.* 128. 5

Eveleigh, Devonsh., between two laurel-branches in orle a stag lodged gardant ppr. 116. 11

Eveleigh, Devonsh., a demi-griffin per pale or and sa. 64. 2

Evelick, Scotland, a sword in pale, on its point a pair of scales, all ppr. *Recta vel ardua.* 179. 1

Evelyn, Bart. (*extinct*), of Long Ditton, Surrey, a griffin passant or, the beak and fore-legs az., ducally gorged of the last. *Durate.* 63. 3

Evelyn, William John, Wotton, Dorking, same crest and motto.

Evens, a demi-lion rampant sa. 10. 1

Everard, Bart., of Much-Waltham, Essex, a man's head couped at the shoulders ppr., on his head a long cap barry wavy of eight or and sa., turned up of the second.

Everard, William Thomas, Bardon Hall, Leics., same crest.

Everard of Gillingham, Norf., a man's head in profile couped at the shoulders ppr., having a cap or, fretty sa. *Say and do.*

Everard, a man's head couped at the shoulders ppr., on his head a cap chequy or and az., tasselled of the last.

Everard, a Moor's head couped at the shoulders in profile ppr., wreathed arg. and az. 192. 13

Everard of Hawkdown, Suff., three annulets conjoined or. 167. 11

Everard, a pelican in her piety ppr. *Virtus in actione consistit.* 98. 14

Everard, Colonel Nugent Talbot, J.P., D.L., of Randlestown, Navan, co. Meath, a pelican in her piety, her wings endorsed and inverted. *Virtus in actione consistit.*

Everdon, on the top of a Doric pillar arg., a terrestrial globe ppr.

Evered, Andrew Robert Guy, Hill House, Otterhampton, Bridgwater, out of a mural coronet gu., an estoile gu., between two wings displayed or. *Vigilans et audax.*

Everest, on the point of a sword a mullet, all ppr. 169. 3

Everest, upon a broken battlement ppr., a stork sa., resting the dexter claw upon a cinquefoil or. *Semper otium rogo divos.*

Everet or **Everett,** an arm in armour couped and embowed, the elbow resting on a chapeau and the hand holding a spear. 197. 4

Everet or **Everett,** a griffin's head erased sa., collared of three pieces, the middle or, the others arg. *cf.* 66. 2

Everett, Wilts, a griffin's head sa., erased gu., charged with three barrulets, the centre one arg., the others or, over all a pallet wavy erm. 66. 3

Evering, a wyvern sejant or, with wings expanded gu.

Everingham, Yorks and Lincs, a demi-lion rampant arg., holding in the dexter paw a rose-branch flowered or, stalked and leaved vert. 12. 1

Everington, the late Mitchell, Esquire, of Denmark Hill, Camberwell, Surrey, in front of the trunk of a tree eradicated fessewise and sprouting to the sinister ppr., a stag current per pale arg. and gu., holding in the mouth a trefoil slipped vert. 118. 14

Everit or **Everitt,** a demi-lady holding in her dexter hand a pair of scales equipoised ppr. 183. 2

Everitt, George Allen, Esquire, J.P., Knight of the Orders of Leopold and of Hanover, of Knowle Hall, near Birmingham, Warw., a griffin's head erased ppr., the neck encircled gemelle of three pieces arg. *Festina lente.* *cf.* 66. 2

Everitt, Nicholas, Esquire, of Oulton Broad, Suffolk, out of the coronet of a marquess a bear's head muzzled and chained.

Everitt, F. W. E., Esquire, of Lincoln's Inn, Middx., a griffin segreant or, winged vairée of the last and gu., supporting a tilting-spear erect ppr. *cf.* 62. 2

Evers, a dexter arm ppr., vested quarterly or and sa., holding a roll of paper arg. 208. 8

Eversfield, Sussex, out of a ducal coronet a camel's head, all or. *cf.* 132. 7

Evershead, Surrey, a mullet of six points or, between two wings arg. 112. 1

Eversley, Viscount (*extinct*), Rt. Hon. the late Charles Shaw-Lefevre, six arrows interlaced saltireways, three and three ppr., and interlacing an annulet or. *Sans changer.*

Everton, Suff., a buck's head erased or, pellettée, attired sa. *cf.* 121. 2

Every, Sir Edward Oswald, Bart., of Egginton, Derbysh., a demi-unicorn arg., guttée-de-sang, armed and crined or. *Suum cuique.* 48. 7

Every, Staffs, Devonsh., and Dorset, a demi-unicorn gu., crined, armed, and unguled or. 48. 7

Every-Halstead, Charles Edward, Esquire, of Mainstone Court, Ledbury, Heref.: (1) Out of a mural crown chequy or and az., a demi-eagle displayed erm., beaked gold (*for Halstead*). (2) A demi-unicorn arg., guttée-de-sang, and crined or (*for Every*).

Evesham, a Moor's head in profile ppr., in a helmet or.

Evett, Worcs., a demi-dragon or, holding a cross formée flory gu. *cf.* 73. 10

Evington and **Evinton,** within a serpent in orle a boar's head erased and erect. 41. 11

Evington, out of a mural coronet az., a unicorn's head ppr., caparisoned and plumed of the first, armed or.

Evington, Middx. and Hants, out of a mural coronet az., a nag's head in armour ppr., on the head three feathers, the centre one arg., between two of the first. *cf.* 50. 14

Evington, Lincs, a horse's head erased arg., collared az. *cf.* 51. 4

Evre, a parrot feeding on a bunch of cherries, all ppr. 101. 8

Evreux, out of a ducal coronet or, a talbot's head sa. 57. 12

Ewan, Scotland, a demi-lion rampant. *Audaciter.* 10. 2

Ewarby, out of a ducal coronet or, a female's bust, the face ppr., vested gu., crined of the first. 182. 9

Ewart, a hand erect gauntleted, holding a cross crosslet fitched in pale. 210. 4

Ewart, a hand holding a dagger, all ppr. *Abest timor.* 212. 9

Ewart, Henry Peter, Felix Hall, Kelvedon, Essex, same crest.

Ewart, Sir William, Bart., of Glenmachan House, co. Down, Ireland, a hand erect gauntleted ppr., holding a cross crosslet fitchée in pale gu. *In cruce spero.* 210. 14

Ewart, John Hoggan, Esquire, M.D., of 23, Clifton Cross, Folkestone, a dexter cubit arm in armour fesseways holding in the gauntlet a sword wavy in pale pierced through a human heart, all ppr. *Pro Deo, Rege et Patria.*

Ewart, a hand holding a cutlass, all ppr. *cf.* 212. 13

Ewart, General Sir John Alexander, K.C.B., Craig Cleuch, Langholm, Dumfriessh., a dexter gauntlet fesseways holding a sword erect, enfiled with a heart distilling blood gu. *Abest timor.* 233. 9

Ewart, a heart ppr., transfixed by a sword arg., hilt and pommel or. 181. 6

Ewbank, Durh., out of a ducal coronet gu., a dragon's head or. 72. 4

Ewbank, out of a ducal coronet a dexter and a sinister hand, each holding an ostrich-feather.

Ewen, on a mount vert, a stork statant ppr. *cf.* 105. 11

Ewen, a curlew ppr.

Ewen, John Norris Frederick, Reydon Hall, Wangford, Suff., same crest.

Ewens, Dorset and Somers., on a mount vert, a curlew rising ppr.

Ewens of Wincanton, Somers., on a mount vert, a curlew ppr.

Ewer and **Ewar,** a pheon or, headed arg., mounted on a broken dart gu., entwined by a serpent ppr.

Ewerby, an eagle displayed per fess vert and arg. 75. 2

Ewers, a staff raguly or. *cf.* 147. 10

Ewers, a demi-heraldic tiger rampant or. 25. 13

Ewes, a quatrefoil vert. 148. 10

Ewing, Bart., *see* Orr-Ewing, Bart.

Ewing, an arm in armour couped and tied at the shoulder embowed, resting the elbow on a chapeau gu., and holding in the hand a sceptre. *cf.* 196. 9

Ewing, Ireland, the moon in her complement ppr. 162. 4

Ewing, Scotland, a demi-lion gardant. 10. 8

Ewing, Major William, of London, a demi-lion rampant gu., armed and langued az., holding in his dexter paw a mullet, also gu. *Audaciter.* 15. 7

Ewing, Archibald Orr, Esquire, of Ballikinrain, Stirlingsh., and Lennoxbank, Dumbartonsh., Scotland, a demi-lion rampant gu., armed and langued az., holding in his dexter paw a mullet, also gu. *Audaciter.* 15. 7

Ewing of Burton Grange, Cheshunt, Herts, a demi-lion rampant holding in the dexter fore-paw a mullet gu. *Audaciter.* 15. 7

Exalt, an eagle's head erased sa., charged on the neck with three étoiles in fess or. *cf.* 83. 2

Exeter, Marquess of (Cecil), of Burghley, near Stamford, Northamp., on a chapeau gu., turned up erm., a garb or, supported by two lions, the dexter arg., the sinister az. *Cor unum, via una.* *cf.* 3. 5

Exeter, out of a ducal coronet two arms in saltier ppr., each hand holding a scimitar in pale, also ppr. *cf.* 92. 5

Exmew, a dove arg., holding in its beak a text R or, from a sprig of laurel ppr.

Exmouth, Viscount (Pellew), of Canonteign, Dunsford, near Exeter, upon waves of the sea the wreck of the *Dutton*, in the background a hill, upon the top of which a tower with a flag hoisted. *Deo adjuvante.—Algiers.*

Exton, the sail of a ship ppr. 160. 9

Eychebald, Yorks, a boar's head in bend couped sa.

Eye, on a chapeau gu., turned up erm., two wings ppr. *cf.* 112. 9

Eyer, a talbot's head erased arg., spotted gu., collared az. 56. 1

Eyland, Lincs, on a chapeau az., turned up or, a martlet gu. 95. 1

Eyles, a lion's gamb erased lying fesseways arg., holding a fleur-de-lis sa.

Eynes, Shropsh., *see* Heynes.

Eynes, Shropsh., Oxon., and Dorset, an eagle displayed standing on a tortoise ppr. 74. 12

Eynes, Shropsh., Oxon., and Dorset, an eagle displayed az., semée of étoiles or. *cf.* 75. 2

Eynford and **Eynsworth,** a hand holding a wheat-ear or. 218. 14

Eyre, Bucks, a phœnix close ppr. 82. 9

Eyre, William Gregory, Esquire, of Eyrecourt Castle, Ballinasloe, an armed leg couped at the thigh ppr., garnished and spurred or. 193. 1

Eyre, Lord Eyre, Ireland, same crest. *Pro rege sæpe, pro patriâ semper.*

Eyre, Frederick James, Esquire, of Barton Terrace, North Adelaide, South Australia, a leg in armour couped at the thigh ppr., garnished and spurred gold, charged with a mullet gu. (*for cadency*), and debruised (*for distinction*) by a baton sinister. *Pro Rege sæpe, pro patriâ semper.*

Eyre, Arthur Hardolph, Esquire, a leg in armour couped at the thigh quarterly arg. and sa., spurred or. *Virtus sola invicta.* 193. 1

Eyre, Colonel Henry, C.B. (late of), Rampton Manor, Lincs, same crest and motto.

Eyre, George Edward Briscoe, Warrens, Bramshaw, near Lyndhurst, same crest. *Sola virtus invicta.*

Eyre, Henry John Andrews, Shaw House, Newbury, same crest.

Eyre, Lieutenant-Colonel Henry Robert, 10, Berkeley Square, W., same crest. *Si je puis.*

Eyre, Vincent Thomas Joseph, of Lindley Hall, Nuneaton, Leics., same crest. *Neminem metue innocens.*

Eyre, Thomas Joseph, of Thorpe Lee, Egham, Staines, same crest and motto.

Eyre, Yorks, a leg in armour couped at the thigh quarterly vair and sa., spurred or. 193. 1

Eyre, Derbysh. and Wilts, a leg in armour couped at the thigh per pale arg. and sa., spurred or. 193. 2

Eyre, Middx., Cambs. and Wilts, a leg in armour couped at the thigh per pale arg. and gu., spurred or. 193. 1

Eyre, Wilts, on a chapeau a booted leg. *Virtus sola invicta.*

Eyre, an antelope sejant or, attired and ducally gorged arg. *cf.* 126. 4

Eyre, an ibex maned, armed, and ducally gorged arg.

Eyre, a lion passant gardant, tail extended gu. *cf.* 4. 3

Eyre, a dexter gauntlet ppr. 209. 8

Eyre-Matcham, William Eyre, Newhouse, near Salisbury, out of an Eastern crown or, a cubit arm habited vert, in the hand ppr. three ears of barley stalked and bladed of the first.

Eyres, Wilts, an armed leg couped at the thigh, garnished and spurred or. *Sola virtus invicta.* 193. 1

Eyres of Dumbleton Hall, Glouc.: (1) Upon a mount ppr., a human leg couped at the thigh in armour quarterly sa. and or, the spur or, on either side three cinquefoils slipped, vert (*for Eyres*). (2) A lion rampant gu., holding in the dexter fore-paw a cross patée fitchée, and resting the sinister hind-paw on a cross patée or (*for Kettlewell*).

Eyres, a lion's gamb sa., holding a sceptre in pale or. *cf.* 38. 7

Eyres, a griffin's head erased, ducally gorged and lined, holding in the beak a laurel-branch. *cf.* 66. 11

Eyringham, on a chapeau ppr., a fleur-de-lis or. *cf.* 148. 2

Eyston, an étoile of eight points or. *cf.* 164. 4

Eyston, two arms embowed vested holding up an escallop.

Eyston of East Hendred, Berks, a lion sejant or. 8. 8

Eyston, John Joseph, of Hendred House, Steventon, Berks, an estoile of eight points or.

Eyton, out of a ducal coronet or, a demi-dragon with wings endorsed arg., holding in the dexter claw a sabre of the last, hilt and pommel of the first.

Eyton, John Prys, Esquire, of Llanerchymor, Holywell, North Wales, a demi-lion rampant holding between the paws a ducal coronet, all or. *Fy nuw fy ngwlad a i gwyrthiau.*

Eyton, Robert Henry, Esquire, same crest and motto.

Eyton, William Henry Plowden, same crest and motto.

Eyton, Leics. and Northamp., a demi-dragon with wings addorsed ppr., collared, winged, and lined arg., holding in the dexter paw a sword of the last, hilt and pommel or, the point embrued gu.

Eyton, a lion's head arg., devouring a tun or.

Eyton, Ralph Aglionby Slaney Eyton, Esquire, of Eyton, near Wellington, Salop, and Walford Hall, near Shrewsbury, a reindeer's head couped and attired or, holding in the mouth an acorn-slip vert, fructed of the first.

Eyton, Shropsh.: (1) A reindeer's head couped and attired or, holding in his mouth an acorn-slip vert, fructed or. (2) A Cornish chough's head erased ppr., holding in his beak a trefoil slipped vert. (3) A lion's head or, devouring a barrel or tun of the same. *Je m'y oblige.—Si Deus est pro nobis quis contra nos.*

Eyvill, D., an arm in armour embowed holding in the hand a spiked club, all ppr. *cf.* 199. 2

Eyvill, a bear sejant muzzled ppr. 34. 8

F.

Faal, Scotland, a pair of scales. *Honestas.* 179. 8

Faber, Hamilton S., Esquire, M.R.C.S., L.R.C.P., of St. George's Hospital, Hyde Park Corner, London, S.W., out of a ducal coronet or, a cubit arm in armour holding in the hand ppr. a rose gu. slipped. *Quisque faber fortunæ suæ.*

Fabian, a lion's gamb erased holding a sceptre in pale or. 38. 7

Fabian, on a chapeau a fleur-de-lis gu., from between the flowers two split flags arg., each charged with an ermine-spot.

Fablye, a cross crosslet gu., between two palm-branches vert.

Faconbridge, a yew-tree vert. 143. 1

Fagan, Ireland, out of a ducal coronet a swan's head and neck between two wings, all ppr. 100. 10

Fagan or **Fargon,** Ireland, a griffin segreant supporting a branch of olive ppr. 62. 5

Fagan of Croydon, a griffin segreant arg., winged and tufted or, supporting between the talons an olive-branch vert, fructed of the second. *Deo patriæque fidelis.* 62. 5

Fage, a cross crosslet in bend, surmounted by a sword in bend sinister point downwards. 166. 12

Fagge, Sir John William Charles, Bart., of Wiston, Sussex, an ostrich with wings expanded arg., beaked, legged, and ducally gorged or, holding in the beak a horse-shoe ppr. 97. 1

Fahie, a dexter arm couped below the elbow grasping a javelin, the point downwards ppr.

Fahy, Ireland, a dexter arm holding a hunting-spear point downwards.

Fair, Ruttledge-: (1) On a mount vert, a dove holding an olive-branch in its beak and charged with a trefoil upon its breast, all ppr. (*for Fair*). (2) An oak-tree ppr., pendent from a dexter branch thereof by a riband az. an escutcheon or (*for Ruttledge*). *Verax atque probus.*

Fair, Charles Edward, Esquire, LL.D., of Athlone, co. Westmeath, a dove with wings expanded and inverted holding in the beak a branch of olive. *Pax et plenitas.*

Fair, Thomas, of Clifton Hall, near Preston, Lancs, a garb or, encircled by two serpents vert. *Veritas vincit.* 153. 3

Fair, Charles Bass, Esquire, of Audit Office, Cape Town, out of a ducal crest coronet a demi-falcon rising ppr. *A tout faire.*

Fair, Rev. Robert Herbert, of the Rectory, Westmeon, Petersfield, same crest and motto.

Fair of Hamilton Terrace, St. John's Wood, London, N.W., a garb or, encircled by two snakes vert. *Vincit veritas.* 153. 3

Fairbairn, Sir Arthur Henderson, Bart., of Ardwick, Manchester, the sun in his splendour or. *Semper eadem.* 162. 2

Fairbairn, Rev. W. M., B.A., of the Rectory, Loxbeare, Tiverton, a sun in splendour ppr. *Semper eadem.*

Fairbairn, John, M.B., University Union, Edinburgh, same crest and motto.

Fairbairn, Sir Andrew, of Askham Grange, Yorks, a dexter cubit arm erect, the hand grasping the worm of a lever-screw in bend sinister, all ppr. *Ne cede arduis.* 214. 8

Fairbairn, a griffin passant sa. 63. 2

Fairbank, Frederick Royston, Esquire, M.D., F.R.C.P., F.S.A., of Westcott, Dorking, on a mount vert, the sun in splendour ppr. *Eterna veritas.*

Fairbeard of Northmore, Oxon., a dexter arm in armour ppr., couped at the shoulder and lying fesseways, erect from the elbow, holding in the gauntlet a cross botonnée fitchée or.

Fairborne, Notts, an arm in arm couped in fess, holding a sword erect enfiled with a Turk's head affrontée with a turban, all ppr. *Tutis si fortis.*

Fairbrother, a cockatrice displayed ppr. 68. 14

Fairclough, a demi-lion rampant sa., holding between the paws a fleur-de-lis az. *cf.* 13. 5

Fairclough, a lion's gamb or, grasping a fleur-de-lis az.

Fairclough, Revell Anthony, Esquire, of 9, Craven Hill, Paddington, in front of a lion's gamb erased or, holding a fleur-de-lis, three fleurs-de-lis fessewise, all az. *Faire sans dire.*

Fairfax, see Ramsay-Fairfax.

Fairfax, Baron (Fairfax), a lion passant gardant gu. *Fare fac.* 4. 3

Fairfax of Ravenswood, Roxburgh, a lion passant gardant ppr. *Fare fac.* 4. 3

Fairfax, Bryan Charles, Esquire, a lion passant gardant sa. *Je le feray durant ma vie.* 4. 5

Fairfax, Rev. Charles Henry, M.A., of Dumbleton, Glouc., same crest and motto.

Fairfax, Guy Thomas, Esquire, of Bilbrough Hall, Yorks, and Steeton Hall, Tadcaster, same crest and motto.

Fairfax, a lion's head erased sa., collared gemelles or. *cf.* 17. 8

Fairfax of London, a lion's head erased sa., charged with three bars gemelles and a mullet or. *cf* 17. 8

Fairfax, Yorks and Norf., a lion's head erased sa., gorged with three bars gemelle and ducally crowned or. *cf.* 18. 8

Fairfax, Yorks, a goat's head erased arg., charged on the neck with three bars gemelle and attired gu., ducally gorged or. 128. 10

Fairfax-Cholmeley, Hugh Charles, Esquire, of Brandsby, Easingwold, a demi-griffin segreant sa., beaked or, holding a helmet ppr., garnished or.

Fairfield, a demi-savage affrontée, handcuffed ppr. 186. 12

Fairford, on a chapeau a talbot sejant, all ppr. 54. 14

Fairford, out of a mural coronet a spear surmounted by two laurel-branches in saltier, all ppr. *cf.* 175. 3

Fairfowl, Scotland, a parrot ppr. *Loquendo placet.* 101. 4

Fairgray, Yorks, an anchor ppr. 161. 1

Fairholm, Scotland, a dove holding in its beak an olive-branch ppr. *Spero meliora.* 92. 5

Fairholm, Scotland, a spur winged or, leathered gu. *Nunquam non paratus.* 111. 12

Fairholme, Scotland, a dove holding in its beak an olive-branch ppr. *Fide et firme.* 92. 5

Fairlie or **Fairly,** Scotland, a lion's head couped or. *Paratus sum.* 21. 1

Fairlie, James Ogilvy, Esquire, J.P., of Myres, Scotland, a lion's head couped gu. *Tak' a thocht.* 21. 1

Fairlie, James, Esquire, of Holms, by Hurlford, Ayr, a lion's head couped ppr. *Meditare.*

Fairlie, Robert Francis, Esquire, of Woodlands, Clapham, Surrey, a lion's head erased sa., langued gu. *Je suis prest.* 17. 8

Fairlie or **Fairly,** Scotland, a unicorn's head couped arg. *I am ready.* 49. 7

Fairlie-Cuninghame, Sir Charles Arthur, Bart., of Robertland and Fairlie, Ayrsh., a unicorn's head ppr., armed or (*for Cuninghame*). *Paratus sum fortitudine.* —*Over, fork over.* 49. 7

Fairn, between two laurel-branches in orle an open book, all ppr. 158. 1

Fairnie, Scotland, a greyhound current ppr. *Quiescens et vigilans.* cf. 58. 2

Fairweather, the sun in splendour or. *Volvitur et ridet.* 162. 2

Faith, on the stump of a tree a crane perched ppr. 105. 12

Faithfull, a key in pale, wards upwards, surmounted by a crosier and a sword in saltier. 171. 11

Faithfull, a talbot statant ppr. cf. 54. 2

Fakenham and **Feckenham,** a square padlock az. 168. 13

Fakeyt, a cockatrice's head erased sa. 68. 12

Falch, three quatrefoils on one branch stalked and leaved ppr. 148. 7

Falcon and **Fawcon,** four arrows, points downwards, and a bow in saltier ppr. 173. 12

Falcon, Ralph, of Camerton Hall, near Workington, a falcon rising ppr. *Vif, coura jeux fier.*

Falconberg of Germany and Ireland, a sword of state unsheathed and erect, environed with an olive-branch ppr. *Germana fides candorque.*

Falconar-Stewart, George Mercer, Esquire, of Binny, Uphall, Linlithgowsh.: (1) A falcon close ppr., between two laurel-branches in orle vert. (2) A dexter hand holding a dagger, point downwards. *Candide.—Armis potentius æquum.*

Falconer, *see* Kintore, Earl of.

Falconer of London and Scotland, a falcon rising ppr. *Fortiter sed apte.* 87. 1

Falconer, John, Esquire, of St. Ann's, Lasswade, Midlothian, Scotland, a falcon rising ppr. *Ad æthera.* 87. 1

Falconer of London, same crest. *Vi et industria.*

Falconer, Henry, Esquire, of Hackhurst, Hellingly, out of a ducal coronet, a falcon rising. 307. 5

Falconer, a falcon perched, hooded and belled, all ppr. *Vive ut vivas.* cf. 85. 1

Falconer, Scotland, a falcon ppr., hooded gu. *Paratus ad æthera.* cf. 85. 1

Falconer, Scotland, between two branches of laurel a falcon perched ppr.

Falconer, Scotland, an angel praying or, within an orle of laurel ppr. *Vive ut vivas.* 184. 2

Falconer, a man's heart gu., winged with two falcon's wings ppr. *Cordi dat animus alas.* 112. 10

Falconer, a garb or, banded arg. 153. 2

Falconer of London, a trefoil slipped or. 148. 9

Faldo, Beds, three arrows gu., headed and feathered arg., two in saltier, one in pale, enfiled with a ducal coronet or. cf. 173. 1

Falkiner, Richard Henry Fitz-Richard, Esquire, J.P., of Mount Falcon, co. Tipperary, Ireland, a falcon's lure erect ppr., charged with a mullet gu., between two wings az. *Fortuna favente.* cf. 110. 10

Falkiner, Sir Frederick Richard, of Inverusk, Lower Killiney, co. Dublin, same crest, but charged with a mullet for difference.

Falkiner, Sir Leslie Edmund Percy Riggs, Bart., of Anne Mount, co. Cork, a falcon's lure ppr., between two wings az. *Fortuna favente.* 110. 10

Falkiner, Ireland, a hawk's lure ppr., the string nowed between a pair of wings arg. cf. 110. 10

Falkiner, Ireland, out of a ducal coronet a cubit arm vested gu., cuffed or, holding the sun ppr. 209. 2

Falkland, Viscount (Cary), of Falkland, Fife, a swan with wings elevated ppr. *In utroque fidelis.* 99. 12

Falkner, on the stump of a tree an escutcheon pendent ppr. 145. 8

Falknor, a garb banded or. 153. 2

Fall, Scotland, a cornucopia ppr. *Honestas.* 152. 13

Fall, a talbot passant. 54. 1

Fallesby, a demi-antelope arg. cf. 126. 5

Fallesley, a dexter arm from the shoulder extended ppr., holding an anchor az. cabled sa.

Fallon, a hand holding a mill-rind.

Fallon, a hawk rising ppr., jessed and belled or. *Fortiter et fideliter.* 87. 1

Fallone, Ireland, a demi-greyhound arg. 60. 11

Fallowfield, Cumb., on a chapeau a lion gardant, collared and ducally crowned, all ppr. cf. 4. 2

Falls of Dublin, a naked cubit arm grasping a dagger ppr., pommel and hilt or. *Dum spiro, spero.* 212. 9

Falmouth, Viscount (Boscawen), of Tregothnan, near Truro, a falcon close ppr., belled or. *Patience passe science.* cf. 85. 2

Falshaw, the late Sir James, Bart. (*extinct*), of Edinburgh, a dexter hand holding a white rose slipped and leaved ppr. *In officio impavidus.* 218. 10

Falstoffe, an oak-tree vert. 143. 5

Falstoffe, Norf. and Suff., a hawk with wings expanded sa., holding in the beak an oak-branch vert, fructed or.

Fanacourt, a chevalier in armour wielding a sword, all ppr. cf. 188. 7

Fancourt, out of a ducal coronet or, a wyvern erect, holding between its claws a staff raguly.

Fancourt, two staffs raguly banded with olive ppr. cf. 147. 11

Fane, Earl of Westmoreland, *see* Westmoreland.

Fane, Ponsonby-, Hon. Sir Spencer Cecil Brabazon, K.C.B., of Brympton Park, Somers.: (1) Out of a ducal coronet or, a bull's head arg., pied sa., armed of the first, charged on the neck with a rose gu., barbed and seeded ppr. (*for Fane*). cf. 44. 11. (2 On a ducal coronet az., three arrows, one in pale and two in saltire, points downwards, entwined with a snake ppr. (*for Ponsonby*). *Ne vile fano.—Pro rege, lege, grege.* 173. 2

Fane of Hempstead, Essex, and Old Lodge, Melton Mowbray, out of a ducal coronet or, a bull's head arg., pied sa., armed of the first, charged on the neck with a rose gu., barbed and seeded ppr. *Ne vile fano.*

Fane, Frederick, Esquire, of Moyles Court, Ringwood, Hants, same crest and motto.

Fane, William Dashwood, Esquire, J.P., of Fulbeck Hall, Lincs, same crest and motto, and *Nec temere nec timide.*

Fane De Salis, Cecil, Esquire, Count Palatine of the Palace of the Lateran, Count of the Holy Roman Empire, of Dawley Court, Uxbridge: (1) Out of a ducal coronet a demi-woman vested ppr., the hair flowing down the back, crowned or, winged in lieu of arms arg. (2) Out of a ducal coronet or, an eagle displayed sa., crowned or. (3) Out of a mural coronet or, a demi-lion rampant, double queued and crowned of the same, brandishing a sword ppr., hilt gold, the lion cotised by two tilting-spears or, from each a banner paly of six arg. and gu., fringed of the first. (4) Out of a ducal coronet or, a bull's head arg., pied sa., armed of the first, charged on the neck with a rose gu., barbed and seeded ppr. (*for Fane*). *Flectit non frangit.—Pro Deo, Rege, et patria.—Pro fructibus arma.*

Fane de Salis, Rev. Preb. Charles, M.A., of the Rectory, Weston-super-Mare, same crests and mottoes.

Fane, Lincs, a gauntlet or, holding a sword ppr., hilt and pommel of the first. 211. 4

Fane, Lincs, a gauntlet or, holding a broken sword arg., hilt and pommel of the first.

Fane, Ireland, a dexter hand holding a laurel-branch ppr. 219. 9

Fannell, a tiger sejant sa., ducally gorged or. cf. 27. 6

Fanner, out of a ducal coronet or, a buck's head of the same. 120. 7

Fanning, a dexter hand ppr., vested sa., holding a mill-rind az. 207. 4

Fanning, a cherub ppr. 189. 9

Fanshaw, Ireland, a greyhound sejant gu. 59. 4

Fanshaw, Derbysh., a dragon's head erased or, charged with two chevrons erm. cf. 71. 2

Fanshaw, Henry Ernest, Dengey Hall, Essex, a dragon's head erased vert, vomiting flames ppr. 72. 5

Fanshawe of Parsloes, Essex, a dragon's head erased arg., vomiting flames of fire ppr. *Dux vitæ ratio in cruce victoria.* —*In cruce victoria.* 72. 5

Fanshawe, Colonel Thomas Basil, same crest and mottoes.

Fanshawe, on a ducal coronet az., a wyvern sa. 70. 9

Fanshawe, a cockatrice's head ppr. cf. 68. 13

Fant, *see* Fauntan.

Fantlaroy, a fleur-de-lis or, between two wings expanded az. cf. 148. 2

Fantleroy, the head of a halbert issuing from the wreath ppr. 172. 1

Faquier, a hand issuant pruning a vine ppr.

Farange, Ireland, a demi-lion rampant gu. 10. 3

Farbridge, Ireland, a parrot gu. 101. 4

Farby, Kent, a cinquefoil or. 148. 11

Fardell of London and Lincs, issuing from a mount vert, a demi-lion or, holding a book expanded ppr., charged on the shoulder with a rose gu. *Non nobis solum.* 9. 13

Fardell, Frederick Charles, Esquire, on a mount vert, a demi-lion erminois, charged on the shoulder with a rose, and holding between the paws an open book ppr. *Non nobis solum.*

Fardell, John Wilson, Esquire, of Ryde, Isle of Wight, same crest and motto.

Fardell, Sir (Thomas) George, of 26, Hyde Park Street, W., same crest and motto.

Farebrother, a greyhound's head couped arg. *cf.* 61. 2

Farell, Heref. and Warw., a boar's head couped sa., gorged with a collar arg., charged with three torteaux *cf.* 41. 1

Farewell, Somers., an heraldic tiger sa., ducally gorged, armed, and tufted or.

Farewell, an heraldic tiger sejant sa.

Farey, a plough ppr. 178. 7

Farie, Allan, of Baronald, Lanark, an eagle displayed ppr., charged on the breast with an anchor arg. *Corde, mente, manea.* *cf.* 75. 2

Farie, Allan James Crawford, of Farme, Lanark, same crest and motto.

Faringham and **Farneham,** out of an earl's coronet or, a Moor's head from the shoulders ppr. 182. 2

Farington, *see* Farrington.

Farington, a wyvern arg., sans wings, ducally gorged gu., chained or. *Domat omnia virtus.* 69. 1

Farington, Lancs, a wyvern statant sans wings, the tail nowed arg., ducally gorged, and the chain reflexed over the back or. 69. 1

Farington of London, a dragon passant ppr. 73. 2

Farington, on a chapeau gu., turned up or, a fox sejant ppr. 32. 12

Farish, Arthur Farish, of 57½, Old Broad Street, London, E.C., upon two horseshoes or, a bugle-horn stringed az. *Forward.* 263. 13

Farish, Claude Reginald Thorne, Esquire, of Aldershot, same crest and motto.

Farish, Edward Garthwaite, Esquire, of 4, Elm Park Gardens, South Kensington, same crest and motto.

Farish, John, Esquire, of Bibiani, West Africa, same crest and motto.

Farish, Leonard Walter, Esquire, of Brooklands, Chesh., same crest and motto.

Farish, Rupert Vaughan, Esquire, Lieutenant Royal Warwickshire Regt., same crest and motto.

Farley, Surrey, on a mount vert, in front of a Calvary cross gu., a lamb passant ppr. *Tollit peccata mundi.* 130. 5

Farley, an antelope's head erased and pierced through the neck by a spear-head, all ppr. 127. 1

Farley, Turner-: (1) A boar's head couped paly of six sa., guttée d'eau, and or, (*for Farley*). (2) A lion gardant sa., charged on the body with three crosses patée fitchée arg., resting the dexter fore-paw upon a shield of the last, charged with a mill-rind, also sa. (*for Turner*). *Aeito viret honore.* 5. 8

Farlough, Lancs, a demi-lion rampant holding in the dexter paw a fleur-de-lis sa. 13. 2

Farlow, a dragon's head ducally gorged and chained. *cf.* 72. 9

Farmar, Ireland, out of a ducal coronet or, a cock's head gu., crested and wattled of the first. *Hora e sempre.* 90. 6

Farmar, William Robert, of Nonsuch Park, near Cheam, same crest and motto.

Farmar, Ireland, a lion's head erased gu. *Fortis et fidelis.* 17. 2

Farmbrough, Francis, Esquire, of Denbigh Hall, Bletchley, a dexter arm embowed vested gu., holding a plough-paddle handled also gu., the blade or, and the arm garnished with a wreath of wheat-ears ppr. *Deus noster refugium.* 298. 7

Farmer, a tiger's face.

Farmer, Norf., a cock's head gu., combed and wattled or, holding in the beak a rose of the first, stalked and leaved vert.

Farmer, William Robert Gamul, of Nonsuch Park, Surrey, out of a ducal coronet or, a cock's head gu., crested and wattled of the first. *Hora e sempre.* 90. 6

Farmer, Bart., of Mount Pleasant, Sussex, out of a ducal coronet or, a cock's head issuing gu., combed and wattled or. *Hora e sempre.* 90. 6

Farmer, Northamp., out of a ducal coronet or, a cock's head gu., crested and jelloped of the first. 90. 6

Farmer, Leics., a dexter arm couped at the elbow, gauntleted, holding a lamp arg., flammant ppr.

Farmer, Leics., out of a ducal coronet or, a salamander in flames ppr. *Esto vigilans.* 138. 1

Farmer, upon the battlements of a tower arg., a salamander statant vert, collared or, in flames ppr. 138. 3

Farmer, Sir William, of Ascot Place, Berks, upon a mount vert, an antelope arg., semée of estoiles sa., armed and ungu. or, resting the dexter fore-foot upon a fountain ppr. *Agendo honeste.* 126. 10

Farmer, Scotland, a cross fleury fitched between two wings, each charged with a crescent. *cf.* 166. 8

Farmingham, a sea-lion rampant or. 20. 5

Farmour, a cock's head erased gu., combed and wattled or, holding in the beak a bunch of flowers arg., leaved ppr.

Farnaby, Bart., Kent, a stork arg. 105. 11

Farnaby, Kent, out of a mural coronet a stork rising ppr., charged with two bars gemelle arg., and holding in the beak a snake vert.

Farnam, out of a ducal coronet a griffin's head, holding in the beak a cross crosslet fitched. *cf.* 67. 9

Farnborough, Baron, *see* Long.

Farncomb of Kennington, Surrey, a cockatrice's head couped sa., combed and wattled or, between two wings of the first, each charged with a cinquefoil of the second. *cf.* 68. 8

Farncombe-Tanner, William Tanner, Esquire, of Fisher's Wakes Colne, Halstead, and More House, Wivelsfield, Burgess Hill, Sussex, a Moor's head in profile couped at the shoulders ppr., between two trefoils slipped vert. 264. 12

Farnden, Sussex, on a mural coronet or, a leopard's face purp.

Farnell, a hawk with wings expanded and inverted, ducally gorged and belled ppr. 87. 2

Farnham, Baron (Maxwell), of Farnham, co. Cavan, Ireland, a buck's head erased ppr. *Je suis prêt.* 121. 2

Farnham, William Edward Basil, 13, Stratton Street, W., an eagle close or, preying on a coney arg. *cf.* 79. 6

Farofeld, a lion passant arg. 6. 2

Farquhar, Bart., *see* Townsend-Farquhar.

Farquhar, Sir Henry Thomas, Bart., of Cadogan House, Middx., an eagle rising ppr. *Mente manuque.* 77. 5

Farquhar, Scotland, a lion rampant. *Sto, cado, fide et armis.* 1. 13

Farquhar and **Ferquhar,** Scotland, issuing out of a cloud ppr., a star arg. *Vertitur in diem.* 164. 11

Farquhar, Scotland, a dexter hand couped apaumée ppr. *Fide et armis.* 222. 14

Farquhar, Admiral Sir Arthur, of Drumnagesk, Aboyne, N.B., out of a naval crown or, a sword erect ppr., the blade encircled by a wreath of laurel, also ppr., and a flag flowing towards the sinister in saltire az., inscribed with the word "Acheron" in letters of gold, surmounted by a dexter hand issuant gu. *Sto, cado, fide et armis.*

Farquhar, Scotland, a dexter hand couped apaumée ppr. *Sto, cado, fide et armis.* 222. 14

Farquhar, Gray-, Scotland, a sinister hand apaumée gu. *Sto, cado, fide et armis.* 222. 9

Farquharson, Scotland, a demi-lion rampant gu. *In memoriam majorum.* 10. 3

Farquharson, Robert, of 2, Porchester Gardens, same crest.

Farquharson, Dorset, a demi-lion rampant holding in the dexter paw a dagger erect ppr., hilt and pommel or. *cf.* 14. 12

Farquharson, Alexander, of Invercauld, a demi-lion gu., holding in the dexter paw a sword ppr. *Fide et fortitudine.* 14. 12

Farquharson, George, Esquire, of Whitehouse, Aberdeen, same crest and motto.

Farquharson, same crest. *Fortitudine.*

Farquharson, the sun in his splendour ppr. *Illumino.* 162. 2

Farquharson of Haughton, the sun rising from behind a cloud ppr. *Illumino.* 162. 5

Farquharson, Scotland, out of a cloud the sun rising ppr. *Non semper sub umbra.* 162. 5

Farquharson and **Farquherson,** a portcullis gu. 178. 3

Farr, on the point of a sword in pale ppr., a maunch gu. 169. 11

Farrand, Norf., in front of a garb or, a pheasant ppr. *Nulla pallescere culpa.*

Farrand, an arm in armour embowed, holding in the hand a battle-axe. *cf.* 200. 6

Farrant, Kent, out of a ducal coronet or, a pelican's head arg., vulning herself gu., between two wings of the last.

Farrant of London and Kent, a cubit arm erect, vested az., cuffed arg., charged with a cross patonce vairée of the last and gu., the hand grasping an anchor cabled ppr. *cf.* 208. 3

Farrant, Surrey and Yorks, a cubit arm erect vested vair, cuffed arg., holding in the hand ppr. a battle-axe of the second. *cf.* 207. 10

Farrant, Henry Gatchell, B.A., of Welland, Worcs., same crest. *Fortiter et fideliter.*

Farrar, Yorks, a horse-shoe sa., between two wings arg. 110. 11

Farrar, Reginald, Esquire, M.A., M.D. Oxon., of 7, Grove Park Gardens, Chiswick, W., a horse-shoe sa., between two wings erect arg. *Ferré va ferme.*

Farrar, a thistle and a cross crosslet fitched in saltier ppr.

Farrel and **Farrell,** Ireland, a bear passant sa., pierced through the shoulder by a hunting-spear arg. *cf.* 34. 4

Farrell, a dexter hand apaumée gu. 222. 14

Farrell, Ireland, on a ducal coronet a greyhound current, gorged with a collar, and affixed thereto by a broken chain a regal crown, all ppr. *Cu re bu.*

Farren, George, Esquire, of Trefenai, Carnarvon, upon a block of dressed gray granite ppr., a lion passant regardant gu., resting the dexter fore-paw on a saltire or. *Perseverantia vincit.* 256. 14

Farrer, Baron (Farrer), a quatrefoil within a horse-shoe between two wings, all arg. *Ferré va ferme.* 234. 11

Farrer and **Farror,** a horse-shoe sa., between two wings or. 110. 11

Farrer, James Anson, of Ingleborough, Yorks, a horse-shoe between two wings ppr. *Ferré va Ferme.* 110. 11

Farrer of Brayfield, Bucks, a horse-shoe arg., between two wings sa. 110. 11

Farrer, Rev. Frederic, M.A., of Bourton-on-the-Hill, Moreton-in-the-Marsh, and Brayfield House, Bucks, same crest.

Farrer, a horse-shoe arg., between two wings or. 110. 11

Farrer, out of a ducal coronet or, between two wings arg., a crescent of the first. *Ferré va ferme.* 294. 14

Farrer, Claude St. Aubyn, Physician, 7, Westbourne Park Road, W., same crest and motto.

Farrer, William, Whitbarrow, Westml.: (1) An acorn slipped and leaved ppr., within a horse-shoe sa., between two wings of the last, each charged with a horse-shoe arg. (2) In front of a demi-tower ppr., thereon a stag's head erased erminois, three spears, one in pale and two in saltire, also ppr. *Ferré va ferme.*

Farrington, a lamb passant arg., bearing a banner pink, the staff ppr., surmounted by a cross or. 131. 2

Farrington, a wyvern vert. 70. 1

Farrington, a wyvern sans wings, the tail extended vert. 73. 2

Farrington, Bart., of Gosford House, Ottery St. Mary, Devonsh., a dragon with wings elevated and tail nowed vert; bezantée, gorged with a mural coronet arg., a chain therefrom reflexed over the back or, and charged on the body with two caltraps fesseways of the last. *Le bon temps viendra.*

Farrow, a lion's gamb holding a thistle ppr. 37. 6

Farside, William, Esquire, of Fylington, Whitby Strand, Yorks, two lion's gambs erect arg., erased gu., holding a bezant, the whole debruised by a sinister bendlet wavy erm. *Furth and fear nocht.*

Farwell, two oak-branches in orle vert, acorned or. 146. 1

Farwell, George, Esquire, of East Marden, Chichester, a talbot sa., ducally gorged. *Semper idem.*

Fasant, a Cornish chough with wings expanded ppr. 107. 3

Fassett, a shark's head issuant regardant, swallowing a negro, all ppr. 139. 2

Fauconbridge or **Fawconbridge,** out of a ducal coronet or, a plume of three ostrich-feathers banded ppr.

Faudel-Phillips, Sir George Faudel, first Bart., of Balls Park, Hertford: (1) Upon a mount vert, a squirrel sejant cracking a nut or, between on the dexter side a trefoil slipped, and on the sinister a branch of hazel fructed extending to the dexter, charged on the shoulder with an acorn leaved and slipped ppr. (*for Phillips*). 280. 3. (2) Upon a mount a peacock regardant in its pride ppr., between two roses arg., leaved and slipped vert. *Ne tentes, aut perfice.* 280. 4

Faudel-Phillips, Samuel Henry, Esquire, J.P., of Mapleton, Edenbridge, Kent, same crests and motto.

Faulder, on a mountain a beacon inflamed, all ppr. 177. 8

Faulkner, a cross moline pierced gu. 165. 1

Faulkner, Suff., a demi-cockatrice with wings addorsed ppr.

Faulkner, Middx., a dragon's head and neck with wings addorsed, couped at the shoulders, all ppr.

Faulkner, Hugh, Esquire, J.P., D.L., of Castletown, co. Carlow, Ireland, on a mount vert, an angel in a praying posture or, within an orle of laurel ppr. *Vive ut vivas.* *cf.* 184. 2

Faulkner, a falcon's lure or, between two falcon's wings ppr. 110. 10

Faulkner, Alexander S., Surgeon-Major, Indian Army, on a dexter hand in fess, couped at the wrist, a falcon close, belled and hooded, all ppr. *Paratus ad æthera.* 86. 8

Faulkner, John, Esquire, of Dunfield, Fairford, Glouc., Lord of the Manor of Kempsford, upon a rock a falcon rising ppr., belled and jessed or, resting the dexter claw on a mullet of six points az., surmounted by a rainbow, also ppr. *Vive ut vivas.*

Faulks, a boar's head couped ppr. 43. 1

Faunce, a demi-lion rampant sa., langued gu., ducally gorged or, between two wings arg. *Ne tentes, aut perfice.* *cf.* 9. 8

Fauntan, Faunt, and **Fant,** a naked boy ppr., crined or, holding in his dexter hand a toy of the last.

Fauntleroy, Cornw., the head of a halberd issuing ppr 172. 1

Fauntleroy, Wilts, a fleur-de-lis or, between two wings expanded az. *cf.* 148. 2

Fausset, Kent, a demi-lion rampant sa., holding in his paws a Tuscan column bendwise, gobonée arg. and gu., the base and capital or.

Faussett, Godfrey-, Godfrey Trevelyan, 17, Belgrave Road, S.W., a demi-lion rampant sa., holding in the paws a Tuscan column inclined bendwise, gobony arg. and gu., the base and capital or. (2) A pelican's head erased vulning itself or. *Fortiter si forsitan.—Post spinas palma.*

Fauze, a tower ppr. 156. 2

Favell, on the point of a sword in pale a maunch, all ppr. 169. 11

Favene of London, on a bale of Piedmont thrown-silk a falcon ppr., beaked, membered, and belled or, gorged with a collar, and therefrom a chain reflexed over the back of the last.

Fawcet, a dolphin naiant ppr. 140. 5

Fawcett, Northumb. and Durh., a demi-lion sa., holding between the paws an arrow erect or, feathered arg. *cf.* 10. 1

Fawcett, a stag's head. 121. 5

Fawcett, Ireland, a mitre. *cf.* 180. 5

Fawcett, Hon. Captain Theodore, J.P., of Binjarrah Park, Murray District, Western Australia, a dolphin naiant arg., finned or. *Officio et fide.* 140. 5

Fawcett, Christopher John Foyle, Somerford, Keynes, Wilts, a demi-lion rampant sa., holding between its paws an arrow or.

Fawcon, *see* Falcon.

Fawconbridge, *see* Fauconbridge.

Fawconer and **Fawkoner,** a tower sa., masoned or. 156. 2

Fawether and **Fayreweather,** a lion's head erased gu., billettée or. *cf.* 17. 8

Fawkes, Yorks, a falcon ppr. *A Deo et rege.* 85. 2

Fawkne, a hawk's head erased. 88. 12

Fawkner and **Fawkenor,** a trefoil slipped or. 148. 9

Fawlconer, Hants and Northamp., a garb or, banded gu. 153. 2

Fawlde, Beds, three arrows, one in pale and two in saltier gu., barbed and flighted arg., enfiled by a ducal coronet or.

Fawset or **Fawsset,** Lincs, a stag's head erased ppr. 121. 2

Fawsitt, Ferguson-, John Daniel, Esquire, of Walkington Hall, Beverley, Yorks: (1) A demi-lion pean supporting a pillar erect gu., thereon a bugle-horn or, stringed az., the lion charged on the shoulder for distinction with a cross crosslet or (*for Fawsitt*). (2) In front of a cubit arm ppr., grasping a dagger erect, also ppr., pommel and hilt or, a buckle arg. (*for Ferguson*). *Arte et marte.—Dominus providebit.*

Fawssett, Thomas, Esquire, 97, Philbeach Gardens, Earl's Court, S.W., a stag's head erased ppr. 121. 2

Fay, Ireland, a dexter cubit arm holding in the gauntlet a dagger, all ppr. 211. 4

Fay, James Henry, Esquire, J.P., of Faybrook and Moyne Hall, co. Cavan, a dragon's head couped or. *Toujours fidèle.* 71. 1

Fayrer, Sir Joseph, Bart., K.C.S.I., M.D., F.R.S., in front of a sword erect, point upward, ppr., pommel and hilt or, a horse-shoe or, between two wings erect gu. *Ne tentes, aut perfice.* 242. 7

Fayreweather of Brissett, Suff., a lion's head erased gu., billettée or. *cf.* 17. 2

Fayting of Woodcote, Bromsgrove, Worcs., on a mount vert, a holly-leaf ppr. *Fideli distillant sanguine corda.*

Fayt, a water-bouget gu. 168. 4

Fazakerley, John Nicholas, Esquire, of 73, Harrington Gardens, London, S.W., on a mount vert, a swan close arg. 100. 7
Fea, a man digging ppr. *Fac et spera.*
Fea, Rev. William Hay, of the Charterhouse, Hull, a demi-man affrontée, wreathed about the temples and waist with leaves, holding a club over his dexter shoulder, all ppr. *I mean well.*
Fead, in front of the sun in splendour ppr., a unicorn rampant arg. 48. 1
Feake and **Feeke,** out of a ducal coronet or, a demi-ostrich with wings expanded arg., beaked gu., holding in its beak a horse-shoe of the first. 96. 8
Fearguson, an arm in armour embowed holding a dagger. 196. 5
Fearguson, Ireland, an arm in armour embowed holding in the hand a broken tilting-spear. 197. 2
Fearnley-Whittingstall, George, Esquire, of 105, Queen's Gate, S.W.: (1) In front of an antelope's head couped at the neck az., armed or, a saltire composed of nine lozenges or (*for Whittingstall*). (2) A mount vert, thereon in front of a bush of ferns ppr., a talbot passant erm., collared and line, reflexed over the back gu., the dexter forefoot resting on a buck's head caboshed or (*for Fearnley*). *Animus tamen idem.*
Fearnly, a talbot passant arg., through fern vert, collared and lined or. *cf.* 54. 5
Fearon, within an annulet or, an escutcheon gu. *cf.* 167. 6
Fearon, a demi-lion rampant ppr., holding between its paws an escutcheon gu., within an annulet or. *cf.* 10. 2
Fearon, Sussex, out of a ducal coronet a falcon's head, all ppr. 89. 4
Feast, Middx., a pheon point upwards gu. 174. 9
Featherston or **Featherstone,** a cross crosslet. 165. 2
Featherston, *see* Fetherston.
Featherstonhaugh, *see* Fetherstonhaugh.
Featherstonhaugh, Durh., a falcon ppr. 85. 2
Featherstonhaugh, E., Esquire, J.P., of 13, Park Place, West Sunderland, an antelope statant ducally gorged.
Featherstonhaugh, Cecil Howard Digby, of Bracklyn, Killucan, same crest and motto.
Feauliteau, Surrey, a squirrel sejant cracking a nut, all ppr. 135. 7
Fecher, a spur-rowel between two wings ppr. *cf.* 164. 8
Feckenham, a square padlock az. 168. 13
Fedelow, an erm. statant ppr., collared and lined sa. *cf.* 134. 6
Feild, *see* Feld.
Feilden, Sir William Leyland, Bart., J.P., of Feniscowle, Lancs, a nut-hatch perched upon a hazel-branch fructed, all ppr., holding in its beak a rose gu., slipped vert. 259. 6. *Virtutis præmium honor.*
Feilding, Earl of Denbigh and **Viscount Fielding,** *see* Denbigh.
Feilding, General Sir Percy Robert Basil, K.C., a nut-hatch with a hazel-branch fructed, all ppr. *Crescit sub pondere virtus.—Virtutis præmium honor.*
Feilding, John Basil, Esquire, of Upper Downing, Holywell, North Wales, same crest and motto.

Felbridg, a man's heart imperially crowned between two wings, all ppr. 110. 14
Felbridge, a tower embattled, thereon a bird rising. 156. 8
Felbridge, from a tower embattled the sun rising ppr.
Felbrigge, out of a ducal coronet gu., a plume of ostrich-feathers erm. 114. 13
Feld, *see* Field.
Feld, Scotland, an eagle's head erased ppr. 83. 2
Feld and **Field,** of East Ardesley, Yorks, issuing out of clouds ppr., a dexter arm in fess, vested gu., holding in the hand, also ppr., a sphere or. *cf.* 198. 14
Feldingham or **Fillingham,** a slip of three teazles or. 154. 9
Feldon, Leics., a wild man ppr.
Felfair, a gem ring. 167. 14
Felix, a covered cup gu.
Fell, a lion sejant ppr. 8. 8
Fell, Northumb., a catherine-wheel ensigned on the top with a cross patée fitched or. 167. 3
Fell, a pelican with wings elevated and addorsed vulning itself, all ppr.
Fell, out of a ducal coronet or, a demi-eagle displayed, ducally gorged. *cf.* 80. 14
Fell of London, a hand holding a clarionet ppr.
Fell of London, out of a mural coronet gu., a dexter arm embowed in armour ppr., garnished or, holding in the hand, also ppr., a tilting-spear of the last. *cf.* 197. 1
Fell, John, Flan How, Ulverston, a dexter arm embowed in armour ppr., garnished or, holding in the hand ppr. a tilting-spear ppr. *Patribus et posteritati.*
Fell, A. Lonsdale, Grosvenor Chambers, Oxford Street, Knells, Cumberland, and Lismore, Ayrshire, upon a rock ppr. a lion sejant per pale arg. and gu., charged on the shoulder with a rose counter-changed, and resting the dexter forepaw on a cross patée fitchée at the foot, also gu. *Vigilate.* 276. 4
Fellgate, Suff., a griffin sejant salient arg., pierced through the breast by a broken spear or, and holding the point in its beak. *cf.* 63. 1
Fellow, Ireland, a lion sejant gardant per fess gu. and or, resting the dexter paw on an escutcheon paly of the first and second. *cf.* 8. 2
Fellowes, Baron De Ramsey, *see* De Ramsey.
Fellowes, Evelyn Napier, Esquire, B.A., of 29, Warwick Square, S.W., a lion's head erased arg., crowned with a mural coronet or. *Patientia et perseverantia.*
Fellowes, Robert, Shotesham Park, Norwich, a lion's head erased or, murally crowned arg., charged with a fess dancettée erm. *Patientia et perseverantia cum magnanimitate.* 18. 3
Fellowes, issuing out of a cloud a dexter hand holding a club, all ppr. 214. 9
Fellowes or **Fellows,** Devonsh., a scaling-ladder ppr., hooked at the top. 158. 14
Fellowes, Ernest Gadesden, Esquire, in front of a lion's head erased ppr., crowned with a vallery coronet, and holding in the mouth the attire of a reindeer, three lozenges conjoined or. *Fac et spera.* 260. 7

Fellowes, Frederick Burmington, Esquire, same crest and motto.
Felt, on a mural coronet or, a stag trippant ppr. *cf.* 117. 8
Felter, a dexter hand ppr., holding up a covered cup or. 217. 11
Feltham of London, an arm in armour holding in the gauntlet a broken spear, the pieces in saltier, all ppr. *Portanti spolia palmâ.* *cf.* 209. 10
Felton of Litcham, Norf., out of a ducal coronet or, two wings inverted gu., quilled of the first.
Felton of London: (1) Out of a ducal coronet two wings or and arg. 109. 8 (2) A stag lodged gu., ducally gorged and lined or, attired vert, on the top of each branch a bezant.
Fencourt, a portcullis sa., the chains az. 178. 3
Feney, out of a heart a dexter hand holding a dagger in pale, all ppr. *cf.* 212. 9
Fenis, a bridge of three arches ppr. 158. 4
Fenkell, a mullet sa. 164. 2
Fenn, Suff., a dragon's head erased az., gorged with a collar arg., charged with three escallops of the first. *cf.* 71. 2
Fenn, a talbot's head erased or, collared az. 56. 1
Fennel or **Fennell,** a hunting-horn sans strings. 228. 9
Fenner, two hands couped and conjoined in fess gu., supporting a cross crosslet fitched az. 224. 11
Fenner, an eagle displayed or, winged arg. 75. 2
Fenning, a lion passant regardant ducally gorged and lined. *cf.* 6. 3
Fennison, Scotland, a crane's head ppr. *Vigilat et orat.* 104. 5
Fennor, a mermaid holding in her dexter hand a dagger, all ppr. 184. 7
Fenouillet of London, a demi-pegasus regardant or, winged gu., holding a banner vert, charged with a bee-hive or, the staff gu. *Industriâ et spe.* *cf.* 47. 8
Fenrother of London, a boar's head couped between two branches in orle ppr. 42. 1
Fentiman, a Cornish chough rising, ducally gorged, all ppr. *cf.* 107. 3
Fenton, Yorks, Notts, and Ireland, a fleur-de-lis sa., enfiled with a ducal coronet or. 148. 1
Fenton of Underbank Hall, Yorks, a fleur-de-lis sa., enfiled by a ducal coronet or. 148. 1
Fenton of Dutton Manor, Longridge, Preston, Lancs, in front of two arrows in saltire or, barbed and flighted arg., a fleur-de-lis sa. *Je suis prest.* 265. 14
Fenton, Scotland, out of a rock a palm-tree growing ppr. *Per ardua surgo.* *cf.* 144. 3
Fenton, Perthsh., out of a ducal coronet a griffin's head holding in the beak a key. *Felix qui pacificus.* 65. 14
Fenton of Fenton, Notts, out of a ducal coronet an arm embowed in armour or, holding in the hand a sword arg., hilted of the first. 195. 10
Fenton, Ferrar, Esquire, F.R.A.S., F.C.A.A., of 8, King's Road, Mitcham, S.E., same crest. *Mon hieur viendra.*

Fenton of Fenton Park, Stafford, out of an Eastern coronet a dexter arm in armour, the hand holding a sword in bend sinister, all ppr., the arm charged with two fleurs-de-lis az.

Fenton, Lieutenant-Colonel Sir Myles, of Redstone Hall, Redhill, Surrey, out of an Eastern coronet a dexter arm in armour embowed, the hand holding a sword in bend sinister, all ppr., the arm charged with two fleurs-de-lis az. *Virtute et fide vinco.*

Fenton-Livingstone, George Frederick James, Esquire, Easter Moffat, Airdrie, Lanarksh.: (1) Out of an antique crown a dexter arm in armour embowed holding in the hand a sword, all ppr. (2) Out of a baron's coronet, a demi-savage wreathed about the head and loins with laurel, holding in his dexter hand a club resting on his shoulder, and a snake entwined around his sinister arm all ppr. *Nec temere nec timide.—Si je puis.*

Fenton-Livingstone, Lanarksh., a demi-savage wreathed about the head and loins with laurel holding in his dexter hand a club resting on his shoulder, and a snake entwined around his sinister arm, all ppr. *Si je puis.* 264. 11

Fenton-Livingstone, John Nigel Edensor, Esquire, of Westquarter, near Falkirk, and Bedlormie, Linlithgow, same crest and motto.

Fentoun, Viscount, *see* Mar and Kellie, Earl of.

Fenwick, a beaver passant ppr., holding in its mouth a sugar-cane or. *cf.* 134. 8

Fenwick or **Fennwick,** a phœnix in flames ppr. *Virtute sibi præmium.* 82. 2

Fenwick, Leics., a phœnix az., winged gu., in flames ppr. 82. 2

Fenwick, Leics., a phœnix arg., wings gu., gorged with a ducal crown or, and issuant from flames ppr. *cf.* 82. 2

Fenwick, George Gerard Charles, Stockerston Hall, near Uppingham, same crest and motto.

Fenwick, Admiral William Henry, of 7, St. Alban's Road, Kensington Palace, W., a phœnix in flames ppr., murally gorged or. *Toujours loyal.* *cf.* 82. 2

Fenwick, Rev. John Edward Addison, same crest and motto.

Fenwick, Charles, Esquire, L.R.C.P. and S. Edin., of Dunsford, Exeter, same crest. *Resurgam.*

Fenwick, Durh., same crest. *Virtute sibi præmium.*

Fenwick, Northumb., same crest. *Perit ut vivat.*

Fenwick - Bisset, the late Mordaunt, Esquire of Lessendrum, Aberdeensh., Scotland: (1) On the dexter side—The trunk of an oak-tree sprouting afresh ppr. (*for Bisset*). 145. 2. (2) On the sinister side—A phœnix in flames gorged with a mural crown ppr. (*for Fenwick*). *Abscissa virescit.—Perit ut vivat.* *cf.* 82. 2

Fenwicke-Clennell, Thomas Clennell, Esquire, of Harbottle Castle, Rothbury, Northumb.: (1) Issuing from flames ppr., a phœnix with wings elevated or, gorged with a ducal coronet az., charged on the breast and on each wing with a martlet sa. (*for Clennel*). (2) A phœnix in flames with wings elevated ppr., supporting with the beak a staff raguly erect sa. (*for Fenwicke*). *Tous jours loyale.*

Ferby, Kent, on a mural coronet or, a plate between two wings sa.

Fergant, a cross crosslet quarterly or and gu. 165. 2

Fergus, Scotland, a dexter arm in armour holding in the hand a sword in pale az.

Fergus, Ireland, a naked hand couped below the elbow holding the upper part of a broken lance ppr., headed or. 214. 13

Fergus, a demi-lion ppr., crowned with a mural crown or. *cf.* 10. 11

Fergushill, Scotland, out of a ducal coronet a cock's head, all ppr. 90. 6

Ferguson-Fawsitt, *see* Fawsitt.

Ferguson-Davie, Sir John Davie, Bart., J.P., D.L., of Creedy, Devonsh.: (1) A paschal lamb regardant gu. *cf.* 131. 2 (2) A halcyon or kingfisher with wings elevated ppr., holding in the beak a branch of olive vert, fructed or. *Auspice Christo.* *cf.* 96. 9

Ferguson, Bart., Ireland, on a thistle leaved and flowered ppr., a bee or. *Dulcius ex asperis.* 150. 9

Ferguson, Scotland, a thistle leaved and flowered, thereon a bee, all ppr. *Industria.* 150. 9

Ferguson, George Bagot, Esquire, M.A., M.D., M.Ch., Oxon., F.R.C.S. Eng., of Altidore Villa, Pittville, Cheltenham, a thistle ppr., passing through a buckle or, alighting thereon a bee or, winged az. *Dulcius ex asperis.—Ut prosim aliis prosim.* 271. 21

Ferguson, Major S. C., of Lowther Street, Carlisle, in front of a demi-lion or, collared vair, holding in the dexter paw a thistle leaved and slipped ppr. three oval buckles in fesse, tongues upwards. *Vi et arte.* 271. 3

Ferguson, a demi-lion ppr., holding between the paws a buckle gu. *Virtutis fortuna comes.* *cf.* 10. 2

Ferguson, Ronald George Munro, of 46, Cadogan Square, same crest and motto.

Ferguson, a demi-lion holding in the dexter paw a scimitar. 14. 10

Ferguson, upon clouds a crescent with the horns upwards ppr. *Virtute.* 163. 9

Ferguson, George Arthur, Esquire, of Pitfour, near Mintlaw, N.B., out of clouds ppr., a crescent or. 163. 9

Ferguson, a hand holding a dagger erect. *Arte et marte.* 212. 9

Ferguson, on a crescent a cock ppr. 91. 10

Ferguson of Craigdarroch, Scotland, a hand holding a spear in bend ppr. *Vi et arte.* 214. 11

Ferguson, a dexter hand grasping a broken spear in bend ppr. *Vi et arte.* 214. 10

Ferguson, James, Esquire, K.C., D.L., 10, Wemyss Place, Edinburgh, issuing from a cloud a dexter hand grasping a broken spear in bend, all ppr. *Arte et animo.* *cf.* 214. 10

Ferguson, William, Esquire, J.P., D.L., of Kinmundy, Mintlaw, N.B., same crest and motto.

Ferguson of London, an arm in armour grasping in the hand a broken spear, all ppr. *True to the last.* *cf.* 210. 9

Ferguson-Fawsitt, John Daniel Esquire, of Walkington Hall, near Beverley: (1) A demi-lion pean supporting a pillar erect gu., thereon a bugle-horn or, stringed az., the lion charged for distinction with a cross crosslet or (*for Fawsitt*). (2) In front of a cubit arm ppr., grasping a dagger erect, also ppr., pommel and hilt or, a buckle arg. *Arte et marte.—Dominus providebit.*

Fergusson, Rt. Hon. Sir James, Bart., P.C., G.C.S.I., K.C.M.G., C.I.E., of Kilkerran, Ayrsh., a bee on a thistle ppr. *Ut prosim aliis.—Dulcius ex asperis.* 150. 9

Fergusson, Sir James Ranken, Bart., of Spitalhaugh, Peebles, and Hever Court, Ifield, Kent, a dexter hand grasping a broken spear in bend sinister, all ppr. *Vi et arte.* 214. 10

Fergusson, Robert Cutlar, of Craig Darroch, Moniaive, Dumfries, same crest and motto.

Fergusson, Hew Dalrymple Hamilton, 35, Elm Park Gardens, same crest.

Fergusson-Buchanan, George James, Esquire, of Auchentorlie, Dumbartonsh., Lt.-Col. 3rd Battalion Royal Scots Fusiliers: (1) On the dexter—An armed dexter hand couped holding up a cap of dignity purpure, faced erm., with two laurel-branches disposed in orle ppr. (*for Buchanan*). 210. 8. (2) On the sinister—A bee on a thistle ppr. (*for Fergusson*). *Clarior hinc honos.—Dulcius ex asperis.* 150. 9

Fergusson - Pollok of Atholl Crescent, Edinburgh: (1) Upon the dexter side—A boar passant shot through with a dart ppr. (*for Pollok*). 40. 14. (2) On the sinister side—On a thistle leaved and flowered a bee ppr. (*for Fergusson*). *Audacter et strenue.—Dulcius ex asperis.* 150. 9

Fergusson, a demi-lion rampant gu. *Virtus sibi præmium.* 10. 3

Fergusson, Joseph Gillon, Esquire, of Isle, Dumfries, an increscent or. *Growing.* 163. 3

Fergusson of London, a palm-tree ppr. *Sub onere crescit.* 144. 1

Fergusson, a dexter hand grasping a broadsword ppr. *Pro rege et patria.* 212. 13

Fergusson, Robert W., Esquire, of Kilquharity, Kirkcudbright, Scotland, a bee on a thistle ppr. *Dulcius ex asperis.*

Fermor, Earl of Pomfret, *see* Pomfret.

Fermor, Sussex, a tiger passant erm. *cf.* 27. 11

Fermour, two oak-branches in saltier ppr. 157. 1

Fermoy, Baron (Roche), co. Cork, standing on a rock ppr., an osprey or sea-eagle with wings displayed arg., collared gemelle az., membered or, holding in its dexter claw a roach, also arg. *Mon Dieu est ma roche.*

Fernandez, on a cloud a celestial sphere ppr. 159. 5

Ferne, issuing out of fern ppr., a talbot's head arg., eared and collared gu., garnished and ringed or.

Ferne, on a mount of fern ppr., a garb or, banded gu. 153. 12

Ferne, Derbysh., Lincs, and Staffs, a garb or, between two wings expanded, the dexter per pale indented of the first and gu., the sinister counterchanged. 153. 14

Fernely or **Fernley,** through fern vert a talbot passant arg., collared and lined or. *cf.* 54. 5

Ferney, Scotland, a crescent arg. 163. 2

Fernie, Scotland, a greyhound current. *Quiescens et vigilans.* *cf.* 58. 2

Ferns, Ireland, out of a cup az., a bouquet of roses ppr. 177. 3

Feron, Scotland, a cross patée erm. *cf.* 165. 7

Ferrall, Ireland, a dagger and a sword in saltier ppr. *cf.* 171. 12

Ferrall, Carmichael- : (1) Out of a ducal coronet or, a dexter hand gu. (*for Ferrall*). *cf.* 222. 14. (2) An arm embowed in armour grasping a broken lance, all ppr., charged with a trefoil or (*for Carmichael*). *cf.* 197. 2

Ferrand, William, Esquire, J.P., D.L., High Sheriff, 1904, of St. Ives and Harden Grange, Yorks, W.R., a cubit arm vair, charged with a cinquefoil gu., in the hand a battle-axe ppr. *Justus propositi tenax.* *cf.* 207. 10

Ferrand, Yorks, an arm in armour embowed holding in the hand a battle-axe ppr. *Justus et propositi tenax.* *cf.* 200. 6

Ferrant, a demi-lion or, semée of hurts. 10. 4

Ferrar, Augustus Minchin, Esquire, of Torwood, Belfast, a dexter arm embowed in scale armour arg., charged with a horse-shoe sa., the hand bare, grasping a broken sword ppr., pommel and hilt or. *Ferré va ferme.*

Ferrar, Benjamin Banks, Esquire, of Armagh, same crest and motto.

Ferrar, Henry Stafford, Esquire, of Nebraska, America, same crest and motto.

Ferrar, John Edgar, Esquire, of Durban, Natal, same crest and motto.

Ferrar, Michael Lloyd, Esquire, of Little Gidding, Ealing, same crest and motto.

Ferrard, Viscount, *see* Masserene, Viscount.

Ferrer, Ireland, a falcon's head erased arg., collared vairée gu. and arg. *cf.* 88. 12

Ferrers, Earl (Shirley), a Saracen's head in profile couped ppr., wreathed about the temples or and az. *Honor virtutis præmium.* 190. 14

Ferrers, of Baddesley, Clinton, Warw., a unicorn passant erm. *Splendeo tritus.* *cf.* 48. 5

Ferrers of Pentreheylin Hall, Oswestry: (1) A unicorn passant erm (*Ferrers*). (2) A dexter cubit arm vested az., cuffed arg., encircled by a wreath of oak, the hand supporting a cross botonnée fitchée or on the dexter side of the wreath (*Croxton*). *Splendeo tritus.* *cf.* 48. 5

Ferrers, Glouc., an ostrich ppr., holding in the beak a horse-shoe or. 97. 8

Ferrers, Herts, two bees volant saltierwise ppr. 137. 3

Ferrers, a leopard passant gardant and ducally gorged, all ppr. *cf.* 24. 3

Ferrie, Scotland, an anchor and a cable, all ppr. *Be firm.* 161. 2

Ferrier, Scotland, a garb or, banded gu. *Diligentia ditat.* 153. 2

Ferrier, Scotland, a plumb-rule or. *In recte decus.* 176. 6

Ferrier, a horse-shoe ppr. *Bon fortune.* 158. 6

Ferrier, Scotland, a horse-shoe az., between two wings or. *Advance.* 110. 11

Ferrier, Alexander Walter, Esquire, of Belsyde, Linlithgow, N.B., a horse-shoe arg., winged ppr. *Advance.*

Ferrier, of Hemsby and Great Yarmouth, Norf.: (1) A falcon's head couped charged with a collar vairé or and gu. 278. 11. (2) A horse's head erased. *In ferro tutamen.* 278. 12

Ferris of Hawkhurst, Kent, and Thackham, Sussex, on a mount vert, an ostrich arg., charged with a horse-shoe sa., and holding in the beak a cross crosslet fitchée of the first.

Ferris, out of a ducal coronet a sinister hand between two wings ppr. 221. 3

Ferron, out of a ducal coronet an arm in armour, brandishing in the hand a cutlass, all ppr. *cf.* 209. 11

Ferry or **Ferrey,** a plough ppr. 178. 7

Fesant, a demi-antelope ppr., collared gu. 126. 3

Fesant, a cock-pheasant ppr. *cf.* 90. 8

Festing, a fire-beacon inflamed ppr. 177. 14

Fetherston, a griffin's head erased, murally gorged. *cf.* 66. 2

Fetherston or **Fetherstone,** Ireland, a cross crosslet fitched arg., and a sword az., in saltier. 166. 12

Fetherston, Cumb., an antelope's head erased gu., attired or. 126. 2

Fetherston, Cumb., an antelope's head erased gu., attired or, charged on the neck with an ostrich-feather and an annulet arg. *cf.* 126. 2

Fetherston of Packwood House, Warw., an antelope's head erased gu., attired and langued vert. *Christi pennatus sidera morte peto.* 126. 2

Fetherston, Rev. Sir George Ralph, Bart., of Ardagh, co. Longford, Vicar of Piddletrenthide, Dorset, an antelope statant arg., attired or. *Volens et valens.* 126. 12

Fetherston-Whitney, Henry Ernest William, Esquire, of New Pass, Rathowen, co. Westmeath: (1) A bull's head couped sa., horned arg., tipped gu., gorged with a collar chequy or and sa. (*for Whitney*). *cf.* 44. 10. (2) An antelope statant arg., attired or (*for Fetherston*). *Volens et valens.* 126. 12

Fetherston-Whitney, Edmund Whitney, Esquire, of Newpass, co. Westmeath, Ireland: (1) A bull's head couped sa., horned arg., tipped gu., gorged with a collar chequy arg. and gu. (*for Whitney*). *cf.* 44. 12. (2) An antelope statant arg., attired or (*for Fetherston*). *Volens et valens.* 126. 12

Fetherstonhaugh-Whitney, Captain Henry Ernest William: (1) A bull's head couped sa., horned arg., tipped gu., gorged with a collar chequy or and sa. (*for Whitney*). *cf.* 44. 12. (2) An antelope statant arg., attired or (*for Fetherstonhaugh*). *Volens et valens.* 126. 12

Fetherstonehaugh, Bart., an antelope statant arg., attired or. 126. 12

Fetherstonhaugh, Ireland, an antelope statant or. 126. 12

Fetherstonhaugh, Charles, Esquire, an antelope's head erased gu., armed or. *Valens et volens.* 126. 2

Fetherstonhaugh, Timothy, Esquire, of the College, Kirkoswald, Cumb., same crest and motto.

Fetherstonhaugh, Shirley Arthur Stephenson, Esquire, of Hopton Court, Worcs.: (1) A heraldic antelope's head erased gu., surmounted by two feathers in saltire arg., charged on the neck for distinction with a cross crosslet or. (2) In front of a garb or, a cornucopia fesseways ppr. *Ne vile velis.* *cf.* 153. 2

Feton, a chevalier in complete armour at full speed wielding a scimitar, all ppr. 189. 10

Fettes, Bart., Scotland, and **Fettas,** Scotland, a bee volant in pale ppr. *Industria.* 137. 2

Fettiplace, Berks, a cock's head erased, dragon's head vert, eared gu. 71. 1

Fettiplace of Denchworth, Berks, a gu., crested and wattled or. 90. 3

Fettiplace, Berks, a griffin's head erased, vert, beaked gu. 66. 2

Fettyplace, a griffin's head erased vert, beaked and eared gu. 66. 2

Feversham, Earl of (Duncombe), out of a ducal coronet or, a horse's hind-leg sa., hoof upwards, the shoe arg. *Deo regi patriæ.* 123. 6

Fewster, out of a ducal coronet or, a key erect, between two elephants' trunks sa. *Animum rege.* 123. 13

Fewtrell, a leopard's head ppr., gorged with a collar arg., charged with three mullets sa. *cf.* 22. 12

Fewtrell, Shropsh., a leopard's head arg., collared sa., and thereon three mullets of the first. *cf.* 22. 12

Feyrey and **Feytrey,** a cross crosslet fitched sa. 166. 2

Feyry, Beds, a griffin segreant holding in the dexter claw a sword ppr. *cf.* 62. 2

Ffarington of Worden Hall, Lancs, a wyvern arg., ducally gorged gu., chained or, and the chain reflexed over the back and resting under the tail. *Domat omnia virtus.*

Ffarrington, Lancs, a wyvern sans wings, and with the tail nowed arg., langued and ducally gorged gu., chained or. *Domat omnia virtus.* 69. 1

Ffinch, Kent, *see* Finch.

Ffinden, Rev. George Sketchley, M.A., Downe Vicarage, Farnborough, Kent, upon a wreath of the colours, upon a mount vert, a bull arg., pied and yoked sa., resting the dexter foot upon an escutcheon az., charged with a cross patée fitchée at the foot arg. *Suchet und ihr werdet finden.* 45. 3

Ffolkes, Sir William Hovell Browne, Bart., D.L., of Hillington, Norf., a dexter arm embowed, vested per pale vert and gu., cuffed erm., holding in the hand a spear ppr. *Qui sera sera.—Principiis obsta.*

Ffolliott, a lion rampant per pale gu. and arg., double-queued and murally crowned or. *Quo virtus et fata vocant.* cf. 1. 14

Ffoulkes, Edmund Andrew, of Eriviatt, Wales, a boar's head erased arg. *Jure non dono.* 42. 2

ffrench, Baron (ffrench), of Castle Ffrench, co Galway, Ireland, a dolphin naiant ppr. *Malo mori quam fœdari.* 140 5

Ffrench, William J. Lowe, Esquire, L.R.C.S.I., L.R.C.P.I., of Barnetby-le-Wold, Lincoln, a dolphin naiant. *Malo mori quam fœdari.*

Ffytche, a leopard's face or, pierced by a sword in bend sinister ppr., hilt and pommel of the first.

Ffytche, Lincs: (1) A leopard passant ppr., resting the dexter paw upon an escutcheon vert, charged with a leopard's face or. 24. 6. (2) A pelican with wings addorsed vuloing herself ppr. *Esperance.*

Fichet, Somers., a demi-lion pean, ducally crowned or. 10. 11

Ficklin, Philip Berney, Esquire, of Tasburgh Hall, near Norwich, an heraldic tiger sejant sa., semée of escallops, crined and gorged with a collar gemel or, resting the dexter paw on a bezant. *Semper fidelis.—Quod bene mancat.*

Fickling, on a chapeau gu., turned up erm., an eagle's head az. 83. 12

Fiddes, a cinquefoil erm. 148. 12

Fiddes, two hands issuing from clouds in fesse grasping a cornucopia ppr. *Industria.*

Fidelow, a dexter hand in fess couped reaching towards a garland of olive, all ppr. cf. 222. 3

Fidler, a dexter hand holding a palm-branch ppr. 219. 11

Field, Ireland, a lily and a holly-branch in saltire ppr. 151. 10

Field, a garb or, banded gu. 153. 2

Field, a dolphin naiant per pale or and gu., in front of two darts in saltire ppr., points upward. cf. 140. 5

Field, Albert Frederick, Esquire, M.D., M.Ch., M.R.C.S. Eng., L.R.C.P. Edin., of Central House, Castle Drive, Falmouth, in front of two darts in saltire ppr., points upward, a dolphin embowed per pale or and gu.

Field, issuing from clouds a dexter arm in fess ppr., vested gu., cuffed az., holding in the hand a javelin of the first.

Field, George H., Esquire, B.A., M.B., of Forest Corner, Chester Road, Bournemouth, a demi-lion rampant holding between the paws a garb.

Field, Baron (Field), of Bakeham, Surrey, on a wreath of the colours issuing from clouds ppr., a cubit arm erect, vested gu., cuff arg., the hand ppr., holding a spear in bend sinister or, the whole between two wings arg. *Sapientia donum Dei.* 207. 12

Field-Hall, J., Esquire, M.B., Ch.M., of Adelphi House, 71 and 72, Strand, W.C., a griffin's head erased erm. *Per ardua ad alta.*

Field, Joshua, Esquire, J.P., D.L., of Latchmere, Ham, Surrey, a slip of oak fructed in front of an arm in armour fesseways issuant from clouds from the sinister, holding in the hand, all ppr., an armillary sphere erect or. *Bis dat qui cito dat.*

Field, Jonathan, of Laceby, Great Grimsby, Lincoln, same crest and motto.

Field, Edwin, Esquire, B.A., of 1, Eardley Road, Streatham, S.W., an arm in armour fesseways issuant from clouds from the sinister, holding in the hand, all ppr., an armillary sphere erect or.

Fielden, John, Esquire, of Dobroyd Castle, Lancs, and Grimston Park, Yorks, on the stump of a tree couped and sprouting ppr., between two ears of wheat stalked and leaved or, a dove holding in its beak an olive-branch, all ppr. *Virtutis præmium honor.*

Fielder, a lion rampant, holding in his dexter paw a fleur-de-lis. 2. 7

Fields, issuing from a cloud a hand erect grasping a cloud ppr. 214. 9

Fiennes, issuing from clouds two hands in fess conjoined and supporting a flaming heart ppr. 224. 5

Fiennes, *see* Saye and Sele, Baron.

Fife, Duke of, 15, Portman Square: (1) A horse in full speed arg., clothed over the neck and body and down to the fetlocks with a mantling gu., charged with six escutcheons of the arms of Macduff, viz.: "or, a lion rampant gu.," on his back a knight in complete armour cap-à-pie with his sword drawn ppr., on his sinister arm a shield charged as the escutcheons, and on his helmet a flowing lambrequin, also gu., doubled and tasselled or, and thereupon a wreath of the colours a demi-lion rampant of the second. 240. 7. (2) A demi-lion rampant gu., holding in the dexter paw a broad-sword ppr., hilted and pommelled or. *Virtute et opera.* 14. 12

Fife, Aubone George, Esquire, of 42, Jermyn Street, W., St. James's Palace, S.W., and 6, Pump Court, Middle Temple, E.C., out of the battlements of a tower ppr., a demi-lion gu., holding in the dexter paw a saltire arg., and resting the sinister paw on an escutcheon or, charged with a thistle slipped and leaved ppr. *Virtute et opera.*

Fife, William Henry, Esquire, J.P., of Langton Hall, Northallerton, Yorks, same crest and motto.

Fife or **Fiffe**, Scotland, a demi-lion rampant sa. 10. 1

Fife-Cookson of Whitehill Park, Durh., and Lee Hall, Wark, North Tyne: (1) A demi-lion ppr., guttée-de-sang, grasping in both paws a club, also ppr. (*for Cookson*). (2) Out of the battlements of a tower ppr., a demi-lion gu., holding in the dexter paw a saltire arg., and resting the sinister paw on an escutcheon or, charged with a thistle leaved and slipped vert (*for Fife*). *Nil desperandum.—Virtute et opera.*

Fifield, Kent, a falcon rising gu. 88. 2

Figes, two anchors in saltier az., stocks gu. 161. 7

Figgins, Wilts, a dexter arm holding in the hand a cross crosslet fitched gu. 221. 14

Filbut and **Filbutt**, an arm in armour holding in the hand a carved shield.

Filled, a cross crosslet fitched between two palm-branches ppr. cf. 166. 5

Filgate, William de Salis, Esquire, J.P., of Lissrenny, near Ardu, co. Louth, a griffin sejant erect arg., pierced through the breast with a broken spear or, holding the point in its beak. *Virescit vulnere virtus.* cf. 63. 1

Filgate of Glenfoot, Fairlie, N.B.: (1) A griffin sejant salient arg., pierced through the breast with a broken spear or, holding the point in its beak (*for Filgate*). cf. 63. 1. (2) A cubit arm erect grasping a rose-branch, all ppr. (*for Macartney*). *Mens conscia recti. Virescit vulnere virtus.* 218. 10

Filioll, Essex and Dorset, a unicorn's head couped sa. 49. 7

Filkin and **Filkyn**, a pair of wings in lure ppr. 113. 3

Fillent, an anchor or, cabled ppr. *Facta non verba.* 161. 2

Fillingham, Norf., a dexter hand gauntleted holding a pheon point towards, all ppr. 211. 7

Fillingham, on a chapeau arg., turned up gu., a boar sa. 40. 7

Fillingham, a slip of three teazles or. 154. 9

Filmer, Sir Robert Marcus, Bart., of East Sutton, Kent, upon a ruined castle or, a falcon with wings expanded and inverted ppr., beaked and legged of the first.

Filshed, a lion rampant regardant and winged ppr. cf. 20. 7

Fincastle, Lord, *see* Dunmore, Earl.

Finch, Earl of Aylesford, *see* Aylesford.

Finch-Hatton, Earl of Winchelsea, *see* Winchelsea.

Finch, Ireland, a griffin passant az. *Bono vince malum.* 63. 2

Finch, Rutl., a griffin passant sa. 63. 2

Finch, Wynne-, Charles Arthur, of Voelas, Denbighsh.: (1) A griffin passant sa. (*for Finch*). 63. 2. (2) A lion rampant arg., armed and langued gu., holding in the dexter paw a rose of the last slipped ppr., seeded or, barbed and leaved vert (*for Wynne*). cf. 1. 13

Finch, George Henry, Esquire, of Burley-on-the-Hill, Oakham, a pegasus courant arg., winged, crined, and ungu. or, debruised by a pallet wavy sa. *Nil conscire sibi.*

Finch, Kent, a griffin passant with wings addorsed sa., ducally gorged or. 63. 3

Finch, Henry, Esquire, of Bergen House, South Godstone, Surrey, and of Willesden, a griffin segreant az., bezantée, wings elevated or, holding between its claws an escutcheon erm., charged with a lion's head erased sa. *Carpe diem.* 62. 3

Finch, Henry Baldwyn, of Cinden Gate, Henley-on-Thames, a griffin passant sa. *Nil conscire sibi.*

Finch-Hatton-Besly, William David, Esquire, of Kensington Gardens Square, London: (1) In front of a tower triple-towered arg., the trunk of a tree fesseways eradicated and sprouting to the dexter ppr. (*for Besly*). (2) A pegasus courant arg., wings endorsed or (*Finch*). *Tandem vi.*

Fincham, a hind's head erased or, holding in the mouth a branch of holly vert, fructed gu. cf. 124. 3

Finche, Surrey, a griffin passant sa., ducally gorged arg. 63. 3

Finchingfield, a dagger and a sword in saltier ppr. *cf.* 171. 12

Finden, upon a mount vert, a bull arg., pied and yoked sa., resting the dexter foot upon an escutcheon az., charged with a cross pattée fitchée arg. *Suchet und werdet findem.* 45. 3

Finderne, an ox-yoke or. 178. 6

Findlater, an eagle regardant ppr. 76. 6

Findlater, Alexander, Esquire, of Dublin, and of the Slopes, Kingstown, co. Dublin, Ireland, on a rock an eagle regardant with wings displayed, all ppr., the breast and each wing charged with an estoile or.

Findlater, Sir William Huffington, Esquire, of Fernside, Killinney, co. Dublin, on a rock an eagle regardant, wings displayed, all ppr., the heart and each wing charged with an estoile or. *Sit mihi libertas.*

Findlay of Easterhill, Lanark, a boar passant arg. *Fortis in arduis.* 40. 9

Findlay, Robert Elmsall, Esquire, of Boturich Castle, Balloch, Dumbarton, same crest and motto.

Findley, Scotland, a boar passant arg. *Fortis in arduis.*

Fineaux, Kent, an eagle's head erased or, ducally crowned arg. *cf.* 83. 2

Finet, Kent, a tower arg., round the top fleurs-de-lis.

Fingall, Earl of (Plunkett), a horse passant arg. *Festina lente.* 52. 6

Finglas, Ireland, a bear statant ppr., muzzled, collared, and chained or *cf.* 34. 5

Finglasse, Ireland, a demi-eagle displayed with two heads per pale or and sa. *cf.* 82. 1

Finlason, Scotland, a stag's head erased [illegible] *Cœlitus datum.* 121. 2

[illegible] a boar passant ppr. *Fortis in arduis.* 40. 9

Finlay, Major John, of Castle Toward, Greenock, a dexter hand couped at the wrist holding a dagger in bend, all ppr. *I'll be wary.* 212. 3

Finlay, Scotland, a naked arm from the shoulder embowed brandishing a scimitar ppr. *Fortis in arduis.* 201. 1

Finlay, Sir Robert Bannatyne, of Newton Nairn, N.B., a hand holding a dagger ppr. *Fortis in arduis.*

Finlay, Scotland, an olive-branch slipped ppr. *Beati pacifici.* 151. 11

Finlayson, a spur-rowel. 164. 8

Finlayson, Scotland, a stag's head at gaze erased ppr. *cf.* 119. 2

Finlayson, Scotland, a stag's head erased, holding in its mouth a serpent. *Cœlitus datum.* *cf.* 121. 7

Finlayson, Scotland, same crest. *Haud on.*

Finley, a dexter hand holding a sword, all ppr. 212. 13

Finmore, *see* Fynmore.

Finn, a unicorn sejant resting his dexter foot against a tree ppr. 48. 3

Finnan, a dove with wings expanded az., holding in its beak an olive-branch ppr. 94. 5

Finney, a bundle of seven arrows ppr. 173. 7

Finnie, Scotland, a dove holding a leaf in its beak, all ppr. *Tandem.* *cf.* 92. 5

Finnis, a cross crosslet fitched gu. and a sword az. in saltier. 166. 12

Finnis of Wanstead Park, Essex, a cross crosslet fitchée gu. and a sword az. in saltire. *Finis coronat opus.* 166. 12

Finny, Henry Leslie, Esquire, L.R.C.P., of Leixlip, Ireland, and of Pinehem, near Alfreston, Sussex, and of Ellesmere Port, Chester, a demi-lion rampant gu., gorged with an antique Irish crown, and holding in the dexter paw a fleam or. *Spes mea Deus.—Fine opus coronat.* 240. 8

Finny, Professor John Magee, M.D., of 36, Merrion Square, Dublin, same crest and motto.

Finny, Thomas George Roecastle, Esquire, R.I.M.S., Port Officer, Madras, same crest and motto.

Finny, William Evelyn St. Lawrence, Esquire, M.D., of Tamesa, Kingston Hill, Surrey, same crest and motto.

Finucane of Ennistymon House, co. Clare, Ireland, a falcon rising ppr., belled or. *Fide et fortitudine.* 87. 1

Finucane, Ireland, a vine-branch leaved vert, fructed ppr. 152. 9

Finzel of Frankfort Hall, Somers., between two buffalo-horns, that on the dexter per fesse or and sa., and that on the sinister per fesse counterchanged, a demi-lion rampant, to the sinister per fesse of the first and az., gorged with a collar vair. *Quod tibi hoc alteri.*

Fiott, a demi-horse arg., charged on the shoulder with a fleur-de-lis sa. *Malgré l'injustice.—Ho'd firm.* *cf.* 53. 3

Firbank, Joseph Thomas, Esquire, J.P., D.L., High Sheriff for Monmouthsh., 1891, of St. Julian's, Newport, Monmouthsh., and of Coopers, Chislehurst, Kent, upon a mount vert, a sun in splendour between two ostrich feathers. *Cœlitus mihi vires.* 240. 6

Firebrace, a flame of fire ppr. *Fideli quid obstat.* 177. 10

Firebrace, Cordell William, Esquire, of Elmstone Court, Preston, Dover, a dexter arm in armour embowed supporting a portcullis chained and resting on the wreath. *Fideli quid obstat.* 300. 14

Firmage, Suff., an ermine sejant ppr., collared and lined or.

Firman, Humphrey Brooke, Esquire, of Gateforth Hall, Selby, Yorks, in front of two cross crosslets fitchée in saltire gu., a sun in splendour or. *Firmus in Christo.* 162. 1

Firmin of London, a demi-dragon with wings addorsed vert, holding between its claws a garb or. *Firmus in Christo.* 299. 5

Firmin, Philip S., of Ladbroke, Kew, same crest and motto.

Firth, issuing out of a ducal coronet a broken battle-axe, the head in bend sinister. *cf.* 172. 7

Firth, Thomas Williams Staplee, of 140, Upper Tulse Hill, out of a ducal coronet a broken battle-axe, all ppr. *Frangas non flectes.*

Firth of Oak Brook, Sheffield, Yorks, on a mount vert, in front of two Danish battle-axes in saltire sa., a demi-lion rampant or. *Deo non fortuna.*

Firth, Bernard Alexander, Esquire, of Norton Hall, near Sheffield, on a mount vert, in front of a demi-lion rampant or, two battle-axes in saltire sa. *Deo non fortuna.*

Firth, Chesh., on a mount vert, a griffin passant sa., in front of a hurst of six trees ppr. *Deus incrementum dabit.*

Firth, Frederic Hand, Esquire, of Place, Ashburton, same crest and motto.

Firth, Charles, Esquire, M.D. Lond., F.R.C.S. Eng., an eagle's head erased. *Ung roy, ung loy, ung foy.*

Firth-Heatley of Waterford, a sword erect entwined by two snakes, all ppr.

Fischer, a lion passant, the tail extended gu. 5. 11

Fish, a tiger's head erased erm., maned and tusked or.

Fish, Middx., on a rock ppr., a stork erm., beaked and legged gu., charged on the breast with an increscent of the last.

Fishacre, Devonsh., issuing from a cloud a dexter hand in fess ppr., holding a ball sa. *cf.* 223. 1

Fishborne of London and Middx., a lion's head arg., gorged with a collar sa., charged with three fleurs-de-lis of the first. *cf.* 18. 6

Fishe, *see* Fish.

Fisher, Staffs, a kingfisher holding in its beak a fish, all ppr. *Veritas vincit.*

Fisher, Joseph Devonsher, Esquire, of 13, Lower Ormonde Quay, Dublin, a kingfisher holding in its beak a fish, all ppr. *Veritas vincit.* *cf.* 96. 9

Fisher, same crest. *Virtutem extendere factis.*

Fisher of London, on the stump of a tree couped and eradicated a kingfisher, all ppr. *cf.* 96. 9

Fisher, John, of 19, Avenue Elmers, Surbiton, same crest.

Fisher of Maidstone, Kent, on a branch of a tree couped and raguly fesseways sprouting, a branch at each end, a peacock in his pride, all ppr. *cf.* 103. 12

Fisher, on a branch trunked and raguly fesseways and sprouting from the dexter a honeysuckle, a kingfisher, all ppr., holding in its beak a fish or. *cf.* 96. 9

Fisher, Charles Edward, Esquire, of Distington Hall, Whitehaven, in front of a kingfisher, holding in the beak a fish ppr., three crosses patée fesseways arg. *Virtutem extendere factis.*

Fisher of Thornton, Surrey, amidst bulrushes a fountain, thereon a kingfisher rising with wings addorsed holding in the beak a fish, all ppr. *Favente Deo.* *cf.* 96. 9

Fisher of London and Derbysh., a kingfisher ppr., holding in its beak a fish or. *cf.* 96. 9

Fisher of Ravenston, Leics., a kingfisher ppr., holding in the dexter claw a fleur-de-lis sa. *cf.* 96. 9

Fisher, Sharples, Esquire, of Helme Edge, Netherton, Yorks, in front of a bulrush erect a kingfisher ppr., resting the dexter claw on a fleur-de-lis or. *Virtute et fide.* *cf.* 96. 9

Fisher, George Gregg, Esquire, Helme Edge, Netherton, same crest and motto.

Fisher of Cossington Leics., a kingfisher ppr., charged on the breast with a fleur-de-lis sa. *Respice finem.* *cf.* 96. 9

Fisher, Staffs, upon a mount vert, the stump of a tree couped, thereon a kingfisher ppr. *cf.* 96. 9

Fisher, a demi-sea-dog quarterly arg. and az.

Fisher of Hartwell Park Northamp., a demi-sea-dog or.

Fisher, Bart. (*extinct*), of Packington, Magna, Warw., a demi-sea-dog az., crined and ungu. or.

Fisher, Warw., a talbot's head erased arg., collared and eared gu. 56. 1

Fisher, an eagle displayed or 75. 2

Fisher, an eagle displayed sa., charged on the breast with a cross arg. *cf.* 75. 2

Fisher, Ireland, a pelican's head erased ppr., vulning itself gu. 98. 2

Fisher, a demi-lion rampant gu., holding between his paws a laurel-branch ppr.

Fisher, Joseph, J.P., Loughbrow, Hexham, same crest.

Fisher, Staffs, a demi-lion rampant gu., holding between his paws an anchor az. *Spe et amore.* 12. 12

Fisher, Frederick, Esquire, of Hill View, Tulse Hill, S.W., a demi-lion rampant per chevron or and gu., holding in the dexter paw a stag's attire of the last, and resting the sinister paw upon an eel-spear ppr. *Fortiter.*

Fisher, out of a ducal coronet a demi-lion rampant holding between the paws a gauntlet. *Virtutem extendere fac.* *cf.* 10. 2

Fisher, Ireland, a demi-lion rampant arg., holding in the dexter paw a hammer ppr. *cf.* 10. 2

Fisher, Middx., a demi-lion rampant guardant or, holding a carved shield of the arms, viz.: gu., three demi-lions rampant or, a chief indented and the carving of the shield of the last.

Fisher, Hants, a demi-heraldic tiger regardant, vulned in the shoulder by a spear held in his mouth, all ppr. *cf.* 25. 13

Fisher, Wilts, a demi-stag ppr., collared and lined or. *cf.* 119. 2

Fisher, Scotland, an anchor cabled ppr. *Spe et amore.* 161. 2

Fisher, Ireland, a fleur-de-lis quarterly arg. and sa. 148. 2

Fisher-Rowe, Edward Rowe, Esquire, of Thorncombe, Guildford, Surrey: (1) A lamb resting the dexter fore-leg on a beehive ppr., and charged on the body with a cross patée or (*for Rowe*). 253. 17. (2) On a fountain between six bulrushes, a kingfisher, all ppr. (*for Fisher*). *Favente deo.* 253. 18

Fisherwick, Baron, *see* Donegal, Marquess of.

Fishwick, Henry, Esquire, of the Heights, Rochdale, a bull's head couped. *cf.* 44. 3

Fiske-Harrison, *see* Harrison.

Fiske, out of a ducal coronet a reindeer's head. 122. 3

Fiske, Suff., a triangle erected sa., on the vertex an étoile ppr. 167. 8

Fison, Frederick William, Esquire, J.P., of Greenville, Burley-in-Wharfedale, Leeds, a demi-heraldic tiger or, collared gu., holding between the paws an escutcheon arg., charged with a battle-axe erect sa. *Deo confide.* 25. 9

Fitch, Kent and Essex, a leopard's face or, holding in the mouth a sword fessewise ppr., hilted gu. *cf.* 22. 2

Fitch, Essex, two swords in saltier gu., enfiled with a leopard's face or. 22. 7

Fitch, Essex, a leopard passant ppr., resting the dexter paw on an escutcheon vert, charged with a leopard's face or. 24. 6

Fitch, Frederick George, Esquire, J.P., of Pines, Enfield, Middx., a leopard's face erminois pierced through the mouth with a sword broken in the middle arg., pommel and hilt or. *Facta non verba.* 235. 19

Fitch, Frederick, Esquire, of Hadleigh House, Highbury New Park, Middx., same crest and motto.

Fitch, Devonsh. and Warw., a sagittarius gu. 53. 2

Fitchet, a cubit arm holding in the hand a dagger, all ppr. 212. 9

Fitchett, a lion rampant erminois ducally crowned or. 1. 12

Fithie, Scotland, a stork's head erased arg. 106. 1

Fithier, a martlet volant sa., winged or. 96. 2

Fithier, an angel, the dexter hand on the breast, the sinister pointing to heaven. *cf.* 184. 12

Fiton, a demi-Moor shooting an arrow from a bow, all ppr. 185. 6

Fitter, an antelope's head erased arg. 126. 2

Fitton, Chesh., a garb or. 153. 2

Fitton, on a chapeau az., turned up erm., a garb erect arg. 153. 10

Fitton, Chesh., on a chapeau az., turned up erm., a lily ppr., stalked and leaved vert. *cf.* 151. 2

Fitton, of Gawsworth, Chesh., on a chapeau az., turned up erm., a cinquefoil arg. *cf.* 148. 12

Fitton, Heref., Chesh., and Lancs, on a chapeau a wyvern sans legs, the wings expanded. 69. 14

Fittz, two elephants' proboscis erect. 123. 10

Fitz, Devonsh., an escallop arg., charged with a centaur gu.

Fitz-Alan-Howard, *see* Norfolk, Duke of.

Fitz-Alan, Sussex and Shropsh., on a mount vert, a horse passant arg., holding in the mouth an oak branch ppr. 52. 11

Fitz-Alan, out of a ducal coronet a gryphon's head between two wings. 67. 1

Fitz-Allan or **Fitz-Alin,** Shropsh., a spear broken in three pieces, one in pale and two in saltier ppr., banded gu. 175. 2

Fitzalan, issuing out of a ducal coronet a bird.

Fitz-Allen, a sword in pale between two laurel-branches in orle ppr. 170. 3

Fitz-Allen, a dexter arm ppr., vested gu., holding in the hand a mill-rind or. 207. 4

Fitz-Amond, out of a ducal coronet or, two wings addorsed ppr.

Fitz-Barnard, a peacock issuant az. 103. 10

Fitz-Barnard and **Fitz-Bernard,** a cup or. 177. 4

Fitz-Clarence, Viscount, *see* Munster, Earl of.

Fitz-Ellis, within a crescent arg., an arrow in pale point upwards ppr. *cf.* 163. 13

Fitz-Eustace, on a chapeau ppr., a cockatrice sejant gu. *cf.* 68. 9

Fitz-Geffrey, Beds and Northamp., out of a ducal coronet or, a demi-bull rampant sa., armed of the first. *cf.* 45. 8

Fitz-Geoffry, a fox current ppr. *cf.* 32. 8

Fitzgerald, Duke of Leinster, *see* Leinster.

Fitzgerald, Baron De Ros, *see* De Ros.

Fitzgerald, Bart., *see* Judkin-Fitzgerald, Bart.

Fitzgerald-Day, *see* Day.

FitzGerald (**Rt.** Hon. John David, LL.D., P.C.), **Baron FitzGerald,** of Kilmarnock, co. Dublin, on the Roman fasces lying fessewise ppr., a boar passant erm., fretty gu. *Fortis et fidelis.—Crom a Boo.* 40. 1

Fitzgerald, Hon. Arthur Southwell, same crest and mottoes.

Fitzgerald, His Honour the Hon. Judge David, of 18, Clyde Road, Dublin, same crest and mottoes.

Fitzgerald, Hon. Edward, same crest and mottoes.

Fitzgerald, Hon. Eustace, of 40, Stanhope Gardens, same crest and mottoes.

Fitzgerald, Hon. Gerald, K.C., B.A., of 6, Fitzwilliam Square, Dublin, same crest and mottoes.

Fitzgerald, Hon. John Donohoe, of 33, Harrington Gardens, Kensington, S.W., same crest and mottoes.

Fitzgerald-Day, Charles E., Esquire, two dexter hands clasped together ppr., each from a wing expanded quarterly or and az. counterchanged, over the hands a mullet gu. *Sic itur ad astra.*

Fitzgerald-Day, Major J., R.E., same crest and motto.

Fitzgerald and Vesci, Baron (Vesey-Fitzgerald): (1) A soldier fully equipped on horseback at full speed and holding a sword erect, all ppr. (*for Fitzgerald*). *cf.* 189. 10. (2) A dexter hand in armour holding a laurel-branch ppr. (*for Vesey*). *Shanet a Boo.* *cf.* 209. 14

Fitz-Gerald, Foster-Vesey-: (1) Out of a ducal coronet or, a boar passant gu., charged with three annulets arg. (*for Fitz-Gerald*). *cf.* 40. 8. (2) A hand in armour holding a laurel-branch, all ppr. (*for Vesey*). *cf.* 209. 14. (3) A stag trippant ppr. (*for Foster*). *Shanet a Boo.* 117. 8

FitzGerald, Hon. Nicholas, J.P., of Moira, St. Kilda, and of Collins Street West, Melbourne, Victoria, Australia, a boar passant. *Honor probataque virtus.* 40. 9

FitzGerald, Wilson-, William Henry, Chacombe, near Banbury: (1) A boar passant gu., bristled and armed or, charged with a saltire of the last (*for Fitzgerald*). 258. 1. (2) On a mount vert, in front of a lion s head erminois, a lion's gamb erased arg. (*for Wilson*). 258. 2. *Shannet a boo.*

FitzGerald, of Kilcarragh, co. Clare, Ireland, a boar passant gu., bristled and armed or, charged with a saltire couped of the last. *Shanet a Boo.* *cf.* 40. 9

Fitzgerald of Furlough Park, co. Mayo, a boar passant. *Honor probataque virtus.* 40. 9

Fitzgerald, Sir Gerald, K.C.M.G., J.P., of 18, Cadogan Gardens, S.W., on a mount ppr., a boar passant or.

Fitzgerald of Adelphi, Clare, on a chapeau a boar passant. *Shanet a Boo.* cf. 40. 8

FitzGerald, a boar passant erm., fretty gu. cf. 40. 1

Fitzgerald, Francis, Esquire, of 43, Ennismore Gardens, Prince's Gate, a boar rampant. *Honor probataque virtus.*

Fitzgerald, Dalton-, Bart., D.L., of Castle Ishen, co. Cork: (1) A boar passant gu., bristled and armed or (*for Fitzgerald*). 40. 9. (2) A dragon's head couped vert, between two wings or (*for Dalton*). *Shanet a Boo.* 72. 7

Fitzgerald, Sir Augustine, Bart., D.L., of Newmarket-on-Fergus, co. Clare, a chevalier in complete armour on horseback at full speed, his sword drawn and beaver up, all ppr. *Fortis et fidelis.* 189. 10

Fitzgerald, Sir Maurice, Bart., Knight of Kerry, of Valencia and Ballinruddery, co. Kerry, an armed knight on horseback, all ppr. *Mullachar a Boo.* 189. 10

Fitzgerald, Sir Edward, Bart., of Cork, on a mount in front of a hurst of trees, a knight in complete armour on horseback all ppr., his shield gu., charged with a civic crown or. 259. 5

Fitzgerald, Suff. and Northamp., a monkey passant gardant sa., collared and chained round the body or. cf. 136. 8

Fitz-Gerald, a monkey statant ppr., environed about the middle with a plain collar and chained or. *Crom a Boo.* 136. 8

Fitzgerald, Frederick Lattin, Esquire, of Rathgar, co. Dublin, and Leccagh, co. K[illegible]e, a monkey passant in front of a cap erm., all ppr. *Crom a brudh.*

Fitzgerald, Bruce, Esquire, of the Royal Farm, Pepperharrow, Surrey, a monkey statant arg., charged on the body with two roses, and resting the dexter foreleg on a saltire gu. *Crom a boo.*

FitzGerald of the Little Island, co. Waterford: (1) On a wreath of the colours a monkey ppr., environed about the middle and chained or, charged with a mullet arg., upon a crescent az. for difference (*for FitzGerald*). cf. 136. 8. (2) On a wreath of the colours a cubit arm vested az., cuffed arg., holding a sword in bend sinister ppr., pommelled and hilted or, pierced through the jaw of a boar's head couped sa., vulned and distilling drops of blood ppr. (*for Purcell*). *Crom a Boo.*

Fitzgibbon, Earl of Clare, *see* Clare.

Fitz-Gibbon, The White Knight, a boar passant gu., charged on the body with three annulets fesseways arg. cf. 40. 8

Fitzgibbon, Augustus Henry, Esquire: (1) A boar passant gu., bristled and armed or, charged with three annulets of the second (*for Fitzgibbon*). (2) A demi-lion rampant gu., holding between the paws an estoile arg. (*for Dillon*). *Nil admirari.*

Fitzgibbon, Clare Valentine, Esquire, same crests and motto.

Fitzgibbon, Louis Theobald, Esquire, same crests and motto.

FitzGibbon, Hon. Gerald Normanby, of Mount Shannon, co. Limerick, Ireland: A boar passant gu., bristled and armed or, charged with two annulets of the second. cf. 40. 8. *Nil admirari.*

FitzGibbon, Philip John, Esquire, of Crohana, a boar passant ppr., fretty arg. *Honore integro contemno fortunam* cf. 40. 1

Fitzgilbert, a hand holding a fleur-de-lis, all ppr. cf. 215. 5

Fitz-Hamon, a dexter hand holding a tilting-spear in bend ppr. 214. 11

Fitz-Harbert, a salamander or, in flames gu. 138. 4

Fitz-Harris, Viscount, *see* Malmesbury, Earl of.

Fitz-Harry, a bear's head erased ppr., muzzled gu. 35. 2

Fitz-Henry, a wyvern vomiting fire at both ends. 69. 9

Fitz-Henry, Evans-, co. Carlow, Ireland: (1) A lion rampant gu. (*for Fitz-Henry*). 1. 13. (2) A demi-lion rampant per fesse or and gu., holding between the paws a boar's head erased az. (*for Evans*).

Fitz-Henry of Ballymackesey, Ireland, a lion rampant gu. *Henricus a Henrico.* 1. 13

Fitzherbert - Brockholes, *see* Brockholes.

Fitzherbert, Rev. Sir Richard, Bart., of Tissington Hall, Derbysh., a cubit arm in armour erect, the hand appearing clenched within the gauntlet, all ppr. *Ung je serviray.* 246. 8

Fitzherbert, Richard Ruxton, Esquire, of Shantonagh, co. Monaghan, and of Black Castle, co. Meath, Ireland, a dexter cubit arm erect, the hand clenched, armed, and gauntleted, all ppr., charged with a crescent gu. *Ung je serviray.* 246. 8

Fitzherbert, Major Walter Hepburn Mellitas, of The Hall, Somersal Herbert, Derby, same crest. *Plain living, high thinking.*

Fitz-Herbert, Derbysh. and Staffs, a cubit arm in armour erect, the hand appearing clenched within a gauntlet, all ppr. *Ung je serviray.* 246. 8

Fitzherbert, Arthur Vesey, Esquire, of Estancia Media Agua, Mercedes, Banda Oriental, South America, same crest and motto.

Fitzherbert, Basil Thomas, Esquire, of Swynnerton Hall, Stone, Staffs, same crest and motto.

Fitzherbert, Francis Edward, Esquire, of Swynnerton Hall, Stone, Staffs, same crest and motto.

Fitzherbert, Henry Corry, Esquire, of Milbrook, Abbey Leix, Queen's Co., Ireland, same crest and motto.

Fitzherbert-Brockholes, William Joseph, Esquire, of Claughton Hall, Garstang, Lancs.: (1) A brock passant sa. (*for Brockholes*). (2) A dexter cubit arm in armour erect, the hand appearing clenched within a gauntlet, all ppr. (*for Fitzherbert*).

Fitz-Hewe or **Fitz-Hugh,** Bucks, a Cornish chough ppr. 107. 14

Fitzhugh, Godfrey, Esquire, of Plas Power, near Wrexham, Denbighsh., a quatrefoil sa., thereon a martlet erminois. *In moderation placing all my glory.* 307. 6

Fitzhugh of Plas Power, Wales, a martlet ppr. *In moderation placing all my glory.* 95. 4

Fitz-Hugh, Yorks and Oxon., on a chapeau gu., turned up erm., a wyvern sans legs, with wings expanded arg. 69. 14

Fitz-Hugh, on a chapeau crimson turned up erm., a demi-griffin segreant arg. cf. 64. 2

Fitz-Humfrey or **Humphrey,** Essex, a dragon's head vert, holding in the mouth a sinister hand gu. cf. 72. 6

Fitzjames, Duke of Berwick, on a chapeau gu., turned up erm., a dragon passant arg., gorged with a collar az., charged with three fleurs-de-lis or. 73. 4

Fitz-James, a dolphin arg., devouring the top of an antique cap az., turned up erm.

Fitz-James, a buffalo passant sa., armed or.

Fitz-John, Lincs, on a chapeau a salamander in flames, all ppr. 138. 2

Fitz-John, a demi-lion rampant. 10. 2

Fitz-John, Ireland, a dexter hand holding an olive-branch ppr. 219. 9

Fitz-Lewis, Essex, a bull statant per pale or and purp., armed and unguled sa. 45. 2

Fitz-Marmaduke, a catherine-wheel arg. 167. 2

Fitz-Maurice, *see* Lansdowne, Marquess of.

Fitzmaurice, Earl of Orkney, *see* Orkney.

Fitz-Maurice, Ireland, a sagittarius ppr. and arg., shooting an arrow from a bow, also ppr. *Virtute, non verbis.* 53. 2

Fitz-Maurice, Ireland, two hands holding a sword in pale ppr. 213. 1

Fitzmore, a parrot issuant.

Fitz-Neel, Bucks, on a chapeau ppr., a cinquefoil or. cf. 148. 11

Fitz-Nicoll, Ireland, a falcon rising arg., belled or, holding in the beak a cross formée fitchée gu. cf. 87. 1

Fitz-Osbern and **Fitz-Osberne,** a demi-eagle displayed with two heads az. cf. 82. 3

Fitz-Osbert, a demi-dragon vert. 73. 10

Fitz-Osborn, two arms in armour embowed or, wielding a battle-axe arg. cf. 194. 12

Fitz-Osborn, a spear-head az. 174. 12

Fitz-Ourse, an anchor and cable sa., and a sword az., hilted or, in saltier. 169. 9

Fitzpaine, a lion passant. 6. 2

Fitz-Patrick, Baron Castletown, *see* Castletown.

Fitzpatrick, Ireland, a dragon regardant vert, surmounted by a lion gardant sa., the tail extended. *Fortis sub forte.* cf. 73. 8

Fitz-Pen, Cornw., a bee volant erect or, winged vert. 137. 2

Fitz-Piers, a bell az. 168. 7

Fitz-Pomeroy, around two hunting-spears in pale a serpent entwined ppr.

Fitz-Ralph, a square padlock az. 168. 13

Fitz-Randolph, of Langton Hall, Notts, and Chesterfield, Derbysh., on a chapeau or, turned up az., a wyvern of the last. *cf.* 70. 4

Fitz-Rause, on a mount vert, a hind statant ppr. 125. 3

Fitz-Raynard and **Raynold,** two wings conjoined ppr. 113. 1

Fitz-Richard, two dolphins haurient addorsed ppr. 140. 1

Fitz-Roger, an eagle's leg erased arg. *cf.* 113. 8

Fitz-Ronard, a dove standing on a serpent nowed ppr. 92. 10

Fitz-Roy, *see* Grafton, Duke of.

Fitz-Roy, *see* Southampton, Baron.

Fitzroy, Cecil Augustus, Esquire, J.P., of Ringstead, Hastings, Hawkes Bay, New Zealand, on a chapeau gu., turned up erm., a lion statant gardant or, crowned with a ducal coronet az., and gorged with a collar countercompony arg. and of the fourth. *Et decus et pretium recti.* 4. 2

Fitzroy, Almeric William, Esquire, of 55, Lower Belgrave Street, S.W., same crest and motto.

Fitz-Simmons, an eagle with wings expanded looking towards the sun, all ppr.

Fitz-Simon, a griffin's head holding in its beak a palm-branch between two wings, all ppr. 65. 9

Fitz-Simond, Ireland, a dove arg. 92. 2

Fitz-Simons, Ireland, a boar passant regardant pulling from his shoulder an arrow.

Fitz-Stevens of Dublin, a wolf's head erased gu., holding in the beak a snake ppr. *cf.* 30. 8

Fitz-Symon, Ireland, a demi-parrot close vert, gorged with a collar gu., beaked of the last.

Fitz-Symon of Dublin, a dove arg., collared gu. *cf.* 92. 2

Fitz-Symon, a dexter and a sinister hand wielding a two-handed sword ppr. 213. 3

Fitz-Symond, issuing from a cloud a hand holding a club, all ppr. 214. 9

Fitz-Thomas, Essex, a dragon's head pierced through the neck by a spear in bend sinister, all ppr. 72. 10

Fitz-Thomas, Ireland, out of a ducal coronet or, a sceptre environed by a serpent between two wings, all ppr. *cf.* 170. 13

Fitz-Urse, out of the battlements of a tower an arm in armour wielding in the hand a scimitar, all ppr.

Fitz-Vrian, two battle-axes in saltier gu. and az., the heads or, between the tops a bird sa. *cf.* 172. 4

Fitz-Walter, Baron (*extinct*), *see* Bridges, Bart.

Fitz-Walter, a heart gu., winged or. 112. 10

Fitz-Warren, Somers., a holy lamb regardant ppr., with a banner sa. *cf.* 131. 2

Fitz-Waryn, a wyvern with wings expanded gu. *cf.* 70. 8

Fitz-Waryne, a wyvern arg., eared and langued gu. 70. 1

Fitz-Water, a lion rampant or. 1. 13

Fitz-Water, issuing from a cloud a hand holding a club ppr. 214. 9

Fitz-Wight, on a chapeau ppr., a lion passant gardant az. 4. 5

Fitzwilliam, Earl (Wentworth Fitzwilliam): (1) Out of a ducal coronet or, a triple plume of ostrich-feathers arg. (*for Fitzwilliam*). 114. 6. (2) A griffin passant arg. (*for Wentworth*). *Appetitus rationi pareat.* 63. 2

Fitz-William of Merrion, Dublin, in front of a peacock's tail ppr., a greyhound's head erased arg., collared and spotted gu.

Fitz-William, Surrey, a tiger passant sa., ducally gorged and lined arg.

Fitz-William, a trefoil stalked raguly and slipped arg. *cf.* 148. 9

Fitz-William, a phœnix az., beaked or, in flames gu. 82. 2

Fitzwygram, Sir Frederick Wellington John, Bart., of Walthamstow, Essex, on a mount vert, a hand in armour in fesse, couped at the wrist ppr., charged with an escallop and holding a fleur-de-lis erect or. *Dulcis amor patriæ.* 259. 8

Fitz-Zimon, or **Zymon** a monkey ppr. banded about the middle. 136. 8

Flacke, a covered cup.

Flacket of Dovebridge, Derbysh., a fox's head erased gu., shot through the neck fesseways with an arrow sa., feathered arg. *cf.* 33 6

Flamank and **Flamock,** Cornw., a Saracen's head ppr., banded or. 190. 5

Flamank, Phillips-, Rev. William, a lion rampant sa., semée of saltires arg., and holding between the paws an escarbuncle or. *Virtus ad astra.*

Flamsted, Northamp., a talbot's head arg., erased gu., eared and gorged with a bar gemelle or. *cf.* 56. 2

Flamvile, Leics., two battle-axes addorsed in saltier, ensigned by a dove, all ppr.

Flanagan, Ireland, a lion's gamb holding a crescent. 39. 15

Flanagan, Ireland, a hand holding a dagger. *Audaces fortuna juvat.* 212. 9

Flanders, a harp gu. 168. 9

Flashman, out of a ducal coronet two arms from the elbow in saltier, each holding a scimitar in pale, all ppr.

Flattesbury, on a mural coronet or, a stag sejant erm. 116. 4

Flavel, Sidney, Esquire, of Bushbury Lodge, Leamington, in front of flames of fire ppr., two keys in saltire wards upwards az. *Tu Deus ale flammam.* 168. 11

Flaxney, Oxon., on a mount vert, a talbot sa., collared and lined or, the end of the line tied in a knot. *cf.* 54. 2

Flay, on a mural coronet gu., a snake nowed ppr. 142. 12

Fleeming, a goat's head erased ppr. 128. 5

Fleeming of Moness, a goat's head erased arg., armed or. *Let the deed shaw.* 128. 5

Fleeming, Scotland, a goat's head erased arg., armed and gorged with a collar az., charged with three cinquefoils arg. *Let the deed shaw.* 128. 7

Fleeming, Scotland, on a mural coronet or, a stag sejant erm. 116. 4

Fleeming, Staffs, on a mount vert, a cross patée fitched or, thereon perched a Cornish chough ppr.

Fleeming, Scotland, a palm-tree ppr. *Sub pondere cresco.* 144. 1

Fleet of London, a sinister arm embowed, vested sa., slashed arg., holding in the hand ppr. a club of the second.

Fleet, a goat holding in its mouth a trefoil ppr. *cf.* 129. 5

Fleete of London, a sea-lion gardant erect, the upper part or, the lower part az., holding between the paws an escallop gu.

Fleetwood, a wolf passant regardant arg., vulned in the shoulder ppr. *cf.* 28. 12

Fleetwood, Hesketh-, Bart., of Rossall Hall, Lancs: (1) A wolf regardant arg., charged on the breast with a trefoil vert (*for Fleetwood*). *cf.* 28. 12. (2) A garb erect or, in front of an eagle displayed with two heads ppr. (*for Hesketh*). *Quod tibi, hoc alteri.* 74. 3

Fleetwood, Hesketh-: (1) A wolf statant regardant arg., charged on the breast with a trefoil vert and on the body with a pale wavy az. (*for Fleetwood*). *cf.* 28. 12. (2) A mount vert, thereon, in front of an eagle with two heads displayed ppr., a garb or, banded gu., the whole debruised by a bendlet wavy sinister az. *Quod tibi, hoc alteri.* *cf.* 74. 3

Flegg, two lion's gambs in saltier sa., enfiled with two branches of laurel in orle vert. *cf.* 39. 14

Fleming, *see* Flemming.

Fleming, *see* Coham-Fleming.

Fleming, a palm-tree ppr. *Sub pondere cresco.* 144. 1

Fleming, Lord Slane, a mortar-piece casting out a bomb with flames, all ppr., chains and rings or. *Bhear na Righ gan* ("*May the King live for ever*"). *cf.* 169. 10

Fleming, Hants, an eagle displayed sa., beaked, legged, and ducally gorged or. [illegible] 2

Fleming, Hon. John, of Riel[illegible] House, Aberdeen, a goat's [illegible] erased arg., armed or. *Let the deed shaw.* 128. 5

Fleming, Henry Contarini, Esquire, of Greenore, Clontarf, co. Dublin, a goat's head erased arg., armed or, between the horns a cinquefoil gu. *Let the Deid Schaw.*

Fleming, Rev. William Alexander, B.A., T.C.D., of St. John's Parish, Bradford, Yorks, same crest and motto.

Fleming, Harry Oliver, of Greenore, Clontarf, co. Dublin, same crest and motto.

Fleming, Alfred Alexander, Esquire, of 68, Victoria Street, London, S.W., same crest and motto.

Fleming, Thomas, Esquire, of Greenore, Clontarf, co. Dublin, same crest and motto.

Fleming of Clayquhat, Perth; Bigadon, Tor Dean, and Hawkbridge Barton, Devonsh., a goat's head erased ppr., collared or. *Let the deed shaw.* *cf.* 128. 9

Fleming, Ireland, a demi-lion rampant ducally gorged. 10. 7

Fleming, a snake nowed ppr. 142. 4

Fleming, Sir Andrew Fleming Huddleston, Bart., of Rydal, co. Westml., a serpent nowed, holding in his mouth a garland of olive and vine, all ppr. *Pax, copia, sapientia.* 142. 7

Fleming, Hughes-Le, of Rydall Hall, Westml.: (1) A serpent nowed holding in the mouth a wreath of olive and vine leaves, all ppr. (*for Le Fleming*). 142. 7. (2) A lion couchant, the dexter paw resting upon a fountain, all ppr. (*for Hughes*). *Pax, copia, sapientia.* cf. 7. 5

Fleming, Willis-, John Edward Arthur, Stoneham Park, Southampton: (1) An eagle displayed sa., beaked, membered, and ducally gorged or. (2) Out of a mural crown or, a demi-lion rampant gu., within a collar gemelle gold, three bezants.

Fleming, a dexter hand gauntleted holding a sword, all ppr. 211. 4

Fleming, Shropsh., a dexter arm in armour holding a sword, all ppr. 210. 2

Flemming of London, a goat's head ppr. *Cave lupum.* 128. 12

Flemyng, a dolphin arg., crowned az., and charged with six pellets.

Flemyng, England, and **Flemynge,** Scotland, a hand issuant plucking a rose. 213. 13

Flesher a squirrel sejant per fesse or and gu. cf. 135. 4

Fletcher-Boughey, see Boughey.

Fletcher, Bernard, Esquire, of Dunans, Glendaruel, Argyllsh., two arms drawing a bow, all ppr. *Recta pete.* 200. 2

Fletcher, Sir Henry, Bart., of Ham Manor, Angmering, Sussex, a horse's head arg., charged with a trefoil gu. *Martis non Cupidinis.* cf. 50. 6

Fletcher, Bart., Ireland, out of a mural coronet or, a horse's head erm., gorged with a wreath of laurel vert.

Fletcher, Charles William Corrie, M.R.C.S., L.R.C.P., of the Gables, Burton Road, Derby: (1) A horse's head erased arg., gorged with a ducal crown az., charged on the neck with a pheon sa. (2) On a cap of maintenance gu., turned up erm., a scaling-ladder in bend sinister or. *Sub cruce salus.*

Fletcher, Frederick Brandstrom, Esquire, M.A., of Stow Thorna, Beauchamp Road, East Molesey, same crests and motto.

Fletcher, Rev. James Michael John, of Tideswell Vicarage, Buxton, Derbysh., same crests and motto.

Fletcher, Thomas Russell, Esquire, of Lawneswood, near Stourbridge, same crests and motto.

Fletcher, Walter John, Esquire, F.R.I.B.A., A.M.I.C.E., of the Chantry, Wimborne Minster, Dorset, same crests and motto.

Fletcher, William Bainbrigge, Esquire, of 78, Thornlaw Road, West Norwood, same crests and motto.

Fletcher, Rev. William George Dimock, M.A., F.S.A., of St. Michael's Vicarage, Shrewsbury, same crests and motto.

Fletcher, William Giffard, Esquire, of Berwood, Erdington, near Birmingham, same crests and motto.

Fletcher, Rev. William Henry, M.A., same crests and motto.

Fletcher of Corsock, Kirkcud, a horse's head arg. *Martis non Cupidinis.* cf. 50. 13

Fletcher, a horse's head erased arg., gorged with a ducal coronet az. cf. 51. 4

Fletcher, England and Scotland, a horse's head erased arg. *Martis non Cupidinis.* 51. 4

Fletcher, Lieutenant-Colonel Henry Arthur, of 17, Victoria Square, S.W., and Engine Court, St. James's Palace, a horse's head couped. *Martis non cupidinis.*

Fletcher, a horse's head couped arg., guttée-de-sang. cf. 50. 13

Fletcher, Ireland, a horse's head erased arg., maned or. 51. 4

Fletcher, Worcs. and Derbysh., a horse's head arg., erased sa., gorged with a collar of the second, charged with three pheons or, points downward, holding in the mouth a rose gu., slipped and leaved ppr. *Sub cruce salus.*

Fletcher, George Hamilton, Esquire, J.P., of the Anchorage, near Christchurch, and Pyt House, Tisbury, Wilts, in front of a fern-brake a centaur ppr., wielding with the dexter hand a spear or. *Droit comme ma flèche.*

Fletcher, a talbot sejant. cf. 55. 2

Fletcher, Sussex, a talbot passant arg., pellettée. cf. 54. 1

Fletcher, Leics. and Warw., a demi-talbot rampant or. cf. 55. 8

Fletcher, Leics. and Warw., a demi-talbot rampant az., ducally gorged or. 55. 12

Fletcher, Rev. William Dudley Saul, B.A., B.D., of Lissadell Parsonage, co. Sligo, a demi-talbot rampant gu., ducally gorged and charged with an escallop or. *Dieu pour nous.* 230. 10

Fletcher, Leics. and Warw., a demi-talbot rampant az., eared or. cf. 55. 8

Fletcher, John, Esquire, of Saltoun Hall, Pencaitland, N.B., a bloodhound az., ducally gorged or. *Dieu pour nous.*

Fletcher, Glouc., a demi-bloodhound az., langued gu., ducally gorged or. *Dieu pour nous.*

Fletcher, Scotland, a demi-lion az., holding in the dexter paw a cross crosslet fitched gu. *Libertate extincta, nulla virtus.* 11. 10

Fletcher of the Lodge, Tiverton, Devonsh., a demi-lion rampant

Fletcher, Scotland, a demi-lion az., holding in the dexter paw a cross crosslet fitched gu. *Fortis in arduis.* 11. 10

Fletcher, Chesh., a pheon point upwards per pale erm. and sa. 174. 9

Fletcher of London and Oxon., a fleur-de-lis or, pellettée. cf. 148. 2

Fletcher, three arrows, two in saltire and one in fess ppr., diverging from each angle a fleur-de-lis az., and surmounted in the centre by a saltire wavy sa. *Alta pete.*

Fletcher, on a cap of maintenance gu., turned up erm., a scaling-ladder in bend sinister or. cf. 158. 14

Fletcher, a dexter arm in armour embowed, holding in the gauntlet ppr. an arrow, also ppr., headed or. cf. 198. 4

Fletcher, Monm. and Lancs, a dexter arm embowed, encircled above the elbow by a wreath of yew ppr., holding in the hand a bow or, stringed sa. *Sperans pergo.*

Fletcher, John Robert, Esquire, of the Uplands, Whitefield, near Manchester, and Kearsley, Stoneclough, Lancs, in front of a naked arm embowed holding a long bow, two arrows in saltire points downwards, all ppr. *Forti nihil difficile.*

Fletcher, a dexter arm in armour embowed holding in the hand an arrow in fess, all ppr., and behind the arm an anchor erect or. cf. 198. 4

Fletcher, Scotland, two arms ppr. shooting an arrow from a bow sa. *Recta pete.* 200. 2

Fletcher, Scotland and Ireland, out of a ducal coronet or, a plume of three ostrich-feathers az., banded of the first. *Dieu pour nous.* 114. 2

Fletcher-Campbell, Henry John, Esquire, of Beech Lodge, Wimbledon Common, a boar's head couped ppr. *Ne obliviscaris.*

Fletcher-Twemlow, George Fletcher, Esquire, of Pitmaston, Worcs.: (1) A paroquet standing on the stump of a tree, a branch sprouting therefrom ppr. (*for Twemlow*). (2) On the dexter side, a plate charged with a pheon per pale erm. and sa., point downwards (*for Fletcher*). (3) On the sinister side, a leopard sa., spotted and collared or, resting its paw on a pheon or (*for Royds*).

Fletewikes, an arm embowed vested and cuffed arg., holding in the hand ppr. an arrow sa., headed and feathered of the first

Fletewood, a heraldic tiger sa. cf. 25. 5

Fletwick, Beds, two lion's gambs supporting an escutcheon arg. 39. 1

Fleury, Ireland, a lion passant holding in the dexter paw a crescent. 5. 6

Flexney, see Flaxney.

Flexney, a dexter and a sinister arm shooting an arrow from a bow, all ppr. 200. 2

Flight, a savage's head from the shoulders ducally crowned, and issuant therefrom a long cap, the top turned forward. 190. 8

Flin and **Flinn,** Ireland, two dexter hands ppr., clasped and conjoined at the wrists to two wings or. 224. 12

Flinn of Dublin, a lion passant holding in his dexter paw a laurel-branch. cf. 6. 2

Flint, Scotland, an étoile. *Sine maculâ.* 164. 1

Flint, a flint ppr., thereon an estoile or.

Flint, out of a cloud az., an étoile arg. 164. 11

Flint, a lion's gamb erect sa., holding a laurel-branch ppr. 37. 4

Flitt, on a mount a dove, all ppr. 92. 3

Flockhart, Scotland, on a mount vert, two harts, one lodged, the other at gaze ppr. 116. 6

Flood, Ireland, a wolf's head erased arg. *Vis unita fortior.* 30. 8

Flood, Devonsh., a demi-lion rampant az., crowned or, holding a cinquefoil of the last. cf. 10. 11

Flood, Ireland, a heart crowned between two wings ppr. 110. 14

Flood, a chevalier on horseback in complete armour, his visor up. 189. 10

Flood, a chevalier in armour on horseback holding in his dexter hand a tilting-spear. 189. 10

Florio, the sun in his splendour or. 162. 2

Flory, Rev. William, Hon. Canon of Worcester Cathedral, of Redland Lodge, Leamington, between two saltires az., a stag's head erased arg., gorged with a collar of the first, therefrom three crescents of the second, and between the attires a fleur-de-lis, also az. *Ut prosimus.*

Flote, out of a ducal coronet a reindeer's head ppr. 122. 3

Flounders, Shropsh. and Yorks, a demi-eagle displayed vert. *Aquila non capiat muscas.* 81. 6

Flowde, out of a tower a greyhound's head erased arg., collared sa., holding in the mouth a hind's leg, also erased ppr. cf. 61. 5

Flower, *see* Ashbrook, Viscount.

Flower, a flower erm., foliated vert.

Flower, Surrey, issuing out of clouds a cubit arm erect, holding in the hand a rose and a lily, each slipped, all ppr. *Flores curat Deus.* 257. 5

Flower, Arthur, Esquire, J.P., of 36, Prince's Gate, S.W., same crest and motto.

Flower of Aston Clinton, Tring, issuing from clouds a cubit arm erect, holding in the hand a rose and a lily slipped, all ppr. *Flores curat Deus.* 257. 5

Flower and **Flowre,** Kent, Northamp., and Yorks, a lion's head erased sa. 17. 8

Flower, a lion's head erased arg., charged with a mullet gu. cf. 17. 8

Flower, Edgar, J.P., Middle Hill, Broadway, Worcs., same crest.

Flower, Bart., Oxon., a demi-lion per pale erm. and ermines, gorged with a chain within a collar gemelle or, and holding in the dexter paw a gilliflower ppr. *Perseverando.* cf. 10. 9

Flower, Ireland, a boar statant az., armed, unguled, and bristled or, langued gu. cf. 40. 7

Flower, Wilts, a unicorn's head couped or. 49. 7

Flower, Hon. Robert Thomas, of Knockatrina House, Durrow, Queen's Co., a raven having on its beak an ermine-spot sa. cf. 107. 5

Flower, Cambs, a stork with wings elevated ppr., beaked and legged gu. cf. 105. 2

Flowerdew of Hetherset, Norf., a demi-man habited az., wreathed about the temples arg. and sa., holding in the dexter hand a sprig of two roses gu., stalked and leaved ppr.

Flowerdew and **Flowerdue,** in a maunch an arm embowed, the elbow resting on the wreath. 203. 1

Floyd, Sir John, Bart., a lion rampant regardant arg., murally crowned gu., bearing a flag representing the standard of Tippoo Sultan, flowing to the sinister ppr. *Patiens pulveris atque solis.*

Floyd, a griffin sejant az., holding in its dexter claw a garland of laurel ppr. 62. 9

Floyer, Devonsh. and Somers., out of a ducal coronet a dexter hand holding a sword wavy in pale, all ppr. 212. 1

Floyer, Dorset, a buck's head erased or, holding in its mouth an arrow arg. *Floret virtus vulnerata.* 249. 3

Floyer, George William, Esquire, of Stafford House, near Dorchester, same crest and motto.

Floyer, Rev. John Kestell, M.A., of Warton Vicarage, Carnforth, same crest and motto.

Fludd, out of a ducal coronet or, an ounce's head arg. 23. 11

Flude, an arm couped and embowed, the elbow resting on the wreath, holding in the hand a sword in pale enfiled with a savage's head couped, all ppr. 201. 7

Fludyer, Sir Arthur John, Bart., Ayston Hall, Uppingham, Rutl., an escallop arg., between two wings elevated, also arg. 141. 7

Fluik, Arthur R., Esquire, of 5, Abbey Green, Chester, a demi-boar rampant or, charged with three billets between two bendlets sa.

Flux, William, Esquire, late of Bibury Court, near Cirencester, Glouc., upon the trunk of a tree fessewise eradicated to the sinister a coney courant arg. *Fluctus fluctu.*

Fly, Hants, an arm in armour erect ppr., holding in the gauntlet a hawk's lure or, stringed gu.

Flynn, a hand couped at the wrist grasping a serpent ppr. *Honor præmium virtutis est.* 220. 2

Flynt, a human heart purp., winged or. 112. 10

Foakes, a dexter arm erect, paly vert and gu., cuffed erm., holding a javelin. *Qui sere sera.*

Foden, upon a mount vert, a unicorn sejant erect arg., armed, maned, and unguled or, supporting with the forefeet a cross-bow sa.

Fodon, Staffs, out of a ducal coronet or, a pike's head az. cf. 139. 14

Fodringay, a crane arg., holding in its beak a bunch of clover ppr. cf. 105. 9

Fodringham, Yorks, a buck ppr. 117. 5

Fogg and **Fogge,** Kent, a unicorn's head arg. 49. 7

Fogg and **Fogge,** Kent, a unicorn's head couped arg., semée of mullets sa. c.f. 49. 7

Fogg-Elliot, John Walton, Esquire, of Elvet Hill, Durh.: (1) A dexter arm holding a cutlass ppr. (*for Elliot*). (2) A unicorn's head couped arg. (*for Fogg*).

Foggo or **Fogo,** Scotland, a cherub's head ppr. 189. 9

Fogo, Scotland, a cross crosslet fitchée gu. *Fuimus.* 166. 2

Fokeram, Berks, a long cross vert. 165. 4

Fokke, a lion's gamb or, holding a cross patée fitched gu. cf. 36. 9

Folborne, a sinister hand couped in fess ppr.

Foleborne, a branch of fir vert, fructed or. 147. 6

Foleborne, three holly-leaves vert, banded gu. 150. 12

Folet, on a chapeau ppr., an escallop or. cf. 141. 11

Foley, Baron (Foley), of Kidderminster, Worcs., a lion rampant arg., holding between the forepaws an escutcheon charged with the arms, viz.: arg., a fesse engrailed between three cinquefoils, all within a bordure sa. *Ut prosim.* 2. 8

Foley, Surrey, a lion rampant arg., holding between the paws a ducal coronet. 3. 6

Foley, Worcs., a lion sejant arg., holding between the paws a ducal coronet or. cf. 8. 13

Foley, Paul Henry, Esquire, J.P., of Stoke Edith Park, Heref., and Prestwood House, near Stourbridge, Staffs: (1) A lion sejant arg., holding between the fore-paws an escutcheon charged with the arms, *i.e.*, arg., a fess engrailed between three cinquefoils sa., with a bordure of the last (*for Foley*). 289. 1. (2) A horse's head erm., pierced through the neck with a spear, the staff broken ppr. (*for Hodgetts*). *Ut prosim.* 289. 2

Foley, a demi-lion rampant gu., holding in the dexter paw a pheon point upwards arg. cf. 10. 2

Foley, Ireland, a griffin segreant gu., winged, legged, and beaked or. 62. 2

Foliot and **Foliott,** a battle-axe ppr. *Hope to come.* 172. 3

Foljamb, an armed leg party per pale or and sa., gartered with a wreath of the first and az., couped at the thigh. cf. 193. 1

Foljambe, Staffs, a leg couped at the thigh quarterly or and sa., spurred of the first, charged on the thigh with a fess gu. cf. 193. 1

Foljambe, Yorks, an armed leg couped at the thigh quarterly or and sa., spurred of the first. 279. 8

Foljambe, George Savile, of Cockglode, Notts, a jamb unarmed excepting the spur quarterly or and sa. *Soies ferme.* 279. 8

Foljambe, Rt. Hon. Francis John Savile, of Osberton, Worksop, same crest and motto.

Folkard, Sussex, out of a ducal coronet a demi-swan with wings expanded. *Sic fidem teneo.* cf. 100. 12

Folkenorth, an ostrich holding in its beak a broken tilting-spear. cf. 97. 2

Folkes, Middx., a dexter arm erect vested per pale vert and gu., cuffed erm., holding in the hand a spear ppr. 207. 14

Folkes, Norf., a dexter arm embowed vested per pale vert and gu., cuffed erm., holding in the hand a spear ppr. *Qui sera sera.—Principiis obsta.*

Folkestone, Viscount, *see* Radnor, Earl of.

Folkeworth, an ostrich holding in the beak a broken tilting-spear, all ppr. cf. 97. 2

Foller, a garb or. 153. 2

Follet, Follett, and **Folliott,** a wolf passant regardant transfixed by an arrow. cf. 28. 12

Follett, Devonsh., a demi-griffin segreant. *Quo virtus ducit scando.* 64. 2

Folliott, out of a ducal coronet or, a nag's head arg. 51. 7

Folliott, a lion rampant per pale gu. and arg., double-queued, murally crowned or. *Quo virtus et fata vocant.* cf. 1. 14

Folliot and **Folliott,** on a chapeau ppr., a wyvern vert. cf. 70. 4

Follye, an escallop or between two olive-branches ppr. cf. 141. 4

Folman, a wolf current per pale arg. and erm. 28. 4

Folshurst, Chesh., a unicorn's head couped or. 49. 7

Folton: (1) On a ducal coronet a pair of wings or and arg. 109. 8. (2) A stag lodged gu., ducally gorged and lined or, attired vert, at the top of each branch a bezant.

Folvill, Chesh., a garb per pale or and vert, banded counterchanged. 153. 2

Folvill and **Folleville**, a griffin's head erased holding in the beak a sword ppr. 66. 10

Fonce, a demi-lion rampant, ducally gorged, between two wings. *cf.* 9. 8

Fonceux, a demi-lioness ppr.

Fondre, a Moor's head ppr. 192. 13

Fonnereau of London and Middx., the sun in splendour or. 162. 2

Fonnereau, William Neal, of the Moat, near Ipswich, same crest.

Fonnereau, a lion rampant supporting a garb ppr. 1. 7

Fontain and **Fontaine**, a raven's nest with young birds ppr. 113. 7

Fontain and **Fontaine**, an eagle's head erased ppr. 83. 2

Fonte, Ireland, a demi-lion sa. 10. 1

Foord, a flag displayed gu. 176. 15

Fookes, Ireland, an arm in armour embowed vert, the hand grasping an arrow ppr. 198. 4

Foord, a demi-lion rampant and crowned or, armed and langued gu. *Noli irritare leonem.* 10. 11

Foot, a demi-griffin regardant gu., winged or, holding a flag displayed of the first, charged with a crescent arg. 64. 14

Foot of Carrigacunna, Ireland, a pelican in her piety ppr. *Virescit vulnere, virtus.* 98. 9

Foote of Harrington Square, London, two crosses patée fitchée in saltire gu., thereon a pelican in her piety arg., per wings fretty of the first. *Excidit amor nunquam.*

Foote, Rev. John Vicars, Seskin Ryan, co. Carlow, a martlet az., charged on the breast with a cross humetté or. *Spes mea Deus.* 253. 16

Foote, Ireland, a greyhound's head per fess arg. and sa., collared gu. 61. 2

Foote, Kent, a lion's head erased arg., charged on the neck with an ermine-spot sa. *Pedetentim.* *cf.* 17. 8

Foote, out of a mural coronet or, a spear sa., headed arg., charged with three plates.

Foote, Kent and Cornw., a lion's head erased arg., charged with an ermine-spot. *cf.* 17. 8

Foote, a naked arm erect ppr., holding a trefoil slipped sa.

Foote, an arm erect vested sa., cuffed arg., holding in the hand ppr. a trefoil slipped sa. 205. 9

Footner of Ladyfield, Wilmston, issuant from clouds ppr., a demi-eagle displayed sa., each wing charged with a morion ppr., and holding in the beak a Passion cross or. *Devoir.*

Foquett, a horse's head arg., in mail az., bridled or, on the head a plume of ostrich-feathers of the first. 50. 14

Forbes, *see* Clinton, Earl of.

Forbes, Earl of Granard, *see* Granard.

Forbes-Semphill, Baron Semphill, *see* Semphill.

Forbes-Mitchell, *see* Mitchell.

Forbes, Baron (Forbes), Scotland, a stag's head couped at the neck ppr. *Grace me guide.* 121. 2

Forbes, Norman Hay, Esquire, J.P., F.R.C.S. (Edin.), of Drumminor, Calverley Park, Tunbridge Wells, Kent, same crest and motto. *Lonach.*

Forbes of Kingerlock, Argyle, a stag's head attired ppr. *Solus inter plurimos.* 121. 5

Forbes of Jolly How, a stag's head erased ppr. *Salus per Christum.* 121. 2

Forbes of Polquhor, a stag's head erased and attired with ten tynes ppr. *Salus per Christum.* 121. 2

Forbes of Ardo, a stag's head couped gu., attired arg. *Cura et candore.* 121. 5

Forbes, Leith-, of Whitehaugh, Aberdeensh.: (1) A pelican vulning herself ppr. 98. 1. (2) A stag's head erased and attired with ten tynes or. 121. 2 (3) A dove holding in its beak an olive-branch ppr. *I die for those I love.* —*Salus per Christum.*—*Fidus ad extremum.* 92. 5

Forbes-Leslie of Rothie and Badenscoth, Scotland: (1) A griffin's head and neck erased ppr. (*for Leslie*). 66. 2. (2) A bear's head and neck couped and muzzled ppr. (*for Forbes*). *Grip fast.*—*Spe expecto.* 34. 14

Forbes of Corsindae, a bear's head. *Spe expecto.* 34. 14

Forbes-Leith, Alexander John, of "Fyvie Castle," Aberdeensh.: (1) On the dexter side—A cross crosslet fitchée sa. (*for Leith*). 166. 2. (2) On the sinister side—A bear's head and neck couped arg., muzzled az. (*for Forbes*). *Trustie to the end.*—*Spe expecto.* 34. 14

Forbes of Milbuy, a bear's head couped arg., muzzled gu., within an orle of olive-branches vert. *Virtute, non ferocia.* 35. 11

Forbes, Major Henry Erskine, a cock ppr. *Watch.* 91. 2

Forbes, Bart., of Craigievar, Scotland, a cock ppr. *Watch and pray.* 91. 2

Forbes of Balgownie, Aberdeen, a cock ppr. *Watch.* 91. 2

Forbes of Robslaw, a dove ppr. *Virtute cresco.* 92. 2

Forbes, Scotland, a falcon ppr. *Altius ibunt, qui ad summa nituntur.* 85. 2

Forbes, Sir Charles Stewart, Bart., D.L., of Newe and Edinglassie, Aberdeensh., a falcon rising ppr. *Altius ibunt, qui ad summa nituntur.* 88. 2

Forbes of Brux, a hawk's head erased ppr. *Nec mons nec substrahit aer.* 88. 12

Forbes, an eagle rising. *Salus per Christum.*—*Spernit humum.* 77. 5

Forbes, an eagle displayed ppr. *Spernit humum.* 75. 2

Forbes of Watertown, an eagle displayed sa. *Virtuti inimica quies.* 75. 2

Forbes of Culloden House, Inverness, an eagle displayed or. *Salus per Christum.* 75. 5

Forbes, a greyhound passant ppr. *Delectatio.* *cf.* 60. 2

Forbes, Scotland, a griffin's head erased. 66. 2

Forbes, Scotland, the sun in his splendour ppr. *Spero.* 162. 2

Forbes of Foveran, a cross patée arg. *Salus per Christum.* *cf.* 165. 7

Forbes of Glasgow, a book expanded ppr. *Virtute me involvo.* 158. 3

Forbes of Corse, a wreath or crown of thorns. *Rosas coronat spina.* 146. 6

Forbes of Echt, a sand-glass ppr. *Fugit hora.* 177. 15

Forbes of Ballogie, a sheaf of arrows ppr. *Concordia praesto.* 173. 3

Forbes of Auchreddy, a sword in bend ppr. *Scienter utor.* 170. 5

Forbes of Balling, a skean piercing a man's heart ppr. *Non deest spes.* 181. 6

Forbes, Bart., of Pitsligo, Aberdeensh., issuing out of baron's coronet a dexter hand holding a scimitar, all ppr., with the motto over: *Nec timide, nec temere.* *Fax mentis honestæ gloria.*

Forbes, Sir William Stuart, of Carterton, Wellington, New Zealand; Pitsligo, Aberdeensh; and of Fettercairn House, Kincardine, Scotland, issuing out of a baron's coronet a dexter hand holding a scimitar ppr., with the motto over: *Nec timide, nec temere* (*for Forbes*). *Fax mentis honestæ gloria.*

Forbes, John Honblon, Esquire, of Medwyn, West Linton, Pee., same crest and motto.

Forbes, His Honour David Grant, B.A., of Sydney, New South Wales, Australia, District Court Judge, an arm in armour ppr., couped at the elbow, lying fesswise, the hand ppr. holding a dagger in pale, thereon a bear's head couped arg., muzzled gu. *Solus inter plurimos.* *cf.* 211. 9

Forbes, Captain, J.G., of King's Shropshire Light Infantry, and Captain J.F. of Avoca, Weston-super-Mare, a dexter cubit arm fesseways holding a sword erect pierced through a bear's head, muzzled and couped, all ppr. *Solus inter plurimos.*

Forbes, Captain J. G., of Shropsh., same crest and motto.

Forbes, John Charles Matthias Ogilvie, Esquire, of Boyndlie, Fraserburgh, N.B., a man's heart ppr., winged or, and in an escroll over the same this motto: *Spes expecto*, and under the arms: *Toujours fidèle.*

Forbes, Scotland, a hand holding a dagger in pale ppr. *Spero.* 212. 9

Forbes of Newe, an arm in armour grasping in the hand a broadsword ppr. *Non temere.* 210. 2

Forbes of Pitscottie, Scotland, out of a ducal coronet a dexter arm in armour holding a scimitar, all ppr. *Scienter utor.* *cf.* 209. 11

Forbes of Skellater, Scotland, a hand holding a dagger erect, and on its point a bear's head couped ppr. *cf.* 212. 6

Forbes, Scotland, a dexter hand holding a battle-axe ppr. *Salus mea Christus.* —*Dinna waken sleepin' dogs.* 213. 12

Forbes-Gordon, Arthur Newton, Esquire, of Rayne, Wartle, Aberdeensh., and Rathwade, Bagenalstown, co. Carlow, a cock ppr. *Watch.*

Forbes-Robertson, late John, Esquire, of 22, Bedford Square, London, an arm erect ppr., charged with a heart gu., the hand holding an imperial crown, also ppr. *Virtutis gloria merces.* cf. 217. 1

Forbes of Allford, issuing out of a cloud a hand holding an anchor ppr. *Non deest spes.*

Forbisher, on a chapeau the sun in splendour ppr. cf. 162. 2

Ford, Sir Francis Colville, Bart., of Ember Court, Surrey, a greyhound's head sa., erased gu., muzzled or. *Omnium rerum vicissitudo.*

Ford, a greyhound's head erased arg. 61. 4

Ford, a greyhound's head issuant ppr. cf. 61. 2

Ford, Scotland, a demi-greyhound arg. *Fortis in arduis.* 60. 11

Ford of Chagford, Ashburton, Bagtor and Nutwell, Devonsh., a demi-greyhound rampant sa., charged with three acorns in bend between two bendlets or, all between as many branches vert, fructed arg. 60. 10

Ford, Glouc., Kent, and Suff., out of a naval coronet a bear's head sa., muzzled. cf. 34. 3

Ford, Edward, Esquire, of Bridgen Place, Bexley, Kent, same crest.

Ford, a lion rampant. 1. 13

Ford, Thomas Benson Pease, J.P., Lower Bentham, Lancaster, a lion rampant crowned.

Ford of Ellell Hall, Lancs, a lion rampant holding a coronet. *Excitat.* 3. 6

Ford, a demi-lion rampant. *Excitat.* 10. 2

Ford, John Walker, of Enfield Old Park, Middx., a demi-lion rampant az.

Ford, William, Esquire, of 50, Coltman Street, Kingston-upon-Hull, a demi-lion per bend or and az., holding in the dexter paw a ship's mast with two sails furled ppr., and pennon flying gu., and resting the sinister on the stern of a ship ppr. *Fortis in arduis.*

Ford, a demi-lion rampant and crowned or. 10. 11

Ford of Abbeyfield, Chesh., a lion's head erased az. 17. 8

Fordam and **Fordham,** on a mount vert, a peacock ppr. cf. 103. 4

Forde, a tiger sejant ppr. 27. 6

Forde, Ireland, a greyhound's head issuant sa. cf. 61. 2

Forde, Rt. Hon. William Brownlow, of Seaford, co. Down, a martlet or. *Incorrupta fides nudaque veritas.* 95. 2

Forder, Surrey, a hawthorn-tree vert.

Fordham, *see* Fordam.

Fordham, Edward Snow, Esquire, of Elbrook House, Ashwell, near Baldock, Herts, a peacock in its pride ppr. *Christus turris, fides telum.*

Fordwich, Viscount, *see* Cowper, Earl.

Fordyce-Buchan, *see* Buchan.

Fordyce, Scotland, a camel's head couped at the neck ppr. *Persevere.* 132. 7

Fordyce, a stag lodged ppr. *In arduis fortis.* 115. 7

Fordyce, Dingwall-, Alexander, of Brucklay and Culsh, Aberdeensh.: (1) An eagle volant ppr., holding in the claws an escroll with this motto, "*Altius ibunt qui ad summa nituntur*" (*for Fordyce*). (2) A stag lodged ppr. (*for Dingwall*). *In arduis fortis.* 115. 7

Foreman and **Forman,** Scotland, a hand holding a scimitar ppr. *True to the end.* 213. 5

Foresight, Scotland, two wings expanded ppr. *Sum quod sum.* 109. 6

Forest, a grenade fired ppr. 177. 12

Forest, a squirrel sejant cracking a nut ppr. 135. 7

Forester, Baron (Forester), of Willey Park, Shropsh.: (1) A talbot passant arg., collared sa., and therefrom a line reflexed or (*for Forester*). 54. 5. (2) A wyvern sa., guttée-d'or, the wings elevated, also, or collared, and therefrom a line reflexed over the back of the same. (*for Weld*). *Semper eadem.* 69. 7

Forester, a talbot passant arg., collared sa., and lined or. 54. 5

Foricall, two lion's gambs endorsed gu.

Forican, an elephant's head erased sa., eared and armed arg. 133. 3

Forington, a dragon sans wings, the tail extended, per fess or and vert.

Forkington, a demi-greyhound sa., collared or. 60. 8

Forman, Scotland, *see* Foreman.

Forman of London and Leics., a demi-dragon vert. 73. 10

Forman, a demi-griffin holding a ducal coronet. cf. 64. 2

Formby, a dove ppr. *Semper fidelis.* 92. 2

Forners and **Forneys,** a wheel az. 167. 1

Forrest, Sir William, Bart., of Comiston, Midlothian, on a mount vert, an oak-tree ppr. *Vivunt dum virent.* 143. 14

Forrest, an oak-tree ppr. *Vivunt dum virent.* 143. 5

Forrest, L. R. W., of Ravensholt, Harrow-on-the-Hill, same crest. *Et virent in undis.*

Forrest, John Clark, Esquire, J.P., of Auchenraith, Lanarksh., an oak-tree fructed ppr. *Live while green.* 143. 2

Forrest, Scotland, a hand couped in fess holding a cross crosslet fitched. 221. 10

Forrest, William, Esquire, of Leschenault, near Banbury, West Australia, a cubit arm erect vested az., cuffed arg., holding in the hand ppr. a cross botony fitchée in bend sinister, also arg. *Vivunt dum virent.* 207. 5

Forrest, Hon. Sir John, K.C.M.G., C.M.G., J.P., F.R.G.S., F.G.S., F.L.S., of Hay Street, Perth, Western Australia, Premier of that Colony, a cubit arm erect vested az., cuffed arg., the hand ppr., holding a cross botony fitchée in bend sinister, also arg. *Vivunt dum virent.* 207. 5

Forrester, Baron, Scotland, *see* Verulam, Earl of.

Forrester, Scotland, a lily growing through and surmounting a thorn-bush ppr. *Spernit pericula virtus.* 151. 9

Forrester of Carbeth, Stirling, a hunting-horn sa., garnished and stringed vert. *Hunter, blow the horn.* 228. 11

Forrester of Kinnaird, Larbert, Stirlingsh., Scotland, a hunting-horn sans strings. *Blow, hunter, thy horn.* 228. 9

Forrester, Scotland, a dexter hand holding a hunting-horn sa., garnished gu. *It is good to be blown.* 217. 4

Forrester, a talbot passant arg., collared sa., lined and ringed or. 54. 5

Forrester of Dundee, Scotland, a greyhound in a leash ppr. *Recreation.*

Forsan, a griffin's head per fess az. and or. 66. 1

Forsaith, Frederic Gregory, Viscount de Fronsac, of Montreal, Canada, a griffin's head between two wings vert. *Loyal à la mort.*

Forser of Kelboe and Haverhouse, Durh., a fox sejant ppr., vulned in the neck by an arrow or, feathered arg. cf. 32. 11

Forset and **Forsett,** Middx., a demi-lion sa., supporting a column gobony arg. and gu., the capital and base or.

Forsham, a talbot's head arg., eared gu., spotted sa. 56. 12

Forstall of Forstalltown, Rochestown, and Ringville, co. Kilkenny, Ireland, a greyhound's head couped arg., collared and chained or. *In corda inimicorum Regis.* cf. 61. 2

Forster, *see* Haire-Forster.

Forster of Alnwick, Northumb., a buck trippant ppr. 117. 8

Forster, Bart. (*extinct*), of Bamborough Castle, Northumb., a stag sa., attired and guttée-d'or. 117. 5

Forster, John Burke, L.R.C.S.I., 27, Breckfield Road, N., Liverpool: (1) A stag trippant. (2) A dexter arm in armour embowed holding in the hand a broken javelin. *Audaces fortuna juvat.*

Forster of Cumnor Hall, a stag lodged regardant gu., charged with a martlet or for difference, and pierced through the neck with an arrow az.

Forster of Trotton, a stag's head erased arg., attired, collared, and lined or.

Forster, Suff., out of a mural coronet chequy arg. and sa., a stag's head ppr., attired or, and holding in the mouth an arrow arg. *Think on.* 121. 6

Forster, Sir Charles, Bart., M.A., D.L., J.P., of Lysways Hall, Staffs, in front of a stag's head erased arg., collared and lined sa., two pheons of the last. *Sit Fors ter felix.*

Forster of Kilgreege, co. Dublin, a hind's head couped arg., collared and chained or.

Forster of Battle, Sussex, a talbot's head erased or, collared and ringed gu.

Forster, Thomas Henry Burton, Esquire, of Holt Manor, Wilts, an arm embowed, sleeved gu., holding a broken tilting-spear. *Redde diem.*

Forster, Sir Thomas Oriel, Bart., C.B., D.L., of Coolderry, co. Monaghan, an arm embowed in armour, the hand bare, grasping a broken spear, all ppr. *Audaces fortuna juvat.*

Forster of London and Cumb., an arm in armour embowed arg., garnished or, holding a broken tilting-spear of the last. 197. 2

Forster, Henry William, Esquire, B.A., of Southend Hall, Catford, S.E., a dexter arm in armour embowed holding in the hand ppr. a broken tilting-spear or. *Sta saldo.*

Forster, James, Esquire, of Welton Garth, near Brough, East Yorks, same crest. *Ante omnia sylva.*

Forster of London, a dexter arm in armour embowed arg., garnished or, and round the arm a sash vert, holding in the hand ppr. an arrow of the third, barbed of the second, broken off at the head.

Forster, an arm embowed habited sa., charged with a pheon or, between two bezants in pale, holding in the hand a bow and arrow arg.

Forster of Forrest, co. Dublin: (1) An arm in armour holding a broken spear ppr. (*for Forster*). 197. 2. (2) A talbot's head erased gu., collared or (*for Hill*). *Vita potior libertas.* 56. 1

Forster-Coull, William Dixon, of North Middleton, Morpeth: (1) In front of a unicorn's head couped arg., gorged with a collar gemelle az., three annulets interlaced or (*for Coull*). (2) Issuant from a wreath of oak vert, a dexter arm embowed in armour, the hand in a gauntlet holding a tilting-spear ppr. (*for Forster*). *Ad finem spero.*

Forsyth-Brown, *see* Brown.

Forsyth, a cup gu. 177. 4

Forsyth, a covered cup gu.

Forsyth, Scotland, a demi-griffin vert. *Instaurator ruinæ.* 64. 5

Forsyth of Leeds, and of Armley, Yorks, a demi-griffin vert, armed and membered gu., and with the tail extended. Motto (over the crest). *Instaurator ruinæ.* 64. 5

Forsyth, Douglas Methuen, Esquire, of Leavington House, Ryde, Isle of Wight, a demi-gryphon vert, gorged with a collar gemel arg., and supporting with the sinister claw, a thistle leaved and slipped ppr. *Instaurator ruinæ.* 268. 6

Forsyth, Thomas Hamilton, Esquire, of Northwold, Cavendish Road, Bournemouth, same crest and motto.

Forsyth, Thomas, Esquire, a gryphon segreant erm., supporting with the claws an anchor sa. *Instaurator ruinæ.*

Forsythe, Scotland, a demi-griffin vert, armed and ducally crowned or. *cf.* 64. 5

Fort or **Forte,** a cock gu., holding in its beak a daisy ppr. *cf.* 91. 2

Fort or **Forte,** on a rock a tower ppr. *Inest clementia forti.* 156. 3

Fort, on a mount vert, a lion sejant gardant, pellettée, collared gu., holding in the dexter paw a cross crosslet fitched of the last.

Fort, Richard, Esquire, of Read Hall, Lancs, a rock ppr., thereon a lion sejant gu., bezantée, gorged with a collar gemelle or, and holding in the dexter fore-paw a cross crosslet fitchée sa.

Forteath, Colonel Frederick Prescott, of Newton House, Elgin, a buck's head erased ppr. *Tam animo quam mente sublimis.* 121. 2

Fortescue, *see* Parkinson-Fortescue.

Fortescue, Earl (Fortescue), a heraldic tiger statant arg., armed, maned, and tufted or. *Forte scutum salus ducum.* *cf.* 25. 5

Fortescue, Archer Irvine, Esquire, of Kingcausie, Aberdeen, Swanbister, Kirkwall, N.B., same crest and motto.

Fortescue, a plain shield arg. *Forte scutum salus ducum.* *cf.* 176. 10

Fortescue, Devonsh., an escutcheon arg. *cf.* 176. 10

Fortescue of Fallapit, Devonsh., a heraldic tiger passant arg., armed and maned or. *Forte scutum salus ducum.* 25. 5

Fortescue, William Blundell, Octon, Torquay, same crest and motto.

Fortescue, a heraldic tiger passant arg., maned, armed, and tufted or. *Forte scutum salus ducum.* 25. 5

Fortescue, Essex and Ireland, a leopard passant gardant ppr. 24. 4

Fortescue, a heraldic tiger passant or. 25. 5

Forth, Viscount, *see* Perth, Earl of.

Forth, Suff., a bear's head erased sa., muzzled or. (*Another,* muzzled gu.) 35. 2

Forth of London, a hind's head couped vert, guttée-d'or, collared and lined of the last. *cf.* 124. 5

Fortibus, De, an escarbuncle or. 164. 12

Fortick of Dublin, a martlet sa. *Forte.* 95. 5

Fortrye, a lion rampant holding a tilting-spear ppr.

Fortun, Scotland, a dolphin haurient az. *Ditat Deus.* 140. 11

Fortune, a demi-lion gardant az., holding in his dexter paw a battle-axe or. 16. 14

Fortune, Scotland, on a chapeau a stag trippant, all ppr. 118. 3

Forty, on a ducal coronet a mullet between two branches of laurel in orle, all ppr. 146. 7

Forty, a lion's gamb erased sa., holding a cross patée fitched gu. 36. 9

Forward, a lion passant gu., charged on the shoulder with an ermine-spot or. *cf.* 6. 2

Forward, John Adams Field Bars House, Chard, an escallop inverted. *Forward.*

Forwood, Sir Dudley Baines, Bart., of the Priory, Gateacre, Liverpool, and 24, Hans Crescent, London, S.W., between two wings arg., the battlements of a tower, thereon in front of a stag's head two hatchets in saltire ppr. 262. 3

Forwood, Sir William Bower, of Bromborough Hall, Chesh., same crest.

Fosbery of Clorane and Curragh Bridge, co. Limerick, Ireland, a pheon supported by two bear's paws erased, all ppr. *Non nobis solum.*

Fosbery, Lieutenant-Colonel George Vincent, of Victoria Square, S.W., two lion's gambs erased, the dexter or, the sinister gu., holding a pheon per pale of the last and the first. *Non nobis solum.*

Fosbery, Major William T. E., 21, Basil's Mansions, S.W., same crest and motto.

Fosbroke and **Fosbrooke** of London and Derbysh., two bear's paws sa., supporting a spear erect ppr.

Fosbrooke, Leonard, Ravenstone Hall, Ashby-de-la-Zouche, same crest.

Foscott and **Foxcote,** a dove on an olive-branch ppr. *cf.* 92. 2

Foskett, a broken spear in pale, the end hanging in bend. 175. 6

Foskett, Herts, an arm in armour embowed holding in the gauntlet a cross-bow, all ppr.

Foss, a thistle and a rose-branch in saltier ppr. 150. 3

Foster, Viscount Ferrard, *see* Ferrard.

Foster, *see* Forster.

Foster and **Forster** of Shropsh., *see* Forester.

Foster of Coomie Castle, co. Cavan, Ireland, a stag trippant ppr. 117. 8

Foster, Harry Seymour, Esquire, in front of a fasces erect, a stag trippant ppr., and pendent from the attires a bugle-horn stringed sa. *Suaviter in modo, fortiter in re.*

Foster, Sir Augustus Vere, Bart., Glyde Court, Ardee, co. Louth, a stag trippant ppr. *Divini gloria ruris.* 117. 8

Foster, Sir William, Bart., D.L., of Norwich, a buck ppr., the dexter foot resting on an escutcheon gu., charged with a castle arg. *Virtute et labore.*

Foster, Hon. William John, of Thurnby, Newtown, New South Wales, Puisne Judge of the Supreme Court of N.S.W., a stag trippant ppr. *Divini gloria ruris.* 117. 8

Foster-Vesey-FitzGerald, James, Esquire, of Myoriesk, co. Clare: (1) On a ducal coronet of five leaves or, a boar passant gu., charged with three annulets arg. (*for FitzGerald*). (2) On a wreath or and sa., a hand in armour holding a laurel-branch, all ppr. (*for Vesey*). (3) A stag trippant ppr. (*for Foster*). *Shannat a boo.* 117. 8

Foster-Vesey-FitzGerald, John Vesey, Esquire, of 56, Stanhope Gardens, S.W., same crests and motto.

Foster, Ebenezer, Esquire, of Anstey Hall, Cambs, a demi-stag or, semée of pheons, and holding between the legs a bugle-horn az. *Præmium honor.* 119. 9

Foster, Rev. Albert John, Wootton Vicarage, Beds, a demi-stag semée of pheons holding between the legs a bugle az. *Virtutis præmium honor.*

Foster, George Edward, B.A., Brooklands, Cambridge, a demi-stag holding between the feet a bugle-horn, all ppr.

Foster, a stag's head erased ppr. 121. 2

Foster, Sir Balthazar Walter, M.P., D.C.L., LL.D., M.D., F.R.C.P., of Ashfield, Edgbaston, and 30, Grosvenor Road, Westminster, S.W., a stag's head erased ppr. *Labore et virtute.* 121. 2

Foster, Joseph, M.D., 10, St. George's Road, Eccleston Square, S.W., same crest. *Cinis æquat.*

Foster, William Joscelyn, M.D., 61, Prince of Wales' Mansions, S.W., same crest. *Cinis æquat.*

Foster, William Edward, F.S.A., Lindum House, Aldershot, and Pipwell House, Moulton, Lincs, a hind's head couped ducally gorged, and lined. *Inconcussa fides.* 301. 7

Foster, a stag's head quarterly sa. and arg., attired or. 121. 5

Foster of Wich, Worcs., an antelope's head erased arg., attired or, collared and ringed, and a line therefrom of the same.

Foster, Richard, Esquire, of Lanwithan, Lostwithiel, Cornw., a horse's head couped az., maned, and charged on the neck with three escallops in fess within a collar gemelle, and holding in the mouth an arrow in bend, the point downwards or. *Advena in sylvis.*

Foster, Henry Durett, Esquire, of Treledan, Bodmin, same crest and motto.

Foster, John Armstrong, Fellow of the Royal Numismatic Society (for life), Member of the British Numistic Society (for life), F.Z.S., Chestwood, near Barnstaple, North Devon, a talbot's head erased. *Spero.* 56. 2

Foster, Lewis Charles, Esquire, V.D., J.P., of Trevillis, Liskeard, Cornw., same crest and motto.

Foster, Thomas Robins, Esquire, of 3, Strangways Terrace, Truro, Cornw., same crest and motto.

Foster, William Henry, Esquire, of Apley Park, Bridgnorth, Salop, and Spratton Grange, Northamp., in front of an antelope's head erased ppr., gorged with a collar vair, ringed and lined or, an escallop between two pheons fessewise of the last. *Exitari non hebescere.* 246. 9

Foster, James, Esquire, of Cranborne Hall, Windsor, same crest and motto.

Foster, John, Esquire, same crest and motto.

Foster, James, Esquire, of Woodcote, Grange, Newport, Salop, same crest and motto.

Foster, Arthur Wellesley, Esquire, M.A., J.P., D.L., of Brockhampton Court, near Ross, Heref., a stag's head erased ppr., attired and guttée-d'or, pierced through the head with an arrow gold, feathered arg. *Justum perficito nihil timeto.*

Foster, William Henry, Esquire, J.P., D.L., of Hornby Castle, Lancs, a stag's head erased ppr., attired and guttée-d'or, pierced through the head with an arrow gold, feathered arg. *Justum perficito nihil timeto.*

Foster, Joseph, Esquire, M.A., of 21, Boundary Road, Finchley Road, London, N.W., a greyhound current arg., gorged with a wreath of hawthorn vert, holding in the mouth by the string gu. a bugle-horn or. *Per se vere.*

Foster, Richard Andrews, Esquire, of Tutshill House, Sidenham, Glouc., a greyhound sejant or, gorged with a collar gemel, therefrom pendant a bugle-horn, stringed gu., between two branches of oak leaved and fructed ppr. *Semper fidelis.*

Foster, Edmund Benson, Esquire, of Clewer Manor, Windsor, Berks, a dexter arm embowed, vested gu., in the hand ppr. a tilting-spear, also ppr., suspended from the wrist a bugle-horn or. *Spectemur agendo.*

Foster, Frederick Durham, Esquire, of the Hall, Thorne, West Riding, Yorks, in front of fern a deer-hound statant ppr., gorged with a collar flory counter-flory, with a chain pendent or. *Vi et visu.*

Foster-Melliar, William Melliar, Esquire, of North Aston Hall, Deddington, Oxford, in front of a lion's gamb erect and couped or, holding a branch of myrtle ppr., two mascles interlaced fesseways az. *Semper eadem.—Cupio meliora.*

Foster, Rev. Frederic Adolphus La Trobe, 34, The Avenue, Folkestone, an arm in armour embowed holding the head of a broken tilting-spear, all ppr. *Si fractus fortis.*

Foston, a gate az. 158. 1

Fotherby, Kent and Lincs, a falcon with wings expanded ppr., beaked or, and holding therein an acorn of the last leaved ppr. *cf.* 87. 1

Fotherby, Henry Arthur, M.R.C.S., Headcorn, Kent, a falcon with wings expanded and elevated ppr., beaked or, in the beak an oak-branch vert, bearing an acorn or. *Per ardua petit alta.*

Fothergill of Aberdare, Glamorgansh., a talbot passant collared. *cf.* 54. 2

Fothergill, George, J.P., Allanbank, Grasmere, a talbot passant.

Fothergill, on a rock a lion rampant ppr., collared and chained or, holding in the dexter paw an arrow sa. 2. 6

Fothergill, a stag ppr. 117. 5

Fotheringham, a pelican in her piety. 98. 14

Fotheringham, a griffin's head erased ppr. *Another,* couped. *Be it fast.* 66. 2

Fotheringham of Powrie, Forfarsh., a griffin segreant ppr. *Be it fast.* 62. 2

Fotherley, a lion's gamb erased or, grasping a wolf's head erased arg.

Fothringham, Walter Thomas James Scrymsoure Steuart, Esquire, of Pourie, Forfarsh., and Grandtully, Perthsh.: (1) On the dexter side—A griffin segreant ppr. (*for Fothringham*). 62. 2. (2) On the sinister side—A lion's gamb erased holding a scimitar ppr. (*for Scrymsoure*). *Be it fast.—Dissipate.* *cf.* 38. 13

Fouk, a cross pattée erm. *cf.* 165. 7

Fouler, Scotland, a stag's head erased gu., attired arg. 121. 2

Foulerton, a Cornish chough sa. 107. 14

Foulis, *see* Liston-Foulis.

Foulis, Scotland, a flower-pot with a branch of laurel springing out of it. *Non deficit.*

Foulis, Yorks, out of a crescent arg., a cross formée of the same. 163. 6

Foulis, Bart., Yorks: (1) Out of a crescent arg., a cross formée fitchée sa. (2) A demi-unicorn winged ppr.

Foulis, Scotland, a dove holding in its beak an olive-leaf ppr. *Pax.* *cf.* 92. 5

Foulis of Ravelston, Scotland, a dove volant, holding in her beak a leaf ppr. *Thure et jure.* *cf.* 93. 10

Foulke, Worcs., a squirrel sejant az., bezantée, collared or, holding an acorn-branch vert, fructed of the second. *cf.* 135. 2

Foulkes, S. G., of Tring, on a rock a demi-lion rampant holding between the paws a mullet. *Nec timide, nec temere.*

Foulkes, a lion's head erased per pale arg. and sa., collared counterchanged. 18. 6

Foulkes and **Foulks,** a boar's head couped in fess sa. 43. 1

Foulks, a boar's head erased arg. *Jure non dono.* 42. 2

Foulks, out of a tower arg., a demi-eagle sa., beaked or, holding therein a fleur-de-lis gu. 156. 6

Fouller, a greyhound's head erased sa., collared or. *cf.* 61. 2

Foulshurst, Chesh. and Lancs, a unicorn's head erminois, armed or. 49. 7

Foulson, Hunt-: (1) A demi-lion gu., gorged with a collar and charged on the shoulder with five mullets saltireways arg., and holding in the mouth a crescent or (*for Foulson*). (2) A leopard's face az., in front of two arrows points downwards in saltire ppr., between two wings or, each charged with a cross potent az. (*for Hunt*). 22. 11

Foulston, Devonsh., a demi-lion rampant arg. 10. 2

Founder and **Foundowre,** out of a ducal coronet a griffin's head between two wings, all ppr. 67. 1

Fountain, Devonsh., an eagle's head erased, holding in the beak a snake. *cf.* 83. 2

Fountain of Lochhill, Scotland, an eagle rising ppr. *Præclarius quo difficilius.* 77. 5

Fountaine, Norf., an elephant ppr. *Vix ea nostra voco.* 133. 9

Fountaine, Algernon Charles, Narford Hall, Swaffham, same crest and motto.

Fountayne, Yorks and Bucks, an elephant's head couped or, armed arg., vulned in the neck. 133. 2

Fountbery, a cross pattée arg., environed by a snake vert. 165. 9

Fouracre, a demi-griffin or, holding between the claws an escallop gu. *cf.* 64. 2

Fourbins, a sheaf of arrows ppr., banded gu. 173. 3

Fourdrinier, on a chapeau a unicorn's head ppr. *cf.* 49. 10

Fournier, a martlet per fess az. and arg. 95. 4

Fovell, Chesh., *see* **Folvill.**

Fowbery, Yorks and Durh., a stag's head arg., attired or, charged on the neck with three trefoils slipped vert, one and two. *cf.* 121. 5

Fowbery, Hunts, a stag's head arg., attired or, charged on the neck with three trefoils slipped vert, one and two, and holding in the mouth a rose gu., stalked and leaved vert.

Fowell, Devonsh., out of a mural coronet ppr., an antelope's head arg., attired gu.

Fowell, a griffin's head erased arg., pierced through the breast by an arrow ppr. *Non ostento sed ostendo.* *cf.* 66. 13

Fowke, an Indian goat's head erased arg.

Fowke, Sir Frederick Thomas, Bart., D.L., of Lowesby, Leics., *uses* a dexter arm embowed habited vert, cuffed arg., holding in the hand an arrow or, barbed and flighted of the second, point downwards. *Arma tuentur pacem.*

Fowke, Ireland, an arm fesseways couped at the shoulder embowed, holding a spear in pale ppr. 201. 11

Fowke of Ardee, co. Louth, Ireland, out of a ducal coronet or, a sword erect entwined with a serpent descending, all ppr.

Fowkes, a golden fleece ppr. 130. 10

Fowkes of Dublin, a lion passant az., charged on the shoulder with a fleur-de-lis or. *cf.* 6. 2

Fowkroy, a lion's gamb holding an ostrich-feather ppr. 37. 3

Fowle, Kent and Sussex, a griffin's head erased arg., pierced through the neck by an arrow gu., barbed of the first, vulned of the second. *cf.* 66. 13

Fowle, Sussex, Wilts, and Berks, out of a ducal coronet or, an arm in armour embowed ppr., garnished of the first, holding a battle-axe of the same.

Fowle, same crest. *Ut seres ita metes.*

Fowle of Market Lavington, Wilts: (1) Out of a ducal coronet or, a dexter arm in armour embowed ppr., garnished and holding in the hand a battle-axe of the first (*for Fowle*). (2) Out of a ducal coronet or, a plume of feathers arg. and az. (*for Legge*). *Boutez en avant.*

Fowle, Norf., an antelope's head pierced by an arrow. *cf.* 127. 1

Fowler-Butler, *see* Butler.

Fowler, Thomas Webb, Esquire, of Wycombe House, Coventry, between two hawk's lures gu., a lion rampant or, charged on the shoulder with a rose also gu., barbed and seeded ppr. *Je me fie in Dieu.*

Fowler, Staffs, a cubit arm vested az., holding in the hand ppr. a hawk's lure vert, feathered arg., the line or, twisted round the arm.

Fowler, Bart., Shropsh.: (1) A cubit arm habited az., holding in the hand ppr. a lure vert, feathered arg., the line or, twisted round the arm. (2) An owl arg., ducally gorged or. *cf.* 96. 5

Fowler, Sir Thomas, Bart., of Gastard House, Wilts, and Bruce Grove, Middx., a dexter arm fesswise couped vested az., cuffed arg., the hand ppr., holding a hawk's lure entwined round the arm or, surmounted by an owl arg. *Possunt quia posse videntur.*

Fowler, Robert Henry, Esquire, of Rahinston, Enfield, co. Meath, out of a ducal crest coronet or, a demi-horned owl, wings expanded ppr. *Esto pernox.*

Fowler, an owl arg., ducally gorged gu. *cf.* 96. 5

Fowler, Scotland, on a chapeau, an owl rising gardant ppr. 96. 6

Fowler, Robert Dashwood, 15, Howard Place, St. Andrew's, N.B., out of a ducal coronet an owl affrontée with wings expanded.

Fowler, Sir John Edward, Bart., of Braemore, Ross-sh., an owl arg., collared and charged on the breast with a cross pattée gu., wreathed about the head with ivy vert, and resting his dexter claw on a cross pattée or. *Sapiens qui vigilat.* 96. 4

Fowler, a stork arg., membered gu., holding in its beak a cross formée fitched or. *cf.* 105. 11

Fowler, Glouc. and Scotland, an ostrich's head or, between two wings arg., holding in its beak a horse-shoe az. *cf.* 97. 10

Fowler of Clifton, an ostrich's head couped or, holding in the beak a horse-shoe sa., between two wings arg., each charged with two cinquefoils in pale az. *cf.* 97. 10

Fowler - Butler, Major-General Robert Henry, of Pendeford Hall, Wolverhampton and Barton Hall, Burton-on-Trent, Staffs: (1) A covered cup or, surmounting two wings quarterly or and sa. (*for Butler*). (2) A crowned owl (*for Fowler*). *Garde le roy* (*for Fowler*). *Depressus extoller* (*for Butler*).

Fowles, a stag's head couped sa. 121. 5

Fowlis, a sword in pale, on the point thereof a garland. 170. 1

Fowlis, a dove holding in its beak an olive-branch ppr. 92. 5

Fowne, an arm in armour embowed, holding in the hand a fleur-de-lis. 199. 5

Fownes, a hawk holding in its dexter claw an ear of wheat ppr. 85. 7

Fownes, Ireland, on a ducal coronet or, an eagle displayed az., armed of the first. *cf.* 75. 2

Fownes, Ireland, a unicorn's head erased gu., armed and bearded or. 49. 5

Fownes, Devonsh., the stump of an oak-tree with a branch on each side ppr. 145. 2

Fownes, out of a ducal coronet a demi-eagle with wings expanded. 80. 14

Fownes-Luttrell, Alexander, Esquire, J.P., Court House, East Quantoxhead, Bridgewater, Somers., out of a ducal coronet or, a plume of five feathers arg. *Quæsita marte tuenda arte.*

Fownes-Luttrell, George, Esquire, of Dunster Castle, Taunton, same crest and motto.

Fownes-Luttrell, Hugh Courteney, Esquire, same crest and motto.

Fowtes, a flower-pot gu., springing thereout an olive-branch ppr.

Fox, a fox statant gu. (confirmed anno. 1623 to Sir Charles Fox of Bromfield, Shropsh.; to Sir Richard Fox of Whichcote, Shropsh.; to Edmund Fox Esquire, of Leighton, Heref.; to Sir Edward Fox of Gwernoge, Montgomerysh.; to Henry Fox, Esquire, of the Hurst, Shropsh.; to Somerset Fox, Esquire, of Kaynham, Shropsh.; to Geo. Fox, Esquire, of the Bower, in the parish of Greet, Shropsh.; to Charles Fox, Esquire, of Greet, Shropsh.; and to Edward Fox, Esquire, of Ludlow, Shropsh.). The motto used by some members of the foregoing families was "*Fidelis esto.*" 32. 2

Fox of Ratcliffe, Leics., same crest.

Fox, Lane-, late Rt. Hon. Sackville George, 12th Baron Conyers: (1) A fox statant gu. (*for Fox*). (2) Out of a ducal coronet or, a demi-griffin sa., winged arg. (*for Lane*).

Fox, Lane-, James Thomas Richard, Esquire, J.P., D.L., of Bramham Park, Yorks: same crests.

Fox-Pitt-Rivers, Lieutenant-General Augustus Henry Lane, of Rushmore, Salisbury, Wilts: (1) A stork ppr. (*for Pitt*). 105. 11. (2) On a five-leaved ducal coronet or, a fox passant ppr. (*for Fox*). *Aquam servare mentem.*

Fox of Chacombe, Northamp., a fox passant regardant per pale arg. and gu., in the mouth a rose-branch flowered of the last, stalked and leaved vert. 32. 3

Fox of Essex, on a chapeau gu., turned up erm., between two crosses potent sa. and vert, a fox passant arg.

Fox, Broomhead-Colton-, Barnard Platts, Esquire, of Wales and of Sheffield, both in the West Riding of the county of York, Solicitor of the Supreme Court of Judicature: (1) In the centre a fox passant gu., guttée-d'or, resting the dexter fore-paw upon an annulet encircling an escallop, both or (*for Fox*). (2) Upon the dexter side—Upon a rock ppr., in front of a cross crosslet erect and fitchée sa., a boar passant arg., charged on the body with two roses gu., barbed and seeded ppr. (*for Colton*). (3) Upon the sinister side—In front of a unicorn's head erased erm., maned, horned, and holding in the mouth a fleur-de-lis or, a staff raguly fessewise, also or. *Perfidem et patientiam.*

Fox, on a chapeau, a fox sejant.

Fox, Samson, Esquire, J.P., of Grove House, Harrogate, Yorks, upon a representation of a corrugated boiler flue lying fessewise ppr., a fox statant gu., resting the dexter paw upon a trefoil slipped vert. *Forti nihil difficile.*

Fox, Baron Holland (*extinct*), on a chapeau az., turned up erm., a fox sejant or. 32. 12

Fox-Strangways (Rt. Hon. Henry Edward, 5th Earl of Ilchester), on a chapeau az., turned up erm., a fox sejant or. *Faire sans dire.* 32. 12

Fox, Charles Henry, of Shuteleigh, Wellington, Somers., a fox sejant or, collared flory, and the dexter paw resting upon a fleur-de-lis, both az. *Faire sans dire.* 33. 3

Fox, Robert, Esquire, of Grove Hill, Falmouth, same crest and motto.

Fox, Sylvanus, Esquire, of Linden, Wellington, Somers., same crest and motto.

Fox, Sylvanus, Linden, Wellington, Salop, same crest.

Fox, Bonneville Bradley, Esquire, of Brislington, Somers., a fox sejant gu., collared and chained or, supporting by his sinister paw a flagstaff ppr., thereon a banner az., semée-de-lis or. *J'ay ma foi tenu à ma puissance.* 33. 1

Fox, Ireland, a fox sejant ppr. 32. 11

Fox, Sir Douglas, 12, Queen's Gate Gardens, S.W., on a wreath of the colours, upon a rock ppr., a fox sejant or, resting the dexter leg on a human heart gu. *Faire sans dire.*

Fox, Francis Douglas, 19, Kensington Square, W., same crest and motto.

Fox, Francis, Esquire, Alyn Bank, the Downs, Wimbledon, same crest and motto.

Fox, Henry, Esquire, Moorfoot, Putney Hill, same crest and motto.

Fox, Colonel Malcolm, 168, Eaton Square, S.W., same crest and motto.

Fox, Arthur Douglas, St. George's Lodge, Eastern Road, Brighton, same crest and motto.

Fox, Rev. Smyth Whitelaw, M.A., of Rathmines, co. Dublin, and of Cupidstown, co. Kildare, on a ducal coronet ppr., a fox sejant or. *Fortitudine et sapientia.*

Fox of London and Yorks, a fox's head erased ppr. 33. 6

Fox, a fox's head erased gu., collared and ringed or.

Fox, Embleton-: (1) A fox's head erased arg., gorged with a collar engrailed sa., within a chain in arch or (*for Fox*). 33. 11. (2) Issuant from clouds ppr., a crescent arg., between the horns a fleur-de-lis or (*for Embleton*). *Non immemor beneficii.* *cf.* 163. 9

Fox of London, out of a ducal coronet a greyhound's head, all or. 61. 7

Fox, Marmaduke, Esquire, of Royds House, Mirfield, Yorks, and Polbae, Wigtownsh., N.B., a mill-rind fessewise sa., thereon a greyhound sejant arg. *Virtute et numine.* 59. 11

Fox of Missenden, Bucks, a lion sejant gardant or, supporting with the dexter paw a book or.

Fox, an eagle displayed sa. 75. 2

Fox or **O'Sionnach** of Kilcoursey, King's Co., and Galtrim House, co. Meath,

Ireland, an arm embowed in armour, holding in the hand a sword, all ppr. *Sionnach aboo.* 195. 2

Fox, Captain B. H. M., Royal Irish Rifles, Trainfield House, Victoria Barracks, Belfast, same crest and motto.

Fox of Fox Hall, co. Longford, Ireland, a sceptre between two wings. *Nec elatus, nec dejectus.*

Fox, on a mount an oak-tree growing among grass ppr. 143. 14

Foxall of London, a griffin's head or, erased and ducally gorged gu. *cf.* 66. 11

Foxall, out of a ducal coronet a greyhound's head or. 61. 7

Foxall, Ireland, two hands couped and conjoined in fess, supporting a cross crosslet fitched. 224. 11

Foxall, Ireland, a horse's head couped sa., pierced through the neck with the shiver of a lance gu.

Foxcote, *see* Foscott.

Foxcote, a cord knotted and tasselled between wings. 113. 2

Foxford, Baron, *see* Limerick, Earl of.

Foxley, Berks, a hawk's leg erased at the thigh sa., belled or. 113. 8

Foxton, a rose arg., barbed vert. 149. 4

Foxwell, a galley ppr. 160. 2

Foxwest of London, a reindeer's head erased ppr. *cf.* 122. 1

Foy, an eel ppr. 142. 7

Foy, William Lowndes Toler, Esquire, of Clayhill, Enfield, Middx., and Manor Gardens, Henley-on-Thames, upon a mount vert, a lion rampant per bend sinister gu. and erm., holding between the fore-paws a cross patonce gu., and resting the dexter hind-leg upon an escutcheon or. *In cruce gloria.*

Foyle, Hants and Dorset, a horse's head arg., crined gu., gorged with two bars compony or and sa. *cf.* 50. 13

Foyle, Hants, a cross crosslet fitched arg., between two dragons' wings chequy or and az.

Foyle, Wilts, a cross crosslet arg., between two dragons' wings chequy or and az.

Foyler, on a ducal coronet a fleur-de-lis. *cf.* 148. 2

Foyster of St. Pancras, Middx., a demi-stag ppr., attired and ungu. or, collared with a bar gemelle gu., sustaining a bugle-horn of the second. *cf.* 119. 9

Fraigneau of London, a stork close arg., beaked and membered gu., holding in its beak a slip of ash ppr. *cf.* 105. 14

Framlingham, a demi-Moor brandishing a scimitar, and therewith attacking a tiger issuing on the sinister side. 185. 7

Framlingham, a lion's head erased gardant or, semée of hurts and torteaux.

Framlingham of Hartlip, Kent, an elephant or, armed gu., gorged with a chaplet vert. *cf.* 133. 9

Frampton, Dorset, a greyhound sejant arg., collared gu., ringed or. *cf.* 59. 2

Frampton, out of a mural coronet a demi-griffin, holding between its claws a mullet. *cf.* 64. 4

Framyngham, Suff., a camel's head erased az., bezantée. *cf.* 132. 7

France, on a mount a stag current ppr. 118. 13

France, on a mount vert, an erm. ppr. 134. 10

France, a stag springing ppr. 117. 2

France, Scotland, on a mount an oak-tree fructed ppr. 143. 14

France, Chesh., on a mount a hurst ppr., from the centre tree a shield pendent gu., charged with a fleur-de-lis or, the strap az. *Virtus semper viridis.* 144. 2

France-Hayhurst, Colonel Charles Hosken, J.P., D.L., of Bostock Hall, Middlewich, Chesh.: (1) A cubit arm ppr., holding in the hand a cross patée fitchée erect or, between two wings sa., each charged with an annulet of the second (*for Hayhurst*). 215. 8. (2) A mount vert, thereon a hurst of five trees ppr., from the centre tree pendent by a strap az., an escutcheon gu., charged with a fleur-de-lis or (*for France*). *Virtus semper viridis.* 144. 2

France-Hayhurst, Edward, Esquire, J.P., same crests and motto.

France-Hayhurst, Henry Howard, Esquire, J.P., of Overley, Wellington, Salop, same crests and motto.

Franceis, *see* Francies.

Franceis of Foremark, Derbysh., a falcon rising or, holding in its beak a vine-branch fructed ppr.

Frances, Scotland, the stump of an oak-tree, shooting forth a branch from the sinister vert.

Franche, a griffin segreant ppr., collared and lined or, the end of the line and ring turned off and held in the beak. *cf.* 62. 2

Francheville, two wings addorsed. *cf.* 109. 12

Francies and **Frances,** a lion passant, resting the dexter paw on an escallop. 5. 4

Francies and **Frances,** issuing from a cloud a hand seizing a stag by the horns, all ppr. 116. 10

Francis, a dove holding in its beak an olive-branch ppr. 92. 5

Francis of Quy Hall, Cambs, upon a mount vert, in front of three ears of wheat or, a dove arg., beaked and membered gu., holding in the beak a sprig of olive ppr. 92. 6

Francis, late George, Esquire, a bugle-horn sa., thereon a dove holding in the beak an olive-branch, both ppr. *Lege et labore.*

Francis, Staffs, out of a ducal coronet or, a demi-eagle displayed gu. 80. 14

Francis, an eagle with wings addorsed, holding in the dexter claw a vine-branch fructed ppr.

Francis, Derbysh. and Herts, on the trunk of a vine-tree fructed, an eagle with wings elevated, all ppr.

Francis, Derbysh., an eagle displayed erm., beaked and membered or. 75. 2

Francis, Kent, an eagle displayed sa. 75. 2

Francis, Captain Thomas John, on a wreath of the colours a falcon rising with wings expanded ppr., guttée-de-sang, holding in the beak a vine-branch fructed, also ppr. *On le sort appelle.*

Francis, out of a ducal coronet or, a demi-lion gu. 16. 3

Francis, Rev. E. H., Bembridge Vicarage, Isle of Wight, an eagle displayed erm., beaked and membered or. *Spectemur agendo.* 75. 2

Francis, late Sir Phillip, K.C.B., out of a ducal coronet or, a demi-lion rampant sa., charged on the shoulder with a shamrock or, and holding in the paws a garb of the last.

Francis, a lamb passant. *cf.* 131. 9

Franck, out of a mural coronet or, a lion's head gu., between two wings erminois. *cf.* 19. 7

Francke of Grimsby, Lincs, on a staff raguly fesseways or, a Cornish chough ppr.

Francklin, a dexter hand ppr., holding a cross crosslet fitched or. 221. 14

Francklin, John Liell, Esquire, J.P., of Gonalston, Notts, and Great Barford, Beds, a dolphin's head or, erased gu., between two olive-branches vert. *Sinceritate.* 140. 12

Francklyn, a dexter hand in fess couped gu., charged with an eye ppr. 221. 4

Franco, a dexter arm embowed, vested purp., cuffed arg., purfled and diapered or, holding in the hand ppr. a palm-branch vert. *Sub pace copia.*

Francois, on the stump of a tree shooting forth branches, a hawk belled ppr. *cf.* 86. 11

Francoys, a bull's head erased sa. 44. 3

Franey, Rev. John, M.A., a fleur-de-lis az., between two quatrefoils or. *Ut vita finis.*

Frank, Suff., a hawk close belled or. 85. 2

Frank, Yorks and Norf., a falcon ppr. 85. 2

Frank, Frederick Bacon, Esquire, of Campsal, Doncaster, Yorks, a morion ppr., thereon a falcon, also ppr., guttée-de-larmes and belled or. *Esse quam videri.* 86. 9

Frank, Scotland, a lion salient queue-fourchée ppr. *Non omnibus nati.*

Frank, a goat's head erased or, armed gu. 128. 5

Franke, Leics., out of a mural coronet or, a dexter arm embowed, vambraced arg., garnished or, holding a falchion, also arg., hilt and pommel of the first. 195. 9

Frankfort De Montmorency, Viscount, (De Montmorency), on a ducal coronet a peacock in his pride ppr. *Dieu ayde.* 103. 12

Frankland, Herts and Wilts, an anchor erect sa., entwined by a dolphin arg. 140. 8

Frankland, Sir Frederick William Francis George, Bart., of Thirkeby, Yorks, a dolphin haurient arg., entwined round an anchor erect ppr. *Franke Lande, Franke Mynde.* 140. 8

Frankland-Russell-Astley, Bertram Frankland, of Chequers Court, Butler's Cross, Bucks: (1) Out of a ducal coronet or, a plume of five feathers arg. (2) On a cap of maintenance, a ducal coronet or, thereout a plume of feathers arg., incased gu. (*both for Astley*). (3) A goat statant arg., gorged with a mural coronet, armed and unguled or (*for Russell*). (4) A dolphin haurient arg., entwined round an anchor erect ppr. (*for Frankland*). 140. 8. *Justitiæ tenax.* *cf.* 129. 5

Frankland of London, a dexter arm embowed in fess ppr., erect from the elbow vested, frilled at the shoulder, holding in the hand a palm-branch. 203. 7

Franklin of Limerick, Ireland, an anchor in pale, the flukes upwards entwined with a dolphin, all ppr. *Anchora labentibus undis.* cf. 140. 8

Franklin, a dolphin's head in pale arg., erased gu., finned or, between two branches vert. 140. 12

Franklin, a conger-eel's head erect or, erased per fess gu., between two branches vert. 139. 7

Franklin, Ireland, a fox's head erased. 33. 6

Franklyn, Suff., a dolphin haurient arg., entwined round an anchor erect sa. 140. 8

Franklyn, Middx. and Herts, a dolphin naiant ppr., finned gu., pierced through the sides by two fishing-spears in saltier or, tied together in a bow-knot at the top.

Franklyn, Yorks, a fish's head in pale or, erased gu., between two sprigs vert. 139. 7

Franklyn, a hind's head erased or, charged with three pellets, between two wings expanded vairée or and az. 124. 9

Franklyn, a greyhound's head brown, collared or, between two wings arg. cf. 61. 2

Franks, Yorks, a falcon ppr. 85. 2

Franks, on the stump of a tree ppr., a falcon or. 86. 11

Franks, on the stump of a tree a hawk ppr., charged on the breast with a torteau. cf. 86. 11

Franks, a stag's head erased ppr. 121. 2

Franks, a demi-lion rampant supporting the rudder of a ship. 11. 11

Franks, Thomas John, Esquire, J.P., of Ballyscaddane Castle, co. Limerick, Ireland, out of a mural coronet or, a griffin's head gu., between two wings erminois, each charged with a mullet sa. *Sic vos non vobis.* cf. 67. 1

Franks, Sir John Hamilton, C.B., of Dalriada, Blackrock, co. Dublin, and Jerpoint Hill, co. Kilkenny, same crest and motto.

Franks, William Whitmore, Esquire, of Carrig Park, Mallow, same crest and motto.

Franks, formerly **Franke** (granted by Thos. St. George, 1689), Leics., out of a mural coronet or, a dexter arm embowed, vambraced arg., garnished or, holding a falchion of the second, hilt and pommel of the first. *Spiritus gladius verbum dei.* 195. 9

Franks, Godfrey Firth, Esquire, M.A., F.G.S., Demerara, same crest and motto.

Franks, Henry Edmund, Rye, Sussex, same crest. *Spiritus gladius verbum dei.*

Fraser, Baron Saltoun, see Saltoun.

Fraser, Baron Lovat, see Lovat.

Fraser, a stag's head erased gu. 121. 2

Fraser of Fingask, a stag's head erased ppr., charged with an annulet. *Ubique paratus.* cf. 121. 2

Fraser of Auchnagarne, a stag's head erased ppr., charged with a star of eight rays issuing from a crescent arg. *Pace et bello paratus.* cf. 119. 8

Fraser of Inveralochy, a stag's head ppr. *Je suis prest.* 121. 5

Fraser, Scotland, a buck's head erased. *Ready.* 121. 2

Fraser of Struy, Inverness, Scotland, a stag's head couped ppr., attired or. *Amicum proba, hostem scito.* 121. 5

Fraser, a buck's head ppr., attired or. *Je suis prest.* 121. 5

Fraser, Sir William Augustus, Bart., J.P., D.L., M.A., F.S.A., of Ledeclune and Morar, Inverness-sh., a buck's head erased gu. *Je suis prest.—Thorough.* 121. 2

Fraser of Piteullain, a stag's head erased, in the ear an annulet. *I am ready.* cf. 121. 2

Fraser, a stag's head erased or, attired arg. *I am ready.* cf. 121. 2

Fraser, William Nathaniel, of Findrack, Aberdeensh., a stag's head erased or. *I am ready.* 121. 2

Fraser of Castle Fraser, Ross: (1) A mount of strawberries fructed ppr. (2) A stag's head couped ppr. *All my hope is in God.—Je suis prest.* 121. 5

Fraser, Scotland, a stag's head erased or, attired arg., between two battle-axes ppr.

Fraser of Strichen, a stag's head couped arg. *Vive ut postea vivas.* 121. 5

Fraser of Eskdale, a stag's head erased ppr., attired or, charged with an increscent and a decrescent interlaced arg. *Vel pax vel bellum.* cf. 121. 2

Fraser, Hugh, Esquire, (Secretary to H.M. Embassy to the King of Italy), a stag's head erased ppr. *Je suis prest.* 121. 2

Fraser, Francis, Esquire, of Tornaveen, Aberdeensh., same crest and motto.

Fraser, Scotland, a buck's head erased ppr. 121. 2

Fraser, Alastair R. L., Esquire, of Findrack Torphius, Aberdeensh., a stag's head erased ppr. *I am ready.*

Fraser, Alexander Edmund, Esquire, of British Legation, Lisbon, a buck's head attired and couped ppr., gorged with an ancient Scots crown or (above the crest). *Je suis prest.—Tout bien ou rien.*

Fraser of Bath, a stag's head erased ppr., charged on its neck with the rod of Esculapius or. *Je suis prest.* cf. 121. 2

Fraser-Mackintosh of Drummond, Inverness-sh., M.P. for that county: (1) On a wreath of the colours a cat gardant ppr., collared gu., resting the dexter paw upon an escutcheon or, charged with a dexter hand couped at the wrist and clenched, also gu. (*for Mackintosh*). 26. 5. (2) A stag's head erased arg., attired and collared gu., holding in the mouth a sprig of fern ppr., and pendent from the collar an escutcheon az., charged with a cinquefoil arg. (*for Fraser*). *Onward.* 120. 8

Fraser of Belladrum, Inverness, Scotland, a stag starting ppr., attired or. *Virtutis laus actio.* 117. 8

Fraser, Scotland, an eagle displayed ppr. *Celus petit.* 75. 2

Fraser, Scotland, on a globe winged, an eagle rising ppr. *In virtute et fortuna.* 159. 9

Fraser of Incheulter, a phœnix in flames ppr. *Ex se ipso renascens.* 82. 2

Fraser of Poppachie, same crest. *Non extinguar.*

Fraser of Fyvie, an ostrich holding in its beak a horse-shoe ppr. *In God is all.* 97. 8

Fraser of Fraserfield, an ostrich ppr., holding in its beak a horse-shoe az. *Quam sibi sortem.* 97. 8

Fraser of Knock, a rose gu. *I am ready.* 149. 2

Fraser, Major-General Sir Thomas, K.C.B., C.M.G., P.S.C., of 83, Onslow Square, S.W., a cherub's head and wings ppr., wreathed round the temples with a garland of frases az. *Tout jour prest.*

Fraser, on a ducal coronet or, an ostrich arg., holding in its beak a horse-shoe ppr. cf. 97. 8

Fraser, Scotland, a sword and an olive-branch in saltier ppr.

Fraser of Farraline, Inverness, Scotland, a sword ppr., hilted and pommelled or, and an olive-branch also ppr., in saltire *Ready.*

Fraser, Allan-, of Hospitalfield, Forfarsh., a talbot's head erased, holding in the mouth a bunch of strawberries ppr. *Nosce teipsum.* 56. 3

Fraser of Kirkton, Forfarsh., Scotland, a bunch of strawberries ppr. *Nosce teipsum.*

Fraser of Inverness-sh., a dexter hand pointing upwards with the forefinger. *Semper parati.* 222. 12

Fraser-Tytler, Edward Grant, of Aldowrie Castle, Inverness-sh.: (1) The rays of the sun issuing from behind a cloud ppr. (*for Tytler*). (2) A stag's head erased ppr. (*for Fraser*). *Occultus non extinctus* (*for Tytler*).—*Je suis prest* (*for Fraser*).

Fraser-Tytler, James William, Esquire, J.P., of Woodhouselee, Roslin, Edinburgh, the rays of the sun issuing from behind a cloud ppr. *Occultus non extinctus.*

Fraunceis, Fraunces, and **Fraunceys,** a hand issuing out of a cloud seizing a stag by the horns ppr. 116. 10

Fray and **Fraye,** a stag pierced in the side by an arrow, all ppr. 117. 10

Frayle, a horse rampant arg.

Frazer, Lord Frazer, a mount full of strawberries, leaved, flowered, and fructed, all ppr. *All my hope is in God.*

Frazer, Edward Fitzgerald, Surgeon, 20, Queen's Road, Brighton, a stag's head erased ppr. *Je suis prêt.*

Frazer, see Fraser.

Freake, Sir Thomas George, Bart., of Cromwell House, Kensington, Fulwell Park, Middx., and Bank Grove, Kingston-on-Thames, Surrey, a bull's head sa., holding in the mouth a mullet of six points or. *Integrity.* 262. 10

Frebody, Sussex, a leopard sejant regardant arg.

Freby, a castle sa., ports and loopholes gu. 155. 8

Frechville, Derbysh., a demi-angel affrontée ppr., crined and winged or, on the head a cross formée of the last, vested in mail, also ppr., holding in both hands an arrow in bend of the first, headed and feathered arg.

Freckelton and **Freckleton,** Hunts, a bear's head arg., muzzled or. 34. 14

Freckelton and **Freckleton,** a camel's head arg., bridled or cf. 132. 9

Frederick, Middx., *on a chapeau gu.*, turned up erm., a dove ppr., holding in the beak a laurel-branch. *Pretium et causa laboris.* cf. 92. 5

Frederick, Sir Charles Edward, Bart., J.P., of Westminster, Middx., on a chapeau az., turned up erm., a dove arg., holding in its beak an olive-branch ppr. *Prudens simplicitas beat.* cf. 92. 5

Free, a fox's head ppr. 33. 4

Freebairn, Scotland, the sun in splendour. *Always the same.* 162. 2

Freebairn, Scotland, a dexter hand holding an eel ppr.

Freeborn, J. C. R., 38, Broad Street, Oxford, a sun in splendour. *Always the same.*

Freeford and **Freford**, out of a ducal coronet an eagle's head cf. 83. 14

Freeke, *see* Freke.

Freeland, a leopard passant arg., pellettée. cf. 24. 2

Freeland, a leopard passant ppr. *Res, non verba.* cf. 24. 2

Freeland of Cornbrook Park, Manchester, a bear's head couped arg., muzzled gu., gorged with a collar compony or and of the second, between two mullets az. *Res, non verba.*

Freeling, a unicorn's head couped arg., maned, horned, and tufted or. 49. 7

Freeling, Sir Harry, Bart., a unicorn's head couped per pale indented erm. and gu., armed, maned, and tufted or. *Nunquam nisi honorificentissime.* 49. 5

Freeling, Hugh Melvil, Esquire, of 66, Elm Park Gardens, S.W., and Bude, North Cornw., an unicorn's head couped per pale indented erm. and gu. *Nunquam nisi honorificentissime.*

Freeman-Mitford, Baron Redesdale, *see* Redesdale.

Freeman-Mitford, Algernon Bertram, Esquire, of Batsford Park, Moreton-in-Marsh, Glouce.: (1) Two hands couped at the wrist ppr., grasping a sword erect arg., the point and hilt or, the blade enfiled with a boar's head erased sa. (*for Mitford*). (2) A demi-wolf arg., supporting between the paws a fusil or, gorged with a collar dancettée gu. (*for Freeman*). *God careth for us.*

Freeman of London, Wilts, and Yorks, a demi-lion rampant erased gu., holding a cross fleury or.

Freeman of Castle Cor, co. Cork, Ireland: (1) A demi-lion rampant gu., holding between his paws a lozenge arg. (*for Freeman*). cf. 10. 2. (2) A tortoise displayed ppr. (*for Deane*). *Liber et audax.—Ferendo non ferendo.*

Freeman, Heref., a demi-lion rampant gu., holding between the paws a rustre or. cf. 10. 2

Freeman, Charles Edward, Esq., Hon. Col., J.P., Oakwood House, Edgerton, Huddersfield, upon a rock a demi-fox ppr., charged with two lozenges in pale, and holding between the paws a mascle, all or. *Liber et audax.* 249. 2

Freeman, Rev. John, of the Vicarage, Woodkirk, Yorks, same crest and motto.

Freeman of Higham Ferrers, Northamp., a demi-lion rampant gu., charged on the shoulder with a lozenge arg. cf. 10. 3

Freeman, Essex, Oxon., and Northamp., a demi-lion rampant gu., gorged with three lozenges in fess arg. cf. 10. 2

Freeman of Waterford, a demi-lion rampant gu., holding between his paws a civic crown or. *Nec temere, nec timide.* cf. 10. 3

Freeman, Williams-: (1) A demi-lion gu., charged with a lozenge or (*for Freeman*). cf. 10. 2. (2) A lion rampant gorged with a chaplet of oak-leaves ppr., and crowned with a naval coronet or (*for Williams*). 1. 8

Freeman, Williams-, Augustus Peere, 3, Egerton Gardens, S.W., same crests.

Freeman of London and Eberton, Worcs., a demi-wolf arg., holding between his paws a lozenge of the same. cf. 31. 1

Freeman, out of a ducal coronet a wolf's head, all ppr.

Freeman, John Robert, Esquire, Barrister-at-Law, of Staines, Middx., and of Lincoln's Inn, a greyhound couchant sa., holding in the mouth an ear of wheat leaved and slipped, and resting the dexter paw upon a lozenge, both or. *Aspiro.*

Freeman, Northamp., out of a ducal coronet az., a boar's head erect arg. 41. 4

Freemantle, out of rays a dexter hand vested, holding up a human skull. 208. 10

Freemantle, Hon. Sir Charles William, K.C.B., J.P., a demi-lion gu., issuing out of a mural crown or, holding a banner quarterly arg. and vert, the staff or, and charged on the shoulder with a plate. *Nec prece, nec pretio.*

Freemantle, Admiral Sir the Hon. Edmund Robert, G.C.B., C.M.G., of 44, Lower Sloane Street, S.W., same crest and motto.

Freer, Norf., *see* Frere.

Freer, a sphere or. 159. 1

Freer, Scotland, a swan ppr. *No sine periculo.* 99. 2

Freer of Stratford-upon-Avon, a dolphin naiant ppr. 140. 5

Freer, Alfred, J.P., Acton Homes, Pedmore, Stourbridge, out of a ducal coronet gu., an antelope's head arg., attired or. *Aime ton frère.* 300. 4

Freer, Major William Jesse, V.D., F.S.A., Stony Gate, Leics., out of a ducal coronet an antelope's head. *Aime ton frere.* 300. 4

Freeston and **Freston**, Norf., a demi-greyfriar ppr.

Freestone, a demi-greyhound arg., collared or. *Stemmata quid faciunt.*

Freeth, issuing from a cloud a hand in fess, holding a club in pale ppr. 223. 5

Freford, out of a ducal coronet an eagle's head, all ppr. cf. 83. 14

Freford, *see* Freeford.

Freke, Evans-, Baron Carbery, *see* Carbery.

Freke and **Freeke**, Dorset and Norf., a bull's head couped sa., attired, collared, and lined or. cf. 44. 12

Freke and Freeke, Ireland, a dexter arm in armour embowed, brandishing in the hand a sword, all ppr. 195. 2

Freke, Hussey-, Ambrose Denis, Esquire, of Hannington Hall, Wilts: (1) A bull's head couped sa., collared and chained or, charged for distinction with a cross crosslet of the last (*for Freke*). cf. 44. 12. (2) A boot sa., spurred or, and turned over erm., surmounted by a heart ppr., supported by two arms embowed in armour, the hands gauntleted, also ppr. (*for Hussey*). 194. 4

Fremantle, *see* Cottesloe, Baron.

Fremantle, Francis Edward, M.A., M.B., the College, Guy's Hospital, S.E., same as above with a crescent for difference.

Fren and **Frene**, a physician's cap. 180. 7

Frenband, a demi-lion gu., holding in the dexter paw a trefoil slipped or. cf. 10. 2

French, Baron De Freyne, *see* De Freyne.

French, Rev. William Day, Yaverland Rectory, Brading, Isle of Wight, a demi-lion rampant.

French, Worcs., a fleur-de-lis sa., seeded or.

French, A. D. Weld, Esquire, of No. 160, State Street, Boston, Massachusetts, a fleur-de-lis. *Nec timeo nec sperno.* 148. 2

French, in a crescent arg., a fleur-de-lis sa. cf. 148. 2

French of Cranfield, Essex, a crescent per pale arg. and or, between the horns a fleur-de-lis counterchanged.

French, Frederick John, Esquire, of Prescott, Grenville, and of Osgoode Hall, Toronto, Canada, Member of the Legislative Assembly of Ontario, Canada, the same crest. *Malo mori quam fœdari.*

French, Ireland, a fleur-de-lis or, charged with a trefoil vert. cf. 148. 2

French of Cloonyquin, Ireland, a dolphin naiant ppr. 140. 5

French of Monavie, Ireland, same crest. *Malo mori quam fœdari.* 140. 5

French of Frenchgrove, Ireland, same crest and motto.

French, Savage French, of Cuskinny, Cork, a dolphin naiant. *Veritas vincit.* 140. 5

French-Brewster, Robert Abraham, Esquire: (1) A leopard's head erased az., bezantée, holding in the mouth a trefoil slipped vert (*for Brewster*). cf. 23. 2. (2) A dolphin naiant ppr. (*for French*). *Verite soyez ma garde.* 140. 5

French, Scotland, a boar's head couped. *Malo mori quam fœdari.* 43. 1

French, an heraldic tiger rampant. *Spere meliora.*

French, Scotland, a ship in full sail ppr. *Par commerce.* 160. 13

Frend, co. Limerick, a buck's head cabossed erm. *Aude e prevalebis.* 122. 5

Frend, a beacon fired ppr. 177. 14

Frere, Bart. (*extinct*), of Water Eyton, Oxon., two arms embowed erect, holding a wheat-sheaf.

Frere, out of a ducal coronet or, an heraldic antelope's head arg., attired, crined, and tufted of the first. 300. 4

Frere, Sir Bartle Compton Arthur, Bart., D.S.O., of Wressil Lodge, Wimbledon, Surrey, out of a ducal coronet or, an antelope's head arg., armed and crined of the first. *Traditum ab antiquis servare.—Frère ayme Frère.* 300. 4

Frere, John Tudor, Esquire, of Roydon Hall, Diss, same crest and motto.

Frescheville, a gem ring or, stoned gu. 167. 14

Frescheville, Lord Frescheville (*extinct*), of Staveley, Derbysh., a demi-angel issuing from the wreath ppr., crined and winged or, on the head a cross formée of the last, vested arg., with the arms in armour ppr., holding in both hands an arrow in bend of the second, feathered and headed, also arg.

Fresell and **Fresill,** a hand issuant from the wreath plucking a rose from a bush ppr. 218. 13

Fresh, out of a ducal coronet a horse's hind-leg erect, all ppr. 123. 6

Freshacre, a savage's head affrontée, ducally crowned, all ppr. 192. 9

Freshfield, on a mount vert, a stag lodged per fess or and gu., attired of the last. 115. 12

Freshfield of Moor Place, Betchworth, and Upper Gatton, Surrey, a demi-angel ppr., winged or, vested arg., the arms in chain-mail, holding a lance in bend point downwards, also ppr., charged on the breast with a cross botonnée, and on the head a like cross gu. *Nobilitatis virtus non stemma character.*

Freshfield, Douglas William, Esquire, M.A., of Kidbrooke Park, East Grinstead, Sussex, same crest and motto.

Freshwater, two trout in saltier, heads downward ppr., enfiled by a ducal coronet or.

Freston, *see* Freeston.

Freston, Norf., a demi-greyhound sa., collared or. 60. 8

Freston, Thomas Westfaling, Esquire, of Eagle's Nest, Prestwich, Lancs, a demi-greyhound sa., collared or, charged with three torteaux. *Prest d'accomplir.* 241. 5

Freston, Suff., a demi-greyhound sa., collared arg., rimmed or. 60. 8

Freston, a talbot's head gu., eared arg. 56. 12

Freston of Altofts, Yorks, a talbot's head erased gu., eared arg., the ears charged with three bars sa., gorged with a collar or. *cf.* 56. 1

Freton, a unicorn's head arg., pellettée. 49. 7

Frevile, Worcs., out of a ducal coronet a garb, all ppr. *cf.* 153. 2

Frevile, on each side of a chapeau gu., turned up arg., a wing addorsed or.

Frevile, out of a ducal coronet or, an old man's head couped below the shoulders ppr., vested gu., turned back erm., on his head a cap of the third, tasselled of the first.

Frew, Scotland, a demi-lion or, holding a mullet az. 15. 7

Frewen, a demi-lion rampant arg., langued and collared gu., holding between the paws a caltrap az. *Mutare non est meum.* *cf.* 10. 2

Frewen, Edward, of Brickwall, Northiam, Sussex, same crest and motto.

Frewke, a goat's head erased sa., armed and bearded arg. 128. 5

Frey, an arm erect, vested vert, holding in the hand ppr. a spiked club of the first. *cf.* 206. 2

Fribourg, a unicorn's head erased erm., maned and armed or. 49. 5

Fridag and **Friday,** out of a ducal coronet or, a plume of three feathers arg. 114. 2

Friend, a stag's head cabossed ppr. 122. 5

Frier, Lincs, out of a ducal coronet or, an antelope's head arg.

Friere, out of leaves vert, five tulips or.

Frisel, Scotland, a stag's head erased ppr. 121. 2

Friskenny, Lincs, a plume of five ostrich-feathers, two arg., three az., banded round the middle with a wreath or and gu., with strings at each end.

Frith, above a grove of trees ppr., the sun in his splendour or, beneath clouds, also ppr. 283. 5

Frith, Walter Halsted, Shenstone House, Sunninghill, Berks, a demi-griffin segreant or, holding in his dexter claw a battle-axe arg. *Frangas non flectes.* 64. 11

Frith, Frederick George, Esquire, of Belmont, Harbledon, Canterbury, a demi-gryphon sa., holding in his dexter claw a pole-axe arg. *Frangas non flectes.* 64. 11

Frith, Rev. W. R., M.A., Swynnerton Rectory, Stone, Staffs, a dexter arm in armour embowed, holding in the hand a dagger fesseways ppr. *Semper fidelis.* 196. 5

Frith, J. B., J.P., the Cross, Enniskillen, Ireland, same crest and motto.

Frith, B. G., Esq., B.A., M.B., Drumgay, Grove Road, Guildford, same crest and motto. 196. 5

Frobisher, William Martin, Esquire, J.P., 6, Campden Hill Square, Kensington, W., a dexter arm embowed in armour, the hand grasping an arrow in bend sinister point downwards.

Frodham, a dexter hand holding a fleur-de-lis. *cf.* 215. 5

Frodsham, Chesh., an escallop or. *Another* arg. 141. 12

Froggat and **Froggatt,** a parrot feeding on a bunch of cherries ppr 101. 8

Frogmer, Worcs., a demi-griffin with wings addorsed arg., holding between the claws a cross crosslet sa. *cf.* 64. 2

Frohock of London and Cambs, a stag ppr., charged on the shoulder with an etoile arg. *cf.* 117. 5

From, a demi-griffin segreant or, holding in the dexter claw a cross crosslet gu. *cf.* 64. 2

Frome, a greyhound couchant between two laurel-branches in orle ppr. 60. 5

Frome of Puncknoll, Dorset, a cross crosslet az., between two wings arg. *cf.* 111. 8

Fromond and **Fromont,** a dexter hand holding an escallop-shell. 216. 2

Fromonds, Kent and Surrey, a tiger passant. *cf.* 27. 11

Frost, George, Esquire, M.D., L.R.C.P., M.R.C.S., of Clovelly, Bournemouth, in front of a trefoil slipped, a serpent nowed, holding in the mouth a like trefoil, all ppr.

Frost, Yorks, an old man's head ppr., between two sprigs of laurel vert. 191. 13

Frost, Norfolk, a trefoil slipped between two wings erect az. *E terra ad cœlum* 110. 12

Frost, Francis Aylmer, Esquire, Meadowslea, Flintsh., between two wings erm., each charged with a trefoil az., a mount vert, thereon a trefoil, also az. *E terra germino ad cœlum expando.* 111. 11

Frost, Sir Thomas Gibbons, of Dolcorsllwyn Hall, Montgomerysh., on a mount vert, between two wings erect az., each charged with a quatrefoil arg., a trefoil slipped of the second. *E terra ad cœlum.* *cf.* 111. 11

Frost, Edmund, Esquire, M.B., C.M., of Chesterfield, Meads, Eastbourne, same crest and motto.

Frothingham, Yorks, a stag trippant ppr., attired gu. 117. 8

Froud, a Saracen's head sa., between two ostrich-feathers arg.

Froude, Devonsh., a stag regardant ppr., attired, collared, and ungul. or, holding in the mouth an oak-sprig vert, fructed of the first.

Frowicke and **Frowyke,** Middx., two arms embowed vested az., holding in the hands ppr. a leopard's face or.

Froyle, a demi-lion per pale gu. and az., collared or. 10. 9

Fructuozo of Langham Place, London, on a mount vert, in front of an orange-tree fructed ppr., two thyrsi in saltire, also ppr. *Fructus per fidem.*

Fruen of London, a demi-lion arg., holding between the paws a caltrap az. *cf.* 10. 2

Fry, Sir Theodore, Bart., a dexter arm embowed in armour ppr., garnished or, the hand grasping a sword, also ppr., pommel and hilt or, between two horse-shoes sa. *Esto fidelis.* 234. 6

Fry, Rt. Hon. Sir Edward, P.C., K.C., sometime a Judge of the High Court of Justice and a Lord Justice of Appeal, of Failand House, Failand, Bristol, a dexter arm in armour embowed, holding in the hand a sword in bend sinister, all ppr. *Libertas virtusque.* 195. 2

Fry, Rt. Hon. Lewis, P.C., of Goldney House, Clifton Hill, Bristol, same crest and motto.

Fryer of London, Essex, and Worcs., out of a ducal coronet or, an heraldic antelope's head arg., armed, crined, and tufted of the first. *Another* gu.

Fryer, John Edward, of Chatteris, Isle of Ely, same crest. *Jamais arrière*

Fryer, on a tower sa., a cock or, the tower environed by a serpent arg., darting at the cock. 156. 14

Fryer, Dorset, on a tower sa., a cock or, the tower encircled by a serpent arg., darting at the cock. *Mea fides in sapientia.* 156. 14

Fryer, Lieutenant-General Sir John, K.C.B., a tower, upon the battlements a cock, the tower entwined by a serpent darting at the cock, all ppr.

Fryer, Staffs, a castle arg., encircled by a branch of oak fructed ppr., thereon a cock sa., combed and wattled gu. *Mea fides in sapientiâ.*

Fryer, Ireland, an heraldic tiger's head couped arg., crined and ducally gorged or.

Fryer, an heraldic antelope's head erased per fess arg. and gu., gorged with a ducal coronet or, attired of the second.

Fryton, an heraldic tiger's head ducally gorged and chained ppr.

Fulborn and **Fulborne,** out of an antique coronet or, a demi-lion az.

Fulcher, a demi-lion holding an anchor ppr. 12. 12

Fulford, Devonsh. and Dorset, a bear's head erased arg., muzzled sa. 35. 2

Fulford, a bear's head erased arg., muzzled gu. 35. 2

Fulford, Francis Drummond, J.P., D.L., Esquire, of Great Fulford, Devonsh., a bear's head erased sa., muzzled or. *Bear up.* 35. 2

Fulham, a greyhound's head ppr. *cf.* 61. 2

Fulham, on a mount vert, a lion sejant or, supporting with the dexter paw an escutcheon arg., charged with a teazle stalked and leaved ppr.

Fulherst and **Fulsherst,** a triangular harrow ppr. 178. 4

Fulkworth, a dexter arm vested erm., holding in the hand ppr. a sword az., hilted or.

Fullarton of that Ilk, Ayrsh., Scotland, a camel's head and neck erased ppr. *Lux in tenebris.* *cf.* 132. 7

Fullarton-Robertson, Archibald Louis Fullarton, Kilmichael, Brodick, Isle of Arran, a camel's head erased ppr. *Lux in tenebris.*

Fullarton of Greenhill, Scotland, a camel's head and neck erased arg. *Ad summum emergunt.* *cf.* 132. 7

Fullarton, Scotland, an otter's head erased gu. *Lux in tenebris.* 134. 3

Fullarton, a tiger's head couped per fesse wavy or and sa., holding in the mouth a cinquefoil slipped vert. 27. 7

Fuller of Ashdown House, Sussex, a horse passant arg. *Currit qui curat.* 52. 6

Fuller, James Franklin, Esquire, F.S.A., of Glashnacree, Kenmare, co. Kerry, a horse passant ppr., charged on the shoulder with a mullet or. *Fortiter et recte.* *cf.* 52. 6

Fuller, co. Kerry, Ireland, same crest and motto. *cf.* 52. 6

Fuller of Rosehill Waldren and Ashdown House, Sussex: (1) A horse passant ppr. 52. 6. (2) Out of a ducal coronet gu., a lion's head arg. 17. 5. (3) A dexter hand in armour couped above the wrist, grasping a scimitar, all ppr., the wrist charged with a key sa. *Currit qui curat.—Fortiter et recte.*

Fuller, Ireland, a horse-shoe az. 158. 6

Fuller of Tanners Waldren, Sussex, out of a ducal coronet or, a lion's head ppr. 17. 5

Fuller, Thomas, M.D., Penryn, 19, Wilbury Avenue, Hove, same crest. *Currit qui curat.*

Fuller, Sussex, out of a ducal coronet gu., a lion's head arg. 17. 5

Fuller, a greyhound's head erased gu. 61. 4

Fuller, Bucks, on a mount vert, a beacon erect, fired ppr. *Fermiora futura.* 177. 8

Fuller, Lieutenant-General the late Sir Joseph, G.C.B., out of a mural coronet or, on a mount vert, a beacon erect, fired ppr., crossed by two swords in saltire ppr., hilts and pommels or. *Semper paratus.* 177. 11

Fuller, Canada, a martlet ppr. *Fidelitas in adversis.* 95. 4

Fuller, Hants, a dexter arm embowed, vested arg., cuffed sa., holding in the hand ppr. a sword of the first, hilt and pommel or. 204. 1

Fuller-Eliott-Drake, Sir Francis George Augustus, Bart., of Nutwell Court, Devonsh.: (1) A ship under sail drawn round a terrestrial globe with a cable rope by a hand issuing from clouds, and on an escroll the words *Auxilio divino* (*for Drake*). 160. 3. (2) A dexter arm in armour couped above the wrist, grasping a scimitar, all ppr., the wrist charged with a key sa. (*for Eliott*). (3) Out of a ducal coronet gu., a lion's head arg. (*for Fuller*). *Fortiter et recte.—Sic parvis magna.—Per ardua.* 17. 5

Fullerton, John Skipwith Herbert, Esquire, of Thibergh Park, near Rotherham, a camel's head erased ppr. *Lux in tenebris.*

Fulleshurst, Chesh., a unicorn's head erm. 49. 7

Fullwood, two laurel-branches in orle vert, fructed gu. 146. 5

Fullwood, Derbysh., Staffs, and Warw., a stag ppr., holding in its mouth an acorn-branch vert, fructed or. *cf.* 117. 5

Fullwood, a demi-stag or. 119. 2

Fullwood, a demi-man in armour arg., holding in his dexter hand a broken tilting-spear or, on his helmet four feathers alternately of the first and gu.

Fulmerston, a goat's head erased az., platée, armed and bearded or, holding in the mouth a branch of eglantine vert, flowered arg. *cf.* 128. 5

Fulmeston or **Fulmerston,** a heraldic antelope's head erased gu., platée, armed or, holding in the mouth a rose-branch ppr.

Fulrich, a tower, on the top a plume of five ostrich-feathers ppr.

Fulthorp and **Fulthorpe,** a horse passant arg., bridled az., bit and tassels or. 52. 4

Fulthorp, an eagle displayed arg., charged on the breast with a cross moline sa. *cf.* 75. 2

Fulton, Sir Forrest, K.C., LL.B., of 27, Queen's Gardens, Lancaster Gate, and the Cottage, Sheringham, Norfolk, a cubit arm erect grasping a broken javelin, point to the sinister, all ppr. *Vi et virtute.*

Fulton, E. M'G. Hope, of Bombay, same crest and motto.

Fulton, Henry, Esquire, of Inkwelo, Lee-on-the-Solent, Hants, same crest and motto.

Fulton, John, Esquire, of Christ Church, New Zealand, same crest and motto.

Fulton, Richard Robert, Esquire, of Parsonstown, King's Co., same crest and motto.

Fulton, Robert Valpy, Esquire, same crest and motto.

Fulton, Sydney Wroughton, Esquire, of Melbourne, same crest and motto.

Fulton, Lieutenant Henry, Lisburn, Sevenoaks, same crest and motto.

Fulton, a stag's head gu., attired or. 121. 5

Fulton, Scotland, on a mount a stag lodged regardant ppr. *Quæ fecimus ipsi.—Parta labore quies.* 115. 9

Fulton, John Williamson, Esquire, J.P., M.A., Barrister-at-Law, of Braidnyle House, near Lisburn, co. Antrim, Ireland, a cubit arm erect grasping a broken javelin, all ppr., the point towards the sinister, the arm charged with a mullet sa. *Vi et virtute.*

Fulwar of Ringrone, co. Cork, Ireland, a pillar arg., crowned and based or, thereon a book gu.

Fulwar, Ireland, a cushion arg., tasselled and garnished or, thereon a book gu. 158. 2

Fulwer, Hants, a dexter arm embowed in armour sa., garnished and holding in the gauntlet a sword arg., pommel and hilt or. 195. 1

Fulwer of London, on a mount vert, a beacon arg., fired ppr. 177. 8

Fulwood, a demi-stag or. 119. 2

Fulwood, Hants and Warw., a buck trippant holding in its mouth an oak-slip, all ppr. *cf.* 117. 8

Fulwood of Tamworth, Warw., a demi-knight in armour arg., holding in the dexter hand a broken tilting-spear or, on the helmet four feathers of the first and gu. *cf.* 187. 13

Funeaux, an arm in armour from the elbow holding up a caltrap, all ppr. 210. 7

Furbisher, out of a ducal coronet gu., a griffin's head arg. 67. 9

Furbisher and **Furbusher,** a unicorn's head erased az., armed arg., ducally gorged or. *cf.* 49. 5

Furguason, a demi-lion holding a torteau, semée d'étoiles. *cf.* 11. 7

Furlong, an eagle's head erased ppr. *Liberalitas.* 83. 2

Furnace, Furnes, Fernese, and **Furness,** Kent, a talbot sejant sa. *cf.* 55. 2

Furneaulx of Paignton and Buckfastleigh, Devonsh., round the stem of a tree erased at both ends in pale, two serpents entwined, all ppr.

Furneaux, Rev. Henry, M.A., 35, Banbury Road, Oxford, same crest.

Furneaux, Rev. William Mordaunt, of Repton Hall, Burton-on-Trent, and Gwyl Annedd, Penmaenmawr, same crest. *Nescit virtus otiari.*

Furnes, Furnese, and **Furness,** out of a ducal coronet a lion's gamb holding a lance, all ppr. 36. 14

Furness, Sir Christopher, of Tunstall Court, West Hartlepool, Durh., and Grantley Hall, Ripon, Yorks, issuant from a wreath of cinquefoils vert a bear's paw erect arg., charged with a torteau grasping a javelin in bend sinister sa., pendent therefrom by the straps ppr. two straps or. *I'll defend.*

Furney of Perristone, Heref., a lion's head erased gu. 117. 2

Furnival and **Furnivall,** an anchor cabled and a sword in saltier, all ppr. 169. 9

Fursdon, Charles, of Fursdon, Devonsh., out of a ducal coronet a plume of five ostrich-feathers, all ppr. 114. 13

Furse, the late Rev. Charles Wellington, of Halsdon, Devonsh., a castle ppr. *Nec desit virtus.* 195. 8

Furse, a lion sejant affrontée holding in the dexter paw a dagger, and in the sinister a fleur-de-lis. 7. 3

Furser and **Furzer,** on a mount a stag lodged, all ppr. 115. 12

Fursland, a savage's head affrontée couped at the shoulders ppr., vested paly of six sa. and arg.

Fursman, a lion passant with wings elevated arg., collared dovetailed gu., reposing the dexter paw on a cross botony or. 20. 10

Fury, a demi-lion rampant. 10. 2

Fury, a demi-lion rampant grasping a thunderbolt or. *cf.* 10. 2

Fussell, *see* Coldham-Fussell.

Fust, Glouc., a horse at full speed arg. *Terrena pervices sunt aliena.* 52. 8

Fust, Jenner-, Herbert, Hill Court, Berkeley, Glouc.: (1) A horse at full speed arg. (2) A covered cup or, standing on two swords saltirewise arg., hilt and pommels gold. *Terrena pervices sunt aliena.*

Futroye, Surrey, two elephants' trunks issuing from the wreath sa. *Tod.* 123. 10

Futter, Norf. and Suff., a goat's head erased or, armed sa., holding in its mouth a holly-branch vert, fructed gu. *cf.* 128. 5

Futter, Isle of Man, a goat's head erased or, armed sa., holding in its mouth a laurel-branch slipped ppr. *cf.* 128. 5

Fyan of Dublin, a demi-woman ppr., habited per pale or and arg., holding in the dexter hand a branch of lily ppr., leaved or, flowered, also arg. *cf.* 183. 4

Fydell, a hind's head couped per chevron sa. and erm. 124. 1

Fydell of Morcott, Rutlandsh., issuing out of rays of the sun gu., a demi-lion arg., gorged with a collar flory counterflory, and holding between the paws an escutcheon or, charged with an anchor sa. *Esto fidelis usque ad finem.* 14. 3

Fyers, a goat passant, holding in its mouth a bunch of ivy. *cf.* 129. 9

Fyfe-Butler, Lancs, an eagle's head erased ppr. 83. 2

Fyfe and **Fyffe,** Scotland, a demi-lion rampant gu. *Decens et honestum.* 10. 3

Fyfe, Andrew Johnstone, B.A., Hayes, Middx., same crest and motto.

Fyffe of Smithfield, Forfarsh., a demi-lion gu., armed and langued az. *Decens et honestum.* 10. 3

Fyffe, Captain John, R.N., issuing out of a naval crown or, the rim encircled with a branch of laurel ppr., a demi-lion gu., supporting in the dexter paw a sword erect ppr., pommel and hilt of the first. *Virtute et opera.*

Fyler, a fox sejant per fess or and gu. 32. 11

Fyler, a dexter arm vested az., cuffed or, holding in the hand ppr. a cross flory of the second. *Volonté de Dieu.*

Fyler, John Arthur, of Woodlands, Surrey, a porcupine ppr. *Volonté de Dieu.* 136. 5

Fyler, John William Townsend, of Hethfelton, Wareham, Dorset, same crest and motto.

Fylkyn, a demi-greyhound between two wings. *cf.* 60. 11

Fylloll, a unicorn's head erased sa. 49. 5

Fynderne, an ox-yoke or. 178. 6

Fynderne of Fyndern, Derbysh., and Nuneaton, Warw., an ox-yoke or, the chain pendent gu. *cf.* 178. 6

Fynes, a peacock's head erased az., crested or. 103. 1

Fyneux, an eagle's head erased or, ducally crowned gu. *cf.* 83. 2

Fynmore, a unicorn sejant resting the dexter foot on a tree ppr. 48. 3

Fynmore and **Finmore,** a bull's head arg., couped sa., charged with two chevronels gu. *cf.* 44. 3

Fynney, Staffs, a staff raguly or. *Fortem posce animum.* *cf.* 147. 10

Fynte, a basilisk or.

Fyres, a dexter hand holding a salamander in flames, the head to the dexter, all ppr. *Ardit virtus non urit.*

Fysh, Hon. Sir Philip Oakley, Esquire, K.C.M.G., of Hobart Town, Tasmania, issuant from a wreath of red coral a cubit arm vested az., cuffed arg., holding in the hand a flying-fish ppr. *Nitor in adversum.*

Fyshe, Suff. and Herts, a triangle arg., voided and surmounted on the top with an étoile or. 167. 8

Fysher of London, a kingfisher ppr. *cf.* 96. 9

Fysher, Wilts, a demi-lion rampant gardant gu., holding a gauntlet arg. *cf.* 10. 8

Fyske, on a chapeau a martlet, all ppr. 95. 1

Fytche, a tower triple-towered arg., masoned sa. 157. 6

Fythey and **Fythie,** Scotland, a crane's head erased. 104. 11

Fyvie, Scotland, a lion's gamb holding up a human heart. 39. 11

G.

Gabb, out of a ducal coronet a harpy with wings expanded and ducally gorged, all ppr. *Nullius in verba.*

Gabb, a griffin's head between two wings holding in the beak a branch of palm, all ppr. 65. 9

Gabell, Hants, a boar's head couped or. 43. 1

Gabell, a savage wreathed about the middle and treading on a serpent, all ppr. 188. 3

Gabbett-Mulhallen, Marshall: (1) An escallop or (*for Mulhallen*). (2) Under an oak-tree ppr., a boar passant sa., armed, bristled, unguled, collared, and chained or (*for Gabbett*). *Parcere subjectis et debellare superbos.—Always ready.*

Gabourel of Jersey, a greyhound's head couped arg., collared and chained or. *cf.* 61. 2

Gabriel of Bath, a chevron gu., surmounted by a label of three points arg. *Arma virumque cano.* 167. 10

Gabriel Bart., of Edgecombe Hall, Surrey, on a mount vert, a boar's head erased and fesseways sa., billettée or. *In prosperis time, in adversis spera.*

Gabriel and **Gabryell,** a demi-savage regardant ppr. 185. 1

Gace, an arm in armour embowed ppr., grasping in the hand a broken falchion arg., hilt and pommel or.

Gaddes and **Gaddez,** a stag's head ppr. 121. 5

Gaddesden, a wyvern ppr. *Decrevi.* 70. 1

Gadsby, a stag trippant arg. 117. 8

Gael, a cock gu. *Vigilate.* 91. 2

Gaff, a demi-antelope or, collared gu. 126. 3

Gage, *see* Baillie-Gage.

Gage, Viscount (Gage), a ram statant arg., armed and unguled or. *Courage sans peur.* 131. 13

Gage, Bart., Suff., a ram passant arg., armed or. 131. 13

Gage, Rokewood-, Bart.: (1) A ram passant arg., armed or (*for Gage*). 131. 13. (2) A chessrook sa., winged arg. (*for Rokewood*). *Bon temps viendra.—Tout est Dieu.* 110. 1

Gage, Herts, a stag trippant ppr. 117. 8

Gahagan, Francis Evatt, M.B., 42, Farnley Road, South Norwood, a greyhound passant arg., collared vert, the collar studded with fleurs-de-lis or. *Manu forti.* 271. 1

Gahn, a stag's head erased ppr. *Si je puis.* 121. 2

Gailie, out of a mural coronet a garb, thereon a bird, all ppr. 153. 9

Gaine, a demi-lion rampant. 10. 2

Gainsborough, Earl of (Noel), Lincs, a buck at gaze arg., attired or. *Tout bien ou rien.* 117. 3

Gainsborough, Surrey, a griffin's head erased az., charged with three chevronels arg. *cf.* 66. 2

Gainsby, out of a mount a sprig of laurel growing vert. 145. 11

Gainsford, William Dunn, Esquire, of Shendleby Hall, Spilsby, a woman emergent holding a wreath and a rose.

Gainsford, London, Kent, and Oxon., a demi-woman vested and crined or, holding in her dexter hand a chaplet vert, and in her sinister a rose ppr. *cf.* 183. 5

Gair, a lion rampant gardant gu., holding in his dexter paw an ox-yoke ppr.

Gair, Scotland, a mill-rind. 165. 11

Gairden, Scotland, a boar passant arg. *Vires animat virtus.* 40. 9

Gairden, Scotland, a dexter hand holding two palm-branches in orle ppr. *Vive le roi.* 218. 7

Gairden, Scotland, a rose slipped ppr. *Sustine, abstine.* 149. 5

Gairden, Scotland, two dexter hands conjoined ppr., supporting a cross crosslet fitched or. 224. 11

Gairdner, Scotland, a demi-leopard rampant ppr. *cf.* 23. 13

Gairdner, a demi-tiger rampant, collared and lined. *cf.* 23. 13

Gairdner, Scotland, a dove holding in its beak an olive-branch ppr. *Jovi confido.* 92. 5

Gaisford, a boar passant per fess or and gu., unguled of the last, bristled of the first. 40. 9
Gaitskill, on a mountain an eagle regardant with wings expanded ppr., collared az., resting the dexter claw on a pellet.
Gaitskell, Lieutenant-Colonel Walter James, Denbigh Lodge, Southsea, same crest. *Fortitudo et integritas.*
Galaad, a demi-greyhound arg. 60. 11
Galay, a snail, the horns erect ppr. 141. 8
Galbraith, John Alexander, Esquire, of 28, Belhaven Terrace, Glasgow, a galley, sails furled sa., flagged gu. *Trust and do good.*
Galbraith, a bear's head erased or, muzzled sa., holding in the mouth a trefoil slipped arg. cf. 35. 2
Galbraith, Scotland, a bear's head couped arg., muzzled or. 34. 14
Galbraith, a bear's head and neck per fess or and gu. 34. 14
Galbraith, Scotland, a lion's head and neck erased ppr. *Vigilo et spero.* 17. 8
Gale, a unicorn's head paly of six or and az., the horn twisted of the second and first. 49. 7
Gale, Yorks, out of a ducal coronet or, a unicorn's head paly of six az. and or, armed of the last. 48. 12
Gale, Henry Richmond Hoghton, Esquire, J.P., of Bardsea Hall, Ulverstone, Lancs, a unicorn's head az., charged with an anchor or, between two pallets arg. cf. 49. 7
Gale, Charles William, Esquire, same crest. *Depressus extollor.*
Gale, Curwen John Zouch, Esquire, same crest and motto.
Gale, James, Esquire, same crest and motto.
Gale, John Cherry, Esquire, same crest and motto.
Gale, Marmaduke Henry Littledale, Esquire, same crest and motto.
Gale, Walter Andrew, Esquire, same crest and motto.
Gale, Roger Edward, of Scruton Hall, Bedall, a unicorn's head or. *Qui semina vertu raccoglia fama.*
Gale, Scotland, a unicorn's head sa. 49. 7
Gale, Dorset, a horse's head erased, bendy wavy of six arg. and sa. 51. 4
Gall, a shank-bone and a palm-branch in saltier ppr. 147. 4
Gall, a lion sejant gu., holding a banner ppr.
Gall, Scotland, a ship ppr., her flags and pennons flying gu. *Patientia vincit.* 160. 13
Gall, a ship in full sail ppr. 160. 13
Gallagher, Ireland, a hand holding a sickle ppr. 219. 13
Galland, a stag lodged per pale or and gu. cf. 115. 7
Gallard, an arm embowed vested gu., holding in the hand ppr. a rose or, slipped and leaved vert.
Gallaway, Scotland, out of a ducal coronet or, a dragon's head between two wings addorsed vert. 72. 1
Gallaway or **Galloway,** Scotland, an arm holding in the hand a dagger ppr. 212. 3
Gallay, Galley, or **Galle,** Somers. and Dorset, a nag's head bendy wavy of six arg. and sa. cf. 50. 13
Gallie, James Butler, Barrister-at-law, 64, Albemarle Road, Beckenham, a horse's head couped. 304. 15
Galliers, an antelope trippant quarterly sa. and arg. 126. 6
Galliez, a savage standing on a serpent ppr. *Divino robore.* 188. 3
Gallightly, a lion's head issuant gu., crowned with an antique crown or. *Hactenus invictus.* cf. 17. 12
Gallimore, a cock ppr. 91. 2
Gallini of Winnal House, Hayward's Heath, Cuckfield, a lyre or, surmounted by a wreath of olive-leaves in bend vert. *Concordia et harmonia.* 168. 8
Galloway, Earl of (Stewart), a pelican in her piety, the nest and young ppr. *Virescit vulnere virtus.* 98. 14
Galloway, Charles John, Esquire, of Thornyholme, Knutsford, a mound surmounted by a cross crosslet between two wheat-ears in saltire ppr. *Higher.* 247. 9
Galloway, David J., J.P., M.D., the Manor House, Singapore, Straits Settlements, a dexter cubit arm erect holding in the hand a dagger, the blade wavy, all ppr. *Deo juvante gero.* 272. 3
Galloway, Baron Dunkeld, a mound or, bespread with rays of the sun ppr., between two ears of corn in saltire and ensigned with a cross crosslet of the first. *Higher.*
Galloway, out of a ducal coronet or, a dragon's head with wings addorsed vert. 72. 1
Galloway, *see* Gallaway.
Gallwey, Bart., *see* Payne-Gallwey.
Gallwey, co. Cork, a cat sejant ppr., collared and chained or. cf. 26. 13
Gallwey, Lieutenant-General Sir Thomas Lionel, K.C.M.G., of 3, Hartfield Square, Eastbourne, upon a mount vert, a cat sejant guardant ppr., gorged with a collar or, charged with two mullets gu., and chain of the third. *Unus rex et una lex.*
Gally, a cock ppr. 91. 2
Galpin, Rev. Arthur John, Headmaster of the King's School, Canterbury, a cock's head erased sa., combed and wattled gu., charged with a galtrap between two cock's feathers or. *Vigilat validus.* 256. 12
Galpin, Rev. Francis William, of Hatfield Vicarage, Harlow, same crest and motto.
Galpine, a plume of feathers banded ppr.
Galsworthy, Sir Edwin H., J.P., of 26, Sussex Place, Regent's Park, a griffin's head erased holding in the beak a sprig of laurel. *Agendo gnaviter.*
Galt, Sir Alexander Tilloch, G.C.M.G., of Seaforth, Caconna, and Montreal, Canada, in front of a demi-archer equipped ppr., habited vert, holding a drawn bow and arrow, also ppr., a thistle leaved and slipped or. *Semper paratus.*
Galt, William Howard Curtis, Esquire, of Coleraine Club, Coleraine, Ireland, on a garb fesseways or, banded gu., a man's head in profile couped at the neck ppr., wreathed az. *Nihil melius virtute.*
Galt, George Moore, Esquire, same crest and motto.
Galton, a bull's head erased gu., ducally gorged or. 44. 2
Galton, Hubert George Howard, Esquire, of Hadzor, Droitwich, Worcs., on a mount vert, an eagle erm., looking at the sun in splendour, and resting the dexter claw on a fleur-de-lis gu. *Gaudet luce.*
Galton, Darwin, Esquire, J.P., D.L., of Claverdon Leys, Warw., same crest and motto.
Galton, Sir Douglas, K.C.B., D.C.L., F.R.S., of Himbledon Manor, Droitwich, same crest and motto.
Galton, Erasmus, Esquire, of Loxton, Weston-super-Mare, same crest and motto.
Galton, Ewan Cameron, Esquire, of Shelsley Grange, Worcs., same crest and motto.
Galton, Francis, Esquire, F.R.S., D.C.L., D.S.C., of 42, Rutland Gate, S.W., same crest and motto.
Galway, Viscount (Monckton-Arundell): (1) On a chapeau az., turned up erm., a swallow arg. (*for Arundell*). cf. 96. 3. (2) A martlet or (*for Monckton*). *Famam extendere factis.* 95. 2
Galwey, a cat sejant ppr., collared and the chain reflexed over the back or. cf. 26. 13
Gamage, Herts, a griffin segreant or. 62. 2
Gamage, a dexter hand holding a pen ppr. 217. 10
Gambell or **Gamble,** a Roman soldier in full costume ppr. 188. 4
Gambell or **Gamble,** a crane holding in its beak a rose stalked and leaved ppr. cf. 105. 9
Gambier, James W., Esquire, J.P., Captain R.N., of Mylncroft, Farnborough, Hants, out of a ducal coronet an eagle displayed. *Sursum.*
Gambier-Parry, Major Ernest, of Highnam, Glouc., and Garing, Oxon., three battle-axes erect ppr. *Tu ne cede malis.*
Gambier of London, Kent, and Bucks, out of a naval coronet or, an eagle displayed erminois, charged on the breast with an anchor sa. *Fide non armis.*
Gambier, an eagle displayed. 75. 2
Gamble, Sir David, Bart., C.B., Windlehurst, St. Helens, Lancs, on a mount between two trefoils slipped vert, a stork arg., holding in the beak a rose gu., stalked, leaved, and slipped ppr. *Vix ea nostra voco.* 255. 3
Gamble, William, J.P., Briars Hey, Ramhill, Lancs, same crest and motto.
Gamble, Mercier, M.B., Arnwood, Wilbraham Road, Fallowfield, Manchester, a stork arg., holding in the beak a rose gu., leaved and slipped vert.
Gambon and **Gamon,** a torteau between two wings ppr. cf. 110. 4
Game, a cross crosslet fitched and a palm-branch in saltier ppr. cf. 166. 11
Gamell or **Gammill,** two lions' heads addorsed gu. 17. 3
Gamell, same crest. 17. 3
Gamell, Gammel, or **Gamonill,** Scotland, a talbot's head sa. 56. 12
Games, Leics., an eagle's head or, between two wings erm. 84. 2
Gamin, an armed arm embowed wreathed with laurel and grasping a sword, all ppr. cf. 195. 2

Gamlin of London, a pelican vulning herself ppr. *Moriens, sed invictus.* 98. 1

Gammell, Sydney James, Esquire, of Drumtochty Castle, Fordoun, Kincardine, and Countesswells, Aberdeen, Scotland, a pelican with wings displayed, pierced from behind by an arrow, all ppr. *Moriens, sed invictus.* cf. 98. 1

Gammell, Scotland, a talbot's head sa. 56. 12

Gammill, *see* Gamell

Gammon and **Gamon,** Middx., a boar passant arg., charged on the body with a pale sa., thereon a leopard's face or. *Virtus in arduis.* 227. 9

Gammon, a boar passant arg. 40. 9

Gamoll, Chesh., a human heart ppr., crowned or, between two wings displayed sa., purfled of the first. 110. 14

Gamul of Buerton, Chesh., out of a ducal coronet or, a trefoil slipped of the same, between two wings sa. cf. 110. 12

Gander, a demi-talbot per chevron arg. and az. cf. 55. 8

Gandey, a saltier gu.

Gandey and **Gandy,** a fox current per pale or and sa. cf. 32. 8

Gandolfi of Richmond, Surrey, a demi-lion gu., crined or, holding in the dexter paw a dagger ppr. cf. 14. 12

Gandolfi, Hornyold-, Thomas Charles Gandolfi, of Blackmore Park, Hanley Castle, Worcs., and Villa Gandolfi, San Remo, Italy, a demi-unicorn gu., armed, crined, and unguled or. *Fidem tene.*

Gandy, James Gandy, Esquire, of Heaves, Kendal, a pen in bend dexter arg., surmounted by a sword in bend sinister ppr., pommel and hilt or, encircled by a chaplet of oak vert, fructed or. *Marte et ingenio.*

Gange, Glouc., a stork drinking out of a horn, all ppr.

Ganlard, a dexter hand brandishing a sabre ppr. 212. 13

Gannoke, Lincs, a stag sejant arg., ducally gorged or. cf. 116. 8

Gannon, a bull's head ducally gorged and crowned. cf. 44. 2

Ganstin, Ireland, a hand holding a dagger. *Gladio et virtute.* 212. 3

Ganstin, out of a ducal coronet a dexter arm armed holding in the hand a dagger. *Gladio et virtute.*

Gant, a mill-rind ppr. 165. 11

Gant, Lincs, a wolf's head or, collared vair. 30. 9

Gant, Dr., of 16, Connaught Square, London, W., *uses:* out of a ducal coronet an eagle displayed. *(Of no authority.)* *Constancy.*

Ganuble, a lion passant with its tail extended ppr. 5. 11

Gape, a lion passant regardant or, pellettée, collared vair. cf. 6. 1

Gapper, out of an antique coronet or, a demi-lion rampant gu. cf. 16. 3

Gapper, a demi-lion rampant gu., holding in the dexter paw a cross crosslet fitchée or. 11. 5

Garbet, a demi-eagle displayed with two heads, an escutcheon suspended from the neck. 82. 3

Garbett, an imperial eagle with two heads displayed sa. *Gare la bête.* cf. 74. 2

Garbridge, Norf., a sheaf of reeds ppr., banded about the middle with a wreath arg. and sa. cf. 153. 2

Gard, a tower arg., between two laurel-branches vert. 157. 4

Garde, Ireland, an antelope's head erased ppr. 126. 2

Garde, a demi-griffin segreant sa. *Toujours fidele.* 64. 2

Garden of that Ilk, Scotland, two dexter hands conjoined ppr., holding a cross crosslet fitchée or. *Cruciata cruce junguntur.* 224. 11

Garden of Borrowfield, Forfarsh., Scotland, a dexter hand holding a palm-branch disposed in orle ppr. *Vive le roi.*

Garden, a rose gu., slipped and leaved ppr. 149. 5

Garden, Francis Alexander, Esquire, of Troup, Troup House, Banff, Scotland, a boar passant arg. *Vires animat virtus.* 40. 9

Garden, Scotland, an open book ppr. 158. 3

Garden, a mallard amongst flags ppr. 102. 5

Gardenar, out of a mural coronet ppr., an armed arm arg., holding in the hand a flag gu., charged with a sword of the second.

Gardener of Himbleton, Worcs., out of a mural crown or, an armed arm embowed ppr., holding in the hand a flagstaff, thereon a split pennon gu., flowing to the sinister, charged with two staves in saltire, fired of the first. cf. 199. 7

Gardener, Lincs, a Turk's head ppr., the turban or and az.

Gardener, Norf., Cambs, and Wilts, a griffin's head erased sa. 66. 2

Gardener, Northumb., on a book sanguine, clasped and garnished or, a falcon rising of the last.

Gardenor, a leopard passant arg., pellettée, holding in the dexter paw a pine-apple or, stalked and leaved vert.

Gardin, Scotland, an otter issuing devouring a salmon ppr. *Ad escam et usum.* 134. 12

Gardiner, Berks and Bucks, a griffin's head erased az., charged with three bends or. cf. 66. 2

Gardiner, Dorset, a griffin's head erased bendy of six or and purp. cf. 66. 2

Gardiner, Essex, a griffin passant regardant sa. 63. 14

Gardiner, a griffin's head or, gorged with a chaplet of laurel vert, between two wings expanded az. *Persevere.* cf. 65. 11

Gardiner, Patrick, 56, Coolhurst Road, Crouch End, N., same crest. *Nil desperandum.*

Gardiner, a demi-griffin, with wings expanded ppr. *Nil desperandum.* 64. 2

Gardiner of Oxford, a griffin's head erased. *Deo, non fortuna.* 66. 2

Gardiner, a griffin sejant, resting the dexter claw on a book sa. cf. 62. 10

Gardiner, an eagle's head erased between two wings. *Nil desperandum.* cf. 84. 2

Gardiner, Oxon., a stork ppr. 105. 11

Gardiner of Oxford, a stork holding in the beak a serpent. cf. 105. 11

Gardiner of London, a Saracen's head in profile ppr., erased at the shoulders gu., wreathed round the temples arg. and of the second.

Gardiner, Smith-Whalley-, Bart., a Saracen's head affrontée couped at the shoulders ppr., wreathed gu. and az., on the head a cap or.

Gardiner of London, a man's head ppr., thereon a cap turned up gu. and az., crined and bearded sa.

Gardiner, a Moor weeping vested in a sailor's dress, kneeling on one knee, the jacket az., and trousers arg.

Gardiner, a stag's head cabossed ppr., between the attires a mullet sa., pierced and pendent from a chain or. cf. 122. 5

Gardiner of King's Brompton, Somers., a stag ppr., the dexter fore-leg supporting an escutcheon arg., charged with four lozenges conjoined in fesse gu., between two barrulets sa.

Gardiner, Herts, two halberds erect, environed by a snake ppr. 172. 6

Gardiner of Madras, out of a mural coronet or, seven battle-axes ppr., one in fesse and six in saltire. *Omnia superat virtus.*

Gardiner of London and Norf., a rhinoceros passant arg. cf. 226. 7

Gardiner, Scotland, a dexter hand grasping a sword ppr. *My hope is constant in thee.* 212. 13

Gardiner, Worcs., out of a mural coronet or, a dexter arm in armour embowed sa., garnished of the first, holding in the hand a pennon gu., charged with a pomegranate or, the staff ppr., headed of the first.

Gardiner, Surrey, out of a ducal coronet or, a goat's head gu., attired of the first. 128. 14

Gardner, *see* Burghclere, Baron.

Gardner, Major Smith Hannington, Broomfield, Tiverton, Devonsh., a demi-lion rampant, holding between the paws a roundel charged with a pale. *Invidia major.* 298. 1

Gardner, Baron (Gardner), a demi-griffin az., collared and chained or, supporting bteween the claws an anchor erect and cabled or.

Gardner, Colonel Alan Coulstoun, of Newton Hall, Dunmow, Essex, and Clearwell Castle, Glouc., same crest. *Valet anchora virtus.*

Gardner, Shropsh., a griffin's head erased sa. 66. 2

Gardner, Kent, a griffin's head erased, gorged with a mural coronet. cf. 66. 2

Gardner, a griffin's head erased ppr., charged with a crescent or. *Virtute et fortunâ.* cf. 66. 2

Gardner, Cambs, a griffin's head erased arg., gorged with two barrulets sa., within two laurel-branches in orle vert. cf. 66. 4

Gardner of Chatteris House, Isle of Ely: (1) A griffin's head erased arg., surmounted by two branches of laurel in saltire ppr. (*for Gardner*). cf. 66. 2. (2) Two swords in saltire, the points upwards ppr., pommels and hilts or, tied with a riband vert, and pendent therefrom a key sa. (*for Dunn*). *Fide et amore.* 177. 4

Gardner, John Sykes, Esquire, of 12, Sunnyside, Devonshire Road, Prince's

Park, Liverpool, in front of two dibbles (half-spades) in saltire a griffin's head erased, all ppr. *Animo et fide.* cf. 66. 2

Gardner, Rev. James Cardwell, of Fluke Hall, Garstang, Lancs, same crest and motto.

Gardner, Benjamin Bamber, Esquire, of Aldingham Hall, Ulverston, same crest and motto.

Gardner, an eagle's head erased ppr. *In virtute et fortunâ.* 83. 2

Gardner, on a ducal coronet or, a lion passant gardant arg. cf. 6. 4

Gardner, Middx., a reindeer's head arg., attired or. cf. 122. 3

Gardner, Lincs, an elephant's head erm., eared sa., armed or. 133. 2

Gardner, Dorset, an elephant's head bendy az. and or. 133. 2

Gardner, Surrey, a demi-unicorn erased or, crined and armed sa., ducally crowned arg.

Gardner, Scotland, on a thistle a bee, all ppr. *Labore et virtute.* 150. 9

Gardner of London and Lincs, a Saracen's head affrontée ppr., erased at the neck gu., wreathed of the last and az., on his head a cap or.

Gardner-Medwin, Frank Medwin, Esquire, upon a mount within a serpent embowed, with tail in mouth, head to dexter ppr., a cinquefoil sa.

Gardyne, Scotland, two dexter hands couped and conjoined in fess, supporting a cross crosslet fitchée or. *Cruciata cruci junguntur.* 224. 11

Garfield, out of a heart a hand holding a sword ppr.

Garfield of Kilsby, Northamp., out of a ducal coronet or, a cross Calvary gu. cf. 166. 1

Garfit of Bromley, Kent, upon a wreath of the colours between two bezants the battlements of a tower or, issuant therefrom a goat's head arg., armed gold, gorged with a collar gemelle sa. *Semper idem.*

Garfit, Thomas Cheney, Esquire, of Kenwick Hall, Louth, Lincs, same crest and motto.

Garfit, William, Esquire, of West Skirbeck House, Boston, Lincs, same crest and motto.

Garfoot, Essex and Suff., out of a mural coronet sa., a goat's head arg., armed or. cf. 128. 14

Garforth, a wolf current ppr. 28. 4

Garforth, Yorks, out of a ducal coronet or, a goat's head arg. 128. 14

Gargate, a lion poisson rampant. 20. 5

Garginton, a vine-branch fructed and leaved ppr. 152. 9

Gargrave, Yorks, a falcon rising ppr. 87. 1

Garioch, Scotland, a dove holding in its beak an olive-branch ppr. 92. 5

Gariochs and **Gariock,** Scotland, a palm-tree and a trefoil slipped, growing out of a mount, all ppr. *Concussus surgo.*

Gariock, a palm-tree ppr. *Concussus surgo.* 144. 1

Garland of Quatre Bras, Dorset, two lances saltireways arg., interlacing a chaplet ppr. cf. 175. 13

Garland, Edward Charles, M.D., Yeovil, Somers., same crest.

Garland, Yorks, on a mural coronet or, a lion sejant regardant arg., supporting with the dexter paw an escutcheon of the second, charged with a garland ppr.

Garland, Ireland, a horse passant arg., unguled or. 52. 6

Garland and **Garlant,** Kent and Sussex, a lion's gamb erased holding a battle-axe ppr. 38. 3

Garlick, a dexter arm in armour erect, holding in the hand a cutlass in pale, all ppr., hilt and pommel or.

Garlies, Viscount, *see* Galloway, Earl.

Garling, a fish's head erased in fess ppr. 139. 6

Garman and **Garmon,** an oak-tree, and therefrom two weights pendent, all ppr. 143. 10

Garmish, Suff., a cubit arm holding in the hand a scimitar, all ppr., hilt and pommel or. 213. 5

Garmoyle, Viscount, *see* Cairns, Earl.

Garmston, Lincs, a shark's head regardant arg., swallowing a negro ppr. *Opera Dei mirifica.* 139. 2

Garnatt, a squirrel sejant, holding in its fore-paws a branch of hazel ppr. 139. 2

Garneshe or **Garnishe,** Suff., a mermaid ppr. 184. 5

Garnet, a demi-lion ducally crowned. 10. 11

Garnett, Henry, Esquire, of Wyreside, near Lancs, a demi-lion arg., gorged with a collar dovetail gu., holding between the paws an escutcheon or, charged with a cross pattée fitched gu. *Fidus et audax.*

Garnett, Captain Charles Henry, of Wyreside, near Lancaster, same crest and motto.

Garnett, of Adrett Court, Westbury-on-Severn, Glouc., same crest and motto.

Garnett, Rev. Lionel, B.A., of Christleton, Chesh., same crest and motto.

Garnett, Robert, Esquire, of the Ridding, Lower Bentham, Lancs, same crest and motto.

Garnett, William, Esquire, of Quernmore Park and Bleasdale Tower, Garstang, Lancs, a demi-lion arg., gorged with a wreath of oak ppr., holding between the paws an escutcheon gu., charged with a bugle-horn or. *Diligentiâ et honore.*

Garnett, a dexter hand holding up a swan's head and neck erased ppr. 220. 9

Garnett-Botfield, William Egerton, Esquire, J.P., F.G.S., of the Hut, Bishop's Castle, R.S.O., Salop, and of Decker Hill, Shifnal: (1) On a rock a stag at gaze, holding in the mouth an arrow fesseways, all ppr. (*for Botfield*). (2) A demi-lion arg., crowned or, gorged with a plain collar vair, and holding between the paws a lozenge gu., charged with a bee gold (*for Garnett*). *The Lord will provide.*

Garnett, Frederick William Rowland, Esquire, of 1, Grosvenor Place, S.W., a gryffon's head erased or. *Viendra le jours.—Omnia vanitas* (over the crest).

Garnett-Orme, George Hunter, Esquire, of Tarn House, Skipton-in-Craven, Yorks, West Riding: (1) In front of a battle-axe in bend, surmounted by a tilting-spear in bend sinister ppr., a dolphin naiant arg. (*for Orme*). (2) A dexter cubit arm erect ppr., grasping two sea-lions' heads erased respectant and saltirewise arg. (*for Garnett*). *Deus refugium nostrum.—Diligentia et honore.*

Garneys or **Garnish** of Laxfield and of Heveningham, Kenton, Mickfield, and Redesham, Suff., and of Gelderton, Norf., a cubit arm erect grasping a scimitar embrued, all ppr., pommel and hilt or. *Goddes grace governe Garneys.—Flectar non frangar.* 213. 5

Garnham, a goat's head erased sa., armed or. 128. 5

Garnier, Carpenter- of Mount Tavy, Devonsh., in front of a lion's head erased az., gorged with an oak-wreath or, three fleurs-de-lis of the last. cf. 17. 10

Garnier of London and Hants, a lion's head erased arg. 17. 8

Garnier, a griffin's head gu., between two wings arg., charged with a torteau. cf. 65. 11

Garnock, Viscount, *see* Lindsay, Earl.

Garnock, Scotland, a greyhound current. cf. 58. 2

Garnon, Sussex, a wolf's head or, collared gu. 30. 9

Garnons, Wales, a demi-lion rampant sa., ducally crowned and gorged or. *Nid Cyfoeth, ond Boddlondeb.* cf. 10. 11

Garnstone, *see* Garmston.

Garnyl, *see* Garnish, Suff.

Garnyl, a mermaid ppr. 184. 5

Garon, a cross crosslet fitched gu. 166. 2

Garrard of London, Kent, and Bucks, a leopard sejant ppr. cf. 24. 13

Garrard, Drake-, of Lamer, Herts: (1) A leopard sejant ppr. cf. 24. 13. (2) A naked dexter arm erect, holding a battle-axe sa., headed arg. 213. 12

Garrard, Cherry- of Denford, Hungerford, Berks: (1) Same crest as (1) above. (2) A demi-lion arg., the neck encircled with an annulet, and holding between the paws a fleur-de-lis within an annulet, all gu. *Cheris l'espoir.*

Garrard of Fellingham, Norf., an heraldic tiger sejant arg., maned and tufted sa., resting the dexter paw on a tun or.

Garrard of Shinfield, Berks, out of a ducal coronet a demi-lion rampant az. 16. 3

Garrard of London, a wyvern, its tail nowed ppr., pierced through the neck by a spear or, headed arg.

Garrat and **Garratt,** a hind sejant regardant, resting her dexter foot on a bee-hive ppr. 125. 1

Garratt of London and Surrey, a lion passant ermines, resting the dexter paw on a fleur-de-lis or. 5. 5

Garratt, Job, Esquire, of Wassell Grove, Stourbridge, a pear fesseways, stalked, leaved, and slipped thereon a rock ppr., holding in the beak a feather sa. *Gradatim.*

Garraway, an escallop between two wings. 141. 10

Garret, a demi-monk holding in his dexter hand a lash. 187. 11

Garrett, Ireland, a lion passant resting the sinister paw upon a trefoil. *Semper fidelis.* cf. 6. 2

Garrett, Frank, Esquire, of Leiston Works, Leiston, and Aldringham House, Aldringham, the sun rising in splendour, the rays alternately or, arg., and sa.

Garrick, Middx., a mullet or. 164. 2
Garrioch, *see* Garioch.
Garrioch, Scotland, on a mount a tree. *Concussus surgit.* 143. 14
Garrioch and **Garrock,** Scotland, a salmon haurient. 139. 11
Garrod, Sir Alfred, of 10, Harley Street, W., in front of a tilting-spear erect ppr., a boar sa., resting the dexter leg on a quatrefoil or. *Altiora spero.*
Garrow, Sussex, on a mount vert, a palm-tree ppr., charged with three torteaux, two and one. *cf.* 144. 3
Garroway, Sussex and Herts, a griffin passant or. 63. 2
Garroway of Netherfield, Lanarksh., a griffin passant or. *Aut vincere, aut mori.* 63. 2
Garroway, Surrey, on a rock a Cornish chough ppr., beaked and legged gu. 106. 9
Garscadden, a hand holding a buckle ppr. 223. 11
Garsett and **Garsed,** Norf., a bow erect gu., stringed sa., with an arrow or, headed az., feathered arg.
Garshore, Scotland, an eagle displayed ppr. 75. 2
Garside, two daggers in saltier ppr. 169. 8
Garstin, John Ribton, Esquire, M.A., J.P., D.L., F.S.A., of Braganstown, Castle Bellingham, co. Louth, out of a ducal coronet or, a dexter arm in armour embowed, holding in the hand a dagger, all ppr., the arm charged with a fleur-de-lis gu. *Gladio et virtute.* *cf.* 196. 5
Garstin, Ireland, a hand holding a dagger. *Gladio et virtute.* 212. 9
Garstin, a dexter hand holding a broken hammer. 221. 13
Garston, on the stump of a tree eradicated, a raven with wings expanded, all or.
Garston, out of a mural coronet arg., a wyvern or, charged on the breast with a fire-ball sa.
Gartside-Spaight, Cavendish Walter, Esquire, of Derry Castle, Killaloe, co. Clare, a jay ppr. *Vi et virtute.*
Gartside-Tipping, Henry Thomas, Esquire, of Quarr Wood, Binstead, Isle of Wight: (1) An heraldic antelope's head erased, gorged with a ducal coronet. (2) A greyhound passant. *Fidelitur vive ut vivas.*
Gartsyde, Yorks, a stag per pale gu. and sa., attired and unguled or. 117. 5
Garter, a caltrap or, embrued on the upper point ppr. 174. 14
Garter, a caltrap per pale gu. and or. *cf.* 174. 14
Garth, a goat passant arg., collared and chained or. *cf.* 129. 5
Garth, Surrey, an Indian goat arg., attired, eared, collared, and lined or.
Garthside, out of a ducal coronet or, a cross pattée az.
Garton, a leopard's face. 22. 2
Garton, Sussex, a leopard's head erased or, ducally gorged gu., on the head two straight horns of the last.
Garton, an antelope's head erased gu., ducally gorged or *cf.* 126. 2
Gartshore and **Garthshore,** Scotland, an eagle displayed ppr. *I renew my age.* 75. 2

Gartside, two daggers in saltier ppr. 169. 8
Gartside, Lancs, a greyhound statant arg. *Vincit qui patitur.* *cf.* 60. 2
Garvagh, Baron (Canning), of Garvagh, co. Londonderry: (1) A demi-lion rampant, holding in the dexter paw a battle-axe. (2) A demi-griffin segreant. (3) A demi-lion rampant arg., charged with three trefoils slipped vert, holding in his dexter paw an arrow pointing downwards or, feathered arg. *Ne cede malis sed contra.* *cf.* 1. 13
Garvey, Ireland, a greyhound's head az., collared arg. 61. 2
Garvey, John W. F., Esquire, of Ballina, co. Mayo, Ireland, a lion passant gardant gu. *Morior invictus.* 4. 3
Garvie, Scotland, a dexter hand pointing with two fingers gu. 222. 11
Garvin, Scotland, a dexter hand holding a dagger in pale, point downwards ppr. *cf.* 213. 6
Garvine, Scotland, a hand holding a fish ppr. *Always helping.* 220. 4
Garway, a leopard's head erased, thrust through the neck by an arrow in fess ppr. *cf.* 23. 10
Garwinton, a vine-branch fructed and leaved ppr. 152. 9
Gascelyn, an arm holding in the hand a broken sword arg., hilted or.
Gascoign, out of a ducal coronet an alligator's head ppr. 138. 7
Gascoigne-Cecil, Marquess of Salisbury, *see* Salisbury.
Gascoigne, Yorks and Norf., out of a ducal coronet a demi-lucy erect or. *cf.* 139. 14
Gascoigne of Parlington, Yorks, and Norf., out of a ducal coronet a demi-lucy erect or, charged with a pellet.
Gascoigne, Rev. W. B., Little Carlton Rectory, Louth, out of a ducal coronet or, a demi-luce erect of the same. *Justus et tenax.*
Gascoigne, Trench-, Frederick Charles, Parlington Park, Aberford, Yorks: (1) A conger's head couped and erect or, charged for distinction with a pellet (*for Gascoigne*). (2) Trench.
Gascoyne, Beds, a lucy's head erect or, between two ostrich-feathers arg. 138. 12
Gaselee, an arm in armour embowed, holding in the hand ppr. a dagger arg., hilt and pommel or. 196. 5
Gaskell, Yorks, a stork ppr., collared or, pendent therefrom an escutcheon az., charged with an annulet or, the dexter foot resting on an escallop gu.
Gaskell, Milnes-, Charles George, Esquire, of Thornes House, Yorks, and Wenlock Abbey, Shropsh.: (1) A stork sa., gorged with a collar or, therefrom pendant an escutcheon az., charged with an annulet or, and resting the dexter claw upon an escallop gu. (*for Gaskell*). (2) A garb or, banded by a fesse dancettée az., charged with three mullets pierced or (*for Milnes*). *Scio cui credidi.* 152. 10
Gaskell, Milnes-, Gerald, Esquire, J.P., D.L., of Lupset Hall, Wakefield, same crest and motto.
Gaskell, Captain Henry Brooks, of Kiddington Hall, Oxon., and Beaumont Hall, Lancs, an anchor in bend sinister entwined by a cable and surmounted by a rainbow, all ppr. *Spes.*

Gaskell, on a mount vert, under an oak-tree ppr., a greyhound couchant sa., collared or, resting the dexter paw on an escutcheon or, charged with a fleur-de-lis az.
Gaskin of London, issuing from the sea an arm embowed, holding in the hand an anchor ppr. *Spes anchora vitæ.* 202. 7
Gason, Kent, on a chapeau az., turned up erm., a goat's head couped arg., bearded and armed or. *cf.* 128. 12
Gason, Kent, a goat's head couped arg., armed or, gorged with three mascles sa. *cf.* 128. 12
Gason, Kent, out of a ducal coronet az., a goat's head couped arg. 128. 14
Gasselyn and **Gasselyne,** an eagle displayed sa. 75. 2
Gasselyn or **Gasselyne,** *see* Gascelyn.
Gaston, an owl sa. 96. 5
Gastrell, Glouc., a lion's head erased ppr., gorged with a chaplet vert. 17. 10
Gatacre, Major-General Sir William Forbes, K.C.B., C.B., D.S.O., of Hazel Mill, Stroud, a raven ppr. *Hic eram in dierum sæculis.* 107. 14
Gataere, Edward Lloyd, of Gatacre, Bridgnorth, Shropsh., same crest and motto.
Gatacre, Major-General John, same crest and motto.
Gatchell, Somers., out of a mural coronet arg., a dexter arm embowed, vested az., cuffed erm., holding in the hand a chaplet of wheat ppr.
Gateford, a demi-antelope ppr., collared or. 126. 3
Gatehouse, George, Esquire, of Bognor Lodge, Bognor, Sussex, in front of two keys saltirewise az., a portcullis arg. *Quæ serata secura.*
Gates, Essex, Yorks, and Lincs, a demi-lion rampant gardant or. 10. 8
Gates, Percy, 5, Monson Place, Queen's Gate, S.W., a stag lodged ppr.
Gates, Devonsh., out of a crescent flames issuant ppr. 163. 12
Gatesden, a dexter arm embowed, vested gu., cuffed arg., and holding a tilting-spear ppr.
Gatfield, on a ducal coronet or, a cross gu.
Gathwaite, a mastiff ppr., chained and collared or.
Gatonby, two swords in saltier ppr. 171. 12
Gattie and **Gatty,** a stork ppr., holding in its dexter claw a stone. 105. 6
Gatty, *see* Scott-Gatty.
Gatty, a pheasant rising ppr. *cf.* 90. 13
Gatty, Hon. Stephen Herbert, Chief Justice of Gibraltar, a fern brake, and rising therefrom a cock-pheasant, all ppr. *Cute at caute.* 290. 8
Gatty, an embattled gateway, thereon a cock-pheasant rising, all ppr. *Non cute sed caute.* 90. 13
Gauden, a peacock's head ppr. 103. 2
Gaudine, Scotland, a savage's head couped ppr. 190. 12
Gauldesborough, Essex, a pelican vulning herself ppr. 98. 1
Gauler, a hawk holding in its dexter claw an ear of wheat ppr. 85. 7
Gaulfield, a dexter hand vested, holding up the sun or. *cf.* 209. 2

Gaunt, Kent and Staffs, a wolf's head or, collared vair. *Dum spiro, spero.* 30. 9

Gaunt, De, a cross pattée fitched sa. 166. 3

Gauntlet, out of a ducal coronet a bear's head muzzled, all ppr. 34. 3

Gaury, a lion passant arg., armed and crowned or. *Recta ubique.* cf. 6. 2

Gausen and **Gaussen,** a bee-hive with bees volant, all ppr. 137. 7

Gaussen, a greyhound's head arg., eared and spotted sa. cf. 61. 2

Gavell, Surrey, a demi-buck regardant or, vulned in the shoulder gu.

Gaven and **Gawen,** a dexter hand holding up a ducal coronet capped between two laurel-branches, all ppr. 217. 3

Gaven, a land tortoise ppr. cf. 125. 5

Gavin, Scotland, a ship in full sail ppr. *Remember.* 160. 13

Gavin, Scotland, in the sea a two-masted ship in full sail ppr. *By industry we prosper.* cf. 160. 13

Gawaine and **Gawayne,** a horse-shoe or. 158. 6

Gawden, an arm in a maunch gu., the hand clenched ppr. 203. 3

Gawdy, Norf. and Suff., on a chapeau gu., turned up erm., two swords erect arg., hilts and pommels or.

Gawdy, Norf., a wolf passant per pale arg. and gu. 28. 10

Gawer, out of a ducal coronet or, a bear's head erect sa., between two ostrich-feathers arg. cf. 41. 14

Gawler, *see* Gauler.

Gawler, a hawk holding in the dexter claw an ear of wheat, all ppr. 85. 7

Gawsworth, a savage's head in profile ppr. 191. 1

Gawthern, Notts, out of a mural coronet or, a wyvern's head sa. 72. 11

Gay, Somers., a greyhound current ppr. *Stat fortuna domus.* cf. 58. 2

Gay, a demi-greyhound ppr. 60. 11

Gay, Kent, a demi-greyhound rampant sa., collared or. 60. 8

Gay, a hand ppr., holding a sword arg., hilt and pommel or. 212. 13

Gay, Norf., a fleur-de-lis or. 148. 2

Gay, James, of Alborough New Hall, Norf., a fleur-de-lis or. *Toujours gai.*

Gay, James, Thurning Hall, East Dereham, Norf., same crest and motto.

Gay, Devonsh., on a chapeau gu., turned up erm., a lion passant gardant or, charged on the breast with an escallop az. cf. 4. 5

Gay, John, Esquire, of 119, Upper Richmond Road, Putney, same crest.

Gay, in front of a fig-tree ppr., a falcon arg., belled or, supporting with the dexter claw an arrow point downwards, also ppr., and charged on its breast with an escallop az. *Gwyr yn erbyn y byd.* 86. 10

Gayer, a lion rampant sa., supporting a spear. cf. 1. 13

Gayford of West Wretham, Norf., a goat's head erased arg., armed or. 128. 5

Gaylard of London, a dexter hand apaumée ppr. *Munifice et fortiter.* 222. 14

Gaylien, a hind's head between two roses, stalked and leaved ppr. 124. 4

Gayner and **Gaynor,** a dexter hand apaumée ppr. 222. 14

Gaynes, out of a ducal coronet a demi-swan with wings expanded ppr., ducally gorged sa.

Gaynor, Ireland, a lion's head erased gu., charged with a trefoil or. cf. 17. 8

Gaynsford and **Gaynsforth,** a rose gu., slipped and leaved vert, and a spear ppr., in saltier. 150. 1

Gaynsford of Idbury, Oxon., a demi-woman vested and crined or, holding in the dexter hand a garland vert charged with four roses gu. cf. 183. 5

Gaynsford, Surrey, a demi-maiden couped below the waist, habited gu., crined or, holding in the dexter hand a wreath vert, and in her sinister a rose-branch ppr. cf. 183. 5

Gays, an eagle with two heads displayed ppr. 74. 2

Gayton, three legs in armour conjoined at the thigh, flexed at the knee, and spurred ppr. 193. 7

Geach, an arm embowed holding in the hand a battle-axe, enfiled with a garland round the elbow, all ppr. cf. 201. 5

Gealagh of Nantes, France, and of Ireland, a naked arm embowed holding a sword, all ppr. *Hæc manus pro patria pugnando vulnera passa.* 201. 4

Geale-Brady, *see* Brady.

Geale, Ireland, out of a ducal coronet or, a hand holding a fleur-de-lis ppr. 215. 2

Geale-Wybrants, William, Esquire, of the City of Dublin: (1) A stag's head erased ppr., charged with a bezant (*for Wybrants*). cf. 121. 2. (2) A unicorn's head erased or, charged with an anchor erect sa. (*for Geale*). *Fortis in arduis.* cf. 49. 5

Gear and **Geare,** Kent and Devonsh., a leopard's head az., ducally gorged or, between two wings gu.

Geary, Sir William Nevill Montgomery, Bart., of Oxon Hoath, Kent, out of a naval crown or, a dexter arm embowed, habited az., cuffed arg., supporting a flagstaff, therefrom flowing to the sinister a banner of the third, charged with a cross couped gu. *Chase.*

Geary, Surrey, a heraldic antelope's head erased quarterly arg. and sa., charged with a lozenge erm.

Geary, Herts, an antelope's head erased quarterly arg. and sa., charged with three mascles, two and one counter-changed. cf. 126. 2

Geary-Salte, a demi-lion per pale or and sa., charged on the shoulder with two mullets in fesse counterchanged. cf. 10. 2

Ged and **Gedd,** Scotland, a pike's head ppr.

Ged, Scotland, a hand ppr., holding up an escutcheon gu. cf. 219. 7

Geddes and **Geddies,** Scotland, a pike's head couped ppr. *Durat, ditat, placet.*

Geddes and **Geddies,** Scotland, a stag's head couped ppr. *Fato prudentia major.* 121. 5

Geddes and **Geddies,** Scotland, a stag's head. *Veritas vincit.* 121. 5

Geddes and **Geddies,** Scotland, on a mural coronet a bundle of seven arrows banded.

Gedding and **Geding,** a demi-savage holding a scimitar ppr. 186. 3

Gedeney, *see* Gedney.

Gedney, a bird perched on an oak-plant ppr. 107. 10

Gedney, Lincs, two lucies in saltire arg.

Gee, *see* Pearson-Gee.

Gee, a gauntlet erect arg., garnished at the wrist or, holding a sword of the first, hilt and pommel of the second.

Geekie of London, a dexter hand holding a sickle ppr. 219. 13

Geering, Sussex, a savage's head affrontée, ducally crowned ppr. 192. 9

Geff of Huborne, Berks, on a chapeau gu., turned up erm., a tiger couchant arg., tufted and maned sa., armed or, and charged on the body with a martlet of the fourth.

Geffery of London, a lion's head erased or, billettée sa. cf. 17. 8

Geffry, a lion's head erased arg., ducally crowned or. 18. 8

Geffrys, Worcs., on a mount vert, a sea-pie rising ppr., beaked and legged gu.

Geike, Scotland, a boar's head erased sa. *Vigilo.* 42. 2

Geils, a demi-chevalier holding in his dexter hand a sword. 187. 1

Geldart, Cambs, a demi-lion rampant regardant or, crowned of the same, and holding an oak-branch ppr.

Gell, Sir James, C.V.O., Clerk of the Rolls of the Isle of Man, of Castletown, Isle of Man, a stag's head caboshed. *Shee ec y jerrey* (Manx: *Peace at the last*). 122. 5

Gell, Henry Willingham, Esquire, of 36, Hyde Park Square, London, W., a greyhound trippant pean, about the neck a collar arg., and thereon a rose between two mullets of six points gu. *Vocatus obedivi.* 230. 14

Gell, Philip Lyttelton, Esquire, J.P., of Hopton Hall, and of Kirk Langley, Derbysh., and Langley Lodge, near Oxford, same crest and motto.

Gell, Derbysh., a greyhound's head collared or. 61. 2

Gell of Hopton, Derbysh., a greyhound statant sa., collared or. cf. 60. 2

Gellatly, Peter, of Loughton, Essex, a lion's head erased gu., armed and langued az., crowned with an antique crown or. *Hactenus invictus.* cf. 17. 12

Gellatly, Edward, of Uplands, Sydenham Hill, London, S.E., a lion's head erased gu., armed and langued az., crowned with an antique crown or. *Hactenus invictus.* cf. 17. 12

Gellibrand of Hobart, Tasmania, out of a ducal coronet a stag's head and neck affrontée. *Retinens vestigia famæ.* 119. 13

Gellie or **Gelly,** Scotland, a man standing on a serpent ppr. *Divino robore.* 188. 3

Gelling, on a chapeau a lion passant gardant, the tail extended and ducally crowned, all ppr. cf. 4. 4

Gelstable, a dexter hand holding a sword in pale, all ppr. 212. 9

Gem, a dexter hand holding a gem-ring ppr., stoned gu.

Gemell, Gemill, and **Gemmell,** a flame of fire between two palm-branches, all ppr. 146. 12

Gemell, Gemill, and **Gemmell,** a demi-peacock ppr. 103. 10

Gemmel, Scotland: (1) A dexter arm holding in the hand a dart. 214. 4. (2) A laurel-branch and a sword in saltier ppr.

Geneville, out of a cloud a dexter hand holding a broken tilting-spear, all ppr. *cf.* 214. 10

Geney or **Genny,** out of a cloud a hand issuing in fess holding a cross patée fitched. 223. 6

Genn, between two spear-heads in pale, a Cornish chough rising, all ppr. 108. 7

Gennett, a chevalier on horseback wielding a scimitar, all ppr. 189. 10

Gennys, an eagle per pale az. and gu. with wings raised, each charged with a bezant, and from the beak a scroll arg., thereon the words, *Deo gloria.* 78. 3

Gennys, Henn-, John Croad, Esquire, of Whitleigh, Devonsh.: (1) An eagle per pale az. and gu., the wings elevated, each charged with a bezant, from the beak an escroll arg., thereon the words, *Deo gloria* (*for Gennys*). 78. 3. (2) A hen-pheasant ppr. (*for Henn*).

Genor, a dexter hand holding a baton gu., tipped or.

Gent of Norton and Muscott, Northumb., a demi-griffin gu., with wings addorsed or, holding a gilliflower of the first, stalked and leaved vert. *cf.* 64. 2

Gent, Essex, out of a ducal coronet or, a demi-eagle displayed erm. 80. 14

Gent, out of a ducal coronet a phœnix or, in flames ppr. 82. 5

Gent-Wood, A'Deane, 6, Gordon Road, Clifton, a branch of oak, fructed and leaved all ppr. *Diu virescit.*

Gentill, Scotland, two lion's gambs holding a bezant. *cf.* 39. 4

Gentle, Scotland, a bee erect ppr. *Industria.* 137. 2

Gentle, on a ducal coronet or, an étoile of twelve points. *cf.* 164. 4

Gentleman, Robert George, Esquire, of Ballyhorgan and of Mount Coal, co. Kerry, Ireland, a demi-eagle displayed with two heads sa., on each wing a trefoil or. *Truth, honour, and courtesy.* 230. 12

Geogham, an arm in armour embowed holding in the hand a dagger. *Manu forti.* 196. 5

Geoghegan, England and Ireland, on a ducal coronet or, a dolphin naiant az. 140. 4

Geoghegan, Ireland, a greyhound passant arg., collared vert, the collar studded with fleurs-de-lis or.

George, Ireland, a stag's head erased ppr. 121. 2

George, Scotland, the sun shining on a sunflower ppr.

George, Bart., Middx., a falcon rising az., beaked, legged, and belled or. 87. 1

George, Georges, and **Gorges** of London and Middx., a greyhound's head ppr. *cf.* 61. 2

George or **Georges** of Baunton, Glouc., a demi-talbot salient sa., collared and eared or. *cf.* 55. 8

George, Robert, Esquire, of Ballyhorgan, near Listowel, a demi-eagle displayed with two heads sa., on each wing a trefoil or. *Truth, honour, and courtesy.*

George of Trenouth, Cornw., a demi-talbot sa., collared, indented, and eared or, between two fir-branches vert. 57. 2

George, Frederic Brand, Esquire, of Wells, Somers., a demi-talbot per fesse indented sa. and gu., charged on the shoulder with a bezant, thereon a lion's head erased of the second, and resting the sinister paw on a garb vert. *Strive to attain.* 230. 9

George, John Daniel, Esquire, of Norfolk House, Norfolk Crescent, Bath, same crest and motto.

George, William Edwards, Esquire, of Downside, Stoke Bishop, Bristol, a demi-talbot rampant sa., eared and collared, indented or, between two fir-branches vert. *Magna est veritas et prevalebit.* 57. 2

Georges of the Island of St. Christopher, a boar passant az., armed and bristled or. 40. 9

Gepp, a griffin's head, collared, between two wings. 67. 7

Gepp, Somers. and Essex, on a mount vert an eagle rising az., the wings erminois, gorged with a collar and holding in the beak a mascle or, the dexter claw supporting a sword in pale ppr., hilt and pommel also or. 78. 6

Gerandot, a demi-lion rampant sa. 10. 1

Gerard, Baron (Gerard), of Bryn, Lancs, a lion rampant erm., ducally crowned or. *En Dieu est mon espérance.* 1. 12

Gerard, Frederick, Esquire, of Kinwarton House, Alcester, a monkey statant ppr., environed round the loins and chained arg. *En Dieu est mon espérance.*

Gerard, Berks, a lion statant gardant, ducally crowned gu. *En Dieu est mon espérance.* *cf.* 4. 1

Gerard, Middx., and of Ince, Lancs, a lion's gamb erased erm., holding a hawk's lure gu., garnished and lined or, tasselled arg.

Gerard, a lion's gamb couped erm., holding a hawk's lure gu., tasselled and garnished or.

Gerard, Major-General Sir Montagu Gilbert, of Rochsoles, Lanarksh., out of a mural crown arg., a lion's gamb erect erm., holding the "Punja," in bend sinister ppr. *Haud inferiora secutus.*

Gerard, Kent, a monkey passant, collared round the middle and chained ppr. *Bono vince malum.* 136. 8

Gerard, Lancs and Derbysh., two wings expanded sa. 109. 6

Gerard-Dicconson, Hon. Robert Joseph, of Wrightington Hall and Blackley Hurst, near Wigan: (1) A bezant charged with a hind's head vert, erased gu., and holding in the mouth a cross crosslet fitchée of the last. (2) A monkey statant ppr., environed about the middle with a plain collar and chained arg.

Gerbridge, a lion's gamb holding a thistle ppr. 37. 6

Gercom, a griffin segreant ppr., collared gu., holding in its beak a line and ring or. *cf.* 62. 2

Gerdelley and **Gerdilly,** a hand holding a sword ppr. 212. 13

Gerdon, a human heart ppr., surmounted by two hands couped and conjoined in fess. 181. 3

Gerebzoff, out of the coronet of a marquis ppr., a cross patée or, surmounted by a human heart gu., flammant ppr., between two wings sa.

Geridot, a demi-lion rampant. 10. 2

Gerling, a unicorn's head erased arg., collared sa. 49. 11

Germain, a dexter arm couped and embowed fesseways holding in the hand a tilting-spear in pale ppr. 201. 6

German, of Preston, Lancs, a demi-lamb ppr. supporting a flagstaff or, therefrom flowing a pennon arg., the ends gu., and charged with a rose, also gu. 227. 5

Germin and **Germyn,** a lion rampant az. 1. 13

Germin and **Germyn,** a unicorn's head between two branches of laurel in orle. 49. 14

Germin, Hunts, three lilies arg., stalked vert.

Germon, three lilies, each stalked and leaved ppr. *Virtus tutamen.*

Gernegan, an allerion displayed gu.

Gerney, on a garb in fess, a cock statant ppr. 91. 4

Gernon, Gernoun, or **Gernun,** a hand issuing from a cloud in fess holding a club ppr. 223. 5

Gernon, Ireland, a horse passant arg., unguled or. *Parva contemnimus.* 52. 6

Gernon, a wolf's head couped az., collared and ringed or. *cf.* 30. 9

Gernon, a wolf's head couped az., charged on the neck with two bars gemelle. *cf.* 30. 5

Gerre, Herts, a lion's head gardant or, gorged with a collar gu., charged with three mascles, also or, between two wings displayed of the same.

Gerson, Lancs, an arm in armour couped at the shoulder in fess holding a helmet in pale ppr. 198. 11

Gervais, Francis Peter, Esquire, J.P., of Cecil, co. Tyrone, Ireland, a lion's head erased arg., charged with a fleur-de-lis az. *Sic sustenta crescit.* *cf.* 17. 8

Gervays, on a mural crown gu., a fire-beacon between two wings ppr. 112. 5

Gervis, Bart., *see* Meyrick.

Gervis, Cambs and Worcs., a tiger's head erased arg.

Gervis, Essex, a demi-lion rampant gardant or, holding a banner arg., charged with a cross gu., on the handle ppr. a mural coronet of the first, and issuing therefrom four small spears az.

Gerwood, a cubit arm ppr., holding in the hand a cross crosslet fitched gu. 221. 11

Gery, Wade-, William Hugh, of Bushmead Priory, Beds, an antelope's head erased quarterly arg. and sa., charged with four mascles counterchanged, attired or. *Mentis honestæ gloria.* *cf.* 126. 2

Gessors, a talbot sejant sa., collared arg. 55. 1

Gessors, a dexter hand holding a battle-axe. 213. 12

Getham, a bustard ppr. 102. 9

Gethin, Ireland, a stag current arg., attired or. *Try.* *cf.* 118. 13

Gethin, Ireland, Wales, Essex, and Wilts, a buck sejant arg., attired or, between two wings of the first. *cf.* 116. 8

Gethin, Sir Richard Charles Percy, Bart., of Hilton, Netley, Hants, on a chapeau ppr. a stag's head erased arg., attired and ducally gorged or. *Try.* cf. 121. 2
Gettens, a sheldrake ppr.
Geynes, a griffin's head erased ppr., holding in the beak a trefoil vert. cf. 66. 2
Geynes, out of a cloud a dexter hand pointing aloft with the forefinger ppr.
Geynton and **Geyton,** the sun in splendour or, at each ray a flame of fire ppr. cf. 162. 2
Ghest, a swan's head and neck erased ppr., between two ostrich-feathers or. cf. 101. 1
Ghrimes, a talbot sejant sa., collared arg. 55. 1
Gib, Scotland, a mullet pierced or. *Spero.* 164. 5
Gib, Scotland, a spur or, between two wings gu. 111. 13
Gibant, Jersey, a tower or, masoned sa. 156. 2
Gibb, Scotland, a dagger in pale sustaining on its point a wreath of laurel ppr. 170. 1
Gibb of Pyrgo Park, Essex, and Sheerwater Court, Byfleet, Surrey, issuant from a wreath of cinquefoils vert, a stag's head or, couped gu., attired arg. 255. 6
Gibball, Ireland, a goat passant arg., armed and unguled sa. cf. 129. 5
Gibbard, an arm couped and embowed, vested and purfled at the shoulder, the part above the elbow in fess, the hand in pale, holding a palm-branch ppr. 203. 7
Gibbe, a Bengal tiger passant gardant ppr. 27. 4
Gibbens and **Gibbins,** an arm holding a fish ppr. 220. 4
Gibbes, Bart., *see* Osborne-Gibbes.
Gibbes, an arm fesseways ppr., vested arg., cuffed and purfled at the shoulder sa., from the elbow in pale, holding a palm-branch of the first. 203. 7
Gibbines and **Gibbins,** on a ducal coronet or, the attires of a stag ppr. cf. 123. 1
Gibbines and **Gibbins,** a lion rampant sa. 1. 10
Gibbings of Gibbings Grove, co. Cork, Ireland, a demi-lion rampant ppr., holding in his paws a fleur-de-lis az. cf. 13. 5
Gibbon, Kent, on a chapeau gu., turned up erm., an escarbuncle or. 164. 14
Gibbon, Kent, a demi-lion rampant gardant arg., ducally crowned or, holding between its paws an escallop of the last. cf. 13. 7
Gibbon, a stork with wings expanded ppr.
Gibbons, Sir Charles, Bart., of Stanwell Place, Middx., a lion's gamb erect and erased gu., charged with a bezant, holding a cross patée fitchée sa. *Gratior est a rege pio.* cf. 36. 9
Gibbons, Oxon., Warw., and Wales, a lion's gamb erased and erect gu., holding a cross formée fitched sa. 36. 9
Gibbons, a demi-lion rampant regardant sa., holding between its paws an escallop arg. cf. 13. 10
Gibbons, a demi-lion rampant sa., holding an escallop arg. 13. 10
Gibbons, Rev. Benjamin, of Poollands, Hartlebury, Worcs., and Waresley House, near Kidderminster, a demi-lion regardant or, gorged with a collar sa., pendent therefrom an escutcheon of the last, charged with a cross potent arg., and holding between the paws an escallop, also arg. *Fide et fortitudine.* 226. 3
Gibbons, John Skipworth, of Boddington Manor, Glouc., same crest and motto.
Gibbons, Robert Alexander, Esquire, M.D., F.R.C.S., of 29, Cadogan Place, Chelsea, London, S.W., and Val des Portes, Alderney, upon a mount vert, a demi-lion sa., holding in the dexter paw a thistle slipped and leaved ppr., and resting the sinister on an escallop or. *Nitor donec supero.* 307. 7
Gibbons, Ireland, a naked arm erect couped below the elbow, holding in the hand a salmon, all ppr. 220. 4
Gibbons, Ireland, a dexter and sinister arm in armour embowed, the hand supporting a heart inflamed ppr. cf. 194. 7
Gibbons, a morion ppr., thereon an escarbuncle or. *Fide Deo et ipse.*
Gibbs of Belmont, Somers., an arm in armour embowed ppr., garnished or, holding in the gauntlet a battle-axe arg 200. 6
Gibbs, in front of a rock a dexter arm embowed in armour, the hand in a gauntlet, all ppr., holding a battle-axe sa. *Tenax propositi.* 231. 1
Gibbs, Henry Martin, Esquire, of Barrow Court, Flax Bourton, R.S.O., Somers., same crest. *En Dios mi amparo.*
Gibbs, Antony, 16, Hyde Park Gardens, same crest and motto.
Gibbs, Henry Hucks, Esquire, of Aldenham House, near Elstree, Herts, in front of a rock a dexter arm in armour embowed, the hand in a gauntlet, all ppr., holding a battle-axe fesseways sa., the head to the sinister. *Tenax propositi.* 231. 1
Gibbs, Warw., three broken tilting-spears or, one in pale and two in saltier, enfiled with a wreath arg. and sa.
Gibbs, co. Derry, Ireland, a griffin's head erased arg., pierced through the back of the neck by an arrow or, barbed and feathered of the first. cf. 66. 2
Gibbs, John, Esquire, of the Yews, Sheffield, Yorks, same crest. *Frapper au but.* cf. 66. 2
Gibbs, Devonsh., a leopard passant gardant erm. 24. 4
Giberne, a plume of feathers. *Tien ta foi.* 115. 1
Giblett, a demi-stag holding in its mouth a cinquefoil slipped. cf. 119. 2
Gibon, out of a ducal coronet or, a lion's head couped gu., bezantée. cf. 17. 5
Gibon, a demi-wolf rampant regardant arg., collared gu. cf. 31. 5
Gibon, a lion's gamb erased gu., holding a cross patée fitched or. 36. 9
Gibson, Baron Ashbourne, *see* Ashbourne.
Gibson-Craig, *see* Craig.
Gibson, Maitland-, *see* Maitland.
Gibson, *see* Milner-Gibson-Cullum.
Gibson-Carmichael, the Rev. Sir William Henry, Bart., M.A., D.L., of Skirling, Peeblessh.: (1) A dexter arm embowed in armour, holding a broken lance in bend, the top pendent ppr. (*for Carmichael*). (2) A pelican in her piety ppr. (*for Gibson*). *Toujours prest.*—*Pandite, cœlestes portæ.* 98. 8
Gibson, a pelican in her piety ppr., gorged with a mural crown or. *Cœlestes, pandite portæ.* cf. 98. 8
Gibson, Right Hon. John George, P.C., of 38, FitzWilliam Place, Dublin, same crest and motto.
Gibson, Ireland, a stork's head sa., crowned or. 104. 7
Gibson, a stork rising ppr.
Gibson, H. C. M., Lowlands, Bungay, same crest.
Gibson, a stork close arg., holding in its beak an oak-leaf. cf. 105. 14
Gibson, a stork rising ppr., holding in its beak an olive-branch vert.
Gibson, Charles, M.D., Woodcote, 5, Beech Grove, Harrogate, a stork holding in the beak a branch of hawthorn.
Gibson, Norf., a stork arg., beaked, legged, and ducally gorged gu. cf. 105. 4
Gibson, of Saffron Walden, Essex, and Balder Grange, Yorks, on a mount vert, a stork arg., beaked, membered, and gorged with a collar gu., pendent therefrom an escutcheon az., charged with a barnacle or. *Recte et fideliter.*
Gibson, Joseph, Esquire, of Whelprigg, Kirkby Lonsdale, Westml., on a mount a stork, wings expanded, holding in the beak a holly-leaf between two holly-branches fructed ppr.
Gibson, Thomas George, Esquire, of Lesbury House, Lesbury, Northumb., a stork rising arg., between two acorns slipped and leaved, and holding in the beak an acorn slipped ppr. *Per ardua ad alta.*
Gibson, William, Esquire, J.P., of Scone, near Launceston, Tasmania, upon the trunk of a tree fesseways, eradicated and sprouting to the dexter, all ppr., a pelican, wings elevated and addorsed arg., vulned and charged on the wings with a key erect, wards to the sinister gu. *Pandite, cœlestes portæ.*
Gibson-Watt, James Miller, Esquire, of Doldowlod, Rhayader, Radnorsh.: (1) Upon a fer-de-moline fesseways or, an elephant statant ppr., charged on the body with a cross moline gold (*for Watt*). (2) Upon a key fesseways, wards downwards az., a pelican in her piety or, wings addorsed az., semée of crescents arg. *Pandite, cœlestes portæ.*—*Ingenio et labore.*
Gibson, of Dublin, an ostrich arg., beaked, legged, and ducally gorged gu. cf. 97. 2
Gibson of London, an arm in armour embowed ppr., garnished or, holding a battle-axe sa. *Ense et animo.* 200. 6
Gibson of London, Essex, Northumb., and Cumb., out of a ducal coronet or, a lion's gamb ppr., holding a club gu., spiked of the first.
Gibson-Wright, a dexter arm in armour issuing out of a cloud and grasping a scimitar ppr. *Pro rege sæpe, pro republica semper.* cf. 210. 12
Gibsone, John, Major, of Pentland, Edinburgh, a pelican in her piety ppr. *Pandite, cœlestes portæ.* 98. 14
Gibthorp or **Gibthorpe,** a naked arm embowed, holding in the hand a dagger ppr.

Giddy, a lion passant gu., holding in the dexter paw a banner az., charged with a cross or, the staff and the point ppr. 5. 13

Gideon, a cock's head erased gu. 90. 3

Gideon, a stag's head arg., ducally gorged or. *cf.* 121. 5

Gideon of London and Lincs, a stag's head erased arg., attired gu., gorged with a palisado coronet or, holding in the mouth an acorn slip fructed ppr.

Gidion of London, a hand in fess gu., supporting an anchor or, environed with clouds ppr. 223. 4

Gidley of Gidley, Devonsh., an eagle issuant or, the wings sa., bezantée.

Gidley, Devonsh., a griffin's head or, between two wings elevated sa., bezantée. *cf.* 65. 11

Gidley, Gustavus George, M.R.C.S., High Street, Cullompton, Devonsh., a dragon's head or between two wings sa., bezantée. 304. 14

Giesque, a stag salient. 117. 2

Giffard, Walter Thomas Courtenay, of Chillington, near Wolverhampton, Staffs: (1) A demi-archer ppr., bearded and couped at the knees, from the middle a short coat paly arg. and gu., at his side a quiver of arrows or, and in his hands a bow drawn to the head, and an arrow, also or. 187. 6. (2) A tiger's head couped or, spotted of various colours, affrontée, fire issuing from the mouth gu. *Prenez haleine, tirez fort.* *cf.* 23. 6

Giffard, Ireland, a sphinx gardant with wings addorsed ppr. *cf.* 182. 12

Giffard, Scotland, a deer's head couped ppr. *Spare nought.* 121. 6

Giffard, Scotland, a dexter hand holding a thistle ppr. 218. 2

Giffard, co. Wexford, a cock's head erased or. 90. 1

Gifford, Earl, *see* Tweeddale, Marquess of.

Gifford, Baron (Gifford), of St. Leonard's, Devonsh., a panther's head couped affrontée, between two branches of oak ppr. *Non sine numine.*

Gifford, Devonsh., a cock's head erased or, holding in its beak a sprig ppr. *cf.* 90. 1

Gifford, Herbert James, Esquire, Civil Engineer, Moseley Lodge, Leamington, a stag's head erased ppr., armed or. *Spare nought.* 121. 2

Gifford, Scotland, a hart's head ppr., attired or. *Spare when you have nought.* 121. 5

Gifford, Shropsh., a goat's head erased arg. 128. 5

Gifford, an arm couped at the elbow, vested or, charged with two bars wavy az., cuffed arg., holding in the hand ppr. a buck's head cabossed gu.

Gifford, Bart. (*extinct*), of Castle Jordan, co. Meath, Ireland, a cubit arm erect, vested gu., slashed and cuffed arg., the hand ppr., holding four roses of the first, seeded or, stalked and barbed vert. *Malo mori quam fœdari.* *cf.* 205. 14

Gifford, Ireland, a dexter cubit arm in armour embowed holding in the hand a gilliflower, all ppr. *Potius mori quam fœdari.*

Gigge, Suff., a lion statant sa.

Gigger, Mace-, of Reading, a cubit arm ppr., holding in the hand a cross crosslet fitchée gu., surmounted by two arrows in saltire or, points downwards, flighted and pheoned ppr. *Gratitude.* *cf.* 221. 14

Gigon, a dexter arm holding in the hand a swan's head erased ppr. 220. 9

Gilbard, a squirrel sejant gu., cracking a nut ppr. 135. 7

Gilberd, on a chapeau sa., turned up erm., a fox sejant ppr. 32. 12

Gilbert, of Tredrea, Cornw., a squirrel sejant gu., cracking a nut or. *Teg Yw Hedwch.* 135. 7

Gilbert-Davies, Carew, of Tressilick, Cornw., and Manor House, Eastbourne, Sussex, a squirrel sejant gu., charged on the shoulder with a cross crosslet or. *Teg Yw Hedwch.* *cf.* 135. 7

Gilbert, Rev. Walter Raleigh, M.A., S.C.L. Oxon., Chaplain R.N., of the Priory, Bodmin, Cornw., a squirrel sejant on a hill vert, feeding on a crop of nuts ppr. *Mallem mori quam mutare.* 135. 5

Gilbert, Devonsh., and Dr. Walter B. Gilbert, of 15, West Twenty-fifth Street, New York, U.S.A., a squirrel sejant upon a mount vert, feeding on a crop of nuts ppr. *Mallem mori quam mutare.* 153. 5

Gilbert, out of a mural coronet a griffin's head ppr. 67. 10

Gilbert, out of a ducal coronet or, a griffin's head gu., beaked of the first. 67. 9

Gilbert, Herts and Kent, a griffin's head az., beaked or, collared erm. *cf.* 67. 7

Gilbert, Derbysh. and Shropsh., out of a ducal coronet or, an eagle's head gu., beaked of the first. *cf.* 83. 14

Gilbert, Sussex and Suff., issuing out of rays or, an eagle's head ppr. 84. 13

Gilbert, Essex and Suff., on a mount vert, a demi-eagle displayed az., charged on the breast with a mullet or.

Gilbert, an eagle displayed az. 75. 2

Gilbert, out of a mural coronet or, a demi-lion rampant and ducally crowned of the first holding a battle-axe sa., headed arg. *cf.* 16. 10

Gilbert of Chedgrave Manor, Loddon, Norf., and Cringleford Lodge, near Norwich, Norf., out of a ducal coronet or, a stag's head erm., attired of the first. 120. 7

Gilbert of Hassingham, Norwich, Norf., a stag's head or, charged on the neck with a fess engrailed and plain cottised gu. *Tenax propositi.* *cf.* 121. 5

Gilbert, a greyhound passant ppr. *cf.* 60. 2

Gilbert, on a mount vert, an arm embowed in armour or, grasping a broken spear of the last headed arg.

Gilbert, Scotland, a hand holding a fleur-de-lis or. *cf.* 215. 5

Gilbert, an arm in armour embowed ppr., holding in the hand a broken tilting-spear or in bend sinister headed arg., point downwards. *cf.* 197. 2

Gilbert, Heref. and Monm., an arm in armour embowed ppr., severed below the wrist, the hand dropping, grasping a broken spear or, headed arg., point downwards.

Gilbertson, a snail in its shell ppr. 141. 8

Gilbey, Sir Walter, Bart., of Elsenham Hall, Essex, in front of a tower ppr., issuant from the battlements thereof a dragon's head gu., a fleur-de-lis or, all between two ostrich-feathers arg. *Honore et virtute.* 250. 20

Gilborne of London and Kent, a tiger salient arg., lined and collared or.

Gilby or **Gilbie,** Lincs, a tower or, a dragon's head issuing from the top, and the tail out of the door vert. *cf.* 71. 11

Gilchrist of London, out of a cloud the sun rising ppr. *I hope to speed.* 162. 5

Gilchrist, Scotland, a crescent arg. *Fide et fiducia.* 163. 2

Gilchrist, Percy Carlyle, Esquire, of Frognal Bank, Hampstead, between the attires of a stag attached to the scalp or, a crescent arg., issuant therefrom an arrow palewise, point downwards, also or. *Fide et fiducia.* (*Recorded in the College of Arms, London.*) 163. 14

Gilchrist, Scotland, a lion rampant holding in the dexter paw a scimitar, all ppr. *Mea gloria fides.* *cf.* 1. 13

Gilchrist, James, Esquire, of 3, Kingsborough Gardens, Kelvinside, Glasgow, a lion rampant arg., supporting in his fore-paws a pennoncelle ppr., the flag az., charged with a horse passant, also arg. *Mea gloria fides.* *cf.* 3. 7

Gilchrist-Clark, late John Henry, Esquire, of Speddoch, Dumfries-sh., within a serpent in circle an estoile pierced or. *Animo et scientia.*

Gildart, Lancs, a demi-lion rampant regardant or, crowned of the last, holding in the dexter paw an oak-branch ppr. *cf.* 14. 4

Gildea, a wolf's head erased ppr., langued gu. *Re e merito.*—*Vincit qui patitur.* 30. 8

Gildea, Sir James, C.V.O., C.B., 11, Hogarth Road, Earl's Court, S.W., a wolf's head erased arg. *Re e merito.*

Gildea, Rev. George Robert, M.A., Provost of the Cathedral Church of Tuam, a wolf's head erased ppr., langued gu., charged on the neck with a cross crosslet fitchée gu. *Vincit qui patitur.* *cf.* 30. 8

Gilded, George Frederick Campbell, Esquire, same crest and motto, with *Re e merito.*

Gilder, an arrow enfiled with a ducal coronet. 174. 3

Gildridge, Sussex, a sinister arm in armour embowed ppr., holding in the gauntlet a club in pale or, and above the gauntlet a dexter hand ppr., couped gu., grasping the club.

Giles of London and Worcs., out of a chalice or, three pansy-flowers ppr. *cf.* 177. 3

Giles, Charles Tyrrell, Esquire, M.P., J.P., of Copse Hill House, Wimbledon, same crest.

Giles, a squirrel sejant gu., bezantée, holding in the paws an oak-branch leaved and fructed ppr. *cf.* 135. 10

Giles, Devonsh., a lion's gamb erect and erased sa., holding an apple-branch of the last leaved vert.

Giles of Bowden, Devonsh., a lion's gamb erect and erased ppr., charged with a bar or, holding an apple-branch vert, fructed, also or.

Giles, Scotland, a demi-chevalier holding in his dexter hand a sword. 187. 1

Giles-Puller, Christopher Bernard, Esquire, of Youngsbury, near Ware, Herts: (1) In front of a mount vert, thereon a dove holding in the beak an olive-branch ppr., three escallops inverted or (*for Puller*). (2) Issuant from an annulet or, a lion's gamb erased az., charged with a cross clechée, voided, also or, holding a branch of a peach-tree leaved and fructed ppr. (*for Giles*).

Gilfillan or **Gilfillian**, Scotland and Ireland, an eagle's head erased sa., langued gu. *Armis et animis.* 83. 2

Gilford, Lord, *see* Clanwilliam, Earl.

Gilford, an angel couped at the breast ppr.

Gilham and **Gillham,** three savages' heads conjoined in one neck, one looking to the dexter, one to the sinister, and one upwards, all ppr.

Gill, David, Esquire, C.B., LL.D., F.R.S., of Blairythan, Aberdeensh., a demi-eagle rising ppr. *Sursum prorsusque.—In te, Domine, spes nostra.* 80. 2

Gill, Wallace, Major, Knaresborough, a demi-eagle rising with wings expanded and elevated or, fretty vert.

Gill, James Bruce, Esquire, of Runnymede, Casterton, co. Normanby, Victoria, and Greenvale, Dalrymple, North Kennedy District, Queensland, Australia, a demi-eagle rising ppr. 80. 2. *Sursum prorsusque* above the crest, and below the shield, *In te, Domine, spes nostra.*

Gill, Mitchell-, Andrew John, of Savock, Aberdeensh., and Auchinsouth, Elginsh.: (1) Same crest as above (*for Gill*). (2) Three blades of wheat conjoined in one stalk ppr. (*for Mitchell*). *Sapiens qui assiduus* (*for Mitchell*).

Gill, a demi-eagle arg., with wings expanded fretty az. *cf.* 80. 2

Gill, a demi-eagle rising az., the wings or, fretty vert. *cf.* 80. 2

Gill of London, a falcon's head erased az., between two wings elevated vert, fretty or. 227. 3

Gill, Herts, a hawk's head az., between two wings or, fretty vert. *cf.* 227. 3

Gill, Charles Frederick, Esquire, K.C., of Monks, Ockley, Surrey, issuant from a mural crown or, a falcon, wings expanded ppr., holding in its beak an ostrich-feather arg. *Re e merito.*

Gill, Sir David, K.C.B., of Blairythan, Aberdeensh., a demi-eagle rising ppr. *Sursum prorsusque.—In te, Domine, spes nostra.*

Gill of London, a falcon's head couped az., between two wings or. 89. 1

Gill of Eshing House, Surrey, a falcon's head couped arg., charged with three mullets palewise sa., between two wings vair. 227. 1

Gill, out of an Eastern coronet a demi-lion vert, holding a sword ppr.

Gill, a griffin's head, collared, with wings addorsed. *cf.* 67. 11

Gill of London, a salamander gu., in flames of fire ppr. 138. 4

Gill, Devonsh., a boar passant sa., resting its dexter foot on an increscent or. *In te, Domine, spes nostra.*

Gillam, a demi-griffin vert, winged and beaked or. 64. 5

Gillam, Essex, out of a ducal coronet or, a dragon's head ppr. 72. 4

Gillan and **Gilland,** a dexter arm embowed ppr., vested and cuffed az., holding in the hand a covered cup or. 203. 4

Gillanders, Scotland, a hand holding a sword ppr. *Durum sed certissimum.* 212. 13

Gillbanks, formerly of Whitefield House, Cumb., a stag's head or. *Honore et virtute.* 121. 5

Gille, *see* Gill.

Gille of London and Warw., a demi-parrot with wings expanded vert.

Gilles, a hand holding an escallop-shell, all ppr. 216. 2

Gillespie, Scotland, a unicorn's head arg., armed or. *Fidelis et in bello fortis.* 49. 7

Gillespie, David, Esquire, J.P. and D.L., of Mountquhanie, Cupar, Fife, Scotland, an anchor ppr. *Tu certá salutis anchorá.* 161. 2

Gillespie of Torbanehill, a cat sejant. *Touch not the cat, but a glove.* 25. 2

Gillespie, Scotland, a demi-cat ppr. *Touch not the cat, but a glove.* 26. 11

Gillespie-Stainton, Robert William, Esquire, of Bitteswell House, Leics., a wild cat salient ppr. *Qui me tangit pœnitebit.* *cf.* 26. 3

Gillet, a hand holding a dagger in pale pp. 212. 9

Gillet, a lion rampant holding in its dexter paw a battle-axe ppr.

Gillett, *alias* **Chandler,** of Ipswich, Suff., and Broadfield, Norf., a lucy's head erased and erect gu., collared with a bar gemelle or. 139. 3

Gillett, Rear-Admiral Arthur Woodall, of Waltham House, West Cowes, Isle of Wight, same crest. *Spes mea in Deo.*

Gilliat, John Saunders, Esquire, of 18, Princes Gate, London, S.W., on a mount vert, in front of a garb or, two fronds of fern in saltire ppr.

Gillies of Kintrocket, a gray cat passant ppr. *Touch not the cat bot a glove.* 26. 4

Gillies and **Gillis,** Scotland, a cat current ppr. *Touch not the cat, bot a glove.* *cf.* 26. 6

Gillingham, a dexter arm couped and embowed fesseways ppr., vested sa., cuffed arg., holding a sword in pale entiled with a leopard's face ppr. 204. 4

Gilliot, a garb or. 153. 2

Gillis, Scotland, a cat courant ppr. *Touch not the cat, but a glove.* *cf.* 26. 6

Gillman, *see* Gilman.

Gillman, Major Bennett Watkins, of the Retreat, Clonakilty, co. Cork, Ireland, a griffin's head erased sa., charged with an annulet or, and holding in the beak a bear's paw of the last. *Non cantu sed actu.* 226. 12

Gillman, John St. Leger, Esquire, J.P., of the Retreat, Clonakilty, co. Cork, a griffin's head erased sa., charged with an annulet or, holding in the beak a bear's paw of the last. *Non cantu sed actu.*

Gillon, Henry, Esquire, of Wallhouse, Bathgate, Linlithgowsh., on the face of a rock a raven ppr. *Tutum refugium.* 106. 9

Gillon, a dexter hand holding up a bomb fired ppr. 216. 6

Gillot, a garb or. 153. 2

Gillow, a horse passant sa., saddled and bridled gu. *Alis et animo.* 52. 4

Gillson, a leopard's head erased erm., ducally gorged az. *cf.* 23. 2

Gillum of Middleton Hall, Northumb., a dolphin haurient ppr. 140. 11

Gilly of Hawkdon, Suff., a demi-griffin segreant with wings erect arg., holding in the dexter paw a saltire or. *Ab aquila.* *cf.* 64. 2

Gilman, Norf., on a chapeau gu., turned up erm., a demi-lion rampant arg. 15. 14

Gilman, Herbert Francis Webb, Esquire, an eagle's head sa., holding in the beak gu. a brand sa., fired ppr. *Non cantu sed actu.*

Gilman, Thomas Herbert, Esquire, same crest and motto.

Gilman, Sir Charles Rackham, of Stafford House, Eaton, Norwich, issuing from a cap of maintenance gu., turned up erm., a demi-lion rampant or. *Esperance.*

Gilman, Kent, a man's leg couped at the thigh in pale sa., issuing out of rays or, the foot in chief. 193. 6

Gilman, Ireland, a Bengal tiger sejant ppr. 27. 6

Gilmer, Sussex, a unicorn's head arg., couped gu., attired or. 49. 7

Gilmer and **Gilmour,** Scotland, a dexter hand holding a scroll of paper within a garland of laurel ppr. *Nil penna sed usus.* 215. 3

Gilmore and **Gilmour,** Scotland, a dexter arm embowed vested gu., brandishing a sword ppr. 204. 1

Gilmore and **Gilmour,** Scotland, a dexter arm from the shoulder vested az., brandishing a sword ppr. 204. 1

Gilmour, *see* Gordon-Gilmour.

Gilmour, Allan, Esquire, of Eaglesham, Renfrewsh., Scotland, a dexter hand fesseways couped holding a writing-pen ppr. *Nil penna sed usus.* 307. 8

Gilmour, Sir John, Bart., of Lundin and Montrave, Fifesh., and of South Walton, Renfrewsh., a dexter hand fesseways couped holding a writing-pen ppr. *Nil penna sed usus.* 307. 8

Gilmour, Gordon-, Major Robert Gordon, 104, Eaton Square, S.W. (1) Between two branches a cubit arm grasping a roll, all ppr. (2) Out of a crest coronet a stag's head affrontée ppr. *Nil penna sed usus.—Bydand.*

Gilmour of Craigmillar, Scotland, a garland of laurel ppr. *Perseverantidabitur.* 146. 5

Gilmour of Townsend, Lanarksh., an old Gothic church window ppr. *In limine ambulo.*

Gilpin, *see* Brown-Gilpin.

Gilpin, Westml. and Cumb., a pine-branch vert.

Gilpin, an arm in armour embowed ppr., holding in the hand ppr. a laurel-sprig vert.

Gilpin, out of a ducal coronet or, a swan with wings expanded ppr., collared and lined. 99. 5

Gilpin of Bungay, Suff., three halberds, two in saltire and one in pale ppr., bound with a ribbon; thereon the word "*Foy.*"

Gilpin, three spears or, bound with a ribbon, thereon the word "*Foy.*" *Une joy mesme.*

Gilpin, Bart. (*extinct*), of Hockliffe Grange, Beds, in front of three tilting-spears, points upwards, one in pale and two in saltire ppr., as many mascles interlaced fessewise or. 227. 12

Gilpin of Hockliffe Grange, Leighton Buzzard, and Halverstown House, co. Kildare, in front of three tilting-spears, points upwards, one in pale and two in saltire ppr., as many mascles interlaced fesseways or. *Une joy mesme.* 227. 12

Gilpin Brown, George Thomas, Esquire, of Sedbery Park, Richmond, Yorks, and Scar House, Arkengarthdale, Richmond, Yorks, a lion's gamb erased arg., armed and charged with a bar gemel gu., the paw holding two eagle's wings conjoined sa. *Dictis factisque simplex.*

Gilpin-Brown, William Dundas, Esquire, of Shilston House, Leamington, same crest and motto.

Gilroy, James, Esquire, M.B., C.M. (Glasg.), of Waterbeck, Ecclefechan, Dumfriessh., a winged heart in flames ppr., the wings or. *Ad finem fidelis.* 110. 6

Gilsland, a dexter arm ppr., vested arg., cuffed az., holding up a caltrap of the first. *cf.* 206. 14

Gilson, *see* Gillson.

Gilstrap of Northgate, Newark-on-Trent, Notts, upon a rock a cubit arm erect in armour ppr., grasping an escutcheon gu., charged with a caltrap arg. (2) A mail arm embowed grasping a Turkish scimitar ppr. (*for MacRae*). *Candide secure.*—*Fortitudine.*—*Nec curo nec curo.*

Gimber, a bear's head erased, muzzled. 35. 2

Ginger, a savage's head affrontée ppr., between two laurel-branches vert. 101. 13

Ginkell, De, Earl of Athlone, *see* Athlone.

Gipp, Suff., out of a ducal coronet or, two wings expanded az., semée of estoiles of the first. *cf.* 109. 8

Gipps, issuing out of a cloud a dexter hand holding a garb, all ppr. 218. 3

Gipps, General Sir Reginald, G.C.B., of the Sycamore House, Farnborough, Hants., out of a mural coronet or, two wings elevated az., each charged with three estoiles in pale of the first.

Girandot, Jersey, a lion rampant sa. *Nil desperandum.* 1. 10

Girdler, a hand plucking a rose ppr. 218. 13

Girdlestone of Chester Terrace, Regent's Park, London, a griffin's head erased az., gorged with a collar dancettée or, thereon three crosses patée gu., and holding in the beak two arrows in saltire, the pheons downwards of the second. 226. 10

Girdwood, Scotland, a cock's head between two wings.

Girflet, an arm in armour embowed fesseways ppr., bound round the shoulder with a sash gu., holding a club sa., spiked or. 199. 3

Girle, a garb or. 153. 2

Girling, Norf., a demi-griffin az., holding between the claws a fleur-de-lis gu. *cf.* 64. 2

Girling, Norf., on a ducal coronet or, a wolf's head erased arg. *cf.* 30. 8

Girlington, Lancs and Yorks, a demi-griffin with wings addorsed or, holding a bezant. *cf.* 64. 2

Giron, a horse ppr. 52. 5

Girvan of Achairne, Scotland, a dove holding in her beak an olive-branch ppr. *Home.* 5 92.

Gisborne, Staffs, out of a mural coronet arg., a demi-lion rampant erm. gorged with a collar dove-tailed or.

Gisborne, Hon. William, J.P., of Allestree Hall, Derby, Lingen, Brampton Bryan, Heref., same crest.

Gisborne, Matthew Babington, Esquire, same crest.

Gisborne, Hartley, Esquire, of P.O. Box 405, Qu'Appelle Station, same crest. *Labor omnia vincit.*

Gisborne, Ireland, a horse's head az., bridled gu. 51. 5

Gise, a dexter hand couped in fess, holding a rose stalked and leaved, all ppr.

Gisland, a lion's head ppr. 21. 1

Gissing and **Gissinge,** an arm in armour brandishing a sword, all ppr. 210. 2

Gist and **Gest,** a swan's head and neck erased, between two ostrich-feathers, all arg. *cf.* 101. 1

Gist, Samuel, Wormington Grange, Glouc., a swan's head and neck erased erm., collared gu., between two palm-branches vert. *Benigno numine.*

Given, John, Aigburth Lodge, Liverpool, a sword in pale ppr., supporting on the point a mullet arg. *Depechez.*

Given, John Cecil Mackmurdo, M.D., Farloe, Mossley Hill, Liverpool, same crest and motto.

Gladdish of Gravesend, a mount vert, thereon an eagle rising regardant or, holding in the beak and the dexter claw a tilting-spear in bend sinister sa. 227. 4

Gladhill, England and Scotland, a demi-lion sa., holding a mullet or. 15. 7

Glading, Sussex, a unicorn's head. *Nil time.* 49. 7

Gladstanes or **Glaidstanes,** Scotland, a demi-griffin holding in its dexter claw a sword, all ppr. *Fide et virtute.* 64. 6

Gladstone, Sir John Robert, Bart., D.L., of Fasque and Balfour, Kincardinesh., issuant from a wreath of holly ppr., a demi-griffin sa., supporting between the claws a sword, the blade entiled by a bonnet of oak, also ppr. *Fide et virtute.* 64. 8

Gladstone, Walter Longueville, Esquire, of Court Hey, Broad Green, Liverpool, same crest and motto.

Gladstone, Robert, Esquire, of Woolton Vale, near Liverpool, same crest and motto.

Gladstone, the Right Hon. Herbert John, of Hawarden, Chesh., issuant from a wreath of holly vert, a demi-griffin sa., supporting between the claws a sword, the blade entiled by a bonnet of holly and bay, also vert. *Fide et virtute.* 64. 8

Gladstone, Rev. Stephen Edward, of Hawarden Rectory, Chester.

Gladwin, *see* Goodwin-Gladwin.

Gladwin, Derbysh., on a mount ppr., a lion sejant arg., guttée-de-sang, holding in its dexter paw a sword erect or.

Gladwin, Hamilton Fane, Esquire, of Seven Springs, near Cheltenham, Glouc., same crest.

Glamis, Lord, *see* Strathmore, Earl of.

Glandine, Viscount, *see* Norbury, Earl of.

Glanton, a dexter hand in armour throwing a dart, all ppr.

Glanusk, Baron, (Bailey), of Glanusk Park, Crichowell, Breconsh., a griffin sejant arg., semée of annulets gu. *Libertas.* *cf.* 62. 10

Glanvile and **Glanville,** Devonsh., on a mount vert, a stag trippant ppr. 118. 2

Glanvile and **Glanville,** Cornw., a buck trippant ppr. 117. 8

Glanvile and **Glanville,** a dexter arm, the hand clenched ppr., in a maunch or. 203. 3

Glasbrook, a demi-lion gu., ducally crowned or. 10. 11

Glasco, Ireland, a demi-lion rampant or, holding a battle-axe gu. 15.

Glascock of Felstedbury, Essex, and Wormley, Herts, an antelope's head arg., attired or, gorged with a garter sa., garnished and buckled or. *cf.* 126. 2

Glascock of Trenchfoile, Chignal, and Smealy, Essex, a dragon's head couped per pale arg. and gu., langued az. 71. 1

Glascock of Much Dunmow and Roxwell, Essex, out of a ducal coronet or, a dragon's head per pale arg. and az. 72. 4

Glascock, Essex, out of a ducal coronet or, a dragon's head per pale arg. and vert. 72. 4

Glascock of Duary and Ballyroan, Queen's Co., Ireland, a cock az., beaked, wattled, combed, and legged or, holding in the beak an annulet gu. *Vigil et audax.* *cf.* 91. 2

Glascock of Hertshobury, Essex, an antelope's head erased arg., collared sa., attired or. *cf.* 126. 2

Glascock, Essex, an antelope's head arg., attired or, gorged with a belt sa., rimmed of the second.

Glascott of Aldertown, co. Wexford, Ireland, an eagle displayed with two heads gu., armed and beaked sa. *Virtute decoratus.* 74. 2

Glascott of Killowen, Ireland, on a ducal coronet or, an eagle displayed with two heads gu., armed and beaked sa. *Virtute decoratus.* *cf.* 74. 2

Glasford, Scotland, issuing from clouds two hands conjoined grasping a caduceus ensigned with a cap of liberty, all between two cornucopiæ, all ppr. *Prisca fides.* 224. 14

Glasfurd of Borrowstounness, Scotland, a bugle-horn gu., stringed and garnished sa. *Mente et manu.* 228. 11

Glasfurd, Charles Lamont Robertson, Lieutenant-Colonel Bombay Staff Corps, a bugle-horn gu., stringed and garnished sa. 228. 11

Glasgow, Earl of (Boyle), an eagle displayed with two heads per pale embattled arg. and gu. *Dominus providebit.* 74. 2

Glasgow, Scotland, a demi-negro holding in his dexter hand a sugar-cane, all ppr. *Parcere subjectus.*

Glasgow, Robert Purdon Robertson, Montgreenan, Ayrsh., Scotland, same crest and motto.

Glasgow, Scotland, a cubit arm erect, holding in the hand an imperial crown, all ppr. *Quo fas et gloria.* 217. 1
Glasgow, Scotland, a martlet sa. *Lord, let Glasgow flourish.* 95. 5
Glasgow, Cork, an eagle rising from a rock ppr. *Dominus providebit.*
Glasier, Chesh., out of a ducal coronet gu., a dragon's head and neck between two wings displayed or. *cf.* 72. 7
Glasier and **Glazier,** a man's heart ppr., charged with a cinquefoil. 181. 1
Glass, Scotland, a mermaid with her mirror and comb ppr. *Luctor non mergor.* 184. 5
Glass, a unicorn rampant arg. 48. 2
Glasscott, an eagle displayed with two heads or. *Virtute decoratus.* 74. 2
Glasse, a demi-lion or, maned gu. 10. 2
Glastenbury, a griffin's head between two wings, each charged with three bezants. *cf.* 65. 11
Glastings, an arm in armour embowed ppr., holding a baton sa. *cf.* 200. 3
Glaston, an arm embowed holding a laurel crown ppr. 202. 4
Glastonbury, a garb ppr. 153. 2
Glazebrook, in front of a bear's head erased or, muzzled az., an eagle's leg erased fesseways of the last. 253. 23
Glazebrook, Francis Kirkland, Esquire, of Hayman's Green, West Derby, Liverpool, same crest.
Glazebrook, Frederick Edward de Twenebrokes, Esquire, same crest and motto.
Glazebrook, Hamilton, Esquire, of Hayman's Green, West Derby, Liverpool, same crest.
Glazebrook, Henry George Twanbrook, Esquire, same crest.
Glazebrook, Herbert Ernest, Esquire, same crest.
Glazebrook, James Francis Walmisley, Esquire, of Oxton, Birkenhead, same crest.
Glazebrook, Michael George, same crest.
Glazebrook, Nicholas Smith, Esquire, of Bombay, India, same crest.
Glazebrook, Philip Kirkland, Esquire, same crest.
Glazebrook, Richard Tetley, Esquire, of Bushy House, Teddington, Middx., same crest.
Glazebrook, Thomas Twanebrook, Esquire, of Palatine Club, Liverpool, same crest.
Glazebrook, William Hall, Esquire, same crest.
Glazebrook, William Rimington, Esquire, of 17, Kingsmead Road, South Birkenhead, same crest and motto.
Glazebrook, of Glazebrook, Lancs, a demi-lion rampant gu., ducally crowned or. *Dum spiro, spero.* 10. 11
Glazebrook, Lancs, a bear's head or, muzzled sa., charged on the neck with a fleur-de-lis in fess az. *Dum spiro, spero.* *cf.* 34. 14
Glazebrook, Harter Kirkland, Esquire, of Exchange Buildings, Liverpool, same crest.
Gleadow, Yorks and Shropsh., a lion's head erased az., charged on the neck with a cross patée or, between two wings of the last, each charged with a cross patée of the first. 225. 2
Gleame and **Gleane,** Norf., a Saracen's head affrontée ppr., wreathed arg., and sa. 190. 5
Gleave, Cupid with his bow and arrow ppr. 189. 7
Gledstanes, Moutray Vance, Esquire, of Fardross, Clogher, Robert Gledstanes, Esquire, Junior, his brother, and Robert Gledstanes, Esquire, Senior, of Twickenham, King's Co., Ireland: (1) A demi-griffin sa., holding a spear ppr., transfixing a savage's head couped, distilling drops of blood and wearing a bonnet composed of bay and holly leaves, all ppr. (*for Gledstanes*). (2) Out of park palings ppr., a demi-huntsman affrontée, habited gu., belt and cap sa., winding a horn or, and in an escroll above the crest the motto. *Virtutis laus actio* (*for Hornidge*).
Gledstanes, Scotland, an arm in armour embowed holding in the hand a sword ppr. 195. 2
Gledstanes of Upton, a demi-griffin holding in its dexter claw a sword. *Fide et virtute.* 64. 6
Gleg and **Glegge,** a demi-eagle with wings expanded ppr. 80. 2
Gleg and **Glegg,** Scotland, a falcon with wings expanded preying on a partridge, all ppr. *Qui potest, capere capiat.* 77. 1
Glegg, Birkenhead-, of Blackford Hall, and Irbie Hall, Chesh.: (1) A hawk with wings expanded preying on a partridge, all ppr. (*for Glegg*). 277. 1 (2) A goat salient arg., armed or, resting the fore-feet on a garb ppr. 277. 2
Glegg, Baskervyle-, John, of Old Withington and Gayton Hall, Chesh.: (1) A hawk with wings expanded preying on a partridge, all ppr. (*for Glegg*). 77. 12. (2) A forester habited vert, edged or, holding over his dexter shoulder a cross-bow of the last, and with the other hand in a leash a hound passant arg. (*for Baskervyle*). *Qui potest capere capiat.*
Gleig, Scotland, a dexter hand brandishing a sword ppr. 212. 13
Gleig, Scotland, a rose gu., seeded or, barbed vert. 149. 2
Glemham, a falcon volant arg., beaked and belled or. 88. 3
Glen and **Glenn,** a ferret collared and lined. 134. 9
Glen and **Glenn,** Scotland, a martlet sa. *Alta pete.* 95. 5
Glen and **Glenn,** an arm embowed vested sa., holding in the hand ppr. a heart gu.
Glen and **Glenn,** out of a ducal coronet a hand holding a swan's head and neck erased, all ppr. 220. 7
Glen-Coats, Sir Thomas Glen, Bart., of Ferguslie Park, Paisley, N.B.: (1) An anchor in pale ppr. *Be firm* (*for Coats*). (2) A Cornish chough sa., beaked and membered gu. *Deus alit corvos.* (*for Glen*).
Glencross, George Poole Norris, Esquire, M.A., J.P., of Luxstowe, Liskeard, Cornw., a greyhound arg., charged on the body with a cross patonce az., and resting the dexter fore-foot upon a chaplet of oak ppr., fructed or. *A cruce salus.*
Glendenning, a sword and a wheat-ear in saltier ppr. 154. 11
Glendenning and **Glendonwyn,** Scotland, on the point of a sword a maunch ppr. *Have faith in Christ.* 169. 11
Glendonyn of Glendonyn, Ayrsh., two arms dexter and sinister erect and embowed in armour ppr., grasping a cross crosslet fitched or. *In cruce glorior.*
Glendowing, on the point of a sword in pale a maunch ppr. *Have faith in Christ.* 169. 11
Gleneagles, Scotland, an eagle's head erased or. *Suffer.* 83. 2
Glenelg, Baron (Grant): (1) A burning mountain ppr. 179. 2. (2) A banyan-tree ppr. *Stand suir.—Revirescimus.*
Glenesk, Baron (Borthwick), on a staff raguly fessewise sa., a blackamoor's head in profile couped ppr. *Qui conducit.* 299. 15
Glenester, a boar passant sa., charged with a pale arg., thereon a leopard's face ppr. 227. 9
Glengall, Earl of (Butler), Ireland, out of a ducal coronet or, a plume of five ostrich-feathers arg., and therefrom a demi-falcon rising of the last. *God be my guide.*
Glenham, Suff., a hawk with wings expanded arg., beaked and legged gu., belled or. 87. 1
Glenlyon, Baron, Scotland, a demi-savage wreathed about the head and waist with oak-leaves, holding in his dexter hand a dagger, all ppr., hilt and pommel or, and in his sinister a key erect of the last. *Furth fortune, and fill the fetters.* 186. 2
Glenn, James Ferguson, Esquire, of Fairmount, Agkadowey, co. Londonderry, on a mount vert, under an oak-tree ppr., a winged lion passant or, charged on the shoulder with an estoile gu., and holding in his dexter fore-paw a battle-axe ppr. *Deus fortitudo mea et salus.* 209. 20
Glennie, Brazil, an eagle preparing to rise ppr. *Eirich as a ghleannan.*
Glennon of Tyrawley, co. Mayo, a mullet pierced between two wings, all sa. *Generosus et animosus.* *cf.* 112. 1
Glenton, Warw., a cubit arm erect ppr. 222. 14
Glentworth, Lord, *see* Limerick, Earl.
Glerawly, Viscount, *see* Annesley, Earl of.
Glin, a lion's head ppr. 21. 1
Gloag, Scotland, an eagle with wings addorsed ppr. *Nunquam senescit.*
Gloag, Scotland, an eagle with wings expanded. *Qui vult capere capiat.* 77. 5
Glocester and **Gloucester,** a swan's head between two wings ppr. 101. 6
Glodredd, Wales, a sheaf of arrows banded, points upwards.
Glodrydd, Wales, an eagle rising, holding in its beak a trefoil slipped. *cf.* 77. 5
Glossop, out of an Eastern coronet gu., a griffin's head or.
Glover of London, Kent, and Warw., a cross-bow az., between two wings or. 112. 13
Glover, Scotland, within the horns of a crescent a cock ppr. *Surgite, lumen adest.* 91. 10
Glover, Sir John, Merton Lodge, West Hill, Highgate, N., a cock between two buffalo-horns.

Glover, Rev. Frederick Augustus, M.A., of Witherne Rectory, Alford, Lincs, an eagle displayed arg., charged on the breast with three spots of erminites. *cf.* 75. 2

Glover, out of a mural crown a demi-lion rampant holding between the paws a crescent.

Glover, Wilts, a talbot passant sa., collared arg. *cf.* 54. 5

Glover, a dragon passant az. 73. 2

Glover, on a chapeau sa., turned up arg., two wings expanded of the first.

Glover, a fleur-de-lis or, between two wings sa.

Glubb, a demi-lion az., bezantée. *cf.* 10. 2

Glyd of Brightling, Sussex, and London, a griffin sejant, the dexter claw elevated sa., the wings also elevated and plain collared and lined gu.

Glyn, an eagle's head and neck erased. 83. 2

Glyn, Sir Richard George, Bart., of Gaunts, Dorset, an eagle's head erased sa., guttée-d'or, holding in the beak an escallop arg. *Firm to my trust (Fidei tenax).* 268. 11

Glyn, Sir Gervas Powell, Bart., same crest. *Pro libertate lege sancta.*

Glyn, Carr Stuart, of Wood Leaze, Wimborne, Dorset, same crest. *Fidei tenax.*

Glyn, Clayton Louis, Esquire, of Durrington House, Essex, Sherring Hall, Harlow, Essex, same crest. *Firm to my trust.*

Glyn, General Sir Julius Richard, K.C.B., of Sherborne House, Sherborne, Dorset, same crest.

Glyn, a demi-lion sa., charged with three bezants, one and two. *cf.* 10. 1

Glyn and **Glynn** of Glynn, Cornw., a demi-talbot erm., eared or. *Dry weres agan dew ny.* *cf.* 55. 8

Glynn, Lieutenant-Colonel T. G. Holbery, of 2, Templeton Place, South Kensington, S.W., a demi-talbot erm., eared or. *Dry weres agan dew ny.—Aut viam inveniam aut faciam.*

Glynn, Ireland, a lion's head erased, collared sa. 18. 6

Glynne, Shropsh., a cock arg., crested, armed and wattled or. 91. 2

Goadefroy, an arm in armour embowed holding in the gauntlet a sword, all ppr. 195. 1

Goat and **Goate,** a goat passant arg., armed or. *cf.* 129. 5

Goater, a wolf sejant or, grasping a cross crosslet fitched gu.

Goatham, a hunting-horn sa., garnished and stringed gu. 228. 11

Goatley and **Goatly,** Kent, a sphinx couchant or, winged arg., the face and breast ppr. *cf.* 182. 14

Goband, a mermaid holding a dagger ppr. 184. 7

Gobel, a wyvern vert. 70. 1

Gobion, in water a swan naiant with wings elevated ppr. 99. 9

Goble, a lion passant charged on the shoulder with a fleur-de-lis. *cf.* 6. 2

Goche, a talbot passant per pale arg. and sa. 54. 1

Godard, Hants and Wilts, a stag's head couped at the neck and affrontée gu., attired or. 119. 12

Godard of London, Berks, and Hants, a hawk's head erased or, holding in the beak a lure gu., garnished of the first, stringed of the second.

Godard, Norf., an eagle's head between two wings or. 84. 2

Godbold, Surrey, an arm in armour embowed holding in the hand an arrow ppr. 198. 4

Godbold of Hatfield, Essex, and Westhall, Suff., an arm in armour ppr., wreathed about the arm or and az., the ends flotant, holding in the gauntlet an arrow sa., feathered and headed arg.

Godbow, out of a mural coronet or, a griffin's head between two wings gu.

Godby, a tree. 143. 5

Godby, a chevalier on horseback in complete armour, his visor closed, all ppr.

Goddard of London and Eastwood Hay, a hawk's head or, holding in the beak a lure gu., capped vert, garnished of the first, stringed of the second.

Goddard, a salamander in flames ppr. 138. 4

Goddard, Wilts, a stag's head erased at the neck and affrontée ppr. 119. 10

Goddard, of Cliffe House, Wilts, a stag's head affrontée, couped at the neck gu., attired or. *Cervus non servus.* 119. 12

Goddard, Rainald William Knightley, of 133, Denmark Hill, London, S.E., same crest and motto.

Goddard, Charles E., M.D., Harrowdene House, Wembley, same crest and motto.

Goddard, Rev. Charles Frederick, of Clearwell Vicarage, Coleford, Glouc., same crest.

Goddard, Edward Hesketh, Esquire, same crest.

Goddard, Fitzroy Pleydell, Esquire, of the Lawn, Swindon, Wilts, and the Comedy, Christian Malford, Chippenham, Wilts, same crest.

Goddart, Scotland, a stag's head affrontée, couped gu., attired or. 119. 12

Godden, Kent, on a garb in fess a bird close, holding in its beak a wheat-ear, all or. 93. 3

Goddin, a winged heart ppr. 112. 10

Goderich, Viscount, *see* Ripon, Earl of.

Godeston, a buffalo's head sa. *cf.* 44. 1

Godfray, a demi-griffin or. *Deus est pax.* 64. 2

Godfrey, Sir William Cecil, Bart., of Bushfield, co. Kerry, a griffin passant sa., holding in the dexter claw a sceptre or. *God fried.—Deus et libertas.*

Godfrey, A. C., M.D., Freemantle, Southampton, same crest. *Deus et libertas.*

Godfrey, a demi-griffin or. 64. 2

Godfrey, Kent and Middx., a pelican's head erased or, vulning gu. 98. 2

Godfrey, an eagle displayed sa. 75. 2

Godfrey, Staffs and Warw., a pelican with wings addorsed or, gorged with an Eastern coronet az., holding in its beak a cross crosslet fitched gu.

Godfrey, Ingram Fuller, Brook St. House, Ash-next-Sandwich, Kent, a demi-negro ppr., holding in the dexter hand a cross crosslet fitched arg.

Godfrey, William Bernard, Old Quarry Hall, Blechingley, a sea-lion erect ppr. *Deus et libertas.* 20. 5

Godfrey, a leopard's head couped az. 22. 10

Godin, an ox-yoke in bend sa., stapled az. 178. 6

Goding of London, on a garb fessewise a bird close, holding in its beak an ear of wheat, all or. *Dominus providebit* 93. 3

Godley, Sir Arthur, K.C.B., of Killigar, Belturbet, co. Leitrim, a unicorn's head erased arg., horned gu., charged with three trefoils slipped vert. *Sans Dieu rien.* *cf.* 49. 5

Godley, Ireland, a demi-lion gardant or, holding in its dexter paw a fleur-de-lis gu. *cf.* 10. 8

Godman, on a mount vert, a blackcock with wings displayed ppr. *Cœlum quid quærimus ultra.* 89. 8

Godmanstone, a man's leg couped at the thigh ppr. *cf.* 193. 10

Godolphin, Baron, *see* Leeds, Duke of.

Godolphin, Devonsh. and Cornw., a dolphin naiant sa., finned or. 140. 5

Godsal of Iscoyd Park, Wales, a griffin's head erased paly of six indented arg. and sa., beaked or. 66. 2

Godsale, a griffin's head erased per pale arg. and sa., beaked or. 66. 2

Godsall, Godsell, Godsel, and **Godseel,** an arm erect holding in the hand a spade ppr.

Godsall and **Godsell,** a griffin's head erased paly indented of six arg. and sa. 66. 2

Godsalve, a griffin's head erased paly wavy of four arg. and sa., holding in the beak a branch vert. *cf.* 66. 11

Godschall, a lion's gamb holding a crescent. 39. 15

Godson of Westwood Park, Droitwich, a dexter arm in armour embowed holding in the hand a sword, and pendent therefrom a wreath of thorn. *Forward.*

Godstone, on a chapeau ppr., a talbot's head arg. *cf.* 56. 12

Godweston, out of a ducal coronet a plume of five ostrich-feathers alternately arg. and sa. 114. 13

Godwin, Somers., a hawk's leg erased ppr., belled or, jessed gu. 113. 8

Godwyn, a griffin sejant or, guttée-de-poix. 62. 10

Goff or **Goffe,** Ireland, a stag's head erased gu., armed arg. 121. 2

Goff or **Goffe,** out of a ducal coronet or, a rod raguly vert. 147. 10

Goff, Thomas Clarence Edward, Esquire, of Carroweve Park, co. Roscommon, Ireland, a squirrel sejant ppr., charged on the shoulder with a fleur-de-lis or, and holding in its fore-paws a nut, also ppr. *Honestas optima politia.* *cf.* 135. 7

Goff, Gerald Lionel Joseph, Esquire, of Hale Hall, Salisbury, Hants, a squirrel sejant ppr. *Fier sans tache.* *cf.* 135. 4

Goff, Davis-, of Horetown, Ireland, a squirrel sejant arg. *Honestas optima politia.* *cf.* 135. 4

Goff, Robert, Esquire, of Summers Place, near Billingshurst, Sussex, same crest.

Gofton, Surrey, on a chapeau gu., turned up arg., a rose or, between two wings expanded az.

Gogarty, Surgeon - Major Henry Alexander, M.D., of Thwaite House, Canterbury, a talbot passant gu., its fore-paw supported by a fleam or. *Fidelis.*

Going of Traverstown, co. Tipperary, Ireland, an arm embowed in armour ppr., charged on the fore-arm with three estoiles in pale gu., holding a palm-branch, all ppr. *Dum spiro, spero.*

Gokin of Ickham, Kent, on a mural coronet arg., a cock or, beaked, barbed, and membered gu. *cf.* 91. 2

Golborn and **Golborne,** Chesh., a man's leg couped above the knee vert, spurred or. 193. 8

Golbourn, a dove holding in its beak an olive-branch ppr. 92. 5

Gold, Wilts, a demi-lion rampant or. 10. 2

Gold, Charles, Esquire, of the Limes, Birchange, Essex, in front of a demi-lion gu., gorged with a collar or, supporting with the paws a branch of three roses leaved and slipped, all arg., a bezant. *Non deerit alter aureus.*

Gold, Alfred G., Rawdon House, Holyport, Maidenhead, same crest and motto.

Gold, Wilts, an eagle's head erased az., holding in its beak a pine or. *cf.* 83. 2

Golden, Lincs, a dragon's head erased vert, collared and lined or. *cf.* 71. 2

Golden, a cinquefoil ppr. 148. 12

Golder, Berks, a demi-lion rampant gardant or. *Semper erectus.* 10. 8

Goldesborough and **Goldsbrough,** a dexter hand holding a trident ppr. 214. 12

Goldesburgh, Yorks and Essex, a pelican with wings addorsed vulning herself, all ppr.

Goldesburgh of London, a demi-lion rampant. 10. 2

Goldfinch, Kent, a camel passant ppr. 132. 2

Goldfinch, a goldfinch ppr.

Goldfrap, a wolf's head erm. 30. 5

Goldie - Scot, Archibald Murgatroyd Goldies, Esquire, of Craigmuie, Kirkcudbrightsh., Scotland: (1) A stag trippant ppr. (*for Scot*). 117. 8. (2) A garb or (*for Goldie*). *Fideliter amo.*—*Quid utilius.* 153. 2

Goldie, Scotland, a garb or. *Honestas.* 153. 2

Goldie, Scotland, an antique crown or. *Nil solidum.* 180. 12

Goldie, a hand holding a thistle ppr. 218. 2

Goldie-Taubman, John Leigh, the Nunnery, Douglas, Isle of Man: (1) A garb (*for Goldie*). *Quid utilius.* (2) A wolf's head erased (*for Taubman*). *Diligentia ditat.*

Golding, Essex and Suff., a garb or. 153. 2

Golding, a hind's head couped, holding in its mouth an acorn-branch, all ppr. *cf.* 124. 1

Golding of Colson Bassett, Notts, a griffin's head erased gu., collared or. *cf.* 66. 2

Golding, Essex, and of Cavendish and Postingford, Suff., a dragon's head erased vert, collared and lined or. *cf.* 71. 2

Golding, Ireland, an arm in chain armour embowed ppr., garnished at the wrist or, tied with ribbons arg. and sa., the hand ppr., holding an arrow gu., point of the second.

Golding-Bird, Frederic, Fairholme, Torquay: (1) A ring-dove ppr., resting its dexter claw on a rose or. 271. 5. (2) A hind's head with oak-branch in mouth, all ppr. *Tentanda via est.* 271. 6

Goldingham, Norf. and Suff., a lion's gamb erect and erased or. 36. 4

Goldington, out of a ducal coronet or, a cock's head ppr. 90. 6

Goldman, Scotland, a fox current ppr. *cf.* 32. 8

Goldney, Sir (Gabriel) Prior, Bart., of Beechfield, near Chippenham, and Bradenstoke Abbey, Wilts, in front of a garb sa., banded or, three cinquefoils fesseways of the last. *Honor virtutis præmium.* 275. 12

Goldney, Hon. Sir John Tankerville, of Trinidad, West Indies, same crest and motto.

Goldsmid, Bart. (*extinct*), of Wick House, Brighton, Sussex, East Titherley House, Hants, and Somerhill, Kent: (1) Out of the coronet of a Baron of Portugal ppr., a demi-dragon with wings elevated or, holding in its claws a rose gu., slipped ppr. (2) A demi-lion arg., holding in the paws a bundle of reeds erect or, banded az. 243. 2. *Quis similis tibi in fortibus Domine.*—*Concordia et sedulitate.*

Goldsmid-Stern-Salomons, Sir David Lionel, Bart., of Broomhill, Tunbridge Wells, Kent: (1) On a mount vert, thereon issuant out of six park pales or, a demi-lion double-queued gu., holding between the paws a bezant charged with an erm. spot (*for Salomons*). 243. 3. (2) A demi-unicorn gu., armed, maned, and ungu. or, charged on the shoulder with a cross crosslet arg. (*for Stern*). 243. 1. (3) A demi-lion arg., in the paws a bundle of twigs erect or, banded az., charged on the shoulder with a cross crosslet gu. *Deo adjuvante.* 243. 2

Goldsmid, Osmond Elim D'Avigdor, Esquire, J.P., B.A., LL.B. (Cambs.), of Somerhill, Tonbridge, Kent: (1) A demi-lion arg., supporting with the paws a bundle of twigs erect or, banded az. (*for Goldsmid*). 243. 2. (2) Two demi-greyhounds respecting each other sa., supporting between the paws a bezant charged with a demi-lion rampant and couped, holding in the dexter paw an anchor erect, both sa.

Goldsmidt, a demi-lion rampant holding between its paws a pillar.

Goldsmidt, two lions' gambs erased supporting a crescent or. 39. 6

Goldsmith, a bird close sa.

Goldsmith, Hants, a stork sa., bezantée or. *cf.* 105. 11

Goldsmith, on a mount a kingfisher ppr. 96. 9

Goldson, Norf., a leopard's head erased arg., collared and chained sa., the collar charged with three bezants. *cf.* 22. 12

Goldston and **Goldstone,** a Minerva's head ppr. 182. 1

Goldsworthy, a griffin's head erased sa., holding in the beak a holly-leaf vert. *cf.* 66. 11

Goldsworthy, an eagle's head erased per pale or and arg., holding in the beak a holly-leaf vert. *cf.* 84. 10

Goldthorpe, William, Esquire, J.P., of Brook House, Levenshulme, Manchester, and Gorst House, Chorley, Chesh., a rock and volant above an eagle ppr., in the beak a billet or, surmounted by a rainbow, also ppr. *Endeavour.* 238. 3

Goldtrap, Kent, a lion's gamb erased az., holding a baton or, between two wings elevated of the last. 37. 14

Goldwell, out of a well or, a vine and two columbine-branches ppr.

Golever, a mermaid ppr. 184. 5

Golightley, out of an antique crown a lion's head.

Gollop, an antelope trippant ppr. 126. 6

Gollop, of Strode, Dorset, a demi-lion bendy or and sa., holding in the dexter paw a broken arrow gu. *Be bolde, be wyse.* *cf.* 10. 2

Golofer, an eagle's head couped arg. 83. 1

Goloner, a demi-griffin ppr., collared and sustaining an anchor az. *cf.* 64. 7

Goloner, a lion passant gardent arg., ducally crowned or. *cf.* 4. 3

Golston, an eagle's head couped arg. 83. 1

Goltshed, two wings conjoined or, thereon a dove statant ppr.

Gom, two scimitars in saltier ppr.

Gomeldon, a demi-griffin arg., holding between the claws a mullet or.

Gomeldon, issuing out of a cloud an arm in armour embowed and gloved wielding a spiked mace, all ppr.

Gomersall, out of a crescent or, a dexter gauntlet arg., grasping a battle-axe gu., pointed and headed of the second.

Gomm, Middx. and Bucks, two lions' gambs in saltier sa., erased gu., each holding a seax erect arg., hilt and pommel or. *Per constanza e speranza.* 39. 5

Gomm, Sir William, same crest and motto. 39. 5

Gonne, on a glove a falcon, all ppr. 86. 12

Gonor, a stag's head ppr., holding in the mouth a cinquefoil or, leaved vert. *cf.* 121. 5

Gonston of London and Essex, an antelope's head arg., guttée-de-sang. *cf.* 126. 2

Gonton and **Gunton,** out of an earl's coronet a Moor's head affrontée, all ppr.

Gonvill, Norf., a dove arg., beaked and membered gu., and holding in the beak a flower-gentle stalked vert. 92. 5

Gooch, out of a ducal coronet a stag's head collared. *cf.* 120. 7

Gooch, Norf., a greyhound passant arg., spotted and collared sa. *cf.* 60. 2

Gooch, Sir Thomas Vere Sherlock, Bart., of Benacre Hall, Suff., a talbot statant per pale arg. and sa. *Fide et virtute.* *cf.* 54. 2

Gooch, Sir Daniel Fulthorpe, Bart., of Clewer Park, Windsor, Berks, a talbot passant per pale sa. and arg., gorged with a wreath of oak, and resting the dexter paw on a wheel or. *Fide et virtute.* 54. 8

Gooch, Charles Fulthorpe, Kingsmead, Matfield, Kent, same crest and motto.

Gooch, Charles C., Esquire, of 8, Porchester Gate, Hyde Park, London, W., a talbot passant per pale or and sa., charged on the body with two annulets counterchanged, and holding in the mouth a baton, also sa. *Memor et gratus.*

Gooch, Middx. and Lincs, a cubit arm erect, vested per pale, embattled or and arg., grasping in the hand ppr. a dragon's head erased az. 208. 7

Gooche, on a ducal coronet or, a leopard arg., spotted sa.

Good, on a ducal coronet or, a leopard arg., spotted sa

Good, an antelope's head erased, holding in its mouth a laurel-branch. *cf.* 126. 2

Good, the Holy Bible closed.

Goodacre, Ireland, a unicorn's head erased sa., armed and maned or. 49. 5

Goodacre, Hugh George, 78, Gloucester Terrace, Hyde Park, W., same crest. *I live and die in loyalty.*

Goodair, Lieutenant-Colonel William Henry, of Ashton Park, Preston, a partridge holding in its beak a wheat-ear. *Possunt quia posse videntur.* *cf.* 89. 10

Goodale and **Goodalle**, Scotland, a cup arg. *Good God increase.* 177. 14

Goodall, Suff., an eagle displayed arg., beaked and membered or, gorged with a chaplet of grass ppr. *cf.* 75. 2

Goodall, Scotland, an eagle displayed. *Toujours fidele.* 75. 2

Goodall, a dexter arm embowed, vested vert, holding in the hand ppr. two arrows in saltier arg., feathered or.

Goodbridge, Devonsh. and Yorks, a thrush ppr.

Goodchild, a parrot vert, beaked and legged gu. *Vincit omnia veritas.* 101. 4

Goodchild, a parrot ppr., holding in the beak an annulet gu. 101. 11

Goodchild of London, and of Valetta, Malta, a pellet, and thereon a parrot ppr., holding in its beak an annulet gu. *cf.* 101. 11

Gooddage, Essex and Suff., a greyhound sejant erm., collared and lined or. *cf.* 59. 2

Goodden, John Robert Phelips, Compton House, Sherborne, Dorset, a griffin's head erased or, with wings endorsed vairé arg. and gu., holding in its beak an olive-branch ppr. *Jovis omnia plena.*

Goode of London and Cornw., a talbot's head erased gu., ducally crowned or. 56. 9

Goode, a lion passant. 6. 2

Goodear and **Goodyear**, a lion's head erased imperially crowned ppr *cf.* 17. 14

Gooden and **Gooding**, Somers., a dexter arm ppr., vested arg., charged with three bars gu., and holding a palm-branch vert.

Gooden and **Gooding**, Suff., a griffin sejant with wings expanded or, guttée-de-poix, beaked and armed sa. 62. 10

Gooden-Chisholm, Chisholm, Esquire, "The Chisholm," of Canada, a dexter hand couped at the wrist, holding a dagger erect, on which is transfixed a boar's head couped. *Feros ferio.* 212. 2

Goodenough, a demi-wolf rampant ppr., holding between the paws an escallop arg. *cf.* 31. 2

Goodenough, a hand holding a dagger in pale, all ppr. 212. 9

Goodenough, on a chapeau gu., turned up erm., a lion couchant or. 7. 12

Goodere, Glouc., a partridge holding in its beak a wheat-ear, all ppr. *Possunt, quia posse videntur.* *cf.* 89. 10

Gooderick, of Kirkby, Lincs, a demi-lion rampant sa., collared or, supporting a battle-axe arg., handled gu. *cf.* 15. 4

Goodfellow, a horse rampant gu.

Goodfellow, a demi-female figure representing Temperance, vested arg., mantle az., in the dexter hand a palm-branch, and in the sinister a bridle ppr. *Temperance.* 249. 1

Goodford, Arthur John, of Chilton Cantelo, Somers., a boar's head arg., langued gu., charged on the neck with a pellet. *cf.* 34. 14

Goodhall, Lincs, a boar's head erased and erect sa., patée, ducally gorged or.

Goodhand, an arm in armour embowed ppr., holding in the hand a sword arg., hilt and pommel or. 195. 2

Goodhard or **Goodhart**, on a ducal coronet a lion passant, all ppr. 6. 6

Goodhart, Charles Emanuel, Esquire, of Langley Park, Beckenham, Kent, a beehive or, between two bees, all within a rainbow terminating in clouds ppr. 227. 8

Gooding, *see* Gooden.

Gooding, a hedgehog ppr. 135. 8

Gooding, on a mount vert, a hedgehog ppr. *cf.* 135. 8

Gooding of Whershed, Deback, and Chetfield, Suff. and Norf., a griffin sejant with wings expanded or, guttée-de-sang, claws and beak sa. *cf.* 62. 10

Goodison, a peacock's head ppr. 103. 2

Goodlad of London, a wing arg. 109. 7

Goodlad, in a frame a globe ppr. 159. 4

Goodlake, a savage kneeling on his sinister knee, holding over the sinister shoulder a club, and tied round his loins.

Goodlake, Berks, on a mount vert, a wood witt or wild man ppr., holding up his club or. *Omnia bona desuper.*

Goodlaw, Lancs, a griffin sejant arg., supporting with his dexter claw a column az.

Goodman of London, Chesh., and Herts, the battlement and upper part of a tower arg., thereon a woman couped at the knees, vested az., hair dishevelled or, holding in her dexter hand a rose gu., stalked and leaved vert.

Goodman, an eagle with two heads displayed sa. 74. 2

Goodman, Wales, out of a ducal coronet or, a demi-eagle displayed with two heads erm.

Goodrich, a lion's head couped ppr. 21. 1

Goodrich, Essex, a demi-lion rampant arg., holding in the dexter paw a cross crosslet or. 11. 10

Goodrick, Middx., Lincs and Camb., a demi-lion rampant sa., collared or, supporting a battle-axe arg., the handle gu. *cf.* 15. 4

Goodrick and **Goodricke**, a demi-lion rampant gu., collared or, holding in its paw a battle-axe az. *cf.* 15. 4

Goodricke, Bart., Yorks, out of a ducal coronet or, a demi-lion erm., armed and langued gu., holding between the paws a battle-axe ppr., helved of the first. *Fortior leone justus.*

Goodricke, Holyoake-, Bart. (*extinct*): (1) Issuing out of a ducal coronet or, a demi-lion rampant erm., holding between the paws a battle-axe ppr., helved of the first, and charged upon the shoulder with a cross crosslet of the last for difference (*for Goodricke*). (2) On a mount vert, an oak fructed ppr., around the lower part of the stem an escroll, thereon a cross patée gu., between the words *Sacra quercus* (*for Holyoake*).

Goodridge of Totnes, Devonsh., a blackbird ppr. *cf.* 106. 2

Goodrood, a unicorn's head gu., collared or. *cf.* 49. 11

Goodsir, Scotland, an eagle's head erased ppr. *Virtute et fidelitate.* 83. 2

Goodsir, Scotland, a cock holding in its beak a bunch of keys. *Fortitur et fideliter.* 91. 3

Goodson, a wolf's head erm., collared gu. 30. 9

Goodwin, Herts, a griffin's head arg., with wings addorsed vair. *cf.* 67. 11

Goodwin, Cambs, out of a ducal coronet arg., a nag's head or, maned and bridled of the first. 51. 7

Goodwin, Devonsh. and Suff., a griffin sejant with wings expanded or, guttée-de-poix. 62. 10

Goodwin of Upper Winchingdon, Bucks, a demi-lion rampant arg., gorged with an heraldic coronet gu. *De bon volore.* *cf.* 10. 2

Goodwin, a demi-lion rampant holding a bezant. 11. 7

Goodwin, a demi-lion rampant gardant sa., holding a bezant.

Goodwin, Ireland, out of a ducal coronet or, a demi-lion rampant az., holding between the paws a fleur-de-lis of the first. *Lilia candorem pectus Leo nobile monstrax.* *cf.* 16. 3

Goodwin, Goodwin Charles, Esquire, a demi-lion arg., ducally gorged gu., charged on the body with three lozenges az., and holding between the paws a fleur-de-lis of the second.

Goodwin of London, a lion sejant gardant erect sa., holding between the paws a lozenge vair.

Goodwin - Gladwin of Hinchleywood House, Mappleton, Derbysh., a mount vert, thereon a lion sejant arg., guttée-de-sang, holding in the dexter paw a sword erect or.

Goodwin or **Goodwyn**, Surrey and Sussex, an arm embowed vested or, cuffed arg., holding in the hand ppr. a lozenge of the second.

Goodwing of Dublin, an ostrich arg., legged sa., and charged on the breast with a crescent gu. *cf.* 97 2.

Goodwright, a dove holding in its beak an olive-branch ppr. *Pro bono ad meliora.* 92. 5

Goodwyn, Derbysh., a griffin sejant with wings expanded or. *Fide et virtute.* 62. 10

Goodwyn, Henry, L.R.C.P., Church Style, Bovey Tracy, a griffin sejant erm. *Fortes, Fortuna, adjuvat.* 62. 10

Goodwyn, a griffin sejant or, guttée-de-poix. *cf.* 62. 10

Goodwyn of East Grinstead, Sussex, an arm embowed vested gu., the hand ppr., resting on a lozenge arg.

Goodyer, *see* Goodear.

Googe, a rose stalked and leaved ppr. *Audaces juvat.* 149. 5

Goold, Ireland, a demi-lion rampant ppr. 10. 2

Goold, Sir Henry Valentine, Bart., of Old Court, co. Cork, a demi-lion rampant or. *Deus mihi providebit.* 10. 2

Goold, the Venerable Frederic Falkener, of Dromadda and Rosbrien, co. Limerick, Archdeacon of Raphoe and Rector of Paymochy, co. Donegal, a demi-lion rampant or, charged on the shoulder with a crescent gu. *Deus mihi providebit.* *cf.* 10. 2

Goold - Verschoyle, Esquire, Hamilton Frederick Stuart, of Athea House, Athea, co. Limerick: (1) As above (*for Verschoyle*). (2) A demi-lion rampant or, charged on the shoulder with a crescent gu. (*for Goold*). *Temperans et constans.*

Goold, on a mount vert, an erm. passant ppr. 134. 10

Goold, Scotland, within the horns of a crescent arg., a buckle or. 163. 15

Goorick, a nag's head erased. 51. 4

Gooseling, a lion's gamb erased gu., holding a fleur-de-lis or.

Goostrey, Bucks, a stag's head erased or. 121. 2

Gophill, Surrey, out of a ducal coronet per pale az. and gu., a demi-leopard rampant gardant or, collared and lined of the second.

Gordnee, on a mural coronet gu., a griffin's head erased arg. *cf.* 66. 2

Gordon, Duke of, *see* Richmond and Gordon.

Gordon, *see* Huntly, Marquess of.

Gordon, Viscount, *see* Aberdeen, Earl of.

Gordon, Viscount Kenmure, *see* Kenmure.

Gordon-Canning, *see* Canning.

Gordon-Cumming, *see* Cumming.

Gordon, *see* Hay-Gordon.

Gordon, *see* M'Haffie-Gordon.

Gordon, *see* Wolrige-Gordon.

Gordon, Scotland, a stag lodged ppr. *Nunc mihi grata quies.* 115. 7

Gordon, Scotland, a hart at gaze ppr. *Dum vigilo paro.* 117. 3

Gordon, Sir Robert Glendonwyn, Bart., D.L., J.P., of Letterfourie, Banffsh., a stag at gaze ppr. *Dum sisto vigilo.* 117. 3

Gordon of Faskine, a stag lodged ppr. *Bydand to the last.* 115. 7

Gordon of Terpersie, Aberdeensh., Scotland, a hart at gaze ppr. *Non fraude sed laude.* 117. 3

Gordon of Knockespock, Aberdeen: (1) A stag's head erased ppr., attired or. 121. 2. (2) A stag at gaze ppr. *Non fraude sed laude.—Dum vigilo, tutus.* 117. 3

Gordon, Bart., of Lesmore, Scotland, a hart's head couped ppr. *Bydand.* 121. 5

Gordon, Henry, Manar, by Inverurie, Aberdeensh., same crest and motto.

Gordon of London, a stag's head erased ppr. *Vigilando.* 121. 2

Gordon, John Patrick, Cairnfield, Buckie, a stag's head erased or. *Bydand, Ryh.—Dum vigilo tutus.*

Gordon of Birkenburn, a hart's head couped ppr., charged with a crescent arg. *Bydand.* *cf.* 119. 8

Gordon of Millrig, a stag's head erased ppr. *Bydand.* 121. 2

Gordon, Scotland, a buck's head and neck affrontée ppr. *Truth prevails.* 119. 12

Gordon of Gight, a buck's head and neck affrontée ppr. *Bydand.* 119. 12

Gordon of Torquhon, a stag's head erased ppr. *Fear God.* 121. 2

Gordon, Charles Edward Grant, of Newtimber Place, Hurstpierpoint, a buck's head erased ppr., ducally gorged per pale arg. and or.

Gordon, a buck's head affrontée ppr., attired and ducally gorged or. *Truth prevails.* 119. 14

Gordon, Conway-, Colonel Francis Ingram, Lynewode Manor, Market Rasen, Lincs, issuing out of a mural crown or, a stag's head at gaze ppr., attired and charged on the neck with a crescent of the first. *Bydand.—Animo non astutia.*

Gordon of South Carolina, a hart's head affrontée ppr. *Animo.* 119. 12

Gordon-Gilmour, Major Robert Gordon, Esquire, of Craigmillar: (1) On the dexter side, on a wreath of the proper liveries a dexter hand holding a scroll of paper within a garland of laurel ppr. (*for Gilmour*). 215. 3. (2) On the sinister, issuing from an earl's coronet a hart's head affrontée ppr. (*for Gordon*). *Nil penna sed usus.—Bydand.*

Gordon, Scotland, a hart's head cabossed ppr. *Bydand.* 122. 5

Gordon, More-, of Charlton, Forfarsh., a buck's head cabossed ppr. *I byd my time.—Deo favente.* 122. 5

Gordon of Badenscoth, a hart's head cabossed ppr. *Still bydand.* 122. 5

Gordon of Sorbie, Scotland, out of a mural crown a boar's head erect and erased, all ppr. *Forward, and fear not.*

Gordon, a boar's head couped or. *Do well, and let them say.* 43. 1

Gordon of Glenbucket, a boar's head couped and erect, surrounded by an adder in orle. *Victrix patientia.* 41. 11

Gordon of Ardmeally, a boar's head erased or. *Byde be.* 42. 2

Gordon of Edinglassie, a boar's head erased, holding in the mouth a sword ppr. *Aut mors, aut vita Deus.* 42. 6

Gordon, Bart., of Embo, co. Sutherland, a boar's head erased or. *Forward without fear.* 42. 2

Gordon, Scotland, a boar's head erased or. *Byde.* 42. 2

Gordon, a boar's head gu. 43. 1

Gordon, James Gillespie, Esquire, M.P., of Clifton, Hawke's Bay, New Zealand, a boar's head erased or, armed and langued gu.

Gordon, Hon. John Edward, of 61, Prince's Gate, S.W., and East Dene, Bonchurch, Isle of Wight, same crest.

Gordon, Scotland, a boar's head couped or, holding in the mouth four arrows gu., feathered and headed arg. *Doe well, and let them say.* *cf.* 42. 9

Gordon, Ireland, a boar's head erased and erect sa., armed and eared or. 43. 3

Gordon, a boar's head couped gu., encircled by two serpents internowed, the heads respecting each other in chief ppr.

Gordon of Cairnfield, Banff, a boar's head erased or. *Dum vigilo, tutus.* 42. 2

Gordon-Oswald, James William, Esquire, of Aigas, Inverness-sh., and Roughgrove, co. Cork: (1) A hand pointing to a star. (*for Oswald*). (2) A dagger erect piercing a boar's head erased, all ppr. (*for Gordon*). *Non mihi commodus uni.—Non astutia.*

Gordon of Craig, Scotland, a boar's head erased or. *Byde.* 42. 2

Gordon, William, C.I.E., 9, Tavistock Road, Croydon: (1) A boar's head erased close. (2) A stag's head couped. *Dum vigilo tutus.*

Gordon of Auchintoul, Scotland, a demi-boar ppr. *Bydand.* 40. 13

Gordon, Scotland, a sword in pale enfiled with a boar's head couped ppr. 42. 4

Gordon, Scotland, a dexter hand couped in fess, holding a sword in pale enfiled with a boar's head erased, all ppr. *Aut mors, aut vita decora.*

Gordon, Archibald Alexander, Esquire, J.P., of 1, Coates Gardens, Edinburgh, a dexter cubit arm vested paly arg. and gu., the hand grasping a scimitar ppr. *Dread God.*

Gordon, Captain William Eagleson, V.C., Gordon Highlanders, same crest.

Gordon, Bart., of Niton, Isle of Wight, out of a mural coronet a dexter arm in armour embowed ppr., charged with a mullet gu., garnished or, the hand grasping a falchion, also ppr., enfiled with a boar's head erect and erased of the third. *Animo non astutiâ.*

Gordon of London, a demi-savage wreathed about the head and middle with laurel, holding over the dexter shoulder a club, all ppr. *Dread God.* 186. 1

Gordon of Lochinvar, a demi-savage wreathed about the head and middle. *Dread God.*

Gordon, Bucks and Notts, a demi-savage wreathed about the head and middle with laurel, and holding over the dexter shoulder a club, all ppr. 186. 1

Gordon, James Rollings, 19, Victoria Road, Upper Norwood, same crest. *Dread God.*

Gordon, George Henry, Wincombe Park, Shaftesbury, same crest and motto.

Gordon, Scotland, a demi-savage wreathed about the head and middle with leaves, and holding in the sinister hand over the shoulder an arrow, point downwards, all ppr.

Gordon, of Rothiemay, a demi-man presenting a gun, all ppr. *Vel pax, vel bellum.* 187. 2

Gordon of Shirmers, Kirkcudbright, Scotland, a demi-savage holding in his dexter hand a baton erected on his shoulders, and in his sinister an ear of wheat ppr. *Tam pace quam prœlio.*

Gordon, Scotland, a savage's head erased ppr. *Fear God.*

Gordon, two arms drawing a bow and arrow ppr. 200. 2

Gordon of Cairnbulg, Aberdeensh., two naked arms holding a bow with an arrow at full stretch, all ppr. *Fortuna sequatur.* 200. 2

Gordon, Duff-, Sir Cosmo Edmund, Bart., of Halkin, co. Ayr: (1) Two arms naked holding a bow and ready to let fly an arrow, all ppr. (*for Gordon*). 200. 2. (2) A demi-lion gu., holding in the dexter paw a sword erect ppr., hilt and pommel or, charged on the breast with a mullet gu. for difference (*for Duff*). *Deo adjuvante.* cf. 14. 12

Gordon, Cameron, Bentley Priory, Stanmore, Middx., a sinister arm from the shoulder and a dexter hand holding a bent bow, and in the act of letting fly an arrow ppr. *Fortuna sequatur.* 200. 2

Gordon, Duff-, Thomas Duff, Esquire, of Drummuir, Keith, and Park House, Banff., a heart ppr., winged or. *Kind heart.—Be true, and you never shall rue.*

Gordon, Scotland, issuing out of a cloud a dexter hand holding six darts. *Majores sequor.* cf. 214. 3

Gordon of Gordonbank, a dexter hand issuing out of a cloud, and grasping a sheaf of arrows, all ppr. *Legibus et armis.* cf. 214. 3

Gordon of Braco, a dexter hand holding a dart ppr. *Sequor.* 214. 4

Gordon of Nethermuir, a dexter hand issuing out of a cloud holding a dart, all ppr. *Majores sequor.* 214. 1

Gordon of London, a dexter hand holding a dagger, all ppr. *Time Deum.* 212. 3

Gordon, Scotland, issuing out of a cloud a dexter naked arm grasping a flaming sword, all ppr. *Dread God.*

Gordon of Dalpholly, a dexter hand issuing from a heart and holding a flaming sword. *Corde manuque.*

Gordon, a cubit arm erect holding a dagger ppr. 212. 3

Gordon, Scotland, a dexter hand holding a scimitar. *Dread God.* 213. 5

Gordon, Sir William, Bart., of Earlston, Kirkcudbrightsh., a dexter hand grasping a sabre ppr. *Dread God.* 212. 13

Gordon, Scotland, out of a heart a dexter hand holding a sword wavy, all ppr.

Gordon, out of a ducal coronet or, a cubit arm erect in armour ppr., and holding in the hand a sword arg., hilted and pommelled, also or.

Gordon, Wilts, a hand holding an open book ppr. *Veritas ingenio.* 215. 10

Gordon of Denguech, a hand holding a baton erect ppr. *Maneo non fugio.*

Gordon of Holm, Scotland, a hand holding a writing-pen ppr. *Time Deum.* 217. 10

Gordon, Bart., of Park, Banffsh., a sinister gauntlet ppr. *Sic tatus.*

Gordon, Taylor-: (1) An oak-tree (*for Gordon*). 143. 5. (2) A stork ppr., supporting with the dexter claw an anchor az. (*for Taylor*). *I bide.—Dum spiro, spero.* 105. 10

Gordon of Tobago, an oak-tree ppr. *Sub tegmine.* 143. 2

Gordon of Cluny, Scotland, a spreading oak-tree gu. *Sub tegmine.* 143. 5

Gordon of Glasgow, a palm-tree ppr. *Deo fidens.* 144. 1

Gordon-Cuming-Skene, Alexander, Esquire, a dove ppr. *I hope.*

Gordon-Cuming-Skene, of Pitlurg, Aberdeensh., a dove arg., beaked and membered gu., holding in its beak an olive-branch ppr. *I hope.* 92. 5

Gordon of Clunie, a dove volent arg., holding in its beak an olive-branch. *Pax et libertas.* 93. 10

Gordon of Glastirim, a lion's head erased and langued ppr. *Divisa conjungo.* 17. 8

Gordon of Gordonstone, a catamountain salient arg., armed az. cf. 26. 3

Gordon, Scotland, a cat statant gardant ppr.

Gordon, Hugh Mackay, of Abergeldie Castle, Ballater, N.B., a deer-hound arg., collared gu. *God for us.*

Gordon, Scotland, a greyhound passant cf. 60. 2

Gordon, Scotland, a greyhound passant arg., collared az. *God with us.* cf. 60. 2

Gordon of Beldorny, a cross crosslet fitched gu. *In hoc spes mea.* 166. 2

Gordon, Rafael, Wardhouse, Insch, Aberdeensh., same crest and motto.

Gordon, Xeres le Frontera, a cross crosslet fitchée gu., between two wings expanded or. *In hoc spes mea.* 111. 3

Gordon, Scotland, a cross Calvary gu. *Spero.* 166. 1

Gordon of Buthlaw, Aberdeensh., Scotland, a Doric pillar or. *In recto decus.* 176. 3

Gordon of Newark, Scotland, a crescent arg. *Gradatim pleno.* 163. 2

Gordon, Scotland, in the sea a ship under sail, all ppr. *Fertur discrimine fructus.* 160. 13

Gordon, Scotland, same crest. *Nil arduum.*

Gordon-King, James Alexander, Esquire, of Tertowie, Kinaldie, Aberdeensh., a demi-lion rampant gu., crowned with an antique crown or. *Fear na.*

Gore, Earl of Arran, *see* Arran.

Gore-Langton, *see* Langton.

Gore, Ormsby-, Baron Harlech, *see* Harlech.

Gore, *see* Saunders-Knox-Gore and Pery-Knox-Gore.

Gore, Ireland, a wolf rampant arg., collared gu. *Sola salus servire Deo.* 28. 2

Gore, Sir Ralph St. George Claude, Bart., of Manor Gore, co. Donegal, a wolf rampant arg., collared gu. *Sola salus servire Deo.* cf. 28. 2

Gore, a wolf passant collared and lined. cf. 28. 10

Gore, Middx., Herts, and Surrey, a wolf rampant ppr., ducally gorged or. cf. 28. 2

Gore, Ireland, on a mount vert, a wolf salient ppr., ducally gorged or.

Gore, Knox-, Sir Charles James, Bart., D.L., of Belleek Manor, co. Mayo: (1) A wolf salient or (*for Gore*). cf. 28. 1. (2) A falcon close perched on a rest ppr. (*for Knox*). *In hoc signo vinces.* 85. 13

Gore-Booth, Bart., Sir Henry William, of Lissadell, co. Sligo: (1) A lion passant pean resting the dexter fore-paw upon a chaplet of roses (*for Booth*). (2) A wolf rampant arg. (*for Gore*). *Quod ero spero.—In hoc signo vinces.—Genti æquus utrique.* 28. 2

Gore of London and Herts, on a mount vert, an heraldic tiger salient arg., tufted and maned sa., ducally gorged or.

Gore, Ormsby-, Shropsh.: (1) An heraldic tiger rampant arg., ducally gorged or, tufted sa., langued gu. (*for Gore*). (2) An arm in armour embowed ppr., charged with a rose gu., holding in the hand, also ppr., a man's leg in armour of the same, garnished and spurred or, flexed at the knee, couped at the thigh, and dropping blood gu. (*for Ormsby*).

Gore, Ireland, an heraldic tiger rampant arg., collared gu., and charged on the shoulder with a trefoil slipped vert. *In hoc signo vinces.*

Gore, Wilts, a bull's head couped sa. cf. 44. 3

Gore-Langton, Hon. Henry Powell, of Hatch Park, Taunton: (1) An eagle or, and wyvern vert, their necks entwined regardant (*for Langton*). (2) On a mount vert, an heraldic tiger salient arg., collared gu. (*for Gore*). (3) On a ducal coronet a martlet or (*for Temple*). *In hoc signo vinces.*

Gorely and **Gorley,** a hand in armour holding a cross crosslet fitched in pale ppr. 210. 14

Gorge, a greyhound's head couped arg., collared az., studded or. 61. 2

Gorges, Lord Dundalk, (*extinct*), a greyhound's head couped arg., gorged with a bar gemelle gu. cf. 61. 2

Gorges, Somers., a greyhound's head couped ppr., collared or. 61. 2

Gorges, John Arthur Howard, Esquire, of 15, Royal Terrace, East Kingstown, co. Dublin, a greyhound's head couped ppr., collared gu., bezantée. *Prend moy tel que je suis.*

Gorges, Ireland, a salmon haurient ppr. 139. 11

Gorges and **Gorgis,** a gem-ring or, stoned az. 167. 14

Gorham, a sword in pale and on its point a garland of laurel, all ppr. 170. 1

Gorham of St. Neots, Hunts, a griffin's head couped between two wings, all or. *Ready and faithful.* 65. 11

Goring, Sir Harry Yelverton, Bart., of Highden, Sussex, a lion rampant gardant sa. *Renascentur.*

Goring, Rev. John, of 55, Eaton Place, S.W., same crest.

Goring-Thomas, Rhys, Esquire, J.P., of Plas Llannon, Llanelly, Carmarthensh., a heron's head arg., gorged with a garland and erased gu. *A Deo et patre.*

Gorley, Kent, a hand in armour holding a cross crosslet fitchée in pale, all ppr. 210. 14

Gorm, Scotland, an eagle's head erased sa., beaked or. 83. 2

Gorman, a horse at full speed saddled ppr. 52. 1

Gorman, Ireland, a naked arm holding a sword ppr. 212. 3

Gorman, Ireland, a dexter armed arm embowed, the hand bare, grasping a sword, the blade wavy, all ppr. *Primi et ultimi in bello.* cf. 195. 2

Gormanston, Viscount (Preston), on a chapeau gu., turned up erm., a fox statant ppr. *Sans tache.*

Gorney, on a chapeau gu., turned up erm., a lion passant arg., resting the dexter paw on a cinquefoil or. cf. 4. 9

Gorney, a merman ppr., holding a target or.

Gorrey and **Gorie,** Scotland, an eagle's head sa. 83. 1

Gorst, Right Hon. Sir John Eldon, of Howes Close, Cambs, a pheon or, the shaft entwined by a serpent ppr. *Quod adest gratum.* 241. 6

Gort, Viscount (Vereker), out of a mural coronet gu., a stag's head ppr. *Vincit veritas.*

Gorton, out of an earl's coronet a Moor's head affrontée ppr.

Gorton of Gorton, Lancs, a goat's head erased arg., ducally gorged or. *cf.* 128. 5

Gorwood and **Gurwood,** a unicorn's head ppr. *Pour jamais.* 49. 7

Goschen, Viscount (Goschen), on an arrow fesswise, a dove, wings addorsed, all ppr. *Pacem.* 283. 3

Gosell and **Gossell,** Norf., out of a ducal coronet or, a talbot's head erm. 57. 12

Gosford, Earl of (Acheson), a cock gu., standing upon a trumpet or. *Vigilantibus.* 91. 6

Goshall, out of a ducal coronet or, a lion's gamb gu., holding an arrow of the first, headed of the second.

Goskar, a Cornish chough holding in its beak a mullet. *Spes mea in Deo.*

Goslett, Glouc., a stalk of wheat and a palm-branch in saltier ppr. 154. 10

Goslett, George A. D., of Highfields, East Grinstead, Sussex, same crest. *Deus spes mea est.*

Goslike, a griffin's head couped between two wings gu., plattée. 65. 11

Gosling and **Gosolyn,** an eagle's head erased sa., charged with a crescent erm. *cf.* 83. 2

Gosling, an eagle's head erased erm., charged on the neck with a bezant, and over it a cross formée arg. *cf.* 83. 2

Gosling, Robert Cunliffe, Hassobury, Bishop Stortford, in front of a bear's paw erased ppr., holding a fleur-de-lis a crescent, both or.

Gosnall and **Gosnold,** a bull's head affrontée per pale or and vert, armed counterchanged. 44. 8

Gosnall and **Gosnold,** of Ipswich and Otley, Suff., a bull's head gardant per pale or and az. 44. 8

Gospatrick, an antique ship of one mast, the sail furled sa., the flag gu. 160. 6

Goss, William Henry, Esquire, F.G.S., etc., Stoke-upon-Trent, Staffs, a falcon with wings expanded and inverted ppr., ducally gorged or. *Se inserit astris.* 291. 10

Goss, Samuel, Physician and Surgeon, Burlington Lodge, Southsea, on a mount a falcon with wings expanded and elevated ppr., ducally gorged or. *Se inserit astris.*

Gosse of Epsom, Surrey, a pheon sa., entwined by a branch of oak or, between two wings of the last, guttée-de-sang. 227. 10

Gosse, Radnorsh., a sword in pale ppr., pommel and hilt or, between two branches of laurel vert. *En Dieu est ma foy.* 170. 3

Gosselin or **Gosselyn,** an antelope's head erased ppr. 126. 2

Gosselin, Sir Martin Le Marchant Hadsley, K.C.M.G., C.B., of Blakesware, Herts, a Moor's head ppr. 192. 13

Gosselin, Hellier Robert Hadsley, Esquire, of Bengeo Hall, Herts, a Moor's head couped at the neck ppr., wreathed about the temples arg. and sa.

Gosset or **Gossett,** a hand couped at the wrist erect holding a dagger in pale ppr. 212. 9

Gosset, a greyhound's head erased arg., collared gu., ringed and garnished or. *cf.* 61. 2

Gossip, a martlet sa. 95. 5

Gossip of Hatfield, Yorks, two goats' heads erased and addorsed, the dexter az., the sinister arg. *Prospice, respice.* 268. 4

Gost of London, a pheon or, between two wings arg.

Gostling, a phœnix in flames ppr. 82. 2

Gostomes and **Goston** of Stockwell, Surrey, on a chapeau gu., turned up arg., a rose or, between two wings az.

Gostwick or **Gostwyke,** Beds, a griffin's head between two wings expanded gu. 65. 11

Gostwick, Beds, a griffin's head between two wings expanded gu., plattée. *cf.* 65. 11

Gostwyck, William Gostwyck, Esquire, a griffin's head couped gu., on the neck a bend cotised arg., between two wings of the first, each charged with a mullet of six points of the second.

Gostwyck, C. H. G., Chartham Down, Canterbury, same crest.

Gotham, on the stump of a tree an eagle with wings addorsed ppr. 79. 12

Gothard, Northumb., out of a ducal coronet or, a buck's head ppr. *Aquila non captat muscas.* 120. 7

Gotley, a demi-lion rampant holding a sword-blade wavy, all ppr. *cf.* 10. 2

Gotobed, a pelican in her piety gu. 98. 14

Gott of London and Sussex, a griffin's head erm., between two wings expanded erm. 65. 11

Gottes, Cambs, a greyhound's head erased arg., collared and lined or. *cf.* 61. 2

Gottington, a horned owl ppr. 96. 5

Goucell, a unicorn passant or. *cf.* 48. 5

Gouch, a griffin's head erased ppr. *Semper eadem.* 66. 2

Goudie, Scotland, a garb or. *Honestas.* 153. 2

Gouge, Wales, on a dexter gauntlet in fesse a hawk with wings expanded, all ppr. *cf.* 86. 13

Gough, Viscount Gough, of Goojerat: (1) In the centre a boar's head couped at the neck or. 41. 2. (2) On the dexter side, of honourable augmentation, on a mural coronet arg., a lion passant gardant or, holding in the dexter paw two flag-staves in bend sinister ppr., the one bearing the Union flag of Great Britain and Ireland, surmounting the other the staff thereof broken, with a triangular banner flowing therefrom, being intended to represent a Chinese flag, having thereon the device of a dragon and in an escroll above the word "*China.*" (3) On the sinister side, also of honourable augmentation, a dexter arm embowed in the uniform of the 87th Regiment, being gu., faced vert, the hand grasping the colours of the said regiment displayed and a representation of a French eagle reversed and depressed, the staff broken ppr., and in an escroll above, the word "*Barossa.*" (Over the family crest) *Faugh a Ballagh.*—(Under the arms) *Goojerat.*

Gough, Somers. and Ireland, a boar's head couped arg. 41. 1

Gough, General Sir Charles John Stanley, of United Service Club, S.W., a boar's head couped at the neck or, tusked arg. *Faugh a Ballagh.* 41. 1

Gough, General Sir Hugh Henry, of 40, Gloucester Street, S.W., same crest and motto.

Gough, Major-General Hugh Sutlej, C.B., of Caer Rhûn, Conway, North Wales, Llechweddygarth Hall, Montgomerysh., same crest. *Gradu diversa via una.*

Gough, Somers. and Ireland, a boar's head couped arg., holding in the mouth a broken spear gu. *Domat omnia virtus.*

Gough, Admiral Frederick William, Esquire, R.N., C.B., J.P., a boar's head couped or, devouring a broken spear gu. *Domat omnia virtus.*

Gough, George, Clensmore House, Woodbridge, Suff., a boar's head close, pierced through the head by a tilting-spear. *Domat omnia virtus.*

Gough, Ireland, a wyvern with the tail nowed ppr. *cf.* 70. 1

Gough, Shropsh., a horse's head erased arg. 51. 4

Goughton, a rose slipped gu., leaved and stalked ppr., between two wings.

Gouin of Brighton, a lion rampant or, gorged with a collar az., holding in the dexter forepaw a javelin in bend ppr., and resting the sinister on a cross couped, also az. *Je tiens.*

Goulborne, Chesh., a stag's head or, gorged with a chaplet of laurel ppr. 120. 3

Goulburn, a dove holding in its beak an olive-branch ppr. 92. 5

Gould of Fleet House, Dorset, an arm embowed vested gu., cuffed or, holding in the hand ppr. a banner paly of six az. and or, on a canton arg. a cross, also gu., the staff of the second.

Gould of Upwey, Dorchester, Dorset, an arm embowed vested vert, holding in the hand a flagstaff ppr., therefrom flowing a banner or, charged with three barrulets wavy az., on a canton arg. a cross gu. *Aperto vivere voto.*

Gould, Ireland, a martlet or. 95. 2

Gould, a demi-lion rampant or, holding a scroll arg.

Gould, Devonsh., a demi-lion rampant az., bezantée. *Probitate et labore.* 10. 4

Gould, Rev. Sabine Baring, of Lew Trenchard, same crest. *Gold bydeth ever bright.—Toujours sans tache.*

Gould, Hon. Albert John, of Enesbury, Edgecliffe, Sydney, a demi-lion erm., grasping with the dexter paw a saltire arg. and resting the sinister on a bezant. 238. 2

Gould, Scotland, between the horns of a crescent arg., a buckle or. 163. 15

Gould, Scotland, a stag's head ppr. 121. 5

Gould, Joseph, of Hambledon, Christchurch, New Zealand, on a mount vert, a demi-lion arg., holding in the hott dexter paw a hurt, resting the sinister on a saltire az. *Honore et labore.*

Goulden, a lion's head erased ppr. 17. 8
Gouldie, Scotland, a garb or. *Quid utilius.* 153. 2
Goulding, William Joshua, Esquire, of Ballyrosheen and Summerhill House, co. Cork, and Roebuck Hill, co. Dublin, and of Millicent, Sallius, co. Kildare, a dexter hand couped at the wrist and apaumée, encircled by a wreath of oak in bend pierced with an arrow in bend sinister, point downwards, all ppr. *Virtute et valore.*
Goulding, Ireland, a hawk ppr., jessed, belled, and hooded or. 85. 1
Goulding, Kent, a lion sejant sa., supporting with the dexter paw an escutcheon or. *cf.* 8. 1
Gouldingham, a lion's gamb erased. 36. 4
Gouldney, a quatrefoil ensigned with a lion's head erased.
Gouldsmith, Kent, a Cornish chough ppr., guttée-d'eau. 107. 14
Gouldwell of Wisbeach, Camb., and Bury St. Edmunds, Suff., out of a well or, a branch of columbines stalked and leaved vert, flowered ppr.
Goulstone, an ostrich's wing of five feathers alternately arg. and gu., charged with a bend sa., thereon three plates. 113. 6
Goulter, Thomas Morse, Esquire, of Aldmondsbury, Glouc., a cubit arm vested gu., cuffed arg., the hand ppr. holding a battle-axe sa., suspended from the wrist by a chain an escutcheon or, charged with an anchor, also sa. *Animo et fide.*
Goulter, Cyrus, Esquire, of New Zealand, five annulets fessewise interlaced or, thereon a crescent arg.
Goulton, Yorks, a fleur-de-lis sa. 148. 2
Gouring, a lion rampant. 1. 13
Gourlay, Scotland, a salmon naiant arg., *Ditat et alit.* 139. 12
Gourlay, Gourley, and **Gourlee,** a boar's head erased ppr. 42. 2
Gourlay and **Gourley,** Scotland, a mullet of six points or. 164. 3
Gourlay, Austin-, of Kincraig, Fife, Scotland: (1) A demi-eagle displayed arg., armed and beaked gu. (*for Gourlay*). 81. 6. (2) An eagle displayed with two heads per pale or and gu., charged on each wing with a crescent counterchanged (*for Austin*). *Profunda cernit.*—*Virtute non vi.* *cf.* 74. 4
Gourlie, Scotland, two hands couped and conjoined in fess ppr., supporting a cross crosslet fitched gu. 224. 11
Gourney, Essex, on a chapeau gu., turned up erm., a lion statant, tail extended arg., the dexter paw resting upon a cinquefoil or. *cf.* 4. 8
Govan, Scotland, a sword in pale ppr., on the point thereof a mullet arg. *Dépêchez.* 169. 3
Gove, out of a mural coronet or, a demi-monkey sa. 136. 13
Gover, in a maunch or, a dexter hand apaumée ppr. 203. 1
Govesy and **Govisy,** a demi-woman ppr., richly attired az., holding in her dexter hand a balance of the first. 183. 2
Govett, a demi-savage holding in his dexter hand a sheaf of arrows and pointing with the sinister to a crown. 186. 13
Gow, Scotland, a hand holding an escallop ppr. 216. 2
Gow, Thomas, West Grange, Cambo, Northumb., an arm embowed in armour holding a broadsword (*Gow*). A demi-lion rampant or (*Steuart*). *Caraid ann am fheum.*—*Hinc orior.*
Gow-Steuart of Little Colonsay, Argyllsh.: (1) A demi-lion holding in his dexter paw a Lochaber-axe in pale (*for Steuart*). (2) A dexter arm in armour embowed holding a broadsword enfiled with a boar's head, all ppr. (*for Gow*). *Firm.*—*Caraid ann am fheum.*
Gowan, Samuel H., 6, Duncain Terrace, Belfast, a demi-lion rampant holding in the dexter paw a fleur-de-lis.
Gowan, Major R. W., 14, Helena Road, Southsea, out of a Viscount's coronet a naked hand couped at the shoulder holding a drawn sword.
Gowan, Scotland, a lymphad, her oars in action sa., flag gu. 160. 7
Gowan, Scotland, a sword in pale ppr. 170. 2
Gowans, Scotland, a lion's head erased ppr., collared or. 18. 6
Gowcell, Norf., a unicorn passant arg. *cf.* 48. 5
Gower, *see* Sutherland, Duke of.
Gower, *see* Granville, Earl of.
Gower, *see* Cromartie, Earl of.
Gower, *see* Leveson-Gower.
Gower, Yorks, a demi-eagle or. 80. 2
Gower, Essex and Worc., a wolf's head erased or. 30. 8
Gower, Berks and Yorks, a wolf passant arg., collared and lined or. *Frangas, non flectes.* *cf.* 28. 10
Gower of London, a talbot sejant. *cf.* 55. 2
Gower, Ireland, two wings displayed or. 109. 6
Gowland, Durham, a bezant charged with a mount vert, thereon a stag trippant ppr. *cf.* 116. 11
Gowshell, Norf., a bull's head caboshed ppr. 43. 8
Goylin, a greyhound's head per pale arg. and or, between two roses gu., stalked and leaved ppr. 61. 11
Graben, an eagle displayed or, gorged with a chaplet of leaves vert. *cf.* 75. 2
Grabham, Somers., on a mount vert, a boar's head erased or, guttée-de-sang, and entwined by a snake ppr. *L'Espérance du salut.*
Grabham, George Wallington, M.D., Mathyns, Witham, Essex, a boar's head erased or. *L'Espérance du salut.*
Graby and **Greby,** out of a ducal coronet or, a demi-eagle displayed ppr. 80. 14
Graby and **Greby,** out of a ducal coronet or, an eagle displayed or, armed gu. 80. 14
Grace, *see* Hamilton-Grace.
Grace, Sir Valentine Raymond, Bart., B.A., J.P., D.L., of Grace Castle, co. Kilkenny, a lion rampant per fesse arg. and or. *Concordant nomine facta.* 10. 2
Grace, a demi-lion rampant arg. *En grace affie.* 10. 2
Gracie, Scotland, a fox current. *cf.* 32. 8
Graden, Scotland, a bull's head erased ppr 44. 3
Graden, Scotland, a demi-otter erect sa., devouring a fish ppr. *Ad escam et usum.* 134. 12
Gradock and **Gradocke,** a horse-shoe az., between two eagle's wings ppr. 110. 11
Gradwell, Robert Bernard George Ashhurst, Esquire, J.P., of Dowth Hall, co. Meath, Ireland, a stag trippant ppr., collared and chained or, charged with a rose gu. *Nil desperandum.* *cf.* 117. 8
Gradwell, George Fitzgerald, Esquire, of Platten Hall, Drogheda, co. Meath, Ireland, same crest and motto.
Grady, Ireland, a horse's head arg. *cf.* 50. 13
Grady, a demi-lion rampant ppr. 10. 2
Græme, Perthsh., an eagle volant ppr. *Ardenter prosequor alis.*
Græme, Colonel R. C., Brackenhurst, Camberley, Surrey, an eagle rising with wings expanded and elevated.
Græme of Garvock, Dunning, Perthsh., a lion rampant gu. *Noli me tangere.* 1. 13
Græme, Scotland, a stag lodged ppr. *Cubo ut excubo.* 115. 7
Græme of Inchbrakie, Perthsh., a hand holding a garland ppr. *A Deo victoria.* 218. 4
Græme, Alexander Malcolm Sutherland, a lion couchant lying before a sword in pale ppr.
Græme, Durh., a cubit arm holding a laurel-chaplet ppr. 218. 4
Græme, Laurence Anthony Murray, Esquire, of Fonthill, Shaldon, Devonsh., a mailed hand holding a garland ppr. *A Deo victoria.*
Græme, Hamond-: (1) Two arms erect issuing from clouds in the act of removing from a spike a human skull, above the skull a marquess's coronet, all between two palm-branches ppr. (*for Græme*). (2) Out of a naval crown or, an eagle's head sa. (*for Hamond*). *Sepulto viresco.* 83. 7
Grafton, Duke of (Fitzroy), Northamp., on a chapeau gu., turned up erm., a lion statant gardant or, crowned with a ducal coronet az., and gorged with a collar compony-countercompony arg. and of the fourth. *Et decus et pretium recti.* 4. 2
Grafton of London, Bucks, Worc., and Shropsh., on the trunk of a tree couped and eradicated an eagle rising, all or. 79. 12
Graham, Earl and Baron Graham, *see* Montrose, Duke of.
Graham, Baron Lynedoch, *see* Lynedoch.
Graham, *see* Murray-Graham.
Graham, *see* Savage-Graham.
Graham-Toler, *see* Toler.
Graham, Sir Richard James, Bart., D.L., of Netherby, Cumb., two wings addorsed or. *Reason contents me.* *cf.* 109. 12
Graham, Sir Reginald Henry, Bart., J.P., D.L., of Norton-Conyers, Yorks, two wings addorsed or. *Reason contents me.* *cf.* 109. 12
Graham, Sir Robert James Stuart, Bart., of Esk, Cumb., two wings addorsed or. *Reason contents me.* *cf.* 109. 12
Graham, Scotland, a vol ppr. *Reason contents me.* 113. 1

Graham, James, 39, Ennismore Gardens, an eagle ppr., beaked and armed ppr., and killing a stork of the last armed gu. *Ne oublie.*

Graham, Donald, of Airthrey Castle, Bridge of Allan, N.B., same crest and motto.

Graham, George Marshall, of Toronto, Canada, an eagle's head erased ppr. *Right and reason.*

Graham, Scotland, an eagle's head ppr., beaked or. *Right and reason.* 83. 1

Graham, John James, of Newlands, Cape Town, a phœnix in flames ppr. *Bon fin.* 82. 2

Graham, an eagle's head erased gu. *Right and reason.* 83. 2

Graham, Scotland, a demi-eagle with wings expanded ppr. *Right and reason.* 80. 2

Graham, Robert Bontine Cunninghame, of Ardoch, Dumbartonsh., a demi-eagle issuing out of a ducal coronet ppr. *Copiose et opportuna.*

Graham of Gartmore, an eagle displayed holding in its dexter talon a sword in pale ppr. *For right and reason.* 75. 7

Graham-Stirling, an eagle displayed ppr., holding in dexter talon a sword and in sinister a pistol of the last. *For right.—Noctes diesque præsto.* cf. 75. 7

Graham of Orchill, an eagle volant ppr. *Prosequor alis.*

Graham of Glasgow, an eagle regardant rising from the top of a rock, all ppr. *Souvenez.* 79. 9

Graham-Maxwell, Scotland: (1) Same crest as above. 79. 9. (2) A stag's head cabossed. *Souvenez.—Prospere sed cura.* 122. 5

Graham of Morphie, an eagle devouring a crane. *Ne oublie.* 79. 7

Graham of Dalkenneth, Lochearnhead, Perthsh., an eagle preying on a heron, both ppr. *Ne oublie.* 79. 7

Graham of Burntshiels, Renfrew, an eagle devouring a stork, all ppr. *Ne oublie.* 79. 7

Graham of Killern, a falcon killing a stork ppr. *Memor esto.* 79. 7

Graham, Donald, Esquire, C.I.E., of Airthrey Castle, Bridge of Allan, a falcon ppr., beaked and armed or, killing a stork arg., armed gu. *Ne oublie.*

Graham, James Noble, Esquire, of Carfin, Carluke, Lanarksh., same crest and motto.

Graham, Robert Chellas, Esquire, of Skipness, Argyllsh., same crest and motto.

Graham, Douglas William, Esquire, of Hilston Park, St. Maughans, Monm., an eagle ppr., beaked and armed arg., and killing a stork of the last, armed gu. *Ne oublie.*

Graham, Robert Gore, Southmead, Westbury-on-Trym, between two roses gu., stalked and leaved, an eagle preying on a stalk ppr., the wing charged with a cross crosslet fitchée or. *Quod Deus trahit virtus secura sequitur.*

Graham of Drynie, a falcon ppr., armed and beaked or, standing on a heron. *Ne oublie.*

Graham of New Wark, Scotland, a pelican's head couped ppr. *Fides et amor.* cf. 98. 2

Graham, a falcon's head ppr. *Right and reason.* cf. 88. 12

Graham, Scotland, a falcon ppr. *Prædæ memor.* 85. 2

Graham, a falcon ppr., beaked and membered gu. *Prædiæ memor.* 85. 2

Graham of Balgowan, a dove ppr. *Candide et secure.* 92. 2

Graham of Gartur, Stirling, a dove rising with a twig of palm in her beak ppr. *Peace and grace.*

Graham of Garvoch, Perth, a lion rampant gu. *Noli me tangere.* 1. 13

Graham of Grahamshall, Scotland, a lion couchant in front of a sword in pale ppr. *Nec temere, nec timide.* cf. 7. 5

Graham of Breckness, a lion's gamb erect and erased gu., grasping a sword in pale ppr. *Nec temere, nec timide.* 38. 8

Graham, a greyhound passant. cf. 60. 2

Graham of Balchlave, a stag lodged gu. *Cubo ut excubo.* 115. 7

Graham of Callander, Stirlingsh., an escallop or. *Spero meliora.* 141. 12

Graham of Dougalstoun, an escallop or. *Pignus amoris.* 141. 12

Graham of Duntroon, a flame of fire ppr. *Recta sursum.* 177. 10

Graham of Potento, Forfarsh., same crest. *Semper sursum.* 177. 10

Graham of Monargan, Scotland, same crest. *Nunquam deorsum.* 177. 10

Graham of London, a blade of thistle and a fig-leaf ppr. in saltire. *Hinc decus inde tegmen.*

Graham, an oak-branch erect ppr., bearing one acorn or. 152. 1

Graham of London, an oak-sprig with an acorn ppr. *Alteri proses sæculo.* 152. 1

Graham of Meiklewood, Stirling, a star ppr. *Auxiliante, resurgo.* 164. 3

Graham, Sir Cyril Clerke, Bart., C.M.G., of Kirkstall, Yorks, two arms in armour embowed issuing out of the battlements of a tower, all ppr., holding in the hands ppr. an escallop sa. *Fideliter et diligenter.*

Graham, John Davenport, same crest. *Ne oublie.*

Graham, Thomas Henry Boileau, of Edmond Castle, Carlisle, Cumb., same crest and motto.

Graham of Braco, two hands issuing out of a cloud, in each a sword flourished, the dexter over the sinister. *Defendendo vinco.*

Graham of Gorthey, two arms issuing from a cloud erect, and holding up a man's skull encircled with two branches of palm-tree, and over the head a marquess's coronet, all ppr. *Sepultu vi resco.*

Graham, within a wreath of cypress vert, out of clouds, two arms embowed ppr., holding a skull arg., crowned or.

Graham, Robert, Esquire, of Drumgoon, co. Fermanagh, and of Ballmakill, co. Galway, Ireland, on a wreath of the colours an arm embowed, vested az., cuffed arg., the hand ppr. grasping a staff raguly gu. *Ratio mihi sufficit.*

Graham, Francis John, Esquire, of Drumgoon, Maguiresbridge, co. Fermanagh, and Ballmakill, Letterfrack, co. Galway, same crest and motto.

Graham, William, Esquire, of Crosbie, Ayrsh., a naked arm brandishing a spear, all ppr. *Pro rege.* 212. 9

Graham, Scotland, a hand holding a sword in pale ppr. *Non immemor.*

Graham of Inchbraikie, Scotland, a dexter hand holding a garland ppr. *A Deo victoria.* 218. 4

Graham, Murray-, Henry Stuart, Murrayshall, Perth: (1) A dove ppr. (with motto *Candide et secure*). (2) A buck's head couped ppr. (*for Murray*). *Macte virtue.*

Graham, issuing out of a cloud in fess a hand reaching to a garland, all ppr. *Numen et omnia.* 223. 3

Graham, Ireland, a hand in fess couped holding a fleur-de-lis or. 221. 9

Graham of Airth Castle, Stirling, a dexter hand holding a sword erect ppr. *Non immemor.* 212. 9

Graham-Barns-Graham, Allan, Esquire, of Craigallian, Stirlingsh.; Kirkhill, Ayrsh., Lymekilns and Cambuslang, Lanarksh., and Fereneze, Renfrewsh.: (1) On the dexter side a naked arm, the hand brandishing a spear ppr. (*for Graham*). 214. 11. (2) On the sinister side a garb ppr., banded gu. (*for Barns*). *Pro rege.—Peace and plenty.*

Graham, Westm., an arm in armour embowed brandishing a cutlass ppr. 195. 2

Graham, Thomas Henry Boileau, Edmond Castle, Carlisle, Cumb., two armed arms issuing out of the battlements of a tower ppr., holding an escallop sa. *N'oublie.*

Graham-Campbell, Robert Charles, Esquire, of Shirvan, Lochgilphead, N.B.: (1) A hart's head erased ppr. (*for Campbell*). (2) An escallop or (*for Graham*). *Pignus amorus.—Pro aris et focis.*

Graham-Clarke, Leonard John, Esquire, of Frocester Manor, Stonehouse, Glouc., and Glanrhos, Breconsh., an escallop quarterly gu. and or (*for Clarke*).

Graham-Foster-Pigott, Esquire, G.E., of Cheriton House, Hants.: (1) A mount vert, thereon in front of a pickaxe or, a greyhound passant sa., gorged for distinction with a collar or (*for Pigott*). (2) In front of a stag's head couped or, attired sa., gorged for distinction with a mural crown gu., a bugle-horn, also sa., garnished or (*for Foster*). (3) An escallop or, with the words "*Spero meliora*" above it (*for Graham*). *Hoc age.*

Graham-Foster-Pigott, Thomas, Esquire, of Abington Pigotts, Royston, same crests and motto.

Graham-Wigan, John Alfred, Esquire, of Oakwood, Maidstone, Kent, and Duntrune, Dundee, N.B.: (1) On a mount vert, a mountain-ash tree under a rainbow ppr. (*for Wigan*). (2) A flame of fire ppr., charged with a cross crosslet sa., for difference (*for Graham*). *Recta sursum.*

Grahame, Francis Barclay, Spyland Bank, Midlothian, a cross patée.

Grailly, a man's head in profile with ass's ears arg. cf. 190. 6

Grainger, Essex, a dexter arm couped, vested az., purfled or, cuffed arg., holding in the hand ppr., by the chains of the second, a portcullis gu.

Grainger, *see* Stewart-Grainger.

Grainger, co. Waterford, Ireland, a dexter arm embowed, vested az., bezantée, cuffed arg., the hand ppr., holding by the chains or, a portcullis gu.

Graison, a stag lodged regardant ppr. *cf.* 115. 9

Grammer, Herts, a demi-lion rampant az., billettée or. *Fax mentis incendium gloria.* 10. 2

Gramshaw, Farbrace Sidney, M.D., F.R.C.S., 9, St. Leonard's, York, a demi-griffin segreant. *Amicitia.*

Granado, a pomegranate slipped ppr. 152. 4

Granard, Earl of (Forbes), a bear passant arg., guttée-de-sang, muzzled gu. *Fax mentis incendium gloriæ.*

Granby, Marquess of, *see* Rutland, Duke of.

Grance, a holly-branch vert, fructed gu. 147. 7

Grance, a demi-bear rampant ppr. 34. 13

Grandford, a hawk perching on a fish ppr. 86. 6

Grandgeorge, Lincs, a stag's head arg., gorged with a bar gemelle gu. *cf.* 121. 5

Grandgeorge, Lincs, a stag's head couped per pale sa. and or, guttée, counter-changed. 121. 5

Grandison, Viscount, *see* Jersey, Earl of.

Grandison and **Granson,** a female supporting a portcullis ppr. 183. 7

Grandiville and **Granville,** a griffin's head between two wings endorsed, all ppr. *cf.* 67. 11

Grandorge or **Grain d'Orge,** Yorks: (1) A hawk ppr. 85. 2. (2) A stag's head arg., gorged with a bar gemelle gu. *cf.* 121. 5

Grandorge, Lincs, a stag's head couped, guttée, holding in the mouth an ear of barley vert.

Grandson, out of a heart gu., a hand holding a scimitar ppr. 213. 4

Grandson, a poplar-tree ppr. 144. 12

Grandvell, a greyhound's head sa., collared and ringed or. 61. 2

Grandville, a griffin passant or. 63. 2

Grane, Yorks, a wolf passant paly of four or and sa., holding in his mouth a pen of the first. 227. 7

Grane, a boar passant sa., collared and lined or. *cf.* 40. 9

Granell, round a pheon shafted, a serpent entwined ppr.

Grange of London, a lion's gamb erect and erased ppr., holding a branch of pomegranates or.

Grange, Norf. and Cambs, a demi-antelope or, attired, maned, and ungu. sa. *cf.* 126. 5

Grange, a griffin's head erased sa., beaked and eared or, charged with three bezants. *cf.* 66. 2

Granger, *see* Grainger.

Granger, Staffs, a griffin passant arg. *Honestas optima politia.* 63. 2

Granger, a dexter arm embowed, holding in the hand three wheat-ears, all ppr.

Granger, Thomas Colpitts, His Honour, of Pencair, Falmouth, an arm embowed to the sinister, the hand grasping a vested az. and cuffed arg., the elbow portcullis gu., by the chains or.

Granson, Kent, out of a ducal coronet gu., a plume of feathers arg. 114. 13

Grant, Baron Glenelg, *see* Glenelg.

Grant-Dalton, *see* Dalton.

Grant, Scotland, a burning hill ppr. *Stand sure.—Stand fast.* 179. 2

Grant, Murray-, Ian Robert James, Glenmoriston, Inverness, same crest. *Stand firm.*

Grant, Scotland, a burning hill, all ppr. *Stand fast, craig Elachie.* 179. 2

Grant, James, Esquire, late of Tullochgorum, Fingal, Tasmania, Member of Council of Education, a mount fire ppr. *Stand fast.* 179. 2

Grant-Thorold, Alexander William, 3, Grosvenor Gardens: (1) A buck arg., charged on the body with a quatrefoil vert, resting a dexter foot on an escutcheon arg., thereon a martlet or. (2) On a rock a burning mountain surmounted by a rainbow, all ppr.

Grant of Aberlour, Banffsh., Scotland, a burning mountain ppr. *Stabit.* 179. 2

Grant, Colonel A. C., same crest. *Stand fast.*

Grant, Cardross, Brentsfield, Beckenham, same crest. *Stand sure.*

Grant of Glenmoriston, Inverness, a mountain in flames ppr. *Stand firm.* 179. 2

Grant of Glenlochy, same crest. *Ferte cito flammas.* 179. 2

Grant, Edward, Esquire, of Litchborough Hall, Weedon, a conical hill fired at the summit ppr., issuant therefrom a cross Calvary or. *Stand sure.*

Grant, Charles Eustace, Esquire, same crest and motto.

Grant of Lurg, Scotland, a hill, on the top of which is a forest, all ppr. *Stabilis.*

Grant, Scotland, a rock ppr. *Immobile.* 179. 7

Grant, Sir Ludovic James, Bart., of Dalvey, the trunk of an oak-tree sprouting out leaves with the sun shining thereon, all ppr. *Te favente virebo.* 145. 5

Grant of Gartenbeg, Scotland, on the trunk of an oak-tree sprouting the sun shining, all ppr. *Wise and harmless.* 145. 5

Grant, Scotland, an oak-tree ppr. *Suo se robore firmat.* 143. 5

Grant of Shewglie and Redcastle, Scotland, a banyan-tree ppr. *Recrescimus.*

Grant of Corrimony, Scotland, a demi-savage ppr. *I'll stand sure.* 232. 5

Grant, Sir James Alexander, K.C.M.G., M.D., F.R.C.S., F.R.C.P., of 150, Elgin Street, Ottawa, Canada, Inverness-sh., Scotland, same crest and motto.

Grant, Francis James, Esquire, W.S., Rothesay Herald, of Lyon Office, Edinburgh, and 106, Thirlestane Road, Edinburgh, N.B., same crest and motto.

Grant, Rev. Roderick John Archibald, of 41, Brook Green, Hammersmith, W., same crest and motto.

Grant-Ives, Wilfrid Dryden, Esquire, M.A., J.P., of Bradden House, Towcester: (1) Issuant from a rock ppr., a blackamoor's head in profile couped at the shoulders ppr., the temples and the neck each encircled by an annulet or (*for Ives*). (2) A conical hill fired at the summit ppr., issuant therefrom a cross Calvary or (*for Grant*). *Stand sure.*

Grant of Preston Grange, Scotland, a demi-Hercules with a lion's skin ppr. *Non inferiora secutus.*

Grant of Cullen, a book expanded. *Suum cuique.* 158. 3

Grant, Sir Arthur Henry, Bart., D.L., of Monymusk, Aberdeensh., a Bible displayed ppr. *Suum cuique.—Jehovah Jireh.* 158. 3

Grant, Ireland, a cat-a-mountain rampant. 26. 2

Grant, Ireland, a cat rampant gardant. *cf.* 26. 2

Grant of Invereshie, a cat sejant erect ppr. *Parcere subjectis.* 25. 2

Grant, Macpherson-, Sir George, Bart., D.L., of Ballindalloch, co. Elgin: (1) On the dexter side a hand erect issuing from the wreath, and holding a dirk in pale ppr. 212. 9. (2) On the sinister side, a cat sejant erect gardant ppr. *Ense et animo.—Touch not the cat, but a glove.* 26. 9

Grant, John Peter, Esquire, of Rothiemurchus, Inverness-sh., Scotland, a hand and arm holding a broadsword ppr. *In God is all my trust.—Pro patria.* 210. 2

Grant of Blackburn, an arm in armour embowed holding in the hand a sword, all ppr. *Fortitudine.* 195 2.

Grant, Scotland, a dexter hand holding a dagger in pale ppr. *Ense et animo.* 212. 9

Grant of Darlway, a dexter hand holding a branch of oak ppr. *Radicem firmant frondes.* *cf.* 219. 9

Grant of Chelsea, a two-handed sword in bend ppr., hilted and pommelled or, over a man's head of the first. *Have at you.*

Grant, John Patrick, Esquire, Captain Seaforth Highlanders, of Kilgraston and Drummonie House, Bridge of Earn, Perthsh., Scotland, the Roman fasces erect ppr. *Leges juraque serva.* 171. 4

Grant of Achnanie, Scotland, a cock ppr. *Audacia.* 91. 2

Grant of Carron, Banffsh., an adder nowed with the head erect ppr. *Wise and harmless.*

Grant of Easter Elchies, Banffsh., Scotland, a unicorn's head and neck arg. *Audentior ito.* 49. 7

Grant, Major, of Willow Hyrst, Chiddingly, Hellingly, out of a ducal coronet a demi-eagle displayed ppr.

Grant, Warw., a fleur-de-lis az. 148. 2

Grant, Scotland, a boar's head couped ppr. *Stabit conscius æqui.* 43. 1

Grant of London and Hants, a demi-lion arg. *Tanquam despicatus sum, vinco.* 10. 2

Grantham, Lincs, a demi-griffin segreant gu. *Honore et amore.* 64. 2

Grantham of Ketton Grange, Rutland, a demi-griffin gu. *Honore et amore.* 64. 2

Grantham, Hon. Sir William, Judge of the High Court of Justice, King's Bench Division, J.P., of Barcombe Place, near Lewes, and 100, Eaton Square, a demi-griffin segreant gu., charged on the body with two cross crosslets palewise or, and holding between the claws an escutcheon of the last charged with a cross crosslet sa. *Comme Dieu grantit.*

Grantham, Lincs., a Moor's head couped at the shoulders ppr., crined or. 192. 13

Grantham, Middx., a Mercurial cap placed above a scimitar, edge downwards, and a caduceus in saltier, thereon a Turk's head affrontée, erased at the shoulders, ensigned with a turban, all ppr. 171. 3

Grantham, Scotland, a hand erect couped at the wrist holding a dagger ppr. 212. 9

Grantley, Baron (Norton), a Mooress's head affrontée couped at the shoulders ppr., wreathed round the temples with laurel, and round the neck a torse arg. and az. *Avi numerantur avorum.*

Granville, Earl (Leveson-Gower), a wolf passant arg., collared and lined or, charged with a crescent for a difference. *Frangas non flectes.* *cf.* 28. 10

Granville, Warw., on a chapeau ppr., a griffin passant or. *Deo, patriæ, amicis.* *cf.* 63. 2

Granville, Somers., on a mural coronet arg., a serpent nowed vert. 142. 12

Granville, a griffin's head between two wings endorsed ppr. *cf.* 67 11

Granville, Bevil, Esquire, of Wellesbourne Hall, Warw., and the Cottage, Northchurch, Herts, on a cap of maintenance ppr., a griffin or. *Deo, patriæ, amicis.*

Grape, Berks, on a mount vert, a stag grazing erminois, collared gu. *cf.* 116. 9

Grassal and **Grassall,** an arm in armour embowed holding in the hand a dagger ppr. 106. 5

Grassick, Scotland, a dexter hand holding three arrows. *Defend.* *cf.* 214. 2

Grassick of Buchuam, a lion's head gu. *Fear God, and spare not.* 21. 1

Grattan - Guinness of Beaumont, co. Dublin, Ireland: (1) A boar passant quarterly or and gu. (*for Guinness*). 40. 9. (2) On a mount vert, a falcon with wings elevated holding in the dexter claw a sceptre, all ppr. (*for Grattan*). 248. 7. (3) On a pillar arg., encircled by a ducal coronet or, an eagle preying on a bird's leg erased ppr. (*for Lee*). *Spes mea in Deo.—Esse quam videre.* 248. 1

Grattan, a dove ppr. standing on a tun and holding in its dexter claw a sceptre, also ppr.

Grattan, on a tun or, a falcon arg., wings elevated, holding in the dexter claw a sceptre of the first.

Grattan-Bellew, Thomas Arthur, Esquire, of Mount Bellew, co. Galway, Ireland: (1) An arm embowed in armour ppr., charged with a crescent or for difference, and grasping in the hand a sword, also ppr., pommel and hilt or (*for Bellew*). *cf.* 195. 2. (2) A dove ppr., holding in its dexter claw a sceptre or, and standing on a barrel or (*for Grattan*). *Tout d'en haut.* 248. 2

Gratton, on a heart an eagle's leg ppr. 113. 14

Gratwick, Sussex, an ostrich's head or, holding in the beak a horse-shoe arg.

Gratwick, *see* Challen-Gratwick.

Gravatt, a wolf passant per pale erminois and arg. 28. 10

Grave, Berks, within an annulet az., an escutcheon sa., charged with a lion rampant arg. 9. 1

Grave, Ireland, a cock sa., combed and wattled gu. 91. 2

Grave, Sussex, Yorks, and Cornw., a demi-eagle erased or, beaked gu., environed round the body with a ducal coronet arg.

Graveley, Richard, of Newick, Lewes, and Graveley, Herts, a mullet. 164. 2

Gravell, out of a ducal coronet or, a demi-eagle displayed ppr. 80. 14

Graves, Baron (Graves), of Gravesend, co. Londonderry, a demi-eagle displayed and erased or, enfiled round the body and below the wings by a ducal coronet arg. *Aquila non capit muscas.*

Graves, Glouc., a demi-eagle erased or, environed with a ducal coronet gu., holding in its beak a cross crosslet fitched of the last. *Graves disce mores.*

Graves, John Hicks, Esquire, of Bradenham, High Wycombe, Bucks.

Graves, Robert Kennedy Grogan, Esquire, of Cloghan Castle, Banagher, King's County, same crest and motto.

Graves, Robert Wyndham, Esquire, British Consulate-General, Canea, Crete, same crest and motto.

Graves, Alfred Perceval, Esquire, a demi-eagle displayed and erased or, enfiled round the body and below the wings with a ducal coronet gu., each wing charged with a cross patonce, also gu. *Aquila non capit muscas.*

Graves-Sawle, Sir Charles Brune, Bart., M.V.O., Capt. R.N., of Penrice, Cornw., and of Barley House, Devonsh., an eagle displayed or, supporting in the dexter claw a staff erect ppr., thereon hoisted a pennon forked and flowing to the sinister gu., with the inscription, "*Per sinum Codanum,*" in letters of gold (*for Graves*).

Graves, a squirrel sejant ermines. *cf.* 135. 4

Graveshend or **Gravesend,** Kent, a lion's gamb gu., charged with a bezant and holding up a cross patée fitchée or. *cf.* 36. 9

Gravett, Ireland, an arm in armour gu., the hand ppr. holding a sword of the same. *Per varios casus.* 210. 2

Gray, Baron, Scotland, an anchor in pale or. *Anchor, fast anchor.* 161. 2

Gray, O. Harrison, Esquire, of The Chantry, Ingatestone, same crest and motto.

Gray, Walter Wingate, Esquire, J.P., D.L., of Nunraw, near Prestonkirk, East Lothian, same crest and motto.

Gray, Lord, *see* Moray, Earl of.

Gray-Farquhar, Scotland, a sinister hand apaumée gu. *Sto, cado, fide et armis.* 222. 9

Gray, Edmond Archibald, Esquire, of Gray, Forfarsh., Kinfauns, Perthsh., and of Balmerino, Fifesh., an anchor or. *Anchor, fast anchor.* 161. 1

Gray, an anchor erect or, cabled ppr. *Anchor, fast anchor.* 161. 2

Gray, an anchor, the cable waved ppr. *Anchor, fast anchor.* 161. 2

Gray, George, Esquire, of 7, Doune Gardens, Kelvinside, Glasgow, *claims* an anchor sans cable in pale or. *Anchor, fast anchor.* (*Of no authority.*) 161. 2

Gray of Carntyne, formerly of Dalmarnock, Lanarksh., Scotland, an anchor cabled stuck fast in the sea, all ppr. *Fast.* 161. 8

Gray of Carse, Forfar, Scotland, an anchor fesseways fastened to a cable ppr. *Anchor fast.*

Gray of Charleville House, Rathmines, Ireland, an anchor erect sa., entwined with a ribbon az., with the word "*Vartry*" inscribed thereon in letters of gold. *Anchor, fast anchor.*

Gray, Robert, Esquire, of Armagh, an anchor in pale az., timbered ppr., and fluked or. *Anchor, fast anchor.*

Gray, Scotland, an anchor cabled in the sea, all ppr. *Fast.* 161. 8

Gray-Buchanan of Scotstoun and Eastfield, Cambuslang, Lanarksh., Scotland: (1) On the dexter side, two hands grasping a two-handed sword ppr. (*for Buchanan*). 213. 5. (2) On the sinister side, an anchor in the sea ppr. (*for Gray*). *Clariora sequor.—Fast.*

Gray, Hamilton-: (1) An anchor cabled in the sea, all ppr. (*for Gray*). 161. 8. (2) Out of a ducal coronet or, an oak-tree ppr., fructed of the first and penetrated transversely through the main stem by a frame-saw, also ppr. (*for Hamilton*). *Fast.—Through.* 143. 8

Gray, Hon. Samuel Brownlow, Clermont, Bermuda, a dragon's head erased sa., ducally gorged, scaled, and chained or. *Animo et fide.*

Gray of Ballincor, King's Co., Ireland, a demi-lion rampant or, holding in his mouth an annulet gu. *Præstare et prodesse.* *cf.* 10. 2

Gray of Durham, a lion's gamb erased holding a serpent, all ppr. 35. 3

Gray, John Robin, Esquire, of Farley Hill Place, Reading, Berks, upon a rock ppr., a bear's paw erect and erased sa., grasping a snake entwined around it ppr. *Tenebo.* 35. 6

Gray, Robert, Esquire, of Hughenden, Queensland, a bear's paw grasping a snake.

Gray, Herbert, Esquire (formerly Miers), of The Limes, Frisby, near Melton Mowbray, Leics., on a mount vert, a hedgehog statant ppr., charged on the body with a rose gu., barbed and seeded ppr., in front of a holly-bush fructed, also ppr. 256. 11

Gray, Scotland, a heart gu. *Constant.* 181. 2

Gray, out of a mural coronet a phœnix in flames ppr. *Clarior e tenebris.* *cf.* 82. 5

Gray, Northumb., out of a ducal coronet or, a phœnix in flames ppr. 82. 5

Gray, same crest. *Clarior e Glammis.*

Gray, Northumb., out of a ducal coronet a demi-swan ppr.

Gray, on a chapeau ppr., a wyvern gu. *cf.* 70. 4

Gray, a scaling-ladder of two rows in bend ppr.

Gray, William Martello, Esquire, F.C.A., of Graythwaite Manor, Grange-over-Sands, North Lancs, and of Sefton Lodge, Bradford, Yorks, a tower ppr., surmounted by an escutcheon az., charged with a rose arg., barbed and seeded ppr. *Veritas vincit.* 255. 5

Gray, a scaling-ladder ensigned with a ram's head couped, all ppr. *De bon vouloir servir le Roy.*

Gray, Essex, a ram's head couped arg. 130. 1

Gray, in front of the sun in splendour or, a unicorn passant erm.

Gray of Warriston, a lily, slipped, bladed, and seeded, all ppr. *Vigет in cinere virtus.* 151. 2

Gray, Ireland, a hand holding a dagger in pale ppr. 212. 9

Gray of Haystoun, Scotland, a fox regardant ppr. *Concussus surgo.*

Graydon, two lion's gambs erect supporting an escutcheon. 39. 1

Grayhurst, a dove az., holding in its beak an olive-branch ppr. 92. 5

Grayley, Essex, a hand holding a fish ppr. 220. 4

Grayrigge, Robert Stockdale, Wood Broughton, Grange-over-Sands, Carnforth, Lancs, a sheldrake ppr., in its beak an escallop arg. *Festina lente.* 291. 7

Grayson, out of a tower a demi-lion ducally crowned, holding a grenade fired, all ppr. *cf.* 157. 10

Grazebrook and **Grazerbrook,** a bear's head or, muzzled sa., charged on the neck with three fleurs-de-lis in fess az. *Nec sinit esse feros.* *cf.* 34. 14

Gream, Yorks, two wings addorsed or. *cf.* 109. 12

Greathead, a savage's head ppr. 190. 12

Greathead, on a chapeau gu., turned up erm., a martlet with wings addorsed sa. *cf.* 95. 1

Greathead, Warw., on a mount vert, a fleur-de-lis or. *cf.* 148. 2

Greathed, Edward Archer, Esquire, of Armstrong Point, Winnepeg, Canada, out of bulrushes ppr., a stag's head per pale engrailed arg. and gu., attired or, in the mouth an arrow of the first. *Work with a will.*

Greathed, Hervey, Esquire, same crest and motto.

Greatheed, Bertie-: (1) On a mount vert, a fleur-de-lis or, the top of each leaf surmounted by a torteau, and the centre one charged for distinction with a fusil gu. (*for Greatheed*). (2) The bust of a man couped and affrontée ppr., ducally crowned or, the breast charged for distinction with a fusil of the same (*for Bertie*). *cf.* 192. 9

Greatorex, a goat's head ppr. 128. 12

Greatorex, H. A., Esq., of Rowney Bury, Harlow, Essex, a leopard's head erased or, pelettée. *Vivat Greatrakes semper virescat.* 302. 1

Greaves-Bagshawe, *see* Bagshawe.

Greaves, Staffs, an eagle displayed or, winged gu. *Aquila non capiat muscas.*—*Suprema quæro.*—*Dum spiro, spero.* 75. 2

Greaves, Warw., an eagle with two heads displayed sa., beaked and membered or. 74. 2

Greaves of Glen Etive, Argylesh., an eagle displayed with two heads sa., resting each claw on a pellet, each charged with a lion's head erased or, and either wing charged with two escallops or. *Aquila non capiat muscas.*

Greaves, John Ernest, Esquire, of Bron Eifion, Criccieth, and Glan Gwna, Carnarvonsh., same crest and motto.

Greaves, Richard Methuen, Esquire, of Wern, Tremadoc R.S.O., Carnarvonsh., same crest and motto.

Greaves, Derbysh., Kent, and Sussex, a demi-eagle displayed or, winged gu. 81. 6

Greaves, Robert Bond, M.D., Cemetery Road, Sheffield, same crest. *Aquila non capiat muscas.* 81. 6

Greaves, Sir George Richards, K.C.M.G., G.C.B., of Netherwood, Saundersfoot, Pembrokesh., South Wales, same crest and motto.

Greaves, a demi-eagle displayed or, winged and langued gu. *Aquila non capiat muscas.* 81. 6

Greaves of Sheffield, Yorks, a demi-eagle displayed or, the wings chequy of the last and gu., holding in the beak three quatrefoils slipped vert.

Greaves, Lancs, out of the battlements of a tower ppr., a demi-eagle or, the wings expanded gu., holding in the beak a cross crosslet fitched arg., charged on the breast with a rose of the third, leaved vert. *Spes mea in Deo.*

Greaves-Banning: (1) Upon a key fesseways, wards downwards, or, an ostrich arg., charged on the breast with an escallop sa. (*for Banning*). (2) Out of the battlements of a tower ppr., a demi-eagle displayed or, the wings gu., holding in the beak a cross crosslet fitchée arg., and charged on the breast with a rose of the second, and the battlements of the tower charged for distinction with a cross crosslet, also gu. (*for Greaves*). *A Deo non fortuna.*

Greaves of Page Hall and Elmsall Lodge, Yorks, on a mount vert, a stag trippant or, holding in the mouth a slip of oak ppr. *Deo non fortuna.* *cf.* 118. 2

Greaves, Francis Edward, 15, Powis Square, Brighton, same crest and motto.

Greaves, George Richard, Western House, Winslow, Bucks, same crest. *In veritate triumpho.*

Greaves, an arm in armour embowed thrusting a dagger ppr. 196. 5

Greaves, Ireland, a cubit arm in armour, holding a cross crosslet fitched ppr. 210. 14

Grebell, a greyhound's head erased arg., pellettée, collared and ringed or. *cf.* 61. 2

Greby, a demi-eagle holding in its dexter claw a branch of laurel ppr. 80. 3

Greeke of London, the trunk of a tree eradicated and sprouting branches ppr., pendent from the trunk a circular shield or, thereon a sun az.

Greeke of London, the trunk of a tree couped at the top and erased at the root ppr., issuing from towards the top two branches vert, thereon suspended, by a belt gu., a Grecian target or, charged with a star az.

Green-Price, Bart., *see* Price.

Green, Sir Edward, Bart., M.P., of Nunthorpe Hall, York, and Ken Hill, King's Lynn, Norf., in front of a mount ppr., thereon a stag trippant or, gorged with a collar gemelle vert, three roses fessewise arg. *Waste not.* 117. 11

Green, Capt. C. Fiddian, Sutton Coldfield, near Birmingham, same crest and motto. 117. 11

Green, Edward Lycett, Esquire, of Ken Hall, King's Lynn, and Dringhouses, York, same crest and motto.

Green, a stag trippant ppr. 117. 8

Green of Pavenham Bury, Beds, a buck trippant or. *Semper viridis.* 117. 8

Green of Chiddingly, Sussex: (1) In front of a spear erect ppr., therefrom pendent a bugle-horn sa., stringed gu., a stag statant or (*for Green*). 117. 4. (2) A mount vert, thereon an antelope erm., attired or, the dexter foot resting on a hurt charged with a cross crosslet gu. (*for Verral*). 126. 9

Green, Chesh., a demi-stag salient or. 119. 2

Green, Thomas, of Poulton Hall, Chesh., a demi-buck springing per fesse or and az., charged with two crescents counterchanged. 119. 6

Green, Everard, Esquire, Rouge Dragon Pursuivant of Arms, in front of a buck's head couped or, between the attires an annulet az., a fleur-de-lis and two annulets az. *Spiritu principali.*

Green, Rev. John Henry, the Rectory, Mowsley, same crest and motto.

Green, Norf. and Oxon., a stag's head erased az., attired or. 121. 2

Green, Shropsh., a stag's head erased or. 121. 2

Green, Richard Spurgeon, Esquire, of Stonylands, Dedham, Essex, same crest. *Virtute non verbis.*

Green, Oxon., a buck's head or, charged with a mullet sa. *cf.* 121. 5

Green, Herts, Somers., Berks, and Essex, a buck's head erased erm., attired or. 121. 2

Green, out of a ducal coronet a buck's head, all ppr. 120. 7

Green of London and Berks, a stag's head erased and attired or, charged on the neck with a pheon sa., and under it three guttes-de-sang. *cf.* 121. 2

Green, James Sullivan, Esquire, of Air Hill, Glanworth, co. Cork, and 83, Lower Leeson Street, Dublin, a buck's head erased or. *Nec timeo nec spurno.*

Green, Norf. and Essex, a buck's head erased az., attired or. *Vive valeque.* 121. 2

Green, a stag's head arg., attired or, gorged with a chaplet of laurel ppr. 120. 3

Green of London and Norf., a buck's head erased or, attired arg., murally gorged and chained of the last. *cf.* 121. 2

Green, an antelope's head couped ppr. *cf.* 126. 2

Green, Bart., of 74, Belsize Park Gardens, London, N.W., issuant from the battlements of a tower gu., a horse's head or, between two ears of wheat stalked and leaved ppr. *Æquam servare mentem.* 285. 12

Green, Bucks, out of a mural coronet arg., a demi-lion rampant purp., holding in the dexter paw a slip of laurel vert. *cf.* 16. 11

Green, out of a mural coronet gu., a demi-lion rampant erminois. *cf.* 16. 11

Green, John Tindell, Solicitor, the Esplanade, Sunderland, a demi-lion rampant. *I flourish.*

Green, Essex, a lion sejant per pale or and sa. 8. 8

Green of Milnrow, Yorks, a griffin's head erased sa., langued gu., collared gemelle or, and between the collars a cinquefoil erm., and holding in the beak a key or. *Æquam servare mentem.* *cf.* 66. 6

Green, a griffin's head erased quarterly or and sa., holding in the beak a trefoil slipped of the last. *cf.* 66. 2

Green, Norf., a dragon sans wings passant per fess or and vert.

Green, Ireland, an eagle displayed ppr., charged on the breast with a quadrangular lock arg. *Memor esto.* *cf.* 75. 2

Green, on a mount vert, a squirrel sejant ppr., holding an escallop az.

Green, Herts, a squirrel sejant bendy sinister arg. and sa., holding in its paws an escallop or. 135. 9

Green, a demi-greyhound. 60. 11

Green, Ireland, a sinister arm in armour embowed ppr., holding a shield or. 194. 8

Green, a cubit arm erect vested vert, cuffed or, holding in the hand a holly-branch fructed ppr. *Virtus semper viridis.*

Green, C. E., 7, Gordon Terrace, Edinburgh, a dexter hand in a gauntlet couped at the wrist and holding a branch of holly ppr. *Erst wägen den wagen.*

Green, Arthur, Esquire, of Windarra, Launceston, Tasmania, and the other descendants of the late Richard Green, Esquire, of Herts, England, in front of a cubit arm erect ppr., the hand grasping an anchor in bend sinister sa., a cross patée between two escallops or. *Je feroi bien.* 229. 1

Green, Alfred, Esquire, of 51, George Street, Launceston, Tasmania, same crest and motto.

Green, Edwin Jackson, Esquire, of 28, Buxton Street, North Adelaide, South Australia, same crest and motto.

Green, Richard, Esquire, of 194, Cimitiere Street, Launceston, Tasmania, same crest and motto.

Green, Kent, out of a mural coronet gu., a horse's head arg., maned or. *cf.* 51. 7

Green, G. R., Park Street, Ripon, same crest. *Æquam servare mentem.*

Green, Herts, Notts, and Yorks, a woodpecker pecking at a staff raguly, couped and erect ppr.

Green, a rose gu., barbed vert, seeded or, environed by two laurel-branches ppr.

Green, Herts, on a mount vert, an escallop az. *cf.* 141. 14

Green-Emmott, Walter Egerton John, Esquire, of Emmott Hall, Colne, Lancs, and the Old Hall, Rawdon, Yorks: (1) Out of a ducal coronet composed of five leaves erminois, a demi-buffalo sa., and ungu. or (*for Emmott*). (2) A stag's head arg., erased or, attired sa., gorged with a collar gemel gu., holding in the mouth a sprig of holly fructed ppr. (*for Green*). *Tenez le vraye.—Nec in arido defit.*

Greenall, Sir Gilbert, Bart., of Walton Hall, County Palatine of Chester, between two wings or, a pommé surmounted by a bugle-horn of the first. *Alta peto.* 305. 3

Greenaway, a demi-eagle issuant with wings expanded ppr. 80. 2

Greenaway, a lion sejant or, holding with its fore-paws a scaling-ladder gu.

Greenaway, Glouc., a griffin's head erased az., holding in its beak an annulet or. *cf.* 66. 2

Greene, Sir Edward Walter, Bart., in front of a griffin's head erased or, holding in its beak a sprig of three trefoils slipped vert, two annulets interlaced az. between as many bezants. *Non sine numine.* 242. 1

Greene, late Benjamin Buck, of Midgham, Berks, in front of an eagle's head erased or, holding in the beak a sprig of three trefoils slipped vert, two annulets az. between as many bezants.

Greene, Dawson Cornelius, Esquire, of Whittington Hall, Kirkby Lonsdale, a stag ppr., gorged with a collar invected or, with an escutcheon, also or, pendent therefrom, and charged with a rose gu.

Greene, Charles John, Esquire, of Slyne, near Lancaster, same crest and motto.

Greene of Milton, Clifton, Somers., an arm erect habited vert, holding in the hand a branch of holly ppr., fructed gu.

Greene, Ireland, a horse's head sa., between two wings or. 51. 3

Greene, a stag trippant arg. 117. 8

Greene, Henry Dawson, of Slyne, Lancs, a stag ppr., gorged with a collar invecked vert, with an escutcheon or pendent therefrom, and charged with a rose gu.

Greene, Leics., out of park pales in a circular form, a stag's head ppr., attired or.

Greene, New England, a buck's head or. 121. 5

Greene of Kilmanahan Castle, Waterford, out of a ducal coronet a stag's head, all or. *Nec timeo, nec sperno.* 120. 7

Greene, W. T., M.A., M.D., 282, Portobello Road, W., same crest and motto.

Greene, Molesworth Richard, Esquire, J.P., of Greystones, Bacchus Marsh, Victoria, Australia, out of a ducal coronet a stag's head or. *Nec timeo, nec sperno.* 120. 7

Greene, Richard, F.R.C.P., the Shelleys, Lewes, issuant from a ducal coronet gu., a buck's head or. *Nec timeo, nec sperno.*

Greene, Staffs, a stag's head erased or. 121. 2

Greene, a buck's head couped or, charged with a mullet for difference. *cf.* 121. 9

Greene, John, Esquire, of Shamrock, Kyneton, Victoria, Australia, out of a ducal coronet gu., a buck's head or. *Nec timeo, nec sperno.*

Greene, Reginald Latimer Wellington, Esquire, of Tregara House, Stratford-on-Avon, same crest and motto.

Greene, Richard Massy, Esquire, of Smithstown, Rathore, Cappagh, Brittas, and Coolebela, co. Kilkenny, same crest and motto.

Greene, Thomas, Esquire, of Millbrook and Hallahoise, co. Kildare, issuant from a ducal crest coronet gu., a buck's head or, charged with a crescent gu. for difference. *Nec timeo nec sperno.*

Greene, Edward Jonas, Esquire, of Newstead, Clonskeagh, Dublin, a dragon's head erased az., gorged or. *Nescia fallere vita.*

Greene, George Arthur, Esquire, of 23, Pembroke Gardens, Kensington, W., same crest and motto.

Greene, Rev. Jonas, of Mount Temple Rectory, Moate, Westmeath, same crest and motto.

Greene, Rev. Joseph, of Rostrevor, Clifton, Glouc., same crest and motto.

Greene, Herbert W., 49, St. Stephen's Green, Dublin, same crest and motto.

Greene, Richard Jonas, Esquire, of 49, St. Stephen's Green, Dublin, same crest and motto.

Greene, Very Rev. William Conyngham, Dean of Christ Church, Dublin, of 49, St. Stephen's Green, Dublin, same crest and motto.

Greene, Walter Raymond, Esquire, M.P., of Nether Hall, Bury St. Edmunds, Cambridge, in front of a gryphon's head erased or, holding in the beak a branch of trefoil vert, two annulets interlaced fesseways az., between as many bezants. *Non sine numine.*

Greenfield, a branch of oak vert, and a cross crosslet fitched gu., in saltier. 166. 11

Greenfield, on a chapeau gu., turned up erm., a griffin statant arg., beaked and membered or. *cf.* 63. 13

Greenfield, on a ducal coronet or, a griffin sejant ppr., resting the dexter claw on an escutcheon. 62. 11

Greenfield, of Rhyddgaer, a griffin passant with wings elevated or, resting its dexter claw on a clarion gu. *Injussi virescunt.*

Greenfield, Thomas Challen, Esquire, of 6, Albion Road Sutton, Surrey, same crest and motto.

Greenford of Levanton, Kent, out of a ducal coronet or, a boar's head and neck az., between two wings arg. *Fide sed cui vide.*

Greenhalgh and **Greenhaugh,** a stork sa. 105. 11

Greenhalgh, a bugle-horn sa., stringed or. 228. 11

Greenhall, a bugle-horn between two wings arg. *Alta pete.* 112. 3

Greenhaugh, a greyhound passant. *cf.* 60. 2

Greenhill of London and Middx., a demi-griffin segreant gu., powdered with thirty-nine mullets or. *Honos alit artes.* *cf.* 64. 2

Greenhill, a demi-griffin segreant arg. *Another,* or. 64. 2

Greenhill, Christophe William Moor, Esquire, J.P., of Puriton Manor Estate, Puriton Manor, Bridgwater: (1) A swan with wings elevated and endorsed, ducally gorged and lined. (2) Out of a ducal coronet a man's head. *Toujours prêt.*

Greenhow, *see* Greenhalgh.

Greening, a nag's head arg. *cf.* 50. 13

Greenland, a dexter arm embowed holding a bomb fired ppr. *cf.* 202. 5

Greenlaw, Scotland, an eagle's head erased sa., holding in its beak an acorn-slip ppr. 84. 10

Greenlaw, on a mount a cubit arm in armour ppr., environed by a snake vert, holding in the hand, also ppr., a spear in bend.

Greenlees and **Greenless,** Scotland, out of a mount a sprig growing ppr. *Viresco.* 145. 11

Greenlogh, a griffin's head erased. 66. 2

Greenly, Heref., a demi-stag springing per fess erm. and erminois charged on the shoulder with an escallop az. *Fall-y-gallo.* *cf.* 119. 2

Greenly, Edward Howarth, M.A., Titley Court, Titley, R.S.O., a demi-stag rampant per fesse erm. and erminois charged on the shoulder with an escallop az., and on the neck with a cross crosslet sa. (for distinction). *Fall-y-gallo.*

Greenock, Lord, *see* Cathcart, Earl.

Greenough of London: (1) The sun in splendour ppr., within the circumference of a bugle-horn sa., stringed gu., rimmed and mounted or. (2) A stag's head erased per fess indented arg. and gu., attired or, holding in its mouth a fleur-de-lis az. *cf.* 121. 2

Greenough, a cock crowing between two adders in orle, their tails in saltier. 91. 1

Greensmith, Derbysh., a dove close arg., beaked and legged gu. 92. 2

Greensmith of Steeple Grange, Derbysh., a dove close arg., beaked and legged gu., holding in its beak an ear of wheat or, and standing upon a pig of lead az.

Greenstreet, Kent, a dragon's head erased arg., guttée-de-sang, ducally gorged az. *cf.* 71. 8

Greenvile, Cornw., out of a ducal coronet or, a plume of feathers, thereon a dove rising arg.

Greenvile, a griffin's head with wings addorsed or. *cf.* 67. 11

Greenvile, a griffin passant or, collared sa. *cf.* 63. 2

Greenway, Warw.: (1) A griffin's head erased az. (*for Greenway*). 66. 2. (2) A lion sejant or, holding in the dexter paw a scaling-ladder gu. (*for Kellynge*).

Greenway, Surrey, a griffin's head. 66. 1

Greenway, Warw., a griffin's head erased az. 66. 2

Greenway, Edward Maurice, Esquire, of Greenway, near Honiton, Devonsh., a griffin's head az., erased per fess gu., holding in the beak an arrow in bend dexter ppr., headed or. *Nil desperandum.* 66. 8

Greenway, Devonsh., a griffin's head erased az., holding in its beak an anchor gu.

Greenwell, Durh., a stork ppr., beaked and legged gu., gorged with a chaplet of laurel vert. *cf.* 105. 11

Greenwell, Rev. William, of 27, North Bailey, Durh., a stork ppr., gorged with a chaplet of laurel vert.

Greenwell, a crane's dead couped arg., beaked gu., gorged with a wreath of laurel vert. *Viresco.*

Greenwell of London and Durh., an eagle's head arg., beaked gu., gorged with a chaplet of laurel vert. *cf.* 83. 1

Greenwood, a tiger sejant or. 27. 6

Greenwood, a demi-lion sa., holding between the paws a saltier humettée or.

Greenwood, F. R., Surgeon, Glenden House, 21, St. George's Square, Portsea, a demi-lion rampant holding between the paws a saltire couped. *Fortiter ferre crucem.*

Greenwood, Charles Staniforth, Esquire, of Swarcliffe, Birstwith, Leeds, a leopard sa. or, resting the dexter foreleg on an escutcheon sa., thereon a saltire couped arg. 300. 7

Greenwood, Hubert John, Esquire, of 28, Chapel Street, Belgrave Square, London, S.W., same crest and motto.

Greenwood, Derbysh. and Yorks, a demi-lion or, holding between the paws a saltire arg.

Greenwood, W. De R. Croylands, Spring Grove, Isleworth, a horse's head couped erm., gorged with a ducal coronet.

Greenwood, Frederick, J.P., of Edgerton Lodge, near Huddersfield, a demi-lion rampant, holding between the paws a saltire. *Viret et semper virebit.*

Greenwood, Suff. and Oxon., a lion sejant erect sa., holding a saltier arg.

Greenwood, Norf. and Yorks, a mullet sa., between a pair of ducks' wings expanded of the same. *Ut prosim.* 300. 11

Greenwood, Arthur, Esquire, Greenholme, Burley-in-Wharfdale, Yorks, a mullet sa., between a pair of ducks' wings expanded of the same. *Ut prosim.* 300. 11

Greer, a hand vested gu., cuffed or, holding a trefoil vert. 205. 9

Greer, Thomas, Esquire, J.P., of Sea Park, Carrickfergus, Ireland, an eagle displayed ppr., charged on the breast with a quadrangular lock arg. *Memor esto.* *cf.* 75. 2

Greer, Frederick, Esquire, J.P., of Tullylagan Manor, Dungannon, co. Tyrone, same crest and motto.

Greer, a round padlock ppr. 168. 14

Greerson, a fetterlock arg. 168. 12

Greet, a cock's head erased or. 90. 1

Greete, a demi-greyhound arg., collared az. 60. 8

Greetham, two hands issuing holding a two-handed sword ppr. 213. 3

Greethead, a fleur-de-lis arg. 148. 2

Greg, an arm in armour embowed ppr., holding in the hand a scimitar az., hilt and pommel or. 196. 10

Greg, Robert Philips, Esquire, of Coles Park, Buntingford, same crest. *Ein doe, and spair not.—S' Rioghal mo dhream.*

Gregg, a lion passant gardant az. 4. 3

Gregg, Derbysh., a stork's head and neck ppr., holding in the beak a trefoil slipped vert.

Gregg, Chesh., out of a ducal coronet or, a stork's head and neck per pale arg. and sa., holding in the beak a trefoil slipped of the last.

Gregg, Huband George, Esquire, of Old town (Rathallard), co. Longford, and Clonmore, Stillorgan, co. Dublin, out of a ducal coronet a griffin's head holding in the beak a sprig of shamrock slipped vert. *Memor esto.*

Gregg, out of a ducal coronet or, an eagle's head and neck per pale arg., guttée-de-sang, and sa., holding in the beak a trefoil slipped of the last.

Gregg of London, out of a ducal coronet or, an eagle's head and neck per pale erm. and sa., holding in the beak a trefoil of the last.

Gregge-Hopwood, out of a ducal coronet or, a griffin's head per pale arg. and sa., holding in the beak a trefoil vert. *cf.* 67. 9

Gregor, Scotland, a hand holding a dagger point downwards ppr. *Pro patriâ.*

Gregor, a hind's head erased gu. 124. 3

Gregor, Cornw., a garb or. 153. 2

Gregor, Cornw., a Saracen's head affrontée, surmounting a javelin in bend, all ppr.

Gregorie, Notts, a garb or, banded gu. 153. 2

Gregorie of Dunkirk, Scotland, the trunk of an old fir-tree fallen, from which issues a vigorous shoot ppr. *Non deficit alter.*

Gregorson, Scotland, a lion's head erased, crowned with an antique crown. *E'en do and spare not.* *cf.* 17. 12

Gregory, *see* Welby-Gregory.

Gregory, three garbs or. 153. 13

Gregory of Harlaxton Manor, Notts, three garbs or, banded together gu. *Crux scutum.* 153. 13

Gregory of Buscott, Berks, a demi-boar salient or. 40. 13

Gregory, Leics. and Warw., a demi-boar rampant sa., collared and crined or. *Vigilanter.* *cf.* 40. 13

Gregory, Francis Hood, Esquire, of Styvechale, near Coventry, same crest and motto.

Gregory, Middx., a demi-boar salient arg., armed and crined or, collared az. *cf.* 40. 13

Gregory, Kent, a demi-boar rampant sa., langued gu., ungu., crined, and collared or. *cf.* 40. 13

Gregory of London, a demi-boar erect sa. 40. 13

Gregory of Greenwich and Westminster, out of a mural coronet per pale or and az., a demi-boar salient arg., crined and armed of the first, collared of the second, valued in the breast gu., with an arrow of the first feathered of the second.

Gregory, Augustus Charles, C.M.G., of Rainworth, Brisbane, Queensland, out of a ducal coronet a bull's head.

Gregory, Rev. John George, M.A., 2, Clarence Terrace, Leamington, a demi-lion rampant. *Be just and fear not.*

Gregory, Ireland, a lion's head erased, collared or. 18. 6

Gregory, Lancs and Shropsh., two lion's heads addorsed and erased az. and arg., collared, counterchanged. 18. 2

Gregory of Hanbury Mount, Worcs., two lions' heads erased and addorsed az., semée of cross crosslets arg., in front of a garb fessewise or. *Nil desperandum.—Crux scutum.*

Gregory, Scotland, a sphere ppr. *Altius.* 159. 1

Gregory, Lincs, out of a ducal coronet or, a maiden's head ppr., vested gu. 182. 9

Gregory, Scotland, the trunk of an oak-tree sprouting. *Nec deficit alter.* 145. 2

Gregson, Durh. and Derbysh., an arm couped at the elbow, vested bendy wavy of six arg. and gu., holding in the hand ppr. a battle-axe or, the handle sa., tied round the wrist with a ribbon. *Vigilo.* *cf.* 207. 10

Gregson, a cubit arm in armour ppr., charged with three bendlets wavy sa., holding in the gauntlet a battle-axe of the last, headed or.

Gregson, Colonel Lancelot Allgood, of Burdon, near Sunderland, a cubit arm erect, vested bendy sinister of six arg. and gu., a riband around the wrist also gu., the hand ppr., holding a battle-axe or, the handle sa., between two roses of the second, barbed and seeded ppr. *Vigilo.*

Gregson, Francis Robert, Esquire, of Place of Tilliefour, Kemnay, Aberdeensh., same crest and motto.

Gregson of Lowlyn, Durh., a cubit arm in armour couped arg., charged with a bendlet wavy az., between two others gu., tied round the wrist with a riband of the same colours, and holding in the hand ppr. a battle-axe or, the staff sa., entwined with a wreath of oak fructed, also ppr.

Greham, Ireland, a demi-bull sa., armed or. *cf.* 45. 8

Grehan of Mount Plunkett and St. John's, co. Roscommon, Ireland, a demi-lion gu., gorged with three escallops or. *Ne oubliez.* *cf.* 10. 3

Greiden, Scotland, a demi-otter sa., devouring a fish ppr. 134. 12

Greig, Scotland, a boar's head ppr. *Persevere.* 41. 1

Greig, Thomas Watson, Esquire, of Glencarse, a falcon rising belled and ducally gorged, all ppr. *Certum pete finem.* 87. 2

Greig, a falcon rising ppr., jessed, belled, and ducally gorged or. 87. 2

Greig of Lethangie, a martlet sa. *Nec sorte, nec fato.* 95. 5

Greig, Scotland, an arm in armour embowed holding a scimitar ppr. *Strike sure.* 196. 10

Greinvile, a demi-griffin or. 64. 2

Greir and Grier, Scotland, a fetterlock az. *Hoc securior.* 168. 12

Greive, Scotland, an arm in armour brandishing a scimitar ppr. *Hoc securior.*

Greive, Scotland, an arm in armour holding a dagger point downwards. *Quâ fidem servasti.*

Greive, Northumb., a martlet sa. *J'ai la clef.* 95. 5

Greive, Scotland, a ram's head ppr. *Pro rege et grege.* 130. 1

Grelley, a hand holding a fish ppr. 220. 4

Grellier, a demi-eagle displayed or. 81. 6

Gremiston, out of a crescent arg., a lion's face sa., crowned with an antique crown or. 21. 6

Grendall, a lion passant gardant or, holding a flag arg., the staff sa.

Grendon, a decrescent or. 163. 1

Grene of Cappamurra, Tipperary, a wolf's head erased. 30. 8

Grenehalgh, Notts, a bugle-horn sa., stringed or. *Omnia debeo Deo.* 228. 11

Grenewell, Durh., a stork close ppr., beaked and legged gu., gorged with a chaplet vert. *cf.* 105. 11

Grenfell, William Henry, Esquire, M.P., of Taplow Court, Taplow, Bucks, on a chapeau gu., turned up erm., a griffin passant or. *cf.* 63. 13

Grenfell, Major-General Sir Francis Wallace, G.C.B., G.C.M.G., of the Palace, Malta, same crest.

Grenfell, Charles Seymour, Esquire, of Elibank, Taplow, Bucks, and 46, Pont Street, S.W., same crest.

Grenfell, a griffin passant ppr. 63. 2

Grenford, a hunting-horn gu., veruled or. *cf.* 228. 9

Grensby, a sinister hand holding a bow ppr. 214. 5

Grentmesnell, a plume of ostrich-feathers arg. 115. 1

Grenvele of London, a sinister arm couped and embowed ppr., vested gu., holding a bow bent sa. *cf.* 204. 11

Grenville, Baron Grenville, a garb vert. 153. 2

Grenville, Baron Glastonbury, a garb vert. *Uno œquus virtute.* 153. 2

Grenville, Duke of Buckingham and Chandos, *see* Buckingham.

Grenwelle, a swan's head and neck couped arg., beaked gu., gorged with a branch of laurel vert. *cf.* 101. 5

Greseley, an owl ppr. 96. 5

Gresham, on a mount of grass vert, a grasshopper or. 137. 8

Gresham of London, a grasshopper ppr., about the neck a collar gemelle or, and holding in the mouth a pawnce flower ppr.

Gresley, Sir Robert, Bart., of Drakelow, Derbysh., a lion passant arg. *Meliore fide quam fortuna.* 6. 2

Gresley, Staffs, a lion passant erm., collared gu. *cf.* 6. 2

Gresley-Douglas, *see* Douglas.

Gresoun, Scotland, a fetterlock. *Hoc securior.* 168. 12

Gresque, Lincs, a lion passant arg., guttée-de-poix, collared gu. *cf.* 6. 2

Gressey, a talbot sejant sa., collared and lined or. 55. 5

Gresswell, Albert, M.D., Louth, Lincs, a lion gu.

Gretton, Suff., an arm couped at shoulder holding a truncheon.

Gretton, John, Esquire, of Stapleford Park, Melton Mowbray, and 66, Ennismore Gardens, London, S.W., an arm embowed ppr., vested above the elbow arg., holding in the hand a torch erect fired, a sickle in bend sinister, both also ppr. *Steadfast.*

Greve, Herts, a squirrel sa., charged with two bends sinister arg., holding an escallop or. 135. 9

Grevile, Warw., out of a ducal coronet gu., a demi-swan with wings expanded arg., beaked of the first. *cf.* 100. 12

Grevile, a greyhound's head erased sa., collared and ringed or. *cf.* 61. 2

Greville, Earl of Warwick and Brooke, *see* Warwick.

Greville, Baron, Rt. Hon. Algernon William Fulke Grevile, out of a ducal coronet gu., a demi-swan rising with wings expanded arg. *Vix ea nostra voco.* *cf.* 100. 12

Greville-Nugent, Rt. Hon. the late Fulke Southwell, first **Baron Greville,** of Clonyn Castle and Clonhugh, co. Westmeath, and of North Myms Park, Herts: (1) A cockatrice ppr., charged on the breast with a pellet for difference (*for Nugent*). *cf.* 68. 4. (2) Out of a ducal coronet gu., a demi-swan with wings expanded and elevated arg. (*for Greville*), and in an escroll over the first crest, *Decrevi.—Vix ea nostra voco.* *cf.* 100. 12

Greville, a greyhound's head erased sa., bezantée, gorged with a collar arg., charged with three pellets. *cf.* 61. 2

Grevis, the sun in his splendour or. 162. 2

Grevis, Kent, a squirrel holding between its paws an escallop or. *cf.* 135. 9

Grevis-James, Lieutenant-Colonel Demetrius Wyndham, of Ightham Court, Ightham, Sevenoaks: (1) Out of a ducal coronet or, a demi-swan with wings expanded arg., beaked gu. (*for James*). (2) A squirrel holding between the paws an escallop or. *Fide et constantia.*

Grey, Earl of Stamford, *see* Stamford.

Grey de Wilton, Viscount, *see* Wilton, Earl of.

Grey, Earl (Grey), a scaling-ladder in bend sinister or, hooked and pointed sa. *De bon vouloir servir le Roy.* 158. 14

Grey de Ruthyn, Baron (Clifton), a dexter arm embowed in armour holding a sword ppr. *Mortem aut triumphum.* 195. 2

Grey, Sir Edward, Bart., M.P., of Fallodon, Northumb., a scaling-ladder in bend sinister or, hooked and pointed sa. *De bon vouloir servir le Roy.* 158. 14

Grey, George, Esquire, J.P., of Milfield, Wooler, Northumb., a scaling-ladder in bend. *De bon vouloir servir le Roy.*

Grey, a scaling-ladder in bend sinister or, hooked and pointed arg. *De bon vouloir servir le Roy.* 158. 14

Grey, Northumb., a scaling-ladder arg. 158. 14

Grey, Northumb.: (1) A scaling-ladder arg. 158. 14. (2) A ram's head arg. 130. 1

Grey, a demi-lion rampant holding a scaling-ladder.

Grey-Egerton, Sir Philip Henry Brian, Bart., D.L., of Egerton and Oulton Park, Chesh.: (1) Three arrows, two in saltire arg., and one in pale sa., banded with a ribbon gu. (*for Egerton*). 173. 1. (2) On a dexter glove arg., a falcon rising or (*for Grey*). *Virtuti non armis fido.* *cf.* 87. 1

Grey, Durh., on a sinister glove in fess arg., a falcon rising or, encircled with a branch of honeysuckle ppr.

Grey, Suff., a unicorn passant gu., bezantée, crined, armed, unguled, and ducally gorged or. *cf.* 48. 6

Grey, on a hand lying fesseways, couped at the wrist arg., thereon a bracelet or, a falcon of the last with wings expanded.

Grey, a unicorn passant erm., armed, maned, tufted, and unguled or, in front of a sun in splendour. *A ma puissance.*

Grey, Chesh., in front of the sun in splendour ppr., a unicorn erect erm., armed, crested, and unguled or. 48. 1

Grey, Beds, Essex, and Herts, a demi-woman couped at the waist ppr., her hair flotant or, holding in each hand a sprig of laurel vert.

Grey, out of a ducal coronet or, a demi-swan arg., beaked gu. *cf.* 100. 12

Grey, Northumb., out of a ducal coronet or, a swan rising wings elevated arg., charged on breast with a trefoil gu. *De bon vouloir servir le Roy.* *cf.* 100. 12

Grey, Scotland, an anchor entwined with a cable ppr. 161. 2

Grey, out of a ducal coronet gu., a demi-eagle ppr. 80. 4

Grey of Wolbeding, Sussex, and Barton, Yorks, out of a ducal coronet per pale or and gu., a demi-eagle with wings elevated arg.

Grey, Leics., out of a ducal coronet az., a demi-peacock in pride ppr.

Grey, Ireland, a griffin's head erased arg., beaked or, and holding in the beak an annulet gu. *cf.* 66. 2

Grey, a wyvern with wings addorsed supporting with the dexter claw a staff raguly.

Grey, on a chapeau gu., turned up erm., a wyvern or. *Foy en tout.* cf. 70. 4
Grey, on a chapeau gu., turned up erm., a wyvern with wings elevated and addorsed or. *A ma puissance.* cf. 70. 4
Grey, Norf. and Yorks, a dragon's head or. 71. 1
Grey, Scotland, a badger ppr. 33. 10
Grey, Northumb., a ram's head arg. 130. 1
Grey, a fox passant regardant ppr. cf. 32. 3
Greyndour, a squirrel sejant cracking a nut, all ppr. 135. 7
Greysbrook, a bear's head or, muzzled sa., charged on the neck with three fleurs-de-lis fesseways az. cf. 34. 14
Greystock, a lion passant gardant or. *Volo non valeo.* 4. 3
Gribble, a greyhound's head erased sa., collared or.
Gribble, George James, Esquire, of Henlow Grange, Biggleswade, in front of a greyhound's head couped sa., collared and ringed or, three mullets of six points fesseways of the last. *Veritas prevalebit.* 235. 7
Gribble, James Byng, Esquire, of 5, Wetherby Gardens, London, S.W., same crest and motto.
Gribble, John Charles, Esquire, of 12, Park Road, Richmond, same crest and motto.
Grice, Norf., a boar passant sa., ducally gorged or. cf. 40. 9
Grice, between two wings or, a blackamoor's head couped sa., ear-rings or, and ducally gorged of the last.
Gridley, out of a ducal coronet a demi-lion rampant or, holding between the paws a pheon ppr. *Devant si je puis.* cf. 16. 3
Grierson, Ireland, a demi-lion rampant holding in the dexter paw a rose. 12. 1
Grierson, a dolphin naiant az. 140. 5
Grierson, Ireland, a phœnix in flames ppr. 82. 2
Grierson, Scotland, a branch of fir ppr. *Spem renovat.* 147. 6
Grierson, Sir Alexander Davidson, Bart., of Lag, Dumfries, a fetterlock arg. *Hoc securior.* 168. 13
Grierson of Milton Park, Kirkcudbright, a fetterlock or. *Hoc securior.* 168. 12
Grierson, out of a ducal coronet or, an arm erect ppr., holding a key of the first.
Griesdale, a dexter hand in fess, couped and frilled, holding a sword in pale ppr.
Grieve, Scotland, a cock regardant ppr. 91. 9
Grieve, Scotland, an anchor in pale ppr. *Candide et caute.* 161. 1
Grieve, an escallop or, between two wings gu. 141. 10
Grieve, Roxburgh, Scotland, an arm in armour embowed, the hand grasping a dagger fesseways point to the dexter ppr. *Hoc securior.* 196. 5
Grieve, Russia, a dexter arm armed holding a dagger ppr. *Quia fidem servasti.*
Grieve, Scotland, an arm in armour holding a dagger point downwards ppr. *Hoc securior.*
Grieve, Frederick John Mackenzie, Esquire, Commander R.N., a dexter arm in armour embowed, the hand grasping a dagger ppr. *Qua fidem servasti.* 196. 5
Grieve, John Andrew Mackenzie, Esquire, Major, Royal Artillery, a dexter arm in armour embowed, the hand grasping a dagger ppr. *Qua fidem servasti.* 196. 5
Grieves, a pelican's head erased vulning itself ppr. 98. 2
Grieves, James Percy, M.R.C.S., 61, Fairlop Road, Leytonstone, N.E., out of a mural coronet a demi-eagle displayed holding in the beak a cross crosslet fitchée.
Grieveson, of Nevill Holt, Leics., an escallop or, surmounted by a mascle az., between two wings, also az., each charged with an escallop of the first. *Celeriter sed certe.*
Griffen, a unicorn's head erased az., bezantée. cf. 49. 5
Griffeth, a griffin's head erased or. (*Another*, ppr.) *Non crux, sed lux.* 66. 2
Griffin, London, Northamp., Warw., a talbot's head erased sa. *Vincam.*
Griffin, Marten Harcourt, Esquire, of the Pell Wall Estates, Market Drayton, Salop, a talbot's head erased sa. *Vincam.* 56. 2
Griffin, James Whitehouse, Esquire, J.P., of Towersey, Bucks, a talbot's head erased sa. *Ne vile velis.*
Griffin, a talbot's head erased ppr. 56. 2
Griffin, Staffs, a woman's head couped at the breasts ppr., the hair flotant or.
Griffin of London, out of a ducal coronet or, a demi-griffin erm., membered or. 64. 4
Griffin, Edward Lysaght, Esquire, Barrister-at-Law, of Violet Hill, Bray, co. Wicklow, Ireland, a demi-griffin segreant arg., charged on the shoulder with a fleur-de-lis az. *Fide et fortitudine.* cf. 64. 2
Griffin, Patrick, Esquire, of Woodhill Terrace, Tivoli, Cork, and Laharden, co. Kerry, a demi-griffin segreant arg., charged on the shoulder with a cross patée az. *Fide et fortitudine.* cf. 64. 2
Griffin, Richard Michael, Esquire, of Quorn House, Milverton, Warw., same crest and motto.
Griffin, Sir Lepel Henry, K.C.S.I., a griffin segreant or, between two ostrich-feathers arg. *Judge not.* cf. 62. 2
Griffinhoofe, a griffin's head or. 66. 1
Griffis, a peacock in his pride ppr. 103. 12
Griffith, late Francis Robert, Esquire, of Corsley and Crofton, Nilgiri Hills, South India, a demi-woman affrontée ppr., vested arg., supporting with the dexter hand a cross crosslet erect of the last, and resting the sinister hand on an escutcheon, also arg., charged with a rose gu., barbed and seeded ppr. *A fin.*
Griffith, a woman's head couped at the breasts ppr., hair flotant or.
Griffith, Glouc., a woman's head affrontée ppr. 182. 3
Griffith, Wales, a buck's head cabossed per pale or and arg. 122. 5
Griffith, a stag's head erased holding in its mouth a sprig of laurel ppr. cf. 121. 2
Griffith, a lion rampant sa. 1. 10
Griffith, Wales, a lion passant sa. 6. 2
Griffith of Bangor, Carnarvonsh., upon a mount vert, a lion statant, tail extended erm., charged on the body with three crosses patée in fesse gu.
Griffith, Shropsh., a demi-lion rampant holding in his dexter paw a pheon point downwards. cf. 10. 2
Griffith, a demi-lion rampant gu. *Gryf yn y fydd.* 10. 3
Griffith of Castell March, Wales, out of a mural coronet a demi-lion holding in the dexter paw a palm-branch. *A fynno Duw deued.* 16. 11
Griffith, Somers., a wolf's head couped sa., semée of estoiles or. cf. 30. 5
Griffith, Waldie-, Sir Richard John, Bart., of Munster Grillagh, co. Londonderry, on a ducal coronet a griffin segreant or, charged on the shoulder with a trefoil vert. *Jovis omnia plena.* 62. 2
Griffith, Rev. George Octavius, B.A., of St. Barnabas Vicarage, Beckenham, a demi-woman affrontée, habited gu., crined or, supporting with the dexter hand a cross crosslet, the sinister hand resting on an escutcheon arg. charged with a rose gu., barbed and seeded ppr. *A fin.* 255. 20
Griffith, Ralph Thomas Hotchkin, Esquire, M.A., C.I.E., of Corsley, Kotagiri, South India, same crest and motto.
Griffith, Herbert Edward, Esquire, of 11, St. Bride's Avenue, Fleet Street, E.C., same crest and motto.
Griffith, Richard William Smith, Esquire, of Eyeworth Lodge, Lyndhurst, Hants, a demi-maiden affrontée ppr., vested az., holding in the dexter hand a cross flory fitchée or, and resting the sinister on a lozenge, also or, charged with a martlet gu. *Fidèle à fin.*
Griffith, Rt. Hon. Sir Samuel Walker, G.C.M.G., of Merthyr, Brisbane, Queensland, a wyvern wings endorsed ppr., semée of trefoils or, the dexter foot supporting an escutcheon of the last, charged with a cross flory gu. *Esperance sans peur.* 253. 4
Griffith, late Charles Marshall, Esquire, of Llwynduris, Cardigansh., Wales, a griffin regardant sa., wings elevated or, holding in the beak an arrow, the barb downwards ppr., the dexter claw resting upon a man's head in profile armed in a helmet, the visor up, also ppr., garnished or. *Le bon temps viendra.* 63. 12
Griffith, John, Esquire, of Park Twad, near Newcastle Emlyn, same crest and motto.
Griffith, on a ducal coronet a griffin sejant. cf. 62. 10
Griffith, a griffin's head erased sa., guttée-d'or. cf. 66. 2
Griffith, on a mount vert, a squirrel sejant gu., holding a hazel-branch fructed, cracking a nut ppr. 135. 5
Griffith, Ireland, a dexter arm embowed holding in the hand a dagger.
Griffith, Gideon de Gorrequer, M.R.C.S., 34, St. George's Square, Belgravia, S.W., a bear's head, erased. *Acting rightly, trust in God.*
Griffith, Darby-, Christopher William, Padworth House, Reading: (1) A stag's head cabossed per pale gu. and az., attired or, between the attires an

estoile of the last (*Griffith*). (2) A garb arg., charged with an anchor erect sa. (*Darby*).

Griffiths, Worcs., a demi-lion rampant gu. 10. 3

Griffiths, Heref., a wolf's head couped sa., semée of estoiles or. *Firmitas et sanitas.* cf. 30. 5

Griffiths, a demi-Moor affrontée, charged on the breast with three suns ppr., girt round middle with a band rayonnée, and holding in the dexter hand a spear.

Griffiths, a stag's head cabossed per pale gu. and az., between the attires an étoile of eight points or. cf. 122. 5

Griffiths, Edward St. John, Esquire, of Upton House, Nursling, Southampton, a lion rampant gu., charged with a chevron or, holding between the fore-paws an escutcheon arg., thereon a stag's head caboshed of the first, and resting the hind-leg on a cinquefoil of the second. *Usque ad aras amicus.* 292. 6

Grigby, an ounce's head erased ppr., collared arg., charged with two mullets gu.

Grigg, a horse's head erased arg. *Ut prosim.* 51. 4

Grigg, out of a ducal coronet a dexter hand holding up a swan's head, all ppr. 220. 7

Griggs, a sword in pale enfiled with a leopard's face, all ppr. 22. 1

Griggs, Joseph, Esquire, D.L., of Mountfields, Loughborough, in front of two ostrich-feathers in saltire gu., a sword in pale enfiled with a leopard's face ppr. *Secondo curo.* 22. 13

Grigson, a ram's head erased ppr. 130. 6

Grigson, of Saham Toney, Norf., out of a ducal coronet or, a griffin's head chequy arg. and sa. 67. 9

Grigson, a griffin's head couped chequy arg. and sa., encircled by an annulet or. *Vincit qui se vincit.*

Grigson, Rev. William Shuckforth, Pelynt Vicarage, Duloe, R.S.O., Cornw., same crest.

Griles, Devonsh., a hedgehog arg. 135. 8

Grill, a demi-chevalier in armour holding in his dexter hand a scimitar, all ppr. 187. 4

Grilles, Cornw., a porcupine passant arg. cf. 136. 5

Grills, Devonsh. and Cornw., a hedgehog arg. 135. 8

Grimaldi, a demi-griffin segreant ppr. *Deo juvante.*

Grimes of London, a martlet vert. 95. 4

Grimes, Warw. and Hants, two wings addorsed or. cf. 109. 12

Grimes, a horse's head couped or, between two wings arg. 51. 3

Grimké-Drayton: (1) On a rock ppr. a raven sa., guttée d'eau, supporting with the dexter foot a cross engrailed gu. (*for Drayton*). (2) On a mount vert, a demi-lion or, charged on the shoulder with a cinquefoil of the first, between two palmetto-trees ppr. (*for Grimké*). *Hac iter ad astra.*

Grimond, a camel's head erased or, collared gu., and belled arg.

Grimsbie and **Grimsby,** Leics., a demi-ram salient sa. 130. 13

Grimshaw, Lancs, a griffin segreant sa., beaked and membered or. 62. 2

Grimshaw, Captain John, of Hutton Lodge, Kirkby Stephen, J.P., D.L., a griffin segreant sa., beaked and membered or, ducally crowned of the last. *Candide et constanter.*

Grimshaw, Robert, of Hanover, a griffin segreant holding in the dexter claw a rose slipped and leaved.

Grimshaw of High Bank, Lancs, a demi-griffin sa. *Tenax propositi, vinco.* 64. 2

Grimshaw, Ireland, a dexter arm in armour ppr., holding in the hand a cross crosslet fitched in pale az. cf. 210. 14

Grimshaw, two lions' heads erased, collared and addorsed ppr. 18. 2

Grimstead and **Grimsted,** a dexter arm embowed ppr., the elbow on the wreath, holding a bow towards the sinister ppr.

Grimston, a stag's head with a ring round its neck arg. *Faitz proveront.* cf. 121. 5

Grimston, Essex, a stag's head erased ppr., attired or. *Mediocria firma.* 121. 2

Grimston and **Grimstone,** a stag's head arg., attired or. 121. 5

Grimston, Earl of Verulam, *see* Verulam.

Grimthorpe, Baron (Beckett), of Grimthorpe, Yorks, a boar's head couped or, pierced by a cross patée fitchée erect sa. *Prodesse civibus.*

Grimwood, on the top of a tower an eagle issuing with wings addorsed, holding in its beak an acorn slipped ppr. 76. 10

Grimwood: (1) A demi-wolf rampant, collared, and holding between the paws a saltire. (2) A lion's gamb erased and erect sa., charged with a cross crosslet arg., and holding a buckle or. *Auxilio divino.*

Grindal and **Grindall,** an arm in armour embowed, holding by the blade a sword, point downwards, ppr. 195. 6

Grindal and **Grindall,** a demi-lion rampant per pale or and az. 10. 2

Grindlay and **Grindley,** a buffalo's head erased gu. 44. 1

Grindlay and **Grindley,** a dove ppr. 92. 2

Grindlay and **Grindley,** a pea-hen ppr.

Gringfield, Sussex, a gauntlet or. 209. 8

Grinlinton, Sir John Joseph, C.E., F.R.G.S., F.S.A., of Rose Hill, Middle Wallop, Hants, a sword erect ppr., pommel and hilt or, surmounting a pen fesseways arg., interlaced by a spur or. *Fide et fortitudine.* 246. 10

Grisewood of London, a demi-lion gardant arg., environed with laurel vert, holding a garb az., banded or. *Nil desperandum.*

Grislay, a dexter hand ppr., holding a lozenge or. 219. 10

Grissell, Hartwell Delagarde Esquire, of Brasenose College, Oxford, on a wreath or and gu., a greyhound's head erased sa., around the neck a double chain or, and pendent therefrom an escutcheon of the last, charged with a bugle-horn stringed sa. 61. 1

Grissell, Frank De la Garde, Esquire, of Army and Navy Club, S.W., same crest.

Grissell, Thomas De la Garde, Esquire, of Norbury Park, Dorking, same crest and motto.

Gritton, a lion's face between two wings ppr. 21. 4

Grive, a martlet sa. *J'ai le clef.* 95. 5

Groat of Newhall, Scotland, an anchor ppr. *Anchor fast.* 161. 2

Groat, Middx. and Kent, on a mount vert, a dexter arm in armour embowed ppr., garnished or, holding in the hand a javelin surmounted by two oak-branches.

Grobham, Wilts, a boar's head couped or. 43. 1

Grogan, Ireland, a hawk holding in its dexter claw a wheat-ear ppr. 85. 7

Grogan of Johnstown, Wexford, Ireland, a lion's head erased sa. *Honor et virtus.* 17. 8

Grogan, Sir Edward Ion Beresford, Bart., a lion's head erased sa., charged with a mullet or. *Honor et virtus.* cf. 17. 8

Grogan-Morgan: (1) A reindeer's head cabossed or (*for Morgan*). 122. 4. (2) A lion's head erased sa. (*for Grogan*). *Honor et virtus.—Fidus et audax.* 17. 8

Grogan, a hind trippant or. 124. 12

Grome, Suff., an arm in armour ppr., garnished or, holding in the hand a gauntlet, also ppr.

Gronow, a lion rampant. 1. 13

Gronow of Ash Hall, Glamorgan, a lion rampant. *Gronwi hil Gwerninion.* 1. 13

Grooby, Wilts, out of a ducal coronet or, an eagle displayed ppr., charged with a label.

Groom, Grome, and **Groome,** on a torteau winged gu., an eagle with wings displayed or. cf. 79. 1

Groom, a dexter arm in armour embowed ppr., garnished or, holding in the hand of the first a gauntlet, also ppr., and suspended from the wrist by a pink ribbon an escutcheon, also or, thereon a pile gu., charged with a cross patée fitched arg. 199. 11

Groombridge, out of a mural coronet a garb, thereon a crow perched, all ppr. 153. 9

Grose, Surrey, on a mount vert, a lamb sa., holding with the dexter foot a banner erm., charged with a cross clechée gu. cf. 131. 14

Groseth, Scotland, a dexter hand holding a sword ppr. *Pro patriâ.* 212. 13

Grosett, *see* Grossett.

Gross, on a ducal coronet or, a talbot passant ppr., collared and lined of the first. 54. 9

Grosse, out of a ducal coronet a hand holding a dagger ppr. 212. 11

Grosset and **Grossett,** four arrows, points downwards, and a strung bow in saltier, all ppr. 173. 12

Grossett-Muirhead, *see* Muirhead.

Grossett, Wilts, two hands holding a sword erect ppr., hilt and pommel or. 213. 1

Grosvenor, Duke of Westminster, *see* Westminster.

Grosvenor, Glouc., a talbot statant or. cf. 54. 2

Grosvenor, William Clayton, Esquire, of Hungersheath, Arnside, Westml., same crest.

Grosvenor, Randolph Lea, Esquire, 75, Oakley Street, Chelsea Embankment, S.W., same crest. *Virtus non stemma.*

Grosvenor of Bushbury, Staffs, a talbot passant or, collared gu. cf. 54. 5

Grosvenor, Dorset, a horse current saddled and bridled, all ppr. 52. 1
Grosvenor, George William, Esquire, of Broome House, Stourbridge, a garb erminois surmounting three battle-axes, one in pale and two in saltire ppr. *Virtus non stemma.*
Grote of London and Surrey, between two elephants' probosces erect, a pine-tree, all ppr. *Prodesse quam conspici.*
Grotrian, Frederick Brent, Esquire, M.P., a dragon's head between two wings expanded arg. *Animo et fide.* 72. 7
Grout, on a mount vert, a dexter arm in armour embowed ppr., garnished or, holding a javelin surmounted by two oak-branches, also ppr.
Grove, Ireland, a lion rampant gu. *Gloria finis.* 1. 13
Grove, John M. C., Esq., of Castle Grove, same crest and motto.
Grove of Shenston Park, Staffs, on a mount vert, a dragon statant ppr., collared and chained or, and charged on the shoulder with an estoile gu. *Laudo manentem.* 235. 10
Grove, John William, Esquire, J.P., of Coldbrook, Long Bay, D'Entrecasteaux Channel, Tasmania, Member of Licensing Bench and Educational Board of Advice, etc., a mount, thereon a dragon, with wings elevated vert, collared and chain reflexed over the back, and charged on the shoulder with an estoile or. *Laudo manentem.* 235. 10
Grove, a stag trippant ppr. 117. 8
Grove, a hand holding a glove ppr. 220. 5
Grove, a hand holding a thistle ppr. 218. 2
Grove, Dorset and Wilts, a talbot passant sa., collared or. *cf.* 54. 1
Grove, Dorset and Wilts, a talbot passant sa., collared arg. *cf.* 54. 1
Grove, Troyte-Chafyn-, George, Zeal's House, near Mere, Wilts, a talbot passant sa., collared and tirreted arg. *Grow as a grove.—Ni dessous ni dessoux.*
Grove, a talbot passant sa., gorged with a collar engrailed arg. *cf.* 54. 5
Grove of Dunhead, Wilts, a talbot passant sa., ducally gorged or. *cf.* 54. 1
Grove, Sir Thomas Fraser, Bart., M.P., of Ferne, Wilts, a talbot statant sa., collared arg. *Ny dessux, ny dessoux.* 54. 2
Grover, issuing out of a cloud in the sinister an arm embowed holding a garland of flowers ppr. 200. 12
Grover of Porth-y-Glo, near Cardiff, out of a cloud in the sinister an arm embowed holding a garland of flowers, all ppr. 200. 12
Grover of the Bury, Hemel Hempstead, Herts, and Bovenay Court, Burnham, Bucks, a demi-lion gu., gorged with a collar gemel, holding in the dexter paw a palm-branch slipped and resting the sinister on a mullet, all or. *Le Roy, la loy, la foy.* *cf.* 15. 10
Groves, John Percy, Esquire, of Candie, Guernsey, a talbot sejant collared. *Gaudet tentamine virtus.*
Groves, out of a ducal coronet or, a cock's head combed and wattled gu. 90. 6
Groves, Ireland, a greyhound passant sa., ducally gorged or. *cf.* 60. 2
Groves, Staffs, on a mount vert, a dragon statant ppr., collared and chained or, charged on the shoulder with an estoile gu.
Groves of Bridge House, Beaminster, Dorset, a talbot passant.
Growtage or Goutrige, an ostrich's head holding in the beak a horse-shoe ppr.
Groyn, a bear's head sa. 34. 14
Groze, a mullet or. *Deo juvante.* 164. 2
Grubb, Scotland, a lion's head erased. *Strength is from heaven.* 17. 8
Grubb, Herts, a griffin's head erased per pale arg. and gu., charged with a rose counterchanged.
Grubb, Edward Walter, Esquire, a griffin's head erased per pale arg. and gu., charged with a rose counterchanged. *cf.* 66. 2
Grubb, Wilts, a lion's head az., ducally crowned or. *cf.* 18. 8
Grubbam and **Grubham,** a cock ppr. 91. 2
Grubbe, Charles Walter, Esquire, a griffin's head erased per pale arg. and gu., charged with a rose counterchanged.
Grubbe, Rev. Charles Septimus, M.A., same crest.
Grubbe, Francis William, Esquire, of Shellow, Ongar, Essex, same crest.
Grubbe, John Eustace, Esquire, of Southwold, Suff., same crest. *Factis dictisque merere.*
Grubbe, Robert William, Esquire, same crest.
Grubbe, a lion's head az., murally crowned or.
Grubbe, Wilts, a lion's gamb sa., holding a rose gu., stalved and leaved ppr. *cf.* 37. 10
Gruben, an acorn slipped and leaved vert. 152. 1
Grubham, a rose gu., stalked and leaved vert. 149. 5
Grudgfield, Suff., a gauntlet or 209. 8
Grueber, Stephen Henry, Esquire, J.P., of Ormley, Fingal, Tasmania, a rose between two wings erect, each charged with a rose. *Honor virtutis præmium.*
Gruffeth, Staffs and Warw., a demi-woman vested gu., crined or. 182. 8
Grumley, Ireland, a vine-branch ppr. 152. 9
Grumstead, an antelope's head couped arg., attired or. *cf.* 126. 2
Grundie, Notts, a demi-leopard rampant gardant sa., bezantée. 23. 4
Grundin, a stag trippant erm. 117. 8
Grundy, a demi-leopard rampant gardant sa., bezantée. *Scio cui confido.* 23. 4
Grunhut, Victor Phillip James, Westcote, Westoe, a helmet fan arg., rayonnée, and charged with a chevron gu. *Semper constanter.* 300. 12
Gryce, Norf., a boar arg., ducally gorged, armed and ungu. or. *cf.* 40. 9
Grylls, Cornw., a porcupine passant arg. *Vires agmenotis unus habet.* *cf.* 136. 5
Gryme, the Roman fasces ppr. 171. 4
Grymes, issuing out of a cloud a hand seizing a stag by the attires, all ppr. 116. 10
Grymes, a griffin's head erased sa., semée of escallops or. *cf.* 66. 2
Grymsby, Essex, a sinister hand holding a bow ppr. 214. 5
Grys, a lion sejant sa., collared and lined or. 7. 4
Gubbay, Moses, Esquire, of Poona, East India, a pelican arg., standing on a rose-branch slipped ppr., and charged on the wing with a key gu. *Probitas fons honoris.* 98. 5
Gubbay, Maurice Elias, Esquire, of Grosvenor Gardens, London, S.W., a bird of paradise, in the beak a branch of fern, and resting the dexter leg on a lotus flower, all ppr. *Toujours ou jamais.*
Gubbins, an arm from the elbow vested, holding a branch of holly vert.
Gubyon, a demi-lion rampant sa., charged with three escallops arg. *cf.* 10. 1
Gucheres, a water-bouget sa. 168. 4
Guernsey, Lord, *see* Aylesford, Earl of.
Guest, *see* Wimborne, Baron.
Guest, Scotland, a swan ppr. 99. 2
Guest, a swan with wings expanded ppr. *Nec temere, nec timide.* *cf.* 99. 12
Guest, a swan's head erased ppr., between two ostrich-feathers or. *cf.* 101. 1
Gueva, Lincs, a plume of four ostrich-feathers, the two outside ones or, and the two centre ones gu. *cf.* 114. 1
Guidott, Hants, a gerfalcon ppr., with wings elevated, beaked, and membered or, holding in the beak a branch of olive vert, fructed or. *Pax optima rerum.*
Guildford, Earl of (North), a dragon's head erased sa., ducally gorged and chained or. *La vertue est la seule noblesse.—Animo et fide.* *cf.* 71. 8
Guilford, Kent, a tree raguly couped and trunked or, flammant gu.
Guilford, on a chapeau gu., turned up erm., an ostrich-feather erect or.
Guillam, a dolphin haurient ppr. 140. 11
Guillamore, Viscount (O'Grady), of Cahir Guillamore, Kilmallock, co. Limerick, a horse's head erased arg., charged with a portcullis az. *Vulneratus non victus.* *cf.* 51. 4
Guille, Jersey, and Guernsey, a mullet of seven points or, between two wings arg. *Raptim ad sidera tollar.* *cf.* 111. 5
Guille, Jersey a mullet of seven points or. *E cœlo lux mea.*
Guillemard, Francis Henry Hill, M.D., a dexter arm embowed in armour ppr., the hand grasping a mullet arg.
Guillim, Glouc., an arm in armour embowed, holding in the hand a broken sword, all ppr.
Guinners, Ireland, out of a mural coronet az., a demi-lion or, holding in his dexter paw a palm-branch vert. 16. 11
Guinness, Baron Ardilaun, *see* Ardilaun.
Guinness, *see* Grattan-Guinness.
Guinness, *see* Lee-Guinness.
Guinness, Richard Seymour, Esquire, of 16, Rutland Gate, London, S.W., a boar passant quarterly or and gu. *Spes mea in Deo.* 40. 9
Guinness, John Cecil Jenkinson, Esquire, of San Francisco, U.S.A., same crest.
Guinness, Sir Reginald Robert Bruce, J.P., D.L., of 134, Ashley Gardens, S.W., same crest and motto.
Guinness, Rev. Robert, M.A., of the Vicarage, Market Harborough, same crest and motto.

Guinness, Captain Benjamin Lee, D.L., of Ballard, Combe, Kingston-on-Thames, and 25, Cadogan Gardens, London, S.W.: (1) Guinness. (2) On a pillar arg., encircled by a ducal coronet or, an eagle preying on a bird's leg erased ppr. (*for Lee*). 248. 1. *Spes mea in Deo.*

Guion and **Guyon,** a cock az., combed and wattled or. 91. 2

Guise, Sir William Francis George, Bart., J.P., D.L., of Elmore Court, Glouc., out of a ducal coronet or, a swan rising ppr., collared and chained of the first, and charged with a lozenge vair. *Quo honestior eo tutior.* 247. 3

Guise, Francis Edward, Esquire, M.A., of Dean Hall, Little Dean, Newnham, same crest.

Gulby, a naked arm embowed, thrusting a sword, point downwards.

Guldeford, a firebrand flammant ppr.

Gull, Sir William Cameron, Bart., M.A., of Brook Street, in the parish of St. George, Hanover Square, Middx.: (1) On the dexter side, of honourable augmentation, a lion passant gardant or, supporting with the dexter paw an escutcheon az., thereon an ostrich-feather arg., quilled or, enfiled with the coronet, encircling the badge of the Prince of Wales. 279. 1. (2) On the sinister side, two arms embowed vested az., cuffs arg., the hands ppr. holding a torch or, fired ppr. *Sine Deo frustra.* 279. 2

Gull, Kent, a dexter arm in armour embowed in fess ppr., the elbow on the wreath, holding in the hand a battle-axe arg., the handle or.

Gullan, Scotland, a stag lodged ppr. 115. 7

Gulland, Scotland, a dove within a serpent in orle ppr. *Innocence surmounts.* 92. 11

Gulline, Scotland, a dove ppr. 92. 2

Gulline, Scotland, a falcon belled ppr. *cf.* 85. 2

Gulliver, a lion passant gardant arg., ducally crowned or. *Non dormit qui custodit.* *cf.* 4. 3

Gullon, in a cavity of a rock a Cornish chough sitting, all ppr. *Tutum refugium.* 102. 6

Gully, Rt. Hon. William Court, P.C., K.C., M.P., of Speaker's House, Westminster, S.W., and Sutton Place, Seaford, Sussex, a cubit arm vested sa., cuff arg., the hand grasping a sword erect ppr., between two wings each per pale nebuly, the dexter of the last and gu., and the sinister gu. and or.

Gully, two keys in saltier. *Nil sine cruce.*

Gulman, a man's leg in armour couped and embowed, the thigh in fess, the leg in pale, the foot in chief, spurred, all ppr.

Gulston, Alan Stepney, Esquire, of Derwydd, Llandebie R.S.O., Carmarthensh., an ostrich's wing, five feathers alternately arg. and gu., charged with a bend sa., thereon three plates. Over crest, "*Crescent sub pondere virtus.*" 113. 9

Gumbleton, Middx., a demi-griffin with wings addorsed arg., beaked and legged gu., holding a mullet or. *cf.* 64. 2

Gun-Monro, *see* Monro.

Gun, co. Kerry, a dexter hand erect and apaumée ppr. *Vincit amor patriæ.* 222. 14

Gun, a dexter arm in mail embowed, holding in the hand a sword ppr. *cf.* 195. 2

Gun of Fethard, Tipperary, Ireland, two swords in saltire, points upwards, ppr., pommels and hilts or. *Dum spiro, spero.* 171. 12

Gun, Scotland, a wolf passant sa. 28. 10

Gun-Cunningham, Cornwallis Robert Ducarel, Esquire, of Mount Kennedy, Newtownmountkennedy, co. Wicklow, Ireland, the stump of an oak-tree fructed with a single acorn ppr., surmounted by a scroll inscribed with the word "*Tandem.*" *Over, fork over.*

Gundry, a demi-lion holding in the dexter paw a sword, all or. 14. 12

Gunman, Kent, out of a naval coronet arg., an anchor erect sa., cabled or.

Gunn, on a chapeau az., a fox sejant or. 32. 12

Gunn, Scotland, a hand holding a sword ppr. *Aut pax, aut bellum.* 212. 13

Gunn, Scotland, a dexter hand holding a musket.

Gunn, Norf., a lion rampant gu., holding a bezant.

Gunner, a lion's head erased or. 17. 8

Gunning, Sir George William, Bart., J.P., M.A., of Eltham, Kent, a dove holding in the dexter claw a caduceus ppr. *Imperio regit unus æquo.* 283. 15

Gunning, Kent, on a wreath of the colours a dove az., the dexter claw supporting a sword wavy and radiated in bend ppr., hilt and pommel or. *Verité sans peur.*

Gunning, Somers., an ostrich holding in the beak a horse-shoe ppr., charged on the breast with a cross patée gu. *cf.* 97. 8

Gunson, Gonson, and **Gonston,** an antelope's head couped arg., guttée-de-sang, attired or. *Non aqua solum.* *cf.* 126. 2

Gunston, Ireland, a tower triple-towered arg. 157. 6

Gunter of Milton, Wilts, and Kintbury, Berks, an antelope's head erased per pale or and sa. 126. 2

Gunter, Sussex, a stag's head erased per pale sa. and gu., attired or. 121. 2

Gunter, Sussex, a stag's head couped per pale gu. and sa., attired, counter-changed. 121. 5

Gunter, Wales, a stag's head per pale gu. and sa. 121. 5

Gunter, Sir Robert, Bart., on a gauntlet fessewise or, a stag's head erased proper. 284. 12

Gunthorpe, Norf., a lion's head erased, collared. 18. 6

Gunthorpe, a unicorn's head arg. 49. 7

Gurdon, Hants, Suff., and Wilts, a goat arg., attired or, salient against a mountain vert. 238. 1

Gurdon, Norf. and Suff., a goat climbing up a rock, all ppr. *In arduis viget virtus.* 238. 1

Gurdon, Sir William Brampton, K.C.M.G., of Assington Hall, Suff., same crest and motto.

Gurdon, Major-General Evelyn Pulteney, of 12, Norton Road, Hove, Sussex, same crest and motto.

Gurdon, Philip, Esquire, of 6, Conduit Road, Bedford, same crest and motto.

Gurlin, on a mural coronet gu., an eagle with wings addorsed or, holding in the beak an acorn stalked and leaved ppr. *cf.* 76. 10

Gurney, a lion's head erased or, gorged with a palisado coronet composed of spear-heads az.

Gurney, Alexander Cecil, M.B., 5, Gildridge Road, Eastbourne, out of a baronial coronet a lion's head. *A Deo nutritus.—Sit Deo gloria.*

Gurney, John Henry, Esquire, of Keswick Hall, Norwich; Richard Hanbury Joseph Gurney, Esquire, of Northrepps Hall, Norwich; and Somerville Arthur Gurney, Esquire, of Northrunceton Hall, Norf.: (1) On a chapeau gu., turned up erm., a gurnard fish in pale head downwards. 139. 1. (2) A wrestling-collar or. 165. 12.

Gurney, Richard Hanbury Joseph, Esquire, D.L., of Northrepps Hall, Norwich, on a chapeau gu., turned up erm., a gurnard fish in pale head downwards.

Gurteen of Bleane, Kent, a demi-heraldic antelope sa., attired, ungu., and crined or, supporting between the legs a tilting-spear of the last. 127. 12

Gurwood, out of a mural coronet a castle ruined in the centre, and therefrom an arm in armour embowed, holding a scimitar, all ppr.

Gurwood, a unicorn's head. 49. 7

Guscotte, a demi-gryphon arg., guttée-de-sang, wings elevated vair, holding in the dexter paw a goutte gu., and supporting with the sinister by the blade a sword in bend point upwards ppr., pommel and hilt or. *Constantia et labore.*

Gush, William Frederick, Esquire, late of 53, Sussex Gardens, Hyde Park, an owl arg., holding in the beak a balance or. *Sapiens et justus.*

Gusthart, an eagle displayed sa., pierced through with an arrow bendwise arg. *Avitos novit honores.* *cf.* 75. 2

Guston, a demi-wolf gu. 31. 2

Gutch, John, Esquire, M.A., M.D., of 28, Fonnereau Road, Ipswich, on a wreath of the colours, arg. and gu., in front of three roses arg., stalked and leaved ppr., a boar's head erased, also arg. *Persevere.* 252. 20

Guthrie, *see* Lingard-Guthrie.

Guthrie, a salmon naiant arg. *Ditat et alit.*

Guthrie, an eagle displayed sa., holding in its dexter claw a sword ppr. 75. 7

Guthrie of Halkertoun, Kincardine, Scotland, a falcon with wings elevated standing on a dexter hand in fess couped behind the wrist ppr. *Ad alta.*

Guthrie, Scotland, a cross crosslet fitchée az. *Ex unitate incrementum.* 166. 2

Guthrie of Craigie, Forfarsh., Scotland, a demi-lion rampant gu., holding in his dexter paw a cross crosslet fitchée gu. *Sto pro veritate.* 11. 10

Guthrie, a demi-lion rampant gu., armed and langued az., holding in his dexter paw a cross crosslet fitchée of the last. *Sto pro veritate.—Nec timidus nec timidus.*

Guthrie, Scotland, a dexter arm in armour embowed brandishing a sword ppr. *Sto pro veritate.* 195. 2

Guthrie, John Douglas Maude, Esquire, of Guthrie Castle, Guthrie, N.B., and Gagie House, Dundee, N.B., a dexter arm issuing holding a drawn sword ppr. Above the crest, *Sto pro veritate.*

Guthrie, Scotland, a hand holding a sword ppr. *Sto pro veritate.* 212. 13

Guthry, Scotland, a lion's gamb issuant grasping a palm-branch ppr. *Sto pro veritate.* 36. 7

Guthry, Scotland, a cross crosslet fitched az. *Ex unitate incrementum.* 166. 2

Gutteridge or **Guttridge,** a swan ppr., crowned with an antique crown or. *cf.* 99. 2

Guy, Northamp. and Wilts, between two wings expanded or, a lion's head az., collared arg. *cf.* 19. 7

Guy, a man's face affrontée bearded ppr., crowned with an antique crown or. *Dare quam accipere.*

Guyan, Essex, a demi-lion rampant gardant or, gorged with a collar per pale az. and sa. *cf.* 10. 8

Guybyon, an eagle's head erased erm. 83. 2

Guylemin, Herts and Wales, an eagle's head erased sa., beaked gu., holding in the beak a lion's gamb or, erased of the second. *cf.* 83. 2

Guyling, an arm embowed ppr., vested arg., the hand, also ppr., holding a scimitar.

Guyon, Gardiner Frederic, Col. retired, late Royal Fusiliers, of Egerton House, Richmond, Surrey, out of a mural crown arg., charged with three pellets, a demi-lion rampant ppr. *Vis unita fit fortior.*

Guyot, an eagle displayed. 75. 2

Gwatkin, a garb or, banded. 153. 2

Gwatkin, Alexander George Stapleton, Esquire, on a mount vert, a garb or, in front thereof a Cornish chough with wings expanded sa. *Duw a bortha y brain.*

Gwatkin, Arthur John Campbell, Esquire, M.A., same crest and motto.

Gwatkin, Frederick Stapleton, Esquire, same crest and motto.

Gwatkin, Hugh Fortescue Wilmshurst, Esquire, same crest and motto.

Gwatkin, Joshua Reynolds Gascoigne, Esquire, of the Manor House, Potterne, in front of a beehive ppr., a bee volant between six points fesseways or. *Industria.*

Gwatkin, Stewart Beauchamp, Esquire, in front of a beehive ppr., charged with a cross crosslet or, a fern-brake, also ppr. *In recto glorior.* 253. 8

Gwillam, a dolphin haurient ppr. 140. 11

Gwillanne, an eagle ppr. 76. 2

Gwilt, of London, a cubit arm couped ppr., holding in the hand a saltire or, surmounted by a fleur-de-lis sa.

Gwilt of Westminster, on a saltire or, interlaced by two amphisbœna az., langued gu., a rose of the last barbed and seeded ppr.

Gwilt of Icklingham, Suff., from a mount vert, the sun rising in its splendour ppr., therefrom issuant a unicorn's head couped sa., armed and crined or, holding in the mouth a cross pattée fitchée of the last. 49. 3

Gwinnell, a sinister arm in fess vested gu., embowed, holding a bow towards the sinister ppr. 204. 4

Gwinnell, an arm couped at the shoulder, vested gu., embowed and resting the elbow on the wreath, the hand towards the sinister holding a bow ppr. 204. 11

Gwinnett of Moreton Hall, Heref., and Penlline Castle, Glamorgansh., a horse's head sa., gorged with a wreath of oak or, holding in the mouth a broken spear in bend sinister, point downwards, embrued ppr.

Gwinnett, Glouc., a horse's head couped sa., holding in the mouth a spear in bend, head downwards, embrued ppr.

Gwydyr, Baron (Burrell), of Gwydyr, Carnarvonsh., a naked arm embowed ppr., holding a branch of laurel vert. *Animus non deficit æquus.* 228. 6

Gwyer, Wales, a wolf passant ppr. 28. 10

Gwyn, Ireland, a lion rampant arg. 1. 13

Gwyn, formerly of Baron's Hall, Norf., a lion rampant or. 1. 13

Gwyn, Reginald Preston Jermy, Stanfield Hall, Wymondham, Norf., same crest. *Retribue servo tuo.*

Gwyn, a cannon mounted ppr. 169. 12

Gwyn, two laurel-slips in saltier ppr.

Gwyn, a stag's head erased ppr., between the attires a cross crosslet fitched. 120. 12

Gwyn, Wales, a gauntlet holding a sword arg., pierced through a dragon's head erased or, vulned ppr.

Gwyn, Wales, a sword in pale, point downwards, ppr., pierced through a boar's head sa. *cf.* 42. 4

Gwyn of Dyffryn, Wales, a hand holding a dagger thrust through a boar's head couped arg. *Vim vi repellere licet.* 212. 6

Gwyn, *see* Moore Gwyn.

Gwyn, Berks, London, and Wales, an arm in armour embowed ppr., holding in the hand a sword below the hilt in bend sinister arg., hilt and pommel or. 195. 6

Gwynne, Wales, a hand in armour couped at the wrist ppr., holding a dagger arg., hilt or, pierced through a boar's head erased sa.

Gwynne, Wales, a lion rampant regardant supporting between its paws a boar's head, all or.

Gwynne, England and Ireland, a dolphin naiant az. 140. 5

Gwynne, Sussex and London, a bear and a ragged staff. 34. 9

Gwynne-Holford, James Price William, Esquire, of Kilgwyn, Carmarthensh., Buckland, Bwlch, and Tre Holford, Brecon: (1) From the sun in splendour or, rising from behind a hill vert, a greyhound's head issuant sa. (2) A dexter arm in armour ppr., issuant from a crescent arg., holding a sword erect, also ppr., hilt and pommel or, entiled by a boar's head or, erased and vulned ppr. Over the second crest *Vim vi repellere licet.* Under the arms—*Toujours fidèle.*

Gwynne-Hughes, John Williams, Esquire, of Tregil, Llandilo, Carmarthensh.: (1) A talbot passant (*for Hughes*). (2) A goat passant (*for Williams*). (3) A raven ppr. (*for Gwynne*).

Gwynne-Vaughan of Guildfa House, Penybont, Radnorsh., upon a mount vert, in front of a boy's head affrontée, couped at the shoulders ppr., crined or, a snake nowed, also ppr. *Asgre lan diogel ei pherchen.*

Gybbon, a demi-lion arg., crowned or, holding in its dexter paw an escallop of the first.

Gybbons, a demi-lion rampant sa., charged with three escallops in pale arg. *cf.* 10. 2

Gybons, Oxon., Warw., and Wales, a lion's gamb erect and erased gu., holding a cross formée fitched sa. 36. 9

Gyfford, a lion's head erased gu., gorged with a collar or, charged with three roses of the first. *cf.* 18. 6

Gyles or **Gylls,** a hand holding a club ppr., spiked or. *cf.* 214. 6

Gyles, a pelican in her piety ppr. 98. 8

Gyles, Devonsh., a lion's gamb erect and erased gu., entiled by a bar gemelle or, holding a branch of apples of the last, leaved ppr.

Gyll, Durh. and Yorks, the head of an Eastern king couped at the shoulders in profile ppr., crowned and collared or, a chain passing from the rim of the crown behind to the back of the collar, also or.

Gyll of Wyrardisbury, Bucks, a hawk's head az., between two wings vert, fretty or. *Virtutis gloria merces.* 227. 3

Gyll, a falcon's head az., between two wings or. 89. 1

Gymber of London, an arm in armour ppr., holding a spiked club or.

Gynn, Herts, on a garb or, a bird close az. *cf.* 93. 3

Gypses, a dove holding in its beak an olive-branch ppr. 92. 5

Gyrlyn, Norf., a demi-griffin az., wings, beak, and legs or, holding a fleur-de-lis per pale of the first and gu. *cf.* 64. 2

Gysors, a fox's head erased gu. 33. 6

Gysseling, Lincs, a lion rampant az., winged or. 20. 7

Gyssinge, a lion passant erm., collared gu. *cf.* 6. 2

Gytties, Kent, an arm in armour embowed ppr., garnished or, holding a battle-axe arg. 200. 6

Gyttings, Shropsh., two tilting-spears in saltier.

Gyves, a unicorn's head couped at the neck. 49. 7

H.

Habeck, out of a mural coronet a cubit arm vested az., cuffed arg., holding in the hand a mullet gu. *cf.* 206. 12

Habgood, a sword and a quill in saltier ppr. 170. 4

Habgood, A. E., Solicitor, Clifton, Bristol, a pen in bend surmounting a sword in bend sinister, point upwards, both ppr.

Habgood, Henry, M.D., Stafford House, Upperton Road, Eastbourne, same crest. *Per aspera virtus.*

Habingdon, Worcs., an eagle displayed or, ducally crowned az. *cf.* 75. 2

Habingdon, a horse's head erased arg., bridled sa., between two wings ppr. *cf.* 51. 3

Haccomb, an arm holding a bow and arrow, all ppr.

Haccombe, a dragon's head erased vert, scaled or. *cf.* 71. 2

Hachet, Warw., a hawk's head couped gu. *cf.* 89. 1

Hachet or **Hacket** of London and Bucks, a demi-panther arg., spotted az., or, and gu., holding a branch vert, flowered of the fourth. 23. 14

Hackbeck, a cross pattée erm. *cf.* 165. 7

Hacker, on the trunk of a tree in fess, a moor-cock ppr.

Hacker-Heathcote of East Bridgford, Old Hall, Notts: (1) On a mural coronet az., a pomeis charged with a cross or, between two wings displayed erm. (*for Heathcote*). (2) A woodpecker standing on the top of a tree eradicated ppr. (*for Hacker*).

Hacket, Warw., an eagle's head erased ppr. *Fides sufficit.* 83. 2

Hacket, Bucks and London, a demi-panther arg., spotted az., or, and gu., holding a branch vert, flowered of the fourth. 23. 14

Hacket, Scotland, an arm in armour embowed holding a sword, all ppr. 195. 2

Hackett, Charles, Esquire, J.P., of Riverstown, near Parsonstown, co. Tipperary, a demi-panther arg., spotted az., collared gu., charged on the shoulder with a trefoil slipped vert, and holding in the dexter paw a branch of the last. *Virtute et fidelitate.* *cf.* 23. 14

Hackett, a demi-eagle with two heads displayed per pale gu. and or, wings counterchanged, each head ensigned with a coronet. *cf.* 82. 7

Hackett of Dublin, on a mural coronet arg., an eagle displayed with two heads sa. *Spes mea Deus.* *cf.* 74. 2

Hackett, co. Tipperary, Ireland, an eagle displayed with two heads per pale az. and gu., and between the heads a trefoil slipped vert. *Spes mea Deus.* *cf.* 74. 2

Hackett of Hackettstown, co. Carlow, Ireland, an eagle displayed with two heads ppr., issuing from a ducal coronet and surmounted by a tiara resting on two snakes. *Fortitudine et prudentia.*

Hackford, on a trumpet or, a swan with wings addorsed arg. 100. 6

Hacklet of London, a demi-lion gu. 10. 3

Hacklet and **Hackluit,** a hand holding a hunting-horn ppr. 217. 4

Hackney, out of a ducal coronet a nag's head. 51. 7

Hackote, on a ducal coronet a martlet, all ppr. 95. 12

Hackshaw, Shropsh., a heron's head erased arg., ducally gorged gu. *cf.* 104. 11

Hackvill, on a mount a greyhound passant *cf.* 60. 2

Hackvill, on a chapeau a fox sejant, all ppr. 32. 12

Hackwell and **Hakewill,** Lincs and Devonsh., a trefoil slipped purp., between two wings displayed or. 110. 12

Hackwell, between two wings displayed or, a human heart gu. *cf.* 110. 14

Hacon, Suff. and Norf., a falcon barry of six arg. and vair. 85. 2

Hacote, on a ducal coronet a martlet ppr. 95. 12

Hadaway, Lieutenant-Colonel George Rowley, of Grenville, Godalming, a tower, out of the battlements an eagle rising, wings elevated and addorsed. *Virtus sola nobilitas.*

Hadd, Kent, on a mount vert, a talbot sejant arg., eared sa., ducally gorged gu., on the dexter side of the mount a laurel-branch ppr.

Hadden, an arm embowed brandishing a scimitar ppr. 201. 1

Hadden, Scotland, an eagle's head erased or. *Suffer.* 83. 2

Hadden, Major Charles Frederick, R.A., same crest and motto.

Hadderwick, Scotland, a dexter arm from the elbow holding a roll of paper ppr. *Ne timeas recte faciendo.* 215. 6

Haddington, Earl of, in Scotland (Baillie-Hamilton-Arden): (1) In the centre—Out of a ducal coronet or, a plume of six ostrich-feathers, three and three, also or (*for Arden*). (2) On the dexter side—Two dexter hands issuing out of clouds conjoined fessewise, and holding betwixt them a branch of laurel erect, all ppr. (*for Hamilton*). (3) On the sinister side—A crescent or (*for Baillie*). *Præsto et persto.—Major virtus quam splendor.* 163. 2

Haddo, Lord, *see* Aberdeen, Earl of.

Haddock, a hand holding a fish, all ppr. 220. 4

Haddon of Grandholme, Scotland, a leg in armour couped at the thigh, the foot upward. *Parta tueri.* 193. 3

Haddon, a man's leg couped at the middle of the thigh in armour ppr., garnished and spurred or, flexed at the knee, the foot upwards, the toe pointing to the dexter side. 193. 3

Haden-Best, *see* Best

Haden, *see* Barrs-Haden.

Haden, J. Poynton, Esquire, J.P., of Egremont, Trowbridge, Wilts, a lion's gamb erased grasping a plume of three ostrich-feathers, all ppr. *Integer mens augustissima possessio.* 37. 5

Hadestock, on the stump of an oak-tree sprouting new leaves, the sun shining all ppr. 145. 5

Hadeswell or **Hadiswell,** a demi-lion rampant gu., holding in his paws a battle-axe az. 15. 4

Hadfield, an escallop or. 141. 12

Hadfield, an arm embowed vested az., holding in the hand ppr. a trefoil slipped or.

Hadfield, an arm in armour embowed holding in the gauntlet a crane's head and neck erased. 198. 13

Hadiswell, a demi-lion rampant gu., holding between the paws a battle-axe az. 15. 4

Hadley of London, and of Cranbrook Park, Essex, upon a mount vert, a falcon belled arg., supporting in the dexter claw a buckle, the tongue erect or, and holding in the beak three ears of wheat, also or. *God is my help.* 85. 10

Hadley of London and Heref., a falcon arg., beaked, legged, and belled or, holding in its beak a buckle of the last.

Hadlow, Scotland, a lion's gamb holding a thistle, all ppr. 37. 6

Hadly, a falcon. 85. 2

Hadokes, a talbot's head erased sa., collared arg. 56. 1

Hayson, on a ducal coronet or, a lion rampant gu. *cf.* 1. 13

Hadsor, out of a ducal coronet gu., a dragon's head or, holding in its mouth some leaves ppr.

Hadwen, the bust of an angel with wings elevated ensigned with a cross.

Hadwen, Sidney John Wilson, Esquire, of Dean House, Sowerby, Yorks, a rock overgrown with heath, thereon a grouse holding in its beak a thistle, all ppr. *Had on and win.*

Hadwen, Lancs, out of a mural coronet or, an eagle's head ppr. *Perfero.* 83. 9

Haffenden, Kent, an eagle's head couped. 83. 1

Haffenden of Homewood, Kent, same crest.

Haffenden of Bloomsbury, a griffin's head erased holding in its beak an arrow. *cf.* 66. 8

Haffenden, Rev. John Stillington, Yorks: (1) A gryphon's head erased sa., pendent from the beak an escutcheon arg., charged with a mullet of the first (*for Haffenden*). (2) A demi-wolf or, guttée-de-sang, holding between the paws a cross patée gu. (*for Wilson*).

Haffey, a demi-lion rampant az., armed and langued gu., grasping in the dexter paw a cross patée or. *Avise la fin.*

Hagan, *see* Mahon-Hagan.

Hagan, Ireland, out of a naval coronet or, a demi-negro affrontée with broken manacles depending from each wrist, grasping in the dexter hand the Union Jack displayed on a flagstaff, and in the sinister hand on a similar staff the cap of liberty, all ppr. *Vota vita mea.*

Hagar, a garb in fess ppr. 153. 6

Hagart, a lion rampant ppr. *Sans peur.* 1. 13

Hagarty, Ireland, a dexter hand ppr., holding up an escallop or. 216. 2

Hagell, an olive-branch slipped ppr. 151. 11

Hagen, a stork's head erased ppr. 106. 1

Hagen, a dove rising arg. 94. 2

Haggar, Essex and Cambs, a talbot passant arg., collared and lined gu. 54. 5

Haggar, Essex and Cambs, on a mount vert, a talbot passant or, collared and lined gu. *cf.* 54. 5

Haggard, a cock's head erased ppr. 90. 1

Haggard, Kent, a cubit arm erect holding in the hand a truncheon. *Dux mihi veritas.* 214. 6

Haggard of Bradenhall, Thetford, Norf.: (1) A mullet of six points arg. 164. 3. (2) Out of a mural coronet per pale or and az., a snake erect ppr., holding in the mouth a trefoil slipped vert. *Micat inter omnes.—Modeste conabor.*

Haggard, Henry Rider, Esquire, of Ditchingham House, Norf., same crests. *Per ardua ducit.*

Haggarth, a bugle-horn arg., stringed. 228. 11

Hagger, a demi-lion gu., supporting a long cross az. 11. 14

Haggerston, Edward de Marie Charlton, Esquire, of Ellingham Hall, Chathill, R.S.O., a lion passant arg. 6. 2

Haggerston, Sir John de Marie, Bart., of Haggerston Castle, Northumb., a lion rampant arg. 1. 13

Haggerston, a talbot erm. *cf.* 54. 2

Hagges, Scotland, an arm in armour embowed brandishing a scimitar ppr. 106. 10

Haggie, David Henry, Esquire, of Seaforth, Sunderland, and Hutton Hall, Marston, Yorks, a dexter arm in armour embowed, holding in the gauntlet a scimitar. *Semper paratus.*

Hagley, a dexter arm in armour embowed holding in the gauntlet a battle-axe, all ppr. 200. 6

Hagne, issuing from a tower a leopard's head collared gu. 157. 9

Hagthorpe, Durh., a dexter hand ppr., the sleeve bendy arg. and gu., holding three leaves vert. *cf.* 205. 14

Hague, Yorks, a griffin's head erased arg. 66. 2

Hague, Yorks, a martlet arg. 95. 4

Hahn, on a ducal coronet a swan with wings addorsed and ducally gorged.

Haig, Lieutenant-Colonel Arthur Balfour, C.M.G., of Bemersyde, St. Boswells, N.B., a rock ppr. *Tyde what may.* 179. 7

"Tyde what may betyde,
Haig shall be Haig of Bemersyde."

Haig, Oliver, of Ramornie, Fife, Scotland, same crest and motto. 179. 7

Haig, Alexander Price, Esquire, of Blairhill, Perthsh., and Coldon, Kinross-sh., same crest and motto.

Haig, Alexander Ritchie, Esquire, care Miss Haig, 30, Meeting Street, Charleston, South Carolina, U.S.A., same crest and motto.

Haig, George Ogilvy, Esquire, of 65, Brook Street, W., same crest and motto.

Haig, Henry Alexander, Esquire, of 43, Kensington Park Gardens, W., same crest and motto.

Haig, William James, Esquire, of Dollarfield, Clackmannansh., same crest and motto.

Haig, George Augustus, Esquire, J.P., of Pen Ithon, Radnorsh., a rock ppr. *Tyde what may.* 179. 7

Haig-Smellie, Thomas, Esquire, of 26, St. Charles Square, North Kensington, London, W.: (1) A dexter hand holding a crescent erect, all ppr. (*for Smellie*). 216. 8. (2) A rock ppr. (*for Haig*). *Industria, virtute et fortitudine.—Tyde what may.* 179. 7

Haig and **Haigh,** a demi-savage holding over his dexter shoulder a hammer. 186. 11

Haigh, George Henry Caton, Esquire, of Gainsby Hall, Merionethsh., same crest and motto; and *Sola virtus invicta.*

Haigh, Charles Thomas Ernest, Esquire, of Colne Bridge, Bradley, near Huddersfield, in front of a demi-man affrontee ppr., holding in the dexter hand a crescent or, a rock, also ppr. *Tyde what may.*

Haigh, Arthur Samuel, Esquire, of Cat Cay, Bahamas, same crest and motto.

Haigh, Yorks, a talbot's head erased gu. 56. 2

Haighton of Chaigeley, Lancs, out of a ducal coronet or, a bull's head arg. 44. 11

Hailes, a wheel or. 167. 1

Hailes, Colonel Walter, Cintra, Surbiton Hill Park, Surbiton, a dexter arm in armour embowed holding in the hand an arrow.

Hailes, Major-General John Clements, of 43, Wynnstay Gardens, Kensington, W., same crest.

Hailly, Scotland, a galley sa., the flag gu. 160. 6

Hailstones, Scotland, a rose-branch flowered, all ppr. 149. 8

Hailstone, Rev. Samuel, M.A., of Walton Lodge, Broughton Park, Manchester, a rose-branch bearing roses, all ppr. 149. 8

Haines, on a crescent an arrow in pale ppr. 163. 13

Haines, Field-Marshal Sir Frederick Paul, G.C.B., G.C.S.I., C.I.E., United Service Club, Pall Mall, London, S.W., a stork with wings displayed arg., beaked and legged or. *There is no difficulty to him that wills.*

Haines, an eagle displayed az., semée d'étoiles arg. *cf.* 75. 2

Haines of the Buses, Edenbridge, Kent, an eagle's head erased, gorged with a ducal coronet.

Hains, an antelope's head ppr., collared sa. *cf.* 126. 2

Hair, Scotland, two daggers in saltier ppr. 169. 8

Hair, a hare couchant. *cf.* 136. 12

Haire, James, Esquire, Barrister-at-Law, of Armagh Manor, co. Fermanagh, Ireland, a lion rampant arg., supporting the Roman fasces ppr. *In te Domine speravi.*

Haire, William Hamilton, Esquire, of Armagh Manor, co. Fermanagh, same crest and motto.

Haire-Forster, Rev. Arthur Newburgh, of Ballynure, co. Monaghan, a hind's head erased gu., collared and chained or, holding in the mouth an arrow point downwards arg. (*for Forster*). (2) A demi-lion rampant couped arg., gorged with a collar dancettée gu., and between the paws a cross crosslet of the last (*for Haire*). *Odi profanum.*

Hairstanes, Scotland, a dexter arm holding a key, all ppr. *Toujours fidèle.* 217. 7

Haitlie, a hand holding four arrows points downwards, all ppr. *cf.* 214. 3

Haize of London, a wolf's head ppr., erased gu., charged on the neck with an escallop or. *cf.* 30. 8

Hake, a sword in pale arg., hilt and pommel or, enfiled with a boar's head couped in fess az. 42. 4

Hake, out of a ducal coronet two pot-hooks addorsed between two wings.

Hakellott, out of a ducal coronet or, a plume of four ostrich-feathers sa. 114. 1

Hakewood, on a chapeau a garb, all ppr. 153. 10

Halberdyn, a wolf rampant regardant ppr. 28. 3

Halcro, Scotland, two hands holding a sword in pale ppr. 213. 1

Haldane-Duncan, Earl of Camperdown, *see* Camperdown.

Haldane-Oswald, *see* Oswald.

Haldane, *see* Chinnery-Haldane.

Haldane and **Halden,** Scotland, an eagle's head erased or. *Suffer.* 83. 2

Haldane, James, of 15, Atholl Crescent, Edinburgh, same crest and motto. 83. 2

Haldane, James, Esquire, of Grosvenor Crescent, Edinburgh, same crest and motto.

Haldane, James Alexander, Esquire, W.S., of St. Catherine's, Fortrose, Scotland, same crest and motto. 83. 2

Haldane, James Alexander, Esquire, of St. Catherine's, Fortrose, N.B., same crest and motto.

Haldane, James Aylmer Lowthorpe, Esquire, same crest and motto.

Haldane-Duncan-Mercer-Henderson, Hon. Hew Adam Dalrymple Hamilton, of Fordell, Fifesh., Scotland: (1) A cubit arm erect ppr., the hand holding an estoile or, surmounted by a crescent az. (*for Henderson*). 216. 12. (2) The head and neck of a heron erased holding in its beak an eel seizing the neck of the former, all ppr. (*for Mercer*). *cf.* 104. 2. (3) On waves of the sea a dismasted ship, all ppr. (*for Duncan*). (4) An eagle's head erased or (*for Haldane*). *Sola virtus nobilitat.—The grit poul.—Disce pati.—Suffer.* 83. 2

Haldane, a terrestrial globe ppr. 159. 1

Haldenby, Yorks, a swan close arg., beaked and legged gu., holding in its beak a sprig of laurel ppr. *cf.* 99. 2

Halderman, a dexter arm embowed vested holding in the hand ppr. a broken spear in bend.

Haldimand, a sea-lion sejant ppr. 20. 2

Haldon, Baron (Palk), of Haldon House, Devonsh., on a semi-terrestrial globe of the northern hemisphere ppr., an eagle rising arg., beaked and membered or. *Deo ducente.*

Hale, a heron's head erased ppr. 104. 11

Hale, Major-General Robert, Alderley, Wootton-under-Edge, same crest.

Hale, a lion's gamb erased az., holding two arrows in saltier or, flighted arg.

Hale, on the battlements of a castle arg., a wyvern sa., with wings endorsed guttée-d'or, gorged with a ducal coronet, therefrom a chain reflexed over the back, also or, and holding in the dexter claw a sword erect az.

Hale of Somerton Hall, upon a rock a tower ppr., surmounted by a sun in splendour or, and resting upon the battlements a scaling-ladder in bend sa. *Turris fortis mihi Deus.* 157. 14

Hale of Plymouth, a snake ppr., entwined round five arrows or, headed sa., feathered arg., one in pale and four in saltier. *Vera sequor.*

Hale, an arm embowed vested az., fretty arg., cuffed or, the hand ppr. grasping two arrows, also ppr. *Cum principibus.*

Hales and **Hale** of London and Herts, five arrows, one in pale and four in saltier or, headed sa., feathered arg., environed with a snake ppr.

Hales, a dexter arm in armour embowed holding in the hand an arrow. 198. 4

Hales, a dexter arm in armour embowed ppr., garnished or, holding in the hand, also ppr., an arrow arg., headed of the second, and round the arm a scarf vert. *cf.* 198. 4

Hales, Eli George, Esquire, Major 1st Sussex Royal Engineers, of St. George's Place, Brighton, a dexter arm embowed in armour grasping a sword in bend, a spade in bend sinister, and an arrow in pale point upwards, all ppr. *Vis unita fortior.* 256. 10

Hales, a griffin sejant arg. 62. 10

Hales-Tooke, Baseley, Esquire, of Salhouse, a griffin's head erased sa., charged on the neck with two bendlets arg., and holding in the beak a sword in pale point upwards, also arg., pommel and hilt or. 66. 12

Hales, Edward, Esquire, of North Frith, Kent, upon a mount a garb vert, in front thereof an escutcheon or, charged with a griffin's head couped sa. *Vis unita fortior.* 152. 12

Hales, a dexter arm in armour embowed ppr., garnished or, holding in the hand an arrow of the second, round the shoulder a ribbon tied gu. *cf.* 198. 4

Haley of London and Middx., a goat's head erased arg., gorged with a chaplet gu. *cf.* 128. 5

Haley, Sussex, on a crescent arg., a cross patonce gu.

Halfhead, out of a ducal coronet or, a demi-man in armour couped at the thighs ppr., garnished of the first, the vizor up, brandishing a pole-axe, also of the first, between two wings, each charged with two decrescents arg., and three étoiles pierced sa. 185. 10

Halfhide, a greyhound sejant or, collared az., garnished and ringed of the first. *cf.* 59. 2

Halford, Sir Henry St. John, Bart., C.B., D.L., of Wistow Hall, Leics.: (1) Of honourable augmentation, a staff entwined by a serpent ppr., and ensigned by a coronet composed of crosses patée and fleurs-de-lis or. (2) A greyhound's head couped at the neck sa., collared or. *Mutas inglorius artes.* 61. 2

Halford, a greyhound's head erased at the neck sa., collared or. *cf.* 61. 2

Halford, a demi-greyhound sa., collared or. 60. 8

Halfpenny, a lion sejant ppr., holding in the dexter paw a cross crosslet fitched or, and resting the sinister on a triangle gu.

Halgoet, a thistle ppr. *cf.* 150. 2

Halhead, a falcon with wings expanded arg., beaked and belled or. 87. 1

Haliburton, Baron (Haliburton), a stag at gaze between two sprigs of maple, and gorged about the neck with a wreath of the same ppr. *Watch well.* 285. 2

Haliburton of Pitcur, Scotland, a negro's head couped at the shoulders, helmeted. 192. 7

Haliburton, Scotland, a tree ppr. *Majora sequor.* 143. 5

Haliday of Carnmoney, co. Antrim, Ireland, a boar's head couped arg., langued and tusked or. *Virtute parta.* 41. 1

Haliday, Scotland, a boar's head couped ppr. *Virtute parta.* 43. 1

Halifad, on the stump of a tree erased at the top and couped at the root, lying in fess, a bird. 94. 12

Halifax, Viscount (Wood), of Hickleton Hall, Doncaster, Yorks, a savage ambulant ppr., holding in his dexter hand a club resting upon his shoulder, and upon the sinister arm an escutcheon sa., charged with a griffin's head erased arg. *I like my choice.* 250. 4

Halke, Kent, a dexter arm in armour embowed holding a battle-axe, all ppr. 200. 6

Halkerston, Scotland, a hawk's head erased gu. *In ardua nitor.* 88. 12

Halkerston, Scotland, a falcon's head erased gu. 88. 12

Halket, a dexter arm embowed brandishing a scimitar, all ppr. 201. 1

Halkett, a lion passant. 6. 2

Halkett, Craigie-, of Cramond, Edinburgh, a falcon's head erased ppr. *Fides sufficit.—Honeste vivo.* 88. 12

Halkett, Sir Peter Arthur, Bart., D.L., of Pitfirrane, Fife, same crest and motto. 88. 12

Hall-Gage, Viscount Gage, *see* Gage.

Hall-Dare, *see* Dare.

Hall, Kent, a horse's head in armour ppr., garnished and bridled or, on his head a plume of feathers arg. 50. 14

Hall, Kent, a horse's head sa., in armour ppr., bridled and armed or, on the head a plume of two feathers or and az. *cf.* 50. 14

Hall of Ashford, Kent, a horse's head couped sa., maned arg., bridled of the last, tasselled or, upon the head armour ppr., with a spike upon the forehead, also or, and therefrom issuant two ostrich-feathers, the dexter gu., the sinister of the third.

Hall, a horse's head between two ostrich-feathers. 50. 2

Hall, Percy Craven, Esquire, of Beldornie Tower, Ryde, Isle of Wight, and Purstone Hall, Purston-cum-South-Featherston, Yorks, a gryphon's head erased arg., gorged with a wreath of cinquefoil gu., holding in its beak a cross crosslet fitchée palewise or, between two wings gu., each charged with a fesse, also or. *Vis veritatis magna.* 67. 5

Hall, Bart., of Monm., a palm-branch in bend sinister ppr., in front of a griffin's head erased or, charged with a bar gemelle gu., and holding in its beak a hawk's lure or, tasselled arg. *Turpiter desperatur.*

Hall, Staffs, a griffin's head erased erm. 66. 2

Hall, Scotland, a demi-griffin ppr. *Per ardua ad alta.* 64. 2

Hall, a demi-eagle with wings endorsed sa., collared or.

Hall, Leics., a dragon's head couped az., collared arg. *cf.* 71. 2

Hall, Worcs., a dragon's head az., collared or. *cf.* 71. 2

Hall, Shropsh., on a castle with four towers arg., a wyvern with wings endorsed gu., guttée-d'eau, ducally gorged and lined or, holding in his dexter foot a sword erect arg., hilt and pommel or.

Hall, Shropsh., on the stump of a tree couped or, a wyvern with wings endorsed sa., guttée-d'eau, ringed and lined of the first, the line reflexed over the back, grasping in his dexter claw a sword arg., hilt and pommel or.

Hall of Durham and Oxon., a talbot's head erased sa. 56. 2

Hall, Sir John, K.C.M.G., of Hororata, Canterbury, New Zealand, two fronds of fern ppr., therefrom issuant a talbot's head erased sa., guttée-d'or, gorged with a collar gemelle, also or. *By industry and honour.*

Hall, Leics., a talbot's head sa., spotted or. *Remember and forget not.* 56. 12

Hall, Worcs. and Yorks, a talbot's head sa. 56. 12

Hall, William Wellfitt, Park Hall, Nottingham, a talbot's head erased sa., semée of bezants.

Hall, Durh., a talbot's head erased arg., collared chequy or and az. 56. 1

Hall, a talbot's head erased or, pellettée. *cf.* 56. 2

Hall, a talbot's head erased sa., eared arg., gorged with a chaplet or, garnished with roses gu. *cf.* 56. 2

Hall of London and Yorks, on a chapeau gu., turned up arg., a greyhound sejant erm. *cf.* 59. 4

Hall of Sawforth and Harborough, Lincs, a greyhound's head erased gu., collared or. *cf.* 61. 2

Hall, Yorks, out of a ducal coronet or, a demi-greyhound sa., collared of the first. *cf.* 60. 8

Hall, Ireland, a fox's head paly of six or and gu. 33. 4

Hall, a bear's head muzzled, all ppr. 34. 14

Hall, James Campbell, Esquire, of Rowan tree House, Monaghan, a bear's head couped and muzzled or, charged with a trefoil slipped or. *Remember and forget not.*

Hall, Shropsh., a demi-stag salient or. 119. 2

Hall, Norf., a demi-buck saliant sa., attired or, gorged with a collar of the last, charged with three chaplets of the first. *cf.* 119. 2

Hall, a demi-buck salient or, eared sa., gorged with a fesse wavy between two cottises of the last. *cf.* 119. 2

Hall of Chester, a stag's head ppr., collared or. *cf.* 121. 5

Hall, Shropsh., a buck's head or, collared sa. *cf.* 121. 5

Hall, Edward Kirkpatrick, Esquire, of Kevin, Nairn, N.B., a gryphon's head couped az., semée of cross crosslets or.

Hall of Gretford, Lincs, out of a ducal coronet or, a plume of feathers arg., thereon a demi-lion rampant of the first.

Hall, Frederick Charles Northcote, Esquire, a palm-branch in bend sinister vert, in front of a griffin's head erased or, charged with a gemel gu., holding in the beak a hawk's lure arg., lined and ringed or. *Turpiter desperatur.*

Hall, Rev. Herbert, M.A., of the Rectory, Glemsford, Suff., same crest and motto.

Hall of Celgwyn, Cardigansh., Wales, a demi-lion rampant holding a flaming sword imbrued, all ppr. *Vive ut vivas.* *cf.* 14. 12

Hall of London, a demi-lion gu., supporting a cross moline fitchée or.

Hall of Moundesmere, Southampton, a demi-wolf rampant arg., holding in his dexter paw a heart ppr., transpierced by two darts in saltier of the first.

Hall, Ireland, on a mount vert, a stork arg., holding in its dexter claw a pellet. *Cura quietum.*

Hall, Sir Basil Francis, Bart., D.L., of Dunglass, Haddington, upon a mount a stork holding in its dexter claw a stone, all ppr. *Dat cura quietum.*

Hall, on a mount vert, a stork or, holding in his dexter claw a flint-stone. *cf.* 105. 6

Hall, Musgrave Robert, Esquire, of Foscott Manor, Bucks, same crest. *Cura quietum.*

Hall of Culverwood, Hawkhurst, Sussex, upon a mount a stork arg., holding in her dexter claw a pellet. *Cura quietem.*

Hall, Rev. William John, M.A., of Brecton House, Eltham, and 29, Martin's Lane, Cannon Street, E.C., upon a staff raguly fesseways sa., a dove holding in the beak a Passion-nail ppr. *Non sine numine.*

Hall of Littlebeck, Westml., on a wreath the battlements of a tower, thereon a cock entwined by a snake, all ppr. *Perseverantia et cura quies.*

Hall, a dove holding in its beak an olive-branch, all ppr. 92. 5

Hall, Wilts, an arm in armour embowed ppr., garnished or, holding a battle-axe arg. 200. 6

Hall, Shropsh., a dexter arm embowed, vested az., cuffed or, holding in the hand an arrow arg.

Hall of London, out of a mural coronet arg., a dexter arm embowed habited az., fretty of the first, cuffed or, holding in the hand ppr. a dagger of the last, hilt and pommel or.

Hall of London, a hand gu., holding a ball sa. 206. 3

Hall, a dexter cubit arm in bend vested az., semée of escallops arg., grasping a dagger sheathed, point downwards ppr. *Always ready.*

Hall of Clifton, Yorks, and Grange Hall, Chesh., a tilting-spear erect surmounted by a sword and a laurel-branch saltireways, all ppr. *Aut pax, aut bellum.*

Hall, John, Esquire, of the Grange, Hale, Altrincham, same crest and motto.

Hall, Scotland, a hunting-horn az., veruled arg. *cf.* 228. 11

Hall, William, Esquire, a hunting-horn ppr., garnished and stringed gu. *Forward.*

Hall, Rev. Richard Augustus, M.A., of Tully House, co. Monaghan, Incumbent of Quivey, Diocese of Kilmore, co. Cavan, a bear's head couped and muzzled, all ppr. 253. 10

Hall, Montagu Haffenden, Whatton Manor, Notts, a crescent arg., surmounted by a griffin's head erased sa., in the beak three ears of wheat or. *Persevere.*

Hall, Rev. Frederick Dickinson, M.A., of Broughton Sulney, Notts, same crest and motto.

Hall-Say, Richard, Esquire, of 69, Finchley Road, N.W.: (1) A stag's head erased arg., guttée-de-larmes, holding in the mouth a cinquefoil slipped vert (*for Say*). (2) A talbot's head erased sa., charged with four bezants in cross, holding in the mouth a feather arg. *Fare et age.*

Hall-Watt, Ernest Richard Bradley, Esquire, of Bishop Burton Hall, Beverley, Yorks, and Carhead, near Keighley, Yorks, a greyhound sejant arg., semée-de-lis az. resting its dexter forepaw upon two arrows in saltire ppr. *Vigeur de dessus.* 256. 9

Hallam, on a mount vert, a bull gu. *cf.* 45. 2

Hallen the late Rev. Arthur Washington Cornelius, M.A., F.S.C., of the Rectory, Alloa, Scotland, a demi-lion rampant or, crowned, langued, and armed, and charged on the shoulder with a hammer az., between two antique wings sa. Cri-de-guerre, *Mirabello. Sine Deo nil.* 225. 1

Halles, Herts and London, a snake ppr., entwined round five arrows, one in pale and four in saltier or, headed sa., feathered arg.

Hallet, Kent, out of a ducal coronet or, a demi-lion rampant arg., holding between the paws a bezant. *cf.* 16. 3

Hallet, Somers., a demi-lion holding a bezant. 11. 7

Hallett, a dexter hand holding a key ppr. 217. 7

Halleweel, a boar's head erect sa., between two ostrich-feathers arg. 41. 14

Halley, a boar's head erased and erect between two ostrich-feathers ppr. *cf.* 41. 14

Halliburton, Scotland, a stag at gaze. *Watch well.* 117. 3

Halliday, late John, of Chapel Cleeve, Somers., a demi-lion rampant or, supporting an anchor az. *Quarta saluti* 12. 12

Halliday, an oak-tree fructed ppr. 143. 5

Halliday, Scotland, a boar's head couped arg., armed or. *Virtute parta.* 43. 1

Halliday, a boar's head erased sa. 42. 2

Halliday of Castledykes, Kirkcudbright, Scotland, a dexter arm in armour embowed couped below the shoulder, grasping a dagger, also ppr., hilted and pommelled or, and distilling drops of blood from the point. *Merito.* *cf.* 196. 5

Halliday, Shropsh. and Scotland, a dexter arm in armour embowed in fess, holding in the hand a sword embrued, all ppr. *cf.* 195. 2

Hallifax, a mountain ppr.

Hallifax, Essex, a moorcock with wings expanded per bend sinister sa. and gu., combed and wattled of the second, ducally gorged and charged on the breast with a cross crosslet or. *cf.* 89. 5

Halliley, an arm couped, vested az., the shirt apparent, holding in the hand a flagon or.

Hallington, out of a ducal coronet or, a greyhound's head sa. 61. 7

Halliwell, Lancs, a griffin passant with wings expanded arg., beaked and armed gu. 63. 2

Hallman or **Halman,** Devonsh., a cross-bow erect or, between two wings gu. 112. 13

Hallom, a hand gu., holding a grenade fired ppr. 216. 6

Hallow, an eagle displayed regardant or, holding in its dexter claw a sword in pale ppr. 75. 7

Halloway of London, a demi-lion rampant gardant purp. 10. 8

Hallowes, Derbysh., a demi-griffin segreant sa., winged arg. 64. 2

Hallowes, Thomas Richard Francis Brabazon, of Glapwell Hall, Chesterfield, same crest.

Hallowtown, out of a ducal coronet or, a greyhound's head sa. 61. 7

Halls, an arm vested gu., cuffed or, holding in the hand an anchor ppr. 208. 3

Hallwell, Halwell, and **Halywell,** a hunting-horn az., stringed gu., between two wings or. 112. 3

Hallyburton, Scotland, a Moor's head couped, helmeted ppr. *Watch well.* 192. 7

Halman, *see* Hallman.

Halpen and **Halpin,** on a ducal coronet an eagle displayed. *cf.* 75. 2

Halpin, Ireland, out of a tower arg., a demi-griffin segreant with wings addorsed sa. 157. 5

Halsbury, Earl of (Giffard), of Halsbury, Devonsh.: (1) Out of a coronet a demi-lion or, holding between the paws a lozenge erm. (2) A moorcock's head ppr., holding in the beak a trefoil vert. *Ne vile velis.*

Halsbury, Devonsh., a demi-lion rampant az. 10. 2

Halse and **Halsey,** Devonsh. and Norf., a griffin sejant with wings addorsed arg. 62. 10

Halsey, Rt. Hon. Thomas Frederick, P.C., M.P., of Great Gaddesden Place, Hemel Hempstead, Herts, a dexter cubit arm erect, vested gu., cuffed arg., the hand ppr., holding a griffin's claw erased or. *Nescit vox missa reverti.*

Halsey, a sword erect arg., hilt or, on the blade a boar's head couped sa. 42. 4

Halsey, Surrey, on a garb lying fesseways or, a griffin's head sa., guttée-d'eau, ducally gorged arg.

Halstead, Berks and London, out of a mural coronet chequy or and az., a demi-eagle erm., beaked or.

Halswell, an ounce sejant ppr., resting the dexter fore-paw on an escutcheon gu.

Halton, Essex, a lion sejant arg., holding in the dexter paw a broken lance ppr. 8. 11

Halton, John, Esquire, 4, Norfolk Road, Carlisle, same crest. *Tam pace quam bello.*

Halton, out of a ducal coronet gu., a griffin's head sa., between two wings the dexter or and the sinister az. 67. 1

Haltridge, an ostrich ppr. 97. 2

Halxton, a dexter hand holding a dagger in pale, embrued at the point, all ppr. 212. 9

Haly of Ballyhally, Cork, Ireland, a mermaid with a comb and mirror, all ppr. *Sapiens dominabitur astris.* 184. 5

Haly, Ireland, a savage's head in profile couped ppr. 191. 1

Haly, Scotland, a greyhound current. *Gang forret.* cf. 58. 2

Halyburton, Scotland, a stag at gaze ppr. *Watch well.* 117. 3

Halyburton, Scotland, a boar's head couped and erect ppr. *Watch well.* cf. 43. 3

Halyburton, Scotland, a boar's head couped and erect ppr. *Majores sequor.* cf. 43. 3

Halyburton, Scotland, a greyhound's head couped ppr. *Fidele.* cf. 61. 2

Halyburton, Scotland, a Moor's head sa., banded arg. *Watch well.* 192. 13

Halyburton of Pitcur, Forfarsh., Scotland, a negro's head and neck in profile, couped at the shoulders and armed with a helmet ppr. *Watch weel.*

Halyfad, on the stump of a tree erased at the top and couped at the root lying in fesse, a bird. 94. 2

Halys, a spur rowel az., between two eagle's wings or.

Ham, on a chapeau a unicorn's head erased, all ppr. 49. 10

Hambleton, a bundle of quills ppr. 113. 6

Hambley and **Hambly,** a dolphin haurient az. 140. 11

Hambro, Charles Eric, Esquire, of 70, Prince's Gate, S.W., a falcon with wings displayed and belled or, semée of annulets, and resting the dexter claw upon a crescent. *In Deo.*

Hambro, Everard Alexander, Esquire, of Hayes Place, Hayes, Bromley, Kent, same crest and motto.

Hambro, Henry Charles, Esquire, of Milton Abbey, Dorset, same crest and motto.

Hamborough, on a mount vert, a horse courant arg. cf. 52. 2

Hamborough, Holden- of Steephill Castle, Isle of Wight, and Pipewell Hall, Northamp., on a mount vert, a horse courant arg., semée of cross crosslets az. and guttée-de-sang. *Foresight.—Honestum utili præfer.*

Hambro, Everard Alexander, Hayes, Bromley, Kent, a falcon billed and wings elevated or, semée of annulets, and resting the dexter claw on a crescent or. *In Deo.*

Hambro: (1) A lion rampant holding a battle-axe. (2) As above.

Hambrough, a horse at full speed ppr. 52. 8

Hamby, Lincs, a hawk volant ppr., beaked, legged, and the insides of the wings or. 88. 3

Hamden, Bucks, an eagle's head erased az. 83. 2

Hamel and **Hamell,** a crescent or. 163. 2

Hamelen, Hamelin, and **Hamelyn,** a hand pulling a rose from a bush, all ppr. 218. 13

Hameley, Cornw., a talbot's head erased az., ducally gorged and chained arg. cf. 56. 2

Hamelyng, a sea-horse couchant, resting the dexter paw on a cross pattée arg.

Hamer, on a chapeau az., turned up erm., a lion's head arg. cf. 17. 9

Hamersley, Edward Samuel, Pyrton Manor, Watlington, Oxon, a demi-griffin segreant or, holding in the claws a cross crosslet fitchée gu. *Honore et amore.* 291. 1

Hamerton, Chisnall, of the Peel, Hellifield, Yorks, and Claremont Terrace, Sunderland, a greyhound couchant. *Fixus adversa sperno.* 61. 1

Hamerton, a hand holding a broken hammer ppr. 221. 13

Hamerton, issuant from the wreath a swan with wings addorsed and distended arg. 100. 2

Hames, on a ducal coronet a lion passant, all ppr. 6. 6

Hames, Hayter-, Colville George, of Chagford House, Newton Abbott: (1) a bull's head couped pierced through the neck with a broken spear in bend dexter point. (2) On a ducal coronet a lion passant. *Honor virtutis præmium.*

Hamigston, a dragon's head erased gu., ducally gorged arg. cf. 71. 8

Hamill, Ireland, a demi-lion sa. 10. 1

Hamill, Ireland, a demi-lion sa., collared or. 10. 9

Hamill, Ireland, on a ducal coronet a leopard sejant, all ppr. 24. 11

Hamill, a palm-tree fructed ppr. 144. 1

Hamill-Stewart, John Thomas, Esquire, of Ballyatwood House, co. Down, Ireland: (1) A unicorn's head couped or, horned and crined arg., charged with a crescent gu. for difference (*for Stewart*). cf. 49. 7. (2) A fleur-de-lis or (*for Hamill*). *Forward.* 148. 2

Hamilton, *see* Abercorn, Duke of.

Hamilton, *see* Dufferin and Ava, Marquess of.

Hamilton-Gordon, *see* Aberdeen, Earl of.

Hamilton-Russell, Viscount Boyne, *see* Boyne.

Hamilton, *see* Barrett-Hamilton.

Hamilton, *see* Nisbet-Hamilton-Ogilvy.

Hamilton, *see* Stephenson-Hamilton.

Hamilton, *see* Shaw-Hamilton.

Hamilton and Brandon, Duke of (Douglas-Hamilton): (1) In a ducal coronet or, an oak fructed and penetrated transversely in the main stem by a frame-saw ppr., the frame or (*for Hamilton*). 143. 8. (2) On a chapeau gu., turned up erm., a salamander in flames ppr. (*for Douglas*). *Through.—Jamais arrière.* 138. 2

Hamilton, Baron (Rt. Hon. John Glencairn Carter Hamilton, J.P., D.L.), of Dalzell, Lanarksh., an antelope ppr., armed and ungu. or. *Quis occursabit.* 126. 12

Hamilton, Sir Charles Edward, Bart., in a ducal coronet or, a mount vert, and issuing therefrom an oak-tree penetrated transversely in the stem by a frame-saw ppr., frame arg. *Through.*

Hamilton, Shropsh., out of a ducal coronet or, an oak-tree ppr., fructed of the first and penetrated transversely by a frame-saw of the second, the frame or. *Nec timeo, nec sperno.* 143. 8

Hamilton, John Claude Campbell, of Sundrum, Ayrsh., out of a ducal coronet or, an oak-tree fructed, penetrated transversely in the main stem by a frame-saw ppr. *Through.* 143. 8

Hamilton, Hugh, of Pinmore, Daljarrock, Ayr, same crest and motto.

Hamilton of Bardowie, Lanarksh., Scotland, issuing out of a ducal coronet an oak-tree fructed and penetrated transversely in the stem by a frame-saw ppr., the frame or. 143. 13

Hamilton, G. W. Finlay, Mount View, Portscathe, Cornw., same crest. *Through.*

Hamilton - Hoare of Oakfield Lodge, Three Bridges, Sussex: (1) An eagle's head erased arg., charged with an ermine spot sa. (*for Hoare*). cf. 83. 2. (2) Of honourable augmentation, a mount vert, thereon a castle with the wall on either side broken, and from the battlements the flag of Spain flying ppr., and in an escroll above the motto, "*Alba de Tormes.*" (3) Out of a ducal coronet or, an oak-tree ppr., charged with a crescent sa., a frame-saw through the stem fessewise, also ppr (*for Hamilton*). 143. 8

Hamilton-Grace, Lieutenant-Colonel Sheffield, of Knole, Frant, Tunbridge Wells, Sussex: (1) A demi-lion rampant arg., and on an escroll above the motto, "*En grace affie*" (*for Grace*). 10. 2. (2) Of honourable augmentation, a mount vert, thereon a castle with the wall on either side broken, and from the battlements the flag of Spain flying ppr., and above it upon an escroll the words, "*Alba de Tormes*" (*for Hamilton*). (3) Out of a ducal coronet or, an oak-tree ppr., charged with a crescent sa., traversed with a frame-saw through the trunk fessewise, also ppr., and on an escroll above the motto, "*Through*" (*also for Hamilton*). *Concordant nomine facta.* cf. 143. 8

Hamilton, His Excellency Sir Robert George Crookshank, K.C.B., LL.D., of Hobart, Tasmania, issuing out of a ducal coronet or, an oak-tree fructed and penetrated transversely by a frame-saw, all pr. *Through.* 143. 8

Hamilton, Bart., of the Mount, Middx., out of a ducal coronet or, an oak-tree fructed and traversed with a frame-saw ppr., the frame or, the blade inscribed with the word "*Through.*" *Through.* 143. 13

Hamilton, Sir Edward Archibald, Bart., of Trebinshun House, Breconsh., out of a ducal coronet or, an oak-tree ppr., fructed or, traversed with a frame-saw, also ppr., the frame or, and the blade inscribed with the word "*Through.*" *Sola nobilitas virtus.* 143. 13

Hamilton, Charles Robert, Esquire, of Hamwood, Dunboyne, co. Meath, out of a ducal coronet or, an oak-tree fructed ppr., the frame or., hanging from the tree a shelf arg., charged with a trefoil slipped vert. Over: *Through.*—Under the arms: *Sola nobilitas virtus.*

Hamilton of Riseland, Tobago, issuing from a ducal coronet an oak-tree penetrated transversely by a frame-saw, all ppr., on the blade thereof the word "*Through.*" 143. 13

Hamilton, out of a ducal coronet or, charged with three bombs fired ppr., an oak-tree transfixed with a frame-saw ppr., and in an escroll above the crest the motto, "*Through.*" *cf.* 143. 13

Hamilton, John, Esquire, of Sunningdale House, Silver Hill, St. Leonards-on-Sea, and Sorbie, Broadwater Down, Tunbridge Wells, an oak-tree issuing from a ducal coronet having a saw across it, all ppr. *Through.*

Hamilton, Archibald, Esquire, of Oakthorpe, Windermere, an oak-tree fructed or, transfixed with a frame-saw inscribed with the word "*Through.*"

Hamilton, Sir James, J.P., of Belfast, on a mount vert, an oak-tree ppr., the trunk surmounted by an escutcheon gyronny of eight or and sa. *Virtus acquirit honorem.* 143. 3

Hamilton-Tittle, Isaac, Esquire, M.A., LL.D., of Panonia, Silchester Road, Glenageary, co. Dublin: (1) In front of two battle-axes in saltire an oak-tree fructed, all ppr., the trunk transfixed with a frame-saw or (*for Hamilton*). (2) On a mural crown ppr., a lion rampant or, collared gu., and charged on the shoulder with an escallop sa., and in an escroll, "*In te Domine speravi*" (*for Tittle*).—*Through.*

Hamilton, James, Esquire, J.P., of Cornacassa, co. Monaghan, Ireland, out of three cinquefoils conjoined in fesse or, an oak-tree fructed and penetrated transversely in the main stem by a frame-saw ppr., frame and handles of the first. *Semper virescens.* *cf.* 143. 8

Hamilton of Fyne Court, Somers.: (1) On a mount vert, between two wings arg., an oak-tree penetrated transversely by a frame-saw ppr. (*for Hamilton*). (2) A cross patée fitchée gu., between two wings arg., each charged with a cross crosslet of the first (*for Crosse*). *Se inserit astris.*

Hamilton, Captain John Andrew Charles, of Howden, Tiverton, same crests and mottoes.

Hamilton, Devonsh.: (1) An oak-tree ppr., the trunk surmounted by an escutcheon per pale gu. and az., charged with a cinquefoil or. *cf.* 143. 7. (2) Two spears in saltier issuing through an Eastern coronet or, and between the spears a bugle-horn sa.

Hamilton of Dublin, out of a mural crown an oak-tree ppr., the trunk thereof transfixed with a sword in fesse, the blade wavy arg., pommel and hilt or. *Through.*

Hamilton, Charles William, Esquire, J.P., of Hamwood, co. Meath, Ireland, out of a ducal coronet or, an oak-tree fructed and penetrated transversely in the main stem by a frame-saw ppr., the frame or, and the blade inscribed with the word "*Through,*" suspended from one of the branches a shield arg., charged with a trefoil slipped vert. *Sola nobilitat virtus.* *cf.* 143. 13

Hamilton of St. Peter Port, Guernsey, out of a ducal coronet or, an oak-tree fructed ppr., and penetrated transversely in the main stem by a frame-saw, also ppr., frame and handles or, suspended from the tree by a ribbon az., an escutcheon quarterly arg. and gu., charged with a mullet counterchanged. *cf.* 143. 8

Hamilton, Buchanan- of Spittal, Dumbartonsh.: (1) A dexter hand holding up a duke's coronet within two laurel-branches disposed orleways vert (*Buchanan*). (2) A bent bow held in a hand sinister. (3) A lion's paw erased ppr. (4) Out of a ducal coronet or, an oak-tree fructed penetrated transversely in the main stem by a frame-saw ppr., frame of the first (*Hamilton*).

Hamilton, out of a mural crown or, an oak-tree ppr., the trunk thereof transfixed with a sword in fess, the blade wavy arg., pommel and hilt or. *Through.* *cf.* 143. 11

Hamilton, Scotland, an oak-tree growing out of a torse and fructed ppr. *Obsequio non viribus.* 143. 2

Hamilton, on a mount vert, an oak-tree traversed by a frame-saw, both ppr. *cf.* 143. 8

Hamilton, Sidney Graves, Esquire, J.P., of Kiftsgate Court, Campden, Glouc., out of a ducal coronet gu., an oak-tree fructed and penetrated transversely in the main stem by a frame-saw ppr., and pendent from a branch on the sinister side thereof by a riband arg., an escutcheon gu., charged with a cross crosslet or. *Through.* *cf.* 143. 8

Hamilton of Edinburgh, a fir-tree with a frame-saw across the trunk ppr. *Through.*

Hamilton of Neilsland, Scotland, an oak-tree fructed ppr. *Obsequio non viribus.* 143. 5

Hamilton of Dalziel, Scotland, an oak-tree ppr. *Requiesco sub umbra.* 143. 5

Hamilton of Cambuskeith, Scotland, an oak-tree ppr. *Viridis et fructifera.* 143. 5

Hamilton, Hon. Thomas Ferrier, J.P., of Elderslie, New Gisborne, Bourke, Victoria, Australia, President of the West Bourke Agricultural Society, two branches of oak crossing each other in saltire ppr. *Addunt robur stirpi.* 151. 1

Hamilton, John Ferrier, Esquire, same crest and motto.

Hamilton, Claude William, Esquire, same crest and motto.

Hamilton, John Wallace, of Cairn Hill, Ayrsh., same crest and motto.

Hamilton of Barnton, Scotland, the branch of a tree growing out of an old stock. *Through God revived.* 145. 2

Hamilton of Blair, Scotland, an oaken plant ppr. *Dum in arborem.*

Hamilton of Blanterferm, Scotland, the trunk of an oak-tree couped sprouting two fresh branches ppr. *Non deficit alter.* 145. 2

Hamilton of Westport, Scotland, two branches of oak in saltier fructed ppr. *Addunt robor.* 151. 1

Hamilton, Scotland, an oak-plant or. *Tandem fit arbor.*

Hamilton of Inverdovat, the trunk of an oak-tree sprouting ppr. *Hinc orior.* 145. 2

Hamilton of Broomhill, Scotland, a horse's head. *Ride through.* *cf.* 50. 13

Hamilton, Sir Frederic Harding Anson, Bart., of Silverton Hill, Lanarksh., a horse's head couped arg., maned or. *Through.*—*Sola nobilitas virtus.*—*Stimulis marjoribus ardens.* *cf.* 50. 13

Hamilton, Scotland, a horse's head arg., bridled gu. 51. 5

Hamilton of St. Ernans, co. Donegal, a nag's head couped arg., bridled gu. *Ride through.* 51. 5

Hamilton-Tyndall-Bruce of Grangehill and Falkland, Fifesh., a horse's head erased arg., bridled gu. *Be trew.* *cf.* 51. 5

Hamilton, Scotland, a demi-goat, holding between the fore-feet a human heart, all ppr. 128. 4

Hamilton, Scotland, a demi-goat affrontée, holding between the fore-legs a human heart, all ppr. 128. 4

Hamilton, Robert, Esquire, M.D., of Clifton Mount, Jamaica, a demi-antelope affrontée arg., armed and ungu. or, charged with a crescent gu., and holding between the fore-legs a heart of the last. *Qualis ab incepto.* *cf.* 128. 4

Hamilton, Rt. Hon. Ion Trant, P.C., D.L., of Abbotstown, Castleknock, co. Dublin, a demi-antelope affrontée erm., attired and ungu. or, and holding between the legs a heart gu. *Qualis ab incepto.* *cf.* 128. 4

Hamilton of Orbistown, Scotland, an antelope ppr. *Quis accursabit.* 126. 12

Hamilton-Starke, James Gibson, Esquire, J.P., of Troqueer Holm, Kirkcudbright: (1) On the dexter side, a dexter hand ppr., gripping by the lug and the horn a bull's head downwards erased arg., distilling drops of blood ppr. (*for Starke*). (2) On the sinister side, an antelope's head ppr., gorged and attired gu. (*for Hamilton*). *Fortiorum fortia facta.*—*In via virtuti pervia.* Below the arms, *Auxilio Dei.* *cf.* 126. 2

Hamilton of Olivestob, Scotland, an antelope's head and neck ppr., gorged with a collar and attired gu. *In via virtuti pervia.* *cf.* 126. 2

Hamilton, Gawin William Rowan, Esquire, of Killyleigh Castle, co. Down, and Shangannagh Castle, co. Dublin, a demi-antelope arg., attired or, holding between the fore-legs a heart gu. 307. 9

Hamilton, Colonel Henry Blackburne, M.A., a demi-antelope arg., armed and langued or, charged with a mullet gu., holding between the fore-legs a heart gu. *Qualis ab incepto.*

Hamilton of Vessington, Dunboyne, co. Meath, a demi-antelope erm., attired or, holding between the fore-legs a human heart gu. *Qualis ab incepto.*

Hamilton of Orbiston, Lanarksh., Scotland, an antelope's head ppr., armed and unguled or. *Quis accusabit.* *cf.* 126. 2

Hamilton, Scotland, an antelope's head and neck ppr., collared and attired gu. *In via virtuti pervia.* cf. 126. 2

Hamilton, Stirling-, Sir William, Bart., of Preston, an armed man from the middle brandishing a sword aloft ppr. *Pro patriâ.* 187. 1

Hamilton of Colquot, Scotland, a Cupid with his bow, quiver, and arrows ppr. *Quos dedit arcus amor.* 189. 7

Hamilton-Dalrymple, Sir Walter, Bart., of North Berwick, Haddingtonsh., a rock ppr. *Firm.* 179. 7

Hamilton of Byres, Scotland, two dexter hands issuing out of clouds conjoined in fess, holding a branch of laurel ppr. *Præsto et persto.* cf. 224. 3

Hamilton, Buchanan-Baillie-, John Bailie, Arn Prior, Perthsh.: (1) Same as above. (2) A crescent or (*Baillie*). (3) A sword erected in pale ppr., hilted and pommelled or. *Præsto et persisto.*

Hamilton, Scotland, within two branches in orle two hands conjoined issuing out of clouds, all ppr. *Perstando præsto.* cf. 224. 1

Hamilton-Campbell, William Kentigern, Esquire, of Netherplace, Ayrsh., a hand issuing from a cloud holding a signet letter ppr. *Optime quod opportune.*

Hamilton of Redhouse, Haddington, Scotland, two dexter hands issuing out of clouds conjoined fesseways and holding two branches of laurel disposed in orle ppr. *Perstando præsto.*

Hamilton of Aikenhead, a hand holding an oak-slip ppr. *Virebo.*

Hamilton, a hand holding a seax. cf. 213. 9

Hamilton of Wishaw, Scotland, a hand holding a seax and a quill in saltier ppr. *Tam virtus quam honos.*

Hamilton of Newton, a dexter hand holding a seax. *Fideliter.* cf. 213. 9

Hamilton of Westburn, a hand holding a lance in bend ppr. *Et arma et virtus.* 214. 11

Hamilton of Daichmont, Scotland, a hand holding a heart ppr. *No heart more true.* 216. 9

Hamilton of London, between two cornucopiæ or, filled with fruit and grain ppr., a hand holding a dagger erect, also ppr., hilted and pommelled or. *Through —Ser libre o morir.*

Hamilton of Glasgow, a dexter hand grasping a lance in bend sinister ppr., the hand charged with a star gu. *Et arma et virtus.* cf. 214. 11

Hamilton of Presmenaw, a hand holding a pen ppr. *Tam virtute quam labore.* 217. 10

Hamilton, James, Esquire, of Gresham Road, Staines, a heart gu., charged with a cinquefoil arg. *Fidelis in adversis.*

Hamilton of Pencaitland, Scotland, issuing out of clouds a hand holding a pen. *Tam virtute quam labore.* cf. 217. 10

Hamilton of Gilkerscleugh, a dexter hand issuing out of a human heart ppr., grasping a sword. *In arduis fortitudo.* cf. 213. 4

Hamilton, late Claud Hamilton, Cochna House, Dumbartonsh., and Robert Bruce Hamilton, Esquire, of Dunmore Park, near Larbert, N.B., a man's heart gu., charged with a cinquefoil arg. *Fidelis in adversis.* 181. 1

Hamilton of Kilbrachmonth, a hand pulling up a cinquefoil ppr. *Et neglecta virescit.* 219. 14

Hamilton, a cubit arm erect holding a scimitar. 213. 5

Hamilton, a cubit arm erect holding a tilting-spear. 214. 11

Hamilton, Scotland, a hand holding a holly-leaf ppr. *Semper virescens.*

Hamilton, Scotland, a hand holding a dagger in pale. 212. 9

Hamilton of Bangour, Ayrsh., a ship in distress ppr. *Immersabilis.* 160. 14

Hamilton, Scotland, a ship in distress ppr. *Littora specto.* 160. 14

Hamilton, Scotland, same crest. *Littore sistam.*

Hamilton, Scotland, same crest. *I gain by hazard.*

Hamilton, Scotland, same crest. *Per varios casus.*

Hamilton of Udstoun, Scotland, a boar's head erased ppr. *Ubique fidelis.* 42. 2

Hamilton, Scotland, same crest. *Non metuo.*

Hamilton, Scotland, a greyhound's head and neck couped ppr., collared gu., garnished or. 61. 2

Hamilton, Scotland a salmon hauriant arg., an annulet through its nose or.

Hamilton of Ardoch, Ayrsh., Scotland, a dolphin pursuing another fish in the water ppr. *Honestum pro patria.*

Hamilton, William Malcolm Fleming, of Craighlaw, Kirkcowan, Wigtownsh., same crest and motto.

Hamilton of Barncluith, Scotland, a sphere ppr. *Dat Deus originem.* 159. 1

Hamilton, Scotland, a heart gu., charged with a cinquefoil arg. *Faithful in adversity.* 181. 1

Hamilton of Cairnes, Scotland, a Bible expanded ppr. *Ore lego, corde credeo.* 158. 3

Hamilton, Stevenson-, James, Fairholme, Larkhall, N.B.: (1) A hawk rising ppr., belled or, holding in the dexter foot a sword, also ppr., hilted and pommelled or (*Hamilton*). (2) A dexter hand issuing from a cloud and holding a wreath of laurel, all ppr. *Thankful. —Cœlum non solum.*

Hamilton, Scotland, a crescent gu. *J'espère.* 163. 2

Hamilton of Little Earnock, Lanarksh., Scotland, a boar's head erased ppr. *Non metuo.* 42. 2

Hamilton of Cubardie, a cinquefoil arg. *Non mutat genus solum.* 148. 12

Hamilton of Smaliston, a mascle or. *I'll deceive no man.* 167. 9

Hamilton of Mount Hamilton, Armagh, Ireland, within an adder disposed in a circle a cock, all ppr. *Adest prudenta animus.* cf. 91. 1

Hamilton of Castle Hamilton, co. Cavan, Ireland, a sheaf of seven arrows or, headed and feathered arg., banded gu., surmounted by a morion ppr. cf. 173. 10

Hamilton, Scotland, a sword in pale. 170. 2

Hamilton, Scotland, a crescent arg. 163. 2

Hamley, a garb in fess. 153. 6

Hamlin, seven arrows, points upward, ppr.

Hamlin, James, Buckfastleigh, Devonsh., same crest.

Hamlyn, a swan with wings addorsed ppr. 99. 12

Hamlyn, Devonsh., a demi-swan with wings expanded bezantée.

Hamlyn, a swan close, holding in its beak a baton. cf. 99. 2

Hamlyn, Frederick, Esquire, of the Old Hall, Langham, Oakham, Rutl., and Clovelly Court, Bideford, a demi-swan displayed ppr., on each wing expanded sa., a white rose of the first, and on the breast a bird-bolt erect, the head downwards of the second, and charged on the neck for distinction with a cross crosslet, also sa. *Mea virtute, mea involvo.*

Hamlyng, a hand pulling a rose from a bush ppr. 218. 13

Hamme, on a chapeau a unicorn's head erased, all ppr. 49. 10

Hammersley, two lion's gambs holding up a crescent. 39. 6

Hammersley, a demi-griffin segreant or, holding in the dexter claw a cross crosslet fitched gu. cf. 64. 2

Hammes, on a ducal coronet a lion passant ppr. 6. 6

Hammet, from the battlements of a castle of three towers ppr., a demi-lion double-queued issuant erminois, holding between the paws a pellet.

Hammick, Sir St. Vincent Alexander, Bart., a demi-lion per pale or and vert, holding between the paws an escarbuncle of the first. *Laudari a laudato.*

Hammil of Roughwood, Ayrsh., Scotland, a fleur-de-lis or. 148. 2

Hammill, a palm-tree fructed ppr. 144. 1

Hammington, Kent, a dragon's head erased gu., ducally gorged arg., charged on the neck with three guttes-d'eau in fess. cf. 71. 8

Hammon of Ellingham, Norf., an elephant's head arg., ducally gorged and eared or. cf. 132. 2

Hammond, Baron (*extinct*), Rt. Hon. the late Edmund Hammond, between the attires of a stag a falcon rising ppr., each wing charged with a mullet or. *Per tot discrimina rerum.* 87. 6

Hammond, Kent, an eagle with wings expanded arg., beaked and legged or, between the attires of a stag ppr. cf. 87. 6

Hammond, Kent, a hawk's head collared gu., rays issuing or. *Pro rege et patriâ.*

Hammond, Colonel Arthur George, of Sherborne House, Camberley, Surrey, same crest and motto.

Hammond, out of a ducal coronet or, a demi-eagle with wings expanded sa., charged on the breast with a rose gu.

Hammond, William Oxenden, of St. Alban's Court, near Wingham, Kent, an eagle's head erased sa., charged with a rose gu., the rose issuing rays or. *Pro rege et patriâ.* cf. 83. 2

Hammond, out of a ducal coronet an eagle's head between two wings. 84. 3

Hammond, Joseph Hutchinson, Esquire, out of a naval crown an eagle's head.

Hammond, an eagle's head gorged with a collar indented. cf. 83. 1

Hammond, a wolf's head erased quarterly or and az. 30. 8

Hammond, Henry Lewis, Esquire, of the Vinery, Bury St. Edmunds, Suff., a wolf's head erased per pale indented or and az. *cf.* 30. 8

Hammond of Wistaston Hall, Chesh., a boar passant ppr. 40. 9

Hamon, Jersey, a lion rampant gardant or. *En tout loyal.* 2. 5

Hammond, Basil Edward, Esquire, of Trinity College, Cambs, a dove close ppr., between two ears of wheat stalked and leaved or, supporting with the dexter leg a tilting-spear erect ppr., therefrom flowing to the sinister a banner gu., charged with a cock's head erased or.

Hamond, Vice-Admiral Richard Horace, of the Abbey, Westacre, Norf., on a rock ppr., a dove rising arg., holding in its beak an olive-branch vert. *cf.* 94. 7

Hamond, a crescent arg., within an annulet az., charged with eight estoiles or.

Hamond-Græme, Sir Graham Eden William Græme, Bart., J.P., D.L., of Holly Grove, Berks: (1) Two arms issuing from a cloud erected and lifting up a man's skull encircled with two branches of palm, over the head a marquess's coronet, all ppr. (*for Græme*). (2) Out of a naval crown or, the sails arg., an eagle's head sa. (*for Hamond*). *Paratus et fidelis.* 83. 7

Hamond, a wolf's head erased quarterly or and az. 30. 8

Hamond, Robert Thomas, late of Pampisford Hall, Cambs, same crest.

Hamond, Sir Charles Frederick, of 20, Lorain Place, Newcastle-on-Tyne, a wolf's head erased quarterly or and az., surmounted by some wonderful kind of a coronet. *Industria honore et perseverantia.*

Hamond, Kent, a wolf's head erased quarterly per fesse indented or and az. *cf.* 30. 8

Hampden, Hobart-, *see* Earl of Buckinghamshire.

Hampden, a peacock's head couped az. 103. 2

Hampden, Bucks and Scotland, an eagle's head erased az. 83. 2

Hampden, Bucks and Northamp., a talbot passant erm., collared and lined, the line tied in a bow-knot over his neck gu. 54. 5

Hampden, Captain Osbert Renn Leigh, of Ewelme Old Mansion, Wallingford, Oxon., upon a mount vert, a talbot erm., gorged with a collar gemel, and resting the dexter foot upon a cross patée az. *Vestigia nulla retrorsum.*

Hampson, Sir George Francis, Bart., of Taplow, Bucks, out of a mural crown arg., a greyhound's head sa., collared of the first, rimmed or. *Nunc aut nunquam.* 61. 6

Hampstead and **Hampsted,** a demi-chevalier in full armour brandishing a scimitar, all ppr. 187. 4

Hampton, Baron (Pakington), of Hampton Lovett, and of Westwood, Worcs., a demi-hare gu., charged on the shoulder with a quatrefoil arg. *Par viribus virtus.* *cf.* 136. 6

Hampton, a greyhound sejant holding in his mouth a hare. *cf.* 59. 4

Hampton, a wyvern vert, in bulrushes ppr. *A Deo et rege.* *cf.* 70. 1

Hampton of London, Middx., and Staffs, a wolf's head erased sa. 30. 8

Hampton, Staffs, a wolf's head arg. 30. 5

Hampton, Middx., a tiger's head erased arg.

Hampton, a demi-eagle displayed or. 81. 6

Hanam, a demi-griffin arg., holding between its claws a close helmet az. *cf.* 64. 1

Hanbury, Bateman-, Rt. Hon. William Bateman, **Baron Bateman,** of Shobdon Court, Heref.: (1) Out of a mural crown sa., on a wreath or and vert, a demi-lion or, holding in the dexter paw a battle-axe of the last, helved of the first (*for Hanbury*). *cf.* 16. 13. (2) A duck's head and neck between two wings ppr. (*for Bateman*). *Nec prece, nec pretio.*

Hanbury-Kincaid-Lennox, Bateman-, Hon. Captain Charles Spencer, D.L., A.D.C., of Woodhead and Kincaid: (1) Two broadswords in saltire behind an imperial crown, all ppr. (*for Lennox*). (2) A castle triple-towered arg., masoned sa., and issuing therefrom a dexter arm embowed grasping a sword ppr. (*for Kincaid*). *cf.* 155. 3. (3) Out of a mural crown sa., on a wreath or and vert, a demi-lion or, holding in the dexter paw a battle-axe of the last, helved of the first (*for Hanbury*). *cf.* 16. 13. (4) A duck's head and neck between two wings ppr. (*for Bateman*). *I'll defend.—Nec prece, nec pretio.*

Hanbury-Tracy, Rt. Hon. Charles Douglas Richard, **Baron Sudeley,** of Toddington: (1) On a chapeau gu., turned up erm., an escallop sa., between two wings or (*for Tracy*). 141. 11. (2) Out of a mural crown sa., on a wreath or and vert, a demi-lion or, holding in the dexter paw a battle-axe of the last, helved of the first (*for Hanbury*). *cf.* 16. 13. (*Badge*) In front of a fire-beacon flammant ppr., a leopard passant ducally gorged and chained, the chain reflexed and passing behind the beacon and over the back. *Memoria pii æterna.*

Hanbury, John Capel, of Pontypool Park, Monmouth: (1) A unicorn's head erased arg., armed and crined or (*for Leigh*). 49. 5. (2) Out of a mural crown sa., on a wreath or and vert, a demi-lion or, holding in the dexter paw a battle-axe of the last, helved of the first (*for Hanbury*). *Nec prece, nec pretio.* *cf.* 16. 13

Hanbury, out of a mural crown sa., upon a wreath or and vert, a demi-lion gold, holding in the dexter paw a battle-axe of the last, helved of the first, and charged upon the shoulder with a trefoil slipped vert. (*Granted and confirmed by William Camden, Clarenceux King of Arms, to John Hanbury of Pursell-Greene, in the county of Worcester.*) 16. 13

Hanbury, Sir Thomas, Esquire, F.L.S., Knight of the Order of St. Maurice and St. Lazarus, and Knight Commander of the Cross of the Crown of Italy, of La Mortola, Ventimiglia, Italy, and **Sampson Hanbury,** Esquire, of Langford Park, Maldon, Essex, are sons, and **William Allen Hanbury,** Esquire, is the nephew of the late Daniel Bell Hanbury, Esquire, of Clapham, Surrey, to whom and to the descendants of whose father the following crest was granted, viz.: Out of a mural crown sa., a demi-lion or, charged on the shoulder with three trefoils slipped one and two, and gorged with a collar gemel vert, holding in the dexter paw a battle-axe, the staff sa., the head gold. *Nil desperandum.* 225. 11

Hanbury, Adalbert William Allen, Esquire, same crest and motto.

Hanbury, out of a mural crown gu., charged with two estoiles or, a demi-lion rampant gardant erm., holding in the dexter paw a battle-axe ppr.

Hanbury, late Rt. Hon. Robert William, P.C., of Ilam Hall, Dovedale, Staffs, and Bolehall House, Tamworth, out of a mural coronet a demi-lion holding in the dexter paw a battle-axe. *Nec prece, nec pretio.*

Hanbury, Lionel Henry, Esquire, of Hitcham Grange, Taplow, *uses* out of a mural coronet sa., a demi-lion rampant or, holding in the dexter paw a battle-axe, also or, the handle of the first. (*This is the crest confirmed by Camden as mentioned above, but Mr. Lionel H. Hanbury appears to have established no right to bear or use it.*) *Industria et providentia.* *cf.* 16. 13

Hanbury-Sparrow, Alan Bertram Hanbury, Esquire, of the Uplands, Tettenhall, Staffs: (1) Out of the battlements of a tower ppr., a unicorn's head arg., horned and crined or, semée of pheons az. (*for Sparrow*). (2) Out of a mural crown sa., a demi-lion or, holding in the dexter paw a battle-axe sa., headed or (*for Hanbury*). *In Deo solo salus est.*

Hanby, two arms in armour embowed holding a heart, all ppr. *cf.* 104. 7

Hance, a hand holding a sword in pale enfiled with a Saracen's head couped, all ppr. 212. 12

Hanchett, the sun shining on a sunflower ppr.

Hanckford, a demi-Cupid holding in his dexter hand a torch, all ppr. 185. 8

Hancock, a cock ppr. 91. 2

Hancock, a cock or, combed and wattled gu., armed sa., supporting a palm-branch vert.

Hancock, Leics., a cock's head erminois, combed, wattled, beaked, and ducally gorged gu. *cf.* 90. 1

Hancock, a demi-lion holding between its paws a lozenge sa.

Hancock, an arrow point downwards ppr. 173. 5

Hancocke, Devonsh., a demi-griffin arg., armed or. 64. 2

Hancocks, Alfred John, Esquire, of Woodfield House, Wolverley, near Kidderminster, and Blakeshall House, Kidderminster, on a mount vert a cock gu., holding in the dexter claw an ear of wheat or. *Redeem time.*

Hancocks, Annesley John, Esquire, same crest and motto.

Hancocks, Augustus Talbot, Esquire, of Wolverley Court, Kidderminster, same crest and motto.

Hancome of London, a lion sejant or, collared gu., charged with two étoiles of the first. *cf.* 7. 4

Hancox, an arrow point downwards. 173. 5

Hand, an arm embowed holding in the hand three ears of wheat ppr. 202. 6

Hand, Hunts, a dexter hand apaumée ppr. 222. 14

Hand, a stag trippant ppr. 117. 8

Hand, George, Esquire, in front of a cubit arm holding a marigold leaved and slipped ppr., an escutcheon gu., charged with a golden fleece. *Perseverantia.*

Handasyd, a dexter hand couped and erect ppr. 222. 14

Handby, a hind's head per chevron az. and arg. 124. 1

Handcock, Baron Castlemaine, *see* Castlemaine.

Handcock of Portleek, co. Westmeath, Ireland, a demi-lion rampant az., holding between the paws a fusil arg., charged with a cock gu. *cf.* 10. 2

Handcock, a cock gu. 91. 2

Handcock, Ireland, the stump of a holly-bush shooting out new leaves ppr. 145. 10

Handcock, out of the sea an arm embowed holding in the hand a bait spade. 202. 15

Handcock of Cole Hill House, co. Longford, Ireland, a goat passant sa., armed, unguled, and bearded or. *Perseverando.* *cf.* 129. 5

Handcome of London and Warw., a lion sejant or, gorged with a collar gu., thereon two estoiles of the first. *cf.* 7. 4

Handfield, a hand holding a bombshell fired ppr. 216. 6

Handfield, Cumb., a phœnix's head ppr., crowned or.

Handfield of Ashford, Kent, an eagle's head couped erm., between two wings elevated ppr., and ducally crowned or. *cf.* 84. 2

Handfield, Rev. Henry Hewett Paulet, of St. Peter's Parsonage, Melbourne, Victoria, Minister of St. Peter's Church, Canon of St. Paul's Cathedral, Melbourne, and Rural Dean of that city, *uses an eagle's head couped,* wings elevated, and ducally crowned. *Justus nec timidus.* *cf.* 84. 2

Handford, two ears of wheat in saltier ppr. 154. 4

Handford, Colonel John Compton, C.B., B.A., of Flood Hall, Thomastown, co. Kilkenny, of Wollashall, Pershore, Worcs., on a chapeau gu., turned up erm., a wyvern of the first, wings expanded arg. *Memorare novissima.* *cf.* 70. 4

Handley, *see* Davenport-Handley.

Handley, a sceptre in pale ppr. 170. 19

Handley, a goat current sa., bearded, unguled, and armed or.

Handley, a hand holding a bunch of quills ppr. *Equity.*

Hands, a goat's head erased gu. 128. 5

Handvile of Ulcombe, Kent, an eagle's head erm., ducally crowned or, between two wings ppr. *cf.* 84. 2

Handy, two arms in armour embowed holding a battle-axe, all ppr. 194. 12

Handyside and **Handysyde,** a dexter hand apaumée ppr. *Munifice et fortiter.* 222. 14

Hanercroft, Ireland, a demi-lion rampant gu., collared sa., holding between the paws an open book ppr. *Vita more fide.*

Haney, a stag's head ppr., collared or, and between the attires a cross patée gu. *cf.* 120. 9

Hanford of Watton, Lincs, a cubit arm erect vested or, cuffed arg., holding in the hand ppr. an estoile of the first.

Hanger, Baron Coleraine (*extinct*), a demi-griffin segreant or, holding between the paws an escarbuncle of the same. *Artes honorabit.*

Hanger, a griffin segreant holding between its claws a sun in splendour or. 62. 6

Hanham, Sir John Alexander, Bart., M.A., J.P., of Dean's Court, Dorset, a griffin's head erased or, beaked sa. 66. 2

Hanham, Phelips Brooke, Esquire, care Messrs. Cox, Charing Cross, same crest. *Lex reipublicæ vita.—Pro aris et focis.*

Hankey of London, a demi-wolf erminois. 31. 2

Hankey, John Barnard, Esquire, of Fetcham Park, Leatherhead, Surrey, a wolf's head erased erminois.

Hankey, Rodolph Alexander, Esquire, of 54, Warwick Square, S.W., same crest.

Hankin, a boy pulling a branch from a tree ppr. 189. 6

Hankins, a Moor affrontée, with a bow hung over the sinister shoulder and a quiver of arrows, and holding in the hands extended a snake, all ppr.

Hankinson, Middx., a phœnix with wings elevated or, issuant from flames ppr. *Vi et animo.* 82. 2

Hankinson, Robert Chatfield, Esquire, of Red Lodge, North Stoneham, Hants, an eagle displayed sa., charged on each wing with a cinquefoil and resting each claw on a saltire couped, all or. *Propositi tenax.*

Hankley, out of a ducal coronet or, a triple plume of ostrich-feathers arg. 114. 6

Hankwood, on the stump of a tree sprouting anew ppr., an escutcheon pendent charged with the arms, viz.: arg., on a chevron sa., three escallops of the field. *cf.* 145. 8

Hanlaby, on a mount an oak-tree ppr. 143. 14

Hanley, a sceptre in pale ppr. 170. 10

Hanly, Ireland, three arrows points downwards, one in pale and two in saltire, banded. 173. 1

Hanman, a lion sejant erm. *Per ardua ad alta.* 8. 8

Hanmer, Sir Wyndham Charles Henry, Bart., of Hanmer, Flint, of Stockgrove, Bucks, and Rushmere Lodge, Beds, on a chapeau az., turned up erm., a lion sejant gardant arg. *Gardez l'honneur.* 7. 6

Hanmer of Porkington, Shropsh., out of a mural coronet or, a cubit arm erect vested quarterly arg. and az., cuffed erm., on the hand ppr. a falcon close of the first, beaked, winged, and legged of the third, belled, also or.

Hanmer, on a ducal coronet a peacock close ppr. 103. 8

Hanmer, Shropsh., a falcon rising. 87. 1

Hanna, a wolf's head erased sa. 30. 8

Hannam, a demi-griffin holding between his claws a close helmet ppr. *cf.* 64. 1

Hannay of Rusko, Ulverston, between the horns of a crescent a cross crosslet fitched in pale sa. *Per ardua ad alta.* 166. 9

Hannay, George, Kingsmuir, Pittenweem, same crest. *Cresco et spero.*

Hannay or **Hanney,** Scotland and England, same crest.

Hannen, Hon. James Chitty, B.A., of 207, Gloucester Terrace, London, a demi-lion sa., gorged with a collar, and therefrom pendent from a chain an escutcheon or, charged with a portcullis sa. *His truth shall be thy shield.*

Hanney, Rainsford-, Ramsay William, Kirkdale, Kirkcudbright, same crest. *Per ardua ad alta.*

Hanney, a stag's head ppr., collared or, between the attires a cross patée gu. *cf.* 120. 9

Hanning, a stag's head erased or. 121. 2

Hanny, *see* Hannay and Hanney.

Hanrott of London, an eagle displayed with two heads sa. *Perseverando.—Humani nihil alienum.* 74. 2

Hansard, a martlet sa. 95. 5

Hansard, a falcon volant az. 88. 3

Hansard of Lifford, co. Donegal, Ireland, an arm in armour embowed holding in the gauntlet a broken sword, all ppr. *Fractus pugnatu.* *cf.* 195. 1

Hansard, Victor Hansard, Esquire, of Silverheys, Port Talbot, Glamorgansh., a cubit arm erect, vested az., cuffed or, the arm charged with a fesse arg., thereon a bee volant ppr., and in the hand a mullet, also or. *Probitas verus honos.*

Hansard, an arm in armour couped at the shoulder and embowed, the part from the shoulder to the elbow in fess and bound with a ribbon, the other part in pale, and holding in the hand a broken sword.

Hansard of London, a cubit arm erect vested or, cuffed arg., holding in the hand ppr., a mullet of the second. *Probitas verus honos.*

Hansard, an antique crown or. 180. 12

Hansby, Yorks, a pheon or. 174. 11

Hansfell, the trunks of two trees erect, each sprouting forth a new branch, the two branches in saltier. 145. 4

Hanslap and **Hanslop,** Northamp. and Warw., a leopard sejant ppr. *cf.* 24. 12

Hanson of Abingdon, Berks, and Lord Mayor of London 1675, a lion rampant sa., holding a mascle arg. *cf.* 1. 13

Hanson, Charles Augustin, Esquire, J.P., of Fowey Hall, Fowey, Cornw., and 39, Hans Mansions, Hans Crescent, S.W., a lion rampant az., holding in the dexter fore-paw an antler or, and resting the sinister paw upon two mascles fesseways, and interlaced of the last. *Semper parare.* 307. 10

Hanson of Gilstead Hall, Essex, on a ducal coronet or, a dove close, holding in the beak a sprig of olive, all ppr. *cf.* 92. 5

Hanson, Sir Reginald, Bart., LL.D., D.L., **J.P.**, of Bryanston Square, Middx., on a fasces fessewise or, a martlet with wings endorsed sa. *Deo favente et sedulitate.* 283. 8

Hanson, on a chapeau az., turned up arg., a martlet, wings addorsed sa.

Hantvile and **Handville,** Devonsh. and Kent, an eagle's head erm., ducally crowned or, between two wings. *cf.* 84. 2

Hantvill, an ox-yoke in pale gu., bows to the sinister or. *cf.* 178. 6

Hanwell, a hand holding a club in pale ppr. *cf.* 214. 6

Hara or **O'Hara** of Coolany, co. Sligo, Ireland, a demi-lion rampant pean, armed and langued gu., holding in the paws a chaplet of oak-leaves ppr. *Virtute et claritate.* *cf.* 10. 2

Harbe or **Harbey** of Ashby, Northamp., an eagle's head erased or, between two wings sa., bezantée. *cf.* 84. 2

Harben, Sir Henry, of Seaford Lodge, Hampstead, and Warnham Lodge, Horsham, a cubit arm in armour, the hand in a gauntlet ppr., holding a spur leathered or, between two roses gu., leaved and slipped, also ppr. *Summis viribus.* 210. 5

Harber, a hand holding three arrows, points downwards. *cf.* 214. 3

Harbert, two wings expanded ppr. 109. 6

Harberton, Viscount (Pomeroy), of Carbery, co. Kildare, a lion rampant gu., holding between the paws an apple slipped ppr. *Virtutis fortuna comes.*

Harbin, Henry Edward, Esquire, of Newtown, Surmaville, near Yeovil, Somers., a gauntleted hand couped above the wrist az., holding a spur or, leathered sa. *cf.* 210. 5

Harbin, Somers., a horned owl arg. 96. 5

Harbord, Baron Suffield, *see* Suffield.

Harbord, on a chapeau gu., turned up erm., a lion couchant arg. *Æquanimiter.* 7. 12

Harborne, two lion's gambs sa., holding up a bezant. *cf.* 39. 4

Harborne, on a chapeau gu., turned up erm., an eagle displayed or.

Harborne of Sheen Lane, Middx., on the stump of a tree couped and eradicated ppr., an eagle displayed or, beaked and legged gu.

Harborne of Thackley, Oxon., a lion sejant or, resting the dexter paw upon a bezant. *Deus industriam beat.* *cf.* 8. 8

Harborne, Shropsh.: (1) On the stump of a tree couped and eradicated ppr., an eagle displayed or, armed and membered gu. (2) A lion sejant or, resting his dexter paw on a bezant. *cf.* 8. 8

Harborough, Earl of (Sherard), out of a ducal coronet or, a peacock's tail erect ppr. *Le roi et l'estat.—Hostis honori invidia.* 115. 6

Harbottell, a goat's head erased sa., armed and collared or. *cf.* 128. 7

Harbottle, a demi-falcon or, wings displayed sa.

Harbottle, Suff., a demi-falcon or, with wings expanded barry wavy of six arg. and az.

Harbottle of Brecknock, a dexter arm embowed vested az., cuffed arg., holding in the hand ppr. a club or.

Harbour, Somers., two hands couped holding a cutlas erect, all ppr. 224. 9

Harbron, a hand holding an anchor ppr.

Harby of Atweston, Northamp., a heron's head erased or, between two wings expanded sa.

Harby of Aldenham, Herts, Adston, and Astley, Northamp., a demi-eagle erased with wings expanded sa., bezantée. *cf.* 80. 2

Harbye of Canons Ashby and London, a heron's head erased or, beaked sa., between two wings expanded of the last, bezantée.

Harcla, De, and **Harcle,** a fret az. 165. 10

Harcla and **Harcle,** out of a ducal coronet or, a reindeer's head ppr. 122. 3

Harcourt, Aubrey, Esquire, of Nuneham Park, Abingdon, and **Stanton Harcourt,** Eynsham, both Oxon., on a ducal coronet or, a peacock close ppr. *Gesta verbis prævenient.—Le bon temps viendra.* 103. 8

Harcourt, Guy Elliot, of Ankerwycke, Berks, same crest and motto.

Harcourt, Augustus George Vernon, Esquire, F.R.S., LL.D., of St. Clare, Isle of Wight, same crest and mottoes.

Harcourt, Leveson Francis Vernon, Esquire, of Haddon House, Weybridge, same crest and mottoes.

Harcourt-Vernon, Edward Evelyn, Esquire, of Grove Hall, Retford, Notts: (1) A boar's head erased sa., ducally gorged or (*for Vernon*). (2) A wyvern arg., standing on a weir of the last, banded az., pierced through the body in fesse by an arrow, and devouring a child ppr. (*for Venables*). (3) On a ducal coronet or, a peacock close ppr. (*for Harcourt*). *Ver non semper viret.*

Harcourt, George Elliot, of Ankerwycke House, Berks, on a ducal coronet or, a peacock close ppr. *Le bon temps viendra.* 103. 8

Hard, on a chapeau a greyhound ppr. 58. 4

Hardacre, on a rock an eagle rising regardant, all ppr. 79. 9

Hardcastle of Netherhall, Suff., and of the Lodge, Holt, Norf., a castle arg. *Deus mihi munimen.* 155. 8

Hardcastle, a female attired az., holding in her dexter hand the sun and in her sinister the moon ppr. 184. 4

Hardel or **Hardell,** a sheaf of arrows ppr., banded gu. 173. 3

Hardeley, a soldier firing a gun ppr.

Harden, a dexter hand issuing from a cloud in fess, holding an anchor ppr. 223. 4

Harden, Richard James, Esquire, of Harrybrook, Tandragee, co. Armagh, a dexter arm embowed, holding in the hand a dagger. *Tu ne cede malis, sed contra audentior ito.*

Hardey of London, a cock's head bendy arg. and sa., between two wings, the dexter or, the sinister gu., holding in the mouth a sceptre of the last. 90. 4

Hardgrave and **Hardgrove,** a water-bouget gu. 168. 4

Hardie, a lion passant gardant or, collared az., supporting an anchor of the last. *cf.* 5. 10

Hardie, Scotland, a hand holding a dagger erect ppr. *Tout hardie.* 212. 9

Hardie, Scotland, a dexter arm holding a dagger in pale, point downwards, ppr. *cf.* 213. 6

Hardie, Scotland, an arm in armour embowed, holding in the hand a scimitar ppr. *Sera deschormais hardie.* 196. 10

Hardie, Scotland, a spur-rowel. 164. 8

Hardieman, on a serpent nowed, a hawk perched, all ppr. 86. 3

Hardin, a dexter hand issuing from a cloud in fess, supporting an anchor ppr. 223. 4

Harding of Baraset, Warw., on a chapeau az., turned up erm., a boar passant or. *cf.* 40. 8

Harding, Rev. John Taylor, M.A., of Pentwyn, near Monmouth, on a staff raguly fessways sa., a dexter arm embowed in armour and holding a sword, the blade wavy, all ppr., charged with two escallops, also sa.

Harding, Ireland, a martlet or, billettée gu. *cf.* 95. 2

Harding, Devonsh., a falcon rising ppr. 87. 1

Harding, John Stafford Goldie, the Pines, Westward Ho, Devon, a falcon displayed ppr.

Harding, a demi-stag ppr., attired or, supporting between its fore-feet an anchor of the last.

Harding, Ireland, an arm embowed in fess couped, holding a sword in pale enfiled with a leopard's face.

Harding, Thomas Walter, Esquire, of the Abbey House, Kirkstall, Leeds, and Doddington, Cambs, and Hartholme Hall, Lincoln, on a rock ppr., in front of a tilting-spear erect or, a porcupine, also ppr. *Per ardua surgo.* 292. 9

Harding, of St. Ann's Tower, Headingley, Leeds, and of the Hermitage, Doddington, March, Cambs, upon a rock ppr., in front of a tilting-spear erect or, a porcupine statant, also ppr. *Per ardua surgo.* 292. 9

Harding of Coaley, Glouc., and Rockfields, Monmouthsh., a demi-leopard rampant erased erm., gorged with a collar az., bezantée, chained or. *cf.* 23. 13

Harding, William Derisley, Esquire, of Islington Lodge, King's Lynn, a demi-lion rampant, holding between the paws a cross patée fitchée. *Non durus sed durans.*

Harding of King's Newton, Derbysh., a mitre gu., banded and stringed or, charged with a chevron arg., fimbriated or, and thereon three escallops sa. *Audax omnia perpeti.* 180. 5

Hardinge, Viscount (Hardinge), of Lahore and King's Newton, Derbysh., a mitre gu., thereon a chevron arg., fimbriated or, charged with three escallops sa. *Mens æqua rebus in arduis.* 180. 5

Hardinge, Sir Arthur Henry, K.C.M.G., C.B., of Bencombe House, Dursley, Glouc., a mitre gu., thereon a chevron arg., fimbriated or, charged with three escallops sa. *Mens æqua rebus in arduis.*

Hardinge, Sir Edmund Stracey, Bart., D.L., of Boundes Park, Kent: (1) Of honourable augmentation, a hand fessewise couped above the wrist habited in naval uniform, holding a sword erect, surmounting a Dutch and a French flag in saltier, on the former inscribed "*Atalanta*," on the latter "*Piedmontaise*," the blade of the sword passing through a wreath of laurel near the point and a little below through another of cypress, with the motto, "*Postera laude recens.*" (2) A mitre gu., charged with a chevron arg., fimbriated or, thereon three escallops sa. 180. 5

Hardinge of Monkstown, co. Dublin, Ireland, a raven rising ppr. *Non melior patribus.* 107. 3

Hardisty, two hands issuing from clouds conjoined in fess. 224. 1

Hardisty, Yorks, a boar's head couped ppr., pierced through by an arrow.

Hardman of Liverpool and Rochdale, a naked arm embowed, couped at the shoulder, holding a mill-pick, all ppr.

Hardman, a hand issuant pulling a rose ppr. 218. 13

Hardres, Kent, a stag's head couped ppr. 121. 5

Hardres, a buck's head couped or and erm., attired gu. and az. 121. 5

Hardress, a reindeer's head cabossed ppr., attired or. 122. 4

Hardware, Chesh., out of a ducal coronet or, a cubit arm az., cuffed arg., holding in the hand an oak-branch ppr., fructed or.

Hardwicke, Earl of (Yorke), a lion's head erased ppr., gorged with a collar gu., charged with a bezant. *Nec cupias, nec metuas.* cf. 18. 6

Hardwick of Hardwick, Derbysh., on a mount vert, a stag courant ppr., gorged with a chaplet of roses arg. cf. 118. 13

Hardwicke of Diamond Hall, Bridgnorth, Shropsh., on a mount vert, a stag current gorged with a chaplet of roses, all ppr., charged with a crescent for difference. *Cavendo tutus.* cf. 118. 13

Hardwicke, William Wright, Esquire, J.P., M.D., Staffs, East Molseley, and 32, Cyril Mansions, S.W., same crest. *Cavendo tutus.*

Hardwicke, Herbert Junius, M.D., Southfield Mount, St. Leonard's-on-Sea, same crest and motto, but without the crescent.

Hardwicke, Hardwicke Lloyd, Esquire, J.P., of Tytherington, Glouc., a stag ppr., supporting with the dexter foreleg a scaling-ladder sa. *Cervus non servus.*

Hardwicke, a leopard's face or, jessant-de-lis gu. 22. 5

Hardwike, an ostrich-feather enfiled with a ducal coronet, all ppr. 114. 12

Hardy, Gathorne-, *see* Cranbrook, Baron.

Hardy of Greenfields, co. Dublin, Ireland, a griffin's head erased or, charged with an escallop gu. *Spes in Domino.* cf. 66. 2

Hardy, Bart., Northamp., on a naval coronet or, a griffin's head erased arg., langued gu. cf. 66. 2

Hardy, Admiral Sir Thomas Masterman, Bart, G.C.B., out of a naval coronet or, a dragon's head ppr. cf. 71. 1

Hardy, Edmund Armitage, Esquire, of 1, Oakfield Road, Clifton, Bristol, in front of a lion's head az., gorged with a collar invected arg., thereon three magpies ppr., an escallop between two quatrefoils fesseways or. *Fear one.* 260. 5

Hardy of London, an eagle's head bendy of four arg. and sa., between two wings, the dexter or, the sinister gu., holding in the beak a pansy-flower ppr., stalked and leaved vert. 84. 8

Hardy of Wetwang, Yorks, a demi-eagle arg., with wings displayed gu., charged on the breast with two bendlets sa., holding in the beak a rose-branch ppr.

Hardy, Sir Reginald, Bart., J.P., of Dunstall Hall, Staffs, a dexter arm embowed in armour ppr., garnished or, entwined by a branch of oak vert, charged with two catherine-wheels, the one above and the other below the elbow gu., the hand grasping a dragon's head erased ppr. *Armé de foi hardi.* 198. 12

Hardy, Charles Stewart, Esquire, J.P., D.L., of Chilham Castle, Canterbury, same crest and motto.

Hardy, Laurence, Esquire, of 42, Lowndes Square, S.W., and Sandling Park, Hythe, Kent, same crest and motto.

Hardy, Cozens-, Clement William Hardy, Esquire, of Letheringsett Hall and Cley Hall, Norf.: (1) A dexter arm embowed ppr., charged with a pellet between two chevronels or, and grasping an eagle's head fesseways, also ppr. (*for Hardy*). (2) A lion rampant or, guttée-de-sang and fretty gu. (*for Cozens*). *Fear one.*

Hardy, Cozens-, Herbert Hardy, Esquire, of 50, Ladbroke Grove, W., and 7, New Square, Lincoln's Inn, W.C., same crest and motto.

Hardy, an arm embowed in armour and gauntleted ppr., garnished or, holding a griffin's head erased sa.

Hardy of Toller Wilmer, Dorset, a dexter arm embowed in armour, holding in the hand ppr. a dragon's head erased sa. cf. 198. 12

Hardy of Letheringsett Hall, Norf.: (1) A dexter arm embowed ppr., charged with a pellet between two chevronels or, and grasping an eagle's head fesseways, also ppr. (*for Hardy*). 202. 11. (2) A lion rampant or, guttée-de-sang and fretty gu. (*for Cozens*). *Fear one.* 3. 3

Hardy, Guernsey, an ostrich-feather or. cf. 114. 12

Hardy or **Hardye,** a heart within a fetter-lock.

Hardyman, on a serpent nowed, a hawk perched, all ppr. 86. 3

Hardyman, an arm in armour embowed, grasping in the hand a boar's head erased at the neck.

Hare, Earl of Listowell, *see* Listowell.

Hare, Baron Coleraine (*extinct*), a demi-lion rampant arg., ducally gorged gu. 10. 7

Hare, Sir George Ralph Leigh, Bart., of Gressenhall House, Norf., a demi-lion rampant arg., gorged with a ducal coronet or. *Non videri sed esse.* 10. 7

Hare, John Hugh Montague, Esquire, of Docking Hall, King's Lynn, same crest.

Hare, same crest. *Odi profanum.*

Hare, Norf., a demi-lion arg., gorged with a naval coronet gu. cf. 10. 10

Hare, a demi-lion arg., holding a cross crosslet fitched gu. 11. 10

Hare of Beeston, Yorks, and of Etchingham, Sussex, a demi-lion rampant arg., semée of mullets gu., supporting a flagstaff ppr., therefrom flowing to the sinister a pennon gu., charged with a mullet arg. *By watchfulness, by steadfastness.*

Hare, Scotland, a parrot gu., holding in its beak an annulet or. 101. 11

Harebread, Yorks, an ostrich-feather in pale arg. cf. 114. 12

Harestains, Scotland, a dexter arm holding in the hand a key. *Toujours fidèle.* 217. 7

Harewell, Suff. and Worcs., a hare's head erased or.

Harewood, Earl of (Lascelles), Harewood House, Leeds, Yorks, a bear's head couped at the neck erm., muzzled gu., buckled or, collared of the second, rimmed and studded of the third. *In solo Deo salus.* cf. 34. 14

Harfett, Kent, a demi-dolphin erect ppr.

Harford of Bosbury, Heref., out of flames ppr., a phœnix or, the wings az., fire issuing from the beak ppr. cf. 82. 2

Harford, John Charles, Esquire, of Blaise Castle, Glouc., and Falcondale, Cardigansh., issuing from flames a dragon's head between two wings. *Inter utrumque tene.*

Harford, out of a ducal coronet or, two flags, one of the first, the other sa., both the staves gold.

Hargil, Yorks, out of a mural coronet gu., a lion's head or. 19. 12

Hargrave, a buck's head erased per fesse or and az., attired arg. 121. 2

Hargrave, a buck's head erased per fesse or and gu., fretty az., attired of the second. 121. 11

Hargraves, out of a ducal coronet two branches of laurel in orle, all ppr. 146. 9

Hargreaves, John Reginald, of Arborfield Hall, Reading, a buck's head erased vert, attired or, collared arg., charged with a fret gu., holding in the mouth a sprig of oak ppr. *Fortitudine et prudentiâ.*

Hargreaves, Reginald Gervis, Esquire, of Cuffnells, Lyndhurst, Hants, same crest and motto.

Hargreaves of Bank Hall, Lancs, a buck's head erased az., attired or, gorged with a collar arg., fretty gu., holding in the mouth a sprig of heath ppr. *Vincit amor patriæ.* 121. 10

Hargreaves, Richard Tattersall, Esquire, a stag's head couped az., gorged with a collar nebuly or, within the attires a rose arg., barbed and seeded ppr., the whole between two like roses. *I die in harness.*

Harington-Stuart, Colonel Robert Edward Stuart, of Torrance, East Kilbride, Lanarksh., Scotland: (1) A dexter hand holding a sword, all ppr. *Avant.* (2) A lion's head erased or, gorged with a thong gu., buckled or, the end pendent (*for Harington*). *Nodo firmo.* 212. 13

Harington, His Honour Sir Richard, Bart., of Ridlington, Rutl., and of Whitbourne Court, Worcs., a lion's head erased or, collared with a thong gu., buckled or, the end pendent. *Nodo firmo.* 18. 1

Harington, a lion's gamb holding a thistle ppr. 37. 6

Harison of London, a snake vert, entwined round a broken column or.

Harker, John, Esquire, M.D., of Hazel Grove, near Carnforth, Westml., a dexter arm embowed vested per pale sa. and gu., charged with two escallops or, cuffed arg., the hand ppr. holding a bugle-horn stringed sa. *Audio et juro.* 204. 5

Harneis of Hawerby Hall, Lincs, a stag's head couped. *Que rien ne vous étonne.*

Harkness, Scotland, a ship in distress ppr. *Trust in God.* 160. 14

Harkness of Cragbeg and Garryfine, co. Limerick, Ireland, a dove close per pale or and vert, holding in the beak an olive-branch, also vert, fructed or. *Hope in God.* 92. 5

Harkness, Rev. Robert, formerly Rector of Stowey, Somers., a dove close per pale or and vert, holding in the beak an olive-branch of the second, fructed of the first. *Hope in God.* 92. 5

Harkness, Rev. George Law, M.A., of Netherwood, Southwater, Horsham, Sussex, same crest and motto.

Harkness, William Henry, Esquire, of Temple Athea, co. Limerick, same crest and motto.

Harlakenden of Woodchurch and Tunstall, Kent, and of Earl's Colne, Essex, between the attires of a stag or, an eagle regardant with wings expanded arg.

Harland, a demi-sea-horse ppr., charged on the shoulder with an escallop gu., holding in its claws a buck's head cabossed ppr.

Harland, formerly of Sutton Hall, Yorks: (1) A demi-sea-horse ppr., charged on the shoulder with an escallop gu., and holding in the claws a buck's head cabossed or (*for Harland*). (2) An eagle's head erased sa., charged on the neck with an ermine-spot or, pendent from the lower member of the beak an annulet of the same (*for Hoare*). *Constantia in ardua.* *cf.* 83. 2

Harland, Bart., Suff., a sea-lion sa., supporting an anchor ppr. *Per juga, per fluvios.*

Harland, a sea-lion erect on its tail az., ducally crowned or, holding between its paws an anchor of the last, fluked sa.

Harland, Bart., J.P., of Ormiston, co. Down upon a rock ppr., a sea-lion erect sa., supporting an anchor ppr., suspended from the neck by a chain or, an escutcheon erm., charged with a sun in splendour. *Semper vigilans.* 20. 3

Harlaw, a Moor's head ppr. 192. 13

Harlech, Baron (Ormsby-Gore), of Harlech, Merionethsh.: (1) A heraldic tiger rampant arg., ducally gorged or (*for Gore*). (2) A dexter arm embowed in armour, charged with a rose gu., holding in the hand a man's leg, also in armour and couped at the thigh, all ppr. (*for Ormsby*). *In hoc signo vinces.*

Harleston of South Kendon, Essex, out of a ducal coronet a stag's head browsing a hawthorn, all ppr., cerried or. *cf.* 120. 7

Harlewen, a tower, on the top thereof a crescent. 156. 4

Harley, Heref., a castle triple-towered arg., out of the middle tower a demi-lion rampant gu. *Virtute et fide.* 155. 10

Harley, Robert William Daker, Brampton Bryan, Heref., same crest and motto.

Harley, Shropsh., a buck's head ppr. 121. 5

Harley, a spear-head in pale entwined with an olive-branch.

Harling and **Harlingham,** a bombshell inflamed ppr. 177. 12

Harliston and **Harlston,** a cannon mounted ppr. 169. 12

Harlow of Preston, Northamp., a cinquefoil or, issuing from between the horns of a crescent vair.

Harlstone, Essex, out of a ducal coronet or, a stag's head erm., attired of the first, bearing between the attires a hawthorn-bush fructed ppr. *cf.* 120. 7

Harly, Ireland, a demi-lion gardant gu., holding in his dexter paw a battle-axe ppr. 16. 14

Harman, Ireland, a water-bouget or. 168. 4

Harman, late Lieutenant-General Sir George Byng, K.C.B., of 64, Courtfield Gardens, S.W., a stag's head erased. *Ora et labore.* 121. 2

Harman of Moore Hall, Warw., out of a ducal coronet sa., a buck's head arg. 120. 7

Harman of Taynton, Oxon., an arm erect vested arg., cuffed or, holding in the hand ppr. a halbert, also or, handled gu. *cf.* 207. 10

Harman of Harman Hall, Sussex, out of a ducal coronet or, an arm embowed in armour ppr., garnished of the first, grasping two sprigs of roses arg., stalked and leaved vert, seeded of the first.

Harman of Palace, co. Wexford, Ireland, out of a ducal coronet or, a sinister arm erect, vested az., cuffed arg., the hand ppr., grasping a rose-branch stalked and leaved vert, bearing two roses, the one arg. and the other gu., seeded of the first. *Dieu défend le droit.*

Harman, Thomas Edwards, of Carrig, Byrne, co. Wexford, same crest and motto.

Harman of Antigua, West Indies, a demi-man ppr., crowned with an Eastern coronet or, chained round the waist and holding the end in the sinister hand of the last, the dexter hand holding a withered tree torn up by the root ppr.

Harman of Rendlesham and Mulford, Suff., a demi-old man ppr., beard and hair arg., wreathed about the head with leaves vert, holding in the dexter hand the stump of a tree erased of the last, fructed or, chained round the body with the end of the chain in the sinister hand of the last.

Harmar, David James, Esquire, late of Bath, in front of a cubit arm vested sa., cuffed or, holding in the hand two rose-branches leaved and slipped vert, that on the dexter gu., that on the sinister arg., both barbed and seeded ppr., a portcullis with chains or. 206. 4

Harmer, a book expanded ppr. 158. 3

Harmer, Frederic William, Esquire, J.P., F.G.S., of Oakland House, Cringleford, Norf., in front of a dexter arm embowed vested sa., cuff arg., the hand ppr., holding three roses gu., barbed, seeded, leaved, and slipped, also ppr., as many lozenges conjoined fessewise or. *Esse quam videri.*

Harmon, Glouc., an arm vested sa., cuffed arg., holding in the hand ppr. two rose-branches vert, one arching to the dexter and flowering on the top with a white rose, the other to the sinister in like manner with a red rose.

Harnage, Bart. (*extinct*), of Belswardyne, Shropsh.: (1) Out of a ducal coronet or, a lion's gamb ppr., holding up a torteau (*for Harnage*). *cf.* 39. 13. (2) A demi-griffin or, semée of crescents az., collared gu. (*for Blackman*). *Fide et fiduciâ.* *cf.* 65. 8

Harnet, a hornet-fly wings elevated ppr. 137. 4

Harnet, Ireland, a demi-lion gardant az. 10. 8

Harnett, Major-General E. Meredith, 35, Piccadilly, a demi-lion rampant guardant az. *Certavi et vici.*

Harneys and **Harnous,** Beds, a stag's head sa., guttée-d'or, and attired of the same. 121. 5

Harokins, a griffin's head chequy arg. and sa., between two wings, the dexter or, the sinister gu. 65. 11

Harold and **Harould,** a hawk's lure ppr. 178. 11

Harold, Ireland, a gate ppr. 158. 9

Harpden, Glouc., a hind's head or. 124. 1

Harper, Scotland, an old Scottish harp or, with nine strings arg. *Te Deum laudamus.*

Harper of Edinburgh, a harp sa., stringed or. *Te Deum laudamus.*

Harper of London, upon a crescent or, charged with a fret between two martlets az., an eagle displayed of the last.

Harper, a lion's head erased quarterly or and gu. 17. 8

Harper, a lion's head erased per fesse or and gu., collared of the last and lined of the first. *cf.* 18. 6

Harper of New Ross, co. Wexford, Ireland, a lion's head erased per pale or and gu. 17. 8

Harper, Scotland, a boar passant or. *Et suavis et fortis.* 40. 9

Harper, George Povey, Esquire, M.A., of 19, Mecklenburg Street, Leicester, a boar passant or, ducally gorged. 279. 15

Harpur, Derbysh. and Scotland, a boar passant or, ducally gorged gu. *cf.* 40. 9

Harpur of Berianherbert, Devonsh., a boar passant or, chained and collared gu. *cf.* 40. 9

Harpur, Warw. and Northamp., on the battlements of a tower masoned ppr., a boar's head erased fesseways.

Harpur, Rev. Henry, of Burton Latimer Hall, Kettering, a tower ppr., and on the battlements thereof a boar's head erased close.

Harpur-Crewe, *see* Crewe.

Harpway and **Harpwaye,** an ostrich with wings addorsed holding in its beak a horse-shoe, all ppr. *cf.* 97. 1

Harrance, Kent, a stork holding in the beak a herring, all ppr.

Harreys of Guernsey, a hare couchant arg., between two bushes ppr.
Harridge, a lion's head erased ppr., langued gu. 17. 8
Harrie, Cornw., a demi-sea-dog rampant gu., erased and finned or, holding between the paws a Cornish chough ppr.
Harries of Cruckton, Shropsh., a hawk arg., beaked and belled or, preying on a pheasant of the first. cf. 77. 1
Harries of Benthall: (1) A hawk arg., beaked and belled or, preying on a pheasant of the first. cf. 77. 1. (2) Out of a ducal coronet a dexter arm in armour embowed ppr., garnished or, grasping in the hand ppr. a dagger of the last, hilted or. cf. 196. 5
Harries, George James, of Tregwynt, Pembroke, a mullet pierced or. *Integritos semper tutamen.* 164. 5
Harries, an oak-tree growing out of a mount among long grass, all ppr. 143. 14
Harrington, Earl of (Stanhope), Elvaston Castle, Derbysh., a tower az., from the battlements thereof a demi-lion rampant issuant, holding between the paws a grenade fired ppr. *A Deo et rege.* 157. 10
Harrington of Bishton, Shropsh., a lion's head erased or, gorged with a collar gu., between two trefoils slipped vert, to the collar a line and ring arg. cf. 18. 6
Harrington, a lion's head erased or, gorged with a label of three points gu., charged with nine bezants. cf. 18. 8
Harrington, Lancs, a lion's head erased or, gorged with a belt and buckle gu. 18. 1
Harrington, Middx., a leopard's head couped ppr. 22. 10
Harrington, Ireland, a talbot's head gu. 56. 12
Harringworth, an antique crown or. 180. 12
Harris, Earl of Malmesbury, *see* Malmesbury.
Harris, Baron (Harris), of Seringapatam and Mysore, East Indies, and of Belmont, Faversham, Kent, on a mural coronet or, the royal tiger of Tippoo Sultan passant gardant vert, striped and spotted of the first, pierced in the breast with an arrow of the last, vulned gu., charged on the forehead with a Persian character for Hyder, and crowned with an Eastern coronet, both also or. *My Prince and my country.*
Harris, Shropsh., a hedgehog or. 135. 8
Harris, same crest. 135. 8
Harris, Claudius Shirley, Esquire, in front of two battle-axes saltireways sa., a hedgehog erminois. *Fortis quia paratus.*
Harris, a hedgehog or, charged on the side with a key in pale az. *Ubiqui patriam reminisci.* cf. 135. 8
Harris, Walter Henry, Esquire, late of Elm Tree House, Macaulay Road, Clapham, Surrey, upon a rock ppr., a hedgehog az., between on the dexter side a decrescent and on the sinister side an increscent or. *Ubique patriam reminisci.* 256. 8
Harris, Alfred, Esquire, of Wharfenden, Frimley, Surrey, in front of a demi-pelican displayed arg., collared gemelle az., and charged on the breast with three guttes-de-sang, a faggot fesseways ppr., banded vert. *Fide sed cui vide.* 252. 19
Harris, Frederick Leverton, Esquire, M.P., of 4, Green Street, Park Lane, London, W., and Camilla Lacey, Dorking, same crest.
Harris, Charles Edward, Esquire, of Tylney Hall, Winchfield, Southampton; West Court, Finchampstead, Berks; and Pikeley, Allerton, Yorks, in front of a demi-pelican rising arg., vulning herself, charged on the neck with three guttes-de-sang, and gorged with a collar gemel az., a bundle of reeds fesseways ppr., banded vert.
Harris of Abcot, Shropsh., a pelican in her piety ppr. *Ubique patriam reminisci.* 98. 14
Harris of Radford, Devonsh., an eagle displayed or. 75. 2
Harris of Hayne, Devonsh., an eagle rising erm., beaked and spurred or. *Kur Deu res pub trar.* 77. 5
Harris of Rosewarne, Cornw., a falcon rising erm., belled and spurred or. cf. 87. 1
Harris of Cornw., Eyston, Devonsh., and Herts, on the stump of a tree raguly lying fesseways vert, a falcon rising erm., beaked and legged or.
Harris, Leics., rising from a fern-brake ppr., a dove regardant az., beaked and membered gu., holding in the beak a trefoil vert. *Virtute et operâ.*
Harris, Scotland, on a mount vert, a crane holding in his dexter claw a stone ppr. cf. 105. 6
Harris, Shropsh., a double plume of ostrich-feathers az. and arg. cf. 114. 4
Harris of Cherston, Devonsh., a demi-antelope saliant arg., attired and crined or. cf. 126. 5
Harris, a demi-antelope ppr., attired or. cf. 126. 5
Harris, Essex, a buck's head chequy arg. and az., attired or. 121. 5
Harris, a buck's head or, attired with ten tynes arg. *Dominus dedit.* 121. 5
Harris, Charles Frederick, Esquire, of the Gate House, Rugby, a talbot sejant. *Nil admirari.*
Harris of Maldon, Essex, a talbot sejant or. 55. 2. (*Another,* a buck's head chequy arg. and az., attired or.) 121. 5
Harris, a talbot sejant or. *Nil admirari.* 55. 2
Harris, Sir George David, of 32, Inverness Terrace, W., in front of a rock ppr., a demi-sea-dog or, gorged with a collar gemel sa., and grasping a Cornish chough, also ppr. *True and fast.*
Harris, Samuel, of Westcotes, Leics., out of the battlements of a tower or, a bull's head sa., charged on the neck with a cinquefoil of the first. *In Deo solum robur.*
Harris, William Cecil, Esquire, M.A., of 50, Campden House Court, W., same crest and motto.
Harris, Ireland, a monkey passant, banded round the middle. cf. 136. 8
Harris, William Prittie, Esquire, of Lakeview, Blackrock, co. Cork, a demi-lion rampant or, holding between the paws a cinquefoil pierced gu. *Industria veritas et hospitalis.*
Harris of Windsor, Berks, a demi-pegasus gu., the wings endorsed or. 47. 5
Harris, Herbert James, of Bowden Lacock, Wilts, a demi-pegasus wings addorsed or, guttée-de-poix, holding in the mouth two ears of barley, also or, and resting the sinister leg on an increscent gu. *Ubique patriam reminisci.* 244. 8
Harris of Loudon, a winged heart gu., imperially crowned or.
Harris, Worcs., an arm grasping in the hand a dart. 214. 4
Harrison, *see* Broadley.
Harrison, *see* Rogers-Harrison.
Harrison, *see* Slater-Harrison.
Harrison, Derbysh., a demi-lion or, supporting a chaplet of roses vert.
Harrison, Yorks, a demi-lion rampant arg., holding a laurel-branch vert.
Harrison, Surrey, a demi-lion rampant erminois, erased gu., holding between the paws a garland of laurel ppr., encircling a mascle of the second.
Harrison, John, of Snelston Hall, Ashbourne, Derbysh., on a mount vert, a demi-lion couped or, semée of lozenges az., holding between the paws a chaplet of roses ppr.
Harrison, James, Esquire, M.A., J.P., Barrister-at-Law, of Newby Bridge House, Ulverston, in front of a demi-lion rampant erased or, gorged with a collar gemelle az., and holding between the paws a wreath of oak ppr., three mascles interlaced, also az. *Pro rege et patria.*
Harrison, Gilbert Henry Wordsworth, of Seascale, Cumb., a demi-lion arg., resting the sinister fore-paw on a clarion or, on the shoulder three hurts, each charged with a cross patée, also arg. *Vincit qui patitur.* 241. 9
Harrison of Gouldhurst, Kent, a demi-lion rampant ppr., holding in the paws a lozenge erm. cf. 10. 2
Harrison of Hendon, Middx., out of a mural coronet az., a demi-lion rampant or, crowned with an Eastern crown arg., and in the paws a laurel garland adorned with four damask roses ppr. *Absque virtute nihil.*
Harrison, William Bealey, Esquire, of Aldershaw, Lichfield, a demi-lion per saltire or and arg., holding in the dexter paw a branch of alder slipped ppr., and within a chain in arch of the first. *Sat cito si sat bene.*
Harrison of Galligreaves Hall, Blackburn, within a wreath or and az., a talbot's head erased of the last, collared of the first. *Not rashly nor with fear.* 56. 7
Harrison of Reading, Berks, out of a ducal coronet or, a talbot's head ppr., collared gu. *Amicitia permanens et incorrupta.* cf. 57. 12
Harrison of Hurst and Finchampstead, Berks, out of a ducal coronet or, a talbot's head of the last, guttée-de-poix. 57. 12
Harrison, Mohun-, Rev. Henry Walpole Frederick, of Cross House, Bishopsteignton, Devonsh., same crest.

Harrison, Fiske-, a stork with wings expanded arg., beaked and membered or. *Ferendo et feriendo.*

Harrison of Rutland, an ostrich holding in its beak a snake. *Deo non fortuna.* cf. 97. 2

Harrison, Rt. Rev. William Thomas, D.D., of Copford Hall, Colchester, a stork, wings expanded arg., beaked and membered or. *Ferendo et feriendo.*

Harrison of London, on a chapeau az., turned up and indented erm., a bird with wings addorsed sa.

Harrison, Græme, Esquire, of Easthorpe House, Ruddington, Notts, on an escallop gu., between two roses of the last, barbed and seeded ppr., a dove or. *Vincit virtus omnia.*

Harrison, R. Charlton, Esquire, of St. Mary's Vale, Chatham, on a chapeau gu., turned up erm., an eagle close ppr. *Animus et fata.* 76. 4

Harrison, a double-headed eagle displayed. 74. 2

Harrison of Dublin, a demi-eagle displayed, murally gorged or. cf. 81. 6

Harrison, out of a ducal coronet a demi-eagle with wings displayed, holding in his beak a columbine ppr.

Harrison, Haryson, and **Heryson** of Great Plumstead, Norf., out of a ducal coronet or, a harpy ppr., crined sa., gorged with a lax of the first.

Harrison of London, out of a coronet or, a plume of ostrich-feathers of the same and arg. cf. 114. 8

Harrison, Frederick James, Maer Hall, Staffs, in front of park pales a hare ppr., resting the fore-paw on a garb fessewise and to the dexter or. *Vigilantia.*

Harrison of Downe Hill, Kent, a chapeau gu., turned up erm., on either side a wing expanded arg.

Harrison, a griffin's head erased. 66. 2

Harrison, Ireland, a coney holding between the feet three ears of wheat, all ppr.

Harrison of Winscales and Stainburn, Cumb.: (1) Upon a mount vert, a stag courant regardant sa., semée of quatrefoils attired and ungu. or, holding in the mouth an arrow in bend sinister ppr. (*for Harrison*). 118. 10. (2) Upon a fret sa., a falcon rising ppr., belled or, and holding in the beak a lure of the last (*for Falcon*). *Vite courageux fier.* 87. 4

Harrison of Linethwaite, Cumb., a Roman fasces fessewise ppr., banded gu., surmounted by an anchor erect entwined by a cable, all or. 161. 4

Harrison, Ireland, a cubit arm in armour erased and in fess, holding a scimitar in pale, enfiled with a boar's head couped ppr. cf. 211. 9

Harrison of Atcliffe, Lancaster, and Elkington, Northamp., an arm vested az., purfled or, cuffed arg., holding in the hand a broken dart ppr., pheoned of the second.

Harrison, Sir Richard, G.C.B., C.M.G., a cubit arm, habited az., cuffed arg., holding in the hand an arrow in bend sinister ppr., headed or. 300. 3

Harrison-Broadley, Henry Broadley, Esq., of Welton House, Brough, East Yorks, Tickton Grange, near Beverley, and Hon Gate, Beverley, Yorks: (1) Within a chaplet of roses gu., a cross patée fitchée at foot sa. (*for Broadley*). 243. 13. (2) A demi-lion or, charged with a bend vair arg. and gu., supporting with the sinister paw a shield arg., thereon two branches of laurel saltire-ways vert (*for Harrison*). *Nihil viget simile.* 243. 14

Harison of Poulton-le-Fylde, Lancs, an arm embowed in armour ppr., garnished or, holding a broken spear, the head dependent, also ppr. 197. 2

Harrison of London, a snake vert, entwined round a broken column or.

Harrison-Topham, Major Thomas, D.S.O., of Springfield, Old Charlton and Caldbergh, Middleham, Yorks: (1) Two crosses patée fitchée in saltire or, interlaced with as many serpents vert (*for Topham*). (2) In front of a dexter cubit arm habited az., cuffed or, encircled by a wreath of oak or, holding in the hand a broken arrow-point downwards ppr., two pheons or. *Persevere.*

Harrisson, Charles Millns, Easton Hall, Stamford, an ostrich with a serpent in its mouth, all ppr. *Deo non fortunâ.*

Harrold of Limerick, Ireland, a demi-angel ppr., vested gu., crined and winged or. cf. 183. 12

Harrold, a hawk's lure ppr. 178. 11

Harrold, Ireland, a gate ppr. 158. 9

Harrop, *see* Hulton-Harrop.

Harrow, a hand vested gu., cuffed or, holding a baton az.

Harrowby, Earl of (Ryder), Sandon Hall, Staffs, out of a mural coronet or, a dragon's head arg., charged on the neck with an ermine spot sa. *Servata fides cineri.* cf. 72. 11

Harrower, a garb ppr. 153. 2

Harrower, Scotland, a garb ppr. *Sedulo numen.* 153. 2

Harrowing, J. H., J.P., C.C., of Low Stakesby, Whitby, a hand vested gu., cuffed or, holding a baton az. *Sedulo numen.* 300. 13

Harruse, a bull's head gorged with a chaplet ppr. cf. 44. 3

Harry, an angel's head couped below the breast ppr., vested az., the wings expanded.

Harryson, out of a ducal coronet or, a bull's head. 44. 11

Harryson, a serpent vert, entwined round a broken pillar or.

Harsnet, a dexter hand holding a sword-blade wavy ppr.

Harswell, Warw., out of a ducal coronet a coney's head couped, all or.

Hart, Sir Robert, Bart., 38, Cadogan Place, S.W., on a mount vert, a hart trippant ppr., holding in the mouth a four-leaved shamrock or. *Audacter tolle.*

Hart, Sir Israel, of Ashleigh Knighton, near Leicester, upon a fasces a hart trippant or, the dexter fore-leg resting on a crown vallary az. *Via trita via tuta.* 249. 16

Hart, a hart's head ppr. *Via una, cor unum.* 121. 5

Hart, Lincs, a stag's head erased, holding in the mouth a branch of oak, all ppr. cf. 121. 2

Hart-Synnot, Major-General Arthur FitzRoy, C.B., C.M.G., of Ballymoyer, co. Armagh: (1) A swan issuant, wings expanded sa., ducally crowned or, and vulned in the breast with an arrow gold, feathered arg. (*for Synnot*). (2) A stag's head between two antlers, all ppr. (*for Hart*). 231. 8. *Sine macula.*—*Celer atque fidelis.*

Hart, Major-General Reginald Clare, V.C., K.C.B., Government House, Chatham, a stag's head between two antlers, all ppr. *Celer atque fidelis.* 231. 8

Hart, Colonel Horatio Holt, same crest and motto.

Hart of London, a buck trippant ppr. *Via una, cor unum.* 117. 8

Hart, late Samuel Hopgood, Esquire, of Mulgrave House, Sutton, Surrey, upon a mount vert, a sword fessewise, point to the sinister ppr., pommel and hilt or, thereon a stag trippant arg., attired or, charged on the body with three fleurs-de-lis fessewise gu., and holding in the mouth a sprig of olive slipped and fructed ppr. *Hedduch.* 118. 5

Hart-Davis, Captain Henry V. (late R.E.), of Court Hayes, Limpsfield, Surrey, a fawn lodged ppr. *Dum spiro, spero.* 124. 8

Hart, a camel kneeling ppr. 132. 5

Hart, Ireland, a camel couchant ppr. 132. 1

Hart, Kent, a lion's head couped erm., ducally crowned or. cf. 18. 8

Hart, Shropsh., a lion's head erminois, ducally crowned gu. cf. 18. 8

Hart, William Edward, Esquire, of Kilderry, co. Donegal, Ireland, a heart inflamed issuing out of a castle triple-towered ppr. *Cœur fidèle.*

Hart of Yarnacombe, Devonsh., a fleur-de-lis arg., issuing from a cloud ppr. *Deo adjuvante vincam.*

Hart, Scotland, a sundial or, on a pedestal gu. 176. 7

Hart of Edinburgh, a dexter arm grasping a scimitar ppr. *Fide et amore.* 213. 5

Hart of Baltully, Fifesh., Scotland, a dexter arm grasping a spear, all ppr. 214. 11

Hartagan, Ireland, a hand gauntleted holding a sword ppr. 210. 4

Hartcup, a head in profile helmeted between two wings.

Hartcup, Herbert James, of Upland Hall, Suff., same crest.

Hartcup, William Thomas, Esquire, of Upland Hall, Bungay, Suffolk, and Eastwood, Old Catton, Norfolk, a warrior's head in profile couped at the shoulders, helmeted ppr., garnished or, between two wings arg., in front thereof a short bow stringed of the first.

Harte or **O'Hart,** Ireland, a hand holding a sword. 212. 13

Harte, Kent, a lion's head erminois, murally crowned gu.

Harte, Leics., a stag ppr. 117. 5

Harte, a hart ppr. *Validus.* 117. 5

Harte, Middx. and Norf., a stag's head erased sa., attired arg., in the mouth a flower of the last, stalked and leaved vert. cf. 121. 2

Harter of Broughton Hall, near Manchester, a stag springing from a fern-brake ppr., and gorged with a collar az. *Deo omnia.* 268. 5

Harter, James Francis Hatfield, Cranfield Court, Woburn Sands, Beds, same crest and motto.

Harter, George Loyd Foster, Esquire, J.P., of Salperton Park, Hasellon R.S.O., Glouc., same crest and motto.

Harter, Walter George Hatfeild, Esquire, of the Bury, Kempston, Beds, same crest and motto.

Hartford, a tent ppr. 158. 7

Hartford, a parrot's head gu., between two wings vert. 101. 10

Hartford of London and Hunts, a dexter arm erect couped at the elbow, vested per pale arg. and gu., holding in the hand ppr. a stag's attire sa. 208. 6

Hartgrave, a demi-man in armour royally crowned, wielding in his sinister hand a scimitar, all ppr.

Hartgule and **Hartgull,** a buck's head erased sa., attired or. 121. 2

Hartigan, an armed hand erect holding a sword ppr. 210. 4

Hartill, John Thomas, Esquire, of Manor House, Willenhall, on a wreath of the colours, upon a mount vert, a hart lodged and regardant gu., holding in the mouth an arrow in bend sinister arg., and resting the dexter fore-leg on a heart, also gu. *Diligentes Deus ipse juvat.* 290. 12

Hartill, Alfred, Esquire, of Walsall, same crest and motto.

Hartill, Frederick William, Esquire, of Lonsdale House, Willenhall, same crest and motto.

Hartington, Marquess, *see* Devonsh., Duke of.

Hartland, Baron (Maurice-Mahon), Ireland, an heraldic tiger statant, holding in the dexter paw a broken spear. *Periculum fortitudine evasi.* 25. 8

Hartland, Devonsh., a buck's head erased or. 121. 2

Hartley, Yorks, a stag lodged regardant arg. *cf.* 115. 9

Hartley, Scotland, a demi-antelope collared sa. 126. 3

Hartley, Captain Richard Wilson, J.P., of Beech Park, Clonsilla, co. Dublin, out of a mural coronet or, a stag's head ppr., holding in the mouth a rose gu., barbed and seeded ppr. *Spectemur agendo.* 271. 20

Hartley, Ireland, a dexter arm in armour embowed fesseways couped ppr., holding a club sa., spiked or. 199. 4

Hartley, Thomas, of Armathwaite Hall, Cumb., a martlet sa., holding in its beak a cross crosslet fitched or. *cf.* 95. 5

Hartley, Sir Charles Augustus, Kt., K.C.M.G., M.I.C.E., F.R.S.E., F.R.G.S., of 26, Pall Mall, S.W., a martlet sa., holding in its beak a cross crosslet fitchée or. *Vive ut vivas.*

Hartley, Captain James, D.L., of Ashbrooke, Bournemouth, upon a mount vert, a martlet sa., holding in the beak a cross patée fitchée or. *Sub hoc signo vinces.* 95. 8

Hartley, George Thompson, of Wheaton Aston Hall, Stafford, same crest and motto.

Hartley, Rev. John Thorneycroft, of the Vicarage, Burneston, near Bedale, Yorks, same crest and motto.

Hartley of Settle, Giggleswick, Yorks, a human heart gu., ensigned with a crown vallery or, between two wings barry of six az. and or, the heart charged with an ermine spot of the last for difference. *cf.* 110. 14

Hartman, out of a ducal coronet or, a demi-man in armour couped at the thighs ppr., garnished or, the visor open, brandishing a pole-axe sa., between two wings gu., each charged with a bend wavy, thereon between two decrescents arg., three étoiles pierced sa. 185. 10

Hartop, Leics., out of a ducal coronet or, a demi-pelican with wings addorsed arg., vulning herself gu.

Hartopp, Cradock-, Sir Charles Edward, Bart., of Freathby, Leics.: (1) Out of a ducal coronet or, a demi-pelican with wings endorsed arg., vulning herself ppr. (*for Hartopp*). (2) An arm in armour couped at the elbow lying fesseways, the hand holding a sword erect transfixed with a boar's head couped, all ppr. (*for Cradock*).

Hartopp, Captain James Burns, Dalby Hall, Melton Mowbray: (1) Out of a ducal coronet or, a pelican issuing arg., charged on the neck with a cross crosslet sa. for distinction, vulning herself ppr. (*Hartopp*). (2) A dexter hand ppr. holding a hunting-horn.

Hartree, a stag's head erased ppr., in front of a saltire engrailed gu. *De quo bene speratur.* *cf.* 121. 2

Hartridge, Kent and Surrey, on a portcullis sa., lined and studded arg., a lion passant of the last. 5. 9

Hartridge, Gustavus, Esquire, F.R.C.S., of 12, Wimpole Street, and Marden, Kent, on a portcullis chained a lion passant. *Sorte sua contentus.*

Hartshorn, a wolf passant collared and lined, all ppr. *cf.* 28. 10

Hartshorn, a demi-wolf ppr., gorged with a collar, therefrom pendent a bugle or, and supporting a sword, point downwards, also ppr. *Fortiter in angustis.*

Hartshorne, a buck's head erased sa. 121. 2

Hartsink, a demi-lion holding between his paws a ragged staff. *cf.* 15. 1

Hartstonge and **Hartstronge,** Ireland, a fleur-de-lis or, entwined by a serpent vert. 148. 8

Hartstronge, Dublin, a demi-savage ppr., capped arg., holding in his dexter hand a sword hilted or, point downwards, and in his sinister hand a battle-axe or, the hilt ppr. *Sub libertate quietem.*

Hartwell, in a park paled or, a stag lodged arg.

Hartwell, Sir Brodrick Cecil Denham Arkwright, Bart., of Dale Hall, in Essex, on a mount vert, surrounded with seven pales, the second and fifth charged with a spear's head ppr., embrued gu., a hart lodged arg., resting the dexter foot on a well of the last, and holding in the mouth a sprig of oak vert. *Sorte suâ contentus.* 291. 15

Hartwell, on a mount vert, paled or, a hart current ppr., attired of the second.

Hartwell, Kent, Northumb., and Northamp., a beetle passant gu., with wings addorsed sa., horned arg.

Harty, Ireland, a demi-savage wreathed round the head and middle, and holding a club over his shoulder erect, all ppr. 186. 1

Harty, Sir Henry Lockington, Bart., of Prospect House, co. Dublin, Ireland, and Clarendon House, Tunbridge Wells, a falcon's head erased ppr., charged with a trefoil slipped vert, between two wings erect or, each charged with a hurt. *Malo mori quam fœdari.*

Harty of Birchington, Kent, a falcon's head erased ppr., between two wings expanded or. *cf.* 89. 1

Harvard, a bull's head cabossed. *In Deo spes est.* 43. 8

Harvey-Hawke, *see* Hawke, Baron.

Harvey, Sir Robert Grenville, Bart., of Langley Park, Bucks, a lion passant regardant ppr., resting the dexter paw upon an escutcheon arg., charged with a bat's wing sa., the lion debruised by a bendlet sinister wavy or. *Probitas verus honos.*

Harvey, Sir Charles, Bart., of Crown Point, in the parish of Trowse, Norf., out of a mural coronet or, a dexter cubit arm erect ppr., and above the hand a crescent arg., between two branches of laurel in orle, also ppr. *Alteri sic tibi.*

Harvey, John Robert, Holmwood, Thorpe, Norf., over a dexter cubit arm erect ppr., a crescent arg., between branches of laurel, also ppr. *Alteri sic tibi.*

Harvey of Chigwell, Essex, a dexter hand apaumée ppr., over it a crescent reversed arg. *Téméraire.* 222. 5

Harvey, C. B., between an oak and a laurel-branch, a dexter cubit arm erect ppr., the hand holding a trident or, on the staff thereof a flag az., and thereon the word "*Rosario*" in letters of the second.

Harvey, a cubit arm holding a trefoil ppr.

Harvey, late Sir George, President R.S.A., a dexter hand ppr., holding a trefoil slipped vert. *Delectat et ornat.*

Harvey, a cubit arm holding a trefoil slipped and erect, all ppr.

Harvey, a cubit arm holding a trefoil ppr., issuing from a crescent or.

Harvey, issuant from a crescent or, charged with a stag's head caboshed az., a cubit arm erect holding a trefoil slipped ppr. 216. 13

Harvey, Shand-, James Widdington, of Castle Semple, Renfrew, Scotland, out of a crescent or, charged with a buck's head caboshed sa., a cubit arm ppr., the hand grasping a trefoil slipped and erect vert, the arm charged with an ermine spot or. *Omnia bene.* 216. 13

Harvey, Surgeon-General Robert, c.o. Messrs. Coutts and Co., 59, Strand, W.C., a cubit arm ppr., issuing from a crescent or, charged with an eagle's head erased az., the hand holding a trefoil slipped vert. 238. 6

Harvey of London and Essex, an arm embowed vested az., holding up a garb or.

Harvey of Bargy Castle, Wexford, a dexter arm embowed in armour grasping a sword ppr., pommel and hilt or. *Semper eadem.* 195. 2

Harvey, John Bald, of Tormankin, Glendevon, Perthsh., a dexter arm in armour embowed, holding in the hand a sword, all ppr. *Garde bien.* 195. 2

Harvey, Charles Pigott, Esquire, of Sudborough House, Thrapston, and Guilsborough House Northants a demi ounce guardant or, between two trefoils and holding in the dexter paw a like trefoil, each slipped vert *Honor ab arvis* 256 7

Harvey, Hants and Yorks a leopard passant ppr cf 24 2

Harvey of Alvington Isle of Wight and Wormersley, Yorks, a leopard passant ppr, gorged with a collar engrailed gu cf 24 2

Harvey, Suff and Devonsh, a leopard passant sa bezantée, collared and lined or holding in the dexter paw a trefoil slipped vert

Harvey of London and Essex, a leopard passant arg, ducally gorged and lined or

Harvey of Audley New Barnet a leopard passant, ducally gorged and chained, and holding in the dexter paw a trefoil slipped *Deo non fortuna*

Harvey, Middx, a leopard passant arg, spotted sa, ducally collared and chained or, charged on the shoulder with a trefoil slipped vert

Harvey of London a lion passant ppr, holding a trefoil vert cf 6 2

Harvey, William Marsh Esquire, Barrister-at-Law of Goldington Hall Goldington, Beds and of the Carlton Club, a lion passant gardant ppr, holding in the dexter paw a trefoil slipped vert *Je n'oublieray jamais* 6 5

Harvey, William Francis, Esquire, of Parbrook, Hants same crest and motto

Harvey, George Miller Esquire Malin Hall Malin, co. Donegal same crest *Je n'oublierai jamais*

Harvey of Mintiagho, Innishowen co Donegal Ireland, a lion passant gardant ppr, holding in the dexter paw a trefoil slipped vert 6 5

Harvey, Ireland, a demi lion rampant sa holding in the dexter paw a crescent or cf 10 2

Harvey, Cambs and Suff a demi-leopard arg, spotted sa, holding between the paws an increscent erm

Harvey, Suff a demi leopard sa, bezante holding in the dexter paw a trefoil vert

Harvey, Beds, a leopard's head couped gardant

Harvey of Killiane Castle co Wexford Ireland a bear rampant supporting himself on a staff raguly, all ppr 34 9

Harvey, Kent two bear's paws erased and erect ermines supporting a crescent erminois 39 6

Harvey of Broadley Aberdeen, a trefoil vert *Delectat et ornat* 148 9

Harvey, Essex, Sussex Norf, and Northamp, a sheaf of trefoil vert, banded or

Harvey, Sir Robert, of Trenowth Cornw, Dundridge Devonsh and of Palace Gate, London, W. upon a mount vert a cockatrice ppr, holding in the beak three ears of wheat slipped gorged with a chain and suspended therefrom a harrow all or *Semper eadem*

Harvey, Ireland, two wings in lure ppr 113 3

Harvie, Scotland, a trefoil vert *Delectat et ornat* 148 9

Harvie, a boar[illegible] outnd neck sa 41 1

Harvie-Brown, J[illegible] arg e[illegible]xander Esquire J P F R S E out, Dunipace House Larbert N B a[illegible] on rampant holding a fleur-de lis in his dexter paw gu charged on the shoulder with a trefoil slipped or *Floreat majestas*

Harvill, a goat passant sa, armed or cf 129 5

Harvy of London, a demi-tiger sa, ducally gorged or

Harvy, Norf and Suff, a lion couchant gu 7 5

Harvy, Suff, a leopard passant arg, pellettée, collared and lined or holding in the dexter paw a trefoil slipped vert

Harvye, Somers a squirrel sejant arg, the tail or cracking a nut of the last 135 7

Harward, Surrey a demi stag erm, ducally gorged and attired gu cf 119 2

Harward, of Hayne Devonsh a leopard statant erm, collared or, in front of a cross crosslet fitchee sa, from the collar a chain or, reflexed and attached to the cross

Harwarden, Viscount, *see* De Montalt Earl

Harware of Stoke Warw out of palisadoes or a stag's head gu attired of the first and gorged with a wreath or and az cf 121 5

Harwine of London, a hatchet ppr 172 3

Harwood, out of a ducal coronet or a triple plume of twelve ostrich feathers, three four and five 114 6

Harwood, an owl arg 96 5

Harwood of Battisford Hall, upon a mount vert a wreath of oak or, thereon perched a martlet arg *Vincit pericula virtus*

Harwood, Berks and Shropsh, a stag's head caboshed gu holding in its mouth an oak-branch ppr, acorned or cf 122 5

Harwood of the Cloisters, Bath a stag's head cabossed gu, between the attires a fret arg, and on either side a palm-branch ppr *Generosus et paratus*

Harwood, Henry Harwood Penny, Esquire of Cromarty House, a stag's head caboshed gu holding in the mouth a slip of oak ppr, fructed or, and between the attires a bugle horn stringed also gu *Suaviter*

Harwood, Sir John James of Ash Villa, Northumberland Street Higher Broughton, Manchester, in front of a rock ppr a stag's head caboshed per pale arg and gu, between the attires an escutcheon of the last charged with an owl arg and pendent from a riband, also gu *Strive diligently, hope always*

Harwood of Woodhouse Glouc on a mount between two trefoils slipped a stag's head cabossed between the attires an acorn leaved all ppr

Hasard, Glouc, a bear's head and neck sa, muzzled or 34 14

Hase of Great Melton, Norf, a falcon rising erminois belled arg charged on the breast with an etoile of sixteen points of the last, in the centre thereof an ermine spot

Hase, Herts, from a bush a hare current, all ppr cf 136 3

Haselden, Lincs a talbot's head arg, charged on the neck with a mullet gu cf 56 12

Haselden, Lincs, a talbot's head arg 56 12

Haselerton, a sword in pale ensigned with a cross patee gu 169 5

Haselerton, a flag az charged with a cross arg cf 176 13

Haseley, a leopard's face or 22 2

Haselfoot or **Hassellfoot,** of Boreham Manor, Essex a demi-peacock or, with wings expanded az holding in the beak a snake ppr entwined round the neck 103 6

Haselfoot, *see* Paske-Haselfoot

Hasell, John Edward, of Dalemain Cumb a squirrel sejant cracking a nut between two oak-branches, all ppr cf 135 7

Hasellwood and Haselwood, Northamp, Oxon, and Worcs, a squirrel sejant arg collared or charged with three bezants in pale, holding a hazel branch ppr cf 135 2

Haskell, on a mount an apple-tree fructed, ppr

Haskins, Surrey a lion's head erased ppr 17 8

Haskins, two hands issuing from clouds conjoined, supporting a heart inflamed all ppr 224 5

Haslam, Ireland, a boar passant sa gorged with a laurel crown or 40 6

Haslam, Ireland, on a mount a lamb couchant in front of a hazel tree fructed all ppr

Haslam, Sir Alfred Seale of Breadsall Priory Derby an eagle rising regardant holding in the beak a hazel-leaf slipped ppr pendent from the neck by a ribbon arg, an escutcheon gu charged with a lamb statant ppr *Agnus Dei salvator meus* 77 7

Haslatine, a talbot's head couped arg 56 12

Haslefoote, two wings addorsed erm 109 12

Haslen, a squirrel sejant cracking a nut ppr, collared gemelle az between two branches of palm, also ppr *Qui nucleum vult, nucem frangat*

Haslett of Londonderry and Summerhill co Donegal Ireland, a talbot's head couped sa gorged and chained or *Semper fidelis* cf 56 12

Haslewood, *see* Hasellwood

Haslewood, Rev Frederick George LL D of Chislet Vicarage, Canterbury and Highley Shropsh a squirrel sejant az, collared or charged with three bezants in pale, holding a hazel branch ppr, fructed or *Quod me mihi reddit amicum* 296 14

Hasling, Kent an ostrich holding in its beak a broken tilting spear, all ppr cf 97 2

Hassal, Chesh an arm embowed vested or, turned down at the wrist arg, holding in the hand a dart point downwards or feathered of the second, barbed sa

Hassall and Hassell, a hand holding three arrows points downwards cf 214 3

Hassall and Hassell, out of a ducal coronet a hand holding three arrows points downwards 214 2

Hassard, an escallop or *Vive en espoir* 141 12

Hassard, Edward Hassard, of Edlington Manor, Horncastle, Lincs, an escallop or. *Sinceritas.*

Hassard, an arm in armour embowed holding in the gauntlet a crane's head and neck erased. 198. 13

Hassard of Gardenhill, an escallop or. *Vive en espoir.* 141. 12

Hassell, a dexter arm erect vested gu., cuffed arg., holding in the hand a branch of olive ppr.

Hassell, G. C., Esquire, of Newcastle-on-Tyne, and Colonel J. W. Hassell, Junior United Service Club, London, same crest. *Hæc manus ob patriam.*

Hassell, J. G. T., of Mount Cross, Bramley, Yorks, a dexter cubit arm erect vested gu., cuffed arg., holding in the hand a branch of olive ppr. *Hæc manus ob patriam.*

Hassell, Cumb., between two oak-branches a squirrel sejant cracking a nut, all ppr.

Hassellwood, a squirrel sejant az., collared or, and charged with three bezants in pale, holding a nut-branch ppr. *cf.* 135. 2

Hast, Norf., a stag's head erased gu., attired arg., ducally gorged or. *cf.* 121. 2

Hastaline, a talbot's head couped arg. 56. 12

Hastday, Kent, on a mount vert, a hare in her form ppr. 136. 12

Hasted, a wheel ppr. 167. 1

Hasted of Sunnings, Berks, on a mural coronet az., an eagle displayed erm., beaked or. *cf.* 75. 2

Hasted, same crest. *Fidem servabo.*

Hastie, Scotland, a palm-branch vert. *Pro patriâ.* 147. 1

Hastings, Lord, *see* Huntingdon, Earl of.

Hastings, Abney-, *see* Donington, Baron.

Hastings, Baron, *see* Loudoun, Earl of.

Hastings, Rawdon-, *see* Loudoun, Earl of.

Hastings, Marquess of (*extinct*) (Rawdon-Hastings): (1) A bull's head erased sa., armed and ducally gorged or (*for Hastings*). 44. 2. (2) On a mural coronet arg., a pheon sa., and issuant therefrom a laurel-branch ppr. (*for Rawdon*). *Et nos quoque tela sparsimus*

Hastings, Baron (Astley), out of a ducal coronet or, a plume of five feathers arg. *Justitiæ tenax.* 114. 13

Hastings, Ireland, a dexter arm couped and embowed holding in the hand a fireball, all ppr. 202 5

Hastings, a bull's head erased sa., attired or, gorged with a ducal coronet of the last. *In veritate victoria.* 44. 2

Hastings, Rev. John Parsons, M.A., of Martley, Worcs., a bull's head couped gu., armed or.

Hastings, a mermaid gu., her mirror and comb ppr., crined or. 184. 5

Hastings, Northamp., a demi-panther gardant ppr., supporting a lozenge or.

Haswell, William Cyril, Esquire, M.B. B.S. Durh., of the Hall, Strensall, Yorks, a talbot's head erased, gorged with a collar, charged with three ermine spots. *Fidelité.*

Haswell, John, Esquire, M.A., D.C.L., of the Esplanade, Sunderland, on a wreath of the colours, in front of a talbot's head erased gu., eared or, a fountain ppr. *Mors janua vitæ.* *cf.* 56. 2

Haswell, a talbot[illegible]rased az., collared erm. 56. 1

Hatch, issuant fro[illegible]mes a demi-leopard holding in the [illegible]ter paw a grenade fired, all ppr.

Hatch, Devonsh., a lion's face arg. 21. 12

Hatch of Sutton, Surrey, a demi-lion rampant or, holding a mound.

Hatch, William, Esquire, J.P., M.D., of Ardee Castle, Ardee, co. Louth, Ireland, a demi-lion rampant or, armed and langued gu., charged on the breast with a pile of shot ppr., and holding in his paws a staff, also ppr., thereto affixed a flag arg., charged with a cross of the second. *Fortis valore et armis.*

Hatch, John Anthony Freeman, Esquire, of Ardee Castle, Ardee, co. Louth, same crest and motto.

Hatch, a flag in bend. 176. 12

Hatch, Ireland, out of a ducal coronet a hand holding three arrows points downwards, all ppr. 214. 2

Hatcher, Lincs, an arm embowed, vested az., charged with three bars arg., holding in the hand ppr. a branch of olives vert.

Hatchet and **Hatchett,** a thunderbolt ppr. 174. 13

Hatchet, a blade of a hatchet ppr. 172. 1

Hatcliff, a lion rampant arg., guttée-de-poix. *cf.* 1. 13

Hatcliffe, Lincs, a lion passant gu., holding in the dexter paw a cutlass erect arg., hilt and pommel or. *cf.* 6. 2

Hately, Scotland, an otter's head erased sa. 134. 3

Hatfeild, Captain Charles Taddy, Hartsdown, near Margate, a dexter cubit arm erect vested sa., cuffed arg., holding in the hand ppr. a cinquefoil slipped or. *Pax.* 268. 3

Hatfield of Twickenham, Middx., an arm erect couped below the elbow, vested sa., cuffed arg., holding in the hand ppr. a cinquefoil slipped or. 268. 3

Hatfield, John Randall, of Thorp Arch, Tadcaster, Yorks: (1) A dexter cubit arm vested sa., cuffed arg., the hand ppr., holding a cinquefoil slipped or (*for Hatfield*). 268. 3. (2) Two goats' heads erased and addorsed, the dexter az., the sinister arg. (*for Gossip*). 268. 4. *Pax.*

Hatfield of Hatfield Hall, Yorks, a buffalo's head erased or. 44. 1

Hatfield of Dublin, Ireland, a talbot's head erased arg., collared or. 56. 1

Hatfield and **De Hatfield,** on the stump of a tree couped and sprouting new branches, an eagle with wings inverted and addorsed, all ppr.

Hatfield, an ostrich-feather enfiled with a ducal coronet. 114. 12

Hathaway and **Hatheway,** a demi-lion rampant gu., holding in his dexter paw a fleur-de-lis. 13. 2

Hatherell, Charles Edward Grey, Radford House, near Leamington, an antelope's head couped ppr., gorged with a collar chained or, charged with two mascles az., in the mouth a rose gu., slipped vert. *Probitas verus honos.*

Hatherton, Baron (Littleton), of Hatherton, Staffs, a stag's head cabossed sa., attired or, between the attires a bugle-horn of the first, garnished and pendent from two annulets conjoined, also or. *Ung Dieu et ung roy.*

Hathorn, Scotland, a lion rampant gu., armed and langued az., grasping a hawthorn-tree fructed, and in the dexter paw a scimitar defending the same ppr.

Hathorn, Hugh Fletcher, Castle Wigg, Whithorn, a hawthorn-tree ppr. *Stabo.*

Hathway, a leopard sejant or, collared az., resting his dexter paw on an escutcheon sa., charged with the arms.

Hatley, Bucks, Cambs, and Hunts, out of a ducal coronet an antelope's head or, attired, tufted, and maned sa., pierced through the neck by a broken spear gu.

Hatsell, Middx., on a mount vert, a viper's head erect and erased ppr., holding in the mouth a branch of rue of the last.

Hatt, Essex, Berks, and London, a falcon's head quarterly arg. and gu., between two wings sa. 89. 1

Hatton, Finch-, *see* Winchelsea, Earl of.

Hatton, a hawk close arg., holding in its beak an ear of wheat or. *cf.* 85. 2

Hatton, Shropsh.: (1) A hawk close arg., holding in his beak an ear of wheat or. *cf.* 85. 2. (2) A hind trippant or. 124. 12

Hatton, Chesh., Cambs, Shropsh., and Glouc., a hind trippant or. 124. 12

Hatton, Colonel Villiers, a hind statant or, charged with an annulet gu. *Virtus tutissima cassis.* *cf.* 125. 3

Hatton-Ellis, Joseph Alfred, Esquire, of May Bank, St. Annes-on-Sea, a demi-lion between two garbs, all or. *Fide et amore.* 295. 1

Hatton of London, a demi-bear rampant sa. 34. 13

Hatton, Ireland, a demi-griffin ppr., winged gu., holding between its claws an esquire's helmet or. *cf.* 64. 1

Hatworth, a hat sa., charged with a cinquefoil or.

Haugh, a lion rampant per fess or and az., holding in his dexter paw a fleur-de-lis gu. 2. 7

Haughton, a pelican's head and neck vulning itself ppr. *cf.* 98. 2

Haughton, Chesh., a bull's head couped arg., charged on the neck with three bars sa. *cf.* 44. 3

Haughton of London, a bull's head erased arg., armed sa. 44. 3

Haule, out of a ducal coronet gu., a triple plume of ostrich-feathers or. 114. 6

Hault, Kent, an ermine passant ducally gorged or. *cf.* 134. 6

Haultain, Canada, out of a ducal coronet a ram's head, holding in the mouth a branch of olive. *Satis imperat qui sibi est imperiosus.* *cf.* 130. 1

Haulton, a moon in her complement arg.

Haulton, two hands conjoined. 224. 2

Haulton, issuing out of clouds two hands conjoined, all ppr. 224. 1

Haunton, *see* Hautten.

Haussonville of Lorraine, a tortoise sa., between two pennons, the dexter or, the sinister az.

Hauston, Scotland, a sand-glass winged ppr. *In time.* 113. 11

Hautten and **Haunton,** Oxon., between two sprigs of thistle arg., stalked and leaved vert, an ass's head erased ppr.

Havard, Wales, a bull's head cabossed gu. 43. 8

Havelock-Allan, Sir Henry Spencer Moreton, Bart., Blackwell Hall, Darlington, Yorks: (1) A demi-lion rampant arg., ducally crowned gu., holding in the dexter paw a cross potent or, and supporting with the sinister a rudder of the second, and charged upon the shoulder for distinction with a cross crosslet (*for Allan*). 245. 11. (2) A lion rampant gu., semée of ermine-spots, and charged upon the shoulder with a castle arg., sustaining a Danish battle-axe ppr. (*for Havelock*). 245. 12. *Fortiter gerit crucem.—Fideliter.*

Havergal, Chesh., a greyhound current ensigned by an arrow in flight. *Scité citissimé certé.* *cf.* 58. 2

Haverfield, Francis John, Christchurch, Oxford, a wreath of oats ppr.

Havering, a lion rampant holding a spear sa., the flag gu. *cf.* 3. 7

Havers of London and Norf., a griffin sejant erm., ducally gorged and chained gu. *cf.* 62. 10

Havers of Thelton Hall, Norf., a griffin sejant arg., the beak and claws or, ducally gorged and lined of the last. *cf.* 62. 10

Havers of London and Norf., a griffin sejant arg., the beak and fore-legs or, ducally gorged and lined of the last. *cf.* 62. 10

Haversham, on a ducal coronet or, a mullet sa.

Haviland-Burke, Edmund, Esquire, M.P., of 70, Wellington Road, Dublin: (1) A cat sejant gardant ppr., collar and chain reflexed over the back or (*for Burke*). 26. 13. (2) Out of a coronet sa., a tower triple-towered arg., the portcullis gu. (*for Haviland*). *Vinctus sed non victus.—Dominus fortissima turris.*

Havilland or **De Havilland,** out of a coronet sa., a tower triple-towered arg., the portcullis gu. *Dominus fortissima turris.*

Havilland, John, Kinellan, Kingsley Park, Northants, same crest and motto.

Haw, a poplar-tree growing out of a mount ppr. *cf.* 144. 12

Haward, Kent, an arm vested sa., cuffed or, holding in the hand ppr. a human heart gu.

Haward, on the stump of a tree couped and eradicated ppr., a falcon with wings elevated and displayed, also ppr., belled or. *cf.* 87. 12

Hawarden of Widnes, Lancs, out of a ducal coronet or, a stag's head erm., attired of the first. 120. 7

Hawberke, a hand holding a dart ppr. 214. 4

Hawden, Scotland, a lion's head erased gu. *Ferio, tego.* 17. 2

Hawdon, Cyril Goodricke, Esquire, J.P., of Westerfield, Ashburton, New Zealand, *uses:* a lion's head erased. *Ferio, tego.* 17. 8

Hawe, Norf., a griffin's head erased erm., collared and lined or. *cf.* 66. 2

Hawes, Suff., Surrey, and London, out of a mural coronet az., a lion's head or. 19. 12

Hawes, Dorset, a greyhound's head sa., ducally gorged and lined or. *cf.* 61. 2

Hawes of London, out of a ducal coronet or, a stag's head arg., attired or. 120. 7

Hawes of London, out of a ducal coronet or, a stag's head ppr., holding in the mouth a sprig of laurel vert. *cf.* 120. 7

Hawes, a buck's head erased ppr., attired or, holding in its mouth an oak-branch vert, fructed gu. *cf.* 19. 11

Hawes, Dorset, a goat's head sa., holding in its mouth a holly-branch vert. *cf.* 128. 12

Hawk, a hawk belled ppr. *cf.* 85. 2

Hawke, Baron (Hawke), of Towton, Yorks, a hawk rising erm., beaked, belled, and charged on the breast with a fleur-de-lis or. *Strike.*

Hawke, a falcon rising ppr., charged on the breast with a fleur-de-lis or. *cf.* 87. 1

Hawke, a hawk close ppr. 85. 2

Hawkens, on a hawk's lure, a hawk statant with wings endorsed.

Hawker, a dexter hand ppr., holding a hawk's lure or. 217. 8

Hawker, Devonsh., on the stump of a tree lying in fess a hawk ppr.

Hawker, Hants, a hawk's head erased or. *Accipiter prædam, nos gloriam.* 88. 12

Hawker, P. T. R., of Longparish House, Whitchurch, same crest and motto.

Hawkes, a hind's head erased. 124. 3

Hawkes, Ireland, on a chapeau ppr., an owl with wings expanded arg. 96. 6

Hawkesbury, Baron (Foljambe), Kirkham Abbey, Yorks: (1) A seaweed rock ppr., thereon a sea-lion sejant az., resting the dexter paw on an escutcheon per fesse wavy arg. and az., in chief a cormorant sa., beaked and legged gu., holding in the beak a branch of seaweed called laver, inverted vert (*for Liverpool*), and in base a hawk, wings elevated and addorsed arg. (*for Hawkesbury*). *Démoures ferme.* 2797. (2) A man's leg unarmed, except the spur, couped at the thigh, quarterly or and sa., spurred of the first. *Bee fast.—Soyes ferme.* 279. 8

Hawkes-Cornock, John, Esquire, of Cromwellsfort, co. Wexford, Ireland: (1) A dexter cubit arm fessewise, the hand grasping a sword erect, all ppr., the arm charged with two crescents in fess az. (*for Cornock*). (2) On a branch of oak lying fesswise a hawk rising, all ppr., jessed and belled or, with the motto over, "*Virtute non vi*" (*for Hawkes*). *Animo et fide.*

Hawkesford, a griffin passant sa. 63. 2

Hawkesworth and **Hawksworth,** a sinister hand in fess, issuing from a cloud in the dexter, and reaching to a serpent ppr. 223. 8

Hawkesworth, Thomas, Esquire, M.B., Royal Societies Club, London, a hawk close belled ppr. *Moveo et proficior.*

Hawkewood, a hawk's head or. *cf.* 88. 12

Hawkeworth, a cubit arm erect vested or, cuffed arg., holding in the hand ppr. a cross crosslet gu.

Hawkey, a hand couped holding a curling-stone. 221. 2

Hawkings, a lion's gamb gu., charged with a chevron or. *cf.* 39. 2

Hawkins, Scotland, a falcon jessed and belled ppr. *Providence with adventure.* *cf.* 85. 2

Hawkins of Rathfriland, co. Down, Ireland, a falcon rising ppr., belled or, and perched on a lure of the last. *Providence with adventure.*

Hawkins of Hawkesnest, Warw., a dexter arm couped at the shoulder fesseways and erect from the elbow habited vair, holding in the hand ppr. a falcon perched arg., beaked, legged, and belled or.

Hawkins, Shropsh., a falcon's head chequy arg. and sa., beaked or, between two wings expanded, the dexter or, the sinister gu. 80. 1

Hawkins, Heref. and Glouc., a falcon's head chequy arg. and sa., beaked or, between two wings gu. 89. 1

Hawkins, Berks, a demi-eagle arg. 80. 2

Hawkins, Ireland, out of a naval coronet an antelope's head, all ppr. 127. 6

Hawkins, Monm., on a mount vert, a hind lodged or. *Toujours prêt.* 125. 4

Hawkins, Rev. Sir John Cæsar, Bart., M.A., of Kelston, Somers., same crest. *Pro Deo et Rege.*

Hawkins, Devonsh., a demi-Moor manacled ppr., with annulets on the arms and in the ears or. *Nil desperandum.*

Hawkins of Lewell, Dorset, a demi-naked man ppr., wreathed about the temples arg. and az., the hands extended and manacled at each arm with a rope passing behind his back, also ppr.

Hawkins, Cornw., a cubit arm erect, vested arg., charged with two fleurs-de-lis az., holding in the hand ppr. a baton or, tipped sa.

Hawkins, Christopher Henry Thomas, Trewithen, Probus, R.S.O., Corow., same crest.

Hawks, in the sea a column ppr. 176. 3

Hawkshaw, a hawk's head. *cf.* 88. 12

Hawkshaw, late Sir John, F.R.S., J.P., issuant from the battlements of a tower sa., a hawk's head or, gorged with a collar gemelle, also sa. *My lure is truth.* 89. 3

Hawkshaw, Rev. William, Rector of Fermonamorghan, a hawk's head erased ppr., gorged with a ducal coronet or. *Perseverance.* *cf.* 88. 12

Hawkshaw, Rev. Edward Burdett, of Weston, Ross-sh., same crest and motto.

Hawksley, a falcon with wings addorsed. 88. 2

Hawksley, Bourchier Francis, Esquire, of 14, Hyde Park Gardens, London, W., upon a perch a hawk regardant holding in the beak an ear of wheat, slipped or, between two ostrich-feathers. *Vigilant.*

Hawksley, Randall Plunkett Taylor, Esquire, of Caldy Island, Tenby, Pembrokesh., upon three mascles interlaced fessewise az., a hawk ppr., collared of the first. *Garde l'honneur.* 86. 1

Hawksmore, Notts, a hawk preying on a moorhen, all ppr. *cf.* 77. 12

Hawksworth, a hawk rising. 88. 2

Hawksworth, a hand issuing out of a cloud, and reaching to a serpent ppr. 223. 8

Hawle, out of a ducal coronet or, a mullet gu., between two laurel-branches in orle vert. 146. 7

Hawles, Hants, a greyhound's head sa., ducally gorged, ringed and lined or. cf. 61. 2

Hawley of West Green House, Hants, a winged thunderbolt ppr. *Et suivez moy.* 174. 13

Hawley, Hants, a thunderbolt ppr. 174. 13

Hawley, on a ducal coronet an étoile of sixteen points or. cf. 164. 4

Hawley, a falcon with wings addorsed ppr. 88. 2

Hawley, an Indian goat's head holding in the mouth a three-leaved sprig of holly, all ppr. *Suivez moi.*

Hawley, Sir Henry Michael, Bart., of Leybourne Grange, Kent, *uses:* a dexter arm in armour ppr., garnished or, holding in the hand a spear in bend sinister, point downwards, also ppr. 210. 11

Hawleys, *an arm embowed throwing a dart ppr.* 201. 14

Hawling, an arm embowed ppr. holding a scimitar arg., pommel or. 201. 1

Haworth-Booth, *see* Booth.

Haworth, a wolf passant collared, holding in his dexter paw a trefoil.

Haworth of Churchdale Hall, Derbysh., a stag's head couped, gorged with lozenges in fess. *Quod ero spero.* 122. 6

Haworth of Haworth, Lancs, a stag's head couped gu., attired or, around the neck two twisted cords arg. cf. 121. 5

Haws and **Hawse,** a sphinx statant with wings expanded. cf. 182. 12

Hawtayne of the Ley, Oxon., an ass's head erased or, between two sprigs of thistles arg., stalked and leaved vert

Hawte, a dragon's head and wings per pale or and gu., charged on the breast with a cinquefoil. cf. 72. 7

Hawthorn or **Hawthorne,** a demi-antelope ppr., collared gu. 126. 3

Hawthorn, Scotland, a hand holding a star of six points. cf. 216. 12

Hawthorn of Castlewig, Wigtown, a hawthorn-tree ppr. *Stabo.*

Hawtin, John Nelms, L.R.C.P., etc., of Sturdie House, Roundhay Road, Leeds, Yorks, an ass's head erased between two sprigs of thistles arg., sprigged and leaved vert. *Honor virtutis prœmium.* 290. 14

Hawton of London, a bull's head erased arg., armed sa. 44. 3

Hawtre, Middx., a lion's head erased or, fretty sa. 17. 8

Haxford, a lion rampant sustaining an arrow point downwards. 2. 4

Haxton, Scotland, a decrescent. *Resurgo.* 163. 1

Hay, Marquess of Tweeddale, *see* Tweeddale.

Hay, Earl of Errol, *see* Errol.

Hay, Earl of Kinnoul and **Baron Hay,** *see* Kinnoul.

Hay, *see* Paterson-Balfour-Hay.

Hay, *see* Baird-Hay.

Hay, Robert Mordaunt, of Dunse Castle, Berwick, a goat's head erased arg. *Spare nought.* 128. 5

Hay, Scotland, a goat's head erased or, armed arg. 128. 5

Hay of Mordington, a goat's head erased arg., armed or. *Spare nought.* 128. 5

Hay of Spott, same crest and motto. 128. 5

Hay of Linplum, a goat's head erased arg., armed or, and charged with a crescent az. *Malum bono vince.—Spare nought.* cf. 128. 5

Hay of Drumelzier, a goat's head erased arg., armed or. *Spare nought.* 128. 5

Hay of Newhall, a goat's head and neck erased arg., charged with a crescent. *Spare nought.* cf. 128. 5

Hay, Sir Hector Maclean, Bart., of Alderston, Haddington, Scotland, a goat's head erased arg., armed or. *Spare nought.* 128. 5

Hay of Laxfirth, Scotland, a goat's head arg., armed or, charged on the neck with a mullet az. *Malum bono vincitur.* cf. 128. 12

Hay of Rannes, a goat passant arg., armed and ungu. or. *Spare nought.* cf. 129. 5

Hay of Letham, an ox-yoke entwined with laurel and olive ppr. *Fert laurea fides.*

Hay of Faichfield and Cocklaw, Scotland, as recorded for Charles Hay, Lord Newton, a Judge of the Court of Session, a goat passant arg., armed and unguled or. *Spare nought.* cf. 129. 5

Hay of London, an ox-yoke in bend or. *Pro patriâ.* 178. 6

Hay of Cardenie, an ox-yoke in pale with bows gu. *Hinc honor et opes.* cf. 178. 6

Hay, Scotland, the yoke of a plough in pale with two bows gu. *Serva jugum sub jugo.* cf. 178. 6

Hay, Sir David, Physician (1692), an ox-yoke with a serpent entwined around it, all ppr. *Fortius dum juncta.*

Hay of Strowie, Perthsh., Scotland, an ox-yoke in pale gu., ensigned with a crescent arg. *Cresco sub jugo.*

Hay of Lochloy, Elgin, Scotland, an ox-yoke erected in pale or, with bows gu. *Serva jugum.* cf. 178. 6

Hay of London, a dexter hand holding an ox-yoke ppr., with bows gu. *Valet et vulnerat.* 217. 6

Hay of Woodcockdale, a demi-man ppr., holding an ox-yoke or, with bows gu. *Hinc incrementum.* 217. 6

Hay of Ranfield, a dexter arm embowed holding in the hand an ox-yoke ppr. 202. 9

Hay, Scotland, a demi-arm holding aloft an ox-yoke ppr. *Hoc vince.* 217. 6

Hay, Scotland, an arm from the elbow holding an ox-yoke with bows gu. *Laboranti palma.* 217. 6

Hay of Königsberg, two arms from the shoulder embowed, vested in russet, grasping an ox-yoke or, the bows gu. *Pro patriâ.*

Hay of Newhall and Pitfour, Scotland, a naked arm in pale, holding three stalks of wheat ppr., between the hand and the wheat-ears an ox-yoke in fess gu. *Diligentia fit ubertas.*

Hay of Balhousie, a demi-man vested, holding a blue cap on his head, and holding over his shoulder the yoke of a plough gu. *Renovato animo.* 187. 14

Hay, Rev. Frederick Drummond, M.A., of Lyncombe Lodge, Bath, an aged Lowland Scots country-man couped at the knees, vested in gray, waistcoat gu., bonnet az., bearing on his shoulder an ox-yoke ppr. *Renovate animos.*

Hay of Seggieden, Perthsh., a demi-husbandman ppr., holding over his shoulder an ox-yoke or, bows gu. *Diligentia fit ubertas.* 187. 14

Hay, Scotland, an ox's head couped ppr. *Nec abest jugum.* cf. 44. 3

Hay, Scotland, a plough ppr. *Nil desperandum.* 178. 7

Hay, Ireland, a dexter hand holding an olive-branch ppr. 219. 9

Hay, a hand ppr., holding an annulet or. 216. 1

Hay, the sun in his splendour ppr. 162. 2

Hay, Ireland, a falcon ppr. 85. 2

Hay, Scotland, a falcon perched on the stump of a tree, sprouting a branch before and behind in orle ppr. *Speravi in Domino.*

Hay, Scotland, a falcon volant ppr., armed, jessed, and belled or, gorged with a label. *Propter obedientiam.*

Hay, a falcon rising ppr. 87. 1

Hay, Sir Arthur Graham, Bart., of Park, Wigtownsh., Scotland, *uses:* a falcon displayed ppr. *Serva jugum.*

Hay, Dalrymple-, Admiral the Rt. Hon. Sir John Charles Bart., P.C., K.C.B., F.R.S., D.C.L., Craigenveoch, Glenluce, N.B.: (1) A hawk ppr., charged on the breast with an escutcheon gu. (*for Hay*). 85. 3. (2) A rock ppr. (*for Dalrymple*). *Serva jugum.—Firm.* 179. 7

Hay of Tacumshane and Ballinkeele, co. Wexford, and Hay of St. Malo, a falcon arg., the wings expanded ppr., belled or. *Serva jugum.* 87. 1

Hay, Scotland, a dove with wings expanded ppr. *Serva jugum.* 94. 2

Hay-Gordon, James Robert, Esquire: (1) A stag's head cabossed within two branches of laurel conjoined at the top, all ppr. (*for Gordon*). (2) A goat trippant ppr. (*for Hay*). *Byde together.* *Spare nought.* cf. 122. 5

Hay, Scotland, a buck's head cabossed ppr. *Venter and gain.* 122. 5

Hay-Newton, William Drummond Ogilvy of Newton, Haddingtonsh., Scotland, a demi-lion rampant or, brandishing a scimitar ppr., hilted and pommelled of the first. *Pro patria.* 14. 10

Hay, Macdougal-, Bart., of Mackerston, a lion passant gardant ppr., holding in the dexter paw a cross crosslet fitched gu. *Dread God.* cf. 4. 3

Hay, Scotland, an increscent ppr. *Donec impleat orbem.* 163. 3

Haycock, on a ducal coronet per pale gu. and or, a lion passant per pale counterchanged. 6. 6

Haycock, Henry Edward, Esquire, of Ironville House, Alfreton, Derbysh., same crest. *Fortior leone justus.* 290. 9

Haydock of Banyton, Oxon., a swan rising arg., beaked or, ducally gorged and lined gu.

Haydock, Haidocke, and **Heydock** of Greywell, Hants, a demi-swan with wings expanded arg., ducally gorged, lined and beaked gu.

Haydon, a mastiff ppr.

Haydon, Norf., a talbot arg., spotted sa. cf. 54. 2

Haydon of Grove, Watford, and Oxley, Herts, a talbot statant az. cf. 54. 2

Haydon of Bowood, Epford, and Cadhay, Devonsh., a lion arg., seizing on a bull courant sa.

Haydon or **Haidon** of London, a lion arg., seizing on a bull courant sa. *Ferme en foy.*

Haye, a dexter arm embowed, vested gu., turned up and indented arg., holding in the hand ppr. a scythe in bend or, the blade arching to the dexter.

Hayes, a falcon with wings addorsed ppr. 88. 2

Hayes of Great Badgebury, Kent, a falcon volant ppr., jessed and belled or, gorged with a ducal coronet per pale of the last and gu.

Hayes, Bart. (*extinct*), on a perch ppr., a falcon with wings addorsed or, pendent from the beak an escutcheon gu., charged with a leopard's face or. *Nil desperandum.*

Hayes of London, a fox passant erminois. 32. 1

Hayes, Herts, a leopard's head sa. 22. 10

Hayes, William, Esquire, B.A., of Gloucester House, Highgate, London, N., a leopard's head couped.

Hayes of Nowton and Kettleburgh, Suff., a demi-leopard rampant regardant ppr., collared and chained or, supporting an escutcheon gu.

Hayes, a demi-lion rampant or, holding in the paws a flagstaff or, the pennon arg. *cf.* 15. 2

Hayes, Henry, Esquire, of Stratford, Rathgar, co. Dublin, a demi-lion rampant or, holding in his paws a flagstaff, therefrom a pennon gu., and charged upon the shoulder with a pheon sa. *Renovate animos.* *cf.* 15. 2

Hayes, Sir Samuel Hercules, Bart., of Drumboe Castle, co. Donegal, Ireland, a griffin's head erased between two dragon's wings sa. *Dieu me conduise.* *cf.* 65. 11

Hayhurst, *see* France-Hayhurst.

Hayles, a demi-lion holding a pheon arg., staff or.

Hayles, a hand upholding a torteau.

Hayley of Cleobury Mortimer, Shropsh., a crescent arg., charged with a cross patée gu. *cf.* 163. 2

Hayman, a scimitar and a caduceus in saltier, ensigned with a round hat. *cf.* 171. 1

Hayman, Ireland, a demi-lion rampant sa., holding in the dexter paw a fleur-de-lis. *Virtute non sanguine.* 13. 2

Hayman of Myrtle Grove and South Abbey, Youghal, co. Cork: (1) A demi-Moor affrontée, wreathed round the temples, holding in the dexter hand a rose slipped and leaved, all ppr. (2) A martlet sa. *Cœlum non solum.* 95. 5

Hayne of Gryer Waddon, Dorset, on a tortoise arg., an eagle displayed or. 74. 12

Hayne, Devonsh., a tortoise arg., thereon an eagle displayed ppr., charged on each wing with a plate and on the breast with a rose arg. *cf.* 74. 12

Hayne of Gloucester Square, Hyde Park, London, on a tortoise ppr., an eagle displayed bendy of six sa. and arg., holding in the beak a rose, also arg., slipped ppr. *Labore et honore.* *cf.* 74. 12

Haynes, a stork rising.

Haynes of Thimbleby Lodge, Northallerton, Yorks, a stork with wings displayed ppr., holding in the beak a snake of the last.

Haynes, an eagle preying on a tortoise, all ppr. 79. 8

Haynes, Stanley, M.D., of Malvern, an eagle with wings addorsed and inverted preying on a tortoise. *Semper paratus.*

Haynes, an eagle displayed az., semée of estoiles or. *cf.* 75. 2

Haynes, a demi-hind arg.

Haynes, three Moors' heads conjoined in one neck, facing dexter, sinister, and upwards. 191. 5

Haynes, Ireland, a lion sejant or, collared az. *cf.* 7. 4

Hays, a monkey passant ppr., collared round the loins and chained or. *cf.* 136. 8

Hays of Dallamore, Devonsh., a swan's head ppr.

Hays, a hawk with wings displayed erminois.

Hayter of Salisbury, a bull's head couped or, pierced through the neck with a broken spear arg.

Hayter, Rt. Hon. Sir Arthur Divett, Bart., of Southill Park, Berks; Trevena, Tintagel, Cornw.; and Linslade Manor, Leighton, Bucks, a bull's head erased sa., *semée* of escallops or, and pierced through the neck with a broken spear in bend sinister point upwards ppr. *Via vi.* 273. 6

Hayter, Henry Heylyn, Esquire, C.M.G., of Winterbourne, Malvern Road, Armadale, near Melbourne, Victoria, Government Statist of Victoria, a bull's head erased sa., semée of escallops or, and pierced through the neck with a broken spear in bend sinister point upwards ppr. *Via vi.* 273. 6

Hayter-Hames, Captain Colvile George Hayter, Chagford House, Newton Abbot: (1) On a ducal coronet, a lion passant (*for Hames*). (2) A bull's head couped pierced through the neck with an arrow in bend.

Hayton, Heref., a cock gu., combed, wattled, and legged or, holding in the beak a heart's-ease slipped ppr. *cf.* 91. 5

Hayton, a hand holding a sickle. 219. 13

Hayward, John Frederick Curtis, of Quedgeley House, Glouc., out of a mural coronet or, a demi-lion rampant sa., holding in the dexter paw a fleur-de-lis gold. *cf.* 13. 2

Hayward of Dewes Grove, Sandhurst, Glouc., out of a mural coronet or, a demi-lion rampant sa., charged on the shoulder with a rose, and holding in the dexter paw a rose of the second barbed and seeded ppr.

Hayward, Shropsh., a lion passant ducally crowned. *cf.* 6. 9

Hayward of Acton Round, Shropsh., two cross crosslets fitchée or, saltireways, enfiled with a bull's head caboshed sa.

Hayward, Surrey, a talbot's head arg., collared and ringed of the first. *cf.* 56. 1

Hayward, Rev. Samuel Curling, Timahoe Rectory, Stradbally, Queen's Co., a talbot's head couped arg., collared and ringed sa. *I byde my tyme.* 307. 2

Haywood, a tiger's head arg., armed and maned or, pierced through the neck with a broken spear sa., headed of the first, vulned gu.

Haywood, Staffs, in front of the stump of a tree, thereon a hawk rising ppr., charged on the breast with a pellet, three trefoils slipped vert. *cf.* 87. 12

Haywood, on the stump of a tree a falcon rising ppr. 87. 12

Hazard, Rowland, Esquire, of Oakwoods, in Peace Dale, Rhode Island, U.S.A., and Rowland Gibson Hazard of the Acorns, Peace Dale, Rhode Island, *use* an escallop. *Sinceritas.* 141. 14

Hazard, on an anchor in the sea a dove holding in the beak an olive-branch, all ppr. 94. 4

Hazel, James, Esquire, J.P., Commander R.N., Rowstock, Steventon, Berks, a squirrel sejant between two oak-branches ppr. *Nec myrtus vincet corylos.*

Hazel, a dexter arm vested holding in the hand an olive-slip.

Hazledine, Shropsh., a lion rampant or, charged on the breast with a cross flory sa., holding in his paws a shield arg., charged with the planet Mars sa. *Per juga, per fluvios.*

Hazlerigg, Sir Arthur Grey, Bart., of Noseley Hall, Leics., on a chapeau gu., turned up erm., a man's head ppr. *Pro aris et focis.*

Hazlewood, of Belton, Rutl., a squirrel sejant az., bezantée, cracking a nut *cf.* 135. 7

Hazlewood, a hand holding a bunch of grapes ppr 219. 6

Heacock of Newington, Middx., a hind sejant regardant erminois, collared gu., resting the dexter foot on a bee-hive or. *cf.* 125. 1

Head, a unicorn's head arg. 49. 7

Head, Charles Arthur, Esquire, of Hartburn Hall, Stockton-on-Tees, a unicorn's head couped ermines. *Study quiet.*

Head, Berks and London, a unicorn's head erased arg. 49. 5

Head of Grange Road, West Hartlepool, a unicorn's head erased. *Study quiet.* 49. 5

Head, Sir Robert Garnett, Bart., 2, Sussex Place Hyde Park, W., out of an Eastern crown or, three ostrich-feathers arg. *Study quiet.*

Head, James, Esquire, of Inverailort, Loch Ailort, Inverness-sh., and 40, Lowndes Square, W., same crest and motto.

Head (late Cameron), James, of Inverailort, Inverness-sh., same crest and motto.

Headfort, Marquess of (Taylour), a naked arm embowed holding in the hand an arrow fesseways, all ppr. *Consequitur quodcunque petit.*

Headlam of Kexby, Yorks, a demi-griffin segreant holding a spear, all arg. *cf.* 64. 2

Headlam, Francis John, Esquire, J.P., M.A., Barrister, Stipendiary Magistrate for Manchester, of Chelford, Crewe, a unicorn's head erased. *Innocentia et intellectu.*

Headlam, Charles, Esquire, J.P., of Egleston, Macquarie River, Ross, Tasmania, a unicorn's head erased arg., armed and crined or. *Intellectu et innocentia.* 49. 5

Headley, *see* Balls-Headley.

Headley, Baron (Winn), Aghadoe House, Killarney: (1) A demi-eagle displayed or, ducally gorged erm. (*for Winn*). (2) On a mount vert, a demi-lion rampant gardant or, holding between the paws a cross gu. (*for Allanson*). *Virtute et labore.*

Headley, London, on the stump of a tree a falcon all ppr. *Celere et vigilans.*

Headley, Hunts, a martlet or. 95. 2

Headley, on a sphere a martlet with wings expanded.

Headon, Herts and Lincs, a talbot passant or, spotted sa. 54. 1

Heald, a sword and a key in saltier ppr. 171. 10

Heald of Parr's Wood, Didsbury, Lancs, on a mount vert, a bundle of arrows fesseways, the points towards the dexter ppr., bound gu., thereon an eagle with wings elevated erminois, holding in the beak a sprig of oak, also ppr., the dexter claw resting on a cross patée gu. *Mea gloria crux.* 76. 12

Healey and **Healy,** on a chapeau gu., turned up erm., a lion statant gardant ppr., ducally gorged or. 4. 7

Healy, Ireland, a hand couped at the wrist holding a buck's attire.

Healy, Ireland, a physician's quadrangular cap. 180. 7

Heap, John, Esquire, of Nabbs House, Bury, Lancs, a demi-stag regardant ppr., gorged with a collar gemelle sa., resting the sinister fore-foot on an escutcheon gu., charged with a boar's head erased or. *Nihil sine labore.* 119. 13

Heap, Harold S., M.B., Ch.B., of Crofton House, Hathershaw, Oldham, a cross crosslet fitchée gu., between two palm-branches in orle vert. *Ad finem fidelis.*

Heaps, a cross crosslet fitched, between two branches of palm in orle ppr.

Heard of Manchester, a swan with wings expanded ppr. *Recte et sapienter.*

Heard, Somers., a swan with wings elevated arg., beaked and membered sa., charged on the breast with a rose gu., barbed and seeded ppr., ducally crowned, collared, and chained or. *Naufragus in portum.* 99. 6

Heard, Samuel Thomas, Esquire, J.P., of Rossdohan, Tahilla, co. Kerry, a demi-antelope ppr., ducally gorged or, and charged on the shoulder with a water-bouget sa. *Audior.* 265. 13

Heard, Francis George, L.R.C.P., L.R.C.S., L.F.P., L.F.S.Glas., L.M.Rotunda, of Denton Well, Eccleshill, Bradford, Yorks, a demi-goat salient, gorged with a ducal coronet. *Toujours fidèle.*

Heard, a demi-antelope collared. 126. 3

Hearing of Eye, Suff., a griffin segreant with wings expanded ducally gorged. cf. 62. 2

Hearle, a hand holding a crosier in bend sinister. 219. 4

Hearn and **Hearne,** on a mount vert, a horse at full speed, saddled and bridled ppr. 52. 10

Hearn, Ireland, a greyhound sejant sa. 59. 4

Hearn, William Edward Le Fanu, Esquire, M.D., of Hamilton, Victoria, Australia, on a mount vert a heron arg. *Ardua petit ardea.* 271. 12

Hearn, Rev. Robert Thomas, LL.D., of Youghal, co. Cork, on a mount vert, a heron arg. *Ardua petit ardea.* 271. 12

Hearn, Charles Richard Mont Orgueil, Esquire, J.P., of Templenew, Belleek, co. Fermanagh, and of Caledon, co. Tyrone, same crest and motto. 271. 12

Hearne of London and Maidenhead, Berks, a heron's head ducally gorged, all ppr. *Leges juraque servat.*

Hearne, Ireland, a rose-branch and a spear in saltier ppr. 150. 1

Heart, a leopard passant gardant and spotted ppr. 24. 4

Heart, out of a ducal coronet or, a demi-lion arg., holding in the dexter paw a heart gu. cf. 16. 3

Heart, Scotland, a dexter hand erect grasping a couteau sword. *Fide et amore.* 213. 5

Heath of Brasted, Kent, and of Lyndsfield and Tanridge, Surrey, a wolf's head erased per pale sa. and or, ducally gorged arg., holding in the mouth a broken spear of the second, headed of the third.

Heath of Shelwell, Oxon., a tower arg., flammant ppr. 155. 9

Heath, a parrot's head erased holding in the beak a mullet of five points. 101. 12

Heath, a cock's head sa., crested and jelloped gu., between two branches vert.

Heath of Little Eden, Durh., of Twickenham, Middx., and Lynn, Norf., a cock's head erased or, wattled and combed gu. 90. 1

Heath of Kepyer, Durh., a heathcock's head erased sa., wattled gu. *Espère mieux.*

Heath, George Poynter, Esquire, of Hanworth, Brisbane, Queensland, and 10, Barkston Gardens, South Kensington, W., a heathcock's head erased sa., combed and wattled gu., holding in the beak a mullet pierced or. *Franc et loyal.*

Heath of Tidderington, Chesh., a heathcock holding in the beak a branch of heath, all ppr.

Heath, Robert, Esquire, J.P., of Biddulph Grange, Congleton, and Greenway Park, Stoke-on-Trent, upon the battlements of a tower gu., a heathcock ppr., resting the dexter claw on a pheon sa. *Industriæ præmium.*

Heath, Arthur Howard, Esquire, of Newbold Revel, Rugby, same crest and motto.

Heath, James, Esquire, of Ashorne Hall, Leamington, same crest and motto.

Heath, Middx., a pheasant ppr. cf. 90. 10

Heathcote-Hacker, see Hacker.

Heathcote, Rev. Sir William Arthur, Bart., on a mural crown az., a pomeis charged with a cross or, between two wings displayed erm.

Heathcote of Chesterfield, Derbysh., of Normanton, Rutl., of Stamford, Lincs., of Durdans, Epsom, Surrey, of Hursley Park, Hants, of Brampton and Cutthorp, Derbysh., of Conington Castle, Hunts, of Longton Hall and of Apedale Hall, Staffs, all, same crest.

Heathcote, Colonel Charles George, of Beechwood, Totten, Southampton, same crest. *Deus prosperat justos.*

Heathcote, John Moyer, Esquire, of Conington Castle, Peterborough, same crest.

Heathcote, Justinian Heathcote Edward, Apedale Hall, Staffs, same crest.

Heathcoat-Amory, Major Sir John Heathcoat, Bart., J.P., D.L., of Knightshayes Court, Devonsh.: (1) The battlements of a tower or, therefrom issuant a talbot's head az., charged with two annulets fessewise and interlaced of the first (*for Amory*). 56. 11. (2) Upon a mount vert, between two roses springing from the same gu., stalked and leaved ppr., a pomeis charged with a cross or (*for Heathcoat*). *Amore non vi.* 150. 6

Heather, a lion's gamb sa., holding up a heart gu. 39. 11

Heathfield, Devonsh., a greyhound's head arg., collared gu. 61. 2

Heathfield, an arm embowed ppr., vested vert, and cuffed arg., holding in the hand a sword, also ppr. 204. 1

Heathfield, a garb or, banded gu. 153. 2

Heathorn of Charlton Park, Glouc., on a mount vert, a hawthorn-tree ppr., pendent therefrom by a ribbon gu., an escutcheon az., charged with a pigeon's head erased or.

Heatley, see Firth-Heatley.

Heaton of Mount Heaton, King's Co., Ireland, a lion ducally crowned, plain collared and chained, all ppr.

Heaton - Armstrong, William Charles, Esquire, of 30, Portland Place, W., and Roscrea, Ireland: (1) A dexter arm vambraced and embowed ppr., and a hand grasping an armed leg couped at the thigh and bleeding, also ppr. (*for Armstrong*). (2) A lion ducally crowned, plain collared and chained, all ppr. (*for Heaton*). *Vi et armis.*

Heaton, Colonel Wilfred, of Plas Heaton, Denbighsh., a buck's head arg. *Er cordiad y cœra.* 121. 5

Heaton, a buck's head cabossed arg. 122. 5

Heaton, a nag's head erased arg. 51. 4

Heaven, a boar's head or. *Non omnis moriar.* 43. 1

Heaven, Joseph Robert, Esquire, of 24, Grosvenor Square, and the Forest of Birse, Aboyne, Aberdeen, a boar's head couped or, semée of cross crosslets az. *Non omnis moriar.* 265. 12

Heaven, Rev. Hudson Grosett, of Lundy Island, Tristow, North Devonsh.: (1) A boar's head couped ppr., langued gu., tusked or (*for Heaven*). 43. 1. (2) Two arms holding a double-handed sword, all ppr. *Pro patria auxilio Dei.* 213. 3

Heaven, John Cookesley, Esquire, L.R.C.P., M.R.C.S., L.S.A., D.P.H.Lond., a boar's head couped. *Non omnes moriar.*

Heaviside of Terenure, co. Dublin, a Saracen's head affrontée, couped at the shoulders ppr., and charged on the breast with a trefoil slipped or. *Virtute et industria.* cf. 190. 5

Hebbes, Scotland, a lion's head or, charged on the neck with three roses sa. cf. 21. 1

Hebbs of Corton, Dorset, a lion's head erased or, gorged with a chaplet of roses gu. cf. 17. 8

Hebden of Hebden, Yorks, a Triton holding in his dexter hand a trident, all ppr. *cf.* 185. 12
Hebden, from out of a cave a lion passant ppr.
Hebden of Easthope Park and Appleton, Yorks, a demi-lion rampant az., supporting between the paws a crescent or. *Re e merito.* *cf.* 10. 2
Hebdon, Oxon., out of a ducal coronet or, a leopard's face between two wings az.
Heber, a lion's gamb holding a palm-branch, all ppr. 36. 7
Heber of Marton, Yorks, out of a five-leaved ducal coronet or, a female head and shoulders in profile ppr., heir dishevelled, also or.
Heber - Percy, Algernon, Esquire, of Hodnet Hall, Shropsh., and of Airmyn Hall, Yorks: (1) On a chapeau gu., turned up erm., a lion statant az., tail extended (*for Percy*). 289. 8 (2) Out of a ducal coronet or, a lady's head and shoulders in profile ppr., hair dishevelled or (*for Heber*). 289. 7 *Esperance en Dieu.—Prêt d'accomplir. Badge,* a crescent and fetterlock. 295. 15
Heberden, Charles Buller, Esquire, M.A., of Brasenose College, Oxford, same crest. *Fortunæ sapientia victrix.*
Heberden, William Buller, Esquire, C.B., of Elmfield, Exeter, same crest and motto.
Hebert, a fish naiant ppr. 139. 12
Heblethwayte of Sedbergh and Malton, Yorks, out of a ducal coronet or, a demi-wolf rampant ermines. *cf.* 31. 2
Heborne, Chesh., a round buckle or, the point of the tongue in chief.
Hechins of Hole, Cornw., a lion's head or, issuing from the centre of a rose gu., barbed vert. *cf.* 19. 9
Hector, out of a mural coronet arg., masoned sa., a demi-lion az., holding in his dexter paw a palm-branch vert. 16. 11
Hedderwick of Piteullo, Fifesh., Scotland, a dexter cubit arm, the hand holding an escroll by one end ppr. *Ne timeas recte faciendo.*
Heddle, a leopard's head erased. *Virtute et labore.* 23. 10
Heddle of Melsetter, Orkney, same crest and motto. 23. 10
Hede of Kent and London, an escallop or, between two branches vert. 141. 4
Hedges-White, Earl of Bantry, *see* Bantry.
Hedges, a pomegranate or, stalked and leaved vert. 152. 4
Hedges of London, a swan's head erased ppr. *cf.* 101. 5
Hedges, Charles Edward, Esquire, M.A., M.D., of Fairlight, Mayfield, Sussex, a swan's head and neck erased ppr. *Semper fidelis.*
Hedley, Hunts, a martlet or. 95. 2
Hedworth of Harraton, Durh., a female's head affrontée, couped at the breasts ppr., the hair flowing or, wreathed about the temples with a garland of cinquefoils gu., pierced or.
Hedworth, Durh., in front of an oak-tree ppr., a lion couchant sa.
Heegnie, Scotland, a dove seated on a rock holding in the beak a twig of olive ppr. *Firmé dum fidé.*
Heelas, Walter W., Esquire, M.R.C.S., L.R.C.P., of 8, Tettenhall Road, Wolverhampton, a leg in armour couped at the thigh ppr., spurred or.
Heeley and **Heely,** a dexter hand brandishing a scimitar ppr. 213. 5
Heely, a cockatrice wattled. *Res non verbum.* 68. 4
Heffer of London, a gauntlet holding a sword. *Ut sanem vulnero.* 211. 4
Hefferman, Ireland, a gauntlet holding a broken sword.
Heigham, an escallop-shell or, charged with a mullet gu. 141. 6
Heigham, Clement John Malcolm, Esquire, of Hunston Hall, Suff., a horse's head erased arg. 51. 4
Heigham, Rev. Arthur Linzel, of Matlock House, Torquay, same crest.
Heighington, Durh., a demi-wolf erased erminois, supporting between the paws a cross crosslet fitched az.
Heighington, Durh., a demi-boar erased erm., holding a cross crosslet fitched.
Heilyn, Shropsh., *see* Heylin.
Heingrave, a dragon's head erased gu., collared or. 71. 2
Heisham, a lion rampant wielding in his dexter paw a battle-axe, all ppr.
Heiton, Lancs, out of a ducal coronet or, a bull's head arg., armed of the first. 44. 11
Helard, a demi-Hercules ppr.
Helbert of Gloucester Place, Portman Square, London, W., a mount vert, thereon a stag trippant ppr., holding in the mouth a rose gu., slipped of the first, the dexter fore-foot resting on an escutcheon gu., charged with three arrows, one in pale and two in saltire, the pheons downwards, also ppr. 117. 12
Helborne, Durh., a fiend's head couped ppr., winged or.
Hele of Hele, Devonsh., on a chapeau gu., turned up erm., an eagle close or. 76. 4
Hele or **Heale** of Bovey Tracey, Devonsh., on a chapeau gu., turned up erm., an eagle with wings expanded or. 77. 14
Heley, an arm in armour holding a broken spear ppr. *cf.* 210. 9
Helias, a leg in armour couped at the thigh ppr., garnished and spurred or. 193. 1
Hellam, on a mural coronet or, an eagle with wings endorsed, holding in the beak an oak-branch fructed, all ppr.
Hellard, a demi-Hercules ppr.
Hellen, Ireland, a dolphin haurient between two wings ppr. 140. 2
Heller, Cornw., a Cornish chough erm. 107. 14
Hellesby of Hellesby and Acton, a demi-lion couped immediately beneath the left arm or, double queued, in dexter paw a cross gu., in the sinister paw a saltire sa., the lion looking upward to the cross.
Hellesby of Hellesby and Elton, Chesh., a banner or, forked pennon, surmounted by a cross gu., the flag or, bearing the arms or, a saltire sa.
Hellier, a cock arg., guttée-de-sang, combed and wattled gu. *Pro republicâ semper.* 91. 2
Hellier, late Rev. Thomas, of Woodhouse, Staffs: (1) Same crest as above (*for Hellier*). 91. 2. (2) A hind's head quarterly arg. and or, pierced through the neck with an arrow headed az., the feather broken and dropping arg. (*for Shaw*). *cf.* 124. 1
Hellis, a hand holding an ear of wheat ppr. 218. 14
Hellord, Devonsh., an escarbuncle arg. 164. 12
Helly and **Heley,** an arm in armour holding in the hand a broken spear ppr. *cf.* 210. 9
Helman-Pidsley, W. E., Esquire, 13, Tierney Road, Streatham Hill, London, S.W., a dragon sejant supporting with the dexter claw a spear erect. 296. 2
Helme, Worcs., a pheon arg. 174. 11
Helme of Standish House, near Stroud, on a mount vert, a demi-dragon az., holding in the dexter claw a cross crosslet fitchée or, and supporting with the sinister an escutcheon or, charged with an Esquire's helmet ppr. *Cassis tutissima virtus.*
Helps, Rev. Charles Leonard, of the Rectory, Clowne, near Chesterfield, on a wreath of the colours, two cross crosslets fitchée in saltire az., surmounted by an eagle's head erased or. *Be thankful.*
Helsby of Helsby, Chesh., a demi-lion rampant or, holding in his dexter paw a plain cross gu., and in his sinister a saltire sa. *Dieu est mon espérance.*
Helsby of Helsby, a lion's head couped or, langued and fanged gu.
Helsham, Gustavus, Esquire, J.P., of St. Mary's Hall, King's Lynn, Norf., on a wreath of the colours an Esquire's helmet ppr., charged with a crescent gu. *Cassis tutissima virtus. cf.* 180. 3
Helsham-Jones, Colonel Henry Helsham, of Redlands, the Holmwood, Surrey, on a heart or, a raven sa., gorged with a collar gemel arg. (*for Jones*).
Helton, Yorks, on a chapeau gu., turned up erm., a sinister wing ppr., charged with a chevron of the first. *cf.* 109. 2
Helwish, a lion sejant holding a lance in pale ppr.
Hely, an arm in armour holding a broken tilting-spear ppr. *cf.* 210. 9
Hely-Hutchinson, out of a ducal coronet a demi-cockatrice with wings elevated az. *Fortiter gerit crucem.*
Helyar of Coker Court, Somers., a cock sa., beaked, combed, and wattled gu., in front of a cross fleury fitchée or. *In labore quies.* *cf.* 91. 2
Helyard, a cock sa., combed and wattled gu. 91. 2
Hemans, Wales, a lion passant gardant ppr. *Vérité sans peur.* 4. 3
Hemenhall, a stag's head erased. 121. 2
Hemery of Jersey, a stag's head arg. *Flecti non frangi.* 121. 5
Heming, Lieutenant-Colonel Dempster, Mancetter Lodge, near Atherstone, on a chapeau ppr., a lion sejant or. *Aut nunquam tentes aut perfice.*
Heming and **Hemming,** on a chapeau gu., turned up erm., a lion statant gardant az., crowned and gorged with a ducal coronet or. *cf.* 4. 7
Hemington, Hemingtone, and **Hemmington,** a hand holding a sealed letter ppr.

Hemming, Sir Augustus William Lawson, G.C.M.G., of King's House, Jamaica, same crest.

Hemming of Bentley and Springrove, Worcs., an eagle with wings expanded arg., charged on the breast with a pheon sa., supporting with the dexter claw an escutcheon erm., thereon a pale az., charged with three leopards' faces or. 78. 7

Hemmings, out of a ducal coronet a demi-lion rampant. 16. 3

Hemmingway, a swan's head and neck couped ppr.

Hempgrave, a young woman's head affrontée ppr., couped below the breasts, vested az. 182. 8

Hemphill of Rathkeany, co. Tipperary, Ireland, a greyhound courant ppr., collared gu. *Constanter ac non timide.* cf. 58. 2

Hemstead or **Hemsted,** the top of a halberd issuing from the wreath. 172. 1

Hemsworth, of Monk Fryston Hall, South Milford, Yorks., a dexter arm in armour embowed, holding in the gauntlet a sword ppr., hilt and pommel or, transfixing a leopard's face sa. cf. 195. 1

Hemsworth, Augustus Noel Campbell, Esquire, of Shropham Hall, Thetford, Norf., same crest. *Manus hæc inimica tyrannis.*

Hemsworth, Rev. William Barker, of Banstead, Epsom, same crest and motto.

Hemsworth, Thomas Gerard, Esquire, of Abbeville, co. Tipperary, same crest and motto.

Henbury, a primrose ppr. cf. 150. 11

Henchman, a buffalo's head erased gu. 44. 1

Henckell and **Henckill,** out of a ducal coronet or, an elephant's proboscis contrary embowed.

Hende, a lion's head erased arg. 17. 8

Henden, a greyhound courant in front of a tree ppr. cf. 58. 5

Hender of Botreaux Castle and Veriam, Cornw., a sword erect arg., the blade wavy and dropping blood, with flames of fire issuing from the sides and top, hilt and pommel or. cf. 170. 11

Henderson, *see* Cleland-Henderson.

Henderson, *see* Haldane-Duncan-Mercer-Henderson.

Henderson, Arthur, Esquire, of Williamfield, Ayrsh., a dexter hand ppr., holding a mullet az., surmounted by a crescent arg. *Sola virtus nobilitat.* 216. 10

Henderson, Colonel George, of Heverswood, Sevenoaks, same crest and motto.

Henderson, Sir William, D.L., J.P., Devenha House, Aberdeensh., same crest and motto.

Henderson, Major-General Kennett Gregg, C.B., of 38, Queen's Gate Terrace, S.W., same crest and motto.

Henderson, Sir James, M.A., of Oakley House, Windsor Park, Belfast, a cubit arm erect between two oaks, branches ppr., the hand grasping an estoile of eight points wavy or, ensigned with a crescent az. *Sola virtus nobilitat.*

Henderson, Bart., of Fordell, Scotland, a dexter hand ppr., holding a star or, surmounted by a crescent arg. *Sola virtus nobilitat.* 216. 12

Henderson, John, Esquire, of Randall's Park, Leatherhead, Surrey, and George Henderson, Esquire, of Heverswood, Kent, a dexter hand ppr., holding a star surmounted by a crescent, both arg. *Sola virtus nobilitat.* 216. 12

Henderson, Sir Alexander, Bart., Buscot Park, Faringdon, Berks, a hand holding a torteau charged with a star arg. 303. 14

Henderson, Scotland, a hand ppr., holding a star az. *Virtus nobilitat.* cf. 216. 12

Henderson, Robert Evelyn, Esquire, of Sedgwick Park, Sussex, a cubit arm erect ppr., holding in the hand a star of eight points wavy arg. *Sola virtus nobilitat.*

Henderson of Leith, a dexter hand ppr., holding a star of six points wavy or, ensigned with a crescent az. *Virtus nobilitat.* 216. 12

Henderson of Eildon Hall, Roxburgh, Scotland, same crest and motto. 216. 12

Henderson, Scotland, an arm embowed holding a mullet surmounted by a crescent.

Henderson of St. Laurence, Scotland, a wheel. *Sic cuncta nobilitat.* 161. 1

Henderson of Stirling, a tilter at the ring. *Practise no fraud.*

Henderson, under a tree a boar passant.

Henderson, late Thomas, Esquire, Merchant and Shipowner, of 14, Blythswood Square, Glasgow, a lion rampant arg., armed and langued gu., supporting in his fore-paws a trident paleways, also arg. *Secure amidst perils.*

Henderson, Richard, of Bidston, Chesh., same crest and motto.

Hendey, the stump of a holly-bush shooting out new leaves, all ppr. 145. 10

Hendley, Ireland, a demi-woman ppr., holding in her dexter hand a garland ppr. 183. 5

Hendley, Kent, a martlet with wings endorsed or. 95. 11

Hendley, Ireland, an heraldic antelope's head erased ppr., attired and collared or. cf. 127. 11

Hendley and **Hendly,** a column entwined with woodbine, all ppr. 176. 4

Hendmarsh, an oak-tree ppr., pendent thereon an escutcheon gu.

Hendrick of Dublin, out of a ducal coronet or, a crescent gu.

Hendrick-Aylmer, Hans Hendrick, Esquire, J.P., of Kerdiffstown, co. Kildare, Ireland, out of a ducal coronet or, a chough with wings displayed rising ppr. (*for Aylmer*). (2) Out of a ducal coronet or, a crescent gu. (*for Hendrick*). *Hallelujah.*

Hendrie and **Hendry,** a demi-Cupid holding in his dexter hand a torch ppr. 158. 8

Hendry, a pelican vulning herself. 98. 1

Hendry, a buck's head. 121. 5

Hendy, the stump of a holly-bush shooting forth new leaves ppr. 145. 10

Hendy, Lancs., a lion's head erased arg. 17. 8

Hene, a demi-lion rampant gardant holding a battle-axe. 16. 14

Heneage, Baron (Heneage), Hainton, Lincs, a greyhound courant sa. *Toujours ferme.*

Heneage, *see* Walker-Heneage.

Heneage, Lincs, a greyhound current sa. *Toujours ferme.* cf. 58. 2

Hengham, among clouds a globe ppr. 159. 5

Hengrave, out of a mural coronet a leopard's head ducally gorged. 23. 7

Hengscott, a stag's head erased and attired or, charged on the neck with two nails in saltier sa., between four pellets.

Hening of London, on a chapeau az., turned up erm., a lion sejant of the last. cf. 7. 6

Heningham, Staffs and Suff., an old man's head in profile ppr., vested round the shoulders gu., on the head a cap or, turned up erm., and charged with three guttes-de-sang.

Henley, Baron (Henley), of Chardstock, Ireland: (1) A lion's head arg., ducally crowned gu., semée of hurts. (*for Henley*). (2) A dexter arm embowed in armour ppr., holding a garb or (*for Eden*) which is used. *Si sit prudentia.* cf. 18. 8

Henley, Hants, a lion's head erased arg., semée of hurts, ducally crowned or. cf. 18. 8

Henley, a horse's foot couped ppr. 123. 9

Henley of Oxford, an eagle with wings displayed or, holding in the dexter claw an anchor and cable sa., and in the beak a trefoil ppr. *Perseverando.* 78. 4

Henley, Joseph John, C.B., of Waterperry, same crest and motto.

Henlock, a demi-lion rampant gu., maned and armed or, holding a mullet az. 15. 7

Henly, a falcon rising ppr. 87. 1

Henn-Gennys, *see* Gennys.

Henn of Paradise, co. Clare, on a mount vert, a hen-pheasant ppr. *Gloria Deo.*

Henne, a demi-lion rampant gardant, holding a battle-axe arg. 16. 14

Hennessy of Ballymacmoy, Cork, an arm embowed in armour holding in the hand a battle-axe ppr. cf. 200. 6

Hennidge, an eagle's head erased ppr. *Deo Duce.* 83. 2

Henniker, Baron (Henniker-Major), Thornham Hall, Eye: (1) A dexter arm embowed habited az., cuffed arg., charged on the elbow with a plate, and holding in the hand ppr. a baton or (*for Major*). (2) An escallop or, charged with an estoile gu. (*for Henniker*). *Deus major columna.* cf. 141. 6

Henniker, Captain Sir Brydges-Powell, Bart., of Newton Hall, Essex, an escallop or, charged with an estoile gu. *Deus major columna.* cf. 141. 6

Henning of Poxwell, Dorset, a sea-horse arg., holding between the paws a plate.

Henning, Captain Charles Maxwell Shurlock, Frome Whitfield, Dorchester, same crest. *Undis undique ditant.*

Henraghty, Ireland, a dolphin naiant. 140. 5

Henrie, Scotland, a pelican's head erased, vulning itself ppr. *Fideliter.* 98. 2

Henrieson, Scotland, a hand holding a mullet of six points ensigned on the top with a crescent, all ppr. *Virtus sola nobilitat.* cf. 216. 10

Henry, on a chapeau gu., turned up erm., a lion's head erased sa., langued gu. 17. 9

Henry, a demi-lion rampant holding between the paws a ducal coronet or, the cap gu.

Henry, Mitchell, Esquire, of Kylemore Castle, Letterfrack, co. Galway, Ireland, and of Stratheden House, Knightsbridge, Middx., out of a ducal coronet ppr., a demi-lion rampant arg., holding between the paws a like ducal coronet. *Vincit veritas.*

Henry, Derbysh., a dexter arm in armour embowed holding in the hand a scimitar ppr. 196. 10

Henry-Batten-Pooll, Robert Pooll, Esquire, D.L., of Road Manor, Bath, in front of a griffin's head erased erm., beaked and langued gu., and charged on the neck with a fountain, a battle-axe fesseways ppr. *Confide recte agens.*

Henryson-Caird, James Alexander, Esquire, Kirkcudbrightsh., a dexter hand fesseways couped at the wrist ppr., holding a star of six points ensigned with a crescent arg. *Virtus sola nobilitat.* 286. 11

Henshall, out of a ducal coronet or, a hand vested arg., cuffed gu., holding a sun ppr. 200. 2

Henshall, Ireland, a cross pattée az., between two wings or. 110. 7

Henshaw, Chesh., a griffin's head couped per pale arg. and az., charged on the neck with three bars counterchanged, and holding in the beak an olive-branch vert, fructed or. 65. 10

Henshaw of Great Marlow, Essex, and Henshaw, Chesh., a falcon belled with wings elevated, preying on a mallard's wing arg., guttée-de-sang. *cf.* 79. 13

Hensley, a beech-tree ppr. 143. 1

Hensley, Charles Ernest, Esquire, Barrister-at-law, M.A., S.C.L. (Oxon.), Pratsham Grange, Holmbury St. Mary, Dorking, in front of two branches in saltire a boar's head couped close. *Dum spiro spero.*

Henslow, an eagle with wings expanded supporting a standard ppr., the flag gu. *cf.* 78. 14

Hensman, Howard, Esquire, of 80, Earlham Grove, Forest Gate, Essex, or, a stag's head erased gu. *Fleet and free.*

Henson, a holy lamb regardant arg., in a glory or, the standard gu.

Henstock of Herbert Lodge, Bonsall, Derbysh., in front of a demi-lion arg., holding between the paws a water-bouget sa., a demi-catherine wheel, also sa. *Nil sine magno labore.* 13. 9

Henty, Arthur, Esquire, of Broadwater Hall, Worthing, upon a mount vert, a lion rampant party per chevron or and az., holding between the paws a lozenge of the last, charged with a bezant. *Per ardua stabilis.*

Henvill, a griffin's head between two wings. *Virtus et nobilitas.* 65. 11

Henville, an eagle's head erased between two wings or. *Virtus vera nobilitas.* *cf.* 84. 2

Hepborne, alias Richardson, of Tottenham High Cross, Middx., a round buckle or, the point of the tongue upwards charged with an annulet gu.

Hepburn-Stuart-Forbes-Trefusis, Baron Clinton, *see* Clinton.

Hepburn, Earl of Bothwell and **Duke of Orkney,** a horse furnished and tied to a tree ppr. *Keep traist.*

Hepburn, W. A., Esquire, M.D., M.R.C.S., L.S.A., of Coxhoe R.S.O., Durh., in front of an oak-tree ppr., a horse passant, saddled and bridled gu. *Keep tryst* (or *traist*).

Hepburn of Clerkington, Haddingtonsh., a horse furnished and tied to a tree ppr. *Keep tryst.*

Hepburn of the Hooke, Sussex, a horse arg., furnished gu., tied to a yew-tree ppr. *Keep tryste.*

Hepburn, Malcolm Langton, Esquire, M.D., F.R.C.S., of 28, Marine Parade, Lowestoft, a horse arg., furnished gu., tied to an oak-tree ppr. *Keep tryste.*

Hepburn, Buchan-, Sir Archibald, Bart., D.L., M.P., of Smeaton-Hepburn, Haddingtonsh.: (1) A horse arg., furnished gu., tied to a yew-tree ppr. (*for Hepburn*). (2) The sun in the dexter chief, with a sunflower in full blow open to it ppr. (*for Buchan*). *Domum antiquam redintegrare.—Keep traist.—Non inferiora secutus.*

Hepburn of Blackcastle, Scotland, a horse's head couped ppr., garnished gu. *I keep tryst.—Prudentiâ et virtute.* *cf.* 50. 13

Hepburn of Edinburgh, Scotland, a mort-head overgrown with moss, all ppr. *Virtute et prudentiâ.*

Hepburn, a rose surmounted by a thistle ppr. 150. 3

Hepburn of Keith, Scotland, an anchor in pale ppr. *Expecto.* 161. 2

Hepburne-Scott, *see* Polwarth, Baron.

Hepden of Burwash, Sussex, a lion passant or, issuing out of a mountain-cave ppr.

Hepenstal, *see* Dopping-Hepenstal.

Hepworth, out of a mural coronet a demi-lion rampant holding a palm-branch, all ppr. 16. 11

Hepworth, J. Sheldon, Lt.-Col., of Buccleuch House, Surbiton, out of a mural coronet a demi-lion rampant holding in the dexter paw a palm-branch. *Dictis factisque simplex.*

Hepworth, Rev. William Henry Francklin, M.A., of Shepshed Vicarage, Loughborough, Leics., a demi-lion arg., charged with two mullets in pale gu., holding in the dexter paw a branch of palm slipped ppr., and supporting in the sinister a shepherd's crook in bend or. *Loyal à mort.* 260. 4

Hepworth of Ackworth, Pontefract, out of a ducal coronet or, a wyvern vert. *Loyal à mort.* 70. 9

Herapath of Bristol, a demi-lion or, holding between the paws an arrow-head az. *cf.* 10. 2

Herbert, Earl of Pembroke, *see* Pembroke.

Herbert, Earl of Carnarvon, *see* Carnarvon.

Herbert, Earl of Powis, *see* Powis.

Herbert, Earl of Carnarvon, Herbert, Earl of Pembroke and Montgomery, and **Herbert, Marquis of Powis** (*extinct*), a wyvern with wings elevated vert, holding in the mouth a sinister hand couped at the wrist gu. *Ung je serviray.* 70. 3

Herbert, Earls of Powis, same crest. *Audacter et sincere.* 70. 3

[*The Herberts, Earls of Powis* (*extinct*) *of the first creation used the motto, "Fortitudine et prudentia."*]

Herbert, Hon. Sir Robert George Wyndham, G.C.B., of Ickleton, Great Chesterford, same crest and motto.

Herbert of Colebrook, Monm., **Herbert** of Muckross, Kerry, **Herbert, Baron Herbert,** of Castle Island and Cherbury (*extinct*), and **Herbert, Baron Herbert,** of Cherbury (*extinct*; motto, *Constantia et fortitudine*), a bundle of seven arrows, six in saltire and one in pale or, headed and flighted arg., banded about the middle with a belt gu., the buckle and point extended or. *cf.* 173. 7

Herbert, Shropsh., a wyvern with wings addorsed vert, holding in the mouth a sinister hand couped at the wrist gu. *Fortitudine et prudentiâ.* 70. 3

Herbert, Edward Arthur Field Whittell, of Glan Hafren, Newtown, Montgomerysh., same crest. *Ung je serviray.*

Herbert, Colonel Edward William, C.B., of Orleton, Wellington, Shropsh., a wyvern vert, holding a sinister hand gu. *Ung je serviray.*

Herbert, Sidney George, Esquire, of Pietermaritzburg, Natal, South Africa, a wyvern vert, holding in the mouth a sinister hand couped at the wrist gu., debruised by a bendlet sinister wavy arg. *Ung je serviray.* *cf.* 70. 3

Herbert, Robert Henry, Esquire, of Lincoln's Inn Fields, London, same crest and motto. *cf.* 70. 3

Herbert of London, a wyvern with wings addorsed sa., wreathed and tied or and gu. *Jure non dono.* *cf.* 70. 1

Herbert, W. H., of Paradise in Painswick, Glouc., in front of a dexter arm embowed holding a dragon's head erased ppr., a demi-catherine wheel az. *Ung je serviray.* 296. 13

Herbert, Kenney-, of Lockarrig, co. Cork: (1) A bundle of twelve arrows in saltire or, headed and feathered arg., belted gu., and buckled or (*for Herbert*). (2) A dexter cubit arm erect vested gu., cuffed arg., the hand grasping a scroll of paper ppr. (*for Kenny*). *Ung je servirai.* 208. 8

Herbert, Colonel Ivor John Caradoc, C.B., C.M.G., of Llanarth, Monm., a Saracen woman's head couped at the shoulders ppr., with long hair sa., and double-earrings or, over a veil az., doubled arg., a wreath of the same. *Asgre lân Diogel ei Pherchen.*

Herbert, William Reginald Fitzherbert, Clytha Park, near Abergavenny, same crest.

Herbert, Edmund Philip, Esquire, of Llansantffraed Court, Abergavenny, and Hartpury, near Gloucester, a Saracen woman's head affrontée, couped at the shoulders, with long hair sa., from the ears double rings pendent or, veil az., doubled arg., encircled with a wreath of the same. *Asgre lân Diogell ei Pherchen.*

Herbert, Arthur, Esquire, of Coldbrook, Abergavenny, same crest and motto.

Herbert, Ireland, a dexter hand holding an eel ppr. *cf.* 220. 2

Herbright, on a tower ppr., a flag flotant to the sinister gu., the staff sa. 157. 13

Hercy of Grove, Notts, and of Oxford, out of a ducal coronet or, a Saracen's head couped ppr., the hair sa., encircled with a wreath arg.

Hercy, out of a ducal coronet or, a man's head in profile, wreathed about the temples arg. and gu.

Herd of London, a demi-goat saliant ppr., armed and ducally gorged or. *cf.* 128. 1

Herdson, Kent, a demi-leopard rampant ppr., ducally gorged and chained or. *cf.* 23. 13

Hereford, Viscount (Devereux), Tregoyd, Three Cocks, Breconsh., out of a ducal coronet or, a talbot's head arg., eared gu. *Virtutis comes invidia.—Basis virtutum constantia.* 57. 12

Hereford, an arm from the elbow ppr., holding in the hand an annulet or. 216. 1

Hereford, James Tudor, of Sufton Court, Heref., an eagle displayed arg. 75. 2

Heriet, a hind's head couped or. 124. 1

Heringe of Shropsh., and Owsley-Minor, Warw., a bull's head sa., ducally gorged and crowned or. *cf.* 44. 2

Heringham, on a chapeau a dolphin haurient, all ppr. *cf.* 140. 11

Heriot of Ramornie, Fifesh., a demi-man in complete armour brandishing a sword ppr. *True and trusty.* 187. 1

Heriot, an arm in armour embowed ppr., garnished or, holding in the hand a dagger of the first, hilt and pommel of the second. 196. 5

Heriot, Scotland, a dexter hand holding a wreath of laurel. *Fortem posce animum.* 218. 4

Heris, on a mount vert, a crane holding in its dexter claw a stone ppr. *cf.* 105. 6

Heritage, a bear's head party per chevron arg. and sa., muzzled of the last, between two wings per fesse of the second and first.

Heriz, a demi-female richly attired between two laurel-branches, holding in her dexter hand a rose-branch, all ppr. 183. 14

Herman of Middleton-Stoney, Oxon., a lion couchant gardant or, under a palm-tree ppr. 263. 16

Hermon of Preston, Lancs, and Wyfold Court, Checkendon, Oxon., in front of two palm-trees ppr., a lion couchant gardant erminois, resting the dexter claw upon a bale of cotton ppr. *Fido non timeo.* 9. 6

Hermon-Hodge, Sir Robert T., Bart., Wyfold Court, Reading, an eagle, wings addorsed and inverted or, supporting with the dexter claw an increscent arg. and looking at the rays of the sun issuant from clouds ppr. *Præmium virtutis gloria.* 273. 5

Hermon, a cubit arm vested and cuffed, holding in the hand a dagger.

Herne, *see* Buckworth-Herne-Soame.

Herne or **Heron** of Tanfield Hall, Essex, of London, and of Shacklewell, Middx., a heron's head erased arg., ducally gorged and beaked or. *cf.* 104. 11

Herne, Burchell-, Rev., Humphrey Frederick, of Bushey Grange, Herts: (1) Out of a ducal coronet or, a heron's head ppr. (*for Herne*). *cf.* 104. 5. (2) A lion rampant az., against a tree vert (*for Burchell*). *Usque ad aras.*

Herne of Godmanchester, Huntingdon, a heron or. 105. 9

Herns, Scotland, a buck's head or, attired with ten tynes. *Dominus dedit.* 121. 5

Heron, a heron ppr. 105. 9

Heron of Chipchase, Northumb., a heron close ppr., holding in the beak a staff, therefrom a banner flotant inscribed with the word *Hastings.*

Heron, Bart., Notts, out of a ducal coronet or, a heron's head ppr. *Ardua petit ardea.* *cf.* 104. 5

Heron, Surrey, a heron's head erased arg., ducally gorged or. *cf.* 104. 11

Heron of Grampoole and Abingdon, Berks, and of Elying, Oxon., a heron's head erased arg., charged on the neck with two chevronels sa. *cf.* 104. 11

Heron-Maxwell, Sir John Robert, Bart., J.P., D.L., of Springkell, Dumfriessh., a dexter hand ppr., holding up an eagle's neck with two heads erased sa. *Revirescat.*

Heron, Ireland, a dove volant holding in its beak an olive-branch ppr. 93. 10

Heron of that Ilk, Kirkcudbright, Scotland, a demi-lion arg., holding in his dexter paw a cross crosslet fitchée gu. *Par valeur.—Ad ardua tendis.* 11. 10

Herrick of Beaumanor Park, Leics., a bull's head couped arg., armed and eared sa., gorged with a chaplet of roses ppr. *Virtus omnia nobilitat.* *cf.* 44. 3

Herrick, Perry-, of Beaumanor Park, Leics.: (1) same crest as above, (*for Herrick*) *cf.* 44. 3. (2) A hind's head erased ppr., semée of annulets or, holding in the mouth a pear-tree branch slipped ppr., fructed or. *Virtus omnia nobilitat.*

Herries, Baron (Constable-Maxwell), of Everingham Park, near York (crest of Maxwell, as used), a stag's head with ten tynes arg. *Dominus dedit.* (Crest of Haggerstone: A lion rampant arg.) 121. 5

Herries, Scotland, a buck's head or, attired with ten tynes arg. *Dominus dedit.* 121. 5

Herries of Scotland, a buck's head erased gu., attired vert. 121. 2

Herries, Alexander Young, of Spottes Hall, Dalbeattie, Kircudbrightsh.: (1) A buck's head or, attired with ten tynes arg. (2) A demi-lion rampant gu., holding in its dexter paw a dagger in pale ppr. *Dominus dedit.—Robori prudentia præstat.*

Herries, a cinquefoil erm. 148. 12

Herring, a boar's head couped in fess, pierced through the snout by four arrows ppr. *cf.* 42. 9

Herring, Scotland, a boar's head couped close sa. 43. 1

Herringham, Rev. William Walton, Old Cleeve Rectory, Taunton, a dove rising. *Æquo animo.*

Herrington, a horse's head furnished ppr. 51. 5

Herriot and **Herriott,** a lion's gamb erect sa., holding a crescent arg. 39. 15

Herris of Woodham Mortimer and Sandon, Essex, a talbot sejant or. 55. 2

Hersay, a hedgehog ppr. 135. 8

Herschel, Sir William James, Bart., Lawn Upton, Littlemore, Oxford, a demi-terrestrial sphere ppr., thereon an eagle with wings elevated or. *Cœlis exploratis.* 285. 5

Herschell, Baron (Herschell), of Durh., on a mount vert, a stag ppr., gorged with a collar gemel az., the dexter forefoot supporting a fasces in bend or. *Celeriter.* 276. 7

Hersey, a stag sejant ppr. *cf.* 116. 8

Herst, a hurst of trees ppr.

Hertford, a parrot's head gu., between two wings vert. 101. 10

Hertford, Marquess of (Seymour), Ragley Hall, Alcester, Warw., out of a ducal coronet or, a phœnix in flames ppr. *Fide et amore.* 82. 5

Hertington, a stag's head or, collared gu., and between the attires a cross pattée az. *cf.* 120. 9

Hertog, out of a ducal coronet or, two wings addorsed az.

Hertslet, Edward Cecil, Esquire, H.M. Consul-General for Belgium, Antwerp, a demi-lion rampant ppr., crowned with an Eastern diadem or, and resting the sinister paw on a closed book sa., clasped and hinged or. *Fato fortior virtus.*

Hervey, Marquess of Bristol, *see* Bristol.

Hervey-Bathurst, Bart., Hants: (1) A dexter arm embowed habited in mail, holding in the hand, all ppr., a spiked club or (*for Bathurst*). 199. 2. (2) A leopard sa., bezantée, collared and lined or, holding in the dexter paw a trefoil slipped vert (*for Hervey*). 254. 12

Hervey and **Hervy,** a leopard passant sa., bezantée. *cf.* 24. 2

Hervey, Matthew Wilson, Esquire, of East Bilney Hall, Norfolk, a demi-lion rampant gu., holding in his dexter paw a trefoil slipped or. *Delectat et ornat.*

Hervey, Valentine Smedley, Esquire, of 33, Hyde Park Gate, London, S.W., same crest and motto.

Hervey, Ireland, a mountain-cat ppr., holding in the dexter paw a trefoil slipped vert. *Je n'oublierai jamais.*

Hervey, a trefoil slipped. *Delectat et ornat.* 148. 9

Hervey, Ireland, a lion rampant erm., supporting a plumb-rule ppr. 3. 2

Hervey, Cornw. and Somers., a squirrel sejant arg., the tail or, cracking nuts ppr. 135. 7

Hervieu of France, a wolf rampant or. 28. 2

Hervy, an ox-yoke in bend gu., the bows or. 178. 6

Herworth of Epplin, Devonsh., a cubit arm erect ppr., holding a snake. 220. 2

Hesding, a dexter hand holding a pistol ppr. 221. 8

Heselrigge, on a chapeau ppr., an escallop between two wings. 141. 11

Heseltine, a swan with wings addorsed arg., crowned with an antique crown or. *cf.* 99. 4

Heseltine, a talbot's head erased between two wings. *cf.* 56. 2

Hesill, on a chapeau gu., turned up arg., a flame ppr. 180. 10

Hesilrige, Bart., *see* Hazlerigg.

Hesketh, a mortar mounted ppr. 169. 10

Hesketh, out of a ducal coronet or, two arms embowed in armour, the hands ppr., supporting a leopard's face or.

Hesketh, Lancs, a garb or, banded az. 153. 2

Hesketh, Fermor-, Sir Thomas George, Bart., of Rufford Hall, Lancs: (1) A garb or, banded az. (*for Hesketh*). 153. 2. (2) Out of a ducal coronet or, a cock's head gu., combed and wattled of the first (*for Fermor*). 90. 6

Hesketh of Gwyrch Castle, Denbighsh.: (1) A garb or, charged with a cross patée (*for Hesketh*). *cf.* 153. 2. (2) A rose arg. *cf.* 149. 2. (3) A dexter arm couped at the shoulder and embowed in armour, holding a scythe, all ppr. *In Deo mea spes.*

Hesketh-Fleetwood, Bart. (*extinct*), of Rossall Hall: (1) A wolf statant regardant arg., charged on the shoulder with a trefoil slipped vert (*for Fleetwood*). (2) A garb erect or, in front of an eagle displayed with two heads ppr. (*for Hesketh*). *Quod tibi hoc alteri.* 74. 3

Hesketh-Fleetwood: (1) A wolf statant regardant arg., charged on the shoulder with a trefoil slipped vert, and on the body with a pale wavy az. (*for Fleetwood*). (2) A mount vert, thereon in front of an eagle with two heads displayed ppr., a garb or, banded gu., the whole debruised by a bendlet sinister wavy az. *Quod tibi hoc alteri.* *cf.* 74. 3

Hesketh, Bibby-, Charles Hesketh, Esq., D.L., the Rookery, South Meols, Southport: (1) A mount vert, thereon in front of an eagle with two heads displayed ppr., a garb or, banded gu. (2) In front of a cubit arm erect, holding a sword in bend sinister ppr., pommel and hilt or, a mullet of six points between two escallops fesseways arg. *Quod tibi hoc alteri.*

Heskett, a garb or, charged with a rose gu., the stalk and leaves twisting round the garb. *cf.* 153. 2

Hesse, a demi-wolf between two wings.

Hesse, Middx., on a chapeau ppr., a cockatrice vert, ducally crowned, combed, beaked, and wattled or, charged on the breast with the sun in splendour of the last. *Superi audi et tace.* *cf.* 68. 9

Hester, a parrot gu., holding in its beak an annulet or. 101. 11

Hetherfield, a sinister wing, charged with a chevron gu.

Hetherington, a lion's head erased gu., within a chain in arch arg., both ends issuing from the wreath. 19. 5

Hetherington, Ireland, out of a ducal coronet or, a tower quarterly arg. and gu. *cf.* 156. 2

Hetherington of Ballyroan, Queen's Co., Ireland, a castle with four towers per fess or and gu. 155. 4

Hethersete or Hethersette, a sinister wing charged with a chevron gu.

Hetherton, a lion's head erased gu., within a chain in arch arg., both ends issuing from the wreath. 19. 5

Hetley of Bulbridge House, Wilts, on the stump of a tree a sparrow-hawk, all ppr. 86. 11

Heuer or **Hever,** a phœnix in flames ppr. 82. 2

Heuer, a cat sejant arg., holding in the mouth a goldfinch ppr. *cf.* 26. 8

Heugh of Holmwood Park, Kent, a unicorn's head arg. *Per arduo.* 49. 7

Heusch, a trefoil slipped or, between two wings arg. 110. 12

Hevell, a lion rampant ppr., supporting an anchor reversed az.

Heveningham, Suff. and Staffs, an old man's head in profile ppr., vested gu., on his head a cap az., guttée-d'or. 192. 11

Heveningham or **Heveringham,** Suff. and Staffs, a man's head in profile ppr., vested gu., on his head a cap or, guttée-de-sang, turned up erm. *cf.* 192. 11

Hever, a leopard sejant or. *cf.* 24. 13

Heward, Ireland, a swan's leg couped à la quise with a wing displayed and conjoined arg.

Heward of Carlisle, a dexter arm embowed in armour ppr., garnished or, entwined by a serpent, the hand in a gauntlet holding a sword, also ppr., pommel and hilt or, the blade piercing a heart gu.

Hewat or **Hewatt,** Scotland, the sun rising out of a cloud ppr. *Post tenebras lux.* 162. 5

Heway, Devonsh., a wolf statant regardant ppr. *cf.* 28. 12

Hewer of Oxborough, Norf., a demi-dragon az., with wings endorsed or, collared and lined or, and holding the line in its claws. 290. 11

Hewer, Cecil McKenzie, Esquire, F.R.C.S., of Tarporley, Chesh., a demi-dragon az., wings endorsed or, collared and lined of the last, holding the line in its forelegs. *Virtuti damnosa quies.* 290. 11

Hewer, E. S. Earnshaw, Esquire, F.R.C.S., of Stratford-on-Avon, Warw., same crest and motto.

Hewes, a peacock's head erased az. 103. 1

Hewet, a cross pattée between the horns of a crescent gu. 163. 6

Hewet and **Hewett,** Hants, on the stump of a tree sprouting ppr., a falcon close arg., legged and belled or. *Ne tu quæsiveris extra.—Une pure foy.* *cf.* 86. 11

Hewetson, a serpent nowed, the head in pale or, holding in the mouth a garland of laurel vert. 142. 7

Hewetson, Ireland, a demi-friar vested ppr., holding in his dexter hand a lash. 187. 11

Hewetson of Thomastown, Kilkenny, a coney sejant sa., collared arg. *cf.* 136. 4. *Another,* a talbot passant arg., holding in the mouth a sword ppr. *Ambo dexter.* *cf.* 54. 1

Hewett of London, a lapwing ppr.

Hewett, a cockatrice with wings expanded or. 68. 6

Hewett, George Edwin, Esquire, 11, Chester Terrace, Regent's Park, London, and of Leasowe, Charlton Kings, Glouc., a cockatrice with wings elevated or, semée of crosses pattée gu., and resting the dexter claw on a fleur-de-lis arg. *Labor omnia superat.*

Hewett, Sir Harald George, Bart., of Netherseale, Leics., out of a mural coronet or, the stump of an oak-tree with branches, thereon a hawk ppr., gorged with an Eastern coronet and belled of the first. *Ne te quæsiveris extra.*

Hewett, late Sir Prescott Gardiner, Bart. (*extinct*), F.R.S., of Chesterfield Street, St. George's, Hanover Square, Middx., on a rock a falcon arg., entwined by a serpent ppr. *Ne te quæsiveris extra.*

Hewgell, on the stump of a tree couped in fess and sprouting afresh, an owl.

Hewgell, on a staff raguly in fess, an eaglet with wings expanded.

Hewgill of Hornby Grange, Yorks, a nag's head erased sa. *Marte et labore.* 51. 4

Hewis, on a chapeau ppr., a water-bouget sa. 168. 2

Hewitson, Northumb., a falcon gu., belled or. *Let them talk.* *cf.* 85. 2

Hewitt, Viscount Lifford, on the stump of a tree, a branch growing therefrom, an owl, all ppr. *Be just and fear not.*

Hewitt of Alveston, on the trunk of an old tree, from which spring fresh branches, a horned owl, all ppr.

Hewitt, Robert Morton, Esquire, M.D., B.A., B.Ch., of Oakham, Rutl., on the stump of a tree sprouting to the dexter an owl. *Be just and fear not.*

Hewitt of Ballylane, co. Wexford, Ireland, on the trunk of a tree an owl perched, all ppr. *After darkness comes light.*

Hewitt of Burgatia, Roscarberry, same crest. *Be just and fear not.*

Hewitt, Ludlow-, Thomas Arthur, the trunk of a tree fessewise eradicated ppr., therefrom rising a falcon belled or, fretty gu., holding in the beak an acorn slipped, also ppr.

Hewitt, on the trunk of an oak-tree a falcon perched, belled ppr. *Ne tu quæsiveris extra.* *cf.* 86. 11

Hewitt of London, a falcon close upon a lure arg., lined and ringed or. *cf.* 85. 14

Hewitt, a demi-huntsman ppr., his coat gu., firing a gun. 187. 2

Hewlett, on a mount vert, semée of weeds, an oak-tree ppr. 143. 14

Hewlett, W. H., Esquire, of Strickland House, Standish, Wigan, out of a mural coronet a demi-owl. *Orate et vigilate.*

Hewlett or **Howlett** of Dublin, an owl's head erased and affrontée arg., ducally gorged or.

Hewsham, an eagle with wings addorsed sustaining a bannerol charged with a fleur-de-lis.

Hewson of Ennismore and Castle Hewson, Ireland, the sun in his splendour ppr. *Nam lumen effugio.* 162. 2

Hewson, J. W. P., of 2, Maryville, Dean Street, Cork, same crest and motto.

Hewson of Hunter Street, Brunswick Square, London, a bull's head couped arg., armed or, holding in the mouth a torch of the last emitting flames of fire ppr.

Hewster, out of a coronet arg., an ostrich's head and wings of the same, holding in the beak a horse-shoe or. 97. 11

Hexman, a yew-tree ppr. 144. 11

Hext, a stag's head affrontée, ducally gorged or. 119. 14

Hext, Lieutenant-Colonel Arthur Staniforth, of Trenarren and Constentin, Cornw., and Stavton, Devonsh., on a tower sa., a demi-lion rampant or, holding in the dexter paw a battle-axe of the first. *cf.* 157. 11

Hext, John, Esquire, R.N., C.I.E., same crest.

Hext, Francis John, Tredethy, Bodmin, Cornw., a demi-lion or, rising from a tower sa., holding in the centre paw a battle-axe of the last. *When Bale is hext Boot is next.*

Hexton, a leopard's face sa., jessant-de-lis or. 22. 5

Heycock, J. H., of East Norton, Leics., a hind's head couped and collared. *Non mihi sed patriæ.* 297. 9

Heydon, Herts and Lincs, a talbot passant arg., spotted sa. 54. 1

Heyes of Ratington, Essex, a snake's head erect and erased vert, ducally gorged or.

Heyford and **Heyforde,** out of a ducal coronet two branches in orle, all ppr. 146. 9

Heygate, Sir Frederick Gage, Bart., of Southend, Essex, a wolf's head erased gu. *Boulogne et Cadiz.* 30. 8

Heygate, Edward Leonard Aspinall, Esquire, of Buckland, Leominster, same crest and motto, and *Souvenez St. Quintin.*

Heygate, William Unwin, Esquire, of Roecliffe, Loughborough, same crest. *Boulogne et Cadiz.*

Heygate, William Nicholas, Esquire, M.R.C.S., 12, Bennett Street, Bath, same crest.

Heyland of Southend, on a chapeau gu., turned up erm., a martlet sa. 95. 1

Heyland, Ireland, out of the battlements of a tower ppr., charged with a cross crosslet gu., a nag's head, also ppr., *Faveat fortuna.* 50. 4

Heyland, Alexander Charles, Esquire, late Judge of Ghazeepore in India, out of battlements of a tower ppr., charged with a cross crosslet gu., a nag's head arg. 50. 4

Heylegair, a sword in fess thrust into a demi-wheel on the sinister.

Heylin, a bear passant sa., collared or, thereto a bell pendent of the same.

Heylin, Shropsh.: (1) A bear passant sa., gorged with a collar and bell or. (2) A bear ascending a vine-tree fructed ppr.

Heylyn, Wales, out of a marquess's coronet or, a demi-lion sa. *In utrumque paratus.* cf. 16. 3

Heylyn, Surrey, out of a ducal coronet or, a demi-lion rampant sa. 16. 3

Heyman, a demi-negro boy wreathed about the temples, holding in his dexter hand a slip of cinquefoils.

Heyman, a Moor affrontée, wreathed about the temples, holding in the dexter hand a rose slipped and leaved, all ppr.

Heynes of Turston, Bucks, an eagle's head erased erm., ducally gorged or. cf. 83. 10

Heynes, Shropsh., Oxon., and Dorset, an eagle displayed on a tortoise. 74. 12

Heynes or **Eynes** of Dorchester, Charlbury, Oxon., and Shropsh., an eagle displayed standing on a tortoise. 74. 12. *Another,* an eagle displayed az., semée d'estoiles or. cf. 75. 2

Heyreck, Leics., a bull's head couped arg., gorged with a chaplet of roses ppr. cf. 44. 3

Heyrick of Manchester, Lancs, a bull's head couped arg., round the neck a garland of laurel vert, armed or, tipped sa., the ears and mouth of the last.

Heyrick, a bull's head couped arg., gorged with a chaplet of roses ppr.

Heys, late John, Esquire, of Woodside, Renfrewsh., and Zecharia John Heys, Esquire, of Stonehouse, Barrhead, Renfrewsh., Scotland, a demi-lion rampant az., armed and langued gu., supporting in his paws a banner arg. *Invictus maneo.* 15. 2

Heysham of East Greenwich, Kent, a mount ppr., thereon a buck in full course arg., guttée-de-sang, attired and ungu. or, and wounded through the neck with an arrow gu., feathered and headed or. cf. 118. 13

Heysham, Mounsey-, George William, Castletown, Carlisle, a demi-griffin gorged with a wreath of oak, and holding with the claws a banner erect. *Semper paratus.*

Heysham, a stag's head affrontée, gorged with a ducal coronet. 119. 14

Heytesbury, Baron (Holmes-A'Court), of Heytesbury, Wilts: (1) Out of a naval coronet or, an arm embowed in armour, the hand ppr., grasping a trident az., headed or (*for Holmes*). 197. 8. (2) An eagle displayed sa., charged with two chevronels or, beaked and legged gu., holding in the beak a lily slipped ppr. (*for A'Court*). *Grandescunt aucta labore.*

Heyton of London and Lancs, out of a ducal coronet gu., a bull's head arg. 44. 11

Heyward, an ibex passant erm., crined and tufted or.

Heyward of Wenlock, Shropsh., an ibex passant erm., armed, crined, and tufted or.

Heyward, a dexter arm embowed habited gu., holding in the hand ppr. a tomahawk of the last.

Heyward, on a wing arg., a pale sa., charged with three crescents of the first. 109. 5

Heywood, on the stump of a tree a falcon rising with wings displayed ppr. 87. 12

Heywood, same crest. *Alte volo.*

Heywood, Henry, Esquire, of Witla Court, via Cardiff, upon the stump of an oak-tree sprouting to the sinister a falcon with wings displayed sa., each wing charged with a bezant, and supporting with the dexter leg a key or, the key resting upon the wreath. *Virtus invicta.*

Heywood, Sir Arthur Percival, Bart., D.L., of Claremont, Lancs, and Manchester, Uttoxeter, Derbysh., on a mount vert, the trunk of a tree with two branches sprouting therefrom and entwined by ivy, thereon a falcon with wings displayed, all ppr. *Alte volo.* 284. 6

Heywood, Thomas, Hatley St. George, Malvern, same crest and motto.

Heywood, a tiger's head arg., armed and maned or, pierced through the neck by a broken spear sa., headed of the first, vulned gu.

Heywood-Jones, late Richard Heywood, Esquire, of Badsworth Hall, near Pontefract: (1) In front of a talbot's head couped sa., collared vaire, two roses arg., stalked and leaved ppr. (*for Jones*). (2) On a mount vert, the trunk of a tree with two branches sprouting therefrom and entwined by ivy, thereon a falcon with wings expanded ppr. (*for Heywood*). *Till then thus.* 284. 6

Heywood-Lonsdale, Captain, of Shavington, Market Drayton, and 22, Hill Street, Mayfair, London, W.: (1) A demi-stag gu., collared, attired, and semée-de-gouttes or. (2) Upon a mount vert, the trunk of a tree, with two branches sprouting therefrom, and entwined by ivy, thereon a falcon, wings displayed ppr. 284. 6

Heyworth, George Frederick, Esquire, of 96, Lancaster Gate, Hyde Park, London, a crescent az., issuant therefrom fire ppr., between two bats' wings sa. *Nil dimidium est.* 244. 20

Heyworth-Savage, Cecil Francis, Esquire, of Elstowe, Ash, Surrey: (1) Out of a ducal coronet or, a lion's gamb erect sa. (*for Savage*). (2) A crescent az., issuant therefrom fire ppr., between two bats' wings sa. *A te pro te.* 244. 20

Heyworth, Heyworth Potter Lawrence, Esquire, of 2nd Batt. North Staff. Regt., a crescent az., issuant therefrom flames of fire ppr., between two bats' wings sa. *Nil dimidium est.* 244. 20

Hiatt, a lion's gamb erased holding a broken spear. 38. 9

Hibbert, *see* Holland-Hibbert.

Hibbert, Chesh., a cubit arm erect, vested az., the cuff erm., holding in the hand ppr. a crescent arg. *Fidem rectumque colendo.* 206. 10

Hibbert, Robert Fiennes, Esquire, Woodpark, Scariff, co. Galway, and Bucknell Manor, Bicester, same crest.

Hibbert of Chorley, Lancs, a dexter cubit arm erect, vested az., cuffed erm., holding in the hand ppr. a crescent arg. *Fidem rectumque colendo.* 206. 8

Hibbert, Alderman Sir Henry Flemming, F.S.A., F.R.G.S., Chairman Education Committee, Lancashire County Council, same crest and motto.

Hibbert, Leicester, and Crofton Grange, Orpington, same crest and motto.

Hibbert, Paul Edgar Tichborne, Ashby St. Ledgers, Northamp., an arm erect couped below the elbow, vested az., cuffed erm., hand ppr. grasping a crescent arg. *Sit prudentia.*

Hibbert, a hand holding a mill-rind.

Hibbins, Shropsh., a stag's head issuing out of a ducal coronet. 120. 7

Hibbs of Tunbridge Wells, Kent, a demi-stork with wings expanded ducally crowned or, holding in the beak a salmon arg.

Hiccocks of London, on a mural coronet arg., a sun in splendour ppr. cf. 162. 2

Hicham, on a mount vert, a stag springing arg., on the dexter part of the mount a branch of laurel of the first.

Hichcoke, in a tower gu., embattled or, a lion's head of the last. cf. 157. 7

Hiching, an anchor in pale sa. 161. 1

Hickes of Shipston-on-Stour, Worcs., and London, a hart's head couped arg., attired or. 121. 5

Hickes of Silton Hall, Yorks, a buck's head couped at the shoulders or, gorged with a chaplet vert. *Tout en bon heure.* 120. 3

Hickey or **Hickie,** Ireland, a dexter arm in armour embowed ppr., garnished or, holding in the hand a truncheon or.

Hickey, Ireland, a lamb regardant holding over its dexter shoulder a flag, charged with an imperial crown.

Hickey, a wyvern with wings expanded, holding in its mouth a human hand, all ppr. 70. 3

Hickford, a demi-swan with wings addorsed ppr. 100. 2

Hickie, Ireland, a lion's head couped arg., between two palm-branches vert.

Hickie of Billing, Northamp., a lion's head erased arg., pierced through the mouth with a cross crosslet fitchée gu.

Hickling, Northamp., a leopard's head erased or, pellettée. cf. 23. 2

Hickman of Gainsborough, Lincs, Bart., (*extinct*), a talbot couchant arg., collared and lined az., at the end of the line a knot. *Toujours fidèle.* cf. 55. 5

Hickman, Henry Richard Belcher, Esquire, M.A., M.B., B.Ch., Oxon., of 5, Harley Street, W., on a wreath a talbot couchant arg., collared and lined, the line ending in a knot az. *Ne cede malis.* 290. 7

Hickman of Oaken, Staffs, a talbot couchant arg., spotted sa., collared gu. cf. 54. 11

Hickman, Francis William, Esquire, of Kilmore House, co. Clare, Ireland, a talbot sejant arg., collared and chained gu., charged on the shoulder with a trefoil slipped vert. *Malo mori quam fœdari.* cf. 55. 5

Hickman of Fenloe, co. Clare, a talbot sejant arg., collared and chained gu. *Per tot discrimina rerum.* cf. 55. 5

Hickman, Sir Alfred, Bart., of Wightwick, Wolverhampton, and 22, Kensington Palace Gardens, London, a phœnix rising out of flames transfixed through the mouth by a tilting-spear palewise ppr., each wing charged with two annulets erect and interlaced or. *Igne et ferro.* 251. 4

Hickman, Colonel Thomas Edgcumbe, D.S.O., of Naval and Military Club, London, S.W., same crest and motto.

Hickman, a buck's head and neck couped at gaze ppr.

Hicks, Ireland, a lion's gamb issuing per chevron or and gu. cf. 36. 4

Hicks of London and Beccles, Norf., a griffin sejant az., gorged with a collar embattled and counter-embattled or, beaked, armed, and holding in the dexter claw an arrow or.

Hicks of Rickols, Essex and London, a stag's head or, gorged with a chaplet of cinquefoils of the last, leaved vert. cf. 121. 5

Hicks of Kilmacanoge, co. Wicklow, Ireland, a stag's head couped arg., attired gu., gorged with a chaplet of trefoils vert. *Donner et pardonner.* cf. 120. 3

Hicks of Campden, Glouc., Bart., a buck's head couped at the neck or, gorged with a wreath of laurel ppr. 120. 3

Hicks, Stanley Edward, Esquire, of Wilbraham Temple, Cambs: (1) A buck's head couped or, gorged with a chaplet of roses leaved vert (*for Hicks*). cf. 121. 5. (2) An ounce's head erased ppr., ducally crowned gu., and charged on the neck with a gauntlet or (*for Simpson*). *Tout bien ou rien.*

Hicks, Reginald Stanley, Esquire, same crests and motto.

Hicks-Beach, Rt. Hon. Sir Michael Edward, Bart., P.C., M.P., D.C.L., J.P., D.L., of Beverston, Glouc.: (1) A demi-lion rampant arg., ducally gorged or, holding between the paws an escutcheon az., charged with a pile of the second (*for Beach*). 236. 4. (2) A buck's head couped at the neck or, gorged with a wreath of laurel ppr. (*for Hicks*). *Tout en bonne heure.* 120. 3

Hickson, George Archibald Erskine, Esquire, J.P., of Fermoyle, co. Kerry, out of a ducal coronet a griffin's head sa., armed and charged with a trefoil or. *Fide et fortitudine.* cf. 67. 12

Hide, Chesh., Herts, Shropsh., and Wilts, an eagle with wings addorsed sa., beaked and legged or. cf. 76. 11

Hide, Shropsh., an eagle with wings endorsed ppr. cf. 76. 11

Hide, Lancs, an eagle's head erased or, beaked sa. 83. 2

Hide, Lancs, a hawk's head erased or. 88. 12

Hide, a hawk close. 85. 2

Hide, Dorset, a martlet rising sa., charged with a mullet or. cf. 95. 11

Hide, Berks, a leopard's head erased sa., bezantée. cf. 23. 10

Hiders, a garb banded 153. 2

Higden and **Higdon,** on a chapeau gu., turned up erm., a phœnix in flames ppr. 82. 11

Higford, Higford, Hartsfield, Bechworth, Surrey, out of a mural crown inscribed with the word *Ternate*, a Malay holding in the dexter hand the colours of Ternate, all ppr. *Virtus verus honor.*

Higgan, Scotland, a dove holding in its beak an olive-branch ppr. *Peace.* 92. 5

Higgans and **Higgens,** out of a tower gu., a demi-lion rampant arg. *Fide et fortitudine.* 157. 11

Higgat, Suff., an anchor az., between two wings or. 161. 12

Higginbotham-Wybrants, Charles Wybrants, Esquire, of Grosvenor Road, Rathmines, co. Dublin, a stag's head erased ppr., charged with a bezant. *Mitis et fortis.*

Higgenbottom or **Higginbottom,** a dexter and a sinister arm shooting an arrow from a bow, all ppr. 200. 2

Higgens, Sussex, out of a tower gu., a demi-lion arg.

Higginbotham of Glasgow, a sinister and a dexter arm shooting an arrow from a bow, all ppr. *By aim and effort.* 200. 2

Higgins, Gustavus Francis, of Turvey House, Beds, a griffin's head erased or, gorged with a collar gu. *Virtuti nihil obstat.* cf. 66. 2

Higgins and **Higgons,** Shropsh., a griffin's head erased or, gorged with a collar gu., ringed and finned arg. cf. 66. 2

Higgins, Shropsh., a gryphon's head erased or, and gorged with a collar sa., charged with a lozenge arg., between two plates, and holding in the beak a lobster's claw erased gu. 67. 2

Higgins, Henry, Esquire, J.P., of Moreton Jeffreys and Thing Hall, Withington, Heref., a griffin's head erased or, gorged with a collar sa., charged with a lozenge arg., between two plates, and holding in the beak a lobster's claw erased gu. *Faithful and true.* 67. 2

Higgins, Platt-, Edward, Esquire, Shropsh.: (1) A gryphon's head erased or, and gorged with a collar sa., charged with a lozenge arg., between two plates, and holding in the beak a lobster's claw erased gu. (*for Higgins*). 67. 2. (2) A demi-wolf gu., armed and langued az., semée of plates, holding in the dexter paw a wreath arg. and gu., and charged on the shoulder with a cross crosslet or (*for Platt*). *Labitur et labetur.* 31. 10

Higgins of Glenary, co. Waterford, a griffin's head erased or, charged with a crescent gu., and gorged with a collar of the last, thereon three bezants. *Pro patria et virtute.* cf. 66. 2

Higgins, Joseph Napier, Esquire, B.A., Barrister-at-Law, K.C., of Winchenden Priory, Aylesbury, and 24, the Boltons, London, S.W., same crest and motto.

Higgins, co. Mayo, out of a tower double-turreted sa., a demi-griffin arg., holding in the dexter claw a dagger sa., hilt and pommel or. *Pro patria.*

Higgins of London, out of a tower double-towered sa., a demi-griffin arg., holding in the dexter paw a sword of the last, hilt and pommel or.

Higgins of Skellow Grange, Yorks, out of a tower sa., a lion's head arg. cf. 157. 7

Higgins, a castle. *Tutemus.* 155. 8

Higgins of Craigforth, Stirling, Scotland, on a rock a dove holding an olive-branch in her beak, all ppr. *Firme dum fide.* 93. 9

Higgins of Eastnor, Heref., a garb ppr., charged with two crosses patée gu. *Patriam hinc sustinet.* cf. 153. 2

Higginson, Colonel Theophilus, C.B., of 23, Campden Hill Road, Kensington, W., out of a tower ppr., a demi-griffin segreant vert, armed and beaked or. *Malo mori quam fœdari.* 157. 5

Higginson, Henry Hartland, Esquire, same crest and motto.

Higginson of Saltmarshe, Heref., a tower arg., in front of the portal thereof, pendent by a riband az., an escutcheon gu., charged with three bezants, two and one. 156. 1

Higginson, Ireland, on a chapeau a dexter arm in armour couped and embowed, holding a tilting-spear, all ppr., tied at the shoulder with a cord and tassels or.

Higginson, Middx., out of a human heart a dexter hand erect between two wheat-ears flexed in saltier, all ppr., holding a closed book sa., garnished or.

Higgs or **Higges,** of Collesborne, Glouc., a buck's head gu., attired or, pierced through the neck with an arrow ppr., headed or, feathered arg. 304. 3

Higgs, of South Stoke, Oxon., and Thatcham, Berks, same crest. *Fide et fortitudine.*

Higgs, W. Miller, Esquire, Braeside, Burghley Road, Wimbledon, same crest.

Higham, a horse's head erased arg. 51. 4

Higham, Suff. and Essex, a talbot passant sa., collared and lined, at the end of the line a coil or, a knot of the same. cf. 54. 5

Higham of Echingham, Sussex, an arm embowed in armour ppr., holding a broken sword arg., hilt and pommel or, tied round the arm with a sash of the last and gu.

Higham of Higham, Chesh., an arm embowed in mail grasping in the hand, all ppr., a sword arg., hilt and pommel or, round the arm a scarf or. *cf.* 195. 2

Highgate, Middx. and Suff., a wolf's head erased gu. 30. 8

Highett, John Moore, Esquire, of Toorak, and Mitiamo Park, Victoria, Australia, Member of the Legislative Assembly, Victoria, a demi-pegasus rampant sa., winged, maned, and tufted or. *Fac et spera.* 47. 5

Highlord, Devonsh., an escarbuncle arg. 164. 12

Highmore of Sherborne, a talbot's head couped at the neck. 56. 12

Highmore of Armathwaite, Cumb., a moorcock ppr.

Highmore of Harby-bron, Cumb., and Strickland, Dorset, an arm in armour ppr., brandishing a falchion arg., hilt and pommel or, between two pike-staves gu., headed, also or.

Higson, a hand couped in fess charged with an eye, all ppr. 221. 4

Hilborne of Kingsdon, Somers., on a mount vert, a sunflower ppr., between two ears of wheat, the stalks interlaced or.

Hildershaw, a swan devouring a fish, all ppr. *cf.* 99. 10

Hildesley of Cromers Gifford, out of a mural coronet a griffin's head between two wings expanded arg. *cf.* 67. 1

Hildyard, Yorks., a cock sa., beaked, legged, and wattled gu. 91. 2

Hildyard, Thoroton-, Thomas Blackborne, Esquire, J.P., of Flintham, Notts, a game-cock sa., beaked, legged, and wattled gu. 90. 2

Hildyard, John Arundel, Horseley House, near Stanhope, Durh., same crest.

Hildyard, a cock ppr. 91. 2

Hill, Marquess of Downshire, *see* Downshire.

Hill-Trevor, Viscount Dungannon and **Baron Hill,** *see* Dungannon.

Hill, Noel-, Baron Berwick, *see* Berwick.

Hill, Viscount (Clegg-Hill), of Hawkestone and Hardwicke, in the same county: (1) A castle triple-towered arg., surmounted with a garland of laurel ppr. (*for Hill*). (2) In front of two branches of oak fructed in saltire ppr., a cross crosslet crossed or (*for Clegg*). *Avancez.* 165. 13

Hill, a wolf's head erased az., holding in the mouth a trefoil slipped vert. *cf.* 30. 8

Hill, a wolf's head erased az., collared arg., holding in the mouth a trefoil slipped vert. *cf.* 30. 11

Hill, a wolf's head erased az., charged on the neck with two bars arg., and holding in the mouth a trefoil slipped vert.

Hill, Joseph, Esquire, J.P., of Park Drive, Heaton, Bradford, Yorks, in front of a talbot's head couped sa., a demi-catherine-wheel or, all between two wings per fesse indented or and gu. *Honore et labore.* 56. 13

Hill, Sidney, Esquire, J.P., of Langford House, Langford, Somers., a talbot's head couped arg., charged with a chevron nebuly, and holding in the mouth a fleur-de-lis az. *Omne bonum, Dei donum.* 56. 8

Hill of London, a talbot's head erased arg., between two laurel-branches vert.

Hill, Shuldham, S. G., of 2, Fabrique Street, Quebec, a talbot's head couped, collared, and chained. *Vi et virtute.*

Hill, a talbot's head erased gu., collared or, charged with a trefoil vert. *Spero meliora.* *cf.* 56. 1

Hill of Teddington, Middx., a talbot's head couped sa., guttée-d'eau, gorged with a collar gu., rimmed and studded or. *cf.* 56. 1

Hill, Yorks, a talbot's head and neck couped sa., eared and semée of cinquefoils arg., gorged with a collar gu., edged, ringed, and studded or. *cf.* 56. 1

Hill, Sir Henry Blyth, Bart., of St. Columbe, co. Londonderry, a talbot's head couped sa., guttée-d'eau, collared gu., studded and ringed or. *Ne tentes aut perfice.* *cf.* 56. 1

Hill, Middx., and of Bromsgrove, Worcs., a talbot passant or, collared gu. *cf.* 54. 5

Hill, Richard, Thornton Hall, Pickering, Yorks, a talbot's head couped sa., eared arg., gorged with a collar gu, rimmed and ringed or, and charged on the neck with three cinquefoils of the second, one above and two below the collar.

Hill of St. Katherine's Hill, Worcs., on a mount in front of a fern-brake ppr., a talbot or, collared az., resting the dexter forepaw on three annulets interlaced, also or. *Avancez.* 54. 7

Hill, Edward Henry, Esquire, on a mount vert, a talbot passant ppr., collared gu., its dexter paw resting on three annulets interlaced. *Avancez.*

Hill of Hacketstown, co. Carlow, Ireland, a greyhound sejant arg., collared az. *cf.* 59. 2

Hill of Hales, Norf., a boar's head and neck sa., holding in the mouth a broken spear ppr., headed arg.

Hill of Bury St. Edmunds, Suff., a boar's head couped sa., holding in the mouth an acorn or, leaved vert. 42. 7

Hill of Knutsford, Chesh., between two branches of palm ppr., a boar's head couped or, holding in the mouth a trefoil slipped vert. *Auxilio divino.*

Hill of Taunton, Somers., a squirrel sejant arg., collared and lined or. *cf.* 135. 4

Hill of Yarmouth and Lynn, Norf., on a chapeau gu., turned up erm., a lion passant or, between two dragon's wings expanded of the first, each charged with as many bars of the second.

Hill of Littlepipe, Staffs, a lion rampant arg., pierced through the breast by a broken spear in bend, the point imbrued ppr.

Hill, Ireland, a lion rampant gardant gu., holding in the dexter paw a sword ppr.

Hill of Graig, Doneraile, co. Cork, a lion rampant arg., pierced through the breast by a broken spear in bend ppr., the head imbrued, also ppr. *Ne tenta vel perfice.*

Hill of St. John's, Wexford, a demi-lion gu. *Candide me fides.* 10. 3

Hill, Rev. Henry Copinger, Buxhall Rectory, Stowmarket, on a chapeau gu., turned up erm., a demi-lion passant or, between two dragons' wings expanded of the first, each charged with two bars erm.

Hill, Edward Smith, Esquire, a demi-leopard ppr., gorged with a collar gemel or, holding between the paws a star of eight points or. *Par negotiis neque supra.*

Hill, a demi-leopard arg., spotted of all colours, ducally gorged or. 25. 10

Hill of Silvington, Shropsh., on the horns of a crescent vairée or and az., a bull's head cabossed of the first.

Hill, Bucks, a goat's head per pale indented gu. and az., collared and armed or. *cf.* 128. 11

Hill, Scotland, a stag's head. *Veritas superabit montes.* 121. 5

Hill of Lewisham, Kent, a stag's head erased ppr., holding in the mouth an oak-slip vert, fructed or. *cf.* 121. 2

Hill of Wye, Kent, a stag's head erased ppr. 121. 2

Hill, Rt. Hon. Alexander Staveley, of Oxley Manor, near Wolverhampton, and 4, Queen's Gate, S.W., two arrows in saltire transfixed through a bull's head caboshed. *Fortiter ac sapienter.*

Hill-Whitson, Captain Charles, of Parkhill, Blairgowrie: (1) A dexter arm in armour embowed, holding in the hand a broken tilting-spear fessewise, the point pendent, all ppr. (*for Whitson*). 197. 2. (2) A stag's head ppr. (*for Hill*). 121. 5

Hill, a martlet. 95. 5

Hill, an owl arg. 96. 4

Hill of Stallington Hall, Stafford, a hawk ppr., belled or. *cf.* 85. 2

Hill, on the trunk of a tree lying fessways or, a falcon ppr., beaked and belled of the first.

Hill of Pounsford, Somers., an eagle with wings expanded ppr., holding in the beak an acorn slipped vert, fructed or. *cf.* 77. 2

Hill, Henry Seymour McCalmont, D.C.L., J.P., of Forest View, East Grinstead, Sussex, and 10, King's Bench Walk, Temple, E.C., on a mount vert, a dove rising with wings elevated, holding in the beak an olive-branch, all ppr. *Stant colles o veteresque campi.*

Hill, Devonsh., Cornw., and Northamp., a dove arg., holding in his beak an olive-branch vert. 92. 5

Hill, Charles Gathorne, Esquire, a dove, in the beak an olive-branch ppr., gorged with two chevronels sa., and resting the dexter claw on a mullet arg. *Perseverantia omnia vincit.*

Hill, Colonel Sir Edward Stock, K.C.B., M.P., of Rookwood, Llandaff, Hazel Manor, Compton Martin, Bristol, and 1, St. James's Street, London, S.W., same crest and motto.

Hill, Ernest Gathorne, Esquire, of Raddery, Fortrose, N.B., same crest and motto.

Hill, a fleur-de-lis az. 148. 2

Hill of Dennis Park, Staffs, and Blaenavon, Monm., a fleur-de-lis arg. *Esse quam videri.* 148. 2

Hill, Ireland, three roses ppr., stalked and leaved vert. 149. 12

Hill of London, Middx., and Herts, on a mount a branch vert, with three cinquefoils arg.

Hill, Thomas, Esquire, J.P., of 5, Newcastle Drive, the Park, Notts, two arms in armour embowed ppr., each charged with a leopard's face az., the hand also ppr., holding a sprig of three cinquefoils vert, stalked and slipped ppr. *Fac recte et nil time.* 104. 5

Hill of Edinburgh and Bengal, and Hill of London, a dexter arm in armour embowed, the hand grasping a dagger, all ppr. *Esse quam videri.* 196. 5

Hill, on a mount a chalice with flames issuant therefrom. *cf.* 177. 6

Hill, upon a mount a castle triple-towered with flames issuing therefrom.

Hill, Sir Clement Lloyd, K.C.M.G., of 9, Grosvenor Place, S.W., a castle triple-turreted, surmounted by a garland of laurel ppr. *Avancez.*

Hill, John, Esquire, of Britannia House, Saltburn-by-the-Sea, a castle tripletowered or, charged with an escutcheon az., thereon a rose arg., all between four ears of wheat bladed and slipped or, two on either side. *Avancez.*

Hill of Lambhill, Scotland, a Bible expanded ppr. *Veritas superabit montes.* 155. 8

Hill-Lowe, Arthur Hill Ommanney Peter, Esquire, of Court of Hill, Tenbury: (1) A demi-gryphon segreant or (*for Lowe*). (2) A castle arg. (*for Hill*). *Spero meliora.—Stant colles veteresque campi.*

Hill-Male, Captain Richard, of Pen-y-coedcae, near Pontypridd, Glamorgan, (1) A spear erect ppr., therefrom pendent by a riband az., an escutcheon gu., charged with two battle-axes saltirewise arg. (2) A demi-leopard arg., spotted of all colours, ducally gorged or. *Cruci dum spiro spero.*

Hillaire and **Hillarie,** a griffin's head holding in the beak a key ppr. *cf.* 66. 6

Hillary, Bart. (*extinct*), of Danbury Place, Essex, and Rigg House, Yorks, out of a mural coronet gu., a cubit arm in armour ppr., garnished or, holding in the gauntlet a caltrap, also or, round the arm a scarf vert. *Virtute nihil invium.* 209. 13

Hillas, Robert William Goodwin, Esquire, of Seaview, Dromore, W., co. Sligo, Ireland, within an annulet or, a mullet pierced sa. *Per ferum obtinui.* 167. 4

Hillersden and **Hillesden,** Devonsh., a squirrel sejant ppr., collared and cracking a nut or. *cf.* 135. 7

Hilliar, a harp or. 168. 9

Hilliard, an arm in armour embowed, grasping in the hand a spear, all ppr. 197. 2

Hilliard or **Hillary,** Warw., and of Maringe, Yorks, a cubit arm erect in armour ppr., garnished or, holding in the gauntlet a caltrap arg., and round the arm a sash vert.

Hilliard, Edward, Esquire, of Ickenham, Middx., a dexter arm in armour embowed, holding in the hand a javelin in bend sinister, all ppr. *In te domine speravi.*

Hilliard, Yorks and Durh., a cock sa., combed, legged, beaked, and wattled gu. 91. 2

Hilliard of Caherslee, co. Kerry, a cock statant sa., combed, wattled, legged, and spurred gu. 91. 2

Hillier, an arm from the elbow erect vested, holding in the hand a branch of palm.

Hillier of Mocollop Castle, Lismore, co. Waterford, in front of two Danish battle-axes in saltire a leopard's face holding in the mouth a scimitar fessewise, all ppr. *Crux mea, lux mea.*

Hillingdon, Baron (Mills), of Hillingdon Court, and of Camelford House, Park Lane, both in the county of Middx., of Wildernesse, Kent, a demi-lion regardant or, gorged with a collar gemel az., holding between the paws a millrind sa. *Nil conscire sibi.* 11. 1

Hillman, a demi-eagle with wings displayed or, holding in the beak a rose gu., stalked and leaved vert. *cf.* 80. 2

Hillocks, Scotland, out of a pheon az., between two ostrich-wings gu., a sprig of laurel ppr. *Nihil sine cruce.*

Hills, a horse current gu., holding in his mouth a broken spear-head sa. *cf.* 52. 7

Hills, Kent, a stag's head erased, holding in the mouth an oak-slip fructed, all ppr. *In cœlo confidemus.* *cf.* 121. 2

Hills of Colne Parke, Essex, a tower with two turrets ppr.

Hills, Arnold Frank, Esquire, D.L., of Monkhams, Woodford, Essex, and Redleaf, Penshurst, Kent, upon a rock ppr., a talbot arg., gorged with a collar nebuly, charged on the body with two cross crosslets az., and resting the dexter fore-leg on a fountain, also ppr.

Hills-Johnes, Lieutenant-General Sir James, G.C.B., V.C., of Dolaucothy, Llanwrda, R.S.O., Carmarthensh.: (1) On two halberds in saltire, the staves gu., headed or, a raven sa., and (for distinction) charged upon the breast with a cross crosslet or (*for Johnes*). (2) On a mount vert, a broken tiltingspear erect ppr., and in front thereof a horse current arg., guttée-de-sang, holding in the mouth the other part of the spear, also ppr. (*for Hills*). *Deus pascit corvos.—In cœlo confidemus.*

Hillsborough, Earl of, *see* Downshire, Marquess of.

Hillyard, a cock ppr. 91. 2

Hilton, a hand vested barry arg. and sa., holding a holly-branch ppr.

Hilton-Simpson, Rev. William, M.A., Rector of Milstead, Kent, an ounce's head pean erased gu., gorged with a collar gemelle arg. (*for Simpson*). *cf.* 23. 10. (2) In front of a javelin erect, a man's head in profile in a helmet, the visor up, and a tilting-spear fessewise resting upon the wreath, all ppr. (*for Hilton*). *Nunquam obliviscar.*

Hilton of Hilton Castle, Durh., on a close helmet Moses' head in profile glorified, adorned with a rich diapered mantle, all ppr. *Tant que je puis.*

Hinchinbroke, Viscount, *see* Sandwich, Earl of.

Hinchley, a leopard couchant ppr. 24. 10

Hinchman, a demi-lion arg., holding in his dexter paw a bugle-horn stringed gu.

Hinckes, Hincks, or **Hinks,** a hand holding a scorpion, all ppr. 220. 1

Hinckes of the Wood House, Tettenhall, Staffs: (1) A lion's gamb erased arg., in front thereof three annulets interlaced and fesseways gu. (*for Hinckes*). (2) A man's head in profile, couped at the shoulders, about the neck a halter ppr., on the breasts two cross crosslets fitchée in saltire or (*for Davenport*). *Mors janua vitæ.*

Hinckley, on a ducal coronet or, a star of twelve points ppr. *cf.* 164. 4

Hincks, Ireland, a demi-chevalier holding in the dexter hand a scimitar. 187. 4

Hincks of Chorlton, Chesh., and of Yorks, a demi-lion rampant gu., guttée-de-larmes, gorged with a collar dancettée arg., the sinister paw resting on an annulet or. *In cruce et lacrymis spes est.*

Hincks, Thomas Cowper, Terrace House, Richmond, Yorks, same crest and motto.

Hincks, late Rev. Thomas Dix, LL.D., Professor of Hebrew at the Belfast Institution, a demi-lion rampant sa., the sinister paw resting on a bezant.

Hind, an ensign in full dress, with a cocked hat, holding the Union standard of Britain, all ppr. 188. 6

Hind, on the trunk of a tree raguled arg., a cockatrice or.

Hind of Calais, a demi-talbot arg., collared sa., holding between the paws a key, wards upwards or.

Hind of London, a hind's head couped ppr., collared or, holding in the mouth a rose gu., stalked and leaved vert. *cf.* 124. 5

Hind, Smithard-, William Hind, on a mount a hind at gaze, in the mouth an arrow fessewise ppr., resting the dexter fore-leg on an annulet encircling a cross patée fitchée or.

Hind, Kent, a griffin's head couped between two wings, collared and charged on the breast with an escallop. *cf.* 67. 7

Hinde of Evelith, Shropsh., a lion's head erased arg. 17. 8

Hinde-Hodgson, Northumb., on a rock a dove az., the wings or, holding in the mouth an olive-branch ppr. *Miseris succurrere disco.* 93. 9

Hinde of Bishopwearmouth, Durh., a demi-pegasus arg., maned or, holding a sword of the first, hilt and pommel or. *Tutum te robore reddam.* *cf.* 47. 5

Hinde of Hodgeworth, Bucks, out of a ducal coronet arg., a cockatrice or.

Hindle, a lyre ppr. *cf.* 168. 8

Hindley of Hindley, Lancs, an arm in armour embowed fesseways, holding a scimitar in pale entiled with a boar's head couped.

Hindlip, Baron (Allsopp), of Hindlip Hall, Worcs., and Alsop-en-le-Dale, Derbysh., upon a pheon a plover close, holding in the beak an ear of wheat, all or. *Festina lente.* 93. 6

Hindman, a buck trippant ppr. 117. 8

Hindmarsh, Hendmarsh, or **Hyndmarsh,** Scotland, a demi-lion rampant. *Nil nisi patria.* 10. 2

Hine of Dartmouth, Devonsh., on a tortoise arg., an eagle rising holding in the beak a sprig of heath, and gazing on the sun, all ppr.

Hines, Ireland, a plough ppr. 178. 7
Hingenson, Bucks, a squirrel sejant cracking a nut, all ppr. 135. 7
Hingham, Norf., a horse's head furnished with waggon-harness, all ppr. 58. 12
Hingley, Sir Benjamin, Bart., Hatherton Lodge, Cradley, Stourbridge, out of the battlements of a tower ppr., a demi-lion gu., gorged with a collar vair, holding between the paws a battle-axe of the first, the whole between two wings of the second. *In hoc signo vinces.* 284. 3
Hingston of Holbeton, Devonsh., a hind's head couped or, holding in the mouth a holly-slip ppr. *cf.* 124. 1
Hinks or **Hincks** of London, a lion's head erased or, between two wings arg. 19. 7
Hinshaw, William, Esquire, of Barrochan House, Renfrewsh., Scotland, a fox's head holding in its mouth an olive-branch ppr. *Vigilantia.* *cf.* 33. 4
Hinson of Fulham, Middx., a fleur-de-lis per pale erm. and az. 148. 2
Hinton, Shropsh., a paschal lamb arg., the glory or, carrying a banner of the first, charged with a cross gu.
Hinton of South Denchworth and Kingston, Lisle, Berks, and Shropsh., an eagle's leg erased encircled by a serpent ppr.
Hinton of Halstone, co. Wexford, Ireland, a mount vert, thereon an eagle's leg erased, the claw pressing down the neck of a serpent entwined round the limb, all ppr. *Assurgam.*
Hinxman of Little Durnford, Wilts, a cubit arm vested quarterly or and vert, the hand ppr., holding the attire of a stag or. 208. 6
Hipkiss, a sphinx gardant with wings addorsed ppr. 182. 12
Hippisley, Bart., of Warfield Grove, Berks, on a ducal coronet or, a hind's head erased sa., gorged with a collar of the first. *Amicitiæ virtutisque fœdus —Non mihi sed patriæ.*
Hippisley of Cameley, Somers., and Stanton, Wilts, on a ducal coronet ppr., a hind's head erased or, gorged with a collar sa., charged with three mullets of the first.
Hippisley, Somers., a hind's head erased ppr., gorged with a collar sa., charged with three mullets pierced or. *cf.* 124. 3
Hippisley, Richard John Bayntun, Esquire, Ston Easton, Somers., same crest and motto.
Hippisley, William Henry, Lt.-Col. late Royal Scots Greys, of Sparsholt Manor, Wantage, same crest.
Hird of Bradford, Yorks, a buck's head erased gu., attired or. 121. 2
Hirme of Heveringland, Norf., a talbot passant sa., collared and lined or, the line coiled at the end. *cf.* 54. 5
Hirst and **Hirste,** a hand holding a seax cutting at a feather. 213. 9
Hirst of Howarth, Yorks, a hurst of trees ppr., pendent therefrom an escutcheon arg., charged with a cinquefoil vert. *Efflorescent.* *cf.* 144. 2
Hirst, Reginald, Esquire, of 8, York Place, Huddersfield, a demi-man affrontée ppr., holding in the dexter hand a bugle-horn, stringed or, and supporting with the sinister hand an escutcheon sa., charged with a sun in splendour or. *Non mutat fortuna genus.*
Hirst, Thomas Julius, Esquire, of Meltham Hall, Meltham Mills, York, a dexter cubit arm in bend, holding an arrow ppr., and a scimitar in saltire engrailed at the back, also ppr., pommel and hilt or. *His regi servitium.* 269. 9
Hislop of Bururig, Prestonpans, N.B., upon a mount a stag standing under a tree, all ppr. *Semper paratus.* 116. 13
Hislop, Bart., Devonsh.: (1) Of augmentation, a soldier of the 22nd Light Dragoons mounted, accoutred, and in the position of attack ppr., over the crest *Deccan.* (2) Out of a mural coronet a buck's head couped ppr., attired or. *Hæc manus ob patriam.*
Hitch of Wendlebury, Oxon., an heraldic antelope's head erased sa., tufted and maned or, vulned through the neck by a bird-bolt of the last, feathered arg., holding the end in his mouth.
Hitchcock of Preshute, Wilts, a lion's head erased or, holding in the mouth a round buckle arg.
Hitchens and **Hitchins,** Oxon., out of a mural coronet a garb, on the top thereof a bird perched ppr. 153. 9
Hitchens and **Hitchins,** on an heraldic rose gu., barbed vert, a lion's head erased or. *cf.* 19. 9
Hitchens, on the top of a tower a martlet. 156. 9
Hitchin-Kemp, Fred, of 6, Beechfield Road, Catford, S.E., on a garb fesseways or, a pelican feeding her young, wings elevated sa., vulned ppr., charged on the breast with three annulets interlaced, and gorged with a collar gemel or. *Honestas et veritas.*
Hitfield, an ostrich-feather enfiled with a ducal coronet. 114. 12
Hixon of Fermoyle, co. Kerry, Ireland, out of a ducal coronet or, a griffin's head sa. beaked and charged upon the neck with a trefoil of the first. *Fide et fortitudine.* *cf.* 67. 12
Hoad, Middx. and London, a stag's head erased arg. 121. 2
Hoadley, on a terrestrial globe or, a dove with wings expanded, holding in the beak an olive-branch ppr. *Veritas et patria.* 94. 6
Hoar, a fox current ppr. *cf.* 32. 8
Hoar, George, Esquire, of Twyford, Hants, an eagle's head erased arg., charged with three ermine spots, pendent from the beak an annulet. *cf.* 83. 2
Hoard, a lamb ppr., holding a flag gu., charged with a saltire arg. 130. 2
Hoare, *see* Hamilton-Hoare.
Hoare, Sir Joseph Wallis O'Bryen, Bart., J.P., of Annabelle, co. Cork, a stag's head and neck erased arg. *Venit hora.—Dum spiro, spero.—Datur hora amori.* 121. 2
Hoare, O'Brien-, Stafford, Esquire, of Turville Park, Bucks, an eagle's head erased arg., charged with an ermine spot. *In ardua.*
Hoare, William, M.A., of Iden Manor, Staplehurst, same crest and motto.
Hoare, Edward Brodie, Tenchleys, Limpsfield, a stag's head couped ppr.
Hoare, Ireland, a stag's head affrontée gu., ducally gorged and attired or. 119. 14
Hoare, Sir Henry Hugh Arthur, Bart., an eagle's head erased arg., charged with an ermine spot. *In ardua.* *cf.* 83. 2
Hoare, Sir Samuel, Bart., Sidestrand, Cromer, in front of a stag's head erased arg., three crosses couped sa. *Venit hora.* 305. 2
Hoare or **Hore,** Glouc., an eagle's head erased sa., gorged with a bar gemelle or. *cf.* 83. 2
Hobart, Earl of Buckinghamshire, a bull passant per pale sa. and gu., bezantée, in the nose a ring or. *Auctor pretiosa facit.* *cf.* 45. 2
Hobart, Norf., a bull passant sa., semée of estoiles or. *Quæ supra.* *cf.* 45. 2
Hobart, Bucks and Norf., a bull's head couped sa., semée of estoiles or. *cf.* 44. 3
Hobart, same crest. *cf.* 44. 3
Hobbes of Sarum, Wilts, between the horns of a crescent arg., an estoile or, all between two wings gu. 112. 6
Hobbins of Redmarsley, Heref., a stag's head ppr. 121. 5
Hobbs, Ireland, an arrow point downwards gu., feathered or, and a palm-branch vert, in saltier. 171. 7
Hobbs, Surrey, on a dexter gauntlet in fess arg., a falcon ppr., beaked, legged, and belled or. 86. 13
Hobbs, Middx., a demi-heron volant sa., beaked gu., holding in the beak a fish arg.
Hobbs of Stoke-Gursy, Somers., a demi-heraldic tiger az., armed, maned, and tufted arg., pierced through the body with a broken spear or, headed of the second, vulned on the shoulders gu., the spear entering the breast and coming out at the shoulder.
Hobbs, Captain Herbert Thomas de Carteret, Barnaboy, Frankford, King's Co., same crest. *Semper paratus.*
Hobbs, Kent, a heraldic tiger rampant regardant arg.
Hoberd and **Hobert,** a demi-lion gu. 10. 3
Hobhouse, Baron (Hobhouse), of Hadspen, Somers., on a mural coronet per pale az. and gu., a crescent arg., and issuant therefrom an estoile irradiated or. *Spero meliora.*
Hobhouse, Sir Charles Parry, Bart., Manor House, Monkton Farleigh, Bradford-on-Avon, Wilts, on a mural coronet per pale az. and gu., a crescent arg., and issuant therefrom an estoile irradiated or. *Spes vitæ melioris.*
Hobhouse, Rt. Hon. Henry, M.P., of Hadspen House, Castle Cary, Somers., same crest. *Melioris spero.*
Hobhouse, Somers., a griffin sejant ppr. 62. 10
Hobleday of Thornton, Warw., out of a ducal coronet or, a demi-lion rampant, bezantée. *cf.* 16. 3
Hoblethwayte of Sedberg, Yorks, out of a ducal coronet or, a demi-wolf erm. *cf.* 31. 2
Hoblyn of Bodreyn and Nanswhyden, Cornw., a tower arg. 156. 2
Hoblyn, Charles Dennis, Esquire, a tower ppr. *Delectant domi, non impediunt foris.* 156. 2
Hoblyn, William Ernest Paget, Esquire, of the Fir Hill, St. Columb, Cornw., same crest and motto.

Hoblyn, William Paget, Esquire, of the Fir Hill, Colan, near St. Columb, Cornw., same crest and motto.

Hobson of Merington, Durh., a griffin's head couped arg., between two wings elevated az. *Fortitudine Dei.* 65. 11

Hobson of Marylebone Park, Middx., a griffin passant per pale erm. and or, beaked, membered, and holding in the beak a key of the last. *cf.* 63. 2

Hobson, Middx., a lion's head affrontée arg., charged with three torteaux.

Hobson of Cambs, on a ducal coronet chequy or and sa., a lion's head erased of the first. *cf.* 17. 5

Hobson, Surrey, a leopard's head arg., semée of torteaux. *cf.* 22. 10

Hobson, a leopard's head gardant erased arg., semée of torteaux.

Hobson of Spalding, Lincs, a panther's head erased and gardant ppr., incensed, gorged with a collar chequy or and az.

Hobson, George Andrew, Esquire, of Coverdale Lodge, Richmond, Surrey, a cubit arm erect ppr., holding a rose arg., barbed, seeded, and slipped of the first, and two lilies in saltire of the second, stalked, leaved, and slipped, also ppr. *Vive ut vivas.* 265. 10

Hobson, John Falshaw, Esquire, A.M.I.E., of South Bailey, Durh., same crest and motto.

Hobson, Richard, Esquire, of the Marfords, Bromborough, Chesh., a panther's head affrontée and erased, with flames issuant from the mouth and ears, ppr., transfixed by an arrow fessewise, the pheon to the sinister arg., gorged with a collar counter company or and az. *Fortitudine Deo.* 258. 9

Hobush, out of a ducal coronet or, a savage's head affrontée couped at the shoulders ppr., vested gu., on the head three ostrich-feathers arg. *cf.* 192. 10

Hoby, out of a ducal coronet a fish's head, all ppr. 139. 14

Hoby of Neath Abbey, Glamorgansh., on a chapeau gu., turned up erm., a heraldic tiger rampant arg.

Hoby, Bart. (*extinct*), of Bisham, Berks, a hoby rising sa., beaked, legged, and belled or 88. 2

Hochpied, *see* De Hochpied-Larpent.

Hockenhull, Chesh., a buck's head and neck erased per fess arg. and or, pierced through the nostrils by a dart in bend of the last, feathered of the first, barbed az.

Hockin, Devonsh., on a rock a sea-gull rising, all ppr. *Hoc in loco Deus rupes.* 108. 9

Hockly of Wickwar, Glouc., a demi-griffin segreant with wings endorsed pean, holding in the claws a mullet gu. *cf.* 64. 2

Hockmore of Buckyate and Buckland, Baron, Devonsh., an eagle close, seizing and preying on a moorcock, all ppr.

Hocknell, a dexter hand holding a sugar-cane ppr.

Hoddenet and **Hoddenot,** a dexter hand holding four arrows points downwards ppr. *cf.* 214. 3

Hodder, Robert E., Esquire, in front of a cross fleury or, a battle-axe in pale sa. *Sapere aude.* 172. 5

Hodder, Moore-, of Hoddersfield, co. Cork: (1) A fire-ship, her courses set, fire issuing from below the rigging, all ppr. (*for Hodder*). (2) Out of a ducal coronet or, a Moor's head in profile ppr. (*for Moore*).

Hodder of Ringabella, Cork, a fire-ship in full sail ppr. *Igne et feris vicimus.*

Hoddy, a trout naiant ppr. 139. 12

Hodge, Scotland and Sunderland, a garb entwined by two serpents ppr. 153. 3

Hodge of Angarrack, Cornw., a talbot's head couped arg., semée of estoiles az., holding in the mouth an oak-branch slipped and fructed ppr. *Savoir pouvoir.* *cf.* 56. 12

Hodge, Edward Grose, Esquire, of 9, Highbury Place, London, N., same crest and motto.

Hodge and **Hodges,** an eagle rising looking at the sun, all ppr.

Hodges, Kent, out of a ducal coronet or, a heraldic antelope's head arg., attired and tufted of the first. *Prævisa mala pereunt.*

Hodges, out of a ducal coronet or, a heraldic antelope's head arg., attired and tufted of the first. *Nosce teipsum.*

Hodges of Hanwell, Middx., an antelope's head couped or. *cf.* 126. 2

Hodges, Ireland, out of a ducal coronet a greyhound's head gu. 61. 7

Hodges of Burton and Sison, Leics., a talbot's head couped or, guttée-de-sang, collared and ringed gu. *Fundamentum gloriæ humilitas.* *cf.* 56. 1

Hodges of Overne, Leics., a talbot's head arg., guttée-de-sang, gorged with a collar gu., rimmed and ringed or, and charged with three bezants. *cf.* 56. 1

Hodges, a man ppr., vested arg., his coat gu., holding a standard, also arg., charged with a canton of the third, thereon a cross of the second

Hodges, a dove regardant holding in its beak an olive-branch, all ppr. 92. 4

Hodges of Spickington, Somers., on a chapeau gu., turned up erm., a crescent arg., between two wings or.

Hodges of London and Middx., on a ducal coronet or, a crescent sa.

Hodges of Shipton Moyne, Glouc., out of clouds az., a crescent arg., and between the horns thereof a star of six points or. *Dant lucem crescentibus orti.* *cf.* 136. 9

Hodges of Broadway, Worcs., on a ducal coronet or, a crescent sa.

Hodgeson of London, a dexter arm erect couped at the elbow habited bendy sinister of four arg. and gu., holding in the hand ppr. a covered cup or.

Hodgetts of Hagley, Worcs., an eagle with wings expanded ppr., holding in the beak an annulet. *Confido, conquiesco.* *cf.* 77. 5

Hodgetts of Prestwood, Staffs, a horse's head erm., pierced through the neck by a spear, the staff broken ppr. 289. 2

Hodgkins, Glouc. and Middx., an eagle rising looking towards the sun, all ppr.

Hodgkinson of Overton Hall, Ashover, Derbysh., a garb or, between two wings expanded vert. 153. 14

Hodgkinson of Preston, Lancs, and Middx., a cinquefoil or, between two dragon's wings displayed vert. *Sans Dieu rien.*

Hodgson, Durh., a dove holding in its beak an olive-branch ppr. *Metuo secundus.* 92. 5

Hodgson, Arthur, Esquire, Clopton House, Stratford-on-Avon, same crest.

Hodgson, Robert Kirkman, Esquire, J.P., of Ashgrove, Sevenoaks, same crest. *Pax et fides.*

Hodgson of Houghton House, Cumb., a dove close az., holding in its beak a sprig of laurel ppr. *Dread God.* 92. 5

Hodgson Cumb., Essex and Middx., a dove az., winged or, beaked and membered gu., holding in its beak an olive-branch ppr. 92. 5

Hodgson, Thomas Hesketh, Esquire, of Newby Grange, near Carlisle, same crest. *Dread God.*

Hodgson, on a rock a dove holding in its beak an olive-branch, all ppr. 93. 9

Hodgson of Elswick House, Northumb., on a rock a dove az., winged or, holding in the beak an olive-branch ppr. 93. 9

Hodgson, Chesh., on a mount vert, a falcon with wings close ppr., beaked, legged, and belled or, collared dancettée and pierced through the breast with a sword arg., hilted, also or, vulned ppr.

Hodgson, a griffin's head erased, murally gorged. *cf.* 66. 2

Hodgson of Framfield, Sussex, a griffin's head erased devouring a hand erased at the wrist gu.

Hodgson, Ireland, a salmon haurient az. 139. 11

Hodgson of Boston, Lincs, a dexter cubit arm holding in the hand a broken and bloody hanger, the pommel and hilt or, the point embrued ppr.

Hodgson, John, Esquire, J.P., Nocton Hall, near Lincoln, same crest. *Labore vinces.*

Hodgson, Yorks and Norf., a cubit arm erect habited in mail holding in the hand, all ppr., a broken falchion gu.

Hodiam, a lion's head erased az. 17. 8

Hodilow, Hoddylowe, and **Hoddelow,** a dragon's head sa., collared or. *cf.* 71. 1

Hodington of Hodington, Worcs., over a tower arg., a bird volant or. *cf.* 156. 9

Hodiswell, Yorks, a well ppr. 159. 15

Hodkinson, a shank-bone and a palm-branch in saltier, all ppr. 147. 4

Hodsall, a well arg. 159. 15

Hodsdon of Hodsdon, Herts, a man's head couped at the shoulders ppr., vested arg., on the head a cap or. 192. 11

Hodsdon of Edgeworth, Middx., a man's head ppr., couped at the shoulders, vested az., collared or, on the head a chapeau gu., turned up erm.

Hodsoll, Charles Maxfield, Esquire, of Loose Court, near Maidstone, Kent, a stone fountain or well arg. *Maintien le droit.* 246. 11

Hodson, a dove on a rock. *cf.* 93. 9

Hodson, Ireland, an antelope's head erased gu. 126. 2

Hodson, a griffin's head erased, murally gorged. *cf.* 66. 2

Hodson, Sir Robert Adair, Bart., of Hollybrooke House, co. Wicklow, a dove az., beaked and membered or, holding in her beak an olive-branch ppr. *Pax et amor.* 92. 5

Hodson, Cambs, a unicorn courant regardant arg., gorged with a chaplet of laurel vert.

Hodson, John, Esquire, of the Archway, Downing Terrace, Cambs., upon water ppr., a swan sa., holding in the beak a lotus flower, slipped, also ppr., between two coral branches gu. *Fait bien.*

Hody, Scotland, a bull passant sa. cf. 45. 2

Hody, a trout naiant ppr. 139. 12

Hoe, a hand holding a hautboy. 219. 1

Hoey, Ireland, a pheasant. cf. 90. 8

Hoey, Cashel-, John Baptist, Esquire, of the Middle Temple, a unicorn sejant arg., armed and unguled or, gorged with an Irish crown gu. *Iterum interumque.*

Hoey of Dunganstown, co. Wicklow, out of a ducal coronet or, a dexter and a sinister arm in armour, the hands grasping a sword, all ppr., pommel and hilt or.

Hoey, issuing out of a ducal coronet or, two dexter arms in armour embowed ppr., grasping a dagger of the last. *Fides fortuna fortior.*

Hoffman, out of the top of a tower a demi-woman issuing ppr., attired az., holding in her dexter hand a garland of laurel vert.

Hoffmann, late James Rix, Esquire, of York Terrace, Regent's Park, a demi-lion double-queued az., holding between the paws a sun in splendour ppr., between two elephants' probosces erect, the dexter per fesse gu. and arg., the sinister per fesse or and az. *Tiens à la verité.*

Hofner, the hind parts of a lion couped in the middle of the back, the legs toward the dexter and sinister, the tail erect.

Hoffnung-Goldsmid, Sidney Francis, of 35, Chesham Place: (1) a demi-lion arg, supporting with the paws a bundle of twigs, erect or, banded az., charged on the shoulder with a cross crosslet gu. (2) A demi-lion or, charged with two bars nebuly, and holding between the paws as many anchors in saltire az., all between two proboscides of the last. *Spes anchora vitæ.*

Hog of Harcarse, Scotland, an oak-tree ppr. *Dat gloria vires.* 143. 5

Hog, Thomas Alexander, of Newliston, Linlithgow, same crest and motto. 143. 5

Hog, Scotland, an oak-tree growing out of a mount vert. 143. 14

Hog of Blairdrum, Scotland, a dexter hand couped ppr. *Dant vires gloriam.* 222. 14

Hogan of London, on a chapeau gu., an escallop-shell or, between two wings ppr. 141. 11

Hogan, Ireland, an ostrich's head between two feathers arg. cf. 97. 12

Hogan, a dexter arm in armour embowed ppr., brandishing a sword, also ppr., pommel and hilt or. *Fulminis instar.* 195. 2

Hogan, Ireland, a dexter arm in armour embowed, the hand grasping a sword, all ppr. 195. 2

Hogan of London and East Bradnam, a lion's gamb couped and erect arg., holding an annulet gu., and charged with an annulet for difference.

Hogarth, R. G., F.R.C.S., of 60, Ropewalk, Nottingham, a horse's head couped between two wings. *Candor dat viribus alas.*

Hogarth or **Howgart,** Scotland, a pegasus's head or, winged arg. *Candor dat viribus alas.*

Hogg, *see* Magheramorne, Baron.

Hogg-Allen, *see* Allen.

Hogg, an oak-tree fructed ppr. *Dat gloria vires.* 143. 5

Hogg of Bishopwearmouth, Durh., against an oak-tree vert, fructed gu., a boar statant arg., pierced in the side by an arrow sa.

Hogg, Sir Frederick Russell, K.C.I.E., C.S.I., out of an Eastern coronet arg., an oak-tree fructed ppr., and pendent therefrom an escutcheon az., charged with a dexter arm embowed in armour, the hand grasping an arrow, also ppr. *Dat gloria vires.*

Hogg, Sir Stuart Saunders, of Villa Celine, Beaulieu, France, same crest and motto.

Hogg of Norton House, Durh., a boar statant ppr., pierced in the side with an arrow or, in front of an oak-tree, also ppr., fructed, also or. *Dat gloria vires.*

Hogg, Devonsh., a wyvern vert. 70. 1

Hogg, Scotland, a hand couped in fess. 221. 6

Hoggeson, a swallow volant sa. 96. 2

Hoggeson or **Hoggson,** a hand couped below the wrist or, the hand ppr., holding a broken cutlass arg., hilted of the first, the broken piece falling from the other.

Hogh, a bull passant arg. cf. 45. 2

Hoghe, Chesh., a lion's gamb holding a cross patee or. cf 36. 9

Hoghton, Bart., *see* De Hoghton.

Hoghton of Park Hall, Lancs, a bull passant arg., armed and unguled sa., collared or. cf. 45. 2

Hogue, Scotland, an oak-tree ppr. *Dat gloria vires.* 143. 5

Hoke, an escallop-shell sa., between two wings arg. 141. 10

Hokeley, a bee volant reversed sa. cf. 137. 1

Hol, six tilting-spears in pale, three on the dexter and three on the sinister.

Holand, an arm holding an arrow arg., feathered or. 214. 4

Holbeach, an escutcheon or, pendent from the stump of a tree ppr. 145. 8

Holbeame, a cross crosslet gu. between two palm-branches.

Holbech, Warw., a maunch vert, semée of escallops arg.

Holbech, Venerable Charles William, Farnborough, Warw., same crest.

Holbech or **Holbeach,** Somers., a lion passant sa. 6. 2

Holbeche or **Holbeance,** out of a ducal coronet or, a pelican's head, also or, vulned gu. cf. 98. 2

Holbeck and **Holbecke,** the sun rising from behind a hill ppr. 162. 7

Holbeck of Whittingham, a demi-griffin or, winged gu., holding in the dexter claw an escallop arg. cf. 64. 2

Holberton, William, Esquire, of Tor House, Devonsh., on a mount vert, in front of two tilting-spears in saltire ppr., a boar's head erect couped gu. *Ora et labora.*

Holbiche, a peacock's head erased az. 103. 1

Holbrook, a lion passant gardant tail extended ppr. cf. 4. 3

Holbrooke, Suff., a lion's head erased sa., charged with a chevron or, surmounted of a cross formée fitchée at the foot of the same. cf. 17. 8

Holbrow, Stanley Charles, Glouc., between a pair of wings elevated arg., three mullets pierced in triangle. 256. 6

Holbrow, Rev. Thomas, of Shaw Well, Corbridge-on-Tyne, Northumb., same crest.

Holburne, Bart., Scotland, a demi-lion holding in his dexter paw a mullet arg. *Decus summum virtus.* 15. 7

Holcomb and **Holcombe,** a serpent nowed, holding in its mouth a garland of laurel ppr. 142. 7

Holcombe of Hull, Devonsh., a man's head affrontée, couped at the breast ppr., wreathed round the temple or and az. 190. 5

Holcombe, Walter, Esquire, Highwick, Arkwright Road, Hants, a Saracen's head in profile, couped at the shoulders or, banded about the temples arg. *Dum spiro spero.*

Holcott, on the point of a sword, a stag's head caboshed, all ppr.

Holcroft of Holcroft, Lancs, an eagle with wings expanded sa., holding in the dexter claw a sword arg., hilt and pommel or. cf. 77. 10

Holcroft of Balkerton, Notts, an eagle gu., holding in the dexter claw a sword in pale arg., hilt and pommel or, charged on the breast with a fleur-de-lis of the last.

Holden-Hambrough, late Oscar William, of Pipewell Hall, Kettering, Northamp., on a mount vert, a horse courant arg., powdered with cross crosslets az. and guttée-de-sang. (Over the crest) *Foresight.*—(Under the arms) *Honestum utili præ fer.*

Holden, Scotland, an eagle's leg erased at the thigh ppr. cf. 113. 8

Holden, Scotland, a cock ppr. 91. 2

Holden, Lancs, a pheasant ppr. cf. 90. 8

Holden of Derby, a moorcock rising sa., winged or. 89. 5

Holden of Holden, Lancs: (1) A double-headed allerion gu. (2) A moorcock sa., winged or. cf. 89. 5

Holden of Darley Abbey, Derbysh., a moorcock sa., combed and wattled gu. cf. 89. 5

Holden, Harry Ralph Lonsdale, Esquire, of Reedly House and Palace House, Lancs, a moorcock ppr., charged on the breast with a cinquefoil or. *Nec temere, nec timide.*

Holden, Colonel Henry, same crest. *Teneo et teneor.*

Holden, John, Nuttall, Notts, a moorcock sa., semée of trefoils or.

Holden, Edward Charles Shuttleworth, Esquire, D.S.O., J.P., of the Cottage, Doveridge, Derbysh.: (1) On a mount vert, a moorcock rising sa., winged or (*for Holden*). 89. 8. (2) A cubit arm in armour ppr., grasping in the gauntlet a weaver's shuttle sa., tipped and furnished with quills of yarn, the threads pendent or (*for Shuttleworth*). cf. 211. 3

Holden, Rev. John Shuttleworth, M.A., of Lackford Manor, Bury St. Edmunds, same crests.

Holden of Cruttenden, an antelope's head ppr. 126. 2

Holden, Sir Angus, Bart., Oakworth House, Keighley, issuant from a chaplet of oak vert, an eagle's head erased or, gorged with a collar gemel az. *Extant recte factis premia.* 276. 12

Holden, Edward Thomas, Esquire, of Glenelg, Great Barr, Staffs, a cubit arm erect vested sa., charged with a pile erminois, the hand ppr., holding a bugle-horn stringed or, between two pheons erect or. *Holden.* 267. 10

Holden, Robert Henry, Esquire, J.P., of Rushall, Walsall, Staffs, same crest and motto.

Holden, William Rose, Esquire, of Weymouth, a dexter cubit arm erect vested sa., the hand ppr., holding a cross crosslet fitchée or, from the wrist a pile erm., the arm charged with a bugle-horn strung or. *Et teneo et teneor.*

Holden, George Herbert Rose, M.A., M.D., B.C., of 168, Castle Hill, Reading, same crest and motto.

Holder, Sir John Charles, Bart., Pitmaston, Moor Green, Birmingham, on the battlements of a tower per pale or and arg., charged with a cross gu., a lion sejant per pale indented az., and of the third, supporting with a dexter paw an anchor arg. *Nisi Dominus frustra.* 276. 6

Holder, on a ducal coronet gu., a lion sejant or. *cf.* 8. 8

Holder, Charles Henry Vane, Esquire, of 45, Clanricarde Gardens, London, W., on a ducal coronet of five leaves a lion sejant, the dexter paw elevated.

Holder, a lymphad per pale or and arg. *Insignia virtutis.* 160. 6

Holderness, between the horns of a crescent or, a cross patée gu. 163. 6

Heldich and **Holdiche,** an arm in armour embowed holding in the gauntlet a scimitar, all ppr. 196. 4

Holdich, Sir Edward Alan, K.C.B., of 19, Onslow Square, London, S.W., a martlet sa., in front of a cross patée fitchée between two branches of palm or. 95. 9

Holdich-Hungerford, Henry Vane Forester, Esquire, J.P., D.L.: (1) Out of a ducal coronet or, a pepper garb of the first between two sickles erect ppr. (*for Hungerford*). (2) A martlet sa. in front of a cross patée fitchée between two branches of palm or (*for Holdich*).

Holding, Middx., a bugle-horn ppr. 228. 11

Holdip of London and Southamp., on a chapeau az., turned up arg., a griffin's head erm., collared of the first, beaked sa., and holding in the beak a broken spear or.

Holdsworth, Thomas Holy, Sandal Hall, Yorks, a raven ppr. *Religione viret fortitudo.*

Hole, Shropsh., an escallop sa., between two wings arg. 141. 10

Hole of Ebberley House, near Great Torrington, Devonsh., out of a mural coronet or, an arm in armour embowed holding a battle-axe, all ppr. *Honor virtutis præmium.*

Hole, William Robert, Esquire, J.P., D.L., of Parke, Bovey Tracy, Devonsh., same crest and motto.

Hole, Very Rev. Samuel Reynolds, Dean of Rochester, of the Deanery, Rochester, and Caunton Manor, Newark, in front of a spear in pale ppr., headed or, between two branches of palm vert, a demi-lion rampant az., holding in the paws a crescent or. *Frœna vel aurea nolo.*

Holebrooke, two dolphins in saltire az. 140. 3

Holerton, a wyvern vert. 70. 1

Holford, Leics. and Rutl., a greyhound's head sa., collared and ringed or. 61. 2

Holford, Glouc., and of Holford, Chesh., a greyhound's head sa. *cf.* 61. 2

Holford, Thomas, of Castle Hill, Buckland Newton, Dorchester, a mount vert, therefrom in front of a greyhound's head sa., gorged with a collar gemelle, holding in the mouth a fleur-de-lis or, the sun rising. *Toujours fidèle.*

Holford, Captain George Lindsay, C.I.E., M.V.O., Dorchester House, Park Lane, W., same crest.

Holford, Gwynne-, Lieutenant-Colonel James Price, of Buckland, Brecknock: (1) From the sun in splendour or, rising from behind a hill vert, a greyhound's head issuant sa., gorged with a collar gemel and holding in the mouth a fleur-de-lis or (*for Holford*). (2) A dexter arm in armour ppr., issuant from a crescent arg., holding a sword erect, also ppr., hilt and pommel or, enfiled by a boar's head or, erased and vulned ppr. *Vim vi repellere licet.—Toujours fidèle.*

Holgrave and **Holgreve,** a hand holding a thunderbolt in pale ppr. 216. 4

Holhead, a falcon rising. 88. 2

Holinshed, a bull's head and neck sa. *cf.* 44. 3

Holker of London, a lion rampant per chevron embattled or and az. 1. 13

Holl, Norf., a sea-lion sejant or, guttée-de-sang. 20. 2

Holland, *see* Knutsford, Baron.

Holland, Duke of Exeter, on a chapeau gu., turned up erm., a lion statant gardant or, ducally crowned of the same, gorged with a collar az., charged with a fleur-de-lis, also or. *cf.* 4. 4

Holland, Baron (Fox), on a chapeau az., turned up erm., a fox sejant or. *Et vitam impendere vero.* 32. 12

Holland of Burwarton, Charlecot, and Pickthorne, Shropsh., a demi-lion rampant gardant grasping in the dexter paw a fleur-de-lis az.

Holland, out of a ducal coronet or, a demi-lion rampant arg. *Vincit qui se vincit.* 16. 3

Holland, of Benhall Lodge, Suff., and Bognor, Sussex, out of a ducal coronet or, a demi-lion rampant arg. *Vincit qui se vincit.* 16. 3

Holland, out of a five-leaved ducal coronet or, a demi-lion queue-fourchée arg.

Holland, Shropsh., a demi-lion rampant gardant holding in his dexter paw a fleur-de-lis az.

Holland of Denton, Lancs, out of a ducal coronet or, a demi-lion rampant gardant arg., collared gu., holding in the dexter paw a fleur-de-lis also arg.

Holland of Sutton, Lancs, out of a ducal coronet or, a demi-lion rampant arg., holding between the paws a fleur-de-lis of the second.

Holland, Lieutenant-Colonel Trevenen, C.B., Mount Ephraim House, Tunbridge Wells, out of a ducal coronet a demi-lion rampant guardant holding between the paws a fleur-de-lis. *Bis vincit qui se vincit.*

Holland of Heaton, Lancs, out of a ducal coronet or, a demi-lion rampant arg., holding in the dexter paw a fleur-de-lis, also or. *cf.* 16. 3

Holland, Thomas Lindsey, Esquire, of Cornwall Terrace, Regent's Park, London, N.W., out of a palisado coronet or, the rim charged with three torteaux, a demi-lion gardant ppr., holding in the dexter paw a plume of three ostrich-feathers arg.

Holland, Chesh., out of a vallery coronet a demi-lion rampant gardant per bend arg. and az., charged with a bendlet engrailed counterchanged, and holding in the dexter paw a fleur-de-lis, also arg.

Holland-Hibbert, Hon. Arthur Henry, D.L., of Munden House, Watford, Herts: (1) In front of a dexter cubit arm erect ppr., vested az., cuffed erm., holding in the hand a crescent arg., a demi-catherine wheel, also arg. (*for Hibbert*). *cf.* 206. 8. (2) Out of a vallery coronet or, a demi-lion gardant per bend arg. and az., charged with a bendlet engrailed counterchanged, and holding in the dexter paw a fleur-de-lis arg. (*for Holland*). *Animum ipse parabo.*

Holland, a horse's head and neck couped, bridled and charged with an escutcheon. *cf.* 51. 5

Holland, out of a ducal coronet or, a plume of ostrich-feathers arg. *cf.* 114. 8

Holland, Francis Dermott, Esquire, J.P., of Cropthorne Court, Pershore, a wolf passant sa., charged on the breast with a mullet. *Malo mori quam fœdari.*

Holland-Corbett, Corbett, Esquire, of Admington Hall, Glouc., a raven sa., charged with three ermine-spots or, holding in the beak a sprig of holly.

Holland, Lincs and Notts, a sinister wing or. 109. 7

Holland, Sussex, a wolf passant sa. 28. 10

Holland of Clifton, Lancs, a wolf passant sa. 28. 10

Holland, Stephen Taprell, Esquire, of Great Otterspool House, Aldenham, Herts, a wolf passant az., charged on the body with a bar engrailed couped, flory counterflory, and resting the dexter paw on a fleur-de-lis arg. *In lumine lutens.*

Holland, Norf., Lincs, and Cambs, a wolf passant sa., charged on the breast with a mullet. *cf.* 28. 10

Holland of Conway, Carnarvonsh., issuant out of flames ppr., an arm vested sa., holding in the hand ppr. a lion's gamb erased and fesseways or, the talons to the sinister side. *Fiat pax floreat justitia.*

Holles, Duke of Newcastle and **Earl of Clare** (*extinct*), a boar passant az., bristled or. *Spes audaces adjuvat.* 40. 9

Holles, Baron Holles, of Ifield (*extinct*), a Moor's head couped below the shoulders in profile ppr., wreathed about the neck and temples arg. and sa. *cf.* 192. 13

Holles, a Moor's head couped ppr., wreathed about the temples arg. and az. 192. 13

Holles, a lion's gamb erased or, holding a heart gu. *cf.* 39. 11

Holles or **Hollis** of Grimsby, Lincs, and Haughton, Notts, a boar passant az., bristled or. 40. 9

Holley, Major-General Edmund Hunt, R.A., J.P.: (1) A sea-lion gu., guttée-d'or, finned of the last (*for Holley*). (2) A lion's head erased and collared (*for Hunt*).

Holleys of London, an arm embowed vested bendy of six arg. and sa., cuffed or, holding in the hand ppr. a branch of holly vert, fructed gu.

Holliam, a harrow gu. 178. 4

Holliday, a grenade fired ppr. 177. 12

Holliday, an esquire's helmet. 180. 3

Holliday, a demi-pegasus arg., winged gu. 47. 5

Holliday of Bromley, Middx., a demi-lion rampant gardant resting the paws on an anchor, all ppr.

Hollier, a dexter hand holding a fish ppr. 220. 4

Holligan of Barbadoes, a demi-lion az., gorged with a collar gemel or, and charged on the shoulder with a bezant, holding in the dexter paw a branch of holly ppr.

Hollingbury, a buck's head cabossed gu. 132. 5

Hollings, a hunting-horn or, stringed gu., between two wings az. 112. 3

Hollingshed of Hollins, Sutton, Chesh., a bull's head gorged with a ducal coronet. *cf.* 44. 3

Hollingworth of Hollingworth, Chesh., and Lincs, a stag lodged arg. *Disce ferenda pati.* 115. 7

Hollingworth, H. G., of Llanbedr, R. S. O., Merionethsh., a stag lodged ppr. *Disce ferenda pati.* 302. 7

Hollingsworth, Durh., a crescent arg. *Lumen accipe et imperti.* 163. 2

Hollins, a dexter hand pointing with two fingers to a star ppr. 222. 2

Hollins of Whitmore Hall, Staffs, and of Oakhill Hall, Stoke-upon-Trent, a dexter hand pointing with two fingers to a star, all ppr. *Sic itur ad astra.* 222. 2

Hollinshed of Hollinshed Hall, Lancs: (1) In front of a bow and arrow in saltire ppr., a heron arg., holding in the beak a cross crosslet fitchée sa., and charged on the breast for distinction with an escallop az. (*for Hollinshed*). (2) A boar's head couped or, between the attires of a stag sa. *Nemo me impune lacessit.*

Hollinsworth and **Hollinworth,** a mount ppr., semée of trefoils.

Hollis of Stoke, near Coventry, Warw., a blackamoor's head couped at the shoulders in profile ppr., wreathed about the temples and tied in a knot arg. and az.

Hollis, George, of Dartmouth House, 47, Dartmouth Park Hill, London, N.W., in front of an arrow erect gu., a chaplet of roses or, surmounted by a boar's head erased az. *Festina lente.* 297. 10

Hollis, a dexter arm in armour embowed ppr., garnished or, holding in the hand a branch of holly-berries, also ppr.

Hollist, Anthony May Capron, Esquire, of Midhurst, Sussex, between two sprigs of strawberry fructed ppr., a dexter arm embowed in armour, the hand within a gauntlet holding a sprig of holly, all ppr. *Currendo.—Gardez-le-Capron.* 235. 1

Hollist, Edward Ommaney, Lodsworth, near Petworth, Sussex, same crest and mottoes.

Holloway, *see* Martin-Holloway.

Holloway, out of a mural coronet arg., a lion's head or, charged with a torteau. *cf.* 19. 12

Holloway of London, a demi-lion rampant gardant purp. 10. 8

Holloway, Samuel Frederick, Esquire, M.R.C.S., L.R.C.P., of Holmwood, Bedford Park, W., a dragon's head erased, holding in the mouth the head of a broken tilting-spear, the lower part pierced through the neck. *Deus lux nostra.*

Holloway, a goat's head erased arg., armed or, holding in its mouth a rose slipped and leaved ppr.

Holloway of London and Oxon., a goat's head erased and armed, all arg., collared and lined gu., on the collar three crescents of the first. *cf.* 128. 7

Holloway of Kensington, Middx., out of a crescent or, an antelope's head gu., attired, collared, and chained of the first. *A Deo lux nostra.*

Hollowell, a goat passant arg., armed or. *cf.* 129. 5

Hollway-Calthrop, *see* Calthrop.

Hollyland or **Holyland,** a demi-savage handcuffed, all ppr. 186. 12

Holman of London, a greyhound's head couped. *cf.* 61. 2

Holman of London, on a chapeau gu., turned up erm., an ostrich's head arg.

Holman of Banbury, Oxon., a bow and arrow, the bow erect, bent and strung, the arrow fesseways on the bow, all or.

Holman of Godstone, Surrey, the same crest between two wings, all or.

Holmden or **Holmeden** of Tenchleys, Surrey, an otter's head erased or. 134. 3

Holme of Gawdy Hall, Norf., a holly-tree vert, fructed gu. *cf.* 145. 6

Holme, Bryan Holme, Esquire, of Paull-Holme, Yorks: (1) A holly-tree fructed ppr. *cf.* 145. 6. (2) On a mural coronet gu., a hound's head erased or. *Holme semper viret.* *cf.* 56. 6

Holme of Tranmere, Chesh., an arm couped and embowed vested barry of six or and az., cuffed erm., holding in the hand a rose-branch ppr.

Holme of London, a lion's head couped or, thereon a chapeau az., turned up erm. *cf.* 21. 10

Holme-Sumner, Frank, Esquire, 17, Queen Anne's Gate, S.W., and New Haw Farm, Addlestone, Surrey: (1) A lion's head erased arg., ducally gorged or. 18. 5. (2) A hawk with wings elevated and addorsed ppr. 87. 10

Holme or **Hulme** of Hulme, Lancs, a lion's head erased gu., langued az., thereon a chapeau ppr. *Fide sed cui vide.* 21. 10

Holme or **Hulme** of Overhulme, Staffs, on a ducal coronet or, a chaplet gu., therein a garb of the first.

Holmes, A'Court-, Baron Heytesbury: (1) Out of a naval coronet or, a dexter arm in armour embowed holding a trident ppr., headed, also or (*for Holmes*). 197. 8. (2) An eagle displayed sa., charged with two chevronels or, beaked and legged gu., holding in the beak a lily slipped ppr. *Grandescunt aucta labore.*

Holmes, *see* Worsley-Holmes.

Holmes of Retford, Notts, out of a naval coronet or, a dexter arm embowed in armour holding a trident ppr., headed, also or. *Justum et tenacem propositi.* 197. 8

Holmes, Hants, and Emra Holmes, F.R.H.S., F.R.S.A.I., Esquire, of Oundle, Northants, late Civil Service, out of a naval coronet or, a dexter arm in armour embowed, holding in the hand, all ppr., a trident-spear or. *Vectis.* 197. 8

Holmes, out of a ducal coronet a stag's head. 120. 7

Holmes, George John, Esquire, of Brook Hall, Norf., out of a vallery coronet or, the rim charged with three annulets in fesse az., a stag's head erm., attired or.

Holmes, Ireland, on the point of a spear issuing, a dolphin naiant ppr. 140. 9

Holmes, a lion's head erased holding in the mouth a sword.

Holmes, Yorks, a lion's head erased or, thereon a chapeau az., turned up erm. 21. 10

Holmes, Rev. William, M.A., of Scole House, Norf., a lion's head erased or. *Ora et labora.* 17. 8

Holmes, Lieutenant-Colonel William Prescod, Ivy Lodge, Aylestone Hill, Hereford, a demi-lion rampant. *Nemo me impune lacessit.*

Holmes of London, a lion rampant or. *Courage sans peur.* 1. 13

Holmes, William James Owen, of Strumpshaw Hall, Norwich, Norf., a lion's head erased or, thereon a chapeau gu. turned up erm. *Ora et labora.*

Holmes of Derby, a demi-griffin. *Quod facio valde facio.* 64. 2

Holmes, John Sancroft, Gawdy Hall, Harleston, a holly-tree vert, fructed gu.

Holmes-Tarn, Harry, Kininvie House, Dufftown, N.B., on a garb fessewise a raven, all ppr. *Viret in æternum.*

Holmesdale, Viscount, *see* Amherst, Earl.

Holmpatrick, Baron (Hamilton), Abbotstown, Castleknock, co. Dublin, a demi-antelope arg., attired or, holding between the forelegs a human heart gu., and charged on the shoulder with a mullet gu. *Qualis ab incepto.*

Holroyd, Earl of Sheffield, *see* Sheffield.

Holroyd, a demi-griffin or. 64. 2

Holroyd, Honourable Edward Dundas, K.C., of Fernacres, Alma Road, Caulfield, near Melbourne, Victoria, Australia, Judge of the Supreme Court of Victoria, a demi-griffin or. 64. 2

Holroyd or **Holroyde,** Yorks, a demi-griffin sa., holding between its claws a coronet or. *Quem te Deus esse jussit.* *cf.* 64. 2

Holstock of Orsett, Essex, a demi-man ppr., chained round the middle and holding the chain in his sinister hand or, and in his dexter a club raguly arg.

Holt, Bart. (*extinct*), of Aston Hall, Warw., a squirrel sejant or, holding a hazel-branch slipped and fructed, all ppr. 135. 2

Holt, Warw., a squirrel sejant or, cracking a nut. 135. 7

Holt, Middx., a spear-head ppr. *Ut sanem, vulnero.* 174. 12

Holt of Enfield, Westml., same crest and motto.

Holt of Swaston, Cambs, a pheon sa. 174. 11

Holt, Middx., a pheon in pale sa. *Quod vult, voldé vult.* 174. 11

Holt of London and Lancs, a dexter arm in armour embowed ppr., garnished or, holding in the gauntlet a pheon sa.

Holt, James Maden, Culverlands, Oakleigh Park, N., same crest.

Holt of Grisselhurst, Lancs, a dexter arm erect habited per pale az. and gu., holding in the hand a pheon sa.

Holt, William Harvey, Esquire, J.P., of the Firs, Parramatta, New South Wales, and of Glenprairie, Rockhampton, Queensland, Australia, *uses* a dexter cubit arm in armour erect holding in the hand ppr. a pheon, also erect.

Holt or **Holte,** Suff., an arm erect couped at the elbow habited per pale az. and gu., the hand ppr. holding a pheon sa.

Holt, late Major Joseph, Esquire, V.D., J.P., of the Grange, Farnborough, Hants, and Ogbeare Hall, near Holsworthy, North Devonsh., a dexter arm embowed in armour ppr., garnished or, holding in the gauntlet a pheon sa. *Animo et fide.*

Holt of Bisham Hall, Edlinge Higher End, Lancs, in front of a cubit arm in armour, the hand in a gauntlet ppr., holding a pheon sa., a fer-de-moline fesseways of the last.

Holt, Edward, Esquire, J.P., of Woodthorpe, Prestwich, Lancs, and Blackwell, Westml., two arms embowed in armour sa., each charged on the forearm with a fleur-de-lis or, and holding in the hands gauntleted, also sa., a mountain ash-tree fructed and eradicated ppr. *Vincere est vivere.*

Holte of Stoke Lyne, Oxon., an arm holding a baton surmounted by a pheon.

Holte, *see* Orford-Holte.

Holtom, Charles John, Esquire, M.R.C.S., of the Willows, Haulgh, Bolton, an eagle displayed. *Labor omnia superat.* 75. 2

Holton, a map ppr. 159. 11

Holway, out of a ducal coronet or, a greyhound's head sa. 61. 7

Holyland and **Hollyland,** a demi-savage handcuffed, all ppr. 186. 12

Holyland, a cross Calvary entwined by a serpent, all ppr. *cf.* 166. 1

Holyngeworthe of Holyngworthe Hall, Chesh., a stag lodged ppr. *Disce ferenda pati.* 115. 7

Holyoake-Goodricke, Bart. (*extinct*), of Ribston Hall, Yorks: (1) Out of a ducal coronet or, a demi-lion ermines, holding a battle-axe, also or, and charged with a cross crosslet of the last for difference (*for Goodricke*). (2) On a mount vert, an oak-tree fructed ppr., and around the trunk an escroll arg., thereon a cross patée gu., between the words *Sacra quercus* (*for Holyoake*).

Holyoake of Tettenhall, Staffs, and Studley Castle, Warw., on a mount vert, an oak-tree fructed ppr., around the lower part of the stem an escroll, thereon a cross patée gu., between the words *Sacra quercus.*

Holyoake, Edmund, Esquire, of the Willows, Redditch, Worcs., and Claybrooke, Mappleborough Green, Warw., an oak-tree ppr. *Sacra quercus.*

Holyoke, a crescent arg. 163. 2

Holyoke, a cubit arm ppr., vested gu., cuffed arg., holding in the hand an oak-branch vert, fructed or.

Homan, Bart., Ireland, a lion's head erased or, thereon a chapeau gu., turned up erm. *Homo sum.* 21. 10

Homan, Ireland, in the sea an anchor in pale, all ppr. 161. 6

Homan-Mulock, William Bury, Esquire, J.P., D.L., of Bellair, Ballycumber, King's Co., a lion passant az., in the dexter paw a cross crosslet fitchée gu. *In hoc signo vinces.* 297. 13

Home, Earl of (Douglas-Home): (1) On a cap of maintenance ppr., a lion's head erased arg., armed and langued gu. (*for Home*). 17. 9. (2) On a cap of maintenance ppr., a salamander vert, encircled with flames of fire, also ppr. (*for Douglas*). *Jamais arrière.*—*A home, a home, a home.*—*True to the end.* 138. 2

Home of Westertoun, Scotland, a lion's head erased arg., gorged with a collar gu., charged with three roses of the first. *True to the end.* *cf.* 18. 6

Home, Scotland, a lion's head erased arg., collared gu. 18. 6

Home of Ninewells, Scotland, a lion's head erased ppr., collared or, charged with three wells ppr. *True to the end.* *cf.* 18. 6

Home of Renton, Scotland, a lion's head erased gu. *True to the end.* 17. 2

Home of Whitfield and Mount Eolus, Midlothian, a lion's head erased arg., armed and langued gu. *True to the end.* 17. 8

Home, Logan-, Major George John Ninian Broomhouse, Edrom, Berwicksh., a lion's head erased arg., gorged with a collar gemel vert, and in front thereof a thistle ppr. *True to the end.*

Home or **Hume** of Crossrigg, a lion's head erased arg., collared gu. *True to the end.* 18. 6

Home of Kimmerham, a lion's head erased arg., gorged with a collar gu., charged with roses and fleurs-de-lis. *True to the end.* *cf.* 18. 6

Home of Linhouse, a lion's head erased ppr., collared gu. *True to the end.* 18. 6

Home, on a chapeau a lion's head erased. 17. 9

Home, Bart., of Well Manor Farm, Hants, a lion's head erased ppr., thereon a label of three points arg., the middle point charged with a fleur-de-lis az., the others with the cross of St. George gu. *True.* *cf.* 17. 8

Home, Archibald Fraser, Esquire, of Cavalry Depot, Canterbury, a lion's head erased ppr., collared sa., charged with a fleur-de-lis or, and in an escroll over the same. *True to the end.*

Home, Fergusson-, of Bassendean, Berwicksh., Scotland, on a chapeau gu., turned up erm., a lion's head erased vert. *A home, a home.*—*True to the end.* 17. 9

Home of Kaimes, Scotland, a pelican's head couped ppr. *True to the end.* *cf.* 98. 2

Home of Renton, Scotland, a pelican's head couped ppr. *True to the end.* *cf.* 98. 2

Home, Bart., Berks, a unicorn's head and neck couped, gorged with an Eastern coronet. *Remember.* *cf.* 49. 7

Home of Wedderburn, Berwicksh., Scotland, a unicorn's head and neck arg., gorged with a ducal coronet, maned and horned or. *Remember.* *cf.* 49. 7

Home, a boar's head and neck erased. 41. 5

Home of that Ilk, Berwicksh., a popinjay's head ppr.

Home-Spiers, Sir James, Bart., of Blackadder, Berwicksh., Scotland, an adder in pale sa., holding in its mouth a rose gu., leaved and stalked vert. *Vise à la fin.* 285. 13

Homer, a lion's gamb holding up a cross patée. *cf.* 36. 9

Homes, an antelope trippant ppr. 126. 6

Homfray, an otter ppr., vulned in the shoulder. *L'homme vrai aime son pays.* *cf.* 134. 5

Homfray, Alfred, Esquire, of Otterbourne Court, Hales Owen, Worcs., an otter ppr., wounded in the shoulder by a spear. *Vulneratur non vincitur.*—*L'homme vrai aime son pays.*

Homfray, Captain John Glyn Richards, J.P., of Penllyn Castle, Cowbridge, Glamorgan, same crest and motto.

Homfray, Herbert Richard, Esquire, J.P., late 1st Life Guards, an otter vulned in the shoulder with a spear, all ppr. *Vulneratur non vincitur.*

Homfray of the Hyde, Staffs; Wollaston Hall, Broadwater's House, and Red Hill House, Worcs.; Cowerth Park, Berks; Penny Darren Place, Rhonda House, and Llandaff House, Glamorgansh.; Great Yarmouth, Norf.; and Yorks: (1) An otter passant, vulned in the sinister shoulder with a spear, all ppr. (2) Out of a ducal coronet or, a dragon's head vert. 72. 4. (3) A dragon's head vert, holding in his mouth a sinister hand couped at the wrist gu. *L'homme vrai aime son pays.*—*Vulneror non vincor.* 72. 6

Homfray-Addenbrooke of Wollaston Hall, Worcs., on the banks of a river ppr., an otter passant per pale arg. and sa., charged with two crescents counterchanged. *Vincit qui patitur.* *cf.* 134. 5

Homfray of Penllyne Castle, Glamorgansh., an otter passant vulned in the sinister shoulder with a spear, all ppr. *Vulneratur non vincitur.*

Hone of Devonsh., a sword in pale ppr., ensigned with a cross patée. 169. 5

Hone of the Spa, Glouc., an arm in armour embowed holding in the hand a scimitar, all ppr. 196. 10

Hone, Ireland, on a mount overgrown with rye-grass, a birch-tree, all ppr. *cf.* 144. 11

Honeywill, a bee-hive with bees volant ppr. 137. 7

Honford, on a chapeau az., turned up erm., a dragon passant gu. *cf.* 73. 4

Hongon of East Bradenham, Norf., a lion's gamb erect az., grasping another gamb erased gu., in bend sinister.

Honnor and **Honor,** a serpent nowed sa., spotted or. 142. 4

Honnyman or **Honyman,** Scotland, an arrow in pale ppr., point downwards. *Progredere, ne regredere.* 173. 5

Honnyton, a hand holding a dart point upwards, all ppr. *cf.* 214. 4

Honor of Honorsborough, co. Cork, an eagle displayed ppr., guttée-de-sang, charged on the breast with a cinquefoil or. *Altiora videnda.* *cf.* 74. 14

Honyman, Rev. Sir William Macdonald, Bart., M.A., of Armadale, Sutherland, an arrow in pale point downwards ppr., flighted arg. *Progredere, ne regredere.* 173. 5

Honywood, Kent, a wolf's head erased erm. 30. 8

Honywood, Sir John William, Bart., of Evington, Kent, a wolf's head couped erm. *Omne bonum desuper.* 30. 5

Hoo, a maiden's head ppr., within an annulet or.

Hoo, a bull passant quarterly arg. and sa. *cf.* 45. 2

Hoo, a hand holding a hautboy. 219. 1

Hood, Viscount Bridport, *see* Bridport.

Hood, Viscount (Hood), of Whitley, Warw.: (1) A Cornish chough sa., in front of an anchor in bend sinister or. 276. 10. (2) A demi-cat-a-mountain guardant az., gorged with a collar gemelle, and charged with three ermine-spots, two and one, or. *Ventis secundis.*

Hood, Fuller-Acland-, Sir Alexander Bateman Periam, Bart., of St. Audries, Somers.: (1) A Cornish chough in front of and holding an anchor on the dexter side in bend sinister ppr. (*for Hood*). 245. 9. (2) A man's hand couped at the wrist in a glove lying fessewise, thereon a falcon perched, all ppr., charged on the breast with a quatrefoil or (*for Acland*). *cf.* 86. 14. (3) Out of a ducal coronet gu., a lion's head arg., charged for distinction with a cross crosslet, also gu. (*for Fuller*). *Zealous.* *cf.* 17. 5

Hood, Donald William Charles, Esquire, C.V.O., M.D., F.R.C.P., of 43, Green Street, Park Lane, London, out of a mural coronet a bull's head gorged with a chaplet of roses. *Nil sine causa.*

Hood, Edward Thesiger Frankland, of Nettleham Hall, Lincs, a hooded crow holding in the beak a Scotch thistle, and in the dexter claw a sword, all ppr. *Esse quam videri.*

Hood, late Archibald, Esquire, of Rosedale, Rosewall, Midlothian, and of Sherwood, Cardiff, a demi-archer clothed and accoutred holding a bow and arrow in full draught ppr. *Olim sic erat.* 187. 6

Hood, of Stoneridge, Berwick, a demi-archer clothed and accoutred ppr. *Olim sic erat.—Swift and sure.* 187. 6

Hood, Cockburn-, same crest. *Swift and sure.—Olim sic erat.* 187. 6

Hood of Bardon Park, a demi-talbot gu., collared and lined arg. *Manners maketh man.* 55. 8

Hoofsteller, a talbot sejant az., collared arg. 55. 1

Hook, a fish haurient. 139. 11

Hook, an arm in armour embowed, and around it a trumpet, holding in the hand a pistol.

Hooke-Child, *see* Child.

Hooke, an escallop sa., between two wings arg. 141. 10

Hooke of Norton Hall, Worcs., a demi-eagle displayed gu., charged on the breast with a ducal coronet or. *cf.* 81. 6

Hooke of Alway, Glouc., a demi-eagle displayed gu., ducally gorged or. *cf.* 81. 6

Hooker of Bramshott, Hants, an eagle displayed gu., charged on the breast with a ducal coronet or. *cf.* 75. 2

Hooker, Surrey, Sussex, Hants, and Glouc., an escallop sa., between two wings arg. 141. 10

Hooker (*alias* **Vowell**) of Exeter, Devonsh., a hind trippant or, holding in the mouth a branch vert, flowered arg. *cf.* 124. 12

Hookham, a covered cup arg.

Hooklay, an arm embowed vested gu., cuffed arg., holding in the hand ppr. a branch of oak vert, fructed, also ppr.

Hoole, a rose gu., barbed vert, seeded or. 149. 4

Hoole of Edgefield, Yorks, an eagle displayed gu., each wing charged with two roses and transfixed through the mouth by a tilting-spear palewise or. *Flectas non franges.*

Hoole, Colonel James, C.M.G., J.P., Lieutenant-Colonel commanding and Hon. Colonel 3rd Battalion (Mil.) Yorks Regiment, of the Manor House, Headington, Oxford, same crest and motto.

Hoole, Henry Elliott, Esquire, of Ravenfield Park, Rotherham, Yorks, an eagle displayed per fesse or and gu., each wing charged with a rose per fesse counterchanged, surmounted by a rainbow ppr. *Spes mea Deus.*

Hoole, Colonel William Wright, J.P., of Chavenage House, Tetbury, Glouc., same crest and motto.

Hooley, out of a mount vert, a tree ppr. 143. 14

Hooley, Ernest Terah, Esquire, of Risley Hall, Derbysh., and Papworth Hall, Cambs, on a mount an oak-tree fructed ppr. *En Dieu est mo foy.*

Hooper of London, an antelope ppr. *Absque metu.* 126. 12

Hooper of Linkinghorne, Cornw., a demi-lion holding between the paws an annulet. *cf.* 10. 2

Hooper, Edmund Huntly, Esquire, of Shelley Hill, Christchurch, in front of a lion's head erased sa., a fret arg. *Garde bien.*

Hooper of London, of Stanmore Cottage, Middx., and of Sarum, Wilts, a boar's head erased at the neck az., bezantée, armed and crined or. *cf.* 41. 5

Hooper, Daniel, Esquire, B.A., M.B., M.R.C.P., of 9, Trinity Square, Borough, S.E., a boar's head erased at the neck az., bezantée, armed and crined or. *Fortis in arduis.*

Hooper of Hendford, Yeovil, Somers., a demi-wolf couped holding in the dexter paw an oak-branch fructed, all ppr. *cf.* 31. 2

Hooper, George Glass, Esquire, of 30, Palace Court, Kensington Gardens, W., an esquire's helmet ppr., between two wings per fesse indented or and sa., each charged with as many fleurs-de-lis paleways counterchanged. *Non nobis solum.* 231. 18

Hooper, James, Esquire, of the Walnuts, Hatherleigh, Devonsh., same crest and motto.

Hoops, a plate charged with a Cornish chough ppr. *Amo.*

Hoord of Park Bromage, Shropsh., a nag's head arg., maned or. *cf.* 50. 13

Hooton of Hooton, Chesh., a chevalier holding his horse by the bridle with his dexter hand ppr. 53. 11

Hopcot, Cornw., a fox's head erased ppr. 33. 6

Hopcroft, a morion ppr. 180. 1

Hope, *see* Hopetoun, Earl of.

Hope, Arthur, Esquire, of Woodbury, Canterbury, New Zealand, of Kaurunui, Timaru, and of Richmond Station, Mackenzie Country, Canterbury, New Zealand, a broken globe under a rainbow, with clouds at each end, all ppr. *At spes non fracta.* 159. 2

Hope, Captain Henry Walter, D.L., J.P., of Luffness, Haddington, and of Rankeillour, Fife, a broken globe surmounted by a rainbow ppr. *At spes infracta.* 159. 2

Hope, James Fitzalan, Esquire, of Heron's Ghyll, Uckfield, Sussex, same crest and motto.

Hope, Scotland, same crest. *Spero suspiro donec.*

Hope, Scotland, same crest. *Solamen.*

Hope, Scotland, same crest. *At spes infracta.*

Hope, Sir Theodore Cracraft, K.C.S.I., C.I.E., Hope Farm, Boothstown, Lancs, and 21, Elvaston Place, Queen's Gate, S.W., same crest and motto.

Hope of Kerse, Scotland, a broken globe ensigned by a rainbow issuing out of clouds at each end. *Spes tamen infracta.* 159. 2

Hope, John, Esquire, of St. Mary's Isle, Kirkcudbright, N.B.: (1) A broken globe surmounted by a rainbow ppr. *At spes infracta* (*for Hope*). (2) On a cap of maintenance, a salamander in flames ppr. *Jamais arrière* (*for Douglas*).

Hope of Granton, Edinburgh, a broken globe surmounted of a rainbow issuing out of clouds at each end ppr. *Spero suspiro donec.* 159. 2

Hope, Adrian Elias, 8, Chesterfield Gardens, W., same crest. *At spes non fracta.*

Hope-Vere, James Charles, of Craigiehall, Linlithgow, Scotland: (1) On the dexter side, a broken globe surmounted by a rainbow issuing out of clouds at each end ppr. (*for Hope*). 159. 2. (2) On a chapeau gu., turned up erm., a lion statant az., armed or (*for Vere*). *At spes non fracta.—Vero nihil verius.* *cf.* 4. 8

Hope, Sir Alexander, Bart., of Craighall, and Pinkie House, Musselburgh, a broken terrestrial globe surmounted by a rainbow issuing out of a cloud at each end, all ppr. *At spes infracta.* 159. 2

Hope-Edwards, Rev. St. Leger Frederick, of Netley, near Shrewsbury, Salop, a broken terrestrial globe between two palm-branches surmounted by a rainbow ppr., and charged with three arrows, two in saltire and one in pale or (*for Hope,* there being no crest for Edwards). *A fyno duw derfid.*

Hope, William Williams, Esquire, of London: (1) A globe fractured ppr., charged with an anchor sa., and surmounted by a rainbow, also ppr. (*for Hope*). *cf.* 159. 2. (2) A cubit arm erect vested sa., charged with a cross crosslet and cuffed or, the hand holding two sprigs of oak in saltire ppr., fructed, also or, on the hand a Cornish chough statant, also ppr.

Hope, Derbysh., a Cornish chough with wings expanded ppr. 107. 3

Hope of Mullingar, co. Westmeath, Ireland, a palm-tree ppr. 144. 1

Hope-Lloyd-Verney, James Hope, Esquire, of Carriden House, Bo'ness, N.B., and 14, Hinde Street, Manchester Square, W.: (1) A demi-phœnix in flames ppr., charged with five mullets in cross or, and looking at rays of the sun, also ppr. (*for Verney*). 278. 14. (2) Out of a mural coronet arg., two spears erect, therefrom two pennons flowing towards the dexter, one erminois, the other pean (*for Calvert*). 278. 15. (3) A lion rampant sa., holding in the mouth a fleur-de-lis or, supporting an antique shield gu., charged with three annulets interlaced in pale or, and upon the shoulder for distinction a cross crosslet or (*for Lloyd*). 278. 16. *Ung sent ung soleil.—Servata fides cineri.*

Hoper, Heref. and Sussex, a dexter arm couped at the elbow vested sa., the cuff turned up arg., holding in the hand a pomegranate seeded and slipped or.

Hopetoun, Earl of (Hope), *vide* Linlithgow.

Hopgood, John, Esquire, of 17, Bolton Gardens, S.W., a cubit arm erect vested per chevron nebuly gu. and or, cuff arg., the hand ppr., holding an anchor in bend of the second, and a cross crosslet fitchée in saltire of the first. *Spes bona dat vires.* 244. 16

Hopkin, a dove holding in its beak an olive-branch. 92. 5

Hopkins, Edric John Murray, of Tidmarsh, Berks, a castle in flames ppr. *Inter primos.* *cf.* 155. 1

Hopkins, Bart., Ireland, a tower arg., fired ppr. 155. 9

Hopkins, a fort in flames ppr., charged with two pellets in fess.

Hopkins of Hackney, Middx.: (1) A castle in flames ppr., charged with two pellets in fesse (*for Hopkins*). (2) A lion sejant erm. (*for Bond*). 8. 8

Hopkins of Oving House, Bucks, and of Coventry, Warw., a tower per bend indented arg. and gu., flames issuing from the loopholes and battlements ppr.

Hopkins, Maryland, U.S.A., a rock, and over the top a battery in perspective, thereon the flag of the kingdom of France hoisted, and upon the said rock an officer of the Queen's Royal American Rangers holding in his dexter hand a sword, all ppr. *Inter primos.*

Hopkins, Lincs, a demi-lion rampant sa. 10. 1

Hopkins of London and Newland, Glouc., an ostrich-head couped erm., holding in the beak a key az.

Hopkins, Ireland, on an oak-plant a bird ppr. 107. 10

Hopkinson of Alford, Lincs, a demi-lion rampant sa., armed and incensed gu. 10. 1

Hopkirk, an arm in armour pointing with one finger to a crescent, all ppr. *Memo rare novissima.*

Hopkirk of Dalbeth, Lanarksh., an arm in armour ppr., pointing with one finger to a crescent in the dexter chief arg. *Spero procedere.*

Hopley of Liverpool, a stag's head affrontée and erased ppr., gorged with a collar gemel az., between two ears of wheat or. *Semper vigilans.*

Hopley, George Augustus, Esquire, of Charlestown, South Carolina, U.S.A., out of a mural coronet gu., a garb or, issuant therefrom a serpent ppr. *In copia cautus.*

Hoppare, Scotland, a lion rampant gu., holding in his dexter paw a fleur-de-lis. 2. 7

Hoppe, a demi-swan with wings addorsed ppr. 100. 2

Hopper of Walworth, Durh.: (1) A tower triple-towered arg., masoned sa. (*for Hopper*). 157. 6. (2) A sword arg., hilt and pommel or, and a sceptre of the last in saltier, enfiled with an oaken civic crown vert, fructed of the second (*for Carles*). 170. 7

Hopper, Rev. Edmund Carles, Starston Rectory, Harleston, Norf., same crests. *Subditus fidelis regis et salus regni.*

Hopper of Silksworth and Hermitage, Durh., a tower triple-towered arg., masoned sa. *Subditus fidelis regis et salus regni.* 157. 6

Hoppey, a dexter hand ppr., holding a fleur-de-lis in pale az. *cf.* 215. 5

Hoppey, a stag's head cabossed gu., and between the attires a cross crosslet fitchée of the same. *cf.* 122. 5

Hopson, a stag lodged ppr. 115. 7

Hopson of Rochester, Kent, on a mount vert, a griffin passant or, the wings elevated chequy of the last and az., the dexter claw resting on a cinquefoil of the first. *Vive, ut semper vivas.* 63. 10

Hopson of Minster, Isle of Sheppey, Kent, a mount vert, thereon a griffin passant or, the wings elevated chequy of the last and az., the dexter claw resting upon a cinquefoil of the first. 63. 10

Hopton of Hopton, Heref., a lion's head erased or, charged with a bend gu., thereon three cross crosslets of the first. *cf.* 17. 8

Hopton, Somers., and of Blithbou, Suff., a griffin passant arg., holding in the dexter claw a stone sa. *cf.* 63. 2

Hopton of Canon Frome, Heref., out of a ducal coronet or, a griffin's head arg., holding in the beak a dexter hand bleeding ppr.

Hopton, Lieutenant-General Sir Edward, K.C.B., of Homend-Stretton, Grandison, Ledbury, out of a ducal coronet or, a gryphon's head arg., in the mouth a dexter hand couped and ensanguined ppr. *Post nullos memorandus.*

Hopton, Harry Chester, Esquire, same crest. *Vi et virtute.*

Hopton, Rev. Michael, M.A., of Holmer Hall, Heref., same crest. *A me absit gloriari nisi in cruce.*

Hopton, Rev. William Cope, of the Vicarage, Bishop Ffrome, Heref., same crest and motto.

Hopton, Shropsh.: (1) Out of a ducal coronet or, a griffin's head arg., holding in the beak a dexter hand bleeding ppr. (2) A lion's head erased or, charged on the neck with a bend gu., and thereon three cross crosslets fitchée or. *cf.* 17. 8

Hopton, Lieutenant-Colonel John Dutton, of Canon-ffrome Court, Ledbury, and Kemerton Court, Tewkesbury: (1) Out of a ducal coronet or, a gryphon's head arg., in the mouth a dexter hand couped and ensanguined ppr., and charged for distinction with a cross crosslet gu. (*for Hopton*). (2) A talbot sejant arg., collared flory and counter-flory and chained gu., and resting the dexter paw upon a saltire or. *Vi et virtute.*

Hopwood, out of a ducal coronet an eagle's head holding in the beak a trefoil slipped, all ppr.

Hopwood, Gregg-, Edward Robert, 37, Hertford Street, W., same crest.

Hopwood, Lancs, a dexter hand in fess, couped at the wrist ppr., holding an escallop or. *Gradatim.*

Hopwood, Cecil Hutchinson, Esquire, M.B., Ch.B., of Moorfield, Heyrod, Stalybridge, a dexter cubit arm fesseways couped, and holding in the hand an escallop. *Gradatim.*

Hopwood, Charles Henry, Esquire, K.C., of 1, Essex Court, Temple, E.C., on a mount vert, a saltire raguly gu., surmounted by an escallop arg. *Sperarem.*

Horan, Ireland, a hand holding a cushion ppr. 215. 9

Horan of Galway, Ireland, a demi-lion rampant or. 10. 2

Hord of Hord's Park and Walford, Shropsh., a nag's head couped arg., maned or. *cf.* 50. 13

Horden, a demi-wolf quarterly sa. and arg., holding in the dexter paw a quatrefoil quarterly of the second and first. 31. 7

Hordern of Oxley House, Staffs, an ox's head cabossed gu., armed or, surmounting two arrows in saltier or, banded and flighted arg. *Fortiter ac sapienter.*

Hordern, of Prestbury, Chesh., a wyvern or, pierced through the neck by an arrow fesseways point to the sinister ppr., and resting the dexter claw upon an escutcheon gu., charged with a child's head couped at the neck, also ppr. *Nabbap hig hordern ac God felt.* 240. 11

Hore, *see* Ruthven, Baron

Hore of Pole-Hore, co. Wexford, a demi-eagle az. *Constanter.* 80. 2

Hore and **Horem,** a hand holding a sickle ppr. 219. 13

Horman, a lizard gardant sa.

Horn, William Austin, Esquire, M.P., J.P., of Holmwood, Adelaide, South Australia, *uses* a heron close ppr., holding in the bill a standard staff, the banner flotant, thereon the word "*Hastings.*" *Nil desperandum.*

Horn of Bishopwearmouth, Durh., same crest and motto.

Horn, Shropsh., an owl ppr. 96. 5

Horn, a hand gu., holding a hawk's lure arg. 217. 8

Horn of Westhall, Aberdeen, two horns conjoined per fesse or and sa. 123. 8. (Originally a bugle-horn az., garnished and stringed arg. 228. 11.) *Moneo et munio.*

Horn and **Horne,** Scotland, a bugle az., garnished and stringed arg. *Monitus, munitus.* 228. 11

Horn, William, Esquire, of Woodcote Park, Blackshiels, Midlothian, a hunting horn or, stringed az. *Monitus, munitus.*

Hornby, Sir William Henry, Bart., Pleasington Hall, Blackburn, a hunting horn sa., pendent from an arrow fessewise or. *Crede cornu.*

Hornby, Edmund Geoffrey Stanley, of Dalton Hall, Westml., a bugle-horn, the mouth to the dexter sa., within the strings a pheon gu. 168. 5

Hornby, Admiral of the Fleet, Sir Geoffrey Thomas Phipps, G.C.B., Principal Naval A.D.C., of Lordington, Emsworth, Sussex, a bugle-horn sa., stringed, and within the string a pheon gu. (*for Hornby*). 168. 5. A lion's gamb sa., holding a trefoil slipped arg. (*for Phipps*). 36. 8

Hornby of Ribby Hall, a bugle-horn stringed sa., an arrow passing through the knot point toward the sinister or. *Crede cornu.* 303. 8

Hornby, a Roman soldier in full armour ppr. 188. 4

Horncastle of Dublin, a unicorn's head erased vert, armed and maned or, charged on the neck with a trefoil of the last. *cf.* 49. 5

Horncastle, on a chapeau a serpent nowed, all ppr. 142. 9

Horncastle, Walter Radcliffe, Esquire, of Taymouth House, Hackney Downs, upon a rock ppr., the battlements of a tower sa., surmounted by a bugle-horn or, stringed vert. *Audaces fortuna juvat.*

Horne, *see* Elphinstone.

Horne, out of a mural coronet a tiger's head. *cf.* 27. 1

Horne, a talbot sejant arg., collared and lined or. 55. 5

Horne, a bull's head couped or. *cf.* 44. 3

Horne, Oxon., a unicorn's head erased az., semée of mascles or. *cf.* 49. 5

Horne, Kent, a hand gu., holding a hawk's lure arg. 217. 8

Horne, Shropsh., an owl ppr. 96. 5

Horne, a bugle-horn arg. 228. 11

Horne, John Fletcher, Esquire, M.D., F.R.S.E., J.P., of the Poplars, Barnsley, within a chaplet of roses arg., leaved vert, a bugle-horn stringed and garnished or.

Horne of Cranage Hall, Holme's Chapel, Chesh., issuant from a chaplet of oak fructed a dexter cubit arm erect ppr., holding in the hand two antlers saltireways or. *Industria et prudentia vincunt.*

Horneck of St. Margaret's, Westminster, the stump of a tree couped ppr., a branch sprouting on the sinister.

Horner of Caleford and Wells, Somers., a talbot sejant arg., collared and lined or. 55. 5

Horner, John Francis Fortescue, Mells Park, Frome, Somers., a talbot sejant arg., collared and lined or. *Tyme tryeth troth.*

Horner, Scotland, a stag's head erased ppr. *Nitor in adversum.* 121. 2

Horner, Captain John, of Fitz Manor, Shrewsbury, a stag's head erased. *Nitor in adversis.* 121. 2

Horner, Christopher, of Middledale and Ripon, Yorks, a bugle-horn garnished or.

Horner, a buck's head erased ppr. 121. 2

Hornes, a griffin sejant ppr., resting the dexter claw upon an escutcheon of the arms, viz.: arg., three bugle-horns in pale gu. *cf.* 62. 10

Horniman, Frederick John, Esquire, M.P., of Falmouth House, 20, Hyde Park Terrace, W., a lion couchant guardant or, under a palm-tree ppr. *Espérance en Dieu.* 263. 16

Horniold or **Hornyold,** Worcs., a demi-unicorn gu., crined and armed or. 48. 7

Hornsby of Grantham, a demi-bear rampant sa. 34. 13

Hornsby, William, Esquire, J.P., D.L., of Elsham House, Grantham, and Burwell Park, Louth, Lincs, a bear's head. *Rebus angustis fertis.*

Hornsey, a rock ppr. *Semper eadem.* 179. 7

Hornyold, Thomas Charles Gandolfi, Duke Gandolfi of Rome, of Blackmore Park and Hanley Castle, Worcs.: (1) A demi-unicorn gu., armed, crined, and unguled or (*for Hornyold*). 48. 7. (2) A demi-lion sa., holding in the dexter paw a dagger in pale ppr. (*for Gandolfi*). *Multi virem durando sæcula vincet.—Quod vult, valde vult. Fidem tene.* 10. 1

Hornyold, John Vincent, Esquire, of Blackmore Park, Worcs., and Elmstead Hall, Essex, same crests and mottoes.

Horrell, a crow feeding ppr. 107. 4

Horrocks, on a mount a stag lodged regardant ppr. 115. 9

Horrocks, on a mount a hawk with wings endorsed ppr. *Spe.* *cf.* 88. 9

Horrocks of Preston, Lark Hill, Lancs, upon a rock an eagle with wings elevated and endorsed ppr., and pendent from the beak an escutcheon gu., charged with a hank of cotton arg.

Horrocks, Edgworth, Esquire, Mascells, Brenchley, Kent, same crest. *Industria et spe.*

Horscote, a chevalier on horseback in full armour holding in the dexter hand a scimitar, all ppr. 189. 10

Horsbrugh of the Pirn, Peebles, a horse's head couped. *Ægre de tramite recto.*

Horseburgh of that Ilk, Scotland, a horse's head arg. *Ægre de tramite recto.* *cf.* 50. 13

Horsefall, *see* Horsfall.

Horsefall, Yorks, a horse's head couped erm. 50. 13

Horsefall, on a ducal coronet a swan or, with wings addorsed arg., ducally gorged gu. *cf.* 99. 5

Horseford, a lion's head az., between two wings or. *cf.* 19. 7

Horseman, issuing from a cup or, flames of fire ppr. 177. 6

Horsenail of Worvill, Berks, out of a mural crown arg., a horse's head of a dun colour, maned sa., gorged with a collar dovetailed az.

Horsey of Honington, Warw., a horse's head couped arg., bridled or, plumed az. *cf.* 51. 5

Horsey, Herts and Wilts, a horse's head arg., in armour ppr., bridled or. 51. 13

Horsfall of Rugeley, a horse's head issuing ppr., bridled or. *Ad finem fidelis.* 51. 5

Horsfall, John, Esquire, M.A. (Oxon.), F.R.C.S. (Eng.), Streate Place, Bournemouth, a horse's head couped erm. (*Granted* 1612.) *Carpe diem.* 50. 13

Horsfall, Michael Heineken, Esquire, Westthorpe, Little Smeaton, Northallerton, same crest. *Labore et honore.*

Horsfall, Thomas Garnett, Esquire, J.P., of Hornby Grange, Northallerton, same crest.

Horsfall, John Cousin, Esquire, J.P., C.A., Hayfield, Glusburn, near Keighley, Yorks, a horse's head couped erm. *Labore et honore.* 50. 13

Horsfall, James, Esquire, of Birmingham, on the stem of a tree leaved vert, a horse's head erased arg., gorged with a collar gemel gu.

Horsfall or **Horsefall,** a stag's head couped, around the neck a garland. 120. 3

Horsford, on the waves of the sea ppr., a horse passant arg. *Benigno numine.* 52. 3

Horsford, late General Sir Alfred Hastings, G.C.B., issuant out of a mural coronet gu., a demi-pegasus with wings addorsed erm., gorged with a collar gemel, also gu., and holding between the paws a tilting-spear erect and resting on the coronet ppr. *Justitia et clementia.*

Horsley, *see* Decies, Baron.

Horsley of Horsley, Northumb., a horse's head erased arg. 51. 4

Horsman, a horse's head in armour, bridled and plumed ppr. 50. 14

Horsman, a castle in flames ppr. *cf.* 154. 1

Horspoole, *see* Horsepoole.

Horspoole of London, a demi-pegasus erased with wings expanded erm., enfiled round the loins with a ducal coronet or. 47. 7

Hort, Sir Arthur Fenton, Bart., of Castle Strange, Middx., *uses* an eagle regardant with wings expanded ppr., holding in the beak a chaplet vert.

Hortford of London and Hunts, a dexter arm erect couped at the elbow vested per pale arg., and holding in the hand a stag's attire sa. 208. 6

Horton, *see* Wilmot-Horton.

Horton of Catton, Derbysh., issuing from waves of the sea ppr., a spear-head in pale or, headed arg., on its point a dolphin, also ppr. 140. 10

Horton of the Holt, Northamp., and Mascalls, Brentwood, Essex, a dolphin naiant arg., in front of three tilting-spears, one in pale and two in saltier, or. *Perseverantia palmam obtinebit.*

Horton of Chadderton, Lancs, a red rose seeded and barbed ppr., between two laurel-branches in orle vert. *Pro rege et lege.*

Horton, Joshua Thomas, of Howroyde, near Halifax, same crest and motto.

Horton of Freshwater Court, Isle of Wight, a rose gu., seeded or, and barbed vert, within an orle of two branches of the last. *Pro rege et lege.*

Horton of Howroyde, Yorks, same crest and motto.

Horton of Hullington, Somers., and Ilford, Wilts, a cubit arm erect vested gu., cuffed arg., holding in the hand ppr. an arrow az., barbed and feathered or.

Horton, an arm couped at the elbow, vested gu., holding in the hand ppr. an arrow point downwards az., barbed and feathered or, and a branch of roses erect arg., leaved vert, the arm charged with a crescent, also or.

Horton of Southwark, Albert Square, Lambeth, Surrey, and of Ystrad, Carmarthensh., a demi-stag gu., semée of cinquefoils or, and resting the sinister foot upon a millrind or. *Vigilo et spero.* 119. 7

Horton-Smith, Richard, Esquire, M.A., K.C., of 53, Queen's Gardens, Hyde Park, London, W., on a wreath of the colours, arg. and sa., in front of a mount vert, thereon a greyhound couchant ppr., two battle-axes in saltire or. *Prêt à tressaillir.*

Horton-Smith, P., of 19, Devonshire Street, Portland Place, same crest and motto.

Horwood, a crow with wings expanded, pierced through the breast by an arrow point upwards, all ppr. cf. 107. 11

Horwood, a hand issuing from a cloud holding a club, all ppr. 214. 9

Hose, a lion's head erased. 17. 8

Hose of Kentish Town, Middx., a reindeer's head couped ppr., attired or, gorged with a collar erminois, fimbriated arg. cf. 122. 1

Hoseason of Jamaica, an eagle regardant rising from a rock ppr. *In recto decus.* 79. 9

Hosier of Cruckton, Shropsh., on a chapeau az., turned up or, a talbot sejant. 54. 14

Hosken, Cornw., a lion rampant or. *Vis unita fortior.* 1. 13

Hoskins, Monm., two limbs of a tree raguled and couped in saltire arg., the sinister surmounting the dexter. cf. 147. 9

Hoskins of Oxted, Surrey, a cock's head erased or, pellettée, combed and wattled gu., between two wings expanded of the first.

Hoskins of Higham, Cumb., same crest. *Virtute non verbis.*

Hoskyns, *see* Wren-Hoskyns.

Hoskyns, a lion's head erased ppr. 17. 8

Hoskyns, Rev. Sir John Leigh, Bart., M.A., of Aston Tyrold Rectory, Berks, a lion's head erased or, vomiting flames of fire from the mouth ppr., ducally crowned of the first. cf. 17. 1

Hoskyns, Henry William, Esquire, of North Perrot Manor, Crewkerne, Somers., a cock's head erased or, pellettée, combed and wattled gu. *Finem respice.*

Host of London, two wings addorsed or, charged with a crescent gu.

Hoste, Suff., two wings addorsed or. 282. 2

Hoste, Sir William Graham, Bart.: (1) Of honourable augmentation—out of a naval coronet or, the rim encircled with a branch of laurel ppr., an arm embowed vested in naval uniform grasping in the hand, also ppr., a flag-staff, and flowing therefrom a flag, inscribed "*Cattaro.*" 282. 1. (2) Two wings addorsed or. *Fortitudine.—Fas est et ab hoste doceri.*—(Over crest) *Cœlum ipsum petimus.* 282. 2

Hoste, Major-General Dixon Edward, C.B., of 23, Sussex Square, Brighton, same crests and mottoes.

Hotblack, John Turner, 45, Newmarket Road, Norwich, a mill-rind fesseways gu., thereon a dolphin naiant arg.

Hotham, Baron (Hotham), of South Dalton, Ireland, and of Scarborough, Yorks, a demi-man issuing out of waves of the sea ppr., holding in his dexter hand a flaming sword arg., hilt and pommel or, and on his sinister arm a shield of the arms of Hotham, viz.: barry of ten arg. and az., on a canton or, a Cornish chough ppr. *Lead on.* 185. 5

Hothfield, Baron (Tufton), of Hothfield, Kent, a sea-lion sejant arg., debruised by a bendlet sinister wavy sa. *Alis volat propriis.* cf. 20. 2

Hotoft or **Hotofte** of Flintham, Notts, a lion's gamb holding a human heart ppr. 39. 1

Hoton, Glouc., a sea-horse couchant arg., ducally gorged sa., sustaining an anchor az. cf. 46. 8

Hotson, Hamilton Andrew, Esquire, of 4, Rothesay Terrace, Edinburgh, a dove ppr., the dexter claw resting upon a bezant. *In fide robur.*

Hotton, Cumb., a martlet rising ppr. cf. 95. 11

Houblon, Essex and Berks, a dexter hand holding up a book expanded ppr. cf. 215. 1

Houblon, Archer-, Lieutenant-Colonel George Bramston, of Hallingbury Place, Essex, and Culverthorpe, Lincs: (1) A lion's head erased or (*for Houblon*) 17. 8. (2) A wyvern arg. (*for Archer*). 70. 1. (3) A leg in armour couped at the thigh ppr., garnished and spurred or (*for Eyre*). 193. 1

Houby, a leopard's head ppr. 22. 10

Houell, a sea-lion sejant erm. 20. 2

Hough, a boar's head erased holding in the mouth a sword in bend sinister. 42. 6

Hougham of Hougham, Wedington, and Barton House, Kent, on a chapeau gu., turned up erm., a falcon arg., with wings expanded or, beaked and belled of the last.

Houghton, Baron (Rt. Hon. Robert Offley Ashburton Milnes), of Great Houghton, in West Riding of Yorks, a garb or, charged with a fesse dancetté az., thereon three mullets arg. *Scio cui credidi.* 152. 10

Houghton, a bull passant arg. *Malgré le tort.* cf. 45. 2

Houghton, C. Hobart, M.B., Ch.B., of Nottingham General Dispensary, a bull's head sa., charged on the neck with three bars arg. *Malgré le tort.*

Houghton, a bull passant arg., armed and unguled or, the tail reflexed over his back and tipped sa. *Malgré le tort.* cf. 45. 2

Houghton, a bull's head couped gu., armed or. cf. 44. 3

Houghton of King's Clyff, Northamp., a bull's head arg., armed or, gorged with three bars sa., the centre one charged with a rose of the second.

Houghton and **Haughton** of Haughton, Chesh., of Petersfield, Hants, and Lancs and Sussex: (1) A bull's head sa., armed arg., charged on the neck with three bars of the last. (2) A bull passant gu. cf. 45. 2

Houghton, Ireland, a stag's head or, collared gu., between the attires a cross formée of the last. cf. 120. 9

Houghton, Yorks, a scimitar erect arg., point upwards, pommel and hilt or.

Houghton, formerly of Gunthorp, Norf., a demi-eagle displayed or, guttée-de-sang. 81. 6

Houison, Scotland, a lion's head erased gu. 17. 2

Houison-Craufurd, Lieutenant-Colonel William Reginald, Esquire, of Craufurdland Castle, Kilmarnock, and Braehead Cramond Bridge, Midlothian, a marble pillar supporting a man's heart ppr. (*for Craufurd*). (2) A dexter hand couped apaumée ppr. (*for Houison*). *Stant innixa Deo* (*for Craufurd*).—*Sursum corda* (*for Houison*).

Houldsworth, Sir William Henry, Bart., M.P., of Reddish, Lancs, and Coodham, Ayrsh., a stag's head erased gu., attired and collared or, the attires banded with a hank of cotton arg. *Flecti non frangi.* 285. 7

Houldsworth, James Hamilton, Esquire, of Gonaldston, Notts, and Coltness, Lanarksh., Scotland, a stag's head erased gu., attired and collared or, the attires bound with a hank of cotton arg. *Honos præmium industriæ.*

Houldsworth, Henry, Esquire, of Glasgow and Cranstonhill, Lanarksh., Scotland, same crest. *Flecti non frangi.*

Houle of London, a sea-lion sejant erm. *Perspicax audax.* 20. 2

Houlton, Somers., a ferret passant ppr. cf. 134. 9

Houlton of Farley Castle, Somers., a talbot's head erased az., gorged with a collar wavy or, charged with three torteaux. *Semper fidelis.* cf. 56. 1

Houndegart, a water fountain in full play ppr. 159. 13

Hounhill, a lion's gamb erased holding a tilting-spear in bend tasselled, all ppr. 38. 11

Hounsell, William, Esquire, of Mount Culd, Bradpole, Bridport, a dexter arm embowed, vested and cuffed, holding in the hand a bird. *Contentus esto.*

Hounston of Boston, Lincs, a nag's head or, holding in the mouth a holly-branch vert, fructed gu.

House, two hands issuing from clouds placing an anchor in the sea ppr. 224. 13

Housson and **Howson** of London, issuing out of clouds ppr., a bull's head az., semée-d'étoiles or.

Houston, on a mount vert, a hind statant ppr., collared or. 124. 14

Houston, Ireland, a dexter hand holding a dagger ppr. 212. 9

Houston, Scotland, a sand-glass ppr. *In time.* 177. 15

Houston, George Ludivic, Esquire, J.P., D.L., of Castle Johnstone, Johnstone, same crest.

Houston, Scotland, a sand-glass with wings ppr. *In time.* 113. 11

Houston, James Flower, Clerkington, Haddington, N.B., same crest and motto.

Houston, Blakiston-, of Orangefield, co. Down, Ireland: (1) A sand-glass ppr. (*for Houston*). 177. 15. (2) A cock gu., charged with an annulet or (*for Blakiston*). *In time.—Do well and doubt not.* cf. 91. 2

Houstoun-Boswall, Sir George Lauderdale, Bart., of Blackadder, Berwicksh.: (1) A cubit arm erect ppr., charged with a cross crosslet sa., grasping a sword, also ppr. (*for Boswall*). 239. 7. (2) A sand-glass winged ppr. (*for Houstoun*). *Fortiter.—In time.* 239. 8

Houton, De, a fox current. cf. 32. 8

Hoveden, Ireland, a dragon's head vert, issuing out of flames ppr. cf. 72. 12

Hovell-Thurlow-Cumming-Bruce, *see* Bruce.

Hovell, a leopard sejant ppr. cf. 24. 13

Hovell, on a ducal coronet or, a leopard sejant ppr. 24. 11

How of London, on a chapeau ppr., a martlet sa. 95. 1

How, Essex and Suff., out of a ducal coronet or, a unicorn's head gu., attired and crined of the first. 48. 12

How of London, a wolf's head erased pean. 30. 8

How, Archibald Wybergh, Esquire, of Droitwich, Worcs., a wolf's head erased.

How of London, a wolf's head sa., holding in his mouth a rose gu., stalked and leaved vert. cf. 30. 12

How of London, and Herse, Somers., out of a ducal coronet or, a demi-wolf rampant sa. cf. 31. 2

How or **Howe,** Glouc. and Notts, out of a ducal coronet or, a plume of five ostrich-feathers az. *Utcunque placuerit Deo.* 114. 13

Howales, a griffin sejant ppr. *Forward.* 62. 10

Howard, Duke of Norfolk, *see* Norfolk.

Howard, *see* Effingham, Earl of.

Howard, *see* Carlisle, Earl of.

Howard, *see* Suffolk and Berkshire, Earl of.

Howard, Earl of Wicklow, etc., *see* Wicklow.

Howard of Glossop, **Baron** (Fitzalan-Howard), Glossop Hall, Derbysh.: (1) Issuant from a ducal coronet or, a pair of wings gu., each charged with a bend between six cross crosslets fitchée arg. (*for Howard*). 109. 9. (2) On a chapeau gu., turned up erm., a lion statant with tail extended or, gorged with a ducal coronet arg. (*for Brotherton*). cf. 4. 8. (3) On a mount vert, a horse passant arg., holding in the mouth a slip of oak fructed ppr. (*for Fitzalan*). *Sola virtus invicta.* 52. 11

Howard, Edward Stafford, Esquire, C.B., of Thornbury Castle, Thornbury, Glouc.: (1) Issuant from a ducal coronet or, a pair of wings gu., each charged with a bend between six cross crosslets fitchée arg. (2) On a chapeau gu., turned up erm., a lion statant, with tail extended or, gorged with a ducal coronet arg. *Sola virtus invicta.*

Howard, Henry Charles, Esquire, J.P., of Greystoke Castle, Penrith, same crests.

Howard, Robert Mowbray, Esquire, J.P., D.L., of Hampton Lodge, Farnham, Surrey, same crests and motto.

Howard, Sir Henry, K.C.M.G., C.B., of the British Legation, the Hague, Netherlands: (1) Issuant from a ducal coronet or, a pair of wings gu., each charged with a bend between six cross crosslets fitchée arg. 109. 9. (2) On a chapeau gu., turned up erm., a lion statant guardant, tail extended or, ducally crowned and charged upon the neck with a label of three points arg *Sola virtus invicta.*

Howard-De-Walden, Baron, (Ellis) Seaford House, 37, Belgrave Square, on a mount vert, a goat's head arg. *Non quo sed quomodo.* cf. 128. 12

Howard, out of a ducal coronet two wings gu., each charged with a bend between six cross crosslets fitched arg. 109. 9

Howard, on a chapeau gu., turned up erm., two wings of the first, each charged with a bend between six cross crosslets fitched arg. *Another,* without the chapeau. 112. 9

Howard, two wings expanded gu., each charged with a bend vairée or and az., between six cross crosslets of the second.

Howard, Colonel Henry Richard Lloyd, C.B., of Wygfair, St. Asaph, same crest. *Watch, ward, win.*

Howard, Philip, John Canning Esquire, J.P., of Corby Castle, Cumb., on a chapeau gu., turned up erm., a lion statant gardant, the tail extended or, ducally crowned arg., gorged with a label of three points of the last. *Volo, non valeo.* cf. 4. 4

Howard of Compton Place, Sussex, on a chapeau gu., turned up erm., a lion statant guardant, the tail extended or, ducally gorged, a mullet sa. for difference. *Volo, non valeo.*

Howard, Major Frederick Compton, of Dacre House, Scarborough, same crest and motto.

Howard, Gerald Richard, Esquire, same crest and motto.

Howard, Fitzalan, Esquire, J.P., of Holyrood House, Spalding, on a chapeau gu., turned up erm., a lion statant guardant, the tail extended. *Sola virtus invicta.*

Howard-Bury, Captain Kenneth; (1) A boar's head couped at the neck or, tusked arg., langued gu., transfixed through the neck by a spear ppr., and charged for difference with a cross crosslet vert (*for Bury*). (2) On a chapeau gu., turned up erm., a lion statant gardant with tail extended or, ducally gorged arg., and charged on the body with a crescent, also gu., for difference, and over the crest the motto, *Nous maintiendrons* (*for Howard*). *Virtus sub cruce crescit.* cf. 4. 7

Howard, Bart., of Bushy Park, co. Wicklow, on a chapeau gu., turned up erm., charged with a crescent sa., a lion statant gardant or, ducally gorged gu., holding in the mouth an arrow in fess ppr. *Inservi Deo, et lætare.* cf. 4. 7

Howard, William Dillworth, Esquire, of Culduff and Redford Glebe, in the Benefice of Cloncha and co. Donegal, Ireland, a lion statant gardant, tail extended arg., resting the dexter fore-paw on a stag's head caboshed or. *Sola virtus invicta.*

Howard of Dublin, on a chapeau gu., turned up erm., a lion statant gardant, the tail extended or, ducally gorged gu., and pierced through the mouth with an arrow ppr. cf. 4 7

Howard of London, a lion couchant erm., holding in the dexter paw a cross pommée fitched or. cf. 7. 5

Howard, Robert Edward, Esquire, of Brinnington, Chesh., in front of a cross botonny fitchée gu., a lion couchant or, charged on the shoulder with an estoile, also gu. *Per fidem omnia.* 7. 5

Howard, Cephas John, Esquire, J.P., same crest and motto.

Howard, Lanes, a lion rampant arg., holding between its paws a cross crosslet fitched of the same. cf. 3. 13

Howard, late Joseph Jackson, Esquire, of Mayfield, Orchard Road, Blackheath, Kent, *Maltravers Herald of Arms Extraordinary,* LL.D., F.S.A., a lion rampant ppr., charged on the body with two annulets in pale vert, holding between the paws a fret as in the arms, and resting the dexter hind-paw on two S's as linked in a herald's collar arg. *Credo Christi cruce.*

Howard, Robert, Esquire, M.A., J.P., of Broughton Hall, Flintsh., a lion's head affrontée between two wings and a cross crosslet fitchée issuing from the head. *Virtus sine metu.* 260. 11

Howard of St. Andrew's, Holborn, a lion couchant erm., holding in the dexter paw a cross botonée fitchée of the second. cf. 7. 5

Howard, William, Esquire, of Kingswode Hoe, Colchester, Essex, a lion passant az., charged on the body with two trefoils, holding in the dexter paw a cross crosslet fitchée, all or. *Nous maintiendrons.* 260. 20

Howard, out of a ducal coronet a wolf's head. cf. 30. 5

Howard of London, a demi-wolf ppr., holding between the paws a cross crosslet fitchée or, gorged with a collar gu., thereon a mullet between two cinquefoils of the second. cf. 31. 5

Howard, Sir Richard Nicholas, of Green Hill House, Weymouth, a demi-wolf or, gorged with a collar gemelle and charged on the body with two quatrefoils sa., holding between the paws an escutcheon gu., charged with a cross patonce fitchée or. *Fide et animus.* 31. 11

Howard of Hackney, Middx., on a chapeau gu., turned up erm., a demi-hind salient ppr., charged on the shoulder with a cross fleury fitched arg.

Howard, Allan Maclean, Esquire, of Toronto, Canada, a catherine-wheel arg., between on the dexter side a branch of palm, and on the sinister a branch of cypress ppr. *Pro fide.* 167. 5

Howard, James Harold, Esquire, J.P., of the Grange, Kempston, Beds, in front of an eagle displayed sa., holding in the beak an ear of wheat slipped or, a tower of the last. *Progress with prudence.*

Howard-Vyse, Howard Henry, Esquire, J.P., D.L., of Stoke Place, Slough, and Boughton Park, Northamp., on a chapeau gu., turned up erm., a lion statant guardant, the tail extended or, ducally crowned and charged on the neck with a label of three points arg., a mullet sa. charged with a crescent or, for difference (*for Howard*). *Virtutis mille scuta.*

Howat, late David Gemmill, Esquire, 2, Kew Terrace, Glasgow, the sun in his splendour rising out of a cloud ppr. *Post tenebras lux.* 162. 5

Howatson, Charles, Esquire, Glenbuck, N.B., and Dornel, Auchinleck, Ayrsh., a dexter hand couped at the wrist apaumée ppr. *Hinc orior.* 222. 14

Howden, Baron (Caradoc), a man in a coat of mail, crowned with a crown of three points, kneeling upon one knee and presenting a sword, all ppr. *Traditus, non victus.*

Howden, Scotland, a castle triple-towered ppr. 155. 8

Howdon, a dragon's head vomiting flames of fire ppr. *Feris tego.* 72. 3

Howe, Earl (Curzon-Howe), Gopsall, Atherstone, Leics.: (1) Out of a ducal coronet or, a plume of five feathers az. (*for Howe*). 114. 13. (2) A popinjay rising or, collared gu. (*for Curzon*). *Let Curzon holde what Curzon helde.*

Howe, *see* **How.**

Howe, Wilts, and Langar, Notts, a gauntlet in fess ppr., lined gu., holding a falchion arg., enfiled with a wolf's head erased of the first. 211. 5

Howe or **How** of London, out of a ducal coronet or, a demi-wolf rampant sa. *cf.* 31. 2

Howe, Somers., an arm erect ppr., vested arg., charged with two bends wavy gu., holding a bunch of broom vert.

Howe, a dexter hand holding a wheat-ear ppr. 218. 14

Howe, Edward Russell James Gambier, 7, New Square, Lincoln's Inn, W.C., out of a ducal coronet or, a unicorn's head gu., crined and attired of the first. *Fide non armis.*

Howel and **Howell,** a camel ppr. 132. 2

Howel and **Howell,** a beaver passant ppr. *cf.* 134. 8

Howell, a camel passant ppr. *cf.* 132. 2

Howell, same crest. *Perseverando.*

Howell, Glouc., a stag lodged sa., holding in the mouth a leaf ppr. *cf.* 115. 7

Howell of Prinknash Park, Glouc.: (1) A stag lodged sa., holding in the mouth a leaf ppr. (*for Howell*). *cf.* 115. 7. (2) Out of a ducal coronet or, a lion's head sa., guttée-d'eau (*for Jones*). 17. 5

Howell of Eynsham, Oxon., a griffin segreant az., holding a broken spear sa. *Virtus in arduo.*

Howell or **Hovell** of Soulgrave, Northamp., Pack, Warw., and Suff., a griffin sejant arg., beaked, legged, and winged az., pierced through the breast with a broken tilting-spear ppr., and holding the bottom part of the broken spear in the sinister claw.

Howell of St. Albans, Herts, issuing out of a ducal coronet or, a rose arg., stalked and leaved vert, between two wings endorsed sa.

Howenden of Killeban, Queen's Co., Ireland, issuing out of flames ppr., a dragon's head arg. *Virtute et prudentia.* *cf.* 72. 12

Howes, a demi-youth ppr., vested az., holding in his dexter hand a heart gu.

Howes, Essex, a dexter hand erect holding an ear of wheat, all ppr. 218. 14

Howes of Morningthorpe, Norf., three ostrich-feathers or, therefrom issuant a unicorn gu., collared, armed, and crined or. *Stat fortuna domus.*

Howetts, a nail erect head downwards ppr., enfiled with a mural coronet arg.

Howgart, Scotland, a horse's head ppr., between two wings arg. *Condor dat viribus alas.* 51. 3

Howick, Viscount, *see* Grey, Earl.

Howison, Ireland, an antelope trippant gu. 126. 6

Howison of Holmfoot, Lanarksh., an eagle rising ppr. *Nulla temerata nube.* 77. 5

Howison of Braehead, Midlothian, Scotland, a dexter hand couped apaumée ppr. *Sursum corda.* 222. 14

Howitt, William Adlington, Esquire, B.A., M.R.C.S., L.R.C.P., of 54, Goldsmith Street, Nottingham, a crested lapwing or plover ppr. *Audax pro suis.* 291. 12

Howland, Baron, *see* Bedford, Duke of.

Howland of London, a leopard passant sa., ducally gorged or. *cf.* 24. 3

Howlet, an owl's head erased ppr., gorged with a mural coronet or.

Howlett of Sydenham, Kent, an owl arg., ducally gorged or, holding in the dexter claw a rose gu., slipped and leaved vert.

Howlett, Major-General Arthur, C.B., a cross crosslet sa., between two branches of laurel ppr. *Fide et vigilantia.*

Howley, late Rt. Rev. William, D.D., Bishop of London, an eagle displayed erm., charged on the breast with a cross fleury gu. *cf.* 75 2

Howman of Norwich, on a mount ppr., a pegasus volant sa. *Labile quod opportunum.* *cf.* 47. 2

Hownd or **Hound** of Collis, Cambs, and Heref., a demi-talbot arg., collared sa., holding a key or.

Howndhile or **Howndhill,** a Saracen's head ppr., wreathed about the temples or and gu. 190. 5

Hownhill, a lion's gamb erased, holding a tilting-spear in bend tasselled, all ppr. *cf.* 38. 11

Howorth, Lancs., a stag's head gu., attired or, gorged with a wreath arg. 120. 3

Howse, a dexter hand holding an ear of wheat ppr. 218. 14

Howson, a falcon belled ppr. *Ad finem fidelis.* *cf.* 85. 2

Howston, Scotland, on a ducal coronet a lion passant. 6. 6

Howth, Earl of (St. Lawrence), Howth Castle, co. Dublin, a sea-lion per fesse arg. and ppr. *Qui panse.* 20. 2

Howton, Oxon., a hind's head erased or, between two branches of roses flowered arg., stalked and leaved vert. *cf.* 124. 4

Hoxton of Sutterton Hoxton, Suff., a tower ppr., ensigned with a flag az., flotant to the sinister, the staff sa. 157. 13

Hoy, Ireland, a pheasant ppr. *cf.* 90. 8

Hoy of Higham Lodge, Suff., a griffin sejant sa., holding in the dexter claw a sword erect ppr., pommel and hilt or. *cf.* 62. 10

Hoy, a demi-lion gu., supporting a long cross or. 11. 14

Hoye, a demi-lion gu., supporting a Passion cross or. 11. 14

Hoyland, Lancs, a dexter hand in fess issuing from a cloud pointing to a crosier in pale issuing ppr. 223. 2

Hoyle, Fretwell William, Esquire, of Eastwood Lodge, near Rotherham, Yorks, on a wreath of the colours an eagle's head erased ppr., charged on the neck with a mullet sa., and holding in the beak a white rose slipped ppr. *Facta non verba.*

Hoyle, a demi-lion rampant regardant or, holding between the paws an escutcheon az., charged with a sun in splendour of the first.

Hoyle, Ireland, a lion couchant or, charged on the shoulder with a mullet sa. *cf.* 7. 5

Hoyles, a youth's head in a helmet affrontée ppr., plumed arg.

Hozier, Baron, *see* Newlands.

Hozier, Sir Henry Montague, K.C.B., of Stonehouse, Lanarksh., and 26a, North Audley Street, W., a bloodhound sejant ppr. *Aye ready.*

Huband, Warw. and Derbysh., a wolf passant or. *Cave lupum.* 28. 10

Hubart, Hubert, or **Hubberd,** a boar's head couped gu., collared, ringed, and lined arg., holding in the mouth a spear sa., headed of the second.

Hubbald of Stoke, Surrey, a leopard's face or, jessant three feathers, the centre one az., the other two gu.

Hubbard, Baron Addington, *see* Addington.

Hubbard of Freeby, Leics., a Saracen's head ppr. 190. 5

Hubbersty, Cantrell-, Colonel Albert, Tollerton Hall, Notts: (1) Upon a wreath of the colours, in front of a griffin's head erased arg., charged with a fesse engrailed vert, a mole fessewise or (*for Hubbersty*). (2) On a wreath of the colours, in front of a tower arg., a rock ppr., thereon a boar passant sa., armed or, charged on the body with two roses arg. (*for Cantrell*). *Propositi tenax.—Pectus fidele et apertum.*

Hubbert, Ireland, a boar's head sa. 43. 1

Hubert of Sunbury, Middx., on a chapeau gu., turned up erm., a lion's head erased or, charged with three étoiles in fess of the first. *cf.* 17. 9

Hubert-Marshall, a demi-heraldic tiger sa., guttée-d'or, armed, crined, tufted, and gorged with a collar gemel, also or, resting the sinister paw upon an escutcheon gu., charged with a pheon or. *Ducit amor patriæ.* 25. 6

Hucks, between the attires of a stag affixed to the scalp a boar's head erased and erect. 43. 2

Hucks, on a ducal coronet or, a fleur-de-lis arg. *cf.* 148. 2

Huddart, Rev. G., Kirklington Rectory, Bedale, Yorks, a stag's head erased. *Fear God.*

Huddersfield and **Huddesfield,** a boar passant or. 40. 9

Huddesdon or **Hudson** of Guy's Cliff, Warw., an eagle's leg sa., joined at the knee to a sinister wing or. *cf.* 113. 5

Huddleston and **Huddlestone,** on a ducal coronet a peacock ppr. 103. 8

Huddleston, Tristram Frederick Croft, Esquire, two arms dexter and sinister embowed, vested erm., cuffed gu., the hands supporting a dexter gauntlet erect ppr., encircled by a chaplet of roses gu.

Huddleston, Andrew John, Esquire, of Hodelston, Yorks, and of Millum Castle and Hutton John, Cumb., two arms dexter and sinister, embowed, vested arg., holding in the hands a scalp ppr., the inside thereof gu. *Soli Deo honor et gloria.* 203. 8

Huddleston, Denys Alexander Lawlor, Sawston Hall, Cambridge: (1) Two arms dexter and sinister, embowed vested, and cuffed arg., the hands ppr., holding a stone sa. 269. 17. (2) On a mount vert, a stag lodged ppr. in front of a spear-head in pale, point upwards ppr. *Soli Deo honor et gloria.—Mea culpa fides.* 269. 18

Huddleston of Sawston, Cambs, same crest. *Soli Deo honor et gloria.*

Huddlestone, Scotland, a hand holding a pen ppr. *Ingenio et viribus.* 217. 10

Huddy, Somers., a bull passant sa., armed or. *cf.* 45. 2

Huddy, Devonsh., a bull passant sa., armed or, collared and lined arg. *cf.* 45. 2

Hudson of London, a dexter hand erect ppr., holding with the thumb and forefinger a bezant.

Hudson, James, Esquire, J.P., of Capenor, Nutfield, Surrey, two escallops in fesse sa., thereon a martlet or. *Animo non astutia.*

Hudson, William Hebard, Esquire, c.o. Messrs Grindlay and Co., 55, Parliament Street, Westminster, c.o. Messrs Grindlay, Groom and Co., Bombay, and Common Room, Lincoln's Inn, W.C., a cock holding in the beak an acorn leaved and slipped, and between two ears of wheat, all ppr. 265. 9

Hudson of Low Hall, Scarborough, a cubit arm erect in a coat of mail, holding in the hand, all ppr., a broken falchion gu.

Hudson, Norf., a fawn's head erased ppr., gorged with a mural coronet or.

Hudson, Ireland, on a chapeau gu., turned up or, an owl with wings expanded arg. 96. 6

Hudson of Preston, Lancs, a lion rampant or, holding between the paws a boar's head couped sa. *cf.* 225. 5

Hudson, George Bickersteth, Esquire, M.P., J.P., D.L., of Frogmore Hall, Hertford, and 15, Gloucester Square, W., a lion rampant holding between the paws a boar's head erased, all ppr. *Fide cui vide.*

Hudson, John Thomas, Esquire, of Glen Beg, Dungarvan, same crest. *Certavi et vici.*

Hudson, Rev. Joseph, M.A., Hon. Canon of Crosby House, Carlisle, a falcon, wings displayed ppr., beaked, membered, and belled or, collared az., reposing the dexter claw on an escutcheon gu., charged with a cross crosslet fitchée arg.

Hudson, Rear-Admiral Joseph Samuel, of Hythe, Southampton, same crest.

Hudson-Kinahan, Bart., of Glenville, co. Cork, of Wyckham, co. Dublin, and of Merrion Square North, Dublin: (1) A demi-lion rampant sa., holding in the paws a battle-axe ppr., and charged on the shoulder with a cross couped or (*for Kinahan*). 15. 5. (2) A lion rampant gu., charged with a cross couped or, and holding between the paws a boar's head couped arg. (*for Hudson*). *Deo fidens persistas.* 225. 5

Hudson, Donaldson-, Ralph Charles, Esquire, of Cheswardine Hall, Chesh.: (1) Upon a millrind fesseways sa., a lion's head erased or, gorged with a bar gemel indented gu. (*for Hudson*). (2) In front of a saltire az., a cubit arm erect grasping a dagger, and charged with a thistle slipped, both ppr. (*for Donaldson*).

Hudson, a martlet az., winged or. 95. 4

Hudson of London, a martlet vert, winged or. 95. 4

Hudson, out of a ducal coronet a griffin's head holding in the beak a trefoil slipped. *cf.* 67. 9

Hudson, Bart., Leics., a griffin's head erased arg., gorged with a mural coronet gu., charged with three escallops of the first. *cf.* 66. 2

Hudspath, a griffin segreant holding between its claws a tilting-spear enfiled with a boar's head erased.

Huet, a crow rising ppr. 107. 3

Huger of South Carolina, a sprig, thereon a Virginian nightingale ppr. *Ubi libertas, ibi patria.* 145. 7

Hugessen, Knatchbull-, Lord Brabourne, *see* Brabourne.

Hugessen, Knatchbull-: (1) An oak-tree ppr., between two wings elevated, pinions az., feathered or (*for Hugessen*). 236. 3. (2) On a chapeau az., turned up erm., an ounce statant arg., spotted sa. (*for Knatchbull*). *Crucifixa gloria mea.*

Hugford, a lion's gamb issuing and resting upon an escutcheon. *cf.* 37. 2

Hugford of Dicklestone, Glouc., Wollas Hall, Worcs., and Warw., same crest. 120. 3

Huggard of Ireland, an estoile of sixteen points arg. *In heaven is my hope.*

Huggerford, Glouc. and Warw., a stag's head or, gorged with a chaplet of laurel vert. 120. 3

Huggins of London, a sword in pale, enfiled with a leopard's face. 22. 1

Hugham, a fox's head arg., semée of torteaux. *cf.* 33. 4

Hughan of Airds, Kirkcudbright, Scotland, an escallop or. *E mare.* 141. 12

Hughes-Le Fleming, *see* Fleming.

Hughes, Hugh Robert, Esquire, of Kinmel Park, Abergele, North Wales, and Glanywern, Denbighsh., out of a ducal crest or, a demi-lion rampant arg., holding between the paws a rose gu., slipped ppr. (*Confirmed by Sir Richard St. George, Norroy, 1620.*) *Heb Dduw heb ddim Duw a digon.* 16. 2

Hughes of Plas yn Diserth and Llewerllyd, Flintsh., out of a ducal coronet or, a demi-lion rampant arg., holding between the paws a rose gu., leaved and slipped vert. 16. 2

Hughes, Hugh Robert, of Ystrad, Denbighsh., a lion couchant sa.

Hughes, Michael James, Esquire, of Sherdley Hall, St. Helen's, Lancs., and Penketh Hall, near Warrington, same crest and motto.

Hughes of Kinmel, Invercauld, Braemar, out of a baron's coronet a demi-lion rampant arg., holding between the fore-paws a rose gu. *Heb Dduw heb ddim Duw a digon.* 16. 6

Hughes, John George Parry, of Alltlwyld, Cardigan, on a chapeau gu., turned up erm., a demi-lion rampant holding in the dexter paw a fleur-de-lis. 307. 11

Hughes, William, Esquire, of 62, Palace Road, Tulse Hill, S.W., in front of a demi-lion or, holding between the paws an eagle's head erased gu., a fleur-de-lis between two roses of the last. *Semper meliora spero.* 265. 8

Hughes, out of a ducal coronet or, a demi-lion rampant sa., armed and langued gu. 16. 3

Hughes of Gwerclas in Edeirnion, Merionethsh.: (1) Out of a ducal coronet or, a demi-lion rampant sa. 16. 3. (2) A boar passant erm., fretty gu. *cf.* 40. 1. (3) On a chapeau az., turned up erm., a dragon gu., gorged with an ancient regal crown. *Kymmer-yn-Edeirnion.* *cf.* 73. 4

Hughes of Ireland, a lion rampant arg. 1. 13

Hughes, a lion rampant or, holding a thistle slipped ppr. *cf.* 1. 13

Hughes, a lion sejant holding in the mouth a dart. *cf.* 8. 8

Hughes, Sir Collingwood, Bart., of East Bergholt, Suff., a lion couchant or. 7. 5

Hughes of the Quadrant, Highbury, London N., in front of a staff raguly fessewise ppr., and thereon a lion couchant az., holding between the paws an escallop gu., a tilting-spear erect or. *Semper vigilans.* *cf.* 7. 5

Hughes, Guy Ferguson, Esquire, of Dunley, Bovey Tracey, Devonsh., in front of a sword paleways, point downwards ppr., pommel and hilt or, an arm in armour couped at the elbow and fesseways, the hand in a gauntlet, all ppr., holding a fleur-de-lis gu.

Hughes-Buller, Ralph Buller, Esquire, of Dunley, Bovey Tracey, Devonsh., same crest and motto.

Hughes, Louis Campbell, Esquire, Dunley, Bovey Tracey, Devonsh., same crest and motto.

Hughes, William Gwynne, Esquire, of Nantgaredig R.S.O., South Wales, a talbot.

Hughes of Middleton, Stoney, Oxon., a heron arg., beaked gu. 105. 9

Hughes, a crane holding in the beak a serpent. 105. 8

Hughes, George Pringle, Esquire, High Sheriff of the County of Northumberland, Middleton Hall, Wooler, a mount vert, thereon between two wings az., a stork arg., beaked and legged gu. *Si Deus nobiscum.* 104. 8

Hughes, Joseph William, Esquire, of 2, Preston Park Avenue, Brighton, same crest and motto.

Hughes of Plas Côch, Anglesea, a Cornish chough ppr. *Duw a ddarpar i'r brain.* 107. 14

Hughes, a Cornish chough ppr., holding in the dexter claw a fleur-de-lis arg. 292. 1

Hughes, James Llewellyn, Esquire, Strangways, Truro, a cough, ppr., holding in his dexter claw a fleur-de-lis gu. *Duw a ddarpar i'r brain.* 292. 1

Hughes of Plas'yn, Llangoed, Beaumaris, a Cornish chough holding in the dexter claw a fleur-de-lis. *Duw aedir, par ir brain.* 292. 1

Hughes of Maidstone, Kent, on a chapeau gu., turned up erm., a demi-eagle with wings elevated ppr. 80. 12

Hughes, Wales, an eagle's head erased sa., holding in the beak a staff raguly inflamed ppr.

Hughes of Bodwryn, Anglesea, an eagle's head erased sa., holding in the beak a brand raguly of the same fired gu. *A fynno Duw derfyd.*

Hughes, Gwynne-, John William, Tregib, Llandilo, Carmarthen: (1) A talbot passant (*for Hughes*). (2) A goat passant (*for Williams*). (3) A raven ppr. (*for Gwynne*).

Hughes of Ely House, Wexford, a griffin's head erased gu. *Verus amor patriæ.* 66. 2

Hughes, Frederic James Robert, Esquire, of Rosslare Fort, and Barntown House, co. Wexford, a griffin's head erased gu., holding in the beak a fleur-de-lis or. *Verus amor patriæ.*

Hughes, Walter Hastings Frederick, Esquire, of Barnton House, Rosslare, co. Wexford, same crest and motto.

Hughes, Sir Frederic, of Ely House, co. Wexford, Ireland, Knight Bachelor, and Knight of the first class of the Royal Persian Order of the Lion and Sun, same crest and motto. *cf.* 66. 2

Hughes of Nuneaton, Warw., in front of a griffin's head erased sa., a fret or. *cf.* 66. 2

Hughes-D'Aeth, Kent, a griffin's head erased or, holding in the beak a trefoil slipped vert. *cf.* 66. 2

Hughes of Archerstown, co. Tipperary, Ireland, a demi-griffin or. *Non sibi sed patriæ.* 64. 2

Hughes, Ireland, a griffin sejant gu., winged, armed, and beaked or, holding in the dexter claw a laurel-garland vert. 62. 9

Hughes, a boar's head erased in fesse. 42. 2

Hughes, Scotland, out of a ducal coronet or, a unicorn's head arg. 48. 12

Hughes of Brecon, a hand in armour ppr., couped above the wrist in fess, holding a fleur-de-lis arg.

Hughes, Wales, an arm in armour ppr., holding a fleur-de-lis arg. 210. 6

Hughes, Colonel Sir Edwin, V.D., of Oaklands, Plumstead Common, two horse-shoes az., thereon a stag's head erased or. *Faber quisque fortunæ suæ.*

Hugo, Devonsh., a lion rampant holding in the paws a standard arg., charged with a cross gu. 3. 7

Hugworth, a goat passant arg., armed and ungu. or. *cf.* 129. 5

Hulbert, issuing out of a cloud a hand in pale ppr., holding a garland of laurel. 218. 9

Hulburn, a lion issuant holding in his dexter paw a mullet arg. 15. 7

Hulford, Glouc., a dexter hand holding an oak-branch, all ppr.

Hulgrave, Chesh., a hand grasping a thunderbolt ppr. 216. 4

Hulgrave, Chesh., a hand holding a thunderbolt, all ppr. 216. 4

Hulkes, Cecil James Gladdish, Esquire, Petting's House, Ash, near Sevenoaks, Kent, a buck's head couped at the neck ppr., wreathed vert, attired or, between the attires a sun in splendour of the last. *Utile dulci.*

Hull, Scotland, a talbot's head sa. 56. 12

Hull of Clonakilty, co. Cork, Ireland, a talbot's head couped arg. 56. 12

Hull of Larkbeare, Devonsh, Osterley, Durh., Battersea, Surrey, London and Bucks, a talbot's head erased arg., between two laurel-branches ppr., united at the top. *cf.* 269. 8

Hull, Edmund Charles Pendleton, Esquire, J.P., of Earlswood Mount, Redhill, Surrey, a talbot's head erased arg., gorged with a collar dancettee erminois, between two laurel branches ppr. *Vi et virtute.* 269. 8

Hull, Edward, Esquire, of 20, Arundel Gardens, London, W., same crest and motto.

Hull, Durh., a cubit arm erect ppr., vested, cuffed arg., holding in the hand a fleur-de-lis.

Hull, a hunting-horn az., garnished arg. 228. 11

Hull, Ireland, a pigeon volant az. *cf.* 93. 10

Hull, Surrey, a dragon's head couped sa., eared gu., gorged with a collar or, thereon three torteaux, and charged on the neck with a pale arg., between four plates.

Hulles, Hulse, Huls, and **Hulsey** of Newbury, Berks, and Betherden, Kent, a buck's head couped ppr., attired or, between the attires a sun in his splendour of the last. *cf.* 121. 5

Hulley, Holland, Esquire, of The One House, Rainow, Chesh., and Seisdon, near Wolverhampton, a demi-cat-a-mountain regardant arg., holding between the paws an escutcheon or, charged with a hillock vert. *One house, one faith.* 235. 18

Hulleys and **Hullies,** out of a ducal coronet or, a unicorn's head gu. 48. 12

Hulling or **Hullingey,** a demi-savage holding over the shoulder a tree eradicated and bound round the waist and temples with leaves ppr.

Hully, Ireland, a greyhound's head az., bezantée. 61. 12

Huls of Norbury, Chesh., a buck's head couped ppr., attired sa., gorged with a chaplet vert, and between the attires a sun in splendour or. *cf.* 120. 3

Hulse, Shropsh., a stag's head ppr., attired sa., gorged with a chaplet vert, and between the attires a sun or. *cf.* 120. 3

Hulse, a buck's head gorged with a chaplet ppr. 120. 3

Hulse, Sir Edward Hamilton, Bart., of Breamore House, Hants, a buck's head couped ppr., charged with two bezants and a plate, attired or, and between the attires a sun in splendour of the last. 286. 15

Hulson of London and Yorks, a lion rampant sa., holding an escutcheon arg., having a carved bordure.

Hulton, out of a tower ppr., three arrows sa.

Hulton, out of a mural coronet a stag's head, holding in the mouth a branch of hawthorn. *Mens flecti nescia.*

Hulton, William Wilbraham Blethyn, of Hulton, Lancs, out of a ducal coronet or, a hart's head and neck cabossed arg., between two branches of hawthorn ppr. *Mens flecti nescia.*

Hulton-Harrop: (1) In front of a saltire or, an eagle displayed sa., crusily arg. (*for Harrop*). 246. 17. (2) Out of a ducal coronet or, a hart's head and neck cabossed arg., between two branches of hawthorn ppr., each bearing three roses arg., seeded gu., barbed vert (*for Hulton*). 246. 18. *Terrena pericula sperno.*

Hulton of Bevis Mount, Hants, out of a ducal coronet or, a hart's head ppr., attired of the first, between two branches, also ppr., each bearing three roses gu.

Hulyn, on a lion's head couped or, a chapeau az., turned up erm. *cf.* 21. 10

Humberston, Herts and Norf., a griffin's head erased arg., charged with three pellets in pale. *cf.* 66. 2

Humble, on a chapeau an owl rising, all ppr. 96. 6

Humble a stag's head erased. 121. 2

Humble, Bart. (*extinct*), of London, a demi-buck gorged with a wreath of laurel ppr. *cf.* 119. 2

Humble, Bart., of Cloncoskan, co. Waterford, a demi-stag salient arg., charged with a trefoil slipped vert, and attired or. *Decrevi.* *cf.* 119. 2

Humby of Bedford Row, Middx., an eagle displayed gu., charged on the breast and on each wing with a bee or. *cf.* 75. 2

Hume, Earl of Marchmont, out of a human heart a dexter arm erect holding a scimitar, all ppr. *True to the end.* 213. 4

Hume, Bart., Herts, a lion's head erased arg. *True to the end.* 17. 8

Hume of Humewood, Ireland, same crest and motto.

Hume of Crossrigs, Scotland, a lion's head erased arg., collared gu. *True to the end.* 18. 6

Hume of Polwart, a lion's head erased arg., collared gu., charged with a rose or. *True to the end.* *cf.* 18. 6

Hume, Ross-, James Alexander, Ninewells, Chirnside, Berwicksh., a lion's head erased arg., gorged with a collar gu., charged with eight fountains. *True to the end.*

Hume, Scotland, issuing out of a crescent, the horns thereof upwards, a lion's head.

Hume of Auchindolly, co. Kirkcudbright, Scotland, a lion's head erased gu. *True to the end.* 17. 2

Hume of Whitfield, Edinburgh, a lion's head erased arg., gorged with a collar or, charged with three mullets gu. *True to the end.* cf. 18. 6

Hume, Colonel Archibald, of Auchendolly, Dalbeattie, Kirkcudbrightsh., a lion's head erased gu., armed and langued az. *True to the end.*

Hume of Harries, a lion's head erased ppr. *True to the end.* 17. 8

Hume, John Hume, Esquire, of East Melbourne, Victoria, in front of a cross engrailed az., a lion's head erased arg., charged with two cinquefoils in pale gu. *True to the end.*

Hume of Renton, Scotland, a pelican ppr. 98. 1

Hume, Scotland, a demi-leopard ppr. *Perseverance.* cf. 23. 13

Hume of Willow Terrace Road, Leeds, a demi-heraldic antelope regardant arg., charged on the shoulder with a lozenge az., and resting the dexter fore-leg on an escutcheon or, thereon a popinjay ppr. *Nil desperandum.*

Hume-Cookson of Willow Terrace Road, Leeds: (1) A demi-lion gu., gorged with a collar gemelle or, holding between the paws a leg couped at the thigh in armour ppr., garnished and spurred or (*for Cookson*). (2) A demi-heraldic antelope regardant arg., charged on the shoulder with a lozenge az., and resting the dexter fore-leg on an escutcheon or, charged with a popinjay ppr. (*for Hume*).

Hume of Coldinghamton, a hand issuing from a heart holding a sword, all ppr. *True to the end.* cf. 213. 4

Hume, Scotland, a hand holding a scimitar ppr., issuing from a human heart or. 213. 4

Hume-Campbell, a dexter arm issuing from a heart and grasping a scimitar, all ppr. *True to the end.—Fides probata coronat.* 213. 4

Humffreys, on a chapeau ppr., a boar passant arg., fretty gu. cf. 40. 8

Humffreys of Llwyn, Montgomerysh., on a chapeau ppr., a boar passant arg., fretty gu. cf. 40. 8

Humfrey of Wroxham House, Norf.: (1) On a ducal coronet an eagle with wings elevated holding in the dexter claw a sceptre or, and charged on the breast with a cross crosslet gu. (*for Humfrey*). (2) On a morion a martlet ppr. (*for Blake*). *Cœlestem spero coronatu.*

Humfrey, co. Cavan, on a ducal coronet or, an eagle with wings elevated holding in the dexter claw a sceptre, also or.

Humfrey of Dublin, upon a ducal coronet an eagle with wings endorsed and holding in the dexter claw a broken spear, all or.

Humfrey of Truro, Cornw., on a mount vert, a Cornish chough with wings expanded arg., beaked and legged gu., and gorged with a bar gemelle or.

Humfrey, Leics., and of Barton, Northamp., a harpy arg., the face ppr., crined or, with wings expanded of the last. 189. 4

Humfrey of Cavanacor, co. Donegal, a sphinx sejant. *Sic olim.*

Humfrey of Chaldon-Humphrey, Dorset, a leopard passant or, embrued at the mouth gu. cf. 24. 2

Humfrey, Glouc. and Northamp., a cross botonnée arg., charged with five pellets.

Humfrey of Rottendon, Essex, a dexter arm in armour, holding in the hand, all ppr., a cross batonnée fitchée arg., charged with four pellets.

Humfrey of London, a horse's head or, pellettée, between two wings barry wavy of six arg. and az. cf. 51. 3

Humfreys, Shropsh., a boar arg., in a net gu. cf. 40. 11

Humfreys, Humphreys, Humfrey, or **Humfry** of London and Wales, a lion sejant or, resting the dexter paw upon a nag's head couped ermines.

Humphery, Sir William Henry, Bart., the Cottage, Great Brington, Northamp., a unicorn passant arg., armed, crined, and hoofed or, the dexter forefoot supporting a Roman fasces in bend of the last. *Deus protector meus.* 276. 9

Humphray, a harpy gardant ppr. 189. 1

Humphress, a boar's head couped. 43. 1

Humphrey, Humphrie, and **Humphroy,** a demi-griffin with wings addorsed holding between its claws a ducal coronet ppr.

Humphrey, Humphrie, or **Humphry,** a demi-griffin with wings endorsed holding between the claws a ducal coronet ppr.

Humphrey of Swebston, Liecs., and Barton, Northamp., a harpy arg., crined or, and with wings displayed of the last. 189. 4

Humphrey, Sir William Henry, Bart., C.B., M.A., of Penton Lodge, Hants, a unicorn passant arg., armed, crined, and unguled or, the dexter foot supporting a Roman fasces in bend of the last. *Deus protector meus.*

Humphrey, Blake-, Lieutenant-Colonel Thomas, Heggatt Hall, Horstead, Norwich, same crests and motto.

Humphreys, a boar's head couped in fess. 43. 1

Humphreys, Humphries, or **Humphryes,** three legs conjoined at the thigh, flexed at the knees and spurred, all ppr. 193. 7

Humphreys-Owen, Arthur Charles, Esquire, of Glansevern, Berriew, Montgomerysh., a wolf salient ppr., supporting a scaling-ladder arg. *Toraf cyn plygaf.*

Humphry, Alfred Paget, Esquire, of Foxton House, Royston, Cambs, in front of a rock, thereon a falcon close ppr., belled and jessed or, holding in the beak a key arg., four escallops, also or. *Persiste.*

Humphrys, William, of Ballyhaise House, co. Cavan, Ireland, and of 5, De Vesc Terrace, Kingstown, Dublin, on a ducal coronet an eagle with wings endorsed or, armed and membered gu., holding in the dexter claw a broken spear-head of the first. *Optima sperando spiro.*

Humphrys, Rev. Hugh, of Vicarsfield, Knocktopher, Ireland, same crest and motto.

Hun, Essex, a demi-lion rampant arg., ducally gorged or. 10. 7

Huncks or **Hunkes,** Bucks, Glouc., Warw., and Worcs., a greyhound current erm. cf. 58. 2

Huncks or **Hunkes,** a greyhound courant erm., collared sa. cf. 58. 2

Hungate or **Hungatt,** Bart. (*extinct*), of Saxton, Sandhutten, Burnby, and North Dalton, Yorks, a talbot sejant arg. cf. 55. 2

Hungerford, co. Cork, out of a ducal coronet or, a pepper garb between two reaping-hooks, all ppr. *Et Dieu mon appuy.*

Hungerford, out of a ducal coronet or, a garb between two sickles ppr. *Et Dieu mon appuy.*

Hungerford, Holdich-, Henry Vane Forester, Esquire, of Dingley, Northamp.: (1) same crest as above, (*for Hungerford*). (2) A martlet sa., in front of a cross pattée fitchée, between two branches of palm or (*for Holdich*). *Et Dieu mon appui.* 95. 9

Huninges, Chesh., and of Carsam, Suff., a lion's head erased arg., collared sa. 18. 6

Hunkes or **Huncks,** a greyhound courant erm., collared and ringed sa. cf. 58. 2

Hunloke, Bart., Derbysh., on a chapeau az., turned up erm., a cockatrice with wings expanded ppr., combed, beaked, and wattled or. cf. 68. 6

Hunnis, Middx., between two honeysuckles ppr., a unicorn's head couped or, charged with two bendlets az.

Hunston of Walpole, Norf., a hind's head couped or, holding in the mouth a hollyslip vert, fructed gu. cf. 124. 1

Hunt-Foulson, see Foulson.

Hunt, Sir Frederick Seagar, Bart., 10, Royal Crescent, Ramsgate, on a rock a stork ppr., between two fleurs-de-lis az.

Hunt, see Husey-Hunt.

Hunt, Le, out of a baron's coronet a hand holding a cutlass, all ppr.

Hunt, Le, Ireland, a hand holding a boar's head erased and erect in pale. 220. 6

Hunt, Roland, of Boreatton, Shropsh., a talbot sejant sa., collared or, lined az., the line tied to a halberd in pale of the second, headed of the third. cf. 55. 5

Hunt, Arthur Roope, Esquire, of Southwood, Torquay, on a wreath of the colours a mount vert, thereon a talbot sejant or, guttée-de-sang, collared in front of and attached by a chain of the last to a battle-axe erect sa., headed ppr. *Credentibus nil difficile.*

Hunt, on a mount vert, a talbot sejant or, collared and lined gu., the line fastened by a bow-knot to a halberd erect, the staff of the second, the blade arg. cf. 555

Hunt, John Joseph, Esquire, of Grimston Court and 26, Aldwark, York, a talbot sejant or, charged on the shoulder with a rose, collared, attached by a riband to a battle-axe erect gu., beaded arg., the whole in front of fern-brake ppr. *Vi et virtute.*

Hunt, John Henry, of York, same crest and motto.

Hunt of Ashover, Derbysh., a bugle-horn sa., stringed vert. 228. 11

Hunt, on a chapeau gu., turned up erm., a talbot statant arg.

Hunt, Richard Burges, Esquire, a mount vert, thereon a talbot sejant or, gorged with a collar vair, attached by a riband az. to a spear erect ppr., therefrom flowing towards the sinister a banner sa., charged with a pheon, also or.

Hunt, Edward Frederick, Esquire, of Holmwood, Goldsmith Gardens, Acton, W., on a mount vert, in front of a battle-axe erect, a talbot sejant collared and lined, the line tied to the battle-axe.

Hunt, between two ostrich-feathers sa., a boar's head couped and erect ppr. 41. 14

Hunt, Scotland, a lion's head erased and collared, all ppr. *Vi et virtute.* 18. 6

Hunt, Shropsh., a lion's head erased per pale arg. and sa., collared gu., lined or. *cf.* 18. 6

Hunt, Shropsh.: (1) same crest as above. *cf.* 18. 6. (2) A hind's head and neck arg. 124. 1. (3) A shark or lucy's head erect or, langued gu.

Hunt of Hermyngtoft, Norf. and Suff., a lion sejant erm. 8. 8

Hunt of Stoke, Lindon, and Barradon, Rutl., a leopard's face between two wings, all or. *cf.* 22. 11

Hunt, a stag's head erased ppr. 121. 2

Hunt of Longnor, Shropsh., a hind's head couped arg., vulned in the breast with a pheon sa., dropping blood ppr. *cf.* 124. 1

Hunt, Ireland, out of a ducal coronet or, an arm erect gu., the hand grasping the pommel and hilt of a broken sword of the first.

Hunt, Bart. (now De Vere), of Curragh, co. Limerick, a representation of the Castle of Limerick, being a portway between two towers arg., masoned sa., with the Union Jack of England displayed from a flagstaff erect ppr.

Huntbach, Staffs, a talbot's head erased arg., collared gu., fretty or. *cf.* 56. 11

Hunter-Blair, *see* Blair.

Hunter, two lions' heads addorsed and collared, all ppr. *cf.* 18. 2

Hunter, two lions' heads addorsed ppr. 17. 3

Hunter, a demi-lion rampant ppr., holding between the paws a cross pattée or, charged with an annulet.

Hunter, Sir Charles Roderick, Bart., of London: (1) A demi-lion holding between the paws a cross pattée fitchée at the foot sa. (2) A demi-bear salient sa., muzzled or.

Hunter, Henry Lannoy, Beech Hill, Reading, a demi-lion gu., holding between the paws a cross pattée fitchée sa.

Hunter, Norf., a boar's head erased ppr. 42. 2

Hunter of London, same crest. 42. 2

Hunter, Scotland, a stag's head erased ppr. 121. 2

Hunter of Straidarran, Ireland, a stag's head cabossed ppr. *Arte et marte.* 122. 5

Hunter, a buck's head erased or. 121. 2

Hunter of Bonnytoun and Doonholm, Ayrsh., and Andrew Alexander Hunter, Esquire, of The College, Cheltenham, a stag's head cabossed or. *Vigilantia, robur, voluptas.* 122. 8

Hunter of Durh., a deer's head. *Vigilantia, robur, voluptas.* 121. 5

Hunter-Arundell, of Barjarg, Dumfriessh., a stag's head erased. *Vigilantia, robur, voluptas.* 121. 2

Hunter of Straidarran, co. Londonderry, Ireland, a stag's head cabossed ppr. *Arte et marte.* 122. 5

Hunter, James, Anton's Hill, Coldstream, N.B., a buck's head. *Vigilantia, robur, voluptas.*

Hunter, Richard, Esquire, of Thursten, Innerwick, N.B., a stag's head ppr. *Vigilantia, robur, voluptas.—Deo dale.*

Hunter, Charles Fleeming, Esquire, of Sunnyside, Church End, Finchley, Middx., a greyhound sejant arg., collared or. *Cursum perficio.* *cf.* 59. 2

Hunter of Hunterstoun, Ayrsh., a greyhaund sejant ppr., gorged with an antique crown or. *Cursum perficio.* *cf.* 59. 13

Hunter-Weston, Lieutenant-Colonel Gould, F.S.A., of Hunterston, West Kilbride, Ayrsh., N.B.: (1) An eagle rising regardant sa., charged on the breast and on each wing with a crescent or (*for Weston*). 78. 5. (2) A greyhound sejant ppr., gorged with an antique crown or charged upon the shoulder for distinction with a cross crosslet gu.; but this not to be borne by his descendants (*for Hunter*). 59. 13

Hunter of Abbotshill, Ayrsh., a greyhound in full course arg., collared or. *Expedite.* *cf.* 58. 2

Hunter, Major Charles Fleeming, a greyhound sejant arg., collared gu. *Cursum perficio.*

Hunter, formerly of Croyland Abbey, Lincs, a greyhound's head and neck couped arg. *cf.* 61. 2

Hunter, Scotland, a greyhound's head. *Dum spiro, spero.* *cf.* 61. 2

Hunter, a greyhound's head and neck erased arg. 61. 4

Hunter of Seaside, Perth, a greyhound's head arg., collared gu. *Dum spiro, spero.* 61. 2

Hunter, Charles, Esquire, F.R.S., F.S.A., of Plas Coch, Llanfairpwll, Anglesey, a greyhound's head and neck couped arg., collared gu. *Dum spiro, spero.*

Hunter, a greyhound's head and neck arg. *cf.* 61. 2

Hunter, same crest. *Fecunditate.*

Hunter of Glencarse, Perthsh., Scotland, a greyhound's head and neck arg., collared gu. *Dum spiro, spero.* 61. 2

Hunter of Manchester, a greyhound's head erased ppr. *Dum spiro, spero.* 61. 4

Hunter, William Henry, Esquire, a mount vert, thereon a greyhound's head erased or, collared gu., between two thistles issuant ppr.

Hunter, Scotland, an anchor in pale. 161. 1

Hunter of Hafton, Argyllsh., an anchor in pale ppr. *Spero.* 161. 2

Hunter of St. Lucar, an anchor ppr. *Raised again.* 161. 2

Hunter, Scotland, a hunting-horn vert, stringed gu. *Spero.—In cornua salutem spero.* 228. 11

Hunter, Scotland, a hunting-horn vert, verruled or, and stringed gu. *In cornua salutem spero.* *cf.* 228. 11

Hunter, William George, Esquire, of Burnside, Forfarsh., a hunting-horn vert, stringed gu. *Spero.* 228. 11

Hunter, Scotland, same crest and motto. 228. 11

Hunter, James Ewing, M.B., C.M., of Duncairn, Helensburgh, Dumbartonsh., a falcon rising ppr. *Swift and sure.*

Hunter, Richard Hubbard, Esquire, J.P., of Glentyan, Kilbarchan, Renfrewsh., same crest. *Semper sublime.*

Hunter-Marshall, William, Esquire, of Callander, Perthsh., Scotland, a dove holding in its beak an olive-branch ppr. *Et decerpta dabunt odores.* 92. 5

Hunter, Scotland, two hands shooting an arrow from a bow, all ppr. *Fortuna sequatur.* 200. 2

Hunter, late Andrew Galloway, Esquire, of Dean Burn, Roxburghsh., a dexter and a sinister arm shooting an arrow from a bow, all ppr. *Far and sure.* 200. 2

Hunter of Restennet, Forfarsh., a fir-tree ppr. *Fecunditate afficior.* 144. 13

Hunter, Ireland, an urus's head erased sa. 44. 3

Huntercomb, a sword in pale enfiled with a man's head couped and wreathed about the temples. *cf.* 191. 9

Huntercomb, an arm in armour issuing from a cloud, the hand grasping a sword, all ppr. 210. 12

Huntingdon, Earl of (Hastings), Sharavogue, S.O. King's Co., a bull's head erased sa., armed and gorged with a ducal coronet or. *In veritate victoria.—Honorantes me honorabo.—Post prœlia prœmia.* 44. 2

Huntingdon and **Huntington,** a crosier arg. 170. 14

Huntingdon, William Balle, of Woodlands, Darwin, Lancs, upon a mount vert, a lion's head or, gorged with a collar vair, between two roses gu., barbed, leaved, and stalked ppr. *In veritate victoria.*

Huntingfield, Baron (Vanneck), of Heveningham Hall, Yoxford, Suff., a bugle-horn gu., stringed or, between two wings expanded arg., tipped or. *Droit et loyal.* 112. 3

Huntingfield, a dagger and a sword in saltier ppr. *cf.* 171. 12

Huntingford, a griffin's head erased or, with wings elevated fretty gu., holding in the beak a cross pattée fitchée at the foot arg.

Huntington, William Balle, Esquire, J.P., D.L., and High Sheriff of the Woodlands, Darwen, Lancs, upon a mount vert, a lion's head or, gorged with a collar vair, between two roses gu., barbed, leaved, and stalked ppr. *In veritate victoria.*

Huntingtower, Lord, *see* Tollemache, Bart.

Huntley, Rev. Osmond Currie, M.A., of Boxwell Court, Glouc., a talbot statant ppr., collared and lined or. *cf.* 54. 2

Huntley, on a mount a lizard, all ppr. 138. 5

Huntley of Treowen, Monm., a buck's head caboshed arg., and between the attires a bugle-horn stringed sa. *cf.* 122. 5

Huntley of Boxwell, Glouc., a talbot ppr., collared and lined or. *cf.* 54. 2

Huntly, Marquess of (Gordon), Aboyne Castle, Aberdeensh., in a ducal coronet or, a stag's head and neck affrontée ppr., attired with ten tynes of the first. *By-dand.—Animo non astutiâ.* 119. 13

Huntly, a talbot passant gu., collared and lined or. 54. 5

Hunton, Wilts, a demi-talbot rampant and erased arg. *cf.* 55. 8

Hunton of East Knoyle, Wilts, a demi-talbot gu., collared and eared or, holding between the paws a stag's head cabossed of the last.

Huntsman, Francis, Esquire, of West Retford Hall, Retford, Yorks, a mount vert, thereon a fern-brake in front of two spears in saltire ppr., therefrom pendent a bugle-horn sa., garnished or, stringed gu. *Esto vigilans.*

Hurd, a bear's head sa., muzzled gu., between two wings. *cf.* 35. 5

Hurd, Worcs., a horse's head couped arg., maned or. *cf.* 50. 13

Hurd, Reginald John Wickham, Esquire, LL.B., of 74, Kensington Park Road, Bayswater, W., a horse's head couped. *Deus pascit corvos.*

Hurell and **Hurle,** a lion rampant holding a flag gu., charged with a cross in the dexter chief. *cf.* 3. 7

Hurlblatt of Farnham, Surrey, out of a ducal coronet or, a talbot's head arg., eared gu., collared of the last, ringed and studded of the first. *cf.* 57. 12

Hurlebert, an arm embowed gu., holding a battle-axe the staff of the last, the blade and gauntlet arg., at the wrist a ribbon tied in a knot of the first. *cf.* 200. 6

Hurlestone, a goat's head arg., bearded and armed or, charged on the neck with four ermine spots in cross. *cf.* 128. 12

Hurley, a pillar ppr. 176. 3

Hurley, on a ducal coronet a peacock ppr. 103. 8

Hurlston, Lancs, an ermine passant ppr. 134. 6

Hurly, Robert Conway, Esquire, of Glenduff, Tralee, co. Kerry, Ireland, out of an antique Irish crown or, a naked arm embowed ppr., holding a cross crosslet of the first. *Dextra cruce vincit.*

Hurly, John, Esquire, J.P., of Tralee, co. Kerry, on a wreath of the colours a naked arm embowed holding a sword wavy, all ppr.

Hurly, John Charles Denis, Esquire, of Feuit House, Fenit, Tralee, co. Kerry: (1) A naked dexter arm embowed holding a sword wavy, all ppr. (2) Out of an antique Irish crown or, a naked dexter arm embowed ppr., holding a cross crosslet or. *Dextra vincit cor* (over the first).—*Dextra cruce vincit* (over the second).

Hurnard, Hamilton Hawtrey, Esquire, B.A., of Gurney's Manor, Hingham, Norf., a demi-lion rampant gu., holding in the dexter paw a cross crosslet fitchée or. *Nobilis est ira leonis.*

Hurot, two hands couped and conjoined in fess ppr. 224. 2

Hurr, a harpy with wings expanded ppr. 198. 4

Hurrell, a lion rampant ppr., holding a flag displayed gu., charged with a cross in the dexter chief. *cf.* 3. 7

Hurry, a harpy with wings expanded gu. 189. 4

Hurry, Jamieson B., M.D., Abbotsbrook, Reading, and Arnold Eardley Hurry, B.C.S., Umballa, India, same crest. *Nec arrogo, nec dubito.*

Hurry, Scotland, a lion's gamb. *Sans tache.* *cf.* 36. 4

Hurst of Horsham Park, Sussex, an oak-tree ppr. 143. 5

Hurst of Hurst, Lancs, upon a mount vert, a hurst of trees ppr. *Pro Deo et rege.* *cf.* 144. 2

Hurst, Robert Henry, Horsham Park, Sussex, an oak-tree ppr. *Libertas sine licentia.*

Hurst, Herts, in a wood ppr., the sun or.

Hurst of Welberry, Herts, rising from behind a castle ppr., standing on a mount vert, the sun or.

Hurst, Walter, B.Sc., L.S.A., of Kirkgate, Tadcaster, Yorks, in front of a demi-sun in splendour, the stump of a tree sprouting to the dexter, thereon a song-thrush close. *Virtute et labore.*

Hurst, Joseph Stancliffe, Esquire, J.P., of Copt Hewick Hall, Ripon, a dragon with wings elevated or, semée of crescents sa., and resting the dexter claw on an escutcheon of the last charged with a sun in splendour of the first. *Lux tua vita mea.* 73. 5

Hurst of Hinckley, Leics., a dragon with wings elevated arg., resting the dexter claw on a cross crosslet or, charged on the shoulder with a fleur-de-lis az.

Hurt, Albert Frederick, Esquire, of Alderwasley, Matlock, on a torse or and sa., a hart passant in his proper couller, horned, membryed, and hurt in the hanche with an arrow or, fethyred arg. (*vide* Flower's Grant, September 4, 1565). *Mane prædam, vesperi spolium.*

Hurt, a stag trippant ppr., attired or, vulned in the haunch by an arrow of the last, feathered arg. *cf.* 117. 8

Hurt of Alderwasley, a hart trippant ppr., attired, membered, and pierced in the haunch by an arrow or, feathered arg. *Mane prædam, vesperi spolium.* *cf.* 117. 8

Hurt, two hands couped and conjoined in fess ppr. 224. 2

Hurt-Sitwell, William Willoughby George, of Ferney Hall, Craven Arms, Shropsh., a demi-lion erased sa., holding an escocheon per pale or and vert.

Husband, a demi-griffin holding between its claws a ducal coronet ppr.

Husbands, Harold Wessen, Esquire, of North Town House, Taunton, a demi-griffin segreant holding in the claws a ducal coronet. *Justus sis non timeto.*

Husdell, Durh., a demi-lion ppr. *Trust in God.* 10. 2

Huse, a dexter hand ppr., holding a cross patée in pale or.

Husee, a leopard passant gardant ppr. 24. 4

Husey-Hunt, James Hubert, formerly of Compton Castle, Somers., and of Brighton: (1) An arm embowed vested az., cuffed or, holding in the hand a slip of trefoil in blossom ppr. (*for Hunt*). (2) A boot sa., spurred or, the top erm., surmounted by a heart supported by two hands issuant from clouds ppr., and on an escroll above the motto, "*Cor nobyle, cor immobyle*" (*for Husey*).

Huskisson, *see* Tilghman-Huskisson.

Huskisson, *see* Milbanke-Huskisson.

Huskisson, on a rock a goose perched ppr.

Huson, a ram's head erased arg., armed or. 130. 6

Huson, Narcissus Edmond, Esquire, of Springfield, co. Wexford, Ireland, a harp az., stringed or. *Sursum corda.* 168. 9

Hussey-De Burgh, *see* De Burgh.

Hussey-Freke, *see* Freke.

Hussey-Walsh, Walter, Esquire, of 81, Onslow Gardens, London, S.W., a swan pierced through the back and breast with a dart, all ppr. *Transfixus sed non mortuus.*

Hussey, on a mount vert, a hind trippant arg., in front of a tree ppr.

Hussey, on a mount vert, a hind lodged in front of a hawthorn-tree ppr.

Hussey, on a mount vert, a hind lodged in front of a hawthorn-tree ppr., ducally gorged and lined or.

Hussey, Edward Windsor, Esquire, J.P., of Scotney Castle, Lamberhurst, Sussex, a hind lodged under a hawthorn tree ppr., ducally gorged and chained or. *Vix ea nostro voco.*

Hussey, Dorset, and of Hador, Gowthorp, and Linwood, Lincs, on a mount vert, a hind lodged regardant in front of a hawthorn-tree ppr., ducally gorged and lined or.

Hussey, the late Richard Hussey, Esquire, of Upwood and Wood Walton, Hunts, a hind trippant ppr., gorged with a ducal coronet and chained or. *cf.* 124. 12

Hussey, Ireland, an arm in armour az., holding a cross crosslet fitched in pale or. 210. 14

Hussey, a boot sa., spurred or, topped erm. 193. 12

Hussey of Scotney Castle, Sussex, a boot sa., spurred or, turned down erm. *Ut tibi sic aliis.* 193. 12

Hussey, a boot sa., and thereon a human heart held by two hands issuing from clouds fessewise dexter and sinister.

Hussey of Moslerton and Bredy, near Barton Bradstock, Dorset, a boot sa., spurred or, turned over erm., surmounted by a heart ppr., supported by two arms embowed in armour, the hands gauntleted, also ppr. *Cor immobile.* 240. 15

Hussey of Highcliffe, Lympstone, Devonsh., same crest and motto.

Hussey of Wyrley Grove, near Lichfield, Staffs, a leg couped above the knee, booted sa., the top erm., spurred.

Hustler, Yorks, a talbot sejant arg., gorged with a collar az., charged with three fleurs-de-lis or. *cf.* 55. 1

Hustler, William Thomas, Acklam Hall, Cleveland, Middlesbrough-on-Tees, same crest. *Aut nunquam tentes aut perfice.*

Hustwick, Yorks, a lion passant ppr. *Opera Dei mirifica.* 6. 2

Hutchens, a lion's head erased arg., gorged with a mural coronet az. *cf.* 17. 8

Hutcheson, Scotland, an arm in armour throwing a hammer, all ppr. *Sursum.*

Hutcheson, Scotland, an arm in armour embowed az., throwing a dart pointed gu., feathered arg. *Sursum.* 198. 4

Hutcheson, Thomas Brown, Esquire, M.B., M.S., of the High Street, Saffron Walden, a dexter arm in armour holding in the gauntlet an arrow, all ppr., headed gu. *Sursum.*

Hutcheson of Drummalig, co. Down, and Clifton, Glouc., an arrow point upwards ppr. *cf.* 173. 5

Hutchings, out of a mural coronet a demi-lion holding in the dexter paw a branch of palm vert. 16. 11

Hutchings and **Hutchins,** a lion passant gardant sa. 4. 3

Hutchings, Somers., a lion's head erased gu., ducally crowned or. 18. 8

Hutchings of Telscombe, Sussex, a lion's head erased arg., gorged with a collar sa., thereon three arches, and holding in the mouth a cross crosslet fitchée or.

Hutchins, a branch of a holly-tree vert. 150. 10

Hutchins of London, a lion passant gardant sa. *Nihil humani alienum.* 4. 3

Hutchinson, *see* Donoughmore, Earl of.

Hutchinson, *see* Synge-Hutchinson.

Hutchinson, *see* Parker-Hutchinson.

Hutchinson, Alan, Esquire, of Durham, a bloodhound statant ppr., holding in the mouth a cross crosslet or, and supporting with the dexter fore-paw an escocheon az., thereon a sun rising at the base. 282. 6

Hutchinson of Whitton, Durh., out of a ducal coronet or, a cockatrice az. *Nihil humani alienum.*

Hutchinson, Notts, out of a ducal coronet or, a cockatrice with wings addorsed az., beaked, combed, and wattled gu.

Hutchinson, Durh., a cockatrice with wings expanded az., combed, wattled, and membered or. *Cunctanter, tamen fortiter.* 68. 6

Hutchinson of Owthorpe, Notts, a cockatrice az., combed and legged or. 68. 4

Hutchinson of Skirsgill and Crossfield House, Cumb., out of a ducal coronet or, a cockatrice with wings endorsed az., beaked, combed, and wattled gu. 301. 9

Hutchinson, Frederick William Hutchinson, M.A., Bar.Ch. (Cantab.), of Brooklands Avenue, Cambridge, and Beechy Park, Rathvilly, co. Carlow, a cockatrice combed, wattled, wings expanded, issuant from a coronet. *Fortiter gerit crucem.* 301. 9

Hutchinson, on a mural coronet or, a cockatrice arg., combed and wattled gu., gorged with a wreath of laurel or. *Perseverande.*

Hutchinson - Lloyd - Vaughan, William Piesley, Esquire, of Golden Grove, King's Co., Ireland: (1) A boy's head couped at the shoulders, crined or, round the neck a snake entwined ppr. (*for Vaughan*). (2) A lion rampant arg., holding in the dexter fore-paw a snake ppr. (*for Lloyd*). (3) On a ducal coronet or, a cockatrice with wings addorsed ppr. (*for Hutchinson*). *Vitæ via virtus.—Innocentia infantis, sapientia serpentis.* 301. 9

Hutchinson, Henry Ormerod, Esquire, of Elderslie, Prestwich, Manchester, a Saracen's head affrontée, couped at the shoulders ppr., wreathed about the temples arg. and az., and charged upon the breast with a cross patée sa., between a branch of laurel on the dexter side, and a branch of oak fructed on the sinister, both also ppr. *Perseverando.*

Hutchinson, John Richard, Esquire, J.P., of the Hirsel, Leamington, Warwick, same crest and motto.

Hutchinson, William, Esquire, of North Highfield, Rockferry, Chesh., same crest and motto.

Hutchinson, William Arthur, of the Groves, near Douglas, Isle of Man, same crest and motto.

Hutchinson, a parrot gu., holding in the beak an annulet or. 101. 11

Hutchinson, Durh., a demi-lion rampant. *Cunctanter, tamen fortiter.* 10. 2

Hutchinson of Dublin, a demi-lion rampant az., charged on the shoulder with a trefoil slipped or. *cf.* 10. 2

Hutchinson, out of a ducal coronet a swan's head and neck between two wings, all ppr. 100. 10

Hutchison, an arm in armour throwing a dart ppr. *Surgam.*

Hutchison, same crest. *Sursum.*

Hutchison, a stag trippant ppr. 117. 8

Hutchison of Rockend, Dumbartonsh., a stag's head erased gu., attired or. *Memor esto.* 121. 2

Hutchison, John William, Esquire, D.L., of Laurieston Hall, Castle Douglas, N.B., and Edinghame, Dalbeattie, N.B., same crest and motto.

Hutchison, James Thomas, Esquire, J.P., D.L., of Moreland and Hardiston, Kinross-sh., and of 12, Douglas Crescent, Edinburgh, a stag's head erased ppr., attired or. *Scientiæ laborisque memor.* 121. 2

Hutchison, Thomas Walter, Esquire, of Carlowrie, Kirkliston, N.B., a stag's head erased ppr., collared or. *Scientiæ laborisque memor.*

Hutchon, a stag's head erased affrontée. *Fortis et veritas.* 119. 10

Huth of London, three sprigs of oak erect ppr., each bearing an acorn or. 152. 2

Huth, Edward, Esquire, of Wykehurst Park, Haywards Heath, Sussex, three sprigs of oak ppr., each bearing one acorn or. *Animus non res.* 152. 2

Huth, Alfred Henry, Esquire, of Fosbury Manor, near Hungerford, and 58, Rutland Gate, London, S.W., same crest and motto.

Huth, Ferdinand Marshall, Esquire, of 44, Upper Grosvenor Street, London, W., and Eaglehurst, Fawley, Southampton, same crest and motto.

Huth, Frederick Henry, Esquire, of Oakhurst, Tunbridge Wells, and Beckford House, Lansdown Crescent, Bath, same crest and motto.

Huth, Louis, Esquire, of Passingworth Manor, Waldron, Sussex, same crest and motto.

Huth, Percival, Esquire, of Freshford Manor House, Freshford, Bath, same crest and motto.

Huthwait, a pheon or. 174. 11

Hutt, George William, Esquire, of Appley Towers, Ryde, Isle of Wight, a peewit. *Nil nisi virtute.* 243. 7

Huttoft, a whale's head erect and erased az., gorged with a mural coronet or, thereon three pellets, to the collar a chain and ring of the second. 139. 9

Hutton, a hind statant. *cf.* 125. 3

Hutton, Yorks, a stag's head erased lozengy arg. and az. *Spiritus gladius.* 121. 2

Hutton, Rev. Arthur Wollaston, Rector of St. Mary le Bow, Cheapside, in front of a fern-brake ppr., a stag's head caboshed or. *Post tenebras spero lucem.* 247. 5

Hutton, Edmund Bacon, Esquire, of Bidworth Dale, Notts, a stag's head caboshed or. *Post tenebras spero lucem.*

Hutton, Charles Wollaston, Esquire, of 56, Goldington Avenue, Bedford, same crest and motto.

Hutton, Frederick Wollaston, Esquire, of Christchurch, New Zealand, same crest and motto.

Hutton, George Holden, Esquire, J.P., D.L., of Thorney Hall, Newark, same crest and motto.

Hutton, Rev. Henry Wollaston, of Vicars' Court, Lincoln, same crest and motto.

Hutton, Rev. William Holden, B.D., of the Great House, Burford, Oxon., same crest and motto.

Hutton, George Morland, Gate Burton, near Lincoln, same crest and motto.

Hutton, Rev. Charles Frederick, M.A., of the School House, Pocklington, East Yorks, on two annulets in fesse gu., a crescent or. *Dat deus incrementum.* 246. 12

Hutton of Goldsborough, Yorks, three broad arrows, two in saltire and one in pale, sa., enfiled with a ducal coronet or.

Hutton, William Leak, Esquire, of Moss Bank, Aughton, Ormskirk, three arrows, one in pale and two in saltire, points downwards, enfiled by a ducal coronet. *Pax.* 290. 2

Hutton, Ireland, out of a crescent or, an arrow in pale sa. 163. 13

Hutton, John, of Hutton, Cumb., two eagles' heads erased in saltier addorsed sa., enfiled with a ducal coronet or.

Hutton, Westml., an eagle displayed or, beaked and legged sa., between two branches of laurel vert. *cf.* 75. 2

Hutton of Hemwick, Durh., an ostrich's head between two ostrich-wings arg., holding in its beak a horse-shoe or. *cf.* 97. 10

Hutton, Durh. and Lancs, an American ppr., wreathed round the middle vert, holding in the dexter hand a tobacco-leaf ppr.

Hutton, Durh. and Kent, a blackamoor wreathed about the temples and waist, and holding in the dexter hand a trefoil slipped vert.

Hutton of Bishopwearmouth, Durh., a man ppr., wreathed about the temples and loins vert, and holding in the hand three leaves of the last. *Pax.*

Hutton, Scotland, a serpent catching at the finger of a man's hand issuing from a cloud, all ppr. *Deus, quis contra.* 223. 8

Hutton, a serpent vomiting fire from its mouth and nostrils, all ppr.

Hutton, John Timothy D'Arcy, of Marske, Yorks, on a cushion gu., placed lozengeways, an open Bible, the edges gilt with the words "*Odor vitæ*" inscribed. *Spiritus gladius.* 246. 13

Hutton, Arthur Edward Hill, Esquire, of Houghton Hall, Houghton-le-Spring, Durh., and 107, Gloucester Terrace, Hyde Park, W., same crest and motto.

Huxham of London, and of Plymouth, Devonsh., a demi-lion rampant ermines, holding between the paws an escutcheon arg., charged with a cross crosslet gu.

Huxley of Edmonton, Middx., out of a ducal coronet or, a demi-lion rampant erm., collared of the first, holding between the paws a crescent of the last.

Huxley of Huxley, Chesh., a snake ppr. 142. 4

Huxley, a wolf's head erased sa., gorged with a collar or, charged with three crescents gu. *In Deo omnia.* cf. 30. 11

Huyshe, an elephant's head couped arg., ducally crowned and tusked or. cf. 133. 2

Huyshe, Rev. Francis John, Hon. Canon of Salisbury, of Wimborne Minster, Dorset, and Clisthydon, Exeter, same crest.

Hyatt, a tower gu., and out of the battlements a demi-lion rampant sa. 157. 11

Hyatt, a demi-lion rampant ppr. *Fac et spera.* 10. 2

Hyde, Lord, *see* Clarendon, Earl.

Hyde, Earl of Clarendon (*extinct*), an eagle with wings expanded gu. 77. 5

Hyde, Gustavus Rochefort, Esquire, M.A., of Lynnbury, Mullingar, co. Westmeath, an eagle with wings expanded sa., beaked and membered or. *Soyez ferme.*

Hyde, Shropsh., an eagle with wings addorsed sa., beaked and legged or.

Hyde of Denton, Lancs, an eagle's head erased or, beaked sa. 83. 2

Hyde of Whetstone, Middx., a demi-eagle displayed and erased az., gorged with a collar arg., charged with three lozenges or.

Hyde of Ormston, Lancs, a raven rising. 107. 3

Hyde of Hyde, Beds, a raven volant sa.

Hyde of Castle-Hyde, a lion's head erased sa., bezantée. *De vivis nil nisi verum.* cf. 17. 8

Hyde, Arthur, Esquire, of Holly Wood, co. Kerry, a leopard's head erased sa., bezantée. *De vivis nil nisi verum.* cf. 23. 10

Hyde of Hydon, Dorset, a cock's head erased az., crested and jelloped gu., bezantée, holding in the beak a pansy-flower of the last.

Hyde, a cock's head erased az., combed purp., charged on the neck with a lozenge or, between four bezants, and holding in the beak a pansy-flower ppr., stalked and leaved vert.

Hyde of London and Kent, a unicorn's head erased arg., armed and maned or, collared vair. 49. 11

Hyde of London, a dexter wing gu. 109. 7

Hyde, Ireland, on a mount a holy lamb ppr., the standard az. cf. 131. 2

Hyde, an antelope statant. 126. 12

Hyde, a stag's head arg. 121. 5

Hyde, a standard in pale with a flag gu., and tassels. cf. 176. 15

Hyde of London, seven arrows, six in saltire and one in pale, az., feathered and headed arg., enfiled with an Eastern coronet or. cf. 173. 7

Hyett, *see* Hyatt.

Hyett, a dexter hand holding a thistle in pale ppr. 218. 2

Hyett of Watton, Somers., a demi-pegasus sa., crined or, the wings addorsed of the last. 47. 5

Hyett, Francis Adams, Esquire, J.P., B.A., of Painswick House, Glouc.: Out of a castle ppr., charged with four pellets, a lion's head sa., holding in the mouth a rose slipped gu. (*for Hyett*).

Hyghlord, a ship in the sea in full sail, all ppr. 160. 13

Hyghmore, Cumb., a moorcock ppr.

Hyland, out of a mural coronet a garb, and thereon a bird, all ppr. 153. 9

Hylton, Baron (Jolliffe), of Hylton, Durh., and Petersfield, Southampton, a cubit arm erect couped, vested vert, cuffed, and the sleeve charged with a pile arg., the hand grasping a sword in bend ppr. *Tant que je puis.*

Hyman, a demi-Cupid holding in his dexter hand a torch. 185. 8

Hynd of London, a hand gu., holding an eagle's claw ppr. 220. 12

Hynde, a hind's head couped ppr., collared or, holding in the mouth a rose gu., leaved vert. cf. 124. 5

Hynde, an ostrich's head couped chequy arg. and sa., holding in the beak a horse-shoe az.

Hynde of Hedsore, Bucks, on a ducal coronet or, a cockatrice of the same, combed and legged gu.

Hynde, a griffin's head az., collared and charged with an escallop or, between two wings of the first, guttée-d'eau. cf. 67. 7

Hynde, Ireland, a demi-pegasus rampant arg., maned or, grasping with the feet a sword ppr., pommel and hilt or. cf. 47. 5

Hyndman, the sun shining on a sun-dial. *True as the dial to the sun.*

Hynell, an angel praying. cf. 184. 2

Hynes, Ireland, an elephant passant sa. cf. 133. 9

Hynes, George John, Esquire, Postmaster-General, Punjab, India, a dexter arm in armour embowed grasping in the hand a dagger fessewise, all ppr. *Toujours fort.* 196. 5

Hyrson, issuing out of a cloud a dexter hand holding a club, all ppr. 214. 9

Hyslop of Edinburgh, a bookbinder's folding-stick and polishing-iron crossing each other saltireways ppr. *His parva crescunt.*

Hyslop, Archibald Richard Frith, Lotus, Dumfries, a stag's head caboshed ppr. *Semper vigilans.*

I.

I'Anson, a griffin's head between two wings, all ppr. 65. 11

I'Anson, William Andrew, Esquire, of Denton Hall, Scotswood, R.S.O., Northumb., and Westgate Hill House, Newcastle-on-Tyne, a cubit arm habited per pale, indented az. and or, encircled by an annulet of the last, the hand ppr. holding a cross flory. *Faire mon devoire.*

Ibbetson, Selwin-, *see* Rookwood, Baron.

Ibbetson, a horse's head charged with a pale indented sa. cf. 50. 13

Ibbotson of Crofton Hall, Yorks, a unicorn's head erased arg., armed and crined or, charged on the neck with an escallop gu., between four estoiles az. cf. 49. 5

Ibetson, Yorks, a unicorn's head arg., semée of escallops gu., attired, maned, and erased of the last. *Vixi liber, et moriar.* 49. 6

Ibgrave, Herts, a dexter arm embowed vested bendy of six or and az., cuffed arg., holding in the hand ppr. a cross crosslet fitched sa.

Ichingham and **Ilchingham,** a demi-dragon with wings expanded vert. 73. 10

Ickyll, a horse's head couped arg., crined and bridled sa., studded and tasselled or. *In Deo confido.* 51. 5

Iddesleigh, Earl of (Northcote), on a chapeau gu., turned up erm., a stag trippant arg. *Christi crux est mea lux.* 118. 3

Idle, a helmet ppr., garnished or. 180. 3

Idle, a leopard passant resting his dexter fore-paw upon a helmet, all ppr.

Ifield, out of a ducal coronet or, a dolphin's head az.

Ihones of London and Shropsh., a lion rampant or, supporting an anchor az., the stock of the first.

Ikerrin, Viscount, *see* Carrick, Earl.

Ilam and **Ilamy,** a peacock's head between two wings or, holding in the beak a serpent entwined round its neck ppr. 103. 3

Ilbert, William Roope, of Bowringsley and Horswell House, Devonsh., a cock-pheasant arg., combed and wattled gu., holding in the beak a red rose slipped ppr., and standing on a mount vert. cf. 90. 8. (*Another*, a demi-wyvern vert, collared or.) *Nulla rosa sine spinis.* cf. 69. 12

Ilbery of Biscaya, Spain, Berks, London, and Calcutta, a demi-dragon vert, the wings and belly flesh-coloured, holding between the claws a lozenge az., charged with a fleur-de-lis or. cf. 73. 10

Ilchester, Earl of (Fox-Strangways), on a chapeau az., turned up erm., a fox sejant or. *Faire sans dire.* 32. 12

Ilderton, out of a ducal coronet or, a battle-axe, the handle broken ppr.

Ile or **Isle,** Durh., a demi-lion rampant, holding between the paws an escallop. 13. 10

Iles, a wolf collared and lined, all ppr. *cf.* 29. 2

Iley, a cubit arm erect vested arg., holding in the hand ppr. a fleur-de-lis sa.

Iley, Illey, and **Ilney,** a hand erect holding a cross crosslet fitched in pale. *cf.* 221. 14

Iliff, out of a ducal coronet a peacock's tail ppr 115. 6

Ilinge, a heraldic tiger's head couped gu., maned and ducally gorged or, langued az.

Illnn, a wolf's head erased gu. 30. 8

Illidge, John, Esquire, of Brixton, Surrey, in front of a saltire couped or, an eagle's head erased sa. *Aquila non capit muscas.* *cf.* 83. 2

Illingworth, William, Esquire, of Newfield Hall, Bell Busk, Leeds, on a crescent arg., a cock or, charged on the breast with an escallop sa. *Honesta peto.* 237. 5

Illingsworth and **Illingworth,** Surrey, within a crescent arg., a cock crowing sa. 91. 10

Illingsworth, a demi-lion charged with three roundles holding between its paws a battle-axe. *cf.* 15. 4

Illsley or **Ilsley,** between two serpents in orle, the tails in saltier, a cock, all ppr. 91. 1

Ilney, *see* Iley.

Image, of Whepstead and Bury, Suff., a wolf's head erased az., gorged with a collar arg., charged with three roundles, and holding in the mouth a cross flory fitchée. 253. 22

Image of Herringswell House, Mildenhall, Suff., a boar's head erased quarterly erm. and az., holding in the mouth a cross crosslet fitchée gu.

Imbrie and **Imrie** of Crubie, Scotland, a plough ppr. *Evertendo fæcundat.* 178. 7

Immans and **Inmans,** a basilisk ppr.

Immins, a dragon's head couped. 71. 1

Impey, an ostrich with wings addorsed holding in its beak a horse-shoe ppr. *cf.* 97. 1

Impey-Lovibond, Archibald, Esquire, of Newhall, Ardleigh, Essex: (1) Upon a rock ppr., a boar's head erect and couped gu., within a chain in arch or (*for Lovibond*). (2) A leopard's face or, in front of a sword in pale point downwards ppr., pommel and hilt or, between two wings sa. (*for Impey*). *Leges juraque servo.*

Impey of Yarmouth, Norf., a leopard's face sa., between two wings or. *cf.* 22. 11

Imrey, Scotland, a plough ppr. *Nil desperandum.* 178. 7

Ince, on a mount vert, a horse sejant by an oak-tree ppr. 53. 9

Ince, a goat salient against a tree ppr. 129. 8

Ince of Chester, a tree ppr., fructed or. 143. 5

Ince, John, Esquire, of Montague House, Swanley, Kent, a horse arg., holding in the mouth a trefoil slipped vert, resting the dexter fore-leg on a caduceus erect ppr. *Labore et scientia.* 256. 5

Inchbold, Yorks, a wyvern. *Palladia fama.* 70. 1

Inchiquin, Baron (O'Brien), Dromoland, Newmarket-on-Fergus, co. Clare, Ireland, issuing from a cloud an arm embowed brandishing a sword arg., pommel and hilt or. *Vigueur de dessus.* —*Lamh laidir an vachtar.* *cf.* 201. 4

Inckpen or **Inkpen** of Whitehouse, Hants, a dexter hand holding a club ppr. 214. 6

Incleden, a hand issuing from a cloud in fess, pointing to a serpent ppr. 223. 7

Incledon of Incledon, Devonsh., a falcon ppr., beaked and belled or. *cf.* 85. 2

Incledon-Webber, Edward Chichester, Esquire, St. Brannock's, Braunton, North Devonsh.: (1) A wolf's head couped per pale or and gu. (*for Webber*). (2) A falcon close ppr., jessed or. *Malo mori quam fœdari.*

Inderwick, Frederick Andrew, Esquire, of 8, Warwick Square, S.W., and Mariteau House, Winchelsea, Rye, Sussex, a demi-man affrontée ppr., habited, cap adorned with a feather vert, collar and cuffs arg., and resting the sinister hand upon a knife point downwards, also ppr. *Sapienter et sincere.*

Iners, a dexter arm in armour holding in the hand a scimitar in pale, all ppr.

Inge, a hand holding a glove ppr. 220. 5

Inge of Thorp, Constantine, Staffs, two battle-axes in saltire ppr., enfiled with a ducal coronet or. *cf.* 172. 4

Inge, William Frederick, of Thorpe Hall, Thorpe Constantine, near Tamworth, same crest and motto.

Ingeham or **Ingham,** an arm in armour embowed issuing from a cloud in the sinister holding a sword ppr. 196. 1

Ingerland, on a plate a thistle ppr.

Ingestre, Viscount, *see* Shrewsbury, Earl of.

Ingham, on a chapeau gu., turned up erm., an owl ppr., sitting in holly-leaves vert.

Ingham of Marton in Craven, Yorks, two arms embowed vested, and holding between the hands a maunch. *In veritate victoria.*

Ingham, His Honour Robert Wood, J.P., D.L., of Sugwas Court, Eaton Bishop, Heref., issuant from a cloud in the sinister an arm embowed in armour, entwined by a serpent ppr., charged with two mascles or, grasping a sword, also ppr.

Ingham, Edward Theodore, Blake Hall, Mirfield, a demi-lion gu. holding between the paws an escallop ppr. 295. 3

Ingilby, Sir Henry Day, Bart., M.A., J.P., D.L., of Ripley, in West Riding of Yorks, a boar's head couped and erect arg., tusked or, holding in the mouth an estoile of the last. *Mon droit.*

Ingilby, Amcotts-, Bart. (*extinct*), of Kettlethorpe Park, Lincs, and Ripley Castle, Yorks: (1) A boar's head couped and erect arg., tusked or, and issuant from the mouth an estoile of the last (*for Ingilby*). (2) A squirrel sejant gu., cracking a nut and collared or (*for Amcotts*). *cf.* 135. 7

Ingilby, a boar's head erect and erased arg. 43. 3

Ingilby, Rev. Arthur, Lawkland Hall, Clapham, Lancs, a boar's head erect arg., tusked or. *Mon droit.*

Ingle, a hand erect issuing from a cloud and holding a sword wavy, all ppr. 212. 4

Ingle, George, Esquire, of Socon, Beds, in front of a cubit arm in bend ppr., charged with an acorn leaved and slipped vert, the hand grasping a sword in bend sinister of the first, pommel and hilt or, the trunk of a tree fesseways eradicated, and sprouting to the dexter, also ppr. *Disce pati.*

Inglebert, a greyhound ppr., current towards a tree vert. 58. 11

Ingleby, Yorks, a boar's head arg., tusked or. 43. 1

Ingleby, Clement Mansfield, Esquire, M.A., LL.D., of Valentines, Essex, a boar's head couped erect ppr., tusked or. *Non immemor benefici.* *cf.* 43. 3

Ingleby, Yorks, a boar's head couped and erect arg., armed or. *Mon droit.* *cf.* 43. 3

Ingleden of Newcastle-on-Tyne and Yorks, a phœnix in flames ppr. *Ex flamma lux.* 82. 2

Ingledew, a dexter arm embowed in fess issuing out of a cloud in the sinister, reaching to a garland of laurel, all ppr. *cf.* 223. 3

Ingledew, on a mount vert, an ingle ppr., issuing therefrom an eagle with wings expanded ppr. *Ex flamma lux.*

Inglefield, Warw., an arm embowed vested per pale gu. and or, cuffed arg., holding in the hand ppr. a branch vert.

Inglefield, Henry Beaufort, Esquire, 24, Cadogan Place, London, S.W., and Colthurst, Clitheroe, Yorks, on a naval crown ppr., an eagle displayed per pale az. and gu. *The sun my compass.*

Ingles or **Inglis,** Scotland, a demi-lion rampant arg. *Nobilis est ira leonis.* 10. 2

Ingles, a fetterlock az., the fetter or. 168. 12

Inglesby, Colonel T. J. J., Prince Alfred's Vol. Art., of Harlemere, Seapoint, South Africa, a horse rampant or, holding in its mouth an oak sprig fructed ppr., the sinister fore-foot resting on an escutcheon az., charged with a hand grenade of the first. 307. 12

Ingleton, Devonsh., a hand issuing from a cloud in fess pointing to a serpent ppr. 223. 7

Inglett of Allington, Devonsh., a lion's head erased gu. 17. 2

Inglis, Bart., Beds, a demi-lion rampant ppr., holding in the dexter paw an étoile or. *Nobilis est ira leonis.*—*Recte faciendo securus.* *cf.* 15. 7

Inglis, Scotland, a demi-lion rampant holding in the dexter paw a mullet or. *Nisi dominus frustra.* 15. 7

Inglis, Scotland, same crest. *Recte faciendo securus.*—*Invictus maneo.*

Inglis, a demi-lion arg. *Recte faciendo securus.* 10. 2

Inglis, a demi-lion rampant ppr., holding in his dexter paw a branch of laurel vert. *Invictus maneo.*

Inglis, out of a mural coronet or, a demi-lion rampant arg. *cf.* 16. 11

Inglis of Broomhill, Lanarksh., Scotland, a demi-lion rampant arg., armed and langued gu., holding in his dexter paw a mullet, also gu. *Recte faciendo securus.* 15. 7

Inglis, a demi-lion rampant arg. *Recte faciendo securus.* 10. 2

Inglis, William Raymond, Esquire, a demi-lion rampant arg. *Nobilis est ira leonis.*

Inglis of Manor, and Mannerhead, Peebles, a demi-lion rampant arg. *Nobilis est ira leonis.* 10. 2

Inglis of Murdieston, Scotland, a demi-lion arg., grasping in his dexter paw an oak-branch slipped ppr. *Invictus maneo.* cf. 10. 2

Inglis of Broomhill, Lanarksh., Scotland, a demi-lion rampant arg., holding in his dexter paw a mullet gu. *Recte faciendo securus.* 15. 7

Inglis of Glencorse, Edinburgh, a demi-lion rampant holding in his dexter paw a mullet arg. *Recte faciendo securus.* 15. 7

Inglis of Cramond, a demi-lion rampant arg., holding in the dexter paw a mullet or. *Nisi dominus frustra.* 15. 7

Inglis, Bart., Beds, a cubit arm holding in the hand a scimitar. 213. 5

Inglis of Newtounleys, Haddington, Scotland, a star environed with clouds, all ppr. *In tenebris lucidior.* 161. 11

Inglish, an ear of wheat and a palm-branch in saltier, all ppr. 154. 19

Ingo, Essex, out of a ducal coronet or, a dragon's head with wings addorsed gu. 72. 1

Ingoldesby and **Ingoldsby** of Lethenborough, Waldridge, Bucks, and of Newbottle, Northamp., Bart. (*extinct*), out of a ducal coronet or, a demi-lion gu., charged on the shoulder with an étoile of the first. cf. 16. 3

Ingowville, Jersey, a lion rampant ppr. 1. 13

Ingram, Sir William James, Bart., Swineshead Abbey, Lincs, on a rock ppr., issuant from a wreath of cinquefoils or, a griffin's head erased quarterly gu. and arg., charged on the neck with an escallop counterchanged. *In hoc signo vinces.* 273. 12

Ingram, Viscount Irvine (*extinct*), of Temple Newsom, Yorks, a cock ppr. *Magnanimus esto.* 91. 2

Ingram, *see* Meynell-Ingram.

Ingram, Scotland, a griffin's head erased ppr., collared arg. cf. 66. 2

Ingram, a griffin's head quarterly gu. and arg. 66. 1

Ingram of Glasgow, a phœnix in flames, all ppr. *Ad sidera vultus.* 82. 2

Ingram, a cock ppr. 91. 2

Ingram of Ades, Chailey, Lewes, a cock in his pride ppr. *Magnanimus esto.*

Ingram, a bull's head erased. 44. 3

Inkeldon and **Inkledon** of Buckland, Devonsh., an ibex passant or.

Inkersall, Herts and Middx., a griffin's head gu., gorged with a fess dancettée erm., between two wings displayed or. cf. 65. 11

Inman, R. M., L.R.C.P., F.Z.S., of 7, South Street, South Place, E.C., on a mount vert, a wyvern ppr., ducally gorged and lined or. cf. 69. 11

Inman, Ernest Stobart, Esquire, of Mere Bank, Davenham, Chesh., a wyvern vert, winged fretty or, gorged with a plain collar with a line therefrom reflexed over the body gold, holding in the mouth a rose gu., barbed, seeded, and slipped ppr. *In Domino confido.*

Innes, Earl, *see* Roxburghe, Duke of.

Innes-Ker, *see* Roxburghe, Duke of.

Innes, *see* Mitchell-Innes.

Innes, Middx., a boar's head erased or. 42. 2

Innes of Innes, a boar's head couped or. *Be traist.* 43. 1

Innes, Scotland, a boar's head erased sa. 42. 2

Innes of Edinburgh, two hands conjoined in fess, holding a sword, all ppr. *Ditat servata fides.* 224. 7

Innes, Bart. (*extinct*), of Lochlalsh, Ross-sh., and Coxton, co. Moraysh., a boar's head erased ppr., langued gu. *Be traist.—Exempla suorum.* 42. 2

Innes, Scotland, a bee volant ppr. *Non servit sed laborat.* 137. 1

Innes of Towie, Aberdeensh., and Lichnet, Banffsh., a bee volant ppr. *Provide qui laboriose.* 137. 1

Innes of Gamrie and Belhevie, a bee ppr. *E labore dulcedo.* 137. 1

Innes of Reidhall, Banffsh., a bee volant upwards ppr. *Non servit sed laborat.* 137. 2

Innes of Blairtoum, a primrose ppr., thereon a bee or. *E labore dulcedo.* 150. 11

Innes of Blairtoun and of Balnacraig, a thistle ppr., thereon a bee. *E labore dulcedo.* 150. 9

Innes of Gifford Vale, Haddington, Scotland, a Scotch thistle with a bee thereon sucking ppr. *E labore dulcedo.* 150. 9

Innes, out of a ducal coronet a thistle ppr. 150. 2

Innes, Scotland, a thistle ppr., surmounted by a star arg. *E labore dulcedo.*

Innes, Alexander Berowald, of Raemoir and Dunnottar, Kincardinesh., Scotland, a branch of palm slipped ppr. *Ornatur radix fronde.* 147. 1

Innes, Colonel Thomas, of Learney, Aberdeensh.: (1) On the dexter side—a branch of palm slipped ppr. (*for Innes*). 147. 1. (2) Upon the sinister side—a cubit arm in armour, the hand bare holding a dart in bend sinister point downwards, all ppr. (*for Brebner*). *Ornatur radix fronde.—Per tela, per hostes.*

Innes, Lieutenant-Colonel Francis Newell, R.A., of Learney, Torphins, Aberdeensh. same crests and motto.

Innes, Rev. William Disney, of Cowie House, Stonehaven, N.B., a branch of palm slipped ppr. *Ornatur radix fronde.*

Innes of Thurster, a star of six rays environed with clouds, all ppr. *Dum spiro, cœlestia spero.* cf. 164. 11

Innes, Scotland, a mullet az. *Virtus ad astra.* 164. 2

Innes-Cross, Arthur Charles, Esquire, J.P., D.L., of Dromanline, co. Down: (1) A stork ppr., holding in the beak a cross potent fitchée arg., and resting the dexter claw on a rose gu., seeded or, barbed vert, and charged on the body with a cross patée az., for distinction (*for Cross*). (2) An estoile az., and over it the motto, *Be traiste* (*for Innes*). *Certari et vici.* 164. 1

Innes, Rose-, Thomas Gilzean, Netherdale, Banffsh., N.B.: (1) A rose gu., stalked and leaved ppr. (*Rose*). (2) A branch of palm slipped ppr. *Armat spina rosas.—Ornatur radix fronde.*

Innes of Edinburgh, a star of twelve points arg. *Me duce.*

Innes of Dunkinty, Elgin, a star az. *Virtus ad astra.—Sub tigno salus.* 164. 1

Innes, Scotland, an increscent ppr. *Je reçois pour donner.* 163. 3

Innes, on a ducal coronet or, a wyvern sejant gu. 70. 9

Innes of that Ilk, Elgin, Scotland, within an adder disposed in a circle a castle triple-towered ppr. *Prudentiâ et vi.*

Innes, Scotland, a hind's head erased ppr. *Fortis et fidus.* 124. 3

Innes, Scotland, a cock crowing ppr. *Prudentiâ et vi.* 91. 2

Innes, Scotland, an arm embowed holding a dagger ppr. *Sine crimine fiat.—Pro patria.*

Innes of Leighnot, an arm holding in the hand a sword ppr. *Honos vitâ clarior.* 212. 13

Innes of Chelsea, a dexter arm embowed and vambraced ppr., holding a banner disveloped gu. *Pro patria.*

Innes of Balveny, a dexter arm in armour couped at the elbow holding a broadsword in pale ppr. *Pro patria.*

Innes, Sir John, Bart., D.L., of Balveny and Edengight, Banffsh., a dexter arm armed and couped at the elbow holding a broadsword in pale ppr. *Sine crimine fiat.—Pro patria.*

Innes-Lillingston, Frederick George, Esquire, of Bute Court, Torquay, a demi-wyvern issuant, tail nowed sa., wings expanded and elevated or, charged with an ermine-spot of the first, on the breast two annulets conjoined in pale or. *Pro Deo et patria.*

Insole of Ely Court, Glamorgansh., a gryphon passant or, charged on the body with two pheons, and resting the dexter claw on a leopard's face jessant-de-lis az.

Inverarity, John Duncan, of Rosemount and Hedderwick, Forfarsh., a rose-bush ppr. *Semper floreat.* 149. 14

Inverclyde, Baron (Burns), Castle Wemyss, Renfrewsh., a dexter cubit arm ppr., the hand grasping a bugle-horn sa., garnished vert. *Ever ready.* 297. 8

Inverurie, Lord, *see* Kintore, Earl.

Inwards, on a chapeau gu., turned up erm., an eagle's head ppr. *Invidiâ major.* 83. 12

Inwood of Cobham, Surrey, a demi-lion rampant or, holding a battle-axe az. 15. 4

Inys, on a mount vert, a rabbit ppr., against a tree of the first, fructed or. 136. 10

Iohnson of Aykleyheads, Durh.: (1) A naked dexter arm embowed firing a pistol, all ppr. (*for Iohnson*). 200. 11. (2) A dexter cubit arm erect vested erminois, cuffed arg., holding in the hand ppr. a roundle of the first (*for Dixon*). *Fortiter et sincere.* 205. 13

Ipre, on a mount vert, a leopard couchant gardant gu., ducally crowned or. 24. 9

Ipres, Lancs, a unicorn's head or, collared gu. cf. 49. 11

Irball, Lancs, two halberds in saltier addorsed sa. 172. 4

Irby, Baron Boston, *see* Boston.

Irby, Lincs, a wyvern's head arg., gorged with two bars gemelle gu. cf. 71. 1

Irby, Lincs, a Saracen's head in profile couped at the shoulders ppr., wreathed arg. and sa.

Irby of Boyland Hall: (1) A Saracen's head ppr. (*for Irby*). 190. 5. (2) A cubit arm erased holding in the hand a scimitar embrued, all ppr., the hilt and pommel or (*for Garneys*). *cf.* 213. 5

Irby, Edward, Esquire, of Bolivia, Tenterfield, Clive, New South Wales, Australia, a Saracen's head in profile ppr., wreathed about the temples arg. and sa. *Honor fidelitatis præmium.* 190. 4

Ireby, an antelope trippant ppr. 126. 6

Ireby, a sword in pale enfiled with a savage's head ppr. 191. 9

Ireland, Herts and Shropsh., a fleur-de-lis arg., entwined with a snake regardant vert, perforating the centre leaf.

Ireland, a bird arg., beaked and legged gu. 92. 2

Ireland of Owsden Hall, Suff., a dove holding in its beak an olive-branch, all ppr. 92. 5

Ireland, Chesh., Lancs, and Shropsh., a dove arg., beaked and legged gu., holding in its beak a sprig of laurel vert. 92. 5

Ireland, Ireland, a dove holding in its beak an olive-branch ppr. *Amor et pax.* 92. 5

Ireland of Hutt and Hale, Lancs, same crest and motto. 92. 5

Ireland, Scotland, a lion rampant gardant gu. 2. 5

Iremonger, Lancs and Shropsh., a boar's head arg., collared vairée or and gu. *cf.* 41. 1

Iremonger of the Priory, Wherwell, Hants, a phœnix or, in flames ppr. 82. 2

Ireton, Ireland, a squirrel sejant ppr. *cf.* 135. 4

Ireton, a demi-lion sa., collared arg., holding in the dexter paw a mullet gu. *cf.* 15. 7

Ireton of Little Ireton, Derbysh., a squirrel sejant cracking a nut ppr. *Fay ce que doy advienne que pourra.* 135. 7

Ireys of Ireys, Dorset, on an oak-tree eradicated and erect ppr., a dragon or, pierced through the breast by a sword of the first, hilt of the second 73. 7

Irland, Irrland, or **Ireland** of Albrighton, Shropsh., a dove arg., holding in the beak a sprig of laurel vert. 92. 5

Irnynge, a child's head ppr.

Irons, a cross moline lozenge-pierced az. 165. 1

Ironside of Houghton-le-Spring, Durh., a cross crosslet fitched az. *In hoc signo vinces.* 166. 2

Ironside, a dexter hand couped in fess holding a sword in pale, surmounted by a laurel crown, all ppr. 221. 7

Ironside, Bax-, Henry George Outram, Houghton-le-Spring, Durh.: (1) A cubit arm vested per pale az. and gu., cuffed arg., the hand ppr. holding a cross flory or. (2) A demi-lion gu., charged on the shoulder with three cinquefoils arg., holding between the paws an Eastern crown or. *In hoc signo vinces.—Cavendo tutus.*

Irton of Irton Hall, Cumb., a Saracen's head. *Semper constans et fidelis.* 190. 5

Irton of Inverramsey, a hand holding two holly-branches of three leaves each in saltire ppr. *Color fidesque perennis.*

Irvine, *see* Mervyn-D'Arcy-Irvine.

Irvine, a cock ppr. 91. 2

Irvine, a lion rampant with wings addorsed. 20. 7

Irvine, Scotland, a sheaf of five arrows banded, all ppr. *Sub sole, sub umbra virens.* 173. 3

Irvine of Kingcausie, Aberdeensh., Scotland, a decussis like the letter X within a circle sa. *Deo regi et patriæ.*

Irvine, Robert, Esquire, late of Orchard House, Durh., in front of two anchors saltirewise with cables or, a dolphin embowed ppr.

Irvine, a sword and a palm-branch in saltier.

Irvine of Artamfoord, Scotland, two holly-leaves in saltire vert. *Sub sole viresco.*

Irvine, Scotland, a sheaf of holly-leaves ppr. *Ope solis et umbra.* 150. 12

Irvine, Scotland, a sheaf of holly of seven leaves banded gu.

Irvine of Beilside, Aberdeensh., three holly-leaves conjoined in one stalk ppr. *Moderata durant.*

Irvine of Lairnie, Aberdeensh., a branch of holly and a lily both slipped in saltier ppr. *Candide et constanter.* 151. 10

Irvine, Scotland, a holly-branch gu. 150. 10

Irvine of Cairnfield, Banffsh., Scotland, a cross crosslet fitched gu., and a branch of holly slipped vert, in saltier. *Ferendo feres.* 166. 10

Irvine of Lenturk, Aberdeensh., a sheaf of holly of seven leaves banded gu. *Fideque perennat.*

Irvine of Inchray, Scotland, two holly-branches in saltire ppr. *Sequitur vestigia patrum.*

Irvine, Alexander, of Drum, Aberdeensh., Scotland, a sheaf of nine holly-leaves vert. *Sub sole, sub umbra virens.*

Irvine of Fedderet, Aberdeensh., Scotland, a sheaf of six holly-leaves vert, banded gu. *Ope solis et umbræ.*

Irvine of Bonshaw, Dumfriessh., Scotland, a cubit arm in armour holding in the gauntlet a branch of holly, all ppr. *Haud ullis labentia ventis.* 209. 14

Irvine, Scotland, same crest. *Moderata durant.—Sub sole, sub umbra virens.*

Irvine, Bart. (*extinct*), of Lowtherstown, co. Fermanagh, a gauntlet issuing out of a cloud holding a thistle, all ppr. *Dum memor ipse mei.*

Irvine, John Gerard, Esquire, of Killadeas, co. Fermanagh, issuing from a cloud a gauntlet fesseways holding in the hand a thistle slipped and leaved, all ppr. *Dum memor ipse mei.*

Irvine of Auchinbedridge, Dumfriessh., a hand holding a branch of holly whereon are five leaves ppr. *Nil mihi tollit hyems.*

Irvine of Castle Irvine, co. Fermanagh, a dexter arm in armour fesseways issuant out of a cloud, the hand holding a thistle, all ppr. *Dum memor ipse mei.*

Irvine of Burleigh, Scotland, a dexter hand holding a holly-branch consisting of three leaves ppr. *Sub sole, sub umbra virens.*

Irvine, Thomas, Esquire, of Glen Huntly, Aigburth Road, Liverpool, a holly-wreath ppr. *Sub sole, sub umbra virens.*

Irvine and **Irving,** out of a ducal coronet per pale arg. and az., a lion's gamb per fess or and gu., holding a cross crosslet fitched of the last. 36. 11

Irvine of Gottenburg, a dexter hand holding two holly-branches of three leaves, each crossways ppr. *Color fidesque perennis.*

Irvine, a hand holding a bay rod adorned with nine leaves ppr., with the chemical letters of Terra, Aqua, Ignis, Sal Spiritus, Sulphur, Sol, Venus, Mercurius or. *Auspice summo numine.*

Irving, *see* Winter-Irving.

Irving, *see* Brodribb, formerly Broderip.

Irving, Bart., of Woodhouse, co. Dumfriessh., Scotland: (1) A chapeau gu., turned up erm., wreathed round the crown with holly or. *cf.* 180. 8. (2) A dexter arm in armour embowed ppr., garnished or, holding in the hand two holly-leaves vert, banded gu. *Haud ullis labentia ventis.—Sub sole, sub umbra virens.*

Irving of Hyde Park Square, London, W., a cornucopia fesseways ppr., in front of an arm in armour embowed, also ppr., holding a holly-leaf vert. *Sub sole, sub umbra virens.*

Irving, Major John Beaufin, late of Bickington Lodge, Fremington, Devonsh., an arm in armour gauntleted ppr., charged on the wrist with a crescent gu., and holding a branch of holly consisting of seven leaves fructed ppr. *Haud ullis labentia ventis.*

Irving of Newtown, Lanarksh., Scotland, three arrows ppr., points upwards, two in saltire and one in pale, flighted arg., banded gu. *Sub sole, sub umbra virens.* *cf.* 173. 14

Irving, three arrows bound by a ribbon gu. 173. 1

Irwin, Colonel William John, of St. Catherine's Park, Leixlip, co. Kildare, a dexter arm in armour embowed holding a branch of holly.

Irwin of Justustown, Cumb., a dove holding in its beak an olive-branch ppr. *Haud ullis labentia ventis.* 92. 5

Irwin of Calder Abbey and Justustown, Cumb., a dove holding an olive-branch in its beak. *Haud ullis labentia ventis.* 92. 5

Irwin, Colonel Thomas Angelo, Lynehow, near Carlisle, upon a mount between two holly-leaves vert, a dove arg., holding in the beak an olive-branch ppr., and an ear of wheat or. *Haud ullis labentia ventis.* 92. 13

Irwin, James Daniel, Esquire, a dexter arm in armour fesseways, issuant out of a cloud, the hand holding a sword erect enwreathed with a thistle, all ppr., the arm charged with a cross patée gu. *Dum memor ipse mei.*

Irwin, John Arthur, Esquire, of Derrygore, co. Fermanagh, Ireland, a mailed arm fesseways holding in the hand a thistle and a holly-leaf, all ppr., and charged on the arm with a crescent gu. *Nemo me impune lacessit.* *cf.* 211. 12

Irwin, Rev. Arthur William, of Napton, Rugby, same crest and motto.

Irwin, De la Cherois Thomas, of Carnagh House, Carnagh, co. Armagh, and 170, Cooper Street, Ottawa, Ontario, a hand and arm in armour holding erect a thistle. *Nemo me impune lacessit.*

Irwin, Ireland, an arm couped above the wrist in armour ppr., lying fesseways, holding in the gauntlet a bunch of holly consisting of three leaves vert, tied gu., the strings flotant. *Sub umbra virtutis.—Sub sole, sub umbra virens.—Nemo me impune lacessit.* 211. 13

Irwin, Ireland, issuing out of a cloud a hand grasping a bunch of thistle ppr. *Nemo me impune lacessit.*

Irwin or **Irwine,** Ireland, a mullet pierced or. *cf.* 164. 2

Irwine, an arm in armour couped above the wrist in fess holding in the gauntlet a branch of holly vert, the arm charged with a crescent. *cf.* 211. 12

Irwine, an arm couped about the wrist in armour ppr., lying fesseways, holding in the gauntlet a bunch of holly of three leaves vert, tied gu., the strings flotant, and charged on the arm with a crescent for difference. *cf.* 211. 13

Isaac, a martlet. 95. 4

Isaac of Boughton, Worcs., a dexter arm in armour embowed, the hand holding a sword enfiled with a leopard's face the point downwards and resting on the wreath, all ppr.

Isaac, in the sea a cross patée between two ears of wheat in orle, all ppr. 154. 12

Isaack, of Exeter and Heavitree, Devonsh., a leopard's head erased or, pellettée and ducally collared. *Floreseat.*

Isaacs, a hand holding a mill-rind.

Isaacson, Surrey, a demi-lion rampant az. (*another*, arg.), holding between the paws an escallop. *Θάρσει.* 13. 10

Isaacson of Fifield, Essex, same crest.

Isaacson, two lion's gambs sa., holding up a bezant. *cf.* 39. 4

Isate, Yorks, a stag's head erased per fess arg. and gu., pierced by an arrow ppr. *cf.* 121. 2

Isely or **Isley,** a hand holding a roll of paper between two branches of laurel in orle, all ppr. 215. 3

Isham of Bramston, Northants, a demi-swan with wings endorsed arg., guttée-de-larmes. *cf.* 100. 9

Isham, Sir Vere, Bart., D.L., of Lamport, Northamp., a demi-swan with wings displayed arg., beaked sa. *Ostendo non ostento.—On things transitory resteth no glory.*

Isherwood of Windsor, Berks, a wolf's head per pale ermines and erminois, erased gu. 30. 8

Isherwood, John Henry Bradshaw, of Marple Hall, Chesh., and Bradshaw Hall, Lancs: (1) A wolf's head erased ppr., issuant out of a crescent az. (*for Isherwood*). *cf.* 30. 8. (2) On a mount vert, a stag at gaze ppr. under a vine-branch, also ppr., fructed or (*for Bradshaw*). *Bona benemerenti benedictio.* *cf.* 116. 14

Ismay, Joseph Bruce, Esquire, of Sandheys, Mosley Hill, Liverpool, an esquire's helmet ppr., in front thereof a cross patée fitchée or. *Be mindful.*

Ismay, James Hainsworth, of 30, James Street, Liverpool, same crest and motto.

Ismay, Thomas Henry, Esquire, J.P., of Dawpool, Birkenhead, Chesh., on a wreath of the colours an esquire's helmet ppr., and in front thereof a cross patée fitchée or. *Be mindful.* 180. 2

Israel, the sun rising from behind a cloud ppr. 162. 5

Isted of Ecton, Northamp., a buck's head erased ppr., attired and ducally gorged or. *cf.* 121. 2

Ithell, Cambs, and of Billesden, Leics., on a ducal coronet or, a Cornish chough with wings expanded sa., beaked and legged gu. 108. 6

Ivat and **Ivatt** of London, out of a mural coronet a cubit arm in armour holding in the gauntlet, all ppr., a fleur-de-lis or.

Ive, an arm in armour couped and embowed holding a sword ppr., the elbow resting on the wreath.

Iveagh, Baron (Guinness), of Castleknock, co. Dublin: (1) A boar passant quarterly or and gu., a crescent for difference (*for Guinness*). *cf.* 40. 9. (2) On a pillar arg., encircled by a ducal coronet or, an eagle preying on a bird's leg erased ppr. (*for Lee*). *Spes mea in Deo.*

Iverach of Wideford, Orkney, a boar's head couped arg. *Nunquam obliviscas.* 43. 1

Ivers, a demi-lion rampant or, collared sa. 10. 9

Ives, Northamp., out of a ducal coronet gu., an Indian goat's head arg., guttée-de-sang, attired or.

Ives of Bradwell, Norf., a boar passant ppr., collared and chained or. *cf.* 40. 9

Ives, Grant-, Wilfrid Dryden, Bradden House, Northamp., issuant from a rock ppr., a blackamoor's head in profile couped at the shoulders ppr., the temples and neck each encircled by an annulet or (*for Ives*). (2) A conical hill fired at the summit ppr., issuant therefrom a cross calvary or (*for Grant*).

Iveson of Hedon, near Hull, Yorks, a Moor's head in profile erased at the neck sa.

Ivey, Devonsh., a demi-lion rampant or, supporting a staff raguly vert. *cf.* 15. 1

Ivie, Scotland, the attires of a stag affixed to a scalp ppr. *cf.* 123. 5

Ivory, a lion sejant affrontée, holding in the dexter paw a sword, and in the sinister a fleur-de-lis. 7. 3

Ivye, Oxon., and of West Keynton, Wilts, a lion rampant arg., supporting a staff raguly gu.

Iwarby and **Iwardby,** a cock's head gu. *cf.* 90. 1

Izacke of Exeter, a leopard's head erased sa., ducally gorged or. *cf.* 23. 10

Izod of Tudington and Stainton, Glouc., a man's head in profile ppr., in armour or, on the head a plume of feathers gu. and arg.

Izon, a dexter hand couped in fess, holding a cross crosslet fitched in pale. 221. 10

Izzard, a dolphin naiant ppr. 140. 5

J.

Jack, a pear-tree vert, fructed or. 144. 10

Jack, a horse's head erased, holding in the mouth a broken tilting-spear.

Jack, Scotland, the sun in his splendour or. *Post nubila Phœbus.* 162. 2

Jackaman, Henry Mason, Esquire, J.P., of Ipswich, a griffin's head erased sa., guttée-d'or. *Fortiter qui fide.* 293. 15

Jackerell, on a stand a hawk's lure, and thereon a hawk perched, all ppr. 85. 12

Jacket, issuing out of a cloud a dexter hand ppr., holding a cross patée fitched in pale or. 223. 6

Jackman, a griffin's head erased sa., guttée-d'or. 66. 2

Jacks, William, Esquire, of Crosslet, Dumbartonsh., on a mount a collie-dog. *Treu und fest.*

Jackson, Yorks, and of Cuddesdon, Oxon., a sheldrake ppr. 102. 10

Jackson, Bart. (*extinct*), of Beach Hill, Surrey, a shoveller tufted on the head and breast arg., and charged with a trefoil slipped vert. *Innocentiæ securus.—Malo mori quam fœdari.*

Jackson, Francis Arthur, Esquire, of Jackson Dale Savu Savu, Fiji (other estates, Na Ko, Vadra Vadra, and Wai Ko Vuna, all in Fiji), educated at Rugby, served with H.M. New Zealand Militia during the New Zealand War (for lineage, *see* Burke's "Colonial Gentry," vol. i.), on a wreath of the colours a demi-gryphon gu., collared and chain reflexed over the back or, holding in the dexter claw a shoveller's head erased arg. *Strenue et honeste.* 65. 2

Jackson, Charles Hugh, Esquire, Doncaster, same crest and motto.

Jackson, Freeman Rayney, Esquire, of Wanganui, New Zealand, same crest and motto.

Jackson, Henry Bower, Esquire, of Telau, Savu Savu, West Fiji, same crest and motto.

Jackson, Hugh Rowland, Esquire, of Doncaster, same crest and motto.

Jackson, Clement Nugent, of Hertford College, Oxford, same crest and motto.

Jackson, Sir Keith George, Bart., of Beach House, Walmer, a goat's head couped arg., guttée-de-sang, armed and bearded or, gorged with a collar gu., charged with three bezants ringed, and a line therefrom reflexed of the third.

Jackson, Chesh., a goat's head az., attired or. 128. 12

Jackson, Bart., upon a ragged staff sa., a goat's head couped arg., semée of trefoils slipped vert. *Fortiter, fideliter, feliciter.* 128. 9

Jackson, William, Esquire, J.P., of Forest Road, Birkenhead, same crest and motto.

Jackson, Major-General William, Kirkbuddo, Forfarsh., a griffin issuing out of the wreath, holding in his dexter claw a sword ppr.

Jackson of Laurel Lodge, Toowong, near Brisbane, Queensland, in front of a mount vert, a mullet of six points or, thereon an eagle close ppr. *Confide recte agens.* 228. 3

Jackson, an eagle close ppr. 76. 2

Jackson, Oxon., an eagle rising ppr. 77. 5

Jackson, Scotland, an eagle's head erased ppr. *Dominus fecit.* 83. 2

Jackson, Scotland, same crest. *Sublimiora peto.*

Jackson, Shropsh., an eagle's head erased az., holding in its beak a lily slipped ppr.

Jackson, Heref., on a five-leaved coronet or, a hawk's head and neck erased gu., charged on the breast with a cross patée fitched, also or. *Scuto amoris divini.*

Jackson of Bath, Somers., a dove close ppr., holding in the beak an olive-branch, and charged on the breast with a torteau. *cf.* 92. 5

Jackson, John Thomas, Esquire, of the Hurstead, Rochdale, Treburvaugh, Llangunllo, Radnorsh., two pheons gu., thereon an eagle with wings expanded or, each wing charged with a rose gu., barbed and seeded ppr. *Res non verba.* 235. 8

Jackson, Major-General William, Kirkbuddo, near Forfarsh., a griffin issuing out of the wreath, holding in his dexter claw a sword ppr. *Ausim et confido.*

Jackson of Southgate, Middx., a greyhound passant sa., collared or, resting the dexter paw on a pheon of the last. 58. 8

Jackson, a greyhound passant arg., resting the dexter paw on a pheon of the last. *cf.* 58. 8

Jackson of Bromfield, Middx., a demi-greyhound salient arg., collared or, holding between the feet a pheon sa. *cf.* 60. 8

Jackson, a greyhound's head couped arg., collared gu. 61. 2

Jackson, Rutl., the sun rising or.

Jackson of Keswick, Cumb., and Oxon., a sun or, in flames ppr.

Jackson of Kelwoold's Grove, Yorks, the sun or, between two branches in orle. 162. 6

Jackson, Donald Frederick, Esquire, of King's Lynn, Norf., a demi-horse arg., guttée-de-sang.

Jackson, Northamp., same crest. *cf.* 53. 1

Jackson, Thomas Graham, Esquire, M.A., R.A., Eagle House, Wimbledon, a demi-horse arg., guttée gu., maned and hoofed sa.

Jackson, William Goddard, Esquire, J.P., of Duddington, near Stamford, Northamp., and of Wisbech, Isle of Ely, a demi-horse arg., guttée-de-sang, and charged with a crescent gu. 53. 1

Jackson, Cumb., of Sunderland, Durh., of Bedale, Yorks, and of Combhay, Devonsh., a horse current arg., guttée-de-sang. 52. 8

Jackson, General Sir James, Knight Grand Cross of the Most Honourable Order of the Bath, a horse passant arg., charged on the shoulder with a trefoil slipped vert. *Celer et audax.* *cf.* 52. 6

Jackson, Edwin, Esquire, of Threlkeld Leys, Cockermouth, Cumb., in front of a mount vert, thereon a horse courant arg., three caltraps or. *Celer et audax.*

Jackson of Christchurch, Surrey, a horse passant arg., semée of cinquefoils gu. *cf.* 52. 6

Jackson of Allerton Hall, Chapel Allerton, near Leeds, a horse or, holding in the mouth an ear of wheat slipped vert, resting the dexter fore-leg upon three annulets, one and two, interlaced gu. *Essayez.*

Jackson, of Upwell, Norf., upon the trunk of a tree eradicated and sprouting to the dexter ppr., a horse current arg., guttée-de-poiz, charged on the body with a pale gu., thereon a cinquefoil, also arg. *Jamais arrière.* 53. 7

Jackson, George James Vaughan, Esquire, of Carramore, co. Mayo, a horse passant arg. *Celer et audax.* 52. 6

Jackson, Herbert Francis Vaughan, Esquire, of Potter's Bar, Middx., same crest and motto.

Jackson of London, a hand ppr., holding a boar's head erased and erect sa. 220. 6

Jackson of Torphin, Scotland, a dexter arm in armour embowed, holding in the hand a battle-axe ppr. *Devant si je puis.* *cf.* 200. 6

Jackson of Bubnell, Derbysh., an arm in armour embowed holding a battle-axe ppr. 200. 6

Jackson, Arthur, Esquire, F.R.C.S., of College Hill House, Shrewsbury, a tower ppr., and issuing from the battlements thereof a demi-lion rampant sa.

Jackson, Kent, a demi-lion rampant or, holding between the paws a pheon az. *cf.* 10. 2

Jackson, Sir Thomas, Bart., Stansted House, Essex, upon a fountain ppr., a sheldrake close or. *Aut mors aut victoria.* 283. 13

Jackson, Scotland, a holly-leaf ppr. *Virescit virtus.*

Jackson, Ireland, a fleur-de-lis or, entwined by a serpent vert. 148. 8

Jacob, Bart. (*extinct*), of Bromley and Bow, an heraldic tiger passant ppr., maned and tusked or. *Tantum in superbos.* 25. 5

Jacob, Oxon., same crest and motto. 25. 5

Jacob, Archibald Hamilton, Esquire, J.P., of Raymond Terrace, Sydney, N.S.W., and William Higgins Jacob, Esquire, of 59, Portsdown Road, Maida Vale, London, W., an heraldic tiger passant ppr. *A Deo salus.* 25. 5

Jacob, Wilts, an heraldic tiger passant sa., resting his dexter fore-paw on an escutcheon or. *cf.* 25. 5

Jacob, John Henry, Esquire, J.P., the Close, Salisbury, same crest. *Dum spiro spero.*

Jacob of Tolpiddle, Dorset, and Dover, Kent, a lion rampant or, supporting a cross crosslet fitched gu.

Jacob of Canterbury, Woolavington, Waldershare, Whitfield, and Sextries, Kent, on a mount vert, a lion rampant per fesse or and gu., supporting a cross crosslet botonny fitchée, also gu. *Non nobis solum.*

Jacobs, William Wall, Esquire, L.R.C.P., S.I., of 58, Burnt Ash Road, Lee, S.E., a dexter arm in armour embowed holding in the hand by the blade a sword fesseways, point to the dexter, all ppr.

Jacobs, an arm in armour embowed holding in the hand a sword by the blade, all ppr. 195. 6

Jacobs, Hull, an heraldic tiger passant. 25. 5

Jacoby, John Henry, Esquire, Rope Walk, The Park, Notts, a stag arg., charged on the body with two roses fessewise gu., barbed and seeded ppr., resting the dexter fore-foot on a cross of eight points gu. *Opera bona effulgent.* 118. 8

Jacoby, James Alfred, Esquire, M.P., of Oakhill House, Notts, and 8, Queen's Gate Gardens, S.W., same crest and motto.

Jacoby, Charles Theodore, Esquire, formerly of Lyegrove House, near Chipping Sodbury, Glouc., same crest and motto.

Jacomb, a lion's head erased barry of six arg. and az. *cf.* 17. 4

Jacomb of Burton Lazers, Leics., a hand holding two branches of palm in orle ppr. 218. 7

Jacques, a horse's head couped arg., maned or, struck in the breast with a tilting-spear of the last. *cf.* 50. 11

Jacques, Rev. Kinton, M.A., Brindle Rectory, Chorley, same crest. *Ad mortem fidelis.*

Jacques, a plate charged with a lion's head erased and collared. *cf.* 19. 1

Jacson of Barton Hall, a sheldrake rising ppr. *Innocentiæ securus.*

Jadewin of London, an oak-tree vert, fructed or, supported by two lion's gambs erased of the last, entwined with a scroll inscribed with the motto, "*Robur in vita Deus.*"

Jaffe, Sir Otto, of Belfast, an eagle displayed with wings inverted between two oak-branches, all ppr. *Deus nobiscum.*

Jaffray, Sir William, Bart., of Skilts, Warw., on a mount in front of two palm-branches saltirewise vert, a mullet or. *Post nubila Phœbus.* 272. 4

Jaffray, Scotland, between two branches of palm in orle a mullet, all ppr. *Post nubila Phœbus.* 146. 8

Jaffray, Ireland, a demi-leopard rampant gu. *cf.* 23. 13

Jaffrey of King's Wells, Kincardinesh., Scotland, the sun shining through a cloud. *Post nubila Phœbus.*

Jager, out of a ducal coronet a hand holding a sword, all ppr. 212. 11

Jaggard, William, of 139, Canning Street, Liverpool, issuing from clouds a dexter hand fesseways grasping two olive-branches in saltire and a sceptre erect, surmounted by a portcullis with chains pendent, all ppr., a serpent nowed about the wrist enclosing the motto *Prudentia.* 294. 7

Jago, a talbot couchant ppr. 54. 11

Jago, issuing out of clouds two dexter hands, both grasping the stump of an old tree sprouting afresh, all ppr. 224. 10

Jago-Trelawney, Major-General John, J.P., of Coldrenick, Liskeard, Cornw.: (1) A wolf statant ppr. (*for Trelawney*). (2) Upon a rock ppr., a cormorant rising sa., wings pean, charged upon the breast with a cross crosslet or (*for Jago*). *Sermoni consona facta.*

Jakeman, out of a ducal coronet or, an eagle's head ppr. *cf.* 83. 14

Jakes of London, a horse's head couped arg., maned or, struck in the breast with a tilting-spear of the last. *cf.* 50. 11

Jalabert of Dublin, the figure of Ceres ppr.

Jalfou of Hackney, Middx., on a mount vert, a greyhound courant arg., holding in the mouth a sword in pale, point downwards, ppr., pommel and hilt or. 58. 6

Jalmes, out of a ducal coronet or, five ostrich-feathers, the three inner ones sa., and the two outside ones arg. 114. 13

James, Baron Northbourne, *see* Northbourne.

James, Baron (James), of Heref., a cubit arm erect ppr., pendant from the band by a chain or, an escutcheon erm., charged with a balance or, the hand grasping a sword erect ppr., pommel and hilt or, the blade transfixing a boar's head couped erm. *Vim vi repellere licet.* 276. 13

James, Kent, an ostrich arg. 97. 2

James, Bart., Berks: (1) An ostrich arg., beaked and legged or. 97. 2. (2) On a ducal coronet or, two laurel-branches in saltier vert, environed with a snake ppr. *J'aime à jamais.*

James of Denford, Berks, and Newport, Isle of Wight, an ostrich arg., beaked and legged or. 97. 2

James of Beconsfield, Much Woolton, Lancs, upon the battlements of a tower or, an ostrich sa., holding in the beak a billet, also or. 250. 17

James, Cambs, upon two palm-branches in saltier vert, a dove arg.

James, Walter Culver, Esquire, of Quality Court, Chancery Lane, W.C., a caduceus in bend dexter surmounted by another in bend sinister, thereon perched a wood-pigeon close ppr. *Loyal à jamais.*

James, Frederick Culver, Esquire, of Marloes Road, Kensington, W., same crest and motto.

James, Essex, of Wellsborough, Kent, and Reigate, Surrey, out of a ducal coronet or, a demi-swan with wings expanded arg., beaked gu. *cf.* 99. 5

James, Drevis-, Lieutenant-Colonel Demetrius Wyndham, of Igtham Court, Kent: (1) Out of a ducal coronet or, a demi-swan with wings expanded arg., beaked gu. (*for James*). *cf.* 99. 5. (2) A squirrel holding between the paws an escallop or (*for Grevis*). *Fide et constantiâ.* *cf.* 135. 9

James, Fullarton-, Sir John Kingston, Bart., of the city of Dublin, issuing from a ducal coronet or, a swan ppr., beaked gu., and holding therein a dart of the first feathered arg., pointed towards the breast. *A jamais.—Pro Deo, patria, et Rege.*

James, Rt. Hon. the late Sir William Milbourne James, Lord Justice of Appeal, a cock gu., gorged with a collar gemel or, the dexter claw resting on a portcullis of the last. *Gwna a ddyled doed addel.* 91. 8

James, Bart. (*extinct*), of Park Farm Place, Eltham, Kent, in a naval coronet or, a tower with two port-holes in front of the same, fire issuing from the portholes and top ppr., on the tower a flagstaff of the last, thereon a flag flotant to the sinister gu., in the position of striking being half-way down the mast. *Victor.*

James of Upminster, Essex, and Kent, a garb arg., banded vert. 153. 2

James, Glouc., a garb. 153. 2

James, a demi-lion rampant erminois, holding an escallop gu. 13. 10

James of Haughton Hall, Hanover, Jamaica, same crest. *Malgré le tort.*

James, Cambs and Cornw., out of a ducal coronet or, a demi-lion az., holding an escallop gu. *cf.* 13. 10

James of Astley, Worcs., out of a mural coronet az., a demi-lion rampant regardant or, collared of the first, holding an escallop sa. *cf.* 16. 5

James of Presteign, Radnorsh., a lion rampant arg., collared, and holding between the fore-paws a rose gu., the dexter hind-paw resting on an escutcheon arg., charged with a spear-head sa. *Duw a digon.* 1. 6

James, James George, Esquire, of Ty-Newydd Blackwood, Bedwelty, Monm., and Blaen Nant, Nant-y-glo, Monm., a demi-lion vert, in the mouth a sinister hand, and holding in the dexter paw a pickaxe, both arg. *Ymdrech-i-drechu.*

James, Cornw., two lion's gambs erased sa., supporting an escallop arg., charged with a crescent az. *Nosce teipsum.*

James, Colonel Charles, in front of two spears in saltire and amid flags a tiger couchant, all ppr. *Quæ fecimus ipsi.*

James, Kent, a buffalo arg., armed sa.

James, Kent, a buffalo current sa., attired or.

James, a bull passant. *cf.* 45. 2

James, William, Esquire, of Otterburn, and the Moat, Eastbourne, a buffalo passant gu., armed ppr., resting the dexter fore-foot on an escutcheon arg., charged with a pheon sa. *Deo semper confide.* 45. 10

James, William Wybergh, of Barrock, Cumb., a buffalo passant ppr. *Vincit amor patriæ.*

James of the Close, Exeter, on a mount vert, a bull erm., armed, ungu., tufted, and collared or, the dexter forefoot supporting a water-bouget, and charged on the body with two annulets arg. 45. 4

James of Michbarrow, Somers., a demi-bull or, wreathed round the middle with a chaplet of laurel vert. *cf.* 45. 14

James, a demi-buffalo rampant sa., armed or. 45. 12

James, a demi-buffalo salient, armed and ungu. or. 45. 12

James, Lloyd-, William Frederick, of Pantsaison, Pembrokesh., a demi-bull rampant sa., armed and ungu. or, laugued gu. *Ffyddylon at y gorfin.* *cf.* 45. 8

James, Durh., a bull's head couped sa., armed or. *cf.* 44. 3

James of Barrow Court, Somers., a dolphin naiant ppr. 140. 5

James, a dolphin naiant or. 140. 5

James, Major-General Edward Renouard, R.E., 27, Nevern Mansions, Earl's Court, S.W., same crest.

James, Rev. John Burleigh, M.A., of Vanbrugh Fields, Blackheath, Kent, a unicorn's head erased arg., charged on the neck with an escallop gu., and supporting in the mouth a Passion cross gu., resting upon the wreath. *Memor.* 230. 15

James, Rev. Edward, Peakirk, Peterborough, same crest and motto.

James, Rev. Frank, of the Vicarage, Rossett R.S.O., Denbighsh., same crest and motto.

James, Arthur John, Esquire, of Edgeworth Manor, Cirencester, Glouc., same crest and motto.

James, Rev. Nicholas Hopkins, D.D., of Clonfeacle Rectory, Moy, co. Tyrone, a hart's head erased ppr., charged on the neck with a fleur-de-lis az. *J'aime à jamais.* 120. 5

James, William Dodge, West Dean Park, Chichester, upon the battlements of a tower or, an ostrich sa., holding in the beak a billet, also or. *J'aime à jamais.* 250. 17

James, a dexter naked arm embowed holding a sword. 201. 4

James, of Highfield, near Lydney-on-Severn, Glouc., and Perth, Western Australia, in front of a garb or, charged with an acorn slipped vert, a dolphin naiant ppr. *Tiens foi.* 265. 7

Jameson, an antelope trippant or, attired gu. 126. 6

Jameson, Scotland, a ship in full sail, her flag displayed gu. *Sine metu.* 160. 13

Jameson of Windfield, co. Galway, Ireland, a Roman galley ppr., the sail gu., charged with a lion passant gardant or. *Sine metu.*

Jameson or **Jamieson,** Ireland, a torteau between two wings gu. *cf.* 110. 4

Jamieson of Glasgow, and Croy, Dumbartonsh., a ship under sail ppr. *Ad littora tendit.* 160. 13

Jane, a swan with wings addorsed devouring a trout, all ppr. 99. 10

Janes of Kirtling, Cambs, and Botalock, Cornw., out of a ducal coronet or, a demi-lion az., holding an escallop gu. *cf.* 13. 10

Janes, Kent, out of a naval coronet or, a tower inflamed on the top ppr.

Janns, *see* Dudley-Janns.

Janson, an arm from the elbow erect and vambraced, holding in the hand a falcon's lure.

Janson of Ashby Ledgers, Northants, a cubit arm vested or, cuffed arg., holding a cross patonce of the first.

Janson, on a mount vert, a hind ppr., collared gu. 124. 14

Janssen, the sun in his splendour or. 162. 2
Janssen, Bart. (*extinct*), of Wimbledon, Surrey, a quatrefoil stalked and leaved vert.
Janssen, a rose-slip with a rose in full bloom ppr. 149. 5
Japp, William, Esq., Broom Hall, Alyth, Perthshire, an anchor in pale, entwined by a cable. *Deus me juvate.*
Jaques, Middx., a horse's head couped arg., maned or, struck in the breast by a tilting-spear of the last. *cf.* 50. 11
Jaques, a bezant charged with a lion's head erased ppr., collared or. *cf.* 19. 1
Jaques, Leonard, of Easby Abbey, Richmond, Yorks, a lion's head erased, pierced through the neck by a sword. 17. 13
Jardelay, a dexter arm in armour wielding a scimitar, all ppr.
Jardin or **Jardine,** Scotland, a spur-rowel. *Cave adsum.* 164. 8
Jardin, Scotland, a spur-rowel. *Ex virtute honos.* 164. 8
Jardin and **Jarden,** Scotland, a hand holding a bezant, all ppr. *Ex virtute honos.*
Jardine, an étoile ppr. 164. 1
Jardine, Scotland, a dexter hand holding up a spur-rowel.
Jardine, Sir William, Bart., of Applegirth, Dumfriessh., a spur-rowel of six points arg. *Cave adsum.* 164. 8
Jardine, Sir Robert, Bart., J.P., D.L., M.P., of Castlemilk, Dumfriessh., a spur-rowel gu. *Cave adsum.* 164. 8
Jardine, David Jardine, Esquire, of Jardine Hall, Lockerbie, N.B., and 9, Upper Grosvenor Street, W., same crest and motto.
Jarman, an eagle's leg erased in bend sinister holding a feather in bend dexter.
J'armay, Gustav, Esquire, Hartford Lodge, Hartford, Chesh., out of the coronet of a marquess a demi-lion rampant, double-queued, ducally crowned, holding in the dexter paw a branch of lilies. 307. 13
Jarrat and **Jarret,** an eagle with wings expanded ppr. 77. 5
Jarred of London, a sword in pale, on the point a garland of laurel ppr. *Res non verba.* 170. 1
Jarrett, a lion's head erased and ducally crowned or, collared gu. *cf.* 18. 8
Jarrett, Yorks, in front of a saltier az., a lion's head erased arg., guttée-de-larmes. *Res non verba.* *cf.* 17. 8
Jarrett, a sword in pale, on the point a garland of laurel ppr. 170. 1
Jarrett, a lion passant purp., resting the dexter fore-paw on a fleur-de-lis or. 5. 5
Jarrett of London, a lion's head erased arg., guttée-de-poix, collared gu., ducally crowned or.
Jarveis and **Jarvis,** a lion rampant gu. 1. 13
Jarvie of Glasgow and Singapore, an eagle rising ppr. *Ad littora tendo.* 77. 5
Jarvis, George Eden, of Doddington Hall, Lincs, a unicorn's head arg., gorged with a collar, charged with three cinquefoils. *All for the best.* *cf.* 49. 11
Jarvis, a hawk's head couped holding in the beak a lure arg., between two wings barry of six of the last and gu.
Jary, Robert Herbert Heath, of St. Andrew's House, Burlingham, Norf., issuing out of clouds two arms in armour embowed ppr., the hands also ppr., holding a rose gu. *Mens conscia recti.* 252. 18
Jason, Bart. (*extinct*), of Broad Somerford, Wilts, on a chapeau gu., turned up erm., a pegasus salient with wings addorsed, holding in the mouth a burr ppr.
Jasper of London, a standard arg., charged with a cross gu. 176. 13
Jaudrill, a demi-antelope gu., holding between the feet an escutcheon or. 126. 1
Jaupin, a demi-greyhound salient ppr. 60. 11
Jausselin of London and Essex, a falcon's leg erased at the thigh gu., belled or. 113. 8
Javel, a lion rampant holding in the dexter paw a branch of laurel. *cf.* 1. 13
Jawderill, an antelope's head arg., gorged with a belt and buckle.
Jay, on a ducal coronet or, a griffin sejant az., resting the dexter claw on an escutcheon gu. 62. 11
Jay, Scotland, a lion's gamb holding a thistle, all ppr. 37. 6
Jaye of London and Norf., an otter passant ppr. *cf.* 134. 5
Jaye of Dorking, Surrey, out of a ducal coronet per pale or and az., a camel's head sa., bezantée. *cf.* 132. 6
Jeaffreson of Dallingham House, Cambs, a talbot's head erased arg., eared gu. 56. 2
Jeakes of Taynuilt, Great Malvern, a lion sejant supporting with his dexter paw a lily slipped and leaved. *Labor omnia vincit.*
Jeane, a swan with wings addorsed devouring a trout, all ppr. 99. 10
Jeanes or **Jeans,** a decrescent or. 163. 1
Jebb, Ireland, two rods raguly in saltier, banded. 147. 11
Jebb, on a serpent nowed, a falcon rising, all ppr. *cf.* 86. 3
Jebb, Joshua Gladwyn, Barnby Moor House, East Retford, Notts, a falcon tiring ppr., belled or, standing on a lure fessewise arg.
Jeddon, a leopard's head. 22. 10
Jee, Deputy-Inspector General Joseph, C.B., of Hart's Hill, Warw., a gauntlet arg., garnished at the wrist or, holding a sword of the first, hilt and pommel or. *In fortitudo mea.* 211. 4
Jeffcoat of Newlands, Rochester, Kent, a dovecote within park pales ppr. *Dum spiro spero.*
Jeffcock of Wolverhampton, in front of a mount of coal, therefrom issuant a dexter arm embowed, grasping a coal-pick, all ppr., a cross patée arg. *Persevere.*
Jeffcott or **Jephcott,** Worcs., Northamp., and Ireland, a boar passant. 40. 9
Jefferay of Malling, Sussex, a lion's head erased arg., ducally crowned az. 18. 8
Jeffereys, a demi-lion rampant or, holding between its paws a chaplet vert.
Jefferies, a lion's head erased az., collared arg., charged with three roses gu. *cf.* 18. 6
Jefferis, a lion rampant sa. 1. 10
Jefferis, Arthur Henry, Esquire, Eastbourne, West Didsbury, Lancs, on a rock arg., a castle with two towers domed, all or. *Stand firm.* 283. 7
Jefferson of London and Yorks, a demi-griffin az., collared or, holding between its claws a bezant.
Jefferson, John Ingleby, Standard House, Northallerton, a demi-griffin segreant, collared, and holding between the claws a bezant.
Jefferson, Joseph John Dunnington, of Thicket Priory, Yorks: (1) A griffin sejant with wings endorsed arg., gorged with a collar gemel az., and holding in the beak a lily slipped ppr. (*for Jefferson*). (2) A horse courant arg., gorged with a collar gu., charged with a bezant between two annulets or (*for Dunnington*). *A cruce salus.*
Jefferson, a talbot's head erased arg., eared gu. 56. 2
Jefferson, a wolf's head erased. 30. 8
Jeffery, a demi-lion rampant holding a scimitar ppr. 14. 10
Jefferyes, Worcs.: (1) On a rock arg., a castle or, the two towers domed. 157. 1. (2) On a mount vert, a castle arg.
Jefferyes or **Geffreys** of Clifton and Corncastle, Worcs., on a rock arg., a castle with two towers or, the towers domed. 157. 1
Jefferyes of Little Bursted, Essex, out of a mural coronet or, a lion's head az., ducally crowned of the first. *cf.* 19. 12
Jefferyes of London, a lion's head erased arg., charged with three billets sa. *cf.* 17. 8
Jefferyes or **Jefferys,** a lion's head erased arg. 17. 8
Jefferyes and **Jeffries,** a lily and a holly-branch in saltier ppr. 151. 10
Jefferyes of Earl's Croom, Worcs., on a mount vert, a sea-pie with wings expanded, ash colour, beaked and legged gu.
Jefferys, by a tree ppr., a panther passant resting the dexter fore-paw on an anchor.
Jefferys, a demi-lion rampant or, holding between its paws a chaplet vert.
Jeffrey, on a ducal coronet or, a martlet sa. 95. 12
Jeffrey, Scotland, a star of six rays. *Phœbus, lux in tenebris.* 164. 3
Jeffrey of Edinburgh, the sun rising from a cloud ppr. *Post nubila Phœbus.* 162. 5
Jeffrey, Thomas, Esquire, of 23, Chester Street, Edinburgh, same crest and motto. 162. 5
Jeffreys, a wolf's head couped sa. 30. 5
Jeffreys, Shropsh., a lion's head erased sa., gorged with a wreath. *Supra spem spero.* 17. 10
Jeffreys and **Jeffries,** a demi-lion rampant or, holding a garland of laurel vert.
Jeffreys, John, Esquire, B.A., J.P., of Canterton Manor, Lyndhurst, Hants, a demi-lion rampant or, holding in the dexter paw a laurel wreath ppr.
Jeffreys, Rt. Hon. Arthur Frederick, Esquire, P.C., M.P., J.P., D.L., C.C., of Burkham, near Alton, Hants, a demi-lion rampant or, holding in the dexter paw a laurel wreath ppr. *Pob dawn o Dduw.*
Jeffreys and **Jeffries,** Shropsh., a demi-lion rampant arg. 10. 2
Jeffries, a tower triple-towered or. 157. 6
Jeffryes, *see* Jefferyes and Jeffreys.

Jeffryes of Chiddingley, Sussex, a lion's head erased arg. 17. 8
Jeffryes of London, a lion's head erased arg., charged with three billets sa., two and one. *cf.* 17. 8
Jeffryes of the Priory, Breconsh., on the stump of a tree couped and sprouting out new branches vert, a stork arg. 105. 12
Jeffs, a pelican's head erased vulning itself, all ppr. 98. 2
Jeffson of London, *see* Jephson.
Jeffson or **Jephson** of London, an arm couped at the elbow and erect, habited, paly of four arg. and az., cuffed of the first, thereon a bend gu., holding in the hand a bunch of roses ppr., stalked and leaved vert.
Jegon, a pelican or, vulning itself gu. 98. 1
Jegon or **Jeggings,** an eagle with wings expanded or, beaked arg. 77. 5
Jehangier of Cowasjee, on a mount vert, a low pillar, the base and capital masoned, flames of fire issuing therefrom, all ppr. *Burning I shine.*
Jejeebhoy, Sir Jamsetjee, Bart., C.S.I., a Parsi Merchant, J.P., and a Member of the Legislative Council of Bombay, of Mazagone Castle, Bombay, a mount vert, thereon a peacock amidst wheat, and in the beak an ear of wheat, all ppr. *Industry and liberality.* 103. 9
Jeken and **Jekin** of Dover, Kent, a demi-lion regardant erm., semée of crescents gu., holding between the paws a pheon sa.
Jekyl and **Jekyll** of Castle Hedingham, Essex, a horse's head couped arg., maned and bridled sa., studded and tasselled or. 51. 5
Jekyll, Edward Joseph, Esquire, of Higham, Bury, near Ampthill, Beds, a nag's head couped arg., maned and bridled sa., studded and tasselled or. *In Deo confido.* 267. 9
Jekyll, Herbert, Esquire, C.M.G., of 3, Green Street, Park Lane, W., and Munstead House, Godalming, same crest and motto.
Jekyll, Middx., a horse's head, paly wavy arg. and sa., bridled or. 51. 5
Jelf of Oaklands Park, Glouc., and London, a stork with wings elevated arg., beaked and legged gu., holding in the beak a trefoil slipped vert, and charged on the breast with a cross patée of the second, holding in the dexter claw a fleur-de-lis or.
Jelf, Arthur Richard, Esquire, of Oak House, Carlton Road, Putney Hill, S.W., a stork with wings elevated arg., beaked and legged gu., in the beak a trefoil slipped vert, and on the breast a cross patée of the second, the dexter claw resting on a fleur-de-lis or.
Jelf, Canon of Rochester, same crest and motto.
Jelf, Colonel Richard Henry, C.M.G., R.E., of Governor's House, Woolwich, 9, Egerton Gardens, S.W., and Offcote Hurst, Ashbourne, Derbysh., same crest and motto.
Jelf-Petit, Louis William, Esquire, of Bodhyfyrd, Llanrwst, same crest and motto.
Jelley and **Jelly,** a garb entwined by two snakes ppr. 153. 3
Jellicoe, a cherub or. 189. 9
Jellicoe, Shropsh., a demi-lion rampant holding in his dexter paw a dagger erect. *cf.* 14. 12
Jelter, a cat sejant gardant or. 26. 8
Jemmet, Rev. Francis, B.C.L., M.A., of the Vicarage, Feltham, Middx., and of Ashford, Kent, a unicorn's head erased. *Cui fidas vide.* 49. 5
Jenings, a dove volant az., legged arg. *cf.* 93. 10
Jenins and **Jenyns** of London, a cat's head erased gardant gu., bezantée, holding in the mouth a cross formée fitchée arg.
Jenison, out of a ducal coronet or, a dragon's head az. 72. 4
Jenkens, a wyvern gu., standing on a tilting-spear without bur or vamplate, and broken off at the point or, in its mouth the remaining part of the shaft armed arg. 69. 4
Jenkenson and **Jenkinson** of London, a sea-horse assurgent or, maned az., supporting a cross patée gu.
Jenkes, Shropsh., a dexter arm embowed, vested sa., cuffed arg., enfiled with a ducal coronet or, grasping in the hand ppr. a sword of the second, hilt and pommel of the third. *cf.* 204. 1
Jenkin, Cornw.: (1) A lion rampant regardant sa. 2. 3. (2) On a mural coronet sa., a lion passant regardant or. *cf.* 6. 10
Jenkin of Folkestone, Kent, on a mural coronet arg., a lion passant regardant sa. *cf.* 6. 10
Jenkins, Shropsh., a lion rampant regardant sa. 2. 3
Jenkins of the Grove and of Nant-y-Groes, Radnorsh., a lion rampant or, holding between the fore-paws an escallop gu., and resting the dexter hind-paw on a plate charged with a heart of the second. *Byw a gadael byw.* 225. 8
Jenkins, Shropsh., a lion passant regardant or, armed and langued gu. 6. 1
Jenkins, Shropsh., on a mural coronet sa., a lion passant regardant or. *Perge sed caute.* *cf.* 6. 10
Jenkins, Major-General Charles Vanbrugh Jones, of Cruckton Hall and Charlton Hill, Shropsh., upon a mural coronet sa., a lion passant regardant or, supporting with the dexter paw an escutcheon barry of six az. and erm., charged with an annulet or. *Perge sed caute.* *cf.* 6. 10
Jenkins, Charles Edward, Esquire, of Cruckton Hall, Shrewsbury, on a mural coronet sa., a lion passant regardant or, supporting with the dexter paw an escutcheon barry of six az. and erm., charged with an annulet or. *Perge sed caute.*
Jenkins, Edgar Kynnersley, of Charlton Hill, near Shrewsbury, and 7, Westbourne Crescent, Hyde Park, W., same crest and motto.
Jenkins of Caerleon, Monm., a lion sa., charged with two fleur-de-lis or, and resting the dexter paw on an escarbuncle of the last.
Jenkins, Wales, a battle-axe, the handle or, the head ppr. 172. 3
Jenkins, Ireland, on a ducal coronet or, a talbot statant arg., collared and lined gu. *cf.* 54. 9
Jenkins, a lion's gamb erased ppr., holding a bezant. 39. 13
Jenkins, Sir John Jones, of the Grange, Swansea, a lion's gamb erect and erased arg., holding a pellet charged with a fleur-de-lis or, all between two fleurs-de-lis, also arg. *Perseverance.* 37. 13
Jenkins, seven arrows, one in pale and six in saltier, ppr., encircled with an annulet or. *cf.* 173. 7
Jenkinson, Earl of Liverpool, *see* Liverpool.
Jenkinson of London and Lincs, a sea-horse ppr. 46. 2
Jenkinson of London and Shropsh., a sea-horse assurgent or, maned az., supporting a cross patée gu.
Jenkinson, Norf., a sea-horse or, finned gu. 46. 2
Jenkinson, a sea-horse az., winged or.
Jenkinson, Sir George Banks, Bart., of Hawkesbury, Glouc., a sea-horse assurgent or, maned az., holding between the feet a cross patée gu. *Pareo non servio.* 285. 14
Jenkinson of London, a sea-horse assurgent per pale or and az., crined gu.
Jenkinson, Bart. (*extinct*), of Walton, Derbysh., a sea-horse's head couped az., crined or, gorged with two barrulets of the same.
Jenkinson, a sea-horse's head couped arg., crined gu., gorged with a fess az.
Jenkinson, Derbysh., a sea-horse's head couped az., crined or, gorged with two barrulets of the last.
Jenkinson of Tunstal, Norf., and Oulton, Suff., a bull's head arg., crined sa., the horns twisted or and of the second. *cf.* 44. 3
Jenkinson, Ireland, out of a ducal coronet az., a demi-lion rampant, holding a palm-branch vert. *cf.* 16. 11
Jenks, out of a ducal coronet or, a griffin's head ppr. 67. 9
Jenkyns, Yorks, on a ducal coronet sa., a lion rampant regardant or. *cf.* 2. 3
Jenkyns, a wyvern gu., standing on a tilting-spear without bur or vamplate, and broken off at the point or, holding in its mouth the other part of the shaft armed arg. 69. 4
Jennens of Acton, Suff., a griffin's head couped between two wings inverted ppr., holding in the beak a plummet pendent sa.
Jenner of London, a covered cup or, between two swords in saltier arg., hilts and pommels of the first. 171. 13
Jenner, Hugh, Esquire, of Venn Wood, near Hereford, and Summerfield, Weston Park, Bath, two swords in saltire arg., hilted and pommelled or, supporting a covered cup of the last.
Jenner, Henry, Esquire, of the Old House, Bushey Heath, Herts, same crest. *A Deo Rex, a Rege lex.*
Jenner-Fust, Herbert, Esquire, LL.D., of Hill Court, Glouc.: (1) A horse at full speed arg. (*for Fust*). (2) Two swords in saltire arg., hilted and pommelled or, supporting a covered cup of the last (*for Jenner*). *Terrena per vices sunt aliena.*
Jenner of Wenvoe, Glamorgansh., same crest.

Jenner of London, a greyhound sejant arg. *Constans et fidelis.* 59. 4
Jenner, Essex, same crest. 59. 4
Jenner, Sir Walter Kentish William, Bart., of Harley Street, Cavendish Square, Marylebone, Middx., on a mount vert, a lamp with three branches arg., suspended by three chains or, fired ppr. *Fide et labore.* 272. 6
Jennerson, two swords in saltier supporting a scimitar in fess, all ppr., and between the points of the swords a covered cup or. *cf.* 171. 13
Jennet, out of a ducal coronet or, a dexter arm embowed in mail ppr., holding in the hand a sword arg., hilt of the first. *cf.* 195. 10
Jennet or **Jennett,** Ireland, a hind's head gu. 124. 1
Jenney, on a glove in fesse arg., a hawk or, belled of the last. 86. 12
Jenney, Stewart William, Drayton Lodge, Tring, same crest.
Jenney of Bredfield House, Suff., same crest.
Jenney of Frisby Hall, Derbysh., same crest. *Deus mihi providebit.*
Jenning, Beds, a hawk rising az. 88. 2
Jenning, on a mount vert, a wolf passant erm., in front of a cross calvary gu.
Jenninges and **Jennings,** a jay ppr.
Jennings, Ireland, out of a mural coronet az., a garb or, thereon a sparrow ppr. 153. 9
Jennings of Burton Pynsent, Dorset, a redbreast upon a morion. *cf.* 108. 11
Jennings of Minster Lea, Reigate, Surrey, a falcon rising with wings expanded and inverted, belled ppr. *Heb dduw heb ddim duw a digon.* 87. 1
Jennings of Oldcastle, Chesh., a wolf's head erased per pale arg. and vert. 30. 8
Jennings, Shropsh., same crest. *Ut prosim aliis.*
Jennings, a wolf's head per pale arg. and sa. 30. 5
Jennings of York, a griffin's head couped between two wings ppr., holding in the beak a plummet pendent sa.
Jennings of Ripon and Silsden, Yorks, a griffin's head couped between two wings ppr., holding in the beak a plummet pendent sa.
Jennings, Richard Edward, Esquire, J.P., Barrister-at-Law, of Gellideg, Kidwelly, Carmarthensh., and 15, Palmeira Mansions, Brighton, same crest.
Jennings of London, a demi-dragon erminois, the wings addorsed gu., erased of the last, holding a battle-axe erect az. *Il buon tempo verra.*
Jennings of the Shrubbery, Dover, a dragon passant vair, winged or, the dexter claw resting on an escutcheon az., charged with a toison-d'or.
Jennings, a demi-lion rampant or, holding the upper part of a spear-shaft of the same.
Jennings of Dublin, out of a ducal coronet or, a demi-lion rampant sa., holding in the paws a battle-axe ppr. *cf.* 16. 10
Jennins, a griffin statant gu., holding a buckle or. 63. 7
Jennins, Hants, a demi-griffin ppr., holding in its beak a plummet sa.
Jennoway, a horned owl. *Je pense.* 96. 5
Jenny, Suff., a falconer's hand within a glove in fess ppr., thereon a falcon perched or. 86. 14
Jenny, a falcon rising and belled or. 88. 2
Jenny, out of a ducal coronet or, an arm in armour brandishing a scimitar, all ppr. 209. 11
Jennyns, Middx., Worcs., Cambs, and of Ipsley, Warw., a leopard's head erased and gardant gu., bezantée, holding in the mouth a cross formée fitched arg.
Jenoure and **Jenoyre,** Essex, a greyhound sejant. *In pretium persevero.* 59. 4
Jenssen of London, a quatrefoil stalked and leaved vert.
Jeny, a hand fessewise issuing from a cloud ppr., holding a cross patée fitched arg. 223. 6
Jenynge, Hants, and of Hesse, Middx., a demi-lion erased and rampant or, supporting a spear erect of the first, headed az.
Jenynges, Suff., a demi-savage sa., collared about the neck or, wreathed round the temples of the last and vert, holding in his dexter hand a halberd az., the staff gu.
Jenynges, a demi-man vested sa., cap vert, holding in his dexter hand a battle-axe az.
Jenyns, Shropsh., a wolf's head erased per pale arg. and vert. *Ut prosim aliis.* 30. 8
Jenyns, Roger William Bulwer, Bottisham Hall, Cambridge, a demi-lion rampant or, supporting a spear erect of the first, headed az. *Ignavis nunquam.*
Jephson, Ireland, a hind trippant or. 124. 12
Jephson, Ireland, a lion's head erased arg., between two palm-branches vert. *Virtus sub pondere crescit.* *cf.* 17. 7
Jephson of London, a cubit arm erect, vested paly of four arg. and az., cuffed of the first, thereon a bend gu., holding in the hand a bunch of roses ppr., stalked and leaved vert.
Jephson, Bart., of Spring Vale, Dorset, a cubit arm vested paly arg. and az., cuffed of the second, surmounted of a bend gu., holding in the hand a pansy or heartsease ppr. *Veritas magna est.* 205. 10
Jephson-Norreys, late Sir Charles Denham Orlando, Bart. (*extinct*), upon a mount vert, a raven rising ppr. *Loyalement je sers.*
Jepine, a lion's head erased or, billettée sa., and ducally crowned of the first. *cf.* 18. 8
Jeppe of Sutton's Court, Somers., an eagle displayed ppr 75. 2
Jerard or **Jerrard** of Pamford, Somers., an eagle displayed with two heads or, charged with a saltier sa. 74. 1
Jercy, a phœnix in flames ppr. 82. 2
Jeremy, an arm in armour embowed, gauntleted, and wielding a battle-axe, all ppr. 200. 6
Jermain and **Jermayne,** a gilliflower ppr. 151. 8
Jermin or **Jermyn** of Wickham Bishop, Essex, a buck's head cabossed sa., between two wings arg.
Jermy and **Jermyn,** a griffin passant gu. 63. 2
Jermyn, Earl, *see* Bristol, Marquess.
Jermyn, Sussex and Devonsh., a tiger's head erased gu.
Jermyn, Suff., a talbot passant arg., gorged with a ducal coronet or. *cf.* 54. 1
Jermyn, Suff., out of a ducal coronet or, a greyhound's head ppr., collared of the first. *cf.* 61. 7
Jermyn, Suff., a greyhound's head sa., gorged with a bar gemelle or. *cf.* 61. 2
Jerningham, Baron Stafford, *see* Stafford.
Jerningham, Norf., on a ducal coronet or, a demi-falcon with wings expanded ppr. 88. 10
Jerningham, Sir Hubert Edward Henry, K.C.M.G., of 14, Bruton Street, W., and Longridge Towers, Berwick, out of a ducal coronet or, a demi-falcon with wings displayed ppr.
Jerningham, Norf. and Suff., out of a ducal coronet or, a demi-falcon displayed arg. *cf.* 88. 10
Jersey, Earl of (Villiers), Middleton Park, Bicester, Oxford: (1) A lion rampant arg., ducally crowned or (*for Villiers*). 1. 12. (2) On a rock ppr., an eagle rising arg., ducally gorged or, holding in the beak an adder ppr., and charged on the breast for distinction with an ermine spot (*for Child*). *Fidei coticula crux.* *cf.* 77. 8
Jersey, a phœnix in flames ppr. 82. 2
Jerveis, Worcs., and **Jervis** and **Jervois,** Hants, an heraldic tiger's head sa. 25. 4
Jervis, Viscount St. Vincent, *see* St. Vincent.
Jervis, Swynfen John, Esquire, of Chatcull, Eccleshall, Staffs, and Staff College, Camberley, Surrey, between two wings sa., a griffin's head erased or, gorged with a collar gu., pendent therefrom an escutcheon az., charged with a boar's head couped arg.
Jervis of Petling, Leics., a hawk's head or, between two wings erm. 89. 1
Jervis-White-Jervis, Sir John Henry, Bart., of Ballyclis, co. Wexford: (1) A martlet or (*for Jervis*). 95. 2. (2) Three arrows, one in fesse and two in saltire, gu., headed or, flighted arg., enwreathed (*for White*). *Venale nec auro.*
Jervis-White of Ferns and Gorey, co. Wexford, Ballylenan, co. Cavan, and Heathfield, co. Wexford: (1) A martlet or. (2) Three arrows, two in saltire, one in fesse.
Jervois, the late Sir William Francis Drummond, G.C.M.G., K.C.M.G., C.B., on a wreath of the colours an ostrich-feather erect arg., between two grenades fired ppr.
Jervoise: (1) An heraldic tiger's head sa. (*for Jervoise*). 25. 4. (2) A plume of five ostrich-feathers arg. (*for Ellis*). 115. 1
Jervoise, Francis Henry Tristram, Esquire, J.P., of Herriard Park, Basingstoke, an heraldic tiger's head sa. *Virtutis præmium laus.*
Jervoise, Clarke-, Sir Henry, Bart., of Idsworth Park, Hants: (1) An heraldic tiger's head sa. (*for Jervoise*). (2) Within a gem ring or, set with a diamond ppr., a roundle per pale gu. and az., charged with a pheon arg. (*for Clarke*).

Jervys, a hand ppr., holding an eagle's leg erased at the thigh gu. 220. 12

Jerworth, a crane's head couped ppr. 104. 5

Jesse of Llanbedro Hall, Denbighsh., a lion sejant supporting an escutcheon gu. *cf.* 8. 2

Jessel, Sir Charles James, Bart., M.A., D.L., of Ladham House, Goudhurst, Kent, a torch fessewise fired ppr., surmounted by an eagle volant arg., holding in the beak a pearl, also arg. 284. 4

Jessel, Captain Herbert Merton, of 50, Mount Street, Park Lane, W., same crest. *Persevere.*

Jesson, an arm erect vested paly of six arg. and az., charged with a bend gu., holding in the hand ppr. a cinquefoil purp., leaved vert. *cf.* 205. 10

Jesson, Warw., a dexter arm ppr., vested gu., charged with a bend arg., cuffed or, holding in the hand a rose of the second stalked and leaved vert. *cf.* 205. 10

Jesson of Oakwood, Staffs, a cubit arm erect, vested az., charged with a bend embattled counter-embattled and cuffed arg., holding in the hand ppr. a rose gu., slipped vert. *Consilii taciturnitas nutrix.*

Jessop, Ireland, a goat's head erased sa., armed and collared or. *cf.* 128. 7

Jessop, a moorcock ppr.

Jessop of Doory, Longford, a dove holding in its beak an olive-branch ppr. *Pax et amor.* 92. 5

Jessop, a cockatrice's head erased purp., combed gu., winged ppr. 68. 12

Jessop, John De Burgh, Esquire, of Overton Hall, Ashover, near Chesterfield, a cockatrice's head couped ppr., charged with two bars arg., holding in the beak a trefoil slipped vert, between two wings of the first, each charged with a cross couped of the second. *Pax et amor.*

Jessop of Mount Jessop, co. Longford, Ireland, a cockatrice's head ppr., combed and wattled, and the wings displayed gu., each charged with a trefoil slipped arg. *cf.* 68. 8

Jessop, Walter B., Esquire, of 8, Bushmead Avenue, Bedford, Beds, on a branch fesseways erased at the dexter and couped at the sinister, a dove ppr., within a laurel-branch in orle issuing from the dexter side. *Præmia virtutis honores.*

Jessop of Bromhall, Yorks, a turtle-dove standing on an olive-branch which is bent over its head ppr.

Jessope, Dorset, a cockatrice displayed vert, combed and wattled gu. 68. 14

Jessope, Jessopp, or **Jessup,** a man on horseback at a charge, holding in his hand a broken tilting-spear ppr. 189. 5

Jett of London, out of rays of the sun or, a demi-swan with wings elevated sa., holding in the beak an arrow arg. 189. 5

Jetter of Bayton, Ellowe, and Lowestoft, Suff., out of a ducal coronet or, a cubit arm erect habited in mail, holding in the hand, all ppr., the blade of a broken sword arg.

Jetter, out of a ducal coronet an arm erect holding a broken spear, all ppr. *cf.* 214. 10

Jeudwine, Canon, M.A., of Harlaxton Rectory, Grantham, Lincs, a tower ppr.

Jeune, Rt. Hon. Sir Francis Henry, of Arlington Manor, Newbury, Berks, between the attires of a stag affixed to the scalp an estoile, all arg. *Faire sans dire.* 123. 2

Jeune, Evan Browell, Esquire, J.P., of the Manor House, Lynmouth, Barnstaple, same crest and motto.

Jevers, a demi-lion rampant or, collared sa. 10. 9

Jevon, Staffs, a saltire or, between two palm-branches ppr.

Jewel, an oak-branch fructed ppr. 151. 3

Jewell of Bowden, Devonsh., a cubit arm vested az., cuffed arg., holding in the hand ppr. a gilliflower gu., stalked and leaved vert.

Jewell, Durh., same crest. *Tota gloriosa filia regis intrinsecus.*

Jewell, Scotland, a dexter hand holding a gilliflower ppr.

Jewers, between the horns of a crescent a buckle ppr. 163. 15

Jewitt of Matlock Bridge, Derbysh., a demi-pegasus regardant, wings addorsed arg., holding between the legs a flag-staff, thereon a flag floating to the dexter of the same, charged with a cross of St. George gu. *Non sibi.* 47. 8

Jewkes, Lancs and Warw., a demi-lion ducally crowned. 10. 11

Jewsbury, Glouc., on a mount vert, a martlet or. 95. 7

Jex of Lowestoft, Suff., a horse's head arg., maned or, holding in his mouth a broken spear of the last.

Jex-Blake, F. W., Esquire, of Swanton-Abbots, Norf.: (1) A morion ppr., thereon a martlet arg. (*for Blake*). (2) A horse's head arg., maned or, erased gu., holding in the mouth a broken tilting-spear, also or (*for Jex*). *Bene præparatum pectus.*

Jeyes, Philadelphus, Esquire, Holly Lodge, Boughton, Northamp., out of a ducal coronet a camel's head ppr., bezantée. *Tenax et fidelis.*

Jeynes, an arm erect holding a battle-axe. 213. 12

Jeynor, Essex, a greyhound sejant or. 59. 4

Jeynor, a greyhound sejant collared. *cf.* 59. 2

Jeys, a horse passant arg. 52. 6

Joanes of Brimsey, Somers., a tiger's head erased.

Joanes of London and Worcs., the sun in his splendour or. 162. 2

Joanes, a greyhound's head arg., between two roses gu., slipped and leaved ppr. 61. 11

Joass of Collinwort, Banffsh., Scotland, a sand-glass winged. *Cogit amor.* 113. 11

Job, Lancs, out of a ducal coronet a bull's head. 44. 11

Jobber, Staffs, a fox sejant ppr. 32. 11

Jobling of Newton Hall, Northumb., a demi-lion rampant holding a battle-axe ppr. *For my country.* 15. 4

Jobling, same crest. *Per ardua ad alta.*

Jobson of Snayth, Yorks, on a sinister gauntlet arg., a falcon close or. *cf.* 86. 13

Joce, an antelope trippant ppr. 126. 6

Jocelyn, Earl of Roden, *see* Roden.

Jocelyn or **Jocelyne,** Herts, a falcon's leg erased à la quise ppr., belled or. *Faire mon devoir.* 113. 8

Jockel of Edinburgh, the mast gu., and the sail of a ship arg., with pennon flotant at top az., tackling and yards ppr. *Fiduciâ et labore.* 160. 11

Joddrell, on a chapeau a greyhound sejant ppr. *cf.* 59. 4

Jodrell, *see* Cotton-Jodrell.

Jodrell, Chesh., a cock's head and neck couped or, the wings elevated arg., combed and wattled gu.

Jodrell, Herbert Henry, Esquire, a cock's head and neck couped, the wings erect or, combed and jelloped gu., issuant out of a chaplet of roses of the last, barbed and seeded ppr., and for distinction charged on the neck with a cross crosslet sa. 305. 7

Jodrell, Derbysh., a cock's head and neck couped, wings erect or, combed and jelloped gu., issuing from a chaplet of roses barbed and seeded ppr. 305. 7

Jodrell, Sir Alfred, Bart., D.L., of Sall Park, Norf., a demi-cock with wings erected and endorsed or, combed and wattled gu., issuant out of a wreath of roses of the last, barbed and seeded of the first. *Non sibi, sed patriæ natus.* 305. 7

Joel, a hare lodged among grass ppr. 136. 12

Joel, Solomon Barnato, of Great Stanhope Street, London, W., a lion passant ppr., holding in the mouth a sprig of three roses, slipped, leaved, barbed, and seeded, also ppr., supporting with the dexter fore-paw an antique shield az., ornamented and charged with a rose or. *Facta non verba.*

John, Cornw., an arm in armour embowed holding in the hand a sword. 195. 2

John, on two battle-axes in saltier ppr., the blades or, a Cornish chough sa., beaked and membered gu.

John, a demi-lion rampant ppr. 10. 2

Johnes, Monm., two battle-axes in saltier ppr., the handles or. 172. 4

Johnes, Lancs, out of a ducal coronet a plume of five ostrich-feathers. *Vince malum bono.* 114. 13

Johnes of London, a lion rampant or, supporting an anchor az., the flukes of the first.

Johnes, Hills-, Lieutenant-General Sir James, G.C.B., V.C., Dolaucothy, Carmarthensh.: (1) On two halberts saltirewise gu., headed or, a raven sa. charged on the breast with a cross crosslet or, for difference (*for Johnes*). (2) On a mount vert, in front of the shaft of a broken tilting-spear erect ppr., a horse courant arg. guttée-de-sang, holding in the mouth the other part of the spear, also ppr. *Deus pascit corvos.—In cœlo confidimus.*

Johns, on a mural coronet ppr., a serpent nowed vert. 142. 12

Johns of Trewince, Cornw., two battle-axes in saltier ppr. 172. 4

Johns of Glasgow, Scotland, a crow ppr. *Semper sic.* 107. 14

Johns, Beldam-, of Windmill Lodge, Bishop Stortford, Herts, upon a mount vert, a garb banded or, pendent from the band by a ring, also or, an escutcheon of the first charged with a dexter hand couped at the wrist of the second. *Dat Deus incrementum.*

Johnson, Bart., Middx., an arm embowed, the hand grasping a sword ppr. *Deo regique liber.* 201. 4

Johnson, late Sir William Gilleland, of Belfast, an arm in armour embowed grasping in the hand a sword, all ppr., between two wings erect az. *Nunquam non paratus.*

Johnson of Kittlesworth, Durh., a dexter arm in armour embowed firing a pistol, all ppr. 197. 12

Johnson of Wilmslow, Chesh., a dexter arm embowed firing a pistol, all ppr. *Fugite fures omnes.* 200. 11

Johnson, Dixon-, of Aykleyheads, Durh.: (1) Same as above. (2) A cubit arm erect vested erminois, cuffed arg., in the hand a roundle of the first. *Fortiter et sincere.*

Johnson, Chesh., an arm in armour, holding in the hand, all ppr., an arrow arg., with a pheon's head or.

Johnson of Kennal Manor, Chislehurst, Kent, in front of a dexter arm embowed in armour ppr., the hand, also ppr., grasping a javelin in bend sinister, pheoned or, and entiled with a chaplet of roses gu., two branches of oak in saltire vert. 198. 8

Johnson, Herbert Alfred, Esquire, of Farnah Hall, near Derby, in front of a dexter arm embowed in armour ppr., the hand grasping a javelin in bend sinister, pheoned or, and entiled with a chaplet of roses gu., two branches of oak in saltire vert. *Virtus patientia veritas.* (Granted to the late Richard Johnson, Esquire, of the County Palatine of Lancaster.) 198. 8

Johnson, out of a mural coronet gu., a cubit arm erect vested or, turned up arg., holding in the hand ppr. a scimitar of the third, hilt of the second.

Johnson, Kent, an arm erect vested per pale az. and or, holding in the hand ppr. a cross patonce or. 207. 6

Johnson of Limehouse, Middx., a triangular harrow or. 178. 4

Johnson of Beaconsfield, Bucks, a cubit arm habited or, grasping in the hand ppr. a cross flory, also or. *cf.* 207. 6

Johnson, Bart., of Twickenham, Middx., a hand gu., encircled with a ducal crown or, grasping a sword ppr., pommel and hilt or. *Nec aspera terrent.* 212. 7

Johnson of Luffenham, Rutl., a lion's head gu., crowned or, between two ostrich-feathers arg.

Johnson, Rutl. and Notts: (1) A lion's head erased gu., ducally crowned or, between two ostrich-feathers arg. (2) Out of a ducal coronet arg., a leopard's head or. 23. 11

Johnson, a lion's head gardant erased per pale gu. and sa., bezantée, collared or.

Johnson of London, a demi-lion rampant ppr. 10. 2

Johnson, Durh., a demi-lion rampant regardant, gorged with a palm-branch arg.

Johnson, a lion statant gardant royally crowned. *cf.* 4. 1

Johnson, Honourable George Randall, of Fitzherbert Terrace, Wellington, and the Arai, Poverty Bay, New Zealand, and also of Stalham and Tunstead, Norf., England, Member of the Legislative Council of New Zealand; and James Woodbine Johnson, Esquire, J.P., of Wairakaia, Gisborne, Poverty Bay, New Zealand, Captain in the New Zealand Militia, a lion rampant erminois, holding in the dexter fore-paw a mullet sa., the dexter hind-paw resting on a cross moline gu. *Strenue et prospere.*

Johnson of London, an heraldic tiger's head erminois, maned arg. 25. 4

Johnson, Middx. and Heref., an heraldic tiger's head erased or. *cf.* 25. 4

Johnson of Great Yarmouth, Norf., out of a ducal coronet or, a leopard's head and neck gu. 23. 11

Johnson, Durh., a tiger's head couped sa., bezantée.

Johnson, Durh., a leopard's head sa., bezantée, flames issuing from the mouth and ears.

Johnson of Twyzell, Durh., a leopard's face per pale az. and sa., bezantee, from the mouth and ears flames issuant ppr.

Johnson, a pheon gu., surmounted by a star of eight points or. *cf.* 174. 11

Johnson of Bury, Saxmundham, and Bildeston, Suff., a leopard's head erased ppr., collared or. *Fortiter in re, suaviter in modo.* *cf.* 22. 12

Johnson of Milton Bryant, Beds, on a chapeau gu., turned up erm., an ounce's head erased arg. *cf.* 23. 10

Johnson of Gainsborough, Lincs, a leopard passant gardant sa., platée and bezantée. *cf.* 24. 4

Johnson, a wolf passant, holding in its mouth a sprig of woodbine in full blossom, all ppr. *cf.* 28. 10

Johnson, John William Denne, Esquire, of Temple Belwood, Lincs, and Sarre Court, Westgate-on-Sea: (1) Upon a mount vert, a wolf passant sa., holding in the mouth a branch of woodbine ppr. (*for Johnson*). (2) A man's head affrontée between two bulrushes ppr. (*for Hilton*). *Tant que je puis.*

Johnson, Staffs and Suff., on a mount vert, an ibex sejant erm., ducally gorged, crined, and tufted or, attired arg.

Johnson, Vivian Abbott, Esquire, of Sheffield, Yorks, same crest. *Semper viridis.*

Johnson, Oliver, Esquire, Avondale Road, Hillsborough, same crest and motto.

Johnson, on a mount vert, a talbot couchant arg., collared and chained or.

Johnson, Kent, Worcs., and Glouc., out of a ducal coronet or, a nag's head sa. 51. 7

Johnson, out of a ducal coronet a demi-bear rampant, muzzled and ducally crowned, holding between the paws a sword in pale. *cf.* 34. 10

Johnson, a greyhound's head couped vert, collared or. 61. 2

Johnson, Scotland, a bull's head cabossed sa., armed or. 43. 8

Johnson of London and Yorks, a cock arg., combed and wattled or, charged on the body with three guttés-de-sang. *cf.* 91. 2

Johnson of London, a cock arg., combed and wattled or, standing upon a fasces of the last. *cf.* 91. 2

Johnson, Sir Allen Bayard, K.C.B., of 60, Lexham Gardens, S.W., a tower arg., charged with a crescent for difference, on the battlements thereof a cock ppr. *Vicisti et vivimus.—Nunquam non paratus.* 156. 12

Johnson, Oswald Carnegy, Esquire, B.A., Barrister-at-Law, of the Quillet, Salisbury, a tower arg., thereon a cock ppr. (Above the crest) *Vicisti et vivimus.* (Below the shield) *Nunquam non paratus.*

Johnson of London, out of a ducal coronet a swan's head and neck, all or.

Johnson, Chesh., on a ducal coronet or, an eagle with wings expanded sa.

Johnson of London, an eagle's leg sa. *cf.* 113. 8

Johnson, Charles Plumptre, Esquire, issuant from clouds a serpent nowed holding in the mouth a poppy-head slipped ppr., thereon an eagle rising, also ppr., charged on the breast and each wing with a cross crosslet gu. *In lucem aspiro.*

Johnson, Edward Middleton, Esquire, same crest and motto.

Johnson, Northumb., a stalk of wheat ppr. *Nunquam non paratus.* 154. 1

Johnson of London, a spear-head arg., between two branches of laurel vert, crossing each other over the spear-head.

Johnson of Withcot, Leics., a demi-griffin gu., collared erm., holding between its claws a pheon or.

Johnson, Thomas Fielding, Esquire, of Brookfield, Knighton, near Leics., a demi-griffin gu., holding a pheon in the dexter claw, and resting the sinister on a lozenge or. *Labore et honore.* 252. 17

Johnson, out of a ducal coronet a griffin's head. 67. 9

Johnson of Ulverscroft and Burleigh Field, Leics., a griffin's head erased per fesse arg. and gu., holding in the beak a palmer's scrip of the last.

Johnson of Thwaite, Lincs, Middx., and Norf., out of a ducal coronet per pale arg. and az., two wings expanded counterchanged. 109. 8

Johnson, a man's head couped at the neck affrontée and bearded, all ppr. 190. 12

Johnson of Deanery, Durh., a savage's head couped at the shoulders, bearded and wreathed, all ppr. *Nil admirari.*

Johnson, Northumb. and Durh., in front of a man's head affrontée, couped at the shoulders ppr., wreathed about the temples arg. and gu., two pheons or.

Johnson, late Francis, Esquire, of Low Newton, Northumb., in front of a man's head affrontée, couped at the shoulders ppr., wreathed about the temples arg. and gu., two pheons or. *Nil admirari.*

Johnson, a chevalier in complete armour on horseback at full speed, holding in his dexter hand a sabre. 189. 10

Johnson, a mermaid holding in her dexter hand a sceptre, and in her sinister a mirror, all ppr.

Johnson, Arthur, Esquire, of the Woodlands, Bishop Stortford, Herts, in front of a Passion cross or, an anchor in bend sinister sa. *Fides, spes, caritas.*

Johnson of Long Melford, Suff., and of Tyldesley, Lancs., a spur or, the strap gu., between two wings of the first. 111. 13

Johnson, James, Esquire, of Thurlaston House, Dunchurch, Rugby, in front of two tilting-spears in saltire ppr., a spur or, the whole between two wings, also ppr. *Servabo fidem.*

Johnson of Walton House, Cumb., a spur between two wings, within the spur an estoile, all ppr.

Johnson, Lancs: (1) A spur or, the strap gu., between two wings of the first. 111. 13. (2) A tower in flames. 155. 9

Johnson of Edinburgh, Scotland, a winged spur ppr. *Nunquam non paratus.* 111. 12

Johnson of Rockenham, co. Cork, and Castle Lyons House, Fermoy, on a mural crown ppr., a spur erect or, between two wings expanded arg., each charged with an annulet gu. *Nunquam non paratus.* cf. 111. 13

Johnson, Frederick Ponsonby, Esquire, of Castlesteads, Brampton, Cumb., within a winged spur erect an estoile, all or. *Nunquam non paratus.* cf. 111. 12

Johnson of Runcorn, Chesh., a crescent or, issuant therefrom a pheon sa., all between two wings of the last. *Servabo fidem.*

Johnson, Lancs, a tower in flames. 155. 9

Johnson, Bucks, a castle ppr. 155. 8

Johnson, a sword and a dagger in saltier, the blades arg., hilts and pommels or. cf. 171. 12

Johnson, Ireland, a sword and a key in saltier ppr. 171. 10

Johnson of Ayscough Fee Hall, a ducal coronet. *Onus sub honore.* 228. 10

Johnsonn, a greyhound's head couped vert, collared or. 61. 2

Johnston of Gormack, Scotland, a spur-rowel between two palm-branches in orle, all ppr. *Securior quo paratior.* 146. 13

Johnston of Corehead, a spur or. *Ad arma paratus.* 178. 8

Johnston, Archibald, Esquire, late of 9, Claremont Crescent, Edinburgh, a spur winged or, leathered gu. *Ready, aye ready.* 111. 12

Johnston, Archibald Francis Campbell, Carnsalloch, Dumfriessh., same crest.

Johnston, Bart., Dumfries, a spur with wings or, leathered gu. *Nunquam non paratus.* 111. 12

Johnston of Gartney, a winged spur or, leathered gu. *Cave paratus.* 111. 12

Jhonston of Polton, Edinburgh, a spur ppr., between two wings or. *Sic paratior.* 111. 13

Johnston, Lawson-, George Lawson, Esquire, of Kingswood, Sydenham Hill, Kent, a spur between two wings or. *Nunquam non paratus.*

Johnston, William Elliot Lawson, Esquire, same crest and motto.

Johnston, Scotland, same crest. *Caute et sedulo.*

Johnston, a spur ppr., between two wings arg. 111. 13

Johnston, William, Esquire, of Ballykilbeg, co. Down, same crest.

Johnston of Beaulieu, co. Louth, a winged spur or, leathered gu. *Nunquam non paratus.* 111. 12

Johnston, Rev. George Thompson, Broughton Rectory, Huntingdon, same crest and motto.

Johnston, Andrew, Esquire, J.P., D.L., of Forest Lodge, Woodford Green, a winged spur or. *Nunquam non paratus.—Assiduitate.*

Johnston of Holly Park, co. Down, a winged spur. *Nunquam non paratus.* 111. 12

Johnston of Wardmilnes, Scotland, a hand ppr., holding an escallop gu. *Sine fraude fides.* 216. 2

Johnston of Edinburgh, a hand holding a bezant ppr. *Ex solá virtute honos.*

Johnston of Straiton, an arm in armour, holding in the gauntlet a sword, all ppr. *Semper paratus.* 210. 4

Johnston, Lieutenant-Colonel George Hamilton, Esquire, Kilmore, co. Armagh, Ireland, an arm in armour embowed, holding in the hand a sword in bend sinister, all ppr., the elbow charged with a spur-rowel gu. *Nunquam non paratus.* 195. 5

Johnston, Rev. Richard, M.A., of Kilmore, Richhill, co. Armagh, same crest and motto.

Johnston, Robert H., M.A., M.D., B.Ch., of 8, Marlborough Hill, St. John's Wood, N.W., a dexter arm in armour embowed, holding in the hand a sword ppr. *Nunquam non paratus.*

Johnston and **Johnstone,** Ireland, a dexter arm in armour embowed, the hand apaumée ppr. 200. 1

Johnston of Knappagh and Glenaule, co. Armagh, Ireland, an arm in armour embowed holding a sword. *Nunquam non paratus.* 195. 2

Johnston, Bart., of Johnston, Scotland, a sword and a dagger in saltier, the points upward, all ppr. *Paratus ad arma.—Vive ut postea vivas.* cf. 171. 12

Johnston of Hilltoun, a sword and dagger in saltier, all ppr. *Paratus ad arma.* cf. 171. 12

Johnston, a sword and a dagger in saltier, the points upwards, all ppr., hilted and pommelled or. cf. 171. 12

Johnston, Christian Frederick Charles Alexander James, Esquire, of Hiltoun, Berwick, a sword and a dagger ppr., hilted or, crossing each other saltirewise with the points upwards. *Paratus ad arma.* cf. 171. 12

Johnston of Clathrie, Dumfriessh., Scotland, a star issuing out of a cloud or. *Appropinquat Dies.* 164. 11

Johnston of Johnston and Caskieben, a phœnix in flames ppr. *Vive ut postea vivas.* 82. 2

Johnston, Scotland, a phœnix in flames. *Vive ut vivas.* 82. 2

Johnston, Sir William, Bart., J.P., of that ilk, of Hilton and Caskieben, Aberdeensh.: (1) A phœnix in flames ppr. 305. 10. (2) Two dexter hands clasped in fesse holding a thistle and branch of laurel ppr. *Vive ut postea vivas.* 305. 11

Johnston of Graitney, Dumfriessh., Scotland, a man armed cap-à-pie on horseback brandishing a sword, all ppr. *Cave paratus.* cf. 189. 10

Johnston, a griffin's head erased gu. 66. 2

Johnston of Dublin, a horse passant per fesse arg. and sa. *Festina lente.* 52. 6

Johnston-Stewart, Stair Hathorn, Esquire, of Glasserton and Physgill Whithorn, Wigtown, and Champfleurie, Linlithgowsh., N.B., a demi-lion rampant holding in his dexter paw a buckle or. *Suffibulatus majores sequor.*

Johnstone, see Derwent, Baron.

Johnstone, see Vanden-Bempde-Johnstone.

Johnstone, Sir Frederick John William, Bart., D.L., of Westerhall, Dumfriessh., a spur with wings or, leathered gu. *Nunquam non paratus.* 111. 12

Johnstone, Montague George, Esquire, of Craig-Sanquhar, Cupar, Fifesh., N.B., same crest and motto.

Johnstone of Lathrisk, Fifesh., Scotland, a spur placed upright, the rowel in chief or, winged arg., leathered gu. *Semper paratus.* 111. 12

Johnstone, Edward, Esquire, of Dunsley Manor, Staffs, a spur winged ppr. *Nunquam non paratus.* 111. 12

Johnstone, of Fulford Hall, Hockley Heath, Warw., a spur ppr., winged or. *Nunquam non paratus.*

Johnstone of Alva, Clackmannan, a spur with wings or, leather gu. *Nunquam non paratus.* 111. 12

Johnstone, George Charles Keppel, of Rothsay, West Cowes, Isle of Wight, a spur with wings or. *Nunquam non paratus.*

Johnstone, John Douglas, of Snowhill, Lisbellow, co. Fermanagh, same crest and motto.

Johnstone, John Heywood, Esquire, of Bignor Park, Pulborough, Sussex, a spur with wings or, leathered gu. *Nunquam non paratus.*

Johnstone, Ralph W., M.D., B.A., of 175, New Bond Street, a spur-rowel upwards between two wings. *Nunquam non paratus.*

Johnstone of Pitkeirie, Fifesh., Scotland, a winged spur or. *Assiduitate.* 111. 12

Johnstone of Netherwood, Dumfriessh., a spur with wings or, leathered gu. 111. 12

Johnstone, Hope-, John James, of Annandale: (1) A spur erect or, winged arg. (*for Johnstone*). 111. 12. (2) A globe fractured at the top under a rainbow with clouds at each end, all ppr. (*for Hope*). *At spes non fracta.—Nunquam non paratus.* 159. 2

Johnstone, Scotland, a spur or. 178. 8

Johnstone, Scotland, an arm in armour holding in the gauntlet a sword erect, all ppr. *Semper paratus.* 210. 4

Johnstoun, a winged spur or. *Nunquam non paratus.* 111. 12

Joicey, Sir James, Bart., M.P., D.L., J.P., of Longhirst, Northumb., and of 58, Cadogan Square, London, S.W., a demi-chevalier in armour proper, garnished or, the helmet adorned with three feathers, holding in his dexter hand a scimitar of the first, supporting with the sinister an escocheon arg., charged with three Korteaux within two bendlets inverted of the second between two fleurs-de-lis sa. *Omne solum forti patria.* 284. 2

Joicey-Cecil, Lord John Pakenham: On a cap of maintenance a garb or, supported by two lions, the dexter arg., the sinister az. (*for Cecil*). (2) A demi-man affrontée ppr., the helmet adorned with three feathers gu., arg., and az., resting the dexter hand on an escutcheon of the arms of Joicey, and supporting with the sinister a spiked mace, all ppr. *Cor unum via una.*

Joiner, a greyhound sejant sa. 59. 4

Jokes of London, on a ducal coronet or, a cockatrice displayed gu. *cf.* 68. 14

Jolles of London, out of a mural coronet a nag's head, all or. *cf.* 50. 13

Jolley, Lancs, a cubit arm vested vert, charged with a pile arg., holding in the hand ppr. a sword of the second, hilt and pommel or.

Jolley or Jolly of Hatton Garden, London, a demi-eagle displayed or, holding in the beak a sinister hand arg. *cf.* 81. 6

Jollie, Edward, Esquire, of Waireka, Patea, Taranaki, New Zealand, *uses:* a bird holding in the beak a sprig of olive. *Lætavi.*

Jollie, Scotland a fox's head sa. 33. 4

Jollie, a hand holding a scimitar ppr. 213. 5

Jolliff or Jolleff, an arm holding in the hand a dagger. 212. 9

Jolliffe, *see* Hylton, Baron.

Jolliffe, out of a mural coronet a nag's head. *cf.* 50. 13

Jolliffe, Somers., a cubit arm in armour, holding in the hand a scimitar, all ppr.

Jolliffe, Twyford-, a cubit arm erect, vested and cuffed, the sleeve charged with a pile arg., holding in the hand a sword ppr. *Tent que je puis.*

Jolly, Scotland, a dove holding in its beak an olive-branch. *Lætavi.* 92. 5

Jolly, Samuel Aird, Esquire, L.R.C.P., of Cumberland Park, Acton, W., a dexter cubit arm in armour holding in the hand a scimitar in bend sinister, all ppr.

Jollyffe, an eagle's head erased sa., beaked or. 83. 2

Jonas, on a tower ppr., a crescent or. 156. 4

Jones, Viscount Ranelagh, *see* Ranelagh.

Jones, *see* Tyrwhitt.

Jones, *see* Marsham-Jones.

Jones-Parry, Bart., *see* Parry.

Jones of Caton, Lancs, and London, out of a ducal coronet or, a plume of five ostrich-feathers az. *Vince malum bono.* 114. 13

Jones, Richard, Esquire, Barrister-at-Law, East Wickham House, Welling, Kent, a demi-lion rampant holding in his dexter paw a cross crosslet fitchée.

Jones of Sunningwell, Berks, of Chastleton, Oxon, and Worcs., a demi-lion rampant or, holding between its paws a mullet gu. *cf.* 15. 8

Jones of Gwynfryn, Cardigansh., a demi-lion rampant. *Mors mihi lucrum.* 10. 2

Jones, John Arnallt, Esquire, L.R.C.P., M.R.C.S., J.P., of Heathmont, Aberavon, Port Talbot, Glamorgansh., a demi-lion sa., charged with a cross clechée and pomonetée or, and holding in the dexter paw a cross calvary in bend sinister, also or. *Bydd lew heb lid.*

Jones, Rev. George Ifor Rhys, B.A., of Hursley, Llandovery, same crest and motto.

Jones of Rhiewport, Montgomerysh., a lion rampant gu. *Frangas, non flectes.* 1. 13

Jones, William Charles, Esquire, of the Oaklands, Preston Brook, Chesh., and Thomas Oswald Jones, Esquire, of 26A, Duke Street, St. James's, London, S.W., a demi-lion ppr., holding between the paws a sun in splendour or, and supporting under the sinister paw an increscent arg. *Esto sol testis.* 225. 4

Jones of London, a demi-lion rampant ppr. 10. 2

Jones of Revell, Wilts, out of a ducal coronet or, a demi-lion rampant sa., langued gu., armed of the first. 16. 3

Jones, Admiral Sir Lewis Tobias, Knight Grand Cross of the Most Honourable Order of the Bath, a lion couchant or, armed and langued gu., charged on the shoulder with a trefoil slipped vert. *Periculum ex aliis facito.* *cf.* 7. 5

Jones of Fakenham, Norf., a lion couchant sa. 7. 5

Jones, Admiral Loftus Francis, R.N., of Hylton House, Petersfield, a lion couchant or. *Periculum ex aliis facito.*

Jones, Sir Lawrence John, Bart., M.A., of Cranmer Hall, Norf., in front of a castle a lion couchant arg., gorged with a wreath of laurel ppr., pendent therefrom an escutcheon gu., charged with a representation of the gold medal presented to Sir John Thomas Jones, the first Bart., for his services at Badajoz. *Marte et arte.*

Jones, Burne-, Sir Philip, Bart., North End House, Rottingdean, Sussex, in front of fire ppr., two wings elevated and addorsed purpure, charged with a mullet or. *Sequar et attingam.* 283. 14

Jones, Charles Alfred, District Registrar of H.M. High Court of Justice, Deputy-Constable of Carnarvon Castle, Bron Hendre, Carnarvon, a demi-lion rampant holding in the dexter fore-paw a bunch of arrows. *Gorau meddyg, meddyg enaid.* 293. 5

Jones, Heref., a lion rampant or. 1. 13

Jones, Berks, a lion rampant or, grasping an anchor in pale sa.

Jones, Shropsh., a lion rampant or, supporting an anchor az., timbered of the first.

Jones, Wales, a lion rampant az., holding a shield or, with a carved bordure.

Jones of Laneych, Pembrokesh., a lion rampant regardant sa., armed and langued gu. *Sine numine nihilum.* 2. 3

Jones of Grothkenan, Denbighsh., Wales, a lion's head erased per pale arg. and sa. 17. 8

Jones-Bateman of Pentre Mawr, Denbighsh., a lion's head erased az. *Spes non fracta.* 17. 8

Jones of Chiswick, Middx., a lion's head erased sa., collared or, studded gu. 18. 6

Jones, William, Esquire, of Walsall, Staffs, issuant from a sun rising in splendour ppr., a lion's head vert, bezantée. *Diligentia.*

Jones of Dublin, a wolf statant arg., resting the dexter paw on a human head erased ppr.

Jones of Stratford-by-Bow, Middx., a wolf's head erased or. 30. 8

Jones of Rowe, Middx., and Heref., a tiger's head erased or.

Jones, John, Esquire, J.P., D.L., of Ynysfor, Penrhyndendraeth, Merionethsh., a boar's head couped ppr.

Jones, Heywood-, Richard, Badsworth Hall, Pontefract: (1) In front of a talbot's head couped sa., collared vairée, two roses arg., stalked and leaved ppr. (*for Jones*). (2) On a mount vert, the trunk of a tree with two branches sprouting therefrom and entwined by ivy, thereon a galen, wings expanded ppr. (*for Heywood*). *Till then thus.*

Jones, Wales, a boar's head erased in fess or. 42. 2

Jones, Wales, a boar's head erect and erased or. 43. 3

Jones of Wexford, Ireland, a boar's head erased and erect ermines. *Pawb yn ol ei arfer.* 43. 3

Jones, Wilson Carstairs, Esquire, of Gelli Gynan, Denbighsh., and of Hartsheath, Flintsh., and the Old Hall, Chester, on a mount vert, a boar's head couped gu., in front of an arrow palewise ppr. *Heb nevol nerth nid sicr saeth.*

Jones, Alexander Fair, Esquire, of 55, Northumberland Street, Edinburgh, same crest and motto.

Jones, Captain Valentine, a boar's head erased per bend sinister erm. and ermines. 42. 2

Jones, Frederick Arthur Gerwyn, Esquire, J.P., D.L., of Pantgas, Golden Grove, Carmarthensh., on a mount vert, a representation of a Pembrokesh. ox's head in profile ppr., bezantée. *Da ei flydd.*

Jones, out of a ducal coronet or, a goat's head. 128. 14

Jones of Ystrad, Carmarthensh., a stag's head erased ppr. *Heb Dduw heb ddim.* 121. 2

Jones of London, a buck's head erased sa., attired or, and between the attires a bugle-horn of the first. *cf.* 121. 2

Jones of Esthall, Oxon., a buck trippant arg. 117. 8

Jones, Edward Fielding, of 38, Athole Gardens, Glasgow, a stag trippant ppr., in front of two spears in saltire, the shafts sa., and the heads arg. *Spectemur agendo.* 267. 8

Jones, Wales, on a chapeau gu., turned up erm., a stag arg., attired vert. 118. 1

Jones, Captain Henry Hastings, of Ardnaree, Ballina, co. Mayo: (1) A buck's head erased sa., attired or, and between the attires a bugle-horn of the first. (2) On a chapeau ppr., a stag statant arg., attired vert.

Jones, a stag trippant arg., attired and collared or, from the collar an escutcheon pendent sa., charged with a martlet of the second. *cf.* 117. 8

Jones, Robert, Esquire, M.D., of Claybury, Woodford Bridge, Essex, a stag statant between two arms in armour counter-embowed, each holding in the hand a fleur-de-lis. *A noddo Duw a noddir.* 294. 8

Jones, Robert Hesketh, Esquire, Belfort Park, Hill Rise, Croydon, a boar's head couped close. *Heb nevol nerth nid sicr saeth.*

Jones, the late Rev. Thomas, of Eisteddfa Criccieth, North Wales, same crest and motto.

Jones, Major John Lloyd Thomas, I.M.S., same crest and motto.

Jones, Thomas, Esquire, Chartered Bank of India, Australia, and China, same crest and motto.

Jones of Glanmere House, Forest Hill, Kent, upon a mount vert, between two roses arg., slipped ppr., a stag lodged, also ppr., collared az. *Ex vero decus.* *cf.* 115. 12

Jones, James, Esquire, of Williamstry Park, Fairford, Glouc., a stag lodged and regardant ppr., semée ot acorn-vert, holding in the mouth a fern's branch, also ppr. *Deo adjuvante.* 115. 8

Jones, Hon. Alfred Gilpin, M.P., of Bloomingdale North-West-Arm, Halifax, Nova Scotia, Canada, a stag's head couped.

Jones, Ireland, a greyhound's head erased or, holding in its mouth a stag's foot erased gu. 61. 5

Jones, a talbot's head couped arg., gorged with a chain or. *cf.* 56. 12

Jones, Ireland, a talbot's head couped arg., collared and chained gu. *cf.* 56. 1

Jones of Dublin, a talbot's head couped arg., langued and chained gu. *Deus fortitudo meo.* *cf* 56. 12

Jones, a Cornish chough ppr., holding in its dexter claw an étoile arg.

Jones of Nass, near Lydnay, Glouc., a Cornish chough ppr. 107. 14

Jones, Rev. Preb. H. Jones, M.A., Chaplain-in-Ordinary to the Queen, of Barton Mere, Pakenham, Suff., and Rev. C. W. Jones, M.A., of Pakenham, standing on a heart or, a raven ppr., collared gemelle arg. 107. 8

Jones, Sir William Hollingworth Quayle, of 14, Royal Avenue, Chelsea, S.W., and Pakenham, Bury St. Edmunds, same crest and motto.

Jones, a bird's head sa., holding in the beak a branch reversed vert.

Jones of Penrose, Cornw., and Wilts, a dragon's head erased vert. *cf.* 71. 2

Jones, a dragon's head erased vert, ducally gorged or, holding in its mouth a glove. *cf.* 72. 6

Jones of Shackerley Hall, Shropsh.: (1) The sun in splendour or. 162. 2. (2) On an Eastern coronet or, a dragon passant gardant gu. *Over na ovno angau.—Esto sol testis.*

Jones, Wales, the sun in splendour or, at the end of each ray a flame of fire, all ppr.

Jones, Shropsh., the sun in splendour or. 162. 2

Jones, Inglis-, Wilmot, Derry Ormond, Cardigansh., same crest.

Jones, Norf., a battle-axe and spear in saltier, the handles gu., the heads arg., garnished or.

Jones, Shropsh., a mermaid ppr. 184. 5

Jones, a nag's head erased arg. 51. 4

Jones, Morris Paterson, Esquire, J.P., of Airlie House, Hoylake, Chesh., and 11, Dale Street, Liverpool, and Gungroy, Welshpool, a fasces fessewise or, surmounted by a nag's head erased arg. *Justus ac tenax propositi.* *cf.* 51. 12

Jones, William Brittain, Esquire, C.S.I., of Ash Grove, Knockholt, Kent, upon an acorn erect, slipped and leaved, a lark rising, all ppr. ΑΙΕΝ ΑΡΙΣΤΕΥΕΙΝ.

Jones, of Llanerchrugog, Denbighsh., a garb or. *Look to the past.* 153. 2

Jones of Benada Castle, co. Sligo, Ireland, a wing gu., semée d'étoiles or. *cf.* 109. 7

Jones, William, Esquire, J.P., of Glandenys, Lampeter, and Blaenos, Llandovery, an ox sa., bezantée. *Da-ci-ffyd.*

Jones of Beaver Hill, Derbysh., in front of a spear between two laurel-branches ppr., a cross patée gu. *Esto fidelis usque ad mortem.*

Jones of Uppingham, Rutl., a paschal lamb ppr. 131. 2

Jones of Foy, Heref., a hedgehog passant ppr. *cf.* 135. 8

Jones of Barrow and Filmingham, Lincs. a cubit arm erect vested purp., cuffed arg., holding in the hand ppr. a branch of marigolds of the third, stalked and leaved vert. 205. 14

Jones of London, an arm erect vested or, charged with three étoiles in pale gu., holding a pheon erect arg.

Jones, an arm in fess couped at the elbow, holding in the hand a sword in pale, pierced through a boar's head couped ppr.

Jones of London, a gauntlet in fess or, holding a sword erect arg., hilted of the first, pierced through a boar's head erased vert. *cf.* 211. 9

Jones, Wales, a cubit arm erect in armour ppr., holding in the gauntlet a spear of the first, headed arg., embrued gu. *cf.* 210. 11

Jones-Williams, Howel Richard, Esquire, of Cui Parc, Talybont-on-Usk, Breconsh., a dragon's head erased, holding in the mouth a dexter hand couped at the wrist. *Ar Duw y Gyd.*

Jones of Sugwas, Poulstone, Cleve, and Mountcraig, Heref., a gauntlet lying fesseways holding a spear enfiled with a boar's head erased ppr.

Jones, Oliver Henry, Esquire, of Fonmon Castle, Cardiff, Glamorgansh., a cubit arm erect in armour ppr., holding in the gauntlet a spear of the first, headed arg., embrued gu. *cf.* 210. 11

Jones, Morgan, Esquire, of Kilwendeage, Pembrokesh., in front of a dexter arm in armour embowed ppr., garnished or, the hand within a gauntlet striking with a scimitar, also ppr., the hilt of the second, a boar's head erased az., tusked, also or. *Pro patria et Rege.*

Jones of Littlington, Beds, on a chapeau az., turned up or, an armed arm embowed, tasselled gu., holding in the hand ppr. a spear, the staff of the fourth armed of the second.

Jones of London, a gauntlet fesseways or, holding a sword erect arg., hilt of the first, pierced through a boar's head erased vert. *cf.* 211. 9

Jones of Glan Helen, Carnarvonsh., a dexter arm embowed in armour ppr., garnished or, surmounted by two branches of laurel in saltire vert, the hand grasping a javelin in bend sinister point downwards of the first, pendent from the wrist by a ribbon an escutcheon gu., charged with a scimitar, also ppr., pommel and hilt of the second. *Integritate et fortitudine.*

Jones-Barker, Evan Barker James: (1) A bear's head erased sa., muzzled, gorged with a collar gemel, and between two estoiles, all or (*for Barker*). (2) A cross patée fitchée gu., between on the dexter side an increscent, and on the sinister side a decrescent, both or. *Beneficii memor.*

Jones-Bateman, Burleton, Esquire, of Pentre-Mawr, Abergele, a lion's head erased az. *Spes non fracta.*

Jones-Parry, Sydney Henry, Esquire, of Tyllwydd, Newcastle Emlyn, South Wales: (1) On a chapeau ppr., a demi-lion rampant or (*for Jones*). (2) A nag's head erased sa. (*for Parry*).

Jones-Parry, five battle-axes, staves gu., headed or, three in pale and two in saltire, encircled with a wreath of laurel ppr. *Gofol dyn duw ai gwerid.*

Jones-Williams, Thomas John, of Langhern Hill, Wichenford, Worcester, between two spears erect ppr., a talbot passant per pale erm. and erminois, charged for distinction on the shoulder with a cross crosslet sa.

Jope of Merryfield, Cornw., an antelope sejant erm., supporting with the dexter foot an escutcheon per pale or and arg.

Jopling or **Joppling,** a dexter hand ppr., holding up an escallop-shell or. 216. 2

Jopp of Cotton, Aberdeensh., on a garb in fess a cock crowing arg. *Sic donec.* 91. 4

Jopp, on a garb in fess a cock crowing, all ppr. 91. 4

Jorcey, a hand ppr., holding a swan's head and neck erased arg., beaked gu. 220. 9

Jordan, Somers. and Wilts, a mound or, surmounted by a scroll charged with the motto, "*Percussa resurgo.*"

Jordan, Surrey, an almond-tree ppr., fructed or.

Jordan, Surrey, a lion sejant sustaining a cross crosslet fitched, all or.

Jordan, Surrey, a demi-lion or, the sinister paw resting on the wreath, and holding in the dexter an eagle's head erased sa. 9. 7

Jordan of Mountfield, Sussex, a lion sejant or, holding in the dexter paw an eagle's head erased sa.

Jordan, F. W., Esquire, M.D., of Heaton Norris, Lancs, issuing from a crescent or, a plume of five feathers az., entwined by a serpent of the first.

Jordan, Lancs, a crescent or, and issuing therefrom a plume of five feathers az., entwined by a serpent of the first. *Arte non vi.*

Jordan, Harry Risden Hall, a martlet with wings displayed gu. *Crux dat salutem.*

Jordan or **Jordon,** a cross crosslet fitched. *Percussa resurgo.*

Jordayne of London, on a chapeau gu., turned up erm., a hawk or, the inside of the wings of the second.

Jorden of Wellington, Shropsh., a demi-talbot gu. *cf.* 55. 11

Jordon, Ireland, an arm embowed holding in the hand a dagger ppr. *cf.* 200. 10

Jordon, out of a mural coronet a hand ppr., vested az., brandishing a sword wavy of the first.
Jordon, a boar's head couped in fess. 43. 1
Jorge, a hand ppr., holding a swan's head and neck erased arg., beaked gu. 220. 9
Joselin or **Joselyn,** a talbot passant sa., collared or. cf. 54. 2
Joseph-Watkin, Thomas Morgan, Esquire, of College of Arms, London, in front of three spears, one in pale and two in saltire, sa., a wolf's head ppr., couped, and charged on the neck with a fesse erm. *Ofner na ofno argent.*
Joseph, Arthur Hill, Esquire, M.D., of Glanmor, Bexhill-on-Sea, in front of three spears, one in pale and two in saltire, points upwards or, a wolf's head couped tenné, collared arg., charged with three spears' heads sa. *Peri aur y chalon wir.*
Joskin or **Joskyn,** an antelope's head arg., collared gu., armed sa. cf. 126. 2
Joslin, Walter, Esquire, of the Hunts, Upminster, between two hawks' bells a rock, thereon a falcon's leg erased at the thigh and belled, all ppr. *Faire mon devoir.* 252. 16
Joslin, Clement, Esquire, of High House, Purfleet, same crest and motto.
Joslin, Henry, of Gaynes Park, Upminster, Essex, same crest and motto.
Josselyne, Joseline, or **Josselin,** Essex, a bear's head and neck sa., muzzled or. 34. 14
Josselyn, Lieutenant-Colonel Arthur Henry, J.P., Fornham, near Bury St. Edmunds, a falcon's leg, belled or, erased at the thigh gu. *Faire mon devoir.* 113. 8
Josselyn, Lieutenant-Colonel Frederick John, Chief Constable of Beds, same crest and motto.
Josselyn, Willoughby, Esquire, Bury St. Edmunds, same crest and motto.
Josselyn, John Henry, Esquire, J.P., Ipswich, same crest and motto.
Josselyn, Colonel James Edward, late R.A., same crest and motto.
Josselyn, George Francis, Esquire, J.P., Ipswich, same crest and motto.
Jossey of Westpans, Haddingtonsh., Scotland, an eye ppr. *Je voy.* 193. 13
Jossey of Edinburgh, an eye ppr. *Manuque.* 193. 13
Jouatt, an arm in armour ppr., holding in the hand a fleur-de-lis or. 210. 6
Joubert (de la Ferté), Charles Henry, Esq., of the Ferns, Weybridge, Surrey, two pine-trees in saltire, eradicated and fructed proper. *Omnia virtuti cedunt.*
Joule, out of a ducal coronet or, a stag's head affrontée ppr. 119. 13
Jourdain, late Sir Henry John, K.C.M.G., of the Elms, Watford, Herts, a lion sejant or, charged on the body with two cross crosslets in pale, holding in the dexter fore-paw a cross crosslet, and resting the sinister upon an escallop, all az. *Frangas non flectes.*
Jourdan, two anchors in saltier ppr. 161. 7
Joweles or **Jowles,** Kent and Surrey, a tower gu., surmounted with eight broad arrows interlaced arg.
Jowers, Reginald F., F.R.C.S., of 55, Brunswick Square, Hove, Brighton, out of a ducal coronet a demi-lion rampant double queued. *Virtute et opera.*
Jowitt of Eltofts Thorner, Yorks, a lion sejant gardant gu., the dexter forepaw supporting an escutcheon of the arms, viz.: az., on a chevron arg., between two chaplets of oak in chief and a lion sejant gardant in base or, three bugle-horns stringed sa.
Joy of London and Wilts, a falcon standing on a cinquefoil between two vine-branches, all ppr.
Joy, Ireland, a hand holding an arrow point downwards. 214. 4
Joy, a demi-lion rampant. *Pro patriâ ejusque libertate.* 10. 2
Joy of Hartham Park, Wilts, out of a ducal coronet or, a plume of five feathers arg. *Vive la joye.* 114. 13
Joyce or **Joice,** a demi-chevalier in armour brandishing a scimitar, all ppr. 187. 4
Joyce, an antelope statant. 126. 12
Joyce, Sir Matthew, of 16, Great Cumberland Place, W. (and descendants of the late John Hall Joyce of Blankfordby, Leics.), in front of a lion rampant ppr., collared nebuly, with chain reflexed over the back or, three water-bougets fessewise sa. *Nec temere nec timide.*
Joyce of Galway, Ireland, a demi-wolf ducally gorged, all ppr. cf. 31. 2
Joye, Wilts, a lion rampant arg., supporting a staff raguly or.
Joye of Benefield, Northamp., the trunk of a vine with two branches, thereon a dove statant, all ppr. 93. 4
Joyner of London and Sussex, a dexter arm in armour embowed holding in the gauntlet a battle-axe, the handle or, headed arg. 200. 6
Joyner, Ireland, a demi-lion az., langued gu., holding between the paws a fleur-de-lis or, charged with a mullet, also gu. cf. 13. 5
Joynour, two battle-axes in saltier. 172. 4
Joynson of Liscard, Chesh., on a mount vert, an eagle displayed with two heads az., semée of roses arg. *Ad honorem industria ducit.* cf. 74. 10
Joynson, Tertius, Esquire, same crest and motto.
Joynson, Francis, Esquire, of New Park, Annan, Dumfriessh., same crest and motto.
Joynson, William, Esquire, of the Manor House, Tachbrook Mallory, Leamington, same crest and motto.
Joynt, Christopher, Esquire, M.D., 21, Leeson Park, Dublin, on a mount vert, a boar passant ppr., resting its sinister fore-leg on an escutcheon az., charged with a fleur-de-lis or. *I hope.* 272. 15
Joynt, Henry William, of Westhill, Taunton, same crest and motto.
Joynt, Surgeon-General Francis John, M.D., a cubit arm erect ppr. charged with an escallop arg., and grasping in the hand a battle-axe in bend sinister, also ppr. *Nec temere, nec lente.* cf. 213. 12
Joynt, Alfred Lane, Esquire, B.A., of 4, Pembroke Park, Clyde Road, Dublin, on a wreath of the colours issuant out of a chaplet of oak-leaves vert, two eagles' heads conjoined, the dexter gu., the sinister az. *Nec degenero.* cf. 84. 11
Joynt, Rev. Henry Russell, M.A., of Marksbury Rectory, Bristol, same crest and motto.
Juatt, an arm in armour ppr., holding a fleur-de-lis or. 210. 6
Juba, a heraldic antelope sejant arg., tufted, maned, and armed or, resting the dexter foot on an escutcheon per pale of the second and first.
Juchen, two wings expanded ppr. 109. 6
Juckes-Clifton, Bart., *see* Clifton.
Juckes or **Jukes,** a column ppr. 176. 3
Juckes-Dixon, A., the Marsh, Wellington, Shropsh., an eagle's head couped between two wings.
Judd and **Jude** of London, a ferret passant ppr., collared and lined or. 134. 9
Judd, Francis Savile Harry, Esquire, J.P., of Maces Place, Rickling, Bishop's Stortford, a griffin's head erased per chevron or and vert, charged with three fleurs-de-lis counterchanged, and holding in the beak an ear of wheat of the same crest and motto.
Judge, between two laurel-branches a sword in pale, all ppr. 170. 3
Judge of Mosstown, co. Meath, an escallop or. *Totum est providentia.* 141. 12
Judgson and **Judson,** Scotland, out of a ducal coronet two dexter arms in saltier, vested ppr., holding two scimitars in pale, also ppr. cf. 203. 10
Judkin-Fitzgerald, Bart., of Lisheen, co. Tipperary, a chevalier in complete armour on horseback at speed, his sword drawn and beaver up, all ppr. cf. 189. 10
Judson, a wyvern with wings addorsed. 70. 1
Juge, Leics., two battle-axes in saltier headed ppr., the handles gu., enfiled with a ducal coronet or. cf. 172. 4
Jugg, an oak-leaf vert.
Jugler of Reigate, Surrey, two swords in saltier ppr., surmounted by a cross crosslet in pale sa. 166. 14
Jukes, Shropsh., a dexter arm in armour embowed and vambraced ppr., garnished or, supporting a lance in pale, also ppr., the standard quarterly sa. and arg., bordered or, fringed, bearing the arms of the Holy Trinity.
Julian and **Julion,** on a chapeau a salamander in flames, all ppr. 138. 2
Julian, James Edward John, Esquire, J.P., of Kilflynn, co. Kerry, a star and crescent.
Julien, a lion's gamb erased holding the hilt of a broken sword, all ppr. 38. 2
Julius of Richmond, Surrey, an estoile arg. 164. 1
Jump, Henry, Esquire, late of Woodlands, Little Woolton, Lancs, a demi-stag regardant ppr., charged on the shoulder with three roses chevronwise arg., supporting a Passion cross or. *Fortiter et fideliter.*
Jump, James, Esquire, of Hardwicke House, Bury St. Edmunds, Suff., same crest and motto.
Jumper, a demi-lion ppr., supporting a long cross gu. 11. 14
Jumper of London, a wing arg., charged with two bars gemel sa. cf. 109. 7
Jupp, a griffin passant holding in the dexter claw a buckle ppr. 63. 7

Jury, a cubit arm in armour holding in the hand a caltrap ppr. 210. 7
Justice, a cat sejant erect ppr. 25. 2
Justice of Hinstock, Shropsh., a falcon rising or. *Justitiæ soror fides.* 88. 2
Justice of East Chrichton, Edinburgh, Scotland, a sword in pale ppr. *Non sine causa.* 170. 2
Justice of Coventry, Warw., on a garb or, a cock gu. 91. 4
Justine or **Justyne,** a stag's head erased affrontée or. 119. 10
Jutting, a fleur-de-lis between two elephants' proboscis. 148. 4
Juxon, an Ionic pillar on a base arg. 173. 6

K.

Kadie, Scotland, a lancet expanded ppr. 178. 9
Kadrad, two anchors in saltier az. 161. 7
Kadrohard, Wales, a griffin's head erased sa. 66. 2
Kadye, on a mount vert, a cockatrice arg., combed and wattled gu., ducally gorged and chained or. 68. 7
Kaer, issuing out of a crescent two eagles' heads addorsed. 84. 15
Kagg, a falcon regardant resting the dexter claw on a laurel-crown ppr. *cf.* 85. 4
Kahl, a camel's head arg. 132. 7
Kaines, a wolf current gu. 28. 4
Kandishe, on a chapeau ppr., a dove with wings addorsed az. 94. 10
Kane, Ireland, a pomeis charged with a pale indented arg. 159. 6
Kane, an arm in armour embowed holding in the hand a sword ppr. 195. 2
Kane, William Francis De Vismes, Esquire, J.P., D.L., of Drumcaske, co. Monaghan, a naked arm embowed ppr., charged with an estoile gu., and holding in the hand a sword, also ppr. *cf.* 201. 4
Karben, out of a ducal coronet or, a cubit arm vested gu., cuffed of the first, holding the sun ppr. 209. 2
Karhyll, a stag lodged or. 115. 7
Kardaile and **Kardoyle,** an antelope trippant erm., attired gu. 126. 6
Karkenton and **Karkington,** out of an antique crown or, a demi-lion rampant gu. *cf.* 10. 2
Karnabye, Northumb., a Triton holding in his dexter hand a trident. *cf.* 185. 12
Karr, *see* Seton-Karr.
Karr, a stag's head erased az. 121. 2
Karr, Scotland, a dexter hand holding a dagger. *Sans peur.* 212. 9
Karr, a dexter arm in pale couped below the wrist ppr., holding in the hand a dagger arg., hilt and pommel or. 212. 9
Karrick or **Karricke,** a dexter arm embowed ppr., vested gu., cuffed or, holding in the hand a covered cup of the last. 203. 4
Karvell or **Karvill,** on a ducal coronet or, a wyvern gu. 70. 9
Kassye, Northumb., a dexter hand pointing with two fingers gu. 222. 11
Kateler, Kateller, and **Katherler,** on a chapeau ppr., a lion's head erased arg., ducally crowned or. 21. 3
Kater, Honourable Henry Edward, J.P., of Mount Broughton, Moss Vale, New South Wales, Australia, Member of the Legislative Council of New South Wales, and Member of Licensing Court, a cat rampant gardant ppr., between two elephants' trunks or. *Nil mortalibus arduum.* 253. 2
Katerley and **Katherley,** a hind's head ppr. 124. 1
Katheram, an arm in armour couped and embowed, resting on the elbow, holding in the hand a club ppr. 199. 4
Katherler, *see* Kateler.
Katherler, Katerler, or **Kateller,** on a chapeau ppr., a lion's head erased az., ducally crowned or. 21. 3
Kathrens or **Kathrins,** Ireland, a plume of ostrich-feathers arg., enfiled with a ducal coronet or. *cf.* 115. 1
Kating, Kathyng, Katting, or **Kaytyng,** a demi-angel holding in the dexter hand a griffin's head erased, all ppr. 183. 3
Kavanagh, Ireland, on the point of a sword erect, a mullet. 169. 3
Kavanagh of Coolgreany, co. Wexford, Ireland, a dexter arm embowed vested purp., holding in the hand ppr. a sword arg., pommel and hilt or. 204. 1
Kavanagh of Ballyleigh, co. Wexford, and **Baron of Gniditz** in Bohemia, issuant from the horns of a crescent gu., a garb or. *Mea gloria fides.*
Kavanagh, Walter Macmorrough, Esquire, J.P., D.L., of Borris, co. Carlow, Ireland, issuant from the horns of a crescent gu., a garb or. *Siothchain agus fairsinge.*
Kavanagh of Nantes, France, issuant from the horns of a crescent gu., a garb of the last. *Virtus sola nobilitat.*
Kawston, out of a mural coronet a hand ppr., habited paly of six arg. and sa., holding a mullet of the first. 206. 12
Kay of Woodsome, Yorks, and of Edith-Weston, Rutl., a goldfinch ppr. 108. 8
Kay, Hunts, a goldfinch ppr., charged with a mullet. *cf.* 108. 8
Kay of Battersea, Surrey, on a crescent or, a goldfinch ppr. *cf.* 108. 8
Kay, Rt. Hon. Sir Edward Ebenezer, of 37, Hyde Park Gardens, W., same crest and motto.
Kay, a martlet volant. *In Deo solo spes mea.* 96. 2
Kay, Durh. and Northumb., a griffin's head erased sa. 66. 2
Kay of Milshaw, Dalton, and the Heath, Yorks, a griffin's head erased arg., beaked gu., charged with a martlet sa., holding in the beak a key or. *cf.* 66. 6
Kay of Manningham: (1) A griffin's head collared (*for Kay*). *cf.* 67. 7. (2) A stag's head ppr. (*for Linten*). 121. 5. (3) A greyhound sejant arg., collared sa. (*for Cunliffe*). *cf.* 59. 2
Kay, Alexander, of Cornhill, Lanark, a griffin's head erased vert, holding in his beak a key or. *In Deo solo spes mea.* 66. 6
Kay, Sir Brook, Bart., of Stanley Lodge, Battledown, Cheltenham, and East Sheen, Surrey, a griffin's head erased erminois, gorged with a collar az., charged with three crescents or, and holding in the beak a key ppr. *Fidem parit integritas.* *cf.* 66. 6
Kay of Sunderland, Durh., and of North Shields, Northumb., a griffin's head erased sa., holding in the beak a key az. 66. 6
Kay, James Openshaw, Esquire, formerly of the Elms, Bedhampton, Hants, a demi-griffin with wings elevated sa., holding in the claws three arrows, one in pale and two in saltire ppr., surmounted in the centre by an escutcheon az., charged with an annulet or.
Kay, Thomas, Esquire, of Moorfield, Stockport, an eagle's head arg., erased gu., holding in the beak a key in bend, the wards downwards az., within a chain in arch or. *Clavis felicitatis labor.*
Kay, John Robinson, Esquire, a demi-stag supporting a cornucopia ppr., and gorged with a collar gemel az. *In via recta celeriter.*
Kay, Scotland, a marigold ppr. 151. 12
Kayble, a cubit arm ppr., vested erm., cuffed indented gu., holding in the hand an escarbuncle of the last. 207. 7
Kaye, *see* Lister-Kaye.
Kaye, Bart. (*extinct*), of Woodesham, Yorks: (1) A griffin's head erased arg., holding in the beak a key or. 66. 6. (2) A goldfinch ppr. *Kynd kynn knawne kepe.* 108. 8
Kayle, on a chapeau gu., turned up arg., a greyhound passant of the last. *cf.* 58. 4
Kayle, Cornw., a demi-talbot ducally gorged. 55. 12
Kayle or **Kele** of London, a wyvern arg., with wings expanded or. *cf.* 70. 8
Kaynton, a mountain ppr.
Kealy, John Robert, of Ashley House, Alverstoke, Hants, a demi-lion ppr., charged with a fesse, holding in the dexter paw a battle-axe in bend, both sa., and resting the sinister paw on a quatrefoil or. *Ne time crede tantem.*
Kealy, Rev. Arthur Graham, R.N., H.M.S. *Royal Sovereign*, Home Squadron, same crest. *Garde ta foy.*
Kean, Ireland, a horse's head erased. 51. 4
Kean of Dublin, a cat-a-mountain rampant per fesse az. and gu. *Inclyta virtus.* 26. 2
Keane, Baron (Keane), of Ghuznee, in Affghanistan, and of Cappoquin, co. Waterford: (1) Of augmentation, a representation of the Cabool gate of the fortress of Ghuznee, all ppr., and on an escroll above the word "*Ghuznee.*" (2) A cat sejant ppr., supporting in his dexter paw a flagstaff, thereon a Union Jack ppr. *Deus mihi providebit.* 285. 8

Keane, Sir John, Bart., of Cappoquin House, co. Waterford, a cat sejant ppr., supporting in his dexter paw a flagstaff, thereon the Union Jack, also ppr. *Felis demulcta mitis.* 285. 8

Keane, Frederick Henry, of Tivoli, Cappoquin, co. Waterford, same crest and motto.

Keane, Francis Burton, Esquire, of the Hermitage, near Ennis, co. Clare, Ireland, a wild cat rampant gardant ppr., gorged with an antique Irish crown or, and charged on the shoulder with a trefoil vert. *Felis demulcta mitis.*

Keane, Marcus, Esquire, of Beech Park, Ennis, same crest and motto.

Keane, Ireland, on a chapeau a stag trippant, all ppr. 118. 3

Kearney, *see* Cuthbert-Kearney.

Kearney, *see* Butler-Kearney.

Kearney, *see* Aylward-Kearney.

Kearney of St. Louis and St. Germans, France, a gauntleted hand lying fesseways ppr., holding a dagger erect arg., pommel and hilt or.

Kearney of Blanchville, co. Kilkenny, Ireland, a gauntleted hand or, holding a dagger arg. *Sustine et abstine.* 211. 4

Kearney of Ballyvary, co. Mayo, Ireland: (1) A ruined castle in flames ppr. (2) A gauntleted hand in fesse or, holding a dagger arg. *Sustine et abstine.*

Kearney, Ireland, a ruined castle in flames ppr.

Kearns, Ireland, out of a heart gu., a hand holding a scimitar ppr. 213. 4

Kearsley and **Kearsly** of London and Lancs, a demi-eagle erm., winged or. 80. 2

Keat, a demi-cat gardant. 26. 12

Keate of Woodford, Essex, and of Grovehurst, Kent, a mountain-cat passant sa. 26. 4

Keates, Joseph Andrew, Esquire, Lord of the Manor of Bishop's Nympton, Bishop's Nympton, North Devon, and of Dunstone, Torquay, a tiger passant gardant ppr., charged upon the body with three bezants fesseways, and resting the dexter paw upon an escutcheon sa., thereon a cake of copper ppr. *Esto memor.* 27. 8

Keating and **Keatinge,** Ireland, a Cupid holding in his dexter hand an arrow, and in his sinister a bow, all ppr. *cf.* 189. 7

Keating, on a mount vert, a boar passant sa. 40. 5

Keating of Kilcoan, co. Wexford, a boar statant gu., armed and unguled or, holding in the mouth a nettle-leaf vert.

Keating of Baybush, co. Limerick, a boar statant gu., armed and unguled or, holding in the mouth a nettle-leaf vert. *Providentia Divina.*

Keating, Rev. William, M.A. Oxon, of 177, Queen's Gate, London, S.W., a boar passant gu., holding in the mouth an oak-leaf slipped between two oak-branches ppr. *Amor ducit patriæ.*

Keats, on a naval coronet or, a tiger statant gardant ppr., charged on the body with an anchor sa.

Keats, Glouc. and Berks, a mountain-cat passant sa. 26. 4

Kebell of Homerston, Leics., a demi-griffin with wings displayed arg., gorged with a bar gemelle.

Keble, an elephant's head couped. 133. 2

Keck, Powys-, Harry Leycester, of Staughton Grange, Leics., and of Bank Hall, Lancs: (1) Out of a mural coronet gu., a maiden's head erm., purfled or, hair dishevelled of the same and flotant, adorned with a chaplet vert, garnished with roses ppr. (2) A lion's gamb erased and erect gu., grasping a fleur-de-lis bendways or.

Keddie, Scotland, a lancet open ppr. *Opifer per orbem dicor.* 178. 9

Kedmarston, Suff., a demi-lion rampant arg. 10. 2

Kedslie, an eagle with two heads displayed ppr., charged on the breast with a mullet arg. *Veritas omnia vincit.* *cf.* 74. 2

Keele, Ireland, a lion's gamb party per chevron or and gu. *cf.* 36. 4

Keegan, a dexter hand holding a sheaf of arrows. 214. 3

Keegan, Edward Wells, Esquire, J.P., of Clonavar, Strandtown, co. Down, a dexter hand holding a sheaf of five arrows, all ppr., charged on the wrist with a harp or, stringed arg. *Nunquam non paratus.*

Keeling of Newcastle-under-Lyne, Staffs, out of a mural coronet gu., a demi-lion or, supporting an escutcheon arg., charged with a cross formée fitchée gu.

Keeling, Frederic Hillersdon, Esquire, of St. Mary's Terrace, Colchester, in front of a demi-lion rampant or, holding between the paws an escutcheon gu., charged with a cross patée fitchée arg., a scaling-ladder fesseway sa. *Honneur sans reproche.*

Keeling of Southill, Beds, and Worcs., a lion sejant or, supporting a scaling-ladder gu.

Keeling, Kellyng, Kelyng, and **Kelynge,** a sword erect enfiled with a Saracen's head affrontée, all ppr. *cf.* 191. 11

Keen, Ireland, a bundle of five arrows or, barbed and feathered arg., banded gu. 173. 3

Keen or **Keene,** Suff., a hind's head erased sa., bezantée. *cf.* 124. 3

Keene, a griffin's head ppr. 66. 1

Keene, an eagle's head couped ppr. 83. 1

Keene, Ireland, a martlet or. 95. 2

Keene, Henry George, Esquire, C.I.E., a bundle of five arrows or, barbed and flighted arg., tied with a ribbon gu.

Keenlyside, a beacon lighted ppr. 177. 14

Keep, a weaver's shuttle erect gu., threaded ppr. 176. 13

Keep, a talbot passant. *Keep faith.*

Keet of Canterbury, Kent, a dexter arm embowed, couped at the shoulder vested, az., cuffed arg., holding in the hand ppr., a battle-axe of the second, staff or, entwined with a serpent vert.

Keete of Chellesburne, Dorset, a unicorn's head erased arg., collared gu., buckled and garnished or, armed of the last.

Keighley, a dragon's head erased arg., charged on the breast with a mullet sa. *cf.* 71. 2

Keighley-Peach, Henry Peach, Esquire, of Idlicote House, Shipston-on-Stour, and Alderminster Lodge, Stratford-on-Avon: (1) A demi-lion rampant per fesse arg. and gu., crowned or (*for Peach*). (2) A griffin's head sa., langued gu., charged with three mullets all counterchanged (*for Keighley*). *Quicquid dignum sapiente bonoque est.*

Keightley, Archibald, M.D., 46, Brook Street, Hanover Square, W., a griffin's head erased.

Keignes and **Keynes,** a cross crosslet fitched gu., between two palm-branches vert.

Keignes, a talbot passant sa., collared arg. *cf.* 54. 2

Keigwin of Mousehole, Cornw., a greyhound's head couped or. *cf.* 61. 2

Keiling, *see* Keeling.

Keily, a male griffin statant ppr.

Keinsham, a greyhound's head or, charged with three bars vert, guttée-d'or. *cf.* 61. 2

Keir of Calcutta, a mahout or Indian elephant-driver upon an elephant, all ppr. *Cum grano salis.* 133. 8

Keir-Small-Keir: (1) A branch of palm erect ppr. (*for Small*). 147. 4. (2) A hand holding a sword ppr. (*for Keir*). 212. 13

Keir, Scotland, an arm embowed, vested and cuffed, holding in the hand a sword. *Alterum non lædere.* 204. 1

Keir, Scotland, an arm in armour embowed holding in the hand a sword, all ppr. 195. 2

Keir, Scotland, a pelican vulning herself ppr. *Deus meum solamen.* 98. 1

Keir-Mackintosh of Dalmigavie, Inverness-sh.: (1) On the dexter side—a cat courant gardant ppr. (*for Mackintosh*). 26. 6. (2) On the sinister side—a pelican vulning herself ppr. (*for Keir*). *Touch not the cat but a glove.—Virescit in arduis virtus.* 98. 1

Keirie of Gogar, Edinburgh, Scotland, a hand holding a rose ppr. *Virtute viget.* 218. 10

Keirll of Croft Castle, Heref., a horse's head erased arg., holding in the mouth a palm-branch ppr. *cf.* 51. 4

Keith, *see* Kintore, Earl of.

Keith, a stag's head erased. 121. 2

Keith, Scotland, a stag's head ppr. *Veritas vincit.* 121. 5

Keith, Earl Marischal, a hart's head erased ppr., attired with ten tynes or. *Veritas vincit.* 121. 2

Keith, Scotland, a stag's head couped. *Memento creatorem.* 121. 5

Keith of Bruxie, a stag's head erased arg. *Veritas vincit.* 121. 2

Keith of Craig, Scotland: (1) *Ancient,* a stag at gaze or, under a bush of holly, all ppr. *Fortiter qui sedulo.* 116. 12 (2) *Modern,* an ermine ppr. *Ex candore decus.* 134. 6

Keith of Ostend, a demi-lion rampant ppr. *Recta sequor.* 10. 2

Keith of Tillygone, co. Kincardine, a hawk's lure ppr. *Venit ab astris.* 178. 11

Keith of Ravelston, a dexter arm holding in the hand a dagger ppr. *Pro veritate.* 212. 3

Keith of Auquhorsk, Aberdeensh., a hand holding a pen ppr. *Et loquor et taceo.* 217. 10

Keith of Arthurhouse, a dexter hand holding a pike erect ppr., headed arg. *Justa sequor.*

Keith, a dexter hand holding a scroll of paper ppr. *Et loquor et taceo.* 215. 6

Keith of Ludquhairn, Aberdeensh., Scotland, a dexter hand casting an anchor into the water. *Remember thy end.*

Keith, Scotland, an arm in armour in fess couped holding in the hand a sword in pale ppr.

Keith of Montrose, a hand holding a thunderbolt ppr., winged or. *Fortiter qui sedulo.* 216. 4

Keith, Lord Altrie, Scotland, a rock ppr. *Watch the temptation.* 179. 7

Kekebourne, on a ducal coronet or, a lion sejant holding a sword erect ppr.

Kekewich of Ketchfrench, Cornw., a leopard's head and neck affrontée sa. *cf.* 23. 3

Kekewich, Trehawke, Peamore House, Exeter, same crest.

Kekewich, Sir Arthur, a Judge of the High Court, same crest.

Kelburne, Viscount, *see* Glasgow, Earl of.

Kele of London, a demi-woman ppr., her hair dishevelled or, on her head a chaplet vert. 182. 5

Kelham, a demi-eagle displayed with two heads az., semée of erm. spots or, each wing charged with a covered cup of the last. 82. 1

Kelham, Robert, of Bleasby Hall, Notts, a demi-eagle displayed with two heads az., semée of erm. spots or, and charged on each wing with a covered cup of the same. *Beneficiorum memor.* 82. 1

Kelham, Godfrey Marmaduke, of Boxmore, Herts, same crest and motto.

Kelham, Robert Cecil, Esquire, of Havre, France, same crest and motto.

Keling of Hackney, Middx., out of a mural coronet a demi-lion or, supporting an escutcheon arg., charged with a cross pattée fitched at the foot gu.

Kelk or **Kelke,** a wolf sejant ppr. 29. 3

Kelk, Sir John William, Bart., of Tedworth, Wilts, and 3, Grosvenor Square, Middx., a wolf sejant erect sa., collared or, holding between the paws a leopard's face ppr., jessant-de-lis arg. *Lætus sorte vives sapienter.* 273. 7

Kell and **Kelle,** a boar's head erased az., ducally gorged or. 41. 6

Kellam and **Killome** of Danby, Yorks, a cross crosslet fitched gu., and a palm-branch vert, in saltier.

Kellam or **Kellum,** an otter's head erased ppr. 134. 3

Kellam and **Killome,** out of a mural coronet a griffin's head ducally gorged. 67. 6

Kelland of Painsford, Devonsh., a demi-tiger salient or, maned arg.

Kellaway or **Kelloway** of Stowford, Devonsh., a tiger passant regardant sa.

Kellawaye of Sherborne, Dorset, a cock arg., combed and wattled az. 91. 2

Kelle, *see* Kell.

Kelleher, Ireland, out of a mural coronet az., a lion's head or. 19. 12

Kellet of Ripley, Surrey, a cubit arm vested sa., cuffed and purfled arg., holding in the hand a roll of parchment of the last. 208. 3

Kellet, Ireland, a demi-wolf rampant sa. 31. 2

Kellett, Sir William, Bart., of Lota, co. Cork, an armed arm embowed, garnished or, holding in the hand a baton of the last. *Feret ad astra virtus.* *cf.* 200. 3

Kelley, Ireland, on a mount an apple-tree fructed, all ppr.

Kelley or **Kelly,** Devonsh., Sussex, and Ireland, out of a ducal coronet gu., an ostrich's head arg., holding in the beak a horse-shoe or. *cf.* 97. 11

Kelley, Kelly, and **Keylley,** a boar passant or, wounded by an arrow ppr. 40. 14

Kelley or **Kelly,** Ireland, a hand holding by the horn a bull's head erased.

Kelley of Torrington, Devonsh., a sea-horse in water ppr., holding between the paws a spiked ball.

Kellie, Earl, *see* Mar and Kellie.

Kellock, Scotland, out of a ducal coronet a sinister hand between two wings, all ppr. 221. 3

Kellock, Scotland, between two wings or, a heart. *Gloria in excelsis Deo.* *cf.* 110. 14

Kelloway and **Kellaway,** Devonsh., a tiger passant regardant sa.

Kelloway, a barnacle-bird arg.

Kelloway, Hants, a cock arg., combed, beaked, wattled, and spurred az. 91. 2

Kellum, an otter's head erased ppr. 134. 3

Kelly, Kelley, or **Keylley,** a boar passant or, vulned in the side by an arrow ppr. 40. 14

Kelly, Arthur Dillon Denis, Esquire, of Mucklow, Ballyforan, Ballinasloe, co. Galway, an enfield statant vert, with a bushy tail turned over the back. *Turris fortis mihi Deus.*

Kelly of Castle Kelly and Newtown, co. Galway, an enfield passant vert. *Turris fortis mihi Deus.* 252. 15

Kelly, Edward Festus, Esquire, of Northerwood House, Lyndhurst, Hants, and 49, Charles Street, Berkeley Square, same crest and motto.

Kelly, Ireland, on a chapeau gu., turned up erm., an enfield vert. *Turris fortis mihi Deus.*

Kelly, Francis Hume, Esquire, J.P., M.A., of Glencara, co. Westmeath, Barrister-at-Law, an enfield vert, charged on the shoulder with a mullet or. *Turris fortis mihi Deus.*

Kelly, Rev. Maitland, of Kelly, Lifton, and the Vicarage, Ottery St. Mary, Devonsh., out of a ducal coronet gu., an ostrich's head arg., holding in the beak a horse-shoe or.

Kelly, Reginald, Esquire, J.P., D.L., of Kelly, Lifton, Devonsh., same crest and motto.

Kelly, William Henry, Esquire, of Porchester Terrace, Paddington, Middx., in front of two anchors in saltire sa., a castle or. *Justam perficito nihil timeto.*

Kelly, Sir William Freeman, K.C.B., on a ducal coronet or, a greyhound courant arg. *Turris fortis mihi Deus.*

Kellyng, *see* Keeling.

Kelsey of Chelmsford and Thorpe, Essex, two cubit arms in pale vested sa., cuffed or, holding in the hand ppr. an escutcheon of the last. 208. 2

Kelshaw, a griffin's head erased. 66. 2

Kelso of Kelsoland, Ayrsh., a garb or. (Over the crest) *Otium cum dignitate.* 153. 2

Kelso, Lieutenant-Colonel Archibald, 25, South Street, Thurloe Square, S.W., same crest and motto.

Kelso, Captain Edward Barrington Purvis, J.P., D.L., Horkesley Park, Colchester, a garb supported by two lions rampant. *Lairg.*

Keltie and **Kelty,** a wheat-sheaf ppr. *Industria.* 153. 2

Kelton, Shropsh., a lion passant per pale erm. and ermines, ducally crowned or. *cf.* 6. 2

Kelverton, an eagle's head couped arg., gorged with a chaplet of roses ppr.

Kelvin, Baron (Thomson), Netherhall, Largs, Ayrsh., a cubit arm erect, vested az., cuffed arg., the hand holding five ears of rye ppr. *Honesty without fear.* 205. 5

Kelwich, a lion's head gardant sa.

Kelyng and **Kelynge,** *see* Keeling.

Kemball, Charles Gurdon, Esquire, of Mettingham Castle, Bungay, Suff., in front of a rock ppr., a fasces fesseways, also ppr., thereon a goat salient sa. *Nulla nisi ardua virtus.* 264. 9

Kemball, General Sir Arnold Burrowes, K.C.B., of 62, Lowndes Square, S.W., same crest and motto.

Kemball, Major-General John Shaw, J.P., of Fairseat, Wrotham, Sevenoaks, same crest and motto.

Kemble, between a branch of laurel on the dexter side and one of palm on the sinister, both ppr., a boar's head and neck sa., erased gu., charged with an étoile arg. 42. 3

Kemble, a dexter arm in armour, holding in the hand a broken spear ppr. *cf.* 210. 9

Kemble, Thomas, Runwell Hall, Essex, a wolf's head couped and erect or, the mouth dropping blood.

Kemble, Captain Horatio, R.N., Great Claydons, East Hanningfield, a wolf's head couped and erect or, the mouth dropping blood.

Kemeys-Tynte, Halswell Milborne, Esquire, J.P., D.L., of Cefn Mably, Glamorgansh., Halswell, Somers., and Burleigh Hall, Leics.: (1) On a mount vert, a unicorn sejant arg., armed and crined or (*for Kemeys*). (2) Issuant from a ducal coronet a demi-griffin, all or (*for Halswell*). *Duw dy ras.* 64. 4

Kemeys-Tynte, S. David, 10, Royal Crescent, Bath: (1) Same as (1) above (*for Kemeys*). (2) A demi-griffin erased or (*for Halswell*). *Duw dy ras* (*for Kemeys*) *Tynctus cruore Saraceno* (*for Tynte*).

Kemor, a lion's head erased or, pierced through by arrows sa. 18. 4

Kemp, a goat statant arg. 129. 5

Kemp, a goat passant arg. *cf.* 129. 5

Kemp, Surrey and Cornw., a falcon ppr., beaked and legged or, hooded gu. *cf.* 85. 1

Kemp of Westbrook, Norf., and of South Mallins, Sussex, on a garb in fess or, a falcon with wings addorsed erm.

Kemp, Sir Kenneth Hagar, Bart., B.A., of Gissing, Norf., a pelican vulning herself ppr. upon a garb fesseways or. *Lucem spero.*

Kemp, George Brookes, Esquire, of Goodyers, Hendon, Middx., a garb fesseways or, thereon a pelican in her piety with wings elevated sa., vulned ppr., charged on the breast with three annulets interlaced and gorged with a collar gemel of the first. 98. 10

Kemp, Captain William, of Lyminster House, near Arundel, on a mount vert, a falcon with wings elevated, feeding on a garb or, and charged on the breast with a hurt.

Kemp, on a mount vert, a pelican or, charged on the breast with a pomeis picking at a garb of the second.

Kemp, Ireland, an antelope trippant or, collared az. *cf.* 126. 6

Kemp and **Kempt,** Scotland, a demi-lion holding in the dexter paw a battle-axe, all ppr. *Promptus.* *cf.* 15. 6

Kemp and **Kempe,** Essex and Suff., an arm couped at the elbow, vested arg., charged with two bends wavy az., cuffed of the first, holding in the hand ppr. a chaplet vert.

Kempe, Charles Eamer, Esquire, of Old Place, Lindfield, Sussex, and 28, Nottingham Place, W., on a mount vert, a falcon with wings elevated, feeding on a garb or, and charged on the breast with a hurt.

Kempe, Kent, a demi-griffin or, winged gu., holding a garb of the first.

Kempe, C. M., Chantry House, New Shoreham, Sussex, a falcon belled. *Qui seminat in lachrymis metit in gaudeo.*

Kempenfelt, a demi-man in armour, the sinister arm embowed, the dexter holding a sword above his head, all ppr., between two wings erect vert.

Kempsey, Shropsh., a holly-tree vert, fructed gu. *Sit vult Deus.* 145. 6

Kempson and **Kempston,** Warw. and Staffs, a demi-lion az., gorged with a collar or, charged with three mullets of the first. *cf.* 10. 9

Kempson, a demi-talbot. *cf.* 55. 8

Kempster, a lion's gamb holding a thistle ppr. 37. 6

Kempston, Ireland, a hand holding an olive-branch ppr. 219. 9

Kempt, a hedgehog or. 135. 8

Kempt, the late Lieutenant-General Rt. Hon. Sir James, G.C.B., out of the battlements of a tower arg., a demi-lion erminois, grasping in both paws a battle-axe, the blade and handle thereof arg., the spear-head or. *Promptus.*

Kempthorne, a lion sejant. 8. 8

Kempthorne, Rev. Philip Henry, M.A., F.R.A.S., Wellington College, Berks: (1) A lion sejant. *Karenza whelas karenza.* (2) On a chapeau a dexter arm embowed grasping a scimitar ppr. *Pro rege et patria.* (*for Ainslie*).

Kempton of London, Middx., and Cambs, out of a ducal coronet or, a garb arg. *cf.* 153. 2

Kempton, a cloud ppr. 162. 13

Kempton of London, and Morden, Cambs, a goat erm., armed and ungu. or, collared and lined sa., the collar charged with three bezants, with a ring at the end of the line.

Kemsley, John Cole, on a mount vert, a demi-zebra ppr., gorged with a collar gemel or, resting the sinister fore-leg on an esquire's helmet, also ppr.

Kemyng, a unicorn's head sa., platée. *cf.* 49. 7

Kenah, Lieutenant-Colonel Thomas, C.B., a horse's head erased arg., charged on the neck with a fleur-de-lis az. *Fidelis.* *cf.* 51. 4

Kenan, Dumfries, Scotland, a lion rampant az. *Nostra quæ fecimus.* 1. 13

Kendall, Devonsh., a hand holding a sheaf of arrows points downwards, all ppr. 214. 3

Kendall of Thorpthules, Durh., a wolf's head and neck erased arg. 30. 8

Kendall of Austrey, Warw., an eagle displayed az. *Aquila petit solem.* 75. 2

Kendall of Stourbridge, Worcs., an eagle displayed or. 75. 2

Kendall, a demi-pelican arg., vulning herself ppr.

Kendall of Exeter, a lion statant, the tail coward and passing over his back gu.

Kendall, Osmond Lennox, Pelyn, Lostwithiel, Cornw., a lion passant gu. *Virtus depressa resurget.*

Kendlemarsh, two lions' gambs chevronways ermines, armed gu.

Kendrick, a hawk's leg erased, jessed and belled, all ppr. 113. 8

Kendrick of Warrington, Lancs, on a sheaf of arrows a falcon jessed and belled, all ppr. *Virtue is honour.*

Kene of Starston, Norf., a hind's head erased arg., gorged with a collar gu., charged with three bezants, to the collar a ring or. *cf.* 124. 5

Kene, Suff., a hind's head erased arg., pellettée, charged with a trefoil or. *cf.* 124. 3

Kenerby, a wolf's head erased erm. 30. 8

Keningham, a man's head in profile bearded ppr., on the head a chapeau gu., turned up erm.

Kenisham of Semford, Beds, a greyhound's head couped az., charged on the neck with three bars between as many guttes-d'or. *cf.* 61. 2

Kenlis, Baron, *see* Headfort, Marquess.

Kenmare, Earl of (Browne), Killarney House, Killarney, Kerry, a demi-dragon arg., wings expanded sa., guttée of the first. *Loyal en tout.* 72. 7

Kenmure, Viscount (Gordon), Scotland, a demi-savage wreathed about the head and loins with laurel, all ppr. *Dread God.*

Kenn, Somers., three crescents interwoven arg.

Kenna, Paul Aloysius, Esquire, 21st Hussars, Madras, on a mount vert, a ruined castle in flames ppr. *Age quod agis.*

Kennan, Ireland, out of a crescent az., a cross crosslet fitched gu. 166. 9

Kennard, Sir Coleridge Arthur Fitzroy, Bart., Fernhill, Southampton, a dexter cubit arm erect in armour ppr., charged with a buckle gu., the hand grasping a key in bend or, surmounting a broken sword in bend sinister ppr. *At spes non fracta.*

Kennard, Colonel Edmund Hegan, V.D., F.R.G.S., M.A. (Oxon.), of 25, Bruton Street, W., a dexter cubit arm in armour ppr., charged with a buckle gu., grasping in the hand a key or, in bend, and a broken sword in bend sinister ppr. *At spes non fracta.*

Kennard, Adam Steinmetz, Esquire, of Crawley Court, Winchester, same crest and motto.

Kennard, Edward, Esquire, D.L., J.P., of Junior Carlton Club, same crest and motto.

Kennard, Henry Martyn, Esquire, of Falkirk, Stirlingsh., and 63, Lowndes Square, London, S.W., same crest and motto.

Kennard, Henry Steinmetz, Esquire, of Shopwyke House, Oving, near Chichester, same crest and motto.

Kennard, Robert William, Esquire, of Llwyndu Court, Abergavenny, same crest and motto.

Kennard, a lion's gamb erased vert. 36. 4

Kennard, Ireland, a hand in armour ppr., holding a broken sword gu.

Kennard of Hordle Cliff, Hants, a cubit arm erect in armour ppr., holding a key and a broken sword in saltire or. *At spes non fracta.*

Kennaway, a phœnix in flames ppr. 82. 2

Kennaway, on a chapeau a phœnix in flames, all ppr. 82. 11

Kennaway, Sir John Henry, Bart., D.L., M.A., M.P., of Escot, Ottery St. Mary, Devonsh., an eagle rising ppr., from the beak an escutcheon pendent az., charged with the sun in splendour, also ppr. *Ascendam.* 283. 1

Kenne of Kenne, Somers., a unicorn's head az., bezantee, crined or, the horn twisted of the last and sa. *cf.* 49. 9

Kenneday, an arm in pale grasping a belt, all ppr. 219. 3

Kennedy, Marquess of Ailsa, *see* Ailsa.

Kennedy of Garvin Mains, a dolphin naiant ppr. *Avise la fin.* 140. 5

Kennedy, same crest and motto. 140. 5

Kennedy, Robert John, Esquire, of Cultra Manor, Holywood, co. Down, same crest and motto.

Kennedy, John, of Underwood, Ayrsh., Scotland, and 15, Aldford Street, Park Lane, W., a dolphin haurient, head upwards ppr. *Vincit vim virtus.* 140. 11

Kennedy of Cultra, co. Down, a dolphin naiant ppr. *Avise la fin.* 140. 5

Kennedy of Girvanmains, Ayrsh., same crest and motto. 140. 5

Kennedy, Scotland, a dolphin naiant. 140. 5

Kennedy, Charles George Blagrave, Esquire, J.P., of Mullanteau, Stewartstown, co. Tyrone, a dolphin naiant az. *Avise la fin.*

Kennedy of Knocknalling, Ayrsh., a dolphin naiant or. *Avise la fin.* 140. 5

Kennedy: (1) On the dexter side—a soldier of the 1st Royal Dragoons holding in his dexter hand a sword ppr., and in his sinister a French eagle with a tricoloured flag having thereon the number 105. (2) On the sinister side—a dolphin naiant az. *Avise la fin.* 140. 5

Kennedy, Clark-, John William James, Knockgray, Kircudbrightsh.: (1) A demi-dragoon of the Royal Dragoons holding dexter a sword and sinister an eagle, all ppr. (2) A dolphin naiant ppr. *Avise la fin.*

Kennedy, Scotland, a palm-branch slipped vert. 147. 1

Kennedy of Kirkmichael, Ayrsh., a palm-branch slipped ppr. *Malim esse probus quam haberi.* 147. 1

Kennedy, Ireland, in front of a tree vert, a greyhound courant arg. *cf.* 58. 5

Kennedy, William M'Laughlin, Esquire, of Ellerslie, Eltham, Taranaki, New Zealand, a dove lying upon its back, thereon perched an eagle with wings extended preying on the breast of its victim. *Veritas odium parit.* 77. 1

Kennedy, on a rock a goose, all ppr.

Kennedy, Scotland, a hawk hooded ppr. *cf.* 85. 1

Kennedy of Dublin, a demi-eagle displayed sa., bezantée, holding in the beak a cross formée fitchée gu.

Kennedy of Barclanachan, in the sea an anchor in pale, all ppr. *God be guide.* 161. 6

Kennedy, John Campbell, Dunure, Maybole, Ayrsh., a fleur-de-lis or, issuing out of two oak-leaves ppr. *Fuimus.*

Kennedy of Dunure, a hand holding a sword. *Fuimus.* 212. 13

Kennedy of Clowburn, a dexter hand holding a military girdle with the inscription, *Vires veritas. Non fallo.* *cf.* 219. 3

Kennedy of Kirkhill, a hand holding a dagger ppr. *Fuimus.* 212. 9

Kennedy of Auchterfordle, same crest. *Avise la fin.*

Kennedy of Tombrechan, co. Tipperary, an arm erect couped below the elbow, the hand holding an oak-branch fructed, all ppr.

Kennedy, Sir John Charles, Bart., D.L., B.A., of Johnstown, Kennedy, co. Dublin, an arm embowed in armour ppr., holding in the hand a branch of oak, also ppr. *Adhæreo virtuti.*

Kennedy, Ireland, a hand ppr., holding an acorn between two oak-leaves vert.

Kennedy, Ireland, an arm in scale armour embowed holding in the hand a scimitar, all ppr.

Kennedy, Ireland, out of a cloud an arm in armour embowed in fess, holding in the hand a dagger ppr. *The strongest hand uppermost.*

Kennedy of Romanno House, Peeblesh., a dexter hand grasping a dagger ppr.

Kennedy, Ireland, a hand holding a bloody dagger ppr. *Laugh ladur an aughtar.* *cf.* 212. 9

Kennedy, Roland Fergussone, of Bennane, Ayrsh., and Glenapp, Ayrsh., Scotland, out of two oak-leaves ppr., a fleur-de-lis or. *Fuimus.*

Kennedy-Erskine, Augustus John William Henry, of Dun House, Montrose, N.B.: (1) A griffin's head erased gu., charged with a mullet erm., holding in the beak a sword bendways, point upwards ppr. (*for Erskine*). (2) A dolphin naiant ppr. (*for Kennedy*).

Kennedy-Skipton, Henry Stacy Skipton, Esquire, M.A.: (1) An arm vambraced holding a dagger ppr. (*for Skipton*). (2) A dolphin ppr. *Avise la fin.—Pro patria.*

Kennell, two lions' heads erased and addorsed, the dexter or, the sinister gu. 17. 3

Kennerley, a lion's gamb holding a laurel-branch ppr. 37. 4

Kennet or Kennett, Norf., two branches of palm in orle. 146. 2

Kennett, George Buttler, Esquire, Town Clerk of Norwich, *uses:* a dexter arm in armour embowed, holding in the hand an esquire's helmet (*of no authority*). *Gardez bien.*

Kennett of London, out of a ducal coronet or, an arm embowed in armour ppr., the hand in a gauntlet holding an esquire's helmet ppr.

Kennett-Barrington, Sir Vincent Hunter Barrington, of 57, Albert Hall Mansions, W., and Manor House, Dorchester: (1) A hermit's head in profile, couped below the shoulders ppr., vested paly of six gu. and or, his cowl thrown back (*for Barrington*). (2) Between two branches of palm a dexter arm embowed in armour ppr., garnished or, charged with an estoile gu., holding in the hand a helmet ppr. (*for Kennett*).

Kenney, Ireland, a greyhound couchant between two branches of laurel in orle, all ppr. 60. 5

Kenney, Ireland, an arm in armour embowed holding in the hand a baton, all ppr. 294. 12

Kenney, Edward Herbert, Clifton House, Alleyn Park, London, S.E., same crest. *Tuebor.*

Kenney of Dublin, a cubit arm erect vested gu., cuffed arg., holding in the hand a roll of parchment, all ppr. 208. 8

Kenney, Ireland, out of an earl's coronet or, pearled ppr., a demi-arm erect sleeved gu., with a white ruff, holding in the hand a roll of parchment ppr. *Teneat, luceat, floreat, vi, virtute, et valore.* 208. 11

Kenney of Kilclogher, co. Galway, and Merrion Square, Dublin, out of an earl's coronet or, the pearls arg., a cubit arm erect vested gu., cuffed also arg., the hand grasping a roll of parchment ppr. *Teneat, luceat, floreat.* 208. 11

Kenney, Jacques Louis Lionel, Lieutenant in the Imperial Navy of France, Knight of the Orders of the Legion of Honour and of St. Stanilaus of Russia, issuing from an earl's coronet or, the pearls arg., a cubit arm erect vested gu., cuffed arg., holding in the hand a roll of parchment ppr. *Teneat, luceat, floreat.* 208. 11

Kenney, Arthur Herbert, Esquire, C.M.G., D.S.O., Lieutenant-Colonel Royal Engineers, of 2, Manston Terrace, Heavitree, Exeter, on a wreath or and az., a demi-arm, sleeved gu., with a white ruff, holding in the hand a roll of parchment ppr. 243. 12

Kenney-Herbert, John, Esquire, J.P.: (1) A bundle of twelve arrows in saltire or, headed and feathered arg., belted gu., and buckled of the first (*for Herbert*). (2) A dexter cubit arm erect vested gu., cuffed arg., the hand grasping a paper scroll ppr. (*for Kenney*).

Kennicot, a griffin's head erased. 66. 2

Kenning, a yew-tree growing out of a mount semée of trefoils, all ppr.

Kennion of Liverpool, Lancs, a demi-lion rampant ppr., holding between the paws an anchor erect or. *Ventis secundis.—Deo juvante.*

Kennison, a dove holding in its beak an olive-branch, all ppr. 92. 5

Kennoway, Scotland, an arm embowed in fess couped gu., holding three stalks of wheat or. 202. 6

Kennoway, Scotland, a thunderbolt winged ppr. 174. 13

Kenny, a demi-lion rampant gardant gu., holding a fleur-de-lis or. *cf.* 13. 2

Kenrick, an arm erect and vested, holding in the hand ears of wheat. 205. 7

Kenrick of London, on a sheaf of arrows fesseways or, feathered and headed arg., a hawk close, also arg., beaked and belled of the first.

Kenrick, Shropsh., on a bundle of arrows in fess or, feathered and headed arg., bound sa., a hawk close of the second, beaked and belled of the first.

Kenrick, Flintsh., a falcon rising grasping in the dexter claw three arrows, two in saltier and one in fess. *Virtute ad astra.*

Kensey, Herts, a demi-griffin erased erm., holding between his claws a mullet or.

Kensing, a stag springing ppr. 117. 2

Kensing, on a mount a stag current, all ppr. 118. 13

Kensington, Baron (Edwardes), St. Bride's, Little Haven, Pembrokesh., upon a mount vert, a wyvern with wings expanded arg. *Garde la foi.* 314. 1

Kensington, out of a ducal coronet a demi-eagle displayed, all ppr. 80. 14

Kensit, Thomas Glover, Esquire, of Skinner's Hall, London, the Roman fasces fesseways ppr., thereon an eagle rising regardant or, supporting in the beak a tilting-spear resting upon the fasces in bend sinister, also ppr. 78. 9

Kent, Ireland, a bridge of three arches ppr. 158. 4

Kent, a wolf's head couped. 30. 5

Kent, Northamp., a talbot's head couped gu., charged on the neck with a cinquefoil erm. *cf.* 56. 12

Kent, a lion's head erased or, collared sa. 18. 6

Kent, Egleton-, Bart., Suff., a lion's head erased collared. 18. 6

Kent, George Charles, Esquire, of Park House, Longton, Staffs, a lion's head erased erminois, collared, lined, and ringed az. *Virtute et honore.* 298. 13

Kentish, Somers., a demi-ostrich with wings addorsed, holding in its beak a horse-shoe.

Kenton, on a chapeau gu., turned up or, a lion passant gardant arg., ducally crowned ppr. *cf.* 4. 5

Kenton, a dexter hand couped in fess holding a fleur-de-lis or. 221. 9

Kenwick, an arm in armour holding in the hand an esquire's helmet ppr.

Kenyon, Baron (Kenyon), Gredington, Flintsh., a lion sejant ppr., resting the dexter paw on a cross flory arg. *Magnanimiter crucem sustine.* *cf.* 8. 8

Kenyon, James William, Esquire, of Cecily Hill, Cirencester, a lion sejant ppr., holding in the mouth a cross patonce arg., and resting the dexter fore-paw on a woolpack sa. *Si diligens honorabilis.* 260. 9

Kenyon, Robert Lloyd, Esquire, of Pradoe, Oswestry, Shropsh., a lion sejant ppr., resting the dexter paw on a cross flory arg. *Magnanimiter crucem sustine.*

Kenyon-Slaney, William Slaney, Esquire, of Hatton Grange, Shifnal, Salop: (1) A griffin's head gu., winged erminois, and gorged with a collar gemel or (*for Slaney*). (2) A lion sejant ppr., resting the dexter paw on a cross flory arg. (*for Kenyon*). *Deo duce, comite industria* (*for Slaney*).—*Magnanimiter crucem sustine* (*for Kenyon*).

Kenyon of Easthall, Oxon., and London, a demi-lion rampant ppr., holding a halbert gu., headed or. 15. 4

Kenyon, on a rock a dove holding in its beak an olive-branch, all ppr. 93. 9

Keogh, Ireland, an arm embowed ppr., vested az., holding in the hand a covered cup or. 203. 4

Keogh, Ireland, a boar passant, armed and crined or.

Keogh of Kilbride, co. Carlow, a boar passant ppr. *Resistite usque ad sanguinem.* 40. 9

Keppel, Earl of Albemarle, *see* Albemarle.

Keppel, Hon. Sir Henry, K.C.B., Admiral of the Fleet, of 8, the Mansion, Albany, W., out of a ducal coronet or, a swan's head and neck arg. *Ne cede malis.*

Keppel, William George, Esquire, of Old Buckenham Grange, Attleborough, Norf., same crest and motto.

Kepping, a maiden's head affrontée, the hair dishevelled, the bust vested. *cf.* 182. 5

Ker, Duke of Roxburghe, *see* Roxburghe.

Ker, Earl of Ancrum, a stag's head and neck couped arg., collared gu., charged with three mullets of the first issuing out of an open crown or. *Tout droit.*

Ker, Lord Jedburgh, a stag's head erased or. *Forward.* 121. 2

Ker of Kerhall, a unicorn's head erased arg., armed and crined or. *Pro Christo et patriâ dulce periculum.* 49. 5

Ker of Blackshiels, a unicorn's head erased arg. *Virescit vulnere virtus.* 49. 5

Ker of Morristoun, Roxburghsh., Scotland, a unicorn's head couped arg., gorged with a collar az., charged with three crosses moline of the first. *Dulce pro patria periculum.* *cf.* 49. 11

Ker of Gateshaw, Scotland, a unicorn's head erased arg., armed and maned or. *Pro Christo et patriâ.* 49. 5

Ker of Knock, Banffsh., a unicorn's head erased arg. *Virescit in arduis virtus.* 49. 5

Ker of Cevers, a stag's head erased or. *Tout droit.* 121. 2

Ker, same crest. *Deus solamen.* 121. 2

Ker, Scotland, a stag's head erased ppr., with ten tines or. 121. 2

Ker, Scotland, the sun in his splendour or. *A Deo lumen.* 162. 2

Ker of Abbot-rule, Roxburghsh., the sun rising out of a cloud ppr. *J'advance.* 162. 5

Ker of Chatto, Roxburghsh., the sun in his splendour ppr. *Régulier et vigoureux.* 162. 2

Ker of Sutherland Hall, Roxburghsh., a dexter hand holding a dagger ppr. *Abest timor.* 212. 9

Ker of Linlithgow, a pelican volant ppr. *Deus meum solamen.*

Ker-Seymer, Harry Ernest Clay, Esquire, of Hanford, near Blandford, Dorset: (1) A chapeau turned up erm., winged or. (2) A unicorn's head erased arg. (3) Two wings displayed arg., each charged with a chevron engrailed between three trefoils slipped sa. (*for Clay*). *Dulce pro patria periculum.*

Kerby, a hand in armour holding a pheon ppr. 211. 7

Kercher, Norf., a cross botonnée az., between two wings inverted saltireways or.

Kerchinall, Northamp., a demi-bay-horse ppr., armed and bridled or, on his head three feathers az., or and arg 53. 6

Kercy, a boar's head couped or. 43. 1

Kerdeston, on a mountain ppr., a goshawk sa. 108. 4

Kerdiffe, on a tower ppr., a lion rampant or. 157. 12

Kerdiffe, a hind sejant regardant ppr., resting the dexter foot on a mount vert. *cf.* 125. 1

Kerdiston, issuing out of a tower a demi-griffin, all ppr. 157. 5

Kerdiston and **Kerdston,** a dexter hand apaumée couped in fess ppr. 221. 6

Keresforth, Yorks, a demi-lion rampant gu., holding in its paws a mill-rind in pale arg. *cf.* 10. 3

Kergourdenac, two dolphins addorsed ppr. 140. 1

Kerioll, a mullet or, environed with clouds ppr. *cf.* 164. 11

Kerle, on a mount vert, a hedgehog or. *cf.* 135. 8

Kernaby, a cubit arm ppr., holding in the hand a crescent sa. 216. 8

Kerne of Truro, Cornw., on a mount vert, a greyhound current per pale or and arg., collared gu. *cf.* 58. 2

Kerney, a unicorn sejant sa., armed and maned or.

Kerr, *see* Lothian, Marquess of.

Kerr-Pearse, *see* Pearse.

Kerr, Glasgow, a mullet gu. *Praise God.* 164. 2

Kerr of Westbourne Terrace, Hillhead, Lanarksh., a mullet gu. *Praise God.* 164. 2

Kerr, the late Robert Malcolm, Esquire, LL.D., a mullet arg. *Praise God.*

Kerr of Bughtrigg, Roxburghsh., Scotland, the sun in his splendour ppr. *A Deo lumen.* 162. 2

Kerr, William James, Esquire, Hythe House, Hythe, Southampton, a sun in his splendour ppr. *Sero sed serio.* 162. 2

Kerr, Northamp., a stag's head erased or. *Deus solamen.* 121. 2

Kerr, Russell James, Esquire, J.P., Chairman of Quarter Sessions, of the Haie, Newnham-on-Severn, Glouc., same crest and motto.

Kerr of Prestbury Court, near Cheltenham, a unicorn's head. *Deus solamen.*

Kerr, a chevalier in full armour holding a horse by the head ppr. 53. 11

Kerr-Pearse, Captain Beauchamp Albert Thomas: (1) A dexter arm embowed in armour, the hand grasping a tilting-spear in bend sinister, all ppr., between two estoiles gu. (*for Pearse*). (2) The sun in splendour ppr. (*for Kerr*). *Cadente porrigo dextram.*—*Sero sed serio.*

Kerr, Scott-, Robert, Chatto, Roxburghsh. (1) The sun ppr. (*for Kerr*). (2) A stag trippant armed with ten tines (*for Scott*). *Régulier et vigoureux.*—*Pacem amo.*

Kerrich, Walter Fitzgerald, of Geldeston Hall, Suff., on a mount vert, a galtrap sa. *Nunquam non paratus.* *f.* 174. 14

Kerrich-Walker, Henry Walker, Esquire, of Newker House, Chester-le-Street, Durh.: (1) In front of a greyhound's head couped arg., gorged with a collar gemelle sa., a crescent gu. (*for Walker*). *cf.* 61. 2. (2) In front of two spears in saltire ppr., a galtrap or. (*for Kerrich*). *Faire sans dire.*

Kerrifford of Dublin, a demi-lion rampant sa., holding between the paws a cross moline or.

Kerrison of Birkfield Lodge, Ipswich, Suff., a bundle of sugar-canes ppr., thereon a dove arg., winged or, holding in the beak an olive-branch ppr.

Kerrison of Breckles, Norf., on a mount vert, a tiger passant ppr., collared and lined or, the dexter fore-paw resting on a galtrap of the last. *Rien sans Dieu.*

Kerrison, Bart. (*extinct*), of Hoxne and Brome, Suff.: (1) Of honourable augmentation, out of a mural coronet or, a dexter arm in armour embowed, entwined by a branch of laurel, holding in the hand a flagstaff ppr., therefrom flowing a forked banner gu., fringed or, inscribed with the word "*Peninsula*" in letters of gold. (2) Upon a mount vert, a tiger passant ppr., collared and lined or, the dexter fore-paw resting on a galtrap of the last. *Rien sans Dieu.*

Kerry, Earl of, *see* Lansdowne, Marquess of.

Kerryll, a lion rampant gu., holding a sword erect ppr.

Kers, Scotland, a torteau between two wings or. *cf.* 110. 4

Kersey, a boar's head couped or. 43. 1

Kersey, Robert, Esquire, of Hurst Lodge, Lee, Kent, upon a mount vert, a boar's head couped arg., on either side a branch of three cinquefoils slipped vert. *Peractus conamine.* 42. 8

Kershaw, a ram passant ppr. 131. 13

Kershaw, Lancs, a cock pheasant ppr. *cf.* 90. 8

Kershaw of Savile Green, Yorks, the stump of an oak eradicated and sprouting fesseways ppr., thereon a pheasant holding in the beak a sprig of oak, also ppr.

Kershaw, Edmund William, Esquire, of 10, Hanover Square, London, W., on a mount vert, in front of two trunks of trees erect, sprouting from the sinister a pheasant ppr., holding in the beak two ears of wheat slipped or. *Fide semper Deo.*

Kerslake of Barmer Hall, Norf., on the trunk of a tree a falcon close, all ppr. *Ad finem fidelis.* 86. 11

Kersteman of Canewdon, a demi-man affrontée in armour ppr., the viser up, plumed arg., holding in his dexter hand an arrow palewise or, barbed and flighted az. *cf.* 187. 3

Kervell, on a ducal coronet or, a wyvern gu. 70. 9

Kervyle of Wallington, Norf., two lion's gambs in pale arg., holding between the claws a pile gu.

Kervyle of Wiggenhall, Norf., a goat passant sa., armed and crined or. *cf.* 129. 5

Keryell, an arm in armour embowed couped at the shoulder, the part above the elbow in fess resting on the wreath, the hand erect holding a close helmet, all ppr. 198. 11

Kesstell, an oak-tree ppr. 143. 5

Kestell of Kestell in Manaccan, Cornw., a demi-bull erm., armed, ungu., collared and lined sa. 45. 8

Kestell of Kestell in Eglospayle, Cornw., a tower ppr. 156. 2

Kestell-Cornish: (1) A Cornish chough (*for Cornish*). (2) A tower ppr. (*for Kestell*).

Kesterton of London, a demi-bull rampant ppr., armed and ungu. or, gorged with a chaplet vert. *Timor omnis abest.* 45. 14

Kesteven, Baron (Trollope), of Casewick, Stamford, Lincs, on a mount vert, a stag courant arg., attired or, and holding in the mouth an oak-leaf ppr. *Audio sed taceo.* *cf.* 118. 13

Keswick, William, Esquire, of Eastwick Park, Great Bookham, Leatherhead, upon two wings arg., an arm, vested az., cuffed of the first, the hand holding a thistle ppr. *Ubique.*

Ketchin, Scotland, a pelican's head erased, vulning itself ppr. 98. 2

Keteridge of London, out of a mural coronet a lion's head or. 19. 12

Ketford, a stag's head erased and affrontée arg., attired or. 119. 10

Kething, Ireland, a dexter hand holding a pine-branch ppr.

Ketland, a lion passant az. 6. 2

Ketleby, *see* Kettleby.

Ketson, a lion's head erased, holding in the mouth a trefoil slipped, all ppr. *cf.* 17. 8

Kett, Suff., on a mount vert, a peacock ppr. *Rara avis in terris.* *cf.* 103. 4

Kett, Norf., a leopard's face az. 22. 2

Kett of Kellsall, Suff., on a mount vert, a peacock ppr. *Rara avis in terris.* *cf.* 103. 4

Kettewell of Dumbleton Hall, Glouc., a lion rampant gu., holding in the dexter fore-paw a cross patée fitchée, and resting the sinister hind-paw on a cross patée or.

Kettle, a bundle of five arrows ppr., banded gu., buckled or. 173. 3

Kettle of Dallicott House, Claverly, Shropsh., a reindeer's head erased ppr., collared and chained or. *Bono vince malum.* 122. 1

Kettle, Rupert Edward Cooke, Esquire, of 1, Essex Court, Temple, E.C., Merridale, Wolverhampton, Staffs, and of Glan-y-don, Towyn, Merionethsh., in front of a dexter cubit arm vested az., cuffed arg., the hand ppr. holding a balance suspended or, a portcullis, also arg. *Qui tel.*

Kettleby or **Kettelby,** a lion's head erased gu., holding in the mouth an arrow az., feathered arg. *cf.* 17. 8

Kettleby, Lincs and Shropsh., a lion's head erased gu. 17. 2

Kettlewell, William Wildman, Esquire, of Harptree Court, East Harptree, Bristol, on a wreath of the colours, in front of a demi-bull sa., gorged with a collar and a line therefrom reflexed over the back, and holding between the legs a cinquefoil, three crosses patée fessewise or. *Taurum cornibus prende.* 45. 13

Ketton, a boar's head couped in fess, between two branches of laurel in orle, all ppr. *cf.* 42. 1

Ketton, Robert William, Esquire, of Felbrigg Hall, Norf., out of a ducal coronet a griffin's head between two ostrich-feathers.

Keux, a mound crossed and banded ppr. 159. 12

Kevel, a horse's head couped. *cf.* 50. 13

Keverdon, Lancs, a buck's head per pale arg. and az., attired counterchanged. 121. 5

Kevett of Coventry, Warw., a demi-lion rampant purp., murally gorged, lined and ringed or. *cf.* 10. 2

Kew, Yorks, a demi-lion or, holding between its paws a garb az. 12. 5

Kewley, a stag's head erased az. 121. 2

Key, a greyhound's head arg., charged with three pellets. *cf.* 61. 12

Key, Scotland, a bird volant. *In Deo solo spes mea.* 88. 3

Key, Rev. Sir John Kingsmill Causton, Bart., of Thornbury, Glouc., a mount vert, thereon a hart lodged gardant ppr., charged on the body with three mullets fesseways sa. *In Domino confido.* 285. 3

Keydon, a dolphin charged on the back with an increscent. *Avise la fin.* *cf.* 140. 5

Keye of Milcomb, Oxon., a griffin's head couped at the breast, the wings addorsed arg., holding in the beak a key or. *cf.* 67. 11

Keyes, an open hand couped at the wrist ppr., holding between the forefinger and thumb a key or. *Virtute adepta.*

Keyes, a griffin's head between two wings, holding in the beak a palm-branch, all ppr. 65. 9

Keyle, a woman's head and shoulders ppr., vested az., the hair dishevelled, round the head a chaplet or. 182. 5

Keylley, a boar passant or, vulned by an arrow ppr. 40. 14

Keymer, an ass passant ppr. 125. 7

Keyne, Suff., six arrows in saltier ppr., feathered arg., barbed or, banded with a ribbon sa. 173. 13

Keynes, a talbot passant sa., collared arg. *cf.* 54. 5

Keynes or **Keignes,** a cross crosslet fitchée gu., between two palm-branches vert. *cf.* 166. 5

Keys, a Minerva's head ppr. 182. 1

Keysall, a sinister arm embowed and vested, holding in the hand a lily slipped and leaved.

Keyser, Charles Edward, Esquire, of Aldermaston Court, Reading, a hand holding a carbuncle emitting rays. *Providentia tutamur.* 293. 9

Keyt, Glouc., a kite's head erased or.

Keyte, a unicorn's head erased arg., armed and collared gu. 49. 11

Kibble, Scotland, an antique crown az. 180. 12

Kibble, a Roman fasces erect. 171. 4

Kibble of Whiteford, Renfrewsh., Scotland, a demi-eagle rising ppr. *Illæso lumine solem.* 80. 2

Kidd, a martlet with wings addorsed ppr. *cf.* 95. 11

Kidd of Armagh, on a wreath arg. and vert, an increscent arg., charged with a rose gu. *Donec impleat orbem.* 163. 13

Kidd, Arthur William Lyle, Esquire, an increscent arg., charged with a rose gu. *Donec impleat orbem.*

Kidd of London and Scotland, a crescent arg. *Donec impleat.* 163. 2

Kidd, out of a crescent az., a pine-apple ppr. *Nil sine magno labore.* *cf.* 152. 8

Kidd of Farnworth, Lancs, a goat's head erased arg., attired or. *Nil admirari.* 128. 5

Kiddall of South Ferreby, Lincs, a goat's head erased arg., ducally gorged, armed and bearded or. *cf.* 128. 5

Kiddell, Glouc., a talbot's head arg., gorged with a collar az., studded and rimmed or. *cf.* 56. 1

Kiddell, *alias* **Benner,** of Camden, Glouc., a talbot's head arg., gorged with a collar az., studded and rimmed or. *cf.* 56. 1

Kidder, Ireland, a cubit arm erect vested az., holding in the hand ppr. a packet, thereon the word "*Standard.*" *Boyne.*

Kidderminster, a greyhound's head arg., gorged with a fess dancettée az., charged with three bezants. *cf.* 61. 2

Kidley, Devonsh., a turbot naiant az.

Kidney of London and Leics., on a mount vert, an eagle regardant rising ppr., holding in its beak a kidney gu.

Kidson of Bishop Wearmouth, Durh., a unicorn's head arg., attired and maned or, environed with palisadoes of the last. *Pro rege et lege.*

Kidston, Archibald Glen, Esquire, of Glasgow, a unicorn's head erased arg. *Pro rege et lege.* 49. 5

Kidston, John Pearson, Esquire, of Nyn Park, Herts, a unicorn's head erased arg. *Pro rege et lege.* 49. 5

Kidwell, Wales, a peacock's head couped ppr. 103. 2

Kier, Scotland, on the point of a sword in pale ppr., a garland vert. 170. 1

Kierman, Ireland, a demi-antelope erm., collared gu. 126. 3

Kierzkowski-Steuart, Charles F. de, of Langley House, King's Langley, Herts, and Collingham Road, Kensington, London, S.W.: (1) A lion's head erased gu., langued az. (*for Steuart*). 17. 2. (2) Out of a ducal coronet or, three ostrich-feathers, the centre one arg., the outer ones az. (*for De Kierzkowski*). 114. 8

Kiffin of Knolyrante, Shropsh., on a garland of laurel in orle a lion passant ppr. 5. 15

Kift, a lion's head erased ducally crowned. 18. 8

Kighley, a dragon's head erased sa. *cf.* 71. 2

Kighley and **Kightley,** Yorks and Essex, a dragon's head couped sa. 71. 1

Kighley or **Kightley,** Lancs, of South Littleton, Worcs., and Keighley, Yorks, a dragon's head couped sa., charged with a mullet or, and having three tongues gu.

Kilburne of Hawkchurst, Kent, and London, a bald coot ppr.

Kilby, issuing out of a cloud a hand in fess pointing to crosier erect, all ppr. 223. 2

Kilcoursie, Viscount, *see* Cavan, Earl of.

Kildahl, Sobieski, Esquire, of Dublin, a demi-lion gu., holding between his paws a decrescent az.

Kildare, Marquess of, *see* Leinster, Duke of.

Kilderbee, Suff., a demi-cockatrice or, charged on the breast with an escallop, and on each wing with a cross patée gu.

Kilgour, Scotland, between two wings gu., a mullet or. 112. 1

Kilgour, Scotland, a wyvern with wings addorsed, the tail terminating with a head. *cf.* 69. 9

Kilgour and **Killgowr**, Scotland, a crescent arg. *Gradatim.* 163. 2

Kilkenny, Earl of (Butler), Ireland, out of a ducal coronet or, a plume of five ostrich-feathers arg., therefrom a falcon rising of the last. *Depressus extollor.*

Killach, Scotland, a horse passant arg. 52. 6

Killand, Devonsh., a demi-tiger salient or, maned arg.

Killanin, Baron (Morris), Spiddal, co. Galway, on a fasces fessewise ppr., a lion's head erased arg., guttée-de-sang. *Si Deus nobiscum quis contra nos.* 285. 10

Killeen, Lord, *see* Fingall, Earl.

Killegrew of Killegrew and Arwennick, Cornw., a demi-lion sa., charged with three bezants in pale. *cf.* 10. 4

Killegroue, a hand holding a branch of laurel ppr. 219. 9

Killey, out of a ducal coronet arg., a bull's head sa. 44. 11

Killicke, a swan with wings addorsed arg. 99. 12

Killikelly of Bilbil, Spain, out of a ducal coronet or, an arm in armour embowed, the hand grasping a spear, all ppr.

Killingworth, a sea-horse az., ducally gorged or, holding in the mouth a scroll charged with the motto "*Prate et petago.*"

Killingworth of Killingworth, Northumb., and Sibble, Essex, a sea-horse az., ducally gorged or. *cf.* 46. 2

Killome, out of a mural coronet a griffin's head ducally gorged. 67. 6

Killowe and **Kiloh**, two hands issuing from clouds in chief supporting an anchor, all ppr. *cf.* 224. 13

Kilmaine, Baron (Browne), of the Neale, in Ireland, an eagle displayed vert. *Suivez raison.* 75. 8

Kilmarnock, Baron, *see* Errol, Earl of.

Kilmore, a demi-eagle with two heads, the wings displayed sa., and ducally gorged. *cf.* 82. 1

Kilmorey, Earl of (Needham), Mourne Park, Newry, co. Down, Ireland, a phœnix in flames ppr. *Nunc aut nunquam.* 82. 2

Kilner, an eagle displayed with two heads. *Sursum.* 74. 2

Kilpatrick, a hand holding a dagger erect dropping blood. *I make sure.* *cf.* 212. 9

Kilpin, Ernest Fuller, Esquire, C.M.G., J.P., of Linford, Kenilworth, near Cape Town, in front of an oak ppr., charged with a pheon or, a mount vert, thereon a saltire az. *Firmus in firmis.* 296. 11

Kilvington, a hand erect issuing from a cloud holding a sealed letter, all ppr. 215. 7

Kilworth, Lord, *see* Mountcashell, Earl.

Kimber, a bull's head affrontée. *Frangas non flectes.* 44. 8

Kimberley, Earl of (Wodehouse), Kimberley House, Wymondham, Norf., a dexter arm couped and erect vested arg., and grasping a club in bend sinister or. *Agincourt.—Frappe fort.*

Kimpton, a crescent party per crescent or and gu. 163. 5

Kimpton of Monken Hadley, Middx., a demi-goat erm., armed and ungu. or, collared and chained sa. *cf.* 129. 10

Kinahan, Hudson-, Sir Edward Hudson, Bart., J.P., of Glenville, co. Cork, Wyckham, co. Dublin, and Merrion Square North, Dublin: (1) A demi-lion rampant sa., holding in his paws a battle-axe ppr., and charged on the shoulder with a cross couped or (*for Kinahan*). 15. 5. (2) A lion rampant gu., charged with a cross couped or, and holding between the paws a boar's head couped arg. *Deo fidens persistas.* 225. 5

Kinahan, late of Knock Breda, in the Diocese of Down, a demi-lion rampant sa., holding in his paws a battle-axe ppr., and charged on the shoulder with a cross or. *Deo fidens persistas.* 15. 5

Kinaird, Scotland, a garland of laurel vert. *Qui patitur vincit.* 146. 5

Kinarby, a flag gu., flotant to the sinister. 176. 15

Kinardsly of Warde End, Warw., on a mount vert, a greyhound sejant arg., collared or, under a hawthorn-tree ppr., fructed gu. 59. 10

Kincaid, a dexter hand holding a lancet. *Bis te ici.* 216. 14

Kincaid of Edinburgh, a dexter hand holding a chirurgeon's instrument called a bistoury, all ppr. *Incidendo sano.*

Kincaid of Edinburgh, a dexter arm from the elbow holding a drawn sword ppr. *I will defend.* 212. 13

Kincaid of that Ilk, Stirlingsh., a castle triple-towered arg., masoned sa., and issuing therefrom a dexter arm embowed grasping a sword ppr. *I'll defend.* *cf.* 155. 3

Kinch, Ireland, a demi-lion ppr., holding between the paws a round buckle in fess or.

Kinchant, issuant from a ducal coronet or, a demi-lion arg. *Virtus pyramis.*

Kindelan of Ballinakill, co. Meath, an arm in armour holding a sword, all ppr. 210. 2

Kinder of Ely, Cambs, and Notts, on a column or, a Cornish chough sa., beaked and legged gu.

Kinder, a crane's head erased ppr. 104. 11

Kinder, a crane's head erased holding in the beak a serpent. 104. 2

Kinder of Harrytown Hall, Chesh.: (1) On a column or, a Cornish chough sa., beaked and legged gu. (2) A buck's head ppr., couped at the neck. 121. 5

Kindon and **Kingdon**, an eagle's head erased ppr. 83. 2

Kinchant of Park Hall, Shropsh., out of a ducal coronet or, a demi-lion arg. *Virtus pyramidis.* 16. 3

King-Noel, *see* Lovelace, Earl of.

King-Tenison, Earl of Kingston: (1) In front of a crosier and a cross crosslet in saltire sa., a leopard's face or, jessant-de-lis az. (*for Tenison*). 22. 9. (2) Out of a five-leaved ducal coronet or, a dexter hand erect, the third and fourth fingers turned down ppr. (*for King*). *Spes tutissima cœlis.* *cf.* 222. 11

King, Viscount Lorton, *see* Lorton.

King, Baron King, a dexter arm erect couped at the elbow, vested az., thereon three ermine spots in fess or, cuffed arg., the hand ppr., grasping a truncheon sa., the top broken off, the bottom couped of the third. *Labor ipse voluptas.*

King, Bart., *see* Dashwood.

King, a lion's gamb erased charged with a crescent holding a cross patée fitched. *cf.* 36. 9

King, Rev. Louis Henry, Vicar of North Newton, Bridgwater, a demi-griffin per fesse arg. and sa., holding in the claws an arrow point downwards. *Byddwch barod.*

King, Sir James, Bart., Carstairs House, Lanarksh., a redbreast ppr. *Honos industriæ præmium.*

King, Duckworth-, Sir Dudley Gordon Allan, Bart., of Bellevue, Kent: (1) A lion's gamb erased and erect sa., grasping a cross patée fitchée at the foot or. 280. 1. *Jamais sans espérance.* (2) A tower, the battlements partly demolished, from the top flames issuant ppr., on the sinister side a sea-lion erect az. 281. 2

King, Hon. Philip Gidley, of Banksia, Double Bay, Sydney, Gonoo Gonoo, and Tamworth, New South Wales, Australia, Member of the Legislative Council of New South Wales, a lion rampant. *Labor ipse voluptas.* 13. 1

King of London, on a ducal coronet a lion rampant or, holding in the dexter paw a lance arg., on the point thereof an annulet of the first.

King, Sir Henry Seymour, K.C.I.E., F.R.G.S., M.A., of 25, Cornwall Gardens, South Kensington, W., a lion rampant or, gorged with a collar gemel az., holding in the dexter fore-paw a trefoil slipped vert. *Floreo in ungue leonis.*

King, King-, William Edward, of Staunton Park, Heref., a lion rampant bendy or and az., holding two branches composed of two roses gu. and three cinquefoils vert, slipped and leaved of the last. *Floreo in ungue leonis.*

King, Leics., a lion passant erm., ducally crowned or. *cf.* 6. 2

King, a lion sejant erect ppr., holding between its paws an escallop arg.

King of Highbury Crescent, Middx., a lion sejant per chevron engrailed or and az., supporting with the dexter paw a spear erect of the first enfiled with a gauntlet of the second. *Altiora peto.*

King of Broomfield, Essex, in front of a lion couchant gu., a woolpack ppr. *cf.* 7. 5

King of Umberslade, Warw., out of a ducal coronet a demi-lion rampant. 16. 3

King of Chad's Hunt, near Warwick, out of a ducal coronet a demi-lion rampant or.

King, James Alexander Gordon, Tertowie, Kinaldie, Aberdeensh., a demi-lion rampant gu., on the head a Swedish crown arg.

King of Bickenhill, Warw., a demi-lion rampant double-queued or, billettée az., ducally crowned of the first, holding in the dexter paw a sword arg.

King of Saxlingham, Norf., a demi-lion rampant gu., crowned with an antique crown or, and holding in its dexter paw a rose ppr. *Richt do and fear na.* *cf.* 12. 1

King of Exeter, Devonsh., out of a mural coronet arg., a lion's head and neck sa., charged with three ducal coronets or. *cf.* 19. 12

King, out of a ducal coronet or, a dexter hand couped at the wrist pointing upwards with two forefingers. *cf.* 222. 11

King of North Petherton, Somers.: (1) On a mount vert, an arm in bend dexter couped at the elbow, the hand supporting a tilting-spear erect, the head broken, the arm surmounting a branch of oak in bend sinister, all ppr. (*for King*). (2) A demi-griffin az., with wings elevated erm., holding in the dexter claw a fleur-de-lis or (*for Meade*). *Cadenti porrigo dextram.*

King, an arm couped at the elbow in pale ppr., holding in the hand a broken spear. 214. 10

King, Ireland, a cubit arm holding a dagger in pale, all ppr. 212. 9

King, Sir Charles Simeon, 3rd Baronet, of Corrard, co. Fermanagh, Ireland (descended from the house of Barra, Aberdeensh.), a dexter cubit arm erect, the hand holding a dagger in pale, all ppr. 212. 9. The crest as borne by the family in Scotland and after its settlement in Ireland in the seventeenth century was "a demi-lion rampant gu." *Audaces fortuna juvat.* 10. 3

King, a dexter arm couped below the elbow and erect, vested and cuffed, the hand holding a roll. 208. 8

King of Newmilne, Elginsh., a hand holding a dagger ppr *Audaces fortuna juvat.* 212. 9

King of London, a dexter arm embowed in armour holding a broken spear, all ppr. 197. 2

King, Walter George, M.A., Junior Carlton Club, W., a dexter arm in armour embowed holding in the gauntlet the lower part of a broken tilting-spear. *Si Deus nobiscum quis contra nos.*

King of Campsie, Stirlingsh., a dexter hand ppr. *Honos industriæ præmium.* 222. 14

King, Lucas White, Esquire, C.S.I., a dexter hand couped at the wrist and erect, the third and fourth fingers turned down ppr., charged on the wrist with an estoile arg. *Spes tutissima cœlis.*

King, Ireland, a dexter hand couped at the wrist and erect ppr., holding a cross crosslet fitchée gu. 221. 14

King of Ashby Hall, Lincs, a talbot's head erased sa., eared arg., ringed and collared gu. 56. 1

King of London, a talbot's head erased sa., collared and eared or. 56. 1

King, same crest. 56. 1

King, Wilts, a talbot's head couped sa., collared or. *cf.* 56. 1

King, Reeve-, Neville Henry, Ashby-de-la-Laund, Lincs: (1) same crest as above. (2) A horse's head erased per fesse nebuly arg. and gu., charged with two mullets palewise counter-changed (*for Reeve*). *Virtute fortuna cedit.*

King, Meade-, William Oliver, Walford, near Taunton: (1) A mount vert, thereon an arm in bend dexter couped at the elbow, the hand supporting a tilting-spear erect, the head broken, the arm surmounting a branch of oak fructed in bend sinister, all ppr. (*for King*). 246. 19. (2) A demi-griffin az., wings elevated erm., in the dexter claw a fleur-de-lis or (*for Meade*). 246. 20. *Cadenti porrigo dextram.*

King, a greyhound's head couped, ducally gorged. *cf.* 61. 2

King (formerly Mahon), of Ballylin, Ireland, an escallop gu. *Spes tutissima cœlis.* 141. 14

King, Sir Gilbert, Bart., D.L., of Charlestown, co. Roscommon, an escallop-shell gu. *Spes tutissima cœlis.* 141. 14

King, Devonsh., and of Towcester, Northamp., out of a ducal coronet or, a demi-ostrich with wings addorsed arg., beaked of the first. 96. 11

King, George Anthony, Esquire, a Master of the Supreme Court, Croydon, out of an earl's coronet or, a demi-ostrich with wings addorsed arg., beaked of the first, and holding in its beak a horse-shoe.

King, Sussex, an ostrich-head arg., ducally gorged or. *cf.* 97. 9

King, an ostrich-head erased arg., gorged with an earl's coronet ppr.

King, an ostrich-head erased arg., ducally gorged and holding in the beak a key or.

King of Eltham, Kent, an ostrich's head couped arg., ducally gorged or, between two ostrich-feathers ppr. 97. 9

King of the Hyde, Middx., on a rock ppr., a duck's head erased arg., collared az., holding in the beak an ostrich-feather, also arg.

King, Sir James, Bart., LL.D., J.P., D.L., of Campsie, Stirlingsh., and of Claremont Terrace, Glasgow, a redbreast ppr. *Honos industriæ præmium.* 108. 11

King, a cock ppr. 91. 2

King, a demi-griffin or. 64. 2

King, Hants, a helmet in profile ppr., garnished or, the vizor open.

King-Harman, Wentworth Henry, Esquire, of Newcastle, Ballymahon, co. Longford: (1) Out of a ducal coronet or, a dexter arm armed and erect in pale ppr., cuffed arg., the hand also ppr. grasping two slips of roses, one gu., the other arg., stalked, seeded, and leaved ppr. (*for Harman*). (2) Out of a ducal crest coronet or, a dexter hand erect, the third and fourth fingers turned down ppr. (*for King*).

King-Harman, Charles Anthony, Esquire, C.M.G., M.A., of Government House, Castries, St. Lucia, same crests.

King-Noel, Captain the Hon. Lionel Fortescue, of Horsley Towers, Leatherhead, and Ben Damph Forest, Auchnasheen, Ross-sh., N.B.: (1) A buck statant arg., attired or, charged for distinction with a cross crosslet gu. (*for Noel*). 306. 7. (2) A dexter arm erect, couped at the elbow, vested az., the hand ppr., grasping a truncheon sa., the top broken off, the bottom couped of the third (*for King*). *Labor ipse voluptas.* 306. 8

Kingdom, out of a ducal coronet or, a griffin's head gu., holding in the beak a key of the first. 65. 14

Kingdom, a dolphin naiant ppr. *Tentando superabis.* 140. 5

Kingdon, Ireland, a dolphin naiant or. 140. 5

Kingdon of Launcells, Cornw., and Castle Hartley, Devonsh., an eagle displayed with two heads sa. *Regis donum gratum bonum.* 74. 2

Kinge, a talbot's head erased sa., eared and collared or. 56. 1

Kinge of London, same crest. 56. 1

Kinge of Gainsborough, Lincs, a talbot's head sa., eared gu., collared and ringed or. *cf.* 56. 1

Kinge, Dorset, a lion sejant ppr., resting the dexter paw on an escallop arg.

Kinge, an arm in armour couped at the elbow ppr., garnished or, holding in the gauntlet a broken spear of the second, headed arg., girt round the arm with a scarf of the last. *cf.* 210. 9

Kingeston, on a mount vert, a goat arg., armed or, leaping against a tree of the first. *cf.* 129. 8

Kingford of Youlkston, Cornw., an eagle displayed per fess gu. and arg., crowned or, holding in the beak a rose arg., slipped and barbed vert, seeded of the first. *cf.* 75. 2

Kinghan of Finaghy House, Dunmurray, Belfast, co. Antrim, Ireland, two dexter hands clasped and conjoined and couped at the wrists, the third finger of that on the dexter side ringed with the royal signet ppr., thereon a lion rampant gardant or. *A favore regis nomen.*

Kinghan of Silverstream, Greenisland, co. Antrim, Ireland, two dexter hands clasped and conjoined, couped at the wrists, the third finger of that on the dexter side ringed with the royal signet ppr., thereon a lion rampant or. *A favore regis nomen.*

Kinglake of Saltmoor, Stoke St. Gregory, Somers., an eaglet perched and looking up to the sun in its splendour. *Non degener.* 76. 1

Kingley, a cross crosslet fitched sa., and a sword ppr. in saltier. 166. 12

Kingley, a cock's head between two wings ppr. *cf.* 90. 7

Kingsale, Baron (de Courcy), on a ducal coronet or, an eagle displayed with two heads arg. *Vincit omnia veritas.* *cf.* 75. 2

Kingsborough, Viscount, *see* Kingston, Earl of.

Kingsbury, Ireland, a snail issuing from its shell ppr. 141. 8

Kingsbury, Ireland, a wyvern vert. *Prudens et innocuus.* 70. 1

Kingscote, Sir Robert Nigel Fitzhardinge, K.C.B., of Kingscote, Glouc., and 19, South Audley Street, W., an escallop sa. 141. 14

Kingscote, Fitzhardinge, Esquire, of Furlough, co. Galway, same crest.

Kingscote, John Bloomfield, Esquire, of Stratton Audley, Bicester, same crest.

Kingsdown, Baron (Pemberton-Leigh): (1) A demi-lion rampant gu., holding in the dexter paw a lozenge arg., charged with a rose of the first (*for Leigh*). (2) A dragon's head erm., erased gu., ducally gorged or, transfixed by an arrow in fess ppr. (*for Pemberton*). *Ut tibi sic alteri.*

Kingsford, a rose-branch ppr. 149. 8

Kingsley of Canterbury and Herts, a goat's head couped arg. 128. 12

Kingsmill, Hants, a Moor's head in profile couped at the shoulders ppr., wreathed about the temples or and gu. 192. 13

Kingsmill, Andrew de Portal, of Millbrook and Sydmonton Court, Newbury, a cubit arm in pale vested arg., charged with a bendlet az., cuff ermines, holding in the hand ppr. a fer-de-moline, also az. *Do well and doubt not.* 207. 4

Kingsmill of Correndoo Park, co. Galway, and of Hermitage Park, co. Dublin, Ireland: (1) A cubit arm erect, vested arg., cuffed ermines, holding in the hand ppr. a fer-de-moline pierced sa., the arm charged with a Maltese cross gu. for difference (*for Kingsmill*). *cf.* 207. 4. (2) Out of an earl's coronet or, the pearls arg., a cubit arm erect, vested gu., ruffed arg., the hand grasping a roll of parchment ppr., the arm charged with a crescent arg. for difference (*for Kenney*). *Do well, doubt not.* *cf.* 208. 4

Kingston, Earl of (King-Tenison): (1) In front of a crosier and a cross crosslet fitchée in saltire sa., a leopard's face or, jessant-de-lis (*for Tenison*). 282. 14. (2) Out of a five-leaved ducal coronet or, a dexter hand erect, the third and fourth fingers turned down ppr. (*for King*). *Spes tutissima cœlis.—Malo mori quam fœdari.* 282. 15

Kingston, Glouc., a goat salient arg., against a tree vert. 129. 8

Kingston of London, out of a mural coronet counter-componée or and sa., a unicorn's head az., crined arg., armed gobonée of the second and first.

Kingston of Charlton House, Somers., on a crescent az., five guttes-d'or, between two sprigs of myrtle ppr. 163. 10

Kingstone, Frederick, Esquire, of 107, Homeville Avenue, Toronto, Canada, a swan holding in its beak a thistle slipped ppr. *Dei gratia.*

Kingswell, a parrot gu., holding in its beak an annulet or. 101. 11

Kington-Oliphant, Thomas Laurence, Esquire, of Gask, Auchterarder, a falcon perched ppr. *A tout pouvoir.*

Kinloch, Scotland, a mermaid holding in her dexter hand a mirror and in her sinister a comb, all ppr. *Ut olim.* 184. 5

Kinloch, Charles Young, Esquire, of Gourdie, Perthsh., Scotland, an eagle soaring aloft. *Yet higher.*

Kinloch and **Kinlock** of London, an eagle rising ppr. *Non degener.* 77. 5

Kinloch, Scotland, an eagle looking at the sun in his splendour. *Altius tendo.* 76. 1

Kinloch of that Ilk and Nevay, Forfarsh., Scotland, an eagle perched, looking at the sun in splendour. *Non degener.* 76. 1

Kinloch, Sir Alexander, Bart., D.L., of Gilmerton, Edinburgh, an eagle rising ppr. *Altius tendo.* 77. 5

Kinloch, Sir John George Smyth, Bart., M.P., B.A., J.P., D.L., of Kinloch, Perthsh., a young eagle perched, looking up to the sun in his splendour, all ppr. *Non degener.* 76. 1

Kinloch of Kilrie, Forfarsh., an eagle regardant with wings endorsed sa., armed gu., looking at the sun ppr. *Altius tendo.*

Kinlock, Scotland, an eagle with wings extended and addorsed. *Altius tendo.* *cf.* 76. 11

Kinnaird, Scotland, a garland of laurel vert. *Qui patitur, vincit.* 146. 5

Kinnaird, an otter's head erased sa. 134. 3

Kinnaird, Viscount, *see* Newburgh, Earl of.

Kinnaird, Baron (Kinnaird), of Inchture, Perthsh., Scotland, a mullet between the horns of a crescent or, issuing out of a cloud within two branches of palm in orle ppr., and over the crest the motto, *Errantia lumina fallunt.* *Patitur qui vincit.—Certa cruce salus.* 146. 11

Kinnear, *see* Balfour-Kinnear.

Kinnear of Edinburgh, an anchor in pale az. *Spem fortuna alit.* 161. 2

Kinnear, Baron (Kinnear), of Spurness, Orkney, an anchor ppr. *Spem fortuna alit.*

Kinnear of that Ilk, Fifesh., Scotland, two anchors in saltier with cables, all ppr. *I live in hope.* 161. 7

Kinnear, Scotland: (1) Two anchors in saltier cabled ppr. 161. 7. (2) A crescent or. *I live in hope.—Honesty is the best policy.* 163. 2

Kinnear, Robert Hill, Esquire, of Brookong House, Toorak, Melbourne, Victoria, *uses:* two anchors cabled saltireways ppr. *I live in hope.* 161. 7

Kinnedar, Scotland, a greyhound current arg. *Gang forret.* *cf.* 58. 2

Kinnerby, on a chapeau gu., turned up erm., a lion passant of the first. 4. 9

Kinnersley of Binfield Manor, Berks, a mount vert, thereon, before an oak-tree fructed ppr., a greyhound sejant erm., collared or, the dexter fore-paw supporting a cross crosslet of the last. *Timor omnis abesto.* *cf.* 59. 10

Kinninmond of that Ilk, Fifesh., Scotland, an oak-tree vert. *Stabo.* 143. 5

Kinnoull, Earl of (Hay), an aged Lowland Scots countryman couped at the knees, vested in gray, the waistcoat gu. and the bonnet az., bearing on his shoulder an ox-yoke ppr. *Renovate animos.* 187. 14

Kinross, Baron (Blair Balfour, P.C.), on a rock a mermaid holding in the dexter hand an otter's head erased, and in her sinister hand a swan's head, also erased, all ppr. *Nil temere.* 285. 6

Kinsellagh of Dublin, a demi-eft or lizard salient ppr.

Kinsey, out of the top of a tower ppr., an arm embowed, vested vert, holding in the hand a spear fesseways, also ppr.

Kinsman of Loddington, Pipwell Abbey, and Broughton, a buck ppr., lodged in fern vert. *cf.* 115. 12

Kintore, Earl of (Keith-Falconer), an angel in a praying posture or, within an orle of laurel ppr. (*for Falconer*). *Vive ut vivas.* 184. 2

Kippen, William James, Esquire, an eagle with wings expanded issuing out of a tower, all ppr. *Liberty.*

Kirby and **Kirkby** of Hawthorn, Durh., and Kirby Thore, Westml., an anchor gu., entwined with a serpent vert. 161. 3

Kirby and **Kirkby,** between two branches of palm in orle vert, a flaming heart gu. 181. 12

Kirby of London, and Meoptham's Bank, Tunbridge, Kent, out of a ducal coronet per pale or and arg., an elephant's head gu., eared of the second, tusked of the first. 133. 1

Kirby, on a chapeau crimson, turned up erm., a cross moline arg., within a wreath of the last and gu.

Kirby of London, a hand gauntleted holding a pheon. *Marte non arte.* 211. 7

Kirby of Blandford Square, Middx., a dexter arm in armour embowed grasping a scimitar, and in front thereof a chaplet of roses, all ppr. *Firm.* *cf.* 196. 10

Kirch, on a pillar arg., a heart gu. 176. 5

Kirch, a talbot's head sa., collared and lined gu.

Kirk, a church ppr. *Votis et conamine.* 158. 10

Kirk, Scotland, a fox sejant gu. 32. 11

Kirk of Retford, Notts, a boar's head erect and erased sa. 43. 3

Kirk of Aberfoil, Scotland, a crosier and a dagger in saltier, all ppr. *Optimum quod primum.*

Kirk, George Edmonstone Kirk, Esquire, and Cyril Gage Pardo Kirk, Esquire, of Carrickfergus, co. Antrim, Ireland, a crosier or, and a sword ppr. hilted and pommelled of the first, in saltire enfiled by a garland of thistles and trefoils, also ppr. *Optimum quod primum.* 265. 6

Kirk of Norton, Stockton-on-Tees, out of the battlements of a tower a demi-dragon or, charged on the shoulder with a trefoil slipped gu., holding in its claws a flagstaff in bend sinister, therefrom flowing a pennon, also or. *For Kirk and King.* 73. 11

Kirk, Thomas Lascelles, of Norton Green, Stockton-on-Tees, same crest and motto.

Kirkaldie or **Kirkaldy** of Grange, Scotland, a man's head, the face looking upwards ppr. *Fortissima veritas.* 190. 10

Kirkby, David William, Esquire, J.P., late Captain of Denbigh and Merioneth Militia: (1) On a chapeau ppr., a plate charged with a cross moline gu. (2) On a chapeau ppr., a wild boar pass within a net. *Crux nostra corona.*

Kirke of Eastham, Essex, a dexter arm in armour embowed ppr., garnished or, holding in the hand a cutlass arg., hilt and pommel of the second. *cf.* 105. 2

Kirke of Edinburgh, a temple ppr. *Conamine.*

Kirke of Markham Hall, Notts, a boar's head erect couped sa. *cf.* 43. 3

Kirke, Henry, of the Eaves, Derbysh., a wild boar passant sa. 40. 9

Kirkenton, Kirkton, or **Kerton** of Kirton, Lincs, a fox passant ppr. 32. 1

Kirkham of Fynnshed and Cutterstock, Northamp.: (1) A Saracen's head affrontée couped at the shoulders ppr., gorged with a ducal coronet or, wreathed arg. and sa. (2) A popinjay vert, beaked and collared gu. *cf.* 101. 4

Kirkham of Ashcombe and Blagdon, Devonsh., a lion's head erased arg. 17. 8

Kirkhoven, Earl of Bellomont (*extinct*), a demi-negress couped at the waist in profile ppr., wreathed about the temples az. and arg., winged of the last.

Kirkhoven, a beacon fired ppr. 177. 14

Kirkland, Scotland, a leopard's face ppr. *Pro aris et focis.* 22. 2

Kirkland or **Kirkeland,** on a ducal coronet a falcon belled, all ppr. 85. 9

Kirkland, an owl arg. 96. 5

Kirkland, Kirkeley, Kirklay, Kirkley, Kirklayne, or **Kirkaton,** a church environed with trees ppr. 158. 11

Kirkley or **Kirkly,** two eagles' heads erased and addorsed ppr. 84. 11

Kirkman, a crosier and a sword in saltier, all ppr. *In Deo confido.*

Kirkman, a demi-lion rampant arg. 10. 2

Kirkpatrick, Ireland, a mount in flames ppr. 179. 2

Kirkpatrick, a stag's head arg. 121. 5

Kirkpatrick of Culloch, Kirkcudbrightsh., a hand holding a dagger in pale distilling drops of blood. *I mak sicker.* *cf.* 212. 9

Kirkpatrick-Howat of Mabie, Kirkcudbrightsh., a dexter armed hand holding a dagger in pale distilling drops of blood ppr. *I mak sicker.*

Kirkpatrick, Sir Charles Sharpe, Bart., of Closeburn, Dumfriessh., a hand holding a dagger in pale embrued and distilling drops of blood, all ppr. *I make sure.* *cf.* 212. 9

Kirkpatrick of Allanshaw, Lanarksh., Scotland, a dexter hand in armour holding a dagger erect distilling drops of blood, all ppr. *I'se mak sicker.* *cf.* 212. 9

Kirkpatrick, Lieutenant-Colonel George Airey, Q.C., LL.D., of Closeburn, Kingston, Ontario, Canada, a hand holding a dagger in pale distilling drops of blood ppr. *I mak sicker.* *cf.* 212. 9

Kirkpatrick, William Trench, Esquire, of Donacomper, Celbridge, Ireland, same crest. *I make sicker.*

Kirkpatrick-Howat, of Mabie, Dumfriessh., a dexter armed hand holding a dagger in pale distilling drops of blood ppr. *I mak sicker.*

Kirkton and **Kirton,** an arm embowed resting the elbow on the wreath, holding in the hand three ears of wheat ppr. 202. 6

Kirkwall, Viscount, *see* Orkney, Earl of.

Kirkwood, Thomas Yaden Lloyd, Esquire, J.P., D.L., of Woodbrook, co. Roscommon, Ireland, a pheon erect point downwards sa., charged with a mullet or. *Spes mea in Deo.* *cf.* 174. 11

Kirkwood, John Townsend, Yeo Vale, Bideford, a pheon sa.

Kirkyn, a demi-griffin ppr., holding in its claws an escallop or. *cf.* 64. 2

Kirsopp, James Joseph, Esquire, J.P., of the Spittal, Northumb., a mount vert, thereon a crane arg., the dexter claw resting on an escutcheon of the last charged with the letter *K* sa. *Credo.*

Kirtland, two dexter hands conjoined supporting a scimitar erect. *cf.* 224. 9

Kirton of Thorpe Mandevil, Northamp., a falcon with wings expanded arg., beaked, jessed, and belled or, reposing the dexter claw on a hawk's hood gu.

Kirton, William Ferdinand, Esquire, B.A. Oxon., a falcon, wings endorsed and inverted ppr., guttée-de-sang, resting the dexter claw on an escutcheon arg., charged with a mullet sa. *Ad altiora.*

Kirton, *see* Kirkton.

Kirwan, issuing out of a cloud a hand in pale holding a broken spear ppr. *cf.* 214. 10

Kirwan of Baunmore, Clare, and Galway, a Cornish chough sa. *Mon Dieu, mon Roi, et ma patrie.* 107. 14

Kirwan, co. Galway, Ireland, and the Island of Martinique, a Cornish chough ppr. 107. 14

Kirwan of Moyne, co. Galway, Ireland, same crest. *J'aime mon Dieu, mon Roi, et ma patrie.* 107. 14

Kirwan of Burdigala, France, same crest *J'aime mon Dieu, mon Roi, et mon pais.* 107. 14

Kissock, Scotland, between two wings an arm erect vested az., cuffed arg., holding in the hand a thistle ppr.

Kitchen, issuing out of a cloud in the sinister an arm in armour embowed holding in the hand a sword ppr. 196. 1

Kitchener, Viscount (Kitchener), G.C.B., G.C.M.G.: (1) (Of augmentation) Issuant from a mural crown or an elephant's head ppr., holding in the trunk a sword erect of the first. 287. 1. (2) A stag's head erased, the neck transfixed by an arrow ppr., between the attires a horseshoe or. *Thorough.* 287. 2

Kitchener, Francis Elliott, Esquire, of Oulton Old Hall, Staffs, a stag's head erased, transfixed through the neck by an arrow in bend, point to the dexter, all ppr., and between the attires a horse-shoe or.

Kitchener, between two flags displayed az., each charged with a cross or, a bull's head cabossed sa. *cf.* 43. 5

Kitchener, Arthur Buck, Esquire, of Waihemo Grange, Dunback, Otago, New Zealand, *uses:* a stag's head pierced with an arrow.

Kitchin of London, a pelican's head erased az., beaked or, vulning itself gu. 98. 2

Kitchiner, a buck's head erased pierced through the neck by an arrow in bend, all ppr. *cf.* 121. 2

Kitching, Heref., on a ducal coronet or, a wyvern vert. 70. 9

Kite or **Keyte** of Ebrington, Glouc., a kite's head erased or.

Kite, a unicorn's head erased arg., armed and collared gu. 49. 11

Kitson of Hengrave, Suff., a unicorn's head sa., armed and maned or. 49. 7

Kitson or **Kittson,** Suff., a unicorn's head arg., attired and maned or, environed by palisadoes of the last.

Kitson, upon a mount or, a unicorn's head sa., in flames ppr.

Kitson, Sir James, Bart., J.P., of Gledhow Hall, Yorks, issuant from park pales ppr., a demi-unicorn arg., gorged with an annulet az. *Palmam qui meruit ferat.* 244. 9

Kitson, William Henry, Esquire, J.P., Shiphay House, near Torquay, a griffin's head couped.

Kittelby or **Kittleby,** Shropsh., a lion's head erased gu. 17. 2

Kittermaster, on a chapeau arg., turned up erm., an eagle with wings expanded erminois. *cf.* 77. 5

Kitto or **Kittoe,** a lion sejant gu., collared arg. *cf.* 7. 4

Kivilioc, an Indian goat's head arg.

Klee of London, within a serpent in orle vert, a boar's head erect and erased. 41. 11

Knaplock, Hants, a boar's head couped or, the mouth embrued. 43. 1

Knapman, a sword erect, enfiled with a Saracen's head couped ppr. 191. 9

Knapp of Needham and Washbroke, Suff., and Tuddenham, Norf., an arm in armour embowed ppr., garnished or, the hand of the first grasping by the blade a broken sword arg., hilt and pommel of the second, with a branch of laurel vert.

Knapp, John Mathew, Esquire, of Linford Hall, Wolverton, Bucks, upon a laurel-branch vert, an arm embowed in armour ppr., garnished or, grasping a broken sword in bend sinister, blade downwards ppr., pommel and hilt gold, and charged with two frets, one above and one below the elbow sa. *In bello aut in pace.*

Knapp, Robert Bruce, Esquire, of Mount Lebanon, Natal, South Africa, same crest and motto.

Knapp, a demi-lion rampant sa., holding between his paws an esquire's helmet arg. *En Dieu est ma confiance.*

Knapton, out of a ducal coronet two arms dexter and sinister in saltier, in each hand a scimitar erect, all ppr.

Knapton, Augustus Lempriere Knapton, Esquire, of Boldre, Hants, a garland gu., floretted or, about a lance arg.

Knatchbull-Hugessen, Lord Brabourne, *see* Brabourne.

Knatchbull-Hugessen, *see* Hugessen.

Knatchbull, Sir Wyndham, Bart., of Mersham Hatch, Kent, on a chapeau az., turned up erm., a leopard statant arg., spotted sa. *In crucifixa gloria mea.*

Kneeshaw, Henry, Penmaenmawr, Carnarvon, out of an Eastern crown a dexter arm embowed in armour, the hand grasping a dagger. *Sublimiora petimus.—Forte manu.*

Knell, Oxon. and Glouc., a demi-lion or, holding in the dexter paw a cross crosslet fitched az. 11. 10

Kneller, Wilts, on a mount vert, a stag statant ppr., beside a vine-tree of the first. 116. 14

Knevet, a nest with young birds ppr. 113. 7

Knevet, in the sea a ship in full sail, all ppr 160 13

Knevett or **Knevit** of Rosemaryn, Cornw, Norf and Suff, a dragon's head between two wings sa 72 9

Kneysworth or **Knesworth**, a buffalo's head erased gu 44 1

Knife, a dove regardant holding in the beak an olive branch all ppr 92 4

Knight-Bruce, *see* Bruce

Knight, Rev Charles Rumsey J P, Tythegston Court, Bridgend, Glamorgansh on a ducal coronet an eagle displayed

Knight, Shropsh., on a ducal coronet gu, an eagle displayed or cf 75 2

Knight of Congresbury, Somers, on a ducal coronet an eagle displayed all or *Gloria calcar habet* cf 75 2

Knight, on a ducal coronet or, an eagle displayed erm cf 75 2

Knight, Hants on a ducal coronet gu, an eagle displayed or cf 75 2

Knight, Shropsh, on a spur lying fesse ways or, an eagle per fesse arg and az, with wings expanded of the first, beaked and legged gu

Knight of Shrewsbury and Baschurch Shropsh and Wolverley Worcs on a spur lying fesseways or an eagle per fesse arg and az, with wings expanded of the first, beaked and legged gu

Knight, Boughton-, Andrew Johnes Rouse, Esquire, of Downton Castle, Ludlow (1) In the centre—on a spur fesseways or an eagle rising ppr, holding in the beak a spear erect of the first (*for Knight*) (2) On the dexter side—a stork's head erased chevronny of four sa and arg holding in the beak or, a snake ppr (*for Boughton*) (3) On the sinister side—the bust of a man couped at the shoulders ppr, the hair, beard and whiskers sa, the head surrounded and crossed by a ribbon knotted at the top, the ends flowing from either temple arg (*for Rouse*) *Eques sit semper æquus*

Knight of Charlecote, Upper Avenue Road N W an esquire's helmet in profile *Cadenti porrigo dextram* 302 11

Knight, Northamp, between two wings gu a spur leathered or 111 13

Knight of the Manor House Glen Parva, Leics, between two wings a spur in pale standing on its rowel, with leather and buckle *Nunquam non paratus*

Knight, Sir Henry Edmund of Stain Hill Park, Hampton and 41 Hill Street, Mayfair W, upon the Roman fasces fessewise or a spur erect, rowel upwards, of the same, between two wings gu each charged with a wreath of oak of the first *Virtute et labore* 111 14

Knight of Santa Cruz, in the West Indies, and of Cloncorrich Castle, co Leitrim Ireland, a spur or, between two wings arg, each charged with a rose gu seeded or, barbed vert *Virtus sibi aureum calcar* cf 111 13

Knight, Scotland, a winged spur buckled and strapped or *Te digna sequere* 111 12

Knight, a talbot sejant sa, bezantee or cf 55 2

Knight, Glouc and Yorks, a talbot's head erased sa, bezantee cf 56 2

Knight, Hants a griffin's head gu the beak and the dexter ear arg, the sinister sa gorged with a collar or cf 66 1

Knight, Kent and Hants on a mural coronet or, a buck sejant arg, attired or 116 4

Knight, Kent and Hants, on a mural coronet or, a buck sejant arg, attired of the first 116 4

Knight of Baldock and Weston Herts, and Betsford, Notts, a goat's head or attired and erased per fess gu, holding in the mouth a sprig of laurel vert cf 128 5

Knight, Ireland, on a chapeau sa turned up arg, a serpent nowed or spotted vert 142 9

Knight, Scotland, a ship in full sail all ppr *Darcen* 160 13

Knight, Richard Solicitor Morecambe a knight in armour *Excelsior*

Knight of London and Kent, a demi friar ppr, vested and hooded arg, having an upper mantle or, holding in his dexter hand a lantern ppr, purfled or, and in his sinister a paternoster gu with a crucifix hanging at the end

Knight, Montague George, Chawton House, Alton, Hants (1) A demi-friar habited ppr, holding in his dexter hand a cinquefoil arg, and suspended from the sinister wrist a rosary sa the breast charged with a rose gu (*Knight*) (2) On a mural crown or, a stag sejant arg, attired or (*Austen*)

Knight of Chawton Hants, a demi-grey friar ppr, holding in the dexter hand a cinquefoil slipped arg, and from the sinister wrist a bracelet of beads pendent sa

Knight of Godmersham, Kent, a demi-greyfriar ppr, holding in the dexter hand a cinquefoil slipped arg, and in the sinister a cross sa suspended from the wrist, the breast charged with a rose gu *Suivant St Pierre*

Knight, Hants and Northamp, a dexter arm in armour embowed ppr holding in the hand a sword of the last, hilt and pommel or, the point resting on the wreath

Knight, issuing out of a cloud a dexter hand holding a club all ppr 214 9

Knight, an arm couped at the elbow habited bendy of four or and az holding in the hand ppr the lower half of a fish couped in the middle of the second

Knight of Clopton and Althorpe, Northamp, a dexter arm embowed, vested bendy wavy sinister of four or and gu supporting with the hand a sword in pale the point resting on the wreath, the pommel surmounting a pair of spurs, all ppr

Knight-Erskine, Henry William, Esquire, J P, D L of Pittodrie, near Pitcaple, Aberdeensh, a demi-lion rampant gu, armed and langued az, holding in the dexter paw a thistle ppr, and in the sinister a fleur-de lis az (Over the crest) *Je pense plus* —(Below the shield) *Fisus et fidus et regia duxit*

Knightley, a stag's head erased arg, attired or. 121 2

Knightley of Kingston on-Thames, Surrey, a stag's head arg, attired or, charged on the neck with a trefoil vert 121 8

Knightley, Sir Charles Valentine Bart, of Fawsley, Northamp, a buck's head couped arg, attired or *Invita fortuna* 121 5

Knightly, Warw and Northamp, a buck's head arg, attired or 121 5

Knightly, Worcs, a dragon's head sa, having three tongues gu

Knightly, Lancs, a goat's head arg 128 12

Knightly of Chorley Lancs, a goat's head arg, charged with a mullet for difference cf 128 12

Knighton of Bayford, Herts, and Suff, out of a ducal coronet or two dragons' heads and necks in saltier ppr cf 72 13

Knighton of London, out of a ducal coronet gu two dragons' heads and necks twisted in each other

Knighton, late Sir William Wellesley, Bart (*extinct*), two dragons' heads in saltire couped at the shoulders, the dexter gu the sinister or wreathed about the necks by a chain of the last cf 72 13

Knill, Sir John, Bart of the Crosslets, the Grove, Blackheath, S E and Fresh Wharf, London Bridge, Alderman and Justice of the Peace for the City of London and Justice of the Peace for the County of London, a demi lion rampant or, holding in the dexter paw a cross botony fitchee az, and supporting with the sinister a fasces in bend ppr *Nil desperandum* 304 7

Knipe of London and Lancs a wolf's head arg pierced through the breast by a broad arrow or, feathered and headed of the first 29 6

Knipell, between two laurel branches vert a tiger's face or

Kniphausen, Prussia out of a coronet with seven pearls on the rim, a demi lion rampant sa between two wings or

Kniveton of Mercaston Derbysh between two wings an eagle's head, all ppr 84 2

Knoell, Knoll, and **Knolle**, a parrot feeding on a bunch of cherries, all ppr 101 8

Knolas, a ram's head couped arg armed or 130 1

Knolles, on a cloud a sphere, all ppr 159 5

Knolles, Hants a griffin segreant or 62

Knollis, an elephant statant arg 133 9

Knolls or **Knowles**, a ram's head arg, armed or 130 1

Knollys, Berks and Warw, an elephant arg 133 9

Knollys, Bart (*extinct*), of Thame, Oxon, same crest *In utrumque paratus* 133 9

Knollys, Clement Courtenay, Esquire C M G Barbadoes West Indies, same crest and motto

Knot or **Knott**, a lion's head erased gu 17 2

Knotshull, issuing out of a cloud a hand holding a broken spear, all ppr cf 204 10

Knott, a wolf collared and chained ppr. cf 29 2

Knott of London, a unicorn's head arg., armed and crined or. *Liberté tout entière.* 49. 7
Knott, Sussex, same crest. 49. 7
Knotwood, a boar regardant sa., seizing an arrow fixed in his shoulder.
Knowell, between two wings vert, a parrot's head gu. 101. 10
Knowler, Kent, issuing out of reeds a demi-heron volant ppr.
Knowler, Kent, out of a ducal coronet or, a demi-heron erm.
Knowles, Norf., a ram's head arg., attired or. 130. 1
Knowles, out of a ducal coronet gu., a ram's head arg., armed or. *cf.* 130. 8
Knowles, Robert, Esquire, of Ednaston Lodge, Derby, and of Swinton, near Manchester, in front of a ram's head couped arg., armed or, three roses fessewise gu., barbed and seeded ppr. *Nec diu, nec frustra.*
Knowles, Andrew, Esquire, of Newent Court, Glouc., in front of a ram's head couped arg., armed or, three roses fessewise gu., barbed and seeded ppr. *Nec diu, nec frustra.* 130. 3
Knowles, Robert Millington, Esquire, of Colston Basset, Bingham, Notts, same crest and motto. 130. 3
Knowles, Lees, Esquire, M.A., LL.M., M.P., of Westwood, Pendlebury, same crest and motto.
Knowles, Charles Henry Gough, Solicitor, Oakdene, Castle Street, Luton, a boar's head couped close holding in the mouth the upper part of a broken tilting-spear. *In Deo spes.*
Knowles of Cole Ashby, Northamp., and Walton, Suff., out of a ducal coronet gu., an elephant's head arg. 133. 1
Knowles, an elephant arg. 133. 9
Knowles, Bart., of Lovel Hill, Berks, an elephant statant arg., in front of an anchor sa. *Semper paratus.*
Knowles, a unicorn rampant ppr. 48. 2
Knowles, Scotland, a parrot feeding on a bunch of cherries ppr. 101. 8
Knowles of Downton and Winchester, a griffin segreant or. 62. 2
Knowling of Exeter and Harburton, a falcon with wings displayed ppr. *cf.* 87. 12
Knowlys, a unicorn rampant ppr. 48. 2
Knowlys of Heysham Hall, Lancs, and Stockwell, Surrey, out of a ducal coronet gu., an elephant's head arg. *Lento sed certo et recto gradu.* 133. 1
Knows, Scotland, a hand erect ppr., holding a crescent or. 216. 8
Knowsley, a leopard's head couped, collared and lined, a ring at the end of the line. 22. 14
Knox, *see* Ranfurly, Earl of.
Knox-Gore, *see* Gore.
Knox-Gore, *see* Saunders-Knox-Gore and Pery-Knox-Gore.
Knox, Edmond Francis Vesey, Esquire, M.A., M.P., of Shimnagh House, Newcastle, co. Down, of 39, Leinster Square, Bayswater, London, W., and 2, Garden Court, Temple, London, E.C., a falcon close on a perch, all ppr. *Moveo et proficior.* 85. 13
Knox, Captain William, of Clonleigh, Strabane, Ireland, same crest and motto.
Knox, Major-General William George, of United Service Club, London, W., same crest and motto.
Knox of Rappa Castle, Mayo, on a perch a falcon close, all ppr. 85. 13
Knox-Browne, Hervey Browne, Esquire, Aughentain Castle, Fivemiletown, co. Tyrone: (1) An eagle displayed with two heads vert, charged on each wing with a fleur-de-lis or (*for Browne*). *cf.* 74. 2. (2) A falcon on a perch close ppr. charged on the breast with a pheon sa. (*for Knox*). And on an escroll over the second crest the motto, *Moveo et proficio.—Suivez raison.* *cf.* 85. 13
Knox, Scotland, a falcon close ppr. *Moveo et proficior.* 85. 2
Knox, an eagle rising. 77. 5
Knox, a griffin's head between two wings or, each charged with a torteau. *cf.* 65. 11
Knox, a griffin's head between two wings or, each charged with three torteaux. *cf.* 65. 11
Knox, a demi-lion arg., holding in the dexter paw a key gu.
Knox-Browne, Lieutenant-Colonel John Hervey, of Aughentaine Castle, Fivemiletown, co. Tyrone: (1) An eagle displayed with two heads vert, charged on each wing with a fleur-de-lis or (*for Browne*). (2) A falcon on a perch charged on the breast with a pheon sa. (*for Knox*). *Moveo et proficio.—Suivez raison.*
Knox-Wight of Ravenspoint, Ascot, a dexter cubit arm erect, holding in the hand a dagger in bend sinister, point downwards, all ppr. *Fortiter.*
Knutsford, Viscount (Holland), of Knutsford, Chester, out of a vallery coronet or, a demi-lion gardant per bend arg. and az., charged with a bendlet engrailed counterchanged, holding in the dexter paw a fleur-de-lis arg. *Respice, aspice, prospice.*
Knylton, Reginald Benett, of Uphill, Somers., between two wings sa., an eagle's head erased or. *In te Domine confido.* *cf.* 84. 2
Knyvett, a demi-dragon az., langued gu. 73. 10
Knyvett, a demi-dragon vert, the wings az. 73. 10
Knyvett, Sir Carey John, of 62, Eccleston Square, London, S.W., a demi-dragon with wings addorsed az. *Ni plus ni moins.*
Knyvett, Felix Sumner, Esquire, J.P., of Aswellthorpe, Watford, Herts, same crest and motto.
Knyvett, a sword and an ear of wheat in saltier ppr. 154. 11
Knyvett, issuing out of a cloud a hand in pale pointing to a star, all ppr. 222. 7
Koehler, two coulters endorsed in pale az.
Kognose, Northumb., a cock sa., combed and wattled gu., beaked and legged or. 91. 2
Koke of Broxbourne, Heref., an ostrich holding in its beak a horse-shoe arg. 97. 8
Kokefield, De, out of a ducal coronet a lion's gamb. 36. 12
Kokington, a unicorn's head erased or. 49. 5
Kollands, a dexter hand couped in bend, holding a dagger. *Spes juvat.*
Kolon, a bird's head arg., winged az., holding in the beak three ears of wheat or.
Kough, Shropsh. and Ireland, a boar passant. *Resistque ad sanguinem.* 40. 9
Krag or **Kragg,** a dexter hand ppr., holding a garland of laurel vert. *Juvat dum lacerat.* 218. 4
Kragg, a cubit arm holding in the hand a sabre, all ppr. 212. 13
Kramer, Ireland, a fleur-de-lis between two wings expanded or, penned arg. *Inevitabile fatum.* *cf.* 148. 2
Krampton and **Kranton,** a dexter hand vested az., holding a palm-branch ppr.
Kriery, *see* McCririe.
Krog or **Kroge,** a hand holding a garland of roses slipped and leaved ppr. 218. 6
Kroge, a plough ppr. 178. 7
Krowton, an arm holding in the hand a broken spear ppr., the top pendent. 214. 10
Kuckfield, a demi-lion rampant sa., holding in its dexter paw a sword or. 14. 12
Kuelley or **Kewly,** issuing out of waves ppr., the head of a sea-horse.
Kuerden of Preston, Lancs, a stag's head couped quarterly or and az. 121. 5
Kukefield, a demi-lion rampant sa., brandishing a scimitar or. 14. 10
Kullingwike, a cubit arm in pale vested sa., cuffed erm., holding in the hand ppr. a chaplet of laurel vert.
Kumerson, a griffin's head erased or. 66. 2
Kutchin, a crane's head erased arg. 104. 11
Kyan of Ballymurtagh, co. Wicklow, Ireland, a wild cat rampant ppr., gorged with an antique Irish crown or. *cf.* 26. 2
Kychard, a wolf's head or, collared gu., holding in the mouth a trefoil vert. *cf.* 30. 9
Kyd, David Hope, Esquire, of 23, Prince's Gardens, S.W., a hunting-horn stringed or, garnished vert. *Quam non torret hyems.*
Kyd, John Normansell, Esquire, of Rosendael, Broughtey Ferry, Forfarsh., same crest and motto.
Kyd or **Kyde,** Scotland, a hunting-horn. *Doneo impleat orbem.* 228. 11
Kyd, Captain Alexander, of Graz, Styria, Austria, in front of a dexter cubit arm ppr., holding three ears of wheat on one stalk, an increscent or, the whole debruised by a bendlet sinister wavy erm. 241. 3
Kyd, Scotland, an increscent ppr. *Donec impleat orbem.* 163. 3
Kydd, Scotland, a crescent. *Donec impleat.* 163. 2
Kydermaster, Sussex, on a chapeau gu., turned up erm., an eagle arg., with wings addorsed. 77. 14
Kydermaster, Warw. and London, on a chapeau az., turned up erm., a cockatrice erminois, with wings addorsed. *cf.* 68. 9
Kyffin and **Kyffyn,** Shropsh., a lion rampant per fess arg. and sa. *Cais y gorn chaefedd syddo duw unig.* 1. 13
Kyle, a deer's head ppr. 121. 5
Kyle, Scotland, an anchor and cable ppr. 161. 2
Kyle, out of a ducal coronet or, a bull's head sa. 44. 11

Kyle, William Blacker Hamilton, Esquire, of 7, Pembroke Road, Dublin, Ireland, a lion rampant per fesse sa. and or, supporting in his paws a cross formée fitchée arg. *Tibi soli.* 3. 3

Kyle, Colonel Samuel, R.A., a lion rampant per fesse sa. and or. *Nec temere nec timide.*

Kyllachy, Lord (Mackintosh), of Kyllachy, Inverness-sh., a cat-a-mountain salient ppr., charged on the breast with a crescent gu. *Touch not the catt butt a glove.*

Kylle, a rock sa. 179. 7

Kyllingbeck, on a ducal coronet a talbot collared and lined, all ppr. 54. 9

Kylom, a buck's head couped gu., attired or, charged on the neck with a fess of the second, between three annulets arg. *cf.* 121. 5

Kymberlee and **Kymberley,** a cock regardant gu. 91. 9

Kyme, De, a sagittarius shooting an arrow from a bow, all ppr. 35. 2

Kyme, a pole-cat ppr. 135. 13

Kymer of West Shelburgh, Dorset, a cat's head couped gu.

Kymes, on a mount vert, a tortoise ppr. 125. 5

Kympton of Weston, Herts, a demi-goat erm., armed and unguled or, collared and lined sa. *cf.* 129. 10

Kynardesley, Derbysh., Somers., Staffs, and Warw., on a mount vert, a greyhound sejant arg., collared or, under a holly-tree of the first, fructed gu. 59. 10

Kynardsley or **Keynardsley,** Kent, a leopard's face or, holding in the mouth a sword ppr.

Kynaston of Oteley Park, Shropsh., a lion's head erased sa., guttée-d'or. 225. 10

Kynaston, Bart. (*extinct*), of Hardwick, Shropsh., the sun in splendour surmounted of a dexter arm in armour embowed ppr., holding in the hand a sword arg., hilt and pommel or. 195. 7

Kynaston, Walter Roger Owen, of Hardwick, Ellesmere, Salop, in front of a sun in splendour a dexter arm embowed in armour the hand grasping a sword, all ppr., the arm charged above the elbow for distinction with a cross crosslet gu. *Deus est nobis sol et ensis.* *cf.* 195. 7

Kynaston, Essex and Shropsh., an eagle's head erased sa., ducally gorged arg., holding in its beak a laurel-sprig vert. *cf.* 83. 10

Kynaston, Shropsh., an eagle's head erased sa., ducally gorged arg., holding in its beak a trefoil slipped ppr. *cf.* 83. 10

Kynerby, on a chapeau arg., turned up gu., and charged with four fleurs-de-lis or, a lion passant of the second. 4. 9

Kyneston, a demi-greyhound az. 60. 11

Kyngesley, out of a ducal coronet gu., a goat's head arg. 128. 14

Kynn, an eagle's head couped or. 83. 1

Kynnaird, Viscount, *see* Newburgh.

Kynnelmarch, two lion's gambs arg. and sa., united at the bottom guttée counterchanged, holding a wolf's head erased, also sa.

Kynnersley, Thomas, Esquire, on a mount vert, a greyhound sejant arg., collared or, under a hawthorn-tree fructed ppr. 59. 10

Kynnersley, Thomas Frederick, Esquire, J.P. (Shropsh.), of Leighton Hall, Leighton, near Ironbridge, Shropsh.: (1) On a mount vert, a greyhound sejant arg., collared or, under a hawthorn-tree fructed ppr. (*for Kynnersley*). 59. 10. (2) A wyvern wings expanded sa. *Dread shame* (*for Leighton*). 70. 8. (3) A griffin's head erased sa. *Fide sed cui vide* (*for Gardner*). 66. 5. (4) A dolphin haurient or, between two wings gu., each charged with as many bars arg. (*for Panting*). 140. 7

Kynnersley, Sneyd-, Clement, of Loxley Park, Staffs: (1) On a mount vert, a greyhound sejant arg., collared or, under a hawthorn-tree ppr., fructed gu. (*for Kynnersley*). 59. 10. (2) A lion statant gardant tail, extended sa. (*for Sneyd*). *Nec opprimere, nec opprimi.* *cf.* 4. 1

Kynnerton, between two wings ppr., a chess-rook sa. 110. 1

Kynsey, Sir William Raymond, C.M.G., a squirrel sejant gu., cracking nuts or, stalked and leaved vert. *Nulla deditio.* 297. 15

Kynynmound, *see* Minto, Earl of.

Kyrby, out of a ducal coronet per pale or and arg., an elephant's head gu., eared of the second, tusked of the first. 133. 1

Kyrby and **Kyrkby,** out of a tower arg., a demi-lion gu., holding between its paws a bomb fired ppr. 157. 10

Kyrby and **Kyrkby,** a demi-savage affrontée, holding in his dexter hand three sprigs ppr. 186. 4

Kyrell of Sutton, Kent, a bull's head cabossed sa. 43. 8

Kyrell, a talbot's head erased arg. 56. 2

Kyrke, Richard Henry Venables, Esquire, of Nantyffrith, near Wrexham, a boar passant sa.

Kyrklot, a dexter hand holding a sword erect, all ppr. 212. 9

Kyrle, *see* Money-Kyrle.

Kyrle, Heref., on a mount vert, a hedgehog or. *Nil moror ictus.* *cf.* 135. 8

Kyrrelorde, an antique lamp or, flammant ppr. 177. 5

L.

Laban, Ireland, an antelope trippant per pale or and gu. 126. 6

La Barthe, Ireland, a cinquefoil arg. 148. 12

Laborer or **Labruer,** a hand couped in fess, charged with an eye, all ppr. 221. 4

Labouchere, Henry, Esquire, of 5, Old Palace Yard, S.W., and Pope's Villa, Twickenham, a stork arg., holding in its beak a lotus flower. *Passibus citis sed æquis.*

Lace, a talbot's head sa. 56. 12

Lace of Ingthorpe Grange, Yorks, a demi-eagle displayed purp., issuing out of a wreath of oak or, and holding in the beak an ear of wheat ppr. *Dum exspiro spero.*

Lacey, a bear's paw erased holding a rose-branch ppr., leaved vert. 37. 10

Lachlan, Scotland, a swan with wings addorsed arg. *Divina sibi canit.* 99. 12

Lachlan, a demi-savage wreathed about the head and middle, holding in his dexter hand a club erect, all ppr. 185. 2

Lackerstein of Calcutta, a Latin cross in pale or, surmounted by an anchor sa., cabled arg. *Deo et virtute.*

La Cloche, Jersey, an Eastern coronet or. 180. 12

Lacock, on a bear's paw a cock statant.

Lacock of Stourton and Burton, and of Southwell, Notts, a cock arg., combed, jelloped, and legged gu., supporting with the dexter claw a gauntlet sa., garnished or.

Lacon, a falcon ppr., beaked and belled or. *cf.* 85. 2

Lacon, Shropsh., a falcon close ppr., beaked and belled or. *Connois vous même.* *cf.* 85. 2

Lacon, Sir Edmund Beecroft Francis Heathcote, Bart., of Great Yarmouth, Norf., a mount vert, thereon a falcon ppr., beaked and belled or, charged on the breast with a cross flory and gorged with a collar gu. *Probitas verus honos.*

Lacon, Henry Edmund, Esquire, of Ackworth House, East Bergholt, Suff., same crest and motto.

Lacy, Leics. and Yorks, a fret-knot arg. and purp.

Lacy of Stamford, Lincs, a demi-lion rampant gu. 10. 3

Lacy of Enfield, Middx., of Skipton-under-Whichwood, Oxon., and Somers., on a ducal coronet or, a lion sejant erm. *cf.* 8. 8

Lacy of Lane House, Feckenham, Worcs., on a ducal coronet or, a demi-lion rampant arg. 16. 3

Lacy of Beverley, Yorks, a buck's head cabossed per pale arg. and or, attired counterchanged. 122. 5

Lacy, Ireland, a hawk close sa. 85. 2

Lacy, Ireland, an eagle with wings expanded arg. 77. 5

Lacy of Ballingarry, co. Limerick, an eagle rising or. *Meritis augentur honores.* 77. 5

Lacy of Walsham-in-the-Willows, Norf., and Suff., out of a ducal coronet gu., a demi-eagle with wings expanded or, holding in the beak an arrow of the first, headed and feathered arg.

Lacy, C. J., Esquire, Fleet, Hants, on a chapeau ppr., a boar's head erased close.

Ladbroke of London, an arm in pale couped at the elbow, vested gu., cuffed arg., holding in the hand ppr. five quatrefoils in cross, stalked of the second, pierced of the first.

Ladbrook or **Ladbrooke,** a hawk rising ppr., ducally gorged and belled or. 87. 2

Ladbrooke, a stag's head erased. 121. 2

Ladd or **Ladde,** on a cloud a crescent ensigned with a star, all between two palm-branches in orle, all ppr. 146. 11

Lade of Barham, Kent, a panther's head erased gardant sa., spotted or. 23. 3

Lade, Bart., Sussex, out of a ducal coronet or, a leopard's head regardant sa., bezantée.

Lade of Broughton House, Kent, a leopard's head ppr. 22. 10

Ladkin, a savage's head crowned with a garland of laurel, all ppr. 190. 7

Lado of Glasgow, a panther's head erased and gardant ppr. *Constant et ferme.*

Laery, Robert, Esquire, of Willis Street, Wellington, New Zealand, upon a mount vert, in front of a fir-cone slipped and erect or, a martlet az., between two feathers of the last.

Laffan, Bart., out of a ducal coronet or, an eagle displayed sa., semée-de-lis of the first. *Vincit omnia veritas.* cf. 75. 2

Laffan, Rev. Robert S. de Courcy, M.A., of 119, St. George's Road, South Belgravia, S.W., same crest and motto.

Laffan, Lieutenant-Colonel H. D., Royal Engineers, same crest and motto.

Laffer, an eagle rising, resting its dexter claw on a flint-stone, all ppr. 77. 6

Lafone, Alfred, Esquire, of Hanworth Park, Hanworth, Middx., a lion sa., charged on the body with a fleur-de-lis arg., gorged with a collar nebuly and ducally crowned or, resting the dexter fore-paw on a mullet arg., pierced az. *Fidus ut olim.*

La Font of Hinxworth, Herts, a bull's head or, armed az., ducally gorged gu. *Prenez en ire.* cf. 44. 2

La Forest and **Le Forest,** a unicorn sejant arg., armed and tufted or.

Laforey, Bart., of Whitby, Devonsh., a lion rampant regardant holding in the dexter paw a firebrand, all ppr. *Loyal à mort.*

Lagenham, out of a ducal coronet or, a serpent in pale nowed vert. 142. 11

Lagford, a dexter arm gu., holding in the hand a sabre erect az., hilted or.

Laid, *see* Lade, Bart.

Laidlaw, issuing from a heart a dexter hand holding a dagger in pale, all ppr. *Fides probata coronat.*

Laidlay, Andrew, Esquire, D.L., of Seacliffe, Haddingtonsh., a dexter hand issuing from a heart holding a scimitar, all ppr. *Fides probata coronat.* 258. 19

Laing of Hawick, a dove holding in its beak a sprig of olive, all ppr. *Misericordia est mea cupido.* 92. 5

Laing, Scotland, same crest. *Mercy is my desire.* 92. 5

Laing, Sir James, of Thornhill, Sunderland, in front of a demi-catherine wheel sa., a dove holding in the beak two sprigs of olive slipped ppr.

Laing, on a chapeau az., turned up arg., a cock gu. 91. 12

Laing, Scotland, a cock gu. *Vigilant.* 91. 2

Laing, a cock ppr. *Vigilance.* 91. 2

Laing, Scotland, a bear's head and neck ppr., muzzled arg. *Labor omnia superat.* 34. 14

Lainson of Euston Square, London, in front of a rock surmounted by a castle a ship in full sail, all ppr.

Laird of Glenhuntley, Scotland, a buck's head ppr. *Spero meliora.* 121. 5

Laird, a hand holding a covered cup ppr. 217. 11

Lake, Viscount and **Baron** (Warwick-Lake), a horse's head couped arg., charged on the neck with a bar gemelle gu.

Lake, Sir St. Vincent Atwell, Bart., of Edmonton, Middx.: (1) A cavalier in complete armour on a horse courant arg., bridle and trappings, all ppr., holding in his dexter hand a sword embrued, and holding the bridle in his mouth, the sinister arm hanging down useless, round his body a scarf in bend gu. 189. 2. (2) A sea-horse's head arg., finned or, gorged with a fess cottised gu. *Un Dieu, un Roy, un cœur.*

Lake, a sea-horse's head and neck couped arg., holding in the mouth an annulet or.

Lake, George, Esquire, of Rushey, Herts, *uses:* a seahorse's head and neck couped arg., holding in the mouth an annulet or. *Fonte puro.*

Lake, Hants, a cannon mounted ppr. 169. 12

Lake of Welston and Buckland, Bucks, Herts, and Staffs, a cross formée fitched in a crescent, all within an annulet or.

Lakin, Michael Henry, Esquire, J.P., of the Cliff, Warwick, a dexter arm holding a palm-branch, all ppr. *Un Dieu, un Roy, un cœur.*

Lakin and **Laking,** a dexter arm ppr., vested sa., holding a palm-branch vert.

Laking, Sir Francis, Bart., G.C.V.O., 62, Pall Mall, S.W., a dexter cubit arm vested az., cuffed erm., the hand holding a palm-branch, both ppr., between two falcons respecting each other belled and jessed or. *Palmam qui meruit ferat.* 284. 10

Lakington of Washbourne, Devonsh., a pelican in her piety, all ppr. 98. 14

Lakinleech, Lakenlyche, and **Lakinlich,** a harp or. 168. 9

Lalande, a dove couped at the legs with wings addorsed and expanded arg., holding in the beak three wheat-ears or.

Laleman, Ireland, a dexter arm embowed holding in the hand a club, all ppr. 202. 10

Lally, a buck trippant ppr. 117. 8

Lally of Tullindally, co. Galway, an eagle displayed gu., holding in the beak a sprig of laurel ppr. cf. 75. 2

Lalor, *see* Power-Lalor.

Lalor of Cregg, co. Tipperary, Ireland, on a wreath of the colours an arm embowed, vested gu., cuffed vert, the hand ppr., grasping a short sword, also ppr. *Fortis et fidelis.* 204. 1

Lalynde, a maiden's head affrontée couped at the breast ppr., attired az. cf. 182. 5

Lamb, Baron Beauvale, *see* Beauvale.

Lamb, Viscount Melbourne (*extinct*), a demi-lion rampant gu., holding between the paws a mullet sa. *Virtute et fide.* cf. 15. 8

Lamb, Scotland, a holy lamb with a staff, thereon a flag charged with a cross, all ppr. 131. 2

Lamb, on a mount vert, a gate, on the top a paschal lamb ppr., the staff of the banner entwined with laurel, all ppr.

Lamb, Wilts, on a mount vert, a lamb arg. cf. 131. 9

Lamb of West Denton, Northumb., a paschal lamb ppr. *Palma non sine pulvere.* 131. 2

Lamb, Robert, Esquire, Dundee, same crest. *Virtus sine macula.* 31. 2

Lamb, William Rutherford, Goldsborough Hall, York, same crest. *Palma non sine pulvere.*

Lamb, Sir Archibald, Bart., of Burville, Berks: (1) A lamb passant sa., charged on the body with a bezant, thereon a trefoil slipped vert (*for Lamb*). 131. 11. (2) A camel's head ppr., bezantée, erased gu. (*for Burges*). *Levius fit patientiâ.* cf. 132. 7

Lamb, a lion rampant. 1. 13

Lamb, a demi-lion rampant erminois, holding in the dexter paw a mullet vert. 15. 7

Lamb, same crest. *Per mare, per terras.*

Lamb, Kent, and of Barham, Suff., a demi-lion gu., collared or, holding in the dexter paw a mullet sa. cf. 15. 7

Lamb, Audouin-, of East Hill, co. Wicklow, Ireland, a stag's head erased, ppr. *Chassé pour foi.* 121. 2

Lamb, a rhinoceros's head couped sa. 226. 5

Lamb, Charles Edward, Kettering, same crest.

Lamb, a hand holding a sword in pale enfiled with a savage's head ppr. 212. 12

Lambard of Sevenoaks, Kent, a reindeer's head erased sa. *Deo patriæ tibi.* cf. 122. 1

Lambard, a horse's head erased or, bridled gu. cf. 51. 5

Lambard of London and Ledbury, Heref., a trogodice's head erased az., maned or, eared and horned arg., langued gu.

Lambard or **Lambarde,** a garb in fess ppr. 153. 6

Lambarde, William Gore, Esquire, of Bradbourne Hall, Riverhead, and Beechmont, Sevenoaks, Kent, a reindeer's head erased arg. *Deo patriæ tibi.*

Lambart, Earl of Cavan, *see* Cavan.

Lambart, Francis William Gustavus, Esquire, of Beau Parc, Meath, and Kilbeggan, co. Westmeath, a centaur ppr. drawing his bow gu., arrow or. *Ut quocunque paratus.* 53. 2

Lambart, a hand holding a glove. 220. 5

Lambe, *see* Lamb.

Lambe, a demi-lion rampant erm., holding between the paws a mullet arg. cf. 15. 8

Lambe, Herts, a demi-lion rampant erminois, holding in the dexter paw a mullet vert. 15. 7

Lambe, a lion's gamb erased holding a palm-branch vert. cf. 36. 7

Lambe, two bear's paws erased in saltier ppr. cf. 39. 14

Lamberby, on a ducal coronet a lamb sejant ppr.

Lambert, Sir Henry Foley, Bart., of London, out of a ducal coronet or, three ostrich-feathers gu., arg. and az. *Sequitando si giunge.* cf. 114. 8

Lambert, Ireland, a centaur per pale gu. and or, charged with a trefoil vert, shooting an arrow from a bow of the second. *cf.* 53. 2

Lambert, Arthur Oliver, Esquire, of East London, South Africa, a mount vert, thereon a centaur per pale ppr. and arg. *Ut quocunque paratus.*

Lambert, Colonel Frederick Arthur Heygate, J.P., F.S.A., Knight of Justice of the Order of St. John of Jerusalem in England, of Garratt's Hall, Banstead, and Fairlawn House, Woodmansterne, Surrey, on a mount vert, a centaur passant regardant, the human parts ppr., the other erm., girt about the loins with a garland of laurel of the first, drawing a bow and arrow gu. 53. 5

Lambert, Ireland, on a mount vert, a centaur ppr., the bow gu., arrow or. *cf.* 53. 2

Lambert, John, Foxearth Hall, Essex, same crest. *Ut quicunque paratus.*

Lambert, Henry Charles Miller, Esquire, of Colonial Office, S.W., same crest. *Optima quæque honesta.*

Lambert, Colonel Joseph Alexander, of Brookhill, co. Mayo, Ireland, a centaur ppr., charged on the shoulder with a cross crosslet or. *Ut quocunque paratus.* *cf.* 53. 2

Lambert, George Henry, Esquire, of Carnagh, co. Wexford, and Tan-y-Craig, Anglesey, a sagittary per pale gu. and arg., charged with a trefoil vert, the bow and arrow or. *Deus providebit.*

Lambert, a sagittarius passant or, the head of the bow wreathed az. *Ne mireris homines mirabiliores.* 53. 2

Lambert of Carnagh, co. Wexford, Ireland, a sagittarius passant per pale gu. and arg., charged with a trefoil vert, the bow and arrow or. *Deus providebit.* *cf.* 53. 2

Lambert, Surrey, a female centaur ppr., crined or, holding a rose-branch vert, flowered arg. 53. 8

Lambert of Woodmansterne, Surrey, and Rev. William Lambert, 19, Christchurch Road, Winchester, Hants, a centaur ppr., shooting a bow and arrow gu.

Lambert of Boyton House, Wilts, a demi-pegasus erm. 47. 5

Lambert, Bucks and Yorks, a sphinx passant gardant or, the face ppr., holding in the dexter foot a rose gu., seeded and leaved vert. *cf.* 182. 12

Lambert, a sphinx couchant arg., crined or, holding in the dexter paw a cinquefoil of the first, stalked and leaved vert. 182. 14

Lambert, a lion rampant arg. 1. 13

Lambert of Pinchbeck, Bucks, a lion's head erased arg., gorged with a fess chequy or and az. *cf.* 17. 8

Lambert of Brixton, Surrey, in front of a gate or, a stag's head couped ppr., attired of the first, holding in the mouth a slip of oak vert, fructed, also or, the neck charged with a bend az., thereon three acorns or. 120. 11

Lambert, a reindeer's head az., attired arg., maned or. *cf.* 122. 1

Lambert, Kent, a reindeer's head erased sa. *cf.* 122. 1

Lambert, a reindeer's head erased, collared sa. *cf.* 122. 1

Lambert, two lobster's claws in pale gu., holding in each a fish or. 141. 3

Lambert, Durh., a demi-lamb rampant supporting a shield erminois.

Lambeth, a talbot's head arg. 56. 12

Lambeth, a badger or. 33. 10

Lamblord or **Lamford,** a dexter hand ppr., wielding a scimitar arg. 213. 5

Lamborn or **Lamborne,** a demi-lion rampant gu., supporting a ship's rudder sa. 11. 11

Lamborne, out of a tower ppr., a lion's head or, collared sa. *cf.* 157. 9

Lambsey or **Lamesey,** a savage's head ppr., wreathed arg. and sa. 190. 5

Lambton, Earl of Durham, *see* Durham.

Lambton, Yorks and Durh., a ram's head cabossed arg., armed sa. 130. 7

Lambton, Major-General Arthur, C.B., of Guards' Club, S.W., same crest and motto.

Lambton-Dawson, Durh., a torteau charged with a ram's head couped at the neck erm., within two branches of oak or. *cf.* 130. 12

Lamford, a dexter hand ppr., holding a scimitar arg. 213. 5

Lamington, Baron (Cochrane-Baillie): (1) In the centre—a boar's head erased ppr. 42. 2. (2) On the dexter side—issuing out of a naval crown or, a dexter arm embowed, vested az., cuffed arg., the hand holding a flagstaff ppr., thereon hoisted the flag of a rear-admiral of the white—being arg., a cross gu., and thereon the words "*St. Domingo*" in letters of gold. (3) On the sinister side—a horse trotting arg. *Quid clarius astris.* 52. 2

Lammie, Scotland, a hand holding a crosier ppr. *Per varios casus.* 219. 4

Lammin, a paschal lamb passant arg. *Agnus Dei mihi salus.* 131. 2

Lamond, Scotland, a hand holding a dagger ppr. *Ne parcas, nec spernas.* 212. 9

Lamond, a dexter hand couped ppr. *Ne parcas, nec spernas.* 222. 14

Lamont, John Henry, Esquire, J.P., D.L., of Westward Ho, Bideford, a hand couped at the wrist ppr. *Ne parcas, nec spernas.* 222. 14

Lamont, a dexter hand holding a baton ppr. *Ne parcas, nec spernas.*

Lamont, Henry, Esquire, J.P., of Greelaw, Ayrshire, and Gribton, Dumfriessh., a dexter hand ppr., holding a fleur-de-lis gu. *Ne parcas, nec spernas.* 215. 5

Lamont, James, Esquire, of Knockdow, Toward, Argyllsh., and Palmiste, Trinidad, a dexter hand couped at the wrist holding a dagger erect in pale ppr. *Ne parcas, nec spernas.*

Lamont of Lamont, Argyllsh., a hand apaumée couped ppr. *Ne parcas, nec spernas.* 222. 14

Lamorley, on a naval coronet or, a lion rampant gu. *cf.* 1. 13

Lampard, a cinquefoil az. 148. 12

Lampen of Paderda, Cornw., a ram's head cabossed arg., armed or. 130. 7

Lampet and **Lampeth,** a Doric pillar arg., entwined with a branch of laurel vert, and surmounted by a flame ppr.

Lamplugh, Rev. David, M.A., Rokeby Rectory, Barnard Castle, on a wreath of the colours in front of a goat's head couped arg., armed or, gorged with a collar nebuly sa., two roses gu., barbed, leaved, and seeded ppr. *Providentia Dei stabiliuntur familiæ.*

Lamplugh, Charles Edward, Esquire, D.L., J.P., City of London Club, Old Broad Street, London, in front of a cubit arm erect ppr., encircled about the wrist with a wreath of oak, and holding in the hand a sword, also ppr., pommel and hilt or, an escutcheon arg., charged with a goat's head couped sa. *Through.—Providentia Dei stabiliuntur familiæ.* 213. 2

Lamplugh of Lamplugh Hall, Cumb., a goat's head couped sa., armed and bearded or. 128. 12

Lamprey, Ireland, a hand holding a cross crosslet fitched in pale ppr.

Lampson, Sir Curtis George, Bart., of Rowfant, in the parish of Worth, Sussex, a gryphon's head erased gu., charged with an escarbuncle arg., between two wings, each paly of four arg. and gu. *Persevera et vince.* *cf.* 65. 11

L'Amy, William Ramsay, of Dunkenny, Forfarsh., a dexter hand erect ppr., holding a crosier or. *Per varios casus.* 219. 4

Lanburn, two lions' heads addorsed ppr., collared or. *cf.* 18. 2

Lancashire, a demi-lion rampant arg., gorged with a chaplet vert, holding in the paws an escutcheon charged with two bendlets or, the uppermost engrailed.

Lancaster, De, a lion couchant or. 7. 5

Lancaster, Edward Snow, Esquire, J.P., of 27, Dorset Square, London, N.W., a lion rampant or, charged on the shoulder with three fleurs-de-lis chevronways az., grasping in the dexter fore-paw a scimitar ppr., pommel and hilt or, and supporting with the sinister an antique shield of the first, thereon a rose gu., barbed and seeded ppr. *Semper paratus.* 230. 6

Lancaster, Cumb. and Lancs, a lion's head erased arg., charged with a crescent gu. *cf.* 17. 8

Lancaster, Cumb. and Lancs, a sea-horse ppr. 46. 2

Lancaster, Ireland, a hand brandishing a sabre ppr. 212. 13

Lancaster, William John, Esquire, J.P., of South Lynn, Putney Hill, and Snettisham, Norf., two cinquefoils fesseways, that on the dexter sa., that on the sinister or, surmounted by a third cinquefoil per pale of the last and first. *Ornat forem prudentia.* 302. 5

Lance, a hand ppr., holding a covered cup or. 217. 11

Lancelot, an astrolabe. 167. 7

Lancey, De, a demi-leopard gardant supporting an anchor ppr. 23. 1

Land, a church with a spire environed with trees ppr. 158. 11

Landal, Landel, and **Landell,** Scotland, a dexter arm embowed holding in the hand a laurel crown ppr. 202. 4

Landale, Scotland, a dexter arm embowed holding up two branches of laurel in orle ppr. *Pax aut defensio.* 202. 4

Landale, David Guild, Esquire, of Limpsfield Grange, Limpsfield, Surrey, same crest and motto. 202. 4

Landell of Southwark, Surrey, on a mount vert, a garb or, thereon an escutcheon sa., charged with a tau of the second.

Landen, Lincs, a dexter hand apaumée ppr. *Ero quod eram.* 222. 14

Lander, Devonsh., an elephant's head sa., armed and ducally crowned or. *cf.* 133. 2

Lander, a hand issuing from a cloud holding a sword wavy. 212. 4

Landeth, a winged heart ppr. 112. 10

Landle, Scotland, a cock crowing ppr. 91. 2

Landon of Cheshunt, Colonel Aislabie Landon, and Perceval Landon, Esquire, of Sella Park, Carnforth, *use:* (1) A lizard vert. *cf.* 138. 5. (2) A demi-tiger rampant gardant arg., semée of pellets hurts and torteaux, flames issuant from the mouth and ears, and holding a palm-branch, all ppr. *Vera sequor.—Ma force d'en haut.—Palma virtuti.* 23. 12

Landon, a demi-pegasus gardant arg., supporting a pennon gu., tasselled or. 47. 9

Landor of Rugeley, Staffs, and Warw., an arm in pale vested bendy of six or and gu., cuffed arg., holding in the hand ppr. a fleur-de-lis az.

Landsay or **Landsey,** a dexter hand holding a sword erect supporting a pair of scales.

Landsborough, *see* McLandsborough.

Landwath, a demi-pegasus arg., guttée-de-poix. 47. 5

Lane, John Henry Hervey Vincent, Esquire, of King's Bromley, Staffs, and Lily Hill, Bracknell, Berks, of augmentation, a strawberry roan horse salient, couped at the flanks, bridled sa., bitted and garnished or, supporting between the feet an imperial crown ppr. *Garde le Roy.* 53. 4.

Lane, Henry Murray, Esquire, Chester Herald of Arms, of Herald's College, E.C., a strawberry-roan horse salient, couped at the flanks, bridled sa., bitted and garnished or, supporting between the feet an imperial crown ppr. *Garde le Roy.* 53. 4

Lane, Ven. Archdeacon Ernald, M.A., of Leigh Rectory, Stoke-on-Trent, same crest and motto.

Lane, William Jenner, Esquire, the Firs, Poulton, Fairford, Glouc., a demi-horse bridled holding between the feet a crown. *Mitis et fortis.*

Lane-Fox: (1) A fox statant gu. (*for Fox*). 32. 2. (2) Out of a ducal coronet or, a demi-griffin sa., winged arg. (*for Lane*). 64. 4

Lane, Suff., a demi-griffin segreant gu., bezantée, holding between the claws a bezant. *cf.* 64. 2

Lane of Roscommon, Ireland, out of a ducal coronet or, a demi-griffin sa., winged arg. 64. 4

Lane of Twickenham, Middx., a demi-griffin arg. 64. 2

Lane, Major-General Charles Powlett, Glanden, Wimborne, two griffin's heads, one gu., the other az., issuing out of a crescent or. *Nec degenero.*

Lane, a bezant charged with two griffin's heads erased and addorsed between two branches, one of palm, the other of laurel. 226. 8

Lane, Charles Pelham, Esquire, of Moundsley Hall, King's Norton, Worcs., two griffins' heads couped and addorsed, the dexter az. and the sinister gu., in front thereof a crescent between two saltires fesseways arg. *Tenax et fidelis.* 296. 3

Lane, Henry Charles, Esquire, J.P., of Middleton, Hassocks, Sussex, two gryphon's heads erased, addorsed or, in the beak of each a sprig of laurel ppr. *Loyal jusqu'à la mort.* 296. 1

Lane, out of a crescent or, two eagle's heads addorsed, the dexter gu., the sinister az. 84. 15

Lane, a dexter arm vested erm., turned up and indented arg., holding in the hand ppr. a mullet az. 206. 13

Lane, Smith Edward, Esquire, of Union Club, Fifth Avenue, New York, U.S.A., a dexter cubit arm erect vested erm., turned up indented arg., holding in the hand ppr. a mullet az. *Perseverando.* 206. 13

Lane, issuing out of the sea a spear-head, on its point a dolphin naiant, all ppr. 40. 1

Lane, W. A., Esquire, of Lyons Farm House, Broadwater, Worthing, out of a crescent or, two griffins' heads addorsed, the dexter gu., the sinister az. *Mitis sed fortis.*

Lanesborough, Earl of (Butler): (1) A wyvern with wings elevated and tail nowed or, the dexter claw supporting an escutcheon arg., thereon a bend gu., charged with three martlets, also or (*for Danvers*). 312. 5. (2) A demi-cockatrice couped vert, with the wings elevated arg., combed, beaked, wattled, and ducally gorged or (*for Butler*). *Liberté toute entière.* 312. 6

Lanford and **Langford,** an heraldic tiger passant, the tail coward. *cf.* 25. 5

Lang, Ireland, a hand erect holding a broken spear. 214. 10

Lang, Ireland, a hand holding a hautboy. 219. 1

Lang, a savage's head issuing ppr. 190. 12

Lang, Scotland, a tower arg., masoned sa. *Une stay.* 156. 2

Lang, three sprigs of oak bearing acorns. 152. 2

Lang, Scotland, a dove holding in its beak an olive-branch ppr. *Mercy is my desire.* 92. 5

Lang and **Langan,** Ireland, out of a mural coronet or, a spear ppr., between two palm-branches in orle vert. 175. 1

Langdale, Baron (Bickersteth), a dexter arm in armour embowed ppr., garnished or, about the elbow a wreath of oak vert, holding in the hand a roll of paper ppr. *Suum cuique.* 266. 1

Langdale, Henry Joseph Grattan, Esquire, of Houghton Hall, R.S.O., Yorks, an estoile arg. *Post tenebras lucem.*

Langdale of Langdale, Yorks, an étoile or. 164. 1

Langdale, Philip, Esquire, of 31, Curzon Street, W., and Houghton Hall, R.S.O., Yorks, same crest and motto.

Langdale, Rev. Horace Marmaduke, M.A., of Compton House, Compton, near Petersfield, Sussex, on a mount vert, an estoile arg., between two oak-branches ppr. *Post tenebras lux.*

Langdell, a star arg. 164. 2

Langdon of London, a dove holding in its beak an olive-branch ppr. *Mercy is my desire.* 92. 5

Langdon of Wolferton, Norf., on a mount vert, a lynx of the last, gorged with a bar gemel or. *cf.* 127. 2

Langeford or **Langford** of London, a demi-shoveller with wings displayed arg., charged with a crescent for difference.

Langer, upon a globe or, winged sa., a maiden balancing herself ppr., the hair or, her eyes covered with a bandage arg., the dexter arm embowed and extended grasping the end of a veil sa., passing in an arch above her head and held around the loins by her sinister hand. *Ora et labora.* 184. 3

Langespear, *see* Langspear.

Langford, Baron (Rowley), of Summerhill, co. Meath, Ireland, a wolf's head erased arg., collared or, langued gu. *Bear and forbear.* 30. 11

Langford, Bart. (*extinct*), of Kilmackedret, co. Londonderry, a demi-lion rampant holding in the dexter paw a truncheon, all or.

Langford, Derbysh., Shropsh., and Notts, an heraldic tiger passant, coward gu., maned and tufted or. *cf.* 25. 5

Langford-Nibbs of Antigua, West Indies, a stag's head cabossed gu., pierced in the scalp with an arrow or, feathered arg. *cf.* 122. 5

Langham, out of a ducal coronet gu., a bear's paw sa., holding a sword arg., pommelled or. *cf.* 38. 5

Langham, J. G., Esquire, Westdown, Eastbourne, a bear's head erased sa., muzzled or. *Nec sinit esse feros.*

Langham, Sir Herbert Hay, Bart., of Cottesbrooke Park, Northamp., a bear's head erased sa., muzzled or. *Nec sinit esse feros.* 35. 2

Langhans, Johann Gottlieb Julius, Esquire, B.A., of Hertford College, Oxford, in flags on the sinister side the stump of an oak-tree in bend sinister, one branch sprouting to the dexter, thereon a kingfisher, all ppr. *Ich wart der Stund.*

Langholme, a holy lamb ppr., the standard gu. *In cruce salus.* 131. 2

Langhorn or **Langhorne,** a bugle-horn sa., stringed gu., between two wings expanded arg. 112. 3

Langlands of that ilk, Scotland, in the sea an anchor erect, all ppr. *Spero.* 161. 6

Langley, Beds, Heref., and Shropsh., out of a ducal coronet or, a plume of five ostrich-feathers, three arg. and two vert. 114. 13

Langley, Yorks, out of a ducal coronet or, five ostrich-feathers arg. 114. 13

Langley, Shropsh.: (1) A pheon or, between two laurel-branches vert. *cf.* 174. 11. (2) Out of a ducal coronet or, a plume of five ostrich-feathers, three arg. and two vert. 114. 13

Langley of Brokley, Shropsh., between two sprigs of laurel vert, a pheon or. *cf.* 174. 11

Langley, Alfred Francis Claringbold Chichester, Esquire, of Golding, Peterston-super-Ely, a pheon or, between two sprigs of laurel vert, fructed ppr.

Langley, Yorks, Lancs, and Suff., a cock arg., combed, legged, and wattled gu. 91. 2

Langley of London, Lincs, and Shropsh., a cockatrice sa., beaked or, combed and wattled gu. 68. 4

Langley, Henry, Esquire, J.P., D.L., of Queen's Gate Terrace, Kensington, London, a cockatrice with wings addorsed sa., combed, wattled, and spurred gu. *Fide sed cui vide.* 68. 4

Langley, Shropsh., a cockatrice sa., beaked, combed, wattled, and legged gu. 68. 4

Langley, Shropsh., on a garb lying in fesse or, a dove close arg., beaked and legged gu. *Bear and forbear.* cf. 93. 3

Langley, Glouc., Shropsh., and Warw., on a garb lying fesseways or, a dove close arg., beaked and legged gu. *Beare and forbeare.* cf. 93. 3

Langley, Shropsh., on a garb lying in fesse or, a dove with wings endorsed arg., beaked and legged gu. cf. 93. 3

Langley, Shropsh., same crest. *Sustine et abstine.*

Langley, Ireland, a boar passant sa., bristled, ungu., and armed or. 40. 9

Langley, Glouc., a dexter gauntlet in fess holding a sword in pale, all ppr., the blade enfiled with a dragon's head sa., couped at the neck gu.

Langlois, a rock ppr. 179. 7

Langman, John Lawrence, Esquire, of Stanhope Terrace, Hyde Park, London, and Great Marlow, Bucks, in front of a mount vert, thereon a portcullis with chains sa., three water-bougets fesseways of the last. *Justus esto et non metue.*

Langman, Philip Lawrence, Esquire, same crest and motto.

Langmead, between two wings a spur. 111. 13

Langmeade, Devonsh., a boar's head and neck erased gu., gorged with a chaplet of oak ppr. cf. 41. 5

Langmore, on a chapeau a greyhound statant, all ppr. 58. 4

Langmore of Dundaire, College Road, Upper Norwood, London, S.E., out of the battlements of a tower two tilting-spears in saltire, all ppr., tied by a riband az., pendent therefrom an escutcheon or, charged with a trefoil slipped vert. *Labor vincit omnia.* 175. 5

Langrish or Langrishe, Ireland, a dragon's head gu., vomiting fire ppr. 72. 3

Langrishe, Sir James, Bart., J.P., D.L., of Knocktopher, co. Kilkenny, on a wreath of the colours a lion rampant per fesse or and sa. *Medio tutissimus ibis.*

Langrishe, Richard, Esquire, of Dundrum House, Dundrum, co. Dublin, same crest and motto.

Langspear, a talbot's head, holding in the mouth a demi-hind couped.

Langstaff, Joseph, Esquire, of Newcastle, on a serpent nowed or, in front of two palm-branches in saltire vert, a stork rising ppr. 104. 14

Langston, issuing from waves of the sea vert, a demi-dolphin haurient or, holding in its mouth a rose-branch, also issuant leaved vert and bearing three roses gu., barbed and seeded. *De tout mon cœur.* 139. 10

Langston or **Langstone,** a lion rampant gu., supporting a pillar.

Langthorne, a tun sa., in the bung-hole three roses gu., stalked and leaved vert. cf. 150. 4

Langton, Baron of Newton, Lancs, the head of a maiden affrontée, couped below the shoulders ppr., vested gu., the cap and necklace or.

Langton of Broughton Tower, Lancs, an eagle displayed with two heads vert, charged on the breast with a trefoil or. *Loyal au mort.* cf. 74. 2

Langton, Bennett Rothes, Esquire, of Langton Hall, Spilsby, Lincs, an eagle or, and a wyvern vert, interwoven and erect on their tails. 310. 2

Langton, Hon. Edward, of 10, Bruce Street, Toorak, Melbourne, Victoria, an eagle or, and a wyvern vert, their necks entwined regardant. *Loyal à mort.* 310. 2

Langton of Danganmore, co. Kilkenny, Ireland, a heart gu., between two wings arg. *Sursum corda.* cf. 110. 14

Langton, Francis Albert Romuald, Esquire, of 11, Exhibition Road, London, S.W., same crest and motto.

Langton of Stanton and Stanmore, Middx., out of a ducal coronet gu., a demi-lion rampant or, holding in its paws a battle-axe arg. cf. 15. 4

Langton, a greyhound's head couped, collared, and chained. cf. 61. 2

Langton and **Launton,** a dexter arm in armour embowed wielding a sword, all ppr. 195. 2

Langtree, Lancs, an eagle with wings expanded gu., beaked and legged or. 77. 5

Langworthy of Bath, Somers., a demi-stag ppr. 119. 2

Lanigan-O'Keeffe, Stephen Martin, Esquire, of Delville, Glasnevin, co. Dublin, upon an antique crown a gryphon segreant or, holding in the dexter claw a sword erect arg., pommelled or. *Forti et fideli nihil difficile.*

Lanis, out of a crescent two eagle's heads addorsed ppr. 84. 15

Lankin, two wings addorsed arg., one on each side of a chapeau ppr., issuing from the rim.

Lannoy or **Lanoy** of Bletsoe, Beds, a chevalier's head in a helmet plumed, all ppr.

Lanphier of Parkstown, co. Tipperary, a demi-lion rampant gu. *Virtute et fidelitate.* 10. 3

Lansdowne, Marquess of (FitzMaurice): (1) A bee-hive beset with bees diversely volant ppr. 137. 7. (2) A centaur drawing a bow and arrow ppr., the part from the waist arg. *Virtute non verbis.* 53. 2

Lansford, a savage's head couped ppr. 190. 12

Lansley, a griffin's head erased ppr. 66. 2

Lant, a swan's head and neck couped bendy of six arg. and sa., charged with a rose between two rose-branches leaved vert.

Lant, Devonsh., Northamp., and Staffs, a dove arg., beaked and legged gu., standing on a serpent nowed ppr. 92. 10

Lant of Thorp Underwood, Northamp., on a serpent nowed az., a dove arg., charged on the breast with a mullet of the first. *Prudentia et simplicitate.* cf. 92. 10

Lante, a serpent nowed vert. 142. 4

Lany, Norf., a talbot's head guttée. 56. 12

Lany of London, Leics., and Suff., a merman ppr., the tail arg., the fins and hair or, wreathed round the temples arg. and az., holding in the hand a hawk's bell ppr., suspended from a string vert, tasselled arg.

Lanyon, Cornw., a falcon rising wings extended and belled. 87. 1

Lanyon, of Belfast, on a mount vert, a falcon rising ppr., belled and jessed or. *Vive ut vivas.*

Lanyon of Northleigh, Fortwilliam Park, Belfast, same crest and motto.

Lanyon of Lanyon, Cornw., on a mount vert, within a castle in perspective with four towers arg., a falcon rising on waves of the sea az.

Lapington, a pelican in her piety ppr. *Innocue ac provide.* 98. 14

Lapp, a dexter hand holding a battle-axe ppr. 213. 12

Lapp, a demi-mermaid ppr., holding in her dexter hand a purse gu., and in her sinister a comb or.

Lapsley and **Lapslie** of Campsie, Scotland, a Passion-cross gu. *Corona mea Christus.* 165. 4

Lapthorne, a lion's head erased or, collared vair. 18. 6

Lapworth, Cambs, a stork ppr., resting its dexter claw on a fleur-de-lis or. cf. 105. 11

Larayne and **Lareyn,** out of a cloud a hand holding a garland of laurel ppr. 218. 9

Larcom, Sir Thomas Percival, Bart., 9, Anglesey Crescent, Alverstoke, Hants, on a cap of maintenance az., turned up erm., a martlet sa., holding a fleur-de-lis in its beak or. *Le Roy, la loy.* cf. 95. 1

Larder of Upton Payne, Devonsh., a woman's head couped at the shoulders ppr., vested gu., garnished or, and crined of the last. 182. 3

Larder of Loders, Dorset, an elephant's head sa., armed and ducally crowned or. cf. 133. 2

Lardner, on a chapeau a bull, all ppr. cf. 45. 9

Large, a demi-savage holding in his dexter hand a sheaf of arrows, pointing with the sinister to a coronet, all ppr. 186. 13

Large of London, a demi-savage holding in his dexter hand a sheaf of arrows, pointing with the sinister to a ducal coronet, all ppr. *Loyal en tout.* cf. 186. 13

Lark or **Larke,** a hand issuing from a cloud in fess, lifting a garb ppr. 223. 12

Larkan or **Larken,** a greyhound sejant az. 59. 4

Larke, Lincs, a lark with wings endorsed. 139. 2

Larken, Francis Rop Esquire, of Cantilupe Chantry, Lincoln, upon a mount in front of three ears of barley stalked and leaved, a lark holding in the beak a columbine ppr. *Surget alauda.* 230. 19

Larkin and **Larkins,** a lark with wings addorsed holding in its beak a columbine, all ppr.

Larkin, John, Esquire, of Delrow, Aldenham, Herts, in front of a rock an escallop, thereon a lark ppr., holding in the beak two ears of wheat or. *Fidelis et constans.*

Larking, Cuthbert, Esquire, of Layston Lodge, Buntingford, a lark rising, holding in the beak a sprig of leaves.

Larkworthy, Devonsh., a demi-stag ppr. *Perseverando.* 119. 2

La Roche, Bart. (*extinct*), of Over, Glouc., a crow ppr. 107. 14

Larpent, *see* De Hochpied-Larpent.

Larpent of London, a unicorn's head erased arg., attired or, charged on the neck with a fleur-de-lis az. *cf.* 49. 5

Larping, a unicorn's head arg., attired or, charged on the neck with a fleur-de-lis az. *cf.* 49. 7

Larra, an elm-tree ppr. 143. 9

Lart, Charles Edmund, B.A., of Charmouth, Dorset, a lion rampant sa., armed and langued gu. *Croyc.*

Lascelles, Earl of Harewood and **Viscount Lascelles,** *see* Harewood.

Lascelles, Rt. Hon. Sir Frank Cavendish, K.C.M.G., a bear's head erm., muzzled gu., buckled, collared, rimmed, and studded or. *In solo Deo salus.*

Lascelles, Walter Richard, Esquire, of Norley, Frodsham, Chesh., and 55, Hans Road, S.W., same crest and motto.

Lascells, Notts and Yorks, out of a ducal coronet or, a griffin's head vert. 67. 9

Lascells of Sturton and Gaytford, Notts: (1) A buck's head arg. 121. 5. (2) Out of a ducal coronet or, a griffin's head vert, beaked of the first, and charged on the neck with a mullet for difference. *cf.* 67. 9. (3) Out of a ducal coronet or, a griffin's head vert, beaked of the first. 67. 9

La Serre of Guernsey, a stag ppr., attired or, semée of estoiles of the same, and resting the dexter foot on a bezant. *L'Eternel règne.* *cf.* 117. 8

Lashmar, a boar's head erased and erect sa. 43. 3

Laslett, Emerson-, Worcs.: (1) A demi-lion rampant holding a battle-axe. 15. 4. (2) A bear's head couped at the neck. 34. 14

Laslett of Aberton Hall, Worcs., a demi-lion rampant sa., charged with five bezants. *Finem respice.* *cf.* 10. 4

Lasley, a griffin's head erased ppr. 66. 2

Lasman, a squirrel sejant or, holding between its paws a branch of laurel vert. *cf.* 135. 2

Latch of Woodhouse, Leics., and Elston, Notts, a lion's head or, gorged with a fess wavy az. *cf.* 21. 1

Lateward, a demi-hawk with wings expanded sa., having on the head two horns bent or.

Latham, Essex and Lancs, an eagle preying on a child, all ppr., the child in swaddling-clothes gu., bound arg., at the head of the child an oak-branch of the second.

Latham, Alexander Mere, Barrister, 3, King's Bench Walk, Temple, E.C., and 7, Cheyne Gardens, Chelsea, S.W., an eagle preying on a child in swaddling-clothes.

Latham of Bradwall, Chesh., and London, an eagle with wings elevated erminois, preying on a child ppr., swaddled az., banded arg., exposed on a rock of the second.

Latham, A. M., B.A., 7, Cheyne Gardens, Chelsea, S.W., same crest. *Expertus fidelem.*

Latham of the Priory, Frensham, Surrey, an eagle rising with wings expanded and inverted, holding an olive-branch in its claw. *Æquanimitate.*

Lathom, Earl of (Bootle-Wilbraham), of Lathom: (1) A wolf's head erased arg. (*for Wilbraham*). 30. 8. (2) A demi-lion regardant ppr., holding between his paws an escutcheon gu., charged with a cross flory arg. (*for Bootle*). *In portu quies.*

Lathom of Parbold and Allerton, Lancs, an oak-branch fesseways, truncated and leaved ppr., thereon a heron rising or. *cf.* 105. 2

Lathom of Lathom, Lancs, an eagle regardant or, rising from a child's cradle gu. *cf.* 77. 13

Lathom of Moosborough, Ormskirk, Lancs, on a chapeau gu., turned up erm., an infant ppr., swaddled gu., banded arg., thereon an eagle preying or. 79. 3

Lathum, on a hank of cotton or, an eagle regardant of the first, the wings expanded.

Latimer, on a mount vert, a hind sejant arg., collared and chained or, under a tree ppr.

Latimer, an Eastern crown gu. 180. 12

Latimer, a plume of feathers or. 115. 1

Laton, out of a ducal coronet or, a stork's head arg.

Latouche or **La Touche,** a hand couped and gauntleted in fess, holding a scimitar entiled with a boar's head couped. *cf.* 211. 9

La Touche, John, Esquire, of Harristown, Brannockstown, Newbridge, co. Kildare, a mullet of five points pierced arg. *Quid verum atque decens curo et rogo.*

La Touche, Major Octavius, of Bellevue, Delgany, co. Wicklow, and Drumhearney, Leitrim, a mullet or. *Quid verum atque decens curo et rogo.*

Latouche, Ireland, on a heart gu., an eagle's claw erased ppr. 113. 14

Latouche, a mullet of six points pierced or. 164. 5

Latouche, Ireland, an étoile pierced or. *cf.* 164. 1

La Touche, a bezant charged with a mullet gu.

La Trobe-Bateman, Rev. William Fairbairn, M.A., of Ascot Rectory, Berks: (1) An eagle's head between two wings displayed or, charged on the neck with a mullet within the horns of a crescent gu., and upon each wing with an escallop of the last (*for Bateman*). (2) Out of clouds a dexter cubit arm erect ppr., the hand grasping an anchor fesseways or, the flukes to the dexter or (*for La Trobe*). *Sidus adsit amicum.*

Latta, Scotland, an oak-tree ppr. *Dum vivo, vireo.* 143. 5

Latter, out of a foreign coronet having nine balls visible upon the rim, a greyhound's head arg., collared and chained or. *Pour trois.—A tôt bien estrain.*

Lattin and **Latton** of Upton, Berks, and Esher, Surrey, a cross-bow or.

Lattin of Morristown Lattin, co. Kildare, an eagle's leg erased arg., charged with a crescent gu. *cf.* 113. 8

Lauchlan or **Lawchlan,** Scotland, a swan. *Divina sibi canit.* 99. 2

Lauder, a hand couped at the wrist in fess holding a sword in pale, on the point a leopard's face.

Lauder of Winepark, Scotland, a dexter hand holding a scimitar, and on the point thereof a Saracen's head, all ppr.

Lauder of Belhaven and Westbarnes, Scotland, the trunk of an old tree sprouting anew. *Repullulat.* 145. 2

Lauder, Scotland, the trunk of an old tree budding ppr. *Repullulat.* 145. 2

Lauder of Bass, Scotland, on a rock ppr., a solan goose sejant. *Sub umbrâ alarum tuarum.*

Lauder or **Lawder,** a tower and issuing from the battlements a demi-griffin. *Strike alike.* 157. 5

Lauder of Newington, Scotland, a balance equilibriated or. *Mediocria firma.* 179. 8

Lauder, Dick-, Sir Thomas North, Bart., of Fountain Hall, Haddingtonsh.: (1) A tower with the portcullis down, and the head and shoulders of a sentinel appearing above the battlements in a watching posture ppr. (*for Lauder*). (2) A stag's head erased ppr., attired or (*for Dick*). *Turris prudentia custos.—Virtute.*

Lauderdale, Earl of (Maitland), a lion sejant affrontée gu., ducally crowned ppr., holding in the dexter paw a sword of the last, pommel and hilt or, and in the sinister a fleur-de-lis az. *Consilio et animis.* *cf.* 7. 3

Laugharne, issuing out of a cloud a hand in pale pointing with one finger to the sun, all ppr.

Laugher, a plough ppr. 178. 7

Laughlin, Ireland, a talbot sejant arg., resting its dexter paw on an escutcheon gu.

Launce of Halesworth, Suff., a hand in armour ppr., in fess, grasping a lance or, headed arg.

Launce, Cornw., a demi-bull erm., armed or, pierced by a broken spear sa., headed arg., embrued gu.

Launder, Lancs, a demi-unicorn sa., armed, ungu., and crined or, the body charged with three mullets of six points in bend arg. *cf.* 48. 7

Laungton of Wilford, Wilts, a dexter arm in armour embowed brandishing a sword, all ppr. 195. 2

Laurel, issuing out of an antique crown a cubit arm vested, holding in the hand a bird and a garland of laurel.

Laurence, Ireland, a griffin sejant with wings addorsed, holding in its dexter claw a garland of laurel ppr. 62. 9

Laurence of Lisreaghan, co. Galway, a demi-turbot, the tail erect ppr. *Pro rege sæpe, pro patria semper.*

Laurence of Sherdington, Glouc., a demi-fish erect, tail upwards, per pale arg. and gu.

Laurence, G. Herbert, Esquire, the Grange, Norwood Green, Middx., a demi-turbot erect, tail upwards ppr. *Loyal au mort.*

Laurenson, Scotland, a dexter arm in armour embowed, holding in the hand a scimitar. *Justitia et veritas.* 196. 10

Laurie, a hill ppr.

Laurie or **Lawrie,** Scotland, the trunk of an oak-tree sprouting new branches ppr. *Repullulat.* 145. 2

Laurie, Craig-, Colonel John, the Red Castle, Castle Douglas, Kircudbrightsh.: (1) The trunk of an oak-tree sprouting ppr., and above the same a cross patée fitchée gu. (*for Laurie*). (2) A chevalier on horseback in full career grasping a broken lance in bend ppr. (*for Craig*). *Benedictio Dei ditat.—Vive Deo ut vivas.* 189. 5

Laurie of Redcastle, Kirkcudbrightsh., the trunk of an oak-tree sprouting ppr., above the same a cross patée fitchée gu. *Benedictio Dei ditat.*

Laurie, out of a mural coronet or, the stump of an oak-tree sprouting out leaves ppr.

Laurie, Rev. Sir John Robert Laurie Emiluis Laurie, B.D., Bart., of Maxwelton, Dumfriessh., Scotland, a garland of laurel between two branches of the same, all ppr. *Virtus semper viridis.*

Laurie of London, a wreath of laurel ppr. *Virtus semper viridis.* 146. 5

Laurie, Scotland, two branches of laurel in saltier ppr. *Virtus semper viridis.*

Laurie of London, an arm in armour embowed ppr., garnished or, holding in the hand a wreath of laurel vert. *cf.* 199. 12

Laurie, Lieutenant-General John Wimburne, C.B., M.P., 47, Porchester Terrace, London, W., and Oakfield, Halifax, Nova Scotia, and Peter George Laurie, Esquire, Heron Court, Herongate, near Brentwood, Essex, a dexter arm in armour embowed ppr., garnished or, holding in the hand a wreath of laurel vert. *Deeds shew.*

Laurie of Polmont, Linlithgowsh., Scotland, a dexter arm holding a slip of laurel ppr. *Virtutem coronat opus.* 219. 9

Laurin, on a chapeau ppr., an eagle's head az. 83. 12

Lauriston, an arm in armour embowed holding in the hand a scimitar, all ppr. *Justitia et veritas.* 196. 10

Lautour of Hexton House, Hitchin, Herts, an arm in armour embowed to the sinister ppr., garnished or, supporting with the gauntlet an escutcheon erminois, charged with a fess, embattled, cottised gu.

Lauty, Scotland, a dexter hand holding a spear erect ppr.

Lauzon, a mermaid with a mirror and a comb, all ppr. 184. 5

La Vach, a bull's leg reversed erm.

Lavelis of Castleharnock, Cornw., a tower triple-towered or. 157. 6

Lavell, a fox current ppr. *cf.* 32. 8

Laven of Poole, Scotland, a buck's head couped or. 121. 5

Lavender of London and Herts, a demi-horse arg., gorged with a wreath of lavender. *cf.* 53. 3

Laver, a talbot's head erased gu., ducally crowned or. 56. 9

Laverick or **Laverike,** two lion's gambs sa., supporting a pillar or. 39. 8

Laverin and **Lavering,** a shepherd's flute erect ppr.

Laverock, Laverick, or **Laverike,** two lion's gambs erased ppr., supporting a pillar or. *cf.* 39. 8

Lavers, a hand holding a crosier in bend sinister. 219. 4

Laverye, a savage's head affrontée ppr. 190. 12

Lavie, out of a ducal coronet or, a lion's gamb ppr., holding a cross crosslet fitched az. 36. 11

Lavington, a covered cup arg.

Law, Rt. Hon. Edward Downes, **Baron Ellenborough** of Ellenborough, Cumb., and 65, George Street, Portman Square, W., a cock gu., chained round the neck and charged on the breast with a mitre or. *Compositum jus fasque animi.* *cf.* 91. 2

Law, a cock gu., charged on the breast with a mitre pendent from a chain round the neck or. *Compositum jus fasque animi.*

Law, Edward Downes, Esquire, of 65, George Street, Portman Square, W., same crest and motto.

Law, James Adeane, Esquire, J.P., of the Caves, Banwell, Somers., same crest and motto.

Law, a cock gu. *Lex summa ratio.* 91. 2

Law, Scotland, a cock crowing. *Sat amico si mihi felix.* 91. 2

Law, William Thomas, Esquire, M.D., of 5, Duchess Street, Portland Place, a cock gu. *Lex ratio summa.* 91. 2

Law of Newton, Scotland, a cock's head erased ppr. *Nec obscura, nec ima.* 90. 1

Law of Burntoun, Fifesh., Scotland, a unicorn's head ppr. *Nec obscura, nec ima.* 49. 7

Law of Lauriston, Edinburgh, Count of the Empire of France, same crest and motto.

Law of East Kinevie, Scotland, a unicorn's head erased ppr., charged with a crescent or. *Non obscura, nec ima.* *cf.* 49. 5

Law, Ireland, a dexter hand holding a battle-axe ppr. 213. 12

Law, out of a tower a demi-griffin segreant. 157. 5

Law of Rochester, Kent, a dove holding in its beak an olive-branch, all ppr. 92. 5

Law, on a wreath, arg. and vert, a dove close arg., beaked and legged gu., holding in the beak an olive branch slipped ppr., between two wings sa., each enfiled with a wreath of olive vert.

Law of Stanmore and Newington, Middx., a wolf's head erased gu., ducally gorged or. *cf.* 30. 8

Laward, Laware, and **Lawarre,** out of a ducal coronet or, a griffin's head az., beaked of the first. 67. 9

Laward, a demi-bird sa., on the head two small horns or, the wings expanded, the dexter the outside gu., the inside arg., the sinister the outside of the last, the inside of the third.

Lawder, Scotland, a balance ppr. *Mediocria firma.* 179. 8

Lawder, Scotland, the trunk of an old tree budding ppr. *Repullulat.* 145. 2

Lawder of Lawderdale, Ballinamore, co. Leitrim, a gannet standing on one leg on a rock ppr. *Sub umbra alarum tuarum.*

Lawe, Drinkwater- of Kirby, Isle of Man: (1) In front of a spear erect ppr., a demi-eagle displayed with two heads vert, and charged on each wing with a fleur-de-lis arg. (*for Lawe*). (2) Three ears of wheat, one in pale and two in saltire enfiled with a ducal coronet, all or (*for Drinkwater*). *Sapiens qui assiduus.*

Lawes, Sir Charles Bennet, of Rothampstead Manor House, Herts, Kent, and Norf., on a ducal coronet or, an ermine passant ppr.

Lawes of Rothampstead, Herts, a mount vert, thereon the trunk of a tree fessewise, eradicated and sprouting to the dexter, surmounted by an ermine passant ppr. *Pour la foi.*

Lawes, *see* Wittewrong.

Lawford, a demi-lion holding between the paws a naval coronet.

Lawford, a demi-lion rampant erm., holding between the paws a naval coronet or, and in the mouth a laurel-branch ppr. *In utrumque paratus.*

Lawford of London, a lion rampant ppr., ducally crowned or, charged on the shoulder with a mullet arg. *In Deo confido.* *cf.* 1. 12

Lawford, an arrow, point downwards, and a palm-branch in saltier, all ppr. 171. 7

Lawful, a cornucopia or, the flowers and fruit ppr., and a trident az., in saltier.

Lawful, a helmet arg., plumed or. 180. 4

Lawler, on a dexter hand couped in fess a falcon rising ppr.

Lawler, Ireland, a bull's head gu. *cf.* 44. 3

Lawless, Baron Cloncurry, *see* Cloncurry.

Lawless, Ireland, out of a ducal coronet a demi-man in armour and in profile ppr., on his head a helmet of the same, visor up, garnished or, thereon a plume of feathers gu., holding in his dexter hand a sword erect of the first, hilt and pommel also or. *Virtute et numine.* 229. 3

Lawless, Scotland, a boar's head couped az. 43. 1

Lawless, a demi-lion rampant ducally crowned. 10. 11

Lawley, Baron Wenlock, *see* Wenlock.

Lawley-Thompson (Baron Wenlock): (1) An arm embowed quarterly or and az., gauntleted ppr., grasping the truncheon of a tilting-spear or (*for Thompson*). (2) A wolf statant sa. (*for Lawley*). *Je veux de bonne guerre.* 29. 2

Lawley, Shropsh., a wolf statant sa. 29. 2

Lawley, a wolf passant sa. *Auspice Christo.* 28. 10

Lawlor, Huddleston-, Denys Alexander, Esquire, of Sawston Hall, Sawston, Cambs., and of Grenagh, co. Kerry: (1) Two arms embowed, dexter and sinister, vested and cuffed arg., the hands ppr. holding a stone sa. (*for Huddleston*). 269. 17. (2) On a mount vert, and in front of a spear-head in pale, point upwards, a stag lodged, all ppr. (*for Lawlor*). *Mea culpa fides.—Soli Deo honor et gloria.* 269. 18

Lawnde, a hand in armour couped ppr., holding a cross crosslet fitched gu. 210. 14

Lawrence, Baron (Lawrence), of the Punjaub, and of Grately, Southamptonsh., out of an Eastern coronet or, a cubit arm entwined by a wreath of laurel and holding a dagger, all ppr. *Be ready.* 272. 2

Lawrence, Sir Henry Waldemar, Bart., J.P., of Alenho, Wimbledon, and 2, Mitre Court Buildings, Inner Temple, same crest. *Never give in.*

Lawrence, Bart., of Westbourne Terrace, Middx., on a wreath of the colours a wolf's head erased arg., crusilly and charged with a pair of compasses extended sa. *Per ardua stabilis.* 249. 15

Lawrence, Alfred Henry, Esquire, same crest and motto.

Lawrence, Glouc., a wolf's head ppr., charged on the neck with a crescent or. *cf.* 30. 5

Lawrence of Foxhall, Glouc., a wolf's head arg., charged on the neck with a cross crosslet gu. *cf.* 30. 5

Lawrence, a wolf's head couped ppr. 30. 5

Lawrence of Foxcote, Glouc., a fox's head ppr., charged with a bezant. *cf.* 33. 4

Lawrence, Sir James John Trevor, Bart., F.R.G.S., F.R.H.S., of Ealing Park, Middx., a gryphon's head couped arg., in front thereof a serpent nowed ppr. *Mente et labore.* *cf.* 66. 1

Lawrence, Ireland, a griffin sejant holding in the dexter claw a garland of laurel ppr. 62. 9

Lawrence of Cirencester, Glouc., a griffin's head erased. 66. 2

Lawrence, Hants, on a chapeau gu., turned up erm., a talbot sejant gu. 54. 14

Lawrence of London, a dolphin naiant ppr. 140. 5

Lawrence, Glouc., the lower part of a fish in pale, couped ppr.

Lawrence, a demi-turbot arg., tail upwards.

Lawrence, Rev. Charles, of Lisreaghan, Lawrencetown, co. Galway, a demi-turbot, tail erect ppr. (*for Bellevue*). *In cruce salus.*

Lawrence, Christian William, Esquire, J.P., of Sandywell Park, and Sevenhampton Manor, both near Andoversford, R.S.O., Glouc., same crest and motto.

Lawrence, Rev. Anthony Cocks, of Whittington, Glouc., same crest and motto.

Lawrence, Middx., Bucks, and Hunts, a demi-turbot in pale gu., the tail upwards.

Lawrence, a sea-lion party per fesse arg. and ppr. *Que pensez.* 20. 2

Lawrence of Rugby, a lion's gamb erased or, holding a branch of dates vert, fructed, also or, the husks arg.

Lawrence, two laurel-branches vert, in orle. 146. 5

Lawrence, Joseph, Esquire, of 2, Whitehall Court, S.W., on a mount vert, a gridiron ppr. *Ardent.*

Lawrence, Scotland, an acorn slipped and leaved vert. 152. 1

Lawrence of London, two trunks of trees raguly in saltier, environed with a chaplet vert. *cf.* 147. 9

Lawrence of London, a saltire raguly arg., encircled by two branches of laurel vert.

Lawrence of Iver, Bucks, and Hants, a stag's head erased sa., platée, attired or, ducally gorged arg. *cf.* 121. 2

Lawrence, Freeling Jones, Esquire, the Lodge, Eliot Vale, Blackheath, S.E., a demi-talbot arg. *Chwennych anrhydedd.*

Lawrens, Dorset and Winchester, on a chapeau gu., turned up erm., a talbot sejant of the first. 54. 14

Lawrie, *see* Laurie.

Lawrie of the Moss, Stirling, Scotland, the stump of an oak-tree with a branch sprouting from either side ppr. *I'll be wary.* *cf.* 145. 2

Lawrie of London and Kent, the trunk of a laurel-tree eradicated sprouting fresh branches ppr.

Lawrie, Scotland, the trunk of an oak-tree in fess couped and raguly ppr., ensigned with a cross patée fitched arg., entwined with a laurel-branch vert, fructed gu. *Industria atque fortuna.*

Lawrie, Scotland, a fox current ppr. *Ingenio innumerato habe.* *cf.* 32. 8

Lawrie, a monk holding in his dexter hand a crucifix and in his sinister a rosary. *Industria atque fortuna.* *cf.* 187. 7

Lawrie, Scotland, a dolphin naiant, and behind it a laurel-tree fructed ppr. *Industria atque fortuna.* *cf.* 140. 5

Laws, an elephant statant ppr. 133. 9

Laws, Durh. and Scotland, a cock ppr. *Compositum jus fasque animi.* 91. 2

Lawse, Kent and Norf., on a ducal coronet or, an ermine passant ppr.

Lawson of Hall Barn, Bucks, *see* Levy.

Lawson of Brayton, Northumb., and Durh., issuing out of clouds ppr., two arms embowed vested erminois, cuffed sa., supporting the sun ppr. *Quod honestum, utile.* 276. 11

Lawson, De Cardonnel-, of Cramlington Hall, Northumb.: (1) Two arms embowed vested erm., supporting the sun ppr. (*for Lawson*). (2) A goldfinch ppr., charged on the breast with a trefoil vert (*for De Cardonnel*). *Rise and shine.* *cf.* 108. 8

Lawson, Northumb., two arms couped at the elbow, habited erm., cuffed arg., holding in the hands ppr. a ring or, gemmed gu., within the ring the sun in splendour ppr.

Lawson, Sir Wilfrid, Bart., of Brayton, Cumb., out of clouds ppr., two arms embowed vested erminois, cuffed sa., holding in the hands a sun in splendour, also ppr. *Quod honestum, utile.*

Lawson, Sir Arthur Tredgold, Bart., of Weetwood Grange, Leeds, between two arms embowed ppr., holding a sun in splendour, a trefoil slipped, the whole surmounted by a rainbow, also ppr. *Surge et fulge.* 299. 12

Lawson-Smith, Edward Maule, Esquire, of Colton Lodge, Tadcaster: (1) On a mount vert, a stork arg., holding in the beak a serpent ppr. (*for Smith*). (2) On a mount vert, two arms embowed, couped at the elbow, vested erm., cuffed or, supporting between the hands ppr. a sun in splendour, also or (*for Lawson*).

Lawson, Staffs, an arm in armour embowed ppr., garnished or, holding in the gauntlet a battle-axe, the handle gu., the head arg. 200. 6

Lawson, Ireland, an arm from the elbow vested gu., the cuff indented or, holding a holly-branch ppr.

Lawson, Sir John, Bart., D.L., of Brough Hall, Yorks, on a cap of maintenance gu., turned up erm., a martlet sa. *Leve et reluis.* 95. 1

Lawson, Bart., a ram passant arg., his foot resting on a quatre-foil, in mouth a trefoil slipped vert. *Of old I hold.* 257. 8

Lawson, Yorks, a wolf's head erased ppr., collared vert, charged on the neck above the collar with three bezants. *Loyal secret.* *cf.* 30. 11

Lawson, Andrew Sherlock, Aldborough Manor, near Boroughbridge, a wolf's head erased ppr., collared vert, charged on the neck with three bezants, one above and two below the collar.

Lawson, Scotland, a leopard's head erased ppr. *Surgo, lumen adest.* 23. 10

Lawson, a demi-lion rampant holding between the paws a mullet of six points. *cf.* 15. 8

Lawson of Halbercot, Edinburgh, a garb or. *Dominus providebit.* 153. 2

Lawson, Alexander, Esquire, of Annfield, Fifesh., N.B., a garb or, banded gu. *Te splendente.*

Lawston, Ireland, a cubit arm vested gu., the cuff indented or, holding in the hand a holly-branch ppr.

Lawton, a wolf passant. 28. 10

Lawton of Lawton, Chesh., a demi-wolf salient regardant arg., vulned in the shoulder gu., and licking the wound.

Lawton, John William Edward, Esquire, a demi-wolf rampant arg., licking a wound in the right shoulder.

Lawton, a demi-lion arg., ducally crowned or. 10. 11

Lax of St. Ibbs, Herts, on a mount vert, a catharine-wheel or. *cf.* 167. 2

Laxton, issuing out of a tower ppr., a demi-griffin or. 157. 5

Lay, an escallop or, charged with a saltier gu., all between two wings of the first. *cf.* 141. 7

Lay, Horatio Nelson, Esquire, a demi-unicorn arg., collared vair, resting the sinister foot on a cross patonce sa. *Through.*

Layard of St. George's, Westminster, Middx., out of a ducal coronet or, a mullet of six points of the same. *Juvante Deo.*

Laycock, Joseph Frederick, Wiseton, Bawtry, Notts, a cock arg., combed, jellopped, and legged gu., supporting with the dexter claw a gauntlet sa. *Semper paratus.*

Layer, a mullet of six points gu. 164. 3

Layer, Norf., a unicorn's head erased arg. 49. 5

Layfield, Essex, a bull's head cabossed sa. 43. 8

Layland, on a terrestrial globe a ship sailing, all ppr. 160. 1

Layland-Barratt, Francis, Esquire, of 68, Cadogan Square, London, S.W., and Tregarne Lodge, St. Austell, Cornw., a bear sa., muzzled, semée of escallops, and resting the dexter fore-paw on an escallop, all or. *Cui debeo fidus.* 271. 15

Layman, a demi-bull rampant ppr. *cf.* 45. 8

Layton of Delmayne, Cumb., a lion's head erased arg., gorged with a collar sa., charged with three bezants. *cf.* 18. 6

Layton, Scotland, a demi-lion rampant. *In omnia paratus.* 10. 2

Layton, Lincs and Yorks, out of a mural coronet two wings expanded arg., each charged with a cross crosslet fitched sa. 227. 11

Layton, issuant from a mural coronet two wings displayed arg., each charged with a cross crosslet fitchée sa. *Dat cura quietem.* 227. 11

Layworth, Oxon., a lapwing ppr., resting his dexter claw on a fleur-de-lis or.

Lazarus, a hand ppr., holding a dragon's head erased vert.

Lea, Sir Thomas, Bart., in front of a mount vert, thereon a demi-heraldic antelope arg., supporting a bird-bolt erect or, three pheons fessewise sa. *Semper fidelis.*

Lea, Scotland, a lion rampant or. *Another,* arg. 1. 13

Lea, Rev. Thomas Simcox, M.A., of Astley Hall, Worcs., a beaver ppr., semée-de-lis or, holding in the mouth a branch of willow ppr. *Spe vitæ melioris.*

Lea, a stag's head erased or. 121. 2

Lea, a stag's head erased arg. 121. 2

Lea of Halesowen Grange, Worcs., a unicorn arg., guttée-de-poix, gorged with a double tressure flory and counterflory gu. *Contentus paucis.*

Lea, His Honour Judge George Harris, of Longworth, Heref., in front of a mount vert, thereon a demi-heraldic antelope arg., supporting a bird-bolt erect or, three pheons fesseways sa. *Semper fidelis.* 284. 10

Leach and Leache, out of a ducal coronet or, a lion's gamb holding a cross crosslet fitched sa. 36. 11

Leach, a swan with wings expanded arg., standing on a trumpet. *cf.* 100. 6

Leach, Cornw., a hand couped at the wrist grasping a snake. 220. 2

Leach of Stoke Climsland, Cornw., out of a ducal coronet or, a dexter cubit arm grasping a serpent, all ppr. *cf.* 220. 2

Leacroft, Captain Edward Ranulph, Esquire, 3rd Derby Regiment, Rowberrow Manor House, Congresbury, Somers., a dexter hand holding a wreath, all ppr. *Fari quæ sentiat.*

Leadbetter, Greenshields-, Thomas, Esquire, of Stobieside, Strathaven, N.B., and Edmonston, Biggar, N.B., issuing out of a mural coronet gu., a demi-unicorn erm., armed, crined, and ungu. or. *Tuta timens.* 296. 6

Leadbitter of Deptford, near Sunderland, Durh., on a mural coronet gu., a demi-unicorn erminois, erased of the first, armed and crined or.

Leadbitter, Gibson-, of Warden House, near Hexham, Northumb.: (1) A griffin's head sa., erased gu., pierced through the mouth by an arrow fesseways or, and charged upon the neck for distinction with a cross crosslet of the last (*for Leadbitter*). *cf.* 296. 8. (2) In front of a stork rising arg., holding in the beak an olive-branch ppr., between two ears of wheat or, a water-bouget sa. (*for Gibson*). *Fidelis.*

Leadbitter, Thomas Francis, of Warden, Northumberland (postal address, and Auckland House, Willesden Lane, N.W.), a griffin's head sa., erased gu., pierced through the mouth with an arrow fesseways or, point to the sinister. 296. 8

Leadbitter-Smith, Matthew Edward, Esquire, of Flass Hall, Durh.: (1) A stag lodged arg., semée of estoiles az., attired and gorged with an Eastern crown, the chain reflexed over the back or (*for Smith*). (2) A griffin's head sa., erased gu., pierced through the mouth with an arrow fesseways or (*for Leadbitter*). *Vigilans.* 296. 8

Leader, a demi-black negro holding in his dexter hand an arrow and a quiver of arrows at his back, all ppr. 185. 6

Leader of Much Stoughton, Hunts, an arm embowed vested vert, with two pallets gu., the hand holding a sprig of rosemary flowered ppr.

Leader of Buntingford, Herts, and of Moor End, Sheffield, an arm embowed issuing from an annulet and vested or, charged with two pallets engrailed sa., the hand holding a sprig of three roses ppr. *Virtus salus ducum.*

Leader, Holland Waterhouse, Esquire, of 34, Prussia Road, Hoylake, near Birkenhead, same crest and motto.

Leader, Robert, Esquire, of 138, Manchester Road, Sheffield, same crest and motto.

Leader of Ashgrove, co. Cork, Ireland, an arm embowed habited paly wavy of six vert and gu., the hand grasping a branch of three roses gu., barbed and leaved, all ppr. *Probum non pœnitet.*

Leader, William Nicholas, Esquire, J.P., D.L., of Dromagh Castle, Kanturk, co. Cork, an arm habited paly of six vert and gu., holding in the hand ppr. a branch of three roses barbed and leaved ppr.

Leaf of Park Hill, Streatham, a dove rising ppr., resting the dexter claw on a staff-tree leaf or.

Leahy, Ireland, a demi-savage holding over his shoulder a club, all ppr. 186. 5

Leahy of Shanakiel House, co. Cork, Ireland, out of a mural coronet ppr., a demi-lion rampant grasping in his dexter paw a sceptre, all or, and charged on the shoulder with a tower gu. *Tout vient de Dieu.*

Leak, a hand holding up a heart, all ppr. 216. 9

Leak and Leake, on each side of a garb a bird pecking at it with wings endorsed.

Leake, Robert, Esquire, of Little Missenden Abbey, Bucks, a garb ppr., supported by two popinjays rising or, and pecking at it. *Versus æternum viator.*

Leake of Mile End, Middx., a ship gun-carriage, and on it a piece of ordnance mounted, all ppr. *Pari animo.*

Leake, late Sir Luke Samuel, of Perth, in the colony of Western Australia, Speaker of the Legislative Council of that colony, a tilting-spear erect between four peacock's feathers ppr., encircled by an annulet or. *Perseverando.*

Leaky, Ireland, a horse-shoe ppr. 158. 6

Leale, Leall, or **Lealle,** out of a ducal coronet a sceptre entwined by a serpent between two wings, all ppr. *cf.* 170. 13

Lear of London, two hands issuing from clouds and grasping the trunk of an oak-tree ppr. 224. 10

Lear-Cholwich, *see* Cholwich.

Lear, Rev. Canon Francis, Bishopstone Rectory, near Salisbury, a demi-unicorn holding between the feet a staff raguly in pale. *Quicquid agis age.*

Learmont and **Learmonth,** of Balcomie, Scotland, a rose gu., stalked and leaved vert. *Spero.* 149. 5

Learmonth, Scotland, a dove holding in its beak an olive-branch ppr. *Dum spiro, spero.* 92. 5

Learmonth, John Livingstone, of 11, Gloucester Gardens, Hyde Park, London, W.: (1) On the dexter side, a dove holding in its beak an olive-branch ppr. (*for Learmonth*). 92. 5 (2) On the sinister side, a dexter hand grasping a sabre ppr. (*for Livingstone*). *Dum spiro, spero.—Si possim.* 212. 13

Learmonth, Andrew James Livingstone, and Somerville Livingstone Learmonth, both of Ercildoun, Victoria, Australia; Thomas Livingstone Learmonth of Parkhall, Stirling, Scotland: (1) On the dexter side, a dove holding in its beak an olive-branch ppr. (*for Learmonth*). 92. 5. (2) On the sinister side, a dexter hand grasping a sabre ppr. (*for Livingstone*). *Dum spiro, spero.—Si possim.* 212. 13

Leary, Ireland, a dexter hand ppr., holding an oak-branch vert, fructed or.

Leash, Scotland, a demi-lion rampant gu., holding in his dexter paw a thistle ppr., and in the sinister a fleur-de-lis or. 13. 12

Leash of that ilk, Scotland, a crescent arg. *Virtute cresco.* 163. 2

Leash, out of a mural coronet a beacon inflamed between two wings. 112. 5

Leatham, a dexter arm in armour brandishing a scimitar. *Maintien le droit.*

Leatham, Arthur William, Yorks, and of Misarden Park, Cirencester, on a nest an eagle with wings elevated or, the nest and wings fretty vert. *Virtute vinces.*

Leatham, Samuel Gurney, Esquire, of Hemsworth Hall, Yorks, same crest and motto.

Leatham, Claude, Solicitor, Wentbridge, Pontefract, Yorks, same crest and motto.

Leather, Gerard Frederick Towlerton, of Middleton Hall, Northumb., and Leventhorpe Hall, Yorks, a demi-lion rampant sa., charged on the shoulder with three mullets of six points, two and one or, and holding between the paws a fountain ppr. *Nil nisi quod honestum.* 296. 5

Leather-Culley, Arthur Hugo, Esquire, of Fowberry Tower, near Belford, Northumb.: (1) In front of an oak-tree ppr., a talbot statant per pale az. and or, gorged with a collar gemelle arg., and holding in the mouth a lily slipped ppr., and charged for distinction upon the shoulder with a cross crosslet or (*for Culley*). 278. 3. (2) A demi-lion sa., holding in the paws a fountain, and charged on the shoulder with three mullets of six points, two and one or (*for Leather*). *Amicos semper amat.* 278. 4

Leathes of Leathes and Dalehead, Cumb., a lion's head affrontée ppr.

Leathes, Hill Mussenden, Herringfleet Hall, Suff.: (1) A demi-griffin rampant armed and langued gu. (*for Leathes*). (2) A dove with an olive-branch in its beak, all ppr. (*for Mussenden*). *In ardua virtus.—Tending to peace.*

Leaton Blenkinsopp, Northumb. and Durh.: (1) A lion rampant or (*for Blenkinsopp*). 1. 13. (2) Out of a mural coronet ppr., two eagle's wings expanded arg., each charged with a cross crosslet fitched sa. (*for Leaton*). *Dieu défende le droit.* 227. 1

Leatt of London, on a mural coronet or, a fire-beacon sa., inflamed ppr., between two wings az. 112. 5

Leaver, an arm embowed holding a club, all ppr. 202. 10

Le Bailly, Jersey, a demi-lion ppr. *Deus fortissima turris.* 10. 2

Le Bareu, a mullet ppr. 164. 2

Le Blanc of London and Middx., and Rouen, an eagle displayed sa., ducally crowned or, charged on the breast with a cinquefoil of the last. *Sans tache.* 74. 14

Le Blond, *see* Blond.

Le Bon, out of a ducal coronet or, a plume of ostrich-feathers ppr. *Confido.* *cf.* 114. 8

Lecawell, a unicorn arg., armed gu. *cf.* 48. 5

Leche, two lion's gambs erased sa., holding up a crescent arg. 39. 6

Leche, John Hurleston, of Carden Park, Chesh., out of a ducal coronet a cubit arm ppr., the hand grasping a snake vert. *cf* 29. 6

Leche of Chatsworth, Derbysh., out of a ducal coronet or, an arm erect ppr., grasping a leech or snake environed round the arm vert. *cf.* 220. 2

Leche, out of a ducal coronet or, an arm in pale ppr., the hand grasping a snake entwined round the arm vert. *cf.* 220. 2

Lechford, Surrey, a leopard's head per pale arg. and sa., between two wings counterchanged.

Lechford of Shelwood, Surrey, a unicorn's head erased arg., armed and maned or, and bearing on the horn a serpent ppr. *cf.* 49. 5

Lechingham of Wendover, Bucks, and Beds, a ram's head cabossed or. 130. 7

Lechmere, Baron Lechmere (*extinct*), out of a ducal coronet a pelican or, vulning herself ppr.

Lechmere, Sir Edmund Anthony Harley, Bart., of Rhydd Court, Worcs., a pelican az., vulning herself ppr. *Christus pelicano.* 98. 1

Lechmere of Hanley, a pelican ppr. 98. 1

Lechmere, Edmund Henry Scudamore, of Fownhope Court, Heref., a pelican az., vulning herself ppr. *Ducit amor patriæ.* 98. 1

Lechmere, Middx. and Heref., a pelican az., vulning herself ppr. 98. 1

Leck of Hollybush, Ayrsh., and of Woodend, Lanarksh., a wolf's head erased ppr. *Virtutis præmium.* 30. 8

Leckey of Craigavoran, Queen's Co., Ireland, an anchor in pale ppr., cabled or and gu., surmounted by a boar's head erased and erect az. *Gubernat navem Deus.*

Leckie, Scotland, an anchor in pale, cabled ppr. *Deus gubernat navem.* 161. 2

Leckie, Scotland, in the sea vert, a ship in distress ppr. *At spes non fracta.* 160. 14

Leckie or **Lecky,** an arm embowed holding a club ppr. 202. 10

Leckie, two arms, dexter and sinister, couped at the wrist issuing, holding between them a two-handed sword, all ppr. 213. 3

Lecky, *see* Browne-Lecky.

Lecky of Castle Lecky, co. Derry, and Ballyholland House, co. Down, a wild boar's head erased ppr. *Semper paratus.* 42. 2

Lecky, Sir Thomas, of Greystone Hall, Limavady, co. Londonderry, a boar's head erased. *Utere dum potes.*

Lecky, Ireland, a fawn trippant ppr. 124. 12

Lecky, the late William Edward Hartpole, Esquire, of Ballyvale, co. Carlow, and Kilbracken, Queen's Co., an anchor in pale ppr., cabled or and gu., surmounted by a boar's head erased and erect az. *Gubernat navem Deus.*

Le Cocq of Jersey, Guernsey, and Alderney, a cock crowing with wings extended sa.

Leconfield, Baron (Wyndham), of Leconfield, in the East Riding of the county of York, a lion's head erased or, within a fetterlock, the lock or, and the bow countercompony or and az., the head charged with a saltire wavy gu. *Au bon droit.* 282. 5

Le Couteur, Jersey: (1) A dove holding in the beak an olive-branch, all ppr. 92. 5. (2) A sword and a sprig of laurel in saltire ppr. *Toujours prest.*

Le Couteur of St. John la Hougue Boete, Jersey, on an ivy-wreath erect or, an owl sa. *La vita il fin e'l di loda la sera.* *—Boni virtutis amore.*

Le Cronier, Jersey, a mastiff ppr. *Je garde ma foy.*

Lecton of Wilborne, Lincs, a savage's head couped at the shoulders affrontée ppr., wreathed round the temples gu. and or. 190. 5

Leder of Great Stoughton, Hants, a dexter hand holding a sheaf of arrows ppr. 214. 3

Leder, a cubit arm vested bendy sinister of six gu. and vert, holding in the hand ppr. a bunch of leaves of the second.

Le Despencer, a griffin's head ppr. 66. 1

Le Despencer, Baron (Stapleton), out of a ducal coronet or, a Saracen's head affrontée ppr., wreathed arg. and sa. *Pro magna charta.—Ne vile fano.*

Ledgcomb, an elephant's head erased. 133. 3

Ledger, an escarbuncle az. 164. 12

Ledger, Walter Edwin, A.R.I.B.A., of 5, Wilton Road, Wimbledon, an escarbuncle az., fleurette arg.

Lediard of Cirencester, Glouc., a wolf's head erased per pale pean and gu. 30. 8

Ledlie, a ram's head couped arg., armed or, and behind it a crosier in bend sinister ppr. *cf.* 130. 1

Ledsam, a bull's head erased or. 44. 3

Ledsam of Chad Hill, Warw., a Cornish chough ppr. *Fac et spera.* 107. 14

Ledwich, Ireland, an eagle displayed gu. 75. 2

Ledwich, Ireland, a lion rampant gu. 1. 13

Lee, Viscount Dillon, *see* Dillon.

Lee, Earl of Lichfield (*extinct*), out of the coronet of a marquess or, a demi-stone column arg., on its capital an eagle's leg erased at the thigh and preyed upon by a falcon, all ppr. *Fide et constantia.*

Lee of Quarendon, Bucks, and Ditchley, Oxon., a falcon or, with wings close gu., preying on an eagle's leg lying fesswise az.

Lee, Gordon Ambrose de Lisle, Esquire, Bluemantle Pursuivant of Arms, of Selwood Lodge, Elm Place, South Kensington, upon an eagle's leg fesseways erased at the thigh, the claw to the sinister az., a falcon belled or, legged gu., twined round the body and neck by a hawk's lure sa. *Fide et constantia.*

Lee, Scotland and Calcutta, the upper part of a column, thereon a falcon preying on a heron's leg erased arg. *Fide et constantia.*

Lee, William Blackstone, Somerset House, Seend, Melksham, Wilts, on a staff raguly a squirrel cracking a nut, from the dexter end of the staff an oak-branch fructed, all ppr. *Ne incautus futuri.*

Lee-Guinness: (1) A boar passant quarterly or and gu. (*for Guinness*). 40. 9. (2) On a pillar arg., encircled by a ducal coronet or, an eagle preying on a bird's leg erased ppr. (*for Lee*). *Spes mea in Deo.* 248. 1

Lee of Fitchworth, Sussex, a stag's head erased or. 121. 2

Lee, Middx., a cock arg., combed and wattled or, beaked and legged gu. 91. 2

Lee-Norman, Luke Alexander, Esquire, M.A., J.P., D.L., of Corbollis, Ardee, co. Louth: (1) A lion passant gardant ppr. (*for Norman*). 278. 2. (2) A demi-lion rampant grasping a sceptre, all ppr. (*for Lee*). *Honor virtutis præmium.* 278. 1

Lee-Dillon, Hon. Harry Lee Stanton, of Ditchley, Enstone, Oxon., a demi-lion rampant gu., holding between the paws an estoile arg. *Dum spiro spero.*

Lee, Ireland, a demi-lion rampant erminois, navally crowned az., holding between the paws a sceptre sa. *Courageux.*

Lee of Tralee, co. Kerry, Ireland, on a ducal coronet or, a lion rampant sa., holding in the dexter paw a sword ppr., pommel and hilt of the first. *Fide et fortitudine.*

Lee, Cornw. and Wilts, a lion sejant or. 8. 8

Lee of Ebford, Devonsh., a bear sejant ppr., muzzled and chained or. *cf.* 34. 8

Lee, Lennox Bertram, Esquire, of How Caple Court, Heref., a bear passant arg., collared and chained az., charged upon the body with two cinquefoils of the last, resting the dexter fore-paw on an escutcheon or, thereon a fleur-de-lis, also az. *Patitur qui vincit.* 256. 4

Lee of Hartwell, Bucks: (1) A bear passant sa., muzzled, collared, and chained, the chain reflexed over the back arg. (*for Lee*). *cf.* 34. 1. (2) A demi-horse rampant arg., charged on the shoulder with a fleur-de-lis for difference (*for Fiott*). *Verum atque decens.* *cf.* 53. 2

Lee, Thomas, Esquire, J.P., of Alder House, Atherton, Lancs, a bear passant arg., muzzled, collared, and chained or. *Patitur qui vincit.*

Lee of Holborough Court, Kent, a bear statant ppr., muzzled gu., collared and chained arg. *Verum atque decens.* *cf.* 34. 1

Lee, Bart. (*extinct*), of Hartwell, Bucks, a bear passant sa., muzzled, collared, and chained, the chain reflexed over the back arg. *cf.* 34. 1

Lee of London, a bear statant ppr., muzzled gu., collared and chained arg., charged on the shoulder with a bezant. *cf.* 34. 1

Lee of Coldrey, Hants, on a mount vert, a bear passant ppr., muzzled and chained or. *cf.* 34. 5

Lee of Lee, Wincham, and Darnhall, Chesh., on a ducal coronet or, a leopard's face sa. *cf.* 22. 2

Lee, Major-General Henry Herbert, of Dynas Powis, Glamorgansh., on a ducal coronet or, a leopard's face sa. *Fortiter sed suaviter.* *cf.* 22. 2

Lee of London, a talbot's head arg., collared az., to the collar a ring and a line nowed of the last. *cf.* 56. 1

Lee, out of a ducal coronet a ram's head holding in its mouth a branch, all ppr.

Lee, Shropsh., a squirrel sejant cracking a nut. 135. 7

Lee, Shropsh., on a staff raguly a squirrel cracking a nut, from the dexter end of the staff an oak-branch bearing acorns issuing, all ppr.

Lee, Shropsh., the stem of an oak-tree lying fesseways couped and raguly, sprouting out one branch fructed ppr., on the tree a squirrel sejant cracking an acorn, all ppr. *Fidei virtutem adde.*

Lee of Fishburn, Durh., an heraldic antelope's head erased arg., pellettée, maned, tufted, and attired sa., holding in the mouth a white lily slipped ppr.

Lee, a leopard passant, bezantée. *cf.* 24. 2

Lee, Somers., a leopard passant ppr., supporting an escutcheon, thereon between four cotises arg. three leopard's faces sa. *cf.* 24. 5

Lee, Vaughan-, Major Arthur Vaughan Hanning, Dillington, near Ilminster: (1) On a mount vert, a leopard passant ppr., supporting with the dexter fore-paw a shield az., charged with two bars gemelle arg. (*for Lee*). (2) In front of a boy's head affrontée, around his neck a snake entwined ppr., a bugle-horn sa. (*for Vaughan*).

Lee of Dulce, Kent, and Southwell, Notts, a demi-Moor ppr., vested gu., the sleeves arg., rimmed round the collar with two bars or, tied round the waist with a ribbon arg., wreathed about head of the last and gu., and holding in his dexter hand a gem ring of the third. 185. 9

Lee of London, a dexter hand in fess, holding a sword in pale ppr. *Forte non ignave.* *cf.* 223. 10

Lee of Liverpool, a cubit arm erect vested gu., cuffed arg., holding in the hand a spear, point downwards. 207. 14

Lee, Ireland, issuing out of a cloud a hand erect holding a sealed letter. 215. 7

Lee, out of a ducal coronet or, an arm in armour embowed, holding a dart ppr. *cf.* 198. 4

Lee of Lady-hole, Derbysh., an arm in armour embowed ppr., bandaged or, gauntleted az., and holding a battle-axe ppr., the staff also or. *cf.* 200. 6

Lee of the Abbey, Knaresborough, an arm in armour holding a battle-axe, all ppr. *Dum spiro, spero.*

Lee, Herts, a dexter arm in armour embowed, holding in the hand a sword arg., hilt and pommel or, from the blade flames of fire issuing ppr. 195. 8

Lee, Essex and Leics, an arm embowed habited gu., cuffed arg., holding in the hand ppr. a sword in pale of the second, the hilt or, on the blade a snake entwined vert. *cf.* 24. 1

Lee-Grattan-Guinness, Arthur William,: (1) A boar passant quarterly or and gu. (*for Guinness*). (2) On a mount vert, a falcon, wings elevated, holding in the dexter claw a sceptre, all ppr. (*for Grattan*). 248. 7. (3) On a wreath of the colours on a pillar arg., encircled by a ducal coronet or, an eagle preying on a bird's leg erased ppr. (*for Lee*). Under the arms (*for Guinness*): *Spes mea in Deo.*—Over the crest (*for Grattan*): *Esse quam videri.* 248. 1

Lee-Warner, Henry, Esquire, of Walsingham Abbey, Norf., a squirrel sejant gu., between two branches of oak fructed ppr., cracking a nut or. *Non nobis tantum nati.*

Lee-Warner, Rev. James, M.A., of Thorpland Hall, Fakenham, Norf., same crest and motto.

Leech or **Leeche,** on a glove a hawk, all ppr. 86. 12

Leech of Clooncorra, co. Mayo, Ireland, out of a ducal coronet or, charged with a trefoil vert, an arm erect ppr., grasping a snake environed about the arm, also vert. *Virtute et valore.* *cf.* 220. 2

Leech, John Henry, Esquire, of Kippure House, Kilbride, co. Wicklow, Ireland, on a wreath of the colours a cubit arm erect grasping a snake entwined about the arm, all ppr. 220. 2

Leech, John Cyril, Esquire, of Hurdcott House, Wilts, an arm erect ppr., grasping a snake vert. *Virtus est venerabilis.*

Leech, Stephen, Esquire, of San Martino, Portofino, Italy, same crest and motto.

Leechman and **Leeshman,** Scotland, a pelican ppr. *Industriæ munus.* 98. 1

Leeds, Duke of (Osborne): (1) An heraldic tiger passant or, tufted and maned sa. (*for Osborne*). 25. 5. (2) A dolphin naiant sa. (*for Godolphin*). 140. 5. (3) On a chapeau gu., turned up erm., a bull sa., armed or (*for D'Arcy*). *Pax in bello.* *cf.* 45. 9

Leeds or **Leedes,** Berks, Lincs, Middx., and Yorks, on a staff raguly vert, a cockatrice with wings addorsed or, combed and wattled gu. *cf.* 68. 4

Leeds, Sir Edward Temple, Bart., of Croxton Park, Cambs, a staff raguly fesseways vert, thereon a cock with wings expanded gu., combed, wattled, beaked, and legged or, the whole debruised by a bendlet sinister wavy erm. *Vigilate.* 305. 4

Leeds, on a chapeau a cock statant, wings elevated.

Leeds, a bombshell sa., fired ppr. 177. 12

Leek, a demi-lion gardant, holding in its dexter paw a fleur-de-lis.

Leeke of Newark-on-Trent, Notts, a peacock's tail erect, the plume displayed ppr., supported by two eagles with wings expanded arg.

Leeke, Colonel Ralph, late Grenadier Guards, of Longford, Shropsh., a leg couped at the thigh encircled by a garter az., charged with two fleurs-de-lis. *Agendo gnaviter.*

Leeke, Shropsh., a leg arg., couped at the thigh, gartered az., passing through several blades of grass vert.

Leeke, Shropsh., a tuft of long grass and thereon a leg flexed at the knee ppr., and couped at the middle of the thigh gu., gartered below the knee az., ends pendent, charged on this thigh with a fleur-de-lis or. *Agendo gnaviter.*

Leeke of Edmonton, Middx., a leg couped at the thigh arg., gartered below the knee az.

Leeks, a tree ppr. 143. 5

Leeky, Ireland, a dexter hand holding a dagger ppr. 212. 9

Leeming of Greaves House and Lentworth Hall, Lancs, upon a rock ppr., a cross patonce or, between two ostrich-feathers arg.

Leeming, John Fishwick, Esquire, of Whalley Range, near Manchester, between two crosses potent az., a dexter arm embowed in armour, the hand grasping a sword, all ppr., charged with two oak-leaves, the one above and the other below the elbow vert. *In hoc signo vinces.* 255. 9

Leeper or **Leper,** co. Donegal, a leopard's face per pale or and sa. *Regi patriæque.* 22. 2

Lees, Eric Brown, J.P., of Thurland Castle, Kirkby Lonsdale, Lancs, in front of two cross crosslets fitchée saltirewise gu., a falcon belled arg. *Fide sed cui vide.* 85. 5

Lees, a serpent erect, the tail nowed, holding in its mouth a garland of laurel vert. 142. 7

Lees, Sir Harcourt James, Bart., of Black Rock, co. Dublin, a dexter hand couped above the wrist and erect ppr., grasping a crescent or. *Exegi.* 216. 8

Lees, Sir Elliott, Bart., South Lytchett Manor, Poole, Dorset, on a millrind fessewise sa., an owl arg. *Without haste, without rest.*

Lees of Acomb Park, Yorks, a lion rampant gu., supporting a flagstaff entwined by a wreath of oak fructed ppr., thereon a banner of the arms, namely, per fesse or and gu., a fesse dovetailed per fesse embattled between two falcons belled in chief and a lion rampant in base, all counterchanged. *In dubiis rectus.*

Lees, Francis Gerald, Esquire, of Werneth, Oldham, Lancs, a lion rampant gu., supporting a flagstaff entwined by a wreath of oak fructed ppr., therefrom flowing a banner of the arms, viz., per fesse or and gu., a fesse dovetailed per fesse embattled between two falcons belled in chief and a lion rampant in base, all counterchanged. *In dubiis rectus.*

Lees, William, Esquire, of Brooklands, Sale, Chesh., in front of a cotton-hank fesseways or, thereon an owl close holding in the beak a branch of a cotton-tree, a distaff fesseways, also ppr. *Perge sed caute.* 249. 18

Lees, Joseph, Esquire, J.P., of Werneth Grange, Oldham, and Bank Hall, Preston, same crest and motto.

Lees, Joseph Crompton, Esquire, of Newtown Manor, co. Sligo, a mount, thereon amidst wheat a mower, in his hands a scythe in the attitude of mowing, all ppr. *Ein doe and spare nought.*

Lees, Joseph Arthur, Esquire, J.P., B.A., same crest and motto.

Lees-Milne, James Henry, Esquire, J.P., of Crompton Hall and Park House, Shaw, near Oldham: (1) In front of five palm-leaves ppr., a lamb couchant arg., holding in the mouth a trefoil slipped or, and supporting with the dexter fore-foot a flagstaff in bend sinister ppr., therefrom flowing a banner arg. charged with a cross crosslet gu. (*for Milne*). (2) A mount, thereon amidst wheat a mower, in his hand a scythe in the attitude of mowing, all ppr. *Prudenter qui sedulo.*

Leeshman, Scotland, a pelican ppr. *Industriæ munus.* 98. 1

Leeson, Earl of Milltown, *see* Milltown.

Leeson-Marshall Markham Richard, Esquire, of Callinafercy House, Killorglin, co. Kerry: (1) a demi-man in armour affrontée ppr., holding in the dexter hand a baton sa., tipped or, charged on the breast with a rose gu., girded with a sash, also gu., a crescent gu. for difference (*for Marshall*). (2) A demi-lion rampant gu., holding in the paws a sun or, partially eclipsed by clouds ppr. (*for Leeson*). (3) A winged lion sejant guardant arg., wings addorsed, holding between the fore-paws a harp or, the head encircled by a plain glory of the last (*for Markham*).

Leeson, on a ducal coronet three arrows, points downward, wreathed about with a serpent ppr. 173. 2

Leeson, on a chapeau gu., turned up or, a phœnix in flames ppr. 82. 11

Lee-Steere, H. C., Esquire, of Jayes Park, Ockley, Surrey: (1) An arm embowed, vested gu., cuffed arg., holding in the hand ppr. a sword erect of the second, hilted or, on the blade a snake entwined vert. (2) Out of a mural coronet per pale gu. and sa., a lion's gamb erect arg., armed of the first (*for Steere*). *Tu ne cede malis.*

Leet or **Lete,** of Eversden and Kingston, Cambs, and Southoe, Hunts, on a ducal coronet an antique lamp or, the flames ppr. 177. 7

Leete, William John, Esquire, of 38, Eaton Terrace, London, S.W., a lion rampant quarterly or and gu., holding between the paws a sun in splendour ppr., and resting the dexter hind-leg on an escutcheon gu., charged with a lamp or, fired az. *Fide et amore.*

Le Fleming, Stanley Hughes, Esquire, J.P., D.L., of Rydal Hall, Ambleside: (1) A serpent nowed, holding in the mouth a wreath of olives and vine-leaves, all ppr. (*for Le Fleming*). (2) A lion couchant resting the dexter paw on a fountain (*for Hughes*). *Pax, copia, sapientia.*

Leete, of Bury St. Edmunds, Suff., a demi-bull gu., gorged with a chaplet of laurel vert. *cf.* 45. 14

Leeth, a demi-griffin segreant gu., winged az., charged on the body with two fleurs-de-lis or. *cf.* 64. 2

Leeves of Tortington, Sussex, on a mount vert. a swan with wings elevated arg., ducally crowned and gorged or, a chain reflexed over the back therefrom of the same, charged on the breast with three pellets, two and one, beaked and membered sa.

Le Febvre, Jersey, and scallop or. 141. 12

Le Feuvre, Jersey, a triple-eared stem of corn ppr. 154. 4

Lefever or **Lefevre,** the trunk of a tree couped and eradicated in fess, between the branches a fleur-de-lis. 145. 13

Lefevre, Middx., a trefoil or. 148. 9

Lefevre of Old Ford, Middx., six arrows interlaced saltierways, three and three, ppr., and interlacing an annulet or.

Le Forest, a unicorn sejant arg., armed, crined, and tufted or.

Lefroy, Rt. Hon. Thomas Langlois, of Carrickglass, co. Longford, Ireland, a demi-wyvern gu., langued az. *Mutare sperno.* 69. 12

Lefroy, Charles James Maxwell, Esquire, same crest and motto.

Lefroy, Augustine Hugh, Esquire, of the Lodge, Boxted, Colchester, same crest and motto.

Lefroy, Augustus Henry Fraser, Esquire, of Toronto, Canada, a demi-wyvern gu., gorged with a collar dancetty arg., fretty vert. *Mutare sperno.*

Lefroy, a greyhound's head erased arg. 61. 4

Leftwich of Leftwich, Chesh., five leaves conjoined at the base vert.

Leg, a fountain of three basons throwing up water ppr. *cf.* 159. 13

Le Gallais, Jersey, a cock statant, the dexter foot uplifted. *cf.* 91. 2

Legard, Leics. and Yorks, a greyhound or, collared gu., charged with three bezants.

Legard, Bart., of Ganton, Yorks, a greyhound or, collared sa., studded arg. *Per crucem ad stellas.* *cf.* 60. 2

Legard, Colonel James Digby, Welham, Malton, Yorks, same crest and motto.

Legard, Albert George, Esquire, of Gibraltar Cottage, Monm., same crest and motto.

Legat or **Leggatt** of Edinburgh, Scotland, a cherub's head ppr. *Jesus Hominum Salvator.* 189. 9

Legat, two lion's gambs in pale gu., supporting a mitre or.

Legatt, a sea-lion sejant arg. 20. 2

Leger, a pheon with part of the shaft therein. 174. 10

Legett, two lion's gambs supporting a regal crown, all ppr.

Le Geyt, Jersey, a lion's head couped ppr. *Quo fata vocant.* 21. 1

Leggat or **Leggatt,** an arm from the elbow habited counter-compony gu. and or, holding in the hand a mill-rind. 207. 4

Legg, Rev. William, M.A., of Newbury, Berks, a dexter arm in armour sa., garnished or, holding in the hand a roll of paper arg., between roses or. *Tolle, lege.* 267. 7

Legg, *see* Rowan-Legg.

Legge, Earl of Dartmouth, *see* Dartmouth.

Legge, Baron Stawell (*extinct*), out of a ducal coronet or, a plume of five ostrich-feathers, three arg. and two az. *En parole je vis.* 114. 13

Legge, Rev. Augustus George, M.A., of Bramdean House, Alresford, out of a ducal coronet or, a plume of five ostrich-feathers alternately arg. and az. *Gaudet tentamine virtus.*

Legge, Kent and Sussex, same crest and motto.

Legge, Lieutenant-Colonel William Vincent, of Cullenswood House, St. Mary's, Break o' Day River, Tasmania, a man's leg couped at the middle of the thigh standing on a triple-tower, all ppr. *Se defendendo.*

Legge, Kent, on a triple-tower a man's leg couped at the thigh, all ppr.

Legge, Cambs, a unicorn's head erased arg., crined, armed, and ducally gorged or. *cf.* 49. 5

Legget, Scotland, a mermaid holding in her dexter hand a sword, all ppr. 184. 7

Legh, *see* Leigh.

Legh of Lyme, Chesh., out of a ducal coronet or, a ram's head arg., armed of the first, holding in the mouth a laurel-sprig vert.

Legh of Lyme, Chesh., issuant out of a ducal coronet or, a ram's head arg., armed or, holding in the mouth a laurel-sprig vert, and over all a pellet wavy gu. *Another,* the pallet az., and a third with the pallet vert. 303. 9

Legh of Preston, Lancs, out of a ducal coronet or, a ram's head arg., holding a sprig of laurel vert, and charged on the neck with a trefoil gu.

Legh, Chesh., a unicorn's head couped arg., armed and crined or, charged on the neck with a cross patonce gu.

Legh, Arthur Masterton Robertson, Esquire, of Adlington Hall, Macclesfield, co. Chester, same crest.

Legh, Lieutenant Colonel Henry Martin Cornwall, J.P., D.L., of High Legh Hall, near Knutsford, co. Chester: (1) A demi-lion rampant gu., langued az., collared or (*for Legh*). (2) A Cornish chough ppr. (*for Cornwall*). *Pour Dieu, pour terre.—La vie durante.* 10. 9

Legh, Lieutenant-Colonel H. C., Chyknell, Bridgnorth, Salop: (1) A demi-lion rampant gu., collared or. (2) A Cornish chough ppr. *La vie durante.*

Legh, Devonsh. and Somers., a demi-greyhound sa., holding a stag's head arg., attired or.

Legh, Chesh., a bear passant ppr., chained or. *cf.* 34. 1

Legh, Chesh., a cubit arm in pale vested paly of six or and sa., cuffed arg., holding in the hand ppr. the top of a broken tilting-spear of the third, point downwards.

Legh, an arm in armour embowed, holding in the hand a sword with a serpent entwined thereon, all ppr.

Legh of Norbury Booths Hall, Chesh., an arm embowed, couped at the shoulder, vested gu., the hand ppr. holding a sword erect, also ppr., a snake twisted round the same arg. *Prudens, fidelis et audax.*

Legham and **Leigham,** an arm couped at the shoulder, the part above the elbow lying in fess, the hand in pale holding a bombshell fired ppr.

Le Grice of Treriefe, Cornw., a boar passant sa., collared or. *cf.* 40. 9

Legrosse, an arm embowed ppr., vested gu., holding a sword by the blade, point downwards, arg., hilted or.

Legryle, of Brockdish, Norf., a boar passant sa. 40. 9

Le Hardy of St. Peter, Jersey, a dexter arm embowed in armour ppr., garnished or, holding a griffin's head sa. *Le hardy ne guerre pas querelle.—Sic donec.*

Lehoop, a rose ppr. 149. 5

Le Hunt, Ireland, a demi-chevalier brandishing a sword ppr. 187. 1

Le Hunt, Ireland, a hand holding a boar's head erased and erect in pale. 220. 6

Le Hunt of Little Bradley, Suff., and Huntshall, Essex, out of a baron's coronet or, the pearls arg., a dexter hand holding a cutlass, all ppr.

Le Hunt, Bainbrigge-, of Burgh, Lincs, and Ashbourn, Derbysh., on a mount vert, a goat sa., collared, armed, and unguled arg. *Deus mihi providebit.* 129. 3

Le Hunte, George Ruthven, Esquire, of Artramont, co. Wexford, a lion sejant arg. *Parcere prostratis.* 8. 8

Leicester, Earl of (Coke), of Holkham, Norf., on a chapeau az., turned up erm., an ostrich arg., holding in its beak a horse-shoe or. *Prudens qui patiens.* 97. 13

Leicester, Sir Peter Fleming Frederick, Bart.: (1) A wyvern's head couped vert. (2) A swan's head arg., guttée-de-sang. (3) A mermaid ppr., in the dexter hand a mirror, and charged on the body with five escallops or.

Leicester, a swan's head and neck arg.

Leicester of Tabley, Chesh., a swan's head and neck arg., guttée-de-sang.

Leicester, Chesh., a stag's head per pale or and gu., attired of the second, holding in the mouth an oak-branch vert, fructed of the first. 110. 11

Leich, out of a ducal coronet a cubit arm erect, the hand grasping an adder entwined round the arm. *cf.* 220. 2

Leichman, Major-General John Thomas, of Rodwell Lodge, Weymouth, a pelican in her piety ppr. *Industria munus.*

Leids, an eagle's head gu., between two wings or. 84. 2

Leigh, Baron (Leigh), a unicorn's head couped or. *Tout vient de Dieu.* 49. 5

Leigh, *see* Pemberton-Leigh.

Leigh, *see* Hanbury-Leigh.

Leigh of Ridware, Staffs, a unicorn's head or. *Tout vient de Dieu.* 49. 7

Leigh, a unicorn's head erased arg., armed and crined or. 49. 5

Leigh, Chesh. and Derbysh., a unicorn's head arg., couped gu., crined and armed or. 49. 7

Leigh of Rushall, Staffs, a unicorn's head erased sa., armed or, crined and collared arg. 49. 11

Leigh of Egginton, Derbysh., a unicorn's head arg., crined or, armed gobony gu. and or. 49. 7

Leigh, Austen-, Cholmeley, Esquire: (1) A unicorn's head or (*for Leigh*). 49. 7. (2) On a mural coronet or, a stag sejant arg., attired of the first (*for Austen*). *Tout vient de Dieu.—Qui invidet minor est.* 116. 4

Leigh of Belmont, Chester, a lozenge gu., charged with a unicorn's head couped arg., crined or. *Leges juraque servo.* 302. 12

Leigh, John Dickinson, M.D., Cockton Hill, Bishop Auckland, same crest and motto.

Leigh, a nag's head erased. 51. 4

Leigh, Shropsh., a demi-lion rampant gu., collared arg. 10. 9

Leigh, Egerton, Esquire, of West Hall, in High Leigh, Chesh., of Jodrell Hall, Holmes Chapel, and Twenlow Hall, Holmes Chapel, Chester: (1) A cubit arm vested paly of five pieces or and sa., cuffed arg., the hand ppr. grasping the upper and lower fragments of a broken tilting-spear, point downwards. (2) A demi-lion rampant gardant or, holding a flagstaff ppr., headed arg., therefrom flowing to the sinister a forked pennon displayed az., charged with two pallets arg., fimbriated or, inscribed with the motto of the family, *Force avec vertue,* and having an escutcheon of the arms of Leigh, viz.: "or, a lion rampant gu.," upon which are three escutcheons of pretence with the arms of the three husbands of Agnes de Leigh, viz.: *for Lymme,* "gu., a pale lozengy arg."; *for Venables,* "az., two bars arg., over all a bend gu."; and *for Haywarden,* "gu., a cross engrailed arg.," the escutcheon surmounted by "a lion rampant gu."; as a crest the whole of the banner adorned with scroll-work or and arg.

Leigh, Arthur Egerton, Esquire, B.A., of the Manor House, Sherborne, Dorset, same crest as first above, and motto.

Leigh, Edward Egerton, Esquire, of Broadwell Manor House, Stow-on-the-Wold, Glouc., same crest.

Leigh, Major-General Robert Thomas, of Hill Cottage, Ilfracombe, North Devonsh., a demi-lion rampant arg., armed and langued gu. *Legibus antiquis.*

Leigh of Whitley, Lancs, a demi-lion rampant gu., holding between the paws a lozenge erm.

Leigh of Bardon, Somers., a demi-lion rampant or, armed and langued gu. *Legibus antiquis.* 10. 2

Leigh, Chesh., a demi-lion rampant gu. 10. 3

Leigh, Bart., Lancs, same crest. *Prodesse quam conspici.* 10. 3

Leigh of Drogheda, Ireland, out of a ducal coronet a demi-lion holding between the paws a sceptre surmounted of a fleur-de-lis, all gu., armed and langued az.

Leigh, Roger, Esquire, of Hindley Hall, Wigan, of Barham Court, Kent, and 70, Courtfield Gardens, S.W., a demi-lion gu., holding between the paws a lozenge arg., charged with a rose gu., and upon the shoulder for distinction with a cross patée or.

Leigh of Borough of Northam, Devonsh., a demi-lion rampant erminois, holding an escallop arg. 13. 10

Leigh, Bart. (*extinct*), of Hindley Hall, Lancs, a demi-lion rampant gu., holding between the paws a lozenge arg., charged with the rose of Lancaster gu.

Leigh, a lion rampant. 1. 13

Leigh of Stockwall, Surrey, on a mount vert, a lion couchant gardant arg., charged on the breast with an annulet sa.

Leigh, Alexander Haslop, Mayfields, Shortlands, Kent, a hind passant arg. *Legibus antiquis.*

Leigh of Wells, Somers., a demi-greyhound sa., holding a stag's head cabossed arg., attired or.

Leigh, a greyhound's head arg., between two roses gu., slipped and leaved ppr. 61. 11

Leigh, Chesh., out of a ducal coronet or, a ram's head arg., attired of the first, holding in the mouth a sprig of laurel vert.

Leigh, Surrey, a cockatrice az., combed and wattled gu. 68. 4

Leigh of Northcourt, Isle of Wight, Hants, a hind trippant arg. 124. 12

Leigh of Southwell, Notts, a demi-Moor vested gu., sleeved arg., holding in the dexter hand a gem ring and about the neck a collar or, wreathed round the temples of the second and az. 185. 9

Leigh, Lancs, a dexter arm embowed habited gu., cuffed arg., holding in the hand ppr. a sword of the second, hilt and pommel or, environed with a snake vert.

Leigh, Berks, Chesh., and Derbysh., an arm in armour couped at the shoulder or, girt with a scarf az., the hand grasping a halberd ppr.

Leigh of Oughtrengton, Chesh., and Shropsh., a cubit arm erect vested paly of six or and sa., cuffed arg., holding in the hand ppr. a broken tilting-spear of the third.

Leigh, Bart., of South Carolina, a cubit arm erect vested, the hand grasping a tilting-spear in fess, all ppr.

Leigh of Standishgate, near Wigan, Lancs, a cubit arm erect, grasping in the hand a serpent entwined about the arm ppr., between two antlers gu. *Hæc manus inimica tyrannis.*

Leigh of Rathbride, co. Kildare, a dexter arm embowed vested company-counter-company or and gu., the hand holding a sword ppr., pommel and hilt of the first. 204. 1

Leigh-Bennett, Rev. George Spencer, J.P., the Vicarage, Long Sutton, Lincs, out of a mural crown a lion's head arg., charged on the neck with a bezant. *Dux vitæ ratio.*

Leigham, within a fetterlock az., a human heart gu.

Leigham, *see* Legham.

Leight, Hants, a wolf passant gu. 28. 10

Leighton, Sir Bryan Baldwin Mawddwy, Bart., of Watlesborough, Shropsh., a wyvern with wings expanded sa. *Dread shame.* 70. 8

Leighton, David C. R., Esquire, of Charlton Kings, Cheltenham, out of a mural crown arg., a tiger's head vert, striped and crowned with an Eastern crown or. *Light on.* 306. 15

Leighton, Clarence F., Esquire, of Manorfield, St. Albans, Herts, same crest and motto.

Leighton, Shropsh.: (1) A wyvern with wings expanded sa. 70. 8. (2) A stag's head couped at the neck. *Dread shame.* 121. 5

Leighton, Parker, Sweeney Hall, Oswestry, a wyvern expanded sa. (*for Leighton*). *Dread shame.*

Leighton, the late Sir Frederick (Baron Leighton), LL.D., D.C.L., of Holland Park Road, Kensington, Middx., President of the Royal Academy, upon a staff raguly sessewise sa., a wyvern ppr., gorged with a chain or, suspended therefrom an escutcheon arg., issuant from the base flames of fire ppr. *Dread shame.*

Leighton of Ulishaven, Forfarsh., Scotland, a palm-tree vert. *Per adversa virtus.* 144. 1

Leighton, Scotland, a lion's head erased gu. *Light on.—Dread shame.* 17. 2

Leighwood, a banyan-tree ppr.

Leighwood of London, same crest.

Leinster, Duke of (FitzGerald), a monkey statant ppr., environed about the middle with a plain collar and chained or. *Crom a boo.* 136. 8

Leir of Ditcheat, Somers., and Jaggard's House, Wilts, a demi-unicorn rampant holding between the legs a staff raguly. 278. 8

Leir, Rev. Lewis Randolph Marriott, of Charlton Musgrove, Wincanton, same crest.

Leir, Somers., a quill and a sword in saltier, all ppr. 170. 4

Leir-Carleton, Major-General Richard Langford, J.P., of Ditcheat Priory, Somers.: (1) A dexter arm embowed ppr., vested above the elbow gu., edged arg., the hand grasping an arrow in bend sinister, point downwards, also ppr. (*for Carleton*). 278. 7. (2) A demi-unicorn rampant holding between the legs a staff raguly (*for Leir*). 278. 8. *Quondam his vicimus armis.*

Leishman, a pelican in her piety ppr. *Industriæ munus.* 98. 14

Leitch, Scotland, a hand holding a serpent ppr. 220. 2

Leith, *see* Forbes-Leith.

Leith, Norf., a cross crosslet fitched sa. 166. 2

Leith of Leith Hall, Aberdeen, Scotland, a cross crosslet fitched sa. *Trustie to the end.* 166. 2

Leith, General, K.B.: (1) Out of a mural coronet a demi-lion rampant regardant, all ppr. 16. 5. (2) A cross crosslet fitched. *Trusty to the end.* 166. 2

Leith of Over Barns, Scotland, a turtle-dove ppr. *Semper fidus.* 92. 2

Leith of Whitehaugh, Aberdeen, Scotland, a dove holding in its beak an olive-branch ppr. *Fidus ad extremum.* 92. 5

Leith, a stork holding in its beak a staff and banner.

Leith of Freefield, Scotland, a hart at gaze ppr. *Trusty to the end.* 118. 3

Leith, Alexander Henry, of Glenkindie, Aberdeensh., same crest and motto. *Non timeo sed caveo.*

Leith-Buchanan, Sir George Hector, Bart., of Burgh St. Peter's, Norf., a lion passant gu., charged on the body with three mullets in fesse or. *Trusty to the end.* *cf.* 6. 2

Leith-Ross, John, Esquire, of Arnage Castle, Ellon, N.B., and Bank House, Elton, Bury, Lancs, on a cap of maintenance a water-bouget sa. *Agnoscar eventu.—Virtue hare virtue.*

Leitrim, Earl of (Clements), a hawk ppr., belled or. *Patriis virtutibus.* *cf.* 85. 2

Leivy, a naked arm embowed holding in the hand a sword, all ppr. 201. 4

Leke of Sutton, a peacock's tail erect, the plume displayed ppr., supported by two eagles with wings expanded arg.

Lelam, Northamp. and Yorks, on a mount vert, a cock gu., combed, wattled, and legged or, charged on the breast with a saltire of the last. *cf.* 91. 7

Leland, a crow rising transfixed by an arrow. 107. 11

Lello or **Lelo,** Heref., a gem ring or, entwined and fretted with two serpents ppr.

Lelon, Lellow, Lelou, and **Lelow,** on a rock a fort in flames, all ppr. 155. 1

Lely, a cornucopia ppr. 152. 13

Le Maire of London, a Moor's head couped ppr. *Tempora te tempori.* 192. 13

Leman or **Lemmon,** Bart. (*extinct*), of Northaw, Herts, in a lemon-tree ppr., a pelican in her piety or, vulned, also ppr.

Leman, Naunton Robert Twysden, Brampton Hall, Suff., same crest.

Lemarch, an arm in armour embowed striking with a dagger, all ppr. 196. 5

Lemarchand, Michael Joseph, Esquire, of Ghazepoor, Bengal, out of an Eastern coronet or, a horse's head arg., charged with a bee volant ppr.

Lemarchant, issuing out of a ducal coronet an owl's leg in pale, all or.

Le Marchant, Sir Henry Denis, Bart., of Chobham Place, Surrey, out of a ducal coronet gu., an owl's leg erect or.

Le Marchant, Guernsey, same crest.

Le Master, a lion's head affrontée or, pierced with a pheon in pale issuant from the mouth.

Le Mesurier, a demi-savage wreathed about the middle with leaves, holding in the hand three oak-sprigs, all ppr. 136. 4

Le Mesurier, a hawk ppr., with wings expanded or. 87. 1

Lemitaire or **Lemitare** of Westminster, Middx., a demi-griffin sa., holding a catherine-wheel arg.

Lemmington, a savage's head erased and affrontée ppr. *cf.* 190. 12

Lemoine, a dove holding in its beak an olive-branch. 92. 5

Lemon, Cornw., a lion passant gu. 6. 2

Lemon, Bart. (*extinct*), of Carclew, Cornw., a lion passant gu., charged with three mullets or. *cf.* 6. 2

Le Mottée, Guernsey, a boar's head sa. 43. 1

Lempriere, a dove ppr. 92. 2

Lempriere, a dove with wings expanded ppr. *Non generant aquilæ columbas.* 94. 2

Lemprière of Jersey, an eagle rising ppr. *Timor Dei nobilitas.* 77. 5

Lemprière, Reginald Raoul, Rozel Manor, Jersey, same crest and motto.

Lemprière, Major-General Arthur Reid, Collingwood Mount, Camberley, Surrey: (1) An eagle rising ppr. (2) An elephant and castle. (3) A squirrel sejant.

Lemster, a demi-Cupid holding in his dexter hand an arrow and in his sinister a bow bent, all ppr.

Lenaghan, Ireland, an antelope trippant or, armed gu. 126. 6

Lench or **Lenche** of Wych, Worcs., a tiger sejant or, collared gu., resting the dexter paw on an escutcheon per chevron of the second and first.

Lenche, an ounce couchant ppr. 24. 10

Lenderick, between two elephants' trunks or, a lion's head erased gu.

Lendon, an eagle issuing holding in its dexter claw a branch of laurel ppr. 80. 3

Lendrum, George Cosby, Esquire, J.P., of Magheracross, Ballinamallard, co. Fermanagh, on a mount vert, a dove close holding in its beak an olive-branch, all ppr. *La paix.* *cf.* 92. 5

Le Neve, out of a ducal coronet or, a lily arg., stalked and leaved vert, bladed and seeded of the first 151. 5

Le Neve of London, on a mount vert, three lilies arg., conjoined in one stalk, leaved and seeded, all ppr.

Lenigan of Castle Fogerty, co. Tipperary, a lion rampant or, leaning on a sword arg., hilted or.

Lenihan of Limerick, a buck trippant gu., attired or, holding in the mouth a trefoil slipped vert, and resting the dexter fore-foot on an escutcheon of the Burke arms, viz.: or, a cross gu., in the first quarter a lion rampant sa., and in the second a sinister hand couped of the last. *Patriæ infelici fidelis.*

Lenington or **Lennington,** a savage's head erased and affrontée ppr. *cf.* 190. 12

Lennard of Chevening and Knoll, Kent, a demi-lion rampant ducally gorged holding in the dexter paw a rose gu. *cf.* 12. 1

Lennard, Kent and Essex, out of a ducal coronet or, a heraldic tiger's head arg. 25. 3

Lennard, a heraldic tiger's head quarterly or and az. 25. 4

Lennard, Sir Henry Arthur Hallam Farnaby, Bart., J P., D.L., of Wickham Court, Kent: (1) Out of a ducal coronet or, a heraldic tiger's head arg., the whole debruised by a bendlet wavy sinister sa. (*for Lennard*). *cf.* 25. 3. (2) A lion's head erased erminois, charged on the neck with two bars engrailed gu. (*for Cator*). *cf.* 17. 8

Lennard, Barrett-, Sir Thomas, Bart., of Belhus, Aveley, Essex, out of a ducal coronet or, an Irish wolf-dog's head per fesse arg. and erm., charged with an escallop-shell per fesse nebuly gu. and sa. *La loi le veut et moi ni mot.—Pour bien désirer.—La bondad para la medra.*

Lennie, Scotland, a dexter arm ppr., holding a covered cup or. 217. 11

Lennington, a savage's head erased affrontée ppr. *cf.* 190. 12

Lennon, Ireland, on a mount vert, a buck browsing ppr. *Prisco stirpe Hibernico.* 116. 9

Lennos or **Lenos,** a pennon party per pale gu. and or, tasselled of the last.

Lennox, Scotland, a lion sejant collared and lined. 7. 4

Lennox, Gordon-, Duke of Richmond and Gordon, *see* Richmond.

Lennox, John Maitland, Esquire, of 49, Lupus Street, Pimlico, S.W., on a chapeau gu., turned up erm., a lion guardant or, ducally crowned gu., and gorged with a collar compony of four pieces arg. and gu., charged with two roses of the last. *En la rose je fleurie.*

Lennox of Woodhead, Scotland, two broadswords in saltire behind an imperial crown, all ppr. *I'll defend.*

Lent, a horse passant arg. 52. 6

Lentaigne, John Nugent, Esquire, J.P., of Tallaght, co. Dublin, Ireland, a dove with wings endorsed ppr., holding in its bill a fleur-de-lis or, and charged on the breast with a mullet az., and on an escroll over the crest, *Pro fide, rege, et patria pugno. Dieu ayde.*

Lenthall of Leynthall and Hampton Court, Heref., of Lachford, Oxon., and Monkton, Devonsh., a greyhound saliant sa., collared or.

Lenthall, Edmund Kyffin, of Besselsleigh Manor, Abingdon, same crest. *Azincourt.*

Lenthorp and **Lenthrop,** a lady ppr., richly vested vert.

Lenton of Aldurnkle, Northamp. and Bucks, a heraldic tiger's head erased az., tufted, armed, collared, and ringed or.

Leny, Scotland, a cubit arm ppr., the hand holding up a covered cup or. 217. 11

Leonard, Earl of Sussex, out of a ducal coronet or, a heraldic tiger's head arg., maned and tufted or. *Pour bien désirer.* 25. 3

Leonard, out of a ducal coronet or, a heraldic tiger's head arg. 25. 3

Lepard, a fox current or. *cf.* 32. 8

Le Poer-Trench, *see* Clancarty, Earl of.

Lepper, Alfred John Adolphus, Esquire, of Rhanbury, Carrickfergus, co. Antrim, Ireland, out of a crown vallary or, a demi-leopard gardant ppr., holding between the paws a rose gu., barbed and seeded, also ppr. *Ducente Deo.* 294. 4

Leppington of Louth, Lincs, and Haverstock Hill, Finchley, Middx., upon a mount vert, a garb or, banded az., within a chain in arch of the second. *Avito non sine honore.*

Lepton, Yorks, out of a castle tripletowered a demi-lion, all ppr. 155. 10

Lermitte of Knightons, Middx., J.P., a hermit habited in russet resting the dexter hand upon a staff ppr., holding in the sinister hand a cross patée, and pendent from the wrist a rosary or. *Dieu le veut.*

Le Roache, a rock ppr. 179. 7

Le Roulx, Jersey, a falcon rising ppr. 88. 2

Leroux, a plume of feathers arg. 115. 1

Le Roy-Lewis, Colonel Herman, D.S.O., J.P., D.L., B.A., of Westbury House, Petersfield, Hants, and 31, Hill Street, Berkeley Square, W., out of a ducal coronet or, a cross crosslet patée and fitched gu., between two wings arg., each charged with a bend gu.

Lerrier, Jersey, a chapel ppr. *Pugna pro aris.—Bonus justus et utilis.* 158. 10

Leschallas, Pigé- of Page Green, Tottenham, Middx., on a mount vert, a column arg., thereon flames of fire ppr., and entwined by a vine-branch, also ppr.

Lescher, Joseph Francis, Esquire, of Boyles, Essex, in front of a bugle-horn sa., a dexter arm in armour embowed ppr., garnished or, entwined by a serpent, the hand grasping a dagger fesseways point towards the dexter, also ppr., pommel and hilt, also or. *Singulariter in spe.* 196. 7

Lescomb, on a mount vert, a greyhound current, between two branches of laurel, all ppr. *cf.* 58. 2

Le Scot, two battle-axes in saltier az., hafted sa. 172. 4

Leslie-Melville, Earl of Leven, *see* Leven.

Leslie, Forbes-, *see* Forbes.

Leslie, Lord Lindores, a demi-angel with wings or, holding in her dexter hand two greyhounds' heads erased ppr. *Stat promissa fides.* *cf.* 183. 3

Leslie, Robert Charles Leslie, Esquire, of Ballybay, co. Monaghan, Ireland, and 22, Cornwall Gardens, S.W., an angel affrontée ppr. 184. 12

Leslie, Colonel Edmund Douglas, J.P., D.L., of Leslie Hill, Ballymoney, co. Antrim, same crest. *Grip fast.*

Leslie, Scotland, a demi-angel vested az., winged or, holding in her dexter hand a griffin's head erased ppr., beaked or. *Stat promissa fides.* 183. 3

Leslie, Bart., out of a ducal coronet arg., a griffin's head gu., beaked of the first. *Grip fast.* 67. 9

Leslie, a griffin's head erased ppr. *Firma spe.* 66. 2

Leslie of Glasslough, Monaghan, a griffin's head erased gu. *Grip fast.* 66. 2

Leslie of Balquhain, Aberdeensh., Scotland, same crest. *Grip fast.* 66. 2

Leslie of Kineraigie, Aberdeensh., Scotland, a griffin's head couped ppr., charged with a cross crosslet fitchée arg. *Firma spe.* *cf.* 66. 1

Leslie, Sir John, Bart., of Glaslough, co. Monaghan, a griffin's head erased gu. *Grip fast.* 66. 2

Leslie, Arbuthnot-, William, Warthill, Aberdeen, a griffin's head erased ppr. *Grip fast.*

Leslie, John, Esquire, of Ballyward Lodge, co. Down, a griffin's head couped ppr., charged with a cross crosslet fitchée az. and with a crescent. *Firma spe.* *cf.* 66. 1

Leslie William, Esquire, of Nethermuir, Aberdeen, a demi-griffin ppr. *Grip fast.* 64. 2

Leslie, Major John Henry, R.A. (retired list), Army and Navy Club, Pall Mall, S.W., a demi-griffin.

Leslie, Scotland, same crest. 64. 2

Leslie of Dunlugas, Banffsh., Scotland, a demi-griffin segreant ppr., holding in its claws a buckle or. *Grip fast.* *cf.* 64. 2

Leslie, Sir Charles Henry, Bart., of Wardis and Findrassie, co. Moray, a demi-griffin ppr. *Grip fast.* 64. 2

Leslie of New Leslie, Aberdeensh., Scotland, a griffin ppr., winged or, holding in its dexter claw a buckle of the last. *Probitas et firmitas.* 63. 7

Leslie, Archibald Young, of Kininvie, Aberdeensh., Scotland, a griffin ppr., holding in the dexter talon a buckle or. *Quæ juncta firma.* 63. 7

Leslie of Burdsbank and Torry, Scotland, a buckle or. *Keep fast.* 178. 4

Leslie of Findrassie, Elgin, Scotland, a buckle arg. *Firma durant.* 178. 4

Leslie of Colpnay Shiels, Aberdeensh., Scotland, between the horns of a crescent a buckle, all arg. *Commoditas augeam.* 163. 15

Leslie of Powis, Aberdeensh., Scotland, a crescent arg. *Crescat, Deo promotore.* 163. 2

Leslie of Tulloch, Aberdeensh., Scotland, an eagle's neck with two heads erased sa. *Hold fast.—Firma spe.* 84. 11

Leslie, a demi-lion rampant gu. double-queued. 10. 6

Leslie, Bart., Surrey, a camel's head erased or, bridled, lined, ringed, and gorged with a ducal coronet sa. *Mens cujusque is est quisque.* 132. 9

Leslie-Duguid, Charles Stephen, Esquire, of Auchenhove, Aberdeensh., a dove holding an olive-branch in her beak ppr. *Patientia et spe.* 92. 5

Leslie of Oustens, Scotland, a hand holding a pen ppr. *Soli Deo gloria.* 217. 10

Leslie-Ellis, Lieutenant-Colonel Henry, of Magherymore, co. Wicklow: (1) A dolphin naiant embowed arg., charged with an escallop az. (*for Ellis*). 289. 4. (2) A griffin's head erased with wings addorsed ppr. (*for Leslie*). *Non sine jure.—Grip fast.* 289. 5

Leslie, a cubit arm erect holding a sword in pale ppr., on its point a boar's head erased in fess. 212. 6

Leslie, a chevalier in complete armour holding in his dexter hand a flagstaff, the pennon flotant overhead and held by the sinister hand.

Leslie, Ireland, a fox sejant or. 32. 11

Lesly, Scotland, a griffin's head erased ppr. *Grip fast.* 66. 2

Lesly, Scotland, a griffin's head. *Grip fast.* 66. 1

Lesly, Scotland, a griffin's head couped ppr., charged with a cross crosslet fitched arg. *cf.* 66. 1

Lesly, Scotland, an eagle's neck with two heads erased sa. *Hold fast.* 84. 11

Lesly, a demi-lion rampant gu., double-queued. 10. 6

Lesly, Scotland, out of a crescent arg., a man in armour ppr., holding a buckle, also arg.

Leson or **Lesone** of Wheatfield and Soulgrave, Northamp., out of a cloud the sun rising in splendour, all ppr. 162. 5

Lesone of Dublin, a demi-lion rampant gu., holding between the paws the sun rising out of clouds ppr. *Clarior e tenebris.*

Lessingham, a martlet sa. 195. 5

Lessington, on a baron's coronet or, a lion rampant gu.

Lessler, a Minerva's head couped at the shoulders ppr. 182. 1

Lesslie, a griffin's head *Grip fast.* 66. 1

Lester, Chesh., a demi-griffin segreant gu. 64. 2

Lester of Wimborne Minster, Dorset, a demi-gryphon with wings elevated erm., beaked and membered or, holding between the claws a trident erect az., headed of the second. *Favente Deo.*

Leston, a lion passant az., ducally gorged and chained or. *cf.* 6. 2

Lestrange, Norf., Suff., and Middx., a lion passant gardant or. 4. 3

Lestrange, two hands couped and conjoined in fess. 224. 2

L'Estrange, a lion's gamb sa., holding a dagger ppr. 38. 5

Le Strange, a lion statant tail extended or. *cf.* 4. 8

le Strange, Hamon of Hunstanton Hall, Norf.: A lion statant tail extended or (*for Le Strange*).

Le Sueur of Grouville, Jersey, a bezant charged with a rose gu. *Sure.*

Le Taylor of Lidgate and Stechworth, Suff., a lynx ppr. 127. 2

Letch, a harp gu. 168. 9

Letchworth, Edward, Esquire, of Enfield, Middx., in front of three ears of wheat, two in saltire and one in pale, or, a leopard's face ppr., all between two wings arg., each charged with a rose gu., barbed and seeded ppr. *Ut sibi sic alteri.*

Lete, out of a ducal coronet or, a lamp of three branches of the same, fired ppr. 177. 7

Letemps, the emblem of Time passing with his scythe over his shoulder, all ppr.

Letham or **Lethem,** a griffin's head between two wings, holding in the beak a feather, all ppr. *cf.* 65. 11

Letham or **Lathem,** on a mount vert, a peacock ppr. *cf.* 103. 4

Lethbridge, a bear's paw erased and erect holding a spear-head point downwards between two wings.

Lethbridge, Devonsh., a stag's head erased per fess arg. and sa., attired or, holding in the mouth a rose of the first, stalked and leaved vert. *cf.* 121. 2

Lethbridge, Sir Wroth Perian Christopher, Bart., D.L., of Sandhill Park, Somers., out of an embattled arch gu., a demi-eagle displayed sa., the wings erminois, and charged on the breast with a leopard's face or. *Spes mea in Deo.—Truth.*

Lethbridge, late Christopher, Esquire, of Prospect, Homebush, New South Wales, Australia, from a bridge embattled of one arch gu., a demi-eagle issuant sa., the wings elevated erminois, and charged on the breast with a leopard's face or. *Spes mea in Deo.*

Lethbridge, Sir Roper, of Exbourne Manor R.S.O., Devonsh., of the Lodge, Lynsted, Kent, and of the Inner Temple, Barrister-at-Law, K.C.I.E., M.A., M.P., in front of a demi-tower ppr., issuant therefrom a demi-eagle displayed sa., each wing charged with a rose arg., a lotus-flower leaved and slipped ppr. *Spes mea in Deo.* 231. 11

Lethbridge, Edward Galton, Baron, Esquire, J.P., of Tregeare, Egloskerry R.S.O., Cornw., an eagle displayed ppr. *Spes mea in Deo.*

Lethieullier, Essex, and **Lethulier,** Middx., a parrot ppr. 101. 4

Lethim, Scotland, a dove within a serpent in orle, all ppr. 92. 11

Lethoop, a rose ppr. 149. 5

Lett, three organ-pipes, two in saltier, surmounted by the third in pale ppr., banded vert.

Letton, a dexter hand in fess couped gu., holding a cross crosslet fitched az. 221. 10

Letton, Herts, a bittern in flags, seeded, all ppr.

Le Touzel, Jersey, out of a ducal coronet or, a demi-rose gu., and a demi-fleur-de-lis of the first conjoined. *Deus ab inimicis me defendit.*

Leukenor, a unicorn's head couped az., platée, armed or. 49. 7

Levall, a Cornish chough with wings expanded issuing from the top of a tower, all ppr. 156. 13

Le Vavasour, Yorks, a cock gu. 91. 2

Leveale and **Levealis,** Cornw., a tower ppr., masoned sa. 156. 2

Leveland, a dexter hand holding a dagger in pale with a laurel-wreath pendent therefrom, all ppr.

Levelis of Trewoof, Cornw., a tower masoned sa. 156. 2

Leven, Earl of, and **Earl of Melville, Viscount Kirkaldie, Baron Balgonie, Melville,** and **Raith,** of Monimail and Balwearie, in Scotland (Rt. Hon. Ronald Ruthven Leslie-Melville): (1) The head of a ratch-hound erased sa. (*for Melville*). (2) A demi-chevalier in complete armour holding in his dexter hand a dagger erect ppr., the pommel and hilt or (*for Leslie*). *Denique cœlum.—Pro rege et patria.* 187. 1

Levens, on a chapeau a wyvern with wings addorsed. 69. 14

Levens of Oxford, a squirrel sejant ppr., within a wreath of hazel-leaves vert.

Lever, Lancs, a hare ppr.

Lever of Arlington, Lancs, on a trumpet in fess, a cock, all ppr. 91. 6

Lever, Lancs, on a trumpet nowed, a cock with wings extended. 91. 6

Leveret, Ireland, a dove arg., holding in the beak an olive-branch vert. 92. 5

Levermore of Exeter, Devonsh., an arm embowed holding in the hand a scimitar erect ppr. 201. 1

Leversage of Leversock, Whelock, Kinderton, and Bechton, Chesh., a leopard's face jessant-de-lis or. 22. 5

Leversedge of Vallis, Somers., same crest. 22. 5

Leversey and **Levesey,** a lion's gamb issuing ppr. supporting an escutcheon gu. *cf.* 37. 2

Leverton, a hare sejant arg.

Leverton of London and Surrey, a pelican arg., vulning herself ppr. 98. 1

Levesay or **Levesey,** Kent, Lancs, and Surrey, a lion's gamb erased gu., holding four trefoils slipped vert.

Leveson, *see* Cromartie, Earl of.

Leveson, *see* Sutherland, Duke of.

Leveson, Lord, *see* Granville, Earl.

Leveson, Edward John, 6, Queen's Mansions, Westminster, in front of a sun rising or, a red deer trippant ppr. *Spero.* 293. 11

Leveson, Kent and Shropsh., a goat's head erased erm., armed or. 128. 5

Leveson, Staffs, an arm in armour embowed ppr., garnished or, holding in the gauntlet a battle-axe, the handle gu., the head arg. 200. 6

Leveson-Gower, Arthur Francis Gresham, Esquire, M.A., of British Legation, the Hague: (1) A wolf passant arg., collared and lined or (*for Gower*). (2) A goat's head erased erm., attired or (*for Leveson*). *Fiat voluntas tua* (*for Gresham*).—*Frangas non flectes* (*for Gower*).—*Defende le droit* (*for Leveson*).

Leveson-Gower, Granville Charles, Esquire, of Titsey Place, Limpsfield, Surrey, (1) and (2) same crests and mottoes as above. (3) A grasshopper ppr. (*for Gresham*).

Levesque, on a fish a sparrow-hawk, all ppr. 86. 6

Levet or **Levett,** a gad-fly with wings addorsed ppr.

Levett of Salehurst, Sussex, a lion rampant arg., crowned or, holding between the paws a cross crosslet fitched of the first.

Levett, William Swinnerton Byrd, of Milford Hall, Stafford, a demi-lion or, ducally crowned, entwined with a sprig of laurel vert, supporting a cross crosslet fitched sa.

Levett, Theophilus Basil Percy, of Wichnor Park, Burton-on-Trent, a demi-lion arg., ducally crowned or, gorged with a collar az., holding in the dexter paw a cross crosslet fitched sa., the sinister resting on an escutcheon of the third, charged with a fleur-de-lis of the second. 302. 3

Levett, Robert Thomas Kennedy, Esquire, J.P., D.L., of Packington Hall, Lichfield, a demi-lion rampant, ducally crowned, and holding in the dexter paw a cross crosslet fitched. *Hoc age.* 301. 1

Levett-Prinsep, Thomas, Esquire, of Croxall Hall, Lichfield: (1) An eagle's head erased gu., guttée-d'or, in the beak a bird bolt erect (the bolt downwards) ppr. (*for Prinsep*). (2) A demi-lion arg., ducally crowned or, gorged with a collar az., in the dexter paw a cross crosslet fitchée sa., the sinister paw resting on an escutcheon of the third, charged with a fleur-de-lis or (*for Levett*).

Levin of Cleveland Square, Hyde Park, London, on a mount a squirrel passant ppr., resting the dexter foot on an escallop or. *Certavi et vici.*

Leving, Ireland, an oak-tree fructed ppr. 143. 5

Leving and **Levinge,** a sword and a garb in saltier ppr. 153. 7

Leving and **Levings** of Baddesley, Warw., within a chaplet vert, an escallop arg.

Levinge, Ireland, a bell az. 168. 7

Levinge, Sir Richard William, Bart., of High Park (now Knockdrin Castle), co. Westmeath, an escallop arg., within a garland ppr. *Vestigia nulla retrorsum.*

Levingstone, Scotland, a demi-savage holding over his shoulder a club ppr. 186. 5

Levins, a bull's head sa., charged with a crescent gu. *cf.* 44. 3

Levinz, a torteau charged with a squirrel sejant ppr

Levinz of London, Northamp., and Oxon., on a vine-branch a squirrel sejant, all ppr. *cf.* 135. 1

Levy, Benn Wolfe, Esquire, of 8, Pembridge Square, Kensington, a demi-wolf or, holding in the dexter paw a mullet of eight points arg., and resting the sinister on a woolpack ppr. *Honore et labore.*

Lew, a dexter arm holding a roll of vellum ppr. 215. 6

Leward, a demi-lion rampant or, holding between the paws a mullet arg. *cf.* 15. 8

Lewcas, on a chapeau a heraldic tiger passant, all ppr. *cf.* 25. 5

Lewellin of Silvermines, co. Tipperary, out of a ducal coronet or, a man's head couped at the shoulders and affrontée ppr. *Virtus et nobilitas.*

Lewellyn, a pheon ppr. 174. 11

Lewen of Siston, Leics., the moon in her complement arg.

Lewes, Earl of, *see* Abergavenny, Marquess of.

Lewes of London, an eagle displayed sa., the claws resting upon the wreath, holding in the beak a snake entwined round the body ppr. *cf.* 75. 11

Lewes, William Price Llewellyn, Llysnewydd, Llandyssil, South Wales, an eagle displayed, holding in the beak a serpent entwined round the body ppr.

Lewin, a buck trippant or, gorged with a chaplet vert. *cf.* 117. 8

Lewin, Herts, a buck trippant quarterly or and az. 117. 8

Lewin and **Lewins,** a demi-lion rampant sa., supporting a lozenge or, charged with a trefoil slipped vert.

Lewin, Kent, a sea-lion ppr., the tail nowed, holding between its paws an escutcheon gu., charged with an escallop or.

Lewin, Honourable James Davies, of Lancaster, St. John, New Brunswick, Senator of the Dominion of Canada, a sea-lion ppr., tail nowed, holding in the paws an escutcheon gu., charged with an escallop or.

Lewin of Horsfall, a demi-lion holding between its paws a trefoil.

Lewin of Cloghans, co. Mayo, a demi-lion sa., holding between the paws a trefoil slipped vert. *Spes mea in Deo.* *cf.* 10. 1

Lewins, a demi-lion rampant ppr. 10. 2

Lewis-Barned, *see* Barned.

Lewis, Sir Herbert Edmund Frankland, Bart., D.L., of Harpton Court, Radnorsh., in a coronet vallery or, a mount vert, thereon a heraldic tiger statant or. *Expertus fidelem.*

Lewis, Bart., of Hyde Park Gate, Kensington, Middx., a boar's head az., in front thereof three roses in fesse arg. *Non nobis nascimur.*

Lewis, Sir William Thomas, Bart., of the Mardy, Aberdare, South Wales, an eagle displayed az., charged on the breast with a bee volant or, and holding in the beak a roll of paper arg. (Over the crest) *Hirbarhad.*—(Under the arms) *Gwna a ddylit doed a ddel.* 75. 12

Lewis, Wales, on a chapeau gu., turned up erm., a heraldic tiger ppr.

Lewis, Wales, on a chapeau gu., turned up erm., a tiger statant. *Expertus fidelem.*

Lewis, Lancs, on a chapeau gu., turned up erm., a heraldic tiger passant. *Hæc olim meminisse juvabit.* *cf.* 25. 5

Lewis, Shropsh., a demi-griffin segreant or. 64. 2

Lewis, Charles Bassett, of Gwinfe, Carmarthensh., same crest. *Facta, non verba.* 64. 2

Lewis, Charles Edward, of St. Pierre, Monm., a griffin segreant sa. *Ha persa la fide, ha perso l'honore.* 62. 2

Lewis, Yorks, out of a ducal coronet a plume of five ostrich-feathers, two or and three sa., charged with a chevron of the first. *Spe tutiores armis.* *cf.* 114. 13

Lewis of Kilcullen, co. Kildare, Ireland, out of a ducal coronet ppr., a plume of five ostrich-feathers alternately gu. and az., charged with a chevron or. *Bidd llu hebb llydd.* *cf.* 114. 13

Lewis, Henry Owen, Esquire, B.A., J.P., D.L., of Inniskeen, co. Monaghan, and 62, Lancaster Gate, Hyde Park, London, S.W., out of a ducal coronet ppr., a plume of five ostrich-feathers alternately gu. and az., charged with a chevron or, thereon a crescent gu. *Bidd llu hebb llydd.* *cf.* 114. 13

Lewis, Essex, Herts, and Yorks, out of a ducal coronet or, a plume of five ostrich-feathers arg. 114. 13

Lewis of Gilfach and Llwyncefu, Carmarthensh.: (1) A stag trippant arg., between the attires an imperial crown ppr. (2) An eagle's head erased or. *Byddwch gyfiawn ac nag ofnwch.*

Lewis, Scotland, a stag's head erased affrontée. 119. 10

Lewis of Stoke, Dorset, and Somers., an heraldic antelope's head erased sa., attired, maned, tufted, and ducally gorged or.

Lewis, Ireland, on the top of a spear issuing a dolphin naiant, all ppr. 140. 9

Lewis, John Michael Aylward, Esquire, J.P., of Ballinagar, Loughrea, co. Galway, and 42, Morehampton Road, Dublin, a lion rampant ppr. *Amicus omnibus.*

Lewis, Ireland, a lion rampant gu. 1. 13

Lewis, John Penry, Esquire, of the Ceylon Civil Service, Ceylon, a lion rampant erm., holding in the dexter paw a leek erect or, and supporting with the sinister an escutcheon arg., charged with a dragon's head erased gu. *Ymlaen.* 301. 3

Lewis, Walter Llewellyn, M.A., of Belsize, British Honduras, Central America, same crest and motto.

Lewis, Wales, a lion sejant erect arg. 8. 13

Lewis of the Van, Glamorgansh., a lion sejant arg. *Patriæ fidus.* 8. 8

Lewis of Green Meadow, Glamorgansh.: (1) A lion sejant arg. (*for Lewis*). 8. 8 (2) A Paschal lamb glorified or, bearing a pennon of St. George (*for Price*). *cf.* 131. 2

Lewis of Plas-Draw, Aberdare, a lamb passant ppr., semée of crescents arg., holding in the mouth three cinquefoils slipped vert, and resting the dexter fore-paw on a staff in bend sinister ppr., therefrom a flag flying to the sinister arg., charged with a cross couped gu. *Duw fo; O fy rhan.*

Lewis, Evan, Esquire, J.P., of Brynderwen, Llandaff, Cardiff, same crest and motto.

Lewis, a greyhound's head arg., between two roses gu., slipped and leaped ppr. 61. 11

Lewis, on a mount vert, a greyhound couchant gu., collared or. *cf.* 60. 1

Lewis, on a chapeau gu., turned up erm., a greyhound sa., collared or. *cf.* 58. 4

Lewis, a demi-wolf rampant arg. 31. 2

Lewis of Llanarchayron, Cardigansh., out of a mural coronet gu., a demi-wolf salient arg. *Libertas.*

Lewis of Clynflew, Pembrokesh., a horse's head bridled ppr. 51. 5

Lewis, Kent, an ermine passant ppr. 134. 6

Lewis, Kent, a demi-beaver ppr.

Lewis of Rossenden in Bleane, Kent, a demi-beaver ppr.

Lewis, Hampton-, Thomas Lewis, of Bodior and Henllys, Anglesea, Wales: (1) A Cornish chough ppr., holding in the dexter claw a fleur-de-lis az. (*for Lewis*). (2) A wyvern amidst bulrushes ppr. (*for Hampton*). *A Deo et rege.*

Lewis of Stanford, Notts, out of a mural coronet or, a boar's head erect erm., langued gu. *cf.* 41. 10

Lewis of Lampeter Velfry, Pembrokesh., an arm embowed holding an arrow. *Sors est contra me.* 201. 14

Lewis, Sir George Henry, Bart., 88, Portland Place, W., a stock of a tree eradicated ppr., thereon an owl, wings expanded sa., holding in the dexter claw a flaming sword erect ppr., pommel and hilt or. *Je meurs ou je m'attache.* 283. 6

Lewisham, Viscount, *see* Dartmouth, Earl.

Lewkenor or **Lewknor,** Suff., Sussex, and Worcs., a greyhound current arg., collared gu. *cf.* 58. 2

Lewknor, Sussex and Worcs., a unicorn's head erased az., bezantée, armed and crined or. *cf.* 49. 5

Lewsell, an antelope's head gardant or, attired sa.

Lewthwait or **Lewthwaite,** an heraldic tiger's head erased gu. *Tiens à la vérité.*

Lewthwaite of Broadgate, Cumb., a garb bound by a serpent ppr., holding in the mouth a cross crosslet fitched gu. *Tendens ad æthera virtus.* 153. 1

Lewthwaite, George, of Littlebank, Settle, Yorks, same crest and motto.

Lewyn, Kent, a buck trippant quarterly or and az. 117. 8

Lewys, out of a ducal coronet a plume of feathers. *Spe tutiores armis.* *cf.* 114. 8

Lexinton, Yorks, a demi-lady between two branches of palm in orle, holding in her dexter hand a thistle ppr. *cf.* 183. 14

Lexton, out of a castle triple-towered a demi-lion issuing, all ppr. 155. 10

Ley of Ley, Devonsh., a lion sejant or. *Vincendo victus.* 8. 8

Ley, Francis, Esquire, of Epperstone Manor, Nottinghamsh., in front of a cubit arm in armour holding in the hand a broken tilting-spear in bend sinister ppr., four lozenges conjoined fesseways gu. *Post mortem spero vitam.*

Ley, on an escallop between two wings or, a saltier gu. 141. 7

Leyborne, an eagle regardant with wings expanded az., beaked and legged or. 77. 4

Leybourn, a buck's head erased ppr. 121. 2

Leybourne, an eagle volant regardant az., beaked and legged or. 79. 5

Leycester, a demi-lion rampant sa., holding in the dexter paw a fleur-de-lis or. 13. 2

Leycester, Shropsh., a stag trippant per pale or and gu., attired of the last, and holding in its mouth an oak-branch ppr., acorned or. *cf.* 117. 8

Leycester, Rafe Oswald, of Toft, Chesh., a roebuck trippant per pale or and gu., attired of the second, holding in his mouth an oak-branch fructed vert. *cf.* 117. 8

Leycester, Ernest Gerard, Esquire, of Moberley Old Hall, Knutsford, Chesh., same crest.

Leycester of Nether Tabley, Chesh., a swan's head and neck couped arg., guttée-de-sang.

Leycester of Worleston, Chesh., a fleur-de-lis per fesse or and az. 148. 2

Leycroft, a hand in pale ppr., vested az., holding a chaplet gu. *cf.* 205. 6

Leye, an arm in armour embowed holding in the gauntlet a battle-axe, all ppr. 200. 6

Leyham, a ship in full sail ppr. 160. 13

Leyland, Lancs, a demi-dove arg., with wings addorsed az., holding in the beak three ears of wheat or.

Leyland of the Grange, Hindley, near Wigan, Lancs, on a mount vert, amid flags a corn-crake, all ppr., holding in the beak three ears of wheat or. *God feedeth ye land.*

Leyland, Christopher John, Haggerstone Castle, Northumb., a mount vert, thereon an escallop arg., surmounted by a demi-eagle erminois, wings endorsed az., bezantée, in the mouth three ears of barley. *Fidus et audax.* *cf.* 279. 4

Leynys, a hand holding an oak-branch ppr., fructed or.

Leyson, a goat's head erased erm., attired or. 128. 5

Leyver, a leveret couchant ppr.

Liard, an antelope trippant ppr., collared or. 126. 6

Libby, out of a paling or, a dexter arm ppr., vested gu., holding in the hand a baton az., tipped of the first.

Liberton, a stag's head couped az. 121. 5

Liberty, Arthur Lasenby, Esquire, J.P., D.L., of the Lee Manor, near Great Missenden, Bucks, in front of a tower gu., a lion passant, holding in the dexter fore-paw a fleur-de-lis, both or. *Libertas.* 309. 15

Lichfield, Earl of (Anson): (1) Out of a ducal coronet or a spear-head ppr. (2) A greyhound's head erased erm., gorged with a collar double gemelle or. *Nil desperandum.*

Lichfield, *see* Randolph-Lichfield.

Lichfield, Oxon., an arm embowed vested arg., holding in the hand ppr. a bow or, strung gu. *cf.* 204. 9

Lichfield, on a chapeau gu., a garb ppr. 153. 10

Lickie, Scotland, two hands issuing, couped below the wrist, and holding a sword ppr., hilt and pommel or. 213. 3

Lidcott of Rushcombe, Berks, a catherine-wheel or, surmounted by a boar's head couped sa., ringed of the first.

Liddel of Edinburgh, Scotland, a rose slipped gu. *Hinc odor et sanitas.* 149. 5

Liddell, *see* Ravensworth, Earl of.

Liddell or **Lidell,** Scotland, a demi-lion or, holding in his dexter paw a mullet gu. 15. 7

Liddell, Durh. and Northumb., a lion rampant sa., billettée or, crowned with an Eastern crown of the last. *Unus et idem.*

Liddell, Charles Oswald, Esquire, of Shirenewton Hall, Chepstow, a lion rampant purp., billettée, surmounted on the head by a mullet of six points pierced or, and resting the dexter hind-leg on a like mullet. *Unus et idem.* 241. 8

Liddell, John, Esquire, J.P., of Prudhoe Hall, Northumb., a cross crosslet gu., surmounting two clasped hands ppr., between a pair of wings or. *Constans et fidelis.* 250. 11

Lidderdale of St. Mary Isle, Kirkcudbrightsh., Scotland, an eagle's head erased ppr. *Foresight is all.* 83. 2

Lidderdale of London, same crest. *Per bello qui providet.*

Lidderdale, Rt. Hon. William, P.C., late Governor Bank of England, of 42, Lancaster Gate, W., an eagle's head erased ppr. *Foresight is all.* 83. 2

Liddiard, Wilts, a demi-lion rampant arg., holding in his dexter paw a mullet gu. 15. 7

Liddiat of Humley and Walsall, Staffs, and Wollaston, Worcs., a wolf's head erased per pale erminois and gu. 30. 8

Liddle, two lion's gambs erased supporting a column ppr. 39. 8

Lidel, two hands conjoined in fess, each hand united to a wing at the wrist. 224. 12

Lidgbird of Plumstead, Kent, and Rougham, Suff., a mural coronet, therein the trunk of a tree ppr., sprouting vert, surmounted by a pelican vulning herself and ducally crowned.

Lidiard, a wolf's head. *Gardez vous.* 30. 5

Lidsey of London, a demi-griffin segreant az., beaked and legged gu., holding in its dexter claw a trefoil slipped or. *cf.* 64. 2

Lidwill, Captain George, J.P., of Dromard, co. Tipperary, Ireland, a demi-lion rampant sa., crowned with an Irish crown or, and charged on the shoulder with a fleur-de-lis of the last. *Vis unita fortior.*

Lidwill, Robert Atkins, Esquire, of Clonmore, Kilmanogue, co. Tipperary, of Rosemount, Australia, and 3, Stafford Terrace, Phillimore Gardens, Kensington, W., a lion rampant sa., crowned with an Irish crown or. *Vis unita fortior.—Malo mori quam fœdari.*

Liebenrood of Prospect Hill Park, Reading, Berks, out of an Eastern coronet gu., charged with a cross crosslet or for difference, two unicorn's horns arg., wreathed vert.

Lienis and **Lienys,** an arm couped at the elbow in pale, vested arg., holding in the hand ppr. a bunch of acorns vert, fructed or.

Lievre, a hare courant ppr. *Il y a de ma vie.—Gardez bien.* *cf.* 136. 3

Lifeilde or **Lifield,** Surrey and Herts, a bull's head caboshed arg., armed or, charged on the forehead with three ermine spots, one and two. *cf.* 43. 8

Lifford, Viscount (Hewitt), of Lifford, co. Donegal, Ireland, on a stump of a tree with one branch growing thereon, an owl, all ppr. *Be just and fear not.*

Ligh, a cubit arm in pale in armour ppr., garnished or, holding in the hand a tilting-spear, also ppr., headed arg. 210. 11

Lightbody, Scotland, a star issuant from a cloud, all ppr. *Clarior e tenebris.* 164. 11

Lightbody, Scotland, same crest. *E tenebris lux.*

Lightborne or **Lightbourne** of Manchester, Lancs, an eagle displayed az., ducally gorged, beaked, and membered or. *cf.* 75. 2

Lightbourne, Ireland, out of a ducal coronet a cockatrice's head between two wings. 68. 11

Lightfoot, a human heart pierced by a Passion nail in bend. 181. 4

Lightfoot, a griffin's head erased, gorged with a collar, charged with three escallops. *cf.* 66. 2

Lighton, Sir Christopher Robert, Bart., B.A., of Merville, co. Dublin, a lion's head erased crowned with an Eastern crown or, langued az. *Fortitudine et prudentia.* *cf.* 17. 12

Lighton, Scotland, a lion's head erased gu. *Light on.* 17. 2

Lighton, Scotland, an eagle's head erased ppr., holding in the beak an acorn or, stalked and leaved vert. 84. 10

Lighton, Scotland, a Minerva's head affrontée ppr. 182. 1
Ligo of Burcot, Weston Turville, and Stoke Manderville, Bucks, on a chapeau az., turned up arg., an étoile between two wings or. *cf.* 112. 1
Ligon, Worcs. and Glouc., an old man's heap ppr., the hair and beard sa.
Ligon, Glouc. and Worcs., a Saracen's head ppr., wreathed arg. and gu. 190. 14
Ligonier of London and Surrey, out of a mural coronet gu., a demi-lion rampant erminois, holding in its dexter paw a branch of palm vert. 16. 11
Ligonier, Ireland, out of a mural coronet gu., a demi-lion erminois, holding in its dexter paw a palm-branch vert. *A rege et victoriâ.* 16. 11
Lilburne or **Lilborne** of Thickley and Pincherdon, Durh., a castle triple-towered ppr., flagged sa. *Vis viri fragilis.* 155. 8
Lile and **Lille,** on a chapeau ppr., a lion couchant or. 7. 12
Lilford, Baron (Powys), of Lilford, Northamp., a lion's paw erased and erect gu., holding a sceptre in bend sinister headed with a fleur-de-lis or. *Parta tueri.*
Lill, Ireland, a hand erect issuing out of a cloud and holding an anchor in pale, all ppr. 219. 2
Lillan, a hand holding a dagger, on the point thereof a Moor's head couped at the shoulders.
Lilley, an oak-tree ppr. 143. 5
Lilley, Joseph Edward, Esquire, J.P., of the Chestnuts, Wealdstone R.S.O., Middx., a cubit arm erect ppr., charged with a fleur-de-lis arg., and holding in the hand two lilies of the valley leaved and slipped in saltire, also ppr. *In foris ardutior.*
Lillie, between the attires of a stag or, a rose gu. 140. 9
Lillie, Scotland, issuing out of a cloud a dexter hand grasping a club, all ppr. 214. 9
Lillingston, Ulverscroft, Leicester, a griffin's head erased per fesse arg. and gu., holding in the beak a Palmer's scrip of the last.
Lillingston of Ulverscroft: (1) A demi-wyvern issuant, tail nowed sa., wings expanded and elevated or, charged with an ermine spot of the first, on the breast two annulets conjoined in pale gold. (2) A boar's head transfixed with a spear, gutté-de-sang. *Pro Deo et patria.*
Lillingston, Innes-, Frederick George, Bute Court, Torquay, a demi-wyvern issuant, tailed nowed sa., wings expanded and elevated or, charged with an ermine spot of the first, on the breast two annulets conjoined in pale or.
Lilly, Ireland, a lion rampant regally crowned. *cf.* 1. 12
Lilly, a dexter hand apaumée gu. 222. 14
Lilly or **Lighly** of Newhall, Yorks, a dexter hand apaumée gu. 222. 14
Lilly of Stoke Prior and Bromsgrove, Worcs., a swan's head erased arg. *cf.* 101. 5
Limbery and **Limbrey,** Dorset, a unicorn passant gu., crined, armed, and ungu. or. *cf.* 48. 5
Limborne, a dexter hand holding a hunting horn sans strings, all ppr. 217. 4
Limerick, a demi-savage affrontée, holding in his dexter hand a hatchet and in his sinister a club resting on his shoulder.
Limerick, Earl of (Pery), a hind's head erased ppr. (*for Pery*). *Virtute non astutiâ.* 124. 3
Limesey, the stump of an oak-tree sprouting new branches ppr. 145. 2
Limesie, a rose-bush bearing roses ppr. 149. 8
Limsay and **Limsey,** out of a ducal coronet gu., a dexter arm holding a sword ppr. 212. 11
Linacre of Linacre Hall, Derbysh., a greyhound's head erased quarterly arg. and sa., charged with four escallops counterchanged. 61. 10
Linch, a lynx passant arg. *cf.* 127. 2
Lincoln, Earl of, *see* Newcastle, Duke of.
Lincolne, out of a ducal coronet or, a demi-lion ppr., crowned with an antique crown of the first. *cf.* 16. 3
Lincolne, a lion rampant sa., ducally gorged or. *cf.* 1. 13
Lincolne of Dublin, a leopard's head erased arg., spotted sa., between two oak-branches vert, acorned or. *Non vi sed mente.*
Lind of Gorgie, co. Edinburgh, Scotland, two branches of laurel in saltier ppr. *Semper virescit virtus.*
Lindear of Dublin, on a mount a stag statant charged on the shoulder with a trefoil slipped, all ppr. *cf.* 117. 1
Lindley of Skigby, Notts, a griffin's head erased arg., gorged with a bar gemel sa. *cf.* 66. 2
Lindley, Baron, Rt. Hon. Sir Nathaniel, Lord of Appeal, of 19, Craven Hill Gardens, Hyde Park, London, W., in front of a pelican in her piety ppr., charged on the breast with a pheon gu., three quatrefoils fessewise or. *Sis fortis.* 305. 6
Lindon, Ireland, an arm embowed brandishing a scimitar, all ppr. *Patria cara carior libertas.* 201. 1
Lindon, Ireland, a dragon. 73. 2
Lindow of Ingwell, Cumb., a lion rampant gu., semée of buckles or, and holding between the paws a fountain. *Vi et virtute.*
Lindow, Burns-, Isaac William, Ireton Hall, Cumb., same crest and motto.
Lindsay, Lord Wantage, *see* Wantage.
Lindsay, Earl of Balcarres (merged in Crawford), *see* Crawford.
Lindsay (Bethune): (1) A swan with wings expanded ppr. (2) An ermine ppr. 134. 6. (3) An otter's head erased ppr. *Live but dreid.—Je ayme.—Sine labe nota.—Debonnaire.* 134. 3
Lindsay, Rt. Hon. James Ludovic, LL.D., F.R.S., **Earl of Crawford** (also Earl of Balcarres): (1) Issuing from an antique ducal coronet or, the head, neck, and wings of a swan ppr., also an ostrich ppr., holding in its beak a key or. 100. 8. (2) A tent az., fringed and semée of stars or, ensigned with a pennon gu. (*for Balcarres*). *Endure fort.—Astra castra numen lumen munimen.* 158. 13
Lindsay, William Alexander, Esquire, (Portcullis), 17, Cromwell Road, S.W., and the other issue of the late Hon. Colin Lindsay, as Earl of Crawford.
Lindsay Bart., of Westville, Lincs, and Leuchar, Fifesh., a tent az., fringed and semée of stars or, ensigned with a pennon floating to the sinister gu. *Astra castra numen lumen munimen.* 158. 13
Lindsay of Glasnevin, co. Dublin, as Earl of Balcarres.
Lindsay, Scotland (**Viscount Garnock**), an ermine ppr. *Sine labe nota.*
Lindsay, Lord Spynie, an ostrich's head erased ppr., with a horse-shoe or in its beak, and a label of three points about its neck. *cf.* 97. 8
Lindsay of Cavill, Kinross, Scotland, an ostrich's head erased ppr. *Sis fortis.*
Lindsay of Maryville, co. Cork, an ostrich holding a key ppr. *Endure furth.* 97. 5
Lindsay of Wormistone, Fifesh., Scotland, an ostrich ppr. *Patientia vincit.* 97. 2
Lindsay of Edzell, Forfarsh., an ostrich ppr., holding in its beak a horse-shoe or.
Lindsay, Rev. Thomas, of 116, St. James's Road, Croydon, Surrey, an ostrich ppr., holding in the beak a key or, the dexter leg supported by a fusil gu. *Endure fort.*
Lindsay of Kirkforthar, Fifesh., an ostrich holding a key in its beak. *Live but dread.* 97. 5
Lindsay of Perth, an ostrich ppr., holding a key in its beak. Below shield, "*Endure furth.*" Above in scroll, "*Love but dread.*" 97. 5
Lindsay of Cahoo, co. Tyrone, Ireland, a swan ppr. *Live but dread.* 99. 2
Lindsay of Glenview, Wicklow: (1) A swan statant ppr., wings close. 99. 2. (2) A negro's head in profile ppr., crowned with an Eastern crown or (*for Brocas*). *Live but dread.—Vincit veritas.* 191. 4
Lindsay of Loughoy, co. Tyrone, a swan ppr., standing with wings closed. *Love but dread.* 99. 2
Lindsay of Dunrod, Renfrewsh., Scotland, a duck with wings expanded ppr.
Lindsay of Hollymount, co. Mayo, Ireland, a double-headed eagle displayed gu. *Endure fort.* 74. 2
Lindsay, co. Mayo, an eagle displayed with two heads gu. 74. 2
Lindsay of Dowhill, Kinross, Scotland, a castle ppr. *Firmus maneo.* 155. 8
Lindsay of Culsh, Aberdeensh., Scotland, a tower ppr., ensigned with a crescent arg. *Firmiter maneo.* 156. 4
Lindsay, Scotland, an otter's head and neck erased sa. 134. 3
Lindsay of Pitcarlies and Cairn, Forfarsh., Scotland, two stalks of wheat bladed and eared in saltire ppr. *Non solum armis.* 154. 4
Lindsay, Scotland, two stalks of wheat in orle ppr. 97. 5
Lindsay of Blacksolme, Renfrewsh., and of Balquharrage, Stirlingsh., Scotland, a withered branch of oak sprouting forth green leaves ppr. *Et mortua virescunt.* 151. 3
Lindsay, Scotland, a dexter hand holding a branch of olive ppr. *Mutus amore cresco.* 219. 9

Lindsay of Evelick, Perthsh., Scotland, a sword in pale, on the point a balance and scale ppr. *Recte vel ardua.* 179. 11

Lindsay of Virginia, U.S.A., a mailed hand supporting on a dagger's point a pair of balances ppr. *Recta vel ardua.*

Lindsay, Scotland, a griffin's head arg., beaked gu. *Je ayme.* 66. 1

Lindsay of the Mount, Fifesh., Scotland, and **Sir David Lindsay,** Lyon King of Arms, a man's heart in flames gu., surmounted by a scroll. *Je ayme.—Cantor cantar cantas.* 181. 13

Lindsay-Bucknall, of Turin Castle, co. Mayo, a buck's head cabossed sa., attired or. 122. 5

Lindsay-Smith, John Lindsay, Esquire, an ostrich ppr., holding in the beak a horse-shoe or. *Tu ne cede malis.*

Lindsey, Earl of (Bertie), a Saracen's head affrontée couped at the breast ppr., ducally crowned or. 192. 9. (*The paternal crest of Bertie is a pine-tree ppr.*) *Loyaulté me oblige.* 144. 13

Lindsey of Bucksted, Sussex, an eagle displayed sa., beaked and legged or, charged on the breast with a cross patée of the last. *cf.* 75. 2

Lindsey of Colby, Norf., a unicorn sejant regardant or, armed, ungu., maned, and ducally gorged az.

Line, Scotland, a griffin's head erased gu. 66. 2

Linesley of Linesley, Lancs, an arm in armour embowered, holding in the gauntlet a sabre, all ppr. 195. 1

Linford, a talbot passant arg. 54. 1

Ling and **Lingue,** Lincs, on a mount vert, a lion sejant gardant or, resting the dexter paw on a caltrap az.

Lingard, a stag's head affrontée gorged with a ducal coronet ppr. 119. 14

Lingard, Thomas Dewhurst, Esquire, of Burnside, Windermere, a wolf's head erased sa., charged on the neck with an escallop arg., and holding in the mouth a branch of three cinquefoils slipped vert. 247. 17

Lingard-Monk, Richard Boughey Monk, Esquire, of Broome House, Lancs: (1) A dragon sa., charged on the wing with a cross patée or, and resting the dexter claw upon an escutcheon gu., thereon a lion's head erased of the second (*for Monk*). 247. 16. (2) A wolf's head erased sa., charged with an escallop or, holding in the mouth three cinquefoils slipped vert (*for Lingard.*) *Tout d'en haut.* 247. 17

Lingard-Guthrie, Rev. Roger Rowson, of Taybank, Forfarsh., Scotland, a demi-lion rampant gu., armed and langued az., holding in his dexter fore-paw a cross crosslet fitchée, also az. *Sto pro veritate.* 11. 5

Lingen, Baron (Lingen), out of a ducal coronet or, a garb vert. *Dominus providebit.*

Lingen, Shropsh., out of a ducal coronet or, seven leeks, roots upwards, ppr. 147. 5

Lingen-Burton of Logner Hall, near Shrewsbury: (1) On a wreath of the colours a dexter gauntlet az., couped at the wrist (*for Burton*). 209. 5. (2) Out of a ducal coronet or, seven leeks, roots upwards, ppr. (*for Lingen*). *Dominus providebit.* 147. 5

Lingen-Burton, Edward Robert, Esquire, of Four Sisters, East Bergholt, Suff.: (1) On a wreath of the colours a dexter gauntlet az., couped at the wrist (*for Burton*). 209. 8. (2) Out of a ducal coronet or, seven leeks, roots upwards, ppr. (*for Lingen*). 147. 5

Lingham, two branches of oak in saltier ppr. 157. 1

Linghooke, Norf., a griffin's head erased gu., gorged with a collar dancettée or, holding in the beak a violet az., stalked and leaved vert.

Lingwood, an antelope's head erased erm. 126. 2

Lingwood of Braintree, Essex, a talbot's head or, pellettée, gorged with a mural coronet az.

Linley, Scotland, out of a ducal coronet gu., a demi-boar or. *cf.* 40. 13

Linlithgow, Marquess of (Sir John Adrian Louis Hope), K.T., G.C.M.G., G.C.V.O., a globe fracted at the top under a rainbow with clouds at each end, all ppr. *At spes non fracta.*

Linnet, out of a ducal coronet or, a double plume of ostrich-feathers arg., five and four. *cf.* 114. 4

Linning, Scotland, a dexter cubit arm wielding a broadsword, all ppr. 212. 13

Linque or **Link,** Lincs, on a mount vert, a lion sejant gardant or, resting his dexter paw on a caltrap az.

Linskill, a demi-eagle displayed with two heads or, holding in the beak a scroll with the motto, "*Victor.*" *cf.* 82. 3

Lint, a dexter hand gu., holding a cross crosslet fitched sa 221. 14

Linton, Scotland, an eagle's head erased holding in the beak an acorn stalked and leaved, all ppr. 84. 10

Linton, Cambs, a griffin's head erased. 66. 2

Lintot, two lion's gambs holding a garb.

Linwood, a demi-talbot holding in the mouth an arrow ppr. 55. 10

Lionnel, an antique crown. 180. 12

Lippincot, Bart. (*extinct*), of Stoke Bishop, Glouc., out of a mural coronet gu., a plume of six ostrich-feathers in one row alternately arg. and az. *Secundis dubiisque rectus.*

Lippitt, Alfred Joseph George, Esquire, M.A., of 11, King's Bench Walk, Temple, E.C., and Schloss Pernegg, Styria, Austria, a talbot sejant or, charged on the shoulder with two annulets interlaced fesseways gu., resting the dexter fore-leg on a rose gu., barbed and seeded ppr. *Stet fortuna domus.* 241. 1

Lipscomb, a cubit arm in armour holding in the hand an oak-branch ppr.

Lipton, Sir Thomas Johnstone, Bart., K.C.V.O., Osidge, Southgate, Middx., two arms in saltire, the dexter surmounted by the sinister, holding a sprig of the tea-plant erect, and the other a like sprig of the coffee-plant, both slipped and leaved ppr., vested above the elbows arg. *Labor omnia vincit.* 283. 2

Lisbone and **Lisborne,** a boar passant or. 40. 9

Lisburne, Earl of (Vaughan), an armed arm embowed ppr., holding a fleur-de-lis arg. *Non revertur inultus.* 199. 4

Lisgar, Baron (Young), a demi-lion gu., charged on the shoulder with a trefoil slipped, and holding in the dexter paw a sprig of three maple-leaves slipped or. *cf.* 10. 3

Lisle, Baron (Lysaght), of Mountnorth, co. Cork, in Ireland, a dexter arm embowed in armour, the hand holding a sword, all ppr. *Bella, horrida bella.* 195. 2

Lisle, William Beresford, Esquire, of Narrowgate House, Alnwick, Northumb., a lion passant gardant az., resting the dexter fore-paw on a fret, and charged on the body with two pheons, all or. *In cruce non in leone fides.*

Lisle, Hants, a lion's head couped. 21. 1

Lisle of St. Martins-in-the-Fields, Middx., a lion's gamb az., holding an escallop or.

Lisle, Ireland, a marigold slipped and leaved ppr. 151. 12

Lisle, a stag arg., collared, chained, and attired or. *cf.* 117. 5

Lisle, Hants, a stag trippant arg., attired or. 117. 8

Lisle of Wodyton, Thruxton, and Moyles Court, Hants, a stag trippant ppr., attired or. 117. 8

Lisle, a millstone arg., charged in the centre with a mill-rind sa. *cf.* 180. 14

Lismore, Viscount (*extinct*) (O'Callaghan), a naked dexter arm embowed holding bendwise a sword entwined with a snake, all ppr. *Fidus et audax.* 201. 3

Lister, Baron Ribblesdale, *see* Ribblesdale.

Lister, Scotland, a buck's head erased ppr. *Malo mori quam fœdari.* 121. 2

Lister, Staffs, a buck's head party per fess ppr. and or, charged with a crescent. *Retinens vestigia famæ.* *cf.* 119. 8

Lister, a stag's head erased ppr. 121. 2

Lister, George Spofforth, Esquire, of Finningley Park, Bawtry, Yorks, same crest.

Lister of Burwell Park, Lincs, same crest. *Est modus.* 121. 2

Lister, Shropsh., Derbysh., and Yorks, a buck's head erased ppr. 121. 2

Lister, Sir Villiers, K.C.M.G., of 64, Cadogan Square, London, S.W., and Armitage Hill, Ascot, Berks, on a ducal coronet a stag's head erased per fesse ppr. and gu. *Retinens vestigia famæ.* *cf.* 120. 7

Lister of London, a stag's head erased per fesse ppr. and or, attired of the last. 121. 2

Lister of Hirst Priory, Lincs, a stag's head issuing from a ducal coronet. *Retinens vestigia famæ.* 120. 7

Lister, Staffs, on a five-leaved ducal coronet or, a buck's head erased per fess arg. and gu. *cf.* 120. 7

Lister, John, of Shibden Hall, Southowram, Halifax, Yorks, a stag's head erased ppr., charged on the neck with a trefoil slipped gu. *Justus propositi tenax.* 121. 8

Lister, Baron (Lister), of Park Crescent, in the parish of St. Marylebone, Middx., in front of a stag's head erased ppr., three mullets arg. *Malo mori quam fœdari.* 304. 5

Lister-Kaye, Sir John Pepys, Bart., D.L., of Denby Grange, Yorks: (1) A goldfinch ppr., charged on the breast with a rose gu. (*for Kaye*). *cf.* 108. 8. (2) A buck's head ppr., erased wavy or, attired sa., holding in the mouth a bird-bolt bendways of the third, flighted arg. *Kynd kynn knawne kepe.*
Lister-Empson of the Hall, Ousefleet, Goole, Yorks: (1) A tent arg., adorned or, lined az., charged in the interior with a cross formée of the first (*for Empson*). (2) Out of a five-leaved ducal coronet a stag's head (*for Lister*). *Corona mea Christus.*
Lister-Foulis, Reginald John, Esquire, of Curry-Rivel, Somers., same crest and motto.
Liston, Scotland, a demi-lion gu., holding a gilliflower ppr.
Liston, Scotland, two hands couped and conjoined ppr. 224. 2
Liston, an antique plough ppr. *Poco a poco.* 178. 8
Liston-Foulis, Sir James, Bart., of Colinton and Ravelston, a dexter hand couped holding a sword in pale, sustaining a wreath of laurel, all ppr. *Mente manuque præsto.—Non jure deficit.—Thure et jure.* 235. 17
Listowel, Earl of (Hare), a demi-lion arg., ducally gorged or. *Odi profanum.* 10. 7
Litchfield, a goat's head couped affrontée. 128. 13
Litchfield, an arm in armour embowed holding in the hand a sword ppr. *Semper pugnare paratus.* 195. 2
Litcott, an old man's head ppr., vested sa., ducally crowned or. 192. 1
Lithgow, Scotland, a palm-branch vert. 147. 1
Litler or **Littler,** a filbert-tree ppr., the trunk raguly, on each side a squirrel salient gu.
Litster, Scotland, a deer's head couped ppr. *Labore et fiduciâ.* 121. 5
Litster, a stag at gaze ermines, ducally gorged and attired or. *cf.* 117. 3
Litster, Lincs, an anchor cabled sa. *Sine Deo nihil.* 161. 2
Litt, Lyte, and **Lytte,** a bear rampant sa., muzzled gu., supporting a ragged staff. 34. 9
Littell, two daggers in saltier ppr. 169. 8
Littell, Essex, on an arrow or, a cock statant, combed and wattled gu. *cf.* 91. 2
Little, a demi-bull. *cf.* 43. 8
Little of Liberton, Edinburgh, a leopard's head or. *Magnum in parvo.* 22. 10
Little of Llanvair Grange, Monm., a leopard's head ppr. *Magnum in parvo.* 22. 10
Little, Archibald Cosmo, Esquire, J.P., of Upton House, Tetbury, Glouc., a leopard's face ppr. *Magnum in parvo.*
Little, George Arthur Knightley Howman, Esquire, of Newbold Pacey, Warw., a boar sa., armed, tusked, and maned or, charged on the body with two estoiles fessewise or. *Sua gratia parvis.*
Little, Ernest Knightley, Esquire, of Newbold Pacey, Warwick, a boar sa., armed, maned, and tusked or, charged on the body with two estoiles fessoways of the last. *Sua gratia parvis.*
Little of Meikledale and Langholme, Dumfriessh., Scotland, a tiger's head affrontée ppr. *Magnum in parvo.*
Littleboy, a goat's head erased gu. 128. 5
Littlebury, a lion's gamb per fess gu. and az., holding a spear sa., the point or. *cf.* 38. 11
Littlebury of Stensby, Lincs, a man's head couped at the shoulders, armed in mail, all ppr.
Littledale, two lion's gambs in saltier ppr. 39. 14
Littledale, Henry William Assheton, Esquire, Captain R.N., of Bolton Hall, Yorks, a demi-lion gu., gorged with a collar gemelle arg., holding in the dexter paw a cross crosslet of the same. *Fac et spera.* *cf.* 11. 10
Littledale, Rev. Godfrey Armytage, M.A., of the Vicarage, Chipping Norton, same crest and motto.
Littledale, Willoughby Aston, Esquire, of 26, Cranley Gardens, London, S.W., same crest and motto.
Littledale, Fletcher Castell Hungerford, Esquire, of Cookham End, Berks, same crest. *Crux mihi dux.*
Littlefield, on a garb or, a bird arg., holding in its beak an ear of wheat vert. 93. 3
Littlehales, Sussex, between two wings or, an arm in armour embowed ppr., garnished of the first, holding in the gauntlet an arrow entwined with an olive-branch vert. 198. 10
Littlehales, an arm in armour embowed ppr., garnished or, a garland tied round the wrist with a ribbon vert, holding in the hand a dart in bend, point downwards ppr., all between two wings or. *cf.* 198. 10
Littlejohn, Alexander, Esquire, of Invercharron, Ardgay, N.B., three arrows, one in pale and two in saltire, points downwards ppr. *Virtute tutamen.*
Littlejohn, Camphill, Peterculter, Aberdeensh., three arrows, one in pale and two in saltire, the points downwards or, barbed and flighted ppr., banded arg., therefrom pendent a bugle-horn or. *In virtute tutamen.*
Littlejohn of Woodston, Scotland, two naked arms issuing from a cloud holding a bow bent to the full to let an arrow fly, all ppr. *Ferio.* *cf.* 200. 2
Littler, *see* Litler.
Littler, Middx., a squirrel sejant cracking a nut, all ppr. 135. 7
Littler, General the late Sir John Hunter, G.C.B., on a mount vert, in front of a palm-tree, an elephant statant ppr., the trappings gu., fimbriated or, and charged with a sun in splendour, the girth az., also fimbriated or, the trunk grasping a lotus-flower slipped, also ppr. *Astra et castra.* 133. 12
Littleton, Baron Hatherton, *see* Hatherton.
Littleton, a stag's head cabossed sa., attired or, between the attires a bugle-horn arg., suspended from a bend gu. *Ung Dieu, et ung Roy.*
Littleton, Shropsh.: (1) A stag's head cabossed sa., attired or, between the autlers a bugle-horn arg., stringed of the last. *cf.* 122. 5. (2) A wyvern's head. 71. 1
Littleton, Staffs and Shropsh., same crest as (2) above. 71. 1
Littleton, Worcs., a Moor's head in profile ppr., wreathed arg. and sa. 192. 13
Littlewood, on a mount vert, a peacock ppr. *cf.* 103. 4
Littlewood of the Hyde, Kinver, Staffs, and Burstow Rectory, near Diss, on a mount vert, a peacock in his pride ppr. *Liber et audax.*
Litton, a mountain-cat current ppr. *cf.* 26. 6
Litton of Altmore, co. Tyrone, Ireland, out of a ducal coronet or, an ermine's head erm. *Prudentia gloriam acquirit.*
Litton, Edward de L'Establere, Esquire, J.P., of Ardavilling, co. Cork, same crest and motto.
Litton, Ireland, a goat's head erased vert. 128. 5
Liverpool, Earl of (Jenkinson), a sea-horse assurgent arg., maned az., supporting a cross patée gu. *Palma non sine pulvere.*
Liversidge, Archibald, Esquire, M.A. (Cantab.), F.R.S. (London), Professor of Chemistry, University of Sydney, New South Wales, a leopard's face jessant-de-lis or. 22. 5
Livesay and **Livesey,** of East Church, Kent, a lion's gamb erased gu. 36. 4
Livesay and **Livesey,** a bear's paw erect and erased holding a bunch of trefoils, all ppr.
Livingston, on a mount a bull-dog with a pile of balls in front. *cf.* 57. 10
Livingston, Scotland, a dexter hand wielding a sword ppr. *Ut possim.* 212. 13
Livingston of Counteswells, Scotland, a demi-Hercules wreathed about the head and middle holding in his dexter hand a club in pale, and in his sinister a serpent, all ppr. *Si je puis.* 185. 3
Livingston, Fenton-, John Nigel, Westquarter, near Falkirk, same crest and motto.
Livingston or **Livingstone,** of Baldron, Stirlingsh., Scotland, a gilliflower slipped ppr. *Nativum retinet decus.* 151. 8
Livingstone of Aberdeen, Scotland, a boar's head couped holding in the mouth a pair of scales ppr. *Fortis et æquus.*
Livingstone, a dexter arm holding in the hand an olive-branch. 219. 9
Livingstone, a dexter hand holding a sword, all ppr. *Et domi et foris.* 212. 13
Livingstone of Parkhall, Stirlingsh., Scotland, a dexter hand grasping a sabre ppr. *Si possim.* 212. 13
Livingstone-Learmouth, Somerville Reid, Esquire, of Stakes, Cosham, Hants: (1) A dove holding in the beak an olive-branch ppr. (*for Learmonth*). 92. 5. (2) A dexter hand holding a sabre ppr. (*for Livingstone*). *Dum spiro spero.—Si possim.* 212. 13
Livingstone-Learmonth, Thomas, Esquire, of Parkhall, by Polmont, N.B., same crests and mottoes.
Livingstone of Glentirran, Stirlingsh., Scotland, a dexter hand brandishing a sword ppr. *Ut possim.* 212. 13
Livingstone of Westquarter, Stirling, Scotland, a demi savage, the head

wreathed with laurel holding in his dexter hand a baton erect, and in his sinister a serpent entwined round the arm, all ppr. *Si je puis.* cf. 190. 7

Livingstone of Kinnaird, a Moor's head affrontée couped ppr., wreathed gu. and arg., with pendent arg. at the ears. 192. 4

Livingstone, a demi-man holding in the hand a baton in pale or.

Livingstone, a demi-savage wreathed about the head and middle with laurel, all ppr. *Spe expecto.*

Livingstone, Bart., Stirling, a demi-savage wreathed about the head and loins with laurel-leaves holding in his dexter hand a baton, and in his sinister a serpent entwined round the arm, all ppr. *Si je puis.* cf. 185. 3

Lizars, Scotland, a lion's gamb ppr. cf. 36. 4

Lizars, Scotland, a stag's head erased ppr. *Verus ad finem.* 121. 2

Lizurs, a hand holding a sword ppr. 212. 13

Lizurs, two hands brandishing a sword. 213. 3

Llandaff, Viscount (Matthews), 6, Carlton Gardens, S.W., on a mount vert, a heathcock holding a sprig of broom ppr. *Y fynno Duw y fydd.* 274. 5

Llangattock, Baron (Rolls), the Hendre, Monm., out of a wreath of oak a dexter arm vested or, cuff sa., the arm charged with a fesse dancettée, double cotised of the second, charged with three bezants, in the hand ppr. a roll of parchment arg. *Celeritas et veritas.* 274. 7

Llanover, Baron (*extinct*), Rt. Hon. the late Sir Benjamin Hall, a palm-branch in bend sinister ppr., in front of a griffin's head erased or, charged with a bar gemel gu., and holding in the beak a hawk's lure or, tasselled arg.

Llanwarne, Thomas, Esquire, of Norfolk Place, Heref., a raven ppr. *Virtute securus.* 107. 14

Llewellin, John Charles, M.A., Stow Hill, Newport, a paschal lamb bearing a banner, all ppr. *Vincit qui patitur.*

Llewellin, William, Esquire, J.P., of Upton House, near Poole, Dorset, a lamb passant arg., supporting with the dexter forefoot a flagstaff in bend sinister ppr., therefrom flowing a banner gu., charged with a spear-head or, between two wings of the third, on each a like spear-head. *Duw fo ar fy rhan.*

Llewellyn, a pheon ppr. 174. 11

Llewellyn, a demi-lion rampant arg. 22. 1

Llewellyn, a lamb bearing a banner of St. George with a glory round the head, all ppr. *Vincit qui patitur.* cf. 131. 0

Llewelyn, *see* Dillwyn-Llewelyn.

Lloyd, *see* Mostyn, Baron.

Lloyd, *see* Hutchinson-Lloyd-Vaughan.

Lloyd, *see* Davies-Lloyd.

Lloyd, *see* Whitelocke-Lloyd.

Lloyd of Laques, Carmarthen, an eagle with wings elevated preying on a pigeon 77. 1

Lloyd, William, Esquire, J.P., D.L., of Rockville, co. Roscommon, Ireland, an eagle displayed with two heads sa., armed gu. 74. 2

Lloyd of Plasyndre, Merionethsh., an eagle displayed or. 75. 2

Lloyd of London and Wales, out of a ducal coronet or, a cock's head between two wings gu., combed, beaked, and wattled of the first.

Lloyd, Francis Montagu, Esquire, B.A., J.P., of the Grange, Newnham-on-Severn, and Flexley Grange, Glouc., a cock's head couped arg., combed and wattled gu., charged on the neck with two estoiles in pale az., between two wings erect vair. *Virtus rosa suavior stella clarior.* 90. 11

Lloyd of Cilcen Hall and Plas-yn-Clan, Flintsh., a Saracen's head erased at the neck ppr., wreathed about the temples arg. and sa. *Dial Gwaed Cymro.* cf. 190. 14

Lloyd of Plymog, Denbighsh., a Saxon's head in profile couped ppr. *Heb ddww heb ddym a Duw a digon.*

Lloyd, Wales, a Saracen's head and neck erased ppr., wreathed or and az., gorged with a collar engrailed of the last, charged with two annulets of the second

Lloyd, Lieutenant-Colonel Thomas Edward John, Esquire, of Plas Tregayan, Llangwllog, Anglesey, and Aberdunant, Carnarvonsh., a Saracen's head affrontée erased at the neck ppr., wreathed about the temples or and sa., between two fleurs-de-lis of the last.

Lloyd, a wolf rampant holding between the fore-paws a broken spear. 28. 11

Lloyd, a wolf rampant holding between the fore-paws a dart erect, the point downwards and embrued. 28. 8

Lloyd of Holyrood and Whitnester, Glouc., and Cheam, Surrey, a stag's head erased sa., charged on the neck with a crescent erm. 119. 8

Lloyd, Shropsh., a stag's head erased ppr., attired or. 121. 2

Lloyd, Shropsh. and Glouc., a stag's head couped ppr., attired or, gorged with a chaplet of laurel vert. 120. 3

Lloyd, a stag's head couped arg. 121. 5

Lloyd, Shropsh., a stag's head or, attired of the same. 121. 5

Lloyd of Croghan, co. Roscommon, Ireland: (1) A stag's head couped ppr., the neck charged with a laurel chaplet. cf. 121. 5. (2) On a ducal coronet or, an eagle displayed with two heads sa. cf. 74. 2

Lloyd, a stag trippant ppr., armed and unguled or. *Heb ddww heb ddym ddwwadygon.* 117. 8

Lloyd of Havod Dinas, Denbighsh., Wales, a hart trippant arg., attired or, holding in its mouth a snake vert. cf. 117. 8

Lloyd, Hants, on a mount vert, a lion sejant gardant gu.

Lloyd, Charles Henry, Esquire, of Trallwyn, Chevilo R.S.O., Carnarvonsh., a lion rampant arg., guttée-de-sang, surmounting two spears in saltire ppr. *Instanter perfectus.*

Lloyd of Oswestry, Shropsh., issuing from a five-leaved coronet or, a demi-lion rampant arg. cf. 16. 3

Lloyd, Shropsh., out of a ducal coronet or, a demi-lion rampant sa. 16. 3

Lloyd, Wales, a demi-lion rampant gardant or, holding an arrow erect arg. cf. 10. 1

Lloyd, Shropsh., a lion rampant gu. 1. 13

Lloyd, John Conway, of Dinas House, Llanwrtyd, Breconsh., same crests.

Lloyd, a lion rampant regardant. 2. 3

Lloyd, Thomas William, Esquire, Goodrich House, Heref.: (1) A lion rampant regardant. (2) A goat's head armed arg., issuant out of a ducal coronet or.

Lloyd, a lion rampant regardant holding in his dexter paw a fleur-de-lis. cf. 2. 3

Lloyd, Shropsh., a demi-lion rampant or. 10. 2

Lloyd, Shropsh., same crest. *Retinens vestigia famæ.*

Lloyd, George Butler, Esquire, Shelton Hall, Shrewsbury, a demi-lion rampant regardant.

Lloyd, Shropsh., a demi-lion rampant sa. 10. 1

Lloyd, Edward Pryse, of Glansevin, Carmarthen, a lion rampant. *Fiat justitia, ruat cœlum.* 1. 13

Lloyd, Charles, Esquire, M.A., J.P., D.L., of Waunifor, Maescrugian, South Wales, a lion rampant. *Sic itur ad astra.*

Lloyd, George William, Esquire, Stockton Hall, York, in front of a cubit arm vested az., cuffed arg., the hand grasping a lizard fessewise ppr., a lion dormant sa.

Lloyd, Captain George William David Bowen, Brunant, Llanwrda R.S.O., South Wales, a lion couchant or. *Dum spiro spero.*

Lloyd-Verney, Colonel George Hope, of Clochfaen, Llanidloes, North Wales, Camden House, Bo'ness, N.B., and 14, Hinde Street, Manchester Square, London, W.: (1) A demi-phœnix in flames ppr., charged with five mullets in cross or, and looking at rays of the sun, also ppr. (*for Verney*). 278. 14. (2) Out of a mural coronet arg., two spears erect, therefrom two pennons flowing towards the dexter, one erminois, the other pean (*for Calvert*). 278. 15. (3) A lion rampant sa., holding in the mouth a fleur-de-lis or, and supporting an antique shield gu., charged with three annulets interlaced in pale or, and upon the shoulder for distinction a cross crosslet or (*for Lloyd*). *Ung sent ung soleil.—Servata fides cineri.* 278. 13

Lloyd, Arthur Henry Orlando, of Leaton Knolls, Shropsh., a demi-lion rampant or. *Retinens vestigia famæ.* 10. 2

Lloyd, Llewelyn, M.A., J.P., of Blake House, Winslow, Bucks, on a cap of maintenance a wyvern vert. *Duw ar fy rhan.*

Lloyd, Thomas Edward, of Coedmore, Cardigansh., a lion rampant arg. *Fide et fortitudine.* 1. 13

Lloyd of Swan Hill, Shropsh., a lion rampant gu. 1. 13

Lloyd, Bart. (*extinct*), of Lancing, Sussex, a lion's head erased per bend sinister erm. and pean, gorged with a wreath of oak vert. 17. 10

Lloyd, Francis Thomas, Esquire, of the Castle, Dover, a lion's head couped.

Lloyd of Danyrallt, Carmarthensh.: (1) A wolf rampant arg., holding a spear's head embrued between his paws and piercing the dexter paw distilling drops of blood. 28. 8. (2) A lion rampant regardant sa. *Heb Dduw heb ddym a Duw a digon.* 2. 11

Lloyd, Rev. Torworth Grey, Rural Dean, F.S.A., of Bosherton Rectory, Pembroke, same crests and motto.

Lloyd, Howard Meuric, Esquire, M.A., J.P., Barrister-at-law, of Delfryn, Llanwrda, R.S.O., Carmarthensh., South Wales, a wolf rampant arg., the neck encircled by an annulet or, holding between the paws a broken spear, point downwards embrued, piercing the sinister paw. 313. 3

Lloyd, Hardress-, Ireland, a lion rampant arg., holding in the dexter paw a snake. *Respice, prospice.*

Lloyd, Colonel Edmond George Knapp Piersy, of Passage West, co. Cork, Ireland, and Constitutional Club, S.W., a demi-lion rampant regardant sa., charged on the shoulder with a trefoil slipped or. *Tendit in ardua virtus.* 290. 13

Lloyd, Clifford Bartholomew, Esquire, of Victoria Castle, Killiney, co. Dublin, same crest and motto.

Lloyd of Bradenham House, near Wycomb, Bucks, a lion passant gu., charged with two characters of the planet Venus, one on the shoulder, the other on the hip. *cf.* 6. 2

Lloyd, Wales, a nag's head erased arg. *Fide ne diffide.*

Lloyd, Henry Crampton, Stockton Manor, Chirbury, Salop, same crest.

Lloyd, Charles Westall, Esquire, of Tarramia, Bobinawarrah, Oxleysh., Victoria, Australia, same crest and motto.

Lloyd, Frederick Bianchi, Esquire, of Oakland, California, U.S.A., same crest and motto.

Lloyd, a greyhound's head erased sa. 61. 4

Lloyd, Wales, a horse's head erased sa., maned or. *cf.* 50. 8

Lloyd, Ireland, on a mount a hind statant ppr., collared arg. 124. 14

Lloyd of Marrington, Marton, and Stockton, Chirbury, Shropsh., a nag's head erased arg. *Frangas non flectes.* 51. 4

Lloyd, out of a ducal coronet or, a unicorn's head arg., crined and armed of the first. 48. 12

Lloyd, Edward Owen Vaughan, Rhagatt, Corwen, same crest.

Lloyd, a wolf's head erased arg. 30. 8

Lloyd, Sir Marteine Owen Mowbray, Bart., of Bronwydd, Cardigansh., in front of a holly-tree ppr., a boar passant arg., semée of estoiles az., collared and chained to the tree or. *Iddow Bor diolch* (English, *To God be thanks*).

Lloyd, of Dolobran, Montgomerysh., in front of a fern-brake a goat salient arg., horned and ungu. or, gorged with a collar flory counterflory sa. *Esto vigilans.—Watch.* 258. 17

Lloyd, Henry, Esquire, of Pitsford Hall, Northamp., same crest. *Gwylio.*

Lloyd, Sampson Zachary, Esquire, J.P., of Areley King's, Worcs., same crest and motto.

Lloyd, William Henry, Esquire, of Hatch Court, Somers., same crest and motto.

Lloyd, Wilson, Esquire, of Park Lane House, Woodgreen, Wednesbury, and Honychurch, Hampton-in-Arden, Warw., same crest and motto.

Lloyd, John, Esquire, of Bank House, Shropsh., on a mount vert, amidst heath ppr., a greyhound current arg., collared or. *cf.* 58. 2

Lloyd of Cefndyrrys and Ferney Hall, Shropsh., out of a ducal coronet or, a griffin's head vert. *Gwell angau neu cywilydd.* 67. 9

Lloyd, late Major Sir William, a boar's head erased arg., in front of two flagstaves in saltire ppr., flowing from that on the dexter a banner, tenné inscribed "*Nagpoor*" in letters of gold, and from that on the sinister a banner vert inscribed "*Muckee,*" also in letters of gold. *Heb Dduw heb Ddim.—Jure non dono.* 42. 12

Lloyd, Wales and Kent, a man's head ppr., in armour arg., garnished or, and on a scroll issuing from his mouth and proceeding over his head the motto, *Avonno dio dervid.*

Lloyd of Welcomb House, Warw., *usés:* a cubit arm in scale armour, the hand ppr., the cuff arg., grasping a lizard vert. 209. 3

Lloyd-Price, Meredydd Lewis Willig, Esquire, of Bryn Cothi and Castle Pigyn, Carmarthensh.: (1) A wolf rampant arg. (2) Out of a ducal coronet, a demi-lion rampant. *Spes tutissima cœlis.*

Lloyd-Mostyn, Major-General the Hon. Savage: (1) On a mount vert, a lion rampant or. (2) A Saracen's head affrontée, erased at the neck ppr., wreathed about the temples arg. and sa. (3) A stag trippant ppr., attired or, charged on the shoulder with an escutcheon of the second, thereon a chevron of the first between three men's heads in profile, couped at the neck, also ppr.

Lluellin, Herts, a paschal lamb ppr. 131. 2

Lluellyn of South Withiam, Lincs, on a rock a Cornish chough, all ppr. *Mors mihi lucrum.* 106. 9

Lluellyn of Strethall, same crest.

Loader, on a chapeau gu., two lions rampant, supporting a garb ppr. 3. 5

Loader, a dragon passant ppr. 73. 2

Loades of London, on a wreath a mural coronet arg., and therefrom issuing an arm vested sa., cuffed of the first, holding in the hand ppr. a key or. *Obey and rule.*

Loane, a demi-lion rampant sa., brandishing a scimitar ppr. 14. 10

Loat, between two wings a spur-rowel, all ppr.

Loban, a dexter arm in armour embowed holding in the hand a tilting-spear ppr.

Lobb, a lion's head erased, collared gu. 18. 6

Lobb, a dexter arm in armour embowed holding in the hand a spear-point downwards.

Lobert, a dexter arm embowed, vested az., holding in the hand ppr. a hunting-spear, point downwards sa., headed arg.

Locavel, a unicorn sejant arg.

Loch, Baron (Loch), a swan devouring a perch ppr. *Assiduitate, non desidiâ.*

Loch and **Lock,** Scotland, a swan with wings addorsed and holding in the beak a fish, both ppr. *Assiduitate, non desidiâ.* 99. 10

Loch of Drylaw, Edinburgh, Scotland, a swan with wings addorsed swimming in a loch and devouring a perch, all ppr. *Assiduitate, non desidiâ.* *cf.* 99. 9

Loch, Scotland, a swan with wings addorsed devouring a perch, all ppr. 99. 10

Lochead or **Lochhead,** Scotland, a dexter hand erect pointing to the sun with two fingers. 222. 10

Lochée, William Arthur, Esquire, of Oakenhill House, Canterbury, an eagle regardant, holding in the beak a garland of laurel.

Lochore, Scotland, a fox's head couped gu. 33. 4

Lock, a lion rampant holding between its fore-paws a cushion.

Lock of Mildenhall, Suff., a falcon rising or, ducally crowned arg., holding in the beak a padlock pendent sa.

Lock of Warnford, Southamp., a falcon rising or, collared gu., in its beak padlock sa.

Locke of London, a hand ppr., holding up a cushion or. 215. 9

Locke, co. Kildare, Ireland, an eagle's head ppr., beaked or. 83. 1

Locke of Ashton Gifford, Wilts, and Stourcliffe, Hants, a hawk with wings endorsed holding in the beak a padlock, all or.

Locke, Ernest Dalton Burrough, Ferrum Lodge, Seend, Wilts, same crest.

Locke of Lowndes Square, London, a falcon belled or, with wings elevated chequy of the last and az., and resting the dexter claw upon a padlock sa. *Mente non marte.* 88. 4

Locke, Richard Goord Edwal, Esquire, J.P., D.L., of Dane House, Hartlip, near Sittingbourne, Kent, a pelican vulning herself, wings elevated and addorsed sa., two olive-branches in orle vert. *Plenitudo.*

Locker, a buck's head erased ppr. 121. 2

Locker of London, in front of a stag's head erased ppr., attired or, two keys in saltire of the last. *cf.* 121. 2

Lockett, George Alexander, Esquire, of 58, Prince's Gate, Kensington, S.W., upon a rock a stag's head ppr., gorged with a collar engrailed vair, and holding in the mouth a padlock gu. *Non nobis solum.* 297. 2

Lockett, Charles Harrison, Esquire, of Redcliffe, New Brighton, co. Chester, same crest and motto.

Lockett, Richard Robertson, Esquire, of Enmore, Alexandra Drive, Liverpool, same crest and motto.

Lockett, William Jeffery, Esquire, of Grassendale House, Grassendale, Lancs, same crest.

Lockett, Garstang Bradstock, Esquire, of Barnston Towers, Heswall, Chester, same crest and motto.

Lockett, Chesh., a dexter arm in armour embowed ppr., purfled, and holding in the hand a key in fess or. *Teneimus.*

Lockett of Clonterbrook, Chesh., West Houghton and Liverpool, Lancs and Derby, a stag's head couped ppr. 121. 5

Lockey, Herts, Yorks, and Wales, an ostrich's head couped at the neck arg., holding in the beak a key sa.

Lockhart, a dexter hand holding a boar's head erased and erect, all ppr. *Sine labe fides.* 220. 6

Lockhart, Sir Simon, Bart., D.L., of the Lee and Carnwath, Lanarksh., a boar's head erased arg. *Corda serrata pando.* 42. 2

Lockhart of Birkhill, Lanarksh., Scotland, same crest. *Feroci fortior.* 42. 2

Lockhart of Cleghorn, Lanarksh., Scotland, same crest. *Sine labe fides.* 42. 2

Lockhart, Scotland, a boar's head erased ppr. *Corda serrata pando.* 42. 2

Lockhart, a dexter hand holding up a boar's head erased ppr. *Sine labe fides.* cf. 220. 6

Lockhart, Major-General David Blair, Milton Lockhart, Carluke, Lanarksh., same crest. *Feroci fortior.—Corda serrata pando.*

Lockhart, Elliott-, of Borthwickbrae, Selkirk: (1) A boar's head erased arg. 42. 2. (2) A dexter hand holding a spear, all ppr. *Sine labe fides.—Hoc majorum opus.* 214. 11

Lockhart, Elliott-, William, Clegg Hall, Lanarksh., same crests and mottoes.

Lockhart-Wishart, Count: (1) In the centre, in front of two flags, each party per fesse arg. and gu., flotant to the dexter and sinister, a boar's head erased ppr. (2) On the dexter side, on a ducal coronet an eagle displayed regardant. (3) On the sinister side, out of a ducal coronet a demi-lion holding in the dexter paw a sword. *Corda serrata pando.*

Lockhart, Scotland, a fetterlock. *Hoc securior.* 168. 12

Lockhart of Kirktoun, Lanarksh., Scotland, a dexter hand holding a boar's head erased, all ppr. *Feroci fortior.* 220. 6

Lockhart, Scotland, a dexter hand holding a key in bend, all ppr. *Corda serrata pando.* 212. 7

Lockley, James Henry, Esquire, of Avonmore, Stoke Bishop, Bristol, on a wreath of the colours, issuing from a rock two arms embowed in saltire ppr., each holding in the hand an anchor erect sa. *Ex fide fortis.* 200. 5

Locksmith, out of a mural coronet or, a griffin's head ppr. 67. 10

Lockton of Swinsted, Lincs, out of a ducal coronet or, a griffin's head az. 67. 9

Lockton, George Upton, Esquire, of 6, St. Paul's Road, Thornton Heath, in front of a griffin's head couped per pale arg. and az., gorged with a chain, pendent therefrom a padlock, two mullets of six points, all counterchanged. *Concordia tutissima sera.*

Lockwood of Lockwood, Staffs, a camel's head couped sa. 132. 7

Lockwood of Dews Hall, Essex, of Gayton, Northamp., and Surrey, on the stump of a tree erased ppr., a martlet sa.

Lockyer, an astrolabe arg. 167. 7

Lockyer, Plymouth, Devonsh., on the sea a ship, the three topsails hoisted ppr., the main-topsail charged with a lion rampant gu., the fore and mizen topsails each charged with an ant fesseways ppr., a red ensign flying and a pennant arg., at the main top-gallant masthead charged with a cross az. *Sedule et secunde.*

Lockyer, Edmund Stoughton Braithwaite, Esquire, same crest and motto.

Lockyer, Walter Nevill, Esquire, same crest and motto.

Locock, Sir Charles Bird, Bart., on a mount vert, a cock arg., guttée-de-sang, the dexter claw resting on a gauntlet or. *Victoria.* 286. 9

Lodbrook or **Lodbrooke,** a unicorn rampant. 48. 2

Lodder, Captain William Philip James, a demi-griffin charged with a chevron and supporting a Passion cross in bend az. *In Deo confiteor.*

Loder, a stag's head couped at the neck az., between the attires a cross crosslet. cf. 20. 12

Loder, Sir Edmund Giles, Bart., M.A., of Leonardslee, Sussex, a buck's head cabossed, transfixed with an arrow bendwise, the point to the sinister, all ppr., between two escallops or. *Murus aëneus conscientia sana.* 122. 12

Loder, Alfred Basil, Esquire, of Aldwickbury, Harpendon, same crest and motto.

Loder, Gerald Walter Erskine, of Wakehurst Place, Ardingly, Sussex, and Abinger House, Brighton, same crest and motto.

Loder, Reginald Bernhard, Esquire, B.A., of Maidwell Hall, Northampton, and 47, Grosvenor Square, S.W., same crest and motto.

Loder, Wilfrid Hans, Esquire, of High Beeches, Crawley, same crest and motto.

Loder-Symonds, F. C., Esquire, of Hinton Manor, Faringdon, Berks, in front of a well sa., a dolphin naiant embowed vorant a fish arg. *Miseris succurrere disco.* 267. 6

Lodge, Ireland, a talbot's head erased az., collared or. 56. 1

Lodge of Nettlested, Suff., a demi-lion double-queued az. 10. 6

Lodge of London, a demi-lion rampant sa., holding in the paws a cross patée fitchée gu.

Lodge-Ellerton of Bodsilin, Cornw.: (1) A reindeer trippant or, attired and ungu. gu., gorged with a wreath of oak-leaves vert (*for Ellerton*). cf. 125. 9. (2) A demi-lion erased sa., semée-de-lis or, supporting a cross patée fitched gu. (*for Lodge*).

Lodington, a demi-lady ppr., richly attired az., holding in her dexter hand a garland of laurel vert. 183. 5

Lodwich and **Lodwick,** a cock ppr. 91. 2

Loe, a wolf's head couped arg., gorged with a collar gu., thereon three bezants. cf. 30. 9

Lofft, Henry Capel, Esquire, of Glemham House, Suff., a boar's head couped and erect arg., holding in the mouth a cross crosslet fitchée gu., between two branches of oak fructed ppr. *Fide et fortitudine.*

Lofft, Robert Emlyn, of Troston, Bury St. Edmunds, Suff., a demi-lion rampant holding in his paws a cross crosslet fitchée. *Fide et fortitudine.* cf. 11. 10

Loft of Healing, Lincs, a wolf's head couped gu., charged on the neck with a pheon, and transfixed through the mouth by a broken spear or.

Lofthouse, between two wings a spur, all ppr. 111. 13

Loftie of Tanderagee, co. Armagh, Ireland, a boar's head erect and erased arg., tusked or. *Prend moy tel que je suis.—Loyal au mort.* 43. 3

Loftus, *see* Ely, Marquess of.

Loftus, Ireland, a boar's head erect and erased arg., armed or, langued gu. *Loyal à mort.—Prend mois tel que je suis.* 43. 3

Loftus, a dexter hand holding a dagger, all ppr. 212. 3

Loftus of Woolland, Dorset, a boar's head couped and erect arg., langued gu. cf. 43. 3

Loftus, Ireland, same crest. *Loyal au mort.* cf. 43. 3

Logan, Ireland, a demi-lion rampant vert. 10. 2

Logan of Restalrig, co. Edinburgh, Scotland, a bugle-horn stringed ppr. 228. 11

Logan of that ilk, Scotland, a Passion nail piercing a man's heart, all ppr. *Hoc majorum virtus.* 181. 4

Loges, a swan collared and lined, all ppr. 99. 1

Loggan and **Logon** of Staverton, Berks, and Bucks, a stag's head erased gu., attired, collared, and lined or. cf. 121. 2

Loggie, a goat's head az. 128. 12

Loggie, Scotland, a dexter hand holding a rose gu., stalked and leaved vert. 218. 10

Loghlan, Scotland, a swan. *Divina sibi canit.* 99. 2

Loghlin, an anchor cabled ppr. 161. 2

Logie of Boddam, Aberdeensh., a dexter hand pointing with two fingers ppr. *Tam marte quam arte.* 222. 11

Login, Sir J. S., of Southend, Orkney, a dexter arm in armour embowed and gauntleted ppr., garnished or, holding erect a tilting-spear, also ppr., therefrom flowing a pennon gu., charged with a cross patée or. *By the grace of God.*

Logy, Scotland, a dexter hand holding a rose stalked and leaved, all ppr. 218. 10

Lomas, on a chapeau a pelican vulning herself, all ppr. 98. 7

Lomax of Parkhurst, Surrey, a demi-greyhound arg., collared gu. 60. 8

Lomax of St. George's, Hanover Square, Westminster, issuing from a heart a dexter hand brandishing a scimitar, all ppr. 213. 4

Lomax of Clayton Hall, Lancs, out of a mural coronet a demi-lion gu., collared, holding an escallop. *Fato prudentia major.*

Lomax, Herts, out of a ducal coronet or, a demi-lion gu., holding an escallop or. cf. 13. 10

Lomax, Richard, Esquire, of the Inner Temple, London, a demi-lion erased per bend or and gu., charged with two fleurs-de-lis counterchanged, and holding between the paws an escallop gu., within an annulet or. *Nil nisi de jure.*

Lombe, Edward Henry Evans, of Bylaugh and Great Melton, Norf., two tilting-spears in saltire or, each having a small pennon gu. *Propositi tenax.* 175. 10

Lombe, Alexander Francis, Esquire, same crest and motto.

Lombe, Rev. Henry Evans, B.A., of Melton Hall, Great Melton, Norf., and Melton Lodge, Great Yarmouth, same crest and motto.

Lomelying, a demi-lion rampant arg. *Fortiter et recte.* 10. 2

Lomener, Lomneir, and **Lomnyer,** between two wings arg., a unicorn's head sa., armed and crined or.

Lomner, a unicorn's head sa., winged arg., armed or, holding in the mouth a rose ppr.

Lomond, out of a coronet or, a tower ppr. *cf.* 156. 2

Londesborough, Earl of (Denison): (1) Issuant from clouds an arm in bend ppr., vested gu., cuffed erm., and charged with a covered cup or, the forefinger pointing to an estoile radiated or (*for Denison*). (2) A unicorn's head erased arg., maned and armed or (*for Conyngham*). *Adversa virtute repello.* 49. 5

Londeth, a winged heart ppr. 112. 10

Londham, on a chapeau ppr., an escallop sa. *cf.* 141. 11

London, William, of Quay House, Woodbridge, out of a tower a demi-man in armour in profile, holding in the dexter hand a sword by the blade erect.

Londonderry, Marquess of (Vane-Tempest-Stewart): (1) In the centre a dragon statant or (*for Stewart*). *cf.* 73. 2. (2) A griffin's head erased per pale arg. and sa., beaked gu. (*for Tempest*). 66. 2. (3) A dexter gauntlet erect holding a sword ppr., pommel and hilt or (*for Vane*). *Metuenda corolla draconis.*

Lone of London, a demi-buck salient. *I am lone.* 119. 2

Lone, Kent, and of Warlingham and Elloure, Suff., a demi-buck salient arg., attired or. 119. 2

Lonesby, a coney arg. 136. 1

Loney, a cubit arm vested compony or and gu., holding in the hand an anchor ppr., ringed sa. 208. 3

Long, Baron Farnborough (*extinct*), out of a ducal coronet or, a lion's head arg., guttée-de-sang. *Ingenuas suscipit artes.* *cf.* 17. 5

Long, Captain Samuel, Esquire, R.N., same crest. *Pieux quoique preux.*

Long of London, a lion's head erased per pale arg. and sa., charged with three guttes counterchanged two and one. *cf.* 17. 8

Long, out of a ducal coronet of five leaves or, a demi-lion rampant arg. *cf.* 16. 3

Long, Rt. Hon. Walter Hume, 97, Lennox Gardens, S.W., out of a ducal coronet or, a demi-lion rampant arg. *Pieux quoique preux.*

Long of Draycot, Wilts: (1) Out of a ducal coronet or, a demi-lion rampant arg. 16. 3. (2) A lion's head arg., holding in the mouth a hand erased gu.

Long, Colonel William, C.M.G., D.L., J.P., of Woodlands, Congresbury, Somers., and Newton House, Clevedon, Somers., a lion's head arg., erased or, charged with two crosses crosslet sa., holding in the mouth a dexter hand erased at the wrist. *Pieux quoique preux.*

Long, Rev. Thomas, M.A., of Castle Roberts, Jamestown, Finglas, co. Dublin, and 16, Appian Way, Dublin, a demi-lion rampant per fesse erm. and erminois, holding between the paws a cross crosslet arg. *Virtute et probitate.*

Long of Potterne, Little Cheverell, Melksam, and of Collingbourne Kingston, Wilts, out of a ducal coronet or, a demi-lion rampant arg. *Pieux quoique preux.* 16. 3

Long, Ireland, out of a ducal coronet or, a lion's head gu. 17. 5

Long of Clerkenwell, London, a lion's head erased per pale arg. and sa., charged with three guttes counterchanged. *cf.* 17. 8

Long of Trowbridge, Wilts, out of a crescent or, a lion's head sa., guttée-d'eau.

Long, Walter, Esquire, of Preshaw House, Bishop's Waltham, Hants, out of a ducal coronet or, a demi-lion rampant arg.

Long of London, a lion's head erased gu. *Iram leonis noli timere.* 17. 2

Long of Longville, Jamaica, and Hampton Lodge, Surrey, out of a ducal coronet or, a lion's head arg., guttée-de-sang. *Pieux quoique preux.* *cf.* 17. 5

Long, William Evelyn, Esquire, of Hurts Hall, Saxmundham, same crest and motto.

Long of Rowde Ashton, Wilts, on a ducal coronet a lion's head erased sa., guttée-d'eau. *cf.* 17. 5

Long of West Hackney, Middx., upon a mount in front of a tree ppr., a wyvern couchant vert. *Confide recte agens.*

Long of Swinthorpe, Norf., on a mount vert, a greyhound courant sa., collared and lined erm. *cf.* 58. 2

Long, Fortescue Walter Kellet, Esquire, of Dunston, Norf., same crest.

Longbottom, a horse's head ppr. *cf.* 50. 31

Longchamp or **Longchampe,** a tower triple-towered ppr. 157. 6

Longcroft, Charles Beare, Esquire, of Hall Place, Havant, a demi-lion rampant arg., holding between the paws three annulets interlaced or, and charged on the shoulder with a saltire gu. *Nunc ut olim.*

Longcroft, Worcs., a bull's head couped. *cf.* 44. 3

Longden, on a chapeau gu., turned up or, a dove with wings addorsed az. 94. 10

Longden of Bramcote Hills, Notts, an eagle with wings expanded ppr., charged on the breast and on either wing with an escallop az., and supporting with the dexter claw a buck's head cabossed, also ppr. 78. 11

Longden, Rev. Henry Isham, Rector of Shangton, Leics., a lizard ppr. *Spem longum reseces.*

Longe, Glouc., in a ducal coronet a phœnix in flames, all ppr. 82. 5

Longe, Robert Bacon, of Spixworth Park, Norf., a lion sejant erect gu., holding between the paws a saltier engrailed or. *Pro fide ac patriæ.*

Longe of New Ross, co. Wexford, Ireland, on a ducal coronet or, a lion rampant sa., armed and langued gu. *cf.* 1. 13

Longevile, on a mural coronet a stag sejant, all ppr. 116. 4

Longeville, Bucks and Hants, a talbot's head gu., eared and gorged with a fesse dancettée arg. *cf.* 56. 12

Longeville, Thomas, of Penyllan, Oswestry, Shropsh., same crest.

Longfield, Viscount Longueville, Ireland, same crest and motto.

Longfield, Richard Edmund, Esquire, J.P., of Longueville, Mallow, co. Cork, out of a ducal coronet or, a demi-lion rampant gu. *Parcere subjectis.* 16. 3

Longfield, Mountifort John Courtenay, Esquire, J.P., D.L., of Castle Mary, Cloyne, Ireland, same crest and motto.

Longfield, H. F., of Grange Erin, Douglas, Cork, out of a ducal coronet of five leaves a demi-lion rampant gu.

Longford, Earl of (*extinct*), *see* Aungier.

Longford, Earl of (Pakenham), out of a mural crown or, a demi-eagle displayed gu. *Gloria virtutis umbra.* 80. 8

Longford, a boar's head erased az. 42. 2

Longham, Scotland, a bear's head erased ppr., muzzled or. 35. 2

Longhurst, out of a ducal coronet or, a griffin's head holding in the beak a key ppr. 65. 14

Longland, an anchor in pale. 161. 1

Longland, in the sea an anchor in bend sinister. 161. 8

Longland, an arm couped, vested or, pellettée, holding in the hand ppr. a cross crosslet fitched gu.

Longland, on the stump of a tree eradicated and couped or, a dove arg. *cf.* 92. 2

Longland of Toymoke, Bucks, on a mount vert, a garb or. 153. 13

Longlands, Scotland, an anchor. 161. 1

Longley, an arm embowed, couped at the shoulder, resting on the elbow, holding a sword in pale enfiled with a savage's head couped ppr. 201. 7

Longman, a dexter hand in fess holding an anchor in pale environed with clouds, all ppr. 223. 4

Longman, William Churchill, Esquire, in front of an oak-tree ppr., a greyhound sejant erm., holding in the mouth a trefoil or, and resting the dexter forepaw on a rose gu. 59. 14

Longmore, John Constantine Gordon, Esquire, of the Paddock, Woolstone, Hants, a caduceus erect or, in front of two flagstaves in saltire ppr., flowing from each a banner gu., charged with a lozenge erm., thereon a cross couped, also gu. *In omnibus caritas.*

Longmore, Charles Elton, Porthill House, Hertford, a laurel-branch in bend surmounted by a sword, point upwards, in bend sinister, all ppr. *In utrumque paratus.*

Longridge of Wallbottle, an arm embowed vested, holding in the hand a garb.

Longsdon, a fox's head erased arg. 33. 6

Longsdon, an eagle displayed with two heads or. 74. 2

Longspeare, a talbot's head couped paly of four or and gu., holding in the mouth a demi-hare erased az.

Longspee, on a sphere sa., winged or, an eagle with wings displayed ppr. 159. 9

Longstaff, a stag at gaze under a tree, all ppr. 116. 12

Longstaff, a demi-lien rampant supporting between its paws a quarterstaff, all ppr.

Longstaff, Lieutenant-Colonel Llewellyn W. Longstaff, of Ridgelands, Wimbledon, two arms, dexter and sinister, embowed vested sa., semée-de-lis arg., cuffed of the last, holding in the hands ppr. a quarterstaff fessewise or. *Vigilate.* 203. 13

Longstaff, George Blundell, Esquire, of Highlands, Putney Heath, London, S.W., and Twitchen, Morthoe R.S.O., Devonsh., two arms embowed vested sa., semée-de-lis and cuffed arg., the hands ppr. grasping a quarterstaff fessewise or. *Vigilate.* 203. 13

Longueuil, Baron de, of Longueuil, in the Province of Quebec, Canada (Charles Colmore Grant), a burning hill ppr. *Stand sure.* 179. 2

Longueville, Thomas, Esquire, J.P., of Llanforda, Oswestry, a talbot's head couped gu., eared and charged with a fesse dancettée arg. *Till then thus.* cf. 56. 12

Longueville, Thomas, of Penylan, Shropsh., a talbot's head gu., eared arg., gorged with a collar dancettée of the last. *Till then thus.* cf. 56. 12

Longworth of Longworth, Lancs. a boar's head couped, holding in the mouth a sword ppr. cf. 42. 6

Longworth, Thomas James, Esquire, of Walworth House, Cheltenham, on a mount vert, a talbot's head erased sa., holding in the mouth a sword in bend ppr., point downwards, pommel and hilt or, between two trefoils slipped vert. *Fidèle pour toujours.* 267. 5

Lonsdale, Earl of (Lowther), Westml., a dragon passant arg. *Magistratus indicat virum.* 73. 2

Lonsdale, a bull passant gu. cf. 45. 2

Lonsdale, Yorks, a demi-stag salient erased gu., charged on the body with a crescent sa., attired, ungu., and collared of the last, the collar charged with three crescents.

Lonsdale, Captain Henry Heywood, Shavington, Market Drayton: (1) A demi-stag gu., guttée-d'or, attired and collared or (*for Lonsdale*). cf. 119. 2. (2) Upon a mount vert, the trunk of a tree with two branches sprouting therefrom and entwined by ivy, thereon a falcon with wings displayed ppr. (*for Heywood*). cf. 87. 12

Lonyson of London, between two ostrich-feathers or, a swan issuant ppr.

Looker, a pillar ensigned with a heart gu. 176. 5

Lopes, Rt. Hon. Sir Massey, Bart., of Maristow, Devonsh.: (1) A lion sejant erminois, gorged with a collar gemelle gu., resting the dexter paw on a lozenge az. (*for Lopes*). 282. 10. (2) A dexter arm couped and embowed, habited purp., purfled or, the cuff arg., holding in the hand ppr. a palm-branch vert (*for Franco*). *Quod tibi, id ali.—Sub pace copia.* 282. 11

Lorain of Angelraw, Berwicksh., Scotland, an armed dexter arm, from the elbow erect, holding a branch of laurel ppr. *Lauro resurgo.*

Loraine, *see* Lorrayne.

Loraine, Sir Lambton, Bart.: On the dexter side, on a mount, a bay-laurel tree ppr., depending from a branch thereof by a belt gu., edged and buckled or, and surmounting the trunk a shield az. (*for Loraine*). On the sinister side, issuant from a naval crown or, a dexter arm embowed, encircled by a wreath of laurel ppr., the hand grasping a trident erect of the first (*crest of honourable augmentation granted to Sir Philip Broke of Nacton*). *Sævumque tridentem servamus.—Lauro scutoque resurgo.*

Lorance of St. Ives, Hunts, an antelope's head erased ppr., attired or, and ducally gorged arg. cf. 126. 2

Lorand, on a tower arg., a martlet sa. 156. 9

Lord, in a maunch az., cuffed or, a dexter arm, the hand clenched ppr. 203. 3

Lord, John Courtenay, Esquire, J.P., F.R.G.S., Cotsford, Solihull, Warw., same crest. *Dominus salus mea.*

Lord, Ireland, a sword and a garb in saltier, all ppr. 153. 7

Lord, Ireland, a dove or, holding in its beak an olive-branch ppr. 92. 5

Lord, Sir Riley, J.P., of Highfield Hall, Gosforth, Northumb., upon a rock ppr., in front of a tower sa., a hind arg., resting the dexter leg on a pheon gu. *Virtute et labore.*

Lorimer, a mascle gu. 167. 9

Lorimer, Scotland, a lion's head erased. 17. 8

Lorimer, Scotland, a lion rampant ppr., holding in the dexter paw a fleur-de-lis or. 2. 7

Lorimer, a horse current arg. *Nulla salus bello.* 52. 8

Lorimer of Edinburgh, a horse courant arg. *Virtutis gloria merces.* 52. 8

Lorimer, Scotland, issuing out of a cloud a hand in fess pointing to a crosier erect issuing from the wreath. 223. 2

Lorimer, in a maunch an arm embowed and couped at the shoulder, the elbow resting on the wreath. 203. 1

Lorimer of Kellyfield, Forfarsh., Scotland, two eagle's wings conjoined and expanded ppr., surmounted of a cross crosslet fitchée gu. *Upward.—Onward.* cf. 113. 1

Loring and **Loringe,** a hand holding a mill-rind.

Loringe of Chalgrave, Beds, the leaves of a plant issuing from a flower-pot.

Lorn, Scotland, a boar's head erased. *Ne obliviscaris.* 42. 2

Lorne, Marquess of, *see* Argyll, Duke of.

Lornie, Guthrie-, John, Birnam, Perthsh., a dexter arm issuing holding a drawn sword ppr. *Sto pro veritate.*

Lorrayne and **Lorreyne,** an escutcheon az., suspended from a palm-tree, all ppr.

Lorsor of Kellow, Durh., a wolf sejant ppr., holding in the mouth an arrow erect or, barbed and feathered arg.

Lort, Bart. (*extinct*), of Stacpoole Court, Pembrokesh., an Ionic pillar and base arg. 176. 3

Lort, same crest. *Steady.*

Lorton, Viscount, *see* Kingston, Earl of.

Losack, out of a cloud a dexter hand holding an anchor in pale, all ppr. 219. 2

Losada, *see* Lousada.

Loscombe of Bristol, Somers., a demi-leopard ppr., collared gu., holding in the dexter paw a cross moline or.

Losh, a cubit arm ppr., the hand holding up a crescent or. 216. 8

Losse of Cobdock, Suff., a cubit arm in pale vested gu., holding in the hand ppr. a fleur-de-lis per pale arg. and sa.

Losse of Stanmore, Middx., a lion's head erased per saltire arg. and sa., charged with four guttes counterchanged. cf. 17. 8

Loten of St. James's, Westminster, Middx., a gilliflower ppr., between two wings erect, the dexter or, the sinister vert.

Loterel, Scotland, a lion passant ppr. 6. 2

Loth and **Lothe,** an arrow and a bow in saltier ppr. cf. 173. 12

Lothian, Marquess of (Kerr): (1) The sun in splendour ppr. (2) A stag's head cabossed arg. *Sero sed serio.* 162. 2

Lothian of Edinburgh and Overgogar, Scotland, a bugle-horn arg., garnished or, stringed az. *Non dormit, qui custodit.* 228. 11

Lotysham, Somers., on a ducal coronet gu., an otter's head erased or, holding in the mouth a fish ppr.

Loubis, Devonsh. and Cornw., a bear rampant sa., muzzled and lined arg.

Loudon, Scotland, a bugle-horn. *Non dormit, qui custodit.* 228. 9

Loudon, Scotland, a hand plucking a rose ppr. 218. 13

Loudon, Scotland, a phœnix with two heads in flames, all ppr. *I byde my time.* 82. 12

Loudoun, Earl of (formerly Abney-Hastings, now Rawdon-Hastings): (1) A bull's head erased ermines, armed and ducally gorged arg. (*for Hastings*). 44. 2. (2) A demi-lion rampant or, the sinister paw resting upon an antique shield charged with the arms of Hastings, viz.: "arg., a maunch within a bordure engrailed sa." (*for Abney*). *In veritate victoria.—Trust winneth troth.*

Loudoun, Scotland, an eagle displayed arg., charged on the breast with a cinquefoil gu. cf. 74. 14

Loughborough, Lord, *see* Rosslyn, Bart.

Loughnan, Ireland, a castle triple-towered ppr. *Fortis et fidus.* 155. 8

Louis of Colyton House, Devonsh., in front of clouds ppr., a decrescent or. *Doucement mais fermement.* cf. 163. 1

Louis, Sir Charles, Bart., of Chelston, Devonsh., a griffin's head erased az., between two wings elevated or, holding in the beak a fleur-de-lis, and charged on the breast with a trident erect gold. *In Canopo ut ad Canopum.* 284. 8

Louis, a wolf rampant arg. 28. 2

Louis of Merchiston, Scotland, a hand holding a lance in bend ppr. *Nos aspera juvant.*

Lounde, a hind sejant regardant ppr., resting the dexter foot on a bee-hive ppr. 125. 1

Louris, Devonsh., and of Ogbery, Beardo, and Trantock, Cornw., a bear rampant sa., muzzled and lined arg.

Lousada, Colonel Horace de, **Duke de Losada,** of Losada, a Grandee of the first class in the Kingdom of Spain,

upon a mount vert, a dove regardant arg., wings expanded or, holding in the beak a sprig of olive ppr. *El honor es mia guia.*

Lousada of Peak House, Devonsh., on a mount vert, a dove regardant arg., with wings expanded or, charged on the neck with a bar gemel of the last, and holding in its beak a sprig ppr. *Honneur me guide.*

Louth, Baron of (Plunkett), a horse passant arg. *Festina lente.* 52. 6

Louthfuttis, Scotland, a swan naiant in water with wings addorsed, all ppr. *Addicunt aves.* 99. 9

Louthian, a bugle-horn stringed ppr. *Non dormit, qui custodit.* 228. 11

Lovaine, Lord, *see* Northumberland, Duke of.

Lovat, Baron (Fraser), a buck's head erased ppr., attired arg. *Je suis prêt.* 121. 2

Lovatt of Clayton Hall, Staffs, a demi-wolf rampant sa. 31. 2

Lovatt, Henry, Esquire, of Low Hill, Bushbury, Wolverhampton, a lion rampant. 1. 13

Lovatt, James, J.P., the Cloughs, Newcastle-under-Lyme, in front of a tower triple-towered arg., a wolf passant sa., supporting with the dexter leg an anchor, also arg. *Spe.* 200. 15

Lovayne, *see* Loveyne.

Love, Scotland, a buffalo's head erased gu., armed or, eared arg. 44. 1

Love of Aynho, Northamp., and of Broughton, Oxon., a demi-greyhound rampant arg., collared and lined sa., the end of the line coiled. *cf.* 60. 8

Love of Basing, Hants, on a cross formée fitchée gu., a bird arg.

Love of Norton and Goudhurst, Kent, and Oxon., out of a ducal coronet or, a cross formée gu., thereon a bird arg.

Love of Kirksted, Norf., a heraldic tiger's head erased vert, maned arg. *cf.* 25. 4

Love of Sevenoaks, Kent, a demi-buck. 119. 2

Love, a hand holding an annulet ppr. 216. 1

Love, Kent, on a chapeau gu., turned up erm., a lion passant arg. 4. 9

Loveband, Captain John Edgcombe, a boar's head erect and erased. *Sapere aude incipe.*

Loveday, Suff. and Norf., a squirrel ppr. *cf.* 135. 7

Loveday, John Edward Taylor, of Williamscote, Oxon., an eagle displayed wih two heads per pale sa. and arg., armed, membered, and ducally gorged or. *Cum prima luce.* *cf.* 74. 2

Loveden of Fyfield and Buscot, Berks, a leopard sejant or, ducally gorged arg. *Manus juxta nardus.* *cf.* 24. 3

Loveis of Hennock, Devonsh., a bear sejant sa. 34. 8

Lovejoy, a cubit arm in armour holding in the hand a caltrap. 210. 7

Lovelace, Earl of (formerly Rt. Hon. William King-Noel, now Milbanke): (1) A buck at gaze arg., attired or (*for Noel*). 117. 3. (2) A dexter arm erect couped at the elbow, vested az., adorned wth three ermine-spots in fesse or, the cuff turned up, grasping the truncheon of a spear, the head arg. (*for King*). (3) A lion's head couped gu., charged with a bend erm. (*for Milbanke*). *Pensez à bien.*

Lovelace of Hurley, Berks, and of Lovelace and Canterbury, Kent, a staff raguly vert, surmounted by an eagle displayed arg. 75. 3

Loveland, Norf., a boar's head and neck couped sa. 41. 1

Loveland of Nettleswell, near Marlow, Essex: (1) A dexter cubit arm in armour ppr., charged with a fret sa., encircled by a wreath of oak, and holding in the hand a scimitar, also ppr. (2) A stag lodged ppr., guttée-de-larmes, and resting the dexter foot on a bezant. *Opes industria parit.*

Lovelass, out of a ducal coronet or, a dexter arm ppr., vested purp., cuffed arg., holding up the sun in splendour. 209. 2

Lovelass, a dexter arm ppr., issuing from a ducal coronet or.

Loveless, a demi-talbot ppr. *cf.* 55. 8

Loveley, Northamp. and Norf., an estoile pierced or. *cf.* 164. 1

Lovell, a garb ppr., banded gu. 153. 2

Lovell, Worcs., a garb vert, banded or. 153. 2

Lovell, Peter Audley David Arthur, Esquire, of Cole Park, Malmesbury, Wilts, a garb fessewise or, thereon a squirrel sejant gu., cracking a nut ppr. (*for Lovell*). (2) On a rock ppr., a lion passant gardant sa., semée-de-lis, and holding in the dexter paw a fleur-de-lis or (*for Pugh*). *Propositi tenax.*

Lovell, Norf., a squirrel sejant ppr., cracking a nut. 135. 7

Lovell, Dorset, a wolf passant az., bezantée, collared and lined or. 28. 10

Lovell of Terant, Dorset, same crest. *cf.* 28. 10

Lovell, a talbot passant arg. *Tempus omnia monstrat.* 54. 1

Lovell of Chilcote Manor and Dinder and Skelton, Yorks, a talbot current arg.

Lovell of Laxfield, Suff., a greyhound passant sa., collared, ringed, and lined or, a cubit arm erect ppr., vested purp., holding the line.

Lovell of Barton and Harling, Norf., a peacock's tail erect ppr., belted sa., rimmed and buckled arg., the end pendent.

Lovelock, a greyhound passant sa. *cf.* 60. 2

Loveney, a griffin sejant the wings addorsed ppr. 62. 10

Lovetot and **Lovetoft,** a demi-lady holding in her dexter hand a pair of scales. 183. 2

Lovett, Bart. (*extinct*), of Liscombe, Bucks, a wolf's head erased sa. 30. 8

Lovett, Percival Cosby Ernest, Liscombe House, Leighton Buzzard, Bucks, same crest.

Lovett, Major Hubert Richard, Esquire, of Henlle Hall, Ruabon, a wolf passant ppr. *Spe.*

Loveyne, a cross crosslet fitched or. 166. 2

Lovibond, *see* Impey-Lovibond.

Lovibond, Bucks, a buck's head. 121. 5

Lovibond of Hatfield, Peverell, Essex, a boar's head couped and erect gu. *cf.* 43. 3

Lovis, a lion's head erased gu., on the head a chapeau arg., turned up erm. 21. 10

Lovise, a mound gu., the band and cross or. 159. 12

Low, a wolf passant ppr. 28. 10

Low, a wolf passant arg. 28. 10

Low of Galbally, co. Limerick, Ireland, a wolf's head erased or, charged with an annulet gu. *Facta non verba.* *cf.* 6. 8

Low, Francis Wise, Esquire, of Kilshane, co. Tipperary, Sillaherdane, Kilgarvin, co. Kerry, and 37, Cadogan Square, S.W., a wolf's head erased or, charged with an annulet gu. *Facta non verba.*

Low, Lieutenant-Colonel John Maxwell, of Sunvale, Killmallock, co. Limerick, same crest and motto.

Low, Scotland, a falcon regardant holding in its dexter claw a laurel crown, all ppr. 85. 4

Low, William Malcolm, Esquire, of Clatto Cupar, Fifesh., N.B., and 22, Roland Gardens, S.W., out of a mural crown a dexter arm vambraced, the hand grasping a scimitar ppr. *Fortitudine et fide.*

Low of Aberdeen, Scotland, a leaf between two thistles stalked and leaved, all ppr. *Aspera me juvant.*

Lowcay of Lipson Terrace, Plymouth, Devonsh., a boar's head erect and erased ppr., charged with a bar arg., thereon a trefoil vert. *Virtute et valore.* *cf.* 43. 3

Lowde of Kirkham, Lancs, a bugle-horn sa., stringed or. 228. 11

Lowdell, a sphinx couchant gardant with wings endorsed. *cf.* 182. 14

Lowdell, Edward Lohet, Esquire, of Junior Army and Navy Club, issuant from a bugle-horn or, a demi-lion sa., holding between the paws an escallop or. *Nemini obesse sed omnibus prodesse.*

Lowdell, Hubert Henry, Esquire, of Baldwin's Hill, Surrey, near East Grinstead, same crest and motto.

Lowdell, Sydney Poole, Esquire, of Baldwin's, Lingfield, Surrey, near East Grinstead, same crest and motto.

Lowdell, Edward, of 18, Randolph Road, Maida Hill, W., same crest and motto.

Lowden, on a ducal coronet a wyvern vomiting fire at both ends, all ppr. *cf.* 69. 9

Lowder, out of a mural coronet seven halberds facing outwards ppr.

Lowdes, a wyvern arg. 70. 1

Lowdham, Suff., between two palm-branches an escallop, all ppr. 141. 4

Lowe, *see* Sherbrooke, Viscount.

Lowe, a wolf passant arg. (*Another*, ppr.) 28. 10

Lowe, a wolf passant arg., collared and chained gu., the chain reflexed over back. *cf.* 28. 10

Lowe, Drury-, William Drury Nathaniel, of Locko Park, Derbysh.: (1) A wolf passant ppr. (*for Lowe*). 28. 10. (2) A greyhound current sa., collared, and charged on the body with two mullets in fess or (*for Drury*). *Duty leads me.*—*Droyt et devaunt.*

Lowe, Derbysh., a wolf passant arg. 28. 10

Lowe of Highfield, Notts, a wolf passant arg., collared and chained gu., the chain reflexed over the back. *Innocentia quamvis in agro sanguinis.* cf. 28. 10
Lowe, Arthur Courtald Willoughby, Esquire, of Gosfield Hall, Halstead, Essex, same crest and motto.
Lowe, Wilts, a wolf's head couped arg., collared or. 30. 9
Lowe of Walden, Essex, a wolf's head couped ppr., collared and ringed or. cf 30. 9
Lowe of Clifton Reynes, Bucks, a wolf's head erased arg. 30. 8
Lowe of Bromsgrove, Worcs., a demi-griffin segreant or. *Spero meliora.* 64. 2
Lowe, H. B., Esquire, the Grey House, Barnt Green, Worcs., a wolf's head erased, collared. *Spero meliora.*
Lowe, Staffs, a demi-griffin segreant erased arg. cf. 64. 2
Lowe of Lowe, Worcs., a demi-griffin segreant or. *Spero meliora.* 64. 2
Lowe, George Sidney Strode, Esquire, of 1, Collingwood Villas, Stoke, Devonport, same crest and motto.
Lowe, a wyvern vert. 70. 1
Lowe, Derbysh., on a mount vert, a heath-cock ppr., winged or. 89. 8
Lowe of Bromley, Kent, and London, a falcon with wings extended or. 87. 1
Lowe of Westminster, Middx., two keys in saltier or, interlaced with a chaplet ppr.
Lowe, Frederick Carnegie, Whitehall, Devonsh., same crest.
Lowe, of Shrewsbury, Shropsh., and Calne, Wilts, an erm. passant ppr., collared or, lined and ringed gu. 134. 9
Lowe of Southmills, Beds, Middx., and Herts, out of a mural coronet gu., a wolf's head arg., transfixed by a spear or, headed of the second.
Lowe, a lion's head erased regardant. cf. 17. 6
Lowe, Hill-, Arthur Ommanney, Court of Hill, Tenbury, a demi-griffin rampant or. *Spero meliora.*
Lowen of London, a stag statant quarterly per pale indented or and az., the dexter attire of the last, and the sinister of the first. 117. 5
Lower of Trelaske, Cornw., a unicorn's head erased arg. 49. 5
Lower of St. Winnow Barton, Polmawgan, Tremeere and Lezant, Cornw., a unicorn's head erased quarterly arg. and sa. 49. 5
Lowfield, a bull's head erased sa. 44. 3
Lowis, Scotland, a hand holding a spear in pale ppr. cf. 214. 11
Lowle, Somers., and of Yardley, Worcs., a stag's head cabossed or, between the attires a pheon az. cf. 122. 5
Lowman of Whitstone and Brokeland, Devonsh., a lion's gamb erect and erased sa., holding a battle-axe or. 38. 3
Lownde, a hind regardant ppr., resting its dexter foot on a bee-hive ppr. 125. 1
Lownde of Jekesford, Cambs, on a mount vert, a griffin sejant with wings addorsed or. cf. 62. 10
Lownde, Lincs, on a ducal coronet or, a hawk close of the same, beaked and legged arg. 85. 9
Lowndes of Palterton, Derbysh., a lion's head erased or, gorged with a chaplet vert. 290. 1
Lowndes or **Lownds,** England and Scotland, a dove volant over water holding in the beak an olive-branch ppr. 93. 11
Lowndes, the Bury, Chesham, Bucks, a leopard's head erased at the neck, gorged with a laurel-branch ppr. cf. 23. 10
Lowndes, Stone-, Bucks and Oxon.: (1) A leopard's head and neck erased or, gorged with laurel ppr. (*for Lowndes*). cf. 23. 10. (2) Out of a ducal coronet or, a griffin's head erm. (*for Stone*). *Mediocra firma.* 67. 9
Lowndes, George Allan, of Barrington Hall, Essex: (1) A lion's head erased or (*for Lowndes*). 17. 8. (2) A dexter arm embowed in armour, the hand in a gauntlet grasping a sword in bend sinister, the point downwards ppr., pommel and hilt or, pendant from the wrist by a riband, an escutcheon gold, charged with a griffin's head erased az. (*for Clayton*). cf. 201. 4
Lowndes, Selby-, William, Selby House, Bletchley, Bucks: (1) A leopard's head erased at the neck or, gorged with a laurel-branch ppr. (*for Lowndes*). (2) A Saracen's head affrontée ppr., wreathed round the temples or and sa., at the back a quiver with arrows, also ppr., slung across the left shoulder by a belt az., studded with bezants (*for Selby*). *Ways and means.*
Lowndes, William, Chesham, Bucks, same crests.
Lowndes, F.S.A., 140, Ashley Gardens, Westminster, S.W., a lion's head erased gorged with a wreath of laurel. *Macte virtute esto.* 290. 1
Lowndes of Hassall Hall, Chesh., a lion's head erased or. 17. 8
Lowndes, Oxon., a leopard's head erased at the neck or, gorged with a laurel-branch ppr. cf. 23. 2
Lowndes of Morden, Surrey, a goat arg., armed, unguled, collared, and the line reflexed over the back or, charged on the shoulder for difference with a rose gu. cf. 129. 5
Lowndes, Edward Chaddock, Castle Combe, Chippenham: (1) A lion's head erased or, gorged with a wreath of laurel vert. 290. 1 (2) A pheon or, the shaft entwined with a serpent ppr. (*for Gorst*).
Lownes, a hydra with seven heads. 73. 3
Lowrie or **Lowry,** a cat current gardant ppr. 26. 6
Lowrs, Devonsh. and Cornw., a bear rampant sa., muzzled and lined or.
Lowry, *see* Belmore, Earl.
Lowry, *see* Rowton, Baron.
Lowry, Ireland, between two branches of laurel, a garland of the same ppr. *Virtus semper viridis.—Floreant lauri.* 257. 12
Lowry, Robert William, Esquire, B.A., of Pomeroy House, Pomeroy, co. Tyrone, two laurel-branches interfretted ppr. *Floreant lauri.—Virtus semper viridis.*
Lowry, Cumb., two laurel-sprigs in orle ppr. 146. 5
Lowry, Ireland, a fox's head couped gu. 33. 4
Lowry-Corry, Hon. Henry William, of Edwardstone Hall, Boxford, Suff.: (1) A cock ppr., charged with a crescent gu. (*for Corry*). (2) A garland between two laurel-branches of the same, all ppr. (*for Lowry*). 257. 12
Lowry, Lieutenant-General Robert William, C.B., of Aughnablaney, co. Fermanagh, and of 25, Warrington Crescent, London, W., between two branches of laurel a garland of the same. 257. 12
Lows, Scotland, a lion rampant or. 1. 13
Lowsley, Barzillai, Esquire, Lieutenant-Colonel Royal Engineers (retired), of Linnholm, the Thicket, Southsea, Hants, on a chapeau gu., turned up erm., a millstone arg., with millrind or. *An I may.*
Lowsley, Lionel Dewe, Esquire, of Hampstead Norreys, near Newbury, Berks, same crest and motto.
Lowste, a dexter hand ppr., holding up a fleur-de-lis 215. 5
Lowten of Manley, Chesh., a demi-griffin per fess, indented erminois and erm., the wings elevated sa., holding in the dexter claw a cross crosslet fitched az. cf. 64. 2
Lowtham, an antelope's head gu., collared erm. cf. 126. 2
Lowthen, a dragon's head with wings addorsed, pierced through the breast by a spear.
Lowther, Earl of Lonsdale, *see* Lonsdale.
Lowther, Sir Charles Bingham, Bart., of Swillington, Yorks, a dragon passant arg. *Magistratus indicat virum.* 73. 2
Lowther, Rt. Hon. James, P.C., M.P., of 59, Grosvenor Street, London, W., same crest and motto. 73. 2
Lowther, Gorges St. George Beresford, same crest and motto.
Lowther, Rear-Admiral Marcus, J.P., of 2, Ependen Road, St. Leonards-on-Sea, same crest and motto.
Lowther, Hon. William, of Lowther Lodge, Kensington Gore, S.W., and High House, Campsea Ashe, Wickham Market, same crest.
Lowther, a dexter hand ppr., holding up an escallop or. 216. 2
Lowthian, Edinburgh, a bugle-horn gu., garnished. *Non dormit qui custodit.* 228. 11
Lowthorpe, James William Frederick, Esquire, of 14, Bryanston Street, Portman Square, W., upon a lion's gamb erased fesseways, a wyvern with wings elevated ppr., charged with a trefoil or. *Fortior leone fides.* 265. 5
Lowyn, Herts and Kent, a crab sa. 141. 5
Loxam, a stork's head couped arg., holding in the beak an escallop sa.
Loxdale Shropsh., a bull's head couped ppr. (*Another*, arg., armed or.) cf. 44. 3
Loxdale, Reginald James Rice, Castle Hill, Aberystwyth, same crest and motto.
Loxdale, Shropsh., a bull's head erased arg. 44. 3
Loxton, Samuel, Esquire, of Fern Dell, Cannock, Staffs, in front of a mount

vert, thereon a beacon fired ppr., entwined by a serpent, the head to the sinister gu., three trefoils slipped, also vert. *Fiat lux.*

Loxton, C. A., Esquire, of Shoal Hill House, Cannock, Staffs, in front of a mount vert, thereon a beacon fired ppr., entwined by a serpent, the head to the sinister gu., three trefoils slipped, also vert. *Fiat lux.*

Loxton, S. E., of Fern Dell, Cannoch, Staffs., same crest and motto.

Loyd-Lindsay, *see* Wantage, Baron.

Loyd, Wales, a stag's head erased ppr., attired or 121. 2

Loyd of Havering, Essex, a stag's head couped ppr., attired or, gorged with a chaplet of laurel vert. 120. 3

Loyd, Frederick Edward, Albyns, Romford, Essex, a buck's head ppr., attired or, erased sa., charged on the neck with a fess engrailed of the third, thereon three bezants. *Non mihi, sed patriæ.*

Loyd, Edward Henry, Esquire, J.P., of Langleybury, Herts, same crest and motto.

Loyd, Colonel Lewis Vivian, Esquire, of 55, Egerton Gardens, S.W., same crest and motto.

Loyd, a lion rampant holding between the paws a boar's head couped. *cf.* 225. 5

Loyd or **Lloyd** of Keyswin, Merionethsh., Marrington, Shropsh., and Staffs, a demi-lion rampant sa. 10. 1

Loyd, Wales, a wolf salient arg., holding a broken arrow ppr., the point dropping blood.

Loyd, Thomas Edward John, Esquire, of Aberdunant, Carnarvonsh., a Saracen's head affrontée erased at the neck ppr., wreathed about the temples or and sa., between two fleurs-de-lis of the last.

Luard, a heart gu., charged with a rose arg. *Prospice.* *cf.* 181. 1

Luard, Major-General Charles Edward, of Ightham Knoll, Sevenoaks, Kent, a demi-lion rampant holding between the paws a mullet. *Prospice.*

Lubbock, a stork with wings elevated erm., resting the dexter claw on an antique shield az., bordered or, charged with a lion rampant gardant arg. *Auctor pretiosa facit.* 236. 12

Lubbock, Sir Neville, K.C.M.G., 65, Earl's Court Square, London, S.W., a stork close, resting his dexter claw on a lozenge charged with a lion rampant.

Lubé, *see* Rockliff-Lubé.

Lubienski, Count Louis Pomian Bodenham, Esquire, J.P., D.L., of Rotherwas, Heref., and Bullingham Manor, Heref., hand and arm armed, grasping a falchion rising from a count's coronet.

Lucan, Earl of (Bingham), on a mount vert, a falcon rising with wings expanded ppr., armed, membered, and belled or. *Spes mea Christus.*

Lucar of Madenbrook, Somers., a cubit arm erect vested per pale az. and gu., cuffed arg., holding in the hand a hawk's lure, also arg., stringed gu.

Lucas-Clements, *see* Clements.

Lucas, Baron Lucas (*extinct*), of Shenfield, Essex, out of a ducal coronet or, a dragon's head and shoulders with wings erect gu. 72. 1

Lucas, Essex and Suff., out of a ducal coronet or, a dragon's head gu. 72. 4

Lucas, out of a ducal coronet or, a dragon's head gu., and on the head a baron's coronet ppr.

Lucas, Bart., of Ashtead Park, Surrey, issuing from a wreath of oak or, a dragon's head with wings endorsed gu., semée of annulets arg. *Spes et fides.*

Lucas of Wateringbury, Kent, out of a vallery coronet or, a dragon's head az., gorged with a collar arg., charged with three annulets gu., with wings elevated of the third

Lucas, Charles Davis, Esquire, of 48, Phillimore Gardens, Kensington, W., a demi-griffin arg., beaked and membered or. *Stat religione parentum.*

Lucas, Robert William, Esquire, B.A., of Brighton Road, Carrickmines, co. Dublin, same crest and motto.

Lucas, Richard Clement, of Oaklands House, West Lavington, Sussex, and 50, Wimpole Street, W., a dragon's head couped at the neck gu., issuant from two annulets or, and holding in the mouth a torch fired ppr. *Fortis et fidelis.*

Lucas, Shadwell-, William, Esquire, of the Hall, Fairlight, Hastings: (1) An escallop within an annulet (*for Shadwell*). (2) On a mount vert, a wyvern arg., wings elevated or, charged on the body with six annulets or.

Lucas, Kent, a camelopard passant sa., attired or. *cf.* 132. 8

Lucas-Scudamore, Edward Scudamore, Esquire, of the Cap House, Pontrilas R.S.O.: (1) Out of a ducal coronet or, a bear's paw sa. (*for Scudamore*). (2) A demi-griffin arg., beaked and membered or.

Lucas, Joseph, Esquire, of Foxhunt Manor, Waldron, Sussex, in front of three caltraps or, on a mount vert, a fox passant in front of three oak-leaves ppr. *Respice finem.*

Lucas, Cornw., a lamp or, the flame ppr. 177. 5

Lucas, Cornw., a sword in pale arg., hilt and pommel or, between two wings gu. 112. 4

Lucas, Derbysh., an arm embowed to the sinister, vested sa., bezantée, cuffed arg., holding in the hand ppr. a cross crosslet gu.

Lucas, an arm embowed ppr., vested arg., charged on the elbow with a quatrefoil sa., holding in the hand a cross crosslet fitched gu.

Lucas, Lincs, an arm embowed vested sa., bezantée, cuffed arg., holding in the hand ppr. a cross crosslet gu.

Lucas of Hasland, Derbysh., out of battlements or, a dexter arm embowed ppr., charged on the elbow with five annulets in cross sa., holding in the hand a cross crosslet gu.

Lucas, John Seymour, Esquire, R.A., F.S.A., of New Place, Woodchurch Road, Hampstead, N.W., and Blythburgh, Suff., issuant from the battlements of a tower ppr., a cubit arm erect vested and cuffed or, the hand ppr., holding an antique lamp sa., fired ppr. 296. 15

Luce, an eagle regardant with wings displayed holding in the dexter claw a sword erect. 77. 6

Lucey, out of a ducal coronet a boar's head and neck between two wings displayed.

Lucie of London, a crescent arg. 163. 2

Lucie-Smith, Major-General, C.B., the Acacias, Worthing: (1) A dexter arm in armour embowed holding in the hand a broken tilting-spear, all ppr. 291. 6. (2) A lion's head erased arg., between two laurel-branches vert, and above the head an antique coronet or. *Christo adjuvante.* 291. 5

Luck, a hawk hooded and belled, perched on the stump of a tree. *cf.* 86. 11

Luck of Rotherfield, Sussex, a pelican with wings elevated and endorsed sa., between two branches in orle vert.

Luckin, Essex, a demi-griffin or, issuing from a tower paly of six of the last and sa. 157. 10

Lucy, William, Esquire, of Birmingham, on a mount vert, a boar's head gu., issuant from a wreath of oak ppr., between two wings barry of six arg. and gu. *En avant.*

Lucy, William Charles, Esquire, of Palace Yard, Glouc., same crest.

Lucy, out of a ducal coronet or, a boar's head between two wings sa., billettée of the first.

Lucy, Charlecote, Warw., out of a ducal coronet gu., a boar's head erect arg., guttée-de-poix, between two wings erect sa., billettée or. *By truth and diligence.*

Ludford, Newdigate-, Warw.: (1) A boar's head couped erminois, holding in the mouth a cross patée gu. (*for Ludford*). (2) A fleur-de-lis arg. (*for Newdigate*). 148. 2

Ludgater, of Eltham, Kent, a demi-greyhound couped sa., gorged with a collar or, pendent therefrom an escutcheon of the last charged with a leopard's face jessant-de-lis az. 60. 6

Ludgershall, a talbot passant az., collared or. *cf.* 54. 5

Ludham of London, a demi-dragon erm., with wings elevated, holding between its claws a key or, and charged on the shoulder with a cinquefoil gu.

Ludington, Lincs, a palmer's staff in pale sa.

Ludington of Shrawley, Worcs., a swan sejant holding in the beak a branch ppr.

Ludkin, Suff., a bird with wings expanded az., beaked and legged or.

Ludlow, Baron (Lopes), Heywood, Westbury, Wilts: (1) A lion sejant erminois, collared with a collar gemelle gu., the dexter forepaw resting on a lozenge az. 282. 10. (2) A dexter arm couped and embowed habited purpure, purfled and diapered or, cuffed arg., holding in the hand ppr. a palm-branch vert. 282. 11.

Ludlow, Earl of (*extinct*), (Ludlow), a lion rampant sa., bezantée. *Spero infestis, metuo secundis.* *cf.* 1. 10

Ludlow, a lion rampant sa. 1. 10

Ludlow, Ireland, a lion rampant sa., bezantée. *cf.* 1. 10

Ludlow, a parrot holding in the dexter claw a pear. 101. 13

Ludlow, Edwin, Esquire, of the Firs, Wimbledon, Surrey, a demi-otter couped sa. 134. 11

Ludlow, Edwin, Esquire, a demi-marten couped sa.

Ludlow, John Malcolm Forbes, Esquire, C.B., of 35, Upper Addison Gardens, Kensington, same crest.

Ludlow-Bruges, Richard Heald Esquire, of Seend, Melksham: (1) An anchor erect sa., charged with a saltire or, entwined by a cable ppr. (*for Bruges*). (2) A demi-marten couped sa. (*for Ludlow*). *Mihi cœlum portus* (*for Bruges*). *Omne solum forti patria* (*for Ludlow*).

Ludlow-Hewitt of Clancoole, near Bandon, the trunk of a tree fesseways eradicated ppr., therefrom rising a falcon belled or, fretty gu., in the beak an acorn slipped ppr.

Lufers, a hedgehog ppr. 135. 8

Luff, an elephant passant sa. *cf.* 133. 9

Luffnan, a saltier charged with a crescent.

Lugdon, a lion's head erased or, ducally gorged az. 18. 5

Lugg, a cherub's head ppr. 189. 9

Lugg, out of a ducal coronet or, a pelican's head vulning between two wings, all ppr.

Luke, an archer shooting with a bow ppr. 188. 9

Luke, Cornw., an escallop ppr. 141. 14

Luke of Glasgow and Greenfield, Scotland, a bull's head ppr., winged or. *Strenue insequor.*

Luke of Copley, Beds, Paxton, Durh., and Hunts, a bull's head az., armed or, between two wings addorsed of the last.

Luke, P. V., Esquire, C.I.E., Albert Gate Mansions, S.W., a bull's head couped between two wings addorsed.

Luker of Drangan, Tipperary: (1) An arm erect couped at the elbow, vested per pale az. and gu., cuffed arg., holding in the hand a hawk's lure ppr. (2) Out of a ducal coronet or, a demi-horse gu. *cf.* 53. 3

Lukin, Lincs, a demi-lion gu., collared gobony or and az. 10. 9

Lukin, Rev. Arthur Charles Napier, M.A., of The Vicarage, Ashley Green, Berkhamsted, a demi-lion rampant gu., collared, gobony or and az. *Inspice.*

Lukin, Rev. James, B.A., of Felbrigge Lodge, Romsey, same crest and motto.

Lukin, Colonel Frederick Windham, of 8, New Bond Street, London, and Banksea Cottages, Datchet, Bucks, same crest and motto.

Lukin of Oxford, out of a tower a dragon issuant.

Lukis, Guernsey, a cubit arm vested gu., cuffed vert, garnished or, holding a sprig of three holly-leaves ppr., between two wings or, each charged with a cross crosslet az. *Esse quam videri.*

Lum, Yorks, a Moor's head in profile ppr., wreathed about the temples or and sa. 192. 13

Lumb, a sceptre in pale or. 170. 10

Lumb, James, Esquire, of Homewood and Brigham Hall, Whitehaven, a blackamoor's head in profile couped at the shoulders ppr., wreathed about the temples or and sa., charged upon the neck with a mullet of six points of the second within a wreath in arch, also or and sa. *Respice finem.* 267. 4

Lumisden, Scotland, a naked arm holding a sword ppr. *Dei dono sum quod sum.* 212. 13

Lumley, Viscount, *see* Scarborough, Earl.

Lumley of Harbling, Lincs, a pigeon arg., holding in its beak a laurel-sprig vert. 92. 5

Lumley, Yorks and Middx., a pelican in her piety, all ppr. 98. 14

Lumley, an eagle displayed with two heads. 74. 2

Lumley, Bart. (*extinct*), of Great Bradfield, Essex, an eagle displayed sa., crowned or. *cf.* 74. 14

Lumm, Ireland, a Moor's head in profile ppr., wreathed about the temples or and vert. 192. 13

Lumsdain, Sandys-, Edwin Robert John Blainerne, Edrom, Berwick: (1) An erne devouring a salmon, all ppr. (2) A griffin per fesse or and gu. *Beware in time.*—*Probo non pœnitet.*

Lumsdean and **Lumsden,** Scotland, a heron devouring a fish ppr. *Beware in time.*

Lumsden of Ferryhill, near Aberdeen, an eagle preying on a salmon ppr. *Fide et perseverantia.* 265. 4

Lumsden, James David, Esquire, of Huntingfield, Perthsh., same crest and motto.

Lumsden, a heron devouring a salmon ppr. *Beware in time.*

Lumsden, Henry, of Pitcaple Castle, Aberdeen, Scotland, a naked arm holding a sword ppr. *Dei dono sum quod sum.* 212. 13

Lumsden, Colonel Sir Peter Stark, G.C.B., of Buchromb, Dufftown, N.B., a dexter arm embowed holding a sword. *Dei dono sum quod sum.*

Lumsden of Balgowan, Perthsh., Scotland, a dexter hand grasping a sword in bend sinister ppr. *Dei dono sum quod sum.* 212. 13

Lumsden, James, of Arden, Dumbartonsh., a hand grasping a sword in bend sinister ppr. *Dei dono sum quod sum.* 212. 13

Lumsden of Cushnie, Aberdeensh., a dexter arm embowed holding in the hand a sword in bend sinister, all ppr. *Dei dono sum quod sum.*

Lun or **Lunn,** a greyhound's head erased sa., holding in the mouth a stag's foot or, also erased. 61. 5

Lund and **Lunde,** two laurel-branches in saltier vert.

Lund, Frederick James, Esquire, of Malsis Hall, Kildwick, Yorks, W.R., in front of a crescent or, a fountain ppr. *Secundo flumine.*

Lund, Thomas, Esquire, of Lovely Hall, Blackburn, Lancs, a demi-lion rampant gu., charged with two covered cups in pale or, and holding between the paws a plate thereon a cross patée throughout, also gu. *Semper fidelis.* 11. 4

Lund, Edward, Esquire, of Leighton Villa, Northgate, Edgley, Stockport, a demi-pegasus couped or, the wings charged with five horse-shoes, two one and two, and resting the sinister leg on a lion's head erased gu. *God's my Guide.*

Lund, Herbert, Esquire, of Fern Hill, Pendleton, Manchester, same crest and motto.

Lunden, a cross moline sa. 165. 1

Lundie, Scotland, a boar's head erased and erect sa. 43. 3

Lundin, Scotland, a cross moline gu. *Justitia.* 165. 1

Lundin of Auchtermairnie, Fifesh., a hand ppr., holding up a cushion in pale or. *Tam genus quam virtus.* 215. 9

Lundin of Baldester, Fifesh., Scotland, a dexter hand apaumée, charged with an eye, all ppr. *Certior dum cerno.* 222. 4

Lundin of that Ilk, Scotland, from an antique coronet or, a lion issuing affrontée gu., holding in the dexter paw a sword erect, and in the sinister a thistle slipped, all ppr. *Dei dono sum quod sum.*

Lunn, a demi-pegasus regardant. *cf.* 47. 8

Lunsford, a boar's head or, couped gu. 43. 1

Luntley, a lion's head or, charged with a martlet sa. *cf.* 21. 1

Luppincote, on a cross patée arg., four hearts gu.

Lupton of Thame, Oxon., and Yorks, a wolf's head erased sa. 30. 8

Lurford, a boar's head erased at the neck. 41. 5

Lurgan, Baron (Brownlow), on a chapeau az., turned up erm., a greyhound statant gu., collared or. *Esse quam videri.* *cf.* 58. 4

Lurty, a dexter hand holding a dagger in pale, all ppr. 212. 9

Lusado, on a mount vert, a dove regardant with wings expanded arg., holding in the beak a sprig ppr., charged on the neck with a bar gemelle or. *Honneur me guide.*

Luscombe of Havelock House, Lewisham, a demi-leopard ppr., semée of estoiles az., and holding between the paws an escutcheon or, charged with a cross patonce az.

Luscombe of Comb Royal, Devonsh., a demi-lion rampant gardant crowned or. *cf.* 10. 8

Luscombe, Tooke Cumming, Esquire, of Frankfort, Dundrum, co. Dublin, a demi-lion rampant gardant, crowned or and collared az., pierced through the neck from behind with an arrow ppr., and charged on the neck with a cinquefoil gu. *Deo duce ferro comitante.*

Luscombe of Totnes, Devonsh., a demi-lion rampant gardant and crowned or, collared az., and pierced through the neck with an arrow ppr., charged on the shoulder with a cinquefoil gu. *Deo duce ferro comitante.*

Lusher, Surrey and London, a martlet or. 95. 2

Lusher of London, a demi-lion gu., laying his paws on a gauntlet or. 9. 12

Lushington, Sir Arthur, Bart., of South Hill Park, Berks, a lion's head erased vert, charged on the erasure with three ermine spots or, ducally gorged arg. *cf.* 18. 5

Lushington, Rev Thomas Godfrey Law, M A, of Sittingbourne Vicarage, Kent same crest *Fides nudaque veritas*

Lushington, Sir Godfrey, K C M G, of 34, Old Queen Street, Westminster, and Stokke Great Bedwyn, Hungerford, Wilts same crest

Lushington, Sir Franklin, of Templehurst, Southborough, Kent, same crest and motto

Lushington, His Honour Judge Vernon of 36, Kensington Square W and Pyparts, Cobham, Surrey, same crest and motto

Lushington, *see* Wildman Lushington

Lusk, Sir Andrew Bart of Colney Park, in the parishes of St Stephen, St Albans and Shenley Herts an ancient ship with three masts the sails furled ppr and pennons gu, surmounted by a rainbow ppr *Laus Deo*

Luson, on a ducal coronet a dolphin naiant, all ppr 140 4

Lusy, out of a ducal coronet or, a dexter hand holding a rose stalked and leaved, all ppr 218 11

Lutefoote of Orchill, Perthsh Scotland, a swan ppr, on its head a crescent *Addicunt aves*

Lutefoote, a hand vested holding a mill rind ppr 207 4

Luther, Essex two arms in armour em bowed, holding in the hands a round buckle

Luther, on a rose a long cross gu *Lætitia per mortem*

Lutley, John Habington Brockhampton, Worcs, a lion couchant guardant sa *Virtute non vi*

Lutman of Bentley, Hants, and Langley Sussex out of a mural coronet arg a demi-lion rampant az, holding between its paws a mullet or cf 15 8

Lutteley of Bromscroft Shropsh and Worcs, on a plate an eagle displayed sa

Lutterell, *see* Luttrell

Lutterford, Staffs, a spear or, embrued gu, between two wings expanded sa 112 11

Lutton, in the sea a rock ppr 179 5

Lutton of Knapton, Yorks, on the stump of a tree eradicated or, a peacock close ppr

Luttrell, a dexter hand holding a garland of roses all ppr 218 6

Luttrell-Olmius, Earl of Carhampton (*extinct*) Ireland, a demi-Moor in armour ppr, garnished or, between two branches of laurel vert round the temples a wreath arg and gu, on the breast a fess counter embattled of the second *En Dieu est ma fiance*

Luttrell of Luttrellstown Ireland an otter passant, holding in the mouth a fish all ppr *En Dieu est ma fiance*

Luttrell or Four Oaks, Warw, an otter sa holding in the mouth a fish ppr

Luttrell, Fownes-, George of Dunster Castle Somers out of a ducal coronet or a plume of five feathers arg *Quæsite marte tuenda arte* 114 13

Luttrell of Hanbury Somers, and Hartland Abbey Devonsh, a boar passant arg, bristled and charged on the shoulder with a rose or cf 40 9

Lutwich, a dexter arm in armour holding in the hand a sword, both ppr 210 2

Lutwidge, between two branches of laurel in orle a hand holding a scroll of parchment, all ppr 215 3

Lutwidge, Charles Robert Fletcher Esquire, J P D L. of Holm Rook Hall, Whitehaven Cumb and Shandon Tunbridge Wells Kent on a wreath of the colours a lion rampant per pale arg and gu, collared or *Deo patria amicis.* cf 1 13

Lutwyche, an arm in armour wielding a sword, all ppr 210 2

Lutwyche of Lutwych Shropsh an heraldic tiger's head erased gu tufted and maned or cf 25 4

Lutwyche, Hudson Latham, Esquire J P D L, of Kynaston Ross Heref, same crest

Lutyens, a serpent erect on its tail

Luxford, a dexter arm embowed, holding in the hand a dagger both ppr cf 201 4

Luxford of Wartling and Higham Sussex a boar's head arg erased at the neck gu, holding in the mouth a spear or headed of the first

Luxford, Sussex a wolf rampant supporting an arrow in pale, point downwards or flighted arg

Luxford, Robertson-, John Stewart Odiame, Higham, Sussex (1) Upon a rock ppr, a wolf rampant or, collared with line reflexed over the back az, supporting an arrow az point downwards (2) A cubit arm erect holding an imperial coronet all ppr

Luxford, a boar's head couped or 43 1

Luxmoore, Charles Frederick Coryndon, of Ashbrook Hall, Middlewich (1) A boar statant ppr (*for Brooke*) (2) In front of a battle axe a moorcock all ppr (*for Luxmoore*) *Faste without fraude*

Luxmoore or **Luxmore**, a sea lion rampant ppr 20 2

Luxmore of Witherdon and Kerslake Devonsh a battle-axe erect ppr *Securis fecit securum* 172 3

Lyal or **Lyall**, Scotland, a swallow volant ppr *Sedulo et honeste* 96 2

Lyall, Henry Claud, of Hedley, Epsom a cock or, combed and wattled gu *An I may*

Lybb, Oxon, a naked arm erect holding in the hand an oak-branch fructed all ppr

Lybbe, an arm in armour ppr, holding in the hand a spear of three points

Lybbe, Oxon, a dexter arm embowed in mail supporting a halberd ppr

Lychefield and **Lychfeld**, an arm embowed vested arg, holding in the hand ppr a bow or, strung gu

Lychfeld and Lychfield, Shropsh, a boar's head couped az 43 1

Lychford of Charlwood, Surrey a leopard's face per pale arg and sa, between two wings counterchanged

Lydall or **Lyddall** of Sunning and Didcot, Berks, and Ipsden and Uxmore, Oxon on a mural coronet chequy or and az, a heron's head erased of the first holding in its beak a scroll with the motto, *Et patribus et posteritate* 104 10

Lydcotte, Bucks, of Woodburcot, Northamp and Surrey on a ducal coronet a boar's head couped, all or

Lyddel, a lion rampant arg, ducally crowned or 1 12

Lyde, a stag's head erased erminois *Non sibi* 121 2

Lyde, Ames-, Lionel Neville Frederick Esquire of Ayot St Lawrence and the Hyde, Herts and Thornham Hall, Brancaster, Norf (1) A buck's head erased erminois, attired or (*for Lyde*) 121 2 (2) A rose arg, slipped and leaved ppr in front thereof an annulet or (*for Ames*) *Non sibi* cf 49 5

Lydiard of Meadsfield Surrey, out of a naval coronet or a Moor's head affrontee ppr, wreathed round the temples with laurel vert, round the neck a torse arg and az, thence pendent from a ribbon arg, fimbriated az, a representation of a gold naval medal *Virtute et prudentia*

Lydown, an anchor in pale environed with a serpent 161 3

Lye, an antelope's head arg attired or, collared gu cf 126 2

Lye, Heref and Wilts, an eagle displayed arg, beaked and legged gu 75 2

Lyell, Scotland, a swallow volant ppr *Sedulo et honeste tutela* 96 2

Lyell, Scotland, a unicorn's head erased *At all tymes God me defend* 49 5

Lyell of Kinnordy, Angus, a hand in armour holding a sword ppr, hilt and pommel or *Forti non ignavo* 212 4

Lyell of Murthill, Aberdeen Scotland, a dexter hand holding a sword erect all ppr *Forti non ignavo* 212 9

Lyell of Gardyne Castle, Forfarsh, a dexter hand holding a sword erect ppr, between two sprigs of laurel, also ppr *Tutela*

Lyell of Dysart Scotland, same crest and motto

Lyell, Bart (*extinct*), of Kinnordy Forfarsh, upon a rock a dexter cubit arm erect in armour ppr, charged with a cross parted and fretty gu the hand grasping a sword also ppr *Forti non ignavo* 274 9

Lyfield of Stoke Dabernon Surrey a bull's head caboshed arg, charged with three guttes-de-poix cf 43 8

Lyford, a fox's head erased or 33 6

Lyggins, a greyhound sejant ppr 59 4

Lygon, *see* Beauchamp, Earl

Lygon, a savage's head affrontee couped at the shoulders *Ex fide fortis*

Lyle or **Lyell** of Woodhead Scotland a swallow volant ppr *Sedulo et honeste* 96 2

Lyle, De, Lord Lyle, a cock or, crested gu *An I may* 91 2

Lyley of Fulham, Middx, a cubit arm in armour the hand within a gauntlet grasping a war mace, all ppr, from the handle of the mace a chain pendent encircling the arm or

Lylgrave, a peacock's head couped at the neck gobony or and az holding in the beak a lily arg cf 103 2

Lymesey or **Lymesy**, a demi-bear rampant sa 34 13

Lymington, Viscount, *see* Portsmouth, Earl

Lymme of Lymm Chesh a lion's head couped per pale arg and gu 21 1

Lynacre or **Lynaker**, Derbysh, a greyhound's head erased arg 61 4

Lynam, Ireland, a demi-savage brandishing a scimitar ppr. 186. 3
Lynan, a rose charged with a thistle. 149. 3
Lynch-Power, *see* Power.
Lynch, on a ducal coronet or, a lynx passant gardant arg.
Lynch of Teddington, Middx., a lynx passant gardant ppr. 302. 9
Lynch-Blosse, Bart., *see* Blosse.
Lynch, Ireland, two ears of wheat in saltier ppr. 154. 4
Lynch, James Beverley, Esquire, of Weston Wood, Newport, Shropsh., a wolf passant coward ppr., collared or, charged with a hurt, and chained of the second. *Semper fidelis.*
Lynch of Barna, Galway, a lynx passant gardant ppr. *Semper fidelis.* 302. 9
Lynch, George Staunton, Esquire, J.P., of Clydagh House, co. Galway, Ireland, a lynx passant ppr., charged on the shoulder with a mullet gu. *Semper fidelis.* cf. 127. 2
Lynch of Clogher House, co. Mayo: (1) A lynx passant gardant ppr. (*for Lynch*). cf. 127. 2. (2) A demi-wolf holding between the paws a heart (*for Crean*).
Lynch-Staunton, Charles Rushworth, Esquire, of Clydagh, Headford, Tuam, co. Galway: (1) Upon a mount vert, a fox statant ppr. (*for Staunton*). (2) A lynx passant ppr., charged with a mullet gu. (*for Lynch*). *En Dieu ma foy.*
Lyndergreen, out of a foreign coronet a sprig.
Lyndhurst, Baron (*extinct*), Rt. Hon. the late Sir John Singleton Copley, a dexter arm embowed in armour ppr., charged with an escallop or, grasping a sword and encircled with a chaplet of laurel, also ppr. *Ultra pergere.*
Lyndley of Lyndley, Yorks, and Skegby, Notts, a griffin's head arg., gorged with a bar gemel sa. cf. 66. 1
Lyndon, Somers., five arrows, one in pale and four in saltier, banded and buckled ppr. 173. 3
Lyndon, Ireland, a sea-dragon flying, gorged with a mural coronet or.
Lyndon, George Frederick, Esquire, J.P., of Brandwood House, King's Heath, Worcs., a leopard's head couped and affrontée. *Ung roy, ung foy, ung loy.*
Lyndown, on a pillar a man's heart ppr. 176. 5
Lyndsay of the Mount, Fifesh., amidst flames a heart transfixed by a dart, all ppr. 181. 11
Lyndsey, a demi-bear rampant sa. 34. 13
Lyndsey of London, and Bucksted, Sussex, an eagle displayed sa., beaked and legged or, charged on the breast with a cross patée of the last. cf. 75. 2
Lyndsey of Colby, Norf., a unicorn sejant regardant arg., armed, ungu., crined, and ducally gorged or.
Lyndwood, a fleur-de-lis per pale arg. and sa. 148. 2
Lyne, a griffin's head erased sa. 66. 2
Lyne, John, Esquire, J.P., of Gala, Cranbrook, Tasmania, *uses:* a griffin's head erased sa. *Aperto vivere voto.* 66. 2
Lyne-Stephens of Weymouth: (1) In front of a raven's head couped erm., beaked az., between two wings or, a tower of the last (*for Stephens*). (2) A griffin's head erased sa., charged on the neck with an ermine spot arg., surmounting a cross crosslet in bend sinister or (*for Lyne*). *Recte et suaviter.*
Lynecar or **Lynegar,** Ireland, on a mount a stag, all ppr. 117. 1
Lynedoch, Baron (Graham), an eagle or. *Candide et secure.*
Lynegar, Ireland, on a mount a stag, all ppr., charged with a trefoil. cf. 117. 1
Lynell or **Lineall,** Shropsh. and Chesh., a garb or, between two trefoils sa.
Lynes, an elephant's head erased purp. 133. 3
Lynes of Tooley Park, Leics., and Hatton, Warw., in front of a fleur-de-lis arg., a lion rampant gu. *Foi, roi, droit.*
Lynes, Samuel Parr, Esquire, of Garthmeilio, Corwen, North Wales, same crest and motto.
Lynes, Rev. John, M.A., of Sandesfort House, Wyke Regis, Dorset, same crest and motto.
Lyngard and **Lyngharde,** Northamp., a lion sejant gardant sa., holding in the dexter paw a key in pale or.
Lyngard and **Lyngharde,** Northamp., a lion's gamb erased and erect arg., holding three roses gu., stalked and leaved vert. cf. 37. 12
Lyngarde, Warw., an heraldic tiger's head maned and tufted sa. 25. 4
Lynn, Middx. and Surrey, a lion's head erased arg. 17. 8
Lynn, a demi-lion. 10. 2
Lynn of Woodbridge, Suff., a demi-eagle erm., with wings addorsed and erect az., bezantée, charged on the breast with a martlet gu., and holding in the beak an annulet, also of the last.
Lynn of Southwick Hall, Northamp., a lion's head erminois, erased gu., ducally crowned or, and gorged with a collar sa., charged with four bezants. cf. 18. 8
Lynne, Yorks, a squirrel sejant ppr., supporting a cross crosslet fitched gu. 135. 1
Lyon, *see* Strathmore and Kinghorne, Earl of.
Lyon-Stewart, *see* Blakeney-Lyon-Stewart.
Lyon, Ireland, out of a ducal coronet a demi-savage, the arms embowed.
Lyon, Ireland, out of a ducal coronet a demi-savage, the dexter arm embowed, pointing with forefinger, the sinister elbow resting on the coronet.
Lyon, Scotland, within two branches of laurel a lady to the girdle vested, holding in her dexter hand the royal thistle, all ppr. *In te, Domini, speravi.* 311. 2
Lyon, William Francis Henry, Goring Hall, Worthing, same crest and motto.
Lyon, John Stewart, Kirkmichael, Dumfries, same crest and motto.
Lyon of London and Surrey, a demi-lady ppr., vested arg., the stomacher fretty az., holding in her dexter hand a key or, and in her sinister a thistle slipped and leaved ppr., all within two branches of oak in orle, fructed of the last.
Lyon, a demi-lady ppr., attired or and az., holding in her dexter hand a thistle, and in her sinister a chaplet of laurel ppr. *Lauro redimita quiescam.*—*Speravi.*
Lyon of Heref., London, and West Twyford, Middx., on a pink flowered gu., leaved vert, a lion's head erased per fesse erm. and ermines, charged with a pale counterchanged.
Lyon, Ireland, a lion's head erased sa., charged with a bar gemelle or. cf. 17. 8
Lyon, Thomas Henry, of Appleton Hall, Chesh., a lion's head erased ppr. *Pro rege et patria.* 17. 8
Lyon of Bishop's Caudle, Dorset, a lion rampant az., charged on the body with three crosses patee arg., and resting the sinister paw on a cross moline or. *Innixus vero validus.*
Lyon, Ireland, a hand holding a sword ppr., enfiled with a boar's head erased or. 212. 6
Lyon-Moore, Robert, Esquire, of Molenan, co. Londonderry, and Cliff, Belleek, co. Fermanagh, a Moor's head ppr. *Duris non frangor.*
Lyons, Rt. Hon. the late Sir Richard Bickerton Pemell, G.C.B., **Viscount Lyons** of Christchurch, Southampton (*extinct*), on a chapeau gu., turned up erm., a sea-lion's head erased arg., gorged with a naval coronet az., holding in the mouth a flagstaff in bend sinister ppr., therefrom flowing a banner, also az., having inscribed thereon "*Marack*" in letters of gold. *Noli irritare leones.*
Lyons, Admiral of the Fleet Sir Algernon M'Lennan, G.C.B., of Kilvrough, Glamorgansh., on a chapeau gu., turned up erm., a sea-lion's head erased arg., gorged with a naval crown az.
Lyons of Ledestown, Westmeath, on a chapeau gu., turned up erm., a lion's head erased arg. *Noli irritare leones.* 17. 9
Lyons of Brookhill, Lisburn, co. Antrim, Ireland, a demi-lion rampant holding in the dexter paw a fleur-de-lis arg. *In te, Domine, speravi.* 13. 2
Lyons, William Henry Holmes, Esquire, J.P., of Richmond Lodge, Strandtown, co. Down, same crest and motto.
Lyons, Robert Colvill Jones, same crest and motto.
Lyons, James Bristow, Esquire, same crest and motto
Lyons of Cork, Ireland, a demi-lion rampant sa. *Virtute et fidelitate.* 10. 1
Lyons, William Henry, Esquire, J.P., same crest and motto.
Lyons of Cork, a woolpack arg., thereon a lion passant gu.
Lysaght, Baron Lisle, *see* Lisle.
Lysers, between two wings or, an anchor sa. 161. 12
Lysle of Cambridge, and Compton Davrill, Somers., on a chapeau gu., turned up erm., a millstone arg., charged with a mill-rind or. 180. 14
Lysley, out of a ducal coronet or, a fleur-de-lis arg.
Lysley, William Lowther, Pewsham, Chippenham: (1) On a chapeau gu., turned up erm., a millstone arg. charged with a millrind or. (2) A cubit arm in armour, the hand in a gauntlet grasping

a war-mace, all ppr., from the handle of the mace a chain pendant encircling the arm or. *Forward.*

Lysons, two greyhounds' heads erased, addorsed, and collared. 60. 12

Lysons of Hempsted Court, Glouc., the sun rising out of a bank of clouds ppr. *Valebit.* 162. 5

Lyssers, a dolphin haurient ppr. 140. 11

Lyster, Ireland, on the point of a sword in pale a garland of laurel ppr. 170. 1

Lyster of Rowton Castle, Shropsh., a stag's head erased ppr. *Loyal au mort.* 121. 2

Lyster of Carlow, out of a ducal coronet a stag's head, all ppr. *Retinens vestigia famæ.* 120. 7

Lyster of Waye, Ashburton, Devonsh., out of a ducal coronet or, charged with a cross humettée gu., a stag's head ppr. *Retinens vestigia famæ.*

Lyster of Roscommon, out of a ducal coronet a stag's head, all ppr. 120. 7

Lyster of Fort William, co. Roscommon, a stag's head erased ppr. 121. 2

Lyster-Smythe, Colonel William, of Barbavilla, Collinstown, co. Westmeath, out of a ducal coronet or, a unicorn's head az. *Exaltabit honore.*

Lyte, a bear rampant sa., muzzled gu., supporting a staff. 34. 9

Lyte of Lytescary, Somers., a demi-swan arg., with wings extended gu., against a plume of three ostrich-feathers, the middle one of the first, the other two of the second.

Lyttel, Ireland, a pot of flowers ppr. *Magnum in parvo.*

Lyttelton, Rt. Hon. Sir Charles George, **Viscount and Baron Cobham, Baron Lyttelton,** and **Baron Westcote,** a Moor's head in profile couped at the shoulders ppr., wreathed about the temples arg. and sa. *Ung Dieu, ung roy.* 192. 13

Lyttelton-Annesley, Sir Arthur Lyttelton, K.C.V.O.: (1) On a wreath of the liveries a Moor's head in profile ppr., wreathed about the temples arg. and az. (*for Annesley*). (2) On a wreath of his liveries, a bull'shead caboshed ppr., between two flags gu. (3) Upon a wreath of the colours a Moor's head in profile, couped at the shoulders ppr., wreathed about the temples arg. and sa. (*for Lyttelton*). Under the arms, *Hic murus aheneus.*—Over the Annesley crest, *Virtutis amore.*—Over the MacLeod crest, *Hold fast.*—Over the Lyttelton crest, *Ung Dieu, ung roy.*

Lytton, Surrey, Derbysh., and Herts, a bittern in flags, seeded, all ppr.

Lytton, Earl of (Bulwer-Lytton): (1) A bittern in flags ppr., charged with a rose gu., barbed and seeded ppr. (*for Lytton*). (2) An heraldic tiger's head erased erm., crined and armed or (*for Bulwer*). *cf.* 25. 4. (3) A dove gardant arg., holding in the beak an olive-branch ppr., fructed or (*for Wiggett*). *Hoc virtutis opus.* 92. 4

Lyveden, Baron (Vernon): (1) A boar's head erased sa., ducally gorged or (*for Vernon*). 309. 12. (2) A cubit arm erect in armour ppr., charged with a battle-axe sa., the hand grasping two wreaths of laurel pendent on either side, all ppr. (*for Smith*). *Vernon semper viret.* 274. 11

Lyzzers, a dolphin haurient ppr. 140. 11

M.

Mabb and **Mabbe** of London, a wyvern with wings addorsed or, pellettée. *cf.* 70. 1

Mabball and **Mabbatt,** a wyvern passant vert, at the tail another head, and each head vomiting flames, all ppr. 69. 9

Maberley or **Maberly,** out of a ducal coronet or, a demi-lion gu. 16. 3

Maberley, Thomas Astley, Mytten, Cuckfield, a cross crosslet fitchée or.

Macabe, Ireland, a demi-lion rampant arg., holding between the paws an arrow, point downwards, gu., headed and feathered, also arg.

M'Aben of Knockdohan, Scotland, a swallow ppr. *Nulli præda.* *cf.* 96. 1

Macadam, Scotland, a cross crosslet fitched, and a sword in saltier gu. 166. 12

MacAdam, Lieutenant-Colonel Thomas Stannard, of Blackwater, co. Clare, Ireland, on a mount vert, a cock ppr., holding in his bill a cross Calvary or. *In hoc signo vinces.*

MacAdam-Smith, William Esquire, J.P., Abbotsfield, Wiveliscombe, Somers., in front of a dolphin haurient or., three chess-rooks az. *Generosity with justice.* 235. 2

McAdam, Scotland, a dexter hand holding a hawk's lure. 217. 8

McAdam or **Macadam,** Scotland, a stag's head couped ppr. *Calm.—Crux mihi grata quies.* 121. 5

M'Adam of Waterhead and Ballochmorrie, Ayrsh., a stag's head erased ppr. *Calm.—Crux mihi grata quies.* 121. 2

M'Adam of Craigengillan, Ayrsh., Scotland, same crest. *Steady.* 121. 2

Macalister, Charles Somerville, of Loup and Kennox, a dexter arm in armour erect, holding a dagger in pale, all ppr. *Per mare, per terras.—Fortiter.* 210. 4

McAlister, Scotland, an arm in armour in fess, holding in the hand a cross crosslet fitched gu. *Per mare, per terras.* 211. 14

MacAlister, Donald, Esquire, of Barrmore, Cambs, same crest and motto.

M'Alaster or **Macalister,** Scotland, a dexter hand holding a dirk in pale, both ppr. *Fortiter.* 212. 9

McAlla or **M'Aulay,** Scotland, a boot couped at the ankle ppr., and spurred. *Dulce periculum.* 193. 9

M'Allister, Scotland, a dexter arm in armour embowed, holding in the hand a dagger, both ppr. 196. 5

M'Allum, Scotland, a tower arg., masoned sa. *In ardua tendit.* 156. 2

Macalpin, Scotland, a Saracen's head couped at the neck dropping blood, all ppr. *Cuinich bas alpan.* 190. 11

MacAlpine, Ireland, out of a ducal coronet or, a thistle erect, flowered and leaved ppr. *E'en do baite spare not.* 150. 2

M'Alpin, a man's head bearded, affrontée, crowned with an antique crown, all ppr.

M'Anaspog, Ireland, out of a ducal coronet or, a rock ppr. *cf.* 171. 9

M'Andrew, Scotland, an eagle with wings displayed. *Fear God.* 77. 5

M'Andrew of Ceylon, a lion's head erased ppr., crowned with an antique crown or. *Righ gu brath.* *cf.* 17. 12

M'Andrew of London, a galley with her oars erect in saltire sa., and flags gu. *Fortuna juvat.* 160. 10

McAndrew, James Child, Esquire, of Grafham Grange, Guildford, same crest and motto.

McAndrew, James Johnston, of Lukesland, Ivybridge, Devonsh., same crest and motto.

Macandrew, William, Esquire, of Westwood House, near Colchester, same crest and motto.

M'Ara, a thistle stalked and leaved in front of a dexter arm from the elbow erect, holding a sword in bend sinister, all ppr.

Macarmick, Cornw., an arm in armour embowed ppr., holding in the hand a cutlass. *cf.* 195. 2

MacArtain, Ireland, a bear rampant sa., muzzled or.

McArther or **M'Arthur,** Scotland, two laurel-branches in orle. 146. 5

Macarthur, Rev. George Fairfowl, of Wyandra, Ashfield, near Sydney, New South Wales, Senior Chaplain to the Volunteer forces of New South Wales, two laurel-branches in orle. *Fide et opera.* 146. 5

M'Arthur, Alexander, Esquire, of 79, Holland Park, London, W., in front of a greyhound couchant sa., collared, and line reflexed over the back arg., a billet erect or, the whole between two branches of vert, fructed ppr. *Fide et opera.* 268. 13

M'Arthur, William Alexander, of 12, Buckingham Gate, S.W., and 4, Third Avenue, Hove, same crest and motto.

McArthur, Allen Gordon, Esquire, of 28, Linden Gardens, W., same crest and motto.

MacArthur or **Macarthur,** an escallop or, charged with a mullet gu. 141. 6

MacArthur, Scotland, two wings addorsed. *cf.* 109. 12

M'Arthur, Scotland, two laurel-branches in saltier. *Fide et opera.*

M'Arthur-Stewart of Miltoun and Ascog, Butesh., Scotland, a greyhound couchant within two branches of bay ppr. *Fide et opera.* 60. 5

Macartney, a stag lodged erm. 115. 7

Macartney of Lissanoure, co. Antrim, Ireland, a hand in pale couped above the wrist ppr., holding a rose gu., stalked and leaved vert. *Mens conscia recti.* 218. 10

Macartney of Belfast, Ireland, a cubit erm erect ppr., holding a rose-branch vert, flowered gu. *Stimulat sed ornat.* 218. 10

Macartney, Carthanach George, Esquire, J.P., of Lissanoure Castle, co. Antrim, a cubit arm erect, the hand grasping a rose-branch in flower, all ppr. *Mens conscia recti.*

Macartney, Ellison-: (1) A cubit arm erect, the hand grasping a rose-branch flowered, all ppr. (*for Macartney*). 218. 10. (2) A buck's head erased ppr., charged on the neck with a trefoil slipped vert (*for Ellison*). *Spe gaudeo.* 121. 8

Macartney, Sir John, Bart., of Lish, co. Armagh, and Jolimont, Mackay, Queensland, Australia, a hand holding a slip of a rose-tree with three roses thereon, all ppr. *Stimulat sed ornat.* *cf.* 218. 12

Macartney, Carlile Henry Hayes, Esquire, B.A., of Foxhold, Thatcham, Berks, a cubit arm vested and cuffed bendy gu. and or, the hand holding a rose-branch, both ppr. *Mens conscia recti.* 268. 8

Macartney, Rev. Sydney Parkyns, M.A., of Shalesbrooke, Forest Row, Sussex, same crest and motto.

Macartney-Filgate, Townley Patten Hume, Esquire, J.P., of Lowtherstone, Balbriggan, Dublin, a griffin segreant salient arg., pierced through the breast with a broken spear or, holding the point in its beak.

Macarty, Ireland, an arm embowed vested holding a lizard, all ppr.

M'Carty or **M'Cartie,** Frederick Fitzgerald, of Carrignavar, co. Cork, a dexter arm in armour erect and couped, holding in the hand a newt, all ppr.

Macaul, Scotland, a fleur-de-lis arg. *Pour le roi.* 148. 2

M'Aul, Scotland, a hand wielding a sword. *Ferio, tego.* 212. 13

Macaulay, Baron Macaulay, on a rock a boot ppr., with a spur or. *Dulce periculum.*

Macaulay-Anderson, Francis Adam, Esquire, of Roshnashane, co. Antrim, Ireland: (1) In front of an oak-tree ppr., an escutcheon arg., charged with a boar's head erased az. (*for Anderson*). (2) In front of two arrows in saltire ppr., a boot, also ppr., spurred or, with the motto over, *Dulce periculum* (*for Macaulay*). *Stand sure.*

Macaulay of Edinburgh, a boot couped at the ankle, thereon a spur, all ppr. 193. 9

M'Aully, Scotland, a dexter hand holding a scimitar. *I will.* 213. 5

M'Auliffe, Ireland, a boar's head couped or. 43. 1

M'Auslane of Wandsworth Common, Surrey, a dexter hand charged with a bezant holding up a ducal coronet within two laurel-branches disposed orleways. *Audaces juvo.* *cf.* 217. 3

MacAwley, Ireland, a demi-lion rampant gu. 10. 3

MacBain, Hon. Sir James, K.C.M.G., of Scotsburn, Toorak, near Melbourne, Victoria, Australia, a wolf's head. *Vires in arduis.* 30. 5

MacBain, Scotland, a wolf's head ppr. *Vires in arduis.* 30. 5

McBarnet, Lieutenant-Colonel A. C., of 2, Roland Houses, S.W., a dexter hand grasping a sword in bend ppr., and in an escrol over, *Sic ad astra.*

M'Barnet of Torridon, Ross-sh., Scotland, a hand grasping a sword in bend ppr. *Sic ad astra.* 212. 13

Macbean and **M'Bean,** Scotland, a demi-cat rampant gu. 26. 11

M'Bean, Scotland, a mountain-cat rampant sa. 26. 2

M'Bean of Inverness-sh., Scotland, a cat sejant ppr. *Touch not the cat bot a glove.* 26. 8

Macbeath, Scotland, a dexter arm in armour embowed, holding in the hand a sword, all ppr. 195. 2

M'Beth of London, a serpent's head couped ppr. *Conjuncta virtuti fortuna.* 142. 8

MacBrady, Count of the Holy Roman Empire, a cherub ppr., winged or. 189. 9

M'Braid, Scotland, a dexter hand gu., holding a billet sa. 215. 11

M'Brair, Scotland, or **M'Braire,** a unicorn's head erased arg. 49. 5

M'Braire of Netherwood, Dumfriessh., a lion rampant gu. *In defiance.* 1. 13

MacBrayne of Glenbranter, Cowall, Argyllsh., Scotland, issuing from a ducal coronet a dexter arm, the hand grasping a sword in bend sinister, all ppr. *Fortis ceu leo fidus.* 212. 11

M'Brayne of Summerlee, Lanarksh., a demi-lion rampant or, issuing from a ducal coronet ppr. *I hope in God.—The righteous are bold as a lion.* 16. 3

M'Brayne, David, J.P., of Glenbranter, Strachur, Argyllsh., out of a ducal coronet a dexter arm issuing grasping a sword, all ppr. *Fortis ceu leo fidus.* 212. 11

M'Breid, Scotland, a dexter hand holding a broadsword, all ppr. *I am ever prepared.* 212. 13

Macbride, on a chapeau a salamander in flames, all ppr. 138. 2

Macbride, a raven ppr., wings expanded. 107. 3

M'Caa, Scotland, a hand holding a dagger erect, all ppr. *Manu forti.* 212. 9

M'Cabe, Ireland, on a mount vert, a stag current regardant ppr. 118. 12

Maccabe, Sir Francis Xavier Frederick, M.R.C.S., F.R.C.P.I., of Park Cottage, Sandyford, co. Dublin, a demi-griffin. *Aut vincere aut mori.*

McCall, of Edgbaston, Warw., a griffin's head betwixt two wings ppr. *Dulce periculum.* 65. 11

M'Call, Ireland, a goat's head erased az. 128. 5

M'Call, George, of Daldowie, Lanarksh., Scotland, a leg in armour couped at the calf ppr., and spurred or. *Dulce periculum.* 193. 4

M'Call, a griffin's head between two wings. 65. 11

M'Call, Scotland, a hand holding a broadsword, all ppr. *Ferio, tego.* 212. 13

M'Call, James, Esquire, of Caitloch, Moniaive, N.B., a hand holding a dagger. *Ferio, tego.*

McCallum, Kellie-, of Braco, Perthsh., a tower or, masoned sa. *In ardua tendit.* 156. 2

M'Callum, Scotland, a castle arg., masoned sa. *In ardua tendit.* 155. 8

M'Callum, a tower ppr., cupola and flag gu. 157. 15

MacCalmont, Major-General Sir Hugh, of Abbeylands, co. Antrim, a griffin's head erased ppr., charged with a fleur-de-lis or. *Nil desperandum.*

McCalmont, James Martin, of Holywood House, Belfast, same crest and motto.

M'Cammond, Major Walter Edwin Carson, 4th Battalion Royal Irish Rifles, of Innisfayle, Donegall Park, Belfast, out of a mural crown a lion's head gu., charged on the neck with a bell arg. *Justus ac tenax.* 295. 4

M'Cammond, James Napier, of Ormisdale, Fortwilliam Park, Belfast, and Arnside, Whitehead, co. Antrim, same crest and motto.

M'Cammond, William Alfred, Esquire, of Belfast, Ireland, same crest and motto.

MacCan, Lords of Clan Crassel, co. Armagh, Ireland, a salmon naiant ppr. *Crescit sub pondere virtus.* 139. 12

M'Candlish, a demi-lion vert. 10. 2

McCandlish, George Glennie Leslie, Esquire, 6, Manor Place, Paddington, a demi-lion rampant vert.

M'Candlish, a snake nowed ppr. *Cavendo tutus.* 142. 4

M'Cann, Ireland, a bull's head cabossed sa. 43. 8

M'Carin, Scotland, a swallow ppr. *Nulli præda.* *cf.* 96. 1

M'Carlie, placed on the dexter side of a mount vert, a cross crosslet fitched sa. *cf.* 166. 4

M'Carlie, the sun or, shining on a cross crosslet fitched sa., placed on the dexter side of a mount vert. *In hoc signo vinces.* 166. 4

MacCarthy, Ireland, out of a ducal coronet or, an arm embowed vested az., cuffed arg., the hand holding a lizard ppr. *Lamh laidir a-buagh.*

McCarthy of Springhouse, co. Tipperary, a dexter arm erect, couped at the elbow, vested az., cuffed arg., holding in the hand a lizard, both ppr. *cf.* 209. 3

McCarthy of Carrignavar, Cork, a dexter arm in mail arg., holding in the hand a lizard, both ppr. 209. 3

McCarthy, Earl of Clancarty and **Viscount Muskerry** (*attainted*), a dexter arm vested in mail armour ppr., cuffed arg., erect, holding in the hand a lizard, both also ppr. *Forti et fideli nihil difficile.* 209. 3

McCarthy-Reagh, a dexter arm erect couped at the elbow, vested az., cuffed arg., holding in the hand ppr. a lizard vert. *Fortis ferox et celer.* *cf.* 209. 3

Maccartney, a dexter hand holding a slip of rose-tree ppr. *Mens conscia recti.* 218. 10

Maccartney, Ireland, a dexter hand holding a branch of laurel ppr. *Mens conscia recti.* 219. 9

MacCartney, Scotland, a griffin segreant az., the wings erm., holding between the claws an étoile or. *cf.* 62. 2

M'Cartnay, Scotland, a dexter hand holding a slip of a rose-tree ppr. *Stimulat sed ornat.* 218. 10

M'Cartney, Scotland, same crest. *Sua præmia virtus.*

M Casker and **M Caskill,** Scotland, a hand holding a dagger erect *Manu forti* 212 9

M'Casland of Newlandmuir, Lanarksh., Scotland a dexter hand erect ppr, holding up a ducal cap tufted on the top with a rose gu within two branches of laurel disposed orleways, also ppr *Audaces juvo* 217 2

M Caul, London, a fleur-de-lis arg *Pour le roi* 148 2

MacCausland, Conolly Thomas, J.P D L., of Drenagh (formerly Fruit Hill), Limavady, co Londonderry, Ireland a boar's head erased az armed or, langued gu, and charged with a crescent of the second *Virtus sola nobilitat*

MacCausland of Bessbrooke co London derry, Ireland, on a chapeau gu, turned up erm, a boar's head erased az cf 42 5

M Causland, Ireland, on a chapeau gu turned up erm, a greyhound sejant ppr cf 59 4

Maccaunach, Ireland, a ferret passant ppr cf 134 9

M Cay and **M Coy,** Scotland, a talbot's head erased or, collared sa 56 1

M Chlery, of Kildrochit Wigtonsh, Scotland a thistle ppr *Labore et honore* cf 150 2

M Clauchlan or **M Claughlan,** Scotland, a castle triple towered *Fortis et fidus* 155 8

M Clean, Ireland, a bull's head erased gu 44 3

M Clean, Scotland a tower embattled arg *Virtue mine honour* 156 2

M Cleay, a stag's head 121 5

M Cleish of Maryfield Edinburgh, Scotland, a cross crosslet fitched gu *Love* 166 2

M'Clellan, Scotland, a cubit arm holding a sword, both ppr, on the point a Moor's head or cf 212 12

M'Clellan, Bart., Scotland a Moor's head couped and wreathed ppr. *Sapit qui reputat* 192 13

M'Clellan, Scotland, a dexter arm embowed fesseways, holding in the hand a sword in pale the point enfiled with a man's head, all ppr *Think on* 201 7

McClelland, Ireland, an arm in armour embowed, the hand holding a sword piercing a negro's head, couped all ppr *Think on.* cf 195 2

M'Clelland, Scotland a negro's head couped ppr *Sapit qui reputat* 191 3

M Clen, Scotland, a castle *Virtue mine honour* 155 8

M Cleod, Scotland the sun in splendour *I burn weil, I see* 162 2

M Cleod, Scotland a bull's head cabossed between two flags barry of three gu, az and arg 43 5

Macclesfield, Earl of (Parker), of Shirburn Castle, Wallingford, a leopard's head, affrontée and erased or, ducally gorged gu *Sapere aude* 23 8

Macclesfield of Maer Staffs, out of a ducal coronet or, a goat's head arg, armed or holding in the mouth a sprig of rose-tree vert cf 128 14

M Clesh, Scotland, a dexter hand holding a cross crosslet fitched *Love* 221 14

M Cleverty, a cross crosslet fitched and a palm-branch in saltier

McClintock-Bunbury, *see* Bunbury

McClintock, Baron Rathdonnell, *see* Rathdonnell

M'Clintock of Trintagh co Donegal of Hampstead Hall co Londonderry and of Drumcar, Louth, a lion passant ppr *Virtute et labore* 6 2

McClintock, Charles Edward, of Glenderagh, Crumlin S O, co Antrim same crest and motto

McClintock, Admiral Sir Francis Leopold K C B, of 8 Atherstone Terrace, London, S W, same crest and motto

McClintock, Arthur George Florence, Esquire, J P of Rathvinden Leighlinbridge co Carlow, and Hillsborough, co Down same crest and motto

M'Clintock, Frederick Robert Esquire, of Kilwarlin, Hillsborough, co Down, same crest and motto

M'Clintock, Scotland, a lion passant ppr 6 2

McClintock, Major John Knox, J P, D L of Seskinore Omagh Tyrone, a lion passant arg *Virtute et labore*

M'Cloud, Ireland a fox current ppr cf 32 8

M'Clure, a doomed tower, on the top a flag ppr 157 15

M'Clure, Bart, of Belmont and Dundela co Down a tower domed ppr from the top a flag arg thereon a rose gu *Spectemur agendo* cf 157 15

M'Clymont, out of a mural coronet a lion's head charged with a roundle cf 19 12

McCoghlan of Cloghan, King's Co, Ireland, a dexter arm embowed vested gu, holding in the hand a sword both ppr 204 1

MacColgan of Kilcoglan, Ireland, and the island of Teneriffe, a dexter arm in armour embowed, the hand grasping a spear thrust through a stag's head couped all ppr

M'Coll, Scotland between the horns of a crescent an etoile *Justi ut sidera fulgent* 163 4

M Combie, *see* Duguid-M'Combie

M Combie, a gray cat sejant erect *Touch not the cat bot a glove* 25 2

Mac Conach and **Mac Conachie,** a demi savage wreathed ppr, holding in the dexter hand a sheaf of arrows arg, and pointing with the sinister to an antique crown ppr *Defend and spare not —Ard choille* cf 186 13

Mac Concaled, Ireland two trees couped and raguled in saltier ppr, bound by a garland of leaves vert

M'Connel, Edinburgh and Queensland Australia, a kangaroo sejant erect regardant on the ground under an Australian grass tree, all ppr *Vis in vita Deus* 136 9

M'Connel of Carsriggan co. Wigtown, and Cressbrook Derbysh, a stag's head erased gu, charged on the neck with a trefoil slipped or *Victor in arduis* 121 8

McConnell, Sir Robert John, Bart the Moat, Strandtown co Down, a stag's head erased az, attired and charged on the neck with a bee volant or *Victor in arduis* 265 3

McConnell, Dublin, a stag's head erased arg, charged on the neck with a trefoil slipped vert 121 8

M Connell, Scotland, a dexter arm in fess couped ppr, holding in the hand a cross crosslet fitched *Toujours pret* 221 10

McConnell, William Robert 35, Montagu Place W C, same crest and motto

M'Corda, Ireland a demi savage holding in his dexter hand a barbed arrow, and in his sinister a heart *Via una, cor unum* 186 9

MacCormac, the late Sir William, K C B K C V O, of 13, Harley Street W an arm couped grasping three tilting-spears, all ppr *Sine timore*

M'Cormack and **M Cormick,** Scotland on a rock ppr, a martlet sa *Sine timore* cf 95 7

M Cormick, Ireland, a dexter hand holding a spear in pale ppr cf 214 11

M Corquodale, Scotland a stag at gaze ppr *Vivat rex* 117 3

M Corquodell of that ilk and Phantillans, Scotland a stag at gaze ppr, attired gu *Vivat rex* 117 3

MacCostello, Ireland, a falcon ppr, belled and jessed or cf 85 2

McCowan, David, Esquire J P of 7 Lynedoch Crescent Glasgow, an eagle rising with wings expanded and inverted *Tendimus ad cœlum* 290 6

M Coul, Scotland, a dexter arm in armour embowed wielding a cutlass ppr *Vincere* cf 195 2

M Coy, Scotland, a talbot's head erased or, collared sa 56 1

M Cracken, Scotland a nag's head bridled, the reins broken *Omnia recte* cf 51 6

M'Crae, Scotland a hand holding a sword *Fortitudine* 212 13

M'Crae, Scotland an oak-tree ppr *Delectat et ornat* 143 5

M'Craw, Scotland, a griffin sejant per pale or and gu, winged of the first 62 10

M Cray, Scotland, a hand holding a sword *Fortiter* 212 13

McCreagh-Thornhill, Major Michael, 24, Eccleston Square, S W (1) A thorn-tree ppr, on the trunk a mascle or and with a cross crosslet sa on the branches (*for Thornhill*) (2) A demi-lion gu gorged with a collar gemel, and charged on the shoulder with two mullets of six points fessewise or, holding between the paws a bezant, thereon two mascles interlaced sa (*for McCreagh*) *Mors ante dedecora*

M Cree or **M Crie,** Scotland an arm in armour couped and embowed fessewise, holding in the hand a scimitar *Delectat et ornat* cf 196 10

M Crire, M Cririck, M Rerik, or **Creirie,** and the Rev T W McCririck, of the Hill House, Stockton on Tees originally of McCririck's Cairn, Dumfriessh a bee-hive with bees volant ppr *Industria* 137 7

M'Crobie, Scotland, a hawk rising ppr *Despicio terrena* 88 2

M'Crummen, Scotland, a hand holding a flute 217 9

M'Crummen or **M'Crummin,** Scotland a demi lion rampant gu armed az, holding in the dexter paw a thistle ppr *Permitte cætera divis* cf 13 12

M'Cubbin, Scotland, an arm in armour embowed, holding in the hand a scimitar. *Pro rege et patria.* 196. 10

M'Cubbin, Scotland, a martlet sa. 95. 5

M'Cull, Scotland, a leg in armour spurred and couped above the knee, all ppr. 193. 1

M'Culloch, Scotland, a horse passant. *Sine macula.* 52. 6

M'Culloch of Piltoun, co. Edinburgh, an ermine ppr. *Sine macula.* 134. 6

M'Culloch of Barholm, Kirkcudbrightsh., a hand throwing a dart, all ppr. *Vi et animo.* 214. 4

M'Culloch, Andrew Jameson, Esquire, of Ardwall, Gatehouse-on-Fleet, N.B., and 14, Moray Place, Edinburgh, a hand throwing a dart ppr. *Vi et animo.*

M'Culloch, Scotland, a naked arm embowed throwing a dart. 201. 14

M'Cullock, a triangular harrow gu. 178. 4

M'Cullum, Scotland, a greyhound's head or. *cf.* 61. 2

MacCurdy of London and Ireland, a leopard passant ppr., resting its dexter paw on an escutcheon vert, thereon a leopard's face or. 24. 6

McCurten, Ireland, in front of two lances in saltire arg., headed or, an Irish harp sa.

M'Daniel, Ireland, a hand couped in fess, holding a cross crosslet fitched in pale. 221. 10

McDaniel, of Woodlands, Bandon, a dexter cubit arm in armour, holding in the hand ppr. a cross crosslet fitchée erect. *Per mare, per terras.*

MacDeargan, a peewit ppr.

MacDermot or **MacDermott,** Ireland, a greyhound current sa. *cf.* 58. 5

MacDermot, a demi-lion az., holding in its dexter paw a sceptre surmounted by a crown or. *Honore et virtute.*

MacDermot of Coolavin (Rt. Hon. Hugh Hyacinth O'Rorke MacDermot), of Coolavin and Clogher, Monaster-Aden, co. Sligo, a boar's head erased az. *Honore et virtute.*

MacDermot of Dublin, a demi-lion az., holding between the paws a tower arg. *Honor virtutis præmium.*

MacDermot of Moylurg, co. Roscommon, Ireland, a demi-lion rampant az., holding in the dexter paw a sceptre crowned or. *Honor et virtus.—Honor probataque virtus.*

McDermot of Carrig, co. Roscommon, Ireland, a boar's head erased az. 42. 2

McDermott, Henry Thomas, Esquire, of Trinity House, Gensing Gardens, St. Leonards-on-Sea, Sussex, a demi-lion rampant or, holding between the paws a boar's head erased at the neck az. *Honor virtutis præmium.* 14. 8

MacDermott, Thomas Charles, Esquire, of Alderford House, Ballyfarnow, co. Roscommon, same crest and motto.

McDermott, John Joseph, Esquire, M.D., F.R.C.S., out of an Eastern crown or, a demi-lion rampant az., charged on the shoulder with a cross crosslet of the first, and holding between the paws a sceptre erect, surmounted by a regal crown, all ppr. *Honore et virtute.*

Macdiarmid, Scotland, a lion rampant arg., holding between its paws a garland of flowers ppr. *Non immemor beneficii.*

M'Diarmid, Scotland, a lion rampant or. 1. 13

McDiarmot, Ireland, a lion rampant arg., holding a sceptre or.

Macdona, J. Cumming, Esquire, M.P., of Hilbre House, West Kirby, Chesh., a dexter arm embowed holding a sword in bend sinister environed with a serpent, all ppr. *Virtutis gloria merces.* 302. 15

M'Donagh, Ireland, a dexter arm embowed, holding in the hand a sword environed with a serpent, all ppr. *Virtutis gloria merces.* 201. 3

Macdonald-Lockhart, *see* Lockhart.

Macdonald-Steuart, *see* Steuart.

Macdonald, Baron (Macdonald), of Slate, co. Antrim: (1) A dexter arm in armour fessewise, holding a cross crosslet fitchée gu. (*for Macdonald*). 211. 14. (2) An ox arg., issuing from a hurst of oak-trees ppr. *Per mare, per terras.*

Macdonald, Rt. Hon. John Hay Athole, P.C., C.B., LL.D., F.R.S.S., M.I.E.E., Lord Justice Clerk of Scotland, and Lord President of the Second Division of the Court of Session, Brigadier-General of the Royal Company of Archers (H.M. Bodyguard), and Brigadier General Forth Infantry Brigade, of 15, Abercromby Place, Edinburgh, *uses*: a dexter arm in armour fesseways, holding in the hand ppr. a cross crosslet fitchée in pale gu. (*incorrect*). *Per mare, per terras.*

Macdonald of Craig-na-Gower, Argyllsh., a dexter arm in armour fesseways, couped below the elbow ppr., the hand holding a cross crosslet fitchée gu. *Per mare, per terras.* 211. 14

Macdonald, out of a mural crown or, in front of an arm in armour fesseways, the hand ppr. holding a cross crosslet sa., flames issuing from the top, also ppr., a flagstaff, therefrom flowing to the sinister a banner gu., inscribed "*Arolla*" in letters of gold, the staff entwined with a branch of laurel vert. *Per mare, per terras.*

Macdonald, Sir Archibald John, Bart., of East Sheen, Surrey, a hand in armour holding a cross crosslet fitchée gu. *Per mare, per terras.* 210. 14

Macdonald, William Rae, Esquire, Carrick Pursuivant of Arms, a dexter hand holding a dirk erect ppr. *Nec tempore, nec fato.* 212. 9

Macdonald, William Stone, Esquire, of Blinkbonny, Gananogue, Ontario, Canada, a dexter arm in armour grasping a dagger ppr. *Perseverantia.* 210. 4

Macdonald, Scotland, a dexter hand holding a dagger in pale ppr. *My hope is constant in thee.* 212. 9

Macdonald, William Bell, of Rammerscales, Dumfriessh.: (1) A hand holding a dagger ppr. (*for Bell*). (2) A dexter hand in armour ppr., holding a cross crosslet fitchée gu. (*for Macdonald*). *I beir the bel.—Nec tempore, nec fato.* 212. 3

Macdonald of Edinburgh, a dexter hand holding a dirk erect ppr. *Nec tempore, nec fato.* 212. 9

Macdonald, Moreton-, John Ronald, of Largie, Scotland, a dexter arm embowed holding a dagger in pale, all ppr. *Semper pugnare paratus.—Pro patria.*

Macdonald, out of an Eastern coronet or, a cubit arm erect ppr., encircled by a laurel-wreath vert, holding in the hand a dagger erect, also ppr., hilted and pommelled or.

Macdonald, Allan Douglas, a castle triple-towered arg., masoned sa., and issuing from the centre tower a dexter arm in armour embowed grasping a sword, all ppr., and in an escroll above the motto, *My hope is constant in thee.* —*Dhandeon co heiragha.* *cf.* 155. 3

Macdonald, John Andrew, C.B., Glenaladale, Inverness-sh., same crest and motto.

Macdonald, Hon. Andrew Archibald, of Government House, Charlottetown, Prince Edward Island, Canada, a castle triple-towered arg., masoned sa., and issuing from the centre tower a dexter arm in armour embowed grasping a sword, all ppr. *My hope is constant in thee.* *cf.* 155. 3

Macdonald, William Kid, Esquire, J.P., of Windmill House, Arbroath, and Ballintuim, Perthsh., N.B., a raven ppr., perched on a rock az. *Nec tempore, nec fato.* 107. 2

Macdonald (ancient Lords of the Isles), a raven sa., on a rock az. 107. 2

Macdonald, Durh., in a bush a lion's face and fore-paws sa. *Toujours prêt.* 21. 7

Macdonald, Scotland, a demi-lion rampant arg., regally crowned ppr., holding in its dexter paw a sword wavy of the last, hilt and pommel or. *Pro rege in tyrannos.* 14. 14

Macdonald, Montagu William Colquhoun Farquharson, Esquire, of St. Martins, Perthsh., a demi-lion gu., holding in his dexter paw a hand ppr. *Per mare, per terras.*

Macdonald-Bowie, of Holland, the Holy Bible expanded ppr. *Cœlestia sequor.* 158. 3

MacDonald of M'Donald, on a rock az., a raven sa. *Nec tempore, nec fato.* 107. 2

MacDonald, Scotland, on a rock ppr., a tower. *Sure.* 156. 3

M'Donald, Scotland, a castle ppr. *My hope is constant in thee.* 155. 8

M'Donald, Scotland, on a rock inflamed a raven sa. *Nec tempore, nec fato.* 106. 11

M'Donald, a hind trippant or. 124. 12

M'Donald, Scotland, a hand holding a cross crosslet fitched. *My hope is constant in thee.* 221. 14

M'Donald, Scotland, a hand in armour holding a cross crosslet fitched gu. *Per mare, per terras.* 210. 14

M'Donald, Scotland, an arm in armour gauntleted in fess, couped ppr., holding a cross crosslet fitched sa. *Nec tempore, nec fato.* 211. 14

M'Donald, Scotland, a dexter hand holding a dirk erect. *Nec tempore, nec fato.* 212. 9

M'Donald, Scotland, an arm in armour embowed, holding in the hand a sword, all ppr. *Per mare, per terras.* 195. 2

M'Donal, Ireland, a talbot's head az. 56. 12

M'Donald of Lee, a boar's head erased. *Corda serrata pando.* 42. 2

M'Donall of Logan, two lion's gambs in saltier ppr. *Victoria vel mors.* 39. 14

Macdonell, Rt. Hon. Alexander, M.A., P.C., a dexter arm embowed fesseways, the elbow upon the wreath vested or, cuffed arg., the hand holding a cross crosslet fitchée erect az., the arm charged with a trefoil slipped ppr. *Toujours prêt.* cf. 203. 9

MacDonell, C. R. Armstrong, J.P., D.L., New Hall, Ennis, co. Clare: (1) Same as above, but charged with a crescent. (2) A dexter arm vambraced fesseways and embowed ppr., charegd with a mullet gu., the hand grasping an armed leg couped at the thigh and bleeding, also ppr. *Toujours prest.*

Macdonell of Morar, Inverness-sh., Scotland, a raven perching on a rock ppr. *Faicilleach.—Per mare, per terras.* 106. 9

Macdonell of Glengarry, on a rock az., a raven perched ppr. *Cragan an fhithich.—Per mare, per terras.* cf. 107. 2

Macdonell, Arthur Anthony, of Lochgarry, Banbury Road, Oxford, Esquire (Prof. of Sanscrit, etc., Oxford University), a raven ppr., perching on a rock gu. *Craggan an fhithich.* cf. 107. 2

MacDonell, Scotland, a raven ppr. perching on a rock az. *Craggan an fhithich.* 107. 2

McDonell, Æneas Ranald, Esquire, 49, St. Anns Street, Salisbury, a raven ppr. perching on a rock az. *Cragan an fhithich.* 107. 2

M'Donell, Macdonell, or **M'Donnell,** a hand couped in fess holding a fleur-de-lis. 221. 9

MacDonnel, Ireland, a dexter arm couped at the shoulder, holding in the hand a cross crosslet fitched. *Toujours prest.*

MacDonnell, *see* Armstrong-MacDonnell.

MacDonnell, Ireland, a dexter arm in armour couped in fess, holding in the hand a cross crosslet fitched. cf. 211. 14

MacDonnell, Provost of Trinity College, Dublin, a dexter arm embowed fesseways, vested or, cuffed arg., the hand holding a cross crosslet fitchée erect az., the arm charged with a cross patée gu. *Tout jour prêt.* cf. 203. 9

MacDonnell of Peacockstown, co. Meath, a dexter arm embowed fesseways, vested or, cuffed arg., the hand holding a cross crosslet fitchée erect az., the arm charged with a cross patée gu. *Toujours prêt.* cf. 203. 9

MacDonnell, Connaught, a unicorn passant gu. *His vinces.* cf. 48. 5

McDonnell, Bart. (*extinct*), of Dublin, a dexter arm embowed fesseways vested or, cuffed arg., the hand holding a cross crosslet fitchée erect az., the arm charged with a trefoil slipped ppr. *Toujours prêt.* cf. 203. 9

McDonnell of Murlough and Kilmore, co. Antrim, a dexter arm embowed fesseways couped at the shoulder, vested or, cuffed arg., holding in the hand ppr. a cross crosslet fitchée erect az. *Toujours prêt.* 203. 9

M'Donnell, Earl of Antrim, *see* Antrim.

MacDonogh of Annagh, co. Sligo, a dexter arm erect, couped at the elbow, vested az., cuffed arg., holding in the hand a sword erect entwined with a lizard, all ppr. *Virtutis gloria merces.*

McDouall, James, Esquire, of Logan, near Stranraer, Genoch Dunragit, N.B., a tiger's head erased crowned with an imperial crown, with a lion's paw issuing from a cloud grasping the crown from the tiger's head. *Usurpari nolo.*

M'Dougal, Scotland, a lion's gamb erect and erased ppr. *Vincere vel mori.* 36. 4

M'Dougal of Lorn, an arm in armour embowed ppr., holding a cross crosslet fitchée gu. *Vincere vel mori.*

M'Dougal of Makerstown, Roxburghsh., Scotland, a lion issuing gardant ppr., holding in the dexter paw a cross crosslet fitchée gu. *Fear God.*

Macdougale, a fawn's head couped, collared and lined ppr. 124. 5

Macdougall, a lion's gamb erased sa., holding a sceptre in pale or. 38. 7

MacDougall, Scotland, an arm in armour embowed, holding in the hand a sword ppr. *Virtutis laus actio.* 195. 2

MacDougall, Stewart, of Lunga and Daill, Ardfern, Argyllsh., an arm in armour embossed ppr., holding a cross crosslet fitchée erect sa. *Vincere vel mori.*

MacDougall, Captain Alexander James of MacDougall, Dunollie, Oban, Argyllsh., a dexter arm embowed fesseways resting on the elbow, habited in scale armour, and holding in the hand, all ppr., a cross crosslet fitchée in pale gu. *Vincere vel mori.* or *Buaidh no bas.*

McDougall, Hon. John Frederick, of Rosalie Plains, Jondaryan, Queensland, member of the Legislative Council, *uses:* an arm in armour embowed fesseways, couped ppr., holding a cross crosslet fitchée gu. *Vincere vel mori.*

M'Dougall or **MacDougall,** Scotland, a lion's gamb erased and erect holding a dagger ppr. *Fortis in arduis.* 38. 8

M'Dougall, an arm in armour embowed, holding in the hand a scimitar. 196. 10

M'Dougall, a deer's head erased ppr. 121. 2

M'Dowal, a hand holding a dagger in pale. *Virtus in caducis.* 212. 9

M'Dowal and **McDowall** of Gartland, Wigtonsh., Scotland, a lion's gamb erased and erect. *Vincere vel mori.* 36. 4

M'Dowal, Scotland, and **M'Dowall** of London, a lion's gamb erased holding a branch of olive vert. *Vincam vel moriar.* cf. 37. 4

M'Dowal, Scotland, a demi-lion issuing ppr., holding in its dexter paw a sword az., hilt and pommel or. 14. 12

MacDowall, Henry, Esquire, J.P., of Garthland and Carruth, Renfrewsh., N.B., a lion's paw erased holding a dagger, all ppr. *Fortis in arduis.—Vincere vel mori.*

M'Dowall-Hay, Bart., Scotland, a lion passant gardant ppr., holding in the dexter paw a cross crosslet fitched gu. *Fear God.* cf. 4. 3

M'Dowall, Scotland, a demi-lion arg., crowned with an imperial crown or, holding in its dexter paw a flaming sword, all ppr. *Pro rege in tyrannos.* cf. 14. 14

M'Dowall of Edinburgh, a demi-lion arg., regally crowned or. *Vincere vel mori.*

M'Dowall, Portugal, a lion rampant holding in his dexter paw a sword erect ppr. *Sic itur ad astra.*

M'Dowall and **M'Dowell,** Scotland, two bear's paws erased in saltire. cf. 39. 14

M'Dowall of Castle Semphill, Scotland, a lion's gamb erased holding up a dagger ppr. *Fortis in arduis.* 38. 8

MacDowall, Henry, of Garthland, Lochwinroch, same crest. *Fortis in arduis.—Vincere vel mori.*

M'Dowall of Freugh, Wigtonsh., Scotland, a lion's gamb erased and erect ppr. *Vincet vel mori.—Pro Deo, rege, et patria.* 36. 4

M'Dowall of Stodrig, Roxburghsh., a lion's gamb. *Vincere vel mori.* cf. 36. 4

M'Dowall, Andrew Kenneth, of Logan, Wigtonsh., a tiger's head erased crowned with an imperial crown, and with a lion's gamb issuing from a cloud grasping the crown from the tiger's head ppr. *Usurpari nolo.—Victoria.*

M'Dowall, Scotland, an arm in armour embowed in fess, couped ppr., holding a cross crosslet fitched. *Vincere vel mori.*

M'Dowall, Scotland, on a ducal coronet or, an arm in armour embowed in fess, couped ppr., holding a cross crosslet fitched. *Vincere vel mori.*

M'Dowell, a lion's gamb erased holding a dagger in pale. 38. 8

M'Dowgal, Scotland, two lion's gambs in saltier ppr. *Victoria vel mors.* 39. 14

Macduff, Viscount, *see* Fife, Duke of.

Macduff, Scotland, a demi-lion rampant gu. 10. 3

Macduff, Alexander, Esquire, of Bonhard, Perthsh., a demi-lion gu., armed and langued az., holding in his dexter paw a dagger ppr. *Deus juvat.* cf. 14. 12

McDuff, Scotland, a demi-lion gu., holding a dagger. *Deus juvat.* 14. 12

Mace-Gigger, *see* Gigger.

Mace, a hand erect holding a scimitar in pale ppr. 213. 8

McEacharn, Sir Malcolm Donald, Esquire, of Goathland, Yorks, and of Strathfield Station, Burke, Queensland, an arm in armour, the hand bare ppr. holding a cross crosslet paleways fitchée or. *Per mare, per terras.*

MacEgan of Bally-mac-Egan, co. Tipperary, Ireland, a tower arg., and issuant from the battlements thereof a demi-man in armour, couped at the knees, holding in the dexter hand a battle-axe, all ppr. *Fortitudine et prudentia.*

Macelester, Scotland, a dexter arm in armour couped, holding in the hand a dagger. *Per mare, per terras.* 210. 2

MacElligott, Colonel Henry Richard, Union League Club, New York City, U.S.A., and Norman L. McElligott, Esquire, Calumet Club, New York, a falcon rising, wings expanded and endorsed. *Si Deus quis contra.* 87. 10

M'Emery, MacEmery, and **MacEniery,** Ireland, a falcon belled ppr. cf. 85. 2

M'Entire, Scotland, a dexter hand holding a dagger erect ppr. *Per ardua.* 212. 9

M'Evers, a boar's head couped in fess. 43. 1

Macevoy of Tobertinam, co. Meath, a cubit arm erect vested gu., cuffed erminois, holding in the hand a sword ppr. *Bear and forbear.*

McEvoy, Captain Edward, of Tobertinam, co. Meath, Ireland, on a wreath of the colours a cubit arm erect vested gu., cuffed erminois, holding in the hand a sword in bend sinister ppr. *Bear and forbear.*

Macevoy-Netterville, Joshua James, Esquire, of Villa Rita, Biarritz: (1) A demi-lion rampant guardant gu., bezantée, and charged with a lozenge or for difference (*for Netterville*). (2) A cubit arm erect vested gu., cuffed erminois, holding in the hand a dagger ppr. (*for Macevoy*). *Bear and forbear.*

McEwan, William, Esquire, M.P. for Central Division of Edinburgh, of 16, Charles Street, Berkeley Square, W., the trunk of an oak-tree with a branch sprouting forth on either side ppr. *Reviresco.* 145. 2

M'Ewan of Glasgow, Scotland, the trunk of an oak-tree shooting a young branch ppr. *Reviresco.* 145. 2

M'Ewan of Glenboig, Stirlingsh., a dexter arm couped at the shoulder, the elbow resting upon the wreath and grasping a scimitar, all ppr. *Pervicax recte.*

M'Fadyen and **M'Faiden,** Scotland, a talbot passant gu. 54. 1

M'Fall, Scotland, an eagle's head erased. *Resurgo.* 83. 2

Macfarlan of that ilk and Arroquhar, Dumbartonsh., a demi-savage grasping in his dexter hand a sheaf of arrows, and pointing with the sinister to an imperial crown or. *This I'll defend.* 186. 13

Macfarlan, Lieutenant-Colonel John Warden, Ballancleroche, Lennoxtown, Stirling, same crest and motto.

Macfarlane, seven darts, points upwards, six in saltier and one in pale, enfiled with a ducal coronet.

Macfarlane, Sir Donald Horne, a demi-savage wreathed about the temples and waist with leaves, holding in his dexter hand three arrows, and pointing with his sinister to a crown resting upon the wreath, all ppr. *Lochsloy.*—*This I'll defend.*

Macfarlane, Scotland, an eagle rising ppr. *Laboranti numen adest.* 77. 5

Macfarlane, a bird sitting on a tree.

M'Farlane, of Keithtoun, Scotland, a demi-naked man holding forth a sheaf of arrows ppr., a crown or standing upon the wreath. *This I'll defend.* 186. 13

Macfarlane-Grieve: (1) A demi-savage wreathed about the middle with laurel, grasping in his dexter hand a sheaf of arrows, and pointing with the sinister to an imperial crown or. (2) A dexter arm in armour embowed, the hand grasping a dagger, point downwards, hilted and pommelled or. *This I'll defend.*—*Hoc securior.*

MacFarquhar, Scotland, a dexter hand couped ppr. *Sto pro fide.* 222. 14

M'Farquhar, Scotland, a demi-lion rampant holding in its dexter paw a sword. *Fide et fortitudine.* 14. 12

M'Farquhar, Scotland, a dexter hand ppr. 222. 14

M'Farquhar, on a winged globe an eagle rising, all ppr. 159. 9

M'Fayden, a talbot passant, collared and lined, all ppr. 54. 5

M'Fell, Scotland, an eagle's head erased ppr. *Aspiro.* 83. 2

Macfie, a demi-lion rampant ppr. *Pro rege.* 10. 2

Macfie, John William, Esquire, of Dreghorn and Colinton, Midlothian, and Rowton Hall, Chester, same crest and motto. 10. 2

Macfie, William, Esquire, C.B., of Airds, Argyllsh., a demi-lion rampant sa. *Pro Rege.* 10. 1

M'Fingah, Ireland, an arm in armour embowed, holding in the hand a tilting-spear.

M'Gallock, Scotland, a dove ppr. *Industria et labore.* 92. 2

MacGan, Ireland, a boar's head couped az., armed and crined or. 43. 1

McGarel-Hogg, *see* Magheramorne, Baron.

MacGarry, Ireland, a fox's head couped gu., holding in the mouth a snake ppr. *Fear garbh ar mait.*

M'Gassock, Scotland, a dove ppr. *Industria et labore.* 92. 2

M'Gavin, Scotland, a dragon's head or, vomiting flames of fire gu. 72. 3

McGavin, Robert, of Ballumbie, Dundee, N.B., a wyvern's head vert, ducally gorged or, vomiting flames of fire ppr. *God send grace.*

M'Gee or **M'Ghie,** an ostrich arg., holding in its beak a horse-shoe az. 97. 8

M'Gell, Scotland, a terrestrial globe. *Honestum utili prefero.* 159. 1

McGenis or **Magenis, Viscount Iveagh** (*extinct*), a boar passant ppr., langued gu., armed and ungu. or. *Sola salus servire Deo.* 40. 9

MacGeorge, Lieutenant-Colonel William, a dexter cubit arm, the hand grasping a sabre, all ppr., and charged with a fess indented az. *Dread God.* *cf.* 212. 13

MacGeorge, Andrew, Esquire, of Glenarn, Dumbartonsh., Scotland, an antelope's head erased arg., attired or, gorged with a collar dancettée gu. *Pro veritate.* *cf.* 126. 2

M'George, a greyhound's head or, collared gu. 61. 2

M'George, Scotland, a demi-griffin arg. 64. 2

MacGeoghegan of Moyeashell, co. Westmeath, a greyhound statant arg. *Semper patriæ servire presto.* *cf.* 60. 2

McGeough-Bond, *see* Bond.

McGeough of Drumskill, co. Armagh, a naked arm embowed, the hand holding a scimitar, all ppr. 201. 1

MacGeough, Robert John, Esquire, of Silverbridge House, Silverbridge, Ireland, same crest. *Nemo me impune lacessit.*

M'Gerachty, Ireland, on a mount vert, an oak-tree ppr., bent towards the dexter.

M'Gibbon, Scotland, two oars in saltier sa. 179. 3

M'Gie, a leopard's head erased gardant or.

M'Gilchrist of Northbarr, a lion's gamb in bend arg. *Cogit in hostem.*

M'Gilevray, Scotland, a cat sejant. *Touch not the cat without a glove.* 26. 8

M'Gill or **Macgill, Viscount Oxenford** (*extinct*), a phœnix in flames ppr. *Sine fine.* 82. 2

M'Gill, a phœnix in flames ppr. *Sine fine.* 82. 2

M'Gill of Rankeillour, and of Kembach, Fifesh., Scotland, a martlet arg. *In Domino confido.* 95. 4

M'Gill of Rumgally, Fifesh., Scotland, a martlet rising ppr. *In Deo confido.* *cf.* 95. 11

MacGillafoyle, a demi-lion rampant arg., holding between the paws a battle-axe erect gu., the blade also arg. *cf.* 15. 4

M'Gilleoun or **MacGilleoun,** Scotland, an arm embowed in fess, couped, supporting a spear issuing in pale, all ppr. 201. 11

Macgillicuddy, The, of the Reeks, Ireland, a representation of Macgillicuddy's Reeks, co. Kerry, ppr. *Sursum corda.*

McGillikelly, Ireland, an arm in armour, holding in the hand a spear, all ppr., headed or. 210. 11

M'Gillivray of Montreal, Canada, a buck's head and neck ppr., attired or. *Be mindful.* 121. 5

M'Gillivray, on a mount vert, by the brink of a river a beaver in the act of gnawing a tree by the roots represented as nearly falling, the branches entwined with an escroll bearing the motto, *Perseverance,* all ppr. *Touch not the cat but a glove.*

M'Gilvray, Scotland, a camel's head sa. 132. 7

M'Glashan, Scotland, a long cross crossed gu., on three grieces. 166. 6

M'Gouan or **M'Gowan,** of Skeoch, Wigtownsh., Scotland, a thistle ppr. *Juncta arma decori.* 150. 5

M'Gougan, Scotland, an arm couped at the elbow in fess, holding a cross crosslet fitched. *Vincere vel mori.* 221. 10

M'Gowan, a galley with her oars in action ppr. 161. 7

M'Gowan, Scotland, a talbot passant or, collared az. *cf.* 54. 5

M'Gowran, Ireland, an ancient ship or galley. 160. 6

M'Grady, Henry, J.P., D.L., of Arnhall, Dundee, and Kelly Castle, Arbroath, a horse's head erased arg. *Honore et industria.*

Macgregor, Sir Malcolm, Bart., of Edinchip, Lochearnhead, Perthsh.: (1) Of honourable augmentation, two brass guns in saltier in front of a demi-Highlander armed with his broadsword, pistols, and with a target, thereon the family arms of Macgregor, viz.: arg., a sword in bend dexter az., and an oak-tree eradicated in bend sinister ppr., in the dexter chief an antique crown gu., and upon an escroll surmounting the crest the motto, *E'en do and spare not.* *cf.* 187. 8. (2) Issuing from a mural coronet or, a lion's head crowned with an antique crown ppr., and on an escroll above the crest the motto, *Srioghal mo dhream.* *Ard choille.* *cf.* 19. 12

Macgregor, Scotland, a lion's head erased *Spare not* 17 8

Macgregor of Gleney, out of a mural coronet arg, masoned sa, a lion's head gu crowned with an antique crown or *Eadhon dean gus na caomhain —Virtutis regia merces*

Macgregor, Major Cortlandt Alexander, a lion's head erased crowned with an antique crown ppr *E'en do and spair not* cf 17 12

Macgregor, Captain Robert Francis Henry, Staff Officer of Pensioners, a lion's head erased and crowned with an antique crown ppr cf 17 12

Macgregor, Captain Cortland George, a lion's head erased crowned with an antique crown ppr *E'en do and spair not* cf 17 12

Macgregor, Philip Leighton, Major in the Royal Regiment of Artillery, same crest and motto cf 17 12

Macgregor, Scotland, an eagle perched with wings extended ppr *Serioghalmo dhream —In libertate sociorum defendenda* 77 5

Macgregor, Patrick Comyn, Esquire, of Brediland, Renfrewsh, Scotland a pine-tree eradicated ppr *Ard choille* 144 8

Macgregor, Sir William Gordon Bart a human hand couped at the wrist and holding a dagger erect ppr pommel and hilt or *E'in do and spare not* 212 9

Macgregor, issuing out of a heart a hand grasping a scimitar, all ppr *Firrineach gus e chrich* 213 4

MacGregor, Sir William, M D, K C M G, C B, LL D, D Sc formerly Receiver General and Chief Medical Officer for Fiji, of Government House, Lagos, West Africa, a lion's head or, langued gu *E'en do and spare not* 21 1

M Gregor, Scotland, a lion's head erased *E'en do and spare not* 17 8

M'Gregor, Scotland, a lion's head erased on the head an antique crown ppr *E'en do, bait spair nocht* cf 17 12

M'Gregor of Belfast and Carsbank, Isle of Wight, a lion's head erased, crowned with an antique crown ppr *E'en do and spare not —Nunquam non paratus* cf 17 12

M'Gregor or **Murray** of Napier Ruskie, Perthsh, same crest and first motto

M'Gregor, Scotland, a fir-tree 144 13

M Gregor, Patrick C, Esquire of Bredilands Renfrewsh, a pine-tree eradicated ppr *Ard choille* 144 8

M'Gregor of Raigmore a hand holding a dagger erect ppr, pommel and hilt or *E'en do and spare not* 212 9

M'Gregor, Scotland, an arm in armour ppr, wielding a scimitar az, hilted and pommelled or

McGregor, Scotland, a naked arm holding a sword, the blade enfiled with three royal crowns, all ppr

M Grigor, Sir James Rhoderic Duff Bart, of Camden Hill, Middx a lion's head erased ppr crowned with an antique crown or *Srioghal mo dhream* cf 17 12

M Grigor of Cairnoch Carronbridge, N B, and Beechwood Stirling, a demi lion gu holding in his dexter paw a pine-branch ppr *E'en do and spare not*

Macguarie of that ilk, Isle of Ulva out of an antique crown an arm in armour embowed grasping a dagger, all ppr *Turris fortis mihi Deus* cf 196 5

M'Guarie or **Macquarie,** of Ormaig Isle of Ulva Scotland, a nag's head couped arg, bridled gu *Be true* 51 5

M Guarie, Scotland, issuing from an antique crown an arm in armour embowed grasping a dagger, all ppr *Turris fortis mihi Deus*

McGuffie of Crosshill, near Wigton Cumb, and of Crossmichael Kirkcudbrightsh, a boar's head couped sa, armed and langued gu *Arma parata fero* 43 1

M Guffock, Rusco, Kirkcudbrightsh, a dove ppr *Industria et labore* 92 2

McGuire, Baron Enniskillen (*attainted*), a dexter cubit arm in armour grasping in the gauntlet a sword, all ppr *Marte et arte* 210 4

McGuire of Tempo, co Fermanagh, Chief of M Guire, McGuire of Knockaninny co Fermanagh, and McGuire of Carrigbawn, Rostrevor, co Down, on a ducal coronet or a stag at gaze ppr collared and lined of the first *Justitia et fortitudo invincibilia sunt*

M Guire, Ireland, a buck's head erased az 121 2

McGwire, William Walter, Esquire of Clonea House, Dungarvaw, co Waterford, on a ducal coronet or, a stag statant ppr collared and lined or *Fortitudo et justitia —Virtus et fortitudo invincibilia sunt*

M'Hado and **M Haddo,** Scotland, a hand brandishing a scimitar ppr *Vigilo* 213 5

McHaffie-Gordon, George William Gordon, Esquire of Corsemalzie, Whauphill Wigtownsh, a demi-savage holding a club over his dexter shoulder ppr *Dread God* 186 5

M'Hallie, Scotland, a demi-griffin gu 64 2

Macham, a greyhound current sa cf 58 2

M Hardie, Scotland, the sun in splendour or *Luceo non uro* 162 2

McHardy, Coghlan McLean Esquire J P, of 1, Grenville Place, Cromwell Road, London, S W, an arm in armour embowed wielding in the hand a scimitar all ppr *Tout hardi* 196 10

M Hattie, Scotland between two wings ppr, an escallop arg, charged with a cross fleury sa 141 7

Machell of Wendover, Bucks, a camel's head erased or, ducally gorged arg cf 132 9

Machell, Mauchael, or **Mauchel,** a stag's head erased ppr, ducally gorged or *Originally the crest used was a fleur de lys* cf 121. 2

Machell, James Octavius, **Mauchael,** or **Mauchel,** of Crakenthorpe Hall West morland a stag's head erased ppr, ducally gorged or Originally the crest used was a fleur-de lys cf 121 2

Machell of Pennybridge, Lancs, a stag's head erased and ducally gorged ppr *Mauvais chiens* cf 121 5

Machen or **Machin,** on a lion's head erased sa a chapeau or 21 10

Machen, Charles Edward, of Eastbach Court, Glouc, a pelican's head erased or 98 2

Machet of Lambeth, Surrey, a demi lion rampant or, gorged with a collar gu, charged with three fleurs-de-lis arg cf 10 9

Machin, Notts, on a mount vert a pelican's head couped gu in front of rays of the sun or *Auxilium ab alto*

Machin, Henry Vessey, of Gateford Hill near Worksop, same crest and motto

Machonchy of Dublin, a demi-swan with wings expanded ppr cf 100 5

M Hud, Scotland an arm in armour embowed grasping in the hand a dagger ppr *E'en do* 196 5

MacHugh, Ireland, a greyhound's head couped arg cf 61 2

M'Hutcheon, Scotland, a wyvern *For titer gerit crucem* 70 1

M'Ilwham, Scotland, a parrot feeding on the branch of a cherry-tree ppr 101 8

M Indoe, Scotland, a sundial on a stand arg 176 7

M Innes, a bee sucking a thistle ppr *E labore dulcedo* 150 9

MacInroy, Scotland, a lymphad in full sail sa *Sequor*

M'Inroy, Scotland a pelican in her piety *Fidelitas* 98 14

M'Intire, out of a tower a demi greyhound rampant, all ppr cf 157 8

M Intosh, Scotland, a cat current gardant ppr 26 6

M Intosh or **MacIntosh,** a demi-cat salient sa *Prenez garde* 26 11

M'Intosh or **MacIntosh,** Scotland, a cat salient ppr *Touch not the cat bot a glove* cf 26 3

M Intosh, Scotland, a cat current gardant ppr *Touch not the cat bot a glove* 26 6

M'Intyre, Scotland, a dexter hand holding a dagger in pale, both ppr *Per ardua* 212 9

M'Intyre of Glenoe Scotland same crest and motto 212 9

McIver-Campbell, Colonel Aylmer, of Asknish, Argyllsh, a boar's head couped or *Nunquam obliviscar* 43 1

McIver, Sir Lewis, Bart, M P Coldeast Sarisbury, Southampton same crest and motto

M Iver, Lancs, same crest and motto 43 1

Maciver, David of Woodslee Bromborough, Birkenhead Wanlass How, Ambleside, and 11, Caroline Place Birkenhead an escutcheon gu charged with a boar's head couped or *Nunquam obliviscar*

Maciver, Charles, of Rock Mount, Woolton Liverpool, same crest and motto

M Iver, a griffin's head erased az 66 2

Mack, a heart gu, pierced by an arrow in bend sinister arg *Et domi et foris —Cor vulneratum* 181 10

Mack, Scotland a water bouget sa *In spe et labore transigo vitam* 168 4

Mack, Scotland same crest *En esperanza* 168 4

M'Kaile, of Aberdeen, Scotland, a cancer ppr *Nec fero, nec igne* 141 5

M'Kall, Scotland an arm in armour holding in the hand a caltrap, all ppr 210 7

MacKartney, a dexter hand holding a slip of rose bush ppr *Stimulat sed ornat* 218 10

Mackauly, a leg couped at the knee, booted and spurred, all ppr 193 8

Mackauly, a boot couped at the ankle and spurred all ppr *Dulce periculum* 193 9

Mackay, Arthur Leith-Hay, a demi Highlander, vested and plaided, holding in his dexter hand a halbert, all ppr *Fortiter*

Mackay, *see* Reay, Lord

Mackay, Scotland, a dexter cubit arm erect holding in the hand a dagger in pale, all ppr, hilt and pommel or *Manu forti* 212 9

Mackay, George Duncan, of Inveralmond Cramond, Midlothian, a dexter hand couped at the wrist holding a dagger in pale, all ppr *Manu forti*

Mackay, Francis, of Whitehouse, Cramond, Midlothian, N B, same crest and motto

Mackay, George John, of Kimberley House, Chatteris, Cambs, same crest and motto

Mackay, a lion passant or, holding in the dexter paw a crescent gu 5 6

Mackay, a demi-greyhound vert 60 11

M Kay, a demi greyhound ppr 60 11

M Kay, Scotland, a hand holding a scimitar all ppr *Manu forti* 213 5

Mackbeath, Scotland an arm in armour embowed in fess, holding in the hand a sword all ppr

M Kean, Scotland a demi-cat gardant sa 26 12

M Kean, Scotland, a talbot sejant ppr *J'ai bonne esperance* cf 55 2

M Kechnie, Scotland, a dexter hand holding a spur 217 14

Mackeill, Scotland, a cross Calvary gu 166 1

M'Kell, Scotland, issuing out of clouds a dexter hand brandishing a scimitar, all ppr cf 213 5

Mackellar, Alexander, Esquire, of Lawrenny, Goulburn, New South Wales, a dexter arm in armour embowed wielding a scimitar, all ppr *Perseverando* 196 10

MacKellar, Hon Charles Kinnaird M B, C M, of Dunara, Rose Bay, Sydney, New South Wales, Australia, Member of the Legislative Council, N S W, an arm embowed in armour holding in the hand a scimitar, all ppr *Perseverando* 196 10

McKellar, Thomas, Esquire, J P of Strathkellar and Croxton, Hamilton, Victoria, and of Lerags Oban Argyllsh Scotland, a dexter arm embowed in armour holding in the hand a scimitar ppr *Perseverando* 196 10

M Kellar, Scotland, out of a castle tripletowered a demi lion rampant 155 10

M Kellar, a cat rampant gardant gu 26 1

M Kellar and **M Kellor,** Scotland, an arm in armour embowed brandishing a scimitar all ppr 196 10

M Kellip, Scotland a demi-talbot *Non dormit qui custodit* cf 55 8

M Kellip, Scotland a talbot's head *Non dormit qui custodit* 56 12

M Kellip, on a dexter gauntlet a falcon close and belled all ppr 86 13

Macken, a pelican's head gu, issuing from rays or 98 4

Mackenan and **Mackeuan** or **Mackewan,** Scotland, the trunk of an oak-tree shooting new branches ppr *Reviresco* 145 2

Mackenay, Ireland, an arm in armour embowed holding a spear, the top broken and pendent ppr 197 2

MacKenna of Trough, co Monaghan, a salmon naiant ppr 139 12

Mackennal or **Mackannel** of Cloverbank and Merk, Scotland an eagle's head erased ppr *Intrepidus et benignus* 83 2

Mackendrick of Brookfield, Lymm Chesh, a globe ppr, thereon an eagle with wings displayed and inverted *Qualis ab incepto*

M Kenny, Bart (*extinct*) of Dublin, a hand in armour couped at the wrist holding a roll of parchment *Vincit veritas* 211 1

Mackenzie, *see* Wharncliffe, Earl of

Mackenzie, Bart *see* Muir-Mackenzie Bart

Mackenzie, *see* Shaw-Mackenzie

Mackenzie, *see* Stewart Mackenzie

Mackenzie, *see* Burton Mackenzie

Mackenzie of Ardross, Ross sh, Scotland, a rugged rock ppr *Truth will prevail* 179 7

Mackenzie, James Fowler, of Allanbank House by Munlocky, Scotland, a mountain in flames ppr *Luceo, non uro — Vive ut vivas* 179 2

Mackenzie, Austin, of Carradale Argyllsh a burning mountain ppr *Luceo non uro*

Mackenzie, John Tolmie, J P, of Dunvegan, Isle of Skye, N B, same crest and motto.

Mackenzie, Bart, of Fairburne, Scotland a mountain in flames ppr 179 2

Mackenzie, on a rock a stag's head cabossed cf 122 5

Mackenzie, Middx a buck's head cabossed arg attired or 122 5

Mackenzie, Fitz Arundell Esquire, a buck's head caboshed per fesse az and arg *I face all weathers* 122 5

Mackenzie, W Dalziel, Esquire, of Fawley Court, Henley on-Thames, a stag's head caboshed az, within the attires a cross couped or the whole between two stag's horns of the last *Always faithful*

MacKenzie of Gillotts Oxon, the same crest a martlet for difference

MacKenzie of Warmanbie, Dumfriessh, same crest, a mullet for difference

MacKenzie of Auchenskeoch Kirkcudbrightsh., and Craig's, Dumfriessh, same crest a crescent for difference

Mackenzie, Scotland, between the attires of a stag affixed to the scalp sa, a boar's head erect or 43 2

Mackenzie or **M Kenzie** of Redcastle, Ross-sh, Scotland, a man's heart in flames within two branches of palm in orle all ppr *Ferendum et sperandum* 181 12

Mackenzie of Rosehaugh Ross-sh an eagle rising from a rock ppr *Firma et ardua.*

Mackenzie of Findon, Ross-sh, Scotland, a crescent arg *Crescitque virtute* 163 2

Mackenzie, Sir Arthur George Ramsay, Bart, D L, of Coul, Ross-sh, a boar's head erect or, between the attires of a stag affixed to the scalp sa *Pulchrior ex arduis* 43 2

Mackenzie, Bart, of Kilcoy, Scotland, a lady from the waist, with bodice and short sleeves, presenting a rose with her dexter hand, her sinister arm bent outward the hand resting on her side, ringlets loose *Amori vici.*

Mackenzie or **M Kenzie,** of Scotsburn, Scotland, the sun in his splendour *Sans tache* 162 2

Mackenzie, Sir James Kenneth Douglas, Bart, of Scatwell and Tarbat, Ross sh the sun in splendour ppr *Luceo non uro — Sine macula* 162 2

Mackenzie, Bart, of Garloch, a Highlander wielding a sword, all ppr *Virtute et valore* 188 5

Mackenzie of Craig Hall, Scotland, a demi savage wreathed about the head and loins with laurel holding in his dexter hand and on his shoulder a club, all ppr *Virtute et valore* 186 1

Mackenzie, Scotland, an arm embowed holding in the hand a dart, all ppr *Recte ad ardua* 201 13

Mackenzie, Captain Alexander Francis, of Ord House, Muir of Ord a dexter hand grasping a dagger in bend ppr *Sic itur ad astra*

Mackenzie, Sir Allan Russell Bart of Glenmuick, Aberdeensh, Kintail Ross sh, a dexter hand grasping a sword bendways ppr *Itur ad astra* 212 13

Mackenzie of Ord, Ross-sh, a hand holding a dagger in bend ppr *Sic itur ad astra* 212 3

Mackenzie, Roderick, of Foveran House, Aberdeensh and 14, Charles Street, Berkeley Square W, two hands grasping a two-handed sword in bend ppr *Semper fidelis*

Mackenzie, Captain Donald, Glack, Aberdeensh, same crest

Mackenzie of Lechwards, Ayrsh, Scotland, a dexter arm embowed holding in the hand a sword in bend, all ppr *Fide parta, fide aucta* 201 4

Mackenzie, a dexter hand grasping a sword bendways ppr *Sic itur ad astra* 212 13

Mackenzie, late Colin Esquire, W S, of 25, Ainslie Place, Edinburgh, a dexter arm, the hand holding a garland of laurel ppr *Virtute et labore* 218 4

Mackenzie, Colin Charles Forbes a dexter arm holding a garland of laurel ppr *Virtute et labore* 276 12

Mackenzie, Thomas, Esquire, of Dailuaine House Carron Strathspey N B, same crest *Virtute et valor — Luceo non uro*

Mackenzie, Sir Kenneth John, Bart, J P, of Gairloch, Ross-sh, same crest. *Virtute et valore — Non sine periculo* 218 4

Mackenzie, John Hugh Munro, Calgary, Mull, N B same crest and first motto

Mackenzie, Thomas, Innes House Elgin, same crest *Luceo non uro*

Mackenzie, late Sir Evan, Bart (*extinct*), of Kilcoy Ross sh (1) A dexter arm embowed in chain mail holding a broadsword in bend, all ppr cf

195 2 (2) A stag's head cabossed or, pierced with an arrow ppr *Fide parta, fide aucta —Dia's-Mo-Dhuthaich* cf 122 5

M'Kenzie or **Mackenzie**, a burning mount ppr *Luceo non uro* 179 2

M'Kenzie, Scotland a rugged rock ppr *Truth will prevail* 179 7

M'Kenzie of Fairburn Ross sh Scotland, a mountain in flames ppr *Fide parta fide aucta* 179 2

M'Kenzie, a lady from the middle holding in her dexter hand a cinquefoil ppr *Amore vici*

M'Kenzie or **M'Kinzie**, Scotland, a demi lady richly vested holding a rose ppr *Amore vici*

M'Kenzie of Applecross, Ross-sh, a lion couchant gardant ppr *Insult me not —Fide parta, fide aucta* 7 10

M'Kenzie, Scotland, a demi-lion rampant gu *Avito viret honore* 10 3

M'Kenzie, Scotland, a stag's head cabossed *Cuidich in rhi* 122 5

M'Kenzie, Scotland, a dexter arm throwing a dart, all ppr *Recta et ardua* 214 4

M'Kenzie, Scotland a dexter arm holding in the hand a garland of laurel ppr *Virtute et amore* 218 4

M'Kenzie of Glack, Aberdeensh, and of Hilltoun, Inverness-sh, two hands holding a two-handed sword in bend all ppr *Always faithful* 213 3

M'Kenzie of Suddie Ross sh, Scotland, a dexter hand holding a sword in bend ppr *Sic itur ad astra* 212 13

Mackenzie, Colonel Sir Felix Calvert, D L, of Forres, N B, a dexter cubit arm erect holding a sword in bend sinister all ppr *Corde et manu*

M'Kenzie, Scotland, a dexter hand couped and erect holding a dagger, both ppr *Garde* 212 9

M'Kenzie of Portmore, Peebles, an arm couped at the elbow holding a wreath of laurel ppr *Virtute et valore* 218 4

M'Kenzie, Scotland, issuing out of clouds ppr, two hands conjoined *Fides unit* 224 1

Mackenzie-Ashton, Arundell of Howden Court, Tiverton (1) On a mount vert, a mower ppr, vested paly arg and sa, in the act of whetting his scythe also ppr (*for Ashton*) (2) A buck's head caboshed and counterchanged (*for Mackenzie*)

Mackenzie-Gibson, Rev John of 22, Regent Terrace, Edinburgh, a pelican in her piety in a nest ppr *Cœlestes pandite portæ*

MacKeogh, co Roscommon, a boar passant az 40 9

McKeown, Ireland, an arm embowed in chain armour, the hand holding a sword the blade wavy all ppr

Mackerell of Norwich Norf, a horseman's spear erected in pale ppr, behind two mackerel saltireways, heads upwards ppr

M'Kerlie, Scotland on the dexter side of a mount vert, a cross crosslet fitched sa *In hoc signo vinces* cf 166 4

M'Kerrell, Scotland, an ancient warrior in armour, with a shield and spear, over the point of the latter a star *Dulcis pro patria labor*

M'Kerrell of Hillhouse Ayrsh, a Roman soldier on his march, with standard and utensils, all ppr *Dulcis pro patria labor* 240 1

McKerrell-Brown, Edinburgh, a demi lion or, armed and langued gu, holding in his dexter paw a fleur de-lis of the first *Floreat majestas* 13 2

M'Kerrow, Alexander, Esquire Reform Club, S W, two cross crosslets fitched in saltier *Cruce delecta* 166 13

Mackesy, Thomas Lewis, Esquire, M D, J P, a Vice President of the Royal College of Surgeons in Ireland, of Augmacart Queen's Co, Ireland, out of a mural crown ppr, a demi eagle displayed or, charged on the breast with a sword entwined with a snake both ppr *In Deo manuque fides* 263 15

Mackesy, George Ivie, M B M A, of 47 Lady Lane, Waterford, out of a mural crown ppr, a demi-eagle or, charged on the breast with a sword entwined with a snake in pale, also ppr *In Deo manuque fides* 263 15

Mackey, a lion's head erased arg 17 8

Mackey, Lord Mayor of the City of Dublin 1866, of Clonsilla House, Dublin J P out of a mural crown a dexter hand grasping a dagger in pale all ppr *Manu forti* cf 212 9

Mackie, two oak branches in saltier fructed ppr 151 1

Mackie or **M'Kie**, Scotland, a raven ppr *Labora* 107 14

Mackie, John of Bargaly, Kirkcudbright, and Dowloch Scotland, same crest and motto 107 14

Mackie, John Gladstone, J P, D L of Auchencairn, Kirkcudbrightsh, a hand holding a dagger ppr *Labore* 212 9

Mackie, Colonel Edward Alexander, of Kirkthorpe Scarborough, in front of a dexter cubit arm erect grasping a sword, all ppr, a Narcissus arg between two mullets of six points or *Disce et labora*

Mackiegan, Ireland out of a ducal coronet a griffin's head holding in the beak a key all ppr 65 14

Mackillop or **M'Killop**, a demi-eagle regardant ppr 80 10

M'Killop, Scotland a talbot's head erased ppr *Non dormit qui custodit* 56 2

M'Killop, Scotland, a demi-talbot *Non dormit qui custodit* cf 55 8

M'Killop, on a dexter gauntlet a falcon close belled all ppr 86 13

M'Kimmie, Scotland, a deer's head erased ppr *Je suis prêt* 121 2

Mackinder or **M'Kinder**, an elephant statant ppr 133 9

MacKindlay, Scotland a stag trippant ppr *Amo* 117 8

M'Kindlay or **Mackinlay**, Scotland an eagle's head erased ppr *Spernit humum* 83 2

M'Kinlay, Scotland, an arm in armour holding a branch of olive all ppr *Not too much*

M'Kinna, an arm in armour embowed holding in the hand the butt end of a spear ppr *Prudentia et honor* 197 7

Mackinnon, a spear in pale ppr 175 9

Mackinnon of Pottswood Park Hants, and Scotland, a boar's head erased arg, holding in its mouth a deer's shank-bone ppr *Audentes fortuna juvat*

Mackinnon, William Alexander, Esquire of Acryse Park, near Folkestone, and Belvedere, near Broadstairs same crest and motto

Mackinnon, Sir William, Bart, C I E, J P D L, of Strathaird and Loup, Argyllsh, a boar's head erased holding in the mouth a shin-bone, all ppr *Persevere in hope*

Mackintosh, *see* Fraser Mackintosh

Mackintosh, *see* Keir-Mackintosh

Mackintosh of that Ilk, and Tor Castle, Kellachie, Connadge, and of Kinrara, all in Inverness sh, a cat-a mountain salient gardant ppr *Touch not the cat but a glove* 26 3

Mackintosh, Alfred Donald, J P, of 8, Hill Street, Berkeley Square same crest and motto

Mackintosh, George Gordon, Esquire, of Richmond House, King Street, Twickenham, same crest and motto

Mackintosh, Hugh Richard Duncan M D 12, Onslow Gardens, S W, same crest

Mackintosh, Rev William Lachlan, 6 Ardross Street, Inverness same crest and motto

Mackintosh, Scotland, a cat sejant gardant sa *Touch not the cat bot a glove* 26 8

Mackintosh, a cat sejant erect *Touch not the cat bot a glove* 25 2

Mackintosh, William of Kyllachy Inverness-sh, a cat-a-mountain salient ppr, charged on the breast with a crescent gu *Touch not the catt but a glove* cf 26 3

Mackintosh, Fraser-, Charles Drummond Inverness-sh (1) A cat ppr, collared gu, resting the dexter paw on an escutcheon or charged with a dexter hand couped at the wrist and clenched gu (2) A stag's head erased arg, attired and collared gu in the mouth a sprig of fern ppr and pendent from the collar an escutcheon az, charged with a cinquefoil arg *Onwords*

Mackintosh of Aberarder, Inverness sh, a cat courant gardant ppr *Touch not the cat but a glove* 26 6

Mackintosh, a cat's face gu cf 22 2

Mackinzie, a mountain in flames ppr *Luceo, non uro* 179 2

M'Kirdy, William Augustus Scott, Esquire, D L, of Birkwood, Lanarksh, Scotland a demi wyvern displayed ppr *Dieu et mon pays* 69 12

Mackleid, an arm in armour embowed grasping in the hand a sword enfiled with a Moor's head all ppr

Macklellan or **M'Lellan**, Scotland, a Moor's head and neck ppr *Sapit qui reputat*

Macklellan or **M'Lellan**, Scotland, a naked arm supporting a sword, on the point thereof a Moor's head *Think on*

Macklellan, Scotland, a mortar-piece *Superba frango* 169 10

Macklin, an ass's head 125 12

Macklin, an eagle's head issuing from rays of the sun 84 13

Mackloide or **M'Cloud**, Scotland a bull's head cabossed between two flags. *Hold fast* 43 5

Macklow, a dragon's head per pale indented gu and arg, guttee counterchanged, holding in the mouth an eagle's leg erased or

Macklow, a sinister arm holding a bow sans strings. cf. 214. 5
Mackmure, a dolphin naiant. 140. 5
Mackmoragh and **Macmore,** Ireland, on a ducal coronet a griffin sejant ppr., resting its dexter claw upon a shield arg. 62. 11
Macknight-Crawfurd, see Crawfurd.
Macknight, Scotland, an arm in armour holding in the hand a spear in bend ppr. *Fac et spera.* 210. 11
Macknight or **M'Knight,** Scotland, a tower sa., masoned arg. *Justum et tenacem.* 156. 2
MacKnight, a lion's head erased gu. 17. 2
M'Knight, a lion's head erased az. *Omnia fortunæ committo.* 17. 8
Macknyghte of Macknyghte, Scotland, a demi-lion rampant arg. *Omnia fortunæ committo.* 10. 2
Mackorda, a demi-wild Irish savage holding in his dexter hand a heart and in his sinister a dart, all ppr. 186. 9
M'Kowan, two doves billing. *Constancy.* 93. 2
Mackpherson, Scotland, a cat sejant gardant ppr. 26. 8
Mackreth, Hants, a phœnix in flames ppr. 82. 2
Mackwilliams, a phœnix in flames ppr. 82. 2
Mackworth-Dolben, see Dolben.
Mackworth-Praed, see Praed.
Mackworth of Betton Grange, Meole Brace, Shropsh., a cock gu., beaked, combed, and wattled or. 91. 2
Mackworth of Wales and London, a cock ppr. *Gwell angau nachywilydd.* 91. 2
Mackworth, Sir Arthur William, Bart., Glamorgansh., a cock ppr. 91. 2
Mackworth, Sir Arthur William, Bart., J.P., D.L., of Glen Uske, Monm., a cock ppr. *Gwell angau nachywilydd.* —*Better death than shame.* 91. 2
Mackworth of Mackworth Castle, Derbysh., and of Normanton, Rutl. and Norf., a sinister wing erect per pale indented sa. and erm.
Maclachlan, a castle triple-towered. 155. 8
Maclachlan, John, of that Ilk, Argyllsh., and 12, Abercromby Place, Edinburgh, a castle on a rock ppr. *Fortis et fidus.* 155. 4
Maclachlan of Kilchoan, Argyllsh., on a ducal coronet or, a lion's head erased ppr. *Fortis et fidus.* cf. 19. 10
M'Lachlan or **Maclauchlan** of Trinidad, a leopard's face ppr. *Fortiter.* 22. 2
Maclagan, late Sir Douglas, M.D., Edinburgh, a beaver statant ppr. *Principiis obsta.* 134. 8
M'Lagan, Scotland, a mortar-piece or. *Superba frango.* 169. 10
M'Lagan of Edinburgh, Scotland, a beaver ppr. *Principiis obsta.* 134. 8
Maclagan-Wedderburn, Alexander Stormouth, Pearsie, Kirriennie, N.B., an eagle's head erased ppr.
M'Laggan, Scotland, a greyhound sejant collared arg. cf. 59. 2
Maclaine of Kington House, Glouc., in front of a Lochaber-axe erect two branches of laurel and cypress, all ppr. *Vincere vel mori.* 172. 14
Maclaine, Murdoch Gillian, of Lochbuie, Isle of Mull, in front of a branch of laurel and cypress in saltire a Lochaber-axe erect, all ppr. *Vincere vel mori.*
Maclaine, William Osborne, Kyneton, Thornbury, Glouc., same crest and motto.
M'Clambroch, Scotland, a hand holding a dagger. *Fear God and fight.* 212. 3
McLandsborough, a hand holding a dagger in bend sinister, all ppr. *Fear God and fight.* 212. 3
McLannachan of Oriel Cottage, Eskbank, Midlothian, a tower gu. *Virtue is mine honour.* 156. 5
M'Lardy, Samuel, of Basford, Mount Higher Crumpsall, Manchester, a dexter hand couped ppr., beaked and membered of the third, in the dexter chief point an estoile, and in the sinister chief point a dexter hand couped of the last. *In te fido.*
McLaren, Sir Charles Benjamin Bright, Bart., Hilders, Shottermill, Surrey, 43, Belgrave Square, S.W., the Virgin and child ppr., vested az. *Bi'se mac na Cromaig.* 274. 14
Maclaren, Scotland, a cannon mounted ppr. *Forward.* 169. 12
M'Laren, Scotland, a mortar-piece az. *Frango.* 169. 10
M'Larty of Jamaica and Kilcolmkill, a hand ppr., holding up a cross crosslet fitched in pale gu. *In te fido.* cf. 221. 14
M'Lauchlan, Scotland, a castle triple-towered. *Fortis et fidus.* 155. 8
Maclaughlan, Scotland, a salmon naiant ppr. *Fortis et fidus.* 139. 12
McLaughlan, Ireland, out of a ducal coronet or, a lion's head gu. *Fortis et fidus.* 17. 5
M'Laughlan, a horse's head in armour issuing, on the top a plume of ostrich-feathers, all ppr. 50. 14
M'Laurance and **M'Laurin** of Dreghorn, Edinburgh, the Virgin and Child ppr., vested vert. *Bi se machant Slaurie.*
Maclaurin of Balquhidder, a lion's head erased crowned with an Eastern diadem of four points between two laurel-branches in orle, all ppr. *Ab origine fidus.*
Maclaurin of London, a lion's head erased ppr., crowned with an antique coronet or, all between two branches of laurel issuing from the wreath ppr. *Dalriada.* *Ab origine fidus.*
MacLaurin, Henry Norman, Esquire, of 155, Macquarrie Street, Sydney, New South Wales, a lymphad, sails furled and oars in action sa., flags flying gu. *Fidelis.* 160. 7
M'Laws, a garb or, banded gu. *Dominus providebit.* 153. 2
M'Lea, Scotland, two lion's gambs erased in saltier ppr. *Vincere vel mori.* cf. 39. 14
M'Lea of Russia, two arms, dexter and sinister, from the shoulders extended in saltier, the former holding a pair of compasses, also extended, and the latter a sword in pale, all ppr. *Tam arte quam marte.*
Maclean, see Northampton, Marquess of.
Maclean of Pennycross, Argyllsh., and Scotland, a battle-axe in pale crossed by a branch each of laurel and of cypress in saltier, all ppr. *Altera merces.* cf. 12. 127
Maclean, same crest. *Sorti æquus utrique.*
Maclean, Sir Fitzroy Donald, Bart., of Morvaren, Argyllsh., (1) A tower embattled arg. 156. 2. (2) A battle-axe betwixt a laurel and a cypress branch, with the motto, *Altera merces.* —*Virtue mine honor.* cf. 172. 12
M'Lean, Scotland, a laurel and palm branch in saltier ppr. *Fortiter et strenue.*
M'Lean of Coll, Scotland, and **Maclean** of Haremere Hall, Sussex, a battle-axe in pale crossed by a branch of laurel and of cypress in saltire, all ppr. *Altera merces.*—*Virtus durissima ferit.* cf. 172. 12
MacLean, George Alexander, of Westfield House, Spynie, N.B., same crest and motto.
Maclean, Alexander John Hew, of Ardgour House, Ardgour, Argyllsh., same crest and first motto.
M'Lean, Scotland, a salmon naiant. 139. 12
M'Lean, a dragon's head vert. 71. 1
M'Lean, Scotland, a tower arg. *Virtue mine honour.* 156. 2
Macleans, a cypress-branch and a laurel-slip in saltier, surmounted of a battle-axe in pale, all ppr. cf. 172. 12
Maclear, Vice-Admiral John Pearse, Beaconscroft, Chiddingfold, Godalming, a cock ppr. *Clarus ab ortu.*
Macleay of Keiss Castle, Caithness, a buck's head erased ppr. *Spes anchora vitæ.* 121. 2
M'Leay, Scotland, same crest and motto.
M'Leay, Scotland, a demi-lion rampant gardant or. 10. 8
M'Leish, Scotland, same crest. 10. 8
Maclellan, Baron Kirkcudbright (*dormant*), a naked arm supporting on the point of a sword a Moor's head. *Think on.* cf. 212. 14
Maclellan, a Moor's head on the point of a dagger, all ppr., hilt and pommel or. *Think on.*
Maclellan of Barclay, Scotland, a naked arm supporting on the point of a sword a Moor's head. *Think on.* cf. 212. 14
M'Lellan, Scotland, a mortar-piece. *Superba frango.* 169. 10
M'Lellan of Edinburgh, a Moor's head couped ppr. *Sapit qui reputat.*
Macleod, Baron, see Cromartie, Earl of.
Macleod of Lewis, Scotland, the sun in his splendour ppr. 162. 2
Macleod of Rasay, same crest. *Luceo, non uro.* 162. 2
Macleod of Cadboll, Ross-sh., Scotland, same crest. *Loisgim agus soillsighim.* —*Quocunque jecerit stabit.* 162. 2
MacLeod, Roderick Willoughby, of Invergordon Castle, Ross-sh., same crest and motto.
Macleod of Colbecks, an eagle displayed in the midst of flames of fire ppr. *Luceo, non uro.*—*I buke while I see.* cf. 75. 2
MacLeod, Scotland, a phœnix in flames ppr. *Luceo, non uro.* 82. 2
Macleod of Muiravonside, a lion's head erased gu. *Murus aheneus esto.* 17. 2

MacLeod, Scotland, two lions regardant *Hold fast — Murus aheneus esto*

Macleod, a bull's head cabossed between two flags gu *Hold fast —Hic murus aheneus esto* 43 5

MacLeod, a bull's head erased *Murus aheneus esto* 44 3

M Leod, Scotland, an eagle's head ppr *Murus aheneus* 83 1

M'Leod, Scotland an anchor, the flukes uppermost *Vigilando*

MacLeod, Norman Magnus, of that Ilk, of Dunvegan, and of Talisker, Isle of Skye Scotland, a bull's head cabossed sa, between two flags gu, staves of the first *Hold fast —Murus aheneus esto* 43 5

MacLeod, Rev Roderick Charles, of Mitford Vicarage, Morpeth, same crest and motto

M'Leod, a bull's head cabossed gu *Hold fast* 43 8

M Leod, Scotland, the sun in splendour or *Quocunque jeceris stabit* 162 2

M Leod, a lion's head erased az (*Another* ppr) 17 8

M Leod, a lion's head erased gu, langued az *Hic murus aheneus* 17 2

M Leod, a castle triple towered and embattled arg, masoned sa, windows and port gu 155 8

M'Leur or **M Lure,** Scotland an arm in armour holding in the hand a falcon's lure ppr *Spectemur agendo*

M'Leurg, Scotland a demi-archer shooting an arrow from a bow, all ppr *Ad metam* 187 6

M'Lin, an eagle's head issuing from rays 84 13

M Lin, an ass's head couped holding in the mouth a thistle leaved

M Lintock, Ireland, a lion passant ppr *Virtute et labore* 6 2

M'Liver of Bristol, issuing from a mural crown or, a swan sa, collared lined, and crowned with an Eastern coronet also or *Be mindful*

McLoskey of Rothwell, Northamp, in front of two cross crosslets fitchee in saltire sa a dexter cubit arm erect vested arg cuffed erm the hand grasping a dagger in bend sinister point downwards ppr *Sica inimicis*

McLoskie, Ireland, a dexter hand couped at the wrist holding a dagger, all ppr 212 9

M'Lowe, the stump of an oak tree sprouting forth new branches ppr 145 2

MacLulich, Rev John 25, Rue des Cascades, Chantilly, Oise France, a demi-man affrontee ppr, banded round the temples az and or, holding in the hands a bar of iron fesseways also ppr *Caraid san airc* (*A friend in need*)

Maclure, Sir John E S, Bart, of Whalley Range, Manchester, and Stoneycroft, Reading, an eagle's head erased arg between four roses gu, stalked and leaved, two on either side ppr *Paratus sum* 284 13

M'Lure and **Maclure,** Scotland, same crest and motto 83 2

Macmahon, a goat passant arg, armed and unguled or cf 129 5

MacMahon, Ireland an arm in armour embowed holding in the band ppr a roll or.

MacMahon-Creagh, Major Hugh Michell Macnamara, of Dangan co Clare, Ireland a horse's head erased arg, caparisoned gu in the headstall of the bridle a laurel-branch vert and charged on the neck for distinction with a cross crosslet sa *Virtute et numine*

MacMahon of Clonderlaw **MacMahon** of Coaghy and Tuagh, and **MacMahon** of Leadmore, all in co Clare, Ireland, a dexter arm in armour embowed ppr, garnished or holding in the hand a sword, also ppr, pommel and hilt of the second *Sic nos sic sacra tuemur* 195 2

MacMahon, a naked arm embowed holding a sword, all ppr the point pierced through a fleur de lis sa *So dorn dona dhubhfuiltibh —Manus hæc inimica tyrannis* cf 201 4

MacMahon, Marie Edme Patrice Maurice Duc de Magenta, Marshal of France, a dexter arm in armour embowed ppr garnished or, holding in the hand a sword, also ppr, pommel and hilt of the second *Sic nos, sic nostra tuemur* 195 2

MacMahon of Clenagh Ballylean co Clare, a naked arm embowed holding a sword, the blade entwined by a serpent all ppr *Sic nos sic nostra tuemur.* 201 3

McMahon, Sir Aubrey Hope, Bart in front of an arm embowed in armour holding a sword the blade wavy all ppr, a portcullis gu chained or *Sic nos sic sacra tuemur* 273 2

McMahon, Sir William Samuel Bart, of Dublin same crest and motto

McMahon of Hollymount, co Carlow, a demi-griffin segreant arg 64 2

M Mahon, Ireland, two dexter hands in armour conjoined environed with clouds supporting a flaming heart all ppr 211 2

MacManus, co Fermanagh Ireland a hand and arm couped below the elbow erect holding a long cross ppr

MacManus, co Antrim, a dexter hand apaumee couped at the wrist gu 222 14

McManus of Mount Davis co Antrim, a dexter hand apaumee couped at the wrist gu *Cor et manus* 222 14

McMaster, Alexander Anthony, Esquire of Waikaura and Tokarahi, Oamaru New Zealand, *uses* issuing out of a coronet a unicorn's head *Medio tutus*

M Maught, Scotland a dexter band couped gu holding a fleur de-lis az *Pro aris et focis* cf 215 4

MacMaure, Ireland between two branches in orle a dexter hand holding a roll of paper all ppr 215 3

Macmichael of London and Scotland, a talbot's head couped arg charged with a crescent or cf 56 12

MacMichael, Rev C Walpole Rectory, Wisbech, same crest *Vigilante salus*

Macmichael, a battle axe erect surmounted by a branch of laurel on the dexter and of oak on the sinister in saltier all ppr cf 172 12

M Micing, M Michin, M Micking, or **M Mikin,** Ireland, a demi savage holding in his dexter hand an arrow and on his back a full quiver ppr 275 10

MacMicking, Robert of Manus Upper Murray New South Wales, a demi savage bearing in his dexter hand an arrow at his back a quiver full ppr *Res non verba —We hae dune* 275 10

McMicking, Gilbert Miltonsea, Glenwhilly, co Wigton, same crest and motto

Macmillan, Scotland, a dexter hand holding a broadsword ppr 212 13

Macmillan-Scott, Walter, Esquire, of Wauchope, Roxburghsh (1) On the dexter side, a stag's head erased gu (*for Scott*) 121 2 (2) On the sinister side, a dexter and a sinister hand ppr grasping a two handed sword az hilted and pommelled or (*for Mac millan*) *Ardenter amo —Miseris succurro* 213 3

MacMillan of Dunmore, Scotland a dexter and a sinister hand brandishing a two handed sword ppr *Miseris succurrere disco* 213 3

MacMillan, Ireland, a naked arm erect couped below the elbow holding a sword all ppr 212 13

McMillan, Hon William, of Sydney, New South Wales, Australia Colonial Treasurer and Minister for Railways, *uses* a dexter and sinister hand issuing from the wreath, brandishing a two-handed sword ppr *Miseris succurrere disco*

M'Millan of Edinburgh, a lion rampant *Age aut perfice* 1 13

M Millan, a yew tree ppr 143 1

M'Millan a mullet sa. 164 2

M Min, M'Minn, and **M Myne,** Scotland, a stag lodged ppr *Nil certum est* 115 7

MacMoran of Edinburgh, Scotland, a dexter hand couped gu *Virtus virtutis præmium* 222 14

M'More, Ireland a cubit arm in armour holding in the hand a sword ppr 210 2

MacMorogh, Ireland, issuing out of clouds a hand erect holding a crown between two swords in saltire points upwards all ppr

M'Morran, a raven ppr *Virtus virtutis præmium* 107 14

M'Morran, Scotland, a raven ppr *Pro lusu et præda* 107 14

MacMorran, Alexander, K C, of Lavington, Putney Heath, London, S W, a dexter hand couped gu *Virtus virtutis præmium*

M'Morran, Scotland, a hawk belled ppr *Pro lusu et præda.* cf 85 2

MacMurdoch, Scotland a lion's head erased gu *Omine secundo* 17 2

McMurray of Roxborough House Limerick and of Patrickswell, co Limerick a demi lion rampant gardant gu, holding a Lochaber axe, and charged on the shoulder with a rose arg *Virtute fideque* cf 16 12

M Murray, a lion rampant brandishing in his fore paws a battle axe *Virtute fideque* 15 4

M Murray, Scotland, a stag's head ppr 121 5

MacMurrogh, co Carlow and Wexford, Ireland issuant from between the horns of a crescent or, a garb gu

M Nab of Dundurn, Scotland, a savage s head erased ppr *Timor omnis abesto. —Gun eagal*

M'Nab of that Ilk, Scotland, same crest and first motto.

Macnaghten, Baron (Macnaghten), Runkerry, Bushmills, co. Antrim, a tower gu. *I hope in God.* 156. 5

Macnaghten, Bart., of Dundarave, Bushmills, co. Antrim: (1) A tower gu. 156. 5. (2) Out of a crescent quarterly sa. and or, a lictor's fasces erect, the rods or, the axe ppr. *I hope in God.—Non pas l'ouvrage mais l'ouvrier.*

Macnaghton or **M'Naugton,** Ireland, a tower gu. *I hope in God.* 156. 5

M'Nair, a mermaid ppr., holding in her dexter hand a mirror, and in her sinister a comb. 184. 5

M'Nair of Glasgow, a demi-negro holding a sugar-cane over his dexter shoulder, and in his sinister hand a bunch of tobacco-leaves, all ppr. *Labor omnia vincit.*

MacNally, Ireland, a naked arm couped below the shoulder and erect holding a dagger, also erect, all ppr.

Macnamara, a stag's head or. 121. 5

Macnamara, Scotland, out of a ducal coronet or, an arm embowed holding a tilting-spear ppr.

Macnamara, out of a ducal coronet or, an arm embowed holding a lance ppr.

Macnamara of Ayle and Ranna Castle, co. Clare, out of a ducal coronet or, an arm holding a scimitar ppr., hilt of the first. *Firmitas in cœlo. cf.* 213. 5

Macnamara, an arm embowed holding in the hand a dagger, all ppr., hilt and pommel or. 201. 4

Macnamara, Francis Nottidge, a naked arm holding in the hand a scimitar, all ppr. *Firmitas in cœlo.* 213. 5

Macnamara, George Houseman, M.R.C.S., L.A.C., same crest and motto.

Macnamara, Nottidge Charles, of 13, Grosvenor Street, London, W., same crest and motto.

Macnamara of Kilgurtin, co. Clare, and France, a naked arm embowed grasping a scimitar, all ppr. *Firmitas in cœlo.* 201. 1

Macnamara of Doolen and Ennistymon House, co. Clare, Ireland, same crest. *Virtute et valore.* 201. 1

M'Namard, out of a tower a demi-lion rampant, all ppr. 157. 11

M'Naught of Kilquharity, Kirkcudbright, Scotland, a lion's head erased arg., langued gu. *Omnia fortunæ committo.* 17. 8

M'Naughtan or **M'Naughton,** Scotland, a tower embattled gu. *I hope in God.* 156. 5

MacNaughten of that Ilk, Scotland, a tower gu. *I hope in God.* 156. 5

M'Nayr, a mermaid with a mirror and comb ppr. 184. 5

MacNeal, Hector, of Losset Park, Campbelltown, Argyllsh., a dexter hand holding a dagger point upwards, all ppr. *Vincere vel mori.*

MacNeece, Surgeon-Major James Glaussen, an eagle rising ppr., charged on the breast with a cross crosslet sa. *Fiducia non astutia.*

MacNeece, Surgeon-Major Thomas Frederick, same crest and motto.

McNeight, William John, of San Remo, Howth, N.B., out of the battlements of a tower sa., masoned arg., a dexter arm embowed in armour, the hand holding a spear in bend sinister transfixing a lion's head erased, all ppr. *Omnia Deo committo.*

Macneil or **M'Neill,** of Gigha, Argyllsh., Scotland, an arm in armour from the shoulder issuing, holding a dagger point upwards, all ppr. *Vincere vel mori.*

MacNeil or **Macneill** of Barra, Inverness-sh., a rock ppr. *Vincere vel mori.* 179. 7

McNeil, Ireland, a rock gu. *Per virtutem scientiamque.* 179. 7

M'Neil or **MacNeil,** Scotland, a rock ppr. *Per virtutem scientiamque.* 179. 7

M'Neil, Scotland, an arm in armour embowed holding in the hand a sword, all ppr. *Vincere vel mori.* 195. 2

M'Neil, a lion rampant or. 1. 13

Macneill of Barra, Inverness-sh., a rock gu. *Vincere vel mori.* 179. 7

Macneill of Dublin, an arm in armour embowed, the hand holding a sword, all ppr. *Vincere vel mori.* 195. 2

MacNeill of Kirkdale, Creetown, N.B., a dexter arm vambraced holding a sword, all ppr. *Vincere aut mori.*

MacNeill, John Gordon Swift, M.P., of 14, Blackhall Street, Dublin, and 12, Halsey Street, S.W., same crest and motto.

McNeill, the late Major-General Sir John C., St. James's Palace, S.W., same crest and motto.

MacNeill, Ireland, a dexter arm in armour embowed holding in the hand a dagger, all ppr. *Vincere aut mori.* 196. 5

M'Neill, Baron Colonsay, a mailed arm and hand holding a dagger ppr. *Vincere aut mori.*

M'Nelly, Scotland, an arm in armour embowed holding a sword, all ppr. 195. 2

M'Nemara, Ireland, a mermaid holding in her dexter hand a comb ppr. *cf.* 184. 5

McNevins, Ireland, a palm-branch vert. *Vivis sperandum.* 147. 3

MacNicol, a crescent gu. *Gradatim.* 163. 2

M'Nicoll, Scotland, a lion's head erased ppr. *Nil sistere contra.* 17. 8

M'Nish, an arm embowed and couped in fess ppr., vested az., holding an oak-sprig vert, fructed or.

M'Nish, Scotland, an eagle rising ppr. *Animo non astutia.* 77. 5

M'Onald, Scotland, a mountain in flames. 179. 2

Maconchy, John Arthur, Esquire, J.P., of Rathmore, co. Longford, Ireland, a demi-swan with wings elevated arg. *Humani nil alienum.* 100. 2

Maconochie of Meadowbank, Edinburgh, a demi-man holding in his dexter hand three arrows, and pointing with his sinister to an imperial crown placed on the dexter side of the wreath, his head wreathed, having a loose tartan plaid hung over his sinister shoulder, all ppr. *His nitimur et munitur.* 185. 4

Maconochie, Archibald White, of 22, Westbourne Street, Hyde Park, W., a demi-Highlander habited ppr., holding in his dexter hand a sheaf of arrows, also ppr. *Nitimur et munitur.* 232. 2

Maconochie-Welwood, John Allan, Esquire, J.P., of Kirknewton, Midlothian, N.B., and Pitliver House, Dunfermline, N.B.: (1) Dexter, the trunk of an oak sprouting out branches ppr. (2) A demi-Highlandman holding in his right hand a bunch of arrows, all ppr., above an imperial crown or, to which he is pointing with his left. *Reviresco.—Nitimur et munitur.*

M'Onoghuy, Scotland, a dexter hand in fess couped holding a laurel-branch, all ppr. *Certamine summo.*

M'Oul, an arm in armour embowed in fess couped ppr., holding in the hand a cross crosslet fitched. *Vincere vel mori.*

M'Owl, a lion's gamb erased holding a dagger, all ppr. *Vincere vel mori.* 38. 8

MacPeter, Scotland, out of a mural coronet arg., masoned sa., a lion's head gu., crowned with an antique crown ppr. *Pour mon Dieu.—E'en do and spare not.*

M'Phaill, Scotland, a deer's head erased ppr. *Memor esto.* 121. 2

MacPharlane or **M'Pharlin,** Scotland, a naked man holding in his dexter hand a sheaf of arrows ppr. *This I'll defend.*

Macpherson, a cat sejant erect. *Creagn dhubh chloinn Chatain.* 294. 9

Macpherson, Charles Richard, Esquire, of Paddington Station, via Cobar, New South Wales, Australia, a wild cat sejant erect ppr. *Touch not the cat bot the glove.* 25. 2

Macpherson of Invereshie, a gray cat sejant erect. *Touch not the cat bot the glove.* 25. 2

Macpherson, Albert Cameron, Esquire, of Cluny (commonly called Cluny Macpherson), Inverness-sh., a cat sejant ppr. *Touch not the cat but a glove.* 26. 8

Macpherson, Donald D., Esquire, Bexton Croft, Knutsford, Chesh., a cat-a-mountain rampant guardant. *Na bean don chat gun lamhainn.* 26. 1

Macpherson, Sir Arthur George, K.C.I.E., of 51, Gloucester Terrace, Hyde Park, London, W., a cat rampant guardant ppr. *Touch not the cat but a glove.*

Macpherson, a cat rampant ppr. *Qui me tanget pœnitebit.* 26. 2

Macpherson or **M'Pherson,** a black cat's paw issuing holding up a crescent or.

M'Pherson, a cat current sa. *Touch not the cat bot a glove. cf.* 26. 6

Macpherson, Lieutenant-Colonel Lachlan, Glentruim House, and Kingussie, Inverness-sh., same crest and motto.

M'Pherson, Scotland, a cat sejant ppr. *Touch not the cat bot a glove.* 26. 8

M'Pherson, Ireland, a fox's head erased gu. 33. 6

M'Pherson or **Macpherson,** a cat's paw issuing sa., holding up a crescent or.

M'Phie, Scotland, a demi-lion rampant gu. *Pro rege.* 10. 3

M'Quaid, a lion's head erased. 17. 8

Macquaire, out of a coronet ppr., an arm in armour embowed holding in the hand a dagger arg. *Turris fortis mihi Deus.*

MacQuay, McQuay, or **Maquay,** of Dublin, two swords in saltier point downwards ppr., pommels and hilts or. *Licentiam refræna. cf.* 171. 12

Macqueen, Scotland, a wolf's head couped sa (*Another*, ppr) *Vires in arduis* 30 5

Macqueen, Scotland, issuing out of a cloud a dexter arm in fess holding in the hand a laurel garland ppr *Virtus in arduis*

Macqueen of Corrybrough Inverness-sh Scotland, a wolf rampant erm, sup porting an arrow point downwards arg, pheoned gu *Constant and faithful*

M'Queen, a wolf rampant against a broad arrow erect on its point

M Queen, Thomas Potter Esquire of Ridgmount House, Beds a wolf's head erased ppr *Quæ sursum volo videre* 30 8

M'Queen, Scotland, a wolf's head couped ppr *Virtus in arduis* 30 5

M Queen, a hoar's head erect sa cf 43 3

M Quhan, Scotland, issuing out of a cloud a dexter arm from the shoulder in fess holding a garland all ppr

M'Quie, Lancs a dexter hand couped holding a dagger in pale all ppr *Manu forte* 212 9

M'Quilland, John, Esquire of London, Ontario, a cat sejant ppr 26 8

M'Quinn, a wolf's head ppr *Que sursum volo* 30 5

Macquire or **M Quire,** a dagger in pale ppr 169 2

M Rach, Scotland, a dexter hand holding a scimitar, both ppr *Fortitudine* 213 5

Macrae, Scotland, same crest and motto

Macrae of Orangefield a hand grasping a scimitar ppr *Malim esse quam videri* 213 5

MacRae, Stuart, of Handley House Newark-on Trent a mailed arm embowed, the hand grasping a Turkish scimitar ppr *Fortitudine —Nec curo nec coreo*

MacRae, Scotland a dexter hand holding a broadsword ppr *Fortitudine* 212 13

MacRae, Scotland a dexter arm embowed in mail holding a scimitar ppr *Fortitudine*

M'Rae, Scotland, an arm embowed holding in the hand a scimitar ppr *Fortitudine* 201 1

MacRae-Gilstrap, Major John of Balli more, Argyllsh and of Northgate Newark on Trent (1) Upon a rock a cubit arm erect in armour ppr grasping an escutcheon gu, charged with a galtrap arg, for distinction the arm charged with a cross crosslet gu (*for Gilstrap*) (2) A mailed arm embowed grasping a Turkish sicmitar ppr *Candide secure (for Gilstrap) —Fortitudine (for MacRae)*

MacRannell, co Leitrim Ireland on a mount vert, a stag lodged, all ppr 115 12

Macrath of Fallbower, co Mayo, a naked arm couped below the elbow holding in the hand the upper part of a broken lance, all ppr, headed or 214 13

Macrea, Scotland an oak-tree ppr *Delectat et ornat* 143 5

Macreadie or **Macready** of Pearston Ayrsh, a hand holding a sword ppr *Semper paratus* 212 13

M'Rerik, *see* M'Crire

Macrery or **Mackrery,** a savage statant wreathed round the middle with leaves ppr cf 188 3

MacRery, a demi-lion rampant az., crowned or holding in the dexter paw a sword ppr, pommel and hilt of the second cf 14 12

Macritchie, Scotland, a cat sejant erect sa *Prenez garde* 25 2

MacRitchie, David, Esquire of Logie, Perthsh, and of 4, Archibald Place, Edinburgh, same crest and motto 25 2

M'Ritchie, Scotland, a lion's gamb charged with a cheveron, and thereon a crescent cf 39 2

M Robertson, Scotland, a dexter hand holding up a royal crown ppr *Virtutis gloria merces* 217 1

Macrorie, Scotland a lymphad with sails furled and oars in action sa, flagged gu *Res, non verba* 160 7

Macsagan, Scotland, a greyhound's head arg collared sa, ringed or *Nec timide nec temere* 61 2

MacShanly, *see* Shanly

MacShanly of Corcachlan, co Roscommon, a gauntlet erect grasping a broken sword ppr

MacSheehy, Ireland an arm in armour couped below the elbow and erect holding in the hand a sword, the blade entwined by a serpent all ppr

MacSheehy, Thomas Frederick Corbet Donoman the Drive Mount Ararat, Wimbledon same crest *Certavi et vici*

MacSween of Granada, a broadsword and a bow in saltier, all ppr *By the providence of God*

MacSweeney, Ireland, an arm in armour embowed holding a battle axe, all ppr 200 6

MacSweeney, Ireland, a demi griffin segreant or, holding in the claws a lizard ppr

MacSwiney, Peter Paul Esquire, of 37 Upper Mount Street Dublin, a demi-griffin segreant or holding between the claws a lizard ppr and having on the breast two battle-axes in saltire sa *Tuagha tulaig abu*

MacSwiney, Valentine Emanuel Patrick, a demi gryphon segreant holding in the dexter claw a lizard ppr and charged on the breast with a fleur-de-lis az *Malo mori quam fœdari*

M'Taggart, a trefoil ppr *Ditat Deus* 148 9

M'Taggart, Scotland, a lion's head erased ppr *Vi et virtute* 17 8

M'Taggart of Madras, same crest *Ditat Deus* 17 8

M'Taggart, a greyhound's head erased sa 61 4

M'Taggart of London, an owl ppr *Ratione non vi* 96 5

M Tavish, Scotland, a boar's head erased *Ne obliviscaris* 42 2

M'Tavish of Dunarday and Gartbeg, Scotland, a boar's head erased or *Non oblitus* 42 2

Mactier, Scotland, an arm embowed brandishing in the hand a battle-axe, all ppr *Hæc manus ob patriam* 201 5

MacTiernan, a griffin statant gu, with wings erect vert 63 8

M'Turk of Stenhouse, Dumfriessh, Scotland a ram's head cabossed ppr 130 7

MacVais, a hand erect couped at the wrist and grasping a snake, all ppr 220 2

McVeagh of Lurgan, co Armagh an arm embowed in armour holding in the hand a tilting-spear all ppr *Per ardua*

M'Veagh, George Joseph Brooke, J P of Drewstown co Meath, same crest and motto

M'Vean, Scotland, an arm in armour holding in the hand a sword *Fidelis* 210 2

M'Vicar, Scotland an eagle rising ppr *Dominus providebit* 77 5

M'Vicar-Affleck of Edinghame Scotland, a green branch growing out of the trunk of an oak tree ppr *Tandem* 145 2

M'Vittie, Robert Blake, Esquire, of 43, Harcourt Street, Dublin a cat-a-mountain passant gardant ppr resting the fore-paw upon an escutcheon of the arms, viz, arg on a chevron engrailed gu, between in chief two thistles and base a trefoil slipped all ppr, a fret or

M'Whirter, an antique Scottish harp or, with nine strings arg *Te Deum laudamus*

M'Worth, a cock 91 2

Madam of London, Wilts, and Ireland an eagle's head erased or 83 2

Madden, out of a ducal coronet gu a falcon rising or, holding in the beak a cross hatonnee arg

Madden, John Clements Waterhouse, Esquire, of Hilton Park, Clones co Monaghan and Manor Waterhouse co Fermanagh, out of a ducal coronet a falcon rising or holding in its beak a cross batonnee gu *Fortior qui se vincit*

Madden, Ireland a wolf salient gu *Christo duce vincamus* cf 28 1

Madden, co Fermanagh a falcon with wings expanded arg, membered or holding in the dexter claw a cross botonnee gu *Fortior qui se vincit*

Madden, Rt Hon Dodgson Hamilton, of Nutley, Booterstown, co Dublin same crest and motto

Madden, Walter Wilmot of Roslea Manor, Clones, same crest

Madden, Hon Sir John of Cloyne, Chapel Street, St Kilda, Victoria and Yamala, Frankston Victoria a falcon rising out of a garland, holding in its beak a cross botonnée gu *Propria virtute audax*

Madder, Staffs, on the trunk of a tree in fess vert a lion sejant or 7 9

Maddison, a demi-lion gu 10 3

Maddison of Newcastle, Northumb, out of a crown flory an arm in armour ppr, garnished or holding in the gauntlet a battle axe ppr charged with a cross gu, the staff sa

Maddison, T R, Esq, Durkar House, near Wakefield, out of a palisado coronet a dexter arm in armour embowed holding in the hand a battle-axe in bend sinister *Be firm*

Maddison of Unthank Durh, a dexter hand ppr vested erminois, holding a battle axe sa cf 207 7

Maddison of Partney Hall, Lincs out of a coronet flory or a cubit arm in armour ppr grasping a battle axe sa *Væ timido*

Maddison, Rev. Arthur Roland, M.A., F.S.A., of Vicar's Court, Lincoln, out of a crown fleury, a cubit arm in armour ppr., grasping a battle-axe sa., the blade ppr., charged with a cross gu. *Væ timido.*

Maddison, Henry, Partney Hall, Spilsby, Lincs, a cubit arm in armour ppr., grasping a battle-axe sa. *Væ timido.*

Maddock, a lion passant. 6. 2

Maddock, a demi-lion rampant. *Non leoni sed Deo.* 10. 2

Maddock, Ireland, out of a cloud a hand erect holding a club ppr. 214. 9

Maddocks, an elephant's head erased gu. 133. 3

Maddocks, John, J.P., of Heath Royal, Putney Hill, London, S.W., in front of a passion cross gu., a cherub's head or, each wing charged with a rose, also gu. *Justice and gratitude.* 238. 11

Maddocks, a demi-lion holding in the dexter paw a rose. 12. 1

Maddocks, Captain, the Woodlands, near Wem, Shropsh., a demi-lion rampant holding in the dexter paw a rose slipped and leaved.

Maddox, Bart. (*extinct*), of Wormley, Herts, a Bengal tiger passant gardant ducally gorged ppr.

Maddy, Glouc., a garb vert, charged with a fleece or.

Madelley of St. Pancras, Middx., and Shropsh., a hawk ppr., preying on a martlet sa.

Madeley, an eagle preying on a crane ppr. 79. 7

Madeston, a cubit arm in armour erect, per pale crenellée or and arg., holding in the gauntlet a halberd headed and garnished of the last.

Madeston, an ostrich regardant sa., ducally crowned or, resting the dexter claw on a pellet.

Madeston, a cock's head erm., holding in the beak a trefoil slipped vert.

Madock, an eagle displayed holding in its dexter claw a sword, and in the sinister a pistol, all ppr. *cf.* 75. 7

Madock of Harthury, Glouc., a lion's head erased or, pierced through the neck by a sword in pale, the point issuing from the top of the head embrued ppr., hilted and pommelled of the first.

Madock, Ireland, a demi-wolf regardant arg., vulned in the shoulder ppr.

Madocks of Glanywern, Denbighsh., a demi-lion rampant. 10. 2

Madox, a lion's gamb erased holding a dagger, both ppr. 38. 8

Madox, Herts, Shropsh., and London, a lion sejant or, holding in the dexter paw a sword arg., hilt and pommel of the first.

Madreston, a torteau charged with the sun in splendour or.

Madyston, a cubit arm vested erminois holding in the hand ppr. a battle-axe sa. *cf.* 207. 10

Magan of Emoe, co. Westmeath, and of Clonearl, Ireland, a boar's head erased az., armed and bristled or. *Virtute et probitate.* 42. 2

Magan, Percy, Esquire, J.P., of Correal, co. Roscommon, and Kilcleagh Park, Moate, co. Westmeath, same crest and motto.

Magawley, Ireland, a horse's head arg., in waggon harness sa. 50. 12

Magawley, Ireland, a swan with wings addorsed ppr. 99. 12

Magawley, Ireland, a swan ppr. 99. 2

Magawly-Cerati de Calry, Count Valerio, of the Holy Roman Empire; **Count of Viarolo,** in the Duchy of Parma; and **Count of Ceraté,** of Bavaria; **Baron de Calry,** a demi-lion rampant gu. *Lainb deargh aboo.—Rubra manus victrix.* 10. 3

Magee, Ireland, a lion sejant collared. *cf.* 7. 4

Magenis of Waringstown, a boar passant ppr. *Sola salus servire Deo.* 40. 9

Magenis, Henry Cole, of Finvoy Lodge, Ballymoney, co. Antrim, same crest and motto.

Magennis, Ireland, a demi-lion gardant gu., holding a fleur-de-lis or.

Magens of London and Glouc., an arm erect ppr., holding three trefoils vert.

Mageoghegan, Ireland, a bloodhound, passant ppr., collared, indented.

Mager or Major, a greyhound's head gu., collared or. 61. 2

Magheramorne, Baron (McGarel-Hogg), of Magheramorne, co. Antrim: (1) Out of an Eastern coronet arg., an oak-tree fructed ppr., and pendent therefrom an escutcheon az., charged with a dexter arm embowed in armour, the hand grasping an arrow in bend sinister point downwards, also ppr. (*for Hogg*). 282. 13. (2) Upon a mount vert, in front of a branch of oak erect ppr., a greyhound sejant sa., collared and line reflexed over the back or (*for McGarel*). *Dat gloria vires.—Fide et fiducia.* 282. 12

Magill, a savage's head couped ppr. 190. 12

Magill, Ireland, a falcon ppr., upon a hawk's lure of the same, lined arg. and vert. *cf.* 85. 14

Magin, a demi-wyvern vert. 69. 12

Maginn, Ireland, a cockatrice displayed vert. 68. 14

Maginnise, Ireland, a boar passant ppr. 40. 9

Magnall of London and Lincs, on a mount vert, an eagle rising ppr., crowned with an Eastern coronet or. *cf.* 76. 11

Magnay Sir William, Bart., of Postford House, Surrey, a lion rampant sa., billettée erminois, murally crowned, gorged with a chain, reflexed over the back, and holding between the forepaws a leopard's face or. *Magna est veritas.* 286. 3

Magnus, Yorks, a lion's gamb erased or. 36. 4

Magor of Penventon House, Redruth, Cornw., a greyhound's head erased and collared. *cf.* 61. 2

Magounis, Ireland, a demi-lion gardant gu., holding a fleur-de-lis or.

Magrath of Lambeth, Surrey, an arm couped in fess ppr. *Salus in fide.*

Magrath, on a chapeau a lion passant, all ppr. 4. 9

Magrath of Murhill, near Bradford-on-Avon, Wilts, a dexter cubit arm couped and lying fesseways holding in the hand, all ppr., a cross patée fitchée and erect az. *Salus in fide.*

Magrath, Ireland, a crow sa. 107. 14

Maguire, Ireland, an arm in armour embowed holding in the hand a sword, all ppr. 195. 2

Maguire, on a serpent nowed vert, a hawk statant ppr. 86. 3

Maguire, Ireland, out of a ducal coronet a demi-eagle displayed holding in the beak a rose stalked and leaved, all ppr. *cf.* 80. 14

Maguire, Ireland, a stag statant ppr. 117. 5

Maher, Matthias Aidan, Esquire, J.P., D.L., of Ballen Keele, co. Wexford, Ireland, on a mount vert a hawk rising, belled and hooded ppr., charged on each wing with a crescent or. *In periculis audax.*

Maher, an eagle with wings expanded. 77. 5

Maher, Ireland, a bee volant in pale or. 137. 2

Mahewe of Lostwithiel, Cornw., a Cornish chough erm. 107. 14

Mahewe, Cornw., an eagle with wings addorsed or, preying on a snake nowed ppr.

Mahewe, Norf., a unicorn's head erased arg., crined gu., the horn twisted of the first and second, on the neck a cheveron vair. *cf.* 49. 5

Mahon, Ireland, a demi-husbandman holding over his dexter shoulder an ox-yoke, all ppr. 187. 14

Mahon, Viscount, *see* Stanhope, Earl.

Mahon, Baron Hartland, *see* Hartland.

Mahon, *see* Pakenham-Mahon.

Mahon of Cavetown, co. Roscommon, a heraldic tiger passant holding in the dexter paw a broken tilting-spear, all ppr., and charged on the shoulder with a martlet sa. for difference. *Buaidh go bragh.*

Mahon, Ireland, a tiger statant holding in its dexter paw a broken tilting-spear.

Mahon, Ireland, a lion rampant holding in its dexter paw an olive-branch. *Per ardua surgo.*

Mahon-Hagan of New York, co. Clare, Ireland: (1) Out of a naval crown or, a demi-negro affrontée, with broken manacles depending from each wrist, grasping in his dexter hand the Union Jack displayed on a flagstaff, and in his sinister hand, on a similar staff, the cap of liberty, all ppr. (*for Hagan*). (2) On a wreath of the colours and out of a wreath of roses alternately arg. and gu., seeded or barbed vert, a dexter arm in armour embowed ppr., garnished or, holding in the gauntlet a baton in bend arg., and charged on the arm with a rose of the last (*for Mahon*). *Vota vita mea.—Hæc manus inimica tyrannis.*

Mahon, T. G. S., B.A., J.P., Corbally, Quin, co. Clare, a dexter arm vambraced and embowed grasping in the hand a dagger. *Manus hæc inimica tyrannis.*

Mahon, Rev. Sir William Vesey-Ross, Bart., M.A., of Castlegar, co. Galway, a dexter arm in armour embowed ppr., garnished or, holding in the gauntlet a sword wavy arg., pommel and hilt or. *Moniti meliora sequamur.*

Mahon, John Denis FitzJames Ker, Ballydonelan Castle, Loughrea, same crest.

Mahony, George Philip Gun B A of Kilmorna Listowel, co Kerry, Ireland, out of the coronet of a Count of France a dexter arm in armour em bowed grasping in the hand a sword, all ppr, hilt and pommel or the blade piercing a fleur de lis of the last *Lasair romhuin a buadh.*

Mahony, Harold Segerson, B A, of Dromore Castle, Kenmare, co Kerry, same crest and motto

Mahony, John Moore, Esquire, J P, same crest and motto

Mahony, Pierce, Esquire of Grange Con co Wicklow (1) Same crest as above, (2) A naked arm embowed, the hand grasping a sword flammant, all ppr *Lasair romhuin a buadh*

Mahony of Dunloe Castle, co Kerry, a naked arm embowed, the hand grasping a sword flammant, all ppr *Lasair romhuin a buadh*

Maidman, a leopard's head erased gardant, ducally gorged

Maidman, Hants an arm embowed vested per pale, indented az and or, cuffed arg, holding in the hand a dove ppr

Maidstone, Viscount, *see* Winchelsea, Earl of

Maillard, out of a ducal coronet a peacock s tail, all ppr 115 6

Main, Scotland, an escallop or, charged with a mullet gu 141 6

Main, a leopard rampant ppr

Main, Scotland, a negro s head sa, banded arg 192 4

Main of Lochwood, Stirlingsh, Scotland, a hand throwing a dart ppr *Projeci* 214 4

Main, a cubit arm erect and vested party per chevron arg and sa, holding in the hand ppr a cross crosslet fitched in pale

Main, late Rev Thomas John M A, in front of a cubit arm erect ppr, holding a cross botonnee fitchee in pale or, and a sword fessewise, the point to the dexter also ppr, pommel and hilt or three piles reversed az

Maine, out of a mural coronet per pale gu and erm, an arm in armour garnished or, holding a spear point downward *Vincit pericula virtus*

Maingy, a wolf's head erased erminois 30 8

Mainstone of Urchingfield, Heref, and London, a hedgehog arg 135 8

Mainter, out of a mural coronet or, a unicorn's head az armed and crined or cf 49 7

Mainwaring, *see* Milman-Mainwaring

Mainwaring, *see* Massey-Mainwaring

Mainwaring, Chesh and Salop out of a ducal coronet or, an ass's head ppr *Devant si je puis* 125 10

Mainwaring, Shropsh, on a ducal coronet or, an ass's head erased arg cf 125 10

Mainwaring, Shropsh, an ass's head erased ppr, haltered or

Mainwaring, Charles Francis Kynaston, Esq, of Otley Ellesmere, Shropsh (1) Out of a ducal coronet an ass s head ppr (*for Mainwaring*) 125 10 (2) A lion's head erased sa, guttee-d'or (*for Kynaston*) *Devant si je puis* 225 10

Mainwaring, Charles Salusbury, V D, D L, M A, of Galltfaenan, Trefnant North Wales, same crests and motto

Mainwaring, Rev Percy Edward, M A, of Whitmore Rectory, Newcastle under Lyme, same crests and motto

Mainwaring of Whitmore, Staffs, out of a ducal coronet or, an ass's head with a hempen halter, all ppr *Devant si je puis* cf 125 10

Mainwaring of Croxton, Chesh, an ass's head ppr 125 12

Mainwaring of Exeter Devonsh, an ass's head erased arg, maned and haltered or

Mainwaring, Sir Philip Tatton, Bart, of Over Peover, Chester an ass's head erased ppr, bridled or *Devant si je puis*

Mainwaring - Ellerker - Onslow, Charles Vere Townshend, of Ingleby, Wimborne Road Bournemouth (1) An eagle sa preying on a partridge or (*for Onslow*) 230 3 (2) A dolphin haurient and a sea dragon or, emitting flames of fire ppr, embowed and addorsed and enfiled by a ducal coronet for distinction, with a roundle counterchanged (*for Ellerker*) 230 2 (3) On the sinister isode, out of a ducal coronet or, an ass s head ppr (*for Mainwaring*) *Festina lente* 230 4

Mair of London and Scotland a swan ppr *Tempore candidior* 99 2

Mair, a demi pegasus issuing arg, enfiled round the body with a ducal coronet gu 47 7

Mair, Scotland, a negro s head couped at the shoulders sa, banded arg 192 13

Mair of Aberdeen, a lion's head erased arg *Spes et fortitudo* 17 8

Maire, a cubit arm erect vested, holding in the hand a bugle-horn stringed

Mairis of Marston, Wilts on a mount vert, a peacock in pride or, from the beak issuant an escroll inscribed *Esse quam videri,* and resting the dexter claw on an escutcheon az, charged with a cross patee fitched or *Si Deus nobiscum, quis contra nos*

Maister of Wood Hall, in Holderness, Yorks, out of a mural coronet or, a unicorn's head az, armed and crined of the first *Vix ea nostra voco* cf 49 7

Maisterton and **Maisterson,** Chesh, a tiger passant arg cf 27 11

Maitland, Viscount, *see* Lauderdale, Earl of

Maitland, Bart., *see* Ramsay-Gibson-Maitland

Maitland, Scotland a rock in the sea ppr *Attamen tranquillus* 179 5

Maitland, a rock in the sea ppr *Fluctus fluctu* 179 5

Maitland, Scotland, in the sea a rock ppr 179 5

Maitland, David, of Dundrenan, Kirkcudbrightsh, Scotland a demi monk habited in gray, holding in his dexter hand a crucifix arg and in his sinister a rosary ppr *Esse quam videri* 298 9

Maitland, Bart. (*extinct*) of Pittrichie Scotland, a lion's head erased gu *Paix et peu* 17 2

Maitland, a demi lion rampant gu, langued and membered az, holding in his dexter paw a thistle ppr, and in his sinister a fleur-de-lis of the second *Fisus et fides* 13 12

Maitland, on a ducal coronet or a lion sejant affrontee holding in the dexter paw a sword in pale ppr and in the sinister a fleur de lis arg *Deo juvante* cf 7 3

Maitland, Rev J W, Loughton Hall, Essex same crest

Maitland, Alexander Charles Richards, M A of Cliffden Teignmouth, Devonsh and 20 Buckingham Palace Mansions S W a lion sejant erect and affrontee gu, holding in the dexter paw a sword ppr, hilted and pommelled or, and in his sinister a fleur-de-lis arg *Consilio et animis* 298 15

Maitland, William James, C I E, of Witley Manor, Witley, Surrey and 18, Lennox Gardens, S W same crest.

Maitland of Auchlane, Kirkcudbrightsh, a lion sejant affrontee gu, ducally crowned or holding in the dexter paw a sword in pale ppr, and in the sinister a fleur de-lis arg 298 15

Maitland, a lion sejant affrontee gu, ducally crowned or holding in the dexter paw a sword ppr hilt and pommel or, and in the sinister a fleur de-lis az *Consilio et animis* 298 15

Maitland, Sir John Nisbet, Bart, of Clifton Hall, Fifesh, same crest and motto

Maitland of Eccles, Berwicksh, Scotland a demi lion rampant gu, couped in all the joints or, issuing from water ppr *Luctor et emergam*

Maitland, William Fuller, of Stansted Hall, Essex same crest and motto.

Maitland-Makgill-Crichton, C J Esquire of Lathrisk Falkland, Fifesh, and Monzie Perthsh (1) A dragon's head inflamed and erased, and crowned with a coronet —*Sine fine* (*for Crichton*) (2) On a ducal coronet a lion sejant erect affrontee, ducally crowned, holding in his dexter paw a sword in pale ppr and in his sinister a fleur de lis —*Consilio et animis* (*for Maitland*) (3) A phœnix in flames ppr —*Perseverantia* (*for Makgill*)

Majendie, James Henry Alexander J P of Castle Hedingham, Essex an arm in armour embowed holding in the hand a scimitar ppr *Qualis ab incepto* 196 10

Majendie, Colonel Vivian Dering, C B, 17, Whitehall Court, S W, same crest and motto

Major, *see* Henniker Baron

Major of Southampton, and the Isle of Wight Hants, a greyhound's head gu collared or 61 2

Major of Leicester and Brampston Notts, a greyhound rampant sa, collared arg, on the collar three mullets of the first.

Majoribanks, Scotland, a demi-griffin segreant *Et custos, et pugnax* 64 2

Majoribanks, Scotland a lion's gamb grasping a lance in bend ppr *Advance with courage* cf 38 11

Majoribanks, a bear's paw erased grasping a tilting spear in bend sinister cf 38 11

Makareth, Lancs an arm in armour embowed holding in the hand a broken tilting spear, all ppr 197 2

Makepeace, a unicorn's head arg., between two laurel-branches in orle vert. 49. 14

Makepeace, a dove holding in its beak an olive-branch, all ppr. 92. 5

Makepeace of Pensham Court, Yorks, London, and Warfield, Berks, a leopard passant regardant or, resting his dexter paw on an escutcheon gu., charged with a cross crosslet fitched of the first.

Makins, Colonel Sir W. T., Bart., of Rotherfield Court, Henley-on-Thames, a dexter arm embowed in armour ppr., encircled by an annulet or, and holding a flagstaff in bend sinister ppr., therefrom flowing a banner arg., charged with a lion's face gu. *In lumine luce.* 199. 5

Malbanke, on a tortoise an eagle perching ppr. 79. 8

Malbone, an eagle regardant holding in the dexter claw a sword ppr.

Malby, a goat passant or. *cf.* 129. 5

Malcolm, a demi-swan rising arg. 100. 2

Malcolm, Baron (Malcolm), of Pottalloch, Argyllsh., a tower arg. *In ardua tendit* (*extinct*). 156. 2

Malcolm, Sir James William, Bart., Hoveton Hall, Norwich, a pyramid encircled by a wreath of laurel ppr. *Ardua tendo.* 240. 1

Malcolm, late Sir John, G.C.B., on a mount vert, a tower arg., masoned sa., ensigned by the badge of the Persian Order of the Lion and Sun. *In ardua tendit.*

Malcolm, late Sir James, K.C.B., and the late Admiral Sir Pulteney Malcolm, G.C.B., on a mount vert, a tower arg., masoned sa. *In ardua tendit. cf.* 156. 2

Malcolm, William Elphinstone, J.P., D.L., of Burnfoot, Langholm, Dumfriessh., same crest and motto.

Malcom, a demi-swan rising arg. 100. 2

Malcom of Glenmorag, a castle arg., masoned sa., the portcullis gu. *In ardua tendit.* 155. 8

Malden, Viscount, *see* Essex, Earl of.

Malden, Essex, and Henry Charles Malden, Esquire, M.A., Windlesham House, Brighton, a dexter hand apaumée ppr. *Miseris opem fero.* 222. 14

Malden, Charles Edward, 2, Harcourt Buildings, Temple, E.C., same crest. *Miseris auxilium fero.*

Malden, same crest and motto.

Male, *see* Hill-Male.

Male, on a marquess's coronet a Cornish chough, the wings expanded ppr.

Maledoctus, a demi-lion supporting a long cross. 11. 14

Malefont and **Malesaunts**, a demi-lion regardant gu., supporting a spear enfiled with a boar's head couped ppr. 9. 10

Malephant, Scotland, a demi-lion rampant ppr., crowned or. 10. 11

Malet, Rt. Hon. Sir Edward Baldwin, Bart., G.C.B., G.C.M.G., of Wrest Wood, Bexhill, Sussex, and Chateau Malet, Monaco, out of a ducal coronet a heraldic tiger's head erm. *Ma force de en hault.* 231. 12

Malet, a demi-goat rampant. *Nec temere nec timide.*

Maleverer, a nag's head in armour ppr. 51. 13

Maleverer, Yorks, a greyhound passant arg., collared and ringed or. *cf.* 60. 2

Malfit, a dexter arm in armour holding a scimitar in pale, all ppr.

Malherbe of Fenyton, Devonsh., on a tree a demi-naked man ppr., wreathed about the temples arg. and sa., and holding in his hand an oak-branch, also ppr., acorned or.

Malim, Rev. Alfred, M.A., Jesus College, Cambridge, Chaplain to H.M. Forces (*according to Camden the family was settled in Kent from the Conquest until the end of the sixteenth century, and from 1600 to 1762 at Rotherham and Doncaster, and from 1762 until 1868 at Higham Ferrers, in Northamptonshire*), an arm embowed vested sa., holding an anchor or (*granted to William Malim, M.A., Fellow of King's College, Cambridge, son of Henry Malim of Staplehurst, Kent*). *Fide tenes anchoram.—Malim esse probus quam haberi.* 204. 13

Malin, an elephant passant or. *cf.* 133. 9

Maling, out of a ducal coronet a plume of five ostrich-feathers in a case, all ppr.

Malins, a cubit arm in armour erect ppr., grasping a crescent or. *Adjuvante Deo.*

Malins, a cubit arm in armour erect ppr., grasping a crescent or. *Post prœlia prœmia.*

Malkin, a wolf's head sa. 30. 5

Mallabar, a martlet or. 95. 2

Mallake of Axmouth, Devonsh., a cubit arm erect vested or, charged thereon with two bends wavy sa., holding in the hand ppr. a mallet of the first.

Mallam, a dolphin naiant or. 140. 5

Mallard, on a chapeau gu., a stag trippant ppr. 118. 3

Mallard, 176, Albion Road, Stoke Newington, N., on a chapeau gu., turned up erm., a stag trippant ppr. 118. 3

Mallet of Jersey, a cock statant ppr. *In cruce salus.—En Dieu affie.* 91. 2

Malley, a goat's head erased sa., bezantée. *cf.* 128. 5

Malley, a savage ambulant carrying a tree eradicated, all ppr.

Malley, a savage wreathed round the temples and loins, with a club resting on the shoulder, all ppr.

Mallinson of Manchester, an arm embowed vested az., charged with two crescents and cuffed or, the hand ppr. grasping a fasces palewise, also or.

Mallock, Richard, Esquire, of Cockington Court, near Torquay, a cubit arm erect vested or, thereon two bends wavy sa., holding in the hand a mallet of the first. *Dic quid dicere fas est.*

Mallock, Scotland, between two bay-branches in orle, a lion's head crowned with an antique crown ppr. *Court no friend, dread no foe.—E'en do and spare not.*

Mallom and **Mallon**, of Walter-Acton, Norf., an arm in pale vested vert, the cuff turned up erm., holding in the hand ppr. a lure feathered arg., garnished or, stringed and tasselled gu.

Mallory, a nag's head or. *cf.* 50. 13

Mallory, a nag's head couped gu. *cf.* 50. 13

Mallory, Rev. Herbert Leigh, the Manor House, Mobberley, Chesh.: (1) A nag's head couped gu., charged with a cross patée or (*for Mallory*). 278. 6 (2) A hand holding a broken spear (*for Leigh*). 278. 5

Mallory of Woodford, Northamp., a nag's head gu., crined or, charged with a fleur-de-lis of the last. *cf.* 50. 13

Mallory, a horse's head couped per pale gu. and az., ducally gorged or.

Mallow, on a chapeau gu., turned up erm., two sceptres in saltier or. 170. 9

Malmains, a lamb supporting a banner arg. 131. 2

Malmaynes, an arm in armour embowed, the hand apaumée ppr. 200. 1

Malmesbury, Earl of (Harris), of Heron Court, near Christchurch, Hants, a hedgehog or, charged on the side with three arrows, one in pale and two in saltire ppr., and across them barways a key az. *Je maintiendrai.—Ubique patriam reminisci.* 279. 13

Malone, on a mount a lion rampant ppr., collared gu., holding in the dexter paw an arrow sa. 1. 11

Malone, a man in armour holding in his dexter hand a lance, and on his sinister arm a shield, all ppr. *Fidelis ad urnam.* 188. 4

Malone, Dublin, a squirrel sejant arg., holding between the fore-paws an acorn ppr. 135. 7

Malpas of Bickley, Chesh., on a ducal coronet, a wyvern vomiting fire at both ends ppr.

Malpas of Rochestown, Dublin, a demi-lion rampant gu., holding in the dexter paw a pheon point upwards arg.

Maltby of Maltby, Yorks, a garb or, banded gu. 153. 2

Maltby, Essex, a barley-sheaf erect or, banded of the same, pendent therefrom a bugle-horn arg. *cf.* 153. 2

Maltby, late Rt. Rev. Edward, D.D., Bishop of Durham, between two branches of olive ppr. a garb or, charged with a cross patée gu. *Nil sine labore.*

Maltiward of Rougham, Suff., a demi-griffin arg., holding between its claws a saltier sa.

Malton, Lancs, a dolphin haurient devouring a fish, all ppr. 140. 6

Malton, Ireland, on a rock a dove holding in its beak an olive-branch, all ppr. 93. 9

Malton of South Hayne, Devonsh., and Yorks, a snake nowed in pale ppr., ducally gorged arg. 142. 1

Maltravers, Baron, *see* Norfolk, Duke of.

Maltravers, a fountain ppr. 159. 8

Maly, Ireland, a ship. 160. 13

Malynes, a reindeer's head cabossed ppr. 122. 4

Man, on the stump of an oak-tree an eagle perching ppr.

Man, Scotland, a unicorn's head. *Nil time.* 49. 7

Man, five spears ppr., proceeding from the top of a tower or.

Man or **Mann** of Ipswich, Suff., a demi-dragon, with wings addorsed arg., guttée-de-poix. 73. 10

Man of London, a dragon's head between two dragon's wings expanded gu., guttée-d'or. 72. 7

Manaton or **Mannington** of Manaton, Southill, Cornw., a demi-unicorn sa. 48. 7

Manbey, William John de, Esquire, of Boissevain, Manitoba, Canada in front of an anchor in bend sa, a cubit arm in armour erect ppr charged with an escallop shell gu, holding in the hand a dagger in bend sinister also ppr *Fidelis exsulatæ* 303 12
Manbey, Rev George Henley, M A, of 2, Crompton Terrace, Southend, Essex, same crest
Manby of Elsham, Lincs, an arm couped at the elbow erect, vested per pale crenellée or and arg, holding a sword ppr, pommelled of the first
Manby-Colegrave, Thomas, an ostrich-feather erect az, and two arrows in saltire or barbed and flighted arg, banded by a mural crown gu *Fidei constans*
Manchester, Duke of (Montagu), Kimbolton Castle, Hunts, a griffin's head couped with wings expanded or, gorged with a collar arg, charged with three lozenges gu *Disponendo me, non mutando me* cf 67 7
Manchester, a polecat ppr 153 13
Manchester, on a mount an ermine passant, all ppr 134 10
Mandel, out of a ducal coronet an eagle's head cf 83 14
Mander, a swallow volant sa 96 2
Manderne of Penzance Cornw, a lion rampant or, guttee de-sang, crowned of the first 1 12
Manders of Brackdenstown, co Dublin, a plover ppr beaked and legged gu, holding in the beak a slip of oak leaved vert acorned or *Pro omnibus laus Deo*
Manderson, an antelope trippant arg, collared gu cf 126 6
Mandevile, two dexter hands conjoined supporting a scimitar in pale, all ppr
Mandeville, a mural coronet arg, charged with an escarbuncle sa
Mandeville, Viscount, *see* Manchester, Duke of
Mandis, out of a naval coronet or, an arm embowed holding a couteau sword ppr 201 2
Manditt and **Manduyt,** a garland of laurel ppr 146 5
Manduit, a demi lion rampant supporting a long cross 11 14
Mandut, Manduyt, or **Manduit,** a plate charged with a stag statant on a mount ppr 116 11
Maney, Kent a cubit arm couped and erect vested per pale arg and sa, the cuff counterchanged, holding in the hand ppr a battle axe of the last cf 207 10
Manfield, a griffin's head erased 66 2
Manfield or **Mansfield,** Bucks a tiger sejant or, ducally gorged gu
Manfield, Scotland an ostrich's head between two feathers arg 97 14
Manfield, Harry, Esquire, J P of Moulton Grange Northamp, a greyhound sa, charged on the body with two fleurs de-lis in fesse and collared gemel, and resting the dexter fore paw on a fleur-de lis, all arg *Esse quam videri*
Manford, three annulets interlaced or 167 11
Manger of Jersey and Guernsey, a greyhound's head erased gu, collared and ringed or cf 61 2
Mangin of Bath, a crane holding in the beak a fish all ppr
Mangle and **Mangles,** an arm in armour embowed ppr charged with two roses gu grasping in the hand a scimitar, all ppr cf 196 10
Manico, a quatrefoil vert 148 10
Maningham, Cambs and Kent, out of a ducal coronet arg, a talbot's head or, collared and lined gu, at the end of the line a bow knot cf 57 12
Manington of Manington and Combshed, Cornw, a demi-unicorn rampant sa, armed, crined and ungu arg, charged on the shoulder with a crescent or for difference cf 48 7
Maniot, a Saracen's head affrontée ppr, wreathed arg and sa 190 5
Manley, a cross patée az cf 165 7
Manley, a man's head couped at the shoulders affrontée ppr, the hair sa, wreathed vert 190 5
Manley, Beds and Chesh, a Saracen's head affrontee ppr, wreathed arg and sa 190 5
Manley of Manley, Chesh. and Erbistock, Denbighsh a Saracen's head affrontee ppr, wreathed about the temples arg and sa *Manus hæc inimica tyrannis* 190 5
Manlove of Ashborne, Derbysh, and Staffs, out of a mural coronet gu, a cubit arm erect vested erminois, cuffed arg, holding in the hand a flaming sword ppr
Manlovell, five bell flowers in pale ppr, leaved vert
Manly, a cross patee arg cf 165 7
Manmaker of Middleburgh, Zealand, two wings displayed gu 109 6
Mann, a demi man ppr, wreathed about the head and loins vert holding over the dexter shoulder an arrow of the last
Mann, of Round Green near Barnsley, in front of a demi gryphon arg guttee-de larmes three annulets interlaced fesseways sa *Per ardua stabilis*
Mann, Bart (*extinct*), of Linton, Kent, a demi-dragon with wings addorsed sa guttee d'eau, the inside of the wings and the talons ppr *Per ardua stabilis* 73 10
Mann, Cornwallis-, Earl of Cornwallis (*extinct*) (1) A demi-dragon sa, guttee-d'eau (*for Mann*) 73 10 (2) On a mount vert, a stag lodged regardant arg, attired and ungu or, gorged with a chaplet of laurel vert, vulned in the shoulder ppr (*for Cornwallis*) cf 115 9
Mann of Dunmoyle and Corvey Lodge, co Tyrone, Ireland, a tower or, charged with a trefoil vert, and issuant from the battlements five spears ppr *Virtus vincit invidiam*
Mann of Broadoak, Essex and Kent out of a tower or, five spears ppr
Mannell, a horse's head erased arg 51 4
Manners, Duke of Rutland, *see* Rutland
Manners-Sutton, Viscount Canterbury, *see* Canterbury
Manners, Baron (Sutton), Avon Tyrrell, Christchurch, Hants, on a chapeau gu, turned up erm, a peacock in his pride ppr *Pour y parvenir* 103 5
Manners, George Espec John, of Fornham Park, Bury St Edmunds, same crest.
Manners of Hanby Hall and Buckminster, Lincs and Leics, on a chapeau gu, turned up erm, a peacock in pride ppr, each charged with a bendlet sinister wavy gobony or and sa 103 5
Manners of Ethale, Northumb, out of a ducal coronet or, a bull's head gu, armed of the first 44 11
Manners-Wood, of Fairhaven, Sandown, Isle of Wight a stag trippant and between the attires a ducal coronet
Manners - Wood, Rev William, M A, Littleton Rectory, Shepperton, Middlesex, same crest.
Manning, Hon Sir William Montagu, LL D, of Wallaroy Woollahra, Sydney, New South Wales, Australia Member of the Legislative Council of New South Wales, *uses* out of a ducal coronet or an eagle's head sa beaked or, between two ostrich-feathers arg *Vive ut vivas*
Manning of Codham and Downe Kent, and of Diss, Norf, out of a ducal coronet or an eagle's head sa beaked of the first, between two ostrich feathers arg
Manningham-Buller, Bart *see* Buller
Manningham, Kent, out of a ducal coronet or, a talbot's head gu, collared of the first, lined sa cf 57 12
Mannock of Gifford's Hall, Suff, an heraldic tiger's head erased quarterly arg and gu cf 25 4
Manntell of Heyford, Northants a stag's head couped erm 121 5
Mannynge, *see* Manning
Mansbridge of London a dexter cubit arm erect, vested az, cuffed arg holding in the hand ppr a demi-eagle displayed with two heads gu, ducally gorged or
Mansel, on a mount a buck lodged, all ppr 115 12
Mansel of Congrave Hall Northamp, on a chapeau gu turned up erm a falcon rising ppr *Quod vult, valde vult* cf 88 2
Mansel, Robert Henry, Esquire of the Broadtower, Caerleon, Monm and Maindiff Castle, Abergavenny a falcon rising or, holding in the beak a lily, leaved and slipped ppr, and supporting with the dexter leg two swords in saltire, points upwards, also ppr pommels and hilts or *Constanter tamen fortiter* 267 3
Mansel, Sir Courtenay Cecil, Bart, of Muddescombe Carmarthensh, a cap of maintenance enflamed on the top, all ppr *Quod vult valde vult* 180 10
Mansel, Ernest Digby, Esquire, same crest and motto
Mansel, Eustace Gambier Esquire same crest and motto
Mansel, Lieutenant Colonel John Delalynde of Smedmore Corfe Castle Dorset, same crest and motto
Mansell, an eagle rising ppr 77 5
Mansell, a hawk rising ppr *Quod vult, valde vult* 88 2
Mansell and **Mansel,** on a chapeau gu, turned up erm, a flame of fire ppr *Quod vult valde vult* 180 10
Mansell, an arm embowed and vested holding in the hand a pair of scales equally poised
Manser, William Esquire of Penrhyn, Cornw, a leopard's head erased in

front of three arrows, points upwards one in pale and two in saltire, all ppr. *Dum spiro spero.*

Mansergh, James, Esquire, of Lune Lea, 51, FitzJohn's Avenue, Hampstead, London, S.W., a wyvern sejant and erect gu., gorged with a collar wavy arg., and supporting with the claws an arrow erect gu., barbed and flighted arg. *Tout jour prêt.* 248. 8

Mansergh, a demi-lion rampant arg., gorged with a collar raguly gu., holding in the dexter paw an arrow of the last, barbed and flighted or. 13. 6

Mansergh, Richard Southcote, Esquire, **J.P.,** of Grenane, Tipperary, out of a ducal coronet ppr., charged with a label of three points gu., a demi-lion rampant arg., gorged with a collar raguly of the second, and holding in the dexter paw an arrow, point downwards, of the last flighted and barbed or. *Tout jour prêt.* 298. 3

Mansergh, Daniel James, Esquire, of Grallagh Castle, co. Tipperary, same crest and motto.

Mansfield of London, a cross patée fitched erm. 166. 3

Mansfield, a griffin's head erased. 66. 2

Mansfield, Ireland, an arm in armour embowed holding in the hand a short sword, all ppr. *Turris fortitudinis.* 195. 2

Mansfield, *see* Sandhurst, Baron.

Mansfield of Birstall House, Leics., an eagle rising with wings expanded, holding in the beak an annulet. *cf.* 77. 5

Mansfield, George, J.P., D.L., of Morristown Lattin, Naas, co. Kildare, and of Ballynamultinagh, co. Waterford, Ireland, a dexter arm embowed in armour ppr., garnished or, the hand holding a sword, also ppr., pommel and hilt of the second. *Turris fortitudinis.* 195. 2

Mansfield, Earl of (Murray), Comlongon Castle, Dumfriessh., a buck's head couped or, with a cross patée between his antlers arg. *Uni æquus virtuti.—Spero meliora.* 120. 9

Mansham, a griffin's head erased or, between two wings gu. *cf.* 65. 11

Manson, Holland and Scotland, a dexter hand holding a thistle. *Meæ memor originis.* 218. 2

Manson, James Bruce, Kilblean, Oldmeldrum, N.B., same crest and motto.

Manson, on a chapeau ppr., a garb or. 153. 10

Mansted, an arm in armour, holding in the hand a holly-branch fructed, all ppr. 209. 14

Manston, a harp or. 168. 9

Mansuen and **Mansuer,** of Mansuer, Westml., and Norf., a pelican in her piety sa., the nest or. 98. 8

Mant, an antelope trippant or. 126. 6

Mant, Frank, a demi-lion arg., holding between the paws a cross Calvary sa. *Lucerna pedibus meis.*

Mantebey, a boar's head in bend arg., armed or, out of the mouth flames issuing.

Mantell, Hon. Walter Baldock Durant, of Maramarama, Sidney Street, Wellington, New Zealand, Member of the Legislative Council and of the Board of Governors of the New Zealand Institute, a stag's head couped affrontée arg. 119. 12

Mantell, Walter Godfrey, same crest.

Mantell or **Mantle** of Heyford, Northamp., and Kent, a stag's head couped at the neck affrontée arg. *Another,* erm. 119. 12

Mantell of London, a stag's head couped affrontée arg. *Petit alta.* 119. 12

Manton, a unicorn sejant or, resting the dexter foot against a tree vert. 48. 3

Manvers, Earl, Viscount Newark and **Baron Pierrepont** (Pierrepont), Thoresby Park, Ollerton, Notts, a lion rampant sa., between two wings erect arg. *Pie repone te.* 9. 2

Manwell, a ram passant gu. 131. 13

Manwike, a hurt charged with an étoile or.

Manwood, Kent, and of Bramfield, Essex, out of a ducal coronet a lion's head gardant or.

Manyngham, an ostrich with wings addorsed and holding in its beak a horseshoe, all ppr. *cf.* 97. 1

Mapes of Foltham and Rollesby, Norf., an arm in armour embowed or, holding in the hand a spur arg., leathered sa.

Maple, the late Sir John Blundell, Bart., a squirrel sejant or, holding in the dexter paw a sprig of five maple-leaves slipped ppr., and resting the sinister on an escutcheon az., charged with a bee volant or. *Vi et prudentia.*

Maples, a tower or. 156. 2

Maples, Cecil E., of Aughton Springs, Ormskirk, same crest. *Vi et prudentia.*

Maplesden, out of a mural coronet az., two arms in armour embowed ppr., supporting a flag gu. flotant to the sinister, the staff or.

Mapletoft, Spring Hall, Suff., a demi-lion rampant holding a cross crosslet fitched sa. 11. 10

Mappin, Sir Frederick Thorpe, Bart., **J.P., M.P.,** of Thornbury, Yorks, a boar sa., charged with a pale or, and resting the dexter foot upon a spur fessewise, also or. *Cor forte calcar non requirit.* 40. 12

Mar, Scotland, a goat's head erased sa. 128. 5

Mar, Earl of (Goodeve-Erskine), Sunnington Rise, Bournemouth, a dexter hand holding a cutlass arg., hilted and pommelled or. *Je pense plus.*

Mar and **Kellie, Earl of** (Erskine), Alloa House, Alloa, Clackmannansh.: (1) A dexter hand holding a schene in pale arg., hilted and pommelled or. (2) A demi-lion rampant guardant gu., armed arg. *Je pense plus.—Unione fortior.—Decori decus addit avito.* 212. 9

Marbury, Chesh., on a chapeau gu., turned up erm., a man's head in profile ppr., wreathed or and az., on the chapeau five bezants in fess.

Marbury of Walton, Chesh., a mermaid ppr., with mirror and comb or. 184. 5

Marbury of Marbury Hall, Chesh., on a chapeau gu., turned up arg., and semée of plates, a Saracen's head in profile couped ppr., crined and bearded sa., wreathed of the first.

Marbury, on a cap arg., an old man's head in profile of the same, wreathed arg. and sa., on the cap five guttées-d'or.

Marbury of London, a sea-horse assurgent per pale or and az., crined gu.

Marcell of Languedoc, France, and of Waterford, a demi-eagle issuant ppr.

March, Earl of, *see* Richmond, Duke of.

March, a griffin passant with wings addorsed. 63. 2

March, out of a mural coronet sa., a nag's head arg.

March, a demi-lion rampant arg. 10. 2

March, an arm erect vested bendy wavy sinister or and purp., holding in the hand ppr. a flower gu., leaved vert, on the top a goldfinch volant ppr.

March of the Isle of Wight, a cubit arm erect vested barry wavy of six or and gu., cuffed arg., holding in the hand a battle-axe in bend sinister ppr., headed of the third. *cf.* 207. 10

March, Phillipps de Lisle, *see* De Lisle.

Marchall, a mullet or, between two palm-branches vert. 146. 8

Marchant, out of a ducal coronet a nag's head. 51. 7

Marche of Haddenham, Cambs, on a ducal coronet or, a wolf passant arg. *cf.* 28. 10

Marche, London, a griffin's head erased az., holding in the beak a rose gu., stalked and leaved vert. *cf.* 66. 2

Marchmont, out of a ducal coronet an eagle's claw erect. 113. 13

Marckwick, Sussex, a boar passant per pale arg. and az., charged with a saltier counterchanged. *cf.* 40. 9

Marcon, John, J.P., 44, Cadogan Place, S.W., a lion sejant winged, and supporting a lyre with the dexter foot, behind the lion's head the sun in splendour, all or.

Mardake, an eagle displayed or, environed by a serpent vert, the head turned to the dexter over the eagle's head. 74. 7

Marden of Marden, Heref., out of a ducal coronet or, a unicorn's head sa., armed and maned of the first. 48. 12

Mare, a hand apaumée gu. 222. 14

Mare of Blackheath, Chesh., a demi-leopard salient arg., spotted sa. *cf.* 23. 13

Marewood, out of a mural coronet or, a beacon in flames ppr., between two wings arg. 112. 5

Margary of Kensington, upon a mount vert, an arm in bend ppr. holding a daisy slipped arg. *Cherche qui n'a.*

Margary, Alfred Robert, same crest and motto.

Margerison, John Lister, Esquire, of Bradford, Yorks, a gryphon statant az., semée of mullets or, and resting the dexter claw upon a mill-rind, also or. *Industria et probitate.* 63. 4

Margesson of Offington, Sussex, on a ducal coronet or, a lion passant gardant sa., gorged with a ducal coronet or. *Loyalté me lie.* *cf.* 6. 4

Margesson, Lieutenant-Colonel William George, Findon Place, Findon, Sussex, same crest and motto.

Margetson, Ireland, a demi-lion rampant arg., the sinister paw resting on an estoile of eight points gu. *Par Dieu est mon tout.*

Margetson, Yorks and Ireland, on a ducal coronet or, a lion passant gordant sa., ducally gorged of the first. *Par Dieu est mon tout.* *cf.* 6. 4

Margetts, the attires of a stag affixed to the scalp

Margouts, a stag's head vert 121 5

Mariet, a squirrel sejant ppr, supporting a staff raguly sa

Marindin, Captain Arthur Henry Camberley, Surrey a talbot's head arg erased and gorged with a collar of cinquefoils gu *Flyddlawn Bunydd*

Marishall, Scotland, a trefoil ppr *Semper virescit virtus* 148 9

Marjoribanks, Rt Hon Sir Dudley Coutts, **Baron Tweedmouth,** a lion's gamb erect and erased grasping a lance in bend, both ppr *Advance with courage* cf 38 11

Marjoribanks, Bart, Berwick, a lion's gamb erect and erased grasping a tilting lance in bend sinister the point downward ppr *Advance with courage*

Marjoribanks of Marjoribanks a demi-griffin ppr *Custos et pugnax* 64 2

Marjoribanks of Balbeardie, Linlith gowsh., a demi griffin or *Et custos et pugnax* 64 2

Mark, Sir John, of Greystoke, West Didsbury, Manchester, and Leeswood Hall, near Mold, North Wales, a lion sejant winged or, semée of bees volant ppr, resting the dexter paw upon a rose gu, barbed and seeded ppr *Manu et corde*

Marke, a lion's gamb sa, holding a battle-axe or cf 38 3

Marke of Woodhill, Cornw, a demi lion holding in his dexter paw a fleur-de lis 13 2

Marker, an eagle with wings expanded resting the dexter claw on a mount ppr 77 6

Marker, Devonsh, a greyhound statant per pale arg and sa cf 60 2

Marker of Uffculme Devonsh, a greyhound per pale arg and sa resting the dexter paw upon a saltire gu *Festina lente* 58 13

Markham of Markham and Ollerton, Notts, a lion sejant gardant or, winged and circled round the head arg, resting the dexter paw on a harp of the first 20 9

Markham of Becca Hall Yorks, the lion of St Mark sejant gardant supporting a harp 20 9

Markham, Francis, Morland Westml, same crest

Markham of Cufforth Hall, Yorks a lion, sejant gardant winged or, the head radiated arg supporting the hames of a horse's collar of the first *Mitis et audax*

Markham, Sir Clements Robert of 21, Eccleston Square, London, S W a winged lion of St Mark guardant, the fore paw resting on a pair of horse hames, a glory round the head

Markham, Lieutenant General Edwin K C B Government House, Sandhurst, Camberley, same crest

Markham, Christopher Alexander of the Garth, Dallington Avenue, Northamp, a lion of St Mark sejant guardant, winged or, holding a pair of horse-hames of the last

Markham, Henry Philip of Sedgebrooke, Northamp., same crest.

Markham, of Sedgebrooke Notts, a lion of St Mark sejant gardant or, resting the dexter fore paw upon an escutcheon arg

Markham, a lion couchant winged supporting a lyre all or cf 20 9

Markham of Dublin a lion's head erased erm 17 8

Markoe, a demi lion gu, ducally gorged arg 10 7

Marks or **Markes,** a demi-lion rampant erm, holding a fleur de lis or 13 2

Marks, Middx a lion rampant holding in the dexter paw a fleur-de-lis or 2 7

Marks, Harry Hananel, Esquire, of Callis Court, St Peter's, Thanet, between two annulets or, a dexter arm embowed in armour, the hand in a gauntlet grasping a battle axe ppr, and round the wrist a chaplet of cinquefoils vert *Aut inveniam viam aut faciam* 258 11

Marlay, Ireland, on the point of a spear, issuing a dolphin naiant ppr 140 9

Marlay, Ireland, an eagle displayed ppr *Nulli præda sumus* 75 2

Marlborough, Duke of (Spencer-Churchill), Blenheim Palace, Woodstock (1) A lion couchant gardant arg, supporting with the dexter paw a banner gu charged with a dexter hand apaumee of the first, the staff or (*for Churchill*) (2) Out of a ducal coronet or, a griffin's head between two wings expanded, arg, gorged with a bar gemelle and armed gu (*for Spencer*) *Fiel pero desdichado* cf 67 1

Marler of London, on a chapeau purp turned up erm, an eagle with wings addorsed or ducally gorged beaked and legged gu cf 77 14

Marleton, on a tower arg, a lion rampant ppr 157 12

Marley, Ireland, a demi eagle rising ppr 80 2

Marley and **Marlow,** a cross moline pierced erm 165 1

Marley, an eagle with wings expanded 77 5

Marlay-Rochfort, Charles Brinsley, Esquire, of Belvedere co Westmeath and Bawn co Louth St Katharine's Lodge, Regent's Park, N W · (1) A robin redbreast ppr (*for Rochfort*) (2) An eagle displayed ppr *Nulli præda sumus*

Marlion, an ostrich's head and neck gu, the wings addorsed arg and az, holding in the beak a horse shoe of the second

Marling, Sir William Henry Bart D L of Stanley Park, and Sedbury Park, Glouc in front of a tower arg embattled and domed, thereon a flagstaff ppr, with a pennon gu, three bezants *Nulli præda sumus* 286 2

Marlott of Mundham, Sussex, a demi heraldic tiger rampant arg, erased per fess gu cf 25 13

Marlow, a cross moline square-pierced erm cf 165 1

Marlyn, a tower arg, masoned sa, on the top a cupola or cf 157 15

Marm, a goat's head erased 128 5

Marmaduke, three mullets in cheveron arg 164 7

Marmion of Leics, a rose gu, barbed vert 149 2

Marmyon, a tent az, garnished or 158 7

Marnell, a stag trippant or 117 8

Marner of London and England out of a ducal coronet or, a mullet az, between two laurel-branches vert *Quo virtus ducit scando* 146 7

Marney, a grenade inflamed ppr 177 12

Marney, Scotland, a lion rampant sa 1 10

Marney, Cornw, between two wings arg, a chapeau sa, turned up erm

Marnham, between two stalks of wheat in orle or, a cross moline gu 154 14

Marny, a chapeau sa, lined erm, winged on the top arg

Marples, George Jobson, Esquire, J P of Thornbridge Hall, near Bakewell, Derbysh, a griffin segreant or, resting the sinister claw on a cross crosslet fitchee sa between two wings of the latter *Tenax justitiæ* 252 13

Marr, Scotland, a cross crosslet fitched or *In cruce salus* 166 2

Marr, a horse's head erased and bridled, all ppr cf 51 5

Marr of Colchester, Essex, two lion's gambs erased in saltier or, each holding a battle axe, the handles gu, blades arg

Marrable, a lion rampant gardant or, holding in the paws a chaplet of oak vert, encircling a key in bend sinister the wards upwards of the first surmounted by a staff arg *Integritate sola*

Marrant, a crane with wings addorsed regardant arg resting the dexter claw on a pellet 105 5

Marriot or **Marriott,** a talbot passant sa collared and lined or, the line coiled at the end 54 5

Marriot, out of a ducal coronet or, a ram's head arg, armed of the first cf 130 1

Marriott, Charles, J P, Cotesbach, Lutterworth, same crest *Sursum*

Marriott, Norf, on the sun in splendour or, a ducal coronet of the same thence issuing a ram's head arg

Marriott of Northamp, and of Avonbank Worcs a talbot passant sa, collared and chained or *Virtute et fide* cf 54 5

Marriott, Henry Christopher, of Avonbank, Pershore Worcs in front of a rock ppr, thereon a talbot sa, guttee-d'or, collared and chained, reflexed over the back or, resting the dexter fore leg on a bezant charged with a martlet az, a stag raguly fesseways vert *Virtute et fide* 269 12

Marriott, Humphrey Richard George, of Abbots Hall, Shalford, near Braintree Essex, a demi talbot arg, with a collar, and thereto a leash affixed passing between the legs and reflexed over the back az, supporting a shield gu charged with a mascle arg *Mens conscia recti*

Marriott-Dodington, *see* Dodington

Marriott, Bart, *see* Smith

Marriott, Northamp, a talbot passant sa collared and chained or cf 54 5

Marris of Barton, Yorks, a castle ppr 155 8

Marrow, a pillar arg, the base az 176 3

Marrow, Ireland, a maiden's head ppr 182 3

Marrow, Edward Armfield, M.A., LL.M., between two roses arg., seeded or, barbed vert, a maiden's head couped at the shoulders ppr., crined, also or, the neck encircled with a garland of roses arg., barbed or, seeded vert. *Fide et virtute.*

Marrow, Rev. William John Williamson, M.A., same crest and motto.

Marryatt, a lion rampant double-queued ppr. 1. 14

Marryatt, Very Rev. Charles, M.A., of Christ Church Parsonage, North Adelaide, South Australia, on a mount vert, in front of a ram's head arg., the sun rising or. 231. 6

Marsden of Manchester, Lancs, and Chelmorton, Derbysh., a unicorn's head erased arg., guttée-de-sang, gorged with a ducal coronet az. *Mars denique victor est.* cf. 149. 5

Marsden, Rev. Edward, M.A., of Townend, Chelmorton, Derbysh., in front of an anchor sa., a unicorn's head erased arg., guttée-de-sang, ducally gorged az., in the mouth a trefoil slipped vert. *Mars dentalia tutatur.* 235. 9

Marsden, Rev. Maurice Howard, M.A., Rector of Moreton, Dorchester, same crest and motto.

Marsden, Lieutenant-Colonel William, of Cedar Court, Farnham, Surrey, same crest and motto.

Marsden-Smedley, J. B., Esquire, of Lea Green, near Matlock, a unicorn's head erased arg., guttée-de-sang, gorged with a ducal coronet az. *Mars denique victor est.* 298. 2

Marsden-Smedley, A. S., Esquire, of Normanhurst, Matlock, same crest and motto.

Marsh, Middx., a lion's head erased gu., ducally crowned or. 18. 8

Marsh of Darks, Middx., a demi-lion rampant erased sa., bezantée, gorged with a ducal coronet arg.

Marsh of Ramridge, Hants, a lion's head erased or. 17. 8

Marsh of Edmonton, Middx., Fincham, Bucks, and London, a demi-leopard rampant ppr., pellettée, ducally gorged or. cf. 23. 13

Marsh, William, Esquire, of Old Sarum House, Yeovil, same crest.

Marsh of Marton-in-Langden, Snave Manor, and Ivy Church, Kent, and Hants, out of a mural coronet gu., a horse's head arg., ducally gorged or. 293. 13

Marsh, Charles William Earle, Stowe Park, Newport, and Winterbourne, Glouc., same crest.

Marsh, Kent, a ram's head arg., attired and crowned or. 130. 4

Marsh, Jeremy Taylor, Esquire, of 1, Pembroke Road, Kensington, a griffin's head couped az., gorged with a ducal coronet or, holding in the beak a rose arg., seeded or, slipped, leaved, and barbed vert. *Nolo servile capistrum.* 230. 8

Marsh, William Swaine Chisenhale, J.P., of Gaynes Park, Epping, in front of a cross crosslet fitchée gu., a griffin arg., resting the dexter claw on a pheon in bend and erect sa. *In hoc signo vinces.*

Marsh, Bart. (*extinct*), of Dublin, a griffin's head couped az., ducally gorged or, holding in the beak a rose arg., seeded of the second, slipped and leaved vert. *Nolo servile capistrum.* 230. 8

Marsh of Springmount, Queen's Co., Ireland, a griffin's head couped az., gorged with a ducal coronet or, holding in the beak a rose arg., seeded of the second, slipped and leaved vert. *Nolo servile capistrum.* 230. 8

Marshall, *see* Hunter-Marshall.

Marshall, *see* Burt-Marshall.

Marshall, Scotland, a chevalier in armour, holding in his dexter hand a marshal's baton, resting on his side ppr. *Deus providebit.* cf. 188. 7

Marshall of Ardwick, and Penwortham Lodge, Lancs, a man in the armour of a pikeman of the fifteenth century, holding in his dexter hand a cross crosslet fitched in pale. *Utile pete finem.*

Marshall, Ireland: (1) A demi-man in armour affrontée ppr., holding in the dexter hand a baton sa., tipped or, charged on the breast with a rose gu., girded with a sash of the last, and charged with a crescent, also gu., for difference (*for Marshall*). (2) A demi-lion rampant gu., holding between the paws a sun or, partially eclipsed by clouds ppr. (*for Leeson*). (3) A winged lion sejant gardant with wings addorsed arg., holding between the forepaws a harp or, the head encircled with a plain glory of the last (*for Markham*). *Sapere aude.* cf. 20. 9

Marshall, Thomas Bingham, of 4, Sussex Street, Warwick Square, London, W., a demi-man affrontée in armour ppr., holding in his dexter hand a flagstaff, also ppr., therefrom flowing to the sinister a banner or, charged with a horse's head erased gu., and resting the sinister hand on a horseshoe sa. *Causa justa.* 240. 9

Marshall of Marston, Lincs, a man-of-arms from the waist upwards, armed in armour ppr., garnished or, the beaver open with a plume of feathers of divers colours upon the helm, and wearing a scarf az., bawdricewise, tied at the shoulder with a ribbon gu., and holding in his dexter hand a staff gold.

Marshall of Ballymacanan, a demi-man in armour affrontée ppr., girded round the loins with a sash gu., holding a baton sa., tipped or, and charged on the breast with a red rose ppr.

Marshall, Thomas, Esquire, of Roskille, Waverley, near Sydney, and of Fairlight, Elizabeth Bay, near Sydney, New South Wales, Solicitor of the Supreme Court of New South Wales, *uses*: a knight in armour. *Virtute non verbis.*

Marshall, Notts and Yorks, a man in armour ppr., holding in his dexter hand a truncheon or, and over his shoulder a sash gu. cf. 188. 7

Marshall, Julian, of 13, Belsize Avenue, London, N.W., a man affrontée in armour ppr., holding in his dexter hand a javelin in bend or, and supporting with his sinister hand a flagstaff ppr., therefrom flowing to the sinister a banner sa., charged with two horse-shoes fesseways, also or. *Nec cito nec tarde.* 238. 12

Marshall, a man's head couped at the shoulders ppr., wreathed about the temples or and az. 190. 5

Marshall of Broadwater, Surrey, a female figure vested arg., the dexter hand pointing to a rainbow above her head ppr., and with her sinister supporting an anchor in front sa. *Spes mea in cœlo.*

Marshall of Ivythorne, Somers., an arm in armour embowed ppr., garnished or, the scarf of the last and az., holding in the hand ppr. a tilting-spear, also or.

Marshall of Woodwalton, Hunts, an arrow arg., headed and feathered az., enfiled with a ducal coronet or. 174. 3

Marshall, Mark Bell, the Uplands, Stroud, Glouc., two arrows in saltire or, flighted az., surmounted by a Passion nail in fesse ppr., tied with a riband gu., pendent therefrom an escutcheon of the last charged with a horse-shoe of the first. *Vi martiali, Deo adjuvante.* 244. 6

Marshall of Southwark, Surrey, a greyhound sejant arg., gorged with a collar gu., ringed or, resting his dexter forepaw on a buck's head cabossed of the second.

Marshall of Rochester, Kent, upon a mount vert, in front of a Newfoundland dog sejant regardant ppr., an escutcheon arg., thereon in base waves of the sea, and floating therein a naked man, the sinister arm elevated, also ppr.

Marshall of Abbotts Anne, Hants, out of a ducal coronet a stag's head, all or. 120. 7

Marshall, a stag's head erased. *Ex candore decus.* 121. 2

Marshall, same crest. *Veritas vincit.*

Marshall, Connock- of Treworgy House, Cornw.: (1) An antelope's head erased or. (2) Out of a ducal coronet an eagle's head between two wings. *Invidia major.* 126. 2

Marshall of London, a camel's head or, gorged with a coronet. cf. 132. 9

Marshall, Yorks, a lion passant gardant or. 4. 3

Marshall of Carrigonnon, co. Cork, a lion rampant holding a cross patée fitchée. 3. 13

Marshall, Colonel Herbert, a demi-heraldic tiger sa., guttée-d'or, armed, crined, tufted, and gorged with a collar gemel, also or, resting the sinister paw upon an escutcheon gu., charged with a pheon or. *Ducit amor patriæ.* 25. 6

Marshall, a dove holding in its beak an olive-branch, all ppr. 92. 5

Marshall of Hillcairney, Fifesh., Scotland, a dove holding in its beak an olive-branch ppr. *Virtute tutus.* 92. 5

Marshall of Curriehill, Edinburgh, Scotland, a dove ppr. *Alta petit.* 92. 2

Marshall, a beehive with bees volant about it ppr. 137. 7

Marshall or **Marshal,** Scotland, a trefoil slipped ppr. *Semper virescit virtus.* 148. 9

Marshall of Bescott and Walsall, Staffs., and Ward End, Warw., a bezant charged with a horse-shoe az., between two wings barry of six erm. and az. *Vi martiali, Deo adjuvante.* 110. 13

Marshall, George William, Esquire, LL D, F S A, Rouge Croix Pursuivant, same crest and motto. 110 13

Marshall of Blowberry and Windsor, Berks, a griffin's head erased or charged on the neck with a chessrook between two mullets sa

Marsham, Viscount, *see* Romney, Earl of

Marsham, a falcon rising or, winged az 88 2

Marsham, Essex, a griffin's head couped or, between two wings gu. 65 11

Marsham, Major Henry Savill, Rippon Hall Hevingham, Norf, a lion's head erased gu, charged with three cross crosslets fitched or, one and two *Quod adest* cf 17 2

Marsham, George, of Hayle Place, Maidstone, Kent, a lion's head erased gu 17 2

Marsham-Jones, Henry Shovell Esquire, of Hayle Cottage, Kent (1) A talbot's head couped arg, langued and chained gu charged on the neck for distinction with a cross crosslet, also gu (*for Jones*) cf 56 12 (2) A lion's head erased gu, langued az. (*for Marsham*). 17 2

Marsham-Townshend, Hon Robert of Frognal Foot's Cray, Kent and 5, Chesterfield Street, Mayfair W (1) A stag statant ppr (*for Townshend*) (2) A lion's head erased gu (*for Marsham*) *Droit et avant*

Marshe, Hants, a griffin's head sa, holding in the beak a rose gu, leaved ppr cf 66 1

Marshe of Dunstable, Beds, out of a mural coronet az, a horse's head arg, gorged with a chaplet of laurel ppr

Marske, Yorks, a lion's head erased az, charged with a cinquefoil or cf 17 8

Marson, a portcullis az 178 3

Marston, the sail of a ship ppr 160 9

Marston, Shropsh, a demi eagle displayed 81 6

Marston of Eastcot and Heyton Shropsh, a demi-greyhound sa., gorged with a fess indented erm cf 60 11

Marston, Shropsh a demi greyhound sa, gorged with a collar dancettee erm cf 60 11

Marston, H T Grant, Esq, a sword fesseways ppr, pommelled or, surmounted on the blade by a crescent ar *Spero*

Martaine of Bowton, Cambs, an etoile gu 164. 1

Marten, His Honour Judge Sir Alfred George, K C, of 21, Prince of Wales Terrace Kensington London, W, on a wreath of the colours, in front of a griffin segreant per fesse arg, guttee-de-poix and or, winged of the last, a fasces fessewise ppr *Spes super sidera* 244 19

Marten of Bildeston, Suff, an eagle's head between two wings issuing out of a ducal coronet or 84 3

Marten, George Nisbet, of Marshals Wick, Herts, Radford and Rowsham, Oxon, a martin sa., holding in its beak an oval buckle arg

Marten, late of Winchelsea, Sussex (descended from Aquitaine), an escallop shell or *Aquitaine* 141 12

Marten, Charles Peter, Esquire, of Shalmsford Bridge, Canterbury, a leg couped above the knee ppr, spurred az *Tace aut face* 193 8

Marten, Charles Peter, of Shalmford Bridge, Canterbury, an armed leg couped above the thigh ppr *Tace aut face* 255 17

Marter, on a chapeau gu, turned up erm, an eagle rising ppr 77 14

Martham, out of a tower a demi lion holding between the paws a bomb fired all ppr 157 10

Martham of Dublin, a lion's head erased erm 17 8

Martiall, London, a greyhound salient ppr

Martin, *see* Wood-Martin

Martin, Richard Biddulph, Esquire M P, M A, J P, of 10, Hill Street W, a marten ppr *Pejus letho flagitium*

Martin, Waldyve Alexander Hamilton, the Upper Hall, Ledbury same crest and motto

Martin, George Edward Ham Court Upton on-Severn, Worcs, same crest and motto

Martin, London a wood-martin ppr, collared arg

Martin, Bart Suff (1) A cockatrice's head between two wings 68 8 (2) A martin passant ppr *Initium sapientiæ est timor Domini*

Martin, Edward Pritchard J P, of the Hill, Abergavenny, Monm, Glamorgansh, two hammers in saltire ppr, thereon a cock regardant gu *En martelant* 294 5

Martin, Scotland a martin statant ppr *Initium sapientiæ est timor Domini*

Martin, a martin cat passant ppr

Martin of Wivenhoe, Essex, a martin salient against a cannon erect

Martin of Ham Court Worcs, a martin passant ppr *Pejus letho flagitium*

Martin of Wilderness, Reigate, and Lion field, Cumb in front of a garb or a martin cat statant ppr *Fide et clementia* 265 2

Martin, Henry Richmond, Colonel R A of Bitterne Lodge, near Southampton, same crest and motto

Martin, Admiral Thomas Hutchinson Mangles, of Bitterne Lodge, Bitterne, Southampton same crest and motto

Martin, Major General William George of Hemingstone Ipswich Suff, upon the stump of a tree eradicated ppr surmounted by an anchor in bend sinister or, a martin-cat sejant supporting between the paws a mirror also ppr, and gorged with a naval crown, there from a chain reflexed over the back or *Sans tache* 293 3

Martin, Colonel Sir Richard Edward Rowley, K C B, of Aldeburgh, Suff same crest and motto

Martin, George Bohun of Martin's Ranch, Kamloops, British Colombia, same crest and motto

Martin, London and Herts a martin sa., holding in its beak a buckle arg

Martin, Kent a martin entwined with a serpent ppr, holding in its beak a cross crosslet fitched or.

Martin, Wykeham-, Cornwallis Philip, of Leeds Castle, Kent (1) A martin entwined by a serpent ppr, holding in its beak a cross crosslet fitched or (*for Martin*) (2) A bull's head erased sa, armed or, charged with two chevronels of the same (*for Wykeham*) *Manners malyth man* cf 44 3

Martin-Hosken, Wyndham H, Esquire, of Trenewth, Michaelstowe, Camelford, a lion rampant or. *Vis unita fortior* 1 13

Martin of Bangor, Carnarvonsh, and London, a martlet rising arg, charged on the breast with an estoile sa cf 95 11

Martin, Yorks an eagle displayed or 75 2

Martin, Somers and Devonsh, an eagle's head between two wings issuant from a ducal coronet, all ppr *Accendit cantu* 84 3

Martin of Plymouth, Devonsh, on a celestial globe sans frame an eagle ppr, with wings displayed or, and ducally gorged of the same cf 159 7

Martin, Durham, a demi-ostrich erased arg, with wings elevated gu, and holding in the beak a horse-shoe

Martin, Devonsh and Wales, a leopard's head erased ppr 23 10

Martin, Abraham, Esquire, J P, of Cleveragh, co Sligo, Ireland, a lion rampant holding in the dexter paw a crescent, all or, and charged on the shoulder with a thistle ppr *Hinc fortior et clarior* cf 2 2

Martin, Sir Theodore, K C B, of Bryntysilio, Denbighsh, and 31, Onslow Square, Kensington, London, S W, a lion rampant sa, armed and langued gu, holding in his dexter forepaw a crescent arg *Spero* 260 16

Martin, Scotland, a lion rampant holding a sword ppr *Hinc fortior et clarior*

Martin, Scotland, a lion statant ppr, holding in his dexter paw a crescent or 5 6

Martin, a lion rampant holding in his dexter paw a sabre and in his sinister a thistle slipped all ppr *Hinc fortior et clarior*

Martin, a Saracen's head in profile couped at the shoulders wreathed about the temples, charged on the breast with a saltire

Martin, out of a ducal coronet a buck's head couped between two slips of cypress

Martin, Yorks, a buck's head couped ppr 121 5

Martin, Kent and Yorks, a stag's head sa 121 5

Martin, a demi-antelope arg, collared gu 126 3

Martin, Henry Charrington M D, of Salthrop House, Wroughton Wilts a fox statant ppr *Initium sapientiæ est timor Domini*

Martin of Gibliston, Fifesh, Scotland, an adder with young ones bursting through her side ppr *Ingratis servire nefas* 142 3

Martin of Anstey, Leics, out of a mural coronet vert a talbot's head ppr, eared and langued gu, collared of the first *Sure and steadfast* cf 56 6

Martin, Rev John, of Charley Hall Loughborough, Leics, a talbot's head erased arg, crusily eared and langued gu, gorged with a collar vert *Sure and steadfast* 56 1

Martin, Robert Frewin, J P of the Brand Loughborough, Leics, same crest and motto

Martin, a greyhound's head erased arg, collared sa cf 61 2

Martin-Holloway, Sir George, of Tittenhurst, Sunninghill, and 14, King's Gardens, West Brighton, a horse's head erased arg. *In utrumque paratus.* 51. 4
Martin, Ireland, a leg couped above the knee az., spurred ppr. 193. 8
Martin, a cubit arm erect ppr., wielding a scimitar, the blade also ppr., hilt and pommel or. 213. 5
Martin, Scotland, a dexter hand holding a dagger ppr. *Pro patria.* 212. 9
Martin of Upton Gray, Odiham, Hants, a dexter hand brandishing a scimitar ppr., pommel and hilt or. *Auxilium ab alto.* 212. 13
Martin of Liverpool, a dexter arm erect couped at the elbow ppr., the hand holding a crescent arg. *Hinc fortior et clarior.* 216. 8
Martin of Bowton, Cambs, a tower triple-towered chequy or and az. 157. 6
Martin of Exeter, Devonsh., an etoile gu. 164. 1
Martin of Ross House, Galway, an etoile of six points or. *Sic itur ad astra.* 164. 1
Martin, Archer, Esquire, of Winnipeg, Canada, an estoile of six points or. *Sic itur ad astra.* 164. 1
Martin of Galway, Ireland, an estoile or. *Auxilium meum a Domino.* 164. 1
Martin or **Martyn** of Tullyra, co. Galway, same crest. *Spes mea in cruce unica.* —*Sic itur ad astra.* 164. 1
Martin of Martinique, West Indies, a star of six points or. *Auxilium meum a Domino.* 164. 1
Martin of Ballinahinch Castle and Brook Lodge, co. Mayo, an estoile of eight points or. *Auxilium meum a Domino.* cf. 164. 4
Martin, Sir Richard, Bart., J.P., D.L., of Cappagh, co. Dublin, and Merrion Square, in the city of Dublin, in front of an anchor sa., an estoile or. *Sic itur ad astra.*
Martin of Hemingston, Suff., an ape admiring himself in a looking-glass ppr. *Sans tache.*
Martin-Leake, Stephen, Esquire, M.I.C.E., of Marshalls, High Cross, near Ware, Herts, a ship gun-carriage, on it a piece of ordnance mounted, all ppr. *Parti animo.*
Martinal, three organ-pipes, two in saltier and one in pale, ppr.
Martindale, a wolf current ppr. 28. 4
Martine, Scotland, a lion passant holding in the dexter paw a crescent ppr. *Hinc fortior et clarior.* 5. 6
Martineau, a ram's head erased gu. 130. 6
Martineau of Basing Park, Hants, a martin ppr.
Martineau, David, Esquire, of 4, South Road, Clapham Park, S.W., a martlet or. *Marte nobilior pallas.*
Martinius, between two elephants' tusks gu. and sa., a sword in pale, enfiled with a crown or.
Martinson, Northumb., out of a mural coronet or, a plume of five ostrich-feathers arg., charged with a martlet, with wings expanded ppr. *We rise.*
Marton, Colonel George Blucher Heneage, of Capernwray Hall, Lancs, a stag's head ppr., attired sa. *Dieu et ma patrie.* 121. 5
Martyn, a martlet. 95. 4
Martyn, London, a martin passant ppr.
Martyn of Woodford, Essex, Lancs, and London, a wood-martin ppr., collared arg.
Martyn or **Martin,** on the stump of a tree couped and erased arg., a monkey sejant ppr., collared and lined or, looking in a mirror, framed of the last. *He who looks at Martin's ape, Martin's ape shall look at him.*
Martyn, Waddon, Esquire, of Tonacombe Manor, Morwenstow, North Cornwall, on a rock ppr., an ape sejant, collared and lined, holding in the hands a mirror in which he is admiring himself. *Sans tache.*
Martyn of Okingham, Berks, out of a ducal coronet or, a falcon's head az., beaked of the first. 89. 4
Martyn, out of a ducal coronet or, an eagle's head arg., between two wings gu. 84. 3
Martyn, on a celestial globe or, an eagle with wings displayed arg., ducally gorged of the first. cf. 159. 7
Martyn, London, an eagle displayed gu. 75. 2
Martyn of Long Milford, Suff., a cockatrice's head or, beaked and wattled gu., between two wings expanded vert. 68. 8
Martyn, Durh., an ostrich's head arg., between two ostrich's wings gu., holding in the beak a horse-shoe or. cf. 97. 10
Martyn of Staplemorden, Cambs, a griffin segreant per fesse erm. and or, winged of the last. 62. 2
Martyn of Pertenhall, Beds, a leopard's head couped ppr. 22. 10
Martyn-Linnington, Richard, in front of a rock ppr., a leopard's face gu., surmounted by an estoile or.
Martyn of Oxton, Devonsh., an étoile of sixteen points gu.
Martyn, Ireland, an étoile of six points or. *Sic itur ad astra.* 164. 1
Martyr, an ostrich's head arg., collared or, between two palm-branches vert.
Martyr, a griffin segreant or, with wings addorsed az., holding a rose gu., stalked and leaved ppr. cf. 62. 2
Martyre, a demi-lion rampant ppr. 10. 2
Marvel, out of a ducal coronet or, a plume of ostrich-feathers arg. cf. 114. 8
Marwick, a boar passant per pale arg. and az., charged with a saltire wavy counterchanged. cf. 40. 9
Marwick, Sir James David, D.L., J.P., LL.D., F.R.S.E., sometime Town Clerk of Glasgow, and formerly Town Clerk of Edinburgh, Killermount House, Dumbartonsh., 19, Woodside Terrace, Glasgow, Western Club, Glasgow, and Union Club, St. Andrews, a boar passant az. *Firmus et fidelis.* 40. 2
Marwood-Elton, Bart., see Elton.
Marwood of Widworthy, Devonsh., on a mount vert, a ram couchant ppr., armed or.
Marwood-Elton, Rev. Alfred, B.A., of Widworthy Court, near Honiton, Devonsh.: (1) A dexter arm embowed in armour ppr., garnished or, charged with two estoiles gu., adorned with a scarf about the wrist tied vert, the hand in a gauntlet holding a falchion ppr., pommel and hilt or (*for Elton*). (2) On a mount vert, in front of a branch of oak erect ppr., a ram couchant erm., horned or. *Artibus et armis.*
Marwood, William Francis, of Bushby Hall, Carlton in Cleveland, and the Porch House, Northallerton, Yorks, on a mount vert, a ram couchant arg., horned and hoofed or.
Marwood, Bart. (*extinct*), of Little Busby and Northallerton, Yorks, on a mount vert, a ram couchant arg., armed and unguled or.
Marwood of West Marwood and Plymouth, Devonsh., and Worcs., a goat's head erased arg., armed or, charged with a chevron gu. cf. 128. 5
Maryet and **Maryot,** Berks, of Preston, Glouc., Breadfield, Suff., Whitchurch, Warw., and Sussex, a talbot passant sa., collared and lined or, the line coiled at the end. cf. 54. 5
Maryon-Wilson, Sir Spencer Maryon, Bart., of Eastbourne, Sussex: (1) A demi-wolf rampant or (*for Wilson*). (2) A gryphon segreant sa., bezantée, the wings erm., resting the dexter hind leg on an escutcheon per fesse arg. and or, charged with an eagle displayed gu. (*for Maryon*). *Res non verba.—Pro legibus ac regibus.* 31. 2
Mascall, Kent, a lion's head erased and ducally crowned, all ppr. 18. 8
Mascall, Durh., an elephant statant. 133. 9
Mascall, a sea-lion salient sa. 20. 5
Masey or **Masey,** a lion's head couped arg. 21. 1
Mash, issuing from rays a hand vested holding up a skull. 208. 10
Masham, Baron (Cunliffe-Lister), Swinton Park, Masham: (1) A stag's head erased per fesse ppr. and or, attired sa. (2) A greyhound sejant arg., collared sa., and charged on the shoulder with a pellet (*Cunliffe*). *Retinens vestigia famæ.*
Masham, Baron Masham (*extinct*), a griffin's head couped or, between two wings erect gu. *Mihi jussa capessere.* 65. 11
Masham, a griffin's head couped or, between two wings gu. 65. 11
Masham, Suff., a griffin's head per pale or and gu., between two wings az. 65. 11
Mashiter, a greyhound sejant winged and collared. 59. 9
Mashiter of Priests, Essex, on a mount vert, a talbot passant erm., collared and chained or, resting the dexter fore-paw on an escutcheon az., charged with a leopard's face arg. *Spero et vivo.* 54. 12
Maskell, a leopard rampant ppr.
Maskelyne, a demi-lion rampant holding between its paws an escallop. 13. 10
Maskelyne, Edmund Story, Esquire, of Hatt House, Box, Wilts, and Nevil Story Maskelyne, Esquire, F.R.S., M.P., of Bassett Down House and Salthrop Lodge, Wilts: (1) A demi-lion rampant sa., holding between the paws an escallop-shell arg. (*for Maskelyne*). 229. 4. (2) Two arms counter-embowed, habited purpure, cuffed arg., the hands ppr., grasping by the antlers a stag's head caboshed ppr., attired or, transfixed by an arrow in pale point downwards arg. (*for Story*). 229. 5

Mason, a mermaid ppr 184 5
Mason of Greenwich, Kent, a mermaid per fesse wavy arg and az, the upper part guttee-de-larmes, holding in her dexter hand a comb, and in her sinister a mirror, the frame and her hair sa 184 5
Mason of Hemingford and Cuckney Hants, a mermaid holding a comb and a glass, all ppr 184 5
Mason, William Henry, B A J P, Morton Hall, Retford, a mermaid holding a comb and a glass all ppr, the hair vert *Virtus sola nobilitas*
Mason of London, between two wings arg, a lion's head az, charged with a mullet. cf 19 7
Mason, Robert Harvey, Esquire of Necton Hall, Swaffham Norf (1) On a ducal coronet an eagle with wings elevated, holding in the dexter claw a sceptre, all or, and charged on the breast for distinction with a cross crosslet gu (*for Humfry*) (2) A lion's head couped az, holding in the mouth an antler in bend or, between two wings arg, each charged with an annulet, also az (*for Mason*) (3) On a morion a martlet ppr (*for Blake*)
Mason of Beel House near Amersham, Berks, a demi-lion rampant arg, holding in its dexter paw a crescent or cf 10 2
Mason, Ireland three Moors' heads conjoined on one neck ppr, wreathed about the temples vert 191 5
Mason, Scotland, the sun in splendour 162 2
Mason, a deer's head erased ppr 121 2
Mason, a stag's head erased sa attired or gorged with a ducal coronet of the last cf 121 2
Mason, Warw, a talbot passant regardant arg, eared sa., holding in its mouth a hart's attire or
Mason, Shropsh, a tower 156 2
Mason of Ayr and Rosebank, Scotland, a tower ppr, masoned sa. *Demeure par la verite* 156 2
Mason of Dublin, a tower triple-towered gu within a chaplet or *Sola virtus munimentum* cf 157 6
Mason of Inveresk, Edinburgh a house ppr, ensigned on the top with a crescent arg *Dominus providebit*
Mason of Mordun, Edinburgh a fortified house ppr. *Arte firmus*
Masquenay, Ireland, a Roman head helmeted, couped ppr 101 6
Massam, Ireland, a demi griffin with wings addorsed sa holding a pole-axe gu 64 11
Massereene and Ferrard, Viscount (Foster Skeffington), Antrim Castle, Antrim a mermaid holding in either hand a mirror and a comb, all ppr *Per angusta ad augusta* 184 5
Massenden of Helme, Lincs, a Cornish chough sa, beaked and legged gu, holding in the beak a sprig of laurel ppr cf 107 14
Massey, Baron Clarina, *see* Clarina
Massey, Chesh, out of a ducal coronet or, a bull's head gu, armed sa *Pro libertate patriæ* 44 11
Massey, Bart, Ireland, out of a ducal coronet or, a bull's head gu, armed sa *Pro libertate patriæ* 44 11
Massey, John George Albert, of Kingwell House, near Tipperary, a bull's head gu, issuing out of a ducal coronet or *Pro libertate patriæ*
Massey-Mainwaring, Hon William Frederick Barton, of Knaresborough Yorks, and 30, Grosvenor Place, S W (1) An ass's head erased ppr, haltered arg, charged on the neck for distinction with a cross crosslet or (*for Mainwaring*) (2) Out of a ducal coronet or a bull's head gu armed sa, charged for distinction with an annulet or (*for Massey*) 44 11
Massey, on a chapeau gu., turned up erm a boar passant ppr, environed with a net. 40 11
Massey of London, on a mount vert, a lion current arg interlaced with four trees of the first
Massey, a demi-pegasus rampant arg 47 5
Massey, William Francis Elcocke, Pool Hall, Nantwich, Chesh, a demi-pegasus with wings displayed quarterly or and gu 47 5
Massey, Chesh, a heathcock statant sa, legged, combed, and wattled gu
Massey of Dunham-Massey (1) A moorcock sa, combed and wattled gu charged on the breast for distinction with a cross crosslet or (*for Massey*) (2) A lion's gamb erased holding a branch of olive ppr, pendent therefrom by a chain a bugle or (*for Oliver*) *Pro libertate patriæ—Nunquam fallentis termes Olivæ*
Massey of Rixton, Lancs, a covered cup arg
Massey of Isle of Ely Cambs and Podington, Chesh an owl arg 96 5
Massicks of the Oaks, Millom, Cumb, a cross patee az surmounted by a leopard's face jessant-de-lis or *Vestigia nulla retrorsum*
Massie, a horned owl ppr 96 5
Massie, a lion salient arg, between two trees ppr
Massie, a griffin's head erased bendy of six sa and arg 66 2
Massie, Edward Richard, Esquire, J P, of Coddington Chester, a demi-pegasus quarterly or and gu
Massingberd, Rev William Oswald, of Ormsby, Lincs (1) A dragon's head erased quarterly or and gu between two wings az cf 72 7 (2) A lion's head erased az, charged on the neck with two broad arrows in saltier arg, barbed or between four guttes d'or *Est meruisse satis*
Massingberd, Stephen Langton, of Gunby, Lincs a lion's head erased az, charged with two arrows in saltire between four guttes d'eau *Est meruisse satis* cf 17 8
Massingberd - Mundy, Charles Francis, Ormsby Hall, Lincoln (1) A panther's head erased sa, bezantee (*for Mundy*) cf 23 10. (2) A lion's head erased az, charged with two arrows saltireways between four guttes d'eau (*for Massingberd*) *Deus providebit—Est meruisse satis*
Massingbird, Lincs, a laurel branch fructed ppr 151 13
Massingham, a long cross crossed on three grieces gu 161 6
Masson, Scotland, the sun in splendour 162 2
Massue, *see* De Massue
Massue de Ruvigny, De, Earl of, and Viscount Galway (*extinct*) a demi-savage crowned and girt with laurel holding with both hands a club all ppr *Duce Deo*
Massy, *see* Beresford Massy
Massy, Baron (Massy), of Duntrileague, co Limerick out of a ducal coronet or a bull's head gu, armed sa *Pro libertate patriæ* 44 11
Massy, Edward Hugh, Esquire of Ferny Glen, Roch R S O, Pembrokesh, same crest and motto
Massy, Rev George Eyre of Gumfreston, Tenby same crest and motto
Massy, Hugh Hamon George William Caruthurs, of Hazelhurst, near Sway Hants same crest and motto
Massy of Allerborough Chesh, a lion's head erased arg 17 8
Massy of Alford Chesh, an owl sa, gorged with a collar gobony arg and az cf 96 5
Massy-Dawson, George Charles Henry Edward, Esquire J P, of Ballincourte, and Castlered House co Tipperary (1) A dexter arm embowed in armour ppr, garnished or holding in the gauntlet a battle-axe of the last (*for Dawson*) (2) Out of a ducal coronet or a bull's head gu armed sa (*for Massy*)
Massy-Beresford, John George Beresford, of St Huberts Beltarbet, Ireland (1) A dragon's head erased az, charged with a crescent or pierced through the neck with a broken spear, the point thrust through the upper jaw gold (2) Out of a ducal coronet or, a bull's head gu armed sa, charged with a martlet gold *Pro libertate patriæ*
Master of East Langdon, Kent, out of a mural coronet or, a unicorn's head arg, crined and armed gu 261 3
Master, Charles Hoskins, J P, D L of Barrow Green Court Oxted, Surrey, out of a mural coronet or a unicorn's head arg armed and crined gu *Non minor est virtus quam quærere parta tueri* 261 3
Master, Charles Onslow Esquire of Bourton Grange, Flax Bourton, Somers same crest and motto
Master, Rev Henry Streynsham, of Bourton Grange, Somers, same crest and motto
Master, Robert Edward, Esquire, J P of Hillingdon Furze Uxbridge same crest and motto
Master, Charles Gilbert, Esquire C S I of 25, Oxford Square, London W, same crest and motto.
Master, Rev Gilbert Coventry of Springvale, Lansdowne Road Bournemouth, same crest and motto.
Master, John Henry of Montrose House, Petersham, same crest and motto
Master, Rev Oswald, M.A of St. Arvan's Court Chepstow same crest and motto
Master-Whitaker, Alfred Esquire, M A, of the Holme, near Burnley, Lancs (1) In front of a dexter arm embowed in mail armour, the hand ppr grasping a dagger, also ppr, pommel and hilt or, a mascle between two annulets arg, the arm charged for distinction with a

cross crosslet also arg (*for Whitaker*) (2) Out of a mural coronet or, a unicorn's head arg, crined sa (*for Master*) 261 3

Master, Wilts, a cubit arm couped and erect, vested gu cuffed arg, holding in the hand a bunch of honeysuckles, all ppr

Master, Kent Oxon, and of Cirencester, and Thomas William Chester Masters of Knole Park, Glouc within a ring or, gemmed ppr, two snakes entwined erect on their tails and addorsed az

Masterman of Riccal, Yorks a Moor's head in profile ppr, wreathed about the temples arg and gu 192 13

Masters, an arrow erect sa, barbed and feathered arg, enfiled with a leopard's face or

Masters, an arm gu, holding two branches flowered arg, leaved ppr

Masters, out of a mural coronet or, a unicorn's head arg, armed and crined of the first

Masters of Ewdon, Shropsh, a cock's head erased arg, combed and wattled gu, holding in the beak an ear of wheat slipped or between two wings az, semee of estoiles, also or

Masters, Smith-, William Allan, Camer near Gravesend (1) A lion rampant double queued arg, charged with three roses gu and holding between the paws a cross flory, also gu (2) A talbot sa, collared and lined, and charged with three cross crosslets fitchee arg, and resting the dexter foot upon an escutcheon or thereon a martlet az *Manet intemerata fides*

Masterson, a buck trippant az 117 8

Masterson of Ferns Castle, co Wexford, a garb or banded vert 153 2

Masterson of Nantwich, Chesh, an heraldic tiger passant arg 25 5

Masterton and **Mastertown**, of Grange Perth, Scotland a dexter hand issuing holding a scimitar ppr *Pro Deo et rege* 213 5

Masterton, Scotland in front of a fir-tree a stag courant, all ppr *Per ardua*

Masterton of Parkmilne and Gogar Perthsh, a stag courant bearing on the attires an oak-slip fructed, all ppr *Per ardua*

Maston, Kent the sail of a ship ppr 160 9

Matcham, an arm in pale vested vert cuffed arg, holding in the hand three ears of wheat ppr *cf* 205 5

Matcham, Eyre-, William Eyre Newhouse, Salisbury out of an Eastern crown or a cubit arm habited vert in the hand ppr three ears of barley stalked and bladed of the first

Matchell, Bucks, a camel's head erased or, ducally gorged arg *cf* 132 9

Matchet and **Matcheton**, a cross patee fitched gu 166 3

Matchett, Norf, a demi lion or, armed and langued gu 10 2

Mateos, Anthony, Esquire, of Gibraltar, a lion's face or, encircled by two serpents ppr *Perseverantia vincit*

Mather, Scotland, a rock sa 179 7

Mather, a dexter hand apaumée, charged with an eye *Deus providebit* 222 4

Mather, issuing out of a cloud a hand erect holding an arrow, point downwards 214 1

Mather of Lanton, Roxburghsh, Scotland an eagle displayed ppr. *Fortiter et celeriter* 75 2

Mather, Wales, a demi-mower, his habit and cap and hands and face ppr, holding in his dexter hand a bugle horn or and in sinister a scythe ppr *Mowe warilie*

Mather-Jackson, Sir Henry, Bart (1) Upon a ragged staff sa, a goat's head couped arg, semee of trefoils slipped vert 285 9 (2) A cubit arm erect, vested sa, slashed arg, cuffed erm, charged with two mullets in fesse or, grasping in the hand an arrow ppr

Matheson of Bennetsfield Scotland, a dexter hand brandishing a scimitar ppr *Fac et spera* 213 5

Matheson of Ardentoule, Ross sh Scotland a hand holding a scimitar in fess all ppr *Fac et spera*

Matheson, Scotland, an armed hand holding a naked sword ppr *Heart in hand*

Matheson, Sir Kenneth James, Bart D L, of Lochalsh, Ross-sh, issuant from an Eastern crown or, a dexter hand holding a scimitar in fesse all ppr *Fac et spera*

Mathew, Earl of Landaff (*extinct*), on a mount vert, a moorcock ppr *Y fyn duw a fydd* *cf* 89 8

Mathew, Ireland, a heathcock sa

Mathew, Glamorgansh., on a mount vert a moorcock ppr *cf* 89 8

Mathew of Tresunger and Pennytenny, Cornw, on a mount vert a stork ppr, legged and beaked gu *cf* 105 11

Mathew of Castle Menych an eagle displayed per fesse arg and gu 75 2

Mathew, a dexter hand ppr, holding a gem ring or stoned gu *cf* 216 1

Mathew, Scotland, an arm in armour embowed holding in the hand a sword all ppr *Quid non pro patria.* 195 2

Mathew of Coggeshall, Essex, a lion's gamb erect holding a cross crosslet fitched in pale sa *Cruce non leone fides*

Mathew of Billokesby Norf. a unicorn's head erased arg, armed and maned gu, on the neck a chevron vairee of the first and second *cf* 49 5

Mathews, Ireland, an arm in armour wielding a sword ppr 210 2

Mathews, on an escallop gu, between two wings az., a cross fleury or 141 7

Mathews, Rev William Arnold of Bassingham Rectory Lincoln, same crest

Mathews, Suff, a lion's gamb holding a cross patee fitched all sa *cf* 36. 9

Mathews, a greyhound's head arg between two roses gu, stalked and leaved ppr 61 11

Mathews, a dove close 92 2

Mathias, out of a ducal coronet a broken battle axe

Mathias of Llangwarren, Pembrokesh, a stag trippant ppr, attired or 117 8

Mathias-Thomas, Morgan, Esquire, of Tenby House, Tenby, Pembrokesh a demi lion rampant *Sans peur*

Mathie, Scotland, a unicorn's head erased *Esse quam videri* 49 5

Mathieson or **Mathison**, Scotland, a cock gu 91 2

Mathilez, a serpent nowed vert 142 4

Mathison, Scotland, a branch of laurel fructed ppr *Viridis semper* 151 13

Mathisson, Scotland, a lion rampant *Vigilans* 1 13

Matoke, Mattick, or **Mattock**, Yorks and Herts, a bear salient per bend arg and sa, muzzled or

Maton, an arm in armour embowed, holding in the hand an anchor by the middle in fess

Maton, Leonard James Esquire, B A of Grosvenor Lodge, Wimbledon, and Harston, Sidmouth, a sheaf of seven arrows, one in pale and six in saltire, three and three, points downwards, enfiled by a mural coronet *Per sagittas ad coronam*

Maton, a sheaf of seven arrows sa, enfiled with a mural coronet or

Matran, a sinister arm, the hand clenched all ppr

Matson, on a rock a fort in flames ppr 155. 1

Matterson, Robert De Mowbray of Langford Manor, Fivehead Taunton, a cubit arm entwined by a branch of oak grasping a scimitar, all ppr, the pommel and hilt or, between two roses

Matthew of Stansted Sussex an eagle displayed per fess arg and gu 75 2

Matthew, Dorset, on a mount vert, a moorcock ppr *cf* 89 8

Matthew, Ireland a heathcock ppr

Matthews, *see* Donaldson

Matthews, Bart (*extinct*), of Edmonton, Middx, and Essex a bull's head couped gu, between two wings endorsed arg *Omne solum viro patria est*

Matthews, a stork arg 105 11

Matthews, Heref on a mount vert a moorcock holding in the beak a sprig of heather all ppr

Matthews, Scotland a cross crosslet fitched az, and a palm branch vert in saltier

Matthews, a demi-lion rampant or 10 2

Matthews, Shropsh, a lion's gamb erect arg, holding a cross crosslet sa

Matthison, Scotland, a demi lion ppr holding between its paws a cross crosslet gu

Mattock, a bear salient per bend arg and sa muzzled or

Maturin-Baird, Daniel Baird, Esquire, of Newtown Stewart, co. Tyrone, Ireland (1) A boar's head erased ppr, between two branches of shamrocks vert (*for Baird*) (2) A horse in full speed arg (*for Maturin*), and in an escroll above the motto *Minatur Vi et virtute* 52 8

Maturin, Ireland, a horse at full speed arg *Minatur* 52 8

Maturin, Rev Benjamin, M.A of Vicarage, Lymington, Hants, same crest and motto

Maude, Viscount Hawarden, *see* Hawarden

Maude, a lion's head couped gu 21 1

Maude, Yorks a lion's head couped gu, charged with a cross crosslet fitched or *De monte alto* *cf* 21 1

Maude, a lion's head erased gu, charged on the neck with a cross crosslet fitchee or *cf* 17 2

Maude, Charles Henry Esquire, of 90, Elm Park Gardens S W, a lion's gamb erased gu, holding an acorn or, slipped vert

Maude, Francis Sterling De Montalt, same crest.
Maude, Lieutenant Colonel Robert Henry of White Hill Chase Greatham, West Liss, Hants, same crest *Virtute securus*
Maude, Ireland, a hand holding two branches of palm in orle ppr 218 7
Maudele or **Maudell** of Wells, Somers out of a ducal coronet or, an eagle's head arg cf 83 14
Maudit, Scotland, two laurel branches in orle ppr *Pro rege et lege* 146 5
Maudley, Somers, out of a ducal coronet a falcon's head, all arg 89 4
Maudult, out of a five-leaved coronet or, a griffin's head between two wings arg, beaked of the first cf 67 1
Mauger, a sea-lion rampant az 20 5
Maugham and **Maughan,** a lion's gamb erased holding the hilt of a broken sword in pale 38 2
Maughan, Scotland, the sun in splendour or *Resurgo* 162 2
Maul, a hand holding an escutcheon charged with a crescent gu cf 219 7
Maule, Earl of Panmure, *see* Panmure
Maule, a phœnix in flames ppr *Vivit post funera virtus* 82 2
Maule, Scotland, a wyvern vert, with two heads vomiting fire at both ends ppr, charged with a crescent arg *Clementia tecta rigore* cf 69 9
Maule, Scotland a dragon vert with fire ppr issuing out of the mouth and tail *Inest clementia forti* cf 62 2
Maule, Scotland, same crest *Clementia et animus*
Maule of Vange Essex on a chapeau gu, turned up erm, a demi-peacock with wings displayed arg
Mauleverer, Yorks, a greyhound arg, collared or cf 60 2
Mauleverer, Yorks, a maple branch rising out of the trunk of a tree ppr *En Dieu ma foy*
Mauncell, Ireland, a lion rampant vert 1 13
Mauncell, a griffin's head erased per pale indented arg and gu beaked az, and charged on the neck with a rose counterchanged cf 66 2
Maund or **Maunde,** on a mount a deer trippant all ppr 118 2
Maundefield, a comet ppr 164 10
Maundrell, a lion's gamb couped and erect holding a fleur-de lis
Maundrell, an arm couped, embowed in fess, vested arg holding in the hand ppr a cross crosslet fitched sa 203 9
Maundrell, Rev Herbert in front of three palm-branches slipped one in pale and two in saltire, vert an escallop or *Potior potior*
Maundult, out of a ducal coronet or a griffin's head between two wings arg 67 1
Maunell, from the top of a tower issuing from the wreath an eagle with wings addorsed, holding in the beak an acorn slipped and leaved ppr 76 10
Maunsell of Ballywilliam, Rathkeale co Limerick and the Cottage, Burghclere Newbury Hants, a hawk rising ppr *Honorantes me honorabo* 88 2
Maunsell, Rev Cecil Henry M A, of Thorpe Malsor Hall, Kettering Northamp same crest and motto
Maunsell, General Sir Frederick Richard, K C B, of Laleham Middx, and 32 Ashley Gardens, S W, same crest and motto
Maunsell, Richard Mark Synnot Esquire, J P of Oakly Park Celbridge, co Kildare and Blackwater co Clare, same crest and motto
Maunsell, Ven Robert LL D, of Auckland, New Zealand Archdeacon Emeritus of Auckland a hawk rising ppr *Honorantes me honorabo* 88 2
Maunsell of Plassy and Bank Hall co Limerick Ireland a chapeau inflamed at the top ppr *Quod vult valde vult* — *Honorantes me honorabo* 180 10
Maurice, a hawk perching on the stump of a tree or armed and belled gu
Maurice of Brynygwahe, Denbighsh and Bodynfol, Montgomerysh (1) A unicorn's head erased sa winged arg, armed, maned and bearded or, holding in the mouth a shamrock ppr cf 49 13 (2) A lion passant sa 6 2
Maver, on a rock an eagle ppr, the wings close. cf 76 2
Maw, Lancs and Suff, on a mount vert a camel couchant arg the lump on the back and the end of the tail or 132 4
Maw, Lincs and Shropsh, same crest *Virtute non verbis*
Mawbey and **Mawbrey** of Kennington, Surrey, an eagle displayed az, charged on the breast with a bezant 75 1
Mawbey, Bart (*extinct*) of Botleyes Surrey same crest *Auriga virtutum prudentia*
Mawbrey, *see* Mawbey
Mawdesley of Mawdesley, Lancs formerly De Maudesley, an eagle displayed sa *Fidelis ad urnam* 75 2
Mawdesley, Frederick Leyland, of Fulford Cottage, Dorman's Park, Surrey, same crest *Mos legem regit*
Mawdesley of Leyland, Lancs an eagle displayed sa, charged on the breast with an annulet or cf 75 2
Mawdesley, James Platt Esquire 30 Falkner Square Liverpool an eagle displayed sa semee of annulets, and holding in the beak a hammer arg *Fidelis ad urnam* 75 10
Mawdley, Somers out of a ducal coronet or an eagle's head arg cf 83 14
Mawer, a lion's gamb issuing sa resting on an escutcheon erm cf 37 2
Mawgawley, Ireland a horse s head arg, in waggon harness sa 50 12
Mawgyron, a Catherine-wheel sa, embrued gu 167 2
Mawhood, a lion's head erased arg gorged with a collar gu, rimmed studded and ringed or, charged on the neck with a cross crosslet fitched, also gu cf 18 6
Mawle, Suff, on a chapeau gu turned up erm a demi-peacock displayed arg
Mawley, a cross crosslet fitched gu and a palm-branch ppr in saltier
Mawson of London a lion's head or, collared gobony erm and ermines cf 18 6
Maxey or **Maxie** of Bradwell Essex and Shotley, Suff, a talbot's head erased arg collared and ringed gu 56 1
Maxfield, Chesh on a ducal coronet a dolphin naiant 140 4
Maxton, Scotland a cross crosslet fitched az *Fides* 166 2
Maxtone of Coltoquhey Perthsh, a bee volant ppr *Providus esto* 137 1
Maxtone-Graham, Anthony G, Esquire of Coltoquhey, Perthsh, Scotland and Redgorton (1) A bee ppr (*for Maxtone*) 137 2 (2) A dove ppr (*for Graham*) *Providus esto* —*Candide ut secure* 92 2
Maxwell, *see* Herries, Baron
Maxwell, *see* Farnham, Baron
Maxwell, *see* Constable-Maxwell
Maxwell, *see* Constable-Maxwell Stuart
Maxwell, *see* Stirling Maxwell
Maxwell, *see* Heron Maxwell
Maxwell, *see* Wedderburn Maxwell
Maxwell of Cowhill, Dumfriessh, Scotland, a stag ppr, attired of ten tynes arg, lodged in front of a holly bush also ppr *Reviresco*
Maxwell of Carnsalloch, Dumfriessh, a stag rising from a holly-bush ppr *Viresco et surgo* 116 1
Maxwell, Scotland, a hart lodged, the attires wreathed with holly leaves ppr *Semper viridis* cf 115 7
Maxwell, Yorks and Scotland, a stag lodged ppr, attired or under a thicket of holly *Reviresco*
Maxwell of Glengaber, Dumfriessh, Scotland a stag lodged within two branches of laurel in orle all ppr *Curo dum quiesco* 115 11
Maxwell, Scotland, a stag lodged under a bush of holly all ppr *Non dormio* 116 3
Maxwell, Scotland, same crest *Nunquam dormio*
Maxwell, Scotland, a hart lodged, his attires wreathed with holly-leaves, all ppr cf 115 7
Maxwell of Birdstown co Donegal, Ireland, on a mount vert, a holly-bush and in front thereof a stag lodged all ppr *Reviresco*
Maxwell, Sir William Edward, K C M G, of Government House, Accra West Africa same crest and motto
Maxwell of Munches and Terraughty Dumfriessh, Scotland a stag lodged in front of a holly-bush ppr *Reviresco*
Maxwell of Broomholm Dumfriessh, Scotland, a hart courant ppr *Virtutem sic et culpam* —*Peto ac fugio* cf 118 13
Maxwell, Ireland, a buck's head erased ppr *Je suis prêt* 121 2
Maxwell, Scotland a stag's head cabossed ppr *Propero sed curo* 122 5
Maxwell, Theodore Esquire M D of Ballyrolly Downpatrick, co Down and 29 the Common, Woolwich a stag's head erased ppr, a mullet for difference *Je suis prêt*
Maxwell, Ireland a buck's head erased ppr 121 2
Maxwell, Bart Scotland, a deer's head erased ppr *I am ready* 121 2
Maxwell, a buck's head 121 5
Maxwell, Hall-, Commander Thomas Edward Dargavel, Bishopton, Paisley, a stag's head *I am ready*
Maxwell, Perceval-, of Groomsport, co Down a stag's head and neck erased ppr *Je suis prêt* 121 2
Maxwell of Brediland, Renfrewsh a buck's head couped ppr, attired gu *Spero meliora* 121 5

Maxwell, Graham-, of Werksworth, a buck's head couped ppr., attired or. *Spero meliora.* 121. 5
Maxwell, Scotland, a falcon looking at the sun, all ppr. *I'll bide broad Albine.* 76. 1
Maxwell, Scotland, a falcon looking toward the sun. 76. 1
Maxwell of Tealing, Forfarsh., a falcon looking to the sinister ppr. *I'll byde broad Albion.* 85. 6
Maxwell of Lackiebank, Scotland, a falcon looking to the sinister ppr. *Tendit ad astra.* 85. 6
Maxwell, Scotland, a falcon gazing at a star.
Maxwell, a demi-eagle with wings extended ppr. 80. 2
Maxwell, Scotland, an eagle issuing.
Maxwell, Admiral William Henry, R.N., of Holywych, Cowden, Kent, an eagle rising ppr. *Reviresco.*
Maxwell, Rt. Hon. Sir Herbert Eustace, Bart., D.L., of Monreith, Wigtownsh., an eagle rising sa., beaked and membered gu. *Reviresco.* 77. 5
Maxwell of Kirkconnell, Kirkcudbrightsh., a demi-eagle rising ppr. *Spero meliora.* 80. 2
Maxwell, Rt. Hon. Sir Herbert Eustace, Bart., of Monreith, Wigtownsh., Scotland, an eagle rising ppr. *Reviresco.* 77. 5
Maxwell, Scotland, an eagle's talon holding a pen ppr. *Non sine usu.*
Maxwell, Scotland, a man's head affrontée ppr. *Think on.* 190. 12
Maxwell, Scotland, a savage's head affrontée from the shoulders, within two branches of laurel in orle, all ppr. *Think on.* 192. 14
Maxwell, Scotland, a man's head looking up ppr. *Think on.* 190. 10
Maxwell, Sir William Francis, Bart., D.L., of Cardeness, Kirkcudbrightsh., a man's head, looking "foreright," within two laurel-branches in orle ppr. *Think on.* 192. 14
Maxwell, a griffin's head or. 66. 1
Maxwell-Heron, John Heron, J.P., D.L., of 47, Egerton Gardens, S.W., a demi-lion holding in the dexter paw a cross flory. *Ad ardua tendit.—Par valeur.*
May, Ireland, a Triton, holding in his sinister hand a trident. 185. 12
May, Scotland, on a rock a wild goose statant, all ppr.
May, a leopard's head and neck ppr. *Vigilo.* 22. 10
May of Stoke, Suff., out of a mural coronet arg., a leopard's head gu., billettée or. *cf.* 23. 7
May, Hants, and Oxney, Kent, out of a ducal coronet or, a leopard's head and neck ppr. 23. 11
May, Robert G., of Grena Lodge, Sheen Road, Richmond, Surrey, out of a ducal coronet or, a leopard's head gu.
May, Ireland, out of a ducal coronet or, a leopard's head and neck ppr. *Fortis et fidelis.* 23. 11
May of Hadlow Castle, Kent, out of a ducal coronet or, a leopard's head ppr. *Nil desperandum.* 23. 11
May of Faunt, Sussex, out of a ducal coronet or, a leopard's head gu. 23. 11
May of Belfast, Ireland, out of a ducal coronet or, a leopard's head and neck gu., charged with a billet of the first *cf.* 23. 11
May of Sutton Cheney, Leics., out of a ducal coronet or, a leopard's head gu., charged with a crescent for difference. *cf.* 23. 11
May of London, out of a ducal coronet or, a lion's head gu. 17. 5
May, Sussex and Somers., out of a ducal coronet per pale or and gu., a heraldic tiger's head of the first, pellettée maned sa. *cf.* 25. 3
May, Cornw., an eagle devouring a serpent.
May, an arm in mail embowed holding in the hand, all ppr., a truncheon or, tipped sa.
May, William, Esquire, of the Knowle, Brenchley, Kent, out of the battlements of a tower a hawthorn-tree in blossom with white May-flower, in front thereof two tilting-spears in saltire, all ppr *Memor et fidelis.* 144. 6
Mayats, a boar's head couped and erect. *cf.* 43. 3
Maybery, Henry Oxenford Aveline, of the Priory, Brecon, South Wales, on a chapeau gu., turned up erm., a man's head in profile couped at the shoulders ppr. *Estote prudentes.*
Mayce, a pestle in a mortar ppr. 177. 13
Mayce, a swan with wings addorsed arg., ducally gorged and lined sa. *cf.* 99. 3
Maycote of Reculver, Kent, out of a mural coronet gu., a buck's head or.
Maydwell of London and Northamp., out of a ducal coronet or, a pyramid of laurel-leaves vert. *cf.* 151. 14
Maydwell, Henry Lawrence, Esquire, out of a coronet vallery or, the rim charged with two cinquefoils gu., ten bay-leaves, four, three, two, and one vert.
Mayer, an eagle with wings addorsed ppr. *cf.* 76. 11
Mayer of Jersey, a demi-lion rampant regardant, holding in the dexter paw a sword, all ppr., hilt and pommel or.
Mayersbach or **Mayersback,** out of a ducal coronet two laurel-branches erect, between two elephants' trunks addorsed.
Mayfield, Cambs, a lion's head couped gu., holding in the mouth a May-flower or.
Mayhew, three roses gu., stalked, leaved, and barbed vert. 149. 14
Mayhew, Perceval Sumner, Esquire, of Duxbury Park, Chorley, Lancs, a unicorn's head erased. *Sola in Deo salus.*
Mayhew of Woodlands, Lancs, a unicorn's head erased gu., armed and crined or, charged on the neck with a chevron vair. 265. 1
Mayhew, Walter, of Duxbury Park, Chorley, Lancs, a unicorn's head erased gu., armed and maned or, charged on the neck with a chevron vair. *Sola in Deo salus.* 265. 1
Mayhew of Hemington, Suff., a unicorn's head erased gu., armed and crined or, charged on the neck with a chevron vair. 265. 1
Mayhewe of Clippesby, Norf., a unicorn's head erased arg., charged with a chevron vairée arg. and gu. 265. 1
Mayn, an oak-tree ppr. 143. 5
Maynard, Viscount Maynard (*extinct*), a stag statant or. *Manus justa nardus.* 117. 5
Maynard, Leics., Devonsh., and Middx., a stag trippant or, attired ppr. 117. 8
Maynard, Edmund Anthony Jefferson, of Egginton Hall, Burton-on-Trent, a stag trippant or, gorged with a collar invected arg., fimbriated sa. *Manus justa nardus.*
Maynard, Essex and Ireland, a stag or, charged on the breast with a crescent sa. *cf.* 117. 5
Maynard, a stag or, attired ppr. 117. 5
Maynard, Derbysh., a buck trippant or, gorged with a collar invected arg., fimbriated sa. *cf.* 117. 8
Maynard, Herts, a buck ppr. 117. 5
Maynard of Harsley Hall, Yorks: (1) A stag trippant or, gorged with a collar invected arg., fimbriated sa. (*for Maynard*). *cf.* 117. 8. (2) On a mount vert, a catherine-wheel or (*for Lax*). *Manus justa nardus.* *cf.* 167. 2
Maynard of Moseley, Leics., a stag or, attired ppr. 117. 5
Maynard, a stag trippant ppr., attired and ungu. or. *Manus justa nardus.* 117. 8
Maynard of Sherford, Devonsh., a stag trippant arg., attired gu. 117. 8
Maynard, Ireland, a dexter hand holding a palm-branch, both ppr. 219. 11
Maynard of Carriglas, co. Longford, a wolf's head erased, holding in the mouth a broken spear, all ppr. *Tam corde quam manu.*
Mayne, Ireland, a human heart gu., winged or. 112. 10
Mayne, Bucks and Wilts, out of a mural coronet or, a dragon's head erm. 72. 11
Mayne, Warw., and Rowston, Yorks, out of a ducal coronet or, a dragon's head erm. 72. 4
Mayne of London, and Littington, Devonsh., a cubit arm vested az., in the palm of the hand an eye, all ppr.
Mayne of Creslow, Bucks, a dexter hand ppr., between two wings erm. *cf.* 221. 1
Mayne, a cubit arm in pale ppr., vested sa., cuffed arg., holding in the hand a cross crosslet gu.
Mayne of Powis and Logie, co. Clackmannan, a dexter hand holding a plain cross gu. *Virtuti fortuna comes.*
Mayne, Otway, Esquire, of Walton Lodge, Aylesbury, a dexter hand issuing from a horse holding a plain cross gu. *Virtuti fortuna comes.*
Mayne of Farley Hill, Berks, a cubit arm erect in armour holding in the hand ppr. a cross flory arg.
Maynell, a demi-savage holding in his dexter hand a dagger and in his sinister a key, all ppr. *cf.* 186. 2
Mayner, a hand erect ppr., holding a lion's gamb erased arg. 220. 10
Mayneston of London, a hedgehog or. 135. 8
Mayney of Linton, Kent, an arm in armour quarterly arg. and sa., wielding a battle-axe of the second, the handle or.
Maynstone of Langaran, Glouc., and Heref., a reindeer trippant ppr. 125. 9

Mayo, Earl of (Bourke) Palmerston House, Straffan, co Kildare, a cat-a mountain sejant gardant ppr, collared and chained or *A cruce salus* 26 13

Mayo of Avebury, Wilts, and Cheshunt House, Herts, a dove holding an olive-branch in the beak, all ppr *Nuncia pacis oliva* 92 5

Mayo, C R, 16 Weymouth Street, Portland Place, W, same crest

Mayo, Dorset, out of a ducal coronet or, a sinister hand ppr, between two wings arg 221 3

Mayor, on a chapeau ppr, an escallop gu between two wings or 141 11

Mayor of Rugby, a greyhound's head couped gu, collared or *Mea anchora Christus* 61 2

Mayow of Lostwithiel, Cornw, a Cornish chough erm 107 14

Mayow, Wynell-, of Lowe and Bray, Manor House St Germans, Cornw, a falcon erm, devouring a snake ppr

Mays, out of a ducal coronet a dexter arm vambraced, brandishing a scimitar, all ppr 209 11

Maysey, a lion courant in a wood ppr *Pro libertate patriæ*

Maze, on a lion's head erased az, a chapeau or 21 10

Maze, Peter Esquire of Bristol, an eagle displayed erm charged on the breast and on each wing with a cinquefoil gu *Gorde ta bien aimee* cf 74 14

Maze, Blackburne-, of Shaw House Newbury, Berks (1) An eagle displayed ermines, charged on the breast and wings with a cinquefoil gu, plain collared az (*for Maze*) 237 15 (2) On a mount vert, a trumpet or, thereon a cock gu, beaked wattled, armed, and charged on the breast with a cinquefoil, also or (*for Blackburne*) 237 16

Maziere, De la, of Cork, a lion's head erased ppr 17 8

Mazzinghi of London, a demi lion ppr, holding a club arg

Meacham, a falcon with wings extended ppr, belled or 88 3

Mead, Henry John, Esquire, of 116, Jermyn Street, St. James's, S W, and 27, Ladbroke Gardens W a reindeer trippant vert *Toujours prêt* 125 9

Mead, on a ducal coronet an eagle displayed cf 75 2

Mead of Dublin, a pelican in her piety ppr 98 8

Meade, Earl of Clanwilliam, *see* Clanwilliam

Meade of Ballintobber and Ballymartle, co Cork, Ireland, an eagle displayed with two heads sa, armed or *Toujours prest* 74 2

Meade, John Percy, Esquire, D L of Earsham Hall Norwich, and Burren wood co Down, same crest and motto

Meade, Richard John, Esquire, B A, J P, of Ballymartle, Kinsale, co Cork, same crest and motto

Meade of Essex, an eagle displayed or 75 2

Meade-King, Rev Frederick M A of the Vicarage Stoke Courcy Somers (1) On a mount vert, an arm in bend dexter couped at the elbow, the hand supporting a tilting spear erect, the head broken, the arm surmounting a branch of oak in bend sinister, fructed, all ppr (*for King*) 301 6 (2) A demi-griffin az, wings erm, holding in the dexter claw a fleur de-lis or (*for Meade*) *Cadenti porrigo dextram* 301 12

Meade-King, William Oliver, of Walford, Taunton Somers, same crests and motto

Meade-King, the late Henry Warren, Esquire, of West Derby Liverpool, same crests and motto

Meade-King, Henry Herbert of Clifton, Bristol same crests and motto

Meade-King, Walter of Baring Crescent, Exeter, same crests and motto

Meade-Waldo, Edmund Gustavus Bloomfield, Esquire, of Stonewall Park Edenbridge Kent (1) A griffin's head sa, erased erm, gorged with an Eastern crown arg holding in its beak two trefoils slipped of the last (*for Waldo*) (2) A double-headed eagle displayed or, charged on the breast with a quatrefoil sa, resting its claws on two shields of the second, each charged with a trefoil slipped arg (*for Meade*) *Toujours prest —Mens conscia recti*

Meadows, out of a ducal coronet or a demi eagle with wings displayed sa

Meadows of Witnesham Hall, Great Bealings and Burgersh House, Suff a pelican vulning herself ppr *Mea dos virtus* 98 1

Meadows, out of a ducal coronet or a demi-eagle with wings expanded sa 80 14

Meager, a buffalo's head erased or 44 1

Meakin, Worcs, a unicorn's head erased 49 5

Meales, a stag at gaze sa 117 3

Meara, Ireland, a pelican displayed arg beaked membered, and vulning herself gu, and charged upon the breast with a lozenge vert *Virescit vulnere virtus* cf 98 1

Meare, a mermaid ppr, the hair crined or 184 5

Meares, Rev Robert, B A, of Stewartstown co Tyrone, on waves of the sea a mermaid ppr *Omnia providentiæ committo*

Meares, Richard, of New York same crest and motto

Meares of Meares Court Ireland a kingfisher ppr *Omnia providentiæ committo* cf 96 9

Meares, George, C M G of Grosvenor Malvern, Melbourne, and Willowbank, Gisborne, Victoria, same crest and motto

Meares, a bear's paw erased arg 36 4

Mearing, on a ducal coronet or, a griffin segreant gu cf 62 2

Mearns, a peacock in his pride ppr 103 12

Mearns, Rev. Duncan George of Disblair and South Kinmundy Aberdeensh, three Moors' heads conjoined in one neck erased, looking to the dexter, to the sinister, and upwards respectively *Pretio prudentia præstat*

Mears, a cock's head ppr cf 90 1

Measom, Sir George Samuel, of St Margaret's, near Twickenham, a falcon belled *Vive ut vivas*

Measou, Laing-, of Lindertis, Scotland, a castle ppr *Firm.* 155 8

Meath, Earl of (Brabazon), Killruddery House, near Bray Wicklow on a mount vert a falcon rising or, belled or *Vota vita mea*

Meautys, Essex, a unicorn sejant ermines

Meaux, *see* Meux

Mecham of Garrycastle, co Westmeath a dexter cubit arm erect grasping a dagger transfixed through a human heart, distilling drops of blood, all ppr *Animo fortitudo*

Meddop, a box ppr

Meddowes or **Meddus,** a cross formee or, entwined with a snake ppr 165 9

Medewe, De, of Witnesham Hall, a pelican vulning herself ppr *Mea dos virtus* 98 1

Medford, a deer lodged arg 115 7

Medgley or **Midgley,** on a mount an heraldic tiger sejant, resting its paw on a caltrap

Medhop of Ireland a demi-lion rampant az, holding between the paws a coronet or

Medhurst of Kippax Hall, Yorks, a martlet charged with a fleur de lis holding in the beak an acorn and an oak-leaf, all ppr *Adversa virtute repello*

Medland of Launceston, Cornw, a sea-gull rising ppr, charged on the breast with a crescent

Medley of Buxted, Sussex, an heraldic tiger sejant vert, tufted and maned or *In Deo fides*

Medlicott, James Edward, of Dunmurry Kildare out of a mural coronet gu a demi-eagle with wings expanded or *Dat cura quietem* 80 14

Medlycott of Rocketts, Waterford, out of a mural coronet gu, a demi-eagle with wings elevated or *Dat cura quietem*

Medlycott, Sir Mervyn Bradford, Bart, M A of Ven House, Somers, same crest and motto

Mee, a ram's head erased arg, armed or 130 6

Mee of East Retford, Notts, a stag's head erased between two sprigs of oak ppr

Mee, Rev J H, M A, D Mus the Chantry, Westbourne, Sussex, and Holywell House, Oxford, a stag at gaze ppr, charged on the body with two escallops sa resting the dexter foot on a shield or charged with a cross patonce, also sa Χαριτι θεου ειμι ο ειμι

Meech, a greyhound courant arg cf 58 2

Meek, a demi wolf ducally gorged and lined holding between its paws a mullet of six points 31 6

Meek, a demi lion rampant, holding over his head a scimitar *Pro recto*

Meeke, Essex, a lion rampant arg 1 13

Meeking, Charles, Esquire J P of 31 Belgrave Square, London on a mount vert charged with three bezants, a dove between two laurel-branches or *Sola veritas invicta*

Meekins, on an antique earl's coronet a wolf's head erased arg

Meer of Sherborn, Dorset, an eagle's head couped or, the beak embrued gu. 83. 1

Meer, Dorset and Durh., a demi-dogfish.

Meerehurst of Marplestone, Surrey, a rose arg., barbed vert, between two dragon's wings gu.

Meers of Houghton, Lincs, a peacock's tail erect ppr. *cf.* 115. 6

Meers, a lion's gamb erased, holding a rose-branch, all ppr. 37. 10

Meested, on a broken tower arg., a bird or.

Meetekerke, Herts, a unicorn's head erased arg., crined, tufted, and armed or. 49. 5

Megget, Scotland, a square padlock, therein the key, all or. *Lock sicker.*

Meggison, on a mountain a dove, all ppr. 92. 13

Meggs of Whitechapel, London, a griffin sejant per bend gu. and or, beaked, legged, and ducally gorged of the last, the wings addorsed. *cf.* 62. 10

Meggs, Cambs and Kent, a greyhound's head sa., eared arg., collared gemelle or, between three bezants, one and two, the head crowned with three oak-branches ppr.

Meggs, Dorset, a talbot's head erased arg., eared sa., collared or, below the collar two pellets in fess, and three acorns erect issuing from the top of the head ppr.

Meigh, William Mellor, Esquire, of Ash Hall, Staffs, a lion rampant or, holding in the dexter paw a cross patée fitched az., the sinister resting on an anchor ppr., pendent therefrom by a chain or an escutcheon gu., charged with a boar's head erased arg. *Benigno numine.*

Meighan, Ireland, a griffin's head erased with wings endorsed or.

Meignell, a rose-bush ppr. 149. 8

Meik of Leidcassie, Scotland, an increscent and a decrescent respecting and joining the one to the other, all ppr. *Jungor ut implear.* *cf.* 163. 7

Meikle, Scotland, a deer's head or. 121. 5

Meiklejohn, Major John Forbes, R.A., a dexter arm in armour from the shoulder embowed and resting on the elbow, the hand holding a scimitar, all ppr. *Spes magna in Deo.*

Mein, a hand holding a vine-branch ppr. 219. 6

Mein, Scotland, a dexter hand erect charged with an eye ppr. *Deus providebit.* 222. 4

Mein, George Augustus, Esquire, M.D., J.P., of Falkenstein, St. Kilda, Melbourne, Victoria, and Moolpa, New South Wales, Australia, out of a mural coronet or, a dexter hand issuant charged with a human eye ppr., in front of three swords, one in pale and two in saltire, points upwards, also ppr., pommels and hilts or, the upper parts of the blades encircled by a wreath of laurel vert. *Manus hæc inimica tyrannis.* 222. 13

Melborne, on a ducal coronet or, a wyvern, sans legs vert. 70. 9

Melbourne, Viscount (Lamb), (*extinct*), a demi-lion rampant gu., holding between the paws a mullet sa. *Virtute et fide.* *cf.* 15. 8

Melders, Scotland, a lion's head and neck erased and erect ppr. 17. 8

Meldert, a dexter gauntlet apaumée az. 209. 8

Meldon, James Charles William, of 58, Upper Leeson Street, Dublin, and of Newtown House, Blackrock, co. Dublin, a dexter hand apaumée ppr., surmounted by a crescent or, therefrom issuant an étoile arg. *Pro fide et patria.* 222. 8

Meldon, Austin, Esquire, D.L., of 15, Merrion Square, Dublin, same crest and motto.

Meldrum of Crombie, Banffsh., Scotland, a dexter hand holding a book ppr. *Mens immota manet.* 215. 4

Meldrum, Baron, *see* Huntly, Marquess of.

Meles, on the stump of a tree a martlet ppr.

Melfort, Viscount and **Earl of,** and **Duc de,** *see* Drummond.

Melgund, Viscount, *see* Minto, Earl of.

Melhuish of Taunton, Somers., a cubit arm holding in the hand a pheon in pale.

Melhuish, a pelican in her piety, all ppr. 98. 8

Mell, on a chapeau az., turned up or, a martlet with wings addorsed sa.

Meller and **Mellers** of Laiston, Suff., a greyhound passant sa., collared or, resting the dexter paw on an escutcheon az.

Meller, Ireland, a demi-lion az., holding between the paws a mascle or.

Meller, Alfred, Esquire, of 68, Redcliffe Gardens, S.W., an escutcheon sa., thereon a cross couped arg., between two wings arg., each charged with a fesse engrailed, also sa.

Melles, a portcullis sa., the chains or. 178. 3

Melles, Joseph William, Esquire, of Sewardstone, Essex, and Gruline, Aros, Mull, a fir-tree erect and eradicated ppr. *Usque fidelis.* 144. 8

Melliar, Foster-, William Melliar, of North Aston Hall, Oxon., in front of a lion's gamb erect and couped or, holding a branch of myrtle ppr., two mascles interlaced fesseways az. *Cupio meliora.* 37. 7

Mellis, Scotland, the sun in his splendour or. 162. 2

Mellish, out of a ducal coronet a demi-ostrich with wings addorsed, all ppr. 96. 11

Mellish of London, Ragnold, Notts, and Sandersted, Surrey, out of a ducal coronet or, a swan's head and neck arg.

Mellish, formerly of Blyth, Notts, a swans head and neck erased arg., ducally gorged or. 101. 5

Mellish, Henry, J.P., Hodsock Priory, Worksop, same crest.

Melliship, an ibex. *Sedulus et audax.*

Mello, a mullet arg. 164. 2

Mello, Rev. John Magens, M.A., Cliff Hill, Warwick, two water-melons in saltire stalked and leaved.

Mellor, Rt. Hon. J. W., P.C., K.C., of Culmhead, near Taunton, and of 68, St. George's Square, London, S.W., in front of a bull's head erased arg., between the horns a mascle sa., three mascles fesseways of the last. 261. 2

Mellor, William Moseley, Esquire, J.P., of Lingdale, Claughton, Chester, same crest.

Mellor, James Robert, Esquire, LL.M., of 16, Craven Hill Gardens, London, W., same crest.

Mellor, Alfred, Esquire, J.P., of 68, Redcliffe Gardens, S.W., same crest.

Melton, a serpent nowed az. 142. 4

Melton, a lion's head erased az., guttée-d'or, ducally gorged, also or. *cf.* 18. 5

Melveton, a talbot's head and neck erased. 56. 2

Melveton, a lion's gamb gu., holding a key az. *cf.* 35. 1

Melvile of Balgarvie, a talbot's head and neck erased and collared. 56. 1

Melvile, a talbot's head or. *Denique cœlum.* 56. 12

Melvile, Melvill, and **Melville,** of Murdocairnie, Fifesh., Scotland, a crescent ppr. *Denique cœlum.* 163. 2

Melvill of Carnbee, Fifesh., Scotland, an eagle rising ppr. *Ultra aspicio.* 77. 5

Melvill of Cassingray, Fifesh., Scotland, a ratch-head erased ppr., collared gu., charged with a crescent arg. *Denique cœlo fruar.*

Melvill of Auchmoor, Fifesh., Scotland, a sleuth-hound's head couped ppr. *Denique cœlum.* 56. 12

Melvill or **Melville,** Scotland, two eagle's wings conjoined ppr. *Denique sursum.* 113. 1

Melville, Earl of, *see* Leven, Earl of.

Melville, Viscount (Dundas), of Melville Castle, Lasswade, Edinburgh, a lion's head affrontée or, struggling through an oak-bush, all ppr., and over the crest the motto, *Essayez.* *Quod potui perfeci.* 21. 7

Melville, a talbot's head or. 56. 12

Melville, Whyte-, of Bennochy and Strathkinness, Fifesh., Scotland: (1) An arm embowed holding a laurel-wreath, all ppr. *Virtute parta.* 202. 4. (2) A crescent. *Denique cœlum.* 163. 2

Melville, Balfour-, James Heriot, of Strathkinness, Fifesh., Scotland: (1) A dexter hand holding an olive-branch ppr. *Adsit deus.* (2) A crescent arg. *Denique cœlum.* 163. 2

Melville, George Fisher, of Springfield, North Berwick, and Edinburgh, an eagle rising ppr. *Ad altiora tendo.* 77. 5

Memes of London and Kent, an heraldic antelope's head gu., tufted and armed or, issuing from rays of the last. *cf.* 127. 10

Mendes and **Mends,** Wales, out of the top of a tower an arm in armour embowed wielding a battle-axe.

Mendip, a demi-lion ppr. 10. 2

Mendorf, an oak-tree fructed ppr. 143. 5

Menell or **Meynell,** a demi-savage holding in his dexter hand a dagger, and in his sinister a key, all ppr. *cf.* 186. 2

Menell, a unicorn's head couped, gorged with a chaplet of laurel. *cf.* 49. 7

Menell, a Moor's head in profile couped at the shoulders ppr., wreathed or and az. 192. 13

Menet or **Menett,** a demi-lion rampant az. 10. 2

Menil, a boar passant between two trees, all ppr.

Menles, a portcullis sa., the chains or. 168. 3

Menteath, a hand holding a dagger erect, both ppr *Dum vivo spero* 212 9

Menteath of Auldcathie, Linlithgowsh, Scotland, an eagle rising ppr gazing at the sun in his splendour *Sub sole nihil*

Menteth, Stewart-, Sir James, Bart, of Closeburn Dumfriessh, a lymphad ppr, the flag gu with a canton arg charged with a saltire az *Dum vivo spero —Sub sole nihil*

Menys, a lion's gamb erased sa., charged with a chevron or cf 39 2

Menzies, Sir Robert, Bart, D L, of that Ilk Perthsh, a savage's head in profile erased, wreathed round the head ppr *Vil God I zal*

Menzies, a savage's head affrontee couped at the shoulders sa cf 190 5

Menzies of Aberdeen Scotland, a cherub with wings expanded ppr *Scopus vitæ Christus* 189 9

Menzies of Shian, Perthsh, Scotland, a book expanded ppr *Spero* 158 3

Menzies, A J P, of 6, Great King Street Edinburgh same crest and motto

Menzies of Edinburgh, a crescent ppr *Ut crescit clarescit* 163 2

Menzies of Pitfoddel, Aberdeensh, Scotland a demi-eagle with wings expanded ppr *Malo mori quam fœdari* 80 2

Menzies of Culdares Perthsh, Scotland, a demi-lion holding in its dexter paw a baton ppr *Fortem fors juvat* 15 9

Menzies, William George Steuart Esquire of Arndilly Craig Ellachie, North Britain, a demi lion holding in the dexter paw a marshal's baton ppr *Fortem fors juvat*

Menzies, Stewart-, William James Breadalbane, Esquire, of Chesthill House Aberfeldy N B, a rose slipped and leaved

Meoles, Chesh, a lion's head erased sa, winged or 19 7

Merbury, Chesh, a camel's head sa ducally gorged or cf 132 9

Merbury of Walton, Chesh, a mermaid ppr, holding in her dexter hand a mirror, and in her sinister a comb or 184 5

Mercaunt of Seamur, Suff, two lion's gambs erased in saltier or each holding a battle-axe arg, the handles gu cf 39 14

Mercer, *see* Drewe-Mercer

Mercer, *see* Haldane Duncan - Mercer Henderson

Mercer, *see* Tod Mercer

Mercer of London a stork's head erased ppr, holding in the beak a snake vert cf 106 3

Mercer of Huntingtower, Perthsh Scotland, the head and neck of a stork holding in the beak a serpent writhing ppr *Ye great pule —Crux Christi nostra corona* 106 3

Mercer, William Lindsay, Esquire, of Huntingtower House, Perth same crest *Crux Christi nostra corona*

Mercer of Fordel, Fifesh the head and neck of a heron erased holding in its beak an eel seizing the neck of the former, all ppr *The grit pool* 104 2

Mercer of Salineshaw, Scotland a cross patee fitched gu *Crux Christi mea corona* 166 3

Mercer of Aldie, Kinross-sh, Scotland a cross or *Crux Christi nostra corona*

Mercer of Salineshaw, Fifesh, Scotland, a cross fitchee gu *Crux Christi mea corona*

Mercer of Easter Newton, Scotland a dexter hand holding an open Bible ppr. *Jehova portio mea* 215 10

Mercer, Scotland, a naked arm embowed holding a curtal-axe ppr 201 5

Merchand and **Merchant,** Bucks on a mount vert a moorcock ppr cf 89 8

Mercier, Northumb, a demi huntsman winding a horn ppr, vested az *Blow shrill —Toujours fidele* 187 12

Mercy, a dexter hand holding an olive-branch ppr 219 9

Mere of Mere, Chesh, a mermaid ppr, crined or, the tail vert holding in her dexter hand a comb and in her sinister a mirror, also ppr, the frame and handle of the latter of the second cf 184 5

Meredith, co Kerry out of a ducal coronet or, a griffin's head 67 9

Meredith of Dick's Grove, Kerry, same crest *Sapere aude* 67 9

Meredith, on an Eastern coronet or a dragon passant, with the wings expanded gu langued az

Meredith, Sir James Creed LL D, of Cloneevin 83, Pembroke Road Dublin, a goat's head erased or

Meredith, Sir William Ralph, of Toronto, Canada same crest

Meredith, Hon Richard Edmund, of 31, Fitzwilliam Square, Dublin, same crest

Meredith, Warter-, Henry of Pentrebychan Denbighsh, and Oaklawn, Hamlet Road Upper Norwood, S E, a lion's head erased or *Heb Dduw heb ddima Duw a digon* 17 8

Meredith, a lion's head erased ppr 17 8

Meredith of Radnor Wales and Henbury, Chesh, a demi lion sa, collared, and the chain reflexed over the back or 10 12

Meredith, George Campbell a demi-lion rampant sa collared and chained reflexed over the back or *Spes est in Deo*

Meredith of Crediton Devonsh a demi-lion rampant sa., ducally gorged and chained or cf 10 12

Meredith of Upper Weld, Bucks, a demi-lion rampant per pale or and arg, collared and lined sa

Meredith, Edwin, Esquire, of Llandaff, Masterton, New Zealand a demi lion rampant sa, collared and chained and the chain reflexed over the back or *Spes est in Deo* 10 12

Meredith, Edward Phillipps Esquire, of Glenelg, Australia a lion rampant sa, gorged with a mural coronet, and pendent therefrom a chain reflexed over the back or, holding in the dexter fore-paw a pear leaved and slipped ppr, and the dexter hind-paw resting on an escutcheon arg, charged with a mullet of six points gu

Meredyth, Baron, *see* Athlumney, Baron

Meredyth, Sir Edward Henry John, Bart, of Greenhills, co. Kildare, on an Eastern coronet or, a dragon passant gu *Heb Dduw heb ddim*

Meredyth, Sir Henry Bayly, Bart, of Carlandstown, co Meath on an Eastern coronet or a dragon passant gu *Fiat Dei voluntas*

Meredyth, Bucks, a demi lion rampant per pale or and arg, collared and lined sa.

Meredyth, Ireland, a goat's head erased arg 128 5

Meredyth, a yew-tree ppr 143 1

Merefield of London a garb or, banded sa 153 2

Meres, Lincs, a dexter hand holding a sword in bend ppr *Sine metu* 212 13

Meres, a mermaid ppr, crined or 184 5

Mereweather, an arm in armour embowed ppr, garnished or, holding in the hand also ppr, a sword arg, hilt and pommel or, entwined with a serpent vert. *Vi et consilio* cf 195 2

Merick of West Camel Somers, a water-spaniel passant arg 57 7

Merick of London and Wales a sea-horse ppr maned or, holding in its feet a mullet pierced az

Mering of Mering, Notts a horse's head erased sa, bezantee, in the nostrils an annulet or

Merition, a demi savage holding over his shoulder a club ppr 186 5

Merks, Essex an otter's head and neck erased sa 134 3

Merlay, a hind's head or gorged with a collar sa charged with three bezants cf 124 5

Merle, a lion's tail erased 123 14

Merling, a lion's head erased gu 17 2

Merlyon, an eagle's head or between two wings expanded vair 84 2

Mermyon, a unicorn's head erased sa 49 5

Merrey, *see* Merry

Merrey, a thistle and a rose stalked and leaved in saltier, all ppr 150 3

Merrey or **Merry** of Renburne and Barton, Derbysh, out of a ducal coronet ppr, a demi-lion gu, ducally crowned or cf 16 3

Merrick of Norcote Middx, and London a sea lion couchant or between the paws a mullet az

Merrifield, the sun rising ppr

Merrilees, Scotland, in the sea an open boat all ppr

Merrill, a peacock's head erased ppr 103 1

Merriman, a boar passant, collared and bristled vert cf 40 9

Merriman of London an arm in armour embowed ppr, garnished or, wielding a sword arg, hilt and pommel also or 195 2

Merriman of Rodbourne Cheney, Wilts, a serpent nowed therefrom issuant a dexter arm embowed in armour ppr, garnished or the hand grasping a short sword also ppr, pommel and hilt of the second *Terar dum prosim*

Merrington, a lion's head collared cf 18 6

Merriott, Rev J H, Dorney Cottage, Winchester, a greyhound's head erased collared, lined, and charged with an annulet *Meliora spero*

Merritt, out of a ducal coronet a demi salmon ppr 139 14

Merry of Belladrum, Inverness Scotland a demi lion rampant gu, crowned with an antique crown or *Persto et spero* cf 10 3

Merry, a demi lion holding in both paws an anchor, flukes upwards

Merry of London, a demi-lion holding in the paws an anchor. *Vive en espoir.*

Merry of Herringfleet Hall, Norf., the mast of a ship rompu and erect, thereto a yard with the sail furled in bend sinister, above it a round top, three arrows issuing therefrom on each side in saltier, points upward, all ppr.

Merry of Highlands, Berks, out of a mural coronet arg., a demi-lion rampant gu., ducally crowned or, charged on the shoulder with a cross patée of the first, and holding between the paws a water-bouget or. *Persto et spero.*

Merry of Waterford, Ireland, and Seville, Spain, an arm in armour embowed, the hand brandishing a scimitar, all ppr. *Suprema manus validior.* 196. 0

Merryton, a pair of wings arg. 109 6

Merryweather, Meryweather, or **Merriweather,** a hand gauntleted holding a sword entwined with a serpent. *Another,* an arm in armour embowed, holding in the hand a sword entwined with a serpent. *cf.* 195. 2

Mersar, a cross patée or. *Crux Christi nostra corona.* 165. 7

Merser, Lincs, out of a mural coronet gu., a demi-lion or, holding in its paws a battle-axe arg., the handle of the second. 16. 10

Mertens of London, a demi-stork with wings expanded sa., holding in its beak a key.

Merton, a demi-Moor wielding a scimitar ppr.

Mervin, an escutcheon quarterly or and gu. 176. 10

Mervyn-D'Arcy-Irvine of Castle Irvine, co. Fermanagh, Ireland: (1) A gauntlet issuing out of a cloud and lying in fess, holding a thistle erect, all ppr. (*for Irvine*). (2) On a chapeau gu., turned up erm., a bull passant sa., armed or (*for D'Arcy*). 45. 9. (3) A squirrel sejant ppr., cracking a nut gu. (*for Mervyn*). *Un Dieu un Roy.—De Dieu est tout.—Dum memor ipse mei.* 135. 7

Mervyn of Fonthill Giffard, Wilts, a squirrel sejant ppr., cracking a nut or, gorged with a collar of the last, charged with three torteaux. *De Dieu tout.* *cf.* 135. 7

Merydale of Great Brickhill, Salbury, Bucks, an eagle's head arg., erased per fess gu. 83. 2

Meryet, a porcupine's head sa. *cf.* 136. 2

Meryng, Notts, a nag's head erased sa., bezantée, holding in the mouth an annulet or.

Meryon, a bee displayed ppr. 137. 2

Meryweather, Kent, a hand gauntleted ppr., holding a sword arg., hilted or, a snake ppr. entwining the sword and gauntlet.

Meschines, a rose arg., charged with a thistle ppr. 149. 3

Meschines, De, a hand holding a scimitar. 213. 5

Mescow, a buck's head erased sa., attired or. 121. 2

Mesham, Arthur, Esquire, of Pontryffydd, Bodfari, Flintsh., a lion passant gardant ppr., charged on the body with an etoile of eight points, and supporting with the dexter fore-paw a stag's attires or. *Duty.* 4. 12

Messenger, a pegasus current arg., ducally gorged and chained or. *cf.* 47. 1

Messent, out of a ducal coronet gu., a demi-eagle sa., winged or. *Semper sursum.* 80. 4

Messent of London, a lion's gamb erased holding a rose-branch slipped, all ppr. *Pax et libertas.* 37. 10

Messer and **Messing,** an eagle displayed gu. 75. 2

Messewy, Jersey, a cherry-tree ppr. *Au valereux cœur rien impossible.*

Messye, Worcs., a dragon's head quarterly or and az. 71. 1

Mesurier, Le, an ostrich's head between two feathers, all ppr. 97. 14

Metcalf or **Metcalfe,** a talbot sejant arg., spotted liver colour, resting the dexter paw on an escutcheon or. *cf.* 55. 3

Metcalfe of Inglethorpe Hall, Norf., a hound erm., resting the dexter paw on an escutcheon gu. 53. 3

Metcalfe, Sir Charles Herbert Theophilus, Bart, M.A., of Fern Hill, Berks, a talbot sejant sa., the dexter paw supporting an escutcheon or, charged with a hand issuant from clouds on the sinister, and holding a pen, all ppr. *Conquiesco.* 286. 10

Metcalfe, of London, a demi-sea-calf.

Metcalfe, Walter Charles, Esquire, of 10, Lupus Street, London, S.W., a satyr ppr., cinctured vert, bearing over the dexter shoulder a spiked club, or. 189. 3

Metford, a lion rampant gu., supporting with the dexter fore-paw a garb ppr.

Metge, a dolphin naiant. 140. 5

Metham, a bull's head barry of ten arg. and az., armed sa. *cf.* 44. 3

Metham, a bull's head barry of six arg. and az.

Methen, Scotland, a cross patée or, within a crescent arg. *Marte et clypeo.* 163. 6

Methewen, a wolf's head erased ppr., collared vair.

Methold, Frederick John, J.P., Thorn Court, Bury St. Edmunds, a goat's head erased arg., armed and crined sa., charged with an escallop.

Methoulde or **Methwold,** Norf., a goat's head erased arg., armed and crined sa. 128. 5

Methoulde or **Methwold,** Norf., a goat's head erased or. 128. 5

Methuen, Baron (Methuen), Corsham Court, Corsham, Wilts, a wolf's head couped ppr. *Virtus invidiæ scopus.* 30. 5

Methuen, Scotland, a wolf's head erased ppr. *Fortis in arduis.* 30. 8

Methven of Craigtown, Fifesh., Scotland, a cross patée or, within a crescent arg. *Marte et clypeo.* 163. 6

Methwold, a goat's head erased arg., armed and crined sa. 128. 5

Metivier of Guernsey, over the coronet of a Count of France a demi-lion regardant arg. *Virtute.*

Metley, a mermaid ppr. 184. 5

Meurs, a demi-savage with a club over his dexter shoulder and a serpent entwined round his sinister arm wreathed round the middle with leaves, all ppr. 185. 3

Meux, Bart., of Theobald's Park, Herts (*extinct*), two wings inverted and endorsed arg., conjoined by a cord with tassels or. 113. 2

Meverell of Throwley, Staffs, a demi-griffin segreant sa, beaked and legged gu. 64. 2

Meverell of Tidswell, Derbysh., a gauntlet grasping a dagger, all ppr. 211. 4

Mewbery, a cornucopia ppr. 152. 13

Mewess or **Mewsse,** of Woburn, Beds, a demi-eagle displayed or, ducally gorged gu., beaked az. *cf.* 81. 6

Mewburn, William Richmond, 19, Holland Park, Kensington, W., a demi-wyvern with wings addorsed sa. *Festina lente.*

Mewis, a dexter hand couped in fess, charged with an eye ppr. 221. 4

Mexborough, Earl of (Savile), Methley Park, Leeds, Yorks, an owl arg. *Be fast.* 96. 5

Mey of Houldham Abbey, Norf., a demi-savage wreathed round the loins with leaves, and holding over his dexter shoulder a club ppr., and round his sinister arm a serpent entwined vert. 185. 3

Meyer, a lion rampant double-queued. 1. 14

Meyers, a mermaid holding in her dexter hand a comb, and in her sinister a mirror. 184. 5

Meyler, a lion rampant. 1. 13

Meyler, Captain George, on a wreath of the colours a demi-lion rampant gu., holding in the dexter paw an annulet or. *cf.* 10. 3

Meyler, co. Wexford, Ireland, a demi-lion rampant gu., holding in the dexter fore-paw an annulet or. *Amor patriæ vincit.* *cf.* 10. 3

Meymott, three mullets in fess gu., in front of a dexter arm in armour embowed ppr., holding in the hand a wreath of laurel or. *Be just and fear not.* *cf.* 199. 12

Meymott, Sydney, of Bank House, Broadway, Ealing, W., same crest.

Meynell of Kilvington, Yorks, a negro's head couped at the shoulders ppr., wreathed or and az. *Deus non reliquit memoriam humilium.* 192. 13

Meynell, Edgar, Old Elvet, Durh., a negro's head ppr., encircled with a wreath az. and arg. *Deus non reliquit memoriam humilium.*

Meynell of Meynell Langley, Derbysh., a horse's head erased arg. *Virtute vici.* 51. 4

Meynell, Godfrey Francis, of Meynell Langley, Derby, same crest and motto.

Meynell, Derbysh. and Staffs, a horse's head arg. *cf.* 50. 13

Meynell-Ingram, Hugo Charles, Esquire, of Temple Newsom and Hatfield, Yorks: (1) A cock or (*for Ingram*). 91. 2. (2) A horse's head erased arg. (*for Meynell*). *Virtute vici.* 51. 4

Meyrick, Heref., a tower per pale arg. and erminois. *Stemmata quid faciunt.* 156. 2

Meyrick, Sir Thomas Charlton Bart., J.P., D.L., of Apley Castle, Shropsh., and Bush, Pembrokesh.: (1) A tower arg., thereon upon a mount vert a Cornish chough ppr., holding in the dexter claw a fleur-de-lis gu (*for Meyrick*) 106 14 (2) Out of an Eastern coronet or, a leopard's head and neck issuant affrontee gu (*for Charlton*) 246 4

Meyrick, Williams- of the Hermitage Beaumaris, Anglesey (1) A tower arg, thereon upon a mount vert a Cornish chough ppr holding in the dexter claw a fleur-de lis gu, the tower charged for distinction with a cross crosslet sa (*for Meyrick*) cf 106 14 (2) A lion passant sa, semee of quatrefoils and gorged with a collar gemelle arg holding in the dexter fore-paw a fleur-de lis gu (*for Williams*) *Heb Dduw heb ddim a Duw a digon*

Meyrick, Tapps-Gervis-, Sir George Augustus Eliott, of Hinton Arundell, Hants (1) In the centre a tower arg, thereon upon a mount vert a Cornish chough ppr, holding in the dexter claw a fleur-de-lis gu (*for Meyrick*) 309 1 (2) Upon the dexter side upon a mount vert three ostrich feathers one in pale gu and two in saltire sa enfiled with a wreath of laurel or (*for Gervis*) 309 3 (3) Upon the sinister side a greyhound couchant per pale arg and sa charged on the body with two escallop-shells counterchanged (*for Tapps*) *Heb Dduw heb ddim a Duw a digon —Be just and fear not* 309 2

Meysey-Thompson, Bart *see* Thompson

Meysey of Shakenhurst Worcs, a dragon's head quarterly or and az 71 1

Miall, a crane holding in its beak a branch ppr 105 14

Michael, a garb erect banded or 153 2

Michael, Michall, or **Michell,** Berks a leopard's face per pale or and az 22 10

Michael of London, in front of a saltire couped az a leopard's face or

Michel of Kingston Russell and Dewlish, Dorset a dexter hand holding a crane's head erased all ppr *Nil conscire sibi* cf 220 9

Michel, a hand holding a heron's head erased

Michelbourne of Bradhurst and Stanmore Sussex, a tiger or, its mouth embrued ppr

Michelgrove, Sussex, a unicorn's head erased arg 49 5

Michell, Cornw, a pegasus courant 47 1

Michell, John Esquire of St Petersburg a pegasus salient az mane and tail or, resting its fore feet on an antique escutcheon sa, charged with a pheon or *Vouloir c'est pouvoir*

Michell, Robert of Lostwithiel, Cornw, same crest and motto

Michell of Calne Wilts a cubit arm erect ppr holding in the hand a sword arg hilt and pommel or, seven flames issuing from the blade ppr three from each side and one from the point *Crescat amicitia*

Michell of Hamworth and Hawston, Norf an arm in mail embowed holding in the hand all ppr a cutlass arg on the edge of the blade three spikes, hilt and pommel or

Michell of Truro Cornw, an arm in armour embowed holding in the hand a sword dropping blood

Michell, Captain Charles, Forcett Park, Darlington Yorks, on a mount vert a swan ppr *Utile quod honestum*

Michelson of Chester, a fleur de-lis ppr 148 2

Michelston, Micheston, and **Michelstane,** of Michelstowe, Cornw, a banner displayed arg charged with a cross gu, between four torteaux

Michie, Scotland a dexter hand couped in fess holding a dagger in pale ppr hilt and pommel or *Pro patria et libertate*

Micklethwait, *see* Peckham-Micklethwait

Micklethwait, Viscount Micklethwait (*extinct*), a griffin's head erased ppr *Favente numine* 66 2

Micklethwait, Richard Key, Ardsley House, near Barnsley, Yorks same crest *Favente numine*

Micklethwaite, Yorks a griffin's head erased ppr *In cœlo spes mea est* 66 2

Micklethwaite, of Beeston and Taverham Norwich, Norf, and Iridge Place Sussex a griffin's head arg, erased gu, gorged with a collar componee of the second and first cf 66 2

Micklethwaite of London, on a chapeau a talbot sejant 54 14

Mico of London issuing out of clouds a hand holding a sword in pale ppr hilt and pommel or charged on the blade with a Moor's head also ppr the point of the sword embrued gu cf 212 10

Middlecote, Lincs, a demi-eagle displayed erm ducally gorged or, holding in the beak an escallop of the last

Middlehurst of Middlehurst in Appleton Chesh a wolf's head erased arg 30 8

Middlemore or **Midlemore** of Edgbaston Warw, in grass and reeds a moor-cock, all ppr

Middlemore, John Throgmorton Esquire, M P, of Brookfield, Belbroughton near Stourbridge, a moor cock amidst grass and weeds ppr *Mon desire loyalte*

Middlemore, Thomas, Esquire, of Melsetter, Longhope Orkney, same crest and motto

Middleton, Earl of Middleton, Scotland issuing from a tower sa, a lion rampant gu *Fortis in arduis* 157 12

Middleton, Frederick Dobson, C B K C M G St Thomas's Tower, Tower of London same crest and motto

Middleton, Baron (Willoughby) Wollaton Hall Notts the bust of a man couped at the shoulders and affrontee ppr ducally crowned or *Verite sans peur* 192 1

Middleton, a Saracen's head couped at the shoulders and affrontee wreathed round the temples 190 5

Middleton, Sir Arthur Edward Bart, of Belsay Castle Northumb a wild man arg, holding an oak tree fructed ppr cf 188 10

Middleton of Westerham Kent a savage man wreathed about the head with leaves all ppr, holding in the dexter hand a scroll extended, thereon the motto *Servire Deo regnare est* and resting the sinister hand on a club inverted or

Middleton, Northumb a savage holding in his dexter hand an oak tree erased and fructed, all ppr *Laissez dire* cf 188 10

Middleton, Charles Marmaduke, of Myddelton Lodge near Ilkeley, Yorks a lion passant arg

Middleton, Essex, a dexter hand apaumee ppr 222 14

Middleton, Wales a dexter hand ppr, issuing from a ducal coronet or

Middleton, Ireland out of a naval coronet or, a dexter hand ppr pointing to a star of the first

Middleton of Stansted Montfichet Essex, and Middleton, Shropsh a wolf's head erased ppr 30 8

Middleton of Newington Surrey a monkey passant ppr, collared ringed, and lined or cf 136 8

Middleton of Clerkhill, Scotland on the top of a tree an ape sejant, all ppr *Arte et marte*

Middleton, Lancs on the trunk of a tree or, a monkey sejant ppr collared about the loins az

Middleton of Durham and Wintertown, Lincs, on the trunk of a tree raguled a monkey passant, all ppr collared about the loins or

Middleton, Cambs, Lancs and of Middleton Hall Westml a hawk's head arg, beaked or cf 88 12

Middleton of London on a perch ppr, a falcon or *Diis bene juvantibus* 85 13

Middleton, Carver-, of Leam Derbysh and Yorks (1) An eagle's head erased arg, charged on the neck with a saltier engrailed sa (*for Middleton*) cf 83 2 (2) On a mount vert, a cross clechee or charged on the centre with a fleur-de-lis sa (*for Carver*) *Conjunctio firmat*

Middleton-Athorpe of Leam, Derbysh (1) A falcon ppr belled or, the dexter claw resting on an escutcheon of the arms viz per pale nebulee arg and az two mullets in fesse counterchanged (*for Athorpe*) 85 11 (2) An eagle's head erased arg, charged on the neck with a saltire engrailed sa (*for Middleton*) cf 83 2 (3) A mount vert, thereon a cross clechee or, charged in the centre with a fleur-de lis sa (*for Carver*) *Conjunctio firmat*

Middleton, John Shearer, Esquire of Cadamaney Madras (presently at Blackwood, Dumfries), a tower embattled arg masoned sa thereon a lion rampant gu armed and langued az *In arduis fortis*

Middleton, a tower embattled sa and on the battlements thereof a lion rampant gu *Fortis in arduis* 157 12

Middleton, Middx and Scotland on a tower az a lion rampant gu 157 12

Middleton of Seaton Aberdeensh, a tower sa and issuing from the battlements a lion rampant ppr *Fortis in arduis —Je n'oublierai pas* 157 12

Middleton, Scotland issuing from a tower sa, a demi-lion gu holding in his dexter paw a scimitar ppr *Fortis et fidus* cf 157 11

Middleton of Glasgow, issuing from a tower sa, a lion rampant gu *Fortis in arduis* 157 12

Middleton of Cricksey, Essex, a lion's gamb holding a branch of palm ppr *Sobrie, pie juste* 36 7

Middleton, Scotland a boar s head erased and erect az *Guard yourself* 43 3

Middleton of Stockfield Park, Yorks, be tween two wings arg a garb or 153 14

Middleton, Bart, of Crowfield Hall and Shrubland Hall, Suff a garb or banded vert, between two wings sa *Regardez mon droit* 153 14

Middleton, Hastings Burton Bradford Peverell Dorchester same crest

Middleton, Broke-, Bart of Broke Hall Suff (1) A garb erminois, banded vert, between two wings sa (*for Middleton*) 153 14 (2) Of honourable augmentation, out of a naval coronet or a dexter arm embowed encircled with a wreath of laurel ppr and grasping a trident of the first (*for Broke*) (3) A brock or badger passant ppr (*also for Broke*) *Sævumque tridentem servamus* 33 10

Middleton of the Grove Norwich a garb surmounted by an estoile or between two wings arg fretty az *Meret qui laborat* cf 153 14

Midford, Durh, an owl arg 96 5

Midgeley, two keys in saltier az wards downwards

Midgley, an heraldic tiger sejant erect, holding between its paws a caltrap

Midgley, on a mount an heraldic tiger sejant resting the dexter paw on a caltrap

Midleham, on a chapeau vert, turned up or, a wyvern with wings expanded az cf 70 11

Midlemore, Warw and Worcs a moorcock amongst grass and flags, all ppr

Midleton, Viscount (Brodrick), out of a ducal coronet or, a spear head arg, embrued gu *A cuspide corona*

Midwinter, Devonsh, a dexter arm embowed per pale sa and or, holding in the hand ppr a plume of feathers, two sa, one or

Miers, Henry Nathaniel, J P Ynyspenllwch, Clydach, Swansea Valley a plume of peacock feathers ppr *Virtus est vitium fugere*

Mieville, Sir Walter Frederick K C M G, of 68 Wilbury Road Hove Sussex a helmet affrontee with grills and addorned with seven ostrich-feathers 301 11

Mignot, David Esquire, M D, of Kensington Crescent a large diamond set in the midst of a triangle within a double row of brilliants ppr

Mihill, an arm embowed habited in mail, holding in the hand, all ppr a cutlass arg, on the edge of the blade three spikes hilt and pommel or

Miken, Ireland, a demi Moor holding in his dexter hand an arrow, and on his back a quiver all ppr

Mikieson, Scotland, a decrescent ppr *Ut implear* 163 1

Mikieson, Scotland, a crescent ppr *Ut implear* 163 2

Milbank, Sir Powlett Charles John Bart, D L, of Well Yorks, and Hart, Durh, a lion's head couped arg, guttee-de-poix charged with a pale gu, thereon three roses also arg 286 8

Milbanke, *see* Wentworth Baron

Milbanke - Huskisson, Bart, D L, of Halnaby, Yorks (1) An elephant's head erased arg guttee-de sang and pierced in the neck with an arrow ppr (*for Huskisson*) (2) A lion's head couped gu charged with a bend erm (*for Milbanke*) *Resolute and firm*

Milborne, an eagle with wings expanded ppr 77 5

Milborne of Armathwaite Castle, Cumb, a griffin's head erased 66 2

Milborne - Swinnerton - Pilkington, Sir Lionel Bart, D L, of Chevet Hall Yorks (1) A mower with his scythe ppr habited per pale arg and sa (*for Pilkington*) 306 11 (2) On a mount vert, a boar passant arg charged with a cross formee fleurettee sa (*for Swinnerton*) 306 12 (3) A demi lion per fesse arg and gu holding between the paws a leopard's face of the second (*for Milborne*) *Honestæ gloria fax mentis* 306 13

Milburn, a bear's head erased sa, muzzled or 35 2

Milburne, a hand holding a battle-axe ppr 213 12

Milcham, Norf, a griffin's head ppr 66 1

Mildmay, Earl (*extinct*) and **Baron** (*in abeyance*) **Fitzwalter,** a lion rampant gardant az *Alla ta hara* 2 5

Mildmay, Bart, *see* St John Mildmay

Mildmay, a lion rampant gardant

Mildmay, Henry Bingham, Shoreham Place, Kent, a lion rampant guardant az, armed and langued gu

Mildmay, Essex a lion rampant gardant az 2 5

Mildmay, Francis Bingham, Esquire of 46 Berkeley Square W same crest and motto

Mildmay, St John-, Rev Charles Arundell Hazelgrove, Sparkford, Bath a lion rampant guardant az, armed and langued gu *Alla ta hara*

Mildmay, a leopard's head erased or, ducally gorged gu, ringed and lined of the last on the neck below the coronet three pellets

Mildmay, Essex, a demi stag salient ppr, attired and collared or, wings addorsed arg

Mildmay, a chapeau winged, the points of the wings surrounded by a band therefrom pendent a mortar in fess, the whole surmounted by an étoile

Mildred, a bear passant struck through by the head of a broken spear in bend ppr

Mileham of Burmingham Norf, a griffin's head erased or 66 2

Miles, Sir Henry Robert William Bart., of Leigh Court Somers upon a rock a dexter arm embowed in armour ppr, garnished or supporting with the hand an anchor entwined by a cable also ppr

Miles, Philip Napier Esquire J P, of King's Weston near Bristol a dexter arm embowed in armour ppr, garnished or supporting with the hand an anchor, also ppr

Miles, a dove between two ears of wheat ppr

Miles, a dove between two laurel branches in orle all ppr 92 12

Miles of Narborough Leics an eagle rising erminois, collared, therefrom a chain reflexed over the back and charged on the breast with a mill rind sa *Sans crainte* cf 76 14

Miles, William Frederick Keyham Hall, Leics, same crest and motto

Miles, Ireland, out of a ducal coronet or charged on the rim with three bombs fired ppr, a lion's head az ensigned with a mural coronet arg. and gorged with a laurel wreath of the first *Sola virtus invicta*

Miles, a demi lion supporting an anchor, all ppr 12 12

Miles of London a boar's head and neck couped and transfixed by an arrow

Miles, Hants on a mural coronet gu an escallop arg

Mileson of Esthathesley Yorks a heraldic tiger's head sa tufted, tusked collared and lined or

Milford, a lion's gamb holding a trefoil ppr cf 36 8

Mill, Bart (*extinct*) of Camois Court, Essex and Mottisfont, Hants a demi-bear sa muzzled and chained or *Aides Dieu* cf 34 13

Mill, Sussex a demi-bear salient sa., muzzled ringed, and lined or cf 34 13

Mill of Hampton Kent, a demi bear salient sa muzzled ringed, and lined or and charged on the shoulder with three guttes-d'or

Mill of Dublin a demi-lion rampant gardant gu, holding in the dexter paw a sword ppr *Gladium musarum nutrix*

Mill, a bloodhound's head erased arg *Toujours fidele*

Mill, Scotland a greyhound's head issuing arg collared az, ringed or *Toujours fidèle* 61 2

Mill, a greyhound's head erased 61 4

Mill, Scotland a Pallas's head couped and helmeted, the beaver turned up and plumed gu *Tam arte quam marte* 182 1

Mill, Scotland a galley, her oars erect in saltier and flagged all ppr *Dat cura commodum* 160 10

Mill, an eagle's head erased gu, beaked or, and holding in the beak a cross moline erect sa

Millais, Bart in front of a dexter hand gauntleted and couped gu, an estoile of eight points or *Ars longa, vita brevis*

Millan, Scotland, two hands, dexter and sinister issuing, supporting a sword in pale ppr 213 1

Millar of London a wolf's head erased az, collared erm *Regard bien* 30 11

Millar, three ears of wheat issuing or

Millar, a dexter hand holding a book open all ppr *Felicem reddit religio* 215 10

Millar of Cirencester, the half length figure of a lady affrontée vested az, holding before her a portcullis gu. *Keep tryst and trust* 183 7

Millar, a demi Moor drawing an arrow to the head in a bow, all ppr *Non eget Mauri jaculis* 185 6

Millar of the Meadow, Seamill, Ayrsh,, and 5, Claremont Terrace Glasgow issuing from clouds a dexter hand holding up an open book, all ppr *Felicem reddit religio* 297 12

Millard, on a mount vert, a stag feeding ppr 116 9
Millard, Hants, a demi lion rampant az, supporting between the paws a mascle or cf 10 2
Millard, William Joseph Kelson, Esquire, M D, F R C P M R C S Eng, of Es Sahnia Bayshill, Cheltenham, an eagle displayed sa, entwined round the body and neck by a serpent and holding in each claw a fer de moline or
Millbank, a hill vert
Millburn, out of a ducal coronet a demi-lion, all ppr 16 3
Mille, a unicorn's head 49 7
Millear, Thomas Esquire, J P, of Edgarley Wickliffe Road, Victoria Australia, a cross moline or, surmounted by a martlet sa, between two ears of wheat stalked and leaved, also or *Juris cultum legimus*
Miller, *see* Christie Miller
Miller, *see* Riggs Miller
Miller-Morison, *see* Campbell-Miller-Morison
Miller, Sir James Percy, Bart of Manderston, Berwicksh a dexter hand with two fingers pointing upwards issuing out of a cloud, all ppr *Omne bonum superne* cf 222 11
Miller, Sir William Frederic, Bart, of Glenlee Kirkcudbrightsh, a dexter hand couped at the wrist, the two first fingers pointing upwards ppr *Manent optima cœlo* 222 11
Miller, a hand with two fingers pointing upward ppr *Manent optima cœlo* 222 11
Miller, Scotland a dexter hand pointing with two fingers ppr *Spei bonæ atque animi* 222 11
Miller, Bart Scotland, a hand couped at the wrist the third and fourth fingers folded in the palm arg 222 11
Miller of Leithen, Peeblessh, a dexter hand with one finger pointing upwards ppr *Manent optima cœlo* 222 12
Miller of Gourlebank, Scotland two arms their hands joined ppr *Unione augetur*
Miller, Bart, of Chichester, Sussex, a wolf's head erased arg, gorged with a collar wavy az cf 30 11
Miller of Downpatrick, co Down Ireland a wolf's head erased az, charged with a rose or *Nil conscire sibi* cf 30 8
Miller of Dunstable Beds, a wolf's head erased per pale erm and purp, collared or 30 11
Miller, Bart, Ireland, a wolf's head erased arg 30 8
Miller, Bart, Hants, a wolf's head erased arg, gorged with a fess wavy az cf 30 8
Miller, Kent a wolf's head erased az, collared erm
Miller of Singleton Park, Poulton-le Tylde, Preston, a wolf's head erased bendy or and gu, holding in the mouth a ragged staff sa *Sibimet merces industria*
Miller, Bowen-, of Milford, co Mayo, Ireland (1) A wolf's head erased az (*for Miller*) 30 8 (2) A falcon close ppr, belled or (*for Bowen*) *Esse quam videri* cf 85 2
Miller of Werndean Hall Norwood Surrey, a wolf's head erased az, collared erm *Mea spes est in Deo* 30 11
Miller, Hon Henry John M L C J P of Fernbrook, Oamaru, Otago, New Zealand, a wolf's head erased arg gorged with a collar wavy az
Miller, Thomas, Esquire, of Preston, Lancs, a demi-wolf erminois, gorged with a collar gobony arg and az, supporting with the paw a spindle erect ppr
Miller, Scotland, a cross moline sa *Optima cœlo* 165 3
Miller, a caltrap or the upper point embrued ppr 174 14
Miller, a demi-savage shooting an arrow from a bow all ppr *Non eget Mauri jaculis* 185 6
Miller, Scotland, a lion rampant sa hold ing between its paws a cross moline gu *Forward*
Miller, Devonsh and Middx, a demi-lion rampant gardant az, holding a mascle or
Miller, Rev William Sanderson, Whatcote Rectory Shipston-on-Stour same crest
Miller, Warw and Dorset a demi lion az, holding between the paws a mascle or
Miller, a griffin's head erased arg, ducally gorged and chained az
Miller-Cunningham, John, Esquire, of Leithen, Peeblessh, Civil Engineer a unicorn's head sa, maned and armed or *Over fork over* 49 7
Miller, Charles F L Esquire, Acre Valley, Stirling a horse's head erased arg. *Celer* 51 4
Miller, Ireland, a polecat sa 135 13
Millerd of Rathcormuck Glintown, and Monard co Cork Ireland, out of a baron's coronet ppr, a griffin's head gu holding in the beak a rose branch, also ppr *Per mille ardua*
Milles, *see* Sondes Earl
Milles, a cat sejant ppr 26 8
Milles, a demi-bear sa., muzzled, collared and lined or cf 34 13
Milles, a bear passant sa, muzzled and chained or cf 34 1
Milles, Suff, a hare sejant ppr, holding in its mouth three ears of wheat or
Milles, Kent and Norf, a lion rampant or holding between its paws a mill-rind sa
Milles of London, a paschal lamb passant arg, ungu or, holding over its dexter shoulder a banner of St George double pennoned
Millett, Middx, and of Denham, Bucks, out of a mural coronet an arm erect vested or holding in a glove arg a dragon's head erased vert cf 208 7
Milley, Ireland the Holy Bible az, charged on the cover with a fleur-de-lis or
Millidge, Scotland, a griffin's head erased 66 2
Milligan, Scotland, a demi lion holding in his dexter paw a sword *Fide et fortitudine* 14 12
Milligan, a demi-lion rampant gu holding in its dexter paw a sword ppr *Regarde bien* 14 12
Milligan, Lieutenant Colonel Charles, Caldwell Hall Burton-on-Trent a merchant ship under sail, colours flying ppr *Just in time*
Milliken, Scotland a demi-lion royally crowned gu, holding in his dexter paw a sword ppr *Regarde bien* cf 14 12
Milliken of that Ilk, Renfrewsh, Scotland, a demi lion rampant gu *Regarde bien* 10 3
Millington, an ass's head ppr 125 12
Millman, a cross moline gu 165 13
Millman, a stag lodged per pale arg and or attired and ungu of the last, charged on the body with two hurts in fesse cf 115 7
Millman, a gauntlet ppr 209 18
Millman, a sinister gauntlet or
Millner or **Milner**, Yorks, a horse's head sa, crined and bridled or, charged on the neck with a bezant cf 51 5
Millot of Whitehill, Durh a dexter arm in armour embowed and gauntleted, all ppr, grasping a billet sa
Mills, *see* Hillingdon, Baron
Mills, Surrey and Glouc a lion rampant or 1 13
Mills of Knightington Berks, a lion rampant or holding in its mouth a sinister hand gu
Mills, Middx, on a ducal coronet a lion rampant gu *Honor virtutis pretium* cf 1 13
Mills, Essex, a demi-lion rampant regardant or holding between its paws a mill rind sa *Nil conscire sibi* cf 11 1
Mills of Saxham Hall, Suff a lion rampant or *Confido* 1 13
Mills, a demi-lion rampant or, holding in the paws a mill rind sa
Mills, a lion's gamb erased sa 36 4
Mills, on a ducal coronet a lion's gamb erased cf 36 12
Mills, Suff a demi bear rampant sa muzzled collared and chained or cf 34 13
Mills, Beds, and Casnalbery, Herts, a wing barry of ten arg and vert cf 109 7
Mills, on an earl's coronet the sun in splendour cf 162 2
Mills of Lexden Park, Colchester, Essex, a hurt charged with an etoile or
Mills, James, Esquire, late Town Clerk of Beverley and of Bridlington Yorks a windmill ppr *Aura adversa auxiliatrix* 158 5
Mills of London, a holy lamb passant arg, ungu or, bearing on the dexter shoulder a banner of St George double-pennoned
Mills, Rev Cecil, of Bisterne Ringwood, Hants, a demi-lion reguardant or, holding between the paws a mill-rind sa
Mills of Bitterne, Hants, on a mural coronet gu, an escallop arg
Mills of Norton Court, Kent on a chapeau gu, turned up erm, a mill-rind sa between two marlion's wings of the second
Mills, Joseph, Esquire of the Beeches Kingswinford, Dudley Staffs a hind ppr, holding in the mouth an ear of wheat leaved and slipped or resting the dexter fore leg on an escutcheon sa, charged with a mill rind erect also or *Ad finem fidelis*
Milltown, Earl of, Viscount Russborough, of Russellstown co Wicklow and **Baron Russborough**, of Russborough,

co. Wicklow, Ireland (Rt. Hon. Henry Leeson, B.A.), a demi-lion rampant gu., holding between the paws the sun in splendour or. *Clarior e tenebris.*

Millward, a dexter arm in armour embowed, holding in the hand a sabre, all ppr. 195. 2

Milman, Sir Francis John, Bart., of Levaton, in Woodland, Devonsh., a hart lodged per pale erm. and erminois, attired and ungu. or, charged on the body with two hurts fesseways. *Deus nobiscum, quis contra.* cf. 115. 7

Milman, Archibald John Scott, Esq., C.B., of Speaker's Court, Westminster, same crest and motto.

Milman, Lieutenant-General George Bryan, C.B., of Queen's House, Tower of London, E.C., same crest and motto.

Milman, Major-General Gustavus Hamilton Lockwood, of Martins, Heron, Bracknell, Berks, same crest and motto.

Milman-Mainwaring, Charles Egerton Forbes, Esquire: (1) An ass's head erased ppr., haltered arg. (*for Mainwaring*). (2) A hart lodged per pale erm. and erminois, attired or, and charged on the body with two hurts fesseways (*for Milman*). cf. 115. 7

Miln, a garb erect banded ppr. 153. 2

Milne, *see* Stott-Milne.

Milne of Muretoun, Scotland, a dexter hand holding a folded book ppr. *Efficiunt clarum studia.* 215. 4

Milne, Scotland, a Pallas's head couped at the shoulders ppr., vested about the neck vert, on the head a helmet az., the beaver raised, and surmounted by a plume of feathers gu. *Tam in arte quam marte.* 182. 1

Milne, Scotland, a martlet volant arg. *Prudenter qui sedulo.* 96. 2

Milne of Edinburgh, same crest. *Ex industria.* 96. 2

Milne of Balwyllo, Forfarsh., Scotland, in the sea ppr., a cross moline sa., within two ears of wheat in orle. *Clarum reddit industria.* cf. 154. 14

Milne of Blairtoun and Aberdeen, Scotland, a galley, her oars erect in saltier ppr. *Dat cura commodum.* 160. 10

Milne, John Adam, Esquire, of Ardmiddle House, Turriff, N.B., and Melgum, Aberdeensh., Scotland, a galley, her sails furled and oars in saltire ppr., the flags gu. *Suum cuique.*

Milne, Samuel Milne, Esquire, of Calverley House, Leeds, Yorks, a mill-rind fessewise sa., thereon a lion rampant arg., holding between the paws a mill-rind gu.

Milne, Sir Archibald Berkeley, Bart., of Inveresk, Midlothian, out of a naval coronet or, a dexter cubit arm vested az., the hand ppr. grasping a flag-staff, therefrom flying the flag of a rear-admiral of the Blue, inscribed with the word *Impregnable* in letters of gold. *Tam marte quam arte.* 303. 5

Milne-Home, Captain David William, J.P., D.L., of Wedderburn Castle, Duns, Paxton House, Berwick-on-Tweed and Caldra, Duns, N.B.: (1) A unicorn's head couped gorged with an antique crown. (2) A lion's head couped. *Remember.—True to the end.*

Milne, Lees-, James Henry, Crompton Hall, near Oldham: (1) In front of five palm-trees ppr., a lamb couchant arg., holding in the mouth a trefoil slipped or, and supporting with the dexter forefoot a flagstaff in bend sinister ppr., therefrom flowing a banner arg., charged with a cross crosslet gu. (2) A mount, thereon amidst wheat, a mower, in his hands his scythe, in the attitude of mowing, all ppr. *Prudenter qui sedulo.*

Milner, Rev. Gamaliel, St. Mary de Crypt Rectory, Glouc., a horse's head sa., bridled or.

Milner, Viscount (Milner), in front of a stag's head erased ppr., gorged with a bar gemel or, a bit fessewise of the last. *Acer non effrenus.* 304. 4

Milner, Yorks: (1) A greyhound current sa., collared and ringed or (*for Milner*). cf. 58. 2. (2) A lion's head couped arg., charged with a Catherine-wheel gu. (*for Wheeler*). cf. 21. 1

Milner, Cornw. and Yorks, a wolf's head ppr., couped gu., pierced through the neck from behind with a broken sword, the point thereof and the wound embrued ppr., pommel or.

Milner, Sir Frederick George, Bart., D.L., M.P., of Nun-Appleton, Yorks, a horse's head couped sa., bridled and maned or, charged on the neck with a bezant between two wings, also or. *Addit frena feris.* 305. 1

Milner of Sefton Lodge, Newmarket, a horse's head couped arg., bridled and maned or, charged on the neck with a bezant between two wings or. *Addit frena feris.*

Milner, William Aldam, Totley Hall, Sheffield, a horse's head erased az., bridled or, charged on the neck with a bezant.

Milner-Gibson-Cullum, George Gery, Esquire, of Hardwick House, Bury St. Edmunds, Suff.: (1) A lion sejant ppr., holding a column arg., base and capital or (*for Cullum*). (2) A stork holding in its beak a branch of laurel ppr., and resting the dexter claw upon a bridle-bit or (*for Milner-Gibson*). *Sustineatur.*

Milnes, *see* Houghton, Baron.

Milnes-Gaskell, *see* Gaskell.

Milnes, Scotland, a garb ppr. 153. 2

Milnes, Bart., Leics., a garb or, banded by a fess dancettée az., charged with three mullets pierced of the first. 152. 10

Milnes of Alton Manor, Derbysh., a garb erminois between two trefoils vert. *Non sine labore.* 152. 14

Milnes of Aldercar, Dunston, and Cromford, Derbysh., a bear's head couped at the neck sa., charged with a mill-rind or.

Milnes of Stubbing Edge, Derbysh., a demi-lion rampant or, holding in the paws a mill-rind sa.

Milnes of Beckingham Hall, Lincs, an elephant's head erased ppr., gorged with a ducal coronet or.

Milnes of Stirling, Scotland, out of a mural coronet or, an eagle's head sa., gorged with a collar or, charged with three pallets gu. *In cruce salus.* cf. 83. 9

Milroy, Scotland, a leopard's face or. 22. 2

Milroy, Edward Andrew Wallace, of the Oast House, near Farnham, Surrey: (1) On a wreath or and vert, an ostrich ppr. (*for Milroy*). 97. 2. (2) An elephant's head couped erm., between two elephants' proboscis or (*for Rosher*). *Espérance.—Consider the end.* 133. 5

Milroy, Rev. Andrew, of The Vicarage, Carisbrooke, Isle of Wight, same crest and motto.

Milroy, Arthur John Wallace, same crest and motto.

Milroy, George William Winckworth Wallace, same crest and motto.

Milsolm, a heraldic tiger's head sa., tufted, collared, and lined or.

Milton, Viscount, *see* Fitzwilliam, Earl.

Milton of London, and of Milton, near Thame, Oxon., a lion's gamb erect arg., holding an eagle's head erased gu.

Milton of London, an arm in armour ppr., scarfed az., grasping in the hand, also ppr., a broken spear gu., headed arg.

Milvain, Herbert Forsyth, Esquire, of Seaton House, Holderness, East Yorks, a dexter cubit arm in armour holding in the hand a sword in bend sinister ppr. *Fidelis.* 297. 14

Milward, *see* Sayer-Milward.

Milward of Braxted, Essex, out of a palisado coronet or, a lion's gamb sa., grasping a sceptre of the first.

Milward of Linthurst House, near Bromsgrove, a lion's gamb erased holding a sceptre. *Nec timide nec temere.*

Milward, Essex, a lion's gamb sa., holding a sceptre or. 38. 7

Milward, George, Esquire, J.P., of the Manor House, Lechlade, Glouc., a bear's paw erased sa., the claws or, holding a sceptre in bend sinister of the last, entwined by a sprig of oak ppr., between two wings az.

Milward of Ballyharran, co. Wexford, and Tullogher, co. Kilkenny, a dragon's head couped vert, between two wings gu. 72. 7

Minchin, a lion's tail erased ppr. 123. 14

Minchin, James George Cotton, Esquire, of North View, Wimbledon Common, out of a ducal coronet a dexter arm embowed holding in the hand a baton, all ppr. *Regarde la mort.*

Minchin, William Charles, Esquire, M.D., of Headfort Place, Kells, co. Meath, same crest and motto.

Minchin, Edward Corker, Esquire, of Woodburn, Christchurch, Canterbury, New Zealand, *uses*: a dexter naked arm embowed ppr., holding in the hand a baton or. *Regarde à la mort.*

Minchin of Busherstown, Ballynakill, co. Tipperary, Ireland, a naked arm embowed ppr., grasping a baton or. *Regarde à la mort.*

Minet, William, Esquire, of Fountain Court, London, E.C., a wing elevated arg., charged with three barrulets gu. *Quantum est in rebus inane.*

Minett, a mermaid holding in her dexter hand a mirror, and with her sinister combing her hair, all ppr. 184. 8

Minett, a wing erect arg., charged with three bars gu. cf. 109. 7

Mingay or **Mingey** of Gymingham, Norf a lance or, headed arg, environed with a laurel-branch ppr

Miniet, an eagle volant over a ruined castle ppr

Minnitt of Knygh Castle, co. Tipperary, Ireland, a helmet ppr, garnished or *Virtute et armis* 180 3

Minnitt, Rev Francis Allen of Trinity College, Cambridge (1) A helmet ppr garnished or (2) Out of a ducal coronet or, a demi-lion rampant sa *Gearr Augus dogh Aboo—Virtute et armis*

Minne, Rutl, a heathcock ppr

Minnoch of Glasgow an owl ppr *Je pense plus* 96 5

Minns, Rev G W, Weston Cliff, Weston, Southampton, a swan's neck arg, beaked gu, between two wings, each charged with a cross crosslet. *Mens conscia recti* 297 11

Minors, a cubit arm ppr, holding a lion's gamb erased sa 220 10

Minors, a wolf s head erased sa devouring a sinister hand ppr

Minshall, Mynshall, and **Minshull,** Bucks Chesh, Devonsh, Suff, and Sussex a Turk kneeling on one knee vested gu the legs and arms in mail ppr, at his side a scimitar sa hilted or, on his head a turban with a crescent and feathers arg holding in his dexter hand a crescent of the last. cf 188 11

Minshaw, a dexter hand ppr, holding up a cup or 217 11

Minshull, two lions' gambs gu holding a crescent or 39 6

Minster, Baron, *see* Conyngham Marquess of

Minterne, Mintern, and **Minterin,** Surrey and Dorset a bull's head gu, ducally gorged and armed or cf 44 2

Minto, Earl of, Viscount Melgund, of Melgund, Forfaish, **Baron Minto** of Minto Roxburghsh (Rt Hon Sir William Hugh Elliot-Murray-Kynynmound K T), a dexter arm embowed issuant from clouds, throwing a dart, all ppr *Non eget arcu* cf 201 13

Minton of Stoke-upon-Trent, Staffs, upon a mount vert, a heraldic tiger passant or, the dexter paw resting on a garb erect ppr *Pro Deo et patria*

Minton, Thomas William, Esquire J P, of Chase Ridings, Enfield, same crest and motto

Minton, Thomas Powell, Esquire, of the Hurst, Rock Ferry, Chesh and of Clifton House, Ruyton-xi Towns, Shropsh same crest and motto

Minton-Senhouse, Herbert, Esquire, J P, of 21, Sanderson Road, Newcastle-on-Tyne same crest and motto

Mirehouse of Miresike, Cumb, an arm in armour embowed holding in the hand a sword, all ppr. *Qualis ab incepto* 195 2

Mirehouse, Rev John, of Colsterworth Grantham, same crest

Mirehouse, Richard Walter Byrd, the Hall Angler, Pembrokesh, same crest

Mirfin, a demi-lion ppr, holding a flag arg, charged with a saltier sa cf 15 2

Mirrie or **Mirry,** out of a ducal coronet or, a demi lion gu 16 3

Mirtle, a cubit arm erect ppr, encircled with a chaplet of myrtle vert, holding in the hand a scimitar arg, hilt and pommel or, and on the blade a shackle severed sa

Missenden, amongst flags vert, a demi-swan displayed arg, collared gu

Missinnen or **Misserinen,** a battle-axe in pale ppr 172 3

Mitchell, *see* Parry Mitchell

Mitchell, Bart, of Berry and Westshore, in Shetland, descended of Bandeth, Stirlingsh, three ears of barley con joined in one stalk ppr *Sapiens qui assiduus* 154 2

Mitchell, Frank Johnstone, Llanfrechfa Grange, Caerleon, Newport, Monm, in front of a garb or, charged with an escallop sa, two thistles leaved and slipped in saltire ppr *A Deo fasces* 255 14

Mitchell, Arthur Charles, Esquire, J P, of High Grove Tetbury Glouc same crest and motto

Mitchell of Sidmouth, Devonsh, a mascle sa, interlaced by three ears of barley erect slipped and leaved or *Sapiens qui assiduus* 154 5

Mitchell, Edward Charles, care Messrs Henry S King 65, Cornhill, London, E C, same crest and motto

Mitchell, Sir Hugh Sykes, Bart, of Fernie law Colinton N B, same crest and motto

Mitchell, Rev John Francis, same crest and motto

Mitchell or **Mitchael,** of Alderston Midlothian Scotland, a stalk of wheat bladed and erect ppr *Cresco* 154 3

Mitchell, Scott-, of New South Wales, a dexter hand erect holding a garland of laurel ppr motto over the crest *Deo favente,* under the shield ΕΥΡΗΚΑ 218 4

Mitchell-Innes of Parson's Green, Edinburgh (1) An increscent ppr (*for Innes*) 163 3 (2) A hand holding a garland of laurel, all ppr (*for Mitchell*) *Il recoir pour donner—Deo favente* 218 4

Mitchell-Innes, Alexander Harold of Whitehall Chirnside, N B, same crests and mottoes

Mitchell, late Sir Andrew, K B (*family extinct in male line, now represented by Captain Andrew Mitchell Molyneux of Rock Point New Brighton, Chesh*), issuing from behind three ears of barley ppr, a cubit arm vested in naval uniform, the hand grasping a broken staff from which suspends the Batavian flag depressed, also ppr *Illis honos venit* 206 3

Mitchell, Vice-Admiral William R N, between two ears of wheat or, an arm erect vested az, cuffed or, the hand ppr grasping an anchor in bend sinister or *Omnia superat virtus* 208 1

Mitchell, Sir Henry, of Park Field House, Manningham, Yorks, in front of a cubit arm erect ppr, the hand holding a pen in bend arg, and pendent from the wrist by a ribbon gu, a bugle horn or a rock, also ppr *Dante Deo reddam*

Mitchell of Craigend Stirlingsh, some time designed of Mitchell, Scotland a hand holding a writing pen ppr *Favente Deo supero* 217 10

Mitchell-Carruthers, Rev William M A of the Rectory, Holbrook, Ipswich (1) On the dexter side, a cherub's head ppr (*for Carruthers*) 189 9 (2) On the sinister side St Michael the Archangel in armour holding a spear in his dexter hand, his face neck, arms, and legs bare all ppr the wings arg, and hair auburn (*for Mitchell*) *Promptus et fidelis—Virtute cresco* 189 11

Mitchell-Thomson, Sir Mitchell Bart., of Polmood, Broughton Peeblessh, and 6, Charlotte Square, Edinburgh a hand ppr holding a cross crosslet fitchee gu *Deus providebit*

Mitchell, Ireland, an angel kneeling in a praying posture ppr

Mitchell, co Cork, Ireland, an angel in armour holding in the dexter hand a spear ppr *Tout jour prêt* 189 11

Mitchell, Charles, Esquire, of Jesmond Towers Newcastle-on-Tyne, out of flames of fire ppr, a phœnix rising of the same, semee of mascles sa, and holding in the beak an acorn slipped and leaved ppr *Spernit humum* 82 13

Mitchell, Forbes-, Duncan, Esquire, of Thainston Aberdeensh (1) A cock (*for Forbes*) 91 2 (2) A phœnix in flames ppr (*for Mitchell*) *Watch—Nulla pallescere culpa* 82 2

Mitchell of Truro Cornw, a demi pegasus or, winged az, charged on the shoulder with a demi-rose gu divided fesseways rays issuing from the division pendent arg 47 11

Mitchell, a garb vert 153 2

Mitchell of Enderby Hall Leics, a garb or, banded gu, pendent therefrom an escutcheon arg, charged with three slips of laurel vert

Mitchell, John Hanson, Verona, Worthing, Sussex, a phœnix in flames ppr *Nulla pallescere culpa*

Mitchelson of Middleton, Edinburghsh., Scotland an increscent arg *Crescam ut prosim* 163 3

Mitchelson, a hawk rising *Virtute tutus* 88 2

Mitchener, a dove arg 92 2

Mitford, *see* Redesdale Baron

Mitford, Colonel William Kenyon, of Pitshill, Sussex, a dexter and a sinister hand holding a sword in pale arg, pommelled or, on the point thereof a boar's head sa, tusked ppr, couped in fess arg *God caryth for us*

Mitford, Freeman-, Algernon Bertram, 84, Jermyn Street S W, same crest and motto

Mitford, Edward Ledwich Oswaldeston, of Mitford Castle, Northumb, a dexter and sinister hand couped ppr, holding a sword in pale arg, pommelled or on the point a boar's head sa, tusked ppr, couped in fess arg (2) A man in armour on horseback, all ppr, in the dexter hand a sword arg hilt or, and holding an escutcheon bearing a mascle sa, between three pellets (*for Osbaldeston*) *God caryth for us*

Mitford, a mole passant sa., charged with an escallop or

Mittlewell, an eagle's head erased arg 83 2

Mitton, Shropsh and Staffs, a demi eagle displayed with two heads az cf 82 3

Mitton, a demi-eagle displayed per pale arg. and az. 81. 6

Mitton, Staffs, a demi-eagle displayed with two heads per pale or and az. 82. 1

Mitton, a ram's head couped arg., armed or. 130. 1

Mitton, a ram's head couped arg. 130. 1

Mitton, Staffs, a bull's head sa., armed or, charged with three annulets of the last.

Mitton, Oxon., a lion's gamb couped and erect arg., holding an eagle's head erased gu.

Moberley, Moberly, and **Modburley**, a demi-lady holding in her dexter hand a pair of scales. 183. 2

Mocket, Kent, a tiger sejant az., collared arg.

Mocklow, of Broughton Soulney, Notts, a griffin's head per pale indented arg., guttée-de-larmes, and gu., holding in the beak a buck's foot of the first.

Mocklow, Worcs., a griffin's head per pale indented gu. and arg., holding in the beak an eagle's leg erased or. *cf.* 226. 14

Moda, Suff., a demi-lion rampant crowned or. 10. 11

Modburley, a demi-lady, in the character of Justice, holding in her dexter hand a pair of scales. 188. 2

Modder, Staffs, on a staff couped raguly in fess vert, a lion sejant or. *cf.* 7. 9

Moderby, a hand holding a thunderbolt ppr. 216. 4

Modey, out of a ducal coronet or, a demi-lion with wings displayed gu.

Modyford, a garb or. 153. 2

Moels, a mule passant ppr. 125. 7

Moens, William John Charles, Esquire, of Tweed, Hants, two eagle's wings conjoined arg. 113. 1

Moesler of London, a talbot statant ppr., collared. 54. 2

Moffat, a cat sejant gardant erect ppr. 26. 9

Moffat, Scotland, a cross crosslet fitched gu. *Spero meliora.* 166. 2

Moffat, Robert Maxwell, Egyptian Lodge, Jersey, same crest and motto.

Moffat of Goodrich Court, Heref., the sun in his splendour ppr. 162. 2

Moffatt, Alexander, Esquire, 23, Abercromby Place, Edinburgh, *uses*: a cross crosslet fitchée. *Spero meliora.* 166. 2

Mogg, of Farrington Gurney, Somers., a cock ppr., bearing an escutcheon arg., charged with a crescent gu., pendent from its neck by a chain or. *Curæ pii Diis sunt.*

Mogg, Rees-, William, Esquire, of Cholwell House, Somers.: (1) Between two spear-heads erect sa., a cock ppr. (*for Mogg*). (2) A swan arg., with wings elevated or, holding in the beak a water-lily slipped ppr. (*for Rees*). *Cura pii Diis sunt.*

Mohamud (Nowab Ali Mohamud Khan Bahadoor, J.P., Bombay), a demi-lion ppr., charged with two bars or, holding in the dexter paw a sword, also ppr., and resting the sinister upon an escutcheon az., charged with the sun in splendour of the second. *Nil desperandum.* 14. 9

Mohun, a dexter arm vested with a maunch erm., holding in the hand ppr. a fleur-de-lis or.

Moile or **Moill**, on a winged globe an eagle rising, all ppr. 159. 9

Moillict, James Keir, of Abberley Hall, Worcs., and Cheney Court, Heref., a swan arg. *Gaudat in luce veritas.* 99. 2

Moir, Scotland, a Moor's head. *Non sibi, sed cunctis.*

Moir of Abergeldie and Otterburn, Scotland, a negro's head couped ppr. *Mediocriter.*

Moir, Scotland, a Mauritanian's head couped and dropping blood, all ppr. *Major opima ferat.*

Moir of Stoneywood, Aberdeensh., Scotland, a Moor's head couped and distilling drops of blood ppr. *Major opima ferat.* 190. 11

Moir of Scotstoun, Aberdeen, Scotland, a mort-head with two leg-bones in saltier, all ppr. *Non sibi, sed cunctis.*

Moir, Alastair Erskine Graham, of Leckie, Scotland, a falcon ppr., armed and belled or, perching on a heron, lying on its back ppr., beaked and membered gu. *Ne oublie.* *cf.* 79. 7

Moir of Hilton, Aberdeensh., Scotland, issuing out of a cloud an arm from the shoulder, holding in the hand a branch of laurel slipped. *Virtute non aliter.*

Moir-Byres, George, Esquire, of Tonley, Whitehouse, Aberdeensh., a cock regardant ppr. *Marte duo tutus.*

Moira, Earl of, *see* Loudon, Earl of.

Moises, a tuft of reeds vert. *Nisi virtus vilior alga.*

Molant, a demi-mule gu.

Molcaster and **Moncaster**, an old man's head affrontée ppr., ducally crowned or.

Mold, William Henry, Bethersden, Ashford, Kent, a demi-lion rampant guardant.

Moldford, a buck's head gu. 121. 5

Mole of Molton, Devonsh., out of a ducal coronet or, a snake nowed in pale ppr. 142. 11

Mole of Tringeg, Beds, and Northamp., out of clouds ppr., a cubit arm in pale vested gu., the hand apaumée of the first.

Molesworth, Viscount (Molesworth), Lansdowne Crescent, Bath, and 3, Palace Gate, London, W., a dexter arm embowed in armour ppr., holding a cross crosslet fitchée or. *Vincit amor patriæ.* 198. 5

Molesworth, Sir Robert, late of Edlington, Melbourne, Victoria, Australia, Judge of the Supreme Court of Victoria, same crest and motto. 198. 5

Molesworth, Sir Lewis William, Bart., 3, Great Cumberland Place, W., an armed arm embowed ppr., holding a cross crosslet or. *Sic fidem teneo.* 198. 5

Molesworth, George Mill Frederick, North Down Hall, Bideford, a dexter arm embowed in armour ppr., holding a cross crosslet fitchée or. *Vincit amor patriæ.*

Molesworth, His Honour Hickman, a dexter arm in armour embowed ppr., holding a cross crosslet or. *Vincit amor patriæ.*

Molesworth, James Murray, Esquire, J.P., of Comyn Lodge, Leamington, same crest and motto.

Molesworth, Rev. Reynell Francis Wynn, M.A., of the Lodge, Pembury, Kent, same crest and motto.

Molesworth, Sir Guilford Lindsey, K.C.I.E., of the Manor House, Bexley, Kent, same crest and motto.

Molesworth, George Mill Frederick, of Torridge House, Westward Ho, same crest and motto.

Molesworth, Frederick Nassau, of Gale House, Littleborough, Manchester, same crest and motto.

Molesworth, Alexander, of Hamer Hall, Rochdale, same crest and motto.

Molesworth-St. Aubyn, Rev. St. Aubyn, J.P., of Clowance, Cornw., a rock thereon a Cornish chough rising, all ppr.

Moleyns, De, *see* Ventry, Baron.

Moleyns, *see* Eveleigh-De Moleyns.

Molford of South Molton and Cadburie, Devonsh., out of a ducal coronet or, a demi-swan with wings expanded arg., beaked gu.

Molineaux, a cross moline lozenge-pierced az. 165. 1

Molineux of Hawkley, Lancs, a beaver passant ppr. *cf.* 134. 8

Molineux, Notts, a peacock's tail ppr., in bend sinister, affixed to the side of a chapeau gu., turned up erm.

Molineux, Dorset and Notts: (1) A hat gu., turned up in front arg., between the hat and the turned-up front a plume of peacock's feathers ppr. (2) Issuant out of flames a dexter hand holding an eagle's leg erased à la quise, all ppr. *cf.* 220. 12

Molineux, in a chapeau gu., turned up erm., a peacock's feather in bend sinister ppr.

Molineux-Montgomerie, Frederick Butler, Esquire, a palm-branch ppr. *Procedamus in pace.*

Molineux-Montgomerie, Cecil Thomas Crisp, J.P., D.L., of Carboldisham Hall and Carboldisham Manor, East Harling: (1) A palm-branch ppr. (*for Montgomerie*). (2) In front of two peacock's feathers in saltire, a cross moline or (*for Molineux*). (3) A mount vert, thereon a cameleopard arg., armed and ungu. or, semée of pellets and hurts alternately collared and line reflexed over the back gu. (*for Crisp*). *Procedamus in pace.*

Molins of London, a water-wheel or.

Moll, Scotland, a phœnix in flames ppr. *Post funera fœnus.* 82. 2

Möller, D'Osten-: (1) On the coronet of a Danish baron a fleur-de-lis or (*for Möller*). (2) In front of three peacock's feathers erect ppr., two keys in saltier or, between as many eagle's wings arg. (*for D'Osten*). *Die möller salich ihm.* 112. 12

Molleson, Scotland, a Saracen's head erased and dropping blood ppr. *Fax mentis honestæ gloria.* *cf.* 190. 11

Molleson of Lachintilly, Aberdeensh., Scotland, a hart's head cabossed ppr., attired with ten tynes or. *Fax mentis honestæ gloria.* 122. 5

Molling and **Molying**, on a rock a martlet sa. *cf.* 95. 5

Mollington, a demi-man shooting an arrow from a bow all ppr

Molloy, Ireland out of a cloud a hand erect, holding a book expanded ppr 215 1

Molloy of St. Mary-le bone, Midd a greyhound current arg, in front of a tree vert cf 58 5

Molloy, on a ducal coronet a lion rampant all or cf 1 13

Molloy, out of a ducal coronet a demi-lion rampant all or 16 3

Molloy, Laurance Romford, Esquire, J P of Clonbela Parsonstown, King's Co, in front of an oak tree growing out of a mount, all ppr, a greyhound springing sa collared or ᵹeappaᵹıŋ bóc abú

Molloy, a sea-lion sejant 20 2

Molloy, Bernard Charles, M P, a greyhound courant under a tree *Gearaigh agus dogh buiadh*

Molony, an arm in armour embowed holding in the hand a scimitar, all ppr *Perissem, ni perissem* 196 10

Molony, William Beresford, Esquire of Kiltanon, near Tulla, co Clare, an arm in armour embowed holding a dagger all ppr *In Domino et non in arcu meo sperabo*

Molony of Kiltanon, Granahan and Six Mile Bridge House, co Clare a dexter arm embowed in armour, the hand in a gauntlet and grasping a dagger all ppr *In Domino et non in arcu sperabo* cf 196 5

Molony, Henry Esquire, M D, of Odell Ville Ballingarry co Limerick an arm vambraced embowed, the hand gauntleted grasping a short sword all ppr, the forearm charged with a trefoil slipped az *In Domino et non in arcu meo sperabo*

Molony, James Barry Esquire of Bindon St Ennis, co Clare, same crest and motto

Molony, Alfred, of 12, Vincent Square Mansions, Westminster, S W, same crest and motto

Molony, R H of 10 Cambridge Place, Victoria Road, W, a dexter arm in armour embowed holding in the hand a sword in bend sinister ppr *In Domino et non in arcu sperabo*

Molowney, a stag trippant holding in its mouth a branch cf 117 8

Molson, a crescent between two wings expanded arg cf 112 6

Molton or Moulton, Norf a shark's head regardant issuing, swallowing a blackamoor 139 2

Molton or Moulton of Plympton and Collumpton, Devonsh, a cubit arm erect, vested gu cuffed erm holding in the hand ppr a chaplet of roses also gu leaved vert

Molynes, Berks and Leics, a falcon's head between two wings expanded 89 1

Molynes, a savage's head couped ppr 190 12

Molyneux, Earl of Sefton and Viscount Molyneux, *see* Sefton

Molyneux, a peacock's tail erect ppr, banded or and az

Molyneux, Rev Sir John Charles, Bart, the Vicarage, Portisham, Dorchester Dorset an heraldic tiger passant arg, holding in his dexter fore-paw a cross moline or *Stat fortuna domus virtute*

Molyneux-Seel of Huyton Hey Lancs (1) A wolf's head erased per fesse pean and az (*for Seel*) (2) On a chapeau gu, turned up erm a peacock's tail ppr (*for Molyneux*) *Sat vivere vincere* 303 6

Mompesson, Wilts, a jug or, stringed az, tasselled of the first

Mompesson, Norf a plume of ostrich-feathers arg *Ma foy en Dieu seulement* 115 1

Mompesson of Bathampton, Wilts, a plume of ostrich-feathers arg the centre one sa, all turned over or *Ma foy en Dieu seulement* 115 2

Moncaster, an old man's head affrontee couped at the shoulders ppr, ducally crowned or 192 9

Monck, Duke of Albemarle (*extinct*), on a chapeau gu, turned up erm, a cat a mountain statant gardant per pale sa and arg, between two branches of olive vert *Fortiter fideliter, feliciter*

Monck, Viscount (Monck), Charleville Enniskerry co Wicklow a wyvern with wings elevated sa *Fortiter, fideliter, feliciter* 70 1

Monck, W Berkeley, Esquire, of Coley Park Berks a wyvern arg 70 1

Monck, Monk, or Le Moyne of Potheridge Devonsh, a cockatrice arg 68 4

Monckton, *see* Galway, Viscount

Monckton or Monketon of Cavill, Yorks of Egham Surrey and Lincs a martlet or 95 2

Monckton, Francis Stretton Hall, Stafford same crest *Famam extendere factis*

Monckton, Edward Philip, J P Fineshade Abbey Stamford Northamp, same crest and motto

Monckton, Arthur M A, of Hilton, Salop same crest and motto

Monckton, Hon Horace Manners of Whitecairn, Wellington College Station Berks same crest and motto

Monckton, William Parry, Esquire B A of Stone Court, Glouc, same crest and motto

Monckton, Walter J P, Ightham Park, Kent same crest and motto

Monckton, Mongtown, Monkton, Mongdene, and **Mongton,** two arms in armour embowed placing a Saracen's head affrontee on the point of a pheon, all ppr 94 9

Moncreiff, Baron (Moncreiff), Tulliebole Castle, Ross sh a demi lion rampant gu, armed and langued az *Sur esperance* 10 3

Moncreiff, Sir Alexander K C B, Bandirran Perthsh, a lion's head erased gu *Sur esperance* And **Moncreiffe,** Scotland a demi-lion rampant ppr *Sur esperance* 10 2

Moncreiffe, Sir Robert Drummond, Bart D L., of Moncreiffe, Perthsh a demi-lion gu *Sur esperance* 10 3

Moncrief, Scotland a gillflower ppr *Diligentia cresco* 151 8

Moncrief, Scotland, same crest *Firma spes*

Moncrief, Scotland, a stork's head *Virescit* cf 106 1

Moncrieff, *see* Scott Moncrieff

Moncrieff of France and of Readie and Murnipay, Fifesh Scotland a demi lion rampant gu *Sur esperance* 10 3

Moncrieff of Sauchope Scotland, three ears of rye banded together ppr

Moncrieffe, *see* Stewart Moncrieffe

Moncur, a dexter hand holding a garland of roses ppr 218 6

Money of Walthamstow, Essex a bezant between two wings az, semee de lis or *Factis, non verbis*

Money-Coutts, Francis Burdett Esquire of Stodham Park, Southampton and Ancote, Weybridge, Surrey (1) A man from the middle shooting an arrow from a bow all ppr (*for Coutts*) 187 6 (2) A bezant between two wings az semee-de-lis or (*for Money*) *Esse quam videri*

Money, an eagle's head erased holding in the beak three roses slipped all ppr

Money, Kyrle-, Audley Walter, Esquire, J P D L, of Homme House, Dymock Glouc and Whetham Calne Wilts (1) An eagle's head sa erased arg collared gemelle, and holding in its beak a fleur-de lis or (*for Money*) cf 84 12 (2) On a mount vert a hedgehog or (*for Kyrle*) *Nil moror ictus* cf 135 8

Mongredien of Liverpool on a mount vert, an eagle's head erased or between two palm-branches ppr *Sursum* 84 4

Monhalt, a lion's gamb erased arg, holding an oak-branch ppr, fructed or

Monington, a savage's head in profile ppr

Monins, John Henry Ringwould House Dover a crescent *Mediocria maxima*

Monins, Bart (*extinct*) of Waldershare and Dover, Kent an increscent or *Mediocria maxima* 163 3

Monk, Lieutenant Colonel Charles, of Bombay, out of a mural crown ppr two wings expanded or, each charged with a trefoil slipped vert *Fervor non furor* 238 13

Monk-Bretton, Baron (Dodson), of Conyboro Lewes, Sussex two lions' gambs erased and in saltier gu, entwined by a serpent head to the dexter ppr *Benigno numine enisus* 303 7

Monk, Lingard-, Richard Boughey Monk of Fulshaw Chester (1) A dragon passant per pale gu and arg the wings vairee of the same, supporting with its dexter claw an escutcheon of the second, charged with a lion's head erased of the first (*for Monk*) 247 16 (2) A wolf's head erased sa, charged with an escallop, and holding in the mouth a cross crosslet fitchée both arg (*for Lingard*) *Tout d'en haut — Toujours prest* 247 17

Monk, Charles James, 5 Buckingham Gate a dragon passant

Monkhouse, a church ppr 158 10

Monkhouse of Newcastle-on-Tyne, Northumb, out of a tower ppr masoned sa an arm in armour brandishing in the hand a sword also ppr *Monachus salvabor*

Monks of Idrone Terrace, Blackrock co Dublin out of a mural coronet ppr two dragons' wings displayed or, each charged with a trefoil slipped vert *Fervor non furor*

Monkswell, Baron (Collier), of Monkswell Devonsh, a demi man affrontee ppr holding in the dexter hand an oak-branch slipped and leaved ppr., fructed or, and resting the sinister hand on an escutcheon az., charged with two keys saltirewise or. *Persevere.* 274. 10

Monmouth, a hawk's head erased vert, charged on the neck with a cheveron or, holding in the beak a trefoil of the first.

Monnoux, Beds, a dove holding in the beak an oak-sprig fructed, all ppr. 92. 5

Monnoux, Bart. (*extinct*), of Wotton, Beds, a turtle-dove az., winged or, membered and beaked purp., holding in the beak an oak-stalk vert, fructed or.

Monnyngs, three crescents interlaced arg.

Monnypenny, on a dolphin embowed and bridled Neptune astride, holding with his sinister hand a trident over his shoulder.

Monox, Monnox, or **Monoux** of Walthamstow, Essex, a dove arg., holding in its beak three acorns vert, fructed or.

Monox, Notts, a demi-heron arg., winged gu., holding in the beak a flower or, slipped and leaved vert.

Monro, an eagle's head erased ppr. *Alis et animo.* 83. 2

Monro, Captain David, J.P., D.L., of Allan House, Fearn, Ross-sh., Scotland, an eagle perching ppr. *Dread God.*

Monro, Hector, Esquire, of Edmondsham, Cranborne, Salisbury, an eagle displayed ppr. *Non inferiora.*

Monro, Scotland, an eagle looking to the sun in splendour ppr. *Cœlestia sequor.* 76. 1

Monro of Bearcrofts, Scotland, an eagle perched or. *Non inferiora.*

Monro, Bart., an eagle rising ppr. *Dread God.* 77. 5

Monro, K.B., Scotland, an eagle close ppr. *Dread God.* 76. 2

Monro of Edinburgh, Scotland, an eagle rising, holding in its dexter claw a sword ppr. *Alis et animo.* cf. 77. 10

Monro, an eagle with wings addorsed arg. cf. 76. 11

Monro of Ewell Castle, Surrey, an eagle displayed ppr. *Non inferiora.* 75. 2

Monro of Pitlundie, Scotland, an eagle gazing up at the sun in his splendour ppr. *Non inferiora.* 76. 1

Monro of Craiglockhart, Edinburgh, an eagle rising ppr. *Non inferiora.* 77. 5

Monrose, an eagle rising ppr. 77. 5

Monsell, a lion rampant ppr., holding between its paws a mullet sa. cf. 15. 8

Monsell, *see* Emly, Baron.

Monson, Baron (Monson), Burton Hall, Lincoln, a lion rampant ppr., supporting a column or. *Prest pour mon pays.*

Monson, Rt. Hon. Sir Edmund John, G.C.B., G.C.M.G., of the Embassy, Paris, same crest and motto.

Monson, *see* Oxenbridge, Viscount.

Monson, a lion rampant or, supporting a pillar of the last. *Prest pour mon pays.*

Monson of Preston, three Saracens' heads conjoined in one neck, one each to the dexter and sinister, and one looking upwards. *Pretio prudentia præstat.* cf. 191. 5

Montacute, Earl of Salisbury and **Baron Montacute,** out of a ducal coronet gu., a griffin's head between two wings arg. 67. 1

Montacute, De, a griffin's head gu., between two wings or. 65. 11

Montagu, on a chapeau a leopard passant.

Montagu-Douglas-Scott, Duke of Buccleuch, *see* Buccleuch.

Montagu, *see* Samuel-Montagu.

Montagu, Duke of Manchester, *see* Manchester.

Montagu, Duke and **Earl of Montagu** (*extinct*), a griffin's head couped or, the wings addorsed and beaked sa. *Spectemur agendo.* cf. 69. 11

Montagu, Frederick James Osbaldeston, of Ingmanthorpe Hall, near Wetherby, Yorks, and Melton Mowbray, Doncaster, a griffin's head couped or, beak and wings addorsed sa.

Montagu, *see* Sandwich, Earl of.

Montagu, Earl of Halifax (*extinct*), a griffin's head couped or, beaked, winged, and charged on the neck with a portcullis sa. *Otium cum dignitate.*

Montagu - Stuart - Wortley - Mackenzie, (Earl of Wharncliffe), Rt. Hon. Edward Montagu Stewart Granville, **Viscount Carlton**: (1) An eagle rising from a rock ppr., and in an escroll above the motto *Firma et ardua* (*for Mackenzie*). (2) An eagle's leg erased or, issuant therefrom three ostrich-feathers ppr., charged on the thigh with a fesse chequy az. and arg. (*for Wortley*). (3) A demi-lion rampant gu., and in an escroll above the motto *Nobilis ira* (*for Stuart*). 10. 3. (4) A griffin's head couped or, the wings endorsed and beak sa. (*for Montagu*). *Avito viret honore.* cf. 67. 11

Montagu - Stuart - Wortley - Mackenzie, Major Edward James, C.M.G., of Highcliffe Castle, Hants, same crests and mottoes.

Montagu, Baron (Douglas-Scott-Montagu), of Beaulieu: (1) A griffin's head couped or, beaked and the wings endorsed sa. (*for Montagu*). cf. 67. 11. (2) A stag trippant ppr., attired and ungu. or (*for Scott*). 117. 8. (3) A heart gu., winged and ensigned with an imperial crown or (*for Douglas*). *Spectemur agendo.* 110. 14

Montagu-Pollock, Sir Montagu Frederick, Bart., B.A.: (1) A lion rampant gardant arg., crowned with an Eastern coronet or, holding in his dexter paw in bend an Afghan banner displayed gu., bordered or and vert, the staff broken in two, and in his sinister paw a part of the broken staff, and in an escroll over the same this motto, *Afghanistan.* (2) A boar passant quarterly embattled or and vert, pierced through the sinister shoulder with an arrow ppr., and in an escroll over the same this motto, *Audacter et strenue.* 40. 14. (3) A griffin's head couped, with wings endorsed erminois, collared pean, and in an escroll above this motto, *Spectemur agendo.*

Montagu of Montreal, Canada, a griffin's head couped at the neck or, with wings elevated sa., between two fleur-de-lis of the last.

Montagu, Wilts, a griffin's head couped between two wings expanded or, gorged with a collar arg., charged with three lozenges gu. *Disponendo me, non mutando me.* cf. 67. 7

Montagu, General Horace William, C.B., of 9, Oxford Road, Colchester, same crest.

Montague, Rev. Horatio, a griffin's head couped erminois with wings endorsed and elevated pean, collared of the last. *Spectemur agendo.* cf. 67. 11

Montague, Glouc., a griffin's head or, wings endorsed sa., beaked of the last. cf. 67. 11

Montague, Leopold Agar Denys, Penton Crediton, Devonsh., a griffin's head couped or, beaked sa., wings endorsed of the last. *Spectemur agendo.*

Montaguta, a demi-lion rampant or. 10. 2

Montalt, De, Earl, Viscount Hawarden of Hawarden, co. Tipperary, and **Baron de Montalt** in Ireland (Rt. Hon. Sir Cornwallis Maude), of Dundrum, co. Tipperary, a lion's gamb erased and erect ppr., holding an oak-branch slipped vert, acorned or. *Virtute securus.*

Montalt, a dexter arm embowed throwing a dart ppr. 201. 14

Montchantsey and **Mountchansey,** a hand holding a scimitar in pale ppr. 213. 8

Montchency, in the sea a ship, all ppr. 160. 13

Monteagle, Baron (Spring Rice), of Brandon, co. Kerry: (1) A leopard's face gu., ducally crowned or. (2) A demi-stag saliant ppr. *Fides non timet.* 119. 2

Monteath-Douglas, *see* Douglas.

Monteath, Scotland, a hand holding a dagger in bend. *Dum vivo spero.* 212. 3

Monteath, Lieutenant-Colonel Thomas, out of an Eastern coronet or, the rim charged with three bombs fired, an oak-tree, the stem transfixed by a sword in fesse, the pommel and hilt to the dexter, all ppr. 143. 11

Montefiore, Rev. Durbin Brice, M.A., of Mursley Hall, Winslow, on a mount vert, three fleur-de-lis az., in front of a demi-lion or, holding between the paws a cross moline gu. *Video melioro.* 11. 6

Montefiore-Brice, Arthur John, F.R.G.S., F.G.S., Barrister-at-Law, of Newnham Glouc., and 2, Garden Court, Temple, same crest and motto. 231. 17

Montefiore, Edward Brice Stanley, of Newnham, Glouc., same crest and motto.

Montefiore, late Sir Moses, Bart., (*extinct*): (1) An Eastern crown or, charged with two roses gu. (2) Two mounts of flowers ppr., therefrom issuant a demi-lion or, supporting a flag-staff ppr., thereon hoisted a forked pennon az., inscribed "*Jerusalem*" in Hebrew characters or. *Think and thank.* 283. 9

Montefiore, Sir Francis Abraham, Bart., of Worth Park, Sussex, two mounts of flowers ppr., therefrom issuant a demi-lion or, supporting a flagstaff ppr., thereon hoisted a forked pennon flying towards the sinister az., inscribed "*Jerusalem*" in Hebrew characters or. *Think and thank.* 283. 9

Monteique, issuing out of flames ppr, a crane's head or

Monteith, Scotland an eagle looking at the sun in splendour *Sub sole nihil* 76 1

Monteith, Scotland a hand holding a dagger ppr 212 3

Monteith, Scotland a tree ppr *Viresco* 143 5

Monteith, Scotland a wolf's head holding in the mouth a rose 29 7

Monteith, Scotland a lymphad her oars in saltier ppr, flagged gu, and on a canton arg, a saltire az *Dum vivo spero* cf 160 10

Montesey, a sea lion supporting an anchor all ppr

Montford of Kylnhurst, Yorks, a talbot's head sa, eared or gorged with a ducal coronet of the last

Montgomerie, *see* Eglinton and Winton, Earl of

Montgomerie, *see* Edmonstone Montgomerie

Montgomerie, Scotland a lady holding in her dexter hand an anchor and in her sinister a savage's head *Garde bien* 184 9

Montgomerie-Molineux, Cecil Thomas Garboldisham Hall East Harling a palm branch ppr *Procedamus in pace*

Montgomerie, Admiral John Eglinton, C B of Newfield Kilmarnock Ayrsh, a female figure representing Hope ppr, attired az, holding in her dexter hand an anchor or, and in her sinister, by the hair a human head ppr *Gardez bien*

Montgomerie, Samuel Hynman Esquire J P of Southannan, Fairlie, N B and Aucham Castle, Kilmarnock, N B, a female figure (representing Hope) ppr resting az, holding in the dexter hand an anchor or, and in her sinister by the hair a human head also ppr charged upon the breast with a cross crosslet for difference. *Garde bien*

Montgomerie of Annick Lodge, Ayrsh a female figure ppr, anciently attired az, holding in her dexter hand an anchor or, and in her sinister a savage's head ppr *Gardez bien* 184 9

Montgomerie-Fleming, James Brown, of Kelvinside, Glasgow a goat's head erased arg, armed or *Let the deed shaw*

Montgomery, Major-General George Samuel, C S I, a dexter arm in armour embowed holding a broken tilting spear all ppr *Patriæ infelici fidelis* 167 2

Montgomery, an arm in armour holding, in the hand a broken spear the point falling down *Garde bien* cf 210 9

Montgomery, an arm in armour embowed holding in the hand a dagger 196 5

Montgomery, a cubit arm in armour erect holding in the hand a dagger all ppr

Montgomery, Scotland a cubit arm in armour, holding in the hand a broken spear in bend dexter, the point falling

Montgomery, Bart, Ireland a dexter arm in armour embowed holding in the hand a broken spear, all ppr 197 2

Montgomery of Convoy House, Ireland, an arm in armour embowed, holding in the hand a broken spear, the head dropping, all ppr *Patriæ infelici fidelis* 197 2

Montgomery, a dexter arm in armour embowed ppr, holding a broken tilting-spear in bend sinister, the spear-head pendent *Gardez bien* 197 2

Montgomery, Sir Hugh Conyngham Gaston, Bart, of the Hall co Donegal, on a chapeau gu turned up erm, a cubit arm armed grasping a broken tilting spear ppr *Gardez bien* cf 210 9

Montgomery of Newton, Ayrsh, a dexter hand holding a sword indented at the back like a saw ppr *Fideliter*

Montgomery of Grey Abbey, Downsh on a chapeau an arm in armour erect grasping in the hand a sword

Montgomery, Earl of Mount Alexander, (*extinct*) on a chapeau a dexter gauntlet erect holding a dagger, all ppr

Montgomery, Ireland on a chapeau gu, turned up erm, a dexter gauntlet erect holding a dagger ppr *Honneur sans repos*

Montgomery of Belhaven co Leitrim Ireland a cubit arm erect vested gu cuffed arg, grasping a broken tilting spear, the point falling downwards ppr *Patriæ infelici fidelis*

Montgomery, a dexter arm in armour embowed, the hand grasping a broken spear, all ppr 197 2

Montgomery of Beaulieu co Louth, Ireland an arm in armour embowed the hand grasping a broken spear, the head drooping, all ppr *Patriæ infelici fidelis* 197 2

Montgomery, Scotland a hand holding a branch of palm ppr *Procedamus in pace* 219 11

Montgomery of Broomlands, Ayrsh, Scotland, a branch of palm ppr *Procedamus in pace* 147 3

Montgomery, Norf (1) On a chapeau gu turned up erm, a plume of peacock's feathers ppr (2) A palm branch ppr 147 3

Montgomery, Ireland, out of a ducal coronet or, two laurel branches in orle vert 146 9

Montgomery, Scotland a lady ppr, vested az her dexter hand supporting an anchor, and holding in her sinister a Saracen's head erased held by the hair, both ppr *Garde bien* 184 9

Montgomery, Bart, Scotland a female figure vested az, supporting with her dexter hand an anchor, and in her sinister a Saracen's head couped, all ppr *Gardez bien* 184 9

Montgomery, Graham-, Sir Basil Templer, Bart, M P, of Stanhope, Peeblessh (1) A female figure representing Hope hair dishevelled, richly vested az, the train arg, her dexter hand resting on an anchor, and holding in the sinister a man's head, all ppr (*for Montgomery*) 184 9 (2) An escallop or (*for Graham*) *Garde bien —Spero meliora* 141 12

Montgomery, a merman ppr, holding a target or

Montgomery, a Saracen's head affrontée 190 12

Montgomery, a fleur de-lis or *An I may* 148 2

Montgomery of Milton, Northamp, a hind's head 124 1

Montgomery of Skelmorlie, Ayrsh, Scotland, a heart surmounted of an eye ppr

Montgomery, Scotland, an eagle rising 77 5

Montgomery of Lanishaw Ayrsh, a cock rising ppr *An I may* cf 91 7

Montgomery, a lion couchant arg, semee-de-lis az, gorged with a collar or fimbriated of the second cf 7 5

Monthermer, a griffin's head between two wings ppr 65 11

Monthermer, De, a gem ring or, stoned vert 167 14

Montlaby, a demi fleur de-lis issuing

Montmorency, De, *see* Mountmorres, Viscount

Montmorency, De, *see* Frankfort De Montmorency Viscount

Montmorency, Ireland, on a ducal coronet or a peacock in his pride ppr *Dieu ayde* cf 103 12

Montmorency, France a dog courant ppr *Dieu ayde au premier Baron Chrestien*

Montolieu, a fleur de-lis or, between two wings erect sa *Deo et principi*

Monton, a horse's head or, maned sa cf 50 13

Montpenston, Wilts, three ostrich-feathers, two arg, the centre one sa, all turned over or 115 2

Montresor of Denne Hill Kent, a royal helmet or *Mon trésor*

Montriou, Norf a pheasant ppr cf 90 8

Montrose, Duke of (Graham), a falcon ppr, beaked and armed or, preying on a stork lying on its back, also ppr *N'oubliez* 79 7

Montrose, a spur between two wings 111 13

Monyns of Walwarsher, Kent, an increscent or 163 3

Monypenny, Scotland, a dolphin az, finned gu 140 5

Monypenny, Charlton James Blackwell, J P Kent, and Pitmilly, Fifesh, Scotland Neptune bestriding a dolphin naiant in the sea holding in his dexter hand the reins and in his sinister his trident all ppr *Imperat æquor* 267 2

Monypenny, Gybbon- of Maytham Hall, Ashford, Kent (1) Same crest (2) A demi-lion regardant arg, ducally crowned or

Moodie, a demi-pegasus with wings addorsed, the body enfiled with a ducal coronet 47 7

Moodie of Cocklaw, Fifesh, a pheon *God with us*

Moodie or **Mudie** of Melsetter, in the Orkney Islands, and of the Cape of Good Hope, on a naval coronet a lion passant holding a flag and on an escroll above the words, *The reward of valour*

Moody or **Moodye,** two arms embowed in saltier, the dexter vested gu, the sinister vert, and holding in each hand a cutlass arg, hilted or, the blades saltireways

Moody, Scotland a lion's gamb holding a pennon or, charged with a double-headed eagle displayed sa *The reward of valour* cf 35 12

Moody or **Moodye,** Bart of Baresdon, Wilts, a wolf's head erased ppr 30 8

Moody, J F B. Esquire, of 22, Milverton Crescent, Leamington, a demi pegasus holding in the mouth a trefoil slipped *Verus ad finem* 301 10

Moody of Aspley, Beds, two falchions in saltier ppr., the hilts and pommels or, surmounted by a wolf's head erased per pale arg. and az.

Moon, Rev. Sir Edward Graham, Bart., M.A., of Portman Square, and Rector of Fetcham, Leatherhead, Surrey, a crescent arg., in front of a fasces in bend or, surmounting a sword in bend sinister ppr. *Æquam servare mentem.* 171. 6

Moon, Sir Cecil Ernest, Bart., of Corpsewood Grange, Warw., a demi-eagle displayed gu., in front thereof a fleur-de-lis arg., and charged on the breast with an escutcheon of the last, thereon a crescent, also gu. *Vincit omnia veritas.*

Moone, a bear rampant supporting a staff in pale ppr. 34. 9

Moone, an arm erm., holding a fleur-de-lis or. *cf.* 215. 5

Moor, Berks, a griffin sejant regardant or, winged az., beaked of the first and legged of the last. *Nihil utile quod non honestum.*

Moor, George, Esquire, of Java Lodge, near Wickham Market, Suff., a Moor's head in profile couped at the shoulders. *Moribus antiquis.*

Moor, out of a ducal coronet, a Moor's head between two spears, points upward in bend.

Moor of East Grinsted, Sussex, the bust of a Moorish king ppr., vested gu., wreathed about the temples arg. and vert, on the head an Eastern coronet or, surmounting an anchor in bend sinister. *In Deo confido.*

Moor of Bank Hall, Kirkdale, Lancs, a moorcock arg., guttée-de-poix, membered and wattled gu., holding in the beak a branch of carnation ppr.

Moore, Marquess of Drogheda and **Viscount Moore,** *see* Drogheda.

Moore, *see* Mountcashel, Earl of.

Moore, Kent, a Moor's head in profile ppr., wreathed about the temples or and sa., charged on the neck with a crescent.

Moore, Ireland, out of a ducal coronet or, a Moor's head in profile ppr., wreathed or and az. *Fortis cadere, non cedere potest.* 240. 12

Moore, Kent, out of a ducal coronet or, a Moor's head ppr., wreathed round the head az. and or, a jewel pendent in the ears arg. 240. 12

Moore, Joseph Henry, Esquire, A.I.M., of 63, Eccles Street, Dublin, out of a naval crown, a Moor's head, all ppr. *Dura patientia frango.*

Moore of Tara House, co. Meath, out of a ducal coronet or, a Moor's head in profile ppr., filleted round the temples az. and or, in the ear a jewel pendent arg. *Durum patientia frango.* 240. 12

Moore, a Moor's head couped at the shoulders ppr., wreathed about the head arg. 192. 13

Moore of Moore Hall, co. Mayo, Ireland, a Moor's head and shoulders ppr., in the ear an annulet or. *Fortis cadere, cedere non potest.* *cf.* 192. 13

Moore of Thelwall, Chesh., a Moor's head couped ppr., wearing a cap gu., turned up erm.

Moore, Frederick, the Hollies, Alcester Road, Kingsheath, Worcs., a Moor's head between two wings. *Malo mori quam fœdari.*

Moore, Gordon-, of Mooresfort, co. Tipperary, Ireland: (1) A Moor's head and shoulders in profile ppr., wreathed about the temples arg. and az. (*for Moore*). 192. 13. (2) A stag's head couped ppr., attired or (*for Gordon*). *Audaces fortuna juvat.* 121. 5

Moore, Bart. (*extinct*), of Kersant, Berks, out of a ducal coronet or, a Moor's head ppr., wreathed about the temples arg. and az. *Fortis cadere, cedere non potest.* 240. 12

Moore, William, Esquire, K.C., J.P., of Moore Lodge, Ballymoney, co. Antrim, out of a ducal coronet ppr., charged with an annulet gu., a Moor's head in profile, also ppr., the temples encircled with a wreath arg. and az. *Fortis cadere, cedere non potest.*

Moore, William, Esquire, Moore Fort, co. Antrim, Ireland, same crest and motto.

Moore of Frampton Hall, Lincs, a Moor's head affrontée ppr., wreathed about the temples az. and or, in each ear a jewel pendent arg. *Disce mori mundo.* 192. 4

Moore, Count Arthur John, Kt. Commander of the Order of Gregory the Great, of Mooresfort, co. Tipperary, out of a mural crown ppr., a Moor's head, also ppr., wreathed about the temples arg. and az., and charged on the neck with a rose gu., barbed vert. *Fortis cadere, cedere non potest.*

Moore, Sir Thomas O'Connor, Bart., of Ross Carbery, co. Cork, out of a ducal coronet a Moor's head in profile, all ppr. *Fortis cadere, cedere non potest.*

Moore, Sir John William, of 40, Fitzwilliam Square West, Dublin, out of a ducal crest coronet or, charged with a fleam gu., a Moor's head in profile ppr., wreathed about the temples or and az. *Fortis cadere, cedere non potest.*

Moore of Canterbury, a Moor's head in profile ppr., wreathed about the temples or and sa., and charged on the neck with a crescent for difference. *cf.* 192. 13

Moore, Charles, Esquire, J.P., of Mooresfort, co. Tipperary, out of a mural coronet ppr., a Moor's head, also ppr., wreathed about the temples arg. and az., and charged on the neck with a rose gu., barbed vert. *Fortis cadere, cedere non potest.*

Moore, Edmund F., Esquire, a blackamoor's head in profile ppr., the head encircled with a wreath arg. and az., crowned with an Eastern coronet of six points and with ear-rings or, vested in a white drapery fastened upon the shoulder with a gold buckle. *In Deo confido.*

Moore-Carrick of Corswall, Scotland, a Moor's head in profile couped at the shoulders ppr. *Duris nos frangor.* *cf.* 192. 13

Moore, the late Sir John (killed at Corunna), a Moor's head couped at the neck, the turban ppr.

Moore, a Moor's head couped at the neck, wearing a turban, all ppr.

Moore, Hon. Charles, of Moore Court, Springwood, Blue Mountains, New South Wales, member of the Legislative Council, out of a mural coronet gu., a Moor's head in profile couped at the shoulders ppr., wreathed round the temples or and az., and charged on the neck with a cross crosslet of the third. *Perseverando et cavendo.*

Moore, Walter Montagu, Esquire, J.P., of Wierton, Geraldine, New Zealand. Major South Canterbury Rifle Battalion, New Zealand Volunteers, a Moor's head in profile couped at the shoulders ppr., and round the temples a wreath. 192. 13

Moore, of Stockwell, Surrey, a Moor's head affrontée ppr., wreathed round the temples az. and or, and with a jewel pendent in the ears arg. *Resolve well, persevere.* 192. 4

Moore, a naked man sa., holding in his dexter hand a dart or. *cf.* 186. 9

Moore of Wichford, Hants, a mermaid ppr., crined or, her comb and mirror of the same. 184. 5

Moore - Brabazon, Lieutenant - Colonel John Arthur Henry, of 30, Cranley Gardens, S.W., on a mount vert, a falcon rising, belled or. *Vota vita mea.*

Moore of Appleby Parva, Leics., a moorcock sa., guttée-d'or, wattled and legged gu., the wings expanded, and holding in the beak a branch of heath ppr. *Non civiam ardor.* 89. 5

Moore, George John, Esquire, J.P., D.L., of Appleby, Atherstone, a moorcock sa., guttée-d'or, the beak, comb, wattles, and leg gu., the wings expanded, holding in the beak a branch of heath ppr. *Non civiam ardor.*

Moore, George Henry, Esquire, of Glenmark, Canterbury, New Zealand, *uses:* a moorcock rising. 89. 5

Moore of Ballina, co. Mayo, Ireland, and Alicante, Spain, on a ducal coronet or, a moorcock ppr. *Fortis cadere, cedere non potest.*

Moore of Blandford Forum, Dorset, a staff raguly fesseways or, thereon a moorcock ppr., charged on the breast with a trefoil of the first. *Amore floresco.*

Moore, Bart (*extinct*), of Fawley, Berks, on a tuft of grass vert, a moorcock sa., combed and wattled gu. *Nihil utile quod non honestum.*

Moore of Langley Lodge, Gerard's Cross, Bucks, and Liverpool, on a mount vert, a moorcock sa., holding in the beak a sprig of bramble slipped ppr. *Æquabiliter et diligenter.*

Moore-Gwyn (formerly Moore), Joseph Edward, of Dyffryn, Neath, Glamorgansh., and Abercrave House, Ystradgynlais, Breconsh.: (1) Between two antlers sa., a cubit arm erect ppr., charged with two lozenges palewise, also sa., the hand grasping a sword ppr., pommel and hilt or, the blade transfixing a boar's head erect and erased gu. (*for Gwyn*). 277. 5 (2) Upon a mount vert, a moorcock sa., gorged with a collar nebuly arg., and resting the dexter leg on a greyhound's head erased at the neck, also sa. (*for Moore*). *Vim vi repellere licet.* 277. 6

Moore, on a human heart gu, an eagle's leg erased at the thigh sa 113 14
Moore, Shropsh, an eagle arg preying on a hare sa 79 6
Moore, an eagle preying on a rabbit all ppr 79 6
Moore, Stephen, Esquire, of Barne Clonmel, a goshawk seizing a coney, both ppr *Vis unita fortior* 79 2
Moore, a dove with wings expanded holding in its beak an olive-branch ppr 94 5
Moore, Devonsh., Hants, and Surrey, out of a ducal coronet az, a swan's neck arg, beaked gu
Moore, Joseph Hall Esquire Castleton, Derbysh, via Sheffield a swan arg, with wings elevated barry of six or and az, holding in the beak a flower of the cotton-tree slipped ppr *Mores hoc mutati* 99 14
Moore, William Middleton, Esquire, J P, D L, of Grimeshill, near Kirkby Lonsdale, Westml a swan, wings elevated arg, charged on the breast with a pheon sa, in front of bulrushes ppr *Animum rege*
Moore of Grimeshill, Westml in front of bulrushes ppr, a swan with wings elevated arg, charged on the breast with a pheon sa *Animum rege*
Moore of Newington, Surrey, a demi-bull salient erminois, armed sa cf 45 8
Moore of Ipswich, Suff, a stag trippant sa, platce, attired or cf 117 8
Moore of Grantham Lincs, a lion passant gardant gu, ducally gorged and chained arg cf 4 3
Moore of Northaston, Oxon, a demi lion rampant per pale or and arg., collared and lined sa cf 10. 9
Moore of Sandon and Haddon, Herts and London a demi castle arg, and issuing from the battlements thereof a demi lion rampant gardant or holding a flag staff sa., therefrom flowing a banner of the arms, viz, arg, guttee-de sang two chevronels gu 20 11
Moore of Moorehays, Collumpton, Devonsh, a dexter arm embowed ppr, holding a sword arg 201 4
Moore of Cremorgan Queen's Co, Ireland, a hand lying fesseways couped at the wrist holding a sword erect enfiled with three gory heads, all ppr *Semper fidelis et audax*
Moore or **More** of Balyna, co. Kildare, Ireland a hand lying fesseways couped at the wrist holding a sword erect, enfiled with three gory heads, all ppr *Conlan a bu —Spes mea Deus*
Moore of Roscarberry, co Cork, Ireland a heraldic tiger's head couped arg pierced through the neck with a broken spear
Moore of Bristol and Ireland a heraldic tiger's head erased or, thrust through the neck with a broken spear arg *Fortis cadere, cedere non potest*
Moore, Sir Thomas O'Connor, Bart a heraldic tiger's head couped arg pierced through with a broken spear ppr *Fortis cadere, cedere non potest*
Moores, an eagle rising ppr *Juravi et adjuravi* 77 5
Moorhead, a negro's head sa banded arg
Moorhouse, Yorks, a pelican vulning herself ppr 98 1
Moorman, a hand holding four arrows, points downward cf 214 3
Moorside, a demi dragon vert, holding in the dexter claw an arrow, point downward sa. *Insiste firmater* cf 73 10
Moorsom, on a mount vert a moorcock, in front a banner erect ppr *Ad astra*
Moorton, an eagle preying on a hare ppr 79 2
Mootham, a cubit arm in armour holding in the gauntlet the two ends of a broken spear cf 209 10
Moran of Ballinamore, co Leitrim Ireland (1) Out of a mural coronet a demi-Saracen, the head in profile all ppr (*for Moran*) (2) Out of an ancient Irish crown or, a cubit arm in armour holding a scimitar, all ppr (*for O'Rourke*) *Fides non timet*
Morant, on a ducal coronet a stag's head cabossed cf 122 5
Morant, Edward John Harry Eden of Brockenhurst Park, Hants a dove holding in its beak an olive-branch 92 5
Morant, William George 23, Old Elvet, Durham, same crest *Pax amor fides*
Morant of Great Yarmouth Norf, a lion rampant or, charged on the breast with a cross sa cf 1 13
Morar, London a lion's head erased erm collared bendy or and az 18 6
Moray, Earl of (Stuart), a pelican in her piety ppr *Salus per Christum redemptorem* 98 14
Moray, Home-Drummond-, William Augustus, of Abercairney, Scotland, an earl's coronet surmounted of a star of twelve rays arg *Sans tache —Tanti talem genuere parentes*
Morby, an eagle displayed or 75 2
Morcraft, out of a ducal coronet or a bull's head sa, armed of the first 44 11
Mordaunt, Earl of Peterborough (*extinct*), a blackamoor's head affrontee couped at the shoulders ppr, banded around the temples with a wreath or and gu ribbons of the same *Nec placido contenta quiete est* 192 4
Mordaunt, Sir Osbert L'Estrange, Bart, of Massingham Norf a blackamoor's head in profile couped at the shoulders ppr, banded with a wreath round the temples arg and sa *Ferro comite* 192 13
Morden, Kent, a hawk with wings addorsed arg beaked or, preying on a partridge ppr 77 12
More, Scotland, a Moor's head couped ppr *Major opima ferat*
More, a Moor's head ppr, wreathed arg and sa
More of Kittington, Notts, on a Moor's head in profile ppr, a chapeau gu, turned up erm
More, a Moor's head in profile ppr wreathed or and sa, charged on the neck with a crescent cf 192 13
More, Yorks, a Moor's head and shoulders ppr in the ear a ring or 192 13
More, a Moor's head affrontee sa 192 4
More, on a tower triple-towered or, a Moor's head in profile ppr
More, Yorks a demi-Moor ppr, holding in both hands a sword arg, hilt or reclining over the sinister shoulder
More of Buckhall, Lancs, a moorcock with wings expanded arg, guttée-de-poix, holding in its beak an ear of wheat or cf 89 5
More of London a moorcock arg, guttee-de-poix, beaked and legged gu
More, Bart (*extinct*), of More Hall and Bank Hall, Lancs a partridge with wings expanded holding in its beak a stalk of wheat, all ppr *Comme je fus* 89 11
More, a dove with wings expanded ppr 94 2
More of Linley, Shropsh, an eagle arg, preying on a hare sa 79 6
More (1) Same crest as above (2) Out of a ducal coronet or a swan's head and neck ppr
More, out of a ducal coronet az a swan's head and neck arg, beaked gu
More O Ferrall, Ambrose, Esquire, J P D L., of Balyna House Moyvalley co Kildare, and Glenmonnon Ross-on-Wye, out of a ducal coronet or, a greyhound springing sa
More O Ferrall, Dominic Esquire of Kildangan, Monasterevan, co Kildare, same crest
More O'Ferrall, Edward Gerald, of Lissard, co Longford, same crest
More, Suff, a wolf's head erased sa, gorged with a collar dancettee or cf 30 11
More of Taunton, Somers, and Heytesbury, Wilts, a tiger's head erased arg, pierced through the neck with a broken spear or headed of the first
More, a lion passant regardant gu, ducally gorged and lined arg cf 6 3
More of Broadclist Devonsh a demi-lion rampant gardant az, holding between the paws a garb vert banded gu
More, Devonsh, a hand holding a sword 212 13
More, Devonsh, a naked arm couped above the elbow ppr, wielding a sword arg hilt and pommel or 212 13
More, Bart (*extinct*), of Loseley, Surrey on a ducal coronet an antelope, all arg. cf 126 12
More-Molyneux, William, Esquire, of Loseley Park Surrey (residence St Catherine's House, Guildford) (1) On a cap of maintenance turned up erm, a plume of peacock's feathers ppr (*for Molyneux*) (2) Out of a ducal coronet arg, an antelope passant of the last (*for More*). *Vivere sat vincere*
Moreau, on a wreath of the colours a coronet composed of fleurs de-lis or, therein a dexter arm in armour embowed ppr, holding in the hand a scimitar arg, hilt and pommel or
Morehead, Scotland, two hands couped and conjoined supporting a sword in pale, all ppr *Auxilio Dei* 224. 9
Moreiddig, Wales a boy's head couped at the shoulders ppr, having a snake entwined about the neck vert
Moreland, a ship in full sail ppr 160 13
Mores, a demi lion rampant *Deus nobis quis contra* 10 2
Mores of Coxwell Berks, a Moor's head in profile wreathed round the temples or and az cf 192. 13

Mores, Rowe-, Middx., a Moor's head ppr., wreathed arg. and sa. *Either discard the word, or becomingly adhere to it.* cf. 192. 13

Moresby, Admiral John, of Black Beck, Fareham, Hants, a heraldic antelope rampant gu., gorged with a naval coronet, and therefrom a chain reflexed over the back or, supporting a tilting-spear erect sa. *Je le feray durant ma vie.* 255. 11

Moret, a demi-griffin gu., collared or, supporting an anchor az. 64. 7

Moreton, *see* Ducie, Earl of.

Moreton, Chesh. and Sussex, a wolf's head couped arg. 30. 5

Moreton, Shropsh., a cock's head or, between two wings expanded az.

Moreton, a cock's head or, with wings expanded az., gorged with a fess cottised gu., combed of the last, holding in its beak a trefoil slipped of the third.

Moreton, Shropsh., a cock's head or, charged with six barrulets gu., combed and wattled of the last, between two wings expanded az., holding in his beak a trefoil slipped vert.

Moreton or **Morton,** a demi-moorcock displayed sa., combed and wattled gu. *Perseverando.*

Moreton, Chesh., a greyhound's head couped, collared with a twisted wreath vert. cf. 61. 2

Moreton, John, Esquire, J.P., of Wybaston, Fordhouses, and Moseley Court, Bushbury, Staffs, a buckle the tongue erect gu., between two wings vair. *By perseverance.*

Moreton-Macdonald, John Ronald, of Largie Castle, Tayinloan, a dexter arm from the shoulder holding a dagger in pale ppr. *Semper pugnare paratus.—Pro patria.*

Morewood, Derbysh., two arms in armour embowed ppr., holding a chaplet or.

Morewood of Alfreton Hall, Derbysh.: (1) On a torse arg. and vert, two arms in armour embowed ppr., supporting a chaplet of oak-branches of the second, fructed or (*for Morewood*). (2) A greyhound sejant sa., collared (*for Palmer*). cf. 59. 2

Morewood, Rowland, of Pittsfield, New York, U.S.A., a dexter and sinister arm, armed ppr., supporting a chaplet of oak-branches vert, acorned or.

Morfyn, a blackamoor's head couped at the shoulders ppr., vested paly of six erm. and ermines, pendents in his ears or, wreathed about the temples, and bat's wings to his head sa., expanded on either side. 182. 6

Morgan, Captain Francis George Courthorpe Mansel, Plâs Coed Môr, Llanfairpwll, Anglesea, a demi-lion rampant regardant.

Morgan, *see* Muskerry, Baron.

Morgan, *see* Tredegar, Baron.

Morgan, *see* Grogan-Morgan.

Morgan, Charles Peter, Bryn-yr-Hane, near Mold, Flintsh., a Saracen's head.

Morgan, a reindeer's head caboshed arg. 122. 4

Morgan, Howard Spear, Esquire, J.P., D.L., of Tegfynydd, Llanfalteg, South Wales, a reindeer's head couped arg., collared gu., holding in the mouth a tilting-spear bendways ppr. *Fortitudine et prudentia.* 122. 2

Morgan, a reindeer's head or. cf. 122. 1

Morgan, Wales, a reindeer's head or, attired gu. cf. 122. 1

Morgan, Wales, a reindeer's head caboshed or. 122. 4

Morgan, Captain the Hon. Frederic Courtenay, D.L., M.P., of Ruperra Castle, Newport, Monm., a reindeer's head couped or, attired gu. *Deus nobiscum quis contra nos.* cf. 122. 1

Morgan, Hon. Robert Fitzmaurice Tilson Deane, of Springfield Castle, co. Limerick, Ireland: (1) On a wreath of the colours a reindeer's head caboshed or, charged with a mullet az. for difference (*for Morgan*). cf. 122. 4. (2) Out of a ducal coronet or, a demi-sea-otter ppr. (*for Deane*), and in a scroll above the crests the motto *Honor et virtus. Forti et fideli nihil difficile.*

Morgan, Norf., a reindeer's head sa., attired or, charged on the neck with a mullet. cf. 122. 1

Morgan, Gould-, Bart., Monm.: (1) A reindeer's head couped or, attired gu. (*for Morgan*). cf. 122. 1. (2) An eagle rising ppr., holding in its beak a pine-cone (*for Gould*).

Morgan of Waterford, Ireland, a reindeer's head caboshed or. *Fidus et audax.* 122. 4

Morgan, Hon. Arthur John, of 30, Portman Square, W., and Tredegar Park, Newport, Monm., a reindeer's head couped or.

Morgan of Burnham Norton, Norf., and Chalworth, Surrey, a reindeer's head sa., attired or, and charged on the neck with a mullet. cf. 122. 1

Morgan of Lansore, Monm., a reindeer's head couped or, attired gu. *Y drodde-fodd y orfy.—Vincet qui patitur.* cf. 122. 1

Morgan, Ireland, a stag's head caboshed ppr., attired or. 122. 5

Morgan, Christopher Hird, Esquire, J.P., of Tregfynydd, Llanfalteg R.S.O., Carmarthensh., a stag's head couped arg., collared gu., holding in the mouth a tilting-spear bendways ppr. *Fortitudine et prudentia.*

Morgan of London, a dexter hand ppr., holding a swan's head and neck erased arg. 220. 9

Morgan of Golden Grove, Flintsh., Wales: (1) A Saxon's head ppr. 190. 12. (2) A Cornish chough ppr. *Hheb Dhuw hheb ddim a Dhuw digon.* 107. 14

Morgan, a savage's head affrontée wreathed. cf. 190. 5

Morgan, Shropsh., a spear's head erect arg., imbrued ppr. 174. 12

Morgan, on a mount vert, an oak-tree ppr., fructed or, and in front thereof a wolf passant, also ppr.

Morgan-Richardson, Charles E. D., Esquire, of Noyadd Wilym, Cardigan: (1) Out of a ducal coronet a unicorn's head ppr., horned or (*for Richardson*). 48. 12. (2) A lion rampant sa. (*for Morgan*). 1. 10

Morgan, Frederick, Esquire, J.P., of Glengorm Castle, Argyllsh., and 72, Avenue Road, Regent's Park, London, a sea-horse naiant ppr. *Vive ut semper vivas.* 301. 5

Morgan, a lion rampant sa. 1. 10

Morgan of Biddlesdon Park, Bucks, a demi-lion rampant regardant arg. cf. 16. 5

Morgan, an eagle's head erased. 83. 2

Morgan, out of a ducal coronet two eagles' heads addorsed, all or. cf. 84. 11

Morgan of Mellhouse, Durh., out of a ducal coronet or, a demi-eagle displayed with two heads gu. cf. 82. 3

Morgan of Little Hallingbury, Essex, a demi-eagle displayed or, charged on the body with a fesse wavy sa. cf. 81. 6

Morgan, a griffin segreant. 62. 2

Morgan of South Mapperton, Dorset, a griffin's head erased or, charged with two bends sa. cf. 66. 2

Morgan, Somers., a demi-griffin segreant erased sa. cf. 64. 2

Morgan Sussex, a griffin's head erased ppr. 66. 2

Morgan, Nelson Smith, Esquire, of Henfield, Sussex, a fer-de-moline fesseways sa., thereon a griffin's head erased ppr. cf. 66. 2

Morgan, a dragon's head erased gu., langued az., collared or, between two bars gemel wavy arg. cf. 71. 2

Morgan, Devonsh., and Hanbury and Little Comberton, Worcs., an heraldic tiger sejant sa., crined and tufted or, holding in the dexter paw a battle-axe in pale ppr., headed of the second.

Morgan, Captain W. F. Holroyd, Oak Villa, Charlton Kings, Cheltenham, a leopard's head erased and affrontée. 23. 3

Morgan-Stratford of Swindon Manor, Glouc., and Lubenham Hall, Northamp., a dexter arm embowed, vested arg., the hand grasping a falchion ppr., pommel and hilt or.

Morham, a talbot's head erased sa. 56. 2

Moriarty, *see* Crumpe.

Moriarty, Ireland, an eagle with wings addorsed ppr. cf. 76. 11

Moriarty, on a ducal coronet a griffin sejant, supporting an escutcheon gu. 62. 11

Moriarty, an arm in armour embowed holding a dagger, the blade environed with a serpent. cf. 196. 5

Moriarty, Captain Henry Augustus, C.B., R.N., of 35, Manor Park, Lee, Kent, London, S.E., a dexter arm in armour embowed holding a dagger. *Scandit sublima virtus.*

Morice, a lion's gamb holding a crescent. 39. 15

Morier, a greyhound's head ppr., between two roses slipped and leaved. 61. 11

Morin of Jersey, on a chapeau a dolphin naiant, all ppr. *Fortune le veut.* cf. 140. 5

Moring, a greyhound statant. cf. 60. 2

Moris, Suff., a talbot gu., collared and lined or. cf. 54. 5

Moriskines, a stork or, legged and beaked sa. 105. 11

Morison, *see* Brown-Morison.

Morison, *see* Campbell-Miller-Morison.

Morison, *see* Walker-Morison.

Morison, Lennox James Esquire, M A, of 80, Warwick Square, London S W, three Moor's heads conjoined in one neck ppr, the faces looking dexter, sinister, and upwards *Pretio prudentia præstat* 191 5

Morison, of Touch House Stirling, three Saracens' heads conjoined in one neck ppr, the faces looking upwards and to the dexter and sinister *In Deo confido* cf 191 5

Morison of Prestongrange, Edinburgh three Saracen's heads conjoined in one neck the faces looking upwards and to the dexter and sinister *Pretio prudentia præstat* cf 191 5

Morison, Frederick De Lamarre, Esquire, J P D L, of Mountblairy House, Banff, N B, two hands grasping a dagger *Sunt tria hæc unum*

Morison, Duncan-, of Naughton, Fifesh (1) Three Saracen's heads conjoined in one neck erased and wreathed with laurel ppr, looking upwards and to the dexter and sinister (*for Morison*) cf 191 5 (2) A ship in distress in the sea, all ppr (*for Duncan*) 160 14 (3) An eagle's head erased or (*for Haldane*) *Pretio prudentia præstat* — *Disce pati* —*Suffer* 83 2

Morison, Morrison, or **Morryson,** a pegasus or 47 1

Morison of Standor Herts, of Cadby, Lincs, and Lancs out of a ducal coronet or, an eagle's head between two wings arg 84 3

Morison, Edinburgh, a serpent ppr *Prætio prudentia præstat* 142 4

Morkill, John William, Esquire, J P, of Newfield Hall, Bell Busk Yorks, and Austhorpe Lodge near Leeds a martlet or, between two lilies arg, stalked leaved, and slipped ppr *Be true* 293 7

Morland, an arm couped and embowed holding in the hand three stalks of wheat ppr

Morland, a camel's head erased charged with three bars wavy cf 132 7

Morland of the Court Lodge, Kent, a falcon ppr belled or cf 85 2

Morland, Kent a leopard's face jessant de-lis or, between two wings erm

Morland of Kimble Bucks, and Westminster, a griffin's head with wings addorsed az, semee de lis and of cross crosslets or

Morland, William Courtenay, Lamberhurst Court Lodge, Kent an eagle arg, belled or

Morland, Bernard-, Bart, of Nettleham Lincs (1) A griffin's head with wings addorsed az, semee de lis and of cross crosslets alternately or (*for Morland*) (2) A demi-bear sa muzzled and collared or (*for Bernard*) *Bear and forbear* cf 34 13

Morland, a dove or, holding in the beak an olive branch ppr 92 5

Morland, Benjamin Henry, J P, Sheepstead Abingdon same crest *Olitam fronti præpono*

Morland, a lion's head between two wings arg 19 7

Morleigh, Lancs, a unicorn's head erased or 49 5

Morley, Earl of (Parker) a cubit arm erect couped below the elbow the sleeve az, cuffed and slashed arg, holding in the hand ppr a stag's attire gu *Fideli certa merces* 208 6

Morley of Norwich a wolf sejant sa, maned tufted, collared and lined or 29 3

Morley of East Lavant Sussex out of a ducal coronet a griffin's head between two wings expanded all arg 67 1

Morley, out of a mural coronet a griffin's head between two wings cf 67 1

Morley of Marrick Park Yorks out of a ducal coronet a griffin's head between wings, all arg *S'ils te mordent, mordles* 67 1

Morley, John Esquire, of Hackney, Middx, a demi griffin arg, with wings elevated erm, holding between the claws a leopard's face jessant de-lis sa *Tenax propositi* 65 1

Morley, Rt Hon Arnold, P C, of 7, Stratton Street Piccadilly, W, same crest and motto

Morley, Samuel Hope Esquire J P, D L, of Hall Place, Leigh, Tonbridge same crest and motto

Morley, Henry Clervaux Chaytor, Holden House Southborough, Tunbridge Wells a leopard's face or jessant de lis arg *S'ils te mordent mord les*

Morley of Morley, Lancs and of Glynde Sussex a man in armour ppr garnished or holding in his dexter hand a baton of the last across his body a sash az cf 188 7

Morley of Halstead Essex a demi man ppr habited az holding a pole-axe bendways or, and on his head a steel cap having three feathers gu, or, and az *Nec errat nec cessat*

Morley of Halnaker on a chapeau gu turned up erm, a leopard's face arg jessant de lis or

Morley, a talbot passant regardant ermines, collared or

Morley of Barnes Hants, out of a ducal coronet a demi-talbot all or

Mornell, out of a mural coronet az a dragon's head vomiting flames ppr 72 11

Moro, *see* Phillips

Moroney, co Clare Ireland, a lion rampant arg holding a sceptre or

Morony, Edmund, Esquire, of Odell Ville Ballingarry co Limerick, a lion rampant arg, holding a sceptre or

Morow, out of a ducal coronet an eagle's head between two wings 84 3

Morpeth, Viscount, *see* Carlisle Earl of

Morphew, a crane ppr 105 9

Morphew, a crane statant holding in its beak a serpent

Morphew, a stork ppr 105 11

Morral, Cyrus, of Plas Yolyn, Shropsh, a demi griffin *Norma tuta veritas* 64 2

Morrell, the horns of a bull fixed to the scalp ppr 123 8

Morrell, a harpy arg crined or 189 1

Morrell of Wallingford Berks, a demi lion rampant gardant per pale arg and sa holding in the dexter paw a sprig of three roses gu *Bono animo esto* cf 10 8

Morrell, George Herbert, Esquire, M A of Headington Hill, Oxon, a demi lion rampant guardant per pale arg and sa holding in the dexter paw a branch of three roses gu, seeded or barbed and stalked vert, and resting the sinister on a cross crosslet of the last *Bono animo esto*

Morres, Bart (*extinct*), of Kilkreen co Kilkenny Ireland, a demi lion rampant ppr *Deus nobiscum quis contra nos* 10 2

Morrice, a hawk ppr, belled and jessed or cf 85 2

Morrice, Frederick Launcelot Hamilton Esquire J P, formerly of Bettshanger Kent, on a rest a falcon ppr, beaked and belled or 85 8

Morrice or **Morice** of Chipping Ongar Essex a cock gu beaked, combed and wattled or, environed round the neck by a snake ppr

Morrice, a lion rampant regardant 2 3

Morrice of London, a lion rampant or collared gu holding a pellet

Morrice or **Morris,** a lion rampant or charged on the shoulder with a cross gu cf 1 13

Morris, *see* Pollok-Morris

Morris, the late Rt Hon Sir Michael, **Baron Morris,** P C, of Spieldal co Galway, a Lord of Appeal in Ordinary, on a fasces fesswise ppr a lion's head erased arg, guttée de-sang *Si Deus nobiscum quis contra nos* 285 10

Morris, Sir George, K C B, of 48, Lower Leeson Street, Dublin, same crest and motto

Morris of Coxwell Berks, a Moor's head erased in profile erminois, wreathed arg and az

Morris, His Honour William O'Connor, of Gartnamona Tullamore King's Co, in front of a boy's head affrontee, fasces fesseways ppr *Festina lente*

Morris, Ireland a lion's head erased arg, guttee de sang *Virtute et fortitudine* cf 17 8

Morris, Laurence Burke, the Rectory Thornton in Craven, Leeds same crest *Per medias cædes*

Morris, a demi-lion rampant or holding between the paws a plate cf 11 7

Morris of Barnwood, Glouc, a demi lion rampant or, charged on the shoulder with a cross-fleury sa, and holding in its paws an ear of wheat ppr

Morris of Wanstead, Essex, a lion rampant sa, bezantee, ducally gorged or

Morris, a lion rampant or, charged on the shoulder with a cross gu cf 1 13

Morris, Yorks, a lion rampant regardant or *Marte et mare faventibus* —*Irrupta copula* —*Spectemur agendo* 2 3

Morris of Wingfield House, Bath, Somers a lion rampant or 1 13

Morris, Amherst Henry Gage, Nunburnholme Hayton Yorks, same crest

Morris of Peckham, Surrey, upon a mount vert, a lion rampant or semee of quatrefoils and holding in the dexter paw an annulet gu *Pro rege semper*

Morris, Sir Robert Armine Bart D L, of Clasemont Glamorgansh a lion rampant or, charged on the shoulder with a cross couped gu, within a chain in the form of an arch of the first *Scuto fidei* 286 1

Morris, George Byng, Esquire D L of Dany graig, Porthcawl R S O Glamorgansh same crest and motto

Morris of Ferns, co. Wexford, a demi-lion erased or, guttée-de-sang, langued gu.
Morris, a stag trippant ppr. 117. 8
Morris, a fox's head couped ppr. 33. 4
Morris, a tower in flames ppr. 155. 9
Morris, a castle domed arg.
Morris, a tower or, inflamed gu. 155. 9
Morris, Herbert, the Hurst, Clun R.S.O., Salop, an eagle displayed sa.
Morris, Shropsh., a cock arg. 91. 2
Morris, Shropsh., same crest. *Vivens canam.*
Morris, a cock with a serpent enwrapped round his body, and holding the head in his beak. *cf.* 91. 2
Morris, James, Esquire, of Duke Street, St. James's, upon a saltire or, a moorcock sa. *Moderata durant.*
Morris, Thomas Henry, Esquire, of the Lodge, Halifax, Yorks, an heraldic antelope sejant arg., guttée-de-sang, resting the dexter foot on a sealing-ladder or. *Res non verba quæso.*
Morris of the Hurst, Shropsh., an eagle displayed sa. 75. 2
Morris, a boar's head. *Esto quod esse videris.* 43. 1
Morris, Charles Edward, Wood Eaton Manor, Staffs, same crest and motto.
Morris or **Morech** of Galway, Ireland, a fleur-de-lis or. 148. 2
Morris of Ballybeggan and Castle Morris, co. Kerry, a fleur-de-lis. *L'honnete al agreable.* 148. 2
Morris of Ystradmeuric, Cardigansh., a naked arm erect, holding an open Bible ppr., inscribed with the Welsh word "*Bibl.*" *A Gair Duw yn uchaf.* *cf.* 215. 10
Morris, R. W. T., Esquire, of Nirvana, Ivybridge, a Moor's head affrontée couped below the shoulders, wreathed about the temples. *Festina lente.*
Morrison, three men's faces conjoined in one neck, one affrontée, and the others facing the dexter and sinister. 191. 2
Morrison Richard Fielding, Esquire, of Larkfield, Ballybrack, co. Dublin, Ireland, on a mural coronet gu., an eagle's head and neck between two wings displayed arg., the neck and each wing charged with a fleur-de-lis sa. *Utile et dulce.*
Morrison, Lancs, out of a ducal coronet ppr., an eagle's head and neck between two wings arg. 84. 3
Morrison, a pegasus. 47. 1
Morrison, Ireland, an oak-branch fructed ppr. 151. 3
Morrison, a cubit arm in armour holding in the hand a branch of oak, all ppr.
Morrison, two arms dexter and sinister in fess couped, holding a two-handed sword in pale. 224. 9
Morritt or **Morrit,** a griffin's head erased ppr., holding in its beak a rose gu., barbed and slipped vert.
Morritt, Robert Alexander, Rokeby Park, Barnard Castle, same crest. *Ubi libertas ibi patria.*
Morrogh, co. Limerick, a hand couped at the wrist and erect holding a sword in pale, all ppr. 212. 9
Morrogh, James, Esquire, J.P., of Old Court Doneraile, co. Cork, Ireland, a staff ppr., attached thereto a flag flowing to the dexter az., charged with a harp or, stringed arg. *Virtus invicta.*
Morrogh-Bernard, Edward Joseph Bernard, Esquire, J.P., of Fahagh Court, Faha, Killarney, co. Kerry, a staff ppr., with a flag attached az., charged with a harp or. *Virtus invicta.*
Morryson, a pegasus or. 47. 1
Morse, a lion rampant supporting a plumb-rule. 3. 2
Morse, two battle-axes in saltier, banded with a chaplet of roses ppr. 172. 4
Morse, a battle-axe erect. 172. 3
Morse, Rev. Herbert George, M.A., Trin. Coll., Cantab., late Rector of Littleham, near Bideford, 65, Holland Park, W., a demi-man in complete armour ppr., garnished or, his helmet open and surmounted by a plume of three ostrich-feathers az., on his breast a cross-belt sa., and holding in his dexter hand a halberd ppr. *Deo non armis fido.* 187. 5
Morse, Alfred Herbert, Esquire, of Copdock, Ipswich, same crest and motto.
Morse-Boycott, Frederic Augustus, late of Sennoweville, Bushey, Herts: (1) Issuing from a mural coronet arg., a dexter arm vambraced, the fist clenched ppr., from the little finger pendant by a thong gu., an escutcheon of the first, charged with a fireball ppr. (*for Boycott*). 197. 11. (2) A demi-man in complete armour ppr., garnished or, his helmet open and surmounted by a plume of three ostrich-feathers az., on his breast a cross-belt sa., and holding in his dexter hand a halberd ppr. (*for Morse*). *Deo non armis fido.* 187. 5
Morshead, Cornw., a demi-griffin regardant. *cf.* 64. 3
Morshead, Cornw., a demi-griffin regardant holding between its claws an escutcheon arg.
Morshead, Sir Warwick Charles, Bart., J.P., of Trenant Park, Cornw., a demi-wyvern regardant vert, collared or, supporting an escutcheon az., charged with a bezant. 284. 14
Morshead of Lavethan, Cornw., a demi-dragon regardant vert, debruised by a bendlet sinister wavy and collared or, holding between the claws an escutcheon sa., charged with a bezant.
Morskin of London, a stork or, beaked and legged sa. 105. 11
Morson of London, a lion's head erased per fesse erm. and gu., charged with a pale counterchanged. *cf.* 17. 8
Mort of Astley, Lancs, a phœnix in flames ppr. 82. 2
Mortimer, Baron Mortimer and Earl of March, out of a ducal coronet a plume of feathers. *cf.* 114. 8
Mortimer of London, a torteau between two wings or. 110. 4
Mortimer, Norf., a buck's head quarterly or and gu., attired of the first. 121. 5
Mortimer, Scotland, a buck's head cabossed sa. *Acquirit qui tuetur.* 122. 5
Mortimer of London, a buck's head erased quarterly or and gu. *Press forward.* 121. 2
Mortimer, Charles, Esquire, J.P., of Wigmore, Holmwood, Surrey, a stag's head caboshed ppr. *Virtutum avorum æmulus.*
Mortimer of Fonthill Park, Wilts, a stag's head erased and affrontée ppr., attired or. *Acquirit qui tuetur.* 119. 10
Mortimore, on a chapeau gu., turned up erm., a stag's head. *cf.* 121. 5
Mortinius, a sword in pale enfiled with a ducal coronet, all between two elephants' probosces.
Mortlock, a lion's head erased sa. 17. 8
Mortlock, John George, Esquire, of Melbourn and Meldreth, Cambs, *uses* a lion sejant resting the dexter paw on a fleur-de-lis. *Hic labor hoc opus.* 6. 11
Mortoffe and **Mortoft** of Itringham, Norf., a stag's head erased sa., the nose arg., attired or, gorged with a ducal coronet of the second. *cf.* 121. 2
Morton, Earl of (Douglas), a wild boar ppr. sticking between two clefts of an oak-tree fructed vert, a chain and lock az. holding the clefts together. *Lock sicker.* 40. 4
Morton, Scotland, a lion's gamb erect sa. *A te, pro te.* *cf.* 36. 4
Morton of Erbeck, Heref., an eagle with wings expanded erm. 77. 5
Morton, Edward James, Heathfield, Wolverley, Kidderminster, same crest.
Morton of Morton and Ingleton, Staffs, a cock's head or, between two wings az. *Perseverando.*
Morton, a demi-moorcock with wings displayed sa., combed and wattled gu. *Perseverando.*
Morton, a demi-moorcock displayed sa., combed and wattled gu. *Perseverando.*
Morton of Lechlade, Chesh., a greyhound's head arg., collared vert, rimmed or. 61. 2
Morton, a wolf's head arg. 30. 5
Morton of Belmont, Scotland, a wolf's head couped ppr. *Virtutis præmium.* 30. 5
Morton, Scotland, an oak-tree ppr. *Virtutis præmium.* 143. 5
Morton, Scotland, a tree truncated, leaves sprouting therefrom ppr.
Morton of Croydon, Surrey, and Kent, a goat's head erased arg., armed or. 128. 5
Morton, De, a griffin segreant sa. 62. 2
Morton of Greenock, Scotland, a unicorn's head erased arg., armed, maned, and tufted or. *Perseverando.* 49. 5
Mortymer of Attleburgh, Norf., a buck's head erased quarterly or and gu. 121. 2
Morvile, a cat's head affrontée gu. *cf.* 25. 1
Morwell, a demi-griffin segreant. 64. 2
Moseley of Buildwas, Shropsh., an eagle displayed erm. *Honorate, diligite, timete.* 75. 2
Moseley or **Mosley** of Owsden, Suff., out of a mural coronet chequy arg. and sa., a demi-lion holding in the dexter paw a mill-pick of the first.
Moseley, Lofft-, Henry Capell, Esquire, of Glemham House, Suff.: (1) Out of a mural coronet chequy arg. and sa., a demi-lion or, holding in the dexter paw a pickaxe ppr. (*for Moseley*). (2) A boar's head couped and erect arg., holding in the mouth a cross crosslet fitchée gu., between two branches of oak fructed ppr. (*for Lofft*). *Fide et fortitudine.*
Moseley, William Henry, Leaton Hall, Bobington, Staffs, same crest. *Honorate, diligite, timete.*
Moses, a cock regardant ppr 91. 9.

Moseley, Herbert Richard, Buildwas Park, Shrewsbury, same crest and motto

Mosley, Sir Oswald Bart, D L, of Ancoats, Lancs, an eagle displayed erm. *Mos legem regit* 75 2

Mosley, Arthur Rowland Burnaston, House, Etwall Derbysh same crest and motto

Mosley, Tonman, Esquire D L, of Bangor's Park Bucks same crest and motto

Mosman, Hugh of Aughtefardle a hand couped at the wrist and erect, holding a closed book 215 4

Mosman, same crest *Me meliora manent*

Moss, Edwards-, Sir John Edwards Bart, of Otterspool Aigburth Liverpool (1) Issuing from the battlements of a tower or, charged with a rose gu slipped ppr, a griffin's head erm charged on the neck with a cross patee az (*for Moss*) 68 3 (2) A rock ppr therefrom rising a dove arg holding in its beak an olive branch and surmounted by a rainbow ppr (*for Edwards*). *En la rose je fleurie* 94 7

Moss, Horace Edward, Esquire J P, of Middleton, Gorebridge, Midlothian, a dove holding in his beak a sprig of olive ppr *Peace with power*

Moss or Mosse, out of a mural coronet or a griffin's head erm, charged on the neck with a crescent. cf 67 10

Moss, John Snow, Esquire, of Wintershill Hall, Bishop's Waltham, Hants, and Deane House, Sparsholl, Hants, out of a mural coronet a griffin's head charged with a cross patée *In hoc signo vinces*

Moss, Mark, Esquire, of Rosebank, Melbourne, Victoria Australia upon the trunk of a tree fesseways eradicated and sprouting to the dexter ppr, a griffin's head erased sa, charged with two mullets of six points paleways or *Non nobis solum*

Moss, Saul Esquire of Kingston Jamaica, a demi sea-horse ppr collared vair, resting the sinister foot on an escutcheon arg, charged with a pine-apple ppr *Non nobis solum* 46 10

Mosse of Horton Regis Beds out of a mural coronet or a griffin's head erm, charged on the neck with a bezant cf 67 10

Mossman of Auchtyfardell, Lanarksh, Scotland, a hand couped at the wrist erect, holding a book, all ppr *Me meliora manent* 215 4

Mossop, S S, Esquire, Coly House, Long Sutton, Lincs, on a mount a stag lodged *Rem attente*

Moston, a lion's head gu 21 1

Mostyn, *see* Vaux Baron

Mostyn, Baron (Lloyd Mostyn), of Mostyn, Flintsh a stag trippant ppr, charged on the shoulder with an escutcheon gu, thereon a chevron erm, between three men's heads in profile ppr *Heb Dduw heb ddym a Duw a dygon.*

Mostyn-Champneys, *see* Champneys

Mostyn, Sir Pyers Bart, of Talacre Flintsh (1) On a mount vert, a lion rampant or 240 2 (2) A trefoil slipped vert *Auxilium meum a Domine* 240 3

Motham of Dinkston, Suff, on a mount vert, a talbot couchant erm cf 54 11

Motherwell, Scotland, a crescent or 163 2

Motion, Andrew Richard, Esquire, J P, of Faulkbourne Hall, Essex and Upton House Banbury, a mill-rind fesseways or, thereon a badger statant ppr *Sus cipere et finire* 253 7

Motion, Thomas Augustus, Esquire of Chadshuot, Warw, same crest and motto

Mott, a griffin's head erased between two fleurs-de-lis cf 66 2

Mott, Suff and Essex, an étoile of eight points arg cf 164 4

Mott, John Stanley, Esquire, J P of Barningham Hall, Norf an estoile of eight points arg *Spectemur agendo* cf 164 4

Mott, William Henry, Esquire, of Kilving ton Hall Thirsk, an estoile or, surmounted by a rainbow ppr

Mottershed, the stump of a tree ppr, with a branch sprouting vert

Motteux, Norf, a lion passant gardant to the sinister gu, ducally crowned or *Quid vult valde vult*

Motton, a stag statant ppr, vulned by an arrow of the same 117 10

Mouat, a lion passant gardant ppr 4 3

Moubray and Mubray of Barnbougle, Scotland, a demi-lion rampant gu *Fortitudine* 10 3

Moubray, William Henry Hallowell, of Cockairoy, Fifesh, Scotland, a demi lion rampant arg *Fortitudine.—Let the deed shaw* 10 2

Moubray, John James Esquire, of Naemoor Perthsh N B a demi lion rampant holding in his dexter paw a rose arg *Audentes fortuna juvat*

Moubray, Scotland, a heron's head and neck issuing *Let the deed shaw* 104 5

Moubray or Mowbray, a falcon rising belled *Sola nobilitat virtus* 88 2

Moubray, Scotland, a man's head affrontee *Audentes fortuna juvat* 190 12

Moubray, the figure of Fortune holding in her dexter hand an escroll with the motto "*Suivez moi,*" and in her sinister a cornucopia all ppr

Mouchet, a dexter arm in armour embowed the hand holding a sword in bend dexter, the point downwards, ppr, hilt and pommel or 195 4

Moul or Moule, Northamp a lion rampant supporting a broad arrow, point downwards, ppr

Mould, Yorks, a demi lion rampant gardant or 10 8

Moulden of Stalenborough House Kent, a griffin's head erased 66 2

Moule, a lion rampant supporting a broad arrow point downwards ppr

Moule, Beds, issuing out of clouds ppr a cubit arm vested gu, cuffed arg, the hand apaumée and erect, also gu

Mouliin-Browne, Du, *see* Browne

Moulson, an elephant arg, lifting with its proboscis a branch of laurel ppr

Moulson, a lion's head erased per pale embattled or and sa. 17 8

Moult, a fish naiant az, spotted or cf 139 13

Moult, Notts on a mound or, a pelican with wings expanded arg beaked and legged sa, vulning herself gu

Moulton, a shark's head regardant, issuing swallowing a blackamoor 139 2

Moulton, a griffin segreant regardant

Moulton of London a griffin passant per pale gu and az, resting the dexter claw on a mullet or cf 63 2

Moulton of Plympton Devonsh, a cubit arm erect vested gu cuffed erm, holding in the hand ppr a chaplet of roses of the first leaved vert

Moulton, John, J P, the Hall, Bradford on Avon, same crest. *Virtute non astutia*

Moultrie, Scotland, a mermaid ppr *Nunquam non fidelis* 184 5

Moultrie of Aston Hall, Shropsh, same crest and motto

Mounehense, out of a ducal coronet a phœnix in flames 82 5

Mounsey, an arm in armour holding a sword 210 2

Mounsey of Castletown Carlisle, Cumb a demi griffin gu, collared and chained or, holding in the dexter claw a flag staff in bend ppr therefrom flowing to the sinister a pennon az and resting the sinister claw on a mullet sa *Semper paratus* 65 6

Mounsey-Heysham, George William, J P D L, of Castletown Carlisle, and 15, Stanhope Gardens, S W, a demi griffin gu, collared and chained or holding in the dexter claw a flagstaff in bend ppr, therefrom flowing to the sinister a pennon az., and resting the sinister claw on a mullet sa *Semper paratus*

Mounsher, a man's head in profile ppr

Mount, a demi-man in armour brandishing a scimitar ppr 187 1

Mount, Kent a fox salient supporting the trunk of a tree raguled, all ppr

Mount-Stephen, Baron (Rt Hon Sir George Stephen), of Mount Stephen B C, Canada, a horse's head erased arg bridled ppr, holding in his mouth a sprig of three maple-leaves vert, and charged on the neck with a fleur-de lis az *Contra audentior*

Mountain or Montaigne of the Heath Herts a demi lion rampant gardant per fesse wavy arg and sa, supporting between the paws an escallop gu, charged on the breast with a cross crosslet fitchee of the second *Cum cruce salus* 13 7

Mountaine of Westminster Middx, a stork's head issuing out of rays or

Mountaney, a wolf sejant. 29 3

Mountaney, a wolf sejant, collared and lined, the line reflexed over the back ending in a ring

Mountcashell, Earl of, Viscount Mountcashell, co Tipperary and **Baron Kilworth,** of Moore Park co Cork in Ireland (Rt Hon Charles William More-Smyth, D L) a goshawk with wings addorsed preying on a coney all ppr *Vis unita fortior* 79 6

Mountchansey, a hand holding a scimitar in pale ppr 213 8

Mount-Charles, Earl of, *see* Conyngham, Marquess

Mount-Edgcumbe (Edgcumbe), a boar statant arg, gorged with a wreath of oak leaves ppr fructed or *Au plaisir fort de Dieu* cf 40 6

Mount-Somerby: (1) A fox salient sa. (*for Mount*). (2) A dexter arm embowed in armour, holding in the hand a double-barbed rod in bend sinister (*for Somerby*). *In utroque fidelis.*

Mountford, Scotland, a talbot's head. 56. 12

Mountford of Kelnhurst, Yorks, a talbot's head sa., ducally gorged and eared or.

Mountford and **Mountfort,** of Fuwell, Norf., a fleur-de-lis gu. 148. 2

Mountford, Frederick George, Esquire, of 21, Gloucester Terrace, Hyde Park, London, W., in front of two ostrich-feathers in saltire arg., a fleur-de-lis az. *Quod Deus vult volo.* 148. 5

Mountford of Radwinter, Staffs, and Warw., a lion's head couped az. 21. 1

Mountgarret, Viscount (Butler), out of a ducal coronet or, a plume of five ostrich-feathers arg., therefrom a falcon rising of the last. *Depressus extollor.* 282. 8

Mountjoy, a demi-sportsman firing his piece ppr. 187. 2

Mountmorres, Viscount (de Montmorency), a peacock in his pride ppr. *Dieu ayde.* 103. 12

Mountmorris, Earl of (Annesley), a Moor's head in profile couped ppr., wreathed arg. and az. *Virtutis amore.* cf. 192. 13

Mountney, Norf., Essex, and Leics., a wolf sejant arg., collared and lined gu. cf. 29. 3

Mountney, Leics., a greyhound sejant collared and lined. cf. 59. 2

Mountstephen, Baron, see Mount-Stephen.

Mountstephen, a demi-griffin salient with wings addorsed sa. 64. 2

Mountsteven, a demi-griffin salient with wings addorsed sa., armed or. 64. 2

Mountstuart, Baron, see Bute, Marquess of.

Mount Temple, Baron, see Temple.

Mount Temple, Baron (*extinct*; Rt. Hon. the late William Francis Cowper-Temple): (1) A talbot sa., collared or (*for Temple*). 54. 2. (2) A lion's gamb erect and erased or, holding a cherry-branch fructed ppr. (*for Cowper*). *Tuum est.* cf. 37. 4

Mourant, James, Esquire, Gloucester House, Guernsey, a dove holding in its beak an olive-branch, all ppr. *Je ne vis qu'en mourant.*

Mourant, —, 6, Rozel Terrace, Guernsey, a dove holding in the beak an olive-branch, all ppr. *Je ne vis qu'en mourant.*

Mousell, a wolf salient sa. *Mos legem regit.* cf. 28. 1

Mouthwey, a Doric pillar entwined with ivy, and on the top a flame of fire, all ppr.

Moutray, Rev. John Maxwell, M.A., LL.D., of Richmount Glebe, Ballygawley, co. Tyrone, a mermaid. *Nunquam non fidelis.*

Moutrie, Scotland, a talbot's head arg. *Nunquam non fidelis.* 56. 12

Moutry of Seafield and Rescobie, Fifesh., a mermaid ppr. *Nunquam non fidelis.* 184. 5

Mow of that ilk, Scotland, a phœnix in flames ppr. *Post funera fœnus.* 82. 2

Mowat, Bart., of Inglistoun, Scotland, an oak-tree growing out of a rock ppr. *Monte alto.* cf. 143. 14

Mowat, the battlement of a castle or, issuant therefrom a demi-warrior armed and accoutred ppr., holding in his dexter hand a sword, also ppr., hilted and pommelled or, and in his sinister a flagstaff, thereon twisted a banner vert, fringed and charged with an antique crown or. *Monte alto.—Commit thy work to God.*

Mowatt, a demi-lion or. 10. 2

Mowbray, Segrave and Stourton, Baron (Stourton), Allerton Park, Knaresboro, a demi-greyfriar habited in russet ppr., girt or, holding in the dexter hand a scourge of five knotted lashes gold. *Loyal je serai durant ma vie.* 231. 3

Mowbray, Sir Robert Gray Cornish, Bart., M.P., of Mortimer, Berks, and Bishopwearmouth, co. Durham: (1) An oak-tree or, therefrom pendant an escutcheon gu., charged with a lion's head erased arg., the tree charged with a cross crosslet for distinction (*for Mowbray*). 280. 5. (2) Between two branches of laurel in saltire a Cornish chough rising ppr., charged on the breast with a cross patée or (*for Cornish*). *Suo stat robore virtus.—Deus pascit corvos.* 280. 6

Mowbray, on a chapeau gu., turned up erm., a lion passant arg., between the attires of a stag or.

Mowbray of Grangewood House, Leics., an oak-tree ppr., pendent therefrom an escutcheon gu., charged with a lion's head erased. *Suo stat robore virtus.*

Mowbray, Northumb., a mulberry-tree or. 143. 1

Mowbray, a dexter naked arm erect holding a saw.

Mowbray, De, a hand holding a scimitar. 213. 5

Mowbray, De, a fox current ppr. cf. 32. 8

Mowbray, Scotland, a female's head affrontée ppr. *Audentes fortuna juvat.* 182. 3

Mower, a dove holding in its beak an olive-branch, all ppr. 92. 5

Mowles, out of a ducal coronet a demi-savage ppr.

Mowne, Devonsh., two arms in armour embowed ppr., supporting a ball sa. 194. 11

Moxon, a demi-eagle displayed az. 81. 6

Moyes of Canons, Surrey, a dove arg., holding in its beak a laurel-sprig vert. 92. 5

Moyle, of St. Austel, Cornw., two demi-dragons addorsed, their necks entwined round each other, the dexter gu., the sinister arg.

Moyle, a wyvern with wings expanded gu., platée. cf. 70. 8

Moyle of Bowerhall and Lymby, Notts, two demi-dragons addorsed with their necks entwined, the dexter gu., the sinister or.

Moyne of Charter House, Hinton, and Mendip, Somers., out of a ducal coronet a tiger's head. 27. 3

Moynes, Hunts, a lion rampant holding in its dexter paw a battle-axe, all ppr.

Moynley, a hind's head couped. 124. 1

Moyse, a leopard rampant ppr.

Moyser of Farlington, Yorks, a demi-horse rampant erminois, bridled or. cf. 53. 3

Moysey of Henton, Somers., a dragon's head vert, charged on the neck with a cross flory or. cf. 71. 1

Moysey, Rev. Frederick Luttrell, Bathealton Court, Wiveliscombe, Somers. same crest.

Muchell, a camel's head ducally gorged. cf. 132. 9

Muckle, Scotland, a lion passant gu. 6. 2

Muckleston of Marrington, Shropsh., a greyhound's head erased arg., collared gu. *Fideliter.* cf. 61. 2

Mucklewaite, a griffin's head erased ppr. 66. 2

Mucklow of Broughton Sulney, Notts, a griffin's head couped per pale indented arg., guttée-de-larmes and gu., holding in the beak an eagle's leg erased à la quise or. 226. 14

Mucklowe, a griffin's head per pale indented arg. and gu., guttée counter-changed, holding in its beak a buck's leg erased at the knee of the first.

Mudge, a pheon arg. 174. 11

Mudge of Sidney, Devonsh., a cockatrice gu. *All's well.* 68. 4

Mudge, Arthur Thomas, Sydney, Plympton: (1) A cockatrice sa. (2) A phœnix in flames ppr. *All's well.*

Mudie of Arbeckie, Scotland, a pheon arg. *Defensio non offensio.* 174. 11

Mudie of Pitmuies, Forfarsh., same crest and motto.

Mudie, a ship in full sail or. 160. 13

Mueller, see Von Mueller.

Muggeridge, Henry, Esquire, of Streatham, Surrey, upon a mount vert, a buck's head erased ppr., charged with two chevronels az., between four stalks of oats in full grain, two on either side. *Dat Deus incrementum.*

Muhant, a Bourchier knot sa.

Muilman of Debden Hall, Essex, and London, a mullet of six points or, between two wings arg. 112. 1

Muir, Sir John, Bart., a Saracen's head couped, wreathed with laurel ppr., charged on the neck with a mullet az. *Duris non frangor.*

Muir, Scotland, a Moor's head in profile couped at the neck ppr. *Duris non frangor.* cf. 192. 13

Muir, John Gardiner, Esquire, of Farmingwoods Hall, Thrapston, Northamp., a Saracen's head wreathed with laurel ppr. *Duris non frangor.* cf. 190. 7

Muir, Sir William, K.C.S.I., D.C.L., LL.D., Dean Park House, Edinburgh, a Saracen's head affrontée couped at the shoulders and wreathed about the temples with laurel ppr. *Duris non frangor.*

Muir, Scotland, a savage's head couped ppr. *Durum patientia frango.* 190. 12

Muire or **Mure,** Scotland, a dexter hand issuing holding a sword, all ppr. *Help at hand, brother.* 212. 13

Muirhead of Lauchop, two hands conjoined supporting a sword in pale ppr. *Auxilio Dei.* 224. 9

Muirhead, Lionel Bolton Campbell Lockhart, of Haseley Court, Wallingford, Oxon., two hands grasping a two-handed sword, and on an escrol above, *Auxilio Dei.*

Muirhead, Du Vernet-Grossett-, of Bredisholm, a demi-unicorn rampant arg. *Pro patria auxilio Dei.* 48. 7

Muir-Mackenzie, Sir Alexander, Bart D L, of Delvine, Perthsh (1) A palm-branch in bend dexter surmounted of a sword in bend sinister all ppr (*for Muir*) (2) A dexter hand grasping a dart ppr (*for Mackenzie*) *In utrumque paratus*—*Recte ad ardua* 214 4

Muirside, an oak tree ppr *Insiste firmiter* 143 5

Mulbery and **Mulbury**, a lion passant sa holding a crescent or 5 6

Mulcaster of Barham Kent a lion rampant erminois, holding in the dexter fore-paw a sword erect, the dexter hind paw resting on a bomb fired ppr

Mulcaster, Surrey and of Carlisle Cumb, a lion rampant az, ducally gorged or holding a sword erect arg hilt and pommel of the second, the point embrued gu

Mulcaster, Richard Laversdale, Cumb, same crest

Mulchinock of Clogher's House, co Kerry, Ireland, a stag's head erased ppr, charged with a trefoil slipped or and holding in the mouth an olive branch also ppr *Itur ad astra* cf 121 8

Mules of Honiton, Devonsh, and Somers a mule ppr *Misericordia temperet gladium* cf 125 7

Mulgrave, Earl of, *see* Normanby, Marquess of

Mulhall, Ireland and France on an ancient Irish crown or a dexter hand couped at the wrist lying fesseways, holding a sword erect impaling three gory heads, all ppr

Mulholland of Springvale, co Down, an escallop gu *Semper præcinctus* 141 14

Mulledy of Robertstown, co Meath, Ireland on a ducal coronet or, a greyhound current sa cf 58 2

Muller, a swan ppr 99 2

Mullins of Preshute House, Marlborough Wilts an eagle's head between two wings elevated *Mea gloria fides*

Mullins, George Lane Esquire M A M D, of Murong Waverley near Sydney in front of a cross moline or a Saracen's head affrontee couped at the shoulder ppr, wreathed round the temples arg and gu *Ne cede malis*

Mullins, John Francis Lane, Esquire M A of Killountan, Potts Point Sydney New South Wales, same crest and motto

Mullins, Thomas Lane, of Sydney, same crest and motto

Mulloy, Ireland in front of an oak-tree a greyhound courant, all ppr ducally gorged or *Malo mori quam fœdari* cf 58 5

Mulock, Thomas Esquire, J P, of Kilgarna, Athlone a lion passant, in the dexter claw a cross moline *Virtute et fide*

Mulock, Homan-, a lion passant az, holding in the dexter paw a cross crosslet fitchee gu *In hoc signo vinces* cf 6 2

Mulsho or **Mulshoe** of Gothurst, Bucks, a griffin sejant with wings addorsed gu, armed or 62 10

Multon, a savage's head couped wreathed with laurel ppr cf 190 7

Multram, Ireland, a griffin segreant gu, holding in the sinister claw a sword in pale

Mulvihill of Knockanira, co Clare a dexter cubit arm in pale grasping two battle axes in saltire all ppr the blades outwards *Pro aris et focis* 213 10

Mumbee of Bristol, a Peruvian chief affrontee, on his head a plume of five ostrich-feathers, with beads round his neck, all ppr *Faut être*

Mumby, Lincs, on a ducal coronet a lion sejant all ppr cf 8 8

Mumford, a demi-cat rampant gardant ppr 26 12

Mun of Hackney Middx, and Essex a cubit arm in armour ppr, holding a lion's gamb erased gu

Munby, Arthur Joseph, M A, 6, Figtree Court, Temple and Pyrford, Surrey, a dexter arm in armour embowed. the hand grasping a battle axe all ppr *Virtus tutamen suum*

Muncaster, Baron (Pennington), a cata mountain passant gardant ppr *Vincit amore patriæ* cf 26 4

Munday, a leopard's head erased sa flames issuing from the mouth

Munday or **Mundy**, a wolf's head sa 30 5

Munday or **Mundey**, Francis Noel of Markeaton and Shipley Hall Derbysh, a wolf's head erased sa, bezantee, vomiting flames ppr *Deus providebit* 30 1

Mundell, Scotland, an arm in armour embowed striking with a dagger ppr *Strike* 196 5

Mundell, Scotland, a globe fractured ppr *Impavidum ferient ruinæ* cf 159 2

Munden of Chelsea Middx on a naval coronet or, a leopard's head sa, bezantee

Munds and **Muns**, a cubit arm in armour erect ppr, grasping in the hand a lion's gamb erased or

Mundy, *see* Massingberd Mundy

Mundy, Derbysh, a wolf's head erased sa, bezantee, flames of fire issuing from the mouth ppr 30 1

Mundy, Alfred Edward Miller, of Shipley Hall, Derbysh, same crest

Munn, Scotland, a lion's head erased arg 17 8

Munn, a lion's head erased erm 17 8

Munro, an eagle close ppr *Dread God* 76 2

Munro, Scotland, an eagle rising ppr *Dread God* 77 5

Munro, on a mural coronet arg an eagle close or cf 76 2

Munro, Gun-, of Poyntzfield Cromartysh Scotland an eagle rising ppr *Dread God* 77 5

Munro, Sir Hector, Bart, D L, of Foulis Ross-sh, an eagle perching ppr *Dread God.* 76 2

Munro, Sir Campbell, Bart, D L, of 27, Eaton Place, S W an eagle close ppr, having a representation of a silver medal presented by the Hon E I Company to the first Baronet for his services at the assault and capture of Seringapatam pendent from its neck by a ribbon gu the dexter claw resting on an escutcheon, also gu charged with a representation upon a mount vert of an Indian hill fort, and beneath in letters of gold the word *Badamy*, and holding in the beak a sprig of laurel *Dread God* 283 1

Munro-Ferguson, Ronald Craufurd Esquire M P, of Raith, Kirkcaldy, N B, and Novar Evanton, Ross-sh a demi-lion holding between his paws a buckle gu *Virtutis fortuna comes*

Munster, Earl of (FitzClarence) on a chapeau gu, turned up erm a lion statant gardant crowned with a ducal coronet or, and gorged with a collar az charged with three anchors or *Nec temere, nec timide* cf 4 2

Munt, a savage's head couped distilling drops of blood ppr 190 11

Munt of Cheshunt, Herts a bear's head couped arg, muzzled gu, within a chain in arch or cf 34 14

Munton, a cannon mounted ppr 169 12

Muntz, Sir Philip Albert, Bart Dunsmore, near Rugby in front of a demi swan wings expanded arg, semee of trefoils slipped vert, a staff raguly fessewise or 230 7

Muntz, Frederick Ernest of Umberslade Warw in front of a demi swan with wings extended ppr semee of trefoils slipped vert, a staff raguly fessewise or *Fortiter sed suaviter* 230 7

Munyard, Joseph Esquire, of Camden Town Middx a mount vert, issuant therefrom in front of a banch of oak in bend sinister ppr a demi lion erm holding in the dexter paw a sinister hand erased also ppr, the sinister paw resting on a fleur de-lis gu 13 4

Murchison of Tarradale, Ross-sh, a dexter hand holding a ducal coronet of three leaves ppr *Impavido pectore*

Murden, a leopard rampant gardant ppr

Murdoch, a sword in pale enfiled with a savage's head couped ppr 191 9

Murdoch of Rosshall Renfrewsh, Scotland, a lion's head erased gu *Omni secundo* 17 2

Murdoch, of Gartincaber Perthsh, a raven rising transfixed by an arrow, all ppr *Omnia pro bono* 107 11

Murdock, Charles Townshend, Esquire, J P D L of Buckhurst, Wokingham 1 Pall Mall East and 12 Cadogan Gardens a raven flying transfixed by an arrow *Omnia pro bono*

Murdock, Scotland, a raven rising sa, shot through the breast by an arrow gu, headed and feathered arg *Omnia pro bono* 107 11

Murdock, a raven issuing regardant holding in the dexter claw a sword in pale

Mure, Scotland, a Moor's head in profile, wreathed with a garland ppr *Duris non frangor* cf 192 13

Mure, Scotland, a savage's head from the shoulders wreathed with laurel ppr *Duris non frangor*

Mure, William of Caldwell, Ayrsh a Saracen's head ppr *Duris non frangor* 190 14

Mure of Herringswell House, Suff, same crest and motto 190 14

Mure of Riccartoun, Scotland, a Saracen's head and neck from the shoulders wreathed round the temples with palm ppr *Duris non frangor* cf 190 5

Murehead, two hands ppr. issuing and grasping a two-handed sword in pale az., hilted and pommelled or. *Auxilio Dei.* 213. 1

Muriell, a lion passant gardant, the tail extended ppr. *cf.* 4. 3

Muriell, a demi-cat per pale arg. and sa., holding in the claws a branch of roses of the first leaved ppr., gorged with a fess counterchanged. 260. 1

Murphy, O'Murphy, O'Murroughoue, and **Mac Murroughoue,** a demi-lion rampant gu., holding between his paws a garb or. *Fortis et hospitalis.* 12. 5

Murphy, Arthur Mac Morogh, Esquire, of Oulartleigh, co. Wexford, Ireland, on a chapeau gu., turned up erm., a lion rampant, also gu., holding between the paws a garb or. *Vincere vel mori.—Fortis et hospitalis.*

Murphy, William, Esquire, of Kilbrew, co. Meath, and of Upper Mount Street, Dublin, on a mount vert, a lion rampant gu., bezantée, holding in the fore-paws a garb or.

Murphy, William Brudenell, Esquire, of Mount Merrion, Stillorgan, co. Dublin, same crest. *Fortis et hospitalis.*

Murphy, Ireland, a lion rampant gu., holding between its paws a garb or.

Murphy, Edward, of Montreal, Canada, a lion rampant gu., holding in the dexter paw a garb or. *Fortis et hospitalis.*

Murphy, a lion rampant gu., holding in the dexter paw a garb or.

Murphy, Scotland, a hawk's head or. *cf.* 88. 12

Murphy-Eastwood, Major Francis, a boar passant az., charged with a castle arg., and holding in the mouth an oak-branch ppr. *Oriens sylva.*

Murrant of London, a Moor's head ppr., wreathed round the head arg. and gu., between two dragon's wings or.

Murray, Duke of Atholl, *see* Atholl.

Murray, Earl of Dunmore, *see* Dunmore.

Murray, *see* Minto, Earl of.

Murray, Earl of Annandale, an angel ppr. *Noctesque diesque præsto.* 184. 12

Murray, Earl of Mansfield, *see* Mansfield.

Murray, Lord Elibank, *see* Elibank.

Murray, Baron Glenlyon, *see* Glenlyon.

Murray, His Honour Charles Edward Robertson, of New South Wales District Court Judge, a demi-man wreathed about the middle with oak-leaves ppr., winding a horn or. *Superna venabor.*

Murray, John Forbes Pringle Nesbitt, Esquire, J.P., a demi-man winding his horn. *Hinc usque superna venabor.*

Murray, Archibald Charles Philip, same crest and motto.

Murray, Scott-, Charles Aloysius, Manor House, Hambleden, Henley-on-Thames, same crest and motto.

Murray, Alexander Sutherland, Esquire, of Dunrobin, Casterton, Victoria, formerly of Caius College, Cambridge, a demi-savage holding in his dexter hand a dagger ppr., pommel and hilt or, and in his sinister a key of the last. *Furth fortune and fill the fetters.* 186. 2

Murray, Scotland, a demi-man wreathed about the head and loins vert, holding in his dexter hand a dagger arg., hilt and pommel or, and in his sinister a key ppr. *Furth fortune.* 186. 2

Murray, a demi-man couped at the thighs ppr., wreathed about the head and loins vert, holding in the dexter hand a sword, and in the sinister a key, all ppr. 186. 2

Murray-Aynsley, Charles Edward Murray, Esquire, of Sauta Coupa, Mercara, Coorg, India, a man in armour, holding in the dexter hand a sword erect ppr., pommel and hilt or, and in the sinister in front of his breast a shield gu., charged with a bend arg., thereon three mullets of six points or. *Furth fortune and fill the fetters.*

Murray-Aynsley, Hugh Percy, Esquire, of Riverlaw, Christchurch, New Zealand, same crest and motto.

Murray-Aynsley, Rev. John Cruger, J.P., of Great Brampton, Madley R.S.O., Herefordsh., same crest and motto.

Murray-Aynsley, John Francis, Esquire, of Hall Court, Botley, Hants, same crest and motto.

Murray-Aynsley, John Percy Murray, same crest and motto.

Murray of Eriswell Lodge, Suff., a demi-savage ppr., wreathed about the head and waist vert, holding in his dexter hand a dagger, also ppr., pommel and hilt or, and in his sinister a key of the last. *Furth fortune and fill the fetters.* 186. 2

Murray, George Moore, Esquire, of Mexico, out of a crescent or, a demi-savage affrontée ppr., wreathed about the temples or and az., holding in the dexter hand a sword erect, all ppr., and in the sinister a key, the wards upwards of the first.

Murray, a demi-savage ppr., wreathed about the head and middle vert, holding in his dexter hand a dagger ppr., pommel and hilt or, and in his sinister an anchor of the last. *cf.* 186. 2

Murray of Danesfield, Bucks, a demi-savage wreathed about the temples and loins holding a bugle-horn, all ppr. (*for Murray*). (2) A stag trippant (*for Scott*). *Hinc usque superna venabor.* 117. 8

Murray, Scotland, a demi-savage with a club over his dexter shoulder ppr. *Furth fortune.* 186. 5

Murray, a demi-naked man winding a hunting-horn ppr. *Hinc usque superna venabor.*

Murray of Falahill, Edinburghsh., and Philiphaugh, Selkirksh., Scotland, a demi-man vested in green, winding a hunting-horn ppr. *Hinc usque superna venabor.* 187. 12

Murray, Scotland, a mermaid ppr. *Tout prest.* 184. 5

Murray, John, of Polmaise, Stirlingsh., a mermaid holding in her dexter hand a mirror, and in her sinister a comb, all ppr. *Tout prêt.* 184. 5

Murray of Touchadam, Stirlingsh., Scotland, a mermaid holding in her dexter hand a mirror, and in her sinister a comb, all ppr. *Tout prest.* 184. 5

Murray of Pennyland, Caithness-sh., Scotland, a mermaid holding in her dexter hand a sword ppr. *In utrumque paratus.* 184. 7

Murray, William, of Murraythwaite, Dumfriessh., a cherub ppr., winged or. *Noctesque diesque præsto.* 189. 9

Murray, Ireland, on a ducal coronet a martlet ppr. 95. 12

Murray of Spott and Longhermandston, Haddingtonsh., Scotland, a horse arg., furnished gu. *Virtute fideque.* *cf.* 52. 4

Murray, Scotland, a horse salient arg., furnished gu. *Juncta virtute fides.*

Murray of Pilkeirie, Fifesh., Scotland, a ship under sail ppr. *Tutum te littore sistam.* 160. 13

Murray, Scotland, an olive-tree ppr. *Ex bello quies.*

Murray, Bart., of Ochtertyre, Perthsh., Scotland, an olive-branch issuing vert. *Ex bello quies.* 151. 11

Murray, Scotland, an olive-branch ppr. *In bello quies.* 151. 11

Murray of Lintrose, Perthsh., same crest and motto.

Murray, Sir Patrick Keith, of Ochtertyre, Perthsh., an olive-branch or. *In bello quies.* 151. 11

Murray, a branch of laurel erect vert. *Paritur bello.* 151. 13

Murray, late General Sir George, G.C.B., G.C.H., a laurel-branch erect vert. *Paritur bello.—Furth fortune and fill the fetters.* 151. 13

Murray, an eagle's head erased sa., holding in the beak a fleur-de-lis. *cf.* 84. 12

Murray, an eagle's head ppr. *Tout prest.* 83. 1

Murray, Scotland, an eagle ppr. *Noctesque diesque præsto.* 76. 2

Murray of Lochland, Scotland, a greyhound current ppr. *Gloria non præda.* *cf.* 58. 2

Murray of Deuchar, Selkirksh., Scotland, an escallop gu. *Fidei signum.* 141. 14

Murray, Bart., of Stanhope, Scotland, a dove holding in its beak an olive-branch, all ppr. *Pacis nuncia.* 92. 5

Murray, Scotland, a mullet or. *Sans tache.* 164. 2

Murray-Prior, Hon. Thomas Hodge, Esquire, of Maroon Logom River, Queensland: (1) An estoile vert (*for Prior*). 164. 1. (2) A mullet per pale or and gu. (*for Murray*). *Malo mori quam fœdari.* 164. 2

Murray-Prior, Hervey Morris Murray, Brisbane, Queensland, same crests and motto.

Murray of Murrayshall, Perthsh., a buck's head ppr. *Macte virtute.* 121. 5

Murray, Scotland, a stag's head ppr. *Macte virtute.* 121. 5

Murray, Graham-, Henry Stewart, of Murrayshall, Perth: (1) A dove ppr. (*for Graham*). 92. 2. (2) A buck's head couped ppr. (*for Murray*). *Candide et secure.—Macte virtute.* 121. 5

Murray of Broughton, Wigtownsh., Scotland, a griffin salient ppr. *Imperio.* *cf.* 62. 8

Murray, Alfred Alexander, M.A., LL.B., F.R.S.E., of Gardnershall, and Westfield House, Cramond. *Vale vincique.*

Murray of Castle Murray, co. Donegal, a griffin segreant ppr. *Imperio.* 62. 2

Murray-Stewart, Horatio Granville, Esquire, J.P., D.L., of Cally, Gatehouse, N.B.: (1) A pelican in her piety (*for Stewart*). (2) A griffin salient ppr., charged on the shoulder with a cross crosslet az for difference (*for Murray*) *Viresrit vulnere virtue —Imperio*

Murray, Bart, of Blackbarony, Peeblessh Scotland, a dexter hand holding a roll of paper fesseways all ppr *Deum time* cf 215 6

Murray of Cringletie Peeblessh, a dexter hand holding a roll *Deum time* 215 6

Murray, Sir Digby, Bart, of Blackbarony Peeblessh, a dexter hand holding a scroll fesseways ppr *Deum time.*

Murray, Scotland a dexter arm in armour embowed, the hand apaumee 200 1

Murray, Scotland, a hand ppr, holding a fetterlock or *Inde securior*

Murray, Bart., of Glendoick, Scotland, a dexter hand holding a mirror *Nosce teipsum*

Murray, Sir Robert, Bart, D L., of Clermont, Fifesh, a dexter hand brandishing a flaming sword ppr *Deum time*

Murray, Anthony George, Esq J P, of Dollerie, Crieff, N B, two hands clasped fesseways issuing from clouds *Fides servata*

Murray of Melgund, Forfarsh Scotland a burning lamp ppr *Placeam dum peream* 177 5

Murray, Alexander Borthwick, of Murray Park, Adelaide, S A, a galley sa, the flags gu *Noctes diesque præsto* 160 6

Murray, Scotland a lion's head erased crowned with an antique crown cf 17 12

Murray, Scotland, a lion rampant gu, supporting a battle-axe in pale *Virtute fideque*

Murray, a lion rampant gardant gu collared and chained and supporting an anchor or *Virtute fideque*

Murray of Simprin, Forfarsh, a demi-lion gu, holding between its paws a Lochaber-axe ppr *Virtute fideque* cf 16 12

Murray, Scotland a lion's gamb holding a sword ppr *Fortes fortuna adjuvat* 38 5

Murray of Birmingham, Warw, a telescope on a stand or *They by permission shine*

Murray of Drumcairn, Perthsh Scotland a swan's head couped ppr *Malo mori quam fœdari* cf 101 5

Murrell, a griffin's head with wings addorsed cf 67 11

Murrell or **Murrill,** a demi-lion rampant gardant per pale arg and sa, collared counterchanged holding in the dexter paw a bunch of flowers arg stalked vert

Musard, a savage's head couped and distilling drops of blood ppr 190 11

Muschamp of Brotherlee Durh, a lion rampant gu, holding in the dexter paw a banner az, charged with a crescent or *Vulneror non vincor*

Muschamp of Camberwell, Surrey, a cat-a-mountain ppr, tied round the neck with a scarf arg, charged on the breast with a martlet for difference

Muschamp of Dublin and Cork, on a cannon royal mounted or, a cat a mountain passant gardant ppr *Quid gens sine mente*

Muschampe of Barmoor, Northumb and Horsley Surrey, a mastiff dog ppr, collared arg

Musgrave, *see* Sagar Musgrave

Musgrave, Sir Richard John, Bart, D L, of Tourin, co Waterford, two arms in armour embowed ppr, supporting an annulet or *Sans changer*

Musgrave of Shillington Manor, Hitchin, Beds, two arms in mail armour up lifting an annulet or *Sans changer*

Musgrave, Sir Richard George, Bart, of Edenhall, Cumb two arms in armour embowed and gauntleted ppr, grasping an annulet or *Sans changer*

Musgrave, Sir James, Bart, out of a mural crown or, two arms vambraced, embowed and gauntleted ppr, grasping two annulets interlaced of the first *Sans changer*

Musgrave, two arms embowed habited erm cuffed or, holding in the hands ppr an annulet of the second, between the arms a human heart gu

Musgrave, Wykeham-, Wenman Aubrey Thame Park, Oxon, a bull's head sa horned or charged on the neck with two chevronels arg *Manners maketh man*

Musgrove, Musgrove-, of Raworth, near Hadleigh, Suff, a demi-lion ppr, gorged with a collar gemelle sa and holding between the paws a lozenge az, charged with a cross crosslet or *Nil desperandum*

Musgrove, Bart, of Speldhurst, Kent, same crest and motto

Mushat and **Mushet,** a mount vert semée of strawberries ppr

Mushet of Holland and Scotland a twig of rose blooming ppr *Dabunt aspera rosas* 149 5

Mushet, on the top of a Saracen's head affrontee a dove holding in its beak an olive branch ppr

Muskerry, Baron (Deane Morgan), of Muskerry, co Cork in Ireland (1) A reindeer's head caboshed or, charged with a mullet az (*for Morgan*) cf 122 4 (2) Out of a ducal coronet or, a demi sea otter ppr (*for Deane*) *Honor et virtus —Forti et fideli nihil difficile*

Muskett, Suff and Norf out of a ducal coronet or, a demi antelope sa, chained and ringed of the first cf 126 8

Muskett of Clippesby, Yarmouth, out of a ducal coronet or, a demi-antelope sa, ringed and chained or

Musner, out of a ducal coronet or, a camel's head sa cf 132 7

Mussell of Staple Langford, Wilts a wolf salient sa cf 28 1

Mussenden of Heling, Lincs, a Cornish chough ppr, holding in the beak a sprig of laurel vert cf 107 14

Mussenden of Larchfield co Down, a dove holding in the beak an olive branch, all ppr *J'aime la liberte* 92 5

Mustard of East Lodge, Mistley, Essex issuant from a chaplet of olive a dexter hand couped at the wrist ppr, holding a Passion cross gu

Musters, Chaworth-, *see* Chaworth Musters

Muston, on a chapeau ppr, a garb or 153 10

Muterer, Scotland, a castle triple towered ppr, loopholes and portway gu *Patience and resolution.* 155 8

Mutlow, Glouc and Worcs, a griffin's head couped per pale indented arg and gu guttee counterchanged, holding in the beak a buck's foot erased and erect or

Mutter, a castle triple-towered ppr doors and windows gu *Patience and resolution* 155 8

Mutter, Major James Mitchell, of Somenos dale Somenos E and N Railway, British Columbia, Canada, a castle triple towered sa masoned arg from the centre tower a flag flying arg charged with a cross gu *Patience and resolution* 155 8

Muttlebury of Jordaine, Somers, a hare current arg cf 136 3

Mutton of Pickton, Leics, a unicorn rampant 48 2

Myatt, William James, Esquire, of Abchurch Lane, E C upon a rock ppr, a talbot passant per pale sa and ermines, collared and chain reflexed over the back or supporting with the dexter leg a battle axe, also or *J'y suis j'y reste*

Myddelton, Richard, Chirk Castle, Denbigh, out of a ducal coronet a dexter hand ppr *In veritate triumpho*

Myddleton, Wales out of a ducal coronet or, a dexter hand erect ppr cf 222 14

Myddleton, Wharton-, of Old Park, Durh (1) A savage wreathed about the head with leaves holding in the dexter hand and supporting on his shoulders an oak tree erased and fructed all ppr (*for Myddleton*) (2) A bull's head erased arg charged with a trefoil vert (*for Wharton*) *Laissez dire* cf 44 3

Mydhope, Yorks, a demi lion rampant az, holding a ducal coronet or

Myers, *see* Waskett-Myers

Myers, a ducal coronet or, ensigned with three arrows points downwards entwined with a serpent, all ppr 173 2

Myers, a demi-horse rampant erased cf 5 33

Myers, William Henry, Swanmore Hants a demi lion gu, guttee d'or holding in the dexter paw a mullet of six points or, and resting the sinister on two mascles interlaced of the last

Myers-Beswick, William Beswick, 75, Avenue Road Regent's Park, a dexter hand couped at the wrist ppr, the palm charged with an estoile radiated or, between two antlers ppr *Denique cœlum*

Myers, a boar's head erased in fess 42 2

Myers, Bart (*extinct*) of Whitehaven, Cumb, and Monkstown co Dublin, a mermaid ppr, the waist encircled by a mural coronet or *Non dormit qui custodit* cf 184 5

Myggs, a talbot's head sa, eared arg, collared or cf 56 1

Mylbourne, a leopard's head per pale arg and sa 22 10

Mylchreest, Thomas George Esquire, of Eltofts, Thorner, near Leeds, upon a rock ppr, two cross crosslets or, thereon a lark with wings elevated and addorsed ppr *My shegin dy ve bee eh* 252 12

Myleeent, Yorks out of an antique crown or, a dragon's head sa, collared and chained of the first
Myles, Kent a buzzard ppr
Mylie, Scotland, a bull's head erased sa 44 3
Mylles of London, a lion rampant or 1 13
Mylne, Scotland, a martlet volant *Ex industria* 96 2
Mylne, Sir John Bart, a hand grasping a baton ppr *Prudentia et marte*
Mylne of Mylnefield, Perthsh a dexter hand holding a book ppr *Efficiunt clarum studia* 215 4
Mylne, General William Charles Robert, of Stangrove Park Eden Bridge, Kent, same crest and motto 264 1
Mylne, William John Home, of Amwell Grove, Herts, Esquire of Queen's College, Oxford M A at present residing at Sabrina Clevedon Road Weston super-Mare Somers, and the Rev R S Mylne of Great Amwell, near Ware Herts, a Pallas's head couped at the shoulders ppr, vested about the neck vert, on the head a helmet az the beaver turned up and on the top a plumaish gu *Tam arte quam marte* 182 1
Mynde of Mynde Town Shropsh, a heath cock ppr
Mynn of Cratfield Suff a demi pegasus or 47 5
Mynors of Weatherook Worcs a dexter cubit arm in armour holding in the hand a lion's gamb erased all ppr *Fac et spera*
Mynors, Heref., a naked arm couped at the elbow ppr, holding a lion's gamb erased sa *Spero ut fidelis* 220 10
Mynors, Heref a naked arm couped at the elbow ppr, holding in the hand a lion's gamb erased sa 220 10
Mynors Rev Thomas Hassall of Weatheroak Hall Alvechurch Worcester, same crest
Mynors, Willoughby Baskerville, of Treago, Heref, a naked arm embowed the hand holding an eagle's leg erased at the thigh, all ppr *Spero ut fidelis* 220 12
Mynshull, *see* Minshall and Minshull
Mynshull, Chesh, two lion's gambs gu supporting a crescent arg *cf* 39 6
Myreson, a buck's head erased sa, attired or 121 2
Myreton and Myrtoun, Scotland issuing out of a cloud a dexter hand in fess ppr holding a cross formée fitched gu 223 6
Myreton, Scotland, two arms issuing from clouds, and drawing up an anchor out of the sea ppr *Undique fulsus* 224 13
Myrton, Bart (*extinct*), of Gogar Edinburgh Scotland, a pine tree fructed ppr *Virtutis præmium* 144 10
Myrtoun, Scotland, a crescent arg 163 2
Mysters of London, a griffin's head erased sa, charged with two bars gemelle or *cf* 66 2
Mytton, Devereux Herbert Garth, near Welshpool, Montgomerysh, a ram's head couped arg, armed or 130 1
Mytton of Shipton, Shropsh, a bull's head erased bezantee *cf* 44 3
Mytton of Cleobury North a bull's head charged with three annulets *Interno robore* *cf* 44 3

N

Naas, Lord *see* Mayo, Earl of
Nadler, a cross crosslet fitchée and a sword in saltier 166 12
Naesmith, Scotland a hand holding a broken hammer *Non arte sed marte* 221 13
Naesmyth, Sir Michael George Bart, of Posso, Peeblessh, a hand ppr, holding a broken hammer or *Non arte sed marte* 221 13
Nagle, Bart. (*extinct*), Ireland, a goldfinch ppr *Non vox, sed votum* 108 8
Nagle, Chichester-, of Calverleigh Court, Devonsh (1) A goldfinch ppr (*for Nagle*) 108 8 (2) A heron rising holding in its beak an eel ppr (*for Chichester*) *Non vox, sed votum* *cf* 104 13
Nagle, Lieutenant Colonel Richard, of Rose-Mount, Ramsey, Isle of Man, on an Eastern coronet gu, a nightingale or gorged with a wreath of laurel vert, supporting with its dexter claw a spear erect, therefrom a banner flying to the sinister of the second inscribed with the word "*Assaye*" in letters sa *On with you* (over the crest) *Non vox, sed votum* 108 12
Nagle, Ireland, a naval coronet or there on a falcon with wings expanded ppr, belled and jessed or, resting his dexter claw on an anchor sa *Gratitude and loyalty*
Nail, a round buckle gu, between two wings the dexter arg the sinister of the first
Nairn of Seggieden Perthsh, Scotland the trunk of an oak tree sprouting leaves ppr *Sero, sed serio* 145 2
Nairn, a lion rampant supporting a garb ppr 1 9
Nairn, Scotland, a globe on a stand ppr *Spes ultra* 159 4
Nairn of St Fort, Fifesh a celestial sphere or and az, standing upon a foot gu *Spes ultra —L'esperance me confort*
Nairn or Nairne, William, of Dunsinane Scotland, a celestial sphere on a stand ppr *Spes ultra —L'espérance me confort* 159 4
Nairn, Scotland a globe on a stand ppr *Spes ultra* 159 4
Nairne, the sun in his splendour or 162 2
Naish, a dexter hand holding a sword in pale ppr 212 9
Naish of Ballycullen co Limerick, a greyhound sejant ppr collared arg *cf* 59 2
Nalder of Reading Berks a griffin's head erased 66 2
Nallinghurst, a wyvern gu 70 1
Nanby, a lion's gamb sa, holding an ostrich feather arg 37 3
Nandike of Elstone, Yorks, a demi-griffin with wings addorsed arg supporting a spear sa headed of the first
Nanfan or Nanphan, two dolphins addorsed az 140 1
Nanfan of Birtsmorton Court, Berrow and Pendock, Worcs a water-spaniel passant arg 57 7
Nanfant, three pruning hooks, one in pale and two in saltier or, environed in the middle by a wreath 178 12
Nanfant, on a coronet or a bird az
Nangle of Navan, co Meath Ireland, a falcon sa, jessed and belled or *cf* 85 2
Nangothan and Nangotham, a pole-cat arg *cf* 135 13
Nanney, Wales a lion rampant az 1 13
Nanney, Ellis-, Bart (1) A lion rampant az holding in dexter fore-paw a fleur de lis or, and resting the dexter hind leg on a like fleur de-lis (*for Nanney*) 306 5 (2) A lion rampant or, gorged with a collar invected gules holding between the fore-paws an escocheon of the last, charged with an arm embowed in armour, grasping in the hand a javelin all ppr 306 6
Nanphan of Birts Morton, Worcs a water-spaniel passant arg 57 7
Nansolyn, a cross patee fitched az 163 3
Nanson, a peacock in his pride ppr 103 12
Nanson, John Esquire, J P, of Appleby, a ducal coronet surmounted by a martlet
Nanton, Suff, a cockatrice close ppr, the wings sa
Nants, an estoile of eight points or *cf* 164 4
Napean, a goat passant *cf* 129 5
Naper, Devonsh, a demi antelope erased or attired arg *cf* 126 5
Naper or Napper, Ireland, a phœnix ppr 82 2
Naper, Ireland on a mount vert, a falcon ppr 86 7
Naper or Napier, Bucks a dexter cubit arm vested gu, cuffed arg grasping in the hand ppr a crescent of the first 206 10
Naper of Loughcrew Meath, same crest
Naper or Napper of Bawnmore, New Ross, co Wexford a dexter hand couped at the elbow vested gu, turned up arg grasping a crescent, also gu *Sans tache* 206 10
Napier, Baron (Napier), of Magdala, in Abyssinia, and of Caryngton, County Palatine of Chester, on a mount vert a lion passant or gorged with a collar gu, and a broken chain reflexed over the back or supporting with the sinister fore paw a flagstaff in bend sinister ppr therefrom flowing a banner arg charged with a cross couped gu *Tu vincula frange* 282 9
Napier of Blackstone, Renfrewsh, Scotland, a dexter arm grasping in the hand a crescent *Sans tache* 216 8
Napier, Dorset and Beds a dexter arm erect vested gu the hand ppr, grasping a crescent arg 206. 10

Napier, Edward Berkeley of Pennard House Somers, a dexter cubit arm erect, holding in the hand a crescent *Fato providentia major* 216 8

Napier, Sir William Lennox, Bart, 26, Argyll Road Kensington, a dexter cubit arm erect ppr, the hand grasping a crescent arg, the arm charged with a rose gu *Sans tache* cf 216 8

Napier and Ettrick, Baron (Napier), of Merchiston a dexter arm erect couped below the elbow ppr, grasping a crescent arg and over it the motto, *Sans tache.* 216 8

Napier, Archibald Scott, of Wadakancheri Cochin States, India, same crest and motto

Napier, Archibald David Edinburgh two arms in armour embowed and gauntleted ppr, holding a crescent arg *Sans tache* 267 1

Napier, John Gareth Madulkeele, Ceylon, same crest and motto

Napier, Theodore, Balmanno West Castle Road, Merchiston, Edinburgh an arm in chain armour embowed, the hand grasping a battle-axe ppr *Pro Rege et patria* 294 10

Napier of Culcreuch Stirlingsh, Scotland a hand holding an eagle's leg erased ppr, the talons expanded gu *Fides servata secundat* 220 12

Napier, Scotland, a dexter hand holding an eagle's leg erased *Vincit veritas* 220. 12

Napier, Sir Archibald Lennox Milliken, Bart, of Napier and 69, Onslow Square, S W · (1) An arm grasping an eagle's leg ppr (*for Napier*) 220 12 (2) A demi lion rampant gu, holding in his dexter fore-paw a dagger or (*for Milliken*) *Sans tache —Regarde bien* 14 12

Napier of Ballikinrain, Dumbartonsh a dexter hand holding an eagle's leg erased in bend ppr, armed gu *Nil veretur veritas* 220 12

Napier of Falside, Fifesh, Scotland, two hands conjoined and grasping a cutlass in pale ppr *Absque dedecore*

Napier, two dexter hands clasped in amity holding a dagger in pale, all ppr *Absque dedecore* 224 7

Napier of Craigannet, Stirlingsh, Scotland, a hand holding a couteau sword ppr *Sans tache*

Napier of Ballichearne, Dumbartonsh Scotland an eagle's leg in fess erased ppr armed gu *Vincit veritas*

Napier of Balwhapple Dumbartonsh, Scotland an eagle s leg erased in bend ppr armed gu *Usque fideli*

Napier of Kilmachew, Dumbartonsh, Scotland a man's head adorned with laurel ppr *Virtute gloria parta* cf 190 7

Napier of West Shandon, Dumbartonsh, a man's head in profile wreathed with laurel ppr *Virtute gloria parta.* cf 190 7

Napier, Dorset, a heron ppr 105 9

Napier, Bart (*extinct*), of Luton-Hoo, Beds, and Halliwell, Oxon, a greyhound sejant gu, collared and lined or cf 59 2

Napier, a demi antelope erased at the flanks or, armed arg cf 126 5

Napier-Clavering, Rev. John Warren, Axwell Park, Blaydon-on-Tyne, Durh (1) (on the dexter side) A dexter arm from the elbow in pale ppr the hand grasping a crescent arg and above, *Sans tache* (*for Napier*) (2) (on the sinister side) The top of an embattled tower arg, masoned sa, issuing therefrom four lances disposed saltireways ppr, three and three, with pennons az (*for Scott of Thirlestane*) *Ready, aye ready*

Napleton, a griffin statant 63 8

Napper of London, on a mount vert, a falcon close ppr 86 7

Napton, Warw, a lion passant, the tail extended ppr 5 11

Narbon, a dove volant, holding in its beak an olive-branch 93 10

Narboon or **Narhoone,** the golden fleece or banded az 130 10

Nares, Kent, two spears in saltier ppr banded in the middle az (*Another* gu)

Narford, issuing out of a cloud a dexter hand fesseways ppr, holding a cross crosslet fitchee gu cf 223 6

Nash, Ireland, a pelican vulning herself ppr 98 1

Nash, a wolf regardant cf 28 12

Nash, a greyhound sejant arg *Omnia vincit veritas* 59 4

Nash, Ireland a greyhound sejant sa, collared arg, studded or *Omnia vincit veritas* cf 59 2

Nash, Worcs (1) On a mount vert a greyhound current arg, charged on the body with an ermine-spot sa holding in the mouth a sprig of ash ppr cf 58 2 (2) Out of a ducal coronet jewelled and turned up erm, a greyhound's head arg, collared sa, the rim and ring or cf 61 7

Nash of the Noak, Martley, Worcs, upon a mount vert, a greyhound courant arg charged on the body with an ermine spot sa, holding in the mouth a sprig of ash ppr *In utroque fidelis* cf 58 2

Nash of Martley, Claines, and Droitwich, Worcs, a greyhound courant arg cf 58 2

Nash of London, a cubit arm erect vested az, cuffed arg, holding in the hand an oak branch fructed ppr

Nasmyth, Bart, Scotland, a hand holding a broken hammer or. *Non arte sed marte* 221 13

Nasmyth or **Neasmith,** a hand holding a broken hammer *Non arte sed marte* 221 13

Nason, Dr John James Church House, Stratford on-Avon, a ram's head couped *Spe labor levis*

Nassau, Prince of Orange, out of a ducal coronet or, the attires of a buck gu 123 3

Nassau, Earl of Rochford (*extinct*), in a coronet composed of fleurs-de lis and strawberry-leaves or, two single attires of a stag gu. *Ne supra modum sapere* 123 1

Nassau, Earl of Grantham (*extinct*), on a chapeau az turned up erminois, a lion rampant gardant gu, ducally crowned of the first

Nathaley, Nathiley, or **Natheley,** out of a ducal coronet or, a demi swan with wings displayed sa

Nathan, a heart gu pierced by an arrow in bend sinister sa 181 10

Naughton, Scotland, a demi-tower gu *I hope in God*

Naughton, a demi-lion rampant gardant holding in the dexter paw a fleur de-lis

Naunton, an ostrich's head arg ducally gorged az cf 97 9

Naunton of Alderton and Letheringham Abbey, Suff a basilisk ppr *Ut vidi, ut vici —Constant et vray*

Nayler, Benjamin Round, Beechwood, Beech Lanes near Birmingham, a greyhound sejant arg, resting the dexter paw on a passion nail az, and holding in the mouth a trefoil slipped vert *Celer et certus*

Naylor of Wakefield, Yorks, a lark volant or

Naylor or **Naylour** of London, Durh, Oxon, and Hunts, a lion's head erased sa, charged on the neck with a saltier or cf 17 8

Naylor of Leighton Hall Montgomerysh, a lion passant sa, charged on the body with two saltires or, resting the dexter fore paw upon an escutcheon of the arms viz per pale or and arg, a pale sa, fretty or, between two lions rampant also sa *Hoc age* 5 3

Naylor-Leyland, Sir Albert Edward Herbert, Bart, Hyde Park House Albert Gate, W (1) A mount vert, thereon an escallop arg, in front of a demi-eagle erminois wings endorsed az, bezantee and charged with a cross couped wavy or, in the beak three ears of barley banded or (*for Leyland*) 279 4 (2) A lion sa, on the body two saltires or resting the dexter fore-paw on an escutcheon charged with the arms of Naylor, on the shoulder a cross couped wavy or (*for Naylor*) 279 3

Naylor-Leyland, John a lion passant sa charged on the body with two saltires or, resting the dexter fore-paw on an escutcheon per pale or and arg a pale sa, fretty or, between two lions rampant of the third

Naylor-Leyland, Rowland Edward Leyland, same crest

Naylord of Newland, Glouc a goat's head or, attired sa, holding in the mouth a sprig of laurel ppr cf 128 12

Naylour, Kent on a mount vert, an eagle rising ppr 76 11

Neagle, a demi griffin segreant 64 2

Neal, a ram statant ppr 131 13

Neal, a mound gu, banded and crossed or 159 12

Neal, an arm in armour in bend dexter holding in the hand a sword in bend sinister

Neal or **Neale** of Yelden, Beds, Essex, Wollaston and Hanging Houghton, Northamp, a griffin's head erased arg 66 2

Neal of Yeovil Somers, out of a wreath of oak or a dexter cubit arm in armour holding in the gauntlet ppr a sword erect, also ppr, pommel and hilt of the first, transfixing a greyhound's head erased arg 210 3

Neal, William Phené, Esquire C.C, of Cherryhinton Hall, Cambridge and Pinner's Hall, Great Winchester Street, London, E C, a lion rampant *Consilio non impetu*

Neale, a mascle or 167 9

Neale of Warnford, Hants, out of a ducal coronet or, a chaplet of laurel vert 146 9

Neale of Westminster, Middx., a dragon's head or, vulned in the neck gu. *cf.* 71. 1

Neale, a tower gu., from the battlements a pelican rising with wings displayed or, vulning herself ppr.

Neale, on a mount vert, a stag statant. 117. 1

Neale, John Alexander, 42, Half-Moon Street, W., an arm in armour embowed ppr., brandishing a sword arg., pommel and hilt or. *Loyal au mort.*

Neale-Burrard, Bart.: (1) (of honourable augmentation, granted in 1815). Out of a naval coronet or, a cubit arm erect encircled by a branch of oak ppr., the hand grasping a trident in bend sinister point downwards of the first. 214. 14. (2) A dexter arm in armour embowed, the hand grasping a sword, all ppr. 195. 2

Neale, a dexter arm couped at the elbow brandishing a sword ppr. 212. 3

Neale of Deane, Beds, out of a mural coronet or, a demi-lion rampant per fesse erm. and gu., charged with an escallop counterchanged.

Neale of Allesley Park, Warw.: (1) Out of a mural coronet or, a demi-lion rampant per fess erm. and gu., charged on the shoulder with an escallop counterchanged (*for Neale*). (2) On two crosses patée arg., a demi-eagle displayed sa. (*for Vansittart*).

Neale or **Nele,** a fret az. 165. 10

Neame, Arthur, J.P., Woodlands, Selling, Faversham, in front of a staff raguly fessewise az., a demi-heraldic antelope arg., armed or, gorged with a collar gemel, also az., and pierced through the neck with an arrow in bend sinister ppr. *Ne a meta oculos avertam.* 237. 1

Nearn, Ireland, a lion's head or. 21. 1

Neasmith, Scotland, a dexter hand issuing holding a sword, all ppr. *Marte non arte.* 212. 13

Neat, a horse's head bridled ppr. 51. 5

Neat or **Neate** of London, and Swindon, Wilts, a bull's head couped at the neck gu., armed and crined arg., between two dragon's wings vert. 44. 4

Neave, Sir Thomas Lewis Hughes, Bart., of Dagnam Park, Essex, out of a ducal coronet or, a lily stalked and leaved vert, flowered and seeded of the first. *Sola proba quæ honesta.* 151. 5

Neave, Sheffield Henry Morier, Mill Green Park, Ingatestone, out of a ducal coronet or, a lily stalked and leaved vert, flowered and seeded or. *Sola proba quæ honesta.*

Neave, Arthur Thomas Digby, Hutton Hall, Brentwood, Essex, same crest and motto.

Neave of London, a demi-leopard rampant gardant ppr., supporting an anchor or. *Industriâ permanente.* 23. 1

Neaves, Scotland, a demi-lion gardant gu., supporting an anchor or. *Spe et industria.* *cf.* 12. 12

Nechure, a hand holding a rose-branch ppr. 218. 10

Nedham, Herts, a dolphin naiant or. 140. 5

Nedham, Wymondley, Herts, issuing out of a palisado coronet or, a buck's head sa., attired of the first.

Need of Blidworth, out of an Eastern coronet or, a griffin's head sa., charged with an estoile of the first.

Need, Captain Walter, Woodhouse Castle, Mansfield, Notts, same crest.

Need of Fountain Dale, Notts, out of an Eastern coronet or, a griffin's head ppr.

Needes, a buck's head cabossed, pierced through by an arrow, all ppr. *cf.* 122. 5

Needham, Earl Kilmorey, *see* Kilmorey.

Needham, Leics., a phœnix in flames ppr. *Nunc aut nunquam.* 82. 2

Needham of Lenton, Notts, issuing out of flames a phœnix, all ppr. *Soyez ferme.* 82. 2

Needham of Kynoleton, Derbysh., a phœnix in flames ppr., charged on the breast with a trefoil slipped or. *cf.* 82. 2

Needham or **Nedham** of Nedham in the Peak, Derbysh.: (1) A phœnix in flames ppr. 82. 2. (2) On a mount vert, a stag lodged sa., attired or. 115. 12. (3) Out of a palisado coronet or, a buck's head sa.

Needham, Herts, out of a palisado coronet or, a buck's head sa., attired of the first. *cf.* 121. 5

Needham of Alexton and Gadesby, Leics., on a mount vert, a stag lodged sa., attired or, charged with a crescent. *cf.* 115. 12

Needham, a turkey-cock in pride. 108. 5

Neefield and **Nerfield,** two anchors in saltier az. 161. 7

Neeld, Sir Audley Dallas, Bart., of Grittleton House, Wilts, on a mount vert, a wolf's head erased sa., between two branches of palm ppr. *Nomen extendere factis.* 29. 9

Neele, out of a ducal coronet a chaplet of laurel vert. 146. 9

Neele, a mound gu., banded and crossed or. 159. 12

Neels, Jersey, a lion's head affrontée ppr. *Nostre Roy et nostre foy.*

Nefield and **Nesfield,** a pillar arg., supported by two lion's gambs ppr. 39. 8

Neimeneill or **Neimenell,** a dexter hand apaumée ppr. 222. 14

Negus, Norf., a sea-mew resting its dexter claw on an escallop or.

Neil, Scotland, a lion passant gardant sa. 4. 3

Neil, a unicorn's head erased gu. 49. 5

Neill, issuing out of a cloud a hand holding a club, all ppr. 214. 9

Neill, Smith-, James William, of Barnweil, Ayrsh.: (1) An arm in armour, holding in the hand a dagger backhanded. 277. 4. (2) A dexter hand holding a sword ppr. *Vincere vel mori.* —*Steady.* 277. 3

Neill, upon a mount vert, the embattlements of a tower ppr., surmounted by a pheon or. *Floresco favente Deo.*

Neill, Smith-, James William, Swindrigemuir, Dalry, Ayrsh.: (1) A sinister arm in armour, holding a dagger backhanded, all ppr. 277. 4. (2) A dexter hand holding a sword, all ppr. *Vincere vel mori.—Steady.* 277. 3

Neilson, out of a mural coronet az., a lion's head or. 19. 12

Neilson of Corsock, Wigtownsh., Scotland, a demi-man holding over his shoulder a hammer, all ppr. *Præsto pro patria.* 186. 11

Neilson of Maxwood, Scotland, a dexter hand holding a dagger, all ppr. *Virtute et votis.* 212. 3

Neilson of Craigcaffie, Scotland, a dexter hand holding a lance in pale ppr. *His Regi servitium.*

Neilson, a dexter hand holding a spear ppr. *Præsto pro patria.* 214. 11

Neilson, Scotland, a dexter hand ppr., pointing to a crescent or. *His Regi servitium.*

Neish, Cupid with his bow and arrow, all ppr. *Amicitiam trahit amor.* 189. 7

Neke, a lion's gamb az., holding a lozenge in pale arg., charged with a cross crosslet sa. 35. 10

Nele, a fret az. 165. 10

Nell, a stag's head erased arg., attired or. 121. 2

Nelme, out of a ducal coronet or, a demi-dragon of the same with wings addorsed az., holding between the claws a cross crosslet fitched gu.

Nelson, Earl (Nelson), Hiborough, Norf., and of Trafalgar and Merton: (1) On the dexter side, as a crest of honourable augmentation—on a naval coronet or, the chelengk or plume of triumph presented to Horatio, 1st Viscount Nelson, by the Grand Signior or Sultan Selim II.; and on the sinister the family crest, viz.: upon waves of the sea the stern of a Spanish man-of-war, all ppr., thereon inscribed "*San Joseff.*" *Palmam qui meruit ferat.*

Nelson, Durh., out of a ducal coronet or, a demi-lion rampant arg. 16. 3

Nelson of Grimstead, Yorks, a cubit arm quarterly arg. and sa., holding in the hand ppr. a fleur-de-lis per pale of the first and second. 210. 6

Nelson, Ireland, a dexter arm in armour, holding in the hand an oak-branch ppr.

Nelson, a cubit arm in armour, holding in the hand a baton, all ppr. *cf.* 209. 9

Nelson, Kent, a dexter arm erect, holding a tilting-spear, all ppr. 214. 11

Nelson of Beeston, Norf., a hand holding a scimitar, hilt and pommel or. 213. 5

Nelson, a dexter hand erect ppr., the first finger and thumb pointing to a crescent or. *cf.* 222. 12

Nelson, Thomas, Esquire, of St. Leonards, Edinburgh, a dexter arm in armour embowed ppr., the hand grasping a dagger erect, also ppr., hilted and pommelled or. *Virtute et votis.* *cf.* 196. 5

Nelson, William, Esquire, of Salisbury Green, Edinburgh, same crest and motto. *cf.* 196. 5

Nelson, a lion's gamb erect ppr., holding an escutcheon sa., charged with a cross patonce or.

Nelthorpe, Bart., Middx., issuing out of clouds an arm couped in fess ppr., holding in the hand a sword in pale arg., hilt and pommel or. 223. 10

Nelthorpe, Sutton-, Robert Nassau, Scawby Hall, Lincs, a wolf's head erased gu. *Toujours prest.*

Nembhard or **Nempharts,** a demi-lamb salient, bearing over the dexter shoulder the holy banner of the cross, all ppr. *Pax potior bello.* 130. 9

Nepean, a goat passant ppr. *cf.* 129. 5

Nepean, Rev. Sir Evan Yorke, Bart., D.L., of Bothenhampton, Dorset, on a mount vert, a goat passant sa, charged on the side with two ermine-spots in fesse or, attired ungu, and gorged with a collar of the last thereon two mullets gu *Respice* 286 5

Nerberye and **Nerbury,** three organ pipes two in saltier and one in pale, or, banded with leaves vert

Nereford, a glow-worm ppr

Nerfield, two anchors in saltier az 161 7

Nesbett, an arm in armour couped below the wrist, holding in the gauntlet a baton 209 9

Nesbitt, out of a mural coronet a talbot's head, all ppr 56 6

Nesbitt of Lismore House, Cavan, a dexter cubit arm in armour, holding in the hand a truncheon *Je maintiendrai* cf 209 9

Nesfield, a pillar arg, supported by two lion s gambs ppr 39 8

Nesham, Durh (1) A demi-lion rampant ppr, holding in his dexter paw a cross crosslet fitchee gu (*for Nesham*) 11 10 (2) On a rock ppr, a fleur-de lis per pale or and gu (*for Douthwaite*) *Spes, salus, decus*

Ness, Scotland a dexter hand holding a laurel branch ppr 219 9

Netby of Netby, Lancs, a lion's gamb holding a bird bolt sa

Nethercoat of Moulton Grange, Northamp a wolf's head erased 30 8

Nethersall and **Nethersole** of Wingham Would, Kent, an arm in armour embowed ppr, girt with a scarf flotant vert, holding within the gauntlet a broken tilting-spear or cf 197. 3

Nethersole, a stag at gaze 117 3

Netter, a unicorn's head erased gu ducally gorged armed and maned or cf 49 5

Netterville, Viscount Netterville (*extinct*), a demi lion rampant gardant gu, bezantee cf 10 8

Netterville, a demi-lion rampant gu, bezantee *Cruci dum spiro fido* 10 4

Netterville, Joshua James, Esquire (1) A demi-lion rampant gardant gu, bezantee and charged with a lozenge or for difference (*for Netterville*) cf 10 8 (2) A cubit arm erect vested gu, cuffed erminois, holding in the hand a sword in bend sinister ppr (*for M'Evoy*) *Cruci dum spiro fido.*

Nettlefold, a water-bouget gu 168 4

Nettles of Nettleville, Ireland a stag statant under a tree ppr *Nemo me impune lacessit* cf 116 13

Nettleship, a dexter hand ppr, holding a nettle-branch vert.

Nettleship, a demi-bear rampant arg, muzzled or 34 13

Nettleship of London, a lion passant per pale erm and az, holding in the dexter paw a buckle or cf 6 2

Nettleton, a bear s paw erased gu 36 4

Neve, Le, of London and Norf, out of a ducal coronet or a lily arg, stalked and leaved vert, bladed and seeded of the first 151 5

Neve of Tenterden, Kent out of a ducal coronet or, a lily arg, stalked leaved, and seeded or *Sola proba quæ honesta* 151 5

Nevell, an anchor sa, environed by a serpent or 161 3

Nevemenell, a dexter hand apaumee ppr 222 14

Nevett, an arm in armour embowed holding in the hand a battle-axe, all ppr cf 200 6

Nevil, see Abergavenny Marquess of

Nevil, out of a ducal coronet or a bull's head pied ppr, armed of the first charged on the neck with a rose gu seeded, also or barbed vert *Ne vile velis* cf 44 11

Nevile, Bart. (*extinct*), of Ragnale, and of Thorney, Notts (1) Out of a ducal coronet or, a bull's head arg pied 44 11 (2) On a chapeau gu turned up erm, a ship with sails furled sa *Ne vile velis*

Nevile, Ralph Henry Christopher, of Wellingore Hall, Lincoln same crests

Nevile, Percy Sandford of Skelbrooke Park, Doncaster, a bull's head erased sa *Ne vile velis*

Nevill, Earl of Warwick and Salisbury (1) Out of a ducal coronet a swan's head and neck (2) On a ducal coronet a griffin sejant

Nevill, Earl of Westmoreland (*attainted*), out of a ducal coronet or a bull's head pied 44 11

Nevill of Holt, Leics out of a ducal coronet or a bull s head erm, armed of the first 44 11

Nevill, Kent, and of Billingbeare, Berks, a bull passant pied, armed or cf 45 2

Nevill of Llangenneck Park Carmarthensh a pied bull armed and gorged with a collar and a line therefrom reflexed over the back or and supporting with the dexter foot an escutcheon of the last, charged with an anchor erect sa *Ne vile velis* 45 1

Nevill, Essex a demi-lion rampant arg, guttee-de sang holding a sword of the first hilt and pommel or cf 14 12

Nevill, Ireland a lion's head az, royally crowned ppr

Nevill, Ireland, a greyhound's head erased arg, collared gu charged with a harp or cf 61 2

Nevill, Leics, and of Chevet, Yorks a greyhound's head erased or, charged on the neck with a label of three points vert, between as many pellets, one and two

Nevill of Scotton, Lincs, and Yorks, a tiger sejant erm 27 6

Neville, Baron Braybrooke, see Braybrooke

Neville of Bawnmore House, co Kilkenny, and of Borrismore, Ireland, out of a ducal coronet or, a bull's head pied, armed of the first *Ne vile velis* 44 11

Neville of Haselour Staffs out of a ducal coronet or, a bull's head pied ppr *Ne vile velis* 44 11

Neville of Heacham Hall Norf a mount vert, thereon issuant out of a crescent gu a rose arg, slipped vert

Neville, out of a cloud a hand holding up a garb by the band all ppr 218 3

Neville-Bagot, of Ballymoe co Galway issuing from a coronet or a goat's head ermines horned of the first *Antiquum obtinens*

Neville-Grenville, Robert, Butleigh Court, Glastonbury (1) A garb vert (*for Grenville*) (2) A bull statant arg, pied sa collar and chain reflexed over the back or (*for Neville*)

Neville-Rolfe, Charles William (1) A mount vert thereon issuant out of a crescent gu a rose arg, slipped vert (*for Neville*) (2) A lion's head erased arg, fretty gu *Cresco crescendo*

Neville-Rolfe, Rear Admiral Ernest C B, 167 Victoria Street, S W, same crests and motto

Neville-Rolfe, Eustace, J P, Heacham Hall King's Lynn, same crests and motto

Neville-Rolfe, Herbert, same crests and motto

Nevins, Willis, Esquire, on a mount a palm branch vert *Nil desperandum* cf 147 3

Nevinson or **Nevison** of Estrey, Kent a wolf passant arg pellettee, collared, lined, and ringed or

Nevoy, Scotland, a pegasus ppr *Marte et arte* 47 1

New, a dexter arm ppr, vested per chevron or and gu holding in the hand a roll of parchment arg cf 208 8

Newall, a cross crosslet fitched az 166 2

Newall, Major Henry Gerard Fenton, of Hare Hill and Littleborough, Lancs, a Saracen's head affrontee ppr, wreathed about the temples or and gu, suspended from the mouth by a ribbon of the last a shield paly indented of four, also or and gu *Non recedam* 190 2

Newall of Barskeoch, Wigtownsh Scotland, a bustard holding in the dexter claw a writing-pen ppr *Diligentia ditat*

Newark, Viscount, see Manvers, Earl

Newarke of Akham, Yorks, a savage's head in profile looking up ppr

Newbald or **Newbold,** a cross flory fitched az 166 7

Newbegin, G T, Esquire, of Thorpe Norwich, *uses* on a rock an eagle rising with wings expanded and inverted (*of no authority*) *I'll try*

Newbery, an eagle's head erased arg 83 2

Newbery of London, a Moor's head in profile ppr cf 192 13

Newberry and **Newbery,** a dexter arm ppr vested az, cuffed or holding in the hand a truncheon gu tipped or

Newbigging, Scotland a stag's head erased ppr, and between the attires a cross crosslet fitched sa *Cruce vincimus* 120 12

Newbigging, Scotland an eagle rising ppr *I'll try* 77 5

Newbigging, Scotland a date-tree fructed ppr *Fructu noscitur* 144 1

Newbold, a griffin's head erased 66 2

Newbold, Yorks, a boar's head and neck couped, holding in the mouth a broken spear in bend ppr 42 10

Newbold or **Newbald,** Derbysh and London, a cross flory fitchee az 166 7

Newborough, a dexter arm in armour embowed, holding in the hand a sword, all ppr 195 2

Newborough, a blackamoor's head in profile sa cf 192 13

Newborough, Baron (Wynn) Plas Newydd, Trefnant, Denbighsh a dexter cubit arm erect in armour, holding in the hand ppr. a fleur-de-lis or. *Suaviter in modo, fortiter in re.* cf. 210. 6

Newburgh, Earl of (Giustiniani Bandini), Palazzo Albieri, Rome: (1) A Moor's head ppr., banded chequy arg. and gu., and ear-ringed, also arg. (2) A leg erect in armour, per pale arg. and sa., couped at thigh gu., knee-cap and spur or. *Si je puis.*

Newbury, Berks, a demi-eagle displayed or. 81. 6

Newbury, De, a quatrefoil vert. 148. 10

Newby, an arm in armour, holding in the hand a sword, all ppr. 210. 2

Newcastle, Duke of (Pelham-Clinton), Clumber, Worksop: (1) Out of a ducal coronet gu., a plume of five ostrich-feathers arg., banded with a line laid chevronways az. (*for Clinton*). (2) A peacock in his pride ppr. (*for Pelham*). *Loyaulté n'a honte.* 103. 12

Newce and **Newse** of Much Hadham, Herts, and Ditchingham, Norf., and Surrey, on a mount vert, a garb or, banded gu. 153. 12

Newcom, Newcombe, Newcome, and **Newcomen,** a lion's gamb erased sa. 36. 4

Newcombe of Stanton Drew and Exeter, Devonsh., a demi-horse arg., gorged with a chaplet vert. cf. 53. 3

Newcombe, Devonsh., on a mural coronet or, a raven with wings expanded ppr.

Newcome, Francis D'Arcy William Clough, of Hockwold Hall, Brandon, same crest.

Newcome of London, out of a mural coronet or, a Cornish chough with wings expanded ppr.

Newcomen, Viscount Newcomen (*extinct*), a cock or. *Vigilant.* 91. 2

Newcomen of Saltfleetley, Lincs, a lion's gamb erased and erect sa., armed gu. 36. 4

Newcomen of Sutton, Dublin, a lion's gamb erect and erased sa., armed gu., holding a crescent arg. cf. 39. 15

Newcourt of Pickwell, Halesworthy, and Georgeham, Devonsh., a demi-griffin gu., guttée-d'or, beaked and legged or. cf. 64. 2

Newdegate, a fleur-de-lis arg. *Confide recte agens.* 148. 2

Newdegate, a swan arg., beaked and membered gu., gorged with a ducal coronet or, thereto a chain affixed and reflexed over the back vert. cf. 99. 3

Newdich and **Newdick,** Worcs., out of a mural coronet or, a lion's head gu. 19. 12

Newdigate, a fleur-de-lis arg. 148. 2

Newdigate, Alfred, same crest.

Newdigate, a lion's gamb erased arg. 36. 4

Newdigate-Newdegate, Francis Alexander, Weston-in-Arden, Warw., a fleur-de-lis arg. *Foyall loyall.—Confide recte agens.*

Newdigate, George, J.P., 2, Cavendish Place, Brighton, same crest.

Newdigate, Sir Henry Richard Legge, K.C.B., Harefield, Stoke, Coventry, same crest.

Newdigate, Newdegate-, Lieutenant-General Sir Edward, K.C.B., Arbury, near Nuneaton, Warw., same crest. *Confide recte agens.*

Newdigate, a horse current az., flames issuing from his nostrils ppr. cf. 52. 8

Neweke, between two quills arg., a mullet az. 113. 4

Newell, out of a mural coronet az., a lion's head or. 19 12

Newell, Oxon., an Italian greyhound ppr., gorged with a collar dovetailed or, charged on the shoulder with a cinquefoil arg.

Newell or **Newall,** Scotland, a falcon rising, holding in the dexter claw a pen, all ppr. *Diligentia ditat.*

Newenham, Ireland, in the sea an anchor in pale, ensigned with a dove holding in the beak an olive-branch. 94. 4

Newenham of Coolmore: (1) Between two wings gu., a demi-lion rampant arg., charged on the shoulder with three guttes-de-sang (*for Newenham*). 9. 8. (2) An arm in armour embowed, holding a broken tilting-spear (*for Worth*). *Crucem ferre dignum.* 197. 2

Newenham, Notts, and of Everdon, Northamp., between two wings gu., a demi-lion rampant arg., charged on the shoulder with three guttes-de-sang. 9. 8

Newenham, Major William Thomas Worth, Coolmore, co. Cork, a demi-lion rampant between two wings. *Deo adverso leo vincitur.*

Newenham, Herts, a demi-lion rampant arg., charged with a bend vert. cf. 10. 2

Newenham of Pailton House, near Rugby, a demi-lion couped arg. *Deo adverso leo vincitur.*

Newenham and **Nevenham,** a pegasus current ppr. 47. 1

Newenson, Herts and Kent, a wolf passant arg. 28. 10

Neweuton, a sea-lion rampant or. 20. 5

Newenton, Essex and Sussex, on a chapeau az., turned up erm., a demi-eagle displayed arg. cf. 80. 12

Newhouse, a squirrel sejant gu. cf. 135. 4

Newhouse, Lancs, an arm erect ppr., holding in the hand a banner az.

Newington, a reindeer's head caboshed sa., attired or. 122. 4

Newington, Sussex, on a chapeau az., turned up erm., a demi-eagle displayed arg. *Fac justa.* cf. 80. 12

Newland, Devonsh. and Hants, a lion's gamb erect arg., holding a cross formée fitched gu., charged with three bezants. cf. 36. 9

Newland, Herts, a heraldic tiger's head erased arg., maned and tufted or, gorged with a collar sa., charged with three crescents of the first, holding in the mouth a broken spear embrued ppr.

Newland of Newlands, Hants, a wolf's head couped ppr., collared or. *Le nom, les armes, la loyauté.* 30. 9

Newlands, Baron (Hozier), Mauldslie Castle, Carluke, Lanarksh., a bloodhound sejant ppr. *Aye ready.*

Newlands, Scotland, a demi-lion rampant. *Pro patriâ.* 10. 2

Newman, Sir Robert Hunt Stapylton Dudley Lydston, Bart., J.P., D.L., of Mamhead, Devonsh., a lion rampant per chevron az., guttée-d'eau, and arg., guttée-de-sang. *Ubi amor, ibi fides.* cf. 1. 13

Newman, a lion rampant arg., holding in the dexter paw an anchor or, and resting the sinister upon an escutcheon az., charged with a star of eight points of the first. *Firmiter et fideliter.*

Newman, Cornw., between two wings gu., a demi-lion rampant arg., charged on the shoulder with three guttes-de-sang. 9. 8

Newman of Brands House, Bucks, a swallow volant. *Ad te, Domine.* 96. 2

Newman, Rev. George William, of 5, Malvern Place, Cheltenham, same crest. *Lux mea Christus.*

Newman, Henry Ashburnham Toll, same crest and motto.

Newman, a martlet volant ppr. 96. 2

Newman, a martlet rising ppr. *Lux mea Christus.* cf. 95. 11

Newman, a mermaid in the sea ppr., crined or.

Newman of London, on a mount vert, a man, his jacket az. and breeches sa., on his head ppr. a cap gu., on a ladder and lighting a beacon, all ppr

Newman of London, on a plume of five feathers alternately az. and or, a griffin's head of the last.

Newman of Dromaneene, co Cork, Ireland, an eagle's head erased az., charged on the neck with an escallop or. cf. 83. 2

Newman, John Robert Bramston, J.P., Newberry Manor, Mallow, same crest.

Newmarch, in the sea an anchor in pale, ensigned with a dove holding in its beak an olive-branch, all ppr. 94. 4

Newmarch, Yorks, a dove holding in its beak an olive-branch ppr. 92. 5

Newmarch, Northumb., a demi-griffin ppr. 64. 2

Newmarche, a tower triple-towered ppr. 157. 6

Newnes, Sir George, Bart., Wildcroft, Putney Heath, S.W., a demi-otter sa., holding in its mouth a roll of paper arg., and resting the sinister paw upon a boar's head couped or. *Festina prudenter.* 272. 7

Newnham, a ram's head erased arg. 130. 6

Newnham, a demi-lion charged with a pale. cf. 10. 2

Newport-Charlett, *see* Charlett.

Newport, Viscount, *see* Bradford, Earl of.

Newport, Earl of Bradford (*extinct*), a unicorn's head arg., erased gu., armed and ducally gorged or. *Ne supra modum sapere.* cf. 49. 5

Newport, Baron (Newport): (1) A unicorn's head erased arg., armed, maned, and ducally gorged or. cf. 49. 5. (2) A lion's head erased az., between two griffin's wings expanded gu., holding in his mouth a javelin couped arg., headed or.

Newport, Shropsh., a unicorn's head arg., armed and crined or, erased gu. 49. 5

Newport, Shropsh., a unicorn's head erased arg., ducally gorged or. cf. 49. 5

Newport, Bart, Ireland, a unicorn's head erased arg, armed, maned, bearded, and ducally gorged or *Ne supra modum sapere* cf 49 5

Newport, George Bellingham, Rockview Inistiogue, same crest and motto

Newport, Herts and Northamp, a buck gu attired, gorged, and chained or cf 117 5

Newport, Herts, and of Welton, Northamp, a buck statant gu, attired, gorged, and chained or cf 117 5

Newport, Worcs, a bugle-horn sa stringed az 228 11

Newport of Hanley Court Worcs, a fleur de lis arg 148 2

Newport, a dexter arm in armour embowed ppr, garnished or, holding in the hand, also ppr, a sword arg, hilt and pommel or 195 2

Newry, Viscount, *see* Kilmorey Earl of

News, a demi-lion holding a laurel-branch, all ppr

Newsam, Yorks, a sword in pale arg, enfiled with a thistle ppr

Newsam, Warw, a lion's gamb gu, holding a crescent or 39 15

Newsham, Lancs, a boar's head erased or, charged with a cross crosslet gu cf 42 2

Newsham, a dove holding in its beak an olive-branch ppr 92 5

Newsham, a lion's gamb gu, holding a crescent or 39 15

Newsom, a lion s gamb erased sa, holding a bezant 39 13

Newte, a newt ppr *Pugilem claraverat*

Newton-Deakin, *see* Deakin

Newton, Baron (Legh) Lyme Park Disley Chesh issuant out of a ducal coronet or, a ram's head arg armed or in the mouth a laurel-slip vert, the whole debruised by a pallet wavy az *En Dieu est ma foi* 303 9

Newton, Sir Alfred James Bart Kottingham House Burton-on Trent, and 17, Cumberland Terrace, Regent's Park, N W, out of the battlements of a tower an arm erect, the hand grasping a sword in bend sinister ppr suspended therefrom a flag arg charged with a sword erect between two branches of oak ppr *Faveat fortuna*

Newton, Charles Edmund, of Mickleover, Derbysh, a wild man kneeling on his sinister knee presenting a sword, all ppr *Hinc habeo non tibi*

Newton, John Huby North Riding of Yorks, same crest and motto

Newton of Crabaton, Devonsh, an Eastern prince ppr, crowned or, kneeling and delivering up his sword, the blade also ppr, hilted of the second

Newton, Hay-, William Drummond Ogilvy of Newton, Haddingtonsh, Scotland a demi-lion rampant or, brandishing a scimitar ppr *Pro patria* 14 10

Newton, Yorks Lincs, and Derbysh, a lion rampant arg 1 13

Newton of Cheadle Heath, Chester, a lion rampant per fess erm and gu, collared of the last, holding between the paws a cross of the first flory or

Newton of Belsize Court Hampstead London N W two demi griffins segreant and respecting each other sa, and supporting between their claws a cross flory or *Fides cum officio* 65 13

Newton, Andrew, Esquire, of Dungannon co Tyrone, Ireland, a martlet sa charged on the breast with a cross patee arg *Faveat fortuna* cf 95 5

Newton of Carrickfergus, co Antrim, same crest and motto cf 95 5

Newton, Andrew Willoughby, J P, same crest and motto

Newton, Courtenay Howard, 9, Royal Crescent W, same crest and motto

Newton-Deakin, Charles Frederic Royal Thames Yacht Club 7, Albemarle Street W, a dexter arm embowed ppr holding in the hand a battle-axe in bend sinister arg, pendent from the wrist by a riband an escutcheon arg charged with a lion rampant sa, holding between the paws a cross patée fitchée gu *Stryke, Dakyns, the Devil s in ye hempe*

Newton, a bear's head couped arg, muzzled gu 34 14

Newton, Bart (*extinct*), of Charlton, Kent, and Priory, Warw out of a ducal coronet or a boar s head between two ostrich feathers arg

Newton, Scotland a boar's head erased and erect ppr 43 3

Newton of Dunleckny, co Carlow Ireland out of a ducal coronet or, a boar's head between two ostrich feathers arg, the neck charged with a cross crosslet az *Pro patria*

Newton, an eagle's leg erased at the thigh sa environed by a snake or

Newton, George Onslow Croxton Park, Cambridge same crest

Newton of Badenham, Beds Lavendor, Bucks, and Exmouth, Devonsh, two arms counter embowed dexter and sinister vested az, supporting in the hands ppr a garb or

Newton of Newcastle-upon Tyne, Northumb, an arm embowed vested, holding in the hand a shin-bone

Newton, Francis Murray of Barton Grange, Somers, a lion's gamb erased and erect ppr, grasping a key with the chain or

Newtown-Butler, Lord, *see* Lanesborough Earl of

Newville, a dove holding in its beak an olive-branch ppr 92 5

Neylan, Ireland a hand holding a sword 212 13

Nias, Joseph Baldwin M D 5, Rosary Gardens South Kensington, S W, an anchor fesseways with cable sa, thereon a Cornish chough ppr gorged with a collar engrailed or *Juvante Deo*

Nibbs, a buck s head cabossed gu pierced through by an arrow or, feathered arg cf 122 5

Niblet, an eagle with wings extended or 77 5

Niblett of Llanerchydol, Welshpool, late of Haresfield Court, Glouc an eagle rising quarterly or and arg 293 12

Niblett, Arthur, Esquire B A J P, of the Lypiatts, Cheltenham, on a wreath of the colours, an eagle rising quarterly or and az *Sicut aquilæ pennis* 293 12

Niblett, Surrey, on a mount vert, a lion couchant guarding a cross gu *Veritatis assertor*

Niblie, Scotland, a hand holding a scimitar ppr *Honor et amor* 213 5

Niblock, a leopard passant holding in the dexter paw a trefoil slipped

Niblock-Stuart, Rev James, the Manse, Montrose, a demi lion gu, armed and langued az holding in his dexter paw a trefoil slipped vert *Facta non verba*

Niccols, Shropsh, a martlet 95 4

Nichell, a demi-griffin az, holding in the beak a pink flowered gu, leaved vert cf 64 2

Nichol or **Nicholl,** a lion's gamb az, holding an olive-branch ppr 37 4

Nichol or **Nicol,** Scotland a demi-lion gu, armed and langued or *Generositate* 10 3

Nicholas, a lion passant az, semee d'etoiles or cf 6 2

Nicholas, Heygate William 12, Bennett Street Bath a wolf's head erased gu

Nicholas of Ashton Keynes and Roundway, Wilts, and London on a chapeau az, turned up erm, an owl with wings expanded or 96 6

Nicholas and **Nicholls,** Glouc and Wilts, a quatrefoil on a stalk raguly or charged with a martlet sa

Nicholas, William, Esquire J P, of the Nant, Bothwell, Tasmania an owl close *Vincit qui vigilat* 96 5

Nicholas of Winterborne Earls, Wilts, Devonsh, and Somers, a raven with wings elevated sa perched on the battlements of a tower arg 156 13

Nicholas, late Sir Nicholas Harris, G C M G a fetterlock or the fetter passing through a plume of five ostrich-feathers alternately arg and gu *Patria cara carior fides*

Nicholas, John Toup, Titri Waihola Otago, New Zealand, issuing from a naval coronet or a demi eagle displayed sa, with wings elevated erminois, each charged with a cross couped gu

Nicholl, Iltyd Bond, Esquire of the Ham, Cowbridge Glamorgansh (1) A tower arg on the battlements thereof a Cornish chough with wings expanded ppr 156 13 (2) A demi-lion rampant *Heb dhyw heb dhym duw a digon* 10 2

Nicholl Digby Leys Whitlock Usk Monm, same crest as first above

Nicholl of Llantwitt-Major Glamorgansh a Cornish chough with wings elevated ppr perched on the battlements of a tower arg 156 13

Nicholl of Tredunnock, Monm, on the battlements of a tower a Cornish chough with wings addorsed all ppr 156 11

Nicholl, John Iltyd Dillwyn, Merthyr Mawn Bridgend, Glamorgansh, a castle surmounted by a Cornish chough, wings expanded all ppr *Nil falsi audeat*

Nicholl of Penros Cornw a Cornish chough ppr 107 14

Nicholl, Cornw a cubit arm holding a bow all ppr cf 214 5

Nicholl, John, Esquire, F S A, of Theydon Gernon Essex, and Canonbury Place Islington, a demi-lion rampant gardant arg, guttee-de-poix holding in the dexter paw a lily ppr *Fort Fahren und Verharren* 12 10

Nicholl of Islington, Middx., a squirrel sa., holding a pheon arg.

Nicholls, Shropsh., a lion's head erased arg., ducally gorged or. 18. 5

Nicholls of London, out of a ducal coronet or, a demi-lion rampant arg. *Nil sistere contra.* 16. 3

Nicholls of Saffron Walden, Essex, a squirrel ppr. *cf.* 135. 4

Nicholls of Whitgreave, Staffs, a wolf's head erased sa. 30. 8

Nicholls, Bucks, an eagle rising sustaining a cross crosslet fitched, all or.

Nicholls of London and Shropsh., a dove close ppr. *Dum spiro spero.* 92. 2

Nicholls of London, a tiger sejant erm. 27. 6

Nicholls of Manchester, two battle-axes in saltire in front of a castle surmounted of a Cornish chough, all ppr., the dexter claw resting on a pheon sa. *Semper fidelis.* 156. 10

Nichols, Cornw., a hand couped above the wrist holding a bow in fess or, stringed arg.

Nichols, a pheon arg. 174. 11

Nichols, a demi-lion rampant holding between the paws a human heart.

Nichols, out of a ducal coronet or, a demi-lion rampant arg. 16. 3

Nichols, Harry Sidney, a demi-lion couped or, charged with three human hearts gu., between two eagle's legs erased at the thigh sa. *Aquila non capit muscas.*

Nichols, John Bruce, Esquire, of Holmwood, Surrey, a lion's head erased az., gorged with a collar gemel or, between two wings paly of six or and az. *Labor ipse voluptas.* *cf.* 19. 7

Nichols, Francis Morgan, Lawford Hall, Manningtree, Essex, same crest and motto.

Nichols, John Bruce, M.A., Holmwood Park, Dorking, same crest and motto.

Nichols, Norf., a fox's head erased ppr. 33. 6

Nicholson, a demi-lion rampant. 10. 2

Nicholson, Harvey, Esquire, of Roe Park, co. Londonderry, Ireland, out of a mural coronet a demi-lion rampant, all ppr. *Generositate.*

Nicholson of East Court, Glouc.: (1) A demi-lion erased charged with a bomb fired ppr., supporting a flagstaff encircled by an Eastern coronet or, therefrom flowing to the sinister a banner gu. inscribed with the word *Barrach* in letters of gold (*for Nicholson*). 15. 3. (2) Out of a mural coronet ppr., inscribed *Vittoria*, a dexter arm embowed vested gu., entwined by a thistle ppr., the hand in a glove arg. grasping a sword, also ppr., pendent from the guard by a ribbon gu., fimbriated az., a representation of the Waterloo Medal (*for M'Innes*). *Generositate.* — *Post prœlia prœmia.* 204. 3

Nicholson of Roe Park, Londonderry, out of a mural coronet a demi-lion rampant, all ppr. *cf.* 16. 11

Nicholson, Bart., of Glenbervie, Scotland, a lion's head erased gu. *Nil sistere contra.* 17. 2

Nicholson, Arthur Badenach, of Fourdoun, Scotland, same crest and motto.

Nicholson, Ireland, a lion's head erased gu., charged with a fess or. *cf.* 17. 2

Nicholson of Waverley Abbey, Surrey, in front of rays a lion's head erased.

Nicholson, Lothian Demain, 4, Sloane Court, Chelsea, same crest.

Nicholson of Roundhay Park, Yorks, on the branch of a tree in fess ppr., a lion's head erased at the neck or, charged with a cross patée gu. *Providentia Dei.*

Nicholson, Lancs and Cumb., out of a ducal coronet gu., a lion's head erm. 17. 5

Nicholson, Steele-, of Ballow House, Ireland: (1) Out of a ducal coronet gu., a lion's head erm. (*for Nicholson*). 17. 5. (2) A demi-eagle with wings displayed holding in the beak a snake ppr. (*for Steele*). *Deus mihi sol.* *cf.* 80. 2

Nicholson, Patrick Charles, Esquire, a lion's head erased erm., charged on the neck with a flaming heart gu., all between two branches of palm ppr. 17. 7

Nicholson, Lancs, Cumb., and London, a lion's head erased gu., ducally gorged or. *Per castra ad astra.* 18. 5

Nicholson, Sir Charles, Bart., D.C.L., LL.D., M.D., of Sydney and Luddenham, New South Wales, on a rock ppr., a lion's head az., charged with a star of eight points or. *Virtus sola nobilitas.* 19. 11

Nicholson, James, Esquire, Surgeon, of Glasnevin Lodge, co. Dublin, a wolf's head erased ppr., gorged with a collar ingrailed gu., and charged on the neck with a sun in splendour ppr. 30. 6

Nicholson, Scotland, a unicorn's head erased sa. 49. 5

Nicholson, a stag trippant gu., attired or. 117. 8

Nicholson, Joseph, Wheatfield, Headingley, Leeds, same crest. *Generositate.*

Nicholson, between two roses gu., slipped and leaved vert, a greyhound's head arg. 61. 11

Nicholson of South Carolina, U.S.A., a demi-man vested in a close coat az., the buttons and the cuffs of the sleeves turned up or, the face and hands ppr., armed with a head-piece and gorget arg., the beaver open, holding in the dexter hand a sword in pale ppr., hilt and pommel or, and in the sinister a Bible open, clasps of the fourth. *Deus mihi sol.*

Nicholson of Balrath, co. Meath, a leopard sejant arg., spotted sa., thrust through the neck by a demi-lance ppr.

Nicholson, James, Esquire, Broomfield, Sheffield, on the branch of a tree, in fesse ppr., a lion's head erased at the neck or, charged with a cross pattée gu. *Providentia Dei.*

Nicholson, Huntleys, Tunbridge Wells, a lion's head erased gu. *Nil sistere contra.*

Nickels, John Tetley, the Day House, near Shrewsbury, two arms embowed vested sa., cuffs arg., the hands holding a cross bow erect, stringed ppr.

Nickels, Walter Lanyon, of Chenotrie, Noctorum, near Birkenhead, same crest.

Nickelson, Scotland, a demi-lion ppr. *Generositate.* 10. 2

Nickisson, John Leaver, Hinton Manor, Swindon, two bezants fesseways, thereon a demi-lion rampant, and erased per fesse gu. and arg. *Generositate.* 294. 6

Nicklin, a griffin's head erased arg. 66. 2

Nickols, a hand in armour couped above the wrist in fess, holding an arrow in pale ppr., crossed at the top by a bow in fess or, strung arg.

Nickolson, a hawk's head erased sa. 88. 12

Nickson of Coolattin, Munny and Killinure, co. Wicklow, and Ballymur, co. Carlow, a tiger's head or, pierced through the jaw with a dart ppr., feathered arg.

Nicol, William Edward, Esquire, of Ballogie, Aberdeen, a greyhound's head ppr. *Fidèle.* *cf.* 61. 2

Nicol, a demi-lion rampant gu. 10. 3

Nicol, Alexander, Esquire, Shipowner, Aberdeen, a demi-lion rampant az., armed and langued gu. *Nil sistere contra.* 10. 2

Nicol of Alloa, Clackmannansh., a dexter hand holding a quadrant ppr. *Sedulitate.*

Nicolas, out of a count's coronet a wolf's head. *cf.* 30. 5

Nicolas, Cornw., issuing from a naval coronet or, the rim inscribed with the word *Pilot*, a demi-eagle displayed sa., with wings elevated erminois, each charged with a cross couped gu.

Nicoll, a sparrow-hawk sa., beaked and legged gu. 85. 2

Nicoll or **Nicolls,** of Colneyhatch, Middx., a wolf's head sa., charged with five ermine spots in fess or. *cf.* 30. 5

Nicoll, a lion's head erased az., collared arg., charged with three martlets sa. *cf.* 18. 6

Nicoll of Oldfields, Acton, Middx., a greyhound's head erased sa., charged with a mascle or, and holding in the mouth a thistle slipped ppr. *Deo duce comite industria.* 60. 13

Nicolls of Mershland, Norf., a squirrel sejant sa., collared or, holding between the fore-legs a water-bouget arg. 135. 3

Nicolls of Garisker, co. Kildare, Ireland, a naked arm erect ppr., charged with a pheon sa., the hand grasping a bow in bend sinister or, stringed arg. *As an arrow true.*

Nicolls or **Nycolls** of London, a demi-Cornish chough ppr., holding in the beak an ear of wheat or.

Nicolls of Hardwicke, Northamp., a wolf's head erased sa. 30. 8

Nicolson, Sir Arthur Thomas Bennett Robert, Bart., J.P., of that ilk and Lasswade, and of Lyndhurst, Esplanade, St. Kilda, Melbourne, Victoria, Australia, a demi-lion or, armed and langued gu. *Generositate.* 10. 2

Nicolson, Sir Arthur, Bart., K.C.B., K.C.I.E., C.M.G., British Legation, Tangier, and of Carnock, Scotland, a lion's head erased gu. *Nil sistere contra.* 17. 2

Nicolson, Bart., of Clunie, Aberdeensh., a lion's head erased or. *Generositate.* 17. 8

Nicolson, Badenach-, Arthur, Glenbervie, Kincardinesh., same crest. *Nil sistere contra.*

Nicolson, a lion's gamb gu, holding an anchor or

Nicolson of London, on a mount vert, a leopard sejant arg, spotted sa pierced through the breast by a lance ppr the wound dropping blood

Nicolson, Ireland, an arm in armour ppr, holding in the hand a holly-branch vert 209 14

Nielson, Scotland on a mount vert a tower with a cupola and vane ppr *Murus ahenus* cf 157 15

Nielsen, Hans C, Esquire, 12, Cliff Terrace, Hartlepool, a tower ppr *Ret og Sandhed*

Nigell or **Nigill,** an oak tree vert 143 5

Nightingale, Kent a greyhound passant ppr *Mens conscia recti* cf 60 2

Nightingale of Lichfield, London, and Warw a greyhound current erm charged with a crescent for difference cf 58 2

Nightingale, Sir Henry Dickonson, Bart., of Kneesworth Hall, Cambs, an ibex sejant arg, tufted, armed, and maned or

Nightingale, Lieutenant Colonel Charles William, Landscore House Teign mouth, same crest *Pro Rege et patria*

Nightingall of Brome Hall Norf on a mural coronet or an ibex arg horned, maned and tufted of the first gorged with a laurel wreath vert

Nigon, a leopard's face 22 2

Nihell, Ireland, a greyhound arg, collared gu *Vi et fide vivo* cf 60 2

Nimmo, Scotland out of a mural coronet an arm in armour embowed to the sinister, supporting in pale a pennon of two points *I show, not boast* 199 7

Nimmo, W J, Esquire Castle Eden Durh, a crescent *I show not boast*

Nind, a torteau charged with a pale indented arg 159 6

Nind of Reading and Hawthorns Harehatch, Berks out of a mural coronet arg, a dragon's head gu *Fortis et fidelis* 72 11

Nisbet, Scotland a cubit arm in armour erect, holding in the hand a truncheon ppr *I byde it*

Nisbet-Hamilton-Ogilvy, on the dexter side a demi-lion rampant gu, armed and langued az (*for Ogilvy*) 10 3 In the centre, a horse's head and neck couped arg, bridled gu (*for Hamilton*) 51 5 On the sinister side, a dexter hand issuing out of a cloud and holding a balance, all ppr (*for Nisbet*) *Forward —Ride through —Discite justitiam*

Nisbet-Hamilton-Ogilvy, Henry Thomas Bloxholm Hall Lincoln same crests and mottoes

Nisbet of Dirleton Haddingtonsh, Scotland, issuing out of a cloud in fess a dexter hand holding a balance and scales, all ppr *Discite justitiam*

Nisbet, F S of Brooklyn, Westfield Westfield Road Caversham, Reading a cubit arm in armour erect, holding in the hand a truncheon, all ppr *I byde it*

Nisbet (1) An eagle with wings displayed ppr 77 5 (2) A boar passant sa *Non tabes virtuti sors —I byde it* 40 9

Nisbet of Craigentinny Edinburgh a boar passant sa *I byde it* 40 9

Nisbet or **Nisbett** of that ilk, Scotland same crest and motto 40 9

Nisbet of Southbroome House, Wilts a boar's head erased sa *Vis fortibus arma.* 42 2

Nisbet, same crest 42 2

Nisbet of Greenholm Ayrsh, Scotland, same crest. *Vis fortibus arma* 42 2

Nisbet, a stag's head cabossed or 122 5

Nisbet of Bordeaux, a castle sa, and growing beside it a thistle ppr *Hinc ducitur honos* 155 6

Nisbet, Bart, of Dean, Midlothian an eagle displayed ppr *Non obest virtute sors.* 75 2

Nisbett, John More, of Cairnhill, Lanarksh, a boar's head erased sa *Vis fortibus arma* 42 2

Niven, a holly-branch vert 150 10

Niven of Shonsburgh and Windhouse, in Zetland, a branch of palm vert *Vivis sperandum* 147 3

Niven of Kirkbride, Ayrsh same crest and motto 147 1

Niven of Peebles and Thornton, Aberdeensh a pegasus courant arg, winged and crowned or *I hope in God* *Marte et arte* cf 47 1

Nivison, Scotland, a wolf passant sa *Exitus acta probat* 28 10

Nivison of Branch Hill Lodge, Hampstead, a wolf passant sa., collared and lined *Exitus acta probat*

Nix, on a mount a stag lodged, all ppr 115 12

Nixon, a dexter hand holding a sword ppr 212 13

Nixon, Ireland, on the point of a sword in pale a cross patee ppr 169 5

Nixon, Brinsley de Courcy, Esquire, 27, Collingham Gardens S W, a gamecock ppr, charged on the breast with a bezant *Toujours prêt* cf 90 2

Nixon, Edward Atcherley Eckersall, same crest and motto

Nixon, Frederick Eckersall, same crest and motto

Nixon, a moor-cock ppr

Nixon of Blechingdon, Oxon, a leopard rampant gardant ppr

Noakes, Wickham, Esquire of Selsdon Park Croydon, a plate, thereon a leopard's face gu between two roses arg, barbed and seeded ppr *Nil desperandum* 246 2

Nobbes of Houghton Norf, on a chapeau ppr an eagle's head az 83 12

Noble of Reresby Leics, an eagle displayed or *Fide et fortitudine* 75 2

Noble, Ireland a lion's gamb sa holding a cross patee fitched or cf 36 9

Noble, Sir Andrew Bart., K C B, of Ardmore, Dumbartonsh, Scotland, a dexter hand holding a dagger *Virtute et valore* 298 14

Noble, a lion passant az 6 2

Noble, Joseph Horace M A Selby House Ham Surrey, a leopard passant regardant sa semee of annulets or, holding in the dexter fore paw a battle-axe erect ppr *Loyauté n'a peur*

Noble, William James, M A, 1, Paper Buildings, Temple, E C, issuant from a wreath of oak ppr, fructed or a leopard's head couped and affrontee sa, collared or *Nomen et omen*

Noble, a demi greyhound arg 60 11

Noble of Allenstown, co Meath, Ireland, a dove arg, holding in the beak a ring or gemmed az cf 92 2

Noble, Shirley Newcombe same crest

Nock, a dexter hand brandishing a scimitar ppr 213 5

Nodes, two lion's gambs sa holding a garb or

Nodin, a stag's head couped gu 121 5

Noel, *see* Gainsborough, Earl of

Noel, *see* Lovelace Earl of

Noel, Viscount Wentworth (*extinct*), a buck at gaze arg, attired or *Pensez a bien* 117 3

Noel-Cox, H L, Esquire M B, F R A S, of 29 Vicarage Road Eastbourne, a goat's head erased *Fide et fortitudine*

Noel-Hill, Baron Berwick (1) A stag statant arg (*for Hill*) 117 5 (2) On the battlements of a tower ppr, a hind statant arg, collared and chained or (*for Noel*) 124 10 (3) A stag's head cabossed sa in the mouth a sprig of oak ppr (*for Harwood*) cf 122 5

Noel, His Honour Arthur Baptist of Brisbane, Queensland, Australia Judge Northern District Court Queensland, a buck at gaze arg, attired or *Tout bien ou rien* 117 3

Noel, Bart, Rutl, a buck at gaze arg, attired or *Tout bien ou rien* 117 3

Noel, Charles Perrott of Bell Hall, Stourbridge, Worcs same crest and motto

Noel, Ernest, J P, 8 Portman Square same crest and motto

Noel of Moxhul Park Warw same crest and motto.

Noel of Hilcote, Staffs same crest *Jus suum cuique* 117 3

Nolan of London, a demi-lion rampant gu holding a fleur-de lis or 13 2

Nolan, John Philip, of Ballinderry and Portacarron co Galway Ireland a demi-lion rampant gu *Cor unum via una* 10 3

Nolan, co Galway, Ireland, on a mount vert a falcon close ppr

Nolan-Whelan, John, Esquire J P of Milford House co Dublin Ireland, a griffin's head erased az gorged with a collar gemelle and holding in the beak three ears of wheat conjoined in one stalk or (*for Whelan*) (2) On a mount ppr a falcon arg, holding in the beak a sword erect, point upwards, gu (*for Nolan*) *Vincit amor patriæ*

None, an eagle displayed az, charged on the breast with a mullet or cf 75 2

Noneley, Shropsh, a lion rampant or holding in the dexter paw a dagger gu

Nonwers, Norwers, and **Nowers,** a pestle and mortar or 177 13

Nonwike, out of a plume of ostrich-feathers arg a demi-griffin ppr 64 9

Noone, Norf and Suff, a bull's head erased per fesse arg and gu, armed of the last 44 3

Noone of Walton Leics, an eagle displayed with two heads or, the wings vert 74 2

Norbery and **Norbury,** a dove or 92 2

Norborne of Bremhill Wilts, a demi lion erm holding between the paws a ducal coronet or

Norbury, Earl of (Lindesay Graham Toler), Carlton Park, Market Harborough, Leics., on a ducal coronet a fleur-de-lis or. *Regi et patriæ fidelis.*

Norbury of Norbury, Chesh., out of a ducal coronet or, a bull's head sa. 44. 11

Norbury, Coningsby, of Droitwich and Sherridge, Malvern, out of a vallery coronet or, a bull's head sa., armed of the first, holding in the mouth a trefoil vert.

Norcliffe, a buck's head erased az. 121. 2

Norcliffe, Yorks, a lion passant gu., gorged with a chaplet vert. *cf.* 6. 2

Norcliffe, Francis Best, of Langton Hall, Yorks, a greyhound sejant or, collared az., resting the dexter foot on a mascle arg. *Sine macula.*

Norcop, *see* Radford-Norcop.

Norden of London, an arm couped and erect, vested az., cuffed arg., holding in the hand an escarbuncle or. *Providentia tutamur.* 207. 7

Norden of Easthill, Kent, a hawk arg., belled or, preying on a partridge of the first, beaked of the second. *cf.* 77. 12

Norden, a demi-beaver sa., holding in the mouth a branch of five leaves vert.

Nordet, between two wings ppr., a torteau. *cf.* 110. 4

Norfolk, Duke of, Earl Marshal and Hereditary Marshal of England (Fitz-Alan-Howard), Arundel Castle, Sussex: (1) Issuant from a ducal coronet or, a pair of wings gu., each charged with a bend between six cross crosslets fitchée arg. 109. 9. (2) On a chapeau gu., turned up erm., a lion statant with tail extended or, gorged with a ducal coronet arg. *cf.* 48. (3) On a mount vert, a horse passant arg., holding in the mouth a slip of oak fructed ppr. *Sola virtus invicta.* 52. 11

Norgate, a demi-wolf salient arg., charged on the breast with an étoile gu. *cf.* 31. 2

Norhope, Kent and Notts, a cubit arm vested per pale arg. and vert, holding in the hand ppr. a garland of the second.

Norie of Noristone, Stirlingsh., Scotland, on point of a pheon a negro's head couped between two arms in armour embowed and vambraced, all ppr. *Domi ac foris.*

Norie and **Norrie,** a wolf's head erased sa. 30. 8

Norman, Rev. John Burton, M.A., Rectory, Edgeware, Middx., and of Kirkandrews-in-Eden, Cumb., a stag's head erased ppr. *Frangas non flectes.* 121. 2

Norman, Archibald Cameron, J.P., the Rookery, Bromley Common, Bromley, Kent, same crest. *Pluribus assuesce mentem.*

Norman, Henry John, 21, Cadogan Square, S.W., same crest and motto.

Norman, Ireland, out of a ducal coronet a bull's head. 44. 11

Norman, a spear issuing, thrust through a savage's head couped ppr. 191. 7

Norman, Alfred Reynolds, Esquire, of Gweedore, Castle View Road, Strood, Rochester, a dexter arm embowed in armour, holding in the hand a sword ppr., pommelled and hilted or. *Pro fide strictus.*

Norman, Rev. Harry Bathurst, of Iwood Manor, Somerset, and of Chipstable Rectory, Taunton: (1) An arm embowed in armour, holding in the hand a sword ppr., pommel and hilt or. (2) An escallop ppr. *Pro fide strictus.*

Norman of Deucombe, Sussex, a sea-horse sejant resting the dexter foot on an anchor, all ppr. *Deus dabit vela.* 46. 4

Norman, James Earl, Esquire, M.A., LL.D., of Ivy House, St. Albans, a horse's head erased.

Norman, Lee-, of Corballis, co. Louth, Ireland: (1) A lion passant gardant ppr. (*for Norman*). 4. 3. (2) A demi-lion rampant grasping a sceptre, all ppr. (*for Lee*).

Norman of Shepton Mallet, Somers., a demi-lion rampant holding between the paws a fleur-de-lis sa. *cf.* 13. 5

Normanby, Marquess of (Phipps), Mulgrave Castle, near Whitby, Yorks, a lion's gamb erect and erased sa., holding a trefoil slipped arg. *Virtute quies.* 36. 8

Normand, Scotland, a holy lamb and banner ppr. *Auxilium ab alto.* 131. 2

Normanton, Earl of (Agar), Somerley, Ringwood, Hants, a demi-lion rampant or. *Via trita via tuta.* 10. 2

Norreys, Baron, *see* Abingdon, Earl of.

Norreys, Jephson-, Bart. (*extinct*), on a mount vert, a raven rising ppr. *Loyalement je sers.* *cf.* 107. 3

Norreys of Davyhulme, Lancs, on a mount vert, an eagle with wings elevated sa. 76. 11

Norreys of Cockwells, Berks, a falcon sa. *Feythfully serve.* 83. 2

Norreys of Weston-on-the-Green, Oxon., a raven with wings elevated sa., collared or. *cf.* 107. 3

Norrington, a bat displayed ppr. 137. 11

Norris and **Norreys,** a demi-stag or, attired sa., pierced through the body by an arrow of the last, headed and feathered ppr. *cf.* 119. 5

Norris, Colonel Henry Crawley, Swalcliffe Park, Banbury, same crest. *Mors ultima linea rerum.*

Norris, Hugh, South Petherton, Somers., a demi-buck or, attired sa., pierced through the neck with an arrow guttée-de-sang of the last, point and feathered arg.

Norris, a falcon with wings endorsed. *Respice finem.* 88. 2

Norris and **Norreys,** Berks and Lancs, a raven with wings elevated sa.

Norris, William Edward, Esquire, of Guist and Wood Norton, Norf., a talbot sejant gu., collared and ringed or. *Fideliter serva.* 55. 1

Norse, Scotland, a dexter hand holding a pair of scales. 217. 13

North, Earl of Guildford, *see* Guildford.

North, Baron (North), of Kirtling, Cambs, a dragon's head erased sa., ducally gorged and chained or. *Animo et fide.* *cf.* 71. 8

North, Sir Ford, K.C., of 76, Queensborough Terrace, Bayswater, London, S.W., a lion passant. *Animo et fide.* 6. 2

North, Notts, a lion's head erased arg., collared vairée or and az. 18. 6

North, Captain Harry, Lemonwell, Eltham, a lion's head erased arg., gorged with a collar nebuly sa., and between two mullets, also sa. *Animo et fide.* 294. 3

North, Arthur Jewell, Esq., Redcroft, Eltham, Kent, same crest and motto.

North, Gamble, Esq., same crest and motto.

North, a dragon's head erased sa., purfled or, gorged with a ducal coronet and chain or. *cf.* 71. 8

North, Charles, Rougham Hall, Norf., a dragon's head erased sa., ducally gorged and chained or. *Animo et fide.*

North, North, of Newton Hall, Kirkby Lonsdale, a dragon's head erased sa., guttée-d'or, collared and chained or, in front thereof three mascles interlaced fesseways of the last.

North, Middx., a cock's head couped and winged or, each wing charged with two chevronels sa., collared and holding in the beak a branch of holly leaved and fructed ppr.

North of Cubley, Derbysh., a swan ppr., gorged with a ducal coronet and chained gu. *cf.* 99. 3

North, Hants, a stag's head erased ppr., attired or, pierced by an arrow of the last, flighted arg., and holding in the mouth a slip of olive vert.

North-Bomford, John, Gallow Ferrans, Kilcock, co. Meath: (1) A griffin segreant arg., charged on the shoulder with a cross crosslet fitchée gu. (2) A wyvern's head erased vert, langued gu., collared and chained or. *Virtutus et fidelis.*

Northage of London, a stag's head and neck affrontée ppr. 119. 12

Northam, a demi-wolf gu. 31. 2

Northampton, Marquess of (Compton): (1) On a mount a beacon fired ppr. 284. 7. (2) A battle-axe erect in pale, crossed by a branch of laurel and cypress in saltire, all ppr. (3) A sanglier, sticking betwixt two clefts of an oak-tree, with a chain and lock holding them, all ppr.: in a scroll above, *Lock sicker. Nisi Dominus.—Je ne serche qu'un.* *cf.* 177. 8

Northbourne, Baron (James), of Betteshanger, Kent, and Jarrow Grange, County Palatine of Durham, an ostrich arg., beaked and legged or. *J'ayme à jamais.* 97. 2

Northbrook, Earl of (Baring), of Stratton, Southampton, a mullet erminois, between two wings arg. *Probitate et labore.* *cf.* 111. 5

Northcote, *see* Iddesleigh, Earl of.

Northcote, Baron, formerly Hon. Sir Henry Stafford, Bart., C.B., M.A., on a chapeau gu., turned up erm., a stag trippant arg., charged on shoulder with a crescent for difference. *Christi crux est mea lux.* 118. 3

Northcote, Devonsh., on a chapeau gu., turned up erm., a stag trippant arg. *Christi crux est mea lux.* 118. 3

Northcote of Crediton, Devonsh., same crest.

Northcote of Somerset Court, Brent Knoll, Somers., a stag arg., charged on the body with two crosses botonnée gu., resting the dexter forefoot on an escutcheon or, charged with a pale engrailed bendy of six of the first and az. *Cito non temere.* 117. 4

Northcott, Devonsh, a demi unicorn or 48 7

Northen, out of a mural coronet a dragon's head vomiting flames, all ppr cf 72 11

Northesk, Earl of (Carnegie), Ethie Castle, Arbroath Forfarsh (1) Of augmentation, the stern of a French line-of-battle ship on fire ppr 281 4 (2) Out of a naval coronet or a demi leopard ppr *Tache sans tache* 281 3

Northey, a demi unicorn arg 48 7

Northey, Wilts, and of Epsom Surrey a cockatrice flames issuing from the mouth, all ppr

Northey, Rev Edward William, same crest *Steady*

Northey, Lieutenant Colonel George Wilbraham Ashley Manor, Box, Chippenham, a demi-cockatrice flames issuing from the mouth all ppr *Steady*

Northfolke or **Norfolk,** a lion rampant sa 1 10

Northin of London, on a ducal coronet or, a talbot passant az, collared of the last cf 54 9

Northington, Baron, *see* Henley, Baron

Northland, a falcon close, belled ppr cf 85 2

Northland, Viscount, *see* Ranfurly Earl

Northleigh of Northleigh and Matford three savages' heads conjoined in one neck, one looking to the dexter, one to the sinister, and one upwards cf 191 5

Northmore, of Cleve Hall Exeter a lion's head erased gu, crowned with a radiant crown of five points arg, charged on the breast with a rose of the second barbed and seeded ppr *Nec elata, nec dejecta* 17 12

Northmore, Devonsh, a lion's head erased charged with a cinquefoil, crowned with a radiant crown arg cf 17 12

Northover of Allersome and Alercourt Somers, a lion's gamb arg, holding a lozenge az, charged with a cross crosslet or 35 10

Northumberland, Duke of (Percy), Alnwick Castle, on a chapeau gu turned up erm, a lion statant az, the tail extended *Lspérance en Dieu* 4 8

Northway, a unicorn's head arg, charged with a fleur-de lis gu *Successus a Deo est*

Northwick, Baron (Rushout), a lion passant gardant or *Par ternis suppar* 4 3

Northwood, a demi lion az, armed and langued or 10 2

Norton, Baron Grantley, *see* Grantley

Norton, Baron (Adderley), on a chapeau gu turned up erm, a stork arg *Addere legi justitiam decus* 105 3

Norton, Bart (*extinct*), of Rotherfield Hants a Moor's head couped ppr, wreathed about the temples arg, az, and gu

Norton, Lowndes-Stone-, Roger Fletcher Carle, Brightswell Park, Tetworth (1) Out of a ducal coronet or, a griffin's head erm (*for Stone*) (2) A leopard's head erased or gorged with a chaplet vert (*for Lowndes*) *Mediocria firma*

Norton, a Moor's head couped at the shoulders ppr 192 13

Norton, a man's head in profile ppr, bound about the forehead with a fillet, wreathed and tied in a knot arg, az, and gu 190 4

Norton, Kent, a wolf's head erased 30 8

Norton, a griffin's head or 66 1

Norton, Captain Cecil William, 51 Queen's Gate S W, a tiger's head erased or, charged with a trefoil vert, and holding in the mouth a broken spear ppr *Frangas non flectes*

Norton, Worcs, a tiger's head erased holding in the mouth a broken spear or

Norton, Beds, Herts and Bucks, a griffin sejant ppr winged gu, beaked and armed or 62 10

Norton, Suff, a hare sejant gu in grass vert

Norton, Honourable James, of Ecclesbourne Double Bay near Sydney and of Euchora Springwood, Blue Mountains, near Sydney New South Wales Member of the Legislative Council *uses* a dexter arm embowed in armour holding in the hand ppr a sword arg pommel and hilt or *Cogi qui potest nescit mori* 195 2

Norton, a dexter arm embowed grasping in the hand a battle axe, all ppr 201 5

Norton, Norf, a halberd ppr 172 3

Norton, Ireland between two wings or, a spur-rowel az

Norton, a maiden's head ppr garlanded vert

Norton, a buck's head caboshed or 122 5

Norton, Bucks and Cambs a greyhound's head or, gorged with a fess engrailed between two bars gu, the fess ringed behind or

Norton of Chalton, Berks Kent, and Fulham, Middx, out of a ducal coronet az, a demi lion rampant double queued arg cf 10 6

Norton of Ixworth Suff a demi lion rampant gu 10 3

Norton, a demi dragon holding a sword cf 73 10

Norton of London and Shropsh, between two wings expanded or a wreath of laurel vert, tied with a ribbon gu

Norvel, an apple in pale stalked and leaved ppr

Norvill of Boghall Scotland a martlet rising ppr *Spem renovant alæ* cf 95 11

Norway, a lion passant gu 6 2

Norwich, on a mount vert a cock arg, combed legged and wattled gu 91 2

Norwick, a lion's head erased, environed with a circle of peacock's feathers ppr

Norwood, Kent on waves of the sea ppr a lion sejant holding between the paws an anchor flukes upward *Sub cruce vinces* 8 14

Norwood and **Northwood,** a demi-lion rampant erased arg ducally crowned or, holding in the paws a branch of palm ppr 12 7

Norwood, an eagle rising ppr 77 5

Norwood, out of a ducal coronet a boar's head and neck, all or 41 4

Norys, out of an antique crown or a dragon's head gu cf 71 1

Noswarth, out of a ducal coronet or a unicorn's head sa armed and crined arg 48 13

Notley, Marwood of Chillington House Somers out of a mural coronet a lion's head *Noli mentiri* 19 12

Notley, Marwood, Coombe Sydenham Hall, near Taunton, Somers, same crest and motto

Notman, an eagle rising ppr, sustaining a flag gu, the staff sa

Noton, a hind's head or 124 1

Nott, *see* Pyke Nott

Nott, late Rev Richard, of South Molton, Devonsh (1) Two mascles fessewise interlaced arg, thereon a martlet gu, ducally gorged or holding in the beak a sprig of laurel ppr (*for Nott*) 95 3 (2) On a rock a Cornish chough ppr, collared or resting the dexter claw on a cross patee also or (*for Harding*) *Pax vobiscum*

Nott, Frederick Richard Harding, Tordown, Swimbridge, Barnstaple, same crests and motto

Nott of London and Kent, a martlet arg, ducally crowned or, holding in the beak an olive branch ppr

Nott, a stag's head ppr 121 5

Nott or **Notte** of London and Shelsley Beauchamp, Worcs, a talbot sejant erm, collared or *Solus mihi invidus obstat* 55 1

Nottage, a seax ppr 171 2

Nottage, Suff, a cross patee fitched 166 3

Nottidge of Black Notley, Essex a boar's head couped at the neck gu, langued az crined and tusked or, collared erminois *Peace and plenty*

Nottingham, Ireland, a hand holding an escallop ppr 216 2

Nottingham, a dexter hand ppr, holding an annulet or 216 1

Noune and **Nunne** of Tostock, Norf, a bull's head erased per fess arg and gu armed of the last 44 3

Nourse, a stag's head or 121 5

Nourse, Oxon two bears' gambs or holding a fire ball ppr

Nourse of Woodeaton, Oxon, an arm embowed vested az, cuffed arg, holding in the hand ppr a snake of the last environed round the arm

Nove, Leics, an eagle displayed vert 75 8

Novell of London, a buck trippant arg 117 8

Novelle, a bat displayed sa 137 11

Nowell and **Noel,** Leics, a stag trippant arg, attired or 117 8

Nowell, Middx a cubit arm in pale ppr, holding in the hand a snake or 220 2

Nowell, an arm in armour embowed ppr, garnished or grasping in the hand a fire ball of the first cf 197 10

Nowell-Usticke, Robert Michael, of Polsue Philleigh, Grampound Road, Cornw (1) A demi eagle displayed gu, gorged with a plain collar, and pendent therefrom an escutcheon or, charged with a water-bouget sa (*for Usticke*) (2) A dexter arm embowed in armour grasping a sword ppr, between the antlers of a stag sa (*for Nowell*) (3) On a mount vert, in front of rays of the sun ppr, a martlet sa holding in its beak an acorn slipped also ppr (*for Beauchant*) *Semper paratus*

Nowenham, a sturgeon ppr

Nowers, Norwers, Nouwers, or **De la Nouers** of Gothurst, Bucks a pestle and mortar ppr 177 13

Nowlan and **Nowland,** a cock arg, combed and wattled gu 91 2

Nowlan, Ireland an arm in armour embowed az holding in the hand a sceptre or cf 196 8

Nowland, Ireland, a demi-lion rampant gu 10 3

Nowne, a lion rampant or, charged on the shoulder with a crescent gu cf 1 13

Noy, a fir-tree vert 144 13

Noy, Ireland, two daggers in saltier ppr 169 8

Noye, Cornw, on a chapeau gu, turned up erm, a falcon with wings expanded holding in the beak a branch of laurel ppr

Noye of Pendrea, in St Buryan Cornw on a chapeau gu turned up erm a falcon close arg, holding in the beak a laurel-branch vert

Noyes, a deer's head erm 121 5

Noyes of East Mascall's, Sussex, on a chapeau a dove, holding in its beak an olive-branch, all ppr *Nuncia pacis oliva* cf 92 5

Noyes, Rev Frederick Robert Halsey Herbert D D, the Rectory, Long Crichel, St Giles's, Salisbury, same crest and motto

Noyes, a deer's head erased erm 121 2

Nugent, Earl, *see* Buckingham, Duke of

Nugent, *see* Westmeath Earl of

Nugent, Greville-, *see* Baron Greville

Nugent, *see* Greville Nugent

Nugent, Sir Walter Richard, Bart of Ballinlough Castle, co Westmeath a cockatrice with wings addorsed ppr *Decrevi* 68 4

Nugent, Sir Walter George Bart of Denore co Westmeath a cockatrice vert, tail nowed combed and wattled gu charged with a martlet for difference *Decrevi* cf 68 4

Nugent, Sir Edmund Charles, Bart, D L, of Waddesdon Berks, a cockatrice vert, gorged with a plain collar or, pendent therefrom an escutcheon gu charged with a dagger erect ppr, pommel and hilt or *Decrevi* cf 68 4

Nun, an arm in armour vambraced, holding in the hand a hawk's lure, all or

Nun, a bull's head erased per fess vert and or 44 3

Nunn, an arm in armour embowed, holding in the hand a battle axe cf 200 6

Nunn and Nunne, Ireland, a bull's head erased per fess arg and gu armed and crined of the last 44 3

Nunn of St Margaret's, Wexford, a bull's head erased per fesse arg and gu, armed of the last *Suaviter in modo fortiter in re* 44 3

Nunn, Chas Shirley, Esquire of Bury St Edmunds Suff upon a mount vert, in front of an oak-tree ppr, a bee-hive or

Nunn, Rev Samuel the Rectory, Lawton Stoke-on Trent in front of a saltire az, a bull's head erased or *Justi sicut astra lucebunt*

Nurse, Scotland, a pair of balances ppr *Justitia* 179 8

Nusham, a monster with a lion's head, a fish's body and bird's feet all ppr

Nussey, Rev Edward Richard, B A, Vicar of Longney Glouc out of the battlements of a tower ppr, a demi-lion erminois, holding in the dexter paw a cross patée fitchée az and resting the sinister on a billet or *Arbor re careat vince*

Nutbrowne, Essex, a lion sejant sa, holding in the paws a sword arg, hilt of the first, pommel and gripe of the second

Nutcombe, Wilts, on a mural coronet or a falcon close ppr, beaked and belled or cf 85 2

Nuthall, Chesh and Lancs, a talbot statant arg, collared and chained or cf 54 2

Nuthall, Chesh, a falcon rising arg, beaked and ducally gorged or 87 2

Nuthoobhoy of Sirgnam House, Bombay upon a mount vert, an elephant ppr charged on the body with two mullets or holding in the trunk a branch of palm, also ppr *Wisdom above riches* 133 10

Nuton, Shropsh, a demi-talbot rampant and erased arg

Nutt, on a chapeau a cock crowing all ppr 91 12

Nutt, Glouc and Sussex, on a chapeau gu, turned up erm, a pheon or, between two wings arg

Nuttall, a martlet sa 95 5

Nuttall of Kempsay House Worcs, a martlet sa *Serva jugum* 95 5

Nutter, a dolphin naiant or 140 5

Nutting, Sir John Gardiner, Bart of St. Helen's, Booterstown co. Dublin a demi-gryphon segreant enclosed between two nut branches ppr *Mors potior macula* 285 11

Nyssell, a lion rampant per fesse arg and az holding in the dexter paw a fleur-de lis or 2 7

O.

Oak, Somers and Wilts, a demi leopard rampant gorged with an antique crown holding in the dexter paw an acorn branch fructed, all ppr, and supporting with the sinister a cross crosslet fitched vert *Persevere*

Oakeley, Sir Charles William Atholl Bart, of the Oaks, Tunbridge Wells Kent, a dexter arm in armour embowed ppr, charged with two fleur-de-lis or, each in a crescent gu, holding in the hand a scimitar also ppr, hilt and pommel of the second (*for Oakeley*) 196 12. (2) A stag's head erased or (*for Strachan*) *Non timeo sed caveo* 121 2

Oakeley, Salop and Wales a dexter arm in armour embowed ppr holding in the hand a scimitar ppr, hilt and pommel or 196 10

Oakeley, Sir Henry Evelyn, 97, Warwick Road Earl's Court, a dexter arm embowed in armour ppr, charged with two fleurs-de lis or, each in a crescent gu the hand holding a scimitar, also ppr

Oakeley, Sir Herbert Stanley M A, Mus Doc, 38, Marine Parade Dover, same crest *Paterni nominis patrimonium*

Oakes, Sir Reginald Louis, Bart, 93, Rue Jourdan, Brussels, on a mural coronet gu a buck's head erased ppr, gorged with a collar embattled-counter embattled or *Persevere*

Oakes of Newton Court Suff an oak tree ppr fructed or encircled with palisades *Quercus robur salus patriæ*

Oakes or **Okes** of Oundle, Northamp an oak-tree vert fructed or, supported by two lions rampant arg

Oakes, a cock's head erased gu 90 1

Oakes, a serpent erect on its tail, holding in the mouth a sprig

Oakes of Chesh and London, a demi-leopard ppr gorged with an Eastern coronet or holding in the dexter paw a slip of oak of the first, fructed of the second *Esse quam videri*

Oakes, Augustus Henry, Esquire, C B, Tangleland near East Grinstead, same crest and motto

Oakes, Richard Francis, Springhead, Sandhurst Road, Tunbridge Wells, same crest and motto

Oakey, the rising sun ppr

Oakley, a terrestrial globe ppr 159 1

Oates of Leeds Yorks, a cubit arm in armour ppr charged with two bendlets engrailed az the hand grasping a dirk point upwards also ppr, pommel and hilt or *Persevere*

Oates, Charles George, of Meanwoodside, Leeds same crest *Sua dextra cuique*

Oatley, Shropsh, an oatsheaf or, banded vert

Oatly, a garb ppr 153 2

O'Beirne, *see* Beirne

O'Beirne, Ireland, a dexter arm in armour embowed, grasping in the hand a sword, all ppr 195 2

O'Beirne, Spain, same crest *Fuimus* 195 2

O'Bierne, a cockatrice az, winged or 68 4

O'Boyle, a sword point upwards ppr, and a Passion cross or in saltire, surmounted of a heart gu

O'Breanon, Ireland an arm in armour embowed holding in the hand a sword 195 2

O'Brenan of Cloneen and Moneenroe, co Kilkenny Ireland and Malaga Spain an arm embowed in armour grasping a sword, all ppr *Sub hoc signo vinces.* 195 2

O'Brenan of Ossory Leinster, an arm in armour embowed grasping a sword, all ppr 195 2

O'Brenon, Ulster and Connaught, Ireland out of a ducal coronet or, a plume of five ostrich feathers alternately az and of the first 114 13

O'Brien, Earl of Thomond, issuing out of a cloud a dexter arm embowed brandishing a sword, all ppr *Lamh laidir an nachtar — Vigueur de dessus* cf 201 4

O'Brien, issuing from a cloud an arm embowed brandishing a sword arg pommel and hilt or *Lamh laidir an nachtar — Vigueur de dessus* cf 201 4

O Brien, Viscount Clare (*attainted*), a dexter arm embowed vested gu brandishing a sword ppr, pommel and hilt or *Lamh laidir an nachtar* 204 1

O Brien, Sir John Terence Nicholls 88, Eccleston Square S W, same crest

O Brien, *see* Inchiquin Baron of

O Brien, Sir Timothy Carew, Bart, J P, of Borris in Ossory Queen's Co, out of a castle in flames an arm embowed holding a sword, all ppr *Lamh laidir an nachtar* 284 9

O Brien, Rt Hon Sir Peter, Bart, P C, Lord Chief Justice of Ireland, an arm embowed vested az brandishing a sword arg hilt and pommel or and charged on the elbow with a fasces in pale ppr *Vigueur de dessus*

O Brien, issuing out of a cloud a naked arm holding in the hand a sword, all ppr *Vigueur de dessus* cf 212 13

O Brien, Robert Vere, Monare Foynes, Limerick same crest and motto

O Brien, a crane arg, beaked and legged gu 105 11

O Brien, a crane statant arg, beaked and legged gu holding in the beak a serpent 105 8

O Bryen, Marquess of Thomond, *see* Thomond

O Bryne and **O Byrne,** Ireland a mermaid holding in her dexter hand a mirror and with her sinister combing her hair 184 8

O Byrne, Ireland a mermaid ppr, charged on the breast with five escallops in saltire or, holding in the dexter hand a mirror and in her sinister a dart, also ppr *Certavi et vici*

O Byrne of Glenmalure co Wicklow, Ireland a mermaid with a comb and mirror, all ppr 184 5

O Cahan, Ireland, a cat a mountain rampant ppr *Felis demulcta mitis* 26 2

O Cahan of Ballynaclosky, co Londonderry, Ireland a mountain cat saliant ppr *Inclytus virtute* cf 26 3

O Cahane, Ireland a dexter hand embowed purp, holding in the hand a sword ppr 201 4

O Cahill, Ireland, an anchor erect with the cable entwined around the stock, all ppr 162 2

O Callaghan, Viscount Lismore, *see* Lismore

O'Callaghan-Westropp, George Esquire, Coolreagh, Bodyke co Clare (1) Out of an antique crown or an eagle's head sa (*for Westropp*) (2) A naked arm embowed holding a sword in bend sinister entwined with a snake all ppr (*for O'Callaghan*) 201 3 And over the second crest in an escroll the motto, *Fidus et audax Je tourne vers l'occident*

O Callaghan of Maryfort Ireland, a dexter arm embowed holding in the hand a sword, thereon a snake all ppr *Fidus et audax* 201 3

O Callan or **O Cuilean,** a demi griffin segreant gu 64 2

O'Carill, Ireland between two sprigs a falcon rising belled, all ppr

O Carrie, Ireland an arm in armour embowed holding in the hand a spear point downwards, all ppr

O Carroll, Ireland on the stump of an oak-tree a hawk rising all ppr *In fide et in bello fortis* cf 87 8

O'Carroll, Frederick Locke, J P of Athgoe Park, on the stump of an oak tree sprouting on either side, a hawk rising with wings expanded and inverted ppr *In fide et in bello fortis*

O Carroll of Ardagh co Galway, Ireland on the stump of an oak-tree sprouting new branches a hawk rising all ppr belled or *In fide et in bello forte* cf 87 8

Ochterlonie, Scotland an eagle displayed az *Deus mihi adjutor* 75 2

Ochterlony, Bart out of an Eastern coronet or, a cubit arm erect holding in the hand a scroll entwined with laurel all ppr *Prudentia et animo*

Ochterlony of Aberlemno Forfarsh, Scotland, Jacob's ladder and an angel ascending thereon ppr *Sic itur ad astra*

Ochterlony, Scotland a swan rising arg, ducally crowned or collared and chained of the same and charged on the breast with a rose gu cf 99 6

Ochterlony, Sir David Ferguson Bart a swan with wings elevated arg ducally collared and chained or, the chain reflexed over the back and charged on the breast with a buckle gu, the wings and body debruised by a bendlet sinister wavy az *Spe labor levis* 312 7

Ockham, Viscount, *see* Lovelace Earl of

Ockleshaw, Lancs, a flaming sword erect or 170 11

Ockley, Shropsh, a hand holding two palm-branches in orle ppr 218 7

O'Clancy of Downmacfelimy, co Clare, and Newtown co Galway, Ireland, a dexter hand couped at the wrist erect holding a sword in pale pierced through a boar's head couped all ppr cf 212 6

O Clary, an arm in armour embowed the hand grasping a sword, all ppr 195 2

O'Cobthaigs, Ireland a naked boy riding on the back of a dolphin 189 12

O'Collins, a pelican vulning herself with wings elevated, all ppr 98 1

O Conarchy, Ireland, on a ducal coronet az an eagle displayed gu cf 75 2

O Concanon, Ireland an elephant sa tusked or *Con can an* 133 9

O'Connell, Ireland, a stag statant ppr 117 5

O Connell, Ireland a stag's head erased arg 121 2

O'Connell, Ireland on a ducal coronet a stag trippant arg cf 117 8

O Connell of Darrinane Abbey co Kerry Ireland a stag's head erased arg charged with a trefoil slipped vert *Ciall agus neart* 121 8

O Connell of Castle Connell, co Limerick a stag's head erased ppr *Victor in arduis* 121 2

O'Connell, Sir Donal Ross, Bart, J P, D L, of Lakeview, Killarney and Ballybeggan, Tralee, co Kerry a stag's head erased arg, charged with a trefoil slipped vert *Ciall agus neart* 121 8

O'Connor, a cock's head or cf 90 1

O Connor, Ireland, an arm in armour embowed holding in the hand a sword 195 2

O'Connor, Scotland a hand gauntleted throwing a javelin

O Connor, Jeremiah Edward Esquire of Toronto, *uses* an arm embowed in armour ppr, holding a sword arg, hilt and pommel or, entwined with a snake also arg

O'Connor, Sir Nicholas Roderick K C B, C M G of Dundermott co Roscommon out of an Irish crown or an arm embowed in armour the hand grasping a sword in bend sinister, all ppr

O'Connor, Kerry a dexter arm embowed in armour ppr, garnished or, the hand grasping a sword erect, also ppr, pommel and hilt of the second *Nec timeo, nec sperno*

O Connor of Corcomroe, Ireland a hand in a gauntlet erect holding a broken dart all ppr

O'Conor Don the Rt Hon Charles Owen O'Conor, Clonalis, Castlereagh co Roscommon, an arm vambraced embowed, the hand bare grasping a sword ppr pommel and hilt or

O'Conor, Sligo an arm in armour embowed holding a sword, all ppr 195 2

O Conry, a blackamoor's head in profile couped at the shoulders sa, and bound round the temples with a ribbon arg 192 13

O'Conry of Dungarvan co Waterford, Ireland, and Seville Spain, a blackamoor's head in profile couped at the shoulders sa, and bound round the temples with a ribbon arg *Vincit omnia* 192 13

O Cornyn, Ireland, a sagittarius ppr 53 2

O Corrigan, Ireland, two battle axes in saltire in front of a sword in pale point downwards ppr pommel and hilt or

O'Crean, co Mayo and co Sligo Ireland, a demi wolf rampant sa holding between the paws a human heart or *Cor mundum crea in me Deus* cf 31 2

O Crouley, O Crowly, and **O Croly,** Ireland, an arm erect couped below the elbow vested gu, holding in the hand a spear in bend sinister ppr

O Crouley of Limerick, Ireland, and Cadiz Spain a naked arm erect couped below the elbow gu, holding a spear in bend point upwards ppr *Spero in Deo*

O Cuilean, Ireland, a pelican vulning herself 98 1

O'Cuillean of Carbery co Cork a pelican vulning herself ppr 98 1

O'Cullen, a mermaid with her comb and mirror all ppr 184 5

O Daly of Killymore co Galway, in front of an oak tree ppr a greyhound courant sa *Deo fidelis et regi* 58 5

O Daniel, Ireland a bull passant cf 45 2

O Davoren, Ireland a hind statant ppr cf 124 12

Oddie, an otter's head erased, holding in the mouth a fish

Oddie of Colney House Herts, a brock coming out of a rock ppr

Oddy, a goat's head per pale or and az armed counterchanged 128 12

Odehull and **Odell,** an eagle displayed gu 75 2

Odel, an arm in armour embowed holding in the hand a sword 195 2

Odell, Thomas Smijth, Esquire, of Kilcleagh Park, co. Westmeath, Ireland, a dexter arm embowed in armour, the hand holding a sword, all ppr., and the arm charged with two crescents in pale gu. *Pro patria invictus.*

Odell, Herbert Francis Edward, of Carriglea, co. Waterford, Ireland, a dexter arm in armour embowed, the hand grasping a sword, the blade passing through a chaplet of red roses and trefoils, all ppr. *Quantum in rebus inane.*

Odell, George, Esquire (P.O.B. 459), Bogota, Colombia, South America, a dexter arm embowed in armour, the hand holding a sword, all ppr. *Pro patria invictus.* 195. 2

O'Dempsey, Viscount Glenmalier, a demi-lion rampant gu., langued az., supporting in the dexter paw a sword arg., pommel and hilt or. *Elatum a Deo non deprimat.* 14. 12

Odiard, an arm in armour embowed ppr., garnished or, holding in the gauntlet a covered cup or.

Odin, Kent, a horse rampant arg.

Odingsell of Eperston, Notts, and Warw., a wolf passant gu. 28. 10

Odingsells, a wolf passant or, vulned in the neck gu. *cf.* 28. 10

Odingsells of Long Itchington, Warw., a naked arm erect holding in the hand ppr. a mullet gu. 216. 7

O'Dogherty and **O'Doherty,** Ireland, a dexter hand holding a sword. 212. 13

O'Dogherty, Ireland, a hand couped at the wrist erect grasping a sword, all ppr. *Arn Duthchas.—For my inheritance.* 212. 13

O Dogherty, co. Leitrim, Ireland, and Spain, an arm in armour embowed holding a scimitar, all ppr. *Arn Duthchas.* 196. 10

O'Doinn, Ireland, in front of a holly-bush ppr., a lizard passant or. *Mullach a bu.*

O Donagan, Ireland, a greyhound's head couped sa., charged on the neck with an ermine spot arg. *cf.* 61. 2

O'Donavan, Ireland, an eagle rising. 77. 5

O'Donel, Bart. (*extinct*), two armed arms embowed ppr., crossing each other in saltier, the hand on the dexter side holding a heart, and that on the sinister a scimitar, all ppr. *In hoc signo vinces.* 194. 13

O'Donellan, Ireland, on a mount ppr., a lion rampant or. *Omni violentia major.*

O'Donlevy, a lion rampant gu. 1. 13

O Donnel or **O'Donnell,** on a ducal coronet the attires of a stag ppr. *cf.* 123. 3

O'Donnell of Dublin, out of a ducal coronet or, a naked arm embowed holding a spear, point downwards, all ppr. *In hoc signo vinces.*

O'Donnell, Ireland, out of a ducal coronet or, a naked arm embowed grasping a dart, all ppr. *In hoc signo vinces.*

O'Donnell, two arms in armour embowed and crossed, each holding a sword, that on the dexter side transfixing a boar's head, and that on the sinister a heart. *In hoc signo vinces.*

O Donnell, two arms in armour embowed and crossed, that on the dexter side holding in the hand a scimitar, and that on the sinister a heart. *In hoc signo vinces.*

O'Donnell, Austria, out of a coronet or, two arms in armour embowed and crossed ppr., garnished of the first, the hands also ppr., that on the dexter side holding a heart gu., and that on the sinister holding a short sword of the second, hilt and pommel also or. *In hoc signo vinces.*

O'Donnelly, Ireland, out of a naval coronet or, the rim inscribed "1 June, 1794" in sable characters, an arm in armour embowed grasping a sword wavy ppr., thereon a wreath of laurel vert, and over the crest in an escroll the motto, *Justitia tandem.—Lamh dearg eirin.*

O'Donnoghue, Ireland, on a mount vert, a peacock az., spotted or. *cf.* 103. 4

O'Donochoo, Ireland, an arm in armour embowed holding in the hand a sword entwined with a serpent, the head towards the hilt. *cf.* 195. 2

O'Donoghoe of the Glens, a pelican in her piety ppr. 98. 8

O'Donoghoe of Mor, Ireland, an arm in armour embowed holding a sword, the blade entwined by a serpent, all ppr. *cf.* 195. 2

O'Donoghue of the Glens, Flesh, co. Kerry, an arm in armour holding a sword entwined with a snake, all ppr.

O'Donovan, The, Ireland, on a chapeau gu., turned up erm., a falcon alighting arg., the tips of the wings and the tail sa. *Vir super hostem.*

O'Donovan of O'Donovan Street, Cork, a falcon alighting arg. *Crom a boo.* 88. 2

O'Donovan, co. Cork, on a chapeau gu., turned up erm., an eagle rising ppr. *Adjuvante Deo in hostes.* 77. 14

O'Donovan, Morgan William, Liss Ard, Skibbereen, co. Cork, a falcon, wings displayed and elevated or. *Adjuvante Deo in hostes.*

O'Donovan of Malaga, Spain, an eagle alighting or. 77. 5

O'Donovan, Ireland, an eagle rising. 77. 5

O'Dowling, co. Kilkenny, Ireland, a lion's head erased az., collared gemelle or. *cf.* 17. 8

O'Driscoll, Ireland, a cormorant ppr.

O'Duana of Duanahagh, co. Sligo, Ireland, a fox's head couped sa. 33. 4

O'Dugenan, Ireland, an owl ppr. 96. 5

O'Duire or **O'Dwire,** Ireland, a hand holding a sword. 212. 13

O'Dunn, Ireland, a tree ppr., at the foot a lizard passant vert.

O'Dwyer, Ireland, a hand couped at the wrist and erect grasping a sword, all ppr. 212. 13

O'Dwyer, Cadiz, Spain, a hand couped at the wrist and erect grasping a sword, all ppr. *Virtus sola nobilitas.* 212. 13

O'Dyearne, an arm in armour ppr., garnished or, couped at the shoulder in fess, holding in the hand erect from the elbow of the first a covered cup of the second.

O'Fahy or **O'Fay,** Ireland, a naked arm erect couped below the elbow holding a broken spear, all ppr., point downwards or. 214. 10

O'Fallon, Ireland, a demi-greyhound saliant arg. 60. 11

O'Farrall, Ireland, on a ducal coronet or, a greyhound current sa.

O'Farrell or **O'Ferrall,** a greyhound in full course ppr. *cf.* 58. 2

O'Farrell of Glin and Killindowde, co. Longford, a greyhound springing arg., collared gu. *Cu reubha.*

O'Farrell, Charles Richard John, J.P., Dalyston, near Loughrea, co. Galway, on an Eastern crown or, a greyhound courant per pale arg. and sa., gorged with a collar, therefrom a broken chain, both gu. 58. 9

O'Feargus, a broken lance in pale ppr., the head hanging down or, and the ferrule of the same. 175. 6

O'Ferral-More, co. Kildare: (1) Out of a ducal coronet a dexter hand apaumée. *cf.* 222. 14. (2) A dexter arm couped in fess, vested, holding in the hand ppr. a sword in pale. *Spes mea Deus.*

O'Ferrall Buoy, Lords of Annaly, O'Ferrall of Ballintobber, of Tenelick, and of Bawne, all in co. Longford, and of Balyna, co. Kildare, Ireland, on a ducal coronet or, a greyhound springing sa. *Cu reubha.*

Officer, Scotland, a dexter hand holding a cutlass ppr. *Deo juvante, vinco.*

Offley, out of a ducal coronet or, the attires of a stag affixed to the scalp sa. 123. 3

Offley, a demi-lion per pale or and az., collared and lined, holding in the dexter paw a pink ppr., stalked and leaved vert.

Offley, London and Putney, Surrey, a demi-lion rampant or, collared gu., holding between the paws an olive-branch stalked and leaved ppr., fructed of the first.

Offley, Glouc., a demi-lion rampant per pale or and az., collared counter-changed, holding a branch of laurel ppr.

Offord, London, a demi-lion rampant or, collared gu. *Satis est prostrasse leoni.* 10. 9

O'Fienella, an escallop or, surmounted by a cross crosslet az. *cf.* 141. 12

O'Finnegan, Ireland, a falcon alighting ppr. 88. 2

O'Flahertie, a lizard passant ppr. *cf.* 138. 5

O'Flaherty of Lemonfield, co. Galway, Ireland, a lizard passant ppr. *Fortuna favit fortibus.* *cf.* 138. 5

O'Flaherty of Ballynahinch and Bunowen, co. Galway, Ireland, a lizard passant vert. *Fortuna favent.* *cf.* 138. 5

O'Flanagan, Ireland, a dexter cubit arm in armour ppr., garnished or and gu., holding a flaming sword az., pommel and hilt of the second.

O'Flynn, Ireland, an arm erect issuing out of a cloud ppr., holding a newt sa.

O'Flynn, Ireland, a dexter hand erect couped holding a serpent, the tail embowed and the head to the sinister, all ppr.

O'Friell of Kilmacrenan, co. Donegal, Ireland, a garb or. 153. 2

O'Gallagher, Ireland, a crescent gu., and between the horns thereof a serpent erect ppr.

O'Gara of Coolavin, co. Sligo, Ireland, a demi-lion rampant erm., holding between the paws a wreath of oak vert, fructed or. *Fortiter et fideliter.*

Ogden, a griffin's head erased holding in the beak an oak branch fructed ppr cf 66 2

Ogden of the Laurels Iron Acton, Glouc, a griffin's **head erased sa**, holding in the beak an acorn ppr, and charged on the breast with a cross pattée or (*for Ogden*) (2) A pheon az, between two branches of hazel ppr (*for Hassell*) *Ilias in nuce*

Ogden, an oak tree ppr with a lion rampant against it *Et si ostendo non jacto*

Ogden, a boar passant sa, between two branches of oak ppr, fructed or

Ogden, between two branches of oak in orle ppr fructed or a stag's head ca bossed also ppr attired of the second

Ogg, the late Sir William Anderson, of Oakfield Dulwich, S E, within two arms couped at the shoulders erect and embowed vested az cuffed or holding between the hands a thistle ppr, a wreath of oak leaves vert *Fugiendo vincimus*

Ogie, a human heart gu pierced by a Passion nail in bend sinister az

Ogilby, out of a ducal coronet or a cock's head gu 90 6

Ogilby, R J L, Esquire, Pellipar House, Dungiven co Londonderry, a lion rampant gu supporting a tilting-spear entwined with a spring of trefoils ppr

Ogilvie, *see* Seafield Earl of

Ogilvie, Earl of Findlater, a lion rampant gu, holding between its paws a plummet or *Tout jour* 3 2

Ogilvie, Lord Banff, a lion's head erased gu *Fideliter* 17 2

Ogilvie, Scotland, on a garb in fess or a lion passant gardant gu *Quæ moderate, firma* 5 12

Ogilvie, a lion rampant gardant ppr *Nil desperandum* 2 5

Ogilvie of Auchiries Aberdeensh, a lion rampant gu holding between its paws a plummet or *Tout jour fidele* 3 2

Ogilvie of Miltoun Banffsh Scotland, a lion rampant ppr, armed and langued gu, holding in the dexter paw a rose of the last, stalked and leaved ppr *Fortiter et suaviter*

Ogilvie, Hon Edward David Stuart, Yulgilbar Clarence River New South Wales, a lion rampant gu charged on the shoulder with an anchor or gorged with a chaplet of roses arg, holding in the dexter fore paw a plumb-rule erect ppr, and resting the dexter hind-paw on a saltire of the second *Toujours*

Ogilvie, a lion rampant ppr *Nil desperandum* 1 13

Ogilvie, a demi-lion gu, armed and langued az *Forward* 10 3

Ogilvie, Bart of Baldovan, Dundee, a demi-lion rampant gu, armed az *Forward —Terrena pericula sperno* 10 3

Ogilvie, a demi-lion holding in the dexter paw a sword in pale ppr *Ex armis honos* cf 14 12

Ogilvie, a lion's head erased gu crowned with an imperial crown *A fin* cf 17 14

Ogilvie, a lion's head erased gu 17 2

Ogilvie, Scotland, same crest. *Forward* 17 2

Ogilvie, a lion's gamb ppr *Ex unguibus leonis* cf 36 4

Ogilvie, a demi man armed at all points ppr *Præclarum regi et regno servitium* 187 1

Ogilvie, a demi lady holding in her dexter hand a flower ppr cf 183 14

Ogilvie of Edinburgh a lady's dexter arm the hand apaumee and with a bracelet round the wrist ppr *Pro salute* 222 6

Ogilvie, a dexter hand holding a branch of palm ppr *Secundat vera fides* 219 11

Ogilvie, Bart of Boyne Banffsh Scotland a dexter hand holding a sword, all ppr *Pro patria* 212 13

Ogilvie of Jamaica a hand holding a plummet ppr *Tout jour*

Ogilvie, Banffsh Scotland, a dexter hand holding a branch of palm ppr *Secundat vera fides* 219 11

Ogilvie, a dexter arm holding in the hand a scimitar all ppr *Pro patria* 213 5

Ogilvie, a dexter arm couped in bend dexter holding in the hand a plumb-rule

Ogilvie of Raggell, Banffsh Scotland, a sword in bend ppr *Pro patria* 170 5

Ogilvie, a bull issuant sa collared with a garland of roses ppr *Industria* 45 14

Ogilvie of Hartwoodmyres, Scotland, a talbot's head arg *Ad finem spero* 56 12

Ogilvie, a galley ppr *Cum periculo lucrum* 160 6

Ogilvy, Earl of Airlie, *see* Airlie

Ogilvy-Dalgleish, *see* Dalgleish

Ogilvy, *see* Nisbet-Hamilton Ogilvy

Ogilvy of Pitmouies, Forfarsh, Scotland, on a garb in fess or, a lion passant gardant gu *Quæ moderata firma* 5 12

Ogilvy of Logie, Scotland, a lion rampant holding between the paws a sword in pale ppr *Ex armis honos*

Ogilvy of Ruthven Forfarsh Scotland, a lion rampant gardant ppr *Nil desperandum* 2 5

Ogilvy, Sir Reginald Howard Alexander, Bart J P, D L, of Inverquharity, Forfarsh a demi lion rampant gu, armed az *Forward —Terrena pericula sperno.* 10 3

Ogilvy of Cove Dumfriessh, Scotland a demi-lion rampant az holding in his dexter paw a garb or *Quæ moderata firma* 12 4

Ogilvy of Newgrange Scotland a demi lion holding in the dexter paw a garb ppr *Marte et industria* 12 4

Ogilvy, Scotland a lion's head erased gu *Fideliter* 17 2

Ogilvy, Bart of Barras, Kincardinesh, Scotland a demi-man in armour holding forth his dexter hand ppr *Præclarum Regi et regno servitium*

Ogilvy, Scotland, a hand holding a palm-branch ppr *Secundat vera fides* 219 11

Ogilvy, Scotland, a deer's head couped gu, attired or *Bene paratum dulce* 121 5

Ogilvy, John Donald Burnett, of Inshewan, Forfarsh, a stag's head couped at the neck, attired or *Bene paratum dulce* 121 5

Ogilvy, out of a ducal coronet gu a nag's head arg 51 7

Ogilvy of Balbegno, Forfarsh Scotland, a sun-flower ppr *Quo duxeris adsum*

Ogilvy of Cluny, Perthsh, Scotland a demi bull sa gorged with a garland of roses ppr *Industria* 45 14

Ogilvy, Scotland, a sword in bend ppr *Pugno pro patria* 170 5

Oglander, John Henry J P, Nunwell Brading, St Helen's Isle of Wight a boar's head or couped, langued, and mouth embrued gu *Servare munia vita*

Ogle, Newton Charles, of 59, Green Street Grosvenor Square an heraldic antelope's head erased arg, tufted maned and attired or *Prenez en gre* cf 127 10

Ogle, Bart of Worthy Hants an heraldic antelope's head erased arg tufted maned and attired gu charged with a crescent upon a mullet for difference *Prenez en gre* cf 127 10

Ogle, Ireland a demi tiger rampant and ducally gorged, all ppr

Ogle of Pinchbeck, Lincs a bull's head erased or armed gu gorged with a chaplet vert cf 44 3

Ogle, a demi-lion or holding in the dexter paw a truncheon gu

Ogle, Scotland, an arm in armour embowed and couped resting on the elbow ppr, holding in the hand an ancient mace sa, studded arg 199 3

Ogle of Eglingham, Northumb an armed arm in mail issuing from a circle of gold, holding in the hand a sword broken in the middle, the edge embrued ppr, hilted and pommelled or

Oglethorpe, a cock's head or between two wings gu

Oglethorpe, Ireland a lion rampant gu, armed and langued az supporting a cross crosslet fitchee arg

Oglethorpe of Newington Oxon, a boar's head couped gu, holding in the mouth an oak-branch vert, fructed or 42 7

Oglethorpe of Kynnalton, Notts, a boar's head arg, couped and vulned gu, pierced with a broken spear the staff or the point arg, and charged on the neck with a mascle sa

Ognell of Ognell Hall Lancs and Baddesley Clinton Warw a lion's head erased or guttee-de-poix cf 225 10

O Gorman, Count Ferdinand, Knight of the Order of Christ and Knight Commander of the Order of Gregory the Great an arm in armour embowed ppr grasping in the hand a sword the blade wavy, all ppr *Toshac catha agus deineadh air —Primi et ultimi in bello* cf 195 2

O Gorman, Ireland, an arm in armour embowed grasping in the hand a sword, the blade wavy all ppr *Toshac catha agus deineadh air —Primi et ultimi in bello* cf 195 2

O'Gormley, Ireland a martlet az 95 4

O Grady, *see* Guillamore Viscount

O Grady, The, of Kilballyowen Ireland a horse's head erased arg *Vulneratus non victus* 51 4

O'Grady, John Waller de Courcy the Bank of Montreal, Chicago Illinois, U S A, a nag's head erased sa, maned or *Vulneratus non victus*

O Grady, William de Rienzi, same crest and motto

O Grady, Gerald de Courcy, 718 Waterloo Street, London Canada same crest

O Grady, late Thomas Esquire, J P of Carlton Terrace, Drummond Street, Carlton near Melbourne, and of Queenscliff Victoria a horse's head erased arg charged with a portcullis az *Vulneratus non victus* cf 51 4

O'Grady, Gilbert J P, Landscape co Clare, same crest and motto

O'Grady-Haly, Major General Richard Hebden, of Whitegates Frimley Surrey, a mermaid holding in her dexter hand a comb, and in her sinister a mirror, all ppr *Sapiens dominabitur astris*

Ogston, Alexander Milne, Esquire, D L., of Ardoe Kincardinesh, a lion passant arg, armed and langued gu *Vi et animo.* 6 2

Ogston, Alexander, Esquire, D L, LL D, M D of Glendavin, Aberdeensh., same crest and motto 6 2

Ogston, Francis, M D, Dunedin, New Zealand, same crest and motto

Ogston, James, Kildrummy, Aberdeensh, same crest and motto

O'Hagan, Rt Hon the late Sir Thomas, K P Q C 1st **Baron O'Hagan,** on a Roman fasces lying fessewise ppr a cubit arm vested gu, cuffed erm, the hand holding a dagger erect, both also ppr *Vincere aut mori* 286 14

O'Hagan, Baron (Rt Hon Thomas Towneley O'Hagan), of Tullahogue, co Tyrone, same crest *Victory or death*

O'Haharty or **O'Flarty,** Ireland a lizard vert cf 138 5

O'Halloran, a sword erect distilling drops of blood all ppr cf 170 2

O'Halloran, Ireland, a lizard or *Clan-Fergail a boo* cf 138 5

O'Halloran, late Sir Joseph, G C B (1) Of honourable augmentation, out of an Eastern coronet or, an arm in armour ppr garnished or the hand in a gauntlet also ppr, grasping a flag-staff, therefrom flowing a standard az, charged with a monkey statant or, and over the crest the motto *Purswarrie* (2) A lizard passant or, and over it the motto *Clan Fergail a-boo Lothim agus marbhaim* cf 138 5

O'Halloran, Joseph Sylvester Esquire, of Royal Colonial Institute, Northumberland Avenue London formerly of Adelaide South Australia (1) Of augmentation, out of an Eastern crown or, an arm in armour ppr garnished or, the hand in a gauntlet also ppr, grasping a flagstaff, therefrom flowing a standard az charged with a monkey statant also or motto over, *Pursuarrie* (2) O'Halloran (*ancient*) A lizard passant or, motto over, *Clan-Fergail a-boo Lothim agus marbhaim* cf 138 5

O'Haly, an estoile or 164 1

O'Hangherne of Carrigery co Clare, a pelican in her piety or, the nest ppr *Per ardua surgo* 98 14

O'Hanlan, Ireland on a mount a lizard erect ppr 138 6

O'Hanlon, Ireland, a lizard displayed vert

O'Hanly, Ireland three arrows sa flighted arg headed or one in pale and two barways the upper point towards the dexter and the lower point towards the sinister *Saigeadoir collach a-buadh*

O'Hanraghan, Ireland, an arm erect couped below the elbow vested vert, cuffed arg, holding in the hand ppr a holly-leaf vert

O'Hara, Baron Tyrawley and Kilmaine (*extinct*) a demi lion rampant erm holding between the paws a wreath of oak-leaves ppr *Try*

O'Hara of Nymphsfield co Sligo Ireland, a demi-lion rampant erm holding between the paws a chaplet of oak leaves ppr *Virtute et claritate*

O'Hara, Charles William Esquire, J P, D L of Cooper's Hill co Sligo Ireland (1) A demi-lion rampant erm, holding between the paws a chaplet of oak leaves ppr (*for O'Hara*) (2) A man's bust in profile couped at the shoulders ppr, on the head an Irish crown or and charged on the neck with a crescent sa (*for Cooper*) *Virtute et claritate*

O'Hara of Ballyhara, Cursallagh and Mollane co Sligo, a demi-lion rampant arg holding between the paws a chaplet of oak leaves ppr *Virtute et claritate*

O'Hara of O'Hara Brook, co Antrim, a demi-lion rampant pean, holding in the dexter paw a chaplet of oak leaves vert fructed ppr

O'Hara, Rt Rev Henry Stewart Bishop of Cashel and Emly, the Palace, Waterford same crest

O'Hara, Ireland a demi lion rampant erm, holding in the dexter paw a chaplet of laurel ppr fructed gu

O'Hara, Ireland a lion rampant holding in the dexter paw a sprig

O'Hara, Lieutenant-Colonel James, Lenaboy Galway a demi-lion rampant holding between the paws a chaplet *Try*

O'Hara, a crane's head or, beaked gu 104 5

O'Hart, John Esquire, a dexter cubit arm holding a flaming sword, all ppr *Fortiter et fideliter*

O'Hartagan, a gauntlet erect grasping a sword ppr, pommel and hilt or 211 4

O Hegarty of Magherabegin and Clonsillagh, co Donegal Ireland, an arm in armour embowed, the hand grasping a scimitar all ppr *Nec flectitur nec mutant* 196 10

O'Hennessy, Ireland, between the attires of a stag affixed to the scalp or, an arrow, point downwards gu headed and flighted arg

O'Hennessy or **Henessy** of Ballyhenness, co Kerry and Ballymacreedy co Cork Ireland an arm in armour embowed holding a battle-axe, all ppr *Vi vivo et armis* 200 6

O'Heron, co Kerry, Ireland, a pelican in her piety ppr *Per ardua surgo* 98 8

O'Heyne, Ireland a dexter arm in armour embowed, the hand grasping a sword all ppr 195 2

O'Hickey and **O'Hickie,** Ireland, a hand gauntleted holding a baton 209 9

O'Higgin, Ireland, a tower sa, and issuant from the battlements a demi-griffin with wings elevated arg, holding in the dexter claw a sword ppr cf 157 5

O'Higgins of Ballynary co Sligo, Ireland and Spain a tower sa, and issuant from the battlements a demi-griffin with wings elevated arg, holding in the dexter claw a sword ppr *Pro patria* cf 157 5

Ohmann of Hamburgh and Dublin, a globe thereon a representation of Dame Fortune standing on her dexter foot, the sinister thrown back her arms both in bend sinister, holding a scarf overhead cf 184 3

O'Hogan, *see* Hogan

O'Hosan, co Galway, Ireland a demi-lion rampant 10 2

O Kane, Thomas, Esquire, of 1, Florence Terrace, Londonderry, a cat a mountain rampant ppr *Felis demulcta mitis*

O'Kearin, co Clare, Ireland, a demi-lion rampant sa, holding in the dexter paw a sword erect arg pommel and hilt or *Fidens et constans* 14 12

O'Kearney, Ireland, a gauntleted hand fesseways or, holding a dagger erect ppr pommel and hilt of the first

Okebourn, an eagle rising from a winged globe, all ppr cf 159 9

Okeden of Turnworth, Dorset, a bear's paw sa, holding an oak-branch ppr, fructed or

Okeden of Ellingham Hants, between two oak branches in orle a buck's head cabossed all ppr

O'Keefe, Ireland a dove gu 92 2

O'Keefe, Ireland a griffin passant or holding in the dexter claw a sword ppr cf 63 2

O'Keefe of Ballymaguirk, co Cork, Ireland a griffin passant or, holding in the dexter claw a sword ppr *Forti et fideli nihil difficile* cf 63 2

O'Keevan, Ireland, a dagger erect arg, pommel and hilt or the blade entiled with a lizard vert

O'Kelly, Ireland, a demi-savage handcuffed and wreathed about the temples and middle vert cf 186 12

O'Kelly of Barretstown, co Kildare, an enfield *Turris fortis mihi Deus*

O'Kelly, Count, of Gallagh co Galway, Ireland on a ducal coronet or, an enfield vert *Turris fortis mihi Deus*

O'Kelly of Aughrane, Castle Kelly, and Screen, co Roscommon, and of Clonlyon and Aughrim co Galway, Ireland, on a ducal coronet or, an enfield vert. *Turris fortis mihi Deus*

O'Kennedy, Ireland, an arm embowed vested az, holding a scimitar all ppr. *Turris fortis mihi Deus* cf 204 1

O'Kennelly, Ireland, an arm in armour embowed holding in the hand a flaming sword ppr 195 8

O'Kennelly, Ireland an arm in armour embowed, holding in the hand a sword ppr, the blade wavy cf 195 2

Okeover, Oxon and Staffs, out of a ducal coronet or, a demi dragon erm cf 73 10

Okeover, Haughton Charles 6 Upper George Street Bryanston Square W out of a ducal coronet or, a demi dragon erm, langued gu *Esto vigilans* cf 73 10

Okeover of London, an oak-tree vert, acorned or 143 2
O'Kerney, Ireland, a swan's head sa, between two wings or 101 6
Okes, a cockatrice sa 68 4
Okes-Curtis, 4, Inverness Terrace, Regent's Park, N, a demi lion rampant
Oketon or **Okton,** a fleur-de lis or 148 2
Okewold, Glouc a leopard's head erased or, between two wings vert
O'Knealy, Ireland an arm in armour embowed holding a sword fesseways, the blade flammant, all ppr
Old, *see* Ould
Old, a cluster of grapes pendent slipped and leaved vert 152 7
Old of Cornw, and John Cloke Old, Esquire, Pristacott Launcelle a bunch of grapes pendent slipped and leaved vert 152 7
Old of Sherborne Dorset and Rowton, Shropsh, and the late John Old, Esquire, of Layston House, Reading, a lion sejant regardant ppr, its dexter paw resting on an antique shield gu, charged with a fess or 8 5
Old of Piddle Trenthide, and of Hillfield, Dorset same crest
Old, Joseph Hawken, Carnevas House, St Merryn, Padstow, Cornw, a lion sejant regardant ppr, its dexter paw resting on an antique shield
Oldaker, a griffin's head *Observe* 66 1
Oldaker, Kent, a bull's head erased 44 3
Oldbeife, an eagle displayed sa 75 2
Olderbury of London, out of an antique crown or, a demi-lion rampant az *cf* 10 2
Oldershaw, Suff a pheon sa, entwined by a snake ppr 174 8
Oldershaw of Kegworth and Loughborough, Old Parks, Leics, three arrows, one in pale and two in saltire interlaced by a serpent *Certanti dabitur* *cf* 173 2
Oldesworth, Glouc a lion sejant erect gu supporting between the paws a scroll or
Oldfield, Oxon, Leics, and Lincs on a garb or a dove arg, beaked and legged gu., holding in the beak an ear of wheat of the first 93 3
Oldfield, Herbert Rooke, Esquire LL B, of 6, Pembroke Crescent Bayswater, W, and Tregumna Cottage, Henley-on-Thames, out of a ducal coronet a demi-dragon *In cruce vincam* 290 3
Oldfield of Durington, Lincs a dove close arg, holding in the beak an ear of wheat or *cf* 93 3
Oldfield of Bradfield, Chesh, a demi eagle displayed arg 81 6
Oldfield, Sir Richard Charles, of 2, Harewood Place Hanover Square, London, W, a demi eagle displayed arg, the wings semee of crosses patee fitchee gu in front thereof a demi Catherine wheel sa *In Deo tutamen* 258 6
Oldfield of Oldfield, Chesh, out of a ducal coronet or a demi-wyvern with wings displayed arg *In cruce vincam*
Oldgate, out of a mural coronet arg a bull's head sa collared gobony arg and gu
Oldgate, out of a mural coronet or, a bull's head sa *cf* 44 11
Oldham, a dove sa, holding in the beak a sprig of laurel vert 92 5
Oldham of London, an owl in an ivy-bush, both ppr
Oldham of Oldham, Lancs an owl ppr 96 5
Oldham, Joshua Beaumont, of the Poplars, Tollerton, Easingwold, Yorks, an owl charged with a label 275 15
Oldham of Hatherleigh, Devonsh (1) On a mount vert in front of a tree an owl, all ppr (*for Oldham*) (2) A mount vert, thereon a cock, the dexter claw resting on a thistle ppr (*for Laing*)
Oldmixon of Oldmixon, Somers, a battle-axe erect or, headed arg in the middle of the handle a ribbon tied az *cf* 172 3
Oldnall, Roger William, Sion House Stourbridge, a cock ppr charged on the breast with an ermine spot sa, resting the dexter leg on a scull sa *Mortem non dedecus*
Oldsworth of Pulton's Court, Glouc a lion sejant gardant gu, resting the dexter paw on a carved shield or
O'Learie, Ireland, an arm in armour embowed, holding in the hand a sword 195 2
O'Learie, out of a ducal coronet or an arm in armour embowed holding a sword ppr, pommel and hilt of the first *Laidir ise lear Righ —Fortis undis et armis* 195 10
O Leary of Dromcar, co Cork, Ireland, an arm erect couped below the elbow vested az, the hand holding a sword impaling an evet or lizard all ppr
O'Leaury, an arm in armour couped below the elbow and erect grasping a dagger, all ppr
Oliffe, Sir Francis Joseph, M D Physician to the British Embassy in Paris, on a mill rind sa a dove with wings elevated arg holding in the beak a sprig of olive ppr *Est voluntas Dei*
Oliph of London, a cockatrice's head erased quarterly arg and sa, beaked, combed and wattled or 68 12
Oliphant, Lord Oliphant, Scotland, a unicorn's head erased arg, crined and armed or *Tout pourvoir* 49 5
Oliphant, a unicorn's head couped arg, armed and crined or *Tout pourvoir* 49 7
Oliphant of Carpow, Fifesh, a unicorn's head couped arg, armed and crined or *Tout pourvoir* 49 7
Oliphant, Scotland, an elephant's head erased ppr *Quod agis fortiter* 133 3
Oliphant, an elephant's head couped ppr *Quod agis fortiter* 133 2
Oliphant, Scotland, an elephant's head couped arg *Non mutat fortuna genus* 133 2
Oliphant of Culquhir Perthsh, Scotland, an elephant's trunk ppr *cf* 123 10
Oliphant of Broadfield House, Cumb (1) An elephant (*for Oliphant*) 133 9 (2) A falcon (*for Hewitt*) 85 2
Oliphant, Ferguson-, of Broadfield House, Cumb (1) An elephant statant, semee of crescents and holding in the trunk a fer-de-moline (*for Oliphant*) (2) A demi lion rampant per chevron or and az the dexter paw holding a thistle and the sinister resting on a boar's head couped, also az (*for Ferguson*)
Oliphant of Bachiltoun, Perthsh, Scotland a crescent or *What was may be* 163 2
Oliphant of Clashbainie, Perthsh, Scotland the sun in his splendour ppr *Hinc illuminabimur* 162 2
Oliphant of Condie, Perthsh, Scotland, a falcon volant ppr *Altiora peto* 88 3
Oliphant, Scotland, a falcon ppr *A tout pourvoir* 85 2
Oliphant of Rossie Perthsh, Scotland an eagle regardant with wings expanded ppr *Altiora peto* 77 4
Oliphant, Major General Laurence James, 42 Lowndes Square S W, a falcon volant *Altiora peto*
Oliphant, Stuart Esquire, W S, 7, Chamberlain Road Edinburgh, same crest and motto
Oliphant, a camel ppr 132 2
Oliphant, Scotland, a hand issuing pointing ppr *Hope and not rue* 222 12
Oliphant of Prinlis, Fifesh a hand pointing to the clouds ppr *I'll hope and not rue*
Oliphant-Ferguson, George Henry Hewitt, J P Broadfield House Southwaite Station, Carlisle (1) An elephant statant, semee of crescents, holding in the trunk a fer de moline or (*for Oliphant*) (2) A demi lion rampant per chevron or and az the dexter paw holding a thistle and the sinister resting on a bull's head couped az (*for Ferguson*)
Olive of London, a cockatrice's head erased ppr, combed and wattled gu 68 12
Oliver, a martlet arg holding in the beak a sprig vert *Ad fœdera cresco*
Oliver of Lewes, Sussex same crest
Oliver, Vere Langford, Esquire of Whitmore Lodge, Sunninghill, Berks, *uses* a lion's head erased ermines, collared and ringed arg langued gu 225 12
Oliver, Ireland an heraldic tiger's head erased or collared az *cf* 25 4
Oliver of Edinburgh Scotland a dexter arm ppr, vested arg turned up gu holding in the hand an olive branch fructed ppr *Ad fœdera cresco*
Oliver, a dexter naked arm holding in the hand an olive branch fructed ppr 219 9
Oliver, John Stephen, J P, Uplands Hall, Broughton near Preston, same crest
Oliver, Cornw an arm in armour embowed, holding in the hand a sprig of oak ppr fructed or
Oliver of Cherrymount, Ireland, a cubit arm erect vested gu cuffed arg, the hand holding a branch of olive ppr *Ito tu et fac similiter*
Oliver of Castle Oliver co Limerick Ireland, a cubit arm erect vested gu cuffed arg, the hand grasping an olive-branch ppr
Oliver of Cloughanadfoy, co Limerick Ireland, a cubit arm vested gu cuffed arg the hand holding a branch of olive also ppr
Oliver, Scotland a dexter hand couped hurling a curling-stone, all ppr 221 2
Oliverson of the Middle Temple, London three pheons az, thereon a lion's head erased or *Dum spiro spero*

Olivier of Potterne Manor, Wilts an esquire's helmet ppr *Sicut oliva virens lætor in æde Dei* 180 3
Olivier of London and Beds, an esquire's helmet ppr 180 3
Ollney or **Olney,** Glouc, and of Catesby and Staverton, Northamp, out of a ducal coronet or, a phœnix's head in flames holding in the beak an olive-branch all ppr
Olmius, Baron Waltham (*extinct*), a demi Moor habited in armour ppr garnished or, between two laurel branches vert, wreathed about the temples arg and gu, and charged on the breast with a fess embattled and counter-embattled or *Meritez*
Olmius of London between two laurel-branches vert, a demi Moor in armour ppr, garnished or wreathed round the head arg and gu, charged on the breast with a fess counter-embattled of the third
O'Loghlen, Honourable Sir Bryan Bart, Q C. of Manhattan, Barkly Street, St Kilda, Melbourne, Victoria Australia on a ducal coronet or, an anchor erect entwined with a cable ppr *Anchora salutis* cf 161 11
O'Loghlin, Ireland an anchor cabled and erect ppr 161 2
O'Lonargan, Ireland an arrow in pale, point downwards, distilling drops of blood, all ppr cf 173 5
O'Loughlin, Ireland an anchor entwined with a cable ppr *Anchora salutis* 161 11
O'Mahony, Ireland, out of the coronet of a viscount or, an arm in armour embowed holding a sword ppr, pommel and hilt of the first enfiled with a fleur-de-lis az
O'Mallahan, Ireland a horse at full speed 52 8
O'Malley, a hare current cf 136 3
O'Malley, Ireland a ship of three masts with the sails set, all ppr 160 13
O'Malley, Bart, of Rosehill co. Mayo, a horse in full speed arg *Terra marique potens* 52 8
O'Malley, Sir Edward, Denton House, Cuddesden, Oxford a horse rampant arg *Terra marique potens*
O'Malley, Emilius St Clair, Lismore, Waterford, same crest *Terra marique potens*
O'Malley, Lieutenant-Colonel Frederick William Army and Navy Club Pall Mall S W same crest and motto
O'Malley, Colonel George Hunter, 102, Banbury Road, Oxford same crest
O'Mallun, Baron Glen O'Mallun (*extinct*), out of a basket ppr, a greyhound's head and neck affrontee arg collared or the collar adorned with spikes *Gaudet patientia duris*
O'Malone, Ireland, a man in complete armour holding in the dexter hand a spear resting on the ground all ppr *Fidelis ad urnam* cf 188 2
Oman, Charles William Chadwick, All Souls' College, Oxford, a man's head couped in a morion *Festina lente*
O'Mannis, Ireland, a hand ppr holding a long cross in pale gu
O'Meagher, Ireland, a falcon arg., belled or alighting upon a helmet ppr
O'Meara, Ireland a pelican vulning herself ppr 98 1
O'Meara, Ireland a pelican vulning her self ppr *Opima spolia.* 98 1
O'Meighan of Ballaghmeighan, co Leitrim, Ireland a griffin's head erased with wings endorsed or cf 67 11
O'Melaghlin of Ballinderry co Westmeath a swan with wings expanded arg, membered gu *Scuto amoris divini* 99 12
Omer, a dove holding in its beak an olive-branch ppr 92 5
Ommaney, Surrey, a cubit arm erect, holding in the hand a battle axe in bend sinister ppr 213 12
Ommaney, a cubit arm erect per pale arg and sa cuffed of the first the hand holding a battle axe in bend sinister ppr cf 207 10
O'Monaghan, Ireland a knight in complete armour resting the sinister hand on the hip and holding in the dexter a forked pennon arg charged with an escutcheon of the arms viz 'azure a chevron between three mullets or "
Omond, Scotland, a cubit arm in armour erect, holding in the hand a spear in bend, point downwards 210 11
Omond of Carness, Orkney, Minister of Monzie, Perthsh, a dexter arm erect the hand holding a spear in bend sinister ppr *Avise le temps* 214 11
O'Moran, Ireland a star rayed or *Lucent in tenebris*
O'Morchoe, Ireland, on a chapeau gu, turned up erm a lion rampant, also gu, holding between the paws a garb or
O'More of Balyna, co Kildare, out of a ducal coronet or a dexter hand erect apaumee ppr cf 222 14
O'More, of Cremorgan, Queen's County Ireland, a dexter hand lying fesseways couped at the wrist holding a sword in pale pierced through three gory heads, all ppr *Semper fidelis et audax*
O'More, Ireland, same crest *Conlan-a-bu*
O'Moriartie, an arm in armour embowed holding a sword fesseways entwined with a serpent, all ppr
O'Mullan, Ireland, out of a crescent gu, a dagger erect ppr cf 169 4
O'Mulloy of Ughterthiary Lachan and Hughstown co Roscommon in front of an oak tree ppr, a greyhound couant sa, collared or *Malo mori quam fœdari* cf 58 5
O'Mulloy, Standard-Bearers to the Sovereign in the Kingdom of Ireland in front of an oak tree growing out of a mount, all ppr, a greyhound springing sa, collared or *Gearaigh agus dogh buadh* cf 58 5
O'Mulrian of Owney Ireland, a griffin segreant gu holding in the sinister claw a dagger in pale cf 62 2
O'Mulvihill of Knockanira and Kilglassy, co Clare Ireland a dexter arm couped below the elbow and erect holding two battle axes in saltire ppr 213 10
O'Murphy of the Island of Teneriffe a lion passant gu, resting the dexter paw on a garb or
O'Murphy of Dondown, co Waterford, of Armaloghan co Meath Ireland and Nantes France a demi-lion rampant gu, holding between the paws a garb or *Fortis et hospitalis* 12 5
O'Naghten, Ireland a falcon close ppr 85 2
O'Naghten of Thomastown, co Roscommon, Ireland and France, a falcon close ppr *Sagax et audax* 85 2
O'Neal, Major John Carter Ratcliffe House Folkestone an arm embowed in chain-mail, the hand bare grasping a sword ppr, pierced through a dexter hand couped at the wrist gu *Lamh dearg eirin*
O'Neale, Ireland, out of a ducal coronet a cubit arm, holding in the hand a sword 212 11
Oneby of Oneby, Leics, a bear's head couped per pale arg and gu 34 14
O'Neill, Baron (O Neill), Shane's Castle Antrim (1) An arm embowed in armour, the hand grasping a sword all ppr (*for O'Neill*) 195 2 (2) A stork rising with a snake in its beak, all ppr (*for Chichester*) *Lamh dearg Eirin — Invitum sequitur honor* 104 13
O'Neill, *see* Chichester O Neill
O'Neill, Bart of Upper Clanebovs, Ireland, a dexter arm in antique mail embowed holding in the gauntlet a sword all ppr
O'Neill, out of a ducal coronet or a dexter arm in armour embowed ppr, holding in the hand a sword, the blade waved of the first
O'Neill of the Fews co Armagh, Ireland, an arm in armour embowed the hand grasping a sword, all ppr 195 2
O'Neill of Bunowen Castle, co Galway, a sinister arm in armour embowed grasping a sword, all ppr
O'Neill of Claneboy Ireland, an arm in armour embowed the hand grasping a sword, all ppr *Lamb dearg Eirin*
O'Neill of Mullaghgane co Antrim, and Athboy co Meath, Ireland an arm in armour embowed grasping a sword, all ppr *Pro fide Rege et patria pugno* 195 2
O'Neill, Bart (*extinct*) of Killeleagh, an arm couped below the elbow erect gu enfiled with a ducal coronet or and holding in the hand a sword ppr, pommel and hilt of the second 212 7
O'Neill of Newcastle, Foxford, and Carrowry, co Mayo of Cloon, co Leitrim and Spain, a naked arm embowed brandishing a sword, all ppr *Hæc manus pro patriæ pugnando vulnera passa* 201 4
O Neill-Power, Captain John Joseph, Power Hall Snow Hill Waterford Ireland, upon an earl's coronet a stag's head caboshed and between the attires a crucifix *Per crucem ad coronam* 298 5
O'Neley, Northamp out of a ducal coronet or an eagle's head in flames ppr, holding in the beak a sprig vert
O'Neylan, Ireland, a hand holding a sword 212 13
O'Neylan, Ireland, a dexter hand couped below the wrist holding a sword in pale and on the point a boar's head in fess 212 6
O'Neylan, Ireland, a dexter hand couped at the wrist erect and grasping a dagger, all ppr 212 3

Ongley of Old Warden Ireland on a mount vert a demi-pelican with wings elevated or, holding in its beak a fire-ball *Mihi cura futuri*

Onion, a dexter hand gu, holding a spear or 214 11

Onley of Catesby and Pulborough North amp and Suff out of a ducal coronet or, a phœnix's head in flames ppr, holding in the beak a sprig vert

Onley, Savill- of Stisted Hall Essex, and Middx (1) Out of a vallary coronet or, an eagle's head issuing from flames ppr, holding in the beak a laurel-sprig vert (*for Onley*) (2) On a mount vert, an owl arg, charged on the body with three mullets in bend gu (*for Savill*) (3) A dexter cubit arm, the hand apaumée ppr, charged from the wrist with a pile gu, above the fingers a crescent reversed arg (*for Harvey*) *Alter si tibi*

Onmany, Ireland a gate ppr. 158 9

O'Nolan, Ireland, a hawk 85 2

O'Nowlan, Ireland, a martlet arg 95 4

Onslow, Earl of (Onslow), Clandon Park near Guildford, Surrey, an eagle sa preying upon a partridge or *Festina lente —Semper fidelis* 77 12

Onslow, Sir William Wallace Rhoderic, Bart, J P D L, of Hengar House, Cornw and of Chitterne, Wilts, an eagle sa preying upon a partridge or *Festina lente —Semper fidelis* 77 12

Onslow, Andrew Richard, the Furnace, Newent Glouc, same crest and motto

Onslow, Surrey and Shropsh, a falcon ppr, legged and belled or, preying on a partridge of the first *Festina lente* cf 77 12

Openhemer or **Oppenhemer,** a garland of laurel surmounted by a trident in bend

O'Phealan and **Offealam,** out of a ducal coronet a morion with feathers issuant from the top

Opie of Pawton, in St Breock, Cornw, a demi stag erm attired or, pierced through the neck by an arrow sa, feathered and headed arg, the wound and the head of the arrow embrued cf 119 2

Oppenheim, Henry Maurice William D L, 16, Bruton Street W, a horse's head couped arg, charged with a fesse dancettee gu, and holding in the mouth a branch of palm slipped ppr

Oppenheimer, Francis Charles, Esquire, M A, H B M., Consul at Frankfort-on Maine, of 1, Garden Court Middle Temple, E C, two branches of oak in saltire vert fructed or, in front of a flagstaff in bend ppr, therefrom flowing a banner gu, surmounting a trident in bend sinister, also ppr *Nihil sine labore* 303 2

O'Quigley, an estoile arg 164 1

O'Quinn, Ireland, a boar's head erased and erect arg, langued gu 43 3

O'Quinn, Ireland, a wolf's head erased erm *Quo sursum volo videre* 30 8

Oram, a hurt charged with a stag standing on a mount vert 116 11

Orange, a demi-talbot erased or cf 55 8

Oranmore and **Browne, Baron** (Brown-Guthrie), of Carrabrowne Castle in the co of the town of Galway, and of Castle McGarrett, co of Mayo, in Ireland (1) A dexter hand erect holding a sword in bend, all ppr, and over the crest an escroll with the motto *Sto pro veritate* (2) A griffin's head erased sa *Fortiter et fideliter* 212 13

Oray or **Oyry,** a pennon per fess gu and or, the staff in bend counterchanged 176 12

Orby, an ox-yoke erect arg cf 178 6

Orby or **Orreby,** on a chapeau gu, turned up erm a ram's head ppr cf 130 1

Orchard, Devonsh, a crow sa 107 14

Orchard of Hartland Abbey, Devonsh, out of a mural coronet ppr, a dexter arm couped at the elbow vested az, charged with three fleurs de-lis, one and two or the cuff turned up erm, holding in the hand ppr a pear or

Orchard, Scotland, a hand holding a sheaf of arrows points downward ppr 214 3

Ord, Scotland a fish haurient 139 11

Ord, a stag's head erased purp 121 2

Ord, Richard M A, J P Sands Hall Sedgfield, Durh, same crest *Mitis et fortis*

Ord, Northumb, an elk's head erased arg, attired or

Ord (1) An elk's head couped ppr (*for Ord*), (2) On a chapeau purp turned up erm a griffin statant with wings elevated and addorsed of the second, the beak or (*for Craven*) 63 13

Ord, Captain William St. George, of Fornham House, Suff, an elk's head ppr *Mitis et fortis*

Orde-Powlett, Baron Bolton, *see* Bolton

Orde, Campbell-, Sir Arthur John Bart., D L, of Morpeth, Northumb, an elk's head erased or, gorged with a collar invected sa, motto over *Mitis et fortis*

Orde, Hants, an elk's head erased ppr

Orde, William, of Nunnykirk Northumb, an elk's head ppr *Mitis et fortis*

Orde, Northumb a demi lion holding in the dexter paw a fleur de-lis or 13 2

Orde, Northumb, a demi-lion or holding in the dexter paw a fleur-de lis gu 13 2

Ordway, two wings displayed, each charged with a mullet pierced cf 109 6

O'Reilly, Ireland, a pellet charged with a chevron or

O'Reilly, an acorn slipped and leaved vert 152 1

O'Reilly of Scarborough, Yorks, out of an antique Irish crown or, a tree therefrom a serpent descending entwined round the stem, both ppr *Fortitudine et prudentia*

O'Reilly of Heath House Queen's Co, Ireland and East Brefney (1) Out of a ducal coronet or an oak-tree with a snake entwined descendant ppr (2) A cubit arm in armour holding in the gauntlet a dagger, all ppr *Fortitudine et prudentia*

O'Reilly, William Joseph, Knock Abbey Dundalk, co Louth same crests and motto

O'Reilly, Myles George an oak-tree eradicated, the trunk entwined by a snake ascending ppr

O'Reilly, an arm in armour embowed grasping a scimitar all ppr *Fortitudine et prudentia* 196 10

O'Reilly, Bart of Ballinlough co West meath, Ireland, an arm in armour embowed grasping a scimitar, all ppr 196 10

Orfeur of High Close and Plumbland Hall, Cumb, a woman's head couped at the breasts, all ppr, on the head a cross patee fitched or

Orford, Earl of (Walpole), Walterton Park, near Aylsham, the bust of a man in profile couped at the shoulders ppr, ducally crowned or, and from the coronet flowing a long cap turned forwards gu tasselled or, charged with a Catherine-wheel of the last *Fari quæ sentiat* 190 3

Orford-Holte (1) Upon a mount vert a squirrel sejant ppr, charged on the shoulder with a cross patee or, and supporting with the fore paws a pheon mounted on a staff and flighted head downwards or (*for Holte*) (2) Out of rushes ppr, a demi greyhound arg charged on the neck with two chevronels sa. and holding between the paws a fleur de-lis az (*for Orford*)

Orgaine, Berks and Wilts, three organ-pipes, one in pale and two in saltier, or, bound with a chaplet of laurel vert

Organ, same crest

Orgill of Beccles Suff a buffalo's head sa, gorged with a wreath of roses ppr cf 44 1

Oriel, Baron, *see* Massereene Viscount

O'Riley, Ireland, out of a ducal coronet an oak tree, around the stem a serpent entwined all ppr

O'Riordan of Derryroe, co Cork, Ireland, and Nantes, France, a fleur-de lis gu *Pro Deo et patria* 148 2

O'Riordan or **O'Rearden,** Ireland, a fleur de lis gu *Pro Deo et patria* 148 2

Orkney, Earl of (Fitzmaurice), Glanmore, Templemore, out of a ducal coronet or, an oak-tree fructed and penetrated transversely by a frame saw, all ppr the frame of the first *Through* 143 8

Orlebar, Richard, and Richard Rouse-Boughton, of London and of Hinwick House, Beds an eagle's head between two wings erect arg, charged on the neck with two barrulets gu cf 84 2

Ormathwaite, Baron (Walsh), of Ormathwaite, Cumb, a gryphon's head erased per fesse wavy arg and erm, beaked and eared or *Veritas et virtus vincunt* 66 2

Orme, *see* Garnett-Orme

Orme of Hanch Hall Staffs, a dolphin az finned or, holding in the mouth a spear

Orme of Abbeystown, Mayo, a dolphin naiant az, fins and tail or, surmounted by a pole-axe in bend of the same *Fortis et fidelis*

Orme, Northamp, a dolphin naiant arg, the fins, tail, and tusk or 140 5

Orme, Scotland a dragon passant with wings addorsed ppr 73 2

Orme, Scotland, a griffin passant gu 63 2

Orme, Scotland a demi griffin with wings addorsed arg 64 2

Ormerod of London, Glouc, and Tyldesley Lancs, a wolf's head couped at the neck barry of four or and gu holding in the mouth an ostrich-feather in pale ppr

Ormerod, Rev. George Thomas Bailey, of Stroud, Glouc., same crest.

Ormerod, Ernest William, same crest.

Ormesby, Lincs, an arm embowed vested sa., cuffed or, holding in the hand ppr. a leg in armour couped at the thigh of the last, garnished of the second.

Ormiston of Hill View, Dassett Road, West Norwood, an anchor ppr. *Gardez bien.*

Ormistone, Scotland, a cock crowing ppr. *In dubiis constans.* 91. 2

Ormistone, Scotland, an anchor ppr. *Felicior quo certior.* 161. 1

Ormonde, Marquess of (Butler), Kilkenny Castle, Ireland, out of a ducal coronet or, a plume of five ostrich-feathers, therefrom issuant a falcon rising, all arg. *Butler a Boo.—Comme je trouve.*

Ormsby, *see* Harlech, Baron.

Ormsby-Gore, Shropsh., *see* Gore.

Ormsby of Nun Ormesby and Louth, Lincs, an arm couped at the elbow vested sa., holding in the hand a leg in armour couped at the thigh, all ppr. 243. 20

Ormsby, Bart. (*extinct*), of Cloghan, co. Mayo, a dexter arm in armour embowed holding in the hand a leg in armour couped above the knee, all ppr. *Fortis qui prudens.* 243. 20

Ormsby, Rev. William, M.A., same crest and motto.

Ormsby, Anthony, Ballinamore House, Kiltimagh, co. Mayo, same crest. *Fortis qui prudens.*

Ormsby, Rev. Frederick Alexander, the Vicarage, Christ Church, Clapham, same crest and motto.

Ormsby, Henry Magee, M.A., same crest and motto.

Ormsby, Sir Lambert Hepenstal, M.D., of 92, Merrion Square, Dublin, same crest and motto.

Ormsby, John Becher, same crest and motto.

Ormsby of Willowbrook, co. Sligo, and Shropsh., a dexter arm in armour embowed ppr., charged with a rose gu., holding in the hand a leg in armour couped above the knee, also ppr.

Ormsby, Ireland, two globes ppr. 159. 3

Ormsby, a falcon rising or. 88. 2

Ormsby-Hamilton, Alfred Hamilton, J.P., 16, William Square, Dublin: (1) Out of a ducal coronet of five leaves or, charged on the band with three torteaux fessewise, a mount vert, thereon an oak-tree penetrated transversely in the main stem by a frame-saw ppr., the frame or (*for Hamilton*). (2) A dexter arm in armour embowed ppr., charged with a rose gu., holding in the hand a leg in armour couped above the knee, also ppr.

O'Rorke, Charles Dennis, Clonbern Park, Clonbern, co. Galway, out of a ducal coronet or, an arm in armour erect grasping a sword ppr., pommel and hilt of the first.

O'Rorke or **O'Rourke** of Nantes, France, out of a crown or, an arm in armour erect grasping a sword ppr. *Victorious.*

O'Rorke, George Samuel, Esquire, M.A., LL.D., Solicitor, of 9, Magdala Road, Nottingham, an eagle's head erased or. *In cruce salus.*

O'Rorke, Ireland, out of an ancient Irish crown or, an arm in armour erect grasping a sword ppr., pommel and hilt of the first. *Buagh.—Serviendo guberno.*

O'Rourk, Ireland, out of a ducal coronet or, a gauntlet grasping a sword ppr.

O'Rourke, Count, France, out of a royal crown a naked arm erect holding a scimitar, all ppr. *Victorious.*

Orpen of Ardtully, co. Kerry, Ireland, a demi-lion rampant or, charged on the shoulder with a cross crosslet sa. *Veritas vincet.* cf. 10. 2

Orpen, Rev. Edward Chatterton, Exeleigh, Devonsh., same crest and motto.

Orpen of Killowen, co. Kerry, Ireland, a demi-lion rampant or. *Veritas vincet.* 10. 2

Orpwood of Abingdon, Berks, a boar passant quarterly erm. and ermines, bristled, armed, and ungu. or. 40. 9

Orr-Ewing, Sir Archibald, Bart., M.P., D.L., J.P., of Ballikinrain, Stirlingsh., and Gollanfield, Inverness-sh., a demi-lion rampant gu., armed and langued az., holding in the dexter paw a mullet, also gu. *Audaciter.* 15. 7

Orr-Ewing, Charles Lindsay, 38, Bryanston Square, same crest and motto.

Orr, a lion passant ppr., resting the dexter fore-paw on a torteau. cf. 6. 2

Orr of Harvieston, Clackmannansh., a cornucopia ppr. *Virtuti fortuna comes.* 152. 13

Orr, James, Esquire, B.A., of the Villa Antoinette, Cannes, Alpes Maritimes, France, a cornucopia erect ppr., charged with a trefoil slipped vert. *Bonis omnia bona.* cf. 152. 13

Orr of Belfast, a cornucopia ppr., charged with a trefoil slipped vert. *Bonis omnia bona.* cf. 152. 13

Orr of Barrowfield, Scotland, a cornucopia ppr. *Bonis omnia bona.* 152. 13

Orr of Edinburgh, Scotland, a cornucopia ppr. *Virtuti fortuna comes.* 152. 13

Orr, Scotland, issuing out of a heart a dexter hand grasping a scimitar. *True to the end.* 213. 4

Orr of Ralston, Renfrewsh., Scotland, a dexter hand holding a tree ppr. *Ego accedo.*

Orr of Harvieston and Castle Campbell, Clackmannan, Scotland, a tower ppr. *Fortis et vigilans.* 156. 2

Orred, John Cavendish, of Lavant House, Chichester, a hare salient ppr., holding in the mouth three ears of corn or.

Orrell of Turton, Lancs, Cambs, and Chesh., a lion's head erased arg., semée of torteaux and ducally gorged gu. cf. 18. 5

Orrock of that ilk, Scotland, a falcon ppr. *Solus Christus mea rupes.* 85. 2

Orrock, a hawk ppr. *Christus mea rupes.* 85. 2

Orrock, Scotland, a writing-pen thrust through a man's heart ppr. *Arte fideque.*

Orton and **Ortun** of Lea, Leics., a tower ppr., the cupola and flag gu. 157. 15

Orton, a tower arg. 156. 2

Ory, an arm in armour holding in the hand a sword, all ppr. 210. 2

Osbaldeston of Chadlington, Oxon., a knight in complete armour on a horse arg., on his shield the family arms, viz.: arg., a mascle sa., between three pellets. *Constance et ferme.*

Osbaldeston, Heref., a man in armour on horseback, all ppr., holding in his dexter hand a sword arg., hilted or. cf. 53. 10

Osbaldeston, Glouc.: (1) A stag's head erased per pale arg. and sa., guttée counterchanged, attired or. 121. 2. (2) A man in armour on horseback, all ppr., holding in the dexter hand a sword arg., hilted or. cf. 189. 10

Osbaldeston, of Osbaldeston, Lancs, same crests.

Osbaldeston of Humanby, Yorks, same crests.

Osbaldeston, Heref., a stag's head erased per pale arg. and sa., guttée counterchanged, attired or. 121. 2

Osborn, Sir Algernon Kerr Butler, Bart., J.P., of Chicksands Priory, Beds, a lion's head erased arg., ducally crowned or. *Quantum in rebus inane.* 18. 8

Osborn, Ireland, out of a mural coronet gu., a lion's head arg. 19. 12

Osborn or **Osborne,** a lion's head erased arg., ducally crowned or. 18. 8

Osborn of Peppermilne, Edinburgh, a sword in pale ppr. *Je gagne.* 170. 2

Osborn, a lion's head ppr., ducally crowned or. *Quantum in rebus inane.* cf. 18. 8

Osborn, Samuel, J.P., F.R.C.S., Seymour Street, Hyde Park, a unicorn passant or, ducally gorged, ringed, lined, armed, and crined sa. *Malo mori quam fœdari.*

Osborne, *see* Leeds, Duke of.

Osborne, a heraldic tiger passant arg., charged with a label of three points for difference. *Pax in bello.* cf. 25. 5

Osborne of Kirkby Bydon, Norf., and of Cleby, Essex, out of a ducal coronet or, a heraldic tiger's head sa., armed and crined gold. 25. 3

Osborne, Yorks, a heraldic tiger passant arg., crested and tufted sa. *Pax in bello.* 25. 5

Osborne of London, Ashford, Kent, and Keyton, Notts, a heraldic tiger passant or, tufted and maned sa., charged with a pellet. cf. 25. 5

Osborne, George, J.P., Foxlow, Bungendore, New South Wales, a heraldic tiger passant or, tufted and maned sa. *Pax in bello.*

Osborne of Kelmarsh, Northants, a heraldic tiger passant arg., crested and tufted sa. *Pax in bello.* 25. 5

Osborne, Bernal-, of Newtown Anner, co. Tipperary: (1) A sea-lion sejant ppr., supporting with the dexter paw a trident sa., headed or, and charged upon the shoulder for difference with a cross crosslet or (*for Osborne*). (2) A demi-lion per fesse gu. and vair, langued az., holding a torch or, fired ppr. (*for Bernal*). *Pax.*

Osborne of Osborne House, Spondon, Derbysh., a demi-lion rampant gu. 10. 3

Osborne, Sir Francis, Bart., a sea-lion sejant ppr., holding in the dexter paw a trident sa., headed or. *Pax in bello.*

Osborne of Hartlip Place, Kent, a demi-ounce rampant erm., pellettée, collared and lined. cf. 23. 13

Osborne, Derbysh, a pelican in her piety or 98 8

Osborne of Debenham Suff a unicorn passant or ducally gorged, ringed, lined armed and crined sa cf 48 6

Osborne, Beds, a leopard's head ppr, ducally crowned or

Osborne-Gibbes, Sir Edward Bart, an arm embowed in armour ppr, garnished or, the hand in a steel gauntlet grasping a battle axe sa *Tenax pro positi* 200 6

Osbourne, on a rock a castle in flames ppr 155 1

Osbourne, a unicorn passant or, ducally gorged and chained sa, armed of the second and first 48 6

Osbourne, Scotland, a sword erect ppr *Je gagnie* 170 2

O'Selbac, Ireland, a dexter hand pointing with one finger gu 222 12

Osevain, a horse passant, saddled and bridled 52 4

Osgodby, on a chapeau a cross patee fimbriated

O'Shanly, Ireland a hand in armour grasping a broken sword

O'Shaughnessy, Ireland, a nag's head erased sa, bridled or cf 51 5

O'Shaughnessy, Ireland, an arm in chain armour embowed, the hand grasping a spear, shaft broken, all ppr cf 197 2

O'Shee or **O'Shea**, Ireland, a swan rising sa, beaked and membered gu *Vincit veritas* 99 12

O'Shee of Sheestown Kilkenny, a swan rousant sa *Vincit veritas*

O'Sheehan, a dove arg, holding in the beak an olive branch ppr 92 5

O'Sheil of Castle Burg, co Galway and of Nantes France an arm erect couped at the wrist gu, enfiled with a ducal coronet or, and grasping a sword ppr, pommel and hilt of the last *Omne solum forti patria* 212 7

O'Sheill, co Tyrone, Ireland, out of a ducal coronet or an arm erect vested gu holding a sword ppr *Omne solum forti patria*

O'Slatterie or **Slatterie**, Ireland, a cock crowing ppr 91 7

Osmand, Hon William Henry Seville of the Sycamores, Stawell, Victoria, Australia, in front of two battleaxes in saltire arg a bear ppr, resting the dexter forepaw on a cross crosslet gu *Fidem servare* 253 9

Osmaston, F P B, Esquire of Stoneshill Limpsfield Surrey, a unicorn's head arg erased gu, armed and maned or, charged on the neck with three spear heads, one and two, also gu *Ad rem* 250 8

Osmer, a buck's head cabossed ppr 122 5

Osmond of Coventry and Barkeswell, Warw, out of a mount vert a perch sa. thereon an eagle displayed erm 75 4

Osmond of Exeter, Devonsh, an eagle or 76 2

Ossington, Viscount (*extinct*—Rt Hon the late John Evelyn Denison), a sinister cubit arm in bend dexter, vested vert, cuffed erm, charged on the hand ppr with a cross crosslet, and pointing with the forefinger to an estoile

Ossory, Earl of, *see* Ormonde Marquess of.

Ossulston, Lord, *see* Tankerville Earl of

Osten, D', *see* D'Osten Moller

Ostle, a horse's head cf 50 13

Ostler, a nag's head issuing cf 50 13

Ostrich, an ostrich's head erased az, holding in the beak a horse-shoe or

O'Sullivan Mor, Ireland on a ducal coronet or, a robin redbreast holding in the beak a sprig of laurel all ppr *Lamh foistenach abu* cf 108 12

O'Sullivan Beare, Ireland, on a lizard vert a robin redbreast ppr

O'Sullivan of Dunkerron, co Kerry out of a ducal coronet or a lion's head arg, langued gu *Nec timeo nec sperno* 17 5

Oswald, *see* Gordon Oswald

Oswald, John of Dunnikier, Fifesh Scotland a star of six points wavy arg *Monstrant astra viam* 164 1

Oswald, Thomas Ridley Esquire of Milford Haven South Wales an estoile of six points arg *Monstrant astra viam*

Oswald of Dalderne Stirlingsh a comet star or *Monstrant astra viam* 164 10

Oswald of Fingalton, Renfrewsh issuing out of a cloud a dexter hand pointing toward a star of eight rays *Forti favet cœlum* cf 222 7

Oswald, Haldane-, Richard Alexander, of Auchincruive Ayrsh Scotland (1) A dexter hand issuing out of a cloud and pointing to a star ppr (*for Oswald*) 222 7 (2) An eagle's head erased ppr (*for Haldane*) *Sequamur —Suffer* 83 2

Oswald, on a mount a stag lodged under a holly-bush all ppr

Oswald of Scotstown, Renfrewsh Scotland, a ship under sail ppr *Non mihi commodus uni* 160 13

Oswald-Brown, Major Charles Robert, Manchester Regiment Aldershot a lion rampant parted per fesse arg and az, holding in his dexter paw a star wavy of six rays or *Floreat majestas*

Oteley, Shropsh, *see* Oatley and Otteley

Otgher, a martlet with wings expanded arg cf 93 10

Othwell, a dove volant gu cf 93 10

Otley of St Christopher's St Vincent's, and Antigua West Indies, and Shropsh in front of a garb or, three arrows two in saltier and one in pale, points downward sa *Dat Deus incrementum* 153 11

O'Toole, Ireland a boar passant ppr 40 9

O'Toole, Wicklow Ireland, a lion rampant arg, holding a forked pennon gu *Spero*

Otter-Barry, *see* Barry

Otter, Hunts, a crescent or 163 2

Otterington of Dublin, on a tun lying fesseways or, an otter passant sa

Ottley, a demi-lion or, holding a branch vert cf 10 2

Ottley of Ottley, Shropsh, a sheaf of oats or, banded vert

Otto, an otter ppr cf 134 5

Otway, a demi eagle displayed ppr 81 6

Otway, Yorks, out of a ducal coronet or, two wings expanded sa 109 5

Otway, Rt Hon Sir Arthur John Bart, P C, of Brighton Sussex, out of a ducal coronet or, between two wings erect sa a Passion cross or *St Deus nobiscum, quis contra nos* 111 1

Otway of Otway Towers, Herts (1) Out of a ducal coronet a Passion cross or between two wings sa, each charged for distinction with a cross crosslet arg (*for Otway*) 111 6 (2) Upon the battlements of a tower an arm in armour fesseways couped, holding in the hand a sword erect between two branches of oak all ppr (*for Hughes*) *Semper vigilans* 211 10

Otway-Ruthven, of Invernisk, co Galway, a goat's head erased arg, attired or, charged with a mullet gu *Deed shaw*

Ouchterlony, Scotland, an eagle displayed party per pale *Deus mihi adjutor* 75 2

Ouchterlony, a rock ppr *Jamais abattu* 179 7

Ouchton, an eagle's head or 83 1

Oughton, Scotland a tower the sinister side-battlement broken all ppr there out a laurel sprig vert, the tower charged on the centre with a grenade sa fired ppr *Nescit abolere vetustas*

Oughton, a tower ruined on the sinister top, therefrom a laurel-branch issuing ppr *Nescit abolere vetustas*

Ould, Ireland five arrows in saltier banded in the middle 173 3

Ould of the Mount, Chester a bundle of arrows in saltire banded in the middle 173 3

Ould, a sheaf of five arrows ppr banded gu enclosed by two oak-branches vert *Cedite seni*

Ouldesworth, a lion sejant gu, resting the dexter paw on an escutcheon or

Ouldfield, Lincs on a garb or a dove arg holding in the beak an ear of wheat of the first 93 3

Ouldsworth, out of a ducal coronet a plume of ostrich-feathers ppr cf 114 8

Ouldsworth, Glouc, a lion sejant gu resting the dexter paw on a carved shield or

Oulry, an owl sa between two wings the dexter or the sinister sa cf 96 5

Oulton and **Owlton**, a martlet arg 95 4

Oulton, out of a ducal coronet or a demi lion rampant arg 16 3

Ouseley, Bart, Herts, out of a ducal coronet or, a wolf's head erased sa holding in the mouth a dexter hand couped at the wrist gu *Mors lupi agnis vita*

Ouseley, Northamp, same crest

Ouseley, Ireland, out of a ducal coronet or, a wolf's head arg cf 30 5

Outhwaite of Bradford Moor and Southowram, Yorks, and Westfield North Berwick, Haddingtonsh on a mount vert a stag lodged regardant ppr, charged on the body with two fleurs-de-lis in fesse gu, and a like fleur-de-lis resting upon the head between the attires and holding in the mouth two ears of wheat or *Deo et patria* 115 14

Outhwaite, Thomas Roland Craigforth Earlsferry Elie, Fifesh, same crest and motto

Outlawe, Norf, a demi wolf ppr pierced through the side by an arrow or feathered and headed arg the arrow in bend sinister

Outram, Sir Francis Boyd, Bart, Clack nafaire, Pitlochry, N B, out of an Eastern coronet a demi lion or, gorged with a wreath of laurel ppr holding between the paws a cross flory gu *Mutare fidem nescio* 303 4

Outram, or **Owtram,** Herbert H of Newland Hall, Ellel, near Lancaster, a goat's head erased per fess or and sa *Frangas non flectes* 128 5

Ouvry, E C, of 2, Devonport Street, Hyde Park London, W, a lion rampant sa ducally crowned of three leaves gu, socked, armed, and langued of the last. *Fiat justitia ruat cœlum* 2 1

Over, Middx and Herts, a bird rising or, beaked and membered gu, holding in the beak an olive-branch vert, fructed or 94 5

Overbery and **Overbury,** Glouc a lion's gamb erect arg, encircled by a ducal coronet or 36 3

Overend, Ireland, a cherub's head or 189 9

Overman, Norf and Suff, a leopard sejant ppr, holding in the dexter paw a fleur de lis or

Overstone, Baron (*extinct*), a buck's head and neck erased ppr attired or, charged with a fesse engrailed sa, thereon three bezants *Non mihi sed patria* cf 121 2

Overton of Morecot, Rutl, a maiden's head ppr, vested gu, crined or cf 182 5

Overton, on a chapeau ppr, a martlet sa 95 1

Overtoun, Baron (White), Overtoun, Dumbartonsh, a dexter arm embowed the hand grasping a wreath of laurel ppr *Virtute*

Overy, a bull's head az cf 44 3

Ovey, Richard Lockhart, of Badgemore Henley-on-Thames upon a rock ppr, a lamb passant arg, guttee-de sang supporting with the dexter fore foot a flagstaff in bend sinister or, therefrom flowing a pennon of the second the whole within a chain in arch of the third *Semper eadem*

Owen, Shropsh, a spread-eagle's head erased per fess or and gu 84 14

Owen, two eagles' heads conjoined at the neck erased or 84 11

Owen, Shropsh, two eagles' heads and necks displayed and conjoined in one neck or, erased gu. *Auxilium meum a Domino* 84 14

Owen, Bulkeley-, Rev Thomas Mainwaring Bulkeley, of Tedsmore Hall Shropsh (1) Two eagles' heads conjoined in one neck erased party per fess or and gu, membered of the last (*for Owen*) 84 14 (2) Out of a ducal coronet or, a bull's head arg armed of the first (*for Bulkeley*) *Eryr Eryrod Eryri —Nec temere nec timide* 44 11

Owen, Pembrokesh, an eagle's head erased or 83 2

Owen, Henry, Esquire, D L, J P D C L of Poyston, Haverfordwest an eagle's head erased at the neck or *Trwygymmorth Duw*

Owen of Condover Shropsh, two eagles' heads conjoined and erased or, membered gu 84 14

Owen, Mostyn-, Arthur William, of Woodhouse Shropsh two eagles' heads conjoined and erased per fess or and gu, membered of the last 84 14

Owen, Edward, M A, Bradwell juxta-Mare, Southminster, a demi-lion rampant

Owen, Hugh Darby Annesley, Bettys Hall, Newtown, co Montgomerysh (1) A Cornish chough ppr holding in the dexter claw a fleur-de lis arg (2) Two eagles' heads conjoined in one neck erased party per fess or and gu, membered of the last 84 14

Owen, Shropsh, a Cornish chough ppr, holding in the dexter claw a fleur-de-lis arg cf 107 14

Owen of Glynafon Anglesey, a raven ppr, holding in the beak a bait *Deus pascit corvos* cf 107 14

Owen of Garthynghared, Wales a cock's head erased arg, holding in the beak a snake az

Owen, a demi dragon gu, winged or 73 10

Owen, Shropsh, a demi dragon wings expanded or 73 10

Owen, Peter, Esquire, of the Elms, Great Sutton Chester a demi-wyvern arg, semee de lis gu supporting with the dexter claw an escutcheon of the last charged with a crescent, also arg *Deo duce comite industria*

Owen, Wales a lion rampant or *Honestas optima politia.* 1 13

Owen, Sir Hugh Charles Bart, of Orielton, Pembrokesh, a lion rampant or *Honestas optima politia* 1 13

Owen, an anchor sa, on the base thereof a lion statant gu

Owen, Essex, a demi lion rampant gu 10 3

Owen of Dublin a demi lion rampant gu, armed and langued az, supporting an Ionic pillar arg, the base and capital or *Firmitas in cœlo*

Owen, Arthur D, M D, Spring Grove, Hampton on-Thames, same crest and motto

Owen, Charles Astley, B A, 29, Molesworth Street, Dublin, same crest and motto

Owen, Glouc, out of a mural coronet or a lion's gamb sa, holding a fleur-de lis of the first

Owen, Shropsh, a wolf passant arg 28 10

Owen, a wolf saliant ppr, supporting a scaling-ladder arg *Frangi non flecti*

Owen, Arthur Charles Humphreys, Esquire, M A, J P, D L, of Glansevern, Montgomerysh, a wolf saliant ppr, supporting a scaling-ladder arg *Torav cyn plygav —Flecti non frangi*

Owen, a hawk's lure charged with a fleur-de lis

Owen, Ireland a cubit arm vested holding in the hand a lizard cf 209 1

Owen of Godstone Oxon a cubit arm erect vested gu, cuffed erm, holding in the hand ppr a chaplet of laurel vert

Owen of London, out of a ducal coronet sa, a beech tree vert *Repullulat* 145 9

Owens, of Holestone Antrim a boar passant ppr collared and chained or to a holly bush, also ppr *Inutilis vis est*

Owens, out of a ducal coronet sa a beech-tree vert 145 9

Owgan, Ireland a cockatrice close gu, legged and beaked sa, crested or

Owsley, Leics a lion rampant holding in the dexter paw a holly branch cf 1 13

Oxborough and **Oxburgh,** on the point of a sword erect ppr, a cross patee sa 169 5

Oxborough and **Oxburgh,** of King's Lynn and Emneth Norf, on a mount vert a lion rampant or, holding up a spear gu headed arg, under the head two ribbons flotant, one or, the other az 1 9

Oxcliffe, on a mount vert, a bull passant sa 45 7

Oxenbridge, Viscount (Rt Hon Sir William John Monson, J P, D L) of Burton, Lincs, and **Baron Monson** of same place, a lion rampant ppr, supporting a column or *Prest pour mon pais* cf 1 13

Oxenbridge, Bart, a demi lion queue-fourchee arg, langued and armed gu

Oxenbridge, Hants a demi-lion rampant double-queued arg, armed and langued gu holding in the dexter paw an escallop or

Oxenbridge, issuing out of a cloud a hand holding a club all ppr. 214 9

Oxenden, Dixwell-, Bart, of Dene, Kent out of a ducal coronet gu, a lion's head affrontee or

Oxford and **Mortimer, Earl of** (Harley—*extinct*), a castle triple towered arg, out of the middle tower a demi-lion gu *Virtute et fide* 155 10

Oxley, on a ducal coronet a peacock ppr 103 8

Oxley, Rear-Admiral Charles Lister, of Minster House, Ripon, Yorks, an ox's head couped sa, charged with three ermine spots or. *Tam aris quam aratris*

Oxley, Rev William Henry, Petersham Vicarage, Surrey an ox's head couped sa *Tam aris quam aratris*

Oxman, Rutl, a demi-lion rampant regardant gu cf 16 5

Oxmantown, Lord, *see* **Rosse, Earl of**

Oxnam, Cornw, an ox sa

Oxtoby, a dexter hand holding a sword, all ppr 212 13

Oyke, Norf., an ox-yoke erect sa the bows or 178 6

Oyry, a pennon in bend, waving towards the sinister per fess gu and or, the staff counterchanged 168 12

Ozanne of the Landes, Guernsey a demi lion purp., holding in the dexter paw a cross crosslet fitchee or and resting the sinister upon a helmet ppr 229 7

P.

Pace, an arm in armour embowed holding in the hand a sword ppr 195 2

Pace, a boar's head couped and erect sa eared or, charged with an anchor of the last cf 43 3

Pace, Leics, a buck's head cabossed arg, attired or, between the attires a bird with wings expanded sa 122 9

Pachnum, out of a mural coronet a demi-hawk rising ppr cf 88 11

Pack or Packe, a leg in armour couped above the knee, spurred all ppr 193 1

Pack-Beresford, Denis Robert, Fenagh House Bagnalstown (1) Issuant from a mural crown or, a dragon's head per fesse wavy az and gu the lower part of the neck transfixed by a broken spear holding in the mouth the remaining part of the spear, the point upwards or (*for Beresford*) cf 72 11 (2) On a wreath of the colours a mural crown arg, issuing therefrom a lion's head gu gorged with a wreath or (*for Pack*) *Nil nisi cruce*

Pack, Reynell-, Arthur Denis Henry Heber, of Netherton House Newton Abbot out of a mural coronet arg a lion's head gu, gorged with a wreath or *Fidus confido* cf 19 12

Packe, Norf, a lion's head erased or, gorged with a collar sa, charged with three cinquefoils erm cf 18 6

Packe, Hussey of Prestwold, Leics (1) A lion's head erased or, gorged with a collar sa charged with three cinquefoils with an ermine spot on each leaf (2) On a mount vert a hind lodged regardant ppr, gorged with a ducal coronet, therefrom a line reflexed over the back or, in front of a hawthorn-tree, also ppr *Libertas sub Rege pio* cf 18 6

Packe of Harleston Park, Northamp, a lion's head erased or gorged with a collar sa, charged with three mullets arg cf 18 6

Packenham, Hants, a leopard couchant 24 10

Packenham of Tullenally, co Westmeath Ireland, issuing out of a mural coronet or, a demi eagle displayed gu, armed of the first 80 8

Packer of Bucklebury, Berks, a Moor's head couped sa, wreathed round the temples or and gu cf 192 13

Packer of Baddow, Essex a pelican in her piety arg 98 14

Packer, a demi lion rampant or holding in the dexter paw a cross gu

Packington, Surrey, and of Edgeworth, Middx, a demi-lion az, holding in the dexter paw a dagger arg cf 10 2

Packington, Worcs and Bucks an elephant passant or cf 133 9

Packington, Beds Bucks, and Worcs, a demi hare az, charged with three bezants 136 6

Packnam, out of a mural coronet an eagle with wings elevated

Packwood, Warw a demi-lion rampant arg, holding with the dexter paw and supporting with the sinister a bell sa, charged with a canton erm *None is truly great but he that is truly good*

Paddon, a dexter hand ppr, holding a covered cup or 217 11

Paddon of Henton Deweney, Hants, a tower in flames ppr 155 9

Paddon of Thralesend Beds, a tower or, flammant ppr 155 9

Paddye, Lancs on a chapeau gu, turned up erm a lion passant arg 4 9

Pagan, a hand holding a dagger erect ppr *Nec timeo, nec sperno* 212 9

Pagan, Scotland, out of a mural coronet a demi eagle displayed ppr 80 8

Paganell and **Pagnell,** in the sea ppr a column sa 176 2

Page of Holebrook, Somers a demi griffin gu *Honneur pour objet* 64

Page, out of a mural coronet or a demi-griffin gu cf 6, 2

Page of East Sheen, Surrey out of a ducal coronet per pale or and gu, a demi-griffin per pale counterchanged, beaked of the second *Spe labor levis* 64 4

Page, Kent, a demi griffin erm, beaked and legged gu 64 2

Page, Ernest Esquire, K C, of 78, Queen's Gate, S W same crest

Page, Cambs, a demi-griffin holding a ducal coronet or cf 64 2

Page of Little Bromley, Essex, a demi griffin arg, supporting an anchor ppr, and charged on the wing with a cross moline gu *Crux mihi anchora* cf 64 7

Page of London, a demi-griffin erm 64 2

Page or Paige, Devonsh, an eagle displayed erm 75 2

Page of Chester, an eagle displayed or 75 2

Page, Middx, out of a mural coronet gu, a lion's head or 19 12

Page, a demi-lion rampant gu, holding between the paws a pine ppr cf 10 3

Page of Berry Hall, Beds and Blackheath, Kent a demi-horse per pale dancettee or and az 53 3

Page of Gosport Hants, a demi-seahorse assurgent 46 7

Page of Clifton, Glouc and Hadley, Middx. a demi-Catherine wheel or thereon a dove ppr gorged with a collar gemel, and holding in the beak an olive-branch leaved and slipped also or *Seek peace and ensure it* 92 8

Pagelet, a morion ppr 180 1

Paget, *see* Anglesey, Marquess of

Paget, Somers, a demi heraldic tiger rampant sa, tufted and maned arg ducally gorged or *Diciendo y haciendo* 25 12

Paget of London and Staffs, a demi heraldic tiger rampant sa, ducally gorged, tufted and maned arg 25 12

Paget, Howard Francis Elford Hall Tamworth, same crest *Per il suo contrario*

Paget, Captain Victor Frederick William Augustus, same crest

Paget, Fitzroy Richard Clarence, same crest

Paget, William Henry, 129, Victoria Street S W, same crest

Paget-Tomlinson, Wm Smith, Esquire, M A, of the Biggins Kirkby Lonsdale (1) On a wreath of the colours a man wreathed about the waist with oak, supporting in the dexter hand a tilting-spear erect, all ppr, and resting the sinister hand on an escutcheon per pale nebuly arg and vert, charged with a greyhound current counterchanged (*for Tomlinson*) (2) Between two wings gu, a demi-heraldic tiger sa, holding in the mouth a lion's gamb or (*for Paget*) *Vincit veritas*

Paget, Sir Richard Horner, Bart J P D L, M P of Cranmore Hall, Somers, a demi tiger rampant sa, tufted, maned and gorged with a crown vallery arg, holding in the mouth an eagle's leg erased at the thigh or *Diciendo y haciendo* 281 10

Paget, Sir John Rahere, Bart of Harewood Place, Hanover Square, in the county of Middx, a heraldic tiger passant arg, gorged with a collar, and charged upon the body with two escallops fessewise sa *Labor ipse voluptas*

Paget, Sir George Ernest, Bart, Sutton Bonington, Loughborough, a lion rampant sa collared or supporting with its sinister paw a shield arg charged with an escallop of the first *Espere et persévère*

Paget, Thomas Guy Frederick Humberstone, Leics a lion rampant ppr resting the sinister paw on an escutcheon *Espere et persevere*

Paget, William Byerley, Southfield, Loughborough same crest and motto

Paget of Ruddington Grange, Leics, a lion rampant ppr *Honestas* 1 13

Paget of Chipping Norton Oxon, a cubit arm erect vested sa, cuffed arg, holding in the hand a scroll of the second bearing the inscription, *Deo Paget — Post spinas palma*

Paggin of Wandsworth, Surrey two ragged staves in saltire arg chained sa cf 147 9

Pagitt of London Middx, and Northamp a cubit arm erect vested sa, cuffed arg holding in the hand ppr a scroll of the second charged with the motto *Deo Pagit*, a seal affixed thereto pendent gu

Pagrave, a greyhound's head arg cf 61 2

Pagrave, a rhinoceros or 226 7

Pain, Ireland, on a chapeau ppr, a greyhound sejant or cf 59 4

Pain, a lion rampant ppr, supporting a garb or

Pain of Patcham Place, Sussex, a stag's head erased 121 2

Paine, on a mount vert, a lion rampant collared holding in the dexter paw an arrow 1 11

Paine, Sir Thomas, of Broomfield, Westcott, Dorking, and 9, Albert Road, Regent's Park, London, N.W., a lion's head erased ppr., ducally gorged, ringed, and lined or, holding a sprig of laurel in its mouth vert. *Honor virtutis præmium.*

Painter, a goat passant arg., armed, crined, bearded, and ungu. or. *cf.* 129. 5

Painter, Cornw., three pheons arg., handled or, two in saltier and one in pale, banded gu.

Paiton, a griffin or. 63. 2

Pakeman, a cockatrice close gu., combed and wattled or.

Pakenham, a hand holding three arrows, points downward, all ppr. *cf.* 214. 2

Pakenham, a griffin segreant holding an escarbuncle, all ppr. *cf.* 62. 2

Pakenham of London, out of a ducal coronet a demi-eagle displayed. 80. 14

Pakenham-Mahon, Henry, Esquire, D.L., of 35, St. George's Road, London, S.W.: (1) A heraldic tiger passant holding in the dexter paw a broken tilting-spear ppr. (*for Mahon*). (2) Out of a mural crown or, a demi-eagle displayed gu. (*for Pakenham*). *Periculum fortitudine evasi.—Gloria virtutis umbra.* 80. 8

Pakenham, *see* Longford, Earl of.

Pakenham, Ireland, out of a mural coronet or, a demi-eagle displayed gu., beaked or. 80. 8

Pakenham, Gustavus Conolly, Kobe, Japan, same crest. *Gloria virtutis umbra.*

Pakenham, John Richard Arthur, same crest and motto.

Pakenham, Captain Hercules Arthur, same crest and motto.

Pakenham, Lieutenant-General Thomas Henry, Langford Lodge, Crumlin, co. Antrim, same crest and motto.

Pakenham, William Law, Alconbury, Chelmsford, same crest and motto. 293. 10

Pakington, Middx. and Surrey, a demi-lion az., holding in the dexter paw a dagger arg. 14. 12

Pakington, a demi-hare az., bezantée. 136. 6

Pakington, a demi-squirrel erased gu.

Pakington, Bart. (*extinct*), of Aylesbury and Westwood, Bucks, an elephant passant or, armed gu. *cf.* 133. 9

Pakington, *see* Hampton, Baron.

Paley, a hand issuing from a heart and brandishing a scimitar, all ppr. 213. 4

Paley, a boar's head couped in pale. *cf.* 43. 3

Paley of Oatlands, Yorks, a stag's head couped ppr.

Paley of Langcliffe Hall, Yorks, in front of a stag's head couped ppr., a cross crosslet or. *Cervus non servus.*

Palgrave of Bryn-y-gynog, Denbighsh., in front of a leopard's head affrontée erased arg., gorged with a collar gemel az., a crescent, also az. *Pro Rege et patria.*

Palgrave of Norwood Barningham, Norf., a lion's head erased arg. 17. 8

Palgrave, Francis Turner, M.A., D.L., 15, Cranley Place, S.W., between two branches of palm ppr., a leopard's head affrontée erased arg.

Palgrave, Sir Reginald Francis Douce, Salisbury, between two branches of palm ppr., a leopard's head affrontée, erased arg., charged on the neck with an escarbuncle sa. *Laudans invocabo Dominum.*

Palitana, Thakur Saheb of (Gohilshri Mansinghji Sursinghji), K.C.S.I., the Durbar Palace, Palitana, Kathiawar, Bombay, in front of a horse's head couped sa., charged with an Eastern crown or, an Indian sword fesseways point to the dexter or. *Magna est veritas et prevalebit.* 273. 10

Palk, Baron Haldon, *see* Haldon.

Pallant of Redgrave, Suff., between two wings erect ppr., an escutcheon of the arms, viz., barry of six arg. and erminois.

Palles, Rt. Hon. Christopher, LL.D., of Mountanville House, Dundrum, Dublin, a lion sejant erect az., bezantée, holding in his paws a cross patée fitchée or. *Deo duce, comite fortuna.*

Palley, a camel's head sa. 132. 7

Palliser, Bart. (*extinct*), out of a ducal coronet gu., a demi-eagle with wings elevated or. 80. 14

Palliser of the Vatch, Bucks, out of a ducal coronet gu., a demi-eagle with wings elevated erminois, charged on the breast with an anchor in pale az. *cf.* 80. 14

Palliser of Derryluskan, Ireland, out of a ducal coronet gu., a demi-eagle with wings elevated or. *Deo volente.*

Palmer, *see* Selborne, Earl of.

Palmer, Earl of Castlemaine (*extinct*), a demi-panther rampant and incensed holding in the paws a holly-branch with leaves and berries, all ppr. *Palma virtuti.* 23. 12

Palmer, Sussex, a demi-panther rampant gardant and incensed ppr., holding a branch vert, fructed gu. 23. 12

Palmer of Clifton Lodge, Beds, same crest.

Palmer, Frederick Danby, 52, South Quay, Great Yarmouth, same crest.

Palmer, Montague, Esquire, of Stewkley Grange, Leighton Buzzard, Bucks, a demi-panther rampant guardant, spotted all heraldic colours, issuing flames out of his mouth and ears, holding in his paws a palm-branch, all ppr. *Palma virtuti.* 301. 2

Palmer, Bart. (*extinct*), of Wingham, Kent, a demi-panther rampant and incensed holding in the dexter paw a palm-branch, all ppr. *Palma virtuti.* 23. 12

Palmer, Rev. Sir Lewis Henry, Bart., of Carlton, Northamp., a wyvern or, armed and langued gu. *Par sit fortuna labori.* 70. 1

Palmer, Northamp., a wyvern or, armed and langued gu. *Pour apprendre oublier ne puis.* 70. 1

Palmer, Northamp., a wyvern or, with wings addorsed vert. 70. 1

Palmer, Sir Charles Mark, Bart., M.P., of Grinkle Park, Loftus-in-Cleveland, Yorks, in front of a tilting-spear erect ppr., a wyvern statant or, resting the dexter claw upon a crescent arg. *Par sit fortuna labori.* 69. 8

Palmer, James Dampier, Esquire, J.P., of Heronden Hall, Tenterden, Kent, and of Upper Berkeley Street, St. George's, Hanover Square, London, upon the trunk of a tree eradicated and fessewise ppr., a wyvern with wings elevated barry wavy of twelve or and az., semée of escallops erm., holding in the mouth an eagle's leg erased or.

Palmer, Colonel Frederick, of 30, Beaufort Gardens, S.W., a wyvern or, armed and langued gu. *Par sit fortuna labori.* 70. 1

Palmer, Rev. Charles Samuel, the Residence House, Heref., same crest and motto.

Palmer, Edward Geoffrey Broadley, of Burrough, Melton Mowbray, same crest and motto.

Palmer, Major Herrick Augustus, same crest and motto.

Palmer, Thomas, Brook House, Eardisley R.S.O., Heref., same crest and motto.

Palmer, a dragon's head couped or, collared and winged vert, on the collar three plates, the breast guttée-de-poix, the wings fretty arg., and between the frets trefoils of the same. 71. 7

Palmer, Bart., of Castle Lacken, co. Mayo, Ireland: (1) An arm embowed vested az., cuffed or, grasping a tilting-spear ppr. (2) A griffin sejant arg., with wings endorsed gu., charged with three annulets of the second, beaked and membered or. *Sic bene merenti palma.* *cf.* 62. 10

Palmer, a griffin sejant arg., beaked and legged or, charged on the breast with a crescent. *cf.* 62. 10

Palmer of Barton, Warw., and Yorks, a griffin sejant. 62. 10

Palmer, out of a ducal coronet a griffin's head. 67. 9

Palmer, Bucks and Northamp., issuing out of rays ppr., a griffin's head arg.

Palmer of Hyderabad, an eagle volant rising from a mount with a palm-branch in its beak, all ppr., with the motto over, *It shall flourish.—Deeds not words.*

Palmer of Hill, Beds, a greyhound current sa. *cf.* 58. 2

Palmer, Surrey, a greyhound sejant sa., collared or, charged on the shoulder with a trefoil slipped arg. *cf.* 59. 2

Palmer, Sir Archdale Robert, Bart., of Wanlip Hall, Leics., on a mount vert, a greyhound sejant sa., gorged with a collar or, rimmed gu., and charged on the shoulder with a trefoil slipped arg. *cf.* 59. 2

Palmer of Marston, Staffs, a greyhound sejant sa. *Palma virtute.* 59. 4

Palmer of Holme Park, Berks, a talbot sejant erminois. *cf.* 55. 2

Palmer, Scotland, a cat sejant ppr. 26. 8

Palmer, out of a ducal coronet or, an elephant's head sa. 133. 1

Palmer, between two laurel-branches vert, an escallop arg.

Palmer of London, a lion rampant or, holding a palmer's staff sa., the head, end, and rest or.

Palmer, a lion passant sa., armed and langued, and holding in the dexter paw a dagger gu. *cf.* 6. 2

Palmer, Bart., Leics., a lion couchant or. 7. 5

Palmer, Bart., Ireland, an arm in armour embowed ppr., garnished or, holding in the hand a spear ppr. *In Deo est mihi omnis fides.*

Palmer, Kent an ostrich volant arg

Palmer of Winthorpe, Lincs, a cubit arm erect vested az, cuffed arg, holding in the hand ppr a palmer's staff

Palmer of Wadesden, Bucks, and Stockdale Northamp, a cubit arm in mail erect ppr holding in the hand a halberd sa headed arg

Palmer, John Irwin, M R C S, 47, Queen Anne Street Cavendish Square, W, on a dexter mailed arm embowed grasping a palm-branch and a palmer's staff in saltire, all ppr, an escallop or *Palma v rtuti*

Palmer, Honourable Sir Arthur Hunter, K C M G, of Brisbane and of Beaufort, South Kennedy Queensland, Australia, President of the Legislative Council, *uses* a dexter arm embowed in armour, the hand grasping a spear in bend sinister, point upwards, all ppr *Ius pretium melioris œvi —Palma virtuti*

Palmer, Sir Roger William Henry, Bart, D L, of Castle Lackin, co Mayo, an arm embowed vested az, cuffed or, grasping a tilting-spear ppr *Sic bene merent palma*

Palmer, of Rahan House, co Kildare, Ireland an arm in armour embowed ppr, garnished or, the hand grasping a spear, also ppr *Honor virtutis præmium*

Palmer, a cubit arm in armour grasping a trefoil slipped vert

Palmer, George William, J P, 36, Queen Anne's Gate S W, upon a mount vert in front of a palm-tree ppr, three escallops fesseways or *Per crucem ad palmam*

Palmer, S Ernest 10, Grosvenor Crescent S W, same crest and motto

Palmer, Eustace, Esquire, West Bourne, Coley Avenue, Reading, same crest and motto.

Palmer-Douglas, Edward, J P, Cavers, near Hawick, a dexter hand holding a broken lance bendways ppr *Doe or die*

Palmer-Morewood, Charles Rowland 66, Queen's Gate S W (1) Two arms embowed armed ppr, each charged with a trefoil gu, supporting a chaplet of oak-branches vert, fructed or (*for Morewood*) (2) On a mount vert, a greyhound sejant sa, collared or and charged with a trefoil arg (*for Palmer*)

Palmer-Samborne, Lieutenant Frederick Carey Stucley, Army and Navy Club, 36 Pall Mall, S W, a mullet gu, pierced or *Memor et fidelis*

Palmer-Samborne, Samborne Stukeley, Timsbury House, near Bath, same crest and motto

Palmerston, Viscount (Temple), a talbot sejant sa, collared and lined or *Flecti non frangi* 55 5

Palmes, a hand holding a palm-branch *Ut palma justus* 219 11

Palmes, Rev George, of Naburn, Yorks, a hand holding a palm-branch *Ut palma justus* 219 11

Palmes, Rev Arthur Lindsay, M A, the Rectory, Saltwood near Hythe, same crest and motto

Palmes, Bryan William, of Queensland, same crest and motto

Palmes, Guy St. Maur Lingcroft York, same crest and motto

Palmes, out of a ducal coronet gu, a dragon's head sa, encompassed with flames ppr 72 14

Palshed, an arm embowed vested bendy of eight arg and gu holding in the hand ppr three flowers az, stalked and leaved vert

Paltock of Kingston-upon-Thames, Surrey, on a mount vert, a greyhound sejant sa, spotted arg, collared or 59 2

Pamure, a demi-lion rampant az holding in the dexter paw a rose stalked and leaved or 12 1

Pancefoote, a fleur-de lis az. 148. 2

Panellee, out of a ducal coronet or, a heraldic tiger's head gu 25 3

Panmure, Baron, *see* Dalhousie, Earl of

Panmure, Baron (Maule) a wyvern vert, vomiting flames of fire before and be hind *Clementia et animis* 69 9

Pannell, out of an earl's coronet a Moor's head from the shoulders, all ppr *cf* 182 2

Panter, a talbot passant sa, collared and lined 54 5

Panther, a panther passant gardant ppr 24 4

Panting of Dublin a dexter hand arg, between two wings az, guttee-d'eau 221 1

Panting, a dolphin haurient or, between two wings gu, each charged with as many bars arg (*see* Kynnersley) 140 7

Panton, Sussex, same crest and motto 140 7

Panton of Bishopwearmouth, Durh, and Denbighsh, North Wales, a sword ppr, hilt and pommel or, enfiled with a leopard's head of the last 22 1

Panton, Durh a sword ppr hilt and pommel or, enfiled with a leopard's face of the last *Semper eadem* 22 1

Panton, Scotland a spear-head ppr *Firmius ad pugnam* 174 12

Panton, a lion couchant, the tail coward az, bezantee *cf* 7 5

Pape, a dexter hand ppr, holding a clam shell or 216 2

Pape, George, Esquire, of Brixton, *uses* same crest

Pape, a falcon with wings expanded ppr 87 1

Papeworth, a fox's head erased gu 33 6

Papillion of Acrise Kent, a crescent arg *Dilat servata fides* 163 2

Papillon, Pelham Rawston, of Crowhurst Park, Battle Sussex same crest and motto

Papworth, Cambs Dorset, Devonsh and Hunts, a fox's head erased gu 33 6

Paradis or **De Paradis** of Youghal Ireland a bird of paradise ppr

Parama, Conde de, *see* Walrond

Paramore, Kent, two arms embowed vested az, holding between the hands ppr an etoile or

Paramour of St Nicholas in the Isle of Thanet Kent a cubit arm erect vested az, cuffed arg, holding in the hand ppr an etoile or

Paramour, Leics and Salop, an heraldic antelope sejant or, attired, maned, tufted, and armed sa

Parbury of London between two branches of laurel in saltier ppr a pelican in her piety or semee of torteaux the nest also ppr *Cras mihi* *cf* 98 12

Pardoe, a griffin sejant az, winged, legged and beaked or 62 10

Pardoe, Shropsh, an escallop shell erect 141 14

Pardoe of Park House, Bewdley, Worcs two vulture's heads and necks conjoined ppr

Pardoe of Hailes Park Worcs, a tower gu with a doe issuant therefrom ppr

Pardoe of Hitchin, Herts, a tower arg 156 2

Pardoe, Frank Lionel, Gosmore, Hitchin Herts, same crest

Pardoe, a demi lion rampant gardant arg, supporting an escallop sa *cf* 13 10

Pardoe of Nash Court, Shropsh, a lion passant gardant 4 3

Pares, a greyhound current gu *cf* 58 2

Pares, Edward Henry, of Hopwell Hall Derbysh a demi griffin or *Pares cum paribus* 64 2

Parfitt of Dublin, a falcon rising arg winged beaked, and legged or charged on the breast with a trefoil vert, and holding in the beak an ear of wheat bladed of the same *En tout parfait*

Parfitt of Bruton Somers, a falcon rising arg, winged beaked and legged or charged on the breast with a trefoil vert, and holding in the beak an ear of wheat of the same *En tout parfait*

Pargiter of Greetworth, Northamp, a dexter arm embowed ppr vested arg, holding in the hand a covered cup or 203 4

Paris, a quill erect ppr 176 9

Paris of Stone, Hunts and of Hitchin Herts, a sphinx couchant gu the face and breast ppr, the wings addorsed or, crined of the last *cf* 182 14

Paris, 25, Westbourne Grove, West Kirby, a unicorn's head couped *Omnia vincit amor*

Parish, a unicorn's head erased arg 49 5

Parish, Charles Woodbyne, Esquire, of 58, Ennismore Gardens London, S W, upon a rock ppr, a cross crosslet sa (*Granted to the late Sir Woodbine Parish, K C H*) *Justum et tenacem* 165 8

Parish, Charles 5 Gloucester Square W same crest and motto

Parish, Frank, 5, Gloucester Square, W same crest

Park or Parke, on a ducal coronet a lion passant and ducally crowned, all ppr *cf* 6 6

Park, Scotland, a buck's head cabossed *Providentiæ me committo* 122 5

Park, a stag lodged ppr 115 7

Park, Scotland, a dexter hand holding a book closed ppr *Gravite et pie* 215 4

Park, Holland a sinister hand holding an open book ppr *Sapienter et pie* *cf* 215 10

Park, Philip Esquire J P Altadore, Preston, Lancs, upon a mount vert, a stag's head caboshed gu between two marigolds slipped ppr *Providentiæ me committo*

Parke, Lord Wensleydale (*extinct*), a talbot's head couped gu eared and gorged with a collar gemel or and pierced in the breast with a pheon of the last *Justitiæ tenax* *cf* 56 1

Parke of Wisbeach Cambs a talbot's head gu pierced in the breast by a pheon or *cf* 56 12

Parke, on a mount vert, paled in arg., a fox paly of four or and az.

Parke, Sligo and Leitrim, Ireland, a wing az., semée of estoiles or. *cf.* 109. 7

Parke, Cumb., and of Henbury House, Sturminster Marshall, Dorset, a stag's head couped sa., holding in the mouth a key or. *True and fast.* *cf.* 121. 5

Parke, Charles Ethelston, Vines Close, Wimborne, Dorset, same crest and motto.

Parker, *see* Macclesfield, Earl of.

Parker, *see* Morley, Earl of.

Parker, Baron Morley and Monteagle, an heraldic antelope statant or, ducally gorged and chained az.

Parker, *see* Towneley-Parker.

Parker, John, Esquire, F.S.A., Lord of the Manor of Aylesbury, of Desborough House, High Wycombe, Bucks, a dexter arm in armour embowed arg., holding in the hand ppr. a stag's antler gu. *Jus tene nil time.*

Parker, Anthony, Esquire, of Castle Lough, co. Tipperary, Ireland, a stag salient ppr., charged with a mullet or. *Fideli certa merces.* *cf.* 117. 2

Parker-Hutchinson, Standish Grady John, Esquire, of Timoney Park, Roscrea, co. Tipperary: (1) Out of a ducal coronet or, a cockatrice with wings endorsed ppr. (*for Hutchinson*). (2) A stag salient ppr., charged with a mullet or (*for Parker*). *Fideli certa merces.* *cf.* 117. 2

Parker, a stag's head couped ppr. 121. 5

Parker, Rev. James Dunne, LL.D., D.C.L., F.R.Met.Soc., of Bennington House, Stevenage, Herts, a stag's head couped ppr. *Ne tentes aut perfice.* 121. 5

Parker of Arwerton, Suff., on a mount vert, a stag trippant ppr. 118. 2

Parker of Alkincoats, Lancs, a stag trippant ppr. *Non fluctu, nec flatu movetur.* 117. 8

Parker, Sir George Arthur, 26, Whitehall Court, S.W., same crest and motto.

Parker, a buck's head couped arg., attired or, with an arrow through the attires of the first. *cf.* 121. 5

Parker, Middx., a stag trippant ppr. 117. 8

Parker, Lieutenant-Colonel John William Robinson, same crest. *Nec fluctu, nec flatu movetur.*

Parker of Cuerden and Extwistle, Lancs, a buck trippant ppr., pierced by an arrow in pale, point downwards, arg. *cf.* 117. 10

Parker, George, Delamore, Ivybridge, a leopard's head erased and affrontée ducally gorged gu. *Sub libertate quietum.*

Parker, Chesh., a buck's head erased ppr. 121. 2

Parker, Brockholes-, of Hareden, Yorks: (1) On a chapeau a stag trippant, all ppr. (*for Parker*). 118. 3. (2) A brock sa. (*for Brockholes*). *Non fluctu, non flatu movetur.* 33. 10

Parker of Sweeney, Shropsh., a buck's head cabossed sa. 122. 5

Parker, Henry Chute, Esquire, of Bowland, and of Fair Oak, Whitewell, Clitheroe, Lancaster: (1) A stag ppr., gorged with a collar gemel vert, resting the dexter fore-foot on the stump of a tree eradicated and sprouting ppr. (*for Parker*). (2) A leopard's head erased sa., gorged with a collar vair, pendent therefrom an escutcheon arg., charged with a crescent, also sa. (*for Little*). *Non fluctu, non flatu movetur.*

Parker of Moorehouse Hill, Cumb., a mount vert, thereon a stag regardant ppr., collared, and a line therefrom reflexed over the back or, resting its dexter fore-foot on an escutcheon erect az., charged with a garb, also or. *Medio tutissimus ibis.*

Parker of Bradkirke, Lancs, a stag's head couped or. 121. 5

Parker, Sir Melville, Bart., of Harburn, Warw., on a naval coronet az., the sterns and sails ppr., a stag at gaze arg., in front of a slip of oak in pale ppr. 118. 6

Parker, out of a naval coronet az., a demi-stag or, supporting between the feet an anchor erect sa., encircled by a wreath of laurel ppr.

Parker of Upton Cheney, Glouc., a buck's head holding in the mouth an acorn leaved, all ppr. 119. 11

Parker, Edward Milward Seede, Welford House, Keynsham, Somers., same crest. *Fidelis amicis.*

Parker of Browsholme and Newtown, Yorks, on a chapeau gu., turned up erm., a stag trippant ppr. *Non fluctu, nec flatu movetur.* 118. 3

Parker of Willows, Suff., a talbot passant arg., resting the dexter paw on a buck's head cabossed or.

Parker, Chesh., on a mount vert, a talbot sejant ppr., collared or, resting the dexter paw on a buck's head cabossed gu. 55. 4

Parker of Woodthorpe, Yorks, a talbot's head arg., eared and langued gu., collared pean. *cf.* 56. 1

Parker, a talbot's head arg., collared pean, eared gu. *cf.* 56. 1

Parker of Syberswold, Kent, a talbot passant arg., in front of an oak-tree ppr., fructed or.

Parker, Bart. (*extinct*), of Ratton, Sussex, on a chapeau az., turned up erm., a greyhound or. 58. 4

Parker of London, on a chapeau az., a greyhound passant or, collared, ringed, and lined arg. *cf.* 58. 4

Parker of Whitley Hall, Lincs, of Norton Lees, Derbysh., and of Park Hall, Staffs, a leopard's head erased affrontée or, ducally gorged gu. 23. 8

Parker, Charles Arundel, M.D., F.S.A., J.P., Gosforth, Cumb., same crest. *Hurrah, hurrah.*

Parker, Lieutenant-Colonel William, of Hanthorpe House, Lincs, between two oak-branches ppr., a leopard's face or, over which a mullet of six points. *Auctor pretiosa facit.*

Parker, Sir William Lorenzo, Bart., of Blackbrook House, Hants, and Shenstone Lodge, Staffs, a leopard's head affrontée erased or, ducally gorged gu. *Sub libertate quietem.* 23. 8

Parker, Admiral George, Delamore, Ivybridge, Devonsh., same crest and motto.

Parker, a cock's head gu., between two wings of a tawney colour, beaked arg.

Parker of Aldborough, Norf., a demi-cock with wings addorsed gu., combed and wattled arg. 90. 9

Parker, on the trunk of a tree couped at the top ppr., an eagle preying on a bird. 79. 4

Parker of the Ould, Warw., out of a ducal coronet or, a plume of five feathers sa. 114. 13

Parker, Wales, a lion rampant or. 1. 13

Parker of Frith Hall, Essex, a lion's gamb erased or, holding an arrow gu., headed and feathered arg.

Parker, an elephant's head arg., the trunk and tusks or, the ears gu. 133. 2

Parker of Sandwich, Kent, and Margate, Isle of Thanet, Kent, an elephant's head couped arg., gorged with a collar gu., charged with three fleurs-de-lis or. *cf.* 133. 2

Parker, Bart. (*extinct*), of Bassingbourn, Essex, an elephant's head couped arg., gorged with a collar gu., charged with three fleurs-de-lis or. *Try.* *cf.* 133. 2

Parker of Hurstmonceux, Sussex, out of a ducal coronet or, a bear's head sa., muzzled of the first. 34. 3

Parker of Northfleet, Kent, out of a ducal coronet gu., a bull's head or, armed arg. 44. 11

Parker, a horse's head couped per pale indented arg. and az. *cf.* 50. 13

Parker, Stephen Henry, Esquire, of Karrakalta House, Perth, Western Australia, Member of the Legislative Assembly of York, out of a ducal coronet gu., a bull's head or, armed and crined arg. 44. 11

Parker of Finglesham, Kent, out of a mural coronet or, a horse's head gu., maned of the first. *cf.* 50. 13

Parker, five darts, points downwards, one in pale and four in saltier. *cf.* 173. 3

Parker, an arm erect vested az., cuffed and slashed arg., holding in the hand ppr. the attire of a stag gu. 208. 9

Parker, Christopher, Esquire, of Petterell, Green, Cumb., a cubit arm erect vested vert, cuffed arg., holding in the hand the attire of a stag and a bow and arrow in saltier ppr. *Virtutis alimentum honos.*

Parker of Warwick Hall, near Carlisle, a cubit arm erect vested vert, cuffed arg., holding in the hand the attire of a stag and a bow and arrow saltireways, all ppr.

Parker, Francis, J.P., Fremington, Penrith, same crest.

Parker of Honington, Warw., and Plympton St. Mary's, Devonsh., a cubit arm erect vested sa., cuffed arg., holding in the hand ppr. the attire of a stag gu. *Fideli certa merces.* 208. 6

Parker of Whiteway, Devonsh., an arm erect vested az., cuffed arg., holding in the hand the attire of a stag ppr. *Fideli certa merces.* 208. 6

Parker, Rev. Sir William Hyde, Bart., D.L., of Suff., a dexter arm erect vested az., slashed and cuffed arg., holding in the hand ppr. the attire of a stag gu. 208. 6

Parker, out of clouds arg., a dexter arm ppr., vested gu., holding in the hand the hilt of a broken sword ppr. 208. 13

Parker, a hand or, holding a falchion, the blade arg., hilt of the first. 212. 13

Parker, Kent, a cubit arm erect in mail or holding in the hand ppr a falchion arg, hilt and pommel of the first 210 2

Parker-Douglas, William Thomas M A M B, of Holmby, Speen Newbury a human heart crowned ppr, between two wings *Jamais arrière* 110 14

Parker, J, Esquire, C S I, of Trelawny's Cottage, Sompting, near Worthing, a leopard's head erased and affrontee or, ducally gorged gu *Sapere aude*

Parkes of the Mount Clent, near Stourbridge, Worcs, a greyhound sejant ppr, collared sa, resting the dexter paw on a caltrop arg

Parkes, an escutcheon party per chevron gu and or, between two branches of laurel vert 146 14

Parkes of Willingsworth and Wednesbury, Staffs in an oak-tree fructed a squirrel sejant all ppr

Parkes-Buchanan, Bernard-, John, Union Club S W two heads grasping a two handed sword ppr *Clarиora sequor*

Parkhill, Scotland, a cornucopia or, filled with fruit and grain ppr *Capta majora* 152 13

Parkhouse and **Parkhurst** of London, a stag trippant ppr 117 8

Parkhouse of Eastfield Lodge, Hants, a buck ppr charged on the body with three mullets az, the dexter fore foot resting on a cross flory vert *The cross our stay*

Parkhurst, a griffin segreant per fess or and gu 62 2

Parkhurst of Guildford, Surrey, a demi griffin with wings addorsed sa holding in the dexter claw a cutlass arg hilt and pommel or 64 6

Parkhurst of London, out of a palisado coronet or a buck's head erased arg, attired of the first cf 121 2

Parkin, a fox sejant ppr 32 11

Parkin, Major John Robert, Idridgehay Derbysh, same crest. *Fac recte et spera*

Parkin, Lieutenant Colonel (retired) John William Brooke, a greyhound courant *Verus et fidelis* 295 14

Parkin, Frederick, Esquire, of Little Truro Vean, Truro, Cornw, same crest and motto

Parkin, John Samuel, Esquire, M A of Seaton, Cumb, and of 11, New Square Lincoln's Inn, London, an eagle displayed sa, holding in each claw a cross patee fitchée or and charged on either wing with a billet, also or *Honesta audax*

Parkin, Thomas, Fairseat High Wickham, Hastings, same crest and motto

Parkin, Paxton, Esquire, of Barming Place, Maidstone, out of a ducal coronet a fir-cone, all ppr *Honeste audax* 274 13

Parkin-Moore, William, J P, Whitehall, Mealsgate Carlisle (1) A Moor's head couped at the shoulders in profile ppr, wreathed round the temples or and gu, and suspended from the neck by a double chain or an escutcheon arg, charged with a cross crosslet sa (*for Moore*) (2) On a mount vert a fir cone erect slipped and leaved between two wings sa *Aut nunquam tentes aut perfice*

Parkins, Ireland out of a ducal coronet a demi eagle displayed *Honesta audax* 80 14

Parkins, out of a ducal coronet a swan with wings expanded collared and lined holding in the beak an acorn slip

Parkins of London a bull passant az, with wings addorsed or ducally gorged of the last

Parkins, Notts a pine apple ppr, stalked and leaved vert 152 8

Parkinson-Fortescue, Baron Carlingford, see Carlingford

Parkinson, Robert John Hinman of East Ravendale, Lincs an antelope trippant ppr, in the mouth two ostrich-feathers arg cf 126 6

Parkinson, William Henry same crest

Parkinson, an antelope trippant ppr, holding in the mouth two ostrich-feathers arg, and charged on the shoulder with a pellet for distinction cf 126 6

Parkinson of Falsnape, Lancs, a cubit arm vested or charged with five ermine spots in saltire sa cuffed arg the hand ppr holding an ostrich feather gu 208 4

Parkinson, Heref, a cubit arm erect vested erminois, cuffed arg, holding in the hand ppr an ostrich feather in pale gu 208 4

Parkinson, Reginald James Beresford, Ludford Park, Ludlow, same crest

Parkinson, Thomas Frederick Bydowne North Devonsh, a falcon with wings addorsed and inverted ppr

Parkinson, a griffin's head erased, holding in the beak a sword ppr 66 10

Parkyns, Baron Rancliffe (*extinct*) (1) Out of a ducal coronet or a fir cone ppr (2) Out of a ducal coronet or, a demi-eagle displayed az billettee erm *Honeste audax* cf 80 14

Parkyns, Sir Thomas Mansfield Forbes, Bart, of 20, Ashley Place, S W out of a ducal coronet or, a pine cone ppr *Honeste audax* cf 152 8

Parkyns, a bull passant az winged or, ducally gorged of the same

Parkyns, two eagle's heads conjoined in one neck ppr cf 84 11

Parlane, William, of Gartness, Victoria Park, Manchester, and Craigdhu Wig townsh, out of a rock a demi savage, affrontée ppr holding in the dexter hand three arrows two in saltire and one in pale points upwards, or, headed and feathered arg and in the sinister hand a rose gu slipped and leaved ppr *This I'll defend*

Parlar, Middx a Cornish chough sa, beaked and legged gu 107 14

Parlby, Captain Reginald John Hall, of Manadon Devonsh (1) On a ducal coronet a peacock s head erased holding in the beak a serpent (*for Parlby*) (2) A talbot's head erased gu (*for Hall*) *Parle bien* 56 2

Parmiger, Kent and Hants, out of a ducal coronet or, a stag's head gu, attired of the first, transpierced through the neck by an arrow in bend sinister ppr, headed and flighted arg cf 120 7

Parminster of Tockington, Glouc, a dexter arm in armour embowed, the gauntlet grasping above the hilt a sword the point broken off *Deo favente*

Parminter, Cornw, an eagle displayed ppr 75 2

Parnall of the Cottage Llanstephan, Carmarthensh, a griffin's head between two wings gu, each wing charged with an escallop, and holding in the beak another escallop arg *Spero in Deo* cf 65 11

Parnell, see Congleton, Baron

Parnell, Ireland, out of a ducal coronet or, a dexter arm, holding in the hand a sheaf of arrows ppr 214 2

Parnell of Sheephouse Somers, a griffin passant arg, wings elevated gu, holding in the beak an estoile and in the dexter claw an escallop, both also gu *Est modus in rebus*

Parnham, a leopard's head erased arg 23 10

Parnther, a dexter arm in armour ppr, holding in the hand a cross crosslet fitched in pale or cf 210 14

Paroissien of Hardingham, Norf on a ducal coronet or, a dove ppr

Parr, Westml Northamp, Leics Staffs, and Derbysh, a cubit arm in armour ppr, holding in the hand a bar az

Parr of Backford, Chesh, a demi boar rampant az, bristled or, charged with a bend gu, thereon three lozenges of the second cf 40 13

Parr, Major Henry Hallam, C B, C M G a dexter arm in armour embowed holding in the hand a pair of compasses *Nec par nec impar*

Parr of Lythwood, Shropsh a maiden's head couped below the shoulders vested az, on the head a wreath of roses alternately arg and gu *Amour avec loiaulté* 182 5

Parr, Joseph Charlton, Grappenhall Heyes, Warrington, in front of a maiden's head ppr, an escallop or between two bezants *Faire sans dire* 265 16

Parr, Cecil Francis, J P, Kimpton Grange Welwyn Herts, same crest and motto

Parr, Henry Bingham, 27, Rodney Street, Liverpool same crest and motto

Parr of London, a female's head affrontee ppr, vested az, charged upon the breast with three escallops fesseways arg

Parr of Parr, Lancs, a female's head affrontée couped below the shoulders ppr, habited az, on her head a wreath of roses alternately arg and gu 182 5

Parr of Kendal, Westml, same crest *Amour avecque loiaulte* 182 5

Parr, a mount vert, therefrom issuing in front of a pear-tree fructed ppr a rose-tree vert, bearing five roses gu, barbed and seeded also ppr

Parr of Kempnall, Lancs, a horse's head gu maned or cf 50. 13

Parram, Wilts, a lion's gamb erased or, holding a mallet erect gu

Parret and **Perrott,** Kent and Oxon, a parrot close ppr, beaked and legged gu, holding in the dexter claw a pear or charged on the breast with a mullet of the same cf 101 13

Parrot or **Parrott,** a parrot gu 101 4

Parrott, a parrot holding in the dexter claw a pear 101 13

Parry, Heref, three battle-axes erect ppr 172 11

Parry, Jones-, late Sir Love Thomas Duncombe Bart (*extinct*) of Madryn Castle Pwllheli, North Wales (1) A sheaf of battle-axes, three in pale and two in saltire, staves gu, headed ppr and girt with a laurel wreath, also ppr (*for Parry*) 172 8 (2) On a chapeau gu turned up erm, a demi-lion rampant or (*for Jones*) 15 13 (3) A hart trippant arg, attired and ungu or (*for Hughes*) 117 8 (4) A nag's head erased sa (*for Madrin*) 50 8 Badge, a lozenge az (*for Parry*) *Heb Dduw heb ddim, Duw a digon —Gofal dyn duw ai gwerid —Nil desperandum —Madren*

Parry, Jones-, Thomas Parry, of Llwyn Onn, Wrexham, same crests and mottoes

Parry, Wales, a stag at gaze ppr 117 3

Parry, Segar-, Herts (1) A buck's head couped arg, holding in the mouth a sprig ppr (*for Parry*) 119 11 (2) On a ducal coronet or, two snakes vert entwined round a sceptre of the first between two wings, the dexter also or, the sinister arg (*for Segar*) 170 13

Parry, a demi-lion rampant az, on the head a garb or

Parry of Twysog, Denbighsh, a demi lion rampant arg, charged on the shoulder with a cross gu *Si Deus nobiscum* cf 10 2

Parry, Edward William, Esquire, resident in the kingdom of Bavaria, a demi lion rampant arg, charged on the shoulder with a cross couped gu *Si Deus nobiscum* cf 10 2

Parry, Major Llewelyn England Sidney Meillionem, Carnarvonsh, out of a ducal coronet a demi-lion rampant *Gofal dyn duw ai gwerid*

Parry, Denbighsh and Flintsh, on a chapeau gu. turned up erm, a boar's head couped sa, armed or *Vince fide* 42 5

Parry, Sir Charles Hubert Hastings Bart of Highnam Court, Glouc, in front of three battle-axes erect ppr five lozenges conjoined in fess sable *Tu ne cede malis* 284 5

Parry, on a chapeau gu, turned up erm, a boar's head couped sa armed or *Vince fide* 42 5

Parry of London, a griffin sejant ppr 62 10

Parry, Shropsh, same crest *Veritas odit morem*

Parry, Shropsh, a griffin sejant vert langued gu, ducally gorged and chained or cf 62 10

Parry, a lamb arg, bearing a banner or 131 2

Parry, Henry Harrison, Harewood Park, Ross sh three battle axes ppr *Tu ne cede malis*

Parry of Hamsted Marshall Berks, a cubit arm ppr the hand grasping a snake vert, biting the hand

Parry-Mitchell, Rev Henry Digby Merevale Parsonage Atherstone Warw (1) A lion's gamb erased az holding a fret or, between two wings erminois each charged with an anchor erect of the first (*for Mitchell*) (2) A stag's head couped ppr, gorged with a chain or, suspended therefrom resting upon the wreath an escutcheon az charged with a lozenge arg, and between the attires a lozenge or (*for Parry*)

Parry-Okeden, Uvedale Parry Okeden, Turnworth, Blandford (1) A bear's paw erased sa, grasping an oak branch ppr, fructed or (*for Okeden*) (2) Out of a ducal coronet or, a demi-lion gu (*for Parry*) *Tant que je puis*

Parscoe, a castle triple-towered ppr from the centre tower a demi-lion rampant az 155 10

Parsons, Earl of Rosse, *see* Rosse

Parsons, Barbadoes a demi-griffin segreant arg, beaked and armed gu 64 2

Parsons, Bart (*extinct*), of Stanton on-the Wolds Notts, of Langley Bucks, and Epsom Surrey upon a chapeau gu turned up erm a griffin's head erased arg, beaked also gu cf 66 2

Parsons, Bucks, on a chapeau az, turned up erm, an eagle's head erased arg, ducally crowned or, and charged on the neck with a cross gu

Parsons of London, on a leopard's face gu, an eagle's leg erased at the thigh or 229 8

Parsons, Bernard William, the Wrays, Horley, Surrey, upon a mount ppr, an eagle's leg erased or, between two oak-leaves slipped and erect vert *Aude et prevalebis*

Parsons, Heref, a halberd headed arg embrued gu 172 3

Parsons, Ireland out of a ducal coronet or, a cubit arm erect, holding in the hand a sprig of roses, all ppr 218 8

Parsons, a tower arg 156 2

Parsons of Steyning Sussex, a garb of quatrefoils vert banded or 152 11

Parsons of Clanclewedog, Radnorsh a demi-lion rampant gu *Quid retribuam* 10 3

Parsons-Peters, William, Esquire, of Yeabridge, Somers a horse's head arg, crusily az, holding in the mouth a cinquefoil slipped vert

Partheriche and **Partherlcke**, Middx, a dexter arm in armour embowed, holding in the hand a scimitar ppr 196 10

Partington, an arm ppr, vested arg holding in the hand an anchor of the first 208 3

Partington, a hawk with wings expanded ppr 87 1

Partington, Edward, Easton Glossop, Derbysh, out of the battlements of a tower a goat's head ppr, charged on the neck with a mullet of six points and between two escallops sa

Partis, Northumb, a stag's head cabossed 122 5

Partrich, a partridge volant or

Partrick, an arm in armour embowed the hand apaumee ppr 200 1

Partrickson and **Patrickson**, Cambs, on a mount vert a stag current regardant ppr, attired and ungu or 118 12

Partridge, Henry Thomas of Hockham Hall near Thetford, Norf, a partridge with wings displayed or *Dum spiro, spero* cf 89 11

Partridge, George Anthony Bury St Edmunds same crest and motto

Partridge, Rev Walter Henry Caston Rectory Norf, same crest and motto

Partridge, a partridge rising or, holding in the beak an ear of wheat ppr 89 11

Partridge, a demi-lion rampant or, collared gu garnished or 10 9

Partridge and **Partrich**, a lion's head or, issuing from a rose gu, stalked and leaved vert 19 9

Partridge, a demi leopard rampant gardant sa., bezantee, gorged with a collar gu, charged with three plates

Partridge of Cirencester and Wishanger, Glouc, and Finbarrow, Suff, a horse's head sa, crined or, erased per fess gu 51 4

Partridge of Bishop's Wood, Heref (1) Out of a ducal coronet or, a horse's head sa 51 7 (2) A leopard arg, spotted sa 24 2

Partridge, Captain Walter Croker St Ives the Coppice, Bishop's Wood, near Ross same crests

Partridge, Kent, an arm embowed tied round the elbow with a ribbon, holding in the hand ppr a fire-ball of the last

Partridge of Horsenden House, Bucks, an estoile or *Esse quam videri* 164 1

Paruck, Cursetjee Turdoonjee, J P, of Bombay on a mount vert, in front of a palm-tree ppr, a winged lion passant or charged on the shoulder with an estoile gu *A good conscience is a sure defence* 20 12

Parvise of Unsted, Surrey, a Cornish chough rising ppr 107 3

Pascall of Eastwood, Notts on a mount a holy lamb, all ppr, the banner sa 131 14

Pascall or **Paschall** of Much Baddow and Springfield Essex a demi-man couped at the breast vested ppr lined erm, the head, hair, and beard of the first

Pascoe, a wolf regardant cf 28 12

Pascol, a paschal lamb arg, bearing a banner gu 131 2

Pashley and **Pasley**, a balance and scales arg, the beam az 179 8

Paske, a lion rampant arg, supporting a cross patee fitched sa 3 13

Paske-Haselfoot, Thomas, Esquire, of Wandsworth, Surrey, a demi-peacock or the wings expanded az holding in the beak a snake entwined round the neck ppr 103 6

Paslew, Yorks and Suff, a lion rampant gu 1 13

Pasley-Dirom, *see* Dirom

Pasley, Sir Thomas Edward Sabine Bart, B A of Craig Dumfries sh, out of a naval coronet or, a sinister arm in armour ppr, grasping in the hand a staff thereon a flag arg, charged with a cross wavy gu, and on a canton az a human leg erect couped below the knee or *Pro Rege et patria pugnans* cf 210 1

Pasley, Scotland, a dexter arm from the shoulder in armour, holding in the hand a dagger, point downwards, all ppr *Be sure*

Pasmere, Hayes and Exeter, a demi leopard az

Pasmore, out of a mural coronet seven Lochaber-axes addorsed ppr 172 9

Pass, the sun in splendour or 162 2

Passingham, a demi-lion rampant party per fess or and gu charged with two cinquefoils counterchanged cf 10 2

Passingham, a demi lion semee of cinque foils, holding in the dexter paw a sword in pale cf 14 12
Passmere of Passemerehays and Swetton, Devonsh, a demi-sea-dog az, finned arg
Passmore, a stag at gaze arg 117 3
Paston of Paston, Norf, **Earl of Yarmouth** (*extinct*) a griffin sejant with wings endorsed or collared gu *De mieulx je pense en mieulx* cf 62 10
Paston, Norf, a griffin sejant with wings addorsed or, holding in the beak a chaplet gu
Paston of Horton Glouc a griffin passant or collared arg, lined az cf 63 2
Patch, Devonsh, a dexter arm in armour in fess couped ppr holding in the hand a cross crosslet fitched sa
Patch, Frederick Owen, Esquire, of Tiverton Devonsh a cubit arm erect vested az, cuffed arg, surmounting two cross crosslets fitchee in saltire sa, the hand grasping a flagstaff ppr therefrom a flag per pale arg and or, the dexter side charged with a cross sa 206 9
Patchett, Lieutenant-Colonel William Gordon, Broomhall, Greenfields, Shrewsbury a dexter arm embowed couped at the shoulder, vested arg, resting on a mount vert, the hand grasping a pick-axe ppr, and between two dragon's wings az, each charged with a sword erect ppr, pommel and hilt or
Pate of Cheltenham and Masterden Glouc, a demi lion rampant vair, crowned or 10 11
Pate, Ireland a lion's gamb or holding a wolf's head erased gu
Pate of Brin, Leics a stag's head cabossed arg attired or, and between the attires a raven with wings expanded sa 122 9
Pate, Bart (*extinct*) of Sysonby Leics a stag's head cabossed arg attired or, between the attires a raven with wings expanded sa cf 122 9
Pate of Wisbeach Isle of Ely, a stag's head cabossed or, and between the attires a Roman text R cf 122 5
Pateis, a greyhound current towards a tree 58 11
Pater, a leopard's head and neck erased gardant gu
Paterson of Aberdeen, Scotland, a pelican's head couped ppr *Pro Rege et grege* cf 98 2
Paterson, Charles James George, of Castle Huntly Longfargan Dundee, a pelican in her piety ppr *Merui —Je meurs pour ceux que j'aime* 98 8
Paterson, Major-General Adrian Hugh 25, South Road, Weston-super Mare same crest and first motto
Paterson, Thomas John Tildarg Merrion, co Dublin, same crest *Vivescit vulnere virtus*
Paterson of Kinnettles, Forfarsh, Scotland a pelican in her piety arg *Pro Rege et patria* 98 8
Paterson, Scotland, a branch of palm ppr *Virtute viresco.* 147 1
Paterson, out of a mural coronet a demi-savage wreathed round the middle vert, holding in his dexter hand a cock's head erased, and in his sinister on his shoulder a club
Paterson-Balfour-Hay, Edmund de Haya Esquire of Leys and Carpow, Perthsh and of Randerstoun and Mugdrum, Fifesh a half-length figure of a Lowland Scots countryman vested gray, his waistcoat gu, and his bonnet az, and a feather therein ppr, bearing on his dexter shoulder an ox-yoke, also ppr broken at one extremity *Primus e stirpe* cf 187 14
Paterson of Dunmure, Fifesh Scotland, a dexter hand issuing out of a cloud holding a branch of laurel ppr *Hæc tendimus omnes* cf 219 9
Paterson of Seafield, Scotland, a hand holding a sword in pale ppr *Pro Rege et grege* 212 9
Paterson, Bart, of Bannockburn, Stirlingsh a hand holding a quill, all ppr *Hinc orior* 217 10
Paterson of London on a mural coronet arg, a stag's head erased ppr, attired gu, gorged with a collar az, and pendent therefrom a man's heart gu *Hinc orior*
Pateshall of Layford, Heref, a demi-griffin arg 64 2
Pateshall, a peacock's head sa, between two wings or beaked of the last charged on the neck with three bends arg
Pateshall, Burnam-, Heref, out of a ducal coronet or a pelican arg, vulning herself ppr cf 98 1
Pateson, Norf a pelican in her piety ppr 98 8
Patishull and **Pattishall,** a hand holding a billet az 215 11
Patison, Scotland a pelican in her piety *Hostis honori invidia* 98 8
Patmer, Yorks, a hand holding an imperial crown ppr 217 1
Paton, Scotland, in the hand a cubit arm holding a rose slip leaved ppr *Virtute viget* 218 10
Paton, Major James, Crailing, Jedburgh, same crest and motto
Paton, Sir Joseph Noel, H M Limner for Scotland, 33, George Square, Edinburgh, between two dove's wings expanded ppr a cubit arm erect also ppr, charged on the palm with a Passion cross gu *Do right and fear nocht* 268 16
Paton of Grandhome Aberdeensh, Scotland, a sparrow hawk with wings expanded ppr *Virtute adepta* 87 1
Paton, R Johnston Esquire Kilmarnock, N B a sparrow hawk rising with wings addorsed and inverted ppr *Virtute adepta* 88 2
Paton of Kinaldy, Aberdeensh, Scotland a sparrow-hawk perched ppr *Virtus laudanda*
Paton, Scotland, a sparrow hawk rising ppr *Virtute viget* 88 2
Patoun of Richmond, Surrey, a sparrow-hawk close ppr, charged on the breast with a trefoil slipped or cf 85 2
Patriarche, a greyhound passant arg *Honor et honestas* cf 60 2
Patrick, Scotland a dexter hand ppr holding a saltier sa *Ora et labora* 215 12
Patrick, Ralston-, of Roughwood Ayrsh, Scotland (1) A dexter hand erect ppr, holding a saltier sa (*for Patrick*) 215 12 (2) A falcon looking to the sinister (*for Ralston*) *Ora et labora — Fide et marte* 85 6
Patrick, John, Esquire J P of Gledheather (Dunminning), co Antrim Ireland a dexter hand erect ppr, charged with a saltire couped sa, grasping a dagger also erect, ppr *Ora et labora* 212 8
Patrick, William Ralston, of Trearne, Beith, a dexter hand ppr, holding a saltire sa *Ora et labora*
Patrick of Crowneast Worcs a dexter hand ppr, holding a cross crosslet fitched 219 9
Patrick, Scotland, a hand erect ppr *Ora et labora* 222 14
Patrick, Durh, an arm in armour embowed ppr 200 1
Patrick, a stag trippant 117 8
Patrick, Kent a stag trippant *Study quiet* 117 8
Patrickson of Stockhow, Caswell-How and Calder Abbey, Cumb, on a mount vert a stag current regardant ppr attired and ungu or 118 2
Patrickson, George, Scales, near Ulverston same crest *Mente et manu*
Patrickson of Kirklinton, Cumb, same crest and motto
Patte, a lion rampant az 1 13
Patten, *see* Winmarleigh Baron
Patten, Wilson-, of Bank Hall, Lancs (1) A griffin's head erased vert beaked or (*for Patten*) 66 2 (2) A demi-wolf rampant or (*for Wilson*) *Nulla pallescere culpa — Virtus ad sidera tollit* 31 2
Patten, a griffin's head and neck erased vert, beaked or 66 2
Patten, a griffin's head erased vert. *Nulla pallescere culpa* 66 2
Patten, Lancs a tower or issuing flames of fire ppr 155 9
Patten, Lincs and Middx, a tower or, issuing therefrom flames of fire ppr, over which a label charged with this motto *Mal au tour* cf 155 9
Pattenson of Cherry Burton Yorks, out of a ducal coronet a camel's head cf 132 7
Pattenson, Tylden-, William Boys of Ibornden Kent (1) A camel's head erased sa, bezantee (2) A battle axe erect or entwined with a snake ppr *Finem respice* cf 132 7
Patters, a cross crosslet fitched or, and a palm branch vert in saltier
Patterson, Scotland a naked arm erect holding in the hand a pen ppr 217 10
Patterson, a pelican in her piety, all ppr 98 8
Patterson, Sir Robert Lloyd, J P, D L., F L S, Croft House, Holywood co Down a pelican in her piety vulning herself ppr, gorged with a collar dancettee az *Murus aëneus conscientia sana* 301 4
Patteson, Henry Tyrwhitt Staniforth, the Hall Beeston St. Andrew, Norwich, a pelican in her piety or, charged on the body with two fleurs-de-lis in fesse sa, between two roses gu, barbed and seeded ppr *Nemo sibi nascitur* 290 4
Pattinson of West Bolden, Durh, and William Watson Pattinson Esquire, of Felling House near Gateshead in front of flames of fire a dexter hand bendwise holding an ingot of silver, all ppr *Ex vile pretiosa*
Pattison, a hind's head couped or 124 1

Pattison, Scotland, a pelican in her piety, all ppr. *Hostis honori invidia.* 98. 8

Pattison, Ireland, an arm in armour vambraced az., holding in the hand a hawk's lure or.

Pattison, Scotland, out of a ducal coronet a camel's head sa., guttée-d'or, gorged with a collar and crowned with an antique crown, both or. *Hostis honori invidia.* cf. 132. 12

Pattison of Kelvin Grove, Lanarksh., Scotland, out of a ducal coronet or, a camel's head arg., guttée-de-poix, crowned with an antique crown of the first, collared az., charged with three escallops of the second. *Hostis honori invidia.* 132. 12

Pattle, an eagle displayed ppr. 75. 2

Pattle, an eagle displayed or. 75. 2

Patton-Bethune, *see* Bethune.

Patton, on a rock a swan close ppr. 100. 7

Patton, Scotland, a sparrow-hawk ppr. *Virtus laudanda.* 85. 2

Patton of Glenalmond, Perthsh., a sparrow-hawk rising ppr. *Virtute adepta.* 88. 2

Patton of Bishops Hall and Stoke Court, Taunton, a hawk arg. *Virtute adepta.* 85. 2

Paul, Sir James Balfour, Lyon King of Arms, a lion sejant guardant gu., armed aud langued az., his dexter paw resting on an escutcheon of the first. *Pro Rege et republica.* 8. 2

Paul, Sir Edward John Dean, Bart., of Rodburgh, Glouc., an ounce's head ppr., erased gu. *Pro Rege et republica.* 23. 10

Paul of Woodchester, Glouc., a leopard's head ppr., erased gu. *Pro Rege et republica.* 23. 10

Paul, Herbert Woodfield, 46, Cheyne Walk, S.W., a leopard's head or, erased gu.

Paul of High Grove, Glouc., a leopard's head per pale or and az., charged on the neck with a cross crosslet counterchanged. cf. 22. 10

Paul or **Paule,** a garb vert, banded arg. 153. 2

Paul of Lambeth, Surrey, and Norf., on the trunk of a tree raguly in fess, sprigged and leaved vert, a bird close arg.

Paul of London, an elephant arg., on the back a castle gu., tied under the belly on the point of the trunk a falchion in pale of the last.

Paul, Arthur Duncan, Esquire, of Wearne Wyche, High Ham, Somers., a demigriffin regardant or, gorged with a collar gemelle, and holding between the claws a cross crosslet az., the wings addorsed of the last, semée of cross crosslets or. *Per crucem cœlum.*

Paul, Sir William Joshua, Bart., D.L., of Paulville, co. Carlow, a cross patée fitchée or, between two swords in saltier arg., pommels and hilts or, points upwards. *Vana spes vitæ.* cf. 166. 14

Paul, Ireland, a hand issuing from a cloud in fess holding a torteau.

Paul, Scotland, two arms in armour embowed placing a savage's head affrontée on the point of a pheon. 194. 9

Paulet, Duke of Bolton and **Marquess of Winchester** (*extinct*), a falcon with wings displayed or, belled of the same, and gorged with a ducal coronet gu. *Aymez loyaulté.* 87. 2

Paulet, *see* Winchester, Marquess of.

Paulet, Bart., Southampton, a falcon with wings displayed and belled or, ducally gorged gu. *Aimez loyaulté.* 87. 2

Paulet, late Sir Henry Charles, Bart. (*extinct*), a falcon with wings displayed or, belled of the same, and ducally gorged gu. *Aimez loyaulté.* 87. 2

Paulet of Leigh Paulet, Devonsh., and Thornbury., Glouc., an arm in armour embowed, holding in the hand a sword, all ppr. 195. 2

Pauley, within an annulet an eagle displayed.

Paull, a pillar enfiled with a ducal coronet.

Paull, a leopard's head erased at the neck. 23. 10

Paumier, Devonsh., a hawk's leg erased, jessed and belled ppr. 113. 8

Paunceforte-Duncombe, Bart., *see* Duncombe.

Pauncefote, Baron (Pauncefote), of Hasfield, and Preston Court, Glouc., a lion rampant arg., crowned with a ducal coronet or, holding between the paws an escutcheon of the second charged with a wolf's head erased ppr. *Pensez forte.* 1. 12

Paveley of Westbury, Wilts, an anchor and a sword in saltier ppr. 160. 9

Paver, Yorks, a tree ppr. *Faded, but not destroyed.* 143. 5

Pavey, Norf., a lion rampant gardant sa. 2. 5

Pavia, John Charles, Esquire, Dunsinnan, Inglemere Road, South Sydenham Park, S.E., an arrow fessewise pointing to a mullet of five points on the dexter side. *Semper eadem.* 301. 13

Pavier, Russell-, Herbert Arthur, Esquire, of Heaton Manor, Heaton Norris, Lancs, and of Hammerwich, Staffs: (1) Two arms embowed ppr., vested above the elbow arg., that on the dexter side holding a chisel, and that on the sinister a mallet, also ppr. (*for Pavier*). (2) In front of two palmbranches saltireways vert, a fret or, thereon a martlet sa. (*for Russell*). *Quo fata vocant.* 97. 10

Pawle, Shropsh., a garb fesseways vert, banded arg. 153. 6

Pawle, a leopard's head erased ppr. 23. 10

Pawle, Frederick Charles, J.P., Northcote, Reigate, same crest.

Pawlet, Somers., on a mount vert, a falcon rising or, ducally gorged gu. *Aimez loyaulté.* cf. 87. 2

Pawlett of St. James's, Westminster, Middx., a terrestrial orb or, thereon a falcon rising ppr., collared and belled or. 159. 7

Pawlett of Willesden, Middx., on a mount vert, a falcon rising or, pellettée, belled of the second.

Pawson, Yorks: (1) On a mount vert, the sun in his splendour or (*for Pawson*). 162. 3. (2) A buck's head erased quarterly indented arg. and gu., attired sa. (*for Hargrave*). *Favente Deo.* 121. 2

Pawson, William Hargrave, of Shawdon, Alnwick: (1) A buck's head erased at the neck quarterly indented arg. and gu., attired sa., charged with four roundels counterchanged. (2) A mount vert, and thereon a hart charged with the sun in splendour. *Favente Deo.*

Pawson, a griffin's head or. 66. 1

Paxton, on the top of a tower a sea-pyot rising ppr. 156. 2

Paxton, Scotland, a garb ppr. *Industria ditat.* 153. 2

Paxton of Cholderton, Wilts, of Watford, Herts, and Middleton Hill, Carmarthensh., an eagle's head erased az., charged on the neck with two chevrons or, between two wings arg., semée of mullets gu.

Payler, a lion sejant holding in the dexter paw a saltier.

Payne, Baron Lavington (*extinct*), a lion's gamb erased arg., grasping a broken tilting-lance gu. *Malo mori quam fœdari.* 38. 9

Payne-Gallwey, Sir Ralph William, Bart., of Thirkleby Park, Yorks: (1) A catamountain passant gardant ppr., gorged with a collar gemelle or (*for Gallwey*). (2) A lion's gamb erased arg., holding the lower part of a tilting-lance in bend gu. (*for Payne*).

Payne, a lion's gamb erect and erased arg., grasping a broken tilting-spear gu. *Malo mori quam fœdari.* 38. 9

Payne, Thomas Budds, Esquire, J.P., of Maritimo, South Yarra, Melbourne, Victoria, Australia, a lion's gamb erect and erased arg., holding fesseways a broken tilting-spear gu. *Malo mori quam fœdari.* 38. 9

Payne, Bart., Beds, a lion's gamb erect arg., holding a broken tilting-spear gu. *Malo mori quam fœdari.* cf. 38. 9

Payne of Norwich, a lion's gamb or, holding a baton ragulée of the same.

Payne, a lion's gamb holding a cross patée sa. cf. 36. 9

Payne of East Grinstead, Sussex, a lion's head erased per fess sa. and arg. 17. 8

Payne, a lion's head erased ppr., ducally gorged, lined and ringed or, holding in the mouth a laurel-sprig vert.

Payne of Newark, Leics., an heraldic tiger sejant per pale engrailed az. and erm., surmounting a branch of oak fructed ppr., the dexter fore-paw resting on a mascle gu. 25. 11

Payne of Petworth, Sussex, a griffin passant with wings addorsed per pale or and az. 63. 2

Payne of Fulham, Middx., a griffin passant with wings addorsed or. 63. 2

Payne, a griffin passant az., armed and winged or. 63. 2

Payne of Ittingham, Norf., an ostrich's head erased, between two wings az., holding in the beak a horse-shoe arg. cf. 97. 10

Payne, an ostrich's head couped or, between two wings sa. cf. 97. 10

Payne of Dunham, Norf., an ostrich's head or, issuing out of a plume of feathers arg.

Payne of London, and of Wallingford, Berks, a demi-ostrich with wings addorsed arg., holding in the beak a key or.

Payne of Sulby Hall, Northamp., an ostrich's head erased or, holding in the beak a horse-shoe arg., between two wings sa. cf. 97. 10

Payne, Rev John Vaughan, M A, Kempsford House Glouc, same crest

Payne of London, issuing out of clouds ppr, two hands conjoined 224 1

Payne of London, an arm in armour embowed arg holding in the hand a sword ppr, hilt and pommel or enfiled with a boar s head sa, vulned gu cf 195 2

Payne of Stoke Neyland, Suff, an arm in armour embowed holding in the gauntlet a leopard's head, all or

Payne, a demi-man couped at the loins in profile, holding in the dexter hand an arrow

Payne, Dorset and of Medborne Leics, out of a ducal coronet or, a woman s head couped below the shoulders ppr, vested erm the hair dishevelled or, on the head a chapeau az

Payne, out of a plume of ostrich-feathers a leopard's head or

Payne, Denbighsh, and of Westbrooke, Dorset, a leopard's head or gorged with a collar az, rimmed of the first, and charged with three bezants cf 22 12

Payne of Market Bosworth, Leics, and of Paine, Suff a wolf's head erased az, charged with five bezants in saltier cf 30 8

Payne of Midlow, St Neots, Hunts, among grass ppr an otter passant or holding in the mouth a fish arg

Payne, P Marriott Esquire of Holmesdale, the Park Nottingham, a lion's gamb erect and erased arg, grasping a broken tilting spear or *Malo mori quam fœdari*

Paynell, a lion passant vert 6 2

Paynell, a lion rampant vert 1 13

Paynell of Boothby, Lincs, an ostrich s head ppr

Payntell of London an arm erect vested gu cuffed arg, holding in the hand ppr three lilies or, leaved vert

Paynter, an old man's head couped at the shoulders ppr, vested gu, on the head a long cap az 192 11

Paynter of Sprole, Norf, a lapwing arg environed with two branches vert the tops in saltier

Paynter of Twidall, Kent, on the stump of a tree eradicated ppr, a wyvern vert sans wings, the tail entwined round the tree

Paynter of Boskenna Cornw, three broken broad arrows or, points downwards, two in saltier and one in pale, knit with a lace and mantle gu, doubled arg *Nonum prematur in annum*

Paynter, Major George, Hollinhouse Lane Delph, three broken arrows or bent with a lace and mantlet gu, doubled arg *Carpe diem*

Paynter, Surrey, three broken arrows or, points downwards, two in saltier and one in pale banded gu

Paynter, Rev Francis Stoke Hill Guildford three broken broad arrows or, knit with a lance gu *Carpe diem*

Paynter, George, 21 Belgrave Square S W same crest and motto

Paynter, Henry Grosvenor 118, Ebury Street S W same crest and motto

Paytherus, a boar passant gu, bristled and ungu or 40 9

Payton, Suff, a griffin sejant with wings addorsed or 62 10

Peace, a demi lion rampant purp 10 2

Peace, a dove with wings expanded arg, holding in the beak an olive-branch vert 94 5

Peach and **Peache** of Rooksmore Glouc, a demi lion rampant per fess erm and gu ducally crowned or 10 11

Peach, Keighly- of Idlicote House Shipston on Stour, Warw (1) A demi-lion rampant per fesse erm and gu, ducally crowned or armed az (*for Peach*) 10 11 (2) A griffin's head sa, langued gu, charged with three mullets or (*for Keighly*) *Quicquid dignum sapiente bonoque est* cf 66 1

Peache, a lion's head erased ducally crowned or 18 8

Peachey, Baron Selsey (*extinct*), a demi-lion double queued erm holding in the dexter paw a mullet pierced gu *Memor et fidelis*

Peachey, Sussex a demi lion rampant double queued erm holding in the dexter paw a sword in pale arg, hilt and pommel or *Ne quisquam serviat enses*

Peachey, a demi lion rampant erminois ducally crowned or, holding a tower arg

Peachey, a demi-lion rampant, ducally crowned, double-queued cf 10 6

Peachey, a dexter arm holding in the hand a sabre ppr 212 13

Peacock of Stone Hall, Pembrokesh a peacock's head erased ppr, gorged with a mural coronet or, holding in the beak a rose gu slipped and leaved ppr *Be just and fear not*

Peacock, co Down, Ireland, a peacock's head erased, holding in the beak a thistle leaved all ppr

Peacock of Slyne, Lancs, a peacock's head erased az 103 1

Peacock of Burnhall Durh a peacock s head erased az gorged with a mural coronet or 103 11

Peacock of London, a peacock's head and neck or, with wings expanded az, a snake entwined about the neck of the last 103 3

Peacock, Scotland, a plume of peacock's feathers ppr *Naturæ donum*

Peacock of Springfield Place, Chelmsford, a mount vert thereon an eagle displayed erminois holding in the beak a cross crosslet fitchee gu the dexter claw supporting a hurt charged with a cross crosslet or 74 9

Peacock, a wyvern with wings addorsed ppr 70 1

Peacock of Willesden, Middx, a cockatrice az charged with two annulets conjoined palewise arg resting the dexter claw upon an escutcheon arg, charged with a peacock in his pride ppr

Peacock, Warren Thomas, of Efford Hall Hants, a cockatrice with wings erect vert *Vincit veritas* 68 4

Peacocke, Bart (*extinct*), of Barntic co Clare Ireland a cockatrice vert. *Vincit veritas* 68 4

Peacocks, Bligh-, a peacock's head erased az gorged with a mural coronet or *Naturæ donum* 103 11

Peak, a lion's head issuing or 21 1

Peak, Lincs, of Abchurch, Northamp, and London a lion's head or pierced through the side of the head by an arrow in fess, the point coming out of the mouth of the first, feathered and headed arg

Peake of Lutterworth Leics, and London, a human heart gu between two wings expanded arg cf 110 14

Peake, Leics, a human heart gu between two wings arg cf 110 14

Peake of Llweny, Wales, a leopard's face gu, holding in the mouth an arrow ppr, headed and flighted or *Heb Dduw heb ddim* cf 22 2

Peake of London a lion's head or, erased per fess gu, charged on the neck with three guttes de sang one and two pierced through the side of the head by an arrow arg, barbed and feathered of the first, the point issuing from mouth

Peake of Sandwich Kent, a cockatrice volant or, beaked, combed, legged and wattled gu

Pearce, a leopard sejant gardant ppr the dexter paw resting on an escutcheon arg charged with a bee volant sa

Pearce of Parson's Green Fulham, Middx, and of Withingham, Norf, a demi pelican rising or vulned in the breast ppr, crowned gu

Pearce, Cambs, a Cornish chough sa, beaked and membered gu 107 14

Pearce of Ffrwdgreech Breconsh, on rocks ppr, a cross crosslet fitched, transpiercing a mural coronet az *Celer et audax*

Pearce, Yorks a cross crosslet fitchee or, crowned with a mural coronet gu

Pearce, Sir William George Bart M A, LL.B of Cardell House Renfrewsh, in front of a dexter arm embowed in armour, the hand grasping two javelins all ppr, a unicorn's head erased sa *Audax et celer* 286 4

Pearce, a dexter arm in armour embowed holding in the hand a lance pointing to the dexter

Pearce of Penzance Cornw an arm in armour embowed, holding in the hand an arrow in pale the shaft resting on the wreath

Pearce, a dexter arm holding in the hand a dagger ppr 212 3

Pearce-Edgcumbe, Sir Edward Robert, Sandye Place, Sandy, a demi boar supporting between the legs a javelin erect ppr, and gorged with a collar, therefrom suspended a bugle horn stringed both or 255 10

Pearce-Serocold, Charles, Taplow Hill, Maidenhead (1) A castle or with a fleur-de-lis issuing from the battlements az (*for Serocold*) (2) In front of a rose gu, a Cornish chough ppr (*for Pearce*)

Peard, a demi lion rampant erm, collared sa 10 9

Peard, Devonsh a tiger's head or pierced through the neck by a broken spear ppr, headed arg, the wound embrued gu

Peareth of Unsworth House Gateshead, Durh a leopard's head and neck erased ppr holding in the mouth a cross crosslet fitched *Verax et fidelis* cf 23 10

Pearle, a hand holding a thistle ppr. 218. 2

Pearmain, a demi-lion rampant. 10. 2

Pears, a demi-lion or. 10. 2

Pears-Archbold, James Archbold, Esquire, of Fenham Hall, Northumb.: (1) Two lion's gambs erased, each encircled with a wreath of oak ppr., holding an escutcheon arg., charged with a fleur-de-lis az. (*for Archbold*). 39. 9. (2) Upon a rock ppr., a wyvern vert, gorged with a collar gemel or, supporting with the dexter claw an escutcheon of the same charged with an estoile gu. (*for Pears*). *Vi et virtute.* 69. 10

Pearsall, a lion's head erased or. 17. 8

Pearsall, De, of Willsbridge, Glouc., a boar's head erased gu., crined and tusked, and charged with a cross fleurettée or, langued az. *Better deathe than shame.* cf. 42. 2

Pearse of Thurles, co. Tipperary, Ireland, on a wreath of the colours a fern-brake, thereon a pelican in her piety, the wings elevated ppr., charged on the breast with a trefoil vert. *Nihil amanti durum.*

Pearse, General George Godfrey, C.B., Shanklin, Isle of Wight, same crest and motto.

Pearse, a seax az., hilt and pommel or. 171. 2

Pearse of Bradninch, Devonsh., a wyvern gu., with wings displayed arg. cf. 70. 8

Pearse, Somers., and of Court, Devonsh., an arm in armour embowed, holding in the hand a lance by the middle, the point to the dexter, ppr. *Cadenti porrigo dextram.*

Pearse, Kerr- of Ascot, Berks: (1) A dexter arm embowed in armour, the hand grasping a tilting-spear in bend sinister, all ppr., between two estoiles gu. (*for Pearse*). (2) The sun in his splendour ppr. (*for Kerr*). *Cadente porrigo dextram.—Sero sed serio.* 162. 2

Pearse of Harlington, Beds, a lion's head erased arg. *Vi divinâ.* 17. 8

Pearson, a demi-griffin segreant az., beaked or, and charged on the shoulder with a sun in splendour of the last. cf. 64. 2

Pearson of London, a demi-lion rampant gu., holding in the dexter paw a sun or.

Pearson, Honourable Charles Henry, M.A., of Ediowie, Williams Road, Toorak, Victoria, Australia, a demi-lion rampant gu., charged on the neck with three bezants between a double gemelle or, holding in the dexter paw an escutcheon az., charged with a sun in splendour of the second. *Sol et scutum Deus.*

Pearson, Sir Weetman Dickinson, Bart., Paddockhurst, Worth, Sussex, in front of a demi-gryphon couped, wings elevated and addorsed, holding between the paws a mill-stone ppr., thereon a mill-rind sa., a sun in splendour. 286. 12

Pearson of New Sleaford, Lincs, and of Tunbridge Hall, near Godstone, Surrey, a cock's head erased az., combed and wattled gu., charged on the neck with a sun in splendour or, holding in the beak a yellow heart's-ease or pansy flower sprigged and leaved vert, between two branches of palm ppr.

Pearson, Lieutenant-Colonel Henry, Wingfield House, South Wingfield, Derbysh., an eagle's wing sa., semée-de-lis or, pierced by an arrow embrued in bend, point upwards, and vulned ppr. *Ne tentes aut perfice.*

Pearson, Rev. William Carter, Henley Vicarage, Ipswich, same crest (a crescent for difference) and motto.

Pearson, Rev. Arthur Charles, Ringsfield, Beccles, Suff., same crest. *Ne tentes, aut perfice.*

Pearson, Edward, Wilmslow, Chesh., a demi-lion rampant gu., charged on the neck with three bezants between a double gemelle or, holding in the dexter paw an escutcheon az., charged with a sun in splendour of the second. *Sol et scutum Deus.*

Pearson, Edwin James, Millfield, Berkhampstead, same crest and motto.

Pearson, George, the Tythe House, Knutsford, Chesh., same crest and motto.

Pearson, the sun in his splendour ppr. 162. 2

Pearson of Tyers Hill, Yorks, issuing out of a cloud the sun in his splendour ppr. 162. 5

Pearson-Gee, Arthur Beilby, Esquire, of Wadhurst, Sussex, and 4, New Square, Lincoln's Inn, Barrister-at-Law, in front of a sun rising in splendour an arm in armour couped at the elbow and fessewise, the hand in a gauntlet holding a sword erect, all ppr. *Finis coronat opus.* 211. 8

Pearson, an arm in armour embowed, holding in the hand a rose-branch slipped ppr.

Pearson, a cubit arm erect, holding in the hand a wreath of laurel ppr. 218. 4

Pearson, Scotland, an ostrich holding in its beak a horse-shoe ppr. *Nil desperandum.* 97. 8

Pearson of Balmadies, Forfarsh., Scotland, a dove holding in its beak an olive-branch ppr. *Dum spiro, spero.* 92. 5

Pearson, a parrot ppr. 101. 4

Pearson, on a mural coronet or, a paroquet vert, beaked and legged gu.

Pearson of Kippenross, Stirlingsh., Scotland, a tower ppr. *Rather die than be disloyal.* 156. 2

Pearson, Honourable William, J.P., of Kilmany Park, Sale, co. Tanjil, and of Craigellachie, St. Kilda, both in Victoria, Member of the Legislative Council of that colony, same crest and motto. 156. 2

Pearson, three savage's heads conjoined in one neck, one looking to the dexter, one to the sinister, and one upwards. cf. 191. 5

Pearson, Surrey, out of an Eastern coronet or, a stag's head erm.

Pearson, George, Esquire, of Clifton, Bristol, upon a mount vert, in front of two Passion-nails in saltire az., a seax erect ppr., pommel and hilt or. *Perdurat probitas.* 171. 5

Pearson of Tankerton and Maize Hill, Greenwich, Kent, a boar's head couped sa., holding in the mouth an acorn or, leaved vert. *Perdurat probitas.* 42. 7

Pearson of Upper Gloucester Place, London, a horse's head erased sa., billettée, and gorged with a mural coronet or.

Peart, a dexter hand holding a sword ppr. 212. 13

Peart, a lion rampant or. 1. 13

Peart and **Pert,** out of an earl's coronet or, a Moor's head from the shoulders affrontée ppr. 182. 2

Peart, a stork statant ppr., between bulrushes, three on each side. 104. 3

Pease of Ottery St. Mary, Devonsh., a leopard's head gardant, couped at the neck, collared az., holding in the mouth a sword fesseways ppr.

Pease, Joseph Robinson, of Hesslewood, near Hull, Yorks, an eagle's head erased arg., holding in the beak or a pea-stalk vert. *Confide recte agens.*

Pease, Francis Richard, J.P., Hesslewood, Hull, same crest and motto.

Pease of London, on a mount vert, a dove rising arg., holding in the beak gu. a pea-stalk with blossoms and pods ppr., the legs of the third.

Pease, Bart., upon the capital of an Ionic column a dove rising, holding in the beak a pea-stalk, the blossom and pods also ppr. *Pax et spes.* 94. 1

Pease, Arthur Francis, Hummersknott, Darlington, same crest and motto.

Pease, Joseph Albert, M.P., of Headlam Hall, Gainford, and 8, Hertford Street, London, W., same crest.

Pease, Walter Fell, Brinkburn, Darlington, same crest and motto.

Pease, William Edwin, Mowden, Darlington, same crest and motto.

Peasley, Ireland, a dragon sejant vert, advancing a spear or, headed az.

Peat, Scotland, a deer's head ppr. *Prospere si propere.* 121. 5

Peat of Sevenoaks, Kent, in front of a mount of bulrushes ppr., thereon a stork arg., beaked and legged gu., two mascles interlaced in fess az. *Ardens.* 104. 9

Peat, Middx., out of a ducal coronet or, a heron's head ppr.

Peat, a hand holding a fish ppr. 220. 4

Peat, Scotland, a dexter hand holding a book expanded. *Amicus certus.* 215. 10

Peaterson, of Bannockburn Scotland, a pelican's head erased gu. *Pour le Roy.* 98. 2

Peche or **Pechey,** an astrolabe or. 167. 7

Pechell, a Cornish chough ppr. 107. 14

Pechell, Brooke-, Sir George Samuel, Bart., of Paggleshain, Essex, a lark ppr., charged with two fleurs-de-lis or. *Vix ea nostra voco.*

Pechey of Chichester, Sussex, a lion's head erased arg., ducally crowned or. 18. 8

Pechey, Kent, a lion's head erm., crowned or. cf. 18. 8

Peck of Samford Hill, Essex, and Wood Pelling and Methwould, Norf., two lances in saltier or, headed arg., the pennons of the first, each charged with a cross formée gu., the spears entiled with a chaplet vert. 175. 15

Peck of London, a demi-lion rampant ppr., holding an anchor or. 12. 12

Peck, a cubit arm vested in pale, holding in the hand three flowers stalked and leaved. 205. 14

Peck, a dexter arm embowed ppr, holding in the hand a branch 202 3

Peck of Cornish Hall, Denbighsh, out of a ducal coronet a cubit arm erect vested and cuffed, holding in the hand ppr a sprig of three roses *Crux Christi salus mea*

Pecke, Sussex, a close helmet in profile plumed sa 180 4

Peckham and **Peckam**, a hand holding a scroll of paper ppr 215 6

Peckham, a cubit arm holding in the hand a dagger, point downwards, ppr

Peckham, an ostrich ppr *Tentanda via est* 97 2

Peckham, Rev Harry John, Nutley Vicarage, Uckfield, same crest and motto

Peckham, Thomas Gilbert, Hall Place, Harbledown, Canterbury, same crest

Peckham-Micklethwait, Bart (*extinct*) of Iridge Place, Sussex (1) A griffin's head arg, erased gu, gorged with a collar componnee of the second and first (*for Micklethwait*) *cf* 66 2 (2) On a mount between two palm-branches vert an ostrich or, holding in the beak a horse shoe sa (*for Peckham*) *Favente Numine Regina servatur*

Peckover, a lion's head erased or 17 8

Peckover, Alexander LL D, Esquire, of Sibald's Holme, Wisbech Cambs, a lion rampant az, holding in the dexter paw a sprig of oak leaved fructed, and slipped ppr, and resting the sinister fore paw upon an escutcheon of the arms, viz per pale gu and sa, a garb or, on a chief nebuly of the last three lions rampant az *In Christo speravi*

Pecksall Middx, a Moor's head couped ppr *cf* 192 13

Peckshall and **Peshall**, a wolf's head erased arg, collared flory gu *cf* 30 10

Peckwell, a stag's head cabossed 122 5

Peckwell, a griffin's head between two wings ppr 65 11

Pedder of Ashton Lodge, Lancs, two lion's heads erased and addorsed erminois, gorged with one collar gu, between two olive-branches ppr *Je dis la vérite* 260 17

Pedder, Lieutenant Colonel James Henry Worthington, of Gwinfe Llangadock, Carmarthensh, and St Mary's Cottage, Windermere, same crest and motto

Pedder, Charles Edward, same crest and motto

Pedder, John Wilson, of Finsthwaite House Ulverston, Lancs, and the Vicarage, Garstang, Lancs, same crest and motto

Pedder, two branches of palm in orle vert 146 2

Pedder, Sydney Hampden, of 21 Kensington Palace Gardens London, W, same crest *Je dis la vérité*

Peddie of Raehill, Dumfries, a papingo holding in his beak an arrow ppr *Consulto*

Pede of Bury, Suff, a chapeau gu, turned up erm, with an ostrich-feather on each side the dexter or, the sinister az 114 10

Pedler of Mutley House, near Plymouth, Devonsh, a demi-lion rampant sa crowned with an Oriental crown or holding between the paws a lozenge charged with a fleur de-lis, and in the mouth a flag gu *Animo non astutia* 113 3

Pedley, a lion's head gu 21 1

Pedley of Petworth and Abbotsley Hunts a demi-lion rampant arg, holding in the paws a lozenge or, charged with a fleur-de-lis gu

Pedley, Joseph, Esquire, Great Baddon, a demi-lion rampant arg, holding in the paws a lozenge or, charged with a fleur-de-lis gu

Pedyward, a cross crosslet charged on the centre and on each crosslet with a mullet 165 5

Peech, a lion's head erased erm crowned or 18 8

Peek of Hazelwood, near Kingsbridge, Devonsh two hazel nuts slipped ppr 272 5

Peek, Sir Wilfrid, Bart, of Rousdon, Devonsh two hazel-nuts slipped ppr *Le Maître vient* 272 5

Peel, Viscount (Peel), the Lodge Sandy, Beds, a demi-lion rampant arg, gorged with a collar az charged with three bezants and holding between the paws a shuttle or *Industria* 312 2

Peel, a lion rampant 1 13

Peel, Bart, of Drayton Manor, Staffs, a demi lion rampant arg, gorged with a collar az, charged with three bezants, holding between the paws a shuttle or *Industria* 312 2

Peel, of Peel Fold Lancs, and Trenant Park, Cornw, of Knowlmere Manor, Yorks, of Stone Hall, Pembrokesh, of Aylesmore, Glouc, of Brookfield, Chesh, and Singleton Brook, Lancs, same crest and motto

Peel, Archibald, Wertlea, Broxbourne, Herts, same crest and motto

Peel, Lieutenant-Colonel Cecil Lennox, Easthampstead Cottage, Wokingham, same crest and motto

Peel, William, Knowlmere Manor, Clitheroe, same crest and motto

Peel, Rt Hon Sir Frederick, K C M G, 32, Chesham Place, S W, same crest and motto

Peel, Herbert B A, Taliaris, Llandilo R S O, Carmarthensh, same crest and motto

Peel, Hugh Edmund Ethelston, of Bryn y pys, Flintsh (1) A demi-lion rampant arg, gorged with a collar az, charged with three bezants, and holding between the paws a shuttle or (*for Peele*) (2) A ram's head couped sa, charged with three cross crosslets or *Industria.* *cf* 130 1

Peel of Ackworth Park, Yorks, a lion couchant arg charged on the shoulder with a sheaf of arrows ppr, banded az, and resting the dexter paw upon an escutcheon, also az, charged with a bee volant or *Meret qui laborat* 7 14

Peel, Sir Theophilus Bart, of Potterton Hall, Barwick-in-Elmet, Yorks, same crest

Peele, a stag's head erased or 121 2

Peele, Edmund Cresswell Esquire of Cyngfeld, Shrewsbury, a wolf's head ppr, gorged with a collar fleury and counterfleury *Vincit omnia veritas* 30 10

Peer, co Cork, Ireland a mermaid ppr, holding in her dexter hand a pile wavy or, and in her sinister a fleur de-lis az

Peeres or **Perse** of Westdown Kent a sphere, at the north and south poles an etoile, all or

Peeres or **Peers** of Alverston, Warw, issuing out of clouds ppr, an arm in armour embowed of the first garnished or bound above the elbow with a ribbon in a bow gu, holding in the gauntlet a spear of the third headed with a pheon

Peerman, a stag's head couped or collared sa *cf* 121 5

Peers, on a chapeau ppr, a lion's head per chevron or and az *cf* 17 9

Peers of Chiselhampton, Oxon, a demi-griffin segreant arg 64 2

Peers, Cornw, a crossbow

Peers-Adams, Maxwell Richard William, c o Messrs H King and Co, 9, Pall Mall, on a mount vert, a cross crosslet fitchee or, charged with a bleeding heart gu *In cruce salus*

Peerson of London, and Wisbeach, Isle of Ely, Cambs a parrot ppr 101 4

Peerson, out of a mural coronet chequy arg and az a parrot's head vert

Pegg or **Pegge**, Derbysh a demi-sun issuing or rays alternately sa, or and arg

Pegge-Burnell, *see* Burnell

Pegler, Halifax, a griffin's head erased, ducally crowned *Speranza e verita* 66 7

Pegriz, a dexter and a sinister arm holding a two handed sword in pale ppr 213 1

Peile of Broomhill Inverness-sh, N B a mural coronet or, thereon a mullet pierced sa

Peirce, a griffin passant or 63 2

Peirce of Canterbury, Kent, a unicorn's head couped arg, armed and maned or 49 7

Peirce, a stag's head erased 121 2

Peirce, William, Esquire, of the Bank of Ireland and of the Square, Listowel, co Kerry, a pelican in its piety *Ad mortem fidelis*

Peirse, Beresford-, *see* Beresford

Peirse, London out of a mural coronet a cross crosslet fitched

Peirse, Beresforde-, Sir Henry Monson de la Poer, of Bedale, Yorks (1) A cross crosslet fitchee or surmounted by a mural coronet gu 279 5 (2) Out of a naval crown or a dragon's head per fesse wavy arg and gu, the lower part of the neck transfixed by a broken tilting-spear, and in the mouth the remaining part of the spear point upwards, or (*for Beresford*) 279 6

Peirse-Duncombe, Captain George Thomas, 25, Queen's Gate, S W (1) Out of a ducal coronet the hind-leg of a horse sa, the shoe arg (*for Duncombe*) (2) A cross crosslet fitchee or, surmounted by a mural crown gu, the crown charged with a cross crosslet (*for Peirse*) *Deo regi patriæ*

Peirson, Scotland, a lion's gamb az, holding a heart gu 39 11

Peirson, a deer's head or 121 5

Peisley or **Peasley** of Punchestown, co Kildare, a dragon sejant vert holding a spear or, the head az., embrued and garnished gu. *Periculum fortitudine evasi.*

Peit, Scotland, a dexter hand holding a book expanded ppr. *Amicus.* 215. 10

Peitere, Scotland, a hand holding a dagger in pale ppr. *Pour mon Dieu.* 212. 9

Peiters or **Peters,** Scotland, a boar's head between two bay-branches ppr.

Peiton, a griffin sejant, the dexter claw extended. cf. 62. 10

Peke of Horncastle, Lincs, a lion's head erased or, guttée-de-sang, pierced through the side of the head by an arrow of the first, headed and feathered arg., the arrow coming out through the mouth vulned gu.

Pelham, *see* Newcastle-under-Lyne, Duke of.

Pelham, *see* Yarborough, Earl of.

Pelham, *see* Chichester, Earl of.

Pelham-Holles, Duke of Newcastle (*extinct*), a peacock in his pride arg. *Vincit amor patriæ.* 103. 12

Pelham, Sussex: (1) A peacock in his pride arg. 103. 12. *Badge,* a buckle arg.

Pelham, Lincs, Dorset, and Sussex, a peacock in his pride arg. 103. 12

Pelham-Clay, William M. C., Esquire, of Woodlands, Kinson, near Wimborne, Dorset, (1) Two wings arg., semée of trefoils sa. (*for Clay*). 109. 11. (2) A peacock in pride arg. (*for Pelham*). 103. 12. (3) Out of a ducal coronet or, a plume of five ostrich-feathers per pale arg. and gu. (*for Waldegrave*). *Tout un durant ma vie.* 114. 13

Pelham, Thursby-, James Augustine Harvey, Cound Hall, Shrewsbury: (1) A peacock in his pride arg. (*for Pelham*). (2) A curlew with wings expanded arg., beak and legs ppr. (*for Thursby*). *Vincit amor patriæ (Pelham).—In silentio fortitudo (Thursby).*

Pelissier, Ireland, a fleur-de-lis or, surmounting a bezant between a pair of falcon's wings per fesse arg. and az. *Victrix fortunæ sapientia.* 111. 7

Pell, a pelican arg., with wings addorsed, vulning herself, all ppr. 98. 1

Pell, on a mural coronet or, a mullet pierced sa.

Pell, Albert, Hazlebeach, Notts, same crest

Pell of Dimblesby, Lincs, and Dersingham, Norf., on a chaplet vert, flowered or, a pelican of the last, vulned gu.

Pellat, a lion rampant or. 1. 13

Pellate, a lion passant arg., guttée-de-poix, holding in his dexter paw an oak-branch ppr., fructed or. *Devant si je puis.*

Pellew, *see* Exmouth, Viscount.

Pellew of Treverry, Cornw., a ship in distress on a rock ppr. *Deo juvante.—Deo non fortuna.* 160. 14

Pellot of Bignall Park and Bolney, Sussex, a lion passant arg., guttée-de-poix, holding in the dexter paw an acorn slipped vert, fructed or.

Pelly and **Pelley,** out of a ducal coronet or, an elephant's head arg. 133. 1

Pelly, Bart., of Upton, Essex, out of a naval coronet an elephant's head. *Deo ducente, nil nocet.* cf. 133. 1

Pelly, Sir Harold, Bart., of Upton, Essex, issuant from a vallary coronet or, charged on the rim with three hurts, an elephant's head arg. *Deo ducente, nil nocet.* 313. 8

Pelly, Leonard, J.P., Bath Club, Dover Street, W., same crest and motto.

Pelsant, *alias* **Buswell,** Bart. (*extinct*), a lion's head erased gu., langued az., gorged with a collar raguly arg. cf. 17. 2

Pelton, a hand holding a swan's head and neck erased ppr. 220. 9

Pember of Lyons Hall and Tathill, Heref., and of Newport House, Almeley, on a mount vert, a pheasant feeding on a stalk of wheat ppr. cf. 90. 8

Pemberton-Barnes, *see* Barnes.

Pemberton-Leigh, Baron Kingston: (1) A demi-lion rampant gu., holding between the paws a lozenge arg., charged with a rose, also gu. (*for Leigh*). (2) A dragon's head erm., erased gu., ducally gorged or, and transfixed by an arrow fesseways ppr. (*for Pemberton*). *Ut tibi sic alteri.* cf. 71. 8

Pemberton, Major-General Wykeham Leigh, C.B., Abbot's Leigh, Sussex, same crest as second above.

Pemberton, Durh., a dragon's head sa., couped gu., ducally gorged or. cf. 72. 9

Pemberton of London, a dragon's head vert, couped gu. 71. 1

Pemberton of St. Albans, Herts, a dragon's head erased sa. cf. 71. 2

Pemberton, Shropsh., a dragon's head couped sa., langued gu. *Hauri ex puro.* 71. 1

Pemberton of Milton, Northants, a dragon's head sa., couped and langued gu. 71. 1

Pemberton, Sir Edward Leigh, K.C.B., of Torry Hill, near Sittingbourne, a dragon's head erm., erased gu., ducally gorged or, and transfixed by an arrow fessewise ppr. *Ut tibi sic alteri.* cf. 71. 8

Pemberton, Loftus Leigh, 29, Rutland Gate S.W., same crest and motto.

Pemberton, Busick Edmonds, 14, Sussex Square, W., in front of a cross crosslet fitchée arg., a dragon's head couped vert, collared and chained of the first. *Dum anima spes est.*

Pemberton, Charles Seaton, 25, Queen Gardens, W., same crest and motto.

Pemberton, Cyril Warner Lee, 120, Sloane Street, S.W., same crest and motto.

Pemberton, Major Ernest St. Clair, same crest and motto.

Pemberton, Horace Claud, same crest and motto.

Pemberton, Seaton Blanshard, 36, Rosary Gardens, South Kensington, same crest and motto.

Pemberton, Willoughby Arthur, 11, Lower Belgrave Street, S.W., same crest and motto.

Pemberton, Durh., a griffin's head sa. 66. 1

Pemberton of Aislaby, Durh., a griffin's head couped gorged with a ducal coronet, all ppr. cf. 66. 11

Pemberton, John Stapylton Grey, J.P., Bainbridge, Holme, Belmont, Sunderland, Durh., same crest.

Pemberton, Richard Laurence, J.P., Hawthorn Tower, Seaham Harbour, same crest.

Pemberton, Durh., a griffin's head erased sa. *Sunt sua præmia laudi.* 66. 5

Pemberton, Durh., a griffin's head erased sa. *Labore et honore.* 66. 5

Pemberton, Richard Lawrence, of Bainbridge House and Barnes, Durh., a griffin's head couped and gorged with a ducal coronet, all ppr. *Labore et honore.* cf. 66. 1

Pemberton, Childe-, of Millichope Park, Shropsh.: (1) In front of a griffin's head couped sa., a crescent or (*for Pemberton*). (2) An eagle with wings expanded arg., entwined by a snake ppr. (*for Childe*). 77. 8. (3) Upon a mount vert, a cockatrice arg., beaked, combed, and wattled, and ducally gorged and lined or, charged with a crescent for difference (*for Baldwin*). *Per Deum meum transilio murum.* cf. 68. 7

Pemberton, Colonel Arthur Ralph, Travellers' Club, a boar's head erased sa. *Nec temere nec timide.*

Pemberton, Henry Williams, Trumpington, Cambs, same crest. *Audi alteram partem.*

Pemberton, Rev. Thomas Percy, of Trumpington Hall, Cambridge, a dragon's head erect sa., couped and langued gu., charged with a cross patée arg. *Nec temere, nec timide.* 230. 11

Pemberton, a wolf regardant holding in the mouth an arrow, point downwards.

Pemberton, Lancs, on a coney arg., an eagle ppr. 79. 6

Pemberton, Rev. Joseph Hardwick, the Round House, Havering-atte-Bower, Essex, upon the trunk of an oak-tree eradicated and sprouting towards the dexter ppr., a griffin passant or, guttée-de-poix. *Juncti valemus.*

Pemberton-Barnes, W. H., Havering-atte-Bower, Essex: (1) Upon a rock a leopard passant ppr., semée of estoiles, and charged with a cross crosslet for difference (*for Barnes*). (2) Upon the trunk of an oak-tree eradicated and sprouting towards the dexter ppr., a griffin passant or, guttée-de-poix. *Mutare vel timere sperno.*

Pembridge, a bull's head sa., between two wings or. 43. 10

Pembroke, Earl of, and Montgomery (Herbert), of Wilton House, Salisbury, a wyvern with wings elevated vert, holding in the mouth a sinister hand couped at the wrist gu. *Ung je serviray.* 70. 3

Pembroke of St. Albans, Herts, and Chertsey, Surrey, out of a ducal coronet or, a wolf's head gu.

Pembrooke, a heart gu., charged with a rose arg. cf. 181. 2

Penbar, on a mount vert, a moorcock ppr., combed and wattled gu.

Pen-Curzon-Howe, Earl Howe, *see* Howe.

Pendarves of London, a lion sejant collared and lined. 7. 4

Pendarves, Cornw., a demi-bear erm., muzzled. 34. 13

Pendarves, Wynne-, William Cole, of Pendarves, Cornw.: (1) A lion rampant regardant or cf 2 3 (2) A demi-bear erm, muzzled, lined and ringed or 34 13 (3) A saltier raguly or

Pender, Scotland, a demi lion or holding a sabre ppr 14 12

Pender, Bart, a demi lion rampant or charged on the shoulder with a cross crosslet sa., holding in the dexter paw a seax ppr., pommel and hilt of the first, and resting the sinister paw on a terrestrial globe ppr *Persevero* 14 13

Pender, Denison-, Sir John Denison K C M G, 6, Grosvenor Crescent S W (1) A demi lion or, charged on the shoulder with a cross crosslet sa, holding in the dexter paw a seax ppr, pommel and hilt of the first and resting the sinister on a terrestrial globe ppr (2) The crest of Denison *Persevero*

Pendleton of Norwich, Norf, on a chapeau gu, turned up erm, a demi-dragon with wings addorsed or, holding an escallop arg

Pendleton, Lancs, a lion's gamb sa, holding a battle-axe or cf 38 3

Pendleton, Alan O'Bryen George William Esquire, a lion's gamb erect and erased sa, charged with an escallop or and grasping a battle axe in bend sinister of the last *Audaces fortuna juvat* cf 38 3

Pendock, Northamp, on the top of a tower gu, a demi-pelican with wings addorsed or vulning herself ppr

Pendred, Northants, Broghillstown co Carlow, and Barraderry, co Wicklow, Ireland, a helmet with the visor raised *Nosce teipsum*

Pendret, a fox current ppr cf 32 8

Pendreth, Kent, an heraldic tiger sejant erm tufted and maned or, ducally crowned of the last

Peneystone, Bart (*extinct*), of Leigh, Sussex, a griffin passant sa armed arg 63 2

Penfold, a lion rampant double-queued or 1 14

Penfold, Oliver, Esquire M R C S, J P of Bendigo, Victoria, Australia, out of park pales alternately arg and sa, charged with three escallops in fesse or, a pine tree fructed ppr *Pende valde* 144 5

Penfold, Harold Chiswick, same crest *Pende valde*

Penfold, Hugh, J P, Rustington Worthing same crest

Penfold, Marchant Cape Town South Africa same crest and motto

Penfold, Robert, Roundwyck Petworth, Sussex, same crest

Penfold of Cissbury, Sussex, same crest 144 5

Pengelley, Cornw, a wyvern with wings addorsed vert, devouring a dexter arm ppr cf 70 3

Pengelly, Cornw, a lion's gamb holding a palm-branch ppr 36 7

Penhallow, of Penhallow Cornw a goat passant az, armed and ungu or cf 129 5

Penhelleke of Penhelleke, Cornw, a Saracen's head ppr 190 14

Penken, Worcs an heraldic antelope sejant sa, tufted, attired and maned arg

Penkevell or **Penkevill** of Penkevelle Cornw, on a mount vert, a lion couchant ppr cf 7 5

Penleaze of High Cliff Christchurch Hants, a wyvern with wings elevated ppr 70 1

Penley or **Penly,** a lion's head erased gu, ducally crowned or 18 8

Penman, a hart's head cabossed or 122 5

Penman of Gibraltar, issuing out of clouds a dexter arm holding in the hand a hammer over an anvil all ppr

Penmarch, an ostrich regardant murally crowned resting the dexter claw on an escallop ppr

Penn, Richard Poyer Lewis, Camrose R S O, Haverfordwest (1) A lion rampant sa (*for Bowen*) (2) An eagle displayed standing on a rock (*for Webb*)

Penn, a demi lion rampant arg, gorged with a collar sa, charged with three plates cf 10 9

Penn of Stoke Poges, Bucks, same crest *Dum clarum rectum teneam* cf 10 9

Penn, John, M P 22 Carlton House Terrace S W, issuant from clouds a dexter arm embowed holding a smith's hammer all ppr *Non sine labor*

Penn-Gaskell of Shanagarry, co Cork, Ireland (1) A sinister arm embowed in armour ppr, the hand supporting an escutcheon or, charged with an anchor erect and cabled sa (*for Gaskell*) (2) A demi lion arg, gorged with a collar sa, charged with three plates (*for Penn*) *Ses — Pensylvania* cf 10 9

Pennant, *see* Penrhyn, Baron

Pennant of Downing and Bychton, Flintsh, out of a ducal coronet arg an heraldic antelope's head of the last, maned, tufted armed, and crined or cf 127 10

Pennant, Philip Pennant J P, of Nantlys St Asaph Flintsh (1) On a ducal coronet an antelope's head erased (2) On a ducal coronet an eagle displayed

Pennant of Penrhyn Castle, Carnarvonsh Wales (1) Out of a ducal coronet arg an heraldic antelope's head of the last, tufted, attired and crined or (*for Pennant*) cf 127 10 (2) A dexter arm embowed ppr, ensigned with a crescent gu, holding in the hand a battle-axe ppr, the blade arg, charged with a rose gu (*for Dawkins*) cf 201 5

Pennant, a lion passant gardant gu 4 3

Penneck, Cornw an arm embowed vested gu, cuffed or, holding in the hand a wren ppr

Pennefather of New Park, Ireland a lion sejant arg, supporting an oval shield per fess or and gu, charged with a bend erm, and charged on the shoulder with a mullet *I abide my time*

Pennefather, Alfred Richard C B Little Waltham Hall, Chelmsford, a lion sejant arg, the dexter paw resting on an oval shield per fesse or and gu, a bend erm *I abide my time*

Pennefather, Captain Charles Edward De Fonblanque, same crest and motto

Pennefather, De Fonblanque, Calveley Hall, Tarporley, Chesh, same crest and motto

Pennefather, same crest and motto Second motto *Virtute fortes*

Pennel, a griffin sejant 62 10

Pennel or **Pennell,** an arm in armour couped at the shoulder embowed holding in the hand a scimitar, all ppr 196 10

Pennell, an ostrich's head couped

Penney, a demi lion rampant arg collared sa 10 9

Penney of Bedford and Coddicott Herts, a demi lion rampant gu, holding a comb arg

Penniecook or **Pennyeuick,** Scotland, a stag lodged under an oak-tree ppr *Ut resurgam* 116 3

Pennill, a demi heraldic antelope

Pennill, a demi-wolf rampant 31 2

Penniman, out of a mural coronet a lion's head ppr 19 12

Penning of Ipswich Suff a buck's head erased per fesse indented arg and gu, attired of the last 121 2

Pennington, *see* Muncaster, Baron

Pennington, a talbot passant holding in the mouth a pen

Pennington, a man's head and shoulders in armour affrontee

Pennington of Thorncombe, Devonsh a man's head couped below the shoulders in armour affrontee ppr, between two wings

Pennington, Cumb, a mountain cat passant gardant ppr *Vincit amor patriæ* cf 26 4

Pennington, Essex same crest cf 26 4

Penny, a porcupine or 126 5

Penny, Scotland, a demi-lion or holding a fleur-de lis gu 13 2

Penny of Peterborough, Northamp, on a ducal coronet arg a lynx or

Penny, Robert Penny Greenwood Esquire, of Higher Nutwell House, Devonsh, on a vallary coronet gu, a lynx statant or, holding in the mouth a fleur de lis az

Pennycoock and **Pennyeuick,** Scotland a demi-huntsman winding a horn ppr. *Free for a blast* 187 12

Pennycook of Newhall Edinburgh a stag lodged under an oak-tree ppr *Ut resurgam* 116 3

Pennyfather of London a lion sejant arg supporting an oval shield per fess or and gu charged with a bend erm, and charged on the shoulder with a mullet

Pennyman, James Worsley, of Ormsby, Yorks, on a mural coronet gu, a lion's head erased or pierced through the neck by a broken spear in bend all or, the head to the sinister arg *Fortiter et fideliter*

Pennyston of Leigh Sussex and Bucks, a griffin passant sa armed or 63 2

Penrey, two hands conjoined couped at the wrists, holding a sword in pale ppr 224 9

Penrhyn, Baron (Douglas - Pennant) Penrhyn Castle Bangor North Wales (1) Out of a ducal coronet an heraldic antelope's head arg maned and tufted or charged on neck with a cross crosslet for distinction (*for Pennant*) (2) A sanglier sticking between the cleft of an oak-tree fructed with a lock holding the clefts together, all ppr (*for Douglas*) *Æquo animo* 40 4

Penrice of Great Yarmouth, Wilton House and Plumstead Hall, Norf., and of Kilvarnough House, Glamorgansh., a wing elevated, surmounting another arg., the former charged with two mullets of six points in pale gu. *Tuto et celeriter.*

Penrice, Rev. Charles Berners, Plumstead Parva Rectory, Norwich, two wings elevated, each charged with a mullet gu. *Tuto et celeriter.*

Penrith, a fox current ppr. *cf.* 32. 8

Penrose, Cornw., a fish gu. 139. 12

Penrose of Penrose in Sithney and Tregethow in Manaccan, Cornw., a trout naiant or. 139. 12

Penrose, Ireland and Berks, a lion's head erased or, collared gu. 18. 6

Penrose of Bachelor's Quay, Cork, a lion's head erased or, gorged with a chaplet of red roses, and crowned with a civic wreath, both ppr. *Rosa sine spina.*

Penruddock or Penruddocke, a ram's head erased sa., armed or. 130. 6

Penruddock, Cornw., Wilts, and Cumb., a demi-dragon rampant sans wings vert, between two eagle's wings or.

Penruddocke, Charles, Compton Park, Wilts, a lizard's head, armed az., langued gu., between two eagle's wings or. *Gloria soli Deo.*

Pentagrass, an antelope's head erased arg., attired gu. 126. 2

Penteney of Castletown, Jarvagh, co. Meath, and of the Cabragh, co. Louth, Ireland, upon a mount vert, an oak-tree ppr. *Malo mori quam fœdari.* 143. 14

Pentin, Rev. Herbert, M.A., Vicar of Milton Abbey, Dorset, a lion couchant guardant, double-queued az. bezantée. *Fidelis in omnibus.* 301. 8

Pentland, Ireland, a lion's head or, collared az. *cf.* 18. 6

Pentland of that Ilk, Edinburgh, a lion's head erased gu., gorged with a collar arg., charged with three crescents of the first. *Virtute et opera.* *cf.* 18. 6

Penton, a lion's gamb erased. 36. 4

Penton, Frederick Thomas, Chalfont Park, Slough, and Pentonville, a lion couchant gardant double-queued az., bezantée.

Penwarne of Penwarn and Mullyton, Cornw., a demi-lion rampant supporting with both paws the rudder of a ship. *cf.* 11. 11

Penwyn, Cornw., a stag's head couped per fess indented arg. and gu. 121. 5

Penyfather of Barton-under-Needwood, Staffs, and London, a lion sejant arg., sustaining an oval shield per fesse or and gu., charged with a bend erm.

Penyng of Kettleborough and Ipswich, Suff., a buck's head erased per fesse indented arg. and gu., attired of the last. 121. 2

Penyston, Oxon., on a ducal coronet or, an eagle displayed sa. *cf.* 75. 2

Penyston, Norf., two lion's gambs erased arg., supporting a cone gu., standing upon its apex.

Penyston, Antony Francis, of Cornwell, Oxon., a gryphon statant sa., charged for distinction with a cross crosslet arg. *Virtus invicta vigit.* *cf.* 63. 8

Penyston, John Francis, Cornwell Manor, Chipping Norton, same crest and motto.

Penzance, Baron (Wilde), of Penzance, Cornw, on a mount vert, a hart lodged holding in its mouth a rose ppr. *Veritas victrix.*

Peor, Ireland, a mermaid ppr., holding in her dexter hand a musket or, and in her sinister a fleur-de-lis az.

Pepe, Holland, a falcon with wings expanded ppr. 87. 1

Peper of Canterbury, Kent, a cubit arm erect holding in the hand ppr. two snakes, the heads contrariwise, the tails entwined and knotted round the arm az. 220. 3

Peperell, Bart. (*extinct*), of Massachusetts Bay, New England, out of a mural coronet or, an arm in armour embowed between two laurel-branches ppr., holding in the hand a staff, thereon a flag arg. *Peperi.—Fortiter et fideliter.*

Peperwell, on a mount five palm-trees.

Peple, Devonsh., an eagle's head couped arg. 83. 1

Peploe, *see* Webb-Peploe.

Peploe, out of a ducal coronet a reindeer's head, all or. 122. 3

Peploe, Daniel Henry Theophilus, of Garnstone Castle, Heref., and Lancs: (1) A ducal coronet or, thereon a reindeer's head gu., attired of the first, charged on the neck with a human eye shedding tears ppr. (*for Peploe*). (2) An eagle displayed sa., semée de fleurs-de-lis or, in the mouth a trefoil vert (*for Webb*).

Peploe, Fitzgerald Cornewall, J.P., same crests.

Peppard of Cappagh House, co. Limerick, in front of three ostrich-feathers arg. and az., a greyhound current ppr. *Virtute et valore.* 58. 12

Pepper, Ireland, a demi-lion rampant gardant or. 10. 8

Pepper of Thurmarston, Leics., and Yorks, a demi-lion rampant or. 10. 2

Pepper, Charles, of Ballygarth, Drogheda, co. Meath, Ireland, a demi-lion rampant or. *Semper erectus.* 10. 2

Pepper of Thorlesby, Lincs, a stag trippant arg. 117. 8

Pepper, a greyhound's head arg., between two roses gu., stalked and leaved ppr. 61. 11

Peppercorne, James, Esquire, upon a mount vert, a horse's head erased sa., surmounted by two branches of palm in saltire or, tied with a ribbon of the last.

Pepperell, a parrot between two rose-slips.

Pepperell of London, out of a mural coronet arg., with three laurel-leaves ppr., in the embrasures an arm in armour embowed holding a banner arg. *Peperi.*

Peppin, a pegasus courant with wings endorsed arg., charged on the shoulder with a cross avellane vert. *cf.* 47. 1

Pepwall and **Pepwell,** Glouc., a hawk close between two carnations, all ppr.

Pepys, *see* Cottenham, Earl of.

Pepys, Bart., of London, a camel's head erased or, bridled, lined, ringed, and gorged with a ducal coronet sa. *Mens cujusque est quisque.* 132. 9

Pepys, a camel's head erased or, bridled, lined, ringed, and gorged with a ducal coronet sa. 132. 9

Perbo, Middx., a tiger's head arg., maned and langued or, collared vert, thereon three fleurs-de-lis of the last.

Percehay of Ryton, Yorks, a bull's head az., armed per fess of the same and or. *cf.* 44. 3

Perceval, Viscount, *see* Egmont, Earl of.

Perceval, Baron Arden, *see* Arden.

Perceval, Sir Westby Brook, K.C.M.G., 5, Victoria Street, S.W., a horse passant arg., the fore-leg attached to the hind-leg on the near side by a fetter-lock gu. *Per se valens.*

Perceval, a thistle slipped and leaved ppr. *Sub cruce candore.* *cf.* 150. 2

Perceval of Temple House, Sligo, a thistle erect leaved ppr. *Yvery.—Sub cruce candida.* *cf.* 150. 2

Perceval, a squirrel devouring a nut, all ppr. 135. 7

Perceval-Maxwell of Kilmore Hill, co. Waterford, a stag's head and neck erased ppr. *Je suis prêt.*

Perceval-Maxwell, Robert, J.P., Finnebrogue, Downpatrick, a stag's head erased ppr. *Je suis prêt.* 121. 2

Perchard of Jersey and Guernsey, on a mount vert, a pheasant ppr. *En faizant bien.* 90. 8

Percival, a thistle slipped and leaved ppr. *cf.* 150. 2

Percival, Somers., same crest. *Sub cruce candida.* *cf.* 150. 2

Percival of Moorlands House, Kirkby Stephen, Westml., a bull's head couped arg., charged with a cross patée gu., the neck encircled by an annulet or. *Sub cruce vinces.*

Percivall, a nag's head arg. *cf.* 50. 13

Percivall, a demi-lion gu. 10. 3

Percivall, Hants, a demi-lion rampant or. 10. 2

Percy, *see* Northumberland, Duke of.

Percy, Earl of Beverley, *see* Beverley.

Percy, Baron Prudhoe, *see* Prudhoe.

Percy, Ireland, on a chapeau gu., turned up erm., a lion passant with tail extended az., holding in the dexter forepaw a trefoil slipped or. *Espérance en Dieu.*

Percy of Shaftesbury, Bushton, and Manston, Dorset, a demi-lion rampant az., collared or, holding in the dexter paw a spear of the same.

Percy, Heber-, Algernon Charles, Hodnet Hall, Market Drayton: (1) On a chapeau gu., turned up erm., a lion statant, the tail extended (*for Percy*). 289. 8. (2) Out of a ducal coronet or, a lady's head and shoulders ppr. in profile crined or (*for Heber*). *Prêt d'accomplir.—Espérance en Dieu.* 289. 7

Perham, W. E., of Flax-Bourton Court, Somers., two cubit arms holding in the hands a leopard's face. *Periam ni vinco.*

Periam, John, Esquire, of Bampton, Devonsh., two arms gu., issuing out of a crown or, holding in the hands ppr. a leopard's head of the second. *En Dieu est.*

Perigal of London and Devonsh., a helmet affrontée ppr., with five grills or, gorged with a collar and medal or, bordered of the same, lined gu. *Peri —Gal.*

Perin, out of a ducal coronet or, a peacock's head ppr. *cf.* 103. 2

Perins, Shropsh, a fir-apple erect or, stalked and leaved vert cf 152 6
Perkin, a stag lodged ppr 115 7
Perkin, Worcs, an heraldic antelope sejant sa., tufted attired, and maned arg *A spe in spem*
Perkins, Ireland a demi-eagle displayed sa 81 6
Perkins, same crest 81 6
Perkins, out of a five-leaved coronet or, a unicorn's head arg. maned and armed of the first 48 12
Perkins, Duncombe Steele, of Orton Hall, Leics, and Sutton Coldfield, Warw, out of a ducal coronet a unicorn's head *Toujours loyale* 48 12
Perkins, Alfred Thrale, Eastcourt, Wells Somers, out of a ducal coronet a unicorn's head arg, maned ppr *Actis ævum imple*
Perkins of Marston, Warw, out of a ducal coronet or, a unicorn's head erm, armed and maned of the first 48 12
Perkins, Augustus Frederick, Oakdene, Holmwood, Dorking, out of park pales a unicorn's head arg, armed and maned sa., holding in the mouth a thistle leaved and slipped ppr
Perkins, Hugh, 17, Fulwood Park, Liverpool, S, out of a ducal coronet or a unicorn's head ppr, armed and maned of the first *Mos legem regit*
Perkins of Nuneaton, Warw a lion passant sa, holding a fleur de-lis gu *Simplex vigilum veri* cf 6 2
Perkins of Upton Court, Berks, and Northamp, a pine apple ppr, stalked and leaved vert 152 8
Perkins, James, F R G S, 69, Kennington Park Road, S E, in front of a ship's rudder fesseways a dexter arm in armour ppr, charged with two anchors the one above and the other below the elbow or, the hand holding a battle-axe, also or *In Deo confido*
Perkinson, a unicorn's head erased arg 49 5
Perkinson, Durh, a falcon ppr 85 2
Perks, a lion's head erased or 17 8
Perks, Samuel, J P, Dôlanog, Rhyl, a stag's head erased
Perne, Cambs, out of a ducal coronet arg, a pelican's head or, vulned gu cf 98 2
Perott, a bull's head couped sa armed or gorged with two bars of the last
Perott, a stag's head ppr 121 5
Perowne, Rt Rev (Bishop) John James Stewart same crest
Perowne of 66, Princes Gate, S W., a harp *Nil mortale sonans*
Perpont, *see* Pierpont
Perpound, a lion's gamb erased sa holding a cinquefoil gu
Perreau of London, out of a ducal coronet or, a leopard's head gardant couped at the neck arg
Perrier, Anthony, Esquire, J P, of Lota, co Cork, Ireland, a lion's head ppr, issuant from a French ducal coronet or *Consilio et vi*
Perrier, William Lumley Ballinure House, Blackrock, co Cork same crest and motto
Perriman, a wolf passant sa 28 10
Perrin, a cock crowing ppr 91 2
Perring, a dexter hand holding a sword ppr 212 13
Perring, Bart., Devonsh, a fir-cone leaved ppr cf 152 6
Perring, Rev Sir Philip Bart, M A, Llandovery, Exmouth, Devonsh, on a mount a fir cone vert. *Impavidum ferient ruinæ*
Perrings, three organ-pipes, two in saltier surmounted by one in pale az, banded vert
Perrings, Devonsh, a fir-apple erect, leaved ppr
Perrins, Charles William Dyson, Esquire, of Davenham, Malvern, Worcs, and of Ardross, Ross sh, a demi-talbot arg, gorged with a collar nebulee and charged on the shoulder with two annulets interlaced fesse wise gu holding between the paws a pomegranate seeded and slipped ppr *Perenne sub sole nihil* 55 7
Perris of London a demi tiger regardant per chevron gu and arg holding in the dexter paw an arrow of the last
Perrot, a lion's head erased sa 17 8
Perrot or **Perrott**, a parrot vert, holding in the dexter claw a pear or 101 13
Perrot, Oxon, a parrot vert 101 4
Perrott, Ireland (1) On an ancient royal chapeau a lion of Britain imperially crowned (2) A parrot vert, holding in the dexter claw a pear or, with two leaves of the first *Amo, ut invenio* cf 101 13
Perrott, Sir Herbert Charles Bart, of Richmond Surrey a parrot vert, holding in the dexter claw a pear or, the leaves ppr *Amo ut invenio.* 101 13
Perry, a castle arg, masoned sa 155 8
Perry of London, a hind's head erased ppr gorged with a ducal coronet or, holding in the mouth a pear-tree branch vert, fructed of the second
Perry, Walter Copland, 5, Manchester Square, W in front of a hind's head couped or, holding in the mouth a sprig of oak with two acorns vert three calthrops fesseways gu *Hold fast*
Perry of Walter, Devonsh, a hind's head erased or, holding in the mouth a sprig of pear tree vert fructed of the first cf 124 3
Perry, co Clare Ireland, a hind's head couped arg, holding in the mouth a pear branch fructed ppr
Perry of Wootton under-Edge, Glouc, a stag's head ppr, pierced through the neck by an arrow or, feathered arg headed sa cf 121 5
Perry of Moor Hall, Essex (1) A demi-lion ppr, semee of spear-heads sa, holding in the dexter paw an escutcheon of the last charged with a saltier, double parted and fretty arg (2) A lion's head erased or semee of saltiers and ducally crowned gu, holding in the mouth a pear slipped ppr
Perry, a lion's head erased ppr, ducally crowned or 18 8
Perry of Bitham House Warw, a griffin sejant with wings elevated or, the wings fretty vert and resting the dexter claw upon a mascle of the first *Recti agens confido*
Perry, an arm in armour erect ppr, issuing from the top of a tower gu, holding in the hand a dagger sa
Perry, Worcs, a cubit arm in armour ppr, holding in the gauntlet a sword arg, hilt and pommel or, strings and tassels flowing from the pommel gu
Perryman, a wolf passant sa 28 10
Perryman of London, issuing out of clouds ppr, two arms vested vert, cuffed arg, holding in the hands a leopard's head or
Perryman, Charles Wilbraham, of Bifrons Farnborough, Southampton, a wolf's head erm, erased gu, charged with a fesse indented az, surmounted by two pear-branches leaved, fructed, and slipped in saltire ppr *Per ardua stabilis* 301. 14
Perryn, Middx, Glouc, and Shropsh, a pine apple or, stalked and leaved vert 152 8
Pershall and **Peshall** of Doynton, Lincs, and Horsley, Staffs a wolf's head sa, holding in the mouth a marigold ppr
Pershouse of Reynold's Hall and Sedgley Staffs, a mastiff sejant sa., collared or, resting the dexter paw on a caltrap arg
Pershouse, Henry Clifden, Esquire, of Winscombe, Somers, a greyhound sejant, collared, and resting the dexter paw on a mullet of five points. *Nil desperandum*
Person, Felix, Esquire, of Westminster a mount vert, thereon a saltire engrailed gu, charged in the centre with a sun in splendour or
Persse, Captain W A, Roxburgh Roughlea co Galway on a chapeau ppr, a lion statant with tail extended az *Esperance en Dieu*
Pert, out of an earl's coronet or, a Moor's head affrontee ppr cf 182 2
Pert of Fryarne, Middx, a ram's head erased arg armed or, charged on the neck with three bars gemelle gu cf 130 6
Pert of Arnold Essex a stork ppr, beaked or, statant among bulrushes or, leaved vert the heads of the rushes sa 104 3
Perth and Melfort, Earl of, *see* Drummond
Perton, Shropsh, on a mount vert, a pear-tree fructed ppr *Avi numerantur avorum* cf 144 10
Perwiche, a crescent 163 2
Pery, *see* Limerick Earl of
Pery, a spear-head ppr cf 174 12
Pery, Ireland a unicorn's head sa 49 7
Pery-Knox-Gore, Edmond Henry Colayne Esquire the Bury House, Cottingham Rockingham (1) A wolf rampant or (*for Gore*). 28 2 (2) A falcon close perched on a rest ppr (*for Knox*) 85 13 (3) A hind's head erased ppr (*for Pery*) *In hoc signo vinces* 124 3
Peryan, Herts a griffin's head erased gu, charged with three crescents in pale arg cf 66 2
Peryan, Herts, a lion rampant arg, guttee-de sang cf 1 13
Peryent, Herts (1) Same crest as above cf 1 13 (2) A griffin's head erased gu, charged with three crescents in pale arg cf 66 2
Peryns, Shropsh, *see* Perins

Pescod of Newton Valence, Hants, a griffin sejant arg., beaked and membered or, the dexter claw raised. cf. 62. 10

Peshall, Bart. (*extinct*), Staffs, a boar's head couped gu., crined and tusked or. 43. 1

Peshall, Shropsh., a wolf's head gu. 30. 5

Peshall, Shropsh., a boar's head couped at the neck, tusked and crined or. *Suum cuique.* 43. 1

Pestell, a demi-stag sa., attired ppr. 119. 2

Peter or **Petre,** Essex and Devonsh., two lions' heads erased conjoined and addorsed, the dexter or, the sinister az., collared, ringed, and counterchanged. 18. 2

Peter, Frank, Anama Ashburton, Canterbury, New Zealand, same crest. *Sans Dieu rien.*

Peter, Cornw., same crest and motto. 18. 2

Peter, Rev. Robert Godolphin, Chyverton, Truro, Cornw., same crest and motto.

Peter of Bowhay, Devonsh., two lions' heads erased and endorsed, the dexter or, the sinister az., gorged with a plain collar counterchanged. *Sans Dieu rien.—Sub libertate quietem.* 18. 2

Peter of Clan Alpine House, Scotland, out of a mural coronet arg., masoned sa., a lion's head gu., crowned with an antique crown ppr. *Eadhan dean agus na caomhain.*

Peter of Canterland, Scotland: (1) A dexter arm in bend holding in the hand a dagger, both ppr. (2) Out of a mural coronet arg., masoned sa., a demi-lion gu., crowned with an antique crown ppr. *Pour mon Dieu.—Usque fac et non parcas.—Turris fortis mihi Deus.*

Peter of Whitesleed, Scotland: (1) Out of an antique crown a dexter hand holding a dagger in pale, all ppr. (2) a boar's head couped arg. *Pour mon Dieu.—E'en do, and spare not.* 43. 1

Peter of Cookston, Scotland, between two laurel-branches ppr., a boar's head couped. *Usque facet non parcas.*

Peter of Corsbasket, Forfarsh., out of a mural coronet arg., masoned sa., a dexter arm in armour grasping a scimitar ppr. *Pour mon Dieu.*

Peter, Scotland, a hand holding a dagger point upwards ppr. *Pour mon Dieu.* 212. 9

Peter-Hoblyn, Henry Godolphin, Colquite, Washaway, R.S.O., Cornw.: (1) Two lions' heads erased conjoined and addorsed, the dexter or, the sinister az., collared, ringed, and counterchanged. (2) A tower. *Sans Dieu rien.*

Peterborough, a garb ppr. 153. 2

Peterkin, Scotland, a unicorn's head or. 49. 7

Peterkin or **Peterkyn,** a dove ppr. 92. 2

Peterkin, Scotland, a unicorn's head. *Confido in Domino.* 49. 7

Peters, *see* Parsons-Peters.

Peters of London, a buckle arg. 178. 5

Peters, Scotland, a boar's head couped ppr. 43. 1

Peters, Scotland, a boar's head erased arg., in front of a laurel-branch in pale ppr. *Versus.* cf. 42. 2

Peters, Scotland, between two laurel-branches vert, a boar's head erased arg. *Sit sine labe fines.*

Peters, Scotland, between two laurel-branches ppr., a boar's head couped and erect. *Confido.*

Peters, Scotland, a boar's head couped between two laurel-branches ppr. *Deo adjuvante, non timendum.*

Peters, Ireland, an eagle's head erased sa., holding in the beak a key with the wards downwards ppr. 229. 6

Peters, Glouc., an eagle's head erased holding in the beak a key. *Fais ce que dois advienne que pourra.* 229. 6

Peters of London, a swan regardant ppr., gorged with a ducal coronet sa., resting the dexter foot on a mascle or.

Peters of Park Street, Grosvenor Square, a swan regardant with wings endorsed arg., ducally gorged sa., resting the dexter foot on a mascle or. *Invidia major.*

Peters of Kilburn and Westbourne Terrace, Bayswater: (1) A swan regardant with wings endorsed arg., ducally gorged sa., resting the dexter foot on a mascle or (*for Peters*). (2) A griffin's head couped ppr., holding by the string a bugle-horn az. (*for Winpenny*).

Peters, a lion's head erased and collared. 18. 6

Peters of Newcastle-on-Tyne, Northumb., a lion's head erased erm., charged with a bend engrailed between two escallops az. *Absque Deo nihil.*

Peters, Major-General Harry Brooke, Harefield, Devonsh., two lions' heads erased and endorsed, the dexter or, the sinister az., each gorged with a plain collar counterchanged.

Peters, Scotland, out of a heart a hand holding a sword in pale, all ppr. *Verus ad finem.*

Peters, Scotland, out of a cloud a dexter hand holding a dagger in pale, all ppr. *Dieu pour nous.* cf. 212. 4

Peters, Scotland, issuing out of a heart a hand grasping a couteau-sword in pale, all ppr. *Rien sans Dieu.* And another, *Verus ad finem.* cf. 213. 4

Peters of London, out of a heart a hand holding a couteau-sword, all ppr. *Rien sans Dieu.* 213. 4

Peters of Black Friars, Canterbury, Kent, an arm holding in the hand a rose-sprig ppr. 218. 10

Petersham, Viscount, *see* Harrington, Earl of.

Peterson, Scotland, a pelican ppr. *Nihil sine Deo.* 98. 1

Peterson, a dexter hand brandishing a sabre ppr. 212. 13

Peterson, Scotland, a pelican or. 98. 1

Peterswald, William John, Esquire, of St. Heliers, Adelaide, South Australia, Chief Commissioner of Police for the Colony of South Australia, out of a ducal coronet two elephants' trunks erect. cf. 123. 13

Peterswald, William Ernest, Adelaide, South Australia, same crest.

Pether, a rose gu., barbed vert, seeded or. 149. 2

Petit or **Pettyt,** of Dente de Lion, Kent, a lion's gamb erased and erect or, holding a pellet. 39. 13

Petit of Hexstall, Staffs, a demi-wolf salient ppr. 31. 2

Petit, a hand holding a hunting-horn or. 217. 4

Petit, Sir Jejeebhoy Framjee, Bart., and Knight, of Petit Hall, Island of Bombay, son of Manockjee Musserwanjee Cowasjee Petit, was Sheriff of Bombay, 1887, is a cotton-mill owner, and is a Member of the Parsi Punchayet of Bombay, and was a Member of the Supreme Legislative Council of India from 1888 to 1889. *Crest:* a ship under sail at sea, and in front thereof an anchor fessewise, all ppr. *Consequitor quodcunque petit.* 160. 5

Petley, a horse's head or. cf. 50. 13

Petley, Kent, a cubit arm in armour erect ppr., garnished or, the hand holding a scimitar by the blade of the first, hilted or. *Toujours prêt.*

Petley, Charles Ralph Carter, Riverhead, Kent, same crest.

Peto, an ounce sejant ppr., collared gu., resting the dexter paw on an escutcheon az.

Peto, Sir Henry, Bart., M.A. (Camb.), B.A. (Lond.), of the Inner Temple, London, on a rock ppr., a sinister wing or, charged with three annulets in chevron gu. *Ad finem fidelis.* 274. 8

Petoe and **Peyto** of Chesterton, Warw., a sinister wing or. 109. 7

Petre, Baron (Petre), of Writtle, Essex, two lions' heads erased and addorsed, the dexter or, collared az., the sinister counterchanged. *Sans Dieu rien.* 18. 2

Petre, Edward Henry, 24, Cadogan Gardens, S.W., same crest and motto.

Petre, Sir George Glynn, K.C.M.G., of Dunkenhalgh, Clayton-le-Moors, Lancs, same crest and motto.

Petre, Lawrence Joseph, 4, Clanricarde Gardens, S.W., same crest and motto.

Petre, two lions' heads erased and addorsed, the dexter or, the sinister az., collared counterchanged. 18. 2

Petrie, a rope knotted and tasselled between two wings. 113. 2

Petrie of Portlethen, Kincardinesh., Scotland, an eagle soaring aloft ppr., looking to the sun in glory or. *Fide, sed vide.*

Petrie, Scotland, a demi-eagle displayed looking towards the sun, all ppr. *Fide, sed vide.* cf. 81. 6

Petrie, a demi-eagle displayed ppr. *Fide, sed vide.* 81. 6

Petrie, a dove holding in its beak an olive-branch ppr. 92. 5

Petrie, Scotland, an anchor erect az. *Spem fortuna alit.* 161. 1

Petrie, Scotland, a cross crosslet fitched sa. *Fides.* 166. 2

Pett of Chatham, Kent, out of a ducal coronet or, a demi-pelican with wings expanded arg.

Pett of London, and Walworth, Surrey, a demi-greyhound sa., collared and charged on the body with two bendlets or, between as many fern-branches vert. cf. 60. 10

Pettegrew, Scotland, an increscent gu. *Sine sole nihil.* 163. 3

Pettet or **Pettit** of Shalmisford, Kent, a leopard passant, ppr. cf. 24. 2

Pettit or **Petyt,** a bishop's mitre gu cf 180 5

Pettit, Ireland, a raven ppr 107 14

Pettit, Edward, Esquire, of Leighton Buzzard Beds, a demi-eagle displayed with two heads erm, gorged with a vallery coronet or and holding in each beak a cross botonnee fitchee sa

Pettiward, Robert John of Finborough Hall Suff, a cross raguly sa, charged with five estoiles arg

Pettus of Norwich Norf, a hammer erect arg the handle or

Pettus, Norf, out of a ducal coronet or, a demi-lion arg, holding a spear gu, headed of the first

Pettus, Bart (*extinct*), of Rackheath, Norf, out of a ducal coronet or, a demi lion erm, vulned, holding a piece of a broken tilting-spear in pale ppr

Petty-Fitzmaurice, Marquess of Lansdowne, *see* Lansdowne

Petty, Earls of Shelburne, Ireland, a bee hive beset with bees diversely volant ppr *Virtute non verbis* 137 7

Petty, same crest *Ut apes geometricam* 137 7

Petty, Ireland, a bee-hive or fretty az, with bees volant ppr *Virtute non verbis* 137 7

Pettyt of London, a crane ppr holding in the dexter claw a pebble-stone 105 6

Pettyt, Kent, a lion's gamb erased and erect or, grasping a pellet 39 13

Pettyward, out of a ducal coronet or a demi-pelican with wings expanded arg

Petyt of London and Yorks a crane erm holding in the dexter claw a pebble sa *Qui s'estime Petyt deviendra grand* 105 6

Petytt of Shep Meadow, Suff, a demi-swan displayed arg beaked gu, between two battle axes in pale vert

Peusay, a pelican's head vulning its neck ppr cf 98 1

Pevelesdon, a stag's head erased ppr 121 2

Pevensey, Lincs a demi-Moor ppr, holding in the dexter hand a broken tilting-spear or

Pevensey, six laurel-leaves vert issuing from a castle arg

Pevensley, Viscount, *see* Sheffield, Earl of

Peverell, a plume of four ostrich-feathers alternately gu and az., enfiled with a ducal coronet or

Peverell, a hand holding a dagger point downwards *Hinc mihi salus*

Peverell, Cornw, on a mount vert a garb erect or 153 12

Pew, a cock holding in its beak a rose ppr cf 91 2

Pexall, a Moor's head couped ppr cf 192 13

Peyrse of Northwold, Norf, a pelican with wings addorsed arg, vulning herself ppr

Peyton, a griffin sejant or 62 10

Peyton, Tobias, J P, the Hermitage, Newtownforbes co Longford same crest *Patior, potior*

Peyton, Bart, of Islcham, Cambs, and Kent, same crest *Patior, potior* 62 10

Peyton of Driney, Leitrim, same crest and motto.

Peyton, General Francis, C B, United Service Club, same crest

Peyton, Sir Algernon Francis, Bart, of Doddington, Cambs, same crest and motto 62 10

Phaire of Killoughrum, Wexford, a dove holding in its beak an olive branch ppr *Virtute tutus* 92 5

Phayre, Colonel Sir Arthur Purves, Knight Commander of the Most Exalted Order of the Star of India, and a Companion of the Most Honourable Order of the Bath, a dove ppr, gorged with an Eastern crown or, and holding in the beak an olive branch vert *Virtute tutus* cf 92 10

Phelan, Ireland, a stag's head or 121 5

Phelps, William Robert, of Montacute, Somers, of Barrington and Corfe Mullen, Dorset and Briggins Park, Herts, a square beacon or chest on two wheels or filled with fire ppr *Pro aris et focis*

Phelips, Charles James Hunsdon Estate Ware, and Netteswell Estate Herts same crest and motto

Phelps, a talbot's head erased arg, collared or 56 1

Phelps of Salisbury, Wilts, a demi lion erased sa, charged on the shoulder with a chevron arg, holding in the dexter paw a tilting spear ppr, and resting the sinister on a cross patee sa *Toujours pret*

Phelps of London a wolf's head erased az gorged with a collar or, charged with a martlet sa cf 30 11

Phelps, William, Chestal, Dursley, Glouc, same crest. *Frangas non flectas*

Phene, a lion rampant or, gorged with a label of three points gu cf 1 13

Phesant of Tottenham, Middx, a pheasant close or cf 90 8

Phesant, a pheasant ppr, holding in the beak a rose gu, stalked and leaved vert cf 90 8

Phesant of London a pheasant close or, holding in the beak a gilliflower ppr cf 90 8

Phetoplace, Oxon and Berks, a griffin's head erased vert 66 2

Philimore, on a tower a bird close

Philip of Ormistone, Haddingtonsh, Scotland a talbot ppr *Vivis sperandum* cf 54 2

Philip, Suff and London, out of a ducal coronet az, three ostrich feathers arg cf 114 8

Philipoe, out of a mural coronet a demi-lion rampant arg *Quod tibi vis fieri facias* cf 16 11

Philipps, Rev Sir James Erasmus, Bart M A a lion rampant sa ducally gorged and chained or *Ducit amor patriæ* cf 1 3

Philipps, Sir Charles Edward Gregg, Bart, of Picton Castle, Pembrokesh. (1) A lion rampant sa, ducally gorged and chained, the chain reflexed over the back or (*for Philipps*) 312 16 (2) In front of a bulrush erect a kingfisher ppr resting the dexter claw on a fleur-de lis or Motto over *Virtute et fide* —*Ducit amor patriæ* 286 7

Phillipps, Pembrokesh a lion rampant sa, collared and chained or. *Ducit amor patriæ* 1 3

Philipps, Lloyd-, Rhodr Vaughan, Dale Castle, Milford Haven a lion rampant sa, ducally gorged gu, and chained or *Ducit amor patriæ* cf 1 3

Philipps, Charles David, the Gaer Newport, Monm, on a garb a cock ppr *Ducit amor patriæ*

Philipps, Colonel, of Mabws Aberystwith (1) A lion rampant collared and lined or cf 1 3 (2) A tiger rampant holding in the paw a spear in pale head downwards, embrued *Ar dduw y gyd* —*Ducit amor patriæ*

Philips, Ireland, a lion rampant sa, ducally gorged and chained or *Ducit amor patriæ* cf 1 3

Philipps, Grismond, Cwmgwilly, Bronwydd Arms, R S O Carmarthensh, same crest

Philips, Pembrokesh and Shropsh a lion rampant sa, collared and chained or *Ducit amor patri* 1 3

Philips, Laugharne-, Bart Pembrokesh, a lion rampant sa ducally gorged and chained or cf 1 3

Philips, John Capel of Heath House, Staffs, Lancs, and Warw a demi lion rampant erminois, collared sa ducally crowned or holding between the paws a fleur de lis az within a mascle of the third *Simplex munditiis*

Philips, John William, Heybridge Tean Stoke-on Trent, same crest and motto

Philips, William Morton Heybridge Tean, Stoke on-Trent, same crest and motto

Philips, late Sir George Richard, Bart (*extinct*) of Weston Warw a demi-lion erminois collared sa, ducally crowned or, and holding between the paws a fleur de lis az within a mascle of the third *Nil nisi honestum*

Philips of Aberglasney, Carmarthensh (1) A lion rampant sa, holding between the fore-paws an escutcheon or thereon three snakes interlaced ppr the dexter hind-paw resting on a fleur de lis, also or (*for Philips*) (2) An eagle displayed erm, the body entwined by two snakes respecting each other ppr and holding in each claw a rose gu slipped and leaved vert (*for Walters*) *Fy nuw a chynmry*

Philips, Somers, a lion sejant sa, collared and lined or 7 4

Philips, Worcs on a chapeau az, turned up erm, a demi lion rampant gardant arg

Philips of Tamworth, Warw, a leopard sejant or cf 24 13

Philips of Montrose a bear's head erased sa *Bear and forbear* 35 2

Philips, a horse passant erm, a wreath of laurel encircling its neck vert cf 52 6

Philips of Tenterden, Kent, on a mount vert a stag sejant erm, attired or 116 8

Philips or **Phillips** of London, a rose-branch vert bearing three roses gu between two wings arg

Philips, Somers a beacon on two wheels or filled with fire ppr

Philips, a dexter hand gauntleted holding a sword in pale az, hilt and pommel or 211 4

Philipse of Philipsburg, America, out of a coronet a demi lion rampant *Quod tibi vis fieri facias* 16 3

Philipson of Swadderden Hall, Westml., out of a mural coronet or, a plume of seven feathers alternately arg. and gu.

Phillimore, an eagle displayed gu. 75. 2

Phillimore, Oxon., on a tower a falcon with wings elevated ppr. *Fortem post animum.* 156. 11

Phillimore, Sir Walter George Frank, Bart., K.C., D.C.L., of the Coppice, Oxon., in front of a tower arg., thereon a falcon volant ppr., holding in the beak a lure or, three cinquefoils fessewise of the last. *Fortem posce animum.* 283. 4

Phillimore, Richard Fortescue, Shedfield House, Botley, Hants, same crest and motto.

Phillip and **Philps,** Scotland, a bear's head erased sa. *Bear and forbear.* 35. 2

Phillip, out of a flower arg., stalked and leaved vert, a greyhound's head of the first, collared or. 61. 14

Phillip, a lion's gamb sa., holding three branches of flowers az., leaved vert. 37. 12

Phillip, out of a ducal coronet or, a pyramid arg.

Phillipps, late Sir Thomas, F.R.S., F.S.A., Bart. (*extinct*), of Middle Hill, Worcs., on a mount vert, a lion rampant sa., semée-de-lis or, charged with a sinister bendlet wavy erm., and holding in the dexter fore-paw a sword erect ppr. *Deus patria rex.*

Phillipps of Eaton Bishop, Heref., a demi-lion sa., collared, chained, and holding between the paws a leopard's face jessant-de-lis or.

Phillipps, a demi-lion rampant sa., ducally gorged and chained or. *Toujours prest.*

Phillipps of Landue, Cornw., a lion passant tail extended sa., resting the dexter fore-paw on an escutcheon arg., charged with a chevron, also sa. *Ce m'est egal.* 229. 10

Phillipps-Treby, Major-General Paul Winsloe, of Goodamoor, Plympton, South Devonsh.: (1) A demi-lion rampant arg., gorged with a collar vairée erminois and az. (*for Treby*). (2) A lion passant tail extended sa., resting the dexter fore-paw upon an escutcheon arg., charged with a chevron of the first (*for Phillipps*). *Ce m'est egal.—Renovato nomine.* 229. 10

Phillips-Flamank, *see* Flamank.

Phillips, a lion rampant sa., ducally gorged and chained or. *Ducit amor patriæ.* cf. 1. 3

Phillips, John Frederick Lort, of Lawrenny, Pembrokesh., a lion rampant sa., ducally gorged and chained or. *Animo et fide.* cf. 1. 3

Phillips, the late James Orchard Halliwell, Esquire, of Middle Hill, Worcs., on a mount vert, a lion rampant sa., ducally gorged and with a chain reflexed over the back or, holding in the dexter paw a sword erect ppr., charged on the shoulder for distinction with a cross crosslet, also or.

Phillips, Shropsh. and Cornw., a lion rampant sa., collared and chained or. 1. 3

Phillips, on a mount a lion rampant ducally crowned, holding in the dexter paw a sword in pale, and charged on the neck with a fleur-de-lis.

Phillips of Winterdyne House, Bewdley, and Hanbury, Worcs., on a garb in fess or, a lion rampant sa., ducally gorged and chained of the first, holding a cross crosslet fitched of the last.

Phillips, Shropsh.: (1) A demi-horse. 53. 3. (2) A lion rampant collared and chained. *Ducit amor patriæ.* 1. 3

Phillips, a demi-lion arg., crowned or, holding a fleur-de-lis of the same. cf. 13. 2

Phillips, Bart., Worcs., a demi-lion rampant arg., holding in the dexter paw a fleur-de-lis or. *Deus, patria, rex.* 13. 2

Phillips, Wales, a demi-lion rampant sa., collared and chained or. 10. 12

Phillips, Lionel, 33, Grosvenor Square, W., a demi-lion az., charged on the shoulder with two annulets interlaced paleways or, between as many nuggets of gold. *Veritas vincit.*

Phillips, Lisle-, of Garendon Park and Grace Dieu Manor, Leics.: (1) A demi-griffin gu., armed, winged, eared, collared and chained or, holding an escutcheon az., thereon a lion rampant of the second (*for Phillips*). 64. 10. (2) A demi-lion rampant quarterly or and az., holding a cross couped sa., charged with a cross crosslet fitched or (*for March*). (3) A stag trippant ppr. (*for Lisle*). *Quod justum, non quod utile.* 117. 8

Phillips, a demi-lion sa., collared and chained, holding between the paws a leopard's face jessant-de-lis or.

Phillips of Yeovil, Somers., a lion sejant sa., collared and lined or. 7. 4

Phillips, a horse passant erminois, gorged with a chaplet vert. cf. 52. 6

Phillips, Shropsh., a horse passant erminois, gorged with a chaplet of laurel vert, hind-legs couped at the middle of the thigh.

Phillips, Shropsh., a horse passant erminois. 52. 6

Phillips, a tiger sejant collared and chained. cf. 27. 6

Phillips of Birmingham, a leopard sejant collared and lined. *Semper paratus.* 24. 8

Phillips of Whitmore Hall, Coventry, Warw., a garb in fess or, thereon a leopard sejant ppr., holding in the mouth a trefoil slipped vert. *Mens conscia recti.*

Phillips, a garb banded ppr. 153. 2

Phillips, Ireland, an eel naiant ppr. 142. 10

Phillips, an eagle's head erased az. 83. 2

Phillips of Chelmicke, Shropsh., an eagle's head erased az. 83. 2

Phillips, Shropsh., on the trunk of a tree in fess sprouting at the dexter end vert, a Cornish chough ppr.

Phillips, a dog sejant regardant surmounted by a bezant, charged with a representation of a dog saving a man from drowning.

Phillips, Faudel-, Sir George Faudel, Bart., Balls Park, Hertford: (1) Upon a mount vert, a squirrel sejant cracking a nut or, between on the dexter side a trefoil slipped, and on the sinister a branch of hazel fructed, extending to the dexter, charged on the shoulder with an acorn leaved and slipped ppr. (*for Phillips*). 280. 3. (2) Upon a mount a peacock regardant in its pride ppr., between two roses arg., leaved and slipped vert (*for Faudel*). *Ne tentes aut perfice.* 280. 4

Phillips, out of a ducal coronet a bull's head. 44. 11

Phillips, Moro, Esquire, formerly of West Street House, Chichester, out of a ducal coronet a bear's gamb holding a black mulberry, all ppr. (*This crest is borne as the crest of the family of Moro or Morozowig, the father of the above having changed his name from that to Phillips.*) 36. 13

Phillips, out of a ducal coronet or, an arm in armour embowed holding in the hand ppr., a broken spear of the last, semée-de-lis or.

Phillips of Mount Rivers, co. Tipperary, Ireland: (1) An arm in armour embowed ppr., garnished or, grasping a broken tilting-spear, also ppr. 197. 2 (2) A cock grouse rising ppr. *Pro Deo et Rege.* cf. 89. 8

Phillips, Ireland, an arm in armour embowed ppr., purfled or, holding in the hand a broken spear of the first, the arm charged with a fleur-de-lis or.

Phillips of Witston House, Monm., Wales, a boar's head sa., langued gu., ringed or. *Spero meliora.* 43. 1

Phillips, Coleman, Esquire, of Dry River Station, Wairarapa, New Zealand, J.P., Barrister-at-Law, Supreme Court of New Zealand, first cousin to the late Alderman Sir Benjamin Samuel Phillips, Kt., Lord Mayor of London, Commander of the Order of Leopold of Belgium and the Grecian Order of our Saviour. Mr. Phillips belongs to the Jewish family of Cohen, which gives him a genealogy of some 3,400 years. Motto, *Per multos annos.*

Phillips-Conn, Highgate Henry, M.D., Earlham, Kendrick Road, Reading, a falcon's head erased ppr., armed or, holding in its beak a lure gu. *Vincit qui patitur.*

Phillipson, *alias* **Thelwall,** of Crook Hall and Colegarth, Westml., out of a mural coronet or, a plume of seven feathers, four arg. and three gu.

Phillipson, a boar sa. cf. 40. 9

Phillipson, a camel's head couped holding in the mouth an oak-branch slipped with three acorns, all ppr. cf. 132. 7

Phillipson, a greyhound's head couped holding in the mouth a laurel-branch, all vert.

Phillott, a unicorn's head couped. 49. 7

Phillpot, a plume of ostrich-feathers sa. 115. 1

Phillpotts, a dexter arm in armour embowed holding in the hand a sword, all ppr. *Semper paratus.* 195. 2

Phillpotts, Captain Arthur Stephens, R.N., Chelston Cross, Torquay, and Phillpotts Town, Navan, co. Meath, same crest and motto.

Philpot of Faversham, Kent, and London, a lion's head erased arg., between two wings sa., each charged with a bend erm. cf. 19. 7

Philpot, a porcupine passant or, charged with an annulet for difference. cf. 136. 5

Philpot, Herts and Kent, a porcupine passant or 136 5

Phin, Scotland, a phœnix in flames ppr *Perit ut vivat* 82 2

Phine, Scotland, a crane's head couped ppr *Vigilanti securitas* 104 5

Phippes of London a demi lion rampant arg, holding with both paws a palm branch ppr cf 12 7

Phipps, see Normandy, Marquess of

Phipps, Earl of Mulgrave, see Mulgrave

Phipps, a lion's gamb erect and erased sa, holding a trefoil slipped arg 36 8

Phipps, a lion's gamb erased sa, holding a mullet arg

Phipps, Charles Nicholas Paul, Chalcot, Westbury Wilts, same crest

Phipps, two laurel branches issuing ppr

Phipson of Selley Hall, near Birmingham, Warw, a plume of seven feathers alternately arg and gu

Phipson - Wybrants, Captain Temple Leighton (1) A stag's head erased ppr charged with a bezant (*for Wybrants*) cf 121 2 (2) Issuant from a mural crown ppr, a plume of seven ostrich feathers alternately arg and gu, charged with a chevron engrailed erm (*for Phipson*) *Mitis sed fortis*

Phitton, a lion passant arg 6 2

Picard, a dexter hand holding a sword in pale ppr 212 9

Pichford or **Pitchford** of Lee Brockhurst, Shropsh, an ostrich arg, beaked and ducally gorged or cf 97 2

Pickard-Cambridge, see Cambridge

Pickard, an eagle's head erased sa 83 2

Pickard, a lion sejant arg, supporting an antique shield charged with a canton

Pickard of London, a lion sejant arg resting the dexter paw on an escutcheon gu within a carved bordure or, charged with a fleur-de-lis of the last

Pickard-Cambridge, Rev Edward, 10, Gloucester Row Weymouth (1) A griffin's head erased sa, semee of trefoils in the mouth a cross botony fitchee or (*for Cambridge*) (2) A lion sejant arg, charged on the shoulder with an ermine spot, and gorged with a collar gemelle sa, supporting with the dexter fore paw an escutcheon gu, charged with a fleur de lis within a bordure or (*for Pickard*) *Esse quam videri*

Pickard-Cambridge, George Trenchard same crests and motto

Pickard-Cambridge, Rev Octavius, Bloxworth, Wareham Dorset, same crests and motto

Pickas, a demi lion rampant gu supporting in the paws a spear arg, headed and garnished or

Picken, Scotland, a demi-lion arg 10 2

Pickerget, two pomegranates on one slip stalked and leaved ppr

Pickering, a fleur de lis or 148 2

Pickering, Hunts Northamp, Cambs Yorks, and Sussex a lion's gamb erect and erased az, armed or 36 4

Pickering of Wallford, Chesh, a lion's gamb erect and erased az, enfiled with a ducal coronet or cf 36 3

Pickering, Yorks a lion's gamb erect and erased az armed or 36 4

Pickering, Surrey a lion's gamb erased arg 36 4

Pickering of London, a lion's gamb erased ppr 36 4

Pickering, a sword in pale ppr, hilt and pommel or, within two branches of laurel in orle vert 170 3

Pickering, Notts a leopard's head or, semee of hurts cf 22 10

Pickering of Hartford, Chesh, a demi-griffin sa, beaked and membered arg, grasping a garb or

Pickering, Benjamin, Bellefield Sutton, Hull in front of a bear's paw erect and erased arg, encircled with a chaplet of oak vert a demi catherine wheel az *Je garde bien* 255 13

Pickernell, a lion's head erased gu 17 2

Pickersgill-Cunliffe, see Cunliffe

Pickersgill-Cunliffe, Harry, Chesterford Park, Saffron Walden, Essex (1) A greyhound sejant arg, collared sa, and charged on the shoulder with a pellet (*for Cunliffe*) (2) On a rock ppr an eagle with wings elevated sa, bezantee and holding in the beak a cross crosslet fitchee or *Fideliter*

Pickersgill of Blendon Hall, Kent upon a rock ppr, an eagle with wings elevated sa, bezantee and holding in the beak a cross crosslet fitchee or *Quæ recta sequor*

Pickersgill, William Henry, Esquire of Stratford Place, upon a rock a magpie holding in the beak an acorn slipped ppr *Labore et ingenio* 108 1

Pickett, a martlet gu 95 14

Pickett, an arm embowed vested arg, cuffed vert, charged with two bars wavy of the last holding in the hand a pick axe ppr

Pickford, an arm embowed holding in the hand an arrow ppr 201 13

Pickford a lion's head erased 17 8

Pickup, William, Esquire of Spring Hill, Accrington, Lancs in front of a stag's head couped ppr a demi-catherine wheel az *Candide et constanter* 121. 3

Pickwick of Bathford, Somers a hart's head couped erm, attired or, gorged with a collar gu, therefrom a chain reflexed over the neck of the second, all between two wings az 121 1

Picton or **Pickton** of Wyvill Court, Berks, and Chesh, a demi lion rampant gu 10 3

Picton, John Esquire, of Iscoed, Carmarthensh, out of a mural coronet gu between two branches of laurel ppr, a mullet or, charged with a pellet

Pidcock, Derbysh, a bar-shot ppr, thereon a griffin segreant sa, holding between its claws a grenade fired also, ppr *Seigneur, je te prie garde ma vie* 229 9

Pidcock-Henzell, Major Henry Henzell Fraser Pinehurst, Farnborough Hants, same crest and motto

Piddle, a hawk's head arg cf 88 12

Pie, between two wings a cross crosslet fitched 111 3

Pierce, a parrot holding in the beak an annulet 101 11

Pierce, Hugh, Esquire, of Liverpool the battlements of a tower, therefrom issuant a dexter arm in armour embowed grasping a tilting-spear palewise all ppr, and in front of the battlements a bugle horn stringed gu *Sub cruce salus*

Pierce, John Timbrell, J P, D L, 3, Middle Temple Lane, E C, a pelican arg, vulned ppr *Deus mihi providebit*

Pierie, Scotland a hunting-horn az garnished or, and stringed gu *Vesperi et mane* 228 11

Pierpont, Hants, a fox gu 32 2

Pierpont, Shropsh (1) A fox passant gu 32 1 (2) A lion rampant sa between two wings expanded arg 9 2

Pierpont, Shropsh, a lion rampant sa between two wings arg 9 2

Pierpont, Notts, same crest *Pie repone te*

Pierrepont, see Manvers Earl

Pierrepont of Holme Pierrepont Notts, **Duke and Earl of Kingston** (*extinct*), a lion rampant sa, between two wings erect arg *Pie repone te* 9 2

Pierrepoint, a lion rampant sa, between two wings arg 9 2

Pierrepont, a fox passant gu *Pie repone te* 32 1

Pierrie, Scotland, a horse's head between two wings 51 3

Piers, a griffin or winged arg 63 8

Piers, Sir Eustace Fitzmaurice Bart of Tristernagh Abbey, co Westmeath an arm embowed vested az, cuffed arg the hand holding a flag erect per fesse of the last and of the first in chief two torteaux and in base a plate *Nobilis est ira leonis*

Piers, Walter Rumbold the Residency, Peddie, Cape Colony South Africa, an arm embowed vested az, cuffed arg, the hand holding a flag erect

Pierson, three savages' heads conjoined in one neck one looking to the dexter, one to the sinister and one upwards cf 195 5

Pierson, a parrot vert beaked and legged gu 101 4

Pierson, Devonsh, out of a mural coronet chequy or and az, a parrot's head ppr

Pierson, Herts and Middx out of a ducal coronet or, an ostrich's head between two ostrich feathers arg cf 97 14

Pierson, Rev George James Norton Vicarage Baldock, in front of a sun rising in splendour ppr an ostrich's head erased sa, gorged with a collar gemel arg holding in the beak a Passion nail ppr and between two feathers, also arg *Tout viens de Dieu*

Pierson, Wilts, a demi lion ppr holding in the dexter paw a sun or

Pierson of Olney Bucks a hind's head couped arg charged with two chevronels az cf 124 1

Pierson of London an ounce sejant az armed and langued gu cf 24 13

Piesse, an eagle displayed ppr *Per mare per terras* 75 2

Pige - Leschallas, Henry Boscastle Cornw on a mount vert a column or thereon flames of fire ppr and entwined by a vine branch also ppr

Pigeon of Deptford Kent a demi griffin erm beaked and legged or 64 2

Pigeon of Hampton-upon-Thames, Middx., and Hants, on a chapeau gu., turned up erm., a buck's head ppr. *cf.* 121. 5

Pigeon of Beckham and Yockthorpe, Norf., an elephant's head erased gu., eared, tusked, collared, lined, and ringed or.

Pigg, a demi-lion purpure. 10. 2

Piggot, a bull's head erased gu. 44. 3

Piggot or **Piggott,** an ostrich holding in the beak a horse-shoe, all ppr. 97. 8

Piggot, a stag's head erased ppr. 121. 2

Pigot, a greyhound passant per pale sa. and erminois. *cf.* 60. 2

Pigot, a lion rampant supporting an ancient mace in pale.

Pigot, a martlet gu. 95. 4

Pigot, Sir George, Bart., of Patshull, Staffs, *uses:* a wolf's head erased arg. *Tout foys prest.* 30. 8

Pigot, Rev. John Tayleur, the Rectory, Fremington, North Devonsh., a wolf's head erased arg. *Tout foys prest.*

Pigott, Ireland, a wolf's head erased arg., charged with a crescent gu. *cf.* 30. 8

Pigott, Somers., a wolf's head erased sa., charged with three torteaux arg. *cf.* 30. 8

Pigott, Sir Charles Robert, Bart., of Knapton, Queen's Co., Ireland, a wolf's head erased ppr., collared or.

Pigott, Smyth-, J., Esquire, of Brockley Hall, West Town, R.S.O., Somers.: (1) A wolf's head erased sa., gorged with a collar arg., charged with three torteaux. (*for Pigott*). *Qui capit capitur.* 30. 7. (2) A griffin's head erased gu., charged on the neck with a bar gemelle, beaked and eared or (*for Smyth*). *Toujours prêt.* *cf.* 66. 2

Pigott of Dodershall, Bucks, and Braytoft, Lincs: (1) A wolf's head erased arg., langued gu. (2) A greyhound couchant arg., collared sa., charged on the shoulder with three pickaxes of the second. *cf.* 60. 1

Pigott, Berks, Bucks, Cambs, Beds, and Notts, a greyhound passant sa. *cf.* 60. 2

Pigott, Hants, a greyhound statant ppr. *Labore et virtute.* *cf.* 60. 2

Pigott, Rev. Eversfield Botry, Widmoor, Basingstoke: (1) A mount vert, thereon a stag ppr., the dexter fore-foot resting on a shield gu., billety or, the shoulder charged with a rose of the second for difference (*for Conant*). (2) A mount vert, thereon a lion rampant erm., holding between the fore-paws a fleur-de-lis az., the dexter hind-paw resting on a mill-rind sa. (*for Stainsby*). (3) A greyhound statant per pale sa. and erm. (*for Pigott*). *Labore et virtute.—Conanti dabitur.*

Pigott, Frederick William, Bourne Hill, Horsham, Sussex, same crests. *Labore et virtute.*

Pigott, Sir Paynton, Horsford Hall, Norwich, same crests. *Labore et virtute.*

Pigott, Captain William Harvey, R.N., Doddershall Park, Aylesbury, three pickaxes ppr.

Pigott, Graham-Foster-, of Abington Pigotts, Royston, Cambs: (1) A mount vert, thereon in front of a pickaxe or, a greyhound passant sa., gorged for distinction with a collar, also or (*for Pigott*). (2) In front of a stag's head couped or, attired sa., gorged for distinction with a mural coronet gu., a bugle-horn, also sa., garnished or (*for Foster*). (3) An escallop or, and above it the words *Spero meliora* (*for Graham*). *Hoc age.* 141. 12

Pigott, a dove holding in its beak an olive-branch ppr. 92. 5

Pigott, Thomas Digby, Esquire, C.B., 5, Ovington Gardens, S.W., a greyhound statant ppr. *Toute foys prester.*

Pigou, a lion's head erased ppr. 17. 8

Pike, a pike naiant or. *cf.* 139. 5

Pike, Richard Nicholson, Esquire, J.P., Barrister-at-Law, of Glendarary, co. Mayo, Ireland, an arm embowed in armour, the hand gauntleted grasping a broken spear, all ppr., and charged on the elbow with an escallop az. *Vrai a la fin.* *cf.* 197. 2

Pike of Gottenburgh, Sweden, a demi-Moor ppr., in the ears rings and ear-drops arg., holding in the dexter hand a pike-staff arg.

Pike, Shropsh., a demi-man copper-coloured, holding in the dexter hand a three-pronged fork gu.

Pilcher, on a chapeau ppr., a cockatrice with wings addorsed vert, ducally crowned or. 68. 9

Pile, Sir Thomas Devereux, Bart., Kenilworth House, Rathgar, on a crest a coronet or, charged with a cross bourdonnée az., a pelican with wings endorsed and inverted ppr. *Sine labe nota.* 242. 8

Pile, on a ducal coronet or, a pelican with wings addorsed vulning herself ppr. *cf.* 98. 1

Pilfold of Warnham and Newtimber, Sussex, a sea-horse erect per fesse sa. and or, supporting a trident, also sa. *Audaces fortuna juvat.* 46. 3

Pilfold, Captain John, of Horsham, Sussex, a sea-horse erect per fesse sa. and or, gorged with a naval coronet, also or, and by a ribbon arg., fimbriated az., pendent therefrom a representation of the medal presented to him for gallant service in the Battle off Trafalgar, supporting a trident, also sa. *Audaces fortuna juvat.* *cf.* 46. 3

Pilford, an eagle displayed sa. 75. 2

Pilgrim, an arm in armour embowed ppr., garnished or, holding in the hand a cutlass of the first, hilt and pommel of the second.

Pilgrim or **Pilgrime,** an escallop or. 141. 12

Pilkington, Bart., *see* Milborne-Swinnerton-Pilkington.

Pilkington, a mower with a scythe ppr., vested quarterly arg. and gu. *Now thus! now thus!* 188. 12

Pilkington of Bolton, Lancs, a mower with his scythe ppr., the handle or, habited quarterly gu. and arg., his cap per pale of the last and third. *Now thus! now thus!* 188. 12

Pilkington, Henry Mulock, K.C., LL.D., of Tore, co. Westmeath, Ireland, a mower habited throughout quarterly and counterchanged arg. and gu., having on a high-crowned hat with a flap the crown party per pale of the same, the flap also per pale counterchanged, the coat buttoned in the middle, the face and hands bare, holding a scythe in front in bend ppr., and over this crest the motto, *Now thus! now thus!—Pilkyngton Pailedowne, the Master mows the meadows.* 188. 12

Pilland, on a chapeau gu., turned up erm., a garb or. 153. 10

Pillans, Scotland, a dexter hand holding a dagger point upwards, all ppr. *Virtute et robore.* 212. 9

Pillans, of Leith, Scotland, a hand holding a sword ppr. *Virtute et robore.* 212. 13

Pillans, Francis Scott, Esquire, J.P., of Myres, Inch Cutha, Stirling, Otago, New Zealand, *uses:* a dexter cubit arm holding a dagger in bend sinister, all ppr. *Virtute et robore.* 212. 3

Pillett or **Pillott,** a lion sejant erect gu., holding between the paws an escutcheon of the arms, viz.: arg., two bars sa. *cf.* 8. 4

Pilliner, a unicorn's head gu. 49. 7

Pilmure of Coupar Angus, Scotland, a martlet volant az. *Honeste vivo.* 96. 2

Pilter, William Frederick, C.B., the Grove, Addlestone, Surrey, on a wreath of the colours, in front of a fleur-de-lis or, a dolphin naiant ppr. *Fide patientia labore.* 200. 5

Pim, a dexter hand holding a scimitar ppr. 213. 5

Pim, Rev. Henry Bedford, Leaside, Spencer Road, Bromley, Kent, a dexter arm in armour embowed, holding in the hand a dagger, point to the dexter, all ppr. *Deeds, not words.*

Pinchyon of Writtle, Essex, a tiger's head erased arg.

Pinckard of London, an arm embowed ppr., vested az., charged with two bars arg., cuffed of the last, holding in the hand a sword ppr., the point resting on the wreath, hilt and pommel or.

Pinckeney, the sun or, issuing from clouds arg. 162. 5

Pinckney of Middlesex House, Batheaston, Somers., and Tawstock Court, Barnstaple, Devonsh., in front of a griffin's head erased gu., collared or, three fusils of the last. *Deus nobis.* 230. 16

Pinckney, Erlysman, J.P., Wraxhall Lodge, Bradford-on-Avon, same crest and motto.

Pindall of London and Lincs, a lion's head erased or, ducally crowned az. 18. 8

Pindar or **Pinder** of London and Lincs, a lion's head erased arg., ducally crowned az. 18. 8

Pindar, a stork arg., ducally crowned or. *cf.* 106. 11

Pindar or **Pyndar, Earl Beauchamp,** a lion's head erased erm., ducally crowned or. 18. 8

Pindar of Duffield, Derbysh., and of Kempley, Glouc., same crest. 18. 8

Pine, a lion's head arg. 21. 1

Pine-Coffin, Major John Edward, of Portledge, near Bideford, Devonsh.: (1) A martlet az., charged on the breast with two bezants in pale. (2) A pine-tree ppr. *In tempestate floresco.*

Pinfold, Beds, a pine-tree or, leaved vert, fructed ppr., enclosed with pales arg. and sa. *cf.* 144. 5

Pinford, a dove holding in its beak a honeysuckle slipped, all ppr cf 92 5

Pink of Thornton House Clapham Park, London, S W, a cubit arm erect, vested az, cuffed arg, holding in the hand ppr a cross pattee fitched in pale or *Pro cruce audax*

Pink or Pinck, a mullet of six points gu 164 3

Pink or **Pinck**, Oxon a cubit arm erect vested az, cuffed arg holding in the hand ppr a cross pattee fitched in pale or

Pinker of Dinder, Somers, on a mount vert a heathcock rising ppr 89 8

Pinkerton of London and Scotland, a rose gu, stalked and leaved vert *Post nubila sol* 149 5

Pinkney of Upper Sheen Surrey, out of a ducal coronet or a griffin's head ppr 67 9

Pinkton, a dexter hand gauntleted holding a sword ppr 211 4

Pinner, a dexter arm in armour embowed holding in the hand a cross crosslet fitched in bend

Pinner of London, a stork arg, ducally gorged or cf 105 11

Pinney, *see* Pretor Pinney

Pinney, an eagle displayed gu 75 2

Pinney, George Frederic, J P, Brooklands, Beaminster, Dorset, an arm in armour embowed holding a cross crosslet fitchee arg *Amor patriæ*

Pinnock, an arm embowed, vested, holding in the hand a martlet

Pinsent, Hon Sir Robert J Pinsent D C L, Senior Judge of the Supreme Court of Newfoundland, St John's, Newfoundland, a sinister wing ppr, charged with an escutcheon arg, thereon a chevron engrailed between three mullets of six points 109 3

Pipard, a lion sejant ppr, supporting an escutcheon of the arms, viz arg, two bars az, a canton of the last cf 8 4

Pipe-Wolverstan, Egerton Stanley Statfold near Tamworth (1) A wolf under a tree all ppr (*for Wolferstan*) (2) A leopard's head erased or (*for Pipe*) *Qui sera sera*

Piper, a unicorn's head arg 49 7

Piper of Ridgewell, Essex, out of an Eastern coronet or, a demi dove arg, with wings addorsed

Piper of Tresmarrow, Cornw, a magpie sa 108 2

Piper of Culliton Devonsh, and Kent, a cubit arm encircled with a wreath of laurel ppr, holding in the hand a boar's head fesseways erased sa *Feroci fortior*

Piper of Ashen, Essex, a demi-griffin regardant ppr supporting an antique escutcheon charged with a dexter gauntlet fessewise, holding a sword erect, all ppr

Pipon of Noirmont Manor Jersey, a demi lion holding between the paws a mullet or cf 15 8

Pirbright, Baron (De Worms), Henley Park, Guildford, out of a ducal coronet or, a plume of five ostrich-feathers or, gu or, az, and or *Vinctus non victus*

Pirce, a lion's head ppr 21 1

Pirie, Bart, of London, an eagle's head erased sa, holding in the beak an ostrich-feather arg 83 3

Pirie-Gordon, Edward, Esquire of Gwernvale Crickhowel, South Wales, a fawn's head couped holding a pear branch *Virtute non astutia*

Pirie, Alexander Charles Dunecht Aberdeensh a fawn's head with the sprig of a pear tree in its mouth ppr *Virtute non astutia*

Pirie, Duncan Vernon, M P, 35, Eccleston Square S W, same crest and motto

Pirie, Gordon, Château de Varennes, Savennieres Maine et Loire, France same crest and motto

Pirie, Martin Henry Inverness Lodge Porchester Gate, W, same crest and motto

Pirrie, Rt Hon William James, Downshire House, Belgrave Square, a falcon's head erased per saltire arg and gu *Deeds, not words*

Pirrie, Scotland, a hawk s head erased az 88 12

Pirton, a dragon 73 2

Pitcairn of Pitcairn House Perthsh, Scotland, the sun in his splendour or *Spes lucis æternæ* 162 2

Pitcairn of Pitfour, Fifesh, an anchor erect az *Sperabo* 161 1

Pitcairn, Scotland, the moon in her complement arg *Refulget*

Pitcairn of that Ilk Scotland, the moon in her complement ppr *Plena refulget*

Pitcairn of Dreghorn Scotland a star of six points wavy with straight rays between each point within a circle of clouds *Spes lucis æternæ*

Pitcher, a demi-man in a military habit holding in the hand a flag displayed az 187 9

Pitcher, John Southerby, Esquire of London, a griffin's head couped gorged with a wreath of oak ppr between two wings each charged with a roundle

Pitcher, Colonel Duncan George Gwalior Central India, same crest *Perseverentia et labore*

Pitches, a man's head in profile bearded ppr, wearing a long cap with a tassel hanging down behind cf 192 11

Pitchford, Shropsh an ostrich arg beaked and ducally gorged or cf 97 2

Pites, a swan's neck arg, with wings expanded gu, between two branches vert, holding in the beak a trefoil slipped or

Pitfield, Dorset and Middx, a swan-royal arg, ducally gorged and lined, the line reflexed over the back or

Pitman, a catherine-wheel ppr 167 2

Pitman of Dunchideock, Devonsh on a shell a martlet

Pitman, Devonsh, on a wrinkle-shell or, a Cornish chough ppr *Fortiter agendo*

Pitman of Woodbridge Suff a Moor's arm ppr., vested chequy gu and or holding a pole-axe the handle or and headed arg

Pitson of Guildford, Surrey, a peacock's head erased az 103 1

Pitt, Baron Rivers, *see* Rivers

Pitt, Earl of Chatham (*extinct*), a stork ppr, beaked and membered or, resting the dexter claw on an anchor erect and cabled of the last. *Benigno numine* 105 10

Pitt, Earl of Londonderry (*extinct*) a stork arg beaked and membered or holding up its dexter foot *Amitie*

Pitt of Boconnock, Cornw **Baron Camelford** (*extinct*), a stork arg. *Per ardua liberi* 105 11

Pitt, Cornw and Dorset, a stork arg, beaked and legged gu, supporting an anchor or cabled ppr cf 105 10

Pitt, a stork ppr 105 11

Pitt of Cricket Malherby Somers a stork ppr, resting the dexter claw on a bezant cf 105 11

Pitt, Colonel Thomas Henry, Hayle Place Maidstone same crest

Pitt, Fox-, Alexander Edward Lane, Rushmore Salisbury (1) A stork ppr (*for Pitt*) (2) On a five leaved ducal coronet or a fox passant ppr (*for Fox*) *Æquum servare mentem*

Pitt, Cornw, a stork arg beaked and legged or 105 11

Pitt of Ewern Stepleton Dorset, a stork arg beaked and legged ppr 105 11

Pitt, Shropsh and Worcs a dove with wings expanded arg beaked and legged gu, between two ears of wheat or

Pitt, a demi horse salient 53 3

Pitt, Worcs on the trunk of a tree in fess raguly vert, a stag ppr attired or, between two acorn-branches sprouting from the tree of the first fructed, also or

Pitt of London a dexter arm ppr, vested az, cuffed arg holding in the hand two branches of laurel in orle vert, and between them perched upon the hand a martlet sa 205 6

Pitt of Priors Lea and Shifnal, Shropsh. a cubit arm erect ppr erased at the elbow gu holding in the hand a banner or, charged with a human heart of the second

Pitter of Croydon, Surrey, and Middx, on two billets erect or, a stag's head erased and attired ppr, gorged with a collar and chain of the first 120 1

Pittillo, a sword erect, the point upwards, and thereon a fleur de-lis 169 6

Pittman, a rock sa 179 7

Pittman, a Moor's arm ppr, escarroned of the colours advancing a pole-axe the handle or, headed arg

Pitts of London and Somers, a stork arg, beaked and legged gu, resting the dexter claw on a bezant

Piverne, a cubit arm vested gu cuffed arg holding in the hand ppr a sword in pale enfiled with a leopard's head of the second, hilt and pommel or, the point embrued, also ppr

Pix, a tree vert 143 5

Pix of Crayford Kent on a round chapeau gu turned up erm, a cross crosslet fitched or between two wings az

Pixley, A D, of 21, Leinster Gardens Christ Church Lancaster Gate, a cross crosslet fitchee or on a cap of maintenance between two wings az *Per vias rectas* 111 2

Pixley, F W, Esquire in front of a cross crosslet fitchee or a morion ppr, between two wings az, each charged with a dagger point downwards or *Per vias rectas* 111 2

Pixley, Arthur, J P., Prospect Kangaroo Point, Brisbane, Queensland, same crest and motto

Pixt of Hawkhurst, Kent, on a chapeau gu., turned up erm., a cross crosslet fitched or, between two wings az.
Place, a palm-tree vert, fructed or. 144. 1
Place of Dinsdale, Durh., and Weddington Hall, Warw., out of a ducal coronet or, a dexter arm in armour embowed holding in the hand a battle-axe, all ppr. *cf.* 200. 6
Placetis, a lion's head ppr., collared gu. *cf.* 18. 6
Plafair, Scotland, an arm ppr., armed and embowed az., holding in the hand a fleur-de-lis or. 199. 14
Plaine, the trunk of a tree sprouting forth branches ppr. 145. 2
Plaisto or **Plaistow,** out of a ducal coronet a griffin's head ppr. 67. 9
Plaiters or **Platers,** a falcon arg., armed, beaked, and membered or. 85. 2
Plaiz, a lion's head erased, vomiting flames ppr. 17. 1
Plank or **Planke,** an olive-branch ppr. 151. 11
Plant, a stag trippant gu. 117. 8
Planta of London, out of a marquess's coronet or, a black bear's hind-leg erect, couped at the thigh, showing the bottom of the foot, all ppr.
Plantney of Wolverhampton, Staffs, an heraldic tiger's head erased or, tufted and maned gu. *cf.* 25. 4
Plaskett, a swan arg. 99. 2
Plasto, a lion's head erased. 17. 8
Plater, a pheon az. 174. 11
Platt of Deanwater, Chesh., a demi-wolf gu., platée, armed and langued az., holding in the dexter paw a wreath arg. and of the first. *Labitur et labetur.* *cf.* 31. 10
Platt, Frederick, Esquire, of Barnby Manor, Newark, Notts, in front of a demi-lion rampant ppr., semée of plates, and holding between the paws a rose arg., an escallop or. *Virtute et labore.*
Platt, Sydney, J.P., Wargrave Hill, Wargrave, Berks, same crest and motto.
Platt, Colonel Henry, C.B., of Gorddinog, Llanfairfechan, same crest and motto.
Platt, James Edward, J.P., Howbury Hall, near Bedford, same crest and motto.
Platt, John Harold, 31, Pont Street, W., same crest and motto.
Platt, Samuel Radcliffe, Werneth Park, Oldham, same crest and motto.
Platt of London and Kentish Town, Middx., a demi-lion rampant ppr., holding between the paws a plate. *cf.* 11. 7
Platt, John, Esquire, J.P., of Clifton Lodge, Llandudno, Carnarvonsh., and of Warrington, Lancs, on a wreath of the colours a lamb or, resting the dexter fore-leg on a fleur-de-lis az., and holding in the mouth three cinquefoils slipped vert. *Neminem metue innocens.* 131. 8
Platt, a bird volant az., winged arg. and sa., holding in the beak an escallop of the first.
Platt of Plaistow, Essex, a shoveller with wings expanded ppr.
Platt, a garb or, banded vert. 153. 2
Platt-Higgins, Alfred, a griffin's head erased or, gorged with a collar sa., charged with a lozenge arg. between two plates, in the beak a lobster's claw erased gu. (*for Higgins*). (2) A demi-wolf gu., semée of plates, armed and langued az., holding in the dexter paw a wreath arg. and gu., and charged on the shoulder with a cross crosslet or (*for Platt*). *Labitur et labetur.*
Platt-Higgins, Edward, Rathcoole, Fortwilliam Park, Belfast, same crests and motto.
Platt-Higgins, Frederick, Holmleigh, Bowdon, Chesh., same crests and motto.
Platt-Higgins, Henry, Moorside, Heathview Gardens, Putney Heath, S.W., same crests and motto.
Plaunch, De la, a hunting-horn sans strings sa. 228. 9
Playdell, Berks, a tiger's head erased or, charged with hurts, holding in the mouth a cross patée fitched of the first.
Player, Middx., an arm in armour in fess, holding in the hand a broken lance, all ppr. *Servitute clarior.*
Player, an arm in armour in bend couped below the elbow, the hand supporting a broken spear in pale, all ppr.
Playfair, Baron (Playfair), Uffington House, Stamford, on a chapeau turned up arg., a pelican vulning itself ppr. *Dum spiro spero.*
Playfair, Sir Patrick, C.I.E., Ardmillan, Girvan, Ayrsh., a tree. *Firmitas in cœlo.*
Playfair, on a chapeau a pelican vulning herself, all ppr. 98. 7
Playfair, Scotland, a globe ppr. *Sic te non vidimus olim.* 159. 1
Playfair, Scotland, a pelican in her piety ppr. 98. 14
Playford, Kent, Norf., and Suff., a leopard sejant ppr. *cf.* 24. 8
Playne of Sudbury, Suff., a withered tree erased at the root and erect ppr.
Playse of Toft, Norf., a lion's head erased vomiting flames ppr. 17. 1
Playses, a gauntlet in fess ppr., holding in pale a broken tilting-spear or, the top hanging down, headed arg.
Playstow, Essex, out of a ducal coronet or, a griffin's head ppr. 67. 9
Playters, Bart. (*extinct*), of Sotterley, Suff., a hawk regardant or, winged az., belled of the first.
Playters, on a ducal coronet a lion rampant *cf.* 1. 13
Pleasance of Tudenham, Suff., a griffin sejant with wings expanded erm. 62. 10
Pleasaunce, a griffin segreant erm., armed or. 62. 2
Pleckford, a demi-swan rising arg., with wings addorsed and ducally gorged or. *cf.* 100. 2
Pledger of Bottlesham, Cambs, a buck's head erased or, holding in the mouth an oak-sprig ppr., fructed of the first. *cf.* 119. 11
Plenderleath, Rev. William Charles, Mamhead Rectory, Exeter, a hand holding a writ or paper almost rolled, all ppr. *Prompte et consulto.*
Plenderleith of Blyth, Scotland, a hand holding a scroll of paper ppr. *Prompte et consulto.* 215. 6
Plesant, a bird holding in the beak two roses stalked and leaved.
Pleshey, a bull passant gu. *cf.* 45. 2
Plessels, a church with a spire environed with trees, all ppr. 158. 11
Pleydell, *see* Radnor, Earl of.
Pleydell-Bouverie-Campbell, *see* Campbell.
Pleydell-Bouverie-Campbell-Wyndham, Philip Arthur, Corhampton, Bishop's Waltham, Hants: (1) On a fetter-lock or, within the chain thereof of the last and az., a lion's head erased or, charged on the neck for distinction with a cross crosslet az. (*for Wyndham*). (2) Two oars of a lymphad disposed in saltire ppr. (3) A demi-eagle displayed with two heads sa., ducally gorged or, and charged on the breast with a cross crosslet arg. (*for Bouverie*). 302. 2. *Vis et fides* (*for Campbell*).—*Patria cara carior libertas* (*for Bouverie*).
Pleydell-Bouverie-Campbell-Wyndham, Richard Arthur, Dunoon, Argyllsh., same crests and mottoes.
Pleydell, Mansel-, John Clavell, of Whatcombe, Dorset: (1) A panther's head erased sa., bezantée, swallowing a cross patée fitched gu. (2) A cap of maintenance inflamed on the top. *Imitare quam invidere.*
Pleydell, Bart. (*extinct*), of Coleshill and Shrivenham, Berks, and of Cricklade, Wilts, a panther's head erased gu., platée, holding in the mouth a cross formée fitched of the first.
Plomer, Ireland, a lion sa., holding in the dexter paw a dagger gu.
Plomer, within an annulet or, an escutcheon sa. *cf.* 167. 6
Plomer, a demi-lion rampant arg., holding in the dexter paw a sprig vert.
Plomer, Captain William Harry Perceval, R.A., care of Messrs. Cox and Co., Charing Cross, a demi-lion gu., holding a garb ppr. *Erectus non elatus.*
Plomer of Mayfield and Pettingho, Sussex, a demi-lion rampant gu., holding a garb or. 12. 4
Plompton, a mortar mounted on a carriage ppr. 169. 10
Plompton or **Plomton,** a buck's head couped arg., attired or. 121. 5
Plonckett or **Plonkett,** a stag's head affrontée, gorged with a ducal coronet ppr. 119. 14
Plonckett, Ireland, a wolf sejant ppr. *cf.* 29. 3
Plonket, a hand holding a lance in pale ppr.
Plonket and **Plonkett,** a stag's head affrontée gorged with a ducal coronet or. 119. 14
Plott, an arm in armour embowed sa., garnished or, holding in the hand a scimitar ppr. 196. 10
Plott, Devonsh. and Heref., a dexter arm in armour or, purfled sa., holding a falchion arg., hilt and pommel of the first, a scarf flotant from the hilt enfiling the wrist and tied in a knot of the first and second.
Plowden of Ewhurst Park, Hants, on a mount vert, a buck trippant sa. *Quod tibi hoc alteri.* 118. 2
Plowden, a hart's head erased az. 121. 2

Plowden, William Francis, of Plowden, Shropsh, on a mount vert, a buck trippant sa attired or 118 2

Plowden, Arthur Chichele, 18 Cheniston Gardens, W, same crest

Plowden, Sir Henry Meredith Leintwardine Heref, same crest *Quod tibi hoc alteri*

Plowden, Trevor Chichele, J P, 14 Redcliffe Square, S W, same crest and motto

Plowden Chichele, Sir Trevor John Chichele, K C S I, Hazlehurst Orr, Sussex same crest and motto

Plowden, Sir William Chichele K C S I, 5, Park Crescent, Portland Place, W, same crest and motto

Plowden, on a mount vert a stag trippant sa, attired and ungu or 118 2

Plowes, Alexander J, of 12 West Halkin Street, Belgrave Square, S W, a demi griffin arg, winged or, collared az holding an escutcheon gu, charged with an estoile of six points or *Unita fortior* 64 15

Plowman, a demi savage wreathed about the middle holding over his dexter shoulder a club, and round his sinister arm a serpent entwined 185 3

Plucknett of the Manor House, Finchley Middx, the battlements of a tower ppr, and issuant therefrom a demi-eagle regardant with wings expanded or, charged on the breast with a lozenge gu *In Deo fides*

Plues, Samuel Swire, Esquire, Attorney General for Honduras, on a mount vert a mahogany tree ppr, therefrom pendent by a riband a fasces in bend, or *Fiat justitia*

Plum, out of a ducal coronet a plume of ostrich-feathers, all ppr cf 114 8

Plum of Maldon, Essex, a talbot sejant gu collared and lined or 55 5

Plumbe of Marston, Leics, Kent, and Norf, a greyhound sejant arg, collared gu cf 59 2

Plume, out of a ducal coronet or, a plume of ostrich feathers arg cf 114 8

Plumer or **Plummer,** a demi-lion rampant arg, holding in the dexter paw a sprig vert

Plumer, Alfred Saxby in front of a demi lion gu, gorged with a collar flory counterflory arg, and holding between the paws a garb of the last, surmounted by a martlet sa, the trunk of a tree eradicated and sprouting ppr *Loyal*

Plumer, John Bagwill, same crest and motto

Plumerage, a demi lion rampant ppr langued gu, holding in the dexter paw a fleur-de-lis of the last 13 2

Plumerage, a demi lion rampant az, holding between the paws a fleur-de-lis gu cf 13 5

Plumerdon, a magpie ppr 108 2

Plumett, Ireland, a horse passant arg 52 6

Plumleigh and **Plumley** of Dartmouth Devonsh, an arm embowed vested gu cuffed arg, holding in the hand ppr an arrow of the first, sans feathers, headed of the second

Plummer, a water-houget or 168 4

Plummer, Scott-, Charles Henry of Middlestead, Selkirk Scotland a dexter hand issuing out of a cloud and holding a plumb rule within a garland, all ppr (*for Scott*) (2) A demi-lion rampant arg, in the dexter paw a sprig vert (*or Plummer*) *Jus dicere decus*

Plummer, Scotland, a demi lion arg, holding in its dexter paw a branch of palm ppr *Consulto et audacter*

Plumptre, Henry Fitzwalter, Goodnestone Park Kent, a phœnix or, out of flames ppr *Sufficit meruisse*

Plumptre, Reginald Charles Edward, same crest and motto

Plumridge of Hopton Hall, Suff upon a mount vert a boar's head couped or, in front of a flagstaff erect ppr, therefrom flowing to the dexter a flag gu, charged with a naval coronet of the second

Plumstead of Plumstead Norf out of a ducal coronet or, a griffin's head arg. 67 9

Plumstock, a goat's head erased arg, armed or, charged with a chevron gu cf 128 5

Plumtre, Charles John of Fredville Kent, a phœnix or, in flames ppr *Sufficit meruisse* 82 2

Plumtree, Notts, a phœnix or, in flames ppr *Sufficit meruisse*—*Turpi secernare honestum* 82 2

Plumtree, a phœnix in flames ppr 82 2

Plunket, Baron (Plunket), Private Secretary's Lodge, Phœnix Park Dublin and of Newton co Cork a horse passant arg, charged on the shoulder with a portcullis sa *Festina lente* cf 52 6

Plunket or **Plunkett,** Ireland, a horse passant arg 52 6

Plunkett, Sir Francis Richard, K C M G, British Legation, Brussels, same crest *Festina lente*

Plunkett, *see* Fingall Earl of

Plunkett, *see* Louth Baron of

Plunkett, *see* Dunsany Baron

Plunkett, a wolf sejant ppr cf 29 3

Plunkett, a greyhound's head between two rose-slips 61 11

Plunkett of Dublin a dove arg, holding in the beak an olive-branch ppr 92 5

Plymouth, Earl of (Andrews Windsor), a buck's head affrontee couped at the neck arg attired or *Je me fie en Dieu* 119 12

Pocher, a harpy gardant with wings expanded ppr 189 4

Pochin, William Ann of Edmondthorpe Hall, Leics, a harpy with wings addorsed or, the face ppr

Pochin, Captain the Hon Norman Vansittart Stonhurst, Burnmill Hill Great Bowden, Market Harborough, same crest

Poching and **Pocher,** a harpy with wings addorsed or, the face ppr

Pockley of Thorpe Willoughby, Yorks, a dove with wings displayed arg holding in her beak an oak-branch slipped vert 94 5

Pocklington, Lieutenant Colonel George Henry the Barnards, Chelsworth, Bildeston, Suff, a demi-leopard rampant ppr, holding in the dexter paw an ostrich feather arg cf 23 14

Pocock, an antelope's head erased ppr, attired or 126 2

Pocock of Westminster and Durh out of a naval coronet or, an antelope's head ppr attired of the first *Regi regnoque fidelis* 127 6

Pocock, Sir George Francis Coventry Bart, of Hart Durh, issuing out of a naval coronet or, an antelope's head ppr, attired or *Regi regnoque fidelis* 127 6

Pode of Slade Devonsh, issuing out of clouds ppr a demi eagle az, collared or the wings elevated arg, charged on the breast and on each wing with an etoile counterchanged *Altiora sequimui*

Podmore, Ireland, out of a mural coronet arg, a hand ppr, holding a record or roll of parchment of the first cf 215 6

Poe, Arthur, Harley Park Callan, Tipperary a boar's head erased pierced through by a spear, all ppr *Malo mori quam fœdari*

Poer-Trench, Le, *see* Clancarty Earl of

Poger, a demi-eagle displayed with two heads sa, collared or cf 82 3

Poigndester of London, an esquire's helmet ppr 180 3

Poingdester, Jersey, same crest *Nemo me impune lacessit* 180 3

Pointer, a dexter arm bendways vested sa, cuffed or, pointing with the fore-finger ppr

Pointer, a talbot passant ppr 54 1

Pointer, a pointer or cf 57 6

Pointing, a horse's head erased or charged on the neck with a cross patée sa cf 51 4

Points, an arm couped above the wrist, the hand clenched ppr

Polden, a buck trippant ppr attired or *Clariores e tenebris* 117 8

Pole or **De la Pole, Baron de la Pole, Earl of Pembroke and Duke of Suffolk,** a savage's head couped at the shoulders ppr, banded or studded az cf 190 13

Pole-Carew, Charles Edward, of Ceylon a mast of a ship sa, on the round top a demi lion of the last, surrounded with spears ppr

Pole-Carew, Rev Gerald, of Cheviocke Rectory, St Germains same crest and motto

Pole-Carew, Major General Sir Reginald, K C B C V O, of Antony House, Torr Point, Devonport, same crest and motto

Pole, *see* Wellesley Pole

Pole, Sir Edmund Reginald Talbot de la Bart, of Shute House, Devonsh a lion's gamb erased gu, armed or *Pollet virtus* 36 4

Pole, a lion's gamb sa cf 36 4

Pole, Devonsh, out of a ducal coronet or, a griffin's head az, beaked or *Pollet virtus* 67 9

Pole, an eagle rising ppr 77 5

Pole, Bart, Hants, an eagle rising ppr, charged on the breast with a mullet az *Pollet virtus* cf 77 5

Pole, Baron Montagu, an eagle or, preying on a fish ppr 79 14

Pole, Notten-, Sir Cecil Percy Van Bart, of Todenham House Glouc (1) An eagle rising ppr charged with a mullet for difference (*for Pole*) 312 13 (2) A snake in pale wavy the upper half az., the lower sa., between two wings per fesse az. and arg., counterchanged (*for Van Notten*). *Pollet virtus.—Prudens sicut serpens.* 312. 14

Pole, Derbysh., a hawk with wings expanded and distended ppr., belled and jessed or. 87. 1

Pole, Chandos-, Reginald Walkelyne, of Radbourn, Derbysh.: (1) A falcon rising ppr., belled and jessed or. 88. 2 (2) A knight's head in chain armour. (3) A goat passant arg. *cf.* 129. 5

Polewheele or **Polwhill,** Cornw., a bull passant gu., armed or. *cf.* 45. 2

Poley, Weller-, John George, of Boxted Hall, Suff.: (1) A lion rampant sa., collared and chained or (*for Poley*). (2) A greyhound's head erased sa., in his mouth a rose gu., stalked vert (*for Weller*). *Fortior est qui se.* 1. 3

Poley, a lion rampant per pale or and sa., collared and chained or. 1. 3

Polhill, a bear statant, muzzled, collared, and lined, the line reflexed over the back. *cf.* 34. 1

Polhill or **Pollhill,** Beds and London, out of a mural coronet or, a hind's head ppr., between two acorn-branches vert, fructed of the first.

Polhill-Turner, Rev. Arthur Twistleton, Pachow, Szechuen, same crest.

Polhill-Turner, Frederick Edward Fiennes, Howbury Hall, near Bedford, same crest.

Polhill-Turner, Cecil Henry, Sinins, Kausah, near Thibet, same crest.

Polkinghorne of Polkinghorne, Cornw., an arm in armour embowed holding in the hand a battle-axe, all ppr. *cf.* 200. 6

Pollack, Scotland, a boar passant vulned in the body by an arrow. 40. 14

Pollalion, out of a ducal coronet or, a lion's head. 17. 5

Pollard, a stag trippant arg. 117. 8

Pollard, Oxon., Worcs., Devonsh., and Cornw., a stag trippant arg., attired or. 117. 8

Pollard, Rear-Admiral Edwin John, of Haynford Hall, near Norwich, a stag trippant ppr., gorged with a naval coronet, and charged on the shoulder with a cross fleury or. *Fortiter Deo juvante.*

Pollard-Urquhart: (1) A demi-otter rampant ppr., crowned with an antique crown and collared or, the collar charged with three crescents gu. (*for Urquhart*). (2) A stag trippant arg., attired or (*for Pollard*). 117. 8. (3) Out of a mural coronet arg., a greyhound's head sa., gorged with a collar gu., charged with three plates (*for Hampson*). *cf.* 61. 6

Pollard-Urquhart, Lieutenant-Colonel Francis Edward Romulus, Castle Pollard, Westmeath, same crests.

Pollard of Pollard Hall, Durh., and of Brunton and Bierley, Yorks, a falchion erect arg., the grip vert, hilt and pommel or.

Pollen, a pelican in her piety ppr. 98. 8

Pollen, a pelican in her piety or, the nest ppr. 98. 8

Pollen, Sir Richard Hungerford, Bart., of Rodbourne, Malmesbury, Wilts, a pelican in her piety with wings expanded and in her nest per pale or and az., vulning herself ppr., charged on the wing with a lozenge arg., thereon an escallop sa.

Pollen, Boileau-, of Little Bookham, Surrey, same crest. *De tout mon cœur.*

Pollett, an arm in armour embowed holding in the hand a sword, all ppr. 195. 2

Pollexfen, Captain John James, of Bombay, India, upon a mount vert, two swords in saltire ppr., in front of a quiver erect or, filled with arrows arg. *Semper fidelis.*

Polley or **Pooley,** Suff., a lion rampant sa., collared and chained or. *cf.* 1. 3

Polleyne of Kings Weston, Glouc.: (1) A hound couchant or. 54. 11. (2) On a mount vert, a hound current arg., collared and lined, and the line tied in a knot sa.

Pollington, Viscount, see Mexborough, Earl of.

Pollock, Montagu-, Sir Montagu Frederic, Bart., of Hatton, Middx.: (1) A boar passant quarterly or and vert, pierced through the sinister shoulder with an arrow ppr. 312. 10. (2) A lion rampant guardant arg., adorned with an Eastern crown or, holding with his dexter paw in bend an Afghan banner displayed gu., bordered or and vert, the staff broken in two, and in his sinister paw a part of the broken staff, and in an escroll over the same *Afghanistan.* (3) A griffin's head couped erminois, wings endorsed and collared ermines, and in an escroll over the same *Spectemur agendo. Audacter et strenue.* 312. 11

Pollock, Robert Erskine, K.C., Avening Court, Avening, Glouc.: A boar passant quarterly or and vert, pierced through the sinister shoulder with an arrow ppr. *Audacter et strenue.*

Pollock, Walter Herries, 13, Old Square, Lincoln's Inn, W.C., same crests and motto.

Pollock, Rev. Herbert Charles, M.A., same crests and motto.

Pollock, George, Esquire, of Rhindmuir, Lanarksh., a boar passant pierced with a dart bendways or. *Audacter et strenue.* 40. 14

Pollock, an open book. *Delectatio mea.* 158. 3

Pollock, an étoile of eight points or. *cf.* 164. 4

Pollock, a castle triple-towered arg. 155. 8

Pollock, Rev. Bertram, D.D., Master of Wellington College, Berks, a boar passant, pierced in the shoulder with a dart bendways or. *Audacter et strenue.*

Pollock, A. Gordon, Esquire, the Old House, Mickleham, Dorking, a boar passant, quarterly or and vert, pierced through the sinister shoulder with an arrow ppr., guttée and langued gu. *Audacter et strenue.* 314. 2

Pollok, see Ferguson-Pollok.

Pollok, of Overpollock, Renfrewsh., a boar passant pierced through with a dart ppr. *Audacter et strenue.* 40. 14

Pollok-Morris of Craig, Ayrsh.: (1) A lion rampant ppr. (*for Morris*). 1. 13 (2) A wild boar pierced with a dart ppr. (*for Pollok*). *Fide et fortitudine.—Audacter et strenue.* 40. 14

Polson, the late John, a garb ppr. *In ardua tendit.* 232. 6

Polson, late John, a garb ppr. *In ardua tendit.*

Polstrod of Westeley and Albury, Surrey, out of a ducal coronet or, a boar's head and neck sa. 41. 4

Poltimore, Baron (Bampfylde) Poltimore, near Exeter, a lion's head erased sa., ducally crowned or. *Delectare in Domino.* 18. 8

Polton, a hand holding a swan's head and neck erased ppr. 220. 9

Polwarth, Baron (Hepburne-Scott), Mertoun House, St. Boswell's, Berwicksh.: (1) A lady richly attired holding in her dexter hand the sun, in her sinister a half-moon (*for Scott*). 184. 4. (2) A human heart, out of which issues a dexter arm erect grasping a scimitar, all ppr. (*for Hume*). 213. 4. (3) An oak-tree ppr., and in front thereof a horse passant arg., saddled and bridled gu. (*for Hepburne*). *Reparabit cornua phœbe.—True to the end.—Fides probata coronat.—Keep trust.*

Polwhele, Thomas Roxburgh, of Polwhele and Treworgan, Cornw.: (1) A negro's head holding in the mouth an olive-branch. (2) A bull gu., armed or. *Karanza whilas Karanza.* 45. 2

Polwhele, Rev. Edward, Saltash, Cornw., a bull gu., horned or.

Pomeroy, Viscount Harberton, see Harberton.

Pomeroy, a lion's head erased bezantée, ducally crowned ppr. 18. 9

Pomeroy and **Pomery,** Devonsh., and of St. Columb, Cornw., out of a ducal coronet or, a lion's head gardant gu.

Pomeroy, Ireland, a lion rampant gu., holding an apple. *cf.* 1. 13

Pomeroy, John Arthur, St. Angelo, Bally Cassidy, co. Fermanagh, same crest. *Virtutis fortuna comes.*

Pomeroy, a lion sejant gu., holding in his dexter paw an apple or.

Pomeroy, Ireland, a demi-lion vert. 10. 2

Pomeroy of Chalfont St. Giles, Bucks, a fir-cone vert, charged with a bezant. 152. 6

Pomeroy of Epping, a fir-cone erect ppr., charged with a fret or, between two fir-sprigs, also ppr.

Pomery of Berry Pomeroy, Devonsh., and Cornw., same crest.

Pomfree, an arm in armour holding in the hand a sword. 210. 2

Pomfret, Earl of (Fermor), out of a ducal coronet or, a cock's head gu., crested and wattled of the first. *Hora e sempre.* 90. 6

Pomfret, William Pomfret, Mystole, Canterbury: (1) In front of a dexter arm embowed in armour encircled above the elbow with a wreath of oak, the hand grasping a battle-axe, all ppr., two fleurs-de-lis gu. (*for Pomfret*). (2) In front of a griffin's head erased sa., semée of annulets or, a fret of the last (*for Burra*).

Pomfrett, a swan's head and neck erased, ducally gorged. 101. 5

Pomfrett, a dexter hand holding a battle-axe ppr. 213. 12

Ponchardon, a unicorn's head erased gu bezantee, armed or cf 49 5

Pondrell, a fox current ppr cf 32 8

Ponpons, three pruning hooks, two in saltier and one in pale, or, environed in the middle with a wreath 178 12

Ponsford of Exeter Devonsh, a lion sejant erect regardant gu, crowned arg charged on the neck with three escal lops or, holding between the paws an anchor of the last

Ponsonby, Earl of Besborough, *see* Besborough

Ponsonby, *see* De Mauley, Baron

Ponsonby-Barker, *see* Barker

Ponsonby-Fane, *see* Fane

Ponsonby, *see* Talbot Ponsonby

Ponsonby, Ireland, and of Hale Hall, Haugh, Cumb, on a ducal coronet or three arrows environed by a snake ppr 173 2

Ponsonby, Thomas Brabazon, Kilcooley Abbey, Thurles, co Tipperary, same crest *Pro Rege lege, grege*

Ponsonby, Edward-, Viscount Duncannon C B, 17 Cavendish Square W, out of a ducal coronet five arrows one in pale and two in saltire points downwards, entwined with a snake ppr *Pro Rege, lege grege*

Ponsonby-Fane, Sir Spencer Cecil Brabazon, K C B, Stable Yard St James's, S W (1) Out of a ducal coronet or, a bull's head arg pied sa, charged on the neck with a rose gu (2) Five arrows one in pale and four in saltire, points downwards or, entwined with a snake ppr

Ponsonby, Ireland on a ducal coronet or a serpent ppr pierced through with five darts fretty gu *Pro Rege, lege, grege*

Pont of Shyr's Mill, Scotland, a sphere az beautified with six of the celestial signs environing the terrestrial globe all ppr *Perenne sub polo nihil*

Ponten, a lion's gamb erased sa charged with an escallop arg

Pontifex, a tower ensigned with a crescent gu 156 4

Pontifex, late Edmund, Esquire, of Bath, a tower ppr, charged with a cross moline az, and surmounted by a rainbow, also ppr *In hoc signo vinces* 255 8

Pontifex, Edmund Alfred 72, Cornwall Gardens, South Kensington, same crest and motto

Ponton, Scotland, a tree ppr *Stand sure* 143 5

Pool or Poole, Essex Staffs and Derbysh, a hawk with wings expanded ppr 87 1

Pool, Chesh, and of New Shoreham Sussex a mermaid in profile ppr, holding in the hands a Saxon coronet or

Poole of Waltham, Essex a unicorn passant az, tufted maned, and armed or, ducally gorged arg cf 48 6

Poole, Chesh and Ireland, a mermaid ppr, crined or, holding in both hands a naval coronet or

Poole, Bart (*extinct*) of Poole, Chesh, a bull s head cabossed gu, armed barry of five az and or the sinister horn counterchanged *Pollet virtus* 43 8

Poole, Ireland a falcon rising arg 88 2

Poole, Henry Skeffington, F G S Halifax, Nova Scotia, out of a ducal coronet or a griffin's head az, beaked and eared of the first *Pro libertate*

Poole, Reginald of Mackay, Queensland, same crest and motto

Poole, Colonel Arthur, United Service Club same crest and motto

Poole, R, Esquire, Mayfield Bandon, Cork, same crest *Pollet virtus*

Pooler, Rev James Galbraith, incumbent of Newtownards co Down, Ireland, a falcon rising ppr, belled or, and charged on the breast with a lozenge gu *Vi et virtute* cf 88 2

Pooler, Rev Lewis Arthur Trevor, B D Downpatrick, co Down, a falcon rising ppr belled or, and charged on the breast with a lozenge gu *Vi et virtute*

Pooler, Rev C F Knox, same crest and motto

Pooley, Chesh and Suff a lion rampant sa, collared and lined or cf 1 3

Pooley of the Cedars, Sion Hill, Bath, a lion rampant sa, collared and lined or

Pooll, Henry-Batten-, Robert Pooll, Esquire, J P, of Timsbury and Road Manor, Somers, in front of a griffin's head erased erm armed and langued gu, and charged on the neck with a fountain a battle axe fesswise ppr *Confide recte agens* 226 11

Pooly, Ireland a lion rampant sa, collared or cf 1 10

Poor of Darrington, Wilts, a tower sa, masoned arg 156 2

Poore, Ireland, a stag's head cabossed, between the attires a crucifix all ppr 122 13

Poore, Sir Richard Bart of Rushall Wilts a cubit arm erect vested sa slashed arg, cuffed erm charged with two mullets in fesse or grasping in the hand an arrow barbed and flighted ppr *Pauper non in spe*

Pope, a demi-lion vert 10 2

Pope of Wilcote Wroxton, and Dedington, Oxon and Tittenhanger Herts, two griffin's heads erased and addorsed or and az, ducally gorged counterchanged

Pope, Alfred, J P, of Wrackleford House, Stratton, Dorset, and South Court, Dorchester same crest

Pope, of the Middle Temple, E C out of park pales or, two gryphons' heads addorsed sa gorged with an annulet or

Pope, Berks and Ireland a heraldic tiger passant or, tufted and maned sa 25 5

Pope, Cornw a griffin passant arg collared gu cf 63 2

Pope of London an heraldic tiger passant or, collared and lined sa cf 25 5

Pope of Hendall, Sussex on a chapeau gu, turned up erm, an heraldic tiger statant arg, tufted, maned, collared, ringed, and lined or

Pope, Shropsh, a cubit arm erect, habited gu, cuffed arg, holding in the hand ppr a pair of scales or *Mihi tibi*

Pope, Shropsh, the same, but cuffed erm

Pope, General George, C B a demi-lion rampant gu, gorged with an antique coronet or, and holding in the dexter paw a key in bend of the last *Fideliter et fortiter*

Popham, Somers and Wilts a stag's head couped ppr 121 5

Popham of Popham, Hants Middx and of Huntworth and Bagborough Somers, a stag's head erased ppr 121 2

Popham, Leybourne-, of Littlecote, Wilts, same crest *Mens pristina mansit* 121 2

Popingay of Portsmouth a lion's head per pale or and az, ducally crowned, semee of roundles all counterchanged 18 9

Popkin, Scotland a hand holding a writing-pen ppr 217 10

Poppelwell, a lion rampant ppr *Non nobis nascimur* 1 13

Popplewell, a demi-lioness rampant ppr

Popplewell, a falcon belled vert, between two gilliflowers ppr

Porcelli-Cust, Lieutenant Colonel Allan Roger Charles 13 Great Stanhope Street, W a lion's head erased sa, collared paly wavy of six arg and az, and charged on the neck with a cross crosslet arg

Porch, John Albert of Edgarley, Glastonbury, Somers (1) On a mount vert a wolf passant holding in the mouth an arrow, barb downwards, and in the dexter paw a bow stringed, all ppr (*for Porch*) 280 7 (2) On a mount an eagle with wings expanded resting the dexter claw on a cross flory *Cordi dat robora virtus* 280 8

Porch, Montague Phippin B A, Kewstoke near Weston-super Mare, same crests and motto

Porcher of Snare Hill Norf Borough Green, Cambs, and Clyffe Dorset, a lion rampant or, charged with three bars gu, holding between the paws a cinquefoil erm *Pro Rege*

Porchester, Lord, *see* Carnarvon, Earl of

Pordage, Kent a dragon's head erased or vomiting flames of fire ppr 72 5

Porritt, a demi heraldic antelope gu, plain collared or resting the sinister foot upon an escutcheon of the last charged with a lion's head erased gu (*Granted to William Henry Porritt Esquire, of Armley, Yorkshire, and the other descendants of his father David Wright Porritt, Esquire*) *Fortiter et sapienter ferre* 127 14

Port or Porte, Staffs a hand erect holding a pistol ppr 221 8

Port, an eagle's head erased holding in the beak a cross patee fitched or

Portal, a lion's head erased or 17 8

Portal of Ash Park, Overton Hants a castle arg 155 8

Portal, Sir Wyndham Spencer Bart, of Malshanger, Basingstoke Hants, a castellated portal flanked by two towers arg each tower charged with a fleur de lis in chief az and a wreath of laurel in base vert 305 13

Portal of Laverstoke, Hants a portal flanked by two towers arg each tower charged with a fleur-de lis az *Armet nos ultio regem*

Portal, upon a castellated portal flanked by two towers ppr a fleur de-lis or, and on each tower a rose gu

Portarlington, Earl of (Dawson-Damer), Emo Park, Portarlington: (1) Out of a mural crown or, a talbot's head az., eared or (*for Damer*). 56. 6. (2) A cat's head affrontée erased near the shoulders, of a tabby colour, holding in the mouth a rat sa. (*for Dawson*). *Vitæ via virtus.* 25. 1

Porte, a bird holding in the beak a cross crosslet fitched or. 106. 10

Porteen, a pair of wings expanded, the dexter or, the sinister gu. 109. 6

Porteous of Craig Lockhart, Scotland, a turtle-dove holding an olive-branch in its beak, all ppr. *I wait my time.* 92. 5

Porteous, David Scott, Lauriston Castle, Montrose, a hawk rising ppr., jessed and belled or. *Let the hawk shaw.—Ocius properemus.*

Porteous of Hawkshaw, Scotland, a falcon belled ppr. *Let the hawk shaw.—I byde my time.* cf. 85. 2

Porter, Bart., Merrion Square, Dublin, on a fasces fesseways a cherub, all ppr. 279. 14

Porter of Dublin, a cherub's head ppr. *Fear God, honour the King.* 189. 9

Porter, Sir William Henry, Bart., of Merrion Square, Dublin, in front of two cross crosslets fitchée in saltire or, a cherub ppr. *Fear God, honour the King.* 244. 13

Porter of Etington, Warw., a portcullis arg., chained or. 178. 3

Porter, Thomas Cole, Trematon Castle, Saltash, Cornw., same crest. *Vigilantibus.*

Porter, Thomas Stewart, Esquire, a portcullis ppr., therefrom pendent by a chain or a shield of the arms, viz.: sa., three bells arg., a canton of the last charged with a portcullis ppr. *Et fide et virtute.* 178. 1

Porter, John Porter, Esquire, same crest and motto. 178. 1

Porter, H. R. M., Esquire, of Birlingham, Pershore, Worcs.: (1) Upon a mount vert, in front of a portcullis with chains or, a tilting-spear fessewise ppr. (*for Porter*). 178. 2. (2) A demi-lion sa., gorged with a collar or, and pendent therefrom an escutcheon of the same charged with two escallops palewise of the first, and holding between the paws a ducal coronet of the second (*for Taylor*). *Quod vult valde vult.* 14. 5

Porter, Lincs. and of St. Margarets-in-Southernam, Suff., a portcullis arg., nailed and chained or, the chains cast over in fret.

Porter-Burrall of Coppenagh, in the parish of Lurgan and Diocese of Kilmore: (1) A naked arm embowed, holding in the hand two wreaths of oak interlaced, all ppr. (*for Burrall*). (2) A portcullis with chains or, charged with two bells in fesse sa. (*for Porter*). *Otium cum dignitate.*

Porter of Aston, Warw., between two pillars roofed and spired or, a church-bell arg.

Porter of Claines, Worcs., a squirrel sejant holding a bell sa., garnished or.

Porter, a demi-squirrel or, semée of hurts, holding an acorn-branch vert, fructed or.

Porter, Edward Robert, Esquire, of London, an heraldic antelope's head erased arg., attired or, gorged with a collar gu., therefrom on the centre of the neck a bell pendent sa., charged with an ermine spot of the first. 127. 11

Porter, an heraldic antelope's head erased, ducally gorged. cf. 127. 10

Porter, an heraldic antelope's head couped, ducally gorged. cf. 127. 10

Porter, a demi-antelope or, spotted, collared and attired gu. 126. 3

Porter, a stag's head erased arg., attired and ducally gorged or, between two laurel-branches vert.

Porter of Waterford, Ireland, a stag's head couped sa., attired or. 121. 5

Porter of Launcells, Cornw., a demi-goat erect. 128. 2

Porter, Warw., a bull's head couped gu., armed or. cf. 44. 3

Porter, Hants, a dragon's head couped gu. 71. 1

Porter of Troquain, Kirkcudbrightsh., Scotland, a dexter arm in armour embowed, holding in the hand a sword, all ppr. *Vigilantia et virtute.* 195. 2

Porter, Ireland, a cubit arm habited az., cuffed arg., grasping in the hand a battle-axe ppr. cf. 207. 10

Porterfield of that ilk, Renfrewsh., Scotland, a branch of palm slipped erect vert. *Sub pondere sursum.* 147. 1

Portington, Lincs and Yorks, a dexter hand holding a dart, point downwards. 214. 4

Portland, Duke of (Cavendish-Bentinck), Welbeck Abbey, Worksop, Notts: (1) Out of a marquess's coronet or, two arms counter-embowed vested gu., on the hands gloves, also or, each holding an ostrich-feather arg. (*for Bentinck*). cf. 203. 2. (2) A snake nowed ppr. (*for Cavendish*). *Craignez honte.* 142. 4

Portlock, an ostrich holding in the beak two keys ppr. cf. 97. 2

Portman, Viscount (Portman), of Orchard Portman, Somers.: (1) A talbot sejant or (*for Portman*). 55. 2. (2) A unicorn passant gu., armed and crined or. *A clean heart and a cheerful spirit.* cf. 48. 5

Portman, Somers., a talbot sejant or. 55. 2

Portman, Somers., a leopard's face or, with a cross crosslet fitched run through the skull and out of the mouth, between two snake's heads downwards ppr.

Portman-Dalton, Seymour Berkeley, J.P., 18, Eccleston Square, S.W.: (1) A dragon's head with wings displayed vert, outside of the wings or, gorged with a collar nebuly of the last, and charged with a cross patée arg. (2) A talbot sejant or.

Portmore, Earl, a unicorn rampant. 4. 28

Portsmouth, Earl of (Wallop), of Farley Wallop, co. Southampton, a mermaid holding in her sinister hand a mirror, and in her dexter a comb, all ppr. *En suivant la vérité.* 184. 5

Posingworth, Possingworth, and **Posyngworth,** out of a ducal coronet or, a plume of ostrich-feathers ppr. cf. 114. 8

Postlethwaite, on a ducal coronet or, a boar's head sa., couped gu.

Postlethwaite, George Burrow, Esquire, B.A., of Yewhurst, Bickley, Kent, and 14, Gray's Inn Square, W.C., on a ducal coronet or, a boar's head erased close sa.

Postlethwaite of the Oaks, Cumb., out of a ducal coronet or, a boar's head sa. *Semper paratus.* 41. 4

Poston, a demi-lion or, supporting an arch gu.

Posynworth, a lion's head erased gu., collared or. 18. 6

Potkin of Rickmansworth, Herts, Sevenoaks, Kent, and Cambs, a stag's head erased sa., attired or, the nose arg. 121. 2

Pott, a tower ppr., and on the battlements thereof a crescent arg. 156. 4

Pott and **Potts** of London and Norf., a leopard sejant ppr., collared, lined, and ringed az. 24. 8

Pott, Chesh., a wild cat sejant, collared and chained or. cf. 26. 13

Pott, Chesh., and of Stancliffe, Derbysh., on a mount vert, a greyhound couchant gu., collared and ringed or

Pott, Henry Percy, Borthwickshields House, Hawick, N.B., a leopard sejant ppr., collared, lined, and ringed or. *Vive ut vivas.*

Pott of Woodside, Windlesham, an ounce sejant ppr., collared and chained or. *Fortis et astutus.*

Potter, Somers., Devonsh., Oxon., and Kent, a sea-horse or. 46. 2

Potter, William, Esquire, of Liverpool, in front of a cross crosslet fitchée gu., a sea-horse or.

Potter of Buile Hill, Manchester, on a mount vert, a sea-horse erect ppr., gorged with a collar gemel sa., and supporting a rudder or. 46. 1

Potter, Thomas Bayley, 31, Courtfield Gardens, S.W., same crest. *Virtuti fortuni comes.*

Potter, a star of twelve rays or, between two wings arg.

Potter, Norf., an elephant's head erased arg., guttée-de-sang. cf. 133. 3

Pottinger, Sir Henry, Bart., J.P., D.L., a dexter arm embowed in armour ppr., garnished or, the hand gauntleted and grasping a sword, also ppr., hilted and pommelled or, the arm encircled by an Eastern coronet gu. *Virtus in ardua.* cf. 195. 1

Pottinger of Mount Pottinger, Devonsh., a dexter arm in armour embowed ppr., garnished or, the hand gauntleted and grasping a sword, also ppr., hilted and pommelled of the second, the arm encircled by an Eastern coronet gu. *Virtus in ardua.* cf. 195. 1

Pottman, a fleur-de-lis gu. 148. 2

Potts-Chatto, *see* Chatto.

Potts, a lion's head erased az. 17. 8

Potts, on a mount vert, a greyhound couchant arg. cf. 60. 1

Potts, Bart. (*extinct*), of Mannington, Norf., a leopard sejant ppr., collared, lined, and ringed az. 24. 8

Potts, William Trumperant, same crest. *In vinculis etiam audax.*

Poulain, an eagle displayed gu. 75. 2

Poulden, a hand issuing from a cloud holding a book expanded. 215. 1

Poulet, a hawk with wings elevated, ducally gorged and belled.
Poulett, Earl, Viscount Hinton, and **Baron Poulett,** of Hinton St. George, Somers., an arm embowed in armour, holding in the hand a sword, all ppr. *Gardez la foi.* 195. 2
Poulett, a unicorn's head vert. 49. 7
Pouley, Essex, within an annulet or, an eagle displayed az.
Poulter, a ship in full sail ppr. 160. 13
Poultney, Leics. and Yorks, a leopard's head gardant erased sa., gorged with a ducal coronet or.
Poultney, a leopard's head gardant erased sa.
Poulton, an anchor and cable sa. 161. 2
Pound of Drayton, Hants, a castle ppr. 155. 8
Pound of London, same crest. *Firma durant.* 155. 8
Pound, A. J., Esquire, United University Club, a boar's head couped close. *Fidus et audax.*
Pount, Scotland, a buck's head cabossed ppr., attired or. *Dum spiro, spero.* 122. 5
Pountney, a leopard's head and neck erased. 23. 10
Pourie, Powrie, and **Purie,** Scotland, a hunting-horn az., garnished gu. *Vespere et mane.* 228. 11
Povey, a bugle-horn sa., verruled or, stringed gu. 228. 11
Povey of London, out of a mural coronet or, a griffin's head ppr., charged with an annulet for difference. *cf.* 67. 10
Powe, a crescent az. 163. 2
Powell, *see* Sweetman-Powell.
Powell, Surrey, a lion rampant arg., holding a garb vert.
Powell, Shropsh., a lion rampant sa. *Omne bonum Dei donum.* 1. 10
Powell, Bart., Shropsh.: (1) A lion rampant sa., armed and langued gu. (*for Powell*). 1. 10. (2) A dexter arm embowed in armour, the hand ppr. grasping a sword arg., hilted or, all on a sun in splendour ppr. (*for Kynaston*).
Powell, Sir Francis Sharp, Bart., of Horton Old Hall, Bradford, Yorks, a lion rampant sa., gorged with a double chain or, therefrom pendent a pheon arg., and resting the sinister fore-paw on an escutcheon of the second, charged with an eagle's head erased az. *Omne bonum Dei donum.* 3. 12
Powell, Jeffreys-, of Broynllis, Brecknsh.: (1) A lion rampant arg., holding between the paws a garb vert, and supporting with the dexter hind-paw an escutcheon sa., charged with a boar's head, also arg. (*for Powell*). (2) Upon the stump of a tree between two palm-branches ppr., a heron arg., holding in the beak a spear-head ppr. (*for Jeffreys*). *Labore et scientia.*
Powell of Newicke, Sussex, a lion passant or, holding in the dexter paw the broken shaft of a spear in pale ppr.
Powell of Bruton, Somers., a lion passant, resting the dexter paw on a broken tilting-spear arg.
Powell, Nathanael, Luctons, Buckhurst Hill, Essex, a lion passant or, in the paw a broken tilting-spear in bend ppr., therefrom by a ribbon gu. an escutcheon resting on the wreath sa., charged with a pheon or.
Powell, Charles Watson, Speldhurst, Tunbridge Wells, same crest.
Powell, Rev. Clement, the Rectory, Newick, Sussex, same crest.
Powell, same crest. *Edrych i fynw.*
Powell, Hubert John, Lewes, Sussex, same crest.
Powell, James Crofts, 13, Chester Street, Grosvenor Place, S.W., same crest.
Powell, Reginald Henry, Lewes, Sussex, same crest.
Powell, Arthur Crofts, Esquire, J.P., of Milton Heath, Dorking, a lion passant or, holding in the dexter paw a broken tilting-spear in bend ppr., pendent therefrom by a riband gu. an escutcheon resting on the wreath sa., charged with a pheon or. *Ar nid yw puyil pydyw.*
Powell, a lion statant regardant, pierced through the chest by an arrow in bend, point downwards.
Powell, a demi-lion rampant. 10. 2
Powell of Castle Madoc, a lion's head erased arg., gorged with a collar flory-counter-flory gu. *Anima in amicis una.* *cf.* 18. 6
Powell, Sir Richard Douglas, Bart., K.C.V.O., M.D., 62, Wimpole Street, W., same crest.
Powell, William Folliott, Esquire, Sharow Hall, Ripon, a lion's head erased arg., gorged with a collar flory gu. *Anima in amicis una.*
Powell, Rev. Charles Thomas, M.A., 3, College Yard, Worcs., a lion's gamb erased gu., surmounted by a rose of the last, stalked, leaved, and slipped saltireways ppr. *Per devias vias.*
Powell, Robert Henry Wynyard, M.D., Ottawa, Canada, the sun or, above clouds ppr. *Aude.*
Powell of Fulham, Middx., and St. James's, Clerkenwell, a lion's head erased gu. 17. 2
Powell of Penkelly, Heref., a lion's gamb erased or. 36. 4
Powell of Hurdcott House, Wilts, a lion's gamb erect and erased gu. *Spes mea Christus erit.* 36. 4
Powell of Hinton, Heref., and St. Albans, Herts, out of a ducal coronet or, a demi-griffin sa., beaked and armed of the first. 64. 4
Powell, Lieutenant-Colonel Henry Claringbold, J.P., of Banlahan, co. Cork, Ireland, out of a ducal coronet or, a demi-griffin vert, charged on the shoulder with a trefoil slipped or. *Edrych i fynw* *cf.* 64. 4
Powell of London, out of a ducal coronet or, a demi-griffin sa. 64. 4
Powell, Heref., out of a ducal coronet or, a demi-griffin sa., beaked and legged of the first. 64. 4
Powell, a boar passant sa., collared and lined or.
Powell of Llwydarth, Lanharen, and Maesteg, Glamorgansh., Wales, a boar's head. 43. 1
Powell, Wales, a Saracen's head affrontée, couped at the shoulders ppr., wreathed about the temples arg. and sa. 190. 5
Powell and **Powel,** a demi-savage holding in his dexter hand a club. 186. 5
Powell, Wales, a talbot's head ppr. 56. 12
Powell, William Beauclerk, Nanteos, Aberyswyth, a talbot's head ppr., collared.
Powell, Wales, a talbot's head couped arg., collared and ringed or. *cf.* 56. 1
Powell, of Nanteos, Cardigansh., a talbot's head couped ppr. *Inter hastas et hostes.* 56. 12
Powell of Rock Dale, Kent, two arrows in saltire ppr., thereon a sparrow-hawk arg., holding in the beak a sprig of oak slipped fructed, vert.
Powell, Shropsh., an estoile. 164. 1
Powell, a spear broken in two pieces, the upper part in bend surmounted by the lower in bend sinister, all within two branches of laurel disposed orleways vert.
Power, Viscount Valentia (*extinct*), a demi-stag salient sa., attired and unguled or. 110. 2
Power, Scotland, a stag's head, and between the attires a cross patée. *Per crucem ad coronam.* 120. 9
Power, a stag's head cabossed ppr., attired or, and between the attires a crucifix, also ppr. 122. 13
Power-Lalor of Long Orchard, co. Tipperary: (1) A arm embowed vested gu., cuffed vert, the hand grasping a sword ppr. (*for Lalor*). 204. 1. (2) A stag's head cabossed ppr., attired or, and between the attires a crucifix ppr. (*for Power*). 122. 13
Power, Sir James Douglas Talbot, Bart., of Edermine, co. Wexford, a buck's head cabossed quarterly gu. and or, between the attires counterchanged a cross calvary erect gu. *Per crucem ad coronam.* *cf.* 122. 5
Power of Corbeen, co. Galway, a buck's head cabossed arg., attired or, and between the attires a crucifix ppr. 122. 13
Power of Roskeen, co. Cork, same crest. *Per crucem ad coronam.* 122. 13
Power, Mandeville-, of Wilmar, co. Tipperary, Ireland, a stag's head cabossed arg., attired or, between the attires a cross Calvary of the first, thereon a representation of the Crucifixion ppr. *Per crucem ad coronam.* 122. 13
Power, a stag's head cabossed ppr., attired or, on the top of the scalp a cross botonnée gu. *cf.* 122. 5
Power, a buck's head cabossed ppr., between the attires a cross gu., surmounting an escallop arg. *cf.* 122. 5
Power, Sir Adam Clayton, Bart., J.P., D.L., of Kilfane, co. Kilkenny, a stag's head erased ppr. *Pro patriâ semper.* 121. 2
Power, Ambrose William Bushe, J.P., Glencairn Abbey, Lismore, Ireland, same crest and motto.
Power, Manley Kingsmill Manley, of the Hill Court, near Ross, Heref., issuant from a mural coronet or, a stag's head sa., gorged with a laurel-wreath, and attired of the first. *Angelis suis præcipiet de te.*
Power-Lalor, George Richard, Long Orchard, Templemore, Ireland: (1) An arm embowed vested gu., cuffed

vert, the hand ppr. grasping a short sword, also ppr. (*for Lalor*). (2) A stag's head affrontée or, between the horns a crucifix ppr. (*for Power*). *Fortis et fidelis.*
Power, Oxon., a buck's head couped sa., attired or. 121. 5
Power of Kilbolane, co. Cork, Ireland, a stag's head couped sa. 121. 5
Power, Ireland, an antelope's head erased, the neck transfixed by a spear, all ppr. 127. 1
Power, a dexter hand ppr., holding a close helmet az. 217. 12
Power, Henry, M.B., Bagdale Hall, Whitby, an arm vambraced embowed, grasping a sword, all ppr., charged with a cross crosslet az. *Un Dieu, un Roy.*
Powers, a stag's head couped ppr., charged on the neck with a trefoil vert. *cf.* 121. 8
Powerscourt, Viscount (Wingfield), Powerscourt, near Enniskerry, co. Wicklow, a demi-eagle rising with wings expanded arg., looking at the sun in its splendour. *Fidélité est de Dieu.*
Powerton, Essex, a hand ppr., holding a spur or. 217. 14
Powis, Earl of (Herbert), Powis Castle, Welshpool, a wyvern vert, holding in the mouth a sinister hand couped at the wrist gu. *Ung je serveray.* 70. 3
Powis, *see* Powys.
Powis, a demi-lion rampant regardant. *Audacter et sincere.* *cf.* 16. 5
Powis, a lion's gamb erased sa., grasping a sceptre or. 38. 7
Powis of Sutton, Shropsh., a lion's gamb erased gu., grasping a sceptre or, on the top a fleur-de-lis. 38. 7
Powle, a demi-savage brandishing a sabre ppr. *cf.* 186. 3
Powle, Essex, a unicorn passant az., armed and maned or. *cf.* 48. 5
Powles, upon a mount vert, in front of two battle-axes in saltire or, a goat statant sa., armed or. *Qualis vita finis ita.*
Powlett, *see* Cleveland, Duke of.
Powlett, *see* Bolton, Baron.
Powlett, Baron Bayning, *see* Bayning.
Powlett of Llandisil, Cardigansh., a falcon rising and belled or, ducally gorged gu. 87. 2
Powlett, Hants, a sphinx statant with wings expanded ppr.
Pownall, a unicorn's head erm. 49. 7
Pownall of Pownall, Chesh., a lion's gamb erect and erased ppr., holding a key or, from which a chain is reflexed of the same. 35. 1
Pownall of London, a lion's gamb erect and erased sa., charged with two roses arg., holding a key in bend sinister, wards downwards, or, from which a chain is entwined about the gamb of the same. *Grace me guide.* 35. 4
Pownall, John Fish, J.P., 63, Russell Square, W.C., same crest and motto.
Pownall of Liverpool, a lion's gamb erased ppr., charged with two mullets in pale arg., holding a key in bend sinister or, and affixed thereto a chain entwined about the gamb of the same. *Officium præsto.* 35. 7
Pownall, Charles Assheton Whateley, 15, St. John's Park, Blackheath, S.E., same crest.
Powney of Old Windsor, Berks, a demi-eagle with wings expanded sa., charged on the breast with a mascle arg. *cf.* 81. 6
Powney, Cecil Du Pre Penton, formerly of Fyfield House, Andover, Hants, in front of a demi-eagle, wings displayed sa., holding in the beak a mascle pierced, three like mascles fessways and interlaced arg. *Pro Rege.*
Powney, Cecil Du Pre Penton, Fyfield House, Andover, Hants, in front of a demi-eagle, wings displayed sa., holding in the beak a mascle pierced, three like mascles fessways and interlaced arg. *Pro Rege.*
Powrie of Woodcocksholme, Scotland, a hunting-horn az., garnished gu. *Vespere et mane.* 228. 11
Powrie of Reswallie, Forfarsh., Scotland, a hunting-horn az., garnished and stringed gu. *Vespere et mane.* 228. 11
Powtrell, a Saracen's head issuing ppr. 190. 14
Powtrell of West Hallam, Derbysh., a hedgehog gu., collared, chained, and quilled or. *cf.* 135. 8
Powys, *see* Lilford, Baron.
Powys-Lybbe, Reginald Cecil Lybbe, a lion's gamb erect and erased gu., holding a sceptre or. *Parta tueri.*
Powys of Hardwick, Oxon., a lion's gamb erect and erased gu., holding a sceptre in bend sinister headed with a fleur-de-lis or.
Powys of Berwick, Shropsh., a lion's gamb erased and erect gu., holding a sceptre headed with a fleur-de-lis or. 38. 7
Powys, Shropsh.: (1) A lion's gamb erased gu., grasping a sceptre or. 38. 7. (2) A man's hand couped at the middle of the arm and erect in armour ppr., grasping a sceptre or.
Powys-Keck, Harry Leycester, the Knoll, Kingston Hill, Surrey: (1) Out of a mural crown gu., a maiden's head erm., purfled or, her hair dishevelled and flotant of the same, adorned with a chaplet vert, and garnished with roses ppr. (*for Keck*). (2) A lion's gamb erased and erect gu., grasping a fleur-de-lis bendways or (*for Powys*). *En Dieu est ma foi.—Parta tueri.*
Poyle of Castlezance, Cornw., a hemp hackle or.
Poynder, Dickson-, Sir John Poynder, Bart., of Hardingham, Norf.: (1) Over an arm in armour embowed, brandishing in the gauntlet a falchion ppr., a trident and a spear in saltire or. 306. 10. (2) Out of a demi-tower arg., charged with a cross patonce gu., a cubit arm erect vested sa., cuffed or, holding in the hand ppr. a cross patée fitched of the first. *Fortes fortuna juvat.* 306. 9
Poynder, Alfred, Esquire, M.A., of 43, Lee Park, Blackheath, S.E., same crest. *En avant poyn d'erreur.*
Poynder, issuant out of the battlements of a castle arg., charged with a cross flory gu., a dexter cubit arm erect vested sa., charged with a key in pale, wards upwards, and to the sinister or, cuffed of the same, the hand ppr. holding a cross patée fitchée in bend, also arg. *cf.* 207. 3
Poyner of Beslow and Shrewsbury, Shropsh., a demi-buck salient ppr., attired or, holding in his feet a chaplet of laurel vert, charged on the shoulder with a bugle-horn stringed or.
Poynes, a demi-leopard ducally gorged ppr. 25. 10
Poynes of North Okingdon, Essex, and Alderley, Glouc., a hand issuing from clouds ppr.
Poynings, Baron Poynings, a dragon's head between two wings displayed. 72. 7. *Badges:* (1) A key erect, wards downwards, surmounted by an antique coronet. (2) A unicorn statant.
Poynings, Dorset, a dragon's head with wings displayed. 72. 7
Poynings, a pomegranate ppr. 152. 4
Poynten, a pelican's nest with young birds ppr. 113. 7
Poynter, Sir Edward John, Bart., 28, Albert Gate, S.W., in front of a cubit arm erect vested gu., encircled by an annulet or, cuffed arg., the hand ppr. holding two crosses patée fitchée in saltire, also or, a mount vert. 272. 1
Poynter, Middx., a cubit arm vested sa., cuffed arg., holding in the hand ppr. a baton in bend ensigned with a cross formée or.
Poynter, a hand holding a baton.
Poynter, Chesh., an arm in bend vested sa., cuffed or, pointing with the forefinger ppr.
Poynton, a stag's head vert. 21. 5
Poyntz, a sword erect ppr. 170. 2
Poyntz and **Poynes,** of Iron Acton, Glouc., of Midgham, Berks, and Cowdray, Sussex, a cubit arm, the fist clenched ppr., vested in a shirt-sleeve arg.
Poyntz of Acton, co. Armagh, Ireland, a cubit arm erect, the fist clenched ppr., vested in a shirt-sleeve arg.
Poyntz of Havant and Bedhampton, Northamp., out of a naval coronet arg., a cubit arm, the hand grasping two flagstaves in saltire ppr., and flowing from either a French tricolor flag, that on the dexter inscribed *Tiburon,* and that on the sinister *Impeteaux,* in letters of gold. 221. 5
Poyntz-Stewart, Charles, J.P., Chesfield Park, Stevenage, Herts, a man's head couped ppr. *Never unprepared.*
Poyser of London, a stag's head erased gu., attired or, holding in the mouth an olive-branch fructed ppr., charged on the neck with an Eastern crown or.
Poyser, Arthur Horatio, M.A., Sydenham, Kent, same crest.
Praed, a demi-lion az. 10. 2
Praed, Bucks and Oxon., out of a five-leaved ducal coronet or, a unicorn's head arg., armed and maned of the first. *cf.* 48. 12
Praed, Mackworth-, Robert Herbert, of Mickleham Downs, Dorking, out of a five-leaved ducal coronet or, a unicorn's head arg., maned and horned or.
Pranell or **Prannell** of London, and Martin Wothy, Hants, issuing from rays ppr., an eagle's head sa. 84. 13

Prannell, Herts, issuing from rays an eagle's head all or 84 13

Prater of Eton Water Wilts, a pegasus current sa, ducally gorged or 230 20

Prater, Thomas Herbert, the Grange Farnborough, Banbury, same crest *Labor omnia vincit*

Prater, under a palm tree vert, a lion couchant gardant

Pratt, *see* Camden, Marquess of

Pratt, a wolf's head erased quarterly arg and sa 30 8

Pratt, Norf, a wolf's head per pale arg and sa 30 5

Pratt, a wolf's head per pale arg and sa, gorged with a collar, thereon three pellets counterchanged *Tuum est*

Pratt, Kent, an elephant's head erased arg *Judicium parium aut lex terræ* 133 3

Pratt, Rev John, Durris Bantry Ireland same crest

Pratt, Robert, Gawsworth, Carrigrohane, Cork same crest

Pratt, Edward Roger Murray, of Ryston Hall, Norf, between a branch of oak and another of pine ppr, each fructed or, a wolf's head per pale arg and sa, gorged with a collar charged with three roundles, all counterchanged, langued, and erased gu *Rident florentia prata*

Pratt of Youghal and Castlemartyr co Cork, Ireland, an elephant's head erased sa, tusked or 133 3

Pratt, Bickerton, Roughton, Cærleon, Monm, in front of two javelins in saltire an elephant's head couped ppr holding in the trunk a mullet of six points or *Aut fas aut mors*

Pratt, Leics, a demi-unicorn or, holding a lozenge az *cf* 48 7

Pratt of Hathern, Leics and Southwark, Surrey, a demi-unicorn salient or, holding a mascle az

Pratt, Suff, a lizard vert, ducally gorged and lined or *cf* 138 5

Pratt, co Meath, Ireland, a falcon ppr belled and jessed or *cf* 85 2

Pratt, a caltrap embrued gu 174 14

Pratt, Joseph, of Cabra Castle, co Cavan, Ireland, a lion's head erased gu, pierced through the back of the neck with a broken spear ppr *Virtute et armis*

Pratt, Walter Caulfeild, J P, Oving House, Aylesbury, same crest

Pratte, a lion's head erased vert 17 8

Prattenton of Clareland and Hartlebury, Worcs, a goat's head erased or 128 5

Pratter, a horse's head charged with a caltrap *cf* 51 9

Prattinton of Bewdley, Worcs a goat's head erased or *Vim vi repellere licet* 128 5

Prattman, Durh (1) Two lion's gambs erased holding a mullet or *cf* 10 2 (2) A demi lion rampant holding a cross patee fitched gu *Labor omnia vincit*

Preadeaux, a cutlass and a caduceus in saltier, and in chief a Mercury's cap, all ppr *cf* 171 1

Prelate, a garb in fess ppr 153 6

Prendergast, Ireland, a cockatrice with wings expanded ppr 68 6

Prendergast, a man's head couped at the neck ppr 190 12

Prendergast, an antelope's head couped ppr, attired gu *cf* 126 2

Prendergast of Newcastle, co Tipperary, a heraldic antelope trippant ppr, attired and ungu or *Vincit veritas* 127 5

Prendergast, General Sir Harry Norton Dalrymple, G C B, V C, Heron Court, Richmond, Surrey, same crest and motto

Prendergast, Bart (*extinct*), of Gort, co Galway, Ireland, same crest *Vincit veritas* 127 5

Prentice, Scotland a wolf's head erased or 30 8

Prentice, an eagle displayed holding in the dexter claw a dagger and in the sinister a pistol, all ppr

Prentice, Thomas Augustus, Esquire, of Armagh, Ireland, a demi greyhound rampant or collared, ringed and lined sa, and charged on the shoulder with a trefoil slipped vert *Nec timeo nec sperno* *cf* 60 8

Prentice, John George, Oxton, Chesh, same crest and motto

Prentis, a leopard's face gu, spotted or. 22 2

Prentys of Wygenhall and Burston, Norf, a demi greyhound or collared ringed, and lined sa *cf* 60 8

Prescop, a horse's head arg *cf* 50 13

Prescot or **Prescott**, a dexter hand apaumee gu 222 14

Prescot, Lincs, out of a ducal coronet or, a boar's head and neck arg, bristled or 41 4

Prescott, Hants, on a mural coronet a buck sejant 116 4

Prescott, Sir George Lionel Lawson Bagot Bart, of Theobalds Park Herts a cubit arm erect vested gu, cuffed erm holding in the hand ppr a hand beacon sa, fired ppr *Lux mihi Deus*

Prescott, Charles Barrow Clarke Wilmslow Park, Wilmslow, Chesh, same crest and motto

Prescott - Decie, Richard, Bockleton Court, Tenbury (1) A cubit arm erect holding in bend sinister a sword ppr pommel and hilt or between two trefoils vert 243 17 (2) A cubit arm vested gu, guttee-d'or, holding in the hand ppr a beacon sa, fired ppr *Toujours pret* 243 18

Presland and **Prestland**, a man's head couped at the shoulders affrontee sa, ducally crowned or 192 9

Pressly, Wilts, Hants, and London, a cockatrice sejant ppr 68 4

Prest of Sheffield, a demi-terrestrial globe ppr thereon a demi-pegasus regardant erm, semee of mullets gu, supporting an anchor erect sa *Toujours prest* 47 6

Prestage, a porcupine ppr 136 5

Prestley, London and Herts a cockatrice arg, standing on a broken lance or, the top in the mouth, headed of the first

Preston, *see* Gormanston Viscount

Preston, Lord Dingwall, out of a ducal coronet or a unicorn's head sa 48 12

Preston, Campbell-, Robert William Pigott Clarke, of Valleyfield House, Culross N B same crest and motto

Preston, Scotland, out of a ducal coronet a unicorn's head *Præsto, ut præstem* 48 12

Preston, out of a marquess's coronet a unicorn's head ppr *Præsto, ut præstem* *cf* 48 12

Preston, Scotland, an angel ppr *Præsto, ut præstem* 184 12

Preston, Lancs, Cumb, and Westml over a ruined tower a falcon volant both arg, beaked legged, and belled or *cf* 49 7

Preston of West Derby, Lancs (1) On a ruined tower or, a falcon with wings expanded and elevated ppr, beaked legged and belled of the first (2) On a chapeau gu, turned up erm, a wolf or *Si Dieu veult*

Preston, Rev John D'Arcy Warcop Yorks, on a tower or a falcon with wings expanded and elevated ppr beaked legged and belled of the first *Si Dieu veult* *cf* 156 8

Preston, Captain John Norcliffe of Flasby Hall, Gargrave Yorks, same crest and motto

Preston of Preston Richard Preston Patrick Nether Levens, Westml and of the Manor and Abbey of Furness Lancs (1) On a ruined tower arg a falcon volant of the same beaked legged, and belled or (2) On a chapeau gu, turned up erm, a wolf or *Si Dieu veult* *cf* 29 2

Preston of Holker, Lancs, on a tower arg a stork rising of the last, beaked or

Preston, Ireland, on a ducal coronet per pale or and gu, a griffin sejant of the first, resting the dexter claw on an escutcheon of the last 62 11

Preston, Suff and Ireland, between two wings az, a crescent or *cf* 112 6

Preston, Sir Jacob, Bart, of Beeston St Lawrence Norf, a crescent or *Pristinum spero lumen* 163 2

Preston of Bellinter co Meath, Ireland a crescent or, between two wings inverted az *Virtus sui ipsius præmium*

Preston, Nathaniel Francis, Swainston Navan, same crest and motto

Preston of Yarmouth a crescent or between two wings sa *cf* 112 6

Preston of Ardsallagh, co Meath, Ireland a crescent or between two wings inverted az *Sui ipsius præmium*

Preston of Chilwick, Herts, and Beds out of a mural coronet or a demi fox rampant sa, gorged with a collar erm

Preston of Up Ottery Devonsh, and Durh, on a chapeau gu turned up erm, a wolf or

Preston, John Wilby, of Dalby Park Lincs, same crest and motto

Preston, Major General John Ingle 6 the Esplanade Plymouth on a chapeau gu turned up erm a fox passant ppr

Preston of Preston - in - Amounderness, Lancs, a wolf passant ppr 28 10

Preston, an arm in armour embowed holding in the hand a dagger, all ppr, hilted or 196 5

Preston-Hillary, Charles Ernest Richard, out of a mural crown or, a cubit arm in armour ppr, garnished or, encircled by a sash vert, the gauntlet holding a galtrap erect of the first *Virtute nihil invium* 269 13

Prestwick, a leopard's face jessant-de-lis or. 22. 5

Prestwick or **Prestwich,** Bart. (*extinct*), of Holme, Lancs, a porcupine ppr. *In te, Domine, sperabi.* 136. 5

Prestwold, a demi-lion rampant ducally gorged, all ppr. 10. 7

Prestwood of Boterford, North Huish, Devonsh., a griffin's head sa., with wings endorsed or, pellettée, beaked, also or. *cf.* 67. 11

Pretor, Samuel Ashton, Esquire, J.P., Belfield House, near Weymouth, a dexter arm fesseways couped habited, charged with two roundles, holding in the hand a fasces. *Amor patriæ.*

Pretor, an eagle's head couped or, with wings addorsed sa., gorged with a collar arg.

Pretor-Pinney, Frederick Wake, Esquire, of the Grange, Somerton, Somers.: (1) An arm in armour embowed couped at the shoulder, the part from the elbow to the shoulder fesseways lying upon the wreath, holding in the hand ppr. a cross crosslet fitchée in bend sinister arg. (*for Pinney*). 237. 10. (2) A demi-eagle or, the wings endorsed sa., semée of trefoils slipped of the first, and holding in the beak a like trefoil vert (*for Pretor*). *Amor patriæ.* 237. 11

Pretyman, Ernest George, Orwell Park, Ipswich, two lion's gambs erased supporting a mullet, all or. *Vincet veritas.*

Prevost, Sir Charles Thomas Kehle, Bart., M.A., of Belmont, Hants, a demi-lion rampant az., charged on the shoulder with a mural crown or, the sinister paw grasping a sword erect ppr., pommel and hilt or. *Servatum cineri.*

Prevost, Captain William, Elfords, Hawkhurst, Kent, same crest and motto.

Priaulx, Guernsey, an eagle displayed or. *César Auguste.* 75. 2

Price, *see* Rugge-Price.

Price, a lion rampant sa. 1. 10

Price, a lion rampant regardant sa. 2. 11

Price-Williams, a lion rampant regardant or. *Hoeg dy mwyal.* 2. 3

Price of Kingston-upon-Thames, Surrey, on a mural coronet or, a lion rampant regardant sa., holding between the paws a fleur-de-lis of the first.

Price, Wales, a lion rampant or, holding a rose gu., stalked and leaved vert.

Price, Shropsh., a lion rampant gu., holding in his paws a sprig vert, flowered of the first.

Price, Surrey, a lion rampant arg., holding a rose gu., slipped vert. *Vive ut vivas.*

Price, Bart. (*extinct*), of Foxley, Heref., a lion rampant arg., holding in the dexter fore-paw a rose slipped ppr. *Auxilium meum a Domino.*

Price, Leonard C., Ewell, Surrey, a lion rampant arg., in the dexter paw a rose gu., slipped vert. *Vive ut vivas.*

Price, Edward Augustus Uvedale, 17, Penywern Road, Earl's Court, S.W., a lion rampant arg., holding in the dexter paw a rose gu., stalked and leaved vert. *Vive ut vivas.*

Price, Richard John Lloyd, F.R.A., F.Z.S., J.P., D.L., of Rhiwlas, Merionethsh., a lion rampant arg., holding in the dexter paw a rose-sprig ppr. *Vita brevis gloria æterna.*

Price, Ralph George, 26, Hyde Park Gardens, W., same crest.

Price of Marrington Hall, and Brompton Hall, Shropsh., a demi-lion rampant erminois, holding between the paws an escallop sa., and transfixed through the mouth by a tilting-spear palewise ppr. 237. 14

Price-Davies, Stafford Davies, Esquire: (1) Upon a mount vert, between two antlers or, a lion's head erased arg., ducally crowned gu., and charged with an estoile sa. (*for Davies*). 237. 13. (2) A demi-lion rampant erminois, holding between the paws an escallop sa., and transfixed through the mouth by a tilting-spear paleways ppr. (*for Price*). 237. 14

Price of Saintfield, co. Down, Ireland, a lion's head erased or. *Quis timeo.* 17. 8

Price of Barton Regis, Glouc., out of a mural coronet or, a lion's head ppr. 19. 12

Price, James Nugent Blackwood, Saintfield, co. Down, a lion's head erased or. *Quis timet.*

Price of Castle Madoc, Wales: (1) A dragon's head vert, erased gu., holding in the mouth a sinister hand erect couped at the wrist, also gu., dropping blood ppr. (*for Price*). 72. 6. (2) A boar's head erased in fess (*for Powell*). 42. 2

Price, Morgan Philips, Tibberton Court, Glouc., a dragon's head erased vert, transfixed by a broken spear from the sinister in bend sinister ppr., in the mouth an eagle's leg erased arg. *Spe labor levis.*

Price, Sir Francis Caradoc Rose, Bart., of Trengwainton, Cornw., a dragon's head vert, erased gu., holding in the mouth a sinister hand erect couped at the wrist embrued and dropping blood, all ppr. *Arr Dwrr y gyd.* *cf.* 72. 6

Price, John Frederic, C.S.I., same crest.

Price, Green-, Sir Richard Dansey, Bart., J.P., of Norton Manor, Radnorsh., in front of a dragon's head erased vert, holding in the mouth a dexter hand couped at the wrist gu., three escallops arg. *Vive hodie.* 71. 5

Price, a demi-griffin segreant. 64. 2

Price of London, a griffin's head erased arg., holding in the beak a thistle gu., stalked and leaved vert, all between two wings ppr. *Virtus præ numine.* *cf.* 65. 11

Price of Westbury, Bucks, a leopard's head or. 22. 10

Price, Bucks, same crest. 22. 10

Price John, Esquire, of 7, Rue Evrard de Fouilloy, Amiens, France, on a wreath of the colours an antelope holding in the mouth a trefoil slipped or, resting the dexter fore-leg upon an escutcheon of the same, charged with a spear-head sa., imbrued ppr. *Spes unica virtus.* 126. 13

Price, a holy lamb passant bearing a banner charged with a cross. 130. 2

Price of London, a horse's head couped, holding in the mouth a spear arg.

Price, Howel John James, Esquire, D.L., J.P., Greensted Hall, Ongar, Essex, in front of a boy's head affrontée, couped at the shoulders ppr., two serpents saltirewise, heads upward vert, and a spear-head fessewise. *Innocentes sicut pueri sagaces sicut serpentes.*

Price, James Benjamin Garsed, Esquire, of Penscynor, near Neath, South Wales, same crest and motto.

Price, John Bulkeley, of Plas Cadnant, Anglesey, a falcon rising az. *Na fynno Duw ni fydd.* 88. 2

Price, Hugh Bulkeley, J.P., the Moorings, Menai Bridge, Anglesey, same crest and motto.

Price, Ireland, a cock gu., holding in the beak a pea-pod ppr. *In vigila sic vinces.* *cf.* 91. 2

Price of Glangwilley, Carmarthensh., a wolf rampant arg. *Spes tutissima cœlis.* 28. 2

Price, Shropsh., a bugle-horn stringed or. 228. 11

Price, Ireland, a mortar mounted ppr. 169 10

Price, a garb banded or. 153. 2

Price, G. P., Esquire, the Avenue, Elmers, Surbiton, a dragon's head vert, erased gu., holding in the mouth a sinister hand couped at the wrist and dropping blood gu.

Price-Davies, Stafford Davies, Esquire, of Marrington Hall, Chirbury, Salop: (1) Upon a mount vert, between two antlers or, a lion's head erased arg., ducally crowned gu., and charged with an estoile sa. (*for Davies*). (2) A demi-lion erminois, holding between the paws an escallop sa., and transfixed through the mouth by a tilting-spear paleways ppr. (*for Price*). *Dum spiro spero.*

Prichard, Lancs, a dragon's head erased at the neck vert. *cf.* 71. 2

Prichard of London, a horse's head erm., erased gu. 51. 4

Prichard, Captain Hubert Cecil, Pwllywrach, Cowbridge, Glamorgansh., a wyvern's head erased vert, in its mouth a hand sinister couped at the wrist gu. with guttée-de-sang.

Prickard, Rev. William Edward, J.P., same crest.

Prickett, a heart gu., within a fetterlock az.

Prickett, of Bridlington, Yorks, a hind trippant ppr. *Auxilium ab alto.* 124. 12

Prickett, Yorks, a pricket trippant ppr.

Prickley of London, on a chapeau gu., turned up erm., a mural coronet arg., thereon an arm in armour embowed ppr., vambraced or, holding in the hand a battle-axe of the last, armed sa.

Priddle, a demi-lion or. 10. 2

Prideaulx, a horse's head erased per fess or and gu. 51. 4

Prideaux, Devonsh., an eagle volant arg., beaked and legged gu.

Prideaux, Devonsh. and Cornw., an old man's head couped at the shoulders ppr., the hair and beard or, on his head a chapeau gu., turned up arg.

Prideaux, a man's head in profile couped at the shoulders, on his head a chapeau az., turned up arg.

Prideaux, Bart. (*extinct*), of Netherton, Devonsh, a man's head in profile couped at the shoulders ppr, and on the head a chapeau az, turned up arg *Deus providebit*

Prideaux-Brune, Charles Glynn, 10, Grosvenor Gardens, S W (1) A goat passant per pale indented arg and sa, armed and ungu or, pendent from a collar gu a shield, thereon the arms of Brune (2) A man's head in profile couped at the shoulders ppr, and on the head a chapeau az, turned up arg *Toujours prêt*

Prideaux-Brune, Charles Robert, the Grange, Welwyn, Herts, same crests and motto

Prideaux-Brune, Rev Edward Shapland, Rowner Rectory, Gosport, same crests and motto

Pridham, a hand ppr holding a chapeau az, turned up erm, between two branches of laurel in orle vert 217 5

Pridham of Ottery, and 4, Balmoral Place, Plymouth, Devonsh, a lion's gamb erased az, grasping a fetterlock or *Prudhomme et loyal*

Prierse, a unicorn's head gu, collared vert cf 49 11

Priest, a martlet sa 95 5

Priestley, a demi-lion sa 10 1

Priestley of Whitewindows Sowerby, Yorks, a cockatrice arg, standing on the lower part of a broken spear in fess or, and holding the other part in the mouth *Respice finem.*

Priestley, the late Sir W O, in front of a mount, thereon a cockatrice holding an arrow point downwards in its beak, a serpent nowed, all ppr *Ars longa vita brevis* 269 4

Prigion or **Prujean,** a greyhound's head erased sa, gorged with three roses in fess, between two bars arg 61 3

Prime, out of a ducal coronet or, a lion's gamb holding a tilting spear ppr

Prime of Walberton House, Sussex, an owl ppr, gorged with a collar or, charged with two mullets sa, and issuing from the mouth a scroll with this motto, *Nil invita Minerva*

Primout and **Primouth,** Surrey, a demi-buck sa attired or 119 2

Primrose, Earl of Rosebery, *see* Rosebery

Primrose, Scotland, a demi lion gu, holding in the dexter paw a primrose ppr *Fide et fiducia*

Primrose, a demi lion gu holding in the dexter paw a primrose or

Primrose, a lion rampant gu, holding in the dexter paw a primrose ppr

Primrose, Scotland, a demi lion rampant ppr, armed and langued gu *Primus tametsi virilis* 10 2

Primrose, Sir John Ure, Bart, a hand couped at the wrist grasping a primrose slipped ppr. *Fide et fiducia* 274 1

Primrose, a dexter hand holding a sword ppr 212 13

Prin, out of a ducal coronet or, a demi-eagle volant sa.

Prince of Abbey Foregate, Shrewsbury, Shropsh, out of a ducal coronet or, a cubit arm erect vested gu, cuffed erm, holding in the hand ppr three pine-apples of the first, stalked and leaved vert.

Princep, an eagle's head erased ppr 83 2

Pring, out of a ducal coronet or, a demi-eagle displayed sa. 80 14

Pring, a dagger in pale ppr 169 2

Pring, Walter of Northlands, Exeter a sword in pale ppr *Amicitia reddit honores*

Pringle, Sir Norman Robert, Bart, a saltier within a garland of bay leaves ppr *Corona fides—Amicitia reddit honores*

Pringle of Crichton, a saltire arg. *Spero et progredior*

Pringle, an escallop or *Amicitia reddit honores* 141 12

Pringle of Clifton, Roxburghsh, an escallop between two palm-branches in orle *Spero et progredior* 141 4

Pringle, Scotland, an escallop between two branches of palm in orle *Prompte et consel* 141 4

Pringle of Haining Selkirksh, an escallop half opened, and therein a pearl ppr *Præmium virtutis*

Pringle of Caledon co Tyrone, Ireland, an escallop erminois *Amicitia reddit honores* 141 14

Pringle, James Lewis, of Torwoodle, Selkirksh, Scotland, a serpent nowed ppr *Nosce teipsum* 142 4

Pringle of Whytbank and Yair, Selkirksh., Scotland a man's heart ppr, winged or *Sursum* 112 10

Pringle, Alexander, Junior United Service Club, same crest and motto

Pringle of Greenknowe, Scotland, an anchor within a garland of bay leaves ppr *Semper spero meliora* 161 10

Prinne of Worcs, and Allington, Wilts out of a ducal coronet or, a demi eagle displayed ppr, beaked sa 80 14

Prinsep-Levett, Thomas of Croxhall Hall, Lichfield (1) An eagle's head erased gu, guttée-d'or in the beak a bird bolt erect (bolt downwards) ppr (*for Prinsep*) (2) A demi lion arg, ducally crowned or, gorged with a collar az, in the dexter paw a cross crosslet fitchee sa, the sinister paw resting on an escutcheon of the third charged with a fleur de lis or (*for Levett*)

Prior, *see* Murray Prior.

Prior, an escallop arg 141 14

Prior of Paragon House Blackheath, Kent an escallop-shell arg *Speriamo* 141 14

Prior, Ireland, a star of eight points wavy or cf 164 4

Prior of Roding, Essex, a star of eight points wavy or *Malo mori quam fœdari* cf 164 4

Prior, Ireland (1) An estoile vert 164 1 (2) A talbot's head erased arg, charged on the breast with a trefoil slipped ppr *Quis audeat luci aggredi* cf 56 2

Prior-Wandesforde (1) A church ppr., the spire az and over it the motto, *Pour l'eglise* (*for Wandesford*) 158 10 (2) An etoile vert (*for Prior*), and over it the motto, *Quis audeat luci aggrendi?* 164 1

Prior-Wandesforde, Henry Wallis, Crossogne House, co Tipperary, same crests and mottoes

Prior-Wandesforde, Richard Henry Castlecomes, co Kilkenny, same crests and mottoes

Prior, a dexter hand holding a crosier ppr 219 4

Prior, a bird holding in the beak a slip 92 5

Prisett or **Prosset,** Shropsh, a hand gu holding a torteau

Prissick, a porcupine 136 5

Pritchard, a dexter arm ppr, holding in the hand a battle axe az, handled gu 213 12

Pritchard, a horse's head bridled 51 5

Pritchard, a goat's head erased 128 5

Pritchard, an escallop shell arg 141 14

Pritchard, a lion rampant sa 1 10

Pritchard, late John, Esquire J P, of Stanmore Hall, Bridgnorth, and Broseley, Shropsh, a dragon's head erased arg, holding in the mouth an escallop sa the neck charged with two buckles in fesse between as many barrulets az *Labore et fide* 71. 9

Prittie, *see* Dunalley, Baron

Prittie of Kilboy co Tipperary, Ireland, a wolf's head erased arg *In omnia paratus* 30 8

Pritty, a wolf's head erased per pale arg and gu 30 8

Probert, an arm in armour embowed ppr, holding in the hand a sword ppr 195 2

Probert, William Richard, the Lodge, Linton, Cambs, a Cornish chough ppr within a closed fetterlock or

Proby, *see* Carysfort, Earl of

Proby, Hunts, Chesh, and Shropsh, an ostrich's head erased arg, ducally gorged or, holding in the beak a key of the last

Probyn, John Langford, late of Huntley Manor, same crest

Probyn, General Sir Dighton M, K C S I, K C B, C B, of Park House, Sandringham, Norf, an ostrich's head erased ppr ducally gorged or and holding in the beak a key of the last *Manus hæc inimica tyrannis*

Probyn, Clifford, Grosvenor Street, W, in front of two keys in saltire or, an ostrich's head erased at the neck az *Manus hæc inimica tyrannis*

Probyn, Lieutenant Colonel, 55, Grosvenor Street, W, a demi lion holding in the paws a bezant

Procter of Hay, Brecknock and of Iron bridge Shropsh, a cubit arm habited vert cuffed arg, holding in the hand a hammer ppr *Fit via vi* 207 11

Proctor, *see* Beauchamp Proctor

Proctor, Scotland, a greyhound sejant ppr *Toujours fidele* 59 4

Proctor, Cambs and Middx, a martlet gu 95 4

Proctor, on a chapeau ppr, a martlet or 95 1

Proctor, Middx and London, on a mount vert, a greyhound sejant arg, spotted brown collared or 59 2

Proctor, Major, J P, Bank House, Wednesbury, on a mount vert, a greyhound sejant arg

Prodgers, Edwin, of Dane End, Ware, Herts, in front of a cross Calvary or, a wyvern with wings endorsed vert, holding in the mouth a sinister hand couped at the wrist gu, gorged with a collar, and therefrom a line reflexed over the back of the first, the dexter claw resting on a cross patée, also or. *Dévouement sans bornes.* 70. 7

Prodgers, Herbert, Kington House, Kington St. Michael, Chippenham, same crest and motto.

Promoli, Liverpool, out of a ducal coronet a long cross between two ostrich-feathers. *Nil desperandum.* cf. 114. 9

Prosser, on a mount a horse bridled and at full speed, all ppr. cf. 52. 1

Prosser, a wolf's head erased holding in the mouth a sword in bend sinister, point upwards, all ppr. cf. 30. 8

Prosser, Wegg-, Francis Richard, Belmont, Heret.: (1) A wolf's head erased sa., semée of spear-heads arg., pierced through the mouth with a sword ppr. (*for Prosser*). (2) A sinister hand in a gauntlet ppr., holding an escutcheon sa., charged with an annulet or (*for Wegg*). (3) A demi-lynx ppr., semée-de-lis gu., holding a branch of olive, also ppr. (*for Haggitt*).

Prother, on a tower sa., a crescent or. 156. 4

Prothero, Francis Egerton, M.A., Malpas Court, Newport, same crest and motto.

Prothero, a bird volant purp.

Protheroe, E. Shaw, of Dol-Wilym, Hebron, R.S.O., Carmarthensh., a savage holding in his dexter hand a club, all ppr. *I mean weel.*

Protheroe of Hawksbrook and Llangharne, Carmarthensh., a raven ppr. *Deus pascit corvos.* 107. 14

Proud, a buffalo's head erased vair. 44. 1

Proud, M., of Port and Docks Office, Dublin, a cross formée fitchée charged with five pellets, and intertwined with a wreath of laurel. *Deum de Deo.*

Proud, Middx. and Shropsh., a cross formée fitched or, charged with five pellets, a chaplet of laurel entwined round the cross vert.

Proude, a hand holding a club. 214. 6

Proude, Kent, an otter's head erased or, holding in the mouth a fish arg.

Proudfoot, Ireland, an arm in armour embowed holding in the hand an arrow, all ppr 198. 4

Prouse, a demi-lion or. 10. 2

Prout, Middx., issuant from grass ppr. a lion rampant gardant arg., collared and ringed or, supporting between the paws a lighted taper ppr.

Prouze, Devonsh., an ibex sejant or, armed, tufted, and maned arg.

Provender, Wilts, a squirrel current quarterly or and gu.

Provis, on a rock a wild duck ppr.

Provost, a buckle or. 178. 5

Prower, Major John Elton, 3, Gloucester Walk, Kensington, W., in front of an arm embowed in mail armour, the hand grasping a scimitar ppr., suspended from the blade by a ribbon gu., an escutcheon arg. charged with an estoile az., around the arm a riband tied, also gu., an estoile between two escallops of the fourth *Di Dieu tout.*

Prowse, the golden fleece ppr. 130. 10

Prowse, Somers., an ibex's head erased sa., eared, armed, collared, and lined or.

Prowse of Wicklow, Northamp., out of a ducal coronet arg., a demi-lion rampant gardant of the same, collared and ringed or.

Prowze, a dexter hand throwing a dart ppr. 214. 4

Prowze, Glouc., Somers., and Devonsh., out of a ducal coronet arg., a demi-lion rampant gardant of the first, collared and ringed or.

Prudhoe, Baron (Percy), on a chapeau gu., turned up erm., a lion statant az., the tail extended. *Espérance en Dieu.* 4. 8

Prudhome and **Pridham,** Devonsh., a lion's gamb erased ppr. 36. 4

Pruen of Cheltenham, Glouc., a demi-eagle displayed sa., charged on the breast with a fess arg., thereon three crosses patée gu., and holding in the beak a sprig of olive ppr. 81. 9

Prujean, a greyhound's head erased sa., charged on the neck with three roses between two barrulets arg. 61. 3

Pryce, Wales, a lion rampant regardant or. 2. 3

Pryce, Bart. (*extinct*), of Newtown, Montgomerysh., a lion rampant regardant or. *Avi numerantur avorum.* 2. 3

Pryce, a lion rampant regardant holding in the dexter paw a trefoil. cf. 2. 3

Pryce, Edward Stisted Mostyn, Esquire, of Gunley Hall, Chirbury, Shropsh., a demi-lion rampant sa., holding between the paws a fleur-de-lis gu. *In Deo confidemus omnes.* 13. 5

Pryce, Bruce- of Dyffryn, Glamorgansh.: (1) A paschal lamb ppr. (*for Pryce*). 131. 2. (2) A dexter arm in armour ppr., in bend, grasping a sceptre (*for Bruce*). (3) On a spur lying fesseways and leathered or, a falcon with wings expanded erm. (*for Knight*). *Fuimus.—Duw ar fy rhan.*

Pryce, Herts, a cock gu., combed, wattled, and legged or, holding in the beak a violet az., stalked and leaved vert. cf. 91. 2

Pryce-Jones, Edward, M.P., Caerhowel, Montgomerysh., a shuttle fesseways ppr., thereon a goat statant arg., gorged with a collar flory counterflory gu.

Pryce-Jones, Albert Westhead, Tronfelen, Caersws, same crest.

Pryce-Jones, Sir Pryce, M.P., Dolerw, Newtown, North Wales, same crest.

Prydeux, a dexter cubit arm ppr., holding in the hand a billet in pale az. cf. 215. 11

Prydeux of Nutwell, Devonsh., a dove volant arg., membered and beaked gu. cf. 93. 10

Pryer or **Pryor,** an escallop arg. 141. 14

Prynne, Shropsh., on a ducal coronet or, an eagle displayed ppr., beaked sa. cf. 75. 2

Pryse, Sir Pryse, Bart., D.L., of Gogerddan, Cardigansh., a lion rampant regardant sa., holding between the paws a fleur-de-lis or. *Duw Ar bendithio.*

Pryse, Henry Louis Vanneck, Surrey House, Leamington, a lion rampant regardant or, gorged with a wreath of oak vert, holding in the dexter fore-paw a cross botony fitchée in bend sinister, and resting the dexter hind-leg on two spears in saltire ppr. *Duw an digon.* 231. 10

Prytherch, Wales, a stag's head cabossed, and between the attires an imperial crown ppr. *Duw a digon.* cf. 122. 5

Pucke, George Hale, M.A., J.P., same crest.

Puckering, Herts and Warw., a buck rampant or. 117. 2

Puckering, Herts and Warw., a buck current or. cf. 118. 13

Puckle, a cubit arm erect holding in the hand a spear in bend. 214. 11

Puckle of Graffham, Hunts, a dexter hand apaumée charged with a rose, both ppr.

Puddesey, Yorks, a leopard passant ppr. cf. 24. 2

Puddesey, Yorks, a cat passant ppr. 26. 4

Pudsey, Warw., Yorks, Oxon., Lancs, Staffs, and Beds, same crest.

Pudsey, a leopard passant ppr. cf. 24. 2

Pudsey, Thorn-, A. H., Esquire, of Seisdon Hall, Staffs, a mountain-cat passant gardant ppr., charged on the shoulder for distinction, thereon a cross crosslet vert, with a lozenge or. *Fortuna favente.*

Pudsey, De, an eagle's head holding in the beak an acorn stalked and leaved. cf. 84. 10

Puelesdon or **Pulleston,** Chesh. and Wales, a buck trippant ppr., attired or. 117. 8

Puget, a dove holding in its beak an olive-branch and volant over the sea ppr. cf. 93 11

Pugges, a dexter hand ppr., holding up a covered cup or. 217. 11

Pugh, a dolphin naiant ppr. 140. 5

Pugh, a cross moline lozenge pierced erm. 165. 1

Pugh, a lion rampant arg., holding a fleur-de-lis gu. 2. 7

Pugh, a lion passant gardant sa. 4. 3

Pugh of Llanerchydol, Montgomerysh., a lion passant gardant sa., crowned or, holding in the dexter paw a fleur-de-lis gu. *Qui invidet minor est.*

Pughe of Ty Gwyn, Wales, a lion's head erased holding in the mouth a trefoil slipped ppr. *Nid meddyg ond meddyg enaid.*

Pujolas, Middx., a hind at gaze ppr., about the neck a bugle-horn or, stringed gu.

Pulesdon, Chesh., Shropsh., and Wales, a stag trippant ppr., attired or. 117. 8

Puleston, a stag statant ppr., attired or. 117. 5

Puleston, Sir Richard Price, Bart., J.P., D.L., of Emral, Flintsh.: (1) On a mount vert, an oak-tree ppr., pendent therefrom by a band az. an escutcheon gu., charged with three ostrich-feathers arg., within the coronet of the Prince of Wales or. (2) On a chapeau gu., turned up erm., a buck statant ppr., attired or. *Clariores e tenebris.* 118. 1

Pulford, H., Esquire, Clayton Wickham, Hassocks, on a mount a talbot regardant, collared, and resting the dexter fore-paw on a cross flory fitchée. *Be just and fear not.*

Pullar, Sir Robert Tayside, Perthsh, a demi eagle displayed or, beaked and membered gu *Perseverantia et industria*

Pulleine of Crake Hall, Yorks, a pelican in her piety, all or *Nulla pallescere culpa.* 98 8

Pullen or **Pulleyn,** Yorks, same crest 98 8

Puller, a dexter hand holding a trident in bend 214 12

Puller, Giles-, Christopher Bernard, Youngsbury, Ware Herts (1) In front of a mount vert thereon a dove holding in the beak an olive branch ppr, three escallops inverted or (*for Puller*) (2) Issuant from an annulet or, a lion's gamb erased az, charged with a cross clechee voided, also or, holding a branch of a peach tree leaved and fructed ppr (*for Giles*)

Puller, on a chapeau gu, turned up erm, a dove holding in its beak a laurel branch both ppr cf 92 5

Pulley, a palm-tree vert 144 1

Pulleyn or **Pullen,** Yorks, a pelican in her piety, all ppr 98 14

Pulling, a demi eagle displayed gu, charged on each wing with a cross patee fitched and on the breast with a mill rind or cf 81 6

Pullyn of Great Yarmouth, a lion ram pant sa 1 10

Pulse of St Anne's, Westminster an eagle's head erased arg, holding in the beak a trefoil slipped cf 83 2

Pulteney, Earl of Bath (*extinct*) a leopard's head affrontee and erased sa ducally gorged or *Quo virtus* 23 8

Pulteney of Northerwood Hants a leopard's head erased and affrontee sa, gorged with a ducal coronet or and charged with a cross crosslet *Vis unita fortior* cf 23 8

Pulteney, a leopard's head affrontee erased at the neck sa gorged with a ducal coronet or 23 8

Punchard, Rev Canon Elgood George D D, St Mary's Vicarage Ely Cambs, in front of a unicorn's head erased sa, collared vair, three plates 302 4

Punchardon, a unicorn's head erased gu, bezantee, and armed or cf 49 5

Punshon of Killingworth Cottage Northumb, a lamb passant erm, charged with a pallet wavy az, between two oval buckles or, the tongues pointing upwards 131 1

Purcell, Shropsh, a boar's head erased in fess arg 42 2

Purcell of Ouneslow, Shropsh out of a ducal coronet or, a boar's head arg, guttée de sang cf 41 4

Purcell, Ireland, a hand couped above the wrist erect vested az, cuffed arg holding a sword ppr hilt and pommel or, pierced through the jaw of a boar's head couped sa, vulned and distilling drops of blood

Purcell, Sir John Samuel, K C B, Glebe Lodge, Blackheath, S E, same crest

Purcell, Ireland, a dexter arm couped at the elbow ppr vested gu, cuffed indented erm, the hand grasping a sword ppr, hilted and pommelled or pierced through the jaws of a wolf's head couped sa, vulned ppr *Humani nihil alienum*

Purcell, John Poyntz, Esquire, of Glebe Lodge, Blackheath, Kent, a dexter cubit arm erect vested holding in the hand a sword in bend sinister pierced through the mouth of a boar's head couped close *Aut vincam aut peribo*

Purcell-Fitzgerald, Gerald Little Island—co Waterford (1) A monkey ppr, environed about the middle and chained or, a mullet on a crescent for difference (*for Fitzgerald*) (2) Same crest as above *Crom a boo*

Purchas, Yorks, a dexter hand ppr, holding up a cushion sa, tasselled or 215 9

Purchas of London, Essex, and Monm, a demi-lion sa, holding in the dexter paw a bezant

Purchon, Thomas, Esquire of York House, Leeds Yorks in front of a demi woman vested az the mantle gu. flowing over her sinister shoulder, holding in her dexter hand a palm branch ppr, two anchors in saltier or *Prudentia et vigilantia* 183 1

Purdie or **Purdy,** a peacock's head erased gu 103 1

Purdie, Scotland a dexter hand holding a roll of parchment ppr *Fidelitas* 215 6

Purdon, Cumb, a dexter arm in armour holding in the hand ppr a banner gu, fringed or, charged with a leopard's face arg the staff broken above the hand

Purdon of Bedford, same crest. *Pro aris et focis*

Purdon of Tinerana, co Clare and Cuiristown, co Westmeath, Ireland, a dexter arm embowed ppr, holding a banner gu fringed or charged with a leopard's face arg, the staff broken above the hand *Pro aris et focis*

Purefey, a demi talbot rampant sa, ducally gorged or 55 12

Purefoy and **Pureferoy,** Kent, a dexter hand holding a garland of flowers ppr 218 6

Purefoy of Misterton and Drayton, Leics, a dexter gauntlet or, the inside az, holding a broken tilting-spear of the second 210 9

Purefoy, Captain Richard Purefoy, M V O, R N, Shalstone Manor, Bucks same crest *Purefoy ma joye*

Purefoy, Bagwell-, of Greenfield Ireland a dexter gauntlet holding a broken lance all ppr *En bonne foy* 210 9

Purfield, on a ducal coronet sa, a martlet arg 95 12

Purkis, out of a ducal coronet or, a grey hound's head ppr 61 7

Purland of East Walton, Norf, a demi eagle with wings displayed 80 2

Purling, out of a mural coronet sa, an ostrich's head and neck ppr

Purling of London, a lion sejant or, crowned with a naval coronet arg, holding in the dexter paw an anchor sa

Purnell of Dursley Forward Stancombe and Wickselme Glouc, out of a mural coronet arg, a demi griffin segreant erminois, holding in the dexter claw a thunderbolt ppr

Purnell of Stancombe Park, Glouc (1) (*for Purnell*) (2) Out of a mural coronet arg a demi spear erect ppr, fringed or, and surmounted by two palm branches in saltire vert (*for Cooper*) *Fide et virtute* 175 1

Purnell of Boddington Manor, Glouc, out of a mural coronet arg, charged with three lozenges in fess gu, a demi falcon rising ppr, holding in the beak a cinquefoil slipped vert

Purrier, a dolphin naiant sa, under a pear tree ppr, fructed or

Purse, a demi-bull per fess or and gu cf 45 8

Purser, a fox's head erased or 33 6

Purslow of Sudbury and Hoxstow, Shropsh a hare sejant erm

Purslow, Shropsh (1) A hare sejant erm (2) A purse gu, strings drawn tight at the mouth and tasselled or

Purton, an eagle displayed gu 75 2

Purton, Shropsh, on a mount vert a pear tree fructed ppr cf 144 10

Purton, Walter John Faintree Hall, Bridgnorth, same crest *E fructu cognoscitur arbor —Avi numerantur avorum*

Purves, Bart of that ilk, Berwicksh Scotland the sun rising out of a cloud ppr *Clarior e tenebris* 162 5

Purvis, the sun in his splendour rising from clouds, all ppr *Post nubila Phœbus* 162 5

Purvis, Frederick A, of 41, Fairfax Road, Bedford Park Chiswick, London W issuing from clouds a sun in splendour all ppr *Clarior e tenebris*

Purvis, John, of Kinaldy Fifesh, a dexter hand pointing towards the sun in his splendour ppr *Per vias rectas* 222 10

Purvis, Vice Admiral John Child, 16, Hanover Square, W, same crest *Clarior e tenebris*

Pury, on a ducal coronet or a martlet gu 95 12

Pusey, Sidney Edward Bouverie, Esquire, of Pusey, Berks, a cat passant arg 26 4

Put, a demi lion rampant arg, holding a mascle sa

Putland, an elephant's head sa 133 2

Putnam, Bucks and Beds a wolf's head gu 30 5

Putt, Bart (*extinct*), of Coombe, Devonsh out of a mural coronet a leopard's head ducally gorged, all ppr 23 7

Putteman, two bear's gambs erased and erect supporting a caltrap arg

Puttenham of Penn, Bucks Beds, and of Sherfield, Hants, a wolf's head gu 30 5

Puttinger, on the stump of a tree couped at the top and sprouting a fresh branch on either side, a stag's head cabossed ppr

Puxley, Henry Lavallin Esquire, J P, of Dunboy Castle co Cork Ireland, an arm in armour embowed ppr, charged with a lozenge between two annulets in pale gu, the hand grasping a dagger in bend sinister also ppr *Pro libertate patriæ*

Puxty, Yorks, a pelican's head vulning herself ppr cf 98 2

Puxty, Yorks, out of a mural coronet a demi savage wreathed round the middle vert, holding in the dexter hand a cock's head erased and in the sinister on his shoulder a club

Pybus of Greenhill Grove, near Barnet, Herts, an elephant carrying in its trunk some sugar-canes, all ppr.

Pychard and **Pychow,** a hand holding a club in pale ppr. *cf.* 214. 6

Pychelord, Shropsh., an ostrich arg., beaked and ducally gorged or. *cf.* 97. 2

Pycombe, an arm in armour embowed holding in the hand a scythe in bend sinister.

Pycroft, a hand couped in fess apaumée, charged with an eye ppr., lying on the wreath. 221. 4

Pye, Bart. (*extinct*), of Hone, Derbysh., a cross crosslet fitchée gu., between two wings displayed arg. 111. 3

Pye of the Mynde, Heref., and Faringdon, Berks, a cross crosslet fitched gu., between two wings arg. *In cruce glorior.* 111. 3

Pye, Henry John, Clifton Hall, Tamworth, Staffs, same crest and motto.

Pye of Stoke Damerell, Devonsh., on a mount vert, a talbot's head couped arg., charged with a saltire wavy az. *Pietatis causa.* 56. 4

Pye of London, a demi-lion rampant az., gorged with a ducal coronet or, holding an escallop of the last. *cf.* 13. 10

Pyemont of Lofthouse, Yorks, on a mount vert, a knight in armour and on his knees praying, all ppr.

Pyemont: (1) Upon a mount a knight in armour, but bareheaded, kneeling in the attitude of prayer, all ppr. (*for Pyemont*). (2) A dexter hand couped at the wrist in fesse holding a quill-pen in bend sinister also, all ppr. (*for Smith*). *Tu ne cede malis.*

Pygott of Gravenhurst, Stratton, and Holme, Beds, a cubit arm vested bendy of six arg. and vert, holding in the hand ppr. a pick-axe of the first.

Pyke, a boar passant arg., gorged with a garland of laurel vert. 40. 6

Pyke, a lamb couchant ppr.

Pyke, Edward, Esquire, of Merton Bank, Southport, Lancs, in front of a fountain a pike-fish fesseways, all ppr. *Deo favente progredior.* 139. 5

Pyke, Joseph, Devonshire Place House, Regent's Park, W., a demi-wolf ppr., holding in the dexter paw a torch erect or, fired ppr., and resting the sinister paw upon a quatrefoil, also or. *Id solo Deo volente.* 237. 7

Pyke-Nott, John, Esquire, of Parracombe, Devonsh.: (1) Two mascles fessewise interlaced arg., thereon a martlet gu., ducally gorged or, holding in the beak a sprig of laurel ppr. (*for Nott*). 95. 3. (2) On a mount vert, a demi-pike haurient ppr., between two wings gu., each charged with a trefoil or (*for Pyke*). 138. 10

Pykin, a savage's head couped sa. 190. 12

Pylborow, an eagle's head erased, bendy of six arg. and az., bezantée, holding in the beak a branch of three roses gu., leaved ppr.

Pym, Bart. (*extinct*), of Brymmore, Somers., a lion's gamb holding up a human heart ppr. 39. 11

Pym, Francis, of the Hasells, Beds, a hind's head erased or, gorged with a collar flory and counterflory az., and holding in the mouth a trefoil slipped ppr.

Pym, Charles Guy, M.P., D.L., J.P., of Cæsar's Camp, Beds, 35, Cranley Gardens, S.W., same crest. *Nosce te ipsum.*

Pym, Francis, J.P., the Hazels, Sandy, Beds, same crest and motto.

Pym, Rt. Rev. Walter Ruthven, Brisbane same crest and motto.

Pymar of Endsbury, Dorset, a rock, thereon a sea-pye, holding in the beak a sprig of laver, all ppr.

Pyncombe of South Moulton and East Buckland, Devonsh., an arm in armour embowed ppr., purfled or, holding in the hand of the first a Polish mace arg., fastened to the arm with a scarf gu.

Pyndar of Kempley, Glouc., and Worcs., a lion's head erased erminois, crowned arg. 18. 8

Pynde, a lion's gamb erased arg., holding three pines or, fructed vert.

Pyne, a demi-pegasus rampant, enfiled round the body with a ducal coronet. 47. 7

Pyne of Merriott and Currymallet, Somers., an antelope's head or, attired and maned sa. *cf.* 126. 2

Pyne of Ham, Cornw., and Devonsh., a pine-branch with three pine-apples or, leaved vert. (*Another,* a pine-tree ppr.) 145. 13

Pyne, Ireland, a pine-tree fructed ppr., growing on a mount vert.

Pynell, a demi-eagle with two heads displayed gu., winged or. *cf.* 82. 3

Pynsent, Devonsh., a wing erect ppr., surmounted by an escutcheon charged with three mullets arg., two in chief, one in base, parted by a chevron engrailed arg. *Sidus adsit amicum.* 109. 3

Pynson, three leaves or, issuing from an étoile of sixteen points gu.

Pynson, Yorks, on a chapeau az., turned up or, an eagle with wings expanded ppr. *cf.* 77. 5

Pynson, a demi-eagle displayed holding in the beak a branch of pine-apples, fructed or, leaved vert.

Pyot of London and Staffs, a demi-lion gu., charged on the shoulder with three bezants, two and one. *cf.* 10. 3

Pyrke, a hand holding a sickle. 219. 13

Pyrke, Duncombe, of Dean Hall, Glouc., a cock-pheasant holding in its beak a wheat-ear, all ppr.

Pyrry, a hind's head. 124. 1

Pyrry of Baynton, Wilts, a stag's head erased arg., attired or, holding in the mouth a pear-branch vert, fructed of the second.

Pyrton, Essex, on a chapeau gu., turned up erm., a wyvern vert. 69. 14

Pyrton, a wyvern with wings expanded vert. *cf.* 70. 8

Pytches, John Thomas, of The Little Grange, Woodbridge, Suff., a stag's head ppr.

Pytts of Kyre, Worcs., within a circular wreath of wheat or, a dove with wings displayed arg., beaked and legged gu.

Q.

Quadering and **Quadring,** Lincs, a Moor's head affrontée ppr., couped below the shoulders, wreathed about the head arg. and gu. 192. 4

Quain, Bart., on a wreath arg. and az., and out of the battlements of a tower ppr., a demi-lion rampant or, charged on the shoulder with a trefoil slipped vert, and holding between the paws a battle-axe, also ppr., the blade or. *Avorum non immemor.* 16. 8

Quain, John, M.D., same crest and motto.

Quain, an oak-tree with the trunk entwined by a serpent, all ppr., and charged with an escutcheon arg., thereon a fer-de-moline sa. *Je ne plie ni ne rompe.* 143. 4

Quantock, of Norton House, Ilminster, Somers., out of the battlements of a tower gu., charged with two annulets or, a demi-eagle with two heads per pale erminois and erm. *Non immemor beneficii.* 82. 6

Quaplade, on a mount vert, a boar passant ppr. 40. 5

Quarles, Essex and Beds, out of a ducal coronet or, a demi-eagle displayed vert. 80. 14

Quarrell, a wolf courant ppr. 28. 4

Quartermains of Weston, Oxon., a hand holding a sickle ppr. 219. 13

Quarton, in a maunch arg., a hand ppr. 203. 1

Quash of Exeter, Devonsh., a demi-griffin or, with wings addorsed sa., armed of the last, holding between the claws a fleur-de-lis of the first. *cf.* 64. 2

Quatherine, Lincs, a ship in full sail ppr., flagged gu. *Ad littora tendit.* 160. 13

Quayle, Isle of Man, a quail ppr. *Assiduitas.*

Quayle, Rev. Daniel Fleming Wilson, 34, York Street, Portman Square, a quail between two bulrushes, all ppr.

Quayle, George Harrington, Bridge House, Castletown, Isle of Man, same crest.

Quayle, John, Crogga, Port Soderic, Isle of Man, upon a mount vert a quail ppr., between two bulrushes, also ppr. *Qualis ero spero.*

Quayle, Mark Hildesley, M.A., Queen Anne's Mansions, S.W., same crest and motto.

Queade, an arm embowed holding in the hand a dagger ppr.

Queensberry, Marquess of (Douglas), Smedmore, Corfe Castle, Dorset, a human heart gu, ensigned with an imperial crown between two wings or *Forward* 110 14

Quelch of Wallingford Berks an elephant's head erased az charged with a castle arg, fired ppr cf 133 3

Quelch, a stag's head erased and affrontee ppr 119 10

Querleton or **Querlton,** an acorn stalked and leaved ppr 152 1

Querouaille, a dagger and a sword in saltier ppr cf 171 12

Questeed, out of a mural coronet a garb, thereon a blackbird, all ppr 153 9

Quick, John, Newton St Cyres, Devonsh, a demi antelope arg, armed, attired, tufted and maned gu, collared sa, lined or cf 126 3

Quicke, Devonsh, a tent arg, the flag gu 158 7

Quicke, Ireland a demi-swan sans wings with two necks gu, round the necks a riband or

Quilter of Staple, Kent an arm in armour embowed, holding in the hand a battle-axe all ppr, a scarf tied round the wrist arg cf 200 6

Quilter, Sir William Cuthbert Bart., 74 South Audley Street W, in front of an arm vambraced ppr the hand grasping a battle-axe in bend sinister sa, the head arg the wrist entwined by a wreath of the third and second a Cornish chough ppr *Plutot mourir que changer* 285 4

Quin, *see* Dunraven and Mountreal Earl of

Quin, Ireland, a wolf s head erased erm *Quæ sursum volo videre* 30 8

Quin, Ireland a wolf's head erased gu charged with a cinquefoil or cf 30 8

Quin, Ireland a wolf s head erased arg *Quæ sursum volo videre* 30 8

Quin, co Galway Ireland, a demi-pegasus erm 47 5

Quin, an arm in armour embowed holding in the hand a sword all ppr 195 2

Quin, Scotland, a pheon reversed ppr 174 9

Quinan of Dublin, Ireland a squirrel holding in the paws an oak-tree fructed all ppr *Qui non patriam amat*

Quiney of Shottery, Warw and Staffs a cubit arm erect vested or, slashed arg holding in the hand ppr a scimitar arg, hilt and pommel of the first, the blade embrued

Quinlan, Ireland, a stork az pierced through the body with an arrow arg *True to the end* cf 105 11

Quintin, St, out of a ducal coronet or a lion's gamb sa, holding a cross crosslet fitched or 36 11

Quinton, an arm in armour couped and embowed, holding in the hand a sword ppr 195 2

Quirk, Rev James Francis, M A J P the Rectory, Great Coates a stag s head erased ppr *Will God and I shall*

Quyxley, an antelope's head erased gu 126 2

Qyre of London, an ass's head arg gorged with a chaplet vert cf 125 12

R

Raban, on a mural coronet or, charged with three fire balls sa, a boar's head erased in fess of the last, holding in the mouth a sword in pale ppr 42 11

Rabett, Reginald George Frederick, of Dunwich and Bramfield Hall a demi-rabbit rampant sa, guttee-d'or *Superabit omnia virtus* cf 136 6

Raby, a greyhound's head erased holding in the mouth a stag's foot, also erased 61 5

Rackham, a lion's head erased arg 17 8

Rackham, a griffin's head erased ducally gorged cf 66 11

Radborne, a horse's head between two wings arg 51 3

Radcliff, a dragon sans legs and wings ar

Radcliff, a bull's head erased sa armed arg, the points of the horns or, ducally gorged of the second lined and ringed or cf 44 2

Radcliff, a bull's head erased gu, gorged with a ducal coronet or 44 2

Radcliff, Durh Northumb, Warw and Beds, on a ducal coronet or a bull's head erased sa armed of the first cf 44 11

Radcliff, Lancs, out of a mural coronet arg, a bull's head sa, armed and crined or cf 44 11

Radcliff of Warleigh Hockworthy Court, and Franklin, Devonsh, out of a mural coronet a bull's head *Cæteris major qui melior* cf 44 11

Radcliffe, Earl of Derwentwater (*attainted*), out of a ducal coronet ppr, a bull's head sa, armed or 44 11

Radcliffe, General George Trevis, Leamington, same crest

Radcliffe, Lancs, Derbysh and Northumb, a bull's head erased sa, armed arg ducally gorged or 44 2

Radcliffe, Sir Joseph Percival Pickford Bart, of Rudding Park, Yorks Royton Hall Lancs, and Caverswall Castle, Staffs a bull's head erased sa, the horns arg, tipped or, gorged with a ducal coronet and charged with a crescent for difference of the second *Virtus propter se* cf 44 2

Radcliffe, Lieutenant-General Robert Parker, of Balmore, Caversham, near Reading a bull's head erased sa, ducally gorged and chained or

Radcliffe of Radcliffe Tower Lancs, a bull s head erased sa ducally gorged and lined or cf 44 2

Radcliffe of Langley, Yorks, a bull's head erased sa, the horns arg, tipped or gorged with a ducal coronet of the second *Virtus propter se* 44 2

Radcliffe, Sir David Knowsley Prescot, Lancs out of the battlements of a tower a bull's head sa, armed and gorged with a collar gemel or, holding in the mouth a rose gu, stalked, leaved, and slipped ppr *No thorn no rose* 249 17

Radcliffe of Hockworthy, Devonsh, out of a mural coronet arg a bull's head sa armed or

Radcliffe, Delmé-, Francis Augustus, of Hitchin Priory Herts (1) A bull's head sa armed and gorged with a ducal coronet or, holding in the mouth a cross crosslet fitched of the same (*for Radcliffe*) 44 9 (2) In front of an anchor sa a lion passant gu (*for Delmé*) *Caen, Crecy, Calais* cf 6 2

Radcliffe, Pollexfen Colmore Copleston, Esquire, Barrister-at-Law Derriford, near Plymouth out of a mural crown a bull's head

Radcliffe, Devonsh, a battle-axe erect ppr 172 3

Radcliffe, T E, Esquire, Broom Hall, Oswestry, Salop, a bull's head erased sa, armed arg, tipped or, gorged with a ducal coronet of the second

Radclyffe, out of a ducal coronet or, a bull's head sa 44 11

Radclyffe of Ordshall and Foxdenton, Lancs, a bull's head erased sa, ducally gorged and chained or *Caen, Cressie Calais* cf 44 2

Radclyffe, William Frederick, same crest and motto

Radclyffe, Charles Edward of Little Park Wickham, Hants, out of a ducal coronet or a bull's head sa *Sperare timere est*

Radclyffe of Winmarleigh Lancs a bull's head erased sa, armed and collared or cf 44 3

Radclyffe of Todmorden, Lancs, a bull's head erased per pale arg and sa armed and collared or cf 44 3

Radford, Alfred Joseph Vooght of Vacye, North Tamerton Devonsh a lion salient guardant arg, guttee-de-sang, with a human face ppr, holding in the dexter fore paws a rose arg, slipped and leaved, and resting the sinister on the point of a sword erect, also ppr pommel and hilt or 256 3

Radford, Herbert George, Park Cottage, East Sheen S W, same crest

Radford, Ireland an arm in armour embowed holding a dagger ppr 196 5

Radford, an escutcheon per pale arg and sa, between two laurel branches in orle vert 146 14

Radford-Norcop, Alexander William, of Betton Hall, Shropsh (1) Upon a mount vert a boar's head erased sa in front of two ostrich feathers or (*for Norcop*) 42 14 (2) A fret or thereon a partridge ppr (*for Radford*) *Possunt quia posse videntur* 89 7

Radford, Arthur, of Smalley Hall Derbysh, a partridge holding in its beak an ear of wheat all ppr *Possunt quia posse videntur* cf 89 10

Radley of Halton and Yarborough Lincs, a phœnix in flames ppr 82 2

Radnor, Earl of (Pleydell-Bouverie), Longford Castle, Salisbury, a demi-eagle with two heads displayed sa., ducally gorged or, charged on the breast with a cross crosslet arg. *Patria cara carior libertas.* 302. 2

Radnor, a cross crosslet fitched az. 166. 2

Radstock, Baron (Waldegrave), of Castle Town, Queen's Co., out of a ducal coronet or, a plume of five ostrich-feathers per pale arg. and gu., a crescent sa. for difference. *St. Vincent.* cf. 114. 13

Radway, John Symonds, Esquire, of 151, West 72nd Street, New York, U.S.A., and Radway and Rodway, Glouc., a buck trippant ppr. *Dum spiro spero.* 117. 8

Rae, a lion's gamb ppr. cf. 36. 4

Rae, a mountain-cat current gardant ppr. 26. 6

Rae, Scotland, a hand holding an open book. *Hinc laus et honos.* 215. 10

Rae, Scotland, a stag at gaze ppr. *In omnia promptus.* 117. 3

Rae of Govan, Scotland, same crest. *Ever ready.* 117. 3

Rae, a buck at gaze ppr. 117. 3

Rae, Bart., of Esk Grove, Midlothian, a stag at gaze ppr. *In omnia promptus.* 117. 3

Raeburn, Scotland, a pheon az. 174. 11

Raeburn, Scotland, a hand issuing holding a club ppr. *Tutus, si fortis.* 214. 6

Raeburn of St. Bernards, co. Edinburgh, Scotland, a roebuck statant ppr. *Robur in Deo.* 117. 5

Raffles, Lancs, out of an Eastern coronet or, a griffin's head purp., beaked and gorged with a collar gemelle of the first. cf. 67. 4

Raffles, Rev. Thomas Stamford, Langham Rectory, Colchester, out of an Eastern coronet or, a griffin's head purp., beaked and gorged with a collar gemelle of the first, and holding in the beak a cross crosslet, also or. 67. 4

Ragg, Ragge, or **Wragg,** Leics., a mullet az. 164. 2

Raglan, Baron (Somerset), of Raglan, Monm., a portcullis or, nailed az., with chains pendent therefrom, also or. *Mutare vel timere sperno.* 178. 3

Raglan or **Ragland** of Carnllwyd and Llantwit, Glamorgansh., a unicorn statant gu., armed, crined, and ungu. or. cf. 48. 5

Ragon, a hind's head erased arg. 124. 3

Ragout, a leopard passant gorged with a ducal coronet and chained, the chain reflexed over the back.

Raikes, a stag's head erased or. 121. 2

Raikes of Welton House, Yorks, a griffin's head erased sa., beaked ppr., charged on the neck with an ermine spot arg. *Honestum præferro utili.* cf. 66. 2

Raikes, Arthur Hamilton, Old College, Windermere, same crest and motto.

Raikes, Arthur Stewart, Rio de Janeiro, same crest.

Raikes, Major-General Charles Lewis, Olivet, Bridge Road, Torquay, same crest and motto.

Raikes, Francis William, K.C., LL.D., of Bermands, Chertsey, same crest and motto.

Raikes, Lieutenant-Colonel Frederick Duncan, of Aberhafesp Hall, Newtown, North Wales, same crest and motto.

Raikes, Henry St. John Digby, 13, Lower Belgrave Street, S.W., same crest. *Futuri cautus.*

Raikes, same crest. *Honestum præferre utili.*

Raikes, Robert Taunton, of Treberfydd, Breconsh., and of 171, Victoria Street, S.W., same crest and motto.

Raikes, Rev. Thomas Digby, the Vicarage, Marcham, Abingdon, same crest.

Raikes, Rev. Walter Allan, the Vicarage, Ide Hill, Kent, same crest.

Raikes of London and Herts, a griffin's head erased sa. 66. 2

Raikes, Yorks, a griffin's head vert. 66. 1

Raikes of Hill Ash, Glouc., a griffin's head erased sa., charged with an ermine spot arg. *Futuri cautus.* cf. 66. 2

Raikes, General Robert Napier, Stamford Lodge, Watford, same crest and motto.

Railton, of Fakenham, Norf., a hind's head ppr. 124. 1

Rain or **Raine,** a leg erased at the middle of the thigh ppr. 193. 10

Raine, a leg in armour couped at the thigh, spurred. 193. 1

Rainer of Stradeshall Place, Suff., on a mount vert, an ounce passant ppr. cf. 24. 2

Raines of Wyton Hall, Yorks, out of a ducal coronet or, two rows of ostrich-feathers ppr. *Vici.* 114. 4

Raines of Fitling, Flinton, and Burton Pidsea, Holderness, Yorks, a lion rampant arg. *Judicium parium aut leges terræ.* 1. 13

Raines, Sir Julius Augustus Robert, K.C.B., 46, Sussex Gardens, Hyde Park, W., a cubit arm issuing from clouds and holding an olive-branch. *Esse quam videri.*

Raineval, *see* De Massue, Marquis de Ruvigny et Raineval.

Rainey, Major-General Arthur Jacob Macan, of Trowscoed Lodge, Cheltenham, issuant from a mural crown ppr. a lion's head or, guttée-de-larmes *Fuimus.*

Rainey-Robinson, Major Robert Maximilian, Trowscold Lodge, Cheltenham: (1) A buck trippant or, and pellettée (*for Robinson*). (2) Crest as above.—*Fuimus.*

Rainier of Southampton, out of a naval coronet or, a lion's head arg., pellettée, gorged with a wreath of oak, holding in the mouth a flagstaff erect and broken, thereon hoisted the Dutch tricolour flag ppr., inscribed *Reygersberoen. Laurus crescit in arduis.*

Rainier, a lion's head erased arg., pellettée, and charged with three fleurs-de-lis, two and one az., and holding in the mouth a slip of oak ppr. *Laurus crescit in arduis.*

Rains, a dexter hand brandishing a sword ppr. 212. 13

Rainsford, a reindeer's head erased ppr. cf. 122. 1

Rainsford-Hanney, Ramsay William, of Kirkdale, Creetown, Kirkcudbrightsh., N.B., a cross crosslet fitchée issuing out of a crescent sa. *Per ardua ad alta.*

Raising or **Raysyn** of Malton, Yorks, a dexter arm embowed vested paly of four or and az., cuffed arg., holding in the hand ppr. a bunch of grapes of the second stalked and leaved vert.

Raison, a boar's head erased and erect sa. 43. 3

Rait of Halgreen and Drumnagair, Forfarsh., Scotland, an anchor ppr. *Spero meliora.* 161. 1

Rait of Dundee, Scotland, a lily ppr. *Sperandum.* 151. 2

Rait of Pitforthie, Forfarsh., Scotland, an anchor ppr., ensigned on the top with a crescent arg. *Meliora spero sequorque.*

Rait, Lieutenant-Colonel Arthur John, of Anniston House, Forfarsh., an anchor ppr. *Spero meliora.* 161. 1

Raitt, a dolphin naiant or. 140. 5

Rake, an arm in armour embowed brandishing a club, all ppr., at the shoulder a bow of ribbons gu.

Ralegh, a boar's head couped and erect. cf. 43. 3

Raleigh, Devonsh., a roebuck ppr. 17. 51

Raleigh of Farnborough, Warw., a boar's head erect gu. cf. 43. 3

Raley, a lion rampant ppr. 1. 13

Ralli, Pandeli, Esquire, of 17, Belgrave Square, London, a lion rampant arg., guttée-de-larmes, holding between the fore-paws a cross couped az. Βαλανους Δενρρον Βαλλει.

Ralph, a naked arm, holding in the hand an open book, both ppr. *Fideliter.* 215. 10

Ralph, a griffin's head couped or, holding in the beak a serpent entwined round the neck ppr. 65. 7

Ralphson of Dublin, Ireland, a griffin's head erased gu., ducally gorged or. cf. 66. 11

Ralston of that ilk, Renfrewsh., Scotland, a falcon looking to the sinister ppr. *Fide et marte.* 85. 6

Ralston, John, Esquire, J.P., of Hampden, Deddington, Tasmania, a falcon ppr., belled. *Fide et marte.* cf. 85. 2

Ralston, Alexander Gerard, Rathgael, Ashfield, near Sydney, same crest and motto.

Ralston-Patrick, William, Trearne, Hessilhead: (1) A dexter hand erect holding a saltire sa. (*for Patrick*). (2) A falcon looking to the sinister ppr. (*for Ralston*). *Ora et labora.—Fide et marte.*

Ram of Hornchurch, Essex, on a chapeau or, turned up gu., a fox sejant ppr. 32. 12

Ram, Abel John, K.C., 31, Eaton Square, a ram's head erased arg., armed or, charged with a chevron az. *Quod tibi vis fieri fac alteri.*

Ram of Ramsfort and Clonatin, co. Wexford, a ram's head erased arg., charged with a chevron az. *Quod tibi vis fieri fac alteri.* cf. 130. 6

Ram, Rev. Everard Digby Stopford, 59, Courtfield Gardens, S.W., same crest and motto.

Ram, Rev. Robert Digby, the Vicarage, Hampton, Middx., same crest and motto.

Ram, Stephen, 19, Egerton Gardens, S.W., same crest and motto.

Ramadge of London a unicorn's head erased arg, armed and crined or *Consilio et animis* 49 5

Ramage of Edinburgh, Scotland, an increscent arg *Poco a poco — Vitam impendere vero* 163 3

Rampston, a caltrap embrued ppr 174 14

Ramsay, *see* Dalhousie, Earl of

Ramsay, *see* Wardlaw-Ramsay

Ramsay, Scotland a unicorn's head couped arg, armed and crined or *Nil temere* 49 7

Ramsay of Cockpen, Edinburgh, Scotland, a unicorn's head couped arg, armed or, within two branches of laurel in orle vert 49 14

Ramsay, Scotland, a unicorn's head couped ppr, armed or, and charged with a crescent arg *Dum varior* cf 49 7

Ramsay of Barnton, Midlothian a unicorn's head couped arg armed and maned or *Ora et labora* 49 7

Ramsay of Hill Lodge, Enfield, a unicorn's head couped arg, armed, maned, and tufted or *Ora et labora* 49 7

Ramsay of Whitehill, co Edinburgh, Scotland, a unicorn's head erased arg, charged with a rose gu *Semper victor* cf 49 5

Ramsay, Scotland a unicorn's head couped arg, armed and maned or charged with a crescent *Dum vario* cf 49 7

Ramsay of Edingtoun Berwicksh, Scotland a unicorn's head couped ppr, armed or, charged with a crescent or *Dum varior idem* cf 49 7

Ramsay of Kinalty a unicorn's head erased arg gorged with an oak wreath fructed ppr *Fear nought*

Ramsay, France, a unicorn's head *Ora et labora* 49 7

Ramsay, a unicorn's head and neck arg armed and maned or collared gu, and charged with thistles ppr *Virtute me involvo*

Ramsay, Sir James Henry, Bart, D L, M A, of Banff Perthsh a unicorn's head couped arg maned an armed or *Spernit pericula virtus* 49 7

Ramsay, Jain, Kildalton, Islay, Argyllsh same crest *Nunquam sine spe*

Ramsay, Scotland, a horse's head arg, maned or *Avance* cf 50 13

Ramsay, Scotland, a horse's head sa, bridled gu 51 5

Ramsay of Edinburgh, a horse's head and neck couped sa, bridled arg *Avance* 51 5

Ramsay-Denny, Frederick William, Port Elizabeth Cape Colony, a dexter arm ppr, vested arg, and holding five ears of wheat or *Et mea messis erit*

Ramsay-Gibson-Maitland, Sir James, Bart, J P D L, F L S of Clifton Hall, Midlothian a lion sejant affrontee gu, ducally crowned or, and holding in his dexter paw a drawn sword ppr pommelled and hilted or, and holding in the sinister a fleur-de lis az *Consilio et animis* cf 7 3

Ramsay-Fairfax, Sir William George Herbert Taylor, Bart, of Maxton, Roxburghsh a lion passant gardant ppr *Fare fac* 4 3

Ramsay, an eagle rising regardant sa, armed and membered or *Migro et respicio* 77 4

Ramsay, Bart, an eagle displayed sa *Probando et approbando* 75 2

Ramsay, Sir Herbert Bart of Balmain, Kincardinesh, a demi eagle displayed sa *Aspiro* 81 6

Ramsay, Sir George Dalhousie, K C B 7, Manson Place, Queen's Gate, S W same crest and motto

Ramsay, a parrot vert the breast gu, holding in the beak an annulet or 101 11

Ramsay, Scotland a dove within an adder disposed in orle, all ppr *Prudentia decus innocentia* 92 11

Ramsay, Scotland, a griffin's head couped ppr *Ora et labora* 66 1

Ramsay of Brackmont, a battering ram or, headed and veruled az *Perrumpo*

Ramsay, Ireland, a beech tree ppr 143 5

Ramsay, a star of six rays issuing from a crescent arg *Superiora sequor* 163 4

Ramsay, a star of six rays issuing out of a crescent arg *Superna sequor* 163 4

Ramsay-L'Amy, William, Dunkenny near Forfar, a dexter hand erect ppr, holding a crozier or *Per varios casus*

Ramsay-Fairfax-Lucy, Henry William, J P, Charlecote Park Warwick (1) Out of a ducal coronet gu, a boar's head arg, guttee-de poix, between two wings sa, billettee or and charged on the neck for distinction with a cross crosslet sa. (*for Lucy*) 280 1 (2) A lion passant guardant ppr (*for Fairfax*) 309 4 *By truthe and diligence — Fare fac.*

Ramsbotham of the Old Hall Stand and Centre Vale Todmorden Lancs and Crowborough Warren Kent out of a ducal coronet or a ram's head couped ppr *Non vi sed virtute* cf 130 1

Ramsbottom of Woodside near Windsor Berks, a ram s head couped ppr, holding in the mouth a trefoil vert, gorged with a collar engrailed az, charged with a fleur de-lis or, between two plates

Ramsbottom of London out of a ducal coronet or, a ram's head couped ppr

Romsbottom, an eagle's head erased gu 83 2

Ramsden, Sir John William, Bart, M A, J P, D L, of Byrom, Yorks a cubit arm in armour ppr the gauntlet holding a fleur de lis sa 240 14

Ramsden, Algernon Fielding same crest

Ramsden, Robert Charles Plumptre, Carlton Hall Worksop, same crest

Ramsden, Rev Henry Plumptre, of Cottingham Yorks same crest

Ramsden, John Charles Francis, of Willinghurst Guildford, same crest

Ramsden, William John Freschville of Rogerthorpe Manor, Yorks, same crest

Ramsden, Herbert Freschville Smyth, same crest

Ramsden, Richard J P New University Club, 57, St James's Street, S W, same crest

Ramsden, Frederic James of Abbot's Wood, Furness Abbey issuant from the battlements of a tower or, a cubit arm in armour the hand in a gauntlet ppr holding a fleur-de lis arg, suspended from the wrist by a chain or an escutcheon az, charged with a ram's head couped, also arg *Fit via vi* 210 13

Ramsden of Castle Carra, co Kerry, Ireland a ram's head couped ppr in the mouth a trefoil slipped vert *Cœlum non animum mutat* cf 130 1

Ramsey, Scotland a dexter hand holding a covered cup ppr 217 11

Ramsey, a sea lion sejant ppr 20 2

Ramsey, a unicorn's head couped arg, armed and maned or 49 7

Ramsey, a unicorn's head erased arg, crined and armed or 49 5

Ramsey, Robert, Esquire of 14, Park Terrace, Glasgow, a unicorn's head erased ppr, charged with a crescent *Nil timere* cf 49 5

Ramsey of Kenton Hall, Suff a man's hand and arm couped at the elbow supporting a hawk

Ramsey of Eatonbridge, Kent, a griffin's head erased per fesse indented arg and sa, the latter guttee d'or cf 66 2

Ramus, Middx, on a ducal coronet or, an owl ppr cf 96 5

Rand of London and Durh issuing from a coronet a boar's head erect, all arg 41 4

Randal, Kent, an antelope's head or cf 126 2

Randall, Ireland, a demi-griffin gu winged or 64 2

Randall of Bonnington and Wilford, Warw, and Walston Northamp a bat displayed sa 137 11

Randall, Scotland an arm in armour embowed brandishing a scimitar all ppr 196 10

Randall, a dove volant ppr cf 93 10

Randall of London, a buck's head erased az, ducally gorged lined and ringed or cf 121 2

Randall, a buck statant pierced in the back by an arrow 117 10

Randall and **Randolph** of Aylesford Kent, and Wilts, an antelope's head couped or cf 126 2

Randall of Binfield Berks, and Wilts an antelope's head couped or charged on the neck with four mullets in cross, and holding in the mouth a rose gu, slipped and leaved vert *Nil extra numerum*

Randall, out of a ducal coronet or an antelope's head arg, attired of the first

Randall of Kentesbury, Devonsh, a staff couped and raguly in fess vert thereon a wolf passant az, collared or 29 1

Rande of Rowell, Northamp, on a ducal coronet a boar's head couped all arg cf 43 1

Randell and **Randle,** an arm in armour couped at the shoulder and embowed, the hand holding a spiked club all ppr cf 199 2

Randes, out of a ducal coronet or, a lion's gamb gu, holding a cross crosslet fitched arg 36 11

Randes, Lincs, two lion's gambs erect sa, supporting a sword arg, hilt and pommel or

Randill of Northamp., a martlet volant or. 96. 2

Randles, Edward, Esquire, of Port Natal, South Africa, in front of an assegai erect a springbok statant, all ppr. *Semper in tempore.*

Randles, Walter, same crest and motto.

Randolfe, a bat arg., with wings expanded. 137. 11

Randoll, a garb or. 153. 2

Randolph, Scotland, a demi-lion az., holding in the dexter paw a thistle ppr. *Per aspera belli.* cf. 13. 12

Randolph, a greyhound's head arg., semée of torteaux. 61. 12

Randolph, an antelope's head erased or. 126. 2

Randolph-Lichfield, out of a ducal coronet or, an arm embowed habited in mail, holding in the hand the upper part of a broken spear in bend sinister, point downwards, all ppr. *Nil desperandum.* 197. 6

Randolph, of Wallingford, Berks, a bat displayed sa. 137. 11

Rands and **Randes,** a marigold stalked and leaved ppr. 151. 12

Randulph, an antelope's head arg., attired or. cf. 126. 2

Ranelagh, Viscount (Jones), a dexter arm in armour embowed, the hand in a gauntlet ppr. grasping a dart or. *Cœlitus mihi vires.* cf. 198. 4

Ranfurly, Earl of (Knox), a falcon close standing on a perch ppr. *Moveo et proficior.* 85. 13

Ranken, Scotland, an ostrich holding in the beak a horse-shoe, all ppr. 97. 8

Ranken, Scotland, the sun issuing from behind a cloud ppr. *Virtus prevalebit.* 162. 5

Rankin of Orchardhead, Scotland, a lance issuing arg. *Fortiter et recte.*

Rankin, Sir James, Bart., J.P., D.L., of Bryngwyn, Heref., in front of a cubit arm, holding in the hand a battle-axe in bend sinister ppr., three cinquefoils gu. *Prudentia et virtute.* 213. 11

Rankin, Scotland, a ship ppr. *Prudentia et virtute.* 160. 13

Rankin of Perth, Scotland, a ship ppr. *Providentia et virtute.* 160. 13

Rankine, Captain William Macbean, of Dudhope, Forfarsh., a dexter hand ppr., holding a spur or, the strap also ppr. *Forget not.* 217. 14

Ranking of Rochelle, a broken lance and a palm-branch slipped in saltier, surmounted by a crescent. *Utrius auctus auxilio.* 175. 4

Ranking, Devey Fearon de l'Hoste, LL.D., 9, Overstrand Mansions, Battersea Park, S.W., in front of a tilting-spear in bend and a pole-axe in bend sinister ppr., a boar's head erased gu. *Fortiter et recte.* 253. 14

Ranking, George Spiers Alexander, c.o. H. S. King and Co., 45, Pall Mall, same crest and motto.

Ranking, John Ebenezer, Hanover House, Tunbridge Wells, same crest and motto.

Ranking, Robert Archibald, Rockhampton, Queensland, same crest and motto.

Ranking, Philip William, Rockhampton, Queensland, Australia, same crest and motto.

Ranking, a boar's head erased ppr., langued gu. *Fortiter et recte* 42. 2

Ranson, an eagle displayed per fess az. and or. 75. 2

Ranson, Suff., a hawk's head erased az., holding in the beak an annulet or. cf. 88. 12

Rant, on a ducal coronet arg., a lion sejant or, the tail coward.

Rantt, Norf., an heraldic tiger sejant or, tufted and maned sa., ducally gorged of the first.

Raparus, a griffin's head erased sa. 66. 2

Raper, a buck's head. 121. 5

Raper, Yorks and London, an antelope's head erased per fess wavy or and az. 126. 2

Raper of London, an antelope ppr., collared or. cf. 126. 12

Raper, an antelope statant ppr. 126. 12

Raphael of Ditton Lodge, Surrey, out of an Eastern coronet or, a demi-eagle with two heads displayed sa., beaked and charged on the breast with a cross moline or.

Raphael, Herbert Henry, Gidea Hall, Romford, a mount vert, thereon an eagle's head erased az., gorged with a collar gemel or, and between two tulips leaved and slipped or. *Esse quam videri.*

Raphael, Herbert Henry, J.P., 23, Berkeley Square, W., same crest and motto.

Rasdall, two arms in armour embowed supporting in the hands a heart inflamed ppr., charged with a tower arg. 194. 10

Rashleigh, a dexter hand holding a sword. 212. 13

Rashleigh, Cornw., a Cornish chough ppr. 107. 14

Raspér, on a chapeau an étoile of six points. cf. 164. 1

Rasyn and **Rasynge,** an arm erect vested paly of four or and gu., cuffed arg., holding in the hand ppr. a bunch of lavender vert, flowered az.

Ratchett, Chesh., on a chapeau gu. and erm., a lion passant party per pale gu. and or, charged with a label arg., the dexter paw resting on an escutcheon.

Ratcliff, Bart., Kent, a crane ppr. 105. 9

Ratcliff of Wyddrington, Warw., and Ledbury, Heref., in front of a bull's head erased sa., armed or, collared arg., three escallops, also arg. *Fide et fortitudine.* 43. 4

Ratcliffe, Earl of Sussex (*extinct*), on a chapeau gu., turned up erm., two wings of the first connected by a nimbus, pendent therefrom a fetterlock and surmounted by an estoile, all or. *Virtus propter se.*

Ratcliffe, a bull's head erased sa., armed or, charged with three escallops and gorged with a coronet. *Fide et fortitudine.* 44. 7

Ratcliffe of Todmorden, Lancs, and Yorks, a bull's head erased per pale arg. and sa., armed and ducally gorged or. 44. 2

Ratcliffe, Bucks, a bull's head. cf. 44. 3

Ratcliffe of Malory, Derbysh., and Ordeshall, Lancs, a bull's head erased sa., armed or, ducally gorged, lined, and ringed arg. cf. 44. 2

Ratcliffe of Mowgrave, Yorks, on a mount vert, a Cornish chough sa. 107. 9

Ratcliffe, a crane statant holding in the beak a serpent. 105. 8

Ratford, a man holding a banner arg., charged with a saltier. cf. 188. 6

Rathbone, a dove holding in its beak an olive-branch ppr. 92. 5

Rathbone, William, of Greenbank, Liverpool, in front of a lion's head ppr., gorged with a collar arg., charged with two roses gu., a fasces fesseways of the first. *Suaviter et fortiter.* 17. 11

Rathbone, Hugh Reynolds, Oakwood, Liverpool, same crest and motto.

Rathdonnell, Baron (McClintock Bunbury), of Lisnavagh, Rathvilly, co. Carlow: (1) Two swords in saltire arg., hilted and pierced through a leopard's face or (*for Bunbury*). 22. 7. (2) A lion passant ppr. (*for McClintock*). *Vis unita fortior.—Virtute et labore* 6. 2

Rathdowne, Earl of (Monck), a wyvern. *Fortiter, fideliter, feliciter.* 70. 1

Rathlow, a martlet or. 95. 2

Rathmore, Baron (Plunket) of Shanganagh, co. Dublin, a horse passant arg., charged on the body with a portcullis sa. *Festina lente.*

Ratsey, a dragon's head vert, transfixed by a spear-head. 72. 10

Rattary and **Rattray,** Scotland, a dexter hand ppr., holding a cross crosslet fitchée or. *Ex hoc victoria signo.* 221. 14

Ratton, James Joseph Louis, 4, Cresswell Park, Blackheath, S.E., an ibex statant guardant, charged on the body with two fleurs-de-lis fesseways az., and resting the dexter fore-leg on a shield arg. charged with a Passion cross sa. *In Deo spero.*

Rattray, an arm in armour embowed holding a battle-axe, all ppr. 200. 6

Rattray, Scotland, a cubit arm in armour holding in the hand a battle-axe ppr. *Ex hoc victoria signo.*

Rattray, Clark-, Sir James, K.C.B., of Craighall: (1) A star or, and thereon a flaming heart ppr. (*for Rattray*). 181. 8. (2) A demi-huntsman winding a horn ppr., habited vert. *Super sidera votum.—Free for a blast.* 187. 12

Rattray, J., Esquire, the Ferns, Chobham, Surrey, an estoile of six points or, surmounted by a flaming heart ppr. *Super sidera votum.*

Raughtér, of Kilkenny, Ireland, an eagle's head erased and collared. cf. 83. 2

Rauleigh, a boar's head couped and erect. cf. 43. 3

Raven of London and Norf., a raven ppr. 107. 14

Raven of Litcham, Norf., same crest. *La tête plus que l'argent.* 107. 14

Raven, a demi-dragon vert, winged gu. 73. 10

Raven of London, on a mount vert, a caltrap or. cf. 174. 14

Ravencroft, on a chapeau a lion statant gardant. cf. 4. 7

Ravenhill, Heref., and of Strensham, Worcs., a demi-lion rampant arg., supporting a cross crosslet fitched sa. 11. 10

Ravenscroft, Wales, Sussex, Lancs, and Chesh., on a chapeau gu., turned up erm., a lion passant gardant arg. 4. 5

Ravenscroft, Francis, Esquire, of Birkbeck Lodge, 64, Springfield Road St John's Wood N W, and Birkbeck Bank W C same crest *Perseverantia industria et fidelitas* 4 5

Ravenscroft of Pickhill Denbighsh a lion statant sa

Ravenshaw of Richmond Surrey a lion passant ppr the dexter fore paw resting on an escutcheon arg, charged with a raven s head erased sa *Deus pascit corvos*

Ravensholme, a demi lion rampant gu 10 3

Ravensworth, Earl of (Liddell), Ravensworth Castle, Gateshead, a lion rampant sa, billettee, and crowned with an Eastern coronet or *Fama semper vivit*

Ravis, a lion's head erased per fess arg and gu, within a chain in arch or 19 5

Raw of London, and Skipton, Yorks, an arm in armour embowed sa, garnished or, holding in the hand ppr an escallop also or

Rawdon-Hastings, Marquess of Hastings (*extinct*), *see* Hastings, and Loudoun, Earl of

Rawdon, Earl of Moira (*extinct*), on a mural coronet arg a pheon sa and issuant therefrom a laurel-branch ppr *Nisi Dominus frustra* *cf* 174 2

Rawdon, a sprig of broom enfiled with a mural coronet

Rawdon of Rawdon, Yorks, and Ireland, on a mural coronet arg, a pheon sa, with a laurel-branch issuing therefrom ppr

Rawdon, on a mount vert a wyvern sejant or 69 11

Rawe, Kent a dexter arm in armour embowed sa garnished or, holding in the hand ppr a spiked club arg *cf* 199 2

Rawes, an arm in armour embowed holding a spiked club all ppr *cf* 199 2

Rawle of Hennet in St Juliott Cornw an arm in armour embowed ppr holding in the gauntlet a sword arg hilt or 195 1

Rawles of Fifield, Dorset a demi-lion rampant gu, supporting a battle-axe or 15 4

Rawley of Fardell, Devonsh, a roebuck ppr 117 5

Rawlings, a ram passant sa, armed or 131 13

Rawlings of Saunders Hill Cornw an arm in armour embowed, the elbow resting on the wreath holding in the gauntlet a falchion arg, hilt or *Cognosce teipsum, et disce pati*

Rawlins of Wakering, Essex, a bear's head couped or 34 14

Rawlins, Ireland a lion's head erased gu 17 2

Rawlins or **Rawlyns** of London and Kilreige, Heref a bull's leg couped near the body sa, covered to the fetlock arg, on the top an eagle's head erased gu

Rawlins, an arm in armour embowed ppr, holding in the gauntlet a falchion arg, hilted or 195 1

Rawlins, William Donaldson K C, 26 Norfolk Square, Hyde Park, W, a dexter arm in armour embowed holding in the hand an arrow fesseways, point to the dexter, all ppr *Semper fidelis*

Rawlins, Heref, an arm in armour embowed ppr brandishing a sword arg hilted or *Nec mutandus nec metus* 195 2

Rawlins of Beancroft, Wimborne, Dorset, and Bournemouth Hants, an arm embowed in armour ppr, holding in the gauntlet a falchion arg hilt or *Cognosce teipsum et disce pati* 195 1

Rawlins, Lieutenant Colonel Henry de Courcy, Manor House Taunton, in front of an arm embowed in armour, the hand grasping a sword in bend, point downwards ppr, pommel and hilt or, a like sword fessewise point to the dexter between two roses arg *Non timidus pro patria mori*

Rawlinson, Sir Henry Seymour Bart, C B, of Charles Street, Berkeley Square, issuant from an Eastern crown or, a cubit arm in armour, the hand in a gauntlet encircled with a wreath of laurel, and grasping a sword in bend, all ppr pommel and hilt or *Festina lente* 303 1

Rawlinson, Rev George the Oaks Precincts, Canterbury issuant from a wreath of oak a cubit arm in armour, the hand in a gauntlet charged with a cross patée gu, and grasping a sword in bend all ppr, pommel and hilt or

Rawlinson, Abram Creswicke, same crest

Rawlinson, Charles Brooke same crest

Rawlinson, an eagle's head couped 83 1

Rawlinson, Lancs a sheldrake ppr, holding in the beak an escallop arg *Dieu et mon Roi*

Rawlyn of Dublin, Ireland two swords in saltire points upwards arg pommels and hilts or enfiled with a wreath of oak leaves vert

Rawson of Pickborne Yorks, a falcon sa rising from a tower or 156 8

Rawson of Nidd Hall Yorks, and Darley Hall Lancs, a raven's head couped sa guttee d'or, holding in the beak an annulet or *cf* 106 5

Rawson, Captain Richard Hamilton Woodhurst Crawley Sussex an eagle's head erased sa guttée-d'or holding in the beak an annulet, also or *Laus virtutis actio*

Rawson, John, Esquire of Nudercliffe House Bradford, Yorks in front of an eagle's head erased sa, holding in the beak an annulet or, three annulets interlaced fessewise of the last 83 4

Rawson, John Selwyn, Mill House, Halifax, Yorks issuant from an annulet or, a raven's head erased sa guttee-d'or holding in the beak an annulet or *Laus virtutis actio* 235 12

Rawson, Arthur Pelham, same crest and motto

Rawson, Admiral Sir Harry Holdsworth K C B, United Service Club, 116, Pall Mall, S W, same crest.

Rawson, Charles Collinson Gore Lodge Hampton, Middx issuant from an annulet or a raven's head erased sa, guttee-d'or holding in its beak an annulet gold *Laus virtutis actio* 235 12

Rawson, a castle sa, flagged gu 155 8

Rawson, a quadrangular castle ppr *cf* 155 4

Rawson-Ackroyd, John William, Dean Grange near Kimbolton (1) In front of two tilting spears saltireways ppr, the battlements of a tower arg, thereon a stag's head erased gu (*for Ackroyd*) (2) In front of an eagle's head erased sa, holding in the beak an annulet or, three annulets interlaced fesseways or *Satis quod sufficit —In veritate victoria*

Rawson, Ireland a hand az, vested gu, issuing out of a cloud ppr, holding an anchor or

Rawson of Donoughmore, Queen's Co Abingdon, co Limerick, and Belmont, co Wicklow Ireland, a hand az, vested gu issuing out of a cloud ppr, holding an anchor or *Arx et anchora mihi Deus*

Rawson, issuing from clouds ppr, a cubit arm erect vested arg, cuffed gu, charged with a rose or the hand az, grasping an anchor in fess also or *cf* 208 3

Rawson, Sir Rawson William K C M G C B (1) Issuant out of clouds ppr, a cubit arm vested and cuffed gu the hand in a glove az, holding an anchor fesseways, the flukes towards the dexter or the arm charged for distinction with a rose arg (*for Rawson*) (2) A mount vert, thereon an eagle rising regardant towards the dexter ppr, holding in the beak a mullet sa and resting the sinister claw on a crescent reversed or. *Arx et anchora mihi Deus*

Rawson, B Currer, Esquire, Woodcote Lodge, Windlesham Surrey, issuant from an annulet or, a raven's head erased sa, guttee-d'or holding in the beak an annulet or *Laus virtutis actio*

Rawston, out of a ducal coronet a demi-lion rampant supporting a tower tripletowered

Rawstorne, Lawrence of Penwortham Lancs a lion passant or 6 2

Ray, Lincs an ostrich ppr 97 2

Ray of Howleigh, Suff an ostrich or, holding in its beak a horse-shoe az 97 8

Ray, Herbert Reginald, Esquire, of Hyde Park, London (1) On a mount vert, in front of a fern-brake ppr, an ostrich or holding in the beak a mascle of the same (*for Ray*) 97 7 (2) An Angola goat's head erased vert, armed or and holding in the mouth a fleur-de-lis of the last (*for Wheeler*) *Juste et vray*

Ray, Essex and Glouc, an eagle's head couped with wings addorsed and elevated ppr

Rayce, out of a ducal coronet or, a phœnix's head in flames, holding in the beak a branch of palm, all ppr

Raye, a lion's gamb per chevron gu and or *cf* 36 4

Rayleigh, Baron (Strutt), of Terling Place, Essex a demi-lion az gorged with a mural coronet, and holding in the dexter paw a cross crosslet fitchee or and resting the sinister on an escutcheon sa charged with a chevron arg, between three cross crosslets fitchée also or 312 1

Rayley, a savage's head affrontée 190 12

Rayment, a boar's head erased and erect arg 43 3

Raymond, Baron (*extinct*), out of a ducal coronet or, a demi-dragon erm. *Æquam servare mentem.* cf. 73. 10
Raymond, Cornw., out of an earl's coronet ppr., a demi-dragon vert. cf. 73. 10
Raymond, a dragon's head erased or, ducally gorged gu. cf. 71. 8
Raymond, Samuel Philip St. Clere, of Belchamp Hall, Essex, a dragon's head or, langued and ducally gorged gu. cf. 66. 11
Raymond of Kilmurray, Kerry, an eagle displayed ppr. *Renovatur ætas ejus sicut aquilæ.* 75. 2
Raymond of London, out of a mural coronet a demi-eagle displayed erm., beaked sa., charged on the breast with three pellets. cf. 80. 8
Raymond of London, out of a mural coronet a demi-eagle displayed erm., beaked sa., charged on the breast with three torteaux in pale. cf. 80. 8
Raymond, out of a mural coronet a demi-eagle displayed or, charged on the body with three torteaux in pale. cf. 80. 8
Raymond, a leopard sejant per fess or and sa., collared and chained, and spotted counterchanged. 24. 13
Raymond of Exmouth, Devonsh., on a mount vert, a leopard sejant per fess or and sa., spotted counterchanged. 24. 12
Raymond, Kent, Devonsh., and Essex, a dexter arm in armour embowed, the hand grasping a battle-axe, all ppr. cf. 200. 6
Raymont, an antelope's head erm., collared or. cf. 127. 4
Rayner, a dexter hand holding three arrows, points downwards ppr. cf. 214. 3
Rayner, John, Esquire, M.D., of Swaledale House, Highbury Quadrant, London, N., in front of a demi-lion rampant or, holding in the dexter paw a cross crosslet az., a serpent nowed ppr. *Facta non verba.*
Raynes, an arm embowed, the hand holding a club, all ppr. 202. 10
Rayney, Bart. (*extinct*), of Wrotham, Kent, Tyers Hill, Yorks, and London, out of a mural coronet arg., a lion's head or, pellettée. cf. 19. 12
Raynford of Great Tew and Ashfield, Oxon., a Cornish chough sa. 107. 14
Raynford, Ireland, a stag's head cabossed erm., attired or. 122. 5
Raynham, Viscount, *see* Townshend, Marquess.
Raynold, a vol. 113. 1
Raynolds, a fox's head couped sa., collared with two bars gemelle or, and between them three bezants. 33. 9
Raynor, two winged hands conjoined, all ppr. 224. 12
Raynor, on a mount vert, a leopard passant or. cf. 24. 2
Raynsford, Essex, a greyhound current of a dark russet colour, collared and ringed or. cf. 58. 2
Raynsford of Stanmore-Magna, Middx., Dallington, Northamp., Tew, Oxon., and Warw., a roebuck's head erased sa., attired or. 121. 2
Raynsford, a deer's head cabossed az., attired or. 122. 5
Raynton of Enfield, Middx., a griffin's head couped sa., beaked or, charged on the neck with a cinquefoil of the last. cf. 66. 1
Rayson, Oliver Alfred Edgar, Esquire, of Oakleaf Villa, Wakehurst Road, Wandsworth Common, London, S.W.: (1) On a wreath of its colours a raven's head sa., holding in its beak an annulet or. 106. 5. (2) A hart's head erased gu. *Æternitas.—Refero moro aut vito decora.* 121. 2
Rayson, a hart's head erased gu. 121. 2
Rea and **Ree,** Worcs. and London, out of a mural coronet arg., a dragon's head az. 72. 11
Reahurn, Scotland, a hand issuing holding a Hercules' club, all ppr. *Tutus si fortis.* 214. 6
Read, Bucks, a falcon with wings expanded ppr. 87. 1
Read of East Bergholt, Suff., upon a reed lying fesseways vert, a falcon rising ppr., belled or.
Read, the late General Meredith, Knight Grand Cross of the Order of the Redeemer of Greece, F.S.A., F.R.G.S., M.R.I.A., etc., late United States Minister to Greece, of 128, Rue la Boetie, Champs Elysées, Paris: (1) In the centre—on the stump of a tree vert, a falcon rising ppr., belled and jessed or (*for Read*). 87. 11. (2) On the dexter side—a demi-lion rampant ppr., gorged with a coronet or (*for Rose*). 10. 10. (3) On the sinister side—a demi-lion rampant sa., collared and chained or (*for Meredith*). *Cedant arma togæ.—Nobilis ira leonis.—Heb Ddw heb ddim a Duw a digon.* 10. 12
Read, an eagle displayed sa. 75. 2
Read, Crewe-, of Llandinam Hall, Montgomerysh.: (1) An eagle displayed sa. (*for Read*). 75. 2. (2) Out of a ducal coronet or, a lion's gamb arg., charged with a crescent gu. (*for Crewe*). cf. 36. 12
Read, a shoveller bendy of six arg. and sa., beaked or.
Read, Ireland, a leg couped above the knee erect, vested az., spurred or.
Read, a greyhound's head couped arg., between two roses gu., slipped and leaved ppr. 61. 11
Read, a demi-lion rampant. 10. 2
Read of Hayton, Yorks, a lion's gamb erect pean holding a cross moline erminois.
Read of Hitchin, Herts, a buck's head erased sa., attired or, between two palm-branches vert, charged on the neck with two bars gemelle of the second.
Read of Honningham Thorpe, Norf., a garb between two olive-branches, all ppr. *Pax copia.*
Read, Ireland, a griffin segreant or. 62. 2
Read, a buck's head erased sa., bezantée. cf. 121. 2
Read, Rudston-, W. E., Esquire, Carreg Bran, Llanfair, P.G., Anglesey, a lion's gamb erect pean, grasping a cross moline erminois. *Haud lege peritior.*
Reade, on the trunk of a tree vert, a falcon rising ppr. 87. 11
Reade, Sir George Compton, Bart., Howell, Livingstone County, Michigan, U.S.A., on the stump of a tree vert, a falcon rising ppr., belled and jessed or. *Cedant arma togæ.* 87. 11
Reade, Joseph, Esquire, of the Lodge, Shipton, Oxon., upon the trunk of a tree fessewise vert, a falcon rising ppr., belled and jessed gu., and charged upon the breast for distinction with a cross crosslet, also gu.
Reade, Herbert Vincent, Ipsden House, Wallingford, Oxon., on the stump of a tree vert, a falcon rising ppr., belled and jessed or. *Cedant arma togæ.*
Reade, Percy Hamilton, Solicitor, the White House, Leighton Buzzard, on the stump of a tree sprouting on either side a hawk belled with wings expanded and elevated.
Reade of Holbrooke House, Suff., a mount vert, thereon between two reeds a Cornish chough with wings elevated, all ppr. 265. 15
Reade, Colonel James Colquhoun Revell, Crowe Hall, Stutton, Suff., on a mount vert a Cornish chough, wings extended ppr., between two stalks of wheat, also ppr. *Cedant arma togæ.* 265. 15
Reade, Rev. Charles Darby, Prior Bank, Cromer, same crest and motto.
Reade, Lincs, a shoveller close sa.
Reade, Somers., Herts, Cambs, Kent, and Wales, an eagle displayed sa., beaked and legged or. 75. 2
Reade of London, a griffin's head erased az., purfled or. 66. 2
Reade of Kingsteed, Norf., a stag's head erased sa., bezantée, attired or. cf. 121. 2
Reade of Symington, Norf., a goat's head sa., ducally gorged and armed arg. cf. 128. 5
Reade of Wood Parks, Ireland, issuing out of clouds an arm erect, holding in the hand an open book. *Amor sine timore.* 215. 1
Reade, Ireland, a leg couped above the knee in armour ppr., spurred or. 193. 1
Reade, H. Lister, Esquire, West Street, Congleton, Chesh., on the stump of a tree sprouting to either side an eagle rising with wings expanded and inverted, all ppr. *Cedant arma togæ.*
Reader, Ireland, a leopard's head erased and affrontée az., collared or. cf. 23. 3
Reader, a dexter hand brandishing a sabre ppr. 212. 13
Reading or **Reding,** a griffin sejant holding in the dexter claw a garland of laurel, all ppr. 62. 9
Reading of London, a griffin's head erased or. 66. 2
Reading of Lansdown Place, Brighton, upon a mount vert, a hind's head couped ppr., gorged with a collar nebuly sa., and holding in the mouth a branch of cinquefoils vert. *Dieu défend le droit.* 124. 7
Readshaw of Armston, Lancs, a hind's head arg., collared sa. cf. 124. 5
Ready, Colonel John Tobin, of Ellerslie, Hawkhurst, Kent, a cock's head couped ppr. *Toujours prest.*
Reaman, a cushion charged with a dragon's head couped.
Reanolds, Somers. and Devonsh., out of a mural coronet arg., a talbot's head az., bezantée, eared or. cf. 56. 6

Reardon, Ireland, a dolphin naiant az 140 5

Reason, a boar's head erased and erect sa 43 3

Reason, a fox's head erased ppr 33 6

Reaston-Rodes of Bailborough Hall, Derbysh (1) A cubit arm holding in the hand an oak-branch fructed, all ppr (*for Rodes*) (2) A demi lion ppr, collared or holding between the paws a spear of the last, headed ppr, therefrom a banner gu charged with a cinquefoil of the second, and supporting a rudder az (*for Reaston*)

Reath of Edmistoun, Scotland a garb or *Industria ditat* 153 2

Reave of Breade, Sussex, a dragon's head arg, charged on the breast with three escallops az cf 71 1

Reavely, Thomas, Kinnersley Castle, Letton, Heref an estoile of twelve points az *Optima revelatio stella*

Reay, Lord (Mackay), of Reay Caithness-sh a dexter arm from the elbow erect holding a dagger in pale all ppr, pommel and hilt or *Manu forti* 212 9

Reay of Killingworth House, Northumb, out of a mural coronet arg, a griffin's head or 67 10

Reay of Burn Hall, Durb, a griffin's head erased ppr 66 2

Rebeiro, five tulips in pale

Rebow, *see* Slater-Rebow

Rebow of Colchester Essex, out of a mural coronet or, a demi eagle displayed sa, charged on the breast with a bezant, thereon a fleur-de lis az, holding in the beak an arrow of the first headed and feathered arg 81 10

Rebow, Gurdon-, Hector John of Wyvenhoe Park Essex (1) Out of a mural coronet or, an eagle displayed sa, charged on the breast with a bezant thereon a fleur de-lis az, and holding in the beak an arrow of the first headed and flighted arg (*for Rebow*) 81 10 (2) A goat climbing up a rock all ppr (*for Gurdon*)

Reckitt, Sir James, Bart, Swanland Manor North Ferriby, Yorks, in front of a lion sejant rampant sa, collared flory counterflory or, a fleur de lis of the last between two escallops arg 283 12

Redcomyn, a phœnix in flames ppr 82 2

Reddie, an arm in armour couped at the shoulder embowed and resting on the elbow, holding in the hand a scimitar, all ppr cf 196 6

Reddie, an arm in armour couped at the shoulder, embowed and resting on the elbow with a wreath of laurel round the forearm, holding in the hand a scimitar, all ppr *Honeste et constanter* 296 7

Reddingfield, on the point of a sword erect ppr, a cross patee arg 169 5

Reddish, Dorset Wilts, and Lancs a cock's head erased sa, combed and wattled gu, ducally gorged or cf 90 1

Rede, *see* Reid

Rede, Suff, a stag's head erased 121 2

Rede of Norwich and Beccles, Suff a buck's head erased az, attired or, between two reeds of the last charged on the neck with three bars gemelles also or, and as many bezants in pale

Rede or Reed, Kent and Worcs, a garb or, banded gu 153 2

Redege, a hand apaumee thereon an eye ppr 222 4

Redesdale, Lord (Freeman Mitford) (1) Two hands ppr, grasping a sword erect arg, enfiled with a boar's head erased sa (*for Mitford*) (2) A demi wolf arg, holding a fush or, and gorged with a collar dancettee gu (*for Freeman*) *God careth for us* 31 1

Redfern, William Beales, Inveruglas House, Cambridge, a birch tree ppr

Redford, a quatrefoil gu 148 10

Redham, a cross crosslet fitched gu 166 2

Redhead, an eagle's head az 83 1

Redhead, a sinister arm in armour ppr, embowed to the sinister, holding in the gauntlet a sword, point downwards, arg, hilt and pommel or, charged above the wrist with a crescent of the last

Rediche of Rediche, Lancs, a hawk rising arg membered beaked and belled or, standing upon a lure tasselled of the first, corded and ringed of the second

Reding, Kent a gillflower stalked and leaved ppr 151 8

Redingham, a salmon naiant az 139 12

Redington, of Kilcornan, Ireland, a lion rampant gu *Pro Rege, sæpe pro patria semper* 1 13

Redman, out of a ducal coronet gu, a horse's head arg 51 7

Redman, Norf out of a mural coronet or a horse's head arg, maned gu

Redman of Tulford, Yorks, on a cushion gu, tasselled or a horse's head couped arg, crined also or 51 1

Redmayne, John Marriner, Esquire of Harewood, Gateshead-on-Tyne, out of a ducal coronet or, a horse's head gu *Sans sang nul victoris*

Redmond of Killoughter Ireland a beacon ppr *Pie vivere et Deum et patriam diligere* 177 14

Redmond of the Hall and Movilla, co Wexford, Ireland, a beacon fired ppr 177 14

Redmond, William Hoey Kearney M P, Gresham Hotel Dublin, same crest

Redmond, John Edward, 15, Upper Fitzwilliam Street, Dublin, same crest

Redmond, Gabriel O'Donnell Fitzsimon M R C P I a beacon fired ppr a ladder or *Pie vivere et Deum et patriam diligere*

Redpath, Scotland, an ostrich holding in the beak a key ppr 97 5

Redwood, Boverton, Glen Wathen Church End Finchley, N, on a rock an eagle rising ppr, charged on each wing with a mullet of six points or, and holding in the beak a staff raguly of the same *Lumen servimus antique*

Redwood, Boverton of Glen Wathen, Church End, Finchley, N, same crest and motto

Reece, a galley with her oars in action 160 7

Reece, a wyvern sejant vert with wings elevated holding in the mouth a spear head arg embrued gu *Respice futurum* cf 69 4

Reed, a tower 156 2

Reed, a griffin segreant or 62 2

Reed, Northumb, and of London, a griffin segreant or *Memor et fidelis* 62 2

Reed, Charles John, Esquire, the Crag, Reesdale, Northumb, same crest and motto

Reed, Northumb, a demi griffin or, holding an oak-branch ppr *In Deo omnia* cf 64 2

Reed, William, a greyhound's head erased sa, thereon a rose arg leaved and slipped ppr, between two reeds leaved and flowered *Esse quam videri*

Reed, Sir Edward James, K C B, of the Lodge, Ascot and Broadway Chambers Westminster a demi man in profile looking to the sinister supporting in his dexter hand a hammer resting on an anvil, and holding in the sinister hand an iron ship all ppr

Reede, a hand holding a lance in pale ppr

Reede, a fleur de-lis or 148 2

Rees of Killymaenllwyd, Carmarthensh, a talbot ppr *Spes melioris ævi* cf 54 2

Rees or Rhys of Killymaenllwyd Carmarthensh, a talbot or *Spes melioris ævi* 55 2

Rees, David Llanelly, Carmarthensh, a demi-dragon wings elevated and addorsed ppr holding in the dexter claw a fleur de-lis or, and supporting with the sinister claw an escutcheon gu, charged with an annulet or *A barcho a berchir*

Rees of North Crawley Northamp, a lion rampant supporting a plumb rule, all ppr 3 2

Rees of Llandovery, Carmarthensh, a lion rampant sa, crowned gu *Pietate et probitate* 1 12

Rees-Mogg, William of Cholwell House, Somers, and Temple Cloud Bristol (1) Between two spear-heads erect sa, a cock ppr (*for Mogg*) (2) A swan arg with wings elevated or holding in the beak a water lily slipped ppr (*for Rees*) *Cura pii diis sunt*

Reeve, between two wings a caduceus 112 2

Reeve, Suff, a tiger's head erased arg, armed, maned, and collared or

Reeve, Lincs, a horse's head erased per fesse nebulee arg and gu 51 4

Reeve, Lieutenant Colonel Ellis Philip Fox Carlton Club, a horse's head erased per fesse nebulee arg and gu charged on the neck with two mullets in pale counterchanged

Reeve, an eagle's head erased or collared sa cf 83 2

Reeve, an eagle's head erased arg, gorged with a collar gemel gu and charged with an escallop az

Reeve, Suff a griffin's head erased gu 66 2

Reeve of Wigton, Norf a dragon's head couped sa, bezantee holding in the mouth a lily arg slipped ppr

Reeve of Norf, a dragon's head erased ppr, collared or *Animum rege* 71 2

Reeve, John Sherard of Leadenham House, Lincs a horse's head erased per fesse nebuly arg and gu, charged on the neck with two mullets in pale or 50 3

Reeve, Simms, of Brancaster, Norf, same crest and motto

Reeve-King, Nevill Henry, the Hall, Ashby-de-la-Launde, Lincoln: (1) A talbot's head couped sa., collared or (*for King*). (2) A horse's head erased per fesse nebulée arg. and gu., charged on the neck with two mullets in pale counterchanged (*for Reeve*).

Reeves, Sir William Conrad, K.C., Chief Justice of Barbados, of the Eyrie, St. Michael, Barbados. Motto, *Sic volvere parcas.*

Reeves, a demi-griffin sa. 64. 2

Reeves, out of a ducal coronet a griffin's head. 67. 9

Reeves of Burrane, co. Clare, Platten, co. Meath, Athgarveen, co. Kildare, and Vostersberg, co. Cork, a dragon's head erased or, collared az. 71. 2

Reeves, Robert William Cary, of Burrane, co. Clare, same crest.

Reeves, Robert William Cary, of Besborough, Killimer, co. Clare, same crest. *Animum Rege.—Virtute et fidelitate.*

Reeves of Glastonbury, Somers., on a mount vert, an eagle with wings elevated sa., each charged with a cross patée arg., the dexter claw resting on a cross botonnée or.

Reeves, an eagle displayed. 75. 2

Reeves, James Bowles, of Danemore Park, Speldhurst, Kent, a greyhound sejant sa., bezantée, collared and ringed or. *Prius quam factum considera.* cf. 59. 2

Regan, Ireland, a demi-griffin per fesse or and az. 64. 2

Regnold, a wolf's head erased sa., charged on the neck with three bezants between two bars or. *Pro virtute.*

Reichel, late Most Rev. Charles Parsons, D.D., Bishop of Meath, out of a ducal coronet a demi-lion rampant double-queued holding between the paws a sickle, all or. *Vitam impendere vero.*

Reichel, Rev. Oswald Joseph, B.C.L., M.A., F.S.A., A la Ronde House, Lympstone, Devonsh., same crest and motto.

Reichel, Henry Rudolph, same crest and motto.

Reichel, Lucius Hurlock, Beara Court, Black Torrington, Devonsh., same crest and motto.

Reichel of Geising, in Saxony, out of a ducal coronet a demi-lion rampant double-queued holding between the paws a sickle, all or. *Vitam impendere vero.*

Reichenberg of Treveder, Cornw., a naked arm embowed and couped holding in the hand a laurel-branch. 228. 6

Reid, Bart., of Ewell Grove, Surrey, in front of a castle arg., two spears saltirewise ppr., points upwards. *Firm.*

Reid-Cuddon, Rev. John Edward, of Ashow Rectory, Warw.: (1) A dexter arm embowed in armour, the hand supporting a crossbow erect and bent ppr., fitted with an arrow gu., barbed arg. (*for Cuddon*). 235. 13. (2) Between four roses gu., barbed and seeded ppr., two on either side, a tower arg. (*for Reid*). *Fortiter et suaviter.—Firm.* 235. 14

Reid, Scotland, and of Imber Court, Wilts, a tower gu. *Firm.* 156. 5

Reid, a hand holding an open book. 215. 10

Reid, Scotland, issuing out of a cloud a hand holding a book expanded ppr. *Pro virtute.* 215. 1

Reid, Alexander Arthur, Esquire, of Ratho, Bothwell, Tasmania, a hand issuing from a cloud holding a book expanded ppr. *Pro virtute.—Nihil amanti durum.* 266. 16

Reid of Birnes, Aberdeensh., a hand issuing from a cloud holding a book expanded ppr. *Virtute et labore.* 215. 1

Reid of Blegbie, Scotland, a dexter arm issuing from a cloud holding a book expanded ppr. *Fortitudine et labore.* 215. 1

Reid, Andrew, Esquire, of London, and Lionsdown, Herts, a cubit arm erect issuing out of clouds holding the Holy Bible open at Job xix., all ppr., the edges of the leaves or. 266. 16

Reid, Nevile, of Shandwick, Ross-sh. and Cromarty-sh., same crest. *Pro veritate.*

Reid of Dublin, issuant from a rock a dexter cubit arm erect holding a bill, all ppr. *Firm.*

Reid, Scotland, a demi-eagle issuant gu., beaked az. *Fortitudine et labore.*

Reid, Scotland, and London, an eagle rising ppr. *In sublime.* 77. 5

Reid, John, Esquire, J.P., of Elderslie, Oamaru, New Zealand: a demi-eagle with wings elevated. *Fortitudine et labore.* 80. 2

Reid of London, an eagle rising ppr. *Fortitudine et labore.* 77. 5

Reid, Arthur Archibald Alexander, of Ledsham Hall, Chester, a demi-eagle displayed arg. *Fortitudine et labore.* 232. 4

Reid of Straloch, a demi-eagle displayed gu., beaked and armed az. *Fortitudine et labore.* 81. 6

Reid, Ireland, an eagle displayed with two heads sa., gorged with an Eastern coronet or. *Spectemur agendo.* cf. 74. 2

Reid, Bart., of Barra, Aberdeensh., Scotland, a pelican in her piety, all ppr. *Nihil amanti durum.* 98. 8

Reid, Sir James, Bart., G.C.V.O., K.C.B., V.D., of Muirton, Aberdeensh., same crest and motto.

Reid, Sir George, LL.D., 22, Royal Terrace, Edinburgh, a demi-ostrich arg. holding in the beak a sprig of laurel ppr. *Labor ipse voluptas.*

Reid, Ireland, a cock-pheasant ppr. *Semper eadem.* cf. 90. 8

Reid, a lion passant, the tail extended ppr. 5. 11

Reid, Ireland, a sheaf of rye gu. cf. 153. 2

Reidhaven, Viscount, *see* Seafield, Earl of.

Reidheugh of Cultibraggan, Scotland, two turtle-doves respecting each other az. *Nil nequit amor.* 93. 2

Reielly, Ireland, an archer shooting an arrow from a bow ppr. 188. 9

Reignolds, Devonsh. and Somers., out of a mural coronet arg., a talbot's head az., bezantée, eared or. cf. 56. 6

Reilly, Ireland, an archer shooting an arrow from a bow ppr. 188. 9

Reilly, Ireland, the sun gu. 162. 2

Reilly, John, Esquire, of the Inner Temple, London, a dragon's head couped sa., bezantée, and in front thereof an anchor entwined with a cable fessewise or. 71. 6

Reinell of East Ogwell, Devonsh., a fox passant or. 32. 1

Reiseley, a young man's head couped at the shoulders sa., with ear-rings or, crowned with a chaplet of flowers arg.

Relf, Worcs., and of Ashburnham, Sussex, an opinicus-head or, holding in the beak a snake vert, environed about the neck. 65. 7

Relfe of London, a peacock ppr., collared gu., with wings erect arg., semée of mascles of the second.

Relhan, three ostrich-feathers arg. *Naturæ minister.* 115. 1

Remfry of Truro, Cornw., an antelope lodged ppr., gorged with a collar nebuly gu., and supporting with the dexter fore-foot an escutcheon arg., charged with a wreath of ivy vert. 126. 11

Remington of Lund, Yorks, a hand holding a broken tilting-spear, all ppr. 214. 10

Remington, Rev. Reginald, of Crow Tree, Lancs, a hand erect holding a broken tilting-spear, all ppr. 214. 10

Remmington, between two laurel-branches in orle a fleur-de-lis.

Remnant of Billericay, Scotland, a dolphin naiant ppr. *Mind your own business.* 140. 5

Remnant, an eagle displayed sa. 75. 2

Rempston, a caltrap embrued ppr. 147. 14

Renals, Sir Joseph, Bart., 26, Craven Hill Gardens, W., upon a rock a fox sejant regardant ppr., charged on the shoulder with a lozenge or, and supporting with the dexter fore-leg a fasces, also ppr. *Cavendo tutus.* 272. 14

Rendall, Francis Shuttleworth, Esquire, of Brigmerston House, Amesbury, Wilts: (1) An antelope's head couped or, gorged with a collar gemel, holding in the mouth a horse-shoe, and charged for distinction with a cross crosslet, all gu. (*for Rendall*). (2) On a mount vert, a heathcock rising sa., winged or. (*for Holden*).

Rendel, Baron (Rendel), Hatchlands, Guildford, in front of a rock ppr., thereon a wolf passant az., collared arg., and supporting a flagstaff ppr., therefrom flowing to the sinister a banner sa., charged with a demi-lion rampant erased of the second, a staff raguly couped in fesse vert. *Labore et consilio.* 250. 19

Rendel, Rt. Hon. Stuart, Hatchlands, Surrey, same crest and motto

Rendel, Sir Alexander Meadows, K.C.I.E., 44, Lancaster Gate, W., in front of a rock ppr., a staff raguly fesseways vert, thereon a wolf passant az., collared arg., supporting with the dexter fore-leg a flagstaff, therefrom flowing a banner sa., charged with a demi-lion erased. *Labore et consilio.*

Rendlesham, Baron (Thellusson), a demi-greyhound salient arg., collared sa., between two wings of the last, each charged with a trefoil slipped or. *Labore et honore.* 60. 9

Renney, Scotland, two wings conjoined and inverted erm 113 3

Rennie, a parrot gu, feeding on a bunch of cherries ppr 101 8

Rennie, of Wateringbury, Kent, the sun in his splendour ppr, between two flagstaves broken on each, a flag flying to the exterior arg, charged with a saltire az 162 11

Rennie and **Renny,** a dexter hand holding a scimitar *Probitate* 213 5

Renny-Tailyour, Henry Waugh, of Borrowfield, Forfarsh (1) A hand holding a pair of balances ppr 217 13 (2) A hand ppr, holding a Passion cross gu *Probitate consilium perfecitur*

Renny, a dexter hand issuing holding a balance and scales or *Probitate* 217 13

Renny, George Henry, Dieu la Cresse Abbey, Leek, Staffs, issuant from clouds a cubit arm erect ppr, holding a balance or, between two wings gu each charged with a thistle leaved and slipped, also or *Recte faciendo*

Renolds, a portcullis chained 178 3

Renous, a demi griffin segreant regardant erminois, supporting a banner flotant to the dexter or, charged with a mullet az

Renshaw, Sir Charles Bine, Bart, Coldharbour, Wivelsfield, Sussex, in front of a griffin's head erased sa, a decrescent and an increscent arg *Esse quam videri* 284 15

Renshaw, a decrescent arg, and an increscent or, addorsed

Renshaw, Charles Bine J P, Barochan Houston, N B, a griffin's head erased

Renton, John Thompson Esquire J P of Bradston Brook, Surrey, and Hedgecocks, Sussex, a lion rampant az, holding in the dexter fore-paw a sword, point downwards ppr, pommel and hilt or, and resting the sinister fore paw on a tower arg

Renton of Lamberton, Berwicksh, two hands issuant in the one a sword, point downwards, fixed in the earth, the other lifted up to heaven *Trust in God and not in strength*

Renton, James Crawford, Esquire, M D, 1, Woodside Terrace, Glasgow, two arms issuant, habited and cuffed, the dexter cubit arm holding a sword erect, the sinister embowed, holding a sword point downwards *Trust in God, not in strength*

Rentoul, James Alexander, D L 10A, Great Queen Street, Westminster, a tree *Facta non verba*

Renwick, a lion's head erased 17 8

Renwick, Hon Sir Arthur, Clarendon House, Elizabeth Street, Hyde Park Sydney, in front of a stag's head erased ppr, between the attires a saltire or, three estoiles of the last

Reoch, Scotland, a rock ppr *Dieu est ma roche* 179 7

Reoch, Scotland, a dexter hand holding a dagger in pale ppr *Stand* 212 9

Reoch, a mountain in flames ppr 179 2

Repington of Amington Hall, Warw a demi-heraldic antelope gu, maned, bearded, tusked, and ungu or, billettee arg *Virtus propter se*

Repington, A'Court-, of Amington Hall, Warw (1) A demi-heraldic antelope gu billettee arg, attired, ungu, and tufted or (*for Repington*) (2) An eagle displayed sa, charged on the breast with two chevronels or, beaked and legged gu, and holding in the beak a lily ppr (*for A'Court*) *Virtus propter se*

Repley, Surrey a demi-lion rampant or 10 2

Repley, a lion's head erased az, collared or 18 6

Reppes, out of a ducal coronet a plume of feathers arg, the quills or, between two wings or

Reppley, a lion rampant az, collared arg *cf* 1 13

Repps or **Reppes** of West Walton Norf, out of a ducal coronet or a plume of ostrich feathers erm, between two wings of the first

Reresby, on a chapeau vert, turned up erm, a goat arg *cf* 129 5

Reresby, on a chapeau purp, turned up erm, a goat passant or *cf* 129 5

Resbye, Suff an arm couped at the shoulder embowed and erect from the elbow vested az holding in the hand ppr four ears of wheat or, stalked vert

Reskinner, Cornw, a wolf passant 28 10

Reskymer of Reskymer, in Mawgan, and of Murthen, Cornw a lion rampant sa, holding a branch of laurel vert

Resley of Chatwood, Bucks, a greyhound erm, collared az, ringed or, resting the dexter fore-foot on an escutcheon arg

Reson, a fox's head erased ppr 33 6

Reuce, a greyhound passant per pale arg and ppr *cf* 60 2

Reve, an heraldic tiger's head erased arg, collared and maned or

Reve of Malden Suff, a dragon's head erased arg collared or 71 2

Reve of Brede Sussex, a dragon's head arg, charged on the neck with three escallops two and one az *cf* 71 1

Revel, Yorks, and of Newbold Revel, Warw a cubit arm in armour ppr, the hand holding a lion's gamb erased of the last

Revel of Ogston, Derbysh, an arm in armour embowed ppr, garnished or, holding in the hand a dagger ppr, point downwards, between two bat's wings, also or, membraned gu

Reveley of Bryn y Gwyn, Merionethsh., an etoile of twelve points az *Optima revelatio stella*

Reveley, an etoile of sixteen points az

Revelstoke, Baron (Baring), of Membland Devonsh, a mullet erminois between two wings arg *Probitate et labore* *cf* 111 5

Revett, Suff, a dove az, winged or and gu, holding in the beak a branch vert 92 5

Revett, Cambs, and of Crettinge, Suff an arm erect, holding in the hand ppr a broken sword of the first, hilt and pommel or

Revett, Cambs and Suff, an arm, the hand holding a battle axe 213 12

Rew, a griffin passant ppr 63 2

Rewse, *see* Smith Rewse

Rewse of Hedgestone, Middx, a demi lion erm, holding a laurel branch vert

Rewtoure, a seax erect ppr 171 2

Reye, an ostrich feather arg, enfiled with a ducal coronet or 114 12

Reygnales and **Reynolds,** Suff, a wolf's head erased sa, collared or, charged with three guttes de-poix *cf* 30 11

Reymes and **Reynes** of Overswood Kettlestone, Norf, out of a ducal coronet or, a plume of two rows of ostrich-feathers ppr 114 4

Reynall of London and Egginton, Beds on a mount vert, a fox sejant regardant ppr, collared arg, resting the dexter paw on a lozenge or 32 9

Reynard-Cookson, *see* Cookson

Reynardson, on a mount a fox sejant regardant, resting the dexter paw on a lozenge 32 6

Reynardson of London and Plymouth Devonsh, a lion's head erminois, crowned with a mural coronet chequy arg and gu

Reynardson, Birch-, Colonel Charles, of Holywell Hall, Lincs (1) A lion's head erm, murally crowned chequy arg and gu (*for Reynardson*) *cf* 21 1 (2) A fleur de lis arg, and a trefoil vert, entwined by a serpent ppr (*for Birch*) *Virtus est vitium fugere —Prudentia simplicitate*

Reynell, Middx, and Devonsh, a fox statant or *cf* 32 2

Reynell, Bart (*extinct*) a fox statant or, the tail extended *Murus aheneus esto* *cf* 32 2

Reynell of Killynon, co Westmeath, Ireland, a fox passant or *Murus aheneus esto —Indubitata fides* 32 1

Reynell of Reynella co Westmeath Ireland, on a mount ppr, a fox passant or *Murus æneus esto* *cf* 32 1

Reynell-Peck, Arthur Denis Henry Heber, Netherton House, Newton Abbot, Devonsh, a mural crown arg, issuing therefrom a lion's head gu gorged with a wreath or *Fidus confido*

Reynes of Lewes, Sussex, a bird, the breast arg, the back az, holding in the beak a rose ppr

Reynes of Stanford, Notts, an arm issuing out of clouds, the hand holding three roses all ppr 218 12

Reynett, a cubit arm erect, holding in the hand an anchor in bend

Reynham of South Lynn, Norf, a morion between two mallets

Reynhouse, Middx, a demi griffin segreant regardant erminois, holding a banner flotant to the dexter or the point staff and tassels of the last, charged with a mullet az *cf* 64 14

Reynold, an eagle close 76 2

Reynold of Stratford, Warw, a fox's head erased or 33 6

Reynolds-Morton, Earl of Ducie, *see* Ducie

Reynolds, *see* Young Reynolds

Reynolds, Shropsh a fox's head erased ppr collared sa *cf* 33 6

Reynolds, Somers, a fox's head erased or 33 6

Reynolds of Great Yarmouth Norf a fox's head erased per pale arg and sa gorged with a collar or charged with three torteaux *cf* 33 6

Reynolds of Belsted, Suff., a fox's head erased sa., collared or. *cf.* 33. 6

Reynolds of Shotley, Suff., a fox's head erased sa., gorged with a collar or, charged with three torteaux, and on the neck with a martlet. 33. 7

Reynolds, Devonsh., a fox statant ppr. *Jus meum tueor.* *cf* 32. 2

Reynolds, James Emerson, Esquire, M.D., Burleigh House, Burlington Road, Dublin, same crest.

Reynolds of Colchester, Essex, a griffin's head erased per pale or and arg. 66. 2

Reynolds, Wilts and Somers., a griffin's head erased or. 66. 2

Reynolds, a cockatrice with wings addorsed ppr. 68. 4

Reynolds of London, a wyvern with wings elevated vert, holding in the dexter claw a sword in pale ppr. *Fide, sed cui vide.*

Reynolds, a wyvern passant gu. 69. 5

Reynolds, Henry Revell, M.A., 7, the Boltons, South Kensington: (1) Out of a mural coronet a demi-talbot collared and lined. (2) A dexter arm in armour embowed holding in the hand a lion's gamb erased. *Sperat infestis.*

Reynolds of Carshalton, Surrey, out of a mural coronet or, a demi-talbot arg., eared gu., collared and lined, the line ending in a knot or. *cf* 55. 9

Reynolds, Kent, out of a mural coronet or, a demi-talbot arg., collared and lined of the first. 55. 9

Reynolds, Sir Alfred James, Digswell, Welwyn, Herts, in front of a cross crosslet fitchée or, a talbot passant sa., langued gu., with the dexter paw resting on a rose of the first. *Quod verum tutum.* 244. 3

Reynolds, Walter, Hawkswick, St. Albans, Herts, same crest and motto.

Reynolds of London, on a mount vert, a panther couchant gardant arg., spotted of various colours, fire issuing from the mouth and ears ppr., gorged with a collar and lined gu., ringed or.

Reynolds of Attleborough, Norf., a cat couchant ppr., collared and lined or.

Reynolds of Laghnie, co. Leitrim, and Tully, co. Cavan, Ireland, on a mount vert, a stag lodged ppr. 115. 12

Reynolds, an eagle close arg., ducally gorged and lined or. *cf* 76. 2

Reynolds of Milford House, Hants, a cock's head erased gu., beaked or. 90. 1

Reynolds, a dexter arm in armour embowed, holding in the hand a garb, all ppr.

Reynolds, Ireland, a globe mounted ppr. 159. 4

Reynolds, out of a crescent an étoile. 163. 4

Reynous of Stanmore, Middx., a demi-griffin segreant regardant erminois, holding by the staff a banner flotant to the dexter or, the point and tassels of the last, charged with a mullet az. *cf.* 64. 14

Reyny, Yorks and London, out of a mural coronet arg., a lion's head or, pellettée, langued gu. *cf.* 19. 12

Rhan of Bremen and Enfield, Middx., a sprig of three acorns. 152. 5

Rhodes, Notts and Derbysh., a hand holding a bunch of acorns ppr.

Rhodes or **Rodes** of Great Houghton, Yorks, a cubit arm holding a branch of acorns, all ppr.

Rhodes of Bellair and Shapwick, Devonsh., a hand holding an oak-branch, all ppr. *Cœlum non animum.*

Rhodes, Sir Frederick Edward, Bart., of Loventor, Devonsh.: (1) A cubit arm vested az., guttée-d'or, cuffed arg., holding an oak-branch palewise ppr., fructed or, and two trefoils slipped in saltire vert (*for Rhodes*). (2) A dexter arm embowed vested az., charged with three annulets interlaced or, cuffed arg., holding in the hand ppr. an arrow of the last (*for Baker*).

Rhodes of New Zealand, and Kippax, Yorks, a dexter arm erect vested az., cuffed arg., charged with an acorn or, and grasping a fern sapling of New Zealand eradicated ppr. *Robur meum Deus.*

Rhodes, a griffin's head erased, tied round the neck with a ribbon. 66. 7

Rhodes, an eagle displayed per pale or and sa., charged on the breast with a cross patée counterchanged. *cf.* 75. 2

Rhodes of Knaresborough, Yorks, a leopard sejant or, spotted sa., collared and ringed arg. *cf.* 24. 8

Riall, Lewis John Roberts, Esquire, of Old Connâ Hill, co. Dublin, Ireland, a lion's head erased or, charged with an escallop gu., and holding in the mouth a trefoil vert. *Duw au fendith yw fy ngwenwth.*

Riall, William Arthur, Annerville, Clonmel, same crest. *Re alta modestas.*

Ribblesdale, Baron (Lister), Gisburne Park, West Riding, Yorks, a stag's head erased per fesse ppr. and gu., attired or, differenced by a crescent. *Retinens vestigia famæ.* 119. 8

Ribton, Sir George, Bart., of Woodbrook, co. Dublin (*extinct*), a dove close az., holding in his beak a laurel-branch ppr. *J'aime la liberté.* 92. 5

Ribton of Ribton, Cumb., out of an Eastern coronet or, a demi-lion rampant gu. *cf.* 10. 3

Ricard of London, a man's head couped at the shoulders ppr. *cf.* 190. 5

Ricard of Heck, Yorks, two arms embowed in armour or, the gauntlets arg., supporting a leopard's face of the same.

Ricarde-Seaver, *see* Seaver.

Ricardo, Frank, of Bromesberrow Place, Worcs., and Gatcombe Park, Glouc., a bird holding in the dexter claw a flagstaff with a flag, the latter charged with a cross.

Ricardo, Colonel Horace, Bramley Park, Guildford, Surrey, same crest.

Ricardo, Major Gerald Craven, the Elms, Donnington, Newbury, same crest.

Riccard of London, two lion's heads erased and addorsed. 17. 3

Rice, *see* Dynevor, Baron.

Rice, *see* Monteagle, Baron.

Rice, Ireland, an arm in armour embowed, holding in the hand a scimitar, all ppr. 196. 10

Rice of Preston, Suff., a raven's head erased or.

Rice, Wales, a raven ppr. 107. 14

Rice of Llwn-y-brain, Carmarthensh., Wales, a lion rampant ppr., holding in the dexter paw a bar-shot sa.

Rice, Sir Edward Bridges, K.C.B., Dane Court, Dover, a lion rampant ppr., holding in his paw a bar-shot sa. *Cadarn-yw-fy-ffydd-y-portha-duw-y-gigfrain.*

Rice, a spear-head issuing embrued. 174. 12

Rice of Ballymacdoyle, co. Kerry, a leopard's face gu., ducally crowned or. *Fides non timet.* 297. 5

Rice, Lieutenant-Colonel Richard Justice, J.P., of Bushmount, Lixnaw, co Kerry, same crest and motto.

Rich, Earl of Warwick and Holland (*extinct*), on a mount vert, a wyvern rising arg. *Garde la foy.* 69. 11

Rich, Bart. (*extinct*), of London, on a mount vert, a wyvern with wings elevated arg. 69. 11

Rich, on a mount vert, a wyvern arg. *Garde la foy.* 69. 11

Rich, Sir Charles Henry Stuart, Bart., of Shirley House, Hants, a wyvern arg., with wings expanded erm. *Garde la foy.* 70. 1

Rich, a wyvern arg. 70. 1

Rich, Ireland, a demi-sea-lion gu., armed and langued az., finned or.

Rich of Otford, Kent, a demi-lion rampant sa., between two spears erect arg. 9. 11

Rich, Berks, an armed arm and hand ppr., holding a cross crosslet fitched gu. 210. 14

Rich of Lexden, Essex, on the stump of a tree couped and erased or, a hawk with wings addorsed arg., preying on a pheasant ppr.

Richards of Yaverland, Hants, a griffin's head erased arg. 66. 2

Richards of Solsborough Grange and Ardamine, co. Wexford, Ireland, a griffin's head erased arg. *Honore et amore.* 66. 2

Richards of Rathaspick and Park, co. Wexford, a griffin's head erased arg. *In Deo confido.* 66. 2

Richards, an eagle's head couped ppr 83. 1

Richards of Heath, Hants, an eagle with wings expanded ppr. 77. 5

Richard, Scotland, a mountain-cat current ppr. *cf.* 26. 6

Richards of Fringe, Norf., a fleur-de-lis per pale erm. and arg. 148. 2

Richards, a fox's head couped gu. 33. 4

Richards of Rew, Devonsh., Isleworth, Middx., and Somers., a paschal lamb passant arg., the staff and banner ppr. 131. 2

Richards, William, of Grenfell House, Mutley, Plymouth, same crest.

Richards of Hammersmith, Middx., on a chapeau gu., turned up erm., a lamb passant arg., resting the dexter foot on a lozenge or.

Richards, Bart., of Brambletye House, Suff., and Sussex, a lion rampant az. *Honore et amore.* 1. 13

Richards, Rev. Walter John Bruce, D.D., St. Mary's, Westmoreland Road, Bayswater, upon a fleur-de-lis arg., a lion rampant az., collared with oak-leaves or. *Honore et amore.* 260. 18

Richards, Yorks, out of a mural coronet gu., a talbot's head arg., collared vert, ringed or. *cf.* 56. 6

Richards, an anchor erect and cabled sa, in front of two branches of laurel in saltire vert

Richards, a tower triple towered and the sun in splendour rising behind the same from clouds, all ppr *Pro clara de clara—Deo adjuvante non timendum*

Richards, an arm in armour embowed ppr, garnished or holding in the gauntlet a staff raguly sa, the end flaming

Richards, Richard Edward Lloyd, of Caerynwch, Merionethsh., a dexter arm holding in the hand a scimitar all ppr *Ffyddlawn ir Gwrionedd* 213 5

Richards, Ireland, an arm erect vested vert cuffed arg holding in the hand a rose branch, all ppr

Richardson, *see* Castle-Stewart Earl

Richardson, *see* Stuart Richardson

Richardson-Bunbury, *see* Bunbury

Richardson, *see* Hepborne

Richardson, *see* Morgan-Richardson

Richardson, Lord Cramond, out of a ducal coronet or, a unicorn's head erm *Virtute acquiritur honos* 48 12

Richardson, Jonathan, Esquire, J P, of Lambeg co Antrim, Ireland, a lion rampant arg armed and langued gu holding between the paws a laurel garland ppr *Virtute acquiritur honos*

Richardson, Nicholas Gosselin, Esquire Tyaquin Colmanstown Ballinasloe, co Galway, same crest and motto

Richardson, a lion rampant holding between the paws two oak-slips fructed ppr

Richardson, Scotland, a lion rampant per fesse or and az, holding in his dexter fore paw a garland of laurel ppr *Virtuti paret robur*

Richardson, John, Lambeg, Lisburn, same crest and motto

Richardson, Alexander Airth, J P, Aberdelghy Lambeg Lisburn, co Antrim a lion rampant arg, armed and langued gu, holding between the paws a laurel garland ppr *Virtute acquiritur honos*

Richardson of Augher, co Tyrone Ireland a lion rampant erm, holding in the mouth a trefoil slipped vert, and between the fore-paws a torteau charged with a cross crosslet or

Richardson, Middx, a lion of St Mark sejant with wings endorsed and erect arg, collared flory and counterflory gu, resting the dexter paw on a garb or

Richardson of Rotherbithe Surrey out of a mural coronet or, a demi-lion rampant gu, holding between the paws a guidon arg, charged with a slip of oak ppr, fructed or, the staff and tassels of the last

Richardson, Charles Edward, a mount vert, thereon in front of the battlements of a tower a lion's head erased sa, gorged with a collar vair *Virtute acquiritur honos* 252 11

Richardson, William John, same crest and motto

Richardson, Henry same crest and motto

Richardson, Sir Thomas, Kirklevington Grange, same crest and motto

Richardson of Riccall Hall Yorks a demi lion holding in its dexter paw a thistle, all ppr *Firmus infirmis* cf 13 12

Richardson, Durh on a mural coronet or, a lion's head erased ermines, langued gu, crowned with an earl's coronet of the first

Richardson, formerly of the Briary, Shotley Bridge, Durh, a lion's head erased ppr *Virtute acquiritur honos* 17 8

Richardson of Ripon Yorks a lion's head erased or, gorged with a chaplet vert 17 10

Richardson of Painsthorpe, Kirby-under Dale Yorks, out of a naval coronet or the sails arg a lion's head erm, surmounting an anchor in bend sinister of the first *Memores fecere merendo*

Richardson, John Crow, J P, Glanbrydan Park, Manordeilo, Carmarthensh, on a mural crown or, a lion's head erased gu. *Pretio prudentia præstat*

Richardson of Nantle Hall, on a mural coronet or, a lion's head erased erm crowned with an earl's coronet ppr *Trust in God*

Richardson of Albion Street, Hyde Park, London, W in front of a dexter arm in armour embowed grasping a scimitar, all ppr a lion's head erased or *Constans fidei*

Richardson, a hand in armour holding a sword in pale, all ppr *Virtute acquiritur honos*

Richardson of Pitfour, Scotland a dexter cubit arm in armour, holding in the hand a sword in pale, all ppr *Virtute acquiritur honos*

Richardson, Worcs, an armed arm, the hand holding a sword enfiled with a chaplet of roses ppr, hilt and pommel sa

Richardson, Harry Leo Sidney, Warham Road, South Croydon a dexter arm embowed in armour ppr, encircled by an annulet or the hand holding a sword erect, also ppr, transfixing a lion's head erased erm *Virtute acquiritur honos*

Richardson, William Ridley, Esquire M A (Trin Coll, Camb), formerly Lieutenant Camb Univ Rifle Volunteers of Ravensfell, Bromley, Kent, upon a mount vert in front of a tilting spear lying thereon in fess, a dexter arm in armour embowed, holding in the hand and by the blade a sword in bend sinister, all ppr, hilt and pommel or, the arm garnished of the last and encircled by an annulet also or, and pendant from the wrist by a ribbon gu an escutcheon arg, charged with a falcon ppr *Ben ti voglio* 195 11

Richardson of Dunsfold, Hambledon, and Finden Place, Sussex out of a mural coronet or, a cubit arm in armour holding in the gauntlet a falchion arg, the gripe vert, hilt and pommel or *Sibi constet*

Richardson, a dexter cubit arm in armour erect, holding in the hand ppr. a falchion 210 2

Richardson of Chawston, Worcs, and Glouc, a cubit arm in armour arg, holding in the hand ppr a broken sword the blade of the first, hilt and pommel or

Richardson, Richard Taswell, Esquire, J P, Barrister at-Law, of Capenhurst Hall Chester same crest

Richardson, William Henry 2, Lansdown Place Russell Square W C, a cubit arm in armour ppr the hand holding a broken sword, hilt and pommel or

Richardson, Sir James Thomas Stewart Bart, J P, D L, of Pitfour, Perthsh a dexter arm in armour grasping a dagger in pale all ppr *Virtute acquiritur honos*

Richardson of North Bierley Yorks, out of a ducal coronet or, a dexter arm in armour couped at the elbow, brandishing a falchion arg, the grip vert the hilt and pommel or

Richardson of Field House, Whitby Yorks, a dexter arm erect couped at the elbow, holding in the hand a broken sword ppr *Quod honestum est decet*

Richardson of Iron Acton, Glouc a dexter cubit arm erect in armour, holding in the hand ppr a falchion

Richardson of Honingham Norf, on a ducal coronet ppr, a dexter gauntlet fesseways sa, garnished or, holding a sword erect arg, hilt and pommel also or

Richardson, James Wilson Sneaton Hall, Whitby, Yorks a dexter arm erect couped below the shoulder, holding in the hand a broken sword, all ppr *Quod honestum est decet*

Richardson, Thomas Shepperd, Esquire of Hilder's Court Chiddingly, Sussex issuant from a wreath of oak vert, fructed or, a cubit arm erect ppr, grasping a hammer sa *In Deo et in ipso confide*

Richardson of Ferring, Sussex, out of a mural coronet or a cubit arm holding in the gauntlet a falchion ppr, pommel and hilt or

Richardson of Potto Hall, Northallerton, on the battlements of a tower or, in front of an anchor in bend sinister sa a lion's head erased erm *Potius ingenio quam vi*

Richardson, Charles Trusted Monckton Lodge Durh same crest and motto

Richardson, Warw an armed arm holding a sword enfiled with a chaplet of thorns ppr, hilt and pommel sa

Richardson, Hunts, an arm in armour couped at the elbow holding in the hand ppr a sword arg, hilt and pommel or *Virtute acquiritur honos* 210 2

Richardson of Wilton House, Eltham, Kent, out of a mural coronet or, a dexter arm in armour holding a falchion arg, the grip vert, the hilt and pommel or

Richardson of Upper York Street Portman Square, London, W, a mount vert thereon in front of a dexter cubit arm vested in the uniform of the East India Company's Marine, the hand grasping a scimitar ppr pommel and hilt or an anchor in bend sinister cabled of the last *Mea anchora virtus*

Richardson, Ireland, an arm in armour holding a sword with a bush of thorns at the end, all ppr, pommel and hilt sa *Plus spinis quam ferro*

Richardson, John Mervyn Archdall Carleton J P, same crest *Pro Deo et Rege*

Richardson, Norf. and Worcs., on a marquess's coronet a dexter arm in armour couped at the elbow in fess, holding in the gauntlet a sword erect, all ppr.

Richardson of Edinburgh, Scotland, a dexter arm in armour, the hand holding a broadsword in pale ppr. *Virtute acquiritur honos.* 210. 4

Richardson, Ralph, 10, Magdala Place, Edinburgh, same crest and motto.

Richardson of Keithock, Forfarsh., a unicorn's head arg., armed and maned or. *Virtute honor.* 49. 7

Richardson of Ralston, Renfrewsh., Scotland, issuing out of a ducal coronet or, a unicorn's head arg., armed and maned of the first. *Virtute acquiritur honos.* 48. 12

Richardson of Balmoral Villa, Kirn, Argyllsh., a unicorn's head arg., horned and maned or. *Virtute acquiritur honos.* 49. 7

Richardson, Scotland, a unicorn's head couped erm., armed or. *Virtute acquiritur honos.* 49. 7

Richardson, Scotland, out of a ducal coronet or, a unicorn's head ppr. *Virtute acquiritur honos.* 48. 12

Richardson, out of a ducal coronet a unicorn's head erm., armed or. *Virtute acquiritur honos.* 48. 12

Richardson of Aber-Hirnant, Merionethsh., out of a ducal coronet or, a unicorn's head erm., armed or. *Virtute acquiritur honos.* 48. 12

Richardson of Old Broad Street, London, a unicorn's head erased erm., armed, crined, and tufted or, charged with a bend engrailed gu., thereon three plates. *Virtute acquiritur honos.* *cf.* 49. 5

Richardson, George Wood, a unicorn's head arg., horned and maned or.

Richardson of Edinburgh, a bull's head couped ppr. *Virtute et robore.* *cf.* 44. 3

Richardson, a hind's head couped and collared ppr. *cf.* 124. 5

Richardson, Ireland, a hind's head couped or. 124. 1

Richardson, on a chapeau a wyvern with wings addorsed. 69. 14

Richardson, John Maunsell, J.P., Healing Manor, Lincs, a pegasus sejant sa., resting the dexter foot on a pheon or. *Honorantes me honorabo.* 261. 18

Richardson, late Rev. Henry Kemp, M.A., R.D., Rector of Leire, Leics., a stork ppr., charged on the breast with a cinquefoil and resting the dexter claw on an escutcheon gu., thereon a cross patée arg. *Confido in providentia.*

Richardson-Brady, late William Stewart, Manor Richardson, co. Tyrone, a cherub's head and neck ppr., between two wings or. *Claritate dextra.*

Riches, a hand erect issuing from a cloud holding a garb in bend sinister. 218. 3

Richmond, Duke of (Gordon-Lennox), Goodwood, Chichester, Sussex: (1) On a chapeau gu., turned up erm., a lion, statant gardant or, crowned with a ducal coronet gu., and gorged with a collar company arg. and gu., charged with two roses of the last. *cf.* 4. 2. (2) Out of a ducal coronet or, a stag's head and neck affrontée ppr., attired with ten tynes of the first. *En la rose je fleuris.* 119. 13

Richmond-Gale-Braddyll, Hubert Edward, East Court, Oxton, Chesh.: (1) A badger passant or (*for Braddyll*).

Richmond, Sir William Blake, K.C.B., Beavor Lodge, Beavor Lane, Hammersmith, a demi-lion arg., gorged with a collar and chain reflexed over the back az., the collar charged with two annulets or, holding between the paws encircled by a chaplet of oak an escutcheon az., thereon a fleur-de-lis arg. *Ancora impara.*

Richmond, the sun in his splendour ppr. 162. 2

Richmond, Scotland, between two palm-branches in orle vert, a mullet gu. 146. 8

Richmond of Hedenham, Norf., on a mount vert, an eagle with wings expanded erm., the beak and feathers on the back of the head and tip of the tail or.

Richmond of Rodborne, Wilts, and Stewley, Bucks, a tilting-spear arg., headed or, broken in three parts, the one piece erect, the other two in saltier, enfiled with a ducal coronet of the last. *cf.* 175. 2

Richmond, Douglas Close, Esquire, C.B., M.A., 64, Cornwall Gardens, S.W., same crest.

Richter of London, an eagle displayed sa., holding in the dexter claw an olive-branch vert, and in the sinister a thunderbolt ppr.

Richtie, a cubit arm holding in the hand a cross moline.

Rickard, Scotland, a gray cat sejant gardant. *Prenez garde.* 26. 8

Rickards, a lion passant gardant ppr. 4. 3

Rickards, a tower sa., and from the battlements a demi-lion rampant issuing or. 157. 11

Rickards, a castle with two towers, and from the battlements above the gateway a demi-lion rampant issuing. *cf.* 155. 10

Rickards of Evenjobb, Radnorsh., out of the battlements of a tower ppr., a talbot's head arg., collared vert, ringed or.

Rickards of Beeston, Notts, out of the battlements of a tower ppr., a demi-talbot arg., collared gu. *Esto quod esse videris.*

Rickards, of Westminster, a tower masoned ppr., charged with three annulets conjoined in a triangle gu., and within the battlements a talbot couchant, also ppr. 252. 10

Rickards, Arthur Walter, Esquire, of Parsonage Farm, Udimore, Rye, the Bath Club, 34, Dover Street, W., same crest.

Rickart of Rickartown, Scotland, a gray cat passant. *Prenez garde.—Præmonitus, præmunitus.* 26. 4

Rickart, of Auchnacant and Arnage, Scotland, issuing out of a cloud a dexter hand ppr., holding an escutcheon or, two broken arrows lying near ppr. *Præmonitus, præmunitus.*

Rickets and **Ricketts,** a demi-lion rampant gardant, holding in the dexter paw a battle-axe, all ppr. 16. 14

Ricketts, *see* Tempest.

Ricketts of Jamaica, and Combe, Heref., an arm embowed vested erminois, charged on the arm with two roses gu., cuffed az., the hand ppr. holding a scimitar arg., hilt and pommel or. *Quid verum atque decens.*

Ricketts, Bart. (now Tempest), of Beaumont, Leyes, Leics., out of a naval coronet or, in front of an anchor in bend sinister sa., a dexter arm embowed habited az., and charged on the sleeve with two roses arg., the hand grasping a scimitar ppr. *Prend moi tel que je suis.*

Ricketts, Frederick William Rodney, same crest and motto.

Ricketts, Henry Wyndham, same crest and motto.

Ricketts, Rev. Richard Ernest, M.A., Crambe Vicarage, Kirkham Abbey, same crest and motto.

Ricketts, Rev. St. Vincent Fitzhardinge Lennox, Fairholme, Bournemouth, same crest and motto.

Ricketts, William, R.N., same crest and motto.

Ricketts, Charles Aubrey, Esquire, of Dorton House, Bucks, issuant from a wreath of quatrefoils gu., an arm embowed vested arg., charged with two escallops, also gu., the hand holding a scimitar ppr.

Ricketts of Redland Hill, Glouc., out of a chaplet of roses alternately arg. and gu., a dexter arm in armour embowed or, the hand within a gauntlet grasping a sword ppr, pommel and hilt also or.

Rickford of London and Aylesbury, Bucks, a hawk's lure or, stringed sa., between two wings ppr. *Deeds, not words.* 110. 10

Rickthorne or **Rykthorne** of London and Somers., a buck trippant ppr., attired or, holding in the mouth a rose gu., stalked and leaved vert. *cf.* 117. 8

Ricraft, Shropsh., a sinister hand holding three ears of rye.

Ricrott, Lancs, a griffin's head erased. 66. 2

Ridall, Riddall, and **Riddell,** Durh. and Northumb., a demi-lion erminois supporting between the paws a garb az. 12. 5

Riddel, Scotland, a dexter hand ppr., holding an ear of rye slipped and bladed or. *Virtus maturat.* 218. 14

Riddell, a greyhound issuing ppr. *Row and retake.* 60. 11

Riddell of Granton, a greyhound erect ppr. *Row and retake.* 60. 11

Riddell of Glenriddell, Scotland, a demi-greyhound arg. *Hab shar.—Virtus maturat.* 60. 11

Riddell, Scotland, a demi-greyhound collared. *Right to share.* 60. 8

Riddell-Buchanan, Sir Walter, Bart., M.A., of Riddell, Roxburghsh., a demi-greyhound ppr. *I hope to share.* 60. 11

Riddell, a demi-lion rampant. 10. 2

Riddell, Edward Francis, of Cheesburn Grange, Northumb., a demi-lion couped or, holding a sheaf of rye az. *Deus solus auget aristas.* 12. 5

Riddell, John Giffard, Felton Park, Acklington, same crest and motto.

Riddell, *alias* **Bonner,** Glouc. and Oxon., a talbot's head couped arg., collared az., garnished and ringed or. *cf.* 56. 1

Riddell-Carre, Thomas Alexander, of Cavers Roxburghsh, Scotland a stag's head erased ppr, attired with ten tynes or *Tout droit* 121 2

Riddell of Carmeston, Roxburghsh, a demi-greyhound ppr *I hope to share*

Riddell, Sir Rodney Stuart, Bart of Ardnamurchan and Sunart, Argyllsh a hand issuing from the coronet of a French count holding a baton, all ppr *Utile et dulce*

Riddell or **Ridell,** Norf, a martlet arg 95 4

Riddle, a demi greyhound 60 11

Riddock, Scotland and Ireland a hind's head erased *Tu ne cede malis* 124 3

Ridehalgh, Lieutenant Colonel G J M, of Fell Foot, Ulverstone, a demi lion rampant ppr holding between the paws a garb or *Non minuetur* 12 5

Rideout or **Ridout,** Sussex, a trotting-horse arg, bridled gu *Toutz Foitz Chevalier*

Rideout, Arthur Kennedy, 50, the Drive, Hove, on a mount vert, a horse passant ppr bridled gu *Toutz Foitz Chevalier* 52 4

Rider, Middx, out of a ducal coronet or, a dragon's head arg 72 4

Rider, Middx, of Reygate, Surrey, and Staffs, out of a mural coronet or, a dragon's head arg 72 11

Rider of London, an eagle displayed ppr holding in the dexter claw a laurel branch, and in the sinister a thunderbolt of the first

Rider of Lichfield and Warw, out of a mural coronet per pale or and az, a snake in pale ppr, holding in the mouth a trefoil slipped vert

Rider of Manchester, Lancs, a crescent arg *Dum cresco, spero* 163 2

Rider of Beare Ferris, Devonsh, a crescent or 163 2

Ridge, Ireland a stork's head erased arg, holding in the beak a key sa

Ridge, a hand apaumee, thereon an eye ppr 222 4

Ridge of Tyning House, Sussex, out of a mural coronet two arms embowed the hands holding an escutcheon 200 9

Ridge of Chichester, Sussex, a peacock in his pride arg 103 12

Ridgeway, Earl of Londonderry, a dromedary couchant arg, the bridle and trappings or the saddle chequy sa, and of the second *Mihi gravato Deus* 13 12

Ridgeway of Tor, Devonsh, a dromedary couchant arg, maned sa, the bridle and trappings or 132 1

Ridgeway, Devonsh, a hawk ppr 85 2

Ridgeway, Devonsh, on a mount vert, a hawk with wings addorsed ppr, beaked and legged or cf 88 9

Ridgeway, Devonsh, a demi lion gu, holding an eagle's wing arg

Ridgley of London, Staffs, and Albright Hussey, Shropsh, a buck's head erased or 121 2

Ridgway, Bart. Devonsh, a dromedary couchant arg, maned sa the bridle and trappings or 132 1

Ridgway of Brandford, Gondhurst, Kent and Wallsuches Horwich, Lancs, in front of a palm tree a camel couchant ppr, bridled gu burdened on either side with a bale, also ppr, and gorged with a collar gemel or 132 3

Riding, a griffin's head erased arg 66 2

Ridleworth, Norf, a boar's head couped sa 43 1

Ridley, Viscount (Ridley), of Blagdon, Northumb, a bull passant, the tail turned over the back gu *Constans fidei* cf 45 5

Ridley, Hon Sir Edward, 48, Lennox Gardens S W, same crest and motto

Ridley, Thomas, Newcastle upon-Tyne in front of an oak tree sprouting ppr, a greyhound courant arg charged upon the body with two pellets, gorged with a collar, and pendent therefrom a cross patee sa *Constantia et prudentia*

Ridley of Parkend, Northumb, a bull passant, the tail turned over the back gu *Constans fidei* cf 45 2

Ridley, William Wells, Esquire J P of Holme Lea, Dorking Surrey same crest and motto

Ridley of London a bull passant gu cf 45 2

Ridley, Shropsh, a greyhound courant arg, collared and ringed gu cf 58 2

Ridley of Ridley Hall, Chesh, and Willymoteswick, and Waltown, Northumb a greyhound courant arg cf 58 2

Ridley, a buck's head erased or 121 2

Ridout and **Rideout,** a savage's head ppr

Ridout, same crest 52 4

Ridout, on a mount vert a horse passant arg, bridled or *Toutz foitz chevalier* cf 52 4

Ridpath, Scotland, a demi boar gu, bristled and armed or 40 13

Ridsdale, Yorks a lion's head az 21 1

Ridsdale of Old Hall near Wakefield, Yorks, on a mount a lamb passant ppr *Deus est spes* 131 9

Rig, Scotland, a cock sa, beaked and armed gu *Virtute et labore* 91 2

Rigaud, a buck's head erased az 121 2

Rigby of Preston Wiggan, Lancs an antelope's head erased or, guttée de-sang cf 126 2

Rigby of Burgh and Layton, Lancs, a goat's head sa, bezantee armed and bearded or cf 128 12

Rigby of Middleton Lancs, a goat's head erased or 128 5

Rigby, Rt Hon Sir John 16, Chelsea Embankment, S W, three mullets of six points in fesse sa, thereon a goat's head erased or, collared also sa *Esse quam videri*

Rigbye of Horrock Hall, Lancs, an antelope's head erased sa, attired, bearded and crined or 126 2

Rigdon, Lincs, a cock's head ppr, combed and wattled gu, beaked arg cf 90 1

Rigg of Dounfield, Fifesh, and Rigsland Scotland, a cock sa, beaked and armed gu *Virtute et labore* 91 2

Rigg, a cock sa, combed, legged and wattled gu 91 2

Rigg of Chorlton on-Medlock, Lancs, a cock sa, combed and wattled gu *Dum vivo cano* 91 2

Rigg, Herbert Addington, Wallhurst Manor Cowfold, Horsham, same crest *Virtute et labore*

Rigg, Gibson Sagar Esquire, of Motley Bank, Bowdon Chesh, a heart gu surmounted by a rose or, all within a chain in arch of the last *Virtute et labore* 181 5

Rigg, William Robinson, Turton Towers, Turton, Lancs, same crest and motto

Rigge of Wood Broughton Cartmel, Lancs a sheldrake ppr, holding in the beak an escallop arg *Festina lente*

Riggeley, Staffs, a buck's head erased or 121 2

Rigges of Farnham, Surrey, Stanning Sussex, and Southampton Hants, a talbot passant gu, eared or, holding in the mouth a bird-bolt of the last, feathered arg cf 54 1

Rigges of London, a water-spaniel arg, holding in the mouth a bird bolt or cf 57 7

Rigges-Miller, Thomas John, Esquire J P, of Tyone House, Nenagh, co Tipperary Ireland a wolf's head erased gu, gorged with a collar wavy arg, and charged on the neck with a cross patee or *Malo mori quam fœdari*

Riggs and **Rygges,** Middx, and of Strangle Thorpe, Lincs, a talbot passant gu, eared or, holding in the mouth a bird-bolt of the last feathered arg cf 54 1

Righton, Kent, a tree ppr 143 5

Rigley of Nottingham a mount vert thereon a sea-lion sejant ppr the fore foot supporting an antique shield or, charged with a rose gu, barbed vert, seeded of the third 20 1

Rigmaiden of Wedacre, Lancs a buck's head erased sa 121 2

Riky, Ireland, a dexter hand holding a sword ppr 212 13

Riky, John, Mount Hall, Killygordon, co Donegal a demi-lion rampant, holding in the dexter paw a thistle *Hic fructus virtutis* 238 15

Riley, Berks, an oak tree a snake clinging to the trunk ppr 143 6

Riley, William Felix Esquire, J P, D L, of Forest Will, Windsor, Berks out of a mural coronet an oak tree with a snake entwined descending its trunk, all ppr *Fortitudine et prudentia* cf 143 6

Riley, a dragon's head or, pellettee cf 71 1

Riley, a dragon's head erased sa, charged with a plate and two bezants

Riley, Lancs and Lincs, a dragon's head erased gu, bezantee

Riley, John, Esquire of the Inner Temple, London a dragon's head couped sa bezantee, and in front thereof an anchor entwined with a cable fessewise or. *Spero infestis metuo secundis* 71 6

Riley, John, Putley Court, Ledbury, Heref a dragon's head couped sa, bezantee, and in front thereof an anchor entwined with a cable fessewise or *Sans Dieu rien* 261 10

Riley, Hamlet, of Ennim, Penrith same crest and motto

Riley, James Julian Allan, Ewood Hall, Mytholmroyd, Yorks, same crest and motto

Riley, John Athelstan Laurie, 2, Kensington Court, W, and St Petroc Minor, St Issy, Cornw, same crest *Spero infestis metuo secundis*

Rimmer, a dolphin naiant ppr. 140. 5

Rind of Carse, Scotland, and Amsterdam, a flower-pot containing gillyflowers. *Diuturnitate fragrantior.*

Ring, a hand vested sa., cuffed or, holding a roll of paper. 208. 8

Ring, a dragon with wings elevated. cf. 73. 2

Ringer, Nort., a unicorn's head couped or, semée-de-lis az., between two branches of laurel vert. cf. 49. 14

Ringewood or **Ringwood,** a goat courant towards a tree ppr. 129. 6

Ringley, a wolf's head paly or and sa., enfiled round the neck with a coronet arg., holding in the mouth a fish gu.

Ringrose-Voase of Chilworth Tower, near Romsey, and Aulaby House, near Hull: (1) A rose within a gem-ring. (2) An eagle's head erased, ducally gorged. *Rosa sine spina.*

Rintoul, Scotland, an elm-tree ppr.

Ripley of London, a demi Bengal tiger, ducally gorged ppr.

Ripley of London, Middx., Wilts, and of Ripley, Yorks, a demi-lion rampant regardant vert, collared arg., supporting between the paws an escutcheon per chevron or and az.

Ripley, Sir Frederick, Bart., of Acacia and Bowling Lodge, Yorks, and Bedstone House, Shropsh., a demi-lion regardant vert, gorged with a collar gemel and charged on the body with a cross crosslet or, holding between the paws an escutcheon arg., charged with a cock ppr. 14. 1

Ripon, Marquess of (Robinson), Studley Royal, near Ripon, out of a coronet composed of fleurs-de-lis or, a mount vert, thereon a stag at gaze of the first. *Qualis ab incepto.* cf. 118. 7

Rippon, an antelope's head erased or. 126. 2

Rippon, George, Esquire, of Water Ville, Northumb., a lion sejant ducally gorged ppr., holding in the dexter paw a cross patée-fleury fitched sa. *Our hope is on high.—Frangas, non flectes.*

Rippon, Valentine, Rogerley Hall, Frosterly R.S.O., Durh., same crest. *Frangas, non flectes.*

Risdon, Devonsh., an elephant's head erased erm., eared and armed or. 133. 3

Rise, Ireland, a leopard's face arg., langued gu., crowned with a viscount's coronet ppr. *Fides non timet.*

Risebrow of Norwich, a fret between two wings arg.

Rishton of Elswick, Lancs, a lion passant sa. *Reviresco.* 6. 2

Rishton of Pontalghe, Lancs, a demi-lion rampant erminois. 10. 2

Rishton of Dunkinhaw, Sparth, and Antley, Lancs, on a chapeau gu., turned up erm., a demi-lion erminois. cf. 15. 13

Rising, a pelican vulning herself ppr. 98. 1

Risk, S. Tudor, 51, Victoria Street, S.W.: (1) A dexter arm in armour embowed, holding in the hand a dagger fesseways, point to the dexter (*for Risk*). (2) A demi-lion rampant holding in the dexter paw a Tudor rose (*for Tudor*).

Risley of Risley, Lancs, an oak-tree and thereon a raven, all ppr. *Fato prudentia major.*

Ritchie, Daniel Norman, the Holmes, St. Boswells, N.B., a cubit arm and hand ppr., holding a cross fleury or. *Ostendo non ostento.*

Ritchie, James, 14, Sussex Gardens, Hyde Park, W., same crest and motto.

Ritchie, Robert Blackwood, Blackwood, Penshurst, Victoria, same crest and motto.

Ritchie, a demi Bengal tiger ppr., ducally gorged gu.

Ritchie of Craigtown, Scotland, a unicorn's head erm., armed or. *Virtute acquiritur honos.* 49. 7

Ritchie, James Thomson, Esquire, J.P., same crest and motto.

Ritchie, Rt. Hon. C. T., M.P., same crest and motto.

Ritchie, Major-General John, late R.A., 34, Clarence Parade, Southsea, a dexter hand ppr., holding a cross moline gu. *Ostendo non ostento.*

Ritson, a lion rampant. 1. 13

Ritson, Utrick Alexander, 1, Jesmond Gardens, Newcastle-on-Tyne, issuant from the battlements of a tower or, a lion's head sa., in front thereof a hawk's lure fesseways, also or. *Virtute acquiritur honos.* 261. 8

Rivel, a gem-ring or, stoned gu. 167. 14

Rivers, Baron (*extinct*), of Sudley Castle (Pitt), a stork ppr., beaked and membered or, the dexter claw resting on an anchor erect, cabled of the last. *Æquam servare mentem.* 105. 10

Rivers, *see* Fox-Pitt-Rivers.

Rivers of London, out of a bunch of reeds vert, a demi-swan with wings expanded arg., ducally gorged or.

Rivers, a griffin's tail erased sa. 123. 14

Rivers, an arm in armour embowed, the hand grasping a dart. 198. 4

Rivers, De, a land-tortoise ppr. cf. 125. 5

Rivers, Bart., of Chafford, Kent, on a mount vert, a bull passant arg., collared, ringed, lined, and armed or. *Secus rivos aquarum.*

Riversdale, *see* Alcock-Stawell-Riversdale.

Riversdale, Baron, Ireland (Tonson), out of a mural coronet or, a cubit arm in armour, holding in the hand a sword, all ppr. *Manus hæc inimica tyrannis.*

Rives, Dorset, a greyhound sejant sa., bezantée, collared or. cf. 59. 2

Rivett-Carnac, *see* Carnac.

Rivett, Cambs, an arm, holding in the hand a battle-axe ppr. cf. 213. 12

Rivett of Crettinge, Suff.: (1) An arm erect, the hand ppr. grasping a broken sword of the first, hilt and pommel or. (2) An arm, holding in the hand a battle-axe. cf. 213. 12

Rivett, Hants, a cubit arm in armour erect, holding in the hand a sword ppr. 210. 2

Rivett of Stowmarket, Suff., and Chippenham, Cambs, an arm erect couped at the elbow vested per pale arg. and sa., and cuffed counterchanged, holding in the hand ppr. a broken sword of the first, the handle of the second, the pommel and hilt or.

Rivett-Carnac, Sir James Henry Sproule, Bart., 39, Ovington Square, S.W., a sword erect, pomme land hilt or, issuant from a crescent erm., the internal part gu. *Sic itur ad astra.*

Rivett-Carnac, John Henry, C.I.E., V.D., F.S.A., same crest and motto.

Rivington, on a ducal coronet a hawk belled, all ppr.

Rivington, Charles Robert, Castle Bank, Appleby, Westmoreland, on a crown vallary or, a mount vert, thereon a falcon close ppr., belled or, holding in the beak a hawk's lure reflexed over the back az. *Deum timete et regem favete.* 244. 7

Rix, a demi-griffin ppr. 64. 2

Rix, Arthur Henry Geoffrey, Esquire, son of the late Henry William Rix, Esquire, of the Grove, Thorpe Hamlet, Norwich, a demi-unicorn or, gorged with a collar nebuly az., with a chain reflexed therefrom arg., resting the sinister leg on a cross patée within an annulet, also az. *Rix in min mod.* 297. 3

Rixon, out of a mural coronet a tiger's head ducally gorged. 27. 1

Roach, a horse's head erased arg., bridled gu. cf. 51. 5

Roach, on a mount vert, a pelican preying on a roach, all ppr.

Roach, on a rock a stork with wings elevated, holding in the dexter claw a fish, all ppr.

Roachead, Scotland, a naked arm erect ppr. *Pro patria.* 222. 3

Road and **Roades,** an eagle displayed, holding in the dexter claw a dagger ppr. 75. 7

Roaed and **Roald,** out of a ducal coronet two dragon's wings expanded or, with a chapeau between them arg.

Roane, a stag's head erased ppr., attired or, holding in the mouth an acorn or, leaved vert. cf. 119. 11

Robartes, Baron (Rt. Hon. Thomas Charles Agar-Robartes, M.A.), of Lanhydrock and Truro, Cornw.: (1) A lion rampant or, holding a flaming sword erect ppr., the pommel and hilt of the first. (2) A demi-lion rampant or. 10. 2

Robarts, out of a maunch per pale arg. and gu., cuffed of the second, a hand clenched ppr. 203. 3

Robarts, a stag lodged regardant ppr., attired or. cf. 115. 9

Robarts of London, a stag lodged ppr., attired or. 115. 7

Robarts, Abraham John, of Lillingstone, Bucks, a stag lodged regardant ppr. *Nec temere, nec timide.* cf. 115. 9

Robarts of Charlotte Street, Bedford Square, London, a stag's head erased per fess erminois and gu., attired or, gorged with a collar invected per fesse az. and arg., thereon a cross patée between two annulets or. 121. 12

Robb, Scotland, a hand holding a chapeau between two branches of laurel in orle, all ppr. 217. 5

Robe, a pole-cat ppr. 135. 13

Robe of London, Somers., and Scotland, an ermine passant ppr. *Candore.* 134. 6

Robe of London, a cross crosslet fitched or. 166. 2

Robe, a sabre erect arg., hilted and pommelled or, between two branches of laurel ppr., crossing each other at the hilt and point of the sabre.

Roberton, an anchor erect ppr. *Securitate.* 161. 1

Roberton of that ilk, and Earnock Lanark, an anchor ppr *For security* 161 2

Roberton, John, Lauchope, Holytown, N B, same crest and motto

Roberts, *see* Atkin Roberts

Roberts, Ellis, 6, William Street Lowndes Square, S W, a demi Greek maiden vested az ermed or, on her head a cap of the first holding in her dexter hand four ears of barley stalked and leaved or and in her sinister hand a painter s palette and brushes ppr *Per artem lumen*

Roberts, Griffiths Williams M D, Vale St Denbigh in front of a Saracen's head affrontee erased at the neck ppr, wreathed about the temple or and gu five annulets interlaced fessewise of the last *Nec temere, nec timide*

Roberts, Earl (Roberts) a lion rampant or armed and langued gu charged on the shoulder with an Eastern coronet of the last, and holding in the dexter paw a sword, the blade wavy arg, pommel and hilt of the first *Virtute et valore* 288 9

Roberts of Twickenham, Middx and Cornw, a lion rampant or, holding in the dexter paw a sword the blade wavy arg the hilt and pommel of the first

Roberts, Sir Owen, J P D L, M A, F S A, of 44, Albert Court, Kensington Gore London S W and Plas Dinas, Carnarvonsh, North Wales, a lion rampant per fesse sa and or, guttee counterchanged, holding in the dexter fore paw a branch of three roses arg, stalked and leaved ppr and resting the dexter hind-paw upon two annulets interlaced of the second *Dum spiro spero* 2 9

Roberts, William Robert, Esquire, J P, of Milford Haven, Pembrokesh a lion rampant guardant gu, gorged with a collar engrailed or, holding in the dexter fore paw a dagger ppr, and resting the sinister fore paw on an escutcheon of the second, charged with a bull's head caboshed between three mullets of six points also gu

Roberts, Arthur Phillips, of Coeddu, Flintsh, a lion rampant *Dum spiro spero* 1 13

Roberts, on a chapeau az turned up erm, a lion sejant gardant 7 6

Roberts, Lincs, Worcs and Cornw, a demi-lion az holding a mullet arg pierced sa 15 7

Roberts, Rev Ernest Stewart Master of Gonville and Caius College Cambridge, a demi-lion rampant, holding between the paws a mullet of five points *Suaviter sed fortiter*

Roberts of London, a demi-lion az, holding in the dexter paw a mullet sa 15 7

Roberts, Thomas James Scougal, J P, of Drygrange, Melrose N B, a demi-lion rampant az, holding in the dexter paw a fleur-de-lis or *Industria et probitate*

Roberts, Alexander Fowler, Esquire, J P, of Fairnalie, residing at Thornfield, Selkirk, N B, same crest and motto

Roberts, John, Esquire C M G Littlebourne House Dunedin, New Zealand, same crest and motto

Roberts of Corfton Manor Shropsh, a demi-lion per pale erminois and az, holding in the dexter paw a mullet pierced sa, and charged with a bendlet wavy sinister of the second and or *Deo adjuvante fortuna sequatur*

Roberts, William Esquire of Field House Worcs a demi-lion guardant per bend dovetailed or and gu, holding in the dexter paw a sword erect of the last, and resting the sinister upon a pheon of the first *God and my conscience* 226 1

Roberts, Crompton-, Charles Montagu, Esquire of Drybridge, Monm (1) A demi-lion rampant guardant per bend dovetailed or and gu holding in the dexter paw a sword erect of the last and resting the sinister upon a pheon of the first (*for Roberts*) 306 1 (2) A talbot sejant or, pellettee, resting the dexter paw upon an escutcheon az, charged with a lozenge arg (*for Crompton*) 306 2

Roberts, Kent an eagle displayed arg beaked and legged or, gorged with a chaplet of laurel vert, charged with a crescent for difference *cf* 75 2

Roberts, Bart (*extinct*) of Glassenbury Kent, an eagle displayed arg gorged with a chaplet vert *cf* 75 2

Roberts, William Henry Holborough Court, Rochester, same crest *Fide Deo*

Roberts of Beechfield Bromley Kent, an eagle displayed *Dum spiro spero* 75 2

Roberts, Sir Randal Howland Bart, of Brightfieldstown, co Cork, on a mount vert an eagle displayed az wreathed round the neck with ivy ppr *Post funera virtus* 74 10

Roberts, an eagle's head couped 83 1

Roberts, John Richards, Esquire, J P, of Dormstown Castle, co Meath, Ireland an eagle's head couped or charged with an estoile sa *Eu nêr a folant* 261 7

Roberts, William Edward, Hendre Kilbney, co Dublin, same crest *Eu nêr a folant*

Roberts, W R of 51, Cambridge Street Hyde Park W, same crest

Roberts, a griffin's head couped 66 1

Roberts, Ireland an antelope's head erased per fess arg and gu 126 2

Roberts of Sutton Chevell Leics an antelope's head erased party per fess arg and gu

Roberts, Rev Claude William B A of Woodrising, Sproylon Tasmania Chairman of the Devon Hospital Tasmania *uses* a stag's head erased *Se negare est amare* 121 2

Roberts, Shropsh, a stag's head erased or, collared gu *cf* 121 2

Roberts, a stag trippant sa *Successus a Deo est* 117 8

Roberts, Shropsh and Somers, on a mount vert, a buck trippant sa, attired or, ducally gorged and chained of the last *cf* 118 2

Roberts of Ombersley, Worcs, Camberwell Surrey, and Seedley Lancs upon a mount vert, a holly-tree ppr, in front thereof a goat statant arg, armed and ungu or gorged with a collar gemel sa, holding in the mouth a sprig of holly, also ppr *Ewch ymlaen*

Roberts, Shropsh, a boar's head sa 43 1

Roberts, a leopard s head gardant erased arg, semee of torteaux

Roberts, Middx, and of Little Braxsted Essex (1) Out of a ducal coronet or, a demi-greyhound sa *cf* 60 11 (2) A leopard's head gardant and erased arg semee of torteaux

Roberts, out of a ducal coronet or, a demi greyhound sa *cf* 60. 11

Roberts, Bart (*extinct*) of Willesden Middx a greyhound arg, collared gu *cf* 60 2

Roberts, Shropsh a coot ppr

Roberts-Austen, Sir William Chandler, K C B, Blatchfeld Chilworth, Surrey (1) Upon the battlements of a tower or a tilting-spear fesseways ppr, thereon a roebuck sejant arg attired or (2) On the battlements of a tower ppr, a falcon rising ppr supporting with the dexter claw an anchor or (*for Roberts*)

Roberts-West, Charles Robert, out of a ducal coronet or a gryphon's head proan beaked and eared of the first

Roberts-West, Lieutenant James, R N R Alscot Park, Glouc same crest

Roberts-West, Leonard, Mount House, Hythe Hants same crest

Robertson, Baron (Robertson), Forteviot, Perthsh, a dexter arm erect ppr, charged with an ermine spot the hand holding an imperial crown also ppr *Virtutis gloria merces*

Robertson, *see* Forbes Robertson

Robertson, *see* Stewart Robertson

Robertson of Strowan Perthsh, Scotland, a dexter hand holding up an imperial crown, all ppr *Virtutis gloria merces* 217 1

Robertson, Askew-, Watson of Ladykirk Berwick and Pallinsburn, Northumb (1) A dexter hand charged with a cross crosslet gu, holding up an imperial crown, all ppr (2) A dexter hand holding on a poignard erect ppr, hilt and pommel or, a Saracen s head couped and embrued ppr, wreathed about the temples with a torse arg and gu, tied with ribands of the same colours, and above on a scroll the motto, *Fac et spera* (*for Askew*) *Virtutis gloria merces* 217 1

Robertson of Hoe Place Surrey, same crest and motto

Robertson of Edinburgh an arm erect the hand holding an imperial crown ppr *Virtutis gloria merces* 217 1

Robertson of Parson s Green Edinburgh Scotland, a dexter hand ppr, charged with a star az, holding up an imperial crown, also ppr. *Virtutis gloria merces* *cf* 217 1

Robertson of Newbiggin, Scotland, a hand ppr, charged with a crescent arg and holding up an imperial crown or *Virtutis gloria merces* *cf* 217 1

Robertson, Rt Hon James Patrick Bannerman, P C, of Edinburgh, Lord Justice General of Scotland, a dexter arm erect ppr, charged with an er mine spot, the hand holding an imperial crown, also ppr. *Virtutis gloria merces.* cf. 217. 1

Robertson of Foreshores at Kilmun and Strone, Argyllsh., a dexter hand erect ppr., holding an antique crown or. *Virtute acquiritur honos.*

Robertson, Alasdair Stewart, the Barracks, Rannoch, N.B., a dexter arm and hand erect holding a regal crown, all ppr. *Virtutis gloria merces.*

Robertson, Herbert, of Huntington Castle, co. Carlow, and the Cedars, South Hackney, N.E., a dexter cubit arm erect holding a falchion enfiled with an antique crown, all ppr. *Ramis micat radix.*

Robertson, Scotland, a cubit arm erect, the hand holding a falchion enfiled with an antique crown, all ppr. *Ramis micat radix.*

Robertson, Charles, Kindeace, Ross-sh., a dexter arm holding up an imperial crown ppr., also a swan ppr.

Robertson, Edgar William, Auchleeks House, Blair Athol, a dexter arm and hand erect holding a regal crown, all ppr.

Robertson of London, a dagger erect, ensigned on the point with a regal crown ppr. *Intemerata fides.*

Robertson, Scotland, a dexter hand holding a sword in pale ensigned with a royal crown. *Virtutis gloria merces.*

Robertson of Pitmillan, Scotland, a hand from the wrist holding a dagger in pale supporting an imperial crown ppr.

Robertson of Tranent, Scotland, a dexter hand holding a crescent ppr. *Quæque favilla micat.* 216. 8

Robertson of Muirtown, Elginsh., and Gladney, Fifesh., Scotland, a dexter hand issuing from a cloud holding a garb ppr. *Perseveranti dabitur.* 218. 3

Robertson of Kinlochmoidart, Inverness-sh., out of a cloud a dexter hand holding a garb ppr. 218. 3

Robertson, Scotland, a dexter hand holding two laurel-branches slipped ppr. *Hac virtus mercede digna.* 218. 4

Robertson of Edinburgh, Scotland, a dexter hand issuing from a cloud holding a cornucopia ppr. *Perseveranti dabitur*

Robertson of Aberdeen, Scotland, a savage's arm erect and erased ppr. *Intemerata fides.*

Robertson, Scotland, a wolf's head arg., holding in the mouth a rose gu. *Robore et sapore.* 29. 7

Robertson of Lude, Perthsh., a sleeping dog. *Dinna waken sleeping dogs.*—*Ductus non coactus.*

Robertson, a swan ppr. *Vita faciendo nemini timeas.* 99. 2

Robertson of Fascally, Perthsh., a phœnix in flames ppr. *Post funera virtus.* 82. 2

Robertson of London, a Triton holding in his sinister hand a trident ppr. 185. 12

Robertson of Deisaprice, Lincs, a stag trippant or. 117. 8

Robertson of Bishopmilne, Elginsh., a galley sa. *Detur gloria Deo.* 160. 6

Robertson-Fullarton, Archibald Louis, of Kilmichael, Brodick, Isle of Arran, a camel's head erased ppr. *Lux in tenebris.*

Robertson-Ross, Hugh Maynard Eyre, an eagle displayed ppr., charged on the breast with a water-bouget sa., and resting each claw upon a buckle or. *Spes aspera levat.*

Robertson-Macdonald, Admiral David, 1, Mardale Crescent, Edinburgh: (1) A dexter hand issuing out of clouds holding a garb ppr. (2) A castle arg., masoned sa. *Perseveranti dabitur.*—*My hope is constant in thee.*

Robertson-Glasgow, Robert Purdon, Craigmyle, Torphins, Aberdeensh.: (1) A dexter hand holding up an imperial crown, all ppr. (2) A demi-negro holding in the dexter hand a sugar-cane, all ppr. *Quo fas et gloria.*—*Parcere subjectis.*

Robertson-Luxford, John Stewart Odiarne, Higham House, Robertsbridge, Sussex: (1) On a rock ppr., a wolf rampant or, collared, with line reflexed over the back az., supporting an arrow, point downwards. (2) A hand holding up an imperial crown ppr. *Virtutis gloria merces.*

Robin of Grove Hill, Chesh., and Tan-y-graig, Denbighsh., a robin ppr. *Vivit post funera virtus.* 108. 1

Robins of London, a talbot's head or. 56. 12

Robinson, see Ripon, Marquess of.

Robinson, Yorks, in a coronet composed of fleurs-de-lis or, a mount vert, thereon a buck at gaze of the first. *Virtute, non verbis.* cf. 118. 7

Robinson, on a ducal coronet or, a mount vert, thereon a buck of the first. 118. 4

Robinson, Lord Rosmead, on a wreath of the colours and out of a vallary coronet or, a mount vert, thereon a stag at gaze of the first, charged on the shoulder with a fleur-de-lis az. *Legi regi fidus.* 313. 4

Robinson of Aigburth, Lancs, on a vallary coronet a stag at gaze or, supporting with the dexter fore-foot an escutcheon per saltire purp., and of the last, charged with a saltire erm. *Virtute non verbis.*

Robinson, Major Thomas Middleton, of Charlton Musgrove, Somers., and of Western House, Emsworth, Hants, a buck or, supporting with his dexter fore-leg an escutcheon quarterly gu. and or, in the first quarter a cross flory arg. *Post nubila Phœbus.*

Robinson of Bath, Somers., on a mural coronet gu., a buck at gaze or. cf. 117. 3

Robinson of Chapelizod, co. Dublin, Ireland, on a ducal coronet or, a buck trippant ppr. *Faithful.* cf. 117. 8

Robinson, a stag trippant or, charged on the side with an ermine spot sa. cf. 117. 8

Robinson, Ireland, a buck trippant or, pellettée. *Non nobis solum, sed toti mundo nati.* cf. 117. 8

Robinson, Bart. (*extinct*), of Rokeby Park, Yorks, a buck trippant or, pellettée. cf. 117. 8

Robinson, Bart., of Cranford, Northants, and Stretton Hall, Leics., a buck trippant or, collared and lined vert, the collar charged with three trefoils slipped of the first.

Robinson of Boston, Lincs, a buck trippant sa., bezantée. cf. 117. 8

Robinson of London and Yorks, a stag trippant vert, attired or, bezantée. cf. 117. 8

Robinson, Bart. (*extinct*), of Kentwell Hall, Suff., a buck trippant or. 117. 8

Robinson, Kossuth, J.P., Downleaze, Stoke Bishop, near Bristol, a buck trippant. *Id facito summo ope.*

Robinson of Herrington and Hendon Lodge, Durh., a stag trippant or. 117. 8

Robinson of Haveringate Bower, Essex, a stag trippant ppr. 117. 8

Robinson, Sir Ernest William, Bart., a buck trippant arg., attired and ungu. or, in front of park pales ppr. *Spes mea in futuro est.* 288. 6

Robinson, Sir Gerald William Collingwood, Bart., J.P., D.L., of Rokeby Hall, co. Louth, a buck trippant or, pellettée. cf. 117. 8

Robinson, Sir James Lukin, Bart., of Beverley House, in city of Toronto, and of Middle Temple, London, a stag trippant or, semée of lozenges az., and resting the dexter fore-foot on a mill-rind sa. *Propere et provide.* 310. 12

Robinson, Charles Walker, Beverley House, Mitcham Common, Surrey, same crest.

Robinson, Sir Frederick Villiers Laud, Bart., Cranford Hall, near Kettering, a buck trippant or, collared and lined vert, the collar charged with three trefoils slipped of the first.

Robinson, Frederick, Esquire, upon a mount vert, amid fern ppr., a stag trippant or, guttée-d'olive.

Robinson of London, a buck statant or, pellettée. cf. 117. 5

Robinson of Tottenham, Middx., a buck per pale or and vert, resting the dexter foot on an escutcheon of the last, charged with a trefoil slipped of the first. *Virtus pretiosior auro.*

Robinson of London, a buck statant ppr. 117. 5

Robinson, Sir John Charles, of Newton Manor, Swanage, Dorset, a stag ppr., holding in the mouth three cinquefoils slipped vert, and resting the dexter fore-foot upon a chaplet of roses, all ppr. 261. 6

Robinson of London, a stag statant or, pellettée. cf. 117. 5

Robinson, William Grey, of Parklands, Stonehouse, Glouc., and Silksworth, near Sunderland, a buck or, supporting with his dexter fore-leg an escutcheon quarterly gu. and or, in the first quarter a cross flory arg. *Post nubila Phœbus.*

Robinson, James, Esquire, of Sunderland, a mount vert, thereon a stag regardant or, holding in the mouth a cross Calvary in bend sinister gu., the dexter fore-paw resting on a cinquefoil pierced, also or.

Robinson, Francis Edward, Lynbrook, Stanmore, Middx., two arms embowed, the hands holding a stag's head erased, all ppr., between the attires a heart arg. *In omnibus temperantia.*

Robinson, Henry Matthew Cooper, Knapton House, North Walsham, Norf., a cubit arm holding an imperial crown. *Virtutis gloria merces.*

Robinson, Rev Thomas, Ewshot Hurst Hants in front of a mount vert thereon a stag at gaze or, gorged with a collar vair, three escallops reversed or *Qualis ab incepto*

Robinson of Kirby Frith, Leics, a mount vert, thereon a stag statant at gaze or, semee of torteaux, attired gu, between the attires an estoile, also or, the dexter foot resting on a stirrup iron sa

Robinson of Dullingham, Cambs, and Denston Hall, Suff (1) A stag statant or, pellettée, attired arg (*for Robinson*) *cf* 117 5 (2) A talbot's head erased arg, eared gu (*for Jeaffreson*) 56 2

Robinson, out of a mural coronet per pale gu and or, a demi stag per pale of the last and first, attired counterchanged

Robinson of Cransley, Northamp, and Northumb, out of a mural coronet chequy arg and gu., a demi buck or, attired ppr *cf* 119 2

Robinson of Griqualand, West South Africa and of London, a demi-stag or, charged with two chevronels vert, supporting with the dexter leg a flagstaff in bend sinister ppr therefrom a banner vert charged with a bezant

Robinson, Ireland, a stag's head erased or 121 2

Robinson, Sir Frederic Lacy, K C B Board of Inland Revenue, Somers, a stag's head ppr *Adsit Deus confido*

Robinson of Trethevas, Cornw, a buck's head erased 121 2

Robinson of Southwold, Suff, a stag's head erased or 121 2

Robinson of Moore Place, Bucks on a mural coronet chequy arg and az, a stag's head cabossed ppr *Vincam malum bono* *cf* 122 5

Robinson of Mansloe, Cornw a buck's head az erased erm, attired and charged with three lozenges conjoined in fesse or *Loyal au mort* *cf* 121 2

Robinson, Banffsh, Scotland, a talbot's head and neck arg *Intemerata fides* 56 12

Robinson of London and Drayton Bassett Staffs, a goldfinch ppr standing on the sun in splendour or

Robley, a mount semee of cinquefoils *cf* 179 10

Robley, a goat's head erased arg armed ppr 128 5

Robotham, a demi griffin az, guttee d'eau, ducally gorged or *cf* 64 2

Robotham of Raskyle Yorks, a demi tiger az, guttée-d'eau, armed and langued gu

Robottom and Robotham, an eagle or pellettee, preying on a wing arg, vulned gu *cf* 79 13

Robsert, a fish's head erased in fess ppr 139 6

Robson, a boar's head erect or *cf* 43 3

Robson of Bishop Wearmouth, Durh, a boar's head erased and erect or *Justus esto et non metue* 43 3

Robson, Northumb same crest 43 3

Robson of West Morton Durh and Holtby, Yorks, out of a mural coronet az, a boar's head erminois crined of the first 41 8

Robson, same crest *Justus esto et non metue*

Robson, William, Esquire, of Wellington House, Darlington, out of a mural coronet a boar's head and neck *Justus esto et non metue* 41 8

Robson-Scott, John Alexander, Newton, Jedburgh N B, a stag trippant ppr *Patriam amo*

Roby, a garb vert 153 2

Roby, Arthur Godfrey, the Limes, Didsbury, a stag's head couped ppr

Roby, Henry John Oxford and Cambridge Club, same crest

Robyns and **Robbins,** Staffs, and Netherhall, Worcs, between two dolphins haurient and respecting each other or, a fleur-de lis per pale arg and sa

Robynsone or **Robyson,** a cubit arm vested bended wavy of six or and az, cuffed arg, the hand holding a Saracen's head by the beard ppr

Roche, Baron Fermoy, standing upon a rock ppr, an osprey or sea eagle with wings endorsed arg, collared gemelle az, membered or, and holding in its dexter claw a roach, also arg *Mon Dieu est ma roche*

Roche of Granagh Castle Ireland a rock ppr, thereon a fish eagle or osprey with wings displayed arg, membered or, holding in the dexter claw a roach, also arg *Mon Dieu est ma roche*

Roche, Ireland on a rock ppr an eagle purp. with wings displayed *Mon Dieu est ma roche*

Roche, Sir David Vandeleur Bart, D L, of Carass co Limerick, a rock thereon a stork close, charged on the breast with a torteau and holding in his dexter claw a roach, all ppr *Dieu est ma roche*

Roche, a rock *Mon Dieu est ma roche* 179 7

Roche, Ireland, out of a ducal coronet or, the attires of a stag affixed to the scalp gu 123 3

Roche, a lion's head erased per fess or and sa, within a chain issuing in arch az 19 5

Roche-Burrowes, a lion sejant murally crowned or *Et vi et virtute*

Rochead, Scotland a savage's head in profile couped ppr *Fide et virtute* *cf* 190 7

Rochead, Scotland, a savage's head affrontee couped ppr, wreathed vert *Fide et virtute* *cf* 190 5

Rochead of Whitsomhill, Scotland, a savage's arm erect ppr *Pro patria*

Rocheid, Bart of Inverleith, Edinburgh, a savage's head couped ppr *Fide et virtute* 190 12

Rocheid, of Inverleith Edinburgh, Darnchester Berwicksh, and Himmelsthur near Hildesheim, Hanover, a savage's head ppr *Fide et virtute* 190 12

Rochefort, a unicorn's head between two laurel-branches in orle 49 14

Rochefort, on a ducal coronet or, a cock with wings expanded ppr

Rochester, Essex, a crane arg 105 9

Rochester of Loys Hall, Terling, Essex and Sussex, a cubit arm in armour erect issuing out of clouds ppr, holding in the gauntlet a marigold, a rose, and a pomegranate all ppr leaved vert, and environed with a ducal coronet or

Rochester, a crane statant holding in the beak an eel ppr 105 8

Rochford, a cock gu 91 2

Rochfort, Earl of Belvedere (*extinct*) a robin redbreast ppr *Candor dat viribus alas* 108 11

Rochfort of Rochfort Bridge co Donegal, Ireland, same crest *Vi vel suavite* 108 11

Rochfort of Limerick, same crest *Stat fortis in fide* 108 11

Rochfort, Ireland, same crest *Candor dat viribus alas* 108 11

Rochfort of Clogrenane Ireland, a robin ppr *Vi vel suavitate* 108 11

Rochfort-Boyd (1) Out of a ducal coronet or a hand erect with the third and fourth fingers folded ppr (*for Boyd*) *cf* 222 11 (2) On a mural coronet or, a robin redbreast ppr, charged with a cross patee of the first (*for Rochfort*) Over the first crest, *Confido Candor dat viribus alas* *cf* 108 10

Rochfort, a rose branch bearing roses ppr 149 8

Rock, a demi-lion az 10 2

Rock of Dublin, out of the coronet of a marquess a dexter cubit arm in armour grasping in the gauntlet a naked dagger, all ppr *Nil admirari*

Rocke of Abbey Foregate Shropsh on a rock ppr, a martlet or *cf* 95 2

Rocke, John Charles Leveson, of Clungunford House, Shropsh, same crest *In Deo nostra spes est* *cf* 95 2

Rockley of Rockley, Yorks, a stag's head ppr attired or 121 5

Rockliff-Lubé of Liverpool (1) A dexter arm in armour embowed ppr, charged with two mullets in pale gu, grasping in the hand a sword encircled by a wreath of oak fructed, all ppr (*for Lube*) (2) A bull's head erased per pale arg and gu, gorged with a mural coronet ppr (*for Rockliff*) *Virtus propter se*

Rocksavage, Earl of, *see* Cholmondeley, Marquess of

Rockwood or **Rookwood** of Eveston, Suff, a lion sejant supporting a spear erect arg

Rockwood of Weston, Norf, a lion sejant gardant arg, supporting a spear sa, headed of the first

Roclay, a dolphin haurient ppr 140 11

Rodatz, a rose tree ppr 149 5

Rodber, a demi heraldic antelope erased

Rodd, Edward Stanhope, Esquire J P, of Trebatha Hall Cornw, the Pharos or Colossus of Rhodes, over the shoulders a bow, the dexter hand holding an arrow, the sinister raised above the head holding a ball of fire rays surrounding the head, all ppr *Recte omnia duce Deo*

Roddam, a savage's head couped ppr, distilling blood gu 190 11

Roddam, a cross moline 165 3

Roddam, Roddam John of Roddam Hall Northumb the stump of an oak couped, sprouting out leaves ppr *Nec deficit alter* 145 2

Roddam, on a mount vert the trunk of a tree sprouting fresh branches all ppr *cf* 145 2

Rode of Rode Chesh, a wolf's head sa gorged with a ribbon arg *cf* 30 5

Roden, Earl of (Jocelyn), Tullymore Park, Bryansford, co. Down, a falcon's leg erased à la quise ppr., belled or. *Faire mon devoir.* 113. 8

Rodes-Reaston, *see* Reaston.

Rodes, Bart. (*extinct*), of Barlborough, Derbysh., an arm couped at the elbow arg., holding a branch of oak or, fructed az.

Rodes, an arm couped at the elbow arg., holding in the hand an oak-branch or, fructed az.

Rodes of Skyrkett and Halifax, Yorks, a leopard sejant or, spotted sa., collared and ringed arg. *cf.* 24. 8

Rodger, Scotland, a demi-lady ppr., attired az., holding in her dexter hand a pair of scales or. 183. 2

Rodger, Edward, Esquire, of Clairmont Gardens, Glasgow, on a mount a stag courant between two laurel-branches, all ppr. *Nos nostraque Deo.* *cf.* 116. 7

Rodger, John Pickersgill, Hadlow Castle, Tunbridge, same crest and motto. *cf.* 116. 7

Rodgers of Sheffield, a stag's head erased holding in the mouth an acorn slipped and leaved ppr. *Be just and fear not.*

Rodick, two doves respecting each other ppr. 93. 2

Rodie of Liverpool, a roebuck trippant ppr. *Spero meliora.* 117. 8

Rodney, Baron (Rodney), of Rodney Stoke, Somers., on a ducal coronet or, an eagle with wings displayed and inverted purp. *Non generant aquilæ columbas.*

Rodney of Rodney, Devonsh., on a ducal coronet or, an eagle with wings expanded purp.

Rodney, Lennox George, Berrington, Alverstoke, Hants, same crest. *Eagles do not bring forth doves.*

Rodney, Devonsh., a boar's head sa., couped gu. 43. 1

Rodney: (1) On a ducal coronet or, an eagle with wings displayed and inverted purp. (*for Rodney*). (2) Out of a wreath of laurel vert, a lady's head couped at the shoulders ppr., vested gu. (*for Powell*).

Rodney, Bart., Hants, out of a ducal coronet or, a demi-eagle displayed purp. 80. 14

Rodney, out of a ducal coronet a demi-eagle displayed. 80. 14

Rodon, Captain John, J.P. for the co. of Westmeath, Ireland, on a wreath of the colours a wivern ppr., charged on the breast with an annulet or. *Magna est veritas et prævalet.* *cf.* 70. 1

Rodwell, the sun per fess sa. and or. 162. 2

Roe, Ireland, a roebuck springing ppr. 117. 2

Roe of London, same crest. *Tramite recto.* 117. 2

Roe, on a mount a stag current ppr. 118. 13

Roe, Bart. (*extinct*), of Brundish, Suff., on a mount vert, a roebuck at gaze gu., attired and ungu. or, between the attires a quatrefoil or. *Tramite recto.*

Roe of Muswell Hill, Middx., and Higham Hall, Essex, a buck's head erased gu. 121. 2

Roe, a roebuck's head gu. 121. 5

Roe or **Roo** of London, and Dartford, Kent, a stag's head gu., charged on the neck with three bezants. *cf.* 121. 5

Roe of Graton Hall, Devonsh., a stag's head erased gu. *Non progredi est regredi.* 121. 2

Roe of Mount Anneville Park, co. Dublin, a buck's head erased ppr., charged with a cross crosslet or, and holding in the mouth a trefoil slipped vert. *Virtute et valore.*

Roe, Ireland, a demi-lion rampant erm., supporting a crescent gu.

Roe, Richard, Crane House, Cole Park, Twickenham, same crest. *Industria omnia patent.*

Roe, Deputy-Surgeon-General Samuel Black, C.B., Ballyconnell House, co. Cavan, same crest.

Roebuck, Somers., a lion passant gardant gu. 4. 3

Roebuck of Ingress, Kent, a stork arg., beaked and membered gu. 105. 11

Rofey or Rofy, an eagle displayed or. 75. 5

Roffey, on a mural coronet a serpent nowed, all ppr. 142. 12

Roffey of Adelphi Terrace, London, a demi-lion couped erm., murally gorged gu., the sinister paw resting upon an arch sa.

Rofy, an eagle displayed ppr. 75. 2

Roger, Scotland, out of a ducal coronet a dexter hand ppr., holding a crosier in bend or. *Le Roy et l'Eglise.* *cf.* 219. 4

Rogers, Captain John Peverell, late R.A., of Penrose, Helston, Cornw., a stag trippant sa. 117. 8

Rogers, Baron Blachford, on a mount vert, a stag courant ppr., gorged with a ducal coronet or, between two branches of laurel vert. *Nos nostraque Deo.* 116. 7

Rogers, Bart., of Wisdome, Devonsh., on a mount vert, a roebuck courant ppr., gorged with a ducal coronet or, between two branches of laurel vert. *Nos nostraque Deo.* 116. 7

Rogers, Rev. George Edmund, Southwater Vicarage, Horsham, a stag's head erased ppr., suspended from the neck by a ribbon vert a bugle-horn sa., garnished or, stringed vert, the whole within two branches of oak fructed ppr. *Nos utraque Deo.*

Rogers, John Henry, Stonehouse, Forrest Row, Sussex, same crest and motto.

Rogers of Little Nesse, Shropsh., on a mount vert, a buck trippant sa., attired arg., ducally gorged, ringed, and lined of the last. *cf.* 118. 2

Rogers, Rev. Cecil George William, Rector of Kilmoe, Goleen, Skibbereen, a stag courant between two laurel-branches in orle. *Omnia vincit amor.*

Rogers, on a mount vert, a buck sa., ducally gorged arg., over his back a line reflexed, attired or. *cf.* 117. 1

Rogers-Harrison of Hendon, Middx.: (1) Out of a mural coronet az., a demi-lion rampant or, crowned with an Eastern crown arg., holding in the paws a laurel garland adorned with four damask roses (*for Harrison*). (2) On a vallery coronet or, a stag trippant ppr., charged on the shoulder with a trefoil vert (*for Rogers*). *Absque virtute nihil.*

Rogers-Harrison, George Harrison, Windsor Herald and Blanche Lion Pursuivant Extraordinary: (1) Out of a mural coronet az., a demi-lion issuant or, crowned with an Eastern crown arg., and holding between the paws a chaplet of roses ppr. (*for Harrison*). (2) On a ducal coronet or, a lion rampant arg. (3) On a chapeau gu., turned up erm., a stag trippant ppr., gorged with the coronet of a King of Arms, therefrom a chain passing between the fore-legs or (*for Rogers*). (4) Out of a coronet composed of trefoils or, a plume of five ostrich-feathers alternately arg. and or.

Rogers, William Kissane, Esquire, J.P., of Lota, co. Cork, a stag trippant sa., charged with a trefoil or. *Omnia vincit amor.* *cf.* 117. 8

Rogers of Cannington, Somers., a stag sa., bezantée, ducally gorged and attired or.

Rogers, Rev. Edward Henry, of Rainscombe, Wilts, a stag sa., bezantée, chained and collared or. *Nil conscire sibi.*

Rogers of Wrexham, Denbighsh., on a vallery coronet or, a stag trippant ppr., charged on the shoulder with a trefoil slipped vert. *Absque virtute nihil.* *cf.* 117. 8

Rogers, Kent, and of Bradford, Wilts, a stag trippant sa., bezantée, ducally gorged and attired or.

Rogers, Cornw., a buck trippant arg. 117. 8

Rogers of Treassowe, Cornw., a stag trippant sa. 117. 8

Rogers of Coulston, Norf., a demi-stag sa., platée, attired or, ducally gorged per pale or and arg.

Rogers of the Home, Shropsh., a buck's head sa., charged with three ermine-spots or, erased gu., attired of the second. *Celeriter et jucunde.* *cf.* 121. 2

Rogers, a stag's head erased ppr., holding in the mouth an acorn or, stalked and leaved vert. *cf.* 119. 11

Rogers of Bristol, and Eastwood, Glouc., same crest. *cf.* 119. 11

Rogers, Thomas Englesby, of Yarlington, Somers., a buck's head erased sa., attired or, on the neck a bendlet wavy of the last, charged with three acorns vert, holding in the mouth a slip of oak fructed ppr. *Justum perficito nihil timeto.*

Rogers of Chelmsford, Essex, Purton, Glouc., and Evesham, Worcs., a stag's head sa., attired or, holding in the mouth an acorn of the last, stalked and leaved vert. 119. 11

Rogers of Deritend, Warw., and Sunbury, Middx., a stag's head sa., ducally gorged or. *cf.* 121 5

Rogers of Bryanstown, Dorset, and Glouc., a fleur-de-lis or. 148. 2

Rogers, Coxwell-, Godfrey Hugh Wheeler, of Dowdeswell, Glouc.: (1) Same crest. (*for Rogers*). 148. 2. (2) A demi-dragon displayed arg. (*for Coxwell*). *Vigila et ora.*

Rogers of London, an eagle displayed or. *Ut resurgam.* 75. 5

Rogers, Ireland, same crest 75 5

Rogers, Rev J, Lochee, Dundee, a dove holding in the beak a branch of olive ppr *E preteritis futura*

Rogers of Brompton Park, Middx, and Calcutta, East Indies, upon a branch of a tea-plant entwined with three sprigs of flax ppr, an owl arg

Rogers, a griffin's head couped 66 1

Rogers of London, a cubit arm in a coat of mail holding in the hand ppr a banner, the staff and flag or

Rogers, Kent, a man's head in profile in armour ppr, the helmet or, surmounted by a plume of feathers arg

Rogers of Ellerslie, Fareham, Hants, a demi stag

Rogerson, a demi-lion rampant per fess or and purp 10 2

Rogerson of Wamphrey and Duncrieff, Scotland, a leopard passant, holding in his dexter paw a branch of laurel ppr *Mores fingunt fortunam*

Rohan, a dexter arm embowed couped resting on the elbow, vested and cuffed holding in the hand a cross crosslet fitched 203 9

Rohde, Middx, an eagle displayed per pale or and purp, charged on the breast with a cross patee counter-changed cf 75 2

Rokeby, Baron (*extinct*—Rt Hon the late Sir Henry Robinson Montagu G C B), a griffin's head couped or with wings endorsed sa, difierenced with a mullet upon a mullet *Solo Deo salus* cf 67 11

Rokeby, Rev Henry Ralph of Arthingworth Manor, Northamp., a rook ppr cf 107 5

Rokeby of Rokeby and Mortham, Yorks same crest cf 107 5

Rokeby, a dexter hand holding an escutcheon arg, charged with a crescent gu cf 219 7

Rokeston, an arm in armour embowed holding in the hand a sword ppr 195 2

Rokewood-Gage, *see* Gage

Rokley, Yorks a stag s head couped 121 5

Rokwood, a lion's head vert, collared arg cf 18 6

Rolesley of Rewlesley, Derbysh, a demi-lion rampant per pale arg and gu, holding a rose of the last, stalked and leaved vert 12 1

Rolf of Sarum, Wilts, on a staff couped and raguly in fess and sprouting at the dexter end vert a raven close sa

Rolfe, Baron Cranworth (*extinct*), a dove arg, holding in the beak a sprig of olive ppr, ducally gorged gu, and resting the dexter claw upon three annulets interlaced or. *Post nubila Phœbus*

Rolfe, Middx and Kent a raven close sa, holding in the beak a trefoil slipped vert

Rolfe of Hadleigh Suff, a dragon's head couped gu, fretty arg, ducally gorged and chained or

Rolfe, Neville-, Eustace, of Heacham Hall, Norf (1) A lion's head erased arg, fretty gu (*for Rolfe*) cf 17 8 (2) A mount vert thereon issuant out of a crescent gu, a rose arg, slipped vert (*for Neville*) *Cresco crescendo*

Rolland of Gaske, Scotland, a hand issuing holding a dagger ppr *Spes juvat* 212 3

Rolland of Disblair Aberdeensh, Scotland a fleur de-lis arg *Immutabile durable* 148 2

Rolland, Scotland a lymphad, her sails furled and her oars in action ppr, flagged gu *Sustentatus providentia* 160 7

Rollason, Warw, an eagle's head couped ppr *Ainsi et peut-etre meilleur* 83 1

Rolle, Baron (Rolle), a cubit arm erect vested az, charged with a fess indented double cottised or holding in the hand, a flintstone ppr *Nec Rege, nec populo, sed utroque*

Rolle, Oxon, a cubit arm erect ppr, vested az, charged with a fess, and holding in the hand a roll of paper or *Nec Rege nec populo sed utroque* cf 208 8

Rolles, Devonsh, an arm charged with a fess indented and cottised or holding in the hand a baton sa

Rolleston, Notts of Rolleston Staffs, and the Lea and Swarkston, Derbysh, an eagle's head ppr 83 1

Rolleston, Lancelot, of Watnall Hall Notts, an eagle's head erased ppr *Ainsi et peut estre meilleur* 83 2

Rolleston, Christopher Sydney, New South Wales, an eagle's head erased ppr beaked or, with a crescent for difference *Ainsia peut estre mailleur*

Rolleston, Hon William, Kapunatiki, Rangitata Canterbury, New Zealand, same crest and motto

Rollo, Baron (Rollo), Duncrub Park, Dunning Perthsh, a stag's head couped ppr *La fortune passe par tout* 121 5

Rollo, General the Hon Robert Strathderne, Bournemouth same crest

Rollo of Powhouse Scotland a boar passant ppr *Valor et fortuna* 40 9

Rolls, out of a ducal coronet an arm in armour brandishing a sabre, all ppr

Rolls of the Hendre, Monm, out of a wreath of oak a dexter cubit arm vested or cuffed sa the arm charged with a fess dancettee and double cottised of the second, charged with three bezants, holding in the hand ppr a roll of parchment arg *Celeritas et veritas* 247 7

Rolph, a raven ppr, holding in the beak a trefoil slipped vert

Rolston of Watmoll, Notts, an eagle's head erased ppr 83 2

Rolt, John William of Ozleworth Park Glouc, a stork holding in its beak a bulrush, and resting the dexter claw upon a fountain, all ppr *Be and not seem*

Rolt, Bayntun-, Bart (*extinct*), of Spye Park, Wilts, a griffin's head erased sa, beaked or 66 2

Rolt or **Rolte** of Deptford, Kent (1) On a broken tilting spear arg, a griffin sejant gu holding in the mouth the head of the spear (*for Rolt*) (2) Out of a ducal coronet a demi-pelican vulning herself arg (*for Pett*) *Cuspis fracta causa coronæ*

Rolte, Kent on a broken tilting-spear arg a griffin sejant gu, holding in the mouth the head of the spear or

Romaine, an arrow point downwards 173 5

Romanes, Scotland, a dexter hand holding a sword ppr 212 13

Romanes, James, Esquire, of Dunskaith, Ross-sh, a boar's head erased arg langued az *Sero sed serio* 42 2

Romanes, George Ernest, Pitcalzeane Nigg, Ross-sh N B, same crest and motto

Romanis of Wigston Magna, Leics, and Charterhouse, Godalming, Surrey on a mount vert, in front of a thistle slipped and leaved ppr, a Passion cross or *Per incerta certus amor*

Romans, John, of Newton Grange, Edinburgh, an eagle rising holding in its beak a flaming torch ppr *Pergo sursum*

Romayne, a deer's head erased ppr 121 2

Rome of Clowden Scotland, a slip of a rose tree bearing roses ppr *Pungit sed placet* 149 8

Rome of Courtfield, Cheltenham a dexter arm embowed habited az, charged with two bars arg, holding in the hand a caduceus, both ppr *Nunquam non paratus* 204 8

Rome, a lion passant ppr 6 2

Romera, De, a stag's head at gaze ppr

Romerley and **Romilly,** a crescent 163 2

Romilly, Baron (Romilly) upon a rock ppr a crescent arg *Persevere* 311 11

Romilly, Samuel Henry, Huntingdon Park, Kington, Heref, same crest and motto

Romney, Earl of (Marsham), Gayton Hall King's Lynn, a lion's head erased gu *Non sibi, sed patriæ* 17 2

Romney, London, two cubit arms vested az, cuffed arg, the hands ppr, holding an escallop gu

Romney of Middleton Kent, an arm in armour embowed ppr vambraced or, the hand holding a pennon of two streamers gu, thereon three leopards' faces crowned of the third, the staff ppr

Rompney and **Rumpney,** Worcs, on a mount vert, a lion statant gardant gu, in front of a tree ppr

Ronald, Scotland, an oak tree acorned and eradicated ppr *Sic virescit virtus*

Ronald of Montrose, Scotland an oak tree fructed ppr *Sic virescit virtus* 143 2

Ronaldson, Scotland a greyhound's head erased holding in the mouth a deer's foot, also erased 61 5

Ronan of Farenegelagh, co Limerick Ireland, a blackbird ppr *Ipse fecit nos* cf 106 2

Ronan of Kilkenny, Ireland upon a mirror ppr, a cock or

Rone of Longford, Shropsh, a buck's head erased ppr, attired or 121 2

Roney, Sir Patrick Cusack on a wreath of the colours an arm in armour embowed grasping a sword all ppr, charged with a mullet and a crescent in pale gu *Audaces fortuna juvat* cf 195 2

Roney-Dougal, of Ratho Park Midlothian and Ashley House, Leamington (1) A bull's head caboshed ppr charged for distinction with a cross crosslet or (*for Dougal*). (2) An arm in armour embowed grasping a sword, all ppr., charged with a mullet and a crescent in pale gu. (*for Roney*). *Stand fast.*

Roney-Dougal, Rev. James, Castle Donington, Derby, same crest as first above. Same motto.

Ronne, Middx., a buck's head erased ppr., attired or. 121. 2

Rooe, a buck's head couped gu., attired or. 121. 5

Rooe of Markelsfield, Chesh., a swan with wings addorsed naiant in water ppr. 99. 9

Rook of London, on a garb or, a rook feeding ppr.

Rook, a rook ppr. *cf.* 107. 5

Rook and **Rookes,** on a trumpet in fess, a rook ppr.

Rookby, a rook ppr. *cf.* 107. 5

Rooke, a rook feeding. 107. 4

Rooke of Rookes'oth Bridge, Waverton, Akehead, Rookes' Nest Wigtoun and Carlisle, Cumb., on a garb or, a rook feeding ppr. *Efflorescent cornices, dum micat sol.*

Rooke, Alexander Beaumont, the Ivy, Chippenham, Wilts, a garb, thereon a rook feeding, all ppr. *Nos pascit Deus.*

Rooke, a rock ppr., thereon a martlet or. *cf.* 99. 2

Rooke, a demi-eagle displayed arg., charged on the breast with a chess-rook gu. *cf.* 81. 6

Rooke of Horton, Kent, an arm in armour embowed ppr., garnished or, holding in the gauntlet a pistol of the last, the arm environed with a trumpet arg.

Rookes or **Rokes** of Fawley, Bucks, on a trumpet or, a rook sa.

Rookewood, Norf., a dragon's head gu. 71. 1

Rookwood, Baron (*extinct*) (Selwin-Ibbetson): (1) A unicorn's head arg., powdered with escallops, horned, maned, and erased gu. (2) Two lions' gambs erm., erased az., supporting a torch in pale or, fired ppr. *Vixi liber, et moriar.*

Rookwood, Suff., a lion sejant, supporting a spear in pale arg.

Roome of Newport, America, a dexter arm embowed, habited az., charged with two bars arg., holding in the hand a caduceus, both ppr. 204. 8

Roope, a demi-antelope sa., collared or. 126. 3

Rooper, Rev. John George, of Abbott's Ripton, Hunts, on a chapeau gu., turned up erm., a blazing star or. *Lux Anglis, crux Francis.* 164. 6

Roos, on a chapeau gu., turned up erm., a peacock in his pride ppr. 103. 5

Roos of Glouc. and Swinshead, three slips of roses arg., leaved vert. 149. 12

Roos and **Rosse** (now **Rose**) of Lyme Regis, Dorset, a rose gu., seeded or, barbed vert, between two wings erm. *Sursum.—En la rose je fleurie.*

Roos or **Ros** of Bouseley, Yorks, a falcon's head az. *cf.* 88. 12

Roose, Edward Charles Robson, M.D., 49, Hill Street, Berkeley Square, a peacock in his pride ppr., gorged with a collar, and pendent therefrom, a four-leaved shamrock or. *Je ne change qu'en mourant.*

Roots, a tree ppr. 143. 5

Rope, Chesh. and Devonsh., a lion rampant or, holding in the dexter paw a pheon sa.

Roper, *see* Teynham, Baron.

Roper, *see* Trevor-Roper.

Roper, William Oliver, F.S.A., a lion rampant holding in the dexter paw a ducal coronet.

Roper, Viscount Baltinglass (*extinct*), a boar's head couped in bend or, langued and vulned gu. *Deus veritatem protegit.*

Roper, Yorks and London, an antelope's head erased. 126. 2

Roper, Durh., a roebuck's head erased, gorged with a branch ppr. 120. 3

Roper, Norf., a buck's head erased or, attired sa., holding in the mouth a pear, also or, stalked and leaved vert.

Roper of West Dereham, Norf., a stag's head erased ppr. 121. 2

Roper, Dorset, a stag's head erased ppr., attired or. 121. 2

Roper of Newcastle and Saxlingham, Norf., a goat's head erased or, armed sa., holding in the mouth a daffodil of the first, stalked and leaved vert.

Roper, a lion rampant gu., holding up a ducal coronet or. *Spes mea in Deo.* 3. 6

Roper of Turndich and Heanor, Derbysh., on a chapeau gu., turned up erm., a blazing star or. 164. 6

Ropner, Emil Hugh Oscar Robert, J.P., Preston Hall, Stockton-on-Tees, upon three mascles interlaced fesseways, and in front of three tilting-spears, one in pale and two in saltire or, a stag's head erased sa., attired or. *Fides et fortitudo.*

Rorie, a cinquefoil gu. 148. 12

Rorie, Scotland, a galley with her oars in action ppr. 160. 7

Rorie, James, Westgreen House, by Dundee, a galley, oars in action sa., flagged gu. *Terra marique.*

Rorke, Ireland, an eagle's head erased or. 83. 2

Rosborough-Colclough, *see* Colclough.

Rosborough of Mullinagoun and Dromesky, co. Fermanagh, and Edgeworthstown co. Longford, Ireland, on a dexter hand in fesse couped, a dove close holding in the beak an olive-branch, all ppr. *God is my shield.*

Roscarrock of Roscarrock, Cornw., a lion rampant ppr., ducally gorged arg. *cf.* 1. 13

Roscoe, two elephants' proboscis gu. 123. 10

Roscommon, Earl of (Dillon), a falcon arg. *Auxilium ab alto.* 85. 2

Roscow of Summer Place, Kensington, Middx., a staff erect entwined with two serpents ppr., between as many wings erm. *Cautius quam citius.* 112. 2

Roscruge, Cornw., a demi-lion rampant or, holding in the dexter paw a rose gu., stalked and leaved vert. 12. 1

Rose of Ballevit, Ross-sh., a rose gu., slipped and leaved vert. *Armat spina rosas.* 149. 5

Rose, a rose slipped and leaved ppr. 149. 5

Rose of Insch, a rose gu., stalked and barbed vert. *Magnus et adamus.* 149. 5

Rose, between two wings erm., a rose gu., seeded or, barbed vert.

Rose of London, a dexter hand issuing ppr., holding a rose gu., slipped vert. *Constant and true.* 218. 10

Rose, William Molyneux, of Wolston Heath, Northamp., a cubit arm erect, vested sa., cuffed arg., holding in the hand a rose slipped and leaved ppr.

Rose of Markinch, Scotland, a dexter hand holding a slip of a rose-bush ppr. *Quo spinosior fragrantior.* 218. 10

Rose, a pheasant holding in its beak a rose slipped and leaved ppr.

Rose, out of a mural coronet or, an eagle's head ppr., charged on the neck with a rose gu. *Pro patria.* *cf.* 83. 9

Rose, Richard de Ros, of Ahabeg, co. Limerick, and Foxhall, co. Tipperary, Ireland: (1) A demi-lion rampant arg., holding in the dexter paw a rose gu., slipped vert. 12. 1. (2) An eagle with wings elevated sa., preying on a lion's gamb erased ppr. (3) An oak-tree ppr. *Non sine sente rosa.* 143. 5

Rose, of the Ferns, Sussex, a lion holding in his dexter paw a rose.

Rose of Cransley Hall, Northants, out of a mural coronet a demi-lion rampant.

Rose, William, Ballbrook House, Withington, Lancs, a lion rampant sa., gorged with a collar vair, holding between the fore-paws a lyre or, and resting the dexter hind-leg on a rose arg. *Armat spina rosas.*

Rose, a lion rampant sa. 1. 10

Rose, Scotland, a harp az. *Constant and true.* 168. 9

Rose, Bart., of Montreal, Canada, and Queen's Gate, Kensington, Middx., a harp or, stringed az. Above the crest, *Audeo*, and below the arms, *Constant and true.* 168. 9

Rose of London, a harp or, stringed arg., *Constant and true.* 168. 9

Rose, Major Hugh, of Kilravock, Nairnsh., Scotland, a harp az. *Constant and true.* 168. 9

Rose, Hants, a harp az., the figure or. 168. 9

Rose, a hawk ppr. *Audeo.* 85. 2

Rose, Hugh Francis, of Holme, Inverness-sh., same crest. *Constant and true.* 85. 2

Rose, Ireland, a peacock in his pride ppr., beaked or. 103. 12

Rose, Sir Philip Frederick, Bart., of Rayners, Bucks, a stag arg., collared and resting the dexter fore-leg on a water-bouget az. *Probitate ac virtute.*

Rose or **Rosse** of Waddesden, Bucks, a buck trippant arg. 117. 8

Rose, an antelope's head erased. 126. 2

Rose of Innish, Scotland, an étoile az. *Constant and true.* 164. 1

Rose-Innes, Thomas Gilzean, Kinellan, Murrayfield, Midlothiansh.: (1) A branch of palm slipped ppr. (2) A rose gu., stalked and leaved ppr. *Ornatur radix fronde.—Armat spina rosas.*

Rosebery, Earl of (Primrose), Dalmeny Park, Edinburgh, a demi-lion gu., holding in the dexter paw a primrose or. *Fide et fiducia.*

Rosehill, Lord, *see* Northesk, Earl of

Rosevear, a dove holding in its beak a rosebud, all ppr

Rosewarne, a lion's head erased gu, pierced in the neck by an arrow ppr *cf* 18 4

Rosher, an eagle's head sa 83 1

Rosher, an elephant's head couped erm, between two elephants' proboscides or *Consider the end* 133 5

Rosher of Trewyn House, Heref, and Crete Hall, Kent an elephant's head couped erm, between two elephants' trunks or *Consider the end* 133 5

Rosier, Rutl, a pelican in her piety ppr 98 14

Rosington of Scropton, Derbysh, a griffin's head erased gu, beaked or 66 2

Roskell of Gateacre Lancs, issuing from a wreath of oak or a dexter cubit arm in armour ppr, charged with a martlet gu, holding in the hand, also ppr, a cross crosslet fitched of the third *Ros cœli*

Roskruge, Cornw, a demi-lion rampant or, holding in the dexter paw a rose gu, stalked and leaved vert 12 1

Rosmead, Baron (Robinson) Moorlands, Ascot, out of a crown vallory or a mount vert, thereon a buck at gaze or, charged on the shoulder with a fleur-de-lis az *Legi regi fidus* 313. 4

Ross, William Gordon a stag trippant gu, attired and ungu or *Agnoscar eventu*

Ross, Baron, *see* Glasgow, Earl of

Ross, Earl of Ross (*extinct*), an eagle displayed 75 2

Ross, Lord Ross, of Halkhead a hawk's head erased or *Think on* 88 12

Ross, a hawk's head erased ppr *Think on* 88 12

Ross, Colin George 38, Beaufort Gardens, S W same crest and motto

Ross of Rossie, Scotland, a falcon's head erased ppr *Think on* 88 12

Ross, William Augustus, Esquire of Ardnalea, Craigavad, co Down Ireland, on a mural crown gu charged with a water-bouget or a falcon's head erased ppr *Floret qui laborat*

Ross, an eagle's head couped az 83. 1

Ross, Walter Charteris Esquire, of Cromarty, Cromartysh, an eagle close ppr *Dread God* 76 2

Ross-Lewin of Ross Hill Ireland, on a chapeau gu, turned up erm a peacock in his pride ppr *Consilio ac virtute* 103 5

Ross of Kintore, Scotland a dove holding in its beak an olive-branch ppr *Virtus ad astra tendit* 92 5

Ross, a harp az *Constant and true* 168 9

Ross of Auchlossin Aberdeensh., a water-bouget sa *Agnoscar eventu* 168 4

Ross, Yorks, a water-bouget or *Agnoscar eventu* 168 4

Ross, William, Esquire, of the Villa, Nafferton Yorks, a water bouget arg *Agnoscar eventu* 168 4

Ross, Poland, a water bouget az *Agnoscar eventu* 168 4

Ross, Leith-, Colonel John of Arnage Aberdeensh, on a chapeau ppr, a water-bouget sa *Agnoscar eventu* — *Virtue have virtue* 168 2

Ross of Renfrewsh, Scotland, a dexter arm in armour ppr, garnished or, holding in the hand a water bouget sa. *Agnoscar eventu* 209 4

Ross, a dexter arm in armour holding in the hand a sword ppr *Floret qui laborat* 210 2

Ross, Colonel Sir Edward Charles, C S I, same crest

Ross, Ireland, an arm in armour brandishing a sword ppr *Constant and true* 210 2

Ross-of-Bladensburg, Lieutenant-Colonel Sir John Foster George, K C B, of Rosstrevor, co Down (1) Out of a mural coronet an arm embowed vested gu, the cuff az, encircled by a wreath of laurel, the hand grasping a broken staff of the Standard of the United States, all ppr (2) An arm in armour embowed, the hand grasping a dagger all ppr *Per aspera virtus —Bladensburg* 243 4

Ross, Major John James, a hand holding a garland of laurel ppr *Work and wait* 218 4

Ross of Shian Lodge, Penzance, Cornw, same crest and motto 218 4

Ross of Carne, Penzance, same crest and motto 218 4

Ross, a dexter hand issuing, holding a garland of laurel, all ppr *Spem successus alit* 218 4

Ross, Sir Charles Henry Augustus Frederick, Bart of Balnagowan, Ross-sh a hand holding a garland of laurel ppr *Spem successus alit* 218 4

Ross of Priesthill, Scotland, a dexter hand holding a garland of laurel ppr *Nobilis est ira leonis* 218 4

Ross, Scotland, a dexter hand plucking a rose, all ppr *Constant and true* 218 13

Ross, Scotland, a dexter hand holding a slip of a rose-bush ppr *Quo spinosior, fragrantior* 218 10

Ross of Portivoe, Scotland, and Ireland, a rose tree bearing roses ppr *Florat qui laborat* 149 8

Ross, Scotland, a rose gu stalked and barbed vert *Magnes et adamas* 149 5

Ross, three slips of roses arg, leaved vert 149 12

Ross, Scotland, a spear and a rose in saltier ppr *Per aspera virtus* 150 1

Ross, Scotland, a fox issuant, holding in his mouth a rose arg *Rosam ne rode*

Ross, Trelawney-, Rev John, the Vicarage, Paignton, a hawk's head erased ppr, holding in the beak a cross crosslet fitchee or. *Audeo*

Ross of Kindace Ross sh, Scotland, a fox passant ppr *Caute non astute* 32 1

Ross of Balkaill a fox's head erased ppr *Spes aspera levat* 33 6

Ross (1) A fox's head erased ppr 33 6 (2) On a rock a flagstaff erect, thereon hoisted the Union Jack inscribed with the date '*1st June*, 1831,' being that of discovering the place of the magnetic pole and at the foot and on the sinister side of the flagstaff the dipping needle showing its almost vertical position, all ppr

Ross, Rev James Coulman, M A, Wadworth Hall, Doncaster, same crests. *Spes aspera levat*

Ross of Morinchie, Ross sh, Scotland, a fox's head couped ppr *Spes aspera levat* 33 4

Ross, George Ross Williamson, Pitcalnie, Ross sh, an elk's head issuant from a sheaf of corn ppr *Spem successus alit*

Ross of Millcraig, Ross-sh Scotland, a lymphad, her oars in action sa, flagged gu *Pro patria* 160 7

Ross, Scotland, a sprig of laurel in flower ppr *Agnoscar eventu*

Ross of Lamer Park, Heref, a laurel branch erect ppr. 151 13

Ross Scotland a lion's head erased ppr *Per aspera virtus* 17 8

Ross of Craigie, same crest and motto 17 8

Ross, Honourable David Alexander, of Westfield House, St. Foy Road in the Banlieue of the city of Quebec, Canada, Member of the Legislative and Executive Councils, province of Quebec, and Lieutenant-Colonel of Militia, *uses* a lion rampant holding a rose slipped and leaved *Rosam ne rode*

Ross-Lewin, Rev Canon George Harrison, Benfieldside Vicarage Shotley Bridge, Durham, a demi lion sa, holding between the paws a trefoil slipped vert *Consilio ac virtute*

Ross-Lewin, Rev Richard Sargint Sadleir, the Rectory, Kilmurry, co Limerick, same crest and motto

Ross-Lewin, Rev Robert O'Donelan, M A, R N, the Rectory, Wark on-Tyne, Northumb, same crest and motto

Rosse, Earl of (Parsons), Birr Castle, Parsonstown, King's Co, a cubit arm ppr, grasping a pole-axe erect gu, the point or *Pro Deo et Rege*

Rosse of Waddesden Bucks, a roebuck trippant arg 117 8

Rosse, Scotland, a harp stringed or *Constant and true* 168 9

Rosse, Derbysh, on a chapeau gu, turned up erm, a peacock in his pride ppr 103 5

Rosse of Shepton and Somerton, Somers, a demi-leopard rampant gardant gu, eared vert

Rosseline or **Rosselyne,** Norf a spur-rowel az, between two wings or

Rossell, an arm in armour couped at the shoulder and resting on the elbow, the hand holding a club ppr 199 4

Rosselyne, a cross moline or 165 3

Rosser, Suff an arm embowed erect from the elbow, vested or cuffed erm, holding in the hand four leaves vert

Rosseter, a spear-head ppr *cf* 174 12

Rosseter, Lincs, a leopard passant or. *cf* 24 2

Rossetti, of Vasto Naples, and William Michael Rossetti Esquire, 3, St Edmund's Terrace Regent's Park, N W, a tree ppr *Frangas non flectas*

Rossie, Baron, *see* Kinnaird, Lord

Rossie, Scotland, a cross patee gu *cf* 165 7

Rossington of Youlgrave, Derbysh., a griffin's head erased gu 66 2

Rossiter of Rathmacnee, the Bridge of Bargy and Tomhaggard, co Wexford Ireland, an eagle displayed with two heads ppr 74 2

Rosslyn, Earl of (St. Clair-Erskine), Dysart, Fifesh., N.B.: (1) A phœnix in flames ppr., and over it the device, *Rinasco piu glorioso.* 82. 2. (2) An eagle's head erased ppr., with the words, *Illæso lumine solem. Fight.* 83. 2

Rossmore, Baron (Westenra), Rossmore Park, co. Monaghan, a lion rampant ppr. *Post prœlia prœmia.* 1. 13

Rosson, a demi-griffin gu. *Fight.* 64. 2

Roster, a spear-head ppr. *cf.* 174. 12

Rostron, Simpson, Esquire, of the Middle Temple, London, a cubit arm vested az., charged with a saltire or, cuffed arg., and holding in the hand two branches of hawthorn ppr. *Semper vigilans.* 268. 10

Rotchford, a bird close.

Rote, a stork or. 105. 11

Rote, a crane holding in its beak an eel ppr. 105. 8

Rotham, Kent, a bird rising sa., between two spears or, headed arg. 108. 7

Rothe of Kilkenny, Ireland, on a mount ppr., a stag lodged arg., attired or. 115. 12

Rothe of New Ross, co. Wexford, Ireland, same crest. *Virtute non vi.* 115. 12

Rothe, George Walter Charles, Neithrop House, Banbury, same crest. *Solo salus servire Deo.*

Rothe of Kilkenny, Ireland, a stag lodged gu., attired or, in front of an oak-tree vert.

Rotheram, Essex, Beds, and Somers., a stag's head or. 121. 5

Rotheram, between two branches vert, a buck's head couped or.

Rotheram, a stag's head couped ppr., attired or. 121. 5

Rotherham of Farley, Beds, a stag's head or. 121. 5

Rotherham, Scotland, a sword erect thrust through a savage's head affrontée ppr. *cf.* 191. 11

Rotherfield, a lion's gamb erect sa. *cf.* 36. 4

Rothery, out of a tower arg., a demi-lion rampant gu.

Rothery of Littlethorpe, Yorks, a tower arg., charged with two bendlets indented, and issuant out of the battlements a demi-lion gu., holding in the dexter paw three arrows, one in pale and two in saltier ppr. *Festina lente.*

Rothes, Earl of (Leslie), Brandon, Paignton, South Devonsh., a demi-griffin ppr. *Grip fast.* 64. 2

Rothings, a lion's gamb erased holding a spear tasselled ppr. 38. 11

Rothschild, Baron (Rothschild), Tring Park, Herts: (1) In the centre—issuant from a ducal coronet or, an eagle displayed sa. (2) On the dexter—out of a ducal coronet or, between two open buffalo's horns per fesse or and sa. counterchanged, a mullet of six points or. (3) On the sinister—out of a ducal coronet or, three ostrich-feathers, the centre one arg. and the exterior ones az. *Concordia, integritas, industria.* 114. 8

Rothwell of Southampton, out of a mural coronet a stag's head arg., attired or, holding in the mouth a rose ppr., leaved vert.

Rothwell of Sharples Hall, Lancs, a stag's head couped ppr., bezantée, attired or, gorged with a wreath of fern, also ppr. *Virtuti fortuna comes.*

Rothwell, Peter, Esquire, of Sunning Hill, Lancs, issuant out of park palings ppr., an heraldic antelope's head erm., attired or, gorged with a collar engrailed az., holding in the mouth a rose gu., slipped and leaved vert. *Mens conscia recti.* 127. 8

Rotten, between two wings a sinister arm embowed and vested, the hand holding a bow stringed ppr.

Rotten, an oak-tree and pendent therefrom an escutcheon ppr.

Rotton, Major-General Guy, 12, Barkston Mansions, South Kensington, an arm embowed to the sinister, vested and cuffed, holding a bow stringed in bend sinister, all between two wings displayed.

Rouett of Auchindennan, Scotland, a book expanded ppr. *Quærere verum.* 158. 3

Roughead, Scotland, a Saracen's head affrontée. *Fide et virtute.* 190. 5

Roughsedge, a demi-lion. *Res non verba.* 10. 2

Round, a Cupid with his attributes ppr. 189. 7

Round, Essex, a lion couchant arg. 7. 5

Round, James, of Birch, Essex, a lion couchant arg., charged on the body with three annulets interlaced fessewise sa., holding in the mouth a sword in bend point downwards ppr., pommel and hilt or. *Esse quam videri.*

Round, Francis Richard, C.M.G., Sutton Court, Sutton, Surrey, same crest.

Round, Joseph, Lindenhurst, Richmond Hill, Edgbaston, a falcon rising standing on a plough ppr. *Deo favente.*

Round, John Horace, D.L., 35, Alfred Place West, S.W., a lion couchant arg. *Esse quam videri.*

Round-Turner of Bognor, Sussex: (1) A lion passant arg., guttée-de-poix, holding in the dexter paw a millrind sa., and in the mouth a cross patée fitchée in bend or (*for Turner*). (2) A lion couchant arg., charged on the body with three annulets interlaced fessewise sa., holding in the mouth a sword in bend point downwards ppr., pommel and hilt or (*for Round*). *Esse quam videri.*

Round-Turner of Grundisburgh, near Woodbridge, Suff., same crest and motto.

Roundel, an arm in armour embowed in fess ppr., holding in the hand a mace gu., studded or, tied at the shoulder with a scarf arg. *cf.* 199. 3

Roundell, a sword erect arg., hilt and pommel or, the gripe gu. 170. 2

Roundell, Richard Foulis, of Gledstone, Yorks, a sword in pale arg., hilt and pommel or, the grip gu. *Tenax propositi.* 170. 2

Roundell, Charles Savile, J.P., 32, Sussex Square, Brighton, same crest.

Roupell, Sussex, a demi-African, wreathed round the middle with feathers, holding in his dexter hand a bow and in his sinister three arrows ppr. *Fidele.*

Rourk, Ireland, out of a ducal coronet a hand holding a dagger. 212. 11

Rous, Earl of Stradbroke, a pyramid of bay-leaves in the form of a cone vert. 151. 14

Rous of Great Clacton, Essex, a pyramid of laurel-leaves alternately vert and arg. 151. 14

Rous or **Rouse** of London, a demi-lion rampant az., holding between the paws a bezant. 11. 7

Rous of Piercefield, Monm., Wales, of Edmerston, Devonsh., and Halton, Cornw., a dove arg. *Vescitur Christo.* 92. 2

Rous, Devonsh., a demi-eagle regardant with wings displayed ppr.

Rous of Modbury, Devonsh., an eagle displayed gu. 75. 2

Rouse, *see* Boughton-Rouse.

Rouse, *see* Boughton, Rouse-.

Rouse, *see* Boughton-Knight, Rouse-.

Rouse, the bust of a man couped at the shoulders ppr., the hair, beard, and whiskers sa., the head surrounded and crossed by a ribbon knotted at the top, the ends flowing from either temple arg.

Rouse, Rev. Rolla Charles Meadows, M.A., the Rectory, Rayleigh, Suff., same crest. *La fortune passe partout.*

Rouse of Market Harborough, Leics., a demi-lion rampant per pale indented gu. and erm., holding between the paws a crescent arg.

Rouse, a demi-lioness ppr., collared or.

Roushland, Surrey, a nag's head or, erased per fess gu., maned of the last. 51. 4

Routh, the sun in his splendour or. 162. 2

Routh, out of a mural coronet a talbot's head. 56. 6

Routh, John Christopher Cain, of Clint's House, Gayle, near Hawes, Yorks, and Baxterley, Rusthall, Tunbridge Wells, Kent: (1) Out of a mural coronet gu., a talbot's head arg. (2) A lion's head erased or. (3) An elephant's head erased sa. *Ruda non rudis.*

Routledge, a garb vert. 153. 2

Row, Devonsh., a stag's head erased gu., attired or. 121. 2

Row and **Rowe,** of Kingston, Devonsh., a buck's head couped gu., attired or. 121. 5

Row of Conington, Hunts, a roebuck's head couped gu., attired or. 121. 5

Row, Scotland, an arm in armour issuing, holding in the hand a sword ppr. *Non desistam.* 210. 2

Rowan, Scotland, a garb ppr. *Per industriam.* 153. 2

Rowan, Ireland, same crest. *Hæc lucra laborum.* 153. 2

Rowan, on a mount vert, a holy lamb ppr., holding a banner per fess or and gu. *cf.* 131. 14

Rowan, of Oldstone and Mallans, and Mount Davys, co. Antrim, Ireland, a naked cubit arm, holding in the hand a dagger ppr. *Cresco per crucem.* 212. 3

Rowan, John Joshua, Mount Davys, Cullybackey, co. Antrim, same crest and motto.

Rowan-Legg of Carrickfergus, Ireland: (1) Out of a mural coronet ppr., five ostrich-feathers alternately arg. and az., the centre feather charged with a mullet gu and above it on an escroll the motto, *Cresco per crucem* (*for Legg*) (2) A dexter hand and arm couped at the elbow ppr, grasping a dagger in bend sinister, also ppr (*for Rowan*) *Gaudet tentamine virtus* 212 3

Rowand, Ireland, a garb or *Hæc lucra laborum* 153 2

Rowand of Glasgow, a lion couchant ppr *Benigno Numine* 7 5

Rowand of Moscow, a ship under sail ppr *Nil arduum* 160 13

Rowbache of Lytton, Herts, on a wing arg, a bend gobony or and gu cf 109 7

Rowche, a rock ppr *Mon Dieu est ma roche* 179 7

Rowcliffe, William Charles, Esquire, Halsway Manor Taunton, Somers, a lion's head erased gu, in front thereof two chess rooks arg *Volens et valens* 261 6

Rowcliffe, Edward Lee Esquire Hall Place, Cranleigh, Surrey, same crest and motto

Rowdon, *see* Rawdon

Rowdon, of Rowdon Yorks, a cock crowing ppr 91 2

Rowdon, Suff, a bezant cf 159 14

Rowdon of St Giles', Oxon, two swan's necks addorsed and interlaced issuing from a crescent, all arg, and holding in each beak an annulet gu *Unguibus repostis* 100 11

Rowdon, on a ducal coronet a griffin segreant cf 62 2

Rowe, a buck's head couped gu, attired or 121 5

Rowe, Middx and London, a stag's head ppr 121 5

Rowe of London, and Norton Place Sussex, a stag's head erased gu, attired or charged on the neck with a crescent arg 119 8

Rowe of Colchester, Northamp, a stag's head gu, attired or 121 5

Rowe, Devonsh, a holy lamb or, the staff cross and banner arg 131 2

Rowe of Tolesby Hall, Yorks, and Devonsh, a holy lamb or, the staff, cross, and banner arg *Innocens, non timidus* 131 2

Rowe, Fisher-, Edward Rowe, Thorncombe Park, Guildford, Surrey (1) A lamb resting the dexter fore leg on a beehive ppr, charged on the body with a cross patee or (2) On a fountain between six bulrushes a kingfisher rising, in the beak a fish, all ppr *Favente Deo*

Rowe, Sussex, out of a ducal coronet or, a demi lion gu, holding in the dexter paw a Polish mace in pale sa, spiked and pointed arg

Rowe, a hand issuant ppr, holding a cross crosslet fitched az *Auspice Christo* 221 14

Rowe, a dexter arm ppr vested erminois, holding in the hand a trefoil vert 205 9

Rowe of Ballycross, co Wexford, Ireland an arm embowed in armour ppr, round the wrist a scarf gu, holding in the hand a sword arg, hilted or, enfiled with a wreath vert, the arm charged with a cross patee fitchee, also gu *Agendo gnaviter*

Rowed, a hand holding a lion's gamb erased ppr 220 10

Rowell, a hand couped in fess holding a cross crosslet fitched 221 10

Rowell, a hind passant, holding in the mouth a rose leaved ppr

Rowland, Scotland, a demi lion rampant gu, holding a sword by the blade in pale, hilted or

Rowland, two ducks issuing with wings elevated and addorsed, respecting each other

Rowland, a lion's head erased 17 8

Rowland, Shropsh, out of a ducal coronet or a demi talbot arg

Rowlands, a fleur de-lis gu, entwined with a serpent or 148 8

Rowlands, Jacob, Hollyhurst, South Yardley, Birmingham on three fleurs de-lis fessewise gu, a wolf passant ppr, holding in the mouth a staff raguly in bend also gu *Y blaidd yn y blaen*

Rowlatt, a demi lion arg, maned or 10 2

Rowles, Shropsh, a horse current, holding in the mouth the point of a broken spear, all ppr cf 52 7

Rowles, Surrey, out of a ducal coronet a demi-griffin segreant 64 4

Rowlesley, Derbysh, a demi-lion rampant per pale arg and gu, holding between the paws a rose of the last stalked and leaved vert cf 16 2

Rowley, *see* Langford, Baron

Rowley, a mullet arg, pierced sa

Rowley, Sir Joshua Thellusson, Bart J P, D L, of Tendring Hall, Suff, a mullet pierced or *Ventis secundis*

Rowley, Sir George Charles Erskine, Bart, of Hill House, Berks, a mullet pierced or

Rowley, Admiral Charles John, Holmes land, Botley Hants same crest *Ventis secundis*

Rowley, George Fydell, Priory Park, St Neot's, a mullet pierced arg

Rowley, a sword in bend arg hilted or, passing through a mullet sa

Rowley, Shropsh an etoile of eight points pierced gu

Rowley, a wolf's head collared *Bear and forbear* 30 9

Rowley of Lawton Chesh, a wolf's head erased arg *Bear and forbear* 30 8

Rowley of Carrigaveagh, co Tipperary, Ireland a wolf's head erased sa, collared bendy or and gu *La vertue surmonte tout obstacle*

Rowley, Ireland a wolf's head couped sa, collared and ringed arg *La vertue surmonte tout obstacle* 30 9

Rowley of Castle Rowley co Londonderry, Ireland, a wolf's head couped az gorged with a ribbon knotted at the back arg, and charged on the neck with a crescent or, surcharged with another crescent az

Rowly Conwy, Maurice William Glyn Bodrhyddan, Rhuddlan Rhyl a wolf's head couped at the shoulder collared arg *Bear and forbear*

Rowntree of Stockton-on Tees, a tree ppr 143 5

Rowsewell and **Rowswell,** Devonsh, Norf, and Somers., a lion's head couped arg 21 1

Rowsewell of Vasterne, Wilts, a lion's head erased arg 17 8

Rowton, Baron (Lowry-Corry), of Rowton Castle, Shropsh (1) A cock ppr, charged with a crescent gu (*for Corry*) cf 91 2 (2) A garland of laurel between two branches of the same vert (*for Lowry*) *Loyal au mort* 257 12

Roxburgh, late Sir Francis Q C, J P, of the Beach House, Aldeburgh, Suff, Treasurer of the Middle Temple, and Francis Roxburgh, Esquire, of 43, Leinster Gardens, Hyde Park London, W a horse's head couped arg *Tam audax quam fidelis* cf 50 13

Roxburgh, upon a mount vert, in front of a sun rising from behind clouds a palm-tree ppr *Cœli favore*

Roxburghe, Duke of (Innes Ker), Floors Castle, Kelso, Roxburghsh (1) A unicorn's head erased arg, armed and maned or (*for Ker*) 49 5 (2) A boar's head erased ppr, langued gu (*for Innes*). *Pro Christo et patria —Be traist* 42 2

Roxby of Blackwood, Yorks (1) A wolf's head erased per pale arg and vert, gorged with a collar counterchanged, holding in the mouth a branch of hop ppr (*for Roxby*) (2) Issuing from a wreath of laurel vert a lion's head gu, charged on the neck with a cross crosslet fitched or (*for Maude*) *Perseverando —De monte alto*

Roy of Nenthorn Berwicksh, a lymphad with her sails furled and oars in action sa, in the sea ppr *Qua tendis* 160 7

Roycroft, Lancs, a griffin's head erased 66 2

Royden or **Roydon,** Devonsh, out of a ducal coronet or a demi griffin per pale arg and gu 64 4

Royden, Thomas Bland, Esquire J P, D L Frankby Hall, Chesh a stag's head erased or, collared gemel vert, and pendant from the mouth a shield of the Royden Arms *Au roy donne devoir* 307 15

Roydhouse of London a demi-archer ppr vested vert, holding in the dexter hand an arrow arg, and in the sinister a bow or

Roydon of Exeter, out of a ducal coronet or, a demi griffin per pale arg and gu 64 4

Royds of Falinge, near Rochdale, a leopard sejant ppr, bezantee, gorged with a collar arg, resting the dexter fore paw on a pheon *Semper paratus* 290 10

Royds, Rev Francis Tremlow, of Heysham, Lancs same crest and motto

Royds, Clement Molyneux J P, Greenhill near Rochdale same crest and motto

Royer of St James's Westminster, Middx, a dove arg, with wings expanded or gorged with an Eastern coronet of the last, holding in the beak an olive-branch vert cf 94 5

Royle, on a chapeau ppr a lion's head erased gu ducally crowned or 21 3

Roys, Leics., a demi-griffin arg, holding a rose gu barbed vert cf 64 2

Royse of Fredvile, Kent, a demi lion gardant arg 10 8

Royse of Nantinan, co Limerick a demi lion rampant barry arg and gu cf 12 3

Royse, John Macdonald, J P Thornton, Dunlavin, co Kildare, same crest.

Royston, Viscount, *see* Hardwicke, Earl of.

Royston, out of a ducal coronet or, two lion's gambs in saltier ppr. 39. 10

Rubie, John, Bath, an anchor erect, the shank enfiled by a garb, all or. *Que les rubis brillent.*

Rubridge, a dove or, holding in its beak an olive-branch vert. 92. 5

Ruck, an old man's head ppr., bound round the temples with laurel vert. *cf.* 190. 7

Rudall or **Ruddall**, a hawk's head erased or. 88. 12

Rudall, a falcon ppr. 85. 2

Rudd or **Rudde**, Wales, an arm erect vested az., holding in the hand a scroll, all ppr. *cf.* 208. 5

Rudd, Bart. (*extinct*), of Aberglasney, Carmarthensh., an arm erect vested az., charged with a chevron erm., holding in the hand a scroll, all ppr. *cf.* 208. 5

Rudd of Thorne, near Doncaster, Yorks, an arm erect vested az., charged with a chevron erm., holding in the hand a scroll, all ppr. *Pro Rege et grege.—In cruce salus.* *cf.* 208. 5

Rudd, a griffin's head couped ppr., collared arg. *cf.* 66. 1

Rudd, Worcs. a maiden's head affrontée, couped below the shoulders ppr. *cf.* 182. 3

Rudd of Higham Ferrers, Northamp., and of Abergavenny, Wales, a lion rampant or, holding an escutcheon az., charged with a canton or.

Rudd and **Rudde**, Essex and Lincs, a cross botonée or.

Rudde of London, between two wings arg., a cross crosslet fitched gu. 111. 3

Ruddiman, Scotland, a spur ppr. *Vis viri fragilis.* 178. 8

Ruddock, Rev. Noblett Henry Cranmer, M.A., D.D., J.P., Beaconsfield Road, Upper Knowle, Bristol, a redbreast ppr. *Sustinuit et nos sustinebit Deus.*

Rudge, a pelican in her piety ppr. 98. 8

Rudge, Edward Charles, of Evesham, Worcs., out of a mural coronet or, two arms erect vested gu., the hands and cuffs ppr., supporting an escutcheon arg. *In cruce fides.*

Rudge, Walter William Nouaille, of Threekingham, Folkingham, Lincs, same crest and motto.

Rudge, Eustace E., 24, Central Hill, Norwood, S.E., same crest and motto.

Rudge, Rev. S. E., of Kingscote, Glouc., same crest and motto.

Rudge, Lieutenant-Colonel Walter Reginald, of Highlands, Colne, Wilts, same crest and motto.

Rudge, out of a mural coronet two arms in armour embowed, holding an escutcheon charged with a cross engrailed.

Rudger, a Saracen's head affrontée ppr., wreathed about the temples arg. and sa. 190. 5

Rudhall, a falcon ppr. 85. 2

Rudhall of Rudhall and Ross, Heref., a cubit arm erect in armour ppr., the cuffs barry lozengy counterchanged arg. and az., the hand holding three roses gu., stalked ppr.

Rudiard, Leics. and Staffs, a lion's head gardant and erased or.

Rudierd, a lion's head gardant arg.

Ruding, a cross moline pierced az. 165. 1

Rudinge and **Rudings** of Westcott, Leics., and of Martin-Hussingtree, Worcs., a dragon's head sa., collared and chained or, holding in the mouth a lion's gamb erased of the second.

Rudston, Yorks and Cambs, a bull's head sa. *cf.* 44. 3

Rudston, a lion's gamb erect pean holding a cross moline erminois.

Rudston, Calverley-, Trevor Wheler, of Hayton, Yorks, a bear's paw erect pean holding a cross moline erminois.

Rudyerd of Rudyerd, Staffs, a lion's head guardant arg.

Ruff, a stag statant transfixed by an arrow, all ppr. 117. 10

Rufford of Rufford, Bucks, an eagle with wings expanded, holding in the beak a trefoil slipped, all sa.

Ruffy, a demi-archer shooting an arrow from a bow. 187. 6

Rufus, an antique crown or. 180. 12

Rugeley or **Rugelly** of Shenstone and Smallwood, Staffs, and of Downton Rugeley, Warw., a tower or, flames issuant therefrom ppr., in front of four arrows in saltier arg.

Rugeley, Shropsh., a tower superimbattled, pierced in the centre with two arrows in saltire, points downward.

Rugge of Felmingham, and Billingford, Norf., a talbot passant arg., collared, ringed, and eared sa. *cf.* 54. 5

Rugge of North Reps, Norf., an ibex's head sa., armed, maned, and tufted or.

Rugge-Price, Sir Arthur James, Bart., of Spring Grove, Surrey: (1) A lion rampant arg., holding in the dexter paw a rose gu., slipped vert (*for Price*). (2) A talbot passant arg., gorged with a collar, and pendent therefrom an escutcheon sa., charged with the head of an ibex couped, also arg. (*for Rugge*). *Vive ut vivas.* 309. 10

Ruggles of Spain's Hall, Essex, and of Clare, Suff., a tower or, flames issuing from the top ppr., behind the tower four arrows in saltier arg. *Struggle.*

Rule, an arm in armour embowed, holding in the hand a sword, all ppr. 195. 2

Rumbold, a greyhound's head arg., between two roses gu., slipped and leaved ppr. 61. 11

Rumbold, Herts, a demi-lion rampant or. 10. 2

Rumbold, Sir Horace, Bart., K.C.M.G., of Woodhall, Watton, Herts, a demi-lion rampant erminois. *Ut sursum desuper.—Virtutis laus actio.* 10. 2

Rumford, a hand holding a leg in armour couped at the thigh and spurred, all ppr. 220. 11

Rumford, R. Kennerley, Esquire, Compton Lodge, South Hampstead, N.W., a cubit arm erect, holding in the hand a leg in armour couped at the thigh and spurred, all ppr. *Vi non astutia.* 314. 3

Rumney, a lion statant gardant ppr. 4. 1

Rumney, Howard, F.R.G.S., St. Leonard's-on-Sea, same crest. *Mors ærumnarum requies.* 4. 1

Rumney of Lulsley in Suckley, Worcs., on a mount vert, in front of a tree ppr., a lion statant guardant gu. *Mors ærumnarum requies.*

Rump of Swanton, Norf., a demi-lion rampant regardant ppr., holding between the paws an escutcheon az., charged with the sun in splendour or.

Rumsey, a horned owl gu. 96. 5

Rumsey, Wales, a talbot passant az., collared or. *cf.* 54. 5

Rundle, Cornw. and Devonsh., on a mount vert, a squirrel sejant ppr., collared az., chained or, holding in the mouth an oak-branch fructed ppr. *Laus Deo.*

Rundle, Cornw. and Devonsh., a wolf's head ppr. 30. 5

Rundle, Ireland, a sword in pale arg., the gripe gu., pommel and hilt or. 170. 2

Rupe, out of a ducal coronet five ostrich-feathers. 114. 13

Rusby of Thorpe-in-Balne and Pontefract, Yorks, a golden eagle ppr., pierced with a broken dart, also ppr., barbed and flighted or. *Audax et promptus.*

Rush, an arm in armour embowed to the sinister, holding in the hand a Saracen's head by the beard.

Rush, a bear's head couped, bezantée, muzzled, holding in the mouth an ear of wheat.

Rush, a wolf's head erased erm. 30. 8

Rush of Wimbledon, Surrey, and Elsenham Hall, Essex, a wolf's head erased vert, langued gu., guttée-d'or, gorged with a collar of the last, charged with three torteaux. *Un Dieu, un Roi, une foi.* *cf.* 30. 7

Rushbrook, a Catherine-wheel sa., embrued gu. 167. 2

Rushbrooke, a rose or. 149. 4

Rushbrooke, Suff., a lion sejant, holding in its mouth a rose or.

Rushbrooke, Robert Wyndham Jermyn, of Rushbrooke Park, Suff., same crest. *Fluminis ritu ferimur.*

Rushe, Ireland, a wolf's head erased erm. 30. 8

Rushe, a wolf's head erased vert, guttée-d'eau, langued gu. *cf.* 30. 8

Rushe, Suff., a fox's head erased arg., guttée-d'olive. *cf.* 33. 6

Rushe, Suff., a horse's head erased vert, guttée-d'eau. 51. 4

Rushe, Essex, an arm in armour embowed ppr., garnished or, the hand holding by the hair a man's head, the neck distilling blood, also ppr.

Rushout, Baron Northwick, *see* Northwick.

Rushout, a lion passant gardant or. *Paternis suppar.* 4. 3

Rushout, Sir Charles Hamilton, Bart., of Sezincot, Glouc.: (1) A lion passant guardant or. 4. 3. (2) Within a crescent az., a tiger's face ppr., crowned with an Eastern coronet or. *Par ternis suppar.* 21. 8

Rushout, Algeman St. George William Rushout, Burton House, Moreton-in-Marsh, same crests.

Rushton, Lancs, on a chapeau gu., turned up erm., a demi-lion of the last. 15. 14

Rushton, Lancs and Staffs, on a chapeau gu., turned up erm., a demi-lion rampant of the last. *Have patience and endure.* 15. 14

Ruspeni or **Ruspini,** on a serpent nowed, a dove holding in its beak an olive-branch, all ppr *cf* 92. 10

Russborough, Viscount, *see* Milltown, Earl of

Russel, Worcs, a demi-lion, collared, studded or, holding a cross crosslet fitched sa *cf* 11 10

Russell, Duke of Bedford, *see* Bedford

Russell, Hamilton-, Viscount Boyne, *see* Boyne

Russell, Baron Ampthill, *see* Ampthill

Russell, *see* De Clifford, Baron

Russell, *see* Frankland-Russell

Russell, Earl (Russell), Ardsalla House, near Navan, Meath, a goat statant arg, armed and ungu or *Che sara, sara* 129 5

Russell, Thomas John, titular **Baron of Killoc,** of Quoniamstown and Ballystrew, co Down Ireland a goat passant arg *Che sara, sara* *cf* 129 5

Russell, Scotland and Cumb, a goat passant arg, attired or *cf* 129 5

Russell of Blackbraes, Stirlingsh, a goat passant holding in the mouth a thistle, both ppr *Che sara, sara* 129 7

Russell, Richard Harold, the Grange, Chalfont St Peter Bucks, a goat passant holding in the mouth a trefoil slipped, all ppr *Che sara, sara*

Russell, Scotland, a goat passant ppr *cf* 129 5

Russell, a goat passant arg, armed or *Che sara, sara* *cf* 129 5

Russell, George William Erskine, M A, LL D, 18, Wilton Street, S W, same crest and motto

Russell, Harold John Hastings, 16, Beaufort Gardens, S W, a goat statant arg armed or

Russell of Brancepeth Castle, Durh, a goat passant arg *cf* 129 5

Russell, Bucks, a goat passant ppr, armed, ungu, and murally gorged or *cf* 129 5

Russell, Bart (*extinct*), of Chippenham, Bucks, Cambs, and Berks, a goat arg, armed and gorged with a mural coronet or *cf* 129 5

Russell, His Honour Judge 16, Norfolk Square, W a goat passant arg, armed or charged on the body fesseways with three trefoils vert

Russell, Hon Charles, 40, Hyde Park Gate, W, same crest

Russell, Hon Cyril, 13, Hyde Park Street, W, same crest

Russell, a goat passant arg, holding a trident sa

Russell, Derbysh (1) On a mount vert a goat passant erm, armed ppr, collared gu (*for Russell*). *cf* 129 3 (2) A demi lion or, charged with a cross patee az, holding in the mouth an oak branch ppr, fructed of the first, and between the paws an escutcheon, also az, charged with a fess erminois, between three fleurs-de-lis in chief and a cross patee in base, also or, from the escutcheon a scroll bearing the motto, *Amice* (*for Watts*)

Russell, Dorset, a demi Indian goat rampant arg, the horns, ears hoofs, and beard sa

Russell of Badham, Thorpe, and West Burnham, Norf, a demi-goat arg, armed or 128 2

Russell, Lieutenant-Colonel Andrew Hamilton J P, formerly of Manga Kuri, Hawkesbay, New Zealand, and now of Fonthill, Torquay, upon a mount vert, an antelope lodged ppr, gorged with a collar gemel or, supporting a lance ppr, therefrom a flowing pennon arg., charged with a bomb shell also ppr *Dei beneficio sum quod sum* 126 14

Russell, Worcs and Heref, a demi lion rampant arg, holding a cross crosslet fitched sa 11 10

Russell of Killough, co Down, and Sheephouse, co Meath, a demi lion rampant gu *Che sara, sara* 10 3

Russell, Henry Patrick Marie, **Count Russell** of Rome, heir male and representative of the Russells, Barons of Killough, co Down, a demi-lion rampant gu *Che sara sara* 10 3

Russell, Worcs., a demi lion rampant or, holding a cross crosslet fitched sa 11 10

Russell of Southwark, Surrey, Stubbers, North Ockendon, Essex, and Towcester, Northamp., a demi lion rampant arg, collared gu, charged on the body with a chevron sa, thereon an escallop or, holding between the paws a cross crosslet fitched of the third

Russell, Sir George, Bart, D L M P of Swallowfield, Berks, a demi-lion rampant erm, charged on the shoulder with a fasces ppr and bearing in his dexter paw a cross crosslet fitchee sa *Discite justitiam moniti* *cf* 11 10

Russell of Little Malvern Court Worcs, a demi-lion arg, holding between the paws a cross crosslet fitchee sa *Je tiens foy*

Russell of Brownstown and Bringham, Dublin a demi-lion rampant or, holding between the paws an escutcheon arg, thereon a dexter hand couped at the wrist and erect gu, being the arms of O'Neill with the motto over *Nox St Patrick for Ireland* *In solo regit qui degit in cœlo*

Russell, Robert, Esquire of Government Park, Jamaica, a demi-leopard ppr, gorged with a collar gemel or and holding in the dexter paw a spur leathered also or *Suum cuique*

Russell of Ashiesteel, Selkirk, a fountain ppr *Agitatione purgatur*

Russell, Major General John Cecil, of Barton Court, Canterbury, same crest and motto

Russell, Alexander Eliott, Esquire, the Gables, Church Crookham, Winchfield, Hants, same crest and motto

Russell of Kingseat, Peeblessh, Scotland same crest and motto

Russell, Sir William Bart, C B, of Charlton Park, Glouc (1) A fountain 159 8 (2) Out of a ducal coronet or a demi-eagle rising ppr, gorged with a mural coronet or *Nitor donec supero.*

Russell, Ireland, a phœnix in flames ppr 82 2

Russell, on a bezant a Cornish chough with wings expanded sa, beaked and legged gu

Russell of Galway, Ireland on a laurel branch a raven, all ppr *Fortitudo fidelis honore munerata* *cf* 107 10

Russell of Handsworth, Staffs, in front of two palm branches saltireways vert, a fret or, thereon a martlet sa *Quo fata vocant* 95 10

Russell of London, out of a mural coronet arg, the head of a Newfoundland dog sa, collared or, the neck and breast also arg *Eundo*

Russell of Powick Court, Worcs, a talbot passant arg 54 1

Russell of Meiklour and Montcoffer Banffsh., Scotland, issuing out of a cloud a dexter arm in fess, holding in the hand a sword in pale 223. 10

Russell of Longridge, Lanarksh, Scotland a dexter hand sustaining on the point of a sword a pair of balances, all ppr *Virtus sine macula*

Russell, a pyramid of leaves az 151 14

Russell, Essex and Sussex an adder's head erased ppr, collared gu, ringed or

Russell, Bucks, a demi griffin segreant vert 64 2

Russell, Bart (*extinct*), of Strensham Worcs, a chess-rook or, thereon a plume of ostrich feathers of the same and az

Russell of Rathen, Aberdeensh Scotland, a boar's head couped ppr *Memor esto* 43 1

Russell, Major-General Francis Shirley Aden House, Mintlaw, Aberdeensh (1) A demi-lion rampant, holding in the dexter paw a dagger erect (2) Issuing from clouds in the sinister a dexter hand in bend holding a sword erect *Courage —Promptus*

Russell-Pavier, Herbert Arthur (1) Two arms embowed ppr vested above the elbow arg, that on the dexter holding a chisel, and that on the sinister a mallet, also ppr (2) In front of two palm-branches saltireways vert a fret or thereon a martlet sa *Quo fata vocant*

Rust, Suff, a demi lion rampant 10 2

Rust, a wyvern gu 70 1

Rust, Rev Edgar, of Abbot's Hall, Stowmarket, Rector of Drinkston, Suff a demi lion gu, holding in the dexter paw an ivory rod, and charged on the shoulder with three crosses patée fitchee chevronwise or *Veritatis et æqualitatis tenax*

Rusted, an olive-branch slipped vert 151 11

Ruston, John Seward, Monks Manor, Lincoln, in front of a lion rampant erm, holding between the paws an escallop gu, a leopard's face between two roses of the last barbed vert, seeded or *Have patience and endure*

Ruthall of Wolverton, Bucks, and Little Billing Northamp, a demi eagle rising arg the inside of the wings gu, each wing charged with three guttes d'or holding in the beak a rose of the second slipped vert

Rutherford, Lord Rutherford and Earl of Teviot, a mermaid holding in her dexter hand a mirror and in her sinister a comb, all ppr *Per mare, per terras —Provide.* 184 5

Rutherford or **Rutherfurd,** Scotland, a mermaid ppr *Per mare, per terras* 184 5

Rutherford, on a rock a wild goose, all ppr

Rutherford of that ilk, in Teviotdale, Scotland a martlet sa, beaked gu *Nec sorte, nec fato* 95 5

Rutherford, a martlet sa *Amico fidus ad aras* 95 5

Rutherford of Fairningtoun Roxburghsh Scotland a martlet sa, beaked gu *Amico fidus ad aras* 95 5

Rutherford of Edinburgh, a horse's head couped ppr, bridled gu *In pede fausto* 51. 5

Rutherford, a horse's head issuant, bridled gu *Sedulus et audax* 51. 5

Rutherford, John, Esquire, of Blackburn and Summerhill, Annan Dumfriessh, a white horse's head erased ppr. *Sedulus et audax* 51 4

Rutherford or **Rutherfurd**, Scotland, a horse's head and neck *Sedulus et audax* cf 50 13

Rutherfurd, William Edward Oliver, Edgerston, Jedburgh, Roxburghsh, a martlet sa, beaked gu

Rutherfurd, Andrew, Esquire Advocate of 18, Great Stewart Street, Edinburgh, a mermaid holding in her dexter hand a mirror, and in her sinister a comb, all ppr *Per mare, per terras.* 184 5

Rutherfurd, Oliver-, of Edgerston, Roxburghsh a martlet sa *Nec sorte, nec fato* 95 5

Rutherfurd, Henry, of Fairnington, Kelso, a martlet sa, beaked gu *Nec sorte nec fato*

Ruthven, Lord Ruthven and Earl of Gowrie, a ram's head arg armed or *Deeds shaw* 130 1

Ruthven, Baron (Rt Hon Walter James Hore-Ruthven D L) of Freeland Perthsh Scotland a ram's head couped arg armed or *Deeds shaw* 130 1

Ruthven, a goat's head arg., armed and maned or *Deeds shaw* 128 12

Ruthven, a goat's head erased arg, armed or *Deeds shaw* 128 5

Ruthven, a goat's head couped affrontee 128 13

Ruthven, William Bermingham, Esquire J P, of Quansborough co Galway Ireland a goat's head erased arg attired or charged with a mullet gu and over the crest on an escroll the motto *Deeds shaw* cf 128 5

Ruthven, Ayrsh, Scotland issuing out of a ducal coronet or a goat's head arg, armed, also or *Deeds shaw* 128 14

Ruthven, Scotland a ram's head couped ppr 130 1

Rutland, Duke of (Manners), Belvoir Castle Grantham, on a chapeau gu, turned up erm, a peacock in its pride ppr *Pour y parvenir* 103 5

Rutland of Mitcham, Surrey, a nag's head arg erased per fess gu, maned of the last 51 4

Rutland or **Roushland** of Mitcham, Surrey, a nag's head or erased per fesse and maned gu 51 4

Rutland of Richmond, Surrey a horse's head erased sa, semee of annulets or holding in the mouth a branch of fern ppr *Post prœlia prœmia*

Rutledge, Ireland, an antique crown or 180 12

Rutledge, Thomas Forster, Esquire J P, of Werronggurt Warrnambool, Victoria, Australia, *uses* a mural coronet *Coronat fides*

Rutson, Henry, Esquire, J P B A, of Newby Wiske and Nunnington Yorks a griffin's head couped per bend sa and or, entwined by a serpent ppr *Spectemur agendo* 65 7

Rutt, Bucks, the sun in splendour or 162 2

Rutter, a greyhound's head between two roses slipped and leaved 61 11

Rutter, Devonsh an eagle arg 76 2

Rutter of Exeter Devonsh, an eagle arg, perched on the trunk of a tree erased sa

Rutter, Thomas Joshua Esquire, of Eardington, Shropsh, on the trunk of an oak tree sprouting ppr, an eagle with wings elevated arg, gorged with a collar gemel sa and resting the dexter claw upon a cross patee of the last *Melitæ amor*

Ruttledge-Fair, Robert Fair of Cornfield, Hollymount, co Mayo Ireland (1) On a mount vert a dove with an olive branch in its beak and a trefoil on its breast, all ppr (*for Fair*) (2) An oak-tree ppr, pendent from a dexter branch thereof by a riband az an escutcheon or (*for Ruttledge*) *Verax atque probus*

Ruttledge of Cornfield, Mayo and Dublin an oak-tree ppr, pendent from a branch on the dexter side by a ribbon az, an escutcheon or *Verax atque probus*

Ruttledge, David Knox, Barbersfort Tuam, co Galway, same crest and motto

Ruvigny, *see* De Massue, Marquis de Ruvigny et Raineval, and Massue, Earl of Galway

Ruxton, Ireland a hand gauntleted holding an arrow ppr

Ruxton, William, Esquire, J P D L of Ardee House co Louth, Ireland, a bull's head erased sa, armed or *Jam jam* 44 3

Ruxton, Charles Harcourt Vernon, Lumoling, A B R, Assam, same crest and motto

Ruxton, William Vernon Chickering, Ardee House, Ardee Louth, same crest and motto

Ruxton, Julian Henry Hay of Broad Oak Kent, a bull's head sa armed or, charged with a crescent arg cf 44. 3

Ruxton, John Henry Hay, Esquire, J P, D L of Broad Oak, Kent, a bull's head erased sa armed or, charged with a crescent of the second cf 44 3

Ryan, a hand ppr vested az cuffed arg, holding a baton gu, veruled or

Ryan, on a garb fesseways a goat *Malo mori quam fœdari*

Ryan, Ireland, a griffin's head erased ppr 66 2

Ryan of Cadiz, Spain a griffin's head erased or 66 2

Ryan of Kilkeyll, co Tipperary, Ireland, same crest. *Malo mori quam fœdari* 66 2

Ryan, Charles, Esquire, of Derriweit Heights, Upper Macedon, Victoria, Australia *uses* a griffin segreant az, holding in the dexter claw a sword ppr *Malo mori quam fœdari*

Ryan, Edward Francis Maxwell 4 Great James Street, W C, same crest and motto

Ryan, John Henry, 35, Waterloo Road, Dublin, same crest and motto

Ryan of Inch House co Tipperary, a griffin segreant az, holding a sword in pale ppr *Malo mori quam fœdari* cf 62 2

Ryan, the sun rising from behind a hill ppr 162 7

Ryan of Dublin, a horse sa *Malo mori quam fœdari* 52 5

Rycroft, Yorks, a griffin's head erased and erect arg 66 2

Rycroft, a griffin's head erased or 66 2

Rycroft, Sir Richard Nelson Bart, J.P., of Calton, Yorks a griffin's head erased per bend or and az, charged with two fleurs de lis counterchanged *Faythe hathe no fear* cf 66 2

Ryder, *see* Harrowby Earl of.

Ryder, *see* Wood-Ryder

Ryder, out of a mural coronet or a dragon's head arg *Servata fides cinere* 72 11

Ryder, Dudley Henry, J P, Westbrook Hay, Hemel Hempstead out of a mural coronet or, a dragon's head arg charged on the neck with an ermine spot sa *Ut crescent lucent*

Ryder, George Lisle, 16 Palace Gardens Terrace W same crest

Rydon of Pyrland House, Middx, a gryphon segreant gu with wings chequy of the same and arg holding between the claws an escutcheon of the first charged with a bezant *Fortuna et honos ab alto*

Rye of Whitwell, Derbysh an arm vested purp, holding in the hand three ears of wheat or cf 205. 7

Rye, Norf and Suff, a cubit arm erect vested vert, holding in the hand ppr three rye-stalks or *Sui victoria indicat regem* cf 205 8

Rye, Richard Tonson, Ryecourt, Crookstown co Cork same crest. *Fide et amore*

Rye, Walter, St Leonard's Priory, Norwich, a cubit arm erect holding an hour glass in bend sinister all ppr

Ryecroft, a griffin's head erased erm 66 2

Ryed or **Ryede**, a lion couchant gardant ppr 7. 10

Ryland, *see* Smith-Ryland

Ryland of Bearley and Sherborne Warw, issuing from a mount vert, a dexter arm in armour embowed ppr garnished or, the hand also ppr, holding a rose gu, slipped of the first, and three ears of rye, also or *Not the last* 109 8

Ryland, Thomas, Esquire, J P of the Redlands, Erdington Warw, Lord of the Manors of Wisham and Moxhall, and Howard Proctor Ryland, Esquire, of Gravelly Hill House, near Birmingham, a demi-lion rampant sa, charged with a chevron arg, thereon a sheaf of rye between two escallops of the first, holding between the paws an escutcheon also arg, charged with a martlet, also sa *Avorum honori* 225 6

Ryland, John William, Esquire, J P F S A, of Rowington, Warw, on a wreath of the colours a demi-lion sa, charged with a chevron arg thereon a sheaf of rye between two escallops of the first, holding between the paws an escutcheon also arg, charged with a martlet, also sa *Avorum honori* 225 6

Rylands, John Paul, Esquire of Highfields, Thelwall, Chesh, a demi lion rampant az on the shoulder a bezant charged with a fleur de lis, also az, supporting a flagstaff entwined by a branch of oak ppr, therefrom flowing to the sinister a banner gu, fringed and charged with a lion passant or *Dum spiro spero* 225 3

Rylands, William Harry South Bank Lodge, 1, Campden Hill Place W, same crest and first motto

Ryle, a lion's head erased per pale or and gu 17 8

Ryley, a crane's head erased arg 104 11

Ryley, a demi dragon or holding a cross patee fitched sa

Ryley of the Green Lancs a dragon's head erased sa, charged on the neck with three bezants

Rymer, Scotland, a hand holding a sword in pale, all ppr *Ense animus maior* 212 9

Rymer, Thomas Harrison Esquire, Calder Abbey via Carnforth Cumb, in front of a cubit arm in armour holding a sword erect between four ears of rye leaved and two on either side, all ppr, a cross botony gu

Rynd, James Fleetwood, Esquire, J P of Ryndville co Meath Ireland a demi-lion rampant gu holding in the paws a cross crosslet fitchée or, and charged on the shoulder with a crescent of the same *Fide et fortitudine*

Rynd, Robert Fleetwood William, Blackhall, Naas, co Kildare, same crest and motto

Rynd of Carse Scotland, a flower pot containing gilly-flowers ppr *Diuturnitate fragrantior*

Rynell, a hand holding an eagle's leg erased ppr 220 12

Rypon, Lancs and London, a lion sejant arg, ducally gorged or, holding in the paws a cross flory fitched sa

Rythe, a hawk ppr 85 2

Rythrie, De, of Riverstown House, co Kildare out of a mural coronet a dragon's head or 72 11

Ryton, a dolphin naiant az 140 5

Ryvell, a buck's head couped ppr attired or 121 5

Ryves of Damory Court and Ranston, Dorset an escutcheon quarterly or and gu, between two cypress-branches in orle vert

Ryves, a greyhound sejant sa collared or *cf* 59 2

Ryvett of London, Cambs Somers and Suff, an arm erect the hand ppr, grasping a broken sword of the first hilt and pommel or

Ryvett, Suff, an arm in armour erect couped at the elbow per pale arg and sa holding in the hand ppr a broken sword of the first, hilt and pommel or

S.

Sabbe of London and Norf an arm embowed in a coat of mail, holding in the hand ppr a pennon arg, fringed of the last and sa charged with a cross, also sa, the staff of the first, headed of the second *cf* 199 9

Sabben, a demi savage ppr 186 5

Sabin of Towcester Northamp a demi-bull rampant arg *cf* 45 8

Sabine, out of a ducal coronet or, a hand holding a fleur-de lis gu 215 2

Sable, an arm vested purp the hand ppr, holding a streamer, charged with an escutcheon arg thereon a cross sa, the staff also arg

Sacheverell, a goat passant arg, armed or *cf* 129 5

Sacheverell of Hopwell, Derbysh and Barton, Notts a goat statant ppr 129 5

Sacheverell of New Hall Warw, a goat passant arg, collared gu *cf* 129 5

Sacheverell, Derbysh, on a water bouget or, a lure gu the top az thereon a falcon belled arg

Sacheverell of Kirkby-in Ashfield, Notts, and Ibwell Derbysh, upon a hawk's lure or, a hawk close jessed and belled ppr *cf* 85 14

Sacheverell of Morley, Derbysh and Radcliffe Notts, on a lure az charged with a water-bouget or, the top also or, fretty gu the cords of the second, a falcon arg, beaked and belled or

Sackford, a savage's head ppr banded gu *cf* 190 14

Sackvile or Sackvill, a ram's head erased sa armed or, charged on the breast with a cinquefoil arg *cf* 130 6

Sackvill, a ram's head erased sa, armed or 130 6

Sackville-Germain, Duke of Dorset, *see* Dorset.

Sackville, *see* Delawarr, Earl

Sackville, *see* Stopford Sackville

Sackville, Earl and Duke of Dorset (*extinct*) out of a coronet composed of eight fleurs-de-lis or an estoile of eight points arg *Aut nunquam tentes aut perfice* *cf* 164 4

Sackville-Germain, Viscount Sackville (*extinct*), out of a coronet composed of fleur de lis or an estoile of twelve points arg *Aut nunquam tentes aut perfice* *cf* 164 4

Sackville, Baron (Sackville-West), D L, Knowle, Kent (1) Out of a ducal coronet or a griffin's head az beaked, and eared or (*for West*) 67 9 (2) Out of a coronet composed of fleurs de lis or an estoile arg (*for Sackville*) *Jour de ma vie* *cf* 164 4

Sackville, Sackville George Stopford Esquire, M A, M P of Drayton House same crest as (2) above *Toujours loyal*, *cf* 164 4

Sackville of Silscombe Dorset on a coronet composed of fleurs de lis or an etoile of eight rays arg *cf* 164 4

Sacre, Kent, an elephant or in a wood ppr

Sadleir, Bart (*extinct*), of Temple Dinsley Herts, a demi lion az ducally crowned gu 10 11

Sadleir of Sadleir's Wells co Tipperary a demi-lion rampant az ducally crowned or 10 11

Sadleir of Ballinderry and Castletown, co Tipperary Ireland, same crest *Servire Deo sapere* 10 11

Sadleir, Major General Richard R A, Plassy, co Limerick same crest and motto

Sadler of Edmonton, Middx, an eagle's head between two wings sa, beaked arg 84 2

Sadler of Salisbury, Wilts, a tilting spear erect or charged in the middle with an escutcheon gu 175 7

Sadler of Keynsham, Bury, near Cheltenham Glouc a tilting-spear in pale or charged in the middle with an escutcheon gu *Virtus mille scuta* 175 7

Sadler of Standon and Sopwell Herts, a demi-lion az ducally crowned gu 10 11

Sadler, James Henry, Esquire, J P of Lydiard, Swindon, Wilts, same crest *Servire Deo sapere*

Sadler of Fillongley, Warw, a demi lion rampant az, ducally crowned gu, charged on the shoulder with a mullet or *cf* 10. 11

Sadleyr, a beaver or 134 8

Saffin, Somers, on a mural coronet ppr, an etoile of sixteen rays or

Sagar-Musgrave, Captain John Musgrave, J P of Bramley and Red Hall, Yorks, Lord of the Manor of Roundhay, Shadwell and Seacroft, Red Hall Shadwell, Leeds Carlton and Junior Carlton Clubs (1) Two arms embowed ppr holding an annulet or encircling a tilting spear erect also ppr (*for Musgrave*) 200. 8 (2) Upon a rock ppr an eagle regardant or each wing charged with three bendlets gu resting the dexter claw upon a cross moline az *Valde et sapienter* 77 9

Sage, a stag's head erased ppr *Non sibi* 121 2

Sage, a sage's head erased at the neck and affrontee ppr, vested with a skull cap sa

Sagrenor, a cross moline lozenge pierced gu 165 1

Sainsbury, a hand holding a ducal coronet capped, between two branches of laurel in orle ppr 217 3

Sainsbury of Froyle, Hants, a demi antelope ppr, collared or, charged on the body with three lozenges conjoined in bend erminois.

Saint, John James Heath, Esquire, 112, Lexham Gardens, London, W., and 9, King's Bench Walk, Temple, E.C., a demi-eagle rising.

St. Albans, Duke of (Beauclerk), Redbourne Hall, Brigg, Lincs, on a chapeau gu., turned up erm., a lion statant gardant or, crowned with a ducal coronet per pale arg. and of the first, gorged with a collar of the last, thereon three roses, also arg., barbed and seeded ppr. *Auspicium melioris ævi.* cf. 4. 2

St. Albino, co. Tipperary, Ireland, on a ducal coronet or, a heron with wings elevated arg. *Noli me tangere.*

St. Albyn and **St. Aubyn** of Paracombe, Devonsh., and Alfoxton, Somers., a wolf sejant erm., collared, ringed, and lined, the line reflexed over the back or. *Deus meus dux meus.*

St. Amond, Scotland, an arm in armour brandishing a scimitar ppr.

St. Amond, out of a ducal coronet gu., an ass's head arg. 125. 10

St. Amond, a mule's head couped az., collared or, between three bezants, one and two, charged on the neck with a martlet or.

St. Andrea or **St. Andrew**, Leics., a dolphin haurient az. 140. 11

St. Andrew, a cinquefoil. 148. 12

St. Asaph, Viscount, *see* Ashburnham, Earl of.

St. Aubin, on a rock a Cornish chough ppr.

St. Aubin, Somers., a wolf sejant erm., collared, lined, and ringed or.

St. Aubyn, *see* St. Levan, Baron.

St. Aubyn, Bart. (*extinct*), of Clowance, Cornw., a Cornish chough rising ppr. 107. 3

St. Aubyn, Rev. E. L., Trelawny, Rodwell, Weymouth, Dorset, on a rock a Cornish chough rising ppr. 272. 10

St. Aubyn, Molesworth-, Rev. St. Aubyn Hender, of Clowance, Cornw., on a rock a Cornish chough rising ppr. 272. 10

St. Aubyn of Nantes, France, on a ducal coronet or, a heron with wings elevated arg. *Noli me tangere.*

St. Aubyn Farrer, Claude, Esquire, Physician, 7, Westbourne Park Road, out of a ducal coronet or, between two wings arg., a crescent of the first. *Ferré va ferme.* 294. 14

St. Barbe of Lymington, Hants, a wyvern sa. 70. 1

St. Clair-Erskine, Earl of Rosslyn, *see* Rosslyn.

St. Clair, *see* Sinclair, Baron.

St. Clair, Scotland, a dove holding in its beak an olive-branch, all ppr. *Credo.* 92. 5

St. Clair of Herdmanstoun, Haddingtonsh., Scotland, an eagle's head ppr. crowned or. *Entends-toi.* cf. 83. 1

St. Clair, a swan ppr., ducally gorged and chained or. *Fight and faith.* cf. 99. 2

St. Clair of Staverton Court, Glouc., a phœnix in flames ppr. *Renasce piu gloriosa.—Fight.* 82. 2

St. Clere, a fox current ppr. cf. 32. 8

St. Clere, Oxon., a ram statant arg., armed or. 131. 13

St. Denouac, a vol ppr. 113. 1

St. George, Baron St. George, a demi-lion rampant gu., ducally crowned or. *Firmitas in cœlo.* 10. 11

St. George, Sir John, Bart., of Woodsgift, co. Kilkenny, a demi-lion rampant gu., ducally crowned or, armed and langued az. *Firmitas in cœlo.* 10. 11

St. George, General Sir John, G.C.B., a demi-lion rampant gu., ducally crowned or. *Firmitas in cœlo.* 10. 11

St. George of London, Cambs, and Ireland, same crest. 10. 11

St. Germans, Earl of (Eliot), Port Eliot, St. German's, Cornw., an elephant's head couped arg., collared gu. *Præcedentibus insta.* cf. 133. 2

St. Germyn, a demi-otter. 134. 11

St. Helens, Baron (Fitz-Herbert), a hand in a gauntlet erect ppr. *Intaminatis honoribus.* 209. 8

St. Hill, Devonsh., out of a ducal coronet or, two wyverns' heads addorsed vert, langued gu. 72. 2

St. John, *see* Bolingbroke, Viscount.

St. John of Bletso, **Baron** (St. John), Melchbourne Park, Sharnbrook, Beds, on a mount vert, a falcon rising or, belled of the last, ducally gorged gu. *Data fata secutus.* 272. 11

St. John, Frederic Robert, British Legation, Berne, same crest.

St. John, Rev. Harris Fleming, Dinmore Manor, Leominster, same crest and motto.

St. John, Ireland, a Calvary cross gu., upon three grieces arg. 166. 1

St. John, a monkey passant or. cf. 136. 8

St. John-Mildmay, Sir Henry Bouverie Paulet, Bart., D.L., of Dogmersfield Park, Hants, a lion rampant gardant az., armed and langued gu. *Alla ta Hara.* 2. 5

St. John-Mildmay, Rev. Charles Arundell, 72, Chester Square, W., same crest.

St. John-Mildmay, Charles Beague, Hollam, Dulverton, Somers., a lion rampant az. *Alla ta Hara.*

St. John-Mildmay, Wyndham Paulet, Hazelgrove, Sparkford, Bath, same crest and motto.

St. John, Northamp., Hunts, and Wilts, on a mount vert, a falcon rising or, belled of the last, ducally gorged gu. cf. 87. 2

St. John, on a mount vert, a falcon rising or, belled of the last, ducally gorged gu. *Data fata secutus.* 272. 11

St. John, a falcon with wings expanded or, ducally gorged gu. *Data fata secutus.* 87. 2

St. John, Hants and Worcs., on a mount ppr., a falcon rising or, belled of the last, ducally gorged gu. 272. 11

Saint John, Hants, a falcon rising or. 88. 2

St. John, Edward John, Slinfold, Horsham, Sussex, a goat's head.

St. Leger, *see* Doneraile, Viscount.

St. Leger, a mullet of five points pierced gu. cf. 164. 2

St. Leger, Ireland, a mullet arg., between two palm-branches vert. 146. 8

St. Leger, a griffin passant or. 63. 2

St. Leger, John, Park Hill, Rotherham: (1) A griffin passant or, charged with a cross crosslet az. (*for St. Leger*). (2) Out of a ducal coronet a goat's head arg., attired or (*for Bagot*).

St. Leger, an eagle displayed sa., issuing from a plume of feathers arg.

St. Lawrence, Viscount, *see* Howth, Earl of.

St. Levan, Baron (St. Aubyn), of St. Michael's Mount, Marazion, Cornw., a rock, thereon a Cornish chough rising, all ppr., debruised by a bendlet wavy sinister erm. *In se teres.* 308. 3

St. Lize, a globe in its stand ppr. 159. 4

Saint Lo, a Moor's head affrontée ppr. cf. 192. 4

St. Loe, a blackamoor's head in profile wreathed about the forehead arg. and sa. cf. 192. 13

St. Low, a water-bouget sa. 168. 4

St. Lyz, a demi-lion rampant or, holding a mullet sa. 15. 7

St. Maur, *see* Somerset, Duke of.

St. Maur, a falcon's leg and wing conjoined ppr., jessed and belled or. 113. 5

St. Maure, a branch of oak fructed and leaved ppr. 151. 3

St. Michael or **St. Michell**, out of a ducal coronet or, a bear's head sa., muzzled arg. 34. 3

St. Oswald, Baron (Winn), of Nostell Priory, Wakefield, a demi-eagle displayed or, ducally gorged erm. *Tout pour Dieu et ma patrie.*

St. Owen, an escallop or, between two wings gu. 141. 10

St. Owen, a demi-savage holding a club. 186. 5

Saint Owen, a lion's gamb charged with a chevron, and thereon a mullet sa. 39. 2

St. Paul, late Sir Horace, Bart. (*extinct*), of Ewart Park, Northumb.: (1) Out of the coronet of a marquess an arrow in pale point downwards surmounted by two in pale points upwards or, conjoined in the centre with a riband az. (2) Out of the coronet of a marquess or, a plume of five ostrich-feathers alternately arg. and gu. (3) Out of the coronet of a marquess or, a demi-griffin with wings elevated ducally gorged, all or. *Esse quam videri.*

St. Paule, Bart. (*extinct*), of Snarford, Lincs, an elephant and castle ppr. *Esse quam videri.* 133. 11

St. Pere or **St. Pierre** of Runsell, Essex, a spear erect or, headed arg., on the point thereof a dolphin naiant ppr. 140. 9

St. Philibert, out of a mural coronet a leopard's head ducally gorged. 23. 7

St. Quentin, Bart. (*extinct*), of Harpham, Yorks, out of a ducal coronet gu., a pea-rise ppr., on the top of a fluted column between two horns or.

St. Quenton, Devonsh., a Cornish chough between two horns ppr.

St. Quintin, William Herbert, Scampston Hall, York, same crest.

St. Quintin, Yorks, an eagle's head erased vair. 83. 2

St. Quintin, out of a ducal coronet or, a lion's gamb sa., holding a cross crosslet fitchée of the first. 36. 11

St. Vincent, Viscount (Jervis), out of a naval coronet or, encircled by a wreath of laurel ppr., a demi-pegasus arg., maned and hoofed of the first, winged az., charged on the wing with a fleur-de-lis or. *Thus.* 47. 10

Saker or **Sacker** of Faversham, Kent, a bull's head erased or, between two laurel-branches vert. 43. 12

Sale, a demi-chevalier brandishing a sword. 187. 1

Sale of Barrow Derbysh, a pheon sa 174 11
Sale, Richard, Barrow-on-Trent, near Derby, same crest *Virtute non astutia*
Sale-Hill, Rowley Sale, Esquire C B Ellershe House, Earl's Avenue Folkestone a talbot's head couped sa, guttée d'eau, collared gu, studded and ringed or *Ne tentes aut perfice.*
Sales, on a ducal coronet or, a wyvern sejant vert 70 9
Salisbury, Marquess of (Gascoigne Cecil) Hatfield House, Herts (1) Six arrows in saltier or, barbed and flighted arg, girt together with a belt gu, buckled and garnished of the first, and over the arrows a morion cap ppr (2) A conger's head erased and erect or charged with an ermine spot *Sero sed serio* 173 10
Salisbury of Barnstaple and Buckland, Devonsh, two lions rampant combatant arg ducally crowned or supporting a crescent of the last. 3 8
Salisbury of Newton Burgelaine Leics, a lion rampant arg charged on the shoulder with a crescent sa holding in the dexter paw a crescent or cf 2 2
Salisbury of Ravenston, Leics on a mount ppr, a lion rampant arg, holding in the dexter paw a crescent or cf 2 2
Salisbury or Salusbury, Wales, a demi-lion rampant arg, ducally crowned or, holding a crescent of the last
Salkeld of Hull Abbey, Northumb, a demi dragon rampant sans wings vert, charged with a mullet for difference
Salkeld of Fifehead Neville, a demi dragon rampant sans wings vert
Salkyns of London, a lynx sa cf 127 2
Sall of Shardlow, Derbysh, a pheon sa 174 11
Salle of Cashel co Tipperary a stag's head cabossed gu, attired or *Valore et virtute* 122 5
Salle, Devonsh, a demi lion gu *Timere sperno* 10. 3
Salloway, a Saracen's head ppr, banded about the temples or 190 14
Salmon of Wildheath, Chesh, and Hackney Middx, issuing from a cloud ppr, an armed arm sa. purfled or, holding in the hand a falchion of the first 210 12
Salmon, Admiral Sir Nowell G C.B, V C., Curdridge Grange, near Botley Hants, a mailed arm issuing from a cloud and grasping a scimitar *Vita priore frui*
Salmon, Ireland, a dexter hand brandishing a sword 212 13
Salmon, Cumb, an armed arm sa, holding in the hand a falchion or 210 2
Salmon, an estoile arg 164 1
Salmon, a lion passant or, collared and with a line reflexed over the back sa, supporting with the dexter paw an escutcheon az, charged with a cross patée of the first
Salmon of West Barsham Norf a lion passant or holding in the dexter paw a Trojan escutcheon az
Salmond, a dexter arm embowed holding in the hand a spear in bend
Salmond, Henry James of Waterfoot Penrith Cumb, a naked arm ppr, holding a spear or *Optima sapientia probitas* 214 11
Salmond, a salmon haurient ppr 139 11
Salmond, a salmon naiant ppr 139 12
Salomons, Bart (1) a mount vert, thereon, issuant out of six park pales or, a demi lion double queued gu, holding between the paws a bezant charged with an ermine-spot 13 4 (2) A demi unicorn gu, armed, maned and ungu or, charged on the shoulder with a cross crosslet arg 289 6 (3) A demi lion arg., in the paws a bundle of twigs erect or, banded az, charged on the shoulder with a cross crosslet gu. *Deo adjuvante* 289 3
Salt, Yorks on a rock an alpaca statant ppr *Quid non Deo juvante?*
Salt, Sir William Henry, Bart, J P, D L, of Saltaire Yorks, upon a rock an alpaca statant ppr *Quid non, Deo juvante?* 313 2
Salt, Sir Shirley Harris, Bart., Gliffaes Crickhowell, same crest and motto.
Salt, on a chapeau gu turned up erm, a demi ostrich with wings displayed or, holding in the beak a horse shoe sa
Salt of London on a chapeau az turned up erm, a demi-ostrich with wings expanded arg, holding in the beak a horse-shoe sa
Salt of Yoxhall, Staffs, an eagle displayed sa 75 5
Salt, a dove holding in its beak an olive-branch ppr 92 5
Salt, Sir Thomas, Bart of Weeping Cross, Staffs three annulets interlaced sa thereon a dove holding in the beak an olive branch ppr, and charged on the neck with a chevron, also sa 93 7
Salt, a pedestal arg, thereon a figure representing a sphinx of red porphyry with human arms extended, holding in the dexter hand a pyramid or
Salte, Geary-, see Geary
Salter, Shropsh, a cock's head az, combed and wattled gu, charged on the neck with four billets, one, two, and one or
Salter, Essex a cock's head and neck couped az, combed wattled and beaked gu, charged with four billets, one, two, and one
Salter, Warw and Northamp from Oswestry, Shropsh a cock's head and neck couped gu, combed, wattled beaked and billettee or
Salter, Suff a pheasant's head and neck couped gu beaked and charged with ten billets, one, two three, and four
Salter, Shropsh, Dorset, and Bucks same crest
Salter, Dorset Somers, Bucks, Hants and in London an eagle's head and neck couped gu billettee or
Salter, Samuel James Augustus, Basingfield Basingstoke, an eagle's head gu, charged with six billets or *Fide ac diffide*
Salter of Norwich, Norf an eagle's head and neck erased gu, billettee or cf 83 2
Salter, Ireland a dexter hand holding a salter or saltseller
Saltersford, Baron, see Courtown, Earl of
Salthouse, a dexter hand holding an open book 215 10
Saltmarsh, a rudder or 179 1
Saltmarshe, Philip of Saltmarshe, Yorks, Same crest *Ad astra virtus* 179 1
Saltonstall and **Saltonston** of London and Yorks out of a ducal coronet or, a pelican's head az vulning itself gu cf 98 2
Saltoun, Baron (Fraser), an ostrich holding a horseshoe in its beak, all ppr *In God is all —Post tenebras lux* 97 8
Saltren, Cornw, a lion rampant 1 13
Saltren of Petticombe, Cornw, a lion's head erased arg 17 8
Salusbury, Bart (*extinct*), of Llanwern, Monm, a demi lion rampant couped arg, crowned or holding in the dexter paw a crescent of the last *Satis est prostrasse leoni* 252 9
Salusbury, Rev Francis Russell, Ellenhall, Staffs, same crest and motto
Salusbury, Major General Frederic Octavius 19 Waterloo Crescent Dover, same crest and motto.
Salusbury, Rev Norman, Preston Patrick Milnthorpe, Westml, same crest and motto
Salusbury, Piozzi-, Edward Pemberton, of Bachgraig St Asaph Flintsh a demi lion rampant couped arg, collared gu, ducally crowned or holding in the dexter paw a crescent of the last *Sat est prostrasse leoni* 252 9
Salusbury, Bart (*extinct*), of Lleweny, Denbighsh a demi-lion rampant couped arg, ducally crowned or, holding in the dexter paw a crescent of the last *In veritate triumpho* 252 9
Salvesen, Edward Theodore K C, 40 Drumsheugh Gardens, Edinburgh a dragon ship vert mast and tackling ppr flagged gu *Inveni portum*
Salvin, Durh a wyvern vert with wings elevated and addorsed ppr 70 1
Salvin, Gerard Thornton of Croxdale, Durh, a dragon vert with wings elevated and addorsed ppr *Je ne change qu'en mourant* cf 73 2
Salvin, Francis Henry Sutton Place, Guildford Surrey, same crest
Salvin, Bryan John Francis, Burn Hall, Durh, same crest *Je ne change qu'en mourant*
Salvin, Anthony Gerard, Hawksfold Fernhurst, Sussex, same crest and motto
Salway, Worcs, a Saracen's head couped at the shoulders affrontée ppr wreathed about the temples arg and sa 190 5
Salway, Worcs, a demi-Moor sa, wreathed about the head arg and sa, a belt from the sinister shoulder to the dexter hip az
Salwey, Shropsh, a Saracen's head and shoulders couped ppr, vested vert, knotted and bowed on the sinister shoulder, wreathed round the temples or and sa, crined ppr *Fiat voluntas Dei*
Salwey, Staffs Worcs, and Shropsh a demi-Moor sa, wreathed about the temples arg and gu, a belt from the sinister shoulder to the dexter hip az *Fiat voluntas Dei*
Salwey, Alfred, Esquire, the Lodge Overton, Ludlow, same crest and motto
Sambadge, Kent and Chesh, a reindeer's head erminois, attired or cf 122 1

Samborne, a dexter hand holding a sheaf of arrows ppr. 214. 3

Samborne of Timsbury, Somers., a mullet pierced or. *cf.* 164. 5

Samby or **Sandpy, Lincs**, a winged heart or. 112. 10

Samler, an arm in armour embowed ppr., holding in the hand a battle-axe or. *cf.* 200. 6

Samler, a unicorn's head erased arg., armed and ducally gorged or. *cf.* 49. 5

Sammes or **Sams** of Little Totham and Toulson, Essex, a man's head in a helmet ppr., garnished or, on the top thereof a plume of feathers sa.

Sammes, a lion rampant arg., collared and chained or. 1. 3

Samon of Annesley Woodhouse, Notts, out of a coronet gu., a pelican's head or, beaked and vulned, also gu. *cf.* 98. 2

Sampayo, Portugal, a demi-unicorn arg., armed or, maned ppr. 48. 7

Sampson, a demi-lion az., holding in the dexter paw a sword in pale ppr. *Deo juvante.* 14. 12

Sampson, Suff., a demi-lion az., holding in the dexter paw a sword in pale arg., hilt and pommel or. 14. 12

Sampson of Kersey, Suff., a boar's head erased gu., armed and gorged with a collar or, charged with three escallops sa. *cf.* 41. 5

Sampson, Edward, of Henbury, Glouc., a fret or, thereon a wivern's head erased gu., collared and billettée of the first. *Pejus letho flagitium.* 71. 10

Sams of Langford, Essex, a leopard salient sa., spotted or, ducally gorged, ringed, and lined of the last.

Samson, Scotland, a dexter hand issuing, grasping a club, all ppr. *If God will.* 214. 6

Samuel and **Samwell,** Yorks, a wolf current sa., pierced in the breast by an arrow or, feathered arg. *cf.* 29. 5

Samuel-Montagu, Sir Montagu, Bart., 12, Kensington Palace Gardens, a stag statant holding in the mouth a sprig of palm ppr., in front of a flagstaff erect or, therefrom flowing to the dexter a banner az., charged with a lion rampant or. *Swift yet sure.* 304. 1

Samuel, Sir Edward Levien, Bart., the Grange, Strathfield, Sydney, N.S.W., upon a rock in front of three spears, one in pale and two in saltire, a wolf current sa., pierced in the breast by an arrow arg., flighted or. *A pledge of better times.* 29. 5

Samuel, Stuart Montagu, 12, Hill Street, Berkeley Square, W., upon a mount vert, a rose arg., barbed, seeded, stalked, and leaved ppr., between two bees volant, also ppr. *Excel.* 261. 12

Samuel, an eagle displayed arg., and above the head a coronet or. *Habent sua sidera reges.* *cf.* 75. 2

Samuel-De Vahl, Denis, Esquire, of Dublin, late of Rio de Janeiro: (1) Out of a mural coronet az., a demi-lion rampant, ducally crowned, and holding a sceptre erect or (*for De Vahl*). (2) Upon a wreath of the colours an eagle displayed arg., and above the head an imperial crown or (*for Samuel*).

Samuel, Sir Marcus, D.L., Alderman and sometime Lord Mayor of the City of London, of 20, Portland Place, London, W., a dexter naked arm embowed ppr., charged with two fleur-de-lis or, grasping a battle-axe ppr., suspended therefrom by a chain an escutcheon or, thereon a shell, also ppr. *Facta non verba.* 288. 10

Samuels, Arthur, Esquire, M.A.; John Hasler Samuels, Esquire, B.A.; and William Frederick Samuels, Esquire, on the stump of a tree couped ppr., sprouting on each side vert, a squirrel sejant gu., cracking a nut or, stalked and leaved, also ppr., and charged on the shoulder with a cross formée fitchée or. *Licet ex multo parvum.*

Samuels, Arthur Warren, K.C., LL.D., 80, Merrion Square, Dublin, same crest and motto.

Samuelson, Sir Bernard, Bart., 56, Prince's Gate, W., a phœnix in flames holding in the beak a torch fired ppr., each wing charged with a scroll arg. *Post tenebras lux.* 237. 12

Samuelson, Henry Bernhard, Esquire, J.P., of Braywick Grove, Berks, and La Montagne, Beaulieu, France, a phœnix issuant from flames holding in its beak a torch and charged on each wing with a scroll. *Post tenebras lux.*

Samwayes of Brodway, Devonsh., and Chilhampton, Wilts, a lion's gamb erect and erased or, holding a mullet gu.

Samways of Toller Fratrum and Winterborne St. Martin, Devonsh., an eagle's claw erect and erased or, holding a mullet gu.

Samwell, Watson-, of Upton Hall, Northamp.: (1) On the stump of a tree couped or, sprouting on each side vert, a squirrel sejant gu., cracking a nut of the first, stalked and leaved of the second (*for Samwell*). (2) A griffin's head erased arg., ducally gorged or (*for Watson*). *Christus sit regula vitæ.—Spero meliora.*

Samwell, Cornw., a ducal coronet or, thereon a squirrel sejant gu., cracking a nut of the first, stalked and leaved ppr.

Samwell, Bart. (*extinct*), of Upton, Northamp., on a ducal coronet or, a squirrel sejant cracking a nut, all ppr.

Sand, Scotland, a dove holding in its beak an olive-branch. *Virtute duce.* 92. 5

Sand, a dove holding in its beak a laurel-branch. *Virtute duce.* 92. 5

Sandars, John Drysdale, M.A., North Sandsfield, Gainsborough, a demi-bull rampant and erased gu., armed or, charged with a rose arg. *Non bos in lingua.* 272. 13

Sandbach of Sandbach, Chesh., a reindeer's head couped ermines, attired or. *cf.* 122. 1

Sandbach, Samuel, of Hafodunos, Denbighsh., a reindeer's head erased per fess arg., or and attired of the last, gorged with a wreath of oak, holding in the mouth an ear of wheat vert. *Virtutis gloria merces.*

Sandbach, Lieutenant-Colonel Arthur Edmund, Bryn Gwyn, Oswestry, same crest and motto.

Sandbach, Chesh., a garb or. 153. 2

Sandberg, Arthur G., Esquire, M.D., of Arborfield, Streatham Hill, S.W., a pair of wings arg. *Serva fidem.* 109. 6

Sandby, an antelope trippant or. 126. 6

Sandby, a griffin's head erased arg., gorged with a collar az., charged with a fret of the first.

Sandeland, a crescent ensigned with an étoile of six points. 163. 4

Sandell, a flag issuant arg., charged with a cross sa. 176. 13

Sandeman of Perth and Glasgow, Scotland, a rock ppr. *Stat veritas.—Olim cruore nunc candore.* 179. 7

Sandeman, John Glas, Esquire, of Glasgow, same crest and motto. 179. 7

Sandeman, Albert George, Presdales, Ware, same crest.

Sandeman, George Glas, 34, Grosvenor Gardens, S.W., same crest. *Stat veritas.*

Sandeman, John Glas, 24, Cambridge Square, W., same crest and motto.

Sanders, Bucks and Northamp., an elephant's head erased per chevron sa. and arg., armed or. 133. 3

Sanders of Uxbridge, Middx., out of a ducal coronet or, an elephant's head arg., eared of the first. 133. 1

Sanders or **Saunders,** an elephant's head erased sa. 133. 3

Sanders, Benjamin Lawrence, Esquire, J.P., D.L., Street Court, Kingsland R.S.O., Heref., an elephant's head erased sa. *Fidele et loyale.*

Sanders of Sanders' Park, co. Cork, out of a mural coronet an elephant's head ppr., charged with a bezant. *Nil conscire sibi nulla pallescere culpa.*

Sanders, Robert Massy Dawson, 35, Fitzwilliam Square, Dublin, same crest and motto.

Sanders or **Saunders,** an elephant's head erased sa., armed and eared arg. 133. 3

Sanders of Sandersted, Sanders Place, and Charlwood, Surrey, a demi-bull per pale gu. and sa., eared and armed arg. and or, counterchanged, gorged with a collar gemel of the third and supporting between his feet a stalk of alisander leaved vert, budded or.

Sanders of Lullington and Little Ireton, Derbysh., a demi-bull sa. *Non bos in lingua.* *cf.* 45. 8

Sanders, Surrey, Staffs, London, and Derbysh., a demi-bull rampant gu., armed or. *cf.* 45. 8

Sanders, Scotland, an antelope's head erm. *cf.* 126. 2

Sanders, Ireland, a boar's head erased or. 42. 2

Sanders, C. B., Esquire, Monkerton Manor, Pinhoe, near Exeter, a demi-bull rampant gu., armed and ungu. or.

Sanderson, a talbot passant ppr. *Paratus et fidelis.* 54. 1

Sanderson, Frederick James, Esquire, of Killingworth, North Adelaide, South Australia, Collector H.M. Customs, President of Marine Board of South Australia, and Special Magistrate, *uses:* on a mount vert, a talbot passant sa., eared or. *Sans Dieu rien.*

Sanderson, a talbot passant arg., eared and spotted sa. 54. 1

Sanderson, Northamp., on a mount vert, a talbot sa., eared arg., spotted of the last.

Sanderson, Arthur, Esquire, of 5, Carlton Terrace, Edinburgh, *uses* a talbot. *Sans Dieu rien.*

Sanderson, Rev Alfred Poyntz, M A, the Rectory, Aspenden, Herts, upon five annulets interlaced fesseways or, a talbot sa, resting the dexter fore leg on a dagger in bend point downwards ppr *Sans Dieu rien*

Sanderson of Cheetham, Lancs, a demi-talbot or, gorged with a collar vair and supporting a flagstaff, therefrom flowing to the sinister a banner quarterly or and gu, in the first and fourth quarters an annulet of the last *Deo favente non timeo* 55 6

Sanderson, of West Jesmond, Northumb (1) A wolf's head arg, erased gu, collared and a chain therefrom reflexed behind the neck or, between a branch of palm and another of laurel ppr, charged on the neck with a saltier humettee gu for distinction 287 15 (2) A lion rampant standing on his sinister hind foot, supporting himself by a pilgrim's staff *Clarior ex obscuro*

Sanderson, Lincs, a wolf's head sa, devouring a man ppr, the body from the small of the back downwards hanging out of his mouth

Sanderson, Sir Thomas Henry, G C B, K C M G, 65, Wimpole Street, London, W, same crest

Sanderson, Rev. Edward of High Hurst Wood, Sussex in front of a dragon's head erased sa, gorged with a collar engrailed with a chain reflected behind the neck or, a cross patee of the last between a branch of palm and another of laurel ppr *Clarior ex obscuro* 71 12

Sanderson, Samuel, Esquire, of Clover Hill, co Cavan, Ireland (1) On a mount vert an estoile or (*for Sanderson*) *cf* 164 1 (2) A martlet or, charged with a crescent gu (*for Winter*) *Toujours propice* *cf* 95 2

Sanderson of Thorneycroft, Lancaster, a dragon's head erased, ducally gorged, and chained between two branches of laurel in orle *Clarior ex obscuro*

Sandes, *see* Collis-Sandes

Sandes, Surrey and Kent a griffin segreant per fess or and gu 62 2

Sandes, Somers and Westml, same crest *Probum non pœnitet*

Sandes, John Greenville, Listowel, co Kerry on a mount vert a griffin segreant or, collared fleurettee gu *Virtus fortunæ victrix* 275 9

Sandes, Surrey and Cumb, a heraldic tiger az tufted, maned, collared, and lined or the line twisted round the body four times and falling behind the hind-legs

Sandford, Baron Mount Sandford, *see* Mount Sandford

Sandford, Rt Hon. Sir Francis Richard, **Baron Sandford**, P C, K C B C B, M A, LL.D, of 26 Gloucester Terrace Hyde Park, London W, a falcon with wings endorsed preying on a partridge ppr *Nec temere nec timide* 77 12

Sandford, Ven Ernest Grey, M A, Archdeacon and Canon of Exeter, the Close Exeter, same crest and motto

Sandford of West Hill House, St Leonards-on-Sea, a falcon with wings addorsed ppr, belled or, preying upon a partridge of the first *Nec temere nec timide* 77 12

Sandford, George Montagu Warren, Esquire (1) A falcon with wings endorsed preying on a partridge, all ppr (*for Sandford*) 77 12 (2) A boar's head couped arg, armed and langued gu, and charged with a trefoil slipped vert (*also for Sandford*) (3) A cockatrice vert (*for Peacocke*) *Nec temere, nec timide* 68 4

Sandford, Lieutenant Frederick Marmaduke Henry, same crests and motto

Sandford of Sandford, Shropsh, a falcon with wings addorsed ppr, belled or, preying on a partridge of the first *Nec temere, nec timide* *cf* 77 12

Sandford, Westml, a boar's head couped arg 43 1

Sandford of Springfield, Essex, Stow, Glouc, and Shropsh, a boar's head couped, close or, with a broken spear az, headed arg, thrust into the mouth 42 10

Sandford, Humphrey, of the Isle of Rossall Shropsh a boar's head couped, close or, charged with a mullet, and holding in the mouth a pheon *Nec temere nec timide* 253 11

Sandford of Wisbeach, Isle of Ely, Cambs, out of a ducal coronet gu, a boar's head and neck or 41 4

Sandford - Thompson, William James J P, The Villa Montrose, N B, An arm embowed in armour gu, the gauntlet or, grasping the truncheon of a broken lance ppr *Dum spiro spero*

Sandford-Wills, Edward Wills Esquire of Castlerea House co Roscommon Ireland (1) A demi griffin segreant sa, holding in his claws a battle axe ppr (*for Wills*) *cf* 64 11 (2) Out of a ducal coronet a boar's head and neck or langued gu *Cor unum via una.* 41 4

Sandford, Bart (*extinct*) of Howgill and Askham, a boar's head couped or 43 1

Sandford, Herts an arm in armour embowed ppr holding within the gauntlet a broken tilting spear sa., and a laurel-branch vert

Sandhurst, Baron (Rt Hon Sir William Mansfield), of Sandhurst, Berks out of an Eastern coronet arg, a gryphon's head sa, beaked or, between two branches of laurel ppr *Steadfast* 308 7

Sandiford, a boar's head couped in fess holding in the mouth a dagger thrust down the throat hilt foremost

Sandilands, *see* Torphichen Baron

Sandilands, an eagle displayed ppr *Spero meliora* 75 2

Sandilands, Scotland, an eagle displayed or 75 5

Sandilands of Coustoun Linlithgowsh, Scotland, an eagle displayed or, charged on the breast with a crescent gu *cf* 75 2

Sandilands of Hilderstoun, Linlithgowsh an eagle volant ppr *Victoria non præda*

Sandilands, Scotland and Rotterdam a palm-tree ppr 144 1

Sandilands, a mullet between the horns of a crescent or, between two palm branches environed with clouds ppr 146 11

Sandilands, a star issuing from a crescent arg *Justi ut sidera fulgent* 163 4

Sandilands of Craibston, Aberdeensh, Scotland, and Bordeaux, same crest *Justi ceu sidera fulgent* 163 4

Sandom, a boar passant or 40 9

Sandon, Viscount, *see* Harrowby, Earl of

Sandon, out of a ducal coronet a phœnix in flames, all ppr 82 5

Sands, Surrey Kent, Somers, and Westml, a griffin segreant per fess or and gu *Probum non pœnitet* 62 2

Sands, Scotland, out of a ducal coronet or, a lion's gamb erect sa *Audaces juvat* 36 12

Sands, Sandes, or **Sandys** of Wilberton, Isle of Ely Cambs, South Petherton Somers, Petersham, Surrey and Westml a griffin segreant per fesse or and gu 62 2

Sands, Bart (*extinct*), of Blackhall co Kildare a blackamoor's head couped sa *Deo honor et fortuna* *cf* 192 13

Sandwell or **Sandwill** of Minster Isle of Thanet, Kent, a lion's gamb erect and erased gu, enfiled with a ducal coronet erm *cf* 36 3

Sandwich, Earl of (Montagu), a griffin's head couped or beaked sa between two wings endorsed of the last *Post tot naufragia portus* *cf* 67 11

Sandy, a griffin segreant 62 2

Sandy, a demi heraldic antelope or, armed and maned az

Sandys, Baron (Sandys) (1) A griffin segreant per fesse or and gu (*for Sandys*) 62 2 (2) A stag's head couped gu, attired and collared or (*for Hill*) *Probum non pœnitet* *cf* 121 5

Sandys, Colonel Thomas Myles M P, Graythwaite Hall Ulverston Lancs a griffin segreant per fesse or and gu *Probum non pœnitet* 304 11

Sandys, Baron Sandys, a winged goat's head and neck couped at the shoulders arg, armed or, the wings elevated of the same

Sandys of St Minver Cornw, a griffin segreant per fesse erminois and az, holding between the claws a cross crosslet fitchee gu

Sandys of Esthwaite and Graythwaite Lancs, a griffin segreant per fess or and gu *Probum non pœnitet.* 62 2

Sandys, Major Edwin William, Fulford House York, same crest and motto

Sandys, Bayntun-, Bart (*extinct*) (1) A griffin segreant per fess or and gu, (*for Sandys*) 62 2 (2) A griffin's head erased sa, charged with a cross crosslet fitched or (*for Bayntun*) *cf* 66 2

Sandys-Lumsdaine, of Innergelly Fifesh, and of Lumsdaine and Blanerne Berwicksh (1) A heron devouring a salmon ppr (2) A griffin segreant *Beware in time*

Sanford, a bull's head gu *cf* 44 3

Sanford, William Ayshford of Nynehead Court, Somers, a martlet ppr *Ferme en foy* 95 4

Sanford, Hon William Eli, of Hamilton and of Wesanford, Muskota Canada Senator of the Dominion of Canada, out of a ducal coronet gu, a boar's head and neck or *Nec temere nec timide.* 41 4

Sangster, on a rock a blackbird ppr 106 9

Sangster and **Songster,** Scotland, a blackbird ppr. *Providentia divina.* cf. 106. 2

Sankey, Ireland, a peacock's head couped ppr. 103. 2

Sankey of Coolmore, co. Tipperary, a cubit arm vested sa., cuffed arg., holding in the hand a fish ppr.

Sankey of Sankeystown and Newtown, King's Co., Ireland, a cubit arm vested sa., cuffed arg., holding in the hand a fish ppr. *Sancta clavis cœli fides.*

Sankey, Herbert Stuart, Esquire, Barrister-at-Law, Recorder of Faversham, 35, Queensborough Terrace, Hyde Park, W., and 4, King's Bench Walk, Temple, E.C., same crest and motto.

Sankey, Matthew Villiers Elrington, Coolmore, Fethard, co. Tipperary, same crest and motto.

Sanson, a demi-talbot az. cf. 55. 8

Sansun, a lion's head erased or, holding in the mouth a cinquefoil vert.

Sant, James, 43, Lancaster Gate, Hyde Park, W., a demi-lion rampant gu., gorged with a collar vair, holding in the mouth a rose arg., barbed, seeded, and slipped ppr., and holding between the paws an escallop or. *Si sit sanctus felix.*

Santhey of Burton, Denbighsh., on a mount vert, a lion sejant gardant or.

Santon, Devonsh., a swan ppr. 99. 2

Sapcot, a demi-lion rampant az., holding in the dexter paw a sword ppr. 14. 12

Sapcotes, a goat's head erased arg., armed or. 128. 5

Sapcott, a goat's head erased sa., armed or. 128. 5

Saphar, a beacon on fire ppr. 177. 14

Sapie, a plate charged with a lion's head erased gu. cf. 19. 3

Sapte, Herts, a dove holding in its beak a sprig of laurel ppr 92. 5

Sapwell, Benjamin Beckham, Esquire, of Sankence, Aylesham, Norf., upon a mount vert, in front of a Passion cross or, a well between two branches of oak ppr. *Clarior e tenebris.*

Sapy or **Sapye,** a falcon's wing and leg conjoined ppr., jessed and belled or. 113. 5

Sare, Kent, an arm embowed vested with leaves vert, holding in the hand ppr. a dragon's head erased of the first.

Sare, Kent, an elephant or, in a wood ppr.

Sares of Sandwich, Kent, Horsham, Sussex, Titley, Yorks, and London, a goat's head erased arg., armed or. 128. 5

Sarebruche, a horse's head or, couped and bridled gu. 51. 5

Saresbery, a fish haurient. 139. 11

Sargant and **Sargeant,** Staffs, two eagle's wings conjoined and inverted ppr. 133. 3

Sargant, Sargeant, or **Sargent,** Staffs, a dolphin naiant sa. between two wings arg.

Sargant or **Sergeant** of Dynton, Bucks, a dolphin naiant or, guttée-de-larmes. cf. 140. 5

Sargent, a goat's head erased or. 128. 5

Sarjeantson, a cherub's head and wings ppr. 189. 9

Sarmon, an elephant passant arg. cf. 133. 9

Sarre, Jersey, a dexter arm in armour holding a wreath of laurel, all ppr.

Sarsfield, Viscount Kilmallock (*attainted*), a leopard's face or. *Virtus non vertitur.* 22. 2

Sarsfield of Doughcloyne, Ireland, same crest and motto. 22. 2

Sarson, a wolf sa., collared and lined or, holding in the dexter paw a fleur-de-lis az.

Sartoris, Captain Alfred Urban, a lion rampant holding in the dexter paw a sword. *Olim et nunc.*

Sassoon, Sir Edward, Bart., C.S.I., of 25, Park Lane, London, and of Eastern Terrace, Brighton, on a mount vert, a fern-brake surmounted by a dove volant, having in the beak a laurel-branch, all ppr., the wings semée of estoiles or. *Candide et constanter.* 308. 15

Satherthwayte, Lancs, a lion's head erased or, gorged with a collar sa., charged with three roses arg. cf. 18. 6

Sattherthwaite, a Saracen's head couped at the shoulders, on the head a ducal crown and cap. 190. 8

Satterthwaite, a greyhound sejant az. 59. 4

Saul and **Saule,** a swan arg., collared and lined gu. *Fidele certe merces.* 99. 1

Sault, on a ducal coronet gu., a wyvern sans legs or. 70. 9

Saulton, an ostrich holding in the beak a horse-shoe. 97. 8

Saumarez, a falcon displayed ppr. *In Deo spero.*

Saumarez, same crest. *Fidelis et generosus.*

Saumarez, *see* De Saumarez, Baron.

Saunders, Scotland, a spur-rowel az. 164. 8

Saunders - Knox - Gore, Major - General William Boyd: (1) A wolf rampant or (*for Gore*). 28. 2. (2) A falcon close perched on a rest ppr. (*for Knox*). 85. 13. (3) Out of a mural coronet ppr., a bull's head gu., charged with a crescent or (*for Saunders*). *In hoc signo vinces.*

Saunders, a bull's head erased arg. 44. 3

Saunders, a demi-bull salient erased at the loins arg., charged on the neck with a rose gu.

Saunders, out of a naval coronet arg., a demi-bull rampant gu., armed and ungu. or.

Saunders of Down House, Ealing, Hants, a demi-bull gu. cf. 45. 8

Saunders of Pentre, Pembrokesh., and Glanrhwdw, Carmarthensh., a demi-bull erased gu., charged on the shoulder with a rose arg., armed or.

Saunders of Brickesworth, Sibbertoft, and Flower, Northants, an elephant's head erased per chevron arg. and sa. 133. 3

Saunders, William Henry Radcliffe, 33, Prince's Square, W., an elephant's head arg., erased gu., charged on the neck with an annulet az., between two palm-branches slipped vert. *Fide sed cui vide.* 285. 1

Saunders of London, out of a mural coronet ppr., an elephant's head arg., charged on the breast with an ogress.

Saunders of Saunders Court, co. Wexford, and Saunders Grove and Newtown Saunders, co. Wicklow, out of a mural coronet ppr., an elephant's head arg., charged with a torteau. *Nil conscire sibi.*

Saunders, Charles Morley, of Wennington Hall, Lancs, an elephant's head erased arg. *Spes mea in Deo.* 133. 3

Saunders, Clervaux Morley, Esquire, J.P., of Bovacott, Brandis Corner, Devonsh., same crest and motto.

Saunders, Sir Edwin, F.R.C.S., of Fairlawn, Wimbledon Common, same crest. *Pro patria.*

Saunders of Long Marston, Herts, an elephant's head erased sa. 133. 3

Saunders of Harnington and Welford, Northamp., an elephant's head erased sa., eared and armed arg. 133. 3

Saunders of South Weald, Essex, a dexter arm in armour embowed holding in the gauntlet a sword, all ppr. 195. 1

Saunders, Frederick William, Esquire, of Cheriton, Fitz-Paine, Devonsh., an eagle's head arg., gorged with a collar chequy az. and erm., holding in the beak an estoile, also az.

Saunders, a tree, pendent from the branches on either side a hawk's lure. 143. 12

Saunders, Howard, Esquire, F.L.S., F.R.G.S., 7, Radnor Place, Gloucester Square, London, W., out of a mural coronet ppr., an elephant's head arg. *Sans Dieu rien.*

Saunderson, Earl of Castleton (*extinct*), a talbot passant arg., eared sa. 54. 1

Saunderson of Castle Saunderson, co. Cavan, a talbot passant spotted sa. *Je suis veillant à plaire.* 54. 1

Saunderson of Saxby, Lincs, on a mount vert, a talbot sa., eared or, spotted of the last. *Je suis veillant à plaire.—Sans Dieu rien.*

Saunderson of Brancepeth, Headley Hope, Newcastle-upon-Tyne, and Eggleston, Durh., a talbot passant ppr., spotted sa. *Sans Dieu rien.* 54. 1

Saunderson of Little Addington, Northamp., a talbot passant arg., eared sa. 54. 1

Saunderson, Edward James, Castle Saunderson, Belturbet, a talbot passant.

Saunderson, Rev. Robert de Bedick, Belle Vue Road, Ramsgate, a talbot passant sa., charged with a bezant. *Je suis veillant à plaire.*

Saunderson, a greyhound's head erm. cf. 61. 12

Saunderson of West Jesmond, Northumb., a wolf's head arg., erased gu., collared, and a chain reflexed behind the neck or, between a branch of palm and another of laurel ppr., and for distinction charged upon the neck with a saltire humettée gu. *Clarior ex obscuro.*

Saunderson, an arm in armour embowed holding in the hand a scimitar. 196. 10

Saurin, Ireland, an oak-tree ppr. 143. 5

Saurin, Morgan James, Orielton, Pembroke, same crest.

Saurin, Arthur, Paris, same crest.

Saussaye, Sir Richard Frederick de la, Knight, Major-General in the service of H.M. the Queen of Spain, Governor of Carthagena and Commandant of

Murcia, and Sir Matthew Richard Sausse, Knight, M A, Q C and late Chief Justice of the High Court of Judicature at Bombay out of an antique crown or, a cubit arm in armour gauntleted and holding a long cross sa, with a pennon floating therefrom gu, bearing the legend *Foy* in letters of gold *Foy*

Savage, Earl Rivers (*extinct*), out of a ducal coronet or, a lion's gamb erect sa. *A te pro te* 36 12

Savage, Worcs, out of a ducal coronet or, a lion's gamb erect sa, charged with a rose arg *cf.* 36 12

Savage, out of a ducal coronet or, a lion's gamb erect sa 36 12

Savage, Scotland, out of a ducal coronet a lion's gamb erect sa *Fortis atque fidelis* 36 12

Savage, out of a ducal coronet or, a lion's gamb sa *Te pro te* 36 12

Savage of Ballymadun Ireland out of a ducal coronet or a lion's gamb erect sa *Fortis atque fidelis* 36. 12

Savage, a lion's gamb erect sa *A te pro te* *cf* 36 4

Savage-Graham, of Clonboo co Tipperary, Ireland (1) An eagle wings endorsed ppr charged on the breast with an escallop arg, and holding in the beak a trefoil slipped vert (*for Graham*) (2) A lion's gamb erect or, charged with a rose gu, barbed and seeded ppr (*for Savage*) *cf* 36 4

Savage, a lion's gamb erect and erased sa. 36 4

Savage of Brodway Worcs, out of a ducal coronet or, a lion's gamb erect sa 36 12

Savage of Elmley Lovet, Worcs, and Highgate Middx, out of a ducal coronet or a lion's gamb erect sa charged with a crescent or *cf* 36. 12

Savage of Castleton, Derbysh, and Chesh a unicorn's head arg, erased gu 49 5

Savage, a unicorn's head erased per fesse arg and gu, armed and crined and holding in the mouth a fleur-de lis az. 49 12

Savage of Tidminton and Powick, Worcs, Glouc, and Chesh, a unicorn's head erased arg 49 5

Savage, Clavering-, of Elmley Castle, Worcs, a unicorn's head erased per fesse arg and gu, armed and crined or, holding in the mouth a fleur de lis az 49 12

Savage of Midsomer Norton, Somers, a unicorn's head couped at the neck per fesse wavy az and sa, charged with three bendlets arg armed or, holding in the mouth a sprig of oak fructed ppr. 49 4

Savage of Rock Savage and Clifton Chesh, a unicorn's head erased arg *Ware the horn* 49 5

Savage of London, a pheon point upwards az 174 9

Savage Ireland, a savage's head ppr 190 12

Savage of Norelands, co Kilkenny, issuing from waves a mermaid ppr *Fortis atque fidelis*

Savage of Ardkeen Castle, co Down, Lisanoure Castle, co Antrim and Kilcreen co Kilkenny, Ireland, issuing out of waves of the sea a mermaid, all ppr *Fortis atque fidelis*

Savage, Rev Francis Forbes of the Ards, co Down, and Flushing Vicarage, Falmouth, same crest and motto

Savage, a female's head affrontee couped at the breasts, the hair dishevelled

Savage of Hart Street, London issuing out of an Eastern crown or two arms embowed in armour ppr, supporting a pheon sa

Savary of London a cubit arm in armour holding in the hand, all ppr, a sword in pale arg, hilt and pommel or en filed on the blade with a boar's head erased ppr *Nocentes prosequor*

Savery of Great Totnes, Shilston, Willing and Slade Devonsh, a heron's head erased arg, between two wings sa, holding in the beak an olive branch vert *Aut vita libera, aut mors gloriosa.*

Savignac, a lion's head erased devouring a man the body from the small of the back hanging out of its mouth 18 14

Savell, Savill, or Savile, an owl arg *Be fast* 96 5

Savile, *see* Mexborough Earl of

Savile, Marquess of Halifax (*extinct*), an owl arg *Be fast* 96 5

Savile, Baron (Lumley Savile), an owl arg, charged with a bendlet wavy sinister sa *Be fast* *cf* 96 5

Savile of Oxton, Notts, an owl arg, ducally gorged or *cf* 96 5

Savile, Bart (*extinct*), of Thornhill, Yorks, an owl arg *Be fast* 96 5

Savile of Hill top Derbysh, an owl arg charged with a trefoil gu *cf* 96 5

Savile of Oaklands, Devonsh, and Down House, Glouc, an eagle rising per bend sinister or and sa., holding in the beak a fleur-de lis az *Nil conscire sibi*

Savile, Rev Frederick Alexander Stewart, of Hollanden Park, Hildenborough, Tonbridge, same crest and motto

Savile, Notts, out of a ducal coronet or, a pelican's head vulned ppr *cf* 98 2

Savill, Notts, an owl arg charged on the breast with a fleur-de lis gu *cf* 96. 5

Savill-Onley, Charles Alfred Onley, the Priory Ash Priors, Somers (1) Out of a crown vallory or, an eagle's head issuing from flames ppr, holding in the beak a sprig of laurel also ppr (2) On a mount vert an owl arg, charged on the body with three mullets in bend gu (3) The crest of Marsham *Alteri si tibi*

Saville of Blaby Leics an owl arg membered or charged on the breast with a trefoil for difference *cf* 96 5

Saville, the sun or, rising from clouds arg, tinged gu 162. 5

Savory, Rev Sir Borradaile, Bart, 66, Brook Street Grosvenor Square, W, on a mount in front of a cubit arm ppr, the hand holding a chapeau gu turned up arg, a serpent nowed vert between two branches of laurel, also ppr *Esse quam videri* 288 1

Savory, Sir Joseph, Bart., 33, Upper Brook Street, W, a cubit arm ppr, the hand holding a chapeau gu, turned up erminois in front a cross crosslet fitchee sa, and between two branches of laurel saltireways, fructed and slipped, also ppr. *Vincit omnia veritas* 288 2

Savory, a hand holding a chapeau between two branches of laurel in orle, all ppr 217 5

Saward, out of a ducal coronet or, a horse's hind leg az, shod of the first *Olim facimus* 123 6

Sawbridge-Erle-Drax, *see* Drax

Sawbridge of London and Kent a demi-lion az, supporting a saw in pale or

Sawbridge, Edward Henry Bridgman of East Haddon, Northamp, a demi-lion az, charged on the breast with an ermine spot or, supporting a saw in pale of the last.

Sawers, Scotland a dexter hand holding a scimitar, all ppr, hilted and pommelled or *Virtute non verbis* 213 5

Sawers, a mullet pierced gu

Sawrey of Broughton Tower Lancs a Roman fasces fesseways in front of an arm in armour embowed holding in the hand an arrow in bend sinister, all ppr *Dictis factisque simplex*

Sawrey-Cookson, G M, Esquire, of Broughton Tower in Furness *Cookson crest* a demi-lion rampant ppr, gorged with a collar nebuly gu, holding in the dexter paw a club, also ppr and resting the sinister paw upon a spur the rowel upwards or *Sawrey crest,* in front of a dexter arm embowed in armour, the hand grasping an arrow in bend sinister the pheon downwards, the Roman fasces fessewise, all ppr, thereon a cross crosslet gu *Dictis factisque simplex* —*Nil desperandum*

Sawtell, Somers, out of a pallisado coronet sa, a stag's head ppr *Cœlum ipsum petimus*

Sawyer of Kettering, Northamp, on a mural coronet gu, a parrot's head erased vert beaked of the first.

Sawyer, Edmund Charles, of Heywood, Berks, a talbot gardant ppr

Sawyer, Cambs, and of Causton, Norf, on a mount vert, a hound on scent arg, spotted of a liver colour 57 8

Sawyer, Sir James, Haseley Hall Warw, in front of two caduceux in saltire or on a mount vert a hound on scent ppr *Cherche et tu trouveras*

Saxby of Chafford Kent, on a mount vert, a lion rampant erminois, collared dove tailed, with a line thereto reflexed over the back and terminating in a knot az., holding in the dexter paw a dart sa, feathered arg, headed or *Sit saxum firmum* *cf* 2 6

Saxon, a talbot passant sa 54 1

Saxton, Chesh, out of a ducal coronet or a nag's head arg, between two wings gu

Saxton, Bart (*extinct*), of Circourt Berks on a mount vert, a griffin's head erased sa, ducally gorged or, between two wings arg

Say, Devonsh, out of a ducal coronet or, a bull's head sa, armed arg 44. 11

Say, a goat's head gu 128 12

Say of Blechington, Oxon, a buck's head couped or, on a wreath of thorns az and gu

Say, a stag's head erased arg, guttee de larmes, holding in the mouth a cinquefoil slipped vert *Fare et age*

Say, Hall-, of Swaffham, Norf., and Oakley Court, Berks: (1) A stag's head erased arg., guttée-de-larmes, holding in the mouth a cinquefoil slipped vert (*for Say*). (2) A talbot's head erased sa., charged with four bezants in cross, holding in the mouth a feather arg. (*for Hall*). *Fare et age.*

Saye and Sele, Baron (Twisleton-Wykeham-Fiennes): (1) A wolf sejant arg., gorged with a spiked collar, and a line therefrom reflexed over the back or (*for Fiennes*). (2) A dexter arm embowed vested sa., cuffed arg., the hand ppr., holding a mole spade in bend sinister or, headed and armed of the second (*for Twisleton*). *Fortem posce animum.*

Sayer of Michaell-Penkevell, Cornw., on a mount vert, a leopard couchant regardant ppr.

Sayer, John, of Pett, Charing, Kent, an arm in armour embowed ppr., garnished or, the hand grasping a griffin's head erased of the second.

Sayer-Milward of St. Leonards, Wallingford, Berks: (1) Out of a wreath of oak or, a bear's paw erect sa., holding a sceptre in pale and charged with a bar of the first (*for Milward*). (2) A mount vert, thereon out of rays of the sun a dexter arm embowed in armour grasping in the hand a dragon's head, all ppr. (*for Sayer*). *Bear and forbear.*

Sayer, a cubit arm erect ppr., holding in the hand a dragon's head erased arg.

Sayer, out of a naval coronet or, a dexter arm embowed vested az., and encircled by a wreath of oak of the first, the hand grasping a dragon's head erased ppr., the arm charged for distinction with a cross crosslet, also or.

Sayer, a dexter hand ppr., vested and tied at the cuff, holding up a griffin's head erased.

Sayer, a sinister arm in armour embowed, the hand grasping a flagstaff with a pennon flotant to the sinister, ensigned with a cap of liberty.

Sayers, a hand holding a scroll of paper between two branches of laurel vert. 215. 3

Sayle of Leighton House, Cambs, in front of a wolf's head couped sa., gorged with a collar gemel or, three escallops of the same. *Who most has served is greatest.*

Sayle, Charles Edward, M.A., 9, Brookside, Cambridge, same crest and motto.

Sayvell or **Sayvill,** the head and shoulders of an Indian king ppr., ducally crowned or, crined and wearing a necklace of the last, out of the coronet a plume of feathers vert, charged with three cinquefoils arg.

Scaife, Northumb., an escallop reversed ppr.

Scales, Scotland, a lion's gamb holding a branch of palm ppr. 36. 7

Scales, out of a ducal coronet or, a swan's head between two wings sa. 100. 10

Scales of Middleton, Norf., out of a ducal coronet or, a plume of ostrich-feathers arg. *cf.* 114. 8

Scales, Scotland, a chevalier in complete armour scaling a ladder ppr. *Paulatim.*

Scales, a buck's head erased gu. *Celer et audax.* 121. 2

Scambler of Hickling, Norf., out of a ducal coronet gu., a garb or. *cf.* 153. 2

Scantlebury, Arthur John, Wilton Lodge, Boxmoor, Herts, a Cornish chough ppr., holding in the beak an estoile or, and supporting with the dexter leg an antique shield vert, charged with an anchor, also or. *Et probus, et verus.*

Scarborough, Norf., out of a mural coronet gu., a demi-lion or, holding upon the point of a lance of the first a Saracen's head ppr., wreathed az.

Scarbrough, Earl of (Lumley), a pelican in her piety, all ppr. *Murus aëneus conscientia sana.* 98. 8

Scarbrow of Montague Place, London, a demi-lion or, billettée gu., supporting a spear erect ppr., encircled by a mural coronet or.

Scardlow, an oak-tree vert. 143. 5

Scargell or **Skargill** of Knockwell, Cumb., and Yorks, a plume of three feathers arg., encircled with a bend or.

Scarisbrick of Scarisbrick, Lancs: (1) A dove sa., beaked and legged gu., holding in the beak an olive-branch ppr (*for Scarisbrick*). 92. 5. (2) A magpie ppr. (*for Eccleston*).

Scarisbrick, Charles, Esquire, Scarisbrick Lodge, Southport, between two trefoils slipped vert, a falcon close ppr., belled and jessed, and charged on the breast with a mullet of six points or. *Patientia vincit omnia.* 233. 12

Scarisbrick, Blaudos-, Marie Emmanuel Alvar de, **Marquis de Castéja,** of Scarisbrick Hall, Lancs, a dove sa., beaked and legged gu., holding in the beak an olive-branch ppr., charged for distinction with a cross crosslet or (*for Scarisbrick*). *cf.* 92. 5

Scarlet, Essex, two lions' gambs erased erm., supporting a pillar gobony or and gu., the capital and base of the second. 39. 8

Scarlett, William James Yorke, Achamore, Isle of Gigha, a Tuscan column chequy or and gu., supported on either side by a lion's gamb ermines erased, also gu. 239. 10

Scarlett, Baron Abinger, *see* Abinger.

Scarlett, out of a ducal coronet or, a demi-eagle displayed sa. 80. 14

Scarrow, a naked arm embowed brandishing a scimitar, all ppr. 201. 1

Scarsborough, a rock ppr. 179. 7

Scarsdale, Baron (Curzon), a popinjay rising or, collared gu. *Recte et suaviter.*

Scarth, Scotland, on the stump of a tree couped, sprouting a branch from the dexter side and environed with a serpent, the head to the sinister, an eagle rising, all ppr. *Volando reptilia sperno.* 283. 11

Scarth, Robert, Esquire, J.P., of Binscarth by Finstown, Orkney, N.B., same crest and motto.

Scarth, Scotland, a dexter hand holding a dagger ppr. *Pax aut bellum.* 212. 3

Scatchard, on a mount vert, a bezant charged with a stag ppr.

Scawen of Aden, Cornw., a cubit arm vested gu., cuffed arg., the hand holding the trunk of a tree eradicated, near the top a branch issuing, all ppr. 206. 1

Scepter, a demi-lion rampant ppr., langued gu., holding in the dexter paw a scimitar of the first. *Fac et spera.* 14. 10

Schank, Scotland, an eagle rising gu. *Spero.* 77. 5

Schank, Devonsh. and Scotland, an eagle with wings expanded ppr. 77. 5

Schank of Barton House, Devonsh., an eagle rising ppr. *Spero.* 77. 5

Schank of Castlerig, Fifesh., an eagle rising gu. *Spero.*

Schapmar, Scotland, a tower arg., masoned sa. 156. 2

Schardelow, a ship in full sail. 160. 13

Schaw, Scotland, a covered cup or.

Schaw, a rose gu., barbed vert. 149. 2

Schelley, an escallop gu. 141. 14

Scherlis, a castle or. 155. 8

Schilizzi, *see* Vafiadacchi-Schilizzi.

Schindler, an anchor and cable ppr. 161. 2

Schlater, Rev. Francis Saunderson, Newick Park, Lewes, an eagle sa. rising out of a ducal coronet or.

Schneider, from a round turret a Cornish chough volant.

Schneider, on a mount an otter entering water. 134. 5

Schoffield or **Schofield,** a fleur-de-lis or. 148. 2

Scholes, a cross crosslet sa. 165. 2

Scholey, a dexter hand brandishing a sword. 212. 13

Scholey of London, an arm in armour erect ppr., the gauntlet holding a hurt, on the arm a bend or, charged with a swan sa., between two hurts.

Scholton or **Scholten,** an antelope's head couped ppr. *cf.* 126. 2

Schomberg, Duke of Schomberg and Leinster (*extinct*): (1) An arm in armour embowed holding in the hand ppr. a battle-axe arg. *cf.* 200. 6. (2) Out of a ducal coronet and between two elephants' trunks or, a talbot sejant affrontée sa. (3) Out of a ducal coronet or, three peacock's feathers ppr.

Schomberg, General Sir George Augustus, United Service Club, Pall Mall, out of a naval crown or, the sails arg., a demi-lion gorged with a wreath of laurel ppr., supporting a flagstaff, thereon hoisted a pennon gu., charged with an anchor or. *Persevere.* 266. 15

Schomberg, Stepney, Holmwood, Seaford, Sussex, same crest and motto.

Schomberg, on a winged globe a dove rising, all ppr. 159. 9

Schrieber of Winchelsea and Henhurst, an arm in armour embowed ppr., garnished or, the hand holding a dagger point towards the dexter, also ppr., hilt and pommel of the second. *Deutlich und wahr.* 196. 5

Schreiber, Arthur Thomas, Henghurst, Woodchurch, Ashford, Kent, same crest and motto.

Schröder, a castle triple towered ppr. 155. 8

Schröder, Sir John Henry William, the Dell, Old Windsor, out of a foreign ducal coronet ppr., a rose as in the arms, between two buffalo horns arg. *Vincet veritas.*

Schultz or **Schultze**, on the top of an old castle in ruins an eagle volant.

Sciaualuga, an esquire's helmet ppr, garnished or 180 3

Sclater, *see* Basing, Baron

Sclater, Cambs, a hunting horn stringed or 228 11

Sclater, Hants out of a ducal coronet or, an eagle rising with wings displayed sa

Sclater, Philip Lutley, Esquire M A F R S, Barrister-at Law, Odiham Priory, Winchfield, Hants, out of a ducal coronet or, an eagle rising with wings displayed sa. *Ει μη εν τῷ σταυρῷ*

Sclater, Scotland, a lion passant gardant ppr *Vi et virtute* 4 3

Scobell, Cornw a dexter hand holding up a bomb inflamed ppr 216 6

Scobell of Mevagissey and of Polruddon, Tregonnan, and Menagwins Cornw a demi lion rampant arg, holding in the dexter paw a fleur de-lis sa 13 2

Scobell, Lieutenant-Colonel Barton Laud John, J P of Kingwell Hall Somers, and Littleton Lodge, Boscombe, Bournemouth (1) A demi lion rampant arg, holding in the dexter paw a fleur-de lis sa, the sinister paw resting upon the wreath (*for Scobell*) (2) A stag's head caboshed (*for Laud*) (3) A garb (*for Barton*) *In Deo salutem*

Scobell of Nancealverne, Cornw a demi-lion arg, holding in the dexter paw a fleur de-lis gu, and gorged with a label of three points az *In Deo salutem* cf 13 2

Scobell, Major Sandford George Treweeke, J P, the Down House Redmarley, near Gloucester, same crest and motto

Scobie, a sword erect ppr 170 2

Scobie, John, Esquire, D L, J P, of Keoldale, Sutherland, a dexter hand holding a dagger erect ppr *Bi treun.* 212 9

Scofield, Lancs, a bull's head or cf 44 3

Scofield or **Scoffield** of Scoffield Lancs a bull's head gu, collared arg cf 44 12

Scofield of Scofield, Kent, a bull's head gu collared arg, armed or cf 44 12

Scollay, Scotland, a hand pointing with one finger ppr 222 12

Sconce, Stirlingsh a wyvern ppr, collared and chained gu, charged on the breast with a star arg

Scopham of Scopham and **Scopyn**, Lincs an archer shooting an arrow from a bow 188 9

Scopholme, Scotland an eagle displayed ppr *Spero meliora* 75 2

Scopyn, an archer shooting an arrow from a bow ppr 188 9

Scory of Resburne, Herts, out of a ducal coronet a demi-eagle displayed, all or 80 14

Scot, out of a ducal coronet a phœnix in flames ppr 82 5

Scot, Kent and London, an eagle or, preying on a bittern ppr 79 7

Scot of London, out of a ducal coronet or an eagle's head sa, charged with an escallop arg

Scot, Kent Hants, and Sussex a demi griffin segreant sa, beaked and legged or 64 2

Scot or **Scott**, Scotland, a stag trippant ppr *Pacem amo* 117 8

Scot, a stag trippant ppr, charged on the neck with a crescent or *Amo.* cf 117 8

Scot or **Scott**, Scotland, a demi-lion brandishing a scimitar ppr *Aut tace, aut face* 14 10

Scot or Scott, Scotland a demi-lion gardant *Aut tace aut face* 10 8

Scot or Scott, Scotland a demi-lion ppr *Aut tace aut face* 10 2

Scot, Scotland a demi lion ppr holding in the dexter paw a rose gu, slipped and leaved vert *Fortis et placabilis* 12 1

Scot or **Scott**, a lion s head erased per chevron or and arg charged with a chevron az, thereon five bezants cf 17 8

Scot, Scotland a lion's head erased gu langued az *Spes vires augentur* 17 2

Scot or **Scott** of Camberwell, Surrey, a boar's head couped arg vulned in the neck with a pheon in fess sa

Scot, a dexter hand holding a lance all ppr *I am ready* 214 11

Scot, Scotland a hand holding a gem ring ppr *Do well, and let them say*

Scot or **Scott** of Scotstarvit Balcomie, and Pitlochie, Scotland a dexter hand holding up a gem ring carbuncled ppr *In tenebris lux*

Scot, a cherub's head ppr, the wings in saltier or 189 13

Scot, Scotland, a demi lady richly attired holding in her dexter hand a rose ppr *Prudenter amo* cf 183 14

Scot or **Scott**, Scotland, a lady richly attired holding in her dexter hand the sun, and in her sinister the moon *Reparabit cornua Phœbe* 184 4

Scot, a stalk of wheat ppr *I increase* 154 3

Scot, a star of six points *Potior origine virtus* 164 3

Scot or **Scott**, Scotland, a ship, the sails bent and flags displayed all ppr *Mihi lucra* 160 13

Scote, an arm vested gu, holding a roll of paper ppr cf 208 5

Scote, Cumb, a stag trippant ppr attired and ungu or *Amo* 117 8

Scotland, Scotland, a lion's head erased ppr 17 8

Scotland, Sir Colley Harman, 14, Queen's Gate Gardens S W, same crest

Scott, *see* Buccleuch and Queensberry, Duke of

Scott, *see* Polwarth, Baron

Scott, *see* Eldon, Earl of

Scott, *see* Montagu, Baron

Scott, *see* Clonmell, Earl of.

Scott, *see* Macmillan Scott

Scott, *see* Young Scott

Scott, Baron Stowell, a lion's head erased gu charged on the neck with a portcullis or *Sit sine labe* cf 17 2

Scott, a stag statant ppr *Amo* 117 5

Scott of Caeglâs, Llanelly, Carmarthensh, a stag trippant ppr *Amo*

Scott, Erskine-, Ebenezer Esquire, of Linburn, Mid-Lothian, a stag trippant ppr, attired and ungu arg, charged on the shoulder with a star of six points of the last *Amo* cf 117 8

Scott of Mollance, Kirkcudbright, a stag trippant gu, attired and ungu or charged on the shoulder with a horse-shoe, also or *Amo* cf 117 8

Scott, Charles Norman Lindsay Tollemache, same crest *Amo*

Scott of Stourbridge, Worcs, and Staffs, a stag lodged ppr, the dexter foot resting on a billet or charged on the shoulder with a cross crosslet or *Nunquam libertas gratior.*

Scott, Ireland, a buck trippant ppr 117 8

Scott, Sir John Edward Arthur Murray, of Castle House, Lisburn co Antrim, same crest *Fidus et fortis*

Scott, James Robert 6, Cambridge Gate, Regent's Park, N W, upon a mount of bulrushes a stag couchant ppr, the dexter foreleg resting on a billet or *Nunquam libertas gratior*

Scott of Trabrown, Scotland, a stag at gaze ppr *Free* 117 3

Scott of Harden Roxburghsh, Scotland, a stag trippant attired with ten tynes ppr *Pacem amo* 117 8

Scott of Thirlstane, Roxburghsh and Wall, Selkirksh, Scotland Same crest and motto 117 8

Scott of Edinburgh a stag holding in his mouth a blade of grass ppr *Hic tutus nutrior* cf 117 5

Scott of Wooden, Roxburghsh Scotland, a stag trippant ppr *Amo* 117 8

Scott, Robson-, of Ashtrees Roxburghsh, Scotland, same crest *Patriam amo.* 117 8

Scott of Kelly Renfrewsh, Scotland, same crest *Ready, aye ready* 117 8

Scott of London, same crest *Fidus et fortis* 117 8

Scott of Malleny Mid Lothian a stag lodged ppr attired or *Amo probos* 115 7

Scott, a buck's head 121 5

Scott, Charles, Esquire, of Howcleuch Selkirk, a stag's head erased gu *Ardenter amo* 121 2

Scott, Scotland a stag's head arg 121 5

Scott of Burnhead, Roxburghsh Scotland a buck's head erased ppr, collared az, charged with a star between two crescents or, all within an orle of laurel-branches vert *In recto decus — Nemo sibi nascitur*

Scott of Kew Green Surrey a stag's head couped ppr, gorged with a collar az., thereon a mullet arg, between two crescents or

Scott of Harwood, a stag's head erased ppr *Ardenter amo* 121 2

Scott, Holland, a stag's head erased gu *Ardenter amo* 121 2

Scott, Madras a stag's head erased ppr. *Fideliter amo* 121 2

Scott, Macmillan-, Walter of Wauchope, Roxburghsh, Scotland (1) A stag's head erased gu (*for Scott*) 121 2 (2) A dexter and a sinister hand issuing from the wreath brandishing a two-handed sword, all ppr. (*for Macmillan*) *Miseris succurro —Ardenter amo* 213 3

Scott of Oak Bank, Wetherel Cumb, in front of a stag's head erased ppr gorged with a collar gemel or, three crescents fesseways of the same. *Obstando supera.*

Scott of Aldborough, Yorks, a stag's head erased ppr. 121. 2

Scott, Scotland, a stag's head. *Amo.* 121. 5

Scott, Sir John, K.C.M.G., D.C.L., of Ramleh, College Road, Norwood, a stag's head couped ppr.

Scott of Redfordhill, Peeblessh., a stag's head ppr. *Memor et fidelis.* 121. 5

Scott, Scotland, a lion rampant gu., wielding a scimitar az., hilt and pommel or. *Aut tace, aut face.*

Scott of Brotherton, Kincardinesh., Scotland, a lion rampant brandishing a scymitar ppr. *Paterno robore tutus.*

Scott of Balweerie, Fifesh., a demi-lion gu., holding in its dexter paw a cutlass ppr. *Dieu me fait fort.*

Scott of Benholm, Forfarsh., Scotland, a demi-lion holding in his dexter paw a rose slipped ppr. *Fortis et placabilis.* 12. 1

Scott-Plummer, Charles Henry, D.L., of Middlestead and of Sunderland Hall, Selkirk: (1) A lion issuant arg., holding a twig of palm in his dexter paw. (2) A stag trippant armed with ten tynes ppr. *Consulto et audacter.—Pacem amo.*

Scott, Scotland, a demi-lion gu. *Spe vires augentur.* 10. 3

Scott of Horsley Hill, Scotland, a lion's head erased ppr. *Pro patria.* 17. 8

Scott, a lion's head erased gu., langued az. *Tace aut face.* 17. 2

Scott, Scotland, same crest. *Spe vires augentur.* 17. 2

Scott, Scotland, a lion's head erased gu. *Domini factum est.—Spe vires augentur.* 17. 2

Scott, Sir Francis David Sibbald, Bart., of Dunninald, a lion's head erased gu., langued az. *Tace aut face.—Spe vires augentur.* 17. 2

Scott of Logie, Forfarsh., Scotland, a lion's head erased holding in his mouth a cinquefoil ppr. *Aut tace aut face.*

Scott of Hedderwick, a lion's head erased gu. *Me fortem reddit Deus.* 17. 2

Scott, Monteath-, Sir William, of Ancrum, Roxburghsh., a lion's head erased gu., langued az. *Tace aut face.* 17. 2

Scott of Abbethune, Scotland, a lion's head erased gu., and over it a rainbow ppr. *Spe versus.* cf. 17. 2

Scott-Douglas, Sir George Brisbane, Bart., D.L., M.A., of Springwood Park, formerly Maxwell, Roxburghsh.: (1) A lion's head erased. 17. 8. (2) A cubit arm erect grasping a broken tilting-spear, all ppr. *Do or die.—Pro patria.* 214. 10

Scott, Spain, a lion's gamb holding a thistle ppr. *Reddunt aspero fortem.* 37. 6

Scott, Scotland, a boar's head couped gu., holding in the mouth a sheaf of arrows ppr. *Do well, and let them say.* 42. 9

Scott of Orkney, a boar's head couped or, holding in the mouth four arrows gu., feathered and headed arg. *Doe weel and let them say.* cf. 42. 9

Scott, Robert Thomas Charles, Melby, Lerwick, N.B., same crest and motto.

Scott, a griffin's head and wings sa. cf. 67. 11

Scott, Shropsh. and Wales, a demi-griffin segreant sa., membered gu. *Recte faciendo neminem timeas.* 64. 2

Scott, Shropsh.: (1) A demi-griffin segreant sa., beaked and legged or. 64. 2. (2) A lamb couchant. *Recte faciendo nemine timeas.*

Scott of Scott's Hall, Kent, a demi-griffin segreant sa., beaked and legged or. 64. 2

Scott of Betton Strange, Shropsh., a demi-griffin segreant sa., membered gu. *Recte faciendo neminem timeas.* 64. 2

Scott, Colonel Charles Edmund Southouse, of Draycott House, Kempsey, Worcs., a demi-griffin segreant sa. *Tout ou rien.*

Scott, Rev. Richard Curtis Folliott, of Hulcote Rectory, Beds, a demi-griffin segreant holding in his claws a flagstaff, therefrom flying to the sinister a pointed pennon. *Recte faciendo neminem timeas.*

Scott, a gryphon passant sa., gorged with an Eastern coronet or, supporting with the dexter fore-claw a flagstaff ppr., thereon flowing to the sinister a swallow-tailed banner gu., inscribed with the word *Nagpoor* in letters of gold. *Amo.*

Scott-Chad, Joseph Stonehewer, Thursford Hall, East Dereham, a falcon wings expanded ppr., beaked, legged, membered or, supporting in the dexter claw a cross potent.

Scott of the Hague, an eagle rising or, and looking up to the sun appearing from under a cloud ppr. *Amo inspicio.*

Scott-Gatty, Sir Alfred Scott, Garter King of Arms, Herald's College: (1) A fern-brake, rising therefrom a cock pheasant, all ppr. 269. 5. (2) On a mount vert a stag trippant ppr., gorged with a collar gemelle arg., and supporting with the sinister fore-leg a trident in bend sinister or. (*for Scott*). *Cate at caute.* 269. 6

Scott, an owl ppr. 96. 5

Scott of Wood Hall, Yorks, an owl or, resting the dexter claw on an escutcheon gu., charged with a fleur-de-lis of the first. *Non invita Minerva.*

Scott, a dove holding in its beak an olive-branch, all ppr. ΕΥΡΕΚΑ. 92. 5

Scott, Sir Charles Stewart, G.C.B., G.C.M.G., an escallop shell sa., charged with a trefoil or. *Perge.*

Scott, Rev. Thomas Lucas, St. George's, Dublin, same crest and motto.

Scott, William Edward, J.P., Willsborough, Londonderry, same crest.

Scott, Bart., Derbysh., a crescent, above it an étoile of six points gu., between two eagle's wings or. *Sidus adsit amicum.* 112. 6

Scott, Donald Albert, Esquire, of Beaconsfield House, Hingham, Norf., in front of a wing or, semée of bay-leaves ppr., a crescent pean. *Tace aut face.* 109. 1

Scott of Sinton, Scotland, a crescent arg. *Crescendo prosim.* 163. 2

Scott, late Rev. Thomas Seard, M.A., Vicar of Holy Trinity, Penge, Surrey, a sun rising in splendour from behind waves of the sea, surmounted by a rainbow, all ppr. *Surge illuminare.*

Scott-Kerr, Captain Francis Louis: (1) The sun ppr. (2) A stag trippant armed with ten tynes ppr.

Scott-Kerr, Major Robert, of Sunlaws, near Kelso, Roxburghsh., same crests and motto.

Scott-Kerr, William Murray Threipland, of Fingask Castle, Perthsh: (1) A stag's head. (2) A mermaid.

Scott, a star of six points. *Potior origine virtus.* 164. 2

Scott of Balmouth, Scotland, a star or. *Lucet.* 164. 1

Scott, a female figure ppr., vested, holding in her dexter hand the sun, and in her sinister a crescent. 184. 4

Scott, Walter, of Raeburn, Dumfriessh., a lady richly attired holding in her dexter hand the sun, and in her sinister the moon, all ppr. *Reparabit cornua Phœbe.* 184. 4

Scott, William Hugh, Esquire, of Draycott House, near Derby, same crest and motto.

Scott, Hope-, of Abbotsford, Roxburgh: (1) A female figure ppr., couped above the knees, vested gu., with the waist az., and a laced stomacher or, the cuffs and ruffs arg., holding in her dexter hand the sun or, and in her sinister a crescent of the fifth (*for Scott*). (2) A globe fracted at the top, under a rainbow issuing from clouds at each end, all ppr. (*for Hope*). *Reparabit cornua Phœbe.—At spes non fracta.—Watch weel.* 159. 2

Scott, John Henry Francis Kinnaird, of Gala, Selkirksh., Scotland, a lady from the waist affrontée richly attired holding in her sinister hand a rose gu. *Prudenter amo.*

Scott, Essex, out of pales or, an arm erect vested az., cuffed arg., holding in the hand a truncheon of the last.

Scott of Enfield, Middx., in pales or, a dexter arm vested az., cuffed arg., holding in the hand a roll of paper ppr.

Scott, Sir Samuel Edward, Bart., of Lytchet Minster, Dorset, out of park pales erminois, an arm erect vested per pale indented arg. and gu., cuffed az., holding in the hand a scroll ppr.

Scott, Archibald Edward, of Rotherfield Park, Hants, an arm erect couped at the elbow, habited gu., cuffed erm., the hand ppr. holding a roll of paper arg., the arm environed with park pales or.

Scott of Islington, a dexter cubit arm erect vested sa., cuffed arg., holding in the hand a roll of paper ppr. cf. 208. 5

Scott of Bevillaw, Scotland, a hand holding a scroll of paper ppr. *Facundia felix.* 215. 6

Scott, Scotland, a hand holding a closed book ppr. *Fidelitas.* 215. 4

Scott of Edinburgh, a dexter arm holding in the hand a book half expanded ppr. *Fidelitas.*

Scott of Vogrie, Edinburgh, a dexter hand holding a ring ppr. *Nescit amor fines.* 216. 1

Scott, a hand holding up a human heart. 216. 9

Scott, a hand holding a pen. *Vive la plume.* 217. 10

Scott of Whytslaid, Scotland, a dexter hand holding a broken lance gu *Pro amore patriæ* 214 10

Scott of Hassendean Scotland a hand holding a pole-axe ppr *Trustie and true* 213 12

Scott, Berks, out of a ducal coronet arg, a wheat sheaf between two sickles ppr *Domini factum est —Spe vires augentur*

Scott, Ireland, a rock rising out of the sea thereon a beacon fired, all ppr *Regi patriæque fidelis*

Scott, Sir Edward Dolman, Bart, M A, J P, D L, of Hartington, Derbysh and of Great Barr, Staffs, on a mount vert a beacon sa, fired ppr, the ladder gu *Regi fidelis patriæque*

Scott-Moncrieff of Coats and Rynd, Scotland three stalks of wheat growing out of the ground ppr *Inde spes* cf 154 7

Scott-Moncrieff, Sir Colin Campbell, 11 Cheyne Walk Chelsea same crest and motto

Scott-Moncrieff, Major William, the Barracks Hounslow, same crest and motto

Scott of Toderick the head of a lance ppr *Pro aris et focis* cf 174 12

Scott of Gorrenberry, Scotland an anchor in pale and cabled, all ppr *Sperandum* 161 2

Scott, Bart of Thirlstane Selkirksh, issuing out of a mural coronet six lances with pennons, three and three az, disposed in saltire *Ready, aye ready*

Scott, Yorks, a monkey passant collared round the loins and lined cf 136 8

Scougal, Scotland a crescent arg *Tandem implebitur* 163 2

Scougall of Edinburgh Scotland, a writing-pen ppr *Hæc ornant*

Scourfield, Sir Owen Henry Philipps, Bart, M A, D L, of the Mote and Williamston Pembrokesh (1) Upon a mount vert the trunk of a tree eradicated fessewise ppr, thereon a greyhound courant arg, collared or (*for Scourfield*) 287 8 (2) A lion rampant sa, gorged with a wreath of oak and resting the sinister paw upon a fret or (*for Philipps*) *Fideliter fortiter feliciter —Animo et fide* 287 7

Scowles of Charlton Berks, a demi lion erm, holding in his dexter paw an escallop arg

Scrace, a Cornish chough ppr, between two wings gu

Scrace, on the trunk of a tree entwined by a serpent a falcon with wings expanded

Scrase of Bletchington, Sussex a falcon with wings addorsed ppr, beaked membered and belled or standing on the stock of a tree, round the last a snake entwined, all ppr *Volando reptilia sperno*

Scratton of Pennenden, near Maidstone, Kent, a wolf's head erased ppr holding in the mouth a trefoil slipped vert cf 30 8

Screven, Shropsh, a buck trippant ppr attired or 117 8

Screvener, Scrivener, and **Scrivenor** of Ipswich, Suff, and Norf, an arm couped at the elbow and erect holding between the thumb and finger a pen all ppr 217 10

Scrimshaw and **Scrimshire,** Staffs, a demi-man couped at the knees in armour ppr, holding in his dexter hand a sword reclining on his shoulder arg, hilt and pommel or, and on his sinister arm a shield, also ppr

Scrimzeor or **Scrymzeor,** Scotland a lion s gamb erect holding a cutlass, all ppr *Dissipate*

Scriven of Frodesley, Shropsh Stapleford Cambs and Worcs, a buck trippant ppr attired or 117 8

Scrivenor of Sibton, Suff a stag erm, attired or, ducally gorged gu cf 117 5

Scrivenor of Bacton, Norf, an arm couped at the elbow and erect holding between the thumb and first finger a pen, all ppr 217 10

Scrivington, Hants a tun in fess or issuing from the bung-hole an apple-tree vert fructed of the first, the root erased and through the tun 144 9

Scroggs and **Scrugges** of Reynold, Beds, a pewit s head arg collared sa, with wings addorsed bendy of four or and sa

Scroggs or **Screggs,** an eagle's head erased or 83 2

Scrogie, Scotland, the trunk of an oak-tree sprouting leaves and branches ppr *Ero quod eram* 145 2

Scrogie, Scotland, an oak-tree ppr *Tandem fit surculus arbor*

Scroop, Scroope, or **Scrope,** out of a ducal coronet or, a triple plume of ostrich feathers az 114 6

Scroope of Wormsleigh, Oxon, a plume of feathers arg 115 1

Scrope of Bolton, Yorks out of a ducal coronet a plume of ostrich-feathers *Devant si je puis* cf 114 8

Scrope of Castle Combe Wilts out of a ducal coronet gu a plume of feathers arg *Non hæc sed me* cf 114 8

Scroope, Heref. in flames ppr, a phœnix or 82 2

Scrope, Baron Scrope of Masham, out of a ducal coronet a crab

Scrope, issuing out of a ducal coronet a crab

Scrope, Simon Conyers of Danby Yorks out of a ducal coronet or a plume of ostrich feathers ppr *Devant si je puis* cf 114 8

Scrope, Bart (*extinct*), of Cockerington, Yorks, same crest cf 114 8

Scrutevill, Durh an arm embowed vested erminois cuffed arg, holding in the hand ppr a large pistol the stock sa, the barrel of the second, firing of the third

Scrymgeour, Earl of Dundee and **Viscount Dudhope,** a lion's gamb holding a scymitar *Dissipate* 38 13

Scrymgeour of Bowhill, Scotland a lion's gamb holding a sword fesseways ppr *Dissipate*

Scrymgeour-Wedderburn, Henry, Birkhill, Cupar, Fifesh (1) An eagle's head erased ppr (2) A lion's gamb erased in bend holding a cutlass, both ppr *Non degener —Dissipate*

Scrymsoure-Steuart-Fothringham, Walter Thomas James of Fothringham, Forfarsh, N B (1) A griffin segreant ppr (2) Same as (2) above *Be it fast.—Dissipate*

Scrymgeour of Kirktoun, a lion s gamb erased holding a cutlass ppr *Dissipate*

Scrymgeour of Cartmore, Scotland a lion's gamb grasping a sword fesseways ppr *Dissipate*

Scudamore-Stanhope, *see* Chesterfield, Earl of

Scudamore, Heref, out of a ducal coronet or a lion's gamb in pale sa *Scuto amoris divini* 36 12

Scudamore, Heref, out of a ducal coronet a bear's paw in pale sa, armed gu 36 12

Scudamore, Lieutenant Colonel Frederick William of Chelsworth Hall, Suff, out of a ducal coronet or a bear's paw in pale sa armed gu *Scuto amoris divino* 309 9

Scudamore of Kentchurch Court, Heref out of a ducal coronet or a bear's paw ppr *Scuto amoris divini* 36 12

Scully, Vincent Esquire, J P D L Mantle Hill, co Tipperary, and Merrion Square, Dublin out of a mural crown ppr, a phœnix in flames, also ppr charged on the breast with a cross bottonnee or *Sine labe resurgens*

Scurfield, a hand gauntleted ppr, holding a large pistol *Vidi vici*

Scurfield, an arm embowed vested erminois, cuffed arg holding in the hand ppr a large pistol, the stock sa, the barrel of the second, firing of the third

Scurfield, George John, of Ford and Hurworth upon-Tees, Durh, a cubit arm in armour erect ppr encircled by a wreath of oak or holding in the hand a carbine erect also ppr (2) A scaling ladder arg (*for Grey*) *Vidi vici —Deum time regem serva*

Scutte, Dorset a crane with wings elevated az, beaked and legged gu, holding in the beak a rose ppr

Sea, two lobster's claws in pale, and in each claw a fish 141 3

Seabright or **Sebright,** Worcs, a heraldic tiger sejant arg, maned and crowned or

Seabrook, a hand erect holding a cross crosslet fitched in pale gu cf 221 14

Seabry or **Sebry,** a bird with wings addorsed sa, supporting with the dexter claw a quill, inflamed and environed with a serpent all ppr

Seafield, Earl of (Ogilvie Grant) (1) A lion rampant gu holding between the paws a plumb rule erect ppr (*for Ogilvie*) 3 2 (2) A mountain in flames ppr (*for Grant*) *Tout jour —Craigellachie* 179 2

Seaford, Baron (Ellis), on a mount vert, a goat's head erased arg *Non quo, sed quomodo* cf 128 5

Seagar or **Seager,** a dolphin haurient and devouring a fish all ppr 140 6

Seago, William Rix, Oulton Hall, Oulton Suff, a stag's head couped per pale gu and sa *Sine tremore*

Seagrave and **Seagrove,** a dexter hand holding a palm-branch ppr. 219 11

Seagrave of Castle Ashby, Northamp, six arrows interlaced in saltire and three in pale points downwards all ppr also interlaced and bound with a wreath of the colours viz, arg and sa

Seagrim, a long cross gu 165 1

Seaham, Viscount, *see* Londonderry, Marquess.

Seal, a wolf's head or, embrued at the nose and mouth gu. 30. 5

Seale, Northumb., out of a ducal coronet or, a wolf's head arg., embrued at the nose and mouth ppr. *cf.* 30. 5

Seale, Sir John Henry, Bart., of Wonastow Court, Monm., out of a vallery coronet or, a wolf's head arg., the neck encircled with a wreath of oak vert. 289. 12

Seale-Hayne, Rt. Hon. Charles, of 6, Upper Belgrave Street, S.W., same crest. *In cœlo salus.*

Seale of St. Brealade, Jersey, a wolf's head erased sa. *Loyal en tout.* 30. 8

Sealy, co. Cork, out of a ducal coronet or, a wolf's head sa. *Concipe spes certes.* *cf.* 30. 5

Sealy, same crest. *cf.* 30. 5

Sealy, a quatrefoil gu. 148. 10

Sealy, a talbot sejant ppr., collared and chained or. *cf.* 55. 5

Seaman, a demi-sea-horse salient arg. 46. 7

Seaman of London, out of a crescent erminois, a demi-sea-horse barry wavy of six arg. and az.

Seamark, a yew-tree ppr. 143. 1

Searle of London, and Plymouth, Devonsh., a demi-lion rampant or, holding a broken mast sa., the top set off with palisadoes, thereon a flag arg., charged with the cross of St. George gu.

Searle, Cornw., on a mount vert, a greyhound sejant arg., ducally gorged gu. *cf.* 59. 2

Searle of Thanks, Cornw., on a mount vert, a greyhound sejant arg., collared gu. 59. 2

Searles, a gem-ring stoned or. 167. 14

Sears or **Sayer,** an eagle displayed with wings inverted ppr. *Honor et fides.*

Seaton, Baron (Colborne), out of a ducal coronet or, a reindeer's head arg., attired or, between a branch of laurel on the dexter and a branch of palm on the sinister, both ppr. *Sperat infestis.* 288. 7

Seaton, Scotland, a buck's head couped ppr., attired or. *Bydand.* 121. 5

Seaton, Scotland, a swan naiant ppr. *Cum progressu cautus.* 99. 9

Seaton, Scotland, a Cornish chough on the face of a rock. *Hazard warily.*

Seaton, a boar's head couped or. *Forward ours.* 43. 1

Seaton, Scotland, a wolf's head erased. *Forward ours.* 30. 8

Seaton, on a ducal coronet a wyvern with wings addorsed. 70. 9

Seaton, a dragon vert, vomiting flames of fire ppr. *cf.* 73. 2

Seaton, Durh., a lion rampant or. *Dieu defende le droit.* 1. 13

Seaton, Scotland, a soldier from the middle bearing up a banner in bend and displayed, all ppr. *Sustento sanguine signa.* 187. 9

Seaton, an arm in armour embowed in fess from the elbow holding in the hand a sword enfiled with a savage's head couped.

Seaton, a gauntlet ppr. *Majorum vestigia premo.* 209. 8

Seaton, a dexter hand brandishing a sabre. 212. 13

Seaton, Scotland, a star of six points rayed or. *Habet et suam.*

Seaton, Scotland, a crescent gu. *Semper.* 163. 2

Seaton or **Seton,** Scotland, a crescent inflamed. *Habet et suam.* 163. 12

Seaver, Ricarde-, Major Francis Ignatius, F.R.S.E., F.R.G.S., Knight Commander of the Royal Military Order of Christ of Portugal, Knight Commander of the Royal and Distinguished Order of Isabel the Catholic of Spain, and Knight Officer of the Imperial Order of the Rose of Brazil, of Paris, in front of a pick-axe erect a Moor's head affrontée couped at the shoulders ppr., the turban arg., pierced through the head by a sword fessewise point to the dexter, also ppr. *Malo mori quam fœdari* 261. 20

Sebastian, Lewis Boyd, 22, Kensington Court, W., a demi-cat-a-mountain guardant ppr., holding in the dexter paw an eagle's wing sa., and resting the sinister paw on a dexter hand couped at the wrist pointing upwards, thumb and two fingers ppr.

Seborne, Heref., a lion's head gardant and erased arg., collared az.

Seborne of Sutton, Heref., an eagle close vert, holding in the beak a hawk's lure lined and ringed gu.

Sebright, a demi-lion rampant or. 10. 2

Sebright, Guy Thomas Saunders, Hever Castle, Kent, a heraldic tiger.

Sebright of Blakeshall, Worcs., a heraldic tiger sejant arg., tufted and ducally crowned or.

Sebright, Sir Egbert Cecil Saunders, Bart., of Besford, Worcs., an heraldic tiger sejant arg., maned and crowned or.

Seccombe, Sir Thomas Lawrence, G.C.I.E., Sheridan, Newton Abbot, a lion rampant sa. between two elephant's proboscides ppr. *Paratus et fidelis.* 231. 13

Sechion of Milton, Oxon., out of a mural coronet or, a bull's head couped az., armed of the first. *cf.* 44. 11

Seckford or **Seckforde,** Suff., a cock's head erased vert, combed and wattled gu. 90. 1

Seckford, on a mount a greyhound passant ppr. *cf.* 60. 2

Seckham, Major Bassett Thorne, D.S.O., of Whillington Old Hall, near Lichfield, a lion rampant. *Ut ducam spero.* 1. 13

Secretan, on a mount vert, an eagle regardant or, semée of hearts gu., and holding in the beak a laurel-wreath of the first.

Seddon of Outwood and Kersley, Lancs, two lion's gambs erased and erect sa., supporting a cinquefoil or.

Seddon of the Elms, Great Wigston, Leics., same crest. *Non sino, sed dono.*

Seddon of Hartlepool, Durh., two bear's gambs reversed sa., holding a cinquefoil or. *Non sino, sed dono.*

Sedgewick or **Sedgewicke,** two ears of rye in saltier or. 154. 4

Sedgewick, a sunflower.

Sedley or **Sidley,** Kent, out of a ducal coronet ppr., a goat's head arg., attired or. 128. 14

See of Kent, a hand az., holding an arrow point downwards ppr. 214. 4

See, two lobster's claws in pale gu., each holding a fish arg. 141. 3

Seed, a demi-lion holding a cross crosslet fitchée. 11. 10

Seeds of London and Lancs, a demi-cock with wings expanded az.

Seel, Lancs, a wolf's head erased per fesse nebuly erm. and ermines, holding in the mouth a carnation ppr. *cf.* 30. 8

Seel, Molyneux-, of Huyton Hey, Lancs: (1) A wolf's head erased per fesse pean and az. (*for Seel*). 30. 8. (2) On a chapeau gu., turned up erm., a peacock's tail ppr. (*for Molyneux*).

Seely, Sir Charles, Bart., Sherwood Lodge, Arnold, Notts, in front of three ears of wheat banded or, the trunk of a tree eradicated, and sprouting in the dexter ppr. *In Deo spero.* 289. 15

Seeres, a martlet holding in the beak a serpent, all ppr.

Sefton, Earl of (Molyneux), a chapeau gu., turned up erm., adorned with a plume of peacock's feathers ppr. *Vivere sat vincere.* 303. 6

Segar of Wrotham, Kent, and Lancs, on a mount vert, an eagle rising regardant ppr.

Segar, a demi-lion arg., crowned or, holding between the paws a mascle of the last.

Segar, Norf., a tower gu., and issuant from the battlements a demi-lion arg., holding between the paws a firebrand or, fired ppr. *cf.* 157. 10

Segar, on a ducal coronet or, two snakes vert, entwined round a sceptre of the first, between two wings, the dexter or, the sinister arg. 170. 13

Segar, Halsall, Newferry Vicarage, Birkenhead, a wolf's head couped arg., vulned gu. *Vincit veritas.*

Segar-Parry of Little Haddam, Herts: (1) A buck's head couped arg., holding in the mouth a sprig ppr. (*for Parry*). (2) On a ducal coronet or, two snakes vert, entwined round a sceptre of the first, between two wings, the dexter or, the sinister az. (*for Segar*). 170. 13

Segrave, Henry, of Killeghan, co. Meath, and of Kiltimon, co. Wicklow, Ireland, a demi-lion rampant ppr., holding between the paws an oak-branch vert, acorned or. *Dieu et mon Roy.*

Segrave of Dublin, a demi-lion rampant arg., holding between the paws a branch of oak ppr., fructed or, langued and charged on the shoulder for difference with a martlet gu.

Segrave, De, a lion's gamb holding a branch of laurel vert. 37. 4

Segrave, five arrows or, barbed and flighted arg., banded of the first and wreathed of the second and sa. 173. 3

Segrave of Tilney, five arrows or, headed and flighted arg., wreathed of the last and sa., banded of the first. 173. 3

Segrove, a lion rampant or, holding an oak-sprig ppr.

Selborne, Earl of (Palmer), on a mount vert, a greyhound sejant sa., collared or, and charged on the shoulder with a trefoil slipped arg. *Palma virtuti.* *cf.* 59. 2

Selby, Baron de Selby, in the Kingdom of Denmark, a Saracen's head ppr., wreathed about the temples or and sa. *Semper sapit suprema.* 190. 14

Selby, Northumb and Durh, a Saracen's head ppr, wreathed or and sa 190 14

Selby, Walter Arthur, of Earle and Biddleston Northumb and Winlaton, Durh a Saracen's head couped at the shoulders ppr wreathed and tied in a knot behind or and sa *Semper sapit suprema*

Selby of Whitley and Wimbish Hall, Essex, a Saracen's head ppr *Fort et loyal* 190 14

Selby, Beauchamp Prideaux, Esquire J P of Parstow, Cornhill-on-Tweed same crest and motto

Selby of the Mote Kent a Saracen's head ppr, wreathed about the temples or and sa. *Semper sapit suprema* 190 14

Selenger, a griffin's head between two wings 65 11

Selle, His Honour Sir William Lucius 48, Montagu Square, W, out of a ducal coronet a demi-griffin segreant *Constantiam servare*

Selioke of Haselbarrow, Derbysh., out of a mural coronet or a cubit arm erect vested arg, holding in the hand ppr an oak-branch vert fructed of the first

Selkirk, Earl of, *see* Hamilton Duke of

Selkirk, Earl of (Douglas), on a chapeau gu turned up erm, a salamander in flames ppr *Jamais arriere* 138 2

Sellar of Liverpool, a demi-swan with wings elevated ppr *Confido* 100 9

Sellers, a demi swan with wings addorsed arg 100 2

Selsey, Baron (Peachey), a demi lion double queued erm, holding in the dexter paw a mullet pierced gu *Memor et fidelis*

Selward, Wilts and Warw an eagle's head erased sa, collared or *cf* 83 2

Selwin-Ibbetson, Rt Hon Sir Henry John, **Baron Rookwood,** P C, M A M P, of Leeds, Yorks (1) A unicorn's head arg., semee of escallops armed maned, and erased gu (*for Ibbetson*) (2) Two lion's gambs erm, erased arg supporting a torch in pale or, fired ppr (*for Selwin*) *Vixi liber et moriar* 39 7

Selwyn, Essex, and of Freston Bechington, Sussex, two lion's gambs erased or, holding a beacon in pale, fired ppr *cf* 39 7

Selyocke, Herts and Derbysh, out of a mural coronet or a cubit arm vested arg, holding in the hand ppr an oak-branch vert fructed of the first

Semphill, Baron (Forbes-Semphill) (1) Upon the dexter side—a stag's head arg, attired with ten tynes az, and collared with a prince's coronet or (*for Semphill*) (2) Upon the sinister side—a cock ppr (*for Forbes*) *Keep tryst Watch* 91 2

Sempill, a buck's head erased 121 2

Sempill, Scotland, a stag's head couped ducally gorged ppr, charged on the neck with a cross crosslet *cf* 121 5

Semple, a stag's head ppr, attired arg *Diligentia et vigilantia* 121 5

Semple, same crest *Keep tryste* 121 5

Semple of Cathcart Renfrewsh, and Stockholm, Sweden, a stag's head arg, attired az, charged with a crescent gu *Diligentia et vigilantia* 119 8

Semple, Scotland a stag's head erased *Keep tryste* 121 2

Semple, Scotland, a stag's head couped ppr, attired arg gorged with a royal coronet or, charged with a gilliflower *Keep tryste*

Semple, of Belltrees, Scotland, a hand holding a pistol ppr *In loyaltie* 221 8

Semple, Ireland, out of a ducal coronet a broken battle-axe all ppr *cf* 172 7

Senhouse of Seascale and Ellenborough, Cumb, a popinjay holding in its beak a label inscribed with the motto, *Deo gratias* *Væ victis*

Senhouse, Pocklington-, Humphrey, of Netherhall and Barrow House (1) A parrot ppr, holding in its beak a label inscribed with the motto, *Deo gratias* (*for Senhouse*) (2) A demi leopard rampant ppr holding in the dexter paw an ostrich feather arg (*for Pocklington*) *Væ victis*

Senior of Tewin Herts on a mount vert, a leopard couchant gardant ppr, crowned with a Saxon coronet or *Medio tutissimus ibis* *cf* 24 9

Senlize, De, a lion passant gardant with the tail extended gu *cf* 4 3

Sennicots, a rose-branch bearing six roses ppr *cf* 149 8

Senthill, two dragons' heads erased respecting each other enfiled with a ducal coronet

Senton, Lincs, out of a mural coronet or a lion's head az 19 12

Sent-Pier, on a spear or, pointed arg, a dolphin naiant of the first 140 9

Sepham, Kent and Surrey, a mermaid ppr ducally crowned, crined, finned and holding in her dexter hand a comb or, and in her sinister seaweeds vert

Septuans, Kent a dolphin naiant ppr 140 5

Serell or **Serrell,** a covered cup gu

Sergeant, Bucks, a dolphin naiant or guttee de-larmes *cf* 140 5

Sergison, Charles Warden of Cuckfield Park, Sussex, a dolphin naiant sa, pierced transversely by an arrow arg, vulned gu *cf* 140 5

Sermon, a crescent sa, and issuing from between the horns a cross crosslet fitched gu 166 9

Serocold of Cherryhinton Cambs (1) A castle or and issuing from the battlements a fleur de-lis az (*for Serocold*) (2) In front of a rose gu, a Cornish chough ppr (*for Pearce*)

Serocold, Pearce-, Charles Taplow Hill, Maidenhead same crests

Serres, Scotland an arm in armour holding in the hand a sword, all ppr 210 2

Servante, a demi-bull gu *cf* 45 8

Service, Andrew Graham, Esquire, Dalgowrie, Lenzie N B a lion rampant *Malo mori quam fœdari* 1 13

Servington of Tavistock, Devonsh, a pine tree erased vert fructed or enfiled with a tun or

Seth, a hand ppr, holding a cannon-ball sa 216 3

Seton, Earl of Winton, on a ducal coronet a dragon with wings elevated vert, sprouting fire ppr

Seton, Earl of Dunfermline, a crescent gu *Semper* 163 2

Seton, same crest *Set on* 163 2

Seton, Scotland same crest *Semper* 163. 2

Seton, a flaming crescent *Habet et suam* 163 12

Seton, a crescent gu *Set on*—*Virtus duxit avorum* 163 2

Seton of London, a dragon vomiting flames of fire ppr *Hazard zit forward* *cf* 73 2

Seton, George Advocate, M A, F R S E, F S A S on a ducal coronet a dragon vert, wings elevated, sprouting fire ppr and charged with a star arg *Hazard zet forward*

Seton, a wyvern vert *Hazard it forward* 70 1

Seton-Karr, Sir Henry, C M G, M P of Kippilaw, St Boswells, N B (1) Out of an antique coronet a dexter hand erect holding a dagger in pale, all ppr (*for Karr*) (2) On a ducal coronet or a wyvern ppr (*for Seton*) *Avant sans peur* 70 9

Seton of Touch, Stirlingsh, Scotland, a boar's head couped or *Forward ours* 43 1

Seton, Scotland, a man in armour on horseback at full speed, holding on the point of a sword an imperial crown *Inclytus perditæ recuperator coronæ*

Seton, Major Alexander David, Mounie, Old Meldrum, Aberdeensh, a demi man in armour bearing up in his dexter hand the Royal Banner of Scotland gu, on a canton az a saltire arg bendways and displayed, all ppr, scarf over dexter shoulder, plume and waistbelt arg. *Sustento sanguine signa*

Seton, Bart, of Garleton, Scotland, a star of six points rayed ppr *Habet et suam* *cf* 164 3

Seton, Scotland, a Cornish chough on the face of a rock ppr *Hazard warily*

Seton, Sir Bruce Maxwell Bart D L, of Abercorn, Linlithgowsh a Cornish chough in front of a rock all ppr *Hazard warily*—*Forward ours*

Seton, a hawk's head az *cf* 88 12

Seton-Steuart, Sir Alan Henry Bart D L, of Allanton Lanarksh out of an earl's coronet a dexter hand grasping a thistle all ppr *Juvant aspera fortes*—*Virtutis in bello præmium* 288 8

Seton, a gauntlet ppr *Nigarum vestigia premo* 209 8

Seton, a swan naiant ppr *Cum progressu cautus* 99 9

Seton, Sir William Samuel Bart of Pitmedden and Cushnie, Aberdeensh, a demi-man in a military habit holding the banner of Scotland with the motto on an escroll above *Sustento sanguine signa* *Merces hæc certa laborum*

Severn and **Severne,** Worcs, a cinquefoil or 148 11

Severn of Powick, Worcs, same crest 148 11

Severn, Edward Charles Samuel, Thenford near Banbury same crest

Severne of Wallop Hall, Shropsh, same crest *Virtus præstantior auro* 148 11

Severn, a demi-horse salient pierced in the breast by an arrow *cf* 53 3

Seward, out of a ducal coronet or, a horse's hind-leg, the hoof upwards. 123. 6

Seward of Lee Cottage and Douglas, co. Cork, and Newcastle, co. Limerick: (1) Out of a ducal coronet or, the hind-leg of a horse couped at the thigh az., shod of the first. 123. 6. (2) A dexter hand fesseways grasping a sword in pale ppr., enfiled with an imperial crown or. (3) A dexter cubit arm in pale vested gu., cuffed erm., rising from park pales or, the hand ppr. grasping a truncheon arg. *Olim fecimus.*

Sewell, Essex, on a mural coronet or, a martlet sa.

Sewell, Philip, Esquire, of Clare House, Catton, Norwich, *uses*: on a mural coronet a martlet. (*Of no authority.*)

Sewell, in a chaplet of roses arg., leaved vert, a bee volant of the first. 137. 5

Sewell, Frederic Robertson, Brandlingill, Cockermouth, upon a mount vert, a bee volant ppr., within a chain in arch or. 261. 14

Sewell, Thomas Davies, 29, Grosvenor Road, S.W., a pomme charged with a bee volant ppr., encircled by a wreath of oak, fructed ppr. *Non nobis nascimus.* 261. 13

Sewell, an arm in armour in bend dexter, grasping a staff in bend sinister, crowned with a cap of liberty.

Sewell of Newport, Isle of Wight, Hants, an arm in armour embowed ppr., garnished or, holding in the hand an acorn of the first.

Sexton, Ireland, a leopard's face ppr. 22. 2

Sexton, Ireland, a leopard's face az. 22. 2

Sexton, a woman couped at the waist ppr., vested gu., her hair flowing or, holding in her dexter hand a chaplet vert. 183. 5

Sexton of London, out of a ducal coronet or, a dexter arm in armour embowed ppr., garnished, also or, holding in the gauntlet an anchor sa., fluke and cable of the first.

Sexton, Ireland, a pheon az. 174. 11

Seymer, a hawk's leg in fess erased, holding a quill. 113. 12

Seymer of Handford, Dorset, on a chapeau gu., turned up erm., two wings or. *cf.* 112. 9

Seymer, Clay-Ker-, Harry Ernest, Esquire, of Hanford, Dorset: (1) A chapeau gu., turned up erm., winged or (*for Seymer*). (2) A unicorn's head erased arg., gorged with a collar az., charged with three crosses moline of the first (*for Ker*). (3) Two wings arg., each charged with a chevron engrailed between three trefoils slipped sa. (*for Clay*).

Seymour, Lord, *see* Somerset, Duke of.

Seymour, *see* Hertford, Marquess of.

Seymour, Baron Alcester, *see* Alcester.

Seymour of Bury, Devonsh., out of a ducal coronet or, a phœnix in flames ppr. 82. 5

Seymour, Charles Derick, 41, St. James's Place, S.W., same crest. *Fide et amore.*

Seymour of Knoyle House, Wilts, out of a ducal coronet or, a phœnix of the same in flames ppr. *Foy pour devoir.* 82. 5

Seymour, George Evelyn, a phœnix or, in flames ppr. 82. 2

Seymour, Leopold Richard, 9, Grosvenor Gardens, S.W., same crest.

Seymour-Crossley of Castletown, Ireland, out of a ducal coronet or, a phœnix in flames ppr., with wings expanded or. *Foi pour devoir.* 82. 5

Seymour, Sir Albert Victor Francis, Bart., 31, Eccleston Street, S.W., out of a ducal coronet or, a demi-phœnix in flames ppr., charged with a bendlet sinister wavy or. *Foy pour devoir.* *cf.* 82. 5

Seymour, Culme-, Sir Michael, Bart., of Highmount, co. Limerick, on a naval crown or, two brands in saltier inflamed at the ends ppr., thereon an eagle rising, also ppr., gazing at the sun of the first. *Foy pour devoir.* 308. 13

Seymour, Vice-Admiral Sir Edward Hobart, G.C.B., same crest and motto.

Seymour, Culme-, Henry Hobart, Esquire, of Glenville, Bitterne, Hants, on a naval crown or, two brands in saltire inflamed ppr., thereon an eagle rising, also ppr., gazing on the sun or. *Foy pour devoir.* 308. 13

Seymour, Somers., two wings conjoined in leure surmounted by a ducal coronet, all or.

Seymour of Burton, Oxon., a pair of wings conjoined, the dexter or, the sinister gu., surmounted by a ducal coronet per pale counterchanged.

Seymour, Dorset, on each side of a chapeau gu., turned up erm., a wing or.

Seymor, a swan's neck couped.

Seymour, a branch of oak fructed and leaved, all ppr. 151. 3

Seymour, Ireland, a hind trippant ppr. 124. 12

Seymour, a negro's head. *Fide et amore.* *cf.* 192. 13

Seys of Boverton, Glamorgansh., a demi-lion rampant gu. *Crescit sub pondere virtus.* 10. 3

Seys, Godfrey, Wirewood's Green, near Chepstow, same crest and motto.

Shaa of Lanham, Norf., out of a ducal coronet or, a nag's head arg., between two wings expanded sa.

Shackleton, a poplar-tree vert. 144. 12

Shackleton, Ebenezer, Sunnyside, Carlow, a poplar tree ppr., charged with a buckle tongue paleways or. *Fortitudine vincimus.* 237. 9

Shackleton, Henry, Aberdeen House, Sydenham, same crest and motto.

Shackleton, Joseph Fisher, Anna Liffey House, Lucan, co. Dublin, same crest and motto.

Shad, Norf., out of a ducal coronet or, a nag's head arg., between two wings sa.

Shadegrove, a wood or grove, the sun shining thereon.

Shadford, the sun shining on the stump of an oak-tree sprouting fresh branches. 145. 5

Shadford, on a staff raguly in fess or, a lion passant resting the dexter fore-paw on an hour-glass erect, and holding in the mouth a trefoil slipped. 5. 14

Shadford of Red Barns and Darras Hall, Northumb., a lion passant gardant ppr., the dexter fore-paw resting on an hour-glass arg., holding in the mouth a trefoil slipped vert. *Fugit irrevocabile tempus.*

Shadforth, the sun shining on the stump of an oak-tree sprouting anew. 145. 5

Shadwell of Lyndourie, Staffs, a demi-griffin ppr. 64. 2

Shadwell, Lucas-, William, the Hall, Fairlight, Hastings: (1) An escallop within an annulet per pale or and az. (*for Shadwell*). (2) On a mount vert a wyvern arg., wings elevated or, charged on the body with six annulets or.

Shaen of Crix, Essex, a greyhound statant regardant erm., collared gu.

Shaftesbury, Earl of, *see* Ashley-Cooper.

Shafto, R. C. D., of Whitworth Park, Durh., Cumb., and of Bavington, Northumb., a salamander regardant vert, in the midst of flames ppr., pierced through the neck with a spear, point to the sinister, and in the mouth a cross crosslet fitchée. *cf.* 138. 4

Shaftow, Northumb., a salamander vert, in flames ppr. 138. 4

Shairp, J. C., of Houstoun, Linlithgowsh., a steel helmet in profile with a plumage of feathers ppr. *Vivit post funera virtus.* 180. 4

Shakelton, a poplar-tree vert. 144. 12

Shakerley of Holme, a demi-hare rampant arg., supporting a garb or.

Shakerley, Chesh., Lancs, and Berks, a hare sa., supporting a garb or. *Antiquum obtinens.* 308. 12

Shakerley, Sir Walter Geoffrey, Bart., J.P., of Somerford Park, Chesh., a hare ppr., resting her fore-feet on a garb or. *Moriendo vivam.* 308. 12

Shakespear of Langley Priory, Leics., on a mount vert, in front of a falcon with wings elevated per fesse az. and gu., a tilting-spear erect or. 88. 1

Shakespear, Henry Hope, B.A., 4, Pembridge Mansions, Bayswater, W., a falcon with wings elevated and expanded or, supporting a tilting-spear erect ppr. *Fide sed cui vide.*

Shakespeare of Stratford-on-Avon, Warw., a falcon rising arg., supporting with the dexter claw a tilting-spear or, steeled arg. *Non sanz droict.* 88. 5

Shalcross of London, and of Shalcross, Derbysh., a martlet or, holding in the beak a cross patée fitched gu., charged on the breast with a mullet.

Shales, a goat's head erased arg., attired or. 128. 5

Shanan, Ireland, a dove holding in its beak an olive-branch. *Virtute duce.* 92. 5

Shand, Baron (Shand), a dove with an olive-branch in her mouth. *Virtute duce.*

Shand, *see* Smith-Shand.

Shand, a dove holding in its beak an olive-branch, all ppr. *Virtute duce.* 92. 5

Shand of Aberdeen, and Arnhall, Kincardinesh., Scotland, a dove volant above the waters holding in the beak a branch of olive ppr. *Virtute duce, comite fortuna.* 93. 11

Shane, Ireland, an arm in armour embowed holding in the hand and by the hair a human head couped at the neck distilling drops of blood, all ppr.

Shank of Castlerig, Fifesh, Scotland, an eagle rising arg *Spero* 77 5
Shank of Glemston Fifesh, same crest and motto 77 5
Shanke of Rollesby, Norf, on a ducal coronet or, a lion's head erased per fess arg and gu cf 19 10
Shanks, James, 79, Merrion Square, Dublin, on a mural crown ppr, an eagle rising arg, each wing charged with a trefoil slipped gu *Spero*
Shanly or **MacShanly,** co Leitrim, Ireland, on a wreath of the colours an arm in armour embowed ppr, the hand also ppr, grasping a broken sword arg, hilt and pommel or therefrom five drops of blood *Pro patria et religione*
Shanly of Fearnaght, co Leitrim, Ireland an arm in armour embowed ppr, the hand also ppr, grasping a broken sword arg, hilt and pommel or there from five drops of blood
Shann of Hampstwaite, Yorks, in front of an annulet or, a hand erect holding a dagger, all ppr *Fideliter*
Shannon, a demi talbot sa cf 55 12
Shannon, Earl of (Boyle), out of a ducal coronet or, a lion's head erased per pale crenellee arg and gu, charged with a crescent for difference *Vivit post funera virtus—Spectemur agendo* cf 19 10
Shannon, on a gauntlet an eagle close ppr
Shapleigh of Totnes Devonsh, and Cornw an arm vested gu, turned up arg holding in the hand ppr a chaplet vert, garnished with roses of the first
Shard of Horsleydown, Surrey a lion passant per pale or and sa, guttee counterchanged resting the dexter fore paw on a bugle horn of the second
Shardelow of Shardelow, Suff a plume of feathers arg 115 1
Sharman-Crawford, Robert Gordon, of Crawfordsburn, co Down (1) A swan close ppr (2) A dove rising holding in the beak a laurel sprig ppr *Durum patientia frango*
Sharnborne of Sharnborne Hall, Norf, a lion's gamb couped and erect, grasping a griffin's head erased sa
Sharp, Scotland a branch of oak acorned ppr *Progredior* 151 3
Sharp of Hoddom, Dumfriessh, an oak tree ppr *Sub umbra quies* 143 5
Sharp, William, Esquire Barbados, a demi-lion rampant erased ppr gorged with a collar nebuly az, holding be tween the paws a wreath of oak ppr, encircling an escallop or 227 15
Sharp of Kincarrochy, Scotland a celestial crown or *Pro mitra coronam*
Sharp, Bart, of Scotscraig, Fifesh, Scotland, same crest and motto
Sharp of Stonyhill, Edinburgh, Scotland, a pheon ppr *Progredere, ne regredere* 174 11
Sharp, Herbert, Myrtle Grove, Bingley, Leeds, upon three pheons arg an eagle's head erased sa, gorged with a crown, also vallery
Sharp, a steel cap with a plume of feathers ppr *Vivit post funera virtus.*
Sharp of Bishopwearmouth, Durh, an eagle's head erased az, ducally gorged or holding in the beak a pheon arg *Dum spiro, spero.* 83 10
Sharp, John Henry 21 Palmeira Square, Hove, Sussex same crest
Sharp or **Sharpe,** Yorks, same crest
Sharp, a griffin's head erased per pale or and sa, gorged with a ducal coronet counterchanged cf 66 11
Sharp, Russia a plume of ostrich-feathers ppr *Virtute et vigilantia* 115 1
Sharp, out of a ducal coronet per pale or and sa, a wolf's head counterchanged cf 30 5
Sharp, J Fox, Esquire, Treneere, Torquay an eagle's head erased az, ducally gorged or and holding in the beak a pheon point downwards arg *Mens conscia recti*
Sharpe, Wallace William Jessopp, Solicitor and Public Notary, Falmouth, an eagle's head erased az, holding in the beak a pheon arg *Procédez, ne regredez*
Sharpe, a wolf's head erased per pale sa and or 30 8
Sharpe of Brighton, a wolf's head erased sa ducally gorged or
Sharpe, a wolf's head erased per pale or and sa, gorged with a ducal coronet counterchanged cf 30 8
Sharpe, James Birch of Glenturf, Camberley Surrey Major in the Royal Engineers, in front of a wolf's head erased per pale sa and or gorged with a collar vair, three roses fessewise gu, leaved, barbed, and seeded ppr *Knowledge is power* 30 3
Sharpe, Henry Birch, 2, Albert Street, Lower Grosvenor Place, S W, same crest and motto
Sharpe, James William, Woodroffe, Porterlington Road, Bournemouth, same crest and motto
Sharpe of Melton, Suff, a wolf's head erased per pale or and az, and charged on the neck with a horse-shoe arg *En Dieu est tout* cf 30 8
Sharpe, Ireland, a griffin's head erased per pale or and sa., ducally gorged counterchanged cf 66 2
Sharpe, Rev Thomas Wetherhead Beddington, Surrey, in front of an eagle's head erased or, the neck encircled with four plain collars az, a pheon point downwards of the last
Sharpe, on a ducal coronet or, a peacock sejant ppr
Sharpe of Baydon Cumb, a peacock sejant ppr in a ducal coronet or, holding in the beak an ear of wheat of the second, leaved vert
Sharpe of Rolleston Leics, and Winge, Rutl, on a ducal coronet or a peacock sitting ppr, holding in the beak an ear of wheat of the first bladed vert and charged upon the breast with a crescent for difference
Sharpey of Sharpel Kent, a cubit arm vested az, with three puffs arg, holding in the hand ppr three spears, two in saltier and one in pale, headed of the second, the staves or
Sharples of Trickleton, Lancs, a dexter hand brandishing a sword ppr 212 13
Shattock, Wilts, a dexter hand holding a lion's gamb erased ppr 220. 10
Shaunty, Ireland a chevalier brandishing a flaming sword ppr. chained by the neck or
Shaw-Lefevre, *see* Eversley, Viscount
Shaw, Scotland, a phœnix or, in flames of fire ppr 82 2
Shaw, Alexander-, of Caledon, co Tyrone (1) In flames ppr, a phœnix arg (*for Shaw*) 82 2 (2) An arm in armour embowed grasping a sword all ppr, hilt and pommel or (*for Alexander*) *Vincit amor patriæ* 195 2
Shaw-Hamilton, Very Rev Robert James, D D Dean of Armagh, Ireland (1) In front of two battleaxes in saltire an oak tree fructed, all ppr, the trunk transfixed with a frame-saw or (*for Hamilton*) *Through* (2) A pelican in her piety ppr charged with a covered cup gu (*for Shaw*) *I die for those I love*
Shaw of Norton House, Denby, Pembrokesh, on a bugle horn in fess, a swan with wings elevated ppr *Lætitia et spe immortalitatis*
Shaw, William Otho Nicholson, of Arrowe Park, Chesh (1) A dove bendy sinister of six arg and sa, holding in the beak an olive-branch ppr, the dexter claw resting on a lozenge ermines (*for Shaw*) 92 9 (2) Out of a ducal coronet gu a lion's head erm (*for Nicholson*) *Per castra ad astra.* 17 5
Shaw of Heath Charnock, Preston, Hey Side, and Bullhaghe, all in Lancs, a falcon volant ppr 88 3
Shaw, Ireland, a cock's head issuing gu
Shaw, Scotland, a demi-lion rampant gu, armed and langued az *Mens immota manet* 10 3
Shaw, a demi lion gu holding in the dexter paw a sword ppr *Fide et fortitudine* 14 12
Shaw, a lion rampant gu armed and langued az *Mens immota* 1 13
Shaw of Woodhouse, Staffs, a hind's head quarterly arg and or, pierced through the neck by an arrow headed az, the feather broken and drooping arg
Shaw, Sir Eyre Massey, K C B, 114, Belgrave Road a hind's head sa. transfixed through the neck with an arrow or *Te ipsum nosce*
Shaw, Sir Robert, Bart, J P, D L, of Bushy Park, co Dublin, a hind's head couped az, the neck transpierced by an arrow in bend or, flighted *Te ipsum nosce* cf 124 6
Shaw of London, and Colchester, Essex, a hind's head or, pierced through by an arrow of the same, headed and feathered arg cf 124 6
Shaw of Ardesley, Yorks, a talbot passant ermines, eared arg 54 1
Shaw of Woodfield Yorks, same crest 54 1
Shaw, John Lancaster Esquire, B A (Oxon), Redgehill, Torquay, a talbot passant sa, charged on the body with two fleurs-de lis or holding in the mouth a trefoil slipped vert *Prudens qui patiens* 314 5
Shaw-Hellier, Thomas Bradney the Wodehouse, Wombourne, Wolverhampton (1) A cock arg, guttee-de-sang combed and wattled gu (*for Hellier*) (2) A hind's head quarterly arg and or, pierced through the neck with an arrow headed az, the feather broken and dropping arg (*for Shaw*)

Shaw, Charles Edward, Esquire, M.P., of Rickerscote, Staffs, five arrows, one in pale and four in saltire, banded. *Nil desperandum.*

Shaw, Sir John Charles Kenward, Bart., J.P., of Eltham, Kent, six arrows interlaced saltirewise or, flighted, headed, and encircled by a belt gu., buckle and pendant of the first. *Vincit qui patitur.*

Shaw of London, an arrow in pale or, feathered and headed arg., passing through a mascle sa.

Shaw, Shropsh., Chesh., and Surrey, six arrows interlaced in saltier or, flighted and headed arg., and tied together by a belt gu., the buckle and pendant of the first.

Shaw, Bart., Scotland, a demi-savage affrontée, wreathed about the head and waist ppr., holding in the dexter hand a key or, the sinister resting on a club reversed, also ppr. *I mean well.*

Shaw, Scotland, a demi-savage wreathed about the middle ppr. *I mean well.* 186. 1

Shaw-Stewart, Sir Michael Robert, Bart., of Greenock and Blackhall, Renfrewsh.: (1) A lion's head erased gu. (*for Stewart*). 17. 2. (2) A demi-savage wreathed about the head and middle with laurel, and holding a club over his shoulder, all ppr. (*for Shaw*). *Spero meliora.—I mean well.* 186. 1

Shaw-Yates, Ernest Bentley, of Banwell Castle, Somers.: (1) A talbot passant ermines, eared arg. (*for Shaw*). 312. 8. (2) Upon a mount vert, a goat's head erased arg., armed or, charged on the neck with a pellet, and surmounting two branches of oak in saltire ppr., fructed or (*for Yates*). 312. 9. *Mens immotus.*

Shaw, Scotland, a hand holding up a covered cup ppr. *I mean well.* 217. 11

Shaw of Elmwood, Lanark, Scotland, a dexter hand ppr., holding a covered cup or. *Bene denoto.* 217. 11

Shaw of London, issuing from rays of the sun or, an arm ppr., vested sa., the hand holding up a mort-head ppr. 208. 10

Shaw-Mackenzie of Newhall: (1) A stag's head and neck affrontée couped ppr. (*for Mackenzie*). 119. 12. (2) A dexter cubit arm couped and holding a dagger erect, all ppr. (*for Shaw*). *Perseverando.—Fide et fortitudine.* 212. 9

Shaw-Kennedy, John, 1, South Eaton Place, S.W., a palm-branch ppr.

Shawe, five arrows, one in pale and four in saltier, bound by a ribbon. 173. 3

Shawe of Kesgrave Hall, Suff., a falcon volant ppr. 88. 3

Shawe, Henry Cunliffe, Esquire, of Weddington Hall, Nuneaton, Warw., a falcon volant arg. 88. 3

Shawe-Storey of Arcot Hall, Cramlington, Northumb.: (1) A falcon sa., within a chaplet of laurel ppr., charged on the breast with an Eastern cross or, and for distinction charged also with a cross crosslet of the last. (2) A hind's head couped arg., charged with three lozenges, one and two, erm., holding in the mouth an arrow in pale or, flighted arg. *Sola virtus reddit nobilem.*

Shaxton of Buthell, Norf., out of a ducal coronet gu., a talbot's head sa., collared, eared, and ringed or.

Shayer, on the top of a tree a pelican in her piety with wings elevated and addorsed.

Sheaffe, Bart. (*extinct*), of Edswall, co. Clare, out of a mural coronet arg., a cubit arm vested gu., cuffed vert, the hand grasping a sword in bend sinister ppr., the hilt and pommel or, between a branch of laurel and another of oak, also ppr.

Shearer, Scotland, on a chapeau a dexter hand holding up by the band a garb, all ppr.

Shearer, Lieutenant-Colonel Johnston, Simla, India, a garb or, banded with a serpent ppr. *Vive ut postea vivas.*

Shearman of Grange, Ballycarron, and Kilcreene, co. Kilkenny, Ireland, a dove holding in its beak an olive-branch, all ppr. *Fide et amore.* 92. 5

Shears, a talbot's head erased ppr., collared and lined or. *cf.* 56. 1

Shearwood, a raven sa. 107. 14

Sheath of Wyberton, near Boston, Lancs, a lion passant ppr. *Leniter sustineo.* 6. 2

Shebbeare of Shebbeare-Town, Abbotsham, Devonsh., a lion rampant ppr., holding in the dexter paw a laurel-branch vert. *Cum numine benigno.*

Shed, a tent or. 158. 7

Sheddan, Scotland, a dove volant or, holding in the beak an olive-branch vert. 93. 10

Shedden of Spring Hill, Isle of Wight, of Auchingree, Ayrsh., and Paulersbury Park, Northants, a hermit's head and shoulders affrontée ppr., vested in russet, his hood thrown back. *Fidem meam observabo.* 192. 3

Shee, out of a ducal coronet or, a mount vert, thereon a stag at gaze ppr. 118. 7

Shee of Cloran, co. Tipperary, Ireland, a swan rising sa. *Vincit veritas.* 99. 12

Shee, out of a ducal coronet or, on a mount vert, a swan with wings addorsed ppr.

Shee, a swan rising with wings addorsed. *Cruce salus.* 99. 12

Shee, Bart. (*extinct*), Ireland, a swan with wings addorsed sa., beaked gu. *Vincit veritas.* 99. 12

Sheehy, Ireland, an arm in armour couped below the elbow and erect holding in the hand a sword, the blade entwined with a snake, all ppr. *cf.* 210. 2

Sheen, a sword erect, the blade enfiled with a rebel's head, all ppr. 191. 9

Sheen, out of a mural coronet a staff raguly vert. *cf.* 147. 10

Sheepshanks, Rev. Thomas, of Arthington Hall, Leeds, Yorks, on a mount vert, a sheep passant arg. 131. 9

Sheere, out of a ducal coronet a swan with wings addorsed.

Sheffield, Duke of Buckingham and Normanby (*extinct*), a boar's head erased at the neck or. *Comiter sed fortiter.* 41. 5

Sheffield, Earl of (Holroyd), a demi-griffin segreant with wings endorsed sa., holding between the claws a ducal coronet or. *Quem te Deus esse jussit.*

Sheffield, Sir Berkeley Digby George, Bart., of Normanby, Lincs, a boar's head and neck erased or. *Comiter sed fortiter.* 41. 5

Sheffield, Charles Edward, Romford, Essex, a garb in fesse or, surmounted by a boar's head and neck erased az., langued and crined of the first. *Divino tutamine.* 249. 19

Sheffield of Croxby, Lincs, a boar's head and neck erased gu. 41. 5

Sheffield, three ears of rye or. 154. 6

Sheil, Ireland, out of a ducal coronet or, a triple plume of twelve ostrich-feathers, three, four, and five. 114. 6

Sheild of Uppingham, Rutl.: (1) A demi-ram or, semée of mullets gu. (*for Sheild*). *cf.* 130. 13. (2) Upon a mount vert, a demi-wolf ppr., gorged with a collar sa., supporting a javelin erect, also ppr. (*for Gilson*). *Scuto magnis quam gladio.*

Sheill of Nantes, France, an arm couped at the elbow and erect vested gu., encircled by a ducal coronet or, holding in the hand a sword ppr., pommel and hilt of the second. *Omne solum forti patriæ.*

Sheill of Smithfield, Forfarsh., a cubit arm erect surrounded by flames of fire, the hand grasping a dagger, all ppr. *Agere et pati.* *cf.* 212. 3

Sheils-Eccleston, *see* Eccleston.

Sheils, Scotland, a boar's head couped. *Be traist.* 43. 1

Sheils of Drumshallon, co. Louth, Ireland, a cubit arm erect vested gu., enfiled by a ducal coronet or, grasping in the hand a dagger ppr. *Omne solum forti patria.*

Sheircliff of Shirecliffe, Yorks, a cutlass in pale arg., hilt and pommel or, enfiled on the blade with a leopard's face of the last embrued at the mouth gu. 22. 1

Shekell of Pebworth, Glouc., an esquire's helmet ppr. 180. 3

Shelbery or **Shelbury** of London, Surrey, and Colchester, Essex, a lion's head erased per saltire arg. and gu. 17. 8

Shelburne, Earl of, *see* Lansdowne, Marquess of.

Sheldon of Besley, Worcs., Rowley Regis, Staffs, and Henry James Sheldon, Esquire, of Brailes House, Warw., a sheldrake ppr. *Optimum pati.*

Sheldon, John Prince, Esquire, J.P., the Brund, Sheen, Buxton, Derby, same crest. *Esse quam videri.*

Sheldon, Middx., a sheldrake arg., beaked gu., and holding in the beak a rose of the last, seeded or, slipped and leaved vert.

Sheldon of Aberton, Worcs., and Upton-on-Severne, a sheldrake ppr., charged for distinction with an escallop gu.

Sheldrake, a sheldrake ppr.

Shelletoe, a lion rampant arg., ducally crowned or, in flames of fire ppr. *cf.* 1. 12

Shelley, Sir Charles, Bart., of Castle Goring, Sussex, a griffin's head erased arg., ducally gorged or. *Fey e fidalgia.* *cf.* 66. 11

Shelley, Sir John, Bart., J.P., same crest. *Comme je trouve.* *cf.* 66. 11

Shelley or **Shelly,** Sussex, a griffin's head erased arg., ducally gorged or. *cf.* 66. 2

Shelley, Sussex, a griffin's head erased arg., beaked and ducally gorged or. *cf.* 66. 2

Shelley, a wolf's head couped between two wings or, charged with as many bars gu.

Shelly, Suff , a griffin's head erased arg , ducally gorged or cf 66 2

Shelly, John, Princess House, Plymouth, a unicorn's head erased arg *Pro patria ejusque libertate* 49 5

Shelmerdine of Langport, Somers , an escallop ppr *Nil desperandum* 141 14

Shelton, a Saracen's head ppr 190 14

Shelton, Notts and Yorks, a lion passant gu , gorged with a chaplet of laurel vert cf 6 2

Shennan, Watson, Conical Hills, Otago, New Zealand, on a dexter gauntlet or, a falcon close perched ppr *Virtute duce*

Shenton, a dexter hand holding an open book ppr 215 10

Shepard or **Sheppard,** Bucks, two battle axes in saltier or 172 4

Shepard, Sussex, and of Mendlesham, Suff a lion's head sa , issuing from a tower or

Shepard or **Shepperd** of Chelsbury and Roulwright, Oxon , a ram passant arg , armed or, between two branches of laurel vert

Shepard of Battersea Surrey, and Peasmarsh, Sussex, on a mount vert a stag current regardant ppr , attired arg 118 12

Shepard or **Shepherd,** Devonsh , on a mount vert a stag lodged regardant arg , vulned in the shoulder gu cf 115 9

Shepard or **Shepherd,** Kent and Sussex, a stag lodged regardant arg cf 115 9

Sheperd, two halberds in saltier ppr 172 4

Shepheard and **Sheppard,** a dexter hand ppr holding up a cross crosslet fitched sa 221 14

Shepheard of London same crest *Dextra cruce vincit* 221 14

Shepheard of Ixning, Suff , a ram passant ppr cf 131 13

Shepherd, on a mural coronet a wyvern with wings expanded holding in the mouth a broken spear

Shepherd, a cock gu , holding in the beak a cinquefoil stalked vert cf 91 2

Shepherd of London a buck lodged regardant or, wreathed round the neck with laurel vert cf 115 9

Shepherd, Devonsh , on a mount vert, a stag lodged regardant arg , vulned in the shoulder gu cf 115 9

Shepherd-Cross, Herbert, 19, Queen's Gate Gardens, S W (1) A stork ppr , resting the dexter foot on a fountain and holding in the beak a cross crosslet, all between eight bulrushes, four on either side (*for Cross*) (2) On a mount vert a ram passant in front of a gate, and all between two trees

Shepherd, *alias* **Thwaites,** of Miln-Hay in Heanor and Remerston, Derbysh , a hind's head 124 1

Shepherd of Nun Green, Surrey a mount vert, thereon in front of two shepherd's crooks in saltire or, a lamb passant arg 227 2

Shepley, a lion sejant or, collared gu cf 7 4

Shepley, Surrey and Yorks, a buck's head erased ppr 121 2

Sheppard, Captain Henry, J P , of Clifton, Glinrone, Roscrea, Tipperary Ireland a hand holding a shepherd's crook *Deus pastor meus* 219 8

Sheppard, Rev Henry Drought, D D , incumbent of Christ Church Belfast, a demi man girt round the loins with a goat skin holding in the dexter hand a sword, and in the sinister a shepherd's crook all ppr *Dirigo et defendo*

Sheppard, Shropsh , a ram statant arg , attired or 131 13

Sheppard of Frome Selwood, Somers , a ram passant ppr , between two olive-branches vert

Sheppard, Rev Henry Alexander Graham Rednock House Stirling, same crest

Sheppard, Osborne, Glyn Clydach, co Neath on a mount vert, a stag courant regardant

Sheppard, Cotton-, Bart (*extinct*), of Thornton Hall Bucks (1) A lamb passant arg between two laurel-branches vert (*for Sheppard*) (2) On a mount vert a falcon with wings expanded and belled or (*for Cotton*) *Nec timeo, nec sperno*

Sheppard, Bart of Thornton Hall, Bucks same crests and motto

Sheppard, Ireland, a bull's head erased az 44 3

Sheppard, on a mount vert, a stag in full chase regardant or 118 12

Sheppard of Peasmarsh, Sussex, issuing out of the tower of a castle embattled or, a lion's head sa

Sheppard of Campsey Ashe Suff issuing from a tower or a talbot's head sa.

Shepperd of Kirbydon, Norf , a demi buck regardant ppr attired or

Shepperson, on a mural coronet a wyvern displayed *Ligurio rores* 70 6

Shepstone, Sir Theophilus, K C M G , of Cape Colony, in front of two assegais in saltire ppr a demi-eagle displayed arg , gorged with a wreath of oak vert

Sherar of Shrewsbury, on a chapeau gu , turned up erm , a cubit arm in pale vested az , cuffed of the second, holding in the hand ppr a garb or

Sherard, Baron, *see* Harborough

Sherard, Baron (Sherard) out of a ducal coronet per pale nebuly arg and az , a peacock's tail erect ppr banded or and gu *Hostis honori invidia* cf 115 6

Sherard or **Sherrard,** out of a ducal coronet or, a peacock's tail in pale ppr *Hostis honori invidia* 115 6

Sherborne, Baron (Dutton), a plume of five ostrich feathers arg , az , or, vert and gu *Servabo fidem*

Sherborne of Ribleton Lancs, a unicorn's head arg , ermed and armed or 49 7

Sherbrooke, Viscount (Rt Hon the late Sir Robert Lowe, P C , G C B , D C L., LL.D , F R S), of Sherbrooke, Surrey, in front of a wolf's head erased ppr gorged with a collar gemel or, two mullets of the last pierced gu

Sherbrooke, a fleur-de lis *Vi si non consilio* 148 2

Sherbrooke, a horse's head couped arg , charged with three bars gu cf 50 13

Sherbrooke, William, Oxton Hall, South well (1) Same crest as above (2) A wolf's head erased arg *Vi si non consilio.*

Sherburne, Bart (*extinct*), of Stonyhurst, Lancs, a unicorn's head couped arg , armed or 49 7

Sherburne, a unicorn's head erased lozengy or and vert, armed and maned of the first *Nec temere nec timide* 49 5

Sherd, a bugle-horn arg , strung and garnished sa 228 11

Sherfeild, on a rock sa a fire-beacon or, flammant gu cf 177 8

Sherfield, on the top of a tower a Cornish chough rising, all ppr 156 13

Shergold, a demi lion rampant gu holding an escallop az 13 10

Sheridan, a dexter hand gu , holding a cross crosslet fitched or 221 14

Sheridan, Ireland an angel in a praying posture between two laurel-branches, all ppr 184 2

Sheridan, Middx , out of a ducal coronet a stag's head 120 7

Sheridan, Algernon Thomas Brinsley, of Frampton Court Dorset, out of a ducal coronet a stag's head ppr. *Cervus lacessitus leone* 120 7

Sheridan or **Sheriden,** on a chapeau gu turned up erm , a lion's head erased 17 9

Sheriff or **Sherive** of Bogbye, Warw , a lion's gamb erased or, holding a branch of dates, the fruit of the first, in the pods arg the stalk and leaves vert.

Sheriff, Scotland, a lion's gamb erased or holding a laurel branch vert *Esse quam videri* cf 37 4

Sheriffe of London, a dragon rampant gu holding between the claws a chaplet of the last, leaved vert

Sheringley of Dublin, a hand holding a helmet adorned with a plume of feathers arg and sa

Sherington of London, a talbot sa , eared arg cf 54 2

Sherington of Medburne and Lacocke, Wilts, Worcs , and Sherington, Norf., a scorpion in pale or the tail in chief between two elephant's tusks, the upper part chequy arg and az , the bottom gu , each charged with a cross formee sa

Sherland, a bull's scalp arg 123 8

Sherland of Sheppey, Kent, and Norf , a griffin segreant arg , holding in the dexter claw a fleur de lis or cf 62 2

Sherland, Devonsh , a sea horse arg , charged with an anchor sa

Sherley, a crosier or 170 14

Sherlock, Ireland, among flags vert a duck az 102 5

Sherlock of London, a dolphin haurient sa 140 11

Sherlock, Lieutenant-Colonel Wright, Barradaw, co Cork, a pelican in her piety ppr , charged on the breast with a fleur de lis az. *Prest pour mon pais* cf 98 8

Sherlock of Grace Dieu, co Waterford, and Sherlockstown, co Kildare, a pelican in her piety ppr 98 8

Sherlock, Thomas Thierri, 15, Harcourt Street, Dublin, same crest

Sherlock of Cahir co Tipperary, Ireland, a pelican in her piety ppr , charged on the breast with a crescent for difference cf 98 8

Sherlock, Wright, Barradaw, co Cork, a pelican in her piety charged on the breast with a fleur de-lis az *Prest pour mon pais*

Sherman of Littlehinton Cambs, and Croydon, Surrey, a demi lion rampant sa , holding a sprig of holly vert

Sherman of Ipswich, Suff., a sea-lion sejant per pale or and arg., guttée-de-poix, finned of the first. *cf.* 20. 2

Sherman, Devonsh. and London, a sea-lion sejant per pale or and arg., guttée-de-poix, finned of the first, charged on the shoulders with a crescent for difference. *cf.* 20. 2

Sherman, Suff., a sea-lion sejant sa., charged on the shoulder with three bezants, two and one. *cf.* 20. 2

Sherman of Newark, Leics., a sea-lion sejant arg., guttée-de-poix, finned or. *cf.* 20. 2

Sherman of Ottery St. Mary, Devonsh., a sea-lion sejant sa., guttée-d'or, finned ppr. *cf.* 20. 2

Sherman, a lion's head erased gardant erm.

Sherman of Coniral Hills and of Perketoi, New Zealand, at present residing at Eslemont, Moffat, N.B., on a dexter gauntlet or, a falcon perched ppr. *Virtute duce.* 86. 13

Sherman, Norf., an adder nowed ppr., thereon a pigeon arg., membered gu. 92. 10

Sherrard, Lincs and Leics., out of a ducal coronet or, a peacock's tail erect ppr. *Hostis honori invidia.* 115. 6

Sherrif, Scotland, a lion's gamb erased or, holding a branch of laurel vert. *Esse quam videri.* *cf.* 37. 4

Shershall, a lion sejant sa. 8. 8

Sherston, Major Charles Davis, Evercreech House, Bath, Somers., a stag lodged regardant or, armed and hoofed gu., charged on the shoulder with a cinquefoil vert.

Sherwen, Rev. William, Dean Rectory, Cockermouth, a demi-man holding in his dexter hand a sword, and in his sinister a staff, all ppr.

Sherwin, Hants, and of Bramcote Hills, Notts, an eagle or, pellettée, with wings expanded az. *cf.* 77. 5

Sherwin or **Shirwin** of Chichester, Sussex, a demi-man holding in his dexter hand a sword, and in his sinister a staff, all ppr.

Sherwin, Ireland, a demi-man couped holding in his dexter hand a sword, and in his sinister Jacob's staff, all ppr.

Sherwood, a dexter hand ppr., holding a branch of a rose-tree arg., leaved vert. 218. 10

Sherwood of Colchester, Essex, in front of an olive-tree eradicated ppr., two bill-hooks in saltire or. *In via sternere.*

Shettle, Warw. and Dorset, on a rock a wyvern statant with wings elevated and endorsed. *Lente et certus.* 69. 11

Shettow, a cubit arm erect holding in the hand an étoile.

Shevill of Bishop Wearmouth, Durh., out of a naval coronet or, a demi-lion rampant gu., holding between the paws a ship's sail arg., charged with an anchor sa. *Mon privilège et mon devoir.*

Shewen, an antelope trippant vert. 126. 6

Shewersden, Essex, a demi-talbot arg., eared sa., collared gu., holding between the paws a lozenge of the second.

Shiel, Ireland, an eagle's head between two wings ppr. 84. 2

Shield, Northumb., a buck trippant ppr., charged on the breast with an escutcheon sa., thereon an escallop arg. *cf.* 117. 7

Shield, Rutl., a dexter cubit arm grasping a scimitar. *Pro lege Rege grege.* 213. 5

Shields, Scotland, a dexter hand gu. 222. 14

Shields or **Shiells,** Scotland, a dexter hand gu., holding an escutcheon az. *cf.* 219. 7

Shields, an escutcheon az. 176. 10

Shields, a demi-lion rampant or. 10. 2

Shields, Ireland, a demi-lion rampant or, holding with the paws an anchor az. 12. 12

Shields, a demi-leopard rampant or. *cf.* 23. 13

Shiell, Anthony George, Esquire, of Middle Temple, London, a cubit arm erect surrounded by flames of fire, the hand grasping a dagger, all ppr. *Agere et pati.* *cf.* 212. 3

Shiels, Scotland, a boar's head couped ppr. *Be traist.* 43. 1

Shiels, a mullet pierced or.

Shiercliffe, a falchion erect enfiled with a leopard's face or. 22. 1

Shiers, a dexter hand holding a palm-branch ppr. 219. 11

Shiers, Bart. (*extinct*), of Slyfield, Surrey, a demi-lion rampant sa., supporting an escallop or. 13. 10

Shiffner, a greyhound's head erased gu. 61. 4

Shiffner, Rev. Sir George Croxton, Bart., M.A., of Coombe, Sussex, Rector of Hamsey, Sussex, an estoile or, between the rays six annulets az. 313. 15

Shikleworth, a garb or, banded sa., and in the band a sickle arg. *cf.* 153. 2

Shillinglaw, Scotland, a bee-hive with bees volant and counter-volant ppr. 137. 7

Shilton, on a ducal coronet or, a dolphin naiant az. 140. 4

Shinglehurst of London, a battle-axe erect ppr. 172. 3

Shipey or **Shippey,** on a chapeau sa., turned up erm., an escallop of the first between two wings or. 141. 11

Shipham, a demi-reermouse or bat with wings expanded gu. and arg., ducally crowned or, vulned of the first.

Shipley, a hand ppr., holding an olive-branch vert. 219. 9

Shipley of Twyford, Hants, out of an earl's coronet or, the bust of a Moorish prince ppr., habited of the first, wreathed about the temples arg. and sa. *Nec placida contenta quieta est.*

Shipman, Notts, a leopard sejant arg., spotted sa., resting the dexter paw on a ship's rudder az.

Shipman of Welby, Heref., a demi-ostrich with wings expanded arg., ducally gorged and beaked or, holding in the beak a key az., and vulned in the breast gu.

Shippard, Sir Sidney Godolphin Alexander, K.C.M.G., 15, West Halkin Street, Belgrave Square, S.W., a ram passant arg., armed or, between two laurel-branches vert. *Vi et virtute.*

Shippard, out of a ducal coronet a peacock's tail, all ppr. 115. 6

Shipperdson of Pidding Hall, Garth, and Murton, Durh., a hand issuing out of a cloud and grasping a sword ppr. *Nubem eripiam.*

Shipton, an eel naiant ppr. 142. 10

Shipton, Yorks, a lion rampant. 1. 13

Shirley, *see* Ferrers, Earl.

Shirley, Scotland, a crosier or. 170. 14

Shirley, a Saracen's head in profile couped ppr., wreathed or and az. 190. 14

Shirley, Sewallis Evelyn, Esquire, Ettington Park, Warw., a Saracen's head couped at the neck ppr., wreathed or and az. *Honor virtutis præmium.*—*Loyal suis je.* 190. 14

Shirley of Shirley, Derbysh., a Saracen's head in profile couped at the neck ppr., and wreathed about the temples or and az. *Badges:* (1) A horse-shoe. (2) A Bourchier knot.

Shirley of London, three broad arrows, two in saltier and one in pale, or, plumed arg., enfiled with a garland of laurel vert.

Shirley, Sussex, out of a ducal coronet a stag's head, all arg. 120. 7

Shirreff, a lion rampant double-queued az., armed and langued or. 1. 14

Shirt, a griffin's head between two wings. 65. 11

Shivez, a demi-cat ppr. *Virtute non vi.* 26. 11

Shone, a dolphin naiant gu. 140. 5

Shoobridge of Uckfield, Sussex, a leopard's face or, between two wings sa.

Shore, *see* Teignmouth, Baron.

Shore, a stork holding in its dexter claw a stone ppr. *Perimus licitis.* 105. 6

Shore, Derbysh., a stork regardant arg., resting the dexter claw on a pellet.

Shore, Derbysh., a crane ppr., resting the dexter claw on a mullet sa.

Shore of Norton Hall, Derbysh., a stork regardant arg., beaked and membered gu., holding in its dexter claw a pebble, and gorged with a collar gemel sa., holding in its beak a holly-leaf slipped vert. *Non dormit qui custodit.*

Shorrock, Eccles, Esquire, of Law Hill House, Blackburn, Lancs, a demi-stag ppr., semée of mullets and supporting between the legs a cross patée fitchée, all sa. *Persevera*nda.

Short, Scotland, a ship in flames ppr. *Spes in extremum.*

Short of Tenterden, Kent, a griffin's head or, between two wings az., semée-d'étoiles gold. *cf.* 65. 11

Short, a griffin's head arg., holding in the beak a trefoil slipped vert. *cf.* 66. 1

Short of Edington Grove, Lincs, a griffin's head and neck with wings elevated sa., collared erm. *Sinceritas.* *cf.* 67. 11

Short, Essex, a griffin's head between two wings. 65. 11

Short of Newham Hall, Yorks, a griffin's head couped or, between two wings az. 65. 11

Short of Bickham, Devonsh., a griffin's head or, between two wings az., each charged with an estoile of the first. *cf.* 65. 11

Short of Lincs, a griffin's head and neck, wings elevated sa., collared erm. *Sinceritas.*

Short, E. W., Esquire, of 9, Woodside, Sunderland, upon waves of the sea a ship in flames ppr. *Spes in extremum.*

Shortall, John George, Esquire, of Chicago, U.S.A., a stag trippant ppr., supporting with the dexter fore-paw a cross crosslet az *Certavi et vici* cf 117 8

Shorter of London a griffin's head sa between two wings or, collared and beaked of the last 67 7

Shorthose, a wyvern az 70 1

Shorthose, a hand holding a dagger in pale point downwards, all ppr

Shortland, a sea horse az, ducally gorged arg

Shortland, a sea-horse rampant az, ducally gorged or

Shortreed, Scotland, a dexter hand holding a scimitar ppr *Pro aris et focis* 213 5

Shortsey, a wolf passant holding in the mouth a fish

Shotter of Farnham, Surrey, a demi-lion rampant erminois, charged on the shoulder with two arrows in saltier gu, flighted ppr, holding in the paws a slip of oak leaves and acorns, also ppr

Shove of Isle of Sheppey, out of a ducal coronet or, a griffin's head holding in its beak a cross crosslet ppr cf 67 9

Shoyswell, Sussex a horse's head erased arg, gorged with a collar sa, charged with three horse shoes of the first

Shrawley of London, a hind's head arg, pierced through by an arrow in bend or cf 124. 1

Shrewsbury, Earl of (Chetwynd Talbot) (1) On a chapeau gu, turned up erm, a lion statant or the tail extended (*for Talbot*) 4 8 (2) A goat's head erased arg, armed or (*for Chetwynd*) *Prest d'accomplir* 128 5

Shrigley, a hand holding a bull's head erased ppr

Shrimpton, a leopard passant ppr cf 24 2

Shrubb of Merrist Wood and Stoke Surrey, on an oak branch in fess vert fructed ppr, an eagle close regardant of the last charged on the breast with an escallop gu *Sub cruce semper viridis*

Shrubsole of Canterbury, Kent a cubit arm erect vested gu, cuffed arg, holding in the hand ppr a cherry tree branch fructed of the first

Shuckburgh, Sir Stewkley Frederick Draycott Bart, of Shuckburgh Daventry, Warw, a black a Moor couped at the waist ppr, holding in his dexter hand a dart or *Hæc manus ob patriam*

Shuckburgh, Richard Henry, Esquire, of Bourton Hall, Warw, a demi Moor ppr, wreathed about the temples or and sa, habited arg, semée of mullets pierced, also sa, and holding in the dexter hand an arrow point downwards ppr *Vigilate et orate* 264 3

Shuckburgh, Wilts a demi Moor wreathed about the head, holding in the dexter hand an arrow in bend sinister ppr *Hæc manus ob patriam*

Shuckburgh, Blencowe-, Rev Charles a demi-Moor ppr wreathed about the temples or and sa habited arg semee of mullets pierced of the third, and holding in the dexter hand an arrow point downwards ppr *Vigilate et orate* 264 3

Shuckforth, Norf, an eagle's head erased ppr 83 2

Shugborough, Warw, a demi-Moor ppr, wreathed about the head or holding in the dexter hand an arrow of the first

Shugborough and **Shuckburgh,** Warw and Northamp., a demi Moor ppr, wreathed about the head or vested arg, with an under vestment of the second, holding in the dexter hand an arrow of the same

Shuldham, Baron Shuldham (*extinct*), a griffin passant arg *Post nubila Phœbus* 63 2

Shuldham of Shuldham and Kettlestone Norf and Marlesford, Suff, same crest and motto

Shuldham, Edmund Anderson of Dunmanway co Cork, and Ballymulvey and Moig House co Longford, Ireland, same crest and motto

Shuldham, Frank Naunton Quantock, J P, Norton Manor Stoke under-Ham same crest and motto

Shum, a cock regardant ppr collared or from the collar a bugle horn pendent of the last

Shum-Storey of Ham, Surrey (1) A falcon sa, within a chaplet of laurel ppr, charged on the breast with an Eastern crown or, also charged with a saltier gu for difference (*for Storey*) (2) A cock regardant ppr, collared or, from the collar a bugle-horn pendent or (*for Shum*)

Shurland, Ireland, a sea horse arg, charged on the shoulder with an anchor sa

Shurmer, out of a ducal coronet or an arm in armour ppr holding in the hand a cross crosslet fitched sa

Shury, out of a ducal coronet or a dexter arm in armour embowed ppr garnished of the first, holding in the hand, also ppr, a cross crosslet fitched sa.

Shute, Baron, *see* Barrington Viscount

Shute of Shute, near Crediton Devonsh, a griffin sejant or, pierced in the breast by an arrow arg *Ictus non victus — Vertue sans peur* 62 12

Shute, Hants a griffin sejant or, pierced through the breast by a broken spear ppr cf 62 12

Shute, General Sir Charles Cameron K C B, C B, of 12, Brunswick Place Brighton, and Dinsdale, West Cliff, Bournemouth, and Carlton Club a griffin sejant arg, transfixed through the breast with a broken spear ppr *Ictus non victus*

Shute, Cumb and Yorks, a griffin sejant or pierced in the breast by a broken sword-blade arg vulned gu cf 62 12

Shuter of Winterbourne Wilts on a mount vert, a leopard sejant ppr, ducally gorged and lined or cf 24 12

Shuttleworth, Lancs and Durh, a bear passant arg

Shuttleworth, Frank, of Old Warden Park, Biggleswade, issuant from a chaplet of roses gu, a cubit arm in armour the hand in a gauntlet ppr holding a shuttle in bend sinister sa, tipped and furnished or *Esto velocior vita* 211 3

Shuttleworth of Hodsock Park Notts, a cubit arm erect in armour ppr, holding in the gauntlet a weaver's shuttle sa, tipped and furnished with quills of yarn, the threads pendent or *Utile dulce*

Shuttleworth, Ashton John, Hathersage Hall, Derbysh same crest. *In Domino confide*

Shuttleworth of Gawthorp, Lancs same crest

Shuttleworth of Great Bowden, Leics same crest *Æquanimiter*

Shuttleworth, Baron (Kay-Shuttleworth) of Gawthorpe Hall, Lancs (1) A cubit arm in armour ppr, grasping in the gauntlet a weaver's shuttle sa tipped and furnished with quills of yarn, the threads pendent or (*for Shuttleworth*) (2) On a crescent az a goldfinch ppr (*for Kay*) *Kynd kynn knawe kepe —Prudentia et justitia*

Shyer, a tower domed cf 157 15

Sibbald, Scotland two laurel branches in orle ppr *Sae bauld* 146 5

Sibbald, Scotland, two laurel branches in orle vert 146 5

Sibbald of St. Nicholas, Aberdeensh, Scotland, a hand erect apaumee ppr *Ora et labora* 222 14

Sibbald of Westcott, Cornw, a hand erect ppr holding a sword *Sae bauld* 212 13

Sibbald, Sir John 18, Great King Street Edinburgh, a dexter hand couped at the wrist holding a scroll, all ppr *Sursum specto*

Sibbald, Scotland, a hand holding a closed book ppr *Ora et labora* 215 4

Sibbald of Gladswood, Berwick, a dexter arm in armour embowed grasping a scymitar ppr *Sae bauld.* 196 10

Sibbald of Kipps, Scotland a moor head ppr *Me certum mors certa facit* 193 11

Sibbald of Balgonie, Fifesh, Scotland, a cross moline gu *Justitia* 165 3

Sibbald, Berks, out of a ducal coronet arg, a garb between two sickles ppr *Domini factum*

Sibbering, George Thomas, Barry, Glamorgansh, a bear passant through a hoop *Læte disco*

Sibley, Walter Knowsley, Esquire M A, M D 8 Duke Street Mansions Grosvenor Square W, and Châlet Sans-Souci, Puys, Dieppe, France, a demi lion rampant holding in its paws a fleur de-lis or *Suaviter et fortiter*

Siborne of Kilmainham, Dublin, a falcon close az jessed and belled or holding in the beak and passing over the back a lure twined or and gu, the line resting on the wreath *Sine macula*

Sibthorpe, Coningsby Charles of Canwick Hall, Lincs (1) A demi-lion erased arg, collared sa holding in the dexter paw a fleur de-lis of the last (*for Sibthorpe*) (2) A demi leopard gardant ppr debruised with two bendlets az (*for Waldo*) *Nil conscire sibi — Vestigia nulla retrorsum*

Sicklemore, Suff a garb or, banded gu 153. 2

Sicklemore of Nether Court, St Lawrence, Isle of Thanet, same crest *Par pari*

Siddons, two lion's gambs erased sa, holding up a cinquefoil or

Siddons, a boar's head erased erm., tusked or, surmounted by a plume of three ostrich-feathers az. *Thus thou must do if thou have it.*

Sidebotham, Joseph Watson, Merlewood, Bowdon, Chesh., a demi-lion rampant gorged with a collar, and pendent therefrom an escutcheon.

Sidebottom, Tom Harrop, of Etherow House, Hollingworth, Chesh., upon a mount vert, a talbot regardant sable, gorged with a collar vair, resting the dexter forefoot on an escocheon arg. charged with a bugle horn sable. *Labor ipse voluptas.* 261. 19

Sideley, out of a ducal coronet a goat's head. 128. 14

Sideserf or **Sidserf,** Scotland, an eagle's head issuing gu. *Virtute promoveo.* 83. 1

Sideserf or **Sidserf,** Scotland, a cornucopia ppr. *Industria ditat.* 152. 13

Sideserf, Scotland, an eagle's head couped az. *Semper virtute vivo.* 83. 1

Sidey, a tiger sejant regardant arg., maned sa., holding an arrow of the same.

Sidmouth, Viscount (Addington), a cat-a-mountain sejant gardant ppr., bezantée, his dexter paw resting upon an escutcheon az., charged with a mace erect surmounted with a regal crown or, a bordure engrailed arg. *Libertas sub rege pio.* 308. 14

Sidney, *see* De Lisle and Dudley, Baron.

Sidney, Shelley-, Bart., Kent: (1) A porcupine passant az., armed, collared, and chained or (*for Sidney*). (2) A griffin's head erased arg., beaked and ducally gorged or (*for Shelley*). *Quo fata vocant.* *cf.* 66. 2

Sidney, Philip, Royal Societies Club, St. James's Street, S.W., a porcupine statant az., quilled, collared, and chained or. *Quo fata vocant.* 281. 15

Sidney, Henry, Cowper Hall, Morpeth, Northumb., same crest and motto.

Sidney, Frederick Edward, F.S.A., of Moreton, Frognal, N.W., upon a mount vert, a porcupine statant or, semée of mullets az. *Quo fata vocant.*

Sidney of Bowes Manor, Southgate, on a mount vert, a porcupine or, semée of mullets az. *Gratias Deo agere.*

Sier of Ravensden, Beds, upon a staff raguly or, a pelican in her piety sa., semée of mullets arg., the nest ppr. *Virtus in actione consistit.*

Sievewright or **Sievwright,** Scotland, a hand holding a thunderbolt ppr. 216. 4

Sievier, Robert Standish, Toddington Park, Beds, on a rock ppr., a mullet of six points gu. between two ostrich-feathers arg. *Ne cede malis.*

Sikes of Chantry House, Notts: (1) A bull passant. *cf.* 45. 2. (2) Out of a ducal coronet a wyvern. *Ferox inimicis.—Quod facis, valde facis.* 70. 9

Sikes, a bull ppr., resting the dexter foot upon a fountain, also ppr., and charged upon the body with three billets sa. 45. 6

Sikes, Rev. T. B., Warbleton Rectory, Sussex, a swan with wings endorsed arg., issuing out of reeds vert. *Honos.*

Silchester, Baron, *see* Longford, Earl of.

Silk of London, a greyhound current sa., charged with a cross crosslet or. *Post virtutem curro.* 58. 1

Silk, a greyhound current arg., collared az. *cf.* 58. 2

Sill, a demi-griffin ppr., collared arg. *cf.* 64. 2

Sillar, A. M., Esquire, 2, Queen Anne's Gate, Westminster, S.W., a swan's head between two wings. *Toujours fidèle.* 313. 11

Sillesden, a bird's head az., beaked and collared or, between two wings gu.

Sillifant, Arthur Onslow, of Coombe, Devonsh., at the foot of a cross Calvary or, a lizard ppr. *Mens conscia recti.* 237. 8

Silly of Heligan, Cornw., two bull's horns or. 123. 8

Silly, Cornw., a lion sejant. 8. 8

Silva, Edward, Esquire, Testcombe, Stockbridge, Hants, and 14, Cadogan Gardens, London, S.W., a hunting-horn or, stringed gu., between two wings az.

Silver, a hand holding a vine-branch. 219. 6

Silver of Netherley, Scotland, a unicorn's head erased arg., charged with a chevron gu. *Nil desperandum.* *cf.* 49. 5

Silver, Herts and Hants, an heraldic tiger's head erased gu., tusked, tufted, and maned or. *cf.* 25. 4

Silver of Norwich, a demi-lion regardant or, holding three ears of corn ppr., and issuant out of a castle gu.

Silver, a lion rampant holding between the paws a battle-axe.

Silverthorn of Bristol, a dove alighting on a sheaf of barley, all ppr.

Silvertop, Francis Somerled, of Minster-Acres, Northumb., a wolf's head erased arg., langued gu., pierced with a broken spear ppr.

Silvester, a lion's head erased vert. 17. 8

Silvester, Carteret-, Essex: (1) A lion couchant gu. (*for Silvester*). 7. 5. (2) On a mount vert, a squirrel sejant cracking a nut ppr. (*for Carteret*). 135. 5

Sim, Simm, or **Sime,** Scotland, a lion's head erased ppr. 17. 8

Sim of Coombe Wood, Surrey, a Moor's head ppr., banded arg. *Quod verum tutum.* *cf.* 192. 13

Simcoe of Chelsea, Middx., an arm in armour embowed holding in the hand a sword, all ppr. 195 2

Simcoe of Wolford Lodge, Devonsh.: (1) A dexter arm in armour embowed ppr., holding a sword or. 195. 2. (2) Out of a naval coronet a demi-sea-lion rampant charged on the breast with a rose, all ppr. *Non sibi sed patriæ.*

Simcoe, Samuel Palmer, Penheale, Cornw., out of a naval crown or, a demi-sea-lion ppr., holding in the fore-fin a dagger erect arg., pommel and hilt or, and on his shoulder a rose gu., barbed and seeded ppr.

Simeon, out of a mural coronet erm., a lion's head sa. 19. 12

Simeon, Sir John Stephen Barrington, Bart., J.P., D.L., of Grazeley, Berks, a fox passant regardant ppr., holding in the mouth a trefoil slipped vert. *Serviendo.—Nec temere, nec timide.* *cf.* 32. 3

Simeon, Stephen Esquire, Little Bounds, Fleet, Hants, a fox passant regardant ppr., holding in the mouth a trefoil slipped vert. *Nec temere nec timide.*

Simmer, Scotland, a stag lodged ppr. 115. 7

Simminges, a raven sa., holding in the dexter claw a rose gu., leaved and slipped vert.

Simminges of London, a lion sejant gu., resting the dexter paw on an escutcheon or.

Simmonds, a lion's gamb wielding a battle-axe, all or. *cf.* 38. 3

Simmons, the late Field-Marshal Sir John Lintorn Arabin Simmons, G.C.B., G.C.M.G., K.C.B., C.B., a stump of an oak-tree sprouting, in front thereof a mount, thereon a branch of laurel fructed in bend sinister, all ppr. *Stabilitate et Victoria*

Simmons, Winston Churchill, Esquire, of Churchill, Richmond, Tasmania, Chairman of the General Sessions, same crest and motto.

Simmons, a greyhound's head collared. *In recto decus.* 61. 2

Simmons, a greyhound's head gorged with a plain collar, charged with a mullet of five points. *cf.* 61. 2

Simmons, a dolphin naiant. 140. 5

Simmons, a stag's head erased. 121. 2

Simmons, Ireland, a sea-lion rampant gu. 20. 5

Simmons, Kent, a beaver passant, holding in the mouth an olive-branch, all ppr.

Simms, a gad-fly ppr.

Simon of Perth, a lion's gamb holding a battle-axe. *God giveth the victory.* *cf.* 38. 3

Simon, a pegasus current arg., winged gu. 47. 1

Simon, M. St. L., R.E., a griffin passant. *Haut et bon.*

Simonds, on a mount vert, an erm. passant ppr., holding in the mouth a trefoil slipped or.

Simonds, Major H., of Caversham, Reading, on a mount vert, an erm. passant ppr. holding in the mouth a trefoil slipped or. *Simplex munditiis.*

Simono of London, a cock arg., combed, beaked, and legged gu. 91. 2

Simons of Ullesthorpe, Leics., a wing per pale arg. and or, encircled by a chaplet of roses ppr. *Upward.*

Simpson, *see* Hilton-Simpson.

Simpson, Scotland, a dexter hand pointing with the thumb and forefinger. *Confido.* 222. 12

Simpson of Whitburn and Westhouse, Durh., a naked arm holding in the hand a wreath of laurel. *Perseveranti dabitur.* 218. 4

Simpson of Thorntoun, a crescent or. *Tandem implebitur.* 163. 2

Simpson of Easter Ogil, Scotland, same crest and motto.

Simpson, Edward, Esquire, J.P., of Walton Hall, Wakefield, Yorks, in front of a maiden's head ppr., vested gu., wreathed round the temples with oak-leaves, also ppr., a fret arg. *Labor omnia vincit.* 183. 13

Simpson, Charles Henry, the Hemploe, Wreford, Rugby, same crest.

Simpson, Ireland, a lion's gamb issuing erm., holding a branch of olive vert. 37. 4

Simpson of Udoch, Scotland, and London, a falcon volant ppr. *Alis nutrior.* 88. 3

Simpson, on a tower ruined on the sinister side a bird rising

Simpson, on a demi tower ruined, a bird with wings elevated, holding in the beak a sprig

Simpson, an eagle's head erased ppr *Profunda cernit* 83 2

Simpson of London, same crest *Je suis prêt* 83 2

Simpson, an eagle with wings expanded ppr 77 5

Simpson, a snake nowed vert 142 4

Simpson, Sir James Walter Mackay Grindlay, Bart, of Strathavon Linlithgowsh, and of city of Edinburgh a staff erect encircled by a serpent or *Victo dolore* 313 7

Simpson, a cross raguly gu, suspended thereon an escutcheon per bend sinister arg and or charged with a lion rampant az *Regi regnoque fidelis* 227 4

Simpson of Fulham, Middx and Vauxhall Surrey, a lion rampant or 1 13

Simpson of Castle Lodge Yorks a demi-lion rampant or *Nil desperandum* 10 2

Simpson, out of a mural coronet a demi lion rampant, holding in the dexter paw a sword in pale

Simpson, Admiral Cortland Herbert J P, of Rhydian, Stoke-by-Navland, Suff, same crest *Neque lux sine umbra*

Simpson of Foston Hall, Yorks and Mellor Lodge, Derbysh, out of a mural coronet arg a demi lion rampant gardant per pale or and sa, holding in the dexter paw a sword erect ppr

Simpson of Hillview, Bloomfield Devonsh, same crest *Virtute et valore*

Simpson, Francis Charles, of Maypool, South Devonsh same crest

Simpson of Stamford, Lincs, same crest *Nil sine labore*

Simpson, Yorks, out of a tower az a demi lion rampant gardant per pale or and sa, holding in the dexter paw a sword arg, hilt and pommel of the second

Simpson, Albert, Esquire, J P, Burghill Grange, Heref, and Michaelchurch on Arrow Radnorsh, same crest *I byde my tyme*

Simpson, Bucks out of a tower a demi lion rampant, holding between the paws a scimitar, all ppr

Simpson of Lichfield, an ounce's head ppr, erased and ducally crowned gu charged on the neck with a gauntlet or

Simpson, Cecil Woodsley, Skelmorlie, N B, a griffin's head erased *Profunda cernit*

Simpson, Kent, an ounce's head pean erased gu, gorged with a collar gemelle arg *Nunquam obliviscar*

Sims, Scotland a demi lion holding in the dexter paw a battle axe ppr *Ferio tego* cf 15 4

Sims, Arthur, a demi-stag erased az, attired or, charged with a cross indented erm, between four cross crosslets az holding in the mouth a cross crosslet fitchee sa, and resting the sinister leg on an escallop ppr

Simson, Scotland, an eagle's head erased ppr *Profundo cernit* 83 2

Simson, a lion's head erased ducally crowned or 18 8

Simson, of Pitcorthie, Fifesh, a falcon volant ppr *Alis nutrior* 88 3

Sinclair, see Caithness Earl of

Sinclair, Baron (St Clair), a swan arg, ducally gorged and chained or *Fight* cf 99 2

Sinclair, Sir John Rose George Bart, of Dunbeath and Barrock Caithness-sh, a cock ppr *Fidelitas* 91 2

Sinclair, Captain John, M P, 101, Mount Street W, same crest and motto

Sinclair, of Fairmead Cambs (1) On the dexter side—a cock ppr (*for Sinclair*) 91 2 (2) On the sinister side—on a mural coronet az a pomeis charged with a cross or, between two wings displayed erm *Commit thy work to God —Deus prosperat justos*

Sinclair, Bart, of Longformacus, Berwicksh, a cock crowing with wings expanded ppr, having a broken chain or about his neck *Vincula temno*

Sinclair, a phœnix in flames ppr *Fides* 82 2

Sinclair, Scotland a dove holding in the beak an olive branch ppr *Credo* 92 5

Sinclair, Bart, Scotland, a dove ppr *Credo* 92 2

Sinclair, a griffin's head erased with wings addorsed *Candide, sed caute* cf 67 11

Sinclair, a griffin's head erased ppr *Candide, sed caute* 66 2

Sinclair, Sir Robert Charles, Bart J P, D L, of Stevenson, Haddingtonsh, and Murkle, Caithness sh. same crest *Candide sed caute* 66 2

Sinclair of Dun, Caithness-sh, Scotland, a man on horseback ppr *Promptus ad certamen* 53 10

Sinclair, Scotland a savage resting his club on the wreath ppr *Per ardua virtus*

Sinclair of Stemster, Caithness sh, Scotland, a man bearing a flag *Te duce gloriamur* 188 6

Sinclair of Dunbeath Caithness sh a man displaying a banner ppr *Te duce gloriamur* 188 6

Sinclair, Scotland a demi soldier displaying a banner ppr *Te duce gloriamur* 187 9

Sinclair, Scotland, a demi-man holding in one hand a sea chart, and in the other a pair of pencils, all ppr *Sic rectius progredior*

Sinclair of Ratter and Freswick, Caithness sh a cross patee within a circle of stars arg *Via crucis via lucis* 164 9

Sinclair of Harpsdale, an arrow and a branch of palm in saltier ppr *Detur forti palma* 171 7

Sinclair, Bart, of Oldburr, a demi-otter issuing ppr *Quocunque ferar* 134 11

Sinclair, on a mount an otter ppr, entering water 134 5

Sinclair, a pole cat arg 135 13

Sinclair, Scotland, a cross engrailed sa *Crure delector*

Sinclair, Scotland, a naked arm issuing from a cloud, the hand grasping a small sword, all ppr *Me vincit, ego mereo*

Sinclair, Sir John George Tollemache, Bart, D L, of Ulbster Caithness-sh, an estoile of six points waved or *J'aime le meilleur —Ad astra virtus* 164 1

Sinclair, Frederick Granville, of Barrogill Castle, Thurso, Scotland, a swan arg, ducally collared and chained or cf 99 2

Sinclair-Aytoun, Roger, M A, of Inchdairnie, Kirkcaldy, Fifesh, a hand holding a rose ppr (*for Aytoun*) *Decerptæ dabunt odorem*

Sinclair-Lockhart, Major General Sir Græme Alexander, Cambusnethan House, Wishaw, N B, a boar's head erased arg *Corda serrata pando*

Sing, A M, Fernlea, Mossley Hill, Liverpool, out of a ducal coronet or, an eagle's claw arg *Cœlestia canimus*

Singe, Shropsh, out of a ducal coronet or an eagle's claw arg 113 13

Singleton, Ireland, a lion's head affrontee between two wings ppr

Singleton, an eagle rising regardant, holding in the dexter claw a sword in pale, all ppr 77 10

Singleton, Yorks, a camel passant erm, bridled or cf 132 2

Singleton of Fort Singleton, co Monaghan, Ireland, a demi-antelope sa, plattee crined and attired arg, pierced through the breast by a broken spear or headed of the second vulned and embrued ppr *Mutare sperno*

Singleton of Broughton Lancs, and of Dykelborough and Mendlesham, Norf, an arm in armour embowed ppr the hand grasping a sceptre or, on the top an étoile of the same 196 8

Singleton, Rear Admiral Uvedale Corbet, of Aclare co Meath, Ireland (1) An arm in armour embowed ppr, grasping a sceptre terminated by an estoile or (*for Singleton*) 196 8 (2) An elephant arg, armed or, on his back a tower, also arg, the trappings gu, garnished of the second (*for Corbet*) *Bona fide sine fraude* cf 133 11

Sinnott, a swan sa., with wings elevated 99 12

Sipling, Yorks, a leopard's head or gorged with a chaplet vert

Sirr, Edward Joseph Arthur Sandwich, Kent, an estoile or, within two olive-branches ppr *Nautæ Fida —Lyræ nervos aptavi*

Sirr, Harry, 50, Trisden Road, Highgate same crest and mottoes

Sirr, Rev William, St Philip's Mission House, Plaistow E, same crest and motto

Sirringes, an eagle holding a rose-branch gu, leaved vert

Sisson, a stag trippant arg 117 8

Sissons, a griffin's head erased or *Hope for the best —Si monent tubæ paratus* 66 2

Sitlington of Wigton, Cumb a holy lamb regardant erm, gorged with a laurel-branch vert, holding a banner ppr *Have mercy on us, good Lord*

Sitsill, a thistle ppr 150 5

Sitwell, Wilmot-, of Stainsby, Derbysh (1) A demi-lion rampant erased sa, holding between the paws an escutcheon per pale or and vert (*for Sitwell*) 308 8 (2) An eagle's head couped arg, holding in the beak an escallop gu (*for Wilmot*)

Sitwell, Sir George Reresby. Bart., of Renishaw, Derbysh., a demi-lion rampant erased sa., holding between the paws an escutcheon per pale or and vert. 308. 8

Sitwell, Lieutenant-Colonel Claude George Henry, same crest.

Sitwell, Rev. Degge Wilmot, Manor House, Leamington - Hastings, Warw.: (1) Same crest as above. (2) An eagle's head couped arg., holding in the beak an escallop gu.

Sitwell, Edward Sacheverell, Cattistock Lodge, Dorchester, same crests.

Sitwell, Captain Francis Honorius Sisson, same crest as (1) above.

Sitwell, Francis Staunton, same crests as above.

Sitwell, Robert Sacheverell Wilmot, J.P., Stainsby House, Smalley, Derby, same crests as above.

Sitwell, William Willoughby George Hurt, J.P., Ferney Hall, Salop, same crest as (1) above.

Sivedale, a demi-eagle with wings expanded or. 80. 2

Sivright, *see* Bedell-Sivright.

Skae, Scotland, a buck lodged gu. 115. 7

Skea, Scotland, an arm erect grasping a club ppr. 214. 6

Skearne, on a tower a lion rampant, both arg. 157. 12

Skearne or **Skerne** of Bonby, Lincs, and of Portington, Yorks, on a tower or, a lion couchant arg.

Skeels, Rev. Serocold Clarke, Foston Rectory, Leics., a swan arg., charged on the wing with an escallop gu., and resting the dexter foot on a water-bouget of the last. *Fidens Deo confidens.*

Skeels, Edward Ralph Serocold, Brentwood, Essex, same crest and motto.

Skeen, Scotland, a garb ppr. *Assiduitate.* 153. 2

Skeen, Scotland, a birch-tree environed with stalks of oats, all growing out of a mount ppr. *Sub montibus altis.*

Skeen, a wolf's head couped. *Virtutis regia merces.* 30. 5

Skeen, Scotland, a hand holding a dagger arg., hilt and pommel or, surmounted of a wolf's head. *Virtutis regia merces.*

Skeen, Scotland, a hand holding a sword in pale, on the point a wolf's head couped close by the scalp, all ppr. *Virtutis regia merces.*

Skeen, Scotland, a dexter hand ppr., holding a dagger arg., hilt and pommel or. *Virtutis.* 212. 3

Skeen, Scotland, a dexter arm from the shoulder issuing from a cloud, holding forth a triumphal crown or garland ppr. *Virtutis regia merces.* 200. 12

Skeen, Scotland, a dexter hand holding a garland ppr. *Gratis a Deo data.* 218. 4

Skeene, on a tower arg., a lion rampant of the last. 157. 12

Skeet of Wind Hill House, Bishop's Stortford, on a rock ppr., a covered cup or, supported on either side by an eagle with wings elevated and endorsed arg., gutté-de-sang, each holding in the mouth a cross potent gu. *Ad majorem Dei gloriam.*

Skeffington, *see* Massereene, Viscount.

Skeffington, a mermaid with her comb and mirror, all ppr. 184. 5

Skeffington, Bart., Leics., a mermaid ppr., her comb, mirror, and fins or. 184. 5

Skeges, Hunts, a demi-peacock az., with wings expanded or, beaked and crested of the last.

Skelmersdale, Baron, *see* Lathom, Earl of.

Skelton of Armathwaite Castle, Branthwaite, Highhouse, and Papcastle, Cumb., and Yorks, a bird's head erased sa., holding in the beak an acorn or, staiked and leaved vert. 84. 10

Skelton of Plymouth, Devonsh., out of a ducal coronet az., a horse's head arg. 51. 7

Skene, Scotland, a dexter arm embowed issuing from a cloud, the hand holding a triumphal crown ppr. *Virtutis regia merces.* 200. 12

Skene, Thomas, Esquire, J.P., of Marnoo, Victoria, Australia, a dexter arm from the shoulder issuing out of a cloud holding in the hand a garland ppr. *Virtutis regia merces.* 200. 12

Skene, Alexander John, Esquire, M.A., J.P., of St. Kilda, Melbourne, Victoria, same crest and motto. 200. 12

Skene of Skene, Aberdeensh., Scotland, out of a cloud a naked arm from the shoulder, the hand holding a garland of laurel, all ppr. *Virtutis regia merces.*

Skene of Rubislaw, Aberdeensh., out of a cloud a dexter arm from the shoulder holding in the hand a garland ppr. *Gratis a Deo data.* 200. 12

Skene of Easter Fintray, Aberdeensh., issuing out of a cloud a hand reaching to a garland ppr. *Gratis a Deo data.*

Skene, William Baillie, of Halyards, Fifesh., a dexter hand ppr., holding a dagger arg., hilted and pommelled or, surmounted of a wolf's head. *Virtutis regia merces.*

Skene of Newtyle, Forfarsh., a hand holding a laurel crown ppr. *Sors mihi grata cadet.* 218. 4

Skene of Curriehill, Edinburgh, a wolf's head couped gu. *Virtutis regia merces.* 30. 5

Skene of Ramore, Aberdeensh., Scotland, a birch-tree environed with stalks of oats, all growing out of a mount ppr. *Sub montibus altis.*

Skene of Dyce, Aberdeensh., Scotland, a garb ppr. *Assiduitate.* 153. 2

Skene, a hart's head couped or. 121. 5

Skene, Gordon-Cuming-, of Pitlurg, Ellon, Aberdeensh., N.B., a dove ppr. *I hope.*

Skepper, Durh., a lion's gamb erect or, grasping three roses of the same stalked and leaved vert. 37. 12

Skeres, Yorks, a demi-lion rampant sa., holding in the dexter paw three oak-leaves vert.

Skereth, co. Galway, Ireland, a squirrel gu., cracking a nut or. 135. 7

Skerret, a heraldic tiger passant gu. 25. 5

Skerritt of Finavara, Ireland, a squirrel sejant ppr. *Primus ultimusque in acie.* cf. 135. 4

Sketchley, a boar's head couped close az., langued gu., and in front thereof three cinquefoils in fess or. *Quieta non movere.*

Skettew, a cubit arm erect, the hand holding up an étoile. *cf.* 216. 12

Skevington, a mermaid ppr., her comb and mirror or. 184. 5

Skewse, Cornw., a wolf passant ppr., collared and charged on the body with six stars or.

Skey, a dove regardant holding in its beak an olive-branch. 92. 4

Skiddie or **Skiddy** of Castle Skiddie, co. Cork, out of a ducal coronet ppr., a bear's paw sa., armed gu. *Non inferiora secutus.* *cf.* 36. 12

Skidmore, a unicorn's head erased sa., plattée. *cf.* 49. 5

Skillicorne, Lancs, a raven's head erased ppr.

Skilling of Draycot, Wilts, and Hants, a greyhound current or, collared and lined sa.

Skingley of Wakes Colne Hall, Essex, between two branches of oak a demi-lion ppr., charged with a bend arg., thereon two roses gu., barbed and seeded ppr., holding between the paws an escutcheon, also gu., charged with a garb or.

Skinner of Cowley, Devonsh., out of a ducal coronet or, a demi-talbot gu., collared and lined arg. *cf.* 55. 8

Skinner, a griffin's head erased arg., holding in the beak a dexter hand couped at the wrist gu.

Skinner, Allen Maclean, Esquire, C.M.G., Barton Fields, Canterbury, a griffin's head holding in the beak a gauntlet.

Skinner of Le Burtons and Ledbury, Heref., a griffin's head erased arg., holding in the beak a hand couped gu., charged on the breast with a mullet.

Skinner, Captain Cyriac Burrell, Croome House, Camberley, Surrey, a dragon's head erased, collared, gemelle, and semé of roundles. *Espero.*

Skippe of Ledbury, Heref., a demi-lion or, holding in the dexter paw a rose gu. 12. 1

Skipton, on a mural coronet a stag sejant ppr. 116. 4

Skipton of Ballyshasky, Ireland, an armed arm embowed holding in the hand a dagger, all ppr. 196. 5

Skipton of Beechill, co. Londonderry, an armed arm holding a dagger ppr. *Pro patria.*

Skipwith, Sir Peyton d'Estoteville, Bart., of Prestwould, Leics., a turnstile ppr. *Sans Dieu je ne puis.* 313. 14

Skipwith, Colonel Gray Townsend, J.P., Loversal Hall, Doncaster, same crest and motto.

Skipwith, Philip George, Esquire, Barrister-at-Law, J.P., of Hundleby, Spilsby, Lincs, a reel ppr. *Sans Dieu je ne puis.*

Skipwith of St. Albans, Herts, a griffin's head erased per fess gu. and or, guttée counterchanged, holding in the beak a lion's gamb couped erm.

Skipworth, Bart. (*extinct*), of Ormesby, Lincs, and Bart. (*extinct*), of Methringham, Lincs, a reel or turnstile ppr. *Sans Dieu je ne puis.*

Skirrow, Arthur George Walker, Captain South Lancashire Regiment (P.W.V.), Naval and Military Club, Piccadilly, a dove holding in the beak a branch of olive, all ppr. *Mors potior macula.* 92. 5

Skirvin or **Skirving** of Skirving, Scotland a hand holding a buckle ppr *Fit inde firmior* 223 11
Skone of Lanriverie Cornw out of a ducal coronet a demi eagle with wings expanded, all or cf 80 2
Skory of Bilbury, Heref out of a ducal coronet a demi eagle with wings expanded or
Skottow of London, a lion's head erased arg, collared gu 18 6
Skottowe, a wolf's head erm 30 5
Skottowe, Britiffe Constable (Baron in the Peerage of France) M A 17, Manson Place, Queen's Gate S W an arm couped at the elbow, sleeved az, and a hand ppr holding a mullet of eight points or 274 4
Skoulding-Cann, see Cann
Skrine of Warleigh, Somers, and Stubbings, Bucks, a tower arg on the battlements thereof a lion couchant erm, ducally crowned or *Tutamen*
Skrine, Henry Mills Esquire, of Warleigh Manor, Bath, same crest and motto
Skull, a heraldic tiger passant per pale gu and erm 25 5
Skynner of London, Sheffield, Warw, and Worcs, a griffin's head erased arg, holding in the beak a gauntlet or
Skynner of Thornton and Boston, Lincs, on a ducal coronet arg a falcon of the last, beaked and legged gu 85 9
Skynner of Cowley Devonsh out of a ducal coronet or a demi-lion rampant, arg, collared and lined gu cf 16 3
Skynner, a dragon's head erased az, plattée, charged on the neck with a bar gemel or cf 71 1
Skyrme, a deer's head cabossed or 122 5
Skyrne, on a tower arg, a lion rampant of the last 157 12
Slack, Robert, Derwent Hill, Cumb, in front of a crescent or, a snail ppr *Lente sed certe*
Slack of Bank Vale, Hayfield, a lion couchant resting the dexter paw on a quatrefoil *Lente sed certe*
Slack, a bridge of three arches ppr 158 4
Slack, same crest *Ter fidelis*
Slacke, of Ashleigh, co Down a lion couchant ppr, resting his dexter forepaw on a quatrefoil per bend sinister or and erm *Lente sed certe*
Sladden, a unicorn's head az 49 7
Slade, a hart at gaze ppr 117 3
Slade or **Slader**, Beds, Hunts, and Northamp, a horse's head erased sa 50 8
Slade, Sir Cuthbert Bart, of Maunsel House, Somers, on a mount vert, a horse's head erased sa, encircled with a chain in the form of an arch or *Fidus et audax —A bon droit* 308 9
Slade, Wyndham Montys Court, Taunton, same crest and first motto
Slade, Major General Sir Frederick George C B, Artillery House Gibraltar, same crest 230 17
Slade, Major General John Ramsay, 8, Lowndes Street, same crest
Slade of Ash Boleyne, Yeovil Somers, and Kanimbla, Hampstead, Middx, in front of a horse's head erased sa, charged with a horse shoe, three mascles interlaced fessewise all or *Facta non verba* 50 7
Slade, Ireland a lion's head erased gu, pierced by an arrow ppr
Slade of Trevennen, Cornw, a lion's gamb erased holding up a plume of three ostrich-feathers 37 5
Sladen of Hartsbourne Manor, Herts, Lee and Swanage Kent, a mount vert, thereon, between two branches of palm ppr, a lion's gamb erect and erased sa, holding a plume of five ostrich feathers gu *Vive ut vivas* cf 37 1
Sladen, Lieutenant-Colonel Joseph Ripple Court, near Dover, same crest and motto
Sladen, Frederick St Barbe Stanmore, near Bridgnorth, on a mount vert between two branches of palm ppr, a lion's gamb erect and erased sa holding a plume of five ostrich feathers gu *Vive ut vivas*
Sladen, John Ramsay, J P Rhydoldog, Radnorsh, same crest and motto
Slader of Bath and Barham Downs, Kent a lion's gamb erect and erased or, holding five ostrich-feathers, three arg and two az 37 8
Slaney, Shropsh a griffin's head ppr, wings endorsed or beaked of the last cf 67 11
Slaney, Kenyon-, Colonel William of Hatton Grange, Shropsh (1) A griffin's head gu, winged erminois, and gorged with a collar gemel or, charged on the breast for distinction with a cross crosslet or (*for Slaney*) *Deo duce comite industria* (2) A lion sejant ppr resting the dexter paw on a cross flory arg (*for Kenyon*) *Magnanimiter crucem sustine* cf 67 11
Slaning, Devonsh, a demi lion rampant az collared or 10 9
Slanning of Ley, Devonsh., a demi-lion az collared or 10 9
Slanning, Bart (*extinct*), of Waristow, Devonsh, a demi lion rampant az, collared or 10 9
Slany or **Slaney** of London and Staffs a griffin's head ppr between two wings addorsed or, beaked of the last. cf 67 11
Slater, a cock crowing gu 91 2
Slater, out of a ducal coronet a demi-eagle with wings expanded cf 80 2
Slater-Rebow of Wyvenhoe, Essex (1) Out of a mural coronet or, a demi eagle displayed sa, charged on the breast with a bezant, thereon a fleur-de-lis az and holding in the beak an arrow of the first headed arg (*for Rebow*) 81 10 (2) A cubit arm erect in armour holding in the gauntlet a dagger, all ppr, hilted or (*for Slater*)
Slater of Durant Hall Chesterfield a gauntlet ppr *Crescit sub pondere virtus* 209 8
Slater, a cubit arm in armour erect holding in the gauntlet a dagger all ppr
Slater of Chesterfield, Derbysh, a dexter arm in armour couped below the wrist holding in the gauntlet a sword all ppr, hilt and pommel or *Crescit sub pondere virtus* 211 4
Slater, Middx a lion passant gardant ppr 4 3
Slator of Belville House, co Meath Ireland a lion passant per pale gu and sa holding in the dexter paw a trefoil slipped vert. *Garde la loi* cf 6 2
Slaughter, Worcs a falcon with wings expanded 87 1
Slaughter of Slaughter, Glouc, out of a ducal coronet or an eagle's head between two wings az, beaked of the first 84 3
Slaughter, Heref, out of a ducal coronet or an eagle's head arg, with wings addorsed sa
Slaughter, Very Rev Monsignor Edward Henry out of a ducal coronet or, a demi eagle arg, wings expanded az *Despicio terrena*
Slaughter, William Edmund 7, Arundel Street, Strand same crest and motto
Slauter, a monkey's head ppr 136 14
Slayer of Morlick Somers, a stag's head erased or, holding in the mouth an arrow arg cf 121 2
Sleath, a crane or 105 9
Slee, a chapeau sa, with a plume of three ostrich feathers in front
Sleford of Wilsthrop Lincs, a mermaid ppr 184 5
Slegge, Cambs a demi griffin segreant erm, with wings addorsed or armed arg holding a sceptre of the first
Sleggs of Aynesbury, Hunts, a demi-peacock displayed az
Sleigh, Scotland an eagle's head erased sa beaked gu *Unalterable* 83 2
Sleigh of Ashe Derbysh a demi lion rampant arg, holding a cross crosslet fitched or, ducally crowned of the last cf 11 10
Sleigh, Derbysh and London, an arm erect vested vert, holding in the hand ppr a cinquefoil slipped cf 205 2
Slesser, Scotland a dexter arm brandishing a spear, all ppr *Spectemur agendo* 214 11
Sley, Ireland, a cubit arm vested erm holding in the hand a broken sword
Sligo, Marquess of (Browne), an eagle displayed vert. *Suivez raison* 75 8
Sligo of Carmylie Lanarksh and Auldhame, Haddingtonsh., Scotland the sun in his splendour ppr *Vincit omnia veritas* 162 2
Slinger, Matthew Esquire, B A, a stag lodged ppr attired or, gorged with a collar and chain reflexed over the back and encompassing the stag in the form of an arch of the last
Slingsby, a Cornish chough ppr 107 14
Slingsby, Yorks and Bucks, a lion passant vert. 6 2
Slingsby, Thomas, 24, Portland Place W a lion passant vert charged on the shoulder for distinction with a cross crosslet or
Slingsby, Rev Charles Slingsby, Scriven Park Knaresborough, a lion statant vert *Veritas liberavit*
Slingsby, Bart (*extinct*) of Scriven Yorks, a lion passant vert *Veritas liberavit* 6 2
Sloan, Scotland a lion rampant ppr *Fi et veritate* 1 13
Sloan, an eagle displayed ppr 75 2
Sloane, Middx and Ireland a lion's head erased or, collared with mascles interlaced sa cf 17 8
Slocombe, Somers a griffin's head gu between two wings or 65 11
Sloggett, also called **Tresloggett**, Colonel Arthur Thomas, C M G of Tremalyn Paignton Devonsh, on a chapeau gu

turned up erm., a dragon passant sa., bezantée, and the dexter claw resting on a bezant. 73. 6. *Bethon Dur* (Cornish—*Be bold*). *Badge*, within a garter or, charged with the motto *Cala raggi wethlow* (Cornish—*A straw for idle gossip*), a dragon passant or.

Sloper, Kent, on two snakes entwined together ppr., a dove statant arg., holding in its beak an olive-branch vert.

Sloper of West Woodhay, Berks, on two snakes entwined together ppr., a dove statant arg., bearing an olive-branch vert. *In pace ut sapiens.*

Sloper, Wilts, over a rock ppr., a dove volant arg., guttée-de-sang, holding in the beak an olive-branch vert. *Pacis.*

Sloper, a boar's head or, pierced through the neck by a dart.

Slough, a stork's head erased. 106. 1

Sly, a dove az. 92. 2

Smachey, a lion rampant erm., crowned or, holding a cross patée fitched.

Smail, Scotland, an eagle rising ppr. 77. 5

Smale and **Smalley** of Paddington, Middx., on a chapeau gu., turned up erm., a unicorn couchant arg.

Small of Curriehill, Scotland, a branch of palm ppr. *Ratione non ira.* 147. 1

Small, on a chess-rook arg., a wren ppr.

Smallbones, a Cornish chough ppr. 107. 14

Smallbrook, a cock's head erased or. 90. 1

Smallbrook, a martlet with wings displayed.

Smallman, a hand gauntleted holding a sword in pale ppr. 211. 4

Smallman, Herts, Heref., and Shropsh., a heraldic antelope sejant holding up the dexter foot sa., the horns and tail or, gorged with a ducal coronet and lined of the last.

Smallman of Quatford Chantry, Shropsh., same crest. *My word is my bond.*

Smallman, Henry George, Carlton House, Herne Hill, S.E., the stock of an oak-tree eradicated and sprouting on either side ppr., thereon a heraldic antelope sejant gu., bezantée, and armed or, the dexter fore-foot supporting a bee-hive, also ppr. *Industria premium incidit.*

Smallpage of London and Yorks, an antelope arg., supporting a broken spear or, the head downward.

Smallpiece of Hockering, Norf., a wolf's head erased per fesse embattled arg. and sa. 30. 8

Smallpiece of Hockling, Shropsh., and Norf., an eagle rising arg. 77. 5

Smallpeice of Field Lodge, Burley, Ringwood, Hants, an eagle with wings elevated. *Spirans aspiro.*

Smallwood, a cubit arm vested chequy arg. and sa., holding in the hand ppr. a chaplet of oak vert, fructed or. 205. 4

Smallwood, Rupert, Esquire, the Crescent, Bromsgrove, a cubit arm vested chequy arg and sa., cuffed arg., holding in the hand a chaplet of oak vert, fructed or.

Smalman, Shropsh., a heraldic tiger sejant sa., maned, tufted, and ducally gorged or, lined, and the line reflexed of the same.

Smalpece or **Smallpiece** of Worlingham, Suff., a wolf's head erased per fesse embattled arg. and sa. 30. 8

Smart, Scotland, a hand throwing a dart. *Ettle weel.* 214. 4

Smart, Scotland, a pheon sa. 174. 11

Smart, Scotland, a boar's head erased sa. *Vincet virtute.* 42. 2

Smart, an ostrich's head between two palm-branches ppr. *cf.* 96. 10

Smart of London, a hawk's head between two wings arg., holding in the beak a thistle ppr. *cf.* 89. 1

Smart of London and Scotland, a demi-eagle rising with wings displayed arg., holding in the beak a flower of the burdock ppr.

Smart of Trewhit House, Northumb., a demi-eagle rising with wings displayed, holding in his beak a burdock ppr. *Virtus præ nummis.* *cf.* 80. 2

Smart, Francis Gray, J.P., Bredbury, Tunbridge Wells, same crest. *Esse quam videri.*

Smart, Rev. Robert William John, Parkham Rectory, Bideford, North Devonsh., same crest and motto.

Smedley, an eagle's head erased sa. 83. 2

Smellet, Scotland, the stump of an oak-tree shooting a green branch on each side ppr. *Viresco.* 142. 5

Smellie, *see* Haig-Smellie.

Smellie of London and Scotland, a dexter hand holding a crescent ppr. *Industria, virtute, et fortitudine.* 216. 8

Smelt of Kirkby Fleetham and Leases-by-Bedale, Yorks, a cormorant's head erased.

Smerdon, Devonsh., a lion's gamb erased holding a battle-axe or. *Vincit qui patitur.* 38. 3

Smert, Cornw., a beaver's head erased arg., collared gu., holding in the mouth a branch vert.

Smetham, out of a ducal coronet or, a demi-dragon rampant ppr.

Smethurst, of Chorley and Rookwood, Lancs, an eagle's head erased gu., guttée-d'eau, holding in the beak a serpent or. *Alta peto.*

Smethwicke of Smethwicke, Chesh., an arm embowed vested arg., charged with two bars wavy vert, cuffed of the first, holding in the hand ppr. a tulip or, leaved of the second.

Smijth, Bowyer-, Sir William, Bart., of Hill Hall, Essex: (1) A salamander in flames ppr. (*for Smijth*). 138. 4. (2) An eagle holding in the dexter claw a quill arg. (3) On a ducal coronet or, a heraldic tiger sejant arg. (*for Bowyer*). *Qua pote lucet.* 25. 7

Smiley, Sir Hugh Houston, Bart., J.P., of Drumalis House, Larne, co. Antrim, and of Gallowhill, Paisley, Renfrewsh., a lion's gamb erased holding by a shaft a pheon, point downwards or. *Industria virtus et fortitudo.* 288. 12

Smirke, a falcon with wings addorsed and distended preying on a serpent, all ppr.

Smith, *see* Carrington.

Smith-Barry, *see* Barry.

Smith-Dorrien, *see* Dorrien.

Smith, *see* Lawson-Smith.

Smith, Sir Cecil Clementi-, G.C.M.G., the Garden House, Wheathampstead, A. E. Clementi-Smith, Esquire, of Fir Grove, Sunninghill, Ascot, Rev. Herbert Clementi-Smith, and Rev. Percival Clementi-Smith, in front of a lion's head erased arg., gorged with a collar flory counterflory az., on the head a crown vallory or, three mullets fessewise or. *Perseverando.*

Smith, Ernest Octavius, Sydney, New South Wales, in front of a demi-lion gu., charged on the shoulder with a passion cross two trefoils in saltire, slipped or. *Mens conscia recti.*

Smith, Baron and Viscount Carrington (*extinct*), a peacock's head erased ducally gorged or. *cf.* 103. 1

Smith of Dublin, a demi-peacock in his pride ppr., charged on the breast with a trefoil or.

Smith, an eagle rising ppr. 77. 5

Smith, an eagle's head or, depressed with two bends vert, between two wings arg. and sa., beaked gu.

Smith, Devonsh., a demi-eagle displayed erm. 81. 6

Smith, Heref. and Herts, an eagle's head between two wings arg., beaked sa., charged on the neck with three pellets. *cf.* 84. 2

Smith of Yarmouth, Norf., an eagle regardant with wings elevated ppr., beaked, membered, and crowned with a naval coronet or, resting the dexter claw on a quadrant of the last, the string and plummet az.

Smith, Sir Clarence, Esquire, D.L., of Falcon Wood, Shooter's Hill, on a wreath of the colours two pick-axes in saltire sa., thereon an eagle with wings expanded or, each wing charged with a mullet of six points gu. *Quærendo.* 78. 2

Smith of Craigend, Craighead, and Carbeth Guthrie, Stirlingsh., Jordanhill, Renfrewsh., and Skelmorliebank, Ayrsh., Scotland, an eagle's head erased ppr., gorged with a ducal coronet or. *Macte.* *cf.* 83. 10

Smith, James Parker, J.P., D.L., 20, Draycott Place, S.W., same crest and motto.

Smith, Shropsh., an eagle's head erased az., ducally gorged or. *cf.* 83. 10

Smith, a phœnix's head or, in flames ppr.

Smith, Bart., of Hadley, Middx., a falcon with wings addorsed ppr., belled or, holding in the beak an acorn slipped and leaved, also ppr. *Spes, decus, et robur.*

Smith, out of a ducal coronet or, a demi-falcon with wings expanded ppr. 88. 10

Smith, Lancs, an ostrich or, holding in the beak a horse-shoe arg. 97. 8

Smith of London, an ostrich's head quarterly arg. and sa., between two ostrich-feathers of the first, holding in the beak a horse-shoe or. 97. 12

Smith, Bart. (*extinct*), of Upton-in-Westham, Essex, an ostrich's head couped holding in the beak a horse-shoe, all ppr.

Smith of Abingdon, Berks, and London, on a mural coronet or, an ostrich's head erased ppr., beaked of the first, holding in the beak a horse-shoe arg.

Smith, Bart. (*extinct*), of Hough, Chesh., an ostrich gu., holding in the beak a horse-shoe arg. 97. 8

Smith of Bradbury and Nutburch, Chesh., an ostrich's head arg., winged az., gorged with a collar wavy of the last charged with three bezants, and holding in the beak a horse-shoe of the second

Smith of West Ham Essex, and Stoke Prior, Worcs, an ostrich's head quarterly sa and arg, between two wings expanded gu, holding in the beak a horse-shoe or *cf* 97 10

Smith, Worcs, a demi-ostrich arg, with wings expanded gu, holding in the beak a horse-shoe or

Smith or **Smyth,** Sussex and Suff out of a mural coronet an ostrich's head or

Smith of London, an ostrich arg holding in the beak a horse-shoe all ppr 97 8

Smith or **Smyth** of London, an ostrich's head couped holding in the beak a horse-shoe, all ppr 97 8

Smith, Norf, an ostrich with wings expanded arg, holding in the beak a key or

Smith, Lea-, Ferdinando, of Halesowen Grange, Worcs (1) An ostrich's head quarterly sa and arg, between two wings expanded gu, holding in the beak a horse-shoe or (*for Smith*) *cf* 97 10 (2) A unicorn arg, guttee-de-poix gorged with a double tressure flory and counterflory gu (*for Lea*) *In se ipso totus teres*

Smith (1) On an anchor sa, an ostrich erminois, holding in the beak a horse shoe or (2) Of augmentation a mount vert, inscribed with the Greek letters κιρα or, and issuing therefrom a representation of the silphium plant ppr

Smith of London, and Wray, Lancs, out of a mural coronet arg, an ostrich's head of the last.

Smith, an ostrich ppr, holding in the beak a horse-shoe or *Tu ne cede malis* 97 8

Smith, Chesh, an ostrich arg., holding in the beak a horse-shoe or 97 8

Smith-Shand, James William Fraser Esquire, M D, of Templeland, Aberdeen, a dove volant over the waters with an olive branch in its beak ppr *Virtute duce comite fortuna* 264 7

Smith, out of a ducal coronet or, a dove rising arg

Smith of Damagh co Kilkenny, Ireland, a dove close holding in its beak an olive branch, both ppr, gorged with a bar gemel or, beaked and legged gu *cf* 92 5

Smith, Ireland, a martlet sa 95 5

Smith of Old Park, Devizes, Wilts a caduceus erect ppr, thereon a martlet sa *Nil desperandum*

Smith, Alexander Mackenzie, Esquire, of Bolton Hey, Roby Liverpool on a wreath of the colours, issuant from a chaplet of roses arg, a rock ppr, thereon a martlet rising or, holding in the beak a rose as in the chaplet, leaved and slipped ppr *Suaviter sed fortiter* 250 9

Smith, Francis Patrick, Barnes Hall, near Sheffield, same crest and motto

Smith of Windsor, Berks, a martlet purp 95 4

Smith of Newcastle under-Lyne, Staffs, a parrot vert, beaked and legged gu 101 4

Smith of Little Baddow, Essex, a peacock's head erased az, ducally gorged or *cf* 103 1

Smith of Calais France, a stork's head couped or, beaked gu charged with two bends vert, and between two wings endorsed sa

Smith of Overdinsdale Hall Durh, on a mount vert, a stork with wings elevated arg charged on the breast and on either wing with a cross crosslet gu and holding in the beak a snake ppr

Smith of Togston Northumb a stork arg holding in his beak a serpent ppr

Smith, Durh, a stork arg, rising from a mount vert beaked and legged gu, holding in the beak a serpent ppr

Smith of Rybope, Durh, and Carrow borough, Northumb, on a mount vert, a stork with wings elevated arg, charged on the breast and on either wing with a cross crosslet gu, holding in the beak a snake ppr *Tenax et fidelis*

Smith, Joseph, Esquire, J P, of Plas Parciaw, Old Colwyn North Wales a rose gu, barbed and seeded ppr thereon an owl arg *Labore et diligentia*

Smith, Gordon, M R C S, Richmond Road, Barnsbury Middx in front of a mount vert a serpent nowed thereon an owl all ppr *Cænobio salvus*

Smith of Bristol Somers a heron's head per fess or and gu holding in the beak a dart of the first flighted ppr barbed of the second

Smith of Theddlethorpe Lincs a heron's head erased sa, beaked gu, and holding in the beak a fish arg

Smith of London a heron's head erased sa, guttee d'or, holding in the beak gu a fish arg

Smith of Mitcham Surrey, a stag's head erased gu, attired arg 121 2

Smith, Bucks a heron's head erased holding in the beak a fish ppr

Smith, Leadbitter-, John, Esquire, of Bird Hill, Whickham Durh (1) A stag lodged arg, semee of estoiles az, attired and gorged with an Eastern coronet, the chain reflexed over the back or (*for Smith*) (2) A griffin's head sa, erased gu, pierced through the mouth by an arrow fesseways or (*for Leadbitter*) *Fidelis* *cf* 66 8

Smith of Brambridge, Hants a stag's head erased ppr, attired or, gorged with a wreath of laurel, also ppr 120 3

Smith, a stag's head erased gu 121 2

Smith of London, out of a vallary coronet a demi-buck or pierced through with an arrow in bend sinister gu, barbed and flighted arg

Smith, Surrey a demi-stag erm, attired sa, vulned in the shoulder gu *cf* 119 2

Smith, Taylor-, of Colpike Hall, Durh (1) A stag lodged arg, semee-d'etoiles az, attired and gorged with an Eastern coronet and therefrom a chain reflexed over the back or (*for Smith*) (2) A horse's head couped sa gorged with a plain collar, pendent therefrom an escutcheon arg, charged with a cinquefoil vert (*for Taylor*) *Vigilans*

Smith of the Priory, Dudley, Worcs, and of Berry Hill, Staffs, upon a mount vert, in front of a rock a chamois, both ppr *Per saxa per ignes*

Smith-Shenstone, Frederick, Esquire, J P, D L, of Sutton Hall, Barcombe, Lewes on a mount vert, in front of a rock ppr a chamois charged with a crescent *Per saxa per ignes*

Smith, Sir Edwin Thomas, K C M G, M P, J P of the Acacias, Marryatville, South Australia, a goat's head couped arg, gorged with a collar gemelle az, and between two bezants *Dum spiro, spero*

Smith, Bart (*extinct*), of Edmondthorpe, Leics, out of a ducal coronet or, an Indian goat's head arg, eared sa, armed of the first

Smith of Withcote, Leics, out of a ducal coronet or, an Indian goat's head arg eared sa, bearded and armed of the first

Smith, Lincs and Middx, same crest

Smith, Philip Vernon, Esquire LL D, of 116, Westbourne Terrace W, and 4 Stone Buildings, Lincoln's Inn W C, out of a ducal coronet or, an Indian goat's head arg, erased sa, bearded and attired of the first

Smith-Bosanquet, *see* Bosanquet

Smith-Chatterton, *see* Chatterton

Smith-Cunninghame, *see* Cunninghame

Smith-Dorrien, *see* Dorrien

Smith-Gordon, *see* Gordon

Smith-Masters, *see* Masters

Smith, the late Rev Jeremiah Finch M A, F S A, Prebendary of Lichfield Cathedral, late Rector of Aldridge Staffs, and Rural Dean, a lion rampant sa, on the head a crown vallary holding between the fore paws a Passion cross, and resting the dexter hind foot upon an annulet all or *Doctrina ferro perennior*

Smith, Bart, of Aliwal, upon an Eastern coronet or, a lion rampant arg supporting a lance ppr, therefrom flowing to the sinister a pennon gu, charged with two palm branches in saltire or 227 13

Smith, a demi lion rampant supporting a smith's hammer, all ppr

Smith, Shropsh, a lion's head erased arg 17 8

Smith, a lion's head erased or 17 8

Smith, Rev Algernon Emerick Clementi, Rector of Chadwell St Mary Essex in front of a lion's head erased arg, gorged with a collar flory counterflory az, on the head a crown vallary or, three mullets fessewise, also or

Smith of London a talbot passant party per pale or and sa 54 1

Smith, Henry Flesher Esquire J P, of Kyogle Casino, New South Wales, Australia in front of a talbot's head couped gu, a cinquefoil erm, between two trefoils slipped vert

Smith, Thomas Hawkins, Esquire, J P, of Gordon Brook, Grafton, New South Wales, Australia same crest

Smith-Rewse, Major Henry Whistler, of Glenrock, Sydney, New South Wales, Australia (1) A demi lion rampant erm holding in the paws a branch of laurel slipped vert (*for Rewse*) (2) In front of a talbot's head couped gu, a cinquefoil erm, all between two trefoils slipped vert (*for Smith*)

Smith-Rewse, Henry Stinton Esquire, of Manly and Wollongong, in the suburbs of the city of Sydney, New South Wales, Australia, and of 18, Southwell Gardens, South Kensington; Rev. Gilbert Flesher Smith-Rewse, M.A., Rector of St. Margaret's and St. Peter's, South Elmham, Suffolk, England; and Eustace Alfred Smith-Rewse of Manly, Sydney, New South Wales: (1) A demi-lion rampant erm., holding in the paws a branch of laurel slipped vert, and charged on the shoulder for difference with a mullet gu. (*for Rewse*). (2) In front of a talbot's head couped gu., a cinquefoil erm., all between two treifoils slipped vert (*for Smith*).

Smith, on a mount vert, a talbot sejant erm., collared gu. *cf.* 55. 1

Smith of London, a talbot per pale or and sa., holding in the mouth a rose ppr., leaved vert.

Smith of More End, Northamp., a talbot's head couped gu., charged on the neck with a cinquefoil erm. *cf.* 56. 12

Smith, a talbot statant ppr., collared, and a chain therefrom reflexed over the back or. *cf.* 54. 2

Smith, Bart., of Suttons, Essex, a talbot statant sa., collared, and a chain therefrom reflexed over the back or. *cf.* 54. 2

Smith-Ryland, Charles Alston, Esquire, J.P., of Barford Hill, Warw.: (1) Issuing from a mount vert, a dexter arm embowed in armour ppr., garnished or, the hand, also ppr., holding a rose gu., slipped and leaved of the first, and three ears of rye or (*for Ryland*). 199. 8. (2) A talbot passant or, resting the dexter fore-paw upon an escutcheon sa., charged with a saltire couped, also or, and holding in the mouth an acorn slipped and leaved ppr. (*for Smith*). *Not the last.* 54. 13

Smith-Marriott, Sir William Henry Marriott, Bart., of Sydling, St. Nicholas, Dorset: (1) A mount vert, thereon a talbot passant sa., guttée-d'eau, collared, and a line reflexed over the beak or (*for Marriott*). 282. 4. (2) A greyhound sejant gu., collared, and a line reflexed over the back or, charged on the shoulder with a mascle arg. (*for Smith*). *Semper fidelis.* 309. 11

Smith, Sir William, Bart., J.P., D.L., of Eardiston, Worcs., a greyhound couchant sa., collared, and a line therefrom reflexed over the back or, the body charged with a cross crosslet of the last, the dexter paw resting upon a cross flory or. 308. 2

Smith, Wilts, a greyhound current. *cf.* 58. 2

Smith of Exeter, a greyhound sejant gu., collared and lined arg. *cf.* 59. 2

Smith of Ashfield, Suff., a greyhound couchant or, collared and lined sa. *cf.* 60. 1

Smith, Devonsh., a greyhound sejant gu., collared, and a line therefrom reflexed over the back or. *cf.* 59. 4

Smith, His Honour Judge Lumley, M.A., K.C., 25, Cadogan Square, S.W., on a wreath of the colours, sa. and arg., in front of a mount vert, thereon a greyhound couchant ppr., two battle-axes in saltire or. *Prêt à tressaillir.*

Smith of Bombay, a demi-greyhound regardant arg., supporting a flagstaff ppr., therefrom flowing to the sinister a banner sa., charged with a bull's head caboshed between two wings arg. *In Deo fides.*

Smith, Notts, an elephant's head couped or, charged on the neck with three fleurs-de-lis sa., one and two. *Tenax in fide.* *cf.* 133. 2

Smith, Notts, an elephant's head couped or. *Tenax in fide.* 133. 2

Smith, Notts, an elephant's head erased or, eared gu., charged on the neck with three fleurs-de-lis az., two and one. *cf.* 133. 3

Smith of Houghton Castle, Northumb., an elephant ppr. 133. 9

Smith, Notts, an elephant's head erased or, eared gu., and charged on the neck with three fleurs-de-lis, two and one az. *Tenax et fidelis.* *cf.* 133. 3

Smith, Oswald Augustus, D.L., Hammerwood Lodge, East Grinstead, same crest and motto.

Smith, Abel Henry, Woodhall Park, Herts, an elephant's head erased or, charged on the neck with three fleurs-de-lis sa., one and two. *cf.* 133. 3

Smith, Reginald Abel, of Goldings, Herts, same crest.

Smith, Samuel George, of Sacombe Park, Ware, same crest.

Smith, Frederic Chatfield, Bramcote Hall, Nottingham, same crest.

Smith, Rowland, Duffield, Derby, same crest.

Smith, Francis Abel, Wilford House, Nottingham, same crest.

Smith, Robert Claude, Esquire, of Redcliffe Tower, Paignton, Devonsh., a dolphin haurient ppr. *Mediis tranquillus in undis.* 140. 11

Smith of Whitechapel, London, waves of the sea ppr., thereon a dolphin haurient az., guttée-d'eau, holding in the mouth a fish or.

Smith, William Macadam-, Esquire, J.P., Abbotsfield, Wiveliscombe, Somers., in front of a dolphin haurient or, three chess-rooks az. *Generosity with justice.* 235. 2

Smith, an anchor erect or, entwined about the stock by a dolphin spouting water from the mouth and nostrils ppr. *Victor sine sanguine.* *cf.* 140. 8

Smith of Gottenburg, and Aberdeensh., Scotland, an anchor erect or, the stock sa. *Sine sanguine victor.* 161. 1

Smith of Camno, Forfarsh., Scotland, an anchor ppr. *Hold fast.* 161. 1

Smith of Boughton, Somers., a griffin's head erased gu., charged on the neck with two bars or, beaked and eared of the last. *Quid capit, capitur.* 66. 4

Smith of Elford, Staffs, a griffin's head erased per fesse sa. and gu., gorged with a collar arg., charged with three pellets. *cf.* 66. 2

Smith of Shirford, Warw., a griffin's head erased sa., bezantée. *cf.* 66. 5

Smith, Hon. Charles William, of Ballynatray, co. Waterford, Ireland, out of a ducal coronet or, a demi-bull salient arg., armed and ungu. of the first, and charged with a crescent gu. for difference. *Cum plena magis.*

Smith, *alias* **Smithley,** of Brantingham and Beverley, Yorks, out of a ducal coronet gu., a demi-bull arg., armed or.

Smith of Beabeg and Annsbrook, co. Meath, Ireland, a demi-bull salient az., armed and ungu. or. *Delectat amor patriæ.* *cf.* 45. 8

Smith, Michael Edward, same crest and motto.

Smith of Maine, co. Louth, Ireland, same crest. *cf.* 45. 8

Smith, Ireland, a bull's head couped sa., armed or. *cf.* 44. 3

Smith, Baron Strathcona and Mount Royal, on a mount vert, a beaver eating into a maple-tree ppr. *Perseverance.* 134. 14

Smith of Pygon's Hill, Lydiate, Lancs, on a mount vert, a squirrel arg., charged on the body with a fountain, and holding a marigold slipped ppr. *In medio tutissimus.*

Smith of Brindley, Chesh., a demi-wolf erm., holding in the dexter paw a fleur-de-lis or. *cf.* 31. 2

Smith of Tuddenham and Edmondsbury, a wolf's head erased arg., ducally gorged or. *cf.* 30. 8

Smith, a dragon's head erased or, pelletée. *cf.* 71. 2

Smith, Rev. Joseph Denham, of St. Marylebone, Middx., and Vesey Place, Dublin, a dragon's head erased az., charged with a mullet of six points, and collared flory counterflory or, pierced through the mouth by an arrow fessewise, the point to the dexter ppr.

Smith, Bart., of Newland, Yorks, out of a ducal coronet or, a boar's head az., tusked and crined of the second, langued gu. 41. 4

Smith: (1) Issuing from an Eastern coronet or, a leopard's head ppr., gorged with a plain collar, therefrom a line reflexed of the first. (2) Of augmentation, the imperial Ottoman "chelingk," or plume of triumph, from a turban.

Smith, Ireland, a leopard's head erased arg., spotted sa. 22. 10

Smith, a leopard's head erased arg., spotted sa., collared, lined, and ringed or.

Smith of London, an heraldic tiger sejant arg., tufted and maned or, resting the dexter paw on a broken pillar of the last.

Smith of London, an heraldic tiger sejant erm., tufted or.

Smith, Benjamin Brown, Esquire, of Wolverhampton, Staffs, an heraldic tiger arg., vulned in the neck ppr., charged on the body with two pheons, and resting the dexter fore-leg on a pheon gu.

Smith of Binderton, Sussex, a demi-unicorn gu., maned, armed, ungu., and tufted arg., holding between the fore-legs a lozenge or.

Smith-Milnes, William Broughton, Esquire, of Dunston Hall, Chesterfield, Derbysh.: (1) A mount vert, thereon in front of a boar's head couped sa., muzzled or, a mill-rind of the last (*for Milnes*). 34. 12. (2) A unicorn's head erased per pale arg. and az., gorged with a ducal coronet counter changed and armed or (*for Smith*) *Fortiter et recte* *cf* 49 5

Smith, Richard Clifford Ashford Hall Bakewell, upon a mount vert, in front of a rock, a chamois ppr *Per saxa, per ignes*

Smith-Chatterton, William Peters Esquire of Belmont, Raheny co Dublin (1) An antelope's head erased ppr, attired or, pierced through the back of the neck with an arrow, also ppr, gorged with a ducal coronet of the second, and charged on the neck with a cross crosslet gu (*for Chatterton*) (2) Out of a crown vallary or, a unicorn's head az, armed, crined, and tufted of the first, and charged with a crescent of the same (*for Smith*) *Loyal a mort*

Smith, Henry Dolling Esquire of 18, Maida Vale Mansions Maida Vale, N W, a unicorn's head erased quarterly arg and az *Prodesse quam conspici*

Smith, Bart, Ireland out of a ducal coronet or, a unicorn's head az, armed of the first. *En Dieu est mon espoir* 48 12

Smith, Major General Walter Henry, a unicorn's head quarterly arg and az, erased or *C'en est fait*

Smith, Ireland, a unicorn's head couped sa 49 7

Smith, Cusac-, Sir William, Bart (1) Out of a ducal coronet or, a unicorn's head az, armed of the first 48 12 (2) A mermaid sa, crined and garnished or, holding in her dexter hand a mirror ppr *En Dieu est mon espoir* 184 5

Smith of London out of a mural coronet or a horse's head sa, bridled gu, maned arg

Smith of Walsham, Suff, a horse's head per chevron or and sa *cf* 50 13

Smith, a horse's head erased az gorged with a collar or, charged with a fleur-de lis between two crosses patee fitchee sa

Smith, Ireland, a horse's head couped sa, bridled and double reined arg, bitted or *Prêt* *cf* 51 5

Smith, a salamander couchant regardant and ducally gorged in flames, all ppr

Smith of Denby, Derbysh, an escallop party per fess or and az 141 14

Smith of Edinburgh, Scotland, a flame of fire between two branches of palm ppr *Luceo, non uro* 146 12

Smith of Giblston, Fifesh, Scotland, a crescent arg *Cum plena magis* 163 2

Smith of Jamaica and Scotland a sword and a pen in saltier ppr *Marte et ingenio* 170 4

Smith, Sir Charles Cunliffe, Bart, D L of Tring Park, Herts, a pen in bend or feathered arg, surmounted in saltire by a sword ppr, tied by a ribbon gu, pendent therefrom an escutcheon az, charged with an escallop or *Semper fidelis* 170 8

Smith of Apsley House Beds, an oak tree ppr, fructed or *Non deficit alter* 143 5

Smith of Tan-y Graig, Carnarvonsh, on a rock a tower, both ppr, thereon a crescent surmounted by a mullet of six points or *Lux omnibus refulgeat*

Smith-Barry (Lord Barrymore) a castle arg, and issuant from the battlements a wolf's head sa charged with a cross patee fitchee *Boutez en avant* 254 6

Smith-Barry, James Hugh, same crest and motto

Smith of London on a mount vert, a castle or, between two branches ppr

Smith of Oldhaugh Chesh, a fleur-de-lis per pale or and gu 148 2

Smith of Dorchester a fleur de-lis arg *Benigno numine* 148 2

Smith, a fleur-de lis arg, charged with a cross crosslet sa *cf* 148 2

Smith, Glouc a saltier gu, surmounted of a fleur-de-lis

Smith, Sir Thomas Bart, a fret gu, issuant therefrom a fleur de lis or *Dabit qui dedit* 288 5

Smith of Thraxted, Essex, a demi-wild man ppr, holding in his dexter hand four ears of barley vert and in his sinister a flintstone ppr, his hair sa and wreathed about the temples also ppr

Smith, Scotland, a Minerva s head ppr *Non invita* 182 1

Smith, a plume of five feathers *cf* 114 13

Smith of Halesworth Suff, on a chapeau gu, turned up erm, two wings az, billettee or each charged with a bend erm

Smith of Elmsett, Suff a mullet or charged with a crescent between two wings expanded gu *cf* 111 5

Smith of Hammersmith Middx a sword in pale point upwards entwined with an ivy-branch ppr

Smith of Rochester Kent, a sword in pale ppr hilted or entwined with two ivy branches of the last *Rapit ense triumphos*

Smith, on a ducal coronet vert two swords in saltire arg, hilted or *cf* 171 12

Smith of London on the top of a pillar ppr, a sphere or

Smith of Oundle, Northamp, within an annulet gu, a garb or

Smith, Ireland, two battle-axes in saltire gu headed or 172 4

Smith-Gordon, Sir Lionel Eldred, Bart (1) Issuant from the battlements of a tower a stag's head affrontee ppr, between two palm-branches vert (*for Gordon*) 309 5 (2) Of augmentation, a representation of the ornamental silver centre-piece of the service of plate presented to Lieutenant-General Sir Lionel Smith by his European and native friends at Bombay, all ppr (3) Out of an Eastern coronet or, a dexter arm embowed in armour, encircled by a wreath of laurel, the hand grasping a broken sword, all ppr (*for Smith*) *Animo non astutia —Mea spes est in Deo* 309 6

Smith, I P G Esquire of Sweyney Cliff, near Coalport, Ironbridge Shropsh a dexter arm in armour embowed holding in the hand a scimitar, all ppr *Veritas usque ad finem* 196 10

Smith, Scotland, a hand holding a pen ppr 217 10

Smith of Dirleton, Haddingtonsh Scotland, a dexter hand holding a writing pen ppr *Ex usu commodium* 217 10

Smith, two arms armed, couped above the elbow ppr, holding a sword in both hands fesseways arg, pommel or

Smith of Smithfield, a hand grasping a dagger *Ready* 212 3

Smith, Scotland and of London an arm from the shoulder in armour, brandishing a sword ppr *Carid nam fecham* 195 2

Smith, Scotland, a dexter hand holding a hammer ppr *Semper paratus.*

Smith, Scotland a dexter hand in fess, issuing from a cloud in the sinister and holding a pen all ppr *Floret qui vigilat*

Smith, Duff-Assheton, George William, of Vaynol Carnarvonsh (1) Issuant from a mural coronet or two arms embowed vested az, cuffed arg holding in the hands a pheon or (*for Smith*) (2) A mower in the act of mowing vested per pale arg and sa, the sleeves and hose counterchanged the cap quarterly arg and sa, the scythe handle or, the blade ppr (*for Assheton*) *cf* 188 12

Smith, the late Rt. Hon William Henry P C., Lord Warden of the Cinque Ports of Oxey Herts and Greenlands, Hambleden, Bucks, a cubit arm erect habited az cuffed and charged with three mascles in chevron arg holding in the hand ppr three acorn branches vert fructed or

Smith, Hon William Frederick Danvers, 3, Grosvenor Place, S W, same crest *Deo non fortuna fretus*

Smith, a hand ppr, vested chequy arg and az, holding three arrows two in saltier and one in pale or feathered and headed arg

Smith, Suff a dexter arm in armour ppr, garnished or holding in the hand of the first a chaplet vert

Smith of Eastbourne, Sussex, an arm in armour embowed ppr, charged with an escallop or, holding in the hand of the first a sword arg, hilt and pommel of the second, the blade environed with a chaplet of laurel vert

Smith of London two arms embowed vested az, cuffed arg, holding in the hands ppr a pheon or

Smith, Sidney Brooklands 58 West End Lane, West Hampstead N W, on a Roman fasces a pheon, point upwards, or, between two laurel branches fructed ppr *Concedat laurea linguæ* 250 16

Smith of London, an arm in pale vested az cuffed arg, holding in the hand ppr three acorn branches vert, fructed or

Smith of London, a cubit arm erect vested bendy arg and az, holding in the hand ppr a roll of paper *cf* 208 5

Smith, Norf, a naked arm embowed ppr, bound round the wrist with a ribbon az, holding in the hand the cronel of a broken spear or

Smith, Durh a dexter arm embowed vested erminois, cuffed arg, the hand grasping a broken sword ppr, the hilt or

Smith of Braxted, Essex an arm couped at the elbow and erect vested gu cuffed arg, holding in the hand ppr a cross formee sa

Smith, Bart. (*extinct*), of Pickering of Upper Canada, and Preston, Northumb., a sinister hand apaumée erect couped at the wrist gu., the wrist encircled with a wreath of oak or, the palm charged with a trefoil slipped arg., and on an escroll above the hand the motto *Canada*. *Pro Rege et patria.*

Smith of Ballygowan, co. Down, Ireland, a naked arm couped lying fesseways, grasping in the hand a sword erect, all ppr. *Tenebras expellit et hostes.*

Smith, Sir Thomas, Bart., 5, Stratford Place, W., a fret gu., issuant therefrom a fleur-de-lis or. *Dabit qui dedit.*

Smith, Percy Macan, same crest and motto.

Smith, Roandeu Albert Henry Bickford, F.S.A., M.A., in front of a thunderbolt winged arg. and inflamed ppr., a representation of a Cyclops' head affrontée, also ppr. *Mine eye is single.*

Smith, William Robert, M.D., 74, Great Russell Street, W.C., in front of an anvil, thereon a falcon's wings endorsed and inverted ppr., belled and jessed gu., resting the dexter leg on an escutcheon vert, charged with a serpent nowed or, two swords in saltire, points downwards, pommels and hilt or. 252. 6

Smith, Robert Thomas, Esquire, of Burrage Road, Plumstead, Kent, same crest. *Prudentia et constantia.*

Smith, Lieutenant-Colonel William, Binn Cottage, Dundee, a fleur-de-lis arg., interlaced with a horse-shoe sa. *Ready and fit.* 230. 18

Smith, R. F., Ruthven, Esquire, Mount Cottage, Sunningdale, an elephant's head erased charged with three fleurs-de-lis. *Tenax in fide.*

Smith, Colonel Albert, 53, Egerton Gardens, London, S.W., a talbot passant or. *Tenax in fide.*

Smither, a hawk's head erased ppr. 88. 12

Smitherman, a stork or, charged on the neck with two bars gemelle sa., and gorged with a ducal coronet gu.

Smithers, an eagle's head gu. 83. 1

Smithesby, Ireland, a wolf's head erased arg., gorged with a belt gu., the buckle or.

Smithson, a squirrel sejant cracking a nut ppr. 135. 7

Smithson, out of a ducal coronet or, a demi-lion rampant gu., holding a sun ppr.

Smithwick, Herts, an arm embowed vested bendy of six engrailed vert and arg., cuffed of the last, holding in the hand a rose, all ppr.

Smollet, the stump of an oak-tree shooting young branches ppr. *Viresco.* 145. 2

Smollett of Bonhill, Dumbartonsh., the trunk of an oak-tree sprouting out branches ppr. *Viresco.* 145. 2

Smollett of Kirktown and Stenifleet, Scotland, the trunk of a tree sprouting out leaves ppr. *Adhuc viresco.* 145. 2

Smyly of Dublin, an arm in armour embowed ppr., the hand holding by the point a pheon gu.

Smyly, Sir Philip Crampton, 4, Merrion Square, Dublin, same crest. *Viribus virtus.*

Smyly, William Cecil, K.C., St. George's Square, S.W., same crest and motto.

Smyly, Ireland, out of a mural coronet or, a dexter arm in armour embowed ppr., holding a pheon in pale gu.

Smyth, *see* Mountcashell, Earl.

Smyth, Baron Kiltarton and Viscount Gort: (1) A lion's head couped arg. (*for Smyth*). 21. 1. (2) An antelope trippant ppr., attired and ungu. or. *Vincit veritas.* 126. 6

Smyth, Yorks, a unicorn's head erased az. 49. 5

Smyth of Binderton, Sussex, a demi-unicorn gu., armed and crined or, holding between the fore-legs a lozenge of the last.

Smyth, Colonel the Hon. Leicester: (1) Out of a ducal coronet or, a unicorn's head az., armed and charged with a lozenge of the first (*for Smyth*). *cf.* 48. 12. (2) A popinjay rising or, collared gu., charged with a rose gu. for distinction (*for Curzon*). *Exaltabit honore.*

Smyth, Hugh Lyle, Barrowmore Hall, Chester, out of a ducal coronet or, a unicorn's head az.

Smyth, Ross Acheson, of Ardmore, co. Londonderry, same crest and motto.

Smyth, a unicorn's head erased az. *Exaltabit honore.* 49. 5

Smyth, Colonel James, of Gaybrook, Mullingar, Ireland, out of a ducal coronet or, a unicorn's head az. *Exaltabit honore.* 48. 12

Smyth of London, a pegasus az., winged gu., ducally gorged and lined or. *cf.* 47. 1

Smyth of Overton, Shropsh., Herts, Asham, Notts, and Credenhill, Heref., a horse's head erased roan colour, the mane sa., the bridle or. *cf.* 51. 5

Smyth of Walsham and Old Buckenham, Norf., a horse's head erased per chevron nebulée or and sa. *cf.* 51. 4

Smyth, G. E., within a horse-shoe or, a horse's head erased per fesse arg. and az.

Smyth, Hugh, Esquire, of Quickswood, near Baldock, Herts, a horse's head erased az., within a horse-shoe or. *Ferrum equitis salus.*

Smyth, James Hugh, Esquire, of Norton Hall, near Baldock, Herts, same crest and motto.

Smyth, Thomas, Esquire, of Edworth, near Baldock, Herts, same crest and motto.

Smyth, Thomas, Esquire, of Stretley, Beds, same crest and motto.

Smyth, George Edward, of Northfield House, Henlow, Beds, a horse's head arg., erased az., within a horse-shoe or. *Ferrum equitis salus.*

Smyth, George Edward, same crest.

Smyth of Hilton, Bridgnorth, Shropsh., a buffalo's head ppr. *cf.* 44. 1

Smyth, Lieutenant-Colonel George John, of Heath Hall, Yorks, out of a ducal coronet or, a demi-bull rampant arg., armed and ungu. of the first, gorged with a collar az., rimmed and charged with three lozenges, also or. *Nec timeo nec sperno.*

Smyth of Beverley, Yorks, out of a ducal coronet gu., a demi-bull salient arg., armed or.

Smyth, Percy, Esquire, of Headborough and Monatrea, co. Waterford, out of a ducal coronet or, a demi-bull salient arg., armed and ungu. of the first, and charged with a martlet for difference. *Cum plena magis.*

Smyth, Colonel John Henry Graham, C.M.G., of Ballynatry, Youghal, and More Park, Kilworth, co. Cork, same crest and motto.

Smyth, Essex, out of a ducal coronet per pale or and gu., a plume of feathers arg. and vert. *cf.* 114. 8

Smyth of Greenwich and Plompton, Kent, out of a ducal coronet per pale or and gu., a plume of five ostrich-feathers, three vert and two arg. 114. 13

Smyth, out of a coronet per pale or and purp., a plume of feathers arg. and vert. *cf.* 114. 8

Smyth of Halesworth, Suff., on a chapeau gu., turned up erm., two wings az., billettée or, each charged with a bend erm. *cf.* 112. 9

Smyth of Gunton, Norf., on a chapeau gu., turned up erm., two wings expanded az., each charged with a bend erm., between six billets or.

Smyth of Yatley, Hants, and Essex, a demi-wild man ppr., holding in the hand a bunch of barley vert, and wreathed round the temples of the same.

Smyth, Bart. (*extinct*), of Long Ashton, Somers., a stag or, attired arg. 117. 5

Smyth, Surrey, a demi-stag salient erm., attired sa. 119. 2

Smyth of Lenton, Beds, a stag's head erased or, charged on the neck with three mullets. *cf.* 121. 2

Smyth of Wighton, Norf., an antelope's head erased sa., collared gu., rimmed, studded, lined, and ringed or. *cf.* 126. 2

Smyth of London, Berks, and of Bosworth, Leics., out of a ducal coronet or, an Indian goat's head arg., eared sa., armed of the first.

Smyth of Honyngton, Lincs, a talbot passant or. 54. 1

Smyth of Shouldham, Norf., a peacock's head erased az. 103. 1

Smyth, Ireland, a demi-peacock ppr., charged with a trefoil or.

Smyth, Wilts, a peacock's head ppr., ducally gorged or. *cf.* 103. 2

Smyth, Beds, Essex, of Ashby Folville, Leics., and Wotton, Warw., a peacock's head erased ppr., ducally gorged or. *cf.* 103. 1

Smyth of London and Chesh., an ostrich arg., holding in the beak a horse-shoe or. 97. 8

Smyth, Worcs. and Essex, an ostrich's head between two wings gu., holding in the mouth a horse-shoe or. *cf.* 97. 10

Smyth, Bart. (*extinct*), of Upton, Essex, an ostrich's head couped, holding in the beak a horse-shoe, all ppr.

Smyth, Sussex, out of a mural coronet an ostrich's head, all or.

Smyth, Ireland, a dove regardant az., holding in the beak an olive-branch vert. 92. 4

Smyth, William Henry, Elkington Hall, Louth, Lincs, a falcon's head erased sa., guttée-d'or, holding in the beak a fish ppr.

Smyth of Annas, Lincs, and Northamp., out of a ducal coronet or, a demi-falcon ppr., with wings expanded arg. 88. 10

Smyth, William Grenville, Esquire, of Elkington, Louth, Lincs, same crest.

Smyth, Herts, a falcon volant, with wings expanded ppr. 88. 3

Smyth, Christopher, Esquire, of Little Houghton, and Brafield, Northamp., on a ducal coronet or, a falcon with wings expanded ppr. *Crux Christi spes mea.*

Smyth, Glouc. and Lincs, a heron's head erased az., holding in the beak a fish arg.

Smyth, Herts and Heref., an eagle's head between two wings arg., beaked sa. 84. 2

Smyth, Devonsh., an eagle close regardant ppr., beaked and legged or. 76. 6

Smyth, Hants, London, and Staffs, out of a ducal coronet or, a swan close erm., beaked gu.

Smyth, General Sir Henry Augustus, K.C.M.G., St. John's Lodge, Stone, Aylesbury; (1) (Of augmentation) A mount vert inscribed with the Greek letters KTPA or, and issuant therefrom the plant silphium ppr. (2) An anchor fesseways sa., thereon an ostrich erminois, holding in the beak a horse-shoe or. *Vincere et vivere.*

Smyth of Elmford, Staffs, a griffin's head erased per fess sa. and gu., gorged with a collar arg., charged with three pellets. *cf.* 66. 2

Smyth of Tregoneck, St. Germans, Cornw., on a chapeau gu., turned up erm., a griffin's head or, plattée, beaked arg.

Smyth, Sir John Henry Greville, Bart., J.P., of Ashton Court and Wraxall Lodge, Somers., and Heath House, Glouc., a griffin's head erased gu., gorged with a collar gemel and beaked and eared or. *Qui capit capitur.* *cf.* 66. 2

Smyth of London and Crabbett, Sussex, a dragon's head erased or, pellettée. *cf.* 71. 2

Smyth of Newcastle-under-Lyne, a tiger passant arg., vulned in the shoulder ppr. *cf.* 27. 11

Smyth of London, an heraldic tiger erm., armed, maned, and tufted or.

Smyth of London, an heraldic tiger sejant erm., armed, tufted, and maned or.

Smyth, Kent, a leopard's head erased arg., spotted sa., collared and lined or. *cf.* 22. 14

Smyth of Henlow, Beds, a leopard's head arg., pellettée, murally gorged, lined, and ringed gu.

Smyth, a lion's head erased or. 17. 8

Smyth, Ireland, a lion rampant per fesse arg. and sa. 1. 13

Smyth of Tuddenham and Edmondsbury, Suff., a wolf's head erased arg., ducally gorged or. *cf.* 30. 8

Smyth, Ireland, a wolf current gu. 28. 4

Smyth, Essex, a salamander in flames, all ppr. 138. 4

Smyth, on a ducal coronet vert, two swords in saltier arg., hilted or. *cf.* 171. 12

Smyth, Derbysh., on a mount vert, a tower triple-towered or, on the sinister side of the mount a laurel-branch pendent over the tower ppr.

Smyth, on the top of a pillar ppr., a sphere or.

Smyth, an arm erect, holding in the hand ppr. a griffin's head erased.

Smyth, Scotland, a dexter arm embowed vambraced, the hand holding a sword ppr. *Carid nam fechum.* 195. 2

Smyth, John Watt, Esquire, J.P., of Duneira, co. Antrim, Ireland, a dexter arm couped below the elbow and erect charged with a palm-branch, and holding in the hand a scimitar, all ppr. *With thy might.* *cf.* 213. 5

Smyth, Norf., and of Southwark, Surrey, an arm embowed ppr., holding in the gauntlet a broken tilting-spear or. 197. 3

Smyth of Totnes, Devonsh., a dexter cubit arm in armour ppr., garnished or, holding in the hand, also ppr., a chaplet vert.

Smyth, Middx., and of Kelmarch, Northamp., a cubit arm erect habited per pale or and gu., cuffed arg., holding in the hand ppr. a griffin's head erased az.

Smyth, Ireland, a sword erect ppr., pierced through a dexter hand couped gu. *Vera fidelitas fortitudo.*

Smyth of Balharry, Forfarsh., Scotland, a dexter arm in armour embowed brandishing a sword ppr. *Carid nam fechm.* 195. 2

Smythe, Viscount Strangford *(extinct)*, an ounce's head erased arg., pellettée, collared and chained sa. *Virtus incendit vires.*

Smythe, Lieutenant-Colonel David Murray, of Methven Castle, Perthsh., a dolphin haurient head upwards. *Mediis tranquillus in undis.*

Smythe of Braco, Scotland, a dolphin haurient ppr. *Mediis tranquillus in undis.* 140. 11

Smythe of Hilton, Shropsh., a buffalo's head ppr. *cf.* 44. 1

Smythe, Surrey, a demi-stag salient erm., attired sa. 119. 2

Smythe, Hants, a stag's head erased ppr., attired or, gorged with a chaplet of laurel vert. 120. 3

Smythe, Sir Charles Frederick, Bart., J.P., D.L., of Eshe Hall, Durh., a buck's head erased, gorged with a chaplet of laurel, all ppr. *Regi semper fidelis.* 120. 3

Smythe of Boughton, Winchelsea, Kent, on a mount vert, a talbot sejant erm., eared and collared sa., ringed or, on the dexter side of the mount a branch of laurel of the first.

Smythe, Francis C. D., of Girdler's Hall, 39, Basinghall Street, London, E.C., a talbot passant. *Tenax in fide.*

Smythe of Corsham, Wilts, a peacock's head ppr., ducally gorged or. *cf.* 103. 2

Smythe, three holly-leaves vert, banded gu. 150. 12

Smythe of London, a dexter arm couped at the elbow per pale or and gu., cuffed arg., holding in the hand ppr. a griffin's head erased az., beaked and charged with a martlet of the first.

Smythe, Scotland, a sword and a pen disposed in saltire ppr. *Marte et ingenio.* 170. 4

Smythe of Atherny, Perthsh., Scotland, a dexter hand holding a lancet ready for action ppr. *Arte et labore.*

Smythe, two arms holding a bow in full draught to let an arrow fly, all ppr. *Mediis tranquillus in undis.* 200. 2

Smytheman, Shropsh., a stork or, ducally gorged gu. *cf.* 105. 11

Smythesby, a wolf's head erased arg., collared gu., buckled or. *cf.* 30. 11

Smythies of Wilke, Somers., a cubit arm vested az., holding in the hand ppr. an oak-branch leaved and fructed or.

Smythies, Major Raymond Henry Raymond, Army and Navy Club, Pall Mall, an arm in pale, habited az., cuff arg., in the hand ppr. a branch of oak-leaves vert, fructed or. *Laudari a laudato.* 285. 15

Smythson, Kent, an arm embowed vested arg., the hand ppr., holding a battle-axe of the first, the handle or.

Snafford, an elephant passant or, on its back a castle arg. 133. 4

Snagg or **Snagge,** Herts, a demi-goat erm., armed or. 128. 2

Snagg or **Snagge,** Herts, a demi-antelope ppr. *cf.* 126. 5

Snagge, His Honour Judge Sir Thomas William, M.A., J.P., of 14, Courtfield Gardens, London, S.W.: (1) Out of a ducal coronet or, a horse's head arg. 51. 7. (2) A demi-antelope erm., attired or. *Respice finem.* 126. 5

Snape, between two wings an escallop ppr. 141. 10

Snape, Snappe, or **Snepp,** of Standlake, Oxon., a buck's head per pale or and vert, attired counterchanged. 121. 5

Snell, on a chapeau ppr., an owl with wings expanded arg. 96. 6

Snell of Kennicott, Devonsh., Glouc., and Kingston, Wilts., a demi-talbot rampant gu., collared and lined or. 55. 8

Snell, a wolf preying on a lamb, in front of a cross Calvary in pale gu.

Snellgrove, an anchor sa., entwined with a serpent vert. 161. 3

Snelling of Snelling, Surrey, a demi-eagle displayed arg. 81. 6

Snelling, Surrey, of East Horsley, Sussex, and of Wheatfield, Suff., a griffin's head or, collared gu., studded of the first. *cf.* 66. 1

Snelling, Surrey, a demi-dog rampant, with dragon's wings addorsed or.

Snelling, Dorset, and of Portslade, Sussex, an arm embowed vested vert, holding in the hand ppr. a cutlass of the second, hilted or, from the pommel a line round the arm tied to the wrist of the last.

Snepp, between two wings an escallop ppr. 141. 10

Sneyd-Edgworth, *see* Edgworth.

Sneyd-Kynnersley, *see* Kynnersley.

Sneyd, Ralph, of Keel, Bishton, and Ashcombe, Staffs, a lion passant gardant sa. *Nec opprimere, nec opprimi.* 4. 3

Sneyd, John William, Basford Hall, Leek, Staffs, same crest and motto.

Sneyd, Major-General Thomas William, of Finsthwaite House, near Ulverston, Lancs, same crest and motto.

Sneyd, Drydon Henry, Esquire, of Ashcombe Park, near Leek, Staffs, same crest and motto.

Sneyd, Clement, Esquire, of Loxley Park, near Uttoxeter, Staffs, same crest and motto.

Sneyd, Rev. Gustavus Alfred, M.A., of Chastleton, Oxon., same crest and motto.

Snigg or **Snigge** of Bristol, Somers., a demi-stag salient erased or. *cf.* 119. 2

Snigg or **Snigge,** a swallow volant ppr. 96. 2

Snodgrass, Scotland, a phœnix in flames ppr. 82. 2

Snooke of Chichester, Sussex, a rock ppr., thereon an eagle regardant with wings elevated or, the dexter claw resting on an escutcheon arg., charged with a fleur-de-lis gu.

Snotterley, Norf., a crane asleep with its head under its wing, holding under the dexter claw a stone ppr.

Snow of Cricksand, Beds, and Surrey, an antelope's head erased per pale nebulée arg. and az. 126. 2

Snow, on a mount vert, an antelope's head erased per pale nebulée erm. and az. *cf.* 126. 2

Snow, Alexander Duffett, Esquire, of Neston, Combe Park, Bath, in front of a bugle-horn gu., an heraldic antelope's head couped per pale, indented arg. and az., and charged with two crosses patée in pale counterchanged. *Probitas verus honor.* 233. 2

Snow, Chesh., a demi-lion or, holding in his dexter paw a tassel sa.

Snowball, Berks, and Potters, Bury, Northamp., on a plate a horse's head erased sa.

Snowden and **Snowdon,** a peacock in his pride ppr. 103. 12

Snowdon, on a mount vert, a horse current, bridled sa. 52. 10

Snuggs, a salamander in flames ppr. *Vive ut vivas.* 138. 4

Soame, *see* Buckworth-Herne-Soame.

Soame of London and Suff., on a lure arg., garnished and lined gu., a hawk close or. *cf.* 85. 14

Soames, a demi-eagle regardant holding in the dexter claw a sword ppr.

Soaper, a demi-lion rampant gu., holding a billet sa.

Sockwell, on a ducal coronet or, an eagle displayed arg. *cf.* 75. 2

Soden, a parrot gu., holding in its beak an annulet or. 101. 11

Soden and **Sodey,** a stag lodged guardant between two laurel-branches ppr. 115. 11

Sodon, Ireland, same crest. 115. 11

Sohier, Jersey, a cross arg., between the attires of a stag ppr. *Stella Christi duce.*

Solay, a dolphin naiant az. 140. 5

Sole of London, out of a mural coronet or, a demi-lion sa., ducally crowned of the first.

Sole, Rev. Arthur Baron, of St. Thomas's Rectory, Winchester, out of a mural crown or, a demi-lion rampant sa. *Semper eadem.*

Solers, on a ducal coronet a phœnix in flames ppr. 82. 5

Soley, a dolphin naiant az. 140. 5

Soley of Upton-on-Severn, and Lickhill, Worcs., on a crescent or, a sole naiant arg.

Solley and **Solly,** in a lake a swan naiant with wings addorsed ppr. 99. 9

Solly-Flood, Major-General Frederick Richard, C.B., of Eastbridge House, Hythe, Kent, a wolf's head erased arg. *Vis unita fortior.*

Soloman, a crane statant, holding in the beak an eel. 105. 8

Solomon, a heron devouring a fish.

Solomon, a demi-wolf holding in the dexter paw a rose slipped and leaved ppr.

Solomons, a clam-shell or. 141. 14

Solsby, a boar's head erect sa. *cf.* 43. 3

Soltau of Little Efford, Plymouth, Devonsh., a demi-lion arg., between two branches of roses ppr. *Miseris succurrere disco.*

Soltau-Symons, George William, Esquire, of Little Efford and Chaddlewood, Plymouth: (1) Upon a mount vert, in front a saltire gu., an ermine, holding in the mouth a fern-branch ppr. (*for Symons*). (2) A demi-lion arg., within two branches of roses ppr. *Simplex munditus.*

Somaster, Somester, Summaster, and **Sumaister,** Cornw., a portcullis with chains or. *Quasi summus magister.* 178. 3

Somer and **Somner,** Kent and Suff., on a mount a peacock ppr. *cf.* 103. 4

Somer of Newland, Kent, a stork per pale gu. and az., ducally gorged or. *cf.* 105. 11

Somerford, Staffs, on a mount vert a palm-tree ppr. 144. 3

Somerhill, Baron, *see* Clanricarde, Marquess of.

Somers, Baron (Cocks), on a mount ppr., a stag lodged regardant arg., attired sa. *Prodesse quam conspici.* 115. 9

Somers of St. Margaret's and Rochester, Kent, a lion's head erased or, charged with a fess dancettée erm. *cf.* 17. 8

Somers, Dorset, a coat of mail hanging on a laurel-tree, all ppr.

Somers, Benjamin Edward, Mendip Lodge, Langford, Somers., a laurel-tree suspended therefrom a cuirass with tasses ppr., on either side of the tree an escallop or, and in front thereof a tilting-spear fessewise ppr. 240. 13

Somerset, Duke of Beaufort, *see* Beaufort.

Somerset, *see* Raglan, Baron.

Somerset, Duke of (St. Maur), out of a ducal coronet or, a phœnix issuing from flames ppr. *Foy pour devoir.* 82. 5

Somerset, Glouc., a portcullis chained or, nailed az. *Mutare vel timere sperno.* 178. 3

Somerset, Arthur F., of Castle Goring, Worthing, a portcullis chained or. *Mutare vel timere sperno.*

Somerset, Colonel Alfred Plantagenet Frederick Charles, C.B., of Enfield Court, Middx., a portcullis or, nailed az., the chains or.

Somerset, Suff., a panther arg., spotted of various colours, incensed ppr.

Somerset of London, out of a naval coronet or, a hippocampus erect arg.

Somersett, Rev. William, of Woolastone Lydney, Glouc., same crest. *Mutare vel timere sperno.*

Somersett of South Brentin, Somers., a dove ppr., between two oak-branches stalked and leaved vert, fructed or. 92. 14

Somerton, Viscount, *see* Normanton, Earl of.

Somervale, Scotland, a wheel or, surmounted of a dragon vert, vomiting fire before and behind. *Fear God in life.* 69. 3

Somervell, Colin, Esquire, J.P., Tenterfield, Kendal, same crest and motto.

Somervell, James, of Sorn Castle, Ayrsh., an anchor in pale, the stock, ring, and cable all ppr. *Hold fast.*

Somervile or **Somerville,** two dexter hands conjoined, the dexter in armour holding a branch of laurel and a thistle in orle, all ppr. 224. 8

Somervile of Eadstone, Warw., two leopards' faces in fess or, both crowned with one ducal coronet gu.

Somerville, Baron Athlumney, *see* Athlumney.

Somerville, Baron Somerville, on a wheel arg., a dragon vert, vomiting flames of fire ppr. *Fear God in life.* *cf.* 69. 3

Somerville, a wyvern ppr. 70. 1

Somerville, Arthur Fownes, of Dinder House, Somers.: (1) A wyvern with wings elevated vert, langued gu., on a wheel erect arg. (*for Somerville*). 69. 3. (2) The stump of an oak-tree erased at the top, sprouting a branch on each side ppr. (*for Fownes*). *Fear God in life.* 145. 2

Somerville, Phillip Horatio Townsend, Admiral R.N., same crest and motto.

Somerville, Major Thomas Cameron Fitzgerald, Deishane, co. Cork, Ireland, a dragon vert, charged with a trefoil or, spouting out fire behind and before ppr., standing on a wheel or. *Fear God in life.* *cf.* 69. 3

Somerville, Bellingham Arthur, Esquire, of Friar's Hill House, Wicklow, Ireland, a demi-lion rampant sa., charged on the shoulder with a cross crosslet fitchée and two mullets arg. *Crains Dieu tant que tu vivras.* 10. 5

Somerville of Hamiltonsfarm, Ayrsh., Scotland, an anchor in pale cabled ppr. *Hold fast.* 161. 2

Somery, Warw., a sword and an ear of wheat in saltire. 154. 11

Somery, Warw., an olive-branch ppr. 151. 11

Somim and **Somin,** a demi-wolf sa., guttée-d'eau, holding in the feet a cross formée fitched in pale or.

Sommer of Dublin, Ireland, a harvest-fly or, speckled sa.

Sommers, Scotland, a lion rampant or. 1. 13

Sommers, W. Stirling, of 4, Parkhill Road, Hampstead, N.W., a stag lodged. *Tandem tranquillius.*

Sommers, a coat of mail ensigned with an oak-branch acorned, all ppr.

Sommerville, a crescent ppr. *Donec rursus impleat orbem.* 163. 2

Sommerville and **Somervil,** a hand holding a crescent ppr. *Donec rursus impleat orbem.* 216. 8

Sommerville, Scotland, a dexter hand throwing a hand-grenade ppr. *Audacem juvant fata.* 216. 6
Somner, an eagle's head erased or. 83. 2
Somner, a sun-flower.
Somner, Kent, a crane per pale gu. and az., ducally gorged, beaked, and legged or.
Sondes, Earl of Feversham (*extinct*), a lion's head erased gu., and thereon a chapeau ppr. 21. 10
Sondes, Earl (Milles), a lion rampant erminois, holding between the paws a fer-de-moulin in pale sa. *Esto quod esse videris.*
Sone or **Soone,** Derbysh. and Suff., a demi-lion rampant arg., guttée-de-sang, holding in the dexter paw a baton or, tipped at the ends sa. *cf.* 15. 9
Sonibanck of Haseley, Oxon., out of a ducal coronet or, two wings expanded az., each charged with a sun in his splendour or. *cf.* 109. 8
Soote of Reres House, Forfarsh., Scotland, a griffin sejant az. *Fidelis et paratus.* 62. 10
Soper, a demi-Cupid holding a hymeneal torch, all ppr. 185. 8
Soper, Cumb., a demi-lion rampant, holding between the paws a billet, all sa.
Soper, William Garland, Esquire, of Hareston, Caterham, Surrey, a demi-lion per pale or and gu., holding in the mouth a trefoil slipped vert, and supporting a torch erect fired ppr. 12. 9
Sopper, William, Esquire, of 3, Upper Belgrave Street, London, and of Dunmaglass, Inverness-sh., a demi-bull regardant sa., gorged with a collar vair, resting the sinister paw on an escutcheon or, charged with two swords saltireways ppr.
Sorocold of London, and Barton Lancs, on the top of a tower or, a fleur-de-lis az.
Sorel, Jersey, a partridge close or. *Une foy une loy.* *cf.* 89. 12
Sorrell of Waltham and Stebbings, Essex, and Ipswich, Suff., on a ducal coronet a peacock, all ppr. 103. 8
Sotheby, the sun in his splendour or. 162. 2
Sotheby, Essex, a lion rampant or, holding in the dexter paw an apple gu.
Sotheby, Major-General Frederick Edward, of Sewardston, Essex, and of Ecton, Northamp., a demi-talbot ppr. *Ou bien ou rien.* 274. 2
Sotheby, Admiral Sir Edward Southwell, K.C.B., of 26, Green Street, Park Lane, W., same crest and motto.
Sotheby, Rev. Walter Edward Hamilton, of St. Barnabas Vicarage, South Kennington, same crest.
Sotheram, a crane holding in the dexter claw a flint-stone, all ppr. 105. 6
Sotheron-Estcourt, *see* Estcourt.
Sotheron of Kirklington, Notts, an eagle with two heads displayed party per pale arg. and gu., the wings semée of cross crosslets counterchanged, murally crowned, beaked, and membered or. *cf.* 74. 2
Sotheron of Holme-in-Spaldingmore, Yorks, an eagle displayed with two heads per pale arg. and gu., semée of cross crosslets counterchanged and ducally crowned upon each head or. *Deo gratias.*
Sotherton, a leg couped above the knee gu., spurred ppr. 193. 8
Sotherton, Norwich, a cameleopard's head erased arg., spotted sa., horned or, and gorged with a ducal coronet of the last.
Sotwell, of Grenham, Berks, and Chate, Wilts, out of a mural coronet gu., a lion's head or, pierced through the neck by an arrow ppr., headed sa., feathered arg.
Souchay, an eagle displayed. 75. 2
Soulsby of Bessingby, near Bridlington, Yorks, and Northumb., a boar's head in fess erased. 42. 2
Souter, a harpy gardant with wings displayed ppr. 189. 4
Souter, Scotland, a crescent or. *Donec impleat.* 163. 2
South, a griffin's head erased. 66. 2
South, a lion rampant, ducally gorged or, holding in the dexter paw a mullet arg., pierced sa.
South, Wilts, a dragon's head ppr., ducally gorged per pale or and az., issuing from the mouth flames of fire of the last. *cf.* 73. 3
Southall, a rock sa. 179. 7
Southam, Viscount, *see* Ellenborough, Earl of.
Southam, a thistle and a rose in saltier ppr. 150. 3
Southam, H.R.H., Esquire, F.S.A., of Shrewsbury, out of a ducal coronet or, an eagle's leg reversed sa. *Honor veritas et justitia.*
Southam, John, of Holmwood, Chorlton-cum-Hardy, near Manchester, same crest and motto.
Southampton, Baron (Fitzroy), on a chapeau gu., turned up erm., a lion statant gardant or, crowned with a ducal coronet az., and gorged with a collar countercompony arg. and of the fourth. *Et decus et pretium recti.* 4. 2
Southbey or **Southebye,** Suff. and Yorks, a demi-talbot purp. *cf.* 55. 8
Southbey or **Southby** of Carswell, Berks, a lion rampant or, holding in the dexter paw an apple gu.
Southbey, on a gauntlet an eagle close ppr.
Southby, a demi-peacock issuing ppr. 103. 10
Southcomb of Rose Ash, Devonsh., a dove holding in its beak an olive-branch, all ppr. 92. 5
Southcote, a star rising from a cloud ppr. 164. 11
Southern, a serpent nowed vert. 142. 4
Southern, a bull's head erased at the neck. 44. 3
Southerne of London, and Fitz, Shropsh., an eagle displayed with two heads per pale arg. and az., ducally crowned upon each head or. *Alta peto.* *cf.* 74. 2
Southerton, Norf., a goat's head sa., plattée, ducally gorged and armed or.
Southesk, Earl of, *see* Carnegie.
Southey, an oak-tree vert. 143. 5
Southland of Romney, Kent, a lion's gamb erect or, grasping a spear-head arg.
Southouse, out of a ducal coronet a talbot's head. 57. 12
Southwell, Viscount (Southwell), a demi-Indian goat arg., armed, eared, and ducally gorged gu., charged on the body with three annulets in pale of the last. *Nec male notus eques.—Dulce est pro patria mori.* 313. 10
Southwell, a demi-Indian goat arg., eared, ungu., and ducally gorged gu., charged on the body with three annulets sa.
Southwell of Kingston-on-Thames, Surrey, a demi-goat arg., armed or, gorged with a collar vair, and resting the sinister foot on a cinquefoil, also arg. *Exitus acta probat.*
Southwerth, Ireland, out of a ducal coronet arg., a bull's head sa. 44. 11
Southwerth or **Southworth** of Southworth and Samlesbury, Lancs., a bull's head erased sa., armed arg. 44. 3
Southworth of Sandbury, Lancs, and Wecke, Champfloure, and Wells, Somers., a bull's head erased sa., the horns arg., the tips of the first, charged on the neck with a crescent for difference. *cf.* 44. 3
Southworth, a bull's head erased arg. 44. 3
Southy, a stag's head guardant ducally gorged ppr.
Sowdeak or **Sowtheake,** Cumb., a dexter arm erect couped at the elbow, vested gu., cuffed with a frill arg., holding in the hand a heart, all ppr.
Sowdeak of London, a dexter arm erect couped at the elbow, vested gu., cuffed with a frill arg., holding in the hand a heart ppr., and charged with an annulet or for difference.
Sowdon, a lion's head couped arg., collared az., charged with three mullets or.
Sowdon of Barnstaple, Devonsh., a lion's head erased erm., charged with a fesse gu., thereon two escallops or, the whole debruised by a bendlet wavy sinister az.
Sowerby, a peacock's head erased ppr. 103. 1
Sowerby of Old Park, Durh., Northumb., Dalston Hall, Cumb., and Putteridge Bury, Herts, a lion rampant arg., langued gu. 1. 13
Sowter of London, a harpy gardant with wings displayed ppr. *Donec impleat.* 189. 4
Sowter, G. S., Solicitor, of Brigg, Lincs, same crest. *Donec impleat orbem.*
Spafford, a demi-gryphon regardant arg., charged on the breast with a pheon, and resting the sinister claw upon an escallop, both az. *Fidelis ad extremum.*
Spafford, Frederic, M.A., LL.M., of Wilderspool Hall, Ormston, Lancs, same crest and motto.
Spaight of Bunratty, co. Clare, and Derry Castle, co. Tipperary, Ireland, a jay ppr. *Vi et virtute.* 107. 7
Spaight, William Fitzhenry, of Union Hall, Leap, co. Cork, same crest and motto.
Spalding, Scotland and France, a cross crosslet fitched or. *Hinc mihi salus.* 166. 2
Spalding, a bishop's mitre or, banded gu., charged with a chevron arg., and thereon three bezants. *cf.* 180. 5
Spalding, an elephant's head or, crowned gu.

Spalding, a sword in pale point upwards ppr. 170. 2

Spalding, Sydney Thomas, Esquire, of Avenue House, South Darenth, Horton Kirby, Kent, between two thistles leaved and slipped vert, an escutcheon az., charged with a cross crosslet or. *Hinc mihi salus.*

Span, on a mount an apple-tree fructed, all ppr.

Spaney of Tunstall, Norf., the head of a bugle erased arg., maned sa., the horns wreathed or, and of the last.

Spange, an arm in armour embowed, brandishing a sword ppr. *Fata viam invenient.* 195. 2

Sparchford of London and Bucks, a demi-dragon sans wings, the tail entwined round the neck or.

Sparchford of London, a demi-griffin segreant or. 64. 2

Sparrhawk, a hawk close, belled ppr. *cf.* 85. 2

Spark, a swan with wings addorsed, devouring a fish ppr. 99. 10

Spark or **Sparke,** a demi-panther ppr.

Sparke or **Sparkes,** Edward Bowyer, of Gunthorpe Hall, Norf., of Nantwich, Chesh., London, Essex, and Devonsh., out of a ducal coronet or, a demi-panther rampant gardant arg., spotted of various colours, fire issuing from the ears and mouth ppr.

Sparke, a swan with wings addorsed swallowing a fish ppr. 99. 10

Sparkes of Glenham, Suff., a fleur-de-lis or. 148. 2

Sparkes, Devonsh. and Cornw., out of a ducal coronet or, a demi-lion guttée-de-sang. *cf.* 16. 3

Sparkling of the Isle of Thanet, Kent, an heraldic tiger's head erased arg., gorged with a ducal coronet, maned and armed or.

Sparks, A. E., Esquire, of St. Claude, Fleet, Hants, a griffin's head erased.

Sparling of Petton, Shropsh., a cubit arm in pale vested az., cuffed arg., holding in the hand ppr. a dagger of the first, hilt or. *Virtutis præmium honor.*

Sparow of Somersham and Ipswich, Suff., out of a mural coronet or, a unicorn's head arg., maned purp., armed or. *Je me contente.*

Sparrow, Ireland, a rose arg., barbed vert. 149. 4

Sparrow, a yew-tree ppr. 143. 1

Sparrow, W. A., of 49, St. John's Wood Road, N.W., out of a mural coronet a unicorn's head. *Tenax propositi.*

Sparrow of Stanborne, Essex, out of a mural coronet or, a unicorn's head arg., armed and maned of the first.

Sparrow of Worlingham Hall, Suff., out of a mural coronet or, a unicorn's head arg., armed and crined of the first.

Sparrow of Penn, Staffs, and Albrighton Hall, Shropsh., out of the battlements of a tower ppr., a unicorn's head arg., armed and crined or, semée of pheons az. *In Deo solo salus est.*

Sparrow, Arthur, Esquire, of Preen Manor, Salop, and Nyth Aderyn, Tenby, South Wales, same crest and motto.

Sparrow, Cecil Blair, same crest and motto.

Sparrow, William Arthur, Esquire, J.P., of Albrighton Hall, Shrewsbury, Salop, same crest and motto.

Sparrow of Blackburn, Lancs, a unicorn's head erased arg., semée of cinquefoils gu. *Spero.* *cf.* 49. 5

Sparrow, Hanbury-, Alan Bertram, of the Uplands, Tettenhall, Wolverhampton: (1) Upon the battlements of a tower ppr., a unicorn's head arg., armed and crined or, semée of pheons az. (*for Sparrow*). (2) Out of a mural sa., a demi-lion or, charged on the shoulder with a trefoil slipped gu., and supporting a battle-axe erect or (*for Hanbury*). *In Deo solo salus est.*

Sparrow, Bodyehan-, *see* Bodyehan-Sparrow.

Sparshott, a palm-tree vert, fructed or. 144. 1

Spateman of Rode Nook, Derbysh., out of a ducal coronet arg., a griffin's head erminois. 67. 9

Spayne, Norf., a bull's head arg., armed or and sa. *cf.* 44. 3

Speake, Somers., a hedgehog arg., armed sa. 135. 8

Speake, a hedgehog sa. 135. 8

Speake and **Speke,** Wilts, Somers., and Devonsh., a hedgehog passant ppr. *cf.* 135. 8

Spealt of Herweton, Devonsh., out of a ducal coronet or, a demi-dragon with wings addorsed az. *cf.* 73. 10

Spear, a dolphin haurient devouring a fish ppr. 140. 6

Spear, Ireland, a rose gu., stalked and leaved vert, and a spear or, in saltier. 150. 1

Spearing, on a globe a ship under sail ppr. 160. 1

Spearman of Dunnington, Shropsh., a demi-lion rampant holding in the mouth a spear ppr. *Dum spiro, spero.*

Spearman of Old Acres, Durh., and of Thornley, Durh., a demi-lion rampant holding in his mouth a spear ppr. *Dum spiro, spero.*

Spearman, out of a ducal coronet or, a demi-lion grasping a spear.

Spearman of Eachwicke Hall, Northumb., a lion rampant ppr., gorged with a collar arg., pendent therefrom a bell sa., and supporting a tilting-spear arg., headed or, the spear entwined by a laurel-branch ppr.

Spearman, Sir Joseph Layton Elmes, Bart., J.P., of the Hall, Wem, Salop, a lion rampant ppr., gorged with a collar gemelle or, supporting a tilting-spear also ppr., enfiled with a mural crown of the second. *Dum spiro, spero.* 313. 6

Speccott of Anderdon in Launcells, Cornw., an eagle displayed gu. 75. 2

Spedding, a cornucopia or, the flowers and fruit ppr. 152. 13

Spedding, James Wyndham Harrington Percy, of Summer Grove, Cumb., out of a mural coronet or, a dexter arm in armour embowed holding in the hand a scimitar, the arm charged with three acorns, one and two, and entwined by a branch of oak, all ppr. *Utile dulci.*

Spedding, the late Robert Deey, Esquire, M.A., J.P., of Armathwaite, Exmouth, South Devonsh., in front of two battle-axes in saltire ppr., a boar's head erased. *Prompte sed astute.*

Speede of London, a swallow with wings expanded ppr.

Speer of the Grove, Fulham, Middx.: (1) A garb per fesse or and arg., banded vert, with a spear erect issuing from the centre ppr. (*for Speer*). (2) A griffin segreant per fesse erminois and az., holding between the claws a cross crosslet fitchée of the last (*for Sandys*).

Speer, Hannibal, Esquire, of the Manor House, Thames Ditton, and 26, the Grove, Boltons, S.W., same crests.

Speer, Alfred Ernest, Esquire, of Sandown Lodge, Esher, Surrey, late Captain 3rd Battalion Worcester Regiment, an arm embowed, vambraced, the hand bare, and grasping a spear point downwards, all ppr., and charged on the arm with a thistle, slipped or. *Dum spiro spero.* 303. 10

Speght, a dexter arm vested sa., cuffed arg., holding in the hand ppr. a pheon of the second.

Speid of Ardovie, Forfarsh., Scotland, an armed man from the knees upwards drawing a sword ppr. *Speed well.*

Speir, an arm in armour embowed, holding in the hand a lance ppr. *Forward.*

Speir, Robert Thomas Napier, of Burnbrae and Blackstone, Renfrewsh., a dexter arm in armour embowed wielding a tilting-spear ppr. *Advance.* 197. 1

Speirs, Bart., *see* Home-Spiers.

Speirs, Alexander Archibald, Elderslie House, Renfrewsh., an arm in armour embowed wielding a lance, all ppr. *Salvet me Deus.*

Speke, William, of Jordans, Somers.: (1) A porcupine ppr. (2) (Of augmentation) A crocodile ppr. 136. 5

Spelman, a torteau. 159. 14

Spelman of Narburgh, Norf., a wild man ppr.

Spence, Very Rev. Dean Henry Donald Maurice, D.D., of the Deanery, Glouc., a maltster habited about the loins with a plaid skirt, sustaining with both hands a malt-shovel erect ppr.

Spence, Scotland, a bear's head erased sa. *Bold.—Do good.* 35. 2

Spence, Scotland, a boar's head erased ppr. *Felix qui pacificus.* 42. 2

Spence of Berryholl, Fifesh., a wolf's head couped ppr. *Patior ut potiar.* 30. 5

Spence of Wormeston, Fifesh., a demi-lion rampant gu. 10. 3

Spence, Scotland, out of a ducal coronet a demi-lion rampant. *Virtus auget honorem.* 16. 3

Spence, Scotland, a demi-lion rampant gu. 10. 3

Spence, a demi-lion gu. *Virtute acquiritur honos.* 10. 3

Spence, Scotland, a hart's head erased ppr. *Si Deus, quis contra.* 121. 2

Spence, Scotland, a stag's head couped ppr. 121. 5

Spence, James, Esquire, of Liverpool, a demi-stag or, charged on the shoulder with a saltire sa., and resting the sinister foot upon a buckle, also sa. *Fear God only.*

Spence of Brunstane, Aberdeensh., a clam-shell or. *Semper fidelis esto.* 141. 12

Spence, Scotland, three palm-branches slipped vert, banded or. *Felix qui pacificus.*

Spence of Neyland-Lynfield and South Malling, Sussex, out of a mural coronet arg., three palm-branches vert, tied with a ribbon az.

Spence of Bankham, Sussex, out of a mural coronet arg., three palm-branches in pale vert, each encircled by an annulet interlaced one with the other or.

Spence, George, Esquire, of London, a malster vested about the loins with a plaid skirt, sustaining with both hands a malt-shovel in pale ppr.

Spence, Scotland, two hands from the wrist issuing from clouds, letting down an anchor into the sea ppr. *Visa per invisa firma.* 224. 13

Spence of Shetland, an anchor. *Visa per invisa firma.* 161. 1

Spencer, *see* Marlborough, Duke of.

Spencer, *see* Churchill, Baron.

Spencer-Bell, *see* Bell.

Spencer, Earl (Spencer), out of a ducal coronet or, a griffin's head arg., gorged with a bar gemelle gu., between two wings expanded of the second. *Dieu defend le droit.* *cf.* 67. 1

Spencer, William Francis, Esquire, of Eardisland, Pembridge, Heref., same crest and motto.

Spencer of Worsted, Norf., out of a ducal coronet per pale arg. and gu., a griffin's head of the first, gorged with a collar of the second, charged with three plates, all within two wings or.

Spencer, Major Henry Montagu, of Blockley, Worcs., out of a crest coronet or, a griffin's head between two wings expanded arg., gorged with a bar gemelle gu. *Dieu defend le droit.*

Spencer of Bradfield, Norf., and Suff., out of a ducal coronet per pale or and gu., a griffin's head arg., eared and beaked of the second, gorged with a collar per pale also of the second and first between two wings, the dexter also gu., and the sinister arg., each charged with a mullet.

Spencer, Suff., Beds, and Oxon., out of a ducal coronet a griffin's head between wings of the second. 67. 1

Spencer, Notts, out of a ducal coronet or, a griffin's head between two wings endorsed arg., collared gu., beaked of the first. *Dieu defend le droit.*

Spencer, Frederick, Esquire, of Pondsmead, Oakhill, and Southill, West Cranmore, Somers., in front of a dragon's head erased az., holding in the mouth an acorn leaved and slipped or, between two wings per bend arg. and az., a fountain between two escallops of the third. *No hope, no endeavour.*

Spencer, Bart. (*extinct*), of Offley, Herts, out of a ducal coronet per pale arg. and or, a griffin's head of the first, eared gu., collared per pale of the third and second, between two wings also or, charged with three fleurs-de-lis in fess sa., one on each wing and one on the neck.

Spencer of Helmington Hall, Durh., out of a vallary coronet or, a demi-griffin with wings displayed arg., beaked and gorged with a collar gemel of the first, the dexter wing charged with a bend sinister, and the sinister with a bend dexter az., thereon upon each three escallops of the second.

Spencer of Newcastle-on-Tyne, Northumb., an antelope's head couped or, gorged with a collar engrailed az., between two wings arg., each charged with a fret gu.

Spencer, Leics., and of Badby and Everton, Northamp., an antelope's head erased or, attired sa., collared gu., lined and ringed of the first.

Spencer of London and Chard, Kent, a panther's head or, erased at the neck gu., incensed ppr.

Spencer, on the trunk of a tree in fess raguly, at the dexter end thereof a branch erect vert, a talbot sejant gu., eared arg., collared or.

Spencer, Warw., a moor-hen ppr.

Spencer of Bramley Grange and Attercliffe Hall, Yorks, on a rock a sea-mew, all ppr.

Spencer, De, two wings conjoined ppr. 113. 1

Spencer, Ireland, on a ducal coronet a star of twelve rays or.

Spencer, an arm vested or, thereon a bend az., holding in the hand ppr. a chaplet of roses gu., leaved vert.

Spencer, out of a mural coronet an arm erect vested, charged with two bars gemelle, the hand grasping a sword.

Spencer, an arm erect vested or, charged with two chevrons gu., the fist clenched.

Spencer, an arm vested or, thereon a bend az., holding a chaplet of roses gu., leaved vert.

Spencer-Stanhope, Walter Thomas William, of Cannon Hall, near Barnsley: (1) A tower az. with a demi-lion rampant issuing from the battlements or, ducally crowned gu., holding in the paws a fire-grenade ppr. (2) A sea-mew ppr. (*for Stanhope*).

Spencer of Barton, Percy Road, Bournemouth: (1) An eagle regardant with wings addorsed and inverted, holding in the beak a serpent. (2) A wolf's head couped, charged on the neck with two lozenges in fesse, and holding in the mouth a sprig of oak fructed. *Est modus in rebus.*

Spendluff of Falsethorpe, Lincs, a Saracen's head in profile couped at the shoulders ppr., the beard sa., the hair of the head arg., wreathed about the temples or and gu.

Speney of Tonstall, Norf., a bull's head arg., the horns gobony or and sa. *cf.* 44. 3

Spens, Archibald Lockhart, Esquire, J.P., of Dunruadh, Paignton, Devonsh., late of Lathallan, Fifesh., Scotland, a hart's head erased ppr. *Si Deus qui contra.* 121 2

Spens, John Alexander, of 25, Park Circus, Glasgow, and Kippendavie Lodge, Dunblane, Perthsh., same crest and motto.

Spens, Nathaniel, Esquire, of 13, Queen's Gate Terrace, London, S.W., same crest and motto.

Spens of Craigsanquhar, Fifesh., same crest and motto.

Spens of Edinburgh, three branches of palm slipped vert, banded together or. *Felix qui pacificus.*

Spens of Stonelaw, Lanarksh., a demi-man in armour with a stiff bonnet, holding a battle-axe on his shoulder ppr. *Virtus fides fortitudo.*

Sperling of Weston, Herts, on a chapeau az., turned up erm., a greyhound sejant or. *cf.* 59. 4

Sperling, Charles Brogden, of Dynes Hall, Essex, between two wings conjoined and displayed arg., a mullet suspended or. *Sapiens qui assiduus.* *cf.* 111. 5

Sperling, Arthur, of Lattenbury Hill, St. Ives, Hunts, same crest and motto.

Sperling, Charles Frederick Denne, Esquire, of Dynes Hall, Essex, same crest and motto.

Spert of Tetbury, Glouc., a broken mainmast or, the shrouds sa., in the round top six spears in saltier, on the top a flag arg., thereon the cross of St. George.

Spicer, a round tower embattled with a cupola arg. *cf.* 157. 15

Spicer, Devonsh., out of a viscount's coronet ppr., a cubit arm vested, gloved of the first, holding a fire-ball.

Spicer, Edward, Pentland House, 188, Cromwell Road, S.W., same crest. *Spes nostra Deus.*

Spicer of Weare, in Topsham, Devonsh., out of a ducal coronet or, a cubit arm habited and gloved holding a fire-ball, all ppr.

Spickernell, issuing from clouds shedding forth rays a cubit arm erect, holding in the hand a mort-head ppr. *Tutto alfin vola.* 220. 8

Spickernell, George Eastcott, Esquire, of Fernleigh, Redhill, Surrey, same crest and motto. 220. 8

Spied of Ardovie, Scotland, a demi-man in armour resting the dexter hand on his sword-hilt in sinister, the scabbard point downwards. *Speed well.—Auspice Deo.*

Spiers, a sheaf of arrows or, banded az. 173. 3

Spiers of Elderslie, Renfrewsh., an arm embowed holding a spear in bend ppr. *Salvet me Deus.*

Spiers, Scotland, a dexter hand issuing holding a sword, all ppr. *Salvet me Deus.* 212. 13

Spiers, an arm in armour embowed wielding a lance ppr. *Advance.* 197. 1

Spiers of Gloucester Terrace, Hyde Park, London, W., a portcullis with chains pendent or, ensigned with a thistle slipped and leaved ppr. *Chi dura vince.*

Spigernell, a hand issuing from a cloud in pale shedding forth rays, holding a mort-head. 220. 8

Spiller, Wilts, a falcon with wings expanded arg., standing on a snake nowed vert. 88. 7

Spiller of Laleham, Middx., Sutton, Surrey, and of Kingsley, Bucks, a saker or hawk ppr., beaked and legged or.

Spiller, Staffs, an eagle arg., winged or, standing on a snake nowed vert.

Spilman, a hand issuing from a cloud in pale, holding a garland of laurel ppr. 218. 9

Spilman, Norf. and Staffs, a savage ppr., wreathed about the loins and temples vert, holding in the dexter hand a club of the last.

Spilsburie, Worcs., a unicorn's head gorged with a band of four pearls. *cf.* 49. 7

Spilsbury, a garb az. 153. 2

Spilsbury, a garb or, thereon a dove ppr.

Spink of London, a pheon az. *Venabulis vinco.* 174. 11

Spinkes, Northamp., a talbot passant gu., bezantée, gorged with three fusils arg.

Spinks, a pheon az. 174. 11

Spittal, Scotland, two battle-axes in saltier or, hafted gu. *cf.* 172. 4

Spitty of Rettenden, Essex, out of a ducal coronet or, a plume of two rows of ostrich-feathers arg. 114. 4

Splatt-Collins of Brixton, near Yealmpton: (1) A demi-lion rampant arg., guttée-de-sang, holding between the paws an escutcheon also arg., charged with a Cornish chough ppr., standing on a mount vert (*for Collins*). (2) A demi-lion rampant gu., holding between the paws a ducal coronet or (*for Splatt*). *Pro patria sanguis.*

Splidt, on water a man rowing in a boat to the sinister, all ppr.

Spode, a demi-griffin with wings elevated gu., holding between the claws an escutcheon of the arms, viz., per bend indented sa. and erminois, a bend between two mullets counterchanged. *Sub tutela Domini.*

Spode of Hawkesyard Park, Staffs, a demi-griffin gu., holding between the claws an escutcheon of the arms, viz., per bend indented sa. and erminois, a bend between two mullets all counterchanged. *Recte et fideliter.*

Spofforth, a chess-rook gu. *Tempus meæ opes.* *cf.* 110. 1

Spofforth, Markham, Esquire, of 15, St. George's Place, Hyde Park Corner, London, same crest. *Rather deathe than false of faythe.*

Spokes, Russell, of Denmark Lodge, Brighton, and Broad Sanctuary Chambers, Westminster, S.W., a fasces erect between two ostrich-feathers. *Fiat justitia ruat cœlum.* 266. 14

Spokes, Sir Peter, of 25, Chester Terrace, London, same crest and motto.

Sponer or **Spooner** of Wickhamford, Worcs., a boar's head couped or, pierced through the neck by a spear arg., embrued ppr.

Spooks, a swan with wings expanded standing on a trumpet. 100. 6

Spooner, on a chapeau gu., turned up erm., a pelican ppr. 98. 7

Spooner, Lillingston-, Warw., a demi-griffin with wings elevated, holding in the dexter claw a battle-axe, all ppr. 64. 11

Spooner, Rev. Edward, Rural Dean of Hadleigh, of the Deanery, Hadleigh, Suff., a boar's head pierced through the neck with a spear arg., embrued gu. *Optima loquere pulcherimma fac.*

Spoor of Whitburn, Durh., a demi-antelope erm., erased gu., crined and attired or, holding in the mouth a broken spear sa., headed arg., the head downwards. *Semper constans et fidelis.*

Spoore of Trebartha and Northill, Cornw., and Misterton, Somers., a demi-antelope erm., erased gu., crined and attired or, holding in the mouth a broken spear sa., headed arg., point downwards.

Sporhart of London, out of a mural coronet or, a demi-lion rampant sa., supporting a spear of the first, headed arg.

Spotswood, Scotland, an eagle displayed gu., looking towards the sun in his splendour. *Patior ut potior.*

Spotswood or **Spottiswood,** Scotland, a wolf's head couped ppr. *Patior ut potior.* 30. 5

Spottiswood of Dunipace, Stirlingsh., Scotland, two globes ppr. *Utriusque auxilio.* 159. 3

Spottiswood of that Ilk, Berwick, an eagle rising gu., looking to the sun in splendour. *Patior ut potior.*

Spottiswoode, Welbam Hugh, Coombe Bank, Sevenoaks, same crest and motto.

Spottiswoode, John Roderick Charles Herbert, of Spottiswoode, Berwicksh., and 3, Stanhope Place, Hyde Park, same crest and motto.

Spoure or **Spoor,** a demi-heraldic antelope erm., erased per fess gu., crined and attired or, holding in the mouth a broken spear sa., headed arg., the head downwards. *Constans et fidelis.*

Spouse, Cornw., a demi-buck couped, holding in the mouth an arrow. *cf.* 119. 2

Sprackling of Thanet, Kent, a wolf's head erased sa., tufted, armed, and ducally gorged or. *cf.* 30. 8

Spragg, a sword erect ppr., on the point a crown of olive suspended or. 170. 1

Spraggs, a talbot passant arg., resting the dexter paw on a fleur-de-lis gu. *cf.* 54. 1

Sprakling, a griffin's head ducally gorged or. *cf.* 66. 1

Spranger, a cinquefoil erm. 148. 12

Spranger, Essex, on a ducal coronet per pale or and az., a fleur-de-lis between two wings, all counterchanged az., the sinister or.

Spratley, out of a ducal coronet or, a dragon's head vert. 72. 4

Spratt, two battle-axes in saltier ppr. 172. 4

Sprencheaux, a Cornish chough with wings addorsed, between two spear-heads in pale sa. 108. 7

Spreull of Cowden, Haddingtonsh., Scotland, a book displayed with seals, all ppr. *Manet in æternum.*

Sprigg, a laurel-branch vert. 151. 13

Sprigg, Ireland, an arm couped and erect, vested gu., cuffed arg., holding in the hand a sprig of laurel, all ppr.

Sprignell, Yorks and Middx., a demi-lion rampant or, holding in the dexter paw a battle-axe arg., the handle or.

Spring-Rice, Stephen Edward, of 1, Bryanston Place, London, W., a lion's face affrontée gu., ducally crowned or.

Spring of Cockfield, Suff., a demi-stag quarterly arg. and or, holding in the mouth a bunch of flowers of the first.

Spring, a stag's head. 121. 5

Spring, Suff., a demi-antelope quarterly arg. and or, attired counterchanged. *cf.* 126. 5

Springe, Suff., a stag's head ppr. *Non mihi, sed patriæ.* 121. 5

Springet or **Springett,** Kent and Sussex, an eagle displayed arg., membered and crowned gu., standing on a serpent nowed ppr.

Springett, of 1, Albert Road, Dyke Road, Brighton, on a serpent nowed vert, an eagle displayed ppr., armed and crowned or. *Virtus dolum supprimit.* —*Memor et fidelis.*

Springham of Dublin, Ireland, a demi-lion rampant arg., armed and langued gu., holding a book displayed ppr., garnished or, the ribbons vert. *Virtus vera nobilitas.*

Springhose, a Cornish chough with wings addorsed between two spear-heads erect sa. 108. 7

Springman, Emil, Esquire, of Drachenfels, West Derby, Lancs, a demi-man affrontée ppr., habited in a vest, holding in the dexter hand a roll of paper, and resting the sinister arm on a water-bouget, all or. *Sine Deo frustra.*

Sproston, Samuel, Esquire, of Sproston Wood, Wrenbury, Chesh., a female affrontée, couped at the shoulders ppr., crined or. *Vivat honestas.* 305. 14

Sprot, Lieutenant-General John, J.P., of Riddell, Roxburghsh., a heron ppr. *Parce qu'il me plait.* 105. 9

Sprott, a pelican's head erased, vulning herself ppr. 98. 2

Sprott, Shropsh., a boar passant. 40. 9

Sproul, Scotland, a water-bouget or. 168. 4

Sproule, Somers., a falcon belled preying on a partridge ppr. *cf.* 77. 1

Sprules, George Henry, Esquire, of Manse Field, Reigate, Surrey, a bunting-horn vert, garnished or, stringed gu. *Spe ruo.*

Spry, John Samuel, Esquire, of Place, Cornw., upon a mount between two trefoils slipped vert, a dove arg., standing on a serpent nowed ppr., the whole debruised by a bendlet wavy sinister erm. *Soyez sage et semple.*

Spry of Tyllond, Bodmin, Cuterewe, Tencreke, Mawnen and Mevagissey, Cornw., and Millbrook and Ugborough, Devonsh., a dove arg., beaked and legged gu., standing on a serpent nowed ppr. *Soyez sage et semple.* 92. 10

Spry, Tredenham Hugh, Esquire, of Witherdon, Germansweek, Devonsh.: (1) A dove arg., standing on a serpent nowed ppr. (*for Spry*). (2) A demi-lion rampant gu., ducally crowned or, holding between the paws a bezant. *Soyez sage et simple.*

Spry, a greyhound's head arg. *cf.* 61. 2

Sprye, Cornw. and Devonsh., a dove arg., beaked and legged gu., standing on a snake nowed, all ppr. 92. 10

Spurcock, a cock volant arg., crested gu.

Spurdens, Norf., a lion's gamb ppr., holding a cross moline per bend gu. and or. *Denuo fortasse lutescat.*

Spurling, Essex, between two wings conjoined and displayed arg., a mullet of six points suspended or. 112. 1

Spurling, Herts, on a chapeau az, turned up erm a greyhound sejant or cf 59 4
Spurrier, a cross Calvary or 166 1
Spurrier, Rev Horatio Heighington House, Durh a long cross or, on three grieces sa, arg, and gu *Stimulos adde*
Spursell, a cross bow erect
Spurstow and **Spurstowe** of Spurstow and Rumsey, Chesh and London, a demi woman couped below the breasts, the hair flotant all ppr
Spurway of Spurway and Oakford, Devonsh a garb or 153 2
Spurway, Charles, of Cleeve Hall, Cleeve, near Bristol, same crest *Desira ne riposo*
Spurway, Rev Edward Popham, M A of Heathfield Rectory, Taunton, same crest
Spycer of Knapton, Warw, a tower with a dome on top arg cf 157 15
Spycer, out of a mural coronet a cubit arm in armour holding in the hand a fire-ball fired, all ppr
Spyer of Walgrove and Shortletts, Berks and Huntercomb, Oxon, a garb per fess or and vert, banded arg 153 2
Spygernell, a hand issuing from a cloud erect shedding forth rays, holding a mort head 220 8
Spylman, a torteau 159 14
Spyre, a garb or banded vert 153 2
Squarey of Salisbury, Wilts, a cross crosslet or *Pro cruce audax* 165 2
Squibb of Reading Berks, a swan in pride crowned with an antique crown ppr
Squire, an antelope's head erased pierced through the neck by a spear, the handle broken off
Squire of Felstead Essex, and London, an elephant's head arg, ducally gorged and eared or
Squire of Barton Place, Suff, a bear's paw erect holding a plume of three ostrich-feathers ppr *Tiens ferme.* 37 5
Squires, Essex on a wheel a wyvern with wings addorsed ppr. 69. 3
Squirl-Dawson, Major, of the Lodge, Higham, near Colchester (1) A cat's head erased and affrontee ppr, holding in the mouth a rat sa *Vitæ via virtus* (*for Dawson*) (2) A squirrel sejant. *Quo non ascendam* (*for Squirl*)
Srabonne, an arrow point downwards 173 5
Stable, a castle arg, thereon a flag of St George 155 8
Stable, a demi lion rampant gu, holding between its paws a mullet arg 15 8
Stable, Worcs and of London, descended out of Yorks and Henry B Stable, Esquire of Knutsford, Chesh, same crest *Virtute* 15 8
Stable, Daniel Wintringham, Esquire, J P, of Plas Llwyn Owen, Llanbrynmair Montgomerysh, in front of a demi lion gu, holding between the paws a mullet of six points pierced arg, an acorn slipped between two mullets pierced fesseways of the last *Virtute* 299 9
Stable, Russell Loscombe, Esquire, Brevet Major Loyal North Lancashire Regiment Glenhurst, Fulwood Preston, Lancs, same crest and motto
Stable, Alfred Henry Esquire, of Minterne, Swanage Dorset same crest and motto
Stables, John Percy Lister Durell a demi-lion gu, semee of acorns slipped or holding between the paws a plate charged with a mullet of six points az
Stables, a tower or 156 2
Stace, Kent a cubit arm erect charged with three caltraps, holding in the hand a fleur de lis cf 215 5
Stacey, a sword erect supporting a balance and scales equipoised 179 11
Stacey, Kent an antelope's head erased arg, attired or 126 2
Stacey, C, Major, St. Pierre, Chepstow (1) A demi-lion rampant holding in the dexter paw a gem-ring 280 11 (2) A boar's head erect and erased *Deus dat qui vult* 280 12
Stack of Errimore co Kerry, out of a ducal coronet or, a naked arm erect holding in the hand a sword ppr pommel and hilt of the first 212 11
Stack, Colonel Charles, Esquire, West Ashby Manor, Horncastle, a garb pierced by a sword in bend, the point upwards, all ppr *Virtute et valore*
Stackhouse, a ship in full sail 160 13
Stackhouse of Trehane, Cornw a saltier raguly or
Stackhouse, Major William Anthony, of Ingfield Hall Settle Yorks, a saltire raguly erminois charged in the centre with a pellet
Stackpole, on a ducal coronet a pelican in her piety cf 98 8
Stacpoole, Richard John, Esquire, D L, of Strasburgh, Ennis co Clare, a pelican in her piety *I die for those I love —Pro Deo et pro patria*
Stackpoole, on a rock a fort in flames ppr 155 1
Stacye, Bucks, out of a marquess's coronet or, a demi-pegasus az charged with three estoiles, winged and attired of the first holding in the mouth a pansy gu, stalked and leaved vert
Stacye, Bucks, a cubit arm vested az. cuffed arg holding in the hand ppr a fleur de-lis or charged on the arm with three bezants
Staden of London, an angel ppr *Paratus et fidelis* 184 12
Staff, Kent a demi-lion rampant ppr supporting between the paws a staff raguly vert cf 15 1
Stafferton of Wingfield, Berks, and Hants a buck's head erased ppr pierced through the neck by a spear or
Stafford, Marquess of, *see* Sutherland, Duke of
Stafford, Duke of Buckingham and Earl of Stafford (*attainted*), out of a ducal coronet gu, a swan's head erect between two wings elevated arg 100 10
Stafford, Baron (Stafford-Jerningham), Costessey Park, Norf (1) Out of a ducal coronet or, a demi-falcon with wings expanded ppr (*for Jerningham*) 88 10 (2) Out of a ducal coronet per pale gu and sa, a demi swan rising with wings elevated and displayed arg beaked gu (*for Stafford*) *Virtus basis vita*
Stafford-Jerningham, Stafford Henry William Esquire, J P, of Costessey Park, Norwich, Norf (1) Out of a ducal coronet or, a demi-falcon with wings expanded ppr (2) Out of a ducal coronet per pale gu and sa, a demi swan rising with wings elevated and displayed arg, beaked gu
Stafford, Sir Edward William G C M G of Maine, co Louth, and Landsdowne, Christchurch, New Zealand out of a ducal coronet per pale gu and sa, a demi-swan rising, wings elevated and displayed arg beaked gu *Stat nominis umbra* —Over the crest, *Garde la foy*
Stafford, King-Harman-, Edward Charles of Rockingham Boyle, Ireland (1) Out of a ducal crest coronet or a dexter arm armed and erect in pale ppr cuffed arg, the hand also ppr, grasping two slips of roses, one gu the other arg, stalked, seeded, and leaved ppr (*for Harman*) (2) Out of a ducal crest coronet or, a dexter hand erect the third and fourth fingers turned down ppr (*for King*) (3) A swan s head couped at the neck holding in the bill a fleam or (*for Stafford*)
Stafford of Sydenham Devonsh out of a mural coronet gu, a swan's neck with wings expanded arg, ducally gorged of the first.
Stafford, on a ducal coronet per pale sa and gu, a swan rising arg beaked sa
Stafford, out of a ducal coronet a tiger's head 27 3
Stafford, a griffin's head couped ppr 66 1
Stafford, out of a ducal coronet per pale or and gu, a boar's head and neck sa. 41 4
Stafford of Monkwearmouth, Durh a demi-lion rampant holding in the dexter paw a dagger in pale 14 12
Stafford of Ballymacane, co. Wexford, Ireland a lion rampant or, holding a ragged staff sa
Stafford of Blathenwick Northamp, out of clouds a naked arm embowed holding in the hand a sword all ppr *The strongest arm uppermost* cf 201 4
Stagg, a stag's head cabossed or, between the attires a cross patee cf 122 5
Stahlschmidt, Surrey, a demi-warrior couped at the thighs in armour, an open helmet on his head the face affrontee, holding in the dexter hand a battle axe, all ppr, a label upon a label for difference *Deo inspirante Rege favente*
Stainbank of London, out of a ducal coronet or, a demi-dragon regardant with wings expanded az guttee-d'eau, charged on the neck with a bezant
Stainer, late Sir John, M A Mus Doc of 10, South Parks Road, Oxford in front of a cubit arm erect the hand holding a reed pipe in bend sinister a wreath of laurel, all ppr *Onerari est honorari*
Staines, a castle sa 155 8
Staines and Stains, a dexter hand issuing from a cloud ppr holding up a garland vert 218 9
Staines of Margate, Kent out of a naval coronet or, a buck's head quarterly arg and ppr, attired gu

Stainforth, an anchor az. 161. 2

Stainforth, a dexter arm in armour erect holding in the hand ppr. a broken sword arg., hilt and pommel or.

Stainforth, a cubit arm holding in the hand a broken sword in pale, all ppr.

Stainforth, a cubit arm erect grasping a broken sword, all ppr.

Stainsbury, a demi-lion rampant gu., crusuly or. 10. 3

Stainsby-Conant: (1) A mount vert, thereon a stag ppr., the dexter forefoot resting on an escutcheon gu., billettée or, charged upon the shoulder with a rose ppr. for difference (*for Conant*). (2) A mount vert, thereon a lion rampant erm., holding between the fore-paws a fleur-de-lis az., the dexter hind-paw resting on a millrind sa. (*for Stainsby*). (3) A greyhound statant per pale sa. and erm. (*for Pigott*). *Labore et virtute.—Conanti dabitur.*

Stainton, Gillespie-, *see* Gillespie.

Stainton, a covered cup gu.

Stair, Earl of (Dalrymple), Lochinch Castle, Wigtonsh., a rock ppr. *Quiescam.—Firm.* 179. 7

Stair, a cubit arm ppr., the hand holding an arrow. 214. 4

Stalbridge, Baron (Grosvenor), Motcombe House, Shaftesbury, a talbot statant or, charged with a crescent az. *Virtus non stemma.* cf. 54. 2

Staley, a globe on a stand ppr. 159. 4

Stallard of Blandford Square, Marylebone, Middx., a stork's head erased sa., supporting in the beak a sword point downwards ppr., pommel and hilt or.

Staller, a stork's head or. cf. 106. 1

Stalton, a lion's gamb erased holding a rose-branch slipped and leaved ppr. 37. 10

Stamer, Rt. Rev. Sir Lovelace Tomlinson, D.D., Bart., Bishop Suffragan of Shrewsbury, of Cliffville, Stoke-on-Trent, a stag's head erased ppr., attired or, gorged with a mural coronet of the last, and on an escroll over the crest the motto *Jubilee. Virtute et valore.*

Stamfield of Newmills, Scotland, a goat's head erased arg., armed or, within two laurel-branches ppr.

Stamford, Earl of (Grey), a unicorn passant erm., armed, maned, tufted, and ungu. or, in front of a sun in splendour ppr. *A ma puissance.* 310. 4

Stamford of Hadley, Middx., and Staffs., a gauntlet or, grasping a broken sword arg., hilt and pommel sa.

Stamford of Rowley, Staffs, a stag's head arg., attired or, billettée and charged on the neck with a bar gemelle gu.

Stamp, Devonsh., Berks, and Oxon., a demi-colt arg. 53. 3

Stamp of Fyfield, Oxon., a demi-horse rampant arg., charged with a crescent for difference. cf. 53. 3

Stamps, on a ducal coronet a swan with wings addorsed, ducally gorged, all ppr.

Stanard of London, an arm in antique mail ppr., holding in the hand a battle-axe sa., headed and armed arg.

Stanbridge, Hon. William Edward, of Wombat, Dalesford, Victoria, and of Clare, New South Wales, Member of the Legislative Council of Victoria, uses a demi-lion rampant or, holding between the paws an escallop arg. 13. 10

Stanbury of West Stanberie and Cliff, Cornw., a lion rampant per pale or and az. 1. 13

Stancomb, William, Blount's Court, Devizes, upon a rock a paschal lamb ppr., supporting with his sinister forefoot a garb vert. *Do right, fear not.* 253. 3

Stancomb, John Frederick, Esquire, of Shaw House, Melksham, Wilts, a beaver jumping out of water to a willow-tree. *Industria atque fortuna.*

Standard of Whitehill, Oxon., a cubit arm erect vested vert, cuffed arg., holding in the hand a bow strung ppr.

Standbridge, Sussex, and of Birmingham, a demi-lion rampant or, holding an escallop arg. 13. 10

Standen, an angel ppr. 184. 12

Standish, Berks, Lancs, and Leics., a cock arg., combed and wattled gu. 91. 2

Standish, a cock crowing ppr. 91. 2

Standish, Carr-, of Duxbury Park, Lancs, a cock arg., combed and wattled gu. *Constant en tout.* 91. 2

Standish, a griffin sejant erect holding with the claws a battle-axe in pale.

Standish, William Pery, of Standish, Lancs, and Scaleby Castle, Cumb., an owl arg., beaked and legged or, on a rat sa.

Standish, Henry Noailles Widdington, of Standish Hall, Lancs: (1) An owl with a rat in its talons ppr. (*for Standish*). (2) A holly-bush ppr. (*for Strickland*).

Standley, a stag's head erased. 121. 2

Standon, on the stump of an oak-tree shooting new branches a stork, all ppr. 105. 12

Stane, Bramston-, of Forest Hill, Essex: (1) A cubit arm erect ppr., holding in the hand a battle-axe arg., headed or (*for Stane*). 213. 12. (2) A lion sejant or, collared sa., charged with three plates (*for Bramston*). cf. 7. 4

Stanesby, Durh., a hand holding a horse-lock.

Stanfield, Sussex, on a mount a vine fructed, all vert.

Stanford, a buck's head couped, attired or. 121. 5

Stanford, a lion's head erased gu. 17. 2

Stanford of Barkby, Leics., a dexter gauntlet in bend or, grasping a broken sword erect arg., pommel and hilt sa.

Stanford, Benett-, John Montague, Pyt House, Tisbury, out of a mural crown or, a lion's head issuant az., charged with a mullet or.

Stanger, a lion rampant gu. 1. 13

Stanhop, five bell-flowers erect ppr., leaved vert.

Stanhope, *see* Harrington, Earl of.

Stanhope, *see* Chesterfield, Earl of.

Stanhope, Earl (Stanhope), a tower az., thereon a demi-lion rampant or, holding between the paws a grenade fired ppr. *A Deo et rege.* 157. 10

Stanhope, Yorks and Notts, a tower az., and issuing from the battlements thereof a demi-lion az., ducally crowned gu., holding between the paws a grenade fired ppr. cf. 157. 10

Stanhope, James Banks, Esquire, of Revesby Abbey, Boston, Lincs, same crest. *A Deo et Rege.*

Stanhope, Spencer-, Walter Thomas William, of Cannon Hall, Yorks: (1) A tower az., and issuing from the battlements thereof a demi-lion rampant or, ducally crowned gu., holding between the paws a grenade fired ppr. (*for Stanhope*). 157. 10. (2) A seamew ppr. (*for Spencer*). *A Deo et Rege.—Dieu defend le droit.*

Stanhope, out of a mural coronet a dragon's head vomiting flames. cf. 72. 11

Stanier-Philip-Broade, *see* Broade.

Stanier of Bridgnorth, Shropsh., out of a ducal coronet or, a griffin's head ppr. (*Another, sa.*). 67. 9.

Stanier, Shropsh., a griffin's head sa., charged with an escallop-shell gu. cf. 66. 1

Stanier, Beville, Peplow Hall, Market Drayton: (1) On a mount vert, a boar's head erect or, transfixed by an arrow fessewise ppr. (*for Broade*). 243. 5. (2) In front of a griffin's head erased ppr., three escallops or (*for Stanier*). *Pro Deo et Rege.—Pietate fortior.* 243. 6

Stanier, Frank Justice, same crests and mottoes.

Stanier, Francis, Peplow Hall, Market Drayton, same crests.

Staniland, Meaburn, Esquire, J.P., of Old Hall, Langton, Spilsby, Lincs, an eagle displayed ppr., on each wing a pale or, and in either claw a flint-stone ppr. *Stabilis.* 252. 5

Staniland, Alfred Edward, same crest and motto.

Stanley, *see* Derby, Earl of.

Stanley of Bickerstaff, Lord, *see* Derby, Earl of.

Stanley, Bart., now Errington, Bart.

Stanley, Baron, (Stanley) of Alderley, Alderley Park, Chelford, Crewe, on a chapeau gu., turned up erm., an eagle with wings expanded or, preying upon an infant ppr., swaddled of the first, banded arg. *Sans changer.* 79. 3

Stanley, Baron (Rt. Hon. Sir Frederick Arthur Stanley, P.C., G.C.B., J.P.), of Preston, Lancs, on a chapeau gu., turned up erm., an eagle with wings extended or, preying on an infant in its cradle ppr., swaddled gu., the cradle laced of the third. *Sans changer.* cf. 79. 3

Stanley, Kent and Lancs, on a chapeau gu., turned up erm., a cradle or, containing a child swaddled of the first, thereon an eagle preying. *Sans changer.* cf. 77. 13

Stanley, Edward James, Quantock Lodge, Bridgwater, Somerset, same crest and motto.

Stanley, Northamp., an eagle az., preying on a child ppr., swaddled in a basket gu. 77. 13

Stanley of London, Sussex, and Derbysh., an eagle's head couped arg., charged with three pellets, two and one, holding in the beak an eagle's leg erased at the thigh gu.

Stanley, an eagle's head erased or, holding in the beak an eagle's leg erased at the thigh gu.

Stanley of Honford, Chesh an eagle's head couped or holding in the beak an eagle's claw erased gu armed az

Stanley, a griffin's head erased 66 2

Stanley, a griffin's head erased arg charged with three ogresses, holding in the beak a lion's gamb erased cf 226 12

Stanley, a griffin's head erased sa, charged on the breast with three bezants, one and two, holding in the beak a lion's gamb erased gu cf 226 12

Stanley of Willington, Kent, a demi-heraldic wolf erased arg, tufted or

Stanley of Scottoe, Norf, a stag's head erased arg, attired or 121 2

Stanley, Chesh, a stag's head couped arg, attired or 121 5

Stanley, a stag's head ppr 121 5

Stanley, a stag's head couped or 121 5

Stanley, a stag's head couped arg attired or gorged with a mural coronet of the last cf 121 5

Stanley, Bart, Chesh, a stag's head and neck couped arg, attired and collared or the tongue hanging out gu 121 9

Stanley, William, Ponsonby Hall White haven a stag's head arg, attired or, collared vert *Sans changer* 304 2

Stanley of Dalgarth and Ponsonby, Cumb., a stag's head couped arg, attired or, gorged with a bar az, and charged on the neck with a crescent for difference *Sans changer* cf 121 5

Stanley of Lee, Sussex a stag's head couped arg, attired or gorged with a bar vert, and charged on the neck with a crescent for difference cf 121 5

Stanley, Charles Wentworth, of Long stowe Hall, Cambs (1) A demi stag sa, bezantee, holding between the legs a saltire or (*for Stanley*) (2) On a mount vert a griffin erm, winged chequy arg and sa resting the dexter claw on an escallop or (*for Wentworth*) *Frangas non flectes* cf 63 10

Stanley of Arnaby Cumb, a stag statant gu, attired and ungu or 117 5

Stanley, Bart (*extinct*), of Grange Gorman, co Dublin, Ireland, a chaplet of olive pendent from a sword all ppr 170 1

Stanmer, Essex and Chesh a stag's head erm, attired or, gorged with a fess dancettee gu

Stanmore, Baron (Hamilton Gordon) the Red House, Ascot, Berks (1) Two arms from the shoulder naked ppr, holding a bent bow or, letting fly an arrow ppr (2) Out of a ducal coronet or, an oak tree the stem cut transversely by a frame saw blade inscribed with word *Through*, all ppr, body of the tree charged with an escutcheon arg thereon a heart gu for difference

Stannard, an eagle displayed per pale or and sa 75 2

Stannard, on a ducal coronet a dolphin naiant ppr 140 4

Stannow, Norf, a demi-eagle displayed erm, charged on the breast with three guttes de-sang, two and one, holding in the beak a holly leaf vert

Stannus, Thomas Robert Esquire, of Maghraleave, Lisburn, in the Diocese of Connor Ireland a talbot's head ppr, collared and lined or, holding in the mouth a martlet with wings displayed sa *Et vi et virtute* cf 57 3

Stannus, Rev Beauchamp Walter M A, of the Rectory, Arrow, near Alcester, same crest and motto

Stannus of Carlingford, co Louth, a talbot's head couped arg, collared sa, lined and catching a dove volant of the first *Et vi et virtute* cf 57 3

Stannus, issuing from an Eastern coronet or, a talbot's head and neck az, gorged with a collar of the first, a cord gu., affixed to a ring in the same *Vi et virtute*

Stansfeld, a demi lion rampant arg 10 2

Stansfeld, Major-General Henry Hamer, of Manton, Marlborough Road, Bournemouth, same crest *Nosce teipsum*

Stansfeld, Lieutenant General Thomas Wolrich, same crest and motto

Stansfeld of Burley, Yorks, same crest and motto 10 2

Stansfeld, John, Field House, Halifax, Yorks a lion's head erased or

Stansfield, Crompton-, of Esholt Hall, Yorks (1) A lion's head erased encircled by a wreath (*for Stansfield*) cf 17 10 (2) A demi-horse sa vulned in the chest by an arrow ppr (*for Crompton*) *Nosce teipsum.—Love and loyalty* cf 55 3

Stanton, Norf, Warw, and Suff, a wolf sejant arg, guttee de sang collared and lined or

Stanton, General Sir Edward, K C M G, C B of Atcombe Court, Woodchester, Glouc a wolf sejant arg, guttee-de sang, collared and lined or *Dum spiro spero.*

Stanton, General Edward, C B, of Atcombe Court, Woodchester, Glouc, same crest and motto

Stanton, James Thomas Esquire of the Leaze Stonehouse Glouc same crest and motto

Stanton, Rev William Henry, M A, Hon Canon of Gloucester, of the Rectory, Haselton R S O, Glouc, same crest and motto

Stanton, an ermine gu 134 6

Stanton, Beds and Leics, a demi-lion rampant vaire sa and erm, ducally crowned or 10 1

Stanton, a lion rampant gu, holding in his dexter paw a cross crosslet fitchee or

Stanyforth, Edwin Wilfrid, Kirk Hammerton Hall York on a mount vert a lion sejant erm, gorged with a collar az, thereon three plates *Suivez raison*

Stapers of London a lion sejant arg, holding in the dexter paw an etoile sa

Stapilford, a boar's head couped or holding in the mouth a flower branch vert

Staple, a ram arg armed and ungu or *God be our friend* 131 13

Staple, James Dibble, M R C S, L S A, of Clevedon Villa Cheltenham Road Bristol a lion passant ppr *Spes in fide* 6 2

Staple, Middx., a lion rampant collared cf 1 3

Staples, Sydney Francis Esquire, of Camera Club, upon the battlements of a tower or a swan rising arg beaked and legged ppr ducally gorged or, in the beak a staple sa

Staples, out of a vallery coronet arg a lion's head affrontee gu, semee de lis, ducally crowned or

Staples of Norwood Surrey (1) Out of a vallery coronet arg, a lion's head affrontee gu, semee de-lis and ducally crowned or (*for Staples*) (2) An eagle displayed sa, the wings fretty and resting each claw on a mullet or (*for Browne*) *Sans Dieu rien*

Staples, Ireland, a dexter arm couped and embowed fesseways, the hand holding up a grenade fired ppr 202 5

Staples, on a ducal coronet a swan in his pride, ducally gorged ppr

Staples, Sir John Molesworth, Bart, D L, of Lissane, co Tyrone, a demi negro affrontee ppr, holding a bolt staple or *Teneo*

Staples-Browne, Frederick John Esquire of Brashfield House, Bicester, and the Elms Bampton, Oxon (1) An eagle displayed sa, wings fretty, resting each claw on a mullet or (*for Browne*) (2) Out of a crown vallery arg a lion's head affrontee gu, semee de lis, and ducally crowned or (*for Staples*) *Sans Dieu rien*

Stapleton, see Beaumont Baron

Stapleton, Baron, see Le Despencer

Stapleton-Cotton, see Lord Combermere

Stapleton of Milton Yorks, out of a ducal coronet a man's head couped at the shoulders in profile ppr, wreathed about the temples arg and sa.

Stapleton, Essex same crest *Fide, sed cui vide*

Stapleton, Essex and Yorks, a Saracen's head couped at the shoulders in profile ppr, wreathed about the head arg and sa 191 12

Stapleton, Yorks, a Saracen's head in profile ppr 190 14

Stapleton, Sir Miles Talbot, Bart, of the Leeward Islands, *uses* out of a ducal coronet or a Saracen's head affrontee ppr, wreathed about the temples arg and sa *Pro magna charta*

Stapleton, a talbot arg charged on the shoulder with six guttes de-sang *Pro magna charta* cf 54 1

Stapleton-Bretherton, Frederick Annesley Esquire J P, D L of Heathfield House, Fareham Hants and the Hall, Rainhill, Lancs, in front of a demi-unicorn arg a portcullis sa

Stapleton, Essex and Yorks, a unicorn's head erased armed and attired or 49 5

Stapley, Bart (*extinct*), of Patcham Sussex, on a mount vert, a stag at gaze arg, attired or cf 106. 3

Stapley of Framfield, Sussex a demi-hairy savage ppr, girt round the body with a belt gu, rimmed and studded or, thereon a chain or, holding in the hands a staple or the points downward

Stapylton, a Saracen's head affrontee couped at the shoulders ppr 190 5

Stapylton of Wighill Yorks, and Norton Durh, out of a ducal coronet or a Saracen's head affrontee ppr *Fide, sed cui vide* cf 190 5

Stapylton, Miles John, of Myton, Yorks, in a ducal coronet or, a Saracen's head affrontée ppr., wreathed arg. and sa. *Fide, sed cui vide.* cf. 190. 5

Staresmore of Trolesworth, Leics., a starling ppr.

Stark, Scotland, a bull's head erased arg. *Fortiorum fortia facta.* 44. 3

Stark and **Starke,** out of a ducal coronet or, a stag's head affrontée gu., attired of the first. 119. 13

Starke, see Hamilton-Starke.

Starke of Killermont, Scotland, a dexter hand holding by the horns a bull's head erased arg., distilling drops of blood ppr. *Fortiorum fortia facta.*

Starkey of London, a stork's head erased per pale arg. and sa., holding in the beak gu. a snake vert. cf. 106. 3

Starkey or **Starkie** of London and Lancs, a stork sa. 105. 11

Starkey, John Frederick, Esquire, of Bodicote House, Banbury, same crest. *Homo proponit, Deus disponit.*

Starkey or **Starkie** of Stretton, Chesh., a stork's head erased per pale arg. and sa., holding in the beak gu. a snake vert. cf. 106. 3

Starkey, Barber-, William Joseph Starkey, Aldenham Park, Bridgnorth, Shropsh., a stork arg., semée of estoiles az. *Homo proponit, Deus disponit.*

Starkey of Oulton, Chesh., a stork's head erased per pale arg. and sa., holding in its beak gu. a snake vert, and charged upon the neck with a crescent for difference. cf. 106. 3

Starkey of Wrenbury Hall, Chesh.: (1) A stork's head erased per pale az. and gu., gorged with two bars gemel or, and charged with an annulet, also or, holding in the beak a snake ppr., crowned of the third, the stork's head being also crowned or (*for Starkey*). (2) On a mount vert, a stork erm., beaked and legged gu., the dexter claw resting on a cross crosslet of the last, and holding in the beak a plummet sa. (*for Cross*).

Starkey of Tong, Leics., a stork ppr., holding in the beak a snake vert.

Starkey of Dublin, a stork's head erased per fesse gu. and sa., holding in the beak a serpent vert. *Redit expectata diu.* cf. 106. 3

Starkie, Le-Gendre-, of Huntroyde, Lancs, a stork ppr. 105. 11

Starky, a heron's head erased, holding in the beak a snake vert. 104. 2

Starky of Bromham, Wilts, a stork ppr. *Famæ venientis amore.* 105. 11

Starling, a lion's head ppr., collared az. cf. 18. 6

Starling, Norwich, a starling with wings addorsed sa., resting the dexter claw on an étoile of eight points.

Starr of Halifax, Nova Scotia, a lion rampant ppr. *Vive en espoir.* 1. 13

Starr, a demi-lion ppr., holding a mullet or. 15. 7

Starr of Canterbury, Kent, a lion couchant or, charged with an étoile gu. cf. 7. 5

Starr, Wilts, on a mount vert, a catamountain sejant gardant ppr., the dexter fore-paw resting on an estoile or.

Stasam, a bell az. 168. 7

Statham, a lion's head erased within a fetterlock ppr. 19. 4

Stathum, a greyhound's head erased gu. 61. 4

Staunton, Warw., a fox ppr. *Moderata durant.* cf. 32. 2

Staunton, Henry Charlton, of Staunton Hall, Notts, a fox passant ppr. 32. 1

Staunton, Bart. (*extinct*), of Cargins, co. Galway, Ireland, on a mount a fox statant, all ppr. cf. 32. 2

Staunton, Thomas Tufnell, of Longbridge, Warw., a fox statant ppr. cf. 32. 2

Staunton, Lynch-, of Clydagh, co. Galway: (1) Upon a mount vert, a fox statant ppr. (*for Staunton*). cf. 32. 2. (2) A lynx passant ppr., charged with a mullet gu. (*for Lynch*). *En Dieu ma foy.* cf. 127. 2

Staunton of the Thrupp, Glouc., a wolf sejant arg., guttée-de-sang, collared and lined or. *Dum spiro spero.*

Staunton, Lincs, and of Greenfield, Thelwall, Chesh., a lion passant or, holding in the dexter claw a cross formée fitched gu. cf. 6. 2

Staveley, an oak-branch and a cross crosslet fitched in saltier. 166. 11

Staveley of Dublin, a buck's head cabossed per pale gu. and az. *Fidelis ad urnam.* 122. 5

Staveley, Rev. Robert, of Saintville, Killiney, co. Dublin, same crest and motto.

Staveley of Offham, Lewes, Sussex, a stag's head caboshed. *Nil desperandum.*

Staveley, Thomas Kitchingman, Esquire, of Old Sleningford Hall and Stainley Hall, near Ripon, Yorks, within a circular wreath of oak fructed ppr., a buck's head cabossed, also ppr., attired or. *Ut aspirat cervus.*

Stavert, Archibald, of Hoscote, Hawick, N.B., a hand grasping a club ppr. *Stat veritas.*

Staverton, a stag's head erased sa., pierced through the neck by an arrow arg., feathered and headed or.

Staverton of Staverton Manor, Strode Hall, and Waroyle, Berks, and Dreley, Hants, a stag's head erased ppr., transpierced by an arrow in bend sinister or, barbed and flighted arg. cf. 121. 2

Stawell, see Alcock-Stawell-Riversdale.

Stawell, Baron Stawell (*extinct*), on a chapeau gu., turned up erm., an eagle displayed arg., holding in the beak a scroll, thereon the motto, *En parole je vis.*

Stawell of Cothelstone, Somers., out of a ducal coronet gu., a demi-buck or, attired sa. cf. 119. 2

Stawton of Warnill, Berks, a roebuck's head. 121. 5

Stayley, a globe on a stand ppr. 159. 4

Staylton, a lion's gamb erased holding a rose-branch slipped and leaved, all ppr. 37. 10

Staynings of Honycott, Somers., a bull. 45. 2

Stead, on a chapeau a salamander in flames, all ppr. 138. 2

Stead, Scotland, a nag's head. cf. 50. 13

Steade of Beauchieff Abbey, Derbysh., and Onesacre, Yorks, a stag trippant arg. 117. 8

Steadman, a demi-griffin or. 64. 2

Steavenson of Newcastle-on-Tyne, Northumb., and Scotland, on a rock ppr., a lion couchant gardant or. *Cœlum, non solum.*

Steavenson, Rev. R., Wroxeter Vicarage, Shrewsbury, on a rock ppr., a lion couchant gardant or. *Virtus ubique.*

Stebbing of London and Wisset, Suff., a lion's head erased arg. 17. 8

Stebbing of Woodrising, Norf., a lion's head erased arg. *Quiescam.* 17. 8

Stedman, Scotland, a horse's head or. cf. 50. 13

Stedman, a peacock's head between two wings, holding in the beak an adder ppr. 103. 3

Stedman, Glouc., a demi-virgin ppr., the hair dishevelled, holding in the dexter hand a cross crosslet vert.

Stedman, a chevalier in complete armour on horseback at full speed tilting with a lance, all ppr. cf. 189. 5

Stedman, an anchor ppr. 161. 1

Stedman, an anchor and cable ppr. *Cuncta mea mecum.* 161. 2

Steed, a horse's head erased arg. 51. 4

Steede of Hariesham, Kent, a stag trippant arg. 117. 8

Steede, Kent, a reindeer arg., attired or. cf. 125. 9

Steede, Kent, a reindeer current arg., attired or. cf. 125. 9

Steede, Kent, a castle environed with a laurel-branch.

Steedman, Scotland, an anchor az. *For security.* 161. 1

Steel of Derwent Bank, a lion's head erased gu. 17. 2

Steel, William Strang, Esquire, J.P., D.L., of Philiphaugh, Selkirksh., a lion's head erased gu. *Prudentia et animis.* 17. 2

Steel, Rev. Robert, M.A., Ph.D., D.D., of Lewington House, St. Leonards, Sydney, New South Wales, Australia, Minister of St. Stephen's Presbyterian Church, Sydney, *uses:* a lion's head erased. *Ferro non furto.* 17. 8

Steel, Scotland, a horse passant sa. 52. 6

Steel, Bart. (*extinct*), a Doric column arg. *Firmiter et durabiliter.* 288. 15

Steel and **Steele,** out of a ducal coronet or, a demi-ostrich with wings addorsed gu. 96. 11

Steel, Somers. and Suff., a stork arg. 105. 11

Steel and **Steele,** a cubit arm in armour, the hand holding up an esquire's helmet.

Steel of Carfin, Lanarksh., a dexter arm in bend, the hand grasping a broadsword ppr., in bend sinister. *Steel to the back.*

Steele, a lion's head erased gu. 17. 2

Steele or **Steell,** Scotland, same crest. *Prudentia et animis.* 17. 2

Steele, in front of two swords in saltire ppr., a lion's head erased quarterly arg. and gu., charged with four billets counterchanged.

Steele, Frederick Charles, Esquire, J.P., of Carlton House, Carlton, Tasmania, *uses:* on a wreath of the colours a demi-stork with wings expanded holding a serpent in its beak, all ppr. *Mens sibi conscia recti.*

Steele, William Edward, Esquire, M.D., a demi-eagle with wings elevated and displayed holding a serpent in its beak all ppr and charged on each wing with a billet or *Semper fidelis*

Steele of Rathbride co Kildare, a demi-eagle with wings displayed, holding in the beak a serpent, all ppr, and charged on each wing with a billet arg *Semper fidelis*

Steele, Lawrence E, Esquire, M A, of 18, Crosthwaite Park East, Kingstown same crest and motto

Steele, Lieutenant-Colonel William Henry, Esquire, of 18, Mortimer Road, Clifton, Bristol same crest and motto

Steele, Matthew, Esquire, J P, Onger Hill Netherton Frodsham, near Warrington, a griffin s head

Steer, an arm in armour embowed with a shield buckled on ppr 194 8

Steer, two oars in saltier ppr 179 3

Steer, an eagle with wings addorsed preying on a land tortoise ppr 79 8

Steere, Hon Sir James George Lee, of Perth and of Jayes Blackwood, Western Australia, Speaker of the Legislative Council of Western Australia out of a mural crown per pale gu and sa, a lion's gamb erect arg *Tu ne cede malis* 235 15

Steere, Surrey (1) Out of a mural coronet per pale gu and sa, a lion's gamb erect arg, armed of the first (*for Steere*) 235 15 (2) An arm embowed vested gu, cuffed arg, holding in the hand ppr a sword erect of the second, hilted or, on the blade a snake entwined vert *Tu ne cede malis* cf 204 1

Steere of Dorking, Surrey out of a mural coronet per pale gu and sa a lion's gamb erect arg, armed gu *Tu ne cede me* 235 15

Steere of Jayes, Surrey a lion passant gardant gu, the dexter fore-paw resting on an escutcheon of the arms viz erm., two bars sa charged with three bezants, two on the upper and one on the lower

Steerr and **Steerrs,** a horse's head sa, maned or cf 50 13

Steers, Ireland on a chapeau a wyvern sans legs with wings expanded ppr 69 14

Steers, a griffin sejant or 62 10

Steggall of London, on a chapeau an eagle rising ppr *Sursum* 77 14

Stein, Scotland, an eagle's head between two wings *Ad diem tendo* 84 2

Steinman, a demi ibex rampant arg, armed or, charged on the shoulder with a cross patee az. *Ante expectatum diem*

Steinmetz, two elephants' trunks addorsed sa 123 10

Steinthal, Henry Michael Esquire, of Bradford, Yorks, a bird bolt head downwards, ppr, between two wings erm *Excelsior*

Stelton, a yew tree ppr 143 1

Stempe, Herts, a greyhound's head couped sa., guttée-d'eau, ducally gorged, ringed, and lined or

Stenhouse, Anthony Maitland, Esquire, of Comox, British Columbia, Canada, and University Club, Edinburgh N B, *uses* a talbot's head couped arg, gorged with a collar or, charged with five pellets and issuing out of the mouth a dove of the first *Fortis et fidelis* 57 3

Stenhouse, a talbot's head collared, holding in the mouth a martlet ppr cf 57 3

Stenhouse, Vivian Denman, Esquire, of Courtlands Norton Fitzwarren Taunton Somers, a mount vert thereon a rose arg, barbed and seeded ppr, between two demi spears erect sa *Meliora probo*

Stennett or **Stennitt,** out of a ducal coronet a stag's head or 120 7

Stenning, Charles Horace, Esquire J P, Rovindene Playden, Sussex, a squirrel sejant supporting a cross crosslet fitchee 272 9

Stent of Fittleworth, Sussex a colt's head, holding in the mouth a banner

Stenynge of Honycote Somers, and Suff, a ram passant gu attired or cf 131 13

Stephen, Baron **Mount-Stephen,** *see* Mount Stephen

Stephen, Alexander Edward, of Kelly, Wemyss Bay a ship under sail ppr *Vi et arte* 160 13

Stephen, Scotland, a leopard's face or 22 2

Stephen, Hon Sir Alfred, G C M G C B of Dynevor Terrace, College Street, Sydney, New South Wales, an eagle displayed with two heads sa, beaked and legged or *Virtus ubique* 74 2

Stephen, Cecil Bedford, Esquire, same crest and motto

Stephen, Hon Septimus Alfred, same crest and motto

Stephen, Sir Herbert, Bart, an eagle displayed with two heads sa, resting the dexter claw on an increscent, and the sinister on a decrescent, both or *Sursum* 288 14

Stephen, Middx, an eagle displayed with two heads sa, beaked and legged or 74 2

Stephen of Barton-on the-Hill Glouc, out of a ducal coronet or a dolphin's head arg

Stephen, Scotland a dexter hand and arm grasping a dart ppr *Vi et arte* 214 4

Stephens, *see* Lyne-Stephens

Stephens, Bart (*extinct*) of St Faith's, Norf, a demi eagle with wings addorsed or

Stephens of Minsterley, Shropsh, and Tregony, Cornw a demi eagle displayed or, beaked and winged sa 81 6

Stephens, Essex and Glouc, a demi-eagle displayed or 81 6

Stephens, Percy Somers Tyringham, Esquire, J P. Croxdale Woodhouse, Croxdale, Durh., same crest *Deus intersit Alles for ye beste*

Stephens of Little Sodbury, Glouc, same crest and motto 81 6

Stephens of Prospect Hill and Aldermaston, Berks, a demi eagle sa, with wings elevated erminois charged on the breast with a cross crosslet or and holding in the beak an annulet of the last *Je vis en espoir*

Stephens, Frederick Bentworth Lodge, Alton, Hants, a demi-eagle sa, wings elevated erminois, charged on the breast with a cross crosslet or, in the beak an annulet or *Je vis en espoir*

Stephens of Colchester and Arden Essex an eagle or, preying on a lion's gamb erased gu

Stephens, an eagle's head or, between two wings erm 84 2

Stephens, a griffin's head erased erm collared or between two wings expanded of the last cf 67 7

Stephens of Foxfield Wilts, between two wings or a raven's head erm

Stephens, in front of a raven's head couped erm, beaked az between two wings or, a tower of the last

Stephens of Finglas, co Dublin, Ireland, a cock statant or *Vigilans et audax* 91 2

Stephens of Chilculm, Rosbercon co Kilkenny a cock statant or charged with a crescent for difference cf 91 2

Stephens, Pembroke Scott Esquire K C of 30, Cumberland Terrace, Regent's Park, London, N W a cock statant or, holding in his bill a trefoil vert *Vigilans et audax*

Stephens, Edward, Esquire, F R C S, on a mount and in front of a fern brake ppr, a falcon rising arg beaked and membered gu, belled or holding in the beak an ostrich-feather az, quilled of the fourth *Fides Stephani*

Stephens of Trevigoe, Cornw, on a rock ppr a salmon in fess arg, holding in the mouth a rose gu, stalked and leaved vert

Stephens of Tregenna Castle, Cornw, a lion rampant arg guttee-de sang *Virtutis amore* cf 1 13

Stephens of Crychell Radnorsh a naked arm holding a sword ppr, impaling a griffin's head sa *Semper liber*

Stephens of Hinton on the-Green, Glouc a hand holding an open book ppr *Consilio et armis* 215 10

Stephens, Ireland out of a ducal coronet gu a dexter and a sinister arm embowed vested or, holding between the hands ppr a garland of oak leaves vert

Stephens of Waterford, Ireland, a cock gu 91 2

Stephenson, a ship in full sail ppr 160 13

Stephenson of London an eagle displayed holding in the dexter claw a sword in pale, and in the sinister a pistol all ppr *For right* cf 75 7

Stephenson of St Luke's, Middx, a hawk's head erased or *Sub libertate quietem* 88 12

Stephenson, of the Oaks, Windermere, and Parkfield, Berkdale Park, Southport, same crest *Virtutis fortuna comes*

Stephenson, Sir Henry J P, of Glen Endcliffe, Sheffield a rock, thereon a falcon's head erased ppr, gorged with a collar vair, pendent therefrom an escutcheon vert charged with two arrows saltirewise points downwards or

Stephenson, Sir Augustus William Keppel, K C B, Q C, M A, of 46, Ennismore Gardens, S W, a falcon with wings expanded arg, beaked and legged or, within a herald's collar of SS ppr

Stephenson, Vice-Admiral Henry Frederick, R.N., C.B., United Service Club, same crest.

Stephenson, a leopard's head and shoulders ppr., fire issuing from the mouth.

Stephenson, a garb or. 153. 2

Stephenson, between two fleurs-de-lis arg., a cubit arm vested az., cuffed, also arg., the hand holding a roll of paper ppr. *Fidus in Arcanis.*

Stephenson-Hamilton: (1) A hawk rising ppr., belled or, holding in the dexter claw a sword, also ppr., hilted and pommelled of the second (*for Hamilton*). (2) A dexter hand issuing from a cloud, and holding a wreath of laurel, all ppr. *Thankful.—Cœlum non solum.* 218. 9

Stephenson-Fetherstonhaugh, of 14, Warwick Square, S.W.: (1) An heraldic antelope's head erased gu., surmounted by two feathers in saltire arg., charged on the neck for distinction with a cross crosslet or (*for Fetherston*). (2) In front of a garb or, a cornucopia fesseways ppr. (*for Stephenson*). *Nil vile velis.*

Stephenson, between two fleurs-de-lis arg., a cubit arm vested az., cuffed of the first, holding a roll of paper ppr. *cf.* 208. 5

Stephenson, H. K., Esquire, J.P., Bent's Green, Sheffield, a rock, thereon a falcon's head erased ppr., gorged with a collar vair, pendent therefrom an escutcheon vert, charged with two arrows saltireways, points downwards or.

Stephenson, Thomas, Esquire, Kilmeaden, co. Waterford, a garb or.

Stepkins, a stag's head couped arg., attired or. 121. 5

Stepney, Bart. (*extinct*), of Prendergast, Pembrokesh., Wales, a talbot's head erased gu., eared or, gorged with a collar chequy of the last and az., holding in the mouth a buck's attire of the second. *Fide et vigilantia.*

Stepney, Cowell-, Sir Emile Algernon Arthur Keppel, Bart., J.P., of Llanelly, Carmarthensh.: (1) A talbot's head erased gu., eared or, gorged with a collar chequy or and az., holding in the mouth the attire of a stag of the second (*for Stepney*). 313. 5. (2) On a mount vert, a lion passant gardant or, charged on the body with three pallets gu., holding in the dexter paw a chapeau gu., turned up erm. (*for Cowell*). *Facta probant.—Quo fata vocant.* 310. 14

Stepney-Gulston, Alan, Esquire, of Derwydd, Llandebie, R.S.O., Carmarthensh., an ostrich's wing of five feathers alternately arg. and gu., thereon a bend sa., charged with three plates. Over crest—*Crescent sub pondere virtus.*

Stepple, a sword and a laurel-branch in saltier ppr.

Sterling, Ireland, on the point of a sword erect ppr., a maunch gu. 169. 11

Sterling, Herts, a lion passant ppr. 6. 2

Stern, a griffin segreant ppr. 62. 2

Sterndale, William Handley, Esquire, of Ottar, Hindostan, a mullet of six points pierced az., and transpierced by three arrows, two in saltire, points downwards, and one fesseways, the point to the sinister, or, all barbed and flighted arg. 173. 6

Sterndale-McMikin, Henry Percy, Esquire, of Grange and Westland, co. Ayr, a demi-savage, bearing in his dexter hand an arrow, at his back a quiver-full, all ppr. *Res non verba.* 275. 10

Sterne, Norf., Herts, Cambs, Bucks, and Yorks, a cock-starling ppr.

Sterry, a fir-branch fructed or.

Sterry, a sword in bend ppr. 170. 5

Sterry of Eastbury Hall, Barking, Essex, in front of a dexter arm embowed in armour ppr., garnished or, encircled above the elbow with an annulet or, the hand grasping a seax, also ppr., pommel and hilt also or, an estoile between two pheons of the last. *Pro Rege et patria.* 255. 12

Stert of Membland, Devonsh., a cross formée sa., between two wings arg. 110. 7

Steuart, de Kierzkowski-, *see* Kierzkowski.

Steuart, Durrant-, John Nairne, of Dalguise, Perthsh., Scotland, a demi-lion rampant ppr. *Hinc orior.* 10. 2

Steuart, Gow-, of Little Colonsay, Scotland, and Fowler's Park, Kent: (1) A demi-lion holding in his dexter paw a Lochaber-axe ppr. (*for Steuart*). (2) A dexter arm in armour embowed, holding in the hand a broadsword ppr. (*for Gow*). *Firm.—Caraid ann am fheum.* 195. 2

Steuart, Scotland, a lion's head erased gu. *Stat felix, amice Domino.* 17. 2

Steuart, John, Esquire, of Ballechin, Perthsh., a lion's head erased gu., langued az. *Semper fidelis.* 17. 2

Steuart, George Mackenzie, Esquire, W.S., New Club, Edinburgh, a lion's head erased gu. *Lædere noli.*

Steuart-Moncrieff, a unicorn's head and neck arg., maned or, armed gu. 49. 7

Steuart, Scotland, a pelican in her piety ppr. *Salus per Christum redemptorem.* 98. 8

Steuart of Carlow, a pelican arg., winged or, in her piety, the nest and young ppr. 98. 8

Steuart, Bart., of Coltness, Lanarksh., a thistle and a full-blown rose in saltire ppr. *Juvant aspera probum.* 150. 3

Steuart, Drummond-, Bart., of Grandtully, Perthsh.: (1) Two bees counter-volant ppr. (*for Steuart*). 137. 3. (2) A dexter arm embowed, holding in the hand a broadsword, all ppr. (*for Drummond*). *Provyd.—Nil timeo.* 195. 2

Steuart, M'Adam-, of Glenormiston, Peebles, a branch of olive and a branch of Indian palm in saltire ppr. *Pax copia virtus.*

Steuart of Allanton, a dexter hand holding a thistle, both ppr. *Juvant aspera fortes.—Virtutis in bello præmium.* 218. 2

Steuart of Alderston, Haddingtonsh., a hand holding a thistle ppr. *Juvant aspera fortes.* 218. 2

Steuart, Andrew, of Auchlunkart, Banffsh., Scotland, a dexter and a sinister hand holding up a heart ppr. *Corde et manu.* 224. 4

Steuart-Duckett, Charles Edward Henry, of Rutland Lodge, co. Carlow: (1) Out of a ducal coronet or, a plume of five ostrich-feathers arg., a crescent for indifference, head couped affrontée ppr. (2) A cat's head affrontée and erased, of a tabby colour, holding in the mouth a rat sa. *Je veux le droit.*

Steuart-Fothringham, Walter Thomas James, Esquire, of Fothringham, Forfarsh., N.B.: (1) On a wreath of his liveries a griffin segreant ppr. (*for Fothringham*). (2) On a wreath of his liveries a lion's gamb erased holding a scimitar ppr. (*for Scrymscoure*). *Be it fast.—Dissipate.*

Steven, Hugh, Esquire, of Westmount, Kelvinside, Glasgow, a demi-wyvern displayed ppr. *Ferro non ense.*

Stevens of St. Ives, Cornw., a lion rampant arg., guttée-de-sang. *cf.* 1. 13

Stevens, out of a ducal coronet a demi-lion holding a flag.

Stevens, Cornw., a demi-lion rampant arg., guttée-de-sang. *cf.* 10. 2

Stevens, Glouc., an eagle issuing with wings displayed or, charged on the breast with a mullet sa. *Ad diem tendo.* *cf.* 80. 2

Stevens, Sir Charles Cecil, K.C.S.I., B.A., of Honiton, Devonsh., between two sprigs of oak fructed ppr., a demi-eagle displayed sa., charged on each wing with an Eastern coronet or. *Fac et spera.*

Stevens of Edinburgh, an eagle rising looking at the sun ppr. *Ad diem tendo.*

Stevens, an eagle with wings addorsed preying on a talon.

Stevens, Shropsh., a demi-eagle displayed or, beaked and winged sa. 81. 6

Stevens, Rev. Thomas, M.A., F.S.A., Archdeacon of Essex, St. John's Vicarage, Stratford, London, E., a demi-eagle displayed.

Stevens of Cullum and Bradfield, Berks, a demi-falcon displayed or.

Stevens, out of a ducal coronet a cubit arm vested and cuffed, the hand holding a book expanded.

Stevens, Scotland, a dexter hand holding a mason's chisel ppr. *Vi et arte.*

Stevens, a garb or. 153. 2

Stevens, H. W., Esquire, the Firs, Ash, Surrey, a lion's head erased. *Faire mon devoir.*

Stevenson, Cumb., and of London, a garb erminois. 153. 2

Stevenson of Ounston, Derbysh., and Lincs, a garb or. 153. 2

Stevenson, Chesh., a rose-tree in bloom ppr. *Virtus ubique sedem.* 149. 8

Stevenson, out of a ducal coronet an eagle's head between two wings. 84. 3

Stevenson, a griffin's head couped. 66. 1

Stevenson, an antelope's head erased. 126. 2

Stevenson, on the top of a hollow rock a lion couchant.

Stevenson of Uffington, Lincs: (1) A demi-lion regardant gu., charged on the shoulder with a cross crosslet fitched, holding between the paws a mullet or (*for Stevenson*). (2) A lion's gamb per pale gu. and sa. (*for Bellairs*). *Virtus tutissima cassis.* *cf.* 36. 4

Stevenson, a demi-lion arg. 10. 2

Stevenson, Francis Seymour, M.P., D.L., of Playford Mount, near Woodbridge, Suff., a leopard's face. *Justus et tenax.* 22. 2

Stevenson of Mount Grenan, Renfrewsh, Scotland, a hand holding a scroll rolled up ppr *Fidus in arcanis* 215 6

Stevenson, Scotland a dexter hand holding a scroll of vellum ppr *Fidus in arcanum.* 215 6

Stevenson of Glasgow, a dexter hand holding a wreath of laurel ppr *Respice finem* 218 4

Stevenson, John James, Esquire, of 4, Porchester Gardens, London W, a dexter hand holding a wreath of laurel ppr *Sic curre ut comprendas* 218 4

Stevenson of Edinburgh, Scotland, a dexter hand holding a laurel-crown ppr *Cœlum non solum* 218 4

Stevenson, of Tynemouth, Northumb, a dexter hand holding a wreath of laurel ppr *Sic curre ut comprendas* 218 4

Stevenson, James Cochran Esquire, M P of Eltham Court Eltham, Kent, same crest and motto

Stevenson of Edinburgh, Scotland, a dexter hand issuing from a cloud holding a garland of laurel ppr *Cœlum, non solum* 218 9

Stevenson, James, Braidwood, Carluke, N B, same crest and motto

Stevenson, John Horne, Esquire of 9, Oxford Terrace, Edinburgh a dexter hand holding a laurel-wreath ppr *Cœlum non solum* 218 4

Stevenson-Hamilton, James, Esquire, J P, of Fairholm Larkhall and Kirkton, Carluke, N B (1) A hawk rising ppr, belled or, holding in the dexter foot a sword, also ppr, hilted and pommelled or (*for Hamilton*) (2) A dexter hand issuing from a cloud, holding a wreath of laurel, all ppr (*for Stevenson*) *Thankful — Cœlum, non solum*

Steventon, Shropsh, a stag's head couped at the neck ppr 121 5

Steventon of Dothill, Shropsh, a stag's head cabossed ppr 122 5

Stevynson, Derbysh and Lincs, a garb or 153 2

Steward of Nottingham, Dorset, a pelican vulning herself ppr 98 1

Steward, a griffin's head erased gu, beaked arg, charged with a bend raguly or, between three bezants, one and two

Steward, a griffin's head couped gu 66 1

Steward of Okhey, Cambs, Stuntney, Isle of Ely, Gestwait Heseldon, and Swardeston, Norf, and Suff a stag statant ppr, ducally gorged or *cf* 117 5

Steward, Richard Oliver Francis, Esquire, of Nottington, Dorchester (1) A pelican in her piety (2) A bear's gamb erased charged with three billets, and holding a battle-axe in bend sinister *Nobilitas unica virtus*

Steward of Newton Manor, Cumb (1) A stag or charged on the body with a buckle az, and resting the dexter fore leg on a stag's head caboshed ppr. (*for Steward*) (2) On a rock ppr, and within an annulet in front thereof sa, a falcon close arg (*for Falcon*)

Steward, a stag ppr, ducally gorged and attired or *cf* 117 5

Steward, Cambs, Suff, and Norf., a stag trippant ppr, attired arg, ducally gorged gu *cf* 117 8

Steward of Patteshull, Northamp, and Newton Manor, Cumb, a stag ppr, gorged with a collar chequy arg and az *cf* 117 5

Steward of Stoke Park Suff, on a mount vert, within a vallary coronet or a lion rampant gu *Qui invidet minor est*

Steward, a lion rampant gu, ducally gorged or *cf* 1 13

Steward, Major the Hon William Jukes, of Burford, Ashburton, Canterbury New Zealand, a lion rampant ppr *Deo adjuvante fortuna sequatur*

Stewart-Murray, *see* Athole Duke of

Stewart, Vane-Tempest-, Marquess of Londonderry, *see* Londonderry

Stewart, Earl of Galloway, *see* Galloway

Stewart, Baron Blantyre, *see* Blantyre

Stewart, *see* Blakeney Lyon-Stewart

Stewart, *see* Cumbrae Stewart

Stewart, *see* Hamill Stewart

Stewart, Bart., of Grandtully, Scotland *see* Steuart

Stewart, Lord of Lorn and Innermeath and Earl of Athole, a unicorn's head arg, armed or *Quhidder will zie.* 49 7

Stewart, Charles Montague Duncan Esquire, of Achnacone a unicorn's head couped arg, armed and crined

Stewart, Robert Bruce, of Lorn Appin, and Ardsheal, a unicorn's head maned, horned, and bearded or *Quhidder will zie*

Stewart, Earl of Blessington, Ireland, a dexter hand in armour couped below the elbow holding a heart in pale, all ppr *Nil desperandum*

Stewart, Earl of Orkney, Scotland, a king enthroned holding in his dexter hand a sword, and in his sinister a falcon *Sic fuit est et erit*

Stewart, Charles Balfour, Esquire, B A, M P B C, Thompson Yates Laboratories, University College, Liverpool, same crest and motto

Stewart, Colonel John Ardvolich, Perth, a dexter naked arm issuant grasping a sword in bend sinister all ppr pommel and hilt or *Deo juvante vinco*

Stewart, Earl of Carrick, a king enthroned holding in his dexter hand a sword, and in his sinister a falcon, all ppr *Sic fuit est et erit*

Stewart, Earl of Arran, a lion's head erased gu *Dat incrementum* 17 2

Stewart, Earl of Mar, two serpents nowed erect counter respectant ppr

Stewart Earl of Caithness and Earl of Athole, a lion sejant affrontee gu, holding in his dexter paw a sword erect ppr *cf* 7 3

Stewart, Earl of Darnley, Earl and Duke of Lennox, issuing out of a ducal coronet or, a bull's head sa, vomiting forth flames ppr *Avant Darnley* *cf* 44 11

Stewart, Charles Frederick Esquire, B A of Horn Head Dunfanaghy, co Donegal same crest charged for difference with a mullet *Avant Darnley*

Stewart, Earl of Athole, a dexter hand holding a key in bend sinister ppr *Furth fortune and fill the fetters* 217 7

Stewart, Earl of Traquair, a crow ppr *Judge nought* *cf* 107 3

Stewart, Lord Evandale and Ochiltree, a civet-cat passant ppr *Forward.*

Stewart, Scotland, a civet cat couchant ppr *Semper paratus*

Stewart, Scotland, a pelican in her piety all ppr *Virescit* 98 8

Stewart, a pelican in her piety or, the nest vert *Salus per Christum redemptorem* 98 8

Stewart, Scotland a pelican in her piety, ppr *Salus per Christum redemptorem* 98 8

Stewart, Horatio Granville Murray, Esquire of Cally, Gatehouse, N B (1) A pelican in her piety ppr (*for Stewart*) 98 8 (2) A griffin salient ppr, charged on the shoulder with a cross crosslet az (*for Murray*) *Virescit vulnere virtus —Impero* 62 8

Stewart, Sir David, of Banchory, Devenick, Lord Provost of Aberdeen, a pelican in her piety ppr *Salus per Christum* 98 8

Stewart-Mackenzie, James Alexander Francis Humberston Esquire, of Seaforth, Major in 9th Lancers D L, county of Cromarty, etc (1) On the dexter side, a mountain in flames ppr (*for Mackenzie*) 179 2 (2) On the sinister side, a pelican in her piety ppr (*for Stewart*) *Luceo non uro — Virescit vulnere virtus* 98 8

Stewart, Scotland, a pelican arg, winged or, in her piety, the nest and her young ppr *Virescit* 98 8

Stewart, Scotland, a pelican vulning herself ppr *Virescit vulnere* 98 1

Stewart, William John, Esquire of Geneva House, Darlington, a dove ppr, holding in the beak a rose gu slipped and leaved, also ppr *Soli deo honor*

Stewart, a demi lion rampant gu *Nobilis ira — Arido virct honore* 10 3

Stewart, Scotland a demi-lion rampant gu, holding in the dexter paw a dagger in pale ppr *Hinc orior* *cf* 14 12

Stewart, James, Esquire, of Garvocks, Renfrewsh, and of St. Fillans, Ayrsh, a demi lion holding in his paws a battle axe ppr *Audax in recto* 15 4

Stewart, James Stirling Blackhouse, Skelmorlie, Ayrsh, a demi lion or, holding in his paws a battle-axe ppr *Audax in recto*

Stewart, Scotland, a demi-lion rampant gu *Hinc orior* 10. 3

Stewart, General Sir Richard Campbell, K C B, of West Learmouth, Cornhill-on-Tweed, Northumb, same crest *Fuimus*

Stewart, Scotland, a demi-lion rampant gu, langued and armed az *Nobilis ira* 10 3

Stewart, Johnston-, Stair Hathorn Johnston, of Physgill, Wigtownsh Scotland a demi lion gu, holding in the dexter paw a buckle or *Suffibulatus majores sequor*

Stewart, James Esquire, of Alltyrodyn Llandyssil, Cardigansh, a demi-lion rampant ppr, holding between his paws a mullet gu *Hinc orior* *cf* 15 8

Stewart, Hathorn-Johnston-, Robert, of Glasserton and Physgill, Whithorn, Wigtonsh, and Champfleurie, Linlithgowsh, N B a lion rampant gu armed and langued az., grasping a hawthorn-tree fructed, and in the dexter paw a scimitar defending the same ppr. *Fidelitate et amore.—Suffibulatus majores sequor.*

Stewart of Strathdown, Banffsh., a demi-lion rampant ppr. *Nobilis ira.* 10. 2

Stewart of Ballymoran, co. Down, Ireland, a demi-lion rampant gardant ppr., holding in his dexter paw a round buckle or. *Suffibulatus majores sequor.*

Stewart, MacTaggart-, Sir Mark John, Bart., of Southwick, Dumfriessh., N.B., and Blairderry, Wigtownsh., M.P. for Kirkcudbright, same crest and motto.

Stewart of Lower Canada, a demi-lion rampant ppr. *Nobilis ira.* 10. 2

Stewart, Scotland, a demi-lion gardant ppr., holding in his dexter paw a mullet sa. *Suffibulatus majores sequor.*

Stewart, Scotland, a demi-lion holding in the dexter paw a sword, and in the sinister a pair of scales, all ppr. *Honestate vetustas stat.*

Stewart, Robert King, Esquire, of Murdostoun Castle, Newmains, Lanarksh., same crest. *Hinc orior.*

Stewart of Blundeston, Suff., on a mount vert, within a vallary coronet or, a lion rampant gu. *Presto et persto.*

Stewart, a lion's head erased. *Spero meliora.* 17. 8

Stewart, Scotland, a lion's head erased gu. *Nil sistere contra.* 17. 2

Stewart, Scotland, a lion's head erased ppr. *Semper fidelis.* 17. 8

Stewart, Scotland, a lion's head erased gu. *Stat felix, amice Domino.* 17. 2

Stewart, Scotlaud, same crest. *Lædere noli.* 17. 2

Stewart, Bart., Scotland: (1) A lion's head erased gu., armed and langued az. 17. 2. (2) A demi-savage holding a club over his shoulder ppr., wreathed about the head and middle with laurel vert. *Spero meliora.—I mean well.* 186. 1

Stewart, Admiral Sir William Houston, G.C.B., a lion's head erased gu., armed and langued az. *Spero meliora.* 17. 2

Stewart of Newark, Scotland, a lion's gamb and a palm-branch in saltier ppr. *Christus mihi lucrum.*

Stewart of Peebles, a branch of olive and of Indian palm in saltier. *Pax copia virtus.*

Stewart, Scotland, and England, a thistle and a sprig of a rose-tree in saltier ppr. *Juvant aspera probum.* 150. 3

Stewart, Scotland, a gilliflower slipped ppr. *Viresco.* 151. 8

Stewart, Scotland, the trunk of an old oak-tree sprouting a branch on the dexter side acorned ppr. *Resurgam.* 145. 2

Stewart, Scotland, a bee erect with wings expanded ppr. *God will provide.* 137. 1

Stewart of Fingorth, Scotland, a bee volant en arrière ppr. *Providentiæ fido.* 137. 2

Stewart, Scotland, a bee volant ppr. *Parat et curat.* 137. 2

Stewart of Overdowally, Perthsh., two bees counter-volant ppr. *Provyd.* 137. 3

Stewart, Scotland, two bees in saltier ppr. *Providentiæ fido.* 137. 3

Stewart, Scotland, a unicorn's head and neck arg., maned or, armed gu. *Quhadder will ze.* 49. 7

Stewart, Robert Bruce, Esquire, B.A., of 73, Vanbrugh Road, Blackheath, S.E., a unicorn's head arg., maned, horned, and bearded or, on a scroll above, *Quhidder will zie.*

Stewart, Scotland, a unicorn's head issuing arg., maned, armed or. *Quhidder will zie.* 49. 7

Stewart, Scotland, a unicorn's head issuing arg., armed or. *Pass forward.* 49. 7

Stewart, Scotland, a unicorn's head arg., maned and armed or. *Whadder.* 49. 7

Stewart, Sir John Marcus, Bart., D.L., of Athenry, co. Tyrone, a unicorn's head couped or, armed and crined arg. *Forward.* 49. 7

Stewart of Ardsheal, Argyllsh., Scotland, a unicorn's head arg., maned, armed, and bearded or. *Quhidder will zie.* 49. 7

Stewart-Moncrieff, a unicorn's head and neck arg., maned or, and armed gu. *Quidder will zie.—Sur esperance.*

Stewart, a garb or, surmounted of a crow ppr. *Judge nought.*

Stewart, Scotland, a boar's head couped or. *Virtute orta.* 43. 1

Stewart of Scotstown, a boar's head couped arg. *A virtute orta.* 43. 1

Stewart, Scotland, a greyhound couchant within two branches of bay ppr. *Fide et operâ.* 60. 5

Stewart of Kirkhill and Strabrock, Scotland, a phœnix in flames ppr. *Virtute fortuna comes.* 82. 2

Stewart of Shambelly, Dumfriessh., Scotland, a dove holding in his beak a rose stalked and leaved ppr. *Soli Deo honor.*

Stewart, Scotland, an anchor erect az., ensigned with a man's heart ppr. *Fixus ac solidus.*

Stewart of Roslane, Scotland, an anchor in pale az., ensigned with a man's heart ppr. *Tam fidus quam fixus.*

Stewart, Lord Methven, a tower arg. *Forward.* 156. 2

Stewart of Catrine, Scotland, the sun rising from clouds ppr. *Sol tibi signa dabit.* 162. 2

Stewart, a savage's head ppr. *Never unprepared.* 190. 12

Stewart of Dundee, Scotland, a savage's head couped ppr. *Reddunt commercia mitem.* 190. 12

Stewart of Ladywell, Scotland, a man's head couped ppr. *Pro Rege et patria.* 190. 12

Stewart, Charles Edward, of Temple, E.C., same crest and motto.

Stewart, Poyntz-, Charles, Chesfield Park, Stevenage, same crest.

Stewart of Wester Cluny, Scotland, a savage's head ppr. *Never unprepared.* 190. 12

Stewart, Scotland, a man's head affrontée, armed with a helmet ppr. *Pro Rege et patriâ.*

Stewart, a griffin's head couped gu. 66. 1

Stewart, Rev. Henry William, M.A., of Ballymenagh, co. Tyrone, and of Knockbreda Rectory, co. Down, Ireland, a griffin's head couped ppr. *Forward.* 66. 1

Stewart, Rev. Edward Hamilton, of Croxdale Rectory, Durham, same crest and motto.

Stewart of Stranorlar, co. Donegal, Ireland, a griffin's head couped ppr. *Forward.* 66. 1

Stewart, Scotland, a griffin passant. 63. 2

Stewart-Robertson, James, Esquire, D.L., J.P., of Edradynate, Cluny, and Blackhill, Perthsh.: (1) On the dexter side, a griffin passant ppr. (*for Stewart*). 63. 2. (2) Upon the sinister side, an arm erect, the hand holding an imperial crown ppr. (*for Robertson*). *Never unprepared.—Virtutis gloria merces.* 217. 1 (*Matriculated at Lyon Office, May 25, 1885.*)

Stewart, Scotland, a dragon's head vert. *Pass forward.* 71. 1

Stewart, a dragon statant or. *cf.* 73. 2

Stewart of Ards, co. Donegal, a dragon statant or. *Metuenda corolla draconis.* *cf.* 73. 2

Stewart, Alexander Charles Hector, Esquire, J.P., D.L., of Rock Hill, Letterkenny, co. Donegal, same crest and motto.

Stewart, Alexander John Robert, Esquire, of 22, St. Aubyn's, Hove, Sussex, same crest and motto.

Stewart, Charles John, of 32, Eccleston Square, S.W., same crest and motto.

Stewart, Rear-Admiral Hector Brabazon, of 13, Warwick Square, S.W., same crest and motto.

Stewart of Aberdeen, a basket full of fruit ppr. *Deus providebit.*

Stewart, on a mural coronet or, three lances disposed saltireways ppr., the pennoncels gu. *Ready, aye ready.—Resolve is power.*

Stewart, Scotland, a demi-savage wreathed round the loins chequy az. and arg., on his head an antique crown, holding over his dexter shoulder a club, and in his sinister a heart between two wings imperially crowned. *Dant priscæ decorem.*

Stewart-Balfour, a mermaid ppr., holding in her dexter hand an otter's head erased sa. *Omne solum forti patria.* *cf.* 184. 10

Stewart, a hand issuing holding a scimitar. *Avant.* 213. 5

Stewart, Grainger-, late Sir Thomas, Professor, Edinburgh, two hands ppr., grasping a man's heart or. *Corde et manu.*

Stewart, Alexander Arthur Grainger, Esquire, M.A., LL.B., of 23, Northumberland Place, Edinburgh, same crest and motto.

Stewart of Baldorran, Stirlingsh., and Ardvorlich, Perthsh., a dexter arm embowed, holding in the hand a sword in bend sinister ppr., hilt and pommel or. *Deo juvante vinco.* 201. 4

Stewart, Colonel John, Loch Erne Head, same crest.

Stewart of St. Fort, Fife, a dexter cubit arm holding in the hand a dagger in pale, both ppr. *Never fear.* 212. 9

Stewart of Drummin, Banffsh and Belladrum, Inverness-sh, two hands conjoined holding a man's heart ppr *Corde et manu* 224 4

Stewart, Scotland a dexter hand grasping a sword *Avant* 212 13

Stewart, Sir Norman Robert, Bart Junior Army and Navy Club, a dexter arm couped below the elbow and erect vested gu, holding in the hand a dagger ppr, hilted or *Pro Rege et lege*

Stewart, Scotland, a dexter hand holding a dagger erect ppr, hilt and pommel or *Never fear* 212 9

Stewart, John Esquire, of Ardvorlich Lochearnhead, Perthsh, a dexter naked arm issuant grasping a sword in bend sinister, all ppr, pommel and hilt or *Deo juvante vinco*

Stewart, Scotland, a dexter hand holding a thistle slipped, both ppr *Aspera juvant* 218 2

Stewart, Falconar-, George Mercer Esquire of Binny Linlithgowsh Scotland (1) A falcon close ppr, between two laurel branches in orle vert (*for Falconar*) (2) A dexter hand holding a dagger, point downwards, ppr (*for Stewart*). *Candide —Armis potentius æquum*

Stewart, Scotland, a dexter hand holding a dagger ppr *Pro Rege et lege* 212 3

Stewart, a dexter hand in pale grasping a rose and a thistle in saltier

Stewart, Scotland, a hand holding a thistle ppr *Virtutis præmium* 218 2

Stewart of Binny, Linlithgowsh a dexter hand holding a dagger, point downwards ppr *Candide*

Stewart, Sir Harry Jocelyn Urquhart Bart of Fort Stewart co Donegal, a dexter hand in armour ppr holding a heart gu *Nil desperandum est*

Stewart, Sir Norman Robert, Bart, Junior Army and Navy Club, a dexter arm couped below the elbow and erect vested gu, holding in the hand a dagger ppr, hilted or *Pro Rege et lege*

Stewart of Rosyth Fifesh, a dexter arm from the elbow ppr the hand holding a buckle or 223 11

Stewart of Bigtowne, Orkney, Scotland, a holly leaf slipped vert *Sic virescit industria*

Stewart, Scotland, a hand holding a plumb rule ppr *Candide*

Stewekley, Somers, a triple plume of ostrich feathers alternately arg, the others sa

Stewins, a cross moline lozenge pierced gu 165 1

Stibbert, a castle ruined in the sinister tower with flag displayed

Stibbert of London, out of an Eastern coronet or, doubled erm, the second and fourth points vert, an arm in armour embowed of the first grasping a Persian scimitar ppr hilt and pommel also or *Per ardua*

Stiddolph of Norbury and Micklam, Surrey, a wolf's head erased per fess or and gu 30 8

Stieglitz, Frederick Ludwig Von of the Glen co Armagh, Ireland out of a ducal coronet or, a dexter arm in armour embowed ppr, holding in the hand a sword in bend sinister, also ppr, between two eagle's wings, the dexter per fess arg and gu, and the sinister per fess counterchanged *Spes mea in Deo*

Stiffe, a demi eagle rising or, the wings semee of estoiles az, holding in the beak a billet, also az

Stileman-Gibbard, Leonard Gibbard, Esquire J P, B A, a mermaid holding in her dexter hand a comb, and in her sinister a mirror all ppr

Stiles, a wolf's head erased sa, collared or the neck below the collar fretty of the last *cf* 30 11

Stiles of Wantage, Berks, a dexter arm and hand ppr grasping a stork's head erased or the elbow tied with a scarf az

Still of Christian Malford, Wilts Durley and Hutton, Somers, and Suff a stork arg 105 11

Still, a kingfisher ppr *cf* 96 9

Stillingfleet of Stillingfleet, Yorks, a leopard's head and neck ppr collared and chained gu *Magna est veritas*

Stillington, on a ducal coronet or a mullet between two branches of laurel in orle ppr *cf* 146 7

Stilwell, John Pakenham Esquire of Bregsells Surrey and Hilfield Hants, upon water a swan naiant with wings elevated and endorsed ppr, holding in the beak an anchor or *Hold fast* 99 13

Stimson, E, Esquire, Glendwr, 52, Brixton Hill, London, S W, on a mural coronet three arrows, one in pale and two in saltire *Sic fidem teneo*

Stinton of Lurgan, co Armagh, Ireland, a griffin's head erased gu 66 2

Stirlin, a griffin's head erased arg 66 2

Stirling of Keir *see* Maxwell

Stirling, Scotland a lion passant ppr *Fides servata secundat* 6 2

Stirling of Bankell Stirlingsh, same crest and motto 6 2

Stirling, Sir Charles Elphinstone Fleming, Bart, J P, D L, of Glorat, Stirlingsh, a lion passant gu *Semper fidelis* 6 2

Stirling, Rt Hon Sir James Lord Justice of the Court of Appeal of His Majesty's High Court of Justice of Finchcocks, Goudhurst, Kent, a lion passant or, charged on the body with two estoiles, and resting the dexter fore-paw upon a round buckle az *Tenax*

Stirling, Chalmer-, Gilbert Stirling, Sysonby, Melton Mowbray a demi-lion holding in the dexter paw a fleur-de lis gu *Quid non Deo juvante*

Stirling, Patrick, Esquire of Kippendavie, Perthsh., a Saracen's head in profile ppr, banded gu *Gang forward*

Stirling, Charles Esquire of Gargunnock, Stirlingsh, a Saracen's head in profile couped at the neck and wreathed about the temples *Gang forward*

Stirling of Keir, Perthsh, and Herbertshire Stirlingsh, a Moor's head couped ppr. *Gang forward* *cf* 192. 13

Stirling, John Alexander, of Kippendavie, Perthsh, a negro's head in profile wreathed. *Gang forward* *cf* 192 13

Stirling, Bart, Scotland, a demi Moor issuing, at his back a quiver of arrows, the dexter arm stretched out, holding an arrow in fess all ppr *Forward*

Stirling, Bart., Scotland a Moor's head couped ppr *Gang forward*

Stirling, James, of Garden, Kipping, Stirlingsh same crest and motto

Stirling, John Alexander, Esquire of Kippenross, near Dunblane, a Moors' head sa, banded about the temples arg *Gang forward*

Stirling, Gartshore-, of Craigbarnet (1) A lady issuant from the breasts upwards ppr, robed and winged or, ensigned on the head with a cross arg (*for Stirling*) (2) An eagle displayed ppr (*for Gartshore*) 75 2

Stirling, Scotland, a lady issuing from the breasts upwards ppr, attired and winged or, ensigned on the head with a cross gu 183 12

Stirling of Drumpellier, Lanarksh, issuing out of a ducal coronet a hart's head az *Gang forward —Castrum et nemus Strevilense* 120 7

Stirling, Carolus Home Graham, Strohan Crieff, N B (1) A dexter hand holding a sword in pale ppr (2) A Saracen's head couped ppr *Non immemor —Gang forward*

Stirling, James, Esquire, of the county of Dumbarton Scotland issuing from an antique coronet or a hart's head az *Gang forward* 190 14

Stirling, Scotland, a stag's head erased ppr *Hic fidus et robore* 121 2

Stirling, Scotland out of a ducal coronet or, a stag's head ppr *Forward* 120 7

Stirling, Scotland, out of a ducal coronet or, a buck's head az, attired of the first 120 7

Stirling-Home-Drummond, Henry Edward, Esquire, of Blair Drummond Stirling and Ardoch Braco Perthsh, on a wreath of his liveries a sleuth-hound's head ppr *E cura quies*

Stirling-Maxwell, Sir John Maxwell, Bart., D L, of Pollok, Renfrewsh a stag's head erased ppr *I am ready* 121 2

Stirling of Dundee, Scotland, a ship under sail ppr *Faventibus* 160 13

Stirling, Graham-, of Duchray, Scotland an eagle displayed, holding in the dexter claw a sword, and in the sinister a pistol ppr *For right —Noctesque diesque præsto* *cf* 75 7

Stirling of Cadder Stirlingsh a swan's head and neck issuing out of a ducal coronet ppr

Stirling, Scotland, a boar's head couped ppr 43 1

Stirling, Scotland, a lion's gamb holding an oak-branch fructed ppr *Hic fidus et robore*

Stirling, Rt Hon Sir James, of 630, Royal Courts of Justice, W C, a lion statant or, charged on the body with two estoiles in fesse az, and resting the dexter paw on a round buckle in bend *Tenax*

Stirling, Sir Walter George, Bart, of Faskine, Lanarksh, a dexter arm in armour embowed issuing out of a ducal coronet grasping a dagger in fesse, all ppr, the last hilted and pommelled or *Gang forward* *cf* 196. 5

Stirling, Ireland, out of a ducal coronet or, an arm in armour, holding in the hand a sword, the point supporting a crown of laurel, all ppr. *Gang through.*

Stirling, Scotland, a dexter hand pointing a lancet ppr. *By wounding I cure.* 216. 14

Stirrop, an arm in armour embowed to the sinister, garnished or, holding in the gauntlet a tilting-lance ppr., thereon a forked pennon.

Stiven, Scotland, a crescent gu. *Cresco.* 163. 2

Stobart of Picktree, Chester-le-Street, Durh., a cubit arm holding in the hand a dagger, point upwards. 212. 9

Stock, a domed tower with a flag displayed from the top. 157. 15

Stock, Ireland, a pheon ppr., point upwards. 174. 9

Stock, a hawk with wings displayed ppr., belled or, holding in the beak a laurel-branch vert.

Stock of London, a gauntlet fesseways or, thereon a hawk az., holding in the beak an annulet, also or. *Celeriter et audaciter.*

Stock of London, upon a mount vert, a stock of a tree couped and sprouting on either side ppr., surmounted by an estoile irradiated or. *Ex stirpe nil turpe.*

Stockbridge, out of a cloud two dexter hands in armour conjoined holding up a heart inflamed, all ppr.

Stockdale of Bilton, Yorks, a talbot passant ppr. 54. 1

Stockdale, out of a ducal coronet or, a triple plume of ostrich-feathers ppr. 114. 6

Stockdale of Lockington, Yorks, out of a mural coronet or, a griffin's head arg. 67. 10

Stockdale, Henry Minshull, of Mears Ashby Hall, Northants., out of a mural coronet or, a griffin's head arg. *Omnia mei dona Dei.* 67. 10

Stocken of London, a demi-lion rampant. *Renovate animos.* 10. 2

Stockenström, Sir Gysbert Henry, Bart., of Maastrom, Cape of Good Hope, in front of a stump of a tree sprouting to the dexter two swords in saltier, points upwards, ppr., pommels and hilts or. *Fortis si jure ortis.* 313. 12

Stocker, an old man's head in profile ppr., vested gu., wreathed about the temples arg. and sa.

Stocker, a parrot vert, resting the dexter claw on an escutcheon gyronny of six arg. and vert. *Non sibi sed toti.*

Stockes, a demi-lion rampant. *Fortis, non ferox.* 10. 2

Stocket of London, and St. Stephen's, Kent, on the stump of a tree couped and eradicated arg., a lion sejant sa. cf. 7. 9

Stockham, a demi-eagle displayed or, charged on the breast with a thistle ppr. cf. 81. 6

Stockley, a hind's head ppr. 124. 1

Stockley of London, a hind's head ppr. *Sequor nec inferior.* 124. 1

Stockoe, a horse's head erased or, bridled sa. cf. 51. 5

Stocks or **Stokes,** out of a ducal coronet or, a plume of ostrich-feathers arg., in a case gu.

Stockton, a lion rampant supporting an Ionic pillar, all ppr.

Stockton, Alfred Augustus, Esquire, LL.D., D.C.L., Ph.D., Q.C., of Saint John, New Brunswick, Canada, *uses:* a lion rampant resting his fore-paws against an Ionic pillar ppr. *Omnia Deo pendent.*

Stockton, a wolf's head erased, collared. 30. 11

Stockwell of Blackheath, Kent, against the stock of a tree couped and leaved ppr., a lion sejant erect sa., collared or, supporting between the paws a bezant, charged with a cross formée gu.

Stockwood, out of a mural coronet or, a demi-lion rampant supporting a flag gu. cf. 16. 7

Stoddard of Southhouse, co. Edinburgh, Scotland, a star issuing from a cloud ppr. *Post nubes lux.* 164. 11

Stoddard, Suff., a demi-horse erm., environed round the body with a ducal coronet or. cf. 53. 3

Stodart, late Robert Riddle, Lyon Clerk Depute, Lyon Office, Edinburgh, a star of six points arg. issuing out of a cloud ppr. *Post nubes lux.* cf. 164. 1

Stoddart of Kailzie, Peeblessh., and Ormiston, co. Edinburgh, a star of six points arg. issuing out of a cloud sa. *Post nubes lux.* cf 164. 11

Stoddart of Inveralt, Blundellsands, Lancs, same crest and motto.

Stoddart, Northumb., the fasces in bend surmounted by a silver oar (being the official ensign of the Vice-Admiralty Court in Malta), all encircled by a wreath of oak fructed ppr. *Justitiæ tenax.*

Stoddyr, a fleur-de-lis issuant gu.

Stoke, a stork regardant arg., resting the dexter claw on a pellet.

Stokely, an esquire's helmet az. 180. 3

Stoken, Ireland, an arm from the shoulder, the hand holding a garland of laurel ppr. 202. 4

Stokes, a tiger sejant arg., guttée-de-sang, collared and chained or.

Stokes, Cambs, out of a ducal coronet or, an arm embowed vested gu., cuffed arg., holding in the hand ppr. a staff of the second, thereon an imperial crown of the first.

Stokes of Hean Castle, Pembrokesh., a dove with wings expanded holding in the beak an olive-branch, all ppr. *Fortis qui insons.* 94. 5

Stokes, a tiger sejant arg., guttée-de-sang, collared and chained or.

Stokes, Bart., of Lensfield Cottage, Cambs, a fore-staff in pale ppr. *Ire in adversa.* 288. 13

Stokes, Sir Henry Edward, K.C.S.I., same crest.

Stokes, Whitley, Esquire, of 15, Grenville Place, Cromwell Road, S.W., same crest.

Stokewood, out of a mural coronet a demi-lion rampant supporting a flag gu. cf. 16. 7

Stokoe, a horse's head erased or, bridled sa. cf. 51. 5

Stolyon of Warbleton, Sussex, a stag's head erased sa., charged on the neck with a bezant, holding in the mouth an acorn or, stalked and leaved vert. cf. 119. 11

Stompe, Berks, and of Newnham-Murren, Oxon., a demi-horse rampant arg. 53. 3

Stonard, a leopard's head and neck erased gardant ppr.

Stonard of Loughton, Essex, a horse's head erased arg. 51. 4

Stone, *see* Elphinstone-Stone.

Stone, Lowndes, of Brightwell Park, Oxon.: (1) Out of a ducal coronet or, a griffin's head arg., charged with two bars gemelle gu., between two wings or. cf. 67. 1. (2) A leopard's head erased at the neck or, gorged with a laurel-branch ppr. *Mediocria firma.* cf. 23. 10

Stone of Blackmore, Essex, out of a ducal coronet or, a griffin's head between two wings gu., bezantée. cf. 67. 1

Stone of London, out of a ducal coronet a griffin's head erm., between two wings or. 67. 1

Stone, Edward, Esquire, F.S.A., of Lansdowne Place, Blackheath, London, S.E., a griffin's head erased per pale arg. and or, between two wings sa., each charged with a fleur-de-lis between two cinquefoils of the second. *Sto ne per vim sed per jus.* 272. 12

Stone, out of a ducal coronet or, a demi-griffin erm., winged and beaked of the last. 64. 4

Stone, out of a ducal coronet or, a griffin's head between two wings erm. 67. 1

Stone, Samuel Francis, Esquire, Kirby Frith Hall, Leics., on a rock an eagle displayed holding in each claw a flaming sword ppr., and charged on the breast and on each wing with a cross couped gu. *Nil desperandum.* 299. 2

Stone of Framfield, Sussex, a demi-cockatrice rising arg., winged and crested or.

Stone of Wavesdon, Suff., a demi-lion. 10. 2

Stone of London, a sea-horse or, crined gu., the tail ppr., holding between the fore-feet an escallop of the first.

Stone, Warry-, William John Ellis, of Badbury, Wilts, a griffin's head couped sa., between two horse-shoes or. 52. 10

Stone of London, a unicorn's head sa., issuing from rays or, maned and armed of the same, between two wings of the first.

Stone, Sir John Benjamin, the Grange, Erdington, an eagle, wings displayed, supporting with the dexter claw a wing ppr., and charged on the wing with a cross couped sa. *Seek and find.*

Stone, Sir John Benjamin, J.P., of the Grange, Erdington, Warw., an eagle with wings elevated and addorsed ppr., charged on the wings with a cross couped sa.

Stone, Robert Sidney, Esquire, of 2, Ryder Street, St. James's, London, S.W., a horse courant sa., bridled, crined, and hoofed or. *Quid merui meum est.*

Stone, Edward Herbert, Esquire, of Fairlawn, Freshford, Somers., same crest and motto.

Stone, Francis Gleadowe, Esquire, United Service Club, Pall Mall S W, same crest and motto

Stone of Cliff, Sussex, and London out of a ducal coronet a demi peacock with wings expanded or

Stone of Wedmore, Somers, and Kent a spaniel passant arg 57 7

Stone, Dorset a spaniel courant gu *Nil desperandum*

Stone of Trevigo, Cornw, on a rock paly wavy of six arg and az, a salmon ppr, holding in the mouth a rose of the last, stalked and leaved vert

Stonehewer, out of a ducal coronet or, an eagle's head erased ppr, charged on the neck with an escallop arg

Stoner, Hants, out of a ducal coronet sa, a demi eagle displayed or 80 14

Stoner, on a rock ppr, a bird arg, holding in the beak a stone

Stoner of North Stoke, Oxon, on a rock ppr, semee of torteaux, an eagle az, bezantee

Stones, an eagle displuming a wing ppr 79 13

Stones of Mosborough, Derbysh, a demi-dragon pean holding a cross humettee vert gorged with a collar arg, charged with three roses gu

Stones of Westminster, Middx, and Cartmell, Lancs, a demi dragon vert, collared arg, supporting between the claws a cross crosslet sa

Stonestreet, a bull's head cabossed arg between two winsg sa cf 43 8

Stoney, Charles Butler, Esquire, J P, D L, of Portland Park, co Tipperary, Ireland out of a mural coronet ppr a demi lion or holding between the paws a spur erect arg, winged gu *Nunquam non paratus*

Stoney, Rev F M A, of the Vicarage, Waltham Cross, Herts, same crest and motto

Stoney, Francis Goold, Esquire, of Ipswich, same crest and motto

Stoney, Johnstone Thomas, Esquire, of Emell Castle, Cloughjordan, King's Co, same crest and motto

Stoney, Percy Butler, Esquire of Millom, Cumb, same crest and motto

Stoney, Thomas Johnston Esquire of Ballyknockane House, Ballymackey, co Tipperary, same crest and motto

Stonhouse, Sir Ernest Hay, Bart, of Radley, Berks, a talbot's head couped arg, collared sa, lined and catching a dove volant of the first *Sublimiora petamus* cf 57 3

Stonhouse-Vigor (1) A lion's gamb ppr, charged with a fesse, and thereon a leopard's face sa (*for Vigor*) (2) A talbot's head couped arg, collared sa, lined, and catching a dove volant of the last (*for Stonhouse*) cf 57 3

Stonor, *see* Camoys, Baron

Stonor, His Honour Judge Henry James at the base of a rock arg, enriched with amethysts and rubies a bird ppr charged as the rock, holding in its bill a ruby 259 12

Stonor, Rev Edmund, of 27, Via Sistina, Rome, same crest

Stonor, Edward Alexander, Esquire, of Bachelors' Club, same crest

Stopford, *see* Courtown Earl of

Stopford-Blair of Penningham, co Wigtown, Ireland (1) A dove with wings expanded ppr, charged on the breast for distinction with a torteau (*for Blair*) cf 94 2 (2) A wyvern with wings expanded vert (*for Stopford*) cf 70 8

Stopford-Sackville of Drayton House, Northamp (1) Out of a cornet composed of eight fleurs de lis or, an estoile of six points arg (*for Sackville*) cf 164 4 (2) A wyvern with wings expanded vert (*for Stopford*) *Tousjours loyal* cf 70 8

Stopford, Ireland a lamb arg, bearing a banner gu 130 2

Stopham, an escutcheon sa 176 10

Storar and Storer, a crane ppr 105 9

Storer, Anthony Morris, of Purley Park, Berks a crane ppr *Dum spiro spero* 105 9

Storer of Combe Court, Surrey, a stork ppr 105 11

Storey, Sir Thomas, of Westfield, Lancaster, upon a rock ppr, a whelk shell fessewise gu, thereon a stork arg *Deficiam aut efficiam* 233 11

Storey, Dorset, a stork ppr 105 11

Storey, a heron 105 9

Storey, on a garland of laurel a raven ppr

Storey, Shaw-, of Arcot, Northumb (1) A falcon sa, within a chaplet of laurel ppr charged on the breast with an Eastern crown or, and for distinction charged also with a cross crosslet or (*for Storey*) (2) A hind's head couped arg, charged with three lozenges, one and two erm, holding in the mouth an arrow in pale or, flighted also arg (*for Shaw*) *Sola virtus reddit nobilem*

Storey, an escallop or, between two eagle's wings ppr 141 10

Storey, Herbert Lushington, Esquire, of Lancaster upon a rock ppr a whelk-shell fesseways gu, thereon a stork arg 233 11

Storie of Stockholm, two branches of olive in saltier ppr *Moret qui laborat*

Storie of Springfield Lodge, Surrey, a demi lion rampant double queued gu *Courage et esperance* 10 6

Stork, Scotland, a bull's head erased sa *Fortiorum fortia facta* 44 3

Storks, a buffalo's head erased gu 44 1

Stormont, Viscount, *see* Mansfield Earl of

Stormyn, a bear sejant ppr 34 8

Storr, a cubit arm in armour couped in fess, holding in the hand ppr a cross crosslet fitched or 211 14

Story, Lieutenant General Philip, a cock holding a gauntlet in its dexter claw

Story, a Cupid holding in his dexter hand an arrow, and in his sinister a bow and at his back a quiver all ppr

Story, a stork's head erased, holding in the beak a serpent nowed cf 106 3

Story, Durb, a stork's head erased gorged with a mural coronet cf 106 1

Story, Edward John, of Newcastle-on-Tyne and Ilford, Essex, a stork's head couped ppr, gorged with a mural crown *Dei gratia sum quod sum*

Story, Lieutenant-Colonel, Bingfield, Crossdoney, co Cavan, a stork holding in the beak a serpent, all ppr *Fabula sed vera.*

Stote of Jesmond Northumb, a demi lion rampant erminois, holding between the paws a mullet pierced or cf 15 8

Stoteville of Brinkley Hall, Cambs, and Suff, a plume of feathers paly of six erm and ermines

Stother, a camel's head sa 132 7

Stothert of Cargen Kirkcudbrightsh, Scotland, issuing out of a cloud ppr a star of six points arg *Post nubes lux* cf 164 11

Stott, Scotland a martlet az *Alta petit* 95 4

Stott, on a mount a peacock ppr cf 103 4

Stott-Milne of Rochdale Lancs (1) In front of two palm trees a lamb couchant ppr holding with the dexter foot a pennon arg charged with a cross crosslet gu (*for Milne*) 131 4 (2) A cross patee sa therefrom rising a moor cock holding in the beak a sprig of heath ppr (*for Stott*) *Prudenter qui sedulo* 89 9

Stott of Quebec, issuant out of waves of the sea a demi-bulldog ppr, around the neck and reflexed over the back a log-line or, and holding between the paws a wreath of oak fructed, also ppr

Stoughton, *see* Trent Stoughton

Stoughton, a robin redbreast ppr *Hoc signum non onus, sed honor* 108 11

Stoughton of Owlpenn, Glouc, same crest

Stoughton, Bart (*extinct*), same crest 108 11

Stourton, Baron, *see* Mowbray, Baron

Stourton, a demi greyfriar ppr vested in russet girt or holding in his dexter hand a scourge of three lashes with knots or *Loyal je serai durant ma vie* 231 3

Stout, a talbot passant or 54 1

Stoveld, late John Townsend Esquire of Stedham Hall Sussex, a stag's head couped at the neck and affrontee az between two feathers or *Esmi o Esmi* cf 119 12

Stoven or **Stovin,** a bow in fess gu, transfixed by an arrow erect and flighted of the same headed arg

Stovin, a dragon's head vert 71 1

Stowe of Newton Lincs on a ducal coronet a leopard's face or between two wings vert

Stowell of Dublin, a dove with wings expanded arg, holding in the beak an olive branch ppr 94 5

Stowers, a rose gu, seeded and barbed ppr 149 2

Stowers of Hillside Hollyfield, Surbiton, a rose gu, barbed and seeded ppr *Nulla rosa sine spica* 149 2

Stoyt or **Stoit** of Dublin, a demi lion rampant sa, armed and langued gu, holding in the dexter paw a trefoil slipped vert cf 13 13

Stoyte, Captain William J P, of Green Hill Kinsale, same crest

Stoyte, Lieutenant Colonel John J P, of Glendonen co Cork same crest

Stoyte, James C, of Glendonen co Cork, same crest

Stracey, Sir Edward Paulet Bart of Rackheath Hall, Norf a lion rampant erminois, ducally crowned gu supporting a cross patee fitchee of the last cf 3 13

Stracey, Gilbert Hardinge, Esquire, J.P., of Sprowston Lodge, Rackheath, Norwich same crest.

Stracey-Clitherow, Rev. William James, M.A., of Boston House, Middx., and 50, Portland Place, W.: (1) Out of a tower or, a demi-lion rampant sa. (*for Clitherow*). 157. 11. (2) A lion rampant erminois, ducally crowned gu., supporting a cross patée fitchée, also gu. (*for Stracey*). *Loyal yet free.* cf. 3. 13

Strachan, a stag's head erased. 121. 2

Strachan, Bart., of Thornton, Kincardinesh., Scotland, a demi-stag springing or, holding in the mouth a thistle ppr. *Non timeo, sed caveo.* cf. 119. 1

Strachan, Bart., of Inchtuthill, Scotland, same crest and motto. cf. 119. 1

Strachan of Glenkiddie, Aberdeensh., Scotland, a hart at gaze or, attired and ungu. gu. *Non timeo, sed caveo.* 117. 3

Strachan, on a ducal coronet or, a wyvern sans legs vert. 70. 9

Strachan of Tarrie, Forfarsh., Scotland, a ship in full sail ppr. *Juvat Deus impigros.* 160. 13

Strachan of London, an arm and hand holding a scimitar bendways ppr. *Forward.* 213. 5

Strachey, Somers., an eagle displayed gu., charged on the breast with a cross patée fitched arg. cf. 75. 2

Strachey, Sir Edward, Bart., of Sutton Court, Somers., an eagle displayed gu., charged on the breast with a cross crosslet fitchée arg. *Cœlum, non animum.* cf. 75. 2

Stradbroke, Earl of (Rous), Henham Hall, Wangford, Suff., a pyramid of bay-leaves in the form of a cone vert. *Je vive en espoir.* 151. 14

Stradbrooke, a mountain on fire. 179. 2

Stradling, Heref., a stag trippant arg., attired or, collared. *Heb a hyw heb I him dyne a diyon.* cf. 117. 8

Stradling, Wales, a stag at gaze arg. 117. 3

Stradling, Bart. (*extinct*), of St. Donats, Somers., a stag courant sa., around the neck a scarf arg. cf. 118. 13

Strafford, Earl of (Byng), Wrotham Park, Barnet: (1) Of honourable augmentation, out of a mural coronet an arm embowed vested gu., grasping the colours of the 31st Regiment, and pendent from the wrist by a riband the gold cross presented by royal command for Lord Strafford's gallant achievements, and on an escroll the word *Mouguerre.* (2) An heraldic antelope statant erm., attired, tusked, crined, and ungu. or. *Tuebor.* cf. 127. 5

Strafford, an elephant statant sa. 133. 9

Strahan, on a ducal coronet a wyvern sans legs ppr. 70. 9

Strahan, a dexter arm embowed wielding a scimitar, both ppr., hilt and pommel or. 201. 1

Straiton of Montrose, Scotland, a mortar and therein a pestle ppr. *Arduo vinco.* 177. 13

Straiton of Edinburgh, Scotland, a falcon rising ppr. *Resurgere tento.* 88. 2

Straker, Durh., a horse at full speed ppr. *Deus est super domo.* 52. 8

Straker, John Coppin, Stagshawe House, Corbridge-on-Tyne, in front of an arrow in pale, point downwards, barbed and feathered arg., a horse courant of the last, semée of quatrefoils az. *Deus est super domo.* 264. 6

Strang of London, a cluster of wine-grapes ppr. *Dulce quod utile.* 152. 7

Strange, Earl, *see* Atholl, Duke of.

Strange, *see* Le Strange.

Strange, Baron Strange of Knockyn (*dormant*), a lion statant, tail extended or. cf. 4. 8

Strange, Shropsh., on a chapeau gu., turned up erm., a lion statant, the tail extended. 4. 8

Strange, Lancs, and of London, a lion passant arg. 6. 2

Strange, a demi-lion rampant. 10. 2

Strange, Scotland, a castle ppr., masoned sa. *Stet fortuna domus.—Fortes fortuna domus.* 155. 8

Strange, Shropsh., a tree. 143. 5

Strange of London, two hands clasped ppr., couped at the wrists. 224. 2

Strange of Cirencester and Moun's Court, Glouc., and Somerford-Keynes, Wilts, out of clouds two hands clasped, all ppr. 224. 1

Strangebow, a bull's head caboshed between two flags, each charged with a cross. cf. 43. 5

Stranger, a fox current ppr. cf. 32. 8

Strangewayes or Strangways, Lancs, Dorset, and Yorks, a lion passant paly of six arg. and gu. 6. 2

Strangeways, same crest. 6. 2

Strangeways, a lion's head affrontée out of a palisado coronet.

Strangewiche, a lion passant paly of six arg. and gu. 6. 2

Strangford, Viscount (*extinct*—Rt. Hon. the late Percy Ellen Algernon Frederick William Sydney Smythe), an ounce's head erased arg., pellettée, collared sa., bezantée, and chained of the second. *Virtus incendit vires.*

Strangforth, an arm in armour embowed, holding in the hand a scimitar. 196. 10

Strangman, Essex, two ragged staffs in saltire environed with a ducal coronet or. 147. 14

Strangman, of Waterford, a lion rampant sable, plain collared or, pendent therefrom a harp, and holding between the paws a ragged staff of the last. *Verbum vir fortis nulli succumbit dolori.* 314. 4

Strangman, J. Piers, same crest and motto.

Strangman, Essex, a demi-cockatrice rising sa., winged arg., holding in the beak a slip of oak-leaves vert.

Strangways, *see* Ilchester, Earl of.

Strangways, Yorks, a lion passant paly of six arg. and gu. *Ystoyeau et ne doubtero.* 6. 2

Strangways, Swainston-, John, of Alne, Yorks: (1) A lion passant paly of six arg. and gu. 6. 2. (2) Out of a ducal coronet or, a boar's head sa., between two wings az., pellettée or. *Ystoyeau et ne doubtero.*

Strangways of Melberrie Sampford, Dorset, a lion passant paly of six arg. and gu. 6. 2

Strangways, Hon. H. B. Templer, Shapwick, Somers., same crest. *Ystoyeau et ne doubtero.*

Strangways, Thomas Edward, Esquire, Solicitor, 8, Park Parade, Ashton-under-Lyne, Lancs, same crest and motto.

Strangways, of Wells, Yorks, a lion passant paly of six arg. and gu., with the motto *Ystoyeau* in an escroll above. *Ne doubtero.* 6. 2

Strangways, James Howard Percy, of the Shanty, Westcliff-on-sea, Essex, a lion passant paly of six arg. and gu., gorged with a ducal coronet or. *Soys joyeux et ne doubte pointe.*

Strangways, Leonard Richard Ffleming, Merton, Cullenswood, co. Dublin, and the Dorne, Skerries, co. Dublin, same crest and motto.

Stransham, Kent, a demi-ostrich arg., holding in its beak a horse-shoe or.

Stratford, Earl of Aldborough, *see* Aldborough.

Stratford de Redcliffe, Viscount (*extinct*—Rt. Hon. the late Sir Stratford Canning, K.G., G.C.B.), a demi-lion arg., charged with three trefoils slipped vert, holding in the dexter paw an arrow ppr. *Ne cede malis sed contra.* cf. 13. 6

Stratford, Ireland, a goat's head erased ppr. 128. 5

Stratford, Glouc., an arm in armour embowed, holding in the hand a scimitar ppr. 196. 10

Stratford of Coventry, Warw., an arm in armour embowed ppr., grasping a falchion, hilt and pommel or. 195. 2

Stratford of Farnscott, Hawling, and Nether Guiting, Glouc., a dexter arm embowed habited arg., holding a scimitar or.

Stratford of Belan, co. Kildare, a dexter arm in armour embowed ppr., holding in the hand a scimitar arg., pommel and hilt or. 196. 10

Strathallan, Viscount (Drummond), a goshawk with wings expanded ppr., and over it the motto *Virtutem coronat honos.* *Lord have mercy.*

Strathcona and Mount Royal, Baron (Smith), Glencoe, Argyllsh., on a mount vert, a beaver eating into a maple-tree ppr. *Agmina ducens.* 288. 11

Stratheden and **Campbell** (Baron Campbell), of Hartrigge, Roxburghsh., a boar's head erased gyronny of eight or and sa. *Audacter et aperte.* 235. 20

Strathmore and Kinghorne (Bowes-Lyon), of Streatlam Castle, Darlington, within a garland of bay-leaves a lady to the girdle richly habited, and holding in her dexter hand the royal thistle, all ppr., in allusion to the alliance of Sir John Lyon with Jane, daughter of Robert II. *In te Domine speravi.* 311. 2

Strathnaver, Baron, *see* Sutherland Duke of

Strathy, James Brakenridge, Esquire, of the Pines, London, Canada, an eagle displayed, holding in its beak a thistle slipped and leaved ppr. *Audax justum perficere.* cf. 75. 2

Straton, Scotland, a falcon belled ppr., with wings expanded and inverted. *Surgere tento.* 87. 1

Straton, Scotland, an eagle with wings expanded standing on a man's hand in armour couped at the wrist. *Surgere tento.* 78. 12

Straton, on a gauntlet an eagle close ppr *cf* 86 13

Stratoun, Scotland a pelican's head erased vulning its neck ppr 98 2

Stratton, Suff, a hawk belled and jessed ppr *cf* 85 2

Stratton, out of a mural coronet or an eagle's head ppr 83 9

Stratton, on a gauntlet an eagle with wings expanded and inverted ppr *cf* 76 13

Stratton, John Locke, of Turweston House, Brackley Northamp, an eagle with wings expanded standing on a man's hand in armour couped at the wrist, all ppr

Stratton, Colonel John Heathfield, J P, the Gage, Little Berkhampsted, near Hertford, a falcon belled ppr, with wings expanded and inverted

Straubenzee, *see* Van Straubenzee

Straunge, a wolf az, devouring a child ppr

Straus, Percy Weiller of Hatton Cottage, Chislehurst, an ostrich

Stray, an eagle regardant or, with wings expanded arg, holding a sword ppr 77 10

Stray, an owl or with wings displayed gu, charged on the breast with three hurts between two pallets gu

Streatfeild, Rev Champion Wellbank, Stoke Charity Rectory, Micheldever, Hants, a dexter arm couped at the shoulder embowed in armour ppr, garnished or, supporting in the gauntlet a pennon flotant to the dexter and returning behind the staff to the sinister side gu, the front of the pennon arg, thereon the cross of St George, on the back towards the point three bezants, the staff of the fourth, round the arm near the wrist a sash tied with bows gu

Streatfeild, Richard James, Esquire, J P, the Rocks Uckfield Sussex and Rossington Hall Bawtry, Yorks a dexter arm in armour embowed ppr, garnished or, supporting in the hand a pennon flotant to the dexter, and returning behind the staff to the sinister side gu, the front of the pennon arg, thereon the cross of St George, on the back towards the point three bezants, the staff of the fourth, round the arm near the wrist a sash tied with bows gu *Data fata secutus*

Streatfeild, Rev William Champion Chaits Edge, Kent, same crest and motto

Streatfeild, Lieutenant-Colonel Henry of Chiddingstone, Edenbridge, Kent, same crest and motto

Streatfield, *see* Stretfield

Streatfield, a bunch of quills one in bend sinister ppr

Streatfield-Moore, Alexander M'Neill, Esquire, J P, of Woodcock Hill Berkhampstead, Herts (1) An arm in armour ppr, bent from the elbow, the fore arm encircled with a band tied in a knot gu, supporting a spear with a pennon showing arg, St George's cross on the dexter side of the spear and gu, three bezants fesseways on the sinister, the pennon being twined round the spear to show part of both sides (*for Streatfield*) (2) In front of a crown vallary or, a Moor's head in profile ppr wreathed az and arg, a mullet az (*for Moore*)

Street, an esquire's helmet ppr garnished or 180 3

Street of Kilburn, Middx, on a mount vert, a Catherine-wheel or charged with a cup having handles on each side arg

Street of London, an arm embowed vested the hand holding a bell pendent

Street, Captain James Frederick D'Arley (*see* Wright of Mottram Hall), a demi man in armour ppr, his breast plate charged with a cross parted and fretty gu, and supporting with his dexter hand a flagstaff, therefrom flowing to the dexter a banner gu charged with an annulet or *Quo virtus vocat*

Street, H, Esquire, Chesham Place, Brighton, a demi lion rampant gu, holding between the paws a catherine wheel gu *Fidelis inter perfidos* 304 8

Streete, a lion rampant or, holding between the fore paws a Catherine-wheel gu

Streeter, Kent, an eagle with wings expanded arg, beaked and legged gu 77 5

Strelley, Notts, a Saracen's head ppr 190 14

Strelley, a Saracen's head couped at the shoulders ppr, crined and bearded sa, wreathed about the temples arg and az 190 5

Strelley of Strelley Notts, and Beauchieff and Ullanthorpe Derbysh a man's head couped at the shoulders of a swarthy colour crined sa encircled by a band gu, belled or

Strelley, a cock's head arg, combed and wattled gu, gorged with two bars nebulee az

Strelley of Woodborough, Notts, a cockatrice's head vair, beaked combed, and wattled gu *cf* 68 12

Stretchley, Dorset, a demi-lion rampant crowned or supporting between the paws a cinquefoil

Stretfield or **Streatfield,** a dexter arm couped at the shoulder embowed in armour ppr, garnished or, supporting in the gauntlet a pennon flotant to the dexter and returning behind the staff to the sinister side gu, the front of the pennon arg thereon the cross of St George on the back towards the point three bezants, the staff of the fourth round the arm near the wrist a sash tied with bows gu *Data fata secutus*

Strettell, a swan in his pride arg, naiant in water ppr 99 8

Strettell of Dublin, a swan in his pride arg naiant in water ppr *Robur et astutia* 99 8

Stretton, a demi eagle issuing holding in the dexter claw a laurel branch ppr 80 3

Streveling, the sun shining on the stump of an oak-tree ppr 145 5

Strickland, a turkey-cock sa., membered and wattled gu 108 5

Strickland, Sir Charles William, Bart, J P D L of Boynton, Yorks, a turkey-cock in his pride ppr *A la volonte de Dieu.* 108 5

Strickland, Walter Cecil, Esquire, of the Rise, Dawlish, Devonsh, same crest and motto

Strickland, Algernon Augustine de Lille, Apperley Court, Tewkesbury, same crest.

Strickland, Sir Gerald, K C M G of Sizergh Castle, Westml and Villa Bologna Malta a bundle of holly vert fructed gu banded round the middle with a wreath arg and sa *Sans mal*

Strickland of Thornton Bridge, Yorks, a full topped holly bush ppr

Strickland of Dorchester an escallop arg 41 14

Strickland-Constable, Henry, Esquire, of Wassand Hall Hull (1) A ship with tackle guns, and apparel all or (2) A turkey-cock in his pride sa, membered and wattled gu (*for Constable*)

Strickson, from a mural coronet or, a dragon issuing with wings addorsed gu, holding in the dexter claw a thunderbolt of the first

Stringer, a martlet erminois *Celeriter nil crede* 95 4

Stringer, an eagle's head sa, ducally gorged and lined or

Stringer of Norton, Derbysh, an eagle's head erased erminois 83 2

Stringer, Middx a griffin's head or 66 1

Stringer of Eaton, Notts, a griffin's head erased vert, ducally gorged arg, chained or *cf* 66 11

Stringer, Shropsh, a griffin's head erased vert, ducally gorged and lined or *cf* 66 11

Stringfellow, Yorks and of Barton-Peverell, Hants, a cock's head erased or combed and wattled gu gorged with a ducal coronet and lined sa

Strode, George Sydney Strode, of Newnham Park Devon (1) On a mount a savin tree vert fructed gu (*for Strode*) 280 13 (2) A demi griffin segreant or (*for Loue*) *Hyeme viresco —Spero meliora* 280 14

Strode, Chetham-, of South Hill, Somers (1) A demi-lion couped or (*for Strode*) 10 2 (2) A demi-griffin holding a cross potent arg (*for Chetham*) *Malo mori quam fœdari*

Stronach of Glasgow an eagle rising ppr *Sursum specto* 77 5

Strong, Ireland, a lion rampant az, supporting a pillar arg

Strong, Scotland, a cluster of grapes stalked and leaved 152 7

Strong of the Chase Heref, an eagle displayed or 75 5

Strong, an eagle with two heads wings expanded 74 2

Strong, out of a mural coronet a demi eagle with wings displayed all or 80. 8

Strong-Hussey, Anthony Aloysius, Esquire of Westown Balbriggan, co Dublin, a hind passant arg beneath a tree ppr *Cor immobile*

Strongbow, a bull's head cabossed between two flags charged with a cross *cf* 43 5

Stronge Heref, an eagle displayed or 75 5

Stronge, Sir James Henry, Bart, J P of Tynan Abbey, co Armagh, an eagle with two heads displayed sa beaked and legged a.., langued gu *Tentanda via est —Dulce quod utile* 74 2

Stroode or **Stroud** of Parnham, Dorset, and of London, a demi-lion or. 10. 2

Stroode, Devonsh., on a mount a savin-tree vert, fructed gu.

Strother, Scotland, a martlet sa. *Ad alta.* 95. 5

Strother, a greyhound sejant or. 59. 4

Strother, a battle-axe erect entwined by a serpent, all ppr. 172. 2

Strother of Eastfield, Northumb., upon a mount vert, in front of an oak-tree ppr., fructed or, a falcon belled, also ppr. *Accipiter prædam sequitur nos gloriam.*

Stroude, a demi-lion rampant. 10. 2

Strover, a scaling-ladder sa. 158. 14

Strover, Samuel, of Ashburton, Hutton Avenue, West Hartlepool, a scaling-ladder in bend sinister. *Pro Deo et rege.*

Strover, an eagle displayed. *Pro Deo et patria.*

Strut of Westml. and Middx., a dexter arm erect couped at the elbow, vested sa., cuffed erminois, charged on the sleeve with a cross crosslet fitched or, holding in the hand ppr. a roll of parchment of the last. 247. 8

Struth of Bristol, Somers., and Sydney, New South Wales, the trunk of an oak-tree sprouting forth fresh branches ppr. *Ero quod eram.* 145. 2

Struthers, Scotland, an eagle displayed az. 75. 2

Struthers of Calderbank, Lanarksh., a martlet sa. *Ad alta.* 95. 5

Strutt, Baron Belper, *see* Belper.

Strutt, *see* Rayleigh, Baron.

Strutt, a falcon standing on a glove ppr. 86. 12

Strutt, on a dexter gauntlet a falcon close, belled. 86. 13

Strutt, George Herbert, Esquire, of Makeney House, near Derby, a dexter cubit arm habited ppr., charged with a cross crosslet fitchée, the cuff erm., holding in the hand a roll of paper. *Propositi tenax.*

Struve of the Danan, Meath, three roses or.

Stuart, Crighton-, Marquess of Bute, *see* Bute.

Stuart-Richardson, Viscount Stuart, *see* Castle-Stewart, Earl of.

Stuart, *see* Wharncliffe, Earl of.

Stuart, *see* Stuart, Earl of.

Stuart, Earl of Traquair, *see* Traquair.

Stuart, Baron Blantyre, *see* Blantyre.

Stuart, *see* Moray, Earl of.

Stuart, *see* Clinton, Earl of.

Stuart, *see* Constable-Maxwell-Stuart.

Stuart, *see* Harington-Stuart.

Stuart de Decies, Baron (Villiers-Stuart): (1) A demi-lion rampant gu., charged on the shoulder with a martlet for distinction (*for Stuart*). *cf.* 10. 3. (2) A lion rampant arg., ducally crowned or, charged with a crescent for distinction (*for Villiers*). *Nobilis ira.* *cf.* 1. 12

Stuart, De Rothsay, Baron (Stuart), (*extinct*), Scotland, a demi-lion rampant gu. *Avito viret honore.* 10. 3

Stuart, William Dugald, Esquire, Tempsford Hall, Sandy, Beds, and Aldenham Abbey, Watford, same crest and motto.

Stuart, Lord St. Colm, a lion's head erased gu. 17. 2

Stuart, a demi-lion rampant gu. *Nobilis ira.* 10. 3

Stuart, a demi-lion rampant ppr. *Avito viret honore.* 10. 2

Stuart, Bart., a Roman fasces fessewise, therefrom issuant a demi-lion rampant, holding in the dexter paw a thistle slipped and leaved, all ppr. *Justitiæ propositique tenax.* 310. 5

Stuart, Bart., of Tillicoultry, co. Clackmannan, a demi-lion rampant ppr. *Est nobilis ira leonis.* 10. 2

Stuart-Richardson: (1) A lion rampant arg., holding between the paws a wreath of oak-leaves fructed ppr., charged on the shoulder with a cross formée gu. (*for Richardson*). (2) A unicorn's head couped arg., armed, crined, and tufted or (*for Stuart*). *Virtuti paret robur.* 49. 7

Stuart, late James Meliss, Esquire, of Eriska, Argyllsh., and Charles Gordon Stewart, Esquire, of St. Stephen's Club, a pelican feeding her young or, in a nest az. *Vulnere virescens.* 98. 13

Stuart, Charles Gordon, Esquire, same crest and motto.

Stuart of Kilburn, Middx., a pelican in her piety, all ppr. *Virescit vulnere virtus.* 98. 8

Stuart of Prince of Wales' Island, a dove regardant ppr., holding in the beak a rose gu., and resting the dexter claw on a bezant. *Virtute.*

Stuart of Drumearn, Scotland, a pelican in her piety, all ppr. *Salus per Christum redemptorem.* 98. 8

Stuart, Scotland, a bird standing on a wheat-sheaf or. *Judge nought.*

Stuart, Alexander, of Inchbreck, Kincardine, a civet cat couchant ppr. *Semper apparatus.*

Stuart, the descendants of the late William, Esquire, J.P., of Edington, Shropsh., a unicorn's head erased sa., armed and crined or, charged on the neck with a fess chequy arg. and az. *Quhidder.* *cf.* 49. 5

Stuart, Colonel John Alexander Man, C.B., C.M.G., of Dalvenie, Banchory, N.B., on a wreath of his liveries a unicorn's head erased arg. *Nil Time.* 232. 8

Stuart-French, Thomas George, Esquire, Constitutional Club, Northumberland Avenue: (1) A dolphin naiant arg., charged with a crescent sa. (*for French*). (2) A unicorn's head couped arg., armed, crined, and tufted or, charged with a crescent gu. for difference (*for Stuart*). *Veritas.*

Stuart, a unicorn's head between two laurel-branches in orle. *Forward.* 49. 14

Stuart, George John, of Betton Grange, Shrewsbury, and Peniarthucaf, Towyn, Merionethsh., in front of a demi-griffin sa., beaked gu., holding between the claws an escarbuncle or, a demi-Catherine wheel arg. *Recte faciendo neminem timeas.*

Stuart, Sir Simeon Henry Lechmere, Bart., of Hartley Maudit, Hants, a roebuck statant ppr., attired and ungu. arg., ducally gorged gu. *Avito viret honore.* *cf.* 117. 5

Stuart, Thomas Peter Anderson, Esquire, M.D., Professor of Anatomy, etc., in University of Sydney, N.S.W., a lymphad with her sails furled and oars in action sa., and flags flying gu. *En avant.* 160. 7

Stuart-Menteth, Sir James, Bart., of Canandaigua, New York, U.S.A., a lymphad ppr., the flag gu., with a canton arg., charged with a cross of St. Andrew az. *Dum viro spero.*

Stuart of Fettercairn, Scotland, on a chapeau gu., turned up erm., a dexter cubit arm holding in the hand a scimitar ppr. *Avant.*

Stuart, Scotland, a dexter hand grasping a sword ppr. *Avant.* 212. 13

Stuart, Bart., of Castlemilk, Dumfriessh., a dexter hand grasping a sword ppr. *Avant.* 212. 13

Stuart, Stirling-Crawfurd-, William James Crawfurd, of Milton, Glasgow, and Castlemilk, Rutherglen, Glasgow: (1) A crescent arg. (2) A Saracen's head in profile ppr. (3) A dexter arm erect couped below the elbow holding in the hand a sword, all ppr.

Stubb, on a mural coronet a stag's head cabossed ppr., between the attires a pheon arg.

Stubbe, Norf., a bull's head cabossed, between the horns a pheon. 43. 7

Stubbe of Laxfield, Suff., a stag's head ppr., between the attires a pheon arg.

Stubber, on a mural coronet gu., a martlet arg. *Gladio et arcu.*

Stubber, Ireland, on a mural coronet gu., a martlet close arg.

Stubber, Robert Hamilton Hamilton, Esquire, of Moyne, Durrow, Queen's Co., same crest. *Gladio et ercu.*

Stubbes, Essex, an arm embowed vested barry of ten arg. and az., holding in the hand ppr. a lighted match of the first, fired of the third.

Stubbey of Boxton, Norf, out of a ducal coronet or, a heraldic tiger's head sa., tufted, maned, and horned of the first.

Stubbing of West Broughton, Derbysh., a lamb sejant ppr., collared gu., resting the dexter foot on a trefoil slipped vert.

Stubbs or **Stubbes,** a tiger passant per pale arg. and sa.

Stubbs of London, a demi-eagle displayed or, holding in the beak an oak-branch vert, fructed or.

Stubbs of Water Eaton and Bloxwich, Staffs, and Stanford, Lincs, a demi-eagle displayed or, holding in the beak a laurel-branch vert. *cf.* 81. 6

Stubbs, Launcelot Henlock Ascough, Esquire, of 1A, Middle Temple Lane, E.C., a demi-eagle displayed sa., charged on each wing with a pheon, and holding in the beak a tilting-spear erect, point upwards or. *Et dixi nunc cœpi.*

Stubbs, William Walter, Esquire, of Bonny, S. Nigeria, same crest and motto.

Stubbs, Rt. Rev. William, D.D., LL.D., Bishop of Oxford, in front of a demi-eagle displayed sa., each wing charged with a pheon point downwards, a tilting-spear palewise or, transfixed through the beak. *Et dixi nunc cœpi.*

Stubbs, Henry, Esquire, of Danby, Ballyshannon, co. Donegal, a stump of a tree eradicated ppr., thereon a demi-eagle displayed or, collared sa holding in the beak an oak branch also ppr *Dominus exaltatio mea* 310 9

Stubbs, an eagle regardant issuing ppr 80 10

Stubbs of Beckbury, Shropsh, a stag's head cabossed ppr, between the attires a pheon arg c/ 122 5

Stubbs, Durh, on a mural coronet sa, a pheon arg c/ 174 2

Stubs, a demi-eagle displayed or holding in the beak an oak-branch ppr

Stubs, Peter, Esquire, of Statham Lodge, Chesh, issuant from flames a dexter arm in armour embowed grasping a battle axe, all ppr and pendent from the hand by a chain or an escutcheon sa charged with a pheon of the second *Cedant arma labori*

Stuck, *see* Stych

Stuckey, of Weston, Devonsh, a demi-lion rampant double queued erm 10 6

Stuckey, Vincent Esquire, J P, of Hill House, Langport, Somers, a demi lion rampant double-queued erm, charged with a mascle az *Fortitudine et fidelitate* c/ 10 6

Stuckley, Sir William Lewis Stuckley, Bart J P, D L of Affeton Castle, and Hartland Abbey, Devonsh, between a buck's attires affixed to the scalp sa, a lion rampant or the sinister paw holding a battle-axe resting on the shoulder ppr 310 1

Studd of Ipswich, out of a mural coronet two arms embowed in armour the hands gauntleted, holding a tilting-spear fesseways, the head to the sinister, the staff encircled by a chaplet of oak, all ppr

Studd, Edward Fairfax, Oxton, near Exeter, same crest

Studdert, a bull's head erased erm 44 3

Studdert, Richard of Bunratty Castle co Clare, Ireland a demi-horse rampant sa, enfiled round the body by a ducal coronet or *Refulgent in tenebris* c/ 53 3

Studdert, Robert Wogan Esquire of Cullane, Kilkishen, same crest and motto

Studdy, Henry, of Wadditon Court Devonsh, a demi leopard ppr, collared arg, holding between the paws an anchor erect sa *Fide sed cui vide*

Studdy, Thomas James Charles Aylmer, of the Manor House, Clifford Chambers, Stratford-on-Avon same crest and motto

Studholme of Studholme Abbey, Holme Cumb, a horse's head couped arg, bridled or 51 5

Studholme, John, Esquire J P, of Merevale, Christchurch and Coldstream, Ashburton, co Canterbury New Zealand, *uses* a horse's head couped arg, bridled or *Semper paratus* 51 5

Studley, Shropsh, an eagle devouring a turtle ppr 79 8

Studley of Saudrich-Could Park Kent a stag's head cabossed or, pierced through the scalp by an arrow in bend sinister vert, feathered arg, headed sa

Studley, Dorset, a stag's head cabossed sa 122 5

Stukeley of Reeve, Devonsh, a demi-lion rampant arg holding in the dexter paw a battle-axe or, headed of the first, the battle axe lying behind the head as if carried on the shoulder

Stump of Walmesbury, Wilts, a griffin's head erased per chevron arg and sa 66 2

Stupart, Scotland, a rock arg, thereon an eagle regardant with wings displayed ppr, beaked and membered or

Sturdy, an arm in armour embowed and tied at the shoulder holding in the hand a spiked club ppr

Sturgeon of Whipstead, Suff, a sturgeon or fretty gu

Sturges, a talbot sejant arg, collared az 55 1

Sturgis of Clipston Northants, a talbot's head or eared sa 56 12

Sturmer, Von, *see* Von Sturmer

Sturrock, out of a ducal coronet or two elephants' proboscides sa and issuing from each side to the dexter and sinister five flags per fess gu and or the staves sa

Sturt, *see* Alington, Baron

Sturt, Geoffrey Charles Napier, of Winterdyne Bewdley a demi lion gu holding a banner, also gu, charged with a rose arg the staff or *Major providentia fato* 251 2

Sturton, a demi friar ppr, vested in a russet gown, holding a lash or, the thongs embrued with blood 231 3

Sturton of Narbrowe Leics, a demi-friar vested in russet, girt or, holding in the dexter hand a whip of three lashes ppr laying the sinister on a church or the port arg

Stury, issuing out of a wreath a dexter arm in chain armour couped below the elbow holding in the gauntlet ppr the strings from the gauntlet nowed and pendent vert and or a broadsword arg, hilt and pommel or

Stutvile, a camel's head couped ppr 132 7

Stych, Chesh, and **Styche**, Shropsh, an eagle displayed arg collared az, holding in the beak a laurel-sprig vert

Stych, Bart (*extinct*), of Newbury Essex a demi-eagle displayed arg collared az, holding in the beak a sprig of laurel vert

Styche, same crest

Style, a wolf's head erased sa, fretted on the lower part of the neck and gorged with a collar or, charged with a mullet for difference c/ 30 9

Style of Ipswich Suff, and Essex of Hempstead, a wolf's head couped sa, collared or, the lower part of the neck from the collar fretty or

Style, Sir William Henry Marsham, Bart, M A, J P, D L of Glenmore, co Donegal, a wolf's head couped sa, collared or the lower part of the neck fretty of the last c/ 30 9

Styles of Kent and London, on a chapeau an eagle rising, all ppr 77 14

Styles of London, a lion's gamb erased in fess arg holding a fleur-de-lis sa

Styles of Westbourne Terrace, London in front of a dexter arm embowed ppr, grasping a stork's head erased and fesseways or, three annulets interlaced one and two, also or *Perge sed caute*

Stylman of Steeple Ashton, Wilts, a camel's head erased az, billettee, muzzled, collared lined and ringed or the collar charged with three hurts

Strysted of Kisgrave and Ipswich, Suff a palm tree 144 1

Sublet, a mortar-piece on its stand the mouth elevated ppr 169 10

Suckling, an escallop charged with a cross moline between two wings c/ 141 7

Suckling, Norf, a buck current or *Mora trahit periculum* c/ 118 13

Suckling, of Wootton Norf, a buck current or, holding in the mouth a branch of honeysuckle ppr

Suckling, Rev R A J, Barsham, Suff (1) Same crest (2) The battlements of a tower ppr charged with four ermine-spots, thereon a boar's head erased gu *Mora trahit periculum*

Suckling, Thomas, Esquire of Highwood near Romsey, Hants, same crests and motto

Sudell, a long cross or, lozenge pierced the top encompassed with a circle of laurel ppr

Sudell of Preston Lancs, and Yorks, a long cross or, the top encompassed with a circle of laurel ppr

Sudley, Viscount, *see* Arran Earl of

Sueting, a spur-rowel or, between two wings ppr

Suffield, Baron (Harbord), Gunton Park, Norwich, on a chapeau gu, turned up erm., a lion couchant arg *Æquanimiter* 7 12

Suffleld of Wells Norf on a mount vert a lion couchant gardant erminois 7 8

Suffolk and **Berkshire, Earl of** (Howard) Charlton Park, Malmesbury on a chapeau gu, turned up erm, a lion statant gardant the tail extended or, ducally gorged arg, and charged on the body with a crescent for difference *Nous maintiendrons —Non quo sed quo modo* c/ 4 4

Sugden, a dragon's head or, vomiting flames 72 3

Sugden, a lion's head erased or, ducally gorged az 18 5

Sugden, Kent, Sussex, and Shropsh, a leopard's head erased or, ducally gorged az c/ 23 10

Sugden of Bath, Somers (1) A leopard's head erased affrontee arg, billettee, and ducally crowned az (*for Sugden*) (2) Out of a crescent gu, a lion's head erased erm, holding in the mouth a dexter hand couped of the first (*for Long*)

Sugrue, Lieutenant Colonel James Marmaduke Fermoyle House, Cahirciveen, and 9, Sidney Place, Cork, on a ducal coronet a redbreast *Potientia victrix*

Sulivan, Rev Filmer, M A, Meadfoot Rock, Torquay, on a ducal coronet a robin holding in its beak an olive-branch *Lanih Foisdineach an nachter*

Sulliard of Haughley, Suff, and Essex a stag's head ppr, attired or 121 5

Sullivan, out of an antique crown gu, a demi lion rampant or c/ 10 2

Sullivan, Ireland, out of a ducal coronet gu, two arms in saltier ppr, vested az each holding a sabre of the second

Sullivan, Sir Edward, Bart., the Roman fasces fessewise ppr., banded gu., thereon a robin redbreast, also ppr. *Tot præmia vitæ.*

Sullivan, Admiral Sir Francis William, Bart., K.C.B., C.M.G., of Thames Ditton, Surrey, on a ducal coronet or, a robin holding in the beak a sprig of laurel ppr. *Lamh fois-dineach an nachter.* 308. 6

Sully, a goat passant arg. *cf.* 129. 5

Sully, two bull's horns gu. 123. 8

Sulyard, Bart., Suff., a stag's head cabossed ppr. 122. 5

Sulyard, a lion passant erm. 6. 2

Summaster of Haynsford, Devonsh., a portcullis arg., chained or. 178. 3

Summers, on a terrestrial globe winged ppr., an eagle rising or. 159. 9

Sumner, a crozier erect az. 170. 14

Sumner of Puttenham, Surrey, a lion's head erased arg., ducally gorged or. 18. 5

Sumner, Francis John, Park Hall, Hayfield, Derby, same crest.

Sumner, Surrey, a lion's head erased erm., ducally gorged or. 18. 5

Sumner, Holme-, of Hatchlands, Surrey: (1) A lion's head erased arg., ducally crowned or (*for Sumner*). 18. 8. (2) A hawk with wings elevated ppr. (*for Holme*). 87. 10

Sundridge, Baron, *see* Argyle, Duke of.

Sunger, on a ducal coronet or, two bear's paws to the dexter and sinister sa., ensigned with a plume of three ostrich-feathers, two gu., one arg.

Supple, a cubit arm erect armed ppr., holding in the hand an anchor az., flukes upwards.

Surdevile of Dublin, a dove holding in the beak an olive-branch, all ppr. *Le croix de hors mais pais dedans.* 92. 5

Surkas, Durh., out of a ducal coronet or, a plume of five ostrich-feathers arg. 114. 13

Surman of London, an eagle regardant, with wings expanded, holding a sword in pale ppr. 77. 10

Surman of Swindon Hall and Tredington, Glouc., a lion's head erased sa. *Yet in my flesh shall I see God.* 17. 8

Surrey, Earl of, *see* Norfolk, Duke of.

Surridge, a greyhound sejant gu. 59. 4

Surtees, Northumb., a lion passant. 6. 2

Surtees, out of a mural coronet gu., a wyvern's head or. 72. 11

Surtees, H. S. B., of Redworth House, Durh., out of a five-leaved ducal coronet or, three ostrich-feathers arg. *Malo mori quam fœdari.* *cf.* 114. 8

Surtees of Dinsale, Durh., and Northumb., out of a ducal coronet a plume of three feathers. *cf.* 114. 8

Surtees of Silkmore House, Castle Church, Staffs, three ostrich-feathers arg., interlaced by an orle or. *Malo mori quam fœdari.* *cf.* 115. 1

Surtes, out of a five-leaved coronet or, a plume of three feathers arg. *cf.* 114. 8

Sutcliff, a demi-man armed in antique mail or, holding in the dexter hand a spear in pale of the last, and over the shoulder a belt gu. *Foy en tout.*

Sutcliffe, William Pinches St. John, of the Hollies, Maghull, a demi-man in armour supporting in the dexter hand a lance erect. *Foy en toute.*

Sutcliffe, a dexter hand holding up a baptismal cup ppr. *I mean well.* 217. 11

Sutcliffe of Beech House, Lancs, a stag ppr., gorged with a collar gemel, holding in the mouth three ears of wheat slipped, and resting the dexter fore-foot on a garb fessewise or. *Tout en foy.*

Suter, out of a ducal coronet a hand grasping a swan's neck erased ppr. 220. 7

Sutherland, Duke of (Sutherland Leveson-Gower), Trentham Hall, Staffs: (1) A wolf passant arg., collared and chained or (*for Gower*). *cf.* 28. 10. (2) A goat's head erased erminois (*for Leveson*). 128. 5. (3) A catamountain ppr. (*for Sutherland*). *Frangas non flectas.*

Sutherland, Lord Duffus, a stag's head ppr., collared or. *cf.* 121. 5

Sutherland of Kinstearie, Nairnsh., Scotland, a cat salient ppr. *Still without fear.* *cf.* 26. 3

Sutherland, Scotland, a cat sejant ppr. *Without fear.* 25. 2

Sutherland, Robert Mackay, Esquire, of Solsgirth, Dollar, N.B., a cat salient ppr., charged on the shoulder with a lozenge gu. *Still without fear.*

Sutherland, Sir Thomas, G.C.M.G., Coldharbour Wood, East Liss, Hants, and 7, Buckingham Gate, London, a cat salient holding in the mouth a thistle leaved and slipped ppr., between two roses gu., leaved and stalked vert. *Sans peur.* 266. 12

Sutherland, Scotland, a cat sejant erect. *Sans peur.* 25. 2

Sutherland, George, of Forse, Caithnessh., a cat salient ppr. *Sans peur.* *cf.* 26. 3

Sutherland, Evan Charles, Skibo Castle, Sutherland, a cat sejant guardant gorged with a collar dancettée gu., and holding between the paws a mullet of six points, also gu. *Sans peur.*

Sutherland, a camel's head couped or. 132. 7

Suthill of Redburn, Lincs, a lion rampant vert, supporting a staff raguly or.

Sutter, Scotland, a fox's head ppr. 33. 4

Sutter, on a mount vert, a leopard sejant and ducally gorged, all ppr. *cf.* 24. 2

Sutthery, Arthur Melbourne, an eagle displayed or, each wing charged with a fleur-de-lis az., and resting either claw upon a leopard's face, also or. *Sursum.*

Suttie of Adinston, Scotland, the hull of a ship with one mast, tackling ppr. *Nothing hazard, nothing have.*

Suttie, Bart., a ship under sail, flagged and rigged ppr. *Mihi lucra pericula.* 160. 13

Suttie, Grant-, Sir George, Bart., of Balgone, Haddingtonsh., a ship under sail, all ppr. *Nothing hazard, nothing have.* 160. 13

Suttie, Scotland, a hive of bees ppr. *Sponte favos ægre spicula.* 137. 7

Suttie of Inveresk, Scotland, a hive of bees ppr. 137. 7

Sutton, *see* Canterbury, Viscount.

Sutton, *see* Manners, Baron.

Sutton, Baron Dudley, on a ducal coronet or, a lion sejant gardant az.

Sutton, Baron Lexington (*extinct*), a wolf's head erased ppr. 30. 8

Sutton of Scawby Hall, Lincs, a wolf's head erased gu. *Toute jours prest.* 30. 8

Sutton, Francis, Esquire, of 18, Curzon Street, Mayfair, same crest and motto.

Sutton, Bart., of Norwood Park, Notts, same crest. *Toujours prest.* 30. 8

Sutton, Martin John, Esquire, J.P., of Henley Park, Sutton, a squirrel sejant ppr., resting the fore-paws on an escutcheon arg., charged with a wolf's head erased ppr., a canton sa., charged with a fleur-de-lis of the field. *Toujours prest pour y parvenir.*

Sutton of Ediall, Staffs, a demi-lion rampant vert. 10. 2

Sutton of London and Staffs, a demi-lion rampant double-queued vert. 10. 6

Sutton of Sutton and Prestbury, Chesh. and Lincs, out of a ducal coronet or, a demi-lion double-queued vert. *cf.* 10. 6

Sutton, on a ducal coronet or, a lion rampant az. *cf.* 1. 13

Sutton, a lion's head erased per pale arg. and vert, collared gu. 18. 6

Sutton of Longraige, of Bally Keeroge, and Old Court, Ireland, co. Wexford, out of a ducal coronet or, a lion's head az., langued gu. 17. 5

Sutton, a lion's gamb erect and erased az., charged with three bezants, holding a demi-slip of leaves arg.

Sutton, a lion's gamb erased, holding a branch arg., leaved vert. *cf.* 37. 4

Sutton of Burton and Washingborough, Lincs, and Derbysh., a greyhound's head couped erm., gorged with a collar gu., garnished and ringed or, and charged with three annulets of the same. *cf.* 61. 2

Sutton, Henry, Esquire, of Lexham Gardens, South Kensington, W., three annulets interlaced, one and two arg., between two wings sa., each charged with a cross flory, also sa.

Sutton, Ireland, an elephant's head erased arg. 133. 3

Sutton of Rossway, Herts, a griffin's head erased. *Prend moi tel que je suis.* 66. 2

Sutton, Rev. Archdeacon Robert, Pevensey Vicarage, Hastings, same crest and motto.

Sutton, Middx., a crescent arg., charged with an anchor, and between the horns of the crescent a griffin's head erased collared, and holding in the beak an eagle's leg erased at the thigh.

Sutton of Elton House, near Durham, on a mount vert, a stork ppr., charged on the breast with a cross patée gu., the dexter claw supporting a rose of the last, surmounted of another arg. *Fidelis usque ad mortem.—Live to live.*

Sutton, a harpy gardant ppr. 189. 1

Sutton of London, a demi-Cupid holding in his dexter hand a hymeneal torch, all ppr. *Tuto, celeriter, et jucunde.* 185. 8

Sutton of Over Haddon, Derbysh., three annulets conjoined in a triangle, two and one or. 167. 11

Swabey, Maurice John, of Langley Marish, Bucks, a swan regardant arg., beaked and membered sa., with wings elevated, also sa., murally crowned gu., resting the dexter foot on an escallop or. 99. 7

Swaby, Rt Rev William Proctor, D D, Bishop of Barbados Bishop's Court, Barbados, on a mount vert, a swan regardant, wings addorsed sa, guttee-d'eau, on the head a crown vallary gu, and supporting with the dexter foot a crozier erect or *Perseverantia* 286 13

Swail, a greyhound current erminois, collared az cf 58 2

Swain and Swaine, a fetterlock az 168 12

Swainson, a stag's head couped arg, charged with a mullet of eight points, holding in the mouth two ears of barley or *Pro ecclesia Dei*

Swainson, Shropsh (1) A stag's head couped holding in his mouth an ear of barley or (2) On a ducal coronet an estoile of sixteen points ppr

Swainson or Swaynson, on a ducal coronet or, an etoile of sixteen points ppr

Swainston-Strangways (1) A lion passant paly of six or and gu (*for Strangways*) 6 2 (2) Out of a ducal coronet or, a boar's head sa, between two wings az, billettee or (*for Swainston*) *Isoveau et ne doubtero*

Swainston-Strangwayes, John, Esquire J P, Alne Hall, Easingwold, Yorks, same crests and motto

Swale, Bart (*extinct*), of Swale, Yorks, a greyhound current erm, collared az *Jesu esto mihi Jesus* cf 58 2

Swale, Yorks, on a mount vert, a greyhound current erm, collared az cf 58 2

Swallman, Kent, a swan's neck between two wings or, ducally gorged gu cf 101 5

Swallow, a stag standing in front of a tree ppr 116 12

Swallow, issuing from a whale's mouth the mast, rigging, etc, of a ship

Swan, Captain Joseph Percival, of Baldwinstown Castle, co Wexford, Ireland, a swan ppr, crowned or, charged with a trefoil vert *Sit nomen decus*

Swan, Percival Symes, Esquire, of Baldwinstown, Bridgetown, co Wexford, and Garville Avenue, Rathgar, same crest and motto

Swan, Kent, a demi talbot salient gu, collared or 55 11

Swan of Kilrish, co Dublin, a demi talbot gu, gorged with a plain collar or *Spero meliora* 55 11

Swan of Edinburgh, a demi-talbot arg *Fidelitas* cf 55 8

Swan, Rev Percival Fiennes, Bransby Rectory, Yorks, *uses* a demi-talbot salient gu, collared or 55 11

Swan, Robert Clayton, Gallowhill, Morpeth, Northumb, amidst bulrushes ppr, a demi water-spaniel arg, gorged with a collar az, and holding between the paws a fountain

Swan, Scotland, a cockatrice's head erased ppr, ducally gorged or 68 13

Swan, a cockatrice's head erased ppr, ducally gorged, ringed, and lined arg cf 68 13

Swan, Scotland, a hand holding a spear in bend, all ppr 214 11

Swanley, Middx, a unicorn's head erased. 49 5

Swann, out of a ducal coronet gu, a swan's head arg, between two wings or 100 10

Swann, a demi-talbot salient gu, collared or 55 11

Swans, a sword erect ppr, between two cross crosslets fitched sa

Swansea, Baron (Vivian), Singleton Swansea (1) A lion's head erased ppr, charged with two bezants palewise and gorged with a collar gu, thereon three annulets or with a chain of the last 287 11 (2) Issuant from a bridge of one arch embattled, and having at each end a tower ppr a demi hussar (18th Regiment) holding in right hand a sabre, and in left a red pennon flying to the sinister *Vive anima Dei* 287 10

Swanson, two branches of laurel in saltier ppr

Swanston, Scotland a wolf's head issuing *Gesta verbis prævenient* 30 5

Swanzy, Rev Henry Biddall, M A Ivy Lodge, Newry co Down, a unicorn's head or collared with a bar gemel gu *Per Deum et ferrum obtinui*

Swanzy, Rev Robert Archibald, St John's Vicarage New Clee, Lincs, same crest and motto

Swanzy, Rev Thomas Erskine M A, Hibaldstow Vicarage Brigg same crest and motto

Swayne of Gunvile Dorset a ram's head erased sa 130 6

Swayne of Blandford, Dorset a demi-griffin erm, armed or 64 2

Swayne of London, a demi dragon supporting an arrow arg, armed or

Swayne, John Montague Esquire J P, of the Island, Wilton, Salisbury, same crest

Swayne, Somers and London, a maiden's head couped ppr, crined or, between two wings, expanded of the last

Swedenborg, a demi-lion rampant double queued gu, holding a key

Sweet, on the top of a tower issuing ppr, an eagle with wings addorsed or, holding in the beak an oak-branch vert 76 10

Sweet, Devonsh, between two gillyflowers ppr, a mullet or, pierced az 164 13

Sweetaple of London, out of a mural coronet a plain cross gu

Sweeting of Canterbury, Kent, a goat's head erased arg attired or 128 5

Sweeting, Alfred Charles Esquire J P, B A, of Paxton Hall, St Neots Hunts, an arm embowed to the sinister holding a rose all ppr

Sweetingham, Chesh, a porcupine's head erased az, guttee d'or the quills or collared and lined, also or cf 136 2

Sweetland of Exmouth, Devonsh a cubit arm in armour couped ppr, garnished or, holding in the gauntlet two stalks of wheat bladed and eared and a vine-branch fructed also ppr

Sweetland, the same crest differenced by a rose arg, barbed and seeded ppr

Sweetman, a griffin sejant 62 10

Sweetman-Powell, John Michael, Esquire, Lamberton Park Queen's Co (1) A lion rampant arg, charged with a cross crosslet gu, and holding between the paws a garb vert (*for Powell*) (2) Out of an antique coronet or, a griffin's head gu charged with a mullet of the first (*for Sweetman*) under the arms, *Vi et virtute*, and over the second crest, *Spera in Deo*

Sweetman, Edmund Casimir, Longtown, Clane, co Kildare out of an antique crown or, a griffin's head gu, charged with a mullet or *Spero in Deo*

Sweetman of Tyrrellstown, Ireland an heraldic tiger's head couped per pale or and gu maned of the first 25 4

Sweetnam, Ireland an eagle with wings expanded ppr, standing on a plume of ostrich-feathers or

Sweetnam, an eagle with wings expanded ppr, holding up a banner gu, tasselled or cf 78 14

Swellington, a friar's head in profile ppr, couped at the shoulders vested gray

Swertchoff, out of a coronet a plume of ostrich feathers cf 114 8

Swete of Trayne, Devonsh, a mullet or pierced az, between two gillyflowers ppr 164 13

Swete, Edward Horatio Walker, M D, Lower Wyke Lodge, Worcs, same crest

Swete, Frederick George Buller, J P, the Quarry, Oswestry, Shropsh, same crest.

Swete, Horace Lawton, J P, Castle Hill Fishguard R S O South Wales, same crest

Swetenham, of Somerford Booths Chesh a porcupine's head erased az, guttee-d'eau, armed and collared or *Ex sudore vultus* cf 136 2

Swetenham, Clement William, same crest and motto

Swettenham, *see* Warren Swettenham

Swift, Viscount Carlingford (*extinct*) a sinister arm embowed vested vert cuffed arg holding in the hand a sheaf of five arrows or, feathered ppr, barbed az

Swift of Rotherham, Yorks, a sinister arm embowed vested vert, cuffed arg, holding in the hand a sheaf of five arrows or, feathered ppr, barbed az

Swift, a dexter arm embowed, holding in the hand three arrows, one in fess and two in saltier

Swift, a dexter hand gauntleted throwing a dart, all ppr

Swift, Yorks, a cubit arm vested arg, charged with two bendlets az, holding in the hand a laurel wreath vert encircling a martlet or cf 205 6

Swift of London a pegasus at full speed vert, with wings addorsed or

Swift of Blandford, Dorset a demi lion rampant or holding between the paws a helmet of the same

Swift, Ireland, on a chapeau a flame of fire ppr 180 10

Swift, Heref and Yorks, a demi-buck rampant holding in the mouth a honeysuckle ppr, stalked and leaved vert

Swift of Swiftsheath, co Kilkenny, and Lionsden, co Meath, and Lynn, Ireland, same crest *Festina lente*

Swifte, Godwin Butler Meade, J P D L Swiftsheath co Kilkenny, a sinister arm embowed vested az, cuffed arg, in the hand a sheaf of five arrows or barbed az, flighted arg *Festina lente virtute et sanguine*

Swinborne of Hewthwayt, Cumb a boar's head couped and erect arg cf 43 3

Swinburn of Chopwell, Durh., out of a ducal coronet or, a demi-boar arg., crined and armed of the first. *cf.* 40. 13

Swinburne, Sir John, Bart., J.P. of Capheaton, Northumb., out of a ducal coronet or, a demi-boar rampant arg., crined of the first, langued gu. *Semel et semper.* *cf.* 40. 13

Swinburne, Captain Thomas Anthony, R.N., United Service Club, London, S.W., same crest and motto.

Swinburne-Hanham, John Castleman, Esquire, J.P., Barrister-at-Law, 106, Goldhurst Terrace, Hampstead, N.W., same crest and motto.

Swindley, a sword erect ppr., and pendent from the hilt by a chain or an escutcheon vert, charged with a boar's head erased, also or.

Swindley, Major-General John Edward, 60, Pall Mall, S.W., same crest. *A cuspide honos.*

Swiney, John Harris Hazlett, J.P., Moyagh, Carrowcannon, Moyagh, Ransetton, a boar passant ppr.

Swiney, a fox's head ppr. 33. 4

Swinfen of Swinfen Hall, Staffs, a boar's head erased or. 42. 2

Swinford, a weaver's shuttle threaded ppr. 176. 14

Swinhoe of Calcutta, a boar's head erased and erect or. 43. 3

Swinnee or **Swiney,** Ireland, a talbot passant arg., spotted sa. 54. 1

Swinnerton, *see* Pilkington.

Swinnerton of London, and of Butterton Hall, Staffs: (1) On a mount vert, a boar passant sa. 40. 5. (2) A boar's head erased sa., collared arg. *Avaunces et archez bien.* *cf.* 41. 5

Swinny, Kent, a boar passant ppr. 40. 9

Swinton, Scotland, an ear of wheat issuing. *Dum sedulo prospero.* 154. 3

Swinton or **Swynton,** a dove between two branches of laurel in orle. 92. 12

Swinton of Swinton, Berwicksh., a boar chained to a tree ppr. *J'espère.* 232. 1

Swinton, George, Esquire, of 36, Pont Street, S.W., same crest and motto.

Swinton, John Edulf Blagrave, of Swinton Bank, Peebles, same crest. *Je pense.*

Swinton, Campbell-, John Liulf, of Kimmerghame, Berwick, a boar chained to an oak-tree fructed, all ppr. *J'espère.* 232. 1

Swinton-Hunter, Robert Hepburne, 60, Via due Macelli, Rome, same crest and motto.

Swiny of Ballyteige and Clohamon, Wexford, a demi-griffin segreant arg., winged and armed gu. *Buail tre cabhair a buaig.* 64. 2

Swire of Dowgill Hall and Littlethorpe, Yorks, a swan's head and neck couped arg., ducally gorged or. *Esse quam videri.* *cf.* 101. 5

Swithinbank, Harold William, Esquire, J.P., late Lieutenant in H.M. 11th Hussars, and Captain Reserve of Officers, of Denham Court, Denham, Bucks, out of the battlements of a tower arg., a demi-dragon issuant ppr., holding between the claws a grenade sa., fired, also ppr., and pendent from the neck by a ribbon gu. a bugle-horn of the third, garnished or, and stringed of the fourth. *Frana vel aurea nolo.* 73. 12

Swithinbank, Rev. Herbert Spenser, Kingston Vale Vicarage, Putney, S.W., same crest. *Fama semper viret.*

Sword or **Swourd,** a sword in pale ppr., between two wings or. *Paratus.* 112. 4

Sword of Longacre, Lanarksh., Scotland, bewteen two wings expanded or, a sword erect arg., hilted and pommelled or. *Paratus.* 112. 4

Sword of Longacre, Lanarksh., a sword erect arg., hilted and pommelled or. *Paratus.* 170. 2

Sworder, a demi-lion rampant gu., holding in the dexter paw a sword arg., hilt and pommel or. 14. 12

Swourd, a sword in pale ppr., hilted or, between two wings of the same. 112. 4

Swymmer, a demi-lion rampant gu., holding between the paws a bell or.

Swynerton of London, out of a ducal coronet or, a goat's head arg. 128. 14

Swynerton, on a chapeau a dove with wings addorsed, all ppr. 94. 10

Swynfen of Sutton Cheney, Leics., a boar's head erased az. 42. 2

Swynnerton of London, out of a ducal coronet or, a goat's head arg. 128. 14

Swytham, Swyngham, or **Switham,** Herts, out of a ducal coronet or, a demi-dragon gu. *cf.* 73. 10

Sybells, five halberds in pale arg., corded together of the first and gu. 172. 13

Sybsey, Westbarssam, Norf., a griffin's head erased gu. 66. 2

Sybthorp, St. Alban's, Herts, and Ladham, Norf., a demi-lion rampant and erased arg., collared sa., holding in the dexter paw a fleur-de-lis of the last.

Sybyle, out of a ducal coronet or, a swan's head between two wings. 100. 10

Sydenham of Winford-Eagle, Dorset, Aller and Orchard, Combe, Sidenham, and Whitstow, Somers., a ram's head erased sa., armed arg. *Sit Deus in studiis.* 130. 6

Sydenham, Bart. (*extinct*), of Brympton, Somers., same crest. 130. 6

Sydenham of Dulverton, Somers., a pegasus arg., charged on the shoulder with a cross avellant vert.

Sydney, Earl, *see* Townshend, Marquess.

Sydney of the Bourne, Berks, a pheon az. *Quo fata vocant.* 174. 11

Sydney of Richmond, Surrey, and Tamworth, Warw., a porcupine az., quilled or. 136. 5

Sydney, a porcupine az., quilled or, gorged with a collar and chain reflexed over the back of the last. *cf.* 136. 5

Sydney, Ireland, out of a ducal coronet a goat's head, all or. 128. 14

Sydserf, Buchan-, Thomas, of Ruchlaw, an eagle's head couped gu. *Virtute promoveo.* 83. 1

Sydserf of Collegehead, an eagle's head couped az. *Semper virtute vivo.* 83. 1

Sydserf of Antigua, the sun in his splendour ppr. *Parta labore quies.* 162. 2

Sydserfe, Scotland, a cornucopia ppr. *Industria ditat.* 152. 13

Syer, a cock az., holding in the beak a cinquefoil slipped or. *cf.* 91. 2

Syer of Ravensden, Beds, on a staff raguly fesseways or, a pelican in her piety sa., semée of mullets of the first, the nest ppr. *Virtus in actione consistit.*

Sykes, an ox passant, charged on the shoulder with an heraldic fountain ppr.

Sykes, a swan with wings addorsed arg., ducally gorged or. *cf.* 99. 3

Sykes, Frank, of Brookfield, Chesh., upon the trunk of a tree eradicated fessewise and sprouting to the dexter a swan, wings elevated arg., beaked and legged sa., charged on the breast with a fountain ppr. *Puritas fons honoris.*

Sykes, Arthur Henry, J.P., D.L., Lydham Manor, Bishop's Castle, Shropsh., same crest and motto.

Sykes, Frederick William, J.P., Green Lea, Lindley, Huddersfield, a demi-man in profile holding in the dexter hand a fountain and resting the sinister hand on a whelk-shell sa. 274. 12

Sykes, James Nield, Green Lea, Lindley, Huddersfield, same crest, charged on the breast with a fleur-de-lis az., and same motto.

Sykes, Major-General Henry Peters, 45, Hamilton Road, Ealing, W., a bull passant ppr., charged on the shoulder with a fountain. *Quod facis, valeo facio.—Ferox inimicis.*

Sykes, late John, 23, South Parade, Doncaster, in front of a bull's head erased sa., a fountain ppr. *Fontes sint limpidi.*

Sykes, a swan amongst flags.

Sykes, Sir Henry, Bart., of Basildon, Berks, a demi-lady of Bengal in the complete dress of that country, holding in her dexter hand a rose slipped gu., and in her sinister a rosary ppr. *Sapiens qui assiduus.* 311. 6

Sykes, Sir Tatton, Bart., of Sledmere, Yorks, a demi-Triton issuant from flags or reeds blowing a shell and wreathed about the temples with like flags or reeds, all ppr. 186. 8

Sykes, Matthew Carrington, of Sykeshurst, Barnsley, Yorks, issuing from among reeds a demi-Triton in profile, wreathed about the temples also with reeds, and blowing a conch shell, all ppr. *Aut vincere aut mori.* 186. 8

Sylver, co. Cork, a unicorn's head erased gu., charged with a chevron or. *cf.* 49. 5

Sylvester or **Silvester,** a crow with wings expanded transfixed by an arrow ppr. 107. 4

Sym, Scotland, a hand holding a pen ppr. *Fortuna et labore.* 217. 10

Sym, Scotland, a spur-rowel or. 164. 8

Symcoats, Lincs and London, a pheon sa., within a chaplet vert, flowered or. 174. 6

Symcock, Notts, Stoke, Worcs., and Staffs, a beaver passant erm. *cf.* 134. 8

Symcott or **Symcock** of Burleigh, Somers., a beaver passant erm. *cf.* 134. 8

Symcotts of Isleworth, Middx., out of a ducal coronet or, a spear-head arg., encircled with a garland of flowers and roses of the last gu. and vert.

Syme, an eagle's head. *In recto decus.* 83. 1

Syme, Scotland, a demi lion rampant holding between the paws a battle axe *Ferio, tego* cf 15 4

Syme of Culloch Dumfriessh, Scotland, a hand holding a pen ppr *Fortuna et labore* 217 10

Symeon, out of a vallary coronet an arm, holding in the hand an oak branch acorned and leaved, all ppr

Symes or **Symmes** of Chard and Pounsford, Somers, and Devonsh, a demi-hind erased or

Symes, Edward Spence, Esquire, C I E, Rangoon, same crest *Prævalebit veritas*

Symes of Daventry, Northants, a head and face ppr in a helmet or plumed az, the beaver raised cf 191 10

Symes of Ballyarthur and Ballybeg co Wicklow, a head and face ppr in a helmet or, plumed az, the beaver raised *Droit et loyal* cf 191 10

Syminges, a lion sejant gardant supporting an escutcheon or cf 8 2

Symington of that ilk Lanarksh, Scotland, a cross moline lozenge pierced or 165 1

Symmer, Scotland, a stag lodged or, attired gu *Tandem tranquillus* 115 7

Symonds, *see* Loder Symonds

Symonds of Pengethly a dolphin naiant, holding in the mouth a fish arg

Symonds or **Symondes,** Heref, same crest

Symonds, Heref, a dolphin arg 140 5

Symonds, Charles Price, Esquire, J P, of the Hall, Ormskirk, a dolphin naiant arg vorant a fish *Rectus in curvo*

Symonds, J F of Loder Symonds and Oklengle, Heref a dolphin naiant vorant a fish

Symonds, Loder-, Captain Frederick Cleave, Hinton Manor Farringdon Berks a dolphin naiant, holding in the mouth a fish arg

Symonds, Colehy Suffield, Great Ormsby, Norf (1) A demi-swan with wings expanded arg, holding in the beak a trefoil slipped az (2) A dolphin naiant devouring a fish, both ppr (*for the Ormsby branch*) *Rectus in curvo — Dum spiro, spero*

Symonds, a goose arg

Symonds, out of a mural coronet chequy arg and az, a boar's head of the first, crined sa 41 8

Symonds, Shropsh, out of a mural coronet or, a boar's head arg tusked or 41 8

Symonds, Essex, out of a mural coronet chequy arg and az a boar's head of the first, crined sa *Moriendo vive* 41 8

Symonds of London on a mount vert an ermine ppr, holding in the mouth a cinquefoil gu, slipped of the first

Symonds of Exeter, Devonsh, Lyme Regis, Dorset, and Taunton Somers on a mount vert, an ermine ppr, holding in the mouth a cinquefoil or

Symonds of Woodsford Castle, and Pilsdon, Dorset, and Dowlish Wake, Somers (1) On a chapeau gu, turned up erm, a Moor's arm embowed ppr, tied at the elbow with ribbons arg and az, holding in the hand a fire ball ppr (2) On a mount vert, an ermine passant ppr, holding in the mouth a cinquefoil of the first. *Simplex munditiis*

Symonds, on a mount vert a wolf statant, holding in the mouth a rose slipped, leaved, and stalked, all ppr *Simplex munditiis*

Symonds or **Symmonds** of Exeter, Devonsh., a cubit arm erect ppr, holding in the hand a pole axe arg, the handle sa 213 12

Symonds, Glouc, an arm embowed sa, tied at the elbow with ribbons arg and az, holding in the hand a fire ball ppr

Symonds of White Lady Aston, a vine with grapes ppr 152 9

Symonds-Tayler, Richard Herbert Tayler, Penn Grove, Hereford (1) The battlements of a tower, and issuant therefrom a demi lion rampant sa, collared, and charged on the shoulder with a lozenge within an annulet all arg, and holding in his dexter paw an arrow point downwards, ppr (*for Tayler*) (2) In front of a well sa, a dolphin naiant embowed, devouring a fish (*for Symonds*) *Miseris succurrere disco*

Symons, Thomas Raymond of Mynde Park Heref on a mount vert an erm per pale erm and erminois, in the mouth a trefoil slipped, ppr *Nil admirari*

Symons, Soltau-, George William Culme, Chaddlewood, Plympton, Devonsh on a mount vert, in front of a saltire gu, an ermine holding in the mouth a fern-branch ppr *Simplex munditiis* cf 134 10

Symons, Cambs, an otter passant *Fide liter* cf 134 5

Symons of Whitleford Cambs on a mural coronet gu three arrows or, feathered arg, two in saltier and one in pale, tied in the middle with a ribbon az flotant. cf 173 1

Symons-Jeune, John Frederick, Watlington Park, Tetsworth, Oxon, between the attires of a stag affixed to the scalp an estoile, all arg *Faire sans dire*

Sympson of Winkton, Hants, an ounce's head arg, erased gu, ducally crowned or

Sympson of Polton, Beds, on a mural coronet arg, a demi-lion rampant gardant per pale wavy or and sa, holding in the dexter paw a sword erect of the first, hilted of the second

Sympson, Edward Mansel, M A M D, Esquire, of Deloraine Court Lincoln a lion rampant or, guttee de poix holding between his front paws a maunch sa, and with the foremost back paw resting on a serpent nowed vert *Lætus sorte mea* 273 9

Sympson, Kent, a lion's head erased per fesse erm, and gu, ducally crowned or 18 8

Syms, a demi leopard ppr

Syms, a demi leopard, collared, ringed and lined 23 13

Symson of Piddinghall Garth Durh out of a mural coronet az, a demi lion regardant per pale or and sa holding in the dexter paw a sword ppr pommel or cf 16 5

Synge of Glenmore Castle Ireland out of a ducal coronet or, an eagle's claw ppr *Cœlestia canimus* 113 13

Synge of Rathmore, King's Co, Ireland, out of a ducal coronet or, an eagle's talon ppr. *Cœlestia canimus* 113 13

Synge, Sir Francis Robert Millington Bart, of Lislee Court co Cork, out of a ducal coronet or, an eagle's claw ppr *Cœlestia canimus* 113 13

Synge-Hutchinson, Sir Edward Bart, of Castle Sallah, co Wicklow (1) A cockatrice issuing out of a ducal coronet, all ppr (*for Hutchinson*) (2) An eagle's talon issuing from a ducal coronet, all ppr (*for Synge*) *Non sibi sed toti — Cœlestia canimus* 113 13

Synnot, Ireland a swan sejant sa ducally gorged or, pierced in the breast by an arrow or *Ama Deum et serva mandata*

Synnot of Cadiz Spain, a swan issuant sa, ducally gorged or, and pierced in the breast with an arrow ppr *Ama Deum et serva mandata*

Synnott of Drumcondragh co Meath Ireland a swan issuant with wings expanded sa, ducally crowned or vulned in the breast with an arrow of the last feathered arg *Sin not*

Synnott of Ballymoyer co Armagh Ireland, same crest *Sine macula*

Sypher, a griffin's head ppr 66 1

Syseley, a buck's head erased gu, guttee-d'or collared and attired of the same holding in the mouth a branch of fir vert

Sysington, a dexter arm ppr, holding in the hand a covered cup az 217 11

Syward, a sand-glass gu winged az 113 11

Szlumper, Sir James Weeks 17, Victoria Street, Westminster an arm in armour embowed holding a battle-axe, all ppr *Semper paratus*

T.

Taaffe, Viscount (Taaffe), Castle of Ellischau, Bohemia, a dexter arm in armour embowed brandishing a scimitar ppr., hilt and pommel or. *In hoc signo spes mea.* 196. 10

Taaffe of Ballybraggan, co. Louth, an arm in armour embowed, holding in the hand a sword, all ppr., pommel and hilt or. *In hoc signo spes mea.* 195. 2

Taaffe of Ballyneglough, co. Sligo, Grayfield and Brooklawn, co. Mayo, and Smarmore, co. Louth, Ireland, same crest and motto. 195. 2

Taap or **Tapp,** on the point of a sword erect ppr., a mullet or. 169. 3

Taber, Essex, a griffin's head erased ppr. 66. 2

Tabers of Heard's Hill, Essex, a lion's head erased pierced by a dart.

Tabor, a hand holding a sealed letter ppr.

Tabor, James, Esquire, J.P., of the Lawn, Rochford, Essex, a griffin's head erased ppr.

Tabor, a pomeis, thereon a griffin's head erased or, charged with a trefoil slipped vert.

Tabuteau of Tullamore, King's Co., an ermine spot sa. *Toujours sans tache.*

Tabuteau, Lionel Richard Plunket, 48, Park Avenue, Sandymount, Dublin, same crest and motto.

Tackle, two halberds addorsed or, environed by a snake vert. 172. 6

Tacon, Sir Thomas Henry, Red House, Eye, in front of a dexter arm embowed in armour, couped at the shoulder and fessewise or, gauntletted sa., holding a flagstaff ppr., therefrom flowing to the sinister a banner arg. charged with a lyre, also sa., three escallops fessewise or. *Aut vincam aut peribo.*

Tacon, Rev. Richard John, M.A., J.P., the Rectory, Rollesby, same crest and motto.

Tacon, Charles, Eye, Suff., same crest and motto.

Tadcaster, Baron, *see* Thomond, Marquess of.

Taddy, a fleur-de-lis arg. 148. 2

Taddy, issuing from a cloud ppr., the morning-star or. 164. 11

Tadwell or **Tedwell,** Middx., on a piece of battlement arg., an arm in armour embowed ppr., garnished or, holding in the hand a javelin, also ppr.

Tahourdin, 50, Cranley Gardens, London, S.W., a demi-lion rampant.

Tagg, on a mount vert, an ermine collared. 134. 10

Tailbois or **Tailboys,** Durh., a bull's head couped arg. *cf.* 44. 3

Tailboys of Kettleby, Lincs, a bull passant arg. *cf.* 45. 2

Tailby, William Ward, of Skeffington Hall, Leics., on a mount vert, a bull passant erm., gorged with a wreath of laurel ppr., the sinister foot resting on an escallop or. 229. 11

Taileler, Scotland, the trunk of an oak-tree sprouting ppr. *Viresco.* 145. 2

Taller, a demi-lion rampant sa., holding between its paws a ducal coronet or. *Deus est nostrum refugium.* *cf.* 14. 5

Tailour, Canada, a dexter arm issuing ppr., holding in the hand a cross patée fitched in pale az. *Per ardua.* *cf.* 221. 12

Tailyour, *see* Renny-Tailyour.

Tailyour, Bart. (*extinct*), of Lyssons Hall, Jamaica, a dexter hand issuing out of a ducal coronet ppr., holding a cross crosslet fitchée gu. *In hoc signo vinces.* *cf.* 221. 14

Tailyour of Borrowfield, Forfarsh., Scotland, a dexter hand ppr., holding a passion cross gu. *In cruce salus.*

Tait, Middx. a horse's head couped ppr. *cf.* 50. 13

Tait, Colonel John Sprot, Hartford, Chesh., a horse's head arg. *Pro Rege et patria.*

Tait, Scotland, a horse's head couped sa. *Ægre de tramile.* *cf.* 50. 13

Tait, Scotland the rising sun. *God give grace.*

Tait, the stump of a tree couped and eradicated in fess vert, between the branches a fleur-de-lis or. 145. 13

Tait of South Hill, Limerick, upon a wreath of the colours and out of a civic crown an arm in armour embowed, the hand grasping a red rose slipped and leaved, all ppr. *God give grace.*

Tait of Liverpool, Lancs, an arm embowed vested quarterly or and sa., holding in the hand ppr. a bunch of flowers gu., leaved vert. *Toujours la même.*

Tait of Harviestown, a dexter hand grasping a dagger ppr. *Virtute.—Pro Rege et patria.* 212. 3

Talbot, *see* Shrewsbury, Earl of.

Talbot of Malahide, Baron (Talbot), Malahide Castle, co. Dublin: The original crest of this family, as recorded at the Visitation of Dublin in the year 1610, was a 'talbot-dog passant arg., langued gu.' (54. 1), which is now used by Lord Talbot of Malahide as his second crest. But for a first the same crest as that of the Earls of Shrewsbury and Talbot is used, viz., 'on a chapeau gu., turned up erm., a lion statant or, the tail extended' (4. 8), though in the case of Lord Talbot of Malahide this, according to recent exemplifications, should be 'upon a chapeau gu., turned up erm., a lion passant erminois.' 4. 9. *Forte et fidele.*

Talbot, Lieutenant-Colonel Sir Adelbert Cecil, K.C.I.E., the Cottage, Glenhurst, Esher, Surrey: (1) Upon a chapeau gu., turned up erm., a lion statant, tail extended or (*for Talbot*). (2) A goat's head erased arg. (*for Chetwynd*).

Talbot, Lord Edmund Bernard, 1, Buckingham Palace Gardens, S.W., on a chapeau gu., turned up erm., a lion statant, the tail extended or. *Prest d'accomplir.* 4. 8

Talbot, Viscount Lisle (*extinct*), on a chapeau gu., turned up erm., a lion statant, the tail extended or. *Prest d'accomplir.* 4. 8

Talbot, Charles Henry, of Lacock Abbey, Wilts, on a chapeau gu., turned up erm., a lion statant, the tail extended or. 4. 8

Talbot, George, same crest. *Prest d'accomplir.*

Talbot-Ponsonby, Charles William, Esquire: (1) On a ducal coronet or, three arrows, points downwards, one in pale and two in saltire, shafts or, feathered and pointed arg., entwined by a serpent ppr. (*for Ponsonby*). 173. 2. (2) On a cap of maintenance gu., turned up erm., a lion statant, tail extended or, and over this crest the motto, *Prest d'accomplir* (*for Talbot*). *Pro Rege, lege, grege.* 4. 8

Talbot, Bart., Ireland, on a chapeau ppr., a lion statant, the tail extended or. *Humani nihil alienum.* 4. 8

Talbot, Rt. Hon. John Gilbert, of Falconhurst, Edenbridge, Kent, same crest and motto.

Talbot, William John, Mount Talbot, co. Roscommon: (1) On a chapeau az., turned up erm., a lion passant gu. (*for Talbot*). 4. 9. (2) Three swords, one in pale, point upwards, and two in saltier, points downwards, entwined by a serpent, all ppr. (*for Crosbie*). *Prêt d'accomplir.*

Talbot-Crosbie, Lindsay, J.P., Ardfert Abbey, co. Kerry, same crest as (2) above. *Indignante invidia florebit justus.*

Talbot of Salesbury, Yorks, a talbot passant sa. 54. 1

Talbot of Upper Lyne, Devonsh., a talbot arg., collared gu. 54. 2

Talbot, Edward Lister Kaye, J.P., Ballinclea House, Killiney, co. Dublin, a talbot-dog arg., langued gu. *Forte et fidele.*

Talbot of Broadmayne, Dorset, a talbot passant collared and chained. *cf.* 54. 5

Talbot of Bashall, Yorks, a talbot passant sa. *Touts jours fidèle.* 4. 15

Talbot, Shropsh., a roundle per pale sa. and gu., charged with a talbot passant arg.

Talbot, Devonsh. and Suff., a demi-ostrich arg., the wings expanded gu., and ducally gorged of the last.

Talbot of Gonville Hall, Wymondham, Norf., a demi-ostrich arg., with wings expanded or, ducally gorged gu.

Talcott, a demi-griffin segreant sa., gorged with a collar arg., thereon three pellets. *cf.* 64. 2

Talcott of Colchester, Essex, a demi-griffin erased arg., gorged with a collar sa., charged with three roses of the first. *cf.* 64. 2

Tallant, a hind's head couped ppr. 124. 1

Tallantire, two arms in armour embowed ppr., supporting a bezant. *cf.* 194. 11

Tallerton of London a boar's head couped in fess 43 1

Tallis, Ireland, a dove arg, holding in its beak an ear of wheat ppr *cf* 92 1

Tallis, Ireland a dove arg, holding in the beak an olive branch ppr 92 5

Tallon, Rt Hon Daniel, 136, Leinster Road, Rathmines, Dublin a dexter arm embowed vested barry or and az, cuffed of the last, the hand ppr grasping an eagle's leg erased at the thigh ppr *Deo gloria*

Tame, Essex, a wolf's head erased gu ducally gorged or *cf* 30 8

Tame, a plume of feathers 115 1

Tame, a cock regardant ppr 91 9

Tamworth, Viscount, *see* Ferrers, Earl

Tamworth of London, and Leake, Lincs, a cock gu, combed, wattled, and legged or 91 2

Tanered, Sir Thomas Selby Bart, C E, of Boroughbridge, Yorks, an olive-tree fructed ppr

Tanered, George, Weens House Hawick, N B an olive tree fructed ppr, charged for distinction on the trunk with a cross crosslet or

Tandy, on a ducal coronet a martlet sa 95 12

Tane, a plough ppr *Labor et industria* 178 7

Taney or **Tany,** Essex a demi-eagle with two heads gu, ducally gorged or *cf* 82 3

Tanfield and **Tansfield,** Essex, a maiden's head ppr 182 3

Tanfield, Essex Northamp, and Yorks, a woman's head couped at the shoulders ppr, crined or wreathed about the head with roses arg and sa 182 5

Tankard, Yorks, an olive-tree vert, fructed or environed with a ducal coronet of the last

Tankard, Yorks, an olive-tree vert 144 14

Tankarde, a holly tree erased vert *cf* 145 6

Tankarde, five holly branches vert flowered gu *cf* 145 6

Tanke, out of a ducal coronet or two wings az 109 8

Tankerville, Earl of (Bennet), Chillingham Castle, Belford Northumb (1) Out of a mural coronet or a lion's head gu, charged on the neck with a bezant (*for Bennet*) *cf* 19 12 (2) A double scaling-ladder or (*for Grey*) *De bon vouloir servir le Roy* 158 12

Tanner of Salisbury, Wilts King's Nympton Park, Devonsh, Sherborne and Wimborne, Dorset, and Cornw, a Moor's head in profile couped at the neck sa, banded about the temples arg and gu *cf* 192 13

Tanner, Rev John Vowler Chawleigh Rectory, North Devonsh, same crest and motto

Tanner, Major General, C B of Woodside Old Shirley, Hants, same crest

Tanner, Farncombe-, William Tanner, Esquire of East Lenham Kent a Moor's head in profile couped at the shoulders ppr, wreathed about the temples arg and gu, between two trefoils slipped vert 264 12

Tanner of Ashted, Surrey a demi-antelope rampant regardant erm

Tanner of Brannell, Cornw, a demi-talbot or eared arg *cf* 55 8

Tanner, Somers, a talbot's head erased 56 2

Tanner, on a dexter gauntlet a falcon close belled 86 13

Tanqueray of Tingrave Beds, out of a mount vert in front of two battle axes in saltire a pine-apple ppr

Tanqueray, John Samuel, Penybyn Hall, Llangollen, North Wales same crest

Tansley, Scotland a hand holding a branch of laurel, all ppr *Virtutis laus actio.* 219 9

Tany, a greyhound's head erased az, ducally gorged or *cf* 61 4

Tany, a demi eagle with two heads gu ducally gorged or *cf* 82 3

Taplen, a boar's head erased ppr 42 2

Tapp, on the point of a sword erect ppr, a mullet or 169 3

Tapp, Dorset, a greyhound couchant sa, lined and collared or *cf* 60 1

Tapper, a lion's head erased regardant *cf* 17 6

Tapper, a hand erect issuing out of a cloud holding a garb in bend, all ppr 218 3

Tapper, Robert, Esquire, of Wadham House Invercargill, and of Clifden Southland, New Zealand *uses* a hand erect issuing from a cloud holding a garb in bend *Perseveranti dabitur* 218 3

Tappin, a lion rampant or 1 13

Tapps, *see* Meyrick

Tapps, Hants, a griffin passant 63 2

Tapps, Hants, a greyhound couchant per pale arg and sa charged on the body with two escallops in fess counter-changed 60 3

Tarbat, Viscount, *see* Cromartie, Earl of

Tarbock, Suff, a parrot vert, beaked and legged gu 101 4

Tarbock of Tarbock, Lancs, an eagle close vert beaked and membered gu 76 2

Tarell, issuing out of a cloud a hand in pale holding an arrow, point downwards 214 1

Tarleton, between two ostrich feathers arg a leopard's face ppr 22 4

Tarleton, Bart (*extinct*), of Churchill, Lancs on a mural coronet gu a leopard's face ppr between two ostrich-feathers arg *Post nubila Phœbus* 231 21

Tarleton, Alfred Henry, Breakspears Uxbridge, Middx on a mural crown gu a leopard's face ppr, between two ostrich-feathers arg *Post nubila Phœbus* 231 21

Tarley, a boar's head couped in fess sa armed arg 43 1

Tarlton, Hon Robert Alfred J P of Olivedean Glenelg, Fernbrook Stirling East and of Cavendish Chambers Grenfell Street Adelaide, South Australia, a lion rampant collared and chained *Deus, patria, Rex* 1 3

Tarpey, Hugh, Esquire, of Dublin out of a mural crown gu, a demi-eagle displayed or, holding in the beak a civic crown ppr *Firm as a rock*

Tarpley, Northamp, a dove with wings displayed holding in the beak an olive-branch, all ppr 94 5

Tarrant of London a demi eagle displayed gu 81 6

Tarratt, William Stewart, Ellary Argyllsh an eagle displayed arg wings vair holding in the beak an ostrich feather, also arg *Per ardua stabilis*

Tarte of James Street, Westminster an eagle with wings expanded arg, charged on the breast with a crescent, and therefrom an estoile issuant az, standing on a snake ppr

Tasell, Suff a hawk's head erased az, holding in the beak a pine branch vert, fructed gu 88 14

Tash of London, a demi greyhound or collared gu, holding between the feet an escallop of the last *cf* 60 4

Tasker, a boar's head arg, couped gu 43 1

Tassie, out of a tower ppr, a demi-griffin segreant or 157 5

Taswell, a demi-lion rampant arg 10 2

Taswell, a demi lion purp, holding between the paws a chaplet of eight roses gu

Tatam, within a fetterlock or, a heart gu

Tatchell-Bullen, *see* Bullen

Tate, on the point of a sword erect ppr a maunch erm 169 11

Tate, Notts an arm embowed couped at the shoulder vested per pale gu and or holding in the hand ppr a pine branch or

Tate of De la Pre Abbey, Northants and Sutton Bonnington, Notts, an arm embowed and couped at the shoulder vested per pale gu and or holding in the hand ppr a pine branch of the second *Thincke and thancke*

Tate, Sir William Henry Bart, Highfield Woolton Liverpool a dexter arm embowed vested az cuff arg the arm charged with two roses arg the hand holding a pine apple erect slipped and two ears of wheat saltirewise all ppr *Thincke and thancke* 273 11

Tate, Ireland a lion passant az, charged on the shoulder with a fleur de-lis or *cf* 6 2

Tate, E W, Esquire, Brookhurst, Bromborough, Chesh, a dexter arm embowed and vested az, cuffed or, charged with two roses arg, the hand grasping a pineapple erect ppr between two ears of wheat of the second 305 15

Tatenhall, Chesh a buck's head ppr 121 5

Tatham, out of a ducal coronet or, a plume of ostrich feathers ppr *cf* 114 8

Tatham of London on a trumpet or a swan with wings displayed sa *cf* 100 6

Tatham, Stanley, Esquire J P, a dexter arm embowed in armour ppr, garnished or, in hand three arrows, all ppr

Tatler, a demi-eagle displayed with two heads ppr holding in each beak a cross crosslet fitched or *cf* 82 4

Tatlock of London and of Ewell, Surrey a demi lion rampant or 10 2

Tatlock, out of a mural coronet az, an arm embowed holding in the hand a sword wavy ppr

Tatnall and **Tattall,** a cutlas in pale arg, hilt and pommel or, a ribbon tied round the gripe gu *cf* 170 2

Tattersall, a dove holding in its beak an olive-branch ppr. *Good news.* 92. 5

Tatton, a sword and a garb in saltier ppr. 153. 7

Tatton, Thomas Egerton, Esquire, of Wythenshawe, Northenden, Chesh., a greyhound sejant ppr., collared gu., and tied to an oak-tree ppr. *Crescent.* 59. 5

Tatum, an eagle displayed crowned with an antique coronet. *cf.* 75. 2

Tatum, a dexter arm in armour embowed ppr., garnished or, holding in the hand three arrows, all ppr. 198. 3

Taunton, Baron (*extinct*—Rt. Hon. the late Henry Labouchere), a stork arg., holding in its beak a lotus-flower ppr.

Taunton, out of a ducal coronet a dexter arm, holding in the hand a slip of a rose-tree ppr. 218. 11

Taunton of Somerton, Somers., Hilfield, Dorset, Liskeard and Truro, Cornw., and Freeland, Oxon., a Cornish chough ppr. 107. 14

Taunton, William Garnett, Esquire, of New Club, Jersey, five lozenges conjoined fessewise or, thereon a Cornish chough ppr. *Nova sed vera.* 106. 13

Taunton, Rev. Frederick, Kingswood Vicarage, Epsom, Surrey, same crest and motto.

Taunton, George Edwin, same crest and motto.

Taunton, Frank Pyle, Esquire, of Newbold Firs, Leamington, in front of a tree a greyhound sejant, collared and lined, the line tied to the tree, and at its fore-feet a snail passant. 304. 6

Taverner, out of a ducal coronet gu., an oak-tree fructed ppr. *cf.* 143. 13

Taverner, Essex, Kent, and of Hoxton, Herts, a dove with wings expanded arg., beaked and legged gu., holding in the beak a branch of laurel vert. 94. 5

Tavistock, Marquess of, *see* Bedford, Duke of.

Tawke, a dexter hand holding a lion's gamb ppr. 220. 10

Tawse, Scotland, a lion's head erased sa. *Deo juvante.* 17. 8

Tay, on the point of a sword a garland of laurel ppr. 170. 1

Tay, two pruning-hooks in saltier az. 178. 10

Tayler or **Taylor** of London, a demi-otter rampant or. 134. 1

Tayler, a leopard passant arg., spotted sa., charged with a pheon or. *cf.* 24. 2

Tayler of London, a unicorn's head erased arg., armed and maned or, collared sa., thereon three annulets of the second. *cf.* 49. 11

Tayler of London, a greyhound's head quarterly arg. and sa., collared, counter-changed. 61. 2

Tayler, of Grafton, Oxon., a lion's head erased arg., ducally gorged or. 18. 5

Tayleur, John, of Buntingsdale, Shropsh., out of a ducal coronet or, a dexter arm in armour embowed, holding in the hand a sword, the point embrued ppr. 195. 12

Tayleur, Charles William, Sandwell, Totnes, same crest.

Taylor, issuing out of a ducal coronet or, a dexter arm in armour embowed, holding in the gauntlet a sword embrued at the point ppr. *Floreat Salopia.* 195. 12

Taylor, a dexter arm, the hand ppr. holding a broken sword arg., hilt and pommel or.

Taylor, Edward Richard, of Dublin, and Ardgillan Castle, Dublin, a naked arm embowed, holding in the hand an arrow ppr. *Consequitur quodcunque petit.* 201. 14

Taylor, George Noble, Esquire, J.P., 3, Clarendon Place, Hyde Park Gardens, London, W., same crest and motto.

Taylor, General Sir Richard Chambre Hayes, K.C.B., 16, Eaton Place, S.W., same crest.

Taylor of Kirktonhill, Scotland, out of a marquess's coronet or, a dexter hand ppr., holding a cross crosslet fitched gu. *In hoc signo vinces.* *cf.* 221. 14

Taylor, a dexter arm in armour, holding in the hand a spear, all ppr. 210. 11

Taylor, a hand issuing ppr., holding a cross crosslet fitched az. *Victoriæ signum.* 221. 14

Taylor, Scotland, a hand ppr., holding a cross crosslet fitched sa. *Semper fidelis.* 221. 14

Taylor, Scotland, an arm from the elbow in armour, holding in the hand a dagger, both ppr. *Semper fidelis.*

Taylor of Pennington House, Hants, a dexter arm in armour embowed, the hand in a gauntlet grasping a javelin, all ppr., and pendant from the wrist by a ribbon az., and resting on a wreath of the colours, an escutcheon gu., thereon a boar's head couped and erect arg. *Consequitur quodcunque petit.*

Taylor, out of a ducal coronet or, a cubit arm erect ppr., holding in the hand a cross crosslet in pale gu. *In hoc signo vinces.*

Taylor, James Benjamin, Sherfield Manor, Basingstoke, upon the capital of an Ionic column an arm embowed ppr., encircled about the elbow with an annulet or, the hand grasping a sword in bend sinister, also ppr., pommel and hilt or. *Semper fidelis.* 273. 13

Taylor, Watson-, of Erlestoke, Wilts: (1) Out of a ducal coronet of five leaves or, a cubit arm erect ppr., charged with a heart gu., holding in the hand a cross crosslet fitched of the last (*for Taylor*). (2) The trunk of a tree erased at the top with a branch sprouting from each side (*for Watson*). *In hoc signo vinces.* —*Jus floreat.* 145. 2

Taylor, Ireland, a dexter arm in armour embowed, the hand in a gauntlet grasping a sword ppr., the arm encircled above the elbow by an annulet az., and charged with two bombs fired, also ppr. *Fide non timet.* *cf.* 195. 1

Taylor, a dexter arm from the shoulder embowed grasping a sword at the point, all ppr. *Non arte sed marte.*

Taylor of Manchester, issuing out of a ducal coronet or, a dexter hand erect ppr., holding a cross crosslet fitchée in pale gu.

Taylor of Fort St. George, East Indies, a dexter arm issuing from a heart and grasping a scimitar, all ppr. 213. 4

Taylor of West Ogwell and Beaconsfield, near Plymouth, Devonsh., a leopard passant ppr. *cf.* 24. 2

Taylor, Clough-, Lieutenant-Colonel Edward Harrison, Firby Hall, Kirkham Abbey, a leopard passant per pale ppr., and erm., the dexter paw resting on a shield of the arms.

Taylor, Philip Meadows, Esquire, C.S.I., of Old Court, Harold's Cross, co. Dublin, Ireland, a leopard passant ppr., charged on the shoulder with a trefoil slipped vert. *Incorrupta fides.* *cf.* 24. 2

Taylor of Eaton, Beds, a leopard passant ppr., resting the dexter paw on an escutcheon of the arms, viz., arg., on a pale sa., three lions passant of the field. 24. 5

Taylor, Wright-, R., Esquire, of Lincoln's Inn, W.C., and Baysgarth Park, Barton-on-Humber, Lincs, a leopard passant ppr., resting its dexter paw on an escutcheon of the arms, viz., arg., on a pale sa., three lioncels passant of the field. *Fortitudine victor.* 24. 5

Taylor of Portsmouth, Hants, an ounce sejant or, collared az., supporting with the dexter paw an escutcheon sa., charged with two étoiles in chief arg., and in base an escallop or.

Taylor of London, a tiger's head erased sa., ducally gorged or.

Taylor of Athboy, co. Meath, Ireland, a lion passant per pale gu. and az. 6. 2

Taylor of Mythe House, Tewkesbury, Glouc., and London, a lion passant gu. 6. 2

Taylor of Beaconfield, Denbury, and Ogwell, Devonsh., a lion passant sa. 6. 2

Taylor of Tunbridge Wells, a lion rampant gardant ppr., charged with a sun in splendour or, supporting with the sinister fore-paw an escutcheon az., charged with an escallop arg. *Magna vis veritatis.*

Taylor, Arthur James, of Strensham Court, Worcs., a demi-lion rampant ppr., semée of escallops sa., holding between the paws a saltire, also sa., surmounted by an escallop arg. *Fidelisque ad mortem.*

Taylor of Moreton Hall, Yorks, a demi-lion sa., semée of mallets or, holding between the paws an acorn of the last, slipped vert. *Annoso robore quercus.* 233. 15

Taylor of Todmorden Hall, Lancs, and Culverlands, Berks, a demi-lion rampant az., charged on the shoulder with a bezant, holding between the paws an escutcheon or, charged with a tau gu. *Natale solum dulce.*

Taylor, Rev. Arnold Dawes, Church Stanton Rectory, Devonsh., same crest and motto.

Taylor, Charles Howard, Middlewood Hall, near Barnsley, in front of a dexter arm embowed in armour, the hand in a gauntlet grasping a flaming sword, all ppr., a shield erm. charged with a wolf's head couped sa. *Pro Deo, patria et Rege.*

Taylor, William Francis Kyffin, Esquire, K.C., 4, Harcourt Buildings, Temple, Recorder of Bolton, a lion rampant per fesse raguly sa. and arg., holding between the fore paws a pheon and resting the dexter hind leg on three fusils conjoined or *Cenfigen a ladd ei hunan*

Taylor, Bart , of Hollycombe Sussex, a demi-lion erminois, charged on the body with two escallops and holding between the paws another escallop sa cf 13 10

Taylor, a demi lion rampant sa holding between the paws a ducal coronet or cf 14 5

Taylor of London and Lancs, a demi-lion rampant erm , holding between the paws an escallop or 13 10

Taylor of Bifrons, Kent a lion's head erased arg , gorged with a collar gu , charged with three roses of the first *Fama candida rosa dulciore* cf 18 6

Taylor of London, a lion's head erased erm , gorged with a collar gu , charged with three roses arg cf 18 6

Taylor, Herbert Wilbraham Esquire, J P , a lion's head erased per pale arg and gu , gorged with a collar charged with three estoiles counterchanged *Fama candida rosa dulcior*

Taylor of London, a demi-talbot holding in the mouth a buck's attire

Taylor, Seth, Esquire, of Granard, Roehampton, Surrey a demi greyhound gu , holding between the paws an escallop arg , and charged upon the shoulder with two escallops fesseways or *Servabo fidem* cf 60 4

Taylor or **Taylour** of London Sussex, and Worcester Park, Surrey a demi greyhound az , collared and ringed or, holding in the dexter paw an annulet of the last

Taylor of Glenleigh, near Hastings, a greyhound sejant or, gorged with a collar gemel, and resting the dexter foot on three annulets interlaced one and two *Invictus in arduis* 235 16

Taylor of St James's, Westminster, Middx , a greyhound's head quarterly arg and sa gorged with a collar or, charged with a ducal coronet gu cf 61 2

Taylor of Brooms Staffs a greyhound's head couped arg , gorged with a collar sa , within a strap in arch az the buckle resting on the wreath on the sinister side or

Taylor of Radcliffe on Trent, Notts, an oak-tree 143 5

Taylor-Gordon (1) A spreading oak tree ppr (*for Gordon*) 143 5 (2) A stork ppr , holding an anchor az (*for Taylor*) *I byde —Dum spiro spero* 105 10

Taylor, Derbysh , a stork resting the dexter claw on an anchor all ppr 105 10

Taylor, a cock with wings displayed standing on a fish ppr

Taylor, Shropsh , a dove with wings expanded arg , holding in its beak a branch of olive ppr *Non me deserens sed respertans* 94 5

Taylor of Bishopwearmouth Durh on the top of a tower a stag at gaze gorged with a ducal coronet thence a chain reflexed over the back and fastened by a ring to the battlements cf 118 9

Taylor of Padgbury near Congleton, Chesh , a buck's head cabossed ppr 122 5

Taylor, Domville-, of Lymme Hall, Chester, a buck's head cabossed ppr 122 5

Taylor of Marridge Devonsh , of Stretchworth and Lidgate Cambs, a unicorn's head erased or, ducally gorged and armed az cf 49 5

Taylor of Turnham, Kent, a martin statant or *Qui plane sane vadit*

Taylor-Smith (1) A stag lodged arg semée of estoiles az , gorged with an Eastern crown, a chain therefrom reflexed over the back or (2) A horse's head couped sa , gorged with a plain collar, and pendent therefrom a shield arg charged with a cinquefoil vert *Vigilans*

Taylor-Whitehead of Burton Closes Bakewell, on a wreath of the colours in front of a tau gu a pheon arg *Cruce non hasta* 174 5

Taylor of Ballyphilip co Cork Ireland an Irish rebel's head ppr

Taylor, Captain Wilbraham Coxwell Lodge Faringdon, Berks, a lion's head erased arg , gorged with a collar gu , charged with three roses of the first *Fama candida rosa dulcior*

Taylour, *see* Headfort, Marquess of

Taylour of Middleton Cheney, Northamp and Lancs, a lion's head erased sa ducally gorged or 18 5

Taylour of Westminster, Middx , a leopard's head erminois 22 10

Taylour of Bradley, Hants Cambs, and Haleston Grange, Glouc , a leopard passant ppr cf 24 2

Taylour, Kent, a martin passant or *Stat gratia facti*

Taylour of Parkhouse Kent same crest.

Taylour of Steventon, Beds and Devonsh , a buck's head cabossed ppr , pierced through by two arrows in saltier gu , headed and feathered arg

Taylour, Ireland, a naked arm holding in the hand a bird-bolt ppr

Taylour of London and Shropsh a cubit arm erect vested vair, holding in the hand ppr three roses gu , stalked and leaved vert

Taylour of Carrigfergus, co Antrim, a star ppr between two wings expanded az *Stella futura micat divino lumine* cf 111 5

Tayloure, a talbot's head erased arg eared sa 56 2

Tayte, an arm embowed vested quarterly or and sa , holding in the hand ppr a branch of flowers gu , leaved vert

Teale of London, a spaniel sejant ppr 57 9

Teale of London, a spaniel sejant ppr , resting the dexter foot on an antique shield arg , charged with a teale also ppr

Teale, Thomas Pridgin Esquire, F R C S , of Leeds, Yorks, a greyhound sejant arg , guttee de poix the dexter forepaw resting on an escutcheon gu charged with a fleur de lis or *Fide liter*

Tedwell, out of a demi tower ruined in the sinister an arm embowed vested, holding in the hand a spear in bend

Tee or **Tye,** a tiger's head erased arg

Teesdale, out of a ducal coronet a dexter arm in armour embowed, charged below the elbow with an estoile, the hand in a gauntlet holding an arrow fessewise point to the dexter, all ppr *Animæ capaces mortis*

Teesdale, Charles Lennox Moore Esquire, J P St Rumbold's, Worthing same crest and motto

Teevan of Woodside, Croydon, Surrey, a cherub ppr issuing out of a demi-sun or *Patriæ et religione fidelis*

Tegart, a fire-beacon ppr 177 14

Teignmouth, Baron (Shore) of Teignmouth Ireland, a stork regardant arg beaked and membered and holding in its dexter claw a stone sa *Perimus licitis*

Teissier, De, *see* De Teissier

Teller, out of a ducal coronet or a tree vert 145 9

Teller - Smollett, James Drummond Cameron House, Alexandria, Dumbartonsh , a trunk of oak sprouting *Viresco*

Tellau, out of a ducal coronet a griffin's head 67 9

Temmes, a goat's head erased guttee 128 5

Tempest, *see* Londonderry, Marquess of

Tempest, Plumbe-, of Tong Hall, Yorks, and Aughton, Lincs (1) A griffin's head erased per pale arg and sa , beaked or (*for Tempest*) 66 2 (2) A greyhound sejant arg , spotted gu , collared or (*for Plumbe*) *Loyowf as thow finds* cf 59 2

Tempest, Sir Tristram T , Bart of Tong Hall, Bradford, Yorks and Dalguise, Dunkeld, N B (1) A griffin's head erased per pale arg and sa , beaked or, langued gu 306 3 (2) A demi lion rampant 306 4 *Loywf as thow fynds —Hinc orior*

Tempest, Henry Tempest Dufton, Esquire B A , F S A , of Bridge House, Brockford, near Stowmarket, Suff , a griffin's head erased, party per pale arg and sa *Loywf as thow fynds* 66 2

Tempest, Bart , of Boughton Hall, Yorks, a griffin's head erased per pale arg and sa beaked and crined gu , charged with an annulet or *Loyowf as thow fynds* cf 66 2

Tempest of Bracewell, a griffin's head erased arg 66 2

Tempest of Staveley, issuing from a ducal coronet or a griffin's head per pale erm and arg 67 9

Tempest of Derby, a griffin's head erased per pale arg and erm , collared or cf 66 2

Tempest, Major Arthur Cecil of Broughton in Craven, Heaton Lancs Coleby Hall Lincs a griffin's head erased per pale arg and sa , crined and beaked gu , charged with an annulet or cf 66 2

Tempest, Wilfrid Francis, Esquire, J P , Ackworth Grange, York same crest

Tempest, Sir Robert Tempest, Bart , of Tong Hall, Bradford, Yorks (*ancient*) a griffin's head erased arg , with a crescent for difference cf 66 2; (*modern*), a griffin's head erased per pale arg and sa , beaked or, langued gu 66 2

Tempest of Studley, Yorks, a griffin's head erased sa 66 5

Tempest, Sir Charles Henry, Bart , J P , D L of Heaton in the county palatine

of Lancaster, a griffin's head erased per pale arg. and sa., beaked gu. *Loywf as thow fynds.* 66. 2
Tempest of Hertford and Studley (1352), a man's head couped at the neck.
Tempest of Studley (1440), a pilgrim's (?) head in a hood and hat, couped at the shoulders.
Tempest, on a chapeau a martlet. 95. 1
Tempest, Bart., of Stella, Durh., a martlet sa., beaked gu. 95. 5
Templar or **Templer,** a crane's head issuing ppr.
Temple, *see* Buckingham, Duke of.
Temple, *see* Dufferin and Ava, Marquess of.
Temple, *see* Palmerston, Viscount.
Temple, Baron Nugent, *see* Nugent.
Temple, Earl (Temple [Gore-Langton]), Newton Park, near Bath: (1) An eagle or and a wyvern vert, their necks entwined and regardant (*for Langton*). 310. 2. (2) A heraldic tiger salient arg., collared gu. (*for Gore*). *In hoc signo vinces.*
Temple, Sir Grenville Louis John, Bart., of Stowe, Bucks, on a ducal coronet or, a martlet gold. *Templa quam dilecta.* 95. 12
Temple, Sir Richard Carnac, Bart., C.I.E., of the Nash, in the parish of Kempsey, Worcs., on a ducal coronet a martlet or. *Templa quam dilecta.* 95. 12
Temple, Arthur (Ernest) Harris, of Waterstown, co. Westmeath, Ireland, on a ducal coronet a martlet or, charged with a crescent for difference. 241. 7
Temple, on a ducal coronet a martlet, all or. 95. 12
Temple of Revilrig, Scotland, a pillar wreathed about with woodbine ppr. *Te stante virebo.* 176. 4
Temple, Bucks, Leics., Warw., and Kent, and Bishopstrowe, Wilts, a talbot sejant sa., collared and ringed or. 55. 1
Temple, Grenville Newton, Esquire, of Bishopstrow House, near Warminster, same crest.
Temple of Whitney, Oxon., a talbot sejant sa., collared and ringed or, charged on the shoulder for difference with a mullet arg. *cf.* 55. 1
Temple, Bart. (*extinct*), of Sheen, Surrey, a talbot sejant sa., collared and lined or. *Flecti non frangi.* 55. 5
Temple, Cowper-, Hon. William Francis, of Broadlands, Hants: (1) A talbot sejant sa., collared or, and charged for distinction with a cross crosslet of the same (*for Temple*). *cf.* 55. 1. (2) A lion's gamb erect and erased or, holding a branch vert, fructed gu. (*for Cowper*). *Flecti non frangi.* *cf.* 37. 4
Temple of Burton Dassett, Warw., on a mount vert, a talbot sejant sa. *cf.* 55. 2
Temple, A. W., Esquire, Warburton House, Bridport, Dorset, on a ducal coronet a martlet, all or. *Templa quam dilecta.*
Templeman, Dorset, on a chapeau a phœnix in flames ppr. 82. 11
Templeman of Dorchester, Dorset, and Hants, a cubit arm erect vested az., cuffed gu., holding in the hand ppr. a rose of the second, stalked and leaved vert.
Templeman, same crest. *Quæ habet manus tenebit.*
Templemore, Baron (Chichester), of Templemore, co. Donegal, Ireland, a stork with a snake in its bill ppr. *Invitum sequitur honor.*
Templer of Stover Lodge, Devonsh., on a mount vert, a holy lamb arg., holding in the dexter foot a pennon of the second, charged with the cross of St. George, the streamers wavy az. and gu., the staff or, under an oak-tree ppr., fructed gold. *Nihil sine labore.*
Templer, John George Edmund, Lindridge, Devonsh., same crest.
Templer, Devonsh., a beehive with bees diversely volant. 137. 7
Templeton, a holy lamb regardant arg., supporting a banner gu.
Templeton, Scotland, a tree ppr. 143. 5
Templetown, Viscount (Upton), Castle Upton, Templepatrick, co. Antrim, on a ducal coronet or, a war-horse passant regardant sa., bridled, saddled, sans stirrups, and accoutred of the first. *Virtutis avorum præmium.* 240. 10
Tench, Derbysh. and London, a stag statant. 117. 5
Tench of Ballyhaly House, co. Wexford, Ireland, a lion rampant sa., supporting a battle-axe or. *Tenchebrai.*
Tench, Bart. (*extinct*), of Low Leyton, Essex, an arm couped at the elbow erect vested gu., cuffed arg., holding in the hand a tench ppr.
Tenche of London, an arm vested gu., turned up arg., holding in the hand a tench, all ppr.
Tendering or **Tendring** of Tendering, Essex, a ship under sail ppr. 160. 13
Tenison, *see* King-Tenison.
Tenison, *see* Kingston, Earl of.
Tenison of Kilronan Castle, Ireland, a leopard's face jesant-de-lis. 22. 5
Tenison, Ireland, a mitre charged with a chevron. *cf.* 180. 5
Tenison of Hetherset, Norf., a dove ppr. 92. 2
Tenison, Charles MacCarthy, Hobart, Tasmania: (1) A dove ppr., holding in its beak a rose gu. (2) A demi-griffin segreant or, armed and langued gu., charged on the shoulder and wing with two trefoils slipped in fesse vert. *Favente Deo sedulitate.*
Tennant, on a chapeau ppr., a unicorn's head erased or. 49. 10
Tennant, John Robert, of Chapel House, Yorks, between two wings gu., each charged with a bezant, a sword erect ppr., point downwards, pommel and hilt or, transpiercing a human heart gu. *Tenax et fidelis.* 110. 8
Tennant, Charles Coombe, Cadoxton Lodge, Neath, Glamorgansh., a winged heart gu. pierced with a dagger ppr., hilted or.
Tennant, Staffs, a lion passant gardant gu., the dexter fore-paw resting on an escutcheon erm., thereon two bars sa., charged with bezants.
Tennant of Little Aston Hall, Shenstone, Staffs, and the Eades, Upton-on-Severne, Worcs., a lion passant gardant gu., the dexter fore-paw resting on an escutcheon erm., thereon two bars sa., the upper charged with two bezants and the lower with one.
Tennant, Major Charles Richard, St Anne's Manor, Sutton, Loughborough, a lion passant guardant gu., the dexter fore-paw resting on an escutcheon erm., thereon two bars sa., the first charged with two and the other with one bezant.
Tennant, Sir Charles, Bart., J.P., D.L., of the Glen, in the parish of Traquair, Peeblessh., and of St. Rollox, in the city of Glasgow, a mast with a sail hoisted ppr. *Deus dabit vela.* 160. 11
Tennant, of Pool, Lanarksh., a boat-sail ppr. *Pro utilitate.* 160. 9
Tennant, Hon. Sir David, of Cape Town, Cape of Good Hope, Member of the Legislative Assembly, a mast with a sail hoisted ppr. *Deus dabit vela.* 160. 11
Tennant, Scotland, a sail ppr. *Dabit Deus vela.* 160. 9
Tennant of Lennes, Scotland, same crest. *Plena dabit Deus vela.* 160. 9
Tennant, Major Claude Cambridge, Belvidere, Weymouth, Dorset, a demi-lion rampant ppr., holding between the paws an escallop or. *Tenax et fidelis.*
Tennent, *see* Emerson-Tennent.
Tennyson, Baron (Tennyson), of Aldworth, Haslemere, a dexter arm in armour embowed, the hand gauntleted or, grasping a broken tilting-spear enfiled with a garland of laurel ppr. *Respiciens prospiciens.* *cf.* 197. 3
Tennyson-D'Eyncourt, Edwin Clayton, of 56, Warwick Square, S.W.: (1) A lion passant gardant arg., on the head a coronet of fleurs-de-lis or, the dexter fore-paw supporting an escutcheon az., charged with a fess dancettée between ten billets, four and six or (*for D'Eyncourt*). (2) A dexter arm in armour, the hand gauntleted or, holding a broken tilting-spear enfiled with a garland of laurel ppr. (*for Tennyson*). *En avant.—Nil temere.*
Tenterden, Baron (Abbott), of Hendon, Middx., a fox passant per pale or and arg., charged on the shoulder with a water-bouget sa. *Labore.* *cf.* 32. 1
Tenyson, a dexter arm in armour embowed holding in the hand a tilting-spear in bend sinister, enfiled with a garland.
Terell, a sword and a key in saltier ppr. 171. 10
Ternan, Lieutenant-Colonel Henry Breffney, Ashley Cottage, Hersham Road, Walton-on-Thames, a dragon passant ppr., resting the dexter fore-claw upon a fleur-de-lis gu. *Bradhach.* *cf.* 73. 2
Terne of London, a demi-sea-horse ppr., finned or, holding in the paws an anchor of the same.
Terrell, a leopard's face gu. 22. 2
Terrey of London, a dragon's head erased vert, vomiting flames ppr., collared erm., ringed and lined or. *cf.* 72. 5
Terrick, a lion salient or.
Terry, on a rock a swan ppr.
Terry, a demi-lion ppr., holding a fleur-de-lis gu. 13. 2
Terry, Sir Joseph, of Hawthorn Villa, the Mount, York, a demi-lion rampant ppr., gorged with a wreath of roses arg., holding in the dexter paw a fleur-de-lis or, and supporting with the sinister a fasces in bend, also ppr. *Quod tibi hoc alteri.*

Terry, Major-General Astley Fellowes, 123, St George's Road, S W, a lion's head erased arg, guttee-de larmes, between two oak-branches fructed in arch ppr *Perseveranti dabitur* 275 14

Terry, Rev William Arthur, Ladywood House, Jackfield, Salop, same crest and motto

Terry or **Tyrry** of Baghyoghis, co Cork Ireland, a demi-lion rampant gu holding between the paws an escutcheon or

Terry of Cork and Spain, a demi-lion rampant gu, holding between the paws an escutcheon with the representation of a human face thereon *Ex cruce leone*

Tervise, on a mount a stag rising from under a bush ppr

Tery, Ireland, a boar's head erased and erect 43 3

Teschemaker, late William Henry Esquire, J P, of Taipo Hill and Kauro Hill Otago, New Zealand *uses* issuing out of a ducal coronet two wings displayed and between them a mullet *Ohne furcht*

Tetley of Lynn, Norf, a boar's head and neck issuant sa. 41 1

Tetley, Rev James George, Canon's Lodge, 5, Apsley Road, Clifton, Bristol, an escallop or, in front of two cross crosslets fitchee in saltire, the dexter gu, the sinister az *Triumpho cruce.* 266 11

Tetlow, Lancs, on a book erect gu, clasped or, a silver penny, on the top of the book a dove ppr, holding in the beak a crow-quill pen sa *Præmium virtutis honor* 93 5

Tetlow, William Atcherley, Esquire, of 3, Crosshall Street Liverpool a demi-lion rampant holding in the dexter paw a sprig of laurel *Vos Lauri carpam*

Teulon, a cross patee gu, within an orle of seven stars ppr 164 9

Tew, between two wings a spur rowel az

Tew, Edward Grosvenor, Carleton Grange, Pontefract, same crest *Je tue*

Tew, Percy Esquire, M A, D L, J P, Heath Hall, Wakefield, same crest and motto

Tewydall of Staines, Middx, an eagle's head couped sa, holding in the beak an ear of wheat or

Teynham, Baron (Roper-Curzon), of Teynham, Kent (1) A popinjay rising or, collared gu (*for Curzon*) (2) A lion rampant sa, upholding in the dexter paw a ducal coronet or (*for Roper*) *Spes mea in Deo*

Teys of Layer de-la-Hay, Essex, out of a ducal coronet or a heraldic tiger's head arg, maned az 25 3

Thacker, out of clouds a dexter and a sinister arm in armour embowed holding up the sun ppr

Thacker, Ireland, a pelican's head erased vert 98 2

Thackeray, the shaft of a broken tilting-spear in pale surmounted by the two broken pieces in saltire, the whole enfiled by a ducal coronet

Thackeray, Essex, an eagle with wings elevated, charged on the breast with a cherub's head ppr, holding in the beak an arrow in pale sa, barbed and feathered arg *Nobilitas sola virtus* 78 8

Thackeray, Rev Arthur Thomas James, M A, Norton Vicarage, Loddon, Norf, same crest and motto

Thackeray, Charles, Chapel Earl's Colne, Essex, same crest and motto

Thackeray, Sir Edward Talbot, K C B, V C, same crest and motto

Thackeray, Rev Francis St. John Mapledurham Vicarage, Reading, same crest and motto

Thackeray, Frederick Rennell, J P, Yarrow House Dereham, Norf, same crest and motto

Thackray, William, Esquire Fairmont, Manningham, Bradford a falcon holding in its beak an arrow point downwards in bend sinister *Nobilitas est sola veritas* *cf* 78 8

Thackwell, Edward Francis, Rostellan Castle, Rostellan (1) Same crest as above (2) Within a chaplet of oak ppr, a dragon's head erased, paly of six or and gu, the neck transpierced by an arrow barbed and flighted, all ppr *Mihi solicitudo futuri*

Thackwell, Walter Joseph de Rupe, Aghada Hall, Rostellan, co. Cork, same crests and motto

Thackwell, Major-General William de Wilton Roche, Wynstone Place, Brookthorpe, Glouc, same crests and motto

Thackwell, John, Wilton Place, Dymock, Glouc, within a chaplet of oak ppr, a dragon's head erased, paly of six or and gu, the neck transpierced by an arrow barbed and flighted, all ppr *Mihi solicitudo futuri*

Thackwell, within a chaplet of oak ppr, a dragon's head reversed paly of six, transpierced by an arrow barbed and flighted, also ppr *Mihi solicitudo futuri*

Thackwell, John Esquire Wilton Place, Dymocke, Glouc, same crest and motto

Thackwell, out of a mural coronet arg, a dexter arm embowed vested in the uniform of the 15th King's Hussars, and from the wrist pendant by a riband gu, fimbriated az, a representation of the silver medal for Waterloo, the hand grasping and in the attitude of striking with a sword ppr, pommel and hilt or, between two branches of laurel issuing in like manner from the coronet and above upon an escroll the motto *Frappe fort*

Thackwell, William Polson, the White House Pauntley, Newent, Glouc, same crest and motto.

Thaker or **Thacker** of Repton Priory, Derbysh, a bittern setting among reeds ppr

Thanet, Earl of (Tufton), a sea lion sejant arg *Fiel pero desdichado.—Ales volat propriis* 20 2

Tharrold, on the top of a Corinthian pillar arg, a trefoil vert. *Ex merito* 176 1

Tharp of Chippenham Park, Cambs, the figure of *Hope* represented by a demi-woman habited or the mantle purp, and flowing over the sinister shoulder and supporting in her dexter hand an anchor ppr, resting upon the wreath

Thatcher, Essex, a Saxon sword or scax ppr 171 2

Thayer of Thoydon, Essex a talbot's head erased per fess erm and gu 56 2

Theed, Bucks, an eagle's head erased or 83 2

Thellusson, *see* Rendlesham, Baron

Thellusson, Herbert J P, Brodsworth Hall Doncaster a demi-greyhound salient arg, collared sa, between two wings of the last, each charged with a trefoil slipped or *Labore et honore*

Thelwall, on a mount vert, a stag lodged ppr, attired or, pierced in the breast by an arrow arg, vulned gu *cf* 115 12

Theobald, Kent, a phœnix sa. in flames ppr 82 2

Theobald, same crest *Benigno numine*

Theobald, Essex, out of clouds ppr with rays issuing therefrom or a demi-lion with wings displayed sa

Theobald of Barking Hall Suff, a cock with wings endorsed gu *cf* 91 7

Theshmaker, between wings arg, an eagle's head 84 2

Thesiger, Baron Chelmsford, *see* Chelmsford

Thestlethwayte, Wilts, on a ducal coronet or, an eagle displayed arg *cf* 75 2

Thetford, a dagger erect ppr 169 2

Thetford of Batishall, Norf, a heraldic tiger sejant or, maned and tufted sa

Thicknesse of Bartley, Staffs, a cubit arm erect vested paly of six or and gu, holding in the hand a scythe ppr *cf* 209 1

Thicknesse, Rt Rev Francis Henry, Bishop Suffragan of Leicester, of Beech Hill, Lancs, a cubit arm erect vested paly or and gu, charged with a cross crosslet counter changed, cuffed arg, holding in the hand ppr a scythe the handle or, the blade downwards az *Sine clade sterno* *cf* 209 1

Thicknesse, Ralph, 32, Victoria Street Westminster, S W, same crest and motto

Thimbleby of Irnham, Lincs, a boar's head or couped gu 43 1

Thimblethorp of Foulsham, Norf and Henley-on-Thames, Oxon, an ostrich's head erased or, between two wings arg, holding in the beak a horse shoe or *cf* 97 10

Thimblethorp, Glouc, between two wings arg, a greyhound's head erased or

Thin, Scotland a boar's head couped sa 43 1

Thirke, a lion couchant between two laurel-branches in orle

Thirwall, two daggers in saltier ppr 169 8

Thirwell, on a ducal coronet erm, a boar's head and neck arg

Thirwell, Northumb, on a chapeau gu turned up arg, a boar's head couped at the neck of the second

Thiselton-Dyer, Sir William Turner, K C M G, C I E, Royal Botanic Gardens, Kew, out of a crown vallery or, a goat's head sa, armed and gorged with a collar gemel, also or *Spectemur agendo.*

Thistlethwayte, Alexander Edward of Southwick Park, Hants, a demi lion az, supporting a pheon or

Thistlethwayte, a demi-lion az., holding a pheon or.

Thistlethwayte of Winterlow, Wilts, on a ducal coronet or, an eagle displayed arg. *cf.* 75. 2

Thom, Scotland, a hand holding a sword ppr. *Dum vivo spero.* 212. 13

Thomas, Wales, out of a ducal coronet a demi-sea-horse salient.

Thomas, Edward David, of Welfield House, Radnor, out of a mural coronet arg., a demi-sea-horse gu., crined or, charged on the shoulder with a cinquefoil of the first, holding in the paws an anchor erect sa., resting on the coronet. *I Dduw bo'r diolch.* 255. 16

Thomas, Algernon Evan, R.N., Cærwnon, Builth R.S.O., Breconsh., same crest.

Thomas, Charles Evan, Esquire, J.P., D.L., of Gnoll, Neath, Glamorgansh., out of a mural coronet arg., a demi-sea-horse gu., crined or, resting the paws on an anchor erect sa. *Ddw bo'r diolch.* 46. 6

Thomas, Edward David, Welfield, Builth, Breconsh., same crest and motto.

Thomas, Sir Godfrey Vignoles, Bart., a demi-unicorn erm., armed, crined, and ungu or, supporting an escutcheon sa. *Virtus invicta gloriosa.*

Thomas of Blunsdon Abbey, Highworth, Wilts, an eagle displayed erm., holding in the beak an ear of wheat leaved and slipped ppr., in front thereof an escocheon per pale az. and sa., charged with an eagle displayed or. 276. 8

Thomas, Major-General John Wellesley, 25, Eldon Road, Kensington, a demi-unicorn erm. resting its sinister foot on an escutcheon sa.

Thomas of Gellywernew, Carmarthensh., a heron's head erased arg., gorged with a garland of roses gu. *A Deo et patre.* *cf.* 106. 6

Thomas, a heron's head erased arg., gorged with a chaplet of roses gu. *cf.* 106. 6

Thomas, Rhys Goring, of Plas Llannon, Carmarthensh., same crest. *A Deo et patre.* *cf.* 106. 6

Thomas of Selling, Clavering, Britters, Kent, and Islington, Middx., between two spears erect or, a Cornish chough rising ppr. 108. 7

Thomas of Wrotham, Kent, a Cornish chough with wings elevated sa., beaked and legged gu., between two spears erect or, headed arg. 108. 7

Thomas of London, on the branch of a tree in fess, sprouting at the dexter end vert, a raven with wings expanded sa.

Thomas, on a cross aiguise arg., the foot trunked and the middle stem raguled, a bird sa.

Thomas, a dragon's head erased ppr., holding in the mouth a hand couped at the wrist gu. 72. 6

Thomas of Whitwick, Heref., a dragon's head erased ppr. *cf.* 71. 2

Thomas, Sir George Sidney Meade, Bart., of Yapton Place, Sussex, a demi-lion rampant gu. *Honesty is the best policy.* 10. 3

Thomas, out of a ducal coronet a demi-lion rampant holding a flag.

Thomas, Freeman-, Freeman, of Rattan, Sussex, a demi-lion rampant gu., charged on the shoulder with an ermine spot arg. *cf.* 10. 2

Thomas of Bromley, Kent, a demi-leopard rampant ppr., supporting a baton erect or.

Thomas of Lewes, Sussex, a talbot sejant ppr., spotted arg. and sa., eared of the last. *cf.* 55. 2

Thomas, a greyhound's head arg., between two roses gu., slipped and leaved vert. 61. 11

Thomas of Tregolls, Cornw., three arrows, two in saltier and one in pale ppr., banded gu. 173. 1

Thomas, a buck trippant ppr. 117. 8

Thomas, Abraham Garrod, M.D., Clytha Park, Newport, upon a garb fesseways or, an eagle displayed ppr., holding in the beak a staff or, entwined by a serpent vert. *Egni a lwydd.*

Thomas, William, Tregarnedd, Llangefni R.S.O., Anglesey, upon waves of the sea a ship in full sail ppr., between two anchors in bend stocks upwards sa. *Fac recte et nil time.*

Thomas, David Collet, 21, Second Avenue, Hove, a demi-unicorn gu., charged with two chevronels arg., and resting the sinister leg on a plate, thereon a fleur-de-lis gu. *Equus in arduis.*

Thomas-Stanford, Charles, 3, Ennismore Gardens, S.W.: (1) A buffalo's head caboshed sa. within a chain in arch or, the head charged for distinction with a cross crosslet, also or. (2) A demi-unicorn gu. charged on the body with two chevronels arg., and supporting with the sinister fore-paw a plate charged with a fleur-de-lis gu. *Æquus in arduis.*

Thomason, a demi-talbot arg., ducally gorged or. 55. 12

Thomason, on a gauntlet in fess, a falcon close belled. 86. 13

Thomkins, a dove within an adder in orle ppr. 92. 11

Thomlinson of London and Yorks, out of a ducal coronet or, a griffin's head arg. 67. 9

Thomlinson, out of a mural coronet a griffin's head ppr. 67. 10

Thomlinson of Newcastle-upon-Tyne, Northumb., a greyhound per pale arg. and vert. *cf.* 60. 2

Thomlinson of Blencogo, Cumb., a greyhound per pale wavy arg. and vert. *cf.* 60. 2

Thomond, Marquess of (O'Bryen), an arm embowed holding in the hand a sword arg., hilt and pommel or. *Vigueur de desus.* 195. 2

Thompson, Baron Haversham (*extinct*), an arm erect vested gu., cuffed arg., holding in the hand ppr. five ears of wheat or. *In lumine lucem.* 205. 7

Thompson, Northumb., same crest. *In lumine luce.* 205. 7

Thompson of Clonfin, Longford, an arm in armour embowed holding in the hand, all ppr., five ears of wheat or, the arm charged with a trefoil vert. *In lumine luce.*

Thompson, Acheson Quinton Dick Thomas, Esquire, J.P., of Annaverna, co. Louth, Ireland, a cubit arm erect vested gu., cuffed erm., and charged with an Oriental crown or, the hand grasping five ears of wheat ppr. *In lumine lucem.* *cf.* 205. 7

Thompson, Rev. Sir Peile, Bart., of Park Gate, Guiseley, Yorks, in front of the battlements of a tower ppr., a cubit arm vested az., charged with a mullet of six points or, the cuff arg., the hand ppr., holding five ears of wheat slipped or. *Wheare vertue lys, love never dys.* 311. 12

Thompson of Morpeth, Northumb., an arm erect vested gu., cuffed arg., holding in the hand ppr. five ears of wheat or. *In lumine lucem.* 205. 7

Thompson of Lansdown Place, Somers., a mount vert, therefrom in front of a cubit arm vested az., cuffed arg., the hand holding seven ears of wheat ppr., the sun rising or.

Thompson of Borris Castle, Queen's Co., Ireland, an armed arm erect holding in the hand five ears of wheat ppr.

Thompson, Durh., an arm in armour embowed quarterly or and az., holding in the gauntlet ppr. a tilting-spear erect.

Thompson, Sir Henry, Bart., 35, Wimpole Street, W., in front of an arm embowed in armour, the hand in a gauntlet holding a broken tilting-spear, a staff fessewise entwined by a serpent, all ppr. *Je veux de bonne guerre.* 287. 12

Thompson, George, Esquire, of Clonskeagh Castle, co. Dublin, an arm embowed in armour ppr., holding in the hand, also ppr., five ears of wheat or, the arm charged with a trefoil vert. *In lumine lucem.*

Thompson, Robert Wade, Clonskeagh Castle, Dublin, same crest and motto.

Thompson of Bishopwearmouth, Durh., London, Suff., and Yorks, an arm in armour embowed quarterly or and az., holding in the gauntlet ppr. a broken lance of the first. *Dum spiro, spero.* 197. 3

Thompson, Sir Thomas Raikes, Bart., of Hartsbourne, Herts, out of a naval coronet or, an arm in armour embowed ppr., garnished of the first, the hand supporting a lance erect, also ppr. *Non quo sed quomodo.* 308. 4

Thompson, Meysey-, Sir Henry Meysey, Bart., D.L., J.P., of Kirby Hall, Yorks, an arm embowed in armour quarterly or and az., the gauntlet ppr., holding the truncheon of a broken lance of the first. *Je veux de bonne guerre.* *cf.* 197. 7

Thompson of Newcastle-on-Tyne, an arm embowed in armour quarterly or and az., holding in the gauntlet ppr. the truncheon of a broken lance of the first. *Je veux de bonne guerre.* *cf.* 197. 7

Thompson of Broomford Manor, Devonsh., a dexter arm in armour couped in fesse ppr., the hand holding a cross crosslet fitchée arg. *Deus providebit.* 211. 14

Thompson, a demi-griffin segreant. 64. 2

Thompson, a buck's head caboshed ppr. 122. 5

Thompson, Colonel Pearson Scott, C.B., in front of two swords in saltire, points upwards, ppr., pommel and hilt or, a stag trippant per pale of the last and sa. *Fideliter.*

Thompson, a lion rampant gu., ducally gorged or. *cf.* 1. 13

Thompson, John Troughton, a lion rampant az., gorged with a collar vair, holding in the dexter fore paw a swan's head erased arg, and resting the dexter hind leg on three annulets interlaced fessewise or 237 6

Thompson of Thingwell **Hall** Lancs a lion rampant per fesse nebuly arg and sa, holding between the paws a lure or *Nosce teipsum*

Thompson, George Rodie, J P D L., Lynewood, Sunninghill Berks, same crest and motto

Thompson of London, a lion rampant gu 1 13

Thompson, Surrey, a lion sejant or, holding a saltier arg

Thompson of London, Durh, and Cottingham Castle, Yorks, a lion rampant gu ducally gorged or *Go on, and take care* cf 1 13

Thompson, Vincent Thomas, Esquire, M.A, of 195, Belle Vue Road, Leeds same crest and motto

Thompson, Yorks, a demi ounce erminois collared ringed and lined az 23 13

Thompson, Bart (*extinct*), of Virhees, Sussex, on a naval coronet az charged on the rim with three crosses patee arg, a unicorn passant of the last gorged with a wreath of laurel ppr *Dum spiro spero*

Thompson of Clements, Ilford, Sussex on a habick sa a falcon belled or, holding in the beak a teazle ppr 86 4

Thompson of London a hawk with wings expanded ppr, beaked and legged or between two spears erect, the staves of the last headed arg

Thompson, Ireland, an ostrich's head and neck erm, holding in the beak a horse-shoe or *Lucem virtus amat*

Thompson of Boughton, Kent, out of a ducal coronet arg an ostrich's head, holding in the beak a horse shoe all or

Thompson of Pelham Rayton Kent, a greyhound sejant gu, collared and lined or cf 59 2

Thompson of London between two palm-branches in orle a flaming heart all ppr 181 12

Thompson of Hamburgh, a palm branch ppr *Patientia vinco* 147 1

Thoms, the late George Hunter Mac Thomas, Esquire, F R S E F S A Advocate, Sheriff, and Vice-Admiral of Orkney and Shetland Islands, of 13, Charlotte Square, Edinburgh a demi-unicorn erm, armed crined and ungu or supporting an escutcheon also or *Virtutis præmium* 304 9

Thoms, Thomas H, of Tay-Bank, Withington, same crest and motto

Thoms, on a mount an oak-tree fructed, all ppr 143 14

Thomson, *see* Kelvin, Baron

Thomson, a cubit arm erect vested, holding in the hand five ears of wheat 205 5

Thomson, Scotland, a hand holding a bunch of flowers ppr *Industria murus*

Thomson of London, a cubit arm erect vested gu, cuffed arg, holding in the hand ppr a sprig or

Thomson of Trevelyan and St Caroc, Cornw a cubit arm erect vested gu, cuffed arg holding in the hand ppr five ears of wheat or *In lumine lucem* 205 7

Thomson of Clonfin Granard, co Longford, an arm embowed in armour ppr, holding in the hand also ppr five ears of wheat or the arm charged with a trefoil vert *In lumine lucem*

Thomson, Quintin Acheson, Annaverna near Ravensdale, co Louth a cubit arm erect vested gu cuffed erm and charged with an Oriental crown or, the hand grasping five ears of wheat ppr *In lumine lucem*

Thomson of Logie Scotland a dexter hand holding stalks of lint under bloom ppr *Industriæ munus*

Thomson, Herbert Archer Esquire, of Parkwood House, Whetstone, N, same crest and motto

Thomson of Low Wood co Antrim, Ireland a dexter arm embowed in armour ppr the hand also ppr, holding a cross crosslet fitchee gu, and the arm charged with a spur rowel of the last *Honesty is the best policy*

Thomson, Spencer Campbell Esquire, of 10 Eglinton Crescent Edinburgh, a dexter hand ppr, holding a cross crosslet fitchée erect az *Vincit omnia veritas* cf 221 14

Thomson, Scotland, a dexter hand couped in fess ppr, holding a cross crosslet fitched az *Honesty is good policy* 221 10

Thomson, Anstruther-, John, Charleton, Colinsburgh, Fifesh, two arms in armour holding a battle-axe, all ppr (*for Anstruther*) (2) A naked arm couped at the elbow ppr holding a cross crosslet gu (*for Thomson*)

Thomson, an arm couped below the elbow holding in the hand a cross crosslet fitched *Optima est veritas* 221 14

Thomson, late John Turnbull, Esquire of Lennel, Gladstone, Invercargill, New Zealand late Surveyor General of New Zealand, *uses* a dexter naked arm couped at the elbow and lying fessways holding in the hand a cross crosslet fitchee erect *Deus providebit*

Thomson, Mitchell Esquire, of 6 Charlotte Square, Edinburgh a hand ppr, holding a cross crosslet fitchee gu *Deus providebit* 221 14

Thomson, White-, Colonel Sir Robert Thomas, K C B, Broomford Manor Exbourne, North Devonsh (1) A dexter hand and arm in armour couped between the hand and elbow in fess ppr holding erect a cross crosslet fitched or (*for Thomson*) (2) A stork arg and holding in the beak a bullrush, and resting the dexter leg on an hourglass, all ppr (*for White*) *Deus providebit*

Thomson, Robert Charteris, Amisfield Hamilton, Canada, an arm in armour issuing out of a cloud, the hand holding a dagger ppr *Non gladio sed gratia*

Thomson, Buncombe-Poulett-, of Roehampton and Waverley Abbey, Surrey, (1) An arm in armour embowed ppr, garnished or holding in the hand the staff of a broken tilting spear, also ppr (*for Thomson*) 197 7. (2) An arm in armour embowed holding in the gauntlet, all ppr, a sword arg, hilted or (*for Poulett*) 195 1 (3) A demi-lion gu, charged on the shoulder with a water-bouget arg, supporting a spear, thereon a banner of the first, fringed of the second, charged with a cross flory or (*for Buncombe*)

Thomson, Scotland, a dexter naked arm couped at the elbow fesseways ppr, holding a cross crosslet fitchee erect az *Deus providebit*

Thomson, Scotland a dexter hand holding a cross crosslet fitchée sa *Honestie is the best policie* 221 14

Thomson, Deas-, a dexter hand erect ppr holding a cross crosslet fitchee in bend sinister gu *Fortis in arduis* 221 14

Thomson of Camphill, Renfrewsh, Scotland a dexter arm in armour ppr the hand holding a cross crosslet fitchee arg *Deus providebit* cf 210 14

Thomson of Bonaly, co Edinburgh Scotland, a dexter hand ppr, holding a cross crosslet fitchee az *Vincit omnia veritas* 221 14

Thomson, Spencer Thomson, B A, J P Eilean Shona Acharacle Inverness-sh same crest and motto.

Thomson, Scotland a cross crosslet fitchee gu *Optima est veritas* 166 2

Thomson, Scotland a rose gu barbed vert, seeded or *Christus providebit* 149 2

Thomson of Maynes Scotland a branch of palm ppr *Patientia et gratia vinco* 147 1

Thomson of Wester Bogie Fifesh Scotland, a branch of palm ppr *Patentia vinco* 147 1

Thomson, Scotland, a thistle ppr *Pro patria* cf 150 2

Thomson of Portlethen and Banchory, Kincardinesh and Fairley, Aberdeensh a crane holding in the beak a palm branch all ppr *Curæ cedit fatum —Suum cuique*

Thomson of Aberdeen, a crane holding in its beak a twig of palm ppr *Curæ cedit fatum*

Thomson, Samuel John, of Kenfield, Kent (1) On a mount vert, a greyhound sejant arg gorged with a collar az studded or therefrom reflexed over the back a leash of the last charged on the shoulder for distinction with a cross crosslet gu (*for Thomson*) (2) A heart gu encircled by a ducal coronet arg, between two palm-branches ppr (*for Toker*) *Providentia tutamen* cf 181 14

Thomson, a martlet 95 4

Thomson of Dalmuir House, Dumbartonsh, Scotland, a lion rampant ppr *Optima est veritas* 1 13

Thomson, a lion rampant or ducally gorged az cf 1 13

Thomson of Shalfield Essex and Lincs, a lion rampant ducally gorged or cf 1 13

Thomson, Primrose-, a lion passant gardant ppr *Fortis et fidus* 4 3

Thomson of Dalmuir, Dumbartonsh, a lion rampant ppr *Optima est veritas* 1 13

Thomson of Fairleyhope co Edinburgh Scotland, a quill ppr *Fato prudentia major*

Thomson of Grange, Clackmannansh, and Charlevwood, Herts, issuing from a naval coronet or, a stag's head gu, attired of the first, holding in his mouth a slip of oak vert, fructed ppr., and charged on the neck with a cross crosslet fitchée, also or. *Lente in voto.*

Thomson of Buchromb, Banffsh., a stag's head cabossed ppr. *Deus providebit.* 122. 5

Thomson, Ringler-, a stag's head erased gu., attired with ten tynes and gorged with a ring or. *Meminisse juvabit.* cf. 121. 2

Thomson, W. W., Esquire, Hill Farm, Mitcham, on a chapeau ppr., a sword in pale, point upwards, between two wings.

Thorburn, Sir Robert, K.C.M.G., of Devon Place, Saint John's, Newfoundland, a dove holding in her beak an olive-branch. *Vivimus in spe.* 92. 5

Thores of Garniestown, Scotland, a falcon soaring aloft ppr. *Immeritas temnere minas.* 88. 3

Thoresby of Hay, Brecknocksh., a lion rampant sa., supporting a battle-axe or. *In silentio fortitudo.*

Thorlby and **Thorley,** Scotland, a tower ppr. *Fide et fiducia.* 156. 2

Thorley, a lion's gamb erect arg., fretty sa. cf. 36. 4

Thorley, a demi-lion rampant or, holding between the paws a cinquefoil sa.

Thorn or **Thorne,** an owl ppr. 96. 5

Thorn-Pudsey, *see* Pudsey.

Thorn, Henry A. A., Esquire, of Hurworth, Stonebridge Park, London, N.W., a lion rampant ppr. *Factis non verbis.*

Thornagh, Notts, an heraldic tiger's head or, maned, armed, and tufted sa., gorged with a collar wavy az.

Thornborough and **Thornbury,** Hants, Westml., Middx., and Yorks, a tiger sejant arg., pellettée.

Thornbrough of Bishopsteignton, Devonsh., on a naval coronet or, a fox passant ppr. *Spectemur agendo.*

Thornburgh-Cropper, of Swaylands, Kent: (1) Upon a rock ppr., in front of two spears in saltier az., a cropper pigeon or (*for Cropper*). 94. 9. (2) An heraldic tiger arg., semée of torteaux, collared, and therefrom a chain reflexed over the back sa., and resting the dexter fore-paw on a fret, also sa. (*for Thornburgh*). *Love every man, fear no man.* 25. 14

Thornburgh-Copper, Edward Denman, same crests and motto.

Thorndick, Lincs, a demi-lion rampant gardant or, holding a chaplet of laurel vert.

Thorndike of Great Carleton, Lincs, a damask rose ppr., leaves and thorns vert, at the bottom of the stalk a beetle or, scarabæus ppr. 149. 10

Thorne, Suff. and Devonsh., a lion rampant sa. 1. 10

Thorne of London, same crest. *Vincere vel mori.* 1. 10

Thorne, Suff., and Melverley, Shropsh., out of a ducal coronet or, a mermaid ppr., crined of the first, conjoined to a dolphin haurient of the last, devouring her sinister hand.

Thorneloe, Rt. Rev. Bishop of Algoma, Saulte St. Marie, Algoma, Ontario, Canada, upon a mount vert, a hawthorn-tree eradicated ppr., between two buckles, the tongues erect sa. *Deus, noster refugium.*

Thornes, Shropsh., a hand holding a club ppr. 214. 6

Thornex, on a mount vert, a greyhound couchant or, gorged with a label of three points gu.

Thorney of London, a demi-lion rampant ppr., extending his paw wounded by a thorn sticking therein.

Thorneycroft of Hadley Park, Shropsh., over a mural coronet gu., a falcon volant ppr., jessed, membered, and beaked or, between two palm-branches of the same. *Fortis qui se vincit.*

Thornhagh of Fenton, Notts, an heraldic tiger's head or, maned, armed, and tufted sa., gorged with a collar wavy az.

Thornhill, *see* McCreagh-Thornhill.

Thornhill of Woodleys, Oxon., and Lincs, a woman's head couped at the shoulders affrontée ppr., vested, crined, and ducally crowned, all or.

Thornhill of Fixby, Yorks, the bust of a woman ppr., vested gu., fimbriated or, crined and ducally crowned, also or, and issuing from the coronet five thorn-leaves vert, and charged on the breast for distinction with a cross crosslet of the third. 266. 10

Thornhill, Arthur John, Diddington, Hunts, same crest, omitting the cross crosslet for distinction.

Thornhill, Edmund Henry, Esquire, J.P., of the Manor House, Boxworth, Cambridge, same crest.

Thornhill, Compton-, Bart., J.P., D.L., of Riddlesworth Hall, Norf., and Pakenham Lodge, Suff.: (1) three fleurs-de-lis or, in front of the bust of a woman ppr., vested gu., crined, and on the head a vallary coronet or, and issuing from the coronet five thorn-leaves vert. (*Thornhill*). 287. 13. (2) On a rock a beacon fired, in front thereof a helmet, all ppr. (*Compton*). *Be fast.* 287. 14

Thornhill, out of a ducal coronet a hawthorn-tree ppr.

Thornhill, Michael McCreagh, of Stanton, Derbysh.: (1) A mount, and thereon a thorn-tree ppr., charged upon the branches with a mascle or. (2) A demi-lion rampant gu., collared gemelle, and charged on the shoulder with two estoiles or, holding between the paws a bezant, thereon two mascles interleaved sa. *Amantes ardua dumos.*

Thornhill, co. Cork, Ireland, a thorn-bush, and thereon a robin redbreast, all ppr.

Thornhill of Castle Keevin, co. Cork, Ireland, a thorn-bush, and thereon a robin redbreast, all ppr. *Conquer or die.*

Thornhill of Ollernshaw, Derbysh., out of a vallary coronet gu., a demi-eagle displayed or, pendant from the neck a bugle-horn stringed sa.

Thornholme of Thornholme, Yorks, on a mount vert, a tower arg. cf. 156. 3

Thornhull, Wilts, Bucks, and Dorset, a bird sa., legged or.

Thornley of London, a wolf's head erased arg., charged on the neck with a bar gemelle gu. cf. 30. 8

Thornthwaite, Camb., a lion's head erased gu., holding in the mouth a thorn-sprig vert, fructed ppr.

Thornton, *see* Todd-Thornton.

Thornton, out of a mural coronet a demi-lion rampant, holding in the dexter paw a slip. 16. 11

Thornton, Hon. George, of Sydney, Longwood, Darling Point, and Llangollen, Summer Hill, all in New South Wales, Australia, Member of the Legislative Council of New South Wales, Chairman of the City Bank and of the Savings Bank, issuing out of a ducal coronet a lion's head. 17. 5

Thornton of Birkin, Yorks, a lion's head erased ppr., gorged with a ducal coronet or. 18. 5

Thornton of Scarborough, Yorks, out of a ducal coronet or, a lion's head ppr. 17. 5

Thornton, Rev. J., Ewell, Surrey, a lion's head erased purp., gorged with a ducal coronet or.

Thornton, John Knowsley, Hildesham Hall, Cambridge, same crest.

Thornton, Charles Conway, British Consulate-General, Budapest, same crest.

Thornton, Robert Lawrence, Esquire, J.P., Barrister-at-Law, of High Cross, Framfield, R.S.O., Sussex. *Persevere.*

Thornton, Thomas William, of Brockhall and Newnham, Northamp. and Yorks, a demi-lion rampant gu., charged on the shoulder with an escarbuncle or. cf. 10. 3

Thornton of Skerton and Kirkland Hall, Lancs, out of a ducal coronet or, a lion's head gu. *Deo spes mea.* 17. 5

Thornton of Clapham, Surrey, a lion's head erased purp., gorged with a ducal coronet or. *Fideli tuta merces.* 18. 5

Thornton of Brock Hall, Northamp.: (1) A demi-lion rampant gu., charged on the shoulder with an escarbuncle or. cf. 10. 3. (2) Out of a ducal coronet or, a dragon's head with wings elevated. 72. 1

Thornton, Cambs, Norf., and Yorks, out of a ducal coronet or, a dragon's head between two wings arg.

Thornton of Some, Cambs, Windham, Norf., and Yorks, same crest.

Thornton, Rt. Hon. Sir Edward, G.C.B., K.C.B., C.B., P.C., **Count de Cassilhas** in the Kingdom of Portugal, of 90, Eaton Square, S.W.: (1) Out of the coronet of a Conde of Portugal, an arm embowed vested az., the cuff of gold lace or, the hand ppr. supporting a flagstaff, therefrom flowing the royal standard of Portugal. (2) Out of an Eastern coronet or, a dragon's head between two dragon's wings expanded erm., ducally gorged of the first. *Pro Rege pio.—Fit manus aliena sua.*

Thornton of Estnenton, Yorks, out of a ducal coronet or, a cockatrice's head, combed and wattled gu., between two dragon's wings arg. 68. 11

Thornton, Middx., a griffin's head erased sa., beaked or, charged on the neck with an escarbuncle or. cf. 66. 2

Thornton of Grenville, co. Cavan, Ireland, a griffin's head erased sa., beaked or, charged on the neck with an escarbuncle of the last. *Nec opprimere nec opprimi.* cf. 66. 2

Thornton, Scotland, a maiden's head from the shoulders affrontée, vested az. *Vincit pericula virtus.* cf. 182. 8

Thornton of Laughton, Lincs, out of a ducal coronet or, a maiden's head of the same vested gu

Thornton of Willoughby Lincs, a leopard's head erased at the neck gardant or

Thornton, Northumb, a fountain or, playing ppr 159 13

Thornton of Thornton, Chesh out of the top of a tower an arm in armour embowed, all ppr holding in the hand a pennon of St George

Thornton of Whitton Castle, Northumb, a tower encircled by a wall

Thornton, Charles Edmund de More, Welham, Retford, Nottingham *Cervus non servus*

Thornycroft, Charles Edward, of Thornycroft Hall, Chesh, on a mural coronet gu, a falcon volant ppr, jessed, membered, and beaked or between two palm-branches of the last

Thornycroft, John Isaac, Eyot Villa, Chiswick, upon the battlements of a tower gu, a falcon rising ppr, belled and jessed or, between two branches of a thorn tree or

Thornycroft, William Hamo, R A, 2A, Melbury Road Kensington, same crest *Fortis qui se vincit*

Thorogood of Hornchurch Essex, a wolf's head arg 30 5

Thorold of London, Lincs, and of Chesterton, Cambs, a roebuck erm, attired or 117 5

Thorold, Grant-, of Weelsby Lincs (1) A buck arg, charged on the body with a quatrefoil vert, resting the dexter foot on an escutcheon az, thereon a martlet or (*for Thorold*) (2) On a rock a burning mountain surmounted by a rainbow, all ppr (*for Grant*)

Thorold, Sir John Henry, Bart, J P, D L, of Marston, Lincs, a roebuck trippant erm, attired or *Cervus non servus* 117 8

Thorold, Major General Reginald Gother, Belgrave Lodge, Montpelier Terrace, Cheltenham, same crest and motto

Thorold of Boothby Hall, Grantham, a roebuck passant arg, attired or *Cervus non servus*

Thorold, Montague 47, Wilton Crescent, S W, same crest and motto

Thoroton of Thoroton, Great Crophill and Car Colston, Notts a lion rampant per fesse gu and sa., holding between the paws a bugle-horn of the last *Deus scutum et cornu salutis*

Thoroughgood and **Throwgood** of London (1) A demi lion or 10 2 (2) A demi-greyhound salient arg, collared gu 60 8

Thorowgood or **Thorogood** of Thorowgood and Shartfield, Herts, a wolf's head arg, charged on the neck with a lozenge-shaped buckle, the tongue fesseways az cf 30. 5

Thorp, Robert Disney, Esquire, Leeds, a demi-lion gu, resting the sinister paw on an escutcheon arg, charged with a fess gu, thereon another fess nebuly or *Comme a Dieu playra*

Thorp, Lord Mayor of London, 1821, a lion rampant gu holding in the dexter paw a fleur de lis az *Vivit post funera virtus* 2 7

Thorp, Rev Charles Fenwick, Beadnell Vicarage, Chathill Northumb, a lion rampant gu, holding in the dexter paw a fleur de-lis az gorged with a plain collar, and pendent therefrom an escutcheon or, charged with a cross patee quadrate gu

Thorp, Jonathan, Esquire Green Hall, Wilmslow, a martlet with wings elevated or 95 11

Thorp, John Walter Hook Jordangate House, Macclesfield, a martlet, wings displayed or *Viva post funera virtus*

Thorp, an arrow and a palm branch in saltier ppr 171 7

Thorp of Ryton Durh, a lion rampant gu holding in the dexter paw a fleur-de lis az, gorged with a plain collar, and pendent therefrom an escutcheon or, charged with a cross patee quadrate of the first with the motto ονει ει μη εν τωσταυρω *Super antiquas*

Thorp, Edward Ellerton Kirby Park West Kirby Chesh, a reindeer lodged ppr holding in the mouth a trefoil slipped vert, and resting the dexter leg on an escutcheon arg *Semper fidelis*

Thorpe of Gibshaven, Sussex, Suff, and Norf on a chapeau gu, turned up erm, a stag sa 118 1

Thorpe, James, Coddington Hall Newark-on-Trent, same crest.

Thorpe of London, two lion's gambs erect the dexter or the sinister arg, supporting a fleur de-lis az

Thorpe of London and Northamp, a cock gu, beaked, combed legged, and wattled or 91 2

Thorpe, Leics a bull's head couped at the neck quarterly or and sa, armed, counterchanged cf 44 3

Thorpe of Boston, Lincs, a lion sejant or, holding between the paws a lozenge arg, charged with a maunch sa

Thoyts, William Richard Mortimer, Reading, a heath cock rising ppr charged on the breast with the character of Venus or *Pro rege semper* cf 89 5

Thrale, a cross crosslet fitched gu *In cruce confido* 166 2

Thrale, out of a ducal coronet an oak-tree fructed ppr cf 143 13

Thrale or **Threele,** Surrey and Southwark Sussex an oak-tree ppr, fructed or 143 5

Threipland, Bart, of Fingask, Perthsh. (1) A hart's head erased ppr 121 2 (2) A dexter hand gu, holding a dagger ppr *Animis et fato.—Stricta parata neci* 212 3

Threlle, out of a ducal coronet or, an oak-tree arg cf 143 13

Thresher, Richard Frederick Esquire of Marsh House Bentley Hants, a demi buck regardant arg guttee-de-sang between two branches of fern ppr

Thring, Baron (Rt Hon Sir Henry Thring, K C B), of Alderhurst, Surrey, and 5, Queen's Gate Gardens, S W, a cock gu, charged with an escallop on his breast and wing and holding in his beak an ear of barley or 264. 10

Thring, John Huntley, of Alford House, Somers, a cock gu, charged on the breast with an escallop and holding in the beak an ear of barley or 264 10

Thring, Arthur Theodore, Esquire, C B, of 87, St. George's Square, S W, a cock per pale or and gu, charged with two escallops counterchanged, in the beak an ear of barley ppr 264 10

Thring, Christopher Bevan, Ormond House, Sion Hill, Bath, same crest

Thring, Cyril Theodore, Feldberg, Foxrock, co Dublin, same crest.

Thring, George Herbert South Lodge, Balcombe, Sussex, same crest

Thring, Rev Godfrey B A Ploneks Hill, Shamley Green Guildford, same crest

Thring, John Huntley J P Alford House, near Castle Cary Somers, same crest

Thring, John Gale Faileigh, Uppingham, Rutland same crest

Thring, Lawrence Theodore, M A, New University Club, same crest

Thring, Rev John Charles B A, the Park Dunmow, Essex (1) Same crest (*for Thring*) (2) On an Eastern coronet or, a dragon passant gu (*for Meredith*) *Doe right and fear not*

Throckmorton of Molland, Devonsh, an elephant's head 133 2

Throckmorton or **Throgmorton** (1) A falcon rising arg, jessed or 88 2 (2) An elephant's head erased sa, eared or 133 3

Throckmorton, Sir Nicholas William George, Bart, of Coughton Court, Warwick, a falcon with wings expanded and inverted ppr, belled and jessed or *Virtus sola nobilitas — Moribus antiquis* 87 1

Throughston, Worcs, a pelican in her piety arg 98 14

Throughston, Bucks, a lion's head erased per chevron arg and sa., charged on the neck with three roundles counterchanged cf 17 8

Throwgood or **Throgood,** a wolf's head arg, charged on the neck with a buckle, its tongue in fess az. cf 30 5

Throwley, Viscount, *see* Sondes, Earl

Thrupp of Spanish Place, London, on a mount vert, a serpent nowed surmounted by an eagle ppr, the dexter claw resting on an escutcheon az, charged with a bee volant or 76 9

Thruston, a stork arg, beaked az, legged gu *Thrust on* 105 11

Thruston, same crest *Esse quam videri.*

Thruston, Edmund Heathcote, Pennal Tower, Machynlleth, North Wales, a heron arg *Esse quam videri —Thrust on*

Thruxton, Worcs, a pelican in her piety arg, the nest and young ppr, beaked, legged, and vulned gu 98 8

Thuillier, General Sir Henry Edward Landor, C S I, F R S, Tudor House, Richmond, Surrey a lion statant *Vincit amor patriæ*

Thuillier, Sir Henry Ravenshaw, K C I E, 9 the Grove, Boltons, South Kensington, S W, a lion statant gu *Vincit amor patriæ*

Thunder, a cubit arm ppr holding in the hand a trumpet sa *Certavi et vici*

Thunder, Michael, J P, of Lagore, co Meath, Ireland, a cubit arm ppr, grasping a trumpet sa *Certavi et vici*

Thunder, James William Thomas, Bellewstown House, Drogheda same crest and motto

Thunder, Michael Harman D'Alton, Seneschalstown, co. Meath, same crest and motto.

Thunder, Patrick, J.P., Lagore, Dunshaughlin, co. Meath, same crest and motto.

Thurburn of Murtle, Aberdeensh., and London, a dexter arm in armour embowed, the hand throwing a dart ppr. *Certo dirigo ictu.* 198. 4

Thurburn, same crest. *Thor me mittit amico.* 198. 4

Thurcle, a cubit arm erect ppr., vested gu., cuffed arg., holding in the hand a fleur-de-lis or.

Thurgryn, a pelican in her piety or, the nest arg. 98. 8

Thurkettle of Kelvedon Hatch, Essex, a cubit arm erect vested arg., charged with a fleur-de-lis gu., holding in the hand ppr. a fleur-de-lis or.

Thurkill of London, an arm erect vested gu., charged with three fleurs-de-lis arg., holding in the hand ppr. a fleur-de-lis or.

Thurland of Gainston, Notts, Reigate, Surrey, and Yorks, a Capuchin friar's head couped at the shoulders ppr., vested arg. 192. 3

Thurlby or **Thurley** of London and Northamp., a demi-dragon vert with wings addorsed sa., holding between the paws an escallop arg.

Thurlow, Baron (Hovell-Thurlow-Cumming-Bruce), of Thurlow, Suff.: (1) On a cap of maintenance ppr., a dexter arm in armour from the shoulder resting on the elbow, also ppr., the hand holding a sceptre erect or, with the motto over it, *Fuimus* (*for Bruce*). (2) A lion rampant or, holding in the dexter fore-paw a dagger ppr., and the motto over, *Courage* (*for Cumming*). (3) A raven ppr. gorged with a chain and pendant therefrom a portcullis arg., having the motto over, *Justitiæ soror fides* (*for Thurlow*). (4) A greyhound couchant or, collared, and the line reflexed over the back sa., with the motto over, *Quo fata vocant* (*for Hovell*).

Thurlow, Suff., a raven ppr., a portcullis hanging round the neck by a chain or.

Thurlow, a parrot holding in the dexter claw a pear ppr. 101. 13

Thurlow of Burnham Overy, Norf., an anchor gu., cabled or. 161. 2

Thursby, Yorks, seven arrows, one in pale and six in saltier, ppr. 173. 7

Thursby, Harvey- of Abbington Abbey, Northamp., a lion rampant sa., supporting a battle-axe erect or.

Thursby, Shropsh., same crest.

Thursby, Sir John Ormerod Scarlett, Bart., J.P., of Ormerod House, Lancs, and Holmhurst, co. Southampton, a lion rampant sa., holding a battle-axe erect or. *In silentio fortitudino.*

Thursby, Rev. Herbert Edward, Castle Rising Rectory, King's Lynn, Norf., same crest.

Thursby, Sir John Hardy, Bart., J.P., 37, Ennismore Gardens, S.W., same crest.

Thursby-Pelham, James Augustine Harvey, Harnage House, Cound, Shrewsbury: (1) A peacock in his pride arg. (2) A curlew with wings expanded arg., beak and legs ppr. *Vincit amor patriæ.—In silentio fortitudo.*

Thursfield, Shropsh., a horse's head erased. *Certavi et vici.* 51. 4

Thursfield, Thomas William, M.D., J.P., Selwood, Leamington, same crest and motto.

Thursfield, Alfred Spencer, Esquire, of Lea House, Kidderminster, a horse's head erased between two crescents, and holding in the mouth a trefoil slipped. *Certavi et vigi.*

Thurston of Cranbrook, Kent, a demi-griffin segreant vert, issuing from a plume of ostrich-feathers arg. *Thrust on.* 64. 9

Thurston, Suff., a stork arg., legged az. 105. 11

Thurston, Basset, Esquire, a stork ppr, resting the dexter claw upon a mullet of six points or, surmounted by a rainbow issuing from the clouds, also ppr. 233. 13

Thurstone of Elstone, Hunts, a wolf's head or, pierced through the neck by an arrow gu., headed and feathered arg., vulned of the second. 29. 6

Thurwall of Thurwall, Northumb., on a chapeau gu., turned up erm., a boar's head couped at the neck arg. *cf.* 42. 5

Thurxton of Thruxton, Worcs., a pelican in her piety arg., beaked, legged, and vulned gu., the nest and young ppr. 98. 8

Thwaites, Ireland, a chevalier on horseback at full speed, holding a broken spear ppr. 189. 5

Thwaites, late Daniel, Esquire, J.P., D.L., M.P., of Freeby, Leics., Billinge Scarr and Woodfold Park, Lancs, and Addison Lodge, Middx., the battlements of a tower surmounted by a sheaf of seven arrows ppr., banded together gu., between two branches of oak vert.

Thwaites of Marston, Yorks, a cock with wings addorsed ppr., combed, wattled, and legged gu. *cf.* 91. 7

Thwaites, Bucks, and of Newland Hall, Essex, a cock with wings elevated sa., combed, wattled, and legged gu *cf.* 91. 7

Thwaites of Redmerstone, Derbysh., a hind's head erased ppr. 124. 3

Thwaits, on a mural coronet a bundle of seven arrows ppr., banded gu.

Thwaytes, Yorks, and Chipping Wycombe, Bucks, a gamecock ppr., beaked, wattled, and charged on the breast with a fleur-de-lis gu. *cf.* 90. 2

Thweng, a pelican in her piety, all ppr. 98. 8

Thyly, of Lynn, Norf., an escallop or. 141. 12

Thynne, *see* Bath, Marquess of.

Thynne, Baron Carteret, *see* Carteret.

Thynne, Shropsh., a reindeer or. *J'ai bonne cause.* *cf.* 125. 9

Thynne, Charles Ernest, Esquire, 104, Queen's Gate, S.W., same crest.

Thynne, Rev. Arthur Christopher, M.A., Penstowe, Kilkhampton, North Cornw., a reindeer statant or, collared sa. *J'ay bonne cause.*

Thynne, Major-General Reginald Thomas, Guard's Club, same crest.

Thynne, Beds, a squirrel sejant feeding on a nut, all ppr. *Loyal devoir.* 135. 7

Tibbet, a demi-lion ppr. *Vincere vel mori.* 10. 2

Tibbett, a demi-cat rampant gardant az. 26. 12

Tibbitts, a bee in pale sa. *Per industriam.* 137. 2

Tibbits, John Borlace Maunsell, of Barton Segrave, Northants: (1) A demi-cat rampant gardant az. (*for Tibbits*). 26. 12. (2) A falcon rising ppr. (*for Maunsell*). 88. 2

Tibbs, an oak-branch vert. 151. 3

Tichborne, Baron Ferrard (*extinct*), on a chapeau gu., turned up erm., a demi-vol erect per fesse or and vair. *Pugna pro patria.*

Tichborne, Doughty-, Sir Henry Alfred Joseph, Bart., of Tichborne, Hants: (1) A hind's head couped ppr., between a pair of wings gu. (*for Tichborne*). (2) A cubit arm erect vested per pale crenellé or and arg., thereon a Maltese cross gu., cuffed of the first, holding in the hand ppr. a mullet of six points sa., pierced or (*for Doughty*). (3) On a cap of maintenance a wing erect, charged with the arms of Tichborne, viz., vair, a chief or. (*This last crest is said to pertain by right to the eldest son, and has been so borne from temp. Edward III.*) *Pugna pro patria.*

Tickel or **Tickell,** an eagle displayed ppr. 75. 2

Tickell of London, an arm couped below the elbow and erect vested gu., charged with three fleurs-de-lis or, cuffed arg., holding in the hand ppr. a like fleur-de-lis.

Tickell, Major Edward James, D.S.O., the Lypiatts, Cheltenham, same crest.

Tickhill, a cubit arm erect vested gu., charged with three fleurs-de-lis arg., holding in the hand ppr. a fleur-de-lis or.

Tidbury, the point of a spear in pale surmounted by the shaft and hilt in saltier ppr., banded gu. 175. 2

Tidcastle of London, a leopard statant ppr., resting the dexter paw on an escutcheon or. *cf.* 24. 5

Tidcombe of Estcot, Wilts, a dexter cubit arm in armour ppr., garnished or, holding in the hand a broken lance gu.

Tiddeman or **Tideman,** a savage's head couped distilling drops of blood ppr.

Tiderleigh of Tiderleigh, Dorset, a wolf passant erm. 28. 10

100. 11

Tidman, Arthur, Esquire, M.A., Chislehurst, Kent, a Moor's head affronté wreathed, couped and distilling blood. *Vaglia il vero.*

Tidmarsh, a broken lance, the head turned towards the sinister ppr. 175. 6

Tidswell, Richard Henry, 49, Wilton Crescent, S.W., a demi-lion rampant per pale nebuly or and az., holding in the dexter paw a cross moline, and resting the sinister upon an escallop of the last. *Certum pete finem.* 260. 15

Tidswell, Robert Ingham, J.P., D.L., Haresfield Court, Stonehouse, Glouc., same crest.

Tierney, an oak tree ppr 143 5
Tierney, Bart (*extinct*), of Brighthelmstone, Sussex, on a mount vert, a pheasant ppr, ducally gorged or cf 90 8
Tierney of Limerick, Ireland, a pheasant ppr cf 90 8
Tiffin, a greyhound's head erased, holding in the mouth a stag's foot erased ppr 61 5
Tiffin of Whitrigg, Cumb, a demi lion rampant gu gorged with a collar flory counterflory or, supporting a battle axe ppr *Patriæ fidelis*
Tighe, Ireland, a wolf's head erased ppr, gorged with a collar arg, charged with a cross crosslet sa *Summum nec metuam diem nec optem* cf 30 11
Tighe of Mitchelstown, Ireland · (1) Same crest as above (*for Tighe*) cf 30 11 (2) A stag's head (*for Morgan*) 121 5
Tighe, Lieutenant-Colonel, J P, of Rossanagh Ashford, Wicklow, Ireland, a wolf's head erased ppr, gorged with a collar az, thereon a cross crosslet or between two bezants *Summum nec metuam diem nec optem* 30 4
Tighe-Bunbury, Daniel Esquire J P, D L, of Rossana co Wicklow Ireland (1) Two swords saltirewise passing through the mouth of a leopard's face all ppr (*for Bunbury*) 22 7 (2) A wolf's head erased ppr, gorged with a collar az, thereon a cross crosslet or, between two bezants (*for Tighe*) *Firmum in vita nihil —Summum nec metuam diem nec optem* 30 4
Tighe, Ireland, a galley, her oars in saltier sa 160 10
Tilghman-Huskisson of Easham, Sussex (1) An elephant's head erased arg guttee de-sang, pierced in the neck by an arrow ppr (*for Huskisson*) cf 133 3 (2) A lion sejant sa, crowned or (*for Tilghman*) *Spes alit agricolam* cf 8 8
Till, an ounce sejant ppr, resting the dexter fore-paw on an escutcheon az
Tillard, Kent, an esquire's helmet ppr, garnished or 180 3
Tillard of Godmanchester Hunts, out of a ducal coronet or, a griffin's head az, ears and beak or (*This is the crest of West, borne since an intermarriage with that family in 1726, the Tillard crest being a death's head*)
Tillard, Charles, upon a mount vert a dexter hand couped grasping a mascle in bend sinister sa *Audi, vide, sile* 233 14
Tillard, George Henry, same crest and motto
Tillard, Major General John Arthur C B, Caerlaverock, Ootacamond, Madras, same crest and motto
Tillard, Philip Edward J P, the Holme, Godmanchester, Hunts, same crest and motto
Tillard, Philip Francis, R N, Stocken Hall Oakham, Rutl, same crest and motto
Tillard, Richard same crest and motto
Tillard, Rev Richard Henry, the Rectory, Blakeney Thetford, same crest and motto
Tillard, Rev Robert Mowbray, M A, the Rectory Tittleshall, Norf, same crest and motto
Tillard, Rev James, the Glebe Penshurst Kent, out of a ducal coronet a griffin's head
Tiller, on a mural coronet six spears in saltier ppr 175 8
Tiller, Middx, a demi-cat rampant arg 26 11
Tillet or **Tillett**, six arrows in saltier ppr, banded gu, ensigned with a round hat of the first 173 10
Tilley, the head of a battle axe issuing 172 1
Tilley, Hon Sir Samuel Leonard, C B, K C M G, P C, of Fredericton and St Andrews, New Brunswick, Canada, *uses* · the head of a battle-axe issuing from the wreath ppr 172 1
Tilley, a cockatrice's head couped arg, beaked, combed, and wattled gu cf 68 12
Tillney, Norf a griffin's head erased gu, eared or, holding in the beak a gem ring of the same
Tillotson, Yorks and Kent, out of a mural coronet a greyhound's head all ppr cf 61 6
Tillotson, a pelican's head erased ppr 98 2
Tillstone, Rogers-, of Moulescombe Place, near Brighton Sussex (1) A mount vert, thereon a bear's head couped arg murally gorged gu, encircled by a chaplet of roses ppr (*for Tillstone*) (2) An eagle displayed with two heads or, charged on the breast and on each wing with a crescent, and holding in either beak a saltier gu (*for Rogers*) *Dat Deus incrementum*
Tilly, a rose-tree vert, bearing roses arg 149 8
Tilney, George, Esquire late of Watts House, Bishops Lydeard Taunton Somers, in front of a mount vert the battlements of a tower ppr therefrom a griffin's head gu, issuant from leaves alternately arg and az *Sperando spiro* 258 20
Tilney of Wisbeach, Cambs and Norf, a griffin's head erased gu 66 2
Tilney, Norman Eccles, 8, Attwood Road, S W in front of a mount vert the battlements of a tower ppr therefrom a griffin's head gu issuant from leaves alternately arg and az *Sperando spiro* 258 20
Tilsley, a pelican in her piety or *Ne cede malis sed contra* 98 14
Tilson and **Tilston** of Huxleigh Chesh, out of a mural coronet a bear's head, all ppr cf 34 14
Tilson, a dexter hand plucking a rose ppr 218 13
Tilson and **Tilston**, an arm embowed vested arg, ruffled of the last, holding in the hand ppr a crosier gu, the head and point or
Tilson, Ireland out of a ducal coronet or, a bull's head sa armed of the first *Fugit irreparabile tempus* 44 11
Tilyard, Norf, a lion's head erased sa gorged with a collar vert rimmed or, charged with five ermine-spots arg cf 18 6
Timbrell, a phœnix in flames ppr 82 2
Timbrell, in front of a tilting spear erect two swords in saltire points upwards, ppr, pommels and hilts or 169 7
Timewell, a demi eagle gu with wings expanded erm ducally crowned and gorged with a chaplet or
Timins a rose gu, barbed vert, seeded or 149 2
Timmins, a dexter cubit arm holding in the hand a pair of scales, all ppr 217 13
Timmins, on a mural coronet arg, six spears in saltier sa 175 8
Timporin, Herts, on a mount vert a greyhound couchant arg, resting the fore-paws on an escutcheon of the first, charged with a fess wavy az, thereon three etoiles or
Timpson of Exeter Devonsh and Ireland, on a piece of battlement arg, an eagle rising ppr, holding in the beak an oak-slip vert, fructed or 76 10
Tims, a goat's head couped 128 12
Timson, a horse's head gu bridled or 51 5
Tindal-Carill-Worsley, *see* Worsley
Tindal, a dexter hand holding a writing pen 217 10
Tindal of Dickleburgh, Norf a hand ppr, holding a cross of five mascles gu
Tindal of the Manor House, Aylesbury Bucks, in front of five ostrich-feathers arg, a fleur-de lis az, between two crescents gu *Nosce teipsum* 250 2
Tindal, Charles Frederick, same crest and motto
Tindal, Charles Grant, Fir Grove, Winchfield, Hants, same crest and motto
Tindall, a demi lion rampant supporting a garb 12 5
Tindall, Norf, a lion's gamb erect or, holding a cross of five mascles gu
Tindall or **Tindale**, Suff and Norf out of a ducal coronet or, a plume of five ostrich feathers arg 114 13
Tindall, Sussex out of a ducal coronet or, a plume of feathers erm, within a basket gu
Tingey, John Cottingham, Esquire, 31, Surrey Street, Norwich, a griffin's head couped between two wings sa, beaked gu
Tinker, a cross crosslet az. 165 2
Tinker, a griffin passant 63 2
Tinkler, a cross moline az 165 3
Tinline of Adelaide South Australia, a dexter hand holding an ear of wheat ppr *Pax et copia* 218 14
Tinling, an ear of wheat or, bladed vert, and a palm-branch of the last in saltier 154 10
Tinney of Salisbury Wilts, a griffin's head couped, the wings elevated sa, beaked gu cf 67 11
Tipper, a hand couped in fess holding a sword erect, and on the point a garland of laurel cf 221 7
Tippet, a garb or, banded vert 153 2
Tippet of Truro and Falmouth, Cornw, a cubit arm vested, charged with a cross crosslet arg, holding in the hand an anchor by the middle of the shank *Non robore sed spe* cf 208 3
Tippets, a squirrel sejant gu, cracking a nut or 135 7
Tippetts, Devonsh, an eagle's claw erased ppr cf 113 8

Tipping, Bart. (*extinct*), of Wheatfield, Oxon., on a ducal coronet or, an antelope's head erased vert, attired gu., maned of the first.

Tipping of Bolton and Boldhall, Lancs, an antelope's head erased vert, ducally gorged and attired or. *cf.* 126. 2

Tipping, William Fearon, Esquire, J.P., of Brasted Place, Kent, out of a ducal coronet or, a heraldic antelope's head ppr. *Vive ut vivas.*

Tipping of Merton, Oxon., out of a ducal coronet or, an antelope's head vert, attired gu., maned of the first.

Tipping, Gartside-, Henry Thomas, Quarr Wood Lodge, Isle of Wight, an antelope's head erased vert, ducally gorged or.

Tipping, a cubit arm in armour erect ppr., garnished or, holding in the hand a truncheon sa., tipped of the second.

Tipping of Beaulieu, Louth, an arm in armour holding in the hand ppr. a sceptre or.

Tiptoft, Norf., a stag's head erased or, gorged with a garland of roses gu., leaved vert.

Tirrell of Reigate, Surrey, Thornton, Bucks, Gepynge, Suff., and Heron and Springfield, Essex, a boar's head erect arg., and issuing out of the mouth a peacock's tail ppr.

Tirrey of London, out of a mural coronet or, a dragon's head vert, vomiting flames ppr., collared and lined of the first.

Tirrey or **Tirry** of London, Herts, and Heref., a demi-roebuck ppr., attired and ungu. or, holding in the mouth three ears of corn bladed of the first. *cf.* 119. 2

Tirringham, Bucks, a talbot's head gu., billettée or. *cf.* 56. 5

Tirwhit, Lincs, a savage ppr., wreathed about the head and loins vert, holding over his dexter shoulder a club or. *Me stante, virebunt.*

Tirwhit, Hunts, a lapwing's head and neck or.

Tisdale or **Tisdall**, a peacock's head couped ppr. 103. 2

Tisdall, Charlesfort, co. Meath, out of a ducal coronet or, an armed hand erect arg., charged with a pellet, holding an arrow ppr. *Tutantur tela coronam.*

Tison or **Tyson** of Woodland Green, Glouc., a sinister arm in mail or, the hand ppr. defended by an antique shield or, lined vert, with straps gu. 194. 8

Titchfield, Marquess of, *see* Portland, Duke of.

Titford, a demi-lion rampant. 10. 2

Titley and Titteley of Titteley, Shropsh., between two laurel-branches vert, an escallop or.

Titterton, an oak-tree ppr. 143. 5

Tittle, David Ross, Esquire, M.A., and Isaac Tittle, Esquire, M.A., LL.D., on a mural coronet ppr., a lion rampant or, collared gu., and charged on the shoulder with an escallop sa. *In te Domine speravi.*

Titus of Bushby, Herts, a Moor's head couped at the shoulders ppr., the temples wreathed arg. and az. 192. 13

Tiverton of Towerhurst, Leeds, on a mount a stag courant regardant, all ppr. *Forward.*

Tivitoe of London, a demi-Turk affrontée vested ppr., holding in the dexter hand a scimitar arg., hilt and pommel or. *Vigilo et spero.*

Tizard, Hawkins-, of Winterborne St. Martin, Dorset: (1) On a ducal coronet or, between two wings gu., a bugle-horn stringed of the first (*for Tizard*). (2) Out of a mural coronet a cubit arm erect vested az., cuffed gu., charged with a fleur-de-lis or, holding in the hand ppr. a baton, also or, tipped sa. (*for Hawkins*). *Ne timeas recte faciendo.*

Tobin, two battle-axes in pale environed by a serpent ppr. 172. 6

Tobin of Ballincollig, co. Cork, Ireland, on a mount vert, a falcon rising ppr., belled or, and charged on each wing with a nettle-leaf pointing downwards, also ppr. *Noli me tangere.*

Tobin of Cumpshinagh, co. Tipperary, Ireland, a demi-lion gu., holding between the paws an oak-branch ppr.

Tobin, Richard F., Esquire, 60, Stephen's Green East, Dublin, on a mount vert, a falcon rising with wings expanded and inverted ppr., belled or, charged on each wing with a nettle-leaf pointing downwards, also ppr.

Toby, a perch's head issuing ppr.

Tod, Scotland, a fox's head ppr. *Vigilantia.* 33. 4

Tod, Scotland, a fox rampant ppr. *Oportet vivere.*

Tod, Ireland, a fleur-de-lis or. 148. 2

Tod-Mercer of Scotsbank, Selkirksh., and Hope Park, Edinburgh, a cross patée fitchée gu. *Crux Christi mea corona.* 166. 3

Todcastle of London, a leopard statant ppr., resting the dexter paw on an escutcheon or. *cf.* 24. 5

Todd, *see* Wilson-Todd.

Todd, a fox statant ppr., collared, and a chain therefrom reflexed over the back or, supporting with the dexter paw an escutcheon sa., charged with an étoile of the second. 32. 4

Todd of Sturmer, Essex, a fox sejant ppr. 32. 11

Todd, a fox's head couped gu. *Oportet vivere.* 33. 4

Todd-Thornton, Captain James Henry, of Westbrook, co. Donegal, J.P.: (1) A griffin's head erased sa., beaked and collared or, charged on the neck with an escarbuncle of the last (*for Thornton*). (2) A pelican in her piety (*for Patterson*). (3) A fox passant ppr., charged on the shoulder with a torteau (*for Todd*), and over this second crest the motto, *Faire sans dire. Nec temere nec timide.—I die for those I love.* *cf.* 32. 1

Todd of Tranby, Yorks, on a chapeau gu., turned up erm., a fox sejant ppr., *Oportet vivere.* 32. 12

Todd, Northumb., a fox's head erased ppr. 33. 6

Todd of Bray, Berks, a fox's head or, collared flory counterflory gu. *cf.* 33. 4

Todd, a fox courant with a goose over his back, all ppr.

Todd of Belsize House, Hampstead, a mount vert, thereon a fox sejant ppr., resting the dexter fore-paw on a roundle per pale az. and gu., gorged with a collar, and a chain reflexed therefrom or, the chain attached to the pommel of a sword erect on the sinister side of the fox, the point downwards, also ppr. 32. 7

Todd, John Spencer Brydges, Esquire, C.M.G., 24, Cathcart Road, South Kensington, same crest.

Todd, Robert, Harts, Olveston, Glouc., in front of the stump of an oak-tree a mount, and thereon a fox sejant ppr., charged on the shoulder with a mascle gu. *Vigilans.*

Todhunter, late Isaac, Esquire, M.A., F.R.S., St. John's College, Cambs, in front of a gate sa., a foxhound current ppr.

Todman, a cannon mounted ppr. 169. 12

Todrick, Scotland, a griffin's head erased gu. 66. 2

Todrig, Scotland, a sword in pale ppr. 170. 2

Toft or **Tofte**, a phœnix in flames ppr. 82. 2

Toke, Kent, a fox current or. *cf.* 32. 8

Toke, John Leslie, of Goddington, Kent: (1) A griffin's head erased per chevron arg. and sa., guttée counterchanged, holding in the beak a tuck or sword ppr., hilt and pommel or. *cf.* 66. 10. (2) By augmentation, a fox current ppr. *cf.* 32. 8

Toke, Rev. Nicholas Roundel, same crests. *Militia mea multiplex.*

Toke or **Tokey**, Worcs., an ibex's head az., tufted and collared gemel or, langued gu.

Toker of Ospringe, Kent, a heart gu., enfiled by a ducal coronet or, between two branches of palm ppr. *Providentia tutamen.* *cf.* 181. 14

Toker, Major-General A. C., C.B., the Grange, Lansdowne Road, Bedford, a heart gu., encircled by a ducal coronet arg., between two palm-branches ppr. *Providentia tutamen.*

Tokett, a Paschal lamb couchant ppr., the pennon charged with a cross gu. *En Dieu est ma fiance.*

Tolcarne of Tolcarne, Cornw., a wolf sejant arg., gorged with a spiked collar lined and ringed or.

Tolcher, Edward Henry Archer, Primrose Club, London, a dexter arm embowed couped above the elbow, vested az., cuffed arg., the hand ppr. grasping a ragged staff erect of the second charged with two martlets sa.

Toler, *see* Norbury, Earl of.

Toler-Aylward of Shankhill Castle, co. Kilkenny: (1) Out of a ducal coronet or, a dexter arm embowed vested az., cuffed arg., the hand ppr. holding an anchor of the first (*for Aylward*). (2) Out of a mural coronet ppr., a fleur-de-lis or, charged with an ermine spot sa. (*for Toler*). *Verus et fidelis semper.*

Toler-Rowley, Frederick Pelham, Esquire, of 45, Lefevre Terrace, North Adelaide, South Australia, a wolf's head erased sa., collared bendy or and gu. *La Vertue surmonte tout obstacle.*

Tolhurst, Alfred, Esquire, of Gravesend, Kent, upon a mount vert, a wolf regardant sa., collared or, resting the dexter fore-paw on a bell of the last. *Ne cede malis.* 28. 9

Tolhurst, John, J P, Glenbrook, Beckenham, Kent, a cubit arm in armour ppr, between on the dexter side a decrescent and on the sinister side an increscent sa the hand ppr grasping a bull's head erased sa *Alta pete* 304 10

Toll of Perridge, Devonsh, a boar's head erect cf 43 3

Toll or Tolle, a hand couped holding a dagger erect ppr 212. 9

Tollemache, *see* Dysart Earl of

Tollemache, Baron (Tollemache), Helmingham Hall, Suff, a horse's head erased arg, between two wings or, pellettee *Confido conquiesco* cf 51 3

Tollemache, Rev Algernon Edward, same crest

Tollemache, Henry James, J P., 42 Half Moon Street W, same crest and motto

Toller, a mullet gu, charged with an ermine spot or cf 164 2

Toller of Fowey, Cornw, between two wings or, a cinquefoil arg

Tollet of Betley Hall, Staffs, a pyramid on a pedestal arg, the top entwined by a serpent descending ppr *Prudentia in adversis*

Tolley or Tollye, a demi tiger vert, bezantée, collared arg, pellettee

Tolley, an acorn stalked and leaved vert 152 1

Tolliott, a lion rampant per pale arg and gu 1 13

Tolman, two arms in armour embowed wielding a battle axe, all ppr 194 12

Tolson of Bridekirke Cumb, and Woodland Lodge Somers, out of a ducal coronet or a lion's gamb holding two ostrich feathers, the one vert and the other az *Ferro comite*

Tolson, Legh, Dalton Huddersfield, Yorks in front of a demi-tower issuant therefrom a bear's paw grasping four ostrich-feathers in bend sinister arg, an annulet or *Ferro comite*

Tom of Little Petherick, a Cornish chough ppr, holding in its beak an escallop arg

Tomb, between two wings a pegasus' head 51 3

Tombs, S John, Esquire, of the Hollies Droitwich, a tower ppr *Hic jacet quod mortale fuit requiescat in pace*

Tomes or Toms, a Cornish chough volant ppr

Tomkins, out of a ducal coronet a broken battle axe, all ppr cf 172 7

Tomkins of Webley, Heref, a lion rampant or, holding a broken tilting-spear arg

Tomkinson of Reaseheath, Chesh, a wolf's head erased arg, ducally gorged or cf 30 8

Tomkinson, Michael, Franche Hall, near Kidderminster, in front of a cross flory gu a wolf's head erased arg, gorged with a collar flory counterflory, also gu *Sperans pergo* 250 10

Tomlin of Dane Court, Kent, two battle-axes in saltier ppr, surcharged with a dexter hand couped at the wrist, also ppr *Quondam his vicimus armis*

Tomlin, Edward Locke Esquire, of Angley Park, Cranbrook, same crest and motto

Tomlin, out of a mural coronet or, a martlet arg., holding in the beak an oak-branch vert fructed or

Tomlin, a peacock's head erased az, beaked or 103 1

Tomline, Pretyman-, Bart, N S, two lion's gambs erased ppr, supporting a mullet or

Tomlins, Middx and Sussex, on a mount vert a vine stem couped at the top and leaved ppr, on the stem an escutcheon arg 145 3

Tomlins, out of a mural coronet seven Lochaber axes turned outwards ppr cf 172 2

Tomlinson, *see* Paget Tomlinson

Tomlinson, out of a ducal coronet or, a griffin s head arg *Non sibi patriæ*

Tomlinson of Birdford and Huddersfield Yorks, a savage wreathed about the loins ppr, holding in both hands a spear headed at each end or

Tomlinson, Thomas, Esquire on a mount vert, a savage ppr, wreathed about the temples arg and sa charged upon the breast with a cross crosslet gu, and across the sinister shoulder a bear's skin, and holding with both hands in bend a spear headed at either end, also ppr 311 9

Tomlinson, Sir William Edward Murray, Bart of Heysham House, Lancs, and of Richmond Terrace, Whitehall, London, on a mount vert a savage ppr wreathed about the temples arg and sa, charged on the breast with a cross crosslet gu, across the sinister shoulder a bearskin, and holding with both hands in bend a spear headed at either end, also ppr *Propositi tenax* 311 9

Tompkins, a ship under sail ppr 160 13

Tompkins of Monington Heref, and Arundel, Sussex a unicorn's head erased per fess arg and or, armed and maned counterchanged, and gorged with a laurel wreath vert. cf 49. 5

Tompkinson, Lancs, a wolf's head erased arg, ducally gorged or cf 30 8

Tompson of Witchingham Hall, Norf, on a mount vert, a demi lion rampant gardant or cf 10 8

Tompson, a palm-branch slipped ppr 147 1

Toms of St Mary-le bone, Middx., a Cornish chough ppr charged on the breast with a bezant cf 107 14

Toms, a Cornish chough volant ppr

Toncks or Tonkes, two arms in armour embowed issuing from clouds supporting the sun ppr

Tonge-de-Tonge, Asheton-, Henri, Esquire, of Chateau du Ragotin, Avranches, France, in front of an arm embowed in armour, the hand ppr grasping a grappling iron in bend sinister sa., a lion sejant of the last pierced in the sinister shoulder with an arrow ppr *Tenebo* 197 13

Tonge, Christopher J P, Clairville Grove Studios, Kensington same crest.

Tonge, Henry Asheton 16, Quain Mansions Queen's Club Gardens, West Kensington same crest

Tonge, Reginald Arthur Buluwayo Club Buluwayo, South Africa same crest

Tonge, Richard, Staneclyffe, Disley, Chesh, same crest. *Retineo vi leonis*

Tonge, William Asheton, Staneclyffe Disley, Chesh, same crest and motto

Tonge, Captain F H, Highway, Calne, Wilts, on a rock ppr, a martlet rising or *Steady*

Tongue, Ireland on an oak tree a nest with three young ravens fed with the dew of heaven distilling from a cloud, all ppr

Tongue, an escutcheon or between two myrtle-branches in orle ppr

Tonkin, Cornw, a Cornish chough ppr 107 14

Tonkin of Trevannance and Hendra, Cornw, and Devonsh, an eagle's head erased or 83 2

Tonkin of Plymouth, Devonsh, a dragon's head couped *Kensol Tra Tonkein Ouna Dieu Mathern yn* 71 1

Tonson, Baron Riversdale, *see* Riversdale

Tonson of Dunkettle, co Cork, Ireland, out of a mural coronet or, a cubit arm in armour, holding in the gauntlet a sword, all ppr, hilt and pommel or

Tonson, Ireland, out of a mural coronet or, a dexter arm in armour couped at the elbow ppr, brandishing a sword arg, pommel and hilt of the first *Manus hæc inimica tyrannis*

Tonson, three cross crosslets, one in pale and two in saltire, gu, surmounted of an escallop or

Tonstall of Tonstall and Thurland Castle Lancs, a cock arg combed, wattled and legged or, holding in the beak a scroll with the motto *Droit*

Tonyn, a dexter hand holding a sword in pale ppr 212 9

Toogood, an armed hand holding a caltrap ppr

Took or Tooke, a griffin's head erased per chevron arg and sa guttée counterchanged, eared or, holding in the beak a sword erect arg, hilted gu pommelled or, the hilt resting on the wreath

Tooke, *see* Hales Tooke

Tooke, a griffin's head erased sa, holding in the beak by the middle of the blade a sword arg, pommel downwards cf 66 12

Tooke of Hurston Clays, Sussex, a griffin's head erased sa, holding in the beak a sword point upwards, ppr *Militia mea multiplex* cf 66. 12

Tooke, Norf, a griffin's head erased sa., charged on the neck with two bendlets arg, and holding in the beak a sword in pale point upwards, arg, pommel and hilt or 66. 12

Tooker, Somers a whale's head haurient erased sa, charged with a mascle arg *Mirabile in profundis.* cf 139 8

Tooker, a spur-rowel or 164. 8

Tooker, a human heart enfiled with a ducal coronet cf 181 2

Tooker or Tucker, Bart of Maddington, Wilts, a heart gu, enfiled with a ducal coronet or *Tout cœur* cf 181 2

Tooky, Northamp. and of South Luffenham, Rutl a demi-sea-horse rampant quarterly gu and or, gorged with a ducal coronet per pale counterchanged cf 46 7

Toole, Ireland, a lion's head erased gu *Spero* 17 2

Tooley or Towley, within an annulet or, an escutcheon sa. cf 167 6

Toone, a lion's head erased, holding in the mouth a hand couped ppr.

Toone of London, issuing out of an Eastern coronet or, an eagle's head az., semée of mullets of the first.

Tooth of Park Farm, Sevenoaks, Kent, a gryphon segreant gu., semée of mullets, and holding in the sinister claw a feather arg. *Perseverantia palmam obtinebit.* 62. 1

Tooth of Swifts, Cranbrook, Kent, a griffin segreant gu., semée of mullets, and holding in the sinister claw an ostrich-feather arg. *Perseverantia palmam obtinebit.* 62. 1

Toovey, Oxon., on a mount vert, a stag current arg., pierced through the neck by an arrow in fess, the pheon to the dexter ppr., vulned gu.

Topham of Lincoln's Inn, Middx., and Yorks, an anchor cabled and a sword in saltier ppr. 169. 9

Topham of Middleham Hall, Yorks, two serpents vert, entwined round a cross patée fitched or. *Cruce non prudentia.*

Topham of Caldberg, Yorks, same crest. *Ut vivas vigila.*

Topliffe of Somerby, Lincs, a talbot sejant arg., collared or. 55. 1

Topp of Stockton, Wilts, Devonsh., Shropsh., and Glouc., a gauntlet grasping a hand couped at the wrist, all ppr.

Topp, Bart. (*extinct*), of Tormanton, Glouc., a gauntlet clasped grasping a hand couped at the wrist, all ppr.

Topp of Whitton, Shropsh., a gauntlet clasped grasping a naked hand couped at the wrist and embrued, all ppr.

Topper, a man's head issuing in profile ppr., banded or and gu., tied of the colours. 190. 4

Topping, two lion's gambs sa., supporting a roundle vair. 39. 4

Topsfield, Suff. and Norf., a talbot couchant gardant in front of a tree, all ppr.

Torbock, Staffs, and of Torbeck, Lancs, an eagle close ppr., beaked and legged gu., charged on the breast with a mullet arg. *cf.* 76. 2

Torbock, Joseph, Esquire, of Crakenthorpe Hall, Appleby, Westml., an eagle close ppr., beaked and legged gu., charged on the breast with a mullet arg. *In cœlo spes mea est.*

Torbock, a parrot holding in its dexter claw a pear ppr. 101. 13

Toriano of London, an arm in armour from the shoulder in fess, and from the elbow in pale, holding in the hand a helmet. 198. 1

Toriano of London, an eagle displayed sa. 75. 2

Toriu, an eagle's head erased arg. 83. 2

Torings, a martlet between two laurel-branches in orle.

Torkington of Stoughton, Hunts, a spur-rowel between two wings or.

Torlesse, Berks, a stork ppr. 105. 11

Torleste, a heron or, between two branches vert.

Torley, a boar's head couped in fess sa., armed arg. 43. 1

Torney of Bockhill, Kent, a bull's head erased arg., armed and collared or. *cf.* 44. 2

Torphichen, Baron (Sandilands), of Torpichen, West Lothian: (1) An eagle displayed ppr. (2) A plume of three ostrich-feathers. *Spero meliora.* — *Jamais arrière.* 75. 2

Torr of Riby, Lincs, upon a headland ppr., a tower arg. *Altiora spero.* 156. 3

Torr, a griffin passant with wings addorsed ppr. 63. 2

Torr, Rev. William Edward, Carlett Park, Eastham, upon a mount amidst fern ppr., a gryphon passant, wings elevated per pale or and arg., supporting with the dexter claw a mullet of six points sa. *Turris fortissima Deus.*

Torr, Captain Herbert James, same crest and motto.

Torranee, Scotland, a bull's head erased. *I saved the king.* 44. 3

Torre, John James, of Snydale, Yorks, a griffin passant per pale or and arg. *Turris fortissima Deus.* 63. 2

Torre, a lily arg., leaved vert. 151. 2

Torrell, Cambs, a boar's head erased or. 42. 2

Torrenee, two laurel-branches in saltier vert.

Torrens, a martlet or. 95. 2

Torrens, Ireland, a martlet sa., gorged with a collar or, pendant therefrom an escutcheon erm., charged with a candlestick, also or. *Deus lumen meum.*

Torrens, between two branches of laurel ppr., a martlet sa., around the neck a ribbon gu., fimbriated az., therefrom pendent a representation of the gold medal presented to Major-General Sir Henry Torrens, K.C.B., by command of His Majesty King George IV. *Deus lumen meum.*

Torrie, a horse's head arg. *cf.* 50. 13

Torrin of Kelvedon, a griffin's head erased sa. 66. 2

Torrings, a dove between two branches of laurel fructed ppr. 92. 12

Torrington (Byng), Votes Court, Mereworth, Maidstone, a heraldic antelope statant erm., attired, tusked, maned, and ungu. or. *Tuebor.* *cf.* 127. 5

Torvers, a griffin passant. 63. 2

Torway, Ireland, two lion's gambs erect gu., holding a cross flory fitchée arg. *Non nobis nascimur.*

Tory or **Torry,** a horse passant ppr., furnished gu. 52. 4

Tosh and **Tose,** Scotland, a thistle ppr. *Ad finem.* *cf.* 150. 2

Tosh, Scotland, a withered branch of holly sprouting new leaves ppr. 145. 10

Toshach of Monzievaird, Perthsh., on a sinister hand issuing, a falcon rising, all ppr. *Maha an toshach.*

Tot, a demi-lion ppr. 10. 2

Tothill of Peamore, Plymouth, and Exeter, Devonsh., on a mount vert, a turtle-dove ppr., holding in the beak a sprig vert, fructed or. *cf.* 92. 5

Tothill of London, an olive-branch erect ppr. 151. 11

Tothill of Tothill, Cambs, a crescent or, between two wings displayed sa. *cf.* 112. 6

Tottenham, Charles, Esquire, of Mac Murrough, co. Wexford, Ireland, and Major Charles Robert Worsley Tottenham, Esquire, M.A., of Tottenham Green, co. Wexford, of Woodstock, co. Wicklow, Ireland, and of Plâs Berwyn, Denbighsh., a lion rampant gu., armed and langued az. *Ad astra sequor.* 1. 13

Tottenham, Lieutenant-Colonel Frederick St. Leger, J.P., of Mount Callam, Inagh, co. Clare, same crest and motto.

Tottenham, Charles George, Ballycurry, Ashford, co. Wicklow, same crest and motto.

Tottenham, Charles Gore Loftus, Tudenham Park, co. Westmeath, same crest and motto.

Tottenham, Francis Robert, same crest and motto.

Tottenham, Henry Loftus, same crest and motto.

Tottenham, Henry Loftus Alexander, same crest and motto.

Tottenham, John, Ashfield, Rathfarnham, same crest and motto.

Tottenham, Bart., of Tottenham Green, a lion rampant gu., charged on the shoulder with a bar dancettée arg. *Ad astra sequor.* *cf.* 1. 13

Tottenham, Denis-, of Dunmore East, co. Waterford: (1) A lion rampant gu., charged with a crescent or (*for Tottenham*). *cf.* 1. 13. (2) A heraldic tiger's head erased erm. (*for Denis*). *cf.* 25. 4

Tottenham, Ireland, a crescent erm. 163. 2

Touchet, Earl of Castlehaven (*extinct*), out of a ducal coronet or, a swan rising arg., ducally gorged of the first.

Touchet, out of a ducal coronet ppr., a swan rising arg., ducally gorged or. *Je le tiens.*

Touchet, Essex, and Ireland, an old man's head couped ppr., wreathed arg. and gu. 190. 14

Tough, Scotland, a dexter hand pointing with two fingers gu. 222. 11

Touke, Worcs., a leopard's head couped az., spotted or. 22. 10

Toulmin, a dexter arm in armour embowed holding in the hand a sabre, all ppr. 195. 2

Toulmin, a garb in fess ppr. 153. 6

Tounson, Northamp. and Wilts, three cross crosslets fitched gu., two in saltier and one in pale, over all in the centre an escallop or.

Toures, Scotland, a lion rampant ppr. 1. 13

Tournay, a tower arg. 156. 2

Tournay, Bargrave-, of Eastry and Canterbury, Kent, a bull's head erased arg., armed or, gorged with a collar az., charged with three bezants. *cf.* 44. 2

Tournemine, an arm in armour embowed ppr., holding in the hand a fleur-de-lis. 199. 14

Tourner, Scotland, a flaming heart ppr. *Tu ne cede malis.* 181. 13

Tout, on a chapeau, an angel holding in the dexter hand a sword in pale, and supporting with the sinister an escutcheon.

Touzel, Jersey, two wings erect and conjoined quarterly gu. and arg. *Tout zèle.* 113. 1

Tovey, Scotland, an eagle displayed arg. *In Deo confido.* 75. 2

Tovey, an eagle displayed with two heads arg., charged on the breast with a saltier ppr. 74. 1

Tovey, Hamilton, Esquire of Pynacles, Great Stanmore, Middx, on a mural coronet arg an eagle displayed or, holding in the beak a spear bendwise, the staff broken ppr

Tower, Christopher John Hume, of Weald Hall, Essex, and Huntsmire Park, Bucks, a griffin passant per pale or and az, with wings addorsed of the first *Love and dread* 63 2

Tower, Brownlow Richard Christopher, Ellesmere House, Ellesmere Salop a griffin passant per pale or and erm, the dexter claw resting on a shield sa charged with a tower or *Love and dread*

Tower, Egerton Augustus, same crest and motto

Towers-Clark, *see* Clark

Towers, a tower *Bon accord* 156 2

Towers, Berks and Northamp, a griffin passant per pale or and arg, wings addorsed of the first charged on the breast with a mullet sa *cf* 63 2

Towers of Hinton Manor, Isle of Ely, Cambs, a griffin passant per pale or and az, with wings addorsed of the first. 63 2

Towers of Castletown, Borrisokane, co Tipperary, formerly of Kentstown co Meath, Ireland, a griffin passant per pale sa and or, with wings elevated erm *Turris mihi Deus* 63 2

Towers, Scotland, a stag lodged ppr 115 7

Towers of London, a heraldic antelope's head az, attired and maned or 127 10

Towgood of Axminster, Devonsh, an arm vested in russet gray, cuffed erm, holding in the hand ppr a wallet arg, buckles and buttons or

Towker, *alias* **Pennington,** of Thornecombe, Devonsh, a demi angel ppr habited az, with wings extended gu

Towle, a dove holding in its beak an olive branch ppr *Amo pacem* 92 5

Town or Towne, on a rock a tree growing ppr *cf* 143 14

Town or Towne, a spear in pale ppr 175 9

Towneley of Towneley Hall, Lancs, on a perch or a hawk close ppr, beaked and belled of the first round the perch a ribbon gu *Tenez le vraye* *cf* 85 13

Townend of Moss Side Manchester, a lion rampant holding between the forepaws a plain cross arg and resting the hind-paw on an escallop or *Virtute et constantia*

Townley-Balfour, Blayney Reynell M A Townley Hall, Drogheda (1) A mermaid holding in the dexter hand a swan's head and neck erased, and in the sinister an otter's head, also erased, all arg (2) On a perch or, a hawk close ppr, beaked and belled of the first, round the perch a ribbon gu *Omne solum forti patria.*

Townley-Parker, Thomas Townley, Esquire, of Cuerden, Charnock, and Royle, Lancs (1) A buck trippant ppr, transpierced through the body with an arrow paleways, point downwards arg (*for Parker*) *cf* 117 10 (2) On a perch sa, a sparrow-hawk ppr (*for Townley*) 85 13

Townley, Rev Charles Francis, of Fulborne Cambs, on a perch a hawk close ppr, beaked and belled of the first *Probitas verus honos* 85 13

Townrawe and Townroe, Derbysh and Lincs, a tiger sejant per pale erm and sa. 27 6

Townroe, Lionel Edmund, Esquire M A, of the Grove, Upper Norwood, S E, a leopard sejant per pale erm and sa *Dum spiro spero*

Townsend, out of a ducal coronet a demi swan ducally gorged, the line reflexed over back

Townsend, an eye ppr 193 13

Townsend, Frederick, of Honnington Hall Warw, a stag gorged with a wreath of oak ppr resting the sinister forefoot on two annulets interlaced or *Vita posse priore frui* 264 5

Townsend, Thomas Sutton, 68, Queen's Gate S W, same crest and motto

Townsend, G P, Esquire, on a mount vert, a buck sejant ppr, attired or, supporting with the dexter foot a lance erect gu, headed also or *Mihi res non me rebus*

Townsend, Norf, a stag trippant ppr 117 8

Townsend, Surrey, a salamander arg in flames ppr 138 4

Townsend-Farquhar, Sir Robert, Bart, an eagle rising ppr *Mente manuque* 77 5

Townshend, Marquess (Townshend), Raynham Hall Norf, a stag statant ppr, attired and ungu or *Hæc generi incrementa fides* 117 5

Townshend, Richard Baxter, Esquire, 117, Banbury Road Oxford a stag trippant *Hæc generi incrementa fides*

Townshend, Maurice Fitzgerald Stephens, Grove House, Schull co Cork, on a mount vert, a stag trippant ppr attired, hoofed, and charged on the side with an escallop or *Hæc generi incrementa fides*

Townshend, Shropsh a stag trippant arg, differenced by a mullet on his side

Townshend, S Nugent F R G S, of St Kames Island, Skibbereen, co Cork, a stag trippant ppr *Hæc generi incrementa fides*

Townshend of Hem, Wales, a roebuck's head ppr, attired or gorged with a collar az charged with three escallops arg *Huic generi incrementa fides — Vince malum patientia*

Townshend, Marsham-, Hon Robert Frognal, Foot's Cray, Kent (1) A stag statant ppr (*for Townshend*) (2) A lion's head erased gu (*for Marsham*)

Townshend of Coggeshall Magna Essex, on a mount vert, a buck sejant ppr, attired or, supporting with the dexter foot a lance erect gu, headed, also or

Townshend, Stephens-, of Castle Townshend, co Cork Ireland (1) On a mount vert, a stag trippant ppr attired, ungu, and charged on the body with an escallop or (*for Townshend*) *cf* 118 2 (2) A demi eagle rising or (*for Stephens*) *Hæc generi incrementa fides* 80 2

Townshend of Wretham, Norf, a stag statant ppr attired and ungu or *Hinc generi incrementa fides* 117 5

Townshend of Stony Stanton Hinckley, Leics, a buck ppr, resting the dexter fore-foot on an escallop erm, and between the attires a cross crosslet fitchee arg *Hinc generi incrementa fides*

Townshend, Charles William, Trevallyn, Wrexham, Denbighsh, a roebuck's head attired or, gorged with a collar az, charged with three escallops arg

Townshend, Edward Lee, Wincham Hall, Knutsford, a stag's head couped ppr, attired or, gorged with a collar az, charged with three escallops arg

Townshend, Harry Leigh, Caldecott Hall Nuneaton, Warw, same crest

Townshend, Shropsh a fleur de lis 148 2

Towry, of Yorks and Croglin Hall, Cumb, a griffin passant per pale or and az 63 2

Towse of London and Somers an eagle's head erased or pierced through the neck by a sword arg, hilt and pommel of the first

Toy or Toye, Glouc, on a mural coronet gu, a martlet arg

Traby, a demi-lion rampant sa 10 1

Tracy, *see* Sudeley, Baron

Tracy, Viscount Tracy, on a chapeau gu, turned up erm, an escallop sa, between two wings or *Memoria pii æterna* 141 11

Tracy, on a chapeau gu, turned up erm, an escallop arg, between two wings or 141 11

Trafalgar, Viscount, *see* Nelson Earl

Trafford, de, Sir Humphrey Francis, Bart Trafford Park, Manchester a thrasher ppr his hat and coat per pale arg and gu, sleeves counterchanged, breeches and stockings of the third and second, holding in both hands a flail or, uplifted over a garb lying fessewise upon the dexter side of the wreath over the crest an escroll bearing the motto, *Now thus* *Gripe griffin, hold fast* 188 8

Trafford of Oughtrington, Chesh (1) A husbandman per pale arg and az, threshing a garb or, with the motto over, *Now thus* (*for Trafford*) *cf* 188 8 (2) A cubit arm erect vested paly of four pieces or and sa holding the lower end of a broken tilting spear (*for Leigh*) *Gripe griffin, hold fast*

Trafford, Essex and Lancs, a thrasher ppr, his hat and coat per pale arg and gu, holding in both hands a flail in the attitude of striking a garb or *Now thus* 188 8

Trafford, Henry Randolph Michaelchurch Court Hereford same crest

Trafford, William Henry, Wroxham Hall, Norf, same crest

Trafford, Guy Rawson, of Hill Court, Ross Heref, same crest

Trafford of Bridge Trafford, Chesh a demi-pegasus with wings expanded arg 47 5

Trafford-Rawson, Major Henry, Coldham Hall Bury St Edmunds (1) An eagle's head erased per fesse sa and az, guttee-d'or, holding in the beak two annulets interlaced or (*for Rawson*) (2) A thrasher ppr, his coat, breeches and stockings party per pale arg and gu, holding in his hands a flail ppr the head or over a garb fesseways of the last *Now thus*

Tragett of Awbridge Danes, Hants, upon a mount vert, within a chain in arch or, a dexter hand pointing upwards with the forefinger ppr.

Traherne of St. Hilary, Glamorgansh., on a ducal coronet or, a goat's head erased ppr., charged with three plates, two and one. *Ofna Dduw a'r Brenhin.* cf. 128. 5

Traherne, Llewellyn Edmund, Coedarhydyglyn, Cardiff, a goat's head erased ppr. *Ofna Dduw a'r Brenhin.*

Trail, a column in the sea ppr. 176. 2

Traill of Edinburgh and London, a column set in the sea ppr. *In discrimine salus.* 176. 2

Traill of Ballylough House, co. Antrim, Ireland, same crest. *Discrimine salus.* 176. 2

Traill - Burroughs, Lieutenant - General Frederick William, C.B., of Rousay and Viera, Orkney, N.B., a lion passant gu. *Audaces fortuna juvat.*

Traill, W. H., Esquire, Holland House, North Ronaldshay, Orkney, N.B., on a mount a column, all ppr. *Discrimine salus.* 274. 6

Tranckmore, Devonsh., a demi-heraldic antelope transpierced through the neck by an arrow in bend.

Trangmar, a dexter arm embowed in armour holding in the hand ppr. a sword. 195. 2

Transome or **Transam,** Shropsh., a leopard's head erased in profile transpierced through the mouth by an arrow. cf. 23. 10

Trant, a demi-lion supporting an anchor ppr. 12. 12

Trant, Bart. (*attainted*), Ireland, a demi-eagle holding in the beak a rose-sprig, all ppr.

Trant, of Rathmile, co. Roscommon, Ireland, out of a ducal coronet or, an eagle rising ppr., holding in the beak a sprig of laurel vert. *Aquila non capit muscas.*

Trant, Fitzgibbon, J.P., Dovea, Thurles, co. Tipperary, an eagle rising ppr. *Aquila non capit muscas.*

Trapnell, a griffin's head couped az., beaked or. 66. 1

Trappes of London, a man's head couped at the shoulders, attired gu., garnished or, on the head a steel helmet, all ppr., surmounted by a plume of three feathers arg.

Trappes of Stanley House, Clitheroe, same crest. *Cultui avorum fidelis.*

Trappes-Lomax, out of a crown vallary a demi-lion rampant arg., holding an escallop-shell gu., charged across the shoulder with three escallop-shells within two bendlets gu. (2) A man's head couped at the shoulders ppr., attired gu., garnished or, on the head a helmet, also ppr., surmounted by a plume of three feathers arg. *Cultui avorum fidelis.*

Trappes-Lomax, Richard, Esquire, J.P., of the Manor House, Chatburn, Lancs, a demi-man in armour ppr., holding in his dexter hand a staff arg., on the head a helmet, also ppr., surmounted by a plume of three feathers arg. *Cultui avorum fides.*

Traquair, Earl of (Stuart), on a garb in fess a crow with wings expanded and addorsed, all ppr. *Judge nought.*

Traquair, Scotland, the sun shining on the stump of an old tree sprouting new branches ppr. 145. 5

Trasher, Cornw., a demi-talbot rampant regardant arg., eared gu.

Travell, Northamp. and Warw., a greyhound's head sa., charged with three mullets, two and one or. cf. 61. 2

Travers, Cork, a wolf passant. *Nec timide, nec temere.* 28. 10

Travers, co. Cork, Ireland, a heraldic tiger statant gu. cf. 25. 5

Travers, Clarke-, Sir Guy Francis Travers, Bart., Rossmore, co. Cork: (1) A heraldic tiger passant arg. (*for Travers*). cf. 25. 5. (2) On the stump of a tree couped, eradicated, and sprouting on each side, a lark perched ppr., wings expanded, holding in the beak two wheat ears or. *Nec temere, nec timide.—Constantia et fidelitate.*

Travers, Devonsh., a griffin's head erased or, holding in the beak an eft az.

Travers of Monkstown Castle, Dublin, a griffin's head erased or, holding in the beak a lizard vert.

Travers, Ireland, out of a ducal coronet or, an armed arm gu., holding a sword ppr. *Vulnera mihi vita.*

Travers, Ireland, the sun shining on the stump of a broken tree sprouting new branches. 145. 5

Travers, a rock in the sea ppr. 179. 5

Traves, a leopard's head erased gardant.

Travess, a bird arg., holding in the beak a branch vert. 92. 5

Travis, a bear's head erased gu. 35. 2

Trayner, Hon. John, Lord Trayner, of 27, Moray Place, Edinburgh, a lion sejant gu., armed and langued az. *Par loi et droit.* 8. 8

Trayton of Lewes, Sussex, a dapple gray horse passant ppr. 52. 6

Treacher, a griffin's head erased ppr. 66. 2

Treacher of Stamford Hill, Middx., a boar's head couped gu., armed or, holding in the mouth a dragon's sinister wing arg. *Æquam servare mentem.*

Treacy, out of a tower a demi-lion rampant, all ppr. 157. 11

Treadway, a dexter hand couped below the wrist in armour ppr., holding a sword of the last, hilted or, on the point a Turk's head couped at the neck ppr.

Treby, *see* Phillipps-Treby.

Treby of Goodamoor and Plympton House, Devonsh., a demi-lion arg., collared vairée az. and erminois. 10. 9

Tredcroft of Warnham Court, Sussex, a cock's head erased ppr. *Vigilando quiesco.* 90. 1

Tredcroft of Horsham, Sussex, same crest and motto. 90. 1

Tredcroft, Lieutenant-Colonel Charles Lennox, Glen Ancrum, near Guildford, same crest.

Tredegar, Baron (Morgan), Tredegar Park, Newport, Monm., a reindeer's head couped or, attired gu. cf. 122. 1

Tredenock of Tredenock, Cornw., a buck's head and neck couped ppr. 121. 5

Tree, an oak-tree fructed ppr. 143. 5

Treffry, Charles Ebenezer, of Place in Fowey, Cornw., a Cornish chough's head erased sa., holding in the beak a sprig of laurel vert.

Treffry, Rev. Edward Lambert, Aswarby, Lincs, same crest.

Treffry, Rev. Reginald Heber, St. Endellion, Port Isaac, Cornw., same crest.

Trefusis, Baron Clinton, *see* Clinton.

Trefusis of Landew, Cornw., a griffin sejant or, winged az., resting the dexter claw on an escutcheon arg. cf. 62. 11

Tregent, a Triton holding in his hand a trident. cf. 185. 12

Tregoning, John Simmons, Esquire, J.P., D.L., Landue, near Launceston, Cornw., and Llanelly, Carmarthensh., in front of a rock ppr., thereon a castle arg., a stag lodged or. 155. 11

Tregonwell, St. Barbe-, of Anderson, Dorset, a Cornish chough, head and neck sa., holding in the beak a chaplet erm. and sa. *Nosce teipsum.*

Tregonwell of Tregonwell, Cornw., and Milton Abbey, Dorset, a Cornish chough ppr., holding in the beak a chaplet erm. and sa.

Tregonwell of Cranborne Lodge, Cranborne, Salisbury, same crest. *Nosce teipsum.*

Tregore or **Tregour,** Cornw., out of a ducal coronet or, a unicorn's head erm., maned and armed of the first. 48. 12

Tregos, a crescent ensigned with a huckle or. 163. 15

Tregos, an arm in armour embowed holding in the hand a scimitar, both ppr. *Ferro consulto.* 196. 10

Treheron, Cornw., a demi-griffin erased arg., gorged with two bars az., holding between the claws a fleur-de-lis of the last.

Trelawney, a wolf's head erased ppr. 30. 8

Trelawney, an acorn ppr. 152. 1

Trelawny, Salusbury-, Sir William Lewis, Bart., J.P., D.L., of Trelawny, Cornw., a wolf statant ppr. *Sermoni consona facta.—Virtus patrimonio nobilior.* cf. 28. 10

Trelawny, Horace Dormer, of Shotwick, Chesh., a wolf passant ppr. *Sermoni consona facta.* 28. 10

Trelawny, Collins-: (1) A wolf passant ppr. (*for Trelawny*). 28. 10. (2) A camel's head erased ppr. (*for Collins*). *Sermoni consona facta.* cf. 132. 7

Treloar, Alderman Sir William Purdie, Grange Mount, Norwood, Surrey, two arms embowed vested az., cuffed or, the hand grasping a fasces fesseways, head towards the dexter, pendent therefrom by a chain or an escutcheon sa., charged with a bezant. *Honestate vetustai stat.*

Tremayne, an escutcheon erm., between two myrtle-branches in orle ppr.

Tremayne of Collacomb, Devonsh., two arms embowed vested or, holding between the hands a man's head ppr., and on the head a high-crowned hat sa.

Tremayne of Heligan, St. Austell, same crest. *Honor et honestas.*

Tremayne, John, of Heligan and Carclew, Cornw., two arms embowed vested or, holding between the hands a man's head ppr., and on the head a hat sa. *Honor et honestas.*

Tremayne, Arthur, Carclew, Perran-ar-Worthal, Cornw., same crest.

Tremenheere of Tremenheere, Cornw, a Saracen's head in profile ppr *Thrysscryssough ne Deu a nef* 190 14

Tremenheere of Penzance, Cornw, a demi-man in profile ppr, wreathed about the head *Nil desperandum*

Treminell or Tremynell, an eagle rising ppr 77 5

Trenance, Cornw, on a chapeau gu turned up erm, a unicorn's head of the last, maned, armed, and ducally crowned or cf 49 10

Trench, Le Poer-, Earl of Clancarty, *see* **Clancarty**

Trench, *see* Ashtown, Baron

Trench, *see* Cooke-Trench

Trench of Cangort Park, King's Co., Ireland an arm in armour embowed holding in the hand a sword, all ppr *Virtutis fortuna comes* 195 2

Trench, Charles O'Hara, Clonfert, Eyrecourt, co Galway, same crest and motto

Trench-Gascoigne, Frederick Charles, Parlington Park, Aberford, Yorks (1) A conger's head couped and erect or charged for distinction with a pellet (2) An arm in armour embowed, the hand grasping a cutlass, all ppr

Trench of Heywood Ireland, same crest *Consilio et prudentia*

Trench, a cubit arm in armour ppr, garnished or, holding in the hand a scimitar arg, hilt and pommel of the second

Trenchard of Stanton, Wilts, a cubit arm erect vested az, cuffed arg, holding in the hand a battle-axe ppr *Nosce teipsum*

Trenchard of Hordhill and Wolveton, Dorset, a cubit arm erect vested az, cuffed arg, holding in the hand ppr a sword of the second, hilt and pommel or *Nosce teipsum*

Trenchard of Poxwell and Greenhill House, Weymouth, Dorset (1) A dexter arm embowed vested az, cuffed or, holding in the hand a trenching-knife in bend sinister ppr (*for Trenchard*) (2) A lion sejant arg, charged on the shoulder with an ermine-spot and gorged with a collar gemelle sa, the dexter fore paw supporting an escutcheon gu, charged with a fleur-de-lis within a bordure or (*for Pickard*)

Trenchard, Ashfordly-, of Stanton House, Wilts (1) A dexter arm embowed vested az, cuffed or holding in the hand a trenching-knife in bend sinister, the point depressed ppr (*for Trenchard*) (2) An ass's head erased or gorged with a collar sa, thereon three mullets of the first (*for Ashfordly*)

Trenchard, Dillon-, Henry Luke, Cohnshays House, Bruton, Somers. (1) A dexter arm embowed vested az, cuffed or holding in the hand a trenching-knife (*for Trenchard*) (2) On a chapeau gu turned up erm, a hawk rising ppr *Nosce teipsum.*

Trencharde, a hand ppr, vested az, holding a knife arg, handled or

Trendell of the Abbey House Abingdon, Berks, a stag arg attired and ungu or, charged on the body with three crosses patee gu, and resting the dexter foot on a bugle horn sa, garnished of the second *Crucem vide et festina*

Trenfield, a demi antelope pierced through the neck by an arrow in bend cf 126 5

Trent, an arm in armour embowed holding in the hand a scimitar 196 10

Trent, a crescent erm *Augeo* 163 2

Trent, a demi-eagle with wings expanded or, holding in the beak a laurel branch ppr

Trent-Stoughton, of Saltwood, Kent (1) A robin-redbreast ppr, charged for distinction with a cross-crosslet az (*for Stoughton*) (2) A crescent or, between two roses gu, barbed and seeded ppr (*for Trent*)

Trentham of Rocester, Staffs a griffin's head erased sa, beaked gu 66 5

Trenwith, Cornw, a falcon rising, holding in the beak a branch

Tresaher of Trevethan and Budock Cornw, a demi-talbot regardant arg

Tresham of Northamp, a bezant charged with a talbot's head az cf 57 1

Tresham, Bucks, a boar's head erased at the neck sa, ducally gorged or, holding in the mouth a trefoil slipped vert

Tresloggett, *see* Sloggett

Tresse of Newington, Malling, and Hoo, Kent, an eagle's head couped erm, ducally crowned and beaked or, between two wings erect ermines cf 84 2

Tresson, on a mount a lion passant, ducally crowned, supporting with the dexter paw an arrow in pale

Treswell, on a rock a wild goose ppr

Treunwith, Cornw, a hawk or with wings expanded arg, holding in the beak three ashen keys vert

Trevanion of Cærhayes, Cornw, a stag trippant quarterly gu and arg *En Dieu est mon espoir* 117 8

Trevelyan, Thornton Roger of Netherwitton, Northumb, two arms embowed vested az holding in the hands ppr a bezant *Time trieth troth*

Trevelyan, Cornw, two arms in armour embowed, the hands ppr, supporting a bezant, thereon a parrot statant ppr cf 194 11

Trevelyan, Sir Walter John Bart, of Nettlecombe, Somers, two arms counter embowed ppr, habited az, holding in the hands a bezant *Tyme tryeth troth —Salies bien et bien averis*

Trevelyan, Rt Hon Sir George Otto, Bart, P C., D L, of Wallington Northumb, same crest and motto

Trevenen, Sidney Vyvyan, Carlisle, a stag quarterly vert and erminois, attired or *In se teres*

Trevenyon and Trevanion, Cornw, a stag quarterly gu and arg 117 5

Treves, Sir Frederick, Bart, K C.V O, C B of Dorchester, Dorset, and 6, Wimpole Street W an opinicus statant or, wings elevated and addorsed purpure, resting the dexter paw on a fleam fesseways arg *Fortiter, Fideliter, Feliciter* 287 4

Treves, a demi-griffin holding in the dexter claw a sword ppr 64 6

Trevet or Trevett, a castle arg, masoned sa 155 8

Trevithick, Cornw, a unicorn's head couped ppr 49 7

Trevor-Hampden, Baron Trevor and Viscount Hampden (*extinct*) (1) A talbot passant erm, collared and chained gu (*for Hampden*) (2) On a chapeau gu turned up erm a wyvern rising sa (*for Trevor*) *Vestigia nulla retrorsum*

Trevor, Baron (Hill-Trevor), of Brynkinalt, Chirk, Denbighsh (1) A wyvern sa (*for Trevor*) 70. 2 (2) A rein deer's head couped gu, attired and collared or (*for Hill*) cf 122 1

Trevor of Trevallyn, Denbighsh, a cockatrice with wings expanded and tail nowed sa, beaked, wattled, and combed arg 68 6

Trevor, Norf, on a chapeau gu, turned up erm, a wyvern with wings addorsed sa 69 14

Trevor of the Pirn Innerleithen N B same crest *Heb Dduw heb ddim.*

Trevor, Sir Charles Cecil C B, 11, Astwood Road, South Kensington, S W same crest *Heb Dduw heb ddim*

Trevor-Battye, Charles Edmund Augustine Trevor (1) Upon a club fesseways ppr a stork arg, collared and lined sa, holding in the beak a roach ppr (2) On a mount vert the trunk of an oak tree a branch sprouting from its dexter side, acorned ppr, upon the trunk a wyvern tail nowed sa, wings elevated erminois. *Ducat amor Dei*

Trevor-Roper, Charles James, M A, of Plas Teg, Flintsh (1) A lion rampant sa holding in the dexter paw a ducal coronet or (*for Roper*) (2) On a chapeau gu turned up erm a wyvern with wings elevated sa and charged upon the breast for distinction with an escallop arg thereon a cross flory sa (*for Trevor*) *Spes mea in Deo*

Trevors, Ireland, a griffin's head erased or, holding in the beak a snake ppr cf 65 7

Trew, a demi-chevalier in armour holding in his dexter hand a sword ppr 187. 1

Trew, J P, Esquire, Maple Lodge, Surbiton, Surrey, a demi-chevalier in armour, the helmet surmounted by a plume of three ostrich-feathers, holding in his dexter hand a sword ppr *Pietate et bellica virtute*

Trewarthen, a lion's gamb sa, holding a sceptre in pale or cf 38 7

Trewarther, a pillar in the sea ppr 176 2

Trewent, Devonsh, out of a ducal coronet or, an eagle's head between two wings ppr 84 3

Trewick, a buck's head cabushed pierced through the nose by an arrow fesswise, point towards the sinister, all or (*Of no authority*) *A Truewick, a Truewick*

Trewman, Devonsh, a mullet pierced arg

Trewsdale of Hundon, Lincs, a dragon's head vert holding in the mouth a broken spear ppr

Treys, two hands couped and conjoined in fess, supporting a scimitar ppr

Trice of Godmanchester, Hunts, a phœnix in flames ppr 82 2

Trickey, a lion's head couped sa, holding in the mouth a man by the middle, his legs in chief and his head in base embrued ppr

Trigg, a demi-talbot salient. *cf.* 55. 8

Trigge, Henry Samuel, Esquire, of 79, Blackheath, Kent, a lion rampant regardant or, holding in the dexter paw an arrow ppr. *Spes mea in Deo.*

Triggs of Trygg, Devonsh., the sun rising ppr.

Trimlestown, Baron of (Barnewall), of Trimlestown, co. Meath, from a plume of five ostrich-feathers or, gu., az., vert, and arg., a falcon rising of the last. *Malo mori quam fœdari.*

Trimmer, a dove holding in its beak an olive-branch, all ppr. 92. 5

Trimnel or **Trimnell,** a harpy close ppr. *Audentis fortuna juvat.* 189. 1

Trimnell, Charles Henry, Esquire, Whitecliff, Woldingham, Surrey, a harpy with wings close ppr. *Lenit victoria mortem.*

Trimwell, a lion's head erased. 17. 8

Trinder, a hawk jessed and belled standing on a fish naiant, all ppr. *cf.* 86. 6

Trinder of Westwell and Holwell, Oxon., out of a ducal coronet or, a stag's head ppr., attired of the first. 120. 7

Tringham, Rev. William, M.A., of Long Cross House, Chertsey, *uses* a talbot's head erased gu., billettée or. *Fideliter.* 56. 5

Tringham, on a chapeau gu., turned up erm., a dexter wing az., charged with a chevron or. *cf.* 109. 2

Trinling, a crescent. 163. 2

Tripconie and **Triponia,** Cornw., a cock's head couped arg., combed, beaked, and wattled gu., holding in the beak a snake ppr., environed round the neck.

Tripp, Charles George, Esquire, J.P., of Orari Gorge Station, Woodbury, Canterbury, New Zealand, Barrister-at-Law, *uses* a hawk ppr. (*The Tripp arms and crest are represented upon an old escutcheon in the possession of the Rev. C. Tripp, D.D., Rector of Silverton, Devonshire, with the following legend: 'This Atchivement was given unto my Lord Howard's 5th Son, at ye Siege of Bullogne, King Harry ye 5th being there, ask'd how they took ye Town and Castle, Howard answer'd "I, Tripp'd up ye Walls," saith His Majesty, "Tripp shall be thy name, and no longer Howard," and honored him with ye scaling ladder for his Bend.'*) 85. 2

Tripp of London and Kent, issuing out of rays or, an eagle's head gu. 84. 13

Trist of Culworth, Northants, on a serpent nowed, a falcon ppr. 86. 3

Trist of Parc Behan, Cornw., a falcon holding in the beak a fish, all ppr. *Nec triste, nec trepidum.*

Trist of Bowdon, Hernaford, and Tristford House, Devonsh., same crest and motto. 76. 8

Trist, George Arthur, Prestwood Cottage, Ifield, near Crawley, Sussex, same crest and motto.

Trist, Warren, of Tristford, Harberton, South Devonsh., on two cinquefoils in fesse or, a Cornish chough ppr. *Nec triste, nec trepide.* 280. 15

Trist, John W., Esquire, F.S.A., F.S.I., etc., on a mount vert an osprey statant, holding in its beak a fish arg. *Nec triste, nec trepide.* 76. 8

Tristram, Cumb., a stag's head ppr., attired or, holding in the mouth a trefoil arg., stalked and leaved vert. *cf.* 121. 5

Tristram of Dunall, Bampton, Devonsh., a buck's head ppr., attired arg., holding in the mouth a trefoil, also arg., stalked and leaved vert. *cf.* 121. 5

Tristram, on a chapeau arg., turned up gu., a martlet with wings addorsed sa.

Tristram of Moor Hall, Worcs., a wolf's head erased sa. 30. 8

Trite, a Triton crowned with an Eastern coronet, holding over his shoulder with his sinister hand a trident. *cf.* 185. 12

Trite, a Triton holding in his sinister hand a trident. 185. 12

Tritton, Joseph Herbert, Esquire, D.L., of Lyons Hall, Great Leighs, Essex, and 36, Queen's Gate Gardens, London, W.C., *uses* a trotting horse. (*Of no authority.*) 52. 2

Tritton, a cross patée erm. *Fortiter gerit crucem.* *cf.* 165. 7

Trivett, Sussex and Suff., a leopard's head couped at the neck ppr. *Salvus in igne.* 22. 10

Trivett or **Tryvett,** an ostrich with wings addorsed arg., holding in the beak a horse-shoe az. *cf.* 97. 1

Trivett of Bradwell, Suff., an eagle rising ppr. *Salvus in igne.* 77. 5

Trobe-Bateman, La, *see* Bateman.

Trogood of Sherborne, Dorset, an arm in armour embowed holding in the hand a caltrap.

Trollop, a buck or, pellettée. *cf.* 117. 5

Trollop, Durh., a buck trippant arg., armed or. *Audio, sed taceo.* 117. 8

Trollope, *see* Kesteven, Baron.

Troogood, a wolf's head couped arg., charged with a buckle az. *cf.* 30. 5

Trosse of Trevollard, St. Stephen's, Cornw., a demi-lion rampant or, supporting an escutcheon.

Trotman, out of a ducal coronet or, a demi-ostrich with wings addorsed sa. 96. 11

Trotman of Cam, Glouc., a garb erect or, banded arg. and az., between two ostrich-feathers of the second, quilled of the first.

Trotter of Ballindean, Perth., a horse trotting arg. *Festina lente.* 52. 2

Trotter, Bart., Lincs, same crest and motto.

Trotter, a horse passant arg. 52. 6

Trotter of Raheen, co. Galway, Ireland, on a ducal coronet or, a horse trotting arg., caparisoned ppr., and resting the dexter fore-hoof on an escutcheon paly of six arg. and gu., and over the crest upon an escroll the motto, *Deed shaw. Toujours prêt.* 52. 12

Trotter of Glenkens, Galloway, a horse trotting ppr., furnished gu. *Festina lente.*

Trotter, Alexander Edmund Coutts, of Bush, Midlothian, a horse trotting ppr. *Festina lente.*

Trotter, Coutts, Dreghorn, Edinburgh, same crest.

Trotter of Horton Manor, Surrey: (1) A horse trotting arg., charged on the neck for distinction with a cross crosslet az. (*for Trotter*). *cf.* 52. 2. (2) A lion rampant gu., armed and langued az., holding in the dexter fore-paw a fleur-de-lis arg., with the motto over, *Fortitudine et fidelitate* (*for Brown*). *Festina lente.* 2. 7

Trotter, Ernest Trotter, same crest and motto.

Trotter, Ireland, on a ducal coronet or, a horse trotting arg., saddled and bridled gu., garnished of the first. *In promptu.* 52. 13

Trotter of Kettleshiel, Berwicksh., Bush, co. Edinburgh, and Shuddy Camp, Cambs, a horse trotting ppr. *Festina lente.* 52. 2

Trotter, William, J.P., King's Beeches, Ascot, same crest and motto.

Trotter of Catchelraw, Berwicksh., a horse passant arg., furnished gu. 52. 4

Trotter, a galley in full course ppr. *Virtutis fortuna comes.* 160. 8

Trotter, Major-General Henry, K.C.V.O., of Mortonhall, Mid-Lothian, and 33, Cadogan Square, a man standing in front of and holding a horse arg., furnished gu. *Impromptu.* 53. 11

Trotter of Ardington, Berks: (1) A horse trotting arg. (2) A lion rampant gu., in his dexter fore-paw a fleur-de-lis arg. *Festina lente.—Fortitudine et fidelitate.*

Trotter, William Sampson, the Hill, Batheaston, Bath, same crests and mottoes.

Trotter, a heraldic antelope's head couped. 127. 10

Trotter-Cranstoun, Joseph Young, of Dewar, Mid-Lothian, a crane dormant holding a stone in his dexter claw, all ppr. *Thou shalt want ere I want.*

Trotter, Morpeth, Northumb., a boar passant ppr. *Nec timidus, nec ferus.* 40. 9

Trotter, Yorks, a lion's head erased arg., collared erm. 18. 6

Trotter of Byers, Durh., and Skelton Castle, Cleveland, Yorks, same crest. *Fortis non ferox.*

Troubridge, a bridge of three arches gu., masoned sa. 158. 4

Troubridge, Sir Thomas Herbert Cochrane, Bart., a dexter arm embowed habited az., cuffed arg., holding a flag-staff, thereon a flag, also az., charged with two keys in saltire or. *Ne cede arduis.* 309. 7

Troughton of Great Lindford, Bucks, Leach Hall, Lancs, and Northamp., a lion's head erased per chevron arg. and sa., charged with three roundles counterchanged. 273. 8

Troughton, Captain Cecil Claude Walter, of 17, Hans Mansions, S.W., a lion's head erased per chevron arg. and sa., charged with three roundles, one and two, counterchanged. *Spero meliora.* 273. 8

Troup, a buck trippant arg. 117. 8

Troup, Scotland, a hind's head erased ppr. 124. 3

Trout, Devonsh., on a mount vert, an ostrich close arg. *cf.* 97. 2

Troutback and **Troutbeck,** a wolf's head erased ppr. 30. 8

Troutbeck, of Dunham, Chesh., a Moor's head couped below the shoulders sa. 192. 13

Trove, a wolf's head erased erm. 30. 8

Trowart, an eagle displayed with two heads, the wings expanded and inverted.

Trowbridge, a bridge of two arches ruined on the dexter side

Trowell, a beaver passant ppr cf 134 8

Trower, a lion passant gardant per pale or and az, charged on the body with three crosses patee counterchanged, holding in the dexter paw a spear ppr

Trower, the stump of an oak-tree ppr, sprouting new leaves vert 145 2

Trower, out of a ducal coronet or a demi eagle displayed with two heads gu cf 82 3

Trowtback, a scaling ladder sa 158 14

Trowtbeck, a naked man sa, holding in his dexter hand a dart or

Trowteback, out of a ducal coronet or, a lion's gamb ppr, supporting a cross crosslet fitched of the first 36 11

Troyhin or **Tryhy,** Ireland, a tiger's head erased or

Troys, a tree erect and raguled sprouting out of the top couped three acorn-branches fructed or leaved vert

Troyte, Hugh Leonard Acland of Huntsham Court Devonsh. (1) An eagle's wing sa, charged with five estoiles or, environed with a snake ppr, the wing charged for distinction with a cross crosslet of the second (*for Troyte*) (2) A man's sinister hand gloved and lying fesseways vested az, thereon a hawk perched ppr (*for Acland*) *A Deo in Deo* 86 14

Troyte-Chafyn-Grove, George, Esquire, F S A, D L, J P, of North Coker House, Yeovil, Somers, and Bonville Manor, Corscombe, Dorchester (1) A talbot passant sa collared arg (*for Grove*) 277 13 (2) An eagle's wing sa, charged with five estoiles or, the wing environed by a snake ppr (*for Troyte*) 277 14 (3) On a mount vert, five blacks bills erect, banded with a wreath of olive ppr, therein pendent an escutcheon az charged with a cross crosslet or (*for Bulloch*) *Ny dessux ny dessoux* 277 15

Troyte of Chidderleigh, Devonsh, an eagle's wing sa charged with five estoiles or environed by a snake ppr

Trubshaw, Middx, a mullet per pale gu and sa 164 2

Truell, a heart gu, between two palm branches vert *Semper fidelis* 268 12

Truell, Rev William Henry Augustus, of Clonmannon, co Wicklow, Ireland on a wreath of the colours a heart gu, between two palm-branches vert and over the crest in a scroll the motto, *Semper fidelis Diligentia fortior* 268 12

Trueman or **Truman,** on a ducal coronet or, a wyvern vomiting fire at both ends ppr cf 69 9

Truesdale, a boar's head couped and erect ppr cf 43 3

Truman or **Trueman** of London and Yorks a human heart gu, ducally crowned or cf 110 14

Trumbull of Easthampstead Berks, a bull's head erased sa, breathing fire ppr cf 44 3

Trump, a cock's head couped az, billettee or

Trumpeter, a demi-savage ppr 186 5

Trumwyn and **Truwill,** Worcs, a Saracen's head ppr, wreathed or and sa, vested on the shoulders, also sa round the neck a sash tied in a bow behind vert

Trundle of Crosby Square and Brunswick Square London, an arm couped at the elbow issuant bendways vested sa, charged with a bezant, cuffed arg, holding in the hand a pen ppr *Be just and fear not*

Truro, Baron (Rt Hon Charles Robert Claude Wilde D L, J P), of Bowes, Middx (*extinct*) on a mount vert, a hart lodged holding a rose in its mouth all ppr *Æquabiliter et diligenter* cf 115 12

Trusbut, a hand issuing in fess from a cloud and lifting a garb ppr 223 12

Truscoat or **Truscott,** an arrow and a palm-branch in saltier ppr 171 7

Truscott, Alderman Sir Francis Wyatt, of Oakleigh, East Grinstead, Sussex, a fasces erect surmounted by a palm-branch slipped and an arrow saltireways, all ppr *In utrumque paratus — Gwir yn erbyn y byd* 171 9

Truscott, George Wyatt, Greatwood, Chislehurst, same crest and mottoes

Truss of Gonville, a sword fesseways ppr, thereon a cross patee az, surmounted by an estoile or *Virtus intaminatis fulget honoribus*

Trussell of Gayton, Northamp, and of Peatling Magna Leics, an ass's head arg, gorged with a collar and bell ppr

Trussell of Warmincham, Chesh, and Notts, out of a ducal coronet gu, an ass's head sa 125 10

Truston, on a mount vert, a lion holding an arrow, the point resting on the wreath or

Truston, out of a ducal coronet gu, a unicorn's head arg, attired or, charged on the neck with three hurts cf 48 12

Tryce of Godmanchester, Hants out of an Eastern coronet arg, a demi-eagle displayed sa

Trydell of Blarney, co Cork, Ireland a stag's head erased ppr 121 2

Trye of Leckhampton, Glouc, a buck's head cabossed gu 122 5

Trye, Henry Norwood, Hartshill, near Atherstone, same crest

Tyre, Rev Reginald Edward, the Rectory, Leckhampton, Glouc, same crest

Trygott of South Kirby Yorks, a lion's head couped sa holding in the mouth a man by the waist, his legs in chief and his head in base ppr, embrued on the body gu

Tryon, an ostrich's head between two ostrich-feathers arg, holding in the beak a horse shoe ppr 97 12

Tryon of London and Essex, a bear's head sa semee d'etoiles or cf 34 14

Tryon, Guy Thomas Lewis, Bulwick Park Wansford, Northamp., same crest

Tryon, Richard, Esquire, the Lodge Oakham same crest

Tubb of Trengoff, Cornw, a beaver passant ppr, holding in the mouth a gurnet gu

Tuberville, a bomb inflamed ppr 177 12

Tuchfield, Devonsh, a hawk supporting an arrow ppr

Tuck, three mullets in chevron 164 7

Tucker of Coryton Park Devonsh, a demi-sea-horse regardant arg holding between his paws a heart gu *Auspice Teucro*

Tucker of Exeter, Devonsh a lion's gamb gu charged with three billets in pale or holding a mace of war handled vert headed arg

Tucker, Pierce Joseph A M I C E Molescroft, Beverley, East Yorks, a lion's gamb erased and erect gu, charged with three billets in pale or, and holding a battle axe or head az *Auspice Teucro*

Tucker of Dublin a cubit arm erect vested or, cuffed dancettee arg holding in the hand an arrow ppr *Patet ingeniis campus*

Tuckey, Ireland a crane with wings expanded holding in the beak a serpent 104 13

Tuckfield of Exeter Devonsh, an eagle supporting an arrow ppr

Tuckfield of Fulford Park, an eagle ppr beaked and legged or, the dexter claw supporting an arrow erect gu barbed and flighted arg, and charged for distinction on the breast of the eagle with a rose gu

Tudman, a demi-fox ppr

Tudor, on a mural coronet or, a serpent nowed vert 142 12

Tudor, Hugh Owen Esquire, J P of Lyndwood, Old Windsor Berks, same crest *Semper eadem*

Tudway, a demi lion rampant gu, holding a rose az slipped ppr 12 1

Tudway, Charles Clement the Cedars, Wells, Somers, same crest *Nil desperandum*

Tudway, Somers, an ostrich-feather sa, enfiled with a ducal coronet or 114 12

Tuffnal and **Tuftnell,** a dexter arm in armour embowed ppr, holding in the gauntlet a cutlass arg, hilted or

Tufnell, Lieutenant Colonel William Neville of Langleys Essex an arm in armour embowed ppr, holding in the gauntlet a cutlass arg hilted or

Tufnell, Rev Frederick Charlton House, Radstock Bath, same crest *Manus hæc inimica tyrannis*

Tufnell, Robert Hutchison Campbell, Lackham House Spring Grove Isleworth, same crest

Tufnell, William Michael 30 Eaton Square, S W, same crest

Tufnell-Tyrell, John Lionel, Esquire, of Boreham, Essex (1) A boar's head couped and erect arg issuant out of the mouth a peacock's tail ppr (*for Tyrell*) (2) A dexter arm embowed in armour ppr, holding in the gauntlet a cutlass arg hilt or (*for Tufnell*) *Manus hæc inimica tyrannis*

Tufton, Earl of Thanet, *see* Thanet

Tufton, *see* Hothfield, Baron

Tufton, Surrey and Kent, a sea lion sejant arg 20 2

Tugwell of Crow Hall Somers a stag's head erased ppr, holding in the mouth a trefoil slipped vert. cf 121 2

Tuite, Ireland a dexter arm embowed throwing a dart all ppr 201 13

Tuite, Sir Morgan Henry Paulet, Bart, of Kilucane, Nenagh co Tipperary, an angel vested arg holding in the dexter hand a flaming sword ppr., the sinister resting on an escutcheon of the arms, viz., quarterly arg. and az. *Alleluiah.* 311. 15

Tuke, a demi-lion rampant gu., ducally crowned or. 10. 11

Tulloch, a mitre gu., garnished and rimmed or, jewelled ppr. *cf.* 180. 5

Tulloch of Tannochy, Elginsh., Scotland, a mitre ppr. *Pietate parentum.* *cf.* 180. 5

Tulloch, Major-General Alexander Bruce, C.B., C.M.G., Woodlands, St. Kilda, Melbourne, same crest and motto.

Tullock, two wings in lure or. 113. 3

Tulloh of Elliestoun, Roxburghsh., Scotland (1808-1893), a tiger courant ppr. *Cui debetur reverentia.*

Tulloh of Ellieston, St. Boswells, Roxburghsh. (prior to 1808 and since 1893), a mitre ppr. *Pietate parentum.*

Tully, Ireland, on a chapeau a serpent nowed, all ppr. 142. 9

Tully of Wetherall Abbey, Cumb., Cupid with his bow and quiver, all ppr. 189. 7

Tully, co. Galway, Ireland, a wolf's head couped arg. 30. 5

Tunnadine, Ireland, the top of a halberd issuing ppr. 172. 1

Tunnard, Charles Thomas, Frampton House, Lincs, a swan with wings elevated erm., beaked or, legged sa., the dexter claw resting on a bugle-horn of the last, stringed gu.

Tunnicliffe, Major George Henry, of Whitgreave, Stone, Staffs, on a chapeau ppr., a griffin passant or, holding in his dexter claw a tun ppr. *Haut et bon.*

Tunstall of Cotham Mundeville, Durh., Northumb., Westml., and Yorks, a cock arg., beaked gu., combed, wattled, and membered or, charged with a mullet. *cf.* 91. 2

Tunstall, Durh., and Thurland, Yorks, a cock arg., combed, wattled, and legged or, holding in the beak a scroll inscribed with the word *Droit.* *cf.* 91. 2

Tunstall, Lancs and Yorks, a cock arg., armed or, beaked and wattled gu. 91. 2

Tupper, Hon. Sir Charles, Baronet, G.C.M.G., C.B., LL.D., M.D., L.R.C.S., of Armdale, Halifax, in the province of Nova Scotia, in the Dominion of Canada, and of 97, Cromwell Road, London, S.W., upon a mount vert, a greyhound statant sa., charged on the body with two escallops or, holding in the mouth a sprig of mayflower slipped and leaved ppr. *L'espoir est ma force.*

Tupper, Basil de Beauvoir, Grange Hill, St. Peter Port, Guernsey, a mount vert, thereon a greyhound passant erm., charged on the shoulder with a slip of oak fructed ppr., the dexter fore-paw resting on an inescutcheon az., thereon pendent from a chain a medal or, bearing the profiles of their Majesties King William III. and Queen Mary II. *L'espoir est ma force.*

Tupper, Gaspard le Marchant, 24, Cornwall Gardens, S.W., same crest and motto.

Turbervill or **Turberville** of Coyty Castle, Glamorgansh., an eagle displayed or. 75. 2

Turbervill, Colonel, J.P., of Ewenny Abbey, Glamorgansh.: (1) An eagle displayed sa., armed, and the tips of the wings or, and charged on the body with a fesse erminois (*for Turbervill*). *cf.* 75. 2. (2) A crossbow erect in front of two swords in saltire ppr., pommels and hilts or (*for Warlow*). *Avi numerantur avorum.*

Turbervile, Berks, an eagle displayed sa. 75. 2

Turbervile of Beere, Dorset, a castle arg., the portcullis or. 155. 8

Turbott or **Turbutt** of Ogston Hall, Derbysh., Yorks, a naked arm holding in the hand ppr. a trident or, armed and headed arg. 214. 12

Turbutt of Arnold Grove, Notts, a naked dexter arm holding in the hand a trident. 214. 12

Turbutt (formerly Errington), Rev. John Launcelot, M.A., the Vicarage, Midgham, Reading, in front of a dexter arm embowed ppr., grasping a trident in bend sinister or, a fountain.

Turfeet of London, on a ducal coronet arg., a stag trippant ppr. *cf.* 117. 8

Turgeis, in a knot of rope a talbot's head or, eared sa.

Turing, Sir Robert Fraser, Bart., of Foveran, Aberdeen, and Chilgrove, Chichester, a hand holding a helmet erect ppr. *Audentes fortuna juvat.* 217. 12

Turisden, between two wings a griffin's head, holding in the beak a palm-branch ppr. 65. 9

Turnbull, Scotland, a bull's head erased sa., armed vert. *Audacior favente fortuna.* 44. 3

Turnbull of Stracathrow, Scotland, same crest. *Audaci favet fortuna.* 44. 3

Turnbull, Thomas Strover, B.A., Woodlands, St. Ann's-on-Sea, a bull's head. *Audaci favet fortuna.*

Turnbull, Scotland, a bull's head erased. *Audaci favet fortuna.* 44. 3

Turnbull, Robert, C.I.E., Continental Hotel, Calcutta, same crest and motto.

Turnbull of Mount Henley, Sydenham Hill, London, and of Wellington, New Zealand, in front of a bull's head erased sa., guttée-d'eau, armed or, four annulets interlaced fessewise of the last. *Fortuna favet audaci.* 44. 5

Turnbull, Alexander Horsburgh, Elibank, Wellington, New Zealand, same crest and motto.

Turnbull, Robert Thorburn, Elibank, Wellington, New Zealand, same crest and motto.

Turnbull of Know, Berwicksh., Scotland, a bull's head cabossed sa., armed vert. *Courage.* 43. 8

Turnbull, a cubit arm erect couped above the wrist, holding in the hand a sword erect ppr., enfiled with a bull's head erased sa. 266. 9

Turnbull, George Gillon, of Abbey St. Bathans, Berwick, Scotland, a dexter hand couped fesseways ppr., holding up a dagger erect, also ppr., hilted and pommelled or, bearing on the point a bull's head erased sa. *I saved the King.* 266. 9

Turnbull, John William, Pietermaritzburg, Natal, South Africa, same crest and motto.

Turnbull of Glasgow, a hand holding a dagger erect ppr., bearing on the point a bull's head erased sa. *Audaci favet fortuna.*

Turnbull of Currie, Scotland, a dexter hand holding up a baxter's pyle charged with three loaves in pale arg., all within two branches of palm vert. *Favet fortuna labori.*

Turner-Farley, *see* Farley.

Turner, *see* Round-Turner.

Turner, Hon. James, of Highfield, Hamilton, Ontario, Canada, Vice-President of the Bank of Hamilton and Director of the Northern and Pacific Railway, a lion passant. *Tu ne cede malis.* 6. 2

Turner, Bart. (*extinct*), of Warham, Norf., a lion passant gu. 6. 2

Turner of Thorverton and Halberton, Devonsh., and Norf., a lion passant gu., holding in the dexter paw a laurel-branch vert.

Turner, a lion passant gardant arg., regally crowned ppr., holding in the dexter paw a fer-de-moline sa. *cf.* 6. 7

Turner of Stanley, Warrington, Lancs, Hunts, and Suff., a lion passant gardant arg., holding in the dexter paw a mill-rind sa. *Pro patria.* 6. 7

Turner, Hunts and Suff., a lion passant gardant sa., holding in the dexter paw a mill-rind arg. 6. 7

Turner, Shropsh., a lion passant gardant, holding in his dexter paw a mill-rind sa. 6. 7

Turner of Chadswell, near Clitheroe, a lion passant guardant holding in the dexter paw a fer-de-moline.

Turner, Lincs, a lion passant arg., gorged with a plain collar or, holding in the dexter paw a mill-rind sa.

Turner of Penleigh, Wilts, a lion passant gardant erminois, charged upon the body with three trefoils in fesse slipped vert, and holding in the dexter paw a fer-de-moline sa. (*see* Beckett-Turner). 6. 8

Turner, George Henry, Littleover, Derbysh., a lion rampant guardant per bend sinister or and erm., holding in the dexter fore-paw a mill-rind sa., and resting the sinister on a spade ppr. *Labore et perseverantia.*

Turner, Page-, Bart., of Ambrosden, Oxon.: (1) A lion passant gardant arg., ducally crowned or, holding in the dexter paw a fer-de-moline pierced sa. (*for Turner*). *cf.* 6. 7. (2) A demi-horse per pale dancettée or and az. (*for Page*). 53. 3

Turner, Glouc., Derbysh., and of Parenden, Essex, a lion passant gardant arg., holding in the dexter paw a fer-de-moline sa. 6. 7

Turner-Farley, Thomas Macnaghten, Wartnaby Hall, Melton Mowbray: (1) A boar's head couped paly of six sa., guttée-d'eau and or (*for Farley*). (2) A lion guardant sa., charged on the body with three crosses patée fitchée arg., resting the dexter fore-paw on a shield of the last charged with a mill-rind, also sa. (*for Turner*). *Avito viret honore.*

Turner of Yarmouth, Norf., a lion passant gu., holding in the dexter paw a fer-de-moline or. *Utile quod facias.* *cf.* 6. 9

Turner, William, Purley Chase, Atherstone, Warw, same crest *Esse quam videri*

Turner of Eastbourne, Sussex a lion sejant arg, holding in the dexter paw a fer-de-moline or

Turner of Bandonbridge, co Cork, Ireland, a lion sejant erm, holding in the dexter paw a fer de-moline or, and charged on the shoulder with a crescent sa

Turner, a demi lion rampant gu, holding between the paws a fer de-moline arg

Turner, Augustus M A, Colerne, St John's Road Sidcup a demi-lion rampant holding between the paws a fleur-de lis *Virtus mille scuta*

Turner of Walden, Essex, a demi-wolf gu collared or, holding between the paws a mill rind of the last

Turner, a wolf's head erased sa, guttee-d'eau holding in the mouth a tulip branch vert.

Turner of London, on a chapeau gu, turned up erm, a greyhound statant sa *Pro patria.* 58 4

Turner, on a chapeau gu, turned up erm, a greyhound statant sa, collared arg cf 58 4

Turner of London, an antelope sejant erm, attired or resting the dexter foot on an escutcheon of the second

Turner of Wakestown Essex a demi-heraldic tiger salient or, tufted and maned sa, armed of the first

Turner, Shropsh, a tower arg with broken battlements.

Turner, on a tower arg with broken battlements an eagle regardant sa, holding in the dexter claw a mill-rind of the last

Turner of Caughley Place, Shropsh, a Cornish chough ppr perched on a mill-rind or

Turner of Dublin, an arm erect vested gu, cuffed arg, holding in the hand ppr a fer-de-moline or 207 4

Turner, a sword and a trident in saltier enfiled with an Eastern coronet

Turner of Swanwick Derbysh, and Surrey two wings conjoined in saltier arg, charged in the middle with a trefoil slipped vert

Turner, a flaming heart ppr. *Tu ne cede malis* 181 13

Turner of Menie, Aberdeensh, same crest and motto

Turner, Colonel John, Turner Hall, Ellon, Aberdeensh, same crest and motto.

Turner, Sir William, of 6, Eton Terrace, Edinburgh, K C B, M B, LL D, D C L., F R S, F R C S, a man's heart gu *Quod potui perfeci* 181 2

Turner, Thomas, Esquire, J P, Devonsh, a fer-de-moline *Recte et vere*

Turner, Rev George Wakefield, St. Jude's, Eldon Vicarage, Sheffield, a lion passant guardant arg, holding in the dexter paw a fer-de-moline sa *Pro patria*

Turner, E T, Esquire the Cedars, Cowley, Middx, a wolf's head erased sa, guttee-d'eau, holding in the mouth a tulip-branch vert *Justus et impavidus*

Turney, a cross patee fitched or 166 3

Turney of Cavenby, Lincs a tower sa towered arg. *In hoc signo vinces* 156 2

Turnley, Joseph, Esquire J P D L, Deputy Governor of the Honourable the Irish Society of the New Plantation in Ulster, out of a mural crown ppr, a Fritillaria meleagris stalked and leaved ppr *Perseverando*

Turnly, on a mount vert, an oak tree ppr, and pendent on the sinister side an escutcheon gu, charged with a cross patee or *Perseverando*

Turnly, John, Esquire, D I of Drumnasole, co Antrim, Ireland on a mount vert, an oak tree ppr, supporting on the sinister side a shield gu, charged with a cross patee or *Perseverando*

Turnor, Edmund, of Stoke, Rochford Lincs, a lion passant arg, crowned or, holding in the dexter paw a fer de-moline sa 6 9

Turnor, Algernon, C B, J P, Goadby Hall Melton Mowbray same crest

Turnor-Fetherstonhaugh, Hon Leith, Uppark Petersfield, Sussex (1) An heraldic antelope s head couped gu, armed or, gorged with a collar vair and holding in the mouth an ostrich-feather in bend arg (2) A lion passant guardant arg holding in the dexter paw a fer-de moline sa, and charged on the breast with a crescent gu *Esse quam videri*

Turnour, Earl of Winterton, *see* Winterton

Turnour, between two laurel branches ppr an escutcheon gu 146 14

Turpin of London, Cambs, and Leics, a griffin passant arg, guttee de sang, with wings addorsed or cf 63 2

Turpin, a griffin with wings inverted or, guttee-de sang, armed az cf 63 2

Turtle, between two wings or, a parrot's head gu 101 10

Turton of Larpoole Hall, near Whitby, Yorks and West Bromwich, Staffs, out of a mural coronet arg, a cubit arm vested vert, cuffed of the first, holding in the hand ppr a banner per fess arg and vert, the fringe counter-changed 206 6

Turton, Edmund Rossborough, Esquire J P D L., of Upsall, Yorks out of a mural coronet or, a cubit arm erect vested vert, cuffed arg the hand ppr holding a banner per fesse, also arg and vert charged with a trefoil, and the fringe counterchanged *Formosa quæ honesta* cf 206 6

Turton, Robert Bell, Esquire, of Kildale Hall, Yorks, and the Cottage, Thorpe Satchville, Melton Mowbray same crest and motto

Turton, Bart., of Starborough Castle, Surrey, out of a mural coronet or, a cubit arm erect vested vert, cuffed arg, holding in the hand ppr a banner per pale, also arg and vert, fringed staffed and headed of the first cf 206 6

Turvile, Leics a gate ppr, charged with a crescent or cf 158 9

Turvile, a gate ppr 158 9

Turvile of Husband's Bosworth, Leics a dove close, holding in the beak an olive-branch, all ppr *Virtus semper eadem* 92 5

Turvile of Normanton Turvile Leics, a dove close ppr, holding in the beak a branch of olive slipped vert, fructed or 92 5

Turyn, a demi lady holding in her dexter hand a garland of laurel ppr, vested gu 183 5

Tuson, a lion's head erased arg 17 8

Tuson, John Edward, M D, F R C S East India United Service Club out of a ducal coronet a lion's head

Tuson, a gadfly ppr

Tusser of Ryvenhall, Essex, a lion's gamb erased or, armed gu, holding a battle axe az, purfled of the last. 38 3

Tuthill, a bee volant in pale ppr 137 2

Tuthill of Dublin (1) Out of a coronet composed of a rose in the centre, two trefoils and two thistles with flowered heads or, a wolf's head sa (*for Tuthill*). (2) Out of a ducal coronet or, a demi lion rampant arg ducally crowned or, armed and langued gu (*for Villiers*) *Fidei coticula crux — Vincere aut mori* cf 16 3

Tuthill, Lieutenant Colonel Phineas Barrett Stockbridge, Chichester on a mount vert, a turtle dove ppr holding in her beak an olive branch vert fructed or *Pacis ac legis jure*

Tutin, a bridge of three arches or 158 4

Tutt, out of a ducal coronet or a griffin's head holding in the beak a key all ppr 65 14

Tutt of Barnstaple Devonsh Wilts and Hants, a talbot sejant or, collared and lined arg 55 5

Tutte of Chichester, Sussex, a talbot sejant or collared and lined arg 55 5

Tweddale, a lion's head erased gu 17 2

Tweddell, a pelican's head couped and vulning itself ppr cf 98 2

Tweddell, Ralph Hart Esquire J P, Meopham's Court, near Gravesend, same crest *Semper spero*

Twedie, Scotland, a demi lion holding in the paws an anchor ppr 12 12

Twedy, Essex a falcon rising ppr 88 2

Tweeddale, Marquess of (Hay), Yester House Haddingtonsh, a goat's head erased arg armed or *Spare nought* 128 5

Tweedie of London a palm and a laurel branch in saltier vert *Aut pax, aut bellum*

Tweedie of Drummelzier, Peeblessh., a bull s head sa. *Thol and think* cf 44 3

Tweedie of Rawlinson, a boar's head erased ppr *Thole and think on*

Tweedmouth, Baron (Marjoribanks) of Edington, Berwicksh a lion's gamb erect and erased grasping a lance in bend, both ppr *Advance with courage* 38 11

Tweedy, Chevalier Hugh D'Oyly Swedish and Norwegian Consul at Port au Prince Hayti, on a chapeau ppr, a dove rising of the same *Thole and think on* 94 8

Tweedy, Arthur Hearne Widmore Lodge, Widmore, Bromley Kent, on a prick-spur fesseways a peewit rising ppr, holding in the beak a trefoil slipped vert 286 6

Tweedy, George Alfred same crest

Tweedy, Hugh James, Junior Constitutional Club, same crest *Thole and think on*

Tweedy, Henry Colpoys 7, Clare Street, Merrion Square Dublin a dove volant arg *Fais ce que doit advienne que pourra* 243 19

Twells, Rev. Henry, M.A., Rector of Waltham, Leics., on a fountain ppr., a swan arg., beaked and legged sa. *Benedicite fontes domino.*

Twells, a swan ppr. 99. 2

Twemlow of Peatswood, Staffs, a parrot perched on the stump of a tree ppr. 101. 9

Twemlow of Hatherton, Chesh., on the stump of an oak-tree erect, a parrot perched ppr. *Teneo, tenuere majores.* 101. 9

Twemlow of Twemlow, Chesh., on the stump of a tree erect and sprouting a parrot, all ppr. 101. 9

Twemlow, Major-General Edward D'Oyly, same crest. *Fideliter.*

Twemlow, Francis Randle, D.S.O., Peatswood, Market Drayton, same crest.

Twemlow of Arclyd, Chesh., a parroquet standing on the stump of a tree sprouting, all ppr. *Nec cunctando, nec temere agendo.* 101. 9

Twentyman, a horse's head arg., bridled gu. 51. 5

Twicket, a lion's head erased sa., holding in the mouth a rose gu. 21. 5

Twigg or **Twigge,** an esquire's helmet ppr. 180. 3

Twigg of Repton, Derbysh., a hand holding a branch ppr. *Suo marte.*

Twinell of Peterborough, Northants, a lion's gamb holding a lozenge arg., charged with a cross crosslet fitchée gu. 35. 10

Twinihaw and **Twinies** of Tunworth, Dorset, a lapwing with wings expanded arg.

Twining, a cubit arm, the hand grasping two snakes, each entwined round the arm, all ppr. 220. 3

Twining, the stump of an oak-tree sprouting new branches ppr., thereon pendent an escutcheon gu. 145. 8

Twinnell, Northamp., a lion's gamb holding a lozenge arg., charged with a cross crosslet gu. 35. 10

Twisden of London and Kent, a cockatrice with wings expanded az., beaked, wattled, legged, and winged or. 68. 6

Twisden of Bradbourne, Larkfield, Maidstone, same crest.

Twisden, Bart., Kent, a cockatrice az., with wings displayed or. *Prævisa mala pereunt.* 68. 6

Twisleton, *see* Saye and Sele, Baron.

Twisleton of Barley, Drax, and Goole, Yorks, and Osbaston, Leics., a dexter arm embowed vested sa., turned up arg., holding in the hand ppr. a mole-spade or, headed and armed of the second. *Vidi, vici.*

Twisleton of Dartford, Kent, on a mount vert, a hind statant or, ducally gorged gu. *cf.* 125. 3

Twiss, an étoile rayed or.

Twiss, a cockatrice. 68. 4

Twiss, a demi-griffin ppr. 64. 2

Twist, a wyvern sejant or. *cf.* 69. 14

Twycross, Norf., a swan rising ppr. *Droit et avant.* 99. 12

Twyford, Leics., and Frostdyke, Lincs, a demi-lion rampant double-queued sa., holding a cinquefoil or.

Twyford of Trotton, Midhurst, Sussex, a demi-lion double-queued sa., guttée-d'or, holding in the dexter paw a trefoil slipped vert.

Twyning of Bryn, Pembrokesh., Ithon, Llandrindod, Radnorsh., the twin brothers Castor and Pollux in their infancy. *Stellis aspirate gemellis.*

Twyre, a hawk's head vair. *cf.* 88. 12

Twysden, a cockatrice or. 68. 4

Twysden, Bart. (*extinct*), of Bradbourne, Kent, a cockatrice az., with wings displayed or, and beaked and legged of the last. *Prævisa mala pereunt.* 68. 6

Twysden, Sir Louis John Francis, Bart., of Roydon Hall, East Peckham, Kent, a cockatrice az., winged and tufted or. 68. 4

Tyas and **Tyes** of London, a griffin's head erased arg., beaked gu. 66. 2

Tyas of Bolton-upon-Dearne, same crest. *Try.*

Tye, Essex, out of a ducal coronet or, an heraldic tiger's head tufted and armed arg. 25. 3

Tye, Notts, a wolf's head erased arg. 30. 8

Tyerman, Yorks, a griffin's head erased ppr. 66. 2

Tyers, a demi-lion rampant gu. 10. 3

Tylden of Wye, Kent, a broken spear erect or, environed by a snake vert. 175. 14

Tylden, Richard James, of Milsted, Kent, a battle-axe erect, environed by a snake ppr. *Truth and liberty.* 172. 2

Tylden-Pattenson, Arthur Henry, Naval and Military Club, a camel's head erased sa., bezantée. *Finem respice.—Truth and liberty.* 256. 2

Tylden-Pattenson, William, J.P., D.L., Ibornden, Biddenden, Kent, same crest and mottoes.

Tylden-Wright, Edward William, Manor Croft, Worksop: (1) Issuant from the battlements of a tower or, a dragon's head ppr., charged with two barrulets, and holding in the mouth an escallop, also or. (2) On a mount vert, in front of a battle-axe erect, entwined by a serpent ppr., between two pheons, a pheon or. *Treu und fest.*

Tyldesley of Tyldesley, Lancs, a pelican in her piety or. *Regis et patriæ tantum valet amor.* 98. 8

Tylee, Wilts, a demi-lion rampant gardant arg., pellettée, holding a crescent gu.

Tyler, Colonel Charles James, Engedi, St. Leonard's Road, Eastbourne, a demi-lion rampant guardant holding between its paws a crescent.

Tyler, a tiger salient gardant ppr., navally crowned or, holding in the dexter paw a flag-staff with the French tricolour flag flowing depressed and reversed. *cf.* 27. 5

Tyler, George William, Cottrell, Cardiff, same crest.

Tyler, Lieutenant-Colonel Charles John Roper, the Lodge, Linsted, Kent, same crest, but without the flagstaff.

Tyler of Newtown-limavady, co. Londonderry, Ireland, an arm embowed in armour charged with two crescents gu., the hand grasping a sword ppr. *Merito.* *cf.* 195. 2

Tyler of Monm., in front of a cross crosslet fitched and mounted on three grieces or, a dexter hand couped grasping a dagger embrued ppr., pommel and hilt of the first. *Crux præsidium et decus.*

Tyler, a hind's head erased or. 124. 3

Tyler, a demi-cat rampant and erased or, charged on the side with a cross-crosslet fitched gu., in a crescent of the last.

Tyler, Sir Frederick Charles, Bart., a demi-cat-a-mountain or, charged on the shoulder with two cross crosslets fitchée in saltire gu., holding between the paws a rose arg. 293. 1

Tylgham, Kent, a demi-lion sa., crowned or. 10. 11

Tylley, Somers., a demi-lion rampant gardant arg., pellettée, holding in the dexter paw a crescent gu.

Tylliot of East Bardsale, Suff., and Yorks, a greyhound passant gu., collared or. *cf.* 60. 2

Tylney, Suff. and Norf., on a ducal coronet or, a griffin's head erased gu., armed of the first. *cf.* 67. 9

Tylson, a dexter arm couped, vested sa., cuffed arg., holding in the hand ppr. a crosier or.

Tymewell of London, a demi-eagle gu., with wings displayed erm., crowned, armed, and gorged with a garland or.

Tyndall, *see* Hamilton-Tyndall-Bruce.

Tyndall, Albert Henry, Esquire, Ballyanne House, New Ross, co. Wexford, out of a ducal coronet or, a plume of five ostrich-feathers arg. *Dante Deo.*

Tynedale of Deane, Northants, Hockwold, Norf., Eastwood Park, Glouc., London, and Bathford, Somers., out of a ducal coronet of five leaves or, a plume of five ostrich-feathers arg., charged with a fess erm. *Confido, non confundor.* *cf.* 114. 13

Tynte, Kemeys-, Charles Theodore Halswell, of Halswell, Somers., and Cefn Mably, Glamorgansh.: (1) On a mount vert, a unicorn sejant az., armed, crined, and ungu. or (*for Tynte*). (2) Out of a ducal coronet a demi-griffin, all or (*for Kemeys*). *Duw Dy Ras.* 64. 4

Tynte, Major Fortescue, a unicorn sejant arg., horned and crined or.

Tyreonel, Earl of, Viscount Carlingford (Carpenter), a globe in a stand, all or. *Per acuta belli.* 159. 4

Tyrell, *see* Tufnell-Tyrell.

Tyrell, Bart. (*extinct*), of Springfield, Essex, a boar's head erect arg., and issuing out of the mouth a peacock's tail ppr. *Sans crainte.*

Tyrell, a demi-lion rampant gu., bezantée. 10. 4

Tyringham, Roger William Gifford, Tyringham, Bucks, a talbot's head couped gu., billettée or.

Tyron, an esquire's helmet az., garnished or. 180. 3

Tyrone, Earl of, *see* Waterford, Marquess of.

Tyrrell, a lion's head az., royally crowned or.

Tyrrell, Ireland, a lion's head erased or, within a chain in orle issuing from the wreath az. 19. 5

Tyrrell, Ireland, a demi-lion rampant az. 10. 2

Tyrrell of Fartullagh, co. Westmeath, Ireland, and Florence, Italy, same crest. *Veritas iræ vitæ.*

Tyrrell of Rushton, Staffs, a boar's head erect arg., issuing out of the mouth a peacock's tail ppr.

Tyrwhitt-Drake, *see* Drake.

Tyrwhitt, Richard, Esquire, of Nantyr, West Gwillimbury, Canada, Lieutenant-Colonel 36th Battalion Active Militia (Peel Regiment), a savage ppr wreathed and cinctured vert holding in both hands a club *Me stante, vire bunt —Tyme tryeth truth*

Tyrwhitt of Nantyr, Denbighsh, Wales a savage man ppr, wreathed vert holding in both hands a club *Me stante, virebunt*

Tyrwhitt, Hon Hugh, R N, same crest

Tyrwhitt of Ketilby, Lincs, and Tyrwhitt, Northumb, a savage man ppr, cinctured and wreathed vert, holding in both hands a club *Me stante, vire bunt —Tyme tryeth truth* 279 11

Tyrwhitt, the late Sir Henry Thomas Bart, of Stanley Hall Shropsh (1) A savage ppr, wreathed and cinctured with oak-leaves vert, and holding in his dexter hand a club ppr (*for Tyrwhitt*) 279 11 (2) On a wreath the sun in splendour each ray inflamed or (*for Jones*) *Time tryeth truth —Esto sol testis* 162 2

Tyrwhitt-Wilson, Sir Raymond Robert, Stanley Hall Bridgnorth, same crest as (1) above

Tyrwhitt, a lapwing's head couped or

Tyser, George Walter J P, Oakfield Mortimer, Berks upon a cotton hank fesseways or, a falcon close collared, also or *Deo volente surgam*

Tysoe, a sinister arm in mail ppr, holding an antique shield lined vert, edged or, strapped gu *Non progredi est regredi*

Tyson, Edward Thomas, Woodhall, Cockermouth a demi lion vert, guttee d'eau, holding in the dexter paw a torch erect fired ppr the sinister paw resting on a rose gu barbed and seeded ppr *Fortiter et vigilanter* 12 6

Tyssen, a demi lion rampant or, ducally crowned gu, holding between the paws an escutcheon az, thereon an etoile of the first.

Tytherley, Hants a wolf passant gu 28 10

Tytler, Fraser-, James William, of Woodhouselee co Edinburgh, Scotland, the rays of the sun issuing from a cloud ppr *Occultus, non extinctus* 162 9

Tytler, Fraser-, Edward Grant Aldourie Castle, Inverness (1) Same crest as above (2) A stag's head erased ppr (*for Fraser*)

Tytler, Major General Robert Francis Christopher Alexander, 40, Emperor's Gate S W same crest and motto

Tytler, Fraser-, of Balnain, Inverness sh (1) The rays of the sun issuing from behind a cloud ppr (*for Tytler*) 162 9 (2) A stag's head erased ppr (*for Fraser*) *Occultus, non extinctus —Je suis prest* 121 5

Tytler, Scotland, two laurel-branches in orle vert. *Virtutis gloria crescit* 146 5

Tytler, Scotland, two laurel branches in orle vert encircling an anchor and an Æsculapius rod on the top of the anchor a plume of three feathers, all ppr *Spes firma —Immortalia spero*

Tyzard, a boar's head couped or 43 1

Tyzdale, Ireland out of a ducal coronet or a dexter arm in armour charged with an etoile holding in the hand an arrow all ppr

U.

Uderaj, Muhtab Chund Moharaj, **Bahadur of Burdwan,** Bengal an iron gray horse's head couped around the neck a ribbon az and pendent therefrom an escutcheon of the last, charged with a lotus-flower ppr *Deo credito justitiam colito* 50 9

Udney of that Ilk and Auchterallan Aberdeen, a fleur-de lis gu *All my hope is in God* 148 2

Udney of Cultercullen, a fleur-de lis or *All my hope is in God* 148 2

Udny, John Henry Fullarton, Udny Castle Aberdeensh a fleur-de lis gu *All my hope is in God*

Udward of Longroft, Scotland a torteau *Nec flatu nec fluctu* 159 14

Uffington, Viscount, *see* Craven, Earl of

Uffleet or **Ufflet,** a lion's gamb erased sa, holding the hilt of a broken sword erect ppr 38 2

Uffleete, on the top of a Doric pillar a heart gu 176 5

Ufford, Earl of Suffolk (*extinct*), a man's head erased ppr, bearded and crowned or

Ufford, De, a demi-eagle displayed sa 81 6

Ufford, an anchor or, in the sea vert 161 6

Ufford, a talbot passant, charged on the shoulder with three guttes de-sang *cf* 54 1

Ugletreight, out of a ducal coronet a buck's head 120 7

Uhthoff, a yew-tree ppr

Umfrevile, Essex and Lincs out of a ducal coronet or, an eagle's head arg *cf* 83 14

Umfreville, a lion's gamb erased gu a sceptre in pale or 38 7

Umfreville, out of a mural coronet gu a griffin's head erm 67 10

Umphray of Zetland an open book ppr *Pax tua, Domine, est requies mea* 158 3

Umpton, a demi-greyhound sa 60 11

Umpton, a demi-greyhound sa, collared and ringed, and holding in the mouth a spear head or

Umpton, on a chapeau az, turned up erm a griffin passant arg *cf* 63 13

Undall, Dorset, a serpent vert, entwined round two halberds addorsed ppr 172 6

Underhay of Holland House, Hornsey, London, an arm embowed in armour, holding in the hand a sword all ppr *Factis non verbis* 195 2

Underhill, Middx, of Wolverhampton, Staffs and of Etington and Hunningham, Warw on a mount vert, a hind lodged or 125 4

Underwood, Ireland a lion's gamb holding a thistle ppr 37 6

Underwood, Ireland, a lion passant az *Noli irritare leonem* 6 2

Underwood, a hind's head 124 1

Underwood, Heref a hind's head erased 124 3

Underwood of Buxley and Haveningham, Norf a hind's head or, gorged with a chaplet vert *cf* 124 3

Underwood, Charles Frederick Weston Esquire, Somerby Hall Brigg, Lancs, same crest

Unett of Woodlands, Harborne, Staffs, a lion's head erased 17 8

Unett, Henry Henzell, Huntingdon Hall, York, a lion's head couped

Unett of Castle Frome, Frean's Court, and Marden Court, Heref, on a chapeau gu, turned up erm, a cockatrice sejant ppr *Disce mori ut vivas*

Unett, on a chapeau a cockatrice sejant with wings addorsed and ducally crowned all ppr

Unett, Shropsh out of a ducal coronet or a griffin's head sa 67 9

Uniacke or **Uniake,** a dexter arm in armour gauntleted ppr, holding a hawk's lure or 237 17

Uniacke, Norman Compton Fitzgerald, Mount Uniacke, co Cork, same crest

Uniacke, Norman James Fyfe, same crest *Unicus est*

Uniacke, Richard Gordon Fitzgerald, Chelsham Lodge, Chelsham, Surrey, same crest

Uniacke, Robert Uniacke Fitzgerald, 3 Pennsylvania Exeter same crest

Uniacke-Penrose-Fitzgerald, Sir Robert Uniacke, 35 Grosvenor Road, S W, a knight in complete armour his sword drawn and beaver up all ppr mounted on a horse courant arg the whole charged with a crescent or *Fortis et fidelis*

Unsworth of Mogul Hall Liverpool, and Lancs, a lion rampant bendy of six or and az, holding in the paws a cross patee fitched of the first 3 13

Untercombe, a sword erect, enfiled with a man's head couped 191 9

Unthank, Clement William Joseph of Intwood Hall Norf, a gryphon's head erased gu gorged with a collar flory and ducally crowned or, holding in the beak an increscent of the last *Esto semper fidelis*

Unton of Wadley, Berks, a demi-greyhound sa collared or, holding in the mouth a broken spear

Unwin, a fleur-de lis or 148 2

Upcher, Rev Arthur Hamilton, M A, the Rectory Baconsthorpe, Norf in front of a plume of five ostrich-feathers arg and or, a unicorn's head couped az gorged with a ducal coronet or *Præstat opes sapientia*

Upcher, Rev Arthur Wilson M A, Hingham Norf, same crest and motto

Upcher, Rev Harry Berners Broom Hall Watton Norf, same crest and motto

Upcher, Henry Morris, Sheringham Hall Norf same crest and motto

Uphaugh, Richard Duppa de, Esquire, of Hollingbourne House, near Maidstone, Kent: (1) In front of a dexter arm embowed in armour, the hand in a gauntlet ppr., grasping a lion's paw in bend sinister couped, a rose between two annulets gu. (*for Duppa*). (2) A cubit arm erect ppr., charged with an anchor sa., encircled by an annulet, and holding in the hand in bend sinister a trident, both or (*for Turbutt*).

Uphill of London and Devonsh., on a mount charged with trefoils slipped vert, a bird volant, holding in the beak a trefoil slipped, also vert.

Upjohn, a stork ppr. 105. 11

Uppleby, Rev. George Crowle, of Wootton and Barrow Hall, Lincs, a buck's head couped quarterly arg. and gu., attired sa., collared az., thereon three martlets or. *Metuo secundis.*

Upton, *see* Templeton, Viscount.

Upton of Clyde Court, co. Louth, on a ducal coronet or, a war-horse current sa., caparisoned of the first. *Semper paratus.* 240. 10

Upton of Ingmire Hall, Westml., on a ducal coronet or, a horse passant sa., furnished of the first. *Semper paratus.* 240. 10

Upton, a lion's gamb az., holding a crescent or. 39. 15

Upton of Gaydon, on a chapeau az., turned up erm., a griffin passant arg. *cf.* 63. 13

Upton of Northolme, Lincs, a demi-wolf rampant arg. 31. 2

Upton, Sussex, two dolphins in saltier or, finned az. 140. 3

Upwood of Lovell's Hall, Norf., a horse's head erased sa. 51. 4

Urby, a man's head couped at the shoulders in profile ppr.

Ure, Scotland, a lion's gamb erect and erased gu. *Sans tache.* 36. 4

Urlin, Richard Denny, of the Middle Temple, 22, Stafford Terrace, Phillimore Gardens, W., a boar's head erased. *Nec temere nec timide.*

Urmestone of Westley, Lancs, and Yorks, a dragon's head erased vert. *cf.* 71. 2

Urquhart of Blyth, Aberdeensh., Scotland, a palm-branch and a sword in saltier ppr. *Weigh well.*

Urquhart, Scotland: (1) A dagger and a branch of palm slipped in saltier ppr. (2) A demi-otter sa., crowned with an antique crown or, holding between the paws a crescent gu. *Weigh well.—Per mare, per terras.*

Urquhart of Cromarty, Scotland, a demi-otter ppr., crowned with an antique crown gu., gorged with a collar or, charged with three crescents of the second. *Will well.*

Urquhart, a demi-otter sa., crowned with an antique crown or. *Mean, speak, and doe well.*

Urquhart, Pollard-, Lieutenant-Colonel Francis Edward Romulus, of Castle Pollard, co. Westmeath, Ireland: (1) A demi-otter rampant ppr., crowned with an antique crown or, gorged with a collar of the same charged with three crescents gu. (*for Urquhart*). (2) A stag trippant ppr., attired or (*for Pollard*). 117. 8. (3) Out of a mural coronet arg., a greyhound's head sa., gorged with a collar gu., charged with three plates (*for Hampson*). *Will well.*

Urquhart, Scotland, a boar's head erased or. *Mean, speak, and doe well.* 42. 2

Urquhart of Newhall, Scotland, a boar's head couped gu. *Per actum intentio.* 43. 1

Urquhart of Meldrum, Aberdeensh., Scotland, a boar's head erased or. *Per mare, per terras.* 42. 2

Urquhart, a lion's gamb holding a human heart ppr. 39. 11

Urquhart of Burdsyards, Elginsh., Scotland, a dexter hand holding a dagger in pale ppr. *Mean, speak, and do well.* 212. 9

Urquhart, out of a mural coronet or, a dexter arm from the shoulder embowed, vested gu., turned up with buff, and suspended from the hand by a ribbon gu., an escutcheon az., charged with a wolf's head erased arg., the arm charged with a crescent of the first. *Dum spiro spero.*

Urren, Wales, a Cornish chough rising with wings displayed ppr., resting the dexter claw on an escutcheon sa., charged with a leopard's face or. 107. 12

Urrie, Scotland, a lion's gamb erased gu. *Sans tache.* 36. 4

Urry, Scotland, a lion's gamb erased sa. *Sans tache.* 36. 4

Urry of Thorley, Afton, and Gatcombe, a demi-lioness ppr.

Urswicke, a lion passant arg. 6. 2

Usborne of Cooling, Sussex, a doe lodged at the foot of a tree, all ppr. *Virtus vincit invidiam.*

Usher, a Doric pillar arg., winged or. 113. 10

Usher, Ireland, a swan with wings addorsed regardant arg., murally crowned or, the dexter foot resting on an escallop gu. 99. 7

Usher of Eastwell, Galway, a cubit arm vested az., cuffed arg., holding in the hand a baton of the last. *Ne vile veles.*

Usher, Sir John, Bart., Norton, Ratho, Midlothian, a dexter arm holding in the hand a baton ppr. *Ne vile velis.* 312. 15

Usher of Donnybrook and Portrane, co. Dublin, Ireland, an arm couped below the elbow and erect vested bendy or and az., holding in the hand ppr. a baton of the first.

Usher of Ballysaggartmore, co. Waterford, a dexter cubit arm in pale vested bendy of six gu. and or, cuffed erminois, holding in the hand ppr. a baton arg. *Ne vile velis.*

Usticke of Woodlane, Cornw.: (1) A demi-eagle displayed gu., gorged with a plain collar and pendent therefrom an escutcheon or, charged with a water-bouget sa. (*for Usticke*). 81. 7. (2) A dexter arm in armour embowed grasping a sword ppr., between the attires of a stag sa. (*for Nowell*). (3) Upon a mount vert, in front of rays of the sun ppr., a martlet sa., holding in the beak an acorn slipped, also ppr. (*for Beauchant*). *Semper paratus.*

Usticke, Nowell-, Robert Michael Polsue Philleigh, Grampound Road, Cornw., same crests and motto.

Utber and **Utker** of Norwich and Hoo, Norf., an arrow erect sa., headed and feathered arg., to the shaft wings expanded or, the barb of the arrow in base. 174. 1

Utermarck, Reginald John Guthrie, Esquire, of Vimiera, Guernsey, a sprig of three rose-leaves slipped vert, between two buffalo-horns per fesse or and az. *Va outre marque.* 261. 4

Utreight, out of a ducal coronet a bull's head couped az., armed or. 44. 11

Utterson of Milland Place, Sussex, a mount vert, thereon a tree, and at the foot thereof a paschal lamb, all ppr.

Uvedale of Wikeham and Horton, Hants, and More Crichell, Dorset, on either side of a chapeau az., turned up erm., an ostrich-feather within the turning up. 114. 10

Uvedell, a pheasant vert, crested, armed, and gorged with a chaplet vert. *cf.* 90. 10

Uvery, an elephant's head. 133. 2

Uxbridge, Earl of, *see* Anglesey, Marquess of.

V.

Vachell, a bull passant arg., armed and collared or, a bell pendent from the collar of the last.

Vachell, a bull's leg embowed couped at the thigh erm., the hoof upwards. 123. 4

Vachell of Colley and Windsor, Berks, Beds, and North Marston, Bucks, a bull's leg in pale couped arg., the hoof in base or. 123. 7

Vade-Walpole, Henry Spencer, of Stagbury, Surrey, the bust of a man in profile, couped at the shoulders ppr., ducally crowned or, and from the coronet flowing a long cap, turned forwards gu., tasselled or, charged with a Catherine-wheel of the last. *Fari quæ sentiat.*

Vafiadacchi-Schilizzi of Paddington, Middx.: (1) In front of a tilting-spear erect ppr., a greyhound sejant arg., resting the dexter fore-paw on a bezant (*for Schilizzi*). 59. 7. (2) A garb or, between two elephant's trunks gu. (*for Vafiadacchi*). *Fidelitas.*

Vahl-Samuel, De, *see* De-Vahl.

Valle, Lawrence William, J.P., South Cliff House, Sion Hill, Ramsgate, a mount vert, thereon in front of two cross crosslets fitchée in saltire gu., a wolf's head erased az, in the mouth three ears of wheat *Semper paratus* 264 4

Vair, Scotland, a boar's head and neck couped arg *Cura atque industria* 41 1

Vaire, a fret gu 165 10

Vaizey, Arthur Reginald, Esquire of 9, John Street Bedford Row, W C, in front of a cubit arm in armour erect the hand in a gauntlet holding an oak-branch, also erect, and slipped, all ppr, a cross crosslet arg *Sub hoc signo vinces*

Vaizey, Robert Edward, Esquire of Attwoods, Essex, and Tilbury Hall, Halstead, in front of a cubit arm in armour, the hand in a gauntlet holding an oak branch slipped and erect, all ppr, a cross crosslet crossed arg *Sub hoc signo vinces*

Valange of Possel Scotland, a rose surmounted by a thistle ppr *In utroque* 149 3

Vale of Mathon Court, Worcs, on a mount vert a swan's head couped at the neck arg, guttee-de-poix, in front of two crosses patee fitched in saltier gu *In te Domine speravi* 101 3

Vale-Martindale, Major Henry Edward Coddington Court, Ledbury, same crest *Semper volens*

Vale, on a tower sa, a crescent gu 156 4

Valence and **Valomess**, between two wings or, each charged with a rose gu, a cross fleury fitched az, charged on the centre with the sun, and ensigned with a demi fleur-de lis of the first cf 112 7

Valence, a greyhound's head gu cf 61 12

Valentia, Viscount (Annesley), co Kerry, a Moor's head in profile couped ppr wreathed about the temples arg and az *Virtutis amore* cf 192 13

Valentine, Heref, a demi pegasus salient and erased erm, enfiled round the body with a ducal coronet or cf 47 7

Valentine, Suff, an ostrich holding in the beak a horse shoe ppr 97 8

Vallack, a dove rising ppr 94 2

Vallado, Marquis de, *see* Walrond

Vallance, Scotland, a garb gu 153 2

Vallance, out of a ducal coronet a demi-ostrich with wings addorsed all ppr 96 11

Vallefort, Viscount, *see* Mount Edgcumbe, Earl of

Valpy, Jersey, a mountain ppr *Valet pietas*

Valpy, Robert Harris, J P, Enborne Lodge Newbury, a fox courant arg *Vulpes haud capitur laqueo.*

Vampage, a demi lion rampant or 10 2

Vampage, a bridge of three arches arg 158 4

Van Allen, *see* Allen

Van Cuellan, *see* Cuellan

Van-Hagen, between two wings arg, a trefoil vert 110 12

Van Jucken, two wings expanded ppr 109 6

Van Koughnet, Captain Barker R N, Tyttenhanger Park St Albans, out of a foreign coronet or, a demi-lion rampant gu, holding a sword transfixing three chess-rooks or

Van Notten-Pole, *see* Pole

Van Straubenzee, Yorks, out of a ducal coronet or, two wings per fess arg and gu, counterchanged 109 8

Van Straubenzee of Spennithorne, Yorks an ostrich holding in the beak a horse-shoe 97 8

Van Streyan, a demi-lion rampant sa 10 1

Van Voorst of London, a demi mermaid holding in her dexter hand a drinking cup and in her sinister a jug 183 11

Van-Whalff, a demi wolf 31 2

Van-Zellar of York Place, Portman Square London, a blackbird ppr, beaked and legged gu, charged on the breast with a star of six points or cf 106 2

Van, a stag lodged ppr 115 7

Van, Wales, a heron with wings expanded arg 105 2

Vanam or **Vannam** of London, a bundle of five arrows sa points upwards, bound by a belt gu, the buckle or

Vanbrug and **Vanburgh** of Ghent Flanders, out of a bridge of three arches reversed a demi lion or

Vance, *see* Balbirnie Vance

Vance, Ireland, an old man's head ppr, the helmet az

Vandeleur, Ireland, five arrows in saltier entwined by a serpent, all ppr

Vandeleur, Colonel Boyle a martlet purpure holding in the beak a trefoil or

Vandeleur, Hector Stewart J P, Kilrush House co Clare, same crest

Vandeleur, Crofton Toler, same crest and motto

Vandeleur of Kilrush, co Clare, Ireland, a martlet purp holding in the beak a trefoil slipped or *Virtus astra petit*

Vanden-Bempde-Johnstone, Baron Derwent, *see* Derwent

Vanden-Bempde-Johnstone (1) A spur erect rowel upwards, with wings elevated or, leather gu, the buckle ppr 111 13 (2) Issuing from the battlements of a tower ppr a demi eagle with two heads displayed sa the wings or, about the neck a pearl collar there from a diamond pendent, and charged on the breast with a sword fesseways ppr, pommel and hilt or *Nunquam non paratus*

Vandeput, Bart (*extinct*), of Twickenham, Middx, between two wings or, a dolphin haurient az 140 2

Vandergucht of London, an etoile arg 164 1

Vanderplank of London, a garb or *Industria ditat* 153 2

Vandyk or **Vandyke**, an eagle's head and neck in a tun the dexter wing elevated, the sinister cut off and lying on wreath 80 9

Vane, Duke of Cleveland, *see* Cleveland

Vane-Tempest-Stewart, *see* Londonderry, Marquess of

Vane, a dexter gauntlet erect holding a dagger, all ppr, pommel and hilt or

Vane, Sir Henry Ralph Fletcher Bart, J P, D L, of Hutton in the Forest Cumb (1) An arm in armour embowed holding in the hand a sword 195 2 (2) A gauntlet holding a dagger ppr, hilt and pommel or

Vane, Baron Barnard, same crest.

Vane, Rev Hon Gilbert Holles Farrer, M A, the Rectory Wem, same crest *Nec temere, nec timide*

Vane, a dexter gauntlet ppr, garnished or, holding a sword of the first, hilt and pommel of the second

Vane of Fair lawn, Ravensbourne Park Catford, Lewisham, Kent, on a rock in front of a cubit arm in armour, the hand in a gauntlet grasping a sword in bend sinister, all ppr, pommel and hilt or, three crosses couped or *Nec temere nec timide*

Vane-Tempest (1) A griffin's head erased per pale arg and sa (*for Tempest*) (2) A dexter gauntlet erect holding a sword ppr, pommel and hilt or (*for Vane*)

Vanheck of London, a rose gu, barbed stalked, and leaved ppr 149 5

Vanhitheson, out of a ducal coronet a dragon's head or, the wings addorsed arg each wing charged with three bars gu cf 72 1

Vanneck, *see* Huntingfield, Baron

Vanneck, between two wings a hunting-horn stringed 112 3

Vanort, Holland and France on a terraqueous globe a ship ppr 160 1

Vans-Agnew, Barnbarrock Scotland, *see* Agnew

Vansittart, Baron Bexley, *see* Bexley

Van Sittart-Neale, Henry James, Bisham Abbey Marlow Berks (1) Out of a mural crown or, a demi lion rampant per fesse erm and gu charged on the shoulder with an escallop counter-changed (*for Neale*) (2) On two crosses patee arg, a demi-eagle displayed sa (*for Van Sittart*)

Van-Sittart, an eagle's head couped at the neck, between two wings sa, all resting on two crosses patee arg *Fata viam invenient*

Vansittart, Major Eden, Abbottabad, Punjaub same crest

Van Straubenzer, Major General Turner, C B Spennithorne, Leyburn Yorks, an ostrich with a horse-shoe in its mouth

Vardon, a dexter hand holding a sheaf of arrows ppr 214 3

Varley, out of a ducal coronet or, a staff raguly sa 147 10

Varley of London and Yorks, out of a palisado coronet or an arm in armour embowed holding a battle axe all ppr *Magna est veritas* cf 200 6

Varlo, a cross moline gu, between two ears of wheat bladed ppr 154 14

Varnham, an eagle with wings elevated preying on a coney 70 2

Varnham, a dexter hand holding up a ducal coronet between two laurel-branches, all ppr 217 3

Varty, Cumb, a man's head affrontee ppr, ducally crowned or 192 9

Vashen, a dexter arm, the hand apaumee ppr vested az from the shoulder paleways from the elbow fesseways

Vass, an ostrich's head between two feathers arg holding in the beak gu a horse shoe az 97 12

Vassall of Milford, Hants (1) On a mount vert a breached fortress ppr thereon a flag hoisted gu, with the words *Monte Video* inscribed thereon in letters of gold (2) A ship with masts and shrouds, all ppr *Sæpe pro Rege semper pro republica —Every bullet has its billet*

Vassall of New England, a ship rigged and masted ppr. *Sæpe pro Rege, semper pro republica.* 160. 13

Vaudin, Jersey, an eagle displayed sa. *Povr ma libertay, povr ma patree.* 75. 2

Vaughan, Lord, *see* Lisburne, Earl of.

Vaughan, *see* Hutchinson - Lloyd - Vaughan.

Vaughan, Earl of Carbery (*extinct*), on a ducal coronet or, a lion rampant per fesse arg. and sa. *Plane et sane.* *cf.* 1. 13

Vaughan, a lion rampant ppr. 1. 13

Vaughan of Chilton Grove, near Shrewsbury, a lion rampant az. 1. 13

Vaughan, Bart. (*extinct*), of Nannau, Merionethsh., a lion rampant az., gorged with an antique coronet or. *cf.* 1. 13

Vaughan, on a garb lying fesseways or, a lion rampant regardant holding in the dexter paw three stalks of barley ppr. 233. 1

Vaughan, Hugh Vaughan, the Castle, Builth, Brecon, on a garb lying fesseways or, a lion rampant regardant arg., holding in the dexter paw two ears of wheat of the first. 233. 1

Vaughan, James, Llansaintfraed House, near Builth, on a garb lying fesseways or, a lion rampant regardant arg., holding in the dexter paw three ears of wheat stalked and leaved, also or.

Vaughan of Penmaen-Dovey, Merioneth, a demi-lion rampant sa. 10. 1

Vaughan, out of a five-leaved ducal coronet or, a demi-lion rampant per fess arg. and sa., ducally crowned or. *cf.* 16. 3

Vaughan, Monmouthsh., a demi-lion rampant per fesse or and gu., holding in the paws an escroll inscribed *Immaculate gens.*

Vaughan of Littleton, Middx., a lion's gamb or, holding a human heart gu. 39. 11

Vaughan of Duddleston, Shropsh., a boar's head gu., couped or. (*Another*, a boar's head couped close gu.) 43. 1

Vaughan, Edward Goldisbrough Chambre, of Burlton Hall, Shropsh., on a chapeau ppr., turned up erm., a boar's head couped gu., armed or, langued az. *Afra pob afraid.* *cf.* 42. 5

Vaughan, Chamber-, of Burlton Hall, Shropsh.: (1) On a chapeau gu., turned up erm., a boar's head couped in fess gu., armed or, langued az. (*for Vaughan*). *cf.* 42. 5. (2) Out of a garland of roses a greyhound's head and neck arg., collared az., chained or (*for Chamber*). (3) A demi-boar rampant ppr., armed, bristled, and ungu. or, pierced in the shoulder by an arrow of the last, feathered arg., embrued gu. (*for Bolas*). *Afrad pob afraid.* *cf.* 40. 13

Vaughan, Wales, a man erect ppr., his arms extended, vested in a jacket arg., the breeches sa., his hair flotant, and in his dexter hand a large knife of the second.

Vaughan of Talgarth, Brecknocksh., a maiden's head, her hair dishevelled, couped below the breasts, all ppr.

Vaughan, Gwynne-, of Cynghordy, Carmarthensh., upon a mount vert, in front of a boy's head affrontée couped at the shoulders ppr., crined or, a snake nowed, also ppr. *Asgre lan diogel ei pherchen.* 182. 11

Vaughan of Rheola, Glamorgansh., a boy's head couped ppr., crined or, enwrapped about the neck with a snake vert, and pendent from the neck a bugle-horn sa. *Asgre lan diogel ei pherchen.*

Vaughan of Court Field, Heref., a child's head couped at the shoulders and entwined round the neck with a snake, all ppr. *Duw a digon.—Simplices sicut pueri sagaces sicut serpentes.* 272. 8

Vaughan of Woodstone, Hunts: (1) An infant's head couped at the shoulders entwined with a snake about the neck, all ppr. (*for Vaughan*). 272. 8. (2) Out of a ducal coronet or, a dragon's head issuant ppr. (*for Wright*). 72. 4

Vaughan of Sutton, Yorks, Heref., and Wales, a boy's head couped at the shoulders ppr., crined or, with a snake entwined about the neck vert. 272. 8

Vaughan, Rev. Henry, Wraxall Rectory, Somers., same crest. *Christus servitus vera libertas.*

Vaughan, Rev. George Henry, of Quilly, co. Down, Ireland, a boy's head couped at the shoulders and entwined round the neck with a snake, all ppr., and charged on the neck with a cross of Ulster (*i.e.*, a cross couped gu.). *Honeste audax.*

Vaughan-Jenkins of Combe Grove, Monkton Combe, Somers.: (1) A fleur-de-lis per pale or and sa., encircled with two branches of oak fructed ppr. (*for Jenkins*). (2) A boy's head couped at the shoulders, around his neck a garland of oak ppr., charged on the breast with a cross patée fitchée gu. (*for Vaughan*).

Vaughan-Lee, Arthur Vaughan Hanning, of Dillington Park, Ilminster: (1) On a mount vert, a leopard passant ppr., supporting with the dexter fore-paw a shield az., charged with two bars gemel arg. (2) Same crest as Vaughan of Rheola.

Vaughan-Lloyd, William Peisley Hutchinson, J.P., Golden Grove, Roscrea, King's Co.: (1) A boy's head couped at the shoulders, crined or, round the neck a snake entwined ppr. (*for Vaughan*). (2) A lion rampant arg., holding in the dexter fore-paw a snake ppr. (*for Lloyd of Glouc.*). (3) On a ducal coronet or, a cockatrice, wings addorsed ppr. *Innocentia infantis, sapientia serpentis.*

Vaughan of Falstone, Wilts, Shapwick, Dorset, and Just, Glouc., an arm erect, the hand grasping a snake entwined round the arm, all ppr. 220. 2

Vaughan of Bradward, Wilts, and Bredwarden and Porthamell, Heref., on a plume of three ostrich-feathers gu., a griffin's head or.

Vaughan of Wigmore, Heref., on a mount vert, a hound sejant arg., collared gu.

Vaughan, Shropsh., a fleur-de-lis arg. 148. 2

Vaughan, three hand-guns erect or, and two serpents az., entwined about the barrels of the last.

Vaughan Lloyd, Edward Owen, Esquire, of Berth and Rhagatt, Corwen, North Wales, out of a ducal coronet or, a unicorn's head arg., crined and armed of the first.

Vault, a demi-ape couped at the shoulders ppr.

Vaulx, an eagle's head erased sa., ducally gorged or. *cf.* 83. 10

Vaulx, a cubit arm erect vested chequy or and gu., holding in the hand ppr. a chaplet vert, fructed.

Vaulx and **Vaus** of Marston-Mairley, Wilts, Corley and Tyermain, Cumb., Storesby, Yorks, and Wipsnot Hall, Beds, an eagle's head sa., beaked or. 83. 1

Vaux, Baron, *see* Brougham and Vaux.

Vaux, Baron (Mostyn), of Harrowden, a lion rampant or. *Hodie non cras.* 1. 13

Vaux, on a ducal coronet a peacock statant ppr. 103. 8

Vaux, a griffin's head erased. 66. 2

Vaux of Catterlyn, Cumb., an eagle's head erased sa., collared or. *cf.* 83. 2

Vavasour of Bushton and Averston, Northamp., and Yorks, a goat's head or, gorged with a collar dancettée sa.

Vavasour of Denton and Weston Hall, Yorks, a cock gu., combed and wattled or. 91. 2

Vavasour, Sir William Edward, Bart., of Hazlewood, Yorks: (1) A cock gu., charged with a fountain (*for Vavasour*). *cf.* 91. 2. (2) A demi-friar habited ppr., and holding in his dexter hand a scourge and in his sinister an open book (*for Stourton*). *cf.* 187. 11

Vavasour, Sir Henry Mervin, Bart., D.L., of Spaldington, Yorks, a cock gu., combed, wattled, and legged, and charged on the breast with a fleur-de-lis arg. *cf.* 91. 2

Vavasseur, Josiah, Rothbury, Blackheath Park, S.E., in front of a dexter cubit arm holding in the hand a , two swords in saltire ppr. *Tout par faveur divine.*

Vavazor of Wisbeach, Isle of Ely, Cambs, a squirrel sejant on a hazel-branch turned up behind his back, and feeding on a slip of the same, all ppr.

Vawdrey, Chesh., a swallow ppr. *cf.* 96. 1

Vawdrey, Rev. Llewelyn Brookes, of Tushingham Hall, Chesh., a cock statant arg., armed, combed, and legged gu. 91. 2

Vazie, Oxon., an arm couped at the shoulder in fess, embowed at the elbow, vested gu., cuffed erm., holding in the hand a bunch of laurel vert.

Veal, Henry James, Esquire, J.P., a garb encircled by a ducal coronet. *Victima Deo.*

Veale, a chevalier standing in front of his horse leaning on the saddle ppr. 53. 11

Veale of London, a chevalier standing in front of his horse. *Nero nihil verius.* 53. 11

Veale, Henry Mallet, of Passaford, Devonsh., out of a ducal coronet or, a battle-axe ppr. *Victima Deo.* *cf.* 172. 3

Veale or **Vele** of Over, Glouc., a garb or, enfiled with a ducal coronet gu. 153. 5

Veel, Colborne-: (1) A garb or, enfiled by a ducal coronet gu. (*for Veel*). 153. 5. (2) A stag's head erased arg., semée of estoiles sa., attired or, and holding in the mouth a fern-branch ppr. (*for Colborne*). *Face aut tace.* *cf.* 120. 8

Veele of Langford, Glouc., a demi-calf or, pellettée.

Veevers, Richard, Esquire, of Woningworth, Fulwood Park, near Preston, *uses*: upon a mural coronet a pheon erect, point downwards, all ppr. *Vie vers vertu.* 174. 2

Veiner, *see* Veyner.

Veitch, George Seton, Esquire, of Friar's Hall, Paisley, Scotland, *uses* a cow's head affrontée. *Famam extendimus factis.* 43. 11

Veitch, George Douglas, Esquire, of Elliock, Sanquhar, co. Dumfries, a bull's head affrontée sa. *Famam extendimus factis.*

Veldon of Rafin, co. Meath, Ireland, a lion's head erased arg., collared az., ringed or. *Virtus probata florescit.*

Venables, *see* Vernon, Lord.

Venables of London, a wyvern wreathed gu. *Venabulis vinco.*

Venables of Woodhill, Shropsh., same crest and motto.

Venables, Chesh., a wyvern gu., issuing from a whelk-shell arg. 303. 15

Venables, Rowland George, B.A., Oakhurst, Oswestry, same crest. *Animo et corpore nitor.*

Venables, a wyvern passant gu., issuing from a weir arg.

Venables of Kinderton, Chesh., a wyvern with wings addorsed gu. on a fish-weir, devouring a child, and pierced through the neck by an arrow, all ppr.

Venables of Antrobus, Chesh., a wyvern passant gu., issuant from a weir arg.

Venables, Ireland, a wyvern with wings elevated and tail nowed arg., beaked and legged or, swallowing an infant in swaddling clothes ppr., swaddled gu.

Venables of Agden and Horton, Chesh., a demi-wyvern erect with wings elevated gu., issuing from a weir-basket erect or.

Venables of Andover, Hants, a dragon gu., issuing from a shell in fess arg. 70. 12

Venant, a bull's head cabossed. 43. 8

Venn of Freston Lodge and Ipswich, Suff., on a mount vert, a lion passant erminois, the dexter fore-paw resting on an escutcheon az., charged with a fleur-de-lis or. *Fide et integritate.*

Venn, out of a ducal coronet an eagle's head ppr. *cf.* 83. 14

Venner, an eagle displayed or, winged arg. 75. 2

Vennor, a boar's head couped or. 43. 1

Venor or **Venour** of London, Kent, and Warw., an eagle displayed arg., charged on the breast with a cross formée gu. *cf.* 75. 2

Venour, an eagle displayed ppr. 75. 2

Ventris of Okkington, Cambs, between two wings az., a sword erect arg., hilt and pommel or. 112. 4

Ventry, Baron (Eveleigh-De-Moleyns), of Ventry, co. Kerry: (1) A savage's head affrontée couped below the shoulders ppr. (*for De Moleyns*). *cf.* 190. 13. (2) A goat's head erased per chevron or and sa., attired of the second, holding in the mouth a branch of laurel ppr. (*for Eveleigh*). *Vivere sat vincere.*

Verdelin, a Roman fasces ppr. 171. 4

Verdier, on a mount vert, a peacock ppr. *cf.* 103. 4

Verdin, Sir Joseph, Bart., Garnstone Castle, Weobley, Heref., upon a mount vert, between six ears of wheat stalked and bladed, three on either side or, a tower sa., issuant from the battlements thereof a demi-lion arg., gorged with a collar gemel, also sa. 280. 13

Verdin, William Henry, Darnhall Hall, Winsford, Chesh., same crest.

Verdon, out of a tower sa., a demi-lion gu. 157. 11

Verdon, Sir George Frederic, K.C.M.G., C.B., F.R.S., of Melbourne, Victoria, *uses* a lion passant ppr., resting the dexter paw upon a fret gu. (*Of no authority.*) *En Dieu se fie.*

Vere, Earl of Oxford (*extinct*), **and Vere, Duke of Ireland and Marquess of Dublin** (*extinct*), a boar passant az., bristled and ungu. or. *Vero nihil verius.* 40. 2

Vere, Baron Vere of Tilbury (*extinct*), on a chapeau gu., turned up erm., a boar az., armed, crined, ungu., and bristled or, and charged with a crescent arg. *Vero nil verius.*—*Verité vient.* *cf.* 40. 7

Vere, De-, Sir Stephen Edward, Bart., D.L., of Currah Chase, co. Limerick: (1) On a chapeau gu., turned up erm., a boar passant az., armed and bristled or. *cf.* 40. 8. (2) The castle of Limerick ppr. *Vero nihil verius.*

Vere of Carlton House, Notts, same crest as (1) above. *Vero nihil verius.* 40. 7

Vere, same crest as (1) above. 40. 7

Vere, Suff., a boar passant az., armed or. 40. 2

Vere-Hope, James Charles, of Craigie Hall, Scotland: (1) A broken globe surmounted by a rainbow issuing out of clouds, all ppr. (*for Hope*). 159. 2. (2) A demi-horse rampant arg., saddled and bridled gu. (*for Vere*). *At spes non fracta.*—*Vero nihil verius.*

Vere of Stanbroke, Suff., a hind's head pierced through the neck by an arrow, all ppr. *cf.* 124. 1

Vereker, *see* Gort, Viscount.

Vereist, on a mount vert, between two probosceides or, a rudder with a handle ppr. 238. 16

Verelst, Harry William, Aston Hall, Rotherham, same crest.

Verhulst, Belgium, a plume of three ostrich-feathers, the two outer ones sa. and the centre one or. 115. 1

Verity, John, of 27, Lowndes Square, S.W., on a rock ppr., in front of a sun rising or, an eagle's head erased ppr. *Verite et foy.*

Vernell of Tavistock Square, London, a demi-lion erased gu., bezantée, the sinister paw resting on an escutcheon arg., thereon on a mount vert, an oak-tree fructed ppr.

Verner of Church Hill, co. Armagh, a boar's head couped sa., fretty or. *Pro Christo et patria.* 43. 1

Verner, Sir Edward Wingfield, Bart., J.P., of Verner's Bridge, co. Armagh, a boar's head couped sa., fretty or. *Pro Christo et patria.*

Verney, *see* Willoughby De Broke, Baron.

Verney, *see* Braye, Baron.

Verney, *see* Lloyd-Verney.

Verney, Viscount Fermanagh, and Earl of Verney (*extinct*), a phœnix in flames beholding a ray of the sun, all ppr. *Ung tout seul.*

Verney of London, Herts, and Bucks, a phœnix in flames ppr. *Un tout seul.* 82. 2

Verney, Bart. (*extinct*), of Middle Claydon, Bucks, a phœnix in flames beholding a ray of the sun, all ppr.

Verney, Sir Edmund Hope, Bart., of Claydon House, Bucks: (1) A demi-phœnix in flames ppr., charged with five mullets in cross or, and looking at rays of the sun, also ppr. (*for Verney*). 278. 14. (2) Out of a mural coronet arg., two spears erect, therefrom two pennons flowing towards the dexter, one erminois, the other pean (*for Calvert*). *Ung sent ung soleil.*—*Serenta fides cineri.* 278. 15

Verney of Compton Verney, Warw., an antelope sejant arg., guttée-de-sang, attired or.

Vernon, *see* Lyveden, Baron.

Vernon, Earl of Shipbrook (*extinct*), a demi-Ceres ppr., vested az., holding in her dexter hand a sickle, also ppr., and in her sinister a garb or, wreathed about the temples with wheat of the last. *Semper ut te digna sequare.*

Vernon, Lord (Venables-Vernon), Sudbury Hall, Derby: (1) A boar's head erased sa., ducally gorged or (*for Vernon*). 41. 6. (2) A wyvern arg. standing on a weir of the last, banded az., pierced through the body in fesse by an arrow, and devouring a child ppr. (*for Venables*). *Ver non semper viret.* 69. 13

Vernon, Borlase-Warren-Venables-, Hon. William, D.L.: (1) A boar's head erased sa., ducally gorged or (*for Vernon*). 41. 6. (2) Same crest as (2) above (*for Venables*). 69. 13. (3) Out of a ducal coronet or, a double plume of ostrich-feathers arg., and in the centre thereof an eagle's leg inverted sa. (*for Warren*). (4) A wolf passant regardant arg., holding in the mouth an arrow or, vulning the neck ppr. (*for Borlase*).

Vernon, Essex and Notts: (1) A boar's head erased per fess sa. and gu., ducally gorged or. 41. 6. (2) A tiger's head erased gu., ducally gorged or, charged on the neck with a martlet of the second.

Vernon, Derbysh. and Shropsh., a boar's head erased sa., tusked arg., ducally gorged or. 41. 6

Vernon, Forbes George, Esquire, of Victoria, in the province of British Columbia, Canada, ten years Member of the Executive Council, and Chief Commissioner of Lands and Works until 1894, Agent-General for the Province in London 1895-1899, a boar's head erased sa., ducally gorged or. *Vernon semper viret.* 312. 4

Vernon, Augustus Leveson, of Hilton Park, Staffs, same crest. 41. 6

Vernon, Wentworth-, of Wentworth Castle, Yorks: (1) A boar's head erased sa., ducally gorged and bristled or (*for Vernon*). 41. 6. (2) A griffin passant (*for Wentworth*). *Vernon semper viret.—En Dieu est tout.* 63. 2

Vernon, Edward Venables, of Clontarf Castle, Dublin, a boar's head and neck erased sa., ducally gorged, and charged on the neck with a mullet or for difference. *Vernon semper viret.* cf. 41. 6

Vernon of Little Beligh, Essex and Notts, a boar's head erased per fesse sa. and gu., ducally gorged or. 41. 6

Vernon, Shropsh.: (1) A lion rampant gu. 1. 13. (2) A boar's head erased at the neck sa., ducally gorged or. *Vernon semper viret.* 41. 6

Vernon, Shropsh., a lion rampant gu. 1. 13

Vernon of Haslington, Chesh., and Yorks, a demi-Ceres affrontée ppr., vested az., holding in her dexter hand a sickle and under her sinister arm a garb or, wreathed about her head with wheat of the same.

Vernon of Herringswell, Suff., a demi-Ceres ppr., vested az., holding in her dexter arm a garb and in her sinister hand a sickle, and about her head a wreath of wheat, all ppr., charged on the breast for distinction with a cross crosslet or.

Vernon of Shipbrook, Chesh., a demi-Ceres affrontée ppr., vested vert, holding three ears of wheat over her sinister shoulder or, and in her dexter hand a sickle, also ppr., handled of the third.

Vernon, Sir Harry Foley, Bart., J.P., D.L., of Hanbury Hall, Worcs., a demi-woman ppr., habited or and purpure, crined, also or, wreathed about the temples with wheat, and holding in her arms a garb of the second. *Ver non semper viret.* 311. 3

Vernon of London, a stag sejant or. cf. 116. 8

Vernon-Harcourt, Augustus George, Esquire, of St. Clare, Ryde, upon a ducal coronet or, a peacock close ppr. *Le bon temps viendra.*

Vernon-Harcourt, Rt. Hon. Sir W. G. Granville, Malwood, Lyndhurst, same crest and motto.

Vernor, co. Armagh, a boar's head couped sa. *Pro Christo et patria.* 43. 1

Verschoyle, a boar's head erased gu. 42. 2

Verschoyle, Rev. Hamilton Stuart, of Castleshauagan, co. Donegal, a boar's head couped gu., charged with a cross patée or. *Temperans et constans.* 258. 13

Verschoyle, Frederick Thomas, Castle Troy, co. Limerick, Ireland, same crest.

Verst, a horse's head erased arg. *Virtus ubique.* 51. 4

Versturme-Bunbury, Adolphus Halkett, Portland Place, Walcot, Somers.: (1) Bunbury. (2) Versturme.

Verthon, De, an arm in armour embowed holding a battle-axe, all ppr. 200. 6

Verulam, Earl of (Grimston), Gorhambury, St. Albans, Herts, a stag's head erased ppr., attired or. *Mediocria firma.* 121. 2

Vesey, *see* De Vesci, Viscount.

Vesey, *see* Colthurst-Vesey.

Vesey-Fitzgerald, *see* Fitzgerald.

Vesey, of Derrebard House, co. Tyrone, a hand in armour holding a laurel-branch, all ppr.

Vessey of Isham, Cambs, a griffin's head or, erased per fess gu., ducally gorged arg. cf. 66. 2

Vessey of Pondhall, Essex, an arm embowed and couped at the shoulder, erect from the elbow, habited gu., cuffed erm., holding in the hand ppr. four leaves vert.

Veyner, a sinister arm embowed in armour arg., garnished or, holding in the hand ppr. a gem-ring or, stoned sa.

Vezay or **Vezey,** on a ducal coronet or, a wyvern sans legs vert. 70. 9

Vialls of Twickenham, Middx., a demi-leopard ppr., sans tail, ducally gorged or.

Vian, Ireland, a demi-lion rampant gu., billettée or, holding between the paws a baton of the last.

Vibert of St. Aubin, Jersey, an eagle displayed per pale or and sa. *Vi et libertate.*

Vicarey or **Vikary,** Devonsh., a peacock close or. 103. 7

Vicars, a dove holding in its beak an olive-branch ppr. *Vincit omnia virtus.* 92. 5

Vicars, Sir Arthur Edward, K.C.V.O., Ulster King of Arms, Office of Arms, Dublin Castle, same crest.

Vicary of Warminster, Wilts, a peacock close or. *Probitas verus honos.* 103. 7

Vickers, C. B., Lieutenant-Colonel King's Royal Rifle Corps, London, a cubit arm ppr., vested gu., holding in the hand a mill-rind az. 207. 4

Vickers, same crest. 207. 4

Vickers of Sheffield, Yorks, two arms embowed vested gu., cuffed arg., the hands ppr., holding a mill-rind or. *Vigore.* 235. 4

Vickers, Albert, 14, Cadogan Square, S.W., same crest.

Vickers, Cuthbert Bainbridge, 5, Lansdowne Terrace, Cheltenham, in front of a demi-leopard ppr., charged with three mullets of eight points paleways and holding between the paws an increscent or, a mount vert. *Vulneror non vincor.* 252. 4

Vickers, Kirsop James Bainbridge, of Wellington, Shropsh., same crest. *Vulneror non vincor.*

Vickers, James Muschamp, Waltham House, Great Waltham, Essex, same crest and motto.

Vickers, Kirsop James Bainbridge, Wellington, Shropsh., same crest and motto.

Vickers, Thomas Edwards, C.B., V.D., 35, Park Street, London, W., two arms embowed vested gu., cuffed arg., the hands ppr., holding a mill-rind or. 235. 4

Vickers, William Henry Playfair, M.D., of Coolroe House, Graiguenamanagh, co. Kilkenny, a dove holding in its beak an olive-branch, and standing on a cornucopia fesseways, all ppr.

Vickery, two dolphins haurient addorsed ppr. 140. 1

Victor, on a ducal coronet gu., a wyvern sans legs or. 70. 9

Vidal of Cornborough, Abbotsham, Dublin, a morion ppr., between two ostrich-feathers, one in front and one behind, arg.

Vidler, out of a ducal coronet or, a demi-griffin ppr. 64. 4

Viel and **Vieler,** out of a tower ppr., a leopard's head gu., collared or. 157. 9

Viell, Glouc., a demi-lion rampant gu., holding a baton gobonated arg. and of the first. 15. 9

Vigne, a rose arg., barbed ppr., between two laurel-branches in orle, the slips in saltier vert. 149. 11

Vigne, Albert, Johannesburg, South Africa, a boar's head ppr.

Vignoles, a unicorn's head per fess gu. and or, erased of the first. 49. 5

Vigor, *see* Stonhouse-Vigor.

Vigors of Erindale and Burgage, co. Carlow, Ireland, a stag's head erased at the neck gu., attired or. *Spectamur agendo.* 121. 2

Vigors, Philip Doyne, Holloden, Bagnalstown, co. Carlow: (1) Same crest as above. (2) A wolf's head erased quarterly per pale dancettée or and sa. *Spectemur agendo.*

Vigors, Rev. Richard William, Newport Hall, Almeley, Eardisley, Heref., a stag's head erased gu., attired or. *Spectamur agendo.*

Vigures, a peacock's head erased az., crested or. 103. 1

Vigurs, a mullet arg. 164. 2

Vikary, *see* Vicarey.

Vilant, Scotland, an arm in armour embowed, holding in the hand a spear ppr. *Firma nobis fides.* cf. 197. 1

Vile, an arm holding in the hand a scimitar ppr. 213. 5

Villages, a unicorn's head erased az. 49. 5

Villeboles, a leopard rampant.

Villebois of Markham, a tiger salient ppr.

Villiers, *see* Clarendon, Earl of.

Villiers, *see* Jersey, Earl of.

Villiers, Duke of Buckingham (*extinct*), a lion rampant arg., ducally crowned or, charged on the shoulder with an annulet sa. *Fidei coticula crux.* cf. 1. 12

Villiers, Earl of Anglesey (*extinct*), same crest and motto. cf. 1. 12

Villiers, Mason-, Earl of Grandison, a lion rampant arg., ducally crowned or. *Fidei coticula crux.* 1. 12

Villiers, Viscount Perbeck (*extinct*), a lion rampant arg., ducally crowned or, charged on the shoulder with a mullet sa. cf. 1. 12

Villiers or **Villers,** a lion rampant arg., ducally crowned or. 1. 12

Villiers, Leics. and Staffs, same crest, but the lion charged with a crescent.

Villiers-Stuart, Henry John Richard, J.P., Castletown, co. Kilkenny: (1) A demi-lion rampant gu. (2) A lion rampant arg., ducally crowned or. *Nobilis ira.—Avito viret honore.*

Villet of London, an heraldic tiger's head erased erm., ducally gorged and tufted or.

Villettes of Bath, Somers., out of a ducal coronet an elephant's head, all or. 133. 1

Vincent, Sir Charles Edward Howard, K C M G, Donnington Hall, Newbury, out of a ducal coronet a bear's head 34 3

Vincent of Thingdon Northamp, out of a ducal coronet or, a bear's head arg, collared with a belt sa

Vincent of Firby and Warmsworth, Yorks, out of a ducal coronet or a bear's head gu 34 3

Vincent, Sir Charles Edward Howard, K C M G, C B, 1, Grosvenor Square, W, out of a ducal coronet or, a bear's head ppr

Vincent, Sir Edgar, K C M G, Esher Place, Esher same crest *Vincenti dabitur —Non nisi vincenti*

Vincent, Sir William, Bart, of D'Abernon Chase Leatherhead, Surrey, out of a ducal coronet or, a bear's head muzzled ppr *Virtute non viribus vincent* 34 3

Vincent, Northants, out of a ducal coronet or, a bear's head arg, collared sa cf 34 3

Vincent of Kempsey, Worcs, a bear's head erased gu, muzzled or 35 2

Vincent of Surrey, a bull's head cabossed arg guttee-de poix, armed or cf 43 8

Vincent, Ireland, on a chapeau a pelican vulning herself, all ppr 98 7

Vincent, William Clarke Esquire of Boston Lodge Boston Spa Yorks out of a ducal coronet or, a griffin's head gu, charged with a trefoil slipped or *Vincent qui se vincent* 67 12

Vincent, John Matson, Hemsworth, Lane Ends, near Wakefield, same crest and motto

Vincent, John, same crest and motto

Vincent of Pinckleton Leics, and Messingham Lincs and Willford Notts a demi-ram couped sa, armed and collared or cf 130 13

Vincent of Thrinkston, Leics, a demi ram arg 130 13

Vincent of Kinver Staffs a talbot statant arg, eared or, collared and lined gu the end of the line tied in a knot.

Vine, out of a ducal coronet or, an heraldic tiger's head ppr 25 3

Vine, Sir J Somers D L of Queen Anne's Mansions S W out of a ducal coronet an heraldic tiger's head all ppr 25 3

Viner, Bart (*extinct*), a dexter arm in armour embowed ppr garnished or, holding in the hand a mullet of six points of the same

Viner, Ellis-, of Badgeworth, Glouc (1) A dexter arm in armour embowed encircled at the elbow by a wreath of vine, and holding in the hand a gem ring, all ppr (*for Viner*) (2) A horse's head erased erm, gorged with a plain collar arg charged with a cinquefoil between two crescents sa holding in the mouth a trefoil slipped ppr (*for Ellis*) *Labore et honore*

Viney, on a chapeau a phœnix in flames ppr 82 11

Viney, Kent, an arm couped at the shoulder holding in the hand a bunch of grapes by the stalk, all ppr

Vinicombe, a greyhound's head sa, bezantee 61 12

Vintris, a sword erect 170. 2

Vipan, John Alexander Stibbington Hall Wansford Hunts out of a ducal coronet or, a swan's head between wings ppr *Vi et armis*

Vipont, Rev David Avenel 19 Millerfield Place, Edinburgh (1) A thistle slipped ppr (2) A demi-eagle displayed gu, charged on the breast with a mascle or *Per aspera ad alta —Vinculis fortior*

Vipont or **Vipount,** out of a ducal coronet or, a swan's head between two wings, all ppr 100 10

Virgin, Ireland, a lion's head erased gu *Nunc aut nunquam* 17 2

Virney, a maiden's head couped at the shoulders affrontee, vested and crowned with an Eastern coronet

Virtue, Berks, a lion's head erased arg 17 8

Virtue, Scotland, a pomegranate stalked and leaved ppr 152 4

Vismes, *see* De Vismes

Viveash of Calne, Wilts, on a mount vert, a tiger statant gardant in front of an oak-tree ppr

Vivian, Baron (Vivian) Glynn, near Bodmin, out of waves a bridge embattled, and at each end thereof a tower, and issuant therefrom a demi hussar of the 18th Regiment, holding in his dexter hand a sabre and in his sinister hand a pennon flying to the sinister gu, and inscribed in letters of gold, *Croix d'Orade —Cor nobyle, cor immobyle —Vive revicturus* 185 11

Vivian, Bart of Singleton Glamorgansh, out of waves a bridge of one arch embattled, and at each end a tower ppr, and issuant therefrom a demi hussar of His Majesty's 18th Regiment of Dragoons, habited, armed, and accoutred holding in his dexter hand a sabre, all ppr, and in his sinister a pennon flying to the sinister gu *Vive revicturus* 185 11

Vivian, Sir Arthur Pendarves, K C B 23 Buckingham Gate, S W (1) A lion's head erased ppr, charged with two bezants paleways, and gorged with a collar gu, thereon three annulets or with a chain of the last 287 11 (2) Same crest as above *Vive revicturus*

Vivian, Arthur Pendarves, C B, Bosahan, St Martin R S O, Cornw, same crests *Vive anima Dei*

Vivian, on a chapeau gu, turned up erm, a serpent nowed ppr 142 9

Vivian, a lion's head erased ppr collared and chained gu cf 18 6

Vivian, a lion's head erased, gorged with a naval coronet cf 17 8

Vivian, Cornw, a horse passant furnished, all ppr 52 4

Vivian of Pencalnenick, Cornw, between two roses gu, slipped vert a dexter cubit arm vested az charged with five plates in saltier cuffed arg holding in the hand ppr an anchor in fess the flukes towards the dexter sa *Vive ut vivas —Non robore sed spe*

Vivian of France an etoile or 164 1

Vivian of France, a spur-rowel or 164 8

Vizard of Dursley, Glouc, out of palisades or, a demi-hind regardant vulned in the neck ppr and holding an arrow point downwards or barbed and flighted arg

Voller, a demi-antelope arg, collared gu 126 3

Von Goetze, Hugo Sanssouci, Linden Road, Clevedon, out of a ducal coronet a demi-lion rampant *Suum cuique*

Von Mueller, Sir Ferdinand K C M G, M D, Ph D F R S **Baron Von Mueller** in the Kingdom of Wurtemberg of Melbourne, Australia, out of a ducal coronet a plume of three ostrich feathers *Virtute ingenioque valemus* cf 114 8

Von Stieglitz, Edgar Boyne Esquire, of Wambo, Brisbane Queensland, out of a ducal coronet or an arm in armour embowed, the hand grasping a sword all ppr between two wings expanded the dexter per fess arg and gu, the sinister per fess counterchanged *Spes mea in Deo* 258 7

Von Sturmer, Reverend Heaton Edward, M A (St John's College, Cambridge), (*This Protestant branch of the noble family of Neustetter genant Sturmer von Unternesselbach settled in England in the middle of the eighteenth century*) (1) A pyramidal Oriental hat arg turned up gu, and surmounted by a double plume of six ostrich feathers alternately of the first and second issuing from a flattened pommel or (*for von Sturmer*) 180 13 (2) A demi stag or, attired and ungu sa and vulned through the breast with a broad arrow of the last headed and feathered arg (*for Norris*) *Vive ut vivas* 119 5

Vosper, of Liskeard and Trewoofe, Cornw, a tower triple-towered or *Utraque fortuna contentus* 157 6

Voules, Francis M, 214, Ashley Gardens, Westminster, S W, a lion's head erased

Vowe of Hallaton, Leics, a lion rampant gu *Vows should be respected* 1 13

Vowell, Devonsh out of a mural coronet gu, an antelope's head arg, attired of the first

Vowell, Norf, between two palm-branches vert, a mullet gu 146 8

Vowill, out of a mural coronet an heraldic antelope's head

Vowler-Simcoe, John Henry Walcot of Penheale Egloskerry, Cornw (1) Out of a naval crown or a demi-sea-lion ppr, holding in his fore-fin a dagger erect, pommel and hilt or, and on his shoulder a rose gu barbed and seeded ppr (*for Simcoe*) (2) Issuant from the battlements of a tower arg a demi-lion gu, holding in the dexter paw a cross crosslet, and resting the sinister on a decrescent both also arg (*for Vowler*) *Non sibi sed patriæ*

Vowles, William Esquire of Brislington, Somers, upon a rock ppr, a cock or, the dexter claw resting on an escutcheon, also or, charged with a rose gu barbed ppr *Perseverantia*

Voysey of Bovy-Tracy and Collumpton, Devonsh, a sea-horse rampant arg, maned and armed or 46 2

Vychan, Wales issuing out of clouds a dexter arm in armour embowed, holding in the gauntlet a sword erect, all ppr, on the point a Moor's head couped in profile sa, dropping blood

Vye[1], Cornw., a greyhound passant ppr. *cf.* 60. 2

Vygor, a demi-lion sa., holding between the paws a staff raguly arg. *cf.* 15. 1

Vylgus, Scotland, a lion's head erased ppr. 17. 8

Vynall, Sussex, a demi-lion erased sa., holding a bezant. *cf.* 11. 7

Vyne, Ireland, an arm couped below the elbow and erect, vested sa., cuffed arg., holding in the hand a vine-branch fructed, also ppr.

Vyner and **Vynor** of London and Gantby, Lincs, and Condover, Shropsh., an arm in armour embowed ppr., garnished or, holding in the hand, also ppr., a gem-ring of the second.

Vyner, Robert Charles de Grey, Newby Hall, Ripon, a dexter arm embowed in armour ppr., garnished or, holding a mullet of six points or. *Labore et honore.*

Vynor and **Vynors,** Wilts, an arm in armour embowed ppr., garnished or, holding in the gauntlet a round buckle the tongue erect, also or.

Vyse, Howard-, Howard Henry, Stoke Place, Slough, on a chapeau gu., turned up erm., a lion statant guardant, the tail extended or, ducally crowned, and charged on the neck with a label of three points arg., a mullet sa., charged with a crescent or, for difference (*for Howard*). (2) A griffin's head arg. (*for Vyse*).

Vyvyan, Rev. Sir Vyell Donnithorne, Bart., of Trelowarren, Cornw., a horse passant furnished ppr. *Dum vivimus vivamus.* 52. 4

W.

Wackett, a stag's head erased arg., attired or. 121. 2

Waddel, a battle-axe in pale ppr. 172. 3

Waddell, two battle-axes in saltier ppr. 172. 4

Waddell of Beach House, Walmer, Kent, a lamb couchant ppr., surmounted by a demi-eagle displayed ppr.

Waddell, Scotland, a lion's head erased gu. *Orna verum.* 17. 2

Waddingham, John, Guyting Grange, Cheltenham, on a mount vert, a stag's head cabossed ppr., between attires a rose arg., barbed and seeded ppr. *Prospicio.*

Waddingham, Thomas James, Hafod, Aberystwth, same crest and motto.

Waddington, an arm holding in the hand a hatchet ppr. 213. 12

Waddington of London, a martlet gu. 95. 4

Waddington, John, Esquire, J.P., of Waddington Old Hall, Yorks, and Ely Grange, Frant, Sussex, a dexter arm embowed, holding in the hand a tilting-spear in bend and a battle-axe in bend sinister, all ppr., the hand surmounted by a fleur-de-lis gu. 276. 15

Waddy, John, Esquire, J.P., of Clough East Castle, co. Wexford, a naked arm embowed ppr., grasping a sword in bend sinister arg., pommelled and hilted or. *Ob ducem ob patriam.* 201. 4

Waddy, Richard Anderson, Morpeth, New South Wales, same crest and motto.

Waddy, His Honour Judge Samuel Danks, 8, Claremont, Sheffield, a dexter arm embowed habited arg., charged with three bars wavy gu., holding in the hand a sword point downwards ppr., all between two mullets pierced gu. *Sequor ut ducam.*

Wade, a dove holding in its beak a branch. *Vincit qui patitur.* 92. 5

Wade of Hilton Castle, Durh., a dove holding in its beak an olive-branch, all ppr., and charged on the breast with a cross crosslet sa. *cf.* 92. 5

Wade, Oxon., a boar salient sa., collared or.

Wade, a griffin's head erased or, holding in the beak a pink ppr.

Wade, Essex, a rhinoceros passant arg. *cf.* 226. 7

Wade of Tottington, Bury, Lancs, a mount vert, thereon in front of a palm-tree ppr. a rhinoceros arg. 226. 4

Wade of Spang, Christianstadt, Sweden, a rhinoceros ppr., resting the dexter fore-foot on a garb fesseways or.

Wade of Gilston Road, Kensington, Middx., upon the trunk of a tree fessewise and sprouting ppr. a rhinoceros statant or. *In spe resto.* 226. 6

Wade, Ireland, an arm in armour embowed, the hand grasping a straight sword, and pendent from the blade the star of the Durannée empire, all ppr. *Pro fide et patria.*

Wade, Carruthers-, of Holmains, Dumfriessh., Scotland: (1) An arm in armour embowed, the hand grasping a straight sword in bend, all ppr. (*for Wade*). 195. 2. (2) A seraph volant ppr. (*for Carruthers*). *Pro fide et patria.—Promptus et fidelis.*

Wade, the late Rev. Frederick Tobias, M.A., Prebendary of Lichfield Cathedral and Vicar of Kidsgrove, Staffs, an arm in armour embowed, the hand grasping a sword in bend sinister, all ppr., the arm charged with an escallop gu. *Pro fide et patria.* *cf.* 195. 2

Wade, an arm in armour embowed, holding in the hand a sword. *Pro fide et patria.* 195. 2

Wade-Dalton, Colonel Hamlet Coote, C.B., of Hawxwell Hall, Yorks: (1) A dragon's head couped vert, the wings elevated or, gorged with a collar nebuly or, and charged on the neck for distinction with a cross crosslet arg. (*for Dalton*). (2) A dexter arm embowed in armour ppr., garnished or, holding in the gauntlet a sword, also ppr., pommel and hilt or, and pendent from the gauntlet by a chain of the same an escutcheon az., charged with an escallop, also or (*for Wade*).

Wade-Gery, Charles Robert, of Wornditch Hall, St. Neot's, Hunts: (1) An antelope's head erased quarterly arg. and sa., charged with four mascles counterchanged, attired or (*for Gery*). (2) On a mount vert a rhinoceros ppr., charged with a battle-axe sa. (*for Wade*).

Wade-Gery, William Hugh, same crest and motto.

Wade-Palmer, Fairfax, Blomfield, Holme Park, Sonning, Berks: (1) Three mullets fesseways az. in front of a talbot's head erased arg., charged on the neck for distinction with a cross crosslet, also az. (*for Palmer*). (2) An arm in armour embowed, the hand grasping a sword, all ppr., the arm charged with an escallop gu. (*for Wade*).

Wadeson, two lion's gambs erased ppr., supporting a crescent or. 39. 6

Wadge of Stradbrook Hall, co. Dublin, an eagle's head erased erm., gorged with a collar gu., therefrom suspended a bugle-horn sa., stringed of the second. *Spes in futuro.* *cf.* 83. 2

Wadham, the scalp of a buck or, and between the attires a boar's head couped and erect. *cf.* 43. 2

Wadham of Merefield, Somers., and Devonsh., the scalp of a buck or, and between the attires a rose arg. 149. 9

Wadham of Cotherstone, Dorset, a stag's head erased or, gorged with a collar, charged with three bezants, all between two rose-branches erect flowered arg., stalked and leaved vert. 121. 4

Wadman of Imber, Wilts, a demi-eagle displayed erm., winged gu. 81. 6

Wadman of London, an eagle displayed ppr. *Rosa sine spina.* 75. 2

Wadsworth, on a terrestrial globe winged ppr., an eagle rising or. 159. 9

Wager, a Moor's head crowned with rush-leaves ppr.

Wager, a dexter arm holding in the hand an annulet or. 216. 1

Wagner, in water a swan naiant, all ppr. 99. 8

Wagner, Henry, out of a ducal coronet a demi-lion rampant holding between the paws a demi-wheel.

Wags, an eagle displayed. 75. 2

Wagstaff, Warw., a demi-lion arg., holding a staff raguly sa. 15. 1

Wagstaffe, James Poole, Manor Park, Potton Sandy, Beds, same crest.

Wagstaffe of Haseland, Derbysh., out of a ducal coronet or, a staff couped and raguly in pale sa. 147. 10

Wahl, Charles Frederic, Lovely, 110, Broadhurst Gardens, Hampstead, N.W., a horse arg., on the body a lozenge az., supporting with the dexter fore-leg an escutcheon, also arg., charged with a wyvern, wings elevated and addorsed vert. *Vincit veritas.*

Wailes-Fairbairn, William Fairbairn, M.A., Askham Grange, Yorks: (1) A dexter cubit arm erect, the hand grasping the worm of a lever-screw in bend sinister, all ppr. (2) Two spurs interlaced rowels upwards and leathered or, between as many wings ppr, each charged with a quatrefoil az *Ne cede arduis*

Wailes, between two wings a spur all ppr 111 13

Wainwright of Dudley, Worcs, a lion rampant arg, holding an ancient battle-axe, the handle of the first headed or

Wait of Woodbrough Somers, a bugle-horn stringed sa garnished or *Pro aris et focis* 228 11

Waite and **Waith,** same crest 228 11

Waithman of Westville, Lancs, a demi-eagle displayed sa 81 6

Waithman, R W, Esquire, J P, D L, of Moyne Park co Galway, a demi eagle displayed *Persevero* 81 6

Waithman, W S, J P Merlin Park Galway, a demi eagle displayed *Per severo* 312 12

Wake, Northamp and Somers a lion passant with the tail extended sa, ducally gorged arg cf 5 11

Wake, Sir Hereward Bart, of Courteen hall, Northamp a knot, commonly called a Wake's knot *Verga et ora*

Wakefield, a bat displayed arg 137 11

Wakefield of Dublin, a bat displayed or 137 11

Wakefield, Jacob, Sedgwick House, Kendal, same crest

Wakefield, Edward William, Esquire of Stricklandgate House, Kendal, same crest *Be just and fear not*

Wakefield, on a ducal coronet or, a wyvern sans legs ppr 70 9

Wakefield, Joseph Colen Esquire, of Eastwood Park, Renfrewsh, a wyvern sans legs vert *Ardua vinco* cf 69 14

Wakeham of Borough, Devonsh, on a mount vert between two trees ppr, a greyhound arg, spotted sa 58 3

Wakehurst, a buckle or 178 5

Wakeling, a wyvern with wings addorsed, holding in his mouth a hand couped ppr 70 3

Wakelyn of Eydon, Northamp, and Hylton, Derbysh, a lion rampant or, holding in the dexter paw a tulip gu, slipped vert 3 9

Wakeman, Ireland a lion's head erased or 17 8

Wakeman of the Craig near Monmouth, a lion's head erased or, vomiting smoke and flames of fire ppr *Ora et labora* 17 1

Wakeman of Beckford, and Withe, Glouc, a lion's head erased or, vomiting flames of fire ppr 17 1

Wakeman, Sir Offley, Bart M A, D L, of Rorrington Shropsh, between two palm branches ppr a lion's head erased arg vomiting flames, gorged with a collar engrailed and cottised vert, and charged with three ermine spots or *Nec temere nec timide* 18 7

Wakeman, Lieutenant-Colonel Edward Maltby, Coton Hall Bridgnorth, same crest

Wakeman of Chaderleigh, Worcs, a cock or, combed, wattled, and legged az, holding in the beak a scroll thereon the motto *Evigila qui dormis*

Wakering, Essex on a mural coronet or a pelican of the same vulning herself ppr 98 3

Wakerley, two daggers in saltier ppr 169 8

Walcher, a talbot's head gu 56 12

Walcot or **Walcott,** Oxon an eagle's head or, guttee-de sang holding in the beak az a fleur-de lis of the first cf 84 12

Walcot or **Walcott,** a bull's head erased arg, armed or, ducally gorged, lined and ringed of the last cf 44 2

Walcot of Walcot, Shropsh, out of a ducal coronet or a buffalo's head erased arg, armed, ducally gorged, lined and ringed of the first

Walcott, Owen Charles Bampfylde Dashwood, of Bitterley Court Shropsh, out of a ducal coronet or a buffalo's head erased arg, armed and ducally gorged or *Nullius in verba magistri*

Walcott, Charles Thomas, same crest and motto

Walcott, a bull's head erased erm, armed or, gorged with a wreath of trefoil vert holding in the mouth an arrow in bend also or 44 6

Waldegrave, *see* Radstock, Baron

Waldegrave, Earl (Waldegrave), Chewton Priory, Bath, out of a ducal coronet or, a plume of five ostrich-feathers per pale arg and gu 114 13

Waldegrave of Smallbridge, Suff of Saninghall Norf, of Borley Hall and Lawford, Essex and Northamp out of a ducal coronet or, a double plume of feathers per pale arg and gu 114 4

Walden, a winged spur, rowel upwards ppr 111 12

Walden, Viscount, *see* Tweeddale, Marquess of

Waldeshescheff, Waldesheff, and **Waldsheff,** two spears in saltier pendent thereto two flags quarterly gu and or surmounted by a garland of laurel, all ppr 175 13

Waldie of Hendersyde Park, Roxburghe a dove holding in its beak an olive branch, all ppr *Fidelis* 92 5

Waldo or **Waldoe,** a griffin's head erased vert 66 2

Waldo, Meade-, Edmund Gustavus Bloomfield Stone Wall Park Kent (1) A griffin's head sa, erased erm, gorged with an Eastern crown arg holding in its beak two trefoils slipped of the last (*for Waldo*) (2) A double headed eagle displayed or charged on the breast with a quatrefoil sa resting its claws on two shields of the second, each charged with a trefoil slipped arg (*for Meade*) *Mens conscia recti — Toujours pres*

Waldoure, a wolf's head erased or 30 8

Waldron, Ireland a lion rampant gardant or 2 5

Waldron, two laurel-branches in saltier ppr

Waldron and **Waldrond,** Devonsh, an heraldic tiger sejant arg, armed, tufted and maned or

Waldron of Clent Stourbridge, Worcs, an heraldic tiger sejant sa, platee, maned and tufted or *Fortis et velox*

Waldy, out of a mural coronet ppr, a demi-lion rampant az, crowned or, holding in the dexter paw a cross crosslet fitched of the last *Fidelis*

Waldy of Egglescliffe Durh, on a mural coronet a dove holding in its beak an olive branch, all ppr *Fidelis*

Waldy, George Alfred de Garmonsway, of Barm Durh, same crest

Wale, a yew-tree ppr

Wale, Northumb, a greyhound current arg cf 58 2

Wale of Shepton Mallet Somers and Essex, a lion rampant or supporting a long cross sa

Walford, two palm branches in orle vert 146 2

Walford of Hatfield Peverel Essex a demi lion rampant, holding in the dexter paw a cross crosslet fitched gu 11 10

Walford of Birdbrook, Essex out of a mural coronet or, an ostrich feather arg *Nosce teipsum* 114 14

Walford, Lionel D, 15, King's Gardens Hove Sussex a cock regardant *Sideus nobiscum quis contra nos*

Walford-Gosnall, John Desborough Pearson, Esquire, of Mount Maskall, Boreham, Chelmsford, a ram's head affrontee, couped at the neck per pale arg and az, charged with two fleurs-de-lis counterchanged

Walkeden of London, a griffin's head erased quarterly arg and vert, beaked, ducally gorged and eared or cf 66 2

Walkelin or **Wakelin** of Rosleston, Bretby, and Hilton Derbysh, a lion rampant or, holding a tulip gu, leaved vert 3 9

Walker, *see* Kerrich Walker

Walker of New Romney, a lion's gamb erect and erased gu, enfiled by a mural coronet or *Ganger* 36 1

Walker of Norton Kirkby and Fowkham, Kent and Uttoxeter, Staffs, a lion's gamb erect and erased gu enfiled by a mural coronet or 36 1

Walker of Norton Villa, Whittington Worcs a lion's gamb erect and erased gu, charged with a mural coronet or, between two plates in pale *In Deo confido*

Walker, Rev George Sherbrooke, Christ Church Vicarage Summerfield, Birmingham, same crest and motto

Walker of Drogheda Ireland, a lion's head erased or, gorged with a wreath of laurel ppr. 17 10

Walker, Cambs, a lion in a wood, all ppr 5 2

Walker, a garb issuing from the coronet of a King of Arms, supported by a lion arg and a dragon gu *Loyaulte mon honneur*

Walker - Aylesbury of Marpool Hall Devonsh (1) Upon the trunk of a tree eradicated ppr a dragon's head erased or, gorged with a collar gemel az (*for Aylesbury*) (2) On a mount vert a crescent az, within a chain in arch or (*for Walker*) *Nil desperandum*

Walker of London and Leighton Buzzard Beds, out of flames of fire or a dragon's head vert crowned with an Eastern coronet of the first cf 72 12

Walker, Shropsh, a demi-lion rampant holding a cross formee fitchee *Loyal au mort* 11 10

Walker, Scotland, a stag at gaze under a nut tree ppr *In omnes casus* 116 12

Walker, Scotland, a stag standing in front of a tree ppr *Semper vigilans* cf 116 13

Walker, Hon. William, of Crescentville, Windsor, New South Wales, Australia, member of the Legislative Council, a stag at gaze under a nut-tree, all ppr. *Semper vigilans.*

Walker of Mansfield, Notts, a buck trippant vert. attired or. 117. 8

Walker, a stag's head erased ppr. 121. 2

Walker, Rear-Admiral Sir Baldwin Wake, Bart., out of a naval coronet az., a stag's head ppr., gorged with an Eastern coronet or. *Ready and faithful.* 308. 16

Walker, General George Warren, Tilehurst, 7, Sion Hill, Bath, out of a ducal coronet or, a greyhound's head arg.

Walker, Robert Crawfurd, Esquire, of Dundee, a stag-hound's head couped ppr., collared or. *Sapere aude.*

Walker, a greyhound's head erased sa., collared and cottised arg., the collar charged with three crescents of the first. *cf.* 61. 3

Walker of Wakefield, Yorks, a greyhound's head couped arg., collared sa. 313. 16

Walker, John William, Esquire, F.S.A., Boyne Hill House, Chapelthorpe, near Wakefield, same crest. *Honesta quam magna.*

Walker, Yorks, out of a ducal coronet or, a greyhound's head couped arg. 61. 7

Walker, Thomas Henry, Berkswell Hall, Warwick, a greyhound's head erased sa. *Passant, cressant en honeur.*

Walker of Hillingdon, Middx., and Wakefield, Yorks, a greyhound's head couped arg., gorged with a collar sa., thereon three crescents of the first. *cf.* 61. 2

Walker-Heneage of Compton-Bassett, Wilts: (1) A greyhound courant sa., charged with a mullet upon a crescent for difference (*for Heneage*). *cf.* 58. 2. (2) A demi-heraldic tiger salient per pale indented arg. and sa., armed and langued gu., maned and tufted or (*for Walker.*) *Walk in the fear of God.* 25. 13

Walker, Arthur George, Esquire, of Addington, Ryde, near Sydney, New South Wales, Australia, *uses*: a greyhound passant. *Fideliter et alacriter.*

Walker of Bow, near Stratford, Middx., on a mount vert, a greyhound sejant per pale arg., semée of crescents az. and sa., bezantée, collared or. *cf.* 59. 2

Walker-Morison, Bethune George, of Falfield, Fifesh.: (1) Three Saracens' heads conjoined in one neck ppr., the faces looking upwards and to the dexter and sinister (*for Morison*). *cf.* 191. 5. (2) A greyhound courant ppr. (*for Walker*). *Pretio prudentia præstat.—Fac et spera.* *cf.* 58. 2

Walker, Scotland, a greyhound sejant, collared or. *cf.* 59. 2

Walker, a greyhound passant arg., collared gu., rimmed and ringed or, the collar charged with three ducal coronets of the first.

Walker of Mitchell Grove, Arundel, Sussex, a greyhound sejant arg., collared and charged on the shoulder with a cinquefoil sa. *cf.* 59. 2

Walker of St. Winnon, Cornw., a greyhound sejant, collared and chained or. *cf.* 59. 2

Walker of Redland, near Bristol, on a mount vert, a falcon close or, collared gu., resting the dexter claw on an escutcheon az., charged with a bezant. *Nec temere, nec timide.*

Walker of Blairtown, Aberdeensh., Scotland, an eagle displayed az. *Deus mihi adjutor.* 75. 2

Walker, James Douglas, 20, Queen's Gate Gardens, S.W., same crest.

Walker of Blythe Hall, Notts, on a mount within a serpent in orle, a dove, all ppr. *cf.* 92. 11

Walker, Alfred Osten, Windham Club, St. James's Square, same crest.

Walker, Frederick Edmund, Ravensthorpe Manor, Thirsk, same crest.

Walker, a dove holding in its beak an olive-branch ppr. 92. 5

Walker, Major-General Albert Lancelot, the Chase Cottage, Enfield, Middx., same crest. *Passant cressent en honeur.*

Walker of Rotherham, on a mount a dove statant within a wreathed serpent, all ppr. *cf.* 92. 11

Walker, Hon. Lancelot, of Four Peaks, Geraldine, New Zealand, member of the Legislative Council of New Zealand, on a mount within a wreathed serpent a dove statant, all ppr. *Juncti valemus.* *cf.* 92. 11

Walker of Portlester, co. Meath, Ireland, a dove rising holding in the beak an oak-leaf, all ppr. *Passant cressant en honneur.*

Walker, William, Esquire, J.P., Kilcadden House, Killygordon R.S.O., co. Donegal, same crest and motto.

Walker, Ireland, a dove close holding in the beak an olive-branch, all ppr. *Pax omnibus.—Dum spiro spero.* 92. 5

Walker of St. Petersburg, a Scotch firtree eradicated ppr. *Passus Rege meos.* 144. 13

Walker of Leeds, Yorks, on a mount vert, a dunghill-cock sa., beaked, legged, combed, and wattled gu.

Walker, Bart. (*extinct*), of Bushey Hall, Herts, an ostrich az., holding in the dexter claw a caltrap or.

Walker, Forestier-, Sir George Ferdinand, Bart., D.L., of Castleton, Monm., a mural coronet or, encircled by a wreath of laurel, thereon an ostrich ppr., resting the dexter claw on a shell exploding, also ppr. *Nil desperandum.* 310. 11

Walker of Newcastle-on-Tyne, Northumb., and Scotland, a swan naiant in a loch ppr. *Non sine periculo.* 99. 8

Walker, Leasowe, Morningside, Scarborough, upon an increscent az., a moorcock ppr., holding in the beak an ear of wheat slipped and leaved or.

Walker, Captain John Charles Arthington, on a mount vert, amidst fern ppr., a moorcock sa., combed and wattled gu., charged on the breast with a billet or.

Walker, Ireland, a cherub's head with wings in saltier ppr. 189. 13

Walker, Yorks, a demi-heraldic tiger per pale indented arg. and sa., holding a branch of wallflowers or, slipped vert.

Walker, George Laurie, of Dalry, Midlothian, St. Fort, Fifesh., and Crawfordtown, Dumfriesh., a cornucopia ppr. *Cura et industria.* 152. 13

Walker, James, Hanley Lodge, Corstorphine, Midlothian, same crest.

Walker, Sir Peter Carlaw, Bart., D.L., of Gateacre, Lancs, and Osmaston Manor, Derbysh., same crest and motto. 152. 13

Walker, Scotland, a rock ppr. *Per varios casus.* 179. 7

Walker, Scotland, same crest. *Cura et industria.* 179. 7

Walker of Barbadoes, West Indies, in the sea a rock, thereon the waves beating all ppr. *Per varios casus.* 179. 5

Walker, Esquire, of Bedford Square, London, a sun in his splendour ppr. *Passibus æquis.* 162. 2

Walker, Lancs, the sun rising out of clouds, all ppr. 162. 5

Walker, Henry Rosenbach, a sun in splendour between two estoiles azures. *Ambula in luce.*

Walker, Sir Robert James Milo, Bart., of Sand Hutton, Yorks, and of Beachampton, Bucks, out of a battlement arg., a dexter arm embowed in armour, holding in the hand ppr. a lizard vert. *Honesta quam magna.*

Walker of Eastwood, Notts, a demipegasus arg., semée of cinquefoils az., winged or. *cf.* 47. 5

Walker of Uppingham, Rutl., a pilgrim's head affrontée, couped at the shoulders, vested in a slouched hat and gown, on the hat and cope of the gown three escallops, all ppr.

Walker, Thomas James, M.D., a rock ppr. *Per varios casus.*

Walker, H. Faure, Esquire, Highley Manor, Balcombe, a demi-lion rampant, ducally crowned, and supporting with its paws a cross formé fitchée.

Walkey of Clyst St. Lawrence, Devonsh., a gryphon's head erased arg., charged with two bendlets engrailed gu., and holding in the beak a sprig of three cinquefoils, also gu., slipped vert. *Vigilate.*

Walkfare, a branch of thistle in pale ppr. 150. 5

Walkfare, a holly-branch in pale ppr. 150. 10

Walkingshaw of that Ilk, Renfrewsh., Scotland, a martlet ppr. *In season.* 95. 4

Walkington, a mullet of six points or. 164. 3

Walkington, Middx., a stag trippant gu. 117. 8

Walkinshaw of Burrowfield, Renfrewsh., Scotland, a martlet sa. *In season.* 95. 5

Walkinshaw of Glasgow and London, a dove holding in its beak an olive-branch ppr. *In season.* 92. 5

Wall, Captain Arthur, Coed Manor Hall, near Conway, North Wales, in front of a demi-boy affrontée resting his dexter hand on a human heart, two torches in saltire fired, all ppr.

Wall, James, Esquire, of Leith, a falcon close arg. *Fide et fiducia.* 85. 2

Wall, an eagle's head couped arg. 83. 1

Wall of Crich, Derbysh., a demi-eagle az., with wings addorsed arg.

Wall, a demi-boar rampant sa. 40. 13

Wall of Preston and Wallrush, Lancs, a boar's head couped sa., holding in the mouth an acorn erect or, stalked and leaved vert. 42. 7

Wall of Worthy Park, Hants out of a mural coronet or, a wolf's head arg, charged on the neck with a fess em battled and counter embattled gu *Firm*

Wall of Leominster and Faintree Hall, Shropsh and Heref, same crest

Wall of Malvern and Worcester, out of a mural coronet or a demi wolf salient ppr, collared, embattled, and counter-embattled of the first

Wall or **Walle** of Resby, Suff, of Bristol, Glouc, Rutl, Alby, Norf, and Essex a lion rampant gardant or, supporting a long cross sa *cf* 3 15

Wall of Hoxton, Middx, a demi lion rampant gardant az, holding a battle axe headed arg, handled gu 16 14

Wall, out of a ducal coronet a swan's head and neck

Wall, Ireland, an arm in armour embowed, holding in the hand a sword ppr 195 2

Wall of Stonepitt, Kent, a cubit arm erect in mail the hand presenting a pistol, all ppr

Wall of Claverton, Somers, an arm embowed ppr, tied below the elbow by a ribbon vert, holding in the hand a lion's gamb erased or

Wall of Johnstown co Carlow Ireland a naked arm holding a scimitar the blade embrued, all ppr *Aut Cæsar aut nihil* 213 5

Wallace, Baron Wallace (*extinct*), out of a ducal coronet or an ostrich's head and neck ppr, holding in the beak a horse-shoe

Wallace, Cumb, out of a ducal coronet or an ostrich's head arg, holding in the beak a horse-shoe az *cf* 97 11

Wallace of Asholme Knaresdale, and Featherstone Castle Northumb, out of a vallery coronet or an ostrich's head arg, holding in the beak a horse-shoe sa *Sperandum est*

Wallace, late Sir Richard Bart (*extinct*), in front of fern vert, an ostrich's head erased arg holding in the beak a horse shoe or *Esperance*

Wallace, Scotland, an ostrich's head couped arg *Esperance*

Wallace of Bergen and Helmston, Ayrsh, Scotland an ostrich ppr, holding in the beak a horse-shoe az *Sperandum est* 97 8

Wallace of Ingleston, Scotland, an ostrich in full flight ppr *Sperandum est* 97 6

Wallace, James Alexander Agnew, Esquire, an ostrich with a horseshoe in its beak, seated in a coronet *Esperance*

Wallace, Paterson-, of Edinburgh, an ostrich holding in the beak a horse-shoe ppr *Sperandum est —Je meurs pour ceux que j'aime* 97 8

Wallace, Frederick William Burgoyne a pelican in her piety arg the nest sa the whole enclosed within two olive branches ppr

Wallace, on a rock ppr, a martlet or collared and lined, and at the end of the line a ring

Wallace, Ayrsh, two eagles' heads and necks conjoined *cf* 84 11

Wallace of Lochwood, Lanarksh, a horse shoe sa *Spe et industria* 158 6

Wallace, a lion's head ppr, collared arg *cf* 18 6

Wallace, a boar's head erased 42 2

Wallace, Ireland, a sword erect, enfiled with a Saracen's head affrontee ppr *cf* 191 11

Wallace, Hugh Robert, Esquire of Busbie and Cloncaird, Ayrsh (1) A dexter arm vambraced brandishing a sword ppr (2) An ostrich, head and neck couped holding a horse shoe in its beak all ppr *Pro libertate* 195 2

Wallace of Kelly, Scotland a dexter arm in armour embowed holding in the hand a sword ppr *Pro libertate* 195 2

Wallange, a rose surmounted by a thistle, both ppr *In utroque* 149 3

Waller, Sir Francis Ernest, Bart of Braywick Lodge, Berks, on a mount vert, a walnut-tree ppr, an escutcheon az pendent by a ribbon, charged with a fleur de-lis or *Hæc fructus virtutis —Azincourt* 311 10

Waller, William Newcome J P D L, Allenstone House Kells, pendent from an oak-tree ppr an escutcheon arg, charged with a saltire gu

Waller, Middx, of Groombridge, Kent Hants, and Sidbury Devonsh, on a mount vert a walnut-tree ppr, on the sinister side pendent an escutcheon az, charged with three fleurs de-lis, two and one or *Hic fructus virtutis* 144 4

Waller, Major General William Nowell Farmington, North Leach Glouc, same crest

Waller of Dublin out of a ducal coronet or, an eagle's leg erect gu, in front of a plume of five ostrich feathers, the first third and fifth arg, the second and fourth az *Honor et veritas*

Waller, George Arthur Esquire, J P, Prior Park, Borrisokane, co Tipperary, same crest and motto

Waller, Sir Charles, Bart, of Newport, co Tipperary, out of a ducal coronet a plume of five ostrich-feathers the second and fourth az the first third and fifth arg, surmounted by an eagle's claw gu *Honor et veritas*

Waller, Robert Jocelyn, of Castle Waller co Tipperary, Ireland, out of a ducal coronet or an eagle's leg and thigh erect gu in front of a plume of five ostrich-feathers alternately arg and az *Honor et veritas*

Waller, Thomas Francis Paynton-Glenmoe Road, Sydney, Australia same crest and motto

Waller, a demi griffin segreant 64 2

Waller of Loughton Essex in front of a saltier or a griffin's head erased sa gorged with a collar of annulets interlaced, also or *Fide sed cui vide*

Waller, a goat's head ppr 128 12

Waller of Boklesham, Suff a fox's head az 33 4

Waller, a dexter arm couped and embowed fesseways, holding in the hand a sword erect enfiled with a Saracen's head dropping blood all ppr wreathed about the head arg and az *cf* 201 7

Walley, an eagle preying on an infant ppr *Nihil desperandum* *cf* 77 13

Walleys, a helmet close ppr 180 3

Wallford, two palm-branches in orle vert 146. 2

Wallford, a griffin's head ermines, beaked and ducally gorged or *cf* 66 1

Wallford of Walton Lodge, Sydenham Rise, Forest Hill, S E, between two wings, each charged with a fire ball, a griffin's head erased ppr, collared sa *Virtutis præmium honor* 67 8

Wallinger, Essex, Beds, and Bucks, out of a ducal coronet or, a falcon's head between two wings of the first

Wallingham, out of a ducal coronet or an antelope's head erm

Wallington, on a ducal coronet a peacock ppr 103 8

Wallington of Cheltenham, Peer's Court and Dursley Glouc, a buck's head ppr, erased gu collared sa charged with a cinquefoil or between two lozenges arg *Non temere sed fortiter*

Wallington, Sir John Williams, K C B, Keevil House Trowbridge, same crest.

Wallis, Hoare-, Bart, see Hoare

Wallis, flames of fire ppr 177 10

Wallis of Mevegesie, Cornw, a bonfire ppr 177 10

Wallis of Portrane, co Dublin Ireland a talbot's head erased arg collared az studded and ringed or 56 1

Wallis, Sussex, a Cornish chough ppr 107 14

Wallis, out of a ducal coronet or an ostrich's head arg

Wallis of Underwoods, Etchingham Sussex an ostrich holding in its beak a horse shoe *Pro libertate*

Wallis of Healing near Grimsby Lincs a wolf's head couped gu charged on the neck with a pheon transfixed through the mouth by a broken spear fesseways or the head of the spear imbrued ppr

Wallis of Killeny Queen's Co, an arm couped below the elbow and erect vested sa, cuffed arg holding in the hand ppr a cinquefoil erm *cf* 205 2

Wallop, *see* Portsmouth, Earl of

Wallop, a mermaid with her mirror and comb all ppr 184 5

Wallop, a mermaid with two tails expanded ppr armed or, holding the tail in her hands

Wallpool or **Walpole,** Norf, a Saracen's head and neck couped at the shoulders ppr, ducally crowned or with a long cap turned forward gu tasselled or, thereon a catherine-wheel of the same *Fari quæ sentiat* 190 3

Wallpool or **Walpole** of Pinchbach Lincs, a stag's head gardant couped at the neck ppr, attired or

Wallpoole, Kent a naked arm couped below the elbow and erect holding up the royal crown, all ppr *Dieu et mon droit* 217 1

Wallscourt, Baron (Blake), Ardfry Oranmore co Galway, a cat a-mountain passant gardant ppr *Virtus sola nobilitat* *cf* 26 5

Walmesley of Westwood House Lancs a lion statant gardant ducally crowned gu *En Dieu est mon esperance* *cf* 4 1

Walmesley of Dunkenhalgh and Sholley, Lancs, same crest. *cf.* 4. 1

Walmesley, Richard Joseph, Pilgrim's Hall, Bruntwood, a lion statant guardant erm., ducally crowned or. *Valet veritas.*

Walmesley of Ince, Lancs, a lion statant gardant, ducally crowned gu. *Spes durat avorum.* *cf.* 4. 1

Walmouth of Myclehead, Lancs, a leopard's face or, cut through on the sinister side to the eye by a cutlass arg., hilt and pommel or, the hilt resting on the wreath. 22. 3

Walmsley, a dexter hand holding a sabre. *Pro patria.* 212. 13

Walmesley, Humphreys Jeffreys, Westwood House, Manor of Ince, Wigan, a lion statant guardant erm., ducally crowned or.

Walmesley, John, of Lucknam, Wilts, a lion statant guardant ducally crowned gu. *Spes durat avorum.*

Walmesley, Richard Joseph, Pilgrim's Hall, South Weald, Essex, a lion statant guardant erm., ducally crowned or.

Walmesley, Humphrey, Inglewood House, Hungerford, Berks, a lion statant guardant erm., ducally crowned gu.

Walmsley of Foston Hall, Derbysh., a lion statant gardant erm., ducally crowned or, charged on the body with a trefoil slipped vert. *cf.* 4. 3

Walmsley, late Sir Joshua, of Wavertree Hall, Lancs, a lion passant erm., crowned with a vallery coronet or, and his dexter fore-paw resting on a knight's helmet ppr.

Walne of Brockdish, Norf., a lion rampant sa. 1. 10

Walpole, *see* Orford, Earl of.

Walpole, Vade-, of Freethorpe, Norf.: (1) A Saracen's head in profile couped ppr., ducally crowned or, from the coronet a long cap turned forward gu., tasselled and charged with a catherine-wheel of the second (*for Walpole*). 190. 3. (2) A dexter arm in armour embowed ppr., garnished or, holding in the hand a dagger, also ppr., hilt and pommel also or (*for Vade*). *Fari quæ sentiat.* 196. 5

Walpole, a stag's head gardant couped at the neck ppr., attired or.

Walpole, a lion passant az. 6. 2

Walpole of Athlone, co. Westmeath, a naked arm couped below the elbow and erect holding up the royal crown, all ppr. *Dieu et mon droit.* 217. 1

Walpole, Sir Charles George, Broadford, Chobham, Woking, a Saracen's head in profile couped at the shoulders ppr., ducally crowned or, from the coronet flowing a red cap turned down in front, tasselled, and charged with a catherine-wheel or.

Walpole, Sir Horace George, K.C.B., 18, Linden Gardens, W., same crest. *Fari quæ sentiat.*

Walpole, Sir Spencer, same crest.

Walron, Ireland, issuant from a fleur-de-lis arg., banded or, a dragon's head gu.

Walrond of Alborne, Wilts, a leopard's face or. 22. 2

Walrond, Henry, Lieutenant-Colonel, 4th Batt. Devon Regiment, **Marquis de Vallado, Conde de Parama,** and **Conde de Valderonda,** in the Kingdom of Spain, of Dulford House, Collumpton, Devonsh., and of 13, Delamere Terrace, London, W., a heraldic tiger sejant sa., crined or, pellettée. *Bienlefatz payeray malfaictz vangeray.* Another crest, On a mural crown a heraldic tiger sa., pellettée, was granted by King Charles I. to Colonel Humphrey Walrond for his services during the civil wars.

Walrond of Sea, Somers., a heraldic tiger sa., platée. *Nec beneficii.*

Walrond of Calder Park, Lanarksh., same crest. *Paix et peu.*

Walrond, Sir William Hood, Bart., M.P., of Bradfield and New Court, Devonsh., a heraldic tiger sejant sa., platée, maned and tufted or. *Sic vos non vobis.*

Walsam and **Walsham,** a fir-tree issuing ppr. 144. 13

Walsh, *see* Ormathwaite, Baron.

Walsh, Johnson-, Sir Hunt Henry Allen, Bart., D.L., of Ballykilcavan, Queen's Co.: (1) A griffin's head erased arg., langued gu. (*for Walsh*). 66. 2. (2) A tower arg., thereon a cock gu., langued az. (*for Johnson*). *Firm.* 156. 12

Walsh, Berks and Worcs., a griffin's head erased arg. 66. 2

Walsh of Ballykilcavan, Queen's Co., Ireland, same crest. *Firm.* 66. 2

Walsh, John, Esquire, J.P., of Fanningstown, co. Kilkenny, Ireland, a swan pierced through the neck from behind with an arrow, all ppr., and charged with an annulet gu. *Dum spiro, spero.*

Walsh, Peter, J.P., Fanningstown, Piltown, same crest and motto.

Walsh of the Walsh Mountains and Castle Hoel, co. Kilkenny, a swan pierced through the back and breast with a dart, all ppr.

Walsh, Hussey Valentine John, 81, Onslow Gardens, S.W., a swan pierced through the back and breast with a dart, all ppr. *Transfixus sed non mortuus.*

Walsh of Ballynecully, co. Kilkenny, and St. Malo, France, a swan pierced through the back and breast with a dart, all ppr. *Transfixus sed no mortuus.*

Walsh, Captain Adolphus Frederick, out of a ducal coronet or, a demi-lion rampant gu., gorged with a collar per pale or and arg., and charged on the shoulder with a crescent of the first. *Noli irritare leonem.* *cf.* 16. 3

Walsh, Rt. Hon. John Edward, P.C., Master of the Rolls in Ireland, out of a ducal coronet or, a demi-lion az., charged on the shoulder with a bezant. *Noli irritare leonem.* *cf.* 16. 3

Walsh, Rev. Canon Robert, D.D., St. Mary's Rectory, Donnybrook, Dublin, out of a ducal coronet or, a demi-lion rampant az., charged on the shoulder with a bezant. *Noli irritare leonem.*

Walsh of Castle Walsh, co. Kerry, Ireland, out of a ducal coronet or, a demi-lion rampant az. *Noli irritare leonem.* 16. 3

Walsh of Belcarrow, co. Dublin, Ireland, a wolf's head couped sa. 30. 5

Walsh, an arm, the part below the elbow in bend dexter, holding in the hand a scimitar in bend sinister.

Walsh, Ireland, a cubit arm holding in the hand a tilting-spear ppr. 214. 11

Walsham, Sir John, Bart., M.A., D.L., of Knill Court, Heref., a demi-eagle with two heads displayed sa., each wing charged with a cross patée fitchée between two ermine-spots or, and pendent from the neck by a gold chain an escutcheon arg., charged with a Saracen's head erased ppr., and wreathed round the temples arg. and az. *Sub libertate quietem.* 308. 1

Walshe of Kilgobbin, co. Dublin, out of a ducal coronet or, a demi-lion rampant arg. 16. 3

Walshe of Beardley and Shaldesley, Worcs., and Wormesley, Heref., a griffin's head erased arg. 66. 2

Walshe, a goat's head erased az., attired or, on the top of the horns two hawk's bells arg., charged on the neck with three bezants, two and one.

Walshe of Catengar, Somers., an antelope's head erased az., attired or, on the end of each horn a bell arg., charged on the neck with a fess gobony arg. and gu., between three bezants one and two.

Walsingham, Baron (de Grey), of Walsingham, Norf., a wyvern's head or. *Excitari non hebescere.* 71. 1

Walsingham, Surrey, Kent, and of Exall, Warw., out of a mural coronet gu., a tiger's head or, ducally gorged az. 27. 1

Walstenholme, on a snake nowed, an eagle with two heads displayed.

Walstonecroft, out of a naval coronet a demi-mermaid, holding in her dexter hand a purse and in her sinister a comb. *cf.* 184. 14

Walter, Shropsh., a garb or. 153. 2

Walter, Shropsh., a garb or, banded gu. 153. 2

Walter, Shropsh., a garb of barley quarterly or and az., banded gu. 153. 2

Walter of London, and Ludlow, Shropsh., a lion's gamb erased arg. 36. 4

Walter, Shropsh., a lion's head erased erm., langued gu. 17. 8

Walter of Ashburie, Devonsh., a stork ppr., dipping the beak into a whelk-shell erect or.

Walter, John Henry Fraser, Drayton House, near Norwich, same crest.

Walter, Arthur Fraser, 40, Upper Grosvenor Street, W., same crest.

Walter, Arthur Fraser, Bear Wood, Wokingham, same crest.

Walter, a cubit arm holding in the hand an anchor.

Walters, Robert, Ware Priory, Herts, a lion's head erased erminois, gorged with a collar indented sa., thereon three plates, all between two demi-lances ppr.

Walters, William Melmoth, Purberry Shot, Ewell, Surrey, on a wreath or and az., a squirrel sejant devouring a nut ppr. 313. 13

Walters, Captain Henry Edward, R.N., Caer Llan, near Monmouth, a squirrel devouring a nut or. *Sit Dux sapientia.*

Walters of Cundall Yorks an arm vested gu, turned up arg holding in the hand ppr a chess rook sa

Walters, a dove holding in its beak an olive-branch ppr 92 5

Walthall of Wistaston, Chesh, an arm embowed vested gu cuffed erm, the hand clenched, thereon a falcon close ppr beaked or 258 3

Walthall, Henry Walthall, Alton Manor Derby (1) A dexter arm embowed couped at the shoulder vested gu, cuffed erm, the hand clenched, thereon a falcon close ppr, beaked or, with lure gu stringed gold 258 3 (2) A garb erminois between two trefoils vert (*for Milnes*) *Dimidium qui cœpit habet —A bird in the hand is worth two in the bush*

Waltham, a peacock's head az. 103 2

Walthew of Deptford, Kent out of a mural coronet or, a demi lion sa, supporting the lower part of a tilting-spear of the last

Walton of Clifton, Glouc a griffin's head erased arg, semee of buckles az, pierced through the mouth by a spear in bend sinister point upwards or *Murus æneus virtus*

Walton, Harold Arthur Gordon, same crest and motto

Walton, late General William Lovelace between two wings each charged with a fire ball, a griffin's head erased ppr, collared sa *Virtutis præmium honor* 67 8

Walton, Somers a dragon's head couped or, vomiting flames of fire ppr charged on the neck with a cross patée sa cf 72 3

Walton of Little Burstead Essex an antelope's head couped at the neck gu, attired or, gorged with a collar arg, charged with three fleurs de-lis of the first holding in the mouth a trefoil ppr

Walton of Chaklack Hall, Durh, a buck current arg, charged on the shoulder with three torteaux attired or, pierced through the neck by an arrow of the last, feathered of the first

Walton of Lacock, Wilts, and of Walton, Lancs, a wild man wreathed about the loins ppr and round the head arg and sa holding in his dexter hand a trefoil slipped or, and in his sinister a tree eradicated vert reclining on his shoulder cf 188 10

Walton of Preston Lancs a wild man wreathed about the temples and waist with oak-leaves over the dexter shoulder a chain in bend sinister supporting with the dexter hand an axe head downwards and holding in the sinister hand an oak sapling eradicated and sprouting, all ppr

Walton, a wild man striding forward ppr holding in his sinister hand the branch of a tree resting on the shoulder and wreathed round the temples with a chaplet of laurel, all vert

Walton, on a chapeau arg, turned up gu, a bugle-horn of the last stringed or cf 228 11

Walworth, out of a ducal coronet or two arms embowed vested gu holding in the hands ppr a cake of bread arg

Walwyn, a pheasant ppr cf 90 8

Walwyn of Longworth, Heref on an embattled wall arg, masoned sa, a wyvern with wings expanded vert, scaled or pierced through the head by a javelin ppr, headed, also or vulned gu *Non deficit alter —Drwy Rynwedd Gwaed*

Walwyn, out of a battlement arg, a wyvern with wings expanded vert pierced through the mouth by an arrow or

Walwyn of Witham, Sussex, on a mural coronet gu a dragon with wings expanded vert, pierced through the mouth by an arrow or

Wandesforde, *see* Prior Wandesforde

Wandesford of Kirklington Yorks, a church ppr, the spire az 156 10

Wandsworth, Baron (Stern), 10, Great Stanhope Street Mayfair W, a lion passant ppr gorged with a collar flory counterflory gu, supporting with the dexter fore paw an escutcheon of the second charged with a horse's head erased arg *Vincit perseverantia* 287 9

Wankford of Berwick Hall, Essex a lion rampant gardant holding between the paws a hurt

Wanklyn, Heref and Worcs, a lion's head erased ppr 17 8

Wanley, a cross surmounted by a crescent or

Wantage, Baron (Loyd Lindsay), of Lockinge Berks (1) A tent az fringed and semée of stars or ensigned with a pennon gu (*for Lindsay*) 158 13 (2) A buck's head ppr erased sa attired or, charged on the neck with a fess engrailed also sa, thereon three bezants (*for Loyd*) *Astra castra numen lumen* cf 121 2

Wanton of Stoughton and Great Yarmouth Norf, a trefoil slipped sa charged with another arg cf 148 9

Wanton, Hunts, a plume of seven ostrich-feathers, three arg, two sa and two vert

Wanton of London an eagle preying on a dove all ppr

Warburton, Chesh Cumb Suff and Notts, a Saracen's head ppr couped at the shoulders, wreathed about the head arg and gu, and issuing there from a plume of feathers or *Je voil droyt avoyre* cf 192 10

Warburton, Rev Canon, the Close Winchester, same crest and motto

Warburton, Egerton-, Piers, of Warburton, Chesh (1) A Saracen's head affrontee couped at the shoulders ppr, the temples wreathed arg and gu issuing therefrom three ostrich feathers or charged on the breast with a cross crosslet sa (*for Warburton*) cf 192 10 (2) Three arrows two in saltier and one in pale or, headed and feathered sa, bound by a ribbon gu (*for Egerton*) 173 1

Warburton, Richard Garryhinch, Portarlington Ireland, a Saracen's head affrontee, couped at the shoulders ppr round the temples a wreath arg and gu, and issuing therefrom three ostrich-feathers or

Warburton, Joseph William same crest

Warburton, Ireland, a mermaid with her mirror and comb ppr 184 5

Warcop, Warcup, and **Warcupp** of English Oxon, Yorks, and Cumb a boar's head couped arg 43 1

Warcop, a dexter hand holding a cross crosslet fitched gu 221 14

Ward, Earl of Dudley, and **Baron Ward,** *see* Dudley

Ward, Viscount Bangor, *see* Bangor

Ward, Lucas-, of Guilsborough a wolf's head erased or *Sub cruce salus* 30 8

Ward, Plumer-, of Gilston Park Herts (1) A wolf's head erased and langued holding in the mouth a key all ppr (*for Ward*) (2) A demi lion gu holding in the jaws a garb (*for Plumer*) *Give the thanks that are due* 12 5

Ward, Ireland, a wolf's head erased arg 30 8

Ward, out of a mural coronet gu a wolf's head or

Ward, Chesh a wolf's head erased or 30 8

Ward, Edmund Grenville, Northwood Park Cowes a wolf's head erased and langued ppr

Ward, of Great Ilford Essex, Warw and Yorks a wolf's head erased or, charged on the breast with a mullet sa cf 30 8

Ward of London, out of a mural coronet or a wolf's head per fess of the same and az

Ward of Bishop Middleton Durh a wolf's head erased per fesse or and az 30 8

Ward of Great Ilford Essex a wolf's head erased or, charged on the breast with a mullet sa for difference cf 30 8

Ward, Admiral Thomas Le Hunt, C B, a man's head couped at the shoulders ppr wreathed about the temples or and az and adorned with three ostrich feathers

Ward, William Erskine, C S I same crest

Ward of London, out of a ducal coronet or, a wolf's head ppr

Ward, Colonel Michael Foster of Upton Park and Ogbourne St Andrew Wilts Bucks a wolf's head erased or gorged with a collar az, charged with an escallop of the first between two bezants (2) An arm embowed in armour, the hand grasping a broken spear, all ppr (*for Foster*) *Garde la croix* cf 30 11

Ward of Calverley, Kent a wolf's head erased ppr, langued gu *Garde la croix* 30 8

Ward of London, out of a mural coronet gu a wolf's head or

Ward or **Warde** of Gorleston, Suff on a mount vert a hind lodged arg 125 4

Ward, a doe trippant 124 12

Ward, Norf, a buck trippant ppr 117 8

Ward, Bart (*extinct*) of Bexley Norf a buck trippant ppr, collared, lined and ringed or cf 117 8

Ward, a heraldic antelope sejant

Ward, Berks and Birmingham Warw an Indian goat ppr collared ringed lined, and armed or

Ward of New Market co Dublin Ireland a lion sejant affrontee gu 7 2

Ward, Arthur John Hanslip V D, Colonel 1st Suffolk and Harwich R G A (Vols) the Gables Dovercourt Essex, out of the battlements of a tower a griffin's head. *Aut nunquam tentes aut perfice.* 273. 1

Ward, a griffin's head erased. 66. 2

Ward of Brooke, Norf., on a mount vert. an eagle displayed erm. *cf.* 75. 2

Ward, a dove holding in its beak an olive-branch, all ppr. 92. 5

Ward of Capesthorne, Chesh., a martlet or, holding in the beak a fleur-de-lis sa. *cf.* 95. 6

Ward, Shropsh., a martlet or. 95. 2

Ward of Shenstone, Staffs, and Willey Place, Surrey, a martlet sa., guttée-d'or, holding in the beak a fleur-de-lis or. *Sub cruce salus.* 95. 6

Ward, Edward Foote, of Walcot and Sallhouse Hall, Norf., a dexter arm erect couped at the elbow, vested quarterly or and vert, cuffed arg., holding in the hand ppr. a pheon of the third. *Usque ad mortem fidus.*

Ward-Boughton-Leigh, Rev. Bridgman George, Harborough Magna, Warw.: (1) A cubit arm vested or, cuffed arg., the hand grasping a broken tilting-spear or (*for Leigh*). (2) A stork's head erased chevronny of four pieces sa. and arg., in the beak a snake ppr. (*for Boughton*). (3) A wolf's head erased or, guttée-d'eau, gorged with a collar gemel az. (*for Ward*).

Ward-Boughton-Leigh, Rev. Theodosius, Newbold-on-Avon, Warw., same crests.

Ward-Boughton-Leigh, Henry Allesley, J.P., Brownsover Hall, Rugby, same crests.

Ward-Boughton-Leigh, John Hugh, 67, Albert Hall Mansions, S.W., same crests.

Ward, His Honour Robert, of the Pines, Wanganui, New Zealand, Judge of the Native Land Court, New Zealand, *uses* a dexter arm embowed, the fist clenched. *Kia kaha ki te mahi tika.* 202. 2

Ward of Dublin, a dexter arm in armour embowed holding in the hand a petronel, all ppr.

Ward, Henry, Rodbaston, Penkridge, Staffs, and of Oakland, Wolverhampton, Staffs, in front of a cubit arm ppr., grasping an arrow in bend sinister or, three crosses patée fessewise of the last. 214. 7

Wardall, a boar's head and neck or. 41. 1

Warde-Aldam, *see* Aldam.

Warde of Hurst, Beds, a wolf's head erased or. 30. 8

Warde of Clopton House, Warw., same crest.

Warde, Lieutenant-Colonel Charles Arthur Madan, of Squerryes Court, Kent, a wolf's head erased or. 30. 8

Warde, Alexander John Walter, Dean Lodge, Sevenoaks, same crest. *Licet esse beatis.*

Warde, Augustus Walter Francis, same crest and motto.

Warde, Major Charles Edward, Barham Court, Maidstone, same crest and motto.

Warde, Lieutenant-Colonel Henry Ashley Murray, same crest and motto.

Warde, Major St. Andrew Bruce, same crest and motto.

Warde, Hamilton Francis, same crest and motto.

Warde, Henry John, same crest and motto.

Warde, Walter Eldred, same crest and motto.

Warde, William Henry, same crest and motto.

Warde-Aldam, William Wright, of Frickley Hall, Doncaster, issuant from a mount vert four ostrich-feathers arg., conjoined at the points by a mill-rind or (*for Aldam*). 280. 9. (2) A wolf's head erased or, charged for distinction with a cross crosslet az. (*for Warde*). 280. 10

Warde of Barford, Warw., a wolf's head ppr. 30. 5

Warde, a wolf's head erased sa., eared and nosed or, charged with a chevron paly of six of the last and az. 29. 10

Warde, a goat's head erased and armed or. 128. 5

Warde of Broke, Norf., on a mount vert. an eagle displayed erm. *cf.* 75. 2

Warde, Warw., an eagle's head erased ppr., ducally gorged or. *cf.* 83. 10

Warde of Pilton, Devonsh., a martlet with wings expanded gu., rising from the battlements of a tower arg. 156. 9

Wardell or **Wardle,** a lion's gamb holding a spear ppr., tasselled or. *cf.* 38. 11

Wardell of London, a hawk arg., charged on the breast with three torteaux in bend.

Wardell-Yerburgh, Rev. Oswald Pryor, Tewkesbury Abbey, a falcon close or, belled of the last, preying on a mallard ppr.

Warden, a peacock's feather and two ostrich-feathers in pale, all enfiled by a ducal coronet.

Warden, Scotland, a fleur-de-lis or. *Industria et spe.* 148. 2

Warden, Thomas Fawcett, of Greta Bridge House, Melling, Lancs, out of a crescent arg., an arrow sa., barbed and flighted or. *Industria et spe.* 163. 13

Wardlaw-Ramsay: (1) A unicorn's head erased arg., charged with a rose gu. (*for Ramsay*). *cf.* 49. 5. (2) A star of six points wavy or (*for Wardlaw*). *Familias firmat pietas.—Semper victor.* 164. 1

Wardlaw, Sir Henry, Bart., of Pitreavie, Fifesh., an estoile or. *Familias firmat pietas.* 164. 1

Wardlaw-Ramsay, Robert George, Whitehill, Rosewell, co. Edinburgh: (1) A unicorn's head erased arg., charged with a rose gu. (2) An estoile or.

Wardman of London, a ram's head armed or. 130. 1

Wardon, a pellet charged with a lion's head erased arg., collared gu. 19. 3

Wardor, Hants, and Westbury, Wilts, a fleur-de-lis arg., enfiled by a ducal coronet or. 148. 1

Wardrop of Strathavon, Linlithgow, and Edinburgh, Scotland, issuing from an antique crown a demi-eagle with wings expanded, all ppr. *Superna sequor.* *cf.* 80. 2

Wardrop or **Wardrope,** Scotland, a husbandman issuing, his bonnet and vestments az., holding a ploughshare over his dexter shoulder ppr. *Revertite.*

Ware, Rt. Rev. Henry, Bishop-Suffragan of Barrow-in-Furness, the Abbey, Carlisle, in front of a demi-lion az., between the paws a mullet within an annulet or, issuant from a basket ppr., a cross crosslet fitchée.

Ware, James Thomas, Tilford House, Tilford, Farnham, same crest.

Ware, a bear passant arg. 40. 9

Ware, Essex, Devonsh., and Ireland, a dragon's head or, pierced through the neck by a broken sword-blade ppr.

Ware, Charles Edward Cumberlege, of Poslingford, Suff., and Hendon Hall, Middx., in front of two spears in saltire ppr., a dragon's head gu., gorged with a collar gemel arg. *Deo favente.*

Ware, Ireland, a dragon's head or, pierced through with the shiver of a lance ppr.

Ware, Yorks: (1) A dragon's head couped or, pierced through with the shiver of a lance ppr. (*for Ware*). (2) A cubit arm erect grasping a mill-rind, all ppr. (*for Hibbert*).

Wareing and **Waringe** of Walmesley, Lancs, a wolf's head couped at the neck holding in the mouth an ostrich-feather, all ppr.

Warham, Hants, and Osmington, Dorset, an arm in armour holding in the hand a sword. 210. 2

Waring of Waringstown, co. Down, Ireland, a crane's head ppr. *Nec vi nec astutia.* 104. 5

Waring of Belfast, co. Antrim, an eagle close regardant ppr. *Mox sese attollit in auras.* 76. 6

Waring, a boar's head erased gu. 42. 2

Waring of Haworth Hall, Yorks, upon a mill-rind fessewise or, a dragon gu., charged on either wing with an annulet of the first.

Waring, Henry, Bernham House, Reading, same crest.

Waringe of Shrewsbury, an arm erect vested gu., cuffed arg., holding in the hand ppr. a lure of the first, garnished or, lined and ringed vert, the line twisted round the arm. *Cavendo tutus.*

Waringe, Ireland, a rose or, barbed vert. 149. 4

Warley, a tree ppr. 143. 5

Warley of London, out of a mural coronet az., a dexter arm in armour embowed ppr., garnished or, holding in the hand, also ppr., a falchion arg., hilt and pommel of the third.

Warmestrey, Worcs., three ostrich-feathers az., banded gu.

Warmouth of Newcastle-on-Tyne, Northumb., a demi-lion rampant erm., armed or, holding between the paws a mullet of six points of the last. *cf.* 15. 8

Warnar of London, a plume of feathers or, bound at the bottom arg.

Warne, a horse-shoe or, between two wings ppr. 110. 11

Warne, C. Holland, 37, the Drive, Hove, Sussex, a horse-shoe reversed between two wings.

Warnecombe, Heref., a caltrap or, environed by a serpent vert.

Warneford of Warneford Place, Wilts, a garb ppr. 153. 2

Warner, Edward Hanley, of Quorn Hall, Leics., a squirrel sejant ppr., holding in the paws a rose gu., slipped and leaved of the first, between two escallops of the second. *Non nobis tantum nati.*

Warner, William Pochin J P, D L, Langton Hall, Market Harborough, a squirrel sejant ppr holding in the paws a rose gu, slipped and leaved of the first between two escallops of the second *Non nobis tantum nati*

Warner, Ireland, a badger passant sa cf 33 10

Warner, Suff, a lizard vert cf 138 5

Warner of Strowd Middx and Ratcliff and Rowington, Warw, a horse's head erased per fess erm and gu, maned of the last 51 4

Warner of Dublin a heraldic tiger passant gu *Deo adjuvante non timendum* 25 5

Warner of London, Norf, Kent, and Northamp, a double plume of feathers or cf 114 4

Warner of Waltham Essex London and Sussex, a man's head ppr couped below the shoulders vested chequy or and az, wreathed about the temples of the second and gu, on the head a cap arg

Warner, Yorks, a Saracen's head affrontee ppr, the temples wreathed or and gu 190. 5

Warner, Thomas Courtenay Theydon, Highams, Woodford Green Essex, a Saracen's head affrontee couped at the shoulders ppr, vested gu, on the head a cap chequy arg and of the second and in front thereof three roses in fesse of the third *Spero* 192 5

Warner, Patrick, of Ardeer Ayrsh, Scotland, an open Bible ppr *Manet in æternum* 158 3

Warr, a cross fleury fitched gu fleury or 166 7

Warrand, William Edmund Westhorpe Hall, Southwell a dexter arm in armour holding in the hand a sword, all ppr, hilted and pommelled or *Fortiter* 210 2

Warrand, Alexander John Cruickshand, Bught, Inverness-sh, same crest and motto

Warrand, out of a ducal coronet az, a demi-lion erm 16 3

Warre of Bindon House, Somers, out of a ducal coronet or, a griffin's head arg, holding in the beak the attire of a stag ppr *Je trouve bien*

Warre of Chipley Somers out of a ducal coronet or a griffin's head arg 67 9

Warre, Arthur Brathwaite, Westcliff House, Ramsgate, same crest

Warre, Bart (*extinct*), of Hestercombe Somers an ostrich's head with wings elevated arg, holding in the beak a key or

Warren, Baron de Tabley, *see* De Tabley

Warren-Darley, *see* Darley

Warren, on a chapeau gu turned up erm, a wyvern arg, with wings expanded chequy or and az 70 11

Warren, Lieutenant-Colonel George Gordon, V D, of Poynton House, Market Drayton, Salop, same crest *Tenebo.*

Warren, John, Esquire, of Handcross Park, Sussex, and Lancaster Gate, Middx., on a chapeau gu, turned up engrailed erm a wyvern with the tail nowed arg the wings displayed chequy or and az *Tenebo* 70 11

Warren, Bart (*extinct*) of Little Marlow Bucks, on a chapeau gu, turned up erm, a wyvern arg with wings expanded chequy or and gu *Leo de Juda est robur nostrum* 70 11

Warren of Ashwell, Herts, a wyvern, the tail nowed arg, and the wings expanded chequy or and az 70 5

Warren of Killiney Castle and Rutland Square Dublin and of Ballydonarea Wicklow on a chapeau gu turned up erm, a wyvern arg, wings expanded chequy or and az on the breast a trefoil ppr *Be just and fear not* cf 70 11

Warren, Middx a wyvern arg, with wings expanded chequy or and az *Virtus mihi scutum* 70 5

Warren-Warren, John Rosier Esquire (1) Same crest as above (*for Warren*) 70 5 (2) A griffin's head erased ppr (*for Tyerman*) *En avant si je puis* 66 2

Warren, on a chapeau gu turned up erm a wyvern arg the wings expanded chequy or and az *Tenebo* 70 11

Warren, Rev Samuel Percival, of Balbriggan, on a chapeau gu, turned up erm, a wyvern arg wings expanded chequy or and az on the breast a trefoil vert *Be just and fear not*

Warren of Hedbury, Devonsh, a lion rampant chequy or and az, holding between the fore paws a ducal coronet of the first 3 6

Warren, Blair-, of Horkesley Hall, Essex (1) On a mount vert, a lion rampant or supporting a spear erect gu, headed arg (2) A demi-greyhound erm, collared chequy or and az (*both for Warren*) 60 8 (3) A falcon's head erased ppr (*for Blair*) *Sublimiora spectemus* 88 12

Warren, Sir Augustus Riversdale, Bart, of Warren's Court, co Cork, a lion rampant holding a crozier ppr *Non mihi sed Deo et Regi* 313 1

Warren, on a mount vert, a lion rampant or holding in the dexter paw a spear gu, headed arg

Warren of St Albans Herts, a lion's gamb erased arg, grasping an eagle's leg erased at the thigh or 38 10

Warren of Aldenham Herts, out of a ducal coronet or, an eagle's leg sa, out of a plume of feathers arg

Warren out of a crescent arg an elephant's head sa, the tusks ppr, charged on the neck with a mascle or *Crescenti luce resurgit*

Warren, Middx and London, out of a mural coronet arg, charged with three torteaux an eagle's leg couped at the knee and erect or, between two laurel branches vert *Omne tulit punctum qui miscuit utile dulci*

Warren of Poynton, Chesh, out of a ducal coronet or a plume of five ostrich feathers arg, in the middle of them a griffin's claw of the first *Tenebo*

Warren, Robert Esquire, out of a ducal coronet or, an eagle's talon also or holding a crescent gu in front of a plume of five ostrich feathers arg *Mox virtute se tollit ad auras*

Warren-Swettenham of Swettenham Hall Swettenham, near Congleton, Chesh (1) A lion rampant az, against an oak tree ppr (*for Swettenham*) (2) Out of a ducal coronet or an eagle's talon of the same holding a crescent gu, in front of five ostrich-feathers arg (*for Warren*) *Ex sudore vultus — Mox virtute se tollit ad auras*

Warren of Sandford's Court, co Kilkenny, out of a ducal coronet or, an eagle's talon of the same, holding a crescent gu, in front of a plume of five ostrich feathers arg *Mox virtute se tollit ad auras*

Warren of Warrenstown, King's Co, Ireland out of a ducal coronet or, a plume of ostrich feathers gu, issuant therefrom an eagle's leg and thigh arg

Warren of London a talbot ppr *Omni liber metu* cf 54 2

Warren, a talbot passant ppr 54 1

Warren of Swanton, Glouc, and Chesh a demi greyhound rampant erm gorged with a collar chequy or and az 60 8

Warren of London, and Walterstaff Devonsh, a greyhound sa seizing a hare ppr

Warren, a coney sejant in a fern bush

Warren of London, out of a ducal coronet or a leopard's head of the same, spotted sa 23 11

Warren of Hopton, Suff, upon a mount vert five palisades conjoined sa in front of a leopard's head couped ppr *Non aspera terrent*

Warren of London a dragon's head couped gu 71 1

Warren, Ireland a goat statant ppr 129 5

Warren, Ireland, an arm in armour embowed ppr, holding in the hand a dart sa, feathered arg, barbed or *Fortuna sequatur* 195 4

Warren, Wright-, of Mespil Dublin (1) Out of the coronet of an earl or, pearled arg, an arm in armour embowed ppr, grasping a dart sa feathered arg, barbed of the first (*for Warren*) cf 198 4 (2) An arm in armour embowed holding a broken tilting-spear az pointed or (*for Wright*) *Fortuna sequatur* 197 2

Warren, a sinister arm in armour embowed ppr holding in the hand a broken spear or headed arg

Warren of Burgh Castle Suff, out of a ducal coronet gu a pyramid of leaves arg

Warrender, Sir George, Bart D L of Bruntisfield House, Edinburgh a hare sejant ppr *Industria evehit* 292 10

Warrington of Aigberth Lancs, out of a ducal coronet gu a demi eagle displayed or 80 14

Warrington, Thomas, Esquire of 10, Montagu Square, W, a demi eagle displayed and erased sa charged on the breast with an escutcheon arg, thereon a bull's head erased sa and holding in the beak a cross patee fitchee gu *Constantia et labore* 81 11

Warry, Ernest Arthur Bragge, B.A., Mona Lodge, Batheaston, Bath, a griffin's head couped sa., between two horse-shoes or.

Warry, Thomas William, Weston-super-Mare, same crest.

Warry-Stone, William John Ellis, M.A., 72, Elm Park Gardens, S.W., same crest. *Cave et felix esto.*

Warter or **Wartur,** a fox sejant ppr. 32. 11

Warter of London and Shropsh., a lion rampant sa., collared arg., holding between the paws a chess-rook or. *Vi victus non coactus.*

Warter, Henry de Grey, Cruck Meole, near Shrewsbury, same crest.

Warter-Tatham, Henry de Grey Warter: (1) (*For Tatham*). (2) A lion rampant sa., collared arg., holding between his fore-paws a chess-rook, also arg. *Vi victus non coactus.*

Warters, Ireland, a lion rampant arg., supporting a tree vert.

Wartnaby, a lion's head erased or. 17. 8

Warton, a winged spur ppr. 111. 12

Warton, an arm in armour erect ppr., supporting a battle-axe in pale arg.

Warton of Beverley, Yorks, on the stump of a tree couped, a squirrel sejant, all ppr., cracking a nut or, and collared of the last. *cf.* 135. 6

Warwick, Earl of (Greville), Warwick Castle, Warw.: (1) Out of a ducal coronet gu., a demi-swan with wings expanded and elevated arg., beaked of the first (*for Greville*). (2) A bear sejant arg., muzzled gu., supporting a ragged staff of the first (*for Beauchamp*). *Vix ea nostra voco. cf.* 34. 7

Warwick, a leopard's face or. 22. 2

Warwick of Warwick, Cumb., a dexter arm in armour embowed, couped at the shoulder, holding in the gauntlet a battle-axe, all ppr. 200. 6

Wase of London, and Rotherby, Leics., and Hickling, Notts, on a wreath clouds ppr., issuing rays or, therefrom an arm in armour embowed of the first, garnished of the second, supporting a battle-axe headed arg., the staff gu., garnished, also or.

Wase of Storrington, Sussex, a demi-lion rampant arg., ducally gorged az., charged on the shoulder with a pellet, thereon a crescent or. *cf.* 10. 7

Wasey, a sinister arm and a dexter hand shooting an arrow from a bow, all ppr. 200. 2

Wasey of Priors Court, Berks, a falcon rising or, beaked, membered, and collared sa., belled of the first, and the collar charged with three bezants.

Washborne, a hand holding a dagger ppr. 212. 3

Washbourn, Henry John, Esquire, of Brockworth, Riccarton, Christchurch, Canterbury, New Zealand, *uses* a coil of flax arg., surmounted with a wreath arg. and gu., thereon flames of fire arg.

Washbourne, Berks, Heref., and of Washbourne and Winchenford, Worcs., on a wreath a coil of flax arg., surmounted by another wreath of the last and gu., thereon flames of fire ppr.

Washbourne of London and Glouc., same crest. *Industria et probitate.*

Washington, Warw., out of a ducal coronet or, a raven with wings addorsed ppr.

Washington, on a ducal coronet or, an eagle with wings addorsed sa.

Waskett of Pentlow Hall, Essex, a lion rampant gu., gorged with a collar flory counterflory or, and holding between the paws a mullet of eight points az. *Incorrupta fides nudaque veritas.*

Waskett-Myers of Pentlow Hall, Essex: (1) A mermaid ppr., her waist encircled by a mural coronet or, and charged upon the breast for distinction with a cross patée az. (*for Myers*). (2) A lion rampant gu., gorged with a collar flory counterflory or, holding between the paws a mullet of eight points az. (*for Waskett*). *Non dormiat qui custodit.—Incorrupta fides nudaque veritas.*

Wason, Eugene, Esquire, M.P., of Blair Girvan, parish of Kirkoswald, Ayrsh., a lion rampant arg., armed and langued gu., holding between his fore-paws a saltire couped sa. *Timere sperno.*

Wasse of Wickham, Bucks, a demi-lion rampant arg., ducally gorged az. 10. 7

Wastell, Northamp., and Wastell Head, Westml., a cubit arm erect vested gu., charged with three guttes-d'or, cuffed arg., holding on the hand ppr. a dove az., collared of the third.

Waster, within a ring or, gemmed sa., two snakes entwined and erect ppr.

Wastfield of London, Somers., and Wilts, a lamp passant sa., holding a banner arg., charged with a catherine-wheel of the first.

Wastley, a dexter hand gu., holding an annulet or. 216. 1

Wastneys, Chesh. and Leics., a demi-lion rampant arg., collared gu. 10. 9

Wastneys, Bart. (*extinct*), of Hedon, Notts, a demi-lion rampant double-queued arg., collared gu. *cf.* 10. 6

Wastoile or **Wastoyle,** a hand ppr., holding a grenade sa., fired, also ppr. 216. 6

Wateis, *see* Waties.

Waterfall, in front of a demi-eagle with wings addorsed and elevated sa., holding in the beak an escallop or, a fountain ppr. *Aqua cadit resurgere.*

Waterfield of Daventry, Northants, upon a line coiled or, a talbot passant ppr., collared gu., holding in the dexter fore-paw a water-lily arg., seeded, leaved, and slipped ppr.

Waterford, Earl of, *see* Shrewsbury, Earl of.

Waterford, Marquess of (Beresford), Curraghmore, Portlaw, co. Waterford: (1) A dragon's head erased az., pierced through the neck with a broken spear or, the broken point arg., thrust through the upper jaw (*for Beresford*). (2) A stag's head cabossed ppr., attired or, between the horns a crucifix ppr. (*for De la Poer*). *Nil nisi cruce.* 122. 13

Waterhouse of London and Yorks, the dexter side of an eagle divided palewise without the head sa.

Waterhouse of Halifax, Yorks, the dexter wing and leg of an eagle couped, displayed and conjoined sa. *Veritas vincit omnia.*

Waterhouse, Ireland, an eagle's leg or, conjoined at the thigh to a wing sa.

Waterhouse, Doherty-, Captain Daniel Henry, of Hope Hall, Halifax, Yorks: (1) In front of an eagle's leg erased at the thigh or, and issuant therefrom a wing in bend sa., a fountain ppr., and charged upon the thigh for difference with a cross crosslet sa. (*for Waterhouse*). (2) An arm in armour embowed ppr., charged with a cross crosslet fitchée, the hand grasping a scimitar, also ppr. (*for Doherty*). *Veritas vincit omnia. cf.* 196. 10

Waterhouse, a demi-swan with wings expanded, murally crowned.

Waterhouse, Middx., Herts, and Lincs, a demi-wolf. 31. 2

Waterhouse, Herts, a demi-talbot erm., collared gu., eared sa. *cf.* 55. 8

Waterlow of Storey's Gate, London, a demi-eagle displayed ppr., langued gu., holding in the beak a cross crosslet fitched or, and charged on the breast with a mullet of five points of the same. *Per ardua ad alta.* 81. 3

Waterlow, Sir Sydney Hedley, Bart., of Fairseat, Kent, and of Highgate, Middx., upon a mount an oak-tree, in front thereof a plough, all ppr. *Labor omnia vincit.* 313. 9

Waterlow, a demi-lion gardant az., holding in the mouth a shin-bone in bend, and holding between the paws a human skull, both or. *Per mortem vinco.*

Waterpark, Baron (Cavendish), of Waterpark, co. Cork, on a ducal coronet or, a snake nowed ppr. *Cavendo tutus.* *cf.* 142. 12

Waters, *see* Dun-Waters.

Waters of Sarnau, Carmarthen, a demi-griffin az. *Honor pietas.* 64. 2

Waters, Ireland, an eagle rising regardant ppr. *Spero.*

Waters, a demi-talbot arg., holding in the mouth an arrow gu. *Toujours fidèle.*

Waters of Newcastle, co. Limerick, Ireland, a demi-heraldic tiger per pale indented arg. and az., holding a branch of three red roses slipped ppr.

Waterton, a goat's head erased or, collared gu. *cf.* 128. 7

Waterton of Waterton, Lincs, and Walton Hall, Yorks, an otter passant holding in the mouth a pike, all ppr. *Better kinde frembd than frembd kyen.*

'Waterton the banner bere
Of famed St. George at Agincourt.'

Watford, two arms in armour embowed, the hands grasping a battle-axe, all ppr. *cf.* 194. 12

Wathe, Herts and Northamp., a dragon's head erased sa. *cf.* 71. 2

Wathen, the late Sir Charles, of Ashley Down, Bristol, a dexter cubit arm erect vested sa., cuffed arg., holding in the hand ppr. a cinquefoil slipped or. *Fortiter fideliter felicite.* 205. 2

Waties, Shropsh., an eagle's head erased or. 83. 2

Watkens, Wilts and Wales, a griffin's head gu. 66. 1

Watkin, a cock's head arg., combed and wattled gu. *cf.* 90. 1

Watkin, Sir Alfred Mellor, Bart., of Rose Hill, Northenden, co. Chester, a cock's head couped, transfixed through the mouth by a tilting-spear palewise, all ppr. *Sais and doe.* 311. 13

Watkins of Shotton Hall, Shropsh., a leopard's face jessant-de-lis or. *Vitæ via virtus.* 22. 5

Watkins, Charles Fitzgerald, of Badby House, Northamp., a griffin's head erased. *In portu quies.* 66. 2

Watkins, out of an Eastern coronet or, a griffin's head gu.

Watkins of Badby House, Northants, a griffin's head erased gu. *In portu quies.* 66. 2

Watkins of Llwyn-y-Brain, Carmarthensh.: (1) A dragon's head erased vert, holding in the mouth a staff raguly sa., inflamed ppr. (*for Watkins*). (2) Upon a mount vert, a lion rampant sa., charged on the neck with three guttes-d'or within a bar gemel, also or, and holding in the dexter paw a bar-shot of the second (*for Rice*). *Sic itur ad astra nec aspera terrent.*

Watkins of Pennoyre, Brecknock, a dragon's head erased vert, holding in the mouth a dexter hand couped at the wrist gu. *Pen aur y chalon wir.* cf. 72. 6

Watkins, Wales, same crest. cf. 72. 6

Watkins, Yorks, a lion rampant gu., holding in the dexter paw a fleur-de-lis or. *Virtute avorum.* 2. 7

Watkins, Yorks and Notts, a lion rampant gu., holding in the dexter paw a fleur-de-lis or. 2. 7

Watkins, same crest. *Virtute.* 2. 7

Watkins of Woodfield, Worcs., a talbot's head arg., erased and gorged with a collar of cinquefoils gu. *Ffyddlawn Bunydd.* cf. 56. 2

Watkins of Lloegyn, Brecon, a wolf rampant regardant arg., langued and ungu. gu. *Primum tutare domum.* 28. 3

Watkins, a cubit arm erect, the hand grasping a tilting-spear in bend sinister ppr. 214. 11

Watkins, Heref., a cubit arm in armour erect holding in the hand the broken shaft of a tilting-spear in bend sinister, all ppr.

Watkinson, an hourglass winged ppr. 113. 11

Watkinson, an eagle's head erased az., beaked or, holding a rose arg., slipped vert.

Watkyns, a lion rampant holding in the dexter paw a battle-axe, all ppr.

Watling, out of a heart a dexter hand grasping a sabre, all ppr. *Corde manuque.*

Watling, Surgeon-Major C. W., A.M.D., of London, a sea-lion couchant ppr. *In pristina via manemus.* 20. 6

Watlington of Moor Hall, Essex, a lion's head ppr., ducally crowned or. cf. 18. 8

Watlington of Caldicot Hill, Aldenham, Herts, a demi-lion rampant holding in the dexter paw a sword, all ppr., hilt and pommel or. 14. 12

Watlington of Reading, Berks, a demi-lion ppr., semée of spear-heads sa., holding in the dexter paw a sword, also ppr., and resting the sinister upon an escutcheon, also sa., charged with a saltire double parted and fretty arg. *Mens conscia recti.* 14. 7

Watlington, Perry-, of Moor Hall, Essex: (1) Same crest as above (*for Watlington*). 14. 7. (2) A lion's head erased or, semée of saltires and ducally crowned gu., holding in the mouth a pear slipped ppr. (*for Perry*). *Mens conscia recti.*

Watmough or **Watmoughe,** a ferret passant sa., collared or, lined gu. 134. 9

Watney, Norman, Esquire, of Valence, Westerham, Kent, upon a mount vert, in front of a garb erect or, a greyhound courant sa., gorged with a collar, and therefrom pendent a bugle-horn of the second. *Vive ut vivas.* 58. 10

Watney of Wandsworth and Mitcham, Surrey, same crest. 58. 10

Watney, Sir John, Shermanbury House, Reigate, same crest and motto.

Watney, Daniel, 2, Endsleigh Street, W., same crest. *Auxilium ab alto.*

Watney, Rev. Henry James, Canwick Vicarage, Lincs, same crest and motto.

Watney, Vernon James, J.P., 11, Berkeley Square, W., same crest. *Virtute et industria.*

Watson, Baron (late Rt. Hon. William Watson, P.C., LL.D., D.L.), of Tankerton, Lanarksh., the stump of an oak-tree with two branches sprouting from it, and grasped on either side by a hand issuing from a cloud, all ppr. *A Deo floruit.* 224. 10

Watson, Sir John, Bart., Earnock, Lanarksh., same crest. *Inspiratur florust.*

Watson, Hon. Thomas Henry, 20, Queen's Gate, S.W., same crest. *A Deo floruit.*

Watson, Earl of Rockingham (*extinct*), a griffin's head erased arg., ducally gorged or. *Mea gloria fides.* cf. 66. 11

Watson, Scotland, a griffin's head erased arg., gorged with a collar sa., holding in the beak a flower gu., leaved vert.

Watson, late John, Esquire, of Whitney Terrace, Bowdon, Chesh., in front of a griffin's head erased az., collared gemelle arg., holding in the beak two white roses slipped and leaved ppr., an escutcheon of the second charged with a martlet of the first. *Esto quod esse videris.* cf. 68. 1

Watson of Kidderminster, Worcs., and of Holland Park, London, in front of a gryphon's head erased az., collared, and holding in the beak a branch of two roses arg., leaved and slipped ppr., an escutcheon, also arg., charged with a martlet az. *Esto quod esse videris.* 68. 1

Watson, James Ronald, in front of four thistles saltirewise, leaved and slipped ppr., a gryphon's head erased arg., holding in the beak a branch of olive slipped, also ppr. *Esto quod esse videris.* 255. 1

Watson of Congleton, Chesh., a griffin's head erased arg., charged on the neck with two chevrons sa., holding in the beak a rose-branch gu., leaved vert.

Watson of Silsden, Yorks, a griffin's head erased arg., holding in the beak a sprig leaved vert. cf. 66. 11

Watson, Yorks, a griffin's head erased arg., ducally gorged or. *Mea gloria fides.* cf. 66. 11

Watson, Durh., same crest. *Esto quod esse videris.*

Watson, Innes, Esquire, J.P., Barrister-at-Law, Swanton House, Melton Constable, Norf., same crest and motto.

Watson, Thomas Wright, Esquire, Lubenham, Market Harborough, a griffin's head erased arg., ducally gorged or, and charged below the coronet with a trefoil vert. *Esto quod esse videris.*

Watson, Lieutenant-General George Vincent, a griffin's head erased ppr. *Mea gloria fides.*

Watson of Conington, Cambs, a griffin's head erased sa., gorged with two bars gemelle arg. 66. 4

Watson of Congleton, Chesh., a griffin's head erased arg., charged with two chevronels gu., holding in the beak a cinquefoil vert. cf. 225. 13

Watson, Sir Wager Joseph, Bart., M.A., a griffin's head erased arg., ducally gorged or. *Esto quod esse videris.*

Watson, Sir Arthur Townley, Bart., M.A., 39, Lowndes Square, W., a gryphon's head erased az., ducally crowned or, between two branches of palm ppr. ΠΑΘΗΜΑΤΑ ΜΑΘΗΜΑΤΑ. 63. 2

Watson of Wath Cottage, Pickering, Yorks, a griffin's head erased arg., between two branches of laurel ppr., holding in the beak a club or.

Watson of Melton, Yorks, issuant from a sun rising in splendour ppr., a gryphon's head sa., semée of estoiles or.

Watson of Muirhouse, co. Edinburgh, Scotland, a demi-gryphon holding in his dexter claw a dagger ppr. cf. 64. 6

Watson, the late Sir Henry Edmund, of Shirecliffe Hall, Sheffield, Yorks, in front of an eagle's head couped gu., gorged with a coronet vallery, three crescents, all or.

Watson, William Scott, Bornhead, Hawick, Roxburghsh., a buck's head and neck erased ppr., collared az., the collar charged with a star between two crescents or, all within two branches of laurel issuing from the torse, and disposed circular ways.

Watson-Taylor, Simon, J.P., Erlestoke Park, Devizes: (1) Out of a ducal coronet or, a dexter cubit arm erect ppr., the hand holding a cross crosslet fitchée gu. (*for Taylor*). (2) The stump of a tree sprouting branches ppr. (*for Watson*). *In hoc signo vinces.—Inspiritur floruit.*

Watson of Low Hall, Shropsh., an ermine passant ppr., vulned on the shoulder gu. cf. 134. 9

Watson of Hughfield, Middx., and Gisborough, Yorks, an ermine passant arg., collared, ringed, and lined or. cf. 134. 6

Watson of Newport, Shropsh., an ermine passant ppr., vulned on the shoulder gu. cf. 134. 6

Watson, Hants, on a chapeau gu., turned up erm., a talbot statant of the last, collared or. cf. 54. 2

Watson of Bengeworth, Worcs., a talbot passant erm., collared or. cf. 54. 5

Watson, Colonel Charles Moore, C.M.G., M.A., 43, Thurloe Square, S.W., same crest. *Mea gloria fides.*

Watson, Sir William, 25, Fitzwilliam Place, Dublin, same crest. *Mea gloria fides.*

Watson of Frendsbury, Kent, and Walpett, Suff., on a mount vert, a demi-dragon rampant. *cf.* 73. 10

Watson of Hardendale, Westml., two arms issuing from clouds holding the stump of a tree fructed at the top, with branches on either side, all ppr. *cf.* 224. 10

Watson of Turin, Scotland, a lily of the Nile ppr. *Sine injuria.* 151. 2

Watson of Glentarkie, Fifesh., Scotland, a ship under sail ppr. *Ad littora tendo.* 160. 13

Watson of Saughton, co. Edinburgh, two hands issuing from clouds holding the trunk of an oak-tree sprouting out fresh branches ppr. *Insperata floruit.* 224. 10

Watson of Broomknowe, Dumbartonsh., a mullet arg. *Super sidera votum.* 164. 2

Watson, an oak-slip ppr. *Florescit.* 151. 3

Watson, William Livingstone, Esquire, of 7, Wetherby Gardens, South Kensington, a cross crosslet fitchée arg., issuing out of a crescent gu. *Lippen to God.* 166. 9

Watson, James, Esquire, of Langley House, Bucks, an oak-tree ppr., growing out of a mount vert. *Florescit.* 143. 14

Watson of London, Kent, and Cumb., on a mount vert, a palm-tree or. 144. 3

Watson, William Spencer, Esquire, F.R.C.S., 7, Henrietta Street, Cavendish Square, W., same crest. *Palma non sine cruce.*

Watson, Cumb., an arm in armour embowed ppr., garnished or, holding in the gauntlet a palm-branch vert. 273. 15

Watson of Edinburgh, a flaming heart ppr. *Ex corde charitas.* 181. 13

Watson, Jonas, Esquire, J.P., the Lodge, Llandaff, Glamorgansh.: (1) A cannon ppr. (2) Out of a mural crown a plume of five ostrich-feathers arg. *Mea gloria fides.*

Watson, John William, Esquire, of 65, Eccleston Square, London, in front of a dexter arm embowed in armour, the hand in a gauntlet ppr., grasping a palm-branch slipped vert, a martlet between two crosses botonny gu. *Deum time Regem honora.*

Watson-Armstrong, William Henry Armstrong Fitzpatrick (Baron Armstrong of Bamburgh and Cragside): (1) A dexter arm embowed in armour ppr., couped at the shoulder, garnished or, resting the elbow upon the wreath, and encircled by a wreath of oak, the hand grasping a banner, all ppr. (*for Armstrong*). 234. 2. (2) In front of a dexter arm embowed in armour, the hand in a gauntlet ppr., grasping a palm-branch slipped vert, a martlet between two crosses botonny gu. (*for Watson*). *Fortis in armis.—Deum time Regem honora.*

Watson-Wemyss, Alexander, Esquire, Denbrae, Arboretum Road, Edinburgh, a swan with wings elevated and addorsed ppr. *Je pense.*

Watson of Croslet, Dumbartonsh., Scotland, a dexter hand erect ppr. *Confisus viribus.* 222. 14

Watson, an arm from the shoulder erect issuing out of the sea ppr., holding in the hand an anchor az., cabled or. 202. 7

Watson, Sir John, Bart., of Neilsland, Lanarksh., Scotland, the stump of an oak-tree with a branch sprouting from either side, each grasped by a hand issuing from a cloud, all ppr. *Insperata floruit.* 224. 6

Watson of Neilsland, Lanarksh., Scotland, two hands issuing from clouds in fess, grasping the trunk of an oak-tree in pale, branches sprouting, all ppr. *Insperata floruit.* 224. 10

Watson, William Henry, Esquire, of Braystones and Steelfield Hall, Gosforth, Cumb., a dexter arm in armour embowed, holding in the gauntlet a palm-branch, all ppr. *Veritas.* 273. 15

Watson, James, 5, Clarendon Terrace, Dundee, a griffin's head erased arg., gorged with a collar gemelle sa., holding a sprig, leaved vert. *Esto quod esse videris.*

Watt, a crescent. 163. 2

Watt, William George Thomas, of Breckness, Skaill House, Breckness, Orkney, a cubit arm erect grasping a sword in bend sinister ppr. *Insperata floruit.—Nec temere nec timide.*

Watt, out of a mural coronet or, a wolf's head sa., charged with a fess embattled arg.

Watt, Heref., out of a mural coronet or, a demi-wolf salient arg., charged on the neck with a fess embattled az., holding between the paws a garb in pale ppr.

Watt of Leominster, Heref., out of a mural coronet or, a demi-wolf saliant arg., charged on the neck with a fesse embattled az.

Watt of Bishop Burton, Yorks, a greyhound sejant arg., semée-de-lis, the dexter paw resting upon two arrows. 256. 9

Watt of Speke Hall, Lancs, a greyhound sejant az., holding with the dexter paw a pheon point downwards or.

Watt, a talbot's head erased arg., collared gu. 56. 1

Watt, Scotland, a hawk ppr. 85. 2

Watt of Denmill, Fifesh., Scotland, a falcon close ppr. *Fide et fiducia.* 85. 2

Watt, John Brown, Eynesbury, Woollahra, New South Wales, on a dexter glove lying fesseways tasselled, a peregrine falcon close ppr., belled or, holding in the beak a falcon's hood gu. *Fide et fiducia.*

Watt-Gibson-, of Doldowlod, Radnorsh.: (1) Upon a fer-de-moline fesseways or, an elephant statant ppr., charged on the body with a cross moline of the first (*for Watt*). 133. 7. (2) Upon a key fesseways, the wards downwards az., a pelican in her piety or, with wings addorsed of the first, and semée of crescents arg. (*for Gibson*). *Pandite cœlestes portæ.* 98. 11

Watte, Kent and Somers., a cubit arm in armour erect holding in the hand a pistol, all ppr.

Watters, Andrew, of Belleville, Edinburgh, a talbot's head erased arg. *Toujours fidele.* 56. 2

Watterton of Gosberkyrke, Lincs, an otter passant ppr., holding in the mouth a fish arg.

Watts, Wilts, of Cotlington, Somers., and Devonsh., a greyhound sejant arg., collared az., studded or, supporting a broad arrow of the last, plumed of the first.

Watts, a seal's head couped arg. 134. 1

Watts, Edward Hanslope, of Hanslope Park, Bucks, a greyhound sejant arg., supporting with the dexter foot an arrow or, barbed and flighted of the first. *Non eget Mauri jaculis neque arcu.*

Watts, William Henry, J.P., of Elm Hall, Wavertree, Liverpool, a greyhound sejant or, gorged with a collar gemelle az., holding in the mouth a sprig of oak leaved, fructed, and slipped ppr., and resting the dexter fore-leg on an antique shield of the second charged with a portcullis of the first. *Labore gaudeo.* 255. 4

Watts, a griffin's head erased holding in the beak an annulet. *cf.* 66. 2

Watts, a demi-lion or, charged with a cross patée az., holding in the mouth an oak-branch ppr., fructed or, supporting an escutcheon of the first, charged with a fess erminois between three fleurs-de-lis in chief, and a cross patée in base of the fourth, and from the escutcheon an escroll bearing the motto *Amice.*

Watts of Blakesley, Northamp., a lozenge gu., between two wings or. 110. 3

Watts of Hawkesdale Hall, Cumb., a lozenge gu., between two wings or. 110. 3

Watts of Norwich, Norf., a lion's gamb erect and erased sa., charged with an annulet between two billets in pale or.

Watts of Vincent Square, Westminster, a greyhound sejant arg., collared az., and resting the dexter paw upon a portcullis or. *Va presto ma sano.*

Watts, James, of Abney Hall, Chesh., a demi-griffin sa., winged chequy or and of the first, the dexter claw grasping a garb of the second. *Fide sed cui vide.* 65. 5

Watts of Hockwold, Norf., a lion's gamb erased gu., supporting an escutcheon or. 37. 2

Watts, John Henry, Esquire, Gold Hill, Gerrard's Cross, Bucks, a demi-hind collared and chained holding in the feet a branch. *Dum vivimus vivamus.*

Watts-Russell, Arthur Egerton, Biggin Hall, Northamp.: (1) Upon a mount vert, a goat passant erm., collared gu. (*for Russell*). (2) A demi-lion rampant or, charged on the shoulder with a cross patée az., the paws supporting an escutcheon of the last, thereon a fess erminois between three fleurs in chief, and a cross patée in base of the first. *Amici.*

Watur, a garb per pale or and arg., banded gu. 153. 2

Wauch, Scotland, a greyhound sejant sa. 59. 4

Wauch or **Waugh,** out of a ducal coronet a dexter hand holding a sword erect, the blade wavy, all ppr. 212. 1

Wauchope of Niddrie, co. Edinburgh, Scotland, a wheat-sheaf or. *Industria ditat.* 153. 2

Wauchope, Don-, Sir John Douglas, Bart M A of Newton (1) A garb or (*for Wauchope*) 153 2 (2) A pomegranate ppr (*for Don*) *Industria ditat* —*Non deerit alter aureus* 152 4
Waud of Manston Hall Yorks, a martlet ppr *Sola virtus invicta* 95 4
Waudby, a demi lion gu, collared vair, holding in the dexter paw a lotus-flower stalked, leaved, and slipped ppr, and supporting with the sinister paw a sword point downwards ppr pommelled and hilted or *Usque ad mortem fidelis*
Waugh, a dexter cubit arm habited chequy arg and gu, and cuffed of the first holding in the hand ppr a chaplet of roses *Malo mori quam fœdari*
Waugh of Larkhall, Roxburghsh, Scotland, a garb vert, banded arg *Industria ditat* 153 2
Wauton, a trefoil slipped and voided sa cf 148 9
Waveney, Baron (Adair), a man's head affrontee couped at the neck ppr, *Loyal au mort* 190 12
Wawn, C Esquire Tan-y-gareg, near Carnarvon, a stag's head erased holding in the mouth a thistle slipped *Quod merui meum est*
Way, Rt Hon Sir Samuel James, Bart, of Montefiore, Adelaide, an eagle displayed gu, each wing charged with a Passion cross, and holding in the beak a balance or *Fit via vi* 287 6
Way, Edward Willis L R C P, Montefiore, North Adelaide, same crest and motto
Way, an eagle [illegible]
Way of Torrington Devonsh, and Denham Place, Bucks, an arm embowed in mail holding in the hand ppr a baton or
Way, Lewis John, Spencer Grange, Great Yeldham, Essex same crest
Way, a dexter arm embowed in chain mail holding in the hand ppr a baton or, the ends sa *Fit via vi*
Way, Rev John Hugh Henbury Vicarage near Bristol, same crest and motto
Way of Kilree, co Kilkenny a dexter arm in armour embowed ppr holding in the hand also ppr, a baton sa, tipped or *Nil desperandum* cf 200 3
Wayer, the attires of a stag or 123 5
Wayland, Kent, two hands conjoined in fess couped at the wrists ppr 224 2
Wayne, Frederick, Esquire, of Milton, Otago, New Zealand, a pelican in her piety or, collared gu, charged on the body with an ermine-spot, the nest az *In Te Domine confido* cf 98 8
Wayne of Quorndon House, Derbysh and Tickwood Hall, Shropsh, a pelican in her piety or, collared gu and charged on the breast with an ermine-spot the nest az *Tempus et casus accidit omnibus* cf 98 8
Wayne, Robert Sewallis, J P, Bryn Llewyn, Corwen, North Wales, same crest and motto
Wayne, Rev William Henry, Willey, near Broseley, Salop, same crest and motto
Wayneman of Fringeford and Thame Park, Oxon a cock's head erased az, combed, wattled and beaked or 90 1
Waynewright, a lion rampant arg, holding in the dexter paw a battle axe the handle of the last, headed or
Waynflete, a griffin's head erased vert *Nulla pallescere culpa* 66 2
Wayte of Southampton and Waytecourt Isle of Wight, Hants, a bugle horn stringed sa garnished or 228 11
Weale, a boar's head erased and erect az 43 3
Weare, Edwin Thomas Clinton, Hampton House, Heref, a demi-lion rampant arg, holding in the dexter paw a cross crosslet fitchee gu *Sumus ubi fuimus*
Weare, Henry Oxenden, 6, Courtfield Gardens Earl's Court, same crest and motto
Wear or **Weare** of Wear Gifford, Devon sh, a stag trippant ppr 117 8
Weare of Denford, Berks, and Boxton Wilts, on a lure in fess gu a falcon with wings addorsed ppr
Wearing, James Williamson, J P Fleet Square Lancaster, a wolf's head couped ppr, semee of crescents arg holding in the mouth two ostrich-feathers in saltire of the last *Tenez le droit* 255 2
Weatherall, a cup or 177 4
Weatherby, an arm embowed, the hand grasping a dagger ppr 201 4
Weatherhead, a pelican ppr 98 1
Weatherley, Northumb, a ram's head erased ppr 130 6
Weatherston, a lion's head erased ppr 17 8
Weaver, a ram's head erased arg, armed or 130 6
Weaver of Presteign, Heref, an antelope trippant erm, attired or, supporting with the dexter foot an escutcheon or
Weaver, James Esquire of Worcs an heraldic antelope sa resting the dexter foot upon a cross patee or, and holding in the mouth a pear slipped ppr *Esto fidelis*
Webb, a demi-eagle displayed holding in the beak a cross crosslet fitched cf 81 3
Webb, a demi eagle displayed arg., the wings pellettee, ducally gorged gu cf 81 2
Webb, Bart (*extinct*) of Oldstock Wilts, out of a ducal coronet or, a demi eagle rising gu
Webb of Harrow Hill, Middx, a demi eagle displayed or, pellettee, ducally gorged gu
Webb of the Berrow, Worcs, the battlements of a tower arg thereon a demi eagle displayed az, winged vair holding in the beak a spur or *Be firm*
Webb, Heref, out of a mural coronet a demi-eagle displayed or 80 8
Webb, Hon Edmund, J P, of Hathrop, Bathurst, New South Wales, member of the Legislative Council of New South Wales, *uses* out of a ducal coronet a demi eagle displayed 80 14
Webb of Motcombe, Dorset and Wilts, out of a ducal coronet a demi-eagle displayed or 80 14
Webb, Robert William, Mitford House, Surrey same crest *In alta tendo*
Webb, Charles Daniel Henry, Esquire, J P, of Woodville co Tipperary, Ireland, a demi eagle displayed gu, the wings erminois, holding in the beak a cross crosslet fitchee or and charged on the breast with a mullet arg *Quid prodest*
Webb, Charles Caleb Coote, J P Kilmore Nenagh, co Tipperary, same crest and motto
Webb, Thomas Stammers a double headed eagle displayed sa, charged on the breast with a cross patee fitchee arg *Festina lente*
Webb-Peploe, John Birch, Esquire, of Garnstone (1) A ducal coronet or, and issuant therefrom a reindeer's head gu attired of the first and charged with a human eye shedding tears ppr (*for Peploe*) cf 122 3 (2) An eagle displayed sa semee-de-lis or, and holding in the beak a trefoil vert
Webb, Glouc, an eagle displayed sa 75 2
Webb of Weobley Heref an eagle displayed sa, beaked and membered gu 75 2
Webb, Stephen Harold, Warborough, Kenton near Exeter a demi eagle displayed issuing out of a ducal coronet or
Webb, a phœnix az, issuing from flames ppr winged arg, collared or therefrom pendent a cross of the same cf 82 2
Webb, a demi stag arg ducally gorged or cf 119 2
Webb of Clifford, Somers, a demi-stag erased salient arg attired or cf 119 2
Webb, Richard Frederick of Donnington Hall, Heref a stag lodged 115 7
Webb, Glouc and Kent a hind's head erased ppr, vulned in the neck gu cf 124 3
Webb of Ballymote, co Sligo, Ireland a lion passant or, pellettee *Victoria a Domino* cf 6 2
Webb of Castle Leckey, co Londonderry, out of a ducal coronet or a demi-lion rampant az collared ringed and holding between the paws a Danish battle-axe of the first, headed ppr
Webb, Ireland, a wolf sejant ppr
Webb of Cowton, Yorks, an elephant's head surmounted by a griffin with wings chequy *In hoc signo vinces* 133 6
Webb, H Gillum, Royal Albert Yacht Club, Southsea (1) A griffin's head erased ducally gorged (2) A dolphin hauriant, head upwards
Webb, Charles Boyer, Elford House Tamworth, a dexter cubit arm in bend grasping a sword in bend sinister all ppr pommelled and hilted or and pendent from the hilt and resting upon the wreath an escutcheon az, charged with a cross patee arg *Tiens a la verite*
Webb-Peploe, Rev Hanmer, 25, Onslow Gardens, S W (1) A ducal coronet or issuant therefrom a reindeer's head gu attired or charged on the neck with a human eye shedding drops of

tears ppr (*for Peploe*) (2) An eagle displayed sa, semee de fleurs-de-lis or, in the mouth a trefoil vert (*for Webb*)

Webb of Gillingham, Kent, a dexter arm embowed, holding in the hand an oak-branch ppr 202 3

Webb of London out of an Eastern coronet or a dexter arm erect couped at the elbow, vested az holding in the hand a slip of laurel all ppr

Webb, a broken spear in three pieces the headpiece in pale and the others in saltier ppr, enfiled with a ducal coronet or *cf* 175 2

Webbe of Bottisham Cambs a griffin's head erased or, ducally gorged arg *cf* 66 11

Webbe of Exeter Devonsh a hind's head erased arg, vulned in the neck ppr *cf* 124 3

Webber, Scotland, a hawk jessed and belled ppr *cf* 85 2

Webber, on a ducal coronet an eagle displayed, all or *cf* 75 2

Webber, Cornw, a wolf's head per pale arg and gu 30 5

Webber, Felix Hussey Esquire, J P, of Glyn Dderwen, near Swansea, same crest

Webber, William Downes, Esquire J P of Kellyville, Queen's Co and of Leckfield, co Sligo, Ireland, a wolf's head couped per pale arg and gu, charged with an annulet counter-changed *Esperance* *cf* 30 5

Webber, Major General Charles Edmund, C B, 17, Egerton Gardens, S W, same crest and motto

Webber, Incledon-, Duncan Harold (1) A wolf's head couped per pale arg and gu (*for Webber*) (2) A falcon ppr, jessed or (*for Incledon*)

Webber-Incledon, Laurence Charles Esquire, the Dene Dunster, Somers (1) A falcon close ppr, jessed or (*for Incledon*) (2) A wolf's head couped per pale arg and gu (*for Webber*) *Non extinguentur*

Webber, a demi lion gardant or, holding a fleur de lis az

Webber of Badialton Court Somers, two arms in armour embowed sa, garnished or holding up a hurt charged with a fleur-de lis of the second *Liliæ prælucent telis* *cf* 194 11

Webbes, a hand couped at the elbow holding an oak branch fructed and leaved ppr

Webley, Essex and Surrey, out of a ducal coronet az a griffin's head or, gorged with a collar of the first, fretty of the second *cf* 67 9

Webley, an antelope trippant ppr 126 6

Webley-Parry-Pryse, Edward John, Noyadd Trefawr, Ben Cath South Wales (1) A lion rampant regardant sa, holding a fleurs de lis or (*for Pryse*) (2) A demi-lion arg gorged with a wreath of oak fructed ppr, on the head an Eastern crown or, the dexter paw resting on an escutcheon az, thereon a cross patee fitchee or, charged for distinction on the shoulder with a cross crosslet sa (*for Parry*) (3) Between a branch of oak and another of palm a cubit arm in armour ppr, garnished or the hand grasping a sword, also ppr, the arm charged for distinction with a cross crosslet sa (*for Webley*)

Webster, *see* Cayley-Webster and Wedderburn Webster

Webster, a weaver's shuttle in pale 176 14

Webster of London a leopard's head affrontee, erased crowned with an antique crown ppr, holding in the mouth a shuttle gu, tipped and furnished with quills of yarn or

Webster of Flamborough, Yorks, a swan's head and neck erased arg, beaked gu, holding in the beak an annulet or *cf* 101 5

Webster, Baron Dickinson, of Harewood, Newton Abbot same crest *Carpe diem*

Webster of Penns, Warw, a swan's head erased arg, beaked gu, holding therein an annulet or *Veritas puritas*

Webster of Murlingden Scotland a wyvern's head erased vert *Vincit veritas* 304 13

Webster, Ernest Alfred, Pallion Hall Sunderland a dragon's head erased quarterly vert and or 304 13

Webster, William Solicitor, Abbotsfield St Helen's, a dragon's head erased 304 13

Webster, Sir Augustus Frederick Walpole Edward, Bart, of Battle Abbey Sussex a dragon's head couped regardant quarterly per fesse embattled vert and or vomiting flames ppr *Fides et justitia*

Webster of Chester a dragon's head erased quarterly per fesse indented or and az

Webster, Scotland, the sun rising from the sea ppr *Emergo.*

Weddall of Stebenheath, Middx the embattlements of a castle az, and issuing therefrom a demi lion or, affixing the banner of St George on the same

Weddel or **Weddell,** a battle axe in pale ppr 172 3

Weddell, a hawk hooded and belled or *cf* 86 8

Weddell, Scotland a horse's head arg *cf* 50 13

Weddell, a lion's head erased gu *Orna verum* 17 2

Wedderbourne or **Wedderburn,** an eagle's head erased ppr *Illæso lumine solem* 83 2

Wedderburn, Alexander, K C., 47, Cadogan Place, S W same crest *Non degener*

Wedderburn, Charles David St Clair Bhavnagarpara, Kathiawar, India, same crest and motto

Wedderburn, Rev John Walter Maurice, Stornoway same crest and motto

Wedderburn-Maxwell of Middlebie Dumfries and Glenlair Kirkcudbright (1) On the dexter side a stag lodged in front of a holly-tree ppr (*for Maxwell*) (2) On the sinister side an eagle's head erased ppr (*for Wedderburn*) *Reviresco —Non degener* 83 2

Wedderburn-Scrymgeour (1) A lion's gamb erect holding a scimitar, all ppr (*for Scrymgeour*) 38 13 (2) An eagle's head erased ppr (*for Wedderburn*) *Aquila non capiat muscas* 83 2

Wedderburn, Sir William Bart 84, Palace Chambers, S W same crest as (2) above *Non degener —Aquila non capiat muscas* 83 2

Wedderburn-Webster of Clapham, Surrey, same crest *In Deo spero.—Non degener* 83 2

Wedderburn-Webster, Arthur Augustus, Jamaica same crest and mottoes

Wedderburn, Bart (*attainted*) of Blackness Linlithgowsh, and **Wedderburn,** Bart, of Ballindean, Perthsh same crest as (2) above. *Aquila non capiat muscas* 83 2

Wedderburn, Ogilvy-, of Ruthven, Scotland (1) Same crest (*for Wedderburn*) 83 2 (2) A lion rampant gardant ppr (*for Ogilvy*) *Aquila non capiat muscas —Nil desperandum* 2 5

Wedderburn, Colville-, of Ochiltree, a talbot's head ppr *Ad finem fidelis* 56 12

Wedgewood, two hands conjoined ppr, issuing from clouds 224 2

Wedgewood, Staffs on a ducal coronet or, a lion passant arg 6 6

Wedson, Notts out of a ducal coronet or a flame ppr

Weeden of Hall Court, Sussex, a martlet sa *Credo — Spes mea Christus* 95 5

Weedon, Bucks, Dorset, and Lancs, a hedgehog sa 135 8

Weedon, Bucks, Dorset, and Lancs, a martlet sa 95 5

Weekes, Sussex, a dexter arm in armour embowed, holding in the hand a battle-axe gu *Cari Deo nihilo carent —Vitæ via virtus —Præsta et persta* *cf* 200 6

Weekes, [illegible] Hampton Carlile, Esquire, Hampton Lodge, Hurstpierpoint, Sussex, same crest and motto

Weekes, William, Esquire, of Willestrew, Tavistock, same crest *Deo Cari nihilo carent*

Weeks, a dexter hand holding a scimitar ppr 213 5

Weeks, out of a marquess's coronet, a demi eagle displayed ppr

Weever of Kingston and Prestine Surrey, an antelope trippant erm, supporting with the dexter foot an escutcheon or

Wegerton or **Weigerton,** the sun shining on a sun flower ppr

Wegg, a mullet vair 164. 2

Wegg of Newcastle, Northumb., an armed hand clenched ppr *Hostis honori invidia*

Wegg, same crest *Vigilanter*

Wegg or **Wegge** of Acton Middx, a sinister gauntlet erect ppr, the fist clenched *Nil conscire sibi*

Wegge, a hand from the wrist in a gauntlet

Wegg-Prosser, Francis Richard, Esquire, Lieutenant Colonel 1st London Art Vols (retired), of Belmont Heref. (1) A wolf's head erased sa semee of spear heads arg, pierced through the mouth with a sword ppr (*for Prosser*) (2) A sinister hand in a gauntlet ppr, holding an escutcheon sa, charged with an annulet or (*for Wegg*) (3) A demi lynx ppr, semee de lis gu, holding a branch of olive, also ppr (*for Haggitt*)

Weightman of East Stoke Notts, on the stump of a tree erased ppr a hart trippant arg, collared, chained and attired or

Weil, Myer, Esquire, of 3, Kensington Garden Terrace, Hyde Park, W, on a mount two stags counter rampant sup porting a tree issuing from the mount *Qui quærit reperit*

Weir of Dublin, a demi-horse in armour ppr bridled and saddled gu *Nihil verius* 53 6

Weir, J Campbell, 51, Albany Street Edinburgh, a demi-horse sa saddled and bridled or, with the sinister hoof resting upon a mullet of six points of the last *Nihil verius* 266 6

Weir, Archibald Munday, St Giles Malvern Link, Worcs, same crest and motto

Weir, William Esquire of Crookedholm House, Kilmarnock Scotland, a demi-horse arg *Vero nihil verius* 53 3

Weir of Damsay, Orkney, Ireland a demi horse arg, saddled and bridled gu *Nihil verius*

Weir of Kildonan, a demi horse arg *Vero nihil verius* 53 3

Weir-Vere of Stonebyres Scotland a boar passant or *Vero nihil verius* 40 9

Weir, a cubit arm erect ppr holding in the hand a sword arg hilt and pommel or charged on the arm with a cross crosslet fitchee gu cf 212 3

Weir, Cosans-, of Bogangreen, Berwicksh, Scotland, a cubit arm erect holding in the hand a sword ppr hilted and pommelled or *Vero nihil verius* 212 3

Weiss, Henry, Esquire, J P, of Ravensburg Edgbaston, Birmingham, on a wreath of the colours a demi man affrontee, face and hands ppr, vested per pale az and or collar and cuffs, and wreathed about the waist with a chaplet of roses all counterchanged, holding in the dexter hand a fleur-de-lis or and in the sinister a mullet of six points az *Patientia et perseverantia*

Welbore of London and Cambs, a spear in pale or, headed arg, enfiled with a boar's head couped of the second, vulned gu

Welborne of Burport, Dorset a hand holding three darts cf 214 3

Welby of Halstide, Berks, Rutl, and Mowlton, Lancs, a naked arm embowed issuing from flames ppr, holding in the hand a sword arg, hilt and pommel or

Welby, Baron (Welby) same crest

Welby (Gregory), Sir Charles Glynne Earle Bart of Denton Manor, near Grantham (1) Three garbs or banded gu, the centre one charged with a cross crosslet sa for distinction (*for Gregory*) cf 153 13 (2) A cubit arm in armour issuing fessewise from clouds, holding a sword pommel and hilt or over flames of fire issuant from the wreath ppr (*for Welby*) *Per ignem per gladium* 311 8

Welby of Welby and Denton Lincs a cubit arm in armour issuing from clouds ppr holding a sword arg, pommel and hilt or over flames of fire also ppr, issuant from the wreath *Per ignem per gladium* 311 8

Welby, Alfred Cholmeley Earle, 26, Sloane Court S W, same crest

Welby, John Earle, Allington Hall, near Grantham same crest and motto

Welby, Rev Walter Hugh Earle, St George's Lodge, Ryde, same crest and motto

Welby-Everard, Edward Everard Earle, Gosberton House Gosberton (1) A man's head in profile couped at the shoulders ppr, on the head a long cap arg, semee of estoiles gu, between a branch of palm and another of olive, both or (*Everard*) (2) An arm embowed in armour issuing fesseways from clouds ppr in front of flames of fire issuing from the wreath also ppr

Welch or **Welsh,** a demi wolf rampant gu 31 2

Welch, Scotland, a cross Calvary az 166 1

Welch, Captain George Asser White, R N of Arle House, Glouc, an antelope's head erased billettee, holding in the mouth a cross crosslet fitched

Welch, an antelope's head erased az, bezantee gorged with a collar gobony arg and gu, on the top of each horn a ring or

Welch or **Welsh,** an antelope sejant arg, attired collared, and lined or cf 126 4

Welch-Thornton, Henry J P, Beaurepaire Park, Basingstoke (1) An eagle's head couped arg in front thereof a demi catherine wheel gu (2) Issuant from a wreath of cinquefoils or, a goat's head arg *Gwell angeu na chywilydd*

Welchman, a dexter wing or 109 7

Welchman, George, Cullompton Devonsh, in front of a goat's head erased at the neck between two wings arg, three mullets of six points fesseways gu *Regia incedere via*

Welchman, William, Birdbeck House, Upwell, Wisbech, in front of a goat's head couped ppr charged on the neck with a mullet of six points arg, an eagle's wing fessewise or *Steadfast* 269 2

Welcome of Market Stanton, Lincs on the stump of a tree ppr, sprouting branches vert, a bird close arg, beaked or 86 11

Weld, *see* Forester

Weld, Reginald Joseph, Lulworth Castle, Dorset, out of a ducal coronet ppr a wyvern sa, guttée d'or *Nil sine numine*

Weld, Humphrey Frederick, Chideock Manor, Bridport, a wyvern sa, guttee-d'or, collared and chained or, issuant out of a ducal coronet ppr

Weld, out of a ducal coronet or, a wyvern's head with wings addorsed gu 72 1

Weld of London and Eaton, Chesh, a wyvern with wings expanded sa, guttee d'or collared, and lined or

Weld of Twickenham, a wyvern sa, bezantee gorged with a collar and chain reflexed over the back or, the wings expanded erm each charged with a crescent of the first

Weld of Dublin, a wyvern displayed vert

Weld, Charles Richard Conal More, Norham Gardens Oxford, a wyvern ducally gorged *Verum atque decens*

Weld-Blundell, Charles Joseph of Ince Blundell Lancs a squirrel sejant gu, collared and holding a nut or cf 135 7

Weldish, Kent, a demi-fox erased gu, guttee d'eau

Weldon of Swanscombe Kent, the bust of Queen Elizabeth ppr *Bene factum*

Weldon, Sir Anthony Arthur, Bart. D L, J P, of Rahenderry, co Kildare, and Kilmorony, Queen's Co, *uses* (1) A demi lion rampant arg, guttee-de-sang cf 10 2 (2) The bust of Queen Elizabeth (*granted by Queen Elizabeth as a special mark of her Royal favour to Sir Anthony Weldon, Clerk of the Spicery*) *Bene factum*

Weldon, a demi lion rampant arg, guttee de-sang cf 10 2

Weldon of Shottisbrook, Berks, a demi-lion rampant arg, guttee de-sang cf 10 2

Weldon, William Henry Esquire, C V O Norroy King of Arms a demi-lion rampant arg guttee de sang, resting the sinister paw upon SS *Bien fait* 260 1

Weldon, Ireland, a cross moline erm 165 1

Weldy, a horse's head issuing gu, furnished with waggon harness or 50 12

Welfitt, a buck's head couped and charged on the neck with two bends invected *Servata fides cineri* cf 121 5

Wellord or **Welsford,** Heref, a leopard's head per pale or and gu *Sic fidem teneo* 22 10

Wellan, a demi lion holding in the dexter paw an estoile, the sinister resting on the wreath

Weller, a demi lion rampant holding in the dexter paw an estoile

Weller, a laurel-branch fructed ppr 151 13

Weller of Kingsgate House, Rolvendon, Kent a greyhound's head erased sa, holding in the mouth a rose slipped gu leaved vert *Steady*

Welles, De, an ostrich's head and wings arg ducally gorged gu, holding in the beak a horse shoe az

Welles of Saltash Cornw, on a chapeau az, turned up erm a horse's head arg, maned or ducally gorged gu

Welles, Cambs, a unicorn's head erased az crined, armed, and ducally crowned or between two wings of the last

Welles of Buckstead, Sussex, a talbot passant arg, collared sa, garnished or cf 54 5

Welles or **Wells,** a well ppr 159 15

Wellesley, *see* Wellington Duke of

Wellesley, *see* Cowley, Earl of

Wellesley, Marquess of Wellesley (*extinct*) (1) Out of a ducal coronet or a demi lion gu, holding a banner purp. charged with an estoile radiated wavy between eight spots of the Royal tiger in pairs saltireways, the staff of the first surmounted by a pennon arg, charged with the cross of St George, with the motto over in Hindostan characters (2) A cubit arm erect vested gu enfiled with a ducal coronet or holding a staff bendways on the top thereof the Union Standard of Great Britain and Ireland, and underneath the Mysore Standard, all ppr., with the motto over, *Virtutis fortuna comes*—*Porro unum est necessarium.*

Wellesley-Pole, Baron Maryborough (*extinct*): (1) A lion's gamb erect and erased gu., armed or (*for Pole*). 36. 4. (2) Out of a ducal coronet or, a demi-lion rampant gu., holding a forked pennon, also gu., flowing to the sinister, one-third per pale from the staff arg., charged with the cross of St. George (*for Wellesley*). 16. 1. (3) A cubit arm erect vested gu., enfiled with a ducal coronet or, cuffed arg., holding in the hand a scimitar ppr., pommel and hilt of the second (*for Colley*). *Pollet virtus.*—*Porro unum est necessarium.*

Wellesley, Long-Tylney-, of Draycot, Wilts: (1) Out of a ducal coronet or, a demi-lion rampant gu., holding a forked pennon of the same, one-third per pale from the staff arg., charged with the cross of St. George (*for Wellesley*). 16. 1. (2) Out of a ducal coronet or, a demi-lion rampant arg. (*for Long*). 16. 3. (3) A lion's head arg., holding in the mouth a hand erased (*also for Long*). *cf.* 21. 2

Wellesley, Admiral Sir George Greville, K.C.B., 17, Chester Square, same crest as (1) above.

Welley, Durh., out of a ducal coronet a reindeer's head. 122. 3

Wellington, Duke of (Wellesley), Stratfieldsaye, near Winchfield, Hants, out of a ducal coronet or, a demi-lion rampant gu., holding a forked pennon of the last flowing to the sinister, one-third per pale from the staff arg., charged with the cross of St. George. *Virtutis fortuna comes.* 16. 1

Wells, Heref., a well ppr. 150. 15

Wells of Piercefield, Chepstow, a fire-beacon ppr. 177. 14

Wells of Holme, Derbysh., a demi-talbot ermines. *cf.* 55. 8

Wells, in front of a horse's head couped sa., bridled or, three mullets fesseways arg. *Fortiter in re.* 51. 14

Wells, a demi-lion rampant sa. 10. 1

Wells of Portlemouth, Devonsh., out of an embattlement ppr., a demi-lion double-queued sa., holding between the paws two annulets interlaced or. *Virtute et honore.*

Wells, Edward, Esquire, J.P., of Wallingford, Berks, on a wreath of the colours issuant from a rock a flame of fire ppr., environed by a chain or. *Semper fidelis.*

Wells of Holm House, Hunts, a demi-ostrich with wings displayed arg., ducally gorged or, charged on the breast with an escallop sa., holding in the beak a horse-shoe of the second.

Wells, Sir Arthur Spencer, Bart., of 32A, Orchard Street, W., and of Golder's Hill, Hampstead, Middx., in front of a demi-ostrich displayed arg., holding in the beak a horse-shoe or, a serpent nowed ppr. *In scientia veritas, in arte honestas.* 310. 13

Wells-Dymoke of the Grange, West Molesey, the two ears of an ass sa. *Pro rege Dimico.*

Wellwood of Garvock, Scotland, the trunk of an oak-tree sprouting branches ppr. *Reviresco.* 145. 2

Welman, Charles Noel, of Poundsford Park, Somers., a demi-lion rampant arg., langued gu., holding between the paws a mullet or. *Dei providentia juvat.* *cf.* 15. 8

Welman, Henry Acton, a demi-lion arg., holding between the paws an apple vert. *Dei providentia juvat.*

Welsh, on the branch of a tree an eagle close, all ppr.

Welsh of Carnbee, Dumfriessh., an eagle perching on the branch of an oak-tree, out of which is growing a small branch sprouting leaves, all ppr. *Auspice numine.*

Welsh of Sheldesley, Worcs., a griffin's head erased arg. 66. 2

Welsh, an antelope sejant arg., collared and chained or, attired and ungu. of the same.

Welsh, Scotland, a naked dexter arm grasping an Oriental scimitar richly mounted, all ppr. *Pretium virtutis.* 213. 5

Welstead, out of a mural coronet or, a dexter hand ppr., vested sa., holding a sword-blade wavy of the second.

Welstead or **Welsted,** a hind trippant arg. 124. 12

Welsted of Ballywalter, co. Cork, a hind trippant arg. *Tutus prompto animo.* 124. 12

Welstod, a hind trippant ppr. 124. 12

Weltden, Northumb., a Moor's head ppr. *cf.* 192. 13

Welwood, Maconochie-, John Allan, Esquire, of Kirknewton, Midlothian: (1) A demi-Highlander holding in the dexter hand a bunch of arrows, all ppr., above an imperial crown (*for Maconochie*). (2) A hand holding a dagger ppr. (*for Welwood*). *Reviresco.*—*Nititur et munitur.*

Wemyss and March, Earl of (Wemyss-Charteris-Douglas), Neidpath Castle, Peeblessh., a swan ppr. *Je pense.*—*This our charter.*—*Forward.* 92. 2

Wemyss, David, Wemysshall, Fifesh., same crest and motto.

Wemyss of Balfarge, a demi-swan with wings expanded ppr. *Cogito.*

Wemyss, Bart., Scotland, a sword ppr. *Je pense.* 170. 2

Wemyss, a dexter hand grasping a scimitar, both ppr. *Nec viribus, nec numero.* 213. 5

Wemyss, an antelope's head erased gu. 126. 2

Wemyss of Fudie, Fifesh., a cross crosslet or, within two branches of palm disposed in orle vert. *Virtus dum patitur vincit.*

Wenard, a mullet pierced gu.

Wendesley or **Wensley** of Wendesley, Derbysh., an old man's head in profile couped at the neck ppr.

Wendey, Cambs, a lion's head erased az., gorged with a collar dancettée or.

Wendover of Salisbury, Wilts, a demi-lion or, holding between the paws an eagle's claw sa., erased gu., the claws in base.

Wenham of Moorhall, Sussex, on a chapeau gu., turned up erm., a greyhound statant sa., collared or. *cf.* 58. 4

Wenington, Lincs, a still arg.

Wenley, James Adams, Esquire, of Glasgow, a gryphon segreant az., charged on the shoulder with five escallops saltireways or, holding between the claws a bezant, and resting the dexter paw on a mascle fessewise of the second. *Vigilans et verus.* 62. 4

Wenlock, Baron (Lawley), of Wenlock, Shropsh.: (1) A wolf statant sa. (2) An arm embowed quarterly or and az., gauntletted ppr., grasping the truncheon of a tilting-spear or. *Je veux de bonne guerre.* *cf.* 28. 10

Wenlock, Shropsh., a griffin passant with wings addorsed or. 63. 2

Wenlock, Glouc., a plume of peacock's feathers ppr.

Wenman, Viscount Wenman (*extinct*), a cock's head erased az., crested and wattled or. *Omnia bona bonis.* 90. 1

Wenman of Carswell, Oxon., a cock's head erased gu., crested and wattled or. 90. 1

Wensleydale, Baron (Parke—*extinct*), a talbot's head couped gu., eared and gorged with a collar gemelle or, pierced in the breast by a pheon gu. *Instituto tenax.*

Wentworth, *see* Fitzwilliam, Earl.

Wentworth, Watson-, Marquess of Rockingham (*extinct*), a griffin passant with wings elevated arg., armed, beaked, and ducally gorged or. *Mea gloria fides.*—*En Dieu est tout.* 63. 3

Wentworth, Baron (Rt. Hon. Ralph Gordon Noel Milbanke, D.L.), of Nettlested, Suff.: (1) A lion's head couped gu., charged with a bend erm. (*for Milbanke*). (2) A dexter arm couped, vested az., cuff sa., the arm charged with three ermine spots in fesse or, and holding in the hand a truncheon sa., headed arg. (*for King*). *Pensez à bien.*

Wentworth, Godfrey Hawksworth, Woolley Park, near Wakefield, a griffin passant arg.

Wentworth, Yorks, a griffin passant with wings addorsed arg. 63. 2

Wentworth, Fitzwilliam, Esquire, J.P., of Vaucluse, near Sydney, New South Wales, Australia, a griffin passant with wings elevated arg. 63. 2

Wentworth, Bart., Lincs, on a mount vert, a griffin passant per pale or and sa., charged with two antique keys erect per fess counterchanged. *En Dieu est tout.*

Wentworth, Vernon-, Thomas Frederick Charles: (1) A griffin passant with wings elevated arg., beaked, armed, and ducally gorged or (*for Wentworth*). 63. 3. (2) A boar's head erased sa., ducally gorged and bristled or (*for Vernon*). *En Dieu est tout.* 41. 6

Wentworth, Fitzwilliam, a griffin passant arg.

Wentworth-Fitzwilliam, George Charles: (1) Out of a ducal coronet or, a triple plume of ostrich-feathers arg. (2) A griffin passant arg.

Wentworth, out of a ducal coronet or, a unicorn's head arg., armed and maned of the first. 48. 12

Wentworth, Suff., a leopard sejant erm., ducally gorged, ringed, and lined or. *cf.* 24. 8

Wentworth-Sheilds of Fitzwilliam Street, Dublin, and Francis Webb Wentworth-Sheilds, Esquire, of Delahay Street,

Westminster a dove with wings expanded, holding in the beak an olive branch all ppr, and charged on the breast with a trefoil slipped vert *Vincit qui patitur* cf 94 5
Wenward, a mullet pierced gu
Wenyeve of Brettenham, Suff, a bird with wings expanded, holding in its beak an olive branch, all ppr 94 5
Weoley of Camden Glouc, on a chapeau az, turned up erm a cockatrice close arg combed and wattled of the first
Werden, Chesh, a pegasus' head gu, between two wings or 51 3
Werdman of Charleton, Berks a bear's head erased arg. muzzled and collared sa, lined and ringed or cf 35 2
Were of Sylverton, Devonsh a dexter arm, the hand holding up a gem ring ppr, stoned gu
Were, Rt Rev Edward Ash D D, St Werburgh's Vicarage, Derby, a demi lion rampant ppr holding a cross crosslet fitchee gu *Fuimus*
Were, Francis, Gratwicke Hall, Barrow Gurney Flaxbourton R S O Somers, same crest and motto
Were, T Kennet, Cotlands Sidmouth, same crest and motto
Werge of Hexgrave Park, Notts, a demi-lion rampant or, holding in the dexter paw a pheon purp, gorged with a collar gu, charged with three bezants
Werkesly or **Werkesley,** a wyvern az, langued and eared or 70 1
Wescombe, Somers, out of a mural coronet ppr, a griffin's head or 67 10
Wescombe, Lincs on the top of a rock ppr a bird close arg 106 9
Wescope or **Westcope,** two hands issuing from clouds conjoined in fess ppr 224 1
Wesley, a wyvern ppr *God is love* 70 1
West, Earl De La Warr, *see* De La Warr
West, *see* Sackville, Baron
West of London a griffin's head crased per fess erm and gu, charged on the first with a fess dancettee sa cf 66 2
West of London, out of a mural coronet or a griffin's head arg, gorged with a fess dancettee sa cf 67 10
West of Masworth Bucks, out of a ducal coronet a griffin's head, all or 67 9
West of Cotton End, Northamp, out of a ducal coronet or, a griffin's head az beaked and eared of the first, charged with a fleur de-lis for difference cf 67 9
West of White Park co Fermanagh, of Sacombe Rectory Herts, of Kilcroney, co Wicklow, late of Loughlinstown co Dublin, late of Ardenode, co Kildare, late of Strokestown, co Roscommon, same crest, without the difference mark *Jour de ma vie*
West of Cliff, Sussex, a griffin's head erased per pale wavy or and az 66 2
West-Erskine, Hon William Alexander Erskine M A, of Hindmarsh Island Lake Alexandrina, South Australia member of the Legislative Council of South Australia (1) A griffin's head erased gu charged with a mullet erm holding in the beak a sword bendwise, point upwards, ppr (*for Erskine*) (2) Out of a mural coronet ppr a griffin's head az, charged with a trefoil slipped or (*for West*) *Jour de ma vie —In Domino confido* cf 67 10
West, Roberts-, James, of Alscot Park Glouc, out of a ducal coronet or, a griffin's head pean, beaked and eared or 67 9
West, Bucks and Sussex out of a ducal coronet or a griffin's head az, beaked and eared of the first 67 9
West, Augustus George White Park Brookeborough co Fermanagh, Ireland, same crest *Jour de ma vie*
West of Ballydugan, co Down Ireland out of a ducal coronet a griffin's head all or *Jour de ma vie* 67 9
West of Fortwilliam, co Roscommon, Ireland out of a ducal coronet or a griffin's head arg *Jour de ma vie* 67 9
West of Darley Abbey Derbysh a demi-griffin sans tail vert, collared or holding in the dexter claw a sword arg
West of London on a coronet composed of ears of wheat or, an eagle displayed gu
West, Cornwallis-, William Cornwallis Ruthin Castle Ruthin, Denbighsh out of a ducal coronet or, a griffin's head az, beaked and eared or *Jour de ma vie*
Westall, a buck's head 121 5
Westbury, Baron (Bethell), out of a vallary coronet or an eagle's head sa between two wings az, and charged on the breast with an estoile or *Ap' Ithel* 250 3
Westbrook of Godalming, Surrey Elsted, Slade, and Lavant, Sussex and Kent an armed leg couped above the knee ppr, garnished and spurred or 193 1
Westby of Whitehall Upper Rawcliffe Lancs, a martlet sa, holding in the beak three ears of wheat or, stalked vert *Nec volenti nec volanti*
Westby of Thornhill, Ireland a martlet sa *Nec volenti nec volanti* 95 5
Westby, Francis Vandeleur, Esquire of Roebuck Castle, co Dublin and of Kilballyowen and Rosroe, co Clare a martlet sa holding in the beak a stalk of wheat ppr, with three ears or, and charged on the breast with a mullet of the last *Nec volenti, nec volanti*
Westby, Yorks, an elephant's head ppr 133 2
Westcar, a crocodile ppr, collared and chained or cf 138 8
Westcombe, Bart (*extinct*), out of a mural coronet a griffin's head, both or *Festina lente* 67 10
Westcote, a Moor's head couped ppr, wreathed about the temples arg and sa. *Renovato nomine* 192 13
Westcott, two hands issuing from clouds conjoined in fess ppr 224 1
Westell of Pinkney Green Maidenhead Berks, a cubit arm erect vested and slashed, the hand clenched ppr, thereon a falcon, also ppr
Westenra, *see* Rossmore Baron
Westenra, Ireland a lion rampant arg 1 13
Westerdale, two anchors in saltier 161 7
Westerman of Castle Grove, Sandal, Yorks, a demi-greyhound per chevron or and sa, holding between the paws a cinquefoil of the last
Western, Baron Western (*extinct*) a demi lion rampant or, holding in the dexter paw a trefoil slipped vert *Nec temere, nec timide* cf 13 3
Western, Sir Thomas Charles Callis, Bart, D L, of Rivenhall Essex a demi lion or, holding in its dexter paw a trefoil slipped vert *Nec temere nec timide* cf 13 13
Westerne of London a demi lion rampant or holding in the dexter paw a trefoil slipped vert cf 13 13
Westerton of London two anchors in saltier *Anchora salutis* 161 7
Westhorp of Cornburgh, Yorks an eagle's head erm, beaked or 83 1
Westlemore, a tent arg, flagged and garnished gu 158 7
Westly, out of a ducal coronet or, a hand gu, holding a fleur-de lis az 215 2
Westmacott, upon a mount a column of the Tuscan order fesseways, thereon a bee all ppr *Extremos pudeat rediisse*
Westmacott, Denham, 54 West Cromwell Road W same crest and motto
Westmeath, Earl of (Nugent) of Pallas, Loughrea, co Galway, a cockatrice with wings elevated and the tail nowed vert, combed and wattled gu *Decrevi* 68 4
Westminster, Duke of (Grosvenor) of Eaton Hall, near Chester, a talbot statant or *Virtus non stemma* cf 54 2
Westmore, Lancs, a lion passant gardant or 4 3
Westmoreland, Earl of (Fane), Apethorpe Hall Wansford Northamp out of a ducal coronet or a bull's head arg, pied sa, armed of the first charged on the neck with a rose gu barbed and seeded ppr *Ne vile fano* cf 44 11
Westmoreland, a fox sejant or 32 11
Weston, *see* Hunter-Weston
Weston, Earl of Portland (*extinct*) an eagle rising regardant sa, beaked and legged or *Craignez honte*
Weston of Rugeley, Staffs, an eagle rising regardant sa
Weston, William Henry Purcell Lane House, Dorset, an eagle rising regardant sa beaked and membered or *Craignez honte*
Weston of Lichfield, Staffs, an eagle's head or beaked gu, charged with a crescent for difference cf 83 1
Weston, Sir Joseph Dodge, of Bristol, upon a mount vert, an eagle's head erased or around the neck a ribbon gu pendent therefrom an escutcheon sa, charged with an estoile of the second *Semper sursum* 83 6
Weston of Colleton, Devonsh a cock ppr wattled gu
Weston, a camel sa, collared or cf 132 2
Weston, Henry Macgregor, of West Horsley Place, Surrey, a wolf passant arg ducally gorged or cf 28 10
Weston of Ockham Surrey, a wolf's head couped sa 30 5
Weston of Dublin, a demi lion rampant arg, holding between the paws a cross crosslet fitchee gu
Weston of Sutton Lincs, a Saracen's head affrontee, wreathed about the temples or and vert *Any boro* 190 5

Westrope, Norf., out of a ducal coronet or, a stag's head ppr. 120. 7

Westropp, *see* O'Callaghan-Westropp.

Westropp, Ireland, an eagle's head sa., issuant from an Eastern crown gu.

Westropp, Yorks and Ireland, an eagle's head erm. 83. 1

Westropp, Major-General George Ralph Collier, same crest. *Post funera virtus.*

Westropp, Hugh Massey, Deer Park, Clonlara, co. Clare, same crest. *Je me retourne vers l'occident.*

Westropp, John Massy, Attyflin, Patrickswell, co. Limerick, same crest and motto.

Westropp, Lionel Erskine, 60, Holland Park, W., same crest. *Post funera virtus.*

Westropp, Ralph Hugh, Springfort, co. Limerick, a falcon's head erm. issuant from a ducal coronet. *Je me tourne vers l'occident.*

Westropp, Major-General Sir Robert, Southsea, a falcon's head erm. *Post funera virtus.*

Westropp, Thomas Johnson, M.A., M.R.I.A., F.R.S.A.I., of Luneburg, Sandymount, Dublin, same crest. *Je me tourne vers l'occident.*

Westropp, William Keily, 6, Shorncliffe Road, Folkestone, an eagle's head ppr. issuing from a ducal coronet or.

Westropp-Dawson: (1) On clouds ppr., an estoile or, and upon an escroll above the motto *Toujours propice* (*for Dawson*). 164. 11. (2) An eagle's head couped erm., charged with an annulet gu. (*for Westropp*). *Tourne vers l'occident.* cf. 83. 1

Westropp-Dawson, Francis Walter, Charlesfort, Ferns, co. Wexford, same crests and mottoes.

Westropp of Attyflin Park, Ireland, out of a ducal coronet an eagle's head. *Je me tourne vers l'occident.* cf. 83. 14

Westropp, Ireland, out of a ducal coronet or, an eagle's head gu. *Post funera virtus.* cf. 83. 14

Wes.ropp, a dragon's head gu. 71. 1

Westwood of London and Worcs., a cubit arm vested with leaves vert, holding in the hand ppr. a club gu., spiked arg.

Wetherall or **Wetherell,** Lincs, a demi-lion rampant sa., holding a covered cup or.

Wetherall, Ernest Victor Albert Astley, Hersham, Walton-on-Thames, a lion's gamb erased holding a covered cup. 303. 11

Wethered, Herts, a goat's head erased. 128. 5

Wethered, Thomas Owen, Seymour Court, Great Marlow, a goat's head erased per bend embattled or and gu. *Virtute et labore.*

Wetherell, a lion's gamb erased sa., holding up a covered cup or.

Wetherly, Northumb., a ram's head erased ppr. 130. 6

Wetherton, a lion's gamb erect and erased ppr. 30. 4

Wetherton, Northumb., a lion's gamb erased gu., charged with a chevron arg. cf. 39. 2

Wettenhall of Wettenhall and Hankilow, Chesh., out of a ducal coronet or, an antelope's head arg., attired of the first.

Wettenhall, Ireland, out of a ducal coronet or, a goat's head ppr. *Haud facile.* 128. 14

Wettyn and **Wettyng,** a lion's head erased or, vomiting flames of fire ppr. 17. 1

Wever, a garb in fess or. 153. 6

Wever, Ireland, an heraldic antelope statant erm., attired or, resting the dexter foot on an escutcheon of the second.

Wey, a mailed arm embowed, the hand grasping a baton.

Weykes, a greyhound's head erased or, gorged with a bar-gemelle gu., holding in the mouth a man's leg couped above the knee arg. 61. 8

Weyland, a dolphin naiant az. 140. 5

Weyland of Woodrising Hall, Norf., a lion rampant sa. 1. 10

Weymouth, Viscount, *see* Bath, Marquess of.

Weymouth, a dexter arm in armour embowed, cuffed paly of six arg. and gu., holding in the hand three arrows ppr., one in fess and two in saltier.

Whadcock of Buckley Place, Warw., a dragon's head per pale or, guttée-de-sang and vert, erased gu. cf. 71. 2

Whale, a lion rampant per fess gu. and arg. 1. 13

Whaley, Kent, two anchors in saltier az. 161. 7

Whaley, Rev. Christopher, M.A., a whale's head. *Spe dives re pauper.*

Whaley, J. H., Esquire, 52, Chepstow Villas, London, W., two anchors cabled in saltire az. *Mirabile in profundis.*

Whalley, a whale's head erased and erect sa. 139. 8

Whalley, Colonel Joseph Lawson, J.P., of Richmond House, Lancaster, a whale's head erect and erased sa. *En Dieu sont nos espérances.* 139. 8

Whalley of Overton, Hunts, and Norton, Leics., a whale's head erased in fess sa.

Whalley of Norton Hall, Somers., a whale's head erect and erased sa., charged with a mascle arg. *Mirabile in profundis.* cf. 139. 8

Whalley of Whalley's Hill, co. Armagh, a whale's head erased and erect per pale gu. and sa. *Gloria Deo in profundis.*

Whalley, Rev. George Cairncross, 120, Queen's Road, Bayswater, same crest and motto.

Whannell, Ayrsh., Scotland, a dove holding in its beak an olive-branch ppr. *Nuncia pacis.* 92. 5

Wharncliffe, Earl of (Montagu-Stuart-Wortley-Mackenzie), Wortley Hall, Sheffield: (1) An eagle rising from a rock ppr., and in an escroll above the crest the motto *Firma et ardua* (*for Mackenzie*). (2) An eagle's leg erased or, issuant therefrom three ostrich-feathers ppr., charged on the thigh with a fesse chequy az. and arg. (*for Wortley*). (3) A demi-lion rampant gu., and in an escroll over it the motto *Nobilis ira* (*for Stuart*). 10. 3. (4) A griffin's head couped or, beaked sa., between two wings endorsed of the last (*for Montagu*). *Avito viret honore.* cf. 67. 11

Wharton, Duke of Wharton (*attainted*), Westml.: (1) A Moor kneeling in a coat of mail, all ppr., crowned or, stabbing himself with a sword of the first, hilt and pommel also or. (2) A bull's head erased arg., armed or, gorged with a ducal coronet per pale of the last. 44. 2

Wharton of Dryburn, Durh., a bull's head erased arg., armed or, charged with a trefoil vert. cf. 44. 4

Wharton, a bull's head erased per pale arg. and sa., ducally gorged per pale gu. and of the first. 42. 3

Wharton, Henry, Esquire, of Highfield, Waiau, Amuri, co. Canterbury, New Zealand, a bull's head erased arg., armed or, charged with a trefoil vert. *Dio volendo lo farò.* cf. 44. 3

Wharton, Cumb., Yorks, and Durh., a bull's head erased sa., armed or. 43. 2

Wharton, Westml., a bull's head erased arg., armed or. 44. 3

Wharton, William Henry Anthony, of Skelton Castle, Yorks, a bull's head erased arg. *Generosus nascitur non fit.* 44. 3

Wharton, Rt. Hon. John Lloyd, Dryburn, Durh., same crest and motto.

Wharton-Myddleton: (1) A savage wreathed about the head and middle with leaves, holding in the dexter hand an oak-tree erased and fructed, all ppr. (*for Myddleton*). cf. 188. 10. (2) A bull's head erased arg., charged with a trefoil vert (*for Wharton*). *Laissez dire.* cf. 44. 3

Wharton, Yorks, on the stump of a tree erased a squirrel sejant, both ppr., cracking a nut or. cf. 135. 6

Wharton, Smith-, Devonport, on a wreath arg. and sa., a lion sejant of the first, armed of the second, langued gu., holding in the mouth a battle-spear reversed ppr., charged on the neck with a plain label of three points or.

Whately, a stag's head ppr. 121. 5

Whatley, a stag's head cabossed ppr. *Pelle timorem.* 122. 5

Whatley, a lion rampant or, holding in the dexter paw a fleur-de-lis sa. 2. 7

Whatman, George Dunbar, Esquire, D.L., of 2, Cranley Gardens, London, S.W., a demi-lion rampant holding between the paws a pheon, point downwards. *Qui sis non unde.*

Whatton, Leics., out of a ducal coronet or, a demi-eagle sa., beaked of the first. *Fidei coticula crux.*

Wheat or **Wheate,** Glouc., a stag's head couped or, holding in the mouth three ears of wheat ppr. cf. 121. 5

Wheat or **Wheate** of Walsall, Staffs, and Warw., a stag's head ppr., charged on the neck with three bars or, and holding in the mouth as many ears of wheat of the same.

Wheathill, a sword ppr., and an ear of wheat or, bladed vert, in saltier. 154. 11

Wheatley, on a rock a fire-beacon ppr. cf. 177. 8

Wheatley of Frome, Somers., a stag's head cabossed ppr. 122. 5

Wheatley of Echingfield, Sussex, two arms embowed vested az., holding between the hands ppr. a garb or.

Wheeler-Cuffe, *see* Cuffe.

Wheeler, Ireland, a rose-branch ppr., flowered gu. 149. 8

Wheeler or **Wheler** of Martin Hussingtre, Worcs, and of Burbury, Warw, on a five leaved ducal coronet or, an eagle displayed gu cf 75 2

Wheeler, Rev William Cheslin, Ridgeway Gardens, Wimbledon, a gryphon s head arg, guttee de sang, erased gu, gorged with a wreath of laurel ppr and holding in the beak a wheel of six spokes per pale or and az *Non omnis moriar*

Wheeler, P C, I C S c/o H S King and Co, 9, Pall Mall out of a ducal coronet a double headed eagle displayed *Facie tenus*

Wheeler, Rev T L, Bromwich House, Worcester, on a ducal coronet or, an eagle displayed gu *Facie tenus*

Wheeler, Edward Vincent Vashon, Newnham Court, Tenbury, Worcs out of a ducal coronet a demi eagle displayed

Wheeler of Stuncarter co Kilkenny Ireland, on a ducal coronet or an eagle displayed gu, charged with a crescent for difference *Facie tenus* cf 75 2

Wheeler of Tottenham, Middx, out of a mural coronet or, a griffin's head arg 67 10

Wheeler, Granville Charles Hastings, Ledston Hall Yorks, out of a mural crown or, a griffin's head issuant arg

Wheeler of Ludlow, Shropsh a lion's head couped arg, charged on the neck with a Catherine wheel gu cf 21 1

Wheeler of Stoke, Surrey, a camel's head erased vert, bezantee cf 132 7

Wheeler of Hyde Park Gardens, London, an Angora goat's head erased vert armed or holding in the mouth a fleur-de lis of the last *Avito jure*

Wheeler of Leyrath, co Kilkenny, a talbot sejant arg, gorged with a plain collar or, and charged on the shoulder with a mullet gu cf 55 1

Wheelton of London and of Haslemere, Surrey out of a vallary coronet or a demi-lion ppr, gorged with a collar gemelle sa, holding between the paws a Catherine wheel of the first *Deo duce sequor* 16 4

Wheelwright of Heathfield, Yorks, a demi-heraldic antelope gu armed, tufted and ungu, and guttee-d'or, holding between the legs an escutcheon arg, charged with a Catherine wheel gu *Res non verba*

Wheelwright, Joseph, Nevill Park, Tunbridge Wells, a gryphon's head couped gu gorged with a collar vair between two trefoils slipped vert *Age et tace*

Whelan, *see* Nolan Whelan

Whelan of Herendon House, Tenterden, Kent on a mount vert a stag lodged regardant erm, attired arg the dexter fore paw resting on an escallop az, holding in the mouth a trefoil ppr

Whelan of Dublin, a boar's head erased and erect az, langued gu, armed or, the jaw transfixed with an arrow and vulned ppr *Turris fortis mihi Deus*

Wheldale, an open book ppr 158 3

Wheler of Otterden, Kent (1) On a mural coronet or, a griffin s head erased arg (*for Wheler*) cf 67 10 (2) A martlet charged with a fleur de lis, holding in the beak an oak leaf and acorn (*for Medhurst*)

Wheler, a camel's head erased az cf 132 7

Wheler of Colchester, Essex, and Lincs, a dove with wings addorsed arg holding in the beak a branch vert fructed or cf 93 12

Wheler, Sir Edward Bart, on a ducal coronet or, an eagle displayed gu *Facie tenus* cf 75 2

Wheler, Edward Galton, J P, Swansfield House, Alnwick, same crest

Whelling, Ireland, a cross crosslet arg, surmounted by a sword in bend sinister ppr

Whelpdale, a hand holding a hawk s lure ppr 217 8

Whetcroft, Suff, a garb or, charged with a martlet sa cf 153 2

Whetenhall, Kent out of a ducal coronet gu an ibex's head arg

Whetham, an eagle displayed sa 75 2

Whetham, a cubit arm in armour holding in the hand a sword all ppr hilt and pommel or *Jehovah* 210 2

Whetham, Boddam-, John Whetham, Kirklington Hall, Southwell, Notts (1) Same crest as above (2) A buck trippant ppr, attired and ungu or *Jehovah*

Whetley of Southbreak, Norf, a leopard's head erased gardant or, flames issuing from the ears and mouth ppr, collared lined and ringed az

Whetnall, out of a cup or a nosegay of flowers ppr 177 3

Whetstone of Woodford Row, Essex, an arm in armour embowed sa garnished or, holding in the hand a broken tilting spear or, head arg 197 2

Whetstone, Essex, a bugle horn sa stringed or 228 11

Whettell of Thetford and Ampton, Suff a talbot's head or, eared, collared and ringed arg cf 56 1

Whettnall of Liege Belgium, out of a ducal coronet vert, a goat s head arg, gorged with a chaplet of roses ppr *Virtute et fortitudo* cf 128 14

Whetwell, a hand holding a sword ppr 212 13

Whewell, a dexter hand in bend couped at the wrist in the act of conveying to another dexter hand arg, issuant from the wreath a torch erect gu, fired ppr

Whewell, Thomas, Esquire, of Fair Elms, Blackburn, a wyvern sejant with wings elevated ppr, gorged with a collar gemel or, and supporting with the dexter leg a torch erect sa, fired, also ppr *For faith and for fatherland*

Whichcote, Sir George, Bart, D L, of Aswarby Park, Lincs, a boar's head erased and erect gu, langued ar, armed or *Juste et droit* 43 3

Whicker, a lion rampant ppr, resting the fore paws on a cross patee fitched or

Whiddon of Chagford Devonsh on a ducal coronet or a swan sitting sa, beaked of the first

Whieldon of Springfield House, Warw, on a mount vert, between two branches of oak ppr, a fer de-moline in fess sa thereon a parrot perched vert, collared gu holding in the dexter claw a pear stalked and leaved, also ppr *Virtus præstantior auro* 101 7

Whieldon, Arthur Edward, Lillington, Leamington same crest and motto

Whight, out of a ducal coronet or a dragon's head vert 72 4

Whineray, Edward Westmead Hoylake, Chesh a mast with a sail hoisted ppr the sail charged with an arrow erect ppr, between on the dexter side a branch of oak fructed of the first and on the sinister a coral branch of the second *In solo Deo salus* 252 3

Whinfield, a horse's head couped gu, bridled or 51 5

Whinyates, Edward Henry, the Rectory, Fretherne, Stonehouse, Glouc, in front of an anchor erect sa a cubit arm holding a sword ppr pommel and hilt or *Loyal en tout* 258 18

Whinyates, Colonel Francis Arthur Berrington House Tenbury, Worcs same crest and motto

Whinyates, Major - General Frederick Thomas Abbotsleigh, Bournemouth same crest *Malignum spernere vulgus*

Whipham, Alfred Guy, Esquire, Barrister at-law, of Gidleigh Park, Chagford Newton Abbot a dexter arm erect couped at the elbow, habited gu, the cuff arg holding a chaplet of myrtle leaves and roses ppr *Nec prodigus nec avarus*

Whippy of London a horse's head erased or *Quod potui perfeci* 51 4

Whippy of Lee Place, Oxon, same crest 51 4

Whirple of Dickleborough, Norf an elephant passant erm cf 133 9

Whishaw, an eagle's head couped per fess sa and or 83 1

Whistler, a harp or, stringed sa 168 9

Whitacre of Althorne, Yorks a cubit arm erect, holding in the hand a sword, all ppr 212 3

Whitacre, Wilts, a horse passant or 52 6

Whitaker, *see* Master Whitaker

Whitaker of Lysson House, Heref a horse passant arg 52 6

Whitaker of Besley Hall, Yorks a horse passant arg, gorged with a collar gemel, and resting the dexter fore-leg on a mascle az *Spes et fides*

Whitaker, George Herbert, 12, Warwick Lane, E C, same crest and motto

Whitaker, Captain James, of Broad clough, Lancs, out of a ducal coronet or, a stag's head ppr 120. 7

Whitaker, William Henry, Totterton, Lydbury North Shropsh, same crest

Whitaker of the Holme, Lancs, a cubit arm in armour the hand grasping a flaming sword, all ppr

Whitaker of Symonstone Hall, Lancs a dexter arm in armour the hand grasping a flaming sword, all ppr *Robur atque fides*

Whitaker, Thomas Stephen, Everthorpe Hall R S O, East Yorks same crest

Whitaker, a tent gu, garnished or the pennon az 158 7

Whitbread, a water-bouget az 168 4

Whitbread, Beds, a hind's head erased gu 124 3

Whitbread, Samuel, of Southill, Beds same crest

Whitbread, Colonel Howard, C.B., of Landham Park, Suff., same crest. *Virtute non astutia.*

Whitbread of London, a fox's head couped gu. 33. 4

Whitbred of Writtle, Essex, a hind's head erased gu. 124. 3

Whitbroke of Water Newton, Hunts, a bull's head erased arg., armed and ducally gorged or. 44. 2

Whitbroke of Bridgenorth, Shropsh., a bull's head caboshed arg., armed az., tipped or. 43. 8

Whitburn, C. J. Sofer, Esquire, of 16, Ennismore Gardens, South Kensington, London, S.W., an eagle's head erased az., charged with a mullet of six points arg., and holding in the beak a bezant. *Virtus difficilia vincit.* 83. 13

Whitby, a talbot's head erased, collared, and lined or. *cf.* 56. 1

Whitby of Cresswell Hall, Staffs, an arrow in pale entwined with a snake, all ppr. *Virtus vitium fugere.*

Whitchurch, a lion's head erased ppr. 17. 8

Whitchurch of Loughbrickland, co. Down, Ireland, a talbot's head erased or, collared az., between two wings expanded arg., guttée-de-sang.

Whitcombe of Wydecombe, Somers., out of a ducal coronet arg., a demi-eagle per pale sa. and of the first, winged counterchanged.

Whitcombe, Shropsh., an eagle displayed per pale or and sa., collared, and the wings counterchanged. *cf.* 75. 2

Whitcombe, Shropsh., out of a ducal coronet arg., a demi-eagle displayed quarterly or and sa., the wings counterchanged, collared per pale sa. and or. 80. 14

White, *see* Bantry, Earl of.

White, *see* Annaly, Baron.

White-Jervis, Jervis-, Bart., *see* Jervis.

White of London, an eagle displayed ppr. *Virescit vulnere.* 75. 2

White, on a ducal coronet an eagle displayed ppr. *cf.* 75. 2

White, Frank Armstrong, Caston House, near Peterborough, same crest.

White, Sir Thomas Woollaston, Bart., J.P., of Walling Wells, Notts, out of a ducal coronet arg., a demi-eagle with wings expanded sa. *Loyal unto death.*

White of Malpis, Middx., and Castor, Northants, out of a ducal coronet or, a demi-eagle with wings expanded sa. *Loyal unto death.*

White of Exeter, Devonsh., an eagle preying on a pheasant, all ppr. 77. 12

White of Hutton and Clement's Hall, Essex, between two wings, the dexter or, the sinister arg., a popinjay's head vert, collared and beaked gu., and holding in the beak a rose-branch of the last, stalked and leaved of the third. *Plus vigila.*

White, William, Esquire, 30A, Wimpole Street, W., same crest and motto.

White of Doncaster, Yorks, an ostrich arg. 97. 2

White of Fyfield, Berks, and Hants, an ostrich arg., beaked and legged or. 97. 2

White, Barrington, M.D., Lyndhurst, Hants, a stork resting its dexter claw on an hourglass. *Watch well.*

White, Edward Egerton Leigh, Bantry House, Bantry, co. Cork: (1) A stork arg., beaked and membered or. (2) A cubit arm vested paly of five or and sa., cuffed arg., the hand ppr. grasping the upper and lower fragments of a broken tilting-spear, the point downwards ppr.; above it, *Force avec vertu. The noblest motive is the public good.*

White, Lynch, Esquire, of Leigham House, Streatham, Surrey, a martlet sa. (*granted* 1685 *to Thomas White, 13th Bishop of Peterborough*). *Vincit qui curat.* 95. 5

White of Bankhead, Lanarksh., same crest and motto. 95. 5

White of Hursley, Northamp., an olive-branch issuing from a mount, thereon a dove holding in the beak a narcissus-flower slipped and leaved, all ppr.

White of Weymouth, Dorset, on a mount vert, a curlew close arg.

White of Redheugh and Old Elvet, Durh., Yorks, and Northumb., a cock's head erased sa., combed and wattled gu. *Vigilans et audax.* 90. 1

White, Arthur, Esquire, Eastwood, King Edward Road, New Barnet, Herts, a peacock in its pride ppr. *Stare super vias antiquas.*

White, John, Esquire, of Lime Street, London, a demi-wolf sa., gorged with a wreath of vine-leaves, and charged on the shoulder with three ermine spots, two and one or, the sinister fore-paw resting on a bezant. 31. 3

White, Corrance-, of Parham and Loudham Hall, Suff.: (1) A wolf's head erased sa. (*for White*). 30. 8. (2) A raven supporting with the dexter claw an escutcheon sa., charged with a leopard's face or (*for Corrance*). *cf.* 107. 12

White of Newton Flatman, Norf., same crest as (1) above. 30. 8

White, Rev. Joseph Henry, Brockdish Rectory, Scole, Norf., a lion rampant. *Vicimus.*

White, Ireland, a demi-lion rampant sa., holding between the paws a flagstaff ppr., thereon a banner arg., charged with the cross of St. George. *Echel agus coruic.*

White, a demi-lion rampant gu., holding a flag arg., charged with a cross of the first, the staff ppr.

White of Redhills, co. Cavan, Ireland, a demi-lion rampant gu., holding between the paws a rose arg., stalked and leaved ppr. *cf.* 16. 2

White, Ireland, a demi-lion rampant arg., semée of pomeis, ducally gorged gu. *cf.* 10. 7

White of London, a lion's head erased quarterly or and az. 17. 8

White, a lion's head erased, collared vair. *Merui candore favorem.* 18. 13

White of London, and Mickleton, Glouc., a lion's head erased or, collared vairé of the same and vert. 18. 13

White of Denham, Bucks, a lion's head couped or, vulned in the neck gu.

White of London, a lion's head erased quarterly az. and or, guttée counterchanged. *cf.* 17. 8

White, a lion's head erased arg., gorged with a wreath of laurel vert, therefrom pendent an escutcheon az., charged with a representation of the gold medal presented to Admiral Sir John Chambers White, K.C.B., by the Grand Signior, in commemoration of his services in Egypt in the year 1801, pendent from a riband tennée.

White, out of a ducal coronet or, a bear's head arg., muzzled sa. 34. 3

White of London, of Hackney, Middx., and Norfolk, Yorks, out of a mural coronet gu., a boar's head arg., crined or. 41. 8

White, Eaton, Esquire, J.P., of Boulge Hall, Woodbridge, Suff., in front of a demi-tower gu., issuant therefrom a boar's head arg., tusked and maned or, charged on the neck with a cross patée, also gu., three crosses patée, also arg. 275. 7

White of Bridgecourt, Isle of Ely, Cambs, and Winchelsea, Sussex, a talbot passant or. 54. 1

White, out of a ducal coronet per pale or and gu., a camel's head az., eared of the first, charged on the neck with a wreath, also of the first and second.

White, Dorset, of Duffield, Derbysh., and Hants, a goat's head gu., armed or, holding in the mouth an acorn of the last, leaved vert.

White, Captain Joseph Henry Lachlan, B.A., J.P., D.L., of Bredfield House, Woodbridge, Suff., and Gracefield, Queen's Co., on a mount vert, a buck trippant per pale arg. and ppr., attired or, the dexter fore-leg bearing a flagstaff in bend sinister, also ppr., thereon hoisted a banner or, fringed, and charged with an escallop gu. *Sedule et prospere.* 308. 11

White of Ashted, Surrey, out of a ducal coronet or, a dragon's head vert. 72. 4

White of St. Stephen's, Cornw., and Sutton, Essex, a griffin's head erased sa. 66. 2

White of Truro, Cornw., an erm. sejant ppr.

White, Ireland, three arrows, one in fess and two in saltier ppr. *Sis justus, et ne timeas.*

White of Ballyellis, co. Wexford, Ireland, on a mount vert, three arrows, two in saltire, points downwards, and one in fesse point to the dexter gu., headed or, flighted arg. *Innocent courageous activity.*

White, a garb ppr. 153. 2

White of Edinburgh, a demi-angel ppr. *Pur sans peur.*

White of Marklo, Scotland, a chevalier on horseback, holding in his dexter hand a sword fesseways ppr. *Vincit qui curat.*

White of Charlton, Dorset, a dexter arm embowed, vested or, cuffed arg., the hand holding by the legs an eagle volant ppr., beaked of the first between two roses gu., slipped ppr. *Virtus omnia vincit.*

White of Poole and Tickleford, Dorset, and Yeovil, Somers., an arm embowed vested or, charged with two bends wavy gu., the hand holding a stork by the legs with wings expanded ppr., beaked and legged of the first.

White, James Maitland Logan, of Kellerstain Midlothian an arm supporting a garland of laurel *Virtute parta* 218 4

White, Ireland a cubit arm erect, holding in the hand a sprig, all ppr, bearing three roses gu cf 218 12

White, Colonel Henry of Woodlands co Dublin and of Rathcline co Longford, a cubit arm erect ppr holding a sprig, also ppr, bearing three roses gu on the arm a chevron engrailed of the last, charged with a cross crosslet or *Vi et virtute* 245 10

White, Field Marshal General Sir George Stuart G C B, Gibraltar a dexter arm embowed vambraced and holding in the hand a sprig of three roses slipped and leaved *Honeste parta*

White, Ireland a dexter arm in armour holding in the hand a sword all ppr 210 2

White, Captain James Grove an arm in armour embowed holding in the hand a dagger all ppr, the arm charged with a cross patee or *Nourissez l'esperance* cf 196 5

White, Hans Thomas Fellwhite R N Springfort Hall, Mallow, same crest and motto

White of Richardstown Queen's Co Ireland, a naked arm holding in the hand a dagger, all ppr *Vicimus* 212 3

White, Ireland and France, an arm in armour embowed, holding in the hand a dagger all ppr *Vicimus* 196 5

White, Major General William Richard, of Twyford, Winchester Hants a dexter arm embowed in armour holding in the hand a baton *The noblest motive is the public good*

White of Benicarloe, Spain, a naked arm embowed holding in the hand a sword, all ppr *Ardua per preceps gloria vadit iter* 201 4

White of Milton Scotland, an arm in armour throwing a spear ppr *Par valeur —Providentia et valore* 210 11

White - Thomson, Remington Walter White, M A, Eton College, Windsor (1) A dexter cubit arm in armour fesseways holding a cross crosslet fitchee erect arg (*for Thomson*) (2) A stork resting his dexter claw upon a sandglass and holding in the beak a bullrush leaved, all ppr (*for White*) *Deus providebit*

White-Thomson, Sir Robert Thomas, K C B, Broomford Exbourne, Devonshire, same crests and motto

Whitebread, Essex, a hind's head gu 124 1

Whitefoord, a garb gu, banded or *Ubique aut nusquam* 153 2

Whitefoord, Scotland on a garb erect or, a dove statant ppr *D'en haut*

Whitefoord, Bart of Blairquhan Scotland a garb erect or, thereon a dove ppr *Tout est d'en haut*

Whitefoord, a garb gu, banded or, and thereon a dove arg *Ubique aut nusquam*

Whiteford of Thornhill, Devonsh, a garb az, banded or, therefrom suspended an escutcheon arg, charged with a bend sa, cottised of the first *Virtute superanda fortuna*

Whitehead, *see* Taylor Whitehead

Whitehead, a cross crosslet gu *Ad finem fidelis* 165 2

Whitehead, Hants, a wolf sejant arg

Whitehead, Henry Esquire Haslem Hay, Bury, Lancs same crest *Je vive en espoir*

Whitehead, Robert, same crest *Ad finem fidelis*

Whitehead, George M A Deighton Grove, York same crest *Semper eadem*

Whitehead, of Uplands Hall Lancs out of a celestial crown or, a bugle horn of the same between two wings az *Dum spiro spero*

Whitehead, Charles Esquire J P, D L, Barming House Maidstone a stag's head couped ppr *Je vive en esperance*

Whitehead, Scotland a man issuing out of the water and laying hold of a Highland mantle ppr *Abyssus tiranum dabat me*

Whitehead, Sir James Bart, F S A, J P D L, of Highfield House Catford Bridge Kent an eagle with wings expanded ppr, each wing charged with a fasces erect or supporting with the dexter claw an escutcheon of the arms, viz, per pale az and sa on a fesse invected, plain cottised or, between three fleurs de lis of the last a fasces erect between two eagles' heads erased ppr *Virtute et labore* 310 3

Whitehead, Rowland Esquire of 14 Old Square, Lincoln's Inn, London W C an eagle with wings expanded ppr, each wing charged with a fasces erect or supporting an escutcheon of the arms, viz, per pale az and sa, on a fesse invected and plain cottised or between three fleurs de-lis of the last a fasces erect between two eagles' heads erased ppr *Fervidus stobilis* 310 3

Whitehorn, five spears sa headed or, one in pale and four in saltier

Whitehouse, a lion's gamb erect and erased ppr 36 4

Whitehurst, a cross crosslet fitched sa, between two palm-branches vert

Whitehurst, Shropsh on a mural coronet arg a knight's helmet plumed and pierced with a javelin the point dropping blood, all ppr *Je crains Dieu*

Whitelaw of that Ilk and Woodhall, Scotland, a bee erect ppr *Solertia ditat* 137 2

Whitelaw, Alexander Gartshore Kirkintilloch, Dumbartonsh, same crest and motto

Whitelaw, Lockhart-, Captain Græme Alexander Strathallan Castle, Perthshire same crest and motto

Whitele, Shropsh a buck's head arg, attired or, holding in the mouth the end of a scroll with the motto, *Live to live*

Whiteley, William, Esquire, of 31, Porchester Terrace, London, W, a triple garb or *Labore et vivere* 153 13

Whiteling, a salmon naiant or holding in the mouth a rose gu, stalked and leaved vert

Whitelock, on a castle arg, an eagle with wings displayed or

Whitelock, a dexter hand holding a dagger ppr 212 3

Whitelocke, between two swords in saltier ppr, a cross crosslet fitched sa 166. 14

Whitelocke-Lloyd, George Esquire of Strancally Castle co Waterford, Ireland (1) A cubit arm erect in scale armour ppr the cuff arg, the hand also ppr, grasping a lizard vert (*for Lloyd*) 209 3 (2) On a tower vairee arg and gu an eagle with wings endorsed or and over it *Quod cunq evenerit optimum* (*for Whitelocke*) *Ar ol gwaith gorphoys* 156 11

Whitelocke, Berks on a mural coronet vair, an eagle with wings expanded or

Whiteman, a tower gu, masoned or 156 5

Whiteman, on the stump of a tree a buck

Whitenhall, Kent a crescent gu charged with three bezants, and between the horns a garb or

Whiterage, a talbot's head couped gu, collared or between six fern slips arg

Whiteside of Scarborough Yorks a demi-lion rampant per fesse arg and gu holding in the dexter paw a rose of the second seeded or, slipped and barbed vert 12 1

Whiteway, out of a tower ppr, a demi-lion gu 157 11

Whiteway, Ireland a hand holding a sword ppr *Dum vivo, spiro* 212 13

Whiteway, Dorset, on a ducal coronet or a lion's gamb erased in fess gu

Whiteway, Augustine Robert Hemingford Grey Hunts, same crest

Whitfield, an anchor az, entwined by a serpent or 161 3

Whitfield of Whitfield Hall, Northumb, out of a palisado coronet arg, a stag's head or

Whitfield, Francis Barry, Offham House Lewes same crest

Whitfield of Brighton out of a palisado coronet arg a buck's head or *Medio tutissimus ibis*

Whitford, a cross Calvary or 160 1

Whitford, Scotland, on a garb or a dove arg beaked gu *Tout est d'en haut*

Whitgift, Surrey, out of a ducal coronet or, a lion's gamb arg, holding a chaplet vert

Whitgrave, Essex and Staffs out of a ducal coronet gu, a demi antelope or 126 8

Whitgreave, Robert, of Moseley Court, Staffs (1) Same crest as above 126 8 (2) Of honourable augmentation out of a ducal coronet a sceptre in pale or, surmounted by a branch of oak ppr and a rose gu, slipped in saltier also ppr *Regem defendere victum* 170 13

Whitham, a rose or, stalked and leaved vert 149 5

Whithering or **Withering,** Staffs a raven with wings expanded sa, beaked and ducally gorged or cf 107 3

Whithers, Wilts, out of a ducal coronet or a staff raguly sa 147 10

Whiting, a demi eagle with two heads displayed ppr cf 82 3

Whitingham, Lancs, and of Whitingham, Yorks a cubit arm erect vested arg, holding in the hand ppr an open book of the first garnished or

Whitingham, a tower ppr 156. 2

Whitington, a wyvern's head bezantée, holding in the month the point of a spear in bend embrued.

Whitington, a dolphin haurient arg. 140. 11

Whitington of Newborough, Staffs, out of a ducal coronet or, a goat's head arg., armed of the first. 128. 14

Whitington of Hamswell, Glouc., a lion's head couped sa. 21. 1

Whitington of Pauntlett, Glouc., a lion's head erased sa. 17. 8

Whitington, same crest. *Sapere aude.* 17. 8

Whitle of Halton Hall, Lancs, two lion's gambs erased bendy sinister of four gu. and or, supporting a rose arg., barbed and seeded ppr.

Whitley-Deans-Dundas, *see* Dundas.

Whitley or **Whitlie,** between two swords in saltier ppr., a cross crosslet fitched gu. 166. 14

Whitlock of Warkley and Frestock, Devonsh., a cross patée between two wings gu. 110. 7

Whitlock, on a castle arg., a bird with wings displayed or.

Whitmarsh, a lion's gamb erased ppr. 36. 4

Whitmore, *see* Wolryche-Whitmore.

Whitmore of London, an arm erect couped at the elbow vested or, turned up az., holding in the hand ppr. a cinquefoil, also or, leaved vert, all between two wings of the fourth. 205. 11

Whitmore of Apley, Shropsh.: (1) A falcon on the stump of a tree with a branch springing from the dexter side, all ppr. 86. 11. (2) An arm couped at the elbow and erect vested or, turned up az., holding in the hand ppr. a cinquefoil, also or, leaved vert, all between two wings of the fourth. 205. 11

Whitmore of London, Chesh., and Shropsh., a falcon on the stump of a tree with a branch springing from the dexter side, all ppr. 86. 11

Whitmore, Thomas Charles Douglas, J.P., 2, Lowndes Square, S.W., same crest.

Whitmore of Thurstaston, Chesh., a lion's head couped at the shoulder arg., bound round the neck and tied with a bow at the back with a ribbon az. *Either for ever.*

Whitney, *see* Fetherston-Whitney.

Whitney, *see* Fetherstonhaugh-Whitney.

Whitney of Merton, Wexford, a bull's head couped sa., the horns arg., the points gu. *cf.* 44. 3

Whitney, Chesh. and Glouc., same crest.

Whitney, Heref., same crest. *Magnanimiter crucem sustine.*

Whitney, Shropsh., a bull's head erased sa. 44. 3

Whitney, Shropsh., a bull's head sa., attired per fesse gu. and arg. *cf.* 44. 3

Whitney, a bull's head couped sa., the horns or, the points gu. *cf.* 44. 3

Whitney, Sir Benjamin, of Upper Fitzwilliam Street, Dublin, Ireland, a bull's head couped sa., armed arg., tipped gu., gorged with a collar chequy or and sa., and charged upon the neck below the collar with a cross crosslet arg. *Magnanimiter crucem sustine.*

Whitney, Ireland, a Roman soldier's head helmeted ppr. *cf.* 191. 6

Whitshed, Hawkins-, Bart. (*extinct*), Ireland, a demi-lion per pale indented arg. and gu., holding in the dexter paw a trefoil slipped vert. *cf.* 13. 13

Whitshed, a demi-lion rampant per pale indented arg. and vert, holding in the dexter paw a trefoil slipped ppr. *Libertas et natale solum.* *cf.* 13. 13

Whitson, *see* Hill-Whitson.

Whitson, Scotland, an arm in armour embowed ppr., holding in the hand a tilting-spear broken in the middle or. 197. 2

Whitson of Parkhill, Scotland, a dexter arm in armour embowed, the hand grasping a broken tilting-spear. *Calitus vires.* 197. 2

Whittaker of Newcastle Court, Radnor, a horse passant arg. 52. 6

Whittaker of Barming Place, near Maidstone, Kent, a horse passant or. 52. 6

Whittaker of Prospect Hill, Walton-le-Dale, and of Birch House, Lees, Lancs, a cubit arm erect in armour, about the arm a wreath of oak, the hand in a gauntlet grasping a flaming sword, all ppr., between two mascles arg. *Robur atque fides.*

Whittaker, Thomas, Birch House, Lees, Lancs, same crest and motto.

Whittaker, a sea-gull with wings expanded ppr.

Whittall, Charlton, Esquire, of Smyrna in the Levant, in front of a talbot's head arg., guttée-de-larmes, a sun rising in splendour ppr. *Persevere* 56. 10

Whitteley, three garbs gu., banded or. *cf.* 153. 13

Whittell or **Whittelle,** and **Whittle,** Lancs, two arms embowed vested az., cuffed erm., holding in the hands ppr. a garb or.

Whittell of London, a talbot's head erased or, collared, eared, and ringed arg. 56. 1

Whitten of Golden Grove, Ireland, an arm erect vested sa., cuffed arg., holding in the hand a sword between two oak-branches, all ppr.

Whitter of Ashurst, Sussex, an arm in armour embowed, the hand grasping a battle-axe ppr. *Esto fidelis.* *cf.* 200. 6

Whittewronge, a Saracen's head affrontée wreathed ppr. *cf.* 190. 5

Whitting of Sandcroft House, Somers., a cubit arm erect vested az., cuffed arg., the hand grasping a whiting fesseways, the arm charged with a cross botonnée, also arg. *Recte agens confide.*

Whittingham, a lion's head couped. 21. 1

Whittingham, a dexter cubit arm vested or, cuffed gu., holding in the hand ppr. an open book sa., leaved and tasselled vert, and on the first page a pomegranate of the first. *Non mihi sed patriæ.*

Whittingham, Durh., a cubit arm erect ppr., vested arg., cuffed az., holding in the hand an open book of the second, the edges of the leaves and the clasps or.

Whittingstall, Fearnley-, George, 105, Queen's Gate, S.W.: (1) In front of an antelope's head couped at the neck az., armed or, a saltire of nine lozenges or. (2) A mount vert, thereon in front of a bush ppr. a talbot passant erm., collared, lined, reflexed over the back gu., the dexter fore-foot resting on a buck's head cabossed or. *Animus tamen idem.*

Whittington, Robert Hugh, 16, Beaufort Street West, Bath, a lion's head erased.

Whittington, a dragon's head sa., bezantée, issuing from a rose gu., holding in the mouth an arrow arg., the point in chief embrued.

Whittington, Staffs, a goat's head erased arg., ducally gorged and armed or. *cf.* 128. 5

Whittington, Lincs, an antelope's head erased arg., ducally gorged and armed or. *cf.* 126. 2

Whittington, a dove holding in its beak an olive-branch ppr. 92. 5

Whittington-Ince, Rev. Edward John Cuming, M.A., Rectory, Warmington, Broadway, Worcs.: (1) Upon a rock ppr., a rabbit sejant arg., gorged with a collar gemelle gu., resting the dexter fore-leg on a cross patée fitchée sa. (*for Ince*). (2) On a mount vert, a lion's head erased sa., semée of mullets or, gorged with a collar invected arg., and holding in the mouth an annulet or (*for Whittington*). *Garde la foi.*

Whittle, a bear's head and neck sa., muzzled gu. 34. 14

Whittlebury, a fountain throwing up water ppr. 159. 13

Whitton, in the sea a ship in full sail ppr. 160. 13

Whittuck of Hanham Hall, Glouc., a boar's head erased or. *Messis ab alto.* 42. 2

Whittuck, William Samuel, Ellsbridge House, Keynsham, Bristol, same crest and motto.

Whittuck, a hand holding a pen, all ppr. 217. 10

Whitwange of Dunson, Northumb., a hedgehog ppr. 135. 8

Whitwell, Staffs, a lion's head erased or. 17. 8

Whitwell, Northamp., a griffin's head erased or. 66. 2

Whitwick, a demi-heraldic tiger arg., crined sa., holding a pheon or.

Whitwicke, Berks and Staffs, same crest.

Whitwike, Staffs, a demi-lion or, gorged with a mural coronet arg., holding a pheon gu.

Whitwong, a hedgehog or, bristled sa. 135. 8

Whitworth, Earl Whitworth, out of a ducal coronet or, a garb gu. *Dum spiro spero.*

Whitworth, Baron Whitworth of Galway (*extinct*), same crest.

Whitworth, same crest.

Whitworth, Thomas, Esquire, 1, Greenbank, Waterloo, near Liverpool, on a chapeau a garb.

Whitworth, late Sir Joseph, Bart., (*extinct*), in front of a mount vert, thereon a garb gu., three mascles interlaced fessewise or. *Fortis qui prudens.*

Whorwood of Bobington, Staffs, a demi-griffin issuing from a tower, all ppr. 157. 5

Whorwood, Oxon, and Sandwell Hall, Staffs a buck's head cabossed sa holding in the mouth an acorn branch vert fructed or

Whorwood of Headington House Oxon, a stag's head cabossed sa holding in the mouth a branch of oak ppr, fructed or *Nunc et semper*

Whydon of Chagford Devonsh, out of a ducal coronet arg a demi swan sa, with wings expanded and beaked or

Whyt, Scotland, a boar's head ppr *Per ardua fama* 43 1

Whyt, a boar's head couped at the shoulders arg, bristled and ungu or 41 1

Whyte of Loughbrickland co Down, a demi-lion rampant holding a flag ensigned with a cross *Echel Coryg*

Whyte, a lion's head couped gu 21 1

Whyte of Stockbriggs Lanarksh, an adder issuing out of marshy ground paleways and nowed ppr *Fortuna favet*

Whyte of Grongar, Ayrsh, and Arddarroch, Dumbartonsh, a dexter arm from the shoulder grasping a wreath of laurel ppr *Virtute* 202 4

Whyte of Newtown Manor, Ireland, a dexter arm the hand holding a long straight sword *Fortiter sed feliciter*

Whytehead of Crayke, Yorks, a fox sejant arg 32 11

Whytehead, Rev Robert Yates, Hormead Rectory, Buntingford, same crest

Whyting, a bear's head ppr 34 14

Whytock, Scotland, a dexter hand holding a pen 217 10

Whytt, Scotland, a dexter arm embowed holding in the hand a wreath of laurel ppr *Virtute parta* 202 4

Whytt, Scotland, a dexter hand erect holding a heart ppr *Candidiora pectora* 216 9

Wiberd, Essex a demi-lion rampant arg, ducally crowned or 10 11

Wichasle of Chudleigh Devonsh an antelope's head erased per pale arg and sa charged on the neck with two crescents counterchanged, and holding in the mouth a branch of laurel ppr

Wichingham and **Witchingham,** Suff, an arm erect ppr, holding in the hand an escallop or 216 2

Wickenden, a dexter hand holding a cross crosslet fitched az 221 14

Wickens, a talbot current arg, spotted sa, between two trees vert fructed or

Wickes, Edmund Caleb Esquire of Liverpool and the other descendants of Charles Wickes, Esquire, of Walton, Leics, in front of a sun in splendour ppr a garb fesseways vert. *Ex lumine lucrum* 162 8

Wickes, Thomas B Pullman Palace Car Co Chicago, U S A, same crest and motto

Wickham, out of a tower sa, a martlet volant or 156 9

Wickham, Kent, Abingdon, Berks, and Oxon a bull's head sa, armed or, charged on the neck with two chevronels arg cf 44 3

Wickham, Lieutenant Colonel Thomas, Fronwnion, Dolgelly, same crest. *Manners maketh man*

Wickham of North Hill Somers, same crest and motto

Wickham, Kent a bull's head erased sa, armed or *Manners makyth man* 44 3

Wickham, a bull's head couped sa armed or, charged on the neck with two bars of the last

Wickham of Swalcliffe Oxon, a bull's head sa, charged on the neck with two chevronels arg cf 44 3

Wickham, Captain William Wickham, J P, Chestnut Grove, Boston Spa, Yorks same crest

Wickliff or **Wyckliffe,** a buck's head ppr, and between the attires a cross crosslet fitched cf 120 12

Wickliffe, an anchor cabled ppr 161 2

Wicklow, Earl of (Howard) Shelton Abbey Arklow, co Wicklow on a chapeau gu, turned up erm, a lion statant gardant or, ducally gorged gu holding in his mouth an arrow fesse-wise ppr *Inservi Deo et lætare — Certum pete finem* cf 4 7

Wicks, on a chapeau gu, turned up erm a garb ppr 153 10

Wickstead or **Wicksted,** two anchors in saltier sa 161 7

Wicksteed, Shropsh, two snakes ppr entwined round a garb or 153 3

Wicksted, George Edmund J P, of Betley Hall, Staffs (1) Two serpents ppr, issuing from and round a garb or (*for Wicksted*) (2) A pyramid erected on a pedestal of one degree arg, the top entwined by a serpent descending ppr respecting an escroll with the motto, *Prudentia in adversis* (*for Tollet*)

Wicksted of Nantwich, Chesh, two serpents vert entwined round a garb or 153 3

Widdevil, an ear of rye and a palm-branch in saltier all ppr 154 10

Widdowson of London an eagle rising ppr *Surgam* 77 5

Widdrington, Baron Widdrington (*attainted*) on a chapeau gu turned up erm a bull's head sa spotted arg

Widdrington, Shallcross Fitzherbert, of Newton Hall, Northumb (1) On a chapeau gu turned up erm a bull's head sa (2) A garb or 153 2

Widdrington, Lincs, and Swinbourne Northumb, a bull's head sa, platée cf 44 3

Widenham, of Court co Limerick, Ireland a lion's head erased ppr 17 8

Widevile, on a chapeau ppr, a wyvern vert 69 14

Wiehe, a short column gu, and issuant therefrom a plume of three peacock's feathers ppr all between two wings, also gu *Omnia fortitudine vincit*

Widope or **Wydop** of Westml three horse shoes interlaced arg

Widson of Loudham, Notts out of a ducal coronet or, flames of fire ppr

Widvile, a demi man in armour ppr wielding a scimitar 187 4

Widworthy, Devonsh an eagle rising ppr 77 5

Wifield, a cinquefoil 148 12

Wigan, Baron, *see* Earl of Crawford and Balcarres

Wigan, Sir Frederick, Bart of Clare Lawn, Surrey upon a mount a mountain ash-tree, surmounted by a rainbow all ppr *Carpe diem* 250 6

Wigan, William Lewis, B A, J P, Clare Cottage East Malling, Kent, same crest and motto 311 5

Wigan, Rev Herbert M A Luddesdowne, Kent same crest and motto

Wigge of London, a dexter gauntlet erect the fist clenched ppr

Wiggett of Geist Norf, a dove regardant holding in the beak an olive branch, all ppr 92 1

Wiggin, Sir Henry Samuel, Bart, Metchley Grange, Harborne, Birmingham, within a spear, the rowel upwards, leathered or, a fleur-de-lis sa, the whole between two wings ppr each charged with a fleur-de lis, also sa *To thine own self be true* 287 4

Wiggins, a spur or between two wings ppr 111 13

Wiggins, Arthur Sandhills Christchurch Hants, in front of a garb or charged with an acorn slipped and leaved ppr, three hurts fesseways *Loyal*

Wiggon, a martlet ppr 95 4

Wight of Brabœuf Manor, Surrey, out of a mural coronet a bear's head arg, muzzled sa cf 34 13

Wight-Boycott, Thomas Andrew, of Rudge Hall Staffs (1) Issuing out of a mural coronet an arm in armour embowed casting a grenade fired all ppr (*for Boycott*) 197 10 (2) Issuing out of the battlements of a tower a bear's head charged on the neck with a mascle (*for Wight*) *Pro Rege et religione*

Wight, Scotland, a dexter hand grasping a dagger point downwards ppr *Fortiter*

Wight, Norf an acorn or, stalked and leaved vert 152 1

Wightman of Harrow Hill Middx a stork arg, winged sa membered gu, holding in the beak a snake vert, entwined round the body

Wightman, Scotland, a demi-savage wreathed round the temple and loins with leaves and holding over the dexter shoulder a club ppr *A Wight man never wanted a weapon* 186 1

Wightman, on the stump of a tree ppr a buck trippant arg attired collared and chained or

Wightwick, Staffs, a demi-heraldic tiger arg, crined sa, holding between the paws a pheon or *Aut viam inveniam aut faciam*

Wiglesworth, a pheon az

Wigley of Wirksworth Derbysh, and Scraptoft Leics, issuing from flames ppr an heraldic tiger's head arg maned and tufted sa gorged with a collar embattled gu

Wigmore, an esquire's helmet az, garnished or 180 3

Wigmore of Stamford Lincs, a greyhound sejant arg collared gu ringed and garnished or cf 59 2

Wigmore, Norf on a mount vert a greyhound sejant arg, collared gu garnished and ringed or 59 2

Wigmore of Shobden, Heref, on a mount vert, a greyhound sejant arg, collared gu, garnished or 59 2

Wigott, a griffin's head or winged gu, charged on each wing with an escallop arg cf 65 11

Wigram, Bart, *see* Fitzwygram

Wigram, Essex, on a mount vert, a hand in armour couped at the wrist in fess ppr., charged with an escallop and holding a fleur-de-lis or. 250. 8

Wigram, Henry James, Esquire, Northlands, Salisbury, same crest.

Wigram, Major-General Godfrey James, C.B., De Albany, Piccadilly, W., same crest.

Wigram, on a mount vert, a hand in armour fesseways couped at the wrist ppr., charged with an escallop and holding a fleur-de-lis erect or. *Dulcis amor patriæ.*

Wigram, E. Money, Esquire, 31, Clarges Street, London, W., on a mount vert, a hand in armour fesseways couped at the wrist ppr., charged with an escallop, and holding a fleur-de-lis erect or. *Dulcis amor patriæ.*

Wigston, a lion's head erased per pale gu. and az., guttée-d'or. *cf.* 225. 10

Wigton, a stag's head holding in the mouth an adder, all ppr. 121. 7

Wikes, Glouc., a demi-lion rampant, holding in the dexter paw a scimitar, all ppr. 14. 10

Wilberforce, Middx., an eagle displayed sa., beaked and legged ppr. 75. 2

Wilberforce and **Wilberfos,** Yorks, same crest.

Wilberforce, William, of Markington, Yorks, same crest. *Nos non nobis.* 75. 2

Wilberforce, Edward, Esquire, 61, Belgrave Road, S.W., an eagle displayed with wings inverted sa., beaked and legged ppr. *Nos non nobis.*

Wilbraham, *see* Lathom, Earl of.

Wilbraham, Bootle-, Baron Skelmersdale, *see* Skelmersdale.

Wilbraham, Chesh., a wolf's head erased arg. *Par fluctus portui.* 30. 8

Wilbraham, Hugh Edward, Delamere House, Northwich, same crest. *In portu quies.*

Wilbraham, Donald Fortescue, same crest and motto.

Wilbraham, Captain Hugh Edward, Delamere House, Northwich, same crest and motto.

Wilby, on the point of a sword a garland of laurel, all ppr. 170. 1

Wilcocks of London, Middx., of Brightlingsea, Essex, and Shropsh.: (1) Out of a mural coronet or, a demi-lion rampant sa., collared vairée arg. and az. (2) An eagle's leg erased at the thigh or, between two wings az.

Wilcocks of Knassington, Leics., a demi-lion rampant az. 10. 2

Wilcotts, a demi-eagle with wings displayed arg., beaked sa. 80. 2

Wilcox, on a mount a dove, all ppr. 92. 3

Wilcox, Leics., a demi-eagle with wings displayed arg., ducally gorged or. *cf.* 80. 2

Wilcoxon of Blackheath, Kent, a lion's gamb erect bendy arg. and sa., holding a fleur-de-lis or, encircled by a wreath of oak ppr. *Semper fidelis.*

Wild, *see* Bagnall-Wild.

Wild of Costock, Notts, a demi-buck springing sa., guttée-d'or, attired and ungu., and resting the sinister foot on an escallop, also or. 119. 4

Wild, Kent, an eagle displayed or, beaked and membered sa. 75. 2

Wild, F. C., Esquire, Whirlow Court, Sheffield, a lion passant resting its dexter paw on an escutcheon.

Wildbore of Burghley, Lincs, a wild boar sa., bristled or. *cf.* 40. 9

Wildbore, Dorset, and Doncaster, Yorks, the upper part of a spear ppr., thrust through a boar's head erased arg., distilling blood gu.

Wilde, *see* Penzance, Baron.

Wilde, *see* Truro, Baron.

Wilde of Nettleworth, Notts, a demi-stag salient sa., attired and ducally gorged or. *cf.* 119. 2

Wilde, Shropsh., a lion passant. 6. 2

Wilde, a lion passant gardant. 4. 3

Wilde, Edward Godfrey, on a mount vert, a stag lodged ppr., in the mouth a rose gu., slipped vert. *Veritas victrix.*

Wilder, a demi-griffin holding between the claws a garland of laurel.

Wilder, Rev. Henry Beaufoy, of Nunhide, Purley Hall, and Sulham, Berks, a savage's head affrontée, couped at the shoulders, wreathed about the temples with woodbine, all ppr. *Virtuti mœnia cedant.*

Wilder, Cambs, a man's bust affrontée, wreathed round the temples arg. and az. 190. 5

Wildgoose of Iridge, Essex, and Sussex, a wild man ppr., wreathed round the temples and loins vert.

Wilding, an oak-tree ppr. 143. 5

Wilding of Hackney, Middx., a dragon's head erased vert. *cf.* 71. 2

Wildman, a griffin's head or, charged with a plate. *cf.* 66. 1

Wildman of Beaucot, Berks, out of a mural coronet arg., a demi-lion ppr., holding a battle-axe or, headed of the first. *cf.* 16. 10

Wildman of Chilham Castle, Kent, out of a mural coronet chequy or and az., a demi-lion arg., supporting a battle-axe of the first, the blade ppr. dropping blood. *cf.* 16. 10

Wildman-Lushington, Francis James, J.P., of Norton Court, Faversham, Kent: (1) A lion's head erased vert, ducally gorged or (*for Lushington*). 18. 5. (2) Out of a mural coronet chequy or and az., a demi-lion rampant arg., supporting a battle-axe of the first, the blade ppr. distilling drops of blood (*for Wildman*). *Prudens qui patiens.* *cf.* 16. 10

Wildman of Newstead Abbey, Notts, out of a mural coronet chequy or and az., a demi-lion arg., supporting a battle-axe of the first, the blade ppr. dropping blood. *Tentanda via est.* *cf.* 16. 10

Wiles, a sheaf of arrows gu., pointed az., feathered and banded or. 173. 3

Wiles, Charles Barsham, Esquire, late of Attleborough, Norf., upon a rock ppr., three arrows, one in pale and two in saltire az., interlaced with a catherine-wheel arg. *Æquam servare mentem.*

Wiley, a rose-bush vert, bearing roses arg. 149. 8

Wilford, Worcs., a stag's head gorged with a laurel crown, all ppr. 120. 3

Willord of Enfield, Middx., a bundle of swans' quills arg., banded gu. *cf.* 113. 6

Wilk, on a mount vert, a cross-bow erect or, round it a scroll inscribed, *Arcui mei non confido.*

Wilkes, a holly-branch vert. 150. 10

Wilkes of Lofts Hall, Essex, a rock ppr., thereon a crossbow erect or, in front of two quarrels or bird-bolts in saltire gu. *Arcui meo non confido.*

Wilkes, a cubit arm vested gu., cuffed arg., the hand holding a cross-bow or.

Wilkes of Wisbeach, Isle of Ely, Cambs, and Yorks, an heraldic tiger sejant gu., tufted and maned or, collared, ringed, and lined of the last.

Wilkie of Blackheath, Kent, a primrose ppr. *cf.* 150. 11

Wilkie, West Indies, a demi-negro wreathed about the head or and gu., girt round the waist vert, having ear-rings pendent arg., holding in the dexter hand a bill, and in his sinister a sugar-cane couped, all ppr. *Favente Deo.*

Wilkin, Kent, a dragon's head per pale arg. and vert. 71. 1

Wilkins, Cann-, of Clifton, Glouc., a wyvern ppr. *Syn ar du hun.* 70. 1

Wilkins, Wales, a wyvern's head erased vert. *cf.* 71. 2

Wilkins of Cole-Orton, Leics., a demi-griffin segreant regardant gu., holding in the dexter claw a sword in pale arg., hilt and pommel or. *cf.* 64. 6

Wilkins of Thong, Kent, a boar passant regardant, pierced through the shoulder by an arrow in bend sinister arg., and biting the arrow.

Wilkins-Leir, Rev. Edward John Paul, B.A., Weston House, Weston, Bath: (1) A unicorn's head couped or, in front of a saltire raguly az. (*for Leir*). (2) Upon a mount a trunk of a tree eradicated fesseways ppr., thereon a boar passant regardant sa., pierced through the shoulder with an arrow in bend sinister, also ppr. (*for Wilkins*).

Wilkinson, Ireland, a fire-beacon inflamed ppr. 177. 14

Wilkinson, Scotland, a demi-talbot arg. *cf.* 55. 8

Wilkinson, on a mount vert, a talbot sejant arg., among rushes ppr.

Wilkinson, same crest. *Ad finem fidelis.*

Wilkinson of White Webbs Park, Middx., a demi-talbot sa., holding a rose-branch vert. *Early and late.*

Wilkinson of Dorrington and Bishop-wearmouth, Durh., a demi-talbot sa., eared erm., charged with three billets, two and one or, holding between the paws a branch vert, thereon three daisies arg., seeded, also or. *Incepta persequor.*

Wilkinson of Wateringbury, Kent, on a mount vert, a greyhound sejant arg., gorged with a collar sa., rimmed and ringed or, on the dexter side of the mount a laurel-branch of the first.

Wilkinson of Winterburn Hall, Yorks, a unicorn's head erased arg. *Tenez le droit.* 49. 5

Wilkinson of Old Buckenham, Norf., and of Rantham, Westml., a unicorn's head erased per chevron or and gu., armed gobony of the first and sa. 49. 5

Wilkinson of Kyo and Harperley Park, Durh., on a mural coronet gu., a demi-unicorn rampant erminois, erased of the first armed and maned or *Nec Rege, nec populo, sed utroque* 276 5

Wilkinson, Lieutenant General Sir Henry K C B, United Service Club, Pall Mall, on a mural crown gu, a demi unicorn rampant erminois, erased of the first *Nec Rege, nec populo, sed utroque* 276 5

Wilkinson, Anthony, 25, Prince's Gardens, same crest

Wilkinson of Coxhoe and Halam, Durh, out of a mural coronet gu, a unicorn's head arg

Wilkinson, Rt Rev Thomas Edward, D D, Anglican Bishop for North and Central Europe, Bradford Court, near Taunton out of a mural coronet a unicorn's head *Nec temere, nec timide*

Wilkinson of Upper Hare Park, Cambs, out of a mural coronet gu, a unicorn s head couped arg *Non mihi sed tibi gloria*

Wilkinson, a wolf's head per pale vert and or holding in the mouth a wing arg, charged on the neck with a trefoil slipped gu

Wilkinson of Pontefract, Yorks, a fox's head erased per pale wavy vert and or holding in the mouth a wing arg

Wilkinson, Henry Edward Thornton, Esquire of Beverley House, Malton, Yorks, and Collingham, East Yorks a stag's head erased az, attired arg, charged on the neck with a sun or 121 14

Wilkinson, Captain William Thornton, D S O, of the King's Own Scottish Borderers same crest

Wilkinson of London, a pelican's head vulning its neck ppr *Gardez bien* cf 98 2

Wilkinson, Bucks and Yorks, a pelican's head vulned ppr cf 98 2

Wilkinson of Charlton Kent, a demi-falcon per pale sa and arg

Wilkinson, a demi-eagle with wings expanded per pale or and arg holding in the beak a rose gu, barbed, leaved and stalked vert

Wilkinson, an arm vested embowed to the dexter, holding between the thumb and forefinger an annulet

Wilks, Sir Samuel Bart, M D, F R S, on a rock a crossbow erect, entwined by two serpents, all ppr *Arcui meo non confido* 287 3

Wilks, an arm couped and embowed fesseways the hand holding up a grenade fired all ppr cf 202 5

Wilks, an heraldic tiger rampant.

Will, John Shiriss 13 West Cromwell Road, S W, a tower arg, charged with a rose gu, between a stag's attires, the scalp in front ppr *Fiat Domine*

Willan of London and Yorks, a demi-lion rampant or holding in the dexter paw a mullet of six points sa cf 15 7

Willans, Yorks a griffin's head with wings expanded ppr, collared or 67 7

Willans, John Bancroft, Dolforgan, Kerry Montgomerysh, a demi man affrontée ppr, supporting with his dexter hand a rod of Æsculapius ppr, and resting his sinister on a catherine-wheel or *Hold on*

Willard of Eastbourne, Sussex, a griffin s head erased or 66 2

Willason, Heref a demi-lion rampant or, charged with three pellets, holding a chaplet vert

Willaston, Shropsh issuing out of a ducal coronet a demi-lion holding in his dexter paw a mullet

Willaume of Tingrave, Beds, on a mount vert a pine-apple or, stalked and crowned of the first 152 8

Willcock, a griffin's head and neck erased ppr 66 2

Willcocks, a fleur-de-lis az 148 2

Willding-Jones, Willding Hampton Hall, Malpas Chesh (1) In front of a talbot's head couped sa collared vert, two roses arg, stalked and leaved ppr (*for Jones*) (2) In front of an oak tree ppr, fructed or a dragon's head erased arg holding in the mouth a cross patee fitchee gu *Till then thus*

Willeigh or **Willeley,** a salmon naiant az 139 12

Willes or **Willis,** a hawk with wings displayed ppr cf 87 12

Willet or **Willett,** out of a ducal coronet a plume of ostrich-feathers, all ppr cf 114 8

Willet of Walthamstow, Essex (1) On a ducal coronet or, a moorcock with wings expanded sa combed and wattled gu (2) Out of a ducal coronet or a cockatrice sa, with wings expanded combed, wattled, beaked, and legged gu

Willett, a heathcock ppr

Willett, Yorks on a ducal coronet or a heathcock ppr, combed and wattled gu *Noli me tangere*

Willett of Brighton, upon a rock a moorcock regardant, both ppr, charged on the body with two fleurs-de lis or and holding in the beak a sprig of heath, also ppr *Dieu et mon devoir*

Willett, Edmund Austen M A, J P Strathwell Whitwell, Isle of Wight same crest

Willey or **Willy** of Houghton, Northumb, out of a ducal coronet or, a reindeer's head erminois, attired arg 122 3

Willey, Francis, Blyth Hall, Blyth, Rotherham same crest *Animum fortuna sequitur*

Willey, Henry Alfred A M I C E, Pennsylvania Park, Exeter, upon a column fesseways the top to the sinister sa, an antique lamp or, fired ppr *Lucet et lucebit* 269 1

Williams, Sir John, Bart, M D of Plas Llanstephan a stag trippant arg attired or between the attires a rose of the second, resting the dexter foot on a serpent nowed ppr *Bydd gyfiawn ac nac ofna* 310 10

Williams, *see* Price Williams

Williams, a boar's head couped gu *Ne cede malis* 43 1

Williams, a boar's head couped gu

Williams, a lion's head erased ppr 17 8

Williams, Devonsh, Sussex and Denton, Lincs, a lion rampant ppr 1 13

Williams of Beaumaris Anglesey a lion passant sa semee of quatrefoils and gorged with a collar gemel arg holding in the dexter fore-paw a fleur-de-lis gu.

Williams, Charles Theodore, Esquire, M A, M D, F R C P, a lion passant

Williams of Lee, Kent, out of a mural coronet ppr a demi lion sa, the head paws, and tip of the tail arg *Suaviter sed fortiter*

Williams, Bart (*extinct*) of Clapton, Northants, a lion rampant ppr 1 13

Williams of Ivy Tower Pembrokesh (1) A lion rampant or, holding in the dexter paw a javelin erect ppr and the sinister resting on an escutcheon pean (*for Williams*) (2) A demi antelope arg, holding between the feet an arrow or (*for Harris*)

Williams of Gwernant Park, Cardigan (1) A lion rampant regardant or 2 3 (2) A scaling-ladder *Of nwn yr Arglwydd* 158 14

Williams, a demi lion rampant arg, charged with three chevronels gu cf 10 2

Williams of Aberystwith a demi-lion rampant arg, holding between the paws an escutcheon of the same, charged with a wyvern's head erased vert, holding in the mouth a sinister hand gu *Cywir in gwlad*

Williams, Dr of Prince of Wales Road, Norwich a demi lion rampant holding between the paws an escutcheon arg charged with a wyvern's head erased vert holding in the mouth a sinister hand gu *Cywir in gwlad*

Williams of Penrose, Monm a dragon's head erased vert, holding in the mouth a hand couped at the wrist ppr 72 6

Williams of Chichester, Sussex a dragon s head arg, semee of hurts vomiting flames of fire ppr cf 72 3

Williams of Dundraeth Merionethsh, a griffin segreant gu beaked and armed or *Nid da onid Duw* 62 2

Williams, a demi-griffin gu, the wings erm, charged on the body with three bezants in pale, holding between the claws the rudder of a ship sa

Williams of Malvern Hall Warw, between two spears erect ppr a talbot passant per pale erm and ermines

Williams, Bart (*extinct*), of Llangibby Castle, a talbot passant per pale erm and or eared of the last 54 1

Williams, Addams-, Rowland of Langibby Castle Monm (1) A talbot passant per pale erm and or (*for Williams*) 54 1 (2) A griffin's head erased erm beaked gu charged on the neck with a chevron vairée or and az (*for Addams*) *En suivant la verite* cf 66 2

Williams, Hon Sir Hartley Supreme Court, Melbourne, Australia same crest as (1) above

Williams, Hon Hartley, of St Leonards, St Kilda, Melbourne, Victoria Australia, senior puisne judge of the Supreme Court of the colony of Victoria, uses a talbot passant per pale erm and or 54 1

Williams, Jones-, of Grovehill, Worcs, between two spears erect ppr a talbot passant per pale erm and erminois, charged for distinction upon the shoulder with a cross crosslet sa

Williams, Jones-, Thomas John Esquire, of Laughern Hill Wichenford near Worcester, same crest and motto.

Williams, a greyhound passant collared and ringed. cf. 60. 2

Williams, Charles Reynolds, Esquire, J.P., D.L., of Dolmelynllyn, Dolgelly, a stag's head caboshed. *Si je puis.*

Williams, Shropsh., on a mount vert, a stag statant arg., attired sa. 117. 1

Williams, a buck statant arg., collared or. cf. 117. 5

Williams-Bulkeley, Sir Richard Henry, Bart., D.L., of Penrhyn, Carnarvonsh.: (1) Out of a ducal coronet or, a bull's head arg., armed of the first, charged with a chevron sa. (*for Bulkeley*). cf. 44. 11. (2) A stag's head cabossed arg. (*for Williams*). *Nec temere, nec timide.* 122. 5

Williams, Hants, a goat passant ppr. cf. 129. 5

Williams of Llanspyddid: (1) A goat's head couped ppr. (*for Williams*). 128. 12. (2) A bull's head couped at the neck sa. (*for Bullen*). cf. 44. 3

Williams, a bull's head erased sa. 44. 3

Williams, a bull's head couped sa. cf. 44. 3

Williams, out of a ducal coronet a demi-eagle with wings expanded ppr., holding in the beak a trefoil sa.

Williams, Griffies-, Bart.: (1) A bull's head erased at the neck pean, armed or, holding in the mouth a spear, the staff broken ppr. (*for Williams*). (2) A griffin segreant az., beaked and armed or, the wings elevated erm., the claws supporting a scaling-ladder of the second (*for Griffies*).

Williams, Greswolde-, Francis Wigley, Greswolde, Bredenbury Court, Heref., a falcon ppr.

Williams, Osmond, J.P., Castle Deudreath, Penrhyndeudreath R.S.O., Merionethsh., a griffin segreant gu. *Nid da ouid Dyd.*

Williams, Sir William Robert, Bart., D.L., of Tregullow, Cornw., a demi-eagle az., with wings elevated sa., each wing charged with four bezants. *Nil desperandum.* cf. 80. 2

Williams, Bertram Leopold, same crest and motto.

Williams, Victor George, same crest.

Williams, William Philpotts, same crest.

Williams, John Charles, Caerhays Castle, St. Austell, Cornw., same crest.

Williams, Edward Harvey, same crest and motto.

Williams, Ernest Martyn, same crest and motto.

Williams, Lieutenant Frederick Law, same crest and motto.

Williams, Michael, 10, Old Burlington Street, W., same crest and motto.

Williams of Boston, America, an eagle with wings expanded ppr., resting the dexter claw on a mound or.

Williams of Minster, Isle of Thanet, Kent, an eagle displayed or. 75. 5

Williams-Wynn, Sir Herbert Lloyd Watkin, Bart., of Wynnstay, an eagle displayed or. 75. 5

Williams of Boons, Kent, a cock ppr. *Deus hæc otia fecit.* 91. 2

Williams of Cwymcynfelin, Cardigansh., same crest. *Duw a'n Bendithio.* 91. 2

Williams, George Checkland, same crest and motto.

Williams, a cock gu., combed and legged or. 91. 2

Williams, Bart. (*extinct*), of Gwernevet, Breconsh., a cock gu. *Deus hæc otia fecit.* 91. 2

Williams of Micklegate, Yorks, a cock gu., guttée-d'or, resting the dexter claw on a spear-head sa., embrued ppr.

Williams of Castle Hill, Surrey, on a mount vert, amidst bulrushes, a moorcock ppr., charged on the breast with a bezant.

Williams of Enfield, Middx., on a mount a branch of the tea-plant, thereon a Chinese golden pheasant, all ppr.

Williams, Cambs, a bustard close.

Williams, Bart. (*extinct*), of Clovelly Court, Devonsh., a swan with wings addorsed arg., beaked and legged or, collared gu., holding in the beak a bird-bolt sa. *Mea virtute me involvo.*

Williams, Sir George, 13, Russell Square, W.C., a dove with wings elevated arg., each wing charged with a rose gu., and encircled around the breast with an olive-branch ppr. *Semper fidelis.*

Williams of Appledore, Devonsh., and St. Edmund's Terrace, Regent's Park, Middx., in front of two spears in saltire ppr., a horse's head erased per pale arg. and az., charged with a trefoil slipped counterchanged. *Nulla dies sine linea.* 50. 6

Williams, a paschal lamb ppr. *Y ddiodde fws y orfu.* 131. 2

Williams, a lion's gamb couped arg. cf. 36. 4

Williams, a garb in fess. 153. 6

Williams, Bart. (*extinct*), out of a mural coronet or, a tilting-spear surmounted by a sword saltirewise, and encircled by a wreath of laurel ppr., and upon an escroll above the word *Kars.*

Williams, Devonsh., a chaplet gu.

Williams, Wales, a fox's head erased gu. 33. 6

Williams, Sir William Grenville, Bart., of Bodelwyddan, Rhuddlan, R.S.O., same crest. *Y cadarn ar cyrfwys.* 33. 6

Williams of Barfield, Berks, and Thame, Oxon., a fish-weir.

Williams, a savage's head affrontée, bearded ppr. 190. 12

Williams, Hon. Henry, J.P., of Pakaraka, Kawakawa, Bay of Islands, Auckland, New Zealand, member of the Legislative Council and Chairman of the Bay of Islands County Council, *uses:* a Saracen's head affrontée, couped at the shoulders ppr., and wreathed round the temples. *A fynno duw fydd.* 190. 5

Williams, out of a ducal coronet a hand holding a sword in pale, the blade wavy ppr. 212. 1

Williams, Rev. Charles Eccles Edmund, Summerfields, Oxford, three arrows, one in pale and two in saltire or, barbed and flighted ppr., between two wings arg., each charged with an annulet az. *Fidus in finem.* 252. 2

Williams of Cowley Grove and the Lodge, Hillingdon, Middx., a cubit arm vested or, charged with a pile sa., thereon three spear-heads arg., cuffed, also arg., the hand holding an oak-branch fructed and slipped ppr. *Deo adjuvante, non timendum.*

Williams, Hon. Joshua Strange, Anderson's Bay, Dunedin, Otago, New Zealand, same crest and motto.

Williams, a cubit arm erect vested sa., charged with a cross crosslet or, cuffed of the same, holding in the hand two oak-sprigs in saltier ppr., fructed of the second, on the hand a Cornish chough statant ppr. cf. 205. 6

Williams, Edward Wilmot, J.P., D.L., of Herringston, Dorset, a man's arm couped at the elbow, vested sa., charged with a cross patée or, the hand ppr., holding an oak-branch vert, fructed of the second. *Nil solidum.*

Williams, Arthur Scott, J.P., M.A., Hill House, Yetminster, Dorset, same crest.

Williams, Herbert Scott, Rothesay House, Dorchester, same crest.

Williams, Robert Hamilton, Esquire, Buckland, East Tilbury, Essex, same crest.

Williams, Montagu Scott, Woolland House, Blandford, Dorset, same crest.

Williams, Montague Scott, J.P., Woolland House, Bradford, Dorset, same crest.

Williams, Colonel Robert, M.P., J.P., of Bridehead, Dorchester, 1, Hyde Park Street, W., the arm of a man, the hand brawny, the sleeve barred with four pieces of sable and arg., having on it a crosslet in form interchanged between four bezants, holding in his hand a branch of oak vert, the acorns or.

Williams, an arm vested arg., cuffed sa., charged with a cross patée az., between four bezants, holding in the hand ppr. an oak-branch leaved vert, fructed or.

Williams of Aswarby, Lincs, a cubit arm erect vested erm., cuffed arg., the hand ppr., holding erect a long cross gu.

Williams, an arm embowed vested sa., holding in the hand ppr. three laurel-sprigs vert.

Williams, Bart. (*extinct*), of Eltham, Kent, a tower arg., out of the battlements an arm in mail embowed, holding in the hand a broken lance point downwards embrued ppr. *Virtus incumbet honori.*

Williams of Helton and Whitelavington, Dorset and Oxon., a cubit arm erect vested sa., charged with a cross formée or, between four bezants cuffed, also or, holding in the hand ppr. an acorn-branch vert, fructed of the second.

Williams, a cubit arm erect habited sa., charged with a cross crosslet or, cuffed of the last, the hand holding two sprigs of oak in saltire ppr., fructed or, and on the hand a Cornish chough statant ppr.

Williams of Plasgwyn, Llanedwen, Llanidan, Anglesey, upon a rock two chaplets of oak interlaced and fructed, all ppr. *Tangnefew i'rty.*

Williams, P. Victor, Hinstock Hall, Market Drayton, a bull's head erased at the neck pean, armed or, holding in the mouth a spear, the staff broken ppr. *Cwella angau na cywillydd.*

Williams of the Chestnuts, Torrington Park, North Finchley, a cubit arm erect, vested arg., cuffed sa., holding in the hand ppr., an oak branch fructed and leaved, also ppr. *Byw yr ydwyf trwy ffydd*

Williams, Jones-, Howel Richard, Esquire, Cui Parc, Talybont-on-Usk, R.S.O., Breconsh., a wolf's head erased, holding in the mouth a dexter hand couped at the wrist. *Ar Duw y Gyd.*

Williamson of Mount Vernon, near Liverpool, Lancs, a demi-eagle displayed or, holding in the beak a trefoil slipped sa. *Murus æneus conscientia sana.* cf. 81. 6

Williamson, Baron Ashton, of Ryelands, Lancaster, and Alford House, Prince's Gate, London, S.W., a demi-eagle displayed or, guttée-de-poix, each wing charged with a fesse, and holding in the beak two trefoils in saltire sa. *Murus æneus conscientia sana.* 81. 8

Williamson, a lion's head ducally crowned between two ostrich-feathers.

Williamson, a buck's head erased az., attired arg., charged on the neck with the sun or. 121. 14

Williamson of Peckham, Surrey, a buck's head couped sa., attired or, charged on the neck with a sun in splendour ppr., and between the attires a trefoil slipped, also sa. *Constare in sententia.* cf. 121. 14

Williamson, out of a mural coronet a dragon's head vomiting flames of fire. cf. 72. 3

Williamson of Gainsborough, Lincs, and Great Markham, Notts, out of a ducal coronet gu., a dragon's head with wings addorsed or. 72. 1

Williamson, Middx., and Denford, Northamp., out of a ducal coronet gu., a demi-wyvern with wings addorsed or.

Williamson, Notts, out of a ducal coronet gu., a dragon's head or. 72. 4

Williamson, Sir Hedworth, Bart., D.L., of East Markham, Notts, out of a mural coronet gu., a demi-wyvern or. 261. 1

Williamson, Durh., Oxon., and Yorks: (1) Out of a ducal coronet or, a griffin's head gu. 67. 9. (2) Out of a mural coronet gu., a demi-dragon arg., collared of the first. *Et patribus et posteritate.*

Williamson of Burton, Notts, out of a mural coronet gu., a demi-griffin segreant or. cf. 64. 2

Williamson of Hutchinfield, Scotland, a garb in fess unbound ppr. *Modice augetur modicum.*

Williamson of Keswick, Cumb., a falcon's head or, between two wings az., each wing charged with a sun in splendour of the first. cf. 89. 1

Williamson, Robert Cochrane, Esquire, 6, Moray Place, Edinburgh, a garb lying on its side unbound ppr. *Modicum modice erit magnum.*

Williamson, William Hopper, Stockburn Hall, Darlington, a tower, triple-towered arg., masoned sa.

Williamson, Andrew, Esquire, formerly of 15, Moray Place, Edinburgh, a wapiti deer's head erased ppr. *Persevere.* 229. 12

Williamson of Lawers, Perth, a hand holding a dagger erect. *In defence.* 212. 9

Williamson, Robertson-, of Balgray, Dumfriessh., a dexter hand holding a dagger erect ppr. *In defence.* 212. 9

Williamson, Robertson-, David, Lawers House, Cumrie, Perthsh., same crest and motto.

Williamson, John, Esquire, Ayrsh., a dexter hand gauntleted holding a broken sword ppr., hilted and pommelled or. *God my hope.*

Williamson, W. H., Esquire, D.L., of Celia Villa, New Cross Gate, London, S.E., a dexter arm embowed ppr., holding in the hand a flagstaff in bend sinister, therefrom pendent a banner arg., charged with a cross gu. *Deo et labore.*

Williamson of Banniskirk, Caithness-sh., a ship under sail in the sea ppr. *Dominus providebit.* 160. 13

Willimot, a demi-leopard gardant ppr.

Willingham, a demi-savage wreathed about the temples and loins with laurel-leaves, all ppr. 186. 1

Willington, Warw., a pine-tree ppr. 144. 13

Willington of Castle Willington, Nenagh, co. Tipperary, a mountain-pine vert, fructed or. *Vigueur de dessus.* 144. 13

Willington of Killoskehane Castle, co. Tipperary, Ireland, same crest and motto. 144. 13

Willington of Umberleigh, Devonsh., and Whateley and Tamworth, Warw., same crest. 144. 13

Willis, Henry Rodolph D'Anyers, of Halsnead Park, Lancs, two lion's gambs erect and erased holding a human heart gu. *Virtus tutissima cassis.*

Willis of Fen Ditton, Cambs, and Horingsley and Bales, Herts, two lion's gambs erased, the dexter arg., the sinister gu., supporting an escutcheon or.

Willis, General Sir George Harry Smith, G.C.B., Stretham Manor, Cambridge, and 118, Eaton Square, London, W.: (1) Two lion's gambs erased ppr., supporting an escutcheon or. (2) A reindeer's head.

Willis-Bund, John Willis, of Wick Episcopi, Worcs.: (1) An eagle's head erased or (*for Bund*). 83. 2. (2) Two lion's gambs erect and erased, the dexter arg., the sinister gu., supporting an escutcheon or (*for Willis*).

Willis of London, a hind trippant ppr., holding in the mouth an oak-branch arg., fructed or, charged on the shoulder with a cross formée of the last.

Willis of London, a hind trippant ppr., holding in the mouth an oak-branch vert, fructed or, charged on the shoulder with a mullet of the last.

Willis of Bewdley, Worcs., a hind trippant ppr., charged on the shoulder with a mullet or, holding in the mouth an oak-branch vert, fructed of the second.

Willis, on a chapeau gu., turned up erm., a unicorn's head couped arg., ducally gorged or.

Willis of Hungerford Park, Berks, a falcon with wings expanded ppr., belled or. 87. 1

Willison, out of a crescent or, flames of fire issuing ppr. 163. 12

Willmott, an eagle's head arg., gorged with a collar engrailed az., holding in the beak an escallop gu.

Willmott, a demi-leopard rampant gardant arg., spotted with hurts and torteaux, holding in the paws an oak-branch fructed or.

Willmott of Littlecomb and Charleton, Wantage, Berks, a demi-panther rampant gardant ppr., holding a battle-axe or.

Willmott, Oxon., a demi-leopard rampant arg., spotted with hurts and torteaux, holding an acorn-branch vert, fructed or.

Willmott, Henry, Esquire, late of Cheltenham, Glouc., a demi-lion gardant sa., gorged with a collar pendent, therefrom an escutcheon or, resting the sinister paw on an escutcheon, also or, charged with a Passion-cross gu. *Migremus hinc.* 14. 11

Willmott, a dexter hand holding a palm-branch ppr. 219. 11

Willmott of Sherborne House, Dorset, a dragon's head erased ppr., gorged with a collar gemel or, in front of a garb fessewise of the last. *Aide toi et le ciel t'aidera.*

Willock, a demi-lion rampant az., holding in the paws a spear inverted gu.

Willoughby, *see* Middleton, Baron.

Willoughby De Eresby, Baron, Earl of Ancaster, and **Baron Aveland** of Aveland, Lincs (Rt. Hon. Gilbert Henry Heathcote-Drummond-Willoughby, P.C.): (1) A Saracen's head affrontée, couped at the shoulders ppr., ducally crowned or (*for Willoughby*). 192. 9. (2) On a ducal coronet or, a sleuth-hound arg., collared and leashed gu. (*for Drummond*). 54. 9. (3) On a mural coronet az., a pomeis charged with a cross or, between two wings displayed erm. (*for Heathcote*). *Loyauté me oblige.*

Willoughby de Broke, Baron (Verney), Compton Verney, Stratford-on-Avon: (1) A man's head couped at the shoulders and affrontée ppr., ducally crowned or. 192. 9. (2) A demi-bear couped sa., muzzled and collared, and holding between the paws a mascle or. *Vertue vaunceth.*

Willoughby, Sir John Christopher, Bart., of Baldon House, Oxon., a Saracen's head affrontée, couped at the shoulders ppr., ducally crowned or. *Verité sans peur.* 192. 9

Willoughby, a man's head affrontée couped at the shoulders ppr., ducally crowned or. 192. 9

Willoughby, Sidney Beaumont, same crest.

Willoughby, Notts, an owl arg. 96. 5

Willoughby, Derbysh., Notts, Northamp., and Staffs, an owl arg., ducally crowned, collared, chained, beaked, and legged or.

Willoughby, Bart. (*extinct*), an owl arg., beaked, legged, and crowned or. cf. 96. 5

Willoughby of Wollaton, Notts, a griffin arg. 63. 8

Willoughby, Ireland, a lion's head couped at the shoulders gardant or, gorged with a label of three points sa., and charged on the breast with a mullet gu., all between two wings expanded of the first, fretty az.

Willoughby, J., Esquire, Riversdale, Goring-on-Thames, Oxon., a Saracen's head affrontée, couped at the shoulders ppr., ducally crowned or. *Vérité sans peur.*

Willoughby of Roseneath, Goring-on-Thames, Berks, a Saracens head affrontée, couped at the shoulders ppr., ducally crowned or. *Vérité sans peur.*

Wills, Ireland, a harp or. 168. 9

Wills, Sir Frederick, Bart., M.P., Manor Heath, Bournemouth, issuant from an annulet or, a demi-griffin gu., charged with a sun in splendour, and holding in the dexter claw a battle-axe, also or. *Quo lux ducit.* 305. 12

Wills, Sir William Henry, Bart., of Blagdon, Somers., same crest. *As God wills.*

Wills, Hon. Sir Alfred, Saxholm Bassett, Hants, upon a sword resting upon the hilt and point an eagle, and pendent from its neck by a ribbon an escutcheon charged with a balance. *Supra nives et rupes.*

Wills, a demi-gryphon az., gorged with a collar gemelle arg., holding in the dexter claw a battle-axe erect ppr., and resting the sinister on an escutcheon of the second charged with a quatrefoil vert. *Sursum.*

Wills, a demi-griffin salient holding between the claws a battle-axe. *cf.* 64. 11

Wills of Landrake, Cornw., a demi-griffin with wings endorsed az., holding with both claws a battle-axe ppr. *Sursum.*

Wills, a demi-griffin segreant az., murally gorged or, sustaining a battle-axe ppr. *Meruisse manu.*

Wills, Sandford-, of Willsgrove and Castlerea, co. Roscommon, Ireland: (1) Out of a ducal coronet a boar's head and neck or, langued gu. (*for Sandford*). 41. 4. (2) A demi-griffin segreant sa., holding between the claws a battle-axe ppr. (*for Wills*). *Cor unum via una.*

Wills-Sandford, Arthur Pakenham, the Priory House, Sherborne, Dorset, same crests and motto.

Willsher, the descendants of the late George Willsher, Esquire, on a chapeau gu., doubled erm., an eagle's leg erased at the thigh or. *Fortiter sed suaviter.*

Willshire, Sir Arthur Reginald Thomas, Bart., 77, Belgrave Road, S.W., a Caffre holding in the dexter hand an assegai in bend sinister, point downwards, and supporting with the sinister three assegais, points upwards, all ppr. *Khelat.—Caffraria.* 311. 1

Willson, a cannon sa., the stock or. 169. 12

Willson of Charlton-Kings and Stroud, Glouc., a wolf's head erased erminois, collared sa., charged with three mullets arg. *cf.* 30. 11

Willson, a wolf's head erased erminois, gorged with a collar sa., thereon three mullets arg. *Ego de meo sensu judico.* *cf.* 30. 11

Willson of Dulwich, Surrey, a demi-wolf rampant sa., gorged with a collar dancettée and chained or, and holding between the paws a branch of the walnut-tree ppr. *Perseverantia palma.*

Willy or **Willey,** a dexter hand holding a battle-axe ppr. 213. 12

Willyams, Edward William Brydges, of Carnanton, Cornw., on a ducal coronet a falcon close ppr., belled or. *In Domino confido.—Meor ras tha Dew.* 85. 9

Willyams, Cornw., on a ducal coronet or, a falcon close ppr. 85. 9

Willymot of Kellshull, Heref., on a chapeau sa., turned up or, an eagle displayed arg., winged of the second, membered and beaked gu. *cf.* 75. 2

Wilmer, Northamp., and Rayton, Warw., an eagle's head or, between two wings expanded vair. 84. 2

Wilmot-Chetwode, *see* Chetwode.

Wilmot, a porteullis az., chained or. 187. 3

Wilmot, out of a mural coronet an eagle's head. 83. 9

Wilmot, Eardley-, Bart., of Berkswell Hall, Warw.: (1) An eagle's head couped arg., holding in the beak an escallop gu. (*for Wilmot*). (2) A buck courant gu., attired and ungu. or (*for Eardley*). *cf.* 118. 13

Wilmot, Sir Ralph Henry Sacheverel, Bart., of Chaddesden, Derbysh., an eagle's head couped arg., gorged with a mural coronet sa., holding in the beak an escallop gu.

Wilmot, Sir Robert Rodney, Bart., D.L., of Osmaston, Derbysh., an eagle's head couped arg., gorged with a collar engrailed az., holding in the beak or an escallop gu. *Quod vult, valde vult.*

Wilmot-Horton, Bart., of Osmaston and Catton, Derbysh.: (1) Issuing out of waves of the sea ppr., a tilting-spear erect or, headed and enfiled with a dolphin arg., finned, also or (*for Horton*). 140. 10. (2) An eagle's head couped arg., gorged with a collar engrailed az., holding in the beak an escallop gu. (*for Wilmot*).

Wilmot of Stodham and Chiselhampton, Oxon., a demi-leopard rampant arg., spotted with hurts and torteaux, holding in the dexter paw an acorn-branch vert, fructed or.

Wilmot, Shropsh., a unicorn couchant or.

Wilney, a lion's gamb erect. *cf.* 36. 4

Wilsey, a demi-griffin with wings elevated, holding in the claws a garland.

Wilsford, Kent, a leopard's face per pale or and gu. 22. 2

Wilshere, Herts, a cup or. 177. 4

Wilshere of Hitchin, Herts, a lion rampant gu., maned ppr. 1. 13

Wilshere of the Forsythe, Herts, a lion rampant gu. *Fidelis.* 1. 13

Wilson-Patten, *see* Winmarleigh, Baron.

Wilson, Sir Alexander, Bart., Archer House, Ecclesall, Yorks, a demi-lion gu., charged on the shoulder with a mullet of six points arg. *Semper vigilans.*

Wilson, Arthur Maitland, of Stowlangtoft Hall, Suff., a demi-wolf or, the sinister paw resting on a pellet, charged with a fleur-de-lis of the first. *Wil sone wil.*

Wilson, Thomas, B.A., Rivers Lodge, Harpenden, same crest. *Vouloir ce que Dieu veut.*

Wilson, Charles Henry, Esquire, M.P., of Warter Priory, Pocklington, Yorks, and of 41, Grosvenor Square, London, a demi-wolf rampant. *Pro legibus et Regibus.* 31. 2

Wilson, Allan Bowes, J.P., Manor House, Hutton Rudby, Yarm, Yorks, same crest. *Res non verba.*

Wilson, George Orr, Danardagh, Blackrock, Dublin, same crest and motto.

Wilson, Lieutenant-General the late Sir Robert, out of a marquess's coronet or, jewelled ppr., a demi-wolf holding between the paws a crescent sa.

Wilson, James, Esquire, J.P., D.L., of Currygrane, Edgeworthstown, Longford, Ireland, a demi-wolf rampant or. *Res non verba.* 31. 2

Wilson, Maryon-, Sir Spencer Pocklington Maryon, Bart., Charlton House, Charlton, Kent, a demi-wolf or. *Pro legibus ac regibus.*

Wilson of Flatt, Northumb., a demi-wolf rampant per fess erm. and erminois. 31. 2

Wilson, Herts, a demi-wolf or, charged with a crescent. *cf.* 31. 2

Wilson, Northumb., Sussex, Lincs, and Yorks, a demi-wolf salient or. *Res non verba.* 31. 2

Wilson, Robert Mackay, J.P., Coolcarrigan, co. Kildare, a demi-wolf rampant per pale indented arg. and az. *Pollet virtus.*

Wilson, Edward Shinells, the Grange, Melton, Brough, East Riding, Yorks, in front of a demi-wolf sa. gorged with a collar gemel a fasces arg. 253. 6

Wilson, Berks, Yorks, and London, a demi-wolf salient or. *Res non verba.—Pro legibus ac Regibus.* 31. 2

Wilson of Waldershaigh, Bolsterstone, Sheffield, same crest. *Vincit qui se vincit.*

Wilson of High Wray, Lancs, and Abbot Hall, Westml., a demi-wolf rampant vert. 31. 2

Wilson, Fountayne-, of Melton Hall, Yorks: (1) A demi-wolf sa., holding an escutcheon (*for Wilson*). (2) On a mount an elephant, all ppr. (*for Fountayne*). *cf.* 133. 9

Wilson of Ives Place, Maidenhead, Berks, a demi-wolf rampant or. *Pro legibus ac Regibus.—Res non verba.* 31. 2

Wilson, Colonel Christopher Wyndham, J.P., D.L., of Rigmaden Park, Kirkby Lonsdale, same crest and first motto.

Wilson, Sir Mathew Wharton, Bart., J.P., D.L., of Eshton Hall, Yorks, a demi-wolf or, gorged with a collar gemel sa., resting the sinister paw on an escutcheon of the last, charged with a mullet of six points of the first. *Res non verba.—Loyal en tout.* 308. 5

Wilson of Western Bank, Sheffield, Yorks, a demi-wolf ppr., charged on the shoulder with an estoile az., and holding between the paws a bugle-horn sa., garnished and stringed or. *Vincit qui se vincit.*

Wilson, Thomas Needham, Oak Lodge, Bitterne, near Southampton, a demi-wolf holding an estoile, all or. *Pro legibus ac Regibus.*

Wilson of Rivington Hall, Lancs, a demi-wolf or. 31. 2

Wilson, Frank, Esquire, J.P., of Ulva, Onslow Villas, Highgate, N., a demi-wolf. *Res non verba.*

Wilson, Rev. Canon James Allen, M.A., J.P., Bolton Rectory, Clitheroe, a demi-wolf rampant or. *Vincit qui se vincit.*

Wilson, John, Esquire, M.P., J.P., Perrycroft, Colwall, Heref., a demi-wolf rampant ppr. *Res non verba.*

Wilson, Robert, Esquire, J.P., of Broughton Grange, Cockermouth, same crest and motto.

Wilson, Thomas Newby, the Landing, Lakeside, Ulverston, a demi-wolf rampant per chevron sa. and arg., holding in the dexter paw a mullet of six points arg., and resting the sinister on a trefoil slipped sa. *Fide sed cui vide.*

Wilson, Thomas Needham, 5, Clarence Terrace, Regent's Park, a demi-wolf holding an estoile, all or.

Wilson of Elsbrock, in the Netherlands, and of Gloucester Square, Hyde Park, London, W., a demi-wolf or, semée of horse-shoes sa., holding between the paws an estoile of the first. *Pro legibus ac Regibus.*

Wilson of Brinckliffe Tower, Yorks, a demi-wolf rampant or. *Vincit qui se vincit.* 31. 2

Wilson, James, Esquire, of Greek Street, Soho, a demi-wolf or, gorged with a collar gemel vert, holding in the dexter fore-paw a branch of oak fructed ppr.

Wilson, Ireland, a demi-wolf salient vert. *Aviumque volatus.* 31. 2

Wilson of Dublin, a demi-wolf per fesse or and gu. *Semper vigilans.* 31. 2

Wilson, Henry Smithson Lee, Crofton Hall, Wakefield, a demi-wolf or, charged on the breast with a chapeau, the front to the sinister az. *Res non verba.*

Wilson, Rev. Joseph Bowstead, Knightwick Rectory, Worcester, same crest as Sir Jacob Wilson, charged with a crescent for difference.

Wilson-Barkworth, Arthur Bromby, the Elms, Kirkella, Hull: (1) A demi-lion arg., holding in the dexter paw a clarion, and resting the sinister on an estoile, both gu. 253. 5. (2) In front of a demi-wolf sa., gorged with a collar gemel, a fasces arg. *Esto quod esse videris.* 253. 6

Wilson, Scotland, a wolf salient or. *Expecta cuncta superne.*

Wilson of Fingach, Scotland, a wolf sejant or. *Expecta cuncta superne.*

Wilson of Knowle Hall, Warw., a wolf's head or. *Fortiter et fideliter.* 30. 5

Wilson, a lion's gamb erect and erased. 36. 4

Wilson, John Gerald, C.B., of Cliffe Hall, Durh., and Seacroft, Yorks, on a mount vert, a lion's gamb erased fesseways arg., thereon a lion's head couped erminois. 258. 2

Wilson, Darcy Bruce, Seacroft Hall, Leeds, same crest.

Wilson-Fitzgerald, William Henry, of Chacombe, Banbury: (1) A boar passant gu., bristled and armed or, charged with a saltire of the last (*for Fitzgerald*). 258. 1. (2) On a mount vert, in front of a lion's head erminois, a lion's gamb fesseways arg. (*for Wilson*). *Shannet a boo.* 258. 2

Wilson, Hon. Andrew Heron, of Doon Villa, Maryborough, Queensland, member of the Legislative Council of Queensland, a lion rampant. *Semper vigilans.* 1. 13

Wilson, a lion rampant gu. *Semper vigilans.* 1. 13

Wilson of Penrith, Cumb., and Welborne, Lincs, a lion's head arg., guttée-de-sang. *cf.* 21. 1

Wilson, Captain William Henry, on a wreath of the colours, out of a mural coronet or, a demi-lion rampant gu., holding in the dexter paw a trefoil, also or. *Semper vigilans.*

Wilson of Plewlands, Scotland, a demi-lion gu. *Semper vigilans.* 10. 3

Wilson, Walter Henry, Maryville, near Belfast, a demi-lion rampant gu. *Semper vigilans.*

Wilson, Sir Samuel, D.L., M.P., of Ercildoun, Anakie, Victoria, of 9, Grosvenor Square, London, and of Hughenden Manor, Bucks, a demi-lion or, charged on the shoulder with an estoile gu., and resting the sinister paw upon an escutcheon per pale sa. and gu., thereon a wolf's head erased, also or. *Semper vigilans.* 252. 1

Wilson, Captain Gordon Chesney, M.V.O., Brookby Hall, Leicester, same crest and motto.

Wilson, Wilfrid, same crest and motto.

Wilson-Todd, William Henry, of Halnaby Hall and Tranby Park, Yorks: (1) On the trunk of an oak-tree fesseways a fox sejant ppr., collared or (*for Todd*). (2) Out of a mural coronet or, a demi-lion rampant gu., holding in the dexter paw a trefoil slipped, also or, with the motto over, *Semper vigilans* (*for Wilson*). *Oportet vivere.*

Wilson of Cumberland Terrace, Regent's Park, Middx., Greenwich, Kent, and of Molesworth House, Brighton, Sussex, a demi-lion gu., holding between the paws an escutcheon arg., charged with a cart-wheel gu., and holding in the mouth three cinquefoils slipped vert.

Wilson of Banner Cross, Eccleshall, Yorks, issuant from flames ppr. a demi-lion az., gorged with a collar gemel, and holding in the dexter paw a mullet, both arg.

Wilson, John, Esquire, J.P., D.L., Hillhead House, Glasgow, a demi-lion rampant holding between the paws a lozenge charged with a crescent. *Semper vigilans.*

Wilson-Haffenden, John: (1) A gryphon's head erased sa., pendent from the beak an escutcheon arg., charged with a mullet sa. (2) A demi-wolf or, guttée-de-sang, holding between the paws a cross patée gu.

Wilson-Slater, Henry Bevan, White Hill, Edgeworthstown, a lion passant per pale gu. and sa., holding in the dexter paw a trefoil slipped vert. *Garde la loi.*

Wilson of Scarr and Sledagh, co. Wexford, out of a mural coronet or, a demi-lion rampant gu., holding in the dexter paw a trefoil of the first. *Semper vigilans.*

Wilson of Kelton, Kirkcudbrightsh., Scotland, an anchor cabled and surmounted by a star ppr. *Pro Deo et libertate.*

Wilson, a crescent or, flammant ppr. 163. 12

Wilson of Dallam Tower, Westml., same crest.

Wilson, Bromley-, Maurice, Dallam Tower, Milnthorpe: (1) A crescent or, therefrom issuing flames of fire ppr. (2) A pheasant sitting ppr.

Wilson of Stratford-le-Bow, Middx., on a cloud ppr., a crescent gu., issuing fire ppr.

Wilson, a globe inflamed at the top ppr.

Wilson, William Wright, Esquire, F.R.C.S., Cottesbrook House, Acock's Green, near Birmingham, an eagle displayed sa., langued gu. *Semper vigilans.*

Wilson, Ireland, a water-bouget or. 168. 4

Wilson, an eagle displayed sa. 75. 2

Wilson of Glenderston, Renfrewsh., Scotland, a negro's head ppr., collared arg. *I will, who will not.—Non dormit qui custodit.*

Wilson of Soonhope and Edinburgh, Scotland, a dexter hand holding a pen ppr. *Virtute et labore.* 217. 10

Wilson, James, Esquire, of Glasgow, a talbot's head erased or. *Semper vigilans.* 56. 2

Wilson, Scotland, a talbot's head erased arg. *Semper vigilans.* 56. 2

Wilson, John, Esquire, K.C., of 9, Drumsheugh Gardens, Edinburgh, a talbot's head erased gu., collared arg. *Semper vigilans.* 276. 14

Wilson of West Wickham, Kent, a talbot's head erased ppr. *Semper vigilans.* 56. 2

Wilson of Sneaton Castle, Yorks, a talbot's head erased az., charged on the neck with three ingots of gold in fess crossed by another in bend ppr.

Wilson of Queensferry, Scotland, a talbot's head erased arg. *Expecta cuncta superne.* 56. 2

Wilson, William Shepley, Tunbridge Wells, an oak-tree eradicated ppr., fructed or. *Virtus sibi premium.*

Wilsone, Charles Ranald, Campfield, Glassel R.S.O., Aberdeensh., a talbot's head erased arg., langued gu. *Semper vigilans.*

Wilsone of Glasgow, a talbot's head ppr. *Semper vigilans.*

Wilton, Earl of (Egerton), Heaton Park, near Manchester, three arrows, points downwards, one in pale and two in saltire, or, headed and feathered sa., tied together with a ribbon gu. *Virtuti, non armis fido.* 173. 1

Wilton, Glouc., issuing from an Earl's coronet a griffin's head, holding an arrow in its beak and vulned in the chest with the same. *Vincit qui se vincit.*

Wilton of London, an owl ppr. *Lux in tenebris.* 96. 5

Wilton of Snaresbrook, Essex, an owl ppr., gorged with a collar or, affixed thereto by a ribbon az. a perpendicular gold line and a plumb sa.

Wilton, Wilts, an arm in armour embowed, holding in the hand a dagger ppr., hilt and pommel or. 196. 5

Wilton, a dexter arm holding in the hand a bludgeon ppr. 214. 6

Wiltshire, a horse's head erased and bridled ppr. *cf.* 51. 5

Wiltshire, Middx., a cross patée or. 165. 7

Wimberley of Bitchfield and Spalding, Lincs, a buck's head ppr., attired or issuing from a garland of bay-leaves of the first.

Wimble of the Friars, Lewes, Sussex, a demi-lion chequy or and az. supporting with the paws an antique shield gu., thereon the chemical character of Mars of the first.

Wimbolt, a dagger erect ppr. 169. 2

Wimborne, Baron (Guest), of Canford Magna, Dorset, a swan's head erased ppr., gorged with a collar or, and charged below with a cross moline sa. between two ostrich-feathers or. *Ferre non gladio.* 101. 1

Wimbush, a friar vested in a russet gown, his paternoster, etc., all ppr., supporting himself on a crotch.

Wimpey, an arm in armour holding in the gauntlet a dagger ppr.

Winall, on a mural coronet gu., a mullet or.

Winans, *see* Wynants.

Winbolt, a dexter arm embowed, habited gu., slashed arg., holding in the hand ppr. a falcon of the second belled or, all between two wings sa.

Winch or **Winche** of Hannes, Beds, a dexter hand holding a spear, all ppr. 214. 11

Winch, out of a ducal coronet or, a lion's head affrontée arg., between two spears of the first headed ppr.

Winch, Ireland, an escallop or. 141. 12

Winch, George, Holcombe, Chatham, Kent, an escallop or, charged on the breast with an escallop, and holding in each claw a rose gu., leaved and slipped ppr. *Vive ut vivas.* 269. 3

Winchester, Marquess of (Paulet), Amport St. Mary's, Andover, a falcon with wings expanded or, belled of the same, and gorged with a ducal coronet gu. *Aymez loyaulté.* 87. 2

Winchester, Scotland, a hand holding a cluster of grapes ppr. *Hoc ardua vincere docet.* 219. 6

Winchester of London, and of Oakfield Lodge, Hawkhurst, Kent, in front of a cross crosslet fitched or, a lion passant az., the dexter fore-paw supporting a mascle gu., and pendent from the mouth a double chain of the first.

Winchilsea, Earl of, (Finch-Hatton): (1) A fawn trippant or (*for Hatton*). (2) A griffin passant sa. (*for Finch*). 62. 2. *Je responderay.* cf. 47. 1

Winckworth, a cinquefoil ppr. 148. 12

Wincold and **Wincoll,** Leics., and of Waldingfield, Suff., an arm in armour embowed, couped at the shoulder erect from the elbow ppr., garnished or, holding in the hand, also ppr., a spear also or, headed arg.

Winde, Norf., a griffin's head erased gu. 66. 2

Winder, a dexter hand throwing a dart ppr. 214. 4

Winder, Cumb., out of a ducal coronet or a bull's head erm., holding in the mouth a cherry-branch slipped and fructed, all ppr.

Winder, Corbett-, William Corbet, of Vaynol Park, Montgomerysh.: (1) A vallary coronet or, therefrom issuant a buffalo's head sa., armed of the first, holding in the mouth a branch of cherry-tree fructed ppr., the neck charged for distinction with a cross crosslet of the first (*for Winder*). (2) A raven ppr., holding in the beak a holly-branch slipped ppr. (*for Corbett*). *Nulla pallescere culpa.*

Windeyer, Hon. William Charles, M.A., LL.D., of Lulworth, Boslyn Gardens, Sydney, and of Tomago, Hunter River, New South Wales, Australia, *uses:* an apple ppr.

Windham of Fellbrig Hall, Norf., a lion's head erased within a fetterlock or, the bow compony-counter-compony of the first and az. *Au bon droit.*

Windham, Charles, same crest and motto.

Windham, John, same crest and motto.

Windham, Reginald, same crest and motto.

Windle, a stag's head cabossed ppr. 122. 5

Windle, Bertram C. A., M.D., F.S.A., F.R.S., the University, Birmingham, a stag's head caboshed ppr. between two crosses patée or. *Non omnis moriar.* 266. 5

Windley, Rev. Francis, of Dethick-Lea, Derbysh., in front of a wolf's head erased or, gorged with a collar nebuly az. three fleurs-de-lis, also az. *Stat sua cuique dies.* 273. 4

Windlove, Winlove, and **Windlowe,** a bunch of leaves vert, enfiled by a ducal coronet or.

Windoute, Herts, a cubit arm vested arg., gloved gu., the hand holding a falcon ppr., beaked and belled or, the whole between two wings of the third.

Windoute or **Windowche** of Radiswell, Herts, a cubit arm erect vested arg., gloved gu., between two wings ppr., holding a falcon, also ppr., beaked and belled or.

Windover of London, a cubit arm vested gu., cuffed arg., holding in the hand ppr. three nails or, all between two wings arg. *Labor omnia vincit.* 207. 9

Window, Glouc., a lion's gamb erect and erased az., holding a cross crosslet fitched or. cf. 36. 11

Windsor, Baron (Windsor-Clive), Hewell Grange, Redditch, Worcs.: (1) A griffin passant arg., ducally gorged gu. (*for Clive*). 63. 2. (2) A buck's head affrontée, couped at the neck arg., attired or (*for Windsor*). *Je me fie en Dieu.* 119. 12

Windsor, Berks and Warw., a stag's head affrontée, couped at the neck arg. 119. 12

Windsor, a sheaf of seven arrows enfiled by a ducal coronet, all ppr. cf. 173. 9

Windus, on a ducal coronet or, a serpent entwining a sheaf of arrows ppr. 173. 2

Winford, a dexter hand holding a sheaf of arrows, all ppr. 214. 3

Winford, Bart. (*extinct*), Worcs., on a ducal coronet a Moor's head in profile erased ppr.

Wing, Rutl., between two wings or, a maunch per pale arg. and vert.

Wingam, out of a ducal coronet a broken halberd.

Wingate, Scotland, an arm in armour embowed, holding in the hand a scimitar ppr. *Suum cuique.* 106. 10

Wingate, on a rock a palm-tree ppr. *Per ardua surgo.* cf. 144. 3

Wingate of Harlington and Sharpenhoe, Beds, a gate or, with the motto over, *Win.*

Wingfield, *see* Powerscourt, Viscount.

Wingfield-Baker, *see* Baker.

Wingfield, Worcs., two wings elevated arg. 109. 6

Wingfield, a swan's neck or, with wings gu. 101. 6

Wingfield, an eagle rising with wings expanded arg., looking at the sun in splendour. *Fidelité est de Dieu.*

Wingfield, Anthony Henry, 11, Queen's Gardens, Hove, Sussex, a demi-eagle rising, wings expanded arg., looking at the sun in his glory. *Fidelité est de Dieu.*

Wingfield, Edward Rhys, same crest.

Wingfield, Ireland, a cap per pale ermines and arg., charged with a fess gu., between two wings, the dexter of the second, the sinister of the first.

Wingfield, Charles Humphrey, same crest.

Wingfield, Sir Edward, K.C.B., 40, Albion Street, W., same crest. *Posse, nolle, nobile.*

Wingfield, Godfrey Lee, same crest and motto.

Wingfield, Harry Robert Shaw, same crest and motto.

Wingfield, John Maurice, Tickencote Hall, Stamford, same crest and motto.

Wingfield of Tickencote, Rutl., a cap per pale sa., guttée-d'eau and arg., charged with a fess gu., between two wings, the dexter of the second, the sinister of the first. *Posse, nolle, nobile.*

Wingfield of Onslow, Shropsh., a high bonnet or cap per pale sa. and arg., between two wings all guttée counterchanged, on the cap a fess gu.

Wingfield, Bart. (*extinct*), of Letheringham, Suff., a cap per pale ermines and arg., charged with a fesse gu., between two wings expanded, the dexter of the second, the sinister of the first.

Wingham, a sword and a feather in saltier ppr. 170. 6

Wingoak, two oaks between wings.

Wingrove, a phœnix in flames ppr. 82. 2

Wingrove of the Grove, Worth, Sussex, on a Roman fasces lying fessewise a phœnix with wings expanded ppr., each wing charged with a cinquefoil or. *Fear God and dread nought.* 82. 8

Winlaw, Rev. George Preston Kelsall, the Rectory, Morden, Surrey, upon a hillock vert, three javelins, one in pale and two in saltire ppr., suspended therefrom by a ribbon or, an escutcheon sa. charged with an acorn leaved and slipped, also or. *What I win I keep.* 269. 10

Winmarleigh, Baron (Rt. Hon. the late John Wilson-Patten; *extinct*), of Winmarleigh, Lancs: (1) A griffin's head erased vert, beaked or (*for Patten*). 66. 2. (2) A demi-wolf rampant or (*for Wilson*). *Nulla pallescere culpa.*—*Virtus ad sidera tollit.* 31. 2

Winn, *see* St. Oswald, Baron.

Winn, *see* Headley, Lord.

Winn, Yorks, and London, a demi-eagle displayed or, ducally gorged erm. *Tout pour Dieu et ma patrie.* cf. 81. 2

Winn, Arthur T., Esquire, Aldeburgh, Suff., a demi-eagle displayed or, ducally gorged erm.

Winnington, Sir Francis Salwey, Bart., D.L., of Stanford Court, Worcs., a Saracen's head affrontée couped at the shoulders ppr., wreathed about the temples arg. and sa. *Grata sume manu.* [illegible]

Winnington, Chesh., a still arg.

Winsloe, a dragon passant with wings elevated, holding in the dexter claw a dagger in pale. *cf.* [illegible]

Winsor, Benyon-, of Greenwich, Denbighsh.: (1) A unicorn's head erased or, charged with an annulet between four cross crosslets az. (for *Winsor*). *cf.* [illegible] (2) A griffin sejant with wings elevated arg., holding in the beak a trefoil slipped vert, and resting the dexter claw upon an escutcheon arg., charged with a mullet sa. (for *Benyon*). *Je ne change qu'en mourant.*

Winspeare, a hand ppr. grasping a key with wards at either end or.

Winstanley, of Braunston House, Leics., a cockatrice displayed or, crested and wattled gu. [illegible]

Winstanley, William Alfred, Chaigeley Manor, Clitheroe, Lancaster, same crest. *Pro rege* [illegible].

Winstanley, of Winstanley, Lancs., an arm embowed vested gu., cuffed arg., holding in the hand ppr. a sword of the last, hilt and pommel or. [illegible]

Winstanton, a boar's head couped sa. [illegible]

Winston or **Winstone,** a dexter hand holding four arrows ppr. *cf.* [illegible]

Winstone, of Stapleton, Glouc., a garb erect or, sustained on the dexter side by a lion rampant arg., and on the sinister by another az. *cf.* [illegible]

Winter, of Agher, co. Meath, a martlet. [illegible]

Winter, Francis Pratt, C.M.G., Port Moresby, British New Guinea, a martlet or.

Winter, James Sanderson, M.A., Agher, Summerhill, co. Meath, a martlet or, charged with a crescent gu.

Winter, Leics., a hawk arg., holding in the dexter claw a fish erect or.

Winter, a demi-griffin gu., winged per pale arg. and az., gorged with a ducal coronet or, holding in the dexter claw a garb of the last.

Winter, of Dyrham, Glouc., Worcs., and Bermingham, Norf., a hind trippant arg., ducally gorged, lined, and ringed or. *cf.* [illegible]

Winter, of Canterbury, Kent, on a mount vert a hind gu., ducally gorged, lined, and charged on the shoulder with an annulet or.

Winter-Irving, Hon. William Irving, J.P., of Noorilim, Goulburn River, Moira, Victoria, Australia, member of the Legislative Council of Victoria: (1) A dexter cubit arm in armour, holding in the gauntlet a branch of holly consisting of seven leaves and fructed, all ppr. (motto over, *Haud ullis labentia ventis*) (for *Irving*). (2) A hind trippant arg., supporting with the sinister fore-foot a saltire gu., gorged with a collar [illegible] over the back sa., and charged on the body with two and all slipped of the last (for *Winter*). *Nil nisi* [illegible] *secus* [illegible].

Winter, Surrey, Glouc., and Worcs., a right arm erect vested or, holding in the hand ppr. three ostrich-feathers, the centre one sa., the others of the first.

Winterbotham, a demi-[illegible] rampant [illegible] per pale or and gu., [illegible] counterchanged. *Pro* [illegible] [illegible].

Winterbotham, Frederick, Esquire, of the Brushes, [illegible], on a ducal coronet a leopard's face. *Prorsum semper perseverans.*

Winterbottom, out of a mural coronet sa., a tower between two palm-branches [illegible] all ppr. [illegible]

Wintersells, a [illegible] arg. [illegible]

Winterton, Earl [illegible], Shillinglee Park, near Petworth, a lion passant guardant arg., [illegible] in the dexter paw a fleur-de-lis az. [illegible] [illegible]

Winthrop, on a mount vert a hare courant ppr. [illegible]

Winthrop, of Groton, Suff., on a mount vert a hare courant ppr. *Spes vincit thronum.* [illegible]

Wintle, two wings expanded ppr. [illegible]

Wintle, [illegible] within an annulet or, thereon perched a martlet az., an escallop arg. [illegible]

Winton, Earl of, see Eglinton, Earl of.

Winton, Scotland, a garb or. [illegible]

Wintoun, Scotland, a dove volant ppr. *cf.* [illegible]

Wintour, Hants and Worcs.: (1) A cock pheasant close ppr. (2) Out of a ducal coronet or a dexter arm in armour embowed ppr., garnished of the first, holding in the gauntlet three ostrich-feathers arg.

Wintringham, of London, a demi-lion rampant az. *Fortis cadere, non cedere.* [illegible]

Wintringham, Bart. (extinct), same crest. *Fortis cadere, non cedere.*—*Esse quam videri* [illegible] [illegible] *imperium.* [illegible]

Winwood, of Ditton Park and [illegible], Bucks., out of a ducal coronet or an eagle's head between two wings sa., holding in the beak a chaplet of laurel vert.

Winwood, Thomas Henry Rickards, Esquire, of Tyglyn Aeron, Cardiganshire, and Wellesford Manor, Wellington, Somerset, upon a mount vert, in front of an eagle's head erased sa., holding in the beak a wreath of laurel ppr., two wings saltirewise arg. *Mereri et* [illegible].

Winyard, a buck's head cabossed ppr. [illegible]

Winziet, Scotland, a tower arg., with a portcullis and flag gu. [illegible]

Wirdnam, of Charlton, Berks., a boar's head erased arg., crined or, between [illegible] sa., ringed and lined of the second. *cf.* [illegible]

Wire, Thomas Barton, of Elstree, Lymington, Hants, son of H.M. Lieutenant [illegible] for the [illegible] of [illegible], a demi-[illegible] horse [illegible] sa. and arg., [illegible] [illegible] the face and mane [illegible] vested, holding in the dexter hand two arrows in saltire points downwards, and resting the sinister hand on a trefoil slipped, and in front of the man a fleur-de-lis, all or. *Sapit qui Deo sapit.* 274. 3

Wiseman, issuing out of a tower a demi-man armed in mail ppr., holding in the dexter hand a dart, and on the sinister arm a shield, the temples wreathed arg. and sa. 311. 7

Wiseman, Essex and Berks, a tower or, the portway arg., on the top a demi-Moor in mail, all ppr., his temples wreathed arg. and sa., holding in the dexter hand a dart of the first, plumed and headed of the second, and in his sinister a Roman shield or.

Wisham, a demi-lion or. 10. 2

Wishart of Pitarrow, Forfarsh., a demi-eagle with wings expanded ppr. *Mercy is my desire.* 80. 2

Wishart of Brechin, Scotland, an eagle displayed gu. *Mercy is my desire.* 75. 2

Wishart of Logie, an eagle displayed sa., armed and membered gu., vulned by an arrow shot through the body ppr. *Avitos juvat honores.—Quid non cor sæpius pro Immanueli.* cf. 75. 2

Wisheart, *see* Belsches-Wisheart.

Witford, eight pens in saltier, four and four banded.

Witham, a cubit arm erect vested az., cuffed arg., holding in the hand ppr a cinquefoil stalked or. cf. 205. 2

Witham, Lincs, out of a ducal coronet or, a demi-peacock of the same. 103. 13

Witham of Lartington Hall, Yorks, out of a ducal coronet or, a demi-woman, her hair dishevelled ppr., holding in her dexter hand a gem-ring of the first. *Optime merenti.*

Witham, T. Maxwell, Esquire, 5, Gray's Inn Square, W.C., same crest and motto.

Wither, a demi-hare quarterly gu. and az., holding in the mouth three ears of wheat or.

Wither, Bigg-, of Manydown, Hants: (1) A demi-hare erect az., holding in the mouth three ears of ripe corn, charged on the shoulder with a mullet or. (2) A rhinoceros ppr. 226. 7

Withering, Essex and Staffs, a raven with wings expanded sa., beaked arg., gorged with a ducal coronet or. cf. 107. 3

Witherington, a bull's head couped sa., platée, armed arg.

Withers of Holt, Norf., a demi-hare salient az., holding in the mouth three ears of wheat or.

Withie of Wotton, Calne, and Berry Norbert, Devonsh., out of a ducal coronet or, a cross Calvary gu., between two wings erect arg. cf. 111. 1

Withington, Thomas Ellames, Esquire, Conservative Club, Liverpool, a lion's head erased sa.

Withypoule, Suff., a demi-mountain cat rampant gardant per pale or and gu., guttée counterchanged. cf. 26. 12

Witmore, out of a ducal coronet a cock's head. 90. 6

Witt, Lincs, a dexter hand couped in fess. 221. 6

Wittewrong, Bucks and Herts, a Saracen's head couped below the shoulders ppr., wreathed round the temples and tied in bows or and gu. 289. 10

Wittewrong, Lawes-, Sir Charles Bennet, Bart., of Rothamstead Manor House, St. Albans, Herts: (1) A Saracen's head couped below the shoulders ppr., wreathed about the temples, and tied in bows or and gu. 289. 10. (2) A mount vert, thereon the trunk of a tree fessewise eradicated and sprouting to the dexter, surmounted by an erm. passant ppr. *Pour la foy.* 289. 11

Wittingham, a lion's head. 21. 1

Witton of London and Yorks, an owl arg., legged sa., ducally gorged or. cf. 96. 5

Witts of London, an eagle with wings elevated sitting on a mount of corn springing, holding in the beak a sprig of broom, all ppr.

Witts, George Backhouse, Esquire, J.P., Hill House, Leckhampton, same crest. *Ante obitum nemo felix.*

Witts, a greyhound current. cf. 58. 2

Witty, out of a ducal coronet or, a dexter hand ppr., holding a sword wavy in pale gu., hilted or. 212. 1

Wix, on a rock ppr., a wyvern sejant gu.

Wodderspoon, Scotland, a dexter hand holding a garland of laurel, all ppr. *Deo juvante.* 218. 4

Wodehouse, *see* Kimberley, Earl of.

Wodehouse, issuing out of a cloud a dexter hand holding a club. *Frappe forte.* 214. 9

Wodehouse, William Herbert, Esquire, of Woolmer's Park, Herts, on a ducal coronet or, a cross crosslet arg. *In hoc signo.*

Wodehouse, Colonel Josceline Heneage, C.B., a dexter cubit arm vested arg., and grasping a club in bend sinister or. *Frappe fort.*

Wodehouse, Edmond Robert, M.A., a cubit arm ppr., vested arg., and grasping a club in bend sinister or. *Frappe fort.*

Wodehouse, Henry Ernest, C.M.G., Hong Kong, a dexter arm couped below the elbow, vested arg., and grasping a club or. *Frappe fort.*

Wodehull, Oxon., on a ducal coronet a vol, all or. cf. 113. 1

Wodeson, of Lowdham and Gunthorpe, Notts, out of a ducal coronet or, a flame of fire issuant ppr.

Wodnester, an eagle's head erased arg., gorged with a ducal coronet or. cf. 83. 10

Wodor, an eagle with wings addorsed arg., preying on a fox ppr.

Wogan of Rathcoffey and Richardstown, co. Kildare, a lion's gamb couped and erect gu. cf. 36. 4

Wogan-Browne, Major Francis William Nicholas, an heraldic tiger az., maned, tufted, and armed or. *Qui non ciconia tigris.*

Wolcot of Knowle House, Devonsh., a hawk's head gu., guttée-d'or, holding in the beak a fleur-de-lis, also or. cf. 84. 12

Wolcott of Wolcott, Chudleigh, Southcott, Biterston, and Lisleigh, Devonsh., a griffin's head erased arg., guttée-de-sang, charged with a fleur-de-lis az., bezantée. cf. 66. 2

Wolf or **Wolfe,** a wolf current erm. 28. 4

Wolf, a gray wolf passant ppr., in front of an oak vert.

Wolf, Wolfe, and **Woof,** Shropsh., a demi-wolf rampant sa., holding between its paws a regal crown ppr. *Fides in adversis.* 31. 12

Wolfall, out of a ducal coronet a dexter hand ppr., holding a rose of the first stalked and leaved vert. 218. 11

Wolfall of London, a wolf's head erased sa., ducally gorged or. cf. 30. 8

Wolfall, out of a ducal coronet gu., a dexter hand ppr., holding a rose of the first stalked and leaved vert. 218. 11

Wolfe, *see* Wolf.

Wolfe, Viscount Kilwarden (*extinct*), a wolf's head erased sa., ducally gorged or. *Pro patriæ amore.* cf. 30. 8

Wolfe of Hatherton, Chesh., out of a ducal coronet a demi-wolf rampant. cf. 31. 2

Wolfe, a wolf passant, collared, and a line therefrom reflexed over the back. cf. 28. 10

Wolfe, Birch-, of Woodhall, Essex: (1) A demi-wolf rampant gu., charged on the body with a chevron or, and holding between the paws a mural coronet of the last (*for Wolfe*). 31. 9. (2) A mount vert, thereon a fleur-de-lis arg., entwined with two snakes ppr. (*for Birch*).

Wolfe, Ireland, a wolf's head erased sa., ducally gorged or. *Pro patriæ amore.* cf. 30. 8

Wolfe, George, of Forenaughts, Blackhall, and Bishop Land, co. Kildare, Ireland, same crest. cf. 30. 8

Wolfe of Arthington, Torquay, a wolf's head erased sa., charged with a bezant, thereon a cross moline of the first. *Lupus non lepus.*

Wolfe-Barry, Sir John Wolfe, K.C.B., 23, Delahay Street, Westminster, a gryphon gu., wings elevated and addorsed, barry of six or and az., in its mouth a rose arg., leaved and slipped ppr., resting the dexter paw on a portcullis with chains sa. *Boutez en avant.*

Wolferstan, Pipe-, Francis Stafford, of Statfold Hall, Staffs: (1) A wolf under a tree, all ppr. (*for Wolferstan*). (2) A leopard's head erased or (*for Pipe*). *Qui sera sera.* 23. 3

Wolff, a wolf regardant holding in the mouth an arrow in bend barb downward.

Wolff of Cams Hall, Hants, Baron of Russia and a baronet (*extinct*): (1) In the centre, out of a ducal coronet or, a demi-wolf salient ppr. (2) On the dexter side, out of a ducal coronet or, a fleur-de-lis arg., between two imperial eagle's wings displayed tawny. (3) On the sinister side, on a ducal coronet or, an eagle displayed sa., ducally crowned gu. *Dante Deo.*

Wolgar, Hants, on a mount vert, a peewit ppr.

Wolin, a lion's head erased sa. *Favente Deo.* 17. 8

Wollacombe of Wollacombe, Devonsh., a spur leathered or, the rowel-points embrued ppr. 178. 8

Wollacombe, Devonsh., a falcon ppr., with wings expanded, charged with three bars gu., belled or.

Wollaston, Shropsh., a demi-griffin segreant, holding in its dexter claw a mullet.

Wollaston, F. E. A., Esquire, of Shenton Hall, Leics., out of a mural coronet or, a demi-griffin salient arg., holding a mullet pierced sa. *Ne quid falsi.*

Wollaston, Arthur Naylor, C.I.E., of Glen Hill, Walmer, Kent, same crest and motto.

Wollcote of Exeter, Devonsh., an eagle's head or, guttée-de-sang, beaked az., holding in the beak a fleur-de-lis of the first. 84. 12

Wollen, a demi-lion holding between the paws a cushion tasselled.

Wolley-Dod, *see* Dod.

Wolley of Woodhall, near Shrewsbury, Shropsh., a lion rampant erminois. 1. 13

Wolley, Oldnall-: (1) A lion rampant erminois, charged on the shoulder with a cross patée fitchée sa. for distinction (*for Wolley*). *cf.* 1. 13. (2) A demi-lion arg., guttée-de-larmes, ducally crowned and resting the sinister paw upon a cross patée fitchée or (*for Oldnall*). *Pieux quoique preux.*

Wolley, Phillips-, of Highgate, Middx.: (1) Same crest as (1) above (*for Wolley*). *cf.* 1. 13. (2) Between two oak-branches ppr., on a garb fessewise vert, a lion rampant sa., gorged with a ducal coronet, and therefrom a chain reflexed over the back or, holding between the paws an escallop gu. (*for Phillips*). *Ducit amor patriæ.* 3. 10

Wolley of Comberworth, Lincs, on a mount vert, a lion couchant arg. *cf.* 7. 5

Wolley, a cubit arm erect vested paly of four arg. and az., holding in the hand ppr. a bunch of leaves vert.

Wolley of Beeston, Notts, a man's head in profile and bearded clad in a hood of mail ppr., and charged on the neck with a cross crosslet sa. for distinction. *Honeste audax.*

Wollstonecraft of Mark's Gate, Essex, and London, out of a naval coronet or, a demi-mermaid holding in her dexter hand a mirror ppr., and in her sinister a comb or. 184. 14

Wolmer, a dexter arm embowed ppr., vested vert, cuffed or, holding in the hand a covered cup, also or. 203. 4

Wolmer, Worcs., between two wings or, a wolf's head erased sa.

Wolmer, Worcs., a griffin's head erased sa., between two wings or. *cf.* 65. 11

Wolmer of Bloxholme and Swinsted, Lincs, two lobster's claws erect or, holding an escallop arg.

Wolrich of Cowling, Suff., a demi-royal tiger ppr.

Wolrige, Arthur Field Wolrige, Esquire, of Sheldons, Hants, and 23, Castletown Road, West Kensington, an oak-tree ppr. *Strong and firm.* 143. 5

Wolrige-Gordon, Henry, Esquire, Barrister-at-law, 53, Queen's Gate, London, S.W., a hart's head ppr. *Bydand.* 121. 5

Wolrige or **Wolridge,** a horse-shoe or, between two wings ppr. 120. 11

Wolryche-Whitmore, Francis Alexander, of Dudmaston, Shropsh.: (1) A falcon close on the stump of a tree with a branch springing from the dexter side, all ppr. (*for Whitmore*). 86. 11. (2) An oak-tree ppr., charged with a cross crosslet or for difference (*for Wolryche*). *Incorrupta fides.* *cf.* 143. 5

Wolryche - Whitmore, Rev. Francis Henry, of Dudmaston, Shropsh., same crest and motto.

Wolseley, Viscount, Farm House, Glynde, Sussex, out of a ducal coronet or, a wolf's head ppr. *Homo homini lupus.*

Wolseley, Sir Charles Michael, Bart., D.L., of Wolseley, Staffs, out of a ducal coronet or, a wolf's head erased ppr. *Homo homini lupus.*

Wolseley, Lieutenant-General Sir George Benjamin, K.C.B., Meean Meer, Punjaub, India, out of a ducal coronet or, a wolf's head ppr. *Homo homini lupus.*

Wolseley, Sir Capel Charles, Bart., of Mount Wolseley, co. Carlow, out of a ducal coronet or, a wolf's head ppr. *Mors mihi vita est.*

Wolseley-Jenkins, Major Charles Bradford Harries: (1) On a mural coronet sa., a lion passant regardant or, supporting with the dexter paw an escutcheon barry of six az. and erm., charged with an annulet or (*for Jenkins*). (2) Out of a ducal coronet or, a wolf's head ppr., with marks of distinction (*for Wolseley*). *Perge sed caute.*

Wolsey of Cottingham, Suff., a naked arm embowed grasping a shin-bone, all ppr.

Wolsey of Newton, Norf., a beast in the shape of a beaver az., with long ears erect, finned down the back or, web-footed.

Wolstenholme of Wolstenholme, Lancs, Dransfield and Horsleygate, Derbysh., and of Winchenden, Middx., an eagle displayed or, standing on a snake nowed az.

Wolstenholme, Bart. (*extinct*), of London, an eagle displayed or, standing on a snake nowed az. *In ardua virtus.*

Wolston or **Wolstone,** an arm in armour embowed wielding a sword ppr. 195. 2

Wolstonecraft, out of a mural coronet or, a demi-mermaid holding in the dexter hand a purse ppr., and in her sinister a comb. *Vigilans.*

Wolton, on a bezant a martlet arg.

Wolverstone, a Minerva's head affrontée ppr. 182. 1

Wolverstone, Suff. and Staffs, a wolf passant or. 28. 10

Wolverton, Baron (Glyn), Iwerne Minster, Blandford, an eagle's head erased sa., guttée-d'or, holding in the beak an escallop arg. *Fidei tenax.*

Wombwell, Sir George Orby, Bart., D.L., of Wombwell, Yorks, a unicorn's head couped arg. *In well beware.* 49. 7

Wombwell, a dragon's head erased or, charged on the neck with a chaplet vert.

Wombwell of Northfleet, Kent, a tiger's head erased or, gorged with a garland of laurel vert.

Womerton of Womerton, Worcs., Hatton, Shropsh., a unicorn's head couped gu. 49. 7

Womphrey, a book expanded ppr. *Pax tua, Domine, et requies mea.* 158. 3

Wondesford, a cross crosslet fitchée gu., surmounted by a sword in bend sinister, point downwards, ppr. *cf.* 166. 12

Wood, *see* Halifax, Viscount.

Wood of Hollin Hall, Yorks, an oak-tree ppr., fructed or. *Pro patria.* 143. 5

Wood of Bishop's Hall, Essex: (1) An oak-tree eradicated ppr. (2) A martlet on the stump of an oak-tree sprouting out branches, all ppr. *Tutis in undis.*

Wood, William Derisley, of Riccarton, Christchurch, New Zealand, an oak-tree fructed. *Semper sursum.* 143. 2

Wood of Woodborough and Nether Colwick, Notts, an oak-tree ppr., fructed or. 143. 2

Wood, Yorks, an oak-tree fructed ppr. 143. 2

Wood, Bart. (*extinct*), of Gatton Park, Surrey, an oak-tree eradicated ppr., fructed vert. *Tutus in undis.* 143. 2

Wood, in front of a mount vert, thereon an oak-tree ppr., three bezants in fesse. *Sicut serimus sic metimus.*

Wood, George Swinford, Esquire, and Albert Wood, Esquire, of Bodlondeb, Carnarvonsh., in front of a mount, thereon an oak-tree fructed ppr., three bezants.

Wood of Enfield, Middx., and Yorks, on a mount vert, an oak-tree ppr., fructed or. 274. 15

Wood of Coxhoe Hall, Durh., and Acton Cantlow, Warw., same crest. *Irrideo tempestatem.*

Wood of Mount House and Hetton, Durh., on a mount vert, an oak-tree fructed ppr. *Irrideo tempestatem.* 274. 15

Wood, John, Esquire, J.P., D.L., Hengrave Hall, Bury St. Edmunds, on a mount in front of an oak-tree fructed the trunk of a tree fessewise eradicated. *Dei donum.* 230. 1

Wood, Samuel Hill, Esquire, J.P., D.L., of Moorfield, Glossop, Derbysh., same crest and motto.

Wood of Grangehaugh, Scotland, an oak-slip fructed ppr. *Diu viresit.* 151. 3

Wood-Burne, a lion rampant gu. *Audax ingenii.*

Wood, Sir Lindsay, Bart., the Hermitage, Chester-le-Street, a wolf's head erased sa., gorged with a collar or, the collar charged on the band with three oak-leaves vert between two acorns slipped and leaved ppr. *Loyal en tout.* 293. 6

Wood, a wolf's head sa., collared or. 30. 9

Wood, Francis John Adelbert, Esquire, J.P., of Hallow Park, Worcester, a wolf's head erased ppr. *Deo duce.*

Wood of London, a wolf's head erased sa., collared gu., rimmed or. 30. 11

Wood of Islington, Middx., out of a mural coronet gu., a wolf's head sa., collared arg.

Wood-Besly: (1) In front of a tower triple-towered arg., the trunk of a tree fessewise eradicated and sprouting to the dexter ppr. (*for Besly*). (2) Upon the stump of a tree eradicated ppr., a wolf's head erased paly of six arg. and gu., holding in the mouth a staff raguly in bend sa. (*for Wood*).

Wood, George William Rayner, Singleton, Manchester, a mount vert, thereon in front of an oak-tree ppr. a boar regardant sa., hoofed, tusked, and gorged with a collar, therefrom a chain reflexed over the back and affixed to the tree or. 258. 12

Wood, Staffs, and of West Cutton and Thorp, Yorks, a wolf's head erased sa., collared and ringed or. 30. 11

Wood of Beadnall, Northumb., a wolf's head sa., erased or, gorged with a collar of the last, charged with three annulets gu. *cf.* 30. 11

Wood, Collingwood Lindsay, Freeland, Forgandenny, Perthsh., a wolf's head erased sa., collared and ringed or, the collar charged on the band with three oak-leaves vert. *Loyal en tout.* 314. 9

Wood, a lion's head erased ducally crowned. 18. 8

Wood of Thoresby, Lincs, a lion's head erased and ducally crowned. *Strenue et audacter.* 18. 8

Wood of Newbold Revel, Rugby, Warw., a demi-lion rampant arg., semée of buckles sa., resting the sinister paw upon an escutcheon of the last, charged with a wolf's head erased of the first. *Virtute et labore.*

Wood, Arthur Herbert Edward, Sudbourn Hall, same crest.

Wood of Codshall, Somers., a demi-lion rampant purp., holding an acorn or, the cup vert. *cf.* 12. 3

Wood of Hiltwood, Staffs, a demi-lion rampant purp., holding an acorn-branch vert, fructed or. *cf.* 12. 3

Wood, Richard Shaw, Bosco Manor, Bermuda, same crest.

Wood, Suff., a demi-lion rampant or, holding a wreath of laurel vert.

Wood, Charles Harcourt Gam, Carleton Lodge, Pontefract, a demi-lion rampant or, gorged with a wreath. *Virtus incumbet honori.*

Wood of Fulborne, Cambs, Sneterley, Norf., and Kent, a demi-lion rampant or, gorged with a wreath az. and gu., tied behind with two bows.

Wood-Martin, Colonel William Gregory of Cleveragh, Sligo, Ireland, A.D.C. to the King: (1) A lion rampant ppr., holding in his dexter paw a crescent or (*for Martin*). 2. 2. (2) A demi-savage ppr., wreathed about the temples and loins vert, and charged on the breast with a crescent gu., holding in his dexter hand an oak-tree fructed, and in his sinister a club resting on his shoulder, both also ppr. (*for Wood*). *Hinc fortior et clarior.—Frutu cognoscitur arbor.*

Wood-Ryder, Andrew Richard, Esquire, of Sydney Place, Cork: (1) A lion passant or, resting the dexter paw upon an escutcheon of the Ryder arms, viz., per fesse az. and gu., three crescents or, and a canton of the last (*for Ryder*). (2) Two wings inverted in saltire arg., surmounted by a cherub's head ppr. (*for Wood*). *Timet pudorem.—Vincit veritas.* 189. 13

Wood, Ireland, a cherub or. 189. 9

Wood, Scotland, a savage from the loins upwards holding in his dexter hand a club erect, wreathed about the temples and loins with laurel, all ppr. *Defend.* 186. 1

Wood, a demi-wild man, on his shoulder a club, all ppr., wreathed about the loins vert.

Wood, Devonsh., a demi-woodman holding in his dexter hand an oak-slip and in his sinister a club resting on his shoulder, all ppr., and wreathed about the middle vert.

Wood of Shynwood, Shropsh., Surrey, and Brize Norton, Oxon., a demi-woodman arg., holding a club over his dexter shoulder or. 186. 5

Wood, James, Esquire, J.P., of Woodville, co. Sligo, Ireland, a demi-savage ppr., wreathed about the temples and loins vert, and charged on the breast with a crescent gu., holding in his dexter hand an oak-tree eradicated and fructed, and in his sinister a club resting on his shoulder, both also ppr. *Fructu cognoscitur arbor.*

Wood of Hareston, Devonsh., a demi-wild man holding in his dexter hand ppr. an oak-tree eradicated vert, fructed or.

Wood of North Taunton, Devonsh., a woodman ppr., wreathed about the temples and loins, and holding in the dexter hand an olive-branch, all vert.

Wood, Lancs, out of a mural coronet arg., a demi-woodman ppr., wreathed about the loins and temples vert, holding in his dexter hand a griffin's head erased and in his other over his sinister shoulder a club, also ppr.

Wood, Joseph Snell, Esquire, 29, Kensington Court, S.W., a demi-man affrontée holding over his dexter shoulder a club, all ppr., and resting his sinister hand upon a saltire or, and issuing from the wreath on the dexter side an acorn slipped and leaved ppr. *Non sibi sed aliis.*

Wood, Francis Hugo Lindley, Hoarcross, Burton-on-Trent, a savage ambulant in fesse ppr., holding in his sinister hand a club resting on his shoulder, all ppr., and on his dexter arm a shield sa., charged with a griffin's head erased arg. 250. 4

Wood, Francis John Woodhouse Wood, Esquire, a savage affrontée ppr., holding in his dexter hand a club head downwards, and on his sinister arm an escutcheon arg., charged with a cross gu. *Parabo me.* 314. 6

Wood, Richard Henry, Belmont, Sidmouth, a blackamoor's head in profile couped at the shoulders ppr., wreathed with cinquefoils or, in front thereof three mascles interlaced fesseways, also or.

Wood, Bart., of Hatherley House, Glouc., out of a mural coronet arg., a demi-wild man wreathed about the temples with oak fructed, holding in the dexter hand an oak-tree eradicated and fructed, and in the sinister a club, all ppr. *Defend.* 311. 4

Wood, Sir Henry Trueman, 16, Leinster Square, W., same crest and motto.

Wood, Rev. Frederick John, M.A., same crest and motto.

Wood, General Sir Henry Evelyn, Salisbury, same crest and motto.

Wood, Charles Page, Wakes Hall, Wakes Colne, near Halsted, same crest and motto.

Wood of Brownhills, Staffs, a demi-man wreathed about the temples and waist with oak-leaves fructed, the dexter hand holding a club in bend, all ppr., the sinister arm extended, the hand grasping a wolf's head erased sa. *Deus robur meum.*

Wood, John Baddeley, M.A., Henley Hall, Ludlow, same crest and motto.

Wood, Captain George Wilding, Nithsdale House, Ingatestone, Surrey, a savage affrontée ppr., wreathed about the head and loins, holding over his dexter shoulder a club, and in his sinister hand a wolf's head erased. *Deus robur meum.*

Wood, Bart., of Bonnytown, Fifesh., a demi-savage wreathed about the head and middle with laurel, and holding in his dexter hand a club erect. *Defend.*

Wood, a demi-woodman holding in his dexter hand an olive-branch, and in his sinister a club, all ppr. *Suaviter sed fortiter.*

Wood, on an Eastern coronet or, a leopard passant regardant ppr., holding in the dexter paw a banner gu., the staff and spear-head also ppr.

Wood, Suff., on a ducal coronet or, an eagle per pale of the same and sa.

Wood, Suff., on a ducal coronet or, an eagle with wings expanded per pale or and sa. *cf.* 77. 5

Wood, Middx., of Nottsgrove, Essex, and Newton, near Middlewich, Chesh., a hawk close arg., jessed and belled or, standing on a lure ppr. *cf.* 85. 14

Wood, Shropsh., a falcon rising.

Wood, Edmund Burke, Moreton Hall, Chirk, Salop, a falcon arg., jessed and belled or, standing upon a lure ppr.

Wood of Norwich, Norf., a martlet with wings expanded arg., holding in the beak a tulip ppr., stalked and leaved vert.

Wood, Oxon., a squirrel sejant sa., holding between the paws a honeysuckle arg., slipped and leaved vert.

Wood of Ottershaw Park, Surrey, a ship in full sail ppr. *Tutus in undis.* 160. 13

Wood, Andrew George, Pittleworth, Hants, a ship in full sail. *Tutus in undis.*

Wood, John Gathorne, Thedden Grange, Alton, Hants, a naked arm embowed, couped at the shoulder, holding a club, all ppr., pendent from the wrist a shield arg., charged with a cross flory gu. *Non ligno crucis.*

Wood, Middx., a gauntlet erect gu., garnished or, between two branches of laurel vert.

Wood of Wateringbury, Kent, and Hamsey, Sussex, a dexter gauntlet erect gu., purfled or, between two ostrich-feathers arg.

Wood of the Whitehouse, Heref., a cubit arm erect vested or, cuffed arg., holding in the hand ppr. a cross crosslet fitchée gu. *Credo cruce Christi.*

Wood, a dexter arm in armour embowed, holding in the hand a sword enfiled with a human heart.

Wood of Sandwich, Kent, an arm embowed vested in green leaves, holding in the hand a spear broken in three pieces, one in pale and two in saltier, all ppr.

Wood, Glouc., an arm in pale vested chequy or and sa., cuffed arg., holding in the hand ppr. a fleur-de-lis gu.

Wood-Wright, William Henry Edward, Esquire, J P D L, of Golagh, co Monaghan, Ireland a cubit arm erect vested az cuffed arg charged with a leopard's face or holding in the hand a broken tilting-spear ppr headed or *Veritas vincit*

Wood of Osmington House, Dorset, an arm embowed in armour the hand grasping a spear paleways

Woodall of London out of a ducal coronet an eagle's head holding in the beak a pullet all ppr *Dissipate* 83 14

Woodall, a Cornish chough with wings expanded sa ducally gorged or cf 107 3

Woodbridge, a chaplet of roses ppr

Woodburgh, a bundle of five arrows banded round the middle by a serpent ppr

Woodburn, out of a ducal coronet an eagle's head, all ppr cf 83 14

Woodburne, a camel's head sa 132 7

Woodburne, Lancs, a lion rampant gu *Audax ingenii* 1 13

Woodburne, George Burgess Lancaster Esquire same crest

Woodcock, Ireland, a phœnix in flames ppr 82 2

Woodcock of London New Timber Sussex and Coventry Warw out of rays issuing from the wreath or, a demi-peacock displayed arg

Woodcock of Newport Shropsh a pelican in her piety or, the nest ppr, the young arg 98 8

Woodcock, a demi lion rampant gu, supporting a cross crosslet fitched or 11 5

Woodcock, Essex, a demi lion rampant or collared az, studded, and holding a cross bottonnee fitchee of the first

Woodcock of Brightwell, Bucks two lion's gambs erect and addorsed, the dexter arg, the sinister sa 36 5

Woodcock of Norwich, a Moor's head sa, between two wings gu *Gesta verbis prævenient*

Woodcock, an arm from the shoulder ppr, vested gu, the cuff vandyked arg, wielding a sword ppr 204 1

Woodd, Rev Trevor Basil 16 Eccleston Street London, a demi woodman affrontee ppr, holding over his dexter shoulder with both hands a club or *Non nobis*

Woodd, Basil Aubrey Hollond, 35, Tite Street, S W, same crest and motto

Woodeson, Middx, out of a ducal coronet or, flames ppr

Woodford, Leics two lion's gambs erased or 36 5

Woodford, a demi-woodman sa, wreathed about the temples or holding in his dexter hand a club vert 186 1

Woodford, Bart (*extinct*), of Carleby, Lincs a naked savage wreathed about the temples and loins holding in his dexter hand a club and in his sinister a palm branch in bend, all ppr *Libertate quietum*

Woodforde, Rev Alexander John, of Ansford House, Somers, a woodman ppr, holding a club arg crowned and girt with oak leaves *Pro aris et focis*

Woodgate, a squirrel sejant holding a nut all ppr 135 7

Woodgate, Rev Reginald Stephen Shaw, of Summerhill and Pembury, Kent, same crest 135 7

Woodgate, a dexter arm in armour embowed, holding in the hand a sword by the blade in fess surmounted by a sprig of laurel

Woodgate, John, Esquire Little Bentley Hall, Colchester, same crest *Esse quam videri*

Woodhall, Beds, Thenford, Northamp, and Chesh out of a ducal coronet or two wings addorsed gu

Woodhall of Walden, Essex a cubit arm vested per pale or and sa, cuffed counterchanged, holding in the hand ppr a sword arg, hilt and pommel of the first

Woodham, an arm in armour embowed the hand holding a sword by the blade, point downwards, ppr 195 6

Woodham of Cotherston, Cornw, between two sprigs of roses a buck's head erased all ppr cf 121 4

Woodhead, a vol or 113 1

Woodhead, Henry, the Gardens, Cape Town an African bush buck's head couped ppr, gorged with the battlements of a tower or between on the dexter side an oak branch fructed ppr, and on the sinister a rose arg, stalked and leaved vert *Æquo animo*

Woodhead, a buck's head erased 121 2

Woodhouse, a demi savage resting a club over his shoulder, all ppr *Frappez fort*

Woodhouse, Norf (1) Issuing from clouds ppr, an arm couped at the elbow and erect vested arg, charged with four sinister bendlets sa holding in the hand ppr a club (2) A savage couped at the knees ppr, crined or, holding a club erect sa, wreathed about loins arg and sa

Woodhouse of Portadown co Armagh of Kerrykeel, co Donegal and of Omeath Park, co Louth, Ireland issuing from clouds a cubit arm vested arg and charged with a cinquefoil gu the hand grasping a club all ppr *Agincourt*

Woodhouse of Hickling Norf, a griffin segreant or 62 2

Woodhouse of Holborough Court Kent a demi griffin segreant holding between the paws an arrow, point downwards *Virtus in arduis*

Woodhouse, on a ducal coronet or, a cross crosslet arg *In hoc signo* cf 165 2

Woodhull of Mollington, Oxon, a mantiger passant gardant arg, horned or

Wooding, a goat passant arg, holding in the mouth a slip of ivy ppr cf 129 6

Woodley, an owl arg 96 5

Woodley, James Esquire, J P, D L, of Halshanger Ashburton Devonsh, an owl arg *Sapere et tacere*

Woodlock of Dublin, a demi-lion rampant az, holding in the dexter paw a sword ppr, and charged on the shoulder with a cross crosslet fitchee or *Vi et virtute* cf 14 12

Woodman, a stork regardant sa, resting the dexter claw on a torteau

Woodman, a buck's head erased ppr 121 2

Woodmas of Avonhurst Warw, an oak tree eradicated ppr *Pro Deo et patria*

Woodmas of Green Hill, Compstall, Stockport, Chesh, in front of an oak tree eradicated ppr, fructed or, a cross crosslet gu

Woodnester of Bromyard, Heref, an eagle's head erased arg, ducally gorged or cf 83 10

Woodnoth of Wistanton, Chesh and Shavington St Clere, Cornw, a squirrel sejant or, cracking a nut ppr 135 7

Woodriff, a hind's head ppr 124 1

Woodrof and **Woodrow,** a bull's head erased gu 44 3

Woodrof and **Woodrow,** Yorks a woodcock ppr

Woodroffe, Derbysh and Yorks a woodcock ppr

Woodroffe, a demi lady ppr, vested arg, holding in the dexter hand a civic crown or 183 5

Woodroffe and **Woodruff** of London and Surrey a dexter arm embowed vested with leaves vert holding in the hand a branch of honeysuckle all ppr

Woodroffe of Dublin, an open dexter hand between two branches of honeysuckle all ppr and in an escroll over the crest the motto *Cor ac manus concordant* *Sit dux sapientia*

Woodroffe of St Edmundsbury, Suff a dexter arm embowed vested ermines, cuffed arg holding in the hand ppr a buck's head of the last

Woodroffe, Ireland, a dexter hand couped and apaumee ppr *Sit dux sapientia* 222 14

Woodrooffe, Rev Henry Reade M A, Canon of Grahamstown, Cape Colony a woodcock close ppr *Quod transtuli retuli*

Woodrooffe, S M 100, Pembroke Road Clifton, Bristol a woodcock close ppr *Quod transtuli retuli* 281 13

Woods of Milverton, Dublin a demi-woodman holding in his dexter hand an oak-slip *Fortis in procella*

Woods, the late Sir William Garter King of Arms (1) Out of a ducal coronet or, a demi woodman ppr, supporting over his shoulder a club of the first (2) Out of a ducal coronet or a mount vert, thereon a lion statant gardant of the first in front of an oak-tree ppr, fructed or *Robur* 6 12

Woods, Sussex between two ostrich-feathers erect arg a gauntlet ppr

Woods of Norwich Norf, a martlet with wings addorsed sa, guttee d'or

Woods, William of Wigan, Lancs and of Warnford Park, Bishop's Waltham a staff raguly in fess sa, thereon a martlet with wings elevated of the last, guttee d'eau *Labor et perseverantia*

Woods, Lancs, a martlet sa with wings addorsed, holding in the beak a tulip ppr

Woods, Ireland an arm in armour, the hand holding two pieces of a broken spear 209 10

Woods, Matthew Snooke Grosvenor Mountfield Bonchurch Isle of Wight a rock ppr thereon an eagle regardant, wings elevated or the dexter claw resting on an escutcheon arg., charged with a fleur-de-lis gu. *Integritate tutus.*

Woods, Thomas, Rose Cottage, Lowestoft, Suff., and Llandaff Place, South Wales, a horse's head couped arg., maned or, issuant from a chaplet of roses gu., and holding in the mouth a broken spear in bend, also or. *Ora et labora.*

Woods, the late Sir Albert William, G.C.V.D., K.C.B., K.C.M.G., Garter King of Arms, issuant from a crown vallory or, a mount vert, thereon in front of an oak-tree ppr., a demi-man affrontée resting the dexter hand on a terrestrial globe ppr. *Deus robur meum.*

Woodside, Robert, Esquire, Liswyn, Osborne Park, Balmoral, Belfast, a wolf's head erased, collared, and ringed. *Tiens à la vérité.*

Woodstock of Town, Oxon., out of a ducal coronet or, an oak-tree vert, fructed of the first. *cf.* 143. 13

Woodstock, a sand-glass ppr. 177. 15

Woodthorpe, a camel's head ppr. 132. 7

Woodville, an ear of rye and a palm-branch in saltier ppr. 154. 10

Woodward, on a ducal coronet or, a greyhound sejant arg. *Virtus semper viret.*

Woodward of Avon Dassett and Butler's Marston, Warw., same crest. *cf.* 59. 4

Woodward, Rear-Admiral Robert, C.B., of Hopton Court, a squirrel sejant ppr., holding in its paws a nut or. *Gardez bien.* 135. 7

Woodward of Hampstead, Midds., a heraldic tiger's head erased arg., maned or. *cf.* 25. 4

Woodward, a wolf's head couped arg., gorged with a collar sa., thereon three bezants between two oak-branches vert, fructed or.

Woodward, a wolf's head couped arg., collared sa. 30. 9

Woodward, Beds, and of Upton, Bucks, a wolf's head arg., collared sa., studded or, between an acorn-branch and a branch of fern ppr.

Woodward, Bucks, a wolf's head couped arg., gorged with a collar sa., charged with three plates. *cf.* 30. 9

Woodward of London, on a ducal coronet or, a boar's head couped arg. 41. 4

Woodward of Little Walsingham, Norf., a buck's head erased ppr., attired, and charged on the neck with three billets or, holding in the mouth a mulberry-leaf vert.

Woodward of Dean, Glouc., and Worcs., a demi-lion rampant sa., supporting between the paws a pheon or.

Woodward of Woodmarsh, Kent, a demi-woman couped at the knees vested gu., her hair dishevelled or, holding in her hand a honeysuckle of the first, stalked and leaved vert.

Woodward, Robert, Arley Castle, near Bewdley, a dexter arm embowed in armour holding a falchion, all ppr.

Woodward, Lawrence, a stag's head and neck erased, gorged with a mural coronet between two rose-sprigs, all ppr. *Æquo animo.*

Woodyeare, Yorks, a demi-griffin regardant per pale gu. and sa., semée-de-lis or. *cf.* 64. 3

Woodyeare of Crookhill, Yorks, a demi-griffin segreant regardant with wings inverted sa., beaked, membered, and semée-de-lis or. *cf.* 64. 3

Wool, Edward, Esquire, of South View, Ironbridge, Shropsh., a demi-wolf rampant sa., holding between the paws a regal crown ppr. *Fides in adversis.* 31. 12

Wool, Warw., a lion couchant or. 7. 5

Woolaston of London, Leics., and Staffs, out of a mural coronet or, a demi-griffin segreant arg., holding between the claws a mullet sa., pierced of the second.

Woolcot of Morston, Devonsh., an eagle's head erased arg., charged on the neck with three guttes-de-sang, holding in the beak a fleur-de-lis of the last. 84. 12

Wooldridge, out of a ducal coronet or, an ass's head gu. 125. 10

Wooler of Whitfield House, Durh., a demi-lion rampant ppr., holding between the paws a tassel or. *Confide recte agens.*

Wooley, a hind's head erased erm. 124. 3

Woolfall of Woolfall, Lancs, a wolf's head erased sa., ducally gorged or. *cf.* 30. 8

Woolfe of Madeley, Shropsh., a demi-wolf rampant sa., holding between the paws an imperial crown ppr. *Fides in adversis.* 31. 12

Woolfe, a wolf's head ppr., ducally gorged or. *cf.* 30. 5

Woolhouse of Glapwell, Derbysh., an eagle's head erased ermines, ducally gorged arg. *cf.* 83. 2

Wooll of Rugby, Warw., a lion couchant or. 7. 5

Woollan, Benjamin Minors, in front of a palm-tree, on a rock ppr., a lion couchant regardant per pale indented az. and gu., supporting with the dexter fore-paw an ingot of gold erect. *Laborare et tempus aucupari.* 256. 20

Woollcombe, a falcon ppr., with wings displayed arg., charged with three bars gu., belled and jessed or.

Woollcombe, Captain Charles Belfield, J.P., of Ashbury, North Devonsh., same crest.

Woolcombe, Rev. George Leys, of Homerdon House, Plympton, North Devonsh., same crest.

Woollcombe, Vice-Admiral Henry Bedford, Longridge Road, Earl's Court, S.W., same crest.

Woollcombe, Basil Richard, 36, Theobald's Road, Gray's Inn Road, a falcon rising ppr., each wing charged with three bars gu. *Bear and forbear.*

Woollcombe-Adams, Lieutenant-Colonel, J.P., Ansty Hall, Coventry: (1) A talbot az., bezantée, gorged with a collar and ring, attached arg., and resting the dexter paw on an estoile or. (2) A falcon, wings expanded ppr., each charged with three bars gu. *Sub cruce veritas.*

Woollcombe-Boyce, Rev. William, 26, Imperial Square, Cheltenham: (1) A demi-griffin arg., holding in the beak an acorn leaved and slipped vert, and resting the sinister claw on an escutcheon vert, charged with two cross crosslets fitchée in saltire, also arg. (*for Boyce*). (2) A falcon, wings expanded and inverted ppr., belled and jessed or, on each wing three bars gu., and charged on the breast for distinction with a cross crosslet of the last (*for Woollcombe*). *Cruce robur.*

Woolley, an eagle ppr. 76. 2

Woolley, J. H., Esquire, Kilbourne, Derby: (1) A man's head in chain mail affrontée ppr. (*for Woolley*). (2) Three arrows, two in saltire and one in pale, point downwards ppr. *Honor virtutis præmium.*

Woolridge, out of a ducal coronet arg., an ass's head gu. 125. 10

Woolrych, William Richard, of Croxley House, Herts, an oak-tree ppr. 143. 5

Woolsey, Suff., a naked arm embowed holding in the hand a shin-bone, all ppr.

Woolsey, O'Brien Bellingham, Esquire, Milestown, Castle Bellingham, Ireland, a demi-wolf supporting a battle-axe, all ppr. *Au bon droit.*

Woore of London, out of a ducal coronet or, a demi-heraldic panther rampant arg., spotted vert, gu., and az., holding between the paws a branch of laurel slipped and fructed ppr.

Woorley or **Worley** of Dodington, Kent, out of a mural coronet az., an arm in armour embowed ppr., garnished or, the hand holding a cutlass arg., hilt and pommel of the third.

Woosnam of Newtown, Montgomerysh., in a fern-brake ppr., a snake nowed or, preying on an eagle, also ppr., guttée-de-larmes. 246. 3

Woosnam, Ven. Archdeacon C. Maxwell, St. Margaret's Vicarage, Dunham Massey, Chesh., same crest.

Woosnam, Charles William, Cefullysgwynne, Builth, same crest.

Woosnam, James Bowen, of Borjan, Moheema, Assam, same crest.

Wooton or **Wootton,** out of a ducal coronet arg., a greyhound's head gu. 61. 7

Wootton, a blackamoor's head in profile sa., the forehead wreathed arg. and az., and bat's wings attached to the head of the last.

Worcester, Marquess of, *see* Beaufort, Duke of.

Worden, on a chapeau gu., turned up erm., an eagle rising ppr. 77. 14

Wordesworth, a stag trippant arg. 117. 8

Wordie, Scotland, a sword in pale surmounted by two laurel-sprigs in orle ppr. *Nil indigne.* 170. 3

Wordsworth, Cambs, an antelope's head erased arg. 126. 2

Worge, Sussex, a lion's head erased arg. 17. 8

Worhead, a buck's head cabossed sa. 122. 5

Worke of Bellegrève Villas, Dicq Road, Jersey, a wyvern resting its dexter claw on a salamander. *Virtus triumphat.*

Workesley, a wyvern with wings addorsed az. 70. 1

Workman, out of a crescent quarterly sa. and arg., a lictor's fasces. *Non pas l'ouvrage, mais l'ouvrier.*

Worley, a griffin sejant per fess or and gu. 62. 10

Worley, an eagle's leg erased at the thigh surmounted by three ostrich-feathers

Worlingham, Baron, *see* Gosford Earl of.

Wormald, Harry Wormald, of Sawley and Cookridge Yorks (1) On three mascles interlaced fesseways or, a boar's head erased sa (*for Wormald*) (2) In front of an arm embowed vested az, cuffed arg, the hand grasping by the blade a sword in bend sinister ppr, pommel and hilt or, a gauntlet fessewise of the last (*for Armitage*) *Noli me tangere*

Workman-Macnaghten, Sir Francis Edmund, Bart Dundarave co Antrim (1) A tower gu (2) Out of a crescent quarterly arg and sa, a lictor's fasces, rods or, axe ppr *I hope in God — Non pas l'ouvrage mais l'ouvrier*

Workman-Macnaghten, Sir Steuart, Bittern, Manor House, Southampton, same crests and mottoes

Worme, Northamp, a bull sejant or, armed and attired sa

Wormington, Ireland, a wolf's head erased sa collared or 30 11

Wormleighton, Wormelayton, or **Wormlayton**, an eagle displayed or, charged on the breast with a cross vair *cf* 75 2

Wornack of Norwich, Norf, a goat's head erased arg, semee of cinquefoils slipped gu *Esse quam videri* *cf* 128 6

Worrall, Ireland a goat's head erased ppr 128 5

Worrall, late James, Esquire, J P, of Oldfield, Whalley Range, Lancs of Ordsall, Manchester, and of Midge Hole Halifax Yorks, upon a trunk of a tree eradicated fessewise and sprouting to the dexter ppr, a bear's paw erect and erased arg *Ingenio ac labore*

Worrall, a lion's gamb erect and erased sa 36 4

Worrell, a lion's gamb erect and erased arg holding a cross crosslet of the same

Worrell of London, a lion's gamb erect and erased sa, holding a covered cup or

Worseley, Surrey, Hants, and Lancs, a wolf's head erased or *Ut sursum desuper* 30 8

Worseley of Depingate, Northamp, the trunk of a tree in fess couped and raguled arg, at the dexter end an acorn branch ppr, thereon a pheasant of the first combed and wattled or

Worship of Great Yarmouth Norf, a cock's head erased or, combed and wattled gu *Nil desperandum* 90 1

Worsley, Lord, *see* Yarborough, Earl of

Worsley, a wolf's head erased or 30 8

Worsley-Holmes, Bart (*extinct*), of Pidford House and Newport, Hants (1) Out of a naval coronet or a dexter arm in armour embowed holding a trident ppr, headed, also or (*for Holmes*) 197 8 (2) A wolf's head erased or (*for Worsley*) 30 8

Worsley, Hants, a wyvern with wings addorsed az, armed and legged gu *Ut sursum desuper* 70 1

Worsley of Overton Hall Derbysh out of a mural coronet or, a wyvern gu

Worsley of Platt, Lancs, within a mural coronet or a wyvern sejant vert, the wings endorsed gu *Per castra ad astra*

Worsley of Worsley Booths, Lancs, a wyvern vert. 70 1

Worsley, Sir William Henry Arthington, Bart J P, D L, of Hovingham Hall, Yorks, same crest *Quam plurimus prodesse* 70 1

Worsley, Tindal-Carill-, of Platt Hall, Lancs (1) On a mural coronet or, a wyvern with wings expanded gu, charged on the body for distinction with a cross crosslet arg, and the motto over, *Quod adest gratum juvat* (*for Worsley*) (2) On a mount vert, a stag lodged regardant or charged on the body for distinction with a cross crosslet sa, with the motto over *Per castra ad astra* (*for Carill*) *cf* 115 9 (3) In front of five ostrich-feathers arg, a fleur-de lis az, between two crescents gu, and the motto over, *Nosce teipsum* (*for Tindal*)

Worsley, Shropsh, a bird rising with wings endorsed

Worsley-Taylor, Henry Wilson, K C Moreton Hall, Whalley, Lancs (1) A demi lion rampant sa, semee of mullets or, holding between the paws an acorn or, slipped vert 233 15 (2) A wolf's head erased encircled by a spear fesseways *Annoso robore quercus* 233 16

Worsley and **Wortley**, a lion rampant ppr holding in the dexter paw a fleur-de-lis 2 7

Worsley-Benison, F H, Esquire, Mowbrick Chepstow (1) A wyvern with wings addorsed az, armed and legged gu (2) A wolf's head erased or *Ut sursum desuper*

Worsopp of Dublin, a dexter hand couped at the wrist, and above it a cinquefoil arg

Worster, a griffin segreant gu 62 2

Worsycke, three arrows points downwards banded ppr 173 1

Worth of Worth Devonsh, and Somers. an arm erect vested az gloved erm the hand holding an eagle's leg couped at the thigh or

Worth, Reginald Percy Esquire, the Priory, Holbeach, same crest *Courage sans peur*

Worth and **De Worthe**, Somers and Devonsh, same crest

Wortham, a lion rampant double-queued per fesse gu and arg 1 14

Worthington of the Bryn, Chesh, a goat statant arg armed or *Virtute dignus avorum* 129 5

Worthington, Suff, of Worthington, Lancs Lincs, and Yorks, a goat passant arg, attired or, holding in the mouth an acorn branch vert, fructed of the second

Worthington, Arthur Mason, in front of a trident erect sa a goat passant arg in the mouth an acorn ppr

Worthington, Charles James, the Holme, Hawkshead, Lancaster same crest *Mihi parent æquoris undæ*

Worthington, Godfrey, Parkside, Altrincham same crest

Worthington, Bayley-, of Sparston Hall Chesh, a goat passant arg, semee of estoiles sa, holding in the mouth a sprig of laurel ppr *In optimum sed gratum*

Worthington, a goat browsing on a shrub ppr Αἰὲν ἀριστεύειν

Worthington of Burton-on Trent and Derwent Bank Derbysh, on the trunk of a tree fessewise eradicated and sprouting ppr, a goat passant arg gorged with a collar gemel sa, holding in the mouth a sprig of oak fructed also ppr *Virtute dignus avorum* 129 11

Worthington, Albert Octavius, Maple Hayes, Lichfield, Staffs same crest

Worthom, a lion rampant double queued per fess gu and arg 1 14

Worthy, a griffin passant with wings addorsed or 63 2

Wortley, *see* Wharncliffe, Earl of

Wortley, Bart (*extinct*), of Wortley, Yorks, an eagle's leg plumed on the thigh with feathers arg

Wortling, a greyhound's head arg between two roses gu, leaved and slipped ppr 61 11

Woryndon, on a ducal coronet or, a martlet gu 95 12

Wotherspoon, Ivan, Iverley, St Anne de Bellevue, care Jaques Cartier P Q, a tower gu, and issuant therefrom an eagle displayed or *Per crucem ad lucem* 235 11

Wotton, Baron Wotton (*extinct*), a Moor's bust sa, vested arg, the head wreathed of the last and first and rising from the neck two dragon's wings also sa

Wotton of Marlay, Kent, a satyr's head in profile couped at the shoulders sa, with wings to the side of the head az

Wotton, out of a mural coronet az, a lion's head or 19 12

Wotton, Somers, an ostrich's head or charged on the neck with a cross formee sa

Woulfe, Ireland, a stork with wings elevated sa *Cuilean nasal* 105 2

Wowen of London, a hawk's lure the feathers arg garnished or charged with a fleur-de lis sa, the string and tassel erect and nowed gu

Wragg, a mullet pierced erm

Wrangham, four ostrich-feathers gu enfiled with a ducal coronet or

Wrangham of Langton-on-the-Wolds, Yorks, a dove volant holding in the beak an olive branch ppr *Hyeme exsuperata* 93 10

Wraxall, Sir Morville William, Bart of Wraxhall, Somers, a buck's head erased and affrontee gu, charged on the breast with two lozenges conjoined in fesse, and between the attires an estoile or 310 8

Wray, Bart (*extinct*) of Glentworth and Kelfield, Lincs, an ostrich or *Et juste et vray* 97 2

Wray, Charles Allan Patea Taranaki, New Zealand, same crest and motto

Wray of Bentfield co Antrim, Ireland, an ostrich arg *Et juste et vray* 97 2

Wray, Durh an ostrich or 97 2

Wray, a parrot's head and neck

Wreahoke, Suff, a talbot passant sa 54 1

Wreford of Clawnaborough Bow, North Devonsh, a griffin's head erased *Vrai et tort*

Wren, on a chapeau ppr, a lion's head erased gu 17 9

Wren of Bilby Hall, Durh., a lion's head erased arg., collared gu., pierced through the neck by a broken spear of the last, headed of the first, vulned of the second.

Wren-Hoskyns of Wroxhall Abbey, Warw.: (1) On a ducal coronet a lion's head erased or, crowned of the same, flames of fire issuing from the mouth ppr., and charged with a crescent az. for distinction (*for Hoskyns*). (2) A lion's head erased arg., pierced through the neck from the dexter by a broken spear and collared gu., and charged with a cross crosslet of the last for difference (*for Wren*). *Vinculo da linguæ vel tibi lingua dabit.—Numero pondere et mensura.—Virtuti fortuna comes.*

Wrench, a stag trippant ppr. 117. 8

Wrench, a slip of three acorns ppr., leaved vert. 152. 5

Wrench, an arm in armour embowed holding in the gauntlet a cross crosslet.

Wrentmore, J. H., 27, Parkhill Road, Hampstead, N.W., a double-headed eagle displayed.

Wrey, Sir Robert Bourchier Sherard, Bart., J.P., of Trebitch, Cornw., an arm embowed habited sa., the hand ppr., holding a hatchet arg., helved gu. *Another:* a man's head in profile, couped at the shoulders, on the head a ducal coronet, therein a cap turned forwards and tasselled of the second, charged with a catherine-wheel or. *Le bon temps viendra.* 190. 3

Wright-Taylor, *see* Taylor.

Wright, *see* Wood-Wright.

Wright, Gibson-, *see* Gibson.

Wright-Bruce, Hon. the late Sir Frederick William Adolphus, G.C.B.: (1) A lion passant az. (*for Bruce*). 6. 2. (2) Out of a mural coronet chequy or and gu., a dragon's head vert, charged upon the neck with three leopards' faces, also or, between two bars gemel arg., and also with a cross crosslet of the first for difference. *Faimus.*

Wright, Oxon., out of a mural coronet chequy or and gu., a dragon's head vert, purfled arg., scaled, also or, charged on the neck with three leopards' faces of the first, between two bars gemelle, also arg.

Wright, a dragon's head arg. 71. 1

Wright, a dragon's head couped erm. 71. 1

Wright, Staffs, out of a mural coronet vert, a dragon's head arg. 72. 11

Wright, Essex, out of a ducal coronet or, a dragon's head vert, collared of the first. *cf.* 72. 4

Wright of Kilverstone, Norf., a dragon's head erased arg., pellettée.

Wright of Bradbury, Durh., a dragon's head couped gu., crusuly arg. *cf.* 71. 1

Wright, Bart. (*extinct*), of Dagenhams, Essex, out of a ducal coronet or, a dragon's head ppr. 72. 4

Wright, Bart., of South Carolina, on a mount vert, and within an annulet or, a dragon's head couped at the neck arg., semée of annulets sa., and murally gorged gu. *Mens sibi conscia recti.* *cf.* 71. 4

Wright, a dragon's head couped erm. 71. 1

Wright of Osmaston Manor, Derbysh., a unicorn's head arg., erased gu., armed and maned or, charged on the neck with three spear-heads, one and two, also gu. *Ad rem.* 250. 8

Wright, Charles Ichabod, of Mapperley and Stapleford Hall, Notts, out of a crescent or, a unicorn's head arg., erased gu., armed and maned of the first. *Ad rem.* 253. 24

Wright of Bolton-on-Swale and Plowland-in-Holderness, Yorks, a unicorn passant regardant quarterly arg. and az., armed or.

Wright, Philip Chetwood, of Brattleby, Lincs, on a mount vert, a unicorn passant regardant arg., semée of estoiles az., armed, maned, and ungu. or, gorged with a collar of the third, the dexter foot resting on a cross patée of the fourth. 255. 18

Wright, Rev. Arthur Samuel, 27, Wolverton Avenue, Norbiton, same crest.

Wright, Caleb, Esquire, M.P., of Lower Oak, Tyldesley, Lancs, on a wreath of the colours a demi-unicorn arg., gorged with a collar vair, and supporting between the legs a battle-axe erect and ppr. *Audax et justus.* 48. 11

Wright, Charles Booth Elmsall, of Botton Hall, Yorks, on a mount vert, in front of a garb erect or, a unicorn regardant az., the dexter fore-foot resting upon a mullet of the second.

Wright of Sigglesthorne Hall, Yorks, a unicorn passant per pale or and az., gorged with a collar gemel, and holding in the mouth a feather of the second. *Meritez.*

Wright, Francis Beresford, Wootton Court, Warwick, a unicorn's head arg., erased gu., armed and maned or, charged on the neck with three spear-heads, one and two, also gu. *Ad rem.*

Wright, Fitzherbert, The Hayes, Swanwick, Derby, same crest.

Wright, out of a ducal coronet or, a bull's head arg., armed of the first. 44. 11

Wright, a bull's head cabossed. 43. 8

Wright, out of a ducal coronet or, a bull's head arg., armed of the first. 44. 11

Wright, Edmund, Esquire, of Manchester, a mount vert, thereon a bull's head erased ppr., surmounted by two javelins in saltire, the staves also ppr., headed arg.

Wright, Henry Smith, Averley Tower, Farnham, Surrey, out of a crescent or, a unicorn's head arg., erased gu., armed and maned or.

Wright, William Maurice, Wold Newton Manor, North Thoresby S.O., Lincs, upon a mount vert, a unicorn passant regardant arg., semée of estoiles az., armed, maned, and hoofed or, gorged with a collar, also az., the dexter foot resting on a cross patée or.

Wright, Captain James Frederick Darley Street, of Mottram Hall, Chesh.: (1) A bull's head arg., erased sa., ducally gorged gu., and charged on the neck for distinction with a cross crosslet, also gu. (*for Wright*). *cf.* 44. 2. (2) A demi-man in armour, his breastplate charged with a cross parted and fretty gu., and supporting with his dexter hand a flagstaff, therefrom flowing to the dexter a banner gu., charged with an annulet or (*for Street*). *Sublimiora quæro.—Quo virtus vocat.*

Wright, Philip, Esquire, Marley Mount, Market Drayton, a unicorn's head arg., erased gu., armed and maned or, charged on the neck with three spear-heads, one and two, also gu. *Ad rem.* 304. 12

Wright, Albert Leslie, Butterley Hall, Derby, same crest.

Wright, Harold Stephen Robert, the Grove, Glenorchy, Hobart, Tasmania, same crest. *Mens conscia recti.*

Wright of Southwark, Surrey, a lion's head erased gardant or, ducally crowned az.

Wright, H. Nelson, Esquire, Indian Civil Service, N. Prov., India, a demi-lion rampant, collared and ducally crowned. *Recta breviora.* 312. 3

Wright of London and Hants, on a mount vert, a heraldic tiger passant or, tufted and maned sa., resting the dexter paw on an escutcheon arg.

Wright, a stag trippant.

Wright of Aldington, Kent, and St. Edmundsbury, Suff., a stag's head erased gu., guttée-d'or, attired of the last. *cf.* 121. 2

Wright, a camel's head couped, bridled or, holding in the mouth three ostrich-feathers.

Wright-Armstrong, Henry Bruce, M.A., Killylea, co. Armagh: (1) Out of a mural coronet or, an armed arm embowed, the hand grasping an oak-tree eradicated ppr. (2) Out of a mural crown chequy or and gu., a dragon's head vert, on the neck three leopards' faces or, between two bars gemel a trefoil slipped or. *Invictus maneo.*

Wright of Barne, Hants, on a ducal coronet an eagle displayed sa. *cf.* 75. 2

Wright, Durh., an eagle's head erminois, ducally crowned az. *cf.* 83. 1

Wright, Hon. John Arthur, M.I.C.E., J.P., of Perth, Western Australia, member of the Executive and Legislative Councils, a gamecock's head erased gu. Over the crest, *Quod volo erit.* Below the shield, *Contre fortune bon cœur.*

Wright, Sir Thomas, the Hollies, Stoneygate, Leics., upon a rock a falcon's head erased ppr., holding in the beak a cross botonny fitchée in bend arg., and charged on the neck with a rose gu., barbed and seeded ppr. *Tam arte quam marte.*

Wright of London, a pelican in her piety, all ppr. 98. 14

Wright of London, a martlet arg., gorged with a bar gemelle flory counterflory az.

Wright of London and Surrey, a falcon's head erased ppr. 88. 12

Wright, Chester, a leopard's face arg. 22. 2

Wright of Woodford, Essex, a wheat-sheaf or, environed by an antique crown sa. *cf.* 153. 5

Wright, Ireland, out of a ducal coronet a broken battle-axe, all ppr.

Wright, Scotland, an arm in armour embowed, the hand grasping a battle-axe, both ppr. *Marte et ingenio.* *cf.* 200. 6

Wright of Haston, Middx., a sinister arm in armour holding in the hand a battle-axe ppr. *Marte et ingenio.*

Wright, two arms embowed, the hands holding a battle-axe, all ppr.

Wright, Scotland, a dexter arm holding in the hand a battle-axe ppr *Tam arte quam marte* cf 213 11

Wright of Bickley Chesh, a dexter arm embowed vested az, holding in the hand ppr a sword point downwards arg, hilt and pommel or, enfiled with a leopard's face of the third

Wright, a naked arm couped at the shoulder and embowed, the elbow resting on the wreath, the hand holding a sword in pale, enfiled with a leopard's face

Wright of Bellendon and Hatfield Priory, Essex a dexter arm couped and embowed fesseways, vested az, purfled or, cuffed arg, holding in the hand a sword, both ppr, hilt and pommel also or enfiled with a leopard's face of the last 204 4

Wright, Charles, Anston, Rotherham, Yorks, same crest

Wright, Staffs and Derbysh, a cubit arm erect in a coat of mail ppr, holding in the hand a spear or, headed az

Wright, General Thomas Charles, of Guayaquil, South America out of a ducal coronet or, an arm embowed in armour ppr, grasping a broken tilting-spear az, pointed or *Honor virtute præmium* 314 7

Wright, George Thomas, Esquire, of Longstone Hall, Derbysh, a cubit arm erect vested sa doubled arg, holding in the hand ppr a broken spear or headed az *Tout jours droit*

Wright, Rev Canon Charles Sisum Eyam Derbysh same crest

Wright, Rev Charles Henry Hamilton 90 Bolingbroke Grove, Wandsworth Common, same crest *Honor virtutis præmium*

Wright, Scotland, an arm in armour embowed issuing from a cloud, holding in the gauntlet a sabre ppr *Pro rege sæpe*

Wright, Sydney Evelyn Liardet, Esquire, of Hope Lodge, Hopper Street Wellington, New Zealand, *uses* the bust of a man affrontee couped at the shoulders, a robe flowing over the sinister shoulder and ducally crowned *Danger I court*

Wright, Edward Percival J P, Trinity College, Dublin, an arm in armour embowed ppr holding in the hand a broken tilting spear az, headed or *Honor virtutis præmium*

Wright, Sir F C Cory-, in front of a tilting-spear erect point upwards ppr, a unicorn passant regardant arg, guttee-de-larmes *Dum vivimus vivamus* 288 4

Wright, Rev Ernest Alexanderson M A, 154, Anlaby Road, Hull, same crest and motto

Wrightson, Sir Thomas, Bart, Neasham Hall, Durh in front of a saltire gu, a unicorn salient or *Veritas omnia vincit* 250 1

Wrightson, John, College of Agriculture Downton, same crest and motto

Wrightson, Robert Garmondsway, Ockenden, Cuckfield Sussex, same crest and motto

Wrightson, a unicorn salient or

Wrightson, Battie- of Cusworth, Yorks (1) Upon a rock ppr, a unicorn rampant arg, resting the sinister foreleg on an escutcheon or charged with a gryphon's head erased az 237 4 (2) A stork ppr, holding in the mouth a fish arg

Wrightson of Osbaston Hall Leics a unicorn's head erased quarterly arg and sa, the first and fourth quarters charged with stars and the second and third with crescents counterchanged armed, maned, and tufted or cf 49 5

Wrightsworth, a crane ppr, holding in its beak a fish arg

Wrigley of Timberhurst, Lancs and the Greenways, Leamington, Warw, a stag's head erased or semee of mullets sa, holding in the mouth a trefoil slipped vert *Aquiret qui tuetur*

Wrigley, Oswald Osmond, Bridge Hall, Bury, Lancs same crest and motto

Wriothesley, Earl of Southampton and Chichester (*extinct*) a buffalo sa armed and chained from a ring in the nose, and with a ducal coronet between the horns all or

Wriothesley or **Wriothsley,** a bull passant sa armed and crowned or in the nose an annulet with a line therefrom reflexed over the back

Writington, a demi fox holding in the dexter paw a cross crosslet fitched az 33 2

Writington, a stag at gaze or 117 3

Wrixon-Becher, Sir John, Bart, Ballygiblin, near Mallow out of a ducal coronet or a demi-lion erm gorged with a plain collar vairee *Bis vivit qui bene*

Wrotesley, a boar's head couped erm armed or 43 1

Wroth or **Wrothe** of Blendenhall Kent, Essex, or Woodbery and Youngs Herts and Hempneyshall Suff, a lion's head erased gardant arg, crowned or

Wrottesley, Baron (Wrottesley), Wrottesley Hall, Wolverhampton, out of a ducal coronet or a boar's head erm, armed and crined of the first 41 4

Wrottesley, out of a ducal coronet or, a boar's head arg charged on the neck with an ermine spot cf 41 4

Wrottesley, Staffs, out of a ducal coronet or, a boar's head erm, armed and crined of the first. 41 4

Wrottesley, a boar's head erased and erect 43 3

Wroughton, Philip of Woolley Park, Berks and Stowell Lodge, Wilts, an ibex's head arg pellettee, collared, ringed, and armed or

Wroughton, a stag lodged ppr 115 7

Wryne, a talbot arg, guttee de poix collared gu, between two holly-branches leaved vert, fructed gu

Wyat of Tewkesbury, Glouc a buck sejant regardant ppr

Wyatt-Edgell, *see* Edgell

Wyatt, a boar's head couped in fess 43 1

Wyatt, out of a mural coronet arg, a demi-lion rampant sa, charged on the shoulder with an estoile of the first and holding an arrow ppr

Wyatt, James William, Esquire, Bryn Gwynan, Beddgelert, North Wales, and Eastcourt, Wells, Somers, same crest *Vi attamen honore*

Wyatt, Arthur Norris, Whitegate, near Northwich, Chesh, same crest and motto

Wyatt of Winchead, Somers, a demi-lion per pale crenellee or and sa, holding in the dexter paw an arrow gu, barbed and flighted arg cf 13 6

Wyatt, Essex, a demi lion rampant sa, guttee-d'or holding an arrow or cf 13 6

Wyatt, Kent, a demi lion rampant sa holding an arrow or, barbed and flighted arg

Wyatt, Hugh Richard Penfold, of Cissbury and Court Wick Sussex (1) A demi lion rampant erased az, charged on the shoulder with a pheon or, and holding in the dexter paw an arrow ppr, headed with a pheon arg (2) Out of park pales alternately arg and sa, charged with three escallops in fesse or, a pine tree fructed ppr *Duriora virtus*

Wyatt of Sherwell Devonsh and Bexley Kent, an ostrich ppr holding in the beak a horse-shoe arg 97 8

Wyatt, an ostrich gu bezantee, holding in the beak a horse-shoe sa 97 3

Wyatt, an ostrich gu, bezantee, holding in the beak a horseshoe sa *Suivez raison* 97 3

Wybergh of Clifton Hall Westml, a griffin's head erased or *Hominem te esse memento* 66 2

Wyborn of Hawkwell Place, Kent a swan arg, membered gu *Fama perennis erit* 99 2

Wybrants, *see* Phipson Wybrants

Wybrants, *see* Geale Wybrants

Wybrants of Dublin, a stag's head erased ppr, attired or, and charged on the neck with a bezant *Mitis et fortis* cf 121 2

Wych or **Wyche** of Davenham Chesh a dexter arm embowed vested gu cuffed or holding in the hand ppr a spring vert

Wychcombe, a buck's head erased 121 2

Wyche, Bart. (*extinct*), of Chewton, Somers, a dexter arm embowed habited gu turned up or holding in the hand a sprig vert

Wycherley of Wycherley Shropsh an eagle displayed sa, ducally gorged arg cf 25 7

Wycliffe of London, a dragon's head arg 71 1

Wycliffe of Thorpe, Yorks, a stag's head cabossed and between the attires a cross crosslet cf 122 5

Wycomb, two arrows in pale ppr points upwards

Wycombe, Earl of, *see* Lansdowne, Marquess of

Wycombe of Wycombe, Shropsh, out of a ducal coronet arg, a demi eagle displayed per pale or and sa gorged with a collar counterchanged cf 80 14

Wydent, an arm vested gu the hand ppr, thereon a bird az, all between two wings sa

Wydnell of Tandridge, Surrey a stork or, with wings expanded sa, bezantee, beaked of the second

Wydope and **Wydrope,** three horse shoes interlaced ppr

Wye, Glouc, on a mount a stag trippant, all ppr 118 2

Wye of Lippiat, Glouc, and Ipswich, Suff a griffin's head with wings ad dorsed az., issuing from a plume of five ostrich-feathers, two arg. and three or.

Wyer, an arm ppr., vested az., holding in the hand a holly-branch vert.

Wyke, Herts, a demi-savage holding in his dexter hand an arrow, and at his back a sheaf of arrows ppr.

Wykeham, *see* Saye and Sele, Baron.

Wykeham-Martin, *see* Martin.

Wykeham, Philip James Digby, of Tythrop House, Oxon., a bull's head sa., armed or, charged on the neck with two chevronels arg. *Manners maketh man.* 241. 10

Wykeham-Musgrave, Captain Wenman Aubrey, Barnsley Park, Cirencester: (1) Two arms in armour embowed, the hands gauntleted ppr., grasping an annulet or, and each arm charged for distinction with a cross crosslet arg. (*for Musgrave*). (2) A buffalo's head sa., armed or, charged on the neck with two chevronels arg. (*for Wykeham*). *Sans changer.* 241. 10

Wykes of Moreton Jeffery, a cock gu. 91. 2

Wykes of Dursley, Glouc., a greyhound's head erased or, collared gu., holding in the mouth a man's leg couped at the thigh arg. 61. 8

Wyld of Bordsham, Denbighsh., a hawk or. 85. 2

Wyld of Speen, Bucks, a lion sejant gardant erect ppr., holding between the paws an escutcheon in pale arg., charged with three martlets. *cf.* 8. 7

Wyld of Edinburgh, a stag's head ppr. *Vigilans et promptus.* 121. 5

Wyldbore, a spear-head in pale embrued ppr., thrust through a boar's head erased in fess.

Wylde of Nettleworth Hall and Southwell, Notts, a demi-buck couped sa., ducally gorged, attired, and ungu. or. *Confide recte agens.* *cf.* 119. 2

Wylde-Brown, Shropsh., a griffin's head erased per pale gu. and sa., gorged with a collar or, charged with two trefoils slipped vert.

Wylde, an eagle displayed or. 75. 2

Wylde, Worcs., a stag's head erased erm. 121. 2

Wylde, Shropsh., on a chapeau gu., turned up erm., a lion passant gardant gu. 4. 5

Wylidon, a dexter hand couped in fess holding a cross crosslet in pale. 221. 10

Wylie, on a rock a fort in flames ppr. 155. 1

Wylie of Largs, Ayrsh., Scotland, a stag's head ppr. *Mentes conscia recti.* 121. 5

Wylie, Bart. (*extinct*), a Cossack mounted and in the act of charging at full speed ppr. *Labore et scientia.*

Wylie, John, Esquire, of Glasgow, a knight on a black horse in full armour wielding a battle-axe in his dexter hand ppr. *Fortes fortuna juvat.*

Wylie, Alexander Henry, Esquire, Twynersh, Chertsey, Surrey, a fox courant ppr. *cf.* 32. 8

Wylie, Alexander Henry, 41, Chester Square, W., same crest. *Spes.*

Wylie, a staff entwined with a serpent surmounted by a sabre saltireways, all ppr. *In utroque paratus.*

Wyllie of Forfar, Scotland, a talbot passant arg., spotted liver colour. *Fides.* 54. 1

Wyllie, a fox courant ppr. *Spes.* *cf.* 32. 8

Wyman, on a garb in fess or, a cock gu. 91. 4

Wymond, Sussex, a cubit arm erect in a coat of mail, holding in the hand ppr. a fire-ball or, fired, also ppr.

Wymond, a demi-eagle displayed vert. 81. 6

Wynall, an owl sa. 96. 5

Wynants (modern spelling Winans) of Brabant and Elizabeth, New Jersey, U.S.A., a demi-moor in profile ppr., with collar and fillet arg., habited gu., holding in the dexter hand a bunch of grapes purpure (a younger branch has the grapes vert) leaved and slipped ppr. *Fors non mutat genus.* 303. 13

Wynchcombe of Bucklebury, Berks, a buck's head erased quarterly az. and or, holding in the mouth a laurel-branch ppr.

Wynche, Essex, out of a naval coronet a lion's head erased gardant arg., between two spears or, headed of the first.

Wynche of Woodford, Essex, a lion's head erased gardant arg., ducally crowned, between two spears or, headed of the first.

Wyndham, Earl of Egremont, *see* Egremont.

Wyndham-Quin, *see* Dunraven and Mount Earl, Earl of.

Wyndham, *see* Leconfield, Baron.

Wyndham, William, of Dinton, Wilts, a lion's head erased within a fetterlock or. *Au bon droit.*

Wyndham, Alexander, same crest.

Wyndham of Cromer, Norf., same crest. *Au bon droit.*

Wyndham, Reginald, Esquire, of Leconfield, Branxton, New South Wales, same crest and motto.

Wyndham, Rev. Thomas Heathcote, Kentisbere Rectory, Cullompton, same crest and motto.

Wyndham, Rev. John, of Sutton Mandeville, Wilts, same crest.

Wyndham, John, Dalwood, Branxton, New South Wales, same crest. *Au bon droit.*

Wyndham of London, Somers., Devonsh., Suff., and Norf., a lion's head erased or, within a fetterlock of the same, the bow company counter-company of the first and az.

Wyndham, Campbell-, Colonel Philip Arthur Pleydell Bouverie, of Dunoon, Greenock, Argyllsh.: (1) A lion's head erased or, within a fetterlock of the last, the bow company counter-company of the first and az. (*for Wyndham*). (2) Two oars of a galley in saltire ppr. (*for Campbell*). *Au bon droit.—Vis et fides.*

Wyndham, George, M.P., 35, Park Lane, W., a lion's head erased or, within a fetterlock, the lock or, and the bow counter-company or and az., the lion's head charged with a saltire wavy gu. *Au bon droit.* 256. 10

Wyndham, Hon. Percy Scawen, Clouds, Salisbury, same crest and motto. 282. 5

Wyndham-Quin, Windham Henry, D.S.O., M.P., 5, Seymour Street, W., a wolf's head erased erm.

Wyndowe, Glouc., a lion's gamb erased az., holding a cross crosslet fitchée or. *cf.* 36. 11

Wyneve, an increscent and a decrescent interlaced within a ducal coronet or.

Wynford, Baron (Best), of Wynford Eagle, Dorset, out of a ducal coronet or, a demi-ostrich rising arg., in its beak a cross crosslet fitchée of the first, gorged with a plain collar, and pendent therefrom a portcullis sa. *Libertas in legibus.* 310. 15

Wyngate, of Harlington, Beds, a hind's head or, gorged with a bar-gemelle sa. *cf.* 124. 1

Wyngate of Barnend, Beds, a gate or. 158. 9

Wynill, Yorks, a wyvern with wings elevated arg., vomiting flames of fire ppr. *Par la volonté de Dieu.*

Wynill, Durh., a wyvern with wings addorsed arg., vomiting flames of fire ppr.

Wynington, Chesh., a still arg.

Wynn, *see* Newborough, Baron.

Wynn, a cubit arm vested sa., holding in the hand ppr. a fleur-de-lis arg.

Wynn, a unicorn's head erased arg., maned, armed, and crined ppr. 49. 5

Wynn of Dudleston, Shropsh., a boar's head gu., couped close or. 43. 1

Wynn, an eagle displayed or. 75. 2

Wynne-Finch, *see* Finch.

Wynne of Nerquis Hall, Flintsh., an eagle displayed or. *E rye eryrod erythi.* 75. 5

Wynne-Eyton, Thomas, Esquire, J.P., D.L., the Tower, Wold: (1) A demi-lion rampant arg., holding between the paws a ducal coronet or. (2) A demi-griffin charged with a rose arg.

Wynne of Pengwern, Merionethsh., an eagle displayed or. *Eryr eryrod eryr.—Di ofn Di ymffrost.* 75. 5

Wynne, Jones-, Ven. Archdeacon, M.A., Treiorwerth Valley, Anglesey, a lion's head erased. *Ior ei werth.* 17. 8

Wynne, William Robert Maurice, of Peniarth, Merionethsh., on a chapeau ppr., a boar passant arg., fretty gu. *cf.* 40. 8

Wynne of Haslewood, co. Sligo, a wolf's head erased arg. *Non sibi, sed toto.* 30. 8

Wynne, Llewelyn (late of Mold, Flintsh.), a Saracen's head affrontée, couped at the shoulders, and wreathed about the temples with a torse, all ppr.

Wynne of Garthewin, Denbighsh., Wales, a stag trippant ppr. 117. 8

Wynne, Bart. (*extinct*), of Leeswood, Flint, a dolphin hauriant arg.

Wynne of Coed Coch, Flintsh., a Saracen's head ppr. 100. 5

Wynne of Ashford, Middx., an arm in armour erect ppr., holding in the gauntlet a fleur-de-lis arg. *cf.* 210. 6

Wynniatt of Guiting Grange, Glouc., a lion's head ducally crowned. *cf.* 18. 8

Wynnington of London and Chesh., a still arg.

Wynston of Painswick, Glouc., and Heref., a garb erect or, sustained on either side by two lions rampant, the dexter arg., the sinister az. *cf.* 3. 3

Wynter, Wales, a heath-cock ppr.

Wynter of Aldeburgh, Suff, a cubit arm erect habited or, holding in the hand three ostrich-feathers, the inner one sa, the outer ones or
Wyrall, a cock's head erased gu 90 1
Wyrlay or **Wyrley** of Dodford Northants, and Hampstead Hall, Staffs, out of a ducal coronet or, two wings addorsed ppr
Wyrley, Staffs, a wing erect ppr 109 7
Wyrrall, Glouc, an arm in armour, holding in the hand a sword, all ppr 210 2
Wyrrall, Glouc, a lion's gamb erect gu, holding a cross crosslet fitched arg cf 36 11
Wyrrall, Shropsh, a lion's gamb erect gu, holding a cross crosslet fitchee arg cf 36 11
Wyrrall of Sodersall, Yorks, a lion's gamb erased sa, holding a cup or 38 14
Wyse of Cuddagh, Ireland, a demi-lion rampant gu, guttee-d'eau *Sapere aude* cf 10 3
Wyse, Lucien William Bonaparte, the Manor of St John's, near Waterford, a lion rampant gu guttée-d'eau, holding in the dexter paw a mace or *Sapere aude*
Wyse, a demi lion rampant gu, guttée-d'eau, holding in the dexter paw a mace ppr *Sapere aude*
Wythens of Wantaway, Berks, Eltham, Kent, and London, on a ducal coronet gu, a talbot sejant erm, collared and lined or, and holding out the line with the dexter paw
Wythernewyke of Cloxby, Lincs, a bustard close arg, winged or 102 9
Wythers, a demi-eagle displayed with two heads ppr cf 82 3
Wythers of Colchester, Essex, and of Marydown and Theden, Hants, a demi-hare az, holding in the mouth three stalks of wheat or
Wyvell of Crediton, Devonsh, on a mount vert a peacock ppr cf 103 4
Wyvell of Croydon Surrey, and Yorks, a wyvern with wings addorsed arg, vomiting flames of fire ppr
Wyvill, Marmaduke D'Arcy, of Constable Burton Finghall, R S O and Denton Park, a wyvern arg, vomiting flames of fire ppr *Par la volonte de Dieu* cf 70 10

X.

Ximenes of Bear Place, Berks out of a mural coronet or, an arm in armour embowed ppr, garnished of the first, the hand, also ppr, supporting a trumpet erect and issuant, also or

Y.

Yabsley, Devonsh, a demi lion rampant holding in the paws a serpent ppr *Industria et spe* cf 9 14
Yaldwyn of Blackdown, Sussex on a chapeau sa, turned up erm, a sword in pale arg hilt and pommel or between two wings of the last *Moriendo vivo* 169 1
Yale of Oswestry, Shropsh, on a chapeau gu, turned up erm, a boar az in a net or
Yale - Jones - Parry, William Corbet Madryn, near Pwllheli, a mount vert, thereon a boar az, within a net or, in the mouth an acorn slipped ppr
Yallop, Norf, a caltrap or, between two wings arg
Yarborough, Earl of (Anderson-Pelham), Brocklesly Park, Lincs (1) A peacock in his pride arg (*for Pelham*) 103, 12 (2) A water-spaniel passant or (*for Anderson*). *Vincit amor patriæ* 57 7
Yarborough of Wilmsby, Lincs, a falcon close or belled of the same, preying on a cock-pheasant ppr
Yarborough, Cooke-, George Bryan, Campsmount, near Doncaster (1) A falcon close or, belled or, preying on a mallard ppr (2) Out of a mural crown arg a demi-lion guardant issuing sa gorged with a ducal coronet or *Non sine pulvere palma*
Yarburgh of Heslington Hall, Yorks, a falcon close or, belled of the same, preying on a duck ppr *Non est sine pulvere palma*
Yard, Kent and Staffs an arrow in pale point upwards, enfiled with a ducal coronet ppr
Yarde, *see* Churston Baron
Yarde of Whiteway and Culver House, Devonsh, out of a ducal coronet or a demi ostrich ppr, holding in its beak a horse-shoe of the first *Facta non verba*
Yardeley, a hind trippant ppr 124 12
Yardeley or **Yardley,** a stag in full course or cf 118 13
Yardley, Wales a buck springing
Yardley of Upbery, Kent and Yardley, Staffs, a buck current gu, attired or cf 118 13
Yardly or **Yardley,** a hind's head or 124 1
Yarker, a greyhound current ppr cf 58 2
Yarker, Charles Braddyll, of Leyburn Hall Yorks a stork rising arg, collared, beaked, and legged gu resting the dexter claw on a human heart of the second holding in the beak an oak-branch fructed ppr *La fin couronne les œuvres*
Yarmouth, Earl of, *see* Hertford, Marquess
Yarmouth, Norf and Suff, a pheasant close ppr cf 90 8
Yarner of Ireland, an arm in armour embowed, the hand holding a battle axe or cf 200 6
Yarrow, a buck trippant gu, attired and ungu or 117 8
Yarworth, an arm erect ppr the hand grasping a snake environed round the arm vert 220. 2
Yarworth, Suff, a hawk ppr, belled or cf 85 2
Yate, a horse's head gu cf 50 13
Yate of Hynton Berks, Bentlott Oxon, and of Wootton Wawen, Warw, out of a ducal coronet or a goat's head sa, armed arg 128 14
Yate of Buckland, Berks out of a ducal coronet or a goat's head sa bearded and armed of the first 128 14
Yate of Uppham Wilts, a demi goat rampant per pale sa and arg, armed counterchanged, holding between the feet a gate or 128 3
Yate of Broomsberrow Glouc (1) An elephant's head arg, tusked or 133 2 (2) A falcon volant or *Quo virtus vocat —Quod pudet hoc pigeat* 88 3
Yates, a demi goat holding between its feet a gate, all ppr *Usque ad aras* 128 3
Yates, out of a ducal coronet or, a goat's head sa armed and bearded arg 128 14
Yates of Streetyate Lancs out of a ducal coronet or a goat's head sa armed of the first *Legale judicium parium* 128 14
Yates, Shropsh, same crest. *Quo virtus vocat*
Yates of Oakwood Hall Yorks upon a mount vert, and in front of two oak-branches in saltire ppr, fructed or a goat's head erased arg, armed also or and charged on the neck with a pellet
Yates of Holm Cot, Devonsh, a goat's head erased arg, guttée-de-larmes pierced through the neck fessewise with a sword, point to the dexter, ppr *Pro Rege et patria*
Yates, Park-, a goat's head couped arg crusuly gu, holding in the mouth a cinquefoil slipped vert
Yates, an antelope's head ppr cf 126. 2
Yates, Captain Oswald Vavasour Compton Pauncefote, North Cadbury, Somers, out of a ducal coronet an antelope's head *Legale judicium parium* 273 3
Yates of Bryanston Square, London, a demi-antelope or, gorged with a collar dancettee az, and holding between the feet a mullet pierced sa *Sit quanta cœli*
Yates, a demi-lion rampant az 10 2
Yates, Scotland, a gate ppr *Securus* 158 9
Yatman, William Hamilton of Wellesbourne Warw, and Highgrove Tetbury, Glouc, a gate arg, in front of three ears of wheat slipped or *Fortiter et aperte*
Yawkins, Scotland, a naked arm embowed wielding a scimitar all ppr *Præsto et persisto* 201 1
Yaxley of Boston, Lincs, and Suff, a demi unicorn arg, collared gobony sa and or 48 10
Yaxley, an heraldic antelope sa, bezantee, attired, maned, and tufted or
Yaxley of Yaxley, Suff, an Indian goat arg, pellettee attired or
Yea, a ram passant arg cf 131 13
Yea, Bart (*extinct*), of Pyrland Hall, Somers, a talbot passant arg *Esto semper fidelis* 54 1
Yeamans, Bart (*extinct*) of Bristol and Redland, Glouc, a dexter arm holding a spear, all ppr 214 11
Yeards, an arrow in pale, point upwards, enfiled with a ducal coronet ppr
Yeates or **Yeats,** a lion's head erased arg 17 8
Yeates, Ireland a shark issuant regardant swallowing a man all ppr 139 2
Yeatman-Biggs, *see* Biggs

Yeatman of Stock House, Dorset, a goat's head erased sa., armed, bearded, and charged with a gate or. *Propositi tenax* 243. 11

Yeatman, Harry Farr, same crest and motto.

Yeldham of Great Saling, Essex, a bezant, thereon a lion's head erased az., gorged with a bar-gemelle flory counter-flory arg. *Fides culpari metuens.* cf. 19. 1

Yelloly of Bracklyn, Clare, Suff., within a crescent arg., a caltrap gu. 163. 11

Yellowley, a bat displayed sa. 137. 11

Yelverton, *see* Avonmore, Viscount.

Yelverton, Earl of Sussex (*extinct*), a lion passant regardant gu. 6. 1

Yelverton, same crest. *Foy en tout.* 6. 1

Yenn of London, a lion passant az. 6. 2

Yeo, Devonsh., a peacock ppr. 103. 7

Yeoman, a hand throwing a dart. *Shoot thus.* 214. 4

Yeoman, a dexter cubit arm in armour, holding in the hand a broken spear, all ppr. cf. 197. 1

Yeoman, Rev. Henry Walker, Marsk Hall, Marske-by-the-Sea, same crest.

Yeoman, Thomas Lawrence, Woodlands, Whitby, a dexter arm, holding a broken spear, all ppr.

Yeomans, a dexter arm holding in the hand a spear ppr. 214. 11

Yer, a wolf sejant sa.

Yerburgh of Yerburgh, Lincs, and Willoughby, Notts, a hawk belled or, preying on a mallard vulned in the head ppr. 238. 14

Yerburgh, Robert Armstrong, Woodfold Park, Blackburn, a falcon close or, belled of the last, preying upon a mallard ppr. *Who dares wins.* 281. 14

Yerburgh, Rev. Edmond Rochfort, Wrentham Rectory, Wangford, Suff., same crest and motto.

Yerbury of Shirehampton, Glouc., and Trowbridge, Wilts, a lion's head per fess or and arg. 21. 1

Yester, a ram's head arg., crowned or. 130. 4

Yetsworth of Sunbury, Middx., out of a ducal coronet a buck's head, both or, holding in the mouth a rose gu., stalked and leaved vert.

Yetts, Scotland, a greyhound's head arg. cf. 61. 2

Yeverey, an elephant's head bendy of six arg. and gu. 133. 2

Yles, Scotland, a stag's head erased. 121. 2

Yockney, Algernon, Woodcliffe, St. Lawrence, Isle of Wight, in front of a dexter arm embowed in armour, the hand in a gauntlet grasping a roll of paper, all ppr., a pair of compasses extended or. *Labore et scientia.*

Yockney, Sidney William, Queen Anne's Gate, Westminster, same crest and motto.

Yoe, an anchor sa. 161. 1

Yon of Barrow and Filmingham, Lincs, a cubit arm erect vested purp., cuffed arg., holding in the hand ppr. a bunch of marigolds of the third, stalked and leaved vert. 205. 14

Yong of Midhurst, Sussex, a demi-griffin segreant regardant az., beaked and legged or, charged with a crescent. 64. 3

Yonge, a stork arg., with wings expanded az., holding in the beak a snake ppr. 104. 13

Yonge of London, a dragon's head erased or, ducally gorged arg. cf. 71. 8

Yonge of Kynton and More, Shropsh., a wolf passant sa. 28. 10

Yonge of Trent, Somers., a lion's head erased per fess or and gu., ducally crowned of the first. 18. 8

Yonge, a boar's head erased vert, armed and bristled or. *Fortitudine et prudentia.* 42. 2

Yonge, Devonsh., a demi-unicorn arg. 48. 7

Yonge of Colbrooke, Devonsh., a demi-sea-unicorn arg., armed gu., finned or. 48. 13

Yonge, Rev. Vernon George, of Charnes Hall, Staffs, an antelope's head erased or, guttée-de-sang. *Et servata fides perfectus amorque ditabunt.* cf. 126. 2

Yonge of Puslinch, Devonsh., a buck's head couped between two fern-branches, all ppr. *Qualis vita, finis ita.*

Yonge or **Young** of Basildon, Berks, out of a mural coronet gu., a goat's head or.

York, Edward, of Hutton Hall, Yorks, a demi-lion per fess wavy gu., and barry wavy of four erminois and az., supporting a wool-pack erect ppr., and charged on the breast with a key fesseways or.

York, out of a ducal coronet a dragon's head. 72. 4

York, Yorks, a monkey's head erased ppr. cf. 136. 14

York of Goulthwayt, Yorks, and Lincs, a thistle ppr. cf. 150. 2

Yorke, *see* Hardwicke, Earl of.

Yorke, Philip, of Erddig, Denbighsh., a lion's head erased ppr., gorged with a collar gu., charged with a bezant. *Nec cupias, nec metuas.* cf. 18. 6

Yorke, John Reginald, 2, Chesham Street, S.W., same crest and motto.

Yorke of Burton-Pedwardyn, Lincs, Yorks, and Brackley, Northants, a monkey's head erased ppr. 255. 7

Yorke, Thomas Edward, Bewerley Hall, Pateley Bridge, Yorks, same crest.

Yorke, Dallas-, Thomas Yorke, of Walmsgate, Lincs, the battlements of a tower ppr., therefrom issuant a dragon's head arg., charged with a mullet of six points az. *Lux venit ab alto.*

Yorks, a lion's head erased collared. 18. 6

Yorstone, Scotland, a rose stalked and leaved, all ppr. 149. 5

Yorstoun, Carthew-, Morden, East Tinwald, Dumfriessh., a tower ppr. *Mens conscia recti.* 156. 2

Youl, Scotland, a garb or. *Per vim et virtutem.* 153. 2

Youl, Charles, Esquire, J.P., of Symmons Plains, Perth, Tasmania, *uses* a wheat-sheaf between three crescents.

Young, Baron Lisgar, *see* Lisgar.

Young-Scott of Redfordhill, and Deanshouses, Peeblessh., a stag's head ppr. *Memor et fidelis.* 121. 5

Young, Ireland, a stag's head erased or. 121. 2

Young, out of a ducal coronet a buck's head between two palm-branches.

Young, a buck's head bezantée, between two palm-branches.

Young-Reynolds of Tully, co. Cavan, on a mount vert, a stag lodged ppr. 115. 12

Young, Yorks, out of a ducal coronet or, an ibex's head arg., armed and tufted of the first.

Young, James, Esquire, of Harristown, co. Roscommon, out of a ducal coronet or, an ibex's head arg., horned and tufted or, and charged on the neck with a trefoil vert.

Young, Owen Waller O'Grady, Harristown, Castlerea, co. Roscommon, same crest. *Victoria fortitudo virtus.*

Young, a boar's head couped at the neck ppr.

Young of Orlingbury, Northamp., a boar's head and neck erased ppr. 41. 5

Young, Oliver, Hare Hatch House, Twyford, Berks, a boar's head and neck erased vert.

Young, a squirrel sejant gu., holding a nut-branch vert, fructed or. 135. 2

Young, a squirrel sejant gu., charged on the body with a chevron compony or and az., holding a nut-branch vert, fructed of the second. cf. 135. 2

Young of Tully, co. Cavan, Ireland, a horse's head couped sa. cf. 50. 13

Young, Sir George, Bart., M.A., of Formosa Place, Bucks, a demi-unicorn couped erm., maned, armed, and ungu. or, gorged with a naval coronet az., supporting an anchor erect sa. *Be right and persist.* 310. 6

Young of Hawkhurst, Kent, a griffin's head erased per fess vert and or, charged with two escallops counterchanged. cf. 66. 2

Young, Keays-, of Eylesden Court, Sutton Valence, Maidstone, a gryphon's head erased per fesse vert and or, charged with two escallops in pale counterchanged, the whole between as many fleur-de-lys or. *Quo patria vocat.* 258. 14

Young of Roscommon, out of a ducal coronet or, a dragon's head erect ppr. 72. 4

Young, late Sir Charles George, Garter Principal King of Arms: (1) A dragon couchant with wings elevated gu., collared, and the chain reflexed over the back or, holding in the mouth a rose per pale of the last and arg., seeded and slipped ppr. (2) In water representing the sea, an anchor erect sa., the ring and stock or, the shank entwined by a serpent ppr. *Nullius in verba.*

Young of Lambeth, Surrey, from water ppr., an anchor erect sa., the stock and ring or, the stem entwined by a serpent, also ppr.

Young of Stanhill Court, Charlwood, Surrey, an anchor or. *Dum spiro spero.*

Young of Rosebank, Scotland, an anchor in the sea surmounted by a dove holding in its beak an olive-branch, all ppr. *Sperando spiro.* cf. 94. 4

Young, Scotland, a dolphin haurient. 140. 11

Young, Scotland, a dolphin naiant ppr. *Every point.* 140. 5

Young of Poulton-cum Seacomb, Chesh, and Wales, a demi lion or, collared per pale erm and ermines 10 9

Young, Scotland, a demi-lion gu holding in the dexter paw a sword erect ppr *Robere prudentia præstat* cf 14 12

Young, a lion rampant gardant per fess or and gu, supporting a battle axe of the first

Young, Kent, a lion's head gardant or, between two wings arg, each charged with a fleur-de lis az

Young, Sir William Need Muston, Bart, J P of Bailieborough Castle, co Cavan, a demi lion rampant gu, charged on the shoulder with a trefoil slipped and holding in the dexter paw a sprig of three maple leaves, also slipped or *Prudentia*

Young, William Mackworth C S I, Lahore, Punjaub a demi unicorn couped erm, armed maned and ungu or gorged with a naval crown az, supporting an anchor erect sa

Young of Auldbar, Forfarsh, a lion gu issuing out of the wreath, and holding a sword in pale ppr *Robert prudentia præstat*

Young, Bernard Joseph, of Kingerby, Lincs, a wolf sejant regardant sa, holding between the fore paws the head of King Edmund ppr *Toujours jeune*

Young of Poole House Worcs, a wolf passant sa 28 10

Young of Croome D'Abitot Worcs, and Stratton Audley Oxon, a stork with wings expanded arg beaked gu, holding in the beak a snake ppr 104 13

Young, Scotland, a sword and a writing-pen in saltire ppr *Pro patria semper —Dominus providebit* 170 4

Young of Eastfield, Scotland, a dexter hand holding a pen ppr *Scripta manent* 217 10

Young of Lindbank, Scotland, a dexter hand ppr holding a bezant

Young of Trent, Somers a cubit arm erect habited az, holding a staff or.

Young, Bart., Bucks, a cubit arm erect, the hand grasping an arrow, all ppr *Press through.* cf 214 4

Young, Sir William, Bart, 16, South Eaton Place S W same crest and motto

Young, William, Esquire, J P D L, of Brockley Park, Queen's Co, and of Doohulla Lodge, co Galway, Ireland a cubit arm erect ppr charged with an annulet or, the hand grasping an arrow point downwards, also ppr *Press through* cf 214 4

Young, Sir Frederick K C M G, J P, D L, 5 Queensberry Place, Queensgate, S W a dexter cubit arm erect holding in the hand an arrow in bend sinister, all ppr *Press through*

Young, Rt Hon George, 28, Moray Place Edinburgh same crest and motto

Young, Sir William Lawrence Bart, of North Dean, Bucks, a cubit arm erect, the hand grasping an arrow, all ppr *Press through*

Young of Leny Scotland, a dexter arm holding in the hand a lance in bend ppr *Press through*

Young, William, Cleish Castle, Kinross, a dexter arm, the hand grasping a spear in bend all ppr *Press through*

Young, John Kirkpatrick 25, Earl's Terrace, Kensington an anchor or *Dum spiro spero*

Younge of Raxwell and Roxhall, Essex within a chaplet vert, a griffin's head erased or

Younge of Buckhorne and Colbrooke, Dorset a demi-sea-unicorn arg armed and finned gu 48 13

Younge, Hants a stag's head erased per fess erm and gu 121 2

Younge of London, and Drayton Staffs, on a rock a Cornish chough, all ppr 106 9

Younge of Grenford, Middx and Durnford Wilts, a demi-greyhound erased arg cf 60 11

Younger of Daventry, Northants and Heref, a stag's head or 121 5

Younger, Scotland, an armed leg couped at the thigh az, spurred or 193 1

Younger, George Alloa, N B an armed leg couped at the thigh ppr, garnished and spurred or *Celer et audax.* 255 17

Younger, James Arnsbrae, Alloa, N B, same crest and motto

Younger, William, 29, Moray Place, Edinburgh, same crest and motto

Younger, Robert, 16 Old Square, Lincoln's Inn Fields, W C, same crest and motto

Younger, John, Esquire, Colonel R A, a dexter arm, the hand holding a lance bendways ppr *Tout prest* 214 11

Younger, Henry Johnston of Benmore and Kilmuir Argyllsh, Esquire same crest and motto 214 11

Younger, Colonel John, Langshaw Bush, Moffat, N B, same crest and motto

Younger, William, Esquire, of Auchen Castle, Moffat, Dumfriessh, and Staveley Lodge Leics, a dexter hand holding a lance in bend ppr *Tout prest* 214 11

Younghusband of Wrighton Melbourne, Victoria, on water ppr, a swan sa, beaked gu semee of mullets arg holding in the beak an annulet or *Virtutis conjux —Still und stols gleitend* 99 11

Younghusband of Crossthwaite, Lancaster same crest and motto

Ypres, an eagle with wings expanded ppr 77 5

Yuille of London, an ear of wheat ppr, leaved vert 154 3

Yuille of Darleith, Dumbarton, same crest *Numine et virtute*

Yule, Scotland, a stalk of wheat bladed *Per vim et virtutem* 154 3

Yule, an Indian shield affrontee sa damasked or, with a naked Indian scimitar ppr, and scabbard gu, in saltire behind the same, pommelled and mounted, also gu, and on the margin of the shield is inscribed the Indian word *Hazir Per vim et virtutem*

Yvain, out of a ducal coronet a dexter hand holding a rose-branch, all ppr 218 11

Z.

Zachary of Areley Kings, Worcs, a garb or, charged with an acorn slipped and erect vert *Virtus per se* cf 153 2

Zachert and **Zachet,** three roses, the centre one arg, the outer ones gu, slipped vert 149 12

Zamoyska, a demi Indian goat rampant

Zeal, Senator the Hon Sir William Austin K C M G, M I C E, of Clovelly Lansell Road, Toorak Victoria, Australia, a demi-griffin segreant arg, collared and lined or *Mora trahit periculum*

Zephani of Walton-on Thames, Surrey a demi-man representing Surajud Dowla Subah of Bengal in his complete dress, the sinister hand resting on the head of a tiger enraged the dexter wielding a scimitar in the attitude of striking the blade broken all ppr *Miserrima vidi —Scuto divino*

Zetland, Marquess of (Dundas) Aske Richmond, Yorks, a lion's head affrontee gu, struggling through an oak bush all ppr fructed or *Essayez* 310 7

Zibet of Sweden, a civet cat issuant regardant ppr *Cœlum non animum*

Zinzan, a dove with wings expanded az 94 2

Zorks, an eagle with two heads displayed, surmounted of a saltier gu

Zornlin, Surrey, an arm embowed bare to the elbow holding in the hand a barbel *Fai bien crain rien*

Zouch, an ass's head couped or 125 12

Zouch, Wilts, an ass's head arg, muzzled with cord az, and charged on the neck with a fleur-de lis vert

Zouch, an ass's head tied round the mouth by a cord, all arg

Zouch, out of a ducal coronet gu, a mule's head arg, bridled ppr

Zouch of Pyrton, Wilts and Somers, on a staff couped and raguly or, sprouting at the dexter point, a raven with wings expanded arg

Zouch, Shropsh, a falcon with wings expanded arg, standing on a branch or, leaved az *Prevalet virtus*

Zouche, Baron (Curzon), Parham Park, Pulborough Sussex (1) A popinjay rising or, collared gu (2) A falcon, wings displayed arg standing on the stock of an old tree, from which is sprouting a green leaf or twig ppr, rising or, collared beaked and legged gu *Let Curzon holde what Curzon helde*

Zouche, an ass's head couped erm 25 121

Zurich, on a ducal coronet or, a lion passant gardant gu ducally crowned of the first cf 4 3

Zymon, a cross crosslet and a sword point downwards in saltier cf 106 12

PART II.

(1) MOTTOES.

(2) KEY TO PLATES.

(3) DICTIONARY OF TERMS.

MOTTOES.

A

Motto	Translation	Names
Ab aquila	*From the eagle*	Gilly.
Abest timor	*Fear is far from us*	Ewart, Ker.
Ab origine fidus	*Faithful from the first*	Maclaurin.
Abscissa virescit	*Though lopped off, it flourishes*	Bisset, Bissett.
Absit fraus	*Let all deception be far off*	Gordon.
Absit ut glorier nisi in cruce	*God forbid that I should glory save in the cross*	Clarke.
Absque dedecore	*Without stain*	Napier.
Absque Deo nihil	*Nothing without God*	Peters.
Absque labore nihil	*Nothing without labour*	Edmonds, Steele.
Absque metu	*Without fear*	Dalmahoy.
Absque virtute nihil	*Nothing without virtue*	Harrison, Rogers.
Abstulit qui dedit	*He who gave has taken away*	Howard, Jerningham-Stafford.
Ab uno ad omnes	*From one to all*	Drummond.
Accendit cantu	*He rouses up by crowing*	Cockburn.
Accipe crucem	*Receive the cross*	Gibbons.
Accipe daque fidem	*Receive and give pledges of fealty*	Crickett.
Accipiter prædam nos gloriam	*The hawk seeks its prey, we glory*	Hawker, Strother.
A clean heart and a cheerful spirit		Portman.
A cœur vaillant rien impossible	*To a valiant heart nothing is impossible*	Hartcup.
Actio virtutis laus	*The deed is the commendation of the virtue*	Ashburne.
Acquirit qui tuetur	*He obtains who maintains*	Mortimer.
Acre		Cameron.
A cruce salus	*Salvation from the cross*	Beardsley, Bourke, Burgh, Burke, De Burgh, Glencross, Græme, Jefferson.
A cuspide corona	*From the spear a crown*	Brodrick, Chapman, Midleton.
A cuspide honos	*Honour by the spear*	Swindley.
Ad admissum	*About to be accepted*	Cunningham.
Ad al[illegible]	*To [illegible] high*	Bartholomew, Cairnie, Guthrie, Struther, Struthers.
Ad altiora tendo	*I strive to higher things*	Melville.
Ad amussim	*According to rule*	[illegible]-Cunyngham.
Ad ardua tendit	*He attempts difficult things*	Heron, M'[illegible].
Ad arma paratus	*Prepared for arms*	Johnston, Johnstone.
Ad aspera virtus	*In the face of difficulties, courage*	Sinclair.
Ad astra	*To the stars*	Moorsom.
Ad astra nitamur semper ad optima	*Be the stars, be the best things, always our aim*	Bigsby.
Ad astra per ardua	*To the stars by steep paths*	Drummond.
Ad astra sequor	*I follow to the stars*	Tottenham.
Ad astra virtus	*Virtue leads to heaven*	Saltmarshe, Sinclair.
Ad cœlos volans	*Flying to the heavens*	Clavering.
Ad cœlum tendit	*He aims at heaven*	Booker.
Addecet honeste vivere	*It becomes us to live honourably*	Addison.
Addere legi justitiam decus	*It is an honour to combine law and justice*	Adderley.
Addicunt aves	*The omen is favourable*	Loutfuttes, Lutefoot, Lutefoote.
Ad diem tendo	*I long for day*	Cooch, Stein, Stevens.
Addit frena feris	*He applies the curb to savage natures*	Milner.
Addunt robor	*They give strength*	Hamilton.
Addunt robur stirpi	*They increase the strength of the family*	Hamilton.
A Deo et patre	*From God and my father*	Thomas.
A Deo et rege	*From God and the king*	Fawkes, Hampton, Lewis, Stanhope.
A Deo floruit	*His prosperity came from God*	Watson.
A Deo honor et fortuna	*From God honour and good fortune*	Sands.
A Deo in Deo	*From God in God*	Troyte.
Ad æthera	*To the skies*	Falconar.

A Deo lumen	*Light from God*	Ker, Kerr.
A Deo lux nostra	*Our light is from God*	Holloway.
A Deo, non fortuna	*By God, not by fortune*	Greaves, Greaves-Banning.
A Deo salus	*God is my salvation*	Jacob.
A Deo victoria	*Victory from God*	Græme, Graham.
Ad escam et usum	*For food and use*	Garden, Gardin, Graden.
Adest et visum	*Present to the sight*	Greiden.
Adest prudenti animus	*Courage belongs to prudence*	Hamilton.
Ad finem	*To the end*	Tose, Tosh.
Ad finem fidelis	*Faithful to the end*	Colvil, Colville, Gilroy, Horsfall, Howson, Kerslake, Peto, Wedderburn-Scrymgeour, Whitehead.
Ad finem spero	*I hope to the last*	Ogilvie.
Ad fœdera cresco	*I gain by treaties*	Oliphant, Oliver.
Ad gloriam per spinas	*Through thorns to glory*	Thorn.
Adhæreo virtuti	*I cling to virtue*	Kennedy.
Adhæreo	*I cling fast*	Burrell.
Ad honorem industria ducit	*Industry leads to honour*	Joynson.
Adhuc viresco	*I am still growing green*	Smollett.
Adjuvante Deo	*With God's assistance*	Acton, Malins.
Adjuvante Deo in hostes	*With the assistance of God against our enemies*	Donovan, O'Donovan.
Ad littora tendit	*It makes for the shore*	Jamaieson, Jamieson, Quatherine.
Ad littora tendo	*I make for the shore*	Jarvie, Watson.
Ad metam	*To the goal*	Bower, Combrey, Comrie, Comry, M'Leurg.
Ad mortem fidelis	*Faithful unto death*	Candler, Cheetham.
Adorn the truth		Waddell.
Ad rem	*To the purpose*	Wright.
Adsit Deus	*God be with me*	Balfour.
Adsit Deus non demovebor	*God with me, I shall not be removed*	Baird.
Adsum	*I am here*	Dumas.
Ad summa virtus	*Courage to the last*	Bruce.
Ad summum emergunt	*They rise to the top*	Fullarton.
Ad te, Domine	*To thee, O Lord*	Newman.
Advance		Brand, Ferrier, Speir, Spiers.
Advance with courage		Majoribanks, Marjoribanks.
Advena in sylvis	*A stranger in the woods*	Foster.
Adversa virtute repello	*I repel adversity with courage*	Denison, Dennistoun, Medhurst.
Adversis major, par secundis	*Greater than adversity, a match for prosperity*	Bulwer, Bulwer-Lytton, Forbes.
Adverso fortior	*Stronger than adversity*	Clifton-Dicconson, Dicconson.
Ægis fortissima virtus	*Virtue is the strongest shield*	Aspinall.
Ægre de tramite	*With difficulty along the path*	Tait.
Ægre de tramite recto	*With difficulty along the right path*	Horsburgh, Horseburgh.
Æquabiliter et diligenter	*Constantly and carefully*	Mitford, Moore, Wilde.
Æquam servare mentem	*To preserve a steady mind*	Beckford, Green, Hoyle, Matthew, Moon, [illegible], Preacher, Raymond, Rivers.
Æquanimitate	*With equanimity*	Latham.
Æquanimiter	*With equanimity*	Harbord, Shuttleworth.
Æquitas actionum regula	*Let equity be the rule of our actions*	Bradbury, Montagu.
Æquitate ac diligentia	*With fair play and diligence*	Ashbury.
Æquo adeste animo	*Be ready with constancy*	Bergne, Cope, Copland.
Æquo animo	*With an equable mind*	Pennant.
Æquo pede propera	*Proceed with a steady pace*	East.
Æternitas	*Eternity*	Rayson.
A favore regis nomen	*A name by favour of the king*	Kingan, Kinghan.
Affectat Olympo	*He aspires to heaven*	Bell.
A fin	*To the end*	Griffith, Ogilvie, Ogilvy.
Afrad pob afraid	*All unnecessary things waste*	Vaughan-Chamber.
After darkness comes light		Hewitt.
A fyn Duw a fydd	*What God wills, will be*	Mathew, Williams.
A fynno Duw deued	*Let God's will be done*	Edwards.
A fynno Dwy y fydd	*Let what God wills be*	Hughes, Matthew.
A Gair Duw yn uchaf		Morris.
Age aut perfice	*Act or achieve*	M'Millan.
Age in æternum	*Do what will be for ever*	Conwell.
Agendo gnaviter	*By doing diligently*	Barrows, Leeke.
Agendo honeste	*By doing honourably*	Farmer.
Age omne bonum	*Do all good*	Algood, Allgood.
Agere et pati	*To do and endure*	Shiell.
Agere pro aliis	*To act for others*	Ashton.
Agincourt		Wodehouse.
Agissez honnêtement	*Act uprightly*	Cardwell.
Agitatione paratus	*Prepared by activity*	Russell.
Agitatione purgatur	*It is purified by motion*	Russel, Russell.
Agite pro viribus	*Act according to your ability*	Campbell.
Agnoscar eventu	*Let me be known by the issue*	Ross.

Agnus Dei mihi salus	*The Lamb of God is my salvation*	Lammin
Agnus Dei salvator meus	*The Lamb of God my Saviour*	Haslam
Agnus in pace, leo in bello.	*A lamb in peace, a lion in war*	Edmonds.
A good conscience is a sure defence		Parick
A Home! a Home! a Home!		Home
Aides, Dieu!	*Help, O God*	Aubert, Mill.
Aide toi Dieu t'aidera	*Help thyself and God will help thee*	Caillard
Aide-toi et le ciel t'aidera	*Help thyself and heaven will help thee*	Willmott
Aime ton frère	*Love thy brother*	Freer
Aime le meilleur	*Love the best*	Sinclair
Aimer sans crainte	*Love without fear*	De Massue
Aimez loyauté	*Love loyalty*	Paulet, Pawlet, Orde-Powlet
Ainsi et peut être meilleur	*Thus and perhaps better*	Rolleston
Ainsi il est	*So it is*	Bellingham
A jamais	*For ever*	James
A la bonne heure	*In good time*	Bonnor
A la vérité	*In truth*	Bremer
A la volonté de Dieu	*At the will of God*	Cholmley, Strickland
Alba de Tormes		Hamilton
Albuhera		Lumley
Alert		Croasdaile.
Ales volat propriis	*The bird flies to its own*	Tufton
Algiers		Pellew
Aliis reposita	*Laid by for others*	Cant
Alis aspicit astra	*Flying, he keeps his eye on the stars*	Carnagie, Carnegie
Alis et animo	*With wings and courage*	Gillow, Monro
Alis nutrior	*I am fed by birds*	Simpson, Simson
Alla corona fidissimo	*Most faithful to the crown*	Leche
Alla ta Hara		Mildmay
Alleluiah		Tuite
All is in God		Clovile, Clovyle
All my hope is in God		Fraser, Frazer, Udney
All's well		Mudge
A'lo heco Pecho	*What can't be cured must be endured*	Frankland
Alta pete	*Aim at high things*	Fletcher, Glen, Glenn, Greenall, Greenhall, Tolhurst
Alta petens	*Aiming at high things.*	Hubbard
Alta petit	*He aims at high things*	Marshall, Stott
Alta peto	*I aim at high things*	Greenall, Smethurst, Sotherne
Alte fert aquila	*The eagle soars high*	Rice
Altera merces	*Another reward*	Maclaine, M'Lean, Maclean.
Alteri prosis sæculo	*May you be a blessing to the generation to come*	Graham.
Alteri sic tibi	*Do to another as to thyself*	Harvey
Alteri, si tibi	*To another, if to thee (do to another as to thyself).*	Harvey, Onley
Alterum non lædere	*Not to the injury of another*	Keir
Alte volat.	*He flies high*	Dawson
Alte volo.	*I fly high*	Heywood.
Altiora in votis	*Desire greater things*	Des Vœux.
Altiora pete	*Seek higher things*	Gordon
Altiora petenda	*Higher things must be aimed at*	Burke
Altiora peto	*I seek higher things*	De Cetto, Drummond, King, Oliphant.
Altiora sequimur.	*We follow after higher things.*	Pode
Altiora spero	*I cherish loftier hopes*	Torr
Altiora videnda	*We must look to higher things*	Honor
Altius	*Higher*	Gregory
Altius ibunt qui ad summa nituntur	*They will rise higher, who aim at the highest things*	Forbes, Fordyce
Altius tendo	*I strive higher*	Kinloch, Kinlock
Always faithful		M'Kenzie
Always for liberty		Mawbey
Always helping		Garvine
Always ready		Hall
Always the same		Freebairn
Ama Deum, et serva mandata	*Love God, and obey his commandments*	Synnot
Amantes ardua dumos	*Loving thorny steeps*	Thornhill
A ma puissance	*To the utmost of my power.*	Grey
Amat victoria curam	*Victory loves care; Success is gained by careful attention*	Clark, Clerk
A ma vie	*For my life*	Lievre
Ambo dexter	*Skilful with both hands*	Hewetson
Amice	*In friendship*	Russel, Russell, Watts
Amicitia cum virtute	*Friendship with virtue*	Bradbury
Amicitiæ virtutisque fœdus	*The league of friendship and virtue*	Hippisley.
Amicitiam trahit amor	*Love draws friendship*	Neish
Amicitia permanens et incorrupta	*Friendship constant and incorruptible*	Harrison.
Amicitia reddit honores..	*Friendship gives honours*	Pringle.
Amicitia sine fraude	*Friendship without guile*	Allardice, Allen
Amico fidus ad aras	*Religiously faithful to your friend*	Rutherford, Rutherfurd.
Amicos semper ama	[illegible] *friends*	Leather-[illegible]

Motto	Translation	Names
Amicta vitibus ulmo	*The elm being covered with vines*	Elmsall, Greaves
Amicum proba hostem scito	*Prove a friend, know an enemy*	Fraser
Amicus	*Friendly*	Peit
Amicus amico	*Friendly to a friend*	Bellingham
Amicus certus	*A trusty friend*	Peat
Amicus vitæ solatium	*A friend is the solace of life*	Burton
Amitié	*Friendship*	Pitt
Amo	*I love*	Douglas, Hoops, Mackinlay, Montagu-Douglas Scott, Montagu-Scott, Scott, Scote
Amo honesta	*I love noble deeds*	Thomson
Amo, inspicio	*I love, I look*	Scot, Scott
Amo pacem	*I love peace*	Towle
Amo probos	*I love the virtuous*	Blair, Scot, Scott, Towle
Amœnitas, salubritas, urbanitas	*Amenity, salubrity, and urbanity*	Ryde
Amor Dei et proximi summa beatitudo	*The love of God and our neighbour the greatest blessing*	Dobbs
Amor dulcis patriæ	*The love of dear country*	Wigram
Amore floresco	*I flourish with love*	Moore
Amore non vi	*By love, not by violence*	Amory, Heathcote-Amory
Amore patriæ	*By the love of our country*	Scot
Amor et pax	*Love and peace*	Ireland
Amore vici	*I conquered by love*	M'Kenzie, Mackenzie
Amore vinci	*Vincible by love*	M'Kenzie
Amor patitur moras	*Love endures delays*	Lumsden
Amor patriæ	*The love of country*	Brasier, Pinney, Pretor
Amor patriæ vincit	*The love of country conquers*	Meyler
Amor proximi	*Love one's neighbours*	Craney
Amor sine timore	*Love without fear*	Reade
Amor vincit omnia	*Love conquers all the world*	Usher
Amour avec loyauté	*Love with loyalty*	Parr
Amour de la bonté	*Love of goodness*	Cowell
Amo, ut invenio	*I love as I find*	Perrott
Anchora labentibus undis	*Amid the drifting currents an anchor*	Franklin
Anchora salutis	*The anchor of salvation (hope)*	O'Loghlen, O'Loughlin
Anchor fast		Gray, Groat
Anchor, fast anchor		Gray
Angelis suis præcepit de te	*He has given his angels charge of thee*	Power
Anguis in herba	*A snake in the grass*	Anguish
Angusta ad augusta	*From straitened circumstances to exalted*	Sheffinham
A Nilo victoria	*From the Nile victory*	Gould
Animæ capaces mortis	*Souls capable of death*	Teesdale
Anima in amicis una	*In friends one soul*	Powell
An I may		De Lyle, Lyall, Lyle, Montgomery
Animi fortitudo	*Fortitude of mind*	Mecham
Animo	*With courage*	Gordon
Animo et corpore nitre	*With a strong mind and body*	Venables
Animo et fide	*By courage and faith* *With resolution and fidelity*	Burroughes, Goulten, Grotrian, Guilford, Hawkes-Cornock, North, Phillips, Scourfield
Animo et prudentia	*With courage and prudence*	Jowett
Animo et scientia	*With courage and knowledge*	Clark
Animo non astutiâ	*By courage, not by stratagem*	Gordon, M'Nish, Pedler, Smith Gordon
Animum fortuna sequitur	*Fortune follows courage*	Bedford, Craik
Animum ipse parabo	*I shall myself prepare my mind*	Holland-Hibbert
Animum prudentia firmat	*Prudence strengthens courage*	Brisbane
Animum rege	*Govern your mind*	Beck, Fewster, Keith, Moore, Reeve, Reeves
Animus et fata	*Courage and destiny*	Thriepland
Animus non deficit æquus	*Composure does not desert me.*	Burrell
Animus, non res	*Our soul, not our property*	Huth
Animus tamen idem	*A mind yet unchanged*	Cuffe, Wheeler
Animus valet	*Courage prevails*	Bosworth
A noddo Duw a noddir	....	Jones
Annoso robore quercus	*An oak in full strength*	Aitkenhead, Taylor
Ante expectatum diem	*Before the wished for day*	Steinman
Ante honorem humilitas	*Humility before honour*	Battersby
Antiquum assero decus	*I claim ancient honour*	Arrat, Arrot
Antiquum obtinens	*Possessing what is ancient*	Bagot, Cotgreave, Shakerley
An uachter		O'Hauraghan
Any boro		Weston
Aperto vivere voto	*To live with undisguised devotion*	Finch, Lyne
Ap Ithel		Bethell
A pledge of better times		Samuel
Apparet quod	*It appears that*	Edgar
Apparet quod latebat	*What was hid is now manifest*	Edgar
Appetitus rationi pareat	*Let reason govern desire*	Ashworth, Custance, Fitzwilliam
Appropinquat dies	*Day dawns*	Johnston
Apto cum lare	*With a fit abode*	Elliot
Aqua cadit resurge	*Water falls to rise again*	Waterfall
Aquilæ vitem pocula	[illegible]	Boteler

Motto	Translation	Names
Aquila petit solem	*The eagle soars to the sun*	Kendall
Aquila non capit muscam	*The eagle is no fly-catcher*	Cotton
Aquila non capit muscas Aquila non captat muscas .	*The eagle does not catch flies*	Bacchus, Bedingfield, Buller, Chinn, Drake, Flounders, Gothard, Graves, Greaves, Illidge, Manningham Buller, Wedderburn, Weston
Aquitaine		Martin
Arbor re careat vince		Nussey
Arcui meo non confido	*I trust not to my bow*	Wilk, Wilkes
Arcus, artes, astra	*The bow, arts, and stars*	Birney, Burmey
Ard choille	*The woody hill*	MacConachie, M'Gregor, Macgregor
Ardens	*Burning.*	Peat
Ardenter amo	*I love fervently*	Bell, Scot, Scott.
Ardenter prosequor alis	*On wings I ardently pursue*	Græme
Ardet virtus non urit	*Valour burns but consumes not*	Fyres
Ardua petit ardea	*The heron seeks high places*	Hearn, Heron
Ardua tendo	*I attempt difficult things*	Malcolm
Ardua vinco Arduo vinco	*I conquer difficulties* *I overcome by hardihood*	Straiton, Wakefield
Arduis sæpe, metu nunquam .	*Often in difficulties, never in fear*	Brassey
A rege et victoria	*From the king and conquest*	Barry, Bullen, Ligonier, Tatchell-Bullen
Ariverette		Cameron
Arma parato fero	*I carry arms in readiness*	Campbell, MacGuffie, M'Guffie
Armat et ornat	*For defence and ornament*	Brown
Armat spina rosas .	*The thorn is the defence of the rose*	Rose
Arma tuentur pacem	*Arms are the guardians of peace* .	Fowke
Arma virumque cano	*Arms and the man I sing*	Gabriel
Armé a tous points .	*Armed at all points*	Byrom
Armé de foi hardi	*Armed with hardy faith*	Hardy
Armis et animis	*By arms and courage*	Carnagie, Carnegie, Gilfillan, Gilfillian
Armis et diligentia	*By arms and diligence*	Baskenford, Baskin
Armis et fide	*By arms and fidelity*	Campbell
Armis et industria	*By arms and industry*	Cochran
Armis frango	*I break by arms*	Gib.
Armis potentius æquum	*Justice is more powerful than arms*	Falconer
Arn Duthchas		Doherty, O'Dogherty
Ar nid yw puyil pydyw		Powell
Ar ol gwaith gorphoys		Whitelocke Lloyd
A rore colorem	*Its colour from the dew*	Murray
Arr dwrr v Gyd	*All depends upon God*	Price
Arrivrette		Cameron
Ars bona violentia	*An art requiring exertion*	Baker
Arte et animo	*By stratagem and courage*	Ferguson
Arte et industria	*By art and industry*	Baynes
Arte et labore	*By art and labour*	Smythe
Arte et Marte	*By art and force*	Adair, Drummond, Ferguson Fawsitt, Hunter, Middleton
Arte fideque .	*By art and faith*	Orrock
Arte firmus	*Firm by art*	Mason
Arte non vi	*By art, not by violence*	Jordan
Artes honorabit	*He shall honour the arts*	Hanger
Arte utile facio	*I make what is useful by my art*	Craig
Arte vel Marte	*By art or force*	Deans, Dundas
Artibus et armis	*By arts and arms*	Elton
Artis vel Martis	*Of skill or force*	Eastoft, Eure
Arx et anchora mihi Deus	*God is a stronghold and a security for me*	Rawson
Arx mea Deus	*God is my stronghold*	Castell
As an arrow true		Nicolls
Ascendam	*I will rise*	Kennaway
Asgre lau diogel et pherchen	*A pure conscience is a safeguard to its possessor*	Herbert, Vaughan
A spe in spem	*From hope to hope*	Perkin
Aspera ad virtutem est via .	*Rough is the path to virtue*	Edwardes, Edwards
Aspera juvant	*Dangers delight*	Stewart
Aspera me juvant	*Perils delight me*	Low
Aspera virtus	*Rugged valour*	Sinclair
Aspira	*Aspire*	Feld
Aspire		Edward
Aspire, persevere, and indulge not		Adams
Aspiro	*I aspire*	Curry, Freeman, M'Fell, Ramsay, Caldwell.
Assaye	*Try* .	Dundas
Assiduitas	*Assiduity* .	Beck, Quayles
Assiduitate	*By constant application*	Buist, Johnston, Skeen
Assiduitate non desidia	*By constant application, not by sloth*	Loch, Lock
Assurgam	*I rise up.*	Hinton
Ast necas tu	*But thou killest*	Brook
Astra, castra, numen, lumen	*The stars my camp, God my light*	Lindsay
Astra, castra, numen, lumen, munimen	*The stars my camp, God my light and protection*	Balcarres, Lindsay

Motto	Translation	Names
Astra et castra	*The stars and my camp*	Littler
Atalanta		Hardinge.
At all tymes God me defend		Lyell
A te, pro te.	*From thee, for thee*	Savage
A tot bien estrainz		Latter
A tout jour loill	*Always loyal*	Fenwick
A tout pourvoir	*Provide for all.*	Oliphant.
A tribulacione	*By tribulation*	Cokain
At secura quies	*But in repose is safety.*	Huskisson.
At spes infracta	*But hope is undaunted*	Cunninghame, Dick, Hood
At spes non fracta	*But hope is not lost*	Cawthorne, Hope, Hope Johnstone, Kennard, Leckie, Scott Hope.
At spes solamen	*But hope is comfort*	Hope
Attamen tranquillus	*Tranquil notwithstanding*	Maitland
Attendez vous	*Give attention*	Boyes.
At vincet pauperiem virtus	*But bravery will conquer poverty*	Grey
Au bon droit	*By just right*	Wyndham
Auctor pretiosa facit	*The author makes the value*	Hobart Hampden, Lubbock, Parker
Audacem juvant fata	*The fates assist the bold*	Somerville, Sommerville
Audaces fortuna juvat	*Fortune favours the brave*	Baron, Barron, Bourke, Bowen, Burroughs, Carpenter, Chamberlayne, Columbine, Cosby, Costello, Flanagan, Forster, King, Moore, Pendleton, Roney, Turnbull
Audaces juvat	*She favours the brave*	Campbell, Cleveland, Googe, Sands
Audaces juvo	*I favour the brave*	Buchanan, Campbell, M'Casland, MacCausland
Audacia	*By daring deeds*	Grant
Audacia et industria	*By boldness and diligence*	Buchanan
Audaci favet fortuna	*Fortune favours the brave*	Turnbull
Audaciter	*Boldly*	Buchanan, Euen, Ewan, Ewing, Orr Ewing
Audacter et aperte	*Boldly and openly*	Campbell
Audacter et sincere.	*Boldly and sincerely*	Clive, Herbert, Powis
Audacter et strenue	*Boldly and vigorously*	Crawfurd, Morris, Pollock, Pollok
Audax	*Bold*	Erthe
Audax ero	*I will be brave*	Boldero.
Audax et celer	*Bold and quick*	Pearce
Audax et justus	*Bold and just*	Wright
Audax et promptus.	*Bold and ready*	Douglas, Rusby
Audax et vigilans	*Daring and vigilant*	Currie
Audax ingenii	*Of a bold disposition*	Woodburne
Audax in recto	*Bold in the right*	Stewart
Audax justum perficere	*Bold to perform what is just*	Strathy
Audax omnia perpeti	*Bold to endure all things*	Buchanan, Harding
Audax pro suis	*Bold for himself*	Howitt
Audax vincendo	*Bold by overcoming*	Ashburn
Aude et prevalebis	*Dare and you will prevail*	Frend.
Aude, incipe	*Dare, begin*	Anderton
Audentes fortuna juvat	*Fortune assists the daring*	Burroughs, Mackinnon, Moubray, Mowbray, Trimnell, Turing, Twing
Audentior ito	*Proceed more boldly*	Grant
Audeo	*I dare*	Rose.
Audi alteram partem	*Hear the other side*	Kennett, Ramsbottom
Audio et juvo	*I hear and assist*	Harker
Audio, sed taceo	*I hear, but am silent*	Trollop, Trollope
Audito et gradito	*Hear and advance*	Cruickshank, Cruikshanks.
Augeo	*I increase*	Trent
Augeor dum progredior	*I increase as I proceed*	Durham
Au plaisir fort de Dieu	*At the mighty will of God*	Edgcombe, Edgcume, Edgecumb
Aura adversa auxiliatrix	*The breeze though adverse is helpful*	Mills
Auriga virtutum prudentia	*Prudence is the charioteer of the virtues*	Mawbey
Au roy donne devoir	*To the King give duty*	Royden
Ausim et confido	*I dare and I trust*	Areskine, Erskin, Erskine
Auspice Christo	*Under the guidance of Christ*	Davie, Lawley, Rowe
Auspice Deo	*Under the guidance of God*	Spied
Auspice Deo vinces	*Under the guidance of God thou wilt conquer*	Beley
Auspice Numine	*Under divine direction*	Welsh
Auspice summo Numine	*Under direction of the God most high*	Irvine
Auspice Teucro	*Under the guidance of Teucer*	Tucker
Auspicium melioris ævi	*A pledge of better times*	Beauclerc, Beauclerk; Motto of the Order of St Michael and St George
Aut agere aut mori	*Either to do or die*	Barclay.
Aut Cæsar aut nihil	*Either Cæsar or no one*	Wall
Aut homo aut nullus	*Either a man or no one*	Atkinson
Aut mors aut libertas	*Either death or liberty*	Wall
Aut mors aut vita decora	*Either death or an honourable life*	Gordon
Aut mors aut vita Deus	*Or death or life, God*	Gordon
Aut nunc aut nunquam	*Either now or never*	Lee.

Aut nunquam tentes, aut perfice	*Either do not attempt, or complete*	Bennet, Bennett, Creswell, Germain, Sackvill, Sackville
Aut nunquam testes aut perfice		Ward
Aut pax, aut bellum	*Either peace or war*	Donaldson, Gunn, Hall, Tweedie
Aut tace, aut face	*Either be silent, or act*	Scot, Scott
Aut viam inveniam aut faciam	*I shall either find or make a path*	Wightwick, Wyntwyck
Aut vincam aut peream	*I will either conquer or perish*	Purcell
Aut vincere aut mori	*Either to conquer or die*	Garroway, Sykes
Aut vita libera aut mors gloriosa	*Either a free life or a glorious death*	Savery
Au valeureux cœur rien impossible	*To the brave heart nothing is impossible*	Messeury.
Auxilia auxiliis	*Helps with the help of helps*	Helps
Auxiliante resurgo	*I arise through help*	Graham
Auxilio ab alto	*By aid from above*	Martin
Auxilio Dei	*By the help of God*	Dongall, Ensby, Morehead, Muirhead, Murehead, Stark
Auxilio divino	*By divine assistance*	Drake, Grimwood, Hill
Auxilium ab alto	*Aid from above*	Dillon, Kallet, Machin, Martin, Normand, Prickett
Auxilium meum ab alto	*My help is from above*	Blakeney, Dixon
Auxilium meum a Domino	*My help is from the Lord*	Martin, Mostyn, Owen, Price
Avance	*Advance*	Bristow, Colyear, Collyer, De Colyar Ramsay.
Avancez	*Advance*	Chalmers, Chambers, Churton, Hill
Avant	*Forward*	Adamson, Forbes, Harrington Stuart, Stewart, Stuart, Trefusis
Avant Darley	*Forward Darley*	Stewart
Avant sans peur	*Forward without fear*	Seton Karr
Avauncez et archez bien	*Advance and shoot well*	Swinnerton
Avec ce que je tiens, je suis content	*I am content with that which I have*	Bradshaw
Ave Maria plena gratia	*Hail, Mary, full of grace*	Cusack
Avi numerantur avorum	*The forefathers of our forefathers are numbered*	Hitch, Norton, Perton, Pryce, Rede, Turbervill
A virtute orta	*Sprung from bravery*	Stewart
Avise la fin	*Consider the end*	Cassels, Kennedy, Keydon, Haffey
Avise le temps.	*Consider the times*	Omond
Avito jure	*By ancient right*	Wheeler
Avito non sine honore	*Not without ancestral honour*	Lippington.
Avitos juvat honores	*He maintains his ancestral honours*	Wishart
Avitos novit honores	*He knows the honours he inherits*	Gusthart
Avito viret honore	*He flourishes by ancestral honours*	Creighton-Stuart, Farley M'Kenzie, Mackenzie-Wortley Stuart, Stewart, Stuart, Turner-Farley, Villiers, Wortley
Aviumque volatus	*And a flight of birds*	Wilson
Avonno div dervid	*The all-sufficient God will send*	Lloyd
Avorum honor	*The honour of my ancestors*	Ryland
Avorum honori	*For the honour of my ancestors*	Barne
Avorum non immemor	*Not unmindful of his ancestry*	Quain
Avyno Duw dervid	*What God has willed will be accomplished*	Edwards
Await the day		Mayne
A Wightman never wanted a weapon		Wightman, Wighton
Aye forward		Brand
Aye ready		Hozier
Ayez prudence	*Have prudence*	Biss
Aymes loyauté	*Love loyalty*	Powlett
Aymez loyaute	*Love loyalty*	Carthew, Cowan, Paulett
Azincourt		Billam, Billan, Lenthall, Waller, Wodehouse

B

Badamy		Munro.
Baroach		Nicholson
Barrossa		Gongh
Basis virtutum constantia	*Steadiness is the foundation of the virtues*	Bass, Devereux
Be and not seem		Rolt
Bear and forbear		Barwis, Beare, Bere, Bernard, Burgoyne, Burnard, Grazebrook, Langford, MacEvoy, Milward, Morland Bernard, Philip, Philips, Phillip, Philps, Rowley, Sayer Milward
Beare and forbeare		Langley
Bear thee well		Bardwell
Bear up		Fulford
Be as God will		Praed [illegible]

Motto	Translation	Names
Beati pacifici	*Blessed are the peace-makers*	Stewart, Finlay.
Beati qui durant	*Blessed are they who endure*	Durant.
Beatus qui implevit	*Blessed is he who has finished (his task)*	Bingley.
Be bolde, be wyse		Gollop, Tilly.
Bedhoh fyr ha heb drok		Carthew.
Be ever mindful		Campbell.
Be faithful		Vance, Vans-Agnew.
Be fast		Boutcher, Savill, Saville, Thornhill.
Be firm		Coats, Cotes, Compton, Dalrymple, Ferrie, Webb.
Be hardie		Edmonston, Edmonstone.
Be hardy		Carthew, Dauglish, Edminston, Edmonstone.
Be it fast		Ashby, Atkins, Fotheringham.
Be just and fear not		Ashbee, Ashby, Coleman, Gervis, Hewitt, Payne, Peacock, Tapps, Warren.
Bella dextra	*Wars with the right hand*	Ellis.
Bella ! horrida bella	*Wars! horrid wars!*	Lysaght.
Bello ac pace paratus	*Prepared in peace and in war*	Braikenridge.
Be mindful		Brodie, Calder, Campbell, Ismay, M'Gillivray, M'Liver.
Be mindful to unite		Brodie.
Bene	*Well*	Binney.
Bene denoto	*I indicate well*	Shaw.
Benedicite fontes Domino	*Bless the Lord, ye fountains*	Twells.
Benedic nobis Domine	*Bless us, O Lord*	Bain.
Benedicto Dei ditat	*He enriches with the blessing of God*	Laurie.
Benedictus qui tollit crucem	*He is blessed who bears the cross*	Bennet
Bene factum	*Well done*	Weldon
Beneficii memor	*Mindful of a benefit*	Butler.
Beneficiorum memor	*Mindful of favours*	Kelham, Nicholson.
Bene paratum dulci	*Well prepared for good fortune*	Ogilvy.
Bene præparatum pectus	*A heart well prepared*	Jex-Blake.
Bene qui pacifici	*Blessed are the peace-makers*	Allardice.
Bene qui sedula	*He who acts diligently acts well*	Arkley.
Bene tenax	*With noble tenacity*	Bennet.
Benigno numine	*Under propitious influence*	Barned, Bentley, Copeland, Hicks, Horsford, Meigh, Pitt, Rowland, Smith.
Benigno numine fusis	*Under a propitious Deity I have prospered*	Dodson.
Be not wanting		Baillie, Bazilie, Bazley.
Ben ti voglio	*I wish thee well*	Richardson.
Be ready		Lawrence.
Be right and persist		Young.
Be steadfast		Carvick.
Be strong and of good courage		Beddington.
Be sure		Pasley-Dirom.
Be traist		Innes, Innes-Ker, Sheils.
Be trewe		Hamilton-Tyndal-Bruce.
Be true		Bruce, M'Gaurie, Morkill.
Be true and you shall never rue		Duff.
Better a wee bush than nae bield		Burns.
Better deathe than shame		Pearsall.
Better kinde frembd than frembd kyen		Waterton.
Beware		Cleborne.
Beware in time		Lumisden, Lumsdean, Lumsden.
Beware the reaping		Brookfield.
Be watchful		Daroch, Darroch.
Be wise as a serpent, harmless as a dove.		Lewis.
Bhear na righ gan	*May the king live for ever*	Fleming.
Bidd llu hebb llydd		Lewis.
Bienfaicia paieray malfaictz vangeray	*Benefits I will award, injuries I will avenge*	Walrond.
Bien fait	*Well done*	Weldon.
Bien ou rien	*Well or not at all*	Scott.
Bis dat qui cito dat	*He gives twice who gives quickly*	Bisson.
Bi 'se mac an t-slaurie	*Be thou the son of the crook*	Beacher-Wrixon, M'Laurin.
Bis ti ici	*Once here twice here*	Kincaid.
Bis vincit qui se vincit	*He conquers twice who conquers himself*	Bysse.
Bis vivit qui bene vivit	*He lives twice who lives well*	Becher.
Bi treuu		Scobie.
Bladensburg		Ross.
Blow, hunter, thy horn		Forrester
Blow shrill		Mercier.
Bold		Spence.
Bon accord	*Good harmony*	Towers.
Bonæ virtutis amore	*From love for true valour*	Le Conteur.
Bona fide sine fraude	*In good faith without fraud*	Singleton.
Bon fin	*A good end*	Graham.
Bon fortune	*Good luck*	Ferrier
Bonis omnia bona	*All is good to the good*	Orr.
Bonne et [illegible]elle a[illegible]ez	*G[illegible] and [illegible]and[illegible] [illegible]*	Belasis, Bellasis, Bellasyse, Bowes [illegible].
Bono anim[illegible] [illegible]	*[illegible]*	M[illegible]rr[illegible]ll.

Bono vince malum	*Overcome evil with good*	Finch, Gerard, Kettle
Bon temps viendra	*A good time will come*	Gage, Rokewood-Gage
Bonus justus et utilis	*Good, just, and useful*	Lerrier
Boulogne et Cadiz	*Boulogne and Cadiz*	Heygate
Boutez en avant	*Put forward*	Barry, Barry Garrett Standish, Barry Smith, Fowle
Boyne		Kidder
Breyrgrod Eryri	*The Barons of North Wales*	Wynn Williams
Buaidh go bragh		Mahon
Buail tre cabhavi a buaig		Swiny
Bualim se	*I strike him*	MacCartan
Bua noo bawse	*Victory or death*	O'Hagan
Burning I shine		Jehangier
Butler a boo		Butler
Butt sicker		Sutherland
By aim and by effort		Higginbotham
By assiduity		Byass
Bydand	*Remain*	Gordon, Seaton
Bydand	*Remaining*	Canning, Gordon, Wolrige-Gordon
Bydand to the last	*Remaining for ever*	
Byde		Gordon
Byde be		Brey
By degress		Gordon
Byde together		Cathcart
By faith we are saved		Hall
By industry and honour		Gavin, Gavine
By industry we prosper		Cunard, Moreton
By perseverance		Login
By the grace of God		MacSween
By the providence of God		MacCouach
By these we shine		Atkins
By the sword		Lucy
By truth and diligence		Herin, Heron
By valour		Jenkins
Byw a gadael byw		Hare
By watchfulness, by steadfastness		Stirling
By wounding I cure		

C

Cabool		Burnes
Cadarn ar cyfrwys	*Strong and cunning*	Williams
Cadarn-yw-fy ffydd y portha-duw y gig frain		Rice
Cada uno es hijo de sus obras	*Every man is the son of his works*	Boss
Cadenti porrigo dextram	*I extend the right hand to the falling*	Pearse King, Knight
Cadere non cedere possum	*I can fall, but not yield*	Cottingham
Caen, Crecy, Calais		Radcliffe
Cælitus mihi vires	*My strength is from heaven*	Jones
Cælitus vires	*Strength from heaven*	Whitson
Cæteris major qui melior	*He is greater who is better than the rest*	Radcliff, Radcliffe
Caffraria		Willshire
Cais y gornchaefiedd syddo duw unig		Kyffin, Kyffyn
Cala raggi wethlow		Carminow
Calcar honeste	*A spur with honour*	Crawford
Callide et honeste	*With skill and honour*	Calley
Calm		Macadam, M'Adam
Campo fero præmia belli	*I bear off the rewards of war from the field*	Campbell
Canada		Brock, Prevost, Smith
Candida ma fides	*My faith is serene*	Hill
Candide	*With candour*	Stewart
Candide et caute	*With candour and caution*	Elliot, Elliott, Grieve
Candide et constanter	*Candidly and steadily*	Coventry, Irvine, Pickup, Sassoon
Candide et secure	*Frankly and fearlessly*	Gilstrap
Candide et secure	*Openly and fearlessly*	Graham, Maxtone-Graham, Murray
Candide sed caute	*Candidly, but cautiously*	Sinclair
Candidior	*More dearly*	Mair
Candidiora pectora	*Purer hearts*	Whytt
Candidus cantabit moriens	*The pure man will sing on his deathbed*	Campbell
Candor dat viribus alas	*Candour gives wings to strength*	Boyd, Hogarth, Howgart, Rochfort
Candore	*By candour*	Robe
Candoris præmium honos	*Praise is the reward of sincerity*	Dunbar
Capta majora	*Employed in greater things*	Geddes, Parkhill
Caraid 'an am feum	*A friend in time of need*	Gow, Smith, Smyth, Stewart

Cari Deo nihilo carent	*God's beloved are in want of nothing*	Burton, Weekes
Carid nam fecham		Smith
Carid nam fechm		Smyth
Caritas fructum habet	*Charity yields fruit*	Burnell, Pegge-Burnell
Carn na cuimhne	*The rock of remembrance*	Farquharson
Carpe diem	*Enjoy to day*	Baker, Bradbury, Clarke, Cullen, Finch, Horsfall
Cas ni charo y wlad ai magno		Joseph
Cassis tutissima virtus	*Virtue is the safest helmet*	Armour, Britten, Chamley, Cholmondely, Helme, Helsham
Castra et nemus Strivilense	*The camp and the grove at Stirling*	Stirling
Cate at caute	*Carefully and cautiously*	Gatty
Catius quam citus	*With more shrewdness than dispatch*	Roscow
Cause caused it		Elphinstone
Caute et sedulo	*Cautiously and carefully*	Brown, Johnstone
Caute, non astute	*Cautiously, not craftily*	Ross
Caute, sed impavide	*Cautiously, but without fear*	Cayzer.
Caute sed intrepide	*Cautiously, but fearlessly*	Drummond
Caute, sed strenue	*Cautiously, but vigorously*	Hamlyn.
Cautus a futuro	*Cautious for the future*	Bowen
Cautus metuit foveam lupus	*The wary wolf dreads the pitfall*	Caton
Cave	*Beware*	Cave
Cave, adsum	*Beware, I am here*	Ashmore Jardin, Jardine
Cave, Deus videt	*Beware, God sees*	Cave
Cave et aude	*Beware and dare*	Darwin
Cave lupum	*Beware of the wolf*	Huband
Cavendo	*Being cautious*	Crowfoot
Cavendo tutus	*Safe by being cautious*	Allmack, Awmack, Candlish, Cavendish, Cruckshanks, Cruickshank, Cruikshank, Hardwick, M'Candlish, Waring
Cave paratus	*Be prepared, and beware*	Johnston, Johnstone
Cave ut comprehendas	*Take care you understand*	Drury
Ceart laidir abu		Fitzpatrick
Ceart na suas		MacCochlan
Cedamus amori	*Let us yield to love*	Blunden
Cedant arma	*Arms must give place..*	Barclay
Cedant arma labori	*Let arms give place to labour*	Stubs
Cedant arma togæ	*Arms must give place to the gown*	Reade
Ceidw Owain a Gafodd		Owen
Celer	*Swift*	Miller
Celer atque fidelis	*Swift and faithful*	Dunne, Dun
Celer et audax	*Swift and bold*	Jackson, Scales, Pearce
Celer et vigilans	*Swift and watchful*	Balls-Headley, Douce
Celeritas	*Swiftness*	Becquet
Celeritas et veritas	*Swiftness and truth*	Rolls
Celeriter	*Swiftly*	Lane
Celeriter et jucunde	*Quickly and pleasantly*	Rogers
Celeriter nil crede	*Believe nothing hastily*	Stringer
Celeriter sed certe	*Swiftly but surely*	Grieveson
Ce m'est égal	*This is equal to me*	Phillips Treby
Certa cruce salus	*Sure salvation by the cross*	Garrat, Garritte, Kinnaird
Certamine parata	*Prepared for the contest*	Cairncross, Carncross
Certamine summo	*In the midst of the battle*	Brisbon, Brisbane, M'Onoghuy
Certanti dabitur	*It shall be given to him who strives for it*	Oldershaw
Certavi et vici	*I have fought and conquered*	Byrne, Cross, Levin, O'Byrne, O'Flanagan, Shortall, Thunder, Thursfield
Certior dum cerno	*More sure while I discern*	Lundin.
Certior in cœlo domus	*A surer habitation in heaven*	Adams
Certo dirigo ictu	*I aim with a sure blow*	Thurburn
Certum pete finem	*Aim at a sure end*	Bissland, Corse, Crosse, Greig, Howard, Thompson
Cervus lacessitus leo	*The stag at bay becomes a lion*	Sheridan.
Cervus non servus	*A stag, not a slave*	Goddard, Thorold
César Auguste		Priaulx
Chacun le sien	*To each his own*	Bourke
Chase		Geary
Chassé pour foi	*Persecuted for the faith*	Andovier, Lamb
Cherche et tu trouveras	*Seek and thou shalt find*	Sawyer
Cherche la vérité	*Seek the truth*	De la Rue
Cherche qui n'a	*Let him seek who has not*	Margary
Cheris l'espoir .	*Cherish hope*	Cherry
Che sara sara	*What will be, will be*	Chatferld, Chatfield, Dyer, Russell.
Chescun son devoir	*To each his own*	Cox
Chi dura vince	*He who endures overcomes*	Spiers
Chi la fa l'aspetti	*As a man does, so let him expect to be done by*	Mazzinghi
Chi legge regge	*Who reads rules ..*	Amphlett.
China		Gough
Chi semini vertu raccoglia fama	*He who sows virtue shall reap fame*	Coore
Christi crux [illegible]	*Christ's cross is m*[illegible]	Northcote
Christi [illegible]	*Be Christ my* [illegible]	Stewart

Motto	Translation	Family
Christi pennatus sidera morte peto	*With wings, through the death of Christ, I seek the sky*	Fetherston
Christo adjuvante	*By the help of Christ*	Lucie, Smith
Christo duce feliciter	*Happily, Christ being my conductor*	Binning
Christo duce vincamus	*Let us conquer with Christ as leader*	Madden
Christo suavis odor	*A sweet savour to Christ*	Ross
Christus mihi lucrum	*Christ is my gain*	Stewart
Christus pelicano.	*Christ is like the pelican*	Lechmere
Christus providebit	*Christ will provide*	Thomson
Christus servatus vera libertas	*To serve Christ is true liberty*	Vaughan
Christus sit regula vitæ	*Let Christ be the rule of life*	Samevell Watson
Cia'll agos neart	*Reason ana strength*	O'Connell
Cia'll agus neart	*Reason and strength*	O'Connell
Cio che Dio vuole io voglio	*What God will, I will*	Dormer
Circumspice	*Look round you*	Wise
Cito non temere	*Quickly, not rashly*	Northcote
Civil and religious liberty		Wood
Clan-Fergail a bu	[illegible]	O'Halloran
Clariora sequor	*I pursue more illustrious objects.*	Buchanan
Clarior astris	*Brighter than the stars*	Baillie
Clariores e tenebris	*Brighter after the darkness*	Polden, Puleston
Clarior e tenebris	*Brighter after obscurity*	Bright, Gray, Leeson, Lesone, Lightbody, Purves, Purvis, Sapwell
Clarior ex obscuro	*More glorious from obscurity*	Sanderson
Clarior hinc honos	*Hence the greater honour*	Buchanan, MacCausland,
Clarior virtus honoribus	*Virtue is more illustrious than preferments*	Clay
Claris dextera factis	*Illustrious deeds done by the right hand*	Byam
Claritate dextra	*With a bright light on the right*	Brady, Geale-Brady
Clarum reddit industria	*Industry renders illustrious*	Milne
Clausus mox excelsior	*Shut in, by and by higher*	Close
Clementia et animis	*By clemency and courage*	Maule
Clementia tecta rigore	*Clemency shielded by rigour*	Maule
Clementia in potentia	*Clemency in power*	Compton
Cœlestem spero coronam	*I hope for a heavenly crown.*	Humfrey
Cœlestes pandite portæ	*Open ye heavenly gates*	Gibson
Cœlestia canimus	*We sing of heavenly things*	Synge, Synge Hutchinson
Cœlestia sequor	*I follow heavenly things*	M'Donald, Macdonald Bowie, Monro
Cœli favore	*By the favour of the heavens*	Roxburgh
Cœlis exploratis	*Having searched the heavens*	Herschel
Cœlitus datum	*Granted by heaven*	Borthwick, Finlason, Finlay
Cœlitus mihi vires	*My strength is from heaven*	Firbank, Jones
Cœlitus vires	*Strength is from heaven*	Mallet
Cœlum ipsum petimus	*We aim at heaven itself*	Hoste, Sawtell
Cœlum, non animum	*Heaven, not courage*	Ashworth, Finlayson, Rhodes, Strachy, Waldegrave, Waldgrave, Zibet
Cœlum non animum mutat	*Change of climate does not change the mind*	Ramsden
Cœlum, non solum	*Heaven, not earth*	Barnes, Hamilton, Hayman, Steavenson, Stephenson - Hamilton, Stevenson, Stevenstone
Cœlum quod quærimus ultra	*What seek we more than heaven*	Godman
Cœlum versus	*Heavenward*	Dickson
Cœur fidèle	*Faithful heart*	Hart
Cogadh na sith	*Peace or war*	M'Crummin
Cogit amor	*Love compels*	Joass
Cogit in hostem	*He attacks the enemy*	M'Gilchrist.
Cogito	*I think*	Wemyss
Cogi qui potest nescit mori	*He who can be compelled knows not how to die*	Norton
Cognoies toy-mesme	*Know thyself*	Braddyll
Cognosce teipsum, et disce pati	*Know thyself, and learn to suffer*	Rawlings
Cole Deum	*Worship God*	Coull
Colens Deum	*Worshipping God*	Collins
Colens deum et regem	*Worshipping God and the king*	Collins
Coloony		Vereker
Color fidesque perennis	*Beauty and everlasting faith*	Irton, Irvine
Comiter sed fortiter	*Blandly but determinedly*	Sheffield.
Comme a Dieu playra.	*As shall please God*	Thorp
Comme Dieu grantit	*As God grants*	Grantham
Comme je fus	*As I was*	More, Ward.
Comme je trouve	*As I find it*	Butler, Cary, Shelley
Commit thy work to God		Mowat, Sinclair
Commodum, non damnum	*A gain, not a loss.*	Backie, Baikie
Completur	*It is finished*	Arnot
Compositum jus fasque animi	*Law and equity*	Law, Laws
Conabimur	*We will attempt*	Davies
Conamine	*Make the attempt*	Kirke
Conamine augeor	*I am enriched by the effort*	Leslie, Lesly
Conanti dabitur	[illegible]	[illegible]
Con can an	[illegible]	[illegible]

Motto	Translation	Names
Concipe spes certas	*Indulge sure hopes*	Sealy
Concordant nomine facta	*Our deeds correspond with our name*	Grace
Concordia	*With harmony*	Cobham
Concordia crescimus	*We increase by concord*	Bromhead
Concordia et harmonia	*By concord and harmony*	Gallini
Concordia et industria	*By concord and industry*	Dent
Concordia et sedulitate	*With harmony and diligence*	Goldsmid
Concordia, integritas, industria	*Concord, integrity, and industry*	Rothschild
Concordia præsto	*Concord at hand*	Forbes
Concordia res crescunt	*Public affairs thrive by concord*	Bromhead
Concordia vim dat	*Concord gives strength*	Blumberg
Concordia vincit	*Unanimity overcomes*	Cochran, Cochrane, Cochrin
Concussus surgit	*It rises though shaken*	Garnoch
Concussus surgo	*I arise from the shock*	Garnock, Garnocks, Gray
Condidi	*I have stored up*	Stewart
Conduco	*I lead*	Cowper Essex
Conduct is fate		Brown, Browne, De Beauvoir
Confide recte agens	*Trust in fair dealing*	Broadhead, Jackson, Long, Newdegate, Newdigate, Norton, Pease, Pooll, Wooler, Wylde
Confidimus	*We will trust*	Boyd
Confido.	*I trust*	Bell, Boyd, Le Bon, Mills, Peters, Sellar, Simpson
Confido, conquiesco	*I trust, I am content*	Dysart, Dysert, Hodgetts, Tollemache
Confido in Deo	*I trust in God*	Backhouse, Barrow
Confido in Domino	*I trust in the Lord*	Peterkin
Confido in probitate	*I trust in honesty*	Baillie
Confido in providentia	*I trust in providence*	Richardson
Confido, non confundor	*I trust, I am not put to shame*	Bisco, Tyndale, Tynedale
Confido recte agens	*I trust in honest dealings*	Cozens Newdegate
Confisus viribus	*Trusting in my strength*	Watson
Congoies toy mesme	*Know thyself*	Braddyll
Conjuncta virtuti fortuna	*Fortune joined to bravery*	M'Beth
Conjunctio firmat	*Union strengthens*	Middleton
Conlan a bu		Moore, O'More
Conn can an	*Wisdom without blemish*	Concanon
Connois vous-même.	*Know yourself*	Lacon
Conquer or die		Crosthwaite, Thornhill
Conquiesco	*I am at rest*	Metcalfe
Consequitur quodcunque petit	*He obtains whatever he seeks*	Drummond, Petit, Taylor, Taylour
Conservabo ad mortem	*I will defend and preserve till death*	Jennings
Conservata fides perfectus amorque ditabunt	*Constant fidelity and perfect love will enrich*	Yonge
Consider the end		Milroy, Rosher
Consilio ac virtute	*By wisdom and valour*	Rose Lewin
Consilio et animis	*With prudence and courage*	Maitland, Ramadge, Ramsay-Gibson-Maitland
Consilio et armis.	*With discretion and arms*	Stephens
Consilio et impetu	*By wisdom and vigour*	Agnew, Corrigan
Consilio et prudentia	*By wisdom and prudence*	Le Poer-Trench, Trench
Consilio et vi	*By wisdom and might*	Perrier
Consilio, non impetu	*By wisdom, not by rashness*	Agnew, Vans Agnew
Constance et ferme	*Perseverence and decision*	Osbaldeston, Osboldeston
Constancy		M'Kowan
Constans contraria spernit	*Firmness spurns opposition*	Edgworth
Constans et fidelis	*Constant and faithful*	Brogden, Spoor, Spoure
Constans et prudens	*Firm and prudent*	Campbell
Constans fidei	*Constant in loyalty*	Cogan, Coggan, Colborne, Richardson Ridley
Constans justitiam moniti	*Persevering in justice with moderation*	Russell
Constant		Gray
Constant and faithful		Macqueen
Constant and true		Rose, Ross, Rosse
Constant en tout	*Constant in all*	Standish Carr
Constanter	*With constancy*	Hore
Constanter ac non timide	*Steadily but not timidly*	Hemphill
Constanter et prudentia	*Steadily and with prudence*	Campbell
Constant et ferme	*Constant and firm*	Lade, Osbaldeston
Constantia et fidelitate	*By constancy and fidelity*	Clarke-Travers
Constantia et fortitudine	*With constancy and firmness*	Herbert
Constantia et labore	*By constancy and labour*	Warrington
Constantia et virtute	*By constancy and virtue*	Amherst
Constare in sententia	*To be firm in purpose*	Williamson
Consulit et ornat	*He deliberates and prepares*	Dunbar
Consulto.	*I deliberate*	Peddie
Consulte et audacter	*Deliberately and boldly*	Plummer
Contentement passe richesse	*Contentment surpasses riches*	Bowyer
Contentus paucis	*Content with few things*	Lea
Contra audentior	*In opposition more daring*	Boden, Mount Stephen

Motto	Translation	Names
Contra fortune bon cœur	*Front fortune with a stout heart*	Wright
Copiose et opportune	*In plenty and in time*	Bontine, Bunten
Corda serata	*A heart shut up*	Lockhart
Corda serata fero	*I carry a heart shut up*	Lockhart
Corda serata pando	*I lay open a heart shut up*	Lockhart
Corda sincera principia vera	*Sincere hearts are true principles*	Dudley
Corde et animo	*With heart and soul*	Clayhills
Corde et manu	*With heart and hand*	Gordon, Steuart, Stewart, Stewart-Grainger, Watling
Corde manuque	*With heart and hand*	Gordon, Steuart, Stewart, Stewart-Grainger, Watling
Corde fixam	*Steadfast in heart*	Godfrey
Corde mente manu	*With heart, mind, and hand*	Fane
Cordi dat animus alas	*My spirit gives wings to my heart*	Falconer
Cordi dat robora virtus	*Virtue strengthens the heart*	Porch
Cor et manus	*Heart and hand*	M'Manus
Cor et manus concordant	*Heart and hand are at one*	Bates
Cor forte calcar non requirit	*A strong heart needs no spur*	Mappin
Cor forte suum calcar est	*A stout heart is its own spur*	Mappin
Cor immobile	*A heart immovable*	Hussey, Hyett
Cor mundum crea in me Deus	*Create in me a clean heart, O God*	O Crean, Lynch
Cor nobyle, cor immobyle	*A heart noble, and a heart immovable*	Symons, Vivian
Cornu exaltabitur honore	*His horn shall be exalted with honour*	Smyth
Corona mea Christus	*Christ is my crown*	Chetwoode, Empson, Lapsley, Lapslie, Wilmot-Chetwood
Coronat fides	*Fidelity crowns*	Dall, Pringle
Cor unum, via una	*One heart, one way*	Cecil, Nolan, Sanford, Wills
Cor vulneratum	*A wounded heart*	Mack
Courage		Arrol, Bruce, Cuming, Cummin, Cumming, Cummyng, Dounie, Downie, Gordon-Cumming, Hillson, Turnbull
Courage sans peur	*Courage without fear*	Ainsworth, Anesworth, Aynesworth, Bailie Gage, Gage
Courage et esperance	*Hope and courage*	Stone
Courageux	*Courageous*	Lee
Court no friend, dread no foe		Mallock
Craggan an fhithich	*The rock of the raven*	M'Donel, Macdonell, M'Donnel, Macdonnell
Craigellachie	*The rock of alarm*	Grant, Grant-Ogilvie
Craignez honte	*Dread shame*	Bentinck, Dillwyn, Dillwyn Llewelyn, Weston
Craig dhubh	*The black rock*	Farquharson
Crains Dieu tant que tu viveras	*Fear God as long as thou shalt live*	Somerville
Cras mihi	*To morrow for me*	Parbury
Creag dhubh chloinn Chatain	*The black rock of clan Chattan*	Macpherson
Crede Byron	*Trust Byron*	Biron, Byron
Crede cornu	*Trust in the horn*	Hornby
Crede cruci	*Trust in the cross*	Cross
Crede Deo	*Trust in God*	Atkinson
Crede et vince	*Believe and conquer*	Toash
Credo	*I believe*	Dodson, Kirsopp, Sinclair, Weeden
Credo, amo et regno	*I believe, love, and rule*	Clive
Credo cruci Christi	*I trust in the cross of Chris*	Wood
Credo et amo	*I believe and love*	Crossley
Credo et videbo	*I believe, and I shall see*	Cheslie, Chiesly, Chislie
Credo legi	*I trust in the law*	Hamilton
Credunt quod vident	*They believe what they see*	Elliot
Crescam ut prosim	*I will increase, that I may do good*	Athill, Atthill, Mitchell, Mitchelson
Crescat amicitia	*Let friendship increase*	Michell
Crescat Deo promotore	*Let him prosper under the guidance of God*	Leslie
Crescendo prosim	*Let me do good by increasing*	Scot, Scott
Crescent	*They increase*	Tatton
Crescitque virtute	*And grows by virtue*	Mackenzie, M'Kenzie,
Crescit sub pondere virtus	*Virtue thrives under oppression*	Alison Andrew, Chapman, Feilden, Fielding, Maclean, Pigott, Seys, Slater
Crescitur cultu	*It is increased by culture*	Barton
Cresco	*I increase*	Mitchael, Mitchell, Stiven
Cresco crescendo	*I increase by growing*	Rolfe
Cresco et spero	*I increase and I hope*	Hannay, Auden
Cresco per crucem	*I grow through the cross*	Rowan
Cresco sub jugo	*I grow under the yoke*	Hay
Cressa ne careat		Baker-Cresswell, Cresswell
Croix d'Orade	*The cross of Orade*	Vivian
Crom-a-boo		Bodkin, DeRos, Fitzgerald, O'Donovan
Crom a brudh		FitzGerald
Crow not, croke not		Crockett
Cruce delector	*I joy in the cross*	Sinclair
Cruce duce	*With the cross for guide*	Adams
Cruce dum spiro spero	*While I breathe I hope in the cross*	Cross, Darlington
Cruce glorior	*I glory in the cross*	Pye
Cruce insignis	*Illustrious from the cross*	Beck

Motto	Translation	Names
Crucem ferre dignum	*Worthy to bear the cross.*	Newenham, Worth.
Cruce non hasta	*By the cross, not the spear*	Taylor-Whitehead.
Cruce, non leone fides	*My trust is in the cross, not in the lion*	Mathew.
Cruce, non prudentia	*By the cross, not by wisdom*	Topham.
Cruce salus	*Salvation in the cross*	Shee.
Cruce spes mea	*In the cross is my hope*	Bird.
Cruce vide et festina	*See by the cross and make haste*	Trendall.
Cruce vincimus	*We conquer by the cross*	Newbigging.
Cruciata cruce junguntur	*Afflictions are connected with the cross*	Gairden, Garden, Gardyne.
Cruci dum spiro fido	*While I breathe, I trust in the cross*	Arundel, Dyson, Netterville.
Cruci dum spiro spero	*While I breathe, I hope in the cross*	Hill-Male, Netterville.
Crucifixa gloria mea	*My glory is in the cross*	Knatchbull-Hugessen.
Crux Christi mea corona	*Christ's cross my crown*	Mercer, Tod-Mercer.
Crux Christi nostra corona	*The cross of Christ is our crown*	Barclay, Mercer, Mersar.
Crux Christi salus mea	*My salvation is the cross of Christ*	Peck.
Crux Christi solamen offert	*The cross of Christ gives consolation*	Barclay.
Crux dat salutem	*The cross gives salvation*	Sinclair.
Crux et præsidium et decus	*The cross is both an honour and a defence*	Andros.
Crux fidei calcar	*The cross is a spur to faith*	Brooking.
Crux mea stella	*The cross is my star*	Devlin.
Crux mihi anchora	*The cross is my anchor*	Page.
Crux mihi grata quies	*The cross gives me welcome rest*	Adam, Adamson, Adie, Edie, Macadam, M'Adam.
Crux nostra corona	*The cross our crown*	Austin.
Crux præsidium et decus	*The cross an honour and a defence*	Tyler.
Crux salutem confert	*The cross brings salvation*	Barclay.
Crux scutum	*The cross is my shield*	Gregory.
Crux spes unica	*The cross is my only hope*	Collas.
Cubo, sed curo	*I lie down, but take care*	Dickson.
Cubo, ut excubo	*I rest while I watch*	Græme, Graham.
Cui debeo fidus	*Faithful to whom I am under an obligation*	Craw, Layland-Barratt.
Cui debetur reverentia	*Reverence to whom it is due*	Tulloh.
Cuidich an righ. / Cuidich in rhi	*Assist the king*	M'Donnel, M'Kenzie.
Cuilean uasal		Woulfe.
Cuimhnich bas Alpin	*Remember the death of Alpin*	Alpin, M'Alpin, Macalpin.
Cuimhnig do geallamhnaca		MacLochlin.
Cuislean mo chridhe	*The pulsation of my heart*	M'Donnel.
Cultui avorum fidelis	*Faithful in honouring my ancestors*	Trappes.
Cum corde	*With the heart*	Drummond.
Cum cruce salus	*Safety with the cross*	Mountain.
Cum grano salis	*With a grain of salt (i.e., making allowances)*	Kerr.
Cum periculo lucrum	*Gain with danger*	Ogilvie.
Cum plena magis	*When more full*	Smith, Smyth.
Cum prima luce	*With the dawn of day*	Loveday.
Cum principibus	*With my chiefs*	Hale.
Cum progressu cantus	*Singing while advancing*	Seaton, Seton.
Cum prudentia sedulus	*Careful with prudence*	Beatson, Betson.
Cum secundo flumine	*With the favouring stream*	Lund.
Cum toga honoris	*With the cloak of honour*	Robe.
Cuncta mea mecum	*All my property is with me*	Stedman.
Cunctanter, tamen fortiter	*Leisurely, yet resolutely*	Hutchinson.
Cupio meliora	*I desire better things*	Melliar.
Cupressus honores peperit	*The cypress has procured us honour*	Duff.
Cura atque industria	*By care and industry*	Benn, Vair.
Curaçoa		Brisbane.
Cura dat victoriam	*Foresight gives victory*	Denham.
Curæ cedit fatum	*Destiny yields to care*	Thomson.
Curæ pii Diis sunt	*The pious are the care of the gods*	Mogg.
Cura et candore	*By prudence and sincerity*	Cunningham, Forbes.
Cura et constantia	*By care and constancy*	Cunningham, Cunninghame.
Cura et industria	*By care and industry*	Walker.
Cura quietem	*See to due repose*	Hall.
Cu re bu / Cu reubha	*I have broken my hold*	Farrell, O'Farrell.
Cur me persequeris	*Why do you pursue me*	Eton, Eustace.
Curo dum quiesco	*I am on my guard while I rest*	Maxwell.
Currendo	*By running*	Hollist.
Currit qui curat	*He runs who takes care*	Fuller.
Cursum perficio	*I accomplish my course*	Hunter.
Cuspis fracta causa coronæ	*The broken spear the cause of the coronet*	Rolt, Rolte.
Custos et pugnax	*A vigilant watch and prepared to fight*	Marjoribanks.
Cwell angan neu chwilydd		Phillips.
Cywir im gwlad		Williams.

D

Dabit Deus vela	*God will fill the sails*	Tennant
Dabit otia Deus	*God will give times of leisure*	Brisbane, Brisbane M'Dougall
Dabunt aspera rosas	*Difficulties will yield roses*	Mushet
D'accomplir Agincourt		Dalison
Da ei-fydd		Jones
Da fydd	*Good will come*	Davies.
Dakyns, the devil's in the hempe		Dakyns.
Dalriada		Maclaurin
Danger I court		Wright
Dan ni h andan		Clark
Dant Deo	*They give to God*	Wood
Dante Deo	*By the bounty of God*	Wolff
Dante Deo reddam	*God giving me, I shall restore*	Mitchell
Dant lucem crescentibus orti	*Risen they shed light on things growing*	Hodges
Dant vires gloriam	*Strength gives glory*	Hog, Hogg
Dant vulnera vitam.	*The wounds give life*	Collins
Dare		Darley, Warren Darley
Dare quam accipere	*To give rather than to receive*	Guy
Darien		Knight
Das mo dhuthaich	*For God and my country*	MacKenzie
Data fata secutus	*Following the destiny allotted to me*	Archdale, Archdall, Carpendale, Duthie, Eddington, St John, Streatfield, Stretfield
Dat cura commodum	*Prudence gives profit*	Mill, Milne
Dat cura quietem	*Prudence gives rest*	Hall, Layton, Medlicott, Medlycott
Dat decus origini	*He gives honour to his ancestry*	Hamilton
Dat Deus incrementum .	*God gives the increase*	Crofton, Filstone, Johns, Muggeridge, Otley, Ottley
Dat Deus originem .	*God gives birth (high or low)*	Hamilton
Dat et sumit Deus	*God gives and God takes away*	Ethelston
Dat gloria vires	*Glory gives strength*	Hog, Hogg, Hogue, M'Garell-Hogg.
Dat incrementum	*He gives the increase*	Stewart
Debonnaire	*Kind or gracious*	Bethune, Lindsay, Patton Bethune
De bon vouloir	*With goodwill* ...	Goodwin
De bon vouloir servir le roi	*To serve the king with good will*	Bennet, Bennett, Gray, Grey
Deccan		Hislop
Decens et honestum	*Becoming and honourable*	Broadrick, Fyfe Fyffe
Decerptæ dabunt odorem	*Roses plucked will give sweet smell*	Aiton, Aytoun, Marshall, Hunter Marshall
Decide		Davis
Decide and dare		Dyce
Decore	*With grace*	Baltingall
Decori decus addit avito	*He adds honour to that of his ancestors*	Erskine
Decor integer	*Perfect comeliness*	Mounsey
Decorum pro patria mori	*It is honourable to die for our country*	Ellis
Decrevi	*I have determined*	Gaddesden, Greville Nugent, Humble, Nugent
Decus summum virtus	*Virtue the chief ornament*	Holburn, Holeburn, Hulburn
De Dieu tout	*From God is everything*	Mervyn, Beckford
Deeds not words		Baxter, Dawson, Palmer, Rickford
Deeds shaw		Rutherford
Deeds show		Ruthven
Defend		Grassick, Wood
Defend and spare not		MacConachie
Defendendo vinco	*I conquer by defending*	Graham
Defend the fold ...		Cartwright.
Defensio, non offensio	*Defence, not offence*	Mudie
Deficiam aut efficiam	*I shall fail or accomplish*	Storey
Defying ye field		Cowen
Degenerante genus opprobrium	*Lineage becomes a disgrace to the man who degenerates from it*	Ashurst, Crewe
De hirundine	*Of the swallow*	Arundel
Dei beneficio sum quod sum	*By the grace of God I am what I am*	Russell
Dei dono sum quod sum	*By the gift of God I am what I am*	Drummond, Lumisden, Lumsden, Lundin
Dei donum	*The free gift of God*	Darling
Dei gratia	*By the grace of God*	Kingston
Dei gratia grata	*The grace of God is grateful*	Dixie
Dei memor, gratus amicis	*Mindful of God, grateful to friends*	Antrobus
Dei providentia juva	[illegible]	[illegible]

Motto	Translation	Names
Delectant domi non impediunt foris	*They delight at home and do not hinder abroad*	Hoblyn.
Delectare in Domino	*To rejoice in the Lord*	Bampfylde.
Delectat amor patriæ	*The love of our native land delights*	Smith.
Delectat et ornat	*It delights and adorns*	Brown, Browne-Borthwick, Cree, Harvie, Harvey, M'Crae, M'Crea, M'Cree, M'Crie.
Delectatio mea	*My delight*	Pollock.
Del fuego io avolo	*I escaped from the fire*	Berners.
Delhi		Ochterlony.
Deliciæ mei	*My delight*	Dalgleish.
Demeure par la vérité	*Keep fast by the truth*	Mason.
De mieulx je pense en mieulx	*I think better and better*	Paston, Brooke.
De monte alto	*From a lofty mountain*	Maude, Roxby.
D'en haut	*From above*	Whitefoord.
Denique cœlo fruar	*I will enjoy heaven at last*	Melville.
Denique cœlum	*Heaven at last*	Beswick, Bonar, Melveton, Melvile, Melvill, Melville.
Denique decus	*Honour at last*	Stoddart.
Denuo fortasse lutescat	*May perchance become obscure again*	Spurdens.
Deo ac bello	*By God and war*	Chambers.
Deo adjuvante	*God assisting*	Atkinson, Jones, Mills, Pellew, Salomons, Solomons.
Deo adjuvante fortuna sequatur	*God helping me, good fortune will follow*	Roberts.
Deo adjuvante, non timendum	*When God assists there is nothing to fear*	Fitzwilliam, Peters, Richards, Warner, Williams.
Deo adjuvante vincam	*God helping me, I will conquer*	Hart.
Deo adverso, leo vincitur	*God opposing, the lion is conquered*	Newenham.
Deo confido	*I trust in God*	Fison.
Deo credito justitiam colito	*Practise justice, trusting in God*	Udheraj.
Deo data	*Given to God*	Arundel.
Deo donum	*A gift from God*	Darling.
Deo duce	*Led by God*	Bailey, Cadell, Hennidge, Ricketts.
Deo duce Christo luce	*God my guide, Christ my light*	Butler.
Deo duce comite fortuna	*God for guide, fortune for companion*	Palles.
Deo duce comite industria	*God for guide, industry for companion*	Nicoll, Owen, Slaney.
Deo duce, decrevi	*Under the guidance of God, I have resolved*	Harnage.
Deo duce, ferro comitante	*God my leader, my sword my companion*	Caulfield, Luscombe.
Deo ducente, nil nocet	*God leading, nothing hurts*	Pelly.
Deo duce, sequor	*I follow, God being my guide*	Wheelton.
Deo et gladio	*By God and my sword*	Crealock, Crealocke.
Deo et labore	*By God and with labour*	Williamson.
Deo et patria	*For God and country*	Outhwaite.
Deo et patriæ fidelis	*Faithful to God and country*	Atkinson.
Deo et principe	*For God and my prince*	Lamb, Montolieu.
Deo et regi	*For God and the king*	Stanhope.
Deo et Regi asto	*I stand by God and the king*	Deacon.
Deo et regi fidelis	*Faithful to God and the king*	Atkinson.
Deo et virtuti	*For God and virtue*	Lackerstein.
Deo favente	*By God favouring me*	Alves, Dingwall, Evans, Gordon, Innes, Mitchell, Parminster, Ware.
Deo favente cresco	*I go on increasing by the favour of God*	Bartlett.
Deo favente et sedulitate	*By the favour of God and by assiduity*	Hanson.
Deo favente, florebo	*By the favour of God I shall prosper*	Blenshell, Blinshall.
Deo favente progredior	*I go forward by the favour of God*	Pyke.
Deo favente supero	*Being favoured by God, I overcome*	Cooke.
Deo fidelis et regi	*Faithful to God and the king*	Daly.
Deo fidens	*Trusting in God*	Gordon.
Deo fidens persistas	*Trusting in God, persevere*	Kinahan.
Deo fidens proficio	*I go forward trusting in God*	Chadwick.
Deo gloria	*Glory to God*	Bennet, Gennys.
Deo gratias	*Thanks to God*	Senhouse, Sotheron.
Deo inspirante, rege favente	*God inspiring me, and the king favouring me*	Stahlschmidt.
Deo juvante	*God assisting*	Duff, Groze, Kennion, Maitland, Pellew, Sampson, Shortt, Tawse, Wolderspoon.
Deo juvante gero	*By the help of God I carry on*	Galloway.
Deo juvante, vinco	*I conquer by the help of God*	Duncan, Officer, Stewart.
Deo non arce spes	*My hope is in God, not in my fortress*	Castell.
Deo non armis fido	*I trust in God, not in arms*	Boycott, Morse, Morse-Boycott.
Deo, non fortuna	*Through God, not by chance*	Booker, Chance, Digby, Elwes, Firth, Gardiner, Greaves, Harrison, Harvey, Pellew.
Deo non sagittis fido	*I trust in God, not in arrows*	Cuyler.
Deo omnia	*All things for God*	Harter.
Deo pagit	*He makes a covenant with God*	Pagit, Pagitt.
Deo patriæ amicis	*To God, country, and friends*	Abbot, Binckes, Granville, Lutwidge.
Deo patriæque fidelis	*Faithful to God and country*	Fagan.
Deo, patr[illegible]	[illegible]	Lambard, Sidl[illegible]

Deo patria rege	*For God, my country, and my king.*	Cooper
Deo, regi, et patriæ Deo, regi, patriæ	*For God, my king, and my country*	Irvine Duncombe
Deo regique debeo	*I owe it to God and the king*	Johnson
Deo regi vicino	*For God, king, and neighbour*	Cookes
Deo semper confide	*Trust always in God*	James
Deo spes mea	*My hope is in God*	Thornton
Deo volente	*If God will*	Campbell, Palliser
Depêchez	*Make haste*	Govan.
Depressus extollor	*I am exalted by depression*	Butler
De quo bene speratur	*Whence there is good hope*	Hartree
Desir na repos	*Desire not rest*	Howard
Désormais	*Henceforth*	Clifford
Despicio terrena	*I despise earthly things*	Bedingfield, M'Crobie
Despicio terrena et solem contemplor	*I spurn earthly things and gaze on the sun*	Bedingfield
Despicit quæ vulgus suspicit	*He despises what the vulgar admire*	Ryland
De tout mon cœur	*With all my heart*	Boileau, Langstone, Pollen
Detur forti palma	*Let the reward be given to the brave*	Sinclair
Detur gloria Deo	*Glory be to God*	Robertson
Deum cole, regem serva	*Worship God, save the king*	Cole Ranelagh, Townshend
Deum et regem	*God and king*	Collins
Deum time Deum timete	*Fear God*	Murray Carnegie
Deum time et dedecus	*Fear God and dishonour*	Baddeley
Deum time regem honora	*Fear God, honour the king*	Watson
Deus ab inimicis me defendit	*God defends me from my enemies*	Le Touzel
Deus adesto	*Let God stand by us*	Brown
Deus adjuvat nos	*God assists us*	Booth
Deus alit eos	*God feeds them*	Croker
Deus clypeus meus	*God is my shield*	Biddell, Biddle, Biddelle
Deus dabit	*God will give*	More
Deus dabit vela	*God will fill the sails*	Albertus de Alasco, Campbell, Norman, Tennant
Deus dat qui vult	*God gives what He wishes*	Stacey
Deus dedit	*God gave*	Moir
Deus dexter meus	*God is my right hand*	Dobbyn
Deus dux certus	*God is a sure leader*	Bromage
Deus est libertas	*God is liberty*	Godfrey
Deus est nobis sol et ensis	*God is a sun and sword to us*	Kynaston
Deus est noster refugium	*God is our refuge*	Tailor
Deus est pax	*God is my peace*	Godfray
Deus est spes	*God is my hope*	Ridsdale
Deus est super domo	*God is over the household*	Straker
Deus et libertas	*God and liberty*	Godfrey, Taylor
Deus evehit pios	*God exalts the pious*	Brown
Deus fortissima turris	*God is a very strong tower*	Le Bailly
Deus fortitudo mea	*God is my strength*	Jones, Lee
Deus gubernat navem	*God steers the vessel*	Leckie
Deus hæc otia fecit	*God hath given this season of peace*	Williams
Deus incrementum dabit Deus incrementum dedit	*God will give the increase* *God has given the increase*	Firth
Deus industriam beat	*God blesses industry*	Harborne
Deus intersit	*Let God be in our midst*	Stephens
Deus juvat	*God assists*	Duff, Macduff, M'Duff
Deus lumen meum	*God is my light*	Torrens
Deus major columna	*God a greater pillar of support*	Henniker, Major
Deus me sustinet	*God sustains me*	Arbuthnot
Deus meum solamen	*God is my comfort*	Keir, Ker
Deus meus dux meus	*My God my leader*	St Albyn
Deus mihi adjutor	*God is my helper*	Auchterlonie, Aughterlony, Ochterlonie, Ouchterlony, Walker
Deus mihi munimen	*God is my fortress*	Hardcastle
Deus mihi providebit	*God will provide for me*	Goold, Jenney, Keane, Le Hunt
Deus mihi sol	*God is my sun*	Nicholson, Nicholson Steele
Deus mihi spes et tutamen	*God is my hope and safeguard*	Bradshaw
Deus nobis	*God for us*	Pinckney
Deus nobiscum	*God with us*	Darnell
Deus nobiscum quis contra	*If God be with us, who can be against?*	Milman
Deus nobiscum, quis contra nos	*If God be with us, who can be against us?*	Morgan, Morres
Deus nobis hæc otia fecit	*God hath given us this time of peace*	Boleyn, Bolger, Burrow, Hyde
Deus nobis, quis contra	*God is for us, who can be against us?*	Beddington, Bolgar, Burrow, De Montmorency Mores, Morres
Deus non reliquit memoriam humilium	*God hath not forgotten the humble*	Meynell
Deus noster refugium	*God is our refuge*	Barnes, Farmbrough
Deus pascit corvos	*God feeds the ravens*	Brothers, Brown, Brydges, Corbet, Corbett, Corbin, Cornish Brown, Jones, Mowbray, Owen, Ravenshaw, Williams
Deus pastor meus	C	[illegible]

Deus, patria, rex	*God, native land, and king*	Phillipps, Phillips, Tarlton.
Deus præsidium	*God is our defence*	Bevan.
Deus prosperat justos	*God prospers the just*	Heathcote, Sinclair.
Deus protector noster	*God our protector*	Sweden, Tennant.
Deus protector meus	*God my protector*	Humphery, Berens.
Deus providebit	*God will provide*	Binns, Burton, Drummond, Lambert, Lesly, Marshall, Mather, Mein, Mundy, Prideaux, Stewart, Thompson, Thomson.
Deus quis contra	*God with us, who can be against us?*	Hutton.
Deus refugium nostrum	*God is our refuge*	Garnett-Orme.
Deus robur meum	*God is my strength*	Wood.
Deus salutem disponit	*God orders salvation*	Archer.
Deus scutum et cornu salutis	*God my shield and the horn of my salvation*	Thoroton,
Deus si monet	*If God directs*	Simonet.
Deus solamen	*God my comfort*	Ker, Kerr.
Deus solus auget aristas	*God alone gives the increase*	Riddell.
Deus spes mea	*God is my hope*	Herbertstone.
Deus tuetur	*God protects us*	Davies.
Deus veritatem protegit	*God protects the truth*	Roper.
Deutlich und wahr	*Distinct and true*	Schrieber.
Devant, si je puis	*Foremost if I can*	Allhusen, Gridley, Jackson, Mainwairing, Mainwaring, Mainwarring, Pellate, Scrope, Scroope.
De vivis nil nisi verum	*Of the living nothing but the truth*	Hyde.
Devoir	*Duty*	Footner.
Devouement sans bornes	*Devotion without bounds*	Prodgers.
Dextra cruce vincit	*My right hand conquers by the cross*	Hurley, Hurly.
Dextra fideque	*By my right hand and my faith*	Bell.
Dh'andeon co heiragha	*In spite of who would gainsay*	Macdonald.
Dh' aindheoin co theiradh e	*In spite of who would gainsay*	M'Donald.
Dial Gwaed Cymro		Llyod.
Dia's-mo-Dhuthaich	*For God and country*	Mackenzie.
ΔΙΑ ΤΗΣ ΣΤΕΝΗΣ	*Through the narrow way*	Clarke.
Diciendo y haciendo	*Saying and doing*	Paget.
Dictis factisque simplex	*Simple in words and deeds*	Sawrey.
Die möller salich ihm		Möller.
Dieppe		Harvey.
Dieu aidant	*God assisting*	Balfour.
Dieu a la mer	*God owns the sea*	Dennis.
Dieu avec nous	*God with us*	Barclay, Berkeley, Burroughs.
Dieu ayde	*May God help*	De Montmorency, Lentaigue.
Dieu ayde au premier Baron Chrétien	*God help the premier, Christian Baron*	Montmorency.
Dieu défende le droit	*God defend the right*	Bell, Blenkinsopp, Churchill, Harman, Leston, Reading, Seaton, Spencer, Stanhope.
Dieu donne	*God gives*	Colpoys.
Dieu est ma roche	*God is my rock*	Roche.
Dieu est mon aide	*God is my help*	Band.
Dieu est mon espoir	*God and my hope*	Cusack.
Dieu est tout	*God is all*	Alington.
Dieu et la réligion	*God and religion*	Bondier.
Dieu et ma fiancée	*God aud my affianced*	Latimer.
Dieu et ma foi	*God and my faith*	Favil.
Dieu et ma main droite	*God and my right hand*	Bate.
Dieu et ma patrie	*God and my country*	Marton.
Dieu et mon devoir	*God and my duty*	Bradshaw, Willet.
DIEU ET MON DROIT	*God and my right*	THE SOVEREIGN.
Dieu et mon pays	*God and my country*	M'Kirdy.
Dieu et mon roi	*God and my king*	Rawlinson.
Dieu et mon roy	*God and my king*	Segrave.
Dieu garda Le Moyle	*God protects Le Moyle*	Moyle.
Dieu le veut	*God wills it*	Lermitte.
Dieu m'a fait fort	*God has made me strong*	Scott.
Dieu me conduise	*God guide me*	Delaval, Hayes.
Dieu mon appui	*God is my stay*	Oliver.
Dieu pour la Tranche, qui contre	*God for the Trenches, whoever may oppose*	La Poer-Trench, Trench.
Dieu pour nous	*God for us*	Fletcher, Peters.
Dieu sait tout	*God knows everything*	Lewin.
Dieu, un roi, une foi	*God, one king, one faith*	Rush.
Die virescit	*It flourishes by day*	Wood.
Difficilia quæ pulchra	*What is honourable is difficult*	Craufield, Elford.
Digna sequens	*Pursuing worthy aims*	Botsford.
Dii facientes adjuvant	*The gods help those who exert themselves*	Broughton-Rouse.
Diis bene juvantibus	*By the good help of the gods*	Middleton.
Dilectatio	*Delight*	Forbes.
Diligenter	*Diligently*	Bramwell.
Diligenter et fideliter	*Diligently and faithfully*	Allen.
Diligentia	*Diligence*	Bramwell, Dickman, Jones.
Diligentes Deus ipse juvat	*God Himself helps the diligent*	Hartill.

Diligentia cresco	*I increase by diligence*	Moncrief
Diligentia ditat	*Diligence enriches*	Cruickshank, Ferrier, Newall, Newell
Diligentia et candore	*By diligence and fairness*	Dick
Diligentia et honeste	*By diligence and honourable dealing*	Garnett Orme
Diligentia et honore	*With diligence and honour*	Garnett
Diligentia et vigilantia	*By diligence and vigilance*	Boden, Semple
Diligentia fit ubertas	*Diligence causes fertility*	Hay
Diligentia fortior	*Stronger by diligence*	Truell
Diligentia fortunæ mater	*Diligence is the mother of fortune*	Barkham
Dinna waken sleeping dogs		Robertson, Forbes.
Di ofn Di ymffrost		Wynne
Diovolendo Io faro	*God willing I will do it*	Wharton
Dirigat Deus.	*May God direct*	Allan
Diriget Deus.	*God will direct*	Butter
Dirigo et defendo	*I direct and protect*	Sheppard
Disce et labora	*Learn and labour*	Mackie
Disce ferenda pati ...	*Learn to suffer what must be borne*	Barrs-Haden, De Hollyngworthe, Hollingworth
Disce mori mundo	*Learn to die to the world*	Moore
Disce mori ut vivas	*Learn to die that you may live*	Unett
Disce pati	*Learn to suffer*	Donkin, Dunbar, Duncan
Disciplina, fide, perseverentia	*By discipline, faith, and perseverance*	Duckworth
Discite justitiam	*Learn justice*	Nisbet
Discite justiciam moniti	*Learn justice, having been warned*	Russell
Discrimine salus	*Safety in decision*	Traill
Disponendo me, non mutando me	*By disposing, not by changing me*	Montagu
Dissipate	*Disperse*	Scrimzeor, Scrymgeour, Scrymzeor
Distantia jungit	*He unites things distant*	Case
Ditat Deus	*God enriches*	Fortun, M'Taggart
Ditat et alit	*It enriches and nourishes*	Gourlay, Guthrie
Ditat servata fides	*Faith kept enriches*	Archibald, Arnison, Innes, Papillon
Ditat virtus	*Virtue enriches*	Cheape
Diuturnitate fragrantior	*The more fragrance with lapse of time*	Rind, Rynd
Diu virescit	*He keeps fresh and green for a long time*	Wood.
Divini gloria ruris	*The beauty of the country is from God*	Foster
Divina sibi canit	*She chants to herself divine strains*	Lachlan, Lauchlan, Lawchlan, Loghlan
Divino robore	*By divine strength*	Galiez, Gilliez, Gellie, Gelly
Divisa conjungo	*I heal divisions*	Gordon
Docendo disce	*Learn by teaching*	Brown
Doctrina ferro perennior	*Learning more enduring than the sword*	Smith
Doe well and let them say		Scott
Do good		Spence.
Do it with thy might		Buxton
Doluere dente lacessiti	*Bitten, they felt pain*	Arden
Domat omnia virtus.	*Virtue overcomes all things*	Ffarington, Farington, Gough
Domi ac foris	*At home and abroad*	None
Domine, dirige nos	*O Lord, direct us*	Brome
Domine in virtute tua	*Lord, in thy strength*	Cochrane
Domine, speravi	*O Lord, I have hoped*	Lloyd
Domini factum	*The work of the Lord*	Sibthorpe
Domini factum est	*It is the work of the Lord*	Scott, Sibbald
Domino fides immobilis	*An immovable faith in God*	Barry
Domino quid reddam	*What shall I render to the Lord?*	Blofeld
Dominus a dextris	*The Lord is on my right hand*	Batt
Dominus dedit	*The Lord gave* ..	Harries, Harris, Herries, Herris
Dominus fecit	*The Lord made*	Baird, Jackson
Dominus fortissima turris	*The Lord is a most strong tower*	De Havilland, Haviland, Havilland
Dominus illuminatio mea	*The Lord is my enlightener.*	Brightwen, Leycester
Dominus ipse faciet	*The Lord himself will do it*	Adam
Dominus petra mea	*The Lord is my rock* ..	Dampier
Dominus providebit	*The Lord will provide*	Anderson, Boyle, Burton, Drummond, Fawsitt, Ferguson-Fawsitt, Glasgow, Goding, Lawson, Lingen, MacLaws, M'Laws, M'Vicar, Mason, Williamson, Young
Domum antiquam redintegrare	*To restore an ancient house*	Hepburn
Donec impleat	*Until it fill*	Souter, Kidd, Kyd
Donec impleat orbem	*Until it fill the world*	Hay, Kidd, Kydd
Donec rursus impleat orbem	*Until it again fill the world*	Somervil, Sommerville
Donner et pardonner	*To give and forgive*	Hicks
Do no yll, qouth D'Oylé		D'Oyly
Do, or die		Douglas
Do right and fear nocht		Paton
Do right and fear not		Creswick
Do right, fear not		Stancomb
Doucement, mais fermement	*Kindly but firmly*	Louis
Do well, and doubt not		Blakiston, Brice, Bruce, Bryce, Houston
Do well, and let them say.		Bruce, Elphingston, Elphinstone, Gordon Scot, Scott

Do well, doubt not		Kingsmill.
Do well, doubt nought		Bruce.
Dread God		Carnegie, Carnaghi, Gordon, Hay-Macdougall, Hodgson, Macgeorge, M'Haffie-Gordon, Monro, Munro, Ross.
Dread shame		Leighton.
Drogo nomen et virtus arma dedit	*Drogo us gave name, and virtue arms*	Drew.
Droit	*Right*	Tunstal.
Droit à chacun	*To each his right.*	Dobede.
Droit comme ma flèche	*Straight as my arrow*	Fletcher.
Droit et avant	*Right and forward*	Coey, Townshend, Twycross.
Droit et loyal	*Upright and loyal*	Symes, Vanneck.
Droit et loyauté	*Right and loyalty*	Vannock.
Drwy Rynwedd Gwaed		Walwyn.
Dry weres agan dew ny		Glyn.
Duce Deo	*With God for leader*	De Massue, Massue.
Ducente Deo	*God guiding*	Lepper.
Duci et non trahi	*To be led and not dragged*	Athy.
Ducit amor patriæ	*The love of country leads*	Hubert-Marshall, Lechmere, Marshall, Philips, Phillips, Wolley.
Ducit Dominus	*The Lord leads*	Dirom, Pasley-Dirom.
Ducitur hinc honos	*Hence honour is drawn*	Buchanan.
Ducitur, non trahitur	*He is led, not drawn*	Alexander.
Ductore Deo	*With God for leader*	Peckitt.
Ductus non coactus	*Led, not coerced.*	Robertson.
Dulcedine capior	*I am captivated with pleasantness*	Howlatsone.
Dulce periculum	*Danger is sweet*	Baggally, M'Alla, M'Aulay, Macaulay, M'Call, Mackauly.
Dulce pro patria periculum	*Danger for our country is sweet*	Ker, Seymer.
Dulce quod utile	*That is sweet which is useful*	Strang, Stronge.
Dulces ante omnia musæ	*Music is sweet before all things*	Lowes.
Dulcidine	*By sweetness*	Bogle.
Dulcis amor patriæ	*Sweet is the love of country*	Clifford, Fitz-Wygram, Wigram.
Dulcis pro patria labor	*Labour for our country is sweet*	M'Kerrell, McKerrell.
Dulcius ex asperis	*Sweeter after difficulties*	Bogle, Ferguson, Fergusson.
Dum clarum, rectum teneam	*While I hold to glory, let me hold to right*	Penn.
Dum cresco, spero	*While I grow, I hope*	Rider.
Dum exspiro spero	*In dying I still hope.*	Lace.
Dum in arborem	*While in the tree*	Hamilton.
Dum memor ipse mei	*While he himself is mindful of me*	Irvine.
Dum sedulo prospero	*As yet I prosper by assiduity*	Swinton.
Dum sisto, vigilo	*While I stand, I watch*	Gordon.
Dum spiro, cœlestia spero	*While I breathe, I hope for heavenly things*	Innes.
Dum spiro, spero	*While I breathe, I hope*	Anderson, Appleford, Ascoti, Ascotti, Auchmuty, Aylmer, Baker, Bannatyne, Brabant, Branson, Brook, Bushell, Basement, Cleather, Collet, Colquhoun, Compton, Corbet, Cotton, Coryton, Cotter, Cutler, Davies, Dearden, Dillon, Drummond, Elrick, Elwon, Falls, Gaunt, Glazebrook, Going, Gordon, Greaves, Gun, Hart-Davies, Hensley, Hoare, Hunter, Jacobs, Jeffcoat, Learmonth, Lee, Mason, Manser, Moore, Nicholls, Olwerson, Partridge, Pearson, Pount, Radway, Roberts, Rochdale, Rylands, Salmon, Sharp, Smith, Spearman, Speer, Spry, Stanton, Staunton, Storer, Stover, Symonds, Taylor, Taylor-Gordon, Thompson, Urquhart, Walker, Walsh, Westerman, Whitehead, Whitworth, Young.
Dum tempus habemus operemur bonum.	*Whilst we have time let us do good*	Crisp.
Dum varior	*While I change*	Ramsay.
Dum varior idem	*While I change, the same*	Ramsay.
Dum vigilo curo	*While I watch, I take care*	Cranstoun.
Dum vigilo, pareo	*While I watch, I obey*	Gordon.
Dum vigilo tutus	*While I watch, I am safe*	Canning, Gordon, Buckley-Deakin.
Dum vivo cano	*While I live I sing*	Rigg.
Dum vivo canto	*While I live I sing*	Coghill.
Dum vivo spero	*While I live, I hope*	Dumaresq, Menteath, Menteth, Monteith, Thom-Whiteway.
Dum vivo, vireo	*While I live, I flourish*	Latta.
Durat, ditat, placet	*It sustains, it enriches, it pleases*	Ged, Geddes, Geddies.
Durate	*Endure*	Douglas, Evelyn.
Dureté	*Hardness, stoutness*	Evelyn.
Duriora virt[illegible]	*Virtue, [illegible]*	Penf[illegible]ld, Wyatt.
Duris non [illegible]r.	*I [illegible] not br[illegible]*	Moore-Carrick, Muir, Mure.
Durum p[illegible] [illegible]	*I [illegible]*	Crawford, Crawfurd, Moore, Muir, Mure.

Durum sed certissimum	*Hard, but very sure*	Gillanders
Duty		Brouncker, Mesham
Duw a ddarpar i'r brain	*God feedeth the ravens*	Hughes, Williams
Duw a digon	*God and enough*	James, Nichol, Prytherch, Vaughan
Duw Ar bendithio	*God with us*	Pryse
Duw ar fyrhan	*God for my portion*	Pryce
Duw au bendithi	*God bless them*	Pryse, Williams
Duw au fendith yw fy ngwenwth		Riall
Duw dy ras	*God, thy grace*	Kemeys, Kemeys-Tynte
Duw yd ein cryfdur	*God, that is our strength*	Edwards
Duw yde ein cryfdwr	*God, thou art my strength*	
Dux mihi veritas	*Truth is my guide*	Haggard
Dux vitæ ratio	*Reason is the guide of my life*	Bennet, Boulton, West, West Roberts
Dux vitæ ratio in cruce victoria	*Reason the guide of life, in the cross victory*	Fanshaw

E

Eadhan dean agus na caomhain	*Even do, and spare not*	Macgregor, Peter
Eamus quo ducit fortuna	*Let us go where fortune leads*	Atty
Echel agus		White
Echel Coryg	*The Axle of Corgy*	White
E cœlo lux mea	*My light is from heaven*	Guille
Edrych i fynw		Powell
E'en do		M'Hud
E'en do, and spare not		Greg, Gregorson, Macgregor, M'Gregor, MacPeter, Mallock, Peter, Peters
E'en do, bait spair nocht		M'Gregor, Macgregor
E'en do baite spare not		MacAlpine
E'en do, but spare not		Gregorson
Efficiunt clarum studio	*They make it clear by study*	Milne, Mylne
Effloresco	*I flourish*	Boyle, Cairnes, Cairns
Efflorescent	*They will flourish*	Hirst
Efflorescent cornices dum micat sol	*Crows will abound while the sun shines*	Rooke
Ego accedo	*I assent*	Orr
Ego de meo sensu judico	*I judge from my own sense of things*	Willson.
Ein doe and spair not		Greg
Einch as a ghleannan		Glennie
Either for ever		Whitmore
E labore dulcedo	*Pleasure arises from labour*	Bogle, Innes, M'Innes
Elatum a Deo non deprimat	*Let one not depress him who is exalted by God*	O'Dempsey
El hombre propone, Dios dispone	*Man proposes, God disposes*	Davy
El honor es mi guia	*Honour is my guide*	Lousada
Eloquentia sagitta	*Eloquence is an arrow*	Bland
Elvenaca floreat vitis	*Let the vine of Elvine flourish*	Elvin
Emare	*Have thy price*	Hughan
Emergo	*I rise up*	Glass, Webster
Emeritus	*Honourably retired from active duties*	Emeris
En avant	*Forward*	Lucy, Tennyson-D'Eyncourt
En avant si je puis	*Forward, if I possibly can*	Warren-Warren
En bon espoir	*In good hope*	De Lisle
En bon espoyr	*In good hope*	Cokaine
En bonne foy	*In good faith*	Bonfoy, Chadwick, Purefoy, Purefoy-Bagwell, Sacheverell
En Dieu affie	*Trust in God*	Mallet
En Dieu est ma confiance	*In God is my trust*	Smythe-Owen
En Dieu est ma fiance		Crowder, Luttrell, Luttrell Olmius, Tokett
En Dieu est ma foi	*In God is my confidence*	Chevers
En Dieu est ma foy	*On God is my confidence*	Gosse, Staunton
En Dieu est mon espérance	*In God is my hope*	Gerard, Helsby, Walmesley
En Dieu est mon espoir		Cusack, Cusac-Smith, Smith, Trevanion-Betlesworth
En Dieu est tout	*In God is all*	Chambre, Conolly, Dawes, Sharpe, St Agata, Sturt, Wentworth
En Dieu et mon roy	*In God and my king*	Churchyard.
En Dieu ma foi	*On God is my reliance*	Favell, Favill
En Dieu ma foy		Mauleverer, Staunton
En Dieu se fie	*Trust in God*	Verdon
En Dieu sont nos esperances	*In God are all our hopes*	Whalley
En droyt devant	*Foremost in right*	Molineux
Endure fort	*Suffer bravely*	Lindsay

Motto	Translation	Families
En espérance je vis	*In hope I live*	Carew.
En esperanza	*In hope*	Mack.
En faizant bien	*In doing well*	Perchard.
En foi prest	*Ready in faith*	Barlow.
En grace affie	*Engrafted into grace*	Brudenell, Grace.
En la rose je fleurie	*I flourish in the rose*	Edwards-Moss, Gordon-Lennox, Lennox, Lenox, Moss, Roos, Roose.
En martélant	*Through hammering*	Martin.
Enough in my hand		Cunninghame.
En parole je vis	*I live by the word*	Legge, Stawell.
Ense animus major	*Courage is greater than the sword*	Rymer.
Ense et animo	*With sword and courage*	Grant.
Ense libertatem petit inimico tyrannis	*He demands liberty from tyrants with a hostile sword*	Caldwell.
En suivant la vérité	*By following the truth*	Wallop, Williams.
Entends-toi	*Understand well*	St. Clair.
En tout loyal	*Loyal in everything*	Carne, Hamon.
En tout parfait	*Perfect in everything*	Parfitt.
En vain espère, qui ne craint Dieu	*He hopes in vain who fears not God*	Janssen.
Eo altius quo profundius	*The deeper the higher*	Lloyd.
E perseverantia honor	*From perseverance honour*	Davey.
Eques sit semper æquus	*Let a Knight be alway just and generous*	Knight.
Equity		Handley.
Er cordiad y cæra	*Notwithstanding the agreement of the fortification*	Heaten.
Erectus non elatus	*Exalted, not elated*	Beaumont.
E rege et victoria	*From the king and by victory*	Bullen.
Ernst und treu	*Ernest and true*	Bates.
Ero quod eram	*I will be what I was*	Landen, Scrogie, Struth.
Errantia lumina fallunt	*Wandering lights deceive*	Kinnaird.
Eryr Eryrod Eryri	*The eagle of the eagles of North Wales*	Bulkeley-Owen, Owen, Wynne.
Espana agrad ecida		Evans.
Espérance	*Hope*	Carter, Currey, Ffytche, Milroy, Wallace, Webber.
Espérance en Dieu	*Hope in God*	Atkinson, Beverley, Bullock, Clark, Heber-Percy, Percy.
Espérance sans peur	*Hope without fear*	Griffith.
Espère en Dieu	*Hope in God*	Edgelow.
Espère et persévère	*Hope and persevere*	Paget.
Espère mieux	*Hope better things*	Heath.
E spinis	*From the thorns*	Delap, Dunlop.
Essayez	*Try*	Dundas, Saunders, Whitley-Deans-Dundas.
Essayez hardiment	*Try boldly*	Dundas.
Esse quam videri	*To be, rather than to seem*	Acraman, Anstey, Beadon, Berens, Boevey, Boevy, Bonham, Bourne, Bowen, Bower, Brownlow, Bunbury, Butler, Cambridge, Cook, Coutts, Croft, Cust, Davies, Deline, Frank, Grattan-Guinness, Graves, Hall, Harmer, Hill, Hood, Longley, Lukis, Maitland, Manning, Mathie, Miller, Partridge, Pickard-Cambridge, Round, St. Paul, Savory, Sheriff, Sherrif, Sturges, Swyre, Thruston, Turnour, Woodcock, Wornack.
Essorant victorieux	*Soaring victorious*	Nicolle.
Est concordia fratrum	*It is an alliance of brothers*	Brown.
Estimatione nixa	*Relying on my worth*	Cheyne.
Est meruisse satis	*It is enough to have deserved*	Massingberd.
Est modus	*There is a mean*	Lister.
Est modus in rebus	*There is a measure in things*	Parnell.
Est nec astu	*Nor is it by craft*	Brook, Brooke.
Est nobilis ira leonis	*The rage of the lion is noble*	Stuart.
Est nulla fallacia	*There is no deception*	Carr, Car-Standish.
Esto bonus et pius ne sit leo te magis impavidus	*Be good and pious, let not the lion be more undaunted than thou*	Wintringham.
Esto fidelis	*Be faithful*	Auberton, Weaver, Whittier.
Esto fidelis usque ad finem	*Be faithful unto the end*	Fydell.
Esto fidelis usque ad mortem	*Be faithful unto death*	Jones.
Esto memor	*Be mindful*	Keats.
Esto quod audes	*Be what you dare to do*	Dalway.
Esto quod esse videris	*Be what you seem to be*	Aufrere, Barkworth, Cole, Hall, Hooke, Miles, Morris, Rickards, Southerne, Watson.
Esto semper fidelis	*Be always faithful*	Duffield, Unthank, Yea.
Esto sol testis	*Let the sun be a witness*	Coleman, Jones, Tyrwhitt.
Estote prudentes	*Be prudent*	Couper, Wilkins.
Estote semper parati	*Be always prepared*	Fraser.
Esto velocior vita	*Be swifter than life*	Shuttleworth.
Esto vigilans	*Be watchful*	Farmer, Huntsman, Okeover.

Est pii Deum et patriam diligere	*It is the duty of a pious man to love God and his native country*	Atkinson
Est voluntas Dei	*It is the will of God*	Baldwin, Coates, Oliffe
Et arma et virtus	*Both arms and valour*	Dundas, Hamilton
Et arte et marte	*Both by art and force*	Bain, Bayne
Et custos et pugnax	*Both a keeper and a champion*	Majorebanks, Majoribanks, Marjoribanks
Et decerpta dabunt odorem	*And plucked, they will give forth an odour*	Aiton, Aytoun
Et decus et pretium recti	*Both the glory and reward of integrity*	Disney, Fitzroy
Et Dieu mon appuy	*And God my support*	Hungerford
Et dixi nunc cœpi	*I have said, now I begin*	Stubbs
Et domi et foris	*Both at home and abroad*	Callander, Livingstone, Mack
E tenebris lux	*Light out of darkness*	Alston, Aston, Lightbody
Eternitatem cogita	*Think on eternity*	Boyd
E terra ad cœlum	*From earth to heaven*	Frost
E terra germino ad cœlum expando	*I sprout out of the earth, I expand to heaven*	Frost
Et fide et virtute	*By both faith and virtue*	Porter
Et finem spero	*And I hope for the end*	Bevers
Et juste et vray	*Both just and true*	Kay, Wray
Et loquor et taceo	*I both speak and hold my tongue*	Keith
Et manu et corde	*With hand and heart*	Bates
Et marte et arte	*Both by strength and art*	Bain, Bayn, Drummond
Et mea messis erit	*My harvest also will come*	Denny, Judd
Et mortua virescunt	*And they become green when dead*	Lindsay
Et neglecta virescit	*It flourishes, even when neglected*	Hamilton
Et nos quoque tela sparsimus	*And we also have thrown darts*	Rawdon Hastings
Et patribus et posteritati	*Both for forefathers and posterity*	Lydal, Lydall, Lyddall, Williamson
Et servata fides perfectus amorque ditabunt	*Both faith preserved and perfect love will enrich*	Yonge
Et si ostendo non jacto	*And if I show what I am, I do not boast*	Oakden, Ogden
Et suavis et fortis	*Pleasant and brave*	Harper ✓
Et suives moy	*And follow me*	Hawley
Et teneo et teneor	*I both hold and am held*	Holden
Ettle weel	*Aim well*	Smart
Et vi et virtute	*Both by strength and valour*	Borrowes, Burrowes Burrows, Stamme, Stannus
Et vitam impendere vero	*To sacrifice life for truth*	Fox
Eundo	*By going*	Russell
Eu ner a folant,		Roberts
Eureka	*I have found it*	Robinson
Ever faithful		Gordon
Ever ready		Bryson, Burn, Burns, Rae
Evertendo fœcundat	*It fertilizes while it overturns*	Imbrie, Imrie
Every bullet has its billet		Vassall
Every point		Young
Evigila qui dormis	*Watch thou who sleepest*	Wakemam
Ewch ymlaen	*Go forward*	Roberts
Ewch yn uchae	*Go well*	Wynn Williams
Exaltabit honore	*He will exalt with honour*	Smyth
Exaltavit humiles	*He hath exalted the humble*	Holt
Exaltatio mea	*My exaltation*	Stubbs.
Ex animo	*From the soul*	Boyes.
Ex arduis perpetuum nomen	*From arduous enterprises an undying name*	M'Carthy
Ex armis honos	*Honour from arms*	Oglivies Ogilvy
Ex bello quies	*Rest from war*	Murray
Ex caligine veritas	*Truth out of obscurity*	Calverly
Ex campo victoriæ	*From the field of victory*	Campbell
Ex candore decus	*Honour from sincerity*	Keith, Marshall
Excelsior	*Still higher*	Steinthal
Excidit amor nunquam	*My love never fails*	Foote
Excisa viresco	*Though cut off, I flourish green*	Watson
Excitari, non hebescere	*To be spirited, not sluggish*	De Grey
Excitat .	*He arouses*	Ford
Ex concordia victoriæ spes	*From concord there is hope of victory*	Barnard
Ex corde charitas	*Out of the heart charity*	Watson
Ex cruce leo	*From the cross a lion*	Terry
Excutit inde canit	*He shakes his wings then sings*	Erskine
Exegi	*I have tried*	Lees
Exempla suorum	*The examples of his ancestors*	Innes
Ex fide fortis	*Brave from trust*	Beauchamp, Beddington, Lockley, Lygon, Pindar
Ex flamma lux	*Light is from flame*	Ingledeu, Ingledew
Ex fonte perenni	*Out of everlasting waters*	Brooke.
Ex hoc victoria signo	*Victory by this sign*	Rattary, Rattray
Ex hoc vivo .	*I live from this*	Drummond
Ex industria	*From industry*	Milne, Mylne
Exitus acta probat	*The end proves actions*	Biset, Nivison, Southwell, Stanhope
Ex libertate veritas	*From liberty, truth*	Aspland
Ex lumine lucrum	[illegible]	W[illegible]
Ex merito.		[illegible]

Ex monte alto	*From the high mountain*	Baker.
Expecta cuncta superne	*Expect all things from above*	Wilson.
Expectes et sustineas	*Hope and bear up*	Gwyn.
Expecto	*I expect*	Hepburn.
Expedite	*With despatch*	Hunter.
Expertus fidelem	*Proved faithful*	Latham, Lewis.
Expugnare	*To conquer; to take by storm*	Crawfurd.
Expugnavi	*I have conquered; taken by storm*	Pollock.
Ex recto decus	*Honour is from rectitude*	Durno.
Ex se ipso renascens	*Coming again from himself*	Fraser.
Ex sola virtute honos	*Honour springs from virtue alone*	Johnston, Johnstone.
Ex sudore voluptas	*Pleasure out of hard labour*	Swettenham.
Ex sudore vultus	*Beauty out of hard labour*	Swetenham.
Extant recte factis præmia	*Rewards exist for right actions*	Coffin.
Extinguo	*I extinguish*	Dundas.
Extinctus orior	*I rise when dead*	Douglas.
Extremos pudeat rediisse	*Let the rear feel shame that they have returned*	Westmacott.
Ex undis aratra	*Ploughs from the waters*	Downie.
Ex unguibus leonis	*From the claws of the lion*	Ogilvie.
Ex unitate incrementum	*Increase comes from unity*	Guthrie, Guthry.
Ex urna resurgam	*I shall rise again out of the urn*	Blandy.
Ex usu commodum	*Convenient for use*	Smith.
Ex vero decus	*Honour from the truth*	Jones.
Ex vili pretiosa	*Of great value from what is little worth*	Pattinson
Ex virtute honos	*Honour comes from virtue*	Jarden, Jardin, Jardine.
Ex vulnere salus	*Health, or safety, from a wound*	Borthwick.

F

Face aut tace	*Do but be silent*	Veel.
Fac et spera	*Do and hope*	Armstrong, Arthur, Askew, Ayscough, Caldwell, Campbell, Crommelin, De la Cherios, Donald, Fea, Highett, Hyatt, Ledsam, Littledale, Matheson, Macknight, M'Gee, Morison, Mynors, Richardson, Scepter.
Facies qualis, mens talis	*As the countenance is, so is the mind*	Blair.
Facie tenus	*Even to the face*	Wheeler.
Fac recte et nil time	*Do right and fear nothing*	Jeffries, Hill.
Fac recte nil time	*Do right, fear nothing*	Ashworth.
Facta, non verba	*Deeds, not words*	Chambers, Deedes, De Rinzy, Dickenson, Dunn, Eager, Fillent, Hoyle, Kirkland, Lewis, Low, Rayner, Samuel, Slade, Wilson, Yarde.
Facta probant	*Deeds prove us*	Stepney.
Factis, non verbis	*With deeds, not with words*	Money.
Facundia felix	*Happy eloquence*	Scot, Scott.
Faded, but not destroyed		Paver.
Fai bien, crain rien	*Do good, fear nothing*	Zornlin.
Faicilleach		Macdonell.
Faint yet pursuing		Dickinson.
Faire mon devoir	*To do my duty*	Jocelyn, Josselyn.
Faire sans dire	*To do without saying*	Blamire, Boulton, Fox, Fox-Strangeways, Jeune, Kerrich-Walker, Parr.
Faire son devoir	*To do his duty*	Boulton.
Fais bien crains rien	*Do well, fear nothing*	Tomlin,
Fais ce que dois advienne que pourra	*Do what is right, come what may*	Peters.
Fais ce que doit arrive que pourra	*Do what is right, come what may*	Cure.
Faith and hope		Lindsey.
Faith and works		Nelson.
Faithful		Robinson.
Faithful and true		Higgins.
Faithful in adversity		Hamilton.
Faithful to an unhappy country		Molyneux.
Faith, Hope, Charity		Motto of the Order of the Royal Red Cross.
Faitz proverount	*As he can*	Grimston.
Fal y gallo		Lyle, Greenly.
Fama candida rosa dulcior	*Fair fame is sweeter than the rose*	Taylor.
Famæ studiosus honestæ	*Zealous for an honourable name*	Brown.
Famæ vestigia retinens	*Keeping to the footsteps of fame*	Ennishowen.
Famæ venientis amore	*From a love for future fame*	Starky.

Famam extendere factis	*To extend our fame by our deeds*	Arundell, Monckton
Famam extendimus factis	*We extend our reputation by deeds*	Vach, Veitch
Fama perennis erit	*The fame will be everlasting*	Wyborn
Fama semper viret	*The fame is fresh for ever*	Liddell
Fama semper vivit	*The fame lives always*	Gason, Liddell, Swithinbank
Familias firmat pietas	*Religion strengthens families*	Ramsay, Wardlaw
Far and sure		Hunter
Fare et age	*Say and do*	Say
Fare fac	*Speak, do*	Fairfax, Ramsay Fairfax
Fare wel til then		Goodricke
Fari fac	*Make him speak out*	Fairfax
Fari quæ sentias	*To speak what you think*	Walpole
Fari quæ sentiat	*To speak what he thinks*	Barkas, Wallpool, Walpole
Fari quæ sentient	*To speak what they shall think*	Bretargh
Fast		Gray
Faste without fraude		Brooke
Fast tho' untied		Heneage
Fata viam invenient	*The fates will find a way*	Spange, Van Sittart
Fato fortior virtus	*Virtue is stronger than fate*	Hertslet
Fato providentia major	*Providence is greater than fate*	Napier, Thomson
Fato prudentia major	*Prudence is greater than fate*	Cheney, Cure, Lomax, Risley
Fatti maschi parole femmine	*Deeds masculine, words feminine*	Calvert
Faugh-a-ballagh	*Clear the way*	Gough
Faut être	*It must be*	Numbee
Faveat fortuna	*May fortune favour*	Heyland, Newton
Favente Deo	*By God's favour*	Fisher, Lester, Pawson, Reynolds, Wilkie, Wolin
Favente Deo et sedulitate	*By favour of God and by assiduity*	Collins
Favente Deo supero	*By the favour of God I succeed*	Mitchell
Favente numine	*By the favour of Providence*	Micklethwyatt Peckham, Sombre
Favente numine Regina servatur	*By favour of the Deity the Queen is saved*	Micklethwait
Faventibus auris	*With favouring breeze*	Stirling
Favet fortuna labori	*Fortune favours labour*	Turnbull
Fax mentis honestæ gloria	*Glory is the torch of a noble mind*	Forbes, Lauder, Molleson
Fax mentis incendium gloriæ	*The incitement of glory is the torch of the mind*	Brunton, Forbes, Grammer
Fay bien, crain rien	*Do well, fear nothing*	Benson
Fay ce que doy advienne que pourra	*Do what you ought, come what may*	Ireton
Faythe hathe no feare		Rycroft
Fear garbh ar mait		MacGarry
Fear God		Brisbane, Crum, Crumbie, Gordon, M'Andrew, M'Dougal, MacDougall, M'Dowall, M'Dowell
Fear God and dread nought		Wingrove
Fear God and fight		M'Clambroch, M'Landsborough
Fear God and live		Sinclair
Fear God and spare nought		Grassick
Fear God, honour the king		Bromley-Davenport, Davenport, Porter
Fear God in life		Somervale, Somerville
Fear God in love		Somerville
Fear God only		Spence
Fear not		Dawes
Fear not friendship		Thomson
Fear nought		Ramsay
Fear one		Hardy
Fear to trangress		Scott
Fecunditate	*By fruitfulness*	Hunter
Fecunditate afficior	*I am blessed with fruitfulness*	Hunter.
Felice che puo	*Happy who can*	Carew
Felicem reddet religio	*Religion will render a man happy*	Millar
Felicior quo certior	*The surer, the happier*	Ormistone
Feliciter floret	*It flourishes prosperously*	Crawfurd
Felis demulcta mitis	*The stroked cat is meek*	Keane, O Cahan
Felix qui pacificus	*Happy is the peace maker*	Spence, Spens
Felix qui prudens	*He who is prudent is happy*	Cubitt
Ferendo et feriendo	*By bearing and striking*	Harrison
Ferendo feres	*You will gain by enduring*	Irvine
Ferendo non feriendo	*By bearing not by striking*	Deane, Freeman
Ferendum et sperandum	*Enduring and hoping*	Mackenzie, M'Kenzie
Feret ad astra	*It shall carry to heaven*	Kellet
Feret ad astra virtus	*Virtue shall bear to the stars*	
Fer fortiter	*Bear bravely*	Barnes
Ferio	*I strike*	Littlejohn
Ferio sed sano	*I strike, but I heal*	Sharpe
Ferio, tego	*I strike, I cover*	Hawdon, Hondon, Howdon, M'Aul, M'Call, Sims, Syme
Ferme en foy	*Strong in faith*	Chichester, Haydon, Sanford
Ferme et fidele	*Firm and faithful*	Le Maistre
Fer et perfer	*Bear and forbear*	Barnard

Motto	Translation	Names
Feroci fortior	*Braver than fierce*	Lockhart, Piper.
Feror unus et idem	*I am borne along one and the same*	Collingwood, Mitchell.
Feros ferio	*I strike the fierce*	Chisholm, Gooden-Chisholm.
Ferox inimicis	*Bold against enemies*	Sikes.
Ferre non ferto	*Bear not to bear*	Steel.
Ferré va ferme	*Shod goes steady*	Farrar, Farrer.
Ferro comite	*With the sword for companion*	Clarkson, Mordant, Mordaunt, Tolson.
Ferro consulto	*I appeal to the sword*	Tregose.
Ferro non gladio	*By iron, not by the sword*	Carrington, Guest.
Ferro mea recupero	*I recover my own with my sword*	Bryan.
Ferrum equitis salus	*His sword is the safety of the horseman*	Smyth.
Ferte cito flammas	*Bear fire quickly*	Grant.
Fert lauream fides	*Faith bears the laurel*	Hay.
Fert palmam mereat	*He bears the palm, let him deserve it*	Bates.
Fertur discrimine fructus	*Profit is gained by peril*	Gordon.
Fervor non furor	*Fervour, not fury*	Monks.
Fest		Delafield.
Festina lente	*Hasten with caution*	Allsopp, Barnard, Blaauw, Blaw, Bury, Campbell, Colquhon, Colquhoun, Davies, Evans, Everett, Everitt, Grayrigge, Hollis, Johnstone, Markes, Mewburn, Onslow, Plunket, Plunkett, Rigge, Rothery, Swift, Trotter, Westcombe, Whitaker.
Fey e fidalgia	*Faith and fidelity*	Shelley.
Feythfully serve		Norreys, Norris.
Ffyddlawn ir Gwirionedd		Richards.
Ffyddlon hyd angau		David.
Ffyddylon at y gorfin		James.
Fiat Dei voluntas	*Let God's will be done*	Conolly, Meredith, Meredyth.
Fiat justitia	*Let justice be done*	Bryce, Coker, Plues.
Fiat justitia, ruat cœlum	*Let justice be done, though the heavens should fall in ruins*	Lloyd, Ouvry.
Fiat lux	*Let there be light*	Loxton.
Fiat pax fiat justitia	*Let peace be made, justice be done*	Holland.
Fiat voluntas Dei	*Let God's will be done*	Salway, Salwey.
Fida clavo	*Made sure with a nail*	Carr.
Fide et amore	*With faith and love*	Carden, Conway, Cramp, Dicey, Gardner, Hart, Heart, Seymour, Shearman.
Fide et animus	*Courage with faith*	Howard.
Fide et caritate laboro	*I labour with faith and charity*	Borrer.
Fide et clementia	*Faith and mercy*	Martin.
Fide et amore	*By faith and love*	Hatton-Ellis.
Fide et armis	*By fidelity and arms*	Fairquhar.
Fide et bello fortis	*Strong in faith and war*	Carritt.
Fide et constantia	*By fidelity and constancy*	Dixon, James, Lee.
Fide et diligentia	*With fidelity and diligence*	Crawford, Crawfurd.
Fide et fiducia	*By fidelity and confidence*	Blackman, Chafy-Chafy, Gilchrist, Harnage, James-Grevis, M'Garell-Hogg, Primrose, Thorlby, Thorley, Wall, Watt.
Fide et firme	*With fidelity and steadiness*	Fairholm.
Fide et fortitudine	*By fidelity and rortitude*	Aubert, Barton, Brickdale, Buck, Capel, Capel-Coningsby, Cooper, Cox, Farquharson, Finucane, Gibbons, Griffin, Griffith, Hickson, Higgans, Higgs, Lee, Lloyd, Lofft, M'Farquhar, Milligan, Morris, Noble, Ratcliff, Rynd, Shaw, Sutton.
Fide et integritate	*With fidelity and integrity*	Venn.
Fide et labore	*With faith and labour*	Allan, Jenner.
Fide et Marte	*With fidelity and bravery*	Patrick, Ralston.
Fide et opera	*By fidelity and labour*	M'Arthur, Macarthur, Stewart.
Fide et prseverantia	*By faith and perseverance*	Lumsden.
Fide et sedulitate	*With fidelity and diligence*	Elwood, Elworthy
Fide et spe	*With faith and hope*	Borthwick.
Fide et vigilantia	*With fidelity and vigilance*	Howlett, Stepney.
Fide et virtute	*With faith and valour*	Ashton, Brandling, Collins, Davies-Evans, Evans, Gladstanes, Gladstone, Glaidstanes, Gledstanes, Gooch, Goodwin, Purnell, Rochead, Rocheid, Roughead, Sheppard.
Fidei constans	*Steadfast in faith*	Colegrave.
Fidei coticula crux	*The cross is the touchstone of faith*	Baker, Chevallier, Tuthill, Whatton, Villiers.
Fidei signum	*The sign of my faith*	Murray.
Fidei tenax	*Steadfast in faith*	Glyn.
Fidei virtutem adde	*Add to your faith virtue*	Lee.
Fide laboro	*I labour with fidelity*	Borrer, Geddes, Geddes.
Fidèle	*Trusty*	Halyburton, Nicol, Roupell.
Fidèle p[illegible]	[illegible]	[illegible]
Fideli ce[illegible]	[illegible]	[illegible], Parker-Hutchinson

Fideli certe merces	*Certainly there is a reward to the faithful*	Saul, Saule
Fideli distillant sanguine corde	*Their heart bleeds drop by drop for the faithful*	Fayting
Fideli quid obstat Fideli quod obstat	*What stands in the way of the faithful*	Firebrace, Firebrass Firebrace
Fidelis	*Trusty.*	Blaikie, Crichton, Kenah Leadbitter, MacLawrin, M'Vean, Milvain, Weldie Waldy, Wilshere
Fidelis ad urnam	*Faithful to death*	Malone, Mawdelsy, Mawdesley, O'Malone, Staveley
Fidelis et audax	*Faithful and daring*	Pakington, Russell
Fidelis esto	*Be faithful*	Fox
Fidelis et constans	*Faithful and constant*	Bragge
Fidelis et generosus	*Faithful and generous*	Durell
Fidelis et in bello fortis	*Trusty and brave in war*	Gillespie
Fidelis et paratus	*Faithful and ready*	Soote
Fidelis et suavis	*Faithful and pleasant*	Emery
Fidelis exsulatœ	*Driven into exile by faith* .	Manbey
Fidelis in adversis	*Faithful in adversity*	Hamilton
Fidelis in omnibus	*Faithful in all things*	Collings
Fidelis inter perfidos .	*Faithful amongst the unfaithful*	Street
Fidelisque ad mortem	*And faithful to death*	Taylor
Fidelissimus semper	*Most faithful always*	Keating
Fidelis usque ad mortem	*Faithful even to death*	Buckler, Dowdall, Sutton
Fidelitas	*Fidelity*	M'Invoy, Purdie, Scot, Scott, Sinclair
Fidelitas et veritas	*Fidelity and truth*	Peters
Fidelitas in adversis	*Fidelity in adversity*	Fuller
Fidelitas vincit	*Fidelity overcomes*	Cotton, Deakin, Dunscombe, Scot, Swan, Thompson, Vaffiadacchi
Fidelitate	*With faithfulness* .	Elphinston
Fidelitate et amore	*By fidelity and love*	Hathorn
Fidelité est de Dieu	*Fidelity is from God*	Wingfield
Fideliter ..	*Faithfully* .	Balme, Bow, Cunliffe, Hamilton, Havelock, Henrie, Montgomery Muckleston, Ogilvy, Peale, Pickersgill-Cunliffe, Ralph, Swann, Symons, Thompson, Tringham
Fideliter amo	*I love faithfully*	Goldie Scott
Fideliter et alacriter	*Faithfully and cheerfully*	Walker
Fideliter et diligenter	*Faithfully and diligently*	Graham
Fideliter, fortiter, feliciter	*Faithfully, bravely and successfully*	Scourfield
Fideliter serva	*Serve faithfully*	Norris
Fideli tuta merces	*To a faithful man the reward is sure*	Thornton
Fidel je garderay	*I shall guard faithfully*	Castellain
Fidem meam observabo	*I will keep my plighted word*	Shedden
Fidem parit integritas	*Integrity produces confidence*	Kay, Kaye
Fidem rectumque colendo	*By cultivating fidelity and rectitude*	Hibbert
Fidem servabo genusque	*I will keep true to my word and family*	Browne
Fidem servare	*To keep faith*	Osmand
Fidem servo	*I keep faith*	Alexander
Fidem tene	*Keep faith*	Hornyold
Fide, non armis	*By fidelity, not by arms* .	Gambier
Fidens et constans	*Trusting and steadfast*	O'Kearin.
Fide patientia labore	*By faith, patience and work*	Pilter
Fide parta, fide aucta	*By faith obtained, by faith increased*	Mackenzie, M'Kenzie
Fideque perennant	*And they endure by faith*	Irvine
Fides	*Faith*	Forbes Leith, Maxton, Petree, Petrie, Wylie
Fides amicitiæ periculosa libertas	*Liberty a faith dangerous to friendship*	Dockwra
Fides culpari metuens	*Fidelity fearful of being blamed*	Yeldham, Yildham
Fides cum officio.	*Faith with duty*	Newton
Fide, sed cui vide ..	*Have confidence, but see in whom you place it*	Astley, Bankes, Barker, Beaumont, Birbeck, Coyney, Greenford, Greensugh, Harris, Hulme, Langley, Reynolds, Saunders, Stapleton, Stapylton-Studdy, Wats
Fide, sed vide	*Trust, but observe*	Petrie, Reynolds
Fides et justitia	*Faith and justice*	Webster
Fides et amor	*Faith and love*	Graham.
Fides et libertas	*Faith and liberty*	Dickson
Fides fortuna fortior	*Fidelity is stronger than fortune*	Hoey
Fides in adversis	*Faith in adversity*	Wolf, Woolfe
Fides mihi panoplia	*Faith is my panoply*	Aries
Fides non timet	*Faith does not fear*	Moran, Rice, Rise, Taylor
Fides nudaque veritas	*Faith and naked truth*	Lushington
Fides præstantior auro	*Fidelity is better than gold*	Clapperton, Gibb
Fides probata coronat .	*Approved faith crowns*	Campbell, Hepburn-Scott, Laidlaw, Scott
Fides puritas	*Faith, purity*	Webster
Fides servata ditat	*Tried fidelity enriches*	Baillie
Fides servata secundat	*Faith preserved renders prosperous* ...	Napier, Stirling
Fides Stephani	*The faith of S[illegible]* .	St[illegible]

IF

Motto	Translation	Families
Fides sufficit	*Faith is sufficient*	Hacket, Halket, Halkett-Craigie-Inglis.
Fides unit	*Faith unites*	M'Kenzie.
Fide tenes anchoram	*You hold anchor by faith*	Malim.
Fido Deo et ipse	*I myself, too, trust in God*	Gibbons.
Fido non timeo	*I trust, I do not fear*	Hermon.
Fiducia creat fidem	*Confidence gives rise to fidelity*	Ingoldsby.
Fiducia et labore	*By confidence and industry*	Jockel.
Fidus ad extremum	*Faithful to the end*	Leith.
Fidus ad finem	*Faithful to the last*	Jenkins.
Fidus amicus	*A trusty friend*	Campbell.
Fidus confido	*I as a faithful man confide*	Pack.
Fidus Deo et Regi	*Faithful to God and the King*	De Bary.
Fidus et audax	*Faithful and bold*	Grogan-Morgan, Morgan, O'Callaghan, Slade.
Fidus et fortis	*Faithful and brave*	Scott.
Fidus et suavis	*Faithful and grateful*	Emery.
Fidus in arcanis	*Faithful in secret affairs*	Stevenson.
Fidus in arcanum	*Faithful to a secret*	Stevenson.
Fiel però desdichado	*Faithful though unfortunate*	Churchill, Spencer, Tufton.
Fier sans tache	*Proud but without blemish*	Goff.
Fier et sage	*Proud and wise*	Bradford.
Fight		Ashe, Erskine, Sinclair, St. Clair.
Fight and faith		St. Clair.
Finem respice	*Consider the end*	Bazley, Bligh, Brooks, Burd-Brooks, Close-Brooks, Curling, Hoskins, Laslett, Norris, Patterson.
Fingit premendo	*He fashions by pressing*	Cutliffe.
Finis coronat opus	*The end crowns the work*	Bagley, Baker, Barnett, Bigelow, Finnis.
Finis dat esse	*Death gives life*	Brograve.
Firin		Gow-Steuart.
Firm to my trust		Glynn.
Firm		Dalrymple, Dalrymple-Hay, Elphinstone, Hamilton-Dalrymple, Kirby, Meason, Reid, Steuart, Walch, Wall, Walsh.
Firma durant	*Strong things endure*	Leslie, Lesly.
Firma et ardua	*Firm and arduous*	Mackenzie.
Firm and faithful		Cassidy.
Firma nobis fides	*Our faith is constant*	Vilant.
Firm as a rock		Tarpey.
Firma spe	*By sure hope*	Leslie, Lesly.
Firma spes	*Firm hope*	Moncrief, Moncriff.
Firme	*Firmly*	Dalrymple, Elphinstone, Hay.
Firme, dum fide	*Steadfastly while trustfully*	Heignie.
Firm en foi	*Firm in faith*	Chichester.
Firmiora futura	*Things to come more steadfast*	Fuller.
Firmior quo paratior	*The more prepared the more powerful*	Dunbar.
Firmitas et sanitas	*Strength and health*	Griffiths.
Firmitas in cœlo	*Stability in heaven*	Macnamara, Maher, Owen, St. George.
Firmiter et fideliter	*Steadfastly and faithfully*	Newman.
Firmiter maneo	*I remain steadfast*	Lindsay.
Firmius ad pugnam	*Stronger for battle*	Panton.
Firm to my trust		Glyn.
Firmum in vita nihil	*Nothing in life is permanent*	Bunbury, Dolphin, Tighe-Bunbury.
Firmus in Christo	*Steadfast in Christ*	Firman, Firmin.
Firmus et fidelis	*Steadfast and faithful*	Marwick.
Firmus infirmis	*Strong to the feeble*	Richardson, Kilpin.
Firmus maneo	*I remain constant*	Breek, Breck, Lindsay.
Firm, vigilant, active		Pennington.
Firrinneach gus a chrich	*Faithful to the last*	Macgregor.
Fisus et fidus	*Trusting and faithful*	Maitland.
Fisus et fidus et regia duxit	*Trusting and faithful, and he led the royal bands*	Erskine.
Fit inde firmior	*Thence he becomes stronger*	Skirvin, Skirving.
Fit manus aliena sua	*Another's hand becomes his*	Thornton.
Fit via vi	*The way is made by force*	Campbell, Proctor-Ramsden, Way.
Fixus ac solidus	*Fixed and solid*	Stewart.
Fixus adversa sperno	*Resolute I scorn adversity*	Crump, Hamerton.
Flecti, non frangi	*To be bent, not broken*	Carroll, Hemery, Houldsworth, Temple.
Fleadh agus failte		O'Fogarty.
Flectar non frangar	*I shall bend, not break*	Garneys.
Flectas non frangas	*Bend, you will not break*	Hoole.
Floreant lauri	*Let the laurels flourish*	Lowry.
Floreat majestas	*Let majesty flourish*	Braid, Broun, Brown, M'Kerrell-Brown, Morrison.
Floreat Salopia	*Let Shropshire flourish*	Taylor.
Florescit	*He is flourishing*	Watson.
Florescit vulnere virtus	*Virtue flourishes after a wound*	Bisson.
Floresco favente Deo	*God helping me I flourish*	Neill.
Flores cu[illegible] Deu[illegible]	*God [illegible] for the f[illegible]*	Flower, Flowers.
Floret q[illegible]	*He pro[illegible] who l[illegible]*	Ross.

Motto	Translation	Names
Floret qui vigilat	*He prospers who watches*	Smith
Floret virtus vulnerata	*Virtue though wounded flourishes*	Floyer
Floruit fraxinus	*The ash-tree flourished*	Ashcroft
Fluctuo sed affluo	*I move as a wave, but I flow on*	Arbuthnot
Fluctus fluctu	*Wave on wave*	Flux, Maitland
Fluminis ritu ferimur	*We are borne on as a river*	Rushbrooke
Flyddlawn Bunydd		Watkins
Foi est tout	*Faith is all*	Robinson.
Foi Roi droit	*Faith, king, and right*	Lynes
Follow me		Campbell.
Fonte puro	*From a pure fountain*	Lake
Force avec vertu	*Strength with virtue*	Leigh.
Force d'en haut	*Strength from above*	Mallet
Fordward		Balfour
Foresight is all		Lidderdale
Foresight		Hamborough.
Forget not		Campbell, Campbell-Orde, Davys, Rankine, Ranking
Forget me not		Campbell
Forma, flos, fama, flatus	*Beauty a flower, fame a breath*	Bagshaw, Bagshawe
Formosa quæ honesta	*What is honourable is beautiful*	Tarton, Turton
For my country		Jobling
For my Duchess		Grant
For right		Graham Stirling, Stephenson, Stirling
For right and reason		Graham
For security		Roberton, Robertoun, Steedman
Fors non mutat genus	*Chance does not change a race*	Wynants.
For sport		Cleiland, Cleilland, Cleland
Forte	*By chance*	Fortick
Forte en loyauté	*Brave in my loyalty*	Dacre
Forte et fidele	*Strong and faithful*	Ellis, Furnival, Talbot
Fortem fors juvat.	*Fortune assists the brave*	Menzies,
Fortem posce animum	*Pray for a brave soul*	Crampton, Fiennes, Fynney, Heriot, Twistleton-Wykeham Fiennes, Philimore,
Fortem post animum	*After a brave mind*	Heriot
Fort en loyalté	*Strong in loyalty*	D'Anvers.
Forte non ignave	*Bravely not cowardly*	Lee
Fortes adjuvat ipse Deus	*God himself assists the brave*	Davenport
Forte scutum salus ducum	*A strong shield is the safeguard of our leaders*	Fortescue, Parkinson-Fortescue
Fortes fortuna adjuvat Fortes fortuna juvat	*Fortune assists the brave*	Blennerhassett, Bloomfield, Dickson, Dixon, Goodwyn, Murray, Strange
Fort et loyal	*Brave and loyal*	Danvers, Selby
Fortfahren und verharren	*To go on and persevere.*	Nicholl
Forti et fideli nihil difficile	*Nothing is difficult to the brave and faithful*	Baskcomb, Deane, M'Carthy, Morean, O'Keefe
Forti favet cœlum	*Heaven favours the brave*	Oswald
Forti nihil difficile	*To the brave nothing is difficult*	Disraeli, Fox
Forti, non ignavo	*To the brave, not to the dastardly*	Lyell, Lyle
Fortior est qui se?	*Who is braver than himself*	Poley
Fortior leone justus	*A just man is stronger than a lion*	Broad, Broade, Haycock, Goodricke
Fortior qui melior	*He is the stronger who is the better man*	Buchan
Fortior qui se vincit	*He is stronger who conquers himself*	Madden
Fortior quo mitior	*The milder the stronger*	Buchan
Fortiorum fortia facta	*The brave deeds of braver men*	Stack, Stark, Stork
Fortis atque fidelis	*Brave and faithful*	Savage
Fortis cadere, non cedere potest	*The brave may fall but cannot yield*	Moore
Fortis ceu leo fidus	*Strong as a lion and faithful*	M'Brayne
Fortis esto, non ferox	*Be brave, not ferocious*	Wintringham
Fortis est veritas	*Strong is the truth*	Angus, Barton, Hutchon
Fortis et æquus	*Brave and just*	Douglas, Livingstone
Fortis et celer	*Strong and swift*	Cowell
Fortis et egregius	*Brave and distinguished*	Dowling
Fortis et fide.	*Brave and with faithfulness*	Carfrae
Fortis et fidelis	*Brave and faithful*	Alen, Beton, Bryan, Close, Delacour, Delacourt Douglas, Dunbar, Farmar, Finlay, Findlay, Fitzgerald Fletcher, Lalor, May, Middleton, Nind, Orme, Stenhouse
Fortis et fidus	*Brave and faithful*	Innes, Loughman, M'Clauchlan, M'Lachlan, M'Lauchlan, MacLaughlan, MacLaughlin, Thomson
Fortis et hospitalis	*Brave and hospitable*	Murphy, O'Morchoe, O'Murphy
Fortis et lenis	*Brave and gentle*	Curry
Fortis et placabilis	*Brave, and easily appeased*	Scot, Scott
Fortis et stabilis	*Brave and steadfast*	Kilbkelley
Fortis et velox	*Brave and swift*	Waldron
Fortis et vigilans	*Brave and vigilant*	Orr
Fortis ferox et cele[illegible]	*[illegible], fierce [illegible]*	M[illegible]hy

Fortis fidelis	*Brave, faithful*	Stenhouse
Fortis in arduis	*Brave in difficulties*	Armit, Beaton, Beton, Betton, Clarke, Coghlan, Findlay, Findley, Finlay, Fletcher, Ford, Geale - Wybrants, M'Dougall, MacDougall, MacDowall, M'Dowell, Methuen, Middleton, Thomson
Fortis in armis	*Strong in arms*	Armstrong, Watson-Armstrong
Fortis in bello	*Brave in war*	Cantillon
Fortis in procella	*Strong in storm*	Woods
Fortis non ferox	*Brave, not fierce*	Stockes, Stokes
Fortis qui prudens	*He is brave who is prudent*	Ormsby, Whitworth.
Fortis qui se vincit	*Strong is he who conquers himself*	Thorneycroft, Thornicroft
Fortis, si jure fortis	*Brave, if justly brave*	Stockenstrom
Fortissima veritas	*Truth is the strongest*	Kirkaldie, Kirkaldy
Fortis sub forte	*Brave under the brave*	Fitzpatrick, Fitz Patrick
Fortis sub forte fatiscet	*The brave will yield to the brave*	Fitzpatrick
Fortis valore et armis	*Strong by valour and arms*	Hatch
Forti tene manu	*Hold with a firm hand*	Corry
Fortiter	*Bravely*	Allan, Allen, Balmanno, Balmano, Batten, Beaman, Beauman, Boswell, Clark, Clipsham, Cuthbert, Elliot, Houston, Longbottom, Macalaster, M'Alaster, Macalister, M'Alister, M'Cray, Maclachlan, M'Lachlan Towers-Clark, Warrand, Wight
Fortiter ac sapienter	*Bravely but wisely*	Hordern
Fortiter agendo	*By acting bravely*	Pitman.
Fortiter defendit	*Defends bravely*	Andrews
Fortiter Deo juvante	*Bravely, God helping*	Pollard
Fortiter et aperte	*Bravely and openly*	Yatman
Fortiter et celeriter	*Boldly and quickly*	Mather
Fortiter et fide	*Boldly and with fidelity*	Bontein, Briggs, Bunten
Fortiter et fideliter	*Boldly and faithfully*	Armitage, Briggs, Brodhurst, Brown, Browne, Browne-Guthrie, Cox, Deane Fallon, Goodsir, Guthrie Jump, O'Gara, O'Hart, Pennyman, Peperell, Williams, Wilson
Fortiter et honeste..	*Bravely and honourably*	Abney
Fortiter et recte	*Boldly and rightly*	Allot, Drake, Eliott, Elliot, Fuller, Keay, Lomelying, Rankin, Smith.
Fortiter et sapienter ferre	*To bear bravely and wisely.*	Porritt
Fortiter et sincere	*Boldly and sincerely*	Johnson
Fortiter et strenue	*Boldly and strenuously*	Dempster, M'Lean.
Fortiter et suaviter	*Boldly and with suavity*	Ogilvie
Fortiter et vigilanter	*Boldly and vigilantly*	Tyson
Fortiter, fideliter, feliciter	*Boldly, faithfully, and happily*	Bottomley, Jackson, Monck, Rathdowne, Wathen
Fortiter gerit crucem	*He bears the cross bravely*	Allan, Hely Hutchinson, Hutchinson, Lawrence, M'Hutcheon, Trittou
Fortiter in angustiis	*Bravely in straits*	Hartshorn.
Fortiter in re	*Resolutely in action*	Wells.
Fortiter in re suaviter in modo	*Resolutely in action, suavely in manner*	Johnson
Fortiter qui fide	*Those who act faithfully act bravely*	Hamilton, Jackaman
Fortiter qui sedulo	*Those who act diligently act bravely*	Keith
Fortiter sed apte	*Boldly, but to the purpose*	Falconer
Fortiter sed feliciter	*Bravely but fortunately*	White
Fortiter sed suaviter	*Bravely but gently*	Lee, Muntz, Willsher
Fortiter ubique.	*Bravely everywhere*	Clerk
Fortitudine	*With fortitude*	Adair, Barr, Barry, Boyle, Cuninghame, Cuninghame - Fairlie, Cunningham, Duerryhouse, Erskin, Erskine, Grant, Hobson, Hoste, M'Crae, M'Rach, Macrae, MacRae, Moubray, Ray
Fortitudine crevi.	*I have thriven by fortitude*	Craven
Fortitudine Dei	*By the strength of God*	Hobson
Fortitudine Deo	*By the strength of God.*	Hobson.
Fortitudine et decore.	*With fortitude and grace*	Ballingall
Fortitudine et ense	*By fortitude and the sword*	Crossdell
Fortitudine et fidelitate	*With fortitude and fidelity*	Brown, Stuckey
Fortitudine et labore	*By fortitude and labour*	Reid, Yonge
Fortitudine et prudentia	*With fortitude and prudence*	Campbell, Carson, Halkett, Hargreaves, Lighton, MacEgan, Morgan, O'Reilly, Riley, Stuart, Yonge
Fortitudine et sapientia	*With fortitude and wisdom*	Fox
Fortitudine et velocitate	*With courage and celerity*	Balnaves, Balneaves
Fortitudine victor	*A victor by fortitude*	Taylor
Fortitudine vincit	*He conquers by fortitude*	Doyle
Fortitudini	*To fortitude*	Hoste
Fortitudo	*Fortitude.*	Clark

Fortitudo et justitia invictæ sunt	*Fortitude and justice are invincible*	M'Guire
Fortitudo et prudentia	*Fortitude and prudence*	Egan
Fortitudo fidelis honore munerata	*Faithful fortitude is rewarded with honour*	Russell
Fortitudo in adversis	*Fortitude in adversity*	Cox
Fortius dum juncta	*Stronger while united*	Hay
For true liberty		Renwick
Fortuna audaces juvat	*Fortune assists the daring*	Barron, Cleveland, Cregoe
Fortuna audaces juvat timidosque repellit	*Fortune assists the daring but baffles the timid*	Cregol
Fortuna comes	*Fortune is my companion*	Ferguson
Fortuna et honos ab alto	*Fortune and honour from above*	Rydan
Fortuna et labore	*By fortune and labour*	Brown, Sym, Syme
Fortuna faveat	*May fortune favour us*	O'Flaherty
Fortuna favente	*Fortune favouring*	Falkiner, Pudsey
Fortuna favet	*Fortune favours*	Whyte
Fortuna favet audaci	*Fortune favours the daring*	Turnbull
Fortuna favet fortibus	*Fortune favours the brave*	O'Flaherty
Fortuna juvat	*Fortune furthers* .	M'Andrew
Fortuna parcet labori .	*Fortune will save trouble*	Buchanan
Fortuna sequatur ...	*Let fortune follow*	Gordon, Hunter, Warren
Fortuna sequitur	*Fortune follows*	Dickinson
Fortuna vectem sequitur	*Fortune follows effort*	Wight
Fortuna viam ducit	*Fortune leads the way*	Hassard
Fortuna virtute	*Fortune is from virtue*	Beath, Beith, Bieth
Fortune de guerre .	*Chance of war*	Chute, Chute-Wiggett
Fortune helps the forward		Carmichael
Fortune le veut	*Fortune wills it*	Chaytor, Morin
For valour		Motto of the Victoria Cross
Forward		Balfour, Campbell, Curl, Currel, Currell, Douglas, Farish, Howales, Ker, Maclraen, Millar, Miller, Ogilvie, Ogilvy, Speir, Strachan, Stewart, Stewart Richardson, Stirling, Stuart
Forward, kind heart		Bell
Forward, non temere	*Forward, not rashly*	Balfour
Forward ours		Seaton, Seton
Forward without fear		Gordon
Fovendo foveo	*I cherish by cherishing*	Folville
Foy	*Fidelity*	Gilpin, Sausse
Foy en tout..	*Fidelity in all things*	Grey, Sutcliffe, Yelverton
Foy est tout	*Fidelity is everything*	Babington, Grey, Robinson
Foy pour devoir	*Faith for duty*	Seymour, St Maur
Foys sapience et chevalerie	*Faith, wisdom and chivalry*	A'Beckett
Fractum non abjicio ensem	*I throw not away the broken sword*	Armitage
Fractus pugnatu	*Broken with fighting*	Hansard
Fragrat, delectat, et sanat	*It smells sweet, and delights, and it cures*	Clelland
Fragrat post funera virtus	*Virtue smells sweet after death*	Chesly, Cheisly, Chiesly
Française	*French*	Harris
France et sans dol	*For France and without sorrow*	Cartier
Francha Call Toge		Godolphin
Franco leale toge	*Free and loyal is to thee*	Dolphin
Frangas, non flectes	*You may break, you shall not bend me*	Cassidy, Collins, Frith, Jones, Kimber, Leveson, Leveson Gower, Lloyd, Norton, Rippon, Stanley, Whimper, Whymper
Frangi non flecti	*To be broken, not bent*	Owen
Frango	*I break*	M'Laren
Frango dura patientia	*I break hard rocks by patience*	Cooper
Frapper au but	*To hit the mark*	Gibbs
Frappez avec raison	*Strike with reason*	Parry Mitchell
Frappez fort	*Strike hard* .	Wodehouse, Woodhouse
Free		Scott
Free for a blast		Clark, Clerk, Clerke, Pennycock, Pennycoock, Pennycuick, Rattray
Frere ayme frère .	*Brother loves brother*	Frere
Friendship		Carr
From henceforth		Poore
Fructu arbor cognoscitur	*The tree is known by its fruit*	Purton
Fructu cognoscitur arbor	*The tree is known by its fruit*	Wood, Martin
Fructum habet caritas	*Charity hath fruit*	Buckston
Fructu non foliis	*By the fruit, not the leaves*	Bushby
Fructu noscitur	*It is known by the fruit*	Newbigging
Fructus per fidem	*Fruits of faith*	Fructuozo
Fugiendo vincimus	*We conquer by fleeing*	Ogg
Fugite fures omnes	*Flee from all thieves*	Johnson
Fugit hora	*The hour flies*	Bagnall, Forbes
Fugit irrevocabile tempus	*Time flies beyond recall*	Shadford, Shadforth, Tilson
Fuimus .	*We have been.* . .	Bruce, Bruce-Brudenell, Cartwright, Cumming-Bruce, Fogo, Kennedy, Knight-Bruce, Llewellin, O'Beirn, Pryce, Symons, Were, Wright

Motto	Translation	Families
Fuimus, et sub Deo erimus	*We have been, under God, and shall be*	Coham
Fulcrum dignitatis virtus	*Virtue is the support of dignity*	Bull.
Fulget	*He shines forth*	Belsches.
Fulget virtus	*Virtue shines forth*	Bell.
Fulget virtus intaminata	*Virtue shines unspotted*	Belches, Belsches.
Fulminis instar	*Like lightning*	Hogan.
Functa virtute fides	*Faith having exhibited valour*	Murray.
Fundamentum gloriæ humilitas	*Humility is the foundation of glory*	Hodges.
Furor arma ministrat	*Fury supplies arms*	Baynes.
Furth and fear nocht		Farside.
Furth fortune		Murray, Butter.
Furth fortune and fill the fetters		Aynsley, Glenlyon, Murray, Stewart.
Futuri cautus	*Wary of the future*	Raikes.
Futurum invisibile	*The future is unknown*	Bevill.
Fy ngobaith sydd yu nuw		Carne.
Fy nuw a chymru		Philipps, Walters.

G

Motto	Translation	Families
Gadge and measure		Edmonstone.
Galea spes salutis	*The hope of salvation is our helmet*	Cassells.
Gänger	*A walker*	Walker.
Gang forrit		Haly, Kennedar.
Gang forward		Stirling.
Gang warily		Drummond, Porterfield.
Garde	*Guard*	M'Kenzie.
Garde garde	*Guard carefully*	Edmonstone-Montgomerie.
Garde bien / Gardez bien	*Guard well*	Carrick, Harvey, Montgomerie, Montgomery.
Garde la croix	*Guard the cross*	Ward.
Garde la foi	*Guard the faith*	Edwards, Poulett.
Garde la foy	*Guard the faith*	Stafford.
Garde la loi	*Guard the law*	Slator.
Garde le Roy	*Guard the King*	Lane.
Garde l'honneur	*Guard honour*	Hanmer, Hawksley.
Garde ta bien aimée	*Guard thy well-beloved*	Maze.
Garde ta foy	*Guard thy faith*	Rich.
Gardez	*Guard*	Cave, Verney-Cave.
Gardez bien	*Guard well*	Lievre, Montgomerie, Woodward.
Gardez la foy	*Keep the faith*	Edwardes, Poulett, Rich.
Gardez le capron	*Keep the capron*	Hollist
Gare la bête	*Beware of the beast*	Garbett.
Gare le pied fort	*Clear the way for the strong foot*	Bedford.
Gaudeo	*I rejoice*	Brown, Browne, Chandler-Brown.
Gaudet in luce veritas	*Truth rejoices in the light*	Moilliet.
Gaudet luce videri	*Rejoices to be seen in the light*	Galton, Howard.
Gaudet patientia duris	*Patience rejoices in hardships*	Grimond, O'Mallun.
Gaudet tentamine virtus	*Virtue exults in the trial*	Legg, Legge.
Gaudium adfero	*I bring joy*	Campbell.
Gauge and measure		Edmiston, Edmonstone.
Gearaigh agus dogh buadh		O'Mulloy.
Generosa virtus nihil timet	*Generous valour fears nothing*	Dunphy.
Generositate	*By generosity*	Nichol, Nicholson, Nickelson, Nickisson, Nicol, Nicolson.
Generosity with justice		Smith.
Generosus et animosus	*Noble and courageous*	Glennon.
Generosus et paratus	*Noble and ready*	Harwood.
Generosus nascitur non fit	*A noble man is born, not made*	Wharton.
Genti æquus utrique	*Fair to both families*	Gore-Booth.
Germana fides candorque	*Genuine fidelity and sincerity*	Falconberg.
Gesta prævenient verbis / Gesta verbis prævenient	*Deeds will surpass words*	Eckley. / Harcourt, Swanston, Woodcock.
Giolla ar a-namhuid a-bu		O'Donovan.
Give and forgive		Anderson, Andrew.
Giving and forgiving		Biggar.
Give the thanks that are due		Ward.
Gladio et arcu	*With sword and bow*	Stubber.
Gladio et virtute	*With sword and valour*	Ganstin, Garstin.
Gladium musarum nutrix	*The sword is the nurse of the muses*	Mill.
Gloria calcar habet	*Glory has a spur*	Knight.
Gloria Deo	*Glory to God*	Challen, Henn.
Gloria Deo in excelsis	*Glory to God in the highest*	Leke.
Gloria Deo in profundis	*Glory to God in the depths*	Whalley.
Gloria finis	*Glory the end*	Brooke, Grove.

Gloria in excelsis Deo	*Glory to God on high*	Kellock
Gloria, non præda	*Glory, not plunder*	Murray
Gloria Patri	*Glory to the Father*	Dewar
Gloria sat Deus unus	*One God glory enough*	Weston
Gloria virtutis umbra	*Glory is the shadow of virtue*	Elers, Pakenham, Pakenham-Mahon
Gnaviter	*Actively*	Anderson
Go and do thou likewise		Colston.
God and my conscience		Roberts
God be guide		Kennedy
God be in my bede		Beedham
God be my guide		Blair, Butler
God be our friend		Staple.
God careth for us		Mitford
Goddes grace governe Garneys		Garneys
God feedeth ye land		Leyland
God feeds the crows		Crawford, Crawfurd
God for us		Douglas, Gordon
God fried	*The peace of God*	Godfrey
God give grace		Tait.
God gives increase		Balfour
God giveth the increase		Allen
God giveth the victory		Simon.
God guide all		Leslie, Lesly
God is all		Fraser
God is cortues		Bull
God is love		Wesley
God is my defender		Bream, Breame, Dalton
God is my health		Hadley
God is my safety		Craw
God is my shield		Rosborough, Rosborough-Colclough
God me guide		Crichton
God my trust		Mason
God save the right		Crawford
God send grace		Creighton, Chrichton, Brocklebank
God shaw the right		Crawford, Craufurd, Edmonstone
God's providence is my inheritance		Boyle
God will provide		Stewart
God with my right		Bryson, Buchanan
God with us		Gordon
Gofal dym duw ai gwerid	*A prudent man God will guard*	Jones Parry
Gogoniant yr clethaf	*Glory to the sword*	Gwyn
Good friend		Godfrey
Good deeds shine clear		Minshull
Good God increase		Goodale, Goodalle
Good news		Tattersall
Goojerat		Gough
Go on, and take care		Thompson.
Goren meddyg, meddyg enaid		Jones
Go thou and do likewise		Colston
Go through		Brenton
Grace me guide		Forbes, Pownall
Grace my guide		Forbes
Gradatim	*By degrees*	Anderson, Hopwood, Kilgour, MacNicol
Gradatim plena	*Full by degrees*	Burnside, Gordon
Gradatione vincimus	*We conquer step by step*	Curtis, Duke
Gradu diverso via una	*The same way, by different steps*	Calthorpe, Gough
Grandescunt aucta labore	*What is increased by labour grows great*	A'Court, Holmes
Grata manu	*With a grateful hand*	Call
Grata quies	*Welcome rest*	Vansittart
Grata sume manu	*Take with a grateful hand*	Brisco, Winnington
Gratia naturam vincit	*Grace overcomes nature*	Edwardes
Gratias Deo agere	*Giving thanks to God*	Sidney
Gratior est a rege pio	*It is more agreeable coming from a pious King*	Gibbons
Gratis a Deo data	*Given freely by God*	Skeen, Skene
Gratitude and loyalty		Nagle
Gratitude		Bigland, Gigger, Mace Gigger
Gratitudo	*Gratitude*	Bigland
Graves disce mores	*Learn grave manners*	Graves
Gravis dum suavis	*Grave while sweet*	Graves.
Graviter et pie	*Gravely and piously*	Park
Gripe griffin, hold fast		De Trafford
Grip fast		Forbes, Leslie, Lesly
Gronwi hil Gwerninion	*Goronwy, a descendant of the Gwernin on*	Gronow
Growing		Fergusson
Gryff yu y fydd		Griffith
Guarde la foy	*Keep the faith*	Rich
Guard yourself		Middleton.
Guardez vous	*Guard yourself*	Lidiard
Gubernat navem Deus	*God steers the ship*	Lecky
Gun eagal		[illegible]

Gweithred a ddengys		Ellis
Gwell angau nachywilydd	*Rather death than shame*	Basset, Lloyd, Mackworth, Morris
Gwell augan na gwarth		Fenton
Gwilim		Hatton
Gwir yn erbyn y byd	*Truth against all the world*	Truscott
Gwna a ddylit doed a ddel	*Do thy duty come what may*	James, Lewis
Gwyr yn erbyn y byd		Gay

H

Habent sua sidera reges	*Kings have their stars*	De Vahl-Samuel, Samuel
Habere et dispertire	*To have and share with others*	Bath, Heathcote, Willoughby
Habet et suam	*He has also his own*	Seaton, Seton
Hab shar	*Without offence or a share*	Riddell
Hac ornant	*In this way they adorn*	Scougall
Hactenus invictus	*Hitherto unconquered*	Crawford, Crawfurd, Galightly, Gellatly
Hac virtus mercede digna	*Virtue is worthy of this reward*	Robertson
Had on and win		Hadwen
Hæc dextra vindex principis et patriæ	*This right hand is the avenger of my prince and country*	Ramsey
Hæc fructus virtutis	*These things are the fruits of virtue*	Waller.
Hæc generi incrementa	*These things are accessions to the race*	Townsend-Stephens
Hæc generi incrementa fides.	*Faith has conferred these new honours on our race*	Townshend
Hæc inimica tyrannis	*These are adverse to tyrants*	Riversdale
Hæc lucra laborum	*These are the profits of industry*	Rowan, Rowand
Hæc manus inimica tyrannis	*This hand is hostile to tyrants*	Leigh, Mahon
Hæc manus ob patriam	*This hand for my country*	Castle, Hassell, Hislop, Mactier, Shuckburgh
Hæc manus pro patriæ pugnando vulnera passa.	*This hand has been wounded in defence of my country*	O'Neill, Gealagh
Hæc olim meminisse juvabit	*It will delight us to remember these things some day*	Lewis
Hæc omnia transeunt	*All these things pass away*	Bourne
Hæc origo	*This origin*	Balnaves.
Hæc ornant	*These things adorn*	Scrugall.
Hæc prestat militia	*This warfare excels*	Bannerman
Hallelujah		Aylmer, Hendrick-Aylmer
Ha persa la fide, ha perso l'honore	*He who hath lost his faith hath lost his honour*	Lewis
Hardiment et bellement	*Boldly and handsomely*	Stucley
Hastings		Heron, Horn
Haud facile	*Not with ease*	Wettenhall
Haud inferiora secutus	*Following no lower aims*	Gerard
Haud nomine tantum	*Not in name alone*	Best
Haud ullis labentia ventis	*Yielding under no winds*	Irvine, Irving, Irwin
Hauri ex puro	*To be draw from the pure fountain*	Pemberton
Haut et bon	*High and good*	St Leger
Have at all		Drummond
Have at you		Grant
Have faith in Christ		Glendoning, Glendonwyn, Glendowing
Have mercy on us, good Lord		Sitlington
Have patience and endure		Rushton
Hazard warily		Seaton, Seton
Hazard zet forward		Seton
Heart and hand		Matheson
Heaven's light our guide		Motto of the Order of the Star of India
Heb Dduw, heb ddim	*Without God, without anything*	Evans, Jones, Peake, Price
Heb Dduw, heb ddim, Duw a digon	*Without God, without anything, God and enough*	Beynon, Davies, Edwards, Evans, Hughes, Jennings, Lloyd, Meredith Warter, Meredyth, Meyric, Meyrick, Morgan, Mostyn, Nicoll, Parry, Read, Stradling, Williams
Heb nevol nerth nidd sicr saeth	*Without help from above the arrow flies in vain*	Jones
He conquers who endures		Bath.
Heddwch	*Peace*	Hart
Help at hand, brother		Muire, Mure
Henricus a Henrico	*Henry from Henry*	Fitz-Henry
He seeks high deeds		Marshall
Ἤτοι τὸν λόγον ἄφετε ἢ καλῶς τούτῳ πρόστητε.	*Either discard the word, or becomingly adhere to it*	Mores-Rowe
He who looks at Martin's ape, Martin's ape shall look at him		Martin

Hic fidus et robore	*Here faithful and with strength*	Stirling
Hic fructus virtutis	*This is the fruit of valour*	Waller
Hic hodie cras urna	*Here to-day, to-morrow the urn*	Fletcher
Hic labor .	*This is labour*	Dee, Mortlake
Hic labor hoc opus	*This is labour, this a task*	Mortlock
Hic murus aheneus .	*This is a brazen wall*	Annesley, M'Leod.
Hic tutus nutrior	*I am nourished safe here*	Scott
Higher .		Galloway
Hinc decus inde tegmen	*From this quarter honour, from that protection*	Graham
Hinc delectatio	*Hence delight*	Forbes
Hinc ducitur honos	*Hence honour is derived*	Nisbet
Hinc fortior et clarior	*Hence stronger and more illustrious*	Martin, Martine
Hinc garbæ nostræ	*Hence our sheaves*	Cumine, Cummin, Cumming
Hinc honor et opes	*Hence honour and wealth*	Hay
Hinc honor et salus	*Hence honor and safety*	Lindsay
Hinc illuminabitur	*Hence we shall be enlightened*	Oliphant
Hinc incrementum	*Hence comes increase*	Hay
Hinc laus et honos	*Hence praise and honour*	Rae
Hinc mihi salus	*Hence my salvation*	Spalding, Peverell
Hinc odor et sanitas	*Hence fragrance and health*	Liddel, Liddell
Hinc origo	*Hence our origin*	Balnaves
Hinc orior	*Hence I arise*	Cameron, Hamilton, Howie, Paterson, Steuart, Stewart
Hinc spes effulget	*Hence beams forth our hope*	Aberdour
Hinc usque superna venabor	*Henceforward I will seek after heavenly things*	Murray
Hirbarhad	*Perseverance*	Lewis
His calcabo gentes .	*With these I will tread down nations*	Biddulph - Colclough, Colclough, Rosborough-Colclough
His fortibus arma	*Arms to these brave men*	Nisbet
His gloria reddit honores	*Glory renders honours to them*	Drummond.
His nitimur et munitur	*We rely on these and are strengthened by them*	Maconochie.
His parva crescunt	*By these little things grow great*	Hyslop
His regi servitium	*With these we render service to the king*	Neilson
His securitas	*Safety from these*	Barsane, Bartane, Barton.
History cannot be destroyed by time		Conroy
His vinces	*With these you will conquer*	MacDonnell
Hoc age	*Mind what you are about*	Browne, Levett, Metge, Naylor, Pigott
Hoc ardua vincere docet	*This teaches us to overcome difficulties*	Winchester
Hoc etiam præteribit .	*This also will pass by*	Budgett
Hoc in loco Deus rupes	*Here God is a rock*	Hockin
Hoc majorum opus	*This is the work of my ancestors*	Eliot, Eliot-Lockhart, Elliot
Hoc majorum virtus	*This is the valour of my ancestors*	Logan
Hoc opus	*This is a work.*	Dee, Mortlake
Hoc securior	*Safer by this*	Greson, Grier, Grierson, Grieve, Lockhart
Hoc signum non onus, sed honor	*This banner is no burden, but an honour*	Stoughton
Hoc vinco	*With this I conquer*	Hay
Hoc virtutis opus	*This the work of virtue*	Collison, Lytton
Hodie non cras	*To day, not to morrow*	Mostyn, Vaux
Hoeg dy mwyall	*Sharpen thy battle axe*	Price-Williams
Holden		Holden
Hold fast ..		Ancram, Annesley, Dowine, Leslie, Lesly, M'Leod, MacLeod, Macloide, M'Loud, Smith, Somerville, Stilwell
Hold firm .		Fiott
Holme semper viret	*Holme is always green*	Holme
Hominem te esse memento	*Remember you are a man*	Wybergh
Home .		Girvan
Homo homini lupus	*Man is a wolf to his fellow men*	Wolseley
Homo sum	*I am a man*	Homan
Honesta bona	*Wealth honourably got*	Edgell, Wyatt-Edgell
Honestæ gloria fax mentis	*Glory the torch to an honourable mind*	Pilkington
Honest and fast		Anderson
Honesta peto	*I seek honourable things*	Oliphant
Honesta quam magna	*How great are honourable deeds*	Walker
Honesta quam splendida	*How illustrious are honourable deeds*	Barrington, Critchley, Kennett
Honestas	*Honour* .	Faal, Fall, Goldie, Goudie, Paget
Honestas et veritas	*Honour and truth*	Kemp
Honestas optima politia	*Honesty is the best policy*	Goff Davies, Granger, Owen, Sparrow
Honestas quam splendida	*How illustrious is honourable conduct*	Askwith
Honestate vetustas stat	*Our antiquity stands on honour*	Stewart
Honeste	*Honestly*	Laing
Honeste audax	*Honourably bold ..*	Edingtoun, Lerkin, Parkins, Parkyns, Vaughan, Wolley
Honeste et constanter	*Honourably and constantly*	Reddie
Honeste parta	*Things honourably got*	Whyte.
Honeste vivo	*I live in my honour*	Cr[illegible], [illegible], H[illegible] [illegible]

Honestie is good policie		Thomson
Honesto vivo	*I live by what is honourable*	Halket
Honestum præfero utili	*I prefer what is honourable to what is useful*	Raikes
Honestum prætulit utili	*He has preferred the honourable to the useful*	Emline, Emlyn
Honestum pro patria	*What is honourable for my country*	Hamilton
Honestum utili patria.	*The honourable is the native soil of the useful*	Hamborough.
Honestum utili præfero	*I prefer the honourable to the useful*	M'Gell
Honesty is good policy		Thomson
Honesty is the best policy		Anderson, Kinnear, Thomas, Thomson
Honesty without fear		Thomson
Honi soit qui mal y pense	*Shame be to him who evil thinks*	The motto of the Order of the Garter
Honneur me guide	*Let honour guide me*	Lousada
Honneur pour objet	*Honour for aim*	Page
Honneur sans repos	*Honour without rest*	Montgomery
Honorantes me honorabo	*I will honour those who honour me*	Atthill, Hastings, Maunsell
Honorate, diligite, timete	*Honour, love, and fear*	Moselay
Honorat mors	*Death honours*	Bragge, Broge, Brogg, Broig
Honore et amore	*With honour and love*	Grantham, Richards, Hamersley
Honore et armis.	*By honour and arms*	Campbell
Honore et labore	*By honour and labour*	Hill.
Honore et virtute	*With honour and virtue*	Clark, Gilbanks, Gilbey, MacDermot
Honore integro contemno fortunam	*With honour unstained I despise fortune*	FitzGibbon
Honor et amor	*Honour and love*	Dowglas, Niblie
Honor et fides	*Honour and faith*	Sears
Honor et honestas	*Honour and honesty*	Patriarche, Tremayne
Honor et veritas	*Honour and truth*	Waller
Honor et virtus	*Honour and virtue*	Atkins, Grogan, M'Dermott, Morgan
Honor fidelitatis præmium	*Honour, the reward of fidelity*	Fielding, Irby
Honor me guide		Lusado
Honor, pietas	*Honour, piety*	Waters
Honor post funera vivit	*My honour lives after death*	Broadley
Honor potestate honorantis	*Honour with the power of honouring*	Kynaston
Honor præmium virtutis est	*Honour is the reward of virtue*	Flynn
Honor probataque virtus	*Honour and approved virtue*	Fitzgerald, FitzGerald, MacDermot
Honor rewards industry		Gardiner
Honor sequitur fugientem	*Honour follows him who shuns it*	Chichester
Honor veritas et justitia	*Honour truth and justice*	Southam
Honor, virtus, probitas	*Honour, virtue, and probity*	Barrett
Honor virtute prœmium	*Honour is the reward of virtue*	Wright
Honor virtutem coronat	*Honour crowns virtue*	Davies
Honor virtutis	*The honour of virtue*	Burdon
Honor virtutis præmium	*Honour is the reward of virtue*	Boyle, Ferrers, Goldney, Grueber, Hawtin, Hawtyn, Hickey, Hole, Janns Lee Norman, MacDermott, Norman Paine, Palmer, Shirley, Wright
Honor virtutis pretium	*Honour is the price of virtue*	Mills
Honos alit artes	*Honour cherishes the arts*	Greenhill.
Honos cui honos	*Honour to whom honour*	Brooke
Honos fidelitatis præmium	*Honour the reward of fidelity*	Irby
Honos industriæ præmium	*Honour the reward of industry*	King
Honos virtutis satelles	*Honour the attendant of virtue*	Baker
Honos vitâ clarior	*Honour more glorious than life*	Innes.
Hope and not rue		Oliphant
Hope for the best		Sisson, Sissons
Hope in God		Harkness.
Hope me encourageth		Bushe.
Hope to come		Foliot, Foliott
Hope to share		Riddell
Hope well and have well		Bower
Hope well, love well		Bower
Hora e sempre	*Now and always*	Denys
Hora et semper	*Now and always*	Farmer, Fermor
Hos gloria reddit honores	*Glory has given these honours*	Drummond
Hostis honori invidia	*Envy is an enemy to honour*	Amy, Dickens, Patison, Pattison, Sherard, Sherrard, Wegg
Huc tendimus omnes	*We are all travelling to this bourne*	Paterson
Huic generi incrementa fides	*Loyalty gives increase to this family*	Townshend
Huic habeo	*I hold to this one*	Ellis
Huic habeo non tibi.	*I hold to this one, not to thee*	Greaves
Humani nihil alienum	*Nothing concerning man is indifferent to me*	Atwood, Hanrott, Purcell, Talbot
Humilitate	*By humility*	Carlile, Carlyle.
Hyeme exsuperata	*When the winter is over*	Wrangham
Hunter, blow the horn		Forrester
Hyeme viresco.	*I grow green in winter*	Strode

I

Motto	Translation	Families
I abyde my tyme		Pennefather
I am ever prepared		MacBreid, M'Breid
I am, I am		Ruxton
I am lone		Lone
I am readie		Fraser
I am ready		Fairlie, Fairly, Fraser, Frazer, Maxwell, Scott
I beare in minde		Campbell
I beir the bel		Macdonald
I burn weil, I see		M'Leod
I byde		Gordon, Taylor Gordon.
I byde it		Nisbet
I byde my tyme		Barton, Campbell, Curling Hayward, Gordon, Hastings, Loudon, Porteous
I byde ve fair		Maxwell
Ich dien	*I serve*	H R H the Prince of Wales, K G
I conquer by the wound		Bartholomew
I conquer or die		Lumsden.
Ictus non victus	*Struck, not conquered*	Shute
I dare		Adair, Dalsiel, Dalyell, Dalziel, Dalzel, Dalziell
Iddow Bor Iiolch	*To God be thanks*	Lloyd
I Dduw bo'r diolch		Thomas
I desire not to want		Cranston, Cranstoun
I die for those I love		Forbes-Leith, Shaw, Shaw Hamilton, Stackpoole
I face all weathers		Mackenzie, Mackintosh
If God will		Samson
If I can		Colquhoun
I forget not		Campbell
I gain by hazard		Hamilton
Igne constricto vita secura	*Fire restrained, our lives are secure*	Davy
Igne et ferris vicimus	*We conquer by fire and swords*	Hodder
Igne et ferro	*By fire and sword*	Hickman
I hope		Forrest, Gordon, Joynt, Ogle
I hope for better		Boswell
I hope in God		M'Brayne, Macnaghten, M'Naughtan, M'Naughton, Naughten, Niven
I hope to share		Nisbet, Riddell
I hope to speed		Cathcart, Gilchrist
I increase		Scot
I keep traist		Forbes
Il buono tempo verra	*The good time will come*	Jennings.
Ilias in nuce	*An Iliad in a nutshell*	Ogden
I live in hope		Kennear, Kinnear
Illæso lumine solem	*I can look at the sun with eye uninjured*	Kebble, Kibble, Sharpe, St Clair-Erskine Wedderbourn, Wedderburn
I'll be wary		Finlay, Lawrie
I'll byde broad Albine		Maxwell
I'll deceive no man		Hamilton
I'll defend		Kincaid, Lennox
Ille vincit ego mereo	*He conquers, I deserve*	Sinclair
I'll hope and not rue		Oliphant.
Illis bonos venit..	*Honour comes to them*	Mitchell
I'll stand sure .		Grant
I'll try		Newbegin, Newbigging
Illumino	*I give light*	Farquharson.
Il suffit	*It is enough*	Darker
Il tempo passa	*Time passes*	Boynton
I make sure		Kilpatrick, Kirkpatrick
I mak sicker.		Kirkpatrick
I mean well		Callendar, Callender, Mackenzie, Shaw, Stewart, Sutcliffe
I mean no harm		Gairdner
Imitare quam invidere	*To imitate, rather than to envy*	Child, Hooke Child, Pleydell
Immaculata gens	*An unspotted race*	Vaughan
Immer frey	*Always free*	Austen-Cartmell.
Immeritas temnere minas	*To scorn undeserved threats*	Thores
Immersabilis	*Unconquerable . .*	Hamilton
Immersabilis est vera virtus	*True virtue cannot be overwhelmed*	Codrington
Immobile	*Steadfast*	Grant
Immobilis innocentia	*Steadfast innocence*	Culme

Immortalia spero	*I hope for immortality*	Tytler.
Immotus	*Unmoved*	Alston.
Immutabile, durabile	*Unchangeable, durable*	Rolland.
Impavide	*Undauntedly*	Cabbell.
Impavido pectore	*With undaunted heart*	Murchison.
Impavidum ferient ruinæ	*The ruin shall strike me unappalled*	Mundell, Perring.
Impavidum feriunt ruinæ	*The ruins strike him undismayed*	Perring.
Impegerit fidus	*The faithful man has made fast*	Constable.
Impelle obstantia	*Subdue obstacles*	Arthur.
Impendam, expendar	*I will spend and be spent*	Burket, Burkett.
Imperat æquor	*He commands the wide sea*	Monypenny.
Imperatricis auspiciis	*Under imperial auspices*	Motto of the Order of the Indian Empire.
Imperio	*By command*	Murray.
Imperio regit unus æquo	*One alone governs with just sway*	Gunning.
Impero	*I command*	Murray, Stewart.
Impiger et fidus	*Alert and faithful*	Constable.
Impromptu	*On the spur of the moment*	Trotter.
In adversis etiam fide	*With faith even in adversity*	Dandridge.
In altum	*Toward heaven*	Alston, Alstone.
In arce salus	*In the citadel safety*	Copeman.
In ardua	*In difficulties*	Hoare.
In ardua nitor	*I strive against difficulties*	Halkerston.
In ardua petit	*He aims at difficult things*	Malcolm.
In ardua tendit	*He has attempted difficult things*	M'Allam, M'Callum, Malcolm.
In ardua virtus	*Virtue in distress*	Leathes, Wolstenholme.
In arduis fortis	*Brave in difficulties*	Dingwall, Dingwall-Fordyce, Fordyce Middleton.
In arduis fortitudo	*Firmness in dangers*	Bright, Hamilton.
In arduis viget virtus	*Virtue flourishes in dangers*	Gurdon.
In bello invictus in amore probus	*Unconquered in war, honourable in love*	Steele Steele-Graves.
In bello quies	*Repose in war*	Murray.
In cælo confidemus	*We trust in heaven*	Hill.
In caligine lucit	*It shines in the dark*	Baillie.
In candore decus	*Honour in purity*	Chadwick,
In canopo ut ad canopum		Louis.
Incepta persequor	*I prosecute my undertakings*	Wilkinson.
In certa salutis anchora	*Upon a sure anchor of safety*	Gillespie.
In Christo salus	*Salvation is in Christ*	Abernethy.
In Christo speravi	*In Christ I have hoped*	Peckover.
Incidendo sano	*I cure by incision*	Kincaid.
Inclinata resurgo	*Though bowed down, I rise again*	Cooper.
Inclyta virtus	*Renowned valour*	Kean.
Inclytus perditæ recuperator coronæ	*The glorious recoverer of a lost crown*	Seton.
Inclytus virtute	*Renowned for valour*	O'Cahan.
In cœlo quies	*Rest in heaven*	Bewick, Boscowen, Dolphin, Evans.
In cœlo spero	*I hope in heaven*	Miller.
In cœlo spes mea est	*My hope is in heaven*	Micklethwaite.
Inconcussa fides	*Unshaken faith*	Foster.
Inconcussa virtus	*Unshaken virtue*	Benson, Lane-Fox.
In constantia decus	*Glory in constancy*	Coppard.
In copia cantus	*Amid plenty singing*	Dod, Hopley, Wolley-Dod.
In corda inimicorum Regis	*Into the hearts of the enemies of the king*	Forstall.
In cornua salutem spero	*I hope for safety against the horns*	Hunter.
Incorrupta fides	*Incorruptible faith*	Jones, Taylor, Whitmore, Wolryche-Whitmore.
Incorrupta fides nudaque veritas	*Uncorrupted faith and unvarnished truth.*	Forde, Waskett.
Incrementum dat Deus	*God gives the increase*	Moseley.
In cruce confido	*I trust in the cross*	Thrale.
In cruce et lacrymis spes est	*In the cross and tears there is hope*	Hincks.
In cruce fides	*Faith in the cross*	Rudge.
In cruce glorior	*I glory in the cross*	Cliffe, Pye.
In cruce mea fides	*In the cross is my faith*	Billairs.
In cruce non in leone fides	*In the cross not in the lion is my faith*	Lisle.
In cruce salus	*Salvation from the cross*	Abercrombie, Abercromby, Adam, Adams, Aiken, Aitkin, Aitkine, Baghot-De la Bere, Bourke, Brigham, Carse, Carss, Langholme, Lawrence, Mallet, Marr, Milnes, Renny-Tailyour, Rudd, Tailour Tailyour.
In cruce spero	*I hope in the cross*	Barclay, Ewart.
In cruce spes mea	*In the cross is my hope*	Crossman.
In cruce triumphans	*In the cross triumphant*	Raffles.
In cruce victoria	*Victory through the cross*	Snell.
In cruce vincam	*I shall conquer by the cross*	Oldfield.
In cruce vinco	*I conquer by the cross*	Copley.
In crucifixa gloria mea	*My glory is in the cross*	Knatchbull.
In defence		Williamson.
In defence of the distressed		A'lardice, Allerdice, Barclay, Barclay-Allardice.

In defiance		M'Braire
In Deo confidemus	*In God is our trust*	Pryce
In Deo confido	*I trust in God*	Borton, De St Croix, Ickyll, Kirkman, Lawford, Le Gros, M'Gill, Moor Moore, Morison, Richards, Tovey, Tovy, Walker
In Deo confiteor	*My confession is in God*	Lodder
In Deo est mihi omnis fides	*In God is all my faith*	Palmer
In Deo et in ipso confido	*In God and in myself I trust*	Richardson
In Deo fides	*In God is my faith*	Brady, Medley, Plucknett, Smith
In Deo manuque fides	*In God and my hand is my trust*	Mackesy
In Deo mea spes	*In God is my hope*	Hesketh
In Deo nostra spes est	*In God is our hope*	Rocke
In Deo omnia	*All things are in God*	Bluett, Huxley, Reed
In Deo robur meum	*In God is my strength*	Armstrong
In Deo salus	*In God safety*	Bestick Browning
In Deo salutem	*In God we have safety*	Scobell
In Deo solo spes mea	*In God alone is my hope*	Kay, Key
In Deo solo robur In Deo solum robur	*In God alone is strength*	Harris
In Deo sola salus	*My only salvation is in God*	Grundy
In Deo speravi	*In God I have hoped*	Clark
In Deo spero.	*I hope in God*	Dalby, Saumarez, Webster
in Deo spes	*In God is hope*	Mitchell
in Deo spes est	*In God is hope*	Harvard
in Deo spes mea . .	*In God is my hope*	Beers, Bonython, Couran
in Deo tutamen	*In God is my defence*	Oldfield
nde securior	*Thence the more secure*	Murray
nde spes .	*Thence hope*	Moncrieff
ndignante invidia florebit justus	*Despising envy, the just shall flourish*	Crosbie
in Domino confido . . .	*I trust in the Lord*	Asheton, Ashton, Areskine, Cahill, Cargill, Elmhurst, Erskin, Erskine, Inman, Key, Knyfton, M'Gill, Morris, West Erskine, Willyams
n Domino et non in arcu sperabo	*In God and not in my bow I will hope*	Molony
in dubiis constans	*Steady in doubtful affairs*	Cockburn, Cockburne, Ormistone
in dubiis rectus	*Upright in doubtful affairs*	Lees
ndubitata fides	*Undoubted faith*	Reynell
ndulge not		Edwards
ndustria	*With industry*	Calrow, Crierie, Crisie, Deas, Ferguson, Fettes, Fiddes, Gentle, Keltie, Kelty, Ogilvie, Ogilvy, M'Crire, Peel, Warrender
ndustria atque fortuna	*By industry and fortune*	Lawrie
ndustria ditat	*Industry enriches*	Don, Don Wauchope, Paxton, Reath, Sideserf, Sydserfe, Vanderplank, Wauchope, Waugh
ndustriæ manus	*The hand of industry*	Leechman, Leeshman, Leishman, Thomson
ndustria et labore	*By industry and labour*	M'Gallock, M'Gassock, MacGuffock, M'Guffock
ndustria et perseverantia	*By industry and perseverance*	Cowper
ndustria et probitate	*By industry and probity*	Bell, Margerison, Washbourne
ndustria et spe	*With industry and hope .*	Fenouillet, Warden, Yabsley
ndustria et virtute	*By industry and virtue*	Bolton
ndustria evehit	*Industry promotes*	Warrender
ndustria murus . ..	*Industry is a protection*	Thomson
ndustria permanente	*With unremitting industry*	Neave
ndustria veritas et hospitalitas	*Industry, truth, and hospitality*	Harris.
ndustria virtus et fortitudo	*By industry, virtue, and fortitude*	Smiley
ndustria virtute et fortitudine	*By industry, bravery, and fortitude*	Haig Smellie, Smellie
ndustry and liberality		Jejeebhoy,
nebranlable	*Unshaken*	Acland
nest clementia forti	*Mercy is inherent in the brave*	Fort, Forte, Gent, Maule
nest jucunditas	*Enjoyment is therein*	Elliot, Elliott
nevitabile fatum	*Inevitable destiny*	Kramer
nexpugnabilis	*Impregnable*	Penman
in ferro tutamen	*Defence in the sword* . ..	Ferrier.
n fide et in bello fortes	*Firm in faith and in war*	Bagwell, Carroll, O'Carroll.
n fide fortis	*Strong in faith*	Chambers
nfirmis opitulare	*To help the weak*	Kildahl
ngenio ac labore	*By talent and toil*	Kerr, Worrall.
ngenio et viribus	*By genius and force*	Huddleston
ngenio innumerato habe	*Possess by immense genius*	Lawrie
ingenium innumerata habi	*Justly esteemed a man of genius*	Lawrie.
ngenium superat vires	*Genius surpasses strength*	Adams
ngenium vires superat	*Genius surpasses strength*	Alexander
ngenuas suscipit artes	*He undertakes noble arts*	Long
n God is all		Fraser, Frazer
n God is all my trust		Grant
n God I trust		[illegible]

Ingratis servire nefas	*It is wrong to slave for the ungrateful*	Martin.
In heaven is all my trust		Ambrose.
In heaven is my hope		Huggard.
In hoc plenius redibo	*In this I shall return more full*	Minshull.
In hoc signo	*In this token*	Wodehouse, Woodhouse.
In hoc signo spes mea	*In this sign is my hope*	Taaffe.
In hoc signo vinces	*Under this sign you shall conquer*	Aiscroft, Barreau, Berrie, Berry, Bourke, Bowen, Burke, Colvin, Glasham, Gore, Gore-Booth, Homan-Mulock, Ironside, Knox-Gore, Macadam, M'Carlie, M'Kerlie, Mulock, Newling, O'Donel, O'Donnel, Ormsby-Gore, Perry-Knox-Gore, Pontifex, Stanhope, Taafe, Tailyour, Taylor, Turney, Webb.
In hoc spes mea	*In this is my hope*	Gordon.
In hoc vince	*In this conquer*	Barclay.
In hoc vinces	*In this you shall conquer*	Cross.
Initium sapientiæ est timor Domini	*The fear of the Lord is the beginning of wisdom*	Martin.
In Jehovah fides mea	*In Jehovah is my faith*	Brailsford.
Injussi virescunt	*They grow green unbidden*	Greenfield.
In labore quies	*Repose in labour*	Helyar.
In libertate sociorum defendenda	*In defending the liberty of allies*	Macgregor.
In loyalty		Semple.
In lumine ambulo	*I walk in the light*	Gilmour.
In lumine luce	*Shine thou in the light*	Artindale, Makins, Thompson.
In malos cornu	*My horn against the bad*	Dadley.
In medio tutissimus	*Safest in the middle*	Clarke, Smith.
In memoriam majorum	*In remembrance of our ancestors*	Farquharson.
In misericordia Dei confido	*I trust in the mercy of God*	Durand.
In moderation placing all my glory		Fitzhugh.
In morte quies	*In death peace*	Cust.
In multis, in magnis, in bonis expertus	*Tried in many, great and good exploits*	Bowes.
Innixus vero validus	*Strong depending on the truth*	Lyon.
Innocence surmounts		Gulland.
Innocens non timidus	*Innocence is not afraid*	Rowe.
Innocent and true		Arbuthnot.
Innocent courageous activity		White.
Innocentia quamvis in agro sanguinis	*With innocence though in a field of blood*	Lowe.
Innocue ac provide	*Harmless and with foresight*	Aberbuthnet, Arbuthnot, Bowdler, Lapington, Newbigging.
In officio impavidus	*Fearless in office*	Falshaw.
In omnes casus	*For all chances*	Walker.
In omnia paratus	*Prepared for all things*	Layton, Prittie.
In omnia promptus	*Ready for everything*	Rae.
In omnibus caritas	*In all things charity*	Longmore.
Inopem me copia fecit	*Plenty has made me poor*	Bell.
Inopinum sed gratum	*Unexpected but welcome*	Worthington.
In pace ut sapiens	*In peace as one wise*	Sloper.
In Papam cornua tendo	*I stretch my horns against the Pope*	Aston
In pede fausto	*With a step of good omen*	Rutherford.
In periculis audax	*Bold in dangers*	Maher.
In portu quies	*Rest in the haven*	Bootle-Wilbraham, Watkins, Wilbraham,
In pretium persevero	*I abide my reward*	Jenner. Jenoure, Jenoyre.
In promptu	*In readiness*	Dunbar, Trotter.
In prosperis time, in adversis spera	*In prosperity fear, in adversity hope.*	Gabriel.
In rebus arctis	*In straitened circumstances*	Frye.
In recte decus	*Honour in rectitude*	Ferrier, Simmons.
In recto decus	*There is honour in the right path*	Hoseason, Scott, Syme.
In recto fides	*Faith in rectitude*	Dixon.
In robore decus	*Glory in strength*	Clerk.
In sanguine vita	*In the blood the life*	Cobbe.
In scientia veritas in arte honestas	*In science truth, in art honour*	Wells.
In season		Walkingshaw, Walkinshaw.
In se ipso totus teres	*Quite rounded in itself*	Lea, Smith.
Inservi Deo et lætare	*Serve God and rejoice*	Howard.
In se teres	*Rounded in himself*	St. Aubyn.
Insignia fortunæ paria	*The equal badges of fortune*	Delafield.
In silentio fortitudo	*Fortitude in silence*	Pelham, Thoresby.
Insiste firmiter	*Stand to it stoutly*	Moorside, Muirside.
In solitos docuere nisus	*Unusual efforts have been resorted to*	Babington.
In solo Deo salus	*Safety is in God alone*	Lascelles, Sparrow.
In solo regit qui degit in cœlo	*He who lives in heaven rules on earth*	Russell.
Insontes ut columbæ	*Harmless as doves*	Francis.
In spe et labore transigo vitam	*I pass life in hope and labour*	Mack.
Insperata floruit	*It has flourished beyond expectation*	Cleghorn, Watson.
In spe resto	*I stand firm in hope*	Wade.
In spe spiro	*In hope I breathe*	Sharp.
Inspice	*Examine*	Davis.

Instanta perfectus		Lloyd
Instaurator ruinæ	*A repairer of ruin*	Forsyth
Institutæ tenax	*Holding by the arrangement*	Astley, Parke
In sublime	*Aloft*	Reid
Insult me not		M'Kenzie
Intaminatis fulget honoribus	*It shines with unstained honours*	Seton
Intaminatis honoribus	*With unstained honours*	Fitz-Herbert
In te Deus speravi	*In thee, O God, I have hoped*	Browne.
In te digna sequere	*Follow what is worthy in thyself*	Parnell
In te, Domine, confido	*In thee, Lord, I confide*	Knyfton, Wayne
In te, Domine, speravi	*In thee, O Lord, I have placed my hope*	Abbs, Bowes, Delane, Greenhill, Hame, Haire, Hilliard, Lloyd, Lyon, Lyons, Prestwich, Prestwick, Tittle, Vale
In te, Domine, spes nostra	*In thee, Lord, is our hope*	Gill
In te fido	*I trust in thee*	M'Larty
Integer vitæ	*Upright in life*	Beynon, Christie, Eggington
Integra mens augustissima possessio	*An upright mind is a most glorious possession*	Blaney
Integritas semper tutamen	*Integrity is a constant defence*	Haden, Harries
Integritas tuta virus non capit	*Integrity is safe against poisonous infection*	Holl
Integritate	*By integrity*	Edwards
Integritate et fortitudine	*By integrity and fortitude*	Jones
Integritate sola	*By integrity alone*	Marrable
Integritate stabis ingenuus	*You will stand free by integrity*	Stewart
Integrity		Freake,
Intellectu et innocentia	*By intellect and innocence*	Headlam
Intemerata fides	*Uncorrupted faith*	Aberdeen, Robertson, Robinson
In tempestate floresco	*I flourish in the tempest*	Pine Coffin
In tenebris lucidior	*Brighter in darkness*	Inglis
In tenebris lux	*Light in darkness*	Scot, Scott
Intento in Deum animo	*With a mind directed to God*	Bosvile
Inter cruces triumphans in cruce	*Amid crosses triumphing in the cross*	Dalton
Inter hastas et hostes	*Among spears and enemies*	Powell
Inter lachrymas micat	*Shines amid tears*	Blundell, Blunt
Interna præstant	*Internal things stand fast*	Arburthnet, Arbuthnot
Interno robore	*With inward strength*	Mytton
Inter primos	*Among the first*	Hopkins
Inter utrumque	*Between the two*	Connellan
In the defence of the distressed		Allardice
In time		Hauston, Houston
Intrepidus et benignus.	*Intrepid and kindly*	Mackannel, Mackennal
In uprightness God will support us		Barrett
Inutilis vis est	*Force is useless*	Owens
In utraque fortunâ paratus	*Prepared in all situations*	Cotton, Stapleton-Cotton
In utroque	*In both*	Valange, Wallange
In utroque fidelis	*Faithful in both*	Carey, Cary, Nash
In utroque paratus	*Prepared in both*	Wylie
In utrumque paratus	*Prepared for both*	Caldecott, Deacon Heylyn, Knollys, Lawford, Mackenzie, Martin Holloway, Murray, Truscott
In utrumque utroque paratus	*Prepared for both and in both*	Deacon, Elphingston, Mackenzie, Murray
Inveniam aut faciam	*I shall find a way or make one*	Delmege
In veritas victoria	*Victory in truth*	Blyth
In veritate	*In truth*	Hastings
In veritate triumpho	*I triumph in truth*	Biddulph, Salusbury
In veritate victoria	*Victory in truth*	Abney-Hastings, Akroyd, Hastings, Ingham, Rawson
In via recta celeriter	*Swiftly in the right way*	Kay
In via virtuti pervia	*Virtue finds a way where there is none*	Hamilton
Invia virtuti via nulla	*No path is too hard to virtue*	Seton
Invicta labore	*Unconquered by fatigue*	Armestrang, Armstrang, Armstrong
Invicta veritate	*With invincible truth*	Abell
Invictus maneo	*I remain unvanquished*	Armestrang, Armstrang, Armstrong, Heys, Inglis, Wright
Invictus manes	*Thou remainest unconquered*	Armstrong
Invidere sperno	*I disdain to envy*	Coventon, Saunders
Invidia major	*Above envy*	Drago, Gardner, Inwards, Peters
In vigilia sic vinces	*In watchfulnes thus will you conquer*	Price
In virtute et fortuna	*In valour and fortune*	Fraser, Frazer, Gardner.
Invita fortuna	*In spite of fortune*	Knightley
Invita sortem fortuna	*Fate in spite of fortune*	Knightley
Invitis ventis	*Fate in spite of fortune*	Duport
Invitum sequitur honor	*Honour follows though unsought for*	Chichester, O'Neill
In well beware		Wombwell
I press forward		Croall
Ipse amicus	*He is a very friend*	Baron
Ipse fecit nos	*Himself made us*	Ronan
Iram leonis noli timere	*Fear not the rage of the lion*	Long

Ire in adversa	*To advance against things adverse*	Stokes.
I renew my age		Garshore, Gartshore, Stirling.
I rise by industry		Foulis.
I rise with the morning		Cockburn.
Irrevocabile	*Irrevocable*	Bennett, Bennitt, Bruce.
Irrideo tempestatem	*I deride the storm*	Wood.
Irrupta copula	*An unbroken bond*	Morris.
I rule while I see		MacLeod.
I saved the King		Torrance, Turnbull.
I'se mak' sicker	*I make secure*	Kirkpatrick.
I show not boast		Nimmo.
I soar		Ellidge.
Ita	*Thus*	Cockburn.
Iterum iterumque	*Again and again*	Hoey.
It is fortified		MacConach.
It is good to be blown		Forrester.
Ito tu et fac similiter	*Go thou and do likewise*	Oliver.
It shall flourish		Palmer.
Itur ad astra	*Our way is to the stars*	Mackenzie, Mulchinock.
I wait my time		Porteous.
I will		Davis.
I will defend		Kincaid.
I will never quit		Boulton.
I will not forget		Campbell.
I will who will not		Wilson.

J

Jaculis nec arcu	*With javelins, not with bow*	Bowes.
J'ai bien servi	*I have served well*	Prevost.
J'ai bonne cause	*My cause is good*	Thynne.
J'ai bonne espérance	*I have good hope*	Craig, M'Kean.
J'ai la clef	*I have the key*	Greive, Grive.
J'aime à jamais	*I love always*	James.
J'aime la liberté	*I love liberty*	Ribton, Mussenden.
J'aime la meilleure	*I love the best*	Sinclair,
J'aime mon Dieu, mon Roi, et mon pays.	*I love my God, my King, and my country*	Kirwan.
Jamais abattu	*Never cast down*	Ochterlony.
Jamais arrière	*Never behind*	Campbell, Douglas, Douglas-Gresley, Douglas-Hamilton, Fryer, Gresley, Monteath-Douglas.
Jamais chancelant	*Never wavering*	Le Gallais.
Jamais sans espérance	*Never without hope*	King.
Jam jam	*Just now*	Ruxton.
Jam transit hyems	*Winter is now passing away*	Haig.
J'aspire	*I aim*	De Vismes, Devizmes.
J'avance	*I advance*	Bartram, Bertram, Clayton, East, Gilbert-East, Ker.
J'ay bonne cause	*I have good cause*	Botevile, Boteville, Botfield, Bouteville Thynne.
J'ay espére mieux avoir	*I have hoped for the best*	Dine, Dive.
J'ay ma foy tenu à ma puissance	*I have held to my faith in my power*	Croker, Fox.
J'ayme à jamais	*I love for ever*	James.
Je ayme	*I love*	Lindsay.
Je conduis	*I conduct*	Conder.
Je crains Dieu	*I fear God*	Whitehurst.
Je dis la vérité	*I speak the truth*	Pedder.
Je ferai bien	*I shall do well*	Butler, Green.
Je gagne	*I gain*	Osborn, Osbourne.
Je garde ma foi	*I defend my faith*	Le Cronier.
Je garderay	*I will guard*	Bridges.
Jehovah		Whetham.
Jehovah-Jireh	*The Lord will provide*	Grant.
Jehova portio mea	*The Lord is my portion*	Mercer.
Je le feray durant ma vie	*I shall do it while I live*	Fairfax.
Je le tiens	*I hold it*	Touchet, Tuchet.
Je le vueil	*I wish it*	Binet.
Je loue Dieu grace attendant	*I praise God expecting mercy*	D'Arcy.
Je maintien devrai	*I maintain the right*	Nesbitt.
Je maintiendrai	*I will maintain*	Harris.
Je me contente	*I am content*	Sparrow.
Je me fie en Dieu	*I trust myself in God*	Blois, Clive, Windsor.
J'e m'en souviendray	*I shall remember it*	Nassau.
Je me tourne vers l'occident	*I turn towards the west*	Westropp.

Motto	Translation	Names
Je meurs pour ceux que j'aime	*I die for those whom I love*	Paterson, Wallace
Je mourrai pour ceux que j'aime	*I shall die for those I love*	Coulson, Coulthart
Je m'y oblige	*I bind myself to it*	Eyton
Je ne change qu 'en mourant	*I change only when I die*	Salvin, Winsor
Je ne plie ni ne rompe	*I neither bend nor break*	Quain
Je ne puis	*I cannot.*	Delves
Je ne serche qu'un	*I seek but one*	Compton
Je n'oublierai jamais	*I shall never forget*	Harvey, Hervey
Je n'oublierai pas	*I shall not forget*	Baldwin, Middleton,
Je pense	*I think*	Charteris, Jennoway, Wemyss
Je pense plus	*I think more*	Areskine, Arsking, Frskin, Erskine, Minnoch
Je reçois pour donner	*I acquire that I may distribute*	Innes.
J'espére	*I hope*	Balston, Hamilton, Swinton
J'espére bien	*I hope well*	Carew
Jesu, esto mihi Jesus	*Jesus, be my Jesus*	Swale
Je suis prest	*I am ready*	Fairlie, Fenton, Fraser
Je suis prêt	*I am ready*	Fraser, Frazer, Maxwell, Maxwell Barry, Maxwell Perceval, M'Kimmie, Simpson, Tytler
Je suis veillant à plaire	*I am watching to please*	Saunderson
Jesus		Chipman, Chippengham
Jesu seul bon et bel	*Jesus alone good and beautiful*	Brearey, Breary
Jesus hominum salvator	*Jesus the saviour of men*	Legat, Legatt
Je tiendray ma puissance par ma foi	*I will hold my power by my faith*	Croker
Je tiens ferme	*I hold firm*	Chamberlain
Je tiens foi	*I keep faith*	Russell
Je tourne vers l'occident	*I turn towards the west*	O'Callaghan-Westropp
Je trouve bien	*I find good*	Barnardiston, Warre
Je veux de bonne guerre	*I wish for fair fight*	Lawley-Thompson, Thompson
Je veux le droit	*I wish for the right*	Duckett
Je vive en espoir	*I live in hope*	Rous
Je vive en espérance	*I live in hope*	Akers, Akers-Douglas
Je voil droyt avoyre	*I wish to have my right*	Warburton
Je voys	*I see*	Jossey
Jouir en bien	*To enjoy innocently*	Beckwith
Jour de ma vie !	*Day of my life !*	West
Jovi confido	*I confide in Jove*	Gairdner
Jovis omnia plena	*All things are full of Jove*	Goodden, Griffith
Jubilee		Stamer
Jucundi acti labores	*Past labours are pleasant*	Chater
Jucunditate afficior	*I am greatly delighted*	Hunter
Judge nocht		Stewart
Judge not		Erskine, Stuart
Judge nought		Erskine, Stewart, Stuart
Judicium parium	*The judgment of our peers*	Raines
Judicium parium, aut lex terræ	*The judgment of my peers, or the law of the land*	Pratt, Raines
Juncta arma decori	*Arms united to glory*	M'Gouan, M'Gowan
Juncta virtuti fides	*Fidelity wedded to courage*	Murray
Juncti valemus	*We are strong united*	Walker
Jungor ut implear	*I am joined that I may be complete*	Meik
Juravi et adjuravi	*I have sworn and doubly sworn*	Moores
Jure, non dono	*By right, not by gift*	Ffoulkes, Lloyd.
Jus dicere decus	*It is honourable to dispense justice*	Plummer
Jus floruit	*Right has flourished*	Taylor
Jus meum tuebor	*I will look after my right*	Reynolds
Jus suum cuique	*To every one his right*	Noel
Jussu regis India subacta	*India subdued by the king's command*	Munro
Justam perficito nihil timeto	*Do what is just, fear nothing*	Kelly
Justa sequor	*I will follow just things*	Keith
Juste et droit	*Just and right*	Whichcote
Juste et fortiter	*Justly and bravely*	Blaxland
Juste et vray	*Just and true*	Ray
Justice to all.		Brock
Justi ceu sidera fulgent	*Just men shine as the stars*	Sandilands
Justi terram incolant	*Let the just inhabit the earth*	Coningsby
Justitia	*Justice*	Lunden, Nurse, Sibbald
Justitiæ propositique tenax	*Tenacious of justice and my purpose*	Stuart.
Justitiæ soror fides	*Faith is the sister of justice*	Justice, Thurlow
Justitia et clementia	*By justice and mercy*	Horsford
Justitia et fortitudo invincibilia sunt	*Justice and fortitude are invincible*	M'Guire
Justitiæ tenax	*Tenacious of justice.*	Astley, Lombe, Parke, Stoddart
Justitia et veritas	*Justice and truth*	Lauriston
Justitia et virtus	*Justice and valour*	Charlesworth
Justi ut sidera fulgent	*The righteous shine as stars*	M'Coll, Sandilands
Justum et tenacem	*Just and resolute*	Bowen Colthurst, Colthurst, Macknight, M'Knight, Parish
Justum et tenacem propositi	*Just and firm of purpose.*	Holmes

Motto	Translation	Names
Justum perficito, nihil timeto	*Do justly and fear not*	Rogers.
Justus ac tenax	*Just and firm*	M'Cammond.
Justus ac tenax propositi	*Just and firm to my purpose*	Jones.
Justus esto et non metue	*Be just and fear not*	Charley, Chorley, Robson.
Justus et fidelis	*Just and faithful*	D'Alton.
Justus et tenax	*Just and firm*	Stevenson.
Justus et propositi tenax	*Just and firm of purpose*	Ferrand, How, Howe, Penrice.
Justus nec timidus	*Just and not timid*	Handfield.
Justus propositi tenax	*A just man is firm of purpose*	Ferrand, Lister.
Justus ut palma	*The righteous man is as the palm-tree*	Palmes.
Juvabitur audax	*The bold will be helped*	Buchanan.
Juvant arva parentum	*The field of our ancestors' delight*	Cassan.
Juvant aspera fortes	*Dangers delight the brave*	Seton-Steuart, Steuart.
Juvant aspera probum	*Hardships delight the good*	Denham, Steuart, Stewart.
Juvante Deo	*By the help of God*	Layard.
Juvat Deus impigros	*God assists the diligent*	Strachan.
Juvat dum lacerat	*God helps while he wounds*	Kragg.
Juxta Salopiam	*Near to Shropshire*	Chadwick.

K

Motto	Translation	Names
Karanza whilas karanza	*Love worketh love*	Cavell, Knevitt, Polwhele.
Kar Duw	*For God*	Harris.
Kar Duw, res pub. trar	*For God and the Commonwealth*	Harris.
Keep fast		Leslie, Lesly.
Keep traist		Buchan-Hepburn, Hepburn.
Keep tryst		Belches, Hepburn.
Keep tryst and trust		Millar.
Keep tryste		Belshes, Hepburne-Scott, Sempill, Semple.
Keep watch		Bryden.
Kynd kynn knawe kepe	*Keep to your own kin kind*	Kaye, Kaye-Lister, Lister-Kaye, Shuttleworth, Shuttleworth-Kay.
Khélát		Willshire.
Kia kaha ki te mahi tika	*Be strong to do that which is right*	Ward.
Kind heart		Duff.
Knowledge is power		Sharpe.
Know thyself		Burt.
Kymmer yn Edeirnion		Hughes.

L

Motto	Translation	Names
Labes pejor morte	*Disgrace is worse than death*	Durrant.
Labile quod opportunum	*Opportunity is transient*	Howman.
Labitur et labetur	*It flows and will go on flowing*	Platt, Platt-Higgins.
La bondad para la medra		Lennard.
La bonté de Dieu	*The goodness of God*	D'Olier.
Labora	*Endeavour*	Mackie, M'Kie.
Laboranti numen adest	*Providence is with him that endeavours*	Brownfield, Macfarlane.
Laboranti palma	*The palm to him who strives for it.*	Hay.
Labora ut æternum vivas	*Strive for eternal life*	Aprece, Apreece.
Labore	*By labour*	Abbot.
Labore et amore	*By labour and love*	Horsfall.
Labore et diligentia	*With labour and diligence*	Binns.
Labore et fide	*By labour and loyalty*	Pritchard.
Labore et fiducia	*By labour and trust*	Litster.
Labore et honore	*By industry and honour*	Hayne, M'Chlery, Pemberton, Thelusson, Viner.
Labore et ingenio	*By labour and ingenuity*	Pickersgill.
Labore et perseverantia	*With labour and perseverance*	Campbell, Woods.
Labore et prudentia	*By labour and prudence*	Bartolozzi.
Labore et scientia	*By labour and knowledge*	Powell, Wylie.
Labore et virtute	*By labour and virtue*	Bates, Foster, Gardner, Pigott, Thelusson.
Labore et vivere		Whiteley
Labore omnia florent	*By labour all things prosper*	Drinkwater.
Labore part[illegible]	*[illegible] by labour*	White.
Labor et in[illegible]	*[illegible] and industry*	Tane.

Labor et veritas	*Labour and truth*	Elliott
Labore vinces	*Thou shalt conquer by toil*	Sugden.
Labor improbus omnia vincit	*Unremitting toil overcomes every difficulty*	Mitchell
Labor ipsa voluptas	*Labour itself is a pleasure*	Janvim, King, Nichols, Paget
Labor omnia superat	*Labour overcomes all things*	Campbell, Hewett, Holtom, Laing
Labor omnia vincit	*Labour conquers all things*	Beasley, Beaulands, Beilby, Brown, Burder, Butler, Chaplin, Cromie, Curtler, Edington, Forsyth Brown, M'Nair, Pratman, Simpson, Waterlow
Labor vincit omnia	*Labour conquers all things*	Longmore
La culte en difficulté	*Worship in hardship*	Harrison
Lædere noli .	*Injure no man*	Stewart
Lætavi	*I have rejoiced .*	Jolly
Lætitia per mortem	*Joy through death*	Luther
Lætitiæ et spe immortalitatis	*In the hope of joy and immortality*	Shaw
Læto aere florent	*They flourish in the joyful air*	Ayre
Lætus sorte mea .	*Contented with my lot*	Sympson.
Lætus sorte vives sapienter	*You will live wisely contented with your lot*	Kelk
La fin couronne les œuvres	*The end crowns the works*	Archer, Yarker
La foi me guide	*Faith guides me*	Deane
La fortune passe par tout	*Fortune makes way through everything*	Broughton Rouse, Rollo
Laidir ise lear Righ	*Strong is the king of the sea*	O'Learie
Laissez dire	*Let them speak*	Middleton, Myddleton, Wharton
La liberte	*Liberty*	Ackers
La loi le veut et moi ni mot	*The law wishes it, and I have not a word to say*	Barrett-Lennard.
Lamh dearg aboo	*The Red Hand to victory*	Magawly
Lamh dhearg Eirin	*The red hand of Ireland*	O'Neill
Lamh foisdinneach an uachdar	*The gentle hand uppermost*	Sullivan
Lamh foistenach abu	*The gentle hand to victory*	O'Sullivan Mor
Lamh laidir a buagh	*The strong hand to victory*	MacCarthy
Lamh laidir an uachdar	*The strongest hand uppermost*	O'Brien
L'antiquite ne peut pas l'abolir	*Antiquity cannot abolish it*	Conroy
La paix	*Peace*	Lendrum.
Largs		Currie
Lasair romhuin a buadh .		Mahony
Latet anguis in herba	*A snake lies hid in the grass*	Anguish
La tête plus que l'argent	*The head more than money*	Raven
Laudari a laudato	*To be praised by one in good repute*	Hammick
Laudes cano heroum	*I sing the praises of heroes .*	Dalle, Dalie
Laudo manentem	*I praise him who remains*	Grove
Laurus crescit in arduis	*The laurel grows in steep places*	Rainier
Lauro scutoque resurgo	*I rise again with laurel and shield*	Loraine, Lorraine
Lauro resurgo	*I rise again with the laurel*	Lorain
Laus Deo	*Praise to God*	Arbuthnot, Lusk, Rundle
Laus virtutis actio	*The deed commends the virtue*	Rawson
La vertu est la seule noblesse	*Virtue is the only nobility*	Brown, North
La vertu surmonte tout obstacle	*Virtue surmounts every obstacle*	Rowley
La vie durante	*During life*	Amyand, Cornewall, Cornwall, Legh
La vita al fin e'l di loda la sera	*Praise life when it is at an end, and the day when it is night*	Le Couteur
Lead on !		Hotham
Le beau est le splendeur du vrai	*Beauty is the splendour of truth*	Doulton
Le bon temps viendra	*The good time will come*	Burgess, Farring, Farrington, Griffith, Harcourt, Wilson, Wray, Wrey
Le croix de hors mais pais dedans	*The cross without, but peace within*	Surdevile
Legale judicium parium	*A legal judgment of one's peers*	Yates
Lege et labore	*By law and labour*	Francis
Leges arma tenent sanctas.	*Arms keep the laws sacred*	Benson
Leges juraque serva	*Observe the laws and justice*	Grant
Leges juraque servat	*He keeps the laws and justice*	Hearne
Leges juraque servo	*I keep the laws and justice*	Leigh, Lovibond
Legibus antiquis	*By ancient laws*	Leigh
Legibus et armis	*According to law and arms*	Gordon
Legi regi fidus	*Faithful to the law and the king*	Robinson
Le jong tyra bellement	*He bore the yoke well*	Trosham
Le jour viendra	*The day will come*	Lambton
Le maître vient	*The master comes*	Peck
Le mieulx que je puis	*The best that I can*	Cheney
Leniter sustineo	*I sustain gently*	Sheath
Le nom les armes la loyauté	*The name, the arms, and loyalty*	Newland
Lente in voto	*Deliberate in my vow*	Thomson
Lente sed certe	*Slowly but surely*	Slacke
Lente sed certe et recto gradu	*Slowly, but surely and straightforward*	Knowlys
Lente, sed opportune	*Slowly, but suitably*	Campbell
Leo de Juda est robur nostrum.	*The Lion of Judah is our strength*	Borlace, Warren
Leo inimicis amicis columba	*The lion for my enemies, the dove for my friends*	Dilke
Leoni non sagittis, fido.	*I trust in the lion, and not my arrows*	Egerton
Le Roi et l'état	*The King and the state*	Ashburnham, Sherard

Motto	Translation	Families
Le Roi le veut	*The King wills it*	Clifford, De Clifford, Southwell.
Le Roy et l'église	*The King and the church*	Roger.
Le Roy et l'estat	*The King and state*	Ashburnham.
Le Roy la loy	*The King the law*	Larcom.
L'espérance me comfort	*Hope comforts me*	Berry, Nairn, Nairne.
L'espérance me console	*Hope consoles me*	De Cardonnell.
L'espérance du salut	*Hope of safety*	Grabham.
L'espoir est ma force	*Hope is my strength*	Tupper.
L'homme vrai aime son pays	*The true man loves his country*	Homfray.
Let Curzon holde what Curzon helde		Curzon, Pen-Curzon-Howe.
L'éternel regne	*The everlasting kingdom*	La Serre.
Let the deed shaw		Addison, Fleeming, Fleming, Flemming, Moubray.
Let the hawk shaw		Porteous.
Let them talk		Hewetson.
Leve et reluis	*Arise and re-illumine*	Lawson.
Levius fit patientia	*Patience makes burdens lighter*	Burgess, Lamb.
Lex ratio summa	*Law is the highest reason*	Law.
Lex summa ratio	*Law is the highest reason*	Law.
Liberalitas	*Liberality*	Furlong.
Libera terra liberque animus	*A free land and a free mind*	Frankland, Frankland-Russell, Freeland.
Liber et audax	*Free and brave*	Freeman.
Libertas	*Liberty*	Bailey, Birch, Chatteris, Evans, Evans-A'Arcy, Evans-Freke, Garland, Lewis, Liberty.
Libertas et natale solum	*Liberty and our native soil*	Adams, Freeman, Whitshed.
Libertas in legibus	*Liberty in the laws*	Best.
Libertas sub rege pio	*Liberty under a pious king*	Addington, Packe.
Libertas virtusque	*Liberty and virtue*	Fry.
Libertate extincta nulla virtus	*There is no virtue when liberty is dead*	Fletcher.
Libertate quietem	*Ease in liberty*	Woodford.
Liberté toute entière	*Full liberty*	Butler-Danvers.
Librum cum lampade trado	*I yield the book with the lamp*	Hill.
Licentiam refrœna	*Restrain licentiousness*	MacQuay.
Licet esse beatis	*It is permitted us to be happy*	Warde.
Licet ex multo parvum	*Little though from much*	Samuels.
Lighter than air		Ayre.
Light on		Leighton, Lighton.
Ligurio rores	*I lick up the dew*	Shepperson.
Lilia candorem pectus Leo nobile monstrat	*Lilies show a bright white, the lion a noble heart*	Goodwin.
Liliæ prælucent telis	*Lilies outshine weapons of war*	Webber.
Lippen to God	*Trust God*	Watson.
Littora specto	*I view the shores*	Hamilton.
Littore sistam	*I shall take my stand on the shore*	Hamilton.
Live, but dread		Lindsay.
Live in hope		Coldstream.
Live to live		Bate, Dundas, Sutton, Whitele, Whitley-Deans-Dundas, Witley.
Live while green		Forrest.
Lock sick	*Keep securely*	Erwin.
Lock sicker	*Keep securely*	Douglas, Megget.
Loisgim agus soilleirghim	*I burn and I shine*	M'Leod.
Look and live		St. Barbe.
Look to the past		Jones.
Loquendo placet	*He pleases when he speaks*	Fairfowl.
Lord, have mercy		Beresford-Drummond, Drummond.
Lord, let Glasgow flourish		Glasgow.
Lothim agus marbhaim	*I wound and I kill*	O'Halloran.
Love		M'Cleish, M'Clesh.
Love and dread		Baker, Tower.
Love and loyalty		Crompton.
Love as you find		Tempest.
Love every man, fear no man		Cropper, Thornburgh.
Love, serve		Ashley-Cooper.
Loyal à la mort	*Loyal unto death*	Adair, Barnwell, Chatterton, Drummond, Hepworth, Laforey, Loftus, Lyster.
Loyal à mort	*Loyal to death*	Chatterton, Hepworth, Loftus.
Loyal au mort	*Loyal to the dead*	Adair, Barnwell, Belcher, Brounker, Corry, Drummond, Laforey, Langton, Loftie, Loftus, Lyster, Robinson, Waveney.
Loyal devoir	*Honest duty*	Carteret, De Carteret, Thynne.
Loyalement je sers	*Loyally I serve*	Norreys, Norris.
Loyal en tout	*Loyal in everything*	Brown, Browne, Seale, Wilson, Wood.
Loyal in adversity		Carnegie.
Loyal je serai durant ma vie	*I will be loyal during life*	Stourton.
Loyalle suys	*Be loyal*	Ferrers.
Loyal secret		Lawson.

Loyal suis-je	*Loyal am I*	Shirley
Loyal unto death		White
Loyauté me lie	*Loyalty binds me*	Margesson
Loyauté me oblige	*Loyalty obliges me*	Heathcote-Drummond-Willoughby
Loyauté m' oblige	*Loyalty obliges me*	Bertie, Bertue
Loyauté mon honneur	*Loyalty my honour.*	Walker
Loyauté n'a honte	*Loyalty is not ashamed*	Clinton, Pelham-Clinton
Loyauté sans tache	*Loyalty without spot*	Dare, Hall Dare
Loywf as thow fynds		Tempest
Lucem spero.	*I hope for light*	Kemp
Lucent in tenebris	*In darkness they let their light shine.*	O'Moran
Luceo boreale	*I shine in the north.*	Seton
Luceo et terreo	*I shine and terrify*	Allan
Luceo, non uro	*I shine but do not burn*	Mackenzie, M'Kenzie, Mackinzie, M'Hardie, Macleod, M'Leod, Smith
Luceo non terreo	*I shine, I do not terrify*	Allan
Lucet	*Its light shines*	Scot
Lucrum Christi mihi	*To me Christ is gain*	Forde
Luctor, at emergam	*I struggle, but I shall come out of it*	Maitland.
Luctor, non mergor	*I struggle, but I am not overwhelmed*	Glass
Lumen accipe et imperti	*Receive the light, and communicate it*	Hollingsworth
Lumen cœleste sequamur	*Let us follow heavenly light*	Beatie, Beattie, Beatleys.
Lumen servamus antiquum	*We preserve the ancient light*	Redwood
Lux anglis, crux Francis	*Light to the English, a cross to the French*	Rooper
Lux et salus	*Light and safety*	Brunton
Lux in tenebris	*Light in darkness*	Fullarton, Fullerton
Lux mea Christus	*Christ is my light*	Newman
Lux mihi Deus	*God is my light*	Prescott
Lux mihi laurus	*Light is a laurel to me*	Chalmers, Chambers
Lux omnibus refulgeat	*Let the light shine for all*	Smith.
Lux tua via mea	*Thy light is my path*	Blount, Blunt
Lux tua vita mea.	*Thy light is my life*	Blount, Blunt, Hurst.
Lux venit ab alto	*Light cometh from on high*	Dallas
Lux vitæ	*The light of life*	Burton

M

Mack al sicker	*Make all secure*	Almack
Macte	*Blessed be thou*	Smith
Macte virtute	*Blessings on your valour*	Murray
Macte virtute esto	*Go on and prosper*	Dixon, Lowndes
Ma force d'en haut	*My strength is from on high*	Landon, Malet
Ma foy en Dieu seulement	*My faith is in God alone*	Mompesson
Magistratus indicat virum	*The office shows the man*	Lowther
Magna est veritas	*Great is truth*	Earle, Magnay, Stillingfleet, Varley
Magna est veritas et prævalebit	*Great is truth and will prevail*	George, Rodon, Palitana
Magna in parvo	*Great things in a little*	Congalton
Magnanimiter crucem sustine	*Sustain the cross bravely*	Kenyon, Whitney
Magnanimus esto	*Be magnanimous*	Ingram
Magna vis veritatis	*Great is the force of truth*	Taylor
Magnes et adamas	*The magnet and adamant*	Ross
Magnum in parvo	*Much in little*	Congalton, Congilton, Little, Lyttel
Magnus et animus	*And a great mind*	Ross
Magnus Hippocrates, Tu nobis major	*Great Hippocrates! Thou art greater than we*	Dimsdale
Maha an toshach		Toshack
Maigre l'injustice	*In spite of injustice*	Fiott.
Maintien le droit	*Support the right*	Bridges, Brydges, Leatham.
Maintenant ou jamais	*Now or never*	Barnard
Majora sequor	*I follow greater things*	Haliburton, Halyburton
Majores sequor	*I follow our ancestors*	Gordon, Halyburton
Major optima ferat	*Let the worthier carry off the best*	Moir, More
Majorum vestigia premo	*I follow close on the footsteps of my ancestors*	Seaton
Major virtus quam splendor	*Virtue is greater than splendour*	Auld, Baillie, Baillie Haddington Arden
Make a clean heart and a cheerful spirit		Portman
Mal au tour	*Unaccustomed to artifice*	Patten
Malgré le tort	*In spite of wrong*	De Hoghton, Hoghton-Bold, Houghton, James.
Malim esse probus quam haberi	*I would rather be honourable than merely considered so*	Kennedy, Malim
Malim esse quam videri	*I would rather be than seem*	Macrae
Mallem mori quam [illegible]	[illegible]	[illegible]

Motto	Translation	Names
Malo mori quam fœdari	*I would rather die than be dishonoured*	Adams, Allen, Archer, Athlone, Barnewall, Barnewell, Barnwell, Beale, Casley, De Chastelai, Doeg, Esmond, Ffrench, French, Gifford, Ginkell, Harty, Higginson, Jackson, Lister, Menzies, Mulloy, Murray, Murray-Prior, O'Mulloy, Payne, Penteny, Prior, Riggs-Miller, Ryan, Seaver, Service, Strode, Surtees.
Malo pati quam fœdari	*I would rather suffer than be disgraced*	Duckett.
Malum bono vince	*Overcome evil with good*	Hay.
Man do it		Edgar.
Manent optima cœlo	*The best things abide in heaven.*	Miller.
Manent optima cœlo	*The best things abide in heaven*	Christie-Miller.
Maneo	*I remain*	Gordon.
Maneo et munio	*I remain and defend*	Dalrymple.
Maneo, non fugio	*I remain, I do not fly*	Gordon.
Mane prædam vesperi spolium	*Prey in the morning, spoil in the evening*	Hurt.
Manes non fugio	*I do not shun death*	Gordon.
Manet in æternum	*It remains for ever*	Spreull, Sprevell, Sprewell, Warner.
Manners maketh man		Hood, Wickham, Wykeham.
Manners makyth man		Wickham, Martin-Wykeham.
Manu et corde	*With hand and heart*	Bates.
Manu forti	*With a strong hand*	Clinkscales, Gahagan, Geoghan, M'Caa, M'Casker, M'Caskill, Mackay, Mackey, M'Quie.
Manuque	*And by my hand*	Jossey.
Manus hæc inimica tyrannis	*This hand is an enemy to tyrants*	Dawson, Hemsworth, MacMahon, Mauley, Mein, Proby, Probyn, Tonson, Tufnell-Tyrell.
Manus justa nardus	*A just hand is a balm*	Loveden, Maynard.
Marack		Lyons.
Mar bu mhiann dom		Campbell.
Mar bu mhiann leinn	*As we would desire*	Campbell.
Mars denique victor est	*Mars at last is victor*	Marsden.
Marte et arte	*By war and art*	Drumond, Ferguson, Jones, M'Guire, Nevoy, Niven.
Marte et clypeo	*By offensive and defensive warfare*	Methen, Methven.
Marte et industria	*By bravery and industry*	Ogilvy.
Marte et ingenio	*By war and wit*	Smith, Smythe, Wright.
Marte et labore	*By war and labour*	Hewgill.
Marte et mari faventibus	*War and the sea favouring*	Morris.
Marte non arte	*By bravery, not by knavery*	Neasmith, Nasmyth.
Marte suo tutus	*Safe by his own exertions*	Byers, Byres.
Martis non Cupidinis	*Of Mars, not Cupid*	Fletcher.
Mature	*In good time*	Barttelot.
Mauvais chiens	*Wicked dogs*	Machell.
Maya		Cameron.
Mea anchora Christus	*Christ is my anchor*	Mayor.
Mea anchora virtus	*Virtue is my anchor*	Richardson.
Mea culpa fides	*Fidelity is my fault*	Lawlor.
Mea dos virtus	*Virtue is my dowry*	Meadows, Medewe.
Mea fides in sapientia	*My faith is in wisdom*	Fryer.
Mea gloria crux	*The cross is my glory*	Heald.
Mea gloria fides	*Fidelity is my glory*	Addagh, Ainsworth, Ardagh, Barnard, Gilchrist, Kavanagh, Watson, Wentworth.
Meæ memor originis	*Mindful of my descent*	Manson.
Mean, speak, and do well		Urquhart.
Mea spes est in Deo	*My hope is in God*	Smith, Smith-Gordon.
Mea spes in Deo	*My hope is in God*	Miller.
Mea virtute me involvo	*I wrap myself up in my integrity*	Hamlyn, Williams.
Me certum mors certa facit	*Certain death makes me determined*	Sibbald.
Mecum habita	*Dwell with me*	Dun, Dunn.
Mediis tranquillus in undis	*Calm in the midst of the waters*	Smith, Smythe.
Mediocria firma	*Mediocrity is stable*	Bacon, Grimston, Lauder, Lawder, Lowndes-Stone.
Mediocria maxima	*Moderate things are the greatest*	Monins.
Mediocriter	*With moderation*	Moir, Murison.
Medio tutissimus ibis	*Thou wilt go safest in the middle course*	King, Laugrishe, Parker, Senior, Whitfield.
Medio tutus	*Safe in the middle*	M'Master.
Meditare	*Meditate well*	Fairlie.
Me duce	*Under my leadership*	Innes.
Me fortem reddit Deus	*God renders me brave*	Scot, Scott.
Me juvat ire per altum	*I delight to bridge an abyss*	Bridge.
Meliora sequentur	*They will pursue better things*	Kelsall.
Meliora sperando	*Hoping for better things*	Douglas, Douglass.
Meliora spero sequorque	*I hope for better things, and follow them*	Rait.
Meliore fi[illegible]	[illegible]	D[illegible]-Gresley, Greseley, Gresley.

Melitæ amor	*Love for Melita* . ..	Rutter
Me meliora manent	*Better fortune awaits me* .	Mosman, Mossman
Memento Creatorem	*Remember thy Creator*	Keith
Memento mei	*Remember me*	L'Estrange
Memento mori	*Remember death*	Gumbleton
Me Minerva lucet	*Minerva is my light* .	Le Marchant
Memini	*I remember* .	Campbell
Meminisse juvabit	*We shall delight in remembering*	Thomson
Memor	*Mindful* . .	James, Russell
Memor amici	*Mindful of my friend* . ..	Russell
Memorare novissima	*An unchangeable mind*	Hanford, Hopkirk
Memores fecere merendo	*Their deserts made them to be remembered*	Richardson
Memor esto	*Be mindful*	Campbell, Graham, Green, Greer, Hutchinson, Hutchison, M'Fell, M'Phail, Russell
Memor esto majorum.	*Be mindful of your ancestors*	Farquharson
Memor et fidelis	*Mindful and faithful*	May, Peachey, Reed, Scott, Young Scott
Memor et gratus	*Mindful and grateful*	Gooch
Memoria pii æterna	*The memory of the pious is eternal*	Hanbury-Tracey, Tracy
Memor virtutis avitæ	*Mindful of ancestral virtue*	De Windt
Mens æqua in arduis	*An equal mind in difficulties*	Hastings
Mens æqua rebus in arduis	*An equal mind in difficulties*	Hardinge.
Mens conscia recti .	*A mind conscious of rectitude*	Boulton, Chrisop, Chrisp, Collis, Filgate, Flower, Flower Macartney, Jary, Macartney, Minns, Nightengale, Phillips, Rothwell, Sillifant, Watlington, Wright, Yorstoun
Mens cujusque est quisque	*As the mind of each, so is the man*	Leslie, Pepys
Mens et manus	*Mind and hand*	Duncanson.
Mens flecti nescia	*A mind that knows not how to yield*	Hulton
Mens immota	*An immovable mind*	Shaw
Mens immota manet	*My mind remains immovable*	Meldrum, Shaw
Mens pristina mansit	*The former mind remained*	Popham
Mens sibi conscia recti	*A mind conscious of its own rectitude*	De Crispigny, Steele, Wright
Mente et labore	*With mind and labour*	Lawrence
Mente et manu	*With the mind and the hand*	Glasfurd, Glassford, Patrickson
Mente manuque	*With the mind and the hand*	Benshaw, Bonshaw, Borthwick, Farquhar, Townsend
Mente manuque præsto	*I am ready with mind and hand*	Foulis
Mente non Marte	*By the mind, not by war*	Locke
Mentes consciæ recti	*Minds conscious of their rectitude*	Wylie
Meor ras tha Duw	*The great grace of God who is good*	Willyams,
Merces hæc certa laborum	*This sure reward of our labours*	Seton
Merces profundo pulchrior evenit	*A recompense is fairer from a depth*	Davison
Mercie		Paterson
Mercie is my desire		Abercrombie
Mercy is my desire		Abercrombie, Laing, Lang, Wishart
Merere	*To deserve*	Currer
Merere et confide	*Deserve and trust*	Winwood
Meret qui laborat	*The labourer is worthy of his hire*	Stone
Meret qui laborat	*He who toils earns*	Middleton, Peel
Meritas augentur honores	*Honours are enhanced by deserts*	Lacy
Merite	*Deserve*	Currer
Méritez . .	*Deserve*	Olmins, Wright
Merito	*Deservedly*	Delap, Delop, Dunlop, Elphinstone, Halliday, Tyler
Merui	*I have deserved*	Paterson
Merui candore favorem	*I have deserved favour from my fairness*	White
Meruisse manu	*To have earned by my handiwork*	Wills
Messis ab alto	*Our harvest is from the deep*	Whittock
Me stante, virebunt	*While I stand they will flourish*	Tyrwhitt
Metuenda corolla draconis	*The dragon's crest is to be feared*	Stewart, Vane Stewart, Vane Tempest-Stewart
Metuo secundis	*I fear in prosperity* .	Hodgson, Uppleby
Me vincit, ego mereo	*He hath conquered me—I am the gainer*	Sinclair
Mihi parta tueri	*To protect what is provided for me*	Styleman-Le Strange
Mihi res subjungere conor	*My aim is to subject things to myself*	Crackanthorpe
Mihi robore robor	*I have strength through strength*	Cunninghame
Micat inter omnes	*He shines illustrious among all*	Haggard
Mieux être que paraître .	*Better to be than to seem*	Barclay
Mieux je serai	*Better I will be*	Beaumont, Stapleton
Mieux serra	*Better I will be*	Beaumont
Migremus hinc	*We shall migrate hence*	Willmott
Migro et respicio	*I go away, and look back*	Ramsay
Mihi cœlum portus .	*Heaven is my haven*	Brages, Bruges, Crawley
Mihi consulit Deus	*God consults for my good*	Bennett
Mihi cura futuri	*I am carefnl for the future* .	Ongley
Mihi gravato Deus	*Let God lay the burden on me*	Ridgeway
Mihi jussa capessere	*To execute what is laid on me*	Masham

Motto	Translation	Families
Mihi lucra	*My great gain*	Scot, Scott.
Mihi lucra pericula	*My dangers are profitable to me*	Suttie.
Mihi solicitudo futuri	*I am anxious for the future*	Thackwell.
Mihi terraque lacusque	*I have lands and waters*	Fullerton.
Mihi tibi	*For me for you*	Pope.
Milis et fortis	*Mild and brave*	Orde.
Minatur	*He threatens*	Maturin.
Mind your own business		Remnant.
Min, sicker, reag		Connor.
Mirabile in profundis	*Wonderful in the depths*	Tooker, Whalley.
Mirior invictus	*More wonderful unconquered*	Garvey.
Miserere mihi Deus	*God be merciful to me*	Hynde.
Misericordia temperet gladium	*Let mercy temper the sword*	Mules.
Miseris auxilium fero / Miseris opem fero	*I bring help to the wretched*	Malden.
Miseris succurrere disco	*I learn to succour the unfortunate*	Diamond, Hinde-Hodgson, Loder Symonds, MacMillan, Soltan.
Miseris succurro	*I succour the wretched*	Macmillan-Scott, Scott.
Miserrima vidi	*I saw most miserable things*	Zephane, Zephani.
Misneach	*Courage*	Campbell.
Mitis et audax	*Mild and bold*	Markham.
Mitis et fortis	*Mild and brave*	Orde, Wybrants.
Mitis sed fortis	*Mild but brave*	Orde, Phipson-Wybrants.
Moderata durant	*Moderate things are permanent*	Bushe, Irvine, Staunton.
Moderata manent	*Moderate things remain*	Gillespie-Staunton.
Modeste conabor	*I will attempt with modesty*	Haggard.
Modico augetur modicum	*Little is made larger by little*	Williamson.
Modicum modico erit magnum	*A little will be great by a little*	Williamson.
Mœnibus crede ligneis	*Have faith in wooden walls*	Clarke.
Mœret qui laborat	*He is sad who labours*	Storie.
Monachus salvabor	*Being a monk, I shall be saved*	Monkhouse.
Mon Dieu est ma roche	*My God is my rock*	Roche, Rowche.
Mon Dieu, mon roi, et ma patrie	*My God, my king, and my country*	Broadley, Kirwan.
Mon droit	*My right*	Ingilby.
Moneo et munio	*I warn, and I protect*	Dalrymple, Elphinstone, Horn.
Mone sale	*Advise with prudence*	Monsell.
Moniti meliora sequamur	*Being warned, let us follow better things*	Mahon.
Monitus munitus	*Forwarned, forearmed*	Horn.
Mon privilége et mon devoir	*My privilege and duty*	Shevill.
Monte alto	*On a high mountain*	Mowat.
Monte de alto	*From a high mountain*	Atthill.
Monstrant astra viam	*The stars show the way*	Oswald.
Montjoye et St. Dennis		France.
Mon trésor	*My treasure*	Montresor.
Mora trahit periculum	*Delay causes danger*	Suckling, Zeal.
Mores fingunt fortunam	*Manners mould fortune*	Rogerson.
Mores hoc mutato	*Let this change manners*	Moore.
Mores meliore metallo	*Morals of a better character*	Smith.
Moribus antiquis	*With ancient manners*	Throckmorton.
Moriendo modulor	*I sing dying*	Mitchell.
Moriendo vive	*In dying live*	Symonds.
Moriendo vivo	*In dying I live*	Yaldwin.
Moriens cano	*I sing dying*	Cobbe.
Moriens sed invictus	*Dying, but unconquered*	Gammell.
Mors ærumnarum requies	*Death is a rest from afflictions*	Rumney.
Mors aut vita decora	*Death or a life of honour*	Dempster.
Mors Christi mors mortis mihi	*Christ's death is to me the death of death*	Boothby.
Mors gloria forti	*Death is glory to the brave*	Bradney.
Mors janua vitæ	*Death is the gate of life*	Haswell.
Mors lupi agnis vita	*The death of the wolf is life to the lambs*	Ouseley, Ousley.
Mors meta laborum	*Death is the goal of our labours*	Cromwell.
Mors mihi lucrum	*Death is gain to me*	Jones, Lluellyn.
Mors mihi vitæ fide	*Death to me by faith in life*	Ellis.
Mors mihi vita est	*Death is life to me*	Wolseley.
Mors omnibus communis	*Death is common to all*	Luscombe.
Mors potior macula	*Death rather than disgrace*	Barker, Chamberlayne, Skirrow
Mors potius macula	*Death rather than disgrace*	Ffrench.
Mortale non opto	*I do not wish for what is mortal*	Dyson.
Mort dessus	*Death is hanging over us*	Bunney, Bunny.
Morte leonis vita	*Life by the death of the lion*	Vaux.
Mortem aut triumphum	*Death or triumph*	Clifton.
Mort en droit	*Death in right*	Drax, Sawbridge-Erle-Drax.
Mortua vivescunt	*Dead things become alive*	Lindsay.
Morum certus amor		Cotton.
Mos legem regit	*Custom regulates the law*	Mawdesley, Mosley, Mousell.
Mot pour mot	*Word for word*	Harries.
Moveo et proficior	*I proceed and am more prosperous*	Knox, Knox-Browne.
Mowe warilie		Mather.
Mox sese attolit in auris	*He will soon rise in ethereal heights*	Waring.
Mox virtute se tollit ad auras	*Soon he will raise himself by his valour to the empyrean*	Swettenham, Warren.

Mullac a boo.	" "	Dunne
Mullach a boo	" "	Doyne
Mullach a-bu		O'Doinn
Mullachara boo.		Fitzgerald
Multa tuli fecique	*I have borne and done many things*	Arkwright
Multum in parvo	*Much in little*	Congalton, Congilton
Munifice et fortiter	*Bountifully and bravely*	Handasyd, Handyside
Murus aheneus	*A brazen wall*	Bannatyne, Macleod, M'Leod, Nielson
Murus aeneus esto	*Be thou a wall of brass*	Reynell
Murus aeneus virtus	*Virtue is a wall of brass*	Walton
Murus aeneus conscientia sana	*A sound conscience is a wall of brass*	Lumley, Patterson, Williamson
Mutabimur	*We shall be changed*	Brinkley
Mutare fidem nescio	*I know not how to change my fealty*	Outram
Mutare non est meum . . .	*It is not in my line to change*	Frewen
Mutare sperno	*I disdain to change .*	Graham
Mutare vel timere sperno	*I scorn to change or fear*	Barnes, Beaufort, Bythsea, Somerset
Mutas inglorius artes	*To practise, unambitious of glory, the silent arts*	Halford
Muthig vorwarts .	*Forward with courage*	Prance
Mutuo amore cresco.	*I increase by mutual love.*	Lindsay
Mutus inglorius	*The dumb is without glory*	Halford
Mutus inglorius artis	*The dumb in an art is without glory*	Halford
My defence		Allardice, Allerdice
My hope is constant		Donaldson
My hope is constant in thee		Cramnond, Donaldson, Gardiner, M'Donald Macdonald, Steuart
My hope is in God		Middleton
My prince and my country		Harris
My word is my bond		Smallman
My lure is truth		Hawkshaw

N

Na fynno Duw ni fydd	*What God wishes not will not be*	Price.
Natale solum dulce	*Sweet is our native soil*	Taylor
Nativum retinet decus	*He retains his native honour*	Livingston, Livingstone
Naturæ donum	*The gift of nature*	Peacock, Peacocks.
Naturæ minister	*A servant of nature .*	Relham, Relhan.
Nec abest jugum	*There is always some yoke*	Hay
Nec ab oriente nec ab occidente	*Neither from the East nor from the West*	Jermyn
Nec arrogo nec dubito	*I neither question nor doubt*	Assheton
Nec aspera terrent	*Difficulties do not dismay us.*	Motto of the Royal Hanoverian Guelphic Order Johnston
Nec avarus nec profusus	*Neither greedy nor lavish*	Bryan
Nec beneficii immemor, nec injuriæ	*Unmindful neither of benefits nor injuries*	Walrond
Ne cadem insidiis	*Let me not fall into snares*	Cleland, Clelland
Nec careo nec curo	*I have neither want nor care.*	Craw
Ne cede arduis	*Yield not to difficulties* -	Fairbairn
Nec cede malis	*Yield not to adversity*	Berry, Doig, Keppel, Stratford, Tolhurst, Williams
Ne cede malis	*Yield not to adversity*	Hickman
Ne cede malis, sed contra	*Yield not to adversity, but the contrary*	Canning
Nec cito, nec tardo	*Neither fast nor slow*	Ballantyne, Bannatyne, Marshall
Nec cunctando nec temere agendo	*Neither by delaying nor by acting rashly .*	Twemlow
Nec cupias, nec metuas	*Neither desire nor fear*	Crowhall, Yorke
Nec deerit operi dextra	*My right hand will not fail at my work*	Borthwick
Nec deficit alter	*Another succeeds*	Algeo, Gregory, Roddam
Nec deficit animus	*Courage does not fail me*	Eccles
Nec degenero	*I do not lose caste*	Joynt, Lane
Nec diu nec frustra	*Neither for long nor in vain ..*	Knowles
Nec elata, nec dejecta	*Neither elated nor depressed*	Northmore
Nec elatus nec dejectus	*Neither elated nor depressed*	Atherton, Fox
Nec errat nec assat.		Morley
Nec ferro, nec igne	*Neither by sword nor fire*	M'Kaile
Nec flatu, nec fluctu	*Neither with wind nor tide*	Edward, Udward
Nec flectitur nec mutant	*They neither bend nor change.*	O'Hegarty
Nec fluctu, nec flatu	*Neither with tide nor wind*	Burnet, Burnett
Nec improvidus	*Not improvident*	Danskine
Nec male notus eques	*A knight not badly known*	Southwell.
Nec me qui cætera vincit	*Nor does he who conquers all other things conquer me.*	Bruce
Nec metuas nec optes	*Neither fear nor wish.*	Coddington
Nec minus fortiter	[illegible]	Cuthbert, C[illegible]hbertson

Nec mireris homines mirabiliores	*Do not wonder at more wonderful men*	Lambert.
Nec mons, nec substrahit aer	*The mountain is not moved, nor does the blast subside*	Forbes.
Nec mutandus, nec metus	*Neither change nor fear*	Rawlins.
Nec obscura, nec ima	*Neither obscure nor low*	Law.
Nec opprimere nec opprimi	*Neither to oppress nor to be oppressed*	Sneyd, Sneyd-Kynnersley.
Nec parvis sisto	*Neither do I hesitate at trifles*	De Bathe, De Burgh, Eales.
Nec placida contenta quiete est	*No content with quiet repose*	Mordaunt, Shipley.
Nec prece, nec pretio	*Neither by prayer nor bribery*	Bateman, Fremantle, Hanbury, Hanbury-Leigh.
Nec quærere, nec spernere honorem	*Neither to seek nor despise honour*	Boughey, Fletcher, St. John.
Nec rege nec populo, sed utroque	*Neither for king nor people, but for both*	Rolle, Rolley, Wilkinson.
Nec sinit esse feros	*Nor doth he suffer them to be savage*	Grazebrook, Langham.
Nec sorte, nec fato	*Neither by chance nor fate*	Brown, Greig, Rutherford.
Nec sperno, nec timeo	*I neither despise nor fear*	Ellames.
Nec temere nec lente	*Neither rashly nor slowly*	Joynt.
Nec temere, nec timide	*Neither rashly nor timidly*	Abbot, Aldworth, Arabin, Bailey, Barne, Barnes, Beadnell, Bent, Blair, Blosse, Bridgeman, Buckley, Bulkeley, Chinnery, Chinning, Clarke-Travers, Cottrell, Cradock, Fitz-Clarence, Forbes, Freeman, Graham, Guest, Haldane, Holden, Joynt, Ludlow, Lynch-Blosse, Milward, Owen, Rashleigh, Robards, Sandford, Sherburne, Simeon, Travers, Trefusis, Vane, Walker, Wakeman, Western, Williams.
Nec tempore, nec fato	*Neither by time nor fate*	M'Donald, MacDonald, Macdonald.
Nec te quæsiveris extra	*Do not seek thyself outside of thyself*	Carr-Ellison, Ellison.
Nec timeo, nec sperno	*I neither fear nor despise*	Brown, Cooke, Daniel, Danyell, Greene, Hamilton, Hamilton-Russell, O'Connor, O'Sullivan, Pagan, Pagen, Prentice, Shepphard-Cotton, Shippard.
Nec timide, nec temere	*Neither timidly nor rashly*	Barne, Barnes, Buckley, Bulkeley-Williams, Forbes, Graham, Hepburn-Stuart-Forbes-Trefusis Macsagan, Rashleigh, Sanford, Travers.
Nec timidus nec ferus	*Neither timid nor fierce*	Trotter.
Nec triste nec trepide	*Neither sad nor fearful*	Trist.
Nec triste, nec trepidum	*Neither sad nor fearful*	Trist.
Nec tumidus, nec timidus	*Neither tumid nor timid*	Guthrie.
Ne cuiquam serviant enses	*Let not your swords be the slaves of any one*	Peachy.
Nec vi, nec astutia	*Neither by violence nor cunning*	Maxwell, Waring.
Nec viribus nec numero	*Neither by power nor numbers*	Wemyss.
Nec vi standum nec metu	*We must stand neither on force nor on fear*	Rawlins.
Nec volenti, nec volanti	*Neither to me wishing nor flying*	Westby, Westley.
Ne desit virtus	*Let valour not fail*	Furse.
Neminem metue innocens	*Being innocent, fear no one*	Eyre, Platt.
Nemo me impune lacessit	*No one provokes me with impunity*	Motto of Scotland and of the Order of the Thistle. Bond, De Teissier, Hollinshed, Irwin, M'Geough-Bond, Nettles, Poingdestre.
Nemo sibi nascitur	*No one is born for himself*	Scott, Patteson.
Nemo sine cruce beatus	*None is happy but by the cross*	Baker, Collier.
Ne m'oubliez	*Forget me not*	Carsain, Corsair.
Ne nimis altus	*Not too high*	Perkins.
Ne nimium	*Not too much*	Gordon, Hamilton-Gordon.
Ne obliviscaris	*Do not forget*	Bannerman, Campbell, Cleborne, Colvil, Colville, Lorn, M'Tavish.
Ne parcas, nec spernas	*Neither spare nor despise*	Lamond, Lamont.
Ne quid falsi	*Nothing false*	Wollaston.
Ne quid nimis	*Not too much of anything*	Austen, Cookson, Drinkwater, Fouler, Lowe, Reynard-Cookson.
Nescit abolere vestutas	*Antiquity cannot abolish it*	Oughton.
Nescit amor fines	*Love knows no boundaries*	Scot, Scott.
Nescitur Christo	*He is not known by Christ*	Rous.
Nescit vox missa reverti	*A word once uttered cannot be recalled*	Culleton, Halsey.
Ne supra	*Not beyond*	Catsnellage, Catznellage.
Ne supra modum sapere	*Be not over wise*	Nassau, Newport.
Ne tenta vel perfice	*Attempt not, or else accomplish*	Hill.
Ne tentes aut perfice	*Do not attempt, or else accomplish*	Davis, Davison, Faunce, Hill, Parker.
Ne te quæsiveris extra	*Do not seek thyself outside of thyself*	Hewett, Hewit, Hewitt.
Ne timeas recte faciendo	*Fear not doing what is right*	Hadderwick, Hedderwick, Tizard-Hawkins.
Ne traverse pas le pont	*Do not cross the bridge*	Briggs.
Never fear		Stewart.
Never give in		Lawrence.
Never unprepared		Stewart.

Ne vile	*Nothing base*	Nevill
Ne vile fano	*Nothing to disgrace the altar*	Fane, Neville, Ponsonby Fane, Stapleton
Ne vile velis	*Wish nothing base*	Esler, Fetherstonhaugh, Giffard, Griffin, Nevil, Nevill, Neville, Ussher
Nid cyfoeth and boddlondeb	*Not wealth but contentment*	Garnons
Nid da onid Duw	*No good but God*	Williams
Ni ddawd da o hir arofyn	*No good comes from long intending*	Hall
Ni dessus ni dessous	*Neither above nor below*	Griffin
Nid meddyg, ond meddyg enaid	*Not a physician, but a soul-physician*	Fraser, Pughe
Nigrarum vestigia premo	*I track the footprints of the dark ones*	Seton
Nihil alienum	*Nothing strange*	Rice
Nihil amanti durum	*Nothing hard to one who loves*	Pearse, Reid
Nihil desperandum	*Nothing to be despaired of*	Walley
Nihil humani alienum.	*Nothing human is alien to me*	Hutchinson
Nihil nisi labore	*Nothing without labour*	Emerton
Nihil obstabit eunti	*Nothing will resist you if you proceed*	Arden
Nihilo nisi cruce	*With nothing but the cross*	Barbour
Nihil quod obstat virtuti	*Nothing which obstructs virtue*	Higgins
Nihil sine cruce	*Nothing without the cross*	Beresford, Hillocks
Nihil sine Deo	*Nothing without God*	Peterson, Crooks
Nihil sine labore	*Nothing without labour*	Attenborough, Berry, Cator, Heap, Oppenheimer, Templer, Templer
Nihil utile quod non honestum	*Nothing is useful which is not honourable*	Benyon, Moor, Moore.
Nihil verius	*Nothing more true*	Weir
Nil admirari	*To be astonished at nothing*	Carew, Fitzgibbon, Harris, Johnson, Kidd, Rock, Shapland Carew
Nil arduum	*Nothing arduous*	Cumming, Gordon, Rowand
Nil certum est	*Nought is certain*	M'Min, M'Minn, M'Myne
Nil clarius astris	*Nothing clearer than the stars*	Baillie
Nil conscire sibi	*Conscious of no wrong*	Anderson, Biss, Bullock, Carew, Collingwood, Finch-Hatton, French, Hatton, Michel, Miller, Mills, Rogers, Saunders, Savile, Saville, Sibthorpe, Wegg
Nil conscire sibi, nulla pallescere culpa	*Conscious of no wrong, pale from no crime*	Sanders.
Nil desperandum	*Never despairing*	Anson, Arnold, Beevor, Bullock, Carr, Chard, Chawner, Coddington, Cookson, Crosbie Gardiner, Eastwood, Fife Cookson, Gardiner, Girandot, Grad well, Greenway, Grisewood, Hanbury, Hawkins, Hawxwell, Hay, Haves, Hayse, Heron, Hill, Horn, Hume, Imrey, Knill, May, Mohamud, Musgrove, Nevins, Noakes, Ogilvie, Ogilvy, Parry, Pearson, Promoli, Radway, Randolph-Lichfield, Shelmerdine, Silver, Simpson, Smit, Stewart, Stone, Tremenheere, Tucker, Walker, Walley, Way, Wedderburn, Williams, Worship
Nil desparandum, auspice Deo	*Nothing is to be despaired of under God's guidance*	Anderson, Barstow
Nil desperandum crux scutum	*Nothing to be despaired under shield of the cross*	Gregory
Nil desperandum est	*Nothing is to be despaired of*	Stewart.
Nil dimidium est	*The half is nothing*	Heywood
Nil durum volenti	*Nothing is hard to a willing man*	Arthur, Crawfurd
Nil extra numerum	*Nothing is beyond reckoning up*	Randall
Nil fatalia terrent	*Things decreed by fate do not dismay us*	Carse
Nil impossibile	*Nothing impossible*	Du Bisson, Dubisson
Nil indigne	*Nothing unworthily*	Wordie
Nil invita Minerva	*Nothing against the grain*	Prime
Nil magnum, nisi bonum	*Nothing is great unless it be good*	Cooper
Nil metuens superavi	*Fearing nothing I have overcome*	Bushe
Nil mihi tollit hyems	*No bad weather takes anything from me*	Irvine
Nil moror ictus	*I delay not when struck*	Kyrle, Money Kyrle
Nil mortalibus arduum	*Nothing is too hard for mortals*	Kater
Nil nequit amor	*Love is all-powerful.*	Reidheugh
Nil nisi cruce	*Nothing without the cross*	Beresford, Beresford-Pack, Beresford Peirse
Nil nisi de jure	*Nothing unless by right*	Lomax
Nil nisi honestum	*Nothing unless honourable*	Philips
Nil nisi patria	*Nothing but one's country*	Hindmarsh, Hyndmarsh
Nil nisi quod honestum	*Nothing unless what is honourable*	Leather
Nil obliviscar	*I shall forget nothing*	Collvile
Nil penna, sed usus	*Not the pen, but custom*	Gilmer Gilmour
Nil sine causa	*Nothing without a cause*	Brown
Nil sine cruce	*Nothing without the cross*	Gully

Nil sine Deo	*Nothing without God*	Awdry.
Nil sine labore	*Nothing without labour*	Atkinson, Beecham, Brind, Maltby, Simpson.
Nil sine magno labore	*Nothing without great labour*	Kidd, Henstock.
Nil sine numine	*Nothing without the Deity*	Banner, Weld.
Nil sistere contra	*Nothing to stand against*	M'Nichol, Nicol, Nicholson, Nicolson, Stewart.
Nil solidum	*Nothing is permanent*	Goldie, Williams.
Nil temere, neque timore	*Nothing either rashly or in fear*	Berney.
Nil temere tenta nil timide	*Try nothing rashly or timidly*	Buckle.
Nil tibi	*Nothing for you*	Campbell.
Nil time	*Fear nothing*	Man.
Nil timeo	*I fear nothing*	Drummond, Steuart.
Nil timere	*To fear nothing*	Balfour, D'Eyncourt, Ramsay, Tennyson.
Nil timere nec temere	*To fear nothing nor thoughtlessly*	Combe.
Nil veretur veritas	*Truth fears nothing*	Napier.
Nisi Dominus	*Unless the Lord*	Compton,
Nisi Dominus frustra	*It is in vain without the Lord*	English, Inglis, Rawdon.
Nisi paret, imperat	*Unless he obeys, he commands*	Bernard.
Nisi virtus vilior alga	*Viler than the sea-weed without virtue*	Moises.
Niti facere experire	*To strive, to do, to test*	Caldwell.
Nitimur et munitur	*We strive and are protected*	Wellwood.
Nitor donec supero	*I strive till I overcome*	Russell, Gibbons.
Nitor in adversis	*I strive against*	Horner.
Nitor in adversum	*I strive against*	Bredel, Fysh, Horner.
Nobilis est ira leonis	*The lion's anger is noble*	Buchanan, Crichton-Steuart, Ingles, Inglis, Piers, Ross.
Nobilis ira	*Noble indignation*	Creighton-Stuart, Stewart, Villiers-Stuart.
Nobilis ira leonis	*The lion's anger is noble*	Ross.
Nobilitas est sola virtus	*Virtue is the sole nobility*	Thackeray, Thackray.
Nobilitatis virtus, non stemma, character.	*Virtue, not lineage, is the mark of nobility*	Freshfield, Grosvenor.
Nocentes prosequor	*I prosecute the guilty*	Dumbreck, Savary.
Nocet differre paratis	*When ready it is injurious to delay*	Elliot.
Noctes diesque	*Nights and days*	Stacy.
Noctes diesque præsto	*I perform night and day*	Graham-Stirling, Murray, Stirling.
Nocte volamus	*We fly by night*	Bateson, Yarburgh.
Nodo firmo	*In a firm knot*	Harington, Harrington.
No heart more true		Hamilton.
Noli irritare leonem	*Don't rouse the lion*	Abbs, Cooper, Foord, Underwood Walsh,
Noli irritare leones	*Do not irritate lions*	Lyons.
Noli mentiri	*Do not lie*	Noteley, Notley.
Noli me tangere	*Do not touch me*	Græme, Graham, St. Albino, St. Aubyn, Willett, Wormald.
Nolo servile capistrum	*I do not wish a slave's halter*	Marsh.
Nomen extendere factis	*To perpetuate one's name by deeds*	Neeld.
Non abest virtute sors	*Good fortune follows virtue*	Nisbet.
Non aliunde pendere	*Not to depend on another*	Coke.
Non aqua solum	*Not water only*	Gunson.
Non arbitrio popularis auræ	*Not at the will of the popular breath*	Dale.
Non arte, sed marte	*Not by art, but by arms*	Naesmith, Nasmyth, Neasmith, Taylor.
Non aspera terrent	*Difficulties don't dismay us*	Warren.
Non astutia	*Not by craft*	Gordon, Oswald.
Non cantu sed actu	*Not by singing but by doing*	Gillman.
Non cate sed caute	*Not cunningly but cautiously*	Gatty.
Non cito nec tarde	*Neither quickly nor slowly*	Bannatyne.
Non civium ardor	*Not the ardour of the citizens*	Moore, Spurgeon.
Non crux, sed lux	*Not the cross, but the light*	Black, Blair, Cramer, Griffeth, Griffiths.
Non deerit alter aureus	*Another golden branch will succeed*	Don, Don-Wauchope.
Non deest spes	*Hope is not wanting*	Forbes.
Non deficit	*He does not fail*	Foulis, Hamilton.
Non deficit alter	*Another succeeds*	Algeo, Aljoy, Auldis, Gregorie, Hamilton, Smith, Walwyn.
Non degener	*Not degenerate*	Grindlay, Kinglake, Kinloch, Kinlock, Maxwell, Webster, Wedderburn, Williams.
Non desistam	*I will not desist*	Row.
Non dormio	*I do not sleep*	Maxwell.
Non dormiat qui custodit	*Let not him who guards sleep*	Myers, Waskett.
Non dormit qui custodit	*He does not sleep who keeps guard*	Cramer, Coghill, Gulliver, Lothian, Loudon, Louthian, Lowthian, M'Kellip, M'Killop, Shore, Wilson.
Non eget arcu	*He needs not the bow*	Elliot-Murray-Kynynmound.
Non eget jaculis	*He needs not javelins*	Clark.
Non eget Mauri jaculis	*He needs not the Moorish javelins*	Miller.
Non eget Mauri jaculis neque arcu	*He needs neither the javelins of the Moors nor the bow*	Watts.
None is truly great but he that is truly good		Packwood.
Non est mortale quod opto	*What I wish is not mortal*	Brooke, Burnett.
Non est sine pulvere palma	*There is no palm without wrestling for it.*	Yarborough, Yarburgh.

Non extinguar	*I shall not be extinguished*	Fraser, Frazer
Non fallor	*I am not deceived*	Kennedy
Non fecimus ipsi	*We have not done it ourselves*	Duncombe
Non fluctu, non flatu movetur	*Is moved neither by wind nor wave*	Brockholes-Parker, Parker
Non fluctuo fluctia		Maitland
Non fraude, sed laude	*Not with deceit, but praise*	Gordon
Non frustra	*Not in vain*	Barron
Non generant aquilæ columbas	*Eagles do not bring forth doves*	Lempriere, Rodney
Non gladio, sed gratia	*Not with the sword, but kindness*	Charteris, Charters
Non hæc, sed me	*Not these, but me*	Scrope
Non hæc sine numine	*These things are not without the Deity*	Agar Ellis, Ellis
Non immemor	*Not forgetful*	Graham
Non immemor beneficii	*Not unmindful of kindness*	Broadley, Embleton-Fox, Fitzgerald, Fox, Graham, Macdiarmid, Quantock
Non inferiora	*Not inferior things*	Monro
Non inferiora secutus	*Not following meaner things*	Bromley, Buchan, Fordyce Buchan, Grant, Hepburn, Skiddie
Non inferiora sequenda	*We must not follow meaner things*	Butler
Non invita	*Not by constraint*	Smith
Non in vita	*Not in life*	Smith
Non invita Minerva	*Minerva not unwilling*	Scott
Non jure deficit	*He is not without the right*	Foulis
Non leoni sed Deo	*Not for the lion, but for God*	Maddock
Non lumen effugio	*I do not shun the light*	Hewetson
Non major alio non minor	*Not greater than another, not less*	Clark
Non melior patribus	*Not better than my ancestors*	Hardinge
Non metuo	*I fear not*	Hamilton
Non mihi commodus uni	*Of service not to me alone*	Gordon, Oswald
Non mihi, sed Deo et regi	*Not for myself, but for God and the King*	Booth, Warren
Non mihi sed patriæ	*Not for myself, but for my country*	Heycock, Hippisley, Jones Loyd, Lloyd, Springe, Whittingham
Non mihi sed tibi gloria	*Glory to thee, not to me*	Warren, Wilkinson
Non minima sed magna prosequor	*I follow not small but great things*	Dobie, Dobbie
Non minor est virtus quam quærere parta tueri	*To guard what we have got is no less a merit than to seek what we have not*	Masters
Non modo sed quomodo	*Not in a manner but how*	Ellis
Non moritur cujus fama vivat	*He does not die whose fame may survive*	Congreve
Non multa sed multum	*Not many things, but much*	Caswall.
Non mutat fortuna genus	*Fortune does not change the nature*	Oliphant
Non mutat genus solum	*The country does not alter the nature*	Hamilton
Non nobis	*Not for ourselves*	Woodd
Non nobis Domine	*Not unto us, O Lord*	Willis
Non nobis esti	*Be it not unto us*	Gould
Non nobis nascimur	*We are not born for ourselves*	Lucy, Torway
Non nobis nati	*Born not for ourselves*	Frank
Non nobis, sed omnibus	*Not for ourselves but for all*	Ash, Ashe
Non nobis solum	*Not for ourselves alone* ...	Blayney, Drayton, Eardley, Fardell, Fosbery, Jacob, Lawless, Lockett, Moss, Wilson.
Non nobis solum nati sumus	*We are not born for ourselves alone*	Bradshaw
Non nobis tantum nati	*We are not born for ourselves alone*	Warner
Non nobis solum, sed toti mundo nati	*Born not for ourselves but for the whole world*	Robinson
Non obest virtute sors	*Our lot is not adverse to our virtue*	Nisbet
Non oblie	*Do not forget*	Graham
Non oblitus	*Not forgetting*	M'Tavish
Non obliviscar	*I shall not forget*	Colvil, Colville
Non obscura	*Not obscure*	Law
Non obscura nec ima	*Not obscure nor very low*	Law
Non obstante Deo	*If God oppose not*	Cunningham
Non omnibus dormio	*I am not asleep to everybody*	Balvaird
Non omnibus nati	*We are not born for all*	Frank
Non omnis frangar	*I shall not be all broken*	Colby
Non omnis moriar	*I shall not all die*	Bettescombe, Heaven
Non opes, sed ingenium	*Not wealth, but mind*	Ross
Non ostento sed ostendo	*I do not show off, but merely show*	Fowell
Non parvum est teipsum noscere	*It is no small thing to know thyself*	Cooper
Non pas l'ouvrage, mais l'ouvrier	*Not the work, but the workman*	Macnaghten, Workman
Non præda sed victoria	*Not the spoil, but victory*	Chambers
Non progredi est regredi	*Not to advance is to go back*	Roe, Tyson
Non providentia sed victoria	*Not in providence but in victory*	Coffy
Non quo, sed quomodo	*Not by whom, but in what manner*	Ellis, Howard, Thompson
Non rapui, sed recepi	*I did not plunder, but I received*	Cotterell.
Non recedam	*I shall not recede*	Newall
Non revertar inultus	*I will not return unavenged*	Vaughan
Non robore, sed spe	*Not with strength, but with hope*	Tippet, Vivian
Non sanz droict	*Not without right*	Shakespear
Non semper sub umbra	*Not always under the shade*	Farquharson
Non servit sed laborat	*Does not serve but labours*	Innes
Non sibi	[illegible]	Aillen Cleland Connell, Cullen, Jewitt, [illegible]

Motto	Translation	Names
Non sibi, cunctis	*For all, not for himself*	Moir.
Non sibi, patriæ	*Not for himself, for his country*	Tomlinson.
Non sibi, sed patriæ	*For his country, not for himself*	Baker, Filgate, Heppesley, Hughes, Marsham, Simcoe.
Non sibi, sed cunctis	*Not for self, but for all*	Moir.
Non sibi, sed patriæ natus	*Born not for himself, but for his country*	Joddrell, Jodrell.
Non sibi, sed toti	*Not for self, but for the whole*	Hutchinson, Stocker, Synge, Wynne.
Non sine	*Not without*	Oliver.
Non sine anchora	*Not without an anchor*	Drysdale.
Non sine causa	*Not without cause*	Drury, Justice.
Non sine Deo	*Not without God*	Eliot, Eliott.
Non sine industria	*Not without industry*	Bevan.
Non sine jure	*Not without right*	Charter, Leslie-Ellis.
Non sine labore	*Not without labour*	Milnes.
Non sine numine	*Not without high sanction*	Gifford.
Non sine periculo	*Not without danger*	Freer, M'Kenzie, Mackenzie, Walker
Non sine præda	*Not without prey*	Echlin.
Non sine pulvere palma	*The palm not won without wrestling for it*	Beresford-Peirse.
Non sine sente rosa	*The rose not without a thorn*	Rose.
Non sine usu	*Not without use*	Maxwell.
Non sino, sed dono	*I do not permit, but I give*	Seddon.
Non solum armis	*Not by arms only*	Lindsay.
Non solum pane	*Not by bread alone*	Drisdale.
Non sufficit orbis	*The world is not enough*	Bond, White.
Non temere	*Not rashly*	Chalmers, Forbes.
Non terra, sed aquis	*Not by land, but by water*	Dunnet.
Non timeo, sed caveo	*I do not fear, but am cautious*	Oakeley, Strachan, Strauchan.
Non timere sed fortiter	*Not with fear, but boldly*	Bloxsome, Wallington.
Non tua, te moveant, sed publica voto	*Let not thine own but the public wishes actuate thee*	Alleyne.
Non videri sed esse	*Not to seem but to be*	Hare.
Non vi sed mente	*Not by force but by mind*	Lincolne.
Non vi sed virtute	*Not by force but by virtue*	Burrowes, Elphinstone, Ramsbotham.
Non vi, sed voluntate	*Not by force but free will*	Boucher.
Non vi virtute	*Not by force but by virtue*	Borrowes.
Non vox, sed votum	*Not a voice, but a wish*	Nagle.
Norma tuta veritas	*Truth is the safe rule*	Morrall.
Nos aspera juvant	*Difficulties are helpful to us*	Louis.
Nosce teipsum	*Know thyself*	Buck, Cranmer, Fraazer, Fraser, Fraser-Allan, James, Murray, Pendred, Pringle, Stanfield, Stansfeld, Stansford, Thompson, Tindal, Tregonwell, Trenchard, Walfeld, Walford.
Nos non nobis	*We not for ourselves*	Cookson, Wilberforce.
Nos nostraque Deo	*We and ours to God*	Rodger, Rogers.
Nos pascit Deus	*God feeds us*	Rooke.
Nostra quæ fecimus	*What we have done is our own*	Kenan.
Nostre roy et nostre foy	*Our King and our faith*	Neel.
Notandi sunttibi mores	*You must take note of their manners*	Dallaway.
Nothing hazard, nothing have		Suttie.
Nothing venture, nothing have		Boswell.
Not in vain		Aylet, Aylett, Branfill.
Not rashly, nor with fear		Harrison.
Not the last		Smith-Ryland.
Not too much		Mackinlay, M'Kinlay.
N'oublie	*Do not forget*	Graham, Haldane, Moir, Joynt.
N' oublié	*Not forgotten*	Graham, Moir, Mour.
N'oublies	*Do not forget*	Grehan.
N'oubliez	*Do not forget*	Graham.
Nourissez l'espérance	*Cherish hope*	White.
Nous maintiendrons	*We will maintain*	Howard, Howard-Bury.
Nous travaillerons en l'espérance	*We will labour in hope*	Blacket, Blackett.
Now thus		De Trafford, Trafford.
Now thus, now thus		Pilkington.
Nox nulla secuta est	*No night followed*	Tupper.
Nubem eripiam	*I will snatch away the cloud*	Shipperdson.
Nufragus in portum	*Shipwrecked brought to harbour*	Heard.
Nulla deditio	*No giving up*	Kynsey.
Nulla dies sine linea	*No day without its task*	Lefroy, Singleton, Williams.
Nulla fraus tuta latebris	*No fraud is safe in any lurking-place*	Ellacombe.
Nulla pallescere culpa	*To turn pale at no crime*	Farrand, Forbes-Mitchell, Mitchell, Patten, Pulleine, Waynflete, Wilson-Patten, Winder.
Nulla rosa sine spica	*No rose without a thorn*	Stowers.
Nulla rosa sine spinis	*No rose without thorns*	Ilbert.
Nulla salus bello	*No safety in war*	Lorimer.
Nulla temerata nube	*No profane thing under a cloud*	Howison.
Nulli fraus tuta latebris	*Fraud is safe in no place of concealment*	Ellacombe, Ellicombe,
Nulli inimicus ero	*I will be an enemy to none*	Donaldson.
Nulli præda	*A prey to none*	Arundel, M'Aben, M'Cabin.

Nulli præda sumus	*We are a prey to none*	Marlay, Marley, Marling
Nullis inimica ero	*I will be an enemy to none*	Donaldson
Nullius in verba	*At the dictation of no one*	Bankes, Banks, Gabb, Young
Nullius in verba magistri	*By the words of no master*	Walcot
Nul q'un	*Only one*	Cayley
Numen et lumen effugio	*I shun the Deity and light*	Hewson
Numen et omnia	*Authority and all things*	Graham
Numero pondere et mensura	*I reckon by weight and measure*	Hoskyns
Numine et arcu	*By the Deity and my bow*	Bowman
Numine et patria asto	*I stand by God and my country.*	Aston
Numine et virtute	*With authority and virtue*	Yuille, Yule
Nunc aut nunquam	*Now or never*	Barnard, Hampson, Needham, Virgin
Nunc et olim	*Now and formerly*	Longroft
Nunc et semper	*Now and always*	Whorwood
Nuncia pacis	*The messenger of peace*	Buchanan, Whannell
Nuncia pacis oliva	*The olive the messenger of peace*	Mays, Moyes
Nunc mihi grata quies	*Now is there pleasant repose for me*	Gordon
Nunc ut olim	*Now as before*	Longcroft
Nunquam deorsum	*Never down*	Graham
Nunquam dormio	*I never sleep*	Maxwell
Nunquam fallentis termes olivæ	*A branch of the olive which never deceives*	Massey
Nunquam libertas gratior	*Liberty never more welcome*	Scott
Nunquam mutans	*Never changing*	Bowring
Nunquam nisi honorificentissime	*Never unless most honourably*	Freeling
Nunquam non fidelis	*Never unfaithful*	Moultrie, Moutrie, Moutry
Nunquam non paratus	*Never unprepared*	Bethune, Betton, Brandreth, Bright, Carlton, Crabbie, Domenichetti, Fairholm, Johnson, Johnston, John stone, Johnstoun, Kerrick, Knight, M'Gregor, Maxwell, Skinner, Stoney, Vanden-Bempde Johnstone
Nunquam obliviscar	*I will never forget*	Campbell-M'Iver, Hilton-Simpson, M'Iver, Simpson
Nunquam senescit	*It never grows old*	Gloag
Nunquam se præponens	*Never presuming*	Duntze
Nunquam victus	*Never conquered*	Buchanan
Ny dessux ny dessoux	*Neither above nor beneath*	Grove, Troyte Chafyn Grove

O

Ob ducem ob patriam	*On account of our leader and country*	Waddy
Obduram adversus urgentia	*Not yielding to pressure*	Bothwell
Obey and rule		Loades
Oblier ne puis	*I cannot forget*	Colville
Obliviscar	*I shall forget*	Colvil, Colville.
Obliviscaris	*Forget*	Campbell
Ob patriam vulnera passi	*Having suffered wounds for our country*	Burnes
Obsequio, non viribus	*By yielding, not by force*	Hamilton
Observe		Achieson, Aitcheson, Aitchison, Atcheson, Oldaker
Obstando supera	*Overcome by resisting*	Scott
Occultus, non extinctus	*Hidden, not extinguished*	Tytler
Occurrent nubes	*Clouds will intervene*	Eliot, Elliott
O Dhia gach an cabhair		O'Conar Don
Odi profanum	*I hate whatever is profane or vulgar*	Forster, Haire Forster, Hare
Odor vitæ	*The sweet breath of life*	Hutton
Officio et fide	*By duty and fidelity*	Fawcett
Officium præsto	*I perform my duty*	Pownall
Ofna Dduw a'r Brenhin		Traherne
Ofner na ofno angau		Bruce, Lewis
Ofnwn yr Arglwydd	*Let us fear the Lord*	Williams, Williams Lloyd
Of old I hold		Levy
Ohne Furcht	*Without fear*	Teschemaker
Ohne Rast zum Ziel	*Without resting to the goal*	Abel
Olet et sanat	*It smells and cures*	Dunbar
Olim fecimus	*We did so at one time*	Saward, Seward
Olim florebat	*It flourished at one time*	Landel
Olim sic erat	*Thus it was formerly*	Hood
Omine secundo	*Under favourable auspices*	MacMurdoch, Murdoch.
Omne bonum ab alto	*All good from above*	Crossley
Omne bonum Dei donum	*Every good thing is the gift of God.*	Boughton, Checkland, Edwards, Hill, Powell, Wood

Motto	Translation	Names
Omne bonum desuper	*All good is from above*	Burney, Honywood.
Omne bonum superne	*All good from above*	Miller.
Omnes arbusta juvant	*All find delight in woods*	Underwood.
Omne solum forti patria	*Every land is a native country to a brave man*	Balfour, Bruce, Bruges, Eccleston, Joicey, O'Sheill, Sheill, Stewart.
Omne solum patria	*Every land is our native country*	Bill.
Omne solum vivo patria est	*Every land is a living man's country*	Matthews.
Omne tulit punctum qui miscuit utile dulci	*He has gained every point, who has mixed the useful with the sweet*	Warren.
Omnia bene	*All is well*	Harvey.
Omnia bona bonis	*All things are good to the good*	Wenman.
Omnia bona desuper	*All good things are above*	Goodlake.
Omnia certa fac	*Make everything certain*	Ashpitel.
Omnia debeo Deo	*I owe all things to God*	Grenehalgh,
Omnia Deo confido	*I trust all things to God*	M'Neight.
Omnia Deo juvante	*I can do all things with God's help*	Crawfurd.
Omnia Deo pendent	*Everything depends on God*	Stockton.
Omnia fert ætas	*Time brings all things*	Cheese,
Omnia firmat	*It strengthens all things*	Colquhoun.
Omnia fortitudine vincit	*He conquers everything by his bravery*	Wiehe.
Omnia fortunæ committo	*I commit all things to fortune*	Duff, M'Knight. M'Naught.
Omnia mei dona Dei	*All my goods are the gift of God*	Done.
Omnia mundana turbida	*All earthly things are full of confusion*	White.
Omnia pro bono	*All things for the good*	Murdoch, Murdock.
Omnia providentiæ committo	*I commit all things to Providence*	Meares.
Omnia recte	*All things rightly*	M'Cracken.
Omnia superat diligentia	*Diligence overcomes all difficulties*	Mitchell.
Omnia superat virtus	*Virtue conquers all*	Gardiner.
Omnia vincit amor	*Love conquers all things*	Bruce, Rogers.
Omnia vincit labor	*Labour overcomes everything*	Cook.
Omnia vincit veritas	*Truth conquers everything*	Eaton, Munn, Naish, Nash.
Omnibus amicus	*A friend to everybody*	Chatto.
Omnibus optimus	*The best for all*	Aveling.
Omni liber metu	*Free from all fear.*	Birley.
Omni secundo	*Everything prosperous*	Murdock.
Omnium rerum vicissitudo	*All things are subject to change*	Ford.
Omni violentia major	*Greater than all violence*	Donelan, O'Donellan.
One King, one faith, one law		Burke.
On in the right		Cardarwine.
On things transitory resteth no glory		Isham.
Onus sub honore	*Burden under honour*	Johnston.
Onward		Atherton, Bowring, Fraser-Mackintosh, Lorimer.
Onward ever		Bessemer.
On with you		Nagle.
Opera bona effulgent	*Good works shine forth*	Jacoby.
Opera Dei mirifica	*The works of God are wonderful*	Garmston, Hustwick.
Opera illius mea sunt	*His works are mine*	Cust.
Opera mundi	*The works of the world*	Sanderson.
Ope solis et umbræ	*By the help of the sun and shadow*	Irvine.
Opes parit industria	*Industry produces wealth*	Benson.
Opiferque per orbem dicor	*I am called a helper throughout the world.*	Kadie, Keddie.
Opima spolia	*The richest of the spoil*	O'Meara.
Opitulante Deo	*With the aid of God*	Brereton.
Oportet vivere	*We must live*	Tod, Todd.
Optima cela	*Conceal what is best*	Millar.
Optima est veritas	*Truth is best*	Thompson, Thomson.
Optima quæque honesto	*To the man of honour everything best*	Lambert.
Optima revelatio stella	*A star the best revelation*	Reveley.
Optima sapientia probitas	*The best wisdom is integrity*	Salmond.
Optima sperando spiro	*Hoping for the best I live*	Humphrys.
Optime merenti	*To the most meritorious*	Witham.
Optime quod opportune	*What is done opportunely is best*	Campbell.
Optimum pati	*To bear is best*	Sheldon.
Optimum quod primum	*What is first is best*	Kirk.
Optimus est qui optime facit	*Best is he who does best*	Best, Beste.
Optivo cognomine crescit	*He becomes great by the wished-for name*	De Hochpied-Larpent.
Ora e sempre	*Now and always*	Farmer.
Ora et labora	*Pray and labour*	Alexander, Harman, Holherton, Holmes, Langar, Mure, Orlebar, Patrick, Ramsay, Sibbald, Wakeman.
Orando te aspiciam	*By prayer I shall behold thee*	Foster.
Orate et vigilate	*Pray and watch*	Hewlett.
Orbe circum cincto	*The world being girt around*	Saumarez.
Ore lego, corde credo	*I speak with the mouth, I believe with the heart*	Hamilton.
Oriens sylvia	*The East wood*	Eastwood.
Ornat fortem prudentia	*Prudence adorns the brave man*	Dunbar, Lancaster.
Ornatur radix fronde	*The root is adorned with the foliage*	Innes.

Orna verum	*Adorn the truth*	Waddell, Weddell
Ostendo, non ostento	*I show, not boast*	Betts, Isham, Ritchie
Otium cum dignitate	*Leisure with dignity*	Kelso, Montagu, Porter Burrall
Ou bien ou rien	*Either well or not at all*	Sotheby
Oublier ne puis	*I cannot forget*	Colvil, Colville
Où le sort appelle	*Where destiny calls*	Francis
Our hope is on high		Rippon
Over fork over		Conyngham, Cuninghame, Cunningham, Dick, Gun Cunningham, Miller Cunningham
Ovner na ovno angau		Jones

P

Pace et bello paratus	*Prepared for peace and war*	Fraser, Frazer
Pacem amo	*I love peace*	Columball, Columbell, Ker, Scot, Scott
Pace vel bello	*In peace or war*	M'Turk
Pacis nuncia	*The messenger of peace*	Murray
Paix et peu	*Peace and a little*	Maitland, Walrond
Palladia fama	*Palladian fame*	Inchbold
Palmam qui meruit ferat	*Let him who has deserved the palm bear it*	Kitson, Nelson
Palma non sine pulvere	*The palm not without wrestling for it*	Archibald, Doughty, Jenkinson, Lamb
Palma virtuti	*The palm is for virtue*	Laudon, Palmer
Pandite	*Open*	Gibson
Pandite, cœlestes portæ	*Open, O ye heavenly gates*	Gibson, Gibsone, Watt
Parabo me		Wood
Parat et curat	*He prepares and cures*	Stewart.
Paratus	*Prepared*	Fraser, Sword, Swourd
Paratus ad æthera	*Prepared for heaven*	Falconer, Faulkner
Paratus ad arma	*Prepared for war*	Johnson, Johnston
Paratus et fidelis	*Ready and faithful*	Carruthers, Hamond, Sanderson
Paratus sum.	*I am ready*	Campbell, Fairlie, Fairlie-Cuninghame, Fairly, Maclure, M'Lure
Parce qu'il me plait	*Because it pleases me*	Sprot
Parcere prostratis	*To spare the fallen*	Le Hunte
Parcere subjectis	*To spare the vanquished*	Glasgow, Grant, Longfield
Par ce signe à Agincourt.	*By the watchword at Agincourt*	Entwistle
Par commerce	*By commerce*	French
Par Dieu est mon tout	*My all is from God*	Margetson.
Pareo non servio	*I obey, but not as a slave*	Jenkinson
Parere subjectus	*To be obedient*	Glasgow
Pares cum paribus	*Equals with equals*	Pares
Par fermesse du quesne	*By firmness of the cane*	Du Cane
Par fluctus portui	*The wave equal to the haven*	Wilbraham
Pari animo	*Of courage adequate to the occasion*	Leake
Paritur bello	*It is obtained by war*	Murray
Paritur pax bello	*Peace is obtained by war*	Blane,
Par la volonté de Dieu	*By the will of God*	Wynill, Wyvill
Parle bien	*Speak well*	Parlby
Par loi et droit	*By law and right*	Trayner
Par negotiis neque supra	*Equal to our business and not above it*	Hill
Par pari	*Equal to equal*	Sucklemore
Par sit fortuna labori	*Let the fortune equal the labour*	Buchanan, Lowman, Palmer
Parta labore quies	*Rest obtained by labour*	Fulton, Sydserf
Parta tueri	*I will defend what I have won*	Haddon, Jacob, Powys.
Par ternis suppar .	*Almost equal to three at a time*	Bowles, Rushout
Parum sufficit	*Little sufficeth*	Barrow
Parva contemnimus ..	*We despise small things*	Gernon
Par valeur	*By valour*	Heron, White
Par viribus virtus	*Our virtue is a match to their strength*	Pakington
Passant cressant en honneur	*Progressing in honour*	Walker
Passes avant	*Pass before*	Waldegrave
Pass forward		Stewart
Passibus æquis	*With equal steps*	Walker
Passibus citis sed æquis	*With rapid but equal steps*	Labouchere
Passus rege meos.	*Guide my steps*	Walker
Paterni nominis patrimonium	*The patrimony of a paternal name*	Oakeley
Paternis suppar	*Nearly equal to ancestral glory*	Rushout
Paterno robore tutus	*Secure in ancestral strength*	Scott
Patet ingeniis campus	*The field lies open to talent*	Tucker
Patience		Dow, Dowie
Patience and resolution		Muterer
Patience makes everything light		Lamb
Patience passe science	*Patience surpasses knowledge*	Boscawen, Boscowen

Motto	Translation	Names
Patiens	*Patient*	Dow.
Patiens pulveris atque solis	*Patient of dust and sun*	Floyd.
Patienter	*Patiently*	Bulman.
Patientia casus exsuperat omnes	*Patience overcomes all misfortunes*	Askew, Robertson of Ladykirk.
Patientia et gratia vinco	*I conquer by patience and grace*	Thomson.
Patientia et perseverantia	*By patience and perseverance*	Dent, Weiss.
Patientia et perseverantia cum magnanimitate	*Patience and perseverance with magnanimity*	Fellowes.
Patientia et spe	*By patience and hope*	Duguid, Duiguid, Duniguid, Dwigwid, Leslie-Duguid.
Patientia victrix	*Victor through patience*	Dalton.
Patientia vinces	*You will conquer by patience*	Alvanley, Arden.
Patientia vincit	*He conquers by patience*	Chein, Cheine, Cheyne, Dalton, Gall, Lindesay, Lindesey, Lindsay, Napier.
Patientia vinco	*I conquer by patience*	Thompson, Thomson.
Patiently persevere		Wills.
Patior et spero	*I suffer and hope*	Baillie.
Patior, potior	*I suffer, I obtain*	Maundrell, Peyton.
Patior ut potiar	*I suffer that I may obtain*	Spence, Spottiswood, Spotswood.
Patitur qui vincit	*He who conquers suffers*	Kinnaird.
Patria cara, carior fides	*My country is dear, but my religion is dearer*	Nicholas, Nicolas, Thomson.
Patria cara, carior libertas	*My country is dear, but liberty is dearer*	Bouverie, Cay, Lindon, Pleydell-Bouverie-Campbell.
Patriæ et religioni fidelis	*Faithful to country and religion*	Teevan.
Patriæ fidelis	*Faithful to fatherland*	Bannerman.
Patriæ fidus	*Faithful to fatherland*	Lewis.
Patriæ infelici fidelis	*Faithful to my unhappy country*	Lennard, Molyneux, Montgomery, Sackville, Stopford.
Patriæ non sibi	*For his country, not for himself*	Argles.
Patria fidelis	*A faithful country*	Tiffin.
Patriam amo	*I love my country*	Scott.
Patriam hinc sustinet	*Hence he sustains his country*	Higgins.
Patriis virtutibus	*With the virtues of his ancestors*	Clements.
Pauca suspexi pauciora despexi	*Few things I have looked up to, and fewer looked down upon*	Berkeley.
Paulatim	*By little and little*	Scales.
Pauper non in spe	*Not poor in hope*	Poore.
Pawb yn ol ei arfer		Jones.
Pax	*Peace*	Almack, Foulis, Hatfield, Hutton, Osborne.
Pax alma redit	*Bountiful peace returns*	Domville.
Pax armis acquiritur	*Peace is acquired by arms*	Arnot, Arrat, Arrot.
Pax aut bellum	*Peace or war*	Blain, Blaine, Blane, Blean, Scerth.
Pax aut defensio	*Peace or defence*	Landale.
Pax copia	*Peace, plenty*	Read.
Pax copia sapientia	*Peace, plenty, wisdom*	Fleming, West.
Pax copia virtus	*Peace, plenty, valour*	Steuart.
Pax et amor	*Peace and love*	Dalbiac, Hodson, Jessop.
Pax et copia	*Peace and plenty*	Chandlee, David.
Pax et libertas	*Peace and liberty*	Gordon.
Pax et spes	*Peace and hope*	Pease.
Pax finis bello	*Peace the end of war*	Ellis.
Pax in bello	*Peace in war*	Osborne, Smith.
Pax justa	*A just peace*	Newington.
Pax optima rerum	*Peace is the best of things*	Guidott.
Pax potior bello	*Peace is better than war*	Bastard, Nembhard.
Pax quæritur bello	*Peace is sought by war*	Cromwell.
Pax tua, Domine, est requies mea	*Thy peace, O Lord, is my rest*	Umphray.
Pax vobiscum	*Peace be with you*	Nott.
Peace		Dixon, Higga.
Peace and grace		Graham.
Peace and plenty		Barns, Nottidge.
Peace with power		Moss.
Pedetentim	*Step by step*	Foote.
Pejus letho flagitium	*Disgrace is worse than death*	Martin, Sampson.
Pelle timorem	*Drive away fear*	Whatley.
Pen-aur-y-chalon wir	*A true heart will make gold*	Watkins.
Pende valde	*Weigh well*	Penfold.
Penses comment	*As you think*	Deyvelle.
Pensez à bien	*Think of good*	King-Noel, Milbanke, Noel.
Pensez à moi	*Think of me*	Giles.
Pensez comment	*As you think*	Davell, Deyvelle.
Pensez forte	*Think firmly*	Bromley, Pauncefote.
Peperi	*I have brought forth*	Peperell, Pepperell.
Per	*Through*	Bindlosse.
Per actum intentio	*The intention is judged of by the act*	Urquhart.
Per actus conamine	*You attempt by doing it*	Kersey.
Per acuta belli	*By the stratagems of war*	Bellgough, Belli, Carpenter.
Peradventure		Cockburn, Eliot, Elliott, Fogg-Elliott.

Motto	Translation	Names
Per adversa virtus.	*Virtue through opposition*	Leghton, Leighton, Lighton
Per angusta ad augusta	*Through dangers to honour.*	Christall, Davidson, Devereux, Skeffington
Per angustum	*Through danger*	Fletcher
Per antiquam cartam	*By an ancient charter*	Adlington
Per ardua	*Through difficulties*	Berry, Bervy, Clarkson, Crookshank, Curtis, Drake, Fuller, Heugh, Masterton, M'Entire, M'Intyre, M'Neagh, Stibbert, Tailour, Wright
Per ardua ad alta.	*Through difficulties to heaven*	Achanye, Ahanny, Hall, Hanman, Hannay, Jobling, Waterlow
Per ardua Deo favente	*Through difficulties, God helping*	Butterworth
Per ardua fama	*Fame through difficulties*	Whyte
Per ardua liberi	*Free through difficulties*	Pitt
Per ardua stabilis	*Steady in difficulties*	Harty, Lawrence, Mann, Perryman.
Per ardua stabilis esto	*Be steadfast in difficulties*	Dendy.
Per ardua surgo	*I rise through difficulties*	Draffen, Fenton, Harding, Hardinge, Mahon, O Haugherne, O'Heron, Wingate
Per ardua surgam	*Through difficulties I shall rise*	Beetham, Betham.
Per ardua virtus	*Virtue through difficulties*	Sinclair
Per aspera ad dulcia crucis	*By rugged paths to the sweet joys of the cross*	Bretherton
Per aspera belli	*Through the hardships of war*	Hopkins, Randolph
Per aspera virtus	*Virtue through hardships*	Ross
Per bellum qui providet	*He who provides through war.*	Lidderdale.
Per callem collem	*Over a mountain road*	Collins.
Per castra ad astra	*Through the camp to the stars*	Nicholson, Shaw, Worsley
Per cœli favorem	*By the favour of heaven*	Cowie
Per constanza et speranza	*Through constancy and hope*	Gomm.
Per crucem ad castra	*Through the cross to the camp*	Davies
Per crucem ad cœlum	*Through the cross to heaven*	Paul
Per crucem ad coronam	*Through the cross to the crown*	De la Poer, Le Poer, Poe, Poer, Power, O'Neill-Power
Per crucem ad lucem	*Through the cross to the light*	Campbell.
Per crucem ad stellas	*By the cross to the stars*	Legard
Per crucem confido	*I trust through the cross.*	Crosley.
Percussus resurgo	*When struck down I rise again*	Jordan
Percussus elevor	*Smitten down I am lifted up*	Dovaston
Per damna per cædes	*Through losses, through carnage*	Bosanquet, Boyton
Per Dei providentiam	*Through the providence of God*	Dennett
Per Deum et ferrum obtinui	*By God and my sword I have obtained*	Hill
Per Deum meum transilio murum	*Through my God I leap over a wall*	Pemberton
Perdurat probitas	*Integrity endures*	Pearson.
Per ecclesiam ad cœlum.	*Through the church to heaven*	Eccles
Perenne sub polo nihil	*Nothing is everlasting under heaven*	Pont.
Perenne sub sole nihil	*Nothing is enduring under the sun*	Perrins
Per ferrum obtinui	*I have got possession by my sword*	Hillas
Per fidem et patientiam	*Through faith and patience*	Broomhead Colton-Fox
Per fidem omnia	*All through faith*	Howard
Per fidem vinco	*I conquer through faith*	Eastwood
Perforatus	*Perforated, bored*	Board
Perge sed caute	*Go on, but cautiously*	Jenkins, Styles
Pergo sursum	*I advance upward*	Romans
Periculum fortitudine evasi	*Fortitude preserved me from danger*	Mahon, Pakenham-Mahon, Peisley
Peri-Gal		Perigal
Per ignem ferris vicimus	*We conquer by our swords through fire*	Hodder
Per ignem, per gladium	*By fire, by sword*	Welby, Welby-Gregory
Perissem, ni persitissem	*I would have perished, had I not persisted*	Anstruther, Molony, Thomson
Perissemus, nisi persitissemus	*We had perished, had we not persisted*	Anstruther
Per il suo contrario	*By its opposite*	Paget
Perimus licitis	*We are ruined by permitted things*	Cann, Shore.
Per incerta certus amor	*A sure love in doubtful circumstances*	Romanis
Per industriam .	*By industry*	Rowan
Perit ut vivat	*He loses his life that he may gain it*	Bissett, Fenwick, Phin
Per juga, per fluvios	*Through precipices and torrents*	Harland, Hazledine
Per lucem ac tenebras mea sidera sanguine surgent .	*Through light and darkness my star will arise in blood*	Cayley
Per mare	*By sea*	Anderson
Per mare, per terras.	*By sea and land*	Alexander, Courtayne, Darley, Drummond, Dupré, Durham, Lamb, Macalister, M'Alister, Macdonald, M'Donald, Macdonnell, M'Eachern, M'Eachran, Macelester, Piessf, Rutherford, Rutherfurd, Urquhart, Warren Darley
Per mille ardua	*Through a thousand difficulties*	Millerd
Permitte cætera divis	*Leave the rest to the care of the gods*	M'Crummen, M'Crummin.
Per mortem vinco.	*I conquer through death*	Waterlow
Per multos annos	*Through many years*	Phillips.
Per orbem	*Throughout the globe*	Clay
Perrumpo	[illegible]	[illegible]sey

Motto	Translation	Names
Per saxa per ignes	*By rocks, by fires*	Smith.
Persevera Deoque confide	*Persevere and trust in God*	Brown.
Persevera et vince	*Persevere and conquer*	Lampson.
Perseverance		Burrard, Hawkshaw, Hume, Smith.
Perseverando	*By persevering*	Abbot, Banks, Brinckman, Broadhead, Brooks, Cammell, Cope, Dawson, Denison, Drake, Duncan, Edwards, Elliott, Flower, Frampton, Handcock, Hanrott, Henley, Howell, Hutchinson, Lane, Larkworthy, Leake, M'Kellar, Mackellar, Mackenzie, Moreton, Morton, Reynolds-Moreton, Roxby, Shorrock, Turnly, Wood.
Perseverando et cavendo	*By perseverance and caution*	Moore.
Perseverantia	*Perseverance*	Bell, Crichton, Macdonald, Swaby, Vowles.
Perseverantia ad finem optatum	*By perseverance to the wished-for end*	Jones.
Perseverantia dabitur	*It will be given by perseverance*	Terry.
Perseverantia et cura quies	*Rest by perseverance and care*	Hall.
Perseverantia et labore	*By perseverance and labour*	Pitcher.
Perseverantia industria et fidelitas	*Perseverance, industry, and fidelity*	Ravenscroft.
Perseverantia omnia vincit	*Perseverance conquers all things*	Cooper.
Perseverantia palma	*By perseverance the palm*	Willson.
Perseverantia palmam obtinebit	*Perseverance will obtain the palm*	Horton, Tooth.
Perseverantia victor	*Victor through perseverance*	Campbell.
Perseverantia vincit	*Perseverance conquers*	Alexander, Bamford, Burness, Mateos.
Perseveranti dabitur	*It will be given to the persevering*	Gilmore, Gilmour, Robertson, Simpson, Tapper, Williamson.
Persevere		Baker, Burrard, Collier, Colvile, Comer, Congreve, Dupuis, Edmond, Farnall, Ford, Fordyce, Gardiner, Greig, Hall, Jeffcock, Oak, Oakes, Oates, Romilly, Simpson, Whittall.
Persevere in hope		Mackinnon.
Persevero	*I persevere*	Baker, Pender, Waithman.
Per sinum Codanum	*Through the Gulf of Codanus*	Graves-Sawle.
Persist		Humphry.
Perspicax, audax	*Sharp-sighted, bold*	Erskine.
Persta et præsta	*Stand fast and step ahead*	Bramhall.
Perstando præsto	*I step ahead by standing fast*	Hamilton.
Persto et spero	*I stand fast and hope*	Merry.
Per tela per hostes	*By arrows, by enemies*	Bremner, Brymer, Innes.
Per tela per hostes impavidi	*Undaunted through arrows and enemies*	Borron.
Per tot discrimina rerum	*Through so many critical junctures*	Hammond, Hickman.
Per varios casus	*By various fortunes*	Casey, Cunninghame, Douglas, Drysdale, Gravett, Hamilton, Lammie, L'Amy, Walker.
Per vias rectas	*By right ways*	Blackwood, Pixley, Purvis.
Pervicax recte	*Steadfast in the right*	M'Ewan.
Per vim et virtutem	*By strength and courage*	Bebb, Youl, Yule.
Per virtutem et scientiam	*By courage and knowledge*	MacNeil, M'Neil.
Pestis patriæ pigrities	*Sloth is the plague of one's country*	Dugdale.
Petit alta	*He aims at high things*	Abercrombie, Abercromby.
Petit ardua virtus	*Courage aims at hard things*	Douglas.
Phœbo lux	*Light from the sun*	Kinnaird.
Phœbus, lux in tenebris	*Phœbus, light in darkness*	Jeffrey.
Pie et fortiter	*Piously and bravely*	Bennet.
Piedmontaise		Hardinge.
Pie repone te	*In pious confidence*	Mordey, Pierpoint, Pierrepont.
Pietas et frugalitas	*Piety and thrift*	Guthrie, Guthry.
Pietas tutissima virtus	*Piety is the surest virtue*	Ainsley, Ainslie.
Pietate	*By piety*	Brown.
Pietate et probitate	*By piety and uprightness*	Rees.
Pietate fortior	*Stronger by piety*	Broade, Stanier-Philip-Broade.
Pietate parentum	*By the piety of my forefathers*	Tulloch.
Pietatis causa	*For the sake of piety*	Pye.
Pieux quoique preux	*Pious though valiant*	Long, Wolley.
Pie vivere et Deum et patriam diligere	*To live piously, and love God and our country*	Redmond.
Pignus amoris	*The pledge of love*	Graham.
Pilkyngton Pailedowne; the Master mows the meadows		Pilkington.
Pille mise gu muir	*I will return to sea*	M'Laurin.
Placeam	*Be mine to please*	Murray.
Placeam dum peream	*Let me find favour as long as I live*	Murray.
Plane et sane	*Simply and sensibly*	Vaughan.
Playsyr vaut Payn	*Pleasure costs pain*	Payn.
Plena dabit Deus vela	*God will fill our sails*	Bontine, Tennant.
Plena refulget	*The full moon shines*	Pitcairn.
Plus spinis quam ferro	*More by thorns than the sword*	Richardson.
Plus vigil	*Be more watchful*	White.

Plus ultra	*More beyond*	Elliott, Nabbs, Nairne
Plutot rompe que plie	*Break rather than bend*	De Ponthieu
Pob dawn o Dduw		Jeffreys
Poco a poco	*Little by little*	Liston, Ramage
Pollet virtus	*Virtue avails*	Pole, Poole, Snowden, Wellesley
Por dysserver	*To deserve*	Carr
Porro unum est necessarium	*Moreover, one thing is needful*	Wellesley
Portanti spolia palma	*The prize is to him that carries off the booty*	Feltham
Posce teipsum	*Ask thyself*	Hodges
Posse, nolle, nobile	*To have the power without the wish is noble*	Wingfield
Possunt qui posse videntur	*They are able who believe they can*	Attwood, Butt, Fowler, Goodere, Keightley, Norcop, Radford
Postera crescam laude .	*I shall grow in the esteem of posterity*	Melbourne
Postera laude recens	*Fresh in the praise of posterity*	Hardinge
Post est occasio calva	*Opportunity is bald behind*	Chapman
Post funera fœnus	*Interest after death*	Moll, Mow
Post funera virtus	*Virtue survives death*	Roberts, Robertson, Westropp
Post hominem animus durat	*After a man our courage is strengthened*	Bridge
Post mortem virtus virescit	*Our virtue flourished after death*	Tyssen
Post nubes	*After clouds*	Blunstone Steddert, Stodart, Stothart
Post nubes lux	*Light after clouds*	Blunstone, Blundestone, Steddert, Stodart, Stoddart, Stothart, Stothert
Post nubila	*After clouds*	Jack
Post nubila Phœbus	*After clouds sunshine*	Ahrends, Cranworth, Jack, Jaffray, Jaffrey, Jeffrey, Purvis, Rolfe, Shuldham, Tarleton
Post nubila sol	*After clouds sunshine*	Pinkerton
Post prælia præmia	*After battles rewards*	Cunninghame, Malins, Nicholson, Rutland, Westenra.
Post spinas palma	*After the thorns the palm*	Paget
Post tenebras lucem	*After darkness light*	Bright
Post tenebras lux	*After darkness*	Hewat, Hewatt
Post tot naufragia portum	*After so many shipwrecks I find a port*	Montagu
Post virtutem curro	*I run after virtue*	Blome, Brisco, Briscoe
Potior origine virtus	*Virtue rather than lineage*	Bland, Scot, Scott
Potius ingenio quam vi	*Rather by genius than strength*	Edgar
Potius mori quam fœdari	*Death rather than disgrace*	Gifford
Pour apprendre oublier ne puis	*I cannot forget to learn*	Palmer
Pour bien désirer	*To wish well*	Barrett Lennard, Bolden, Brand, Dacre, Leonard
Pour bien fort	*Strong for good*	Preston.
Pour deservir	*To deserve*	Carr
Pour deservyr	*To deserve*	Carr
Pour Dieu et mon Roi	*For God and my King*	Bagot
Pour Dieu, pour terre	*For God, for the land*	Leigh
Pour jamais	*For ever*	Gorwood
Pour la foi	*For the faith*	Lawes
Pour l'eglise	*For the church*	Wandesford
Pour le Roy	*For the King*	Macaul
Pour loyaulté maintenir	*For maintaining loyalty*	De Massue
Pour ma libertay pour ma patree	*For my liberty, for my country*	Vaudin
Pour ma patrie	*For my country*	Cooper
Pour mon Dieu	*For my God*	Macpeter, Peitere, Peter
Pour mon Roy	*For my King*	Janvim
Pour quoy non	*Why not*	Maundy
Pour trois	*For three*	Latter
Pour y parvenir	*In order to accomplish*	Manners, Manners-Sutton
Poussez en avant	*Push forward*	Barry, Barrow
Pracedentibus insta	*Urge your way among the leaders*	Eliot, Eliot Craggs
Practise no fraud		Henderson
Præcipitatus, attamen tutus	*Headstrong, yet in safety*	Dunbar
Præclarior, quo propinquior	*The more illustrious, the nearer*	Constable
Præclarum regi et regno servitium	*Honourable service to king and country*	Ogilvie, Ogilvy
Præclarius quo difficilius	*The harder, the more honour*	Fountain
Prædæ memor	*Mindful of the prize*	Graham
Præmium honor	*The reward is honour*	Foster
Præmium, virtus, gloria	*Reward, courage, glory*	Corsane
Præmium, virtus, honor .	*Reward, courage, honour*	Boreland, Brown, Cox
Præmium virtutis.	*The reward of virtue*	Pringle
Præmium virtutis honor	*Honour is the reward of virtue*	Bebb, Brown, Cheere, Chere, Corsane, Cox, Tetlow
Præmonitus præmunitus.	*Forewarned, forearmed*	Rickart
Præsta et persta	*Undertake and persevere*	Weekes
Præstando præsto	*Having taken the precedence, I hold it*	Hamilton
Præstare et prodesse	*To outstrip and do good*	Gray
Præstat auro virtus	*Virtue is better than gold*	Cunningham
Præstat tuto quam cito	*Better safely than quickly*	Bonar
Præsto et persisto	*I undertake and persist*	Hamilton, Yawkins

Motto	Translation	Names
Præsto et persto	*I undertake and persevere*	Baillie-Hamilton-Arden, Coe, Crawhall, Hamilton.
Præsto pro patria	*I undertake for my country*	Neilson.
Præsto ut præstem	*I undertake that I may perform*	Preston.
Prævisa mala pereunt	*Foreseen misfortunes come to nothing*	Hodges, Twisden, Twysden, Winterbotham.
Praise God		Kerr.
Prato et pelago	*By sea and land*	Killingworth.
Preignes haleine tire forte	*Take breath, pull strong*	Dorrien, Smith-Dorrien.
Premium virtutis honor	*The reward of virtue is honour*	Bebb.
Prend moi tel que je suis	*Take me such as I am*	Bell, Loftie, Loftus, Rickett, Sutton.
Prenez en gré	*Take in good will*	Ogle.
Prenez en ire	*Take it in anger*	La Font.
Prenez garde	*Be on your guard*	Elmsley, Elmslie, Elmsly, M'Intosh, Macintosh, Macritchie, MacRitchie, Rickard, Rickart, Winstanley.
Prenez haleine tirez fort	*Take breath, pull strong*	Giffard.
Press forward		Mortimer.
Press through		Boreland, Borelands, Cockburn, Young.
Prest d'accomplir	*Ready to accomplish*	Aston, Freston, Heber, Talbot.
Presto et persto	*I undertake and persevere*	Stewart.
Presto ut præstem	*I undertake that I may perform*	Preston.
Prest pour mon pais	*Ready for my country*	Mouson, Sherlock.
Prest pour mon pays	*Ready for my country*	Mouson.
Prêt	*Ready*	Aston, Smith.
Prêt d'accomplir	*Ready to accomplish*	Talbot, Heber-Percy.
Pretio prudentia præstat	*Prudence excels reward*	Monson, Morison, Richardson.
Pretiosum quod utile	*What is useful is valuable*	Affleck, Auchinleck.
Pretiosum quod utile est	*What is useful is valuable*	Auchinleck.
Pretium et causa laboris	*The reward and cause of labour*	Frederick.
Pretium victoribus corona	*The reward to the conquerors is a crown*	Knapton.
Pretium virtutis	*The prize of bravery*	Welsh.
Prêt pour mon pays	*Ready to serve my country*	Monson.
Prevalet virtus	*Virtue prevails*	Zouch.
Prima voce salutat	*Salutes with the first voice*	Boucherett.
Primi et ultimi in bello	*First and last in war*	Gorman, O'Gorman.
Primum tutare domum	*First defend home*	Watkins.
Primus	*First*	Ellis.
Primus e stirpe	*First of the race*	Hay.
Primus tametsi virilis	*First although manly*	Primerose.
Primus ultimusque in acie	*First and last in battle*	Sherritt.
Principiis obsta	*Oppose beginnings*	Bateman, Ffolkes, Folkes, M'Laggan.
Prisca fides	*Ancient faith*	Glassford.
Prisco stirpe Hibernico	*Of an ancient Irish stock*	Lennon.
Prist en foyt	*Ready in faith*	Barlow.
Pristinum spero lumen	*I hope for ancient lustre*	Preston.
Prius frangitur quam flectitur	*Is sooner broken than bent*	Dykes-Ballantine.
Prius mori quam fidem fallere	*Yield to death rather than betray trust*	Drummond.
Prius quam factum considera	*Think before you act*	Reeves.
Pro amore patriæ	*For love of country*	Scot, Scott.
Pro aris et focis	*For our homes and altars*	Ayrton, Blomefield, Campbell, Hasilrigge, Hazlerigg, Hesilrigge, Kirkland, M'Naught, Mulvihall, Philips, Purdon, Scot, Serjeantson, Shortland, Shortreed, Wait, Woodforde.
Pro arte non marte	*For art, not strength*	Blagrave.
Pro avita fide	*For ancestral faith*	Brooke.
Probando et approbando	*Trying and approving*	Ramsay.
Pro bello vel pace	*For war or peace*	Anderson, Anderton.
Probitas cum fortitudine	*Honesty with fortitude*	Brewster.
Probitas sibi ipsi securitas	*Integrity is its own security*	Carr.
Probitas veritas honos	*Integrity, truth, and honour*	Browne.
Probitas et firmitas	*Integrity and firmness*	Leslie, Lesly.
Probitas fons honoris	*Integrity is the fountain of honour*	Gubbay.
Probitas verus honos	*Integrity is true honour*	Bateson, Chetwynd, Hansard, Harvey, Lacon, Newman, Townley, Vicary.
Probitate	*By integrity*	Rennie, Renny.
Probitate ac virtute	*By integrity and valour*	Rose.
Probitate consilium perficitur	*An undertaking is achieved by integrity*	Renny.
Probitate et labore	*By probity and labour*	Baring, Gould.
Probitate et virtute	*By probity and valour*	Rose.
Probitatem quam divitias	*Probity rather than riches*	Claydan, Claydon, Clayton.
Pro bona ad meliora	*For good to better*	Goodwright.
Probum non pœnitet	*The upright man does not repent*	Leader, Sands, Sandes, Sandys.
Procedamus in pace	*Let us proceed in peace*	Montgomery.
Pro Christo et patria	*For Christ and country*	Innes-Ker, Ker, Verner, Vernon.
Pro Christo et pro patria	*For Christ and for country*	Car.
Pro Christo et patria dulce periculum	*For Christ and our country danger is* [illegible]	Ker.
Pro cruce audax	[illegible] *for the cross*	Squarey.

Motto	Translation	Families
Pro Deo certo	*I strive for God*	Anderson
Pro Deo et catholica fide	*For God and the Catholic faith*	Altham
Pro Deo et ecclesia	*For God and the Church*	Bisshopp
Pro Deo et libertate	*For God and liberty.*	Wilson
Pro Deo et patria	*For God and country*	Botheras, Mackenzie, Minton, O'Riordan, Woodmas
Pro Deo et pro patria	*For God and for my country*	Stacpoole
Pro Deo et Rege	*For God and the King*	Bickerton, Blacker, Broade, Golding, Hawkins, Hurst, Masterton, Mastertown, Parsons, Phillips, Stanier Philip-Broade, Zigno
Pro Deo, patria, et Rege	*For God, my country, and my King.*	Beugo, James
Pro Deo, pro Rege, pro patria, et lege.	*For God, for the King, for the country, and the law*	Blakemore
Pro Deo, Rege, et patria	*For our God, our King, and country*	Benga, Bickerton, Blaydes, Blaydes Marvel, De Salis, M'Dowall
Prodesse civibus	*To do good to one's fellow citizens*	Beckett
Prodesse quam conspici	*To do good rather than be famous*	Chamberlayne, Cocks, Cookesey, Coxs, Grote, Leigh
Prodigiose qui laboriose	*Who acts laboriously acts marvellously*	Innes
Pro ecclesia Dei	*For the Church of God*	Swainson, Swainston
Pro fide	*For the faith*	Howard
Pro fide ac patria	*For my faith and country*	Longe
Pro fide et patria	*For our faith and country*	Daniell, Meldon, Wade
Pro fide Rege et patria pugno	*I fight for the faith, King, and country*	Lentaigne, O'Neill
Pro fide strictus	*Drawn for the faith*	Norman
Profunda cernit	*He penetrates into deep things*	Austin-Gourlay, Gourlay, Gourley, Simpson, Simson
Progredere, ne regredere	*Go forward, not back*	Honnyman, Honyman, Sharp
Progredior	*I go forward*	Sharp
Progress with prudence		Howard
Projeci	*I have thrown away*	Main
Pro lege, Rege, grege	*For the law, the King, the people*	Shield
Pro lege senatuque Rege	*For law, senate, and King.*	Dodsworth
Pro legibus ac regibus	*For our laws and kings*	Wilson
Pro legibus et regibus	*For laws and kings*	Wilson
Pro libertate	*For liberty*	Wallace
Pro libertate lege sancta	*For liberty ratified by law*	Glyn
Pro libertate patriæ.	*For the liberty of my country*	Beresford, Massey, Massy, Maysey, Puxley
Pro lusu et præda	*For sport and plunder*	MacMoran, M'Morran
Pro Magna Charta	*For Magna Charta*	Dashwood, Stapleton
Pro me ipso et aliis	*For myself and others*	Carmichael
Pro mitra coronam	*A crown for a mitre*	Sharpe
Prompte et consel	*Quickly and advisedly*	Pringle
Prompte et consulto	*Quickly and with advice*	Plenderleith
Promptus	*Ready*	Donaldson, Kemp, Kempt, Russell
Promptus ad certamen	*Ready for the contest*	Sinclair
Promptus et fidelis	*Ready and faithful.*	Carruthers, Chalmers, Croudace, Mitchell Carruthers, Wade.
Pro patria	*For my country*	Alherley, Bannerman, Beatson, Betson, Bonsall, Borrowman, Bullman, Bulman, Douglas, Grant, Gregor, Groset, Groseth, Hamilton, Hastie, Hay, Hay-Newton, Higgins, Innes, Macdonald, Manby, Newlands, Newton, Ogilvie, O'Higgins, Provan, Roachead, Rochead, Rose, Ross, Scott, Skipton, Thomson, Turner, Walmsley, Wood
Pro patriæ amore	*For the love of my country.*	Wolfe
Pro patria auxilio Dei	*For my country, by the aid of God*	Grossett, Heaven, Muirhead
Pro patria ejusque libertate	*For my country and its liberty*	Joy, Shelly
Pro patria et libertate	*For our country and liberty*	Michie
Pro patria et Rege	*For country and King*	Crofton, Jones, Thomas
Pro patria et religione.	*For my country and religion.*	Shanly
Pro patria et virtute	*For my country and virtue*	Higgins.
Pro patria invictus	*Invincible for my country*	Odell
Pro patria mori	*To die for my country*	Manly
Pro patria non timidus perire	*Not afraid to die for my country*	Champneys
Pro patria sæpe, pro Rege semper	*For my country often, for my King always*	Ainslie
Pro patria sanguis	*My blood for my country*	Splatt
Pro patria semper	*For my country always*	Campbell, Collow, Power
Pro patria uro	*I burn for my country*	Costerton
Pro patria vivere et mori	*To live and die for my country*	Grattan
Propere et provide	*Quickly and cautiously*	Robinson
Propositi tenax	*Tenacious of purpose*	Hankinson, Lowell, Strutt, Tomlinson, Yeatman.
Propria virtute audax	[illegible]	M[illegible]den

Motto	Translation	Names
Proprio vos sanguine pasco	*I feed you with my own blood*	Cantrell.
Propter obedientiam	*Because of obedience*	Hay.
Pro recto	*Because of right*	Meek.
Pro Rege	*For the King*	Aberkirdor, Burnaby, Christie, Graham, Le Boutillier, Macfie, M'Phie, Porcher.
Pro Rege Dimico	*For King and Dymoke*	Dymoke.
Pro Rege et grege	*For the King and people*	Glendee, Grieve, Paterson, Rudd.
Pro Rege et lege	*For the King and law*	Blanckley, Horton, Kidson, Kidston, Maudit, Stewart.
Pro Rege et limite	*For the King and his dominions*	Elliot, Elliott.
Pro Rege et patria	*For King and country*	Aberherdour, Aberkerdour, Ainsley, Ainslie, Bell, Cameron, Carr, Cooke, Crofton, Fergusson, Franklin, Franklyn, Hammond, Harrison, Leicester, Leslie, Leslie-Melville, Lyon, M'Cubbin, Napier, Paterson, Palgrave, Smith, Sterry, Stewart, Tait, Yates.
Pro Rege et patria pugnans	*Fighting for King and country*	Pasley.
Pro Rege et populo	*For King and people*	Basset.
Pro Rege et pro patria semper	*For my King and country always*	Lawrence.
Pro Rege et religione	*For my King and my religion*	Boycott.
Pro Rege et republica	*For King and commonwealth*	Paul.
Pro Rege in tyrannos	*For the King against tyrants*	Macdonald, M'Dowall.
Pro Rege, lege, grege	*For the King, for the law, for the people*	Brougham, Fane, Ponsonby.
Pro Rege pio	*For a pious King*	Thornton.
Pro Rege sæpe	*For the King often*	Wright.
Pro Rege sæpe, pro patria semper	*For our King often, for our country always*	Eyre, Laurence, Redington.
Pro Rege sæpe, pro republica semper	*For the King often, for the commonwealth always*	Gibson.
Pro Rege semper	*For the King always*	Morris, Thoyts
Pro republica semper	*For the commonwealth always*	Hellier.
Pro salute	*For safety*	Ogilvie.
Prosequor alis	*I pursue with wings*	Casson, Graham.
Prospere qui sedulo	*The diligent prosper*	Cunninghame.
Prospere, si propere	*Prosperously if speedily*	Peat.
Prospero, sed curo	*I make haste, but am cautious*	Graham, Maxwell.
Prospice	*Look forward*	Andrew, Luard.
Prospice respice	*Look forward, look back*	Gossip.
Pro utilitate	*For use*	Tennant.
Pro veritate	*For truth*	Keith, MacGeorge,
Provide		Rutherford, Stewart.
Providence		Craick, Craik.
Providence with adventure		Hawkins, Whitshed.
Providentia	*By Providence*	Anderson.
Providentia Dei	*By the providence of God*	Nicholson.
Providentia Dei conservet	*Let the providence of God preserve it*	De la Motte.
Providentia Dei stabiliuntur familiæ	*Families are established by the providence of God*	Lamplugh.
Providentia divina	*By divine providence*	Keating, Keching, Sangster.
Providentiæ fido	*I trust in Providence*	Stewart.
Providentiæ me committo	*I commit myself to Providence*	Kyle, Park.
Providentia et industria	*By providence and industry*	Anderson..
Providentia et virtute	*By providence and virtue*	Hepburn, Rankin, Rankine.
Providentia in adversis	*Providence in adversity*	Tollet.
Providentia tutamen	*Providence is our protection*	Thomson, Toker.
Providentia tutamur	*We are protected by Providence*	Beardmore, Nerden, Keyser.
Provide qui laboriose	*He who labours acts prudently*	Innes.
Providus esto	*Be careful*	Maxton, Maxtone.
Pro virtute	*For virtue*	Regnold, Reid.
Provyd		Stewart.
Prudens et innocuus	*Prudent and harmless*	Kingsbury.
Prudens, fidelis, et audax	*Prudent, faithful, and bold*	Legh.
Prudens qui patiens	*He is prudent who is patient*	Coke, Lushington, Shaw.
Prudens sicut serpens	*Wise as the serpent*	Pole, Van Notten-Pole.
Prudens simplicitas beat	*Prudent simplicity blesses*	Frederick.
Prudenter amo	*I love wisely*	Scot, Scott.
Prudenter qui sedulo	*He who acts diligently acts prudently*	Milne.
Prudenter vigilo	*I watch prudently*	Donaldson.
Prudentia	*With prudence*	Young, Jaggard.
Prudentia decus innocentia	*Prudence, grace, innocence*	Ramsay.
Prudentia et animis	*With prudence and spirit*	Steel, Steele.
Prudentia et animo	*With prudence and courage*	Antram, Ochterlony, Steele, Steell.
Prudentia et constantia	*By prudence and constancy*	Denman, Denmark, Tichbourne.
Prudentia et honor	*Prudence and honour*	M'Kinna.
Prudentia et justitia	*With prudence and justice*	Kaye-Shuttleworth.
Prudentia et marte	*With prudence and courage*	Mylne.
Prudentia et simplicitate	*By prudence and simplicity*	Denman, Lant.
Prudentia et vi	*By prudence and might*	Innes.
Prudentia et vigilantia	*Prudence and vigilance*	Purchon.

Prudentia et virtute	*By prudence and virtue*	Rankin
Prudentia fraudis nescia	*Prudence incapable of deceiving*	Elphinstone
Prudentia gloriam acquirit	*Prudence obtains glory.*	Litton
Prudentia in adversis	*Prudence in adversity.*	Tollet, Wicksted.
Prudentia me sustinet	*Prudence holds me up*	Boyd
Prudentia præstat	*Prudence excels*	Morison, Morrison, Morryson,
Prudentia simplicitate	*By prudence and simplicity*	Birch, Reynardson
Prudhomme et loyal	*Man of honour and loyal*	Pridham
Publica salus mea merces	*The public safety is my reward*	Dick
Pugilem claraverat	*He hath ennobled the champion*	Newte
Pugna pro patria	*Fight for your country*	Ogilvie, Tichborne, Tichbourne
Pugno pro aris	*I fight for our altars*	Le Vrier
Pugno pro patria.	*I fight for my country*	Ogilvy
Pugno pugnas pugnavi	*I have fought battles with my fist*	Despard
Pulchra pro libertate	*In defence of glorious liberty*	Vane
Pulchrior ex arduis	*Fairer from difficulties*	Mackenzie, M'Kenzie
Punget sed placet	*It is painful but pleasing*	Rome
Puro de fonte	*From a pure fountain*	Casborne
Pur sans peur	*Pure without fear*	White.

Q

Qua duxeris adsum	*Where you lead there I am*	Ogilvy
Quæ amissa salva	*What was lost is safe*	Keith, Keith-Falconer
Quæ fecimus ipsi	*What we ourselves have performed*	Fulton, James
Quæ habet manus tenebit	*My hand will hold fast what it has*	Templeman
Quæ immemor beneficii		Ingleby
Quæ juncta firma	*Union is strength*	Leslie, Lesly
Quæ moderata firma	*Moderate things are permanent*	Ogilvie, Ogilvy
Quæque flavilla micat	*Every spark shines*	Robertson
Quæ recta sequor	*I follow the things which are right*	Campbell, Pickersgill
Quærendo	*By seeking*	Smith
Quærere verum	*To seek the truth*	Bowes, Carleton, Holway Calthrop, Rouett
Quære sic est	*Seek, so it is*	Stanhope
Quære verum	*Seek truth*	Birchall
Quæ serata secura	*The things which are locked are safe*	Douglas, Gate House, Monteath-Douglas
Quæsita marte tuenda arte.	*What has been gained by force of war should by skill be guarded*	Luttrell
Quæ supra	*Which things are above*	Hobart, Robartes
Quæ sursum volo	*I wish those things which are above*	M'Quinn
Quæ sursum volo videre	*I wish to see the things which are above*	Macqueen, M'Queen, O'Quin, Quin, Wyndham Quin
Quæ vernant crescent	*The things which are green will grow*	Burnet, Burnett
Quæ vult valde vult	*What things he wishes he wishes fervently*	Wilmot
Qualis ab incepto.	*The same as from the beginning*	De Grey, Hamilton, Majendie, Mirehouse, Robinson, Weddell
Qualis ero spero	*Such as I will be I hope to be.*	Quayle
Qualis vita, finis ita	*Such as the life, so its end*	Coleridge, Powles, Yong, Yonge
Quam non torret hyems.	*As much as winter does not scorch...*	Caunter
Quam plurimis prodesse	*To do good to as many as possible*	Worsley
Quam sibi sortem	*Any condition to him*	Fraser.
Quantum est in rebus inane	*What vanity is in human affairs*	Minett.
Quantum in rebus inane	*What vanity in human affairs..*	Osborn, Osborne.
Qua panditur orbis	*Where the world extends.*	Campbell
Quarta saluti	*A fourth to salvation*	Halliday
Quasi summus magister	*As if supreme master*	Somaster
Qua tendis	*Wherever you go.*	Roy
Que je surmonte	*That I may overcome*	Chanceler, Chancellor
Quem non torret hyems	*Which winter does not scorch*	Kyd
Quem te Deus esse jussit	*What God has commanded you to be*	Holroyd, Holroyde
Que pensez?	*What do you think?*	Lawrence,
Quercus	*The oak*	Wright
Quercus glandifera amica porcis	*The acorn bearing oak is kind to pigs*	Allen
Quercus robur salus patriæ	*The strength of the oak is the safety of the country*	Oakes
Quhidder will ye,	*Whither will ye*	Stewart
Quhidder will zie	*Whither will ye*	Stewart
Quia fidem servasti	*Because you have kept faith*	Grieve
Qui capit, capitur	*He who takes is taken*	Smyth
Qui conducit	*He who leads*	Borthwick
Quicquid crescit, in cinere perit	*Whatever grows, perishes in ashes*	Aserburne, Ashburne, Asherburne, Ashburner

Motto	Translation	Names
Quicquid dignum sapiente bonoque est	*Whatever is worthy of a wise man and a good*	Peach.
Quid capit, capitur	*What takes is taken*	Smith.
Quid clarius astris?	*What is brighter than the stars?*	Baillie, Bayly, Cochrane-Baillie.
Quidder will zie?	*Whither will ye?*	Moncrieff.
Quid gens sine mente?	*What would the clan do without mind?*	Muschamp.
Quid leges sine moribus?	*What are laws without morals?*	Edwards.
Quid leone fortius?	*What is braver than the lion?*	Clayton.
Quidni pro sodali?	*Why not for a companion?*	Burnet, Burnett.
Quidni tandem?	*What pray?*	Hatton.
Quid non cor sæpius pro Immanueli?	*Why is the heart not oftener for Immanuel?*	Wishart.
Quid non, Deo juvante?	*What may not be done by the help of God?*	Chalmers, Salt.
Quid non pro patria?	*What will a man not undergo for his country?*	Campbell, Dewar, Lockhart, Mathew.
Quid non resolutio?	*What cannot resolution achieve?*	Ashton.
Quid prodest?	*What advantage is it?*	Webb.
Quid pure tranquillis?	*What gives pure tranquility?*	Elliot.
Quid retribuam?	*What shall I repay*	Parsons.
Quid utilius?	*What more useful?*	Bell, Goldie, Goldie-Scot, Gouldie.
Quid verum atque decens	*What is true and honourable*	Rickets, Trevor.
Quid verum atque decens curo et rogo	*What is true and honourable is what I care and ask for*	La Touche.
Quid vult, valde vult	*What he wishes he wishes ardently*	Motteux.
Quiescam	*I shall be at rest*	Dalrymple.
Quiescens et vigilans	*Resting and watching*	Fairne, Fairnie, Fernie.
Quieta non movere	*Not to disturb things at rest*	Sketchley.
Qui honeste, fortiter	*Who acts honourably acts bravely*	Anderson.
Qui invidet minor est	*He who envies is inferior*	Cadogan, Leigh, Pugh, Steward.
Qui me tangit pœnitebit	*He who touches me will repent it*	Gillespie, Gillespie-Stainton, Macpherson.
Qui non ciconia tigris	*Who is not a stork is a tiger*	Browne.
Qui non patriam amat?	*Who does not love his country?*	Quinan.
Qui nos vincet?	*Who shall conquer us?*	Beugo.
Qui nucleum vult, nucem frangat	*Whoso wishes the kernel must crack the nut*	Haslen, Hasler.
Qui patitur, vincit	*He who endures patiently, conquers*	Kinaird, Kinnaird.
Qui panse	*Which heals*	St Lawrence.
Qui pense?	*Who thinks?*	Lawrence, St. Lawrence.
Qui potest capere, capiat	*Let him take who can take*	Clegg, Gleg.
Qui plane sane vadit	*Who goes plainly goes safely*	Taylor.
Quis accursabit?	*Who shall assail?*	Hamilton.
Quis accusabit?	*Who shall accuse?*	Hamilton.
Quis audeat luci aggredi	*Assail the light who dares*	Prior.
Quis separabit?	*Who shall separate?*	Motto of the Order of St. Patrick.
Qui sera sera	*What will be will be*	Betenson, Bettenson, Bettinson, Bettison, Edgell, Ffolks, Folkes, Wolferstan.
Qui s'estime petyt deviendra grand	*Who esteems himself little, will become great*	Petyt.
Quis occursabit	*Who shall assault us?*	Hamilton.
Quis similis tibi in fortibus, Domine?	*Who is like to Thee among the mighty, O Lord?*	Goldsmid.
Qui sis non unde	*What you are, not whence*	Whatman.
Qui stat caveat ne cadat	*Let him who stands take care lest he fall*	Dunville.
Qui stat caveat	*Let him who stands take care*	Domville.
Quis timet?	*Who fears?*	Price.
Qui tel?	*Who such?*	Kettle.
Qui uti scit ei bona	*Let wealth be his who knows how to use it.*	Hill, Noel-Hill
Qui vit content tient assez	*He that lives content has got enough*	Bradshagh, Bradshaigh, Bradshaw, Johnson.
Qui vult capere, capiat	*Who wishes to take, let him take*	Gloag.
Quocunque ferar	*Whithersoever I may be carried*	Sinclair.
Quocunque jeceris stabit	*Wherever you shall throw it, it shall stand*	M'Leod.
Quod adest	*What is present*	Marsham.
Quod agis fortiter	*Which you do bravely*	Oliphant.
Quodcunque evenerit optimum	*Whatever happens is best*	Lloyd.
Quod Deus vult fiat	*Let that which God wills be done*	Chetwynd.
Quod Deus vult fiet	*What God wishes will be done*	Dimsdale.
Quod Deus vult volo	*What God wishes I wish*	Mountford.
Quod dixi, dixi	*What I have said, I have said*	Dixie, Dixon.
Quod ero, spero	*I hope what I shall be*	Barton, Booth, Bough, Galbraith, Gore-Booth, Gowans, Haworth, Haworth-Booth.
Quod facio, valde facio	*What I do, I do with all my might*	Holmes.
Quod facit, valde facit	*What he does, he does with all his might*	Sikes.
Quod honestum est decet	*What is honourable is becoming*	Richardson.
Quod honestum utile	*What is honourable is profitable*	Annand, Annandale, Lawson.
Quod justum, non quod utile	*What is just, not what is useful*	De Lisle, Philips.
Quod me mihi reddit amicum	*What restores me to myself befriends me*	Haslewood.
Quod non pro patria?	*What shall we not do for our country?*	Bowie, Bowrie, Campbell.
Quod potui, perfeci	*What I could, I have done*	Dundas, Turner.

Motto	Translation	Families
Quod pudet hoc pigeat	*Let that which causes shame be irksome*	Dobyns, Yate
Quod severis metes	*What you have sown you will reap*	Bliss
Quod sors fert, ferimus	*What fate brings we bear*	Clayton
Quod sursum volo videre	*I am resolved to look upwards*	Quin
Quod tibi, hoc alteri	*That is for thee, this for the other*	Crawford, Crawfurd, Finzel, Fleetwood, Hesketh, Plowden, Terry
Quod tibi, id alii	*That for thee, this for another*	Lopas, Lopes
Quod tibi, ne alteri	*That is for thee, not for the other*	Alexander
Quod tibi vis fieri fac alteri	*Do to another what you would be done to yourself*	Ram
Quod tibi vis fieri, facias	*What you wish done, do yourself*	Philipoe, Philipse
Quod transtuli retuli	*What I have taken I have restored*	Woodroofle.
Quod tuum tene	*Keep what is your own*	Cheetham, Chetham
Quod utilius?	*What is more useful?*	Bell, Goldie, Gouldie
Quo duxeris, adsum	*Whither you shall lead, I follow*	Ogilvy
Quod verum atque decens	*What is true and honourable*	Trevor
Quod verum tutum	*What is true is safe*	Courtenay, Sim
Quod volo erit	*What I wish will be*	Wright
Quod vult, valde vult	*What he wishes, he fervently wishes*	Holt, Mansel, Mansell, Maunsell, Porter, Wilmot
Quo fas et gloria	*Whither right and glory point*	Glasgow
Quo fata vocant	*Wherever fate may call*	Bland, Bruce, Burtchall, Chadborn, Cowell Stepney, Cumming, Le Geyt, Pavier, Russell, Russell-Pavier, Shelley, Sidney, Thurlow
Quo honestior eo tutior	*The more honourable the more safe*	Guise
Quo major, eo utilior	*The greater the more useful*	Neilson
Quo me cunque vocat patria	*Wherever my country calls me*	Arden
Quondam his vicimus armis	*Formerly we conquered with these arms*	Bowman, Broadbent, Carleton, Leir, Carleton, Tomlin
Quo paratior	*The readier we are*	Coats
Quorsum vivere mori? mori vita	*Why live to die? To die is life*	Blencowe
Quos dedit arcus amor	*The bows which love hath given*	Hamilton
Quo spinosior fragrantior	*The more thorns, the greater fragrance*	Rose, Ross
Quo veritas?	*Whither is truth fled?*	Pulteney
Quo virtus et fata vocant	*Where virtue and destiny call.*	Ffolliott
Quo virtus ducit scando	*I climb where virtue leads*	Follett
Quo virtus vocat	*Where virtue calls*	Street, Whimper, Whymper, Yate Yates

R

Motto	Translation	Families
Radicem firmant frondes	*Leaves strengthen the root*	Grant
Radii omnia lustrant	*The rays illuminate all things*	Brownhill
Raised again		Hunter
Ramis micat radix	*The root quivers with the branches*	Robertson
Rapit ense triumphos	*Wins triumphs with the sword*	Smith
Raptim ad sidera tollar	*I shall be snatched aloft to the stars*	Guille
Rara avis in terris	*A rare bird in the world*	Emerton, Kett
Rara bonitas	*Goodness is scarce*	Bennet, Bonnet
Rather die than be disloyal		Pearson
Ratio mihi sufficit	*Reason is sufficient for me*	Graham
Ratione non ira	*By reason, not by rage*	Small
Ratione non vi	*By reason, not by force*	M'Taggart
Ready		Archever, Fraser, Smith
Ready and faithful		Gorham, Walker
Ready, aye ready		Carmichael, Johnston, Napier, Scot, Stewart
Reason contents me		Graham, Brooke.
Rebus angustis fortis	*Brave in adversity*	Cobbold.
Rebus in arduis constans	*Constant in difficulties*	Pembroke
Recreat et alit	*It refreshes and cherishes.*	Duddingstoun
Recreation		Forrester
Recta ad ardua	*Act rightly in difficulties*	Mackenzie, M'Kenzie
Recta pete	*Seek what is right*	Fletcher
Recta sequor	*I follow right on*	Campbell, Keith
Recta sursum	*Things are right which are above*	Graham
Recta ubique	*Things right everywhere.*	Gaury
Recta vel ardua	*Right or difficult*	Evelick, Lindsay
Recte ad ardua	*Straight at difficulties*	MacKenzie
Recte agens confido	*I trust doing rightly*	Perry, Whitting
Recte et fideliter	*Rightly and faithfully*	Gibson, Spode
Recte et sapienter	*R[illegible]htly and [illegible]*	Heard
Recte et suaviter	*Rightly and mildly*	Curzon, Lyne Stephens

Motto	Translation	Names
Recte faciendo neminem timeas	*Fear no one in doing right*	Harvey, Scott.
Recte faciendo neminem timeo	*I fear none in doing right*	Cairncross, Scott.
Recte faciendo securus	*Safe in doing right*	Inglis.
Recte ferio	*I strike straight*	Bedell-Sivright, Sivright.
Recte omnia duce Deo	*With God for guide all is right*	Rodd.
Recte quod honeste	*What is done honourably is right*	Anderson.
Recte sequor	*I follow rightly*	Campbell, Keith.
Recto cursu	*In a right course*	Corsar, Corser.
Rectus in curvo	*Right in bending*	Symonds.
Redde diem	*Restore the day*	Foster.
Reddie aye reddie		Reddie.
Reddunt aspera fortem	*Dangers render brave*	Scot, Scott.
Reddunt commercia mitem	*Commercial intercourses render man sociable*	Stewart.
Redeem time		Hancocks.
Re Deu		Bolitho.
Redit expectata diu	*The long expected returns*	Starkey.
Redoutable et fougueux	*Formidable and fiery*	Harvey.
Re é merito	*This through merit*	Dobbin, Gildea, Hebden, Vassal-Fox.
Refero	*I call to mind*	Campbell.
Refero moro aut vita decora		Rayson.
Refulgent in tenebris	*They glitter in the dark*	Stodart, Studdart, Studdert.
Refulget	*Is resplendent*	Pitcairn.
Regarde à la mort	*Consider death*	Milward, Minchin.
Regarde bien	*Look well*	Milligan, Milliken, Napier.
Regardez mon droit	*Regard my right*	Middleton, Middleton-Foule.
Regardez mort	*Consider death*	Bastable.
Regem defendere victum	*To defend a conquered King*	Whitgreave.
Regi et patriæ fidelis	*Faithful to King and country*	Scott, Toler.
Regi fidelis	*Faithful to the King*	Moulson.
Regi legi fidelis	*Faithful to the King and the law*	Barry.
Regi patriæque	*To the King and country*	Leeper.
Regi patriæque fidelis	*Faithful to King and country*	Scott.
Regi regnoque fidelis	*Faithful to the King and kingdom*	Pocock, Simpson.
Regis donum gratum bonum	*A gift from the King is a welcome boon*	Kingdon.
Regi semper fidelis	*Ever faithful to the King*	Smythe.
Regis et patriæ tantum valet amor	*So much does love of King and country avail*	Tyldesley.
Regit omnia tempus	*Time rules all things*	Boag.
Regulier et vigoureux	*Regular and vigorous*	Ker.
Remember		Motto of the Order of the White Rose.
Remember		Allen, Gavin, Home.
Remember and forget not		Hall.
Remember thy end		Keith.
Renascentur	*They will revive again*	Skiffington, Yelverton.
Renovate animos	*Renew your courage*	Drummond, Hay, Hayes.
Renovato nomine	*The name renewed*	Westcote.
Renovatur ætas ejus sicut aquilæ	*His age is renewed like the eagle's*	Raymond.
Reparabit cornua Phœbe	*The moon shall fill again her horns*	Hepburne-Scott, Hope, Scot, Scott.
Repetens exempla suorum	*Pursuing the examples of his ancestors*	Grenville.
République	*The state*	Harris.
Repullulat	*It sprouts forth anew*	Bisset, Lauder, Laurie, Lawder.
Requiesco sub umbra	*I rest under the shade*	Hamilton.
Rerum sapientia custos	*Wisdom is the guardian of things*	Affleck, Auchinleck.
Resistite usque ad sanguinem	*Resist unto blood*	Keogh.
Res non verba	*Deeds, not words*	Duberley, Freeland, Heely, Jarrett, Macmicking, Macrorie, M'Rorie, Roughsedge, Sterndale - McMikin, Wheelwright, Wilson.
Res non verba quæso	*I seek deeds, not words*	Mountford.
Resolute and firm		Huskisson, Milbank, Milbanke.
Resolutio cauta	*Prudent resolution*	Bethune.
Resolve is power		Stewart.
Resolve well, persevere		Moore, Coleman.
Respice	*Consider*	Nepean.
Respice aspice prospice	*Look back, look around, and look forward.*	Brooks, Holland.
Respice finem	*Consider the end*	Dixon, Fisher, Lucas, Lumb, Norris, Priestley, Snagge, Stevenson.
Respice futurum	*Regard the future*	Reece.
Respice, prospice	*Look behind, look before*	Hardress, Lloyd.
Respiciens prospiciens	*Looking behind, looking before*	Tennyson.
Respicio sine luctu	*I look back without sorrow*	Dendy.
Resurgam	*I shall rise again*	Crosbie, Crosby, Stewart.
Resurgere tento	*I strive to rise again*	Straiton.
Resurgo	*I rise again*	Cooper, Haxton, M'Fall, Maughan.
Retinens vestigia famæ	*Following in the footsteps of our fame*	Lister, Lloyd, Lyster.
Revertite	*Return ye*	Wardrop.
Revirescam	*I shall flourish again*	Dalgleish.
Revirescat	*May it flourish again*	Gould, Maxwell.
Revirescimus	*We grow green again*	Glenelg, Grant.

Revirescit	*It grows green again*	Belches, Belsches, Belshes, Bisset, Maxwell
Reviresco	*I flourish again*	Bisset, Constable Maxwell, Hepburn, M'Ewan, Mackenan, Mackeuan Mackewan, Maxwell, Rishton, Wellwood
Revise		Dundas.
Revocate animos	*Rouse your courage*	Hay
Rex non verba	*The King, not words*	Wilson
Richt do and fear na		King
Rident florentia prata	*The flowery meadows smile*	Pratt
Ride through		Hamilton, Nisbet
Rien sans Dieu	*Nothing without God*	Kerrison, Peters
Righ gu brath		M'Andrew
Right and reason		Dalyell, Graham
Right can never die		Toler
Right to share		Riddell
Rinasco piu gloriosa.	*I rise again more glorious*	Erskine, St Clair-Erskine
Rise and shine		Lawson
Rix in min mod		Rix
Robore et sapore	*With strength and taste*	Robertson
Robore et vigilantia	*By strength and watchfulness*	Aitken
Robori prudentia præstat	*Prudence excels strength*	Young
Robur	*Oaken strength*	Woods
Robur atque fides	*Strength and faith*	Whitaker, Whittaker
Robur et astutia	*Strength and astuteness*	Strettell
Robur in cruce	*Strength in the cross.*	Anketill
Robur in Deo	*Strength in God*	Raeburn
Robur in vita Deus	*God is the strength of life*	Jadewine
Robur meum Deus	*God is my strength*	Rhodes
Rosam ne rode	*Do not speak ill of the rose*	Cashen, Ross
Rosario	*In a bed of roses*	Harvey
Rosas coronat spina	*Roses are crowned with thorn*	Forbes
Rosa sine spina	*A rose without the thorn*	Penrose, Wadman
Ros cœli	*The dew of heaven*	Roskell
Row and retake		Riddell
Rule be ours		Byres
Rumor acerbe, tace	*Harsh rumour, be thou silent*	Echlin
Rupto robore nati	*We are born with weakened strength*	Aikenhead, Aitkenhead, Akenhead, Sibbald.
Rycht and reason		Graham

S

Sacra quercus	*The holy oak*	Holyoake, Holyoake-Goodricke
Sacrificium Deo cor contritum	*A contrite heart is a sacrifice to God*	Coker
Sae bauld	*So bold*	Sibbald
Sæpe pro Rege, semper pro republica	*Often for the King, always for the state*	Vassall
Sævumque tridentem servamus	*Let us preserve the dread trident*	Broke, Loraine
Sagax et audax	*Shrewd and bold*	O'Naghten
Sagesse sans tache	*Wisdom without spot*	Concanon
Saie and doe		Watkin
Saigeadoir collach a buadh	*The valiant archer for ever*	O'Hanly
Sail through		Hamilton
Salamanca		Cotton
Salix flectitur sed non frangitur	*The willow bends but does not break*	De Salis.
Salus in fide	*Salvation by faith*	Magrath
Salus mea Christus	*Christ is my salvation*	Forbes
Salus per Christum	*Salvation through Christ*	Abernethy, Christian, Courtayne, Forbes, Stewart
Salus per Christum Redemptorem	*Salvation through Christ the Redeemer*	Steuart, Stewart, Stuart
Salutem disponit Deus	*God administers salvation*	Edgar
Salve me Deus	*God save me*	Spicrs
Salvus in igne	*Safe in the fire*	Trivett
Sancta clavis cœli fides	*Faith is the sacred key to heaven*	Sankey
Sanctitas	*Sanctity*	Cowan
Sanguine Christe tuo	*By thy blood, O Christ*	Bramhall
Sanguine inscribam .	*I will inscribe it with blood*	Buchanan
Sanguis et vulnera	*Blood and wounds*	Skinner
San Josef	*Without Joseph*	Nelson
Sans changer	*Without changing*	Burton, Cartwright Enery, Clark, Enery, Lefevre, Musgrave, Stanley, Wykeham
Sans changer ma vérité	*With changing my word*	Le Strange, L'Estrange
Sans charger	*Without overloading*	Eddisbury, Enery

Motto	Translation	Names
Sans crainte	*Without fear*	Gordon-Cumming, Sanderson, Tyrel, Tyrell.
Sans Dieu, je ne puis	*Without God I cannot*	Skipwith, Skipworth.
Sans Dieu rien	*Without God nothing*	Elsley, Godley, Hodgkinson, Peter, Petre, Petrie, Sanderson, Saunderson, Staples.
Sans mal	*Without evil*	Strickland.
Sans mauvais désir	*Without evil desire*	Constable.
Sans peur	*Without fear*	Arneel, Arneil, Arnied, Hagart, Hogart, Karr, Sutherland.
Sans reculer jamais	*Without ever drawing back*	Brackenbury.
Sans tache	*Without stain*	Hurry, Le Blanc, Mackenzie, Martin, Moray, Murray, Naper, Napier, Preston, Ure, Urie, Urrie, Urry.
Sans variance et mon droit	*Without change, and for my right*	Bowes.
Sans varier	*Without change*	Charlton, Cunningham.
Sapere aude	*Dare to be wise*	Amos, Caldwell, Hodder, Marshall, Meredith, Parker, Walker, Whitington, Wise, Withington, Wyse.
Sapere aude et tace	*Dare to be wise, and say nothing*	Hesse.
Sapere aude, incipe	*Dare to be wise, begin*	Birney, Burney, Burnie, Claxson.
Sapere et tacere	*Be wise and say nothing*	Broadhurst.
Sapiens dominabitur astris	*The wise man shall rule over the stars*	Comber, Haly.
Sapiens et justus	*Wise and just*	Gush.
Sapiens non eget	*The wise man wanteth not*	Dunbar.
Sapiens qui assiduus	*He is wise who is assiduous*	Drinkwater, Lawe, Mitchell, Sperling, Sykes.
Sapiens qui vigilat	*He is wise who watches*	Fowler.
Sapienter et pie	*Wisely and piously*	Park.
Sapienter si sincere	*Wisely, if sincerely*	Davidson.
Sapienter uti bonis	*Wisely to enjoy blessings*	Butler.
Sapientia donum Dei	*Wisdom is the gift of God*	Field.
Sapientia domus erecta est	*The house is built up by wisdom*	Clippingdale.
Sapientia et veritas	*Wisdom and truth*	Akers-Douglas, Douglas.
Sapientia et virtus	*Wisdom and virtue*	Douglas.
Sapientia tutus	*Safe by wisdom*	Crewdson.
Sapit qui Deo sapit	*He is wise who is wise through God*	Wiseman.
Sapit qui laborat	*He who labours is wise*	Dunbar.
Sapit qui reputat	*He who considers is wise*	M'Clellan, M'Clelland, Macklellan, Maclellan, M'Lellan.
Sat amico si mihi felix	*Enough for my friend, if happy for me*	Law.
Sat cito si sat bene	*Quick enough if well enough*	Colman.
Sat cito si sat tuto	*Quick enough if safe enough*	Clerk.
Satis est prostrasse leoni	*It is enough to have crouched to the lion*	Salusbury.
Satis imperat qui sibi est imperiosus	*He commands enough who has dominion over himself*	Haultain.
Save me, Lord		Corbet.
Savoir pouvoir	*Knowledge is power*	Hodge.
Saw through		Hamilton.
Say and do		Everard.
Scandit sublimia	*It scales great heights*	Crumpe.
Scandit sublimia virtus	*Virtue scales great heights*	Crumpe.
Scientiæ laborisque memor	*Mindful of knowledge and labour*	Hutchison.
Scienter utor	*I use skilfully*	Forbes.
Scio cui confido	*I know in whom I trust*	Grundy.
Scio cui credidi	*I know in whom I have believed*	Milnes, Milnes-Gaskell.
Scire sapere facere	*To know, to be wise, and to do*	Cobham.
Scite citissime certe	*Skilfully, quickly, surely*	Havergal.
Scopus vitæ Christus	*Christ is the aim of my life*	Menzies.
Scripta manent	*What is written remains*	Young.
Scuto amoris divini	*By the shield of divine love*	Jackson, O'Melaghlin, Scudamore.
Scuto amoris divino	*By the shield of divine love*	Scudamore.
Scuto divino	*With the divine shield*	Kay, Zephane, Zephani.
Scuto fidei	*With the shield of faith*	Morris.
Scuto magis quam gladio	*With the shield more than the sword*	Shield.
Scutum meum Jehova	*Jehovah is my shield*	Corry.
Sea or land		Essington.
Secret et hardi	*Secret and resolute*	Rice.
Secum cuique	*To everyone with himself*	Thomson.
Secunda alite	*Under a favourable omen*	Latham.
Secundat vera fides	*Real fidelity prospers*	Ogilvie, Ogilvy.
Secundis dubiisque rectus	*Upright in prosperity and in perils*	Duncan, Fitz Roy, Lippincott.
Secundo curo	*I further, I am careful*	Buchanan.
Secura frugalitas	*Frugality is secure*	Mitchell.
Secura quæ prudentes	*What prudent people do is secure*	Gray.
Secure amid perils		Henderson.
Secure vivere mors est	*To live carelessly is death*	Dayrell.
Securior quo paratior	*The better prepared, the more secure*	Johnston, Johnstone,
Securis fecit securum	*The axe makes secure*	Luxmore.
Securitate	*By security*	Roberton, Robertstown.
Securum præsidium	*The fortress is secure*	Craigdaillie, Craigie.

Securus	*Secure*	Yates
Secus rivos aquarum	*By rivers of waters*	Rivers
Se defendendo	*By defending himself*	Beebee, Eccles, Ecles, Ekles, Legge
Sed sine labe decus	*But it is honour without a stain*	Scott
Sed soli Deo	*But to God alone*	Buckley
Sedule et prospere	*Diligently and prosperously*	White
Sedule et secunde	*Diligently and successfully*	Lockyer
Sedulitate	*By diligence*	Divie, Divvie, Elphingston, Nicol
Sedulo et honeste	*With diligence and honour*	Baker, Lyal, Lyall, Lyle
Sedulo et honeste tutela	*Guardianship with honour and diligence*	Lyell
Sedulo numen	*God is with the diligent*	Harrower, Harrowing
Sedulo numen adest	*God is with the diligent*	Cunninghame, Harrower
Sedulus et audax	*Diligent and resolute*	Mellship, Rutherford, Rutherfurd, Seaton
Seek peace and ensure it		Page
Seek quiet		Deacon
Seigneur je te prie, garde ma vie	*Lord, I beseech thee, save my life*	Brettell, Henzell, Pidcock, Tyzack
Se inserit astris	*He installs himself among the stars*	Crosse, Goss, Hamilton
Semel et semper	*Once and always*	Allcard, Swinburne
Semi mortuus qui timet	*He is half dead who fears*	Cromwell
Semni ne semni	*I can do nothing without God*	Dering
Semper apparatus	*Always prepared*	Stuart
Semper constans	*Always constant*	Dymond
Semper constans et fidelis	*Always constant and faithful*	Irton, Lynch, Mellor, Spoor
Semper constanter	*Always with constancy*	Greenhut
Semper eadem	*Always the same.*	Carrol, Colamore, Collomore, Dockrell, Fairbairn, Forester, Gouch, Harvey, Hornsey, Panton, Reid
Semper erectus	*Always erect*	Pepper
Semper et ubique fidelis	*Always and everywhere faithful*	De Burgh
Semper fidelis	*Always faithful*	Arding, Barbenson, Barbeson, Bonner, Broadmead, Brown, Bruce, Cairns, Carnegie, Chesterman, Cuthbert-Kearney, Dick, Dickins, Duffield, Edge, Formby, Frith, Garrett, Haslett, Houlton, Kearney, Lund, Lynch, Marriott, Nicholls, Onslow, Pollexfen, Smith, Steele, Stewart, Stirling, Taylor, Tiuell, Wilcoxon
Semper fidelis esto	*Be always faithful*	Spence
Semper fidelis et audax	*Always faithful and brave*	Moore, O'More
Semper fidus	*Always true*	Garvine, Leitch, Leith
Semper floreat	*Let it flourish for ever*	Inverarity
Semper idem	*Always the same*	Garfit, Harvey
Semper in tempore	*Always in time*	Randles
Semper liber	*Always free*	Stephens
Semper meliora spero	*Always for better things I hope*	Hughes
Semper otium rogo divos	*I always ask leisure from the gods*	Everest
Semper parere	*To be obedient always*	Hanson.
Semper parati	*Always prepared*	Fraser, Frazer
Semper paratus	*Always ready*	Armitage, Armytage, Clifford, Constable, Dallas, Dodds, Elphinstone, Fuller, Galt, Hislop, Johns, Johnston, Johnstone, Knowles, Lecky, Macreadie, Macready, Mounsey, Phillips, Phillpots, Postlethwaite, Purchas, Roydes, Royds, Smith, Stewart, Stuart, Studholme, Upton, Usticke, Welles, Wells
Semper paratus pugnare pro patria	*Always ready to fight for my country*	Lockhart
Semper patriæ servire præsto	*Be always ready to serve your country*	MacGeoghegan
Semper præcinctus	*Always girt*	Mulholland
Semper pugnare paratus	*Always ready to fight*	Litchfield, Macdonald
Semper sapit suprema	*Is always supremely wise*	Selby
Semper sic	*Always thus*	Johnson
Semper sitiens	*Always thirsty*	Drought
Semper spero meliora	*I always hope for better things*	Pringle
Semper sursum	*Always upward*	Graham, Messent, Weston, Wood
Semper ut te digna sequare	*That you may always follow things worthy of you*	Vernon
Semper verus	*Always true*	Home, Howe
Semper victor	*Always a conqueror.*	Ramsay
Semper vigilans	*Always watchful*	Bourne, Harland, Hopley, Hughes, Otway, Rostron, Walker, Williams, Wilson
Semper virens	*Always flourishing*	Broadwood
Semper virescens.	*Always flourishing*	Hamilton
Semper virescet virtus	*Virtue will always flourish*	Marishall, Marsball.
Semper virescit virtus	*Virtue always flourishes*	Lind
Semper viridis	*Always green*	Green, Maxwell
Semper virtute constans	*Always constant in virtue*	Beaven, Bevan
Semper virtute vivo	[illegible]	[illegible]
Sempre fidèle	[illegible]	[illegible]
Sempre in un modo	[illegible]	[illegible]

Motto	Translation	Names
Se negare est amare	*To love is to deny one's self*	Roberts.
Sepulto viresco	*I grow green when buried*	Græme, Graham, Messent.
Sequamur	*Let us follow*	Oswald.
Sequere me est voluntas Dei	*Follow me, it is the will of God*	Baldwin.
Sequitando si giunge	*By pursuing one attains*	Lambert.
Sequitur patrem non passibus æquis	*He follows his father with unequal steps*	Wilson.
Sequitur vestigia patrum	*He follows the steps of his fathers*	Irvine.
Sequitur victoria fortes	*Victory follows the brave*	Campbell.
Sequor	*I follow*	Campbell, Gordon, MacInroy.
Sequor, nec inferior	*I follow, yet am not inferior*	Crewe.
Sera deshormais hardi	*Be always courageous*	Hardie.
Ser libre o morir	*Freedom or death*	Hamilton.
Sermoni consona facta	*Actions in harmony with our words*	Collins, Trelawney, Trelawny.
Sero sed serio	*Late, but in earnest*	Cecil, Gair, Ker, Kerr, M'Donnell, Nairn, Romanes.
Serpentes velut et columbæ	*Like serpents and doves*	Enys.
Servabit me semper Jehova	*Jehovah will always preserve me*	Barclay.
Servabo fidem	*I will keep faith*	Dutton, Johnston, Taylor.
Serva fidem	*Keep faith*	Corfield, Sandberg.
Serva jugum	*Keep the yoke*	Hay, Hay-Dalrymple, Nuttall.
Serva jugum sub jugo	*Keep the yoke under the yoke*	Hay.
Servare modum	*To observe the middle way*	Earle, Folke.
Servare munia vitæ	*To observe the duties of life*	Oglander.
Servata fides cinere	*The promise made to the ashes of my forefathers has been kept*	Calvert, Lloyd-Verney, Minors, Ryder, Verney, Welfitt, Wellfitt.
Servatum cineri	*Faith kept with the dead*	Prevost.
Serve the King		Bennet.
Serviendo	*By serving*	Simeon.
Serviendo guberno	*I govern by serving*	O'Rorke.
Servire Deo aspere	*To serve God severely*	Sadleir.
Servire Deo regnare est	*To serve God is to rule*	Middleton.
Servitute clarior	*More illustrious by serving*	Player.
Servus servorum Dei	*Servant of the servants of God*	Connell.
Set on		Campbell, Seton.
Seur et loyal	*Sure and loyal*	Colbarne.
Sfida e commanda	*He challenges and commands*	Metaxa-Anzolato.
Shanet a boo		Dalton-Fitzgerald, Fitzgerald, Fitz-Gerald, Vesey-Fitzgerald.
Shee ec y jerrey	*Peace at the last*	Gell.
Shenichun Erin	*The tradition of Ireland*	M'Carthy.
Sherwoode		Hood.
Shoot thus		Yeoman.
Sibi constet	*Let him be firmly resolved*	Richardson.
Sic ad astra	*This way to the stars*	M'Barnet.
Sica inimicis	*A dagger to his enemies*	M'Loskey.
Sic bene merenti palma	*The palm to him who so well merits it*	Palmer.
Sic cuncta caduca	*All things are thus fading*	Henderson.
Sic cuncta nobilitat	*Thus he ennobles all*	Henderson.
Sic curre ut comprendas	*So run that you may obtain*	Stevenson.
Sic donec	*Thus until*	Egerton, Jobb, Jopp, Le Hardy.
Si celeres quatit pennas	*If he shakes his swift wings*	Parkinson-Fortescue.
Sic fidem teneo	*Thus I keep my faith*	Molesworth, Welford, Welsford.
Sic fidus et robor	*Thus true and strong*	Stirling.
Sic fuit, est, et erit	*Thus it was, is, and shall be*	Stewart.
Sic his qui diligunt	*Thus to those who love*	Norris.
Sic itur ad astra	*This is the way to the stars*	Ballenden, Davies-Lloyd, Day, Fitzgerald-Day, Hollins, M'Dowall, Mackenzie, M'Kenzie, Martin, Martyn, Ochterlony, Rivett-Carnac, Watkins.
Sic itur in altum	*This is the way to heaven*	Cowan.
Sicker		Douglas.
Sic limina tuta	*In this way our homes are safe*	Elliott.
Sic, nos sic sacra tuemur	*Thus we guard our sacred rights*	Macmahon, M'Mahon.
Sic olim	*Thus formerly*	Humphrey.
Sic paratior	*Thus more ready*	Johnston, Johnstone.
Sic parvis magna	*Thus great things from small*	Drake.
Sic rectius progredior	*Thus I go more honourably*	Sinclair.
Sic sustenta crescit	*Thus supported it grows*	Gervais.
Sic te non videmus olim	*We did not see thee thus formerly*	Playfair.
Sic tutus	*Thus safe*	Gordon.
Sicut aquilæ pennis	*As on eagle's wings*	Niblett.
Sicut iris florebit	*He will flourish as the lily*	Bor.
Sicut oliva virens, lætor in æde Dei	*Like the green olive-tree, I rejoice in the house of God*	Oliver.
Sicut quercus	*As the oak*	Challoner.
Sicut serimus sic metimus	*Just as we sow we reap*	Wood.
Sic virescit industria	*Thus industry flourishes*	Stewart.
Sic virescit virtus	*Thus virtue flourishes*	Ronald.
Sic viresco	*Thus I flourish*	Christie, Christie-Miller, Christy, Miller
Sic viret virtus	*So virtue flourishes*	Anderson.

Sic vita humana	*Such is life*	Capel
Sic vivere, vivetis	*Thus to live, ye shall live*	Bunce
Sic volvere parcas	*So the Fates determine*	Reeves
Sic vos, non vobis	*So you, not for yourselves*	Franks, Walpole, Walrond
Si Deus nobiscum	*If God be with us*	Hughes, Parry
Si Deus nobiscum, quis contra nos?	*If God be with us, who can be against us?*	Donaldson, Mairis, Morris, Otway
Si Deus pro nobis, quis contra nos?	*If God be for us, who can be against us?*	Caldicote
Si Deus, quis contra?	*If God is for us, who is against us?*	Benson, Dawson, M'Elligott, Spence, Spens
Si Dieu veult	*If God wishes*	Preston
Sidus adsit amicum	*Let a friendly star be with you*	Bateman, La Trobe Bateman, Pynsent Martindale, Scott
Si fractus fortis	*Though broken, brave*	Foster
Signantur cuncta manu	*All things are sealed with the hand*	Greig
Signum pacis amor	*Love is the token of peace.*	Bell
Signum quærens in vellere	*Seeking a sign in a fleece*	Clarke
Si je n'estoy	*If I were not*	Curwen
Si je pouvois	*If I could*	Cleland
Si je puis	*If I can*	Cahun, Colquhoun, Fyre, Eyres, Gahn, Livingston, Livingstone, Radcliffe
Silentio et spe	*With silence and hope*	Brandei
S'ils te mordent mord les	*If they bite you, bite them*	Morley
Similis frondescit virga metallo	*The twig grows covered with leaves like metal*	Calmady
Si monent tubæ, paratus	*Prepared when the trumpets warn*	Sissons
Simplex munditiis	*Plain and neat*	Philips, Symonds, Symons-Soltan
Simplex vigilium veri	*The simple defence of truth*	Perkins
Simplices sicut pueri sagaces sicut serpentes	*Simple as boys, wise as serpents*	Vaughan
Sinceritas.	*Sincerity*	Short, Hazard
Sinceritate	*With sincerity*	Francklin
Sine clade sterno	*I prostrate without injuring*	Thicknesse
Sine crimine fiat	*Let it be done without crime*	Innes
Sine Deo frustra	*Without God, in vain*	Gill, Gull
Sine Deo nihil	*Nothing without God*	Hallen, Litster
Sine dolo	*Without guile*	Lewis
Sine fine	*Without end*	M'Gill
Sine fraude fides	*Faith without deceit*	Johnston, Johnstone
Sine injuria	*Without injury*	Watson.
Sine labe decus	*Honour without stain*	Allen
Sine labe fides	*Faith without dishonour*	Lockhart
Sine labe lucebit	*He shall shine without dishonour*	Crawford, Crawfurd
Sine labe nota	*Noted without dishonour*	Crawford, Crawfurd, M'Kenzie, Pollok
Sine macula	*Without stain*	Carey, Cary, Clough, Flint, M'Culloch, Mackenzie, Norcliffe, Siborne, Synnott
Sine macula macla	*Stained without stain*	Clough
Sine metu	*Without fear*	Jameson, Meres
Sine numine nihilum	*Without the Deity nothing*	Jones
Sine pondere sursum	*Upwards without weight*	Panton
Sine sanguine victor	*A conqueror without blood*	Smith
Sine sole nihil	*Nothing without the sun*	Pettegrew
Sine stet viribus	*Can stand with power*	Abinger
Sine timore	*Without fear*	Cormack, M'Cormack, Owers.
Singula cum valeant sunt meliora simul	*When they are strong separately they are more so together*	Stuart
Singulariter in spe	*Singly in hope*	Leacher
Sin not		Synnott
Si non consilio impetu	*If not by stratagem by assault*	Agnew
Si non datur ultra	*If more is not permitted*	Williams
Sionnach aboo	*The fox to victory*	Fox
Sioth chain agus fairsinge	*Peace and plenty*	Kavanagh
Si possim	*If I can*	Learmonth, Livingstone
Si pouvois	*If I could*	Cleland
Si recte facies	*If you will do rightly*	Drummond
Sis fortis	*Be thou brave*	Lindsay
Si sit prudentia	*If there be prudence*	Brown, Eden
Sis justus nec timeas	*Be just, and fear not*	Garvey
Sis justus, et ne timeas	*Be just and fear not*	White
Si sonent tubæ paratus	*If the trumpets sound I am ready*	Sisson
Sis pius in primis	*Be pious first of all*	Barlow
Sit Deus in studiis	*Let God be amid my studies.*	Sydenham
Sit dux sapientia	*Wisdom be our guide*	Woodroffe
Sit fors ter felix	*May your fate be thrice happy*	Forster
Sit laus Deo	*Let praise be to God*	Arbuthnot.
Sit mihi libertas	*Liberty be mine*	Findlater
Sit nomen decus	*Let the name be a glory*	Swan
Sit ordo in omnibus	*Let there be order in all things*	De Teissier.
Sit saxum firmum	*Let the stone be firm*	Saxby

Motto	Translation	Names
Sit sine labe	*Let it be without stain*	Scott
Sit sine labe fides	*Let faith be without stain*	Lockhart, Peters
Sit sine labe fines	*May my end be without stain*	Peters.
Sit sine spina	*Let it be thornless*	Cay
Sit vita nomini congrua	*May our life be like our name*	Christie
Sit vult Deus	*Be it, God wills it*	Kempsey
Skagh M'Enchroe		Crowe
Slabo	*I shall stand*	Hawthorn
Sobrie, pie, juste	*Soberly, piously, righteously*	Middleton
Sobrii este vigilantes	*Be well advised by watching*	Geekie
So dorn dona dhubhfuiltibh		MacMahon
So fork forward		Cunninghame.
So ho ho dea ne		Comerford
Soies content	*Be content*	Downes
Sola bona quæ honesta	*These things alone are good which are honorable*	Archer, Colebrook, Colebrooke
Sola cruce	*In the cross only*	Best
Sola cruce salus	*Safety in the cross only*	Barclay
Sola in Deo salus	*Safety in God alone*	Montague, Robinson
Sola juvat virtus	*Virtue alone avails*	Stewart, Stuart
Solamen	*Consolation*	Hope.
Sola meus turris Deus	*God is my only fortress*	Baker
Sola nobilitat virtus	*Virtue alone ennobles*	Hamilton, Moubrav, Mowbray
Sola proba quæ honesta .	*The things which are honourable alone are good*	Neave
Sola salus servire Deo .	*To serve God is the only salvation .*	Gore, M'Genis, Magenis
Sola virtus invicta	*Virtue alone is invincible*	Eyre, Eyres, Haig, Haige, Howard, Miles, Waud
Sola virtus munimentum	*Virtue alone is our stronghold.*	Mason
Sola virtus nobilitat	*Virtue alone ennobles*	Henderson, Mitchell
Sola virtus reddit nobilem	*Virtue alone renders noble*	Storey
Sola virtus tedit nobilem		Shaw-Storey
Sola virtus triumphat	*Virtue alone triumphs*	Carvile
Solem contemplor, despicio terram	*I gaze on the sun, and despise the earth.*	Bedingfield
Solem fero	*I endure the sun*	Aubrey, Berrington
Solem ferre possum	*I can endure the sun*	Davies
So'ertia ditat	*Skill enriches*	Whitelaw
Sol et scutum Deus	*God is a sun and shield*	Pearson
Soli Deo gloria	*Glory to God alone*	Bontein, Bonteine, Lesly
Soli Deo honor	*Honour to God alone*	Stewart
Soli Deo honor et gloria	*Honour and glory to God alone*	Huddleston
Sol meus testis	*The sun my witness*	Boehm
Solo Deo gloria	*Glory through God only*	Beste, Digby Beste
Solo Deo salus	*Safety through God only*	Montagu
Sol re mi fa		Bull
Sol tibi signa dabit	*The sun will show signs to thee*	Stewart
Solus Christus mea rupes	*Christ alone is my rock*	Orrock
Solus inter plures	*I am alone among many*	Forbes
Solus inter plurimos.	*I am alone among very many.*	Forbes
Solus mihi invidus obstat	*He alone enviously withstands me*	Nott
Solus per Christum Redemptorem	*Alone by Christ the Redeemer .*	Stewart
Sors est contra me	*Fate is against me*	Lewis.
Sors mihi grata cadet	*A pleasant lot shall fall to me*	Skeen, Skene
Sors omnia versat	*Fate whirls everything about*	Philip
Sorte contentus	*Content with my lot*	Welby
Sorte sua contentus	*Content with his lot*	Hartwell.
Sorti æquus utrique	*Equal to each condition*	Maclean
So run that you may obtain		Baker
Souvenez	*Remember*	Graham
Soyez compatissant soyez courtois	*Be pitiful, be courteous*	Curtoys
Soyez content	*Be content*	Charnocke
Soyez courtois	*Be courteous*	Curtoys
Soyez ferme	*Be steadfast*	Butler, Foljambe, Hyde, Needham
Soyez sage	*Be wise*	Eliott.
Soyez sage et semple	*Be wise and simple*	Spry
Spare not		Giffard, Macgregor
Spare nought		Baird Hay, Gifford, Hay
Spare when you have nought		Gifford
Spe	*By hope*	Horrocks, Lovatt
Spe aspera levat	*He eases difficulties by hope*	Ross
Spectemur agendo .	*Let us be judged by our actions*	Agar Boyle, Browne, Dale, Drumson, Duckett, Elles, Elvin, Francis, Hartley, Hussey, Lloyd, M'Clure, M'Leur, M'Lure, Montague, Montagu Scott, Morris, Mott, Pollock, Reid, Rutson, Scott-Montagu, Slesser, Thornbrough, Vigors
Speed		Garnock
Speed well		Spied
Spe et am[illegible]	*[illegible]*	Fisher
Spe et in[illegible]	*[illegible]*	[illegible], Wallace

Spe et labore	*By hope and labour*	Bladen, Jebb
Spe expecto	*I wait in hope*	Forbes, Leslie, Livingstone
Spe gaudeo	*I rejoice in hope*	Macartney
Spei bonæ atque animi	*Of good hope and courage*	Millar, Miller
Spe labor levis	*Labour is light by hope*	Hill, Page
Spe meliore vehor	*I am borne along by a better hope*	Bogle
Spem fortuna alit	*Fortune nourishes hope*	Balfour - Kinnear, Kinnear, Petree, Petrie
Spem pretio non emam	*I will not purchase mere hope*	Beck
Spem renovant alæ	*Its wings renew its hope*	Norvill
Spem renovat	*It renews hope*	Grierson
Spem renovat anni	*It renews the hope of the year*	Grierson
Spem sequimur	*We follow hope*	Ellison
Spem successus alit	*Success nourishes hope*	Ross
Spem vigilantia firmat	*Vigilance strengthens hope.*	Dunbar
Spe posteri temporis	*In the hope of the future.*	Atcherly
Sperabo	*I will hope*	Annand, Pitcairn
Sperando spiro	*I breathe by hoping*	Silney, Young
Sperandum	*To be hoped for*	Rait, Scot
Sperandum est	*It is to be hoped.*	Crothers, Wallace
Sperans	*Hoping.*	Ellis
Sperans pergo	*I go hoping*	Fletcher, Tomkinson
Speranza e verita	*Hope and truth*	Pegler
Sperare timere est	*To hope is to fear*	Ratcliff
Sperate et vivite fortes	*Hope and live as brave men*	Bland
Sperate futurum	*Hope for the future*	Altree
Sperat infestis	*He hopes in adversity*	Colborne, Seaton
Speratum et completum	*Hoped for and realised*	Arnet, Arnot, Arnott, Arnut
Speravi	*I have hoped*	Lyon
Speravi in Domino .	*I have hoped in the Lord*	Hay
Speriamo		Prior
Spernit humum	*He despises the earth*	Forbes, M'Kindley, Mackinlay, Mitchell
Spernit pericula virtus	*Valour despises dangers*	Forrester, Ramsay
Sperno	*I despise*	Elleis, Ellis
Spero	*I hope*	Allan, Brown, Calderwood, Chalmers, Cuthbert, Dolling, Douglas, Forbes, Foster, Gib, Gordon, Hunter, Hutton, Langlands, Learmont, Learmonth, Leveson, Martin, Menzies, O'Toole, Schank, Shank, Sparrow, Warner, Waters
Spero dum spiro	*I hope while I breathe*	Chambers
Spero et captivus nitor	*I hope and as a captive strive.*	Devenish
Spero et progredior	*I hope and advance*	Pringle.
Spero et vivo	*I hope and live*	Mashiter
Spero in Deo	*I hope in God*	Blackie, O'Crauley, Parnall, Powell
Spero infestis, metuo secundis	*I hope in adversity, and fear in prosperity*	Ellerton, Ludlow, Riley, Stewart
Spero meliora	*I hope for better things*	Ainsworth, Baillie, Blyth, Darby, Douglas, Eccleston, Fairholm, French, Graham, Greaves, Hill, Hobhouse, Kirkwood, Laird, Lowe, Maxwell, Moffat, Moffatt, Montgomery, Murray, Philips, Phillips, Rait, Rhet, Rodie, Roper-Curzon, Samwell-Watson, Sandilands, Shaw, Stewart, Swan, Troughton
Spero procedere	*I hope to prosper*	Hopkirk
Spero suspiro donec	*While I breathe I hope*	Hope
Spero ut fidelis	*I hope as faithful*	Baskerville-Mynors, Mynors
Spes	*Hope*	Gaskell, Wyllie
Spes alit	*Hope nourishes*	Child
Spes alit agricolam	*Hope sustains the husbandman*	Huskisson
Spes anchora tuta	*Hope is a safe anchor*	Dunmore, Dunmure, Dunsmure
Spes anchora vitæ.	*Hope is the anchor of life*	M'Leay
Spes aspera levat	*Hope lightens dangers*	Ross
Spes audaces adjuvat	*Hope assists the brave*	Holles, Hollis
Spes dabit auxilium	*Hope will give help*	Dunbar
Spes decus et robor	*Hope, honour, and strength*	Eardley, Smith
Spes durat avorum	*The hope of my ancestors endures*	Nassau, Walmesley
Spes est in Deo	*Hope is in God*	Bagge, Meredith
Spes et fides	*Hope and faith*	Chamberlain, Clauson, Lucas, Whitaker
Spes et fortuna	*Hope and fortune*	Thesiger
Spes et fortitudo .	*Hope and fortitude*	Mair
Spes firma	*My hope is firm*	Tytler
Spes in Domino	*My hope is in the Lord*	Hardy
Spes in extremum	*Hope in extremity*	Short
Spes in futuro	*My hope is in the future*	Wadge
Spes juvat.	[illegible]	[illegible]

Motto	Translation	Families
Spes labor levis	*Hope is light labour*	Bigland, Ouchterlony
Spes lucis æternæ	*The hope of eternal life*	Black, Pitcairn
Spes magna in Deo	*Great hope is in my God.*	Meiklejohn
Spes mea Christus	*Christ is my hope*	Bingham, Weeden
Spes mea Christus est	*Christ is my hope*	Powell
Spes mea cœlo	*My hope is in heaven*	Abbey
Spes mea Deus	*God is my hope.*	Broke, Brooke, Borlace, Borlacy, Hackett, Hoole, Moore, O'Ferral
Spes mea in cœlis	*My hope is in Heaven*	Boyd, Mellor
Spes mea in cœlo	*My hope is in Heaven*	Marshall
Spes mea in cruce unica	*My hope is in the cross alone*	Martin
Spes mea in Deo	*My hope is in God*	Blewitt, Brooke, Dewhurst, Gaskell, Gillett, Goskar, Grattan-Guinness, Greaves, Guinness, Kirkwood, Lethbridge, Lewin, Roper, Roper Curzon, Saunders, Stieglitz, Wainwright, Ward
Spes mea in futuro est	*My hope is in the future*	Robinson
Spes mea, res mea	*My hope, my estate*	Drummond
Spes mea superne	*My hope is from above*	Bruce
Spes melioris ævi	*The hope of a better time*	Rees
Spes meum solatium	*Hope is my consolation*	Cushney
Spes non fracta	*Hope is not broken*	Jones-Bateman
Spes, salus, decus	*Hope, safety, honour*	Nesham
Spes sibi quisque	*Every one has his own hope*	Bulwer
Spes tamen infracta	*Yet hope is unbroken*	Hope
Spes tutissima cœlis	*The safest hope is in Heaven*	King, King-Tenison, Price, Tenison
Spes ultra	*Hope is beyond*	Nairn, Nairne
Spes unica virtus	*Hope my only virtue*	Price
Spes vincit thronum	*Hope wins a throne*	Winthrop
Spes vitæ melioris	*The hope of a better life*	Broughton, Hobhouse
Spe tutiores armis	*Safer with hope than with arms*	Lewis, Lewys
Spe verus	*True in hope*	Scott.
Spe vires augentur	*Strength is increased by hope*	Black, Scott
Spe vitæ melioris	*In hope of a better life*	Lea
Spe vivitur	*Lives on hope*	Dobree, Dorrel
Spiritus gladius	*The sword of the Spirit*	Hutton
Spiritus gladius verbum Dei	*The sword of the spirit is the Word of God*	Franks
Splendeo tritus	*I shine by being rubbed*	Ferrers
Sponti favus, ægro spicula	*Honey to the willing, thorns to the unwilling*	Suttie
S'rioghal mo dhream	*My race is royal*	Greg, M'Alpin, Macgregor, M'Gregor, M'Grigor
Stabilitate et victoria	*By steadfastness and victory*	Simmons
Stabilis	*Firm*	Grant
Stabit	*He shall stand*	Grant
Stabit conscius æqui	*He shall stand that is conscious of rectitude*	Charlton, Dalton, Grant
Stabo	*I shall stand*	Accorne, Hawthorne, Kinninmond
Standard		Kidder
Stand fast		Dougal, Grant, Grant-Ogilvie
Stand fast Craig Elachie		Grant
Stand sure		Adson, Anderson, Crechton, Crichton, Glenelg, Grant, Ponton
Stans cum Rege	*Standing with the King*	Chadwick
Stant cætera tigno	*The rest stand on a beam*	Gordon
Stant innixa Deo	*They stand depending upon God*	Crawford, Crawfurd
Stare super vias antiquas	*To stand upon the old paths*	Angell, Bayning, Docker, Powlett, Townshend
Stat felix amico Domino	*His happiness is established under the favour of the Lord*	Steuart, Stewart
Stat fortis in fide	*He stands firm in faith*	Rochfort
Stat fortuna domus	*The good fortune of the house stands*	Gay, Guy, Howes, Howse
Stat fortuna domus virtute	*The fortune of the house stands by its virtue*	Molyneux
Stat gratia facti	*It stands for the sake of the deed*	Taylour
Stat nominis umbra	*Stands the shadow of a name*	Stafford
Stat promissa fides	*Promised faith abides*	Leslie, Lesly
Stat religione parentum	*Stands in the religion of parents*	Lucas.
Stat sua cuique dies	*Each has his day*	Windley
Stat veritas	*Truth stands*	Sandeman
St. Domingo		Louis
Steadfast		Mansfield, Mansel.
Steady		Aylmer, Dalrymple, Hood, Lort, Mac Adam, M'Adam, Northey, Verelst, Weller, Yonge
Steel to the back		Steel
Steer steady		Donaldson
Stella Christi duce	*With the star of Christ for guide*	Sohier
Stella futura micat divino lumine	*The star of the future twinkles with a divine light*	Taylour
Stellis aspirate gemellis	*Aspire to the twin stars*	Twyning

Stemmata quid faciunt?	*What does lineage avail?*	Baggallay, Meyrick, Stewart, Windsor
Stet	*Let it stand*	Standbridge
Stet fortuna domus	*May the fortune of the house remain*	Arthur, Strange, Wintle
Stet non timeat	*Let him stand and not fear*	Bindon
Still bydand		Gordon
Still without fear		Sutherland
Stimulat, sed ornat	*It stimulates, but it adorns*	M'Cartnay, MacCartney, Mackartney
Stire steddie		Donaldson
Sto cado fide et armis	*I stand and fall by faith and arms*	Farquhar Farquhar Gray
Sto mobilis	*I stand movable*	Drummond.
Sto ne per vim sed per jus	*I stand not by strength, but by right*	Stone
Sto pro fide	*I stand for the faith*	MacFarquhar
Sto pro veritate	*I stand for truth*	Guthrie, Guthry, Lingard Guthrie
Strength		Armstrong
Strength is from heaven		Grubb
Strenue et audacter	*Strenuously and bravely*	Wood
Strenue et honeste	*Strenuously and honourably*	Jackson
Strenue et prospere	*Strenuously and prosperously*	Eamer
Strenue insequor	*I follow strenuously*	Luke
Stricta parata neci	*Drawn and ready for death*	Budge
Strike		Dasent, Hawke, Mundell
Strike alike		Lauder
Strike, Dakyns, the devil's in the hempe		Dakyns, Deakin.
Strike sure		Greig, Grieg
Strioghal mo dhream	*My race is royal*	M'Gregor
Strong and firm		Wolrige
Struggle		Brise Ruggles.
Studendo et contemplando inde fessus	*Wearied by study and contemplation*	Cardale
Studiis et rebus honestis	*By learning and virtue*	Dunning
Study quiet		Head, Heady, Patrick
St Vincent		Radstock, Waldgrave
Sua gratia parvis	*Little things have a beauty of their own*	Little
Sua præmia virtus	*Virtue is its own reward*	M'Cartney
Suaviter	*Gently*	Harwood
Suaviter et fortiter	*Mildly and firmly*	Daubeney, Elliot-Murray Kynynmound, Rathbone
Suaviter in modo	*Gently in manner*	Churchward
Suaviter in modo, fortiter in re	*Mildly in manner, boldly in action*	Beevor, Caron, Nunn, Rathbone, Wynn
Suaviter sed fortiter	*Mildly but firmly*	Adams, Busk, Dennis, Williams, Wood
Sub cruce candida	*Under the white cross*	Arden, Perceval, Percival
Sub cruce candor	*Sincerity under the cross*	Perceval
Sub cruce copia	*Plenty under the cross*	Cross
Sub cruce glorior	*I glory under the cross*	Astell
Sub cruce lux	*Light under the cross*	Donaldson
Sub cruce salus	*Salvation under the cross*	Capron, Fletcher, Pierce, Ward
Sub cruce semper viridis	*Under the cross always green*	Shrubb
Sub cruce veritas	*Truth under the cross*	Adams
Sub cruce vinces	*Under the cross you shall conquer*	Norwood, Perceval
Subditus fidelis regis et salus regni	*A subject faithful to the King and the safety of the kingdom*	Carlos, Hopper
Sub hoc signo vinces	*Under this sign you shall conquer*	Brenan, Hartley, Helman-Pidsley, O'Brenan, Vaizey, Vassey, Vesey
Subimet merces industria	*Industry is its own reward*	Miller
Subito	*Suddenly*	Crinan, Cringan
Sub lege libertas	*Under the law, liberty*	Daniel
Sub libertate quietem	*Rest under liberty*	Burrel, Carter, Cay, Cosby, Hartstronge, Kay, Keay, Peter, Walsham
Sublime petimus	*We aim at high things*	Cleghorn
Sublimia cures	*Care for high things.*	Bowman
Sublimiora petamus	*Let us aim at loftier things*	Biddulph, Stonehouse, Stonhouse
Sublimiora peto	*I aim at higher things*	Jackson
Sublimiora quæro	*I seek higher things*	Wright
Sublimiora spectemus	*Let us look to higher things*	Warren
Sub montibus altis	*Under high mountains*	Skeen, Skene
Sub onere crescit	*He thrives under the burden*	Fergusson
Sub pace, copia	*Under peace, plenty*	Francklyn, Franco, Lopes
Sub pondere cresco	*I increase under weight*	Fleeming, Fleming
Sub pondere sursum	*In difficulty I look upward*	Porterfield
Sub robore virtus	*Virtue under strength*	Aikin, Aikman
Sub sole nihil	*Nothing under the sun*	Monteith, Menteth
Sub sole patebit	*It shall open under the sun*	Ellies, Ellis
Sub sole, sub umbra, crescens	*Increasing both in sunshine and in shade*	Irvine, Irving
Sub sole, sub umbra virens	*Flourishing both in sunshine and in shade*	Irvine, Irving, Irwine, Winter-Irving
Sub sole viresco	*I flourish under the sun*	Irvine
Sub spe	*In hope*	Cairns, Dunbar
Sub tegmine	*Under covert*	Gordon
Sub tegmine fagi	*Under the covert of the beech*	Beaufoy, Beech
Sub tigno salus	*Safety under the roof-tree*	Innes
Sub tutela Domini	*Under the protection of the Lord*	Spode
Sub umbra	[illegible]	[illegible]

Motto	Translation	Names
Sub umbra alarum tuarum	*Under the shadow of thy wings*	Lauder, Lawder, Williamson.
Sub umbra quies	*Rest under the shade*	Sharpe.
Sub umbra quiescam	*I will rest under the shade*	Fairn.
Successus a Deo est	*Success comes from God*	Roberts.
Suchet und werdet finden	*Seek and ye shall find*	Finden.
Suffer		Chinnery-Haldane, Gleneagles, Hadden, Haldane, Halden, Morison.
Suffibulatus majores sequor	*Harnessed I follow my ancestors*	Hawthorn, Stewart.
Sufficit meruisse	*It is enough to have deserved*	Plumptree, Plumtree.
Sui ipsius præmium	*His own reward*	Preston.
Sui oblitus commodi	*Forgetful of his own interest*	Asgile, Asgill.
Suis ducibus ubique fidelis	*Faithful everywhere to his chiefs*	Le Quesne.
Suis stat viribus	*He rests on his own strength*	Scarlett.
Suivant St. Pierre	*Following St. Peter*	Knight.
Suivez la raison	*Follow the right*	Armistead, Barberie, Barberrie, Brown, Browne.
Suivez moi	*Follow me*	Borough, Brown, Hawley.
Suivez raison	*Follow reason as your guide*	Armistead, Barberrie, Brown, Browne Dixon, Wyatt.
Sui victoria indicat regem	*Victory over self points out the king*	Rye.
Summis viribus	*With all one's might*	Harben.
Summum nec metuam diem nec optem	*Let me neither fear nor wish for the last day*	Tighe, Tighe-Bunbury.
Sum quod sum	*I am what I am*	Coldicott, Foresight.
Sumus ubi fuimus	*We are where we were*	Weare.
Sunt aliena	*They are foreign*	Fust.
Sunt sua præmia laude	*His rewards are with praise*	Barberrie, Brown, Pemberton.
Sunt tria hæc unum	*These three are one*	Morison.
Suo se robore firmat	*He strengthens himself by his own might*	Grant.
Suo stat robore virtus	*Virtue stands by its own strength*	Mowbray.
Supera audi et tace	*Hear celestial things and keep silence*	Hesse.
Superabit omnia virtus	*Virtue will conquer all things*	Rabett.
Superb		Keats.
Superba frango	*I humble proud things*	Macklellan, MacLagan, M'Lagan.
Superiora sequor	*I follow higher things*	Ramsay.
Superna quærite	*Seek things above*	Graves.
Superna quæro	*I seek heavenly things*	Greaves.
Superna sequor	*I follow heavenly things*	Ramsay, Wardrop.
Super sidera votum	*My desires extend beyond the stars*	Rattray, Watson.
Supra spem spero	*I hope beyond hope*	Jeffreys.
Suprema manus validior	*A hand stronger than the highest*	Merry.
Suprema quæro	*I seek the highest*	Greaves.
Sure		Le Sueur, Macdonald.
Sure and steadfast		Martin.
Sur espérance	*Upon hope*	Moir, Moncrief, Moncrieff, Moncrieffe, Steuart.
Sur et loyal	*Sure and loyal*	Wild.
Surgam	*I shall rise*	Hutchison.
Surge illuminare	*Rise to shine*	Scott.
Surgere tento	*I strive to rise*	Straton.
Surgite, lumen adest	*Arise, the light is near*	Glover.
Surgit post nubila Phœbus	*After clouds, rises the sun*	Constable.
Surgo, lumen adest	*I arise, light is near*	Lawson.
Sursum	*Upward*	Alston, Calandrine, Douglas, Hutcheson, Hutchison, Kilner, Marriott, Mongredien, Pringle, Roos, Rosse, Wills.
Sursum corda	*Hearts upward*	Howison, Huson, Langton, MacGillicuddy.
Sursum prorsusque	*Upward and onward*	Gill.
Sursum specto	*I look upwards*	Stronach.
Suscipere et finire	*To undertake and finish*	Bolckow.
Suspice	*Look up*	Edlin.
Sustentatus Providentia	*Upheld by Providence*	Rolland.
Sustento sanguine signa	*I bear the standards with blood*	Seaton, Seton.
Sustine, abstine	*Sustain, abstain*	Gairden.
Sustineatur	*Let him be sustained*	Cullum.
Sustine et abstine	*Sustain and abstain*	Garden, Kearney, Langley.
Sustineo sanguine signum	*I keep the standard in the midst of blood*	Seton.
Suum cuique	*To every one his own*	Bickersteth, Don, Every, Grant, Milne, Peshall, Russell, Thomson, Wingate.
Suum cuique tribue	*Give to every man his own*	Dunbar.
Suum cuique tribuens	*Giving to every man his own*	Younger.
Swift and sure		Hood.
Syn ar du hun	*Wonder at thyself*	Dewing, De Winton, Wilkins, Wilkins-Cann.

T

Motto	Translation	Names
Tace	*Keep silence*	Abercromby
Tace aut face	*Keep silence or do*	Burges, Marten, Scot, Scott
Tache sans tache .	*Spot without spot*	Carnagie, Carnegie, Carnegy-Watson, De Balinhard, Patterson.
Tak a thocht		Fairlie
Tak tent	*Take heed*	Crockat, Crockatt
Tam animo quam mente sublimis	*Exalted in soul as in mind* .	Forteath
Tam aris quam aratris	*As well by altars as ploughs*	Oxley
Tam arte, quam marte . .	*As well by art as strength*	Mill, Milne, M'Lea, Wright
Tam audax quam fidelis.	*As brave as faithful*	Roxburgh
Tam corde quam manu	*With the heart as well as with the hand*	Maynard
Tam fidus, quam fixus	*As faithful as firm*	Stewart
Tam genus, quam virtus	*Lineage as well as virtue*	Lunden, Lundin
Tam in arte, quam marte	*Both in skill and in force*	Milne
Tam interna, quam externa	*As well internal as external*	Arbuthnet, Arbuthnot.
Tam marte quam arte	*As much by war as by skill*	Logie, Milne
Tam pace quam prœlio	*In peace as well as in war*	Gordon
Tam virtus, quam honos	*As well virtue as honour*	Hamilton
Tam virtute, quam labore	*As well by virtue as labour*	Hamilton
Tandem	*At length*	Affleck, Cunningham, Cunninghame, Finnie, M'Vicar
Tandem fit arbor	*At length it becomes a tree*	Cuthbert, Hamilton
Tandem fit surculus arbor	*At length the sprig becomes a tree*	Burnet, Cuthbert, Douglas, Scrogie
Tandem implebitur	*At length he shall be filled*	Scougal, Simpson
Tandem licet sero	*It is allowed at length, but late*	Brown, Campbell
Tandem tranquillus	*Tranquil at length*	Symmer
Tanquam despicatus sum, vinco.	*Though I am despised, I conquer*	Grant
Tanti talem genuere parentes	*So mighty parents produced such a noble man*	Moray
Tant que je puis	*Such as I can*	Hilton, Johnson, Joliffe, Lawson
Tantum in superbos	*Only against the proud*	Jacob
Taurum cornibus prende	*Take the bull by the horns* .	Kettlewell
Te Deum laudamus.	*We praise thee, O God*	Harper, M'Whirter
Te digna sequere	*Follow things worthy of you* .	Borlase, Parnell
Te duce, gloriamur	*We glory under thy guidance*	Sinclair
Te duce, libertas	*Liberty under thy guidance*	Crosby
Te favente virebo	*Thou favouring me, I shall flourish*	Grant
Teg Yw Hedwsh	*Peace is pleasing*	Gilbert, Gilbert Davies
Teipsum nosce	*Know thyself*	Shaw
Téméraire	*Rash*	Harvey
Temere ne sperne	*Do not scorn rashly*	Bramble
Temperans et constans	*Temperate and steady*	Verschoyle
Temperat æquor	*The sea is calm*	Monypenny
Tempera te tempori	*Temper thyself to the times*	Le Maire
Templa quam delecta	*How lovely are thy temples*	Brydges, Grenville, Temple
Tempore candidior	*Become fairer by time*	Mair
Tempus et casus accidit omnibus	*Time and chance happen to all*	Wayne
Tempus meæ opes	*Time is my wealth*	Spofforth
Tempus omnia monstrat	*Time shows all things*	Lovell
Tempus omnia revelat	*Time reveals all things*	Atkinson
Tenax	*Firm*	Stirling
Tenax et fide	*Persevering and with faith*	Smith
Tenax et fidelis	*Persevering and faithful*	Abdy, Carington, Lane, Smith, Tennant
Tenax et fidus	*Firm and faithful*	Bookey
Tenax in fide	*Steadfast in the faith*	Bosanquet, Smith
Tenax propositi ...	*Tenacious of purpose* .	Carnduff, Gibbes, Gibbs, Gilbert, Elgood, Morley, Osborne Gibbes, Roundell, Taylor
Tenax propositi, vinco	*Firm in resolve, I conquer* .	Grimshaw
Tenche-brai		Tench
Tendens ad æthera virtus	*Virtue tending to the sky*	Lewthwaite
Tendimus	*We push forward*	Craik
Tendimus ad cœlum	*We press forward to heaven* .	McCowan
Tending to peace		Leathes
Tendit ad astra	*He presses towards heaven*	Maxwell
Tendit ad astra fides	*Faith extends to heaven*	Burn, Burne
Tendit in ardua virtus	*Virtue aims at difficulties*	Lloyd
Teneat luceat floreat	*Let him hold, shine, and flourish*	Kenney
Teneat, luceat, floreat, vi, virtute, et valore	*Let it hold, shine, and flourish, by strength, courage and valour*	Kenney
Tenebo	*I will hold*	Gray, Tonge, Warren

Tenebras expellit et hostes	*He drives forth darkness and the foe*	Smith.
Tenebras meas	*My darkness*	Abney-Hastings.
Tenebris lux	*Light in darkness*	Scot.
Teneo	*I hold*	Staples.
Teneo et credo	*I hold and believe*	Carson.
Teneo, tenuere majores	*I hold what my ancestors have held*	Arthur, Curzon, Twemlow.
Tenez le droit	*Keep the right*	Clifton, Wilkinson.
Tenez le vraye	*Keep the truth*	Towneley, Townley.
Tentanda via est	*The way is to be tried*	Peckham, Stronge, Wildman, Golding-Bird.
Tentando superabis	*You will conquer by trying*	Kingdom.
Tenuimus	*We have held*	Lockett.
Te pro te	*Thee for thee*	Savage.
Terar dum prosim	*Let me wear if only I do good*	Merriman.
Ter fidelis	*Thrice faithful*	Slack.
Ternate		Burr.
Terra, aqua, ignis, sal, spiritus, sulphur Sol, Venus, Mercurius	*Land, water, fire, salt, spirit, sulphur, Sun, Venus, Mercury*	Irvine.
Terra, mare, fide	*By the earth, sea, and faith*	Campbell.
Terra marique	*By land and sea*	Cuninghame.
Terra marique fides	*Fidelity by land and sea*	Campbell.
Terra marique potens	*Valiant by sea and land*	O'Malley.
Terrena pericula sperno	*I despise earthly dangers*	Hulton-Harrop, Ogilvie, Ogilvy.
Terrena per vices sunt aliena	*Earthly things change hands*	Fust.
Terrere nolo, timere nescio	*I do not wish to frighten, and know not to fear*	Dering, Dyer.
Terris peregrinus et hospes	*A stranger and pilgrim on the earth*	Bonnell.
Te splendente	*Thou being illustrious*	Carstairs.
Te stante virebo	*I shall flourish, while you stand*	De Valmer, Temple.
Thankful		Hamilton, Stephenson-Hamilton
The cross our stay		Parkhouse.
The grit poul		Mercer.
The Lord will provide		Botfield.
The noblest motive is the public good		Hedges-White, White.
There is no difficulty to him that wills		Haines.
The reward of integrity		Cree.
The reward of valour		Moodie, Moody.
The righteous are bold as a lion		M'Brayne.
The strongest arm uppermost		Stafford.
The strongest hand uppermost		Kennedy.
The time will come		Clarke.
The truth against the world		Byam.
They by permission shine		Murray.
Thincke and thanke		Tate.
Think and thank		Brudenell, Brudenell-Bruce, M'Lellan, Montefiore.
Think on		Forster, McClellan, M'Clelland, Macklellan, Maclellan, M'Lellan, Maxwell, Ross.
Think well		Erskine.
This I'll defend		Dorward, Durnard, Macfarlane, M'Farlin, MacPharlane, M'Pharlin.
This our charter		Chartres, Douglas, Wemyss-Charteris.
Thol and think		Tweedie.
Thole and think on		Tweedy.
Thournib 'crev 'th	*I give you the branch*	Creagh.
Thou shalt want ere I want		Cranstoun, Trotter.
Through		Beckford, Coldham-Fussell, Fitz Maurice, Hamilton, Lamplugh, Lay.
Through God revived		Hamilton.
Thrust on		Thruston.
Thryscryssongh ne Deu a nef		Tremenheere.
Thure et jure	*By frankincense and right*	Foulis.
Thurst on		Thurston.
Thus		Jervis.
Thus far		Campbell.
Thus thou must do if thou have it		Siddons.
Tibi soli	*To thee alone*	Kyle.
Tien le droit	*Maintain the right*	Clench.
Tiens à la vérité	*Hold to the truth*	Blaquier, Courtauld, Crook, De Blaquiere, Hoffman, Lewthwait, Lewthwaite.
Tiens ferme	*Hold fast*	Squire.
Tien ta foy	*Keep thy faith*	Bathurst, Giberne.
Tien ta foy	*Hold to thy faith*	Bathurst.
Till then thus		Jones, Longueville.
Time Deum	*Fear God*	Gordon, Monro, Ross.
Time Deum et ne timeas	*Fear God and fear no other fear*	Burnham.
Timere sperno	*I scorn to fear*	Salle, Wason.
Timet pudorem	*He dreads shame*	Burton, Dawnay, Ryder.
Time tryeth troth		Trevelyan, Tyrwhitt

Timor Dei nobilitas	*The fear of God is nobility*	Lemprière
Timor Domini fons vitæ	*The fear of the Lord is a fountain of life*	Arcedeckne Butler, Butler
Timor omnis abest	*All fear is far away*	Craigie
Timor omnis abesto	*Let all fear be far away*	Craigge, Craigie, Craigy, Kinnersley, Macnab, M'Nab
Tod	*Death*	Futroye
Together		Burrows
Tollit peccata mundi	*He bears the sins of the world*	Farley
Toshac catha agus deineadh air		O'Gorman
Tota gloriosa filia regis intrinsecus	*The daughter of the King is all glorious within*	Jewell
Tot præmia vitæ	*So many are the rewards of life*	Sullivan
Totum est providentia	*Everything is by providence*	Judge
Touch not a cat, but a glove		M'Bean
Touch not the cat, bot the glove		Gillies, MacPherson, M'Gilleray
Touch not the cat, but a glove		Gillespie, Gillies, Gillis, Grant, Keir Mackintosh, M'Bean, McCombie, M'Combie, M'Crombie, M'Gillivray, M'Intosh Mackintosh, Macpherson, MacPherson, Macpherson-Grant
Touch not the cat without a glove		M'Gilevray
Toujours	*Always*	Le Feuvre
Toujours ferme	*Always firm*	Heneage
Toujours fidèle	*Always faithful*	Beauchamp, Bladen, Dun Waters, Fay, Fenwick, Garde, Gillis, Goodall, Grant-Macpherson, Hairstanes, Hair stans, Harestans, Hickman, Holford, Macbean, M'Bean, Mercier, Mill, Proctor-Beauchamp, Waters
Toujours fort	*Always strong*	Hynes
Toujours gai	*Always lively*	Gay
Toujours jeune	*Always young*	Young
Toujours le même	*Always the same*	Tait
Toujours loyal	*Always loyal*	Fenwick, Lindsay, Perkins, Sackville
Tonjours loyale	*Always loyal*	Perkins
Toujours prest	*Always ready*	Anstruther, Carmichael, Dayman, Le Couteur, MacDonel, McDonnell, Meade, Monk, Murray, Prest, Sutton, Temple
Toujours prêt	*Always ready*	Amherst, Chadwick, Daniel, Dease, Deasy, Donald, Hawkins, Macdonald, M'Connell, McDonnell, Meade, Nixon, Petley, Phelps, Philps, Pigott, Smyth, Trotter
Toujours propice	*Always propitious*	Dawson, Sanderson
Toujours sans tache	*Always without a stain*	Tabutean
Tourne vers l'occident	*Turn towards the west.*	Dawson, Westropp Dawson
Tous jours loyal	*Always loyal*	Fenwick
Tous jours loyale	*Always loyal*	Craufurd, Benwick-Clennelll
Tout bien ou rien	*All good, or none*	Barham, Compton, Hicks, Montgomery, Noel
Tout d'en haut	*All from above*	Bellew, Bellew Dillon, Monk, White foord, Whitford
Tout droit	*All right*	Carling, Carr, Carre, Ker, Riddell Carr
Toute foys preste	*Always ready*	Pigott
Tout en bonne heure	*All in good time*	Hicks, Hicks-Beach
Tout en foy	*All in faith*	Sutcliffe
Tout est de Dieu	*All is from God*	Gage
Tout est d'en haut	*All is from above*	Whilford.
Tout fin fait	*Every contrivance serves*	St Hill
Tout foitz chevalier	*Always a knight.*	Rideout
Tout foys prest	*Always ready*	Pigot
Tout hardi	*Quite bold*	Hardie, M'Hardie.
Tout jour	*Always*	Ogilvie
Tout jour fidele	*Always faithful*	Ogilvie
Tout jour pret	*Always ready*	Mansegh
Tout jours prest	*Always ready*	Anstruther, Carmichael, Donald, Donaldson, Mitchell, Sutton
Tout ou rien	*All or nothing*	Adams
Tout par et pour Dieu	*Everything by and for God*	De Ferriores
Tout pour Dieu et ma patrie	*All for God and my country*	Winn
Tout pour l'Eglise	*All for the church*	Wandesford
Tout pourvoir	*To provide everything*	Oliphant
Tout prest	*Quite ready*	Monk, Murray, Younger
Touts jours fidele	*Always faithful.*	Talbot
Tout un durant ma vie	*All one during my life*	Pelham Clay
Tout ung durant ma vie	*All one during my life*	Barrington
Tout vient de Dieu	*All comes from God*	Cooper, Leahy, Leigh, Trefusis
Tout zele	*All zeal*	Touzel
Toutz foitz chevalier	*Always a knight*	Ridout

Motto	Translation	Family
Traditus, non victus	*Yielded not conquered*	Cardoc, Cradock, Dangar
Traditum ab antiquis servare	*To preserve what is handed down from antiquity*	Frere
Traducere ævum leniter	*To pass life gently*	Browne
Trafalgar	...	Codrington, Harvey, Nelson, Tyler
Tramite recto	*By a right path*	Roe
Transfigam	*I shall pierce*	Colt, Coult
Transfixus sed non mortuus	*Transfixed but not dead*	Walsh
Tria juncta in uno	*Three joined in one.*	Motto of the Order of the Bath [The motto "Ich Dien" also appears upon the military badges and stars]
Trial by jury		Erskine
Tristis et fidelis	*Sad and faithful.*	D'Alton
Triumpho morte tam vita	*I triumph in death as well as in life*	Allen
Troimh chruadal	*Through hardships*	M'Intyre
Trop hardi	*Too bold*	Hardie
True		Bruce, Home Everard
True and fast		Harris, Parke
True and trusty.		Heriot
True as the dial to the sun		Hyndman
True to the end		Campbell, Douglas Home, Elphinstone Stone, Ferguson, Foreman, Forman, Hanway, Hepburne-Scott, Home, Hume, Orr, Quinlan.
True to the last.		Ferguson
True unto death		Baker
Trustie and bydand.		Leith
Trustie and true		Scott
Trustie to the end		Forbes Leith
Trust in God		Hardness, Husdell, Richardson
Trust in God and not in strength		Renton
Trust winneth troth		Hastings, Rawdon-Hastings
Trusty and bydand.		Leith.
Trusty and kind		Law
Trusty and true.		Scot
Trusty to the end		Leith
Truth		Lethbridge
Truth and liberty		Tylden
Truth, honour, and courtesy		Gentleman
Truth prevails		Gordon
Truth will prevail		Mackenzie, M'Kenzie
Try		Gethin, O'Hara, Parker
Try aud tryst		Clark
Tuagha tulaig abu		MacSwiney
Tu certa salutis anchora	*Thou a sure anchor of salvation*	Gillespie
Tu Deus ale flammam	*Thou, God, nourish the flame*	Flavel.
Tu digna sequere	*Follow thou worthy things.*	Knight.
Tu Domine gloria mea	*Thou, O Lord, art my glory*	Leicester
Tuebor	*I will defend*	Byng, Cranmer-Byng, Kenney
Tuemur	*We defend*	Higgins
Tuens tutissime virtus	*Thou, Virtue, defendest me most safely*	Carlyon
Tulloch ard	*The high hill*	M'Kenzie
Tu meliora spera	*Hope thou for better things*	Donkin
Tum pace, quam prælio	*As well in peace as in war*	Gordon
Tu ne cede malis	*Yield not to misfortunes*	Amery, Amory, Damer, D'Amery, Davenport, Parry, Pyemont, Riddock, Smith, Steere, Tourner, Turner
Tu ne cede malis, sed contra audentior ito	*Yield not thou to misfortunes, but march boldly against them*	Cooke
Tu ne cede me	*Yield not thou to me*	Steere.
Turpi secernere honestum	*To separate the honourable from the base*	Plumpre
Turpiter desperatur	*Despair is base*	Hall
Turris fortis mihi Deus	*God is a strong tower to me*	Clark, Clogstoun, Clugstone, Hale, Kelly, M'Guarne, Macquaire, O'Kelly, Peter, Towers-Clark, Whelan
Turris fortissima Deus	*God is a most strong tower.*	Torr, Torre
Turris fortitudinis	*The tower of fortitude*	Mansfield
Turris mihi Deus	*God is a tower to me*	Towers
Turris prudentia custos	*Prudence is the safeguard of a fortress*	Dick Lauder, Lauder
Turris tutissima virtus	*Virtue is a very safe tower*	Carlyon
Tuta timens	*Fearing safe things*	Leadbetter
Tutamen	*A defence*	Skrine
Tutamen Deus	*God is a defence*	Bent.
Tutamen pulchris	*A defence to the beautiful*	Chambre
Tutantur tela coronam	*Weapons protect the crown*	Tisdall
Tutela	*Protection*	Lyell, Lyle
Tutemur	*Let us defend*	Higgins
Tute tua tuta.	*Your safe things safely*	Robison
Tuto, celeriter, et jucunde	*Safely, quickly, and pleasantly*	Sutton
Tuto et celeriter	*Safely and quickly*	Penrice
Tutto alfin vola	*Every thing vanishes in the end*	Spickernell

Motto	Translation	Names
Tutto si fa	*Everything gets done*	La Trobe Bateman
Tutum monstrat iter	*He showeth a safe road*	Cook
Tutum refugium	*A safe refuge*	Gillon, Gullon
Tutum te littore robore sistam	*I will plant you safe ashore by my strength*	Crauford, Crawford, Hinde
Tutum te robore reddam	*I will render you safe by my strength*	Crauford, Craufurd, Crawford, Murray, Walford
Tutus in bello	*Safe amid war*	Dobell
Tutus in undis	*Safe amid the waves*	Wood
Tutus prompto animo	*Safe by a ready mind*	Welsted
Tutus si fortis	*Safe, if brave*	Fairborne, Raeburn, Reaburn
Tuum est	*It is thine*	Cooper, Cooper Dodge, Cowper, Fenwick Clennell
Tu vincula frange	*Do thou break the chains*	Napier
Tyde what may		Haig, Haige, Haig Smellie
Tyme proveth truth		Adlam
Tyme tryeth troth		Horner, Trevelyan
Tyrii tenuere coloni	*It was possessed by Tyrian colonists*	M'Lauren

U

Motto	Translation	Names
Ubi amor, ibi fides	*Where there is love there is fidelity*	Belfield, Darbishire, Duckenfield, Dukinfield, Newman
Ubi bene ibi patria	*One's country is where one is well*	Baillie
Ubi fides ibi vires	*Where faith is there is strength*	Hussey
Ubi lapsus? Quid feci?	*Where have I fallen? What have I done?*	Courtenay
Ubi libertas, ibi patria.	*Where there is liberty, there is my country*	Beverley, Collard, Dinwiddie, Hugar, Huger
Ubique aut nusquam	*Everywhere or nowhere*	Whitefoord
Ubique fidelis	*Everywhere faithful*	Hamilton
Ubique paratus	*Everywhere prepared*	Fraser, Frazer
Ubique patriam reminisci	*To remember your country everywhere*	Cass, Harris
Ubi solum ibi cœlum	*Where there is land there is sky*	Anderson
Ulterius	*Farther*	Durham
Ulterius et melius	*Farther and better*	Campbell
Ultra aspicio	*I look farther*	Melville, Melvine
Ultra fert animus	*My mind carries me farther*	Durham
Ultra pergere	*To advance farther*	Copley, Crosland
Unalterable		Sleigh
Un Dieu et un Roi	*One God and one King*	De Jersey
Un Dieu, un Roi	*One God, one King*	D'Arcy, Lyttleton
Un Dieu, un Roy, un cœur	*One God, one King, one heart*	Lake
Un Dieu, un Roy, une foi	*One God, one King, one faith*	Rush
Un Dieu, un Roy, un foy	*One God, one King, one faith*	Curle
Undique fulsus	*Supported all round*	Myrton.
Un durant ma vie	*The same while I live*	Barrington
Une foi	*Once*	Curle
Une foy mesme	*One and the same faith*	Gilpin
Une foy, une loy	*One faith, one law*	Sorel
Une pure foy	*A pure faith*	Hewett
Une stay	*A barrier*	Lang
Ung Dieu ung Roy	*One God, one King*	Billiat
Ung Dieu et ung Roy	*One God and one King*	Littleton, Lyttleton
Ung Dieu ung loy ung foy	*One God, one law, one faith*	Burke, Curll
Ung durant ma vie	*The same while I live*	Barrington
Ung je serviray	*One I will serve*	Fitz-Herbert, Herbert
Ung par tout, tout par ung	*One by everything and everything by one*	Wriothesley
Ung Roy, ung foy, ung loy	*One King, one faith, one law.*	Burke, De Burgh, De Burgho, De Burgo
Ung sent ung soleil	*One faith, one sun*	Lloyd Verney, Verney
Ung tout seul	*A one.*	Verney
Uni æquus virtuti	*Friendly to virtue alone*	Grenville, Murray
Unica spes mea Christus	*Christ is my only hope*	Dishington.
Unica virtus necessaria	*Virtue alone is necessary*	Colley
Unione augetur	*It is increased by union*	Miller
Unione minima vigent	*The smallest things flourish by union*	Coghlan
Unita fortior	*Stronger by union*	Plowes
Unitate fortior	*Stronger from union*	Beck
Unite		Brodie, Brody, Cameron
Un Roy, une foy, une loy	*One King, one faith, one law*	Burke
Un tout seul	*One alone*	Verney
Unus et idem	*One and the same*	Bindley, Liddell
Unus et idem ferar	*Let me be one and the same*	Blundell
Upward		Lorimer, Simons
Usque ad aras	[illegible]	Campbell, Herne, Yates
Usque ad aras amicus	[illegible]	[illegible]

Usque ad mortem fidus	*Faithful even to death*	Ward.
Usque fac et non parcas	*E'en do and spare not*	Peter.
Usque fidelis	*Faithful to the last*	Melles, Napier.
Usurpari nolo	*I do not wish to usurp*	M'Dowall.
Ut amnis vita labitur	*Life glides away like a river*	Brooks.
Ut apes, geometriam	*As bees, geometry*	Petty.
Ut aspirat cervus	*As the hart panteth*	Staveley.
Ut crescit, clarescit	*As it increases, it becomes famous*	Anderson, Menzies.
Utcunque placuit Deo	*As God has seen good*	Darby, How, Howe.
Utcunque placuerit Deo	*Howsoever God pleases*	Darby.
Ut deficiar	*That I may be destitute*	Auchinleck.
Ut ducam spero	*As I hope, I will lead*	Seckham.
Utere dum potes	*Enjoy while you may*	Lecky.
Utile dulci	*The useful with the pleasant*	Bestall, Shuttleworth, Spedding.
Utile et dulce	*Useful and agreeable*	Morrison, Riddell.
Utile quod taceas	*It is useful to keep quiet*	Turner.
Utili secernere honestum	*To separate the honourable from the useful*	Davis.
Ut implear	*That I may be filled*	Mikieson.
Utitur ante quæsitis	*He uses former acquisitions*	Draghorn, Dreghorn.
Ut migraturus habita	*Dwell as ready to depart*	Lauder.
Ut olim	*As formerly*	Kinloch, Kinlock.
Ut palma justus	*The just like a palm*	Palmes.
Ut possim	*That I may be able*	Livingston.
Ut prosim	*That I may be of use*	Foley, Grigg, Greenwood.
Ut prosim aliis	*That I may profit others*	Clerke-Jennings, Fergusson, Greenwood, Jennings, Jenyns.
Ut prosim aliis prosim	*Let me prosper that I may benefit others*	Ferguson.
Ut prosimus	*That we may be of service*	Flory.
Ut quocunque paratus	*As prepared for whatever may happen*	Lambart, Lambert.
Utraque fortuna contentus	*Content with either fortune*	Vosper.
Utraque pallade	*By each art*	Bendish, Bendyshe.
Ut reficiar	*That I may be refreshed*	Archibald.
Ut resurgam	*That I may rise again*	Penniecook, Pennycook, Pennycuick.
Utrinque paratus	*Prepared on all sides*	Cottingham.
Utrius auctus auxilio	*Increasing by the help of both*	Rankine, Ranking.
Utriusque auxilio	*By the help of both*	Spottiswood.
Ut sanem vulnero	*I wound in order to heal*	Holt.
Ut se crescit, clarescit	*He grows illustrious as he increases*	Anderson.
Ut secura quies	*As secure quiet*	Huskisson.
Ut sim paratior	*That I may be the more ready*	Clepan, Clepham, Clephan.
Ut sementem feceris ita et metes	*As you sow you shall reap*	Wilson.
Ut sibi sic alteri	*Do to another as to thyself*	Letchworth.
Ut sursum desuper	*Descend to ascend*	Rumbold, Worseley, Worsley.
Ut tibi sic aliis	*As to thee so to others*	Hussey.
Ut tibi sic alteri	*As I do to thee, so will I do to others*	Bowles, Dobson, Pemberton-Leigh.
Ut vidi ut vici	*As I saw, as I conquered*	Naunton.
Ut vinclo vir verbo ligitur	*A man is bound by his word as by a chain*	Clover.
Ut vivas vigila	*Watch that you may live*	Arnold, Bather.

V

Vade ad formicam	*Go to the ant*	Anketill, Anketell.
Væ duplici cordi	*Woe to the deceitful heart*	Fitton.
Væ timido	*Woe to the timid*	Maddison.
Væ victis	*Woe to the conquered*	Senhouse.
Vaillance avance l'homme	*Valour advances the man*	Acton.
Vaillant et veillant	*Valiant and vigilant*	Cardwell.
Valde et sapienter	*With force and wisdom*	Musgrave, Sagar-Musgrave.
Valebit	*It shall prevail*	Lysons.
Valens et volens	*Able and willing*	Fetherstonhaugh.
Valet anchora virtus	*Virtue is equivalent to an anchor*	Gardner.
Valet et vulnerat	*It avails and wounds*	Hay.
Valet pietas	*Piety is strong*	Valpy.
Validus	*Strong*	Harte.
Vallum aeneum esto	*Be thou a rampart of brass*	Bailey.
Valore et virtute	*By valour and virtue*	Salle.
Valor et fortuna	*Valour and fortune*	Rollo.
Valor et lealdade	*Valour and loyalty*	Croft.
Valour and loyalty		Grant.
Vana spes vitæ	*Vain is the hope of life*	Paul.
Vanus est honor	*Honour is vain*	Bowden, Bowdon.
Va outre marque	*Go beyond the mark*	Utermarck.
Va presto ma sano		Watts.
Vectis	*A lever*	Holmes.
Veilliant et vaillant	*Wise and valiant*	Erskine.
Vel arte vel marte	*[illegible]*	Baines, Deans, Deans-Campbell.
Velis id quod possis	*Aim [illegible] you [illegible]*	Brett.

Velle bene facere	*To wish to do well*	Curtis
Vellera fertis oves	*You sheep carry fleeces*	Elliot, Elliott
Velle vult quod Deus	*To wish what God wishes*	Bankes
Velocitate	*With velocity*	Carse
Vel pax, vel bellum	*Either peace or war*	Fraser, Frazer, Gordon, Gunn
Venabulis vinco	*I conquer with hunting spears*	Venables
Venale nec auro	*Not to be purchased for gold*	Jervis, Jervis White
Venit ab astris	*She came from heaven*	Keith
Venit hora	*The hour has come*	Hoare
Ventis secundis	*By favourable winds*	Hood, Kennion, Rowley
Venture and gain		Hay, Wilson
Venture forward		Bruce
Vera sequor	*I follow truth*	Hale, Landon
Vera tropæa fides	*Fidelity is a true trophy*	Swabey
Vera virtus immersabilis	*True virtue is invincible*	Codrington
Verax atque probus	*Truthful and honest*	Fair, Ruttledge
Verax et fidelis	*True and faithful*	Peareth
Veritas	*Truth*	Liston, Wirgman, Watson
Veritas et patria	*Truth and my country*	Hoadly
Veritas et virtus vincunt	*Truth and valour conquer*	Walsh
Veritas ingenio	*Truth with wit*	Gordon
Veritas liberabit	*Truth shall make free*	Bodenham,
Veritas liberavit	*Truth has made free*	Slingsby
Veritas, libertas	*Truth and liberty*	Abraham
Veritas magna est	*Truth is great*	Jephson, Jepson
Veritas me dirigit	*Truth directs me*	Brocklehurst
Veritas non opprimitur	*There is no crushing the truth*	Calderwood
Veritas odit morem	*Truth hates custom*	Parry
Veritas odium parit	*Truth breeds hatred*	Kennedy
Veritas omnia vincit	*Truth conquers all things*	Kedslie, Kidslie
Veritas premitur, non opprimitur	*Truth may be kept down, but not entirely overwhelmed*	Calderwood.
Veritas, puritas	*Truth and purity*	Webster
Veritas prevalebit	*Truth will prevail*	Gribble
Veritas superabit	*Truth shall prevail*	Hill
Veritas superabit montes	*Truth shall cross mountains*	Hill
Veritas via vitæ	*Truth the way of life*	Tyrrell
Veritas victrix	*Truth is conqueror*	Wilde
Veritas vincit	*Truth conquers*	Ayre, Fair, Fisher, French, Geddes, Geddies, Keith, Marshall Orpen, Wood Wright
Veritas vincit omnia	*Truth conquers all things*	Waterhouse
Veritatem	*Truth*	Tatham
Veritatis assertor	*Assertor of truth*	Niblett
Veritatis et æquitatis tenax	*Steadfast to truth and equity*	Rust
Vérite sans peur	*Truth without fear*	Bedford, Gunning, Hemans, Middleton, Shute, Willoughby
Verité soyez ma garde	*Truth be my guard*	Brewster, French Brewster
Vérité vient	*Truth comes*	Vere
Vernon semper viret	*Vernon always flourishes*	Vernon
Vero nihil verius	*Nothing truer than truth*	De Vere, Hunt, Vere, Weir
Vero nil verius	*Nothing truer than truth*	Vere
Versus	*Towards*	Peters
Vertitur in diem	*It is changing into day*	Farquhar
Vertitur in lucem	*It is changing into light*	Baillie
Vertu cerche honneur	*Virtue seeks honour*	D'Arcy
Vertue vauncet	*Virtue prevails*	Verney
Verum atque decens.	*True and becoming*	Browne, Lee, Wylde
Verus ad finem	*True to the end*	Deuchar, Lizars, Peters
Verus amor patriæ	*True love of country*	Hughes
Verus et fidelis	*True and faithful*	Parkin
Verus et fidelis semper	*Always true and faithful*	Aylward, Toler Aylward
Verus et sedulus	*True and diligent*	M'Culloch
Verus honor honestas	*Honesty is true honour*	Lacock
Vescitur Christo	*Feeds on Christ*	Rous
Vespere et mane	*In the evening and morning*	Pierie, Pourie, Powrie, Purie
Vestigia nulla retrorsum	*There is no going back*	Baily, Coningsby, d'Albani, Hampden, Levinge, Massicks, Sibthorpe, Trevor
Veuille bien	*Wish well*	De Veulle
Via crucis via lucis	*The way of the cross is the way of light*	Black, Sinclair
Via trita est via tuta	*The beaten way is the safe way*	Berryman
Via trita via tuta	*The beaten way is the safe way*	Agar
Vi at tamen honore	*By force, yet with honour*	Wyatt
Via tuta virtus	*Virtue the safe way*	Dick Cunyngham
Via una, cor unum	*One way, one heart*	Hart, M'Corda
Vi aut virtute	*By force or valour*	Chisholm
Via vi	*A way by force*	Hayter
Vici	*I* [illegible]	[illegible]
Vicimus	[illegible]	[illegible]
Vicisti et vivimus	[illegible]	[illegible]

Motto	Translation	Names
Vicit amor patriæ	*Love of country has conquered*	Holles.
Vicit pepercit	*He conquered, he spared*	Draper.
Vi corporis et animi	*By force of body and mind*	Boddy.
Victima Deo	*A sacrifice to God*	Veale.
Victo dolore	*Grief overcome*	Simpson.
Victor	*Conqueror*	James, Linskill.
Victoria	*Victory*	Conqueror, Locock, M'Dowall.
Victoria a Domino	*Victory from the Lord*	Webb.
Victoria concordia crescit	*Concord insures victory*	Amherst.
Victoria fortitudo virtus	*Victory, fortitude, virtue*	Young.
Victoriam coronat Christus	*Christ crowns victory*	Campbell.
Victoria non præda	*Victory, not booty*	Durham, Sandilands.
Victoria signum	*Victory is the sign*	Taylor.
Victoria vel mors	*Victory or death*	Macdonald, M'Donall, M'Dowall, M'Dowgal.
Victor in arduis	*A conqueror amid difficulties*	M'Connel.
Victorious		O'Rourke.
Victor mortalis est	*The conqueror is mortal*	Clark.
Victor sine sanguine	*A victor without blood*	Smith.
Victory or death		O'Hagan.
Victrix fortunæ sapientia	*Wisdom the conqueror of fortune*	Andrew, Andrews, Calthrop, Pelissier, Wylie.
Victrix fortuna sapientiæ	*Fortune is the conqueror of wisdom*	Chalmers.
Victrix patientia	*Patience is victorious*	Gordon.
Victrix patientia duris	*Patience is victorious in hardship*	Carter.
Victrix prudentia	*Prudence is conqueror*	Gordon.
Victus in arduis	*Conquered in difficulties*	Harrison.
Video alta sequorque	*I see and follow high things*	Carnagie, Carnegie.
Video et taceo	*I see and hold my peace*	Fox.
Video meliora	*I see better things*	Montefiore.
Video meliora proboque	*I see and approve of better things*	Smythe-Owen.
Viditque Deus hanc lucem esse bonam	*And God saw the light that it was good*	Rundle.
Vidi, vici	*I have seen, I have conquered*	Scurfield, Twiselton, Twisleton.
Vi divina	*By divine force*	Pearse.
Vi et animo	*By strength and courage*	Hankinson, M'Culloch.
Vi et armis	*By force and arms*	Armstrong.
Vi et arte	*By force and art*	Chisholm, Ferguson, Fergusson, Stephen, Stevens.
Vi et consilio	*By force and counsel*	Merewether.
Vi et fide	*By force and faith*	Campbell.
Vi et fide vivo	*I live by force and faith*	Nihell.
Vi et industria	*By force and industry*	Falconer.
Vi et libertate	*By force and liberty*	Vibert.
Vi et veritate	*By force and by truth*	Sloan.
Vi et virtute	*By force and valour*	Baird, Bolton, Brown, Chambers, Chisholme, Fulton, Hunt, Le Ruez, Lindow, M'Taggart, Pears, Pooler, Powell, Smart, Spaight, White, Woodlock.
Vie vers vertu	*Life towards virtue*	Veevers.
Viget in cinere virtus	*Virtue flourshies after death*	Davidson, Grey.
Viget sub cruce	*He flourishes under the cross*	Colquboun.
Vigila et ora	*Watch and pray*	Rogers, Wake.
Vigilance		Laing.
Vigilando	*By watching*	Campbell, Cotton-Jodrell, Gordon, M'Leod.
Vigilando quiesco	*I am at rest from watching*	Tredcorft, Tredcroft.
Vigilans	*Watchful*	Burton, Johnson, Kadwell, Mathisson, Smith, Taylor, Wolstonecraft.
Vigilans et audax	*Watchful and bold*	Bradley, Coates, Cockburn, Corrie, Corry, Currie, Dunn, Stephens, White.
Vigilans et certus	*Vigilant and sure*	Anderson.
Vigilans et fidelis	*Watchful and faithful*	Wilson.
Vigilans et promptus	*Vigilant and prompt*	Wyld.
Vigilans et verus	*Vigilant and true*	Wenley.
Vigilans non cadit	*Watching, he does not fall*	Calder.
Vigilant		Laing, Newcomen.
Vigilanter	*Vigilantly*	Alcock, Gregory, Stawell, Wegg.
Vigilante salus	*Safety by watching*	Cochran, Cochrane.
Vigilantia	*Vigilance*	Aird, Ard, Carfrae, Hinshaw, Tod.
Vigilantia et virtute	*By vigilance and valour*	Porter.
Vigilantia non cadet	*By watching he shall not fall*	Cadell.
Vigilantia, robur, voluptas	*Vigilance, strength, pleasure*	Blair, Hunter.
Vigilantia securitas	*Security by watching*	Phin, Phine.
Vigilantibus	*By the watchful*	Acheson, Aitcheson, Aitchison, Atchison, Bristow.
Vigilantibus non dormientibus	*By the watchful, not the sleeping*	Bristowe.
Vigilanti salus	*Safety to the watchful*	Cochran.
Vigilate	*Watch*	Alcock, Edwardes, Gael, Leeds, Longstaff, Sconce, Walkey.

Vigilate et orate	*Watch and pray*	Capron, Hancock, Handcock, Shuckburgh
Vigilat et orat	*He watches and prays*	Tennison
Vigilo	*I watch*	Dess, Desse, Gregson, May, M'Haddo, M'Hado
Vigilo et spero	*I watch and hope*	Daunt, Galbraith, Horton, Tivitoe
Vigore	*With vigour*	Vickers
Vigore et virtute	*By vigour and virtue*	Casey
Vigueur de dessus	*Strength from above*	Braidwood, O'Brien, O'Bryen, Willington
Vigueur l'amour de croix	*The love of the cross gives strength*	Darnel
Vil God, I zal		Menzies
Vill God, I sall		Menzies
Vi martiali Deo adjuvante	*By force of war, God helping*	Marshall
Vim da vi honestæ	*Give force by force of honesty*	Davy
Vimiera		Walker
Vim vi repellere licet	*We may repel force by force*	Gwyn, Holford, Prattinton.
Vim vi repello	*I repel force by force*	Baldwin
Vincam	*I will conquer*	Griffin,
Vincam malum bono	*I will conquer evil by good*	Robinson
Vincam vel moriar	*I shall conquer or die*	Benyon, M'Dowal, M'Dowall
Vince fide	*Conquer by faith*	Parry
Vince malum bono	*Overcome evil with good*	Eure, Johnes, Jones, Robinson
Vince malum patientia	*Overcome evil by patience*	Townshend
Vincendo victus	*Conquered in conquering*	Ley
Vincenti dabitur	*It shall be given to the conqueror*	Vincent
Vincent qui se vincent	*They shall conquer who conquer themselves*	Vincent
Vincere	*To conquer*	M'Conl
Vincere aut mori	*To either conquer or die*	M'Neill, O'Hagan, Tuthill
Vincere vel mori	*To conquer or die*	M'Dowal, M'Dowall, M'Dougal, M'Gougan, Maclaine, M'Lea, Macneil, M'Neil M'Neill, M'Nelly, M Oul, M'Owl, Murphy, O'Morchoe, Tibbet
Vincet qui patitur	*He shall conquer who endures*	Morgan
Vincet vel mori	*He shall conquer or die*	M'Dowall
Vincet virtute	*He shall conquer by virtue*	Smart
Vincit amor patriæ	*The love of country prevails*	Gun, Hargreaves, James, Molesworth, Nolan-Whelan, O'Hara, Pelham, Pelham Anderson, Pennington, Shaw, Thuillier
Vincit cum legibus arma	*He represses violence with laws*	Atkins, Atkyns
Vincit labor	*Labour overcomes*	Campbell
Vincit liberavit	*He conquers, he has set free*	Slingsby
Vincit omnia	*He conquers all things*	O'Conry
Vincit omnia veritas	*Truth conquers all things*	De Courcy, Eaton, Goodchild, Laffan, Peele, Savory, Sligo, Thomson
Vincit omnia virtus	*Virtue conquers everything*	Vicars
Vincit pericula virtus	*Virtue conquers dangers*	Brady, Harwood, Maine, Thornton
Vincit qui curat	*He conquers who is cautious*	White
Vincit qui devincit	*He conquers who binds fast*	Griffin
Vincit qui patitur	*He conquers who endures*	Acworth, Addenbrooke, Amphlett, Ashurst, Chester, Clarke, Colt, Dancer, Disney, Gildea, Harrison, Homfray, Homfrey, Llwellen, Llewellyn, Morgan, Shaw, Shields, Smerdon, Turner, Wire
Vincit qui se vincit	*He conquers who conquers himself*	Ackworth, Ellis, Fawsett, Grigson, Holland, Wilson
Vincit veritas	*Truth prevails*	Alison, Allison, Baxter, Boddington, Bulfin, Burn, Coote, Dickin, Edmonds, Fair, Galwey, Gort, Hastings, Henry, Jephson, Jepson, M'Kenny, Napier, Orpen, O'Shee, Paget Tomlinson, Peacock, Prendergast, Ryder, Shee, Smyth, Vereker, Ward, Warde, Webster
Vincit vigilantia	*Watchfulness overcomes*	Wright
Vincit vim virtus	*Virtue conquers force*	Kennedy
Vinctus non victus	*Bound, not conquered*	De Worms
Vinctus sed non victus	*Bound, but not conquered*	Bourke, Burke, Galwey
Vincula da linguæ vel tibi lingua dabit	*Lay restraint on thy tongue or thy tongue will lay it on thee*	Hoskyns
Vincula temno	*I despise bonds*	Sinclair
Vi non astutia	*Force, not cunning*	Rumford
Virebo	*I will become strong*	Hamilton
Vires agminis unus habet	*One has the strength of a regiment*	Gryles, Grylls
Vires animat virtus	*Virtue animates strength*	Garden, Gairden
Virescit	*He flourishes*	Moncrief, Stewart
Virescit in arduis virtus	*Virtue grows amid hardships*	Keir, Keir Mackintosh, Mackintosh Ker
Virescit virtus	[illegible]	[illegible]

Virescit vulnere	*He grows strong by being wounded*	Stewart
Virescit vulnere virtus	*Virtue flourishes from a wound*	Brock, Brodhurst, Brownrigg, Burnet, Burnett, Clutton-Brock, Filgate, Foot, Hepenstal, Ker, Meara, Stewart
Viresco	*I become green*	Douglas, Greenless, Greenwell, Monteath-Douglas, Monteith, Smellet, Smollet, Smollett, Stewart, Tailefer
Viresco et surgo	*I flourish and revive*	Maxwell
Vires et fides	*Strength and faith*	Cowan
Vires in arduis.	*Strength in difficulties*	MacBain
Vires veritas	*Truth is power*	Kennedy
Vir gregis	*A man of the crowd*	Clarke
Viridis et fructifera	*Flourishing and bearing fruit*	Hamilton
Viridis semper	*Always green*	Mathison
Vir super hostem	*A man above an enemy*	O'Donovan.
Virtue		Ferguson
Virtue, have virtue		Ross
Virtue is honour		Kendrick, Kenrick
Virtue is my honour		M'Lannahan
Virtue mine honour		M'Clean, M'Clen, Maclean
Virtus acquirit honorem	*Virtue procures honour*	Hamilton, Spence
Virtus ad æthera tendit	*Virtue tends towards heaven*	Balfour, Cairns
Virtus ad astra	*Virtue to the sky*	Innes, Phillips Flamank
Virtus ad astra tendit	*Virtue tends to the stars*	Ross
Virtus ad sidera tollit	*Virtue exalts to the stars*	Patten, Wilson
Virtus ariete fortior	*Virtue is stronger than a battering-ram*	Bertie
Virtus astra petit	*Virtue aims at the sky*	Vandeleur
Virtus auget honorem	*Virtue increases honour*	Edmonstone, Spence
Virtus auget honores	*Virtue increases honours*	Charles
Virtus auro præferenda	*Virtue is to be preferred to gold*	Allen
Virtus basis vitæ	*Virtue is the support of life.*	Jerningham
Virtus castellum meum	*Virtue is my fortress*	Bence
Virtus constat in actione	*Virtue consists in action*	Norgate
Virtus cura servabit	*Virtue shall preserve by care*	Browne
Virtus dabit, cura servabit	*Virtue shall give, care shall preserve*	Brown
Virtus dedit, cura servabit	*Virtue has given, discretion will preserve*	Brown, Browne
Virtus depressa resurget	*Virtue downtrodden will rise again*	Kendall
Virtus difficilia vincit	*Virtue conquers difficulties*	Whitburn
Virtus dum patior vincit	*Virtue overcomes, while I suffer*	Weems
Virtus durat avorum	*The virtue of ancestry remains*	Seton
Virtus durissima feret	*Virtue will sustain the most severe trials*	M'Lean
Virtus duxit avorum	*The virtue of our ancestry was our guide*	Seton
Virtus est Dei	*Virtue is from God*	Briggs, Brooke
Virtus est vitium fugere	*It is a virtue to shun vice*	Reynardson
Virtus et fortitudo invincibilia sunt	*Virtue and fortitude are invincible*	M'Guire
Virtus et industria	*Virtue and industry.*	Browne
Virtus et nobilitas	*Virtue and nobility..*	Henvill, Llewellin
Virtus et spes	*Virtue and hope*	Caldwell
Virtus fides fortitudo	*Virtue, fidelity, and fortitude*	Spens
Virtus fortunæ victrix	*Virtue is the conqueror of fortune*	Collis-Sandes, Sandes
Virtus impendere vero	*It is virtue to be devoted to truth*	Brown
Virtus in actione consistit	*Virtue consists in action*	Clayton, Craven, Everard, Halford, Sier, Syer
Virtus in ardua	*Virtue in the face of difficulties*	Pottinger
Virtus in arduis	*Valour in difficulties*	Baring, Cockain, Cokaine, Cokayne, Gammon, Harrison, Macqueen
Virtus in arduo	*Valour in difficulty*	Howell
Virtus in caducis	*Valour amid the ruin of things*	M'Dowal
Virtus incendit vires	*Valour stirs up strength*	Smythe
Virtus incumbet honori	*Virtue will rest upon honour*	Williams
Virtus insignat audentes	*Virtue distinguishes the bold*	Beamish, Beamish-Bernard
Virtus intaminatis fulget honoribus	*Virtue shines with untarnished honours*	Truss
Virtus invicta	*Virtue is invincible*	Morrogh
Virtus invicta gloriosa	*Unconquered virtue is glorious*	Thomas
Virtus invicta viget	*Invincible virtue flourishes*	Penyston
Virtus invidiæ scopus	*Virtue is the mark for envy*	Methuen, Methven
Virtus laudanda	*Virtue is praiseworthy.*	Paton, Patton
Virtus, laus, actio	*Virtue, praise, exploit*	Frazer
Virtus maturat	*Virtue ripens*	Riddel, Riddell
Virtus mihi scutum	*Virtue, be thou my shield*	Warren
Virtus mille scuta	*Virtue is equal to a thousand shields.*	Clifford, Dayrell, Howard, Howard Vyse, Sadler
Virtus nobilitat	*Virtue ennobles*	Boyd, Cruso, Henderson
Virtus non stemma	*The virtue not the lineage*	Grosvenor, Taunton
Virtus non vertitur	*Virtue does not turn*	Donegan, Sarsfield
Virtus omnia nobilitat	*Virtue ennobles all*	Herrick
Virtus omnia vincit	*Virtue conquers all*	White
Virtus patientia veritas	*Virtue, patience, truth*	Johnsou
Virtus patrimonio nobilior	*Virtue is more noble than patrimony*	Salusbury, Trelawny

Virtus paret robur	*Virtue shows strength*	Bunbury, Richardson
Virtus post facta	*Virtue after exploits*	Borthwick
Virtus potentior auro	*Virtue is more powerful than gold*	Falconer
Virtus præ numine	*Virtue is preferable to power*	Price
Virtus præ nummis	*Virtue before money*	Smart
Virtus præstantior auro	*Virtue more excellent than gold*	Severene, Whieldon
Virtus præstat auro	*Virtue is better than gold*	Cunninghame
Virtus pretiosior auro	*Virtue is more precious than gold*	Robinson
Virtus prevalebit	*Virtue will prevail*	Ranken
Virtus probata florebit	*Proved virtue will flourish*	Bernard, Bernard Beamish
Virtus probata florescit	*Tried virtue flourishes*	Bernard, Cologan, Mac Colgan, Veldon
Virtus propter se	*Virtue for its own sake*	Lubé, Radcliffe, Ratcliffe, Repington
Virtus Pyramidis	*Virtue of the Pyramid*	Kinchant
Virtus repulsæ nescia sordidæ	*Virtue incapable of mean repulse*	Cuffe, Laurie.
Virtus rosa suavior stella clarior	*Virtue is sweeter than a rose, brighter than a star*	Lloyd
Virtus salus ducum	*Virtue is the safety of leaders*	Leader
Virtus semper eadem	*Virtue always the same*	Dodgson, Turvile
Virtus semper viret	*Virtue always flourishes*	Woodward
Virtus semper viridis	*Virtue is always flourishing*	Cory, English, France, France Hayhurst, Green Laure, Lowry Lowry Corry
Virtus sibi aureum	*Virtue is worth gold to itself*	Knight
Virtus sibi præmium	*Virtue is its own reward*	Calderwood, Fergusson
Virtus sine dote	*Virtue without a dowry*	Davies
Virtus sine macula	*Virtue without a stain*	Lamb, Russell
Virtus sine metu	*Virtue without fear*	Howard
Virtus sola	*Virtue alone*	Henderson
Virtus sola felicitas	*Virtue is the only happiness*	Bliss
Virtus sola invicta	*Virtue alone is invincible*	Dauntesy, Eyre
Virtus sola nobilitas	*Virtue is the only nobility*	Blake, Nicholson, O'Dwyer, Throckmorton
Virtus sola nobilitat	*Virtue alone ennobles*	Blake, Blakes, Henderson, Henrieson, Henrison, Henryson, Kavanagh, Mac Causland
Virtus sub cruce crescit	*Virtue grows under the cross*	Bury, Howard Bury
Virtus sub cruce crescit ad æthera tendens	*Virtue that tends towards heaven increases under trial*	Bury
Virtus sub pondere crescit	*Virtue increases under the burthen*	Feilden, Jephson
Virtus tollit ad astra	*Virtue exalts to the stars*	Innes
Virtus triumphat.	*Virtue triumphs*	Church
Virtus tutamen	*Virtue is a defence*	Cermon
Virtus tutissima	*Virtue is safest*	Conlan
Virtus tutissima cassis	*Virtue is the safest helmet*	Barker, Finch Hatton, Raymond, Stevenson, Willis
Virtus ubique	*Virtue everywhere*	Stephen, Stevenson, Verst
Virtus ubique sidem	*Virtue has its home everywhere*	Stevensone
Virtus vera nobilitas.	*Virtue is true nobility*	Drake, Henville, Springham
Virtus verus honos	*Virtue is true honour*	Burr
Virtus viget in arduis	*Virtue flourishes amid difficulties*	Gurdon
Virtus vincit invidiam	*Virtue overcomes envy*	Bowen, Clebborn, Cornwallis, Mann, Usborne.
Virtus virtutis præmium	*Virtue is its own reward*	MacMoran, Macmorran, M'Moran
Virtus vitium fugere	*It is virtue to shun vice*	Whitby
Virtute	*By virtue*	Bain, Burnet, Burnett, Cheshire, Church, Cooper, Couper, Dick, Dick Lauder, Ferguson, Keane, Metivier, Stable, Stuart, Tait, Watkins, Whyte
Virtute acquiret honos	*He shall acquire honour by virtue*	Richardson
Virtute acquiritur	*It is acquired by virtue*	Robertson
Virtute acquiritur honos	*Honour is acquired by virtue*	Richardson, Richie, Ritchie, Spence
Virtute ad astra	*By virtue to the skies*	Kenwick
Virtute adepta	*Acquired by virtue*	Keyes, Paton, Paton Bethune, Patton
Virtute avorum	*By the virtue of ancestors*	Watkins
Virtute cresco	*I increase by virtue.*	Burnet, Forbes, Leask, Mitchell, Mitchell Carruthers
Virtute damnosa quies	*Inactivity inimical to virtue*	Brisbane
Virtute decoratus	*Adorned with virtue*	Glasscott
Virtute dignus avorum	*Worthy of the virtue of our ancestors*	Worthington
Virtute doloque	*By courage and policy*	Binning
Virtute duce	*Under the guidance of valour*	Elder, Sand, Shanan, Shand, Shannon
Virtute duce, comite fortuna	*Under the guidance of valour, accompanied by good fortune*	Shand, Smith Shand
Virtute et amicitia	*By virtue and friendship*	Jervis
Virtute et amore	*By virtue and love*	M'Kenzie
Virtute et armis	*By virtue and arms*	Minnitt, Pratt
Virtute et claritate	*By virtue and high repute*	Hara, O'Hara
Virtute et constantia	*By courage and perseverance*	Auld, Townend
Virtute et fide	*By bravery and faith*	Harley, Lamb, Marriot
Virtute et fidelitate	*By bravery and fidelity*	Beauvale, Blackie, Blaikie, Crofts, Goodsir, H[illegible], L[illegible], L[illegible], Reeves

Virtute et fide vinco	*I conquer by bravery and fidelity*	Fenton
Virtute et fortitudine	*By bravery and fortitude*	Morris, Whettnall, Cooper
Virtute et fortuna	*By virtue and fortune*	Andrew Andrews, Gardner.
Virtute et honore	*By virtue and honour*	Baird, Blair, Kent, Wells.
Virtute et industria	*By virtue and industry*	Brackenbridge, Heaviside.
Virtute et ingenio	*By virtue and ability*	Master
Virtute et labore	*By virtue and labour*	Allanson, Clark, Cochran, Cochrane, Cunningham, Downfield, Forster, Foster, Gregson, Heddle, Knight, Lowcay, M'Clintock, M'Clintock Bunbury, Mackenzie, M'Lintock, Main, Platt, Reid, Rig, Rigg, Whitehead, Wilson, Winn, Wood
Virtute et non vi .	*By virtue and not by violence*	Bradstreet
Virtute et numine	*By bravery and divine aid*	Creagh, Lawless, MacMahon Creagh.
Virtute et opera	*By virtue and deeds*	Bennie, Benny, Benzie, Bernie Binnie, Binny, Cookson, Duff, Fife-Cookson, Fyffe, Harris, Pentland
Virtute et probitate	*By virtue and honesty*	Magan
Virtute et prudentia	*By virtue and prudence*	Bayles, Hepburn, Howenden, Lydiard
Virtute et robore	*By virtue and strength*	Borough, Pillans, Richardson
Virtute et sapientia .	*By virtue and wisdom*	Brownrigg
Virtute et valore	*By virtue and valour* .	Batt, Carson, Ennis, Leech, Lowcay, Mackenzie, M'Kenzie, Macnamara, Noble, Peppard, Roberts, Roe, Stamer, Whitehead
Virtute et valare luceo non uro	*By virtue and valour I shine, outdo not burn*	Mackenzie
Virtute et vigilantia	*By virtue and vigilance*	Sharp
Virtute et veritate	*By virtue and truth*	Blathwayt
Virtute et votis	*By virtue and vows* .	Neilson, Nelson
Virtute excerptæ	*Conspicuous for virtue*	Cary
Virtute fideque	*By bravery and faith*	McMurray, M'Murray, Murray
Virtute gloria parta	*Renown is obtained by bravery*	Napier
Virtute honor	*Honour by virtue*	Richardson
Virtute invidiam vincas	*Overcome envy by virtue*	Cleborne
Virtutem conorat honos	*Honour crowns virtue*	Drummond
Virtutem coronat opus	*The work crowns the virtue*	Laurie
Virtute me involvo	*I wrap me in my virtue*	Forbes, Ramsay.
Virtutem extendere fac	*Act so as to encourage virtue*	Fisher
Virtutem extendere factis	*To spread virtue by noble deeds*	Fisher
Virtutem sic et culpam	*Virtue thus and blame*	Maxwell
Virtute nihil invium	*No way is impassable to virtue*	Chamberlayne, Hillary
Virtute, non aliter	*By virtue, not otherwise*	Moir
Virtute non armis fido	*I trust in virtue, not in arms*	Egerton
Virtute, non astutia	*By bravery, not stratagem*	Clements, Pery, Whitbread
Virtute, non ferocia	*By bravery, not by cruelty*	Forbes
Virtute, non sanguine	*By virtue, not by blood*	Hayman, Hayward Curtis
Virtute, non verbis	*By virtue, not by words* .	Baxter, Clere, Coulthart, Hoskins, Marshall, Maw, Petty Fitz Maurice, Robinson, Sawers
Virtute, non vi ...	*By virtue, not by force*	Austin-Gourlay, Barneby, Berkeley, Chivas, Coppinger, Lutley, Rotbe, Shivez
Virtute, non viribus	*By virtue, not by force*	Derrick
Virtute, non viribus vincent	*They shall conquer by virtue, not by force*	Vincent
Virtute orta	*Sprung from virtue*	Stewart
Virtute orta occidunt rarius	*What is sprung from virtue rarely fails*	Aiton, Aytoun
Virtute paret robur	*Strength obeys virtue* .	Richardson
Virtute parta	*Produced by virtue*	Haliday, Halliday, Hallyday, Melville-Whyte, White, Whyte, Whytt
Virtute parta tuemini	*You defend what is obtained by valour* .	Blackwood, Peperpell
Virtute probitate .	*By virtue and integrity*	Magan
Virtute promoveo.	*I advance by virtue*	Sideserf, Sydserf, Sydserfe
Virtute quies	*Rest through valour*	Phipps
Virtute securus.	*Secure by virtue*	Maude
Virtute sibi præmium	*Let his reward be in virtue*	Fenwick
Virtute superanda fortuna	*Fortune is to be overcome by virtue*	Whiteford
Virtute tutus	*By virtue safe*	Blair, Burt-Marshall, Marshall, Mitchelson, Phaire Phayre
Virtute vici	*I have conquered by virtue*	Ingram, Meynell
Virtute viget	*He flourishes by virtue*	Keirie, Paton
Virtute vinces	*You shall conquer by virtue*	Leatham.
Virtute vincet	*He shall conquer by virtue*	Cooper
Virtute vincit invidiam	*He overcomes envy by virtue*	Mann
Virtute viresco	*I flourish by virtue*	Paterson
Virtuti	*To virtue*	Dick Lauder
Virtuti comes invidia .	*Envy an attendant on virtue*	Cunninghame, Devereux
Virtuti damnosa quies	*Inactivity is injurious to virtue*	Brisbane, Hewer
Virtuti fido	*I trust in virtue*	Ap-Eynions
Virtuti fortuna comes	*Fortune is the attendant of virtue*	Hoskyns, Mayne, Orr, Rothwell, Stewart

Virtuti inimica quies	*Inactivity is an enemy to virtue*	Forbes
Virtuti mœnia cedant	*Fortifications may yield to bravery*	Wilder
Virtuti nihil invium	*Nothing is inaccessible to virtue*	Chamberlayne, Hillary
Virtuti nihil obstat et armis	*Nothing withstands virtue and arms*	Stratford
Virtuti non armis fido	*I trust to virtue, not to arms*	Egerton, Grey-Egerton
Virtuti omnia parent	*All things obey virtue*	Butter
Virtutis	*Of virtue*	Skeen
Virtutis alimentum honos	*Honour is the aliment of virtue*	Parker
Virtutis amore	*By the love of virtue*	Annesley, Stephens
Virtutis avorum præmium	*The reward of my ancestors' valour*	Upton
Virtutis comes invidia	*Envy is the attendant of virtue*	Devereux
Virtutis fortuna comes	*Fortune the companion of virtue*	Colley, Ferguson, Gyll, Orr, Pomeroy, Stewart, Trench, Trotter Wellesley
Virtutis gloria crescit	*The glory of virtue increases*	Tytler
Virtutis gloria merces.	*Glory is the recompense of valour*	Bewley, Deuchar, Forbes-Robertson, Gyll Lorimer, Macdona, MacDonagh, M'Donegh, Macdonogh, M'Donogh, M Robertson, Robertson, Sandbach
Virtutis gloria parta	*Glory obtained by virtue*	Napier
Virtutis honor præmium	*Honour is the reward of virtue*	Sparling
Virtutis in bello præmium	*The reward of bravery in war*	Robertson, Steuart
Virtutis laus actio	*Deeds are the praise of virtue*	Corbet, Fraser, Gledstanes, MacDougall, Rumbold, Tansley
Virtutis præmium	*Virtue's reward*	De Jersey, Leck, Morton, Myrton, Stewart, Thoms
Virtutis præmium honor	*Honour is the reward of virtue*	Dickinson, Feilden, Hapsburgh, Percy-Fielding, Wallford, Walton
Virtutis regia merces	*A palace the reward of bravery*	Alpin, Feilden, MacGregor, Skeen, Skene
Virtutis regio merces	*A country the recompense of bravery*	Blackadder, Duff
Virtutis robore robur	*Strong in virtue's strength*	Daccome, Dackcombe, Fielding
Virtutis stemmata	*The pedigrees of virtue.*	Cobb
Vir tutus et fidelis	*A man safe and faithful*	Bomford
Visa per invisa firma	*Seen things established by unseen*	Spence
Vis courageux fier		Cooke, Falcon
Vise a la fin	*Look to the end*	Blackader, Home
Vis en espoir	*Live in hope*	Hassard,
Vis et fides	*Power and fidelity*	Campbell, Pleydell Bouverie Campbell, Wyndham
Vis et virtus	*Force and courage*	Chisalme, Chisholme
Vis fortibus arma	*Vigour is arms to brave men*	Barton, Cruikshanks, Nisbet, Nisbett
Vi si non consilio	*By force, if not by contrivance*	Sherbrooke
Vis in vita Deus	*God the strength in life*	M'Connel
Vis super hostem	*Power over the enemy*	O'Donovan
Vis unita fortior	*Force is stronger by union*	Brooke, Bunbury, Eyton, Flood, Hales, Hosken, Lidwell, M'Clintock Bunbury, Moore, Pulteney.
Vis veritatis magna	*The force of truth is great*	Hall
Vis viri fragilis	*Weak is the strength of man*	Lilborne, Lilburne, Ruddiman
Vita brevis gloria æterna.	*The life short, the glory eternal*	Price
Vitæ faciendo nemini timeas	*Fear no one in performing the duties of life*	Robertson
Vita et pectore puro	*By life and a pure heart*	Belloe
Vitæ via virtus	*Virtue is the way of life*	Dawson, Vaughan, Watkins, Weeks
Vitam dirigit	*It guides my life*	Christison
Vitam impendere vero	*To devote life to the truth*	Brown, Ramage, Reichel
Vita more fide	*By hope, custom and faith*	Hanercroft
Vita posse priore frui	*To be able to enjoy the former part of life*	Townsend
Vita potior libertas	*Liberty is better than life*	Forster, Lumm
Vittoria .		Nicholson
Vivam te laudare	*Let me live to praise thee*	Chambers
Vivant dum virent	*Let them live while they are green*	Forrest
Vivat Greatrakes, semper virescat	*Let Greatorex live and always flourish*	Greatorex
Vivat Rex	*Long life to the King*	M'Corquodall, M'Corquodell, M'Corquodill
Vivat veritas	*May truth flourish*	Duncan
Vive Deo	*Live for God*	Durham.
Vive Deo ut vivas	*Live for God that you may live*	Abercromby, Craig, Craigie, Laurie
Vive en espoir	*Live in hope*	Hassard, Starr
Vive et vivas	*Live and let live*	Abercromby
Vive hodie	*Live to day*	Green Price, Price
Vivat honestas	*May honesty flourish*	Sproston
Vive la joye	*Long live joy*	Joy
Vive la plume	*Long live the pen*	Scott
Vive le Roi	*Long life to the King*	Gairden
Vi vel suavitate	*By violence or mildness*	Rochfort
Vive memor lethi, fugit hora	*Live mindful of death, time flies*	Bailhache
Vivens canam	*I shall yet sing while alive*	Morris
Vivere sat vincere	*To conquer is to live enough*	Eveleigh De Moleyns, Molyneux, Mullins
Vive revicturus	[illegible]	[illegible]
Vive ut postea vivas.	[illegible]	[illegible]

Motto	Translation	Names
Vive ut semper vivas	*Live so that you may live for ever*	Hopson, Morgan
Vive ut vivas	*Live, that you may live*	Abercrombie, Abercromby, Bathgate, Bentley, Falconer, Falkner, Faulkner, Fraser, Hall, Hartley, Iliff, Johnston, M'Kenzie, Manning, Price, Rugge-Price, Sladen, Snuggs, Stone, Vivian, Von Sturmer, Watney
Vive valeque.	*Live and farewell*	Green,
Vi victus non coactus	*Conquered, not compelled by force*	Warter
Vivimus in spe	*We live in hope*	Thorburn
Vivis sperandum	*While there is life there is hope*	M'Nevins, Niven, Philip
Vivite fortes	*Live bravely*	Allen
Vivit post funera virtus	*Virtue lives after the grave*	Barrett Hamilton, Boyle, Bryson, Maule, Robin, Sharp, Sharp, Thorp
Vivitur ingenio	*He lives by his wits*	Copen, Darley
Vi vivo et armis	*I live by force and arms*	Hennessy, O'Hennessy
Vivunt dum virent	*They live while they are green*	Forrest
Vix ea nostra voco	*I scarce call these deeds of our ancestors ours*	Campbell, Foster, Fonntaine, Greville, Greville-Nugent, Maister, Techell
Vixi liber, et moriar	*I have lived free, and will die so*	Gray, Ibbetson, Ibetson, Selwin
Vocatus obedivi	*I obeyed when called*	Gell
Volabo ut requiescam	*I will make haste, that I may have rest*	Collens, Collins
Volando, reptilia sperno	*Flying, I despise reptiles*	Scarta, Scarth, Scras, Scrase
Volens et valens	*Willingly and powerfully*	Fetherston, Fetherston - Whitney, Fetherstonhaugh-Whitney
Volenti nil difficile	*Nothing is hard to a willing mind*	Creech
Volo, non valeo	*I am willing, but not able*	Greystock, Howard
Volonté de Dieu	*The will of God*	Fyler
Volvitur et ridet	*He despises dangers*	Fairweather, Fairwether
Vota vita mea	*My life is vowed*	Brabazon, Hagan.
Votis et conamine	*With prayers and strenuous exertion*	Kirk
Votis tunc velis,	*Be favourable to my prayers*	Edmunds.
Vows should be respected		Vowe
Vrai à la fin	*True to the end.*	Pike
Vraye foy	*True faith*	Boswell.
Vulnera ecclesiæ liberorum vita	*Wounds are the life of the children of the Church*	Church.
Vulnera sano.	*I heal up wounds*	Balderston, Balderstone
Vulnera temno	*I despise wounds*	Cramond
Vulneratur non vincitur	*He is wounded, not defeated*	Homfray
Vulneratus non victus	*Wounded, not conquered*	O'Grady
Vulnere viresco	*I flourish from a wound*	Stewart
Vulneror, non vincor	*I am wounded, but not vanquished*	Homfrey, Muschamp
Vultus in hostem	*My face to the foe*	Codrington

W

Motto	Translation	Names
Walk in the fear of God		Walker
Ware the horn		Savage
Waste not		Green
Watch		Forbes, Gordon, Otter, Lloyd
Watch and pray		Forbes
Watchful and bold		Coats, Cotes
Watch the temptation		Keith
Watch weel		Halyburton, Scott
Watch well		Halliburton, Hallyburton, Halyburton.
Watch wiel		Scott
Waterloo		Nicholson
Ways and means		Lowndes
We big you see warily		Cornwall
We hae dune		MacMicking
Weigh well		Urquhart
We live in hope		Thorburn
Wer gutes u boses nit kan ertragan wirt kein grose ehre erjagen	*Who cannot bear good and evil shall obtain no great honours*	Brander
We rise		Martinson.
West Indies		Provost
We stoop not		Anderton
Whadder		Stewart
Whatsoever thy hand findeth to do do it with thy might		Buxton
What was may be		Oliphant.
Wheare vertu lys love never dys		Thompson
Who most h[illegible] served is gre[illegible]		Sayle
Who da[illegible] w[illegible]		[illegible]er[illegible]urgh

Whyll God wyll		Treffry
Whyll lyff lastyth		Cornewall
Will God, and I shall		Ashburnham, Menzies.
Will well		Urquhart
Wil sone wil		Wilson
Wisdom above riches		Nuthoobhoy
Wisdom and strength		Crookes
Wisdom's beginning is God's fear		Campbell
Wise and harmless		Grant
With heart and hand		Dudgeon
Without fear		Campbell, Sutherland
Without God castles are nothing		Castleman
Without help from above the arrow flies in vain		Jones.
With thy might		Smith
With truth and diligence		Lucy
Woodnotes wild		Burns
Work and wait		Ross
Wrth ein ffrwythau y'n hadnabydder	*By our fruits we are known*	Ellis

Y

Y cadarn a'r cyrfwys	*The mighty and cunning*	Williams, Williams-Wynn
Y cyfiawn sydd hy megis Llew		Hughes,
Y ddioddefws y orfu		Morgan, Williams
Ye great pule		Mercer
Yet higher		Kinloch, Kinlock
Yet in my flesh shall I see God		Surman
Y fyn Duw a fydd		Mathew
Y gwir yn erbyn y byd	*The truth against the world*	Edwards.
Ymlaen		Lewis
Ynir o yale		Lloyd
Ystoyeau et ne doublero		Strangeways.
Yvery		Perceval, Percival

Z

Zeal and honour		Blomfield.
Zealous		Hood.

KEY TO THE PLATES.

NOTE.—For purposes of comparison, an asterisk is affixed to names in cases where the engraving does not precisely correspond with the blazon as given in the text [See note at p. 1, Part I.] In cases where a crest is absolutely accurate as regards one or more families of a particular name, while it may vary slightly (in colour lines, for example) from another family of the same name, the name is not repeated with an asterisk; therefore, when it is desired to ascertain the precise blazons for various families of the same name, reference should be made to the text under the particular surname required.

PLATE 1.—1 Laforey

2 Cossen, Cosson, Dyce

3 *Davies, Philipps, Lloyd-Philipps, Philips, *Langharne Philips, Phillips, Poley, Polley, Pooley, Sammes, *Staple, Tarleton

4 *Clark

5 Bagnall

6 *Beynon, James

7 Barlande, Barling, Fonnereau

8 Williams

9 Nairn, Oxborongh, Oxburgh

10 Beynon, Blodlow, Casamajor, Casmajor, Clapham, Gibbines, Gibbins, Girandot, Griffith, Jefferis, Ludlow, Marney, Morgan, Norfolk, Northfolke, Powell, Price, Pritchard, Pullyn, Rose, Thorne, Walne, Webb-Bowen, Weyland

11 Malone

12 Cowan, Fitchett, Gerard, *Lawford, *Lilly, Lyddel, Manderne, Paunce-foot, Pauncefort, Rees, *Shelletoe, Villers, Villiers

13 Adams, Addagh, Aufrere, Baker, *Barrett, Baunceford, Bayley, Beldam, Bentham, Billingham, Blenkinsopp, Bois, Boyce, Boyse, Brompton, Brooke, Brown, Browne, Bruce, Buckingham, Burgess, Canning, Casley, *Chace, Chardin, *Chase, Chritchley, Cliff, *Codd, Corbyn, Coverdale, Coverdall, *Cozens, Crawfield, Crossfield, *Cuming, Cumming, Dancey, Davies, Davis, *De Aguilar, *Dease, *De Bathe, De Rinzy, De Silva, *Devan, Dixon, Donelan, Dowson, Drummond, Dupree, Edridge, Egerton, Farquhar, Fitz Henry, Fitz-Water, Ford, *Gayer, Germin, Germyn, *Gilchrist, *Gordon Cumming, Gouring, Graeme, Graham, Gronow, Grove, Gwyn, *Hadson, Hagart, Haggerston, *Hanson, *Hatcliff, Holker, Holmes, Hosken, Hughes, Ingowville, *Janns, Jarveis, Jarvis, *Javel, Jones, Kenan, King, Kyffin, Kyffyn, Lamb, Lambert, *Lamoiley, Lex, Ledwich, Leign, Lewis, *Lincolne, Lloyd, *Longe, Lovatt, Lows, *Lutwidge, M'Braire, M'Diarmid, M'Millan, M'Neil, Mathisson, Maun-cell, Meeke, Meyler, Mills, *Molloy, Monson, *Morant, *Morrice, *Morris, Mostyn, Mylles, Nanney, *Newman, Newton, *Nowne, *O'Donellan, O'Donlevy, Ogilvie, Owen, *Owsley, Parker, Paset, Paslew, Patte, Paynell, Peart, Peel, Pellat, *Peryan, Peryent, *Phene, *Playters, *Pomeroy, Pop-pelwell, Raines, Raley, Redington, *Reppley, Richards, Ritson, Roberts, *Roscarrock, Saltren, Seaton, Shaw, Shipton, Simpson, Sloan, Smyth, Sommers, Sowerby, Stanbury, Stanger, Starr, Stephens, *Stevens, *Sutton, Tappin, *Thompson, *Thomson, Tolliott, Tottenham, Tours, Vaughan, Vaux, Vernon, Vowe, Westenra, Whale, Williams, Wilshere, Wilson, Wolley, Woodburne, *Wynne.

14 Billingham, *Dudley, *Ffolliott, *Folliott, Marryatt, Meyer, Shirreff, Wort-ham, Worthom

PLATE 2.—1 Ouvry

2 Martin, *Salisbury

3 Jenkin, Jenkins, *Jenkyns, Jones, Lloyd, Morrice, Morris, Price Williams, Pryce, Williams, Wynne Pendarves

4 Ashenden, Ashondon, *Brisbon, *Brisbone, Egerton, Haxford

5 Auverquerque, Baxter, Bloys, Brende, Dalgety, Dalgetty, De Blois, Etty, Goring, Hamon, Ireland, Mildmay, St. John Mildmay, Ogilvie, Ogilvy, Pavey, Waldron

6 *Bayloll, Fothergill, *Saxby

7 Broun, Brown, Browning, Brownrigg, Coxan, Coxen, Dixon, *Durrant, Ensor, Fielder, Haugh, Hoppare, Lorimer, Marks, Nyssell, Pugh, Thorp, Trotter, Watkins, Whatley, Worsley, Wortley

8 Foley

9 Roberts

10 Beddington, *Pooly

11 Lloyd, Lloyd Price, Price

PLATE 3.—1 Creswick

2 Bean, Beane, Cashall, Hervey, Morse, Ogilvie, Rees

3 Cozens, Kyle.

4 Baker

5 Cecil, Chein, Cheine, Chiene, Loader, *Winstone, *Wynston

6 Beseley, Besley, Besly, Craddock, Cradock, Foley, Ford, Roper, Warren

7 Acottis, Acotts, *Adkins, *Audyin, *Conroy, *Gilchrist, *Havering, Hugo, *Hurell, *Hurle, *Hurrell

8 Salisbury

9 Wakelin, Wakelyn, Walkelin

10 Phillips

11 Barbenson

12 Powell

13 *Howard, Marshall, Paske, *Stracey, Unsworth

14 Edmondson

15 Alanson, Allanson, Allaunson, Allenson, *Wall, *Walle

PLATE 4. — 1 Bayley, *Caldicote, *Gerard, *Johnson, *Rumney, *Sneyd, *Walmesley

2 Beauclerk, *Bockingham, *Bohun, *Fallowfield, Fitzclarence, Fitzroy, Gordon-Lennox

3 Angus, Brewes, Brews, Brewse, *Bromfield, Burrow, Cambridge, Cambrige, Cobbold, Coriton, Coryton, *Cowell, Cricket, Crickitt, Croft, Crotts, Crosby, De Garis, *Delamote, De Lisle, De Senlize, *Desmond, De Warren, Disney, Edwards, *Eyre, Fairfax, Garvey, *Goloner, Gregg, Greystock, *Gulliver, Hemans, *Holbrook, Hutchings, Hutchins, Macdougal-Hay, *M'Dowall-Hay, Marshall, *Moore, Mouat, *Muriell, Negus, Norman, Northwick, Pardoe, Pennant, Pugh, Ramsay Fairfax, Rickards, Roebuck, Rushout, Sclater, Slater, Sneyd, Thomson, *Walmsley, West-more, Wilde, Zurich

4 *Gelling, *Holland, *Howard, Le-strange

5 *Chedder, *Cheder *Crutchley, *Ed-

mund, Fairfax, Fitz-Wight, *Gay, *Kenton, Ravenscroft.
7. *Diable, *Dibble, *Dible, Healey, Healy, *Heming, *Hemming, *Howard, *Ravencroft, *Wicklow.
8. Aoluite, *Bruce, *Brotherton, *Colvile, *Cornwall, *Gourney, *Howard, *Le Strange, Norfolk, Percy, Strange, Talbot, *Vere.
9. Beaumont, *Blount, Brett, Cheeke, *Colwell, *Covell, *Cowell, *Desnay, Ellis, *Gorney, Kinerby, Kynerby, Love, Magrath, Paddye, Talbot.
10. Evans.
12. Mesham.

PLATE 5.—1. Barnard.
2. Walker.
3. Naylor.
4. Franceis, Frances.
5. Bruce, Garratt, Jarrett.
6. Butcher, Creping, Crepping, Fleury, Mackay, Martin, Martine, Mulbery.
7. Eastwood.
8. Turner.
9. Hartridge.
10. Bamfield, Baumfield, *Colcleugh, Cross, Ellison, *Hardie.
11. Bartley, Carsewell, Fischer, Gannble, Napton, Reid, *Wake.
12. Clulow, Cobben, Cobbenn, Cobbin, Cobbyn, Cobenn, Cobyn, Ogilvie, Ogilvy.
13. Andin, *Andym, *Audyn, *Carnegy, Giddy.
14. Shadford.
15. Dyas, Kiffin.

PLATE 6. — 1. *Aleston, *Alston, *Bigland, Cotter, *Gape, Jenkins, Yelverton.
2. *Adamson, Athy, Auncell, *Barough, *Barrow, Beaton, Beaumont, Beton, Betton, Betune, *Blount, Booth, Boothe, Gore-Booth, *Bramhall, Brant, Brett, Brooks, Broomhall, Brown, Bruce, Bryden, Burroughs, *Cape, Carew, *Casborne, *Catesby, *Cattesbye, Clement, *Coakley, *Collick, *Compton, Copeland, Coryton, Coxhead, *Creston, *Crispie, *Delme, *Delmie, Depham, *Dongan, *Duncan, *Dungan, *Dymoke, Escot, Esscot, Evans, Farofeld, Fitzpaine, *Flinn, Forward, *Fowkes, *Garrett, *Gaury, *Goble, Goode, *Gresley, *Gresque, Griffith, *Gyssinge, Haggerston, Halkett, *Harvey, *Hatcliffe, Holbeach, Holbech, *Homan-Mulock, Hustwick, *Kelton, Ketland, *King, *Leith-Buchanan, Lemon, *Leston, *Lloyd, Loterel, M'Clintock, M'Lintock, Maddock, Maurice, *Nettleship, *Nicholas, Noble, *Norcliffe, North, Norway, Ogston, *Orr, *Palmer, Paynell, Phitton, Rawstorne, Rishton, Rome, Sheath, *Shelton, *Slator, Slingsby, Staple, Staunton, Sterling, Stirling, Strange, Strangewayes, Strangeways, Strangewicke, Strangways, Surtees, Sulyard, Swainston, *Tate, Taylor, Turner, Underwood, Urswicke, Walpole, *Webb, Wilde, Yenn.
3. Branscomb, Branscombe, Bronscomb, *Fenning, *More.
4. *Balscott, Beatty, Dry, Eastwood, *Gardner, *Margesson, *Margetson, *Wilney.
5. *Bruce, Harvey.
6. Burgone, Burgoyne, *Burroughs, Condie, Goodhard, Goodhart, Hames, Hammes, Haycock, Howston, *Park, *Parke, Wedgewood.
7. Dolphin, Dolphine, Turner, *Turnor, Turnour.
8. Turner.
9. *Hayward, *Turner, Turnor.
10. *Jenkin, *Jenkins.
11. *Borne, *Delmar, Mortlock.
12. Woods.

PLATE 7.—1. Dobbs.
2. Dobbs, Ward.
3. *Campbell, Furse, *Maitland, *Ramsay-Gibson-Maitland, *Stewart.
4. Acham, Achym, Acklame, Boardman, *Bramston, Brough, Calcott, Grys, *Hancome, *Handcome, *Haynes, *Kitto, *Kittoe, Lennox, *Magee, Pendarves, Philips, Phillips, *Shepley.
5. Barrett, Denton, De Lancaster, *Dickens, *Graham, Harvy, Howard, *Hoyle, Hughes, Jones, *King, *Montgomery, Palmer, *Panton, *Penkevell, *Penkevill, Round, Rowand, Silvester, Starr, *Wolley, Wool, Wooll.
6. *Bourke, Hanmer, Roberts.
7. Bales, *Dickins, *Hening.
8. Suffield.
9. Badder, Madder, *Modder, *Stocket.
10. Barneby, Bellasis, Bellassis, Cary, Christian, Cocker, M'Kenzie, Ryed, Ryede.
11. Bourke.
12. Diskens, Goodenough, Harbord, Lile, Lille, Suffield.
14. Peel.

PLATE 8. — 1. Brown, *Browne, *Goulding.
2. *Chelmick, *Chilmick, *Fellow, *Jesse, Paul, *Symington.
3. Cooper.
4. *Dicey, *Edwin, *Pillett, *Pillott, *Pipard.
5. Old.
7. Musters, *Wyld.
8. Bond, Burrowes, Chamond, *Cornwall, *Dickin, *Duval, *Duvall, Elvet, Eyston, Fell, Green, Hanman, *Harborne, *Holder, *Hughes, Hunt, Kempthorne, *Kenyon, Lacy, Lee, Le Hunte, Lewis, Ley, Mnmby, Shershall, Silly, *Tighman, Trayner.
9. Egerton.
10. Domenichetti, Markham.
11. *Bolbeck, *Bolebec, *Bolebeck, *Butt, Drayner, Halton.
12. *Brockas, *Brokas, *Christian, Dee.
13. *Eman, *Foley, Lewis.
14. Norwood.

PLATE 9.—1. Grave.
2. Bain, Baine, Bidon, Castleman, Pierpont, Pierrepoint, Pierrepont.
3. Edwards.
4. Bellasis.
5. Bettesworth.
6. Hermon.
7. Jordan.
8. *Faunce, *Fence, Newenham, Newman.
9. Hammick.
10. Acton, Malefont, Malesaunts.
11. Rich.
12. Lusher.
13. Fardell.
14. Barnard, *Bernard, *Yabsley.
15. *Call.

PLATE 10. — 1. Black, Bonell, Bulimore, *Byrde, *Cowden, Davies, Eam, Eames, Emes, Emme, Evens, *Fawcett, Fife, Fiffe, Fonte, Gerandot, *Glyn, *Gubyon, Hamill, Hopkins, Hopkinson, *Lewin, Lloyd, Lyons, Macfie, Pandolfi, Priestley, Traby, Vaughan, Wells.
2. Agar, Ayloffe, *Badley, *Baett, Barkworth, Barnes, Barron, Basket, Baskett, Batt, *Becher, Beecher, Bell, Bentley, Bernall, Bertram, Bethune, Betton, Blaauw, Black, Bladewell, Bladwell, Blodwell, Blouyle, Blunden, Bond, Bosworth, Botheras, Brashier, Brasier, Breck, Breek, *Brett, *Brooke, Browne, *Caldecott, *Caldwell, Card, *Chapell, Charlton, *Cherry, *Clode, *Coachman, Cobham, *Colchester, *Collison, *Colvile, Cook, Cooper, Coppenger, Coppinger, Corrie, Corry, *Craig, *Crampton, Cromer, *Cromwell, Crosthwaite, Cruice, Cruise, Currie, Curry, *Cuthbert, Dalingrugge, Dallaway, *Dalmer, Davis, Dean, *Deane, De la Faye, Dicey, Dickenson, Diconson, Dixon, *Dockrell, *Dodwell, Dolton, *Donelan, Drane, Drummond, Duncombe, Dyes, *Edgell, *Edgill, *Edwardes, *Edwards, English, *Enoke, Ewan, *Fearon, *Ferguson, *Fisher, Fitz-John, Foley, Ford, Foulston, *Freeman, *Frenband, *Frewen, *Fruen, Fury, Gaine, *Geary-Salte, Geridot, Glasse, *Glubb, Gold, Goldesburgh, *Gollop, *Goodwin, Goold, *Gotley, Grace, *Grady, Grammer, Grant, *Gray, *Griffith, Grindal, Grindall, *Gybbons, Halsbury, *Handcock, *Hara, *Harrison, *Harvey, *Hebden, *Herapath, Hendmarsh, Hindmarsh, *Hooper, Horan, Husdell, Hutchinson, Hyatt, Hyndmarsh, Ingles, Inglis, *Jackson, Jeffreys, Jeffries, John, Johnson, Jones, Joy, *Karkenton, *Karkington, Kedmarston, Keith, *Kevett, Kirkman, Langrishe, Layton, Le Bailly, Leigh, Lewins, Llewellyn, Lloyd, Logan, Lomelying, Lynn, M'Candlish, Macfie, Macknight, Macknyghte, Maddock, Madocks, March, Martyre, *Mason, Matchett, Matthews, Mendip, Menet, Menett, *Millard, Moncreiff, Moncreiffe, Montaguta, Mores, Morres, Mowatt, Moubray, Newenham, Newlands, *Newnham, Nicholl, Nicholsor, Nickelson, Nicol, Nicolson, Northwood, *O'Hara, O'Hosan, *Olderbury, Orpen, *Ottley, *Packington, *Parry, *Passingham, Peace, Pearmain, Pears, Pepper, Percivall, Picken, Pigg, Pomeroy, Poore, Powell, Praed, *Prattman, Priddle, Primrose, Prouse, Read, Repley, Rishton, Robartes, Rock, Rogerson, Roughsedge, Rowlatt,

Rule, Rumbold, Rust, Scot, Scott, Sebright, Shields, Simpson, Stansfield, *Stevens, Stevenson, Steuart, Stewart, Stocken, Stockes, Stone, Strange, Strode, Stroode, Stroud, Stroude, Stuart, *Stuckey, *Sullivan, Sutton, Taswell, Tatlock, Thomas, Thoroughgood, Tibbet, Tilford, Tot, Tyrell, Tyrrell, Vampage, *Weldon, Wilcocks, *Williams, Wintringham, Wisham, Yates

3 Allen, Braid, *Braytoft, Bridges, Cade, Capon, Charlton, Clarke, Coulthard, Cumbrae-Stewart, Cunnington, Durand, Dyer, Eaines, Ermingland, Erskine, Esharton, Fairange, Farquharson, Fergusson, Freeman Fyfe, Fyffe, *Grehan, Griffith, Griffiths, Hacklet, Hill, Hoherd, Hobert, *Keresforth, King, Lacy, Lamphier, Leigh, MacAwley Macduff, M'Kenzie, M'Phie, Maddison, Magawly Cerati de Calry, *Merry, *Meyler, Milliken, Moncreiff, Moncreiffe, Moncrieff, Moubray, Nichol, Nicol, Nolan, Norton, Nowland, Ogilvie, Ogilvy, Osborne, Owen, *Page, Parsons, Percivall, Picton, *Pyot, Ravensholme, *Rihton, Russell Sall, Scott, Seys, Shaw, Spence, Stainsbury, Stewart, Stuart, Thomas, *Thornton, Tyers, Wilson, *Wyse, *Young

4 Dennis, Ferrant, Gould, Killegrew, Laslett, Netterville, Tyrell

5 *Beamish, *Bernard-Beamish, Somerville

6 *Blumberg, *Bromeall, *Burghersh, Cowan, Doxat, Leslie, Lesly, Lodge, *Norton,* Peachey, Stone, Stuckey, Sutton, Wastneys

7 Ameredith, *Anscell, *Ansell, *Anstrell, *Atkins, *Browne, Catchmay, Comb, Combe, *Dayman, Eldershaw, Fleming, Hare, Hun, Markoe, Prestwold, *Wase, Wasse, *White

8 *Abadam, *Adams, Ball, De Beaumont, Champain, Colthurst, *Cook, *Coxe, *Cratford, Damory, *Dundas, Emme, Ewing, *Fysher, Gates, *Godley, Golder, *Guynn, Halloway, Harnet, Holloway, Kellie, *Lloyd, *Luscombe, M'Leay, M'Leish, Morrell, Mould, Netterville, Offley, Pepper, Royse, Scot, Scott, *Tompson

9 *Andrews, *Arderes, Ayloffe, Black, Dales, *Davidge, *Ellis, *Flower, Froyle, Hamill, Jevers, *Kempson, *Kempston, Legh, Leigh, Lukin, *Machet, *Moore, Offord, Partridge, Peard, *Pinn, Penney, Slaning, Slanning, Tarby, Tieby, Wastneys, Young

10 *Hare, Ross

11 Boys, *Bramble, *Brinkhurst, *Carbonell, *Carbonelle, *Carbronel, Carpenter, Cornewall, Cornwall, *Criche, Dampier, Delilers, *Elford, *Fergus, Fichet, *Flood, Foord, Ford, Garnet, *Garnons, Glasbrook, Glazebrook, Jewkes, Lawless, Lawton, Malephant, Moda, Peach, Peache, *Piozzi-Salusbury, Sadleir, Sadler, *Salusbury, Stanton, St George, Tuke, Tylgham, Wiberd

12 Meredith, Phillips

PLATE 11 —1 *Mills

2 *Brogden, Carpenter, Chesbrough,

3 March

4 Lund

5 Berrie, Berry, Boddington, Boddinton, Bodington, Gappei, Lingard Guthrie, Woodcock

6 Montefiore

7 *Abney, Batley, *Bedford, Benett, *Bennett, Bent, Beswick, *Beswicke, *Carlyon, Chubbe, *Comport, *Cooke, Crute, *Dockwra, *Furguason, Goodwin, Hallet, *Leather, *Morris, *Platt, Rous, Rouse, *Vynall

8 Pestick, Boddington

9 Allan

10 Barlow, Barrowe, Bennet, *Bonnell, *Breedon, *Bromhall, Bromilow, Buckworth, Capel, Capell, *Champernowne, Clarke, *Denver, Dodding, Fletcher, Goodrich, Guthrie, Hare, Heron, Knell, Knill, *Littledale, *Lofft, Mapletoft, Nesham, Ravenhill, *Russel, Russell, Seed, *Sleigh, Walford, Walker

11 Allan, Allen, Alleyn, Alltham, *Allyn, Altham, *Ballidon, Barrett, Doe, Franks, Lamborn, Lamborne, Penwarne

12 Makdougal.

13 Allhusen

14 Burke, Dobbin, Dodsworth, Edmond, Hagger, Hoy, Hoye, Jumper, Maledoctus, Manduit

PLATE 12 —1 Ardis, Dunbar, Everingham, *King, *Lennard, Maddocks, Panmure, Rolesley, Roscruge, Roskinge, Scot, Scott, Skippe, Tudway, Whiteside, Wise

2 Elvin

3 *Ackhurst, Cohen, *Royse, *Wood

4 Ogilvy, Plomer

5 Cue, Kew, MacMurroughone, Murphy, O'Murphy, O'Murroughone, Plumer, Ridall, Riddall, Riddell, Ridehalgh, Tindall

6 Tyson

7 Norwood, *Phippes

8 Harrison

9 Soper.

10 *Bayley, Nicholl

11 Davis

12 *Bendall, Blackwell, Blackwill, Bonvill, *Du Cane, Fisher, Fulcher, Halliday, Miles, *Neaves, Peck, *Randolph, Shields, Trant, Twedie

14 Brooks, Burd-Brooks

PLATE 13.—1 *Bent, *Chafe, Dare

2 *Bedford, Bourch, Brown, *Buckmaster, By, Cade, Chalmers, *Crombie, *Crome, *Croome, *Dickinson, Dummer, Farlough, Hathaway, Hatheway, Hayman, *Hayward, *Kenny, Leycester, Lyons, McKerrell - Brown, Marke, Markes, Marks, Nolan, Orde, Penny, Phillips, Plumerage, Scobell, Terry

3 *Dymon

4 Salomons

5 *Candler-Brown, *Fairclough, *Gibbings, *Joyner, *Norman, *Plumerage, Pryce

6 *Brock, *Brocke, *Canning, Mansergh, *Stratford, *Wyatt

7 *Gibbon, Montaigne, Mountain.

9 Henstock

10 Baker, Bulmar, Crossman, Edmondson, Gibbons, Ile, Isle, James, *Janes, Leigh, *Lomax, Maskelyne, *Pardor, *Pye, Shergold, Shiers, Stanbridge, Standbridge, Taylor

11 Bass

12 Bates, Carrick, Erskine, *Ferguson, Leash, *M'Crummen, M'Crummin, Maitland, *Richardson

13 *Bedford, *Brown, *Cowmeadow, Dodson, *Stoit, *Stoyt, *Western, *Westerne, *Whitshed

14 Munyard

PLATE 14 —1 Ripley

2 *Acleham, *Aclehum, Tyssen

3 Fydell

4 Brindley, *Gildart

5 *Tailer, Taylor

6. Benson

7 Watlington

8 Duff, M'Dermott

9 Mohamud

10 Allestry, Arrol, Ferguson, Hay Newton, Jeffery, Kukefield, Loane, Newton, Scepter, Scot, Scott, Wikes

11 Willmott

12 Bergaigne, Bergaine, *Bowie, *Bownder, *Bowne, Chalmers, Clough, *Coghlan, Corben, *Dempster, Duff, Farquharson, *Gandolfi, Gundry, *Hill, *Jellicoe, Kuckfield, M'Dowal, McDuff, *Macduff, M'Farquhar, *Mackery, Milligan, Milliken, *Nevill, O'Dempsey, *Ogilvie, O Kearin, Pakington, *Passingham, Pender, Sampson, Sipcot, Shaw, Stafford, *Stewart, Sworder, Watlington, *Woodlock, Young

13 Pender

14 Ansert, Macdonald, *M'Dowall

PLATE 15 —1 Cookson, *Hartsink, *Staft, *Vigor, Wagstaff

2 *Alington, *Bowen, *Dalway, *Hayes, Heys, *Mirfin

3 Nicholson.

4 Bright, Canning, *Chough, *Close, Clough, Clowes, Cooper, Cutler, Dwaris, Edmondstone, *Emerson, Glasco, *Gooderick *Goodrick, *Goodricke, Hadeswell, Hadiswell, *Illingsworth, Inwood, Jobbing, Kenyon, *Langton, Emerson Laslett, *MacGillafoyle, M'Murray, *Sims, Stewart, Syme, Rawles

5 *Buckminster, Kinahan

6 Caley, Calley, Cayley, Caylley, *Canning, Kemp, Kempt

7 Corker, *Dillon, Elston, Euen, Ewing, Frew, Gladhill, Henlock, Holburne, Hulburn, Inglis, *Ireton, Lamb, Lambe, Liddel, Liddiard, Lidell, Orr Lwing, Roberts, Starr, St Lyz, Willan

8 Cooke, Cramp, *Dillon, *English, *Esdaile, *Jones, *Lamb, *Lambe, *Lawson, *Leward, *Lutman, *Monsell, *Pipon, Stable, *Stewart, *Stote, *Warmouth, *Welman

9 *Batt, *Clark, Ettrick, Menzies, *Sone, *Suoone, Viell

10 *Grover

11 *Dare

12 Davies

13 Bishe, Jones, Rishton

14 Bish, Boys, *Bresingham, *Britley, Davies, Gilman, *Hughes, Penfold, Rushton

PLATE 16.—1. Wellesley.

2. Hughes, *Rowlesley, *White.

3. Alden, Aldon, Beach, *Braunch, Bruse, Bryant, Bunford, Caulkin, Chetwode, Churchill, Clarke, Clavering, *Cleg, Cornell, Cowley, Darley, *Dillon, Dunsford, *Edwards, Francis, *Gapper, Garrard, *Gilbert, *Goodwin, *Gridley, *Hallet, *Heart, Hemmings, Heylyn, *Hobleday, Holland, Hughes, *Ingoldesby, *Ingoldsby, Jones, Kinchant, King, Lacy, *Lincolne, Lloyd, Long, Longfield, Maberley, Maberly, M'Brayne, *Merrey, *Merry, Millburn, Mirrie, Mirry, Molloy, Nelson, Nicholls, Nichols, Oulton, Philipse, *Skynner, *Sparkes, Spence, *Villiers, *Vaughan, Walsh, Walshe, Warrand, Whieldon, *Wrixon-Becher.

4. Whieldon.

5. *Evans, *James, *Morgan, *Oxman, *Powis, *Symson.

6. *Burlinson, Hughes, *Tillotson.

7. *Bellairs, *Bromeley, *Bromley, *Clarke, *Dumaresq, *Dumaresque, Fremantle, *Stockwood, *Stokewood.

8. Quain.

9. Burnaby.

10. *Gilbert, *Jennings, Merser, Wildman.

11. *Green, Griffith, Guinners, Hector, Hepworth, Hutchings, *Inglis, *Jenkinson, Ligonier, *Nicholson, *Philipoe, Thornton.

12. Ayde, *McMurray, *Murray.

13. Hanbury.

14. Chedworth, Doolan, Fortune, Harly, Hene, Henne, Rickets, Ricketts, Wall.

PLATE 17.—1. Aboril, Abrol, *Curtler, *Hoskyns, Plaiz, Playse, Wakeman, Wettyn, Wettyng.

2. Argal, Argles, Bates, Bawtre, Bawtree, Buchan, Burney, Burnie, Chaigneau, *Cogan, *Cole, *Doderidge, Edridge, Ennew, Farmar, *Fayreweather, Hawden, Home, Houison, Hume, Inglett, Kettleby, Kittelby, Kittleby, Knot, Knott, Leighton, Lighton, Long, MacKnight, Macleod, M'Leod, MacMurdoch, Maitland, Marsham, *Maude, Merling, Murdoch, *Nicholson, Nicolson, Ogilvie, *Pelsant, Pickernell, Powell, Rawlins, Romney, Scot, Scott, Monteath-Scott, Smyth, Stanford, Steel, Steele, Steell, Steuart, Stewart, Stuart, Toole, Tweddale, Virgin, Waddell.

3. Atlee, Atley, Damant, Dwyre, Gamell, Gammill, Hunter, Kennell, Riccard.

4. *Bowell, Cater, *Jacomb.

5. Awdry, *Bland, Boyle *Bresier, Bruse, *Byles, *Byng, *Caundis, Davison-Bland, Doran, *Dudley, *Ellis, Fuller, *Gibon, Jones, *Long, McLaughlan, May, Nicholson, O'Sullivan, Pollalion, Sutton, Thornton, Ward, *Wise.

6. A'Court, *Bulbec, *Bulbeck, *De Lapasture, *Lowe, *Tapper, Thornton.

7. *Edwards, *Jephson, Nicholson.

8. *Adyn, *Aiselbie, *Aislabie, Anmers, Anners, Argall, Argell, Argill, Arkybus, Ashton, Atherley, Atherly, Atkinson, Auld, Beal, *Beaurain, Bilesby, Birnie, *Bladerike, *Blumberg, *Bonwick, Bow, Brandon, Brunwin, Buckle, Burdett, Burghill, *Camays, *Camoys, *Carr, Carter, Cator, Chalmers, *Chamberlayne, Cheese, Chevallier, Chiefly, Cinsallagh, *Codenham, *Codham, *Coppull, *Corney, Crokey, Crynes, *Cupplade, Dalrymple, *Dandridge, Davis, Deane, Dedan, Dene, Denham, Dodswall, Dodswell, *Dongall, Dowell, *Dowling, Dusgate, *Earl, *Earle, Edeworth, Edgeworth, Edwards, *Erle, *Fairfax, Fairlie, *Fawether, *Fayreweather, Flower, Flowre, *Foote, Ford, Galbraith, Garnier, *Gaynor, *Geffery, *Gervais, Gordon, Goulden, Grogan, Grubb, Gunner, Harper, Harridge, Haskins, Hawdon, Hawtre, *Hebbs, Hende, Hendy, Hinde, Hodiam, *Holbrooke, Holmes, Home, *Hopton, Hose, Hoskyns, Houblon, Hume, *Hutchens, *Hyde, *Jarrett, Jefferyes, Jefferys, Jeffryes, Jones, Jones-Bateman, *Ketson, *Kettelby, *Kettleby, Kirkham, *Lambert, *Lancaster, *Lighton, *Long, Lorimer, *Losse, Lowndes, Lynn, Lyon, Macgregor, M'Gregor, Mackey, M'Knight, M'Leod, M'Naught, M'Nicoll, M'Quaid, M'Taggart, Mair, Markham, Marsh, *Marske, Martham, *Massingberd, Massy, De la Maziere, Melders, Meredith, Warter-Meredith, *Morris, *Morson, Mortlock, Moulson, Munn, *Naylor, Nicolson, *O'Dowling, Palgrave, Payne, Pearsall, Pearse, Peckover, Perks, Perris, Pickford, Pigou, Plasto, Portal, Potts, Pratte, Price, Rackham, Renwick, Richardson, *Rolfe, Ross, Rowland, Rowsewell, Ryle, Saltren, *Scot, Scotland, *Scott, Scott-Douglas, Shelbery, Shelbury, Silvester, Sim, Sime, Simm, *Sloane, Smith, Smyth, *Somers, Strebbing, Steel, Stewart, Surman, Tawse, *Throughston, Trimwell, *Troughton, Tuson, Unett, Virtue, *Vivian, Vylgus, Wakeman, Walter, Wanklyn, Weatherston, Whitchurch, White, Whitington, Whitwell, Williams, Widenham, Wolin, Worge, Wrey, Wynne, Yeates, Yeats.

9. Atfoe, Atsoe, Bec, Beck, Canton, Colbeck, *Docksey, *Hamer, Henry, Home, Fergusson-Home, *Hubert, Lyons,* Peers, Sheridan, Wren.

10. Cooper, Cowper, *Garnier, Gastrell, Jeffreys, Lloyd, Lowndes, Richardson, Stansfield, Walker.

11. Rathbone.

12. *Burghill, *Dunbar, *Gallightly, *Gellatly, *Gregorson, *M'Andrew, *Macgregor, *M'Gregor, *M'Grigor, *Murray, Northmore.

13. *Alban, *Bludder, *Bluder, *Bluther, Dunfee, Jaques.

14. *Bolter, Egremond, *Goodear, *Goodyear, *Ogilvie.

PLATE 18.—1. *Campbell, Haington, Harrington.

2. *Atlee, Blacker, Collyer, Gregory, Grimshaw, *Hunter, *Lanburn, Peter, Petre.

3. Fellowes.

4. Kemor, *Rosewarne.

5. Crawley, Fuller, *Hobson, Lugdon, Lushington, *Melton, Nicholls, Nicholson, *Nicoll, *Orrell, Sumner, Sugden, Tayler, Taylour, Thornton.

6. Allerton, Archbold, Archebold, Auchterlony, Barr, Barry, Betenson, Bettenson, Betterson, Bettinson, Bettison, *Burr, *Catlin, *Catlyn, *Craig, Currer, Cust, *Cutberd, *Cutbert, *Cuthberd, *Cuthbert, Danncey, Dansey, Dauncey, *Darvall, *Darwall, De Placetes, Drew, *Dunk, *Fishborne, Foulkes, Glynn, Gowans, Gregory, Gunthorpe, *Gyfford, *Harper, *Harrington, Home, Hume, Huninges, Hunt, *Jefferies, Jones, Kent, Lapthorne, *Layton, Lobb, *Mawhood, *Mawson, *Merrington, Morar, North, *Packe, Penrose, *Pentland, Peters, *Placetis, Posynworth, *Powell, Repley, *Rokwood, *Satherthwayte, Skottow, *Starling, Sutton, *Taylor, *Tilyard, Trotter, Veldon, *Vivian, *Wallace, *Yorke, Yorks.

7. Wakeman.

8. *Bamfield, Bampfylde, Barnefield, *Barnfield, *Baumfield, *Braudon, Bull, Cosard, Crown, Crowne, Darwell, Davies, Davis, Difford, Dikens, Dipford, Ditford, Domvile, Duperier, Estwood, *Fairfax, Geffry, *Grubb, *Harrington, *Hart, Henley, Hutchings, *Jarrett, Jefferay, *Jepine, Kift, *Lynn, Marsh, Mascall, Osborn, Osborne, Peache, Pechey, Peech, Penley, Penly, Perry, Pindall, Pindar, Pollimore, Pyndar, Simson, Sumner, Sympson *Watlington, White, Wood, Wynniatt, Yonge.

9. Benyngton, Champernon, Cunningham, Pomeroy, Popingay.

11. *Badd, *Baud, *Baude, *Cambell, *Castilion, *Castillon, *Elton.

13. Bragg, *Broadhurst, Brodhurst, North, White.

14. Savignac.

PLATE 19.—1. *Andrea, *Bowdan, *Jacques, *Jaques, *Yeldham.

2. Davis.

3. *Avenet, *Avenett, *Aynett, Delahay, *Sapie, Wardon.

4. *Carsewell, *Carswell, Statham, Wyndham.

5. Bulcock, Damerley, Duff, Hetherington, Hetherton, Ravis, Roche, Tyrrell.

6. Dalling.

7. Abelhall, Ablehall, Ableshall, Binks *Carrell, Darnall, Darnel, Darnol, *Franck, *Guy, Hincks, Hinks, *Horseford, *Mason, Meoles, Morland, *Nichols, *Philpot.

8. Beckett, à Beckett.

9. *Hechins, *Hitchens, *Hitchins, Partrich, Partridge.

10. *Boyle, *Maclachlan, *Shanke.

11. *Hawes, Nicholson.

12. Anton, *Benett, *Bennet, Boles, Davidson, De Mardeston, *Dwyre, Hargill, Hawes, *Holloway, *Jefferyes, Kelleher, Keteridge, *King, *M'Clymont, *Macgregor, Notley, Neilson, Newdich, Newdick, Newell, Osborn, *Pack, Page, Penniman, Price, *Rayney, *Reyny, Senton, Simeon, Wotton.

PLATE 20.—1 Rigley
2 Chetwode, Haldimand Holl, Houell, Houle Lawrence, Legatt, Lux moore, Luxmore, Molloy Ramsey, St Lawrence, *Sherman, Tufton
3 *Batten Harland
4 Bense, Benst, Benstead, Bensted, Delgarno
5 *Blount, Couldwell, Downe, *Ducie, Farmingham, Gargate, Mascall, Mauger, Newenton, Simmons
6 Watling
7 Copland, *Filshed, Gysseling, Irvine
9 Domenichetti, Markham
10 Fursman
11 Moore
12 Paruck

PLATE 21.—1 *Archbold, *Bennett, *Beuzevill, Boswell, Boughton, Burdett, *Carnaby, *Cartwright, *Clay, *Claye, Cooke, Davies, *Dogget, Dundas, Fairlie, Fairly, Gisland, Glin, Goodrich, Grassick, *Hebbes, *Latch, Le Geyt, Lisle, *Luntley, Lymme, McGregor, Mascy, Masey, Maude, *Milner, Moston, Nearn, Peak, Pedley, Pine, Pirce, *Reynardson, Ridsdale, Rowsewell, Rowswell, *Wheeler, Whitington, Whittingham, Whyte, *Wilson, Wittingham
2 *Behald, Codd, Codde, Dunford, Long
3 Deleval, Kateler, Kateller, Katerler, Katherler, Royle
4 Agruall, Alley, Alye, Cockerell, Grinton
5 Beavan, Bevan, Twickett
6 Gremiston
7 Dundas, Macdonald
8 Rushout
9 Cowell Dundas
10 Boustead, Cowling, Holme, Holmes, Homan, Hulme, *Hulyn, Lovis, Machen, Machin, Maze, Sondes
11 *Brace, Dundas
12 Hatch

PLATE 22.—1 Bishe, *Blanckley, Deycourt, Dunnage, Eardley, Griggs, Huggins, Panton, Sheircliff, Shiercliffe
2 *Ashby, Beilby, *Biggs, Bodkin, Charlton, Cholwell, Cockrell, Covert, Crouchley, Curtis, Eade, *Fitch, Girton, Haseley, Kett, Kirkland, Lee, Leeper, Leper, *Mackintosh, M'Lachlan, Maclauchlan, Milroy, Nigon, *Peake, Prentis, *Rice, Sarsfield, Sexton, Stephen, Terrell, Walrond, Warwick, Wilsford, Wright
3 Walmouth
4 Tarleton
5 Adey, Adry, Ady, Anstie, Cantelow, Cantelupe, Cooley, *Cowley, Dawbeney, Hardwicke, Hexton, Leversage, Leversedge, Liversidge, Prestwick, Tenison, Watkins
6 Cockerell
7 Bunbury, Fitch
8 Du Moulin Browne
9 Tenison
10 Barban, Barbon, Braine, Brayne, Cantwell, Dennis, Godfrey, Harrington, Hayes, *Hobson, Houby, Jeddon, Lade, Little, Martyn, May, Michael, Michall, Michell, Mylbourne, *Paul, *Pickering, Price, Smith, Taylour, Tonke, Trivett, Warton, Welford, Welsford
11 Hunt, *Impey
12 Bury, *Tewtrell, *Goldson, *Johnson, *Payne
13 Griggs
14 Knowsley, *Smyth

PLATE 23.—1 Delancey, De Lancey, Delancy, Neave
2 *Atsley, Beaulands, *Biggs, *Brewsted, *Brewster, Davis, *Eckley, *Gillson, *Lowndes, Wolferstan
3 *Blanch, *Blanchmaynes, *Blanckmaynes, *Brand, *Carnegie, Cosgrave, *Kekewich, Lade, *Reader
4 *Barett, *Bracays, *Bracher, *Brakes, Grundie, Grundy
5 Bowes
6 *Dent, *Giffard
7 Deaken, Deakin, Hengrave, *May, Putt, St Philibert
8 *Atkins, *Champion, *Champney, Close, Croughton, Parker, Pulteney
9 Beasley
10 Burnham, Carnegie, *Cole, Cooke, Garway, *Gowndes, Heddle, *Hide *Hyde, *Johnson, Lawson, *Lowndes, Martin, *Mundy, Parnham, Paul, Paull, Pawle, *Peareth, Pountney, *Simpson, *Sugden, *Transam, Transome
11 Bland, *Brand, Fludd, Johnson, May, Warren
12 Landon, Palmer
13 *Cacher, *Carnegy, *Crucks, *Dickens *Gairdner, *Harding, *Herdson, *Hume, *Jaffray, *Mare, *Marsh, *Osborne, *Shields, Syms, Thompson
14 *Catcher, Hachet, Hacket, *Hackett *Pocklington.

PLATE 24.—1 *Bewet, Bocking, *Bowet, Charlton, Delapoole, Knatchbull, *Lee
2 Beaver, *Bernes, *Blake, *Blick, Bray, Cann, *Catesby, *Freeland, *Harvey, *Hervey, *Hervy, *Humfrey, *Lee, *Mowbray, Partridge, *Pettet, *Pettit, *Puddesey, *Pudsey, *Rainer, *Raynor, *Rosseter, *Shrimpton, *Tayler, *Taylor, *Taylour
3 *Adye, Clements, *Ferrers, *Howland, *Loveden
4 Betts, Catesby, Fortescue, Gibbs, Heart, Husee, *Johnson, Panther
5 *Lee, Taylor, *Tidcastle, *Todcastle
6 Ffytche, Fitch, MacCurdy
7 Brown
8 Phillips, *Playford, Pott, Potts, *Rhodes, *Rodes, *Wentworth
9 *Anderson, *Billingsley, Ipre, *Senior
10 *Averey, *Avery, Barnaby, Bootle, Hinchley, Lenche, Packenham
11 Almiger, Cotell, *Cottell, *Cuthell, *Cuthill, Hamill, Hovell
12 *Berns, Camville, Cockburn, Curtayne, *Hanslap, *Hanslop, Raymond, *Shuter, *Sutter
13 *Chipman, *Dick, *Dixie, *Garrard, *Hever, Hovell, *Pierson, Raymond
14 *Keane

PLATE 25.—1 Amary, Dawson, *Morvile
2 Gillespie, Grant, Justice, M'Combie, Mackintosh, Macpherson, Macritchie, MacRitchie, Sutherland
3 Archdale, Archdall, Archedale, Lennard, Leonard, Malet, *May, Osborne, Panellee, Teys, Tye, Vine
4 *Bulwer, *Bushrudd, *Denis, Jerveis, Jervis, Jervois, Jervoise, Johnson, Lennard, *Lewthwait, *Lewthwaite, *Love, *Lutwyche, Lyngarde, *Mannock, *Oliver, *Plantney, *Silver, Sweetman, *Thornhagh, *Woodward
5 Balfour, *Ben, *Benne, *Brian, *Browne, *Bryen, Budd, Churchar, *Crothers, *Crowder, Derhaugh, *Fletewood, Fortescue, *Forteseque, Jacob, Jacobs, *Lanford, *Langford, *Lewcas, *Lewis, Masterson, Osborne, Pope, Skerret, Skull, *Travers, Warner
6 Hubert-Marshall, Marshall
7 *Boorne, Bowyer, Paget
8 Mahon
9 Fison
10 *Allen, *Bothorpe, *Crooks, Hill, Poynes
11 Payne
12 Armeier, Armiger, *Becton, Biddell, Biddelle, Biddle, Dowley, Paget
13 *Apliard, *Aplegarth, *Aplegath, *Appleyard, *Bourne, Coplestone, *Doore, *Elleston, Ewers, *Fisher, *Marlott, Walker
14 Thornburgh

PLATE 26.—1 *Kiter, M'Kellar
2 *Abbey, Crompe, Denton, Grant, Kean, *Kyan, M'Bean, Macpherson, *O'Cahan
3 Bailey, Bringham, Crump, Crumpe, *Gillespie Stainton, Gordon, *Mac Intosh, *M'Intosh, Mackintosh, O'Cahan, *Sutherland
4 Addington, Blake, Caterall, *Catterall, Cropley, Gillies, Keate, Keats, *Pennington, Puddesey, Pudsey, Pusey, Rickart
5 *Adams, Mackintosh
6 Gillies, Gillis, Mackintosh, *Litton, Lowrie, Lowry, M'Intosh, Mackintosh, *M'Pherson, Rae, *Richard
7 Decker
8 Baillie, Brutton, *Bruzead, *Burke, Dick, *Heuer, Jelter, M'Bean, M'Gilevray, Mackintosh, Mackpherson, Macpherson, M'Pherson, M'Quillard, Milles, Palmer, Rickard
9 Macpherson Grant, Moffat
10 Muriell
11 Gillespie, MacBean, M'Bean, M'Intosh, Macintosh, M'Kean, Shivez, Tiller
12 Arnald, Arnauld, *Cattley, Charteris, Charters, Chartres, *Cooke, Keat, Mumford, Tibbett, Tibbits, *Winterbotham, *Withypoule
13 Bourke, Burgh, Burke, De Burgh, De Burgo, *Gallwey, *Galwey, *Pott
14 Beauchatt

PLATE 27.—1 *Brickhurst, *Brighouse, *Browne, *Horne, Rixon, Walsingham
2 *Cane, *Culmer
3 Bolden, *Collar, Moyne, Stafford
4 Dowland, Gibbe

5. *Tyler.
6. *Blamore, Celey, Cicly, Colbrand, *Cosen, *Dixon, *Fennell, Forde, Gilman, Greenwood, Nevill, Nicholls, *Phillips, *Thornagh, Townrawe, Townroe.
7. Fullarton.
8. Keates.
9. Heberden.
11. Beauchamp, *Chicheley, *Fermor, *Fromonds, *Maisterson, *Maisterton, *Smyth.
12. *Birkat, *Byrchett.

PLATE 28.—1. *Biddulph, *Bidulph, *Davies, Davis, *Gore, *Madden, *Mousell, *Mussell, *Wilson.
2. Barcroft, Beardmore, *Bentley, *Biddulph, Gore-Booth, *Carwarden, *Cleborne, *Davies, Gore, Hervieu, Louis, Price.
3. Halberdyn, Watkins.
4. Ashfield, De Bohun, Damory, Dogherty, Doherty, Folman, Garforth, Kaines, Martindale, Quarrell, Smyth, Wolf, Wolfe.
5. Biddulph.
6. *Borlase, *Croachrod.
7. Oakden.
8. Lloyd.
9. Tolhurst.
10. Arundel, Ashfield, Ashurst, Batt, Blundeston, Blunt, *Bracebridge, Breton, Britten, *Byam, *Chartsey, *Cheyney, Coplestone, Crolly, Darell, Dodingsells, Doolman, Gawdy, *Gore, Gower, Gravatt, Gun, Gwyer, *Hartshorn, Holland, Huband, *Johnson, Lawley, Lawton, Leight, Lovell, Low, Lowe, *Marche, Newenson, Nivison, Odingsell, *Odingsells, Owen, Perriman, Perryman, Preston, Reskinner, Tiderleigh, Travers, Trelawny, *Trelawny-Salusbury, Tytherley, *Weston, *Wolfe, Wolverstone, Yonge, Young.
11. Lloyd.
12. *Barnwell, *Daniell, *Fleetwood, *Follet, *Follett, *Folliott, *Heway, *Nash, Pascoe.

PLATE 29.—1. *Bonsor, Randall.
2. Biddulph, *Carden, *Cardin, Dane, *Iles, *Knott, Lawley, *Preston.
3. *Biddulph, Blenerhasset, Blennerhassett, Buchan, Cudden, De la Fons, Douglas, Kelk, Kelke, Morley, Mountaney, *Mountney-Plouckett, *Plunkett.
4. Beal, Beall, *Charles, Ebsworth, Elmslie.
5. Samuel, *Samwell.
6. *Brewster, *Carden, *Cartwright, *Carwarden, Knipe, Thurstone.
7. Ambrey, Ambry, Bath, Monteith, Robertson.
9. Neeld.
10. Warde.
12. Carden.

PLATE 30. — 1. Munday, Mundey, Mundy.
3. Sharpe.
4. Tighe.
5. Andrade, Bare, Barham, *Barry, Belhouse, *Bletsho, Braham, *Bromflete, Cattle, Chibnall, Cleve, Clive, Clopton, *Cooke, *Cookesey, Delahey, Dewhurst, Dounies, *Dowies, *Downes, *Gernon, Goldfrap, *Griffith, *Griffiths, Hampton, Honywood, Howard, Jeffreys, Jennings, Kent, Lawrence, Lidiard, MacBain, M'Queen, Macqueen, M'Quinn, Malkin, Methuen, Moreton, Morton, Munday, Mundy, Nicolas, Nicoll, Nicolls, *Ouseley, Pratt, Putnam, Puttenham, *Rode, Rundle, Seal, *Seale, *Sealy, *Sharp, Skeen, Skene, Skottowe, Spence, Spotswood, Spottiswood, Swanston, Thorogood, *Thorowgood, *Throgood, *Troogood, Tully, Walsh, Warde, Webber, Weston, Wilbraham, Wilson, *Woolfe, Worsoiley.
6. Nicholson.
7. *Image, Pigott, *Rush.
8. Abrook, Abrooke, Adams, Allix, Atkinson, *Bamburg, Barry, Barton, Beath, Bery, Blackie, Blaikie, Blakie, Booer, Borminghall, Bower, *Brykes, Budworth, Burghall, Burn, *Byrkes, *Cartwright, Causton, *Cawarden, Cleborne, Clerke, Clibborn, Cliffe, *Coddington, *Cooke, Crelie, Culy, Dewhurst, Donne, *Downes, Duane, Ellick, *Fitz-Stevens, Flood, *Gathorne, Gildea, Girling, Gower, Grene, *Haize, Hammond, Hamond, Hampton, Hanna, *Heygate, Highgate, *Hill, Honywood, How, Ilinn, Jefferson, Jennings, Jenyns, Jones, Kendall, *Law, *Lawrence, Leck, Lediard, Liddiat, Lloyd, Lovett, *Low, Lowe, Lupton, M'Queen, Maingy, Methuen, Middlehurst, Middleton, Miller, Moody, Moodye, Nethercoat, Nicholls, Nicolls, Norie, Norrie, Norton, O'Quinn, *Payne, Pigot, *Pigott, Pratt, Prentice, Prittie, Pritty, *Prosser, Quin, Rowley, Rush, *Rushe, *Scratton, Seale, Seaton, Seel, Sharpe, Smallpiece, Smalpece, *Smith, *Smyth, *Sprackling, Stiddolph, Sutton, *Tame, *Thornley, *Tomkinson, Tompkinson, Trelawney, Tristram, Troutback, Trove, Tye, Waldoure, Ward, *Warde, White, Wilbraham, *Wolfall, *Wolfe, *Woolfall, Worseley, Worsley, Wynne.
9. Candishe, Cavendish, Chedworth, *Curteis, Gant, Garnon, Gaunt, *Gernon, Goodson, *Kychard, *Loe, Lowe, Newland, Rowley, *Style, Wood, Woodward.
10. *Peckshall, *Peshall, *Peele, *Phelps.
11. *Barnwell, *Barry, *Bradshaw, *Courteis, *Courteys, Dewhurst, Evans, *Hill, *Huxley, *Lawson, Methewen, Millar, *Miller, *More, *Reygnales, *Reynolds, Rowley, *Smythesby, *Stiles, Stockton, *Tighe, *Ward, *Willson, Wood, Wormington.
12. Bath, *Dewes, *How.

PLATE 31.—1. Freeman, Redesdale.
2. Barwell, *Cooke, Cumberland, Derham, Derule, *Goodenough, Guston, Hankey, *Heblethwayte, *Hoblethwayte, *Hooper, *How, *Howe, *Joyce, Kellet, Lewis, Lovatt, Maryon-Wilson, *Norgate, Northam, *O'Crean, Pennill, Petit, Smith, Upton, Van Whalff, Waterhouse, Welch, Welsh, Wilson, *Wolfe.
3. White.
4. Davis.
5. *Burthogge, *Cook, *Dennett, *Dent, *Gibon, *Howard.
6. Banner, *Bruton, *Brutyn, Meek.
7. Horden.
9. Wolf.
10. Platt.
11. Howard.
12. *Bodley, Western, Wolf, Woolf, Woolfe.

PLATE 32. — 1. *Abbot, Asherst, Blaney, Blayney, Brigges, *Dormer, Hayes, Kerton, Kirkenton, Kirkton, Pierrepont, Reinell, Reynell, Ross, Staunton, *Todd.
2. *Ashhurst, *Ashurst, *Ashworth, *Dunnet, Fox, *Reynell, *Reynolds, Staunton.
3. Fox, *Grey, *Simeon.
4. Todd.
5. Fox.
6. Reynardson, Williams.
7. Todd.
8. *De Houton, De Mowbray, *Fitz-Geoffry, Gandey, Gandy, *Goldman, *Gracie, *Hoar, *Lavell, *Lawrie, *Lepard, *M'Cloud, *Pendret, *Penrith, *Pondrell, *St. Clere, *Stranger, *Toke, *Wylie, Wyllie.
9. Reynall.
11. Bridgeman, Crosthwaite, *Forser, Fox, Fyler, Jobber, Kirk, Leslie, Parkin, Todd, Warter, Westmoreland, Whytehead.
12. Farington, Fox, Fox-Strangways, Gilberd, Gunn, Hackvill, Ram, Todd.

PLATE 33.—1. Fox.
2. Writington.
3. Fox.
4. Adcock, Addcock, Aston, Babington, Bloomfield, Broke, Burry, Bury, Cholwich, Cholwick, Clark, Elderton, Free, Hall, *Hinshaw, Hugham, Jollie, *Lawrence, Lochore, Lowry, Morris, O'Duana, Richards, Ross, Sutter, Swiney, Tod, Todd, Waller, Whitbread.
6. *Flacket, Fox, Franklin, Gysors, Hopcot, Longsdon, Lyford, M'Pherson, Nichols, Papeworth, Papworth, Purser, Reason, Reson, Reynold, Reynolds, Ross, *Rushe, Todd, Williams.
7. Reynolds.
8. Bellet, Bellot, Cleeve.
9. Raynolds.
10. Badger, Braddyll, Bradhull, Brocket, Brockhill, *Brockholes, Brocklehurst, Broke, Brokelsbey, Brokelsby, *Brook, Brooke, Brooks, Gale, Grey, Lambeth, Parker, *Warner.
11. Fox.
12. Brockhill, Brooke.

PLATE 34.—1. *Balcombe, *Balguy, *Barford, *Berford, *Barwis, *Bernard, *Brereton, Brooks, *Chamber, *Chambers, *Lee, *Legh, *Miles, *Polhill.
2. Barnes.
3. Berreton, Brereton, *Ford, Gauntlet, Parker, St. Michael, St. Michell, Vincent, White.
4. *Creting, *Cretinge, Debnam, *Farrel, *Farrell.
5. Brookes, *Chambers, *Dicher, *Dichfield, *Dycher, *Finglas, *Lee.
6. Abot, Cottesford.

7 Algoe, *Beauchamp
8 Alexander *Barker, *Deerham, *Dereham, Eyvill, *Lee, Loveis, Stormyn
9 Algeo, Algio, Algoe, Gwynne, Harvey, Litt, Lyte, Lytte, Moone
10 Barnard, *Johnson
11 Barnard
12 Milnes
13 *Barcroft, Barnard, Bearcroft, Berens, *Bernard, Betune, Clock, Cloke, Cohen Couch, Couche, Craddock, Cradock, Denhany, Grance, Hatton, Hornsby, Laing, Lymesey, Lymesy, Lyndsey, Mill, *Milles, *Mills, Nettleship, Pendarves, Whittle, *Wight, Wynne-Pendarves
14 Ashley, Barker, Barnby, Beare, *Benson, Berkeley, Berkley, Brereton, Brewerton, Cambell, Campion, Campyon, Champayn, Chrisope, Deane, Debaney, De Haney, Desborough, Desbrow, Desbrowe, *Duffield, Emerson-Laslett, Forbes, Freckelton, Freckleton, Galbraith, *Glazebrook, *Goodford, *Grazebrook, *Grazerbrook, *Greysbrook, Groyn, Hall, Hasard, Joseline, Josselin, Josselyne, *Lascelles, *Munt, Newton, Oneby, Rawlins, Tilson, *Tryon, Whyting

PLATE 35 — 1 *Claver, *Cleaver, *Melveton, Pownall
2 Amborow, Anborow, Anbury, Barker, Beaumont, Benson, Bere, *Betenham, *Betnam, Brereton, Chamberlain, *Cheyney, *Craddock, *Cradock, Fitz-Harry, Forth, Fulford, *Galbraith, Gimber, Langham, Longham, Milburn, Philips, Phillip, Philips, Spence, Vincent, *Werdman, *Wirdnam
3 Croone *Dun, *Dunn, Gray
4 Pownall
5 Barker, *Barnack, *Barnake, *Carroll, *Hurd
6 Gray
7 Pownall
8 *Swan
9 Albyn, *Dorington, *Dorrington
10 Ekins, Elkings, Neke, Northover, Twinell, Twinnell
11 Doran, Forbes
12 *Asborne, *Ashborne, *Ashbury, Cameron, *Moody

PLATE 36 — 1 Alwin, *Alwyn, Aylwin, Walker
3 Overbery, Overbury, *Pickering, *Sandwall, *Sandwell, *Sandwill
4 *Angolisme, Austin, *Banard, *Banyard, Bellairs, Bellars, Boothby, *Bromley, Buchanan, Carmarden, Carmarthen, *Deane, *Dodington, Dumas, *Dundas, Golding, Goulding ham, *Hurry, *Keefe, Kennard, Livesay, Livesey, *Lizars, M'Dougal, M'Dowal, McDowall, M'Dowall, Magnus, Meares, Mills, *Morton, Nettleton, Newcom, Newcombe, Newcome, Newcomen, Newdigate, *Ogilvie, Penton, Pickering, Pole, Pole-Carew, Powell, Pridham, Prudhome, *Rae, *Raye, *Rotherfield, Savage, Stevenson, *Thorley, Ure, Urrie, Urry, Walter, Wetherton, *Wogan, Whitehouse, Whitmarsh, *Williams, Wilson, Wogan, Worrall

5 *Charlton, Dunville, Woodcock
6. Alland, *Bruyer, *Bruyeres
7 *Brodie, Core, Guthry, Heber, *Lambe, Middleton, Pengelly, Scales
8 *Milford, Phipps
9 *Angellis, *Angles, Arden, Caston, Dighton, *Ellington, *Fokke, Forty, *Gibbons, Gibon, *Graveshend, Gybons, *Hoghe, *Homer, *King, *Mathews, *Newland, *Noble, *Payne
10 Bewshin
11 Bance, Clements, *Ekins, Irvine, Irving, Lavie, Leach, Leache, Randes, St Quintin, Trowteback, *Window, *Wyndowe, *Wyrall, *Wyrrall
12 Brewes, Brews, Brumpton, Brympton, Brymton, Chesham, Cokfeld, Crew, Crewe, De Brewes, De Kokefield, *Mills, Sands, Savage, Scudamore, *Skiddie, *Skiddy
13 Phillips
14 *Begbie, *Craddock, *Cradock, Furnes, Furnese, Furness

PLATE 37 — 1 *Sladen
2 *Cholwich, *Cholwick, *Coulton, *Danmare, *Hugford, *Leveisey, *Levesey, *Mawer, Watts
3 Bretargh, Fowkroy, Nanby
4 *Badelismere, *Badelsmere, *Cooper, *Cowper, Flint, Kennerley, *M'Dowal, *M'Dowall, Nichol, Nicholl, De Segrave, *Sheriff, *Sherrif, Simpson, *Sutton, *Temple
5 Haden, Slade, Squire
6 Farrow, Gerbridge, Hadlow, Harington, Jay, Kempster, Scott, Underwood
7 Foster Melliar
8 Slader
9 Brown
10. Brickenden, Brunsell, Burnell, *Grubbe, Lacey, Meers, Messent, Stalton, Staylton
11 Brown
12 *Lyngard, *Lyngharde, Phillip, Skepper
13 Jenkins
14 Goldtrap

PLATE 38 — 1 Cardigan
2 Ashenden, Chester, Constantine, Dagworth, Eagle, *Edwardes Tucker, Julien, Maugham, Maughan, Uffleet, Ufflet
3 Coudray, Coudrey, Coudry, *Doran, *Emly, Garland, Garlant, Lowman, *Marke, *Pendleton, Scrymgeour, *Simmonds, *Simon, Smerdon, Tusser
4 *Archer, Earle
5 *Cornsley, Egerton, *Langham, L'Estrange, Murray
6 Earle
7 *Cocke, Donelan, *Eyres, Fabian, Macdougall, Milward, Powis, Powys, *Trewarthen, Umfreville
8. Beiger, Chrystie, Crab, Crabbe, Deaves, Graham, M'Dougall, Macdougall, M'Dowall, M'Owl, Madox
9 Bridall, Brydall, Hiatt, Payne
10 Byford, Byfford, Corner, *Dixwell, Warren
11 Baxter, *Budgen, *Dorman, Hounhill, *Hownhill, *Littlebury, *Majoribanks, *Marjoribanks, Rothings, Tweedmouth, *Wardell, *Wardle

12 Bard, Beard
13 Boddington, Bodington, Browne, Cahill, Scrymgeour, *Scrymsoure
14 *Butler, Wyrrall

PLATE 39 — 1 Broyn, Chaucer, Fletwick, Graydon, Willis
2 Awdrey, Awndye, Breton, Bretton, *Hawkings, M'Ritchie, *Menys, Saint Owen, *Wetherton
3 Bramwell
4 Avery, Cressall, *Gentill, *Harborne, Topping
5 Cliffe, Clyff, Clyffe, Gomm
6 Askentine, Asketine, Coats, Cotes, Dawbeney, Goldsmidt, Hammersley, Harvey, Leche, Minshull, *Mynshull, Wadeson
7 Selwin-Ibbetson, *Selwyn
8 *Comberton, Cotter, Dunn, Dunne, Laverick, Laverike, *Laverock, Liddle, Nefield, Nesfield, Scarlet, *Scarlett
9 Archbold, *De la River, *Delariver
10 Atton, Attone, Bramwell, Dobyns, Royston
11 Byirley, Fales, Fyvie, Heather, *Holles, Hotoft, Hotofte, Peirson, Pym, Urquhart, Vaughan
12 Bradestone, Bradston, Bradstone, Byerley, Byerly, Byorley
13 Brounker, Champney, Clayton, Evatt, *Harnage, Jenkins, Newsom, Petit, Pettyt
14 Bermingham, Birmingham, Dobson, *Dodgson, *Domville, Eagles, *Flegg, *Lambe, Littledale, M'Donall, *M'Dowall, *M'Dowell, M'Dowgal, *M'Lea, *Mercaunt
15 Estoft, Flanagan, Godschall, Herriot, Herriott, Morice, *Newcomen, Newsam, Newsham, Upton

PLATE 40 — 1 FitzGerald, *FitzGibbon, *Hughes
2 Barron, *Bolckow, Marwick, Vere
3 Durant
4 Douglas
5 Close, Closs, Keating, Quaplade, Swinnerton
6 Bradeley, Bradley, Edgcumbe, Haslam, *Mount-Edgcumbe, Pyke
7 *Davie, Fillingham, *Flower, Vere
8 *Arden, Arderne, *Ardyn, *Canton, *Crenway, *Davies, *Fitz-Gerald, *FitzGerald, Fitzgerald, *Fitz Gibbon, *Fitzgibbon, *Harding, *Humffreys, Watkin-Wynne
9 Albalanda, Arden, Arderne, Bacon, Bellew, Bleddyn, Bleeddyn, Bodkin, Calton, Cantlow, Clotworthy, *Colton, Craige, Craigg, Craigge, Craigie, Craigy, Crewe, Crudgington, Crudington, De Teissier, *Durrant, Eastwood, Fuston, Findlay, Findley, Finlay, FitzGerald, *Fitzgerald, Gairden, Gaisford, Gammon, Garden, Georges, *Grane, *Grice, Gryce, Guinness, Hammond, Harper, *Harpur, Holles, Hollis, Huddersfield, Huddesfield, Jeffcott, Jephcott, Keogh, Kirke, Kough, Langley, Le Grice, Legryle, Lisbone, Lisborne, *Luttrell, McGenis, Magenis, MacKeogh, Maginnise, *Marckwick, *Marwick, *Merriman, Nisbet, Orpwood, O'Toole, Paytherus, *Phillipson, Rollo, Sandom, Sprot, Swinny, Trotter, Ware, Weir Vere, *Wildbore

10. Bacon.
11. *Humfreys, Massey, Yale.
12. Mappin.
13. Bacon, *Barrow, *Bolas, *Bolle, *Bolles, *Boultbee, *Boultbie, *Bowles, *Burleigh, *Burley, *Dixon, Gordon, Gregory, *Linley, *Parr, Ridpath, *Swinburn, *Swinburne, Wall.
14. Annat, Annet, Annott, *Bridges, *Brydges, *Dogherty, *Doherty, *Durant, *Kelley, *Kelly, *Kevlley, Montagu-Pollock, Pollack, Pollock, Pollok.

PLATE 41.—1. Baddeley, Badeley, Borton, *Bowler, Brackesby, Burwood, Calthorp, Calthrop, *Farell, Gough, Greig, Haliday, Harvie, *Iremonger, Loveland, Tetley, Vair, Wardall, Whyt.
2. Bacon, *Bunce, *Cracherode.
3. Barlay, Barley.
4. Basset, Bassett, Beathell, Beke, Bethell, Bythell, Blockney, Boxell, Bradeston, Bradston, *Broughton, Bythell, *Dowdal, *Dowdall, *Emeryke, Erdeswike, Freeman, Norwood, Polstrod, Postlethwaite, Prescot, *Purcell, Rand, Sandford, Sandford-Wills, Sanford, Smith, Stafford, Woodward, Wrotteley.
5. Barnaby, *Burbyche, Bushey, Bushy, Home, *Hooper, *Langmeade, Lurford, *Sampson, Sheffield, *Swinnerton, Young.
6. *Botilly, *Botley, *Botteley, *Chilworth, Kell, Kelle, Vernon.
7. Calthrop.
8. Robson, Symonds, White.
9. Emeris.
10. *Lewis.
11. Calder, Dun, Dunn, Evington, Evinton, Gordon, Klee.
12. Alford.
13. Evans.
14. Arel, Arle, Bradbury, *Gawer, Halleweel, *Halley, Hunt, Strickland.

PLATE 42.—1. Bosgrave, Burbage, Fenrother, *Ketton.
2. Baillie, Baird, Barton, Bayley, Bayly, Burnet, Campbell, Chisholme, Clive, Cooke, Cruell, Cruikshanks, Crull, Davis, Dennet, Downie, Duncan, Edwards, Ffoulkes, Foulks, Geike, Gordon, Gourlay, Gourley, Gourlee, Halliday, Hamilton, Hughes, Hunter, *Innes-Ker, Jones, Lecky, Lockhart, Elliott-Lockhart, Longford, McDermot, M'Donald, M'Tavish, Magan, Myers, *Newsham, Nisbet, Nisbett, *De Pearsall, *Peters, Powell, Purcell, Ranking, Romanes, Sanders, Smart, Soulsby, Spence, Swinfen, Swynfen, Taplen, Urquhart, Verschoyle, Wallace, Waring, Whittuck, Yonge.
3. Kemble.
4. *Chitwynde, Erskine, Gordon, *Gwyn, Hake, Halsey, Oswald.
5. Bavant, *MacCausland, Parry, *Strangebow, *Thurwall, *Vanghan.
6. *Clerke, Eaton, Gordon, Hough, *Longworth, Sandiford.
7. Baillie, Hill, Oglethorpe, Pearson.
8. Kersey.
9. Cathery, Dickeson, *Gordon, *Herring, Scott.
10. Alford, Newbold, Sandford.
11. *Breton, Raban.
12. Lloyd.
13. Brocke.
14. Norcop.

PLATE 43.—1. Abercorne, *Adams, Asheton, Ashton, Assheton, Asshetton, Baillie, Bairnsfather, Baker, Barnesfather, Barton, Blair, Bradley, Brodley, Brokesby, Brookesby, Cambell, Campbell, Clipsam, Cruikshank, Cruikshanks, Cunningham, *Davies, Downing, Eel, Faulks, Foulkes, Foulks, French, Gabell, Gordon, Grant, Grobham, Haliday, Halliday, Heaven, Herring, Hubbert, Humphress, Humphreys, Ingleby, Innes, Jordon, Kercy, Kersey, Knaplock, Lawless, Le Mottée, Lloyd, Lunsford, Luxford, Lychfeld, Lychfield, M'Auliffe, M'Evers, MacGan, McGuffie, McIver-Campbell, M'Iver, Morris, Peshall, Peter, Peters, Phillips, Powell, *Rande, Ridleworth, Rodney, Roberts, Russell, Sandford, Seaton, Seton, Sheils, Shiels, Stewart, Stirling, Tallerton, Tarley, Tasker, Thimbleby, Thin, Torley, Tyzard, Urquhart, Vaughan, Verner, Vernor, *Verschoyle, Warcop, Whyt, Williams, Winstanton, Wrotesley, Wyatt, Wynn, Young.
2. Burbidge, Elam, Hucks, Mackenzie, *Wadham.
3. *Bedo, *Bedon, Brooksby, Campbell, *Davies, Delmege, Erskine, Gordon, *Halyburton, Ingilby, *Ingleby, Jones, Kirk, *Kirke, Lashmar, Loftie, Loftus, *Lovibond, *Lowcay, Lundie, *M'Queen, *Mayatz, Middleton, Newton, O'Quinn, *Pace, *Paley, Raison, *Ralegh, *Raleigh, Rauleigh, Rayment, Reason, Robson, *Solsby, *Swinborne, Swinhoe, Tery, *Toll, *Truesdale, Weale, Whichcote, Wrottesley.
4. Ratcliff.
5. *Kitchener, M'Cleod, M'Cloud, Mackloide, Macleod, M'Leod, MacLeod, *Strongbow.
6. Calveley, Calverley.
7. Stubbe.
8. Bradley, *Bull, Carrant, Crofts, Dougal, Gowshell, Harvard, Havard, Johnson, Kyrell, Layfield, *Lifeilde, *Little, *Lyfield, M'Cann, M'Leod, Poole, *Stonestreet, Turnbull, Venant, *Vincent, Whitbroke, Wright.
9. Vach.
10. Bolstred, Bolstrode, Boulsted, Boulstred, Bulstrode, Bulteel, Bultell, De Burg, Pembridge, *Tatchell.
11. Veitch.
12. *Cole, Sacker, Saker.

PLATE 44.—1. Brough, Cosars, Delaney, *Godeston, Grindlay, Grindley, Hatfield, Henchman, Knesworth, Kneysworth, Love, Meager, *Orgill, Proud, *Smyth, *Smythe, *Storks.
2. Bertram, Bockland, Bocklande, *Burnett, *Burney, *Burnie, *Daintry, Galton, *Gannon, Hastings, Haughton, *Heringe, *La Font, Minterin, *Mintern, *Minterne, Radcliff, Radcliffe, *Radclyffe, Ratcliffe, Ruxton, *Torney, *Bargrave-Tournay, Walcot, Walcott, Wharton, Whitbroke, *Wright.
3. Acher, Ager, Auger, Alpe, Ancher, Anchor, Anke, Ankor, Archer, *Aston, Aucher, Awger, *Bailward, Bamber, *Bate, *Baynham, Beaumont, *Beauvons, *Beavons, Beverley, *Bilsland *Bissland, *Bullsland, Bloomfield, Black, *Bodley, *Bolaine, *Boloine, Borman, Buckley, Bulkeley, *Bulkely, Bull, *Bullen, Burnman, *Button, *Carnaby, *Chandler, *Clud, *Cludde, *Cole, *Coleman, *Colvil, *Colville, *Conyers, *Crofts, *Dinnet, *Drew, *Finmore, *Fishwick, Francoys, *Freke, *Fynmore, *Gore, Graden, *Harruse, *Haughton, Hawton, *Hay, *Herrick, *Heyreck, *Hobart, *Holinshed, *Hollingshed, *Horne, *Houghton, Hunter, Ingram, *James, *Jenkinson, *Lawler, Ledsam, *Levins, *Longcroft, Lowfield, M'Clean, MacLeod, *Metham, Mylie, *Mytton, Noone, Noone, Nun, Nunn, Nunne, *Ogle, Oldaker, *Overy, *Percehay, Piggot, *Porter, Radclyffe, *Ratcliffe, Richardson, *Rudston, *Sanford, Saunders, Scofield, Sheppard, *Smith, Southern, Southwerth, Southworth, *Spayne, *Speney, Stark, Stork, Studdert, *Tailbois, *Tailboys, *Thorpe, *Torrance, Trumbull, Turbull, Turnbull, *Tweedie, Wentworth-Blackett-Beaumont, *Wharton, *Whitney, *Wickham, *Widdrington, *Williams, Woodrof, Woodrow, *Wykeham.
4. Neat, Neate, *Walcott.
5. Turnbull.
6. *Walcott.
7. Ratcliffe.
8. Albon, Albone, Allebone, Allibone, *Bull, Gosnall, Gosnold, Kimber.
9. Radcliffe.
10. Ashdown, Aston.
11. *Barber, *Barbor, *Bassingborne, *Baynham, Bettes, *Blunt, Brage, Bragg, Bragge, Buckel, Buckle, Buckley, Bukaleel, Bulkeley, Bullman, Cole, Culman, Delany, Eaton, *Fane, Haighton, Harryson, Heiton, Heyton, Job, Killey, Kyle, Manners, Massey, Massy, Morcraft, *Nevil, Nevile, Nevill, Neville, Norbury, Norman, Oldgate, Owen, Parker, Phillips, *Radcliff, Radcliffe, Radclyffe, Say, *Sechion, Southwerth, *Stewart, Tilson, Utreight, Wright.
12. *Freeke, *Freke, *Scoffield, *Scofield, *Whitney.

PLATE 45.—1. Nevill.
2. *Aldrich, *Bovile, *Bovyle, *Bovyll, Bulbeck, *Bull, *Bullmer, *Bulmer, *Cardington, *Clovel, *Clovell, *Clypesby, *Clypsby, *Dacre, *Daniel, D'Arcy, *De Hoghton, Dumaresq, Fitz-Lewis, *Hallam, *Haughton, *Hobart, *Hobart-Hampden, *Hody, *Hogh, *Hoghton, *Hoo, *Houghton, *Huddy, *James, *Lonsdale, *Nevill, *Neville, *O'Daniel, *Pleshey, *Polewheele, Polwhele, *Polwhill, *Ridley, Sikes, Staynings, Tailboys.
3. Ffinden, Finden.

4 James
5 *Doget, *Dogett, Doggell, *Ridley
6 Sikes
7 Allam, Armit, Armitt, Arnet, Bindon, *Bulman, *Cooper, Ditford, Oxcliffe
8 *Clarke, *Fitz-Geffrey, *Greham, James, Kestell, *Lavman, *Moore, *Purse *Sabin, *Sanders, *Saunders, *Servante, *Smith
9 *Agall, *Aggs, *Ashley, *Ashley-Cooper, *D'Arcy, *Lardner
10 James
11. Abingdon
12 *Barrowcourt, Bulmer, Cantelow, James
13 Kettlewell
14 *Burke, Cahil, Cahill, *Dolben, *James, Kesterton, *Leete, Ogilvie, Ogilvy

PLATE 46 — 1 Potter
2 Jenkinson, *Killingworth, Lancaster, Potter, Voysey
3 Pilfold
4 Norman
5 *Astel, *Astle, Brudenell, Brudnell, Clarke, Coyne, Dansie
6 Thomas
7 De Capel Brooke, Elliot, Elliott, Page, Seaman, *Tooky
8 Chippingdale, *Hoton.
9 Tucker
10 Moss, Timpson
11 Brudenell
12 Elliot

PLATE 47 — 1 *Bodyham, Brock, Brownsword, *Calmady, Chamberlayne, Corsar, Corser, Drummond, *Finch Hatton, *Messenger, Michell, Morison, Morrison, Morryson, Nevoy, Newenham, *Niven, *Peppin, *Prater, Simon, *Smyth, Swift
2 *Bourne, *Howman
3 Dove
4 Bourne
5 *Angell, *Anngell, *Bond, Burness, Drummond, Ellyott, Harris, Highett, *Hinde, Holliday, Hyett, *Hynde, Lambert, Landwath, Massey, Mynn, Quin, Trafford, *Walker
6 Prest
7 Chick, Horspoole, Mair, Moodie, Pyne, Valentine
8 *Fenouillet, Jewitt, *Lunn
9 *Bing, Landon
10 *Carnegie Parker Jervis
11 Mitchell
12 Arundale

PLATE 48 — 1 Bickerstaffe, Fead, Grey
2 Berondon, Berondowne, *Butler, Collier, Collyear, Colyear, *Evans, Glass, Knowles, Knowlys, Lodbrook, Lodbrooke, Mutton, Portmore
3 Bracey, Brassy, *Cuninghame, Finn, Fynmore, Manton
4 Blakely
5 *Barkeley, *Berkelev, *Berkley, *Brewin, *Dawtrey, Dudley, *Ferrers, *Goucell, *Gowcell, *Lecawell, *Lambery, *Limbrey, MacDonnell, *Powle, *Raglan, *Ragland
6 Awborn, *Grey, *Osborne, Osbourne, *Poole
7 *Baker, Baynard, Buchanan, Collyer, Criktoft, Culpeck, Cunningham, Du Vernet Grossett, Elder, *Emery, Every, Hornold, Hornyold, *Launder, Manaton, *Manington, Mannington, Muirhead, Northcott, Northey, *Pratt, Sampayo, Yonge
8 Young
9 Alleet, Aylett
10 Abbot, *Barnes, Barret, Brereton, Claude, Yaxley
11 Wright
12 Bromewich, Bromwich, Carleton, Carrington, *Cawson, Charlton, *Christian, *Court, *Covert, Cusac-Smith, Deeves, D'Eureux, Gale, How, Hughes, Hulleys, Hullies, Lloyd, Marden, Perkins, *Praed, Preston, Richardson, Smith, *Smyth, Tregore, *Triston, Wentworth, Younge
13 Noswarth, Yonge
14 Abbot

PLATE 49 — 1 Carrington
2 Brailsford, Steuart Moncrieff
3 Gwilt
4 Savage
5 Abot, *Allett, Beale, Bedingfield, Christopher, Collier, Conyngham, Corre, Cumberdedge, Cumberlege, Cunningham, Curwen, Daniel, Daniell, Davies, Dicome, Discombe, Dobbs, Errington, Errington, Fownes, Free, ling, Fribourg, *Furbisher, *Furbusher, *Gerle, *Godley, Goodacre, *Griffen, Herd, Headlam, *Horncastle, *Horne, *Ibbotson, Jemmet, Ker, Kidston, Kokington, *Larpent, *Law, Layer, *Lechford, *Legge, Leigh, *Lewknor, Lower, Lyell, M'Brair, M'Braire, *Mahewe, *Mathew, Mathie, *Mayhew, *Mayhewe, Meakin, Mecteketke, Mermyon, Michelgrove, Montgomery Cuninghame, Morleigh, Morton, Neill, *Netter, Newport, Nicholson, Oliphant, Perkinson, *Ponehardon, *Punchardon, Ramadge, *Ramsay, Ramsey, *Richardson, *Simler, Savage, Sherburne, *Silver, *Skidmore, *Smith, Smyth, *Sparow, *Sparrow, Stapleton, Swanley, *Sylver, *Taylor, *Tompkins, Vignoles, Villages, Wilkinson, *Winsor, *Wright, *Wrightson, Wynn
6 Ibetson
7 Abbat, *Abbett, *Abett, *Belyn, *Bonnet, Carrington, Castellain, Conyngham, Creese, Cullowe, Cuninghame, Cunningham, Cunynghame, Daniel, Daniell, Danyell, Dobbs, Dunmill, Ersoi, Fairlie, Fairly, Filioll, Flower, Fogg, Fogge, Folshurst, Foulshurst, Freeling, Freton, Fulleshurst, Gales, Geale, Gillespie, Gilmer, Glading, Gorwood, Grant, Gunthorpe, Gurwood, Gyves, Head, Heugh, Home, *Kemyng, Kitson, Knott, *Larping, Law, *Legh, Leigh, Leukenor, *Mainter, *Maister, Man, *Menell, Mille, Miller Cunningham, Oliphant, Peirce, Pery, Peterkin, Phillott, Pillmer, Piper, Poulett, Pownall, *Preston, Ramsay, Ramsey, Richardson, Ritchie, Sherborne, Sherburne, Sladden Smith, Spilsburie, Stewart, Stuart, Trevithick, Wombwell, Womerton
8 Head
9 Basset, *Bassett, *Kenne
10 Emmet, Emmett, *Fourdrinier, Ham, Hamme, Tennant, *Trenance
11 *Alate, Allatt, *Allett, Christian, *Clarke, Conradus, *Cuninghame, Gerling, *Goodrood, Hyde, *Ipres, *Jarvis, *Ker, Keyte, Kite, Leigh, *Prierse, *Tayler
12 Clavering Savage
13 Cooke, *Cosker, *Gregory, *Maurice
14 Bradstreet, Chads, Cherwood, Dench, Germin, Germyn, Makepeace, Ramsay, *Ringer, Rochefort, Stuart

PLATE 50 — 1 Easthope
2 *Creagh, Hall
3 Reeves
4 Heyland, *Hogge
5 See 51, 13
6 *Fletcher, Williams
7 Slade
8 *Atkins, Berryman, Blaney, Clarke, *Lloyd, Madrin, Slade, Slader
9 Uderay
10 Carey
11 Boodle, Devon, *Hodgetts, *Jacques, *Jakes, *Jaques
12 Avern, Binning, *Breres, Magawley, Mawgawley, Savage, Weldy
13 *Basto, *Benett, *Blackburne, Bryers, Colt, *Cook, *Croall, *Dethick, *Fure, *Fletcher, *Foyle, *Gallay, *Galle, *Galley, *Grady, *Greening, *Hamilton, *Hepburn, *Hoord, *Hord, *Horseburgh, Horsefall, Horsfall, *Hurd, *Ibbetson, *Jolles, *Jolliffe, *Kevel, *Longbottom, *Mallory, *Meynell, *Monton, *Ostle, *Ostler, *Parker, *Parr, *Percivall, *Petley, *Prescop, *Ramsay, *Roxburgh, *Rutherford, *Rutherfurd, *Sherbrooke, *Smith, *Stead, *Stedman, *Steerr, Steerrs, *Tait, *Torrie, *Weddell, *Yate, Young
14 Butt, Butts, Cavaler, Davey, *Evington, Foquett, Hall, Horsman, M'Laughlan

PLATE 51 — 1 Redman.
2 Baker.
3 Clive, Cother, *Edgar, Greene, Grimes, *Habingdon, Howgart, *Humfrey, Pierrie, Radborne, *Tollemache, Tomb, Werden
4 *Almericus, *Barrett, *Barrow, *Barstow, Bodelsgate, *Bruce, Butler, *Clarke, Coleman, Dethick, Earl, Earle, Essington, *Evans, *Evington, Fletcher, Gale, Goorick, Gough, Grigg, Heaton, Heigham, Hewgill, Higham, Horsley, Jones, Kean, *Keirll, *Kenah, Leigh, Lloyd, Mannell, Martin Holloway, Meynell, Miller, *O'Grady, Partridge, *Pointing, Prichard, Prideaulx, Reeve, Rotland, Roushland, Rushe, Rutherford, Rutland, *Smyth, Steed, Thursfield, Verst, Upwood, Warner, Whippy
5 Acford, Ackford, *Affordbie, Alexander, Belches, Belhaven, Belshes, Bennie, Benny, Benzie, Binnie, Binny, Blacker, Blaker, Blaney, Bowen, Cockburn, *Coleman, *Collings, *Collins, *Collyngs, *Coltman, *Cookson, Copeland, *Copland, *Creagh, Dance, *Dannsey, Dansey, Darley, Daunsey, Dauvergeue, *Dawnsey, De Cowey, Dick, Dunbar,

Elmeet, Gisborne, Hamilton, Hamilton-Tyndall-Bruce, Herrington, *Holland, *Horsey, Horsfall, Ickyll, Jekyl, Jekyll, *Lambard, Lewis, M'Guarie, Macquarie, *Marr, *Millner, *Milner, Neat, *O'Shaughnessy, Pritchard, Ramsay, *Roach, Rutherford, Sarebruche, *Smith, *Smyth, *Stockoe, *Stokoe, Stonard, Studholme, Timson, Twentyman, Whinfield, *Wittshire.
6. Dancey, M'Cracken.
7. Allen, Alleyne, *Assent, Bayley, Chalkhill, Elrick, Folliott, Goodwin, *Green, Hackney, Johnson, Marchant, Ogilvy, Redman, Skelton, Stubs, Snagge.
8. Clarke.
9. Davies, *Davis, *Pratter.
10. Hall.
11. *Athwat.
12. Curtis, *Jones.
13. Blaney, Blayney, Boston, Cary, Coulthart, Darley, Dartey, Horsey, Maleverer.
14. Wells.

PLATE 52. — 1. *Bagenholt, Bolton, Boltone, Boltoun, Boulton, Bretrook, Gorman, Grosvenor, *Prosser.
2. *Cochrane-Baillie, *Coles, Dear, Deare, *Hamborough, Tritton, Trotter.
3. Horsford.
4. Bensay, Cossar, Cosser, Danrey, Daubie, *Dod, *Dodd, Fulthorp, Fulthorpe, Gillow, *Murray, Osevain, Rideout, Ridout, Trotter, Vivian, Vyvyan.
5. *Bathurst, Giron, Kyan.
6. *Butler, Cochran, Cochrane, Colt, Craddock, Cradock, Crocker, East, Fuller, Garland, Gernon, Jackson, Jeys, Johnston, Killach, Lent, M'Culloch, *Philips, Phillips, Plumett, Plunket, *Plunkett, Steel, Trayton, Trotter, Whitacre, Whitaker, Whittaker.
7. Colt, Hills, *Rowles.
8. Amosley, *Bayons, *Bayos, *Benningham, Colt, *Colthurst, Fust, Hambrough, Jackson, Lorimer, Maturin, *Newdigate, O'Mallahan, O'Malley, Straker.
9. *East.
10. Dewell, Dewelle, Hearn, Hearne, Snowdon, Stone.
11. Fitz-Alan, Fitzalan, *Norfolk.
12. Trotter.
13. Cooper, *Dering, Trotter, Upton.
14. Braddick.

PLATE 53. — 1. Jackson.
2. Ackelom, Bendlowes, Cromie, De Kyme, Fiott, Fitch, Fitz-Maurice, *Gould-Lambart, Lambart, Lambert, O'Cornyn.
3. Aslin, Bayard, *Bindlosse, *Blaker, Brixton, Brixtone, Challen-Cratwick, *Cox, *Crompton, Dickman, *Fiott, *Lavender, *Luker, Metcalfe, *Moyser, Myers, *Newcombe, Page, *Petty-FitzMaurice, Pitt, *Cheesment-Severn, Stamp, *Stoddard, Stompe, *Studdert, Weir.
4. Lane, Tory, Torry.
5. *Disker, *Diskers, *Elsley, Lambert.
6. *Benning, Kerchinall, Weir.
7. Jackson.
8. Snell.
9. Ince.
10. *Dawson, Sinclair.
11. Bentick, Cromer, Hooton, Kerr, Trotter, Veale.
12. *Duff.

PLATE 54. — 1. Alington, *Allen, Allington, Anderson, Barwell, Bell, Boniface, Broadley, *Bronker, Broughton, *Carnsew, *Carter, Cartiles, Chaffin, Chafin, Clapperton, Cochet, *Cockle, Cookesey, Dawson, Echlin, Edwards, Eure, Fall, *Fletcher, Goche, *Grosvenor, *Grove, Headon, *Hewetson, Heydon, Jermyn, Linford, Lovell, M'Fadyen, M'Faiden, Pointer, *Rigges, *Riggs, Russell, Sanderson, Saxon, Shaw, Smith, Smyth, *Spraggs, *Stapleton, Stockdale, Stout, Swiney, Swinnee, Talbot, *Ufford, Warren, White, Williams, Wreahoke, Wyllie, Yea.
2. Alexander, *Allington, *Brudenell, *Cheere, *Chere, Church, Colwell, *Dawson, Dugan, Duggan, *Ebury, *Faithfull, *Flaxney, *Fothergill, *Gooch, *Grosvenor, Grove, *Haggerston, *Haydon, *Huntley, *Joselin, *Joselyn, *Keignes, Moesler, *Nuthall, Temple, *Philip, *Rees, Saunderson, *Sherington, *Smith, Talbot, Temple, *Warren, *Watson.
3. Aubert.
4. Durban.
5. *Adam, *Adams, *Adamson, *Allen, *Baynbrigge, *Bollen, *Hampden, Calton, Cogan, Coggan, *Cokyll, *Dancer, *Dibdin, Druitt, *Duffield, *Echlin, *Fearnly, Fernely, Fernley, Forester, Forrester, *Glover, *Grosvenor, *Grove, Haggar, *Hampden, *Higham, *Hill, *Hirme, Huntly, *Keynes, *Ludgershall, M'Fayden, *M'Gowan, Marriot, Marriott, *Maryet, *Maryot, *Moris, Panter, *Rugge, *Rumsey, *Talbot, *Watson, *Welles.
6. Dawson.
7. Hill.
8. Gooch.
9. *Allen, Bunton, Dobree, Drummond, Gross, *Jenkins, Kyllingbeck, *Northin.
10. Attelound.
11. *Cheselden, *Cheseldon, *Cheseldyne, *Cheselton, *Chiseldine, Coneley, Conelly, Connelley, Connelly, Connely, Connolly, Conolly, Jago, *Motham, Talbot.
12. Mashiter.
13. Smith.
14. Buckland, Buckle, Comyns, Crake, Craker, Fairford, Hosier, Lawrence, Lawrens, Micklethwaite.

PLATE 55. — 1. Burgoyne, Colne, Colney, *Eggington, Gessors, Ghrimes, Hoofsteller, *Hustler, Norris, Nott, Notte, *Smith, Sturges, Temple, Topliffe, *Vaughan, *Wheeler.
2. *Brugh, *Croft, *Crofts, *Crompton, Cruchley Crutchley, *Fletcher, *Furnace, *Furnes, *Furnese, *Furness, *Gower, Harris, *Heneage, Herris, *Hungate, *Hungatt, *Knight, *M'Kean, Portman, *Rees, *Temple, *Thomas.
3. Arsike, Arssick, Arsycke, Arsyke, *Carter, *Cheshire, Coock, Cook, Cook, *Crompton, Laughlin, *Metcalf, *Metcalfe.
4. *Devenport, Parker.
5. Gressey, Horne, Horner, *Hunt, Plum, *Sealy, Temple, Tutt, Tutte.
6. Sanderson.
7. Perrins.
8. *Casey, *Compion, *Courteene, *Fletcher, *Gander, *George, *Georges, *Glyn, *Glynn, Hood, *Hunton, *Kempson, *Loveless, *M'Kellip, *M'Killop, Orange, *Sanson, *Skinner, *Sotheby, *Southbey, *Southebye, *Tanner, *Trigg, *Waterhouse, *Wells, *Wilkinson.
9. Reynolds.
10. Beston, Bestoricke, Bestorike, Dunning, Dun-Waters, Linwood, Waters.
11. *Bowser, *Bowssar, *Casey, *Dagget, *Jorden, Swan.
12. Aber, Campbell, Fletcher, Kayle, Purefey, *Shannon, Thomason.

PLATE 56. — 1. Alexander, *Barritt, *Blood, *Bonner, *Clark, Conarton, *Cotrel, *Cotrell, *Cottrell, *Cramphorne, Duncombe, Egleston, Fyer, Fenn, Fisher, *Freston, Hadokes, Hall, Haswell, Hatfield, *Hayward, Hill, *Hodges, *Houlton, *Huntbach, Jones, *Kiddell, Kiddell (*alias* Benner), King, Kinge, *Lee, Lodge, M'Cay, M'Coy, Martin, Maxey, Maxie, Melvile, *Myggs, *Parke, Phelps, *Powell, *Riddell, Shears, Wallis, Watt, *Whettell, Whitby, Whittell.
2. *Aldham, Allan, Blades, Blaydes, Blaydes-Marvel, Chittinge, Clark, Clarke, Clifford, Desbrowe, *Flamsted, Griffin, Haigh, Hall, *Hameley, *Haswell, *Heseltine, Jeaffreson, Jefferson, *Knight, Kyrell, M'Killop, Melveton, Morham, Parlby, *Prior, Robinson, Tanner, Tayloure, Thayer, *Watkins, Watters, Wilson.
3. Allan-Fraser.
4. Pye.
5. *Tirringham, Tringham.
6. Amery, Amorie, Brampton, Bromige, Damer, D'Amorie, Holme, *Martin, Nesbitt, *Reanolds, *Reignolds, *Richards, Routh.
7. Harrison.
8. Hill.
9. Benson, Bosum, *Davie, Davy, *Etelum, Goode, Laver.
10. Whittall.
11. Amory.
12. *Aselock, *Aslake, Aslack, Asloke, Baron, Barrel, Barrell, *Baskcomb, Bonest, Bonus, Bower, Bowre, Bukill, Carter, Chitty, *Clarke, Colvil, Colville, *Conney, *Cony, *Cotterell, *Cottrell, *Dopping, Forsham, Freston, Gamell, Gammel, Gamonill, Gammell, *Godstone, Hall, Harrington, Haselden, Hasfatine, *Haslett, Hastaline, Highmore, *Hodge, Hull, *Jones, *Kent, Lace, Lambeth, Lany, *Longeville, *Longueville, M'Donald, M'Kellip, *Macmichael, Melvile, Melvill, Mountford, Moutrie, Ogilvie, *Parke, Powell, Robins, Robinson,

*Smith, Sturgis, *Tirringham, Walcher, Wedderburn
13 Hill
14 Collin

PLATE 57 — 1 Allen, *Anguilla, *Tresham
2 *Arguilla, George
3 *Brins, *Stannus, Stenhouse, *Stonhouse
4 Allen
5 Amerex, Americe, Brain, Braine
6 *Pointer
7 Anderson, *Bentley, Merick, Nanfan, Nanphan, *Rigges, Stone
8 Sawyer
9 Allibane, Anderson, Boyes, Boys, Conerley, Teale
10 *Livingston
11 *Atteloound, *Attelounde, *Broughton
12 Bendish, Bendyshe, Campion, Cramer, D'Eureux, Devereux, Doran, *Edwards, Evreux, Gosell, Gossell, Harrison, *Hurlblatt, *Manningham, *Manningham, Southouse
13 Ackeroyd, Ackroyd, Akeroyd, Akroyd, Arkroyd, Crockat, Crockett

PLATE 58 — 1 Calcraft, Silk
2 Ashmole, *Belders, *Boldero, *Bolders, *Boldorne, *Boldron, *Bryan, *Cabytott, *Calcraft, *Calebot, *Cave, *Chelsum, *Christian, *Cochran, *Cochrane, *Cope, *Crawshaw, *Crowgey, *Drewry, Drury, *Duffe, *Fairnie, *Fernie, *Garnock, *Gay, *Haly, *Havergal, Hemphill, *Heneage, *Huncks, *Hunkes, *Hunter, *Kerne, *Kinnedar, *Lescomb, *Lewkenor, *Lewknor, *Lloyd, *Long, *Macham *Meech, *Mulledy, *Murray, Nash, *Nightingale, *O'Farrell, *O'Ferrall, *Palmer, *Pares, *Raynsford, *Ridley, *Silk, *Smith, *Swail Swale, *Wakeham, *Wale, *Walker, *Watts, *Yarker
3 *Wakeham
4 Allwright, Alwright, *Brownlow, Chesterfield, Hard, *Kayle, Langmore, *Lewis, Parker, Turner, *Wenham
5 *Ashmole, Daly, *Hendon, *Kennedy, *MacDermot, *MacDermott, *Molloy, *Mulloy, O'Daly, *O'Mulloy
6 Jalfou
7 Calcraft
8 Jackson
9 Farrell
10 Watney
11 Aberdwell, Abredrobell, Inglebert, Pateis
12 Hingham, Peppard
13 Marker
14 Biscoe, *Brisco

PLATE 59 — 1 Baldock
2 Bourcher, *Butler, *Cunliffe, *Delaber, *Edmonds, *Frampton, *Gooddage, *Halfhide, *Hill, *Hunter, *Jeynor, *M'Laggan, *McGard, *Morewood, *Mountney, *Naish, *Napier, *Nash, *Palmer, Paltock, *Plumbe, Proctor, Proctor-Beauchamp, *Reeves, *Rives, Ryves, *Searle, *Smith, *Thompson, Tritton, *Walker, Wigmore
3 Arkinstall
4 Boldero, *Boucher, *Bouchier, *Bourchier, *Burchir, Burnett, *Cave, *Chinn, Clarke, Cooper, *Cottingham, Cresswell, Dellaber, *Devall, Donelan, Donnelan, Fanshaw, *Hall, *Hampton, Hearne, Jenner, Jenoure, Jenoyre, Jeynor, *Joddrell, Joiner, Larkan, Larken, Lyggins, *M'Causland, Nash, *Pain, Palmer, Proctor, Satterthwaite, *Smith, *Sperling, *Spurling, Strother, Surridge, Waugh, *Woodward
5 Tatton
6 Boatcher
7 Schilizzi
8 Ahlfeldt
9 Benwell, Benwell, *Burghley, *Burgly, Mashiter
10 Kinardsly, *Kinnersley, Kynardesley, Kynnersley
11 *Allen, Fox
12 Butler, *Walker
13 *Hunter
14 Longman

PLATE 60 — 1 *Braithwait, *Brathwayte, *Lewis, *Pigott, *Potts, *Smith, *Tapp
2 *Alençon *Bradley, *Drummond, *Duncan, *Ellison, *Forbes, *Gartside, *Gell, *Gilbert, *Gooch, *Gordon, *Graham, *Greenhaugh *Groves *Hackvill, *Legard, *Lovelock, *MacGeoghegan, *Maleverer, *Marker, *Mauleverer, *Moring, *Nightingale, *Nihell, *Patriarche, *Pigot, *Pigott, *Reece, *Roberts, *Seckford, *Thomlinson, *Tylliot, *Williams
3 Tapps
4 *Tash, *Taylor
5 Boot, Boote, Frome, Kenney, Stewart, M'Arthur Stewart
6 Ludgater
7 See No 9
8 *Barrett, Bradsay, Bradsey, Coleman, Duncan, Elphingston, Forkington, Freston, Gay, Greet, Halfour, *Hall, Jackson, Lomax, *Love, *Prentice, *Prentys, Kiddell, Thoroughgood, Warren
9 Thellusson
10 Ford, *Pett
11 *Brothers, Cruck, Elphingston, Fallone, Ford, *Fylkyn, Galaad, Gay, Green, Jaupin, Kyneston, M'Kay, *Marston, Noble, O'Fallon, Riddell, Riddle, *Roberts, Umpton, *Younge
12 *Atkin, Atkins, Atkyns, Bratt, Lysons
13 Nicoll
14 Atkins

PLATE 61 — 1 Grissell, Hamerton
2 *Adams, *Awston, *Barwell, *Belcher, Belches, Belsches, Berington, Blayne, *Bode, *Chambers, *Chambre, *Churche, *Colman, *Cooke, Creasy, *Cutts, Danet, Dannat, *Dannant, *Dannett, *Day, *De Vallance, *Dewing, *Douglas, *Drywood, Earlsman, *Engledue, *Farebrother, Foote, *Ford, *Forde, *Forstall, *Fouller, *Franklyn, *Fulham, *Gabourel, Garvey, *Gaussen, Gell, *George, *Georges, Gorge, Gorges, *Gosset, *Gottes, Grandvell, *Grebell, *Grevile, *Greville, Halford, *Hall, *Halyburton, Hamilton, *Hawes, *Hawles, Heathfield, Holford, *Holman, Hunter, Jackson, *Jermyn, Johnson, Johnsonn, *Keigwin, *Keinsham, Kemisham, *Kidderminster, *King, Langton, M'Cullum, M'George, MacHugh Macsagan, Mager, *Magor, Major, Manger, *Martin, Mayor, Mill, *Moreton, Morton, *Muckleston, *Nevill, *Nicol, *O'Donaghan, *Pagrave, Simmons, *Spry, *Sutton, *Taylor, *Travell, Walker, *Yetts
3 Prigion, Prujean, *Walker
4 Adams, Banger, Bladen, Bordell, Carpenter, *Chambers, *Clerke, Colvile, Cruice, Cruise, Drury, Ford, Fuller, Hunter, Lefroy, Lloyd, Lynacre, Lynaker, M'Taggart, Mill, Shiffner, Stathum, *Tany
5 Bacon, *Flowde, Jones, Lun, Lunn, Raby, Ronaldson, Tiffin
6 Hampson
7 *Arablester, *Arblester, *Areblaster, *Berrington, Berring, Bird, Coleman, Fox, Foxall, Hallington, Hallowtown Hodges, Holway, *Jermyn, *Nash, Purkis, Walker, Wooton, Wootton
8 Weykes, Wykes
9 *Durant.
10 Linacre
11 Bernil, Birnal, Birnall, Clayley, Colthurst, Curtis, Dickenson, English, Goylin, Joanes, Leigh, Lewis, Mathews, Morier, Nicholson, Pepper, Plunkett, Read, Rumbold, Rutter, Thomas, Wortling
12 Algar, Alger, Burgess, *Cleaveland, *Cleavland, *Comber, Duddingston, Dudingstoun, Hully, *Key, Randolph, *Saunderson, *Valence, Vinicombe
13 Nevill
14 Cave, Phillip

PLATE 62 — 1 Tooth
2 Ackworth Aldrich, Annand, *Bailey, *Barrett, *Bashe, *Basset, *Bassett, Bayley, *Benon, Bold *Bomford, *Bonten, Chisenal, Chisenhall, Clifford, Collet, Colley, Colly, Cooke, Cooling, *Cornfoot, *Cosby, Cross, Culling, Davies, De Morton, Duffin, *Everitt, *Feyry, Foley, Fotheringham, Fothringham, *Franche, Gamage, *Gercom, *Griffin, Waldie Griffith, Grimshaw, *Hearing, Knolles, Knowles, Lewis, *MacCartney, Martyn, *Martyr, *Maule, *Mearing, Morgan, Murray, *O'Mulrain, *Pakenham, Parkhurst, Pleasance, Read, Reed, *Rowdon, *Ryan, Sandes, Sands, Sandy, Sandys *Sherland, Stern, Walshe, Williams, Woodhouse, Worster
3 Finch
4 Wenley
5 Fagan, Fargon
6 Campbell, Hanger
7 *Elphingston
8 Murray
9 Arkell, Arkle, Elphingston, Floyd, Hughes, Laurence, Lawrence, Reading, Reding
10 *Abbot, Aboat, *Bailey, *Beley, *Benyon, *Brady, Chamond, Chaumond, Chew, Clamond, *Clement, *Copley, Creevey, Crevy, Dollen *Gardiner, Godwyn, Gooden, Good

ing, Goodwin, *Goodwyn, Griffith, Hales, Halse, Halsey, *Havers, Hobhouse, *Hornes, Howales, *Hoy, Loveney, *Lownde, M'Craw, *Meggs, Mulsho, Mulshoe, Norton, *Palmer, Pardoe, Parry, Payton, *Peiton, Pennel, *Pescod, Peyton, Pleasance, Soote, Steers, Sweetman, Worley.
11. Banworth, *Bishoppe, Bisshop, Bisshopp, *Brady, Colis, Greenfield, Jay, Mackmoragh, Macmore, Moriarty, Preston, *Trefusis.
12. Shute.

PLATE 63.—1.*Fellgate, *Filgate.
2. Ashfield, Bevan, Bevin, Bevill, Beville, Bevin, *Bladen, *Chilton, Collin, Cross, Cudmore, Cudnor, *Devlin, Dines, Egioke, Fairbairn, Finch, Garroway, Grandville, *Granger, *Granville, *Greenfield, *Greenvile, Grenfell, Halliwell, Hawkesford, *Hobson, *Hopton, Jermy, Jermyn, March, *Moulton, Murray, *Nevill, *O'Keefe, Orme, Paiton, *Paston, Payne, Peirce, Peneystone, Pennyston, *Pope, Rew, St. Leger, Shuldham, Stewart, Tapps, Tinkler, Torr, Torre, Torvers, Tower, Towers, Towry, Turpin, Wentworth, Wenlock, Windsor-Clive, Wingfield, Worthy.
3. Cleve, Cliffe, Clive, Evelyn, Finch, Finche, Wentworth.
4. Margerison.
5. Bevan.
6. Aveling.
7. Charley, Charnley, Jennins, Jupp, Leslie.
8. Bandenell, Catharines, Catherens, Catherns, *Catheryns, Eckford, MacTiernan, Napleton, *Penyston, Piers, Willoughby.
9. Tower.
10. Hopson, *Stanley.
11. Bevan.
12. Griffith.
13.*Collin, *Collins, Craven, Fulwar-Craven, *Greenfield, *Grenfell, *Umpton, *Upton.
14.*Chetham, Gardiner.

PLATE 64.—1.*Beaufey, *Beaufoy, *Chamley, *Cholmeley, *Cholmondeley, Cholmley, *Cholmondley, *Hanam, *Hannam, *Hatton.
2. Adams, Akarys, Akaster, *Allen, Antram, Aunger, Ballard, Bannatine, Bannatyne, *Blackman, *Blackmore, *Blunden, *Bonde, Boyer, Bradfoot, Braidfoot, Brenlee, *Bright, *Brumstead, Canning, Cater, Chadborn, Chatterton, Chester, Chesterman, *Chetum, *Clark, *Clarke, Cockshutt, *Cole, *Coling, Collins, *Cory, *Cosens, Cuff, Dalby, *Derwin, Diddier, Didear, Ditton, Dodson, Dolby, Dolseby, *Duke, Dupuy, Eveleigh, *Fitz-Hugh, Follett, *Forman, *Fouracre, *Frogmer, *From, Garde, Gardiner, *Gent, *Gilly, *Girling, *Girlington, Godfray, Godfrey, Grantham, Greenhill, Greinvile, *Griffin, Grimshaw, *Gumbleton, *Gyrlyn, Hall, Hallowes, *Hamersley, *Hammersley, Hancocke, *Headlam, *Hockly, *Holbeck, Holmes, Holroyd, *Holroyde, Hughes, King, *Kirkyn, Lane, *Leeth, Leslie, Lester, Lewis, *Lidsey, Lowe, *Lowten, Lucas, M'George, M'Haffie, McMahon, Majoribanks, Marjoribanks, Meverell, *Morgan, Morral, Morwell, Mountstephen, Mountsteven, Neagle, *Newcourt, Newmarch, *Nichell, O'Callan, Orme, Page, Pares, Parsons, Pateshall, *Pearson, Peers, Pigeon, Price, *Quash, Randall, *Reed, Reeves, Regan, Rix, *Robotham, Rosson, *Roys, Russell, Scot, Scott, Shadwell, *Sill, Sparchford, Steadman, Swayne, Swiny, *Talcott, Thompson, Twiss, Waller, Waters, *Williamson.
3.*Morshead, *Woodyeare, Yong.
4. Besney, Bestney, Connocke, Coppin, *Correy, *Frampton, Griffin, Hopton, Kemeys, Lane, Page, Powell, Rowles, Royden, Roydon, Stone, Tynte, Vidler.
5. Browne, Forsyth, *Forsythe, Gillam.
6. Areskine, Ballantyne, Ballentine, Bannatyne, *Beckingham, *Duke, Erskine, Gladstanes, Glaidstanes, Gledstanes, Parkhurst, Treves, *Watson, West.
7. Goloner, Moret.
8. Gladstone.
9.*Aldersey, Alderson, Nonwike, Thurston.
10. Phillips.
11. Aeth, Brond, *Bround, Brounde, M'Call, Massam, *Sandford-Wills, Spooner, *Wills.
12. Darwin.
13. Plowes.
14. Barclay, *Breant, Foot, *Reynhouse, *Reynous.

PLATE 65.—1.*Adams, Morley.
2. Jackson.
3. Ballard, *Charles.
4. Cheetham.
5.*Byde, Watts.
6. Mounsey.
7. Ralph, Relf, Rutson, *Trevors.
8*Collen, *Collin, *Collins, *Cutting, *Blackman, Zeal.
9. Fitz-Simon, Gabb, Keyes, Turisden.
10. Henshaw.
11. Bastable, Beauvoir, Buckley, Coleridge, *Cookman, *Corie, *Cory, Cowbrough, Cowbrugh, *Crawford, De Montacute, *Gardiner, *Garnier, *Gidley, *Glastenbury, Gorham, Goslike, Gostwick, Gostwyke, Gott, Harokins, *Hayes, Heuvill, Hobson, I'Anson, *Inkersall, *Knox, *Lampson, *Letham, *Lethem, M'Call, *Mansham, Marsham, Masham, Monthermer, *Parnall, Peckwell, *Price, Selenger, Shirt, Short, Slocombe, *Wigott, *Wolmer.
13. Newton.
12. See 67 1, and 67 3.
14. Bamme, Baum, Baume, Fenton, Kingdom, Longhurst, Mackiegan, Tutt.

PLATE 66.—1. Adcane, Akarys, Akeris, Akers, Akiris, Akyris, Alder, Alred, Auverquerque, Belmour, Berry, Beteuson, *Byer, *Byers, Campbell, Chaderton, Clegg, *Collis, Collins, Cooke, Corry, Cress, Cresse, Cressy, Croste, Cruden, Cudmore, Cyfer, *Death, Douglas, Forsan, Greenway, Griffinhoofe, Ingram, Keene, *Keighly, *Knight, *Lawrence, Le Despencer, *Leslie, Lesly, Lesslie, Lindsay, *Lyndley, *Marshe, Maxwell, Milcham, Norton, Oldaker, Pawson, Pemberton, Raikes, Ramsay, *Raynton, Rogers, Roberts, *Rudd, Short, *Snelling, *Sprackling, Stafford, *Stanier, Stevenson, Steward, Stewart, Stringer, Sypher, Tilney, Trapnell, Treacher, *Wallford, Watkins, Whitwell, *Wildman, *Williams.
2. Acheley, Ackworth, Acworth, Adams, Allen, Aveline, Baird, Ball, Ballard, Bannatyne, Barton, Bayntun, Bayntun-Rolt, Beardmore, Benton, *Bereseth, Berry, Bery, Birde, Blesby, Blesbie, Bligh, Blythe, Bollardt, Braynton, *Brooke, Brown, Browne, Bryce, Bund, Burgess, *Burland, *Burra, Burry, *Cambridge, Campbell, Carkettle, *Cartwright, Chaplin, Clark, *Collen, *Collin, *Collings, Collins, *Collyn, *Cooke, Cotton, Cumby, *Curry, *D'Aeth, Dane, Dangerfield, Dashwood, Dean, Deane, Dennis, Dermott, Dimsdale, *Edmonds, Ednor, *Edwards, *Ellison, *Elliston, *Everet, *Everett, *Everitt, *Fetherston, Fettiplace, Fettyplace, *Leslie, Forbes, Fotheringham, *Gainsborough, Gardener, *Gardiner, Gardner, *Geynes, *Gibbs, Godsal, Godsale, Godsall, Godsell, *Golding, *Gordnee, Gouch, *Grange, *Green, *Greenaway, Greenlogh, Greenway, *Grey, Griffeth, *Griffith, *Grubb, *Grymes, Hague, Hall, Hanham, *Hardy, Harrison, *Hawe, *Higgins, *Higgons, *Hodgson, *Hodson, *Hudson, Hughes, *Hughes-D'Aeth, *Humberston, *Ingram, Jackman, Johnston, Kadrohard, *Kay, Kelshaw, Kennicot, Kumerson, Lansley, Lasley, Lawrence, Leslie, Lesly, *Lightfoot, *Lindley, Line, Linton, Lyne, M'Iver, Manfield, Mansfield, *Marche, Massie, *Mauncell, Micklethwait, Micklethwaite, *Millidge, Milborne, Mileham, Morgan, *Mott, Moulden, Mucklewaite, *Mysters, Nalder, Neal, Neale, Newbold, Nicklin, *Ogden, Ormathwaite, *Parsons, Patten, *Peryan, Peryent, Phetoplace, Raikes, *Ramsey, Raparus, Reade, Reading, Reay, Reeve, Reynolds, Richards, Ricroft, Riding, Rosington, Rossington, Roycroft, Ryan, Ryecroft, *Sharpe, *Shelley, *Shelly, Sinclair, Sissons, *Smith, *Smyth, South, Stanley, Stinton, Stirlin, Stump, Sutton, Subsey, Taber, Tempest, *Thornton, Todrick, Torrin, Tyas, Tyes, Tyerman, Vaux, *Vessey, Waldo, Walsh, Ward, Warren, Watkins, *Watts, Waynflete, Welsh, Winde, Wilcock, Willard, White, West, *Wolcott, Wybergh, *Wylde-Brown, Young.
3. Everett.
4.*Brown, Cooke, Gardner, Smith, Watson.
5.*Baynton, *Bayntun, *Rolt-Bayntun, Best, Beynton, Browne, Gardner, Pemberton, *Smith, Tempest, Trentham.
6. Cay, Channsy, Chansey, *Green, Hillaire, Hillarie, Kay, Kaye.
7. Rhodes.

8 Greenway, *Haffenden, *Leadbitter
9. Collins, Pegler
10 Areskine, Chase, Erskine, Folvill, Folleville, Parkinson, *Toke
11 Boyle, Camp, Campe, *Dycer, *Elletson, *Elliot, *Eyres, *Foxall, *God salve, *Goldsworthy, *Marsh, *Pemberton, *Rackham, *Ralphson, *Raymond, *Sharp, *Shelley, *Stringer, Watson, *Webbe
12 Hales-Tooke, *Tooke
13 Coldham, *Cox, *Fowell, *Fowle
14 Cross

PLATE 67 —1 *Bold, *Bolde, *Bould, *Boulde, Bowles, Chancey, Chauncy, Chausy, *Churchill, *Core, Corey, Corry, Cory, Cox, *Curry, *De spencer Fitz-Alan, Founder, Foundowre, *Franks, Halton, *Hildesley, *Maudult, Montacute, Morley, Spencer, *Stone, *Stonne
2 Higgins, Maunduit
3 Cure
4 Raffles
5 Hall
6 Amond, Ashton, Ayson, Bythesea, Kellam, Killome
7 *Adam, *Adams, *Addams, Adeane, *Ashbrenham, *Ashburnham, *Brett, *Browne, Gepp, *Gilbert, *Hind, *Hynde, *Kay, *Montagu, Shorter, *Stephens, Willans
8 Wallford, Walton
9 Archdall, Archdell, Barker, Bausefield, Bausfield, Bray, Cotsford, *Craye, Estercombe, *Farnam, Furbisher, Gilbert, *Gregge-Hopwood, Grigson, *Hudson, Jenks, Johnson, Lascells, Laward, Laware, Lawarre, Leslie, Lloyd, Lockton, Meredith, Palmer, Pinkney, Plaisto, Plaistow, Playstow, Plumstead, Pole, Reeves, *Shove, Spateman, Stanier, Stone, Tellau, Tempest, Thomlinson, *Tylney, Unett, Warre, *Webley, West, Williamson
10 Amond, Basquer, Bishop, *Boraston, *Borastor, *Coggs, Essex, Gilbert, Locksmith, Moss, Mosse, *Povey, Reay, Stockdale, Thomlinson, Umfreville, Wescombe, *West, Westcombe, Wheeler, Wheler
11 *Bland, Danbus, Dingdale, Dugdale, *Eliot, *Elliot, *Elliott, *Elyot, *Elyott, *Gill, *Goodwin, *Grandiville, *Granville, *Greenvile, *Keye, *Montagu, *Montague, *Murrell, *O'Meighan, *Prestwood, *Scott, *Short, *Sinclair, *Slaney, *Kenyon-Slaney, *Slany, Tinney
12 *Hickson, *Hixon, Vincent

PLATE 68 —1 Watson.
2 *Tilley, Watson
3 Moss
4. Ashe, Baker, Cordall, Cosens, Eshe, Heely, Hutchinson, Langley, *Leedes, *Leeds, Leigh, Monck, Monk, Le Moyne, Mudge *Nugent, O'Bierne, Okes, Peacock, Peacocke, Pressly, Reynolds, Twiss, Twysden
5 Ash, Ashe, Baird, Boucherett, Broome, *Curson
6. Baillie, Benger, Cooke, Hewett, *Hunloke, Hutchinson, Prendergast, Trevor, Twisden, Twysden

7 *Baldwin, *Baldwyn, Cadye, Kadye
8 *Big, *Bigg, *Bigge, *Botteler, Bottiller, *Farncomb, *Jessop, Martin, Martyn
9 *Dawson, *Fitz-Eustace, *Hesse, *Kydermaster, Pilcher
10 Botteler, Butler
11 Brand, Callis, Lightbourne, Thornton
12 Ash, Babthorp, Cooper, *Cowper, Fakeyt, Jessop, Oliph, Olive, *Strelley
13 *Browning, Fanshawe, Swan
14 Bosne, Bosney, Brunet, Buggen, Buggin, Buggine, Daunt, Duckett, Fairbrother, Jessope, *Jokes, Maginn, Winstanley

PLATE 69 —1 Farington, Ffarrington
3 Copildike, Copledike, Copledyke, Somervale, Somerville, *Somerville, Squires
4 Jenkens, Jenkyns, Reece
5 Archer, *Bignell, Reynolds
6 Bageley, Bagley, *Dawes
7 Weld
8 Palmer
9 Crookshank, Fitz-Henry, *Kilgour, *Lowden, Mabball, Mabbatt, *Maule, Panmure, *Trueman, Truman
10 Brickenden, Pears
11 Chettle, Edwards, *Inman, *Montagu, Rawdon, Rich, Shettle, Wix
12 Bevers, Croker, D'Oiley, D'Oyley, Drax, *Ilbert, Lefroy, M'Kirdy, Magin
13 Borlase, Venables
14 *Desney, Fitton, Fitz-Hugh, Levens, Pyrton, Richardson, Steers, Trevor, *Twist, Widevile

PLATE 70 —1 Archer, *Barratt, *Barrett, Bursted, Buthall, Collier, Cornwall, Croft, Crofts, Danvers, De Boys, De Winton, Dine, Dive, Drake, Dunock, Estanton, Farrington, Fitz-Waryne, Gaddesden, Gobel, *Gough, Griffith, *Hampton, *Herbert, Holerton, Hogg, Inchbold, Judson, Kingsbury, Lowdes, Lowe, *Mabb, *Mabbe, M'Hutcheon, Monck, Nollinghurst, Palmer, Peacock, Penleaze, Rathdowne, Rich, *Rodon, Rust, St Barbe, Salvin, Seton, Shorthose, Somerville, Werkesley, Werkesly, Wesley, Wilkins, Wills, Workesley, Worsley, Wyvill, Worsley
2 *Ashfield, Collyer, *Croft, *Dawes, De Anvers, Dungannon (Viscount), St Barbe
3 Brindley, Brinley, Herbert, Hill Trevor, Trevor, Wakeling
4 *Audley, Bromflet, Bronslet, *Folliot, *Folliott, *Gray, *Grey, *Hanford
5 *Fitz-Randolph, Warren
6 Shepperson
7 Prodgers
8 Dormere, *Drake, Edwards, *Fitz Waryn, *Kayle, *Kele, Leighton, *Moyle, *Pearse, *Pyrton, *Stopford
9 Ayre, *Burton, Bushnell, Clifford, Elmen, Fanshawe, Hepworth, Innes, Karvell, Karvill, Kervell, Kitching, Melborne, Sales, Sault, Seaton, Seton, Karr, Sikes, Strachan, Strahan, Vezay, Vezey, Victor, Wakefield.

10 Aldewinckle, Aldewincle, Aldewinkell, Aldwinckle, Aldwinkle, *Crichton
11 *Beecroft, *Midleham, Warren, Warre
12 Venables

PLATE 71 —1 Aske, Aspall, Barton, Beath, Beith, Bieth, *Bonham, Bright, Castell, *Constable, Cosworth, Creed, Croft, *Crofts, Cross, Draycot, Draycott, Elloway, Fay, Fettiplace, Glascock, Grey, *Hardy, *Hodilow, *Hoddelow, *Hoddylowe, Immins, *Irby, Kighley, Kightley, Littleton, M'Lean, Messye, Meysey, *Moysey, *Neale, *Norys, Pemberton, Porter, *Reave, *Reve, *Riley, Rookewood, *Skynner, Stewart, Stovin, Tonkin, Walsingham, Warren, West ropp, Wilkin, Wright, Wycliffe
2 *Armeston, *Armestone, *Bagenhall, *Bagnall, *Banks, Bee, Beke, *Besville, *Bicknoll, *Blake, *Bodenham, *Borodaile, Bringhurst, *Carbery, *Carmalt, *Carthew, *Caulfeild, *Clark, *Crichton, Crosley, *Cross, *Cutler, *Dannsey, *Dauntesey, *Dauntesy, *Davis, *De Winton, *Draycot, *Draycote, *Draycott, *Dyndy, Edmondes, *Fanshaw, Fenn, *Golden, *Golding, *Haccombe, *Hall, Heingrave, *Jones, *Keighley, *Kighley, *Morgan, *North, *Pemberton, *Prichard, Reeve, Reeves, Reve, *Smith, *Smyth, *Thomas, Urmestone, *Wathe, *Webster, *Whadcock, *Wilding, *Wilkins, *Wright
3 Buckler
4 *Wright
5 Price-Green
6 Reilly, Riley
7 Dennis, Palmer
8 *Cadurcis, Cutler, *Greenstreet, Hamigston, *Hammington, *North, *Pemberton, *Raymond, Yonge
9 Pritchard
10. Sampson
11 Gilbey, *Gilbie, *Gilby
12 Sanderson

PLATE 72 —1 *Ballenger, Butterfield, Chisholme, *Cunningham, Gallaway, Galloway, Ingo, Thornton, Vanhitheson, Weld, Williamson
2 St Hill
3 Beath, Beith, *Bright, Chrighton, Crichton, Crighton, Howdon, Langrish, Langrishe, M'Gavin, Sugden, *Walton, Williams, *Williamson
4. Baily, *Benyon-De Beauvoir, Wright-Biddulph, Brailsford, Cadogan (Earl), Carrier, Chandos, Clarke, Cooke, Deering, Dingley, Dyneley, Ewbank, Gillam, Glascock, Homfray, Jenison, Mayne, Rider, Spratley, Vaughan, Whight, White, William son, Wright, York, Young
5 Fanshaw, Fanshawe, Pordage, *Terrey
6 Byam, *Jeffreys, Davies, *Fitz Humfrey, Homfray, *Humphrey, *Jones, *Price, Thomas, *Watkins, Williams
7 Babington, *Baptist-Browne, *Boron, *Brent, Browne, Castleton, Coxwell, Dalton, *Dewe, *Glasier, Grotrian, *Hawte, Kenmare, Man, *Massingberd, Milward, Poynings
8 Carlile, Carlyle
10.*Blackie, *Blackley, *Blakey, *Chib-

nall, *Colnet, *Farlow, Knevett, Knevit, *Pemberton.
10. Bridger, Briger, Budd, Coldham, Fitz-Thomas, Ratsey.
11. Archer, Brawne, *Deynes, Gawthern, Mayne, Mornell, Nind, *Northen, Rea, Ree, Rider, Ryder, De Rythrie, *Stanhope, Surtees, Williamson, Wright.
12. *Croughton, *Hoveden, *Howenden, *Walker.
13. *Knighton.
14. Baptista, Palmes.

PLATE 73.—1. *Douglas.
2. *Barnsley, Castleton, Chester, *Creeton, *Cathrow, *Durant, Farington, Farrington, Glover, Lindon, Loader, Lowther, Orme, Pirton, *Ring, *Salvin, *Seaton, *Seton, *Stewart, *Ternan, *Winsloe.
3. Barrett, Crespin, Crespine, Crispin, Lownes, *South.
4. *Brereton, Fitzjames, *Honford, *Hughes.
5. Hurst.
6. *Compton, Sloggett (or Tresloggett).
7. Ireys.
8. *Fitzpatrick.
9. *Monk.
10. *Appleyard, *Ashpitel, Beauvoir, Briggs, Bury, Castleton, *Cole, *Coles, Dalton, De Beauvoir, D'Oley, Drax, *Evett, *Firmin, Fitz-Osbert, Forman, *Hewer, Ichingham, Ilchingham, *Ibery, Knyvett, Man, Mann, *Moorside, *Norton, *Okeover, Owen, Raven, *Raymond, *Spealt, *Switham, *Swyngham, *Swytham, *Watson.
11. Kirk.
12. Swithinbank.

PLATE 74.—1. Badham, *Borthwick, Brignall, Jerard, Jerrard, Tovey, Zorks.
2. Ashbee, *Ascotti, Asscoti, Atkinson, Ballingall, Blaxland, Boyle, *Brograve, *Browne, Cassy, Crumbie, De Vismes, *Garbett, Gays, Glascott, Glasscott, Goodman, Greaves, *Hackett, Hamrott, Harrison, *Kedslie, Kilner, Kingdon, *Langton, Lindsay, Lloyd, Longsdon, *Loveday, Lumley, Meade, Noone, Reid, Rossiter, *Sotheron, *Southerne, Stephen, Strong, Stronge.
3. Hesketh, *Hesketh-Fleetwood.
4. *Austin, Browne.
5. See No. 2.
6. Campbell.
7. Mardake.
8. Carritt.
9. Peacock.
10. *Coles, *Colles, *Joynson, Roberts.
11. *Brown, *Dickson.
12. *Eynes, Hayne, Heane, Heynes.
13. De Massue.
14. *Abingdon, *Brown, *Cipriani, *Honor, Le Blanc, *Loudoun, *Lumley, *Maze.

PLATE 75.—1. Acres, Acris, Dagger, Ernst, Mawbey, Mawbrey.
2. Acheson, Anwyt, Auchterlonie, Auchterlony, Aughterlony, Baker, Barker, Barne, Bedingfeld, Benge, Bigby *Billinghurst, Bleset, Blesset, Bras-De-Fer, Brendon, Broadbelt, Brotherton, Brown, Browne, *Brownlee, *Brownlie, Bussie, Buttress, Byshoppe, *Bythesea, Charles, Cheslie, Cheurcuse, Chiesly, Chislie, Chipperfield, Clervaux, Cole, *Cook, Cornish, Cotton, Crombie, Crumb, Cullen, *Cussans, Cuttes, *Davison, *De Courcy, Delane, De Visme, Dixon, Dobbie, Dobie, Drake, Dumbleton, Edwards, Englefield, Ernle, Ernley, Ethelstan, Ewerby, *Eynes, Farie, *Fenner, Fisher, *Fleming, *Forbes, *Fownes, Fox, Francis, Fraser, Fulthorp, Gambier, Garshore, Garthshore, Gartshore, Gasselyn, Gasselyne, Gilbert, *Glover, Godfrey, Goodall, *Graben, Greaves, *Green, *Greer, *Gusthart, Guyot, *Habingdon, *Haines, *Halpen, *Halpin, Harris, *Hasted, *Haynes, Hereford, *Heynes, Hooker, *Howley, *Humby, *Hutton, Jeppe, Kendall, Kingford, *Knight, *Laffan, *Lally, Ledwich, *Lightborne, *Lightbourne, *Lindsey, Lloyd, Lye, *Lyndesey, Macleod, Marlay, Martin, Martyn, Mather, Mathew, Matthew, Mawdesley, *Mead, Meade, Messer, Messing, Mouro, Morby, Morris, Moseley, Mosley, Nisbet, Noble, *None, Ochterlonie, *O'Conarchy, Odehull, Odell, Oldbeife, Ouchterlony, Page, Paige, Parminter, Pattle, *Penyston, Phillimore, Piesse, Pilford, Pinney, Poulain, Priaulx, Prynne, Purton, Ramsay, Ranson, Raymond, Read, Reade, Reeves, Remnant, *Rhodes, *Rohde, Ross, Rous, *Samuel, Sandilands, Scopholme, Sloan, *Sockwell, Souchay, Stannard, *Strachey, *Strathy, Struthers, Tatum, *Thestlethwayte, *Thistlethwayte, Tickel, Tickell, Toriano, Tovey, Turbervill, Turberville, Vaudin, Venner, *Venor, Vencour, Vibert, Wadman, Wags, Walker, *Ward, *Warde, Way, Webb, *Webber, *Wheeler, *Wheler, Whetham, *Whitcombe, White, Wilberforce, Wild, Williams, *William-Browne, Williams-Wynn, *Willymott, Wilson, Wishart, *Wormleighton, *Wright, *Wycherley, Wylde, Wynn.
3. De Breteville, Dobbins, Dobins, Lovelace, Roberts.
4. Osmond.
5. *Bacchus, Crook, Forbes, Rofey, Rofy, Rogers, Salt, Sandilands, Strong, Stronge, Wynne.
6. Balmanno, Balmano.
7. Bomford, Cromuel, Graham, *Graham-Stirling, Guthrie, Hallow, *Madock, Road, Roades, *Stephenson, *Stirling.
8. Brown, Browne, Copwood, Nove.
10. Mawdesley.
11. *Lewes.
12. Lewis.

PLATE 76.—1. Baldock, *Corsane, Kinglake, Kinloch, Maxwell, Monro, Monteith.
2. Abingdon, Ahrends, *Ashby, Bure, Carrington, Chappeace, Cosyn, Dapifer, Devenshire, Gwillanne, Jackson, *Mayer, Monro, Munro, Murray, Osmond, Reynold, *Reynolds, Ross, Rutter, Tarbock, Torbock, Woolley.
4. Harrison, Hele.
6. *Brown, Claridge, Findlater, Smyth, Waring.
7. Osmond.
8. Trist.
9. Thrupp.
10. Bowne, Bowyn, Grimwood, *Gurlin, Maunell, Sweet.
11. *Hide, *Kinlock, *Magnall, *Mayer, *Monro, *Moriarty, Naylour, Norreys.
12. Heald.
13. Antwisel, Antisell, Clegg, Stratton.
14. *Miles.

PLATE 77.—1. Gleg, Glegg, *Harries, Kennedy, Lloyd, *Sproule.
2. *Brandford, Bridge, *Child, *Hill.
3. Adams.
4. Agnew, Barker, *Bouvier, Bruse, Candler, Chalmers, *De Breos, Dethicke, Drever, Leyborne, Oliphant, Ramsay, Weston.
5. Affleck, Allan, Allen, Anelche, Ashby, Atkinson, Aubyn, Balfour, Baud, *Bingham, *Blathwaite, *Blathwayt, Borough, Borthwick, Boyson, Buchanan, Burch, Burche, Burgh, Burrough, Busteed, *Carus, Chalmers, Clarke, Clogston, Coton, Comming, Curle, D'Acre, Dacre, Daulbeny, Dormman, Dudley, Dudly, Dugmore, Farquhar, Forbes, Fountain, Gloag, *Glodrydd, Harris, *Hodgetts, Howison, Hyde, Jackson, Jarrat, Jarret, Jarvie, Jeggins, Jegon, Kinloch, Kinlock, *Kittermaster, Knox, Lacy, Laffer, Langtree, Lemprière, M'Andrew, Macfarlane, Macgregor, M'Nish, M'Vicar, Maher, Mansell, *Mansfield, Marley, Maxwell, Melvill, Melville, Milborne, Monro, Monrose, Montgomery, Moores, Morton, Munro, Newbigging, Niblet, Niblett, Norwood, O'Donavan, O'Donovan, Pole, *Pynson, Reid, Richards, Schank, Shank, *Sherwin, Simpson, Smail, Smallpiece, Smith, Streeter, Stronach, Townsend-Farquhar, Trivett, Trominell, Tromynell, Widdowson, Widworthy, *Wood, Ypres.
6. Luce, Marker.
7. Haslam.
8. Child, Childe.
9. Sagar.
10. Agnew, *Baillie, Baratty, Barron, *Holcroft, *Monro, Singleton, Stray, Surman.
11. Thackeray.
12. Bice, Biss, Glegg, *Hawksmore, Morden, *Norden, Onslow, Sandford, White.
13. Darrell, Du Mouline, *Lathom, *Stanley, *Walley.
14. Heale, Hele, Kydermaster, *Marler, Marter, O'Donovan, Steggall, Styles, Worden.

PLATE 78.—1. *Bell, *Bingham, *Burrowes, *Burrows.
2. Smith.
3. Gennys.
4. Henley.
5. Weston.
6. Gepp.
7. Hemming.

8 Thackeray, *Thackray
9 Kensit
10 Barne
11 Longden
12 *Birket, *Birkett, Clinch, Clynch, Straton
13 Chalmers
14 Agbury, *Birch, *Boger, Byrch, *Cranford, *Henslow, *Sweetnam

PLATE 79 — 1 *Grome, *Groom, *Groome
2 Moore, Moorton, Varnham
3 De Ferras, Lathom, *Stanley
4 Parker
5 Adams, Levbourne
6 Cludde, *Farnham, Moore, More, Pemberton
7 *Acland, Graham, Madeley, *Mon, Scot
8 Cockfield, Haynes, Malbanke, Steer, Studley
9 Graham, Graham Maxwell, Hard acre, Hoseason, Sagar Musgrave
10 *Roche
11 *Gammell
12 Boreman, Cockfield, Cokefield, Gotham, Grafton
13 Browne, *Henshaw, *Robotham, *Robottom, Stones
14 Lumsden Pole

PLATE 80 —
2 *Adler, Allanson, Alston, *Alstone, *Atkinson, Bedingfeld, *Bethell, Birch, *Bissell, *Broome, Buckley, Cartland Clack, *Cook, *Cooke, Cousins, *Crux, Curle, *Egleby, *Eglionby, Gill, Gleg, Glegge, Gower, Graham, Greenaway, *Harby, Hawkins, *Hillman, Hore, Kearsley, Kearsly, Kibble, Marley, Maxwell, Menzies, Paston Bedingfeld, Purland, Reid, Sivedale, *Skorie, Slater, *Smart, *Steele, *Stevens, Stephens, *Wardrop, Wilcotts, *Wilcox, *Williams, Wishart
3 Anderson, Greby, Lendon, Stretton
4 Bolourd, Connack, Grey, Messent
5 Baxter
6 Blakeney, Cauley, Cawley, *Cloake
7 Blower, *Brenan
8 Ballett, *Burns, Essex, Estcourt Packenham, Pagan, Pakenham, Raymond, Strong, Webb
9 Vandyk, Vandyke
10 Agneu, Agnew, Egan, Mackillop, M'Killop, Stubbs
11 Barlow
12 *Ashcomb, Hughes, *Newenton, *Newington, *Vishcomb,
13 Chambers, *Cornish, *Cotton
14 Babington, *Bebington, Bowdon, Casey, Casse, Channy, *Charlton Charnell, *Cotton, Cressy, Delves, *Fell, Fownes, Francis, Gent, Graby, Greby, Gravell, Kensington, *Maguire, Meadows, Medlicott, Pakenham, *Palliser, Parkins, *Parkyns, Pring, Prince, Quarles, Rodney, Scarlett, Scory, Stoner, Warrington, Webb, Whitcombe, *Wycombe

PLATE 81 — 1 Estcourt
2 *Colclough, *Webb, *Winn
3 *Custance, Waterlow, *Webb
4 Bairstow, Bristow
5 Addison
6 Aglionby, Aidgmam, Baron, Booker, *Browne, Bruch, Carnegie, Cheltenham, Chipchase, Cockman, De Barentine, Delamain, De Lisle, De Ufford, Dixon, Dopping, *Drago, Elson, Flounders, Gourlay, Greaves, Grelher, Hampton, *Harrison, *Hooke, Houghton, *Jolley, *Jolly, Marston, *Mewess, *Mewsse, Mitton, *Morgan, Moxon, Newbury, Oldfield, Otway, Perkins, Petrie, *Powney, *Pulling, Ramsay, Reid, *Rooke, Smith, Snelling, Stephens, Stevens, *Stockham, *Stubbs, Tarrant, *Tryce, Ufford, Wadman, Waithman, *Williamson, Wymond
7 Ustiche
8 Williamson
9 Pruen
10 Rebow
11 Warrington
13 Darby
14 Calandrine

PLATE 82 — 1 Aisincourt, Ashmore, *De Boyville, *Charles, *Coe, *Coop, *Coope, *Finglasse, Kelham, *Kilmore, Mitton
2 Aldridge, Aldnge, Anderson, Baddeley, Baker, Bindley, Bingley, Bingly, *Fenwick, Biander, Calderwood, Christie, Cooper, Courtis, Crawford, Crawfurd, Davidson, Eddington, Fenwick, Lennwick, Fitz-William Fraser, Gostling, Graham, Grierson, Hankinson, *Harford, Heuer, Hever, Ingledon, Ingram, Iremonger, Jercy, Jersey, Johnston, Kennaway, M'Gill, Macgill, Mackreth, Mackwilliams MacLeod, Maule, Mitchell, Moll, Mort, Mow, Needham, Phin, Plumtre, Plumtree, Radley, Redcomyn, Robertson, Russell, St Clair, Scroope, Seymour, Shaw, Sinclair, Snodgrass, Stewart, Theobald, Timbrell, Toft, Verney, Webb, Wingrove, Woodcock
3 *Fitz-Osbern, *Fitz-Osberne, Garbet, *Linskill, *Mitton, *Morgan, *Poger, *Pynell, *Tancv, *Tany, *Trower, *Whiting, *Wythers
4 Tatler
5 Custance, Dickenson, Gert, Gray, Longe, Monnehense, Sandon, Scot, Seymour, Seymour Crossley, Solers
6 Quantock, Treys, Vanden Bempde Johnstone
7 *Bromell, *Chamber, *Hackett
8 Wingrove
9 Christie, Eyre
10 Campbell
11 Dring, Higden, Higdon, Kennaway, Leeson, Templeman, Viney
12 *Blockley, *Bockley, Loudon
13 Mitchell
14 *Ongley

PLATE 83 — 1 Andlaw, Armory, Banks, Baxter, Bruce, Challenge, Dallender, Davie, Delawar, Dixie, Dixie, Dobell, Dykes, Elfe, Elingham Elphe, *Essex, Golofer, Golston, Gorrey, Gorrie, Graham, *Greenwell, Haffenden, *Hammond, Keene, Kynn, Locke, M'Leod, Murray, Ouchton, Peple, Rawlinson, Redhead, Richards, Roberts, Rollaston, Rolleston, Rosher, Ross, *St Clair, Sideserf, Sidserf, Smithers, Sydserf, Syme, Vaulx, *Vaus, Wall, Westhorpe Whishawe, *Weston, *Westropp, Wright
2 Abbey, Abday, Abdey, Abdy, Ainslie, Alison, Allison, Amler, Argentre, Atkinson, Aubrey Awbrey, Baird, Bishop Bisshop, Brown, *Browne, Bruneck, Bund, *Cheales, Haldane, Cleveland, *Clerke, Datmer, Donaldson *Edwards, Ellison, Evans, *Exall, Feld, *Fineaux, Fontain, Fontaine, *Fountain, Furlong, Fyfe-Butler, *Fyneux, Gardner, Gilfillan, Gilfillan, Gleneagles, Glyn, *Gold, Goodsir, Gorm, *Gosling, *Gosolyn, Graham, Guybyon, *Guylemin, Hacket, Hadden, Haldane, Halden, Hamden, *Hoare, *Hammond, Hampden, *Harland, Hennidge, Hide *Hoar, *Hoare, *Hoie, Hyde, *Illidge, Jackson, Jollyffe, Kindon, Kingdon, Lidderdale, M'Fail, M'Fell, Mackannel, Mackennal, M'Kindlay, Mackinlay, Maclure, M'Lure, Madam, Meer, Merydale, *Middleton, Mittlewell, Monro, Morgan, Newbery, *Newman, Norreys, Owen, Phillips, Pickard, Princess, *Pulse, Ramsbottom, *Raughter, *Reeve, Rolleston, Rolston, Rorke, St Clair Erskine, St Quintin, *Salter, Screggs, Scroggs, *Selward, Shuckforth, Simpson, Simson, Sleigh, Smedley, Somner, Stringer, Theed, Tonkin, Torin, *Wadge, Waties, Wedderbourne Wedderburn, *Wilmot, *Woolhouse, Wyberg
3 Pirie
4 Rawson
5 See No 2
6 Weston
7 Hamond
8 Peters
9 Cooke, Dunsford, Hadwen, *Milnes, *Rose, Stratton, Wilmot
10 Binks, Crofton, Elliston, *Heynes, *Kynaston, Sharp, *Smith, *Vaulx, *Warde, *Wodnester, *Woodnester
11 Burd, Byrde, Elston, Ellison
12 Fickling, Inwards, Laurin, Nobbes
13 Whitburn
14 *Alphe, *Bousfield, Dalston, *Drax, *Freeford, *Freford, *Gilbert, *Jakeman, *Mandel, *Maudele, Maudell, *Mawdley, *Umfrevile, *Venn, Westropp, Woodall, *Woodburn

PLATE 84 — 1 Barlow
2 Aysingcourt, Aysyngcourt, *Beathell, *Beckwith, *Beckworth, Bercy, *Bethell, *Bigg, *Bigge, *Biggs, *Bonenfield, *Clegat, Craford, *Deacons, De St Martin, *Evans, Gaimes, *Gardiner, Godard, *Handfield, *Handvile, *Hantvile, *Harbe, *Harbey, *Henville, *Hundville, Kniveton, *Knyfton, Leids, Merlyon, *Oilebar, Sadler, Shiel, *Smith, Smyth, Stein, Stephens, Theshmaker, *Tresse, Wilmer
3 Connock, Hammond, Marten Martin, Martyn, Morison, Morow, Morrison, Slaughter, Stevenson, Trewent
4 Mongredien
5 Deedes
6 Baddiford
7 Baddiford

8. Hardy.
9. Banks.
10.*Adney, *Arnold, *De Pudsey, Eaton, *Goldsworthy, Greenlaw, Lighton, Linton, *De Pudsey, Skelton.
11. Barlow, Bride, *Browne, *Dale, *Joynt, Kirkley, Kirkly, Leslie, Lesly, *Morgan, Owen, *Parkyns, *Wallace.
12. Aguilar, *Money, *Murray, *Walcot, *Walcott, *Wolcott, Wollcote, Woolcot.
13. Gilbert, Macklin, M'Lin, Pranell, Prannell, Tripp.
14. Owen.
15. Kaer, Lane, Lanis.

PLATE 85.—1*Craufuird, *Crawford, *Crawfurd, *Drummond, *Falconer, Goulding, *Hawkins, *Kemp, *Kennedy.
2. Akeland, Ashoe, Atherton, Athorpe, Atterton, Bather, *Baxter, Beilby, Bell, Bielby, Blagrave, Bolton, Boscawen, Bowen, Brabant, *Bradney, Chalmers, Chambers, Clements, Cooper, Costello, Cotton, Cousins, Culpeper, *Drummond, *Du Bois, Enery, Fawkes, Featherstonhaugh, Forbes, Frank, Franks, Graham, Grain d'Orge, Grandorge, *Gulline, Hacon, Hadly, *Hatton, *Hawk, Hawke, Hay, *Hewitson, Hewitt, Hide, *Hill, *Howson, *Incledon, Knox, *Lacon, Lacy, *MacCostello, M'Emery, *MacEmery, MacEniery, *M'Morran, *Bowen-Miller, *Morland, *Morrice, *Nangle, Nicoll, *Northland, *Nutcombe, Oliphant, O'Naghten, O'Nolan, Orrock, *Patoun, Patton, Perkinson, Plaiters, Platers, *Porteous, *Pratt, *Ralston, Ridgeway, Rose, Rudall, Rudhall, *Rythe, Sparhawk *Stratton, Tripp, Wall, Watt, *Webber, Wyld, *Yarworth.
3. Hay.
4. Banbury, Bandbury, Cassel, Cassell, Chapman, Drummond, *Kagg, Low.
5. Lees.
6. Maxwell, Ralston.
7. Blundell, Boterwike, Fownes, Gauler, Gawler, Grogan.
8. Morrice.
9. Belfarge, Belfrage, Dighton, Kirkeland, Kirkland, Lownde, Skynner, Willyams.
10. Hadley.
11. Athorpe.
12. Jackerell.
13. Atherton, *Balfour, Dillington, Knox, Middleton, Ranfurly, *Towneley, Townley.
14. Barker, *Hewitt, *Magill, *Sacheverell Soame, *Wood.

PLATE 86.—1. Hawksley.
2. Bell.
3. Burg, Hardieman, Hardyman, *Jebb, Maguire, Trist.
4. Thompson.
5. Bradney.
6. Bottonley, Edridge, Grandford, Leves que, *Trinder.
7. Barker, Du Port, *Enery, Naper, Napper.
8.*Boswell, *Brabourne, *Brabon, *Bryan, *Connell, Drummond, Faulkner,
9. Frank.
10. Gay.
11.*Carrol, *Carroll, *Chapple, *Cowie, *Dickins, *Francois, Franks, Hetley, Hewet, Hewett, *Hewitt, Kerslake, *Luck, Welcome, Whitmore.
12. Bott, Cleland, Gonne, Jenney, Leech, Leeche, Strutt.
13.*Clealand, Dormer, *Gouge, Hobbs, *Jobson, M'Kellip, M'Killop, Sherman, *Straton, Strutt, Tanner, Thomason.
14.*Acland, Akeland, Akland, Clifton, Jenny, Troyte.

PLATE 87. — 1. Ainsworth, Anesworth, *Atkinson, Aynesworth, Aynsworth, Bolton, Bowyer, *Brown, Burrow, Carpenter, Chalmers, Chambers, Chapan, Chesham, Chirnside, Clagstone, Clark, Cleland, Colepeper, *Colthurst - Brabazon, Congrave, Congreve, Cooke, *Crawe, *Culpepper, Cunliffe, *Dillon, Doig, Drummond, Eastfield, *Eld, Ellicott, Falconer, Fallon, Finucane, *Fitz-Nicoll, *Fotherby, Gargrave, George, Glenham, *Grey, Halhead, Hanmer, Harding, *Harris, *Hawke, Hay, Henly, Jennings, Lanyon, Le Mesurier, Lowe, Pape, Partington, Paton, Pepe, Pole, Pool, Poole, Read, Slaughter, Straton, Throckmorton, Willis.
2. Beckquet, Borough, Burgh, Carthew, Colquitt, Farnell, Goss, Greig, Ladbrook, Ladbrooke, Nuthall, Paulet, *Pawlet, Powlett, *St. John.
3. Aldhouse.
4. Falcon.
5. Bell.
6. Hammond.
7.*Boulton, Edgell.
8. Carroll, O'Carroll.
9. Abberbury, Aberbury.
10.*Atkinson,, Holme, McElligott.
11.*Bird, Read, Reade.
12.*Basset, *Bassett, *Bell, Blacket, *Carroll, *Donavan, *Donovan, *Douglas, *Haward, Haywood, *Heywood, *Knowling.

PLATF 88.—1. Shakespear.
2. Abercromby, Arthur, *Crees, Drummond, Forbes, Hawksley, Hawksworth, Hawley, Hayes, Hoby, Holhead, Jenning, Jenny, Justice, Le Roulx, M'Crobie, *Mansel, Mansell, Marsham, Maunsell, Mitchelson, Moubray, Norris, O'Donovan, Ormsby, Paton, Patton, Poole, *Pooler, Price, Saint John, *Smith-Fifield, Straiton, Trockmorton, Throgmorton, Twedy.
3.*Arthur, *Brabazon, Dobyns, Glemham, Hamby, Hansard, Key, Meacham, Oliphant, Shaw, Shawe, Simpson, Simson, Smyth, Thores, Yate.
4. Locke.
5. Shakespeare.
6. Cunard.
7. Spiller.
8. Anderson, Tibbits.
9. *Horrocks, *Ridgeway.
10. Jerningham, Smith, Smyth.
11. Belcher, *Pachnum.
12. Alison, Allison, Blackett, Blair, Blakit, *Brakyn, *Bridon, *Bryden, *Carpendale, *Carse, Collison, Collisone, Cotton, Crafford, Craford, Craigie-Halkett, Cruickshank, Daisie, Deasie, Elmsey, Fawkne, *Ferrer, Forbes, *Graham, Halkerston, Halkett, Hawker, *Hawkewood, *Hawkshaw, Hide, *Middleton, *Murphy, Nickolson, *Piddle, Pirrie, *Ranson, *Roos, *Ros, Ross, Rudall, Ruddall, *Seton, Smither, Stephenson, *Twyre, Wright.
13. Anderson.
14. Tasell.

PLATE 89. — 1. *Baker, *Blacket, *Blackett, Couchtree, *Couttry, Darlston, *Davidson, Gill, Gyll, *Hachet, *Harty, Hall, Hawkins, Jervis, Molynes, *Smart, Willes, *Williamson.
2. Bartlett.
3. Hawkshaw.
4. Alphe, Dalston, *Dam, Fearon, Martyn, Maudley.
5.*Hallifax, Holden, Moore, *More, *Thoyts.
6.*Charley, Chorley.
7. Radford.
8. Godman, Holden, Lowe, *Mathew, *Matthew, *Merchand, *Merchant, *Phillips, Pinker.
9. Degge, Stott.
10. Goodair, Goodere, *Radford.
11. More, Partridge.
12.*Caillard, *Sorel.

PLATE 90.—1. Alephe, Blund, Brebner, Bremner, *Cockburn, Cooper, Dicom, Dicons, Giffard, *Gifford, Greet, Haggard, *Hancock, Heath, Law, *Mears, Oakes, *O'Connor, *Reddish, Reynolds, *Rigdon, Seckford, Seckforde, Smallbrook, *Thwaytes, Tredcroft, *Watkin, Wayneman, Wenman, White, Worship.
2.*Delamere, Hildyard, Le Blond, *Nixon.
3. Cockain, Cockaine, Cockayn, Cockayne, Cokayne, Fettiplace, Gideon, Wyrall.
4. Hardey.
6. Bownes, *Branch, Branche, Brews, Brewis, Brooke, Charlesworth, Downie, Farmar, Farmer, Fergushill. Goldington, Groves, Fermor, Ogilby, Witmore.
7. Caldwall, *Kingley.
8.*Bateman, *Bramley, *Brislay, *Bromley, *Brysilly, *Coventry, *Ecleston, *Fesant, *Hoey, *Holden, *Hoy, *Ilbert, *Kershaw, *Montriou, *Pember, Perchard, *Phesant, *Reid, *Tierney, *Walwyn, *Wintour, *Yarmouth.
9. Caldwell, *Jodrell, Parker.
10. Browne, *Heath, *Uvedell.
11. Lloyd.
12. Allison.
13. Gatty.
14. Darnell.

PLATE 91.—1. Donaldson, Greenough, *Hamilton, Illsley, Ilsley.
2. Acheson, Adys, Aird, Airth, *Aitche-

son, Aitkenson, Aitkinson, Akenhead, Alcock, Alexander, Alicock, Allen, Allicock, Allicocke, Ard, Atchison, Barloss, Beltoft, Beltofts, Blackiston, Blackstone, *Blakeston, Blakiston, Blind, Bolles, Bolls, Brown, *Bryce, Burgon, *Chambre, Clutton, Coates, Coats, Cock, Cockburn, Cockburne, Cocke, *Cockeine, Cockridge, Cocks, *Cocksedge, Cockworthy, *Coghill, Cookworthy, *Coppin, Corrie, Corry, Cotes, *Cox, Coxon, Coxson, *Craster, Crow, Currie, Cush, Cushe, De la Fosse, Delaite, Dewar, Dounie, Downfield, Downie, Ducarel, Emmerson, Erington, Errington, Erthe, Forbes, *Fort, *Forte, Gael, Gallimore, Gally, *Glascock, Glynne, *Gokin, Grant, Grave, Grubbam, Grubham, Guion, Guyon, Hancock, Handcock, Hellier, Helyar, Helyard, Hildyard, Hilliard, Hillyard, Holden, Ingram, Innes, Irvine, *Johnson, Kellawaye, Kelloway, King, Kognose, Laing, Landle, Langley, Law, Laws, Lee, *Le Gallais, Le Vavasour, *Littell, Lodwich, Lodwick, Mackworth, M'Worth, Mallet, Mathieson, Mathison, Morris, Norwich, Nowlan, Nowland, Ormistone, Perrin, *Pew, *Price, *Pryce, Rig, Rigg, Rochford, Rowdon, *Shepherd, Simons, Sinclair, Slater, Standish, Carr Standish, Stephens, *Syer, Tamworth, Thorpe, Tunstall, Vavasour, Vawdrey, Weston, Williams, Wykes

3 Goodsir

4 Churchman, Cocksey, Cookesey, Cooksey, Coventry, Gerney, Jopp, Justice, Wyman

5 Bidlake, Cocksedge, *Cokseged, Duberley, Duberly, *Hayton

6. Acheson, Aitchison, Atcheson, Blackburn, Blackburne, Lever

7 Baber, *Brome, *Coghill, Cramer, *Dewar, *Lelam, *Montgomery, O'Slatterie, Slatterie, *Theobald, *Thwaites.

8 James

9 Byers, Byres, Grieve, Kymberlee, Kymberley, Moses, Tame

10. Ferguson, Glover, Illingsworth, Illingworth

11 Brocklebank

12. Almewake Alnwick, Laing, Nutt, *Vavasour

14 Balam, Conway

PLATE 92 —1 Alsop, *Tallis

2 Atwood, Ball, Cant, Chardin, Charnock, Collens, Collins, *Columbine, Cooper, Dakeman, Dassett, De Cardonnel, Dilke, *Dove, Dow, Dowd, Dowdal, Dowdall, Dowds, Dowson, Dylke, Fitz-Simond, *FitzSymon, Forbes, Formby, *Foscott, *Foxcote, Graham, Greensmith, Grindlay, Grindley, Gulline, Ireland, Leith, Lempriere *Longland, M'Gallock, M'Gassock, M'Guffock, Marshall, Mathews, Mitchener, Nicholls, *Nohle, Norbery, Norbury, O'Keefe, Peterkin, Peterkyn, Rous, Sinclair, Sly, Tenison

3 Botreaulx, Botreaux, *Crathorne, Dellee, *Drummond, Flitt, Wilcox

4 Brander, Burye, Durie, Dury, Hodges, Knife, Skey, Smyth, Wiggett.

5 Albeney, Alberry, Albery, Alderson, Allardice, Allen, Allsop, Allsup, Alsope, Ardington, Arthington, Baldwin, Balston, Barclay, *Barker, *Barrow, *Beckwith, Blanckagam, Bradston, Brasier, Brazier, Brummel, Brummell, Buchanan, Burt-Marshall, *Calderwood, Campbell, Chalmers, Clayton, Collingwood, Cowcher, Creed, Dabetot, Dabitot, Daniels, Darroch, David, Davy, *D'Olier, *Dowdall, Duffield, Duguid, Durie, Dury, Dylkes, Edwards, *Exeter, Fairholm, Fairholme, *Finnie, Leith Forbes, *Foulis, Fowlis, Francis, *Frederick, Gairdner, Garioch, Girvan, Golbourn, Gonvill, Goodwright, Gordon Cumming-Skene, Goulburn, Grayhurst, Gypses, Hall, *Hanson, Harkness, Higgan, Hill, Hodgson, Hodson, Hopkin, Hunter-Marshall, Ireland, Irland, Irrland, Irwin, *Jackson, Jessop, Jolly, Kennison, Laing, Lang, Langdon, Law, Learmonth, Leith, Lemoine, *Lendrum, Leslie Duguid, Leveret, Lord, Lumley, Makepeace, Marshall, Mayo, Monnoux, Morant, Morland, Mower, Moyes, Murray, Mussenden, *Newmarch, Newsham, Newville, Noyes, Oldham, Omer, O'Sheehan, Pearson, Petrie, Phaire, Pigott, *Pinford, Plunkett, Porteous, Prior, *Puller, Rathbone, Revett, Ribton, Ross, Rubridge, St Clair, Salt, Sand, Saptie, Scarisbrick, Scott, Shanan, Shand, Shearman, Sinclair, Skirrow, *Smith, Southcomb, Stuart, Surdevile, Tattersall, Tallis, Thorburn, *Tothill, Towle, Travess, Trimmer, Turvile, Vicars, Wade, Waldie, Walker, Walters, Walkinshaw, Ward, Warner, Whannell, Whittington

6 Francis

7 Elphingston.

8 Page

9 Shaw

10. Borough, Fitz-Ronard, Lant, *Phayre, *Ruspini, Sherman, Spry, Sprye

11 Aberbuthnet, Arbuthnot, Deale, Gulland, Lethim, Ramsay, *Walker

12 Boston, Cam, Camm, Miles, Swinton, Swynton, Thomkins, Torrings

13 Irwin, Meggison

14 *Dacres, Somersett

PLATE 93 —1 Thesiger

2 Burgace, Burgas, Burgase, Burgass, Conran, M'Kowan, Reidheugh, Roddick

3 Godden, Goding. *Gynn, *Langley, Littlefield, Oldfield, Ouldfield.

4 Joye

5 Tetlow

6 Allsopp

7 Salt

8 Duxbury

9 Charney, *Higgins, Hinde-Hodgson, Hodgson, *Hodson, Kenyon, Malton

10 Baillie, Bevil, Bevile, *Bookey, *Boswell, Comberford, Dowie, *Foulis, Gordon, Heron, *Hull, *Jenings, Narbon, *Otgher, *Prydeux, *Randall, Sheddan, *Wintoun, *Wrangham

11 Apsey Elliot, Lowndes, Lownds, *Puget, Shand, Smith-Shand

12 Larke, *Wheler

13 *Bolron, *Dopping

14 *Caryer

PLATE 94 —1 Pease

2 Archbold, Blair, Burns, Collins, Delaport, Hagen, Halifad, Hay, Lempriere, More, Vallack, *Wirgman, Zinzan

3 Baird

4 *Allaway, *Alloway, Colwick, Colwyke, Hazard, Newenham, Newmarch, *Young

5 Ackers, Andrews, Blair, *Burges, *Clarke, Cobbett, Colvile, Colwall, Dalbiac, *Davy, Delafield, Doughty, Dove, Finnan, Moore, Over, Peace, Pockley, *Royer, Stokes, Stowell, Tarpley, Taverner, Taylor, *Wentworth-Shields, Wenyeve.

6 Hoadley

7 Edwards, *Hamond

8 Tweedy

9 Cropper

10 Brock, Corby, Edgell, Kandishe, Longden, Swynerton

11 Cardale

12 Halifad, Hoadley

13 Duxbury

14 *Bradbury

PLATE 95 —1 Arundel, Blake, Bourdelain, Bourdillon, Cardiffe, Duperon, Eland, Elland, Eyland, Fyske, *Greathead, Heyland, How, *Larcom, Lawson, Overton, Proctor, Tempest

2 *Adams, Anstay, Anstee Anstey, Anstie, Applebee, Argenton, *Bell, Bickerton, Blesson, Blessone, *Brady, *Carlile, *Coffyn, Forde, Gould, *Harding, Headley, Hedley, Jervis, Keene, Lusher, Mallabar, Monckton, Monketon, Rathlow, *Rocke, Torrens, Ward, *Winter

3 Nott

4 Balls-Headley, Binns, Birdwood, Blackwell, *Blake, Bonney, Bostock, *Cairns, Cargill, Chadock, Crymes, *Dowdall, Fitzhugh, Fuller, Grimes, Hague, Hudson, M'Gill, Martyn, Niccols, O'Gormley, O'Nowlan, Oulton, Pickett, Pigot, *Pine Coffin, Proctor, Sanford, Smith, Stott, Stringer, Thomson, Waddington, Walkingshaw, Waud, Wiggon

5 *Adams, Adderstone, *Addreston, Aderston, Aderstone, *Asen, Bidwell, Bigot, Bigott, *Bird, Camac, Camic, Coe, Crimes, Denton, Douglas, Drysdale, *Edwards, Fortick, Fournier, Glasgow, Glen, Glenn, Gossip, Greig, Greive, Grive, Hansard, *Hartley, Hayman, Hill, M'Cubbin, *Molling, *Molyng, *Newton, Nutt, Nuttall, Oliver-Rutherfurd, Priest, Rutherford, Sandford, Smith, Strother, Struthers, Tempest, Walkinshaw, Weeden, Weedon, Westby, White

6 Ward

7 Adlyn, *Cormac, *Cormack, Dewsbury, Jewsbury, *M'Cormack, M'Cormick

8 *Bradley, Hartley.

9 Holdich

10. Russell

11 *Allen, *Bird, Hendley, *Hide, *Hotton, *Kidd, *M'Gill, *Martin, *Newman, *Norvill, Thorp

12 Chaddock, Chadock, Chadwick, Darnley, Dighton, Hackote, Hacote, Jeffrey, Murray, Purfield, Pury, Tandy, Temple, Woryndon

PLATE 96.—1. *M'Aben, *M'Carin, *Vawdrey.
2.*Cunninghame, Fithier, Hoggeson, Kay, Lyal, Lyall, Lyell, Lyle, Mander, Milne, Mylne, Newman, Pilmure, Randill, Snigg, Snigge.
3.*Arundel.
4. Fowler, Hill.
5. Apleyard, Appleyard, Barton, Bayford, *Bermingham, Boucher, Bouchier, Bredel, Broughton, *Burton, Bayford, Byford, Calverley, Catt, Catton, *Clutton, Dover, Esmond, *Fowler, Gaston, Gottington, Greseley, Harbin, Harwood, Horn, Horne, Jennoway, Kirkland, M'Taggart, Massey, Massie, *Massy, Midford, Minnoch, Nicholas, O'Dugenan, Oldham, *Oulry, *Ramus, Rumsey, Savell, Savile, Savill, *Saville, Scott, Thorn, Willoughby, Wilton, *Witton, Woodley, Wynall.
6. Band, *Battie, Dess, Desse, Fowler, Hawkes, *Hudson, Humble, Nicholas, Snell.
7.*Woodrof, *Woodroffe, *Woodrow.
8.*Baker, Champernonne, Champernowne, Clabrock, Cleybrooke, *Dandern, *Edgar, Feake, Feeke.
9.*Elliot, Ferguson - Davie, *Fisher, *Fysher, Goldsmith, *Meares, *Still.
10. Beckman, *Bereford, *Bond, *Bunn, *Smart.
11. Dease, King, Mellish, Steel, Steele, Trotman, Vallance.
12. Edgar.

PLATE 97.—1. Cock, Fagge, *Harpway, *Harpwaye, *Impey, *Manyngham, *Trivett, *Tryvett.
2.*Brown, Caldecot, Carrick, *Carvick, *Clonvyle, *Clovell, *Clovile, *Clovyle, *Folkenorth, *Folkeworth, *Gibson, *Goodwing, Haltridge, *Harrison, *Hasling, James, Lindsay, Milroy, Peckham, *Pichford, *Pitchford, *Portlock, *Pycheford, Ray, *Trout, White, Wray.
3. Wyatt.
4. Walker.
5. Banning, Dickman, *Echard, Lindsay, Redpath.
6. Wallace.
7. Ray.
8. Cock, Cook, Cooke, Davys, Digby Eden, Escott, Ferrers, Fraser, *Gunning, Koke, Lindsay, M'Gee, M'Ghie, Pearson, Piggot, Piggott, Ranken, Ray, Saulton, Smith, Smyth, Valentine, Van Straubenzee, Wallace, Wyatt.
9. Alfrey, Allfrey, *King, *Naunton.
10.*Contry, *Dewelles, *Espeke, *Fowler, *Hutton, *Martyn, *Payne, Russell, *Smith, *Smyth, *Thimblethorp.
11.*Best, Hewster, *Kelley, *Kelly, *Wallace.
12. Davey, Delamote, Delamotte, *Hogan, Smith, Tryon, Vass.
13. Coke, Cooke.
14. Alfrey, Allfrey, Le Mesurier, Manfield, *Pierson.

PLATE 98.—1. Aguillan, Atkins, *Bambell, *Beck, Borthwick, Bromhead, Buckston, Buxton, Clavedon, *Cooper, Cramond, Culverton, Gamlin' Gammell, Gauldesborough, Hendry, Hume, Jegon, Keir, *Lechmere, Leechman, Leeshmam, Leith-Forbes, Leverton, Meadows, *Meara, De Medewe, Moorhouse, Nash, O'Collins, O'Cuilean, O'Cuillean, O'Meara, *Burnham-Pateshall, Pell, Peterson, *Peusay, *Pile, Rising, Steward, Tweddell.
2. Ainsley, Ainslie, Beggar, Begger, *Biggar, *Bigger, Bill, *Cobbe, Fisher, Godfrey, *Graham, Grieves, *Haughton, Henrie, Holbeance, *Holbeche, *Home, Jeffs, Ketchin, Kitchin, Machen, *Paterson, Peaterson, *Perne, *Puxty, *Saltonstall, *Saltonston, *Samon, *Savile, Sprott, Stratoun, Thacker, Tillotson, Wakering, *Wilkinson.
3. Cooper, Couper, Cupper.
4. Macken.
5. Gubbay.
6. Briggs.
7. Bagne, Bague, Cromwell, Lomas, Playfair, Spooner, Vincent.
8. Aillen, Chandler, Chaundler, *Sneyd-Edgeworth, Gibson, Gyles, *Lindley, Lumley, Mackenzie, Mansuen, Mansuer, Mead, Melhuish, O'Donoghoe, O'Heron, Osborne, Paterson, Pateson, Patison, Patterson, Pattison, Pollen, Pulleine, Pullen, Pulleyn, Reid, Rudge *Shaw, Sherlock, *Stackpole, Steuart, Stewart, Stuart, Thruxton, Thureng, Thurgryn, Thurxton, Tyldesley, *Wayne, Woodcock.
9. Arthur.
10. Hinchin-Kemp, Kemp.
11. Gibson-Watt.
12. Daniell, *Parbury.
13. Stuart.
14.*Ambrose, Apilston, Arthur, Coulson, Cullen, Dixon, *Dunphy, Ellice, Everard, Fotheringham, Gibson, Gibsone, Gotobed, Harris, *Hepenstal, Lakington, Lapington, Leishman, Lumley, M'Inroy, O'Hangherne, Packer, Playfair, Pullen, Pulleyn, Reid, Rosier, Stewart, Stuart, Throughston, Tilsley, Wright.

PLATE 99.—1. Booker, Eastman, Loges, Saul, Saule.
2. Atherton, *Athurton, *Atterton, Bolden, Brenton, Brough, *Campbell, Cary, *Clark, Clarke, Clerke, Creck, *Crossley, Dale, Dolphin, Enderbie, Enderby, Freer, Guest, *Gutteridge, *Guttridge, *Haldenby, Hamlyn, Lauchlan, Lawchlan, Lindsay, Loghlan, Magawley, Mair, Moilliet, Muller, Plaskett, Robertson, *Rooke, *St. Clair, Santon, *Sinclaire, *Terry, Twells, Wemyss, Wyborn.
3.*Carniquet, *Clarke, *Copland, *Mayce, *North, *Sykes.
4. Calder, Cambell, Campbell, Chamberlain, Chamberlayne, *Heseltine.
5. *Acock, Alcock, *Atherton, *Crommelin, Gilpin, *Horsefall, *James.
6. Heard, *Ochterlony.
7. Adger, *Coupland, Swabey, Usher.
8. Calder, Donithein, Strettell, Wagner, Walker.
9. Chalie, Coldstream, Donithorn, Gobion, *Lech, Louthfuttis, Rooe, Seaton, Seton, Solley, Solly.
10. Atkinson, *Hildershaw, Jane, Jeane, Loch, Lock, Spark, Sparke.
11. Younghusband.
12. Boden, Carey, Cary, *Ellis, *Guest, Hamlyn, Killicke, Lachlan, Magawley, O'Melaghlin, O'Shea, O'Shee, Shee, Sinnott, Twycross.
13.*Buist, Shee, Stilwell.
14. Moore.

PLATE 100.—1. Bartlett.
2. Emerton, Hamerton, Hoppe, Maconchy, Malcolm, Malcom, *Pleckford, Sellers.
3. Eastwood.
4. Barttelot.
5. Attwood, *Machonchy, *Muntz.
6. Hackford, *Leach, Patton, Spooks, *Tatham.
7.*Angell, Dand, *Dendy, Fazakerley.
8. Lindsay.
9. Benvil, Benvill, Blachford, Brodhurst, Sellar.
10. Coote, Copeland, *Copland, Crost, *Edmonstone, Fagan, Hutchinson, *Keppel, Scales, Stafford, Swann, Sybyle, Vipont.
11. Blount (*alias* Croke), Croke, Rowdon.
12.*Chalke, *Folkarde, *Grevile, *Greville, *Grey.

PLATE 101.—1.*Ghest, Guest.
2. Beecham, *Gist, *Gest,
3. Torbock, Vale.
4. Abernethy, Boreston, Borreston, *Danvers, Desbrisay, *Dunnage, Fairfowl, Farbridge, Goodchild, *Kirkham, Lethieullier, Lethulier, Parrot, Pearson, Peerson, Perrot, Pierson, Smith, Tarbock.
5. Baker, Blackwell, *Charlton, *Daile, *Grenwelle, *Hedges, *Lilly, Mellish, *Murray, Pomfrett, *Swire, *Webster.
6. Abden, Beauchamp, *Blatchford, *Borough, *Bruget, Coates, Coats, Dolphin, Dunstable, Edlin, Glocester, Gloucester, O'Kerney, Swallman.
7. Whieldon.
8. Abernethy, Bowring, Eyre, Froggat, Froggatt, Knoell, Knoll, Knolle, Knowles, M'Ilwham, Rennie.
9. Tremlow, Twemlow.
10. Avagour, Avougour, *Copinger, Curran, Curren, Hartford, Hertford, Knowell, Turtie.
11. Danvers, Goodchild, Hare, Hester, Hutchinson, Kingswell, Pierce, Ramsay, Soden.
12. Heath.
13. Aberneathy, Ludlow, *Parret, Parrott, Perrot, *Perrott, Thurlow.
14. Avenant, Avenon,

PLATE 102.—1. Ash, Breyton.
2. Becke, *Bruges.
3. Barnes.
4. Brassey.
5. Baines, Garden, Sherlock, Wise.
6. *Boreley, *Borseley, *Borsley, Cornwall, Donand, Gullon, Wingfield.
7. Calder.
8. Sheldon.
9. Getham.
10. Carthew, Coote, Jackson.
11. See No. 5.
12. Coote.

PLATE 103 — 1 Aberbuthnot, *Carrington, *Clarke, Dirwyn, Fynes, Holbiche, Merill, Peacock, Pitson, Purdie, Purdy, *Smith, Smyth, Sowerby, Tomlin, Vigures
2 *Aiburthnet, Arbuthnot, Banaster, Banester, Bew, *Comerford, Currell, Douglas, Eberstein, Gauden, Goodison, Hampden, Kidwell, *Lylgrave *Perin, Sankey, *Smyth, Tisdale, Tisdall, Waltham
3 *Beck, Bourn, Bourne, *Bradford, Carver, Ilam, Ilmy, Peacock, Stedman
4 *Fordam, *Fordham, *Kett, *Lathem, *Letham, *Littlewood, O'Donoghue, *Somer, *Sommer, *Stott, *Verdier, Wyvell
5 Denne, De Ros, Manners, Roos, Ross-Lewin, Rosse
6 Haselfoot, Hasselfoot
7 Abeleyn, Aberbuthnet, Aberbuthnot, Arburthnet, Arbuthnot, Banastre, Banester, Bartelott, Beck, *Blithe, Charnell, Douglas, Vicarey, Vicary, Vikary, Yeo
8 Callow, Durrant, Hanmer, Harcourt, Hiddleston, Huddlestone, Hurley, Martin, Oxley, Sorrell, Vaux, Wallington
9 Jejeebhoy
10 Aberbuthnet, Brounlee, Brownlee, Bronlie, Burley, Burly, Fitz Barnard, Gemell, Gemill, Gemmell, Southby
11 *Carington, Peacock, Bligh Peacocks
12 Allison, Comberford, Comerford, De Montmorency, *Fisher, Griffis, Mearns, *Montmorency, Nanson, Pelham, Pelham Holles, Ridge, Rose, Snowden
13 *Juckes Clifton, Cotgrave, Cressey, De Montmorency, Witham
14 Chafy Chafy

PLATE 104—1 Banks
2 Baighton, *Boughton, Brisbane, Brisbon, Kinder, *Mercer, Starky
3 Barham, Barnardiston, *Lytton, Peart, Pert
4 De Butts
5 Fennison, *Herne, *Heron, Jerworth, Moubray, O'Hara, Phine, Waring,
6 Drysdale
7 Cadman, Gibson, Hanby,
8 Hughes
9 Teat
10 *Browne, Lydall, Lyddall
11 Bowden, *Bowdon, Bussell, Codd, *Cranmer, *Cranmore, Cranston, Cranstoun, Fythey, Fythie, *Hackshaw, Hale, *Herne, *Heron, Kinder, Kutchin, Ryley
12 Chambers
13 Chichester, Tuckey, Yonge, Young
14 Langstaff

PLATE 105 — 1 Crews, Crewse, Cruse, Cruwys
2 Beaumont, Flower, *Gun, *Lathom, Van, Woulfe
3 Accerley, Atherley, Browne, *Crosse, Dale
4 Bankes, *Gibson
5 Brett, *Dalbie, *Dalby, Marrant
6 *Angesteen, Broese, Brookman, Denham, Gattie, Gatty, *Hall, *Harris, *Heris, Pettyt, Petyt, Shore, Sotheram
7 Lumsdean
8 Chichester, *Eastoft, Hughes, O Brien, Ratcliffe, Rochester, Rote, Soloman
9 Amson, Boult, Brooke, Clerveaux, Crane, Cranstoun, Cramwell, *Crawley, *Crosse, Eldrington, *Fodringay, *Gamble, *Gambell, Herne, Heron, Hughes, Morphew, Napier, Ratclin, Rochester, Sleath, Sprot, Storar Storer, Storey
10 Borrowes, Borrows, Coe, Coo, Pitt, Taylor
11 Anderton, Bolt, Boult, Brooke, Bunch, Browne, Campbell, Chater *Cracroft, *Cross, *Crosse, Dale, Denton, *Laton, Elrington, *Ewen, Farnaby, *Fowler, Gardiner, *Goldsmith, Greenhalgh, Greenhaugh, *Greenwell, *Grenewell, *Hearn, *Lapworth, *Mathew, *Matthews, Morishmes, Morphew, Morslin, O Brien, Pinnei, Pitt, *Quinlan, Roebuck, Rote, *Smytheman, *Somer, Starkey, Starkie, Starky, Steel, Still, Storer, Storey, Thurston, Torlesse, Thruston, Thurston, Upjohn, *White
12 Andby, Andev, Andy, Banck, Banke, Colthurst, Faith, Jeffryes, Standon
13 See Plate 79, No 7
14 *Browne, Dawn, Dawne, Fraigneau *Gibson, Miall

PLATE 106 — 1 Bill, *Charteris, *Choke, *Dotchen, Fithie, Hagen, *Moncrief, Slough, *Staller, Story
2 *Bisson, *Goodridge, *Ronan, Sangster, *Songster, *Vanzellar
3 Boughton, *Brisbane, Mercer, *Rouse, *Stapley, *Starkey, *Story
4 *Cardonnell
5 *Rawson, Rayson
6 *Thomas
7 Sangster
8 Cawthorne
9 *De Ferneres, Garrowav, Gillon, Lluellyn, Macdonell, Sangster, Wescombe, Younge
10 Porte
11 M'Donald, *Pindar
13 Taunton
14 Meyrick

PLATE 107 —
2 *Adams, Aubin, Crowhall, Donaldson, Macdonald, MacDonald, *Macdonell, MacDonell, McDonell, St Aubin
3 Barsane, Bartane, Barton, *Beckett, *Cornish, Fasant, *Fentiman, Hardinge, Hope, Huet, Hyde, Macbride, *Norreys Parvise, St Aubyn, *Whithering, *Withering, *Woodall
4 Asadam, Booker, Bushby, Cassy, Cornwall, Horrell, Rooke, Sylvester
5 *Coringham, *Coryngham, *Corneille, Cowtherne *Craster, Craw, *Cromer, Laens, *Flower, *Rokeby, *Rook, *Rookby, *Stewart
6 *Croker, Fgerley, Fggerly
7 Spaight
8 Jones
9 Bowdler, Chitwood, Ratcliffe
10 Corbett, Gedney, Hopkins, *Russell
11 Agnew, Boyton, *Horwood, Leland Murdock
12 Corrance, *Corrance White, Urren
14 Amyand, Aletse, Averinges, Baillie, Bazilie, Bazely, Becket, Beggs, Bennet, Beynham, Blondevill, Blonville, Bosvargus, Busvargus, Cawthorne, Cornewall, Cornish, Cornwall, Craister, Crastein Craster, Crockett, Croker, Crook, Donnithorn, Edwin, Elmore, Fitz Hewe, Fitz-Hugh, *Flower, Foulerton, Gatacre, Gouldsmith, Heller, Hughes, Johns, Jones, Kirwan, La Roche, Ledsam, Llanwarne, Mackie, M'Kie, M'Morran, Magrath, Mahewe, *Massenden, Mayow, Morgan, *Mussenden, Nicholl, Orchard, *Owen, Parlar, Pearce, Pechell, Protheroe, Rashleigh, Raven, Raynford, Rice, Shearwood, Slingsby, Smallbones, Taunton, *Toms, Tonkin, Wallis

PLATE 108 —1 Pickersgill
2 Piper, Plumerdon
4 Kerdeston
5 Campion, Campyon, Champion, Needham, Strickland
6 Aylemer, Aylener, Aylmer, Bunnell
7 Genn, Rotnam, Sprencheaux, Springhose, Thomas
8 De Cardonnel, Kay, Kaye, Nagle
9 Hockin
10 *Rochford, Donegan
11 *Jennings, King, Robin, Rochfort, Stott, Stoughton
12 Nagle, *O Sullivan Mor

PLATE 109 —1 Scott
2 Brooke, *Helton, *Tringham
3 Pinsent
4 Dyne, Dynne
5 Heyward, Otway
6. Addison, Adelsorf, Affleck, Auchinleck, Blomefield Blomfeild, Bloomfield, Blow, Brinckman, *Clay, Coin, De Ginkell, Foresight, Gerard, Gower, Harbert, Juchen Manmaker, Merryton, *Ordway, Porteen, Sandberg, Van Jucken, Wingfield, Wintle
7 *Bay, Calshill, Clarke, *Conyers, Dawney, Dawny, Dean, *Edmonds, Goodlad, Holland, Hyde, *Jones, *Jumper, *Mills, *Minett, *Parke, Petoe, *Rowbache, *Welchman, Wyrley
8 Bass, *Bulteel, Eredy, Folton, *Gipp, Johnson, *Sombanck, Tanke, Van Straubenzee
9 Howard
10 and 11 Clay, Claye, Cley
12 *Bagg, Bagge, *Blomberg *Bor, Borough, *Brydges, Burrowes, Burrows, *Englebert, *Francheville, *Graham, *Gream, *Grimes, Haslefoote, *Hoste, *MacArthur

PLATE 110 —1 Kynnerton, Rokewood, *Spofforth
2 Van Allen
3 Anthonisz, Bareth, Watts
4 *Acton, *Allardace, *Allardice, *Allerdyce, *Gambon, *Gamon, *Jameson, *Jamieson, *Kers, Mortimer, *Nordet
5 *Apeele, *Apsley, *Cassan, Chamond, *Chaumond, *Crag, *Cragg, *Delins, *Edmonds
6 Amerdley, Gilroy
7 *Ainge, Ange, Beckley, Beckly, Bickley, Beykle, Bistley, Bystley, Camden,

Clark, Clarke, Collier, *Collyer, Delafield, Dugnall, Henshall, Whitlock.
8.*Blencowe, Tennant.
9. Camber.
10.*Brook, *Brooke, Falkiner, Faulkner, Rickford,
11. Farrar, Farrer, Farror, Ferrier, Gradock, Gradocke, Warne, Wolridge, Wolrige.
12. Frost, *Gamul, Hackwell, Hakewill, Heusch, Van Hagen.
13. Marshall.
14. Alchorn, Barrett, *Constant, *De Veulle, Douglas, Elsworth, Felbridg, Flood, Gamoll, *Hackwell, *Hartley, *Kellock, *Langton, *Peake, *Trueman, Truman.

PLATE 111.—1. Otway, Withie.
2. Pixley.
3. Askwith, Gordon, Pie, Pye, Rudde.
4. Brackenridge.
5.*Baring, Clauson, *Davies, Duntze, *Guille, *Smith, *Sperling, Taylour.
6. Austin, Otway.
7. Pelissier.
8. Bingley, *Frome.
9.*Bayne, *Beaghan, Greenall.
10. Capel, Cappell.
11. Frost.
12. Annandale, Beeching, Bempde, Burchett, Capp, Champion, Johnstone, Fairholm, Johnson, Johnston, Johnstone, Johnstoun, Knight, Walden.
13. Bonniman, Gibb, Johnson, Johnston, Knight, Langmead, *Lofthouse, Montrose, Vanden, Wailes, Wiggins.
14. Knight.

PLATE 112.—1. *Asterlley, *Astery, Audeley, De Bary, *Esterley, Evershead, *Glennon, Kilgour *Ligo, Muilman, Spurling.
2. Reeve, Roscow.
3. Cumberland, Greenhall, Hallwell, Halwell, Halywell, Hollings, Langhorn, Langhorne, Vanneck.
4. Lucas, Sword, Swourd, Ventris.
5. Elham, Gervays, Leath, Leatt, Marewood.
6. Hobbes, *Molson, *Preston, Scott, *Tothill.
7. Bentham, *Valence, *Valomess.
8. Bateman.
9.*D'Eye, *Eye, Howard, *Seymer, *Smyth.
10. Bell, Chirbrond, Dickson. Douglas, Driver. Duff, Falconer, Fitz-Walter, Flynt, Goddin, Landeth, Londeth, Mayne, Pringle, Samby, Sandpy.
11. Lutterford.
12. D'Osten.
13. Glover, Hallman, Halman.

PLATE 113.—1. Aifler, Aigler, Ayler, Brand, Campbell, Daccomb, Fitz-Raynard, Graham, *Lorimer, Melvill, Melville, Moens, Raynold, St. Denouac, De Spencer, Tonzel, *Wodchull, Woodhead.
2. Foxcote, Meux, Petrie.
3. Ayler, Filkin, Filkyn, Harvey, Pedler, Kenney, Tullock.
4. Neweke.
5. Bock, Cawodley, Cawoodley, *Clark, Copenger, *Huddesdon, *Hudson, St. Maur, Sapy, Sapye.
6. Ceely, Cely, Deraw, Hambleton, *Wilford.
7. De Chandew, Drummond, Fontain, Fontaine, Knevet, Poynton.
8. Codd, Codde, *Craik, *Drayton, Dukley, *Dunkley, *Fitz-Roger, Foxley, Godwin, *Holden, Jausselin, Jocelyn, Jocelyne, *Johnson, Kendrick, *Lattin, Paumier, *Tippetts.
9. Goulstone, Gulston, Gulstone.
10. Aime, Aine, Binckes, Bincks, Binks, *Darlington, Dean, Usher.
11. Aher, Aldworth, Cleather, Clunie, Hauston, Houston, Houstoun, Joass, Syward, Watkinson.
12. Boxall, Boxell, Brittain, Brittaine, Seymer.
13.*Browne, Marchmont, Singe, Synge, Hutchinson-Synge.
14. Aberton, Aburton, Cuthbert, Cuthburt, Gratton, Latouche, Moore.

PLATE 114.—1. Cardew, Copleigh, *Dabridgcourt, *Gueva, Hakeliott.
2. Delius, Fletcher, Fridag, Friday.
3. Arden, Brigham, Delabere, Denis.
4. Arderne, *Harris, *Linnet, Raines, Reymes, Reynes, Spitty, Waldegrave, *Warner.
5. Delius.
6. Brownell, Fitzwilliam Hankley, Harwood, Haule, Scroop, Scroope, Scrope, Sheil.
7. Reppes, Repps.
8.*Harrison, *Holland, De Kierzkowski, *Lambert, *Le Bon, *Lewys, *Marvel, *Mortimer *Ouldsworth, *Philip, *Plum, *Plume, *Posingworth, *Possingworth, *Posyngworth, *Promoli, Rothschild *Scales, *Scrope, *Smyth, *Surtees, *Surtes, *Swertchoff, *Tatham, *Von Mueller, *Willet, *Willett.
9. Promoli.
10. Pede, Uvedale.
11. Astley.
12. Alabaster, Albaster, Allebaster, Arblaster, Bragg, Burke, *Cow, *Cowe, *Cowee, *Cowey, *Cowie, Hardwike, *Hardy, *Harebread, Hatfield, Hitfield, Reye, Tudway.
13. Aldam, Anstis, Arderne, Astley Braham, *Braye, *Brooke, *Cann, Clere, *Clinton, Dellabere, Denny, Dennys, *De Worms, Dollabe, Dowker, *Druitt, *Dutton, Felbrigge, Fursdon, Godweston, Granson, Hastings, How, Howe, Jalmes, Johnes, Jones, Joy, Langley, Legge, Lewis, Luttrell, O'Brenon, Parker, Rupe, *Smith, Smyth, Surkas, Tindale, Tindall, *Tynedale, Waldegrave.
14. Waldegrave, Walford.

PLATE 115.—1. Blofeld, Bonamy, Boyd, Capel, Capell, De Costa, De la Barr, Douglas, Dyne, Dynne, Eden, Edon, Edwards, Egerton, Ellis, Giberne, Grentmesnell. Kathrens, Kathrins, Latimer, Leroux, Mompesson, Phillpot, Relhan, Scroope, Shardelow, Sharp, *Surtees, Tame, Verhulst.
2. Broughton, Enys, Mompesson, Montpenston.
3. De Cetto.
4. Balm, Balme, Bollingbroke, Bollingbrook, Bollinsbrook.
5. Athill.
6.*Blome, Conyston, Eldridge, Iliff, Maillard, *Meers, Sherard, Sherrard, Shippard.
7. Agmondisham, Agmundesham, Anderson, Balberney, Beetham, Blair, *Brocket, Brun, Buck, Cocks, Coggeshall, Crickman, De Hollyngworthe, *Den, *Denne, Denholm, *Dickson, Dingwall-Fordyce, Downes, Fordyce, Fordyce - Blair, *Galland, Gordon, Græme, Graham, Gullan, Hollingworth, Holyngeworthe, Hopson, *Howell, *Karbyll, Macartney, M'Min, M'Minn, M'Myne, *Maxwell, Medford, *Millman, *Milman, Park, Perkin, Robarts, Scott, Simmer, Skae, Symmer, Towers, Van, Webb, Wroughton.
8.*Dodington, Jones, *Smyth.
9. *Carill, Carrell, Carrol, Cocks, *Cornwallis, Cox, Den, Denne, Fulton, *Graison, *Hartley, Horrocks, *Robarts, *Shepard, *Shepherd.
10.*Bowen, Dickson.
11. Badcock, Cavanagh, Cavenagh, *Dickson, Maxwell, Soden, Sodey, Sodon.
12. Addey, Addy, *Adey, *Adrey, *Ady, Anderson, Balderney, Barkeley, *Bowen, Buckland, *Claxson, Cocks, *Dobell, Freshfield, Furser, Furzer, *Jones, *Kinsman, Mackannell, Mansel, *Nedham, Needham, Nix, Reynolds, Rothe, *Thelwall, *Truro, Young-Reynolds.
13. Arnison.
14. Outhwaite.

PLATE 116.—1. Brandt, De Clinton, Maxwell.
3. Austen, Maxwell, Penniecook, Pennycuick.
4. Anncey, Anncy, Clark, Ellwood, Flattesbury, Fleeming, Knight, Longevile, Prescott, Skipton.
5.*Burnby, *Burneby.
6. Flockhart.
7.*Rodger, Rogers.
8.*Gannoke, *Gethin, Hersey, Philips, Somervil, Sommerville, Vernon.
9. Bell, De Clinton, D'Engaine, Dengaine, *Grape, Lennon, Millard.
10. Crawford, Crawfurd, Dealtry, Frances, Francies, Frаunceis, Fraunces, Frannceys, Grymes.
11. Ellard, Eveleigh, *Gowland, Manduit, Mandut, Manduyt, Oram.
12.*Bradshaw, Bucke, *Collingwood, Drought, Keith, Longstaff, Swallow.
13.*Banks, Bradshaw, *Brand, Hislop, *Nettles, Walker.
14. Bradshagh, Bradshaigh, Bradshaw, Kneller.

PLATE 117.—1. Barwick, Ellard, *Lindear, Lynecar, Lynegar, Neale, *Roe, *Rogers, Williams.
2. Bunyard, Delavere, Elcock, France, Furney, Giesque, Kensing, *Parker, Puckering, Roe, Yardley.
3. Anables, Annabell, Annable, Annables, Brees, Breeze, Brockbank, Busk, Clelland, Cochran, Cochrane, Compton, Coppendale, Gordon, Halli-

burton, Halyburton, *Litster, M'Corqudell, M'Corquodale, Meales, Nethersole, Noel, Parry, Passmore, Rae, *Robinson, Scott, Slade, Strachan, Stiadling, Writington
4 Green
5 Armony, *Barfoot, *Bayning, *Browne, Bush, Champ, Eustace, Fodringham, Forster Fothergill, *Frohock, *Fullwood, Garstyde, Harte, Hill, Lisle, Lowen, Maguire, Maynard, *Newport, O'Connell, Puleston, Raeburn, Raleigh, Rawley, *Robinson, Scott, *Scrivenor, Smyth, Stanley, *Steward, *Stuart, Tench, Thorold, Trevanion, Trevenyon, Townshend, *Trollop, *Williams
6 Eustace
7 *Shield
8 Agmondesham, Almard, Audry, Billing, Billinge, Boddam, Bolland, Bowen, *Bowman, Brice, Burrowes, Burrows, Busk, Corns, Creake, Denovan, Devereaux, Devereux, Duvernet, Duvernette, *Ellerton, Ersey, I vans, *Felt, Forster, Foster, Fraser, Frothingbam, *Fulwood, Gadsby, Gage, Glanvile, Glanville, *Gradwell, Green, Greene, Grove, Grundin, Hand, Hart, Hindman, Hughes, *Hurt, Hutchison, Jones, Lally, *I a Serre, Lewin, Lewyn, *Leycester, Lisle, Lloyd, MacKindlay, Marnell, Masterson, Mathias, Maynard, *Molowney, *Moore, Nicholson, Noel, Novell, Nowell *O'Connell, Parker, Parkhouse, Patrick, Pepper, Plant, Polden, Pollard, Puelesdon, Pulesdon, Pulleston, Radway, Rickthorne, Roberts, Robertson, Robinson, Rodie, *Rogers, Rose, Rosse, *Rykthorne, Scot, Scote, Scott, *Erskine-Scott, Screven, Scriven, *Shortall, Sisson, Steade, Steede, *Steward, *Stradling, Thomas, Thorold, Townsend, *Townshend, Trevanion, Trollop, Troup, *Turfeet, Urquhart, Walker, Walkington, Ward, Wear, Weare, Wordesworth, Wrench, Wynne, Yarrow
9 Cage,
10 Bowen, Boydell, Fray, Fraye, Motton, *Parker, Randall, Ruff
11 Green
12 Helbert
13 Pollard.
14 Pettit

PLATE 118 — 1 Jones, Puleston, Thorpe
2 *Greaves, Glanvile, Glanville, Maunde, Patrickson, Plowden, *Roberts, *Rogers, *Townshend, Wye
3 Densy, Fortune, Keane, Leith, Mallard, Northcote, Parker
4 Barne
5 Hart
6. Parker
7 Chilcote, Chilcott, Don, Donn, *Ripon, *Robinson, Shee
8 Jacoby
9 *Taylor
10. Harrison
11 Edwards
12 De Mandevile, M'Cabe, Partrickson, Patrickson, Shepard, Sheppard, Windsor, *Yardeley, *Yardley
13 *Benolt, *Buckeridge, Cathrope, Drew, *Eardley, France, *Gethin, *Hardwick, *Heysham, Kensing, *Maxwell, *Puckering, Roe, *Stradling, *Suckling, Trollope, *Yardley
14 Everington

PLATE 119 — 1 Cayle, Colvil, Colville, *Strachan
2 Allwood, Alwood, *Barley, Barnevelt, Bridgewater, *Cannock, Chittock, *Courthope, *Finlayson, *Fisher, Fullwood, Fulwood, *Giblett, Green, *Greenly, Hall, *Harward, *Humble, Langworthy, Larkworthy, Lone, *Lonsdale, Love, *Opie, Pestell, Power, Primout, Primouth, *Robinson, *Smith, Smyth, Smythe, *Snigg, *Snigge, *Spouse, *Stawell, *Tirrey, *Webb, *Wilde, *Wylde
3 Heap
4 Wild
5 Norreys, Norris, Von Sturmer
6 Green
7 Horton
8 Andrewes, Andrews, *Fraser, *Gordon, *Lister, Lloyd, Rowe, Semple
9 Foster, *Foyster
10. Goddard, Hutchon, Justine, Justyne, Ketford, Lewis, Mortimer, Quelch
11 *Belasyse, Leicester, Parker *Pledger, *Roane, Rogers, Stolyon
12 *Calibut, *Crosell, De Romara, Godard, Goddard, Goddart, Gordon, Mackenzie, Mantell, Mantle, Northage, *Stoveld, Windsor
13 *Anderson, *Austyn, Braylesford, Braylford, *Davison, Gellibrand, Gordon, Heap, Joule, Richmond, Stark
14 *Anncell, Auncell, Gordon, Hext, Heysham, Hoare, Lingard, Plonckett, Plonket, Plonkett

PLATE 120.—1 Pitter
2 Dillwyn
3 Bellingham, Blyth, Blythe, Goulborne, Green, Haworth-Booth, Hicks, Horsefall, Horsfall, Howorth, Hugford, Huggerford, *Huls, Hulse, Lloyd, Roper, Smith, Smythe, Wilfoord
4 Chaytor
5 *Bellingham, James, Wylie
6 Bates
7 *Baspoole, *Bedell, *Bettes, Betts, Boorne, *Brown, *Bulworth, *Colbarne, Doyle, Fanner, Gilbert, *Gooch, Gothard, Green, Greene, *Harleston, *Harlstone, Harman, Hawarden, *Hawes, Hibbins, Holmes, Lister, Lyster, Marshall, *Parmiger, Sheridan, Shirley, Stennett, Stennitt, Stirling, Trinder, Ugletreight, Westrope, Whitaker
8 *Cadell, *Colborne, Fraser
9 Chandois, Chandos, Clendon, Craford, Crawford, *Haney, *Hanney, Herting ton, *Houghton, Murray, Power
10 Ackroyd, *Betts
11 Lambert.
12 *Ballenden, Bellenden, Cairns, Craufurd, Crawford, Crawfurd, Gwyn, *Loder, Newbigging, Wickliff, Wyckliffe
13 Elwon
14 Dudley

PLATE 121. — 1 *Andrews, Pickwick, Power
2 *Amias, Andrew, Andrews, Apted, Astrie, Audouin, Aurd, Bailey, Basevi, Bayley, Baynbridge, Baynbrigge, *Beadle, Beckwith, *Bedle, *Bedell, Belasis, Bell, *Bellas, Bellasis, *Bellasis, *Bellewe, Bellingham, *Bene, Bickwith, *Blythe, *Boardman, *Boorne, Boultbee, Boyse, Bradford, Broadley, Brockdon, Browne, Budorshide, Budoxhead, Bulworth, Burleigh, *Busby, *Bushby, Byrdall, Cahan, Cahn, Cahun, *Cantis, Carling, Carr, Carre, *Chapman, *Clavel, *Clavell, *Claville, *Clotworthy, Colbran, Colleton, Collington, Colquhoun, Couts, Crawfurd, Creketot, Dear, Dick, Dickson, Dirom, Dixon, Doling, *Dorington, Dorn, Downes, *Draper, Edington, Egerton, *Ellacombe, *Ellicomb, *Ellicombe, *Lverton, Fawset, Fawsset, Finlason, *Floyer, Forbes, Forteath, Foster, Fouler, Franks, Fraser, Frisel, Gahn, George, *Gethin, Gifford, Goff, Goffe, Goosbrey, Gordon, Green, Greene, *Greenough, *Griffith, Grimston, Gunter, Hanning, Hargrave, Harman, *Hart, *Harte, Hartgule, Hartgull, Hartland, *Hartree, Hartshorne, *Hast, Hemenhall, Hernes, Hill, *Hills, Hird, Hoad, Hoare, Horner, Humble, Hunt, Hunter, Hunter-Arundel, Hutchison, Hutton, Jones, Karr, Keith, Ker, Kerr, Kewley, *Kitchiner, Knightley, Ladbrooke, Audouin-Lamb, *Lawrence, Lea, Lee, Leith-Forbes, Lethbridge, Leybourne, Lister, Lizars, Lloyd, Locker, *Loggan, Logon, Lovat, Loyd, Lyde, Lyster, M'Adam, M'Dougall, M'Guire, *Machell, *Mauchael, *Mauchel, M'Kimmie, Macleay, M'Phaill, Marshall, Mason, Maxwell, Perceval-Maxwell, Mescow, Mortimer, *Mortoffe, *Mortoft, Mortymer, Myreson, Nell, Norcliffe, Norman, Noyes, O'Connell, Ord Osbaldiston, *Overstone, Pain, Parker, *Parkhurst, Peele, Peirce, Penning, Penyng, Pevelesdon, Piggot, Plowden, Popham, Leybourne Popham, Polken, Raikes, *Randall, Raynsford, Rayson, *Reade, Rede, Riddel Carre, Ridgley, Ridley, Rigaud, Riggeley, Rigmaiden, Roberts, Robinson, Roe, *Rogers, Romayne, Rone, Ronne, Roper, Row, Sage, Scales, Scott, Sempill, Semple, Shepley, Simmons, *Slayer, Smith, *Smyth, Spens, Standley, Stanley, Stirling, Stirling-Maxwell, Strachan, *Thomson, *Tugwell, Trydell, Verulam, Vigors, Walker, Woodhead, Woodman, *Wright, Wybrants, Wychcombe, Wylde, *Wynchcombe, Yles, Young, Younge
3. Marshall, Pickup
4 Wadham, *Woodham
5 Amos, Annesley, Arundel, Barrow, Beckwith, *Bedall, *Bedell, Bell, Bellingham, Blyth, *Bois, Bolles, Bondiville, Bonvile, Boteshed, Botockshed, Bowles, Brackshaw, Bridge, Broadockshaw, Brodockshaw, Buck, Buckley, *Buxton, Caddell, Cadell, Cahurta, Campbell, Cathie, Chapman, Charlett, *Churchward,

Clapcott, Collingwood, Colquhon, Colquhoun, Copenger, Crawford, Crowton, Cuerden, Cureton, Dalrymple, *Dancastle, Denny, Dirom, *Dolling, *Doncastle, Done, Downes, *Doyle, *Draper, Duff, Edward, Fawcett, Forbes, Foster, *Fowbery, Fowles, Fraser, Fulton, Gaddes, Gaddez, Geddes, Geddies, *Gibb, *Gideon, Gifford, *Gilbert, Gillbanks, *Gonor, Gordon, Gould, Grandgeorge, *Grandorge, *Grain d'Orge, *Green, Greene, *Grimston, Grimstone, Gunter, *Hall, Hardres, Harley, Harneys, Harnous, Harris, Hart, *Harware, *Haworth, Heaton, Hemery, Hendry, Herns, *Hicks, *Higgs, Hili, Hobbins, *Hulles, *Huls, *Hulse, *Hulsey, Hunter, Hyde, Keith, Keverdon, Kinder, Kirkpatrick, Knightley, Knightly, Kuerden, Kyle, *Kylom, Laird, Lascells, Laven, Leighton, Libby, Linten, Litster, Lloyd, Lockett, Lovibond, M'Adam, Macadam, M'Gillivray, *Machell, M'Murray, M'Nally, Manntell, Margonts, Martin, Marton, Maxwell, Graham-Maxwell, Meikle, Moldford, Mortimer, Morgan, Mortimore, Murray, Nodin, Nott, Nourse, Noyes, Ogilvy, Paley, *Parke, *Parker, Peat, *Peerman, Peirson, Penwyn, Perott, *Perry, Phelan, *Pigeon, Plompton, Plomton, Popham, Porter, Power, Poynton, Raper, Rockley, Roe, Rogers, Rokley, Rollo, *Roo, Rooe, Rotheram, Row, Rowe, Ryvell, Scott, Seaton, *Sempill, Semple, Skene, Snape, Snappe, Snepp, Spence, Spring, Springe, Stanford, Stanley, Stawton, Stepkins, Steventon, Sulliard, *Sutherland, Tatenhall, Trideneck, *Tristram, Uppleby, Welfitt, Westall, Whateley, *Wheat, *Wheate, Wolrige-Gordon, Wyld, Younger, Young-Scott.

6. *Boulstree, *Bulstree, Forster, Giffard.
7. Borthwick, Cart, Caw, *Finlayson, Tipper, Wigton.
8. Connell, Ellison, Knightley, Lister, M'Connell, McConnell, *Mulchinock, O'Connell, Powers.
9. *Cottington, Errington, *Greene, Stanley.
10. Hargreaves.
11. Hargrave.
12. Adenstoun, Adingstoun, Adinstoun, Alms, Robarts.
13. Bushby.
14. Eure, Wilkinson, Williamson.

PLATE 122. — 1. *Black, *Drake, Edge, *Foxwest, *Hill, *Hose, Kettle, Lambard, *Lambert, Morgan, *Rainsford, *Sainbadge, *Sandbach.
2. *Basset, *Bassett, Court, Morgan.
3. Colborne, Dodds, Fiske, Flote, *Gardner, Harcla, Harcle, Peploe, Welley, Willey, Willy.
4. Brignac, Clench, Clenche, De Carteret, Dowhiggin, Hardress, Malynes, Morgan, Newington.
5. Adean, *Agan, Anne, Austyn, Avenayne, Avenar, Avenel, Avenele, Aveneyle, Avenyle, Averill, *Bencler, Bispleam, Bucknall, Busbridge, Calder, Christopher, Clare, Crozier, Domville, D'Oyley, Frend, Friend, *Gardiner, Gell, Gordon, Graham-Maxwell, Griffith, *Griffiths, *Harwood, *Hay-Gordon, Hay, Heaton, Hollingbury, *Hoppey, Hunter, Hunter-Blair, *Huntley, Hutton, Lacy, *Langford-Nibbs, Lindsay-Bucknall, *Littleton, *Lowle, M'Cleay, Mackenzie, M'Kenzie, Maxwell, Molleson, *Morant, Morgan, Mortimer, *Needes, *Nibbs, Nisbet, Norton, Osmand, Park, Parker, Partis, *Pate, Peckwell, Penman, Pount, *Power, *Prytherch, Raynford, Raynsford, *Robinson, Salle, Skyrme, *Stagg, Steventon, Studley, *Stubbs, Sulyard, Taylor, Thompson, Thomson, Trye, Whatley, Wheatley, Williams, Windle, Winyard, Worhead, *Wycliffe.
6. Haworth.
7. Chapman.
8. Beech, Hunter.
9. Byrde, Pace, *Pate.
10. Baker.
11. Badger, Baghot, Cely.
12. Loder.
13. De la Poer, Eustace, Poore, Power, Waterford.
14. Ellis.

PLATE 123.—1. *Dietz, Egg, *Gibbines, *Gibbins, Nassau.
2. Jeune.
3. Crisp, Nassau, *O'Donnel, *O'Donnell, Offley, Roche.
4. Vachell.
5. Catznellage, Chauster, *De Waetor, *Dunlop, Wayer.
6. Duncombe, Dunscombe, Fresh, Saward, Seward.
7. Delafeld, Delafield, Vachell.
8. Cheney, Cheyney, Crownall, Horn, *Horne, Morrell, Sherland, Silly, Sully.
9. Henley.
10. Callander, Callendar, Cleves, Culliford, Fittz, Futroye, *Oliphant, Roscoe, Steinmetz.
11. Dymoke, Wells-Dymoke.
12. De la Vach, Delavache.
13. Fewster, *Peterswald.
14. Merle, Minchin, Rivers.

PLATE 124. — 1. Alford, Barrow, *Bolton, Cassie, Colclough, Colcloughe, *Collvile, Colvil, Colville, *Colvin, Dicconson, Dickens, Fydell, *Golding, Handby, Harpden, *Hellier, Heriet, *Hingston, *Hunston, Hunt, Jennet, Jennett, Katerley, Katherley, Montgomery, Moynley, Noton, Pattison, *Pierson, Pyrry, Railton, Richardson, Shepherd (*alias* Thwaites), *Shrawley, Stockley, Talland, Underwood, *Vere, Whitebread, Woodriff, *Wyngate, Yardley, Yardly.
2. Conran.
3. *Boulton, Clements, *Collett, Coyle, *Fincham, Gregor, Hawkes, *Hippisley, Innes, *Keen, *Keene, *Kene, *Perry, Fery, Ragon, Riddock, Thwaites, Troup, Tyler, Underwood, *Webb, *Webbe, Whitbread, Whitbred, Wooley.
4. Gaylien, *Howton.
5. *Bickley, *Cocks, *Forth, *Hind, *Hynde, *Kene, Macdougale, *Merlay, *Readshaw, *Richardson.
6. Anderson, *Shaw.
7. Reading.
8. *Brocket, Hart-Davis.
9. Franklyn.
10. Hill, Noel.
11. *Byne.
12. *Amys, Bisshe, Collet, Crotty, *Davoron, *Dottin, Eamer, Grogan, Hatton, Hooker (*alias* Vowell), *Hussey, Jephson, Lecky, Leigh, M'Donald, *O'Davoren, Prickett, Seymour, Ward, Welstead, Welsted, Welstod, *Winter, Yardeley.
13. Bonython.
14. *Amyas, *Cornwallis, Enswell, Entwissel, Houston, Janson, Lloyd.

PLATE 125.—1. Emmot, Emmott, Garrat, Garratt, *Heacock, *Kerdiffe, Lounde, Lownde.
2. Benn.
3. Fitz-Rause, *Hatton, *Hutton, *Twisleton.
4. Crew, *Davies, *Dobell, *Doble, Eastday, Estday, Hawkins, Underhill, Ward.
5. *Chauser, *Chawcer, Deane, *De Rivers, *De Ryvers, *Edward, *Gaven, Kymes, *De Rivers.
6. Crossley.
7. Ascough, Aysscough, Keymer, Moels, *Mules.
8. Davis.
9. *Boteville, *Boteville, *Bouteville, Clesby, Da Costa, *Ellerton, Maynstone, Mead, *Steede, *Thynne.
10. *Ascough, *Ascue, Chamberlain, Chamberlaine, Chamberlayne, Mainwaring, St. Amond, Trussell, Wooldridge, Woolridge.
11. *Ascough, *Askew, *Askue, *Ayscough, *Craycraft, *Crecroft.
12. *Ashfordby, Asken, Askene, Aston, Astonne, *Ayscough, Barnardiston, Chamberlain, Chamberlayn, *Chambers, *De la Chambre, *Delechambre, Macklin, Mainwaring, Millington, *Qyre, Zouch, Zouche.

PLATE 126.—1. Jaudrill.
2. *Amenton, *Arnold, *Atwood, Barwell, Blackburn, *Bicknor, *Bykenor, Calamount, Chyner, Clobery, *Colburn, *Dorrell, *Douce, *Dunning, Fetherston, Fetherstonhaugh, Fitter, Garde, *Garton, *Geary, *Gery, *Glascock, *Gonson, *Gonston, *Good, Gosselin, Gosselyn, *Green, *Grumstead, *Gunson, Gunter, *Hains, *Hamilton, *Hodges, Hodson, Holden, *Joskin, *Joskyn, Lingwood, *Lorance, *Lowtham, *Lye, *MacGeorge, Marshall, Pentagrass, Pocock, *Prendergast, *Pyne, Quyxley, *Randal, *Randall, *Randolph, *Randulph, Raper, *Rigby, Rigbye, Rippon, Roberts, Roper, Rose, *Sanders, *Scholten, *Scholton, *Smyth, Snow, Stacey, Stevenson, *Tipping, Wemyss, Whittington, Wordsworth, *Yates, *Yonge.
3. Baylis, Burra, Cain, Caine, Fesant, Gaff, Gateford, Hartley, Hawthorn, Hawthorne, Heard, Kierman, Martin, Porter, *Quick, Roope, Voller.
4. Bagnall, *Breach, *Buggine, *Burgoigne, *Burgoyne, *Fyre, *Welch, *Welsh.

5 *Capps, *Durning, *Fallesby, *Grange, *Harris, *Naper, *Napier, *Snagg, *Snigge, *Spring, *Trenfield
6 Adshade, Adshead, *Aype, Byfield, Cadwoodley, Caldwoodley, Calwodley, Carew, Chittock, *Chrisope, Coxton, Delaney, Delany, Delatune, *Denby, Edwards, Galliers, Gollop, Homes, Howison, Ireby, Jameson, Joce, Kardaile, Kardoyle, *Kemp, Laban, Lenaghan, Liard, *Manderson, Mant, *Parkinson, Sandby, Shewen, Smyth, Webley
7 Edwards
8 *Muskett, Whitgrave
9 Verral
10 Farmer
11 Remfry
12 Beckwith, Binge, Board, Bostock, Fetherston, Fetherstonehaugh, Fetherstonhaugh, Hamilton, Hooper, Hyde, Joyce, *More, Raper, Vane
13 Price
14 Russell.

PLATE 127 —1 Chatterton, Cox, Farley, *Fowle, Power
2 *Cropley, *Langdon, Le Taylor, *Linch, *Lynch, *Salkyns
3 Copinger
4 *Cooke, *Dax, Raymont
5 Byng, Dennis, *Dighton, Prendergast, *Torrington
6 *Cranfield, Hawkins, Pocock
7 Crosley
8 Rothwall
9 Bagnall
10 Agad, *Bermingham, *Chapman, *Chatfeild, *Chatfield, *Darby, *Memes, *Pennant, *Potter, Towers Trotter
11 *Adlington, *Dyne, *Hendley, Porter
12 Gurteen
13 *Bellew
14 Porritt

PLATE 128 —1 *Herd
2 *Anthony, *Chevers, Russell, Snagg, Snagge
3 Porter, Yate, Yates
4 Hamilton
5 Addlington, Adlington, *Baggalay, *Baily, Baird-Hay, Bawtre, Bennet, Berkhead, *Bewicke, Birmingham, Bowerman, Bowreman, Brooke, Brownlow, Buckton, *Bulwer, *Bunney, *Bunny, Bush, Bushe, Catty, Chetwynd, Clebury, Clobery, Clowberry, Cokeningham, *Copoldyke, Coppinger, Cox, Crutenden, Cuyet, Darrell, Dayrell, *Deton, *Detton, Dorrell, *Dyer, *Eveleigh, Fleeming, Fleming, Frank Frewke, *Fulmerston, *Futter, Garnham, Gayford, Gifford, *Gorton, *Haley, Hands, Hay *Jackson, Kidd, Kiddall, *Knight, Leveson, Leyson, Littleboy, Litton, M'Call, *Malley, Mar, Marm, *Marwood, Meredyth, Methoulde, Methwold, Morton, Outram, *Plumstock, Prittenton, Prattinton, Pritchard, *Reade, Rigby, Robley, Ruthven, Sapcotes, Sapcott, Sares, Sargent, Shales, Stratford, Sevrson, Sweeting, Temmes, Traherne, Warde, Wethered, *Whittington, Wornack, Worrall, *Yeatman

6 Hollway
7 *Bettie, *Betty, *Brownlow, Fleeming, *Fleming, *Harbottell, *Holloway, *Jessop, *Waterton
8 Crossman
9 *Fleming, Jackson
10 Fairfax
11 *Hill, Louthian
12 Anthony, Antonie, Antony, *Bayly, *Boughton, *Bover, Bushe, Candeler, Candler, *Copley, *Cox, Craik, Crawford, Crawfurd, *Dance, *De Buckton, *Edington, *Ellis, Flemming, *Gason, Greatorex, *Hawes, *Hay, *Hurlestone, Jackson, Kingsley, Knightly, Lamplugh, Loggie, *Naylord, Oddy, *Rigby, Ruthven, Say, Tims, Waller, Williams
13 Litchfield, Ruthven
14 Athanray, Bagot, *Dayrell, Delaval, Dyer, Gardiner, *Garfoot, Garforth, Gason, Jones, Kyngesley, *Macclesfield, Ruthven, Sedley, Sideley, Sidley, Swynerton, Swynnerton, Sydney, Wettenhall, *Whettnall, Whitington, Yate, Yates

PLATE 129 —
2 Burkett, Lloyd
3 Bainbridge, Bainbrigg, Bainbrigge, Bainbrigge Le Hunt, Bambridge, Baynbrigge, *Button, *Russell
5 *Amyat, *Amyatt, *Apletree, *Battersbee, *Battersby, *Baynton, *Blaxton, Board, Boord, Borde, *Boynton, *Brune, Bruyin, Bruyn, *Carvill, *Crow, *Chandos Pole, Fstewer, Fstower, *Fleet, *Garth, *Gibball, *Goat, *Goate, *Handcock, *Harvill, Hay, Hollowell, *Hugworth, Kemp, *Kervyle, *Lowndes, *Macmahon, *Malby, *Napean, *Nepean, *Painter, *Penhallow, *Reresby, *Russell, Sacheverell, *Sullivan, Warren Williams, Worthington
6 Connel, Connell, Ringewood, Ringwood
7 Russell
8 Clark, Clarke, Ince, *Kingeston, Kingston
9 Campbell, *Fyers, *Wooding
10. Bardwell, *Bartholomew, *Bartolomew, *Kimpton, *Kympton
11 Worthington

PLATE 130 —1 Ashby, *Aspland, Baggeley, Belgrave, Bilsdon, *Boade, *Capper, Chester, Clerke, Copinger, *Cromer, *Curtis, Dalavall, Dalton, Dreux, *Ethelston, Gray, Greive, Grey, Knolas, Knolls, Knowles, *Ledlie, *Marriot, *Marriott, Mitton, Mytton, *Orby, Orreby, *Peel, *Ramsbotham, *Ramsden, Ruthven, Wardman
2 Currey, Currie, *Davy, *Dewar, Evans, *Haultain, Hoard, Price, Stopford
3 Knowles
4 Marsh, Yester
5 Farley
6 Birket, Capper, Cousen, Cousin, Cremer, Cupholme, De Dreux, Delavall, Dusseaux, Grigson, Huson, [illegible]

dock, Penruddocke, *Pert, *Ram, *Sackvile, Sackvill, Swayne, Sydenham, Weatherley, Weaver, Wetherly
7 Lambton, Lampen, Lechingham, M'Turk
8 *Bertram
9 Nembhard, Nemphartz
10 Deschamps, Fowkes, Narboon, Narboone, Prowse
11 Baggeley, Bigelow
12 *Lambton-Dawson
13 Clarke, Grimsbie, Grimsby, *Sheild, Vincent

PLATE 131 —1 Punshon
2 Austin, Beaufice, Beawfice, Boggie, Bogie, Borron, *Cork, Crosbie, Crosby, Davidson, Delature, Dowdal, Dowdall, *Dyson, Farrington, *Ferguson Davie, *Fitz Warren, *Hyde, Jones, Lamb, Lammin, Langholme, *Lewis, *Llewellyn, Lluellin, Malmains, Normand, Parry, Pascol, Pryce, Richards, Rowe, Williams
3 Davy
4 Milne
5 Llewelyn
6 Brandram
7 Sidebottom
8 Platt
9 *David, *Davie, *Francis, *Lamb, Ridsdale, Sheepshanks
10 Battersby
11 Lamb
12 *Biggs, *Brandreth, *Crouch, *Crowch, *Davis, Llfred,
13 Arbuckle, *Blossome, *Blossun, Budds, *Colde, *Colfe, *Colt, Elliot, Elliott, Gage, Kershaw, Manwell, Neal, Pascall, Rawlings, St Clere, *Shepheard, Sheppard, Staple, *Stenynge, *Yea
14 Benton, Clack, *Grose, *Rowan

PLATE 132. —1 Hart, Ridgeway, Ridgway
2 Amphlet, Amphlett, *Cardinal, Cawton, Derby, Goldfinch, *Hammon, Howel, Howell, Oliphant, *Parker *Singleton, *Weston
3 Ridgway
4 *Appelton, *Appolton, Maw
5 Hart
6 *Jaye
7 Abberbury, *Bourges, Bradford, Burges, Burgis, Butter, Camel, Campbell, Carron, Clove, Clynch, *Collins, Columball, Courthope, *Cowsfield, Crichton, *Crow, *Crowe, Darwen, Darwin, Daughish, *Denn, *Draper, Edmiston, Edmistone, Edmondstone, Eldres, *Eversfield, Fordyce, Framyngham, *Fullarton, Kahl, Lockwood, M'Gilvray, *Morland, *Musner, Palley, *Pattenson, *Phillipson, Stother, Stutvile, Sutherland, *Wheler, Woodburne, Woodthorpe
8 Crisp
9 *Betagh, Clere, Coffin, *Freckelton, *Freckleton, Leslie, *Machell, *Marshall, *Mitchell, *Merbury, *Muchell, Pepys
10 Cammell
11 Crisp
12 [illegible]

PLATE 133.—1. Betham, Bethome, *Davy, Kirby, Knowles, Knowlys, Kyrby, Pelley, Pelly, Sanders, Villettes.
2. Anderson, *Apleton, *Appleton, Bastard, Clarke, Eliot, Elliot, Elliott, Ellyot, Ellyott, Fountaine, Gardner, *Huyshe, Keble, *Lander, *Larder, Oliphant, Parker, Putland, Smith, Throckmorton, Uvery, Westby, Yate, Yeverley.
3. Bestroe, Bestrow, *Carington, *Carson, Dawbeney, Doleman, *Elliot, Forican, *Huskisson, Ledgcomb, Lynes, Maddocks, Oliphant, *Potter, Pratt, *Quelch, Risdon, Sanders, Sargant, Sargeant, Saunders, *Smith. Sutton, Throckmorton, Throgmorton.
4. Snafford.
5. Rosher.
6. Webb.
7. Watt.
8. Keir.
9. Alexander, *Brander, Carson, *Cobb, Concanon, Crooks, De Betum, Fountaine, *Framlingham, *Hynes, Knollis, Knollys, Knowles, Laws, *Luff, Mackinder, M'Kinder, *Malin, Mascall, O'Concannon, Oliphant, *Packington, *Sarmon, Smith, Strafford, *Whirple, *Fountayne-Wilson.
10. Nuthoobhoy.
11. Astley-Corbett, Beaumont, Corbet, *Corbett, St. Paule.
12. *Burdus, *Burduss, Littler.

PLATE 134. — 1. Balfour, Bethune, Watts.
2. *Bygan.
3. Bethune, Brewster, Burdenbroke, Fullarton, Hately, Holmden, Holmeden, Kellam, Kellnm, Kinnaird, Bethune-Lindsay, Lindsay, Merks.
4. *Bariff, *Barriff, *Beriffe, Cooke.
5. *Alexander, *Aprece, Homfray, Homfray-Addenbrook, *Jaye, *Otto, Schneider, Sinclair, *Symons.
6. Attye, Aty, Atye, Blayney, De Butts, Chawner, Craufurd, Crawford, Ermine, *Fedelow, Hault, Hurlston, Keith, Lewis, Bethune-Lindsay, M'Culloch, Robe, Stanton, *Watson.
7. Coleridge.
8. Alexander, Baynham, Beaver, *Beevor, Bell, *Besook, Bevers, Beynham, Brookes, Brooks, *Coram, *Corham, *Danskine, Dimsdale, *Eaton, *Fenwick, *Howel, *Howell, Maclagan, M'Lagan, *Molineux, Sadleyr, *Symcock, *Symcott, *Trowell.
9. Abarough, Abarow, *Atbarough, *Atborough, Crew, Dalley, Daly, *Dickey, *Dickie, Glen, Glenn, *Houlton, Judd, Jude, Lowe, *Maccaunach, Watmough, Watmoughe.
10. Aberigh, Aermine, Airmine, Armine, Bradwarden, Elworth, France, Goold, Manchester, *Soltau-Symons, Tagg.
11. Barrie, Bethune, *Beveridge, Ludlow, St. Germyn, Sinclair, Tayler.
12. Gardin, Graden, Greiden.
13. *Dodds, *Dods.
14. Smith.

PLATE 135.—1. *Levinz, Lynne.
2. *Ash, Baldwin, Foulke, *Hasellwood, *Hasel[illegible], *H[illegible]lewood, Hassellwood, Holt, *Lasman, *Mervyn, Young.
3. Nicolls.
4. Amcots, Ayncotts, *Baldwin, *Broughton, Corbet, *Davis-Goff, *Des Vœux, *Edmondstone, *Flesher, *Goff, *Graves, *Hill, *Ireton, *Newhouse, *Nicholls, *St. Aubyn, *Skerrit.
5. Carteret, Corbet, Gilbert, Griffith, *Rundle.
6. *Warton, *Wharton.
7. Amcot, Amcotes, Amcots, Amcotts, Barrow, Barzey, Billesworth, Blewitt, Bloundell, Blundell, Burles, *Collinson, Creswell, *Dennistoun, *Dighton, Dowsing, Feaulitean, Forest, Gilbard, Gilbert, Gilbert-Davies, *Goff, Greyndour, Harvye, *Hasell, *Hazlewood, Hervey, *Hillersden, *Hillesden, Hingenson, Holt, Ireton, Lee, Littler, *Loveday, Lovell, Malone, *Mervyn, Perceval, Skereth, Smithson, Thynne, Tippets, *Weld-Blundell, Woodgate, Woodnoth, Woodward.
8. Abrahall, Albam, Birom, Byrom, Calamy, Claxton, *Curle, Gooding, Griles, Grills, Harris, Hersay, *Jones, Kempt, *Kerle, *Kyrle, Lufers, Mainstone, Mayneston, *Powtrell, Speake, Speke, Weedon, Whitwange, Whitwong.
9. Green, Greve, *Grevis.
10. *Giles.
11. Cresswell, Bethune.
12. See Plate 134, Nos. 6, 9, 13.
13. Clermont, Du Fou, Kyme, Manchester, Miller, *Nangotham, *Nangothan, Robe, Sinclair.
14. Claxton.

PLATE 136.—1. *Carpenter, *Coney, *Cony, Lonesby.
2. *Booth, *Meryet, *Sweetingham, *Swetenham.
3. *Birch, Brown, Browne, *Byrch, Cranwell, *Hase, *Lievre, *Muttlebury, *O'Malley, Winthrop.
4. Conesby, Coningesby, Coningsby, Conisbie, Coney, *Conney, Cony, *Hewetson.
5. Dessen, Dychfield, Fyler, *Grilles, Grylls, Penny, Philpot, Prestage, Prestwich, Prestwick, Prissick, Speke, Sydney, Woodford.
6. Packington, *Pakington, *Rabett.
7. Black.
8. *Berners, Fitzgerald, FitzGerald, Fitz-Gerald, Fitz-Zimon, Gerard, *Harris, *Hays, *Middleton, *St. John, *Scott, Zymon.
9. *Hodges, M'Connel.
10. Inys.
11. Alderford.
12. Abriscourt, Abuscourt, Abustourt, *Hair, Hastday, Joel.
13. *Cadicott, Cranage, Dan, Dann, Gove.
14. Aldirford, Slauter, *York, *Yorke.

PLATE 137. — 1. Beatson, *Busbie, Byres, Connel, Connell, *Hokeley, Innes, Mastone.
2. Abercrombie, Abercromby, Bathgate, Beatson, Betson, Fettas, Fettes, Fitzpen, Gentle, Innes, Maher, Maxtone, Meryon, Stewart, Tibbitts, Tuthill, Whitelaw.
3. Ferrers, Steuart, Stewart.
4. Abram, Congalton, Congilton, Harnet.
5. Sewell.
6. Allatt.
7. *Beebee, Brade, Browne, *Bullock, Calderwood, Creirie, Cririe, Gausen, Gaussen, Honeywill, M'Crire, M'Cririck, M'Rerik, Marshall, Petty, Petty-FitzMaurice, Shillinglaw, Suttie, Templer.
8. Gresham.
9. Daubeney.
10. Bateson.
11. *Baxter, Bogg, Bouge, Bugge, Colwich, De Rivers, Norrington, Novelle, Randall, Randolfe, Randolph, Wakefield, Yellowley.
12. Babington.

PLATE 138.—1. Farmer.
2. Campbell, Douglas, Fitz-John, Julian, Julion, Macbride, Selkirk, Stead.
3. Farmer.
4. Delaval, Douglas, Dundas, Ebhert, Fitz-Harbert, Gill, Goddard, *Shafto, Shaftow, Smijth, Smyth, Snuggs, Townsend.
5. Huntley, *Landon, *O'Flahertie, *O'Flaherty, *O'Flarty, *O'Haharty, *O'Halleran, *Pratt, *Warner.
6. O'Hanlan.
7. Gascoign.
8. *Westcar.
10. Pyke.
11. *Carpenter.
12. Gascoyne.

PLATE 139.—1. Gurney.
2. Buckton, Buketon, Fassett, Garmston, Garnatt, Molton, Moulton, Yeates.
3. Clarke, Gillet (*alias* Chandler).
4. Cron, Crone.
5. *Pike, Pyke.
6. Candler, Garling, Robsert.
7. Franklin, Franklyn.
8. *Tooker, Whalley.
9. Huttoft.
10. Langston.
11. Garrioch, Garrock, Gorges, Hodgson, Hook, Ord, Salmond, Saresbery.
12. Britweesil, Clapp, Corbally, Couper, Crab, Dudman, Gourlay, Hebert, Hoddy, Hody, MacCan, MacKenna, Maclaughlan, M'Lean, Penrose, Redingham, Salmond, Willeigh, Willeley.
13. *Moult.
14. Archard, Busk, Buske, *Fodon, *Gascoigne, Hoby, Merritt.

PLATE 140. — 1. Durham, Fitz-Richard, Kergourdenac, Nanfan, Vickery.
2. Hellen, Vandeput.
3. Bennet, Holebrooke, Upton.
4. Brickdale, *Durham, Geoghegan, Luson, Maxfield, Shilton, Stannard.
5. Arnold, Askeam, Askeham, Bertwhistle, Birtwesill, Brown, Byrtwhysell, *Caesar, Carmenow, Carminow, Carmynow, Cassels, Colston, Coulson, Coulston, Courtenay, Courtney, *Curtis, Delves, Durham, Fawcet, Fawcett, Ffrench, *Field, Freer, French, Godolphin, Grierson, Gwynne, Henraghty, James, Kennedy, *Keydon, Kir[illegible]m, Kingdon, Lawrence,

*Lawrie, Mackmure, Mallam, Metge, Monypenny, *Morin, Nedham, Nutter, Orme, Pugh, Raitt, Reardon, Remnant, Rimmer, Ryton, *Sargant, *Sargeant, Septuans, *Sergeant, *Sergison, Shone, Simmons, Solay, Soley, Symonds, Weyland, Young
6 Anderley, Crafton, Malton, Seagar, Seager, Spear
7 Panting, Panton
8 Frankland, *Franklin, Franklyn, *Smith
9 Blunden, Earl, Holmes, Lewis, Marlay, St Pere, St Pierre, Sent-Pier
10 Bellismo, Horton, Lane
11 Albany, Beresford, Casaer, *Degon, De Rouillon, Dolphin, Durham, Fortun, Gillum, Guillam, Gwillam, Hambley, Hambly, *Herringham, Kennedy, Lyssers, Lyzzers, Roclay, St Andrea, St Andrew, Sherlock, Smith, Smythe, Whitington, Young
12 Francklin, Franklin

PLATE 141—1 Ellis
2 Ballantine-Dykes, Banester, Dikes, Dykes.
3 Lambert, Sea
4 Aunsham, Awnsam, Bullingham, Bustin, Cenino, *Follye, Hede, Lowdham, Pringle
5 Banester, Bridger, Danby, Lowyn, M'Kaile
6 Crowder, Heigham, *Henniker, Mac-Arthur, Macarthur, Main
7 Flndyer, *Lay, *Ley, M'Hattie, Mathews, *Suckling
8 Abbot, Billers, Carpenter, Galay, Gilbertson, Kingsbury
9 Bolger
10 Aldborough, Aldeborough, Audborough, Bottlesham, Delalynd, De lalynde, Garraway, Grieve, Hoke, Hole, Hooke, Hooker, St Owen, Snape, Snepp, Storey
11 Elston, *Folet, Heselrigge, Hogan, *Londham, Mayor, Shipey, Shippey, Tracy
12 Brock, *Brooking, Cabot, Cowan, Frodsham, Grabam, Hadfield, Hassard, Hughan, Judge, Le Febvre, Marten, *O'Fienella, Pilgrim, Pilgrime, Pringle, Spence, Thyly, Winch
13 Burnard
14 Barnaby, Barnard, Bidwill, Bottell, Bower, Brindesley, *Browne, Brownell, Clarke, Cowan, Curtoys, Dishington, *Green, Hazard, King, Kingscote, Luke, Mulholland, Murray, Pardoe, Prior, Pritchard, Pryer, Pryor, Schelley, Shelmerdine, Smith, Solomons

PLATE 142—1 Malton
2 Aighton
3 Martin
4 Cavendish, Fleming, Honnor, Honor, Huxley, Lante, M'Candlish, Mathilez, Melton, Morison, Pringle, Simpson, Southern
5 Van Notten
6 Alexander
7 Bradby, Fleming, Foy, Hewetson, Holcomb, Holcombe, Lees, Le Fleming
8 M'Beth
9 Bamford, Baumford, Horncastle, Knight, Tully, Vivian
10 Arneel, Arneil, Armed, Boors, Delamare, Dunkin, Ellis, Phillips, Shipton
11 Lagenham, Mole
12 Boreham, Borham, *Cavendish, Flay, Granville, Johns, Roffey, Tudor
13 See No 4
14 Hatsell

PLATE 143—1 Brandwood, Durand, Easton, Ellames, Faconbridge, Hensley, M'Millan, Meredyth, Mowbray, Seamark, Sparrow, Stelton
2 Aickman, Aikenhead, Aikman, Anckettill, Forrest, Gordon, Hamilton, O'Keover, Ronald, Wood
3 Hamilton
4 Quain
5 Accorne, Adson, Aikin, Aitken, Aitkenhead, Akenhead, Anderson, Anketell, Asteiby, *Ayliffe, Braidwood, Brantingham, Brentingham, Clerk, Clunie, Cockram, Courtis, Crum, Cunningham, Deinston, De Ponthieu, Dufrene, Elliot, Elliott, Falstoffe, Forrest, Godby, Gordon Grant, Haliburton, Halliday, Hamilton, Hog, Hogg, Hogue, Hurst, Ince, Kesstell, Kinninmond, Latta, Leeks, Leving, Lilley, M'Crae, Macrea, Mayn, Mendorf, Monteith, Morton, Muirside, Nigell, Nigill, Paver, Pix, Ponton, Ramsay, Righton, Roots, Rose, Rowntree, Saurin, Scardlow, Sharp, Smith, Southey, Strange, Taylor, Templeton, Thrale, Threele, Tierney, Titterton, Tree, Warley, Wilding, Wolrich, Wolrige, *Wolryche, Woolrych
6 Riley
7 Hamilton
8 Hamilton
9 Altree, Larra
10 Alison, Anderson, Cooper, Dexter, Garman, Garmon
11 *Hamilton, Monteath
12 Saunders
13 Hamilton, *Taverner, *Thrale, *Threlle, *Woodstock
14 Abercrombie, Abercromby, Ancketill, Anketell, Anlaby, Basnet, Berangner, Berenger, Bosom, Bosome, Bossum, Chambers, Forrest, Fox, France, Garnoch, Hanlaby, Harries, Hewlett, Hog, Hooley, Mowat, Penteney, Thoms, *Town, *Towne, Watson, Wood

PLATE 144—1 Balfour, Blagrove, Dyxton, Fergusson, Fleeming, Fleming, Ganock, Gordon, Hamill, Hammill, Hope, Leighton, Newbigging, Place, Pulley, Sandilands, Sparshott, Stysted
2 France, *Hirst, *Hurst
3 Bellasses, Bellasis, Crouchfield, Crutchfield, *Fenton, Garrow, Somerford, Watson, *Wingate
4 Waller
5 Penfold, *Pinfold
6 May
7 Eimsall
8 Macgregor, M'Gregor, Melles
9 Scrivington
10 Bertie, Jack, Myrton, *Perton, *Purton
11 Asburner, Aserburne, Ashburne, Ashburner, Asherburne, *Ashworth, Corp, Hexman, *Hone
12 Bartolozzi, Bayen, Cockett, Grandson, *Haw, Shackleton, Shakelton
13 Acton, Andson, Ashlin, Bertie, Bradbourne, Bradburne, Broadwood, Christall, Pine-Coffin, Commolin, Hunter, M'Gregor, Noy, *Thrale, Walker, Walsam, Walsham, Wilbington
14 Tankard
15 Cairns

PLATE 145—1 See No 2
2 Air, Aldjo, Aljoy, Auldis, Auldjo, Belches, Biset, Bisset, Bissett, Bough, Crosbey, Crosbie, Cunningham, Cunninghame, Dalgleish, Fownes, Gregory, Hamilton, Lauder, Laurie, Lawder, Lawrie, Limesey, McEwan, Mackenan, Mackeuan, Mackewan, M'Lowe, M'Vicar-Affleck, Nairn, Plaine, Roddam, Scrogie, Smellet, Smollet, Smollett, Stewart, Struth, Tailefer, Trower, Watson, Wellwood
3 Tomlins
4 Hansfell
5 Agnew, D'Urban, Grant, Hadestock, Shadford, Shadforth, Streveling, Traquair, Travers.
6 Conquest, Doyne, *Holme, Kempsey, *Tankarde
7 *Bradley, Huger
8 Bisset, Boughs, Bush, Bushe, Bussche, Falkner, *Hankwood, Holbeach, Twining
9 Ashburnham, Byrom, Owen, Owens, Telfer
10 Christie, Handcock, Hendey, Hendy, Tosh
11 Gainsby, Greenlees, Greenless
12 See Plate 144, Nos 8 and 12
13 Bonham, Boymen, Boynam, Boynan, Copson, Lefever, Lefevre, Pyne, Tait
14 *Brindling

PLATE 146—1 Farwell
2 Canham, Ducie, Duffy, Dunies, Kennet, Kennett, Pedder, Walford, Wallford
3 See No 5
4 Boulby, Bowlby
5 Conroy, Drummond, Fullwood, Gilmour, Kinaird, Kinnaird, Laurie, Lawrence, Lowry, M'Arther, M'Arthur, Manditt, Manduyt, Maudit, Sibbald, Tytler
6 *Bollens, *Boleyn, *Bolleyn, *Bollin, Dunbar, Forbes
7 Alley, Forty, Hawle, Marner, *Stillington
8 Bloye, *Dellatre, Jaffray, Marchall, Richmond, St Leger, Vowell
9 Casey, Hargraves, Heyford, Heyforde, Montgomery, Neale, Neele
10 *Brigham, Broadstone
11 Kinnaird, Ladd, Ladde, Sandilands
12 Aylford, Aylnford, Conran, Gemell, Gemill, Gemmell, Smith
13 Johnston
14 *Blackwood, Parkes, Radford, Turnour.

PLATE 147. — 1. Archbald, Archibald, Crawford, Hastie, Innes, Kennedy, Lithgow, Niven, Paterson, Porterfield, Small, Thompson, Thomson, Tompson, Whithers.
2. Emeric de St. Dalmas.
3. McNevins, Montgomery, *Nevins, Niven.
4. Baines, Bone, Dempster, Gall, Hodkinson, Small.
5. Lingen.
6. Grierson.
7. Bareu, Barew, Grance.
8. Daubeney.
9. Burghersh, Foleborne, *Hoskins, *Lawrence, *Paggin.
10. Aylesbury, *Bracebridge, *Brasbridge, Dymock, Dymok, Dymoke, *Ewers, *Fynney, Goff, Goffe, *Sheen, Varley, Wagstaff, Whithers.
11. *Fancourt, Jebb.
12. Boddy, Body.
13. Coldham-Fussell.
14. Strangman.

PLATE 148. —1. Clepole, Danvers, Fenton, Wardor.
2. Absalem, Absolom, Absolon, Ascum, Barnett, Blizard, Borough, Boutflour, Burgess, Cairnes, Caron, Chastelin, Cheslin, Clarke, *Cleypole, Coape, *Compton, Cope, *Courtauld, Cowie, Dealtry, Deyvil, Docton, Doketon, Dokerton, *Douthwaite, Durant, *Edmond, Ellis, Estote, *Eyringham, *Fantleroy, *Fauntleroy, Fisher, *Fletcher, *Foyler, French, Gay, Goulton, Grant, *Greathead, Greethead, Hamill, Hammil, Hill, Hinson, *Hucks, *Kramer, Leycester, Lyndwood, Macaul, M'Caul, Michelson, Montgomery, Morech, Morris, Mountford, Mountfort, Newdegate, Newdigate, Newport, Oketon, Okton, O'Rearden, O'Riordan, Pancefoot, Pickering, Pottman, Reede, Richards, Rogers, Rolland, Schoffield, Schofield, Sherbrooke, Smith, Sparkes, Taddy, Tod, Townshend, Udney, Unton, Vaughan, Warden, Willcocks.
3. Drewett.
4. Jutting.
5. Mountford.
7. Crompe, Crump, Crumpe, Falch.
8. Birch, Brook, *Buckner, Burgh, *Crooke, Eady, Hartstonge, Hartstronge, Jackson, Newell-Birch, Rowlands.
9. Aphery, Baldrie, Baldry, Balm, Bridgeman, Conyers, Falconer, Fawkenor, Fawkner, *Fitz-William, Harvey, Harvie, Hervey, Lefevre, M'Taggart, Marishall, Marshal, Marshall, *Wanton, Wanton.
10. *Bohun, Caning, Ewes, Manico, De Newbury, Redford, Sealy.
11. Farby, *Fitz-Neel, Severn, Severne.
12. Airey, Andrea, Botiler, Bottiller, Cairnes, Cairns, Caus, *Crawfurd, Curryer, De Mewburgh, De Newburg, *Epitre, Erisey, Fiddes, *Fitton, Golden, Hamilton, Herries, La Barthe, Lampard, Rorie, St. Andrew, *Spranger, Wifield, Winckworth.

PLATE 149. — 1. *Abcot, *Abcott, Anketel.
2. Adderly, Aiton, Aitoune, Aytoun, Bull, Fraser, Gleig, *Hesketh, Marmion, Pether, Shaw, Stowers, Thomson, Timins.
3. Baggs, Lynan, Meschines, Valange, Wallange, Waringe.
4. Currey, Currie, Foxton, Hoole, Rushbrooke, Sparrow.
5. *Ames, Annand, Bogle, Brown, Buchanan, Burkin, Cheisly, Chesly, Chiesly, Clelland, Danbeck, Dorville, Dunbar, Dunlop, Dupre, Gairden, Garden, Googe, Grubbam, Janssen, Learmont, Learmonth, Lehoop, Lethoop, Liddel, *Marsden, Mushet, Pinkerton, Rose, Ross, Vanbeck, Whitham, Vorstone.
6. Dorville, *Dupre.
7. *Aslin, *Aslyn, *Asslan, Currey.
8. Angeville, Angevine, Angevyne, Anvers, Baker, Cashen, Chambre, Clason, Classon, English, Hailstones, Kingsford, Limesie, Meignell, Rochfort, Rodatz, Rome, Ross, *Sennicots, Stevenson, Tilly, Wheeler, Wiley.
9. *Atwater, Ellsworth, Lillie, Wadham.
10. Thorndike.
11. Caltoft, Collinson, Vigne.
12. Bassinges, Hill, Roos, Ross, Zachert, Zachet.
13. Brodribb.
14. Aiton, Aytoun, Baker, Delap, Inverarity, Mayhew.

PLATE 150.—1. *Brabant, Gaynsford, Gaynsforth, Hearne, Ross, Spear.
2. *Arden, *Blaydes, *Dankeck, *Halgoet, Innes, MacAlpine, *M'Chlery, *Perceval, *Percival, *Thomson, *Tose, *Tosh, York.
3. Denham, Foss, Hepburn, Merrey, Southam, Steuart, Stewart.
4. Cervington, *Langthorne.
5. Alles, Allez, *Dobree, *Emslie, *Emsly, M'Gouan, M'Gowan, Perceval, Sitsill, Walkfare.
6. Heathcoat.
7. Burdett, *Elmslie.
8. Cardiff, Carstairs, *Devere.
9. Cossar, Cosser, Ferguson, Fergusson, Gardner, Innes, M'Innes.
10. Barnet, Bland, Burnet, Christie, Hutchins, Irvine, Niven, Wakinshaw, Wilkes.
11. *Henbury, Innes, *Wilkie.
12. Dunn, Dunne, Foleborne, Irvine, Smythe.

PLATE 151.—1. Bie, Bosworth, By, Bye, Hamilton, Mackie.
2. Chadwick, Coane, *Fitton, Gray, Rait, Torre, Watson.
3. *Amidas, Burnside, Coyney, Coyny, Drywood, Jewel, Lindsay, Morrison, St. Maure, Seymour, Sharp, Tibbs, Watson, Wood.
4. Symonds.
5. Neave, Neve, Le Neve.
6. See No. 12.
7. Chadwick.
8. Bourdon, Burdon, Jermain, Jermayne, Livingston, Livingstone, Moncrief, Perkins, Reding, Stewart.
9. Forrester.
10. Bucket, Field, Irvine, Jefferyes, Jeffries.
11. Barr, Bettescombe, Burge, Finlay, Hagell, Murray, Plank, Planke, Rusted, Somery, Tothill.
12. Borgoine, Botell, Bothell, Coryton, Kay, Lisle, Randes, Rands.
13. Colquhon, Colquhoun, Duer, Massingbird, Mathison, Murray, Ross, Sprigg, Weller.
14. *Ardern, *Maydwell, Rous, Russell.
15. Abenhall, Ableshall.

PLATE 152. — 1. *Andrews, Bagshole, Bagshote, Barton, Blackshame, Dupa, Duppa, Graham, Gruben, Lawrence, O'Reilly, Querleton, Querlton, Tolley, Trelawney, Wight.
2. Huth, Lang.
3. Dabbins, *Dobbin.
4. Amand, Amane, Amarme, Don, Granado, Hedges, Poynings, Virtue, Wauchope.
5. Rhan, Wrench.
6. *Perins, *Perring, Pomeroy.
7. Bourden, Champagne, Old, Strang, Strong.
8. Apperley, *Barfoot, *Kidd, Parkins, *Parkyns, Perryn, Willaume.
9. Ahern, Broun, Brown, Burnet, Finucane, Garginton, Garwinton, Grumley, Symonds.
10. Milnes.
11. Parsons.
12. Hales.
13. Craigg, Craigie, Fall, Lely, Mewbery, Orr, Parkhill, Sideserf, Sidserf, Spedding, Sydserfe, Walker.
14. Milnes.

PLATE 153. — 1. *Benwell, *Dod, Dodd, Lewthwaite.
2. Alvas, Alves, Alvis, Alyis, Aust, Auste, Barney, Barns, Baron, Barron, Bell, Berney, Blair, Bliss, Bouling, Brett, *Bunten, *Bunting, Burket, Burkett, Burleton, Burlton, Catcher, Cheap, Cheape, Chelsum, Close, Compson, Comyn, Crawford, Crawfurd, Crump, Cumine, Cuming, Cummin, Dale, Denson, Darby, De Blaquiere, Dodds, *Doe, Dolman, Donald, Donaldson, *Ducket, *Duckett, Ellis, Este, Falconer, Falknor, Fawlconer, Ferrier, *Fetherstonhaugh, Field, Fitton, Foller, Folvill, *Frevile, *Garbridge, Gilliot, Gillot, Girle, Glastonbury, Goldie, Golding, Goudie, Gouldie, Gregor, Gregorie, Grenville, Gwatkin, Harrower, Heathfield, Hesketh, Heskett, Hiders, *Higgins, James, Jones, Kelso, Keltie, Kelty, *Kempton, Lawson, Lovell, M'Laws, Maltby, Masterson, Merefield, Michael, Miln, Milnes, Mitchell, Modyford, Oatly, O'Flaherty, Paul, Paxton, Peterborough, Phillips, Platt, Price, Randoll, Reath, Rede, Reed, *Reid, Roby, Routledge, Rowan, Rowand, Sandbach, Scambler, *Shikleworth, Sicklemore, Skeen, Skene, Spilsbury, Spurwaye, Spyer, Spyre, Stephenson, Stevens, Stevenson, Stevynson, Tippet, Vallance, Vanderplank, Walter, Warneford, Watur, Wauchop, Wauchope, Waugh, *Whetcroft, White, Whitefoord, Widdrington, Winton, *Wright, Youl, *Zachary.
3. Bracey, Bracy, Fair, Hodge, Jelley, Jelly, Wicksted, Wicksteed.

4 Darby
5 Dade, Veale, Veel, Wright
6 Barsham, Denny, Hagar, Hamley, Lambard, Lambarde, Pawle, Prelate, Toulmin, Wever, Williams
7 Couston, Drummond, Leving, Levinge, Lord, Tatton
8 Close
9 Cash, Gaibe, Groombridge, Hitchens, Hitchins, Hyland, Jennings, Questeed
10 Ashwell, Ashworth, Aswell, Birkby, Broadhead, Buckby, Fitton, Hake wood, Lichfield, Manson, Muston, Pilland, Wicks
11 Otley
12 Ferne, Newce, Newse, Peverell.
13 Gregory, Longland, Whiteley
14 Bancroft, Ferne, Hodgkinson, Middleton

PLATE 154.—1 Affleck, Auchinleck, *Horsman, Johnson
2 Le Feuvre, Mitchell
3 Auchinleck, Crofton, Dunford, Mitchael, Mitchell, Scot, Swinton, Youille, Yule
4 Berwick, Cundall, Cundell, Cundill, Cundy, Handford, Lindsay, Lynch, Sedgewick, Sedgewicke
5 Mitchell
6.*Coultman, *Crakenthorp, *Drinkwater, Ducket, Sheffield.
7 *Crofton, Easum, Eston, *Scott-Moncrieff
8 Bradbury
9 Feldingham, Fillingham, Inglish
10 Allardice, Aubemarle, Birkes, Britten, Goslett, Tinling, Widdevil, Wood ville
11 Baskenford, Baskin, Glendenning, Kynvett, Somery
12 Isaac
13 Cherley
14 Crog, Crogg, Ede, Marnham, *Milne, Varlo

PLATE 155.—1 Bedewell, Bedwell, *Hopkins, Lelon, Lellow, Lelou, Lelow, Matson, Osbourne, Stackpoole, Wylie
2 *Anger, *Angier, *Colliray
3 *Bishton, *Kincaid, *Macdonald
4 Angus, Codd, Codde, Danes, Daneys, Domere, Dormere, Hetherington, Maclachlan, *Rawson
5 Jones
6 Alberough, Albrough, *Batley, *Bataley, *Batteley, *Battley, *Dennis, Nisbet
7 Balfour
8 Allingbridge, *Barttelot, *Beatie, *Beatty, *Bence, *Beseley, *Cassels, Challen, Copeland, Copland, Cowp land, *Courtois, *Courtoys, *Craw ford, *Crawfurd, Elkins, *Endas, *Eneas, Freby, Hardcastle, Higgins, Hill, Howden, Johnson, Lilborne, Lilburne, Lindsay, Loughnan, M'Callum, M'Clauchlan, M'Claugh lan, M Clen, M'Donald, Maclachlan, M'Lauchlan, M'Leod, Malcom, Marris, Laing-Meason, Mutter, Perry, Pollock, Portal, Pound, Rawson, Scherlis, Schroder, Stable, Staines, Strange, Trevet, Trevett, Turberville
9 *Bennett, Heath, Hopkins, Johnson, Morris, Paddon, Patten.
10 Anstavill, Capling, *Casstle, *Castlehow, Cheverton, Cosars, Harley, Lepton, Lexton, M'Kellar, Oxford, Parscoe, *Rickards
11 Tregoning
12 Lamson

PLATE 156—1 Higginson
2 Adderbury, Addison, Allmack, Almanerlaval, *Angel, *Angle, *Anegal, Anegall, Awmack, *Bence, Bogle, Caddel Cantrell, Cantrill, Carfrae, *Castelyon, Cheslin, Clemsby, Crammond, Devereux, Fauze, Fawconer, Fawkoner, Gibant, *Hetherington, Hoblyn, Kestell, Lang, Leveale, Levealis, Levelis, *Lomond, M'Allum, Kellie M'Callum, M'Clean, M'Knight, Macknight, M'Lean, Mal colm, Maples, Mason, Meyrick, Orr, Orton, Pardoe, Parsons, Pearson, Poor, Reed, Schapmar, Stables, Stewart, Thorlby, Thorley, Tournay, Towers, Turney, Wintersells, Yorstoun
3 Fort, Forte, MacDonald, *Thornholme, Torr, Vale
4 Deton, Harlewen, Jonas, Lindsay, Pontifex, Pott, Prother,
5 McLannachan, Macnaghten, Macnaghton, M'Naughtan, MacNaughten, M'Naughton, Reid
6 Foulks.
7 Aslakby, Aslakeby, Darby
8 Blundell, *Bridges, Burton, Casson, Dove, Felbridge, Paxton, *Preston, Rawson
9 *Archdeacon, Burdett, Cairnes, Hitchens, *Hodington, Lorand, Warde, Wickham
10 Nicholls
11 Bridges, Dawson, Dove, Nicholl, Phillimore, Whitelock
12 Johnson
13 Levall, Nicholas, Nicholl, Sherfield
14. Fryer

PLATE 157—1 Fermour, Geffreys, Jefferyes, Lingham, Stewart
2 Reid
4 Gard
5.*Bowyer, *Boyare, Bylney, Connell, Halpin, Higginson, Kerdiston, Lauder, Law, Lawder, Laxton, *O'Higgins, Tassie, Whorwood,
6 Ashborne, Ashburne, Burton, Cartell, Castell, Coore, *De Havilland, Fytche, Gunston, Hopper, Jeffries, Lavelis, Longchamp, Longchampe, Martin, *Mason, Newmarche, Vosper
7 Delaland, Deland, *Dickson, *Hichcoke, *Higgins
8 *Boradaile, *Borradaile, *Borrodaile, Colfox, Eaglesfield, Eglesfield, *M'Intire
9 Dekener, Dekewer, Hagne, *Lamborne, Viel, Vieler
10.*Grayson, Kyrby, Kyrkby, Luckin, Martham, *Segar, Stanhope
11 Addis, Ades, Adis, *Betsworth, *Bettesworth, *Bettsworth, Bevers ham, Bottomley, Boyce, Boyse, *Burrish, Ciderowe, Clederow, Clitherow, *Downs, *Hext, Higgans, Higgens, Hyatt, M'Namard, *Middleton, Rickards, Treacy, Verdon, Whiteway
12 Andros, Beyard, *Blithe, Bound, Buchan, Coles, Dore, Kerdiffe, Marleton, Middleton, Skearne, Skeene, Skyrne
13 Almack, Arnett, Arnot, Arnott, Both, Bothe, Castlyn, Dellaber, Duckensfield, Herbright, Hoxton.
14 Hale
15 Cardwell, Dengayne, Engaine M'Callum, M'Clure, *Marling *Marlyn, *Nielson, Orton, Ortun, *Shyer, *Spicer, *Spycer, Stock, Winziet

PLATE 158—1 Fairn, Foston
2 Fulwar
3 Dalgleish, Dunbar, Forbes, Gardenr Grant, Hamilton, Harmer, Macdonald Bowie, Menzies, Pollock, Rouett, Umphray, Warner, Wheldale, Wom phrey
4 Beatson, Betson, Docker, Fenis, Kent, Slack, Troubridge, Tutin, Vampage
5 Mills, Whiteman
6 Beckwell, Bekewell, Ferrier, Fuller, Gawaine, Gawayne, Leaky, Wallace
7 Bartain, Bartan, Bartane, Bouwen, Carrol, Carroll, Dukes, *Empson, Hartford, Marmyon, Quicke, Shed, Westlemore, Whitaker
8 Hendrie, Hendry
9 Babbwell, Babwell, Brew, Harold, Harrold, Onmany, Turvile, Wills, Wingate, Yates.
10 Donelly, Donnelly, Kirk, Lerner, Monkhouse, Wandesford
11 Allingham, Kirkaton, Kirkeley, Kirkland, Kirklay, Kirklayne, Kirkley, Land, Plesseis.
12 Bennet, Grey
13 Balcarres, Lindsay
14 Arfece, Arfois, Arforce, Fellowes, Fellows, *Fletcher, Grey, Strover, Trowtback, Williams

PLATE 159—1 Brutton, Collings, Davall, Davell, Freer, Gregory, Haldane, Hamilton, M'Gell, Oakley, Playfair
2 *Aimgevyne, Hope, *Mundell
3 Croke, Crook, Ormsby, Spottiswood.
4 Carpenter, Goodlad, Nairn, Nairne, Keynolds, Staley, Stayley, Tyrconel
5 Butterworth, *Croad, *Croade, Fernandez, Hengham, Knolles
6 *Amitesly, *Anelshey, *Anmetesley, *Annelshie, *Anteshey, *Antesley, Basceilly, Dixon, Kane, Nind
7 *Abelyn, *Abelyne, Barrett, *Chinnery, Drummond, *Herschel, Martin, *Martyn, Pawlett
8 Maltravers, Russell
9 Case, Casse, Cowen, Crobber, *Denouac, *Eldres, Fraser, Longspee, M'Farquhar, Moile, Moill, *Okebourn, Schomberg, Summers, Wadsworth
10 Bontein, Bonteine, Bunting
11 Bengham, Benham, Bruckshaw, Bruckshow, Cook, Holton
12 Almond, Archer, Athelstane, Keux, Lovise, Neal, Neele
13 Aicken, Aiken, Aikin, Caldwell, Deighton, Dighton, Houndegart, *Leg, Thornton, Whittlebury
14 *Agrevell, Agworth, Alde, Aldworth *Anna, Banister, Barns, *Beechey, *Beechy, *Boldero, *Bolderowe, *Burn, *Burne, *De Anna, Engolisme *Rowdon, Spelman, Spylman, Udward
15 Coucher, Cowcher, Hodiswell, Hodsall Welles, Wells

PLATE 160.—1. Chambley, Chambly, Layland, Spearing, Vanort.
2. Conder, Foxwell.
3. Drake.
4. Campbell, *Constable.
5. Bagnel, Bagnell, Bagnill, Bagnoll, Esclabor, Gospatrick, Hailly, Holder, M'Gowran, Murray, Ogilvie, Robertson.
6. Petit.
7. Bagnell, Campbell, Draper, Gowan, MacLaurin, Macrorie, Milne, Reece, Rolland, Rorie, Ross, Roy, Stuart.
8. Trotter.
9. Angolesme, Boggis, Boggs, De Angolesme, Exton, Marston, Maston, Tennant.
10. Barrat, Barratt, Crichton, Daniel, M'Andrew, Mill, Milne, *Monteith, Tighe.
11. Jockel, Tennant.
12. Pellew.
13. Aberneathy, Abernethy, Anderson, Arbuthnot, Asche, Aschey, Ascher, Asher, Bailhache, Baird, Bennet, Bentick, Bogle, Brown, Bryson, Cairnie, Constable, Delamare, Duncan, Edmonds, French, Gall, Gavin, Gordon, Hyghlord, Jameson, Jamieson, Knevet, Knight, Leyham, Maly, Montchency, Moreland, Mudie, Murray, O'Malley, Oswald, Poulter, Quatherine, Rankin, Rowand, Schardelow, Scot, Scott, Stackhouse, Stephen, Stephenson, Stirling, Strachan, Suttie, Grant-Suttie, Tendering, Tompkins, Vassall, Watson, Whitton, Williamson, Wood.
14. Abernethy, Dick, Dick-Cunyngham, Donkin, Drummond, Duncan, Hamilton, Harkness, Leckie, Pellew, Williamson.

PLATE 161—1. Allaway, Alloway, Ancram, *Brages, Bridges, *Bruges, Brunton, *Campbell, Catesnelboge, Coats, Cotes, Craick, De la Cherois, Dunsmure, Fairgray, Gray, Grieve, Henderson, Hiching, Hunter, Longland, Longlands, Ormistone, Petrie, Pitcairn, Rait, Roberton, Smith, Spence, Stedman, Steedman, Voe, Young.
2. *Cahill, Capell, Clark, Coats, Craik, Dewers, Drakenford, Drysdale, Elliot, Elliott, Ferrie, Fillent, Fisher, Gillespie, Gray, Grey, Groat, Hepburn, Hunter, Kinnear, Kyle, Leckie, Litster, Loghlin, O'Cahill, O'Loghlin, Poulton, Roberton, Schindler, Scott, Somerville, Stainforth, Stedman, Tayler, Thurlow, Wickliffe.
3. Brisban, Brisbane, Cosyn, Duck, Elley, Kirby, Kirkby, Lydown, Nevell, Snellgrove, Whitfield.
4. Harrison.
5. Cartier.
6. Aiskell, Aiskill, Askill, Bledlow, Delalynd, Homan, Kennedy, Langlands, Massingham, Ufford.
7. Betagh, Boxhall, Boxhull, Boxmell, Chalbots, Figes, Jourdan, Kadrad, Kinnear, M'Gowan, Neefield, Nerfield, Westerdale, Westerton, Whaley.
8. Gray, Longland.
9. Braddyll, Cushney, Depden, Deptun, Ennis.
10. Pringle.
11. Balfour-Kinnear, Inglis, *O'Loghlen, O'Loughlin.
12. Camper, Higgat, Lysers.

PLATE 162.—
2. Abbs, Abraham, *Ashwood, Baillie, *Billington, Blunt, Coke, Cooke, Drayton, Fairbairn, Fairweather, Farquharson, Florio, Fonnerean, Forbes, *Forbisher, Freebairn, *Geynton, *Geyton, Grevis, Hay, Hewson, *Hiccocks, Jack, Janssen, Joanes, Jones, Ker, Kerr, M'Cleod, M'Hardie, Mackenzie, M'Kenzie, Macleod, M'Leod, Mason, Masson, Manghan, Mellis, *Mills, Moffat, Nairne, Oliphant, Pass, Pearson, Pitcairn, Reilly, Richmond, Rodwell, Routh, Rutt, Sligo, Sotheby, Stewart, Sydserf, Tyrwhitt, Walker.
3. Blunt, *Crowley, Firbank, Pawson.
4. *Calston, Ewing.
5. Abrahams, Abram, Auld, Barclay, Bright, Bruce, Dallyson, Eastchurch, Eiston, Farquharson, Gilchrist, Hewat, Hewatt, Howat, Jeffrey, Ker, Leson, Lesone, Lysons, Pearson, Pinckeney, Purves, Purvis, Ranken, Saville, Walker.
6. Jackson.
7. Brayne, *Brownhill, Holbeck, Holbecke, Ryan.
8. Wickes.
9. Deveral, Deverel, Emerson, Tytler.
10. Arabin, Firman.
11. Rennie.
12. Blount.
13. Anderson, Church, De Bouche, Kempton.
14. Blount.

PLATE 163. — 1. Archbald, Archibald, Crawford, Dolan, Grendon, Haxton, Jeanes, Jeans, *Louis, Mikieson.
2. Achym, Adam, Alderton, Anderson, Arnet, Arnot, Baillie, Balfour, Batt, Bestow, Blair, Boudier, Burnside, Crawford, *Crawfurd, Crawfurd-Stirling, *Crog, *Crogge, Dalhurst, Dallas, Dobbie, *Etheridge, Ferney, Gilchrist, Gordon, Hamel, Hamell, Hamilton, *Hayley, Hollingsworth, Holyoke, Kidd, Kilgour, Killgour, Kinnear, Kydd, Leash, Leslie, Lucie, Mackenzie, MacNicol, Melvile, Melvill, Melville, Whyte-Melville, Menzies, Mikieson, Motherwell, Myrtoun, Oliphant, Otter, Papillion, Perwiche, Powe, Preston, Rider, Romerley, Romilly, Scott, Scougal, Seaton, Seton, Simpson, Smith, Sommerville, Souter, Stevenson, Stiven, Tottenham, Trent, Tripling, Watt.
3. Crawford, Dallas, Durham, Fergusson, Hay, Innes, Kyd, Mitchelson, Monins, Monyns, Nansolyn, Pettegrew, Ramage.
4. Alston, Alstone, Bateman, Beatie, Beattie, Boyce, Boyse, Cooker, Cooper, Crawford, M'Coll, Ramsay, Reynolds, Sandeland, Sandilands.
5. Kimpton.
6. Ayleward, Aylward, Aylwarde, Berry, Brien, *Cheek, Dax, Dore, Foulis, Hewet, Holderness, Methen, Methven.
7. Baliol, Baylol, Cor, *Meik.
8. Otter.
9. Ferguson, *Fox.
10. *Barnham, Kington.
11. Yellowly.
12. Achard, Cracklow, Gates, Seaton, Seton, Willison, Wilson.
13. Broheir, Brohier, Carter, *Fitz-Ellis, Haines, Hutton, Kidd, Warden.
14. Gilchrist.
15. Aberkirdor, Cannon, Goold, Gould, Jewers, Leslie, Tregos.

PLATE 164.—1. Aston, Atkins, Baillie, Bayne, Berrington, Cousmaker, Coussmaker, Flint, Innes, Jardine, Julius, Langdale, *Latouche, *Loveley, Martaine, Martin, Martyn, Prior, O'Haly, O'Quigley, Oswald, Partridge, Powell, *Rasper, Rose, Salmon, *Sanderson, Scott, Sinclair, *Stodart, Vandergucht, Vivian, Wardlaw.
2. Anderson, Auforus, Beeby, Boyd, Doughty, Dune, Fenkell, Garrick, Graveley, Groze, Innes, Kerr, Langdell, Le Barue, M'Millan, Mello, Murray, Ragg, Ragge, *St. Leger, Scott, *Toller, Trubshaw, Vigurs, Watson, Wegg, Wragg.
3. Alston, Andrew, Arther, Arthur, Bourchier, Bruce, Carnegie, Clark, Dawson, Dayrolles, Dorrely, Gourlay, Gourley, Graham, Haggard, Jeffrey, Layer, Pinck, Pink, Scot, Seton, Walkington.
4. *Boodam, Burard, *Chaffin, *Despard, *Eyston, *Gentle, *Hawley, *Hinckley, Martin, *Mott, *Nants, *Pollock, *Prior, *Sackville, *Sackville-Germain, Trewman.
5. Barnes, Gib, Harries, Latouche, *Samborne, *Wenard, *Wendesley.
6. Rooper, Roper.
7. Drummond, Du Coin, Elliston, Marmaduke, Tuchfield.
8. Bellere, Bryson, Brysoun, Bryssan, Bryssone, *Fecher, Finlayson, Hardie, Jardin, Jardine, Saunders, Sym, Tooker, Vivian.
9. Baylie, *Burmenster, Sinclair, Teulon.
10. Allan, Burcetre, Chivers, *Cotgrave, *Cotgreve, Cotgrieve, Maundefield, Oswald.
11. Baillie, Black, *Bracester, Brigid, *Crioll, Dawson, Farquhar, Ferquhar, Flint, Innes, Johnston, *Keriell, Lightbody, Southcote, Stoddart, *Stothert, Taddy.
12. Andegarvia, Anger, Aunger, Barwicke, Baxter, Breach, De Fortibus, Hellord, Highlord, Ledger.
13. Sweet, Swete.
14. Gibbon.

PLATE 165. — 1. De Bellomont, Faulkner, Irons, Lunden, Lundin, Marley, Marlow, Molineaux, Pugh, Ruding, Sagrenor, Stewins, Symington, Weldon.
2. Abby, Adamson, Atcliff, Atcliffe, Atclyff, Atclyffe, Corbreake, Crosse, Featherston, Featherstone, Fergant, Scholes, Squarey, Tinker, Whitehead, Woodhouse.
3. Clement, Clements, Cranford, Delaplannch, Devonshire, Miller, Roddam, Rosselyne, Sibbald, Tinkler,
4. *Adam, Carry, Coffin, Devendale, Donaldson, Egan, Fokeram, Lapsley, Lapslie, Seagrim.
5. Pedyward,

6 Astell
7 *Acbiche, *Aceck, *Anstead, *Ansted, *Antished, *Anstell, Arbuthnot, *Archdall, *Astrye, *Aswell, *Barclay, Bate, Caesar, Cruso, *Feron, *Forbes, *Fouk, Hackbeck, *Manley, *Manly, Mersar, *Rossie, *Tritton, Wiltshire
8 Parish
9 Fountbery, Meddowes, Meddus
10 Brockholes, Coghlan, Coghlen, Cowan, De Harcla, Harcle, Neale, Nele, Vaire
11 Alverd, Alured, Andre, Andree, *Begbie, *Bellomont, Berringham, Berringham, Boyd, *Carleon, Dilkes, Gair, Gant,
12 Gurney
13 Clegg, Millman
14 Bowker

PLATE 166 — 1 Abercrombie, Abercromby, Ardem, Ardyn, Barbour, Bogley, Christie, Christison, De Bruges, *Garfield, Gordon, *Holyland, Mackeill, St John, Spurrier, Welch, Whitford
2 Abercrombie, Abernethy, Adamson, Aiken, Aiscough, Aitken, Aitkine, Allan, Caddy, Corse, Crosse, Crossing, Dobbie, Dobie, Ellison, Feyrey, Feytrey, Fogo, Garen, Gordon, Guthrie, Guthry, Ironside, Leith, Loveyne, M'Cleish, Marr, Maxton, Moffat, Moffatt, Newall, Peirse, Petrie, Radnor, Redham, Robe, Spalding, Thomson, Thrale
3 *Belt, Chein, Cheine, Cheyne, De Gaunt, Dorward, Durnard, Earnshaw, Mansfield, Matchet, Matcheton, Mercer, Nottage, Tod-Mercer, Turney
4 M'Carlie, *M'Kerlie
5 *Beg, *Begg, *Bifield, *Byfeld, *Byfield, Filfed, *Keignes, *Keynes
6 *Adams, Almears, Almeers, Ameers, Damory, M'Glashan
7 Capes, Castell, De Mardeston, Dereston, Deveston, Donovan, Newbald, Newbold, Warr
8 *Coffield, *Farmer
9 Achany, Ahanny, Ahany, Carse, Carss, Crass, Crasse, Delaleigh, Delegh, Hannay, Kennan, Sermon, Watson
10 Broon, Dudgeon, Irvine
11 *Game, Greenfield, Staveley
12 Adam, Adie, Addie, Aedie, Andesley, Backie, *Chaworth, Constantyne, Dernford, Downie, Edie, Fage, Fetherston, Fetherstone, Finnis, Kingley, Macadam, Nadler, *Wondesford, *Zymon
13 McKerrow
14 Adam, Ambridge, Brine, Coe, Jugler, *Paul, Whitelocke, Whitley, Whitlie

PLATE 167 — 1 Brenan, Brennan, Crane, Du Boys, Forners, Forneys, Hailes, Hasted
2 Bracken, Byres, Cauty, Deards, *Delavere, Dowding, Fitz-Marmaduke, *Lax, Mawgyron, Montgomery, Pitman, Rushbrook
3 Fell.
4 Hillas
5 Howard
6 Brenchesley, Brenchley, *Fearon, *Plomer, *Tooley, *Towley
7 Achieson, Aitchison, Anwell, Anwyl, Atcheson, Lancelot, Lockyer, Peche, Pechey
8 Fiske, Fyshe
9 Ambler, Amerance, Annes, Anness, Annis, Ascon, Askwith, Cayley, Cayly, Hamilton, Lorimer, Neale
10 Gabriel
11 Everard, Manford, Sutton
12 *Clark, *Clarke
13 Camden
14 Acle, Anhelet, Blackhall, Felfair, Frescheville, Gorges, Gorgis, De Monthermer, Rivel, Searles

PLATE 168 — 1 Ashman, Balfour, Beifore, Belfour, Belfoure
2 Abbeford, Hewis, Leith-Ross
3 Abarle, De la Rever, Delariver, Menles
4 Crean, De Burgh, Dixon, Fayt, Gurheres, Hardgrave, Hardgrove, Harman, Mack, Nettlefold, Plummer, Ross, St Low, Sproul, Whitbread, Wilson
5 Hornby
6 Budgett
7 Bell, Boon, Boone, Cairns, Desbrisay, Dynham, Echingham, Fitzpiers, Leving, Starr, Stasam
8 Gallini, *Hindle
9 Byngley, Bynley, Cope, *Crigan, Critchley, Critchlow, Derwell, Flanders, Hilliar, Huson, Lakenlyche, Lakinleech, Lakinlich, Letch, Manston, Rose, Ross, Rosse, Whistler
10 *Brookes, *Brooks, Delapipe
11 *Beaty, Flavel
12 Biest, Brampston, Crucks, Greer, Greir, Grier, Gresoun, Grierson, Ingles, Lockhart, Oyry, Swain, Swaine
13 Bonney, Fakenham, Feckenham, Fitz Ralph, Grierson
14 Greer

PLATE 169 — 1 Yaldwyn
2 Buchanan, Cairncross, Carnwath, Coytmore, Dalzell, Durnford, Macquire, M'Quire, Pring, Thetford, Wimbolt
3 Blanchard, Everest, Govan, Kavanagh, Taap, Tapp
4 Carnac, *O Mullan
5 Cheeke, Claus, Deans, Haselerton, Hone, Nixon, Oxborough, Oxburgh, Reddingfield
6 Pittillo
7 Timbrell
8 Abercorne, Burn, Garside, Gartside, Hair, Littell, Noy, Thirlwall, Topham, Wakerley
9 Aberdour, Ariel, Ariell, Coningham, Fitz-Ourse, Furnival, *Furnivall, Paveley, Rose
10 Binns, *Fleming, Hesketh, Macklellan, M'Lagan, M'Laren, M'Lellan, Plompton, Price, Sublet
11 Chastelon, Farr, Favell, Glendenning, Glendonwyn, Glendowing, Sterling, Tate
12 Busterd, Cannon, Davy, Durham, Gwyn, Harliston, Harlston, Lake, Maclaren, Munton, Todman, Willson

PLATE 170 — 1 Aberkirdor, Aberkirdour, Bagge, Baillie, Dunn, Fowlis, Gibb, Gorham, Jarred, Jarrett, Kier, Lyster, Spragg, Stanley, Tay, Todrig, Wilby
2 Aberherdour, Aberkerdour, Aberkirdor, Allin, Barclay, Blaine, Blane, *Blissett, Bonar, Boyes, *Browne, Cazenove, Cornack, Dalziel, Deans, Dymoke, Gowan, Hamilton, Justice, *O'Halloran, Osborn, Osbourne, Poyntz, Roundell, Rundle, Scobie, Spalding, Sword, *Tatnall, *Tattall, Vintris, Wemyss
3 Anderson, Bowley, Carncross, *Chester, *Crouch, *Crowch, Fitz-Allen, Gosse, Judge, Pickering, Wordie
4 Crosbie, Crosbey, Dall, *Eastoft, *Edgar, Habgood, Leir, Smith, Smythe, Young
5 Aneys, Carbonel, Carbonell, Forbes, Ogilvie, Ogilvy, Sterry, Whitgreave
6 Arnold, Wingham
7 Carles, Carlos, Kirk
8 Smith
9 Mallow
10 Aundeligh, Bawdewyn, Bawdwen, Drought, Hanley, Lumb
11 Hender, Ockleshaw
12 Halford
13 Bownas, Caldwell, *Conwell, *Fitz-Thomas, *Leale, *Leall, *Lealle, Segar, Segar Parry
14 Arnaway, Arneway, Arnold, Arnway, Delapool, Delapoole, De la Poole, Edwards, Huntingdon, Huntington, Sherley, Shirley, Sumner
15 Whitgreave

PLATE 171 — 1 *Allden, *Alldin, *Alldon, *Hayman, *Preadeaux
2 Belsted, Belstede, Belstide, Beltead, Dalton, Nottage, Pearse, Rewtoure, Thatcher
3 Grantham
4 Booth, Brounker, Cockerell, Crampton, Grant, Gryme, Kibble, Verdelin
5 Pearson
6 Moon
7 De Gray, Hobbs, Lawford, Sinclair, Thorp, Truscoat, Truscott
8 Cafe
9 *M'Anaspog, Truscott
10 Bone, Boun, Bounn, Burgin, Duffus, Dunbar, Elrington, Heald, Johnson, Terell
11 Faithfull
12 *Beaghan, *Brerwood, *Brierwood, Cumming, Cummyng, *Dick, *Ferrall, *Finchingfield, Gatonby, Gun, *Huntingfield, *Johnson, *Johnston, *MacQuay, *McQuay, *Maquay, *Querouaille, *Smith, *Smyth
13 Jenner, *Jennerson
14 Dunn, Dunne

PLATE 172 — 1 Akelits, Akelitz, Elmore, Fantleroy, Fauntleroy, Hakelut, Hatchet, Hemstead, Hemsted, Tilley, Tunnadine
2 Strother, Tylden
3 Clark, Drury, Foliot, Foliott, Harwine, Jenkins, Luxmore, Misserinen, Missirinen, Morse, Norton, Oldmixon, Parsons, Radcliffe, Shinglehurst, *Veale, Waddel
4 Aynesworth, Aynworth, Dornford, Fitz-Vrian, *Inge, Irball, Johnes, Johns, Joynour, *Juge, Le Scot,

Morse, Shepard, Sheperd, Sheppard, Smith, Spittal, Spratt, Waddell.
5. Hodder.
6. Dorn, Gardiner, Tackle, Tobin, *Tomkins.
7. Eccles, Ecles, Ekles, Erisby, *Firth, *Semple.
8. Parry.
9. Bigg, Dempsey, Pasmore, *Tomlins.
10. Dale.
11. Parry.
12. Brattle, *Brudenal, *Brudenell, *Maclean, *Macleans, *Macmichael.
13. Bullock, Sybells, Weddel, Weddell.
14. Maclaine.

PLATE 173. — 1. *Bingley, *Davis, Egerton, *Faldo, Hanly, Irving, *Symons, Thomas, Wilton, Worsycke.
2. Dineley, Leeson, Myers, *Oldershaw, Ponsonby, Romaine, Windus.
3. Ap-Enyions, Bowes, Braksdall, Breche, Cameron, Cawdor, Cole, Crow, De Eureux, D'Eureux, Doane, Done, Donne, *Edmeades, Egerton, *Ellaway, Eureux, Forbes, Fourbins, Hardel, Hardell, Irvine, Keen, Kettle, Lyndon, Ould, *Parker, Segrave, Shawe, Spiers, Wiles.
4. Brownsmith.
5. Akenside, Amerle, Aumarle, Aumerle, Colshull, Ealand, Elwell, Hancock, Hancox, Honnyman, Honyman, *Hutcheson, *O'Lonargan, Srabonne.
6. Juxon, Sterndale.
7. Bowditch, *Bullock, Bygot, Cron, Crone, Finney, *Herbert, *Hyde, *Jenkins, Thursby.
8. Ewar.
9.*Arrowsmyth, Boatfield, *Windsor.
10. Cecil, Gascoyne-Cecil, *Hamilton, Tillet.
11. Callore, *Combrey.
12. Bower, Falcon, Fawcon, Grosset, Grossett, *Loth, *Lothe.
13. Bavent, Bowes, Done, Keyne, Segrave.
14.*Irving.

PLATE 174. — 1. Atkinson, Utber, Utker.
2.*Rawdon, Stubbs, Veevers.
3. Anleby, Anselbie, Anselby, Charlewood, Gilder, Marshall.
4. Archer, *Bowman, *Douglas.
5. Taylor-Whitehead.
6. Symcoats.
7. Davis.
8. Oldershaw.
9. Ely, Feast, Fletcher, Quin, Savage, Stock.
10. Allaunson, Alyson, Boneham, Bonham, Broadbent, Brodbent, Chamberlain, Chamberlan, Dancer, Leger.
11. Atkinson, Beavis, Belward, Bevis, Bickenor, Bicknor, Brumfield, Bykenor, Bykenore, Carden, Chabnor, Clark, Clarke, Clerke, Davidson, De Ferrers, Dragoner, Drayner, Drummond, *Ekeney, Hansby, Helme, Holt, Huthwait, *Johnson, *Kirkwood, Langley, Lewellyn, Llewellyn, Mudge, Mudie, Nichols, Plater, Raeburn, Sale, Sall, Sexton, Sharp, Smart, Spink, Spinks, Sydney.
12. Apreece, *Broderwicke, Brodrick, Caslon, Conqueror, Fitz-Osborn, Holt, Morgan, Panton, *Pery, Rice, *Rosseter, *Roster, Scott, Wisemale.
13. Allnett, Allnutt, Almot, Alneot, Alnot, Carnegie, Cobbold, Hatchet, Hatchett, Hawley, Kennoway.
14. Ball, Delahill, De Vic, Garter, *Kerrich, Miller, Pratt, Rampston, *Raven.

PLATE 175. — 1. Beesley, Beesly, Beseley, Besley, Besly, Cooper, Lang, Langan, Purnell, Winterbottom.
2. Adamson, Cassidy, D'Arcy, Darcy, Fitz-Alin, Fitz-Allan, *Richmond, Tidbury, *Webb.
3.*Fairford.
4. Ranking.
5. Langmore.
6. Borelands, Borland, Cuiler, Ethelstan, Ethelston, Foskett, O'Feargus, Tidmarsh.
7. Sadler.
8. Botatort, Botetourt, Tiller, Timmins.
9. Aprece, Colbroke, Colebrock, Colebrook, Mackinnon, Town, Towne.
10. Lombe.
11. Amherst, Amhurst.
12. Allen.
13.*Garland, Waldeshescheff, Waldesheff, Waldsheff.
14. Tylden.
15. Peck.

PLATE 176. — 1. Tharrold.
2. Blennerhasset, Carlyon, Corby, Hawks, Paganell, Pagnell, Traill, Trewarther.
3.*Ackers, Alderson, Bodkin, Cossens, Craig, Craigdallie, Craigie, Crichton, *Embery, Gordon, Hurley, Juckes, Jukes, Lort, Marrow.
4. Buggen, Buggens, Buggin, Conran, Cranston, Hendley, Hendly, Temple.
5. Crakenthorpe, Craufurd, Crawford, Kirch, Looker, Lyndown, Uffleete.
6. Ferrier.
7. Askeby, Askely, Asklaby, Asklakby, Asklakeby, Boyd, Cuppage, Hart, M'Indoe.
8. De Keyser.
9. Paris.
10. Dyce, *Fortescue, Mervin, Shields, Stopham.
11. Elliot, Elliott.
12. Alberton, *Briscoa, Hatch, Oray, Ovray.
13.*Bryant, Deyncourt, *Haselerton, Jasper, Keep, Sandell.
14. Beavins, Bevans, Bloxam, Bloxham, Boddicott, Bodicote, Bodycoat, Swinford, Webster.
15. Dupont, Esdaile, Foord, *Hyde, Kinarby.

PLATE 177. — 1. Croker.
2. Aderson.
3. Ferns, *Giles, Whetnall.
4. Butler, Drew, Dunn, Dyrrwarne, Dyrward, Dyrwarne, Fitz-Barnard, Fitz-Bernard, Forsyth, Weatherall, Wilshere.
5. Corsellis, Kyrrelorde, Lucas, Murray.
6.*Hill, Horseman.
7. Leet, Lete.
8.*Brinton, Carey, *Compton, Faulder, Fuller, Fulwer, *Sherfeild, *Wheatley.
10. Backie, Baikie, Dart, Darte, Dast, Firebrace, Graham, Wallis.
11. Fuller.
12. Collison, Creighton, Forest, Harling, Harlingham, Holliday, Leeds, Marney, Tuberville.
13. Burslam, Burslem, Comberford, Mayce, Nonwers, Norwers, Nouwers, De la Nouers, Nowers, Straiton.
14. Anlet, Anlett, Boak, Brian, Brunton, Bryen, *Burton, Cockerith, Cokerith, Compton, Crumpton, Festing, Frend, Goodale, Goodalle, Keenlyside, Kirkhoven, Redmond, Saphar, Teggart, Wells, Wilkinson.
15. Benley, Bensley, Bensly, Boag, Bogg, Cooper, Ekington, Ekinton, Forbes, Houston, Woodstock.

PLATE 178. — 1. Porter.
2. Porter.
3. Bell, *Buck, Farquharson, Farquherson, Fencourt, Marson, Melles, Porter, Renolds, Somaster, Somerset, Somester, Sommaster, Sumaister, Summaster, Wilmot.
4. Acre, Aker, Crawley, Cropper, Fulherst, Fulsherst, Holliam, Johnson, Leslie, M'Cullock.
5. Astrovel, *Burges, Dacres, Peters, Provost, Wakehurst.
6. Aiken, Albeney, Atkin, Culchech, Dealbeney, *Delavache, Ennis, Finderne, Fynderne, Godin, *Hantvill, Hay, Hervy, *Orby, Oyke.
7. Allvey, Alvey, Farey, Ferrey, Ferry, Hay, Hines, Imbrie, Imrey, Imrie, Kroge, Laugher, Tane.
8. Abbis, Abbiss, Abis, Abys, Johnston, Johnstone, Liston, Ruddiman, Wollacombe.
9. Dallas, Kadie, Keddie.
10. Tay.
11. Blick, Blicke, Cheshire, Chesshyre, Harold, Harould, Harrold, Keith.
12. Nanfant, Ponpons.

PLATE 179. — 1. Burwasch, Burwash, Burwashe, Donaldson, Evetick, Saltmarsh, Saltmarshe.
2. Creveguer, Creveguere, Grant, Kirkpatrick, Mackenzie, M'Kenzie, Mackinzie, M'Onald, Reoch, Stewart, Stradbrooke.
3. Campbell, M'Gibbon, Stanley Steer.
5. Chetham, Lutton, Maitland, Travers, Walker.
6. Aines, Ainge, Ainger, Aitken, Aitkin, Atkin, Atkins, Colston.
7. Bradwell, *Cadiman, Cornick, Dalrymple, Deline, Grant, Haig, Hamilton-Dalrymple, Hay, Hornsey, Keith, Kylle, Langlois, Le Roache, Mackenzie, M'Kenzie, MacNeil, McNeil, M'Neil, Macneill, Mather, Pittman, Reoch, Roche, Rowche, Sandeman, Scarsborough, Southall, Walker.
8. Beamish, Bemish, Cass, Faal, Lauder, Lawder, Nurse, Pashley, Pasley.
10. Billing, *Robley.
11.*Crawford, Crawfurd, Lindsay, Stacey.
12. Baron, Barron, *Cathcart, *Deram, *English, Malcolm, Malcom.

PLATE 180. — 1. Balbirney, Baldberney, Boult, Callagan, Elworthy, Hopcroft, Pagalet.
2. Ismay.

3 *Helsham, Holliday, Idle, Minnitt, Olivier, Poigndestre Shekell, Stokely, Street, Tillard, Twigg, Twigge, Tyron, Walleys, Wigmore
4 Bandinel, Barrett, *Chemere, Lawful, Pecke, Sharp
5 *Abelon, *Abilon, *Barclay, *Barkeley, *Beardmore, *Berdmore, *Berkeley, *Cleveland, *Cocksey, *Fadon, *Eddowes, *Fawcett, Harding, Hardinge, *Pettit, *Petyt, *Spalding, *Tenison, *Tulloch
6 Edwards
7 Bethune, Codd, Fren, Frene, Healy, Ouchterlony
8 *Irving
9 Ames, Amos
10 Benjamin, Cuckborne, Dundas, Hesill, Mansel, Mansell, Maunsell, Swift
11 Cabourne
12 Goldie, Hansard, Harringworth, Kibble, La Cloche, Latimer, Lionnel, Rufus, Rutledge
13 Sciaualuga, Von Sturmer
14 *Lisle, Lysle

PLATE 181 — 1 Cane, Glasier, Glazier, Hamilton
2 *Campbell, *Corderay, *Corderoy, Dingwall, Douglas, Enswell, Entwissell, Gray, *Pembroke, *Tooker, *Tucker, Turner
3 Gerdon
4 *Chetwyn, Lightfoot, Logan
5 Rigg
6 Breawse, Burden, Chatting, Ewart, Forbes
7 *Beeston, *Beestone, *Beiston, *Dockware, *Dockwrae
8 Rattray
9 Coulter
10 Campbell, Mack, Nathan
11 Lyndsay
12 Kirby, Kirkby, Mackenzie, M'Kenzie, Thompson
13 Boileau, Bulley, Clavel, Clavell, Lindsay, Tourner, Turner, Watson
14 Thomson, *Toker, Truell

PLATE 182 — 1 *Braybrooke, Goldston, Goldstone, Keys, Lessler, Lighton, Mill, Milne, Mylne, Smith, Wolverstone
2 Christie, *Cookes, Faringham, Farneham, *Pannell, Peart, Pert
3 Carey, Cary, Carmichael, Griffith Larder, Marrow, Mowbray, *Rudd, Tanfield, Tansfield
4 Amo
5 Anne, *Darcie, Kele, *Kepping, Keyle, *Lalynde, *Overton, Parr, Tanfield
6 *Daunecourt, *Daunscourt, Morfyn
7 Den
8 Cary, Ellis, Gruffeth, Hempgrave, Thornton
9 Elmes, Ewarby, Gregory.
10 *Braybroke
11 Gwynne-Vaughan
12 Argall, Asgile, Badby, *Brett, *Dempsey, Dernford, *Giffard, *Haws, *Hawse, Hipkiss, *Lambert
14 *Goatley, *Goatly, Lambert, *Lowdell, *Paris

PLATE 183 — 1 Purchon
2 Attwood, Cunningham, Cunninghame, Event, Everitt, Govesy, Govisy, Lovetoft, Lovetot, Moberley, Moberly, Modburley, Rodger
3 Bloss, Dalley, Dally, Daly, Kathyng, Kating, Katting, Kaytyng, Leslie
4 *Collingborne, Darcey, Darcy, D'Arcy, *Fyan
5 Barwell, Eland, Flland, Elphingston, *Gainsford, *Gaynsford, Hendley, Keith, Lodington, Sexton, Turyn, Woodroffe
6 Dankyrsley
7 Airlie, Annesley, Grandison, Granson, Millar
8 Aickinson, Bailey, Bailie, Baylee, Elphinstone
9 Ogilvy
10 Witham
11 Van Voorst
12 *Cargill, *Harrold, Stirling
13 Simpson
14 Heriz, *Lexington, Ogilvie, *Scot.

PLATE 184 — 1 Bailey
2 Bicknall, Bicknell, Boughey, Falconer, *Faulkner, Hynell, Sheridan
3 Langer, *Ohmann
4 Duckworth, Hardcastle, Scot, Scott
5 Bonham, Bruer, Brumherd, Byrn, Byrne, Byron, *Challon, Chiswell, Cullen, Ellice, Ellis, Enell, Garneshe, Garnishe, Garnyl, Glass, Glasse, Golever, Haly, Hastings, Jones, Kinloch, Lauzon, M'Nair, M'Nayr, *M'Nemara, Marbury, Mason, Meare, Merbury, *Mere, Meres, Metley, Meyers, Moore, Moultrie, Montry, Murray, *Myers, O'Byrne, O Cullen Rutherford, Rutherfurd, Skeffington, Skevington, Sleford, Cusac Smith, Wallop, Warburton
6 Ellis
7 Broadhurst, *Cusack, Fennor, Goband, Legget, Murray
8 Aitkenson, Anneles, Atmore, Attemore, Biron, Brewer, Minett, O'Bryne, O'Byrne
9 Conelly, Connelley, Conolly, Montgomerie Montgomery
10 Balfour, *Stewart Balfour
11 Carruthers
12 Carruthers, Croudace, Duffy, *Fithier, Leslie, Murray, Preston, Staden, Standen
13 *Ellis
14 *Britain, *Briton, *Britten, *Britton, Cheeke, Denison, *Walstonecroft, Wollstonecraft

PLATE 185 — 1 Curwen, Gabriel, Gabryell
2 *Barr, Corney, Douglas, Lachlan
3 *Coterell, *Cotrell, *Davers, Livingston, *Livingstone, Meurs, Mey, Plowman
4 Maconachie, Maconochie
5 Hotham
6 *Bowman, Chatfield, Fiton, Leader, Millar, Miller
7 Arscot, Framlingham, *Zephani
8 Corrie, Corry, Hanckford, Hyman, Soper, Sutton
9 Durward, Lee, Leigh
10 Halfhead, Hartman
11 Vivian
12 Curtoys, Dawbin, *Hebden, *Karnabye, May, Robertson, *Tregent, Trite

PLATE 186 — 1 Abadain, Abaudain, *Bowerbank, *Emline, *Emlyn, Gordon, Harty, Mackenzie, Shaw, Shaw Stewart, Stewart, Wightman, Willingham, Wood, Woodford
2 *Maynell, *Menell, *Meynell, Murray
3 Allardice, Allerdice, Allieson, Allison, Burland, Gedding, Geding, Lynam, Murray, *Powle
4 *Aikenhead, *Aitkenhead, *Brickwood, *Brigwood, Dansey, Kyrby, Kyrkby, Le Mesurier
5 Auvray, Blaumester, *Brian, Brisbane, *Bryan, Leahy, Levingstone, McIlaffie-Gordon, Meriton, Murray, Powel, Powell, Sabben, St Owen, Trumpeter, Wood
6 Bowyer, Coults
7 *Babeham, *Babehaw
8 Sykes
9 M'Corda, Mackorda, *Moore
10 Bridgen
11 *Albert, *Browne, Comberton, Dorien, Elwin, Elwyn, Elwynn, Haig, Haugh, Neilson
12 Brenton, Fairfield, Hollyland, Holyland, O Kelly
13 Broad, Dox, Doxey, Govett, Large, *MacConach, *MacConachie, Macfarlan, M'Farlane
14 *Appleford, Cleiland, Cleilland, Cordel, Cordell, Cordelle, *Woodville

PLATE 187 — 1 Bake, Bannerman, Bonekill, Borrowman, Brunsfield, Brunsfields, Chassereau, Croasdaile, Durborough, Easton, Geils, Giles, Heriot, Stirling Hamilton, Joicey, Le Hunt, Leslie, Mount, Ogilvie, Sale, Trew
2 Barrowman, Gordon, Hewitt, Mount Joy
3 Capron, *Kersteman
4 Chevalier, Dalsiel, Dalyell, Dalziel, Grill, Hampstead, Hampsted, Hincks, Joice, Joyce, Widvile
5 *Elliot, *Elliott, Morse
6. Althan, Althaun, Comrie, Comry, *Coults, Giffard, Hood, M'Leurg, Ruffy
7 *Bovil, *Bovile, *Lawrie, *Maitland
8 *Macgregor
9 Aikman, Cleveland, Pitcher, Seaton, Sinclair
10. Caldmore
11 Denman, Dunstavile, Dunstaville, Garret, Hewetson, *Stourton, Sturton
12 Clark, Clerk, Daws, Mercier, Murray, Pennycoock, Pennycuick, Rattray
13 Dangar, *Fulwood
14 Curteiss, Curtess, Curteys, Curtois, Curtoys, Dracelow, Drakelow, Hay, Mahon, *Paterson Balfour Hay

PLATE 188 —
2 *Cardwell, Cletherow, Clyderowe, *Clown, *Delamaine, Modburley, *O'Malone, *Tooker
3 Caster, Clermont, *Donand, Gabell, Gillies, Gellie, Geily, *Mackrery, *Macrery
4 Brooke, Cletherow, Clyderowe, Gambell, Gamble, Hornby, M'Kerrell, Malone
5 Campbell, Mackenzie
6. Clesby, *Danford, *Delamaine, Hind, *Ratford, Sinclair

7 Cloun, Clun, *Fanacourt, *Marshall, *Morley
8 Trafford, De Trafford
9 Cliffe, Luke, Reielly, Scopham, Scopyn
10 *Middleton, *Myddleton, *Walton
11 *Minshall, *Minshull, *Mynshall
12 *Asheton, *Ashton, *Assheton, Ety, Pilkington

PLATE 189 —1 *Benbow, Blackeney, Blackeny, Blackney, Blakeny, Colter, Coulter, Humphray, Morrell, Sutton, Trimnel, Trimnell
2 Lake
3 *Aries, *Arris, Metcalfe
4 Colemere, Colmore, Humfrey, Humphrey, Hurry, Pocher, Souter
5 Abrey, Craig, Craige, Estrange, Jessope, Jessopp, Jessup, Jett, *Stedman, Thwaites
6 Bothwell, *Boynell, *Boyville, Hankin
7 Gleave, Hamilton, *Keating, *Keatinge, Neish, Round, Tully
8 Dunn
9 Adye, Adyer, Ambrose, Baird, Brady, Bushell, Bussell, Busshell, Carruthers, Clavering, Courtney, Depham Desanges, Donhault, Edgworth, England, Fanning, Foggo, Fogo, Jellicoe, Legat, Leggatt, Lugg, MacBrady, Menzies, Murray, Overend, Porter, Sarjeantson, Wade, Wood
10 Adelin, Cock, Cocks, Copland, *Cray, Cunningham, Ernelle, Esingold, Feton, Fitzgerald, Flood, Gennett, Horscote, Johnson, *Johnston, *Judkin Fitzgerald, Sowter
11 Mitchell Carruthers, Mitchell.
12 *Coffy, O'Cobthaigs
13 Auld, Aulde, Courtney, Scot, Walker, Wood

PLATE 190 —1 *Darell, Durell
2 Newall
3 Wallpool, Walpole, Wrey
4 Bayn, Chesney, Irby, Jones, Norton, Topper
5 *Alkene, *Askue, *Ayskew, *Barnsley, Blondell, Bouche, Briscoe, Briscowe, Buller, Burwell, *Byfleet, *Carver, Chandos, Charlewood, Charlwood, Cobham, Creswell, Edington, Flamank, Flamock, Gleame, Gleane, *Heaviside, Holcombe, Howndhile, Howndhill, Hubbard, Irby, Irton, Lambsey, Lamesey, Lecton, Mariot, Manley, Marshall, *Menzies, Middleton, *Morgan, *Mure, Powell, *Ricard, Rochead, Roughead, Rudger, Salway, Stapylton, Strelley, Ward, Warner, Weston, Whittewronge, Wilder, Williams, *Wittewrong, Winnington, Wynne
6 Bawde, *Buch, *Grailly
7 *Cresswell, Curling, Dangerfield, Ladkin, *Livingstone, *Muir, *Multon, *Napier, *Rochead, *Ruck
8 *Bourcher, *Bourchier, *Bourchir, Flight, Sattherthwaite
9 Barrington
10 Alpin, Kirkaldie, Kirkaldy, Maxwell
11 Eddington, Edington, Macalpin, Moir, *Molleson, Mint, Musard, Roddam, Tiddeman, Tideman
12 Ashworth, Brackenbury, Crofton, Duston, Dustone, Gaudine, Greathead, Johnson, Lang, Lansford, Laverye, *Lemmington, *Lenington, *Lennington, Magill, Maxwell, Molynes, Montgomery, Morgan, Moubray, Muir, Prendergast, Pykin, Rayley, Rochead, Rocheid, Savage, Stewart, Waveney, Williams.
13 *Boking, *Bokinge, De la Pole, De Moleyns, Rouse
14 *Abilem, Annesley, Audely, Auge, Bruse, Irby, Ligon, *Lloyd, Mure, Penhelleke, Powtrell, *Sackford, Salloway, Selby, Shelton, Shirley, Stapleton, Stirling, Strelley, Touchet, Tremenheere

PLATE 191 —1 Borthwick, Dunston, Duston, Gawsworth, Haly
2 Morrison
3 M'Clelland
4 Brocas.
5 Big, Bigg, Bigge, Campbell Miller Morrison, Haynes, Mason, *Monson, Morison, Morrison, *Northleigh, *Pearson, *Pierson
6 Blair, Dingley, Dinley, Dodson, Masquenay, *Whitney
7 Colston, Cusach, Cusack, Cusacke, *Derrick, Norman
8. Adair
9 Abeline, Ablin, Ablyn, Brooking, Dransfield, *Huntercomb, Ireby, Knapman, Murdoch, Sheen, Untercombe
10 Buckworth, *Symes
11 Adair, *Keeling, *Kellyng, *Kelnyg, *Kelynge, *Rotherham, *Wallace
12 Stapleton
13 Frost, Ginger

PLATE 192 —1 Litcott
2 Cobham
3 Barrington, Shedden, Thurland
4 Coker, Livingstone, Main, Moore, Mordaunt, More, Quadering, Quadring, *Saint Lo
5 Warner
6 Andrews, *Bugge, *Clerke
7 *Bownell, Haliburton, Hallyburton
9 *Achilles, *Achillis, Bertie, Buxhull, Churchill, Freshacre, Geering, Moncaster, Presland, Prestland, Varty, Willoughby
10 *Earnley, *Hobush, *Warberton, *Warburton
11 *Heveningham, *Heveringham, Hodsdon, Paynter, *Pitches
12 Bacche
13 Agas, Agg, Auge, Andrewes, Andrews, Annesley, Annyslay, *Ansley, Ashurin, Blaikie, Borthwick, Carleill, *Carlisle, Clayfield, Cleland, Coker, Colemere, Collamore, Collmore, Collymore, Conway, Conyers, Cosway, Den, *Du Halgoet, Everard, Fondre, Gosselin, Grantham, Halyburton, Harlaw, Holles, Kingsmill, Le Maire, Littleton, Lum, Lumm, Lyttelton, M'Clellan, Mair, Masterman, Menell, Meynell, Moore, *Moore Carrick Mordaunt, *More, *Mores, *Rowe-Mores, *Muir, *Mure, *Newbery, *Newborough, Norton, O'Conry, *Packer, *Pecksall, *Pexall, *St Loe, *Sands, *Seymour, *Sim, *Stirling, *Tanner, Titus, Troutbeck, *Valentia, *Weltden, Westcote
14 Bacche, Bache, Lygon, Maxwell

PLATE 193 — 1 Airey, Allman, Alman, Archer, Ayre, Eyre, *Foljamb, *Foljambe, Helias, M'Cull, Pack, Packe, Raine, Reade, Westbrook, Younger
2 Ayre, Eyre
3 Copinger, Haddon
4 Chelley, M'Call
5 Acton
6 Gilman
7 Gayton, Humphreys, Humphries, Humphryes
8 *Archer De Boys, *Chambers, Golborn, Golborne, Mackauly, Sotherton
9 M'Alla, M'Aulay, Macaulay, Mac kauly
10 Bacheler, Bachelor, Bachelour, Batchellor, Batchelor, *Bower, *Godmanstone, Rain, Raine
11 Bleuett, Blewet, Blewitt, Sibbald
12 Hussey
13 Jossey, Townsend

PLATE 194 —1 Burton
2 Silber
3 Baker
4 Hussey
5 Hill
6 Barkeman, Barkham
7 Algood, Allgood, Belvale, *Gibbons
8 Green, Steer, Tison
9 Briscoe, Briscowe, Monckton, Mongdone, Mongton, Mongtown, Monkton, Paul
10 Algood, Allgood, Rasdall
11 *Auffrick, *Beecroft, *Butler, Mowne, *Tallantire, *Trevelyan, *Webber
12 Anstruther, Brember, Chartnay, Chartney, *Fitz Osborn, Handy, Tolman, *Watford,
13 *Corbyn, O'Donel
14. *Jary

PLATE 195 —1 Areskine, Brouncker, Clifton, Colbey, Engleheart, Erskine, Fulwer, *Hansard, *Hemsworth, Linesley, *Pottinger, Rawle, Rawlins, Saunders, *Taylor, Thomson, Tuffnal, Tufnell, Tuftnell
2 Abbs, Aldworth, Alexander, Armstrong, Ashtown, Baggally, Bagley, Beirne, Bellew, Boteler, Brace, Breanon, Brigden, Cabbell, Cameron, Carnell, Carvile, *Cheffield, Chepstow, Chevil, Chiney, Clifton, Connor, Connour, Conor, *Copley, Crosroe, Curtis, Donald, Donaldson, Dowglas, Drummond, Ellicombe, Fox, Freeke, Freke, Fry, *Gamin, Gledstanes, Goadefroy, Goodhand, *Gorman, Gow, Graham, Grant, Guthrie, Hacket, *Halliday, Harvey, *Higham, Hogan, John, Johnston, Kane, Keir, *Kirke, Langton, Laungton, Lisle, Litchfield, *Macarmick, Macbeath, *McClelland, *M'Coul, M'Donald, MacDougall, MacMahon, M'Neil, Macneill, M Nelly, Maguire, Mansfield, Mathew, *Mereweather, Merriman, *Merriweather, *Merryweather, *Meryweather, Millward, Mirehouse, Neale-Burrard, Newborough, Newport, Norton, *Nowell, O'Beirne, O'Breanon, O'Brenan, O'Clary, O'Connor, O'Conor, *O Conor Don, Odel, *Odell, *O'Donochoo, *O'Donoghoe, *O'Gorman, O'Heyne, *O'Kennelly, O'Learie, O'Neil, O'Neill, Pace, Paulet, *Payne, Phillpotts, Pollett, Porter, Poulet, Probert, Quin, Quin-

ton, Rawlins, Rokeston, *Roney, Rule, Simcoe, Sionnach, Smith, Smyth, Spange, Stratford, Taarie, Thomond, Toulmin, Trangmar, Trench, *Tyler, Underhay, Vane, Wade, Wall, Wallace, Wolston, Wolstone
3 Abel, Abell, Conner, Douglas
4 Bain, Bastard, Bates, Brenan, Clayton Cringan, Crinan, Crinzian, Mouchet
5 Johnston, Lessingham
6 Abingdon, *Bastard, Blyth, *Cantrell, Grindal, Grindall, Gwyn, Jacobs, Woodham
7 Kynaston
8 Delane, Furse, Lee, O'Kennelly
9 Cameron, *Clark, *Cooke, Franke, Franks, Warley
10 Barksteade, De Massue Fenton, *Jennet, O'Leane
11 Richardson
12 *Evans, Tayleur, Taylor

PLATE 196 —1 Ingeham, Ingham, Kitchen
2 Colby
3 Wright
4 *Elton, Heldich, Holdiche
5 Archideckine, *Bickerton, Brig, Campbell, *Colby, Conner, *Creswick, Douglas, Erskine, Fearguson, *Garstin, Gaselee, Geogham, Grassal, Grassall, Greaves, Grieve, *Harries, Henot, Hill, Hynes, Lamarch, M'Allister, *Macguarie, M Hud MacNeill, *Molony, Montgomery, *Moriarty, Mundell, *Nelson, Pasley, Preston, Radford, Schrieber, Skipton, *Stirling, Vade, White, Wilton
6 *Halliday, *Reddie
7 Lescher
8 Nowlan, Singleton
9 Coblegh, Cobleigh, Cobley, *Ewing
10 Aldborough, Amond, Arcedeckne, Archdeckne, Athol, *Backhouse, *Basnett, Birrell, Black, *Bloor, *Bloore, Blundell, Bradstreet, *Bromage, Buck, Bucke, *Chambers, Chisholm, *Clarkson, *Colby Cree, Crewker, Cripps, Crips, Dasent, Davis, *Doherty, Druce, Drummond, Elyard, Greg, Greig Hagges, Hardie, Henry, Hone, *Kirby, Laurenson, Lauriston, *M'Cree, *M'Crie, M'Cubbin, M'Dougall, M Hardie, McHardy, Mackellar, MacKellar, McKellar, M'Kellar, M Kellor, *Mangle, Majendie, Merry, Molony, Oakeley, *O'Dogherty, O'Hegarty, O'Reilly, Partheriche, Parthericke, Pennel, Pennell, Plott, Randall, Rice, Saunderson, Sibbald, Smith, Strangforth, Stratford, Taaffe, Tregos, Trent, *Waterhouse, Wingate
11 Dickson
12 Oakeley

PLATE 197 —1 Auchmuty, *Carhill, *Currie, *Fell, Speir, Spiers, Vilant *Yeoman
2 Achmuty, *Acombe, *Carmichael, Caswell, Cuthbert, Fearguson, Forster, *Gilbert, Harrison, Hilliard, King, Mackenay, Makareth, Montgomery, *O'Shaughnessy, Phillips, *Pike, Warren, Whetstone, Whitson, Worth
3 Carmichael, *Churchyard, *Nethersall, *Nethersole, Smyth, *Tennyson, Thompson
4 *Bruce, Everet, Everett
5 Combe
6 Randolph Lichfield
7 Armistead, Auchmuty, Ciffe, M'Kinna, *Thompson Meysey, *Thompson, Thomson
8 Holmes
9 Combe
10 Boycott *Nowell
11 Boycott
12 *Castlecomb, Johnson
13 Tonge de-Tonge
14 Parr

PLATE 198 —1 Ashawe
2 Caswall
3 Tatum
4 Baker, Carrie, Chaworth, *Clarke, Cleghorn, Cotter, Cubit, Cubitt *Downing, *Fletcher, Fookes, Godbold, Hales, Hurr, Hutcheson, *Lee, *Matthews, Proudfoot, Rivers, Thurburn, Warren
5 Adams, Aitken, Aitkens, Aldred, Molesworth
6 Clarke
7 Braimor, Edmonds
8 Johnson
9 Caddon, Cuddon
10 Littlehales
11 Chevers, Dickens, Dickins, Gerson, Keryell, Toriano
12 Hardy
13 Hadfield, Hassard
14 *Feld, *Field

PLATE 199 —1 Brudenell
2 Bathurst, *Beringham, *Bringhurst, *D Eyvil, *D'Eyvill, *Randell, *Randle, *Rawe, *Rawes,
3 Abingdon, Bult, Covilhoc, Covill, Coville, Girflet, Ogle, *Roundel
4 Beseley, Hartley, Katheram, Rossell, Vaughan
5 Fowne, Malins
6 Cogger, Ellesworth.
7 *Gardener, Nimmo
8 Ryland.
9 *Banner, *Blackmore, *Delancey, *Sabbe
10 *Bamford
11 Groome
12 *Brady, *Gilpin, Champion, Coe, Cother, *Laurie, *Meymott, *Watson,
13 *Diver
14 Bodwida, Bowida, Cassils, Crook, Eastland, Estland, Estlin, Plafair, Tournemine

PLATE 200. — 1 Anderdon, Anderson, Armstrang, Armstrong, *Blackmore, *Burgh, Johnston, Johnstone, Malmaynes, Murray, Partrick
2 *Ap-Griffith, Archer, Archever, Bower, *Butter, Butters, Chipnam, Drummond, Fletcher, Flexney, Gordon, Higgenbottom, Higginbotham, Higginbottom, Hunter, *Littlejohn, Smythe, Wasey
3 *Beckett, *Carhill, *Glastings, Wheeler-Cuffe, *Kellett, *Kenney, *Way
4 *Armstrong
5 Lockley, Weatherby
6 Blacker, Bradley, *Cove, Davis, Dawson, Drake, *Edmond, *Edmonds, *Farrand, *Ferrand, Gibbs, Gibson, Gytties, Hagley, Halke, Hall, Henessy, *Hurlebert, Jackson, Jeremy, Joyner, Lawson, *Lee, Leveson, Leye, MacSweeney, *Nevett, *Nunn, O'Hennessy, Osborne-Gibbes, *Place, Polkinghorne, *Quilter, Rattray, *Raymond, *Samler, *Schomberg, Varley, Verthon, Warwick, *Weekes, *Whitter, *Wright, *Yarner
7 *Burchall, Exeter, Knapton
8 Musgrave
9 Ridge
10 Deasy, *Jordon
11 Johnson, Johnson
12 Birt, Grover, Skeen, Skene

PLATE 201 —1 Ainsley, Ainslie, Bartram, *Charingworth, Dexter, Erskine, Finlay, Hadden, Halket, Hawling, Levermore, Lindon, M'Geough, McGeough, Macnamara, M Rae, Scarrow, Strahan, Yawkins
2 *Bramfell, Bruce, Mandis
3 *Callagan, M'Donagh, MacMahon, *O'Callagan, O'Callaghan, *Tuite
4 *Bindley, Cahan, Cahane, *Cantillion, *Clayton, Dale, *Dickson, Dollar, *Donelly, Drummond, Gealagh, James, Johnson, *Kane, Leivy, *Clayton, *Luxford, Mackenzie, *MacMahon, Macnamara, Moore, O'Brien, O'Cahane, O'Neill, *Stafford, Stewart, Waddy, White
5 Browning, Cooper, *Dakyns, *Dawkins, *Drake, *Geach, Mactier, Mercer, Norton, *Samuel
6 M'Gregor
7 Bolron, Embery, Flude, Longley, M'Clellan, *Waller
8 Deakin
9 Desbarres, Germain
10 Bolhalth
11 Billing, Billinge, Fowke, M'Gilleoun, MacGilleoun
13 Baker, Bowdler, *Carleton, Carlton, Colt, Coult, Elliot-Murray Kynynmound, Mackenzie, Pickford
14 Atfield, Cantillon, *Eliot, Hawleys, Lewis, M'Cullock, Montalt, Taylor

PLATE 202.—1 Baker, Gordon
2 Aile, Ailes, Armestrang, Armstrong, Ayles, Bullo, Bulow, Constable, Ward
3 Peck, Webb
4 Bludworth, Breeton, Chartsey, Glaston, Landal, Landel, Landell, Landale, Stoken, Whyte Melville, Whyte, Whytt
5 Blackburn, Chamberlen, *Greenland, Hastings, Staples, *Wilks
6 *Amyand, Barclay, Bolger, Cressenor, Cressner, Hand, Kennoway, Kirkton, Kirton
7 Bambridge, Colladon, Cox, Gaskin, Watson
8 Darker
9 Hay
10 Burket, Burkett, Burkitt, Chauncey, Davis, Downham Erskine, Laleman, Leaver, Leckie, Lecky, Raynes
11 Hardy
12 Barke
13 Canceller, Cancellor
14 *Broadbent, *Lennie, *Sysington.
15 Handcock

PLATE 203.—1. Barkham, Dabernon, Debenham, Flowerdew, Flowerdue, Gover, Lorimer, Quarton.
2. Barkesworth, Barksworth, Bentinck, Burbridge, Bentinck.
3.*Burney, Cumine, Cumming, Ellacott, Ellicott, Enderbie, Enderby, Gawden, Glanvile, Glanville, Lord, Robarts.
4. Billings, Brisac, Butler, *Chawrey, *Chawsey, *Chenell, Butler, Crosby, Drewell, Gillan, Gilland, Karrick, Karricke, Keogh, Pargiter, Wolmer.
5. Bentinck.
6.*Macarty.
7. Black, Frankland, Gibbard, Gibbes.
8. Huddleston.
9. Austin, Bollers, Devey, *Macdonell, *MacDonnell, *McDonnell, Maundrell, Rohan.
10. Algist, Drewe, *Judgson, *Judson.
12. Davis.
13. Longstaff.
14. Gull.

PLATE 204.—1. Armytage, *Stratford, Fuller, Gilmore, Gilmour, Heathfield, *Jenkes, Kavanagh, Keir, Lalor, Leigh, McCoghlan, O'Brien *O'Kennedy, *Steere, Winstanley, Woodcock.
2. Brisbane.
3. M'Innes.
4. Allot, Allott, Dodgin, Gillingham, Gwinnell.
5. Harker.
6.*Barnes.
7.*Doyle, *Doyley, Dunster.
8. Rome, Roome.
9. *Lichfield.
10. *Knotshull.
11. Barr, Beste, Buchanan, Budworth, *Grenvele, Gwinnell.
12. Adams, Castle.
13. Malim.
14.*Forster.

PLATE 205.—1. Ackerman, Ackermann, Acraman, Akerman, Cordingley.
2.*Sleigh, Wallis, Wathen, *Witham.
3.*Dixon, *Sleigh, Wallis, Wathen, *Witham.
4.*Bowen, *Bray, Smallwood.
5. Denny, *Matcham, Thomson.
6.*Ainlie, *Ainslie, Barnewell, *Conroy, *Leycroft, Pitt, *Swift, *Williams.
7.*Camfield, Kenrick, *Rye, Thompson, Thomson.
8. Rye.
9. Foote, Greer, Rowe.
10. Jephson, *Jesson.
11. Whitmore.
12. Byngham.
13.*Bloer, Dixon.
14.*Carsey, *Cooke, *Gifford, Hagthorpe, Jones, Peck, Yonn.

PLATE 206.—1. Scawen.
2. Clench, *Frey.
3. Mitchell.
4. Harmar.
5. Akers.
6. Turton.
7. Rhodes.
8.*Abbot, Hibbert.
9. Patch.
10.*Downe, Hibbert, Naper, Napier.
11. Walden.
12.*Abech, Abeck, Crowe, *De Courcy, Elton, Habeck, Kawston.
13.*Allott, Bayly, *Doughty, *Douty, *Draper, Lane.
14.*Browne, *Gilsland.

PLATE 207.—1. Brouncker.
2. Bailey, *Crosier.
3. *Poynder.
4. Abeny, Brangan, Corry, Fanning, Fitz-Allen, Kingsmill, Leggat, Leggatt, Lutefoote, Turner, Vickers.
5. Forrest.
6. Johnson.
7. Beche, Dickenson, Kayble, *Maddison, Norden.
8. Daniel, *Daniell.
9. Alfounder, Windover.
10.*Chancey, Cuffe, Farrant, *Ferrand, *Gregson, *Harman, *Madyston, *Maney, *March, *Ommaney, *Porter.
11. Procter.
12. Field.
14. Folkes, Lee.

PLATE 208.—1. Mitchell.
2. Colson, Kelsey.
3. Avison, Byde, *Farrant, Halls, Kellet, Loney, Partington, *Rawson, *Tippet.
4.*Kenney, Parkinson.
5.*Evans, *Rolle, *Rudd, *Scote, *Scott, *Smith, *Stephenson, *Strutt.
6. Hartford, Hinxman, Hortford, Parker.
7.*Bowyer, Gooch, *Millett.
8. Blenman, Cummings, Evers, Kenney, *New, King, Ring, Rudde.
9. Henderson.
10. Aylworth, Bright, Freemantle, Mash, Shaw.
11. Kenney.
12. Elwill.
13.*Blackborn, *Blackborne, *Blackburn, *Blakeborne, Parker.
14. Trundle.
15. Baynes.

PLATE 209.—1.*Owen, *Thickness.
2. Bitterley, Connor, Dockenfield, Dokenfield, Duckinfield, Duckingfield, Dukenfield, Falkiner, Gaulfield, Henshall, Karben, Lovelass.
3. Lloyd, McCarthy, *McCarthy-Reagh.
4. Ross.
5. Burton.
6. O'Hickey, O'Hickie.
7.*Brome.
8. Burton, Cramer, Crammer, Eccles, Eyre, Gringfield, Meldert, Seaton, Seton, Slater.
9. Balfour, Bellett, *Billet, *Billot, *Nelson, Nesbett, *Nesbitt.
10. Bardwell, Cosby, Cottesmore, *Feltham, Grudgfield, *Mootham, Woods.
11.*Bowland, Bywater, Carbinell, *Clarke, *Ferron, *Forbes, Jenny, Mays.
12. Baron.
13.*Fitzherbert.
14.*Acguillum, Arpin, Bellis, Irvine, Mansted, Nicolson, *Vesey.

PLATE 210.—1. *Pasley.
2. Arnott, Beauman, Browne, Brownlee, Browlie, *Caldwell, Cameron, Claydan, Conyngham, *Cookes, Cruikshank, Cunninghame, Curtis, Delap, Delarous, Dewar, Enson, Erskine, Fleming, Forbes, Gissing, Gissinge, Grant, Gravett, Kindelan, Lutwich, Lutwyche, Macelester, M'More, M'Vean, Mathews, Mounsey, Newby, Ory, Parker, Pomfree, Richardson, Rivett, *Rolls, Ross, Row, Salmon, Serres, *Sheehy, Warham, Warrand, Whetham, White, Wyrrall.
3. Neal.
4. Ap-Howell, Blaw, Butler, *Cleather, Cruikshank, *Cruikshanks, Ewart, Hartagan, Hartigan, Johnston, Johnstone, Macalister, Macdonald, McGuire, Richardson.
5. Harben, *Harbin.
6. Busfield, Hughes, Jouatt, Juatt, Nelson, Wynn, *Wynne.
7. Baring, Bushell, Funeaux, Jury, Lovejoy, M'Kall.
8.*Buchanan.
9. Armstrong, Carmichael, *Ferguson, *Heley, *Helly, *Hely, *Kemble, *Kinge, *Montgomery, Purefoy, Bagwell-Purefoy.
10. Bremer.
11.*Carmichael, Chapman, Dowde, Dymock, Hawley, *Jones, Ligh, McGillikelly, Macknight, Omond, Taylor, White.
12.*Barnes, *Gibson-Wright, Huntercomb, Salmon.
13. Ramsden.
14. Ewart, Gorely, Gorley, Greaves, *Grimshaw, Hussey, Lawnde, Macdonald, M'Donald, *Parnther, Rich, *Thomson.

PLATE 211.—1. M'Kenny.
2. Cannynge, Carnegie, M'Mahon.
3.*Shuttleworth.
4. Fane, Fay, Fleming, Heffer, Jee, Kearney, Meverell, O'Hartagan, Philips, Pinkton, Slater, Smallman.
5. Howe.
6. Anstice, Anstis.
7. Barney, Blackwall, *Bremner, Brymer, Ceely, Ceily, Chape, Chappe, Chappes, Darling, Fillingham, Kerby.
8.*Carney, Pearson-Gee.
9.*Bannester, *Bannister, Eeles, *Forbes, *Harrison, *Jones, Kirby, *Latouche, *La Touche.
10. Hughes.
11.*Barre, *Barrey, *Cheston, During.
14. Bonnett, Dunkin, M'Alister, Macdonald, M'Donald, *MacDonnell, Storr, Thompson.

PLATE 212.—1. Burnham, Daviss, Denston, Floyer, Wauch, Waugh, Williams, Witty.
2.*Chisholm, Dumbreck, Gooden-Chisholm.
3. Alexander, Aylet, Baines, Berrey, Budge, Campbell, Charteris, *Chenevix, Clark, Dalmahoy, Dunlop, Erskine, Finlay, Gallaway, Galloway, Ganstin, Gordon, Gorman, Keith, Loftus, Macdonald, Mackenzie, M'Clambroch, McLandsborough, Monteath, Monteith, Neale, Neilson, Noble, O'Neylan, Pearce, Pillans, Rolland, Rowan, Scarth, *Sheill,

*Shiell, Skeen, Smith, Stewart, Tait, Washborne, *Weir, Cosans-Weir, Whitacre, White, Williamson
4. *Caulfield, Chapman, Colles, Colvil, Colville, Ingle, Lander, Lyell, *Peters
5 Chandlee, *Boswall
6. Chapman, Clancy, Coles, Etton, *Forbes, Gwyn, Leslie, Lyon, *O'Clancy, O'Neylan
7 Daniel, Johnson, Lockhart, O'Neill, O'Sheil
8 Patrick
9. Adlard, Arnot, Arrat, Arrot, Bailie, Baines, Barclay, Bayn, Bayne, Binney, Binny, Campbell, Chisholme, Clarke, Coape, Cocke, Coke, Collow, Cookes, Crabtree, Cross Buchanan, Donaldson, Douglas, Dowine, Dunlop, Durno, Eccleston, Eclestone, Erskine, Ewart, Falls, *Feney, Ferguson, Fitchet, Flanagan, *Forbes, Garstin, Gelstable, Gillet, Goodenough, Gosset, Gossett, Graham, Grant, Gray, Halxton, Hamilton, Hardie, Houston, Jolleff, Jolliff, Karr, Kennedy, Ker, *Kilpatrick, King, *Kirkpatrick, Kyrklot, Lamond, Leeky, Lurty, Lyell, M'Alaster, Macalister, M'Caa, M'Casker, M'Caskill, Macdonald, M'Donald, M'Dowal, M'Entire, Macgregor, M'Gregor, M'Intyre, Mackay, M'Kenzie, *Mackey, Mackie, McLoskie, Macpherson - Grant, M'Quie, Martin, Menteath, Morrogh, Naish, Pagan, Paterson, Peitere, Peter, Picard, Pillans, Reoch, Rymer, Scobie, Shaw, Stewart, Stobart, Toll, Tolle, Tonyn, Urquhart, Williamson
10 *Mico.
11 Beltoft, Beltofts, Brougham, Broughan, Bronhan, Brouchan, Grosse, Jager, Limsay, Limsey, MacBrayne, M'Brayne, O'Neale, Rourk, Stack
12 Downton, Grantham, Hance, Lamb, *M'Clellan
13 Alexander, Barclay, Bontein, *Booty, Bragge, Brettridge, Broge, Brogg, Broige, Brown, Bruce, Buchanan, Bunten, Clevland, Coddington, Cumine, Cumming, Dickson, Dixon, Dogherty, Doherty, Donaldson, Dotson, Dunlop, Duthie, Dwire, Erskine, *Ewart, Fergusson, Finley, Ganlard, Gardiner, Gay, Gerdelley, Gerdillv, Gillanders, Gleig, Gordon, Groseth, Gunn, Guthrie, Harington Stuart, Harte, Innes, Keir, Kennedy, Kincaid, Kragg, Lancaster, Linning, Livingston, Livingstone, Lizurs, Lumisden, Lumsden, M'Aul, M'Barnet, M'Breid, M'Call, M'Crae, M'Cray, *MacGeorge, Mackenzie, M'Kenzie, Macmillan, MacMillam, MacRae, Macreadie, Macready, Martin, Meres, More, Muirc, Mure, Neasmith, Neill, Neylan, Nixon, *O'Brien, O'Dogherty, O'Doherty, O'Dwyer, Ogilvie, O'Hart, O'Neylan, Oranmore, Oxtoby, Parker, Peachey, Peart, Perring, Peterson, Pillans, Primrose, Rains, Rashleigh, Reader, Riky, Romanes, Rowan, Salmon, Scholey, Seaton, Sharples, Sibbald, Spiers, Stewart, Stuart, Thom, Walmsley, Whetwell, Whitelock, Whiteway, Whyte
14 *Ascough, *Askew, Athelstan, Athelston, *Ayscough, *Maclellan

PLATE 213 — 1 Choiseul, Fitz-Maurice, Grossett, Halcro, Millan, Murehead, Pegriz.
2 Lamplugh
3 Buchanan, Carthch, Depden, Fitz-Simon, Greetham, Heaven, Leckie, Lickie, Lizurs, M'Kenzie, Macmillan, MacMillan
4 Campbell, *Dudgeon, Grandson, *Hamilton, Hume, Hume Campbell, Kearns, Laidlay, Lomax, Macgregor, Orr, Paley, Peters, Taylor
5 Adderton, Aderton, Ainslie, *Avanet, *Avenel, *Avenett, Balmanno, Blackwood, Brice, Browell, Bruce, Bryce, Buchanan, Campbell, Carsain, Clark, *Clinton, Cobb, Cobbe, Cockburn, *Couper, Cowper, Dale, Dalyell, Dalziel, Dalziell, Damerley, Dammant, *Demeschines, Dickson, *Dixon, Dowglas, Duncan, Elliot, Elliott, Foreman, Forman, Garmish, *Garneys, Garnish, Gordon, Hamilton, Hart, Heart, Heeley, Heely, Inglis, Jollie, Lambford, Lamford, M'Aully, M'Hado, M'Haddo, M'Kay, *M'Kell, *Macnamara, M'Rach, Macrae, Martin, Masterton, Mastertown, Matheson, De Meschines, De Mowbray, Nelson, Niblie, Nock, Ogilvie, Pim, Rennie, Renny, Richards, Sawers, Shield, Shortreed, *Smyth, Stewart, Strachan, Vile, Wall, Wecks, Wemyss, Welsh
6 Abbot, Abbott, *Cauvin, *Creagh, *Crownall, *Edgar, *Garvin, *Hardie
7 *Barwis, Brady
8 Abbetot, *Brice, Mace, Montchantsey, Mountchansey
9 Cusacke, Durward, *Hamilton, Hirst, Hurste
10. King, Mulvihill, O'Mulvihill
11 *Billcliffe, *Bligh, *Blighe, *Drake, Rankin, Wright
12 Blondell, Cadicott, Colet, Drake, Drake-Garrard, Drumson, Forbes, Gessors, Jeynes, *Joynt, Lapp, Law, Milburne, Ommaney, Pomfrett, Pritchard, Revett, *Rivett, Ryvett, Scott, Stane, Symmonds, Symonds, Waddington, Willey, Willy

PLATE 214 — 1 Elliot, Elliott, Gordon, Mather, Tarell
2 Berkenhead, Boland, Cranber, Dennis, *Grassick, Hatch, *Packenham, Parnell
3 *Bliss, Boon, Boone, Brodie, Brody, *Curtis, De Brevill, *Gordon, *Haitlie, *Harber, *Hassall, Hassell, *Hoddenet, *Hoddenot, Keegan, Kendall, Leder, *Moorman, Orchard, Rayner, Samborne, Vardon, *Welborne, Winford, *Winston, Winstone
4 Barberie, Barberrie, Billam, *Brassey, Cantilon, Clerke, Collis, Colt, Cuthbert, Devoike, Edmerston, Elliot, Elliott, Gemmel, Gordon, Harris, Hawberke, Holand, *Honnyton, Joy, M'Culloch, M'Kenzie, Mackenzie, Main, Portington, Prowze, See, Smart, Stair, Stephen, Winder, Yeoman, *Young
5 Buchannan, Colley, Grensby, Grymsby, *Macklow, Nicholl
6 Adderton, Atherton, *Apifer, Baker, *Brotherton, *Cart, Collier, Erskine, *Gyles, *Gylls, Haggard, *Hanwell, Inckpen, Inkpen, Pronde, *Pychard, Raeburn, Reaburn, Samson, Skea, Thornes, Wilton
7 Ward
8 Fairbairn
9 Armestrang, Armstrang, Armstrong, Bigwood, Fellowes, Fields, Fitz-Symond, Fitz Water, Horwood, Hyrson, Knight, Lillie, Maddock, Neill, Oxenbridge, Wodehouse
10 Abadam, Anwick, Cockburn, Despard, Donkin, Douglas, Ferguson, Fergusson, *Genevile, *Jetter, *Kirwan, Krowton, Lang, O'Fahy, O'Fay, Remington, Scott, Scott Douglas
11 Buchanan, Campbell, Cuthbert, *Dalzell, Dinwordy, Donwike, Drummound, Eliot, Eliott Lockhart, Elliot, Elliott Lockhart, Ferguson, Fitz - Hamon, Graham, Hamilton, Hart, *Lowis, *M Cormick, Neilson, Nelson, Omond, Onion, Puckle, Salmond, Scot, Slesser, Swan, Walsh, Watkins, Winch, Yeamans, Yeomans, Younger
12 Baad, Bad, Goldesborough, Goldsbrough, Puller, Turbott, Turbutt
13 Brind, Dobbyn, Fergus, Macrath
14. *Burrard, Hamilton, Neale-Burrard

PLATE 215 — 1 Argum, Argun, Argune, Brewer, Briwere, *Houblon, Molloy, Poulden, Reade, Reid
2 Dauntsey, Dickenson, Geale, Sabine, Westly
3 Dobie, Gilmer, Gilmour, Lutwidge, MacMaure, Sayers
4 Broun, Brown, *M'Maught, Meldrum, Milne, Mosman, Mossman, Mylne, Park, Scott, Sibbald
5 *Albrecht, *Amerie, *Aynscomb, *Aynscamp, *Brown - Borthwick, *Browne Borthwick, *Carnock, Charpentier, *Clifford, Elder, *Fitzgilbert, *Frodham, *Gilbert, *Hoppey, Lamont, Lowste, *Moone, *Stace
6 Bain, Bayne, Corbreake, Corbreyke, Crockford, Dundas, Hadderwick, Keith, Lew, *Murray, Pecham, Peckham, Plenderleith, *Podmore, Purdie, Scott, Stevenson
7 Campbell, Card, *Catley, Colwick, Colwyke, Kilvington, Lee
8 Hayhurst
9 Coombes, Coombs, Horan, Locke, Lundin, Purchas
10 Applewhaite, Brown, Crewe, Gordon, Mercer, Millar, Miller, *Morris, *Park, Peat, Peit, Rae, Ralph, Reid, Salthouse, Shenton, Stephens
11 Ambros, Ambrose, Ambross, Callandar, Callander, Callender, Colditcott, M'Braid, Patishull, Pattishall, *Prydeux
12 Patrick
13 Ambrose, Dixon
14 Calender, Callander

PLATE 216 — 1 Aberdeen, Cantwell, Hay, Hereford, Love, *Mathew, Nottingham, Scott, Wager, Wastley
2 De Bryan, Cheyn, Cheyne, Dennett, Duff, Fromond, Fromont, Gilles, Gow, Hagarty, Johnston, Jopling, Joppling, Lowther, Nottingham, Pape, Wichington, Witchingham
3 Balnaves, Balneaves, Bedford, Erdington, Hall, Seth

4. Bedell-Sivright, Carnegie, Holgrave, Holgreve, Hulgrave, Keith, Moderby, Sievewright, Sievwright.
5. Cowan.
6. Ball, Balle, Gillon, Hallom, Handfield, Scobell, Sommerville, Wastoile, Wastoyle.
7. Dundas, Odingsells.
8. Carson, Cathcart, Clater, Elliot, Elliott, Kernaby, Knows, Lees, Losh, Martin, Napier, Robertson, Smellie.
9. Bruce, Cathcart, Cochran, Cochrane, Darling, Davidson, Douglas, *Douglass, Drummond, Hamilton, Leak, Scott, Whytt.
10. Douglass, Henderson, *Henriesch.
11. Allen, Alleyn.
12.*Hawthorn, Henderson, *Skettew.
13. Harvey.
14. Balderston, Balderstones, Crauford, Craufurd, Crawford, Crawforde, Downman, Kincaid, Stirling.

PLATE 217.—1. Cheeseman, Chesman, *Clayhills, *Forbes-Robertson, Glasgow, M'Robertson, Patmer, Robertson, Wallpoole, Walpole.
2. Buchanan, Buchannan, M'Casland.
3. Brocton, Gaven, Gawen, *M'Auslane, Sainsbury, Varnham.
4.*Bagshawe, Balvaird, Blaverhasset, Bryson, Burn, Burns, Forrester, Hacklet, Hackluit, Limborne, Petit.
5. Bazeley, Bazley, Drew, Pridham, Robb, Savory.
6. Dickenson, Hay.
7. Belson, Britain, Collyear, Crowgay, Crutwell, Dun, Dunn, Hairstanes, Hallet, Harestains, Stewart.
8. Adam, Alderington, Aldrington, *Anley, Aiton, Ayton, Connor, Hawker, Horn, Horne, M'Adam, Whelpdale.
9.*Eliott, Elliot, Elliott, M'Crummen.
10. Alexander, Anderson, Baillie, Carlyle, *Dick, Don, Elphingston, Gamage, Gordon, Hamilton, Huddlestone, Keith, Leslie, Mitchell, Paterson, Patterson, Popkin, Scott, Screvener, Scrivener, Scrivenor, Shaw, Smith, Sym, Syme, Tindal, Whittuck, Whytock, Wilson, Young.
11. Broadbent, Cancelor, Candisheler, Compigne, English, Felter, Laird, Lance, Lennie, Leny, Minshaw, Paddon, Fugges, Ramsey, Shaw, Sutcliffe, Sysington.
12. Armour, Arweil, Arwell, Binns, Clapham, Clepan, Clephan, Clephane, Coats, Eustace, Power, Turing.
13. Alexander, *Chalmers, Cleghorn, Norse, Rennie, Renny-Tailyour, Timmins.
14. Bristed, Campbell, Chuter, M'Kechnie, Powerton, Rankine.

PLATE 218.—1.*Bevens, Elphinstone, Ennys.
2. Bennet, Bennett, Doeg, Giffard, Goldie, Grove, Hyett, Manson, Pearle, Seton-Steuart, Steuart, Stewart.
3. Byrn, Byrne, Dell, Gipps, Neville, Riches, Robertson, Tapper.
4. Cooper, *Couper, Cowper, *Creeck, Graeme, Graham, Heriot, Krag, Kragg, Mackenzie, M'Kenzie, Scott-Mitchell, Mitchell, Pearson, Robertson, Ross, Simpson, Skeen, Skene, Stevenson, White, Wodderspoon.
5. Boxstead, Boxsted, Considine, Craigdallie, Crean, Crosse, Dowler, Durham.
6. Beekenshall, Couper, Krog, Kroge, Luttrell, Moncur, Purefoy, Pureferoy.
7. Bradfield, Corfield, Gairden, Jacomb, Maude, Ockley.
8. Parsons.
9. Bunting, *Dickenson, Hulbert, Larayne, Lareyn, Spilman, Staines, Stephenson, Stevenson.
10. Bain, Champeroun, Falshaw, Keirie, Loggie, Logy, Macartney, M'Cartnay, Maccartney, Mackartney, Nechure, Paton, Peters, Rose, Ross, Sherwood.
11. Brogden, Clutterbuck, Crause, Lusy, Taunton, Wolfall, Yvain.
12. Duheaume, *Macartney, Reynes, *White.
13. Aiton, Aitoun, Aytoun, Flemyng, Flemynge, Fresell, Fresill, Girdler, Hamelen, Hamelin, Hamelyn, Hamlyng, Hardman, Loudon, Ross, Tilson.
14. Crookshank, Dunbar, *Eynford, *Eynsworth, Hellis, Howe, Howes, Howse, Riddel, Tinline.

PLATE 219.—1. Hoe, Hoo, Lang.
2. Brash, Brecknock, Brecknoy, Burmey, Lill, Losack.
3. Copeland, Copland, Cowpland, Kenneday, *Kennedy.
4. Hearle, Lammie, L'Amy, Lavers, Prior, *Roger.
5. Grame.
6. Arnold, Besiles, Besills, Hazlewood, Mein, Silver, Winchester.
7.*Areskin, *Bown, *Coombes, *Coombs, Denistoun, Dennestoun, Dennistoun, *Emenfield, *Enfield, *Ged, *Maul, *Rokeby, *Shields, *Shiells.
8. Sheppard.
9. Andrews, Balfour, Brenchley, Buchanan, Calderwood, *Clerke, Commerell, *Dalling, *Dickinson, Dobbin, Fane, Fitz-John, *Grant, Hay, Kempston, Killegroue, Laurie, Lindsay, Livingstone, Maccartney, Mercy, Ness, Oliver, *Paterson, Patrick, Shipley, Tansley.
10. Cuningham, Cunningham, Essington, Grislay.
11. Burnet, Caldron, Calwood, Caunter, Ecton, Elder, Fidler, Maynard, Montgomery, Ogilvie, Ogilvy, Palmes, Seagrave, Seagrove, Shiers, Willmott.
12. Keith.
13. Cumine, Cumming, Dusautoy, Gallagher, Geekie, Hayton, Hore, Horem, Pyrke, Quartermains.
14. Hamilton.

PLATE 220.—1. Cole, Colle, Crotty, Hinckes, Hincks, Hinks.
2. Biggs, Bowyer, Denis, Flynn, *Herbert, Herworth, Leach, Leche, *Leech, *Leich, Leitch, MacVais, Nowell, Vaughan, Yarworth.
3. Peper, Twining.
4. Butts, Cairne, Garvine, Gibbens, Gibbins, Gibbons, Grayley, Grelley, Haddock, Hollier, Peat.
5. Cotterall, Cotterell, Cotterill, Dunbar, Grove, Inge, Lambart.
6. Cussans, De Cusance, Jackson, Le Hunt, Lockhart.
7. Blossom, Blossome, Chadwell, Dyas, Glen, Grigg, Suter.
8. Spigernell, Spygernell, Spickernell.
9. Andrew, Baker, Garnett, Gigon, Jorcey, Jorge, *Michel, Morgan, Pelton, Polton.
10.*Chattock, Cockes, Cokes, Mayner, Minors, Mynors, Rowed, Shattock, Tawke.
11. Bigberry, Bigbury, Bygbery, Rumford.
12. Bundy, Hynd, Jervys, *Molineux, Mynors, Napier, Rynell.

PLATE 221.—1.*Mayne, Panting.
2. Bidwell, Bydewell, Drummond, Hawkey, Oliver.
3. Ferris, Kellock, Mayo.
4. Batten, Francklyn, Higson, Laborer, Labruer, Mewis, Pycroft.
5. Poyntz.
6. Blacke, Brandeston, Bree, Colliver, Hogg, Kerdiston, Kerdston, Witt.
7.*Bisset, Cormick, De Den, De Dena, Ironside.
8. Bertrand, Blandford, Hesding, Port, Porte, Semple.
9. Albrecht, Albreght, Clifford, Deram, *Entwisle, Graham, Kenton, M'Donell, Macdonell, M'Donnell.
10. Atwood, Blood, Forrest, Letton, M'Connell, M'Daniel, M'Gougan, Rowed, Thomson, Wylidon.
11.*Bewcham, *Bewebam, Gerwood.
12. Adingstoun, Adinston, Anby, Anbley, *Andby, *Aubley, *Aubly, Barber, Bennet, Boyes, Callwell, Corben, Corbin, Corbyn, Edwards, Egmanton, *Tailour.
13. Down, Downs, Garstin, Hamerton, Naesmith, Naesmyth, Nasmyth.
14. Adam, Balsillie, Barber, Bonsall, Burn, Costley, Cromie, Dene, Drayton, Erskine, Figgins, Francklin, *Mace-Gigger, *Iley, *Illey, *Iney, King, Lint, M'Clesh, M'Donald, *M'Larty, Rattary, Rattray, Rowe, *Seabrook, Shepheard, Sheppard, Sheridan, Taylor, *Tailyour, Thomson, Warcop, Wickenden.

PLATE 222.—1. Boyd, Dingham.
2. Hollins.
3. Aaron, Aarons, Aaroons, Aron, *Fidelow, Roachead.
4. Borthwick, Davell, Dawson, Edmunds, Eglefelde, Eglefield, Lundin, Mather, Mein, Redege, Ridge.
5. Harvey.
6. Blizard, Blizzard, Boyer, Boyes, Dymond, Ogilvie.
7. Bumstead, Bumsted, Charrington, Corke, Knyvett, Oswald.
8. Meldon.
9. Gray-Farquhar.
10. Babb, Babe, Boyd, Dennie, Denny, Lochead, Lochhead, Purvis.
11. Bell, Boyd, Garvie, Kassye, *King, Logie, Miller, Tough.
12. Fraser, Miller, *Nelson, Oliphant, O'Selbae, Scollay, Simpson.
13. Mein.
14. Althoun, Bate, Bates, Birn, Brin, Clifford, *Colpoys, Cromie, Duine, Dun, Dunbar, Duncanson, Farquhar, Farrell, *Ferrall, Gaylard, Gayner, Gaynor, Glenton, Gun, Hand,

Handasyd Handyside, Handysyde Hog, Howatson, Howison, King Lamond Lamont Landen, Lilly MacFarquhar, M'Farquhar MacManus McManus MacMoran, Malden Mare Middleton *Myddleton, Neimeneill Neimenell Nevemenell, O Ferral-More, *O'More Patrick, Prescot, Prescott, Shields, Sibbald Watson, Woodroffe

PLATE 223 —1 Bishopston, Bowen, *Bucknel, *Bucknell, *Fishacre
2 Carnie, Constable, Hoyland, Kilby Lorimer
3 Bucton Bunbury, *Cleghorn, Dornvile, Graham *Ingledew
4 Avison, Birnie, Gidion, Harden, Hardin Longman
5 Behethland, Bricken Durban Durbin, Freeth, Gernon Gernoun Gernun
6 Balderstone, Banderston Banderstone, Bennet, Cornelius, Donald Geney, Genny, Jacket, Jeny, Myreton *Narford
7 Broomfield, Browning, Butterworth, Crook Incleden, Ingleton
8 Hawkesworth, Hawksworth, Hutton
9 *Freeth, *Horwood, *Knight *Oxenbridge
10 *Bonshaw, Branfill, *Devetts, *Lee, Netthorpe Russell
11 Ansdell Basier, Basire Bonekill, Cleeve, Clive, Colquhoun Garscadden, Skirvin, Skirving, Stewart
12 Baker, Casey, Cochran, Cochrane, Lark, Larke, Trusbut

PLATE 224 —1 Armesburg, Armesbury, Cridland Hamilton, Hardisty Haulton, M Kenzie, Payne, Strange, Wescope, Westcope, Westcott
2 Alexander, Buchanan, Haulton, Hurot, Hurt Lestrange, Liston Strange, Wayland, Wedgewood
3 *Burns *Bussell, Ducat Duchet, *Hamilton
4 Cox, Deleland, Deland, Desland Dowker, Steuart, Stewart
5 Espinasse, Fiennes, Haskins
6 Watson
7 Cheverell, Cheverill, *Cross, Innes, Napier
8 Dalziel Somervile Somerville
9 Harbour, *Kirtland, Morehead, Morrison, Muirhead, Penrey
10 Cavenagh, Coulthurst, Dowdeswell, Jago, Lear, Watson
11 Cary, Estmerton, Fenner, Foxall Gairden, Garden Gardyne, Gourlie
12 Day, Derham, Downer, Flin, Flinn Lidel, Raynor
13 Anwil, Anwyl, Culchech, Culcheth, House, *Killowe, *Kiloh, Myreton, Spence
14 Glasford
15 Cubit, Cubitt, Dowse

PLATE 225 —1 Hallen
2 Gleadow
3 Rylands
4 Jones
5 Hudson
6 Ryland
7 De Massue
8 Jenkins
9 Edwards
10 Kynaston, Ognell, *Wigston
11 Hanbury
12 Oliver

PLATE 226 —1 Roberts
2 Bigg
3 Gibbons
4 Wade
5 Lamb
6 Wade
7 *Gardiner, Pagrave, *Wade, Wither
8 Lane
9 See Plate 127, No 2
10 Girdlestone
11 Pooll
12 Gillman *Stanley
13 Burroughs, *Watson
14 *Mocklow, Mucklow

PLATE 227 —1 Gill
2 Shepherd
3 Gill, Gyll
4 Gladdish, Simpson
5 German
6 Gist
7 Grane
8 Goodhart
9 Gammon, Gamon, Glenester
10 Gosse
11 *Cooke, Lyaton Leaton
12 Gilpin
13 Smith
14 Simpson
15 Sharp

PLATE 228 —1 Cawthra
2 Anderton
3 Jackson
4 Burt
5 Dyce
6 Bereel Boreel, Burell, Burrell, Reichenberg
7 Bessemer
8 Dyce
9 Delaplaunch, Fennel, Fennell, Forrester, *Grenford, Loudon, De la Plaunch
10 Archer, Dod, Dode Johnson
11 Agard, Aigles, Amiel, *Ankyrsley, Aygle Bagshaw, Bellingham, Billson Billson Bradshaw, *Bryan, Corney, Curle, Currel, Daunt, Done, Dove, Duncan, Forrester, Glasfurd, Goatham, Greenhalgh, Grenehalgh, Haggarth, *Hall, Holding, Horn, Horne *Hornby, Hull Hunt, Hunter Kyd, Kyde Logan, Lothian Lowde Lowthian Newport, Pierie Pourie Povey, Powrie, Price, Purie, Sclater Sherd Wait Waite, Waith, *Walton, Wayte, Whetstone
12 Denison

PLATE 229 —1 Green
2 Brettell
3 Lawless
4 Maskelyne
5 Story
6 Peters
7 Ozanne
8 Parsons
9 Pidcock
10 Phillips, Phillips-Treby
11 Tailby
12 Williamson

PLATE 230 —1 Wood
2, 3, and 4 Mainwaring-Ellerker-Onslow
5 Lancaster
6 Lancaster
7 Muntz
8 Marsh
9 George
10 Fletcher
11 Pemberton
12 Gentleman
13 Crookes
14 Gell
15 James
16 Pinckney
17 Slade
18 Smith
19 Larken
20 Prater

PLATE 231 —1 Gibbs
2 Bathurst
3 Stourton
4 Cox
5 Bedford
6 Marryatt
7 De Worms
8 Hart
9 Dixon
10 Pryse
11 Lethbridge
12 Malet
13 Seccombe
14 Bailey
15 Cloete
16 Dutton
17 Montefiore
18 Hooper
19 Cooper
20 Dunn
21 Tarleton

PLATE 232 —1 Swinton
2 Maconochie
3 Berry
4 Reid
5 Grant
6 Polson
7 Banbury.
8 Stuart
9 Barlow

PLATE 233 —1 Vaughan
2 Snow
3 Baldwin
4 Barrington-White
5 Armstrong
6 Caldwell
7 Crisp
8 Lawson
9 Ewart
10 Batten, Chisholm-Batten
11 Story
12 Scarisbrick
13 Thurston

14. Tillard.
15 and 16. Worsley-Taylor.

PLATE 234.—1. Brunner.
2. Armstrong.
3. Austin.
4. Bellew.
5. Buckley.
6. Fry.
7. Hawkins.
8. Barry.
9. Boehm.
10. Heathcote.
11. Farrer.
12. Barran.

PLATE 235.—1. Hollist.
2. McAdam-Smith.
3. Bell.
4. Vickers.
5. Bird.
6. Emmott.
7. Gribble.
8. Jackson.
9. Marsden.
10. Grove.
11. Wotherspoon.
12. Rawson.
13 and 14. Reid-Cuddon.
15. Steere.
16. Taylor.
17. Liston-Foulis.
18. Hulley.
19. Fitch.
20. Campbell.

PLATE 236.—1. Burrows.
2. Brougham.
3. Hugessen.
4. Beach.
5. Agnew.
6. Handcock.
7. Beevor.
8. Burrard.
9. Cochrane.
10 and 11. Richardson-Bunbury.
12. Lubbock.

PLATE 237.—1. Neame.
2. Bate.
3. Burney.
4. Battie-Wrightson.
5. Illingworth.
6. Thompson.
7. Pyke.
8. Sillifant.
9. Shackleton.
10 and 11. Pretor-Pinney.
12. Samuelson.
13 and 14. Price-Davies.
15 and 16. Blackburne, Maze.
17. Uniacke.
18. Anstruther.
19. Cadman.

PLATE 238.—1. Gurdon.
2. Gould.
3. Goldthorpe.
4. Joubert de la Ferté.
5. Dumas.
6. Harvey.
7. Colfox.
8. Dimsdale.
9. Davies.
10. Culley.
11. Maddocks.
12. Marshall.
13. Monk.
14. Yerburgh.
15. Riky.
16. Verelst.

PLATE 239.—1. Boord.
2. Baring.
3. Gardner.
4. Bagge.
5. Arthur.
6. Crawley-Boevey.
7 and 8. Houston-Boswall.
9. Powlett.
10. Scarlett.
11. Affleck.
12. Arnott.

PLATE 240.—1. McKerrell.
2 and 3. Mostyn.
4. Lockett.
5. Aldersey.
6. Firbank.
7. Duff.
8. Finny.
9. Marshall.
10. Upton.
11. Hordern.
12. Moore.
13. Somers.
14. Ramsden.
15. Hussey.

PLATE 241.—1. Lippitt.
2. Emerson.
3. Kyd.
4. Bates.
5. Freston.
6. Gorst.
7. Temple.
8. Liddell.
9. Harrison.
10. Wykeham.
11. Hanson.
12. Ball.
13. Annesley.
14. Burlton.
15. Crosse.
16. Debenham.

PLATE 242.—1. Greene.
2. Chubb.
3. Dunn.
4 and 5. Fletcher-Boughey.
6. Coppen.
7. Fayrer.
8. Pile.
9. Gibson.

PLATE 243.—1, 2, and 3. Goldsmid-Stern-Salomons.
4. Ross-of-Bladensburg.
5 and 6. Stanier.
7. Hutt.
8. Baggaley.
9. Dundas.
10 and 11. Yeatman-Biggs.
12. Kenney.
13 and 14. Harrison-Broadley.
15 and 16. Moore-Gwyn.
17 and 18. Prescott-Decie.
19. Tweedy.
20. Ormsby.

PLATE 244.—1. Ashworth.
2. Barnard.
3. Reynolds.
4. Abraham.
5. Edwards.
6. Marshall.
7. Rivington.
8. Harris.
9. Kitson.
10. Boulton.
11. Ames.
12. Cookson.
13. Porter.
14. Clegg.
15. Colman.
16. Hopgood.
17. Bancroft.
18. Corbett.
19. Marten.
20. Heyworth.

PLATE 245.—1. Cubitt.
2. Webster.
3. Blackwood.
4. Addington.
5. Bertie.
6. Barrow.
7. Gibbs.
8. Blomefield.
9. Hood.
10. White.
11 and 12. Havelock-Allen.

PLATE 246.—1. Malcolm.
2. Noakes.
3. Woosnam.
4. Charlton.
5. Chance.
6. Edwards.
7. Ebblewhite.
8. Fitzherbert.
9. Foster.
10. Grinlinton.
11. Hodsoll.
12 and 13. Hutton.
14. Wyatt.
15 and 16. Ross.
17 and 18. Hulton-Harrop.
19 and 20. Meade-King.

PLATE 247.—1. Barttelot.
2. De Trafford.
3. Guise.
4. Bond.
5. Hutton.
6. Carnegie.
7. Rolls.
8. Strutt.
9. Galloway.
10, 11, and 12. Bartlett-Burdett-Coutts.
13. Sykes.
14 and 15. Hunter-Weston.
16 and 17. Lingard-Monk.

PLATE 248.—1. Lee.
2. Strutt.
3. Birkbeck.
4. Clarke.

5 De la Rue
6 Buxton
7 Grattan
8 Mansergh.
9 Butler

PLATE 249 —1 Goodfellow
2 Freeman
3 Floyer
4 Ellis
5 Dillon
6 Croxton
7 Cleland
8 Cawston
9 Casement
10 Cartland
11 Byass
12 Body
13 Beridge
14 Arden
15 Durning-Lawrence
16 Hart
17 Radcliffe
18 Lees
19 Sheffield
20 Dawson

PLATE 250 —1 Wrightson
2 Tindal
3 Bethell
4 Wood
5 Willis-Bund.
6 Wigan
7 Stubbs
8 Wright
9 Smith
10 Tomkinson
11 Liddell
12 Sloggett
13 Bushby
14 Bassett
15 Ballingall
16 Smith
17 James
18 Blyth
19 Rendel
20 Gilbey

PLATE 251 —1 Barrington
2 Sturt
3 Burnett
4 Hickman
5 Barlow
6 Berney
7 Aird
8 Abel
9 Bowman
10 Eden
11 Broadbent
12 Littlehales

PLATE 252 —1 Wilson
2 Williams
3 Whineray
4 Vickers
5 Staniland
6 Smith
7 Cosby
8 Saunders
9 Salisbury
10 Rickards
11 Richardson
12 Mylechreest
13 Marples
14 Bateman
15 Kelly
16 Joslin
17 Johnson
18 Jary
19 Harris
20 Gutch

PLATE 253 —1 Barton
2 Kater
3 Stancourt
4 Griffith
5 and 6 Wilson-Barkworth
7 Molion
8 Gwatkin
9 Osmand
10 Hall
11 Sandford.
12 Bolding
13 Carter
14 Ranking
15 Dalby
16 Foote
17 and 18 Fisher-Rowe
19 and 20 Davenport-Handley.
21 Cartwright
22 Image
23 Glazebrook.
24 Wright

PLATE 254 —1 Brocklehurst
2 Cameron
3 Bingham
4 Chamberlain
5 Blois
6 Barrymore
7 Brown
8 Brisco
9 Bazley
10 Beaumont
11 Brodie
12 Hervey

PLATE 255 —1 Watson
2 Wearing
3 Gamble
4 Watts
5 Gray
6 Gibb
7 Yorke
8 Pontifex
9 Leeming
10 Pearce-Edgcumbe
11 Moresby
12 Sterry
13 Pickering
14 Mitchell
15 Bolton
16 Thomas
17 Younger
18 Wright
19 Bourne
20 Griffith

PLATE 256 —1 Martin
2 Tylden Pattenson
3 Radford
4 Lee
5 Ince
6 Holbrow
7 Harvey
8 Harris
9 Hall-Watt
10 Hales
11 Gray
12 Galpin
13 Fisher
14 Farren
15 Clarke
16 Cornwall
17 Bowman
18 Bell
19 Wyndham
20 Woollan

PLATE 257 —1 Eaton
2 Brocklebank
3 Cave
4 Carew
5 Flower
6 Edwards
7 and 8 Levy-Lawson
9 Chisholm
10 Parnell
11 Carbutt
12 Lowry

PLATE 258 —1 and 2 Fitz-gerald-Wilson
3 and 4 Walthall
5 Charrington
6 Oldfield
7 Von Stieglitz.
8 Crossman
9 Hobson
10 Aikenhead
11 Marks
12 Wood
13 Verschoyle
14 Keays-Young
15 Dale
16 Creyke
17 Lloyd
18 Whinyates.
19 Laidlay
20 Tilney

PLATE 259.—1. Bradford
2 Duke
3 Field
4 Backhouse
5 FitzGerald
6 Feilden
7 Clarke
8 Wigram, Fitzwygram
9 Cunard
10 Gurdon
11 Gardner
12 Stonor

PLATE 260 —1 Weldon
2 Bridgman
3 Nickisson
4 Hepworth
5 Hardy
6 Wakeman
7 Fellows
8 Earle
9 Kenyon
10 Carlyon
11 Howard
12 North
13 Barnard
14 À Beckett
15 Tidswell
16 Martin
17 Pedder
18 Richards

19. Buddicom.
20. Howard.

PLATE 261.—1. Robinson.
2. Mellor.
3. Master.
4. Utermarck.
5. Stubs.
6. Rowcliffe.
7. Roberts.
8. Ritson.
9. Tweedy.
10. Riley.
11. White.
12. Samuel.
13. Sewell.
14. Sewell.
15. Woollcombe.
16. Alford.
17. Williamson.
18. Richardson.
19. Sidebottom.
20. Ricarde-Seaver.

PLATE 262.—1. Crossley.
2. Evans.
3. Forwood.
4. Church.
5. Collet.
6. Dorington.
7. Brett.
8. Dixon.
9. Durand.
10. Freake.
11. Dimsdale.
12. Elphinstone.

PLATE 263.—1. Burtchaell.
2. Butler.
3. Boyce.
4. Bewes.
5. Bolster.
6. Allen.
7 and 8. Baghot-de-la-Bere.
9. Campbell.
10. Barcroft.
11. Craig.
12. Darbishire.
13. Farish.
14. Evans.
15. Mackesy.
16. Horniman.

PLATE 264.—1. Mylne.
2. Britton.
3. Shuckburgh.
4. Vaile.
5. Townsend.
6. Straker.
7. Smith-Shand.
8. Colvin.
9. Kemball.
10. Thring.
11. Fenton-Livington.
12. Farncombe-Tanner.
13. Davey.
14. Coulson.
15. Baines.
16. Carruthers.

PLATE 265.—1. Mayhew.
2. Martin.
3. McConnell.
4. Lumsden.
5. Lowthorpe.
6. Kirk.
7. James.
8. Hughes.
9. Hudson.
10. Hobson.
11. Hickman.
12. Heaven.
13. Heard.
14. Fenton.
15. Reade.
16. Parr.

PLATE 266.—1. Bickersteth.
2. Allott.
3. Allenby.
4. Adamson.
5. Windle.
6. Weir.
7. Verdin.
8. Uppleby.
9. Turnbull.
10. Thornhill.
11. Tetley.
12. Sutherland.
13. Stable.
14. Spokes.
15. Schomberg.
16. Reid.

PLATE 267.—1. Napier.
2. Monypenny.
3. Mansel.
4. Lumb.
5. Longworth.
6. Loder-Symonds.
7. Legg.
8. Jones.
9. Jekyll.
10. Holden.
11. Evans.
12. Compton.
13. Dewar.
14. Catt.
15. Cameron.
16. Bower.

PLATE 268.—1 and 2. Cowper-Essex.
3 and 4. Hatfeild.
5. Harter.
6. Forsyth.
7. Chaplin.
8. Macartney.
9. Biddulph.
10. Rostron.
11. Glyn.
12. Truell.
13. McArthur.
14. Prodgers.
15. Porter.
16. Paton.

PLATE 269.—1. Willey.
2. Welchman.
3. Winch.
4. Christie.
5 and 6. Scott-Gatty.
7. Carter.
8. Hull.
9. Hirst.
10. Winlaw.
11. Priestley.
12. Marriott.
13. Preston-Hillary.
14. Newnes.
15 and 16. Chaworth-Musters.
17 and 18. Lawlor-Huddleston.
19. Buchanan.
20. Glenn.

PLATE 270.—1. Cook.
2. Downes.
3. Brown.
4. Abercromby.
5 and 6. Askew-Robertson.
7 and 8. Cary-Elwes.
9 and 10. Jackson-Barstow.
11 and 12. Haden-Best.

PLATE 271.—1. Gahagan.
2. Dalgleish.
3. Ferguson.
4. Cooper.
5 and 6. Golding-Bird.
7. Allen.
8 and 9. Crompton-Roberts.
10. Burney.
11. Bewley.
12. Hearn.
13. Farish.
14. Corrie.
15. Layland-Barrett.
16. Crawford.
17. Billiat.
18. Carlyon.
19. Cayzer.
20. Hartley.
21. Ferguson.

PLATE 272.—1. Poynter.
2. Lawrence.
3. Galloway.
4. Jaffray.
5. Peek.
6. Jenner.
7. Newnes.
8. Vaughan.
9. Stenning.
10. St. Aubyn.
11. St. John.
12. Stone.
13. Sandars.
14. Renals.
15. Joynt.

PLATE 273.—1. Ward.
2. MacMahon.
3. Yates.
4. Windley.
5. Hermon-Hodge.
6. Hayter.
7. Kelk.
8. Troughton.
9. Sympson.
10. Palitana.
11. Tate.
12. Ingram.
13. Taylor.
14. Tomkinson.
15. Watson.

PLATE 274.—1. Primrose.
2. Sotheby.
3. Wiseman.
4. Skottowe.

5 Mathews
6 Traill
7 Rolls
8 Peto
9 Lyall
10 Collier
11 Smith
12 Sykes
13 Parkin
14 McLaren
15 Wood

PLATE 275.—1 Cayley-Webster
2 Caldwell
3 Cooke-Collis
4 Cartwright
5 Carthew
6 Cayley-Webster.
7. White
8 Coats
9 Sandes
10 McMikin Crawford - McMikin Sterndale-McMikin, McMiking
11 Helman Pidsley
12 Goldney
13 Fosbrook
14 Terry
15 Oldham

PLATE 276.—1 Wood
2 Caulfield
3 Lawrence
4 Fell
5 Wilkinson
6 Holder
7 Herschell
8 Thomas
9 Humphrey
10 Hood
11 Lawson
12 Holden
13 James
14 Wilson
15 Waddington

PLATE 277.—1 and 2 Birkenhead-Glegg
3 and 4 Smith Neill
5 and 6 Moore-Gwyn
7 Yerburgh
8 Bateson
9 and 10 Brook
11 and 12 Blake-Humfrey
13, 14, and 15 Troyte-Chaffin-Grove

PLATE 278.—1 and 2 Lee-Norman
3 and 4 Leather Culley
5 and 6 Mallory
7 and 8 Leir-Carleton
9 and 10 Biddulph
11 and 12 Ferrier
13, 14, and 15 Lloyd-Verney

PLATE 279.—1 and 2 Gull
3 and 4 Naylor-Leyland
5 and 6 Beresford-Peirse
7 and 8 Lord Hawkesbury
9 and 10 Christie-Miller
11 and 12 Tyrwhitt-Drake
13 Harris
14 Porter
15 Harper

PLATE 280.—1 and 2 Lucy
3 and 4 Faudel-Phillips
5 and 6 Mowbray
7 and 8 Porch
9 and 10 Warde-Aldam
11 and 12 Stacey
13 and 14 Strode.
15 Trist

PLATE 281.—1 and 2 Duckworth-King
3 and 4 Lord Northesk
5 and 6 De Colyar
7 and 8 Clough
9 Paget
10 Paget
11 and 12 Dixon-Hartland
13 Woodrooffe
14 Yerburgh
15 Sidney

PLATE 282.—1 and 2 Hoste
3 Greene
4 Smith Marriott
5 Wyndham
6 Hutchinson
7 Rawson
8 Butler
9 Napier
10 and 11 Massey-Lopes
12 and 13 M'Garell-Hogg.
14 Tenison
15 King

PLATE 283.—1 Munro
2 Lipton
3 Goschen
4 Phillimore
5 Cockayne-Frith
6 Lewis
7 Jefferis
8 Hanson
9 Montefiore
10 Weldon
11 Scarth
12 Reckitt
13 Jackson
14 Burne-Jones
15 Gunning

PLATE 284.—1 Kennaway
2 Joicey
3 Hingley
4 Jessell
5 Parry
6 Heywood
7 Compton
8 Louis
9 O'Brien
10 Lea
11 Laking
12 Gunter
13 Maclure
14 Morshead
15 Renshaw

PLATE 285.—1 Saunders
2 Haliburton
3 Key
4 Quilter
5 Herschel
6 Balfour
7 Houldsworth
8 Keane
9 Mather-Jackson
10 Morris
11 Nutting
12 Green
13 Home
14 Jenkinson
15 Smythies

PLATE 286.—1 Morris
2 Marling
3 Magnay
4 Pearce
5 Nepean
6 Tweedy
7 Phillips
8 Milbank
9 Locock
10 Metcalfe
11 Henryson-Caird
12 Pearson
13 Swaby
14 O'Hagan
15 Hulse

PLATE 287.—1 and 2 Kitchener
3 Wilks
4 Wiggin
5 Treves
6 Way
7 and 8 Scourfield
9 Stern
10 and 11 Vivian
12 Thompson
13 and 14 Compton-Thornhill
15 Burdon-Sanderson

PLATE 288.—1 Savory
2 Savory
3 Ripley
4 Cory Wright
5 Smith
6 Robinson
7 Colborne
8 Seton-Steuart
9 Roberts
10 Samuel
11 Smith
12 Smiley
13 Stokes
14 Stephen
15 Steel

PLATE 289.—1 and 2 Foley
3 Goldsmid
4 and 5 Leslie-Ellis
6 Stern
7 and 8 Heber-Percy
9 Salt
10 and 11 Lawes-Wittewrong
12 Seale
13 Verdin
14 Salomons
15 Seely

PLATE 290.—1 Lowndes
2 Hutton
3 Oldfield
4 Patteson
5 Pilter
6 McCowan
7 Hickman
8 Gatty
9 Haycock

10. Royds.
11. Hewer.
12. Hartill.
13. Lloyd.
14. Hawtin.
15. Lovatt.

PLATE 291.—1. Hamersley.
2. De la Motte.
3. Cory.
4. Elton.
5 and 6. Lucie-Smith.
7. Grayrigge.
8. Brown.
9. Brigstocke.
10. Goss.
11 and 12. Tyrwhitt.
13. Percy.
14. Heber.
15. Hartwell.

PLATE 292.—1. Hughes.
2. Crump.
3. Boswell.
4. Abbott.
5. Byrne.
6. Griffiths.
7. Brocklehurst.
8. Batten.
9. Harding.
10. Warrender.
11. Clay.
12. Bannerman.
13. Brooks.
14. Elgood.
15. Amphlett.

PLATE 293.—1. Tyler.
2. Chadborn.
3. Martin.
4. Campion.
5. Jones.
6. Wood.
7. Morkill.
8. Jeffries.
9. Keyser.
10. Pakenham.
11. Leveson.
12. Niblett.
13. Marsh.
14. Elworthy.
15. Jackaman.

PLATE 294.—1. Beardsley.
2. Braikenridge.
3. North.
4. Lepper.
5. Martin.
6. Nickisson.
7. Jaggard.
8. Jones.
9. Macpherson.
10. Napier.
11. Cochrane.
12. Kenney.
13. Butler.
14. Farrer.
15. Boutflower.

PLATE 295.—1. Hatton-Ellis.
2. Collett.
3. Ingham.
4. McCammond.
5. Arthur.
6. Barnard.
7. Burns.
8. Butler.
9. Ackers.
10. Cooke-Collis.
11. Bath.
12. Auden.
13. Aitken.
14. Parkin.
15. Percy.

PLATE 296.—1. Lane.
2. Helman-Pidsley.
3. Lane.
5. Leather.
6. Leadbitter.
7. Reddie.
8. Leadbitter.
9. Hilliard.
10. Cammell.
11. Kilpin.
12. McKenzie.
13. Herbert.
14. Haslewood.
15. Lucas.

PLATE 297.—1. Anslow-Alabone.
2. Lockett.
3. Rix.
4. Bodkin.
5. Rice.
6. Hensley.
7. Birdwood.
8. Burns.
9. Heycock.
10. Hollis.
11. Minns.
12. Millar.
13. Homan-Mulock.
14. Milvain.
15. Kynsey.

PLATE 298.—1. Gardner.
2. Marsden-Smedley.
3. Mansergh.
4. Coghill.
5. O'Neill-Power.
6. Cotton.
7. Farmbrough.
8. Cooper.
9. Maitland.
10. Carr.
11. Cottingham.
12. Crickitt.
13. Kent.
14. Noble.
15. Maitland.

PLATE 299.—1. Craigie.
2. Stone.
3. Castleman.
4. Cartwright.
5. Firmin.
6. Carter.
7. Bulman.
8. Crooks.
9. Stable.
10. Cahill.
11. Coleman.
12. Lawson.
13. Colles.
14. Courthope.
15. Glenesk.

PLATE 300.—1. Drake.
2. Edgelow.
3. Harrison.
4. Freer.
5. Crook.
6. Clover.
7. Greenwood.
8. Cripps.
9. Bedford.
10. Ester.
11. Greenwood.
12. Grunhut.
13. Harrowing.
14. Firebrace.
15. Dennis.

PLATE 301.—1. Levett.
2. Palmer.
3. Lewis.
4. Patteson.
5. Morgan.
6. Meade-King.
7. Foster.
8. Pentin.
9. Hutchinson.
10. Moody.
11. Miéville.
12. Meade-King.
13. Pavia.
14. Perryman.
15. Anningson.

PLATE 302.—1. Greatrex.
2. Bouverie.
3. Levett.
4. Punchard.
5. Lancaster.
6. Brown.
7. Hollingworth.
8. Browning.
9. Lynch.
10. Bartholomew.
11. Knight.
12. Leigh.
13. Braye.
14. Bonar.
15. Macdona.

PLATE 303.—1. Rawlinson.
2. Oppenheimer.
3. Smiley.
4. Outram.
5. Milne.
6. Molyneux.
7. Monkbretton.
8. Hornby.
9. Legh.
10. Speer.
11. Wetherall.
12. Manbey.
13. Winans.
14. Henderson.
15. Venables.

PLATE 304.—1. Samuel-Montagu.
2. Stanley.
3. Higgs.
4. Milner.
5. Lister.
6. Taunton.
7. Knill.
8. Street.
9. Thoms.
10. Tolhurst.

1. Sandys.
2. Wright.
3. Webster.
4. Gidley.
5. Galli.

PLATE 305.—1. Milner.
2. Hoare.
3. Greenall.
4. Leeds.
5. Curle.
6. Lindley.
7. Jodrell.
8. Cowen.
9. Brookfield.
10 and 11. Johnston.
12. Wills.
13. Portal.
14. Sproston.
15. Tate.

PLATE 306.—1 and 2. Crompton-Roberts.
3 and 4. Tempest.
5 and 6. Ellis-Nanney.
7 and 8. King Noel.
9 and 10. Dickson-Poynder.
11, 12, and 13. Milborne-Swynnerton-Pilkington.
14. Haycock.
15. Leighton.

PLATE 307.—1. Ampthill.
2. Hayward.
3. De Frece.
4. English.
5. Falconer.
6. Fitzhugh.
7. Gibbons.
8. Gilmour.
9. Hamilton.
10. Hanson.
11. Hughes.
12. Inglesby.
13. J'Armay.
14. Bernard.
15. Royden.

PLATE 308.—1. Walsham.
2. Smith.
3. St. Levan.
4. Thompson.
5. Wilson.
6. Sullivan.
7. Mansfield.
8. Sitwell.
9. Slade.
10. Walker.
11. White.
12. Shakerley.
13. Culme-Seymour.
14. Addington.
15. Sassoon.

PLATE 309.—1, 2, and 3. Tapps-Gervis-Meyrick.
4. Fairfax.
5 and 6. Smith-Gordon.
7. Troubridge.
8. Hassell.
9. Scudamore.
10. Rugge-Price.
11. Smith-Marriott.
12. Vernon.
13. Frith.
14. Edgelow.
15. Liberty.

PLATE 310.—1. Stucley.
2. Langton.
3. Whitehead.
4. Grey.
5. Stuart.
6. Young.
7. Dundas.
8. Wraxall.
9. Stubbs.
10. Williams.
11. Walker.
12. Robinson.
13. Wells.
14. Cowell-Stepney.
15. Best.

PLATE 311.—1. Willshire.
2. Lyon.
3. Vernon.
4. Wood.
5. Wigan.
6. Sykes.
7. Wiseman.
8. Welby.
9. Tomlinson.
10. Waller.
11. Romilly.
12. Thompson.
13. Watkin.
14. Whiteley.
15. Tuite.

PLATE 312.—1. Strutt.
2. Peel.
3. Wright.
4. Vernon.
5 and 6. Lord Lanesborough.
7. Ochterlony.
8 and 9. Shaw-Yates.
10 and 11. Montagu-Pollock.
12. Waithman.
13 and 14. Van Notten-Pole.
15. Usher.
16. Philips.

PLATE 313.—1. Warren.
2. Salt.
3. Lloyd.
4. Robinson.
5. Cowell-Stepney.
6. Spearman.
7. Simpson.
8. Pelly.
9. Waterlow.
10. Southwell.
11. Sillar.
12. Stockenstrom.
13. Walters.
14. Skipwith.
15. Shiffner.
16. Walker.

PLATE 314.—1. Edwardes.
2. Pollock.
3. Rumford.
4. Strangman.
5. Shaw.
6. Wood.
7. Wright.
8. Baker.
9. Wood.

A

DICTIONARY

OF

HERALDIC TERMS AND SUBJECTS

USED OR MENTIONED IN THIS BOOK.

A

ACORN *plate* 152
ACORNED, bearing acorns 151 3
ADDORSED, ADOSSED, or ADOSEE, placed back to back
see 72 8, 140 1, 109 12, 98 13
AFFRONTEE, full faced 7 2, 23 8
ALLERION, an eagle displayed, but without beak or claws.
ALPACA *see* 125 2
ANCHOR *plate* 161
ANGEL *see plates* 183, 184, 189
ANNULET, a plain ring
see 2 9, 115 5, 167 11
ANTELOPE, an animal of the deer kind, with two straight taper horns
plates 126, 127
ANTELOPE, HERALDIC, a fabulous animal, with the body of a stag and the tail of a unicorn, and having a tusk at the tip of the nose, tufts down the back part of the neck, and on the tail, chest, and thighs
see 127 7, 127 9
APAUMEE, a term applied to the hand when the palm is visible and opened
see 222 5, 8, 14
ARCHER 188 9, and *see plates* 185, 186, 187
ARGENT, silver, usually represented and considered as white, and when engraved the surface is left plain
ARM This, and also the hand, occurs in many positions in Heraldry, particularly amongst Crests (*see plates* 194 to 224) The various positions are as follows —

Arm "embowed," 202 2 [It should be mentioned whether the fist be clenched or the hand apaumée, unless holding something] When the elbow points the reverse way it is "embowed to the sinister" (204 13)

Arm "embowed fesseways" or "embowed and resting upon the elbow" (202 13)

Arm embowed fesseways the part above the elbow lying upon the wreath and the part below the elbow in pale (98 11)

Two arms counter embowed (200 8)

Two arms embowed in saltire (200 5)

A cubit arm is couped just below the elbow (*see* 213 10, or 214 13), being slightly shorter than an arm couped at the elbow, and a little longer than a hand couped below the wrist (214 10) When "in bend," a cubit arm is in the position as shown in 208 14, and when "fesseways," as in 221 9, The hand should be couped *at* the wrist It must be stated whether dexter (222 14), or sinister (222 9), and if open, as these, is termed apaumée, and any other position of the fingers must be specially mentioned

All arms, when bare, are termed ppr, but may be in all the foregoing positions when vested (204 5, 205 3), or in armour (195 2) When vested, the cuff must be mentioned if of a different tincture, and if the hand be not bare it is known as "gloved" When in armour, the hand must be mentioned as proper or in a gauntlet An arm may be habited in leaves (198 1), in chain mail (198 2), or in scale armour (199 2) An arm in armour may be garnished—*i e*, with the edges and rivets of a different colour—and is sometimes termed vambraced

When two hands clasp each other they are known as conjoined (224 2)
ARMED, a term used when the horns, teeth of any beast, and the beak or claws, tusks, or talons of any bird, are in colour different from the body, it is then said to be *armed* of that colour
ARMED, occasionally used to mean in armour
ARROW 173 5
ASS *See plate* 125
ASSURGENT, rising out of the sea.
ASTROLABE, an instrument for taking the altitude of the sun or stars 167 7
ATTIRED, a term used when the antlers or horns of a stag, hart, buck, or antelope are mentioned as of a different colour
ATTIRES, the horns of a stag 123 5
ATTIRES, affixed to the scalp
see plate 123 2, 3
AXE
AYLET, a Sea Swallow, or Cornish-chough, 107 5 and 14
AZURE, blue, represented when engraved by parallel horizontal lines *see* 15 2

B

BADGER, or BROCK 33 10
BALL, FIRE *See* GRENADE
BAND, the fillet or bandage, by which a garb, a sheaf of arrows, etc, are bound
BANDED, when the band of a garb, etc, is of a colour different from the garb itself, it is said to be *banded*, and the colour described
BANNER. *see plate* 176
BAR, a straight horizontal band
see 59 12, 14 9

BARBED, a term used when referring to the five green leaves on the outside of a full-blown rose which are the barbs. 149. 2

BARBED AND FLIGHTED, a term applied to an arrow when the head and feathers differ in tincture from the shaft.

BAR-GEMELLE, a double bar, or two narrow bars placed near and parallel to each other. *see* 128. 10

BARNACLE, a water-fowl resembling a goose.

BARRULET, a diminutive of the bar—one half its width.

BARRULY, divided into several equal parts fessways, each part being the width of a barrulet.

BARRY, transversely divided into several equal parts fessways, of two or more tinctures interchangeably disposed; the number of divisions usually specified as barry of six, eight, ten, or twelve. 12. 3

BASE, the lower part.

BASILISK, a fabulous creature like the cockatrice, but with the head of a dragon at the end of its tail.

BAT. 137. 11

BATON, a staff or truncheon. *see* 200. 3; 15. 9

BATTLE-AXE. 172. 3

BATTLEMENTS, the upper works of a castle or tower *see* 50. 4

BEACON, a fire-beacon, used as a signal. 177. 14

BEAK, the bill of a bird; in birds of prey when with the claws of another colour termed *armed.*

BEAKED, birds are termed beaked when the bills are of a different tincture from their bodies. *see* 88. 13

BEAR. *plates* 34 and 35

BEARS' PAWS. *See* 36. 6. *See* under LIONS' GAMBS.

BEAVER. *see* 134. 8

BEES and BEEHIVES. *plate* 137.

BELL. *See* CHURCH-BELL and HAWK'S BELL.

BELLED, a term applied to the hawk or falcon when both legs have bells upon them, 85. 5. If the word be not used in the blazon, the bird will carry only one bell, and that on the sinister leg.

BEND. *See* PER BEND.

BEND, one of the nine ordinaries; it occupies one-third part of the field or crest, and is drawn diagonally from the dexter chief to the sinister base. *see* 8. 7; 120. 11

BENDLET, a diminutive of the bend of one-half its breadth. *see* 60. 10; 66. 12

BEND SINISTER, IN, placed in the opposite position to bendways. The swords in 170. 6, in 170. 4, and in 195. 1 are all in bend sinister.

BENDWAYS, obliquely, or in bend. *see* 170. 5

BENDY, divided into an equal number of pieces in a slanting direction from the dexter chief to the sinister base. *see* 40. 3; 84. 8; 206. 7; 207. 2

BEZANT, a flat circular piece of gold, supposed to represent the gold coin of that name. *See* ROUNDEL. *see* 11. 7; 27. 8: 31. 3; 54. 4; 57. 1.

BEZANTÉE, semée of, or strewn with bezants. *See* SEMÉE) *see* 13. 1; 71. 6; 73. 6; 97. 3.

BIBLE. *See* BOOK.

BILLET, an elongated rectangular figure. *see* 45. 6; 215. 11, 13

BILLETTÉE, semée of billets. *See* SEMÉE. *see* 56. 5; 126. 4

BILLING, a term applied to birds when looking at each other and with the beaks joining. 93. 2

BISHOP'S MITRE. *See* MITRE.

BITTERN, a bird of the heron family. *see* 104. 3

BLACKAMOOR with bow and arrow. 185. 6

BLACKAMOORS' HEADS. *plate* 182. 2, 4, 7; 191. 3, 4, 5; 192. 4, 6, 7, 13

BLACKBIRD. 106. 2

BLADED, a term used when the stalk or blade of grain is shown upon the ear, or when of a tincture different from the ear or fruit; thus an ear of wheat or., *bladed* vert. 154. 3

BLAZON (*n*), the heraldic description, in words, of a coat-of-arms or crest; (*v*) to heraldically describe in words. To represent in colour is to *emblazon.* To outline only, labelling the colours, is to *trick.*

BOAR. *plate* 40

BOARS' HEADS, couped or erased "*close*" (42. 2; 43. 1), are almost without exception the only forms of the head used in Scotland and Wales, and consequently the additional and descriptive term used above is more often omitted than not. When blazoned "*erect*," it is shewn as in 43. 3. When a coronet takes the place of a wreath this form of head must be blazoned as *upon* the coronet (and not issuing from it), and shewn as 42. 11. The head with the neck, as 41. 5, is supposed to be the more general form for English crests, but there is no hard and fast rule that can be observed as to this, for both forms occur; though for distinctive reasons words "and neck" are often added.

BOAT. 179. 6

BONE. *see* 147. 4

BOOK. *see plates* 158, 215

BOOT. 193. 12; 194. 4

BOUGET. *See* WATER BOUGET.

BOW. *See* CROSS-BOW.

BOW should really be always blazoned, either as strung, unstrung, or sans strings, but in the first case this is often omitted (*see* 173. 12; 198. 9; 188. 9; 200. 2), though in the two latter instances the words "shooting an arrow from a bow," or "pulling an arrow to its head," are required.

BOY, naked. *see* 189. 6; 189. 12

BOY'S HEAD. *see* 182. 11

BRIDGE. The number of the arches will usually be stated. *see* 158. 4

BRISTLED, a term used for the hair on the neck and back of the boar, when it differs in tincture.

BROAD-ARROW differs from the pheon by having the inside of the barbs plain.

BROCK. *See* BADGER.

BUCKLER, a term used for a shield.

BUCKLES are borne of various forms, oval, round, square, and lozenge-shaped. The position of the tongue should be stated. *see* 178. 5; 34. 11

BUFFALO. 45. 10

BUGLE, a kind of ox. [The Editor believes the term with this meaning only occurs once within these volumes.]

BUGLE-HORNS are usually stringed, garnished, and veruled, and frequently of different colours (*see* 228. 11), but when not so they must be blazoned as "sans strings." 228. 9

BULLS and BULLS' HEADS. *see plates* 43, 44, 45

BULL'S LEG. 123. 4 and 7

BUSTARD, a kind of wild turkey, of a brownish colour. 102. 9

C

CABLE, a rope affixed to an anchor. *see* 161. 2

CABLED, an anchor is so termed when borne with a cable entwined round the stock. *see* 161. 2

CABOSSED, a term applied to animals having horns, when the face is affrontée and the head is couped so closely behind the ears that no part of the neck is visible. *see* 43. 8, 9; 122. 4, 5, 8; 130. 7

CADUCEUS, Rod of Esculapius or Staff of MERCURY, a slender winged staff, entwined by two serpents, the heads meeting at the top, and the tails at the base of the handle, and winged at the summit. *see* 171. 1 and 3; 224. 14.

CALTRAP, or GALTRAP, an instrument anciently used in war to wound the horses' feet, having four points, so that when placed on the ground, one point was always erect; and in heraldic art this frequently depicted as bloody, when it is termed "*embrued at the point.*" *see* 174. 14

CAMELEOPARD or CAMELOPARD, the heraldic name of the giraffe, which was stated by writers of early days to be a hybrid between the camel and leopard. *see* 132. 8

CAMELS, and CAMELS' HEADS. *plate* 132

CANNON, *see* 187. 8; 169. 12, which latter, however, should properly be blazoned as a "cannon mounted."

CAP, COLLEGIATE. 180. 9

CAP OF LIBERTY, always red but of very rare occurence. 224. 14

CAP OF MERCURY or winged cap. *see* 171. 1

CAP OF DIGNITY or MAINTENANCE, more usually known as a *Chapeau*, when proper is a flat cap of crimson velvet, lined and turned up with ermine, originally and of right appertaining to ducal rank. It is borne by many families below the crest in place of a wreath (*see plate* 4. 2, 5, 8). It is occasionally of other colours, as shewn in 15. 12.

CAP, PHYSICIAN'S. 180. 7

CAP, STEEL. *See* MORION. *plate* 132

CAPARISONED, a term applied to horses when furnished with trappings, but which has no very definite meaning. It is usually employed in conjuncton with the word "bridled"—*e.g.* 52. 13—which is blazoned "upon a ducal coronet, a horse passant, saddled, bridled and caparisoned all ppr.

CASTLE IN FLAMES. *see* 155. 1

CASTLES have always two towers, joined by an intervening wall; when the cement is different in colour from the stones, it is said to be *masoned* of that particular colour; if the loopholes and portway are of a different colour they must be so blazoned, they are supposed to be then closed *see* TOWER 155 2 and 6

CAT, generally understood to be the wild or mountain cat

CATHERINE WHEEL

CENTAUR or SAGITTARIUS, a fabulous figure composed of the upper part of a man, and the lower part of a horse, usually (though not always) represented with a bow and arrow. The latter named, however, could hardly be applied to the figure if the bow and arrow be omitted 53 2

CHALICE, a communion cup *see* CUP

CHAPEAU, a cap, hat, or bonnet *see* CAP OF DIGNITY

CHAPLET, a garland, or wreath of flowers, laurel, olive, oak, etc 175 13, 202 4

CHAPLET OF ROSES is composed of four roses only, the other part of leaves 175 15

CHART 159 11

CHECKY, CHEQUY, divided into small equal squares, of different tinctures 70 5, 205 4

CHERUB, a child's head between two wings 189 9

CHERUB with wings in saltire 189 13

CHESS ROOK, the rook or pawn used in the game of chess 110 1

CHEVALIER, a knight on horseback completely armed 53 10, 189 10

CHEVERON, CHEVRON, one of the ordinaries, resembling two rafters, meeting at the top 167 10, 13

CHIEF, the upper part

CHOUGH, Cornish 107 14

CHURCH *plate* 158

CHURCH BELL. *see* 168 7

CINQUEFOIL *plate* 148 11, 12

CIVIC CROWN, a garland of oak leaves and acorns

CLENCHED, a term applied to the fist when the hand is closed *see* 202 2

CLOSE, a term applied to a bird when the wings are kept close to the body (85 2), and to a helmet with the vizor down 1[illegible] 3

CLOUDS 162 13

CLOUDS, hands out of *plates* 196, 198, 200, 204, 207, 208, 210, 211, 212, 214, 215, 216, 218, 219, 220, 222, 223, 224

CLUB *see plate* 199

COCK *see plates* 90, 91

COCK, game 90 2

COCKATRICE, a fabulous creature, in heraldry depicted as like a wyvern, but with the head, wattles, beak, and legs of a cock 68 4, 68 5

COLLARED, having a collar about the neck *see* 26 5

COLLARED GEMELLE, having a double collar about the neck 228 8, 11

COMBATANT, a term applied to two lions when facing each other 3 8

COMBED, when the comb or crest of a cock or cockatrice, for example, is of a colour different from the body 90. 3

COMET, represented with an illuminated tail streaming from it 164 10

COMPLEMENT, IN HER, applied to the moon, to denote her being full 162 4

COMPONÉE, or COMPONY, composed of one row of small rectangular pieces alternately of different tinctures, if there be two rows it is termed *compony-counter-compony* *see* 4 2

CONEY, or CONY, a rabbit 136 1

CONJOINED, joined together 106 13, 113 3, 224 2

COOTE, a water fowl 102 10

CORNISH CHOUGH, a species of crow or raven, black, with legs and beak red, common in Cornwall 107 14

CORNUCOPIA 152 13, 224 14

CORONET. Coronets, apart from those of the different members of the Royal Family, which vary according to the degree of relationship to the Sovereign, are as follows —

1 The "Ducal coronet" of heraldry, sometimes termed a "Cimier" or crest coronet, when depicted is shewn as 16 2, and unless stated to be otherwise, has only thee leaves visible. The coronet of a duke is similar in shape, but has five leaves

2 The coronet of a Marquess *see* 203 2

3 The coronet of an Earl *see* 182 2

4 The coronet of a Viscount *see* 179 9

5 The coronet of a Baron *see* 16 6

The above illustrations shew the respective coronets as when used with crests issuing therefrom and forming an unchangeable part of the crest but when used as coronets of rank, they must never be shewn without the cap belonging [Foreign coronets are exceptions to this.] *see* 217 3

No coronets (except in a few exceptional cases) require a wreath below them

The following coronets are also used in heraldry

6 Mural coronet 16 5

7 Naval coronet, composed alternately of the sails and sterns of ships 16 9, 204 2

8 Eastern coronet 206 2

9 Vallary coronet 16 4

10 Pallisado coronet 205 1

11 Celestial coronet, the same as an Eastern coronet, but having each point surmounted by a star

12 Antique coronet, usually the same as an Eastern coronet, but occasionally otherwise *see* 100 8, 130 8

There are other coronets in existence, but having no special names they must be minutely described

COUCHANT, lying down but with the head upright (see LODGED) to distinguish from *dormant* 7 12

COUPED, cut clean off 21 1, 47 5

COUNTERCHANGED, an alternate changing of the colours *see* 2 9, 26 10, 50 6, 119 6

COURANT, CURRENT, running at full speed 52 8, 118 13

CRAB 141 5

CRANE 105 9

CRANE'S HEAD 104 5

CRENELLEE, embattled *see* 1 2, 208 7

CRESCENT, a half moon, horns turned upwards 163 2

Decrescent, horns turned towards the sinister 163 1

Increscent, horns turned towards the dexter 163 3

CRESCENT IN FLAMES 163 12

CRESTED, a term applied to the comb of a cock, or other bird, or to the head feathers of a peacock, and to the top of a pine apple

CRINED, relating to the hair

CROCODILE

CROSIER *See* CROZIER

CROSS AVELANE, or AVELLANE, resembles four filberts or hazel nuts, stalk to stalk

CROSS BOW *see* 112 13

CROSS CALVARY, a passion cross mounted on three steps, grieces, or degrees. 166 1

CROSS CROSSLET 165 2

CROSS CROSSLET FITCHED, having the lower part sharpened to a point 166 2

CROSS FLEURY, or FLORY, a cross having a demi fleur de lis at each extremity 166 7

CROSS FORMEE, or PATTEE, spreading like dovetails at each extremity 165 7, 166 3

CROSS MOLINE LOZENGE-PIERCED 165 1

CROSS OF ST ANDREW, a saltire argent upon a field az

CROSS, PASSION *See* LONG CROSS

CROSS PATONCE, as 165 3, but the ends rather wider and terminating in three parts instead of two

CROSS PATTÉE *See* CROSS FORMEE

CROSS POTENT *see* 226 3

CROSS RAGULED 227 14

CROW 107 5

CROWN *See* CORONET

CROWN OF ENGLAND, sometimes termed the Imperial Crown *see* 31 12, 217 1

CROZIER, or CROSIER *see* 170. 14, 219 4

CRUSILLY, or CRUSULY, semee of cross crosslets

CUBIT ARM, is the hand and arm couped a little below the elbow *See* ARM

CUP, covered 171 13, 202 14

CUP, uncovered. 177 1, 2, 3, 4

CUP IN FLAMES 177 6

CUPID 189 7

CUPID, DEMI- *see* 185 8

CUPOLA, dome of a building *see* 157 15

CURLING STONE 221 2

D

DAGGER [illegible]

DANCETTEE, when the teeth or indents of a zigzag line are large and wide (*see* INDENTED)

DART *See* ARROW

DECRESCENT, the half moon with its horns turned towards the sinister 163 1

DEMI, half 10. 2, 34 14, 186 5

DEVOURING, swallowing 139. 2

DEXTER, the right, but as in heraldry the shield is supposed to be borne in front, the dexter side of the escutcheon is that on the left-hand side when looking straight at it, and similarly with crests —*e g*, 25 11—in which the part marked azure is the dexter and the ermine is the sinister

DISPLAYED, a term usually applied to the eagle when in the position shewn in 75 2, which is *an eagle displayed*, but 77 5 (unless blazoned "rising," as is sometimes the case), shews the claws upon the wreath and the body in profile instead of affrontée, and might be described as "*an eagle with wings displayed*"

DOLPHIN *See* NAIANT and HAURIENT *plate* 140

DORMANT, sleeping with the head resting upon the forepaws 7 13

DOUBLE QUEUED, having two tails 3 1, 10. 6

DOVE. 92 2

DOVETAILED. *see* 226. 1

DRAGON, a fabulous animal, differs from the wyvern by having four legs. 73. 2

DUCAL CORONET, frequently used instead of a wreath, or as a collar; it has three leaves, unless blazoned as having a greater number. *See* CORONET. 10. 7; 16. 2; 23. 8

DUCK. 102. 8

E

EAGLE. 76. 2

EAGLE DISPLAYED, when the wings and legs are extended on each side of the body which is placed affrontée. 75. 2

EAGLE RISING. *See* PREFACE.

EARED, a term used when the ears are in colour different from the body.

EEL. 142. 10

ELEPHANTS. *plate* 133

ELEPHANTS' TRUNKS, or PROBOSCES. 123. 10

EMBATTLED, like the battlements of a castle. *See* CRENELLÉE.

EMBOWED, bent at the elbow. *See* ARM.

EMBRUED, dipped in blood; any weapon bloody, or mouths bloody with devouring prey. 174. 12, 14

ENDORSED. *See* ADDORSED.

ENFILED, a charge is so termed when encircled by, or thrust through, anything else—*e.g.*, a fleur-de-lis enfiled with a ducal coronet (148. 1), or a sword enfiled by a savage's head in profile couped at the neck (191. 9).

ENGRAILED, a term applied to a line composed of semicircular indents. *see* 8. 7; 30. 6

ENSIGNED, a term used with crowns, coronets, and other things, when borne on or over charges; as a heart *ensignea* with a crown. 110. 14

ENTWINED, generally with a snake or a cable; sometimes a sword or a flagstaff, etc., with a branch of laurel. 81. 5; 225. 3

ENVELOPED, entwined by a snake, applied to birds and animals. 77. 8

ERADICATED, torn up by the roots.

ERASED, forcibly torn off, leaving the separated parts jagged and uneven (*see* 15. 3; 17. 8). When erased of a different tincture it should be shown as 39. 7; 49. 2.

ERECT, upright or in pale. A sword, *erect* 170. 2

ERMINE, the. 134. 2; 134. 6

ERMINE, white with black tufts or ermine spots. *see* 19. 8

ERMINES, black with white ermine spots. *see* 225. 12

ERMINOIS, gold with black ermine spots. *see* 81. 13

ESCALLOP-SHELL. 141. 14

ESCALLOP-SHELL, reversed. 141. 9

ESCROL, a slip on which crests were formerly placed; now used to receive the mottoes.

The ESCUTCHEON proper is the shield upon which the *Coat-of-Arms* is displayed, and as to which "Fairbairn" does not in any way treat, but an escutcheon frequently appears (1) as the crest (176. 10), or (2) as a part of it (61. 1), and many crests consist of a bird or an animal supporting an escutcheon or banner of the arms of the family. 76. 7; 85. 11

ETOILE, a star with waved rays or points, usually six in number, but this should always be specified. *see* 164. 1, 4

EYE, human. 193. 13

EYED, a term applied to the variegated spots in the peacock's tail, and when the eye of any creature has to be blazoned as of some tincture.

F

FALCHION, a kind of broadsword.

FALCON, a large species of sporting hawk, but very little distinction is made between the different species. 85. 2

FALCON'S LEG. 113. 8

FASCES. 171. 4; *see* 82. 8; 171. 6, 9

FAWN. 124. 12

FEATHERS, always those of the ostrich, unless mentioned as otherwise. *plates* 113, 114, 115

FER-DE-MOLINE, a mill-rind. 165. 11

FERRET. 134. 9

FESS, the space between two horizontal lines drawn across the field, occupying from a third to a fith part of the escutcheon. 8. 5; 81. 8

FESSWAYS, placed in fess; horizontal—*e.g.*, the sword in 118. 5; the lozenges in 106. 13; and the escallops in 60. 3.

FETTERLOCK. 19. 4; 168. 12

FIMBRIATED, edged of another tincture.

FINCH. *See* GOLDFINCH.

FIR BRANCH. 147. 6

FIR CONE. *see* 152. 6

FIRE-BALL, GRENADE, or BALL FIRED, ppr., has always the fire issuing from the top. 177. 12

FIRE-BEACON. 177. 14

FITCHED, or FITCHÉE, sharpened to a point. *see* 166. 2

FLAG. 176. 15

FLAMANT, flaming. *see* 155. 9

FLAME OF FIRE. 177. 10

FLEUR-DE-LIS. 148. 2; *see* 13. 13; 144. 2

FLEURY or FLORY, a term applied to various objects—*e.g.*, a collar, a coronet, a cross, or a tressure, of which the ends or edges are garnished with fleurs-de-lis or demi-fleur-de-lis. *cf.* 33. 3; 166. 7

FLEXED, bent. *see* 193. 1

FLIGHTED. *See* BARBED AND FLIGHTED.

FLOTANT, floating, or flying in the air as the banner in 73. 11.

FLUTE. 168. 3

FOCKED, a term said to be applied to lions. etc., when the hind feet are of a different tincture. *see* 2. 1

FORMÉE, or PATTÉE, *see* CROSS.

FOUNTAIN, a roundle barry wavy arg. and az. 159. 8

FOUNTAIN, playing. 159. 13

FOX. *see plates* 32, 33

FRASIER, a strawberry plant or cinquefoil. 148. 12

FRET, two long pieces in saltier, extending to the extremity of the field, and interlaced within a mascle in the centre. 165. 10

FRETTY, interlacing each other in saltire. 3. 3; 14. 7; 121. 11

FRUCTED, bearing fruit. 151. 3; 152. 9

FUR. *See* ERMINE, ERMINES, ERMINOIS, PEAN, VAIR, and VAIRÉE.

FURCHÉ, FOURCHÉE, forked, usually applied to the tail of an animal when forked at the middle.

FURNISHED, sometimes used to mean supplied with, *See* CAPARISONED.

FUSIL, a figure similar in shape to a lozenge, but slightly narrower. 147. 13

G

GAD, a plate of steel or iron.

GALLEY, an antique vessel. *see* 160. 6, 7

GALTRAP, *See* CALTRAP.

GAMB, the fore-leg of a lion or other beast. 36. 4

GARB, a sheaf of corn or wheat. 153. 2

GARDANT, a term applied to animals when the body is in profile and the face is affrontée. *See* GAZE, at. *plate* 4. 1, 2, 3.

GARLAND, chaplet or wreath of flowers or leaves. 146. 3

GARLAND OF ROSES. *see* 174. 6; 175. 15

GATE. 158. 9

GAUNTLET, an iron glove. 209. 5, 8

GAZE, at, a term applied to the hart, stag, buck, or hind, when standing in profile with the head affrontée, or full faced; all other beasts in this attitude are gardant. 117. 3

GEMEL, or BAR-GEMEL, signifies a double bar or two bars near and parallel to each other. 120. 13; 128. 10; 139. 3

GIRAFFE. *See* CAMELEOPARD.

GLOBE. 159. 1

GLOVE. *see* 86. 12

GOAT. *plates* 128, 129

GOBONY. *See* COMPONÉE.

GOLDFINCH. 108. 8

GOLDEN-FLEECE, a ram stuffed and suspended by a collar round his middle. 130. 10

GOLPES, purple-coloured roundles. *See* ROUNDLE.

GORGED, having a coronet, collar, ribbon, chain, etc., about the neck or throat.

GRAPES, bunch of. 152. 7

GRENADE. *See* FIRE-BALL.

GREYHOUND. *plates* 58, 59, 60, 61

GRIECES, steps or degrees on which crosses are placed. *see* 166. 1

GRIFFIN, a chimercial animal, half-eagle and half-lion. 62 to 68

GULES, red; represented when engraved by perpendicular lines. *see* 15. 8

GUTTE, a drop.

GUTTÉE, semée of drops, varying in colour, according to what is intended to be represented, and named as follows:—

GUTTÉE-D'EAU, drops of water, *argent*. 12. 6

GUTTÉE-DE-HUILE, or GUTTÉE-D'OLIVE, drops of oil, *vert*.

GUTTÉE-DE-LARMES, tear drops, *azure*. 56. 10

GUTTÉE D'OR, drops of gold, *or*. 225. 10

GUTTÉE-DE-POIX, drops of pitch, *sable*. 101. 3

GUTTÉE-DE-SANG, drops of blood, *gules*. 121. 13

GUTTÉE-REVERSED, drops contrary to the natural position. 227. 10

GYRON, the space between two straight lines from the dexter fess and chief point, meeting in an acute angle in the fess point.

GYRONNY, composed of gyrons. The number should be stated. 143. 3

H

HABITED, clothed, vested *see* 183 3, 187 14; 203 8
HALBERDS *See* BATTLE-AXE
HAMMER. *see* 207 11
HAND, must be couped at the wrist
HAND APAUMEE 222 14
HAND SINISTER 222 9
HARE 136. 3
HARP 168 9
HARPY, the head and breasts of a woman conjoined to the body of a vulture 189 1
HARROW, as used in husbandry; is usually triangular 178 4
HAURIENT, a term applied to a fish when erect 139 11, 140 11
HAWK 85 2
HAWK'S BELL. *see* 86 13
HAWK'S HEAD 88 12
HAWK'S LEG. 113 8
HAWK'S LURE, used by falconers, a decoy 110. 10, 178 11
HEART, human *see plate* 181
HEART INFLAMED 181 8, 12, 13
HEART IN FLAMES 181 11
HEDGEHOG, or URCHIN 135 8
HELMET, of an esquire, when used as a crest 180 3
HERALDIC ROSE 149 2
HERALDIC TIGER 25 5
HIGHLANDER 188 5
[illegible] handle of a sword *see* 170. 2
HIND, a doe [illegible] of the stag *see plates* 124, 125
HIPPOCAMPUS, a sea-horse. *see plate* 46
HOLLY-TREE 145 6, 147 7
HOLLY-LEAVES *see* 211 13
HOLY LAMB 131 2
HOODED, when borne with a hood A hawk, *hooded* 86 8
HORN, hunting *See* BUGLE-HORN
HORNS *See* ATTIRES *see* 123 8
HORSE *plates* 50, 51, 52, 53
HORSE, SEA- *plate* 46
HORSE SHOE 158 6, 110. 13
HORSE, winged *See* PEGASUS,
HUNTING-HORN *See* BUGLE-HORN
HUNTSMAN 187 2, 12
HURT, an azure roundle *See* ROUNDLE
HURTEE, or HURTY, semée of hurts
HUSBANDMAN 187 14, 188 8, 12
HUSSAR, *see* 185 11
HYÆNA 127 13
HYDRA, a dragon with seven heads. 73 3

I

IMBATTLED *See* EMBATTLED.
IMPERIAL CROWN *see* 217 1
IN BEND, *see* BENDWAYS. *see* 122 2, 168 8, 170 5
IN CHEVRON, in the position or shape of a chevron 151 15, 164 7
INCRESCENT, a crescent with the horns turned towards the dexter 163 3
INDENTED, notched like a saw 206 13
IN FESS, horizontal *See* Raguly Staff, 5 14, and Tilting-spear, 178 2
INGRAILED *See* ENGRAILED
IN HER COMPLEMENT *See* COMPLEMENT
IN HER PIETY, a term applied to the pelican when in her nest and feeding her young by vulning or wounding her own breast *see* 98 8
IN HIS PRIDE, a term applied to the pea cock when its tail is displayed 103 12
IN HIS SPLENDOUR, a term used to describe the sun when shewn as 162 2
IN LEURE, a term applied to wings when borne in the position of a lure *See* VOL 113 3
IN ORLE, nearly in a circle, used to describe two branches, encompassing any bearing *see* 3 10; 162 6
IN PALE, upright or erect *see* 173 5
INTERLACED *see* 44 5, 120. 13
INVECTED, the reverse of engrailed 121 12
INVERTED, upside down
ISSUANT, coming up, or arising from 19 9, 61 14

J

JAMBE *See* GAMB
JELLOPED, a term applied to a cockatrice or cock, when the wattles are of a tincture different from the head
JESSANT DE-LIS, having a fleur-de-lis shooting through any charge *see* 22. 5
JESSES, leather thongs, with which the bells are tied to the legs of hawks *see* 87 10

K

KANGAROO 136. 7, 9
KEY *see* 168 11
KINGFISHER 96 9
KNIFE *see* 178 9
KNOT. *see plate* 165

L

LABEL, a figure of three points to distinguish the eldest son [and of five points for the grandson], borne during the life of the father, and borne by a ll the members of the Royal Family, and a term applied to the ribbons that hang from a mitre or coronet 61 13, 167 10
LADDER 158 12, 14
LAMB *see plates* 130, 131
LAMB, Holy, *see* 131 2, 7
LAMP, burning *see* 177 5
LANCE, a spear to thrust with *see* 204 10
LANGUED, a term used when the tongue of beasts or birds is borne of a colour different from the body
LAUREL BRANCH 151 13
LEASH, a small leather thong used by falconers, the line attached to the collar of a dog
LEASHED, lined *see* 55 5
LEG *see plate* 193
LEGGED *See* MEMBERED
LEOPARD, borne in most of the positions of the lion *see plate* 24
LEOPARD'S FACE 22 2
LEOPARD'S HEAD 22 10
LETTER, sealed 215 7
LILY 151 2
LION
Couchant 7 5
Couchant guardant. 7 10
Demi lion 10. 2
Dormant 7 13

LION (*continued*)
Passant 6 2
Passant guardant 4 3
Passant regardant 6 1
Rampant 1 13
Rampant guardant 2 5
Rampant regardant 2 11
Sejant. 8 8
Sejant erect 8 13
Sejant guardant 8 2
Sejant guardant erect 8 7
Sejant regardant 8 5
Statant *cf* 4. 1, 8
Statant guardant 4 1
Statant, with tail extended 4 8
LION, sea *plate* 20
LION'S FACE 21 11
LION'S GAMBS. *plate* 36
LION'S HEAD 17 8
LION'S TAIL 123 14
LION OF ST MARK, OR WINGED LION 8 10, 20. 7, 9, 10, 12
LIZARD 138 5
LOBSTER 141 2
LOCUST 137 8
LODGED, the buck, hart, hind, etc., when at rest, or lying, they must not be termed couchant 115 7
LONG CROSS 165 4
LOZENGE *see* 106 13
LOZENGY, composed of lozenges alternately of different colours 120. 4
LUCY, a fish called a pike *see* 138 10, 139. 5
LURE, or LEURE, a decoy *See* HAWK'S LURE Wings conjoined with their tips downward, are *in leure* [illegible] 3
LYMPHAD, an antique ship, with mast a[illegible] oars 160 7
LYNX 127 2
LYRE, a musical instrument 168 8

M

MACE, a club used in war 199 3
MAIDEN'S HEAD, the head and neck of a woman couped at the breasts.
MAIL, chain 198 2
MAMELUKE 189 8
MAN. *see plates* 185, 186, 187, 188, 189
MANED, when the mane is of a colour different from the body, the animal is *maned* of that colour
MAN'S HEAD, unless differently expressed, is usually in profile and bearded, if without a beard, it is a young man's head
MANTLING, the flourishing ornament attached to the helmet
MARTEN, or MARTIN a kind of weasel
MARTIN, a kind of swallow
MARTLET, a bird without feet, representing the martin 95 5
MASCLE, a figure in the form of a lozenge, but always voided 167 9
MASONED, a term used to indicate that the cement or mortar in buildings is of a different tincture
MAST and SAIL *see* 160. 11
MAUNCH, an antique sleeve
MEMBERED, when the legs or beak of a bird are of a colour different from the body they are *beaked* and *membered* of that colour
MERMAID, a figure half woman, half fish, generally with a comb in one hand, and a mirror in the other 184 5
MERMAN, a figure half man, half-fish *see* 185 12

MILL-RIND, or FER-DE-MOLINE, the iron in the centre of the mill-stone, by which it is turned. 165. 11
MILL-STONE. *see* 180. 14
MINERVA'S HEAD. 182. 1
MIRROR, oval and handled *see* 184. 5
MITRE. This is always placed above the escutcheon of the arms by Bishops, none of whom are permitted to use a crest. In such cases no wreath is placed below it. There is no distinctive mitre for an Archbishop. The Bishop of Durham, and he only, encircles the band of his mitre by a ducal coronet. The illustration 180. 5 is charged with a chevron and thereon escallop shells both of which must be omitted except in those cases where they are mentioned in the blazon.
MONK. 187. 11; 192. 3
MONKEY. 136. 8
MOOR-COCK. 89. 5
MOOR'S HEAD, a black's head, generally in profile, and frequently banded or wreathed. 182. 7; 192. 13
MORION, an antique helmet worn by infantry. *See* HELMET. 111. 2; 173. 10; 180. 1
MORTAR. 169. 10
MORTAR and PESTLE. 177. 13
MORT-HEAD, a death's head, or skull. 193. 11
MOUND, a ball or globe, forming part of the regalia of sovereigns. 159. 12
MOUNT, a small hill, on which crests are frequently represented. *see* 60. 7, 121. 13
MOUNT, semée. 179. 10
MOUNTAIN, as a mount, but larger in proportion to the bearing placed upon it (*see* next).
MOUNTAIN, in flames. 179. 2
MOUNTAIN CAT. 25. 2; 26. 5, 13
MULLET, a five-pointed star. 164. 2
MULLET, of six points, 83. 13; pierced, 164. 5.
MURAL, walled. *see* 195. 9
MURAL CORONET. *See* CORONET.
MURREY, a kind of purple-brown colour, of very rare occurrence.
MUZZLED. 34. 13

N

NAIL. 176. 11
NAIANT. Swimming, or in the position of swimming. 99. 8, 11, 13; 139. 13; 140. 5
NARCISSUS, a flower with six petals, like the leaf of the cinquefoil.
NEBULÉE, or NEBULY, a term applied to waved lines intended to represent clouds. *see* 56. 8; 85. 11; 227. 15
NOWED, knotted. 142. 4
NEPTUNE. 185. 12
NIGHTINGALE. 108. 12

O

OAK-BRANCH. 151. 1, 3
OAK TREE. 143. 2
OARS IN SALTIER. 179. 3
OGRESSES, sable roundles. *See* ROUNDLE.
OR, gold, frequently represented by yellow; and when engraved by small points or dots spread over the field or bearing. 14. 8; 55. 2
ORGAN PIPES. 168. 10
ORLE. *See* IN ORLE.
OSTRICH. *plate* 97
OSTRICH-FEATHERS, generally borne in a plume. *plates* 114, 115
OSTRICH'S WING. 113. 9
OTTER. 134. 5
OUNCE, an animal like the leopard, having the upper part of the body tawny white, and the lower part ash-colour, and sprinkled with numerous black spots. *See* LEOPARD.
OWL, always full-faced. 96. 5
OX YOKE. 178. 6

P

PADLOCK. 168. 14
PALE. The space amounting to a third-part in the centre of the escutcheon enclosed by two perpendicular lines reaching from top to bottom. *See* PER PALE and IN PALE. 5. 3; 48. 4; 117. 14; 227. 9
PALLET, a diminutive of the field half its width; when wavy it frequently denotes illegitimacy. 66. 3; 131. 1
PALM-BRANCHES. 146. 2; 147. 1, 2, 3
PALM-TREE. 144. 1, 3
PALMER'S STAFF. *see* 168. 6
PALY, when, by perpendicular lines, a field is divided into any equal number of parts, it is *paly* of so many pieces. *see* 5[illegible] 12
PANSY. 151. 4
PARROT, or POPINJAY. 101. 4
PARTRIDGE. 89. 12
PARTY. *See* PER PALE, ETC.
PASCHAL LAMB, passant, carrying a banner, generally charged with a cross, called the Banner of St. George. 131. 2, 7, 14
PASSANT, passing, walking. *see* 6. 2
PASSANT, with tail extended. 5. 11
PASSION CROSS. *See* LONG CROSS.
PASSION-NAIL. *see* 171. 5
PATTÉE. *See* FORMÉE.
PAW. *See* GAMB.
PEACOCK. *plate* 103
PEAN, a sable fur, with ermine spots of gold.
PEAR TREE. 144. 10
PEGASUS, a winged horse. *see plate* 47
PELICAN, usually represented as like an eagle, with a long neck and wings addorsed, always vulning herself—*i.e.*, pecking at her breast—whence issue drops of blood. *See* IN HER PIETY. *plate* 98
PELLETTÉE, strewed with pellets.
PELLET, or OGRESS, a sable Roundle. *See* ROUNDLE.
PEN. *see* 170. 4
PENDENT, hanging. *see* 144. 4; 196. 2; 199. 11
PENNED a term used when the stem or quill of a feather is of a colour different from the feather.
PENNON, an oblong flag, terminating sometimes in one and sometimes in two sharp points, carried on the point of a spear. *See* BANNER and FLAG. *see* 227. 13
PER BEND, divided into two equal parts of different colours by a diagonal line. 226. 1
PER BEND SINISTER. 227. 14
PER CHEVERON, divided by two lines placed in cheveron.
PER FESS, divided into two equal parts of different colours by a horizontal line. 2. 9; 14. 2
PER PALE, divided into two equal parts of different colours by a perpendicular line. 5. 7; 32. 3; 225. 9; 226. 14
PER SALTIER, divided into four equal parts, by two diagonal lines crossing each other.
PESTLE and MORTAR. 177. 13
PHEASANT. 90. 8
PHEON, the barbed head of a dart or arrow. 174. 2, 11
PHŒNIX, a fabled bird always in flames, with about half of the body visible. 82. 2
PHYSICIAN'S CAP. 180. 7
PICK. *see* 78. 2; 219. 12
PIERCED, an ordinary or charge, perforated, and showing the field under it. *see* 164. 5
PIKE, a fish, the lucy. *see* 138. 10; 139. 5
PILE, an ordinary of a conical or triangular shape. *see* 111. 4; 131. 6
PINE CONE, the fruit of the pine-tree. *see* 152. 6
PINE APPLE STALKED AND LEAVED. 152. 8
PINE-TREE. 144. 8, 13
PISTOL. *see* 200. 11
PLATE, a round flat piece of silver without any impression. *See* ROUNDLE.
PLATÉE, semée of plates. *See* SEMÉE. [illegible]. 10
PLOUGH.
PLUMB RULE. 176. 6
PLUME, consisting of *three* feathers only. If more are in the plume the number must be expressed. Sometimes one plume is placed above another; it is then termed a double plume. If composed of three rows, one above the other, it is termed a triple plume. 115. 1, 2
POINTER. 57. 6
POMEGRANATE, generally stalked and leaved, and the side of the fruit burst. 152. 4
POMEIS, a roundle of a green colour. *See* ROUNDLE.
POMMEL, the rounded knob of the sword's handle.
POPINJAY. *See* PARROT.
PORCUPINE. 136. 5
PORTCULLIS, for the defence of the gateway of a city, castle, or other fortress. *plates* 178. 2, 3
POWDERED, semée of.
PREYING, a ravenous beast or bird, standing on, and in a proper position for devouring its prey. *see plate* 79. 2, 8
PRIMROSE. 150. 8, 11
PROPER, borne in the proper or natural colours.
PURFLED, garnished or ornamented.
PURPURE, purple; represented when engraved by diagonal lines, drawn from the sinister chief to the dexter base. *see* 229. 5
PURSE. *see* 202. 1
PYRAMID, a building or figure coming to a point. 179. 12
PYRAMID OF LEAVES. 151. 14

Q

QUADRANGULAR LOCK. *see* 168. 13
QUARTERLY, divided into four equal parts. *see* 61. 10

Quatrefoil, a figure consisting of four leaves 148 10

Queue, the tail, used as *queue-fourchée*, meaning having a forked tail, and *double queued*, meaning double-tailed

Quiver of Arrows, a case filled with arrows 174 4

R

Rabbit, usually termed a coney 136 1

Raguled, Ragulee, or Raguly, supposed to represent a ragged staff having its branches lopped, but more usually drawn in the conventional style 13 6, 147 10, 11, 12, 14

Rainbow, an arch of its proper colours, rising from clouds at each end 159 2, 227 8

Ram 131 13

Rampant, standing erect on the sinister hind leg 1 13

Rat 136 11

Raven 107 2

Reflexed, bent back, usually applied to a chain or line 10. 12, 118 9

Regardant, looking behind 2 11, 118 11

Reindeer 122 3, 125 9

Respecting, looking at

Reversed, contrary to the usual position 17 6, 141 9

Rhinoceros 226 2, 4

Ring or Gem ring 167 12, 14

Rising, preparing to fly *See* Preface

Robin Redbreast 108 11

Rock 179 7

Rock in sea 179 5

Roll of paper, or parchment *see* 75 12, 208 5, 8

Roman fasces 171 4

Roman soldier 188 4

Rose, consisting of five principal petals or leaves with small ones in the centre, having between each outer leaf a smaller petal or barb, usually of a different colour When blazoned proper, the rose is red, the seeds yellow, and the barbs green 149 2, 4

Rose, slipped and leaved 149 5

Rose-branch, divested of the stiffness of the heraldic rose, and drawn in a more natural matter, and usually having more than one blossom 149 8

Roses, garland of 172 10, 174 6, 225 9

Roundle, a small flat circular piece, but the name roundle must only be used when composed of a fur, when the colour is unknown, or when composed of more than one colour, 32 7 The names vary as follows —

1, Barry wavy arg and az, a fountain 159 8
2 Or, a bezant
3 Argent, a plate
4 Gules, a torteau 159 14
5 Azure, a hurt
6 Vert, a pomme or pomeis
7 Sable, a pellet, or ogress
8 Purpure, a golpe

Rudder of ship 11 11, 179 1

Rustre, a figure like a mascle, only whilst the mascle is voided the rustre is only pierced with a round hole

S

Sable, black; represented when engraved by perpendicular and horizontal lines crossing each other *see* 1 10

Sagittarius *See* Centaur

Sail of a ship, only a small portion of the mast and yard-arm should be shown 160 9

Salamander, a fabulous animal, always represented surrounded with flames ppr 138 1, 2, 3

Salient, leaping or springing, the hind feet down 62 8

Saltier, or Saltire, a diagonal cross in the form of St Andrew's Cross *see* 215 12

Saltierways, when placed in the position of the saltier 81 13, 166 12, 170 4

Sanglier, a wild boar 40 9

Sand glass or Hour glass 177 15

Sans, without

Saracen's head 190 5

Sash, military *see* 219 3

Savage, a wild man, always naked, usually with a beard, affrontee, and frequently wreathed about the temples and loins with leaves 186 5, 188 10

Savage's head 190. 7, 12, 192 14

Scales 179 8

Scaling ladder, hooked at the top to affix it to the wall 158 14

Sceptre, a royal staff, the emblem of justice 170 9, 10

Scimitar, or Scym[illegible] *see* 196 10

Scorpion *see* 220. 1

Scroll *See* Escrol

Scroll of Paper, etc *See* Roll

Scythe 188 12, 209, 1

Sea horse, an animal, the upper part being like the horse, but with webbed feet, conjoined to the tail of a fish *plate* 46

Sea-lion, upper part like a lion, and lower part like the tail of a fish *plate* 20

Seal's head 134 1

Seax, a sword or scimitar, much hollowed out and also notched in the back of the blade 171 2, 5

Seeded, applied to the seed of roses, lilies, etc, when of a tincture different to the flower itself

Segreant, a term applied only to the griffin when in the position of rampant 62 2

Sejant, sitting 8 8

Sejant affrontee 7 2

Sejant-erect (sometimes called sejant-rampant), sitting on the hind legs with the fore paws raised 8 13

Semée, sprinkled evenly over the surface at regular intervals Any surface or charge may be semee of any other charge, though some must have special terms applied to them (*see* Crusuly, Bezantee, Plaiee, Semee de-lis, Pellettee) In emblazoning it is desirable, where the shape of the figure or field will allow, that the smaller charges, of which the other is semee, should be so arranged that the outer edge of the field should cut off and partially deface one or more of the smaller charges in order to distinguish it from a field charged with a particular number of objects *see* 13 1; 14 7, 115 8, 119 7

Semée-de lis, semée of fleurs de-lis 203 13

Serpent *plate* 142

Shark *cf* 139 2

Shield *See* Escutcheon

Ship in full sail 160 13

Shoveller, a water-fowl, somewhat like a duck, but shown with a peculiar beak

Shuttle 176 14

Sickle *see* 178 10

Sinister, the left *Refer to* Dexter

Slipped, having a stalk

Snail 141 8

Snake *plate* 142

Spade *see* 202 12

Spaniel *see* 57 7

Spear, generally a tilting-spear *see plate* 175

Spear heads 14 7, 174 12

Sphere, a globe 159 1

Sphinx, a fabulous creature having the body of a lion, the wings of an eagle, and the face and breasts of a woman 182 12

Splendour *See* Sun

Springing *See* Salient

Spur 178 8

Spur and wings 111 12, 13

Spur-rowel 164 8

Squirrel *see plate* 135

Staff raguly 147 10, 11, 12

Stag *see plates* 115—122

Star *See* Etoile

Statant, standing 117 5

Steel cap *See* Morion

Stork 105 11

Stringed, applied to the bugle-horn when borne with strings, and to the harp when the strings are of a different colour

Sun, when represented with a human face environed in rays, is termed a sun in his splendour 162 2

Sun dial 176 7

Surmounted, placed above or upon

Swan 99 2

Sword 170. 2

Sword inflamed 170. 11

Sword wavy *see* 212 4

T

Talbot, a species of hound *see plates* 54, 55

Tail (of Bull) 123 12, (of Lion) 123 14

Tasselled, adorned with tassels 176 12

Tent *see* 158 7

Terrestrial Globe 159 1

Thistle *plates* 150 2, 5, 7

Thunderbolt 174 13

Tiger, more properly Bengal tiger *see plate* 27

Tiger, heraldic, is represented with a hooked talon at the nose, and a mane formed of tufts 25 5

Tilting spear 175 9

Tincture really means only colour, but frequently used in a more general sense to include the whole range of the heraldic palette — *viz*, colours, metals, stains, and furs

Toison d'or *See* Golden Fleece

Torce or Torse, the *wreath* *see* 1. 13, 31 10

Torteau, a roundle gules *See* Roundle

Tortoise *see* 125 5

Tower [*See* Castle] 156 2

Transfixed, pierced through *see* 124 6

TREES. *plates* 143, 144, 145
TREFOIL, a three-leaved figure. 148. 9
TRIANGLE. *see* 167. 8
TRIDENT, Neptune's emblem, with three barbed prongs. *see* 185. 12; 197. 8
TRIPPANT or TRIPPING, a beast of chase, with the right foot lifted up, as if walking briskly. 117. 8
TRIPLE-TOWERED. *see* 157. 6
TRITON. 185. 12
TRUMPET. *see* 91. 6
TRUNCHEON, a marshall's staff. *See* BATON.
TURK, demi, vested. 187. 10
TURKEY. 108. 5
TURRETED, having small towers or turrets, 155. 10; 157. 6
TYNES, the branches of the horns of beasts of chase.

U

UNDÉE. *See* WAVY.
UNGULED, a term used when the hoofs are of a colour different from the body.
UNICORN, a fabulous animal with the head, neck, and body of a horse, the legs of a buck, the tail of a lion, and a long horn projecting from the forehead. *see plates* 48, 49
URCHIN. *See* HEDGEHOG.

V

VAIR, a fur always composed of spaces arg. and az., placed alternately in little shield-shaped divisions. 229. 2
VAIRÉE, formed the same as vair, with this difference, that it may be of any number of colours, which must be expressed in the blazon. 124. 9; 174. 7
VALLARY CORONET. *See* CORONET.
VAMBRACED, covered with armour. 195. 2
VERT, green, represented when engraved by diagonal lines from the dexter chief to the sinister base.
VERVELS, small rings to which the jesses of the hawk are fastened.
VERULED, having rings or ferrules round; applied to hunting-horns. 228. 9
VESTED, clothed or habited. 183. 8; 204. 13
VINE-BRANCH. 152. 9
VINE-TREE. *see* 116. 14
VOL, two wings conjoined. 113. 1
VOLANT, flying. *see* 93. 13
VULNED, wounded and bleeding.
VULNING, wounding, particularly applied to the pelican, which is always depicted wounding her breast. *See* IN HER PIETY. 98. 1

W

WALLET, a pilgrim's pouch. *see* 196. 2
WATER-BOUGET, an antique vessel used for carrying water by soldiers. 168. 2, 4
WATTLED, a term used in describing the gills of a cock.
WAVED or WANY, called also UNDÉE, formed like waves. *see* 14. 2; 66. 3
WHALE'S HEAD. 139. 8
WHEAT. *plates* 153, 154
WHEEL. 167. 1
WHEEL, CATHERINE. 167. 2
WILD CAT. *See* CAT-A-MOUNTAIN.
WINGS. *see plates* 109—113
WINGED SAND-GLASS. 113. 11
WOLF. *plates* 28, 29, 30, 31
WREATH, a skein of silk twisted with a metal cord. Wreaths upon which crests are placed show six folds in front, three of metal and three of colour, beginning with metal and ending with colour. Crests are upon wreaths when not expressed as borne upon a cap, or chapeau, or issuing out of a coronet. *See* PREFACE.
WREATH OF LAUREL. 146. 3
WREATH OF THORNS. 146. 6
WREATHED, twisted in the form of a wreath or encircled by a wreath.
WYVERN, or WIVERN, a fabled monster like a dragon, but with only two legs, drawn with wings up and addorsed, unless otherwise described. *plate* 70

Y

YOKE, for oxen. 178. 6

END OF VOL. I.

Printed by T. C. & E. C. Jack, Grange Publishing Works, Edinburgh.

CPSIA information can be obtained at www.ICGtesting.com
Printed in the USA
LVOW050820151211

259502LV00003B/31/P